PEACE *of* GOD BIBLE

PRESENTED TO

BY

ON

PEACE OF GOD BIBLE

THOMAS NELSON
NEW KING JAMES VERSION®

PEACE OF GOD BIBLE

JEREMIAH JOHNSTON, PhD
GENERAL EDITOR

www.ThomasNelson.com

Peace of God Bible, NKJV

Published in Nashville, TN, by Thomas Nelson. Thomas Nelson is a registered trademark of HarperCollins Christian Publishing, Inc.

Library of Congress Control Number: 2025932330

Printed in India

25 26 27 28 29 30 31 32 33 34 /BPI/ 10 9 8 7 6 5 4 3 2 1

CONTENTS

THE OLD TESTAMENT

THE NEW TESTAMENT

PREFACE TO THE NEW KING JAMES VERSION®

To understand the heart behind the New King James Version, one need look no further than the stated intentions of the original King James scholars: "Not to make a new translation . . . but to make a good one better." The New King James Version is a continuation of the labors of the King James translators, unlocking for today's readers the spiritual treasures found especially in the Authorized Version of the Holy Bible.

While seeking to maintain the excellent *form* of the traditional English Bible, special care has also been taken to preserve the work of *precision* that is the legacy of the King James translators.

Where new translation has been necessary, the most complete representation of the original has been rendered by considering the definition and usage of the Hebrew, Aramaic, and Greek words in their contexts. This translation principle, known as *complete equivalence*, seeks to preserve accurately all of the information in the text while presenting it in good literary form.

In addition to accuracy, the translators have also sought to maintain those lyrical and devotional qualities that are so highly regarded in the King James Version. The thought flow and selection of phrases from the King James Version have been preserved wherever possible without sacrificing clarity.

The format of the New King James Version is designed to enhance the vividness, devotional quality, and usefulness of the Bible. Words or phrases in italics indicate expressions in the original language that require clarification by additional English words, as was done in the King James Version. Poetry is structured as verse to reflect the form and beauty of the passage in the original language. The covenant name of God was usually translated from the Hebrew as LORD or GOD, using capital letters as shown, as in the King James Version. This convention is also maintained in the New King James Version when the Old Testament is quoted in the New.

The Hebrew text used for the Old Testament is the 1967/1977 Stuttgart edition of the *Biblia Hebraica*, with frequent comparisons to the Bomberg edition of 1524–1525. Ancient versions and the Dead Sea Scrolls were consulted, but the Hebrew is followed wherever possible. Significant variations, explanations, and alternate renderings are mentioned in footnotes.

The Greek text used for the New Testament is the one that was followed by the King James translators: the traditional text of the Greek-speaking churches, called the Received Text or Textus Receptus, first published in 1516. Footnotes indicate significant variants from the Textus Receptus as found in two other editions of the Greek New Testament:

(1) NU-Text: These variations generally represent the Alexandrian or Egyptian text type as found in the critical text published in the twenty-seventh edition of the Nestle-Aland Greek New Testament (N) and in the United Bible Societies' fourth edition (U).

(2) M-Text: These variations represent readings found in the text of *The Greek New Testament According to the Majority Text*, which follows the consensus of the majority of surviving New Testament manuscripts.

The textual notes in the New King James Version make no evaluation but objectively present the facts about variant readings.

HOW TO USE THE *PEACE OF GOD BIBLE*

Peace is one of the great themes of the Bible. It is present in the beginning of Genesis when God fellowships with Adam and Eve in the Garden of Eden. It is there at the end of Revelation when God renews all of this broken creation and His people take up their residence in His eternal realm. When God reigns over a place and a people, it is a kingdom of peace.

But between the peace of Eden and the glory of the new creation, we have this thing called life. Daily struggles, temptations, and sadness chase after us. As David described in Psalm 23, we "walk through the valley of the shadow of death." Oftentimes our daily experiences attempt to pin us down in that shadowy place. But our Lord, who is the Prince of Peace, ushers us on with the reminder that He is with us—that His rod and staff comfort us. Though we face the bleak and dark days of this world, the peace of God is offered continually to those who will have faith and seek the Lord.

We have designed the *Peace of God Bible* for you. We want you to see easily and quickly all that it teaches about peace and how to live in it. We are blessed to have Dr. Jeremiah Johnston bring this to the forefront with his writing of the Devotions and Peace Notes. He has identified hundreds of places in the Bible where we learn peace can be the key element of our lives in Christ. God's peace is the origin of our salvation, and it is God's peace that sustains us in every step of faith we take in this life.

On the pages ahead, you are going to find these important features to help you study the Bible and learn about the peace of God.

- DEVOTIONS. Over the course of this Bible you will find 365 devotions, each one based on a verse or passage. Jeremiah's devotions guide you to receive and live by God's peace. You can start reading devotions on any day and use them as a yearlong plan for daily devotions or simply as a tool to better understand what you read and study in the Bible.
- ARTICLES. In the front matter, Jeremiah has provided you with foundational articles that give you an overview of what the peace of God is, how to find or recover it, and how to experience eternal salvation because of what God has done for you.
- STUDY THEMES. Use these short lists to study how to apply and live out God's peace in specific areas of your life.
- PEACE NOTES. Throughout the Scripture, Jeremiah has provided short, powerful insights about how God offers and works out peace in your life. You will find these in callout boxes all through the Bible.
- BOOK INTRODUCTIONS. Each book of the Bible begins with a one-page introduction. It will help you understand the theme, the author, and the key ideas present in each book of the Bible as well the part peace plays in that book.

- **CROSS-REFERENCES.** One of the best ways to study the Bible is to see how God's truth connects across the Scriptures. You will find small reference markers in the Bible verses that tie to the cross-references at the bottom of the page. Use these cross-references to see how the themes of the Bible tie together and prophecies are fulfilled.

- **CONCORDANCE.** In the back matter you will find this alphabetical listing of key words found in the Bible. The concordance shows where the terms occur through the Scripture so you can see how they're used in different circumstances by different people.

My prayer for you is that the *Peace of God Bible* will be a helpful edition of God's Word that engages your mind and comforts your heart for a lifetime. It is a joy to have our friend Jeremiah Johnston serve as a guide through the mountainous terrain of life. My hope is that you will engage the Scripture, draw near to Christ, and experience the full power of God's peace in your life.

Philip Nation
Publisher, Thomas Nelson Bibles

THE PEACE OF GOD

FIND IT AND KEEP IT

Many times when I could have gone insane from worry, I was in
peace because my soul believed the truth of God's promise.
George Müller, *The Autobiography of George Müller*

The apostle Paul confessed in 2 Corinthians 2:13, "I had no rest in my spirit" during an apparent anxiety attack he experienced on the second missionary journey in the city of Troas (modern-day Turkey). The time was AD 51–52. Paul was searching the city for his friend Titus and could not find him anywhere. As with anyone looking unsuccessfully for a treasured friend, Paul might have succumbed to panic and catastrophic thinking. He left Troas immediately when God called him to (Acts 16:9–10), but he may have done so with a heavy heart and a sense of failure.

You might be able to identify with Paul. Perhaps you've experienced a situation in which fear clouded your vision and caused you to lose your composure. The feeling of failure now triggers an emotional response.

The supernatural peace of God is the result when the Lord turns our triggers (our Troas experiences, if you will) into triumphs. When we experience God's peace, our pain can become our purpose in ministering to others with the comfort that God showers on us (see 2 Cor. 1:3–4). Paul will show us how to move from panic to peace—but first, let's understand what the Bible says *peace* really is.

It's more than the absence of anxiety. The word "peace" (the Hebrew word is *shalom*; the Greek word is *eirene*), along with its variations, appears 614 times in the original languages of Scripture and was a constant theme in Jesus' teachings. And yet it is a neglected topic today. As a result, God's peace has been elusive to many Jesus-followers (which is why so many are stressed and try to manage anxiety in unhealthy ways).

After the name of Jesus itself, there is no finer word or concept than *shalom* (peace). *Shalom* originates in God Himself, and it epitomizes the gospel and the active relationship God initiates, pursues, and perfects with each of us. *Shalom* is a power both active and holistic—active in the sense that it invites us to flourish and holistic in that it affects our whole being—body, soul, heart, mind.

How can we obtain this peace? The first step is a commitment to God's ways. The Scriptures tell us, "There is no peace . . . for the wicked" (Is. 48:22). Peace simply isn't available to anyone living a worldly, God-free life. God and His peace come hand in hand—you can't have one without the other. If you have committed your life to following the Light of the world, God's Son Jesus Christ, you are a candidate for God's beautiful, life-altering peace. (If not, please see "Find God and His Peace: The Plan for Salvation.")

But how do we *know* peace and maintain it?

Paul's Peace Plan

Let's look at the way Paul found to obtain, maintain, and savor peace.

To find this, we need first to finish Paul's Troas experience. Troas may have become a bad memory for Paul (2 Cor. 2). Because "a door was opened to me by the Lord" (v. 12), he may have felt his seemingly anxious response to Titus's absence meant he had failed there. But he did not see his situation from God's perspective. In reading Acts 16, we find it's possible that part of God's purpose was for Paul to meet a new friend named Luke (v. 10, where "we" includes Luke), a medical doctor who became a new missionary traveling companion. Also, later on in 2 Corinthians, Paul's prayers were answered and he reunited with Titus: "For even when we came into Macedonia, we found no relief" until Titus arrived (7:6 author's rendering). So there was a purpose in Titus's delay, and maybe Luke's joining Paul was an aspect of that. The Holy Spirit would use Luke to author a Gospel and the Book of Acts.

What's more, because of his hasty retreat Paul may have thought the door of ministry in Troas was forever closed. Yet God had other plans. Not only did He bring Paul (and Luke) back to minister in Troas during the third missionary journey (AD 57–58), but the Lord also used Paul to perform his greatest miracle there—raising Eutychus from the dead (Acts 20:7–12). My question is, what happened in Paul's life between his Troas visits? He left Troas after an apparently anxious experience, he returned a few years later in the peace of God and evidently "continued speaking" and left his listeners "not a little comforted" (20:9, 12). How did Paul receive freedom from anxiety and see his ministry flourish?

The answer becomes clearer when we study the peace-of-God plan Paul developed. The apostle shared his plan in the greatest anti-anxiety chapter in all the Bible: Philippians 4.

> Be anxious for nothing, but in everything by prayer and supplication, with thanksgiving, let your requests be made known to God; and the peace of God, which surpasses all understanding, will guard your hearts and minds through Christ Jesus. Finally, brethren, whatever things are true, whatever things are noble, whatever things are just, whatever things are pure, whatever things are lovely, whatever things are of good report, if there is any virtue and if there is anything praiseworthy—meditate on these things.
>
> PHILIPPIANS 4:6-8

Paul knew anxiety in Troas with a great door open; Paul knew peace in a prison cell in Rome (closed door) while writing this epistle under the agency of the Holy Spirit. We receive the promise of Philippians 4:6–7 when we, like Paul, follow God's plans for peace in our lives: Be anxious for nothing . . . remind yourself of God's promises . . . know peace.

Discipline Your Thoughts to Maintain Peace

You see, the content of our thinking determines our peace and happiness. God's Holy Word says we have been "given . . . exceedingly great and precious promises" (2 Pet. 1:4). We must lean on those promises and continuously trust Him. With God there are no hopeless situations, and that is why we can be assured of His peace that passes all understanding; His peace *will* guard our hearts and our minds through Christ Jesus. It is wise to often ask ourselves, *Am I trusting what I know is true in my life through Christ, or am I focusing on the problem and factoring God out of my situation?*

As followers of Jesus, we have to *learn* peace and happiness. Mental, physical, emotional, and spiritual health is a never-ending battle. And the peace of God is unleashed when we, like Paul moving from Troas to triumph, are disciplined thinkers about what we know is true of our lives in Christ. Yes, we can learn from everyone and every situation, but we should never allow anyone else to think for us.

Think through your faith. Live your faith as a discipline and the peace of God will be with you. Like Paul, ask the Lord to envelop you in the peace so transforming and so overwhelming it simply surpasses your ability to understand it.

As you might expect, the peace of God results in a state of genuine, meaningful happiness. Having met and embraced the risen Christ, Paul knew that he was forgiven and so could affirm the psalmist's words: *Happy are those whose iniquities are forgiven, and whose sins are covered; happy is the man against whom the Lord will not reckon his sin* (Rom. 4:7–8 paraphrased; see Ps. 32:1–2). Frequent contemplation of these Scriptures and others related to God's peace helps heal our minds and eliminate anxiety.

The only way to live continually in the peace of God is by making a commitment to know God better and then applying the truth about God to our lives. In other words, we have to learn to trust the God we believe in. When we are committed to truth and to becoming more thoughtful Christians, we search out the truth of God as revealed in Scripture and we come triumphantly to the Person of all peace: Jesus.

The Bible promises that Jesus established peace for us! Jesus' peace is an *objective* reality, and the *subjective* feeling of peace will come as we allow Christ to be established in our hearts through communion with Him in His Word. We experience the peace *of* God when we *have* peace with God, and we attain that through faith in Jesus Christ and His finished work on the cross on our behalf.

The Bible teaches it is God's will for every follower of Jesus to experience His peace/*shalom*. It is not God's will for a follower of Jesus to live in conflict, confusion, or anxiety. This is good news, because the peace of God is not something only for "good Christians" but available to all followers of Jesus on the journey of sanctification and growth in Christlikeness.

Is there a problem to which you can apply Paul's peace plan today?

BELIEVERS CAN RECOVER THE PEACE OF GOD

When you are at the brink of an overwhelming problem and confess, "Lord, I cannot do this!" the Lord in His faithfulness always answers, "But I can! I will give you the strength to endure your situation. I will provide every resource necessary for you to meet this tragedy in your life. You must trade your fleeting human strength for My strength!"

Only through Christ can we soar above our issues and find everlasting, moment-by-moment peace. You have already trusted the Lord for the greatest miracle: your salvation in Jesus. Now the Lord wants you to trust Him to deal with all the catastrophes of life because He never leaves you or forsakes you (Heb. 13:5).

At times the peace of God evades every true believer. Our feelings then ruthlessly try to convince us God has abandoned us, and there is no hope. We all have a false teacher in our minds who accuses us and says, "Really? Again? You are certainly not a forgiven child of God!" Like the psalmist (chs. 42–43), we must preach the truth of God to ourselves and not listen to our hearts, which can be deceptive (Jer. 17:9). Thank God we do not rely on our feelings to validate truth. Truth is unchanging because God is unchanging. The Christian faith is what we believe, not what we feel.

Anxiety is not always sin. Sometimes anxiety is suffering. To recover the peace of God, we must first acknowledge this fact by faith: *Anxiety is not dangerous, and the Lord will get me through what I am facing.* And then there are a few steps you can take toward regaining your peace.

Steps Toward Peace

1. Confess All Sin

By faith, invoke 1 John 1:9 and name your sins to the Lord. He is faithful and just to forgive you and cleanse you. Keep a short account with the Lord: when you sin, acknowledge it immediately, seek His forgiveness, and then keep moving forward. Remember, you are forgiven because of God's faithfulness and not the amount of emotion you show or any other work. All forgiveness comes because of God's grace. The peace of God will be absent, though, especially when we're consciously, rebelliously sinning (1 John 1:5–6; Eph. 4:30; Heb. 12:5–11).

2. Mix the Promises of God with Faith

Again, every believer slips out of the peace of God. But we have been blessed with the Holy Spirit, and He combines the Word of God and His presence to give us divine strength. "The Spirit helps us in our weaknesses . . . The Spirit Himself makes intercession for us with groanings which cannot be uttered" (Rom. 8:26). You have only one requirement: trust. I'm talking about a *continuous habit* of putting faith in the Lord. A phrase I say to myself daily is *God's got this!* The Lord may deliver us out of the problem or sustain us through the problem: either way, He promises to help us in our moments of need (Is. 41:10, 13).

Trusting in the Lord does not mean we leave reality and live in denial. Like Paul, we use our minds to trust the Lord continually by filling them with good and true thoughts (see Phil. 4:8). This means we apply a promise of God to our situation and then continually lean on the Lord to solve or see us through that issue.

3. Wait on the Lord

The Lord promises to strengthen you as you wait on Him in faith. Isaiah gave a vivid picture of what it means to trust in the Lord: "Those who wait on the LORD shall renew their strength; they shall mount up with wings like eagles, they shall run and not be weary, they shall walk and not faint" (40:31). King David also recommended faith in Psalm 27:14: "Wait on the LORD; be of good courage, and He shall strengthen your heart; wait, I say, on the LORD!"

The prophet Jeremiah said in Lamentations that the Lord deals favorably with those who hope in Him (Lam. 3:25). We can center our hope incorrectly on persons, or we can focus properly upon God. See what Paul wrote: "Yes, we had the sentence of death in ourselves, that we should not trust in ourselves but in God who raises the dead, who delivered us from so great a death, and does deliver us; in whom we trust that He will still deliver us" (2 Cor. 1:9–10).

You can recover your peace as often as you need to by following these steps and putting your hope in God.

FIND GOD AND HIS PEACE

THE PLAN OF SALVATION

You are not a Christian because you go to church, you are a good person, or you've kept the Golden Rule. Being a Christian is all about being forgiven. You receive this forgiveness when you invite Jesus into your life as your Savior and Lord. In Jesus Christ we find forgiveness for sin, peace with God, and eternal resurrection life.

The Bible calls the way to have peace with God "the gospel" or Good News: "God so loved the world that He gave His only begotten Son, that whoever believes in Him should not perish but have everlasting life" (John 3:16). We were sinners who couldn't save ourselves. Jesus came to bear our sin before God and redeem us.

You may wonder, *Can't we just be good people so God will be pleased with us and let us into heaven?* The fact is "all have sinned" (Rom. 3:23), which means that every person breaks God's commandments. We can be "good" in the eyes of others, but in our hearts we acknowledge that we often fail to do the things we should.

Romans 6:23 explains that our sin, in God's eyes, calls for death. So, even as our heavenly Father deeply loves us, He simply can't overlook our sin. So God sent His Son to redeem us from it. At a specific point in history, Jesus Christ came from heaven to earth, born in a human body to a human mother, to reveal the love of God for us. The sinless Son of God agreed to pay that cost of death for us, which resulted in His death on a Roman cross. In that great act of love, He purchased a place in heaven for us that He now offers as a free gift.

Through *repentance* and *faith* we receive Jesus and His forgiveness. *Repent* describes a change of direction—a switch from living our own way to living Jesus' way. The decision to repent lies is an act of the mind, not the emotions. Placing your personal trust in Jesus' death for you is God's only requirement for salvation. Trusting Christ is personal. The Bible is clear:

> If you confess with your mouth the Lord Jesus and believe in your heart that God has raised Him from the dead, you will be saved. For with the heart one believes unto righteousness, and with the mouth confession is made unto salvation. For the Scripture says, "Whoever believes on Him will not be put to shame" . . . For "whoever calls on the name of the LORD shall be saved."
>
> ROMANS 10:9-11, 13

Have you placed your trust in Jesus Christ for your forgiveness of sin and eternal life with Him? If not, you can do that right now. Tell God you are ready to surrender to Him your entire life—your thoughts, your words, your attitudes, your actions—knowing that as soon as you open the door to your heart, He will readily and gladly come in. It's helpful to pray a simple prayer such as this one:

> Lord Jesus, I am a sinner in need of Your gift of grace. Right now, I turn from trusting in myself and my good works and repent by placing my trust in You alone for the forgiveness of my sins and to receive eternal life with you in heaven. I know that you are God's Son, and You died and rose again for me. Come into my life, Lord Jesus, as my Savior and Lord and Leader and Friend. Amen.

If you meant what you just prayed, you have now become a Christian. Your sin is forgiven—all of it, past, present, and future—and you have a righteous standing before God! God has secured a home for you with Him in heaven because you have done what the Bible said.

Our assurance of salvation is based on the simple promise of the Bible, not on how we feel. Even if you have no special feelings, God promises to save everyone who believes the gospel and confesses Jesus is His Son.

It's important to realize that though you've become a Christian, you will still sin, but when you do an internal alarm will go off. That is God Himself convicting you of your sin. When you feel that conviction, confess that you've sinned to God, ask His forgiveness, and press on.

As a Christian, you are now eligible to experience the wondrous peace of God, today and forever. You experience the peace *of* God because you have peace *with* God. For more information, see "The Peace of God: Find It and Keep It." Welcome to the kingdom!

THE OLD TESTAMENT

THE FIRST BOOK OF MOSES CALLED

GENESIS

AUTHOR

Nowhere in the Book of Genesis is the author named. Although the events of the book end three hundred years before Moses was born, the rest of the Bible and most church historians attribute the authorship of Genesis to Moses. Both the Old and New Testaments have many references to Moses as its author (Ex. 7:14; Lev. 1:1–2; Num. 33:2; Deut. 1:1; Dan. 9:11–13; Mal. 4:4; Matt. 8:4; Mark 12:26; Luke 16:29; John 7:19; Acts 26:22; Rom. 10:19). Both early Jewish and Christian writers name Moses as the author.

TIME

c. 4000–1804 BC

KEY VERSE

Genesis 3:15

THEME

After the initial story of the world's creation, Genesis ("beginnings") covers two basic subjects: God and man. God creates man. Man disobeys God and alienates himself from God. Genesis is the story, then. of the subsequent interactions between God and man that bring them back together into a right relationship. As such, the book points to the beginnings of the way of change, of restoration, and of a new way of life. Genesis sets the tone for the rest of the Bible with clear teaching on following God's call, believing in His promises, and being obedient to His commands. The main characters who dominate the story are the patriarchs: Abraham, Isaac, Jacob, and Joseph.

The Torah (Hebrew "instruction") begins with Genesis, so titled because of 2:4, "This is the book of the origins" (*geneseos*), which appears in the Septuagint, the Greek translation of the Old Testament. From the origin of the universe we are introduced to the God who brings peace out of chaos. His plan for His creation to lack nothing and find completeness cannot be stopped, even by the great catastrophe of sin and death. When human beings forgot God, even willfully disavowing their Creator (ch. 6), the Lord of Peace providentially forgave their sin and established the covenant of peace for all humankind (15:1–16).

Through the remarkable story of the patriarchs (chs. 12–50), we encounter the ways in which God's peace guides sojourners, often despite their poor decisions. For example, released from years in "the dungeon" (41:14), Joseph told the most powerful man on earth that peace came only from the Lord: "It is not in me; God will give Pharaoh an answer of peace" (41:16). This book of origins closes with the promise that only God has the power to bring peace where others brought evil (50:19–20).

The History of Creation

1 In the [a]beginning [b]God created the heavens and the earth. 2 The earth was [a]without
form, and void; and darkness *was*[1] on the
face of the deep. [b]And the Spirit of God was
hovering over the face of the waters.
3 [a]Then God said, [b]"Let there be [c]light"; and
there was light. 4 And God saw the light, that
it was good; and God divided the light from
the darkness. 5 God called the light Day, and
the [a]darkness He called Night. So the evening
and the morning were the first day.
6 Then God said, [a]"Let there be a firmament
in the midst of the waters, and let it divide the
waters from the waters." 7 Thus God made the
firmament, [a]and divided the waters which *were*
under the firmament from the waters which
were [b]above the firmament; and it was so.
8 And God called the firmament Heaven. So the
evening and the morning were the second day.
9 Then God said, [a]"Let the waters under
the heavens be gathered together into one
place, and [b]let the dry *land* appear"; and it
was so. 10 And God called the dry *land* Earth,
and the gathering together of the waters He
called Seas. And God saw that *it was* good.
11 Then God said, "Let the earth [a]bring forth
grass, the herb *that* yields seed, *and* the [b]fruit
tree *that* yields fruit according to its kind,
whose seed *is* in itself, on the earth"; and it
was so. 12 And the earth brought forth grass,
the herb *that* yields seed according to its kind,
and the tree *that* yields fruit, whose seed *is*
in itself according to its kind. And God saw
that *it was* good. 13 So the evening and the
morning were the third day.
14 Then God said, "Let there be [a]lights in the
firmament of the heavens to divide the day
from the night; and let them be for signs and
[b]seasons, and for days and years; 15 and let them
be for lights in the firmament of the heavens
to give light on the earth"; and it was so. 16 Then
God made two great lights: the [a]greater light

> **PEACE NOTE**
>
> God made us, in His image, with emotions. But our emotions can deceive us. Our feelings do not confirm truth and often contradict God's promises in our lives.
>
> GENESIS 1:26

1:1 [a] [John 1:1–3] [b] Acts 17:24 **1:2** [a] Jer. 4:23 [b] Is. 40:13, 14 [1] Words in italic type have been added for clarity. They are not found in the original Hebrew or Aramaic. **1:3** [a] Ps. 33:6, 9 [b] 2 Cor. 4:6 [c] [Heb. 11:3] **1:5** [a] Ps. 19:2; 33:6; 74:16; 104:20; 136:5 **1:6** [a] Jer. 10:12 **1:7** [a] Prov. 8:27–29 [b] Ps. 148:4 **1:9** [a] Job 26:10 [b] Ps. 24:1, 2; 33:7; 95:5 **1:11** [a] Heb. 6:7 [b] 2 Sam. 16:1 **1:14** [a] Ps. 74:16; 136:5–9 [b] Ps. 104:19 **1:16** [a] Ps. 136:8

THE CREATOR OF PEACE

In the beginning God created the heavens and the earth.

GENESIS 1:1

The very first verse in the Bible gives me a great sense of peace and well-being. Why? It affirms that the universe was created by God, not by chance.

In the ancient world almost every culture had a story about the beginning of the universe or "the heavens and the earth," as it was usually called. Only the Hebrew people said God created it. The other versions of creation speak of gods fighting gods. The carcasses of the defeated gods became various parts of the earth; the teeth or drops of blood that fell into the ground became humans; and so forth. The humanistic conclusion is that there is nothing special about the earth or the heavens. They came about more or less by chance. Their futures are uncertain as well. Doesn't that thinking make you nervous?

The ancient stories about the origin of the universe hardly inspire confidence or peace. The story told in Genesis, however, is very different. The most obvious difference is that the world was created by one supreme God and it—and everyone on it—has a purpose. I find this very reassuring. You should too.

to rule the day, and the [b]lesser light to rule the
night. *He made* [c]the stars also. 17 God set them
in the firmament of the [a]heavens to give light
on the earth, 18 and to [a]rule over the day and
over the night, and to divide the light from the
darkness. And God saw that *it was* good. 19 So the
evening and the morning were the fourth day.
20 Then God said, "Let the waters abound
with an abundance of living creatures, and let
birds fly above the earth across the face of the
firmament of the heavens." 21 So [a]God created
great sea creatures and every living thing that
moves, with which the waters abounded, according to their kind, and every winged bird
according to its kind. And God saw that *it was*
good. 22 And God blessed them, saying, [a]"Be
fruitful and multiply, and fill the waters in the
seas, and let birds multiply on the earth." 23 So
the evening and the morning were the fifth day.
24 Then God said, "Let the earth bring forth
the living creature according to its kind: cattle
and creeping thing and beast of the earth, *each*
according to its kind"; and it was so. 25 And God
made the beast of the earth according to its
kind, cattle according to its kind, and everything that creeps on the earth according to its
kind. And God saw that *it was* good.
26 Then God said, [a]"Let Us make man in Our
image, according to Our likeness; [b]let them
have dominion over the fish of the sea, over
the birds of the air, and over the cattle, over

PEACE NOTE

Since we are made in God's image, you could almost say we have been prewired for happiness, hope, and peace.

GENESIS 1:27

all[1] the earth and over every creeping thing
that creeps on the earth." 27 So God created
man [a]in His *own* image; in the image of God
He created him; [b]male and female He created
them. 28 Then God blessed them, and God said
to them, [a]"Be fruitful and multiply; fill the earth
and [b]subdue it; have dominion over the fish
of the sea, over the birds of the air, and over
every living thing that moves on the earth."
29 And God said, "See, I have given you
every herb *that* yields seed which *is* on the
face of all the earth, and every tree whose

1:16 [b] Ps. 8:3 [c] Job 38:7 1:17 [a] Gen. 15:5 1:18 [a] Jer. 31:35 1:21 [a] Ps. 104:25–28 1:22 [a] Gen. 8:17 1:26 [a] [Eph. 4:24] [b] Gen. 9:2 [1] Syriac reads *all the wild animals of.* 1:27 [a] Gen. 5:2 [b] Matt. 19:4 1:28 [a] Gen. 9:1, 7 [b] 1 Cor. 9:27

CREATED FOR PEACE

Then God said, "Let Us make man in Our image, according to Our likeness" . . . So God created man in His own image; in the image of God He created him; male and female He created them.

GENESIS 1:26–27

Given what atheists say these days, the words of the Creator, "Let Us make man in Our image" are very reassuring. Obviously atheists don't think humans are made in the image of God. How could they be? They say there is no God! But Genesis affirms three important things: (1) the existence of God, (2) the creation of the world by God, and (3) the creation of humanity in the image of God. For the atheist, the human being is nothing more than a two-legged animal whose life has no real meaning. For the atheist, there really are no grounds for hope. And if there are no grounds for hope, then there can hardly be any basis for peace. We are nothing more than a cosmic fluke, a mere flicker in the galaxy that in time will cease to exist.

But the Book of Genesis affirms what every human senses down deep in his or her heart: we are not animals; we are special. We do have meaning; we have a sense of right and wrong. We are spiritual beings. Why do we sense these things? Because we were created in the image of God—and that is a very good reason to have hope—and peace.

fruit yields seed; [a]to you it shall be for food.
30 Also, to [a]every beast of the earth, to every [b]bird of the air, and to everything that
creeps on the earth, in which *there is* life, *I
have given* every green herb for food"; and
it was so. 31 Then [a]God saw everything that
He had made, and indeed *it was* very good.
So the evening and the morning were the
sixth day.

2 Thus the heavens and the earth, and [a]all
the host of them, were finished. 2 [a]And on
the seventh day God ended His work which
He had done, and He rested on the seventh
day from all His work which He had done.
3 Then God [a]blessed the seventh day and
sanctified it, because in it He rested from all
His work which God had created and made.
4 [a]This *is* the history[1] of the heavens and
the earth when they were created, in the day
that the LORD God made the earth and the
heavens, 5 before any [a]plant of the field was
in the earth and before any herb of the field
had grown. For the LORD God had not [b]caused
it to rain on the earth, and *there was* no man
[c]to till the ground; 6 but a mist went up from
the earth and watered the whole face of the
ground.
7 And the LORD God formed man *of* the
[a]dust of the ground, and [b]breathed into his
[c]nostrils the breath of life; and [d]man became
a living being.

Life in God's Garden

8 The LORD God planted [a]a garden [b]eastward
in [c]Eden, and there He put the man whom He
had formed. 9 And out of the ground the LORD
God made [a]every tree grow that is pleasant to
the sight and good for food. [b]The tree of life
was also in the midst of the garden, and the
tree of the knowledge of good and [c]evil.
10 Now a river went out of Eden to water
the garden, and from there it parted and
became four riverheads. 11 The name of the
first *is* Pishon; it *is* the one which skirts [a]the

PEACE NOTE

Secular culture declares, "Emotions and experiences are my truth!" So, if I am in love, I am going to marry that person, but if I'm out of love, I am going to leave that person. This is wrong.

GENESIS 2:24

1:29 [a] Gen. 9:3 1:30 [a] Ps. 145:15 [b] Job 38:41 1:31 [a] [Ps. 104:24] 2:1 [a] Ps. 33:6 2:2 [a] Ex. 20:9–11; 31:17 2:3 [a] [Is. 58:13] 2:4 [a] Gen. 1:1 [1] Hebrew *toledoth,* literally *generations* 2:5 [a] Gen. 1:11, 12 [b] Gen. 7:4 [c] Gen. 3:23 2:7 [a] Gen. 3:19, 23 [b] Job 33:4 [c] Gen. 7:22 [d] 1 Cor. 15:45 2:8 [a] Is. 51:3 [b] Gen. 3:23, 24 [c] Gen. 4:16 2:9 [a] Ezek. 31:8 [b] [Gen. 3:22] [c] [Deut. 1:39] 2:11 [a] Gen. 25:18

OUR CONSTANT COMPANION

Then God saw everything that He had made, and indeed it was very good.

GENESIS 1:31

At each stage of creation God "saw that it was good" (vv. 10, 12, 18, 21, 25; see v. 4) In fact, Genesis says this seven times. But the seventh time, in verse 31, it reads, "Indeed it was very good." The creation of our world was not haphazard and accidental—which is the way most ancient Near Eastern stories describe it. In contrast to those stories, the account in Genesis describes God creating the world in a methodical, step-by-step process. Each stage of creation is "good," and the finished product is "very good." So from the outset, the Bible shows that God's plans for us are purposeful. God made each of us on purpose for a purpose and from the beginning to the end, God's desire is to lavish us with His peace.

I find it reassuring that our world—and that includes humanity—was carefully crafted. I don't know about you, but when I find things in good order, working as they should be, I have a sense of stability, even of tranquility. What I must remember as a follower of Jesus is that God's creation shows me that it is His will for me to live in peace. I should never question if it is God's will for *shalom*-peace to be my constant companion.

EVERY WEEK'S REST

God blessed the seventh day and sanctified it, because in it He rested from all His work.

GENESIS 2:3

It's hard to find peace if you never stop and rest. I believe that is one of the problems people have in our modern world. But look at God the Creator, who, I presume, has endless springs of strength and creativity. When He finished His work of creation, "He rested." This rest from His work was precedent-setting. If God, Someone with no limits, rested, so should we in our very limited humanity. We run out of strength and stamina; God doesn't, yet He created and sanctified the day of rest, which suggests rest is very important.

In these days and moments of rest, we can recharge our spiritual batteries. Ceasing from our work and busy activities allows us to meditate on God and His creation. In these moments of quietness we can pray and think deeply about the God who has made us—and ask Him for renewed energy. At times like these we can find what we need to keep going—and we can find peace.

whole land of Havilah, where *there is* gold.
12 And the gold of that land *is* good. [a]Bdellium
and the onyx stone *are* there. 13 The name of
the second river *is* Gihon; it *is* the one which
goes around the whole land of Cush. 14 The
name of the third river *is* [a]Hiddekel;[1] it *is* the
one which goes toward the east of Assyria.
The fourth river *is* the Euphrates.
15 Then the LORD God took the man and put
him in the garden of Eden to tend and keep
it. 16 And the LORD God commanded the man,
saying, "Of every tree of the garden you may
freely eat; 17 but of the tree of the knowledge
of good and evil [a]you shall not eat, for in the
day that you eat of it [b]you shall surely [c]die."
18 And the LORD God said, "*It is* not good that
man should be alone; [a]I will make him a helper comparable to him." 19 [a]Out of the ground
the LORD God formed every beast of the field
and every bird of the air, and [b]brought *them*
to Adam to see what he would call them. And
whatever Adam called each living creature,
that *was* its name. 20 So Adam gave names to
all cattle, to the birds of the air, and to every
beast of the field. But for Adam there was not
found a helper comparable to him.
21 And the LORD God caused a [a]deep sleep
to fall on Adam, and he slept; and He took
one of his ribs, and closed up the flesh in its
place. 22 Then the rib which the LORD God
had taken from man He made into a woman,
[a]and He [b]brought her to the man.
23 And Adam said:

"This *is* now [a]bone of my bones

PEACE NOTE

It is important to recognize that, though our minds have been tainted by the fall of humanity, they can be renewed in and through Christ.

GENESIS 3:1

And flesh of my flesh;
She shall be called Woman,
Because she was [b]taken out of Man."

24 [a]Therefore a man shall leave his father and
mother and [b]be joined to his wife, and they
shall become one flesh.
25 [a]And they were both naked, the man and
his wife, and were not [b]ashamed.

The Temptation and Fall of Man

3 Now [a]the serpent was [b]more cunning than
any beast of the field which the LORD God
had made. And he said to the woman, "Has
God indeed said, 'You shall not eat of every
tree of the garden'?"

2:12 [a] Num. 11:7 **2:14** [a] Dan. 10:4 [1] Or *Tigris* **2:17** [a] Gen. 3:1, 3, 11, 17 [b] Gen. 3:3, 19 [c] Rom. 5:12 **2:18** [a] 1 Cor. 11:8, 9 **2:19** [a] Gen. 1:20, 24 [b] Ps. 8:6 **2:21** [a] 1 Sam. 26:12 **2:22** [a] 1 Tim. 2:13 [b] Heb. 13:4 **2:23** [a] Gen. 29:14 [b] 1 Cor. 11:8, 9 **2:24** [a] Matt. 19:5 [b] Mark 10:6–8 **2:25** [a] Gen. 3:7, 10 [b] Is. 47:3 **3:1** [a] 1 Chr. 21:1 [b] 2 Cor. 11:3

PEACE NOTE

When Scripture and your feelings disagree, first bring Scripture's truth over your life, and then start walking in the direction of Scripture. Let your emotions catch up.

GENESIS 3:1

2 And the woman said to the serpent, "We
may eat the [a]fruit of the trees of the garden;
3 but of the fruit of the tree which *is* in the
midst of the garden, God has said, 'You shall
not eat it, nor shall you [a]touch it, lest you die.'"
4 [a]Then the serpent said to the woman,
"You will not surely die. 5 For God knows
that in the day you eat of it your eyes will be
opened, and you will be like God, knowing
good and evil."
6 So when the woman [a]saw that the tree
was good for food, that it *was* pleasant to the
eyes, and a tree desirable to make *one* wise,
she took of its fruit [b]and ate. She also gave to
her husband with her, and he ate. 7 Then the
eyes of both of them were opened, [a]and they
knew that they *were* naked; and they sewed
fig leaves together and made themselves
coverings.
8 And they heard [a]the sound of the LORD
God walking in the garden in the cool of the
day, and Adam and his wife [b]hid themselves
from the presence of the LORD God among
the trees of the garden.
9 Then the LORD God called to Adam and
said to him, "Where *are* you?"
10 So he said, "I heard Your voice in the garden, [a]and I was afraid because I was naked;
and I hid myself."
11 And He said, "Who told you that you *were*
naked? Have you eaten from the tree of which
I commanded you that you should not eat?"
12 Then the man said, [a]"The woman whom
You gave *to be* with me, she gave me of the
tree, and I ate."
13 And the LORD God said to the woman,
"What *is* this you have done?"
The woman said, [a]"The serpent deceived
me, and I ate."
14 So the LORD God said to the serpent:

"Because you have done this,
You *are* cursed more than all cattle,
And more than every beast of the field;
On your belly you shall go,
And [a]you shall eat dust
All the days of your life.
15 And I will put enmity
Between you and the woman,

3:2 [a] Gen. 2:16, 17 3:3 [a] Ex. 19:12, 13 3:4 [a] [2 Cor. 11:3] 3:6 [a] 1 John 2:16 [b] 1 Tim. 2:14 3:7 [a] Gen. 2:25 3:8 [a] Job 38:1 [b] Job 31:33 3:10 [a] Gen. 2:25 3:12 [a] [Prov. 28:13] 3:13 [a] 2 Cor. 11:3 3:14 [a] Deut. 28:15–20

GOD'S IMAGE FOR OUR PEACE

And the LORD God formed man of the dust of the ground, and breathed into his nostrils the breath of life; and man became a living being.

GENESIS 2:7

In 1:26 we are told that God made humans in His image. Like all other living creatures in our world, our physical bodies consist of the minerals and elements found on earth. But unlike all other living creatures, humans were given life when God "breathed into" Adam "the breath of life" and he "became a living being" (2:7). This is why it's said that we are created in God's image and why it is so wrong to think of ourselves as mere two-legged animals.

You are the crown of God's special creation (Ps. 8:5). Nothing will ever diminish God's love for you or the value of your life in His eyes—and this absolute truth leads to His peace. When you look at the young child learning to take his first steps, to speak her first words, do you think, *Ah, there goes another mammal* or *animal*? When I look at my children, I see the hand of God. I see something beautifully made. I see something given reason, compassion, intelligence, and the ability to create beauty. Humans made in God's image are also made for peace.

And between [a]your seed and [b]her Seed;
[c]He shall bruise your head,
And you shall bruise His heel."

16 To the woman He said:

"I will greatly multiply your sorrow and
your conception;
[a]In pain you shall bring forth children;
[b]Your desire *shall be* for your husband,
And he shall [c]rule over you."

17 Then to Adam He said, [a]"Because you
have heeded the voice of your wife, and have
eaten from the tree [b]of which I commanded
you, saying, 'You shall not eat of it':

[c]"Cursed *is* the ground for your sake;
[d]In toil you shall eat *of* it
All the days of your life.
18 Both thorns and thistles it shall bring
forth for you,
And [a]you shall eat the herb of the field.
19 [a]In the sweat of your face you shall eat
bread
Till you return to the ground,
For out of it you were taken;
[b]For dust you *are,*
And [c]to dust you shall return."

20 And Adam called his wife's name [a]Eve,
because she was the mother of all living.
21 Also for Adam and his wife the LORD
God made tunics of skin, and clothed them.
22 Then the LORD God said, "Behold, the
man has become like one of Us, to know
good and evil. And now, lest he put out his
hand and take also of the tree of life, and eat,
and live forever"— 23 therefore the LORD God
sent him out of the garden of Eden [a]to till the
ground from which he was taken. 24 So [a]He
drove out the man; and He placed [b]cheru-
bim [c]at the east of the garden of Eden, and
a flaming sword which turned every way, to
guard the way to the tree of [d]life.

Cain Murders Abel

4 Now Adam knew Eve his wife, and she
conceived and bore Cain, and said, "I
have acquired a man from the LORD." 2 Then
she bore again, this time his brother Abel.
Now [a]Abel was a keeper of sheep, but Cain
was a tiller of the ground. 3 And in the process
of time it came to pass that Cain brought an
offering of the fruit [a]of the ground to the
LORD. 4 Abel also brought of [a]the firstborn
of his flock and of [b]their fat. And the LORD
[c]respected Abel and his offering, 5 but He did
not respect Cain and his offering. And Cain
was very angry, and his countenance fell.
6 So the LORD said to Cain, "Why are you angry? And why has your countenance fallen? 7 If
you do well, will you not be accepted? And if
you do not do well, sin lies at the door. And its
desire *is* for you, but you should rule over it."
8 Now Cain talked with Abel his brother;[1]
and it came to pass, when they were in the
field, that Cain rose up against Abel his
brother and [a]killed him.
9 Then the LORD said to Cain, "Where *is*
Abel your brother?"
He said, [a]"I do not know. *Am* I [b]my brother's
keeper?"
10 And He said, "What have you done? The
voice of your brother's blood [a]cries out to Me
from the ground. 11 So now [a]you *are* cursed
from the earth, which has opened its mouth
to receive your brother's blood from your
hand. 12 When you till the ground, it shall no
longer yield its strength to you. A fugitive
and a vagabond you shall be on the earth."
13 And Cain said to the LORD, "My punishment *is* greater than I can bear! 14 Surely You
have driven me out this day from the face of
the ground; [a]I shall be [b]hidden from Your
face; I shall be a fugitive and a vagabond on
the earth, and it will happen *that* [c]anyone
who finds me will kill me."
15 And the LORD said to him, "Therefore,[1]
whoever kills Cain, vengeance shall be taken on
him [a]sevenfold." And the LORD set a [b]mark on
Cain, lest anyone finding him should kill him.

The Family of Cain

16 Then Cain [a]went out from the [b]presence
of the LORD and dwelt in the land of Nod on
the east of Eden. 17 And Cain knew his wife,
and she conceived and bore Enoch. And he
built a city, [a]and called the name of the city
after the name of his son—Enoch. 18 To Enoch
was born Irad; and Irad begot Mehujael, and
Mehujael begot Methushael, and Methushael
begot Lamech.
19 Then Lamech took for himself [a]two wives:
the name of one *was* Adah, and the name of
the second *was* Zillah. 20 And Adah bore Jabal.

3:15 [a] John 8:44 [b] Is. 7:14 [c] Rom. 16:20 **3:16** [a] John 16:21 [b] Gen. 4:7 [c] 1 Cor. 11:3 **3:17** [a] 1 Sam. 15:23 [b] Gen. 2:17 [c] Rom. 8:20–22 [d] Eccl. 2:23 **3:18** [a] Ps. 104:14 **3:19** [a] 2 Thess. 3:10 [b] Gen. 2:7; 5:5 [c] Job 21:26 **3:20** [a] 2 Cor. 11:3 **3:23** [a] Gen. 4:2; 9:20 **3:24** [a] Ezek. 31:3, 11 [b] Ps. 104:4 [c] Gen. 2:8 [d] Gen. 2:9 **4:2** [a] Luke 11:50, 51 **4:3** [a] Num. 18:12 **4:4** [a] Num. 18:17 [b] Lev. 3:16 [c] Heb. 11:4 **4:8** [a] [1 John 3:12–15] [1] Samaritan Pentateuch, Septuagint, Syriac, and Vulgate add *"Let us go out to the field."* **4:9** [a] John 8:44 [b] 1 Cor. 8:11–13 **4:10** [a] Heb. 12:24 **4:11** [a] Gen. 3:14 **4:14** [a] Ps. 51:11 [b] Is. 1:15 [c] Num. 35:19, 21, 27 **4:15** [a] Gen. 4:24 [b] Ezek. 9:4, 6 [1] Following Masoretic Text and Targum; Septuagint, Syriac, and Vulgate read *Not so.* **4:16** [a] 2 Kin. 13:23; 24:20 [b] Jon. 1:3 **4:17** [a] Ps. 49:11 **4:19** [a] Gen. 2:24; 16:3

He was the father of those who dwell in tents
and have livestock. 21 His brother's name *was*
Jubal. He was the father of all those who play
the harp and flute. 22 And as for Zillah, she
also bore Tubal-Cain, an instructor of every
craftsman in bronze and iron. And the sister
of Tubal-Cain *was* Naamah.

23 Then Lamech said to his wives:

"Adah and Zillah, hear my voice;
Wives of Lamech, listen to my speech!
For I have killed a man for wounding me,
Even a young man for hurting me.
24 [a]If Cain shall be avenged sevenfold,
Then Lamech seventy-sevenfold."

A New Son

25 And Adam knew his wife again, and she
bore a son and [a]named him Seth, "For God
has appointed another seed for me instead
of Abel, whom Cain killed." 26 And as for Seth,
[a]to him also a son was born; and he named
him Enosh.[1] Then *men* began [b]to call on the
name of the LORD.

The Family of Adam

5 This is the book of the [a]genealogy of
Adam. In the day that God created man,
He made him in [b]the likeness of God. 2 He
created them [a]male and female, and [b]blessed
them and called them Mankind in the day
they were created. 3 And Adam lived one
hundred and thirty years, and begot *a son*
[a]in his own likeness, after his image, and
[b]named him Seth. 4 After he begot Seth, [a]the
days of Adam were eight hundred years;
[b]and he had sons and daughters. 5 So all the
days that Adam lived were nine hundred and
thirty years; [a]and he died.

6 Seth lived one hundred and five years,
and begot [a]Enosh. 7 After he begot Enosh,
Seth lived eight hundred and seven years,
and had sons and daughters. 8 So all the days
of Seth were nine hundred and twelve years;
and he died.

9 Enosh lived ninety years, and begot Cainan.[1] 10 After he begot Cainan, Enosh lived
eight hundred and fifteen years, and had sons
and daughters. 11 So all the days of Enosh were
nine hundred and five years; and he died.

12 Cainan lived seventy years, and begot
Mahalalel. 13 After he begot Mahalalel, Cainan
lived eight hundred and forty years, and had
sons and daughters. 14 So all the days of Cainan
were nine hundred and ten years; and he died.

15 Mahalalel lived sixty-five years, and begot Jared. 16 After he begot Jared, Mahalalel
lived eight hundred and thirty years, and had
sons and daughters. 17 So all the days of Mahalalel were eight hundred and ninety-five
years; and he died.

18 Jared lived one hundred and sixty-two
years, and begot [a]Enoch. 19 After he begot
Enoch, Jared lived eight hundred years, and
had sons and daughters. 20 So all the days
of Jared were nine hundred and sixty-two
years; and he died.

21 Enoch lived sixty-five years, and begot
Methuselah. 22 After he begot Methuselah,
Enoch [a]walked with God three hundred years,
and had sons and daughters. 23 So all the days
of Enoch were three hundred and sixty-five
years. 24 And [a]Enoch walked with God; and
he *was* not, for God [b]took him.

25 Methuselah lived one hundred and
eighty-seven years, and begot Lamech. 26 After he begot Lamech, Methuselah lived seven
hundred and eighty-two years, and had sons
and daughters. 27 So all the days of Methuselah were nine hundred and sixty-nine years;
and he died.

28 Lamech lived one hundred and eighty-
two years, and had a son. 29 And he called his
name [a]Noah, saying, "This *one* will comfort
us concerning our work and the toil of our
hands, because of the ground [b]which the
LORD has cursed." 30 After he begot Noah,
Lamech lived five hundred and ninety-five
years, and had sons and daughters. 31 So all
the days of Lamech were seven hundred and
seventy-seven years; and he died.

32 And Noah was five hundred years old,
and Noah begot [a]Shem, Ham, [b]and Japheth.

PEACE NOTE

If I want to know practical ways to live in God's peace, the Bible offers many!

4:24 [a] Gen. 4:15 **4:25** [a] Gen. 5:3 **4:26** [a] Gen. 5:6 [b] Zeph. 3:9 [1] Greek *Enos* **5:1** [a] Gen. 2:4; 6:9 [b] Gen. 1:26; 9:6 **5:2** [a] Mark 10:6 [b] Gen. 1:28; 9:1 **5:3** [a] 1 Cor. 15:48, 49 [b] Gen. 4:25 **5:4** [a] Luke 3:36–38 [b] Gen. 1:28; 4:25 **5:5** [a] [Heb. 9:27] **5:6** [a] Gen. 4:26 **5:9** [1] Hebrew *Qenan* **5:18** [a] Jude 14, 15 **5:22** [a] Gen. 6:9; 17:1; 24:40; 48:15 **5:24** [a] 2 Kin. 2:11 [b] Heb. 11:5 **5:29** [a] Luke 3:36 [b] Gen. 3:17–19; 4:11 **5:32** [a] Gen. 6:10; 7:13 [b] Gen. 10:21

The Wickedness and Judgment of Man

6 Now it came to pass, [a]when men began to multiply on the face of the earth, and daughters were born to them, 2 that the sons of God saw the daughters of men, that they *were* beautiful; and they [a]took wives for themselves of all whom they chose.

3 And the LORD said, [a]"My Spirit shall not [b]strive[1] with man forever, [c]for he *is* indeed flesh; yet his days shall be one hundred and twenty years." 4 There were giants on the earth in those [a]days, and also afterward, when the sons of God came in to the daughters of men and they bore *children* to them. Those *were* the mighty men who *were* of old, men of renown.

5 Then the LORD[1] saw that the wickedness of man *was* great in the earth, and *that* every [a]intent of the thoughts of his heart *was* only evil continually. 6 And [a]the LORD was sorry that He had made man on the earth, and [b]He was grieved in His [c]heart. 7 So the LORD said, "I will [a]destroy man whom I have created from the face of the earth, both man and beast, creeping thing and birds of the air, for I am sorry that I have made them." 8 But Noah [a]found grace in the eyes of the LORD.

Noah Pleases God

9 This is the genealogy of Noah. [a]Noah was a just man, perfect in his generations. Noah [b]walked with God. 10 And Noah begot three sons: [a]Shem, Ham, and Japheth.

11 The earth also was corrupt [a]before God, and the earth was [b]filled with violence. 12 So God [a]looked upon the earth, and indeed it was corrupt; for [b]all flesh had corrupted their way on the earth.

The Ark Prepared

13 And God said to Noah, [a]"The end of all flesh has come before Me, for the earth is filled with violence through them; [b]and behold, [c]I will destroy them with the earth. 14 Make yourself an ark of gopherwood; make rooms in the ark, and cover it inside and outside with pitch. 15 And this is how you shall make it: The length of the ark *shall be* three hundred cubits, its width fifty cubits, and its height thirty cubits. 16 You shall make a window for the ark, and you shall finish it to a cubit from above; and set the door of the ark in its side. You shall make it *with* lower, second, and third *decks*. 17 [a]And behold, I Myself am bringing [b]floodwaters on the earth, to destroy from under heaven all flesh in which *is* the breath of life; everything that *is* on the earth shall [c]die. 18 But I will establish My [a]covenant with you; and [b]you shall go into the ark—you, your sons, your wife, and your sons' wives with you. 19 And of every living thing of all flesh you shall bring [a]two of every *sort* into the ark, to keep *them* alive with you; they shall be male and female. 20 Of the birds after their kind, of animals after their kind, and of every creeping thing of the earth after its kind, two of every *kind* [a]will come to you to keep *them* alive. 21 And you shall take for yourself of all food that is eaten, and you shall gather *it* to yourself; and it shall be food for you and for them."

22 [a]Thus Noah did; [b]according to all that [c]God commanded him, so he did.

The Great Flood

7 Then the [a]LORD said to Noah, [b]"Come into the ark, you and all your household, because I have seen *that* [c]you *are* righteous before Me in this generation. 2 You shall take with you seven each of every [a]clean animal, a male and his female; [b]two each of animals that *are* unclean, a male and his female; 3 also seven each of birds of the air, male and female, to keep the species alive on the face of all the earth. 4 For after [a]seven more days I will cause it to rain on the earth [b]forty days and forty nights, and I will destroy from the face of the earth all living things that I have made." 5 [a]And Noah did according to all that the LORD commanded him. 6 Noah *was* [a]six hundred years old when the floodwaters were on the earth.

7 [a]So Noah, with his sons, his wife, and his sons' wives, went into the ark because of the waters of the flood. 8 Of clean animals, of animals that *are* unclean, of birds, and of everything that creeps on the earth, 9 two by two they went into the ark to Noah, male and female, as God had commanded Noah. 10 And it came to pass after seven days that the waters of the flood were on the earth. 11 In the six hundredth year of Noah's life, in the second month, the seventeenth day of the month, on [a]that day all [b]the fountains of the great deep were broken up, and the [c]windows

6:1 [a] Gen. 1:28 **6:2** [a] Deut. 7:3, 4 **6:3** [a] [Gal. 5:16, 17] [b] 2 Thess. 2:7 [c] Ps. 78:39 [1] Septuagint, Syriac, Targum, and Vulgate read *abide*. **6:4** [a] Num. 13:32, 33 **6:5** [a] Gen. 8:21 [1] Following Masoretic Text and Targum; Vulgate reads *God;* Septuagint reads *LORD God.* **6:6** [a] 1 Sam. 15:11, 29 [b] Is. 63:10 [c] Mark 3:5 **6:7** [a] Gen. 7:4, 23 **6:8** [a] Gen. 19:19 **6:9** [a] 2 Pet. 2:5 [b] Gen. 5:22, 24 **6:10** [a] Gen. 5:32; 7:13 **6:11** [a] Rom. 2:13 [b] Ezek. 8:17 **6:12** [a] Ps. 14:2; 53:2, 3 [b] Ps. 14:1–3 **6:13** [a] 1 Pet. 4:7 [b] Gen. 6:17 [c] 2 Pet. 2:4–10 **6:17** [a] 2 Pet. 2:5 [b] 2 Pet. 3:6 [c] Luke 16:22 **6:18** [a] Gen. 8:20—9:17; 17:7 [b] Gen. 7:1, 7, 13 **6:19** [a] Gen. 7:2, 8, 9, 14–16 **6:20** [a] Gen. 7:9, 15 **6:22** [a] Gen. 7:5; 12:4, 5 [b] Gen. 7:5, 9, 16 [c] [1 John 5:3] **7:1** [a] Matt. 11:28 [b] Matt. 24:38 [c] Gen. 6:9 **7:2** [a] Lev. 11 [b] Lev. 10:10 **7:4** [a] Gen. 7:10 [b] Gen. 7:12, 17 **7:5** [a] Gen. 6:22 **7:6** [a] Gen. 5:4, 32 **7:7** [a] Matt. 24:38 **7:11** [a] Matt. 24:39 [b] Gen. 8:2 [c] Ps. 78:23

of heaven were opened. 12[a]And the rain was on the earth forty days and forty nights.

13On the very same day Noah and Noah's sons, Shem, Ham, and Japheth, and Noah's wife and the three wives of his sons with them, entered the ark— 14[a]they and every beast after its kind, all cattle after their kind, every creeping thing that creeps on the earth after its kind, and every bird after its kind, every bird of every [b]sort. 15And they [a]went into the ark to Noah, two by two, of all flesh in which *is* the breath of life. 16So those that entered, male and female of all flesh, went in [a]as God had commanded him; and the LORD shut him in.

17[a]Now the flood was on the earth forty days. The waters increased and lifted up the ark, and it rose high above the earth. 18The waters prevailed and greatly increased on the earth, [a]and the ark moved about on the surface of the waters. 19And the waters prevailed exceedingly on the earth, and all the high hills under the whole heaven were covered. 20The waters prevailed fifteen cubits upward, and the mountains were covered. 21[a]And all flesh died that moved on the earth: birds and cattle and beasts and every creeping thing that creeps on the earth, and every man. 22All in [a]whose nostrils *was* the breath of the spirit[1] of life, all that *was* on the dry *land,* died. 23So He destroyed all living things which were on the face of the ground: both man and cattle, creeping thing and bird of the air. They were destroyed from the earth. Only [a]Noah and those who *were* with him in the ark remained *alive.* 24[a]And the waters prevailed on the earth one hundred and fifty days.

Noah's Deliverance

8 Then God [a]remembered Noah, and every living thing, and all the animals that *were* with him in the ark. [b]And God made a wind to pass over the earth, and the waters subsided. 2[a]The fountains of the deep and the windows of heaven were also [b]stopped, and [c]the rain from heaven was restrained. 3And the waters receded continually from the earth. At the end [a]of the hundred and fifty days the waters decreased. 4Then the ark rested in the seventh month, the seventeenth day of the month, on the mountains of Ararat. 5And the waters decreased continually until the tenth month. In the tenth *month,* on the first *day* of the month, the tops of the mountains were seen.

6So it came to pass, at the end of forty days, that Noah opened [a]the window of the ark which he had made. 7Then he sent out a raven, which kept going to and fro until the waters had dried up from the earth. 8He also sent out from himself a dove, to see if the waters had receded from the face of the ground. 9But the dove found no resting place for the sole of her foot, and she returned into the ark to him, for the waters *were* on the face of the whole earth. So he put out his hand and took her, and drew her into the ark to himself. 10And he waited yet another seven days, and again he sent the dove out from the ark. 11Then the dove came to him in the evening, and behold, a freshly plucked olive leaf *was* in her mouth; and Noah knew that the waters had receded from the earth. 12So he waited yet another seven days and sent out the dove, which did not return again to him anymore.

13And it came to pass in the six hundred and first year, in the first *month,* the first *day* of the month, that the waters were dried up from the earth; and Noah removed the covering of the ark and looked, and indeed the surface of the ground was dry. 14And in the second month, on the twenty-seventh day of the month, the earth was dried.

15Then God spoke to Noah, saying, 16"Go out of the ark, [a]you and your wife, and your sons and your sons' wives with you. 17Bring out with you every living thing of all flesh that *is* with you: birds and cattle and every creeping thing that creeps on the earth, so that they may abound on the earth, and [a]be fruitful and multiply on the earth." 18So Noah went out, and his sons and his wife and his sons' wives with him. 19Every animal, every creeping thing, every bird, *and* whatever creeps on the earth, according to their families, went out of the ark.

God's Covenant with Creation

20Then Noah built an [a]altar to the LORD, and took of [b]every clean animal and of every clean bird, and offered [c]burnt offerings on the altar. 21And the LORD smelled [a]a soothing aroma. Then the LORD said in His heart, "I will never again [b]curse the ground for man's sake, although the [c]imagination of man's heart *is* evil from his youth; [d]nor will I again destroy every living thing as I have done.

22 "While the earth [a]remains,
Seedtime and harvest,
Cold and heat,
Winter and summer,
And [b]day and night
Shall not cease."

7:12 [a] Gen. 7:4, 17 7:14 [a] Gen. 6:19 [b] Gen. 1:21 7:15 [a] Gen. 6:19, 20; 7:9 7:16 [a] Gen. 7:2, 3 7:17 [a] Gen. 7:4, 12; 8:6 7:18 [a] Ps. 104:26 7:21 [a] Gen. 6:7, 13, 17; 7:4 7:22 [a] Gen. 2:7 [1] Septuagint and Vulgate omit *of the spirit.* 7:23 [a] 2 Pet. 2:5 7:24 [a] Gen. 8:3, 4 8:1 [a] Gen. 19:29 [b] Ex. 14:21; 15:10 8:2 [a] Gen. 7:11 [b] Deut. 11:17 [c] Job 38:37 8:3 [a] Gen. 7:24 8:6 [a] Gen. 6:16 8:16 [a] Gen. 7:13 8:17 [a] Gen. 1:22, 28; 9:1, 7 8:20 [a] Gen. 12:7 [b] Lev. 11 [c] Ex. 10:25 8:21 [a] Ex. 29:18, 25 [b] Gen. 3:17; 6:7, 13, 17 [c] Gen. 6:5; 11:6 [d] Gen. 9:11, 15 8:22 [a] Is. 54:9 [b] Jer. 33:20, 25

9 So God blessed Noah and his sons, and
said to them: [a]"Be fruitful and multiply,
and fill the earth.[1] 2 [a]And the fear of you and
the dread of you shall be on every beast of
the earth, on every bird of the air, on all that
move *on* the earth, and on all the fish of the
sea. They are given into your hand. 3 [a]Every
moving thing that lives shall be food for
you. I have given you [b]all things, even as
the [c]green herbs. 4 [a]But you shall not eat
flesh with its life, *that is,* its blood. 5 Surely
for your lifeblood I will demand *a reckoning;*
[a]from the hand of every beast I will require
it, and [b]from the hand of man. From the
hand of every [c]man's brother I will require
the life of man.

6 "Whoever [a]sheds man's blood,
By man his blood shall be shed;
[b]For in the image of God
He made man.
7 And as for you, [a]be fruitful and
multiply;
Bring forth abundantly in the earth
And multiply in it."

8 Then God spoke to Noah and to his sons
with him, saying: 9 "And as for Me, [a]behold,
I establish [b]My covenant with you and with
your descendants[1] after you, 10 [a]and with every living creature that *is* with you: the birds,
the cattle, and every beast of the earth with
you, of all that go out of the ark, every beast
of the earth. 11 Thus [a]I establish My covenant
with you: Never again shall all flesh be cut
off by the waters of the flood; never again
shall there be a flood to destroy the earth."
12 And God said: [a]"This *is* the sign of the
covenant which I make between Me and you,
and every living creature that *is* with you, for
perpetual generations: 13 I set [a]My rainbow in
the cloud, and it shall be for the sign of the covenant between Me and the earth. 14 It shall be,
when I bring a cloud over the earth, that the
rainbow shall be seen in the cloud; 15 and [a]I will
remember My covenant which *is* between Me
and you and every living creature of all flesh;
the waters shall never again become a flood
to destroy all flesh. 16 The rainbow shall be in
the cloud, and I will look on it to remember
[a]the everlasting covenant between God and
every living creature of all flesh that *is* on the
earth." 17 And God said to Noah, "This *is* the
sign of the covenant which I have established
between Me and all flesh that *is* on the earth."

Noah and His Sons

18 Now the sons of Noah who went out of
the ark were Shem, Ham, and Japheth. [a]And
Ham *was* the father of Canaan. 19 [a]These three
were the sons of Noah, [b]and from these the
whole earth was populated.

9:1 [a] Gen. 1:28, 29; 8:17; 9:7, 19; 10:32 [1] Compare Genesis 1:28 **9:2** [a] Ps. 8:6 **9:3** [a] Deut. 12:15; 14:3, 9, 11 [b] Rom. 14:14, 20 [c] Gen. 1:29 **9:4** [a] 1 Sam. 14:33, 34 **9:5** [a] Ex. 21:28 [b] Gen. 4:9, 10 [c] Acts 17:26 **9:6** [a] Lev. 24:17 [b] Gen. 1:26, 27 **9:7** [a] Gen. 9:1, 19 **9:9** [a] Gen. 6:18 [b] Is. 54:9 [1] Literally *seed* **9:10** [a] Ps. 145:9 **9:11** [a] Is. 54:9 **9:12** [a] Gen. 9:13, 17; 17:11 **9:13** [a] Ezek. 1:28 **9:15** [a] Lev. 26:42, 45 **9:16** [a] Gen. 17:13, 19 **9:18** [a] Gen. 9:25–27; 10:6 **9:19** [a] Gen. 5:32 [b] 1 Chr. 1:4

GOD'S SIGN OF PEACE

"Behold, I establish My covenant with you . . . I set My rainbow in the cloud, and it shall be for the sign of the covenant between Me and the earth."

GENESIS 9:9, 13

God's judgment upon the generation of Noah gives me a sense of peace. Why is that? Because in this story we see God's gracious forgiveness at its best. Humanity had become so violent and so sinful that God actually regretted that He created it (6:5–6). Can you imagine that? Though made in God's image we had become so wicked, so perverse that God wished He had stopped His work of creation at the end of day five! So God opened the floodgates and brought a dreadful judgment.

Yet a man named Noah found favor in God's sight. That's why the flood story gives me a sense of hope, and with it, a sense of peace. If humanity can be so bad that God regrets creating us—yet gives us a second chance!—then He is truly a God of grace and mercy. And that gives me great peace. With the sign of the rainbow, God assures us that He will never again destroy the earth with a flood. Remember that the next time you see a rainbow.

What gives you a sense of peace? How can you access it more often?

20 And Noah began *to be* [a]a farmer, and he
planted a vineyard. 21 Then he drank of the
wine [a]and was drunk, and became uncovered
in his tent. 22 And Ham, the father of Canaan,
saw the nakedness of his father, and told his
two brothers outside. 23 [a]But Shem and Japheth
took a garment, laid *it* on both their shoulders,
and went backward and covered the nakedness
of their father. Their faces *were* turned away,
and they did not see their father's nakedness.
24 So Noah awoke from his wine, and knew
what his younger son had done to him.
25 Then he said:

[a]"Cursed *be* Canaan;
A [b]servant of servants
He shall be to his brethren."

26 And he said:

[a]"Blessed *be* the LORD,
The God of Shem,
And may Canaan be his servant.
27 May God [a]enlarge Japheth,
[b]And may he dwell in the tents of Shem;
And may Canaan be his servant."

28 And Noah lived after the flood three
hundred and fifty years. 29 So all the days
of Noah were nine hundred and fifty years;
and he died.

Nations Descended from Noah

10 Now this *is* the genealogy of the sons
of Noah: Shem, Ham, and Japheth.
[a]And sons were born to them after the flood.
2 [a]The sons of Japheth *were* Gomer, Magog,
Madai, Javan, Tubal, Meshech, and Tiras.
3 The sons of Gomer *were* Ashkenaz, Riphath,[1]
and Togarmah. 4 The sons of Javan *were* Elishah, Tarshish, Kittim, and Dodanim.[1] 5 From
these [a]the coastland *peoples* of the Gentiles
were separated into their lands, everyone
according to his language, according to their
families, into their nations.
6 [a]The sons of Ham *were* Cush, Mizraim,
Put,[1] and Canaan. 7 The sons of Cush *were* Seba,
Havilah, Sabtah, Raamah, and Sabtechah; and
the sons of Raamah *were* Sheba and Dedan.
8 Cush begot [a]Nimrod; he began to be a
mighty one on the earth. 9 He was a mighty
[a]hunter [b]before the LORD; therefore it is said,
"Like Nimrod the mighty hunter before the
LORD." 10 [a]And the beginning of his kingdom
was [b]Babel, Erech, Accad, and Calneh, in
the land of Shinar. 11 From that land he went
[a]to Assyria and built Nineveh, Rehoboth Ir,
Calah, 12 and Resen between Nineveh and
Calah (that *is* the principal city).
13 Mizraim begot Ludim, Anamim, Lehabim,
Naphtuhim, 14 Pathrusim, and Casluhim [a](from
whom came the Philistines and Caphtorim).
15 Canaan begot Sidon his firstborn, and
[a]Heth; 16 [a]the Jebusite, the Amorite, and the
Girgashite; 17 the Hivite, the Arkite, and the
Sinite; 18 the Arvadite, the Zemarite, and the
Hamathite. Afterward the families of the Canaanites were dispersed. 19 [a]And the border
of the Canaanites was from Sidon as you go
toward Gerar, as far as Gaza; then as you go toward Sodom, Gomorrah, Admah, and Zeboiim,
as far as Lasha. 20 These *were* the sons of Ham,
according to their families, according to their
languages, in their lands *and* in their nations.
21 And *children* were born also to Shem, the
father of all the children of Eber, the brother of
Japheth the elder. 22 The [a]sons of Shem *were*
Elam, Asshur, [b]Arphaxad, Lud, and Aram.
23 The sons of Aram *were* Uz, Hul, Gether, and
Mash.[1] 24 Arphaxad begot [a]Salah,[1] and Salah
begot Eber. 25 [a]To Eber were born two sons:
the name of one *was* Peleg, for in his days the
earth was divided; and his brother's name *was*
Joktan. 26 Joktan begot Almodad, Sheleph,
Hazarmaveth, Jerah, 27 Hadoram, Uzal, Diklah,
28 Obal,[1] Abimael, Sheba, 29 Ophir, Havilah, and
Jobab. All these *were* the sons of Joktan. 30 And
their dwelling place was from Mesha as you
go toward Sephar, the mountain of the east.
31 These *were* the sons of Shem, according to
their families, according to their languages, in
their lands, according to their nations.
32 [a]These *were* the families of the sons of
Noah, according to their generations, in their
nations; [b]and from these the nations were
divided on the earth after the flood.

The Tower of Babel

11 Now the whole earth had one language
and one speech. 2 And it came to pass, as
they journeyed from the east, that they found
a plain in the land [a]of Shinar, and they dwelt
there. 3 Then they said to one another, "Come,
let us make bricks and bake *them* thoroughly."

9:20 [a] Gen. 3:19, 23; 4:2 **9:21** [a] Prov. 20:1 **9:23** [a] Ex. 20:12 **9:25** [a] Deut. 27:16 [b] Josh. 9:23 **9:26** [a] Gen. 14:20; 24:27 **9:27** [a] Gen. 10:2–5; 39:3 [b] Eph. 2:13, 14; 3:6 **10:1** [a] Gen. 9:1, 7, 19 **10:2** [a] 1 Chr. 1:5–7 **10:3** [1] Spelled *Diphath* in 1 Chronicles 1:6 **10:4** [1] Spelled *Rodanim* in Samaritan Pentateuch and 1 Chronicles 1:7 **10:5** [a] Ps. 72:10 **10:6** [a] 1 Chr. 1:8–16 [1] Or *Phut* **10:8** [a] Mic. 5:6 **10:9** [a] Jer. 16:16 [b] Gen. 21:20 **10:10** [a] Mic. 5:6 [b] Gen. 11:9 **10:11** [a] Mic. 5:6 **10:14** [a] 1 Chr. 1:12 **10:15** [a] Gen. 23:3 **10:16** [a] Gen. 14:7; 15:19–21 **10:19** [a] Num. 34:2–12 **10:22** [a] 1 Chr. 1:17–28 [b] Luke 3:36 **10:23** [1] Called *Meshech* in Septuagint and 1 Chronicles 1:17 **10:24** [a] Gen. 11:12 [1] Following Masoretic Text, Vulgate, and Targum; Septuagint reads *Arphaxad begot Cainan, and Cainan begot Salah* (compare Luke 3:35, 36). **10:25** [a] 1 Chr. 1:19 **10:28** [1] Spelled *Ebal* in 1 Chronicles 1:22 **10:32** [a] Gen. 10:1 [b] Gen. 9:19; 11:8 **11:2** [a] Gen. 10:10; 14:1

They had brick for stone, and they had as-
phalt for mortar. 4 And they said, "Come, let
us build ourselves a city, and a tower [a]whose
top *is* in the heavens; let us make a [b]name
for ourselves, lest we [c]be scattered abroad
over the face of the whole earth."
5 [a]But the LORD came down to see the city
and the tower which the sons of men had built.
6 And the LORD said, "Indeed [a]the people *are*
one and they all have [b]one language, and this
is what they begin to do; now nothing that they
[c]propose to do will be withheld from them.
7 Come, [a]let Us go down and there [b]confuse
their language, that they may not understand
one another's speech." 8 So [a]the LORD scattered them abroad from there [b]over the face of
all the earth, and they ceased building the city.
9 Therefore its name is called Babel, [a]because
there the LORD confused the language of all
the earth; and from there the LORD scattered
them abroad over the face of all the earth.

Shem's Descendants

10 [a]This *is* the genealogy of Shem: Shem *was*
one hundred years old, and begot Arphaxad
two years after the flood. 11 After he begot Arphaxad, Shem lived five hundred years, and
begot sons and daughters.
12 Arphaxad lived thirty-five years, [a]and
begot Salah. 13 After he begot Salah, Arphaxad lived four hundred and three years, and
begot sons and daughters.
14 Salah lived thirty years, and begot Eber.
15 After he begot Eber, Salah lived four hundred
and three years, and begot sons and daughters.
16 [a]Eber lived thirty-four years, and begot
[b]Peleg. 17 After he begot Peleg, Eber lived four
hundred and thirty years, and begot sons
and daughters.
18 Peleg lived thirty years, and begot Reu.
19 After he begot Reu, Peleg lived two hundred
and nine years, and begot sons and daughters.
20 Reu lived thirty-two years, and begot
[a]Serug. 21 After he begot Serug, Reu lived two
hundred and seven years, and begot sons
and daughters.
22 Serug lived thirty years, and begot Nahor.
23 After he begot Nahor, Serug lived two hundred years, and begot sons and daughters.
24 Nahor lived twenty-nine years, and begot
[a]Terah. 25 After he begot Terah, Nahor lived
one hundred and nineteen years, and begot
sons and daughters.
26 Now Terah lived seventy years, and [a]be-
got Abram, Nahor, and Haran.

Terah's Descendants

27 This *is* the genealogy of Terah: Terah
begot [a]Abram, Nahor, and Haran. Haran
begot Lot. 28 And Haran died before his father Terah in his native land, in Ur of the
Chaldeans. 29 Then Abram and Nahor took
wives: the name of Abram's wife *was* [a]Sarai,
and the name of Nahor's wife, [b]Milcah, the
daughter of Haran the father of Milcah and
the father of Iscah. 30 But [a]Sarai was barren;
she had no child.
31 And Terah [a]took his son Abram and
his grandson Lot, the son of Haran, and his
daughter-in-law Sarai, his son Abram's wife,
and they went out with them from [b]Ur of the
Chaldeans to go to [c]the land of Canaan; and
they came to Haran and dwelt there. 32 So
the days of Terah were two hundred and five
years, and Terah died in Haran.

Promises to Abram

12 Now the [a]LORD had said to Abram:

"Get [b]out of your country,
From your family
And from your father's house,
To a land that I will show you.
2 [a]I will make you a great nation;
[b]I will bless you
And make your name great;
[c]And you shall be a blessing.
3 [a]I will bless those who bless you,
And I will curse him who curses
you;
And in [b]you all the families of the earth
shall be [c]blessed."

PEACE NOTE

Faith is moving forward through uncertainty. Faith is tolerant of uncertainty. This leads to peace.

GENESIS 12:1-4

11:4 [a] Deut. 1:28; 9:1 [b] Gen. 6:4 [c] Deut. 4:27 **11:5** [a] Gen. 18:21 **11:6** [a] Gen. 9:19 [b] Gen. 11:1 [c] Ps. 2:1 **11:7** [a] Gen. 1:26 [b] Ex. 4:11 **11:8** [a] [Luke 1:51] [b] Gen. 10:25, 32 **11:9** [a] 1 Cor. 14:23 **11:10** [a] Gen. 10:22–25 **11:12** [a] Luke 3:35 **11:16** [a] 1 Chr. 1:19 [b] Luke 3:35 **11:20** [a] Luke 3:35 **11:24** [a] Josh. 24:2 **11:26** [a] 1 Chr. 1:26 **11:27** [a] Gen. 11:31; 17:5 **11:29** [a] Gen. 17:15; 20:12 [b] Gen. 22:20, 23; 24:15 **11:30** [a] Gen. 16:1, 2 **11:31** [a] Gen. 12:1 [b] Acts 7:4 [c] Gen. 10:19 **12:1** [a] Acts 7:2, 3 [b] Gen. 13:9 **12:2** [a] Deut. 26:5 [b] Gen. 22:17; 24:35 [c] Gen. 28:4 **12:3** [a] Num. 24:9 [b] Acts 3:25; [Gal. 3:8] [c] Is. 41:27

LIVING BY THE PROMISE

"I will bless those who bless you . . . and in you all the families of the earth shall be blessed."

GENESIS 12:3

When I move from one city or state to another, I usually have mixed feelings. A big move is unsettling; it can also create anticipation, even excitement. But I never make a move unless I have a very good idea of where I am going and why. Not knowing where or why would rob me of peace.

This is why Abram so impresses me. God called him to take his family and go to a land that He would show him. Only God's call was clear—the destination was completely mysterious. Abram and his family must have wondered, *Who is this God who is telling me to uproot and travel without a clear purpose?* Abram, his late father, Terah, and everybody they knew worshiped many gods. Who was this one God who commanded him to leave his homeland, a rare and risky move?

Perhaps the key is that God didn't just tell Abram to go, He promised to bless him—as well as "all the families of the earth." Abram decided to trust this God. Ultimately, his obedience provided a family line that delivered the Prince of Peace!

If God told you to uproot from everything familiar to serve Him in a distant place, would you do it?

4 So Abram departed as the LORD had spoken to him, and Lot went with him. And Abram
was seventy-five years old when he departed
from Haran. 5 Then Abram took Sarai his wife
and Lot his brother's son, and all their possessions that they had gathered, and [a]the people
whom they had acquired [b]in Haran, and they
[c]departed to go to the land of Canaan. So they
came to the land of Canaan. 6 Abram [a]passed
through the land to the place of Shechem, [b]as
far as the terebinth tree of Moreh.[1] [c]And the
Canaanites *were* then in the land.
7 [a]Then the LORD appeared to Abram and
said, [b]"To your descendants I will give this land."
And there he built an [c]altar to the LORD, who
had appeared to him. 8 And he moved from
there to the mountain east of Bethel, and he
pitched his tent *with* Bethel on the west and Ai
on the east; there he built an altar to the LORD
and [a]called on the name of the LORD. 9 So Abram
journeyed, [a]going on still toward the South.[1]

Abram in Egypt

10 Now there was [a]a famine in the land, and
Abram [b]went down to Egypt to dwell there,
for the famine *was* [c]severe in the land. 11 And
it came to pass, when he was close to entering
Egypt, that he said to Sarai his wife, "Indeed
I know that you *are* [a]a woman of beautiful
countenance. 12 Therefore it will happen,
when the Egyptians see you, that they will say,
'This *is* his wife'; and they [a]will kill me, but
they will let you live. 13 [a]Please say you *are* my
[b]sister, that it may be well with me for your
sake, and that I[1] may live because of you."
14 So it was, when Abram came into Egypt,
that the Egyptians saw the woman, that she
was very beautiful. 15 The princes of Pharaoh
also saw her and commended her to Pharaoh. And the woman was taken to Pharaoh's
house. 16 He [a]treated Abram well for her sake.
He [b]had sheep, oxen, male donkeys, male and
female servants, female donkeys, and camels.
17 But the LORD [a]plagued Pharaoh and his
house with great plagues because of Sarai,
Abram's wife. 18 And Pharaoh called Abram
and said, [a]"What *is* this you have done to me?
Why did you not tell me that she *was* your
wife? 19 Why did you say, 'She *is* my sister'? I
might have taken her as my wife. Now therefore, here is your wife; take *her* and go your
way." 20 [a]So Pharaoh commanded *his* men
concerning him; and they sent him away,
with his wife and all that he had.

12:5 [a] Gen. 14:14 [b] Gen. 11:31 [c] Gen. 13:18 **12:6** [a] Heb. 11:9 [b] Deut. 11:30 [c] Gen. 10:18, 19 [1] Hebrew *Alon Moreh*
12:7 [a] Gen. 17:1; 18:1 [b] Gen. 13:15; 15:18; 17:8; Acts 7:5; Gal. 3:16 [c] Gen. 13:4, 18; 22:9 **12:8** [a] Gen. 4:26; 13:4; 21:33
12:9 [a] Gen. 13:1, 3; 20:1; 24:62 [1] Hebrew *Negev* **12:10** [a] Gen. 26:1 [b] Ps. 105:13 [c] Gen. 43:1 **12:11** [a] Gen. 12:14; 26:7; 29:17
12:12 [a] Gen. 20:11; 26:7 **12:13** [a] Gen. 20:1–18; 26:6–11 [b] Gen. 20:12 [1] Literally *my soul* **12:16** [a] Gen. 20:14 [b] Gen. 13:2
12:17 [a] 1 Chr. 16:21 **12:18** [a] Gen. 20:9, 10; 26:10 **12:20** [a] [Prov. 21:1]

Abram Inherits Canaan

13 Then Abram went up from Egypt, he
and his wife and all that he had, and
[a]Lot with him, [b]to the South.[1] 2 [a]Abram *was*
very rich in livestock, in silver, and in gold.
3 And he went on his journey [a]from the South
as far as Bethel, to the place where his tent
had been at the beginning, between Bethel
and Ai, 4 to the [a]place of the altar which he
had made there at first. And there Abram
[b]called on the name of the LORD.

5 Lot also, who went with Abram, had flocks
and herds and tents. 6 Now [a]the land was not
able to support them, that they might dwell
together, for their possessions were so great
that they could not dwell together. 7 And
there was [a]strife between the herdsmen of
Abram's livestock and the herdsmen of Lot's
livestock. [b]The Canaanites and the Perizzites
then dwelt in the land.

8 So Abram said to Lot, [a]"Please let there be
no strife between you and me, and between
my herdsmen and your herdsmen; for we
are brethren. 9 [a]*Is* not the whole land before
you? Please [b]separate from me. [c]If *you take*
the left, then I will go to the right; or, if *you*
go to the right, then I will go to the left."

10 And Lot lifted his eyes and saw all [a]the
plain of Jordan, that it *was* well watered
everywhere (before the LORD [b]destroyed
Sodom and Gomorrah) [c]like the garden of
the LORD, like the land of Egypt as you go
toward [d]Zoar. 11 Then Lot chose for himself all
the plain of Jordan, and Lot journeyed east.
And they separated from each other. 12 Abram
dwelt in the land of Canaan, and Lot [a]dwelt
in the cities of the plain and [b]pitched *his*
tent even as far as Sodom. 13 But the men of
Sodom [a]*were* exceedingly wicked and [b]sinful
against the LORD.

14 And the LORD said to Abram, after Lot
[a]had separated from him: "Lift your eyes
now and look from the place where you
are—[b]northward, southward, eastward, and
westward; 15 for all the land which you see [a]I
give to you and [b]your descendants[1] forever. 16 And [a]I will make your descendants as
the dust of the earth; so that if a man could
number the dust of the earth, *then* your descendants also could be numbered. 17 Arise,
walk in the land through its length and its
width, for I give it to you."

18 [a]Then Abram moved *his* tent, and went
and [b]dwelt by the terebinth trees of Mamre,[1]
[c]which *are* in Hebron, and built an [d]altar
there to the LORD.

Lot's Captivity and Rescue

14 And it came to pass in the days of Amraphel king [a]of Shinar, Arioch king of
Ellasar, Chedorlaomer king of [b]Elam, and
Tidal king of nations,[1] 2 *that* they made war
with Bera king of Sodom, Birsha king of Gomorrah, Shinab king of [a]Admah, Shemeber
king of Zeboiim, and the king of Bela (that is,
[b]Zoar). 3 All these joined together in the Valley of Siddim [a](that is, the Salt Sea). 4 Twelve
years [a]they served Chedorlaomer, and in the
thirteenth year they rebelled.

5 In the fourteenth year Chedorlaomer
and the kings that *were* with him came and
attacked [a]the Rephaim in Ashteroth Karnaim, [b]the Zuzim in Ham, [c]the Emim in Shaveh
Kiriathaim, 6 [a]and the Horites in their mountain of Seir, as far as El Paran, which *is* by the
wilderness. 7 Then they turned back and came
to En Mishpat (that *is,* Kadesh), and attacked
all the country of the Amalekites, and also
the Amorites who dwelt [a]in Hazezon Tamar.

8 And the king of Sodom, the king of Gomorrah, the king of Admah, the king of Zeboiim, and the king of Bela (that *is,* Zoar) went
out and joined together in battle in the Valley
of Siddim 9 against Chedorlaomer king of
Elam, Tidal king of nations,[1] Amraphel king
of Shinar, and Arioch king of Ellasar—four
kings against five. 10 Now the Valley of Siddim *was full of* [a]asphalt pits; and the kings of
Sodom and Gomorrah fled; *some* fell there,
and the remainder fled [b]to the mountains.
11 Then they took [a]all the goods of Sodom
and Gomorrah, and all their provisions, and
went their way. 12 They also took Lot, Abram's
[a]brother's son [b]who dwelt in Sodom, and his
goods, and departed.

13 Then one who had escaped came and told
Abram the [a]Hebrew, for [b]he dwelt by the terebinth trees of Mamre[1] the Amorite, brother
of Eshcol and brother of Aner; [c]and they *were*
allies with Abram. 14 Now [a]when Abram heard

13:1 [a] Gen. 12:4; 14:12, 16 [b] Gen. 12:9 [1] Hebrew *Negev* **13:2** [a] Gen. 24:35; 26:14 **13:3** [a] Gen. 12:8, 9 **13:4** [a] Gen. 12:7, 8; 21:33 [b] Ps. 116:17 **13:6** [a] Gen. 36:7 **13:7** [a] Gen. 26:20 [b] Gen. 12:6; 15:20, 21 **13:8** [a] 1 Cor. 6:7 **13:9** [a] Gen. 20:15; 34:10 [b] Gen. 13:11, 14 [c] [Rom. 12:18] **13:10** [a] Gen. 19:17–29 [b] Gen. 19:24 [c] Gen. 2:8, 10 [d] Deut. 34:3 **13:12** [a] Gen. 19:24, 25, 29 [b] Gen. 14:12; 19:1 **13:13** [a] Gen. 18:20, 21 [b] Gen. 6:11; 39:9 **13:14** [a] Gen. 13:11 [b] Gen. 28:14 **13:15** [a] Acts 7:5 [b] 2 Chr. 20:7 [1] Literally *seed,* and so throughout the book **13:16** [a] Gen. 22:17 **13:18** [a] Gen. 26:17 [b] Gen. 14:13 [c] Gen. 23:2; 35:27 [d] Gen. 8:20; 22:8, 9 [1] Hebrew *Alon Mamre* **14:1** [a] Gen. 10:10; 11:2 [b] Is. 11:11; 21:2 [1] Hebrew *goyim* **14:2** [a] Deut. 29:23 [b] Gen. 13:10; 19:22 **14:3** [a] Num. 34:12 **14:4** [a] Gen. 9:26 **14:5** [a] Gen. 15:20 [b] Deut. 2:20 [c] Deut. 2:10 **14:6** [a] Deut. 2:12, 22 **14:7** [a] 2 Chr. 20:2 **14:9** [1] Hebrew *goyim* **14:10** [a] Gen. 11:3 [b] Gen. 19:17, 30 **14:11** [a] Gen. 14:16, 21 **14:12** [a] Gen. 11:27; 12:5 [b] Gen. 13:12 **14:13** [a] Gen. 39:14; 40:15 [b] Gen. 13:18 [c] Gen. 14:24; 21:27, 32 [1] Hebrew *Alon Mamre* **14:14** [a] Gen. 19:29

that [b]his brother was taken captive, he armed
his three hundred and eighteen trained *servants* who were [c]born in his own house, and
went in pursuit [d]as far as Dan. 15 He divided his
forces against them by night, and he and his
servants [a]attacked them and pursued them
as far as Hobah, which *is* north of Damascus.
16 So he [a]brought back all the goods, and also
brought back his brother Lot and his goods,
as well as the women and the people.
17 And the king of Sodom [a]went out to
meet him at the Valley of Shaveh (that *is*,
the [b]King's Valley), [c]after his return from the
defeat of Chedorlaomer and the kings who
were with him.

Abram and Melchizedek

18 Then [a]Melchizedek king of Salem brought
out [b]bread and wine; he *was* [c]the priest of [d]God
Most High. 19 And he blessed him and said:

[a]"Blessed be Abram of God Most High,
[b]Possessor of heaven and earth;
20 And [a]blessed be God Most High,
Who has delivered your enemies into
your hand."

And he [b]gave him a tithe of all.
21 Now the king of Sodom said to Abram,
"Give me the persons, and take the goods
for yourself."
22 But Abram [a]said to the king of Sodom,
"I [b]have raised my hand to the LORD, God
Most High, [c]the Possessor of heaven and
earth, 23 that [a]I *will take* nothing, from a
thread to a sandal strap, and that I will not
take anything that *is* yours, lest you should
say, 'I have made Abram rich'— 24 except
only what the young men have eaten, and
the portion of the men who went with me:
Aner, Eshcol, and Mamre; let them take
their portion."

> **PEACE NOTE**
>
> One reason we can experience God's *shalom* and happiness in our lives is that we have God's divine protection.
>
> GENESIS 15:1

14:14 [b] Gen. 13:8; 14:12 [c] Gen. 12:5; 15:3; 17:27 [d] Deut. 34:1 14:15 [a] Is. 41:2, 3 14:16 [a] Gen. 31:18 14:17 [a] 1 Sam. 18:6 [b] 2 Sam. 18:18 [c] Heb. 7:1 14:18 [a] Heb. 7:1–10 [b] Gen. 18:5 [c] Ps. 110:4 [d] Acts 16:17 14:19 [a] Ruth 3:10 [b] Gen. 14:22 14:20 [a] Gen. 24:27 [b] Heb. 7:4 14:22 [a] Gen. 14:2, 8, 10 [b] Dan. 12:7 [c] Gen. 14:19 14:23 [a] 2 Kin. 5:16

TURNING THE TABLES

Then Melchizedek king of Salem brought out bread and wine; he was the priest of God Most High. And he blessed him and said: "Blessed be Abram of God Most High."

GENESIS 14:18-19

As I was walking off the field after a hard-fought high school football game (I was the quarterback), a stranger approached me. I wasn't sure what he wanted. He made me nervous. Then he shook my hand and introduced himself as a scout for a nearby college. I went from being uneasy to feeling self-assured.

I wonder if Abram felt the same way. He had just defeated five tribal chieftains and recovered captives and stolen property. As he was returning home, out of nowhere a stranger appeared. Someone said he was Melchizedek, the king of Salem. What could he want?

Melchizedek brought bread and wine and pronounced a blessing on Abram. At the very least, Melchizedek's actions foreshadowed fulfillment of God's promise, so Abram probably changed from nervous to calm in just seconds.

When have you had an initially frightening encounter turn out to be a blessing? How would you describe the resulting peace?

God's Covenant with Abram

15 After these things the word of the LORD
came to Abram [a]in a vision, saying,
[b]"Do not be afraid, Abram. I *am* your [c]shield,
your exceedingly [d]great reward."
2 [a]But Abram said, "Lord GOD, what will
You give me, [b]seeing I go childless, and the
heir of my house *is* Eliezer of Damascus?"
3 Then Abram said, "Look, You have given
me no offspring; indeed [a]one born in my
house is my heir!"
4 And behold, the word of the LORD *came* to
him, saying, "This one shall not be your heir, but
one who [a]will come from your own body shall
be your heir." 5 Then He brought him outside
and said, "Look now toward heaven, and [a]count
the [b]stars if you are able to number them." And
He said to him, [c]"So shall your [d]descendants be."
6 And he [a]believed in the LORD, and He
[b]accounted it to him for righteousness.
7 Then He said to him, "I *am* the LORD, who
[a]brought you out of [b]Ur of the Chaldeans, [c]to
give you this land to inherit it."
8 And he said, "Lord GOD, [a]how shall I know
that I will inherit it?"
9 So He said to him, "Bring Me a three-year-
old heifer, a three-year-old female goat, a
three-year-old ram, a turtledove, and a young
pigeon." 10 Then he brought all these to Him
and [a]cut them in two, down the middle, and
placed each piece opposite the other; but he
did not cut [b]the birds in two. 11 And when the
vultures came down on the carcasses, Abram
drove them away.
12 Now when the sun was going down, [a]a
deep sleep fell upon Abram; and behold, horror *and* great darkness fell upon him. 13 Then
He said to Abram: "Know certainly [a]that your
descendants will be strangers in a land *that*
is not theirs, and will serve them, and [b]they
will afflict them four hundred years. 14 And
also the nation whom they serve [a]I will judge;
afterward [b]they shall come out with great

PEACE NOTE

God promised Abraham that He would be a shield and protect him, and Abraham believed that He would. That brought peace.

GENESIS 15:6

15:1 [a] Dan. 10:1 [b] Gen. 21:17; 26:24 [c] Deut. 33:29 [d] Prov. 11:18 **15:2** [a] Gen. 17:18 [b] Acts 7:5 **15:3** [a] Gen. 14:14
15:4 [a] 2 Sam. 7:12 **15:5** [a] Ps. 147:4 [b] Jer. 33:22 [c] Ex. 32:13 [d] Gen. 17:19 **15:6** [a] Rom. 4:3, 9, 22 [b] Ps. 32:2; 106:31
15:7 [a] Gen. 12:1 [b] Gen. 11:28, 31 [c] Ps. 105:42, 44 **15:8** [a] Luke 1:18 **15:10** [a] Jer. 34:18 [b] Lev. 1:17 **15:12** [a] Gen. 2:21; 28:11
15:13 [a] Ex. 1:11 [b] Ex. 12:40 **15:14** [a] Ex. 6:6 [b] Ex. 12:36

LOOK TO YOUR REWARD

The word of the LORD came to Abram in a vision, saying, "Do not be afraid, Abram. I am your shield, your exceedingly great reward."

GENESIS 15:1

If you read too quickly through the Genesis account of Abram, you'll miss the contextual fact that in response to God's call, he left behind his heritage, his rightful land, his generational wealth, his extended family, and all his eventual inheritance to follow Yahweh fifteen hundred miles to Canaan (modern-day Israel). Abram was seventy-five years old when the Lord called him to a defining moment of faith.

God brought Abram out under the glistening night sky, challenged him to count the starry host, and vowed, "So shall your descendants be" (v. 5). Abram's response: "He believed in the LORD" (v. 6). Not only did God promise countless descendants, but He also promised Abram His personal peace—*shalom*!—the first time this word appears in Scripture (see v. 15). Abram would finish the course of his life in *shalom*, an inheritance of peace.

As we meditate on this first occurrence of peace, let us recall that it came by faith in the true and living God who blesses us with His peace. Turn your eyes to the heavens and see Him.

possessions. 15 Now as for you, [a]you shall go [b]to your fathers in peace; [c]you shall be buried at a good old age. 16 But [a]in the fourth generation they shall return here, for the iniquity [b]of the Amorites [c]*is* not yet complete."

17 And it came to pass, when the sun went down and it was dark, that behold, there appeared a smoking oven and a burning torch that [a]passed between those pieces. 18 On the same day the LORD [a]made a covenant with Abram, saying:

[b]"To your descendants I have given this land, from the river of Egypt to the great river, the River Euphrates— 19 the Kenites, the Kenezzites, the Kadmonites, 20 the Hittites, the Perizzites, the Rephaim, 21 the Amorites, the Canaanites, the Girgashites, and the Jebusites."

Hagar and Ishmael

16 Now Sarai, Abram's wife, [a]had borne him no *children.* And she had [b]an Egyptian maidservant whose name was [c]Hagar. 2 [a]So Sarai said to Abram, "See now, the LORD [b]has restrained me from bearing *children.* Please, [c]go in to my maid; perhaps I shall obtain children by her." And Abram [d]heeded the voice of Sarai. 3 Then Sarai, Abram's wife, took Hagar her maid, the Egyptian, and gave her to her husband Abram to be his wife, after Abram [a]had dwelt ten years in the land of Canaan. 4 So he went in to Hagar, and she conceived. And when she saw that she had conceived, her mistress became [a]despised in her eyes.

5 Then Sarai said to Abram, "My wrong *be* upon you! I gave my maid into your embrace; and when she saw that she had conceived, I became despised in her eyes. [a]The LORD judge between you and me."

6 [a]So Abram said to Sarai, "Indeed your maid *is* in your hand; do to her as you please." And when Sarai dealt harshly with her, [b]she fled from her presence.

7 Now the [a]Angel of the LORD found her by a spring of water in the wilderness, [b]by the spring on the way to [c]Shur. 8 And He said, "Hagar, Sarai's maid, where have you come from, and where are you going?"

She said, "I am fleeing from the presence of my mistress Sarai."

9 The Angel of the LORD said to her, "Return to your mistress, and [a]submit yourself under her hand." 10 Then the Angel of the LORD said to her, [a]"I will multiply your descendants exceedingly, so that they shall not be counted for multitude." 11 And the Angel of the LORD said to her:

"Behold, you *are* with child,
[a]And you shall bear a son.
You shall call his name Ishmael,

15:15 [a] Job 5:26 [b] Gen. 25:8; 47:30 [c] Gen. 25:8 **15:16** [a] Ex. 12:41 [b] 1 Kin. 21:26 [c] Matt. 23:32 **15:17** [a] Jer. 34:18, 19 **15:18** [a] Gen. 24:7 [b] Gen. 12:7; 17:8 **16:1** [a] Gen. 11:30; 15:2, 3 [b] Gen. 12:16; 21:9 [c] Gal. 4:24 **16:2** [a] Gen. 30:3 [b] Gen. 20:18 [c] Gen. 30:3, 9 [d] Gen. 3:17 **16:3** [a] Gen. 12:4, 5 **16:4** [a] [Prov. 30:21, 23] **16:5** [a] Gen. 31:53 **16:6** [a] 1 Pet. 3:7 [b] Ex. 2:15 **16:7** [a] Gen. 21:17, 18; 22:11, 15; 31:11 [b] Gen. 20:1; 25:18 [c] Ex. 15:22 **16:9** [a] [Titus 2:9] **16:10** [a] Gen. 17:20 **16:11** [a] Luke 1:13, 31

YOU ARE SEEN BY THE LORD

Then she called the name of the LORD who spoke to her, You-Are-the-God-Who-Sees; for she said, "Have I also here seen Him who sees me?"

GENESIS 16:13

Sometimes our greatest moment of adversity will reveal a new aspect of God's faithfulness in our lives, which leads us to a greater measure of God's peace. Hagar was abandoned by those who were supposed to love her the most. I'm quite sure she felt as though no one saw her. I can imagine Hagar filled with anxiety and the isolation the lies of fear bring. Yet, at this wretched moment, she called on the name of the Lord, and He answered her.

It took lonely moments in the desert for Hagar to learn God's faithfulness, and she innovated a new name for the Lord: Hebrew, *El Roi*—"The-God-Who-Sees." Nothing can give us greater peace than knowing God sees us today. He sees everything. No detail in our lives is too small for Him to care about.

Throughout the first five books of the Old Testament, we are reminded that God sees us and even more, He acts. God never abandons His children. In Exodus, "God looked upon the children of Israel, and God acknowledged [saw] them" (Ex. 2:25). That's *El Roi*! Pray today to our great God *El Roi*, and walk forward in His peace.

Because the LORD has heard your
affliction.
12 [a]He shall be a wild man;
His hand *shall be* against every man,
And every man's hand against him.
[b]And he shall dwell in the presence of
all his brethren."

13 Then she called the name of the LORD
who spoke to her, You-Are-the-God-Who-
Sees; for she said, "Have I also here seen
Him [a]who sees me?" 14 Therefore the well
was called [a]Beer Lahai Roi;[1] observe, *it is*
[b]between Kadesh and Bered.
15 So [a]Hagar bore Abram a son; and Abram
named his son, whom Hagar bore, Ishmael.
16 Abram *was* eighty-six years old when Hagar
bore Ishmael to Abram.

The Sign of the Covenant

17 When Abram was ninety-nine years old,
the LORD [a]appeared to Abram and said
to him, [b]"I *am* Almighty God; [c]walk before
Me and be [d]blameless. 2 And I will make My
[a]covenant between Me and you, and [b]will
multiply you exceedingly." 3 Then Abram fell
on his face, and God talked with him, saying:
4 "As for Me, behold, My covenant is with you,
and you shall be [a]a father of many nations. 5 No
longer shall [a]your name be called Abram, but
your name shall be Abraham; [b]for I have made
you a father of many nations. 6 I will make you
exceedingly fruitful; and I will make [a]nations
of you, and [b]kings shall come from you. 7 And
I will [a]establish My covenant between Me and
you and your descendants after you in their
generations, for an everlasting covenant, [b]to
be God to you and [c]your descendants after
you. 8 Also [a]I give to you and your descendants
after you the land [b]in which you are a stranger,
all the land of Canaan, as an everlasting possession; and [c]I will be their God."
9 And God said to Abraham: "As for you,
[a]you shall keep My covenant, you and your
descendants after you throughout their generations. 10 This *is* My covenant which you
shall keep, between Me and you and your
descendants after you: [a]Every male child
among you shall be circumcised; 11 and you
shall be circumcised in the flesh of your
foreskins, and it shall be [a]a sign of the covenant between Me and you. 12 He who is eight
days old among you [a]shall be circumcised,
every male child in your generations, he
who is born in your house or bought with
money from any foreigner who is not your
descendant. 13 He who is born in your house
and he who is bought with your money must
be circumcised, and My covenant shall be in
your flesh for an everlasting covenant. 14 And

16:12 [a] Gen. 21:20 [b] Gen. 25:18 **16:13** [a] Gen. 31:42 **16:14** [a] Gen. 24:62 [b] Num. 13:26 [1] Literally *Well of the One Who Lives and Sees Me* **16:15** [a] Gal. 4:22 **17:1** [a] Gen. 12:7; 18:1 [b] Gen. 28:3; 35:11 [c] 2 Kin. 20:3 [d] Deut. 18:13 **17:2** [a] Gen. 15:18 [b] Gen. 12:2; 13:16; 15:5; 18:18 **17:4** [a] [Rom. 4:11, 12, 16] **17:5** [a] Neh. 9:7 [b] Rom. 4:17 **17:6** [a] Gen. 17:16; 35:11 [b] Matt. 1:6 **17:7** [a] [Gal. 3:17] [b] Gen. 26:24; 28:13 [c] Rom. 9:8; Gal. 3:16 **17:8** [a] Acts 7:5 [b] Gen. 23:4; 28:4 [c] Lev. 26:12 **17:9** [a] Ex. 19:5 **17:10** [a] Acts 7:8 **17:11** [a] Ex. 12:13, 48 **17:12** [a] Lev. 12:3

OUR BELIEVABLE GOD

When Abram was ninety-nine years old, the LORD appeared to Abram and said to him, "I am Almighty God; walk before Me and be blameless. And I will make My covenant between Me and you, and will multiply you exceedingly."

GENESIS 17:1-2

I would find it very hard to continue believing someone's promise—no matter how often it was repeated—if it remained unfulfilled for decades. The anticipation would eat me alive! I would know God but not know peace. After all, God had summoned Abram many years earlier and promised he would be the father of a "great nation" (12:2). Now the man was ninety-nine years old, and his wife was as barren as ever! How could this promise be fulfilled?

In this passage (ch. 17) God seemingly upped the ante by changing Abram's name to the more familiar Abraham. But here's the kicker: the new name was understood to mean "Father of a Multitude." Think of the irony! Here was a man who had but one son through his concubine. Abraham even "fell on his face and laughed" (v. 17).

Mirth notwithstanding, God got the last word by delivering on this promise just one year later. Want to exchange inner conflict for peace? Trust the One who made the promise.

the uncircumcised male child, who is not circumcised in the flesh of his foreskin, that person [a]shall be cut off from his people; he has broken My covenant."

15 Then God said to Abraham, "As for Sarai your wife, you shall not call her name Sarai, but Sarah *shall be* her name. 16 And I will bless her [a]and also give you a son by her; then I will bless her, and she shall be *a mother* [b]of nations; [c]kings of peoples shall be from her."

17 Then Abraham fell on his face [a]and laughed, and said in his heart, "Shall *a child* be born to a man who is one hundred years old? And shall Sarah, who is ninety years old, bear *a child?*" 18 And Abraham [a]said to God, "Oh, that Ishmael might live before You!"

19 Then God said: "No, [a]Sarah your wife shall bear you a son, and you shall call his name Isaac; I will establish My [b]covenant with him for an everlasting covenant, *and* with his descendants after him. 20 And as for Ishmael, I have heard you. Behold, I have blessed him, and will make him fruitful, and [a]will multiply him exceedingly. He shall beget [b]twelve princes, [c]and I will make him a great nation. 21 But My [a]covenant I will establish with Isaac, [b]whom Sarah shall bear to you at this [c]set time next year." 22 Then He finished talking with him, and God went up from Abraham.

23 So Abraham took Ishmael his son, all who were born in his house and all who were bought with his money, every male among the men of Abraham's house, and circumcised the flesh of their foreskins that very same day, as God had said to him. 24 Abraham *was* ninety-nine years old when he was circumcised in the flesh of his foreskin. 25 And Ishmael his son *was* thirteen years old when he was circumcised in the flesh of his foreskin. 26 That very same day Abraham was circumcised, and his son Ishmael; 27 and [a]all the men of his house, born in the house or bought with money from a foreigner, were circumcised with him.

The Son of Promise

18 Then the LORD appeared to him by the [a]terebinth trees of Mamre,[1] as he was sitting in the tent door in the heat of the day. 2 [a]So he lifted his eyes and looked, and behold, three men were standing by him; [b]and when he saw *them,* he ran from the tent door to meet them, and bowed himself to the ground, 3 and said, "My Lord, if I have now found favor in Your sight, do not pass on by Your servant. 4 Please let [a]a little water be brought, and wash your feet, and rest yourselves under the tree. 5 And [a]I will bring a morsel of bread, that [b]you may refresh your hearts. After that you may pass by, [c]inasmuch as you have come to your servant."

17:14 [a] Ex. 4:24–26 **17:16** [a] Gen. 18:10 [b] Gen. 35:11 [c] Gen. 17:6; 36:31 **17:17** [a] Gen. 17:3; 18:12; 21:6 **17:18** [a] Gen. 18:23 **17:19** [a] Gen. 18:10; 21:2; [Gal. 4:28] [b] Gen. 22:16 **17:20** [a] Gen. 16:10 [b] Gen. 25:12–16 [c] Gen. 21:13, 18 **17:21** [a] Gen. 26:2–5 [b] Gen. 21:2 [c] Gen. 18:14 **17:27** [a] Gen. 18:19 **18:1** [a] Gen. 13:18; 14:13 [1] Hebrew *Alon Mamre* **18:2** [a] Heb. 13:2 [b] Gen. 19:1 **18:4** [a] Gen. 19:2; 24:32; 43:24 **18:5** [a] Judg. 6:18, 19; 13:15, 16 [b] Judg. 19:5 [c] Gen. 19:8; 33:10

IN DUE TIME

Then the LORD appeared to him by the terebinth trees of Mamre . . . And He said, "I will certainly return to you according to the time of life, and behold, Sarah your wife shall have a son."

GENESIS 18:1, 10

Up to this point in Scripture, God's promise of a son has never specified a time, only the guarantee that it would happen. In almost identical wording to verse 10, in verse 14, the Lord very specifically told Abraham that Sarah would have a son "according to the time of life," which includes the message "I will return to you." It is as though God had promised to be Sarah's attending physician. Suddenly the promise was linked to a time frame.

We've seen that the specificity of the promise made Sarah and her husband laugh (17:17; 18:12). Sarah may have been rebuked on this occasion because the Lord Himself was present in their very tent! It was no time for doubt; it was a time for faith. God was inviting her to peace—wholeness—*shalom.* Though she was long encumbered by the shame of childlessness, He was about to bestow a miracle!

When have you rejected peace and scoffed at the possibility of deliverance? Your miracle could be right around the corner, so lean into the peace of God today.

They said, "Do as you have said."
6 So Abraham hurried into the tent to
Sarah and said, "Quickly, make ready three
measures of fine meal; knead *it* and make
cakes." 7 And Abraham ran to the herd, took
a tender and good calf, gave *it* to a young
man, and he hastened to prepare it. 8 So [a]he
took butter and milk and the calf which he
had prepared, and set *it* before them; and
he stood by them under the tree as they ate.
9 Then they said to him, "Where *is* Sarah
your wife?"
So he said, "Here, [a]in the tent."
10 And He said, "I will certainly return to
you [a]according to the time of life, and behold,
[b]Sarah your wife shall have a son."
(Sarah was listening in the tent door which
was behind him.) 11 Now [a]Abraham and Sarah
were old, well advanced in age; *and* Sarah
[b]had passed the age of childbearing.[1] 12 Therefore Sarah [a]laughed within herself, saying,
[b]"After I have grown old, shall I have pleasure,
my [c]lord being old also?"
13 And the LORD said to Abraham, "Why
did Sarah laugh, saying, 'Shall I surely bear
a child, since I am old?' 14 [a]Is anything too
hard for the LORD? [b]At the appointed time I
will return to you, according to the time of
life, and Sarah shall have a son."
15 But Sarah denied *it,* saying, "I did not
laugh," for she was afraid.
And He said, "No, but you did laugh!"

Abraham Intercedes for Sodom

16 Then the men rose from there and looked
toward Sodom, and Abraham went with them
[a]to send them on the way. 17 And the LORD
said, [a]"Shall I hide from Abraham what I am
doing, 18 since Abraham shall surely become
a great and mighty nation, and all the nations
of the earth shall be [a]blessed in him? 19 For I
have known him, in order [a]that he may command his children and his household after
him, that they keep the way of the LORD, to
do righteousness and justice, that the LORD
may bring to Abraham what He has spoken
to him." 20 And the LORD said, "Because [a]the
outcry against Sodom and Gomorrah is great,
and because their [b]sin is very grave, 21 [a]I will
go down now and see whether they have done
altogether according to the outcry against it
that has come to Me; and if not, [b]I will know."
22 Then the men turned away from there
[a]and went toward Sodom, but Abraham still
stood before the LORD. 23 And Abraham [a]came
near and said, [b]"Would You also [c]destroy the
[d]righteous with the wicked? 24 Suppose there
were fifty righteous within the city; would You

18:8 [a] Gen. 19:3 **18:9** [a] Gen. 24:67 **18:10** [a] 2 Kin. 4:16 [b] Rom. 9:9 **18:11** [a] Gen. 17:17 [b] Gen. 31:35 [1] Literally *the manner of women had ceased to be with Sarah* **18:12** [a] Gen. 17:17 [b] Luke 1:18 [c] 1 Pet. 3:6 **18:14** [a] Jer. 32:17 [b] Gen. 17:21; 18:10 **18:16** [a] Rom. 15:24 **18:17** [a] Ps. 25:14 **18:18** [a] [Acts 3:25, 26; Gal. 3:8] **18:19** [a] [Deut. 4:9, 10; 6:6, 7] **18:20** [a] Gen. 4:10; 19:13 [b] Gen. 13:13 **18:21** [a] Gen. 11:5 [b] Deut. 8:2; 13:3 **18:22** [a] Gen. 18:16; 19:1 **18:23** [a] [Heb. 10:22] [b] Num. 16:22 [c] Job 9:22 [d] Gen. 20:4

LAUGHABLE HOPE

"Behold, Sarah your wife shall have a son" . . . Now Abraham and Sarah were old, well advanced in age . . . Therefore Sarah laughed within herself.

GENESIS 18:10-12

We all have moments of doubt and skepticism. It's human nature. Perhaps it's because we ourselves fail often and let people down. It seems only natural to project our own foibles and shortcomings onto others, including God Himself. Abraham, now one hundred years old, found it absurd that he and his aged wife, Sarah, age ninety, would ever have a child together. The idea was laughable enough that Sarah snickered in the tent! But it didn't really matter how old Abraham and Sarah became or how much they mocked the promise—their son was on the way.

It is this faithfulness of God—unperturbed by human doubt, fear, and mismanagement—that gives me hope. The hope in turn fills my soul with a sense of peace. Knowing that God will keep His word no matter how things look or how faithless I act at times is hugely reassuring. Our peace rests upon God's faithfulness, not ours—which Abraham and Sarah and you and I prove every day.

Thank God for His faithfulness that brings you peace.

also destroy the place and not spare *it* for the fifty righteous that were in it? 25 Far be it from You to do such a thing as this, to slay the righteous with the wicked, so [a]that the righteous should be as the wicked; far be it from You! [b]Shall not the Judge of all the earth do right?"

26 So the LORD said, [a]"If I find in Sodom fifty righteous within the city, then I will spare all the place for their sakes."

27 Then Abraham answered and said, "Indeed now, I who *am* [a]*but* dust and ashes have taken it upon myself to speak to the Lord: 28 Suppose there were five less than the fifty righteous; would You destroy all of the city for *lack of* five?"

So He said, "If I find there forty-five, I will not destroy *it*."

29 And he spoke to Him yet again and said, "Suppose there should be forty found there?"

So He said, "I will not do *it* for the sake of forty."

30 Then he said, "Let not the Lord be angry, and I will speak: Suppose thirty should be found there?"

So He said, "I will not do *it* if I find thirty there."

31 And he said, "Indeed now, I have taken it upon myself to speak to the Lord: Suppose twenty should be found there?"

So He said, "I will not destroy *it* for the sake of twenty."

32 Then he said, [a]"Let not the Lord be angry, and I will speak but once more: Suppose ten should be found there?"

[b]And He said, "I will not destroy *it* for the sake of ten." 33 So the LORD went His way as soon as He had finished speaking with Abraham; and Abraham returned to his place.

Sodom's Depravity

19 Now [a]the two angels came to Sodom in the evening, and [b]Lot was sitting in the gate of Sodom. When Lot saw *them,* he rose to meet them, and he bowed himself with his face toward the ground. 2 And he said, "Here now, my lords, please [a]turn in to your servant's house and spend the night, and [b]wash your feet; then you may rise early and go on your way."

And they said, [c]"No, but we will spend the night in the open square."

3 But he insisted strongly; so they turned in to him and entered his house. [a]Then he made them a feast, and baked [b]unleavened bread, and they ate.

4 Now before they lay down, the men of the city, the men of Sodom, both old and young, all the people from every quarter, surrounded the house. 5 [a]And they called to Lot and said to him, "Where are the men who came to you tonight? [b]Bring them out to us that we [c]may know them *carnally.*"

6 So [a]Lot went out to them through the doorway, shut the door behind him, 7 and said, "Please, my brethren, do not do so wickedly! 8 [a]See now, I have two daughters who have not known a man; please, let me bring them out to you, and you may do to them as you wish; only do nothing to these men, [b]since this is the reason they have come under the shadow of my roof."

9 And they said, "Stand back!" Then they said, "This one [a]came in to stay *here,* [b]and he keeps acting as a judge; now we will deal worse with you than with them." So they pressed hard against the man Lot, and came near to break down the door. 10 But the men reached out their hands and pulled Lot into the house with them, and shut the door. 11 And they [a]struck the men who *were* at the doorway of the house with blindness, both small and great, so that they became weary *trying* to find the door.

Sodom and Gomorrah Destroyed

12 Then the men said to Lot, "Have you anyone else here? Son-in-law, your sons, your daughters, and whomever you have in the city—[a]take *them* out of this place! 13 For we will destroy this place, because the [a]outcry against them has grown great before the face of the LORD, and [b]the LORD has sent us to destroy it."

14 So Lot went out and spoke to his sons-in-law, [a]who had married his daughters, and said, [b]"Get up, get out of this place; for the LORD will destroy this city!" [c]But to his sons-in-law he seemed to be joking.

15 When the morning dawned, the angels urged Lot to hurry, saying, [a]"Arise, take your wife and your two daughters who are here, lest you be consumed in the punishment of the city." 16 And while he lingered, the men [a]took hold of his hand, his wife's hand, and the hands of his two daughters, the [b]LORD being merciful to him, [c]and they brought him out and set him outside the city. 17 So it came to pass, when they had brought them outside, that he[1] said, [a]"Escape for your life! [b]Do not look behind you nor stay anywhere in the plain. Escape [c]to the mountains, lest you be destroyed."

18:25 [a] Is. 3:10, 11 [b] Deut. 1:16, 17; 32:4 **18:26** [a] Jer. 5:1 **18:27** [a] [Gen. 3:19] **18:32** [a] Judg. 6:39 [b] James 5:16 **19:1** [a] Gen. 18:2, 16, 22 [b] Gen. 18:1–5 **19:2** [a] [Heb. 13:2] [b] Gen. 18:4; 24:32 [c] Luke 24:28 **19:3** [a] Gen. 18:6–8 [b] Ex. 12:8 **19:5** [a] Is. 3:9 [b] Judg. 19:22 [c] Gen. 4:1 **19:6** [a] Judg. 19:23 **19:8** [a] Judg. 19:24 [b] Gen. 18:5 **19:9** [a] 2 Pet. 2:7, 8 [b] Ex. 2:14 **19:11** [a] Gen. 20:17, 18 **19:12** [a] 2 Pet. 2:7, 9 **19:13** [a] Gen. 18:20 [b] 1 Chr. 21:15 **19:14** [a] Matt. 1:18 [b] Num. 16:21, 24, 26, 45 [c] Ex. 9:21 **19:15** [a] Rev. 18:4 **19:16** [a] 2 Pet. 2:7 [b] Luke 18:13 [c] Ps. 34:22 **19:17** [a] Jer. 48:6 [b] Matt. 24:16–18 [c] Gen. 14:10 [1] Septuagint, Syriac, and Vulgate read *they.*

18 Then Lot said to them, "Please, [a]no, my lords! 19 Indeed now, your servant has found favor in your sight, and you have increased your mercy which you have shown me by saving my life; but I cannot escape to the mountains, lest some evil overtake me and I die. 20 See now, this city *is* near *enough* to flee to, and it *is* a little one; please let me escape there (*is* it not a little one?) and my soul shall live."

21 And he said to him, "See, [a]I have favored you concerning this thing also, in that I will not overthrow this city for which you have spoken. 22 Hurry, escape there. For [a]I cannot do anything until you arrive there."

Therefore [b]the name of the city was called Zoar.

23 The sun had risen upon the earth when Lot entered Zoar. 24 Then the LORD rained [a]brimstone and [b]fire on Sodom and Gomorrah, from the LORD out of the heavens. 25 So He overthrew those cities, all the plain, all the inhabitants of the cities, and [a]what grew on the ground.

26 But his wife looked back behind him, and she became [a]a pillar of salt.

27 And Abraham went early in the morning to the place where [a]he had stood before the LORD. 28 Then he looked toward Sodom and Gomorrah, and toward all the land of the plain; and he saw, and behold, [a]the smoke of the land which went up like the smoke of a furnace. 29 And it came to pass, when God destroyed the cities of the plain, that God [a]remembered Abraham, and sent Lot out of the midst of the overthrow, when He overthrew the cities in which Lot had dwelt.

The Descendants of Lot

30 Then Lot went up out of Zoar and [a]dwelt in the mountains, and his two daughters were with him; for he was afraid to dwell in Zoar. And he and his two daughters dwelt in a cave. 31 Now the firstborn said to the younger, "Our father *is* old, and *there is* no man on the earth [a]to come in to us as is the custom of all the earth. 32 Come, let us make our father drink wine, and we will lie with him, that we [a]may preserve the lineage of our father." 33 So they made their father drink wine that night. And the firstborn went in and lay with her father, and he did not know when she lay down or when she arose.

34 It happened on the next day that the firstborn said to the younger, "Indeed I lay with my father last night; let us make him drink wine tonight also, and you go in *and* lie with him, that we may preserve the lineage of our father." 35 Then they made their father drink wine that night also. And the younger arose and lay with him, and he did not know when she lay down or when she arose.

36 Thus both the daughters of Lot were with child by their father. 37 The firstborn bore a son and called his name Moab; [a]he *is* the father of the Moabites to this day. 38 And the younger, she also bore a son and called his name Ben-Ammi; [a]he *is* the father of the people of Ammon to this day.

Abraham and Abimelech

20 And Abraham journeyed from [a]there to the South, and dwelt between [b]Kadesh and Shur, and [c]stayed in Gerar. 2 Now Abraham said of Sarah his wife, [a]"She *is* my sister." And Abimelech king of Gerar sent and [b]took Sarah.

3 But [a]God came to Abimelech [b]in a dream by night, and said to him, [c]"Indeed you *are* a dead man because of the woman whom you have taken, for she *is* a man's wife."

4 But Abimelech had not come near her; and he said, "Lord, [a]will You slay a righteous nation also? 5 Did he not say to me, 'She *is* my sister'? And she, even she herself said, 'He *is* my brother.' [a]In the integrity of my heart and innocence of my hands I have done this."

6 And God said to him in a dream, "Yes, I know that you did this in the integrity of your heart. For [a]I also withheld you from sinning [b]against Me; therefore I did not let you touch her. 7 Now therefore, restore the man's wife; [a]for he *is* a prophet, and he will pray for you and you shall live. But if you do not restore *her,* [b]know that you shall surely die, you [c]and all who *are* yours."

8 So Abimelech rose early in the morning, called all his servants, and told all these things in their hearing; and the men were very much afraid. 9 And Abimelech called Abraham and said to him, "What have you done to us? How have I offended you, [a]that you have brought on me and on my kingdom a great sin? You have done deeds to me [b]that ought not to be done." 10 Then Abimelech said to Abraham, "What did you have in view, that you have done this thing?"

11 And Abraham said, "Because I thought, surely [a]the fear of God *is* not in this place; and [b]they will kill me on account of my wife.

19:18 [a] Acts 10:14 **19:21** [a] Job 42:8, 9 **19:22** [a] Ex. 32:10 [b] Gen. 13:10; 14:2 **19:24** [a] Deut. 29:23 [b] Lev. 10:2 **19:25** [a] Ps. 107:34 **19:26** [a] Luke 17:32 **19:27** [a] Gen. 18:22 **19:28** [a] Rev. 9:2; 18:9 **19:29** [a] Gen. 8:1; 18:23 **19:30** [a] Gen. 19:17, 19 **19:31** [a] Gen. 16:2, 4; 38:8, 9 **19:32** [a] [Mark 12:19] **19:37** [a] Deut. 2:9 **19:38** [a] Deut. 2:19 **20:1** [a] Gen. 18:1 [b] Gen. 12:9; 16:7, 14 [c] Gen. 26:1, 6 **20:2** [a] Gen. 12:11–13; 26:7 [b] Gen. 12:15 **20:3** [a] Ps. 105:14 [b] Job 33:15 [c] Gen. 20:7 **20:4** [a] Gen. 18:23–25 **20:5** [a] 2 Kin. 20:3 **20:6** [a] 1 Sam. 25:26, 34 [b] Gen. 39:9 **20:7** [a] 1 Sam. 7:5 [b] Gen. 2:17 [c] Num. 16:32, 33 **20:9** [a] Gen. 26:10; 39:9 [b] Gen. 34:7 **20:11** [a] Prov. 16:6 [b] Gen. 12:12; 26:7

EVEN IF WE DOUBT

Then Abimelech said to Abraham, "What did you have in view, that you have done this thing?"

GENESIS 20:10

I have had great days where really good things happened only to find myself fumbling the ball the next day. Know what I mean? It's frustrating. We take a big step forward only to take two back. I wonder if Abraham felt that way after he once again lied about his wife in a cowardly manner. You would think that after sharing a meal with God in his tent (see 18:1–8), and then seeing God's power rain down on Sodom and Gomorrah (see 19:15–28), that Abraham would have walked with courage and confidence. Had he learned nothing?

I don't want to be too hard on the great patriarch, but I confess I find it ironic that he became known as a man of faith (see Heb. 11:8–9) when at least twice he lacked faith in God to protect him, on occasion he expressed skepticism about God's promises, and once he even had the nerve to mock an angel's announcement!

When you fumble the ball like Abraham, how do you handle the resulting disappointment and lack of peace? It appears that Abraham had the wisdom, upon realizing his error, to repent—which is a sure road back to peace. Do you need to repent today?

12 But indeed [a]*she is* truly my sister. She *is* the
daughter of my father, but not the daughter
of my mother; and she became my wife.
13 And it came to pass, when [a]God caused me
to wander from my father's house, that I said
to her, 'This *is* your kindness that you should
do for me: in every place, wherever we go,
[b]say of me, "He *is* my brother." ' "
14 Then Abimelech [a]took sheep, oxen, and
male and female servants, and gave *them* to
Abraham; and he restored Sarah his wife to
him. 15 And Abimelech said, "See, [a]my land
is before you; dwell where it pleases you."
16 Then to Sarah he said, "Behold, I have given
your brother a thousand *pieces* of silver;
[a]indeed this vindicates you[1] [b]before all who
are with you and before everybody." Thus
she was rebuked.
17 So Abraham [a]prayed to God; and God
[b]healed Abimelech, his wife, and his female
servants. Then they bore *children;* 18 for the
LORD [a]had closed up all the wombs of the
house of Abimelech because of Sarah, Abraham's wife.

Isaac Is Born

21 And the LORD [a]visited Sarah as He had
said, and the LORD did for Sarah [b]as
He had spoken. 2 For Sarah [a]conceived and
bore Abraham a son in his old age, [b]at the
set time of which God had spoken to him.
3 And Abraham called the name of his son
who was born to him—whom Sarah bore to
him—[a]Isaac. 4 Then Abraham [a]circumcised
his son Isaac when he was eight days old, [b]as
God had commanded him. 5 Now [a]Abraham
was one hundred years old when his son
Isaac was born to him. 6 And Sarah said, [a]"God
has made me laugh, *and* all who hear [b]will
laugh with me." 7 She also said, "Who would
have said to Abraham that Sarah would nurse
children? [a]For I have borne *him* a son in his
old age."

Hagar and Ishmael Depart

8 So the child grew and was weaned. And
Abraham made a great feast on the same day
that Isaac was weaned.
9 And Sarah saw the son of Hagar [a]the
Egyptian, whom she had borne to Abraham,
[b]scoffing. 10 Therefore she said to Abraham,
[a]"Cast out this bondwoman and her son; for
the son of this bondwoman shall not be heir
with my son, *namely* with Isaac." 11 And the
matter was very displeasing in Abraham's
sight [a]because of his son.
12 But God said to Abraham, "Do not let it
be displeasing in your sight because of the
lad or because of your bondwoman. Whatever
Sarah has said to you, listen to her voice; for

20:12 [a] Gen. 11:29 **20:13** [a] Gen. 12:1–9, 11 [b] Gen. 12:13; 20:5 **20:14** [a] Gen. 12:16 **20:15** [a] Gen. 13:9; 34:10; 47:6 **20:16** [a] Gen. 26:11 [b] Mal. 2:9 [1] Literally *it is a covering of the eyes for you* **20:17** [a] Job 42:9 [b] Gen. 21:2 **20:18** [a] Gen. 12:17 **21:1** [a] 1 Sam. 2:21 [b] [Gal. 4:23, 28] **21:2** [a] Heb. 11:11, 12 [b] Gen. 17:21; 18:10, 14 **21:3** [a] Gen. 17:19, 21 **21:4** [a] Acts 7:8 [b] Gen. 17:10, 12 **21:5** [a] Gen. 17:1, 17 **21:6** [a] Is. 54:1 [b] Luke 1:58 **21:7** [a] Gen. 18:11, 12 **21:9** [a] Gen. 16:1, 4, 15 [b] [Gal. 4:29] **21:10** [a] Gal. 3:18; 4:30 **21:11** [a] Gen. 17:18

GOD DOES IT AGAIN

And the LORD visited Sarah as He had said, and the LORD did for Sarah as He had spoken.

GENESIS 21:1

Have you worried excessively that something bad would happen—or that something good wouldn't happen? Our fears get the best of us and then—what a relief!—often the outcome is fine.

God had promised Abraham and Sarah several times that she would give birth to a son, but as the years passed they began to doubt. When you face a trial, adversity, or perhaps what appears to be an unanswered prayer request, remind yourself of this singular biblical truth: "God's got this!" Did you know that can be one of the most powerful prayers you pray? "God's got this!" no matter what. Abraham and Sarah doubted the promise because they had lost hope and didn't realize God had this issue under His complete control.

But God who is faithful gave the couple their promised son; and appropriately they named him Isaac, which in Hebrew means "Laughter" (v. 3). The laughter of cynicism had become the laughter of joy—and peace.

[a]in Isaac your seed shall be called. 13 Yet I will
also make [a]a nation of the son of the bondwoman, because he *is* your seed."
14 So Abraham rose early in the morning,
and took bread and a skin of water; and
putting *it* on her shoulder, he gave *it* and
the boy to Hagar, and [a]sent her away. Then
she departed and wandered in the Wilderness of Beersheba. 15 And the water in the
skin was used up, and she placed the boy
under one of the shrubs. 16 Then she went
and sat down across from *him* at a distance
of about a bowshot; for she said to herself,
"Let me not see the death of the boy." So
she sat opposite *him*, and lifted her voice
and wept.
17 And [a]God heard the voice of the lad. Then
the [b]angel of God called to Hagar out of heav-
en, and said to her, "What ails you, Hagar?
Fear not, for God has heard the voice of the
lad where he *is*. 18 Arise, lift up the lad and
hold him with your hand, for [a]I will make
him a great nation."
19 Then [a]God opened her eyes, and she saw
a well of water. And she went and filled the
skin with water, and gave the lad a drink. 20 So
God [a]was with the lad; and he grew and dwelt
in the wilderness, [b]and became an archer.
21 He dwelt in the Wilderness of Paran; and
his mother [a]took a wife for him from the
land of Egypt.

A Covenant with Abimelech

22 And it came to pass at that time that
[a]Abimelech and Phichol, the commander of
his army, spoke to Abraham, saying, [b]"God *is*
with you in all that you do. 23 Now therefore,
[a]swear to me by God that you will not deal
falsely with me, with my offspring, or with my
posterity; but that according to the kindness
that I have done to you, you will do to me and
to the land in which you have dwelt."
24 And Abraham said, "I will swear."
25 Then Abraham rebuked Abimelech because of a well of water which Abimelech's
servants [a]had seized. 26 And Abimelech said,
"I do not know who has done this thing; you
did not tell me, nor had I heard *of it* until
today." 27 So Abraham took sheep and oxen
and gave them to Abimelech, and the two of
them [a]made a covenant. 28 And Abraham set
seven ewe lambs of the flock by themselves.
29 Then Abimelech asked Abraham, [a]"What
is the meaning of these seven ewe lambs
which you have set by themselves?"
30 And he said, "You will take *these* seven
ewe lambs from my hand, that [a]they may be
my witness that I have dug this well." 31 Therefore he [a]called that place Beersheba,[1] because
the two of them swore an oath there.
32 Thus they made a covenant at Beersheba. So Abimelech rose with Phichol, the
commander of his army, and they returned to

21:12 [a] Matt. 1:2; Luke 3:34; [Rom. 9:7, 8]; Heb. 11:18 **21:13** [a] Gen. 16:10; 17:20; 21:18; 25:12–18 **21:14** [a] John 8:35 **21:17** [a] Ex. 3:7 [b] Gen. 22:11 **21:18** [a] Gen. 16:10; 21:13; 25:12–16 **21:19** [a] Num. 22:31 **21:20** [a] Gen. 28:15; 39:2, 3, 21 [b] Gen. 16:12 **21:21** [a] Gen. 24:4 **21:22** [a] Gen. 20:2, 14; 26:26 [b] Gen. 26:28 **21:23** [a] Josh. 2:12 **21:25** [a] Gen. 26:15, 18, 20–22 **21:27** [a] Gen. 26:31; 31:44 **21:29** [a] Gen. 33:8 **21:30** [a] Gen. 31:48, 52 **21:31** [a] Gen. 21:14; 26:33 [1] Literally *Well of the Oath* or *Well of the Seven*

PEACE THAT INTERVENES

"Arise, lift up the lad and hold him with your hand, for I will make him a great nation."

GENESIS 21:18

Even the very best people can suffer a raw deal. Unable to conceive, Sarai urged her husband to get a son and heir through his concubine Hagar. Hagar conceived, and after that, what peace had existed in Abram's family went out the tent, so to speak. Convinced that Hagar regarded her with contempt, Sarai treated the woman so harshly she fled from the camp. Years later, after Sarai had given birth to Isaac, the matriarch demanded that the concubine be thrown out (see vv. 8–21). Abram and Sarai look faithless and cruel in their treatment of Hagar. Peace and fulfillment look impossible for Hagar.

But God didn't abandon Hagar to futility. He found her in the wilderness and promised that the child she had borne Abram would be the father of a multitude. The Lord showed her that He saw her, heard her, and cared about her complaint. He gave her hope, a promise of family greatness, and peace in the midst of conflict.

This *shalom* is what God can bring to a dark day. Ask Him to intervene when you feel lost and forgotten, as Hagar did.

the land of the Philistines. 33 Then *Abraham* planted a tamarisk tree in Beersheba, and [a]there called on the name of the LORD, [b]the Everlasting God. 34 And Abraham stayed in the land of the Philistines many days.

Abraham's Faith Confirmed

22 Now it came to pass after these things that [a]God tested Abraham, and said to him, "Abraham!"

And he said, "Here I am."

2 Then He said, "Take now your son, [a]your only *son* Isaac, whom you [b]love, and go [c]to the land of Moriah, and offer him there as a [d]burnt offering on one of the mountains of which I shall tell you."

3 So Abraham rose early in the morning and saddled his donkey, and took two of his young men with him, and Isaac his son; and he split the wood for the burnt offering, and arose and went to the place of which God had told him. 4 Then on the third day Abraham lifted his eyes and saw the place afar off. 5 And Abraham said to his young men, "Stay here with the donkey; the lad[1] and I will go yonder and worship, and we will [a]come back to you."

6 So Abraham took the wood of the burnt offering and [a]laid *it* on Isaac his son; and he took the fire in his hand, and a knife, and the two of them went together. 7 But Isaac spoke to Abraham his father and said, "My father!"

And he said, "Here I am, my son."

Then he said, "Look, the fire and the wood, but where *is* the lamb for a burnt offering?"

8 And Abraham said, "My son, God will provide for Himself the [a]lamb for a [b]burnt offering." So the two of them went together.

9 Then they came to the place of which God had told him. And Abraham built an altar there and placed the wood in order; and he bound Isaac his son and [a]laid him on the altar, upon the wood. 10 And Abraham stretched out his hand and took the knife to slay his son.

11 But the [a]Angel of the LORD called to him from heaven and said, "Abraham, Abraham!"

So he said, "Here I am."

12 And He said, [a]"Do not lay your hand on the lad, or do anything to him; for [b]now I know that you fear God, since you have not [c]withheld your son, your only *son*, from Me."

13 Then Abraham lifted his eyes and looked, and there behind *him was* a ram caught in a thicket by its horns. So Abraham went and took the ram, and offered it up for a burnt offering instead of his son. 14 And Abraham called the name of the place, The-LORD-Will-Provide;[1] as it is said *to* this day, "In the Mount of the LORD it shall be provided."

15 Then the Angel of the LORD called to Abraham a second time out of heaven, 16 and said: [a]"By Myself I have sworn, says the LORD, because you have done this thing,

21:33 [a] Gen. 4:26; 12:8; 13:4; 26:25 [b] Deut. 32:40; 33:27 **22:1** [a] Heb. 11:17 **22:2** [a] Gen. 22:12, 16 [b] John 5:20 [c] 2 Chr. 3:1 [d] Gen. 8:20; 31:54 **22:5** [a] [Heb. 11:19] [1] Or *young man* **22:6** [a] John 19:17 **22:8** [a] John 1:29, 36 [b] Ex. 12:3–6 **22:9** [a] [Heb. 11:17–19] **22:11** [a] Gen. 16:7–11; 21:17, 18; 31:11 **22:12** [a] 1 Sam. 15:22 [b] James 2:21, 22 [c] Gen. 22:2, 16 **22:14** [1] Hebrew *YHWH Yireh* **22:16** [a] Ps. 105:9

PEACE FROM THE TESTING

Now it came to pass after these things that God tested Abraham.

GENESIS 22:1

I have been tested; I've had to make hard choices. We all have. But never have I been tested at the level Abraham was or faced what he did. I can only imagine the utter despair and loss of peace Abraham experienced when God said to him, "Take now your son, your only son Isaac, whom you love, and go to the land of Moriah, and offer him there as a burnt offering" (v. 2). I suspect Abraham said nothing about this to Sarah! Their long-promised and finally delivered son was to be given up as a sacrifice to God? And Abraham himself was to lift the knife?

Of course, we all know that everything turned out okay. God provided Abraham with a ram to offer in place of his son. Abraham and Isaac worshiped God and returned home. When we face tests, we don't know how things will turn out any more than Abraham did. But the ram was already in the wings waiting to get caught.

In the face of hard choices, we do our utmost to make decisions rooted in trust. Remember that God's deliverance is already on the way. And from trust in the One who delivers us comes peace.

and have not withheld your son, your only
son— 17 blessing I will [a]bless you, and multiplying I will multiply your descendants [b]as
the stars of the heaven [c]and as the sand which
is on the seashore; and [d]your descendants
shall possess the gate of their enemies. 18 [a]In
your seed all the nations of the earth shall
be blessed, [b]because you have obeyed My
voice." 19 So Abraham returned to his young
men, and they rose and went together to [a]Be-
ersheba; and Abraham dwelt at Beersheba.

The Family of Nahor

20 Now it came to pass after these things
that it was told Abraham, saying, "Indeed [a]Mil-
cah also has borne children to your brother
Nahor: 21 [a]Huz his firstborn, Buz his brother,
Kemuel the father [b]of Aram, 22 Chesed, Hazo,
Pildash, Jidlaph, and Bethuel." 23 And [a]Bethu-
el begot Rebekah.[1] These eight Milcah bore to
Nahor, Abraham's brother. 24 His concubine,
whose name was Reumah, also bore Tebah,
Gaham, Thahash, and Maachah.

Sarah's Death and Burial

23 Sarah lived one hundred and twenty-
seven years; *these were* the years of the
life of Sarah. 2 So Sarah died in [a]Kirjath Arba
(that *is,* [b]Hebron) in the land of Canaan, and
Abraham came to mourn for Sarah and to
weep for her.
3 Then Abraham stood up from before his
dead, and spoke to the sons of [a]Heth, saying,
4 [a]"I *am* a foreigner and a visitor among you.
[b]Give me property for a burial place among
you, that I may bury my dead out of my sight."
5 And the sons of Heth answered Abraham,
saying to him, 6 "Hear us, my lord: You *are* [a]a
mighty prince among us; bury your dead in
the choicest of our burial places. None of us
will withhold from you his burial place, that
you may bury your dead."
7 Then Abraham stood up and bowed himself to the people of the land, the sons of
Heth. 8 And he spoke with them, saying, "If
it is your wish that I bury my dead out of my
sight, hear me, and meet with Ephron the son
of Zohar for me, 9 that he may give me the
cave of [a]Machpelah which he has, which *is* at
the end of his field. Let him give it to me at
the full price, as property for a burial place
among you."
10 Now Ephron dwelt among the sons of
Heth; and Ephron the Hittite answered Abraham in the presence of the sons of Heth, all
who [a]entered at the gate of his city, saying,
11 [a]"No, my lord, hear me: I give you the field
and the cave that *is* in it; I give it to you in

22:17 [a] Gen. 17:16; 26:3, 24 [b] Gen. 15:5; 26:4 [c] Gen. 13:16; 32:12 [d] Gen. 24:60 **22:18** [a] Gen. 12:3; 18:18; 26:4; [Acts 3:25, 26]; Gal. 3:8, 9, 16, 18 [b] Gen. 18:19; 22:3, 10; 26:5 **22:19** [a] Gen. 21:31 **22:20** [a] Gen. 11:29; 24:15 **22:21** [a] Job 1:1 [b] Job 32:2 **22:23** [a] Gen. 24:15 [1] Spelled *Rebecca* in Romans 9:10 **23:2** [a] Josh. 14:15; 15:13; 21:11 [b] Gen. 13:18; 23:19 **23:3** [a] Gen. 10:15; 15:20 **23:4** [a] [Gen. 17:8] [b] Acts 7:5, 16 **23:6** [a] Gen. 13:2; 14:14; 24:35 **23:9** [a] Gen. 25:9 **23:10** [a] Gen. 23:18; 34:20, 24 **23:11** [a] 2 Sam. 24:21–24

the presence of the sons of my people. I give
it to you. Bury your dead!"
12 Then Abraham bowed himself down
before the people of the land; 13 and he spoke
to Ephron in the hearing of the people of the
land, saying, "If you *will give it,* please hear
me. I will give you money for the field; take
it from me and I will bury my dead there."
14 And Ephron answered Abraham, saying
to him, 15 "My lord, listen to me; the land *is*
worth four hundred [a]shekels of silver. What
is that between you and me? So bury your
dead." 16 And Abraham listened to Ephron;
and Abraham [a]weighed out the silver for
Ephron which he had named in the hearing
of the sons of Heth, four hundred shekels of
silver, currency of the merchants.
17 So [a]the field of Ephron which *was* in
Machpelah, which *was* before Mamre, the
field and the cave which *was* in it, and all
the trees that *were* in the field, which *were*
within all the surrounding borders, were
deeded 18 to Abraham as a possession in the
presence of the sons of Heth, before all who
went in at the gate of his city.
19 And after this, Abraham buried Sarah
his wife in the cave of the field of Machpelah,
before Mamre (that *is,* Hebron) in the land of
Canaan. 20 So the field and the cave that *is* in
it [a]were deeded to Abraham by the sons of
Heth as property for a burial place.

A Bride for Isaac

24 Now Abraham [a]was old, well advanced
in age; and the LORD [b]had blessed
Abraham in all things. 2 So Abraham said [a]to
the oldest servant of his house, who [b]ruled
over all that he had, "Please, [c]put your hand
under my thigh, 3 and I will make you [a]swear
by the LORD, the God of heaven and the God
of the earth, that [b]you will not take a wife for
my son from the daughters of the Canaanites,
among whom I dwell; 4 [a]but you shall go [b]to
my country and to my family, and take a wife
for my son Isaac."
5 And the servant said to him, "Perhaps
the woman will not be willing to follow me
to this land. Must I take your son back to the
land from which you came?"
6 But Abraham said to him, "Beware that
you do not take my son back there. 7 The
LORD God of heaven, who [a]took me from
my father's house and from the land of my
family, and who spoke to me and swore to
me, saying, [b]'To your descendants[1] I give this
land,' [c]He will send His angel before you, and
you shall take a wife for my son from there.
8 And if the woman is not willing to follow
you, then [a]you will be released from this
oath; only do not take my son back there."
9 So the servant put his hand under the thigh
of Abraham his master, and swore to him
concerning this matter.
10 Then the servant took ten of his master's
camels and departed, [a]for all his master's
goods *were in* his hand. And he arose and
went to Mesopotamia, to [b]the city of Nahor.
11 And he made his camels kneel down outside
the city by a well of water at evening time,
the time [a]when women go out to draw *water.*
12 Then he [a]said, "O LORD God of my master
Abraham, please [b]give me success this day,
and show kindness to my master Abraham.
13 Behold, *here* [a]I stand by the well of water,
and [b]the daughters of the men of the city
are coming out to draw water. 14 Now let it be
that the young woman to whom I say, 'Please
let down your pitcher that I may drink,' and
she says, 'Drink, and I will also give your
camels a drink'—*let* her *be the one* You have
appointed for Your servant Isaac. And [a]by
this I will know that You have shown kindness
to my master."
15 And it happened, [a]before he had finished
speaking, that behold, [b]Rebekah, who was
born to Bethuel, son of [c]Milcah, the wife of
Nahor, Abraham's brother, came out with her
pitcher on her shoulder. 16 Now the young
woman [a]*was* very beautiful to behold, a virgin; no man had known her. And she went
down to the well, filled her pitcher, and came
up. 17 And the servant ran to meet her and
said, "Please let me drink a little water from
your pitcher."
18 [a]So she said, "Drink, my lord." Then she
quickly let her pitcher down to her hand,
and gave him a drink. 19 And when she had
finished giving him a drink, she said, "I will
draw *water* for your camels also, until they
have finished drinking." 20 Then she quickly
emptied her pitcher into the trough, ran
back to the well to draw *water,* and drew for
all his camels. 21 And the man, wondering at
her, remained silent so as to know whether
[a]the LORD had made his journey prosperous
or not.
22 So it was, when the camels had finished
drinking, that the man took a golden [a]nose

23:15 [a] Ex. 30:13 **23:16** [a] Jer. 32:9, 10 **23:17** [a] Gen. 25:9; 49:29–32; 50:13 **23:20** [a] Jer. 32:10, 11 **24:1** [a] Gen. 18:11; 21:5 [b] Gen. 12:2; 13:2; 24:35 **24:2** [a] Gen. 15:2 [b] Gen. 24:10; 39:4–6 [c] Gen. 47:29 **24:3** [a] Gen. 14:19, 22 [b] Deut. 7:3 **24:4** [a] Gen. 28:2 [b] Gen. 12:1 **24:7** [a] Gen. 12:1; 24:3 [b] Gen. 12:7; 13:15; 15:18; 17:8 [c] Ex. 23:20, 23; 33:2 [1] Literally *seed* **24:8** [a] Josh. 2:17–20 **24:10** [a] Gen. 24:2, 22 [b] Gen. 11:31, 32; 22:20; 27:43; 29:5 **24:11** [a] Ex. 2:16 **24:12** [a] Ex. 3:6, 15 [b] Neh. 1:11 **24:13** [a] Gen. 24:43 [b] Ex. 2:16 **24:14** [a] Judg. 6:17, 37 **24:15** [a] Is. 65:24 [b] Gen. 24:45; 25:20 [c] Gen. 22:20, 23 **24:16** [a] Gen. 12:11; 26:7; 29:17 **24:18** [a] [1 Pet. 3:8, 9] **24:21** [a] Gen. 24:12–14, 27, 52 **24:22** [a] Ex. 32:2, 3

A SIMPLE REQUEST

Then he said, "O LORD God of my master Abraham, please give me success this day, and show kindness to my master Abraham."

GENESIS 24:12

Have you been given tasks that you feared you might not be able to complete? In my role as a pastor in a megachurch, I have had to play ambassador to try to bring about reconciliation in very sensitive matters. Perhaps you have faced daunting challenges that felt like a mountain you feared climbing. And your inner peace crumbled to bits.

Abraham assigned such a task to a servant: the man was to find a suitable wife for the patriarch's son Isaac. Finding Isaac a wife is a part of the great story. The promise that Abraham would be the father of nations could hardly be fulfilled unless a wife for his son was found!

What I like is how the servant prayed. He asked for success and suggested how he might recognize the right woman, and before he finished his prayer it was answered (v. 14). What is the lesson for us? To reassemble our shattered peace, let us pray to the God of the universe. Let us rely on His sure answer. And let us give glory to God when once again He makes our mountains fall and our peace firm.

ring weighing half a shekel, and two bracelets for her wrists weighing ten *shekels* of gold, 23 and said, "Whose daughter *are* you? Tell me, please, is there room *in* your father's house for us to lodge?"

24 So she said to him, [a]"I *am* the daughter of Bethuel, Milcah's son, whom she bore to Nahor." 25 Moreover she said to him, "We have both straw and feed enough, and room to lodge."

26 Then the man [a]bowed down his head and worshiped the LORD. 27 And he said, [a]"Blessed *be* the LORD God of my master Abraham, who has not forsaken [b]His mercy and His truth toward my master. As for me, being on the way, the LORD [c]led me to the house of my master's brethren." 28 So the young woman ran and told her mother's household these things.

29 Now Rebekah had a brother whose name *was* [a]Laban, and Laban ran out to the man by the well. 30 So it came to pass, when he saw the nose ring, and the bracelets on his sister's wrists, and when he heard the words of his sister Rebekah, saying, "Thus the man spoke to me," that he went to the man. And there he stood by the camels at the well. 31 And he said, "Come in, [a]O blessed of the LORD! Why do you stand outside? For I have prepared the house, and a place for the camels."

32 Then the man came to the house. And he unloaded the camels, and [a]provided straw and feed for the camels, and water to [b]wash his feet and the feet of the men who *were* with him. 33 *Food* was set before him to eat, but he said, [a]"I will not eat until I have told about my errand."

And he said, "Speak on."

34 So he said, "I *am* Abraham's servant. 35 The LORD [a]has blessed my master greatly, and he has become great; and He has given him flocks and herds, silver and gold, male and female servants, and camels and donkeys. 36 And Sarah my master's wife [a]bore a son to my master when she was old; and [b]to him he has given all that he has. 37 Now my master [a]made me swear, saying, 'You shall not take a wife for my son from the daughters of the Canaanites, in whose land I dwell; 38 [a]but you shall go to my father's house and to my family, and take a wife for my son.' 39 [a]And I said to my master, 'Perhaps the woman will not follow me.' 40 [a]But he said to me, 'The LORD, [b]before whom I walk, will send His angel with you and prosper your way; and you shall take a wife for my son from my family and from my father's house. 41 [a]You will be clear from this oath when you arrive among my family; for if they will not give *her* to you, then you will be released from my oath.'

24:24 [a] Gen. 22:23; 24:15 **24:26** [a] Ex. 4:31 **24:27** [a] Ex. 18:10 [b] Gen. 32:10 [c] Gen. 24:21, 48 **24:29** [a] Gen. 29:5, 13 **24:31** [a] Judg. 17:2 **24:32** [a] Gen. 43:24 [b] Gen. 19:2 **24:33** [a] John 4:34 **24:35** [a] Gen. 13:2; 24:1 **24:36** [a] Gen. 21:1–7 [b] Gen. 21:10; 25:5 **24:37** [a] Gen. 24:2–4 **24:38** [a] Gen. 24:4 **24:39** [a] Gen. 24:5 **24:40** [a] Gen. 24:7 [b] Gen. 5:22, 24; 17:1 **24:41** [a] Gen. 24:8

42 "And this day I came to the well and said,
[a]'O LORD God of my master Abraham, if You
will now prosper the way in which I go, 43 [a]be-
hold, I stand by the well of water; and it shall
come to pass that when the virgin comes
out to draw *water,* and I say to her, "Please
give me a little water from your pitcher to
drink," 44 and she says to me, "Drink, and I
will draw for your camels also,"—*let* her *be*
the woman whom the LORD has appointed
for my master's son.'
45 [a]"But before I had finished [b]speaking
in my heart, there was Rebekah, coming out
with her pitcher on her shoulder; and she
went down to the well and drew *water.* And
I said to her, 'Please let me drink.' 46 And she
made haste and let her pitcher down from
her *shoulder,* and said, 'Drink, and I will give
your camels a drink also.' So I drank, and
she gave the camels a drink also. 47 Then I
asked her, and said, 'Whose daughter *are*
you?' And she said, 'The daughter of Bethuel, Nahor's son, whom Milcah bore to him.'
So I put the nose ring on her nose and the
bracelets on her wrists. 48 [a]And I bowed my
head and worshiped the LORD, and blessed
the LORD God of my master Abraham, who
had led me in the way of truth to [b]take the
daughter of my master's brother for his son.
49 Now if you will [a]deal kindly and truly with
my master, tell me. And if not, tell me, that
I may turn to the right hand or to the left."
50 Then Laban and Bethuel answered and
said, [a]"The thing comes from the LORD; we
cannot [b]speak to you either bad or good.
51 [a]Here *is* Rebekah before you; take *her* and
go, and let her be your master's son's wife,
as the LORD has spoken."
52 And it came to pass, when Abraham's
servant heard their words, that [a]he worshiped
the LORD, *bowing himself* to the earth. 53 Then
the servant brought out [a]jewelry of silver,
jewelry of gold, and clothing, and gave *them*
to Rebekah. He also gave [b]precious things to
her brother and to her mother.
54 And he and the men who *were* with him
ate and drank and stayed all night. Then they
arose in the morning, and he said, [a]"Send me
away to my master."
55 But her brother and her mother said, "Let
the young woman stay with us *a few* days, at
least ten; after that she may go."
56 And he said to them, "Do not hinder me,
since the LORD has prospered my way; send
me away so that I may go to my master."
57 So they said, "We will call the young
woman and ask her personally." 58 Then they
called Rebekah and said to her, "Will you go
with this man?"

And she said, "I will go."
59 So they sent away Rebekah their sister
[a]and her nurse, and Abraham's servant and
his men. 60 And they blessed Rebekah and
said to her:

"Our sister, *may* you *become*
[a]*The mother of* thousands of ten
thousands;
[b]And may your descendants
possess
The gates of those who hate them."

61 Then Rebekah and her maids arose,
and they rode on the camels and followed
the man. So the servant took Rebekah and
departed.
62 Now Isaac came from the way of [a]Beer
Lahai Roi, for he dwelt in the South. 63 And
Isaac went out [a]to meditate in the field in the
evening; and he lifted his eyes and looked,
and there, the camels *were* coming. 64 Then
Rebekah lifted her eyes, and when she saw
Isaac [a]she dismounted from her camel; 65 for
she had said to the servant, "Who *is* this man
walking in the field to meet us?"

The servant said, "It *is* my master." So she
took a veil and covered herself.
66 And the servant told Isaac all the things
that he had done. 67 Then Isaac brought her
into his mother Sarah's tent; and he [a]took
Rebekah and she became his wife, and he
loved her. So Isaac [b]was comforted after his
mother's *death.*

Abraham and Keturah

25 Abraham again took a wife, and her
name *was* [a]Keturah. 2 And [a]she bore
him Zimran, Jokshan, Medan, Midian, Ishbak, and Shuah. 3 Jokshan begot Sheba and
Dedan. And the sons of Dedan were As-
shurim, Letushim, and Leummim. 4 And
the sons of Midian *were* Ephah, Epher, Hanoch, Abidah, and Eldaah. All these *were* the
children of Keturah.
5 And [a]Abraham gave all that he had to
Isaac. 6 But Abraham gave gifts to the sons
of the concubines which Abraham had; and
while he was still living he [a]sent them eastward, away from Isaac his son, to [b]the country of the east.

24:42 [a] Gen. 24:12 **24:43** [a] Gen. 24:13 **24:45** [a] Gen. 24:15 [b] 1 Sam. 1:13 **24:48** [a] Gen. 24:26, 52 [b] Gen. 22:23; 24:27 **24:49** [a] Josh. 2:14 **24:50** [a] Ps. 118:23 [b] Gen. 31:24, 29 **24:51** [a] Gen. 20:15 **24:52** [a] Gen. 24:26, 48 **24:53** [a] Ex. 3:22; 11:2; 12:35 [b] 2 Chr. 21:3 **24:54** [a] Gen. 24:56, 59; 30:25 **24:59** [a] Gen. 35:8 **24:60** [a] Gen. 17:16 [b] Gen. 22:17; 28:14 **24:62** [a] Gen. 16:14; 25:11 **24:63** [a] Josh. 1:8 **24:64** [a] Josh. 15:18 **24:67** [a] Gen. 25:20; 29:20 [b] Gen. 23:1, 2; 38:12 **25:1** [a] 1 Chr. 1:32, 33 **25:2** [a] 1 Chr. 1:32, 33 **25:5** [a] Gen. 24:35, 36 **25:6** [a] Gen. 21:14 [b] Judg. 6:3

PEACEFUL MEDITATIONS

Isaac went out to meditate in the field in the evening.

GENESIS 24:63

At day's end I often meditate. I think about what's been finished and what still needs to be done. I think about God's mercies as well as the events that didn't go so well. One day Isaac found himself out in a field meditating when he saw camels approaching. Riding on one of them was Rebekah. She saw Isaac, and Isaac saw her. After a detailed explanation from his servant, Isaac "took Rebekah and she became his wife, and he loved her" (v. 67). It was love at first sight. What a great story! What began with a servant's earnest prayer (see v. 12) ended with meditation and love.

Isaac, his servant, and Rebekah let God write their story. They were not perfect people. But they were people of prayer and meditation. They sensed God's presence, they sought Him, and they were blessed.

Prayer and meditation are the instruments of peace. Taking the time to pray, thinking about what we need to pray about, and considering the many blessings God has sent our way create peace. What tool will you use today to find or restore peace?

Abraham's Death and Burial

7 This *is* the sum of the years of Abraham's
life which he lived: one hundred and seventy-
five years. 8 Then Abraham breathed his last
and [a]died in a good old age, an old man and
full *of years,* and [b]was gathered to his people. 9 And [a]his sons Isaac and Ishmael buried him in the cave of [b]Machpelah, which
is before Mamre, in the field of Ephron the
son of Zohar the Hittite, 10 [a]the field which
Abraham purchased from the sons of Heth.
[b]There Abraham was buried, and Sarah his
wife. 11 And it came to pass, after the death
of Abraham, that God blessed his son Isaac.
And Isaac dwelt at [a]Beer Lahai Roi.

The Families of Ishmael and Isaac

12 Now this *is* the [a]genealogy of Ishmael, Abraham's son, whom Hagar the Egyptian, Sarah's maidservant, bore to Abraham.
13 And [a]these *were* the names of the sons
of Ishmael, by their names, according to
their generations: The firstborn of Ishmael, Nebajoth; then Kedar, Adbeel, Mibsam,
14 Mishma, Dumah, Massa, 15 Hadar,[1] Tema,
Jetur, Naphish, and Kedemah. 16 These *were*
the sons of Ishmael and these *were* their
names, by their towns and their settlements,
[a]twelve princes according to their nations.
17 These *were* the years of the life of Ishmael:
one hundred and thirty-seven years; and [a]he
breathed his last and died, and was gathered
to his people. 18 [a](They dwelt from Havilah as
far as Shur, which *is* east of Egypt as you go
toward Assyria.) He died [b]in the presence of
all his brethren.
19 This *is* the [a]genealogy of Isaac, Abraham's son. [b]Abraham begot Isaac. 20 Isaac
was forty years old when he took Rebekah
as wife, [a]the daughter of Bethuel the Syrian
of Padan Aram, [b]the sister of Laban the Syrian. 21 Now Isaac pleaded with the LORD for
his wife, because she *was* barren; [a]and the
LORD granted his plea, [b]and Rebekah his
wife conceived. 22 But the children struggled
together within her; and she said, "If *all is*
well, why *am I like* this?" [a]So she went to
inquire of the LORD.
23 And the LORD said to her:

[a]"Two nations *are* in your womb,
Two peoples shall be separated from
your body;
One people shall be stronger than [b]the
other,
[c]And the older shall serve the younger."

24 So when her days were fulfilled *for her*
to give birth, indeed *there were* twins in her
womb. 25 And the first came out red. *He was*

25:8 [a] Gen. 15:15; 47:8, 9 [b] Gen. 25:17; 35:29; 49:29, 33 **25:9** [a] Gen. 35:29; 50:13 [b] Gen. 23:9, 17; 49:30 **25:10** [a] Gen. 23:3–16 [b] Gen. 49:31 **25:11** [a] Gen. 16:14 **25:12** [a] Gen. 11:10, 27; 16:15 **25:13** [a] 1 Chr. 1:29–31 **25:15** [1] Masoretic Text reads *Hadad.* **25:16** [a] Gen. 17:20 **25:17** [a] Gen. 25:8; 49:33 **25:18** [a] 1 Sam. 15:7 [b] Gen. 16:12 **25:19** [a] Gen. 36:1, 9 [b] Matt. 1:2 **25:20** [a] Gen. 22:23; 24:15, 29, 67 [b] Gen. 24:29 **25:21** [a] 1 Chr. 5:20 [b] Rom. 9:10–13 **25:22** [a] 1 Sam. 1:15; 9:9; 10:22 **25:23** [a] Gen. 17:4–6, 16; 24:60 [b] 2 Sam. 8:14 [c] Rom. 9:12

[a]like a hairy garment all over; so they called his name Esau.[1] 26 Afterward his brother came out, and [a]his hand took hold of Esau's heel; so [b]his name was called Jacob.[1] Isaac *was* sixty years old when she bore them.

27 So the boys grew. And Esau was [a]a skillful hunter, a man of the field; but Jacob was [b]a mild man, [c]dwelling in tents. 28 And Isaac loved Esau because he [a]ate *of his* game, [b]but Rebekah loved Jacob.

Esau Sells His Birthright

29 Now Jacob cooked a stew; and Esau came in from the field, and he *was* weary. 30 And Esau said to Jacob, "Please feed me with that same red *stew*, for I *am* weary." Therefore his name was called Edom.[1]

31 But Jacob said, "Sell me your birthright as of this day."

32 And Esau said, "Look, I *am* about to die; so [a]what *is* this birthright to me?"

33 Then Jacob said, "Swear to me as of this day."

So he swore to him, and [a]sold his birthright to Jacob. 34 And Jacob gave Esau bread and stew of lentils; then [a]he ate and drank, arose, and went his way. Thus Esau [b]despised *his* birthright.

Isaac and Abimelech

26 There was a famine in the land, besides [a]the first famine that was in the days of Abraham. And Isaac went to [b]Abimelech king of the Philistines, in Gerar.

2 Then the LORD appeared to him and said: [a]"Do not go down to Egypt; live in [b]the land of which I shall tell you. 3 [a]Dwell in this land, and [b]I will be with you and [c]bless you; for to you and your descendants [d]I give all these lands, and I will perform [e]the oath which I swore to Abraham your father. 4 And [a]I will make your descendants multiply as the stars of heaven; I will give to your descendants all these lands; [b]and in your seed all the nations of the earth shall be blessed; 5 [a]because Abraham obeyed My voice and kept My charge, My commandments, My statutes, and My laws."

6 So Isaac dwelt in Gerar. 7 And the men of the place asked about his wife. And [a]he said, "She *is* my sister"; for [b]he was afraid to say, "*She is* my wife," *because he thought,* "lest the men of the place kill me for Rebekah, because she *is* [c]beautiful to behold." 8 Now it came to pass, when he had been there a long time, that Abimelech king of the Philistines looked through a window, and saw, and there was Isaac, showing endearment to Rebekah his wife. 9 Then Abimelech called Isaac and said, "Quite obviously she *is* your wife; so how could you say, 'She *is* my sister'?"

Isaac said to him, "Because I said, 'Lest I die on account of her.' "

10 And Abimelech said, "What *is* this you have done to us? One of the people might soon have lain with your wife, and [a]you would have brought guilt on us." 11 So Abimelech charged all *his* people, saying, "He who [a]touches this man or his wife shall surely be put to death."

12 Then Isaac sowed in that land, and reaped in the same year [a]a hundredfold; and the LORD [b]blessed him. 13 The man [a]began to prosper, and continued prospering until he became very prosperous; 14 for he had possessions of flocks and possessions of herds and a great number of servants. So the Philistines [a]envied him. 15 Now the Philistines had stopped up all the wells [a]which his father's servants had dug in the days of Abraham his father, and they had filled them with earth. 16 And Abimelech said to Isaac, "Go away from us, for [a]you are much mightier than we."

17 Then Isaac departed from there and pitched his tent in the Valley of Gerar, and dwelt there. 18 And Isaac dug again the wells of water which they had dug in the days of Abraham his father, for the Philistines had stopped them up after the death of Abraham. [a]He called them by the names which his father had called them.

19 Also Isaac's servants dug in the valley, and found a well of running water there. 20 But the herdsmen of Gerar [a]quarreled with Isaac's herdsmen, saying, "The water *is* ours." So he called the name of the well Esek,[1] because they quarreled with him. 21 Then they dug another well, and they quarreled over that *one* also. So he called its name Sitnah.[1] 22 And he moved from there and dug another well, and they did not quarrel over it. So he called its name Rehoboth,[1] because he said, "For now the LORD has made room for us, and we shall [a]be fruitful in the land."

25:25 [a] Gen. 27:11, 16, 23 [1] Literally *Hairy* **25:26** [a] Hos. 12:3 [b] Gen. 27:36 [1] Literally *Supplanter* **25:27** [a] Gen. 27:3, 5 [b] Job 1:1, 8 [c] Heb. 11:9 **25:28** [a] Gen. 27:4, 19, 25, 31 [b] Gen. 27:6–10 **25:30** [1] Literally *Red* **25:32** [a] Mark 8:36, 37 **25:33** [a] Heb. 12:16 **25:34** [a] Eccl. 8:15 [b] Heb. 12:16, 17 **26:1** [a] Gen. 12:10 [b] Gen. 20:1, 2 **26:2** [a] Gen. 12:7; 17:1; 18:1; 35:9 [b] Gen. 12:1 **26:3** [a] Heb. 11:9 [b] Gen. 28:13, 15 [c] Gen. 12:2 [d] Gen. 12:7; 13:15; 15:18 [e] Gen. 22:16 **26:4** [a] Gen. 15:5; 22:17 [b] Gen. 12:3; 22:18; Gal. 3:8 **26:5** [a] Gen. 22:16, 18 **26:7** [a] Gen. 12:13; 20:2, 12, 13 [b] Prov. 29:25 [c] Gen. 12:11; 24:16; 29:17 **26:10** [a] Gen. 20:9 **26:11** [a] Ps. 105:15 **26:12** [a] Matt. 13:8, 23 [b] Gen. 24:1; 25:8, 11; 26:3 **26:13** [a] [Prov. 10:22] **26:14** [a] Gen. 37:11 **26:15** [a] Gen. 21:25, 30 **26:16** [a] Ex. 1:9 **26:18** [a] Gen. 21:31 **26:20** [a] Gen. 21:25 [1] Literally *Quarrel* **26:21** [1] Literally *Enmity* **26:22** [a] Gen. 17:6; 28:3; 41:52 [1] Literally *Spaciousness*

23 Then he went up from there to Beersheba. 24 And the LORD [a]appeared to him
the same night and said, [b]"I *am* the God of
your father Abraham; [c]do not fear, for [d]I *am*
with you. I will bless you and multiply your
descendants for My servant Abraham's sake."
25 So he [a]built an altar there and [b]called on
the name of the LORD, and he pitched his tent
there; and there Isaac's servants dug a well.
26 Then Abimelech came to him from
Gerar with Ahuzzath, one of his friends, [a]and
Phichol the commander of his army. 27 And
Isaac said to them, "Why have you come to
me, [a]since you hate me and have [b]sent me
away from you?"
28 But they said, "We have certainly seen
that the LORD [a]is with you. So we said, 'Let
there now be an oath between us, between
you and us; and let us make a covenant with
you, 29 that you will do us no harm, since we
have not touched you, and since we have
done nothing to you but good and have sent
you away in peace. [a]You *are* now the blessed
of the LORD.' "
30 [a]So he made them a feast, and they ate
and drank. 31 Then they arose early in the
morning and [a]swore an oath with one another; and Isaac sent them away, and they
departed from him in peace.
32 It came to pass the same day that Isaac's
servants came and told him about the well
which they had dug, and said to him, "We
have found water." 33 So he called it Shebah.[1]
[a]Therefore the name of the city *is* Beersheba[2] to this day.
34 [a]When Esau was forty years old, he took
as wives Judith the daughter of Beeri the
Hittite, and Basemath the daughter of Elon
the Hittite. 35 And [a]they were a grief of mind
to Isaac and Rebekah.

Isaac Blesses Jacob

27 Now it came to pass, when Isaac was
[a]old and [b]his eyes were so dim that he
could not see, that he called Esau his older
son and said to him, "My son."
And he answered him, "Here I am."
2 Then he said, "Behold now, I am old. I
[a]do not know the day of my death. 3 [a]Now
therefore, please take your weapons, your
quiver and your bow, and go out to the field
and hunt game for me. 4 And make me savory food, such as I love, and bring *it* to me
that I may eat, that my soul [a]may bless you
before I die."
5 Now Rebekah was listening when Isaac
spoke to Esau his son. And Esau went to
the field to hunt game and to bring *it*. 6 So
Rebekah spoke to Jacob her son, saying, "Indeed I heard your father speak to Esau your

26:24 [a] Gen. 26:2 [b] Gen. 17:7, 8; 24:12 [c] Gen. 15:1 [d] Gen. 26:3, 4 **26:25** [a] Gen. 12:7, 8; 13:4, 18; 22:9; 33:20 [b] Ps. 116:17 **26:26** [a] Gen. 21:22 **26:27** [a] Judg. 11:7 [b] Gen. 26:16 **26:28** [a] Gen. 21:22, 23 **26:29** [a] Gen. 24:31 **26:30** [a] Gen. 19:3 **26:31** [a] Gen. 21:31 **26:33** [a] Gen. 21:31; 28:10 [1] Literally *Oath* or *Seven* [2] Literally *Well of the Oath* or *Well of the Seven* **26:34** [a] Gen. 28:8; 36:2 **26:35** [a] Gen. 27:46; 28:1, 8 **27:1** [a] Gen. 35:28 [b] Gen. 48:10 **27:2** [a] [Prov. 27:1] **27:3** [a] Gen. 25:27, 28 **27:4** [a] Deut. 33:1

BE THE PERSON OF PEACE

We have certainly seen that the LORD is with you . . . You are now the blessed of the LORD.

GENESIS 26:28-29

Isaac's life was tumultuous. Like Abraham, Isaac lied about his wife to a tribal chieftain named Abimelech (see chs. 6–11). Isaac also bumped into annoying herdsmen who claimed one well after another that Isaac and his men had dug. When Isaac finally found a place he could call his own, Abimelech paid him a visit. What now?

As it turns out, Abimelech wanted no trouble; he wanted to covenant with Isaac for peace between them. Why? "We have certainly seen that the LORD is with you" (26:28). What exactly had Abimelech seen? Verses 12–16 say that Isaac had sowed and greatly prospered in the land he shared with Abimelech, enough that the Philistines envied him.

I suspect Abimelech saw in Isaac much more than farming know-how. Perhaps the clue lay in the way that Isaac and Abimelech parted company: "They departed from him in peace" (v. 31). Abimelech had witnessed something new—a man of peace. For that reason, Abimelech, though more powerful, desired the younger man's friendship. Peace does that. Are you a person of peace?

brother, saying, [7]'Bring me game and make
savory food for me, that I may eat it and bless
you in the presence of the LORD before my
death.' [8]Now therefore, my son, [a]obey my
voice according to what I command you. [9]Go
now to the flock and bring me from there
two choice kids of the goats, and I will make
[a]savory food from them for your father, such
as he loves. [10]Then you shall take *it* to your
father, that he may eat *it*, and that he [a]may
bless you before his death."

[11]And Jacob said to Rebekah his mother,
"Look, [a]Esau my brother *is* a hairy man, and
I *am* a smooth-*skinned* man. [12]Perhaps my
father will [a]feel me, and I shall seem to be
a deceiver to him; and I shall bring [b]a curse
on myself and not a blessing."

[13]But his mother said to him, [a]"*Let* your
curse *be* on me, my son; only obey my voice,
and go, get *them* for me." [14]And he went and
got *them* and brought *them* to his mother,
and his mother [a]made savory food, such as
his father loved. [15]Then Rebekah took [a]the
choice clothes of her elder son Esau, which
were with her in the house, and put them on
Jacob her younger son. [16]And she put the
skins of the kids of the goats on his hands and
on the smooth part of his neck. [17]Then she
gave the savory food and the bread, which she
had prepared, into the hand of her son Jacob.

[18]So he went to his father and said, "My
father."

And he said, "Here I am. Who *are* you,
my son?"

[19]Jacob said to his father, "I *am* Esau your
firstborn; I have done just as you told me;
please arise, sit and eat of my game, [a]that
your soul may bless me."

[20]But Isaac said to his son, "How *is it* that
you have found *it* so quickly, my son?"

And he said, "Because the LORD your God
brought *it* to me."

[21]Isaac said to Jacob, "Please come near,
that I [a]may feel you, my son, whether you *are*
really my son Esau or not." [22]So Jacob went
near to Isaac his father, and he felt him and
said, "The voice *is* Jacob's voice, but the hands
are the hands of Esau." [23]And he did not recognize him, because [a]his hands were hairy like
his brother Esau's hands; so he blessed him.

[24]Then he said, "*Are* you really my son
Esau?"

He said, "I *am*."

[25]He said, "Bring *it* near to me, and I will
eat of my son's game, so [a]that my soul may
bless you." So he brought *it* near to him,
and he ate; and he brought him wine, and
he drank. [26]Then his father Isaac said to
him, "Come near now and kiss me, my son."
[27]And he came near and [a]kissed him; and
he smelled the smell of his clothing, and
blessed him and said:

"Surely, [b]the smell of my son
Is like the smell of a field
Which the LORD has blessed.
[28] Therefore may [a]God give you
Of [b]the dew of heaven,
Of [c]the fatness of the earth,
And [d]plenty of grain and wine.
[29] [a]Let peoples serve you,
And nations bow down to you.
Be master over your brethren,
And [b]let your mother's sons bow down
to you.
[c]Cursed *be* everyone who curses you,
And blessed *be* those who bless you!"

Esau's Lost Hope

[30]Now it happened, as soon as Isaac had
finished blessing Jacob, and Jacob had
scarcely gone out from the presence of Isaac
his father, that Esau his brother came in from
his hunting. [31]He also had made savory food,
and brought it to his father, and said to his
father, "Let my father arise and [a]eat of his
son's game, that your soul may bless me."

[32]And his father Isaac said to him, "Who
are you?"

So he said, "I *am* your son, your firstborn,
Esau."

[33]Then Isaac trembled exceedingly, and
said, "Who? Where *is* the one who hunted
game and brought *it* to me? I ate all *of it* before you came, and I have blessed him—[a]*and*
indeed he shall be blessed."

[34]When Esau heard the words of his father,
[a]he cried with an exceedingly great and bitter
cry, and said to his father, "Bless me—me
also, O my father!"

[35]But he said, "Your brother came with
deceit and has taken away your blessing."

[36]And *Esau* said, [a]"Is he not rightly named
Jacob? For he has supplanted me these two
times. He took away my birthright, and now
look, he has taken away my blessing!" And
he said, "Have you not reserved a blessing
for me?"

[37]Then Isaac answered and said to Esau,
[a]"Indeed I have made him your master, and

27:8 [a] Gen. 27:13, 43 **27:9** [a] Gen. 27:4 **27:10** [a] Gen. 27:4; 48:16 **27:11** [a] Gen. 25:25 **27:12** [a] Gen. 27:21, 22 [b] Deut. 27:18 **27:13** [a] Gen. 43:9 **27:14** [a] Prov. 23:3 **27:15** [a] Gen. 27:27 **27:19** [a] Gen. 27:4 **27:21** [a] Gen. 27:12 **27:23** [a] Gen. 27:16 **27:25** [a] Gen. 27:4, 10, 19, 31 **27:27** [a] Gen. 29:13 [b] Song 4:11 **27:28** [a] Heb. 11:20 [b] Deut. 33:13, 28 [c] Gen. 45:18 [d] Deut. 7:13; 33:28 **27:29** [a] Gen. 9:25; 25:23 [b] Gen. 37:7, 10; 49:8 [c] Gen. 12:2, 3 **27:31** [a] Gen. 27:4 **27:33** [a] Gen. 25:23; 28:3, 4 **27:34** [a] [Heb. 12:17] **27:36** [a] Gen. 25:26, 32–34 **27:37** [a] 2 Sam. 8:14

all his brethren I have given to him as servants; with [b]grain and wine I have sustained
him. What shall I do now for you, my son?"
38 And Esau said to his father, "Have you
only one blessing, my father? Bless me—me
also, O my father!" And Esau lifted up his
voice [a]and wept.
39 Then Isaac his father answered and said
to him:

"Behold, [a]your dwelling shall be of the
fatness of the earth,
And of the dew of heaven from
above.
40 By your sword you shall live,
And [a]you shall serve your brother;
And [b]it shall come to pass, when you
become restless,
That you shall break his yoke from
your neck."

Jacob Escapes from Esau

41 So Esau [a]hated Jacob because of the
blessing with which his father blessed him,
and Esau said in his heart, [b]"The days of
mourning for my father are at hand; [c]then I
will kill my brother Jacob."
42 And the words of Esau her older son were
told to Rebekah. So she sent and called Jacob
her younger son, and said to him, "Surely
your brother Esau [a]comforts himself concerning you *by intending* to kill you. 43 Now
therefore, my son, obey my voice: arise, flee
to my brother Laban [a]in Haran. 44 And stay
with him a [a]few days, until your brother's fury
turns away, 45 until your brother's anger turns
away from you, and he forgets what you have
done to him; then I will send and bring you
from there. Why should I be bereaved also
of you both in one day?"
46 And Rebekah said to Isaac, [a]"I am weary
of my life because of the daughters of Heth;
[b]if Jacob takes a wife of the daughters of Heth,
like these *who are* the daughters of the land,
what good will my life be to me?"

28 Then Isaac called Jacob and [a]blessed
him, and charged him, and said to
him: [b]"You shall not take a wife from the
daughters of Canaan. 2 [a]Arise, go to [b]Padan
Aram, to the house of [c]Bethuel your mother's
father; and take yourself a wife from there
of the daughters of [d]Laban your mother's
brother.

3 "May [a]God Almighty bless you,
And make you [b]fruitful and multiply
you,
That you may be an assembly of peoples;
4 And give you [a]the blessing of Abraham,
To you and your descendants with you,
That you may inherit the land
[b]In which you are a stranger,
Which God gave to Abraham."

5 So Isaac sent Jacob away, and he went to
Padan Aram, to Laban the son of Bethuel the
Syrian, the brother of Rebekah, the mother
of Jacob and Esau.

Esau Marries Mahalath

6 Esau saw that Isaac had blessed Jacob and
sent him away to Padan Aram to take himself a
wife from there, *and that* as he blessed him he
gave him a charge, saying, "You shall not take a
wife from the daughters of Canaan," 7 and that
Jacob had obeyed his father and his mother
and had gone to Padan Aram. 8 Also Esau saw
[a]that the daughters of Canaan did not please
his father Isaac. 9 So Esau went to Ishmael
and [a]took [b]Mahalath the daughter of Ishmael, Abraham's son, [c]the sister of Nebajoth, to
be his wife in addition to the wives he had.

Jacob's Vow at Bethel

10 Now Jacob [a]went out from Beersheba
and went toward [b]Haran. 11 So he came to
a certain place and stayed there all night,
because the sun had set. And he took one
of the stones of that place and put it at his
head, and he lay down in that place to sleep.
12 Then he [a]dreamed, and behold, a ladder
was set up on the earth, and its top reached
to heaven; and there [b]the angels of God were
ascending and descending on it.
13 [a]And behold, the LORD stood above it
and said: [b]"I *am* the LORD God of Abraham
your father and the God of Isaac; [c]the land
on which you lie I will give to you and your
descendants. 14 Also your [a]descendants shall
be as the dust of the earth; you shall spread
abroad [b]to the west and the east, to the north
and the south; and in you and [c]in your seed
all the families of the earth shall be blessed.
15 Behold, [a]I *am* with you and will [b]keep you
wherever you go, and will [c]bring you back
to this land; for [d]I will not leave you [e]until I
have done what I have spoken to you."

27:37 [b] Gen. 27:28, 29 **27:38** [a] Heb. 12:17 **27:39** [a] Heb. 11:20 **27:40** [a] Gen. 25:23; 27:29 [b] 2 Kin. 8:20–22 **27:41** [a] Gen. 26:27; 32:3–11; 37:4, 5, 8 [b] Gen. 50:2–4, 10 [c] Obad. 10 **27:42** [a] Ps. 64:5 **27:43** [a] Gen. 11:31; 25:20; 28:2, 5 **27:44** [a] Gen. 31:41 **27:46** [a] Gen. 26:34, 35; 28:8 [b] Gen. 24:3 **28:1** [a] Gen. 27:33 [b] Gen. 24:3 **28:2** [a] Hos. 12:12 [b] Gen. 25:20 [c] Gen. 22:23 [d] Gen. 24:29; 27:43; 29:5 **28:3** [a] Gen. 17:16; 35:11; 48:3 [b] Gen. 26:4, 24 **28:4** [a] Gen. 12:2, 3; 22:17 [b] Gen. 17:8; 23:4; 36:7 **28:8** [a] Gen. 24:3; 26:34, 35; 27:46 **28:9** [a] Gen. 26:34, 35 [b] Gen. 36:2, 3 [c] Gen. 25:13 **28:10** [a] Hos. 12:12 [b] Gen. 12:4, 5; 27:43; 29:4 **28:12** [a] Gen. 31:10; 41:1 [b] John 1:51 **28:13** [a] Gen. 35:1; 48:3 [b] Gen. 26:24 [c] Gen. 13:15, 17; 26:3; 35:12 **28:14** [a] Gen. 13:16; 22:17 [b] Gen. 13:14, 15 [c] Gen. 12:3; 18:18; 22:18; 26:4 **28:15** [a] Gen. 26:3, 24; 31:3 [b] Gen. 48:16 [c] Gen. 35:6; 48:21 [d] Deut. 7:9; 31:6, 8 [e] Num. 23:19

16 Then Jacob awoke from his sleep and
said, "Surely the LORD is in [a]this place,
and I did not know *it*." 17 And he was afraid
and said, "How awesome *is* this place! This *is*
none other than the house of God, and this
is the gate of heaven!"

18 Then Jacob rose early in the morning,
and took the stone that he had put at his head,
[a]set it up as a pillar, [b]and poured oil on top
of it. 19 And he called the name of [a]that place
Bethel;[1] but the name of that city had been
Luz previously. 20 [a]Then Jacob made a vow,
saying, "If [b]God will be with me, and keep
me in this way that I am going, and give me
[c]bread to eat and clothing to put on, 21 so that
[a]I come back to my father's house in peace,
[b]then the LORD shall be my God. 22 And this
stone which I have set as a pillar [a]shall be
God's house, [b]and of all that You give me I
will surely give a tenth to You."

Jacob Meets Rachel

29 So Jacob went on his journey [a]and
came to the land of the people of the
East. 2 And he looked, and saw a [a]well in the
field; and behold, there *were* three flocks of
sheep lying by it; for out of that well they watered the flocks. A large stone *was* on the well's
mouth. 3 Now all the flocks would be gathered
there; and they would roll the stone from the
well's mouth, water the sheep, and put the
stone back in its place on the well's mouth.

4 And Jacob said to them, "My brethren,
where *are* you from?"

And they said, "We *are* from [a]Haran."

5 Then he said to them, "Do you know
[a]Laban the son of Nahor?"

And they said, "We know him."

6 So he said to them, [a]"Is he well?"

And they said, "*He is* well. And look, his
daughter Rachel [b]is coming with the sheep."

7 Then he said, "Look, *it is* still high day; *it is*
not time for the cattle to be gathered together. Water the sheep, and go and feed *them*."

8 But they said, "We cannot until all the
flocks are gathered together, and they have
rolled the stone from the well's mouth; then
we water the sheep."

9 Now while he was still speaking with
them, [a]Rachel came with her father's sheep,
for she was a shepherdess. 10 And it came to
pass, when Jacob saw Rachel the daughter of
Laban his mother's brother, and the sheep of
Laban his mother's brother, that Jacob went
near and [a]rolled the stone from the well's
mouth, and watered the flock of Laban his
mother's brother. 11 Then Jacob [a]kissed Rachel, and lifted up his voice and wept. 12 And
Jacob told Rachel that he *was* [a]her father's
relative and that he *was* Rebekah's son. [b]So
she ran and told her father.

13 Then it came to pass, when Laban heard
the report about Jacob his sister's son, that
[a]he ran to meet him, and embraced him and
kissed him, and brought him to his house. So
he told Laban all these things. 14 And Laban
said to him, [a]"Surely you *are* my bone and my
flesh." And he stayed with him for a month.

Jacob Marries Leah and Rachel

15 Then Laban said to Jacob, "Because you
are my relative, should you therefore serve
me for nothing? Tell me, [a]what *should* your
wages *be?*" 16 Now Laban had two daughters:
the name of the elder *was* Leah, and the name
of the younger *was* Rachel. 17 Leah's eyes *were*
delicate, but Rachel was [a]beautiful of form
and appearance.

18 Now Jacob loved Rachel; so he said, [a]"I
will serve you seven years for Rachel your
younger daughter."

19 And Laban said, "*It is* better that I give
her to you than that I should give her to another man. Stay with me." 20 So Jacob [a]served
seven years for Rachel, and they seemed
only a few days to him because of the love
he had for her.

21 Then Jacob said to Laban, "Give *me* my
wife, for my days are fulfilled, that I may [a]go
in to her." 22 And Laban gathered together
all the men of the place and [a]made a feast.
23 Now it came to pass in the evening, that he
took Leah his daughter and brought her to
Jacob; and he went in to her. 24 And Laban
gave his maid [a]Zilpah to his daughter Leah
as a maid. 25 So it came to pass in the morning, that behold, it *was* Leah. And he said to
Laban, "What is this you have done to me?
Was it not for Rachel that I served you? Why
then have you [a]deceived me?"

26 And Laban said, "It must not be done so
in our country, to give the younger before the
firstborn. 27 [a]Fulfill her week, and we will give
you this one also for the service which you
will serve with me still another seven years."

28 Then Jacob did so and fulfilled her week.
So he gave him his daughter Rachel as wife
also. 29 And Laban gave his maid [a]Bilhah to

28:16 [a] Ex. 3:5 **28:18** [a] Gen. 31:13, 45 [b] Lev. 8:10–12 **28:19** [a] Judg. 1:23, 26 [1] Literally *House of God* **28:20** [a] Judg. 11:30 [b] Gen. 28:15 [c] 1 Tim. 6:8 **28:21** [a] Judg. 11:31 [b] Deut. 26:17 **28:22** [a] Gen. 35:7, 14 [b] Gen. 14:20 **29:1** [a] Num. 23:7 **29:2** [a] Gen. 24:10, 11 **29:4** [a] Gen. 11:31; 28:10 **29:5** [a] Gen. 24:24, 29; 28:2 **29:6** [a] Gen. 43:27 [b] Ex. 2:16, 17 **29:9** [a] Ex. 2:16 **29:10** [a] Ex. 2:17 **29:11** [a] Gen. 33:4; 45:14, 15 **29:12** [a] Gen. 13:8; 14:14, 16; 28:5 [b] Gen. 24:28 **29:13** [a] Gen. 24:29–31 **29:14** [a] Gen. 2:23; 37:27 **29:15** [a] Gen. 30:28; 31:41 **29:17** [a] Gen. 12:11, 14; 26:7 **29:18** [a] Gen. 31:41 **29:20** [a] Gen. 30:26 **29:21** [a] Judg. 15:1 **29:22** [a] John 2:1, 2 **29:24** [a] Gen. 30:9, 10 **29:25** [a] 1 Sam. 28:12 **29:27** [a] Judg. 14:2 **29:29** [a] Gen. 30:3–5

his daughter Rachel as a maid. 30 Then *Jacob*
also went in to Rachel, and he also [a]loved
Rachel more than Leah. And he served with
Laban [b]still another seven years.

The Children of Jacob

31 When the LORD [a]saw that Leah *was* unloved, He [b]opened her womb; but Rachel
was barren. 32 So Leah conceived and bore
a son, and she called his name Reuben;[1]
for she said, "The LORD has surely [a]looked
on my affliction. Now therefore, my husband will love me." 33 Then she conceived
again and bore a son, and said, "Because the
LORD has heard that I *am* unloved, He has
therefore given me this *son* also." And she
called his name Simeon.[1] 34 She conceived
again and bore a son, and said, "Now this
time my husband will become attached to
me, because I have borne him three sons."
Therefore his name was called Levi.[1] 35 And
she conceived again and bore a son, and
said, "Now I will praise the LORD." Therefore she called his name [a]Judah.[1] Then she
stopped bearing.

30 Now when Rachel saw that [a]she bore
Jacob no children, Rachel [b]envied her
sister, and said to Jacob, "Give me children,
[c]or else I die!"

2 And Jacob's anger was aroused against
Rachel, and he said, [a]"*Am* I in the place of
God, who has withheld from you the fruit
of the womb?"

3 So she said, "Here is [a]my maid Bilhah;
go in to her, [b]and she will bear *a child* on
my knees, [c]that I also may have children by
her." 4 Then she gave him Bilhah her maid
[a]as wife, and Jacob went in to her. 5 And
Bilhah conceived and bore Jacob a son.
6 Then Rachel said, "God has [a]judged my
case; and He has also heard my voice and
given me a son." Therefore she called his
name Dan.[1] 7 And Rachel's maid Bilhah conceived again and bore Jacob a second son.
8 Then Rachel said, "With great wrestlings
I have wrestled with my sister, *and* indeed
I have prevailed." So she called his name
Naphtali.[1]

9 When Leah saw that she had stopped
bearing, she took Zilpah her maid and [a]gave
her to Jacob as wife. 10 And Leah's maid Zilpah bore Jacob a son. 11 Then Leah said, "A
troop comes!"[1] So she called his name Gad.[2]
12 And Leah's maid Zilpah bore Jacob a second son. 13 Then Leah said, "I am happy, for
the daughters [a]will call me blessed." So she
called his name Asher.[1]

14 Now Reuben went in the days of wheat

29:30 [a] Deut. 21:15–17 [b] Gen. 30:26; 31:41 **29:31** [a] Ps. 127:3 [b] Gen. 30:1 **29:32** [a] Deut. 26:7 [1] Literally *See, a Son* **29:33** [1] Literally *Heard* **29:34** [1] Literally *Attached* **29:35** [a] Matt. 1:2 [1] Literally *Praise* **30:1** [a] Gen. 16:1, 2; 29:31 [b] Gen. 37:11 [c] [Job 5:2] **30:2** [a] 1 Sam. 1:5 **30:3** [a] Gen. 16:2 [b] Gen. 50:23 [c] Gen. 16:2, 3 **30:4** [a] Gen. 16:3, 4 **30:6** [a] Lam. 3:59 [1] Literally *Judge* **30:8** [1] Literally *My Wrestling* **30:9** [a] Gen. 30:4 **30:11** [1] Following Qere, Syriac, and Targum; Kethib, Septuagint, and Vulgate read *in fortune.* [2] Literally *Troop* or *Fortune* **30:13** [a] Luke 1:48 [1] Literally *Happy*

WHEN YOU HAVE TO WAIT

And he served with Laban still another seven years.

GENESIS 29:30

We all know the saying, "What goes around comes around." I think of it every time I read the stories about the patriarchs, especially the story of Jacob. His relationship with his uncle Laban was almost a contest to see who could outsmart the other (see ch. 31). How God worked His will through this character is quite a story. Step by step, the faith of Jacob grew.

One of the ways that Jacob's faith grew was through learned patience. He met Rachel, Laban's daughter, and fell in love. He agreed to work for seven years in order to marry her only to wake up and find that Laban had surreptitiously slipped his older, less beautiful daughter, Leah, into Rachel's place. So Jacob worked for his crafty uncle another seven years. That's one way to learn patience!

I have found that peace often works the same way. It doesn't always come all at once; sometimes it enters my life gradually, step by step. With each step I recognize more fully the working of God's will, and with it I gain a deeper sense of God's peace.

When has peace come over you gradually?

harvest and found mandrakes in the field,
and brought them to his mother Leah. Then
Rachel said to Leah, [a]"Please give me *some*
of your son's mandrakes."
15 But she said to her, [a]"*Is it* a small matter
that you have taken away my husband? Would
you take away my son's mandrakes also?"
And Rachel said, "Therefore he will lie
with you tonight for your son's mandrakes."
16 When Jacob came out of the field in the
evening, Leah went out to meet him and said,
"You must come in to me, for I have surely
hired you with my son's mandrakes." And he
lay with her that night.
17 And God listened to Leah, and she conceived and bore Jacob a fifth son. 18 Leah
said, "God has given me my wages, because
I have given my maid to my husband." So
she called his name Issachar.[1] 19 Then Leah
conceived again and bore Jacob a sixth son.
20 And Leah said, "God has endowed me *with*
a good endowment; now my husband will
dwell with me, because I have borne him
six sons." So she called his name Zebulun.[1]
21 Afterward she bore a [a]daughter, and called
her name Dinah.
22 Then God [a]remembered Rachel, and
God listened to her and [b]opened her womb.
23 And she conceived and bore a son, and
said, "God has taken away [a]my reproach."
24 So she called his name Joseph,[1] and said,
[a]"The LORD shall add to me another son."

Jacob's Agreement with Laban

25 And it came to pass, when Rachel had
borne Joseph, that Jacob said to Laban,
[a]"Send me away, that I may go to [b]my own
place and to my country. 26 Give *me* my wives
and my children [a]for whom I have served
you, and let me go; for you know my service
which I have done for you."
27 And Laban said to him, "Please *stay,* if
I have found favor in your eyes, *for* [a]I have
learned by experience that the LORD has
blessed me for your sake." 28 Then he said,
[a]"Name me your wages, and I will give *it.*"
29 So *Jacob* said to him, [a]"You know how I
have served you and how your livestock has
been with me. 30 For what you had before I
came was little, and it has increased to a great
amount; the LORD has blessed you since my
coming. And now, when shall I also [a]provide
for my own house?"
31 So he said, "What shall I give you?"
And Jacob said, "You shall not give me
anything. If you will do this thing for me, I
will again feed and keep your flocks: 32 Let
me pass through all your flock today, removing from there all the speckled and spotted
sheep, and all the brown ones among the
lambs, and the spotted and speckled among
the goats; and [a]*these* shall be my wages. 33 So
my [a]righteousness will answer for me in time
to come, when the subject of my wages comes
before you: every one that *is* not speckled
and spotted among the goats, and brown
among the lambs, will be considered stolen,
if *it is* with me."
34 And Laban said, "Oh, that it were according to your word!" 35 So he removed that day
the male goats that were [a]speckled and spotted, all the female goats that were speckled
and spotted, every one that had *some* white in
it, and all the brown ones among the lambs,
and gave *them* into the hand of his sons.
36 Then he put three days' journey between
himself and Jacob, and Jacob fed the rest of
Laban's flocks.
37 Now [a]Jacob took for himself rods of green
poplar and of the almond and chestnut trees,
peeled white strips in them, and exposed the
white which *was* in the rods. 38 And the rods
which he had peeled, he set before the flocks
in the gutters, in the watering troughs where
the flocks came to drink, so that they should
conceive when they came to drink. 39 So the
flocks conceived before the rods, and the
flocks brought forth streaked, speckled, and
spotted. 40 Then Jacob separated the lambs,
and made the flocks face toward the streaked
and all the brown in the flock of Laban; but
he put his own flocks by themselves and did
not put them with Laban's flock.
41 And it came to pass, whenever the stronger livestock conceived, that Jacob placed
the rods before the eyes of the livestock in
the gutters, that they might conceive among
the rods. 42 But when the flocks were feeble,
he did not put *them* in; so the feebler were
Laban's and the stronger Jacob's. 43 Thus the
man [a]became exceedingly prosperous, and
[b]had large flocks, female and male servants,
and camels and donkeys.

Jacob Flees from Laban

31 Now *Jacob* heard the words of Laban's
sons, saying, "Jacob has taken away
all that was our father's, and from what was
our father's he has acquired all this [a]wealth."
2 And Jacob saw the [a]countenance of Laban,

30:14 [a] Gen. 25:30 **30:15** [a] [Num. 16:9, 13] **30:18** [1] Literally *Wages* **30:20** [1] Literally *Dwelling* **30:21** [a] Gen. 34:1 **30:22** [a] 1 Sam. 1:19, 20 [b] Gen. 29:31 **30:23** [a] Luke 1:25 **30:24** [a] Gen. 35:16–18 [1] Literally *He Will Add* **30:25** [a] Gen. 24:54, 56 [b] Gen. 18:33 **30:26** [a] Gen. 29:18–20, 27, 30 **30:27** [a] Gen. 26:24; 39:3 **30:28** [a] Gen. 29:15; 31:7, 41 **30:29** [a] Gen. 31:6, 38–40 **30:30** [a] [1 Tim. 5:8] **30:32** [a] Gen. 31:8 **30:33** [a] Ps. 37:6 **30:35** [a] Gen. 31:9–12 **30:37** [a] Gen. 31:9–12 **30:43** [a] Gen. 12:16; 30:30 [b] Gen. 13:2; 24:35; 26:13, 14 **31:1** [a] Ps. 49:16 **31:2** [a] Gen. 4:5

and indeed it *was* not [b]*favorable* toward him
as before. 3 Then the LORD said to Jacob,
[a]"Return to the land of your fathers and to
your family, and I will [b]be with you."
4 So Jacob sent and called Rachel and Leah
to the field, to his flock, 5 and said to them, [a]"I
see your father's countenance, that it *is* not
favorable toward me as before; but the God
of my father [b]has been with me. 6 And [a]you
know that with all my might I have served
your father. 7 Yet your father has deceived
me and [a]changed my wages [b]ten times, but
God [c]did not allow him to hurt me. 8 If he
said thus: [a]'The speckled shall be your wages,'
then all the flocks bore speckled. And if he
said thus: 'The streaked shall be your wages,'
then all the flocks bore streaked. 9 So God has
[a]taken away the livestock of your father and
given *them* to me.
10 "And it happened, at the time when the
flocks conceived, that I lifted my eyes and
saw in a dream, and behold, the rams which
leaped upon the flocks *were* streaked, speckled, and gray-spotted. 11 Then [a]the Angel of
God spoke to me in a dream, saying, 'Jacob.'
And I said, 'Here I am.' 12 And He said, 'Lift
your eyes now and see, all the rams which
leap on the flocks *are* streaked, speckled, and
gray-spotted; for [a]I have seen all that Laban is
doing to you. 13 I *am* the God of Bethel, [a]where
you anointed the pillar *and* where you made
a vow to Me. Now [b]arise, get out of this land,
and return to the land of your family.' "
14 Then Rachel and Leah answered and said
to him, [a]"Is there still any portion or inheritance for us in our father's house? 15 Are we not
considered strangers by him? For [a]he has sold
us, and also completely consumed our money.
16 For all these riches which God has taken from
our father are *really* ours and our children's;
now then, whatever God has said to you, do it."
17 Then Jacob rose and set his sons and his
wives on camels. 18 And he carried away all
his livestock and all his possessions which he
had gained, his acquired livestock which he
had gained in Padan Aram, to go to his father
Isaac in the land of [a]Canaan. 19 Now Laban
had gone to shear his sheep, and Rachel had
stolen the [a]household idols that were her
father's. 20 And Jacob stole away, unknown to
Laban the Syrian, in that he did not tell him
that he intended to flee. 21 So he fled with all
that he had. He arose and crossed the river,
and [a]headed toward the mountains of Gilead.

Laban Pursues Jacob

22 And Laban was told on the third day that
Jacob had fled. 23 Then he took [a]his brethren with him and pursued him for seven
days' journey, and he overtook him in the

31:2 [b] Deut. 28:54 **31:3** [a] Gen. 28:15, 20, 21; 32:9 [b] Gen. 46:4 **31:5** [a] Gen. 31:2, 3 [b] Is. 41:10 **31:6** [a] Gen. 30:29; 31:38–41 **31:7** [a] Gen. 29:25; 31:41 [b] Num. 14:22 [c] Job 1:10 **31:8** [a] Gen. 30:32 **31:9** [a] Gen. 31:1, 16 **31:11** [a] Gen. 16:7–11; 22:11, 15; 31:13; 48:16 **31:12** [a] Ex. 3:7 **31:13** [a] Gen. 28:16–22; 35:1, 6, 15 [b] Gen. 31:3; 32:9 **31:14** [a] Gen. 2:24 **31:15** [a] Gen. 29:15, 20, 23, 27 **31:18** [a] Gen. 17:8; 33:18; 35:27 **31:19** [a] Judg. 17:5 **31:21** [a] 2 Kin. 12:17 **31:23** [a] Gen. 13:8

WHEN GOD IS PRESENT

Then the LORD said to Jacob . . . "I will be with you."

GENESIS 31:3

Jacob's secret departure from his uncle Laban and all that resulted from it are almost comical. Neither man was honorable; both can be faulted. Yet in this story and others like it we see the grace of God at work. God's liberality exceeded Jacob's expectations and certainly what he deserved.

It was from this generosity of God that Jacob could have peace. Often our actions lead to conflict and strife. Laban was ready to attack his nephew, but God warned him in a dream to take care how he treated Jacob (see vv. 24, 29). Because of God's intervention, the two men departed on more or less friendly terms.

More importantly, when God protected the errant patriarch, He also protected the great promises He'd made to Abraham. God sometimes has to intervene to guard His people and advance His purposes. When you are erring, do you have peace? Have you seen God's grace despite your actions? When we study the rearview mirror of our lives, we can see how God causes all things to work together for our ultimate good. Only God can do this. The fact that He does it gives us peace.

mountains of Gilead. 24 But God [a]had come to Laban the Syrian in a dream by night, and said to him, "Be careful that you [b]speak to Jacob neither good nor bad."

25 So Laban overtook Jacob. Now Jacob had pitched his tent in the mountains, and Laban with his brethren pitched in the mountains of Gilead.

26 And Laban said to Jacob: "What have you done, that you have stolen away unknown to me, and [a]carried away my daughters like captives *taken* with the sword? 27 Why did you flee away secretly, and steal away from me, and not tell me; for I might have sent you away with joy and songs, with timbrel and harp? 28 And you did not allow me [a]to kiss my sons and my daughters. Now [b]you have done foolishly in *so* doing. 29 It is in my power to do you harm, but the [a]God of your father spoke to me [b]last night, saying, 'Be careful that you speak to Jacob neither good nor bad.' 30 And now you have surely gone because you greatly long for your father's house, *but* why did you [a]steal my gods?"

31 Then Jacob answered and said to Laban, "Because I was [a]afraid, for I said, 'Perhaps you would take your daughters from me by force.' 32 With whomever you find your gods, [a]do not let him live. In the presence of our brethren, identify what I have of yours and take *it* with you." For Jacob did not know that Rachel had stolen them.

33 And Laban went into Jacob's tent, into Leah's tent, and into the two maids' tents, but he did not find *them.* Then he went out of Leah's tent and entered Rachel's tent. 34 Now Rachel had taken the household idols, put them in the camel's saddle, and sat on them. And Laban searched all about the tent but did not find *them.* 35 And she said to her father, "Let it not displease my lord that I cannot [a]rise before you, for the manner of women *is* with me." And he searched but did not find the household idols.

36 Then Jacob was angry and rebuked Laban, and Jacob answered and said to Laban: "What *is* my trespass? What *is* my sin, that you have so hotly pursued me? 37 Although you have searched all my things, what part of your household things have you found? Set *it* here before my brethren and your brethren, that they may judge between us both! 38 These twenty years I *have been* with you; your ewes and your female goats have not miscarried their young, and I have not eaten the rams of your flock. 39 [a]That which was torn *by beasts* I did not bring to you; I bore the loss of it. [b]You required it from my hand, *whether* stolen by day or stolen by night. 40 *There* I was! In the day the drought consumed me, and the frost by night, and my sleep departed from my eyes. 41 Thus I have been in your house twenty years; I [a]served you fourteen years for your two daughters, and six years for your flock, and [b]you have changed my wages ten times. 42 [a]Unless the God of my father, the God of Abraham and [b]the Fear of Isaac, had been with me, surely now you would have sent me away empty-handed. [c]God has seen my affliction and the labor of my hands, and [d]rebuked *you* last night."

Laban's Covenant with Jacob

43 And Laban answered and said to Jacob, "*These* daughters *are* my daughters, and *these* children *are* my children, and *this* flock *is* my flock; all that you see *is* mine. But what can I do this day to these my daughters or to their children whom they have borne? 44 Now therefore, come, [a]let us make a covenant, [b]you and I, and let it be a witness between you and me."

45 So Jacob [a]took a stone and set it up *as* a pillar. 46 Then Jacob said to his brethren, "Gather stones." And they took stones and made a heap, and they ate there on the heap. 47 Laban called it Jegar Sahadutha,[1] but Jacob called it Galeed.[2] 48 And Laban said, [a]"This heap *is* a witness between you and me this day." Therefore its name was called Galeed, 49 also [a]Mizpah,[1] because he said, "May the LORD watch between you and me when we are absent one from another. 50 If you afflict my daughters, or if you take *other* wives besides my daughters, *although* no man *is* with us—see, God *is* witness between you and me!"

51 Then Laban said to Jacob, "Here is this heap and here is *this* pillar, which I have placed between you and me. 52 This heap *is* a witness, and *this* pillar *is* a witness, that I will not pass beyond this heap to you, and you will not pass beyond this heap and this pillar to me, for harm. 53 The God of Abraham, the God of Nahor, and the God of their father [a]judge between us." And Jacob [b]swore by [c]the Fear of his father Isaac. 54 Then Jacob offered a sacrifice on the mountain, and called his brethren to eat bread. And they ate bread and stayed all night on the mountain. 55 And early in the morning Laban arose, and [a]kissed his sons and daughters and [b]blessed them. Then Laban departed and [c]returned to his place.

31:24 [a] Gen. 20:3; 31:29; 46:2–4 [b] Gen. 24:50; 31:7, 29 **31:26** [a] 1 Sam. 30:2 **31:28** [a] Gen. 31:55 [b] 1 Sam. 13:13 **31:29** [a] Gen. 28:13; 31:5, 24, 42, 53 [b] Gen. 31:24 **31:30** [a] Judg. 17:5; 18:24 **31:31** [a] Gen. 26:7; 32:7, 11 **31:32** [a] Gen. 44:9 **31:35** [a] Lev. 19:32 **31:39** [a] Ex. 22:10 [b] Ex. 22:10–13 **31:41** [a] Gen. 29:20, 27–30 [b] Gen. 31:7 **31:42** [a] Ps. 124:1, 2 [b] Is. 8:13 [c] Ex. 3:7 [d] 1 Chr. 12:17 **31:44** [a] Gen. 21:27, 32; 26:28 [b] Josh. 24:27 **31:45** [a] Gen. 28:18; 35:14 **31:47** [1] Literally, in Aramaic, *Heap of Witness* [2] Literally, in Hebrew, *Heap of Witness* **31:48** [a] Josh. 24:27 **31:49** [a] Judg. 10:17; 11:29 [1] Literally *Watch* **31:53** [a] Gen. 16:5 [b] Gen. 21:23 [c] Gen. 31:42 **31:55** [a] Gen. 29:11, 13; 31:28, 43 [b] Gen. 28:1 [c] Num. 24:25

Esau Comes to Meet Jacob

32 So Jacob went on his way, and [a]the
angels of God met him. 2 When Jacob
saw them, he said, "This *is* God's [a]camp." And
he called the name of that place Mahanaim.[1]
3 Then Jacob sent messengers before him
to Esau his brother [a]in the land of Seir, [b]the
country of Edom. 4 And he commanded
them, saying, [a]"Speak thus to my lord Esau,
'Thus your servant Jacob says: "I have dwelt
with Laban and stayed there until now. 5 [a]I
have oxen, donkeys, flocks, and male and
female servants; and I have sent to tell my
lord, that [b]I may find favor in your sight." ' "
6 Then the messengers returned to Jacob,
saying, "We came to your brother Esau, and
[a]he also is coming to meet you, and four
hundred men *are* with him." 7 So Jacob was
greatly afraid and [a]distressed; and he divided
the people that *were* with him, and the flocks
and herds and camels, into two companies.
8 And he said, "If Esau comes to the one company and attacks it, then the other company
which is left will escape."
9 [a]Then Jacob said, [b]"O God of my father
Abraham and God of my father Isaac, the
LORD [c]who said to me, 'Return to your country and to your family, and I will deal well
with you': 10 I am not worthy of the least of
all the [a]mercies and of all the truth which
You have shown Your servant; for I crossed
over this Jordan with [b]my staff, and now I
have become two companies. 11 [a]Deliver me,
I pray, from the hand of my brother, from the
hand of Esau; for I fear him, lest he come and
attack me *and* [b]the mother with the children.
12 For [a]You said, 'I will surely treat you well,
and make your descendants as the [b]sand
of the sea, which cannot be numbered for
multitude.' "
13 So he lodged there that same night, and
took what came to his hand as [a]a present for
Esau his brother: 14 two hundred female goats
and twenty male goats, two hundred ewes
and twenty rams, 15 thirty milk camels with
their colts, forty cows and ten bulls, twenty
female donkeys and ten foals. 16 Then he
delivered *them* to the hand of his servants,
every drove by itself, and said to his servants, "Pass over before me, and put some
distance between successive droves." 17 And
he commanded the first one, saying, "When
Esau my brother meets you and asks you,
saying, 'To whom do you belong, and where
are you going? Whose *are* these in front of
you?' 18 then you shall say, 'They *are* your
servant Jacob's. It *is* a present sent to my
lord Esau; and behold, he also *is* behind us.' "
19 So he commanded the second, the third,
and all who followed the droves, saying, "In
this manner you shall speak to Esau when
you find him; 20 and also say, 'Behold, your
servant Jacob *is* behind us.' " For he said, "I
will [a]appease him with the present that goes

32:1 [a] Num. 22:31 **32:2** [a] Josh. 5:14 [1] Literally *Double Camp* **32:3** [a] Gen. 14:6; 33:14, 16 [b] Gen. 25:30; 36:6–9 **32:4** [a] Prov. 15:1 **32:5** [a] Gen. 30:43 [b] Gen. 33:8, 15 **32:6** [a] Gen. 33:1 **32:7** [a] Gen. 32:11; 35:3 **32:9** [a] [Ps. 50:15] [b] Gen. 28:13; 31:42 [c] Gen. 31:3, 13 **32:10** [a] Gen. 24:27 [b] Job 8:7 **32:11** [a] Ps. 59:1, 2 [b] Hos. 10:14 **32:12** [a] Gen. 28:13–15 [b] Gen. 22:17 **32:13** [a] Gen. 43:11 **32:20** [a] [Prov. 21:14]

LONGING FOR DELIVERANCE

So Jacob was greatly afraid and distressed.

GENESIS 32:7

After successfully escaping Laban, his uncle and father-in-law, Jacob then faced a person whom he'd cheated long before. At the thought of encountering his bitter brother, Jacob had no sense of peace. In desperation, he cried out to God in prayer, "O God of my father Abraham and God of my father Isaac . . . I am not worthy of the least of all the mercies and of all the truth which You have shown Your servant . . . Deliver me, I pray, from the hand of my brother, from the hand of Esau; for I fear him" (vv. 9–11).

Jacob, however, took the time to pray. He reminded God of the promises that He had made to Abraham and Isaac that, among other things, meant many descendants. Jacob reminded God because he believed God would keep His promises. Peace begins when we cry out to our God, the Peace-Giver. So often we don't know how to pray, and it's hard to find the words. But most of the prayers in the Bible are simple and short, not long monologues. Jacob's prayer consisted of one request: *Deliver me!* Perhaps you will have greater peace in this moment if you pray that same prayer!

before me, and afterward I will see his face;
perhaps he will accept me.” 21 So the present
went on over before him, but he himself
lodged that night in the camp.

Wrestling with God

22 And he arose that night and took his
two wives, his two female servants, and his
eleven sons, [a]and crossed over the ford of
Jabbok. 23 He took them, sent them over the
brook, and sent over what he had. 24 Then Jacob was left alone; and [a]a Man wrestled with
him until the breaking of day. 25 Now when
He saw that He did not prevail against him,
He touched the socket of his hip; and [a]the
socket of Jacob’s hip was out of joint as He
wrestled with him. 26 And [a]He said, “Let Me
go, for the day breaks.”
But he said, [b]“I will not let You go unless
You bless me!”
27 So He said to him, “What *is* your name?”
He said, “Jacob.”
28 And He said, [a]“Your name shall no longer be called Jacob, but Israel;[1] for you have
[b]struggled with God and [c]with men, and
have prevailed.”
29 Then Jacob asked, saying, “Tell *me* Your
name, I pray.”
And He said, [a]“Why *is* it *that* you ask about
My name?” And He [b]blessed him there.
30 So Jacob called the name of the place
Peniel:[1] “For [a]I have seen God face to face,
and my life is preserved.” 31 Just as he crossed
over Penuel[1] the sun rose on him, and he
limped on his hip. 32 Therefore to this day the
children of Israel do not eat the muscle that
shrank, which *is* on the hip socket, because
He touched the socket of Jacob’s hip in the
muscle that shrank.

Jacob and Esau Meet

33 Now Jacob lifted his eyes and looked,
and there, [a]Esau was coming, and with
him were four hundred men. So he divided
the children among Leah, Rachel, and the
two maidservants. 2 And he put the maidservants and their children in front, Leah and
her children behind, and Rachel and Joseph
last. 3 Then he crossed over before them and
[a]bowed himself to the ground seven times,
until he came near to his brother.
4 [a]But Esau ran to meet him, and embraced
him, [b]and fell on his neck and kissed him,
and they wept. 5 And he lifted his eyes and
saw the women and children, and said, “Who
are these with you?”
So he said, “The children [a]whom God has
graciously given your servant.” 6 Then the
maidservants came near, they and their children, and bowed down. 7 And Leah also came
near with her children, and they bowed down.
Afterward Joseph and Rachel came near, and
they bowed down.
8 Then Esau said, “What *do* you *mean by*
[a]all this company which I met?”
And he said, “*These are* [b]to find favor in
the sight of my lord.”
9 But Esau said, “I have enough, my
brother; keep what you have for yourself.”
10 And Jacob said, “No, please, if I have
now found favor in your sight, then receive
my present from my hand, inasmuch as I
[a]have seen your face as though I had seen the
face of God, and you were pleased with me.
11 Please, take [a]my blessing that is brought to
you, because God has dealt [b]graciously with
me, and because I have enough.” [c]So he urged
him, and he took *it*.
12 Then Esau said, “Let us take our journey;
let us go, and I will go before you.”
13 But Jacob said to him, “My lord knows
that the children *are* weak, and the flocks and
herds which are nursing *are* with me. And if
the men should drive them hard one day, all
the flock will die. 14 Please let my lord go on
ahead before his servant. I will lead on slowly
at a pace which the livestock that go before
me, and the children, are able to endure,
until I come to my lord [a]in Seir.”
15 And Esau said, “Now let me leave with
you *some* of the people who *are* with me.”
But he said, “What need is there? [a]Let me
find favor in the sight of my lord.” 16 So Esau returned that day on his way to Seir. 17 And Jacob
journeyed to [a]Succoth, built himself a house,
and made booths for his livestock. Therefore
the name of the place is called Succoth.[1]

Jacob Comes to Canaan

18 Then Jacob came safely to [a]the city of
[b]Shechem, which *is* in the land of Canaan,
when he came from Padan Aram; and he
pitched his tent before the city. 19 And [a]he
bought the parcel of land, where he had
pitched his tent, from the children of Hamor,
Shechem’s father, for one hundred pieces of
money. 20 Then he erected an altar there and
called it [a]El Elohe Israel.[1]

32:22 [a] Deut. 3:16 **32:24** [a] Hos. 12:2–4 **32:25** [a] 2 Cor. 12:7 **32:26** [a] Luke 24:28 [b] Hos. 12:4 **32:28** [a] Gen. 35:10 [b] Hos. 12:3, 4 [c] Gen. 25:31; 27:33 [1] Literally *Prince with God* **32:29** [a] Judg. 13:17, 18 [b] Gen. 35:9 **32:30** [a] Gen. 16:13 [1] Literally *Face of God* **32:31** [1] Same as *Peniel,* verse 30 **33:1** [a] Gen. 32:6 **33:3** [a] Gen. 18:2; 42:6 **33:4** [a] Gen. 32:28 [b] Gen. 45:14, 15 **33:5** [a] Gen. 48:9 **33:8** [a] Gen. 32:13–16 [b] Gen. 32:5 **33:10** [a] Gen. 43:3 **33:11** [a] 1 Sam. 25:27; 30:26 [b] Ex. 33:19 [c] 2 Kin. 5:23 **33:14** [a] Gen. 32:3; 36:8 **33:15** [a] Ruth 2:13 **33:17** [a] Josh. 13:27 [1] Literally *Booths* **33:18** [a] John 3:23 [b] Josh. 24:1 **33:19** [a] John 4:5 **33:20** [a] Gen. 35:7 [1] Literally *God, the God of Israel*

PEACE THROUGH FORGIVENESS

Let me find favor in the sight of my lord.

GENESIS 33:15

One of the hardest things a person can do is forgive. I know what it is like to be slandered and maligned—maybe you do too. Forgiving people who try to hurt and defame you is not easy. But living with a bitter heart is even harder: if you do not forgive, you will have no peace. Your forgiveness does not condone something evil that happened to you. But when we forgive, it does start the process by which we free ourselves from pain, and it provides a lost soul with the opportunity for redemption. We can experience the peace of God when we "let it go," forgive, and move on.

I suspect that was Jacob's experience. Jacob had cheated his brother out of birthright and blessing. Esau vowed revenge. Yet, years later, when they finally met face-to-face, Jacob approached Esau with deep humility and called him "my lord" (v. 8). We are told that "Esau ran to meet him, and embraced him, and fell on his neck and kissed him, and they wept" (v. 4). We can only imagine the relief Jacob felt; we can be sure that both brothers enjoyed a great sense of peace.

I have had to do some pretty tough forgiving—I'll bet you have too. Did you find, like Jacob, that with forgiveness came peace?

The Dinah Incident

34 Now [a]Dinah the daughter of Leah,
whom she had borne to Jacob, went
out to see the daughters of the land. 2 And
when Shechem the son of Hamor the Hivite,
prince of the country, saw her, he [a]took her
and lay with her, and violated her. 3 His soul
was strongly attracted to Dinah the daughter
of Jacob, and he loved the young woman
and spoke kindly to the young woman. 4 So
Shechem [a]spoke to his father Hamor, saying,
"Get me this young woman as a wife."
5 And Jacob heard that he had defiled
Dinah his daughter. Now his sons were with
his livestock in the field; so Jacob [a]held his
peace until they came. 6 Then Hamor the
father of Shechem went out to Jacob to speak
with him. 7 And the sons of Jacob came in
from the field when they heard *it;* and the
men were grieved and very angry, because
he [a]had done a disgraceful thing in Israel by
lying with Jacob's daughter, [b]a thing which
ought not to be done. 8 But Hamor spoke with
them, saying, "The soul of my son Shechem
longs for your daughter. Please give her to
him as a wife. 9 And make marriages with
us; give your daughters to us, and take our
daughters to yourselves. 10 So you shall dwell
with us, and the land shall be before you.
Dwell and trade in it, and acquire possessions
for yourselves in it."
11 Then Shechem said to her father and her
brothers, "Let me find favor in your eyes, and
whatever you say to me I will give. 12 Ask me
ever so much [a]dowry and gift, and I will give
according to what you say to me; but give me
the young woman as a wife."
13 But the sons of Jacob answered Shechem
and Hamor his father, and spoke [a]deceitfully,
because he had defiled Dinah their sister.
14 And they said to them, "We cannot do this
thing, to give our sister to one who is [a]un-
circumcised, for [b]that *would be* a reproach
to us. 15 But on this *condition* we will consent
to you: If you will become as we *are,* if every
male of you is circumcised, 16 then we will
give our daughters to you, and we will take
your daughters to us; and we will dwell with
you, and we will become one people. 17 But
if you will not heed us and be circumcised,
then we will take our daughter and be gone."
18 And their words pleased Hamor and Shechem, Hamor's son. 19 So the young man did
not delay to do the thing, because he delighted in Jacob's daughter. He *was* [a]more honorable than all the household of his father.
20 And Hamor and Shechem his son came
to the [a]gate of their city, and spoke with the
men of their city, saying: 21 "These men *are*
at peace with us. Therefore let them dwell
in the land and trade in it. For indeed the
land *is* large enough for them. Let us take

34:1 [a] Gen. 30:21 34:2 [a] Gen. 20:2 34:4 [a] Judg. 14:2 34:5 [a] 2 Sam. 13:22 34:7 [a] Judg. 20:6 [b] 2 Sam. 13:12
34:12 [a] Ex. 22:16, 17 34:13 [a] Gen. 31:7 34:14 [a] Ex. 12:48 [b] Josh. 5:2–9 34:19 [a] 1 Chr. 4:9 34:20 [a] Ruth 4:1, 11

CLAIMING DAILY CALM

Then Jacob came safely to the city of Shechem, which is in the land of Canaan . . . He erected an altar there and called it El Elohe Israel.

GENESIS 33:18, 20

Peace can be experienced, not just occasionally but all the time. Peace is a state of mind and spirit that grows out of a right relationship with God.

Because Jacob had humbled himself and because Esau had forgiven his brother, peace was restored between them. Reconciled, they parted on good terms and Jacob "came safely to the city of Shechem . . . in the land of Canaan" (v. 18). The patriarch had returned to the land that God had promised Abraham long ago.

The word that the NKJV translates "safely" is *shalem*, which is from the root that gives us *shalom*, "peace." Jacob arrived in the Land of Promise "in a state of peace." Accordingly, he "erected an altar there and called it El Elohe Israel" (v. 20), which means "God, the God of Israel." Jacob finally recognized the God of Peace as his God. Is He yours?

their daughters to us as wives, and let us give
them our daughters. 22 Only on this *condition*
will the men consent to dwell with us, to
be one people: if every male among us is
circumcised as they *are* circumcised. 23 *Will*
not their livestock, their property, and every
animal of theirs *be* ours? Only let us consent
to them, and they will dwell with us." 24 And
all who went out of the gate of his city heeded
Hamor and Shechem his son; every male
was circumcised, all who [a]went out of the
gate of his city.
25 Now it came to pass on the third day, when
they were in pain, that two of the sons of Jacob, [a]Simeon and Levi, Dinah's brothers, each
took his sword and came boldly upon the city
and killed all the males. 26 And they [a]killed
Hamor and Shechem his son with the edge
of the sword, and took Dinah from Shechem's
house, and went out. 27 The sons of Jacob came
upon the slain, and plundered the city, because
their sister had been defiled. 28 They took their
sheep, their oxen, and their donkeys, what *was*
in the city and what *was* in the field, 29 and
all their wealth. All their little ones and their
wives they took captive; and they plundered
even all that *was* in the houses.
30 Then Jacob said to Simeon and Levi,
[a]"You have [b]troubled me [c]by making me
obnoxious among the inhabitants of the
land, among the Canaanites and the Perizzites; [d]and since I *am* few in number, they
will gather themselves together against me
and kill me. I shall be destroyed, my household and I."
31 But they said, "Should he treat our sister
like a harlot?"

Jacob's Return to Bethel

35 Then God said to Jacob, "Arise, go up
to [a]Bethel and dwell there; and make
an altar there to God, [b]who appeared to you
[c]when you fled from the face of Esau your
brother."
2 And Jacob said to his [a]household and to
all who *were* with him, "Put away [b]the foreign
gods that *are* among you, [c]purify yourselves,
and change your garments. 3 Then let us arise
and go up to Bethel; and I will make an altar
there to God, [a]who answered me in the day of
my distress [b]and has been with me in the way
which I have gone." 4 So they gave Jacob all
the foreign gods which *were* in their hands,
and the [a]earrings which *were* in their ears;
and Jacob hid them under [b]the terebinth
tree which *was* by Shechem.
5 And they journeyed, and [a]the terror of
God was upon the cities that *were* all around
them, and they did not pursue the sons of
Jacob. 6 So Jacob came to [a]Luz (that *is*, Bethel), which *is* in the land of Canaan, he and all
the people who *were* with him. 7 And he [a]built
an altar there and called the place El Bethel,[1]
because [b]there God appeared to him when
he fled from the face of his brother.
8 Now [a]Deborah, Rebekah's nurse, died,

34:24 [a] Gen. 23:10, 18 **34:25** [a] Gen. 29:33, 34; 42:24; 49:5–7 **34:26** [a] Gen. 49:5, 6 **34:30** [a] Gen. 49:6 [b] Josh. 7:25 [c] Ex. 5:21 [d] Deut. 4:27 **35:1** [a] Gen. 28:19; 31:13 [b] Gen. 28:13 [c] Gen. 27:43 **35:2** [a] Josh. 24:15 [b] Josh. 24:2, 14, 23 [c] Ex. 19:10, 14 **35:3** [a] Gen. 32:7, 24 [b] Gen. 28:15, 20; 31:3, 42 **35:4** [a] Hos. 2:13 [b] Josh. 24:26 **35:5** [a] Ex. 15:16; 23:27 **35:6** [a] Gen. 28:19, 22; 48:3 **35:7** [a] Eccl. 5:4 [b] Gen. 28:13 [1] Literally *God of the House of God* **35:8** [a] Gen. 24:59

and she was buried below Bethel under the
terebinth tree. So the name of it was called
Allon Bachuth.[1]
9 Then [a]God appeared to Jacob again, when
he came from Padan Aram, and [b]blessed
him. 10 And God said to him, "Your name *is*
Jacob; [a]your name shall not be called Jacob
anymore, [b]but Israel shall be your name."
So He called his name Israel. 11 Also God said
to him: [a]"I *am* God Almighty. [b]Be fruitful
and multiply; [c]a nation and a company of
nations shall proceed from you, and kings
shall come from your body. 12 The [a]land which
I gave Abraham and Isaac I give to you; and
to your descendants after you I give this
land." 13 Then God [a]went up from him in the
place where He talked with him. 14 So Jacob
[a]set up a pillar in the place where He talked
with him, a pillar of stone; and he poured
a drink offering on it, and he poured oil on
it. 15 And Jacob called the name of the place
where God spoke with him, [a]Bethel.

Death of Rachel

16 Then they journeyed from Bethel. And
when there was but a little distance to go to
Ephrath, Rachel labored *in childbirth,* and
she had hard labor. 17 Now it came to pass,
when she was in hard labor, that the midwife
said to her, "Do not fear; [a]you will have this
son also." 18 And so it was, as her soul was
departing (for she died), that she called his
name Ben-Oni;[1] but his father called him
Benjamin.[2] 19 So [a]Rachel died and was buried
on the way to [b]Ephrath (that *is,* Bethlehem).
20 And Jacob set a pillar on her grave, which
is the pillar of Rachel's grave [a]to this day.
21 Then Israel journeyed and pitched his
tent beyond [a]the tower of Eder. 22 And it happened, when Israel dwelt in that land, that
Reuben went and [a]lay with Bilhah his father's
concubine; and Israel heard *about it.*

Jacob's Twelve Sons

Now the sons of Jacob were twelve: 23 the
sons of Leah *were* [a]Reuben, Jacob's firstborn,
and Simeon, Levi, Judah, Issachar, and Zebulun; 24 the sons of Rachel *were* Joseph and
Benjamin; 25 the sons of Bilhah, Rachel's
maidservant, *were* Dan and Naphtali; 26 and
the sons of Zilpah, Leah's maidservant, *were*
Gad and Asher. These *were* the sons of Jacob
who were born to him in Padan Aram.

Death of Isaac

27 Then Jacob came to his father Isaac
at [a]Mamre, or [b]Kirjath Arba[1] (that *is,* Hebron), where Abraham and Isaac had dwelt.
28 Now the days of Isaac were one hundred
and eighty years. 29 So Isaac breathed his last

35:8 [1] Literally *Terebinth of Weeping* **35:9** [a] Josh. 5:13 [b] Gen. 32:29 **35:10** [a] Gen. 17:5 [b] Gen. 32:28 **35:11** [a] Ex. 6:3 [b] Gen. 9:1, 7 [c] Gen. 17:5, 6, 16; 28:3; 48:4 **35:12** [a] Gen. 12:7; 13:15; 26:3, 4; 28:13; 48:4 **35:13** [a] Gen. 17:22; 18:33 **35:14** [a] Gen. 28:18, 19; 31:45 **35:15** [a] Gen. 28:19 **35:17** [a] Gen. 30:24 **35:18** [1] Literally *Son of My Sorrow* [2] Literally *Son of the Right Hand* **35:19** [a] Gen. 48:7 [b] Mic. 5:2 **35:20** [a] 1 Sam. 10:2 **35:21** [a] Mic. 4:8 **35:22** [a] Gen. 49:4 **35:23** [a] Ex. 1:1–4 **35:27** [a] Gen. 13:18; 18:1; 23:19 [b] Josh. 14:15 [1] Literally *Town of Arba*

A NEW IDENTITY

"Your name shall not be called Jacob anymore, but Israel shall be your name."

GENESIS 35:10

I am far from perfect. Yet when I least expect it, I sense the assurance that God is with me and all is well. This is in spite of the fact that I fail often, forget to trust, neglect to forgive—but then I remember that the God of *shalom* is *my* God. Do you wonder what God wishes for you when you are at your worst? Comfort. Comfort is God's thought for you when you are at your worst and weakest (see Is. 40:1–2).

Jacob might have burrowed into his failures and never recovered. He could have wallowed in regret and self-reproach and stopped short of pursuing God's plan for him. But he didn't. He persevered, stumbling now and again. After all the near-disasters he'd been part of, Jacob stopped at Bethel and God reiterated the covenant He'd made with Abraham (Gen. 35:11). Do you see how nothing Jacob did nullified God's promise? Do you know exactly how safe you are in God's hands?

I love Jacob's story because he was not a perfect man, yet God blessed him and gave him peace. Forgive yourself as God forgives you, accept His comfort, and experience peace.

and died, and [a]was gathered to his people,
being old and full of days. And [b]his sons Esau
and Jacob buried him.

The Family of Esau

36 Now this *is* the genealogy of Esau,
[a]who is Edom. 2 [a]Esau took his wives
from the daughters of Canaan: Adah the
daughter of Elon the [b]Hittite; [c]Aholibamah
the daughter of Anah, the daughter of Zibeon the Hivite; 3 and [a]Basemath, Ishmael's
daughter, sister of Nebajoth. 4 Now [a]Adah
bore Eliphaz to Esau, and Basemath bore
Reuel. 5 And Aholibamah bore Jeush, Jaalam,
and Korah. These *were* the sons of Esau who
were born to him in the land of Canaan.

6 Then Esau took his wives, his sons, his
daughters, and all the persons of his household, his cattle and all his animals, and all
his goods which he had gained in the land
of Canaan, and went to a country away from
the presence of his brother Jacob. 7 [a]For their
possessions were too great for them to dwell
together, and [b]the land where they were
strangers could not support them because
of their livestock. 8 So Esau dwelt in [a]Mount
Seir. [b]Esau *is* Edom.

9 And this *is* the genealogy of Esau the father of the Edomites in Mount Seir. 10 These
were the names of Esau's sons: [a]Eliphaz the
son of Adah the wife of Esau, and Reuel the
son of Basemath the wife of Esau. 11 And the
sons of Eliphaz were Teman, Omar, Zepho,[1]
Gatam, and Kenaz.

12 Now Timna was the concubine of Eliphaz,
Esau's son, and she bore [a]Amalek to Eliphaz.
These *were* the sons of Adah, Esau's wife.

13 These *were* the sons of Reuel: Nahath,
Zerah, Shammah, and Mizzah. These were
the sons of Basemath, Esau's wife.

14 These were the sons of Aholibamah,
Esau's wife, the daughter of Anah, the daugh-
ter of Zibeon. And she bore to Esau: Jeush,
Jaalam, and Korah.

The Chiefs of Edom

15 These *were* the chiefs of the sons of Esau.
The sons of Eliphaz, the firstborn *son* of Esau,
were Chief Teman, Chief Omar, Chief Zepho,
Chief Kenaz, 16 Chief Korah,[1] Chief Gatam,
and Chief Amalek. These *were* the chiefs of
Eliphaz in the land of Edom. They *were* the
sons of Adah.

17 These *were* the sons of Reuel, Esau's son:
Chief Nahath, Chief Zerah, Chief Shammah,
and Chief Mizzah. These *were* the chiefs of
Reuel in the land of Edom. These *were* the
sons of Basemath, Esau's wife.

18 And these *were* the sons of Aholibamah,
Esau's wife: Chief Jeush, Chief Jaalam, and
Chief Korah. These *were* the chiefs *who de-
scended* from Aholibamah, Esau's wife, the
daughter of Anah. 19 These *were* the sons of
Esau, who is Edom, and these *were* their chiefs.

The Sons of Seir

20 [a]These *were* the sons of Seir [b]the Horite
who inhabited the land: Lotan, Shobal, Zibeon, Anah, 21 Dishon, Ezer, and Dishan. These
were the chiefs of the Horites, the sons of
Seir, in the land of Edom.

22 And the sons of Lotan were Hori and
Hemam.[1] Lotan's sister *was* Timna.

23 These *were* the sons of Shobal: Alvan,[1]
Manahath, Ebal, Shepho,[2] and Onam.

24 These *were* the sons of Zibeon: both Ajah
and Anah. This *was the* Anah who found the
water[1] in the wilderness as he pastured [a]the
donkeys of his father Zibeon. 25 These *were*
the children of Anah: Dishon and Aholibamah the daughter of Anah.

26 These *were* the sons of Dishon:[1] Hemdan,[2] Eshban, Ithran, and Cheran. 27 These
were the sons of Ezer: Bilhan, Zaavan, and
Akan.[1] 28 These *were* the sons of Dishan: [a]Uz
and Aran.

29 These *were* the chiefs of the Horites:
Chief Lotan, Chief Shobal, Chief Zibeon, Chief
Anah, 30 Chief Dishon, Chief Ezer, and Chief
Dishan. These *were* the chiefs of the Horites,
according to their chiefs in the land of Seir.

The Kings of Edom

31 [a]Now these *were* the kings who reigned
in the land of Edom before any king reigned
over the children of Israel: 32 Bela the son of
Beor reigned in Edom, and the name of his
city *was* Dinhabah. 33 And when Bela died,
Jobab the son of Zerah of Bozrah reigned in
his place. 34 When Jobab died, Husham of the
land of the Temanites reigned in his place.
35 And when Husham died, Hadad the son of
Bedad, who attacked Midian in the field of
Moab, reigned in his place. And the name of
his city *was* Avith. 36 When Hadad died, Samlah of Masrekah reigned in his place. 37 And

35:29 [a] Gen. 15:15; 25:8; 49:33 [b] Gen. 25:9; 49:31 **36:1** [a] Gen. 25:30 **36:2** [a] Gen. 26:34; 28:9 [b] 2 Kin. 7:6 [c] Gen. 36:25 **36:3** [a] Gen. 28:9 **36:4** [a] 1 Chr. 1:35 **36:7** [a] Gen. 13:6, 11 [b] Gen. 17:8; 28:4 **36:8** [a] Gen. 32:3 [b] Gen. 36:1, 19 **36:10** [a] 1 Chr. 1:35 **36:11** [1] Spelled *Zephi* in 1 Chronicles 1:36 **36:12** [a] Num. 24:20 **36:16** [1] Samaritan Pentateuch omits *Chief Korah.* **36:20** [a] 1 Chr. 1:38–42 [b] Gen. 14:6 **36:22** [1] Spelled *Homam* in 1 Chronicles 1:39 **36:23** [1] Spelled *Alian* in 1 Chronicles 1:40 [2] Spelled *Shephi* in 1 Chronicles 1:40 **36:24** [a] Lev. 19:19 [1] Following Masoretic Text and Vulgate (*hot springs*); Septuagint reads *Jamin;* Targum reads *mighty men;* Talmud interprets as *mules.* **36:26** [1] Hebrew *Dishan* [2] Spelled *Hamran* in 1 Chronicles 1:41 **36:27** [1] Spelled *Jaakan* in 1 Chronicles 1:42 **36:28** [a] Job 1:1 **36:31** [a] 1 Chr. 1:43

when Samlah died, Saul of [a]Rehoboth-*by*-
the-River reigned in his place. 38 When Saul
died, Baal-Hanan the son of Achbor reigned
in his place. 39 And when Baal-Hanan the son
of Achbor died, Hadar[1] reigned in his place;
and the name of his city *was* Pau.[2] His wife's
name *was* Mehetabel, the daughter of Matred,
the daughter of Mezahab.

The Chiefs of Esau

40 And these *were* the names of the chiefs
of Esau, according to their families and their
places, by their names: Chief Timnah, Chief
Alvah,[1] Chief Jetheth, 41 Chief Aholibamah,
Chief Elah, Chief Pinon, 42 Chief Kenaz, Chief
Teman, Chief Mibzar, 43 Chief Magdiel, and
Chief Iram. These *were* the chiefs of Edom,
according to their dwelling places in the land
of their possession. Esau *was* the father of
the Edomites.

Joseph Dreams of Greatness

37 Now Jacob dwelt in the land [a]where
his father was a stranger, in the land of
Canaan. 2 This *is* the history of Jacob.
Joseph, *being* seventeen years old, was
feeding the flock with his brothers. And
the lad *was* with the sons of Bilhah and the
sons of Zilpah, his father's wives; and Joseph
brought [a]a bad report of them to his father.
3 Now Israel loved Joseph more than all
his children, because he *was* [a]the son of his
old age. Also he [b]made him a tunic of *many*
colors. 4 But when his brothers saw that their
father loved him more than all his brothers,
they [a]hated him and could not speak peaceably to him.
5 Now Joseph had a dream, and he told
it to his brothers; and they hated him even
more. 6 So he said to them, "Please hear this
dream which I have dreamed: 7 [a]There we
were, binding sheaves in the field. Then behold, my sheaf arose and also stood upright;
and indeed your sheaves stood all around
and bowed down to my sheaf."
8 And his brothers said to him, "Shall you
indeed reign over us? Or shall you indeed
have dominion over us?" So they hated him
even more for his dreams and for his words.
9 Then he dreamed still another dream and
told it to his brothers, and said, "Look, I have
dreamed another dream. And this time, [a]the
sun, the moon, and the eleven stars bowed
down to me."
10 So he told *it* to his father and his brothers;
and his father rebuked him and said to him,
"What *is* this dream that you have dreamed?
Shall your mother and I and [a]your brothers
indeed come to bow down to the earth before
you?" 11 And [a]his brothers envied him, but his
father [b]kept the matter *in mind.*

Joseph Sold by His Brothers

12 Then his brothers went to feed their father's flock in [a]Shechem. 13 And Israel said
to Joseph, "Are not your brothers feeding
the flock in Shechem? Come, I will send you
to them."
So he said to him, "Here I am."
14 Then he said to him, "Please go and see
if it is well with your brothers and well with
the flocks, and bring back word to me." So he
sent him out of the Valley of [a]Hebron, and
he went to Shechem.
15 Now a certain man found him, and there
he was, wandering in the field. And the man
asked him, saying, "What are you seeking?"
16 So he said, "I am seeking my brothers.
[a]Please tell me where they are feeding *their
flocks.*"
17 And the man said, "They have departed
from here, for I heard them say, 'Let us go to
Dothan.'" So Joseph went after his brothers
and found them in [a]Dothan.
18 Now when they saw him afar off, even
before he came near them, [a]they conspired
against him to kill him. 19 Then they said to
one another, "Look, this dreamer is coming!
20 [a]Come therefore, let us now kill him and
cast him into some pit; and we shall say,
'Some wild beast has devoured him.' We shall
see what will become of his dreams!"
21 But [a]Reuben heard *it*, and he delivered
him out of their hands, and said, "Let us not
kill him." 22 And Reuben said to them, "Shed
no blood, *but* cast him into this pit which *is*
in the wilderness, and do not lay a hand on
him"—that he might deliver him out of their
hands, and bring him back to his father.
23 So it came to pass, when Joseph had
come to his brothers, that they [a]stripped
Joseph *of* his tunic, the tunic of *many* colors
that *was* on him. 24 Then they took him and
cast him into a pit. And the pit *was* empty;
there was no water in it.
25 [a]And they sat down to eat a meal. Then
they lifted their eyes and looked, and there
was a company of [b]Ishmaelites, coming from

36:37 [a] Gen. 10:11 **36:39** [1] Spelled *Hadad* in Samaritan Pentateuch, Syriac, and 1 Chronicles 1:50 [2] Spelled *Pai* in 1 Chronicles 1:50 **36:40** [1] Spelled *Aliah* in 1 Chronicles 1:51 **37:1** [a] Gen. 17:8; 23:4; 28:4; 36:7 **37:2** [a] 1 Sam. 2:22–24 **37:3** [a] Gen. 44:20 [b] Gen. 37:23, 32 **37:4** [a] Gen. 27:41; 49:23 **37:7** [a] Gen. 42:6, 9; 43:26; 44:14 **37:9** [a] Gen. 46:29; 47:25 **37:10** [a] Gen. 27:29 **37:11** [a] Acts 7:9 [b] Dan. 7:28 **37:12** [a] Gen. 33:18–20 **37:14** [a] Gen. 13:18; 23:2, 19; 35:27 **37:16** [a] Song 1:7 **37:17** [a] 2 Kin. 6:13 **37:18** [a] Mark 14:1 **37:20** [a] Prov. 1:11 **37:21** [a] Gen. 42:22 **37:23** [a] Matt. 27:28 **37:25** [a] Prov. 30:20 [b] Gen. 16:11, 12; 37:28, 36; 39:1

Gilead with their camels, bearing spices,
[c]balm, and myrrh, on their way to carry
them down to Egypt. 26 So Judah said to his
brothers, "What profit *is there* if we kill our
brother and [a]conceal his blood? 27 Come and
let us sell him to the Ishmaelites, and [a]let not
our hand be upon him, for he *is* [b]our brother
and [c]our flesh." And his brothers listened.
28 Then [a]Midianite traders passed by; so *the
brothers* pulled Joseph up and lifted him out
of the pit, [b]and sold him to the Ishmaelites
for [c]twenty *shekels* of silver. And they took
Joseph to Egypt.

29 Then Reuben returned to the pit, and
indeed Joseph *was* not in the pit; and he
[a]tore his clothes. 30 And he returned to his
brothers and said, "The lad [a]*is* no *more;* and
I, where shall I go?"

31 So they took [a]Joseph's tunic, killed a
kid of the goats, and dipped the tunic in the
blood. 32 Then they sent the tunic of *many*
colors, and they brought *it* to their father
and said, "We have found this. Do you know
whether it *is* your son's tunic or not?"

33 And he recognized it and said, "*It is* my
son's tunic. A [a]wild beast has devoured him.
Without doubt Joseph is torn to pieces."
34 Then Jacob [a]tore his clothes, put sackcloth
on his waist, and [b]mourned for his son many
days. 35 And all his sons and all his daughters
[a]arose to comfort him; but he refused to be
comforted, and he said, "For [b]I shall go down
into the grave to my son in mourning." Thus
his father wept for him.

36 Now [a]the Midianites[1] had sold him in
Egypt to Potiphar, an officer of Pharaoh *and*
captain of the guard.

Judah and Tamar

38 It came to pass at that time that Judah
departed from his brothers, and [a]vis-
ited a certain Adullamite whose name *was*
Hirah. 2 And Judah [a]saw there a daughter of
a certain Canaanite whose name *was* [b]Shua,
and he married her and went in to her. 3 So
she conceived and bore a son, and he called
his name [a]Er. 4 She conceived again and bore
a son, and she called his name [a]Onan. 5 And
she conceived yet again and bore a son, and
called his name [a]Shelah. He was at Chezib
when she bore him.

6 Then Judah [a]took a wife for Er his firstborn, and her name *was* [b]Tamar. 7 But [a]Er,
Judah's firstborn, was wicked in the sight of
the LORD, [b]and the LORD killed him. 8 And
Judah said to Onan, "Go in to [a]your brother's
wife and marry her, and raise up an heir
to your brother." 9 But Onan knew that the
heir would not be [a]his; and it came to pass,
when he went in to his brother's wife, that
he emitted on the ground, lest he should
give an heir to his brother. 10 And the thing
which he did displeased the LORD; therefore
He killed [a]him also.

37:25 [c] Jer. 8:22 **37:26** [a] Gen. 37:20 **37:27** [a] 1 Sam. 18:17 [b] Gen. 42:21 [c] Gen. 29:14 **37:28** [a] Judg. 6:1–3; 8:22, 24 [b] Ps. 105:17 [c] Matt. 27:9 **37:29** [a] Job 1:20 **37:30** [a] Gen. 42:13, 36 **37:31** [a] Gen. 37:3, 23 **37:33** [a] Gen. 37:20 **37:34** [a] 2 Sam. 3:31 [b] Gen. 50:10 **37:35** [a] 2 Sam. 12:17 [b] Gen. 25:8; 35:29; 42:38; 44:29, 31 **37:36** [a] Gen. 39:1 [1] Masoretic Text reads *Medanites.* **38:1** [a] 2 Kin. 4:8 **38:2** [a] Gen. 34:2 [b] 1 Chr. 2:3 **38:3** [a] Gen. 46:12 **38:4** [a] Num. 26:19 **38:5** [a] Num. 26:20 **38:6** [a] Gen. 21:21 [b] Ruth 4:12 **38:7** [a] Gen. 46:12 [b] 1 Chr. 2:3 **38:8** [a] Deut. 25:5, 6 **38:9** [a] Deut. 25:6 **38:10** [a] Gen. 46:12

GOD'S SOVEREIGN PLANS FOR PEACE

Please go and see if it is well with your brothers and well with the flocks, and bring back word to me.

GENESIS 37:14

Jacob was a man with worries. They weren't limited to his own welfare; they extended to his family, especially his sons' growing jealousy of Joseph. Joseph's dreams, which implied that someday Jacob and his sons would bow before the young man, led to envy and resentment. It didn't help that Jacob favored Joseph. We all know what Joseph's brothers did: they sold him into slavery and then deceived their father into thinking that Joseph had been killed by a wild animal.

The villainous actions of Jacob's brothers set in motion one of God's greatest acts of redemption. While they had meant it for evil, "God meant it for good" (50:20). Jacob had much to worry about, but in the end he recognized God's sovereign plan and with that recognition he finally discovered the peace that had eluded him. Let that be our prayer.

11 Then Judah said to Tamar his daughter-
in-law, [a]"Remain a widow in your father's
house till my son Shelah is grown." For he
said, "Lest he also die like his brothers." And
Tamar went and dwelt [b]in her father's house.
12 Now in the process of time the daughter
of Shua, Judah's wife, died; and Judah [a]was
comforted, and went up to his sheepshearers
at Timnah, he and his friend Hirah the Adullamite. 13 And it was told Tamar, saying, "Look,
your father-in-law is going up [a]to Timnah to
shear his sheep." 14 So she took off her widow's
garments, covered *herself* with a veil and
wrapped herself, and [a]sat in an open place
which *was* on the way to Timnah; for she
saw [b]that Shelah was grown, and she was not
given to him as a wife. 15 When Judah saw her,
he thought she *was* a harlot, because she had
covered her face. 16 Then he turned to her by
the way, and said, "Please let me come in to
you"; for he did not know that she *was* his
daughter-in-law.
So she said, "What will you give me, that
you may come in to me?"
17 And he said, [a]"I will send a young goat
from the flock."
So she said, [b]"Will you give *me* a pledge
till you send *it?*"
18 Then he said, "What pledge shall I give
you?"
So she said, [a]"Your signet and cord, and
your staff that *is* in your hand." Then he gave
them to her, and went in to her, and she conceived by him. 19 So she arose and went away,
and [a]laid aside her veil and put on the garments of her widowhood.
20 And Judah sent the young goat by the
hand of his friend the Adullamite, to receive
his pledge from the woman's hand, but he did
not find her. 21 Then he asked the men of that
place, saying, "Where is the harlot who *was*
openly by the roadside?"
And they said, "There was no harlot in
this *place*."
22 So he returned to Judah and said, "I
cannot find her. Also, the men of the place
said there was no harlot in this *place*."
23 Then Judah said, "Let her take *them* for
herself, lest we be shamed; for I sent this
young goat and you have not found her."
24 And it came to pass, about three months
after, that Judah was told, saying, "Tamar
your daughter-in-law has [a]played the harlot;
furthermore she *is* with child by harlotry."
So Judah said, "Bring her out [b]and let her
be burned!"
25 When she *was* brought out, she sent
to her father-in-law, saying, "By the man to
whom these belong, I *am* with child." And
she said, [a]"Please determine whose these
are—the signet and cord, and staff."
26 So Judah [a]acknowledged *them* and said,
[b]"She has been more righteous than I, because [c]I did not give her to Shelah my son."
And he [d]never knew her again.
27 Now it came to pass, at the time for
giving birth, that behold, twins *were* in her
womb. 28 And so it was, when she was giving
birth, that *the one* put out *his* hand; and the
midwife took a scarlet *thread* and bound
it on his hand, saying, "This one came out
first." 29 Then it happened, as he drew back
his hand, that his brother came out unexpectedly; and she said, "How did you break
through? *This* breach *be* upon you!" Therefore
his name was called [a]Perez.[1] 30 Afterward his
brother came out who had the scarlet *thread*
on his hand. And his name was called [a]Zerah.

Joseph a Slave in Egypt

39 Now Joseph had been taken [a]down
to Egypt. And [b]Potiphar, an officer of
Pharaoh, captain of the guard, an Egyptian,
[c]bought him from the Ishmaelites who had
taken him down there. 2 [a]The LORD was with
Joseph, and he was a successful man; and he
was in the house of his master the Egyptian.
3 And his master saw that the LORD *was* with
him and that the LORD [a]made all he did to
prosper in his hand. 4 So Joseph [a]found favor
in his sight, and served him. Then he made
him [b]overseer of his house, and all *that* he
had he put under his authority. 5 So it was,
from the time *that* he had made him overseer of his house and all that he had, that
[a]the LORD blessed the Egyptian's house for
Joseph's sake; and the blessing of the LORD
was on all that he had in the house and in
the field. 6 Thus he left all that he had in Joseph's hand, and he did not know what he
had except for the bread which he ate.
Now Joseph [a]was handsome in form and
appearance.
7 And it came to pass after these things
that his master's wife cast longing eyes on
Joseph, and she said, [a]"Lie with me."
8 But he refused and said to his master's
wife, "Look, my master does not know what *is*

38:11 [a] Ruth 1:12, 13 [b] Lev. 22:13 **38:12** [a] 2 Sam. 13:39 **38:13** [a] Josh. 15:10, 57 **38:14** [a] Prov. 7:12 [b] Gen. 38:11, 26 **38:17** [a] Ezek. 16:33 [b] Gen. 38:20 **38:18** [a] Gen. 38:25; 41:42 **38:19** [a] Gen. 38:14 **38:24** [a] Judg. 19:2 [b] Lev. 20:14; 21:9 **38:25** [a] Gen. 37:32; 38:18 **38:26** [a] Gen. 37:33 [b] 1 Sam. 24:17 [c] Gen. 38:14 [d] Job 34:31, 32 **38:29** [a] Gen. 46:12 [1] Literally *Breach* or *Breakthrough* **38:30** [a] 1 Chr. 2:4 **39:1** [a] Gen. 12:10; 43:15 [b] Gen. 37:36 [c] Gen. 37:28; 45:4 **39:2** [a] Acts 7:9 **39:3** [a] Ps. 1:3 **39:4** [a] Gen. 18:3; 19:19; 39:21 [b] Gen. 24:2, 10; 39:8, 22; 41:40 **39:5** [a] Gen. 18:26; 30:27 **39:6** [a] 1 Sam. 16:12 **39:7** [a] 2 Sam. 13:11

with me in the house, and he has committed all that he has to my hand. 9 *There is* no one greater in this house than I, nor has he kept back anything from me but you, because you *are* his wife. [a]How then can I do this great wickedness, and [b]sin against God?"

10 So it was, as she spoke to Joseph day by day, that he [a]did not heed her, to lie with her *or* to be with her.

11 But it happened about this time, when Joseph went into the house to do his work, and none of the men of the house *was* inside, 12 that she [a]caught him by his garment, saying, "Lie with me." But he left his garment in her hand, and fled and ran outside. 13 And so it was, when she saw that he had left his garment in her hand and fled outside, 14 that she called to the men of her house and spoke to them, saying, "See, he has brought in to us a [a]Hebrew to mock us. He came in to me to lie with me, and I cried out with a loud voice. 15 And it happened, when he heard that I lifted my voice and cried out, that he left his garment with me, and fled and went outside."

16 So she kept his garment with her until his master came home. 17 Then she [a]spoke to him with words like these, saying, "The Hebrew servant whom you brought to us came in to me to mock me; 18 so it happened, as I lifted my voice and cried out, that he left his garment with me and fled outside."

19 So it was, when his master heard the words which his wife spoke to him, saying, "Your servant did to me after this manner," that his [a]anger was aroused. 20 Then Joseph's master took him and [a]put him into the [b]prison, a place where the king's prisoners *were* confined. And he was there in the prison. 21 But the LORD was with Joseph and showed him mercy, and He [a]gave him favor in the sight of the keeper of the prison. 22 And the keeper of the prison [a]committed to Joseph's hand all the prisoners who *were* in the prison; whatever they did there, it was his doing. 23 The keeper of the prison did not look into anything *that was* under *Joseph's* authority,[1] because [a]the LORD was with him; and whatever he did, the LORD made *it* prosper.

The Prisoners' Dreams

40 It came to pass after these things *that* the [a]butler and the baker of the king of Egypt offended their lord, the king of Egypt. 2 And Pharaoh was [a]angry with his two officers, the chief butler and the chief baker. 3 [a]So he put them in custody in the house of the captain of the guard, in the prison, the place where Joseph *was* confined. 4 And the captain of the guard charged Joseph with them, and he served them; so they were in custody for a while.

5 Then the butler and the baker of the king of Egypt, who *were* confined in the prison, [a]had a dream, both of them, each man's dream in one night *and* each man's dream with its *own* interpretation. 6 And Joseph

39:9 [a] Prov. 6:29, 32 [b] Ps. 51:4 **39:10** [a] Prov. 1:10 **39:12** [a] Prov. 7:13 **39:14** [a] Gen. 14:13; 41:12 **39:17** [a] Ex. 23:1 **39:19** [a] Prov. 6:34, 35 **39:20** [a] Ps. 105:18 [b] Gen. 40:3, 15; 41:14 **39:21** [a] Acts 7:9, 10 **39:22** [a] Gen. 39:4; 40:3, 4 **39:23** [a] Gen. 39:2, 3 [1] Literally *his hand* **40:1** [a] Neh. 1:11 **40:2** [a] Prov. 16:14 **40:3** [a] Gen. 39:1, 20, 23; 41:10 **40:5** [a] Gen. 37:5; 41:1

WHAT OTHERS SEE

The LORD was with him; and whatever he did, the LORD made it prosper.

GENESIS 39:23

Have you felt forgotten by God? Joseph might have felt that way. As a teenager he was sold in a human trafficking transaction (see 37:1–36) and became a slave in a powerful Egyptian's house. Wrongly accused by the man's wife, Joseph wound up confined in a foreign prison.

Yet the peace of God reaches to all places and people. His peace and His presence are connected, and God never left Joseph. When we live in the presence and peace of God, it is evident to people around us—even critics. In verse 23 we read that the Lord made everything Joseph did prosper. Everyone seemed to notice God's presence in this young man. His dire surroundings made no difference; even in prison and after, when he was coruler of Egypt, Joseph experienced the Lord's nearness and lived in the *shalom*-peace of God.

Perhaps you have been victimized and traumatized and share the scars of rejection with Joseph. You can claim the same proximity to the Lord today by faith and allow God's presence and peace to surround you. Nothing can stop the peace of God in your life.

came in to them in the morning and looked at them, and saw that they *were* sad. 7 So he asked Pharaoh's officers who *were* with him in the custody of his lord's house, saying, [a]"Why do you look *so* sad today?"

8 And they said to him, [a]"We each have had a dream, and *there is* no interpreter of it."

So Joseph said to them, [b]"Do not interpretations belong to God? Tell *them* to me, please."

9 Then the chief butler told his dream to Joseph, and said to him, "Behold, in my dream a vine *was* before me, 10 and in the vine *were* three branches; it *was* as though it budded, its blossoms shot forth, and its clusters brought forth ripe grapes. 11 Then Pharaoh's cup *was* in my hand; and I took the grapes and pressed them into Pharaoh's cup, and placed the cup in Pharaoh's hand."

12 And Joseph said to him, [a]"This *is* the interpretation of it: The three branches [b]*are* three days. 13 Now within three days Pharaoh will [a]lift up your head and restore you to your place, and you will put Pharaoh's cup in his hand according to the former manner, when you were his butler. 14 But [a]remember me when it is well with you, and [b]please show kindness to me; make mention of me to Pharaoh, and get me out of this house. 15 For indeed I was [a]stolen away from the land of the Hebrews; [b]and also I have done nothing here that they should put me into the dungeon."

16 When the chief baker saw that the interpretation was good, he said to Joseph, "I also *was* in my dream, and there *were* three white baskets on my head. 17 In the uppermost basket *were* all kinds of baked goods for Pharaoh, and the birds ate them out of the basket on my head."

18 So Joseph answered and said, [a]"This *is* the interpretation of it: The three baskets *are* three days. 19 [a]Within three days Pharaoh will lift off your head from you and [b]hang you on a tree; and the birds will eat your flesh from you."

20 Now it came to pass on the third day, *which was* Pharaoh's [a]birthday, that he [b]made a feast for all his servants; and he [c]lifted up the head of the chief butler and of the chief baker among his servants. 21 Then he [a]restored the chief butler to his butlership again, and [b]he placed the cup in Pharaoh's hand. 22 But he [a]hanged the chief baker, as Joseph had interpreted to them. 23 Yet the chief butler did not remember Joseph, but [a]forgot him.

Pharaoh's Dreams

41 Then it came to pass, at the end of two full years, that [a]Pharaoh had a dream; and behold, he stood by the river. 2 Suddenly there came up out of the river seven cows, fine looking and fat; and they fed in the meadow. 3 Then behold, seven other

40:7 [a] Neh. 2:2 **40:8** [a] Gen. 41:15 [b] [Dan. 2:11, 20–22, 27, 28, 47] **40:12** [a] Dan. 2:36; 4:18, 19 [b] Gen. 40:18; 42:17 **40:13** [a] 2 Kin. 25:27 **40:14** [a] Luke 23:42 [b] Josh. 2:12 **40:15** [a] Gen. 37:26–28 [b] Gen. 39:20 **40:18** [a] Gen. 40:12 **40:19** [a] Gen. 40:13 [b] Deut. 21:22 **40:20** [a] Matt. 14:6–10 [b] Mark 6:21 [c] Gen. 40:13, 19 **40:21** [a] Gen. 40:13 [b] Neh. 2:1 **40:22** [a] Gen. 40:19 **40:23** [a] Eccl. 9:15, 16 **41:1** [a] Gen. 40:5

ROLE MODEL OF PEACE

Remember me when it is well with you, and please show kindness to me; make mention of me to Pharaoh, and get me out of this house.

GENESIS 40:14

Joseph did everything right, but everything wrong happened to him. More of Genesis is occupied with the problems and affliction Joseph suffered than any other matter in the book. We see that Joseph surrendered to God wherever he found himself. It is a state of surrender to God I greatly desire, but often I am distracted by worries.

I believe that Joseph wholeheartedly gave his situations to God. That would explain how he survived. He was almost murdered by his brothers, he was sold into slavery, he was falsely accused and cast into prison, and then, despite his good service to a former inmate, he was forgotten and abandoned. Yet Joseph never lost his faith. I'm sure he wavered at times; how could he not? Yet he knew God was with him and, I am sure, sensed God's peace.

Remember, *how* we suffer is much more important than *why* we are suffering. This truth leads me to God's peace.

cows came up after them out of the river,
ugly and gaunt, and stood by the *other* cows
on the bank of the river. 4 And the ugly and
gaunt cows ate up the seven fine looking and
fat cows. So Pharaoh awoke. 5 He slept and
dreamed a second time; and suddenly seven
heads of grain came up on one stalk, plump
and good. 6 Then behold, seven thin heads,
blighted by the [a]east wind, sprang up after
them. 7 And the seven thin heads devoured
the seven plump and full heads. So Pharaoh
awoke, and indeed, *it was* a dream. 8 Now it
came to pass in the morning [a]that his spirit
was troubled, and he sent and called for all
[b]the magicians of Egypt and all its [c]wise
men. And Pharaoh told them his dreams,
but *there was* no one who could interpret
them for Pharaoh.

9 Then the [a]chief butler spoke to Pharaoh, saying: "I remember my faults this day.
10 When Pharaoh was [a]angry with his servants, [b]and put me in custody in the house
of the captain of the guard, *both* me and the
chief baker, 11 [a]we each had a dream in one
night, he and I. Each of us dreamed according
to the interpretation of his *own* dream. 12 Now
there *was* a young [a]Hebrew man with us
there, a [b]servant of the captain of the guard.
And we told him, and he [c]interpreted our
dreams for us; to each man he interpreted
according to his *own* dream. 13 And it came
to pass, just [a]as he interpreted for us, so it
happened. He restored me to my office, and
he hanged him."

14 [a]Then Pharaoh sent and called Joseph,
and they [b]brought him quickly [c]out of the
dungeon; and he shaved, [d]changed his clothing, and came to Pharaoh. 15 And Pharaoh
said to Joseph, "I have had a dream, and *there
is* no one who can interpret it. [a]But I have
heard it said of you *that* you can understand
a dream, to interpret it."

16 So Joseph answered Pharaoh, saying,
[a]"*It is* not in me; [b]God will give Pharaoh an
answer of peace."

17 Then Pharaoh said to Joseph: "Behold,
[a]in my dream I stood on the bank of the river.
18 Suddenly seven cows came up out of the
river, fine looking and fat; and they fed in the
meadow. 19 Then behold, seven other cows
came up after them, poor and very ugly and
gaunt, such ugliness as I have never seen
in all the land of Egypt. 20 And the gaunt
and ugly cows ate up the first seven, the fat
cows. 21 When they had eaten them up, no one
would have known that they had eaten them,
for they *were* just as ugly as at the beginning.
So I awoke. 22 Also I saw in my dream, and
suddenly seven heads came up on one stalk,
full and good. 23 Then behold, seven heads,

41:6 [a] Ex. 10:13 **41:8** [a] Dan. 2:1, 3; 4:5, 19 [b] Ex. 7:11, 22 [c] Matt. 2:1 **41:9** [a] Gen. 40:1, 14, 23 **41:10** [a] Gen. 40:2, 3 [b] Gen. 39:20 **41:11** [a] Gen. 40:5 **41:12** [a] Gen. 39:14; 43:32 [b] Gen. 37:36 [c] Gen. 40:12 **41:13** [a] Gen. 40:21, 22 **41:14** [a] Ps. 105:20 [b] Dan. 2:25 [c] [1 Sam. 2:8] [d] 2 Kin. 25:27–29 **41:15** [a] Dan. 5:16 **41:16** [a] Dan. 2:30 [b] Dan. 2:22, 28, 47 **41:17** [a] Gen. 41:1

AGENTS OF PEACE

So Joseph answered Pharaoh, saying, "It is not in me; God will give Pharaoh an answer of peace."

GENESIS 41:16

How do you recognize fellow believers? Is it their confidence? Their giving of the gospel?

The most powerful descriptor Jesus' followers is this: the peace of God is all over them. God's peace can flow through us and influence others. Though friends had forgotten Joseph in prison, he stood ready to trust the Lord and grab an opportunity when it came. The Lord was ready to show Himself strong on Joseph's behalf.

When Pharoah experienced a nightmare and desperately desired an interpretation, Joseph was brought from the dungeon into the ruler's presence. Joseph had no special power of divination and immediately said so: "It is not in me; God will give Pharaoh an answer." And so God did.

Like Joseph, when we are living in the discipline of God's peace, we can share that peace with anyone. Joseph shared the answer Pharaoh sought, and he became an agent of peace. You can too.

withered, thin, *and* blighted by the east wind, sprang up after them. 24 And the thin heads devoured the seven good heads. So [a]I told *this* to the magicians, but *there was* no one who could explain *it* to me."

25 Then Joseph said to Pharaoh, "The dreams of Pharaoh *are* one; [a]God has shown Pharaoh what He *is* about to do: 26 The seven good cows *are* seven years, and the seven good heads *are* seven years; the dreams *are* one. 27 And the seven thin and ugly cows which came up after them *are* seven years, and the seven empty heads blighted by the east wind are [a]seven years of famine. 28 [a]This *is* the thing which I have spoken to Pharaoh. God has shown Pharaoh what He *is* about to do. 29 Indeed [a]seven years of great plenty will come throughout all the land of Egypt; 30 but after them seven years of famine will [a]arise, and all the plenty will be forgotten in the land of Egypt; and the famine [b]will deplete the land. 31 So the plenty will not be known in the land because of the famine following, for it *will be* very severe. 32 And the dream was repeated to Pharaoh twice because the [a]thing *is* established by God, and God will shortly bring it to pass.

33 "Now therefore, let Pharaoh select a discerning and wise man, and set him over the land of Egypt. 34 Let Pharaoh do *this,* and let him appoint officers over the land, [a]to collect one-fifth *of the produce* of the land of Egypt in the seven plentiful years. 35 And [a]let them gather all the food of those good years that are coming, and store up grain under the authority of Pharaoh, and let them keep food in the cities. 36 Then that food shall be as a reserve for the land for the seven years of famine which shall be in the land of Egypt, that the land [a]may not perish during the famine."

Joseph's Rise to Power

37 So [a]the advice was good in the eyes of Pharaoh and in the eyes of all his servants. 38 And Pharaoh said to his servants, "Can we find *such a one* as this, a man [a]in whom *is* the Spirit of God?"

39 Then Pharaoh said to Joseph, "Inasmuch as God has shown you all this, *there is* no one as discerning and wise as you. 40 [a]You shall be over my house, and all my people shall be ruled according to your word; only in regard to the throne will I be greater than you." 41 And Pharaoh said to Joseph, "See, I have [a]set you over all the land of Egypt."

42 Then Pharaoh [a]took his signet ring off his hand and put it on Joseph's hand; and he [b]clothed him in garments of fine linen [c]and put a gold chain around his neck. 43 And he had him ride in the second [a]chariot which he had; [b]and they cried out before him, "Bow the knee!" So he set him [c]over all the land of Egypt. 44 Pharaoh also said to Joseph, "I *am* Pharaoh, and without your consent no man may lift his hand or foot in all the land of Egypt." 45 And Pharaoh called Joseph's name Zaphnath-Paaneah. And he gave him as a wife [a]Asenath, the daughter of Poti-Pherah priest of On. So Joseph went out over *all* the land of Egypt.

46 Joseph was thirty years old when he [a]stood before Pharaoh king of Egypt. And Joseph went out from the presence of Pharaoh, and went throughout all the land of Egypt. 47 Now in the seven plentiful years the ground brought forth abundantly. 48 So he gathered up all the food of the seven years which were in the land of Egypt, and laid up the food in the cities; he laid up in every city the food of the fields which surrounded them. 49 Joseph gathered very much grain, [a]as the sand of the sea, until he stopped counting, for *it was* immeasurable.

50 [a]And to Joseph were born two sons before the years of famine came, whom Asenath, the daughter of Poti-Pherah priest of On, bore to him. 51 Joseph called the name of the firstborn Manasseh:[1] "For God has made me forget all my toil and all my [a]father's house." 52 And the name of the second he called Ephraim:[1] "For God has caused me to be [a]fruitful in the land of my affliction."

53 Then the seven years of plenty which were in the land of Egypt ended, 54 [a]and the seven years of famine began to come, [b]as Joseph had said. The famine was in all lands, but in all the land of Egypt there was bread. 55 So when all the land of Egypt was famished, the people cried to Pharaoh for bread. Then Pharaoh said to all the Egyptians, "Go to Joseph; [a]whatever he says to you, do." 56 The famine was over all the face of the earth, and Joseph opened all the storehouses[1] and [a]sold to the Egyptians. And the famine became severe in the land of Egypt. 57 [a]So all countries came to Joseph in Egypt to [b]buy *grain,* because the famine was severe in all lands.

41:24 [a] Is. 8:19 **41:25** [a] Dan. 2:28, 29, 45 **41:27** [a] 2 Kin. 8:1 **41:28** [a] [Gen. 41:25, 32] **41:29** [a] Gen. 41:47 **41:30** [a] Gen. 41:54, 56 [b] Gen. 47:13 **41:32** [a] Num. 23:19 **41:34** [a] [Prov. 6:6–8] **41:35** [a] Gen. 41:48 **41:36** [a] Gen. 47:15, 19 **41:37** [a] Acts 7:10 **41:38** [a] Num. 27:18 **41:40** [a] Ps. 105:21 **41:41** [a] Dan. 6:3 **41:42** [a] Esth. 3:10 [b] Esth. 8:2, 15 [c] Dan. 5:7, 16, 29 **41:43** [a] Gen. 46:29 [b] Esth. 6:9 [c] Gen. 42:6 **41:45** [a] Gen. 46:20 **41:46** [a] 1 Sam. 16:21 **41:49** [a] Gen. 22:17 **41:50** [a] Gen. 46:20; 48:5 **41:51** [a] Ps. 45:10 [1] Literally *Making Forgetful* **41:52** [a] Gen. 17:6; 28:3; 49:22 [1] Literally *Fruitfulness* **41:54** [a] Acts 7:11 [b] Gen. 41:30 **41:55** [a] John 2:5 **41:56** [a] Gen. 42:6 [1] Literally *all that was in them* **41:57** [a] Ezek. 29:12 [b] Gen. 27:28, 37; 42:3

Joseph's Brothers Go to Egypt

42 When [a]Jacob saw that there was grain
in Egypt, Jacob said to his sons, "Why
do you look at one another?" 2 And he said,
"Indeed I have heard that there is grain in
Egypt; go down to that place and buy for us
there, that we may [a]live and not die."
3 So Joseph's ten brothers went down to
buy grain in Egypt. 4 But Jacob did not send
Joseph's brother Benjamin with his brothers,
for he said, [a]"Lest some calamity befall him."
5 And the sons of Israel went to buy *grain*
among those who journeyed, for the famine
was [a]in the land of Canaan.
6 Now Joseph *was* governor [a]over the land;
and it was he who sold to all the people of
the land. And Joseph's brothers came and
[b]bowed down before him with *their* faces
to the earth. 7 Joseph saw his brothers and
recognized them, but he acted as [a]a stranger
to them and spoke roughly to them. Then he
said to them, "Where do you come from?"
And they said, "From the land of Canaan
to buy food."
8 So Joseph recognized his brothers, but
they did not recognize him. 9 Then Joseph
[a]remembered the dreams which he had
dreamed about them, and said to them, "You
are spies! You have come to see the nakedness of the land!"
10 And they said to him, "No, my lord, but
your servants have come to buy food. 11 We
are all one man's sons; we *are* honest *men;*
your servants are not spies."
12 But he said to them, "No, but you have
come to see the nakedness of the land."
13 And they said, "Your servants *are* twelve
brothers, the sons of one man in the land of
Canaan; and in fact, the youngest *is* with our
father today, and one [a]*is* no more."
14 But Joseph said to them, "It *is* as I spoke
to you, saying, 'You *are* spies!' 15 In this *manner* you shall be tested: [a]By the life of Pharaoh, you shall not leave this place unless your
youngest brother comes here. 16 Send one of
you, and let him bring your brother; and you
shall be kept in prison, that your words may
be tested to see whether *there is* any truth in
you; or else, by the life of Pharaoh, surely you
are spies!" 17 So he put them all together in
prison [a]three days.
18 Then Joseph said to them the third day,
"Do this and live, [a]*for* I fear God: 19 If you *are*
honest *men,* let one of your brothers be confined to your prison house; but you, go and carry grain for the famine of your houses. 20 And
[a]bring your youngest brother to me; so your
words will be verified, and you shall not die."
And they did so. 21 Then they said to one
another, [a]"We *are* truly guilty concerning
our brother, for we saw the anguish of his
soul when he pleaded with us, and we would
not hear; [b]therefore this distress has come
upon us."

42:1 [a] Acts 7:12 **42:2** [a] Gen. 43:8 **42:4** [a] Gen. 42:38 **42:5** [a] Acts 7:11 **42:6** [a] Gen. 41:41, 55 [b] Gen. 37:7–10; 41:43 **42:7** [a] Gen. 45:1, 2 **42:9** [a] Gen. 37:5–9 **42:13** [a] Gen. 37:30; 42:32; 44:20 **42:15** [a] 1 Sam. 1:26; 17:55 **42:17** [a] Gen. 40:4, 7, 12 **42:18** [a] Lev. 25:43 **42:20** [a] Gen. 42:34; 43:5; 44:23 **42:21** [a] Hos. 5:15 [b] Prov. 21:13

FORGETTING AND REMEMBERING

God has caused me to be fruitful in the land of my affliction.

GENESIS 41:52

God is the "One Who Is" (*Yahweh*), everything I need in every circumstance. Jesus proved to be everything Joseph needed in every circumstance. Joseph's faith in the Lord kept him ready and willing to act when God gave opportunity. Then he saw the many blessings roll in. His work on behalf of Pharaoh and the people of Egypt succeeded. He reconciled with his family. He married and had two sons.

The names of the sons of Joseph speak volumes. The first is Manasseh, which means "Making Forgetful," and the second is Ephraim, which means "Fruitfulness." God stood by Joseph, enabling him to endure trials. Here, Joseph's life had become truly fruitful, both professionally and personally. One of the greatest ways to experience the peace of God right now is to declare "Manasseh" over your life—the blessing of forgetting the past. We have to choose to forgive the past, learn from it, and leave it behind. Trust in the "One Who Is," and know His peace. God apparently helped Joseph to forget his hardships and made him flourish in the place of his affliction. He can do this for you, too!

22 And Reuben answered them, saying,
[a]"Did I not speak to you, saying, 'Do not sin
against the boy'; and you would not listen?
Therefore behold, his blood is now [b]required
of us." 23 But they did not know that Joseph
understood *them,* for he spoke to them
through an interpreter. 24 And he turned
himself away from them and [a]wept. Then
he returned to them again, and talked with
them. And he took [b]Simeon from them and
bound him before their eyes.

The Brothers Return to Canaan

25 Then Joseph [a]gave a command to fill
their sacks with grain, to [b]restore every man's
money to his sack, and to give them provisions for the journey. [c]Thus he did for them.
26 So they loaded their donkeys with the grain
and departed from there. 27 But as [a]one *of
them* opened his sack to give his donkey feed
at the encampment, he saw his money; and
there it was, in the mouth of his sack. 28 So
he said to his brothers, "My money has been
restored, and there it is, in my sack!" Then
their hearts failed *them* and they were afraid,
saying to one another, "What *is* this *that* God
has done to us?"

29 Then they went to Jacob their father in
the land of Canaan and told him all that had
happened to them, saying: 30 "The man *who
is* lord of the land [a]spoke roughly to us, and
took us for spies of the country. 31 But we said
to him, 'We *are* honest *men;* we are not spies.
32 We *are* twelve brothers, sons of our father;
one *is* no *more,* and the youngest *is* with our
father this day in the land of Canaan.' 33 Then
the man, the lord of the country, said to us,
[a]'By this I will know that you *are* honest *men:*
Leave one of your brothers *here* with me, take
food for the famine of your households, and
be gone. 34 And bring your [a]youngest brother
to me; so I shall know that you *are* not spies,
but *that* you *are* honest *men.* I will grant
your brother to you, and you may [b]trade in
the land.' "

35 Then it happened as they emptied their
sacks, that surprisingly [a]each man's bundle
of money *was* in his sack; and when they
and their father saw the bundles of money,
they were afraid. 36 And Jacob their father
said to them, "You have [a]bereaved me: Joseph is no *more,* Simeon is no *more,* and you
want to take [b]Benjamin. All these things are
against me."

37 Then Reuben spoke to his father, saying,
"Kill my two sons if I do not bring him *back*
to you; put him in my hands, and I will bring
him back to you."

38 But he said, "My son shall not go down
with you, for [a]his brother is dead, and he
is left alone. [b]If any calamity should befall
him along the way in which you go, then you
would [c]bring down my gray hair with sorrow
to the grave."

Joseph's Brothers Return with Benjamin

43 Now the famine *was* [a]severe in the
land. 2 And it came to pass, when
they had eaten up the grain which they had
brought from Egypt, that their father said to
them, "Go [a]back, buy us a little food."

3 But Judah spoke to him, saying, "The man
solemnly warned us, saying, 'You shall not
see my face unless your [a]brother *is* with you.'
4 If you send our brother with us, we will go
down and buy you food. 5 But if you will not
send *him,* we will not go down; for the man
said to us, 'You shall not see my face unless
your brother *is* with you.' "

6 And Israel said, "Why did you deal *so*
wrongfully with me *as* to tell the man whether
you had still *another* brother?"

7 But they said, "The man asked us point-
edly about ourselves and our family, saying,
'*Is* your father still alive? Have you *another*
brother?' And we told him according to these
words. Could we possibly have known that
he would say, 'Bring your brother down'?"

8 Then Judah said to Israel his father, "Send
the lad with me, and we will arise and go,
that we may [a]live and not die, both we and
you *and* also our little ones. 9 I myself will
be surety for him; from my hand you shall
require him. [a]If I do not bring him *back* to you
and set him before you, then let me bear the
blame forever. 10 For if we had not lingered,
surely by now we would have returned this
second time."

11 And their father Israel said to them, "If
it must be so, then do this: Take some of the
best fruits of the land in your vessels and
[a]carry down a present for the man—a little
[b]balm and a little honey, spices and myrrh,
pistachio nuts and almonds. 12 Take double
money in your hand, and take back in your
hand the money [a]that was returned in the
mouth of your sacks; perhaps it was an oversight. 13 Take your brother also, and arise, go

42:22 [a] Gen. 37:21, 22, 29 [b] Gen. 9:5, 6 **42:24** [a] Gen. 43:30; 45:14, 15 [b] Gen. 34:25, 30; 43:14, 23 **42:25** [a] Gen. 44:1 [b] Gen. 43:12 [c] [Rom. 12:17, 20, 21] **42:27** [a] Gen. 43:21, 22 **42:30** [a] Gen. 42:7 **42:33** [a] Gen. 42:15, 19, 20 **42:34** [a] Gen. 42:20; 43:3, 5 [b] Gen. 34:10 **42:35** [a] Gen. 43:12, 15, 21 **42:36** [a] Gen. 43:14 [b] [Rom. 8:28, 31] **42:38** [a] Gen. 37:22; 42:13; 44:20, 28 [b] Gen. 42:4; 44:29 [c] Gen. 37:35; 44:31 **43:1** [a] Gen. 41:54, 57; 42:5; 45:6, 11 **43:2** [a] Gen. 42:2; 44:25 **43:3** [a] Gen. 42:20; 43:5; 44:23 **43:8** [a] Gen. 42:2; 47:19 **43:9** [a] Gen. 42:37; 44:32 **43:11** [a] Gen. 32:20; 33:10; 43:25, 26 [b] Jer. 8:22 **43:12** [a] Gen. 42:25, 35; 43:21, 22

back to the man. 14 And may God [a]Almighty
[b]give you mercy before the man, that he may
release your other brother and Benjamin. [c]If
I am bereaved, I am bereaved!"
15 So the men took that present and Benjamin, and they took double money in their
hand, and arose and went [a]down to Egypt;
and they stood before Joseph. 16 When Joseph saw Benjamin with them, he said to
the [a]steward of his house, "Take *these* men
to my home, and slaughter an animal and
make ready; for *these* men will dine with
me at noon." 17 Then the man did as Joseph
ordered, and the man brought the men into
Joseph's house.
18 Now the men were [a]afraid because they
were brought into Joseph's house; and they
said, "*It is* because of the money, which was
returned in our sacks the first time, that we
are brought in, so that he may make a case
against us and seize us, to take us as slaves
with our donkeys."
19 When they drew near to the steward of
Joseph's house, they talked with him at the
door of the house, 20 and said, "O sir, [a]we indeed came down the first time to buy food;
21 but [a]it happened, when we came to the
encampment, that we opened our sacks, and
there, *each* man's money *was* in the mouth
of his sack, our money in full weight; so we
have brought it back in our hand. 22 And
we have brought down other money in our
hands to buy food. We do not know who put
our money in our sacks."
23 But he said, "Peace *be* with you, do not be
afraid. Your God and the God of your father
has given you treasure in your sacks; I had
your money." Then he brought [a]Simeon out
to them.
24 So the man brought the men into Joseph's house and [a]gave *them* water, and they
washed their feet; and he gave their donkeys
feed. 25 Then they made the present ready for
Joseph's coming at noon, for they heard that
they would eat bread there.
26 And when Joseph came home, they
brought him the present which *was* in their
hand into the house, and [a]bowed down before him to the earth. 27 Then he asked them
about *their* well-being, and said, "*Is* your father well, the old man [a]of whom you spoke?
Is he still alive?"
28 And they answered, "Your servant our
father *is* in good health; he *is* still alive." [a]And
they bowed their heads down and prostrated
themselves.
29 Then he lifted his eyes and saw his
brother Benjamin, [a]his mother's son, and
said, "*Is* this your younger brother [b]of whom
you spoke to me?" And he said, "God be
gracious to you, my son." 30 Now [a]his heart
yearned for his brother; so Joseph made

43:14 [a] Gen. 17:1; 28:3; 35:11; 48:3 [b] Ps. 106:46 [c] Esth. 4:16 **43:15** [a] Gen. 39:1; 46:3, 6 **43:16** [a] Gen. 24:2; 39:4; 44:1 **43:18** [a] Gen. 42:28 **43:20** [a] Gen. 42:3, 10 **43:21** [a] Gen. 42:27, 35 **43:23** [a] Gen. 42:24 **43:24** [a] Gen. 18:4; 19:2; 24:32 **43:26** [a] Gen. 37:7, 10; 42:6; 44:14 **43:27** [a] Gen. 29:6; 42:11, 13; 43:7; 45:3 **43:28** [a] Gen. 37:7, 10 **43:29** [a] Gen. 35:17, 18 [b] Gen. 42:13 **43:30** [a] 1 Kin. 3:26

HOW IS YOUR PEACE?

Is your father well, the old man of whom you spoke? Is he still alive?

GENESIS 43:27

When you and I see our loved ones or meet new friends, we often ask each other, "How are you?" The people of God had an ancient tradition of asking, "How is your peace?" Isn't this a better question? Doesn't it get to the point, wipe away meaningless chitchat, and immediately deepen the exchange?

Thankfully, we have numerous examples of peace checks throughout the Scriptures. Imagine how difficult it must have been for Joseph to ask the brothers who sold him into slavery "about their well-being" (v. 27). But he reached beyond his potential resentment to ask, *How is your peace?* Seeing his brothers, learning his father was "in good health [*shalom*]" (v. 28), and seeing his youngest sibling caused great emotion in Joseph and led to reconciliation.

This forgotten tradition of heartfelt exchange is one we must recover in our time. Do you need to ask someone today, "Hey, how is your peace?" It's a question worth answering. Like Joseph, we may find that, through the grace of God, we can see past the faults and failures of loved ones and restore their—if not our own—peace and well-being.

haste and sought *somewhere* to weep. And
he went into *his* chamber and [b]wept there.
31 Then he washed his face and came out;
and he restrained himself, and said, "Serve
the [a]bread."

32 So they set him a place by himself, and
them by themselves, and the Egyptians who
ate with him by themselves; because the
Egyptians could not eat food with the [a]He-
brews, for that *is* [b]an abomination to the
Egyptians. 33 And they sat before him, the
firstborn according to his [a]birthright and
the youngest according to his youth; and the
men looked in astonishment at one another.
34 Then he took servings to them from before
him, but Benjamin's serving was [a]five times
as much as any of theirs. So they drank and
were merry with him.

Joseph's Cup

44 And he commanded the [a]steward
of his house, saying, [b]"Fill the men's
sacks with food, as much as they can carry,
and put each man's money in the mouth of
his sack. 2 Also put my cup, the silver cup, in
the mouth of the sack of the youngest, and
his grain money." So he did according to the
word that Joseph had spoken. 3 As soon as the
morning dawned, the men were sent away,
they and their donkeys. 4 When they had gone
out of the city, *and* were not *yet* far off, Joseph
said to his steward, "Get up, follow the men;
and when you overtake them, say to them,
'Why have you [a]repaid evil for good? 5 *Is* not
this *the one* from which my lord drinks, and
with which he indeed practices divination?
You have done evil in so doing.' "

6 So he overtook them, and he spoke to
them these same words. 7 And they said to
him, "Why does my lord say these words?
Far be it from us that your servants should
do such a thing. 8 Look, we brought back to
you from the land of Canaan [a]the money
which we found in the mouth of our sacks.
How then could we steal silver or gold from
your lord's house? 9 With whomever of your
servants it is found, [a]let him die, and we also
will be my lord's slaves."

10 And he said, "Now also *let* it *be* according
to your words; he with whom it is found shall
be my slave, and you shall be blameless."
11 Then each man speedily let down his sack
to the ground, and each opened his sack.
12 So he searched. He began with the oldest
and left off with the youngest; and the cup
was found in Benjamin's sack. 13 Then they
[a]tore their clothes, and each man loaded his
donkey and returned to the city.

14 So Judah and his brothers came to Joseph's house, and he *was* still there; and they
[a]fell before him on the ground. 15 And Joseph
said to them, "What deed *is* this you have
done? Did you not know that such a man as
I can certainly practice divination?"

16 Then Judah said, "What shall we say to
my lord? What shall we speak? Or how shall
we clear ourselves? God has [a]found out the
iniquity of your servants; here [b]we are, my
lord's slaves, both we and *he* also with whom
the cup was found."

17 But he said, [a]"Far be it from me that I
should do so; the man in whose hand the cup
was found, he shall be my slave. And as for
you, go up in peace to your father."

Judah Intercedes for Benjamin

18 Then Judah came near to him and said:
"O my lord, please let your servant speak a
word in my lord's hearing, and [a]do not let
your anger burn against your servant; for
you *are* even like Pharaoh. 19 My lord asked
his servants, saying, 'Have you a father or a
brother?' 20 And we said to my lord, 'We have
a father, an old man, and [a]a child of *his* old
age, *who is* young; his brother is [b]dead, and
he [c]alone is left of his mother's children, and
his [d]father loves him.' 21 Then you said to
your servants, [a]'Bring him down to me, that
I may set my eyes on him.' 22 And we said to
my lord, 'The lad cannot leave his father, for
if he should leave his father, *his father* would
die.' 23 But you said to your servants, [a]'Unless
your youngest brother comes down with you,
you shall see my face no more.'

24 "So it was, when we went up to your servant my father, that we told him the words of
my lord. 25 And [a]our father said, 'Go back *and*
buy us a little food.' 26 But we said, 'We cannot
go down; if our youngest brother is with us,
then we will go down; for we may not see
the man's face unless our youngest brother
is with us.' 27 Then your servant my father
said to us, 'You know that [a]my wife bore me
two sons; 28 and the one went out from me,
and I said, [a]"Surely he is torn to pieces"; and
I have not seen him since. 29 But if you [a]take
this one also from me, and calamity befalls
him, you shall bring down my gray hair with
sorrow to the grave.'

30 "Now therefore, when I come to your

43:30 [b] Gen. 42:24; 45:2, 14, 15; 46:29 **43:31** [a] Gen. 43:25 **43:32** [a] Gen. 41:12 [b] Gen. 46:34 **43:33** [a] Gen. 27:36; 42:7 **43:34** [a] Gen. 35:24; 45:22 **44:1** [a] Gen. 43:16 [b] Gen. 42:25 **44:4** [a] 1 Sam. 25:21 **44:8** [a] Gen. 43:21 **44:9** [a] Gen. 31:32 **44:13** [a] 2 Sam. 1:11 **44:14** [a] Gen. 37:7, 10 **44:16** [a] [Num. 32:23] [b] Gen. 44:9 **44:17** [a] Prov. 17:15 **44:18** [a] Ex. 32:22 **44:20** [a] Gen. 37:3; 43:8; 44:30 [b] Gen. 42:38 [c] Gen. 46:19 [d] Gen. 42:4 **44:21** [a] Gen. 42:15, 20 **44:23** [a] Gen. 43:3, 5 **44:25** [a] Gen. 43:2 **44:27** [a] Gen. 30:22–24; 35:16–18; 46:19 **44:28** [a] Gen. 37:31–35 **44:29** [a] Gen. 42:36, 38; 44:31

servant my father, and the lad *is* not with
us, since [a]his life is bound up in the lad's
life, 31 it will happen, when he sees that the
lad *is* not *with us,* that he will die. So your
servants will bring down the gray hair of
your servant our father with sorrow to the
grave. 32 For your servant became surety for
the lad to my father, saying, [a]'If I do not bring
him *back* to you, then I shall bear the blame
before my father forever.' 33 Now therefore,
please [a]let your servant remain instead of
the lad as a slave to my lord, and let the lad
go up with his brothers. 34 For how shall I
go up to my father if the lad *is* not with me,
lest perhaps I see the evil that would come
upon my father?"

Joseph Revealed to His Brothers

45 Then Joseph could not restrain himself before all those who stood by him,
and he cried out, "Make everyone go out from
me!" So no one stood with him [a]while Joseph
made himself known to his brothers. 2 And
he [a]wept aloud, and the Egyptians and the
house of Pharaoh heard *it.*

3 Then Joseph said to his brothers, [a]"I *am*
Joseph; does my father still live?" But his
brothers could not answer him, for they
were dismayed in his presence. 4 And Joseph
said to his brothers, "Please come near to
me." So they came near. Then he said: "I
am Joseph your brother, [a]whom you sold
into Egypt. 5 But now, do not therefore be
grieved or angry with yourselves because
you sold me here; [a]for God sent me before
you to preserve life. 6 For these two years the
[a]famine *has been* in the land, and *there are*
still five years in which *there will be* neither
plowing nor harvesting. 7 And God [a]sent me
before you to preserve a posterity for you in
the earth, and to save your lives by a great
deliverance. 8 So now *it was* not you *who*
sent me here, but [a]God; and He has made
me [b]a father to Pharaoh, and lord of all his
house, and a [c]ruler throughout all the land
of Egypt.

9 "Hurry and go up to my father, and say to
him, 'Thus says your son Joseph: "God has
made me lord of all Egypt; come down to me,
do not tarry. 10 [a]You shall dwell in the land
of Goshen, and you shall be near to me, you
and your children, your children's children,
your flocks and your herds, and all that you
have. 11 There I will [a]provide for you, lest you
and your household, and all that you have,
come to poverty; for *there are* still five years
of famine." '

12 "And behold, your eyes and the eyes of
my brother Benjamin see that *it is* [a]my mouth
that speaks to you. 13 So you shall tell my
father of all my glory in Egypt, and of all
that you have seen; and you shall hurry and
[a]bring my father down here."

14 Then he fell on his brother Benjamin's
neck and wept, and Benjamin wept on his
neck. 15 Moreover he [a]kissed all his brothers
and wept over them, and after that his
brothers talked with him.

16 Now the report of it was heard in Pharaoh's house, saying, "Joseph's brothers have
come." So it pleased Pharaoh and his servants
well. 17 And Pharaoh said to Joseph, "Say to
your brothers, 'Do this: Load your animals
and depart; go to the land of Canaan. 18 Bring
your father and your households and come
to me; I will give you the best of the land of
Egypt, and you will eat [a]the fat of the land.
19 Now you are commanded—do this: Take
carts out of the land of Egypt for your little
ones and your wives; bring your father and
come. 20 Also do not be concerned about
your goods, for the best of all the land of
Egypt *is* yours.' "

21 Then the sons of Israel did so; and Joseph
gave them [a]carts, according to the command
of Pharaoh, and he gave them provisions for
the journey. 22 He gave to all of them, to each
man, [a]changes of garments; but to Benjamin
he gave three hundred *pieces* of silver and
[b]five changes of garments. 23 And he sent to
his father these *things:* ten donkeys loaded
with the good things of Egypt, and ten female
donkeys loaded with grain, bread, and food
for his father for the journey. 24 So he sent
his brothers away, and they departed; and he
said to them, "See that you do not become
troubled along the way."

25 Then they went up out of Egypt, and
came to the land of Canaan to Jacob their
father. 26 And they told him, saying, "Joseph
is still alive, and he *is* governor over all the
land of Egypt." [a]And Jacob's heart stood
still, because he did not believe them. 27 But
when they told him all the words which Joseph had said to them, and when he saw the
carts which Joseph had sent to carry him,
the spirit [a]of Jacob their father revived.
28 Then Israel said, "*It is* enough. Joseph
my son *is* still alive. I will go and see him
before I die."

44:30 [a] [1 Sam. 18:1; 25:29] **44:32** [a] Gen. 43:9 **44:33** [a] Ex. 32:32 **45:1** [a] Acts 7:13 **45:2** [a] Gen. 43:30; 46:29 **45:3** [a] Acts 7:13 **45:4** [a] Gen. 37:28; 39:1 **45:5** [a] Gen. 45:7, 8; 50:20 **45:6** [a] Gen. 43:1; 47:4, 13 **45:7** [a] Gen. 45:5; 50:20 **45:8** [a] [Rom. 8:28] [b] Is. 22:21 [c] Gen. 41:43; 42:6 **45:10** [a] Gen. 46:28, 34; 47:1, 6 **45:11** [a] Gen. 47:12 **45:12** [a] Gen. 42:23 **45:13** [a] Acts 7:14 **45:15** [a] Gen. 48:10 **45:18** [a] Gen. 27:28; 47:6 **45:21** [a] Gen. 45:19; 46:5 **45:22** [a] 2 Kin. 5:5 [b] Gen. 43:34 **45:26** [a] Job 29:24 **45:27** [a] Judg. 15:19

Jacob's Journey to Egypt

46 So Israel took his journey with all that
he had, and came to [a]Beersheba, and
offered sacrifices [b]to the God of his father
Isaac. 2 Then God spoke to Israel [a]in the visions of the night, and said, "Jacob, Jacob!"
And he said, "Here I am."
3 So He said, "I *am* God, [a]the God of your
father; do not fear to go down to Egypt, for
I will [b]make of you a great nation there. 4 [a]I
will go down with you to Egypt, and I will also
surely [b]bring you up *again;* and [c]Joseph will
put his hand on your eyes."
5 Then [a]Jacob arose from Beersheba;
and the sons of Israel carried their father
Jacob, their little ones, and their wives, in
the carts [b]which Pharaoh had sent to carry him. 6 So they took their livestock and
their goods, which they had acquired in the
land of Canaan, and went to Egypt, [a]Jacob
and all his descendants with him. 7 His sons
and his sons' sons, his daughters and his
sons' daughters, and all his descendants he
brought with him to Egypt.
8 Now [a]these *were* the names of the children of Israel, Jacob and his sons, who went
to Egypt: [b]Reuben *was* Jacob's firstborn.
9 The [a]sons of Reuben *were* Hanoch, Pallu,
Hezron, and Carmi. 10 [a]The sons of Simeon
were Jemuel,[1] Jamin, Ohad, Jachin,[2] Zohar,[3]
and Shaul, the son of a Canaanite woman.
11 The sons of [a]Levi *were* Gershon, Kohath,
and Merari. 12 The sons of [a]Judah *were* [b]Er,
Onan, Shelah, Perez, and Zerah (but Er and
Onan died in the land of Canaan). [c]The sons
of Perez were Hezron and Hamul. 13 The sons
of Issachar *were* Tola, Puvah,[1] Job,[2] and Shimron. 14 The [a]sons of Zebulun *were* Sered, Elon,
and Jahleel. 15 These *were* the [a]sons of Leah,
whom she bore to Jacob in Padan Aram, with
his daughter Dinah. All the persons, his sons
and his daughters, *were* thirty-three.
16 The sons of Gad *were* Ziphion,[1] Haggi,
Shuni, Ezbon,[2] Eri, Arodi,[3] and Areli. 17 [a]The
sons of Asher *were* Jimnah, Ishuah, Isui,
Beriah, and Serah, their sister. And the sons
of Beriah *were* Heber and Malchiel. 18 [a]These
were the sons of Zilpah, [b]whom Laban gave
to Leah his daughter; and these she bore to
Jacob: sixteen persons.
19 The [a]sons of Rachel, [b]Jacob's wife, *were*
Joseph and Benjamin. 20 [a]And to Joseph in

46:1 [a] Gen. 21:31, 33; 26:32, 33; 28:10 [b] Gen. 26:24, 25; 28:13; 31:42; 32:9 **46:2** [a] Gen. 15:1; 22:11; 31:11 **46:3** [a] Gen. 17:1; 28:13 [b] Deut. 26:5 **46:4** [a] Gen. 28:15; 31:3; 48:21 [b] Gen. 15:16; 50:12, 24, 25 [c] Gen. 50:1 **46:5** [a] Acts 7:15 [b] Gen. 45:19–21 **46:6** [a] Deut. 26:5 **46:8** [a] Ex. 1:1–4 [b] Num. 26:4, 5 **46:9** [a] Ex. 6:14 **46:10** [a] Ex. 6:15 [1] Spelled *Nemuel* in 1 Chronicles 4:24 [2] Called *Jarib* in 1 Chronicles 4:24 [3] Called *Zerah* in 1 Chronicles 4:24 **46:11** [a] 1 Chr. 6:1, 16 **46:12** [a] 1 Chr. 2:3; 4:21 [b] Gen. 38:3, 7, 10 [c] Gen. 38:29 **46:13** [1] Spelled *Puah* in 1 Chronicles 7:1 [2] Same as *Jashub* in Numbers 26:24 and 1 Chronicles 7:1 **46:14** [a] Num. 26:26 **46:15** [a] Gen. 35:23; 49:31 **46:16** [1] Spelled *Zephon* in Samaritan Pentateuch, Septuagint, and Numbers 26:15 [2] Called *Ozni* in Numbers 26:16 [3] Spelled *Arod* in Numbers 26:17 **46:17** [a] 1 Chr. 7:30 **46:18** [a] Gen. 30:10; 37:2 [b] Gen. 29:24 **46:19** [a] Gen. 35:24 [b] Gen. 44:27 **46:20** [a] Gen. 41:45, 50–52; 48:1

SENT FOR THEIR PEACE

Moreover he kissed all his brothers and wept over them,
and after that his brothers talked with him.

GENESIS 45:15

Given what Joseph's brothers had done to him and the power that he now possessed, Joseph could have exacted a fearful revenge on them. No wonder when Joseph revealed himself to his brothers, "they were dismayed" (v. 3). What an understatement! I suspect they were terrified! But Joseph invited his brothers to approach without fear or self-reproach, saying, "God sent me before you to preserve life . . . So now it was not you who sent me here, but God" (vv. 5, 8). What a remarkable thing to say!

Joseph recognized that in all his trials, including terrible acts of injustice, God in His sovereignty was at work, saving Jacob and his family and the lives of many people in Egypt. One of the ways we can have peace is by knowing that this is the way God acts. What may on the surface look disastrous could be something God is at work behind the scenes making right.

Can you peek behind something that looks disastrous to see if God's hand is at work? Can you find peace despite how tragic things look—as Joseph did?

the land of Egypt were born Manasseh and
Ephraim, whom Asenath, the daughter of
Poti-Pherah priest of On, bore to him. 21 [a]The
sons of Benjamin *were* Belah, Becher, Ashbel, Gera, Naaman, [b]Ehi, Rosh, [c]Muppim,
Huppim,[1] and Ard. 22 These *were* the sons of
Rachel, who were born to Jacob: fourteen
persons in all.
23 The son of Dan *was* Hushim.[1] 24 [a]The sons
of Naphtali *were* Jahzeel,[1] Guni, Jezer, and Shillem.[2] 25 [a]These *were* the sons of Bilhah, [b]whom
Laban gave to Rachel his daughter, and she
bore these to Jacob: seven persons in all.
26 [a]All the persons who went with Jacob
to Egypt, who came from his body, [b]besides
Jacob's sons' wives, *were* sixty-six persons in
all. 27 And the sons of Joseph who were born
to him in Egypt *were* two persons. [a]All the
persons of the house of Jacob who went to
Egypt were seventy.

Jacob Settles in Goshen

28 Then he sent Judah before him to Joseph, [a]to point out before him *the way* to
Goshen. And they came [b]to the land of Goshen. 29 So Joseph made ready his [a]chariot
and went up to Goshen to meet his father
Israel; and he presented himself to him,
and [b]fell on his neck and wept on his neck
a good while.
30 And Israel said to Joseph, [a]"Now let me
die, since I have seen your face, because you
are still alive."
31 Then Joseph said to his brothers and to
his father's household, [a]"I will go up and tell
Pharaoh, and say to him, 'My brothers and
those of my father's house, who *were* in the
land of Canaan, have come to me. 32 And the
men *are* [a]shepherds, for their occupation has
been to feed livestock; and they have brought
their flocks, their herds, and all that they
have.' 33 So it shall be, when Pharaoh calls you
and says, [a]'What is your occupation?' 34 that
you shall say, 'Your servants' [a]occupation
has been with livestock [b]from our youth
even till now, both we *and* also our fathers,'
that you may dwell in the land of Goshen;
for every shepherd *is* [c]an abomination to
the Egyptians."

47 Then Joseph [a]went and told Pharaoh,
and said, "My father and my brothers,
their flocks and their herds and all that they
possess, have come from the land of Canaan; and indeed they *are* in [b]the land of
Goshen." 2 And he took five men from among
his brothers and [a]presented them to Pharaoh.
3 Then Pharaoh said to his brothers, [a]"What
is your occupation?"
And they said to Pharaoh, [b]"Your servants
are shepherds, both we *and* also our fathers."

46:21 [a] 1 Chr. 7:6; 8:1 [b] Num. 26:38 [c] Num. 26:39 [1] Called *Hupham* in Numbers 26:39 **46:23** [1] Called *Shuham* in Numbers 26:42 **46:24** [a] Num. 26:48 [1] Spelled *Jahziel* in 1 Chronicles 7:13 [2] Spelled *Shallum* in 1 Chronicles 7:13 **46:25** [a] Gen. 30:5, 7 [b] Gen. 29:29 **46:26** [a] Ex. 1:5 [b] Gen. 35:11 **46:27** [a] Deut. 10:22 **46:28** [a] Gen. 31:21 [b] Gen. 47:1 **46:29** [a] Gen. 41:43 [b] Gen. 45:14, 15 **46:30** [a] Luke 2:29, 30 **46:31** [a] Gen. 47:1 **46:32** [a] Gen. 47:3 **46:33** [a] Gen. 47:2, 3 **46:34** [a] Gen. 47:3 [b] Gen. 30:35; 34:5; 37:17 [c] Gen. 43:32 **47:1** [a] Gen. 46:31 [b] Gen. 45:10; 46:28; 50:8 **47:2** [a] Acts 7:13 **47:3** [a] Gen. 46:33 [b] Gen. 46:32, 34

HE'S ALREADY HERE

God spoke to Israel in the visions of the night, and said,
"Jacob! Jacob!" And he said, "Here I am."

GENESIS 46:2

What robs us of peace is uncertainty. The future does often scare us. It frightened Jacob, too. Given his misadventures and misdeeds, I am not surprised. But God spoke to Jacob, then known as Israel, "in the visions of the night" and reassured him, directing him to go to Egypt, where he would be reunited with Joseph. He'd never have to part from this beloved son again.

We can experience God's words and reassurance that way too. We may or may not have visions, but we can read His Word and find the comfort He's stored for us there. The road of life is rough and uncertain but God is with us, and if we listen, He will show us His presence.

In whatever situations you're struggling right now, can you seek God's peace today? Will you seek Him in whatever ways you can—His Word, biblical teaching, time with other believers? See if His tranquility doesn't *find you* as you hunt for His help.

4 And they said to Pharaoh, [a]"We have come
to dwell in the land, because your servants
have no pasture for their flocks, [b]for the
famine *is* severe in the land of Canaan. Now
therefore, please let your servants [c]dwell in
the land of Goshen."
5 Then Pharaoh spoke to Joseph, saying,
"Your father and your brothers have come
to you. 6 [a]The land of Egypt *is* before you.
Have your father and brothers dwell in the
best of the land; let them dwell [b]in the land
of Goshen. And if you know *any* competent
men among them, then make them chief
herdsmen over my livestock."
7 Then Joseph brought in his father Jacob and set him before Pharaoh; and Jacob
[a]blessed Pharaoh. 8 Pharaoh said to Jacob,
"How old *are* you?"
9 And Jacob said to Pharaoh, [a]"The days of
the years of my pilgrimage *are* [b]one hundred
and thirty years; [c]few and evil have been the
days of the years of my life, and [d]they have
not attained to the days of the years of the life
of my fathers in the days of their pilgrimage."
10 So Jacob [a]blessed Pharaoh, and went out
from before Pharaoh.
11 And Joseph situated his father and his
brothers, and gave them a possession in the
land of Egypt, in the best of the land, in the land
of [a]Rameses, [b]as Pharaoh had commanded.
12 Then Joseph provided [a]his father, his brothers,
and all his father's household with bread, according to the number in *their* families.

Joseph Deals with the Famine

13 Now *there was* no bread in all the land;
for the famine *was* very severe, [a]so that the
land of Egypt and the land of Canaan languished because of the famine. 14 [a]And Joseph
gathered up all the money that was found in
the land of Egypt and in the land of Canaan,
for the grain which they bought; and Joseph
brought the money into Pharaoh's house.
15 So when the money failed in the land
of Egypt and in the land of Canaan, all the
Egyptians came to Joseph and said, "Give us
bread, for [a]why should we die in your presence? For the money has failed."
16 Then Joseph said, "Give your livestock,
and I will give you *bread* for your livestock, if
the money is gone." 17 So they brought their
livestock to Joseph, and Joseph gave them
bread *in exchange* for the horses, the flocks,
the cattle of the herds, and for the donkeys.
Thus he fed them with bread *in exchange* for
all their livestock that year.
18 When that year had ended, they came to
him the next year and said to him, "We will
not hide from my lord that our money is
gone; my lord also has our herds of livestock.
There is nothing left in the sight of my lord
but our bodies and our lands. 19 Why should
we die before your eyes, both we and our
land? Buy us and our land for bread, and we
and our land will be servants of Pharaoh;
give *us* seed, that we may [a]live and not die,
that the land may not be desolate."
20 Then Joseph [a]bought all the land of Egypt
for Pharaoh; for every man of the Egyptians
sold his field, because the famine was severe
upon them. So the land became Pharaoh's.
21 And as for the people, he moved them into
the cities,[1] from *one* end of the borders of
Egypt to the *other* end. 22 [a]Only the land of
the [b]priests he did not buy; for the priests
had rations *allotted to them* by Pharaoh, and
they ate their rations which Pharaoh gave
them; therefore they did not sell their lands.
23 Then Joseph said to the people, "Indeed
I have bought you and your land this day for
Pharaoh. Look, *here is* seed for you, and you
shall sow the land. 24 And it shall come to pass
in the harvest that you shall give one-fifth to
Pharaoh. Four-fifths shall be your own, as seed
for the field and for your food, for those of your
households and as food for your little ones."
25 So they said, "You have saved [a]our lives;
let us find favor in the sight of my lord, and
we will be Pharaoh's servants." 26 And Joseph made it a law over the land of Egypt to
this day, *that* Pharaoh should have one-fifth,
[a]except for the land of the priests only, *which*
did not become Pharaoh's.

Joseph's Vow to Jacob

27 So Israel [a]dwelt in the land of Egypt, in
the country of Goshen; and they had possessions there and [b]grew and multiplied
exceedingly. 28 And Jacob lived in the land
of Egypt seventeen years. So the length of
Jacob's life was one hundred and forty-seven
years. 29 When the time [a]drew near that Israel
must die, he called his son Joseph and said to
him, "Now if I have found favor in your sight,
please [b]put your hand under my thigh, and
[c]deal kindly and truly with me. [d]Please do

47:4 [a] Deut. 26:5 [b] Gen. 43:1 [c] Gen. 46:34 **47:6** [a] Gen. 20:15; 45:10, 18; 47:11 [b] Gen. 47:4 **47:7** [a] Gen. 47:10; 48:15, 20 **47:9** [a] [Heb. 11:9, 13] [b] Gen. 47:28 [c] [Job 14:1] [d] Gen. 5:5; 11:10, 11; 25:7, 8; 35:28 **47:10** [a] Gen. 47:7 **47:11** [a] Ex. 1:11; 12:37 [b] Gen. 47:6, 27 **47:12** [a] Gen. 45:11; 50:21 **47:13** [a] Gen. 41:30 **47:14** [a] Gen. 41:56; 42:6 **47:15** [a] Gen. 47:19 **47:19** [a] Gen. 43:8 **47:20** [a] Jer. 32:43 **47:21** [1] Following Masoretic Text and Targum; Samaritan Pentateuch, Septuagint, and Vulgate read *made the people virtual slaves.* **47:22** [a] Ezra 7:24 [b] Gen. 41:45 **47:25** [a] Gen. 33:15 **47:26** [a] Gen. 47:22 **47:27** [a] Gen. 47:11 [b] Gen. 17:6; 26:4; 35:11; 46:3 **47:29** [a] Deut. 31:14 [b] Gen. 24:2–4 [c] Gen. 24:49 [d] Gen. 50:25

not bury me in Egypt, 30 but [a]let me lie with
my fathers; you shall carry me out of Egypt
and [b]bury me in their burial place."
And he said, "I will do as you have said."
31 Then he said, "Swear to me." And he
swore to him. So [a]Israel bowed himself on
the head of the bed.

Jacob Blesses Joseph's Sons

48 Now it came to pass after these things
that Joseph was told, "Indeed your
father *is* sick"; and he took with him his two
sons, [a]Manasseh and Ephraim. 2 And Jacob
was told, "Look, your son Joseph is coming
to you"; and Israel strengthened himself
and sat up on the bed. 3 Then Jacob said to
Joseph: "God [a]Almighty appeared to me at
[b]Luz in the land of Canaan and blessed me,
4 and said to me, 'Behold, I will [a]make you
fruitful and multiply you, and I will make
of you a multitude of people, and [b]give this
land to your descendants after you [c]*as* an
everlasting possession.' 5 And now your [a]two
sons, Ephraim and Manasseh, who were born
to you in the land of Egypt before I came to
you in Egypt, *are* mine; as Reuben and Simeon, they shall be mine. 6 Your offspring whom
you beget after them shall be yours; they
will be called by the name of their brothers
in their inheritance. 7 But as for me, when I
came from Padan, [a]Rachel died beside me
in the land of Canaan on the way, when *there*
was but a little distance to go to Ephrath; and
I buried her there on the way to Ephrath (that
is, Bethlehem)."
8 Then Israel saw Joseph's sons, and said,
"Who *are* these?"
9 Joseph said to his father, "They *are* my
sons, whom God has given me in this *place.*"
And he said, "Please bring them to me, and
[a]I will bless them." 10 Now [a]the eyes of Israel
were dim with age, *so that* he could not see.
Then Joseph brought them near him, and
he [b]kissed them and embraced them. 11 And
Israel said to Joseph, [a]"I had not thought to
see your face; but in fact, God has also shown
me your offspring!"
12 So Joseph brought them from beside
his knees, and he bowed down with his face
to the earth. 13 And Joseph took them both,
Ephraim with his right hand toward Israel's
left hand, and Manasseh with his left hand
toward Israel's right hand, and brought *them*
near him. 14 Then Israel stretched out his
right hand and [a]laid *it* on Ephraim's head,
who *was* the younger, and his left hand on
Manasseh's head, [b]guiding his hands knowingly, for Manasseh *was* the [c]firstborn. 15 And
[a]he blessed Joseph, and said:

"God, [b]before whom my fathers
Abraham and Isaac walked,
The God who has fed me all my life
long to this day,
16 The Angel [a]who has redeemed me
from all evil,
Bless the lads;
Let [b]my name be named upon them,
And the name of my fathers Abraham
and Isaac;
And let them [c]grow into a multitude in
the midst of the earth."

17 Now when Joseph saw that his father [a]laid
his right hand on the head of Ephraim, it
displeased him; so he took hold of his father's
hand to remove it from Ephraim's head to
Manasseh's head. 18 And Joseph said to his
father, "Not so, my father, for this *one is* the
firstborn; put your right hand on his head."
19 But his father refused and said, [a]"I know,
my son, I know. He also shall become a people,
and he also shall be great; but truly [b]his younger
brother shall be greater than he, and his descendants shall become a multitude of nations."
20 So he blessed them that day, saying, [a]"By
you Israel will bless, saying, 'May God make
you as Ephraim and as Manasseh!'" And thus
he set Ephraim before Manasseh.
21 Then Israel said to Joseph, "Behold, I am
dying, but [a]God will be with you and bring you
back to the land of your fathers. 22 Moreover
[a]I have given to you one portion above your
brothers, which I took from the hand [b]of the
Amorite with my sword and my bow."

Jacob's Last Words to His Sons

49 And Jacob called his sons and said,
"Gather together, that I may [a]tell you
what shall befall you [b]in the last days:

2 "Gather together and hear, you sons of
Jacob,
And listen to Israel your father.

3 "Reuben, you are [a]my firstborn,
My might and the beginning of my
strength,

47:30 [a] 2 Sam. 19:37 [b] Gen. 49:29; 50:5–13 **47:31** [a] 1 Kin. 1:47 **48:1** [a] Gen. 41:51, 56; 46:20; 50:23 **48:3** [a] Gen. 43:14; 49:25 [b] Gen. 28:13, 19; 35:6, 9 **48:4** [a] Gen. 46:3 [b] Ex. 6:8 [c] Gen. 17:8 **48:5** [a] Josh. 13:7; 14:4 **48:7** [a] Gen. 35:9, 16, 19, 20 **48:9** [a] Gen. 27:4; 47:15 **48:10** [a] Gen. 27:1 [b] Gen. 27:27; 45:15; 50:1 **48:11** [a] Gen. 45:26 **48:14** [a] Matt. 19:15 [b] Gen. 48:19 [c] Josh. 17:1 **48:15** [a] [Heb. 11:21] [b] Gen. 17:1; 24:40 **48:16** [a] Gen. 22:11, 15–18; 28:13–15; 31:11 [b] Amos 9:12 [c] Num. 26:34, 37 **48:17** [a] Gen. 48:14 **48:19** [a] Gen. 48:14 [b] Num. 1:33, 35 **48:20** [a] Ruth 4:11, 12 **48:21** [a] Gen. 28:15; 46:4; 50:24 **48:22** [a] Josh. 24:32 [b] Gen. 34:28 **49:1** [a] Deut. 33:1, 6–25 [b] Is. 2:2; 39:6 **49:3** [a] Gen. 29:32

The excellency of dignity and the
excellency of power.
4 Unstable as water, you shall not excel,
Because you [a]went up to your father's
bed;
Then you defiled *it*—
He went up to my couch.

5 "Simeon and Levi *are* brothers;
Instruments of cruelty *are in* their
dwelling place.
6 [a]Let not my soul enter their council;
Let not my honor be united [b]to their
assembly;
[c]For in their anger they slew a man,
And in their self-will they hamstrung
an ox.
7 Cursed *be* their anger, for *it is* fierce;
And their wrath, for it is cruel!
[a]I will divide them in Jacob
And scatter them in Israel.

8 "Judah,[a] you *are he* whom your brothers
shall praise;
[b]Your hand *shall be* on the neck of your
enemies;
[c]Your father's children shall bow down
before you.
9 Judah *is* [a]a lion's whelp;
From the prey, my son, you have gone up.
[b]He bows down, he lies down as a lion;
And as a lion, who shall rouse him?
10 [a]The scepter shall not depart from
Judah,
Nor [b]a lawgiver from between his feet,
[c]Until Shiloh comes;
[d]And to Him *shall be* the obedience of
the people.
11 Binding his donkey to the vine,
And his donkey's colt to the choice vine,
He washed his garments in wine,
And his clothes in the blood of grapes.
12 His eyes *are* darker than wine,
And his teeth whiter than milk.

13 "Zebulun[a] shall dwell by the haven of
the sea;
He *shall become* a haven for ships,
And his border shall [b]adjoin Sidon.

14 "Issachar[a] is a strong donkey,
Lying down between two burdens;
15 He saw that rest *was* good,
And that the land *was* pleasant;
He bowed [a]his shoulder to bear *a
burden,*
And became a band of slaves.

16 "Dan[a] shall judge his people
As one of the tribes of Israel.

49:4 [a] Gen. 35:22 **49:6** [a] Prov. 1:15, 16 [b] Ps. 26:9 [c] Gen. 34:26 **49:7** [a] Josh. 19:1, 9; 21:1–42 **49:8** [a] Deut. 33:7 [b] Ps. 18:40 [c] 1 Chr. 5:2 **49:9** [a] [Rev. 5:5] [b] Num. 23:24; 24:9 **49:10** [a] Num. 24:17; Matt. 1:3; 2:6; Luke 3:33; Rev. 5:5 [b] Ps. 60:7 [c] Is. 11:1 [d] Ps. 2:6–9; 72:8–11 **49:13** [a] Deut. 33:18, 19 [b] Gen. 10:19 **49:14** [a] 1 Chr. 12:32 **49:15** [a] 1 Sam. 10:9 **49:16** [a] Deut. 33:22

WHAT GOD WANTS

Bless the lads; let my name be named upon them, and the name of my fathers Abraham and Isaac; and let them grow into a multitude in the midst of the earth.

GENESIS 48:16

Of all the sons of Jacob, it was Joseph who lived a faithful and righteous life. I am not surprised that Jacob pronounced a special blessing on Joseph, a favor he did not confer on his other sons.

But what impresses me the most about this passage is what Jacob said in the blessing itself; he addressed "God, before whom my fathers Abraham and Isaac walked, the God who has fed me all my life long to this day, the Angel who has redeemed me from all evil" (v. 15). The once-crafty patriarch who had connived and contrived had come to recognize that it was God—not his own man-made tricks and lies—who had provided for and protected him. Now near the end of his mortal life, the patriarch confessed God's faithfulness. He was ready to depart this life in peace.

The peace takeaway from the life of Jacob is this: every time I begin to ask myself what I want to do, I need to stop and ask what *God* wants me to do. Jacob could have avoided so much adversity and anxiety had he simply said, "God, what do You have for me today? I will follow You."

17 [a]Dan shall be a serpent by the way,
A viper by the path,
That bites the horse's heels
So that its rider shall fall backward.
18 [a]I have waited for your salvation,
O LORD!

19 "Gad,[a] a troop shall tramp upon him,
But he shall triumph at last.

20 "Bread from [a]Asher *shall be* rich,
And he shall yield royal dainties.

21 "Naphtali[a] *is* a deer let loose;
He uses beautiful words.

22 "Joseph *is* a fruitful bough,
A fruitful bough by a well;
His branches run over the wall.
23 The archers have [a]bitterly grieved him,
Shot *at him* and hated him.
24 But his [a]bow remained in strength,
And the arms of his hands were made strong
By the hands of [b]the Mighty *God* of Jacob
[c](From there [d]*is* the Shepherd, [e]the Stone of Israel),
25 [a]By the God of your father who will help you,
[b]And by the Almighty [c]who will bless you
With blessings of heaven above,
Blessings of the deep that lies beneath,
Blessings of the breasts and of the womb.
26 The blessings of your father
Have excelled the blessings of my ancestors,
[a]Up to the utmost bound of the everlasting hills.
[b]They shall be on the head of Joseph,
And on the crown of the head of him who was separate from his brothers.

27 "Benjamin is a [a]ravenous wolf;
In the morning he shall devour the prey,
[b]And at night he shall divide the spoil."

28 All these *are* the twelve tribes of Israel,
and this *is* what their father spoke to them.
And he blessed them; he blessed each one
according to his own blessing.

Jacob's Death and Burial

29 Then he charged them and said to them:
"I [a]am to be gathered to my people; [b]bury
me with my fathers [c]in the cave that *is* in the
field of Ephron the Hittite, 30 in the cave that
is in the field of Machpelah, which *is* before
Mamre in the land of Canaan, [a]which Abraham
bought with the field of Ephron the Hittite as

49:17 [a] Judg. 18:27 **49:18** [a] Is. 25:9 **49:19** [a] Deut. 33:20 **49:20** [a] Deut. 33:24 **49:21** [a] Deut. 33:23 **49:23** [a] Gen. 37:4, 24 **49:24** [a] Job 29:20 [b] Ps. 132:2, 5 [c] Gen. 45:11; 47:12 [d] [Ps. 23:1; 80:1] [e] Is. 28:16 **49:25** [a] Gen. 28:13; 32:9; 35:3; 43:23; 50:17 [b] Gen. 17:1; 35:11 [c] Deut. 33:13 **49:26** [a] Deut. 33:15 [b] Deut. 33:16 **49:27** [a] Judg. 20:21, 25 [b] Zech. 14:1 **49:29** [a] Gen. 15:15; 25:8; 35:29 [b] Gen. 47:30 [c] Gen. 23:16–20; 50:13 **49:30** [a] Gen. 23:3–20

THE ANTICIPATION OF PEACE

Judah, you are he whom your brothers shall praise; your hand shall be on the neck of your enemies; your father's children shall bow down before you.

GENESIS 49:8

Once when I said goodbye to a grandfather, in a moment of mental clarity he said goodbye to me and blessed me. Jacob did this with his sons. But in his day that parting was often a formal occasion. The final words and blessings became known as *testaments.* In Jewish tradition the blessings Jacob uttered in chapter 49 set the standard. The blessing that has over the centuries garnered the most attention is the one pronounced on Judah (vv. 8–12).

In what proved to be prophetic, Jacob told Judah that his brothers would praise him and even bow down to him. Judah was compared to a lion and assured that the scepter would not depart from him, meaning that he would rule "until Shiloh comes" (vv. 9–10). What "Shiloh" means has intrigued interpreters, with many thinking it refers to the awaited Messiah, to whom shall be "the obedience of the people" (v. 10). The prophet Isaiah would allude to this description in his prophecy of the coming Messiah.

Jacob's final words give all of us the foundation of our hope: the appearance of the Messiah anticipated by Jacob and called the "Prince of Peace" (Is. 9:6). Put your hope in Him today.

a possession for a burial place. [31][a]There they buried Abraham and Sarah his wife, [b]there they buried Isaac and Rebekah his wife, and there I buried Leah. [32]The field and the cave that *is* there *were* purchased from the sons of Heth." [33]And when Jacob had finished commanding his sons, he drew his feet up into the bed and breathed his last, and was gathered to his people.

50 Then Joseph [a]fell on his father's face and [b]wept over him, and kissed him. [2]And Joseph commanded his servants the physicians to [a]embalm his father. So the physicians embalmed Israel. [3]Forty days were required for him, for such are the days required for those who are embalmed; and the Egyptians [a]mourned for him seventy days.

[4]Now when the days of his mourning were past, Joseph spoke to [a]the household of Pharaoh, saying, "If now I have found favor in your eyes, please speak in the hearing of Pharaoh, saying, [5][a]'My father made me swear, saying, "Behold, I am dying; in my grave [b]which I dug for myself in the land of Canaan, there you shall bury me." Now therefore, please let me go up and bury my father, and I will come back.' "

[6]And Pharaoh said, "Go up and bury your father, as he made you swear."

[7]So Joseph went up to bury his father; and with him went up all the servants of Pharaoh, the elders of his house, and all the elders of the land of Egypt, [8]as well as all the house of Joseph, his brothers, and his father's house. Only their little ones, their flocks, and their herds they left in the land of Goshen. [9]And there went up with him both chariots and horsemen, and it was a very great gathering.

[10]Then they came to the threshing floor of Atad, which *is* beyond the Jordan, and they [a]mourned there with a great and very solemn lamentation. [b]He observed seven days of mourning for his father. [11]And when the inhabitants of the land, the Canaanites, saw the mourning at the threshing floor of Atad, they said, "This *is* a deep mourning of the Egyptians." Therefore its name was called Abel Mizraim,[1] which *is* beyond the Jordan.

[12]So his sons did for him just as he had commanded them. [13]For [a]his sons carried him to the land of Canaan, and buried him in the cave of the field of Machpelah, before Mamre, which Abraham [b]bought with the field from Ephron the Hittite as property for a burial place. [14]And after he had buried his father, Joseph returned to Egypt, he and his brothers and all who went up with him to bury his father.

Joseph Reassures His Brothers

[15]When Joseph's brothers saw that their father was dead, [a]they said, "Perhaps Joseph will hate us, and may actually repay us for all the evil which we did to him." [16]So they sent *messengers* to Joseph, saying, "Before your father died he commanded, saying,

49:31 [a] Gen. 23:19, 20; 25:9 [b] Gen. 35:29; 50:13 **50:1** [a] Gen. 46:4, 29 [b] 2 Kin. 13:14 **50:2** [a] Gen. 50:26 **50:3** [a] Deut. 34:8 **50:4** [a] Esth. 4:2 **50:5** [a] Gen. 47:29–31 [b] Is. 22:16 **50:10** [a] Acts 8:2 [b] 1 Sam. 31:13 **50:11** [1] Literally *Mourning of Egypt* **50:13** [a] Acts 7:16 [b] Gen. 23:16–20 **50:15** [a] [Job 15:21]

SHARING PEACE

As for you, you meant evil against me; but God meant it for good, in order to bring it about as it is this day, to save many people alive.

GENESIS 50:20

To die in peace is what all of us hope for when the end comes. In the west the best-known expression is *requiescat in pace*, "rest in peace." In the Jewish tradition it is simply the noun *shalom*, "peace," often written in Hebrew letters (many Jewish epitaphs read this way).

After Jacob's death, his sons feared that Joseph would take revenge on them for their treachery committed long before. I love how Joseph responded to his worried brothers: "You meant evil against me; but God meant it for good . . . Do not be afraid" (vv. 20–21). What a good and gracious soul!

Joseph had forgiven his brothers, and he also recognized that through their actions God had worked His amazing, redemptive will. Joseph entered eternity as a man of peace. A forgiving spirit is a key ingredient to finding peace. Are you a person who feels, exudes, shares peace? Whom can you forgive as you seek to develop this kind of peace?

17 'Thus you shall say to Joseph: "I beg you,
please forgive the trespass of your brothers
and their sin; [a]for they did evil to you."' Now,
please, forgive the trespass of the servants
of [b]the God of your father." And Joseph wept
when they spoke to him.
18 Then his brothers also went and [a]fell
down before his face, and they said, "Behold,
we *are* your servants."
19 Joseph said to them, [a]"Do not be afraid,
[b]for *am* I in the place of God? 20 [a]But as for
you, you meant evil against me; *but* [b]God
meant it for good, in order to bring it about as
it is this day, to save many people alive. 21 Now
therefore, do not be afraid; [a]I will provide for
you and your little ones." And he comforted
them and spoke kindly to them.

Death of Joseph

22 So Joseph dwelt in Egypt, he and his
father's household. And Joseph lived one
hundred and ten years. 23 Joseph saw Ephraim's children [a]to the third *generation.* [b]The
children of Machir, the son of Manasseh,
[c]were also brought up on Joseph's knees.
24 And Joseph said to his brethren, "I am
dying; but [a]God will surely visit you, and
bring you out of this land to the land [b]of
which He swore to Abraham, to Isaac, and
to Jacob." 25 Then [a]Joseph took an oath from
the children of Israel, saying, "God will surely
visit you, and [b]you shall carry up my [c]bones
from here." 26 So Joseph died, *being* one hundred and ten years old; and they embalmed
him, and he was put in a coffin in Egypt.

50:17 [a] [Prov. 28:13] [b] Gen. 49:25 **50:18** [a] Gen. 37:7–10; 41:43; 44:14 **50:19** [a] Gen. 45:5 [b] 2 Kin. 5:7 **50:20** [a] Ps. 56:5 [b] [Acts 3:13–15] **50:21** [a] [Matt. 5:44] **50:23** [a] Job 42:16 [b] Num. 26:29; 32:39 [c] Gen. 30:3 **50:24** [a] Ex. 3:16, 17 [b] Gen. 26:3; 35:12; 46:4 **50:25** [a] Ex. 13:19 [b] Deut. 1:8; 30:1–8 [c] Ex. 13:19

THE SECOND BOOK OF MOSES CALLED

EXODUS

AUTHOR

Exodus has been attributed to Moses since the time of Joshua (Ex. 20:25; Josh. 8:30–32) and there is a great deal of both internal and external evidence that supports Moses as the author. The claims in Joshua are backed by similar testimony from Malachi (Mal. 4:4), the disciples (John 1:45), Paul (Rom. 10:5), and Christ (Mark 7:10; 12:26; Luke 20:37; John 5:46–47; 7:19, 22–23). Portions of the book itself claim the authorship of Moses (Ex. 15; 17:8–14; 20:1–17; 24:4, 7, 12; 31:18; 34:1–27). The author of Exodus must have been a man familiar with the customs and climate of Egypt. Its consistency of style points to a single author and its ancient literary devices support its antiquity.

TIME

c. 1875–1445 BC

KEY VERSE

Exodus 19:5–6

THEME

The main character of Exodus is clearly Moses. God gives him the job of leading the exodus from Egypt. Moses also takes on the job of establishing, at God's direction, the essential elements of the Jewish patterns of life and worship. He is simultaneously God's designated representative of the people to God and God's messenger and representative to the people. The critical events in Exodus are the Passover and the giving of the Ten Commandments. The remainder of the Old Testament continually refers back to God's deliverance of Israel from Egypt and the law as delivered at Sinai. In these events God's identity and purpose are revealed. There are many signs and wonders of His power. Aspects of His nature and His expectations of the people also become increasingly clear.

The Book of Exodus is the story of God's turning the children of Israel's pain into purpose to bring His peace. Moses received a blessing from his father-in-law Jethro to follow God's call: "Go in peace" (4:18). The resurrected Christ echoed that type of *shalom* blessing (John 20:19). Ultimately, through the sacrificial shedding of blood, the children of Israel were saved from generational bondage and set free ("It is the LORD's Passover," Ex. 12:11). The Song of Moses (15:1–18) is a worshipful, emblematic reminder of the Lord's faithfulness to redeem His people and bring His peace when all seems lost.

Israel's Suffering in Egypt

1 Now [a]these *are* the names of the children
of Israel who came to Egypt; each man and
his household came with Jacob: 2 Reuben,
Simeon, Levi, and Judah; 3 Issachar, Zebulun, and Benjamin; 4 Dan, Naphtali, Gad, and
Asher. 5 All those who were descendants[1] of
Jacob were [a]seventy[2] persons (for Joseph was
in Egypt *already*). 6 And [a]Joseph died, all his
brothers, and all that generation. 7 [a]But the
children of Israel were fruitful and increased
abundantly, multiplied and grew exceedingly
mighty; and the land was filled with them.
8 Now there arose a new king over Egypt,
[a]who did not know Joseph. 9 And he said to his
people, "Look, the people of the children of Israel *are* more and [a]mightier than we; 10 [a]come,
let us [b]deal shrewdly with them, lest they multiply, and it happen, in the event of war, that
they also join our enemies and fight against
us, and *so* go up out of the land." 11 Therefore
they set taskmasters over them [a]to afflict them
with their [b]burdens. And they built for Pharaoh
[c]supply cities, Pithom [d]and Raamses. 12 But
the more they afflicted them, the more they
multiplied and grew. And they were in dread
of the children of Israel. 13 So the Egyptians
made the children of Israel [a]serve with rigor.
14 And they [a]made their lives bitter with hard
bondage—[b]in mortar, in brick, and in all manner of service in the field. All their service in
which they made them serve *was* with rigor.
15 Then the king of Egypt spoke to the [a]He-
brew midwives, of whom the name of one
was Shiphrah and the name of the other
Puah; 16 and he said, "When you do the duties
of a midwife for the Hebrew women, and see
them on the birthstools, if it *is* a [a]son, then
you shall kill him; but if it *is* a daughter, then
she shall live." 17 But the midwives [a]feared
God, and did not do [b]as the king of Egypt
commanded them, but saved the male children alive. 18 So the king of Egypt called for
the midwives and said to them, "Why have
you done this thing, and saved the male
children alive?"
19 And [a]the midwives said to Pharaoh, "Because the Hebrew women *are* not like the
Egyptian women; for they *are* lively and give
birth before the midwives come to them."
20 [a]Therefore God dealt well with the midwives, and the people multiplied and grew
very mighty. 21 And so it was, because the
midwives feared God, [a]that He provided
households for them.
22 So Pharaoh commanded all his people,
saying, [a]"Every son who is born[1] you shall
cast into the river, and every daughter you
shall save alive."

Moses Is Born

2 And [a]a man of the house of Levi went and
took *as wife* a daughter of Levi. 2 So the
woman conceived and bore a son. And [a]when
she saw that he *was* a beautiful *child*, she hid
him three months. 3 But when she could no
longer hide him, she took an ark of [a]bulrushes
for him, daubed it with [b]asphalt and [c]pitch,
put the child in it, and laid *it* in the reeds [d]by
the river's bank. 4 [a]And his sister stood afar
off, to know what would be done to him.
5 Then the [a]daughter of Pharaoh came
down to bathe at the river. And her maidens
walked along the riverside; and when she saw
the ark among the reeds, she sent her maid
to get it. 6 And when she opened *it*, she saw
the child, and behold, the baby wept. So she
had compassion on him, and said, "This is
one of the Hebrews' children."
7 Then his sister said to Pharaoh's daughter,
"Shall I go and call a nurse for you from the Hebrew
women, that she may nurse the child for you?"
8 And Pharaoh's daughter said to her, "Go."
So the maiden went and called the child's
mother. 9 Then Pharaoh's daughter said to
her, "Take this child away and nurse him
for me, and I will give *you* your wages." So
the woman took the child and nursed him.
10 And the child grew, and she brought him
to Pharaoh's daughter, and he became [a]her
son. So she called his name Moses,[1] saying,
"Because I drew him out of the water."

Moses Flees to Midian

11 Now it came to pass in those days, [a]when
Moses was grown, that he went out to his
brethren and looked at their burdens. And
he saw an Egyptian beating a Hebrew, one
of his brethren. 12 So he looked this way and
that way, and when he saw no one, he [a]killed
the Egyptian and hid him in the sand. 13 And
[a]when he went out the second day, behold,
two Hebrew men [b]were fighting, and he said
to the one who did the wrong, "Why are you
striking your companion?"
14 Then he said, [a]"Who made you a prince

1:1 [a] Gen. 46:8–27 **1:5** [a] Gen. 46:26, 27 [1] Literally *who came from the loins of* [2] Dead Sea Scrolls and Septuagint read *seventy-five* (compare Acts 7:14). **1:6** [a] Gen. 50:26 **1:7** [a] Acts 7:17 **1:8** [a] Acts 7:18, 19 **1:9** [a] Gen. 26:16 **1:10** [a] Ps. 83:3, 4 [b] Acts 7:19 **1:11** [a] Ex. 3:7; 5:6 [b] Ex. 1:14; 2:11; 5:4–9; 6:6 [c] 1 Kin. 9:19 [d] Gen. 47:11 **1:13** [a] Gen. 15:13 **1:14** [a] Num. 20:15 [b] Ps. 81:6 **1:15** [a] Ex. 2:6 **1:16** [a] Acts 7:19 **1:17** [a] Prov. 16:6 [b] Dan. 3:16, 18 **1:19** [a] Josh. 2:4 **1:20** [a] [Prov. 11:18] **1:21** [a] 1 Sam. 2:35 **1:22** [a] Acts 7:19 [1] Samaritan Pentateuch, Septuagint, and Targum add *to the Hebrews*. **2:1** [a] Ex. 6:16–20 **2:2** [a] Acts 7:20 **2:3** [a] Is. 18:2 [b] Gen. 14:10 [c] Gen. 6:14 [d] Is. 19:6 **2:4** [a] Num. 26:59 **2:5** [a] Acts 7:21 **2:10** [a] Acts 7:21 [1] Literally *Drawn Out* **2:11** [a] Heb. 11:24–26 **2:12** [a] Acts 7:24, 25 **2:13** [a] Acts 7:26–28 [b] Prov. 25:8 **2:14** [a] Acts 7:27, 28

and a judge over us? Do you intend to kill me
as you killed the Egyptian?"
So Moses [b]feared and said, "Surely this
thing is known!" 15 When Pharaoh heard of this
matter, he sought to kill Moses. But [a]Moses
fled from the face of Pharaoh and dwelt in the
land of [b]Midian; and he sat down by [c]a well.
16 [a]Now the priest of Midian had seven
daughters. [b]And they came and drew water,
and they filled the [c]troughs to water their
father's flock. 17 Then the [a]shepherds came
and [b]drove them away; but Moses stood up
and helped them, and [c]watered their flock.
18 When they came to [a]Reuel their father,
[b]he said, "How *is it that* you have come so
soon today?"
19 And they said, "An Egyptian delivered us
from the hand of the shepherds, and he also
drew enough water for us and watered the flock."
20 So he said to his daughters, "And where
is he? Why *is* it *that* you have left the man?
Call him, that he may [a]eat bread."
21 Then Moses was content to live with the
man, and he gave [a]Zipporah his daughter to
Moses. 22 And she bore *him* a son. He called
his name [a]Gershom,[1] for he said, "I have been
[b]a stranger in a foreign land."
23 Now it happened [a]in the process of time
that the king of Egypt died. Then the children
of Israel [b]groaned because of the bondage,
and they cried out; and [c]their cry came up to
God because of the bondage. 24 So God [a]heard
their groaning, and God [b]remembered His
[c]covenant with Abraham, with Isaac, and with
Jacob. 25 And God [a]looked upon the children
of Israel, and God [b]acknowledged *them.*

Moses at the Burning Bush

3 Now Moses was tending the flock of [a]Jeth-
ro his father-in-law, [b]the priest of Midian.
And he led the flock to the back of the desert,
and came to [c]Horeb, [d]the mountain of God.
2 And [a]the Angel of the LORD appeared to
him in a flame of fire from the midst of a
bush. So he looked, and behold, the bush
was burning with fire, but the bush *was* not
consumed. 3 Then Moses said, "I will now
turn aside and see this [a]great sight, why the
bush does not burn."
4 So when the LORD saw that he turned
aside to look, God called [a]to him from the
midst of the bush and said, "Moses, Moses!"
And he said, "Here I am."
5 Then He said, "Do not draw near this
place. [a]Take your sandals off your feet, for
the place where you stand *is* holy ground."
6 Moreover He said, [a]"I *am* the God of your
father—the God of Abraham, the God of

2:14 [b] Judg. 6:27 **2:15** [a] Acts 7:29 [b] Ex. 3:1 [c] Gen. 24:11; 29:2 **2:16** [a] Ex. 3:1; 4:18; 18:12 [b] Gen. 24:11, 13, 19; 29:6–10 [c] Gen. 30:38 **2:17** [a] Gen. 47:3 [b] Gen. 26:19–21 [c] Gen. 29:3, 10 **2:18** [a] Num. 10:29 [b] Ex. 3:1; 4:18 **2:20** [a] Gen. 31:54; 43:25 **2:21** [a] Ex. 4:25; 18:2 **2:22** [a] Ex. 4:20; 18:3, 4 [b] Acts 7:29 [1] Literally *Stranger There* **2:23** [a] Acts 7:34 [b] Deut. 26:7 [c] James 5:4 **2:24** [a] Ex. 6:5 [b] Gen. 15:13; 22:16–18; 26:2–5; 28:13–15 [c] Gen. 12:1–3; 15:14; 17:1–14 **2:25** [a] Ex. 4:31 [b] Ex. 3:7 **3:1** [a] Ex. 4:18 [b] Ex. 2:16 [c] Ex. 17:6 [d] Ex. 18:5 **3:2** [a] Deut. 33:16 **3:3** [a] Acts 7:31 **3:4** [a] Deut. 33:16 **3:5** [a] Josh. 5:15 **3:6** [a] [Matt. 22:32]

THE GOD WHO HEARS

Then the children of Israel groaned because of the bondage,
and they cried out; and their cry came up to God.

EXODUS 2:23

Being buried under oppressive burdens that show no sign of letting up kills hope faster than anything. Some philosophers and scientists believe that human fate really can't be altered: the eventual outcome will be extinction. Not a very cheery thought. Even we believers sometimes factor God out of the situations of our lives. To be sure, without God, life is hopeless. Skeptics believe God plays no part in our lives.

Obviously such a nihilistic worldview would have provided the people of Israel with no hope and no peace. But then God played a hugely obvious part in their lives, and it was the game changer. "God heard their groaning, and God remembered His covenant with Abraham, with Isaac, and with Jacob" (v. 24). The passage goes on to say that "God looked upon the children of Israel" and He "acknowledged them" (v. 25) or better, He "knew them"—that is, God became intimately acquainted with His people's plight.

We can take great comfort in this passage, for it shows that God is aware of His people's needs and He's willing to act. How does this comfort affect your peace?

Isaac, and the God of Jacob." And Moses hid
his face, for [b]he was afraid to look upon God.
7 And the LORD said: [a]"I have surely seen
the oppression of My people who *are* in Egypt,
and have heard their cry [b]because of their taskmasters, [c]for I know their sorrows. 8 So [a]I have
come down to [b]deliver them out of the hand
of the Egyptians, and to bring them up from
that land [c]to a good and large land, to a land
[d]flowing with milk and honey, to the place of
[e]the Canaanites and the Hittites and the Amorites and the Perizzites and the Hivites and the
Jebusites. 9 Now therefore, behold, [a]the cry of
the children of Israel has come to Me, and I have
also seen the [b]oppression with which the Egyptians oppress them. 10 [a]Come now, therefore, and
I will send you to Pharaoh that you may bring
My people, the children of Israel, out of Egypt."
11 But Moses said to God, [a]"Who *am* I that
I should go to Pharaoh, and that I should
bring the children of Israel out of Egypt?"
12 So He said, [a]"I will certainly be with you.
And this *shall be* a [b]sign to you that I have sent
you: When you have brought the people out of
Egypt, you shall serve God on this mountain."
13 Then Moses said to God, "Indeed, *when*
I come to the children of Israel and say to
them, 'The God of your fathers has sent me to
you,' and they say to me, 'What *is* His name?'
what shall I say to them?"
14 And God said to Moses, "I AM WHO I AM."
And He said, "Thus you shall say to the children of Israel, [a]'I AM has sent me to you.' "
15 Moreover God said to Moses, "Thus you shall
say to the children of Israel: 'The LORD God
of your fathers, the God of Abraham, the God
of Isaac, and the God of Jacob, has sent me to
you. This *is* [a]My name forever, and this *is* My
memorial to all generations.' 16 Go and [a]gather
the elders of Israel together, and say to them,
'The LORD God of your fathers, the God of
Abraham, of Isaac, and of Jacob, appeared
to me, saying, [b]"I have surely visited you and
seen what is done to you in Egypt; 17 and I have
said [a]I will bring you up out of the affliction of
Egypt to the land of the Canaanites and the Hittites and the Amorites and the Perizzites and
the Hivites and the Jebusites, to a land flowing
with milk and honey." ' 18 Then [a]they will heed
your voice; and [b]you shall come, you and the
elders of Israel, to the king of Egypt; and you
shall say to him, 'The LORD God of the Hebrews
has [c]met with us; and now, please, let us go
three days' journey into the wilderness, that
we may sacrifice to the LORD our God.' 19 But I
am sure that the king of Egypt [a]will not let you
go, no, not even by a mighty hand. 20 So I will
[a]stretch out My hand and strike Egypt with [b]all
My wonders which I will do in its midst; and
[c]after that he will let you go. 21 And [a]I will give
this people favor in the sight of the Egyptians;
and it shall be, when you go, that you shall not
go empty-handed. 22 [a]But every woman shall
ask of her neighbor, namely, of her who dwells
near her house, [b]articles of silver, articles of
gold, and clothing; and you shall put *them* on

3:6 [b] 1 Kin. 19:13 **3:7** [a] Ex. 2:23–25 [b] Ex. 1:11 [c] Ex. 2:25 **3:8** [a] Gen. 15:13–16; 46:4; 50:24, 25 [b] Ex. 6:6–8; 12:51 [c] Deut. 1:25; 8:7–9 [d] Jer. 11:5 [e] Gen. 15:19–21 **3:9** [a] Ex. 2:23 [b] Ex. 1:11, 13, 14 **3:10** [a] [Mic. 6:4] **3:11** [a] Ex. 4:10; 6:12 **3:12** [a] Gen. 31:3 [b] Ex. 4:8; 19:3 **3:14** [a] [John 8:24, 28, 58] **3:15** [a] Ps. 30:4; 97:12; 102:12; 135:13 **3:16** [a] Ex. 4:29 [b] Ex. 2:25; 4:31 **3:17** [a] Gen. 15:13–21; 46:4; 50:24, 25 **3:18** [a] Ex. 4:31 [b] Ex. 5:1, 3 [c] Num. 23:3, 4, 15, 16 **3:19** [a] Ex. 5:2 **3:20** [a] Ex. 6:6; 9:15 [b] Deut. 6:22 [c] Ex. 11:1; 12:31–37 **3:21** [a] Ex. 11:3; 12:36 **3:22** [a] Ex. 11:2 [b] Ex. 33:6

DYNAMIC PEACE

"The cry of the children of Israel has come to Me, and I have also seen the oppression with which the Egyptians oppress them."

EXODUS 3:9

Here we are reminded again of our God, *El Roi*, the "One Who Sees." Long before Jesus Christ's advent, God stooped down and studied the plight of His people, Israel. When Moses encountered the burning bush, God said, "I have surely seen the oppression of My people who are in Egypt, and have heard their cry because of their taskmasters, for I know their sorrows" (v. 7). God had seen and heard His people's cry, and He was about to take action.

This is who God is. He is not passively standing by. He sees, He hears, and He responds. In the story of the exodus, God's response was awesome. He crushed Pharaoh and his gods, and He liberated the people of Israel. This is our God, and it is in Him that we have hope. It is in Him that we enjoy—not a passive peace—but an active, life-changing, redemptive peace. Peace is dynamic in our lives!

your sons and on your daughters. So [c]you shall
plunder the Egyptians."

Miraculous Signs for Pharaoh

4 Then Moses answered and said, "But
suppose they will not believe me or listen
to my voice; suppose they say, 'The LORD has
not appeared to you.' "
2 So the LORD said to him, "What *is* that
in your hand?"
He said, "A rod."
3 And He said, "Cast it on the ground." So he
cast it on the ground, and it became a serpent;
and Moses fled from it. 4 Then the LORD said to
Moses, "Reach out your hand and take *it* by the
tail" (and he reached out his hand and caught
it, and it became a rod in his hand), 5 "that they
may [a]believe that the [b]LORD God of their fathers, the God of Abraham, the God of Isaac,
and the God of Jacob, has appeared to you."
6 Furthermore the LORD said to him, "Now
put your hand in your bosom." And he put
his hand in his bosom, and when he took it
out, behold, his hand *was* leprous, [a]like snow.
7 And He said, "Put your hand in your bosom
again." So he put his hand in his bosom again,
and drew it out of his bosom, and behold, [a]it
was restored like his *other* flesh. 8 "Then it
will be, if they do not believe you, nor heed
the message of the [a]first sign, that they may
believe the message of the latter sign. 9 And
it shall be, if they do not believe even these
two signs, or listen to your voice, that you
shall take water from the river[1] and pour *it* on
the dry *land*. [a]The water which you take from
the river will become blood on the dry *land*."
10 Then Moses said to the LORD, "O my Lord,
I *am* not eloquent, neither before nor since
You have spoken to Your servant; but [a]I *am*
slow of speech and slow of tongue."
11 So the LORD said to him, [a]"Who has made
man's mouth? Or who makes the mute, the
deaf, the seeing, or the blind? *Have* not I, the
LORD? 12 Now therefore, go, and I will be [a]with
your mouth and teach you what you shall say."

PEACE NOTE

Whom is the Holy Spirit speaking to you about? Now is the perfect time to pick up the phone, arrange to meet for coffee, and check in with that person.

EXODUS 4:12

3:22 [c] Job 27:17 4:5 [a] Ex. 4:31; 19:9 [b] Ex. 3:6, 15 4:6 [a] Num. 12:10 4:7 [a] Deut. 32:39 4:8 [a] Ex. 7:6–13 4:9 [a] Ex. 7:19, 20 [1] That is, the Nile 4:10 [a] Ex. 3:11; 4:1; 6:12 4:11 [a] Ps. 94:9; 146:8 4:12 [a] Is. 50:4

SPARKING YOUR FAITH

"Thus you shall say to the children of Israel, 'I AM has sent me to you.'"

EXODUS 3:14

This beautiful passage presents us with the personal name for God, which is "the LORD" (v. 15), a term used over six thousand times in the original language in Scripture. When Moses met God in the wilderness, he did not know Him, His character, or His ways. In what could be the single most important verse in the Bible, God identified Himself to Moses as "I AM WHO I AM" (v. 14).

The gods of the pagans had various names that sometimes related to the sun or moon or a star. But God's name isn't exactly a name; it is a statement of ultimate being. He is the Creator of the universe. In the plagues to be brought against Egypt, in the exodus and crossing of the sea, and in the sojourn in the wilderness, Moses would learn about God's character. Moses knew none of this when he encountered God at the burning bush, but something about God's being sparked faith in him.

The encounter at the burning bush changed Moses. Perhaps for the first time in his life, Moses found peace. It seems ironic. Look for the burning bush moment in your life today, a new way God reveals Himself to you, and find His peace again.

13 But he said, "O my Lord, [a]please send by the hand of whomever *else* You may send."

14 So [a]the anger of the LORD was kindled against Moses, and He said: "Is not Aaron the Levite your [b]brother? I know that he can speak well. And look, [c]he is also coming out to meet you. When he sees you, he will be glad in his heart. 15 Now [a]you shall speak to him and [b]put the words in his mouth. And I will be with your mouth and with his mouth, and [c]I will teach you what you shall do. 16 So he shall be your spokesman to the people. And he himself shall be as a mouth for you, and [a]you shall be to him as God. 17 And you shall take this rod in your hand, with which you shall do the signs."

Moses Goes to Egypt

18 So Moses went and returned to [a]Jethro his father-in-law, and said to him, "Please let me go and return to my brethren who *are* in Egypt, and see whether they are still alive."

And Jethro said to Moses, [b]"Go in peace."

19 Now the LORD said to Moses in [a]Midian, "Go, return to [b]Egypt; for all the men who [c]sought your life are dead." 20 Then Moses [a]took his wife and his sons and set them on a donkey, and he returned to the land of Egypt. And Moses took [b]the rod of God in his hand.

21 And the LORD said to Moses, "When you go back to Egypt, see that you do all those [a]wonders before Pharaoh which I have put in your hand. But [b]I will harden his heart, so that he will not let the people go. 22 Then you shall [a]say to Pharaoh, 'Thus says the LORD: [b]"Israel *is* My son, [c]My firstborn. 23 So I say to you, let My son go that he may serve Me. But if you refuse to let him go, indeed [a]I will kill your son, your firstborn." ' "

24 And it came to pass on the way, at the [a]encampment, that the LORD [b]met him and sought to [c]kill him. 25 Then [a]Zipporah took [b]a sharp stone and cut off the foreskin of her son and cast *it* at *Moses'*[1] feet, and said, "Surely you *are* a husband of blood to me!" 26 So He let him go. Then she said, "*You are* a husband of blood!"—because of the circumcision.

27 And the LORD said to Aaron, "Go into the wilderness [a]to meet Moses." So he went and met him on [b]the mountain of God, and kissed him. 28 So Moses [a]told Aaron all the words of the LORD who had sent him, and all the [b]signs which He had commanded him. 29 Then Moses and Aaron [a]went and gathered together all the elders of the children of Israel. 30 [a]And Aaron spoke all the words which the LORD had spoken to Moses. Then he did the signs in the sight of the people. 31 So the people [a]believed; and when they heard that the LORD had [b]visited the children of Israel and that He [c]had looked on their affliction, then [d]they bowed their heads and worshiped.

4:13 [a] Jon. 1:3 **4:14** [a] Num. 11:1, 33 [b] Num. 26:59 [c] Ex. 4:27 **4:15** [a] Ex. 4:12, 30; 7:1, 2 [b] Num. 23:5, 12 [c] Deut. 5:31 **4:16** [a] Ex. 7:1, 2 **4:18** [a] Ex. 2:21; 3:1; 4:18 [b] Judg. 18:6 **4:19** [a] Ex. 3:1; 18:1 [b] Gen. 46:3, 6 [c] Ex. 2:15, 23 **4:20** [a] Ex. 18:2–5 [b] Num. 20:8, 9, 11 **4:21** [a] Ex. 3:20; 11:9, 10 [b] John 12:40 **4:22** [a] Ex. 5:1 [b] Hos. 11:1 [c] Jer. 31:9 **4:23** [a] Ex. 11:5; 12:29 **4:24** [a] Gen. 42:27 [b] Num. 22:22 [c] Gen. 17:14 **4:25** [a] Ex. 2:21; 18:2 [b] Josh. 5:2, 3 [1] Literally *his* **4:27** [a] Ex. 4:14 [b] Ex. 3:1; 18:5; 24:13 **4:28** [a] Ex. 4:15, 16 [b] Ex. 4:8, 9 **4:29** [a] Ex. 3:16; 12:21 **4:30** [a] Ex. 4:15, 16 **4:31** [a] Ex. 3:18; 4:8, 9; 19:9 [b] Gen. 50:24 [c] Ex. 2:25; 3:7 [d] Gen. 24:26

MOVING FORWARD WITH PEACE

Now the LORD said to Moses in Midian, "Go, return to Egypt."

EXODUS 4:19

Are you a perfectionist? Are your standards exacting and obnoxious? Do you worry that because you can't serve God flawlessly, you can't serve Him at all?

Moses shows us something important. Though he would become a great leader, Moses was a flawed man. You see, Moses questioned God, but God never questioned him! When he took a step of faith by obeying God and leading His people out of Egypt, he went in peace, not perfection. God's purpose would be carried out by a sinful human, and God accepted that flawed service. This is the way God will use you today. He will send you forth in peace to take the next steps of faith.

Notice that as Moses traveled to Egypt, he "took the rod of God in his hand" (v. 20). You have something even more powerful to take, the Word of God. As you walk forward in peace today, take comfort in God's Word and go!

First Encounter with Pharaoh

5 Afterward Moses and Aaron went in and told Pharaoh, "Thus says the LORD God of Israel: 'Let My people go, that they may hold [a]a feast to Me in the wilderness.' "

2 And Pharaoh said, [a]"Who *is* the LORD, that I should obey His voice to let Israel go? I do not know the LORD, [b]nor will I let Israel go."

3 So they said, [a]"The God of the Hebrews has [b]met with us. Please, let us go three days' journey into the desert and sacrifice to the LORD our God, lest He fall upon us with [c]pestilence or with the sword."

4 Then the king of Egypt said to them, "Moses and Aaron, why do you take the people from their work? Get *back* to your [a]labor." 5 And Pharaoh said, "Look, the people of the land *are* [a]many now, and you make them rest from their labor!"

6 So the same day Pharaoh commanded the [a]taskmasters of the people and their officers, saying, 7 "You shall no longer give the people straw to make [a]brick as before. Let them go and gather straw for themselves. 8 And you shall lay on them the quota of bricks which they made before. You shall not reduce it. For they are idle; therefore they cry out, saying, 'Let us go *and* sacrifice to our God.' 9 Let more work be laid on the men, that they may labor in it, and let them not regard false words."

10 And the taskmasters of the people and their officers went out and spoke to the people, saying, "Thus says Pharaoh: 'I will not give you straw. 11 Go, get yourselves straw where you can find it; yet none of your work will be reduced.' " 12 So the people were scattered abroad throughout all the land of Egypt to gather stubble instead of straw. 13 And the taskmasters forced *them* to hurry, saying, "Fulfill your work, *your* daily quota, as when there was straw." 14 Also the [a]officers of the children of Israel, whom Pharaoh's taskmasters had set over them, were [b]beaten *and* were asked, "Why have you not fulfilled your task in making brick both yesterday and today, as before?"

15 Then the officers of the children of Israel came and cried out to Pharaoh, saying, "Why are you dealing thus with your servants? 16 There is no straw given to your servants, and they say to us, 'Make brick!' And indeed your servants *are* beaten, but the fault *is* in your *own* people."

17 But he said, "You *are* idle! Idle! Therefore you say, 'Let us go *and* sacrifice to the LORD.' 18 Therefore go now *and* work; for no straw shall be given you, yet you shall deliver the quota of bricks." 19 And the officers of the children of Israel saw *that* they *were* in trouble after it was said, "You shall not reduce *any* bricks from your daily quota."

20 Then, as they came out from Pharaoh, they met Moses and Aaron who stood there to meet them. 21 [a]And they said to them, "Let the LORD look on you and judge, because you have made us abhorrent in the sight of Pharaoh and in the sight of his servants, to put a sword in their hand to kill us."

Israel's Deliverance Assured

22 So Moses returned to the LORD and said, "Lord, why have You brought trouble on this people? Why *is* it You have sent me? 23 For since I came to Pharaoh to speak in Your name, he has done evil to this people; neither have You delivered Your people at all."

6 Then the LORD said to Moses, "Now you shall see what I will do to Pharaoh. For [a]with a strong hand he will let them go, and with a strong hand [b]he will drive them out of his land."

2 And God spoke to Moses and said to him: "I *am* the LORD. 3 [a]I appeared to Abraham, to Isaac, and to Jacob, as [b]God Almighty, but *by* My name [c]LORD[1] I was not known to them. 4 [a]I have also established My covenant with them, [b]to give them the land of Canaan, the land of their pilgrimage, [c]in which they were strangers. 5 And [a]I have also heard the groaning of the children of Israel whom the Egyptians keep in bondage, and I have remembered My covenant. 6 Therefore say to the children of Israel: [a]'I *am* the LORD; [b]I will bring you out from under the burdens of the Egyptians, I will [c]rescue you from their bondage, and I will redeem you with an outstretched arm and with great judgments. 7 I will [a]take you as My people, and [b]I will be your God. Then you shall know that I *am* the LORD your God who brings you out [c]from under the burdens of the Egyptians. 8 And I will bring you into the land which I [a]swore to give to Abraham, Isaac, and Jacob; and I will give it to you *as* a heritage: I *am* the LORD.' " 9 So Moses spoke thus to the children of Israel; [a]but they did not heed Moses, because of [b]anguish of spirit and cruel bondage.

10 And the LORD spoke to Moses, saying, 11 "Go in, tell Pharaoh king of Egypt to let the children of Israel go out of his land."

5:1 [a] Ex. 3:18; 7:16; 10:9 **5:2** [a] 2 Kin. 18:35 [b] Ex. 3:19; 7:14 **5:3** [a] Ex. 3:18; 7:16 [b] Num. 23:3 [c] Ex. 9:15 **5:4** [a] Ex. 1:11; 2:11; 6:6 **5:5** [a] Ex. 1:7, 9 **5:6** [a] Ex. 1:11; 3:7; 5:10, 13, 14 **5:7** [a] Ex. 1:14 **5:14** [a] Ex. 5:6 [b] Is. 10:24 **5:21** [a] Ex. 6:9; 14:11; 15:24; 16:2 **6:1** [a] Ex. 3:19 [b] Ex. 12:31, 33, 39 **6:3** [a] Gen. 17:1; 35:9; 48:3 [b] Gen. 28:3; 35:11 [c] Ps. 68:4; 83:18 [1] Hebrew *YHWH,* traditionally *Jehovah* **6:4** [a] Gen. 12:7; 15:18; 17:4, 7, 8; 26:3; 28:4, 13 [b] Lev. 25:23 [c] Gen. 28:4 **6:5** [a] Ex. 2:24 **6:6** [a] Deut. 6:12 [b] Deut. 26:8 [c] Deut. 7:8 **6:7** [a] 2 Sam. 7:24 [b] Ex. 29:45, 46 [c] Ex. 5:4, 5 **6:8** [a] Gen. 15:18; 26:3 **6:9** [a] Ex. 5:21 [b] Ex. 2:23

12 And Moses spoke before the LORD, saying, "The children of Israel have not heeded me. How then shall Pharaoh heed me, for [a]I *am* of uncircumcised lips?"

13 Then the LORD spoke to Moses and Aaron, and gave them a [a]command for the children of Israel and for Pharaoh king of Egypt, to bring the children of Israel out of the land of Egypt.

The Family of Moses and Aaron

14 These *are* the heads of their fathers' houses: [a]The sons of Reuben, the firstborn of Israel, *were* Hanoch, Pallu, Hezron, and Carmi. These are the families of Reuben. 15 [a]And the sons of Simeon *were* Jemuel,[1] Jamin, Ohad, Jachin, Zohar, and Shaul the son of a Canaanite woman. These *are* the families of Simeon. 16 These *are* the names of [a]the sons of Levi according to their generations: Gershon, Kohath, and Merari. And the years of the life of Levi *were* one hundred and thirty-seven. 17 [a]The sons of Gershon *were* Libni and Shimi according to their families. 18 And [a]the sons of Kohath *were* Amram, Izhar, Hebron, and Uzziel. And the years of the life of Kohath *were* one hundred and thirty-three. 19 [a]The sons of Merari *were* Mahli and Mushi. These *are* the families of Levi according to their generations.

20 Now [a]Amram took for himself [b]Jochebed, his father's sister, as wife; and she bore him [c]Aaron and Moses. And the years of the life of Amram *were* one hundred and thirty-seven. 21 [a]The sons of Izhar *were* Korah, Nepheg, and Zichri. 22 And [a]the sons of Uzziel *were* Mishael, Elzaphan, and Zithri. 23 Aaron took to himself Elisheba, daughter of [a]Amminadab, sister of Nahshon, as wife; and she bore him [b]Nadab, Abihu, [c]Eleazar, and Ithamar. 24 And [a]the sons of Korah *were* Assir, Elkanah, and Abiasaph. These are the families of the Korahites. 25 Eleazar, Aaron's son, took for himself one of the daughters of Putiel as wife; and [a]she bore him Phinehas. These *are* the heads of the fathers' houses of the Levites according to their families.

26 These *are the same* Aaron and Moses to whom the LORD said, "Bring out the children of Israel from the land of Egypt according to their [a]armies." 27 These *are* the ones who spoke to Pharaoh king of Egypt, [a]to bring out the children of Israel from Egypt. These *are the same* Moses and Aaron.

Aaron Is Moses' Spokesman

28 And it came to pass, on the day the LORD spoke to Moses in the land of Egypt, 29 that the LORD spoke to Moses, saying, "I *am* the LORD. [a]Speak to Pharaoh king of Egypt all that I say to you."

30 But Moses said before the LORD, "Behold, [a]I *am* of uncircumcised lips, and how shall Pharaoh heed me?"

7 So the LORD said to Moses: "See, I have made you [a]*as* God to Pharaoh, and Aaron your brother shall be [b]your prophet. 2 You [a]shall speak all that I command you. And Aaron your brother shall tell Pharaoh to send the children of Israel out of his land. 3 And [a]I will harden Pharaoh's heart, and [b]multiply My [c]signs and My wonders in the land of Egypt. 4 But [a]Pharaoh will not heed you, so [b]that I may lay My hand on Egypt and bring My armies *and* My people, the children of Israel, out of the land of Egypt [c]by great judgments. 5 And the Egyptians [a]shall know that I *am* the LORD, when I [b]stretch out My hand on Egypt and [c]bring out the children of Israel from among them."

6 Then Moses and Aaron [a]did *so;* just as the LORD commanded them, so they did. 7 And Moses *was* [a]eighty years old and [b]Aaron eighty-three years old when they spoke to Pharaoh.

Aaron's Miraculous Rod

8 Then the LORD spoke to Moses and Aaron, saying, 9 "When Pharaoh speaks to you, saying, [a]'Show a miracle for yourselves,' then you shall say to Aaron, [b]'Take your rod and cast *it* before Pharaoh, *and* let it become a serpent.' " 10 So Moses and Aaron went in to Pharaoh, and they did so, just [a]as the LORD commanded. And Aaron cast down his rod before Pharaoh and before his servants, and it [b]became a serpent.

11 But Pharaoh also [a]called the wise men and [b]the sorcerers; so the magicians of Egypt, they also [c]did in like manner with their enchantments. 12 For every man threw down his rod, and they became serpents. But Aaron's rod swallowed up their rods. 13 And Pharaoh's heart grew hard, and he did not heed them, as the LORD had said.

The First Plague: Waters Become Blood

14 So the LORD said to Moses: [a]"Pharaoh's heart *is* hard; he refuses to let the people go.

6:12 [a] Jer. 1:6 **6:13** [a] Deut. 31:14 **6:14** [a] Gen. 46:9 **6:15** [a] Gen. 46:10 [1] Spelled *Nemuel* in Numbers 26:12 **6:16** [a] Gen. 46:11 **6:17** [a] 1 Chr. 6:17 **6:18** [a] 1 Chr. 6:2, 18 **6:19** [a] 1 Chr. 6:19; 23:21 **6:20** [a] Ex. 2:1, 2 [b] Num. 26:59 [c] Num. 26:59 **6:21** [a] 1 Chr. 6:37, 38 **6:22** [a] Lev. 10:4 **6:23** [a] Ruth 4:19, 20 [b] Lev. 10:1 [c] Ex. 28:1 **6:24** [a] Num. 26:11 **6:25** [a] Num. 25:7, 11 **6:26** [a] Ex. 7:4; 12:17, 51 **6:27** [a] Ps. 77:20 **6:29** [a] Ex. 6:11; 7:2 **6:30** [a] Ex. 4:10; 6:12 **7:1** [a] Ex. 4:16 [b] Ex. 4:15, 16 **7:2** [a] Ex. 4:15 **7:3** [a] Ex. 4:21; 9:12 [b] Ex. 11:9 [c] Deut. 4:34 **7:4** [a] Ex. 3:19, 20; 10:1; 11:9 [b] Ex. 9:14 [c] Ex. 6:6; 12:12 **7:5** [a] Ps. 9:16 [b] Ex. 9:15 [c] Ex. 3:20; 6:6; 12:51 **7:6** [a] Ex. 7:2 **7:7** [a] Deut. 29:5; 31:2; 34:7 [b] Num. 33:39 **7:9** [a] Is. 7:11 [b] Ex. 4:2, 3, 17 **7:10** [a] Ex. 7:9 [b] Ex. 4:3 **7:11** [a] Gen. 41:8 [b] 2 Tim. 3:8 [c] Ex. 7:22; 8:7, 18 **7:14** [a] Ex. 8:15; 10:1, 20, 27

15 Go to Pharaoh in the morning, when he
goes out to the [a]water, and you shall stand
by the river's bank to meet him; and [b]the
rod which was turned to a serpent you shall
take in your hand. 16 And you shall say to him,
[a]'The LORD God of the Hebrews has sent me
to you, saying, "Let My people go, [b]that they
may serve Me in the wilderness"; but indeed,
until now you would not hear! 17 Thus says the
LORD: "By this [a]you shall know that I *am* the
LORD. Behold, I will strike the waters which
are in the river with the rod that *is* in my
hand, and [b]they shall be turned [c]to blood.
18 And the fish that *are* in the river shall die,
the river shall stink, and the Egyptians will
[a]loathe to drink the water of the river." ' "

19 Then the LORD spoke to Moses, "Say to
Aaron, 'Take your rod and [a]stretch out your
hand over the waters of Egypt, over their
streams, over their rivers, over their ponds,
and over all their pools of water, that they
may become blood. And there shall be blood
throughout all the land of Egypt, both in
buckets of wood and *pitchers of* stone.' " 20 And
Moses and Aaron did so, just as the LORD commanded. So he [a]lifted up the rod and struck
the waters that *were* in the river, in the sight
of Pharaoh and in the sight of his servants.
And all the [b]waters that *were* in the river were
turned to blood. 21 The fish that *were* in the
river died, the river stank, and the Egyptians
[a]could not drink the water of the river. So there
was blood throughout all the land of Egypt.

22 [a]Then the magicians of Egypt did [b]so with
their enchantments; and Pharaoh's heart grew
hard, and he did not heed them, [c]as the LORD
had said. 23 And Pharaoh turned and went into
his house. Neither was his heart moved by
this. 24 So all the Egyptians dug all around the
river for water to drink, because they could not
drink the water of the river. 25 And seven days
passed after the LORD had struck the river.

The Second Plague: Frogs

8 And the LORD spoke to Moses, "Go to
Pharaoh and say to him, 'Thus says the
LORD: "Let My people go, [a]that they may serve
Me. 2 But if you [a]refuse to let *them* go, behold,
I will smite all your territory with [b]frogs. 3 So
the river shall bring forth frogs abundantly,
which shall go up and come into your house,
into your [a]bedroom, on your bed, into the
houses of your servants, on your people, into
your ovens, and into your kneading bowls.
4 And the frogs shall come up on you, on your
people, and on all your servants." ' "

5 Then the LORD spoke to Moses, "Say to
Aaron, [a]'Stretch out your hand with your
rod over the streams, over the rivers, and
over the ponds, and cause frogs to come up
on the land of Egypt.' " 6 So Aaron stretched
out his hand over the waters of Egypt, and

7:15 [a] Ex. 2:5; 8:20 [b] Ex. 4:2, 3; 7:10 **7:16** [a] Ex. 3:13, 18; 4:22 [b] Ex. 3:12, 18; 4:23; 5:1, 3; 8:1 **7:17** [a] Ex. 5:2; 7:5; 10:2 [b] Ex. 4:9; 7:20 [c] Rev. 11:6; 16:4, 6 **7:18** [a] Ex. 7:24 **7:19** [a] Ex. 8:5, 6, 16; 9:22; 10:12, 21; 14:21, 26 **7:20** [a] Ex. 17:5 [b] Ps. 78:44; 105:29, 30 **7:21** [a] Ex. 7:18 **7:22** [a] Ex. 7:11 [b] Ex. 8:7 [c] Ex. 3:19; 7:3 **8:1** [a] Ex. 3:12, 18; 4:23; 5:1, 3 **8:2** [a] Ex. 7:14; 9:2 [b] Rev. 16:13 **8:3** [a] Ps. 105:30 **8:5** [a] Ex. 7:19

JUST DO IT

Then Moses and Aaron did so; just as the LORD commanded them, so they did.

EXODUS 7:6

Have you ever deeply dreaded doing something? If I have to do something for which I don't feel qualified, I am sure I will blow it. I think that is exactly how Moses felt when God told him to go to Pharaoh.

The interesting thing, however, is that God told Moses point-blank that Pharaoh wouldn't in fact listen to him (v. 4: "Pharaoh will not heed you")! Then what was the point? Why give Moses a task he already felt unqualified for and then guarantee his words would fail? Still, Moses did as he was instructed, and it is good that he did, for Pharaoh's hardened heart helped accomplish God's purposes.

That is the lesson for us. That dreaded thing we don't want to do, that thing that may fail, is something we should do if God directs us to do it. Behind the uncertainties and apparent failures, *God is at work.* It is easy to have faith when all looks possible; it's a lot harder when circumstances look dire. Did Moses feel afraid of the task before him? Probably. Did he also feel peace because God was with him? Probably!

[a]the frogs came up and covered the land of
Egypt. 7 [a]And the magicians did so with their
enchantments, and brought up frogs on the
land of Egypt.
8 Then Pharaoh called for Moses and
Aaron, and said, [a]"Entreat the LORD that He
may take away the frogs from me and from
my people; and I will let the people [b]go, that
they may sacrifice to the LORD."
9 And Moses said to Pharaoh, "Accept the
honor of saying when I shall intercede for
you, for your servants, and for your people, to
destroy the frogs from you and your houses,
that they may remain in the river only."
10 So he said, "Tomorrow." And he said, "*Let
it be* according to your word, that you may
know that [a]*there is* no one like the LORD our
God. 11 And the frogs shall depart from you,
from your houses, from your servants, and
from your people. They shall remain in the
river only."
12 Then Moses and Aaron went out from
Pharaoh. And Moses [a]cried out to the LORD
concerning the frogs which He had brought
against Pharaoh. 13 So the LORD did according
to the word of Moses. And the frogs died out of
the houses, out of the courtyards, and out of the
fields. 14 They gathered them together in heaps,
and the land stank. 15 But when Pharaoh saw
that there was [a]relief, [b]he hardened his heart
and did not heed them, as the LORD had said.

The Third Plague: Lice

16 So the LORD said to Moses, "Say to Aaron,
'Stretch out your rod, and strike the dust of the
land, so that it may become lice throughout
all the land of Egypt.' " 17 And they did so. For
Aaron stretched out his hand with his rod and
struck the dust of the earth, and [a]it became
lice on man and beast. All the dust of the land
became lice throughout all the land of Egypt.
18 Now [a]the magicians so worked with their
enchantments to bring forth lice, but they
[b]could not. So there were lice on man and
beast. 19 Then the magicians said to Pharaoh,
"This *is* [a]the finger of God." But Pharaoh's
[b]heart grew hard, and he did not heed them,
just as the LORD had said.

The Fourth Plague: Flies

20 And the LORD said to Moses, [a]"Rise early
in the morning and stand before Pharaoh as
he comes out to the water. Then say to him,
'Thus says the LORD: [b]"Let My people go, that
they may serve Me. 21 Or else, if you will not
let My people go, behold, I will send swarms
of flies on you and your servants, on your
people and into your houses. The houses of
the Egyptians shall be full of swarms *of flies,*
and also the ground on which they *stand.*
22 And in that day [a]I will set apart the land of
[b]Goshen, in which My people dwell, that no
swarms *of flies* shall be there, in order that
you may [c]know that I *am* the LORD in the
midst of the [d]land. 23 I will make a difference[1]
between My people and your people. Tomorrow this [a]sign shall be." ' " 24 And the LORD
did so. [a]Thick swarms *of flies* came into the
house of Pharaoh, *into* his servants' houses,
and into all the land of Egypt. The land was
corrupted because of the swarms *of flies.*
25 Then Pharaoh called for Moses and
Aaron, and said, "Go, sacrifice to your God
in the land."
26 And Moses said, "It is not right to do so,
for we would be sacrificing [a]the abomination
of the Egyptians to the LORD our God. If we
sacrifice the abomination of the Egyptians
before their eyes, then will they not stone
us? 27 We will go [a]three days' journey into the
wilderness and sacrifice to the LORD our God
as [b]He will command us."
28 So Pharaoh said, "I will let you go, that
you may sacrifice to the LORD your God in
the wilderness; only you shall not go very far
away. [a]Intercede for me."
29 Then Moses said, "Indeed I am going
out from you, and I will entreat the LORD,
that the swarms *of flies* may depart tomorrow from Pharaoh, from his servants, and
from his people. But let Pharaoh not [a]deal
deceitfully anymore in not letting the people
go to sacrifice to the LORD."
30 So Moses went out from Pharaoh and
[a]entreated the LORD. 31 And the LORD did according to the word of Moses; He removed the
swarms *of flies* from Pharaoh, from his servants, and from his people. Not one remained.
32 But Pharaoh [a]hardened his heart at this
time also; neither would he let the people go.

The Fifth Plague: Livestock Diseased

9 Then the LORD said to Moses, [a]"Go in
to Pharaoh and tell him, 'Thus says the
LORD God of the Hebrews: "Let My people go,
that they may [b]serve Me. 2 For if you [a]refuse
to let *them* go, and still hold them, 3 behold,
the [a]hand of the LORD will be on your cattle

8:6 [a] Ps. 78:45; 105:30 **8:7** [a] Ex. 7:11, 22 **8:8** [a] Ex. 8:28; 9:28; 10:17 [b] Ex. 10:8, 24 **8:10** [a] Ex. 9:14; 15:11 **8:12** [a] Ex. 8:30; 9:33; 10:18; 32:11 **8:15** [a] Eccl. 8:11 [b] Ex. 7:14, 22; 9:34 **8:17** [a] Ps. 105:31 **8:18** [a] Ex. 7:11, 12; 8:7 [b] Dan. 5:8 **8:19** [a] Ex. 7:5; 10:7 [b] Ex. 8:15 **8:20** [a] Ex. 7:15; 9:13 [b] Ex. 3:18; 4:23; 5:1, 3; 8:1 **8:22** [a] Ex. 9:4, 6, 26; 10:23; 11:6, 7; 12:13 [b] Gen. 50:8 [c] Ex. 7:5, 17; 10:2; 14:4 [d] Ex. 9:29 **8:23** [a] Ex. 4:8 [1] Literally *set a ransom* (compare Exodus 9:4 and 11:7) **8:24** [a] Ps. 78:45; 105:31 **8:26** [a] Gen. 43:32; 46:34 **8:27** [a] Ex. 3:18; 5:3 [b] Ex. 3:12 **8:28** [a] Ex. 8:8, 15, 29, 32; 9:28 **8:29** [a] Ex. 8:8, 15 **8:30** [a] Ex. 8:12 **8:32** [a] Ex. 4:21; 8:8, 15 **9:1** [a] Ex. 4:23; 8:1 [b] Ex. 7:16 **9:2** [a] Ex. 8:2 **9:3** [a] Ex. 7:4

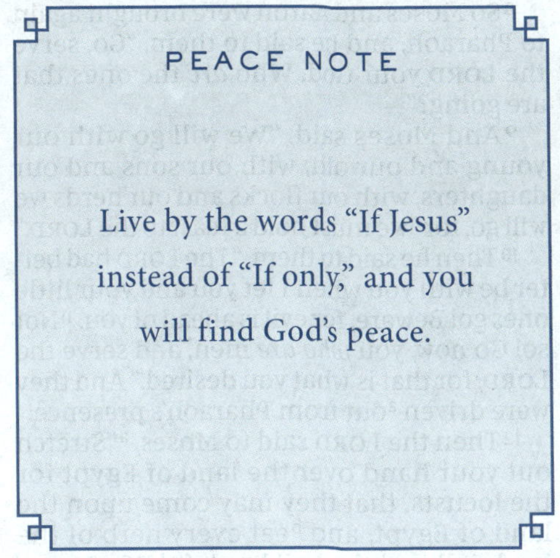

in the field, on the horses, on the donkeys, on
the camels, on the oxen, and on the sheep—a
very severe pestilence. 4 And [a]the LORD will
make a difference between the livestock of
Israel and the livestock of Egypt. So nothing
shall die of all *that* belongs to the children
of Israel.” ’ ” 5 Then the LORD appointed a
set time, saying, “Tomorrow the LORD will
do this thing in the land.”
6 So the LORD did this thing on the next
day, and [a]all the livestock of Egypt died; but
of the livestock of the children of Israel, not
one died. 7 Then Pharaoh sent, and indeed,
not even one of the livestock of the Israelites
was dead. But the [a]heart of Pharaoh became
hard, and he did not let the people go.

The Sixth Plague: Boils

8 So the LORD said to Moses and Aaron,
“Take for yourselves handfuls of ashes from
a furnace, and let Moses scatter it toward the
heavens in the sight of Pharaoh. 9 And it will
become fine dust in all the land of Egypt,
and it will cause [a]boils that break out in
sores on man and beast throughout all the
land of Egypt.” 10 Then they took ashes from
the furnace and stood before Pharaoh, and
Moses scattered *them* toward heaven. And
they caused [a]boils that break out in sores
on man and beast. 11 And the [a]magicians
could not stand before Moses because of
the [b]boils, for the boils were on the magicians and on all the Egyptians. 12 But the
LORD hardened the heart of Pharaoh; and
he [a]did not heed them, just [b]as the LORD
had spoken to Moses.

The Seventh Plague: Hail

13 Then the LORD said to Moses, [a]“Rise early
in the morning and stand before Pharaoh,
and say to him, ‘Thus says the LORD God of
the Hebrews: “Let My people go, that they
may [b]serve Me, 14 for at this time I will send
all My plagues to your very heart, and on
your servants and on your people, [a]that you
may know that *there is* none like Me in all
the earth. 15 Now if I had [a]stretched out My
hand and struck you and your people with
[b]pestilence, then you would have been cut off
from the earth. 16 But indeed for [a]this *purpose*
I have raised you up, that I may [b]show My
power *in* you, and that My [c]name may be
declared in all the earth. 17 As yet you exalt
yourself against My people in that you will
not let them go. 18 Behold, tomorrow about
this time I will cause very heavy hail to rain
down, such as has not been in Egypt since
its founding until now. 19 Therefore send
now *and* gather your livestock and all that
you have in the field, for the hail shall come
down on every man and every animal which
is found in the field and is not brought home;
and they shall die.” ’ ”
20 He who [a]feared the word of the LORD
among the [b]servants of Pharaoh made his servants and his livestock flee to the houses. 21 But
he who did not regard the word of the LORD
left his servants and his livestock in the field.
22 Then the LORD said to Moses, “Stretch
out your hand toward heaven, that there may
be [a]hail in all the land of Egypt—on man, on
beast, and on every herb of the field, throughout the land of Egypt.” 23 And Moses stretched
out his rod toward heaven; and [a]the LORD
sent thunder and hail, and fire darted to the
ground. And the LORD rained hail on the land
of Egypt. 24 So there was hail, and fire mingled
with the hail, so very heavy that there was none
like it in all the land of Egypt since it became
a nation. 25 And the [a]hail struck throughout
the whole land of Egypt, all that *was* in the
field, both man and beast; and the hail struck
every herb of the field and broke every tree of
the field. 26 [a]Only in the land of Goshen, where
the children of Israel *were,* there was no hail.
27 And Pharaoh sent and [a]called for Moses
and Aaron, and said to them, [b]“I have sinned
this time. [c]The LORD *is* righteous, and my
people and I *are* wicked. 28 [a]Entreat the LORD,
that there may be no *more* mighty thundering
and hail, for *it is* enough. I will let you [b]go,
and you shall stay no longer.”

9:4 [a] Ex. 8:22 **9:6** [a] Ps. 78:48, 50 **9:7** [a] Ex. 7:14; 8:32 **9:9** [a] Rev. 16:2 **9:10** [a] Deut. 28:27 **9:11** [a] [Ex. 8:18, 19] [b] Job 2:7 **9:12** [a] Ex. 7:13 [b] Ex. 4:21 **9:13** [a] Ex. 8:20 [b] Ex. 9:1 **9:14** [a] Ex. 8:10 **9:15** [a] Ex. 3:20; 7:5 [b] Ex. 5:3 **9:16** [a] [Rom. 9:17, 18] [b] Ex. 7:4, 5; 10:1; 11:9; 14:17 [c] 1 Kin. 8:43 **9:20** [a] [Prov. 13:13] [b] Ex. 8:19; 10:7 **9:22** [a] Rev. 16:21 **9:23** [a] Josh. 10:11 **9:25** [a] Ps. 78:47, 48; 105:32, 33 **9:26** [a] Ex. 8:22, 23; 9:4, 6; 10:23; 11:7; 12:13 **9:27** [a] Ex. 8:8 [b] Ex. 9:34; 10:16, 17 [c] 2 Chr. 12:6 **9:28** [a] Ex. 8:8, 28; 10:17 [b] Ex. 8:25; 10:8, 24

29 So Moses said to him, "As soon as I have gone out of the city, I will [a]spread out my hands to the LORD; the thunder will cease, and there will be no more hail, that you may know that the [b]earth *is* the LORD's. 30 But as for you and your servants, [a]I know that you will not yet fear the LORD God."

31 Now the flax and the barley were struck, [a]for the barley *was* in the head and the flax *was* in bud. 32 But the wheat and the spelt were not struck, for they *are* late crops.

33 So Moses went out of the city from Pharaoh and [a]spread out his hands to the LORD; then the thunder and the hail ceased, and the rain was not poured on the earth. 34 And when Pharaoh saw that the rain, the hail, and the thunder had ceased, he sinned yet more; and he hardened his heart, he and his servants. 35 So [a]the heart of Pharaoh was hard; neither would he let the children of Israel go, as the LORD had spoken by Moses.

The Eighth Plague: Locusts

10 Now the LORD said to Moses, "Go in to Pharaoh; [a]for I have hardened his heart and the hearts of his servants, [b]that I may show these signs of Mine before him, 2 and that [a]you may tell in the hearing of your son and your son's son the mighty things I have done in Egypt, and My signs which I have done among them, that you may [b]know that I *am* the LORD."

3 So Moses and Aaron came in to Pharaoh and said to him, "Thus says the LORD God of the Hebrews: 'How long will you refuse to [a]humble yourself before Me? Let My people go, that they may [b]serve Me. 4 Or else, if you refuse to let My people go, behold, tomorrow I will bring [a]locusts into your territory. 5 And they shall cover the face of the earth, so that no one will be able to see the earth; and [a]they shall eat the residue of what is left, which remains to you from the hail, and they shall eat every tree which grows up for you out of the field. 6 They shall [a]fill your houses, the houses of all your servants, and the houses of all the Egyptians—which neither your fathers nor your fathers' fathers have seen, since the day that they were on the earth to this day.'" And he turned and went out from Pharaoh.

7 Then Pharaoh's [a]servants said to him, "How long shall this man be [b]a snare to us? Let the men go, that they may serve the LORD their God. Do you not yet know that Egypt is destroyed?"

8 So Moses and Aaron were brought again to Pharaoh, and he said to them, "Go, serve the LORD your God. Who *are* the ones that are going?"

9 And Moses said, "We will go with our young and our old; with our sons and our daughters, with our flocks and our herds we will go, for [a]we must hold a feast to the LORD."

10 Then he said to them, "The LORD had better be with you when I let you and your little ones go! Beware, for evil is ahead of you. 11 Not so! Go now, you *who are* men, and serve the LORD, for that is what you desired." And they were driven [a]out from Pharaoh's presence.

12 Then the LORD said to Moses, [a]"Stretch out your hand over the land of Egypt for the locusts, that they may come upon the land of Egypt, and [b]eat every herb of the land—all that the hail has left." 13 So Moses stretched out his rod over the land of Egypt, and the LORD brought an east wind on the land all that day and all *that* night. When it was morning, the east wind brought the locusts. 14 And [a]the locusts went up over all the land of Egypt and rested on all the territory of Egypt. *They were* very severe; [b]previously there had been no such locusts as they, nor shall there be such after them. 15 For they [a]covered the face of the whole earth, so that the land was darkened; and they [b]ate every herb of the land and all the fruit of the trees which the hail had left. So there remained nothing green on the trees or on the plants of the field throughout all the land of Egypt.

16 Then Pharaoh called [a]for Moses and Aaron in haste, and said, [b]"I have sinned against the LORD your God and against you. 17 Now therefore, please forgive my sin only this once, and [a]entreat the LORD your God, that He may take away from me this death only." 18 So he [a]went out from Pharaoh and entreated the LORD. 19 And the LORD turned a very strong west wind, which took the locusts away and blew them [a]into the Red Sea. There remained not one locust in all the territory of Egypt. 20 But the LORD [a]hardened Pharaoh's heart, and he did not let the children of Israel go.

The Ninth Plague: Darkness

21 Then the LORD said to Moses, [a]"Stretch out your hand toward heaven, that there may be darkness over the land of Egypt, darkness *which* may even be felt." 22 So Moses stretched out his hand toward heaven, and

9:29 [a] Is. 1:15 [b] Ps. 24:1 **9:30** [a] [Is. 26:10] **9:31** [a] Ruth 1:22; 2:23 **9:33** [a] Ex. 8:12; 9:29 **9:35** [a] Ex. 4:21 **10:1** [a] John 12:40 [b] Ex. 7:4; 9:16 **10:2** [a] Joel 1:3 [b] Ex. 7:5, 17; 8:22 **10:3** [a] [1 Kin. 21:29] [b] Ex. 4:23; 8:1; 9:1 **10:4** [a] Rev. 9:3 **10:5** [a] Ex. 9:32 **10:6** [a] Ex. 8:3, 21 **10:7** [a] Ex. 7:5; 8:19; 9:20; 12:33 [b] Ex. 23:33 **10:9** [a] Ex. 5:1; 7:16 **10:11** [a] Ex. 10:28 **10:12** [a] Ex. 7:19 [b] Ex. 10:5, 15 **10:14** [a] Ps. 78:46; 105:34 [b] Joel 1:4, 7; 2:1–11 **10:15** [a] Ex. 10:5 [b] Ps. 105:35 **10:16** [a] Ex. 8:8 [b] Ex. 9:27 **10:17** [a] 1 Kin. 13:6 **10:18** [a] Ex. 8:30 **10:19** [a] Joel 2:20 **10:20** [a] Ex. 4:21; 10:1; 11:10 **10:21** [a] Ex. 9:22

there was [a]thick darkness in all the land of Egypt [b]three days. 23 They did not see one another; nor did anyone rise from his place for three days. [a]But all the children of Israel had light in their dwellings.

24 Then Pharaoh called to Moses and [a]said, "Go, serve the LORD; only let your flocks and your herds be kept back. Let your [b]little ones also go with you."

25 But Moses said, "You must also give us sacrifices and burnt offerings, that we may sacrifice to the LORD our God. 26 Our [a]livestock also shall go with us; not a hoof shall be left behind. For we must take some of them to serve the LORD our God, and even we do not know with what we must serve the LORD until we arrive there."

27 But the LORD [a]hardened Pharaoh's heart, and he would not let them go. 28 Then Pharaoh said to him, [a]"Get away from me! Take heed to yourself and see my face no more! For in the day you see my face you shall die!"

29 So Moses said, "You have spoken well. [a]I will never see your face again."

Death of the Firstborn Announced

11 And the LORD said to Moses, "I will bring one more plague on Pharaoh and on Egypt. [a]Afterward he will let you go from here. [b]When he lets *you* go, he will surely drive you out of here altogether. 2 Speak now in the hearing of the people, and let every man ask from his neighbor and every woman from her neighbor, [a]articles of silver and articles of gold." 3 [a]And the LORD gave the people favor in the sight of the Egyptians. Moreover the man [b]Moses *was* very great in the land of Egypt, in the sight of Pharaoh's servants and in the sight of the people.

4 Then Moses said, "Thus says the LORD: [a]'About midnight I will go out into the midst of Egypt; 5 and [a]all the firstborn in the land of Egypt shall die, from the firstborn of Pharaoh who sits on his throne, even to the firstborn of the female servant who *is* behind the handmill, and all the firstborn of the animals. 6 [a]Then there shall be a great cry throughout all the land of Egypt, [b]such as was not like it *before,* nor shall be like it again. 7 [a]But against none of the children of Israel [b]shall a dog move its tongue, against man or beast, that you may know that the LORD does make a difference between the Egyptians and Israel.' 8 And [a]all these your servants shall come down to me and bow down to me, saying, 'Get out, and all the people who follow you!' After that I will go out." [b]Then he went out from Pharaoh in great anger.

9 But the LORD said to Moses, [a]"Pharaoh will not heed you, so that [b]My wonders may be multiplied in the land of Egypt." 10 So Moses and Aaron did all these wonders before Pharaoh; [a]and the LORD hardened Pharaoh's heart, and he did not let the children of Israel go out of his land.

The Passover Instituted

12 Now the LORD spoke to Moses and Aaron in the land of Egypt, saying, 2 [a]"This month *shall be* your beginning of months; it *shall be* the first month of the year to you. 3 Speak to all the congregation of Israel, saying: 'On the [a]tenth of this month every man shall take for himself a lamb, according to the house of *his* father, a lamb for a household. 4 And if the household is too small for the lamb, let him and his neighbor next to his house take *it* according to the number of the persons; according to each man's need you shall make your count for the lamb. 5 Your lamb shall be [a]without blemish, a male of the first year. You may take *it* from the sheep or from the goats. 6 Now you shall keep it until the [a]fourteenth day of the same month. Then the whole assembly of the congregation of Israel shall kill it at twilight. 7 And they shall take *some* of the blood and put *it* on the two doorposts and on the lintel of the houses where they eat it. 8 Then they shall eat the flesh on that [a]night; [b]roasted in fire, with [c]unleavened bread *and* with bitter *herbs* they shall eat it. 9 Do not eat it raw, nor boiled at all with water, but [a]roasted in fire—its head with its legs and its entrails. 10 [a]You shall let none of it remain until morning, and what remains of it until morning you shall burn with fire. 11 And thus you shall eat it: *with* a belt on your waist, your sandals on your feet, and your staff in your hand. So you shall eat it in haste. [a]It *is* the LORD's Passover.

12 'For I [a]will pass through the land of Egypt on that night, and will strike all the firstborn in the land of Egypt, both man and beast; and [b]against all the gods of Egypt I will execute judgment: [c]I *am* the LORD. 13 Now the blood shall be a sign for you on the houses where you *are.* And when I see the blood, I will pass over you; and the plague shall not be on you to destroy *you* when I strike the land of Egypt.

10:22 [a] Ps. 105:28 [b] Ex. 3:18 **10:23** [a] Ex. 8:22, 23 **10:24** [a] Ex. 8:8, 25; 10:8 [b] Ex. 10:10 **10:26** [a] Ex. 10:9 **10:27** [a] Ex. 4:21; 10:1, 20; 14:4, 8 **10:28** [a] Ex. 10:11 **10:29** [a] Heb. 11:27 **11:1** [a] Ex. 12:31, 33, 39 [b] Ex. 6:1; 12:39 **11:2** [a] Ex. 3:22; 12:35, 36 **11:3** [a] Ex. 3:21; 12:36 [b] Deut. 34:10–12 **11:4** [a] Ex. 12:12, 23, 29 **11:5** [a] Ex. 4:23; 12:12, 29 **11:6** [a] Ex. 12:30 [b] Ex. 10:14 **11:7** [a] Ex. 8:22 [b] Josh. 10:21 **11:8** [a] Ex. 12:31–33 [b] Heb. 11:27 **11:9** [a] Ex. 3:19; 7:4; 10:1 [b] Ex. 7:3; 9:16 **11:10** [a] Rom. 2:5 **12:2** [a] Deut. 16:1 **12:3** [a] Josh. 4:19 **12:5** [a] [1 Pet. 1:19] **12:6** [a] Lev. 23:5 **12:8** [a] Num. 9:12 [b] Deut. 16:7 [c] 1 Cor. 5:8 **12:9** [a] Deut. 16:7 **12:10** [a] Ex. 16:19; 23:18; 34:25 **12:11** [a] Ex. 12:13, 21, 27, 43 **12:12** [a] Ex. 11:4, 5 [b] Num. 33:4 [c] Ex. 6:2

14'So this day shall be to you [a]a memorial;
and you shall keep it as a [b]feast to the LORD
throughout your generations. You shall keep it
as a feast [c]by an everlasting ordinance. 15[a]Sev-
en days you shall eat unleavened bread. On the
first day you shall remove leaven from your
houses. For whoever eats leavened bread from
the first day until the seventh day, [b]that person
shall be cut off from Israel. 16On the first day
there shall be [a]a holy convocation, and on the
seventh day there shall be a holy convocation
for you. No manner of work shall be done on
them; but *that* which everyone must eat—that
only may be prepared by you. 17So you shall
observe *the Feast of* Unleavened Bread, for
[a]on this same day I will have brought your
armies [b]out of the land of Egypt. Therefore
you shall observe this day throughout your
generations as an everlasting ordinance. 18[a]In
the first *month,* on the fourteenth day of the
month at evening, you shall eat unleavened
bread, until the twenty-first day of the month
at evening. 19For [a]seven days no leaven shall
be found in your houses, since whoever eats
what is leavened, that same person shall be cut
off from the congregation of Israel, whether
he is a stranger or a native of the land. 20You
shall eat nothing leavened; in all your dwellings you shall eat unleavened bread.' "

21Then [a]Moses called for all the [b]elders
of Israel and said to them, [c]"Pick out and
take lambs for yourselves according to your
families, and kill the Passover *lamb.* 22[a]And
you shall take a bunch of hyssop, dip *it* in
the blood that *is* in the basin, and [b]strike the
lintel and the two doorposts with the blood
that *is* in the basin. And none of you shall go
out of the door of his house until morning.
23[a]For the LORD will pass through to strike the
Egyptians; and when He sees the [b]blood on
the lintel and on the two doorposts, the LORD
will pass over the door and [c]not allow [d]the
destroyer to come into your houses to strike
you. 24And you shall [a]observe this thing as
an ordinance for you and your sons forever.
25It will come to pass when you come to the
land which the LORD will give you, [a]just as He
promised, that you shall keep this service.
26[a]And it shall be, when your children say to
you, 'What do you mean by this service?' 27that
you shall say, [a]'It *is* the Passover sacrifice of
the LORD, who passed over the houses of the
children of Israel in Egypt when He struck the
Egyptians and delivered our households.' " So
the people [b]bowed their heads and worshiped.
28Then the children of Israel went away and
[a]did *so;* just as the LORD had commanded
Moses and Aaron, so they did.

12:14 [a] Ex. 13:9 [b] Lev. 23:4, 5 [c] Ex. 12:17, 24; 13:10 **12:15** [a] Lev. 23:6 [b] Gen. 17:14 **12:16** [a] Lev. 23:2, 7, 8 **12:17** [a] Ex. 12:14; 13:3, 10 [b] Num. 33:1 **12:18** [a] Lev. 23:5–8 **12:19** [a] Ex. 12:15; 23:15; 34:18 **12:21** [a] [Heb. 11:28] [b] Ex. 3:16 [c] Num. 9:4 **12:22** [a] Heb. 11:28 [b] Ex. 12:7 **12:23** [a] Ex. 11:4; 12:12, 13 [b] Ex. 24:8 [c] Rev. 7:3; 9:4 [d] Heb. 11:28 **12:24** [a] Ex. 12:14, 17; 13:5, 10 **12:25** [a] Ex. 3:8, 17 **12:26** [a] Ex. 10:2; 13:8, 14, 15 **12:27** [a] Ex. 12:11 [b] Ex. 4:31 **12:28** [a] [Heb. 11:28]

SET UP YOUR MEMORIALS

"So this day shall be to you a memorial; and you shall keep it as a feast to the LORD throughout your generations."

EXODUS 12:14

We are forgetful people, which is why memorials are important in our cultures and communities. God's people need memorials. This is what the people of Israel believed, and so they prepared for Passover night, and then in the morning they saw what had happened. They believed what they had not yet seen and then saw what they had believed: God's deliverance was clear!

The greatest holy day in all of Israel's ancient holidays is Passover. It recalls the night when God pounded Egypt with the tenth plague and liberated Israel from several generations of servitude. God told Israel to commemorate that amazing night when the Lord "passed over" (v. 27) the homes with the blood on the doorposts. The faith that caused them to put the blood of the Passover lambs on the doors saved the Israelites from death.

Remembering that night was the spiritual glue that held Israelite—later Jewish—society together. Jesus would later ask the same of His disciples. This is why memorials are so important—they help us remember what God has done. Remembering God's saving deeds gives hope and creates peace.

The Tenth Plague: Death of the Firstborn

29[a]And it came to pass at midnight that
[b]the LORD struck all the firstborn in the
land of Egypt, from the firstborn of Pharaoh who sat on his throne to the firstborn
of the captive who *was* in the dungeon, and
all the firstborn of [c]livestock. 30 So Pharaoh
rose in the night, he, all his servants, and all
the Egyptians; and there was a great cry in
Egypt, for *there was* not a house where *there*
was not one dead.

The Exodus

31 Then he [a]called for Moses and Aaron by
night, and said, "Rise, go out from among my
people, [b]both you and the children of Israel.
And go, serve the LORD as you have [c]said.
32[a]Also take your flocks and your herds, as you
have said, and be gone; and bless me also."

33[a]And the Egyptians [b]urged the people,
that they might send them out of the land
in haste. For they said, "We *shall* all *be* dead."
34 So the people took their dough before it
was leavened, having their kneading bowls
bound up in their clothes on their shoulders.
35 Now the children of Israel had done according to the word of Moses, and they had
asked from the Egyptians [a]articles of silver,
articles of gold, and clothing. 36[a]And the
LORD had given the people favor in the sight
of the Egyptians, so that they granted them
what they requested. Thus [b]they plundered
the Egyptians.

37 Then [a]the children of Israel journeyed
from [b]Rameses to Succoth, about [c]six hundred thousand men on foot, besides children.
38 A [a]mixed multitude went up with them
also, and flocks and herds—a great deal of
[b]livestock. 39 And they baked unleavened
cakes of the dough which they had brought
out of Egypt; for it was not leavened, because
[a]they were driven out of Egypt and could not
wait, nor had they prepared provisions for
themselves.

40 Now the sojourn of the children of Israel
who lived in Egypt[1] *was* [a]four hundred and
thirty years. 41 And it came to pass at the end
of the four hundred and thirty years—on that
very same day—it came to pass that [a]all the
armies of the LORD went out from the land of
Egypt. 42 It *is* [a]a night of solemn observance
to the LORD for bringing them out of the
land of Egypt. This *is* that night of the LORD,
a solemn observance for all the children of
Israel throughout their generations.

Passover Regulations

43 And the LORD said to Moses and Aaron,
"This *is* [a]the ordinance of the Passover: No
foreigner shall eat it. 44 But every man's servant who is bought for money, when you have
[a]circumcised him, then he may eat it. 45[a]A
sojourner and a hired servant shall not eat
it. 46 In one house it shall be eaten; you shall
not carry any of the flesh outside the house,
[a]nor shall you break one of its bones. 47[a]All
the congregation of Israel shall keep it. 48 And
[a]when a stranger dwells with you *and wants*
to keep the Passover to the LORD, let all his
males be circumcised, and then let him come
near and keep it; and he shall be as a native of
the land. For no uncircumcised person shall
eat it. 49[a]One law shall be for the native-born
and for the stranger who dwells among you."

50 Thus all the children of Israel did; as
the LORD commanded Moses and Aaron, so
they did. 51[a]And it came to pass, on that very
same day, that the LORD brought the children
of Israel out of the land of Egypt [b]according
to their armies.

The Firstborn Consecrated

13 Then the LORD spoke to Moses, saying,
2[a]"Consecrate to Me all the firstborn,
whatever opens the womb among the children
of Israel, *both* of man and beast; it is Mine."

The Feast of Unleavened Bread

3 And Moses said to the people: [a]"Remember this day in which you went out of Egypt,
out of the house of bondage; for [b]by strength
of hand the LORD brought you out of this
place. [c]No leavened bread shall be eaten.
4[a]On this day you are going out, in the month
Abib. 5 And it shall be, when the LORD [a]brings
you into the [b]land of the Canaanites and the
Hittites and the Amorites and the Hivites
and the Jebusites, which He [c]swore to your
fathers to give you, a land flowing with milk
and honey, [d]that you shall keep this service
in this month. 6[a]Seven days you shall eat
unleavened bread, and on the seventh day
there shall be a feast to the LORD. 7 Unleavened
bread shall be eaten seven days. And [a]no
leavened bread shall be seen among you, nor

12:29 [a] Ex. 11:4, 5 [b] Num. 8:17; 33:4 [c] Ex. 9:6 **12:31** [a] Ex. 10:28, 29 [b] Ex. 8:25; 11:1 [c] Ex. 10:9 **12:32** [a] Ex. 10:9, 26 **12:33** [a] Ex. 10:7 [b] Ps. 105:38 **12:35** [a] Ex. 3:21, 22; 11:2, 3 **12:36** [a] Ex. 3:21 [b] Gen. 15:14 **12:37** [a] Num. 33:3, 5 [b] Gen. 47:11 [c] Ex. 38:26 **12:38** [a] Num. 11:4 [b] Deut. 3:19 **12:39** [a] Ex. 6:1; 11:1; 12:31–33 **12:40** [a] Acts 7:6 [1] Samaritan Pentateuch and Septuagint read *Egypt and Canaan.* **12:41** [a] Ex. 3:8, 10; 6:6; 7:4 **12:42** [a] Deut. 16:1, 6 **12:43** [a] Num. 9:14 **12:44** [a] Gen. 17:12, 13 **12:45** [a] Lev. 22:10 **12:46** [a] [John 19:33, 36] **12:47** [a] Ex. 12:6 **12:48** [a] Num. 9:14 **12:49** [a] Num. 15:15, 16 **12:51** [a] Ex. 12:41; 20:2 [b] Ex. 6:26 **13:2** [a] Luke 2:23 **13:3** [a] Deut. 16:3 [b] Ex. 3:20; 6:1 [c] Ex. 12:8, 19 **13:4** [a] Ex. 12:2; 23:15; 34:18 **13:5** [a] Ex. 3:8, 17 [b] Gen. 17:8 [c] Ex. 6:8 [d] Ex. 12:25, 26 **13:6** [a] Ex. 12:15–20 **13:7** [a] Ex. 12:19

shall leaven be seen among you in all your
quarters. 8 And you shall [a]tell your son in
that day, saying, '*This is done* because of what
the LORD did for me when I came up from
Egypt.' 9 It shall be as [a]a sign to you on your
hand and as a memorial between your eyes,
that the LORD's law may be in your mouth;
for with a strong hand the LORD has brought
you out of Egypt. 10 [a]You shall therefore keep
this ordinance in its season from year to year.

The Law of the Firstborn

11 "And it shall be, when the LORD [a]brings
you into the land of the [b]Canaanites, as He
swore to you and your fathers, and gives it to
you, 12 [a]that you shall set apart to the LORD all
that open the womb, that is, every firstborn
that comes from an animal which you have;
the males *shall be* the LORD's. 13 But [a]every
firstborn of a donkey you shall redeem with
a lamb; and if you will not redeem *it,* then
you shall break its neck. And all the firstborn
of man among your sons [b]you shall redeem.
14 [a]So it shall be, when your son asks you in
time to come, saying, 'What *is* this?' that you
shall say to him, [b]'By strength of hand the
LORD brought us out of Egypt, out of the
house of bondage. 15 And it came to pass, when
Pharaoh was stubborn about letting us go,
that [a]the LORD killed all the firstborn in the
land of Egypt, both the firstborn of man and
the firstborn of beast. Therefore I sacrifice
to the LORD all males that open the womb,
but all the firstborn of my sons I redeem.'
16 It shall be as [a]a sign on your hand and as
frontlets between your eyes, for by strength
of hand the LORD brought us out of Egypt."

The Wilderness Way

17 Then it came to pass, when Pharaoh had
let the people go, that God did not lead them
by way of the land of the Philistines, although
that *was* near; for God said, "Lest perhaps the
people [a]change their minds when they see
war, and [b]return to Egypt." 18 So God [a]led the
people around *by* way of the wilderness of
the Red Sea. And the children of Israel went
up in orderly ranks out of the land of Egypt.
19 And Moses took the [a]bones of [b]Joseph
with him, for he had placed the children of
Israel under solemn oath, saying, [c]"God will
surely visit you, and you shall carry up my
bones from here with you."[1]
20 So [a]they took their journey from [b]Succoth
and camped in Etham at the edge of the wilderness. 21 And [a]the LORD went before them
by day in a pillar of cloud to lead the way, and
by night in a pillar of fire to give them light,
so as to go by day and night. 22 He did not take
away the pillar of cloud by day or the pillar of
fire by night *from* before the people.

The Red Sea Crossing

14 Now the LORD spoke to Moses, saying:
2 "Speak to the children of Israel, [a]that
they turn and camp before [b]Pi Hahiroth,
between [c]Migdol and the sea, opposite Baal
Zephon; you shall camp before it by the sea.
3 For Pharaoh will say of the children of Israel, [a]'They *are* bewildered by the land; the
wilderness has closed them in.' 4 Then [a]I will
harden Pharaoh's heart, so that he will pursue
them; and I [b]will gain honor over Pharaoh
and over all his army, [c]that the Egyptians may
know that I *am* the LORD." And they did so.
5 Now it was told the king of Egypt that the
people had fled, and [a]the heart of Pharaoh and
his servants was turned against the people;
and they said, "Why have we done this, that
we have let Israel go from serving us?" 6 So he
made ready his chariot and took his people
with him. 7 Also, he took [a]six hundred choice
chariots, and all the chariots of Egypt with captains over every one of them. 8 And the LORD
[a]hardened the heart of Pharaoh king of Egypt,
and he pursued the children of Israel; and [b]the
children of Israel went out with boldness. 9 So
the [a]Egyptians pursued them, all the horses
and chariots of Pharaoh, his horsemen and
his army, and overtook them camping by the
sea beside Pi Hahiroth, before Baal Zephon.
10 And when Pharaoh drew near, the children of Israel lifted their eyes, and behold, the
Egyptians marched after them. So they were
very afraid, and the children of Israel [a]cried
out to the LORD. 11 [a]Then they said to Moses,
"Because *there were* no graves in Egypt, have
you taken us away to die in the wilderness?
Why have you so dealt with us, to bring us up
out of Egypt? 12 [a]*Is* this not the word that we
told you in Egypt, saying, 'Let us alone that
we may serve the Egyptians'? For *it would
have been* better for us to serve the Egyptians
than that we should die in the wilderness."
13 And Moses said to the people, [a]"Do not
be afraid. [b]Stand still, and see the [c]salvation
of the LORD, which He will accomplish for
you today. For the Egyptians whom you see

13:8 [a] Ex. 10:2; 12:26; 13:14 **13:9** [a] Deut. 6:8; 11:18 **13:10** [a] Ex. 12:14, 24 **13:11** [a] Ex. 13:5 [b] Num. 21:3 **13:12** [a] Lev. 27:26 **13:13** [a] Ex. 34:20 [b] Num. 3:46, 47; 18:15, 16 **13:14** [a] Deut. 6:20 [b] Ex. 13:3, 9 **13:15** [a] Ex. 12:29 **13:16** [a] Ex. 13:9 **13:17** [a] Ex. 14:11 [b] Deut. 17:16 **13:18** [a] Num. 33:6 **13:19** [a] Gen. 50:24, 25 [b] Ex. 1:6; Deut. 33:13–17 [c] Ex. 4:31 [1] Genesis 50:25 **13:20** [a] Num. 33:6–8 [b] Ex. 12:37 **13:21** [a] Deut. 1:33 **14:2** [a] Ex. 13:18 [b] Num. 33:7 [c] Jer. 44:1 **14:3** [a] Ps. 71:11 **14:4** [a] Ex. 4:21; 7:3; 14:17 [b] Ex. 9:16; 14:17, 18, 23 [c] Ex. 7:5; 14:25 **14:5** [a] Ps. 105:25 **14:7** [a] Ex. 15:4 **14:8** [a] Ex. 14:4 [b] Num. 33:3 **14:9** [a] Josh. 24:6 **14:10** [a] Neh. 9:9 **14:11** [a] Ps. 106:7, 8 **14:12** [a] Ex. 5:21; 6:9 **14:13** [a] 2 Chr. 20:15, 17 [b] Ps. 46:10, 11 [c] Ex. 14:30; 15:2

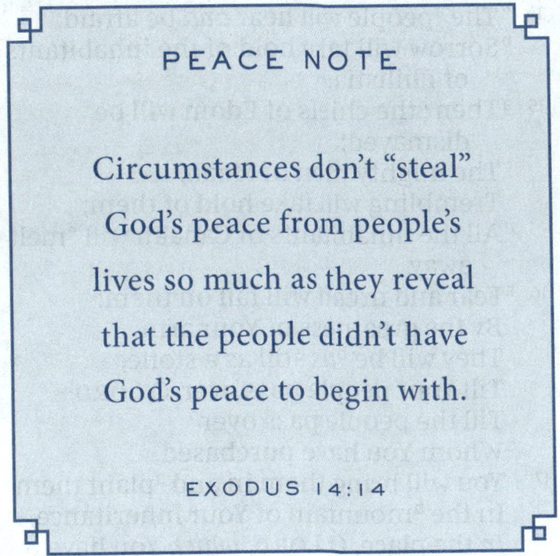

today, you shall [d]see again no more forever.
14 [a]The LORD will fight for you, and you shall
[b]hold your peace."
15 And the LORD said to Moses, "Why do
you cry to Me? Tell the children of Israel to go
forward. 16 But [a]lift up your rod, and stretch
out your hand over the sea and divide it. And
the children of Israel shall go on dry *ground*
through the midst of the sea. 17 And I indeed
will [a]harden the hearts of the Egyptians,
and they shall follow them. So I will [b]gain
honor over Pharaoh and over all his army,
his chariots, and his horsemen. 18 Then the
Egyptians shall know that I *am* the LORD,
when I have gained honor for Myself over
Pharaoh, his chariots, and his horsemen."
19 And the Angel of God, [a]who went before
the camp of Israel, moved and went behind
them; and the pillar of cloud went from before them and stood behind them. 20 So it
came between the camp of the Egyptians
and the camp of Israel. Thus it was a cloud
and darkness *to the one,* and it gave light by
night *to the other,* so that the one did not
come near the other all that night.
21 Then Moses stretched out his hand over the
sea; and the LORD caused the sea to go *back* by
a strong east wind all that night, and [a]made the
sea into dry *land,* and the waters were [b]divided.
22 So [a]the children of Israel went into the midst
of the sea on the dry *ground,* and the waters *were*
[b]a wall to them on their right hand and on their
left. 23 And the Egyptians pursued and went after
them into the midst of the sea, all Pharaoh's
horses, his chariots, and his horsemen.
24 Now it came to pass, in the morning
[a]watch, that [b]the LORD looked down upon
the army of the Egyptians through the pillar
of fire and cloud, and He troubled the army
of the Egyptians. 25 And He took off[1] their
chariot wheels, so that they drove them with
difficulty; and the Egyptians said, "Let us flee
from the face of Israel, for the LORD [a]fights
for them against the Egyptians."
26 Then the LORD said to Moses, "Stretch
out your hand over the sea, that the waters
may come back upon the Egyptians, on their
chariots, and on their horsemen." 27 And
Moses stretched out his hand over the sea;
and when the morning appeared, the sea
[a]returned to its full depth, while the Egyptians were fleeing into it. So the LORD [b]over-
threw the Egyptians in the midst of the sea.
28 Then [a]the waters returned and covered the
chariots, the horsemen, *and* all the army of
Pharaoh that came into the sea after them.
Not so much as one of them remained. 29 But
[a]the children of Israel had walked on dry
land in the midst of the sea, and the waters
were a wall to them on their right hand and
on their left.
30 So the LORD [a]saved Israel that day out of
the hand of the Egyptians, and Israel [b]saw the
Egyptians dead on the seashore. 31 Thus Israel
saw the great work which the LORD had done
in Egypt; so the people feared the LORD, and
[a]believed the LORD and His servant Moses.

The Song of Moses

15 Then [a]Moses and the children of Israel sang this song to the LORD, and
spoke, saying:

"I will [b]sing to the LORD,
For He has triumphed gloriously!
The horse and its rider
He has thrown into the sea!
2 The LORD *is* my strength and [a]song,
And He has become my salvation;
He *is* my God, and [b]I will praise Him;
My [c]father's God, and I [d]will exalt Him.
3 The LORD *is* a man of [a]war;
The LORD *is* His [b]name.
4 [a]Pharaoh's chariots and his army He has cast into the sea;
[b]His chosen captains also are drowned in the Red Sea.
5 The depths have covered them;
[a]They sank to the bottom like a stone.

14:13 [d] Deut. 28:68 **14:14** [a] Deut. 1:30; 3:22 [b] [Is. 30:15] **14:16** [a] Num. 20:8, 9, 11 **14:17** [a] Ex. 14:8 [b] Ex. 14:4 **14:19** [a] [Is. 63:9] **14:21** [a] Ps. 66:6; 106:9; 136:13, 14 [b] Is. 63:12, 13 **14:22** [a] Ex. 15:19 [b] Ex. 14:29; 15:8 **14:24** [a] Judg. 7:19 [b] Ex. 13:21 **14:25** [a] Ex. 7:5; 14:4, 14, 18 [1] Samaritan Pentateuch, Septuagint, and Syriac read *bound.* **14:27** [a] Josh. 4:18 [b] Ex. 15:1, 7 **14:28** [a] Ps. 78:53; 106:11 **14:29** [a] Ps. 66:6; 78:52, 53 **14:30** [a] Ps. 106:8, 10 [b] Ps. 58:10; 59:10 **14:31** [a] John 2:11; 11:45 **15:1** [a] Ps. 106:12 [b] Is. 12:1–6 **15:2** [a] Is. 12:2 [b] Gen. 28:21, 22 [c] Ex. 3:6, 15, 16 [d] Is. 25:1 **15:3** [a] Rev. 19:11 [b] Ps. 24:8; 83:18 **15:4** [a] Ex. 14:28 [b] Ex. 14:7 **15:5** [a] Neh. 9:11

PEACE NOTE

Protection, peace, and even happiness are your portion as a believer.

EXODUS 15:2

6 "Your [a]right hand, O LORD, has become
glorious in power;
Your right hand, O LORD, has dashed
the enemy in pieces.
7 And in the greatness of Your
[a]excellence
You have overthrown those who rose
against You;
You sent forth [b]Your wrath;
It [c]consumed them [d]like stubble.
8 And [a]with the blast of Your nostrils
The waters were gathered together;
[b]The floods stood upright like a heap;
The depths congealed in the heart of
the sea.
9 [a]The enemy said, 'I will pursue,
I will overtake,
I will [b]divide the spoil;
My desire shall be satisfied on them.
I will draw my sword,
My hand shall destroy them.'
10 You blew with Your wind,
The sea covered them;
They sank like lead in the mighty waters.

11 "Who[a] *is* like You, O LORD, among the
gods?
Who *is* like You, [b]glorious in holiness,
Fearful in [c]praises, [d]doing wonders?
12 You stretched out Your right hand;
The earth swallowed them.
13 You in Your mercy have [a]led forth
The people whom You have redeemed;
You have guided *them* in Your strength
To [b]Your holy habitation.

14 "The [a]people will hear *and* be afraid;
[b]Sorrow will take hold of the inhabitants
of Philistia.
15 [a]Then [b]the chiefs of Edom will be
dismayed;
[c]The mighty men of Moab,
Trembling will take hold of them;
[d]All the inhabitants of Canaan will [e]melt
away.
16 [a]Fear and dread will fall on them;
By the greatness of Your arm
They will be [b]*as* still as a stone,
Till Your people pass over, O LORD,
Till the people pass over
[c]Whom You have purchased.
17 You will bring them in and [a]plant them
In the [b]mountain of Your inheritance,
In the place, O LORD, *which* You have
made
For Your own dwelling,
The [c]sanctuary, O Lord, *which* Your
hands have established.

18 "The[a] LORD shall reign forever and ever."

19 For the [a]horses of Pharaoh went with his
chariots and his horsemen into the sea, and
[b]the LORD brought back the waters of the sea
upon them. But the children of Israel went
on dry *land* in the midst of the sea.

The Song of Miriam

20 Then Miriam [a]the prophetess, [b]the sister of Aaron, [c]took the timbrel in her hand;
and all the women went out after her [d]with
timbrels and with dances. 21 And Miriam
[a]answered them:

[b]"Sing to the LORD,
For He has triumphed gloriously!
The horse and its rider
He has thrown into the sea!"

Bitter Waters Made Sweet

22 So Moses brought Israel from the Red
Sea; then they went out into the Wilderness of
[a]Shur. And they went three days in the wilderness and found no [b]water. 23 Now when they
came to [a]Marah, they could not drink the waters of Marah, for they *were* bitter. Therefore
the name of it was called Marah.[1] 24 And the
people [a]complained against Moses, saying,
"What shall we drink?" 25 So he cried out to
the LORD, and the LORD showed him a tree.

15:6 [a] Ps. 17:7; 118:15 **15:7** [a] Deut. 33:26 [b] Ps. 78:49, 50 [c] Ps. 59:13 [d] Is. 5:24 **15:8** [a] Ex. 14:21, 22, 29 [b] Ps. 78:13 **15:9** [a] Judg. 5:30 [b] Is. 53:12 **15:11** [a] 1 Kin. 8:23 [b] Is. 6:3 [c] 1 Chr. 16:25 [d] Ps. 77:11, 14 **15:13** [a] [Ps. 77:20] [b] Ps. 78:54 **15:14** [a] Josh. 2:9 [b] Ps. 48:6 **15:15** [a] Gen. 36:15, 40 [b] Deut. 2:4 [c] Num. 22:3, 4 [d] Josh. 5:1 [e] Josh. 2:9–11, 24 **15:16** [a] Josh. 2:9 [b] 1 Sam. 25:37 [c] Jer. 31:11 **15:17** [a] Ps. 44:2; 80:8, 15 [b] Ps. 2:6; 78:54, 68 [c] Ps. 68:16; 76:2; 132:13, 14 **15:18** [a] Is. 57:15 **15:19** [a] Ex. 14:23 [b] Ex. 14:28 **15:20** [a] Judg. 4:4 [b] Num. 26:59 [c] 1 Sam. 18:6 [d] Judg. 11:34; 21:21 **15:21** [a] 1 Sam. 18:7 [b] Ex. 15:1 **15:22** [a] Gen. 16:7; 20:1; 25:18 [b] Num. 20:2 **15:23** [a] Num. 33:8 [1] Literally *Bitter* **15:24** [a] Ex. 14:11; 16:2

[a]When he cast *it* into the waters, the waters
were made sweet.
There He [b]made a statute and an ordinance for them, and there [c]He tested them,
26 and said, [a]"If you diligently heed the voice
of the LORD your God and do what is right
in His sight, give ear to His commandments
and keep all His statutes, I will put none of
the [b]diseases on you which I have brought
on the Egyptians. For I *am* the LORD [c]who
heals you."
27 [a]Then they came to Elim, where there
were twelve wells of water and seventy palm
trees; so they camped there by the waters.

Bread from Heaven

16 And they [a]journeyed from Elim, and
all the congregation of the children of
Israel came to the Wilderness of Sin, which is
between Elim and [b]Sinai, on the fifteenth day
of the second month after they departed from
the land of Egypt. 2 Then the whole congregation of the children of Israel [a]complained
against Moses and Aaron in the wilderness.
3 And the children of Israel said to them, [a]"Oh,
that we had died by the hand of the LORD in
the land of Egypt, [b]when we sat by the pots of
meat *and* when we ate bread to the full! For
you have brought us out into this wilderness
to kill this whole assembly with hunger."
4 Then the LORD said to Moses, "Behold, I
will rain [a]bread from heaven for you. And the
people shall go out and gather a certain quota
every day, that I may [b]test them, whether they
will [c]walk in My law or not. 5 And it shall be
on the sixth day that they shall prepare what
they bring in, and [a]it shall be twice as much
as they gather daily."
6 Then Moses and Aaron said to all the children of Israel, [a]"At evening you shall know
that the LORD has brought you out of the land
of Egypt. 7 And in the morning you shall see
[a]the glory of the LORD; for He [b]hears your
complaints against the LORD. But [c]what *are* we,
that you complain against us?" 8 Also Moses
said, "*This shall be seen* when the LORD gives
you meat to eat in the evening, and in the
morning bread to the full; for the LORD hears
your complaints which you make against Him.
And what *are* we? Your complaints *are* not
against us but [a]against the LORD."
9 Then Moses spoke to Aaron, "Say to all
the congregation of the children of Israel,
[a]'Come near before the LORD, for He has
heard your complaints.'" 10 Now it came to
pass, as Aaron spoke to the whole congregation of the children of Israel, that they looked
toward the wilderness, and behold, the glory
of the LORD [a]appeared in the cloud.
11 And the LORD spoke to Moses, saying,
12 [a]"I have heard the complaints of the children of Israel. Speak to them, saying, [b]'At twilight you shall eat meat, and [c]in the morning
you shall be filled with bread. And you shall
know that I *am* the LORD your God.'"
13 So it was that [a]quail came up at evening
and covered the camp, and in the morning
[b]the dew lay all around the camp. 14 And when
the layer of dew lifted, there, on the surface
of the wilderness, was [a]a small round [b]sub-
stance, *as* fine as frost on the ground. 15 So
when the children of Israel saw *it,* they said
to one another, "What is it?" For they did not
know what it *was.*
And Moses said to them, [a]"This *is* the bread
which the LORD has given you to eat. 16 This is
the thing which the LORD has commanded:
'Let every man gather it [a]according to each
one's need, one [b]omer for each person, *according to the* number of persons; let every
man take for *those* who *are* in his tent.'"
17 Then the children of Israel did so and
gathered, some more, some less. 18 So when
they measured *it* by omers, [a]he who gathered
much had nothing left over, and he who gathered little had no lack. Every man had gathered
according to each one's need. 19 And Moses
said, "Let no one [a]leave any of it till morning."
20 Notwithstanding they did not heed Moses.
But some of them left part of it until morning,
and it bred worms and stank. And Moses was
angry with them. 21 So they gathered it every
morning, every man according to his need.
And when the sun became hot, it melted.
22 And so it was, on the sixth day, *that* they
gathered twice as much bread, two omers
for each one. And all the rulers of the congregation came and told Moses. 23 Then he
said to them, "This *is what* the LORD has said:
'Tomorrow *is* [a]a Sabbath rest, a holy Sabbath
to the LORD. Bake what you will bake *today,*
and boil what you will boil; and lay up for
yourselves all that remains, to be kept until
morning.'" 24 So they laid it up till morning,
as Moses commanded; and it did not [a]stink,
nor were there any worms in it. 25 Then Moses
said, "Eat that today, for today *is* a Sabbath
to the LORD; today you will not find it in the

15:25 [a] 2 Kin. 2:21 [b] Josh. 24:25 [c] Deut. 8:2, 16 **15:26** [a] Deut. 7:12, 15 [b] Deut. 28:27, 58, 60 [c] Ex. 23:25 **15:27** [a] Num. 33:9 **16:1** [a] Num. 33:10, 11 [b] Ex. 12:6, 51; 19:1 **16:2** [a] 1 Cor. 10:10 **16:3** [a] Lam. 4:9 [b] Num. 11:4, 5 **16:4** [a] [John 6:31–35] [b] Deut. 8:2, 16 [c] Judg. 2:22 **16:5** [a] Lev. 25:21 **16:6** [a] Ex. 6:7 **16:7** [a] John 11:4, 40 [b] Num. 14:27; 17:5 [c] Num. 16:11 **16:8** [a] 1 Sam. 8:7 **16:9** [a] Num. 16:16 **16:10** [a] Num. 16:19 **16:12** [a] Ex. 16:8 [b] Ex. 16:6 [c] Ex. 16:7 **16:13** [a] Num. 11:31 [b] Num. 11:9 **16:14** [a] Num. 11:7, 8 [b] Ps. 147:16 **16:15** [a] 1 Cor. 10:3 **16:16** [a] Ex. 12:4 [b] Ex. 16:32, 36 **16:18** [a] 2 Cor. 8:15 **16:19** [a] Ex. 12:10; 16:23; 23:18 **16:23** [a] Gen. 2:3 **16:24** [a] Ex. 16:20

field. 26 [a]Six days you shall gather it, but on the
seventh day, the Sabbath, there will be none."
27 Now it happened *that some* of the people
went out on the seventh day to gather, but
they found none. 28 And the LORD said to
Moses, "How long [a]do you refuse to keep My
commandments and My laws? 29 See! For the
LORD has given you the Sabbath; therefore
He gives you on the sixth day bread for two
days. Let every man remain in his place; let no
man go out of his place on the seventh day."
30 So the people rested on the seventh day.
31 And the house of Israel called its name
Manna.[1] And [a]it *was* like white coriander
seed, and the taste of it *was* like wafers *made*
with honey.
32 Then Moses said, "This *is* the thing which
the LORD has commanded: 'Fill an omer with
it, to be kept for your generations, that they
may see the bread with which I fed you in the
wilderness, when I brought you out of the land
of Egypt.' " 33 And Moses said to Aaron, [a]"Take
a pot and put an omer of manna in it, and lay
it up before the LORD, to be kept for your generations." 34 As the LORD commanded Moses,
so Aaron laid it up [a]before the Testimony, to be
kept. 35 And the children of Israel [a]ate manna
[b]forty years, [c]until they came to an inhabited
land; they ate manna until they came to the
border of the land of Canaan. 36 Now an omer
is one-tenth of an ephah.

Water from the Rock

17 Then [a]all the congregation of the children of Israel set out on their journey
from the Wilderness of [b]Sin, according to the
commandment of the LORD, and camped
in Rephidim; but *there was* no water for the
people to [c]drink. 2 [a]Therefore the people
contended with Moses, and said, "Give us
water, that we may drink."
So Moses said to them, "Why do you contend with me? Why do you [b]tempt the LORD?"
3 And the people thirsted there for water,
and the people [a]complained against Moses,
and said, "Why *is* it you have brought us up
out of Egypt, to kill us and our children and
our [b]livestock with thirst?"
4 So Moses [a]cried out to the LORD, saying,
"What shall I do with this people? They are
almost ready to [b]stone me!"
5 And the LORD said to Moses, [a]"Go on before the people, and take with you some of
the elders of Israel. Also take in your hand
your rod with which [b]you struck the river, and
go. 6 [a]Behold, I will stand before you there on
the rock in Horeb; and you shall strike the
rock, and water will come out of it, that the
people may drink."
And Moses did so in the sight of the elders
of Israel. 7 So he called the name of the place
[a]Massah[1] and Meribah,[2] because of the contention of the children of Israel, and because
they tempted the LORD, saying, "Is the LORD
among us or not?"

Victory over the Amalekites

8 [a]Now Amalek came and fought with Israel in Rephidim. 9 And Moses said to Joshua,
"Choose us some men and go out, fight with
Amalek. Tomorrow I will stand on the top of the
hill with [a]the rod of God in my hand." 10 So Joshua did as Moses said to him, and fought with
Amalek. And Moses, Aaron, and Hur went up to
the top of the hill. 11 And so it was, when Moses
[a]held up his hand, that Israel prevailed; and
when he let down his hand, Amalek prevailed.
12 But Moses' hands *became* heavy; so they took
a stone and put *it* under him, and he sat on it.
And Aaron and Hur supported his hands, one
on one side, and the other on the other side;
and his hands were steady until the going down
of the sun. 13 So Joshua defeated Amalek and
his people with the edge of the sword.
14 Then the LORD said to Moses, [a]"Write this
for a memorial in the book and recount *it* in the
hearing of Joshua, that [b]I will utterly blot out the
remembrance of Amalek from under heaven."
15 And Moses built an altar and called its name,
The-LORD-Is-My-Banner;[1] 16 for he said, "Because
the LORD has [a]sworn: the LORD *will have* war
with Amalek from generation to generation."

Jethro's Advice

18 And [a]Jethro, the priest of Midian,
Moses' father-in-law, heard of all that
[b]God had done for Moses and for Israel His
people—that the LORD had brought Israel
out of Egypt. 2 Then Jethro, Moses' father-
in-law, took [a]Zipporah, Moses' wife, after he
had sent her back, 3 with her [a]two sons, of
whom the name of one *was* Gershom (for
he said, [b]"I have been a stranger in a foreign
land")[1] 4 and the name of the other *was* Eliezer[1] (for *he said,* "The God of my father *was*
my [a]help, and delivered me from the sword

16:26 [a] Ex. 20:9, 10 **16:28** [a] 2 Kin. 17:14 **16:31** [a] Num. 11:7–9 [1] Literally *What?* (compare Exodus 16:15) **16:33** [a] Heb. 9:4 **16:34** [a] Num. 17:10 **16:35** [a] Deut. 8:3, 16 [b] Num. 33:38 [c] Josh. 5:12 **17:1** [a] Ex. 16:1 [b] Num. 33:11–15 [c] Ex. 15:22 **17:2** [a] Num. 20:2, 3, 13 [b] [Deut. 6:16] **17:3** [a] Ex. 16:2, 3 [b] Ex. 12:38 **17:4** [a] Ex. 14:15 [b] John 8:59; 10:31 **17:5** [a] Ezek. 2:6 [b] Num. 20:8 **17:6** [a] Num. 20:10, 11 **17:7** [a] Num. 20:13, 24; 27:14 [1] Literally *Tempted* [2] Literally *Contention* **17:8** [a] Gen. 36:12 **17:9** [a] Ex. 4:20 **17:11** [a] [James 5:16] **17:14** [a] Ex. 24:4; 34:27 [b] 1 Sam. 15:3 **17:15** [1] Hebrew *YHWH Nissi* **17:16** [a] Gen. 22:14–16 **18:1** [a] Ex. 2:16, 18; 3:1 [b] [Ps. 106:2, 8] **18:2** [a] Ex. 2:21; 4:20–26 **18:3** [a] Acts 7:29 [b] Ex. 2:22 [1] Compare Exodus 2:22 **18:4** [a] Gen. 49:25 [1] Literally *My God Is Help*

of Pharaoh"); 5 and Jethro, Moses' father-in-
law, came with his sons and his wife to Moses
in the wilderness, where he was encamped
at [a]the mountain of God. 6 Now he had said
to Moses, "I, your father-in-law Jethro, am
coming to you with your wife and her two
sons with her."

7 So Moses [a]went out to meet his father-in-
law, bowed down, and [b]kissed him. And they
asked each other about *their* well-being, and
they went into the tent. 8 And Moses told his
father-in-law all that the LORD had done to
Pharaoh and to the Egyptians for Israel's sake,
all the hardship that had come upon them
on the way, and *how* the LORD had [a]delivered
them. 9 Then Jethro rejoiced for all the [a]good
which the LORD had done for Israel, whom
He had delivered out of the hand of the Egyptians. 10 And Jethro said, [a]"Blessed *be* the LORD,
who has delivered you out of the hand of the
Egyptians and out of the hand of Pharaoh, *and*
who has delivered the people from under the
hand of the Egyptians. 11 Now I know that the
LORD *is* [a]greater than all the gods; [b]for in the
very thing in which they behaved [c]proudly,
He was above them." 12 Then Jethro, Moses'
father-in-law, took[1] a burnt [a]offering and *other*
sacrifices *to offer* to God. And Aaron came
with all the elders of Israel [b]to eat bread with
Moses' father-in-law before God.

13 And so it was, on the next day, that Moses
[a]sat to judge the people; and the people stood
before Moses from morning until evening.
14 So when Moses' father-in-law saw all that
he did for the people, he said, "What *is* this
thing that you are doing for the people? Why
do you alone sit, and all the people stand
before you from morning until evening?"

15 And Moses said to his father-in-law, "Because [a]the people come to me to inquire of
God. 16 When they have [a]a difficulty, they
come to me, and I judge between one and
another; and I make known the statutes of
God and His laws."

17 So Moses' father-in-law said to him, "The
thing that you do *is* not good. 18 Both you and
these people who *are* with you will surely
wear yourselves out. For this thing *is* too
much for you; [a]you are not able to perform
it by yourself. 19 Listen now to my voice; I
will give you counsel, and God will be with
you: Stand [a]before God for the people, so
that you may [b]bring the difficulties to God.
20 And you shall [a]teach them the statutes and
the laws, and show them the way in which
they must walk and [b]the work they must
do. 21 Moreover you shall select from all the
people [a]able men, such as [b]fear God, [c]men of
truth, [d]hating covetousness; and place *such*
over them *to be* rulers of thousands, rulers
of hundreds, rulers of fifties, and rulers of
tens. 22 And let them judge the people at all

18:5 [a] Ex. 3:1, 12; 4:27; 24:13 **18:7** [a] Gen. 18:2 [b] Ex. 4:27 **18:8** [a] Ex. 15:6, 16 **18:9** [a] [Is. 63:7–14] **18:10** [a] Gen. 14:20 **18:11** [a] 2 Chr. 2:5 [b] Ex. 1:10, 16, 22; 5:2, 7 [c] Luke 1:51 **18:12** [a] Ex. 24:5 [b] Deut. 12:7 [1] Following Masoretic Text and Septuagint; Syriac, Targum, and Vulgate read *offered.* **18:13** [a] Matt. 23:2 **18:15** [a] Lev. 24:12 **18:16** [a] Ex. 24:14 **18:18** [a] Num. 11:14, 17 **18:19** [a] Ex. 4:16; 20:19 [b] Num. 9:8; 27:5 **18:20** [a] Deut. 5:1 [b] Deut. 1:18 **18:21** [a] Acts 6:3 [b] 2 Sam. 23:3 [c] Ezek. 18:8 [d] Deut. 16:19

HE IS GREATER

Blessed be the LORD, who has delivered you out of the hand of the Egyptians.

EXODUS 18:10

"Seeing is believing," as the old saying goes. I wonder what Jethro thought his daughter was getting into when she became Moses' wife and he returned to Egypt to confront Pharaoh, the mightiest king in the ancient Near East at that time. He may well have wondered if he would ever see Moses or his daughter again. When he did, I can only imagine how amazed he was when he heard what had happened.

When he learned how the gods of the Egyptians were defeated and how Pharaoh himself was humiliated, he confessed, "Now I know that the LORD is greater than all the gods" (v. 11). This is Jethro's first step toward salvation—and it is a big one! Eventually he will learn that the Lord is the only true God, and that all the rest are lifeless idols that can do nothing and provide nothing.

It works for us the same way. Until we confess God and Jesus, His only Son, we are adrift in a sea of idols. Apart from God, life has no purpose and therefore no meaning. Through Christ, we find our meaning, purpose, and ultimate peace.

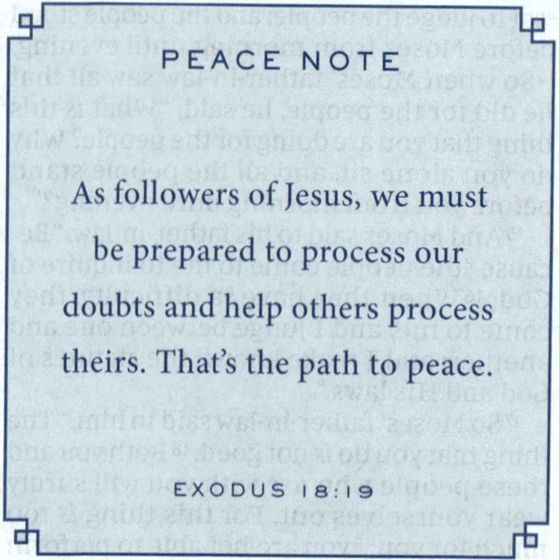

times. [a]Then it will be *that* every great matter they shall bring to you, but every small
matter they themselves shall judge. So it
will be easier for you, for [b]they will bear *the*
burden with you. 23 If you do this thing, and
God *so* commands you, then you will be able
to endure, and all this people will also go to
their [a]place in peace."
24 So Moses heeded the voice of his father-
in-law and did all that he had said. 25 And
[a]Moses chose able men out of all Israel, and
made them heads over the people: rulers
of thousands, rulers of hundreds, rulers of
fifties, and rulers of tens. 26 So they judged
the people at all times; the [a]hard cases they
brought to Moses, but they judged every
small case themselves.
27 Then Moses let his father-in-law depart,
and [a]he went his way to his own land.

Israel at Mount Sinai

19 In the third month after the children
of Israel had gone out of the land of
Egypt, on the same day, [a]they came *to* the
Wilderness of Sinai. 2 For they had departed
from [a]Rephidim, had come *to* the Wilderness
of Sinai, and camped in the wilderness. So
Israel camped there before [b]the mountain.
3 And [a]Moses went up to God, and the LORD
[b]called to him from the mountain, saying,
"Thus you shall say to the house of Jacob,
and tell the children of Israel: 4 [a]'You have
seen what I did to the Egyptians, and *how* [b]I
bore you on eagles' wings and brought you
to Myself. 5 Now [a]therefore, if you will indeed
obey My voice and [b]keep My covenant, then
[c]you shall be a special treasure to Me above
all people; for all the earth *is* [d]Mine. 6 And you
shall be to Me a [a]kingdom of priests and a
[b]holy nation.' These *are* the words which you
shall speak to the children of Israel."
7 So Moses came and called for the [a]elders
of the people, and laid before them all these
words which the LORD commanded him.
8 Then [a]all the people answered together
and said, "All that the LORD has spoken we
will do." So Moses brought back the words
of the people to the LORD. 9 And the LORD
said to Moses, "Behold, I come to you [a]in the
thick cloud, [b]that the people may hear when
I speak with you, and believe you forever."
So Moses told the words of the people to
the LORD.
10 Then the LORD said to Moses, "Go to
the people and [a]consecrate them today and
tomorrow, and let them wash their clothes.
11 And let them be ready for the third day. For
on the third day the LORD will come down
upon Mount Sinai in the sight of all the people. 12 You shall set bounds for the people all
around, saying, 'Take heed to yourselves *that*
you do *not* go up to the mountain or touch its
base. [a]Whoever touches the mountain shall
surely be put to death. 13 Not a hand shall
touch him, but he shall surely be stoned or
shot *with an arrow;* whether man or beast,
he shall not live.' When the trumpet sounds
long, they shall come near the mountain."
14 So Moses went down from the mountain
to the people and sanctified the people, and
they washed their clothes. 15 And he said to
the people, "Be ready for the third day; [a]do
not come near *your* wives."
16 Then it came to pass on the third day,
in the morning, that there were [a]thunder-
ings and lightnings, and a thick cloud on the
mountain; and the sound of the trumpet was
very loud, so that all the people who *were* in
the camp [b]trembled. 17 And [a]Moses brought
the people out of the camp to meet with
God, and they stood at the foot of the mountain. 18 Now [a]Mount Sinai *was* completely in
smoke, because the LORD descended upon [b]it
in fire. [c]Its smoke ascended like the smoke of
a furnace, and the [d]whole mountain[1] quaked
greatly. 19 And when the blast of the trumpet
sounded long and became louder and louder,
[a]Moses spoke, and [b]God answered him by
voice. 20 Then the LORD came down upon

18:22 [a] Deut. 1:17 [b] Num. 11:17 **18:23** [a] Ex. 16:29 **18:25** [a] Deut. 1:15 **18:26** [a] Job 29:16 **18:27** [a] Num. 10:29, 30 **19:1** [a] Num. 33:15 **19:2** [a] Ex. 17:1 [b] Ex. 3:1, 12; 18:5 **19:3** [a] Acts 7:38 [b] Ex. 3:4 **19:4** [a] Deut. 29:2 [b] Is. 63:9 **19:5** [a] Ex. 15:26; 23:22 [b] Deut. 5:2 [c] Ps. 135:4 [d] Ex. 9:29 **19:6** [a] [1 Pet. 2:5, 9] [b] Deut. 7:6; 14:21; 26:19 **19:7** [a] Ex. 4:29, 30 **19:8** [a] Deut. 5:27; 26:17 **19:9** [a] Ex. 19:16; 20:21; 24:15 [b] Deut. 4:12, 36 **19:10** [a] Lev. 11:44, 45 **19:12** [a] Heb. 12:20 **19:15** [a] [1 Cor. 7:5] **19:16** [a] Heb. 12:18, 19 [b] Heb. 12:21 **19:17** [a] Deut. 4:10 **19:18** [a] Deut. 4:11 [b] Ex. 3:2; 24:17 [c] Gen. 15:17; 19:28 [d] Ps. 68:8 [1] Septuagint reads *all the people.* **19:19** [a] Heb. 12:21 [b] Ps. 81:7

Mount Sinai, on the top of the mountain.
And the LORD called Moses to the top of the
mountain, and Moses went up.
21 And the LORD said to Moses, "Go down
and warn the people, lest they break through
[a]to gaze at the LORD, and many of them perish. 22 Also let the [a]priests who come near the
LORD [b]consecrate themselves, lest the LORD
[c]break out against them."
23 But Moses said to the LORD, "The people cannot come up to Mount Sinai; for You
warned us, saying, [a]'Set bounds around the
mountain and consecrate it.' "
24 Then the LORD said to him, "Away! Get
down and then come up, you and Aaron with
you. But do not let the priests and the people
break through to come up to the LORD, lest
He break out against them." 25 So Moses went
down to the people and spoke to them.

The Ten Commandments

20 And God spoke [a]all these words, saying:
2 [a]"I *am* the LORD your God, who brought
you out of the land of Egypt, [b]out of
the house of bondage.
3 [a]"You shall have no other gods before Me.
4 [a]"You shall not make for yourself a carved
image—any likeness *of anything* that *is*
in heaven above, or that *is* in the earth
beneath, or that *is* in the water under
the earth; 5 [a]you shall not bow down to
them nor serve them. [b]For I, the LORD
your God, *am* a jealous God, [c]visiting
the iniquity of the fathers upon the children to the third and fourth *generations*
of those who hate Me, 6 but [a]showing
mercy to thousands, to those who love
Me and keep My commandments.
7 [a]"You shall not take the name of the LORD
your God in vain, for the LORD [b]will not
hold *him* guiltless who takes His name
in vain.
8 [a]"Remember the Sabbath day, to keep it
holy. 9 [a]Six days you shall labor and do
all your work, 10 but the [a]seventh day *is*
the Sabbath of the LORD your God. *In*
it you shall do no work: you, nor your
son, nor your daughter, nor your male
servant, nor your female servant, nor
your cattle, [b]nor your stranger who *is*
within your gates. 11 For [a]*in* six days
the LORD made the heavens and the
earth, the sea, and all that *is* in them,
and rested the seventh day. Therefore
the LORD blessed the Sabbath day and
hallowed it.
12 [a]"Honor your father and your mother, that
your days may be [b]long upon the land
which the LORD your God is giving you.
13 [a]"You shall not murder.
14 [a]"You shall not commit [b]adultery.
15 [a]"You shall not steal.
16 [a]"You shall not bear false witness against
your neighbor.
17 [a]"You shall not covet your neighbor's
house; [b]you shall not covet your neighbor's wife, nor his male servant, nor
his female servant, nor his ox, nor
his donkey, nor anything that *is* your
neighbor's."

The People Afraid of God's Presence

18 Now [a]all the people [b]witnessed the thunderings, the lightning flashes, the sound of
the trumpet, and the mountain [c]smoking;
and when the people saw *it*, they trembled
and stood afar off. 19 Then they said to Moses,
[a]"You speak with us, and we will hear; but [b]let
not God speak with us, lest we die."
20 And Moses said to the people, [a]"Do not
fear; [b]for God has come to test you, and [c]that
His fear may be before you, so that you may
not sin." 21 So the people stood afar off, but
Moses drew near [a]the thick darkness where
God *was*.

The Law of the Altar

22 Then the LORD said to Moses, "Thus
you shall say to the children of Israel: 'You
have seen that I have talked with you [a]from
heaven. 23 You shall not make *anything to be*
[a]with Me—gods of silver or gods of gold you
shall not make for yourselves. 24 An altar of
[a]earth you shall make for Me, and you shall
sacrifice on it your burnt offerings and your
peace offerings, [b]your sheep and your oxen.
In every [c]place where I record My name I will
come to you, and I will [d]bless you. 25 And [a]if
you make Me an altar of stone, you shall not
build it of hewn stone; for if you [b]use your
tool on it, you have profaned it. 26 Nor shall
you go up by steps to My altar, that your
[a]nakedness may not be exposed on it.'

19:21 [a] 1 Sam. 6:19 **19:22** [a] Ex. 19:24; 24:5 [b] Lev. 10:3; 21:6–8 [c] 2 Sam. 6:7, 8 **19:23** [a] Ex. 19:12 **20:1** [a] Deut. 5:22 **20:2** [a] Hos. 13:4 [b] Ex. 13:3 **20:3** [a] Jer. 25:6; 35:15 **20:4** [a] Deut. 4:15–19; 27:15 **20:5** [a] Is. 44:15, 19 [b] Deut. 4:24 [c] Num. 14:18, 33 **20:6** [a] Deut. 7:9 **20:7** [a] Lev. 19:12 [b] Mic. 6:11 **20:8** [a] Lev. 26:2 **20:9** [a] Luke 13:14 **20:10** [a] Gen. 2:2, 3 [b] Neh. 13:16–19 **20:11** [a] Ex. 31:17 **20:12** [a] Lev. 19:3 [b] Deut. 5:16, 33; 6:2; 11:8, 9 **20:13** [a] Rom. 13:9 **20:14** [a] Matt. 5:27 [b] Deut. 5:18 **20:15** [a] Lev. 19:11, 13 **20:16** [a] Deut. 5:20 **20:17** [a] [Eph. 5:3, 5] [b] [Matt. 5:28] **20:18** [a] Heb. 12:18, 19 [b] Rev. 1:10, 12 [c] Ex. 19:16, 18 **20:19** [a] Heb. 12:19 [b] Deut. 5:5, 23–27 **20:20** [a] [Is. 41:10, 13] [b] [Deut. 13:3] [c] Is. 8:13 **20:21** [a] Ex. 19:16 **20:22** [a] Deut. 4:36; 5:24, 26 **20:23** [a] Ex. 32:1, 2, 4 **20:24** [a] Ex. 20:25; 27:1–8 [b] Ex. 24:5 [c] 2 Chr. 6:6 [d] Gen. 12:2 **20:25** [a] Deut. 27:5 [b] Josh. 8:30, 31 **20:26** [a] Ex. 28:42, 43

The Law Concerning Servants

21 "Now these *are* the judgments which you shall [a]set before them: 2 [a]If you buy a Hebrew servant, he shall serve six years; and in the seventh he shall go out free and pay nothing. 3 If he comes in by himself, he shall go out by himself; if he *comes in* married, then his wife shall go out with him. 4 If his master has given him a wife, and she has borne him sons or daughters, the wife and her children shall be her master's, and he shall go out by himself. 5 [a]But if the servant plainly says, 'I love my master, my wife, and my children; I will not go out free,' 6 then his master shall bring him to the [a]judges. He shall also bring him to the door, or to the doorpost, and his master shall pierce his ear with an awl; and he shall serve him forever.

7 "And if a man [a]sells his daughter to be a female slave, she shall not go out as the male slaves do. 8 If she does not please her master, who has betrothed her to himself, then he shall let her be redeemed. He shall have no right to sell her to a foreign people, since he has dealt deceitfully with her. 9 And if he has betrothed her to his son, he shall deal with her according to the custom of daughters. 10 If he takes another *wife,* he shall not diminish her food, her clothing, [a]and her marriage rights. 11 And if he does not do these three for her, then she shall go out free, without *paying* money.

The Law Concerning Violence

12 [a]"He who strikes a man so that he dies shall surely be put to death. 13 However, [a]if he did not lie in wait, but God [b]delivered *him* into his hand, then [c]I will appoint for you a place where he may flee.

14 "But if a man acts with [a]premeditation against his neighbor, to kill him by treachery, [b]you shall take him from My altar, that he may die.

15 "And he who strikes his father or his mother shall surely be put to death.

16 [a]"He who kidnaps a man and [b]sells him, or if he is [c]found in his hand, shall surely be put to death.

17 "And [a]he who curses his father or his mother shall surely be put to death.

18 "If men contend with each other, and one strikes the other with a stone or with *his* fist, and he does not die but is confined to *his* bed, 19 if he rises again and walks about outside [a]with his staff, then he who struck *him* shall be acquitted. He shall only pay *for* the loss of his time, and shall provide *for him* to be thoroughly healed.

20 "And if a man beats his male or female servant with a rod, so that he dies under his hand, he shall surely be punished. 21 Notwithstanding, if he remains alive a day or two, he shall not be punished; for he *is* his [a]property.

22 "If men fight, and hurt a woman with child, so that she gives birth prematurely, yet no harm follows, he shall surely be punished accordingly as the woman's husband imposes on him; and he shall [a]pay as the judges *determine.* 23 But if *any* harm follows, then you

21:1 [a] Deut. 4:14; 6:1 21:2 [a] Jer. 34:14 21:5 [a] Deut. 15:16, 17 21:6 [a] Ex. 12:12; 22:8, 9 21:7 [a] Neh. 5:5 21:10 [a] [1 Cor. 7:3, 5] 21:12 [a] [Matt. 26:52] 21:13 [a] Deut. 19:4, 5 [b] 1 Sam. 24:4, 10, 18 [c] Num. 35:11 21:14 [a] Deut. 19:11, 12 [b] 1 Kin. 2:28–34 21:16 [a] Deut. 24:7 [b] Gen. 37:28 [c] Ex. 22:4 21:17 [a] Mark 7:10 21:19 [a] 2 Sam. 3:29 21:21 [a] Lev. 25:44–46 21:22 [a] Ex. 18:21, 22; 21:30

DINNER WITH THE KING OF KINGS

"An altar of earth you shall make for Me, and you shall sacrifice on it your burnt offerings and your peace offerings."

EXODUS 20:24

Peace doesn't just happen; it is something we choose. To encourage His people to make this choice, God instituted the peace offering. In Hebrew the peace offering is *shelem*, which comes from the same root that gives us *shalom*, "peace." Interestingly, the Greek translation of the Hebrew text uses the word *soteria*, which literally means "things of salvation." God rightly recognized that, in these peace offerings, the people of Israel would maintain their relationship with Him, and they would enjoy His peace.

I love the idea of the peace offering. Simply described, it is a meal one shares with God as celebration and as thanks for being at peace with Him. In essence, God invites His people to have fellowship with Him, to have dinner with Him, and to appreciate all that He has done and will do. Peace and fellowship go hand in hand. Choose communion with the Lord, and know His peace.

shall give life for life, 24[a]eye for eye, tooth for
tooth, hand for hand, foot for foot, 25burn
for burn, wound for wound, stripe for stripe.
26"If a man strikes the eye of his male or
female servant, and destroys it, he shall let him
go free for the sake of his eye. 27And if he knocks
out the tooth of his male or female servant, he
shall let him go free for the sake of his tooth.

Animal Control Laws

28"If an ox gores a man or a woman to death,
then [a]the ox shall surely be stoned, and its
flesh shall not be eaten; but the owner of the
ox *shall be* acquitted. 29But if the ox tended
to thrust with its horn in times past, and it
has been made known to his owner, and he
has not kept it confined, so that it has killed a
man or a woman, the ox shall be stoned and
its owner also shall be put to death. 30If there
is imposed on him a sum of money, then he
shall pay [a]to redeem his life, whatever is imposed on him. 31Whether it has gored a son or
gored a daughter, according to this judgment
it shall be done to him. 32If the ox gores a
male or female servant, he shall give to their
master [a]thirty shekels of silver, and the [b]ox
shall be stoned.
33"And if a man opens a pit, or if a man
digs a pit and does not cover it, and an ox
or a donkey falls in it, 34the owner of the pit
shall make *it* good; he shall give money to
their owner, but the dead *animal* shall be his.
35"If one man's ox hurts another's, so that
it dies, then they shall sell the live ox and
divide the money from it; and the dead *ox*
they shall also divide. 36Or if it was known
that the ox tended to thrust in time past, and
its owner has not kept it confined, he shall
surely pay ox for ox, and the dead animal
shall be his own.

Responsibility for Property

22 "If a man steals an ox or a sheep, and
slaughters it or sells it, he shall [a]re-
store five oxen for an ox and four sheep for
a sheep. 2If the thief is found [a]breaking in,
and he is struck so that he dies, *there shall
be* [b]no guilt for his bloodshed. 3If the sun
has risen on him, *there shall be* guilt for his
bloodshed. He should make full restitution;
if he has nothing, then he shall be [a]sold for
his theft. 4If the theft is certainly [a]found alive
in his hand, whether it is an ox or donkey or
sheep, he shall [b]restore double.
5"If a man causes a field or vineyard to
be grazed, and lets loose his animal, and it
feeds in another man's field, he shall make
restitution from the best of his own field and
the best of his own vineyard.
6"If fire breaks out and catches in thorns,
so that stacked grain, standing grain, or the
field is consumed, he who kindled the fire
shall surely make restitution.
7"If a man [a]delivers to his neighbor money
or articles to keep, and it is stolen out of the
man's house, [b]if the thief is found, he shall
pay double. 8If the thief is not found, then
the master of the house shall be brought
to the [a]judges *to see* whether he has put his
hand into his neighbor's goods.
9"For any kind of trespass, *whether it concerns* an ox, a donkey, a sheep, or clothing,
or for any kind of lost thing which *another*
claims to be his, the [a]cause of both parties
shall come before the judges; *and* whomever
the judges condemn shall pay double to his
neighbor. 10If a man delivers to his neighbor
a donkey, an ox, a sheep, or any animal to
keep, and it dies, is hurt, or driven away, no
one seeing *it,* 11*then* an [a]oath of the LORD
shall be between them both, that he has not
put his hand into his neighbor's goods; and
the owner of it shall accept *that,* and he shall
not make *it* good. 12But [a]if, in fact, it is stolen
from him, he shall make restitution to the
owner of it. 13If it is [a]torn to pieces *by a beast,
then* he shall bring it as evidence, *and* he shall
not make good what was torn.
14"And if a man borrows *anything* from his
neighbor, and it becomes injured or dies, the
owner of it not *being* with it, he shall surely
make *it* good. 15If its owner *was* with it, he
shall not make *it* good; if it *was* hired, it came
for its hire.

Moral and Ceremonial Principles

16[a]"If a man entices a virgin who is not
betrothed, and lies with her, he shall surely
pay the bride-price for her *to be* his wife. 17If
her father utterly refuses to give her to him,
he shall pay money according to the [a]bride-
price of virgins.
18[a]"You shall not permit a sorceress to live.
19[a]"Whoever lies with an animal shall surely be put to death.
20[a]"He who sacrifices to *any* god, except to
the LORD only, he shall be utterly destroyed.
21[a]"You shall neither mistreat a stranger
nor oppress him, for you were strangers in
the land of Egypt.

21:24 [a] Lev. 24:20 **21:28** [a] Gen. 9:5 **21:30** [a] Num. 35:31 **21:32** [a] Zech. 11:12, 13 [b] Ex. 21:28 **22:1** [a] 2 Sam. 12:6 **22:2** [a] Matt. 6:19; 24:43 [b] Num. 35:27 **22:3** [a] Ex. 21:2 **22:4** [a] Ex. 21:16 [b] Prov. 6:31 **22:7** [a] Lev. 6:1–7 [b] Ex. 22:4 **22:8** [a] Ex. 21:6, 22; 22:28 **22:9** [a] Deut. 25:1 **22:11** [a] Heb. 6:16 **22:12** [a] Gen. 31:39 **22:13** [a] Gen. 31:39 **22:16** [a] Deut. 22:28, 29 **22:17** [a] Gen. 34:12 **22:18** [a] 1 Sam. 28:3–10 **22:19** [a] Lev. 18:23; 20:15, 16 **22:20** [a] Ex. 32:8; 34:15 **22:21** [a] Deut. 10:19

22[a]"You shall not afflict any widow or fatherless child. 23 If you afflict them in any way, *and* they [a]cry at all to Me, I will surely [b]hear their cry; 24 and My [a]wrath will become hot, and I will kill you with the sword; [b]your wives shall be widows, and your children fatherless.

25[a]"If you lend money to *any of* My people *who are* poor among you, you shall not be like a moneylender to him; you shall not charge him [b]interest. 26[a]If you ever take your neighbor's garment as a pledge, you shall return it to him before the sun goes down. 27 For that *is* his only covering, it *is* his garment for his skin. What will he sleep in? And it will be that when he cries to Me, I will hear, for I *am* [a]gracious.

28[a]"You shall not revile God, nor curse a [b]ruler of your people.

29"You shall not delay *to offer* [a]the first of your ripe produce and your juices. [b]The firstborn of your sons you shall give to Me. 30[a]Likewise you shall do with your oxen *and* your sheep. It shall be with its mother [b]seven days; on the eighth day you shall give it to Me.

31"And you shall be [a]holy men to Me: [b]you shall not eat meat torn *by beasts* in the field; you shall throw it to the dogs.

Justice for All

23 "You [a]shall not circulate a false report. Do not put your hand with the wicked to be an [b]unrighteous witness. 2[a]You shall not follow a crowd to do evil; [b]nor shall you testify in a dispute so as to turn aside after many to pervert *justice.* 3 You shall not show partiality to a [a]poor man in his dispute.

4[a]"If you meet your enemy's ox or his donkey going astray, you shall surely bring it back to him again. 5[a]If you see the donkey of one who hates you lying under its burden, and you would refrain from helping it, you shall surely help him with it.

6[a]"You shall not pervert the judgment of your poor in his dispute. 7[a]Keep yourself far from a false matter; [b]do not kill the innocent and righteous. For [c]I will not justify the wicked. 8 And [a]you shall take no bribe, for a bribe blinds the discerning and perverts the words of the righteous.

9"Also [a]you shall not oppress a stranger, for you know the heart of a stranger, because you were strangers in the land of Egypt.

The Law of Sabbaths

10[a]"Six years you shall sow your land and gather in its produce, 11 but the seventh *year* you shall let it rest and lie fallow, that the poor of your people may eat; and what they leave, the beasts of the field may eat. In like manner you shall do with your vineyard *and* your olive grove. 12[a]Six days you shall do your work, and on the seventh day you shall rest, that your ox and your donkey may rest, and the son of your female servant and the stranger may be refreshed.

13"And in all that I have said to you, [a]be circumspect and [b]make no mention of the name of other gods, nor let it be heard from your mouth.

Three Annual Feasts

14[a]"Three times you shall keep a feast to Me in the year: 15[a]You shall keep the Feast of Unleavened Bread (you shall eat unleavened bread seven days, as I commanded you, at the time appointed in the month of Abib, for in it you came out of Egypt; [b]none shall appear before Me empty); 16[a]and the Feast of Harvest, the firstfruits of your labors which you have sown in the field; and [b]the Feast of Ingathering at the end of the year, when you have gathered in *the fruit of* your labors from the field.

17[a]"Three times in the year all your males shall appear before the Lord GOD.[1]

18[a]"You shall not offer the blood of My sacrifice with leavened [b]bread; nor shall the fat of My sacrifice remain until morning. 19[a]The first of the firstfruits of your land you shall bring into the house of the LORD your God. [b]You shall not boil a young goat in its mother's milk.

The Angel and the Promises

20[a]"Behold, I send an Angel before you to keep you in the way and to bring you into the place which I have prepared. 21 Beware of Him and obey His voice; [a]do not provoke Him, for He will [b]not pardon your transgressions; for [c]My name *is* in Him. 22 But if you indeed obey His voice and do all that I speak, then [a]I will be an enemy to your enemies and an adversary to your adversaries. 23[a]For My Angel will go before you and [b]bring you in to the

22:22 [a] [James 1:27] **22:23** [a] [Luke 18:7] [b] Ps. 18:6 **22:24** [a] Ps. 69:24 [b] Ps. 109:9 **22:25** [a] Lev. 25:35–37 [b] Ps. 15:5 **22:26** [a] Deut. 24:6, 10–13 **22:27** [a] Ex. 34:6, 7 **22:28** [a] Eccl. 10:20 [b] Acts 23:5 **22:29** [a] Ex. 23:16, 19 [b] Ex. 13:2, 12, 15 **22:30** [a] Deut. 15:19 [b] Lev. 22:27 **22:31** [a] Lev. 11:44; 19:2 [b] Ezek. 4:14 **23:1** [a] Ps. 101:5 [b] Deut. 19:16–21 **23:2** [a] Gen. 7:1 [b] Lev. 19:15 **23:3** [a] Deut. 1:17; 16:19 **23:4** [a] [Rom. 12:20] **23:5** [a] Deut. 22:4 **23:6** [a] Eccl. 5:8 **23:7** [a] Eph. 4:25 [b] Matt. 27:4 [c] Rom. 1:18 **23:8** [a] Prov. 15:27; 17:8, 23 **23:9** [a] Ex. 22:21 **23:10** [a] Lev. 25:1–7 **23:12** [a] Luke 13:14 **23:13** [a] 1 Tim. 4:16 [b] Josh. 23:7 **23:14** [a] Ex. 23:17; 34:22–24 **23:15** [a] Ex. 12:14–20 [b] Ex. 22:29; 34:20 **23:16** [a] Ex. 34:22 [b] Deut. 16:13 **23:17** [a] Deut. 16:16 [1] Hebrew *YHWH,* usually translated *LORD* **23:18** [a] Ex. 34:25 [b] Deut. 16:4 **23:19** [a] Deut. 26:2, 10 [b] Deut. 14:21 **23:20** [a] Ex. 3:2; 13:15; 14:19 **23:21** [a] Ps. 78:40, 56 [b] Deut. 18:19 [c] Is. 9:6 **23:22** [a] Deut. 30:7 **23:23** [a] Ex. 23:20 [b] Josh. 24:8, 11

PEACE NOTE

The result of our obedience to God is always peace due to the protection of God. He truly is an adversary to our adversaries.

EXODUS 23:22

Amorites and the Hittites and the Perizzites
and the Canaanites and the Hivites and the
Jebusites; and I will cut them off. 24 You shall
not [a]bow down to their gods, nor serve them,
[b]nor do according to their works; [c]but you
shall utterly overthrow them and completely
break down their *sacred* pillars.
25 "So you shall [a]serve the LORD your God,
and [b]He will bless your bread and your water.
And [c]I will take sickness away from the midst
of you. 26 [a]No one shall suffer miscarriage
or be barren in your land; I will [b]fulfill the
number of your days.
27 "I will send [a]My fear before you, I will
[b]cause confusion among all the people to
whom you come, and will make all your enemies turn *their* backs to you. 28 And [a]I will
send hornets before you, which shall drive
out the Hivite, the Canaanite, and the Hittite
from before you. 29 [a]I will not drive them out
from before you in one year, lest the land
become desolate and the beasts of the field
become too numerous for you. 30 Little by
little I will drive them out from before you,
until you have increased, and you inherit the
land. 31 And [a]I will set your bounds from the
Red Sea to the sea, Philistia, and from
the desert to the River.[1] For I will [b]deliver
the inhabitants of the land into your hand,
and you shall drive them out before you.
32 [a]You shall make no covenant with them,
nor with their gods. 33 They shall not dwell
in your land, lest they make you sin against
Me. For *if* you serve their gods, [a]it will surely
be a snare to you."

Israel Affirms the Covenant

24 Now He said to Moses, "Come up to
the LORD, you and Aaron, [a]Nadab and
Abihu, [b]and seventy of the elders of Israel,
and worship from afar. 2 And Moses alone
shall come near the LORD, but they shall
not come near; nor shall the people go up
with him."
3 So Moses came and told the people all the
words of the LORD and all the judgments. And
all the people answered with one voice and
said, [a]"All the words which the LORD has said
we will do." 4 And Moses [a]wrote all the words
of the LORD. And he rose early in the morning,
and built an altar at the foot of the mountain,
and twelve [b]pillars according to the twelve
tribes of Israel. 5 Then he sent young men
of the children of Israel, who offered [a]burnt
offerings and sacrificed peace offerings of
oxen to the LORD. 6 And Moses [a]took half the
blood and put *it* in basins, and half the blood
he sprinkled on the altar. 7 Then he [a]took the
Book of the Covenant and read in the hearing
of the people. And they said, "All that the
LORD has said we will do, and be obedient."
8 And Moses took the blood, sprinkled *it* on
the people, and said, "This is [a]the blood of the
covenant which the LORD has made with you
according to all these words."

On the Mountain with God

9 Then Moses went up, also Aaron, Nadab,
and Abihu, and seventy of the elders of Israel,
10 and they [a]saw the God of Israel. And *there*
was under His feet as it were a paved work
of [b]sapphire stone, and it was like the [c]very
heavens in *its* clarity. 11 But on the nobles of
the children of Israel He [a]did not lay His hand.
So [b]they saw God, and they [c]ate and drank.
12 Then the LORD said to Moses, [a]"Come up
to Me on the mountain and be there; and I
will give you [b]tablets of stone, and the law
and commandments which I have written,
that you may teach them."
13 So Moses arose with [a]his assistant Joshua, and Moses went up to the mountain of
God. 14 And he said to the elders, "Wait here
for us until we come back to you. Indeed,
Aaron and [a]Hur *are* with you. If any man
has a difficulty, let him go to them." 15 Then
Moses went up into the mountain, and [a]a
cloud covered the mountain.
16 Now [a]the glory of the LORD rested on
Mount Sinai, and the cloud covered it six

23:24 [a] Ex. 20:5; 23:13, 33 [b] Deut. 12:30, 31 [c] Num. 33:52 **23:25** [a] Deut. 6:13 [b] Deut. 28:5 [c] Ex. 15:26 **23:26** [a] Deut. 7:14; 28:4 [b] 1 Chr. 23:1 **23:27** [a] Ex. 15:16 [b] Deut. 7:23 **23:28** [a] Josh. 24:12 **23:29** [a] Deut. 7:22 **23:31** [a] Gen. 15:18 [b] Josh. 21:44 [1] Hebrew *Nahar*, the Euphrates **23:32** [a] Ex. 34:12, 15 **23:33** [a] Ps. 106:36 **24:1** [a] Lev. 10:1, 2 [b] Num. 11:16 **24:3** [a] Ex. 19:8; 24:7 **24:4** [a] Deut. 31:9 [b] Gen. 28:18 **24:5** [a] Ex. 18:12; 20:24 **24:6** [a] Heb. 9:18 **24:7** [a] Heb. 9:19 **24:8** [a] [Luke 22:20] **24:10** [a] [John 1:18; 6:46] [b] Ezek. 1:26 [c] Matt. 17:2 **24:11** [a] Ex. 19:21 [b] Gen. 32:30 [c] 1 Cor. 10:18 **24:12** [a] Ex. 24:2, 15 [b] Ex. 31:18; 32:15 **24:13** [a] Ex. 32:17 **24:14** [a] Ex. 17:10, 12 **24:15** [a] Ex. 19:9 **24:16** [a] Ex. 16:10; 33:18

days. And on the seventh day He called to Moses out of the midst of the cloud. 17 The sight of the glory of the LORD *was* like [a]a consuming fire on the top of the mountain in the eyes of the children of Israel. 18 So Moses went into the midst of the cloud and went up into the mountain. And [a]Moses was on the mountain forty days and forty nights.

Offerings for the Sanctuary

25 Then the LORD spoke to Moses, saying: 2 "Speak to the children of Israel, that they bring Me an offering. [a]From everyone who gives it willingly with his heart you shall take My offering. 3 And this *is* the offering which you shall take from them: gold, silver, and bronze; 4 blue, purple, and scarlet *thread,* fine linen, and goats' *hair;* 5 ram skins dyed red, badger skins, and acacia wood; 6 [a]oil for the light, and [b]spices for the anointing oil and for the sweet incense; 7 onyx stones, and stones to be set in the [a]ephod and in the breastplate. 8 And let them make Me a [a]sanctuary, that [b]I may dwell among them. 9 According to all that I show you, *that is,* the pattern of the tabernacle and the pattern of all its furnishings, just so you shall make *it.*

The Ark of the Testimony

10 [a]"And they shall make an ark of acacia wood; two and a half cubits *shall be* its length, a cubit and a half its width, and a cubit and a half its height. 11 And you shall overlay it with pure gold, inside and out you shall overlay it, and shall make on it a molding of [a]gold all around. 12 You shall cast four rings of gold for it, and put *them* in its four corners; two rings *shall be* on one side, and two rings on the other side. 13 And you shall make poles *of* acacia wood, and overlay them with gold. 14 You shall put the poles into the rings on the sides of the ark, that the ark may be carried by them. 15 [a]The poles shall be in the rings of the ark; they shall not be taken from it. 16 And you shall put into the ark [a]the Testimony which I will give you.

17 [a]"You shall make a mercy seat of pure gold; two and a half cubits *shall be* its length and a cubit and a half its width. 18 And you shall make two cherubim of gold; of hammered work you shall make them at the two ends of the mercy seat. 19 Make one cherub at one end, and the other cherub at the other end; you shall make the cherubim at the two ends of it *of one piece* with the mercy seat. 20 And [a]the cherubim shall stretch out *their* wings above, covering the mercy seat with their wings, and they shall face one another; the faces of the cherubim *shall be* toward the mercy seat. 21 [a]You shall put the mercy seat on top of the ark, and [b]in the ark you shall put the Testimony that I will give you. 22 And [a]there I will meet with you, and I will speak with you from above the mercy seat, from [b]between the two cherubim which *are* on the ark of the Testimony, about everything which I will give you in commandment to the children of Israel.

The Table for the Showbread

23 [a]"You shall also make a table of acacia wood; two cubits *shall be* its length, a cubit its width, and a cubit and a half its height. 24 And you shall overlay it with pure gold, and make a molding of gold all around. 25 You shall make for it a frame of a handbreadth all around, and you shall make a gold molding for the frame all around. 26 And you shall make for it four rings of gold, and put the rings on the four corners that *are* at its four legs. 27 The rings shall be close to the frame, as holders for the poles to bear the table. 28 And you shall make the poles of acacia wood, and overlay them with gold, that the table may be carried with them. 29 You shall make [a]its dishes, its pans, its pitchers, and its bowls for pouring. You shall make them of pure gold. 30 And you shall set the [a]showbread on the table before Me always.

The Gold Lampstand

31 [a]"You shall also make a lampstand of pure gold; the lampstand shall be of hammered work. Its shaft, its branches, its bowls, its *ornamental* knobs, and flowers shall be *of one piece.* 32 And six branches shall come out of its sides: three branches of the lampstand out of one side, and three branches of the lampstand out of the other side. 33 [a]Three bowls *shall be* made like almond *blossoms* on one branch, *with* an *ornamental* knob and a flower, and three bowls made like almond *blossoms* on the other branch, *with* an *ornamental* knob and a flower—and so for the six branches that come out of the lampstand. 34 [a]On the lampstand itself four bowls *shall be* made like almond *blossoms, each with* its *ornamental* knob and flower. 35 And *there shall be* a knob under the *first* two branches of the same, a knob under the *second* two branches of the same, and a knob under the *third* two branches of the same, according to the six branches that extend from the lampstand. 36 Their knobs and their branches *shall be*

24:17 [a] Deut. 4:26, 36; 9:3 **24:18** [a] Ex. 34:28 **25:2** [a] Ex. 35:4–9, 21 **25:6** [a] Ex. 27:20 [b] Ex. 30:23 **25:7** [a] Ex. 28:4, 6–14 **25:8** [a] Heb. 9:1, 2 [b] [2 Cor. 6:16] **25:10** [a] Ex. 37:1–9 **25:11** [a] Ex. 37:2 **25:15** [a] 1 Kin. 8:8 **25:16** [a] Heb. 9:4 **25:17** [a] Ex. 37:6 **25:20** [a] 1 Kin. 8:7 **25:21** [a] Ex. 26:34; 40:20 [b] Ex. 25:16 **25:22** [a] Ex. 29:42, 43; 30:6, 36 [b] Num. 7:89 **25:23** [a] Ex. 37:10–16 **25:29** [a] Ex. 37:16 **25:30** [a] Lev. 24:5–9 **25:31** [a] Zech. 4:2 **25:33** [a] Ex. 37:19 **25:34** [a] Ex. 37:20–22

of one piece; all of it *shall be* one hammered piece of pure gold. 37 You shall make seven lamps for it, and [a]they shall arrange its lamps so that they [b]give light in front of it. 38 And its wick-trimmers and their trays *shall be* of pure gold. 39 It shall be made of a talent of pure gold, with all these utensils. 40 And [a]see to it that you make *them* according to the pattern which was shown you on the mountain.

The Tabernacle

26 "Moreover [a]you shall make the tabernacle *with* ten curtains *of* fine woven linen and blue, purple, and scarlet *thread;* with artistic designs of cherubim you shall weave them. 2 The length of each curtain *shall be* twenty-eight cubits, and the width of each curtain four cubits. And every one of the curtains shall have the same measurements. 3 Five curtains shall be coupled to one another, and *the other* five curtains *shall be* coupled to one another. 4 And you shall make loops of blue *yarn* on the edge of the curtain on the selvedge of *one* set, and likewise you shall do on the outer edge of *the other* curtain of the second set. 5 Fifty loops you shall make in the one curtain, and fifty loops you shall make on the edge of the curtain that *is* on the end of the second set, that the loops may be clasped to one another. 6 And you shall make fifty clasps of gold, and couple the curtains together with the clasps, so that it may be one tabernacle.

7 [a]"You shall also make curtains of goats' *hair,* to be a tent over the tabernacle. You shall make eleven curtains. 8 The length of each curtain *shall be* thirty cubits, and the width of each curtain four cubits; and the eleven curtains shall all have the same measurements. 9 And you shall couple five curtains by themselves and six curtains by themselves, and you shall double over the sixth curtain at the forefront of the tent. 10 You shall make fifty loops on the edge of the curtain that is outermost in *one* set, and fifty loops on the edge of the curtain of the second set. 11 And you shall make fifty bronze clasps, put the clasps into the loops, and couple the tent together, that it may be one. 12 The remnant that remains of the curtains of the tent, the half curtain that remains, shall hang over the back of the tabernacle. 13 And a cubit on one side and a cubit on the other side, of what remains of the length of the curtains of the tent, shall hang over the sides of the tabernacle, on this side and on that side, to cover it.

14 [a]"You shall also make a covering of ram skins dyed red for the tent, and a covering of badger skins above that.

PEACE NOTE

Paul relied on what was true of His life in Christ to be his only "highlight reel" and to live in the peace of God on the daily.

15 "And for the tabernacle you shall [a]make the boards of acacia wood, standing upright. 16 Ten cubits *shall be* the length of a board, and a cubit and a half *shall be* the width of each board. 17 Two tenons *shall be* in each board for binding one to another. Thus you shall make for all the boards of the tabernacle. 18 And you shall make the boards for the tabernacle, twenty boards for the south side. 19 You shall make forty sockets of silver under the twenty boards: two sockets under each of the boards for its two tenons. 20 And for the second side of the tabernacle, the north side, *there shall be* twenty boards 21 and their forty sockets of silver: two sockets under each of the boards. 22 For the far side of the tabernacle, westward, you shall make six boards. 23 And you shall also make two boards for the two back corners of the tabernacle. 24 They shall be coupled together at the bottom and they shall be coupled together at the top by one ring. Thus it shall be for both of them. They shall be for the two corners. 25 So there shall be eight boards with their sockets of silver—sixteen sockets—two sockets under each of the boards.

26 "And you shall make bars of acacia wood: five for the boards on one side of the tabernacle, 27 five bars for the boards on the other side of the tabernacle, and five bars for the boards of the side of the tabernacle, for the far side westward. 28 The [a]middle bar shall pass through the midst of the boards from end to end. 29 You shall overlay the boards with gold, make their rings of gold *as* holders for the bars, and overlay the bars with gold. 30 And you shall raise up the tabernacle [a]according to its pattern which you were shown on the mountain.

25:37 [a] Lev. 24:3, 4 [b] Num. 8:2 **25:40** [a] [Heb. 8:5] **26:1** [a] Ex. 36:8–19 **26:7** [a] Ex. 36:14 **26:14** [a] Ex. 35:7, 23; 36:19 **26:15** [a] Ex. 36:20–34 **26:28** [a] Ex. 36:33 **26:30** [a] Acts 7:44

31[a]"You shall make a veil woven of blue, purple, and scarlet *thread,* and fine woven linen.
It shall be woven with an artistic design of
cherubim. 32 You shall hang it upon the four
pillars of acacia *wood* overlaid with gold. Their
hooks *shall be* gold, upon four sockets of silver.
33 And you shall hang the veil from the clasps.
Then you shall bring [a]the ark of the Testimony
in there, behind the veil. The veil shall be a
divider for you between [b]the holy *place* and
the Most Holy. 34[a]You shall put the mercy seat
upon the ark of the Testimony in the Most Holy.
35[a]You shall set the table outside the veil, and
[b]the lampstand across from the table on the
side of the tabernacle toward the south; and
you shall put the table on the north side.

36[a]"You shall make a screen for the door
of the tabernacle, *woven of* blue, purple, and
scarlet *thread,* and fine woven linen, made by
a weaver. 37 And you shall make for the screen
[a]five pillars of acacia *wood,* and overlay them
with gold; their hooks *shall be* gold, and you
shall cast five sockets of bronze for them.

The Altar of Burnt Offering

27 "You shall make [a]an altar of acacia
wood, five cubits long and five cubits
wide—the altar shall be square—and its
height *shall be* three cubits. 2 You shall make
its horns on its four corners; its horns shall be
of one piece with it. And you shall overlay it
with bronze. 3 Also you shall make its pans to
receive its ashes, and its shovels and its basins
and its forks and its firepans; you shall make
all its utensils of bronze. 4 You shall make a
grate for it, a network of bronze; and on the
network you shall make four bronze rings at
its four corners. 5 You shall put it under the
rim of the altar beneath, that the network may
be midway up the altar. 6 And you shall make
poles for the altar, poles of acacia wood, and
overlay them with bronze. 7 The poles shall
be put in the rings, and the poles shall be on
the two sides of the altar to bear it. 8 You shall
make it hollow with boards; [a]as it was shown
you on the mountain, so shall they make *it.*

The Court of the Tabernacle

9[a]"You shall also make the court of the
tabernacle. For the south side *there shall be*
hangings for the court *made of* fine woven
linen, one hundred cubits long for one side.
10 And its twenty pillars and their twenty sockets *shall be* bronze. The hooks of the pillars and
their bands *shall be* silver. 11 Likewise along the
length of the north side *there shall be* hangings
one hundred *cubits* long, with its twenty pillars
and their twenty sockets of bronze, and the
hooks of the pillars and their bands of silver.

12"And along the width of the court on the
west side *shall be* hangings of fifty cubits, with
their ten pillars and their ten sockets. 13 The
width of the court on the east side *shall be* fifty
cubits. 14 The hangings on *one* side *of the gate*
shall be fifteen cubits, *with* their three pillars
and their three sockets. 15 And on the other
side *shall be* hangings of fifteen *cubits, with*
their three pillars and their three sockets.

16"For the gate of the court *there shall be* a
screen twenty cubits long, *woven of* blue, purple, and scarlet *thread,* and fine woven linen,
made by a weaver. It *shall have* four pillars
and four sockets. 17 All the pillars around the
court shall have bands of silver; their [a]hooks
shall be of silver and their sockets of bronze.
18 The length of the court *shall be* one hundred
cubits, the width fifty throughout, and the
height five cubits, *made of* fine woven linen,
and its sockets of bronze. 19 All the utensils of
the tabernacle for all its service, all its pegs,
and all the pegs of the court, *shall be* of bronze.

The Care of the Lampstand

20"And [a]you shall command the children of
Israel that they bring you pure oil of pressed
olives for the light, to cause the lamp to burn
continually. 21 In the tabernacle of meeting,
[a]outside the veil which *is* before the Testimony, [b]Aaron and his sons shall tend it from
evening until morning before the LORD. [c]*It*
shall be a statute forever to their generations
on behalf of the children of Israel.

Garments for the Priesthood

28 "Now take [a]Aaron your brother, and
his sons with him, from among the
children of Israel, that he may minister to Me
as [b]priest, Aaron *and* Aaron's sons: [c]Nadab,
Abihu, [d]Eleazar, and Ithamar. 2 And [a]you shall
make holy garments for Aaron your brother,
for glory and for beauty. 3 So [a]you shall speak to
all *who are* gifted artisans, [b]whom I have filled
with the spirit of wisdom, that they may make
Aaron's garments, to consecrate him, that he
may minister to Me as priest. 4 And these *are*
the garments which they shall make: [a]a breastplate, [b]an ephod,[1] [c]a robe, [d]a skillfully woven
tunic, a turban, and [e]a sash. So they shall make
holy garments for Aaron your brother and his
sons, that he may minister to Me as priest.

26:31 [a] Matt. 27:51 **26:33** [a] Ex. 25:10–16; 40:21 [b] Heb. 9:2, 3 **26:34** [a] Ex. 25:17–22; 40:20 **26:35** [a] Ex. 40:22 [b] Ex. 40:24 **26:36** [a] Ex. 36:37 **26:37** [a] Ex. 36:38 **27:1** [a] Ex. 38:1 **27:8** [a] Ex. 25:40; 26:30 **27:9** [a] Ex. 38:9–20 **27:17** [a] Ex. 38:19 **27:20** [a] Lev. 24:1–4 **27:21** [a] Ex. 26:31, 33 [b] Ex. 30:8 [c] Lev. 3:17; 16:34 **28:1** [a] Num. 3:10; 18:7 [b] Heb. 5:4 [c] Lev. 10:1 [d] Ex. 6:23 **28:2** [a] Ex. 29:5, 29; 31:10; 39:1–31 **28:3** [a] Ex. 31:6; 36:1 [b] Ex. 31:3; 35:30, 31 **28:4** [a] Ex. 28:15 [b] Ex. 28:6 [c] Ex. 28:31 [d] Ex. 28:39 [e] Lev. 8:7 [1] That is, an ornamented vest

The Ephod

5"They shall take the gold, blue, purple, and
scarlet *thread,* and the fine linen, 6[a]and they
shall make the ephod of gold, blue, purple, *and*
scarlet *thread,* and fine woven linen, artistically worked. 7It shall have two shoulder straps
joined at its two edges, and *so* it shall be joined
together. 8And the intricately woven band of
the ephod, which *is* on it, shall be of the same
workmanship, *made of* gold, blue, purple, and
scarlet *thread,* and fine woven linen.

9"Then you shall take two onyx [a]stones
and engrave on them the names of the sons
of Israel: 10six of their names on one stone
and six names on the other stone, in order of
their [a]birth. 11With the work of an [a]engraver in
stone, *like* the engravings of a signet, you shall
engrave the two stones with the names of the
sons of Israel. You shall set them in settings
of gold. 12And you shall put the two stones
on the shoulders of the ephod *as* memorial
stones for the sons of Israel. So [a]Aaron shall
bear their names before the LORD on his two
shoulders [b]as a memorial. 13You shall also
make settings of gold, 14and you shall make
two chains of pure gold like braided cords,
and fasten the braided chains to the settings.

The Breastplate

15[a]"You shall make the breastplate of judgment. Artistically woven according to the
workmanship of the ephod you shall make it:
of gold, blue, purple, and scarlet *thread,* and
fine woven linen, you shall make it. 16It shall
be doubled into a square: a span *shall be* its
length, and a span *shall be* its width. 17[a]And you
shall put settings of stones in it, four rows of
stones: *The first* row *shall be* a sardius, a topaz,
and an emerald; *this shall be* the first row; 18the
second row *shall be* a turquoise, a sapphire,
and a diamond; 19the third row, a jacinth, an
agate, and an amethyst; 20and the fourth row,
a beryl, an onyx, and a jasper. They shall be
set in gold settings. 21And the stones shall
have the names of the sons of Israel, twelve
according to their names, *like* the engravings
of a signet, each one with its own name; they
shall be according to the twelve tribes.

22"You shall make chains for the breastplate at the end, like braided cords of pure
gold. 23And you shall make two rings of gold
for the breastplate, and put the two rings on
the two ends of the breastplate. 24Then you
shall put the two braided *chains* of gold in
the two rings which are on the ends of the
breastplate; 25and the *other* two ends of the
two braided *chains* you shall fasten to the
two settings, and put them on the shoulder
straps of the ephod in the front.

26"You shall make two rings of gold, and
put them on the two ends of the breastplate,
on the edge of it, which is on the inner side of
the ephod. 27And two *other* rings of gold you
shall make, and put them on the two shoulder straps, underneath the ephod toward its
front, right at the seam above the intricately
woven band of the ephod. 28They shall bind
the breastplate by means of its rings to the
rings of the ephod, using a blue cord, so that
it is above the intricately woven band of the
ephod, and so that the breastplate does not
come loose from the ephod.

29"So Aaron shall [a]bear the names of the
sons of Israel on the breastplate of judgment
over his heart, when he goes into the holy
place, as a memorial before the LORD continually. 30And [a]you shall put in the breastplate
of judgment the Urim and the Thummim,[1]
and they shall be over Aaron's heart when
he goes in before the LORD. So Aaron shall
bear the judgment of the children of Israel
over his heart before the LORD continually.

Other Priestly Garments

31[a]"You shall make the robe of the ephod
all of blue. 32There shall be an opening for
his head in the middle of it; it shall have a
woven binding all around its opening, like
the opening in a coat of mail, so that it does
not tear. 33And upon its hem you shall make
pomegranates of blue, purple, and scarlet, all
around its hem, and bells of gold between
them all around: 34a golden bell and a pomegranate, a golden bell and a pomegranate,
upon the hem of the robe all around. 35And
it shall be upon Aaron when he ministers,
and its sound will be heard when he goes into
the holy *place* before the LORD and when he
comes out, that he may not die.

36[a]"You shall also make a plate of pure
gold and engrave on it, *like* the engraving
of a signet:

HOLINESS TO THE LORD.

37And you shall put it on a blue cord, that it may
be on the turban; it shall be on the front of the
turban. 38So it shall be on Aaron's forehead, that
Aaron may [a]bear the iniquity of the holy things
which the children of Israel hallow in all their
holy gifts; and it shall always be on his forehead,
that they may be [b]accepted before the LORD.

28:6 [a] Ex. 39:2–7 **28:9** [a] Ex. 35:27 **28:10** [a] Gen. 29:31—30:24; 35:16–18 **28:11** [a] Ex. 35:35 **28:12** [a] Ex. 28:29, 30; 39:6, 7 [b] Josh. 4:7 **28:15** [a] Ex. 39:8–21 **28:17** [a] Ex. 39:10 **28:29** [a] Ex. 28:12 **28:30** [a] Lev. 8:8 [1] Literally *the Lights and the Perfections* (compare Leviticus 8:8) **28:31** [a] Ex. 39:22–26 **28:36** [a] Ex. 39:30, 31 **28:38** [a] [1 Pet. 2:24] [b] Lev. 1:4; 22:27; 23:11

39“You shall [a]skillfully weave the tunic of fine linen *thread,* you shall make the turban of fine linen, and you shall make the sash of woven work.

40[a]“For Aaron’s sons you shall make tunics, and you shall make sashes for them. And you shall make hats for them, for glory and [b]beauty. 41So you shall put them on Aaron your brother and on his sons with him. You shall [a]anoint them, [b]consecrate them, and sanctify them, that they may minister to Me as priests. 42And you shall make [a]for them linen trousers to cover their nakedness; they shall reach from the waist to the thighs. 43They shall be on Aaron and on his sons when they come into the tabernacle of meeting, or when they come near [a]the altar to minister in the holy *place,* that they [b]do not incur iniquity and die. [c]*It shall be* a statute forever to him and his descendants after him.

Aaron and His Sons Consecrated

29 “And this is what you shall do to them to hallow them for ministering to Me as priests: [a]Take one young bull and two rams without blemish, 2and [a]unleavened bread, unleavened cakes mixed with oil, and unleavened wafers anointed with oil (you shall make them of wheat flour). 3You shall put them in one basket and bring them in the basket, with the bull and the two rams.

4“And Aaron and his sons you shall bring to the door of the tabernacle of meeting, [a]and you shall wash them with water. 5[a]Then you shall take the garments, put the tunic on Aaron, and the robe of the ephod, the ephod, and the breastplate, and gird him with [b]the intricately woven band of the ephod. 6[a]You shall put the turban on his head, and put the holy crown on the turban. 7And you shall take the anointing [a]oil, pour *it* on his head, and anoint him. 8Then [a]you shall bring his sons and put tunics on them. 9And you shall gird them with sashes, Aaron and his sons, and put the hats on them. [a]The priesthood shall be theirs for a perpetual statute. So you shall [b]consecrate Aaron and his sons.

10“You shall also have the bull brought before the tabernacle of meeting, and [a]Aaron and his sons shall put their hands on the head of the bull. 11Then you shall kill the bull before the LORD, *by* the door of the tabernacle of meeting. 12You shall take *some* of the blood of the bull and put *it* on [a]the horns of the altar with your finger, and [b]pour all the blood beside the base of the altar. 13And [a]you shall take all the fat that covers the entrails, the fatty lobe *attached* to the liver, and the two kidneys and the fat that *is* on them, and burn *them* on the altar. 14But [a]the flesh of the bull, with its skin and its offal, you shall burn with fire outside the camp. It *is* a sin offering.

15[a]“You shall also take one ram, and Aaron and his sons shall [b]put their hands on the head of the ram; 16and you shall kill the ram, and you shall take its blood and [a]sprinkle *it* all around on the altar. 17Then you shall cut the ram in pieces, wash its entrails and its legs, and put *them* with its pieces and with its head. 18And you shall burn the whole ram on the altar. It *is* a [a]burnt offering to the LORD; it *is* a sweet aroma, an offering made by fire to the LORD.

19[a]“You shall also take the other ram, and Aaron and his sons shall put their hands on the head of the ram. 20Then you shall kill the ram, and take some of its blood and put *it* on the tip of the right ear of Aaron and on the tip of the right ear of his sons, on the thumb of their right hand and on the big toe of their right foot, and sprinkle the blood all around on the altar. 21And you shall take some of the blood that is on the altar, and some of [a]the anointing oil, and sprinkle *it* on Aaron and on his garments, on his sons and on the garments of his sons with him; and [b]he and his garments shall be hallowed, and his sons and his sons’ garments with him.

22“Also you shall take the fat of the ram, the fat tail, the fat that covers the entrails, the fatty lobe *attached to* the liver, the two

PEACE NOTE

God built us to function in four areas: biological, psychological, social, and spiritual. If one area is out of alignment, we are not going to experience God’s peace.

28:39 [a] Ex. 35:35; 39:27–29 **28:40** [a] Ezek. 44:17, 18 [b] Ex. 28:2 **28:41** [a] Lev. 10:7 [b] Lev. 8 **28:42** [a] Ex. 39:28 **28:43** [a] Ex. 20:26 [b] Num. 9:13; 18:22 [c] Ex. 27:21 **29:1** [a] [Heb. 7:26–28] **29:2** [a] Lev. 2:4; 6:19–23 **29:4** [a] Ex. 40:12 **29:5** [a] Ex. 28:2 [b] Ex. 28:8 **29:6** [a] Lev. 8:9 **29:7** [a] Ex. 25:6; 30:25–31 **29:8** [a] Ex. 28:39, 40 **29:9** [a] Num. 3:10; 18:7; 25:13 [b] Ex. 28:41 **29:10** [a] Lev. 1:4; 8:14 **29:12** [a] Lev. 8:15 [b] Ex. 27:2; 30:2 **29:13** [a] Lev. 1:8; 3:3, 4 **29:14** [a] Lev. 4:11, 12, 21 **29:15** [a] Lev. 8:18 [b] Lev. 1:4–9 **29:16** [a] Ex. 24:6 **29:18** [a] Ex. 20:24 **29:19** [a] Lev. 8:22 **29:21** [a] Ex. 30:25, 31 [b] [Heb. 9:22]

kidneys and the fat on them, the right thigh
(for it *is* a ram of consecration), 23 [a]one loaf of
bread, one cake *made with* oil, and one wafer
from the basket of the unleavened bread
that *is* before the LORD; 24 and you shall put
all these in the hands of Aaron and in the
hands of his sons, and you shall [a]wave them
as a wave offering before the LORD. 25 [a]You
shall receive them back from their hands and
burn *them* on the altar as a burnt offering,
as a sweet aroma before the LORD. It *is* an
offering made by fire to the LORD.

26 "Then you shall take [a]the breast of the
ram of Aaron's consecration and wave it *as*
a wave offering before the LORD; and it shall
be your portion. 27 And from the ram of the
consecration you shall consecrate [a]the breast
of the wave offering which is waved, and the
thigh of the heave offering which is raised, of
that which *is* for Aaron and of *that* which is
for his sons. 28 It shall be from the children
of Israel *for* Aaron and his sons [a]by a statute
forever. For it is a heave offering; [b]it shall be
a heave offering from the children of Israel
from the sacrifices of their peace offerings,
that is, their heave offering to the LORD.

29 "And the [a]holy garments of Aaron [b]shall
be his sons' after him, [c]to be anointed in them
and to be consecrated in them. 30 [a]That son
who becomes priest in his place shall put them
on for [b]seven days, when he enters the tabernacle of meeting to minister in the holy *place.*

31 "And you shall take the ram of the consecration and [a]boil its flesh in the holy place.
32 Then Aaron and his sons shall eat the flesh
of the ram, and the [a]bread that *is* in the basket, *by* the door of the tabernacle of meeting.
33 [a]They shall eat those things with which the
atonement was made, to consecrate *and* to
sanctify them; [b]but an outsider shall not eat
them, because they *are* holy. 34 And if any of
the flesh of the consecration offerings, or of
the bread, remains until the morning, then
[a]you shall burn the remainder with fire. It
shall not be eaten, because it *is* holy.

35 "Thus you shall do to Aaron and his sons,
according to all that I have commanded you.
[a]Seven days you shall consecrate them. 36 And
you [a]shall offer a bull every day *as* a sin offering for atonement. [b]You shall cleanse the
altar when you make atonement for it, and
you shall anoint it to sanctify it. 37 Seven days
you shall make atonement for the altar and
sanctify it. And the altar shall be most holy.
[a]Whatever touches the altar must be holy.[1]

The Daily Offerings

38 "Now this *is* what you shall offer on the
altar: [a]two lambs of the first year, [b]day by
day continually. 39 One lamb you shall offer
[a]in the morning, and the other lamb you
shall offer at twilight. 40 With the one lamb
shall be one-tenth *of an ephah* of flour mixed
with one-fourth of a hin of pressed oil, and
one-fourth of a hin of wine *as* a drink offering. 41 And the other lamb you shall [a]offer
at twilight; and you shall offer with it the
grain offering and the drink offering, as in
the morning, for a sweet aroma, an offering
made by fire to the LORD. 42 *This shall be* [a]a
continual burnt offering throughout your
generations *at* the door of the tabernacle of
meeting before the LORD, [b]where I will meet
you to speak with you. 43 And there I will meet
with the children of Israel, and *the tabernacle*
[a]shall be sanctified by My glory. 44 So I will
consecrate the tabernacle of meeting and the
altar. I will also [a]consecrate both Aaron and
his sons to minister to Me as priests. 45 [a]I will
dwell among the children of Israel and will
[b]be their God. 46 And they shall know that [a]I
am the LORD their God, who [b]brought them
up out of the land of Egypt, that I may dwell
among them. I *am* the LORD their God.

The Altar of Incense

30 "You shall make [a]an altar to burn incense on; you shall make it of acacia
wood. 2 A cubit *shall be* its length and a cubit
its width—it shall be square—and two cubits
shall be its height. Its horns *shall be* of one
piece with it. 3 And you shall overlay its top, its
sides all around, and its horns with pure gold;
and you shall make for it a molding of gold all
around. 4 Two gold rings you shall make for
it, under the molding on both its sides. You
shall place *them* on its two sides, and they will
be holders for the poles with which to bear
it. 5 You shall make the poles of acacia wood,
and overlay them with gold. 6 And you shall
put it before the [a]veil that *is* before the ark of
the Testimony, before the [b]mercy seat that *is*
over the Testimony, where I will meet with you.

7 "Aaron shall burn on it [a]sweet incense every
morning; when [b]he tends the lamps, he shall
burn incense on it. 8 And when Aaron lights the

29:23 [a] Lev. 8:26 **29:24** [a] Lev. 7:30; 10:14 **29:25** [a] Lev. 8:28 **29:26** [a] Lev. 7:31, 34; 8:29 **29:27** [a] Num. 18:11, 18 **29:28** [a] Lev. 10:15 [b] Lev. 3:1; 7:34 **29:29** [a] Ex. 28:2 [b] Num. 20:26, 28 [c] Num. 18:8 **29:30** [a] Num. 20:28 [b] Lev. 8:35 **29:31** [a] Lev. 8:31 **29:32** [a] Matt. 12:4 **29:33** [a] Lev. 10:14, 15, 17 [b] Lev. 22:10 **29:34** [a] Lev. 7:18; 8:32 **29:35** [a] Lev. 8:33–35 **29:36** [a] Heb. 10:11 [b] Ex. 30:26–29; 40:10, 11 **29:37** [a] Num. 4:15; Hag. 2:11–13; Matt. 23:19 [1] Compare Numbers 4:15 and Haggai 2:11–13 **29:38** [a] Num. 28:3–31; 29:6–38 [b] Dan. 12:11 **29:39** [a] Ezek. 46:13–15 **29:41** [a] 2 Kin. 16:15 **29:42** [a] Ex. 30:8 [b] Ex. 25:22; 33:7, 9 **29:43** [a] 1 Kin. 8:11 **29:44** [a] Lev. 21:15 **29:45** [a] [Rev. 21:3] [b] Gen. 17:8 **29:46** [a] Ex. 16:12; 20:2 [b] Lev. 11:45 **30:1** [a] Ex. 37:25–29 **30:6** [a] Ex. 26:31–35 [b] Ex. 25:21, 22 **30:7** [a] 1 Sam. 2:28 [b] Ex. 27:20, 21

lamps at twilight, he shall burn incense on it, a perpetual incense before the LORD throughout your generations. 9 You shall not offer [a]strange incense on it, or a burnt offering, or a grain offering; nor shall you pour a drink offering on it. 10 And [a]Aaron shall make atonement upon its horns once a year with the blood of the sin offering of atonement; once a year he shall make atonement upon it throughout your generations. It *is* most holy to the LORD."

The Ransom Money

11 Then the LORD spoke to Moses, saying: 12 [a]"When you take the census of the children of Israel for their number, then every man shall give [b]a ransom for himself to the LORD, when you number them, that there may be no [c]plague among them when *you* number them. 13 [a]This is what everyone among those who are numbered shall give: half a shekel according to the shekel of the sanctuary [b](a shekel *is* twenty gerahs). [c]The half-shekel *shall be* an offering to the LORD. 14 Everyone included among those who are numbered, from twenty years old and above, shall give an offering to the LORD. 15 The [a]rich shall not give more and the poor shall not give less than half a shekel, when *you* give an offering to the LORD, to make atonement for yourselves. 16 And you shall take the atonement money of the children of Israel, and [a]shall appoint it for the service of the tabernacle of meeting, that it may be [b]a memorial for the children of Israel before the LORD, to make atonement for yourselves."

The Bronze Laver

17 Then the LORD spoke to Moses, saying: 18 [a]"You shall also make a laver of bronze, with its base also of bronze, for washing. You shall [b]put it between the tabernacle of meeting and the altar. And you shall put water in it, 19 for Aaron and his sons [a]shall wash their hands and their feet in water from it. 20 When they go into the tabernacle of meeting, or when they come near the altar to minister, to burn an offering made by fire to the LORD, they shall wash with water, lest they die. 21 So they shall wash their hands and their feet, lest they die. And [a]it shall be a statute forever to them—to him and his descendants throughout their generations."

The Holy Anointing Oil

22 Moreover the LORD spoke to Moses, saying: 23 "Also take for yourself [a]quality spices—five hundred *shekels* of liquid [b]myrrh, half as much sweet-smelling cinnamon (two hundred and fifty *shekels*), two hundred and fifty *shekels* of sweet-smelling [c]cane, 24 five hundred *shekels* of [a]cassia, according to the shekel of the sanctuary, and a [b]hin of olive oil. 25 And you shall make from these a holy anointing oil, an ointment compounded according to the art of the perfumer. It shall be [a]a holy anointing oil. 26 [a]With it you shall anoint the tabernacle of meeting and the ark of the Testimony; 27 the table and all its utensils, the lampstand and its utensils, and the altar of incense; 28 the altar of burnt offering with all its utensils, and the laver and its base. 29 You shall consecrate them, that they may be most holy; [a]whatever touches them must be holy.[1] 30 [a]And you shall anoint Aaron and his sons, and consecrate them, that *they* may minister to Me as priests.

31 "And you shall speak to the children of Israel, saying: 'This shall be a holy anointing oil to Me throughout your generations. 32 It shall not be poured on man's flesh; nor shall you make *any other* like it, according to its composition. [a]It *is* holy, *and* it shall be holy to you. 33 [a]Whoever compounds *any* like it, or whoever puts *any* of it on an outsider, [b]shall be cut off from his people.'"

The Incense

34 And the LORD said to Moses: [a]"Take sweet spices, stacte and onycha and galbanum, and pure frankincense with *these* sweet spices; there shall be equal amounts of each. 35 You shall make of these an incense, a compound [a]according to the art of the perfumer, salted, pure, *and* holy. 36 And you shall beat *some* of it very fine, and put some of it before the Testimony in the tabernacle of meeting [a]where I will meet with you. [b]It shall be most holy to you. 37 But *as for* the incense which you shall make, [a]you shall not make any for yourselves, according to its composition. It shall be to you holy for the LORD. 38 [a]Whoever makes *any* like it, to smell it, he shall be cut off from his people."

Artisans for Building the Tabernacle

31 Then the LORD spoke to Moses, saying: 2 [a]"See, I have called by name Bezalel the [b]son of Uri, the son of Hur, of the tribe of Judah. 3 And I have [a]filled him with the Spirit of God, in wisdom, in understanding,

30:9 [a] Lev. 10:1 **30:10** [a] Lev. 16:3–34 **30:12** [a] Num. 1:2; 26:2 [b] [1 Pet. 1:18, 19] [c] 2 Sam. 24:15 **30:13** [a] Matt. 17:24 [b] Num. 3:47 [c] Ex. 38:26 **30:15** [a] [Eph. 6:9] **30:16** [a] Ex. 38:25–31 [b] Num. 16:40 **30:18** [a] Ex. 38:8 [b] Ex. 40:30 **30:19** [a] Ex. 40:31, 32 **30:21** [a] Ex. 28:43 **30:23** [a] Ezek. 27:22 [b] Prov. 7:17 [c] Song 4:14 **30:24** [a] Ps. 45:8 [b] Ex. 29:40 **30:25** [a] Ex. 37:29; 40:9 **30:26** [a] Lev. 8:10 **30:29** [a] Ex. 29:37; Num. 4:15; Hag. 2:11–13 [1] Compare Numbers 4:15 and Haggai 2:11–13 **30:30** [a] Lev. 8:12 **30:32** [a] Ex. 30:25, 37 **30:33** [a] Ex. 30:38 [b] Gen. 17:14 **30:34** [a] Ex. 25:6; 37:29 **30:35** [a] Ex. 30:25 **30:36** [a] Ex. 29:42 [b] Lev. 2:3 **30:37** [a] Ex. 30:32 **30:38** [a] Ex. 30:33 **31:2** [a] Ex. 35:30—36:1 [b] 1 Chr. 2:20 **31:3** [a] 1 Kin. 7:14

in knowledge, and in all *manner of* workmanship, 4 to design artistic works, to work in gold, in silver, in bronze, 5 in cutting jewels for setting, in carving wood, and to work in all *manner of* workmanship.

6 "And I, indeed I, have appointed with him [a]Aholiab the son of Ahisamach, of the tribe of Dan; and I have put wisdom in the hearts of all the [b]gifted artisans, that they may make all that I have commanded you: 7 [a]the tabernacle of meeting, [b]the ark of the Testimony and [c]the mercy seat that *is* on it, and all the furniture of the tabernacle— 8 [a]the table and its utensils, [b]the pure *gold* lampstand with all its utensils, the altar of incense, 9 [a]the altar of burnt offering with all its utensils, and [b]the laver and its base— 10 [a]the garments of ministry,[1] the holy garments for Aaron the priest and the garments of his sons, to minister as priests, 11 [a]and the anointing oil and [b]sweet incense for the holy *place*. According to all that I have commanded you they shall do."

The Sabbath Law

12 And the LORD spoke to Moses, saying, 13 "Speak also to the children of Israel, saying: [a]'Surely My Sabbaths you shall keep, for it *is* a sign between Me and you throughout your generations, that *you* may know that I *am* the LORD who [b]sanctifies you. 14 [a]You shall keep the Sabbath, therefore, for *it is* holy to you. Everyone who profanes it shall surely be put to death; for [b]whoever does *any* work on it, that person shall be cut off from among his people. 15 Work shall be done for [a]six days, but the [b]seventh *is* the Sabbath of rest, holy to the LORD. Whoever does *any* work on the Sabbath day, he shall surely be put to death. 16 Therefore the children of Israel shall keep the Sabbath, to observe the Sabbath throughout their generations *as* a perpetual covenant. 17 It *is* [a]a sign between Me and the children of Israel forever; for [b]*in* six days the LORD made the heavens and the earth, and on the seventh day He rested and was refreshed.'"

18 And when He had made an end of speaking with him on Mount Sinai, He gave Moses [a]two tablets of the Testimony, tablets of stone, written with the finger of God.

PEACE NOTE

The Sabbath, or the Lord's Day, practiced by the believer each week, calibrates the body, soul, and mind with God's peace.

EXODUS 31:13

The Gold Calf

32 Now when the people saw that Moses [a]delayed coming down from the mountain, the people [b]gathered together to Aaron, and said to him, [c]"Come, make us gods that shall [d]go before us; for *as for* this Moses, the man who [e]brought us up out of the land of Egypt, we do not know what has become of him."

2 And Aaron said to them, "Break off the [a]golden earrings which *are* in the ears of your wives, your sons, and your daughters, and bring *them* to me." 3 So all the people broke off the golden earrings which *were* in their ears, and brought *them* to Aaron. 4 [a]And he received *the gold* from their hand, and he fashioned it with an engraving tool, and made a molded calf.

Then they said, "This *is* your god, O Israel, that [b]brought you out of the land of Egypt!"

5 So when Aaron saw *it*, he built an altar before it. And Aaron made a [a]proclamation and said, "Tomorrow *is* a feast to the LORD." 6 Then they rose early on the next day, offered burnt offerings, and brought peace offerings; and the people [a]sat down to eat and drink, and rose up to play.

7 And the LORD said to Moses, [a]"Go, get down! For your people whom you brought out of the land of Egypt [b]have corrupted *themselves*. 8 They have turned aside quickly out of the way which [a]I commanded them. They have made themselves a molded calf, and worshiped it and sacrificed to it, and said, [b]'This *is* your god, O Israel, that brought you out of the land of Egypt!' " 9 And the LORD said to Moses, [a]"I have seen this people, and indeed it *is* a stiff-necked people! 10 Now therefore, [a]let Me alone, that [b]My wrath may

31:6 [a] Ex. 35:34 [b] Ex. 28:3; 35:10, 35; 36:1 **31:7** [a] Ex. 36:8 [b] Ex. 37:1–5 [c] Ex. 37:6–9 **31:8** [a] Ex. 37:10–16 [b] Ex. 37:17–24 **31:9** [a] Ex. 38:1–7 [b] Ex. 38:8 **31:10** [a] Ex. 39:1, 41 [1] Or *woven garments* **31:11** [a] Ex. 30:23–33 [b] Ex. 30:34–38 **31:13** [a] Ezek. 20:12, 20 [b] Lev. 20:8 **31:14** [a] Ex. 20:8 [b] Num. 15:32–36 **31:15** [a] Ex. 20:9–11 [b] Gen. 2:2 **31:17** [a] Ex. 31:13 [b] Gen. 1:31; 2:2, 3 **31:18** [a] [Ex. 24:12; 32:15, 16] **32:1** [a] Ex. 24:18; Deut. 9:9–12 [b] Ex. 17:1–3 [c] Acts 7:40 [d] Ex. 13:21 [e] Ex. 32:8 **32:2** [a] Ex. 11:2; 35:22 **32:4** [a] Ex. 20:3, 4, 23 [b] Ex. 29:45, 46 **32:5** [a] 2 Kin. 10:20 **32:6** [a] Num. 25:2 **32:7** [a] Deut. 9:8–21 [b] Gen. 6:11, 12 **32:8** [a] Ex. 20:3, 4, 23 [b] 1 Kin. 12:28 **32:9** [a] [Acts 7:51] **32:10** [a] Deut. 9:14, 19 [b] Ex. 22:24

burn hot against them and I may consume
them. And [c]I will make of you a great nation."
11 [a]Then Moses pleaded with the LORD his
God, and said: "LORD, why does Your wrath
burn hot against Your people whom You have
brought out of the land of Egypt with great
power and with a mighty hand? 12 [a]Why should
the Egyptians speak, and say, 'He brought
them out to harm them, to kill them in the
mountains, and to consume them from the
face of the earth'? Turn from Your fierce wrath,
and [b]relent from this harm to Your people.
13 Remember Abraham, Isaac, and Israel, Your
servants, to whom You [a]swore by Your own
self, and said to them, [b]'I will multiply your
descendants as the stars of heaven; and all
this land that I have spoken of I give to your
descendants, and they shall inherit *it* forever.' "[1] 14 So the LORD [a]relented from the harm
which He said He would do to His people.
15 And [a]Moses turned and went down from
the mountain, and the two tablets of the
Testimony *were* in his hand. The tablets *were*
written on both sides; on the one *side* and on
the other they were written. 16 Now the [a]tab-
lets *were* the work of God, and the writing *was*
the writing of God engraved on the tablets.
17 And when Joshua heard the noise of the
people as they shouted, he said to Moses,
"*There is* a noise of war in the camp."
18 But he said:

"*It is* not the noise of the shout of
victory,
Nor the noise of the cry of defeat,
But the sound of singing I hear."

19 So it was, as soon as he came near the
camp, that [a]he saw the calf *and* the dancing.
So Moses' anger became hot, and he cast the
tablets out of his hands and broke them at
the foot of the mountain. 20 [a]Then he took
the calf which they had made, burned *it* in
the fire, and ground *it* to powder; and he
scattered *it* on the water and made the children of Israel drink *it*. 21 And Moses said to
Aaron, [a]"What did this people do to you that
you have brought *so* great a sin upon them?"
22 So Aaron said, "Do not let the anger of
my lord become hot. [a]You know the people,
that they *are set* on evil. 23 For they said to
me, 'Make us gods that shall go before us; *as
for* this Moses, the man who brought us out
of the land of Egypt, we do not know what
has become of him.' 24 And I said to them,
'Whoever has any gold, let them break *it* off.'
So they gave *it* to me, and I cast it into the
fire, and this calf came out."
25 Now when Moses saw that the people *were*
[a]unrestrained (for Aaron [b]had not restrained
them, to *their* shame among their enemies),
26 then Moses stood in the entrance of the
camp, and said, "Whoever *is* on the LORD's
side—*come* to me!" And all the sons of Levi
gathered themselves together to him. 27 And
he said to them, "Thus says the LORD God of Israel: 'Let every man put his sword on his side,
and go in and out from entrance to entrance
throughout the camp, and [a]let every man
kill his brother, every man his companion,
and every man his neighbor.' " 28 So the sons
of Levi did according to the word of Moses.
And about three thousand men of the people
fell that day. 29 [a]Then Moses said, "Consecrate
yourselves today to the LORD, that He may
bestow on you a blessing this day, for every
man has opposed his son and his brother."
30 Now it came to pass on the next day
that Moses said to the people, [a]"You have
committed a great sin. So now I will go up to
the LORD; [b]perhaps I can [c]make atonement
for your sin." 31 Then Moses [a]returned to the
LORD and said, "Oh, these people have committed a great sin, and have [b]made for themselves a god of gold! 32 Yet now, if You will
forgive their sin—but if not, I pray, [a]blot me
[b]out of Your book which You have written."
33 And the LORD said to Moses, [a]"Whoever
has sinned against Me, I will [b]blot him out
of My book. 34 Now therefore, go, lead the
people to *the place* of which I have [a]spoken
to you. [b]Behold, My Angel shall go before
you. Nevertheless, [c]in the day when I [d]visit
for punishment, I will visit punishment upon
them for their sin."
35 So the LORD plagued the people because
of [a]what they did with the calf which Aaron
made.

The Command to Leave Sinai

33 Then the LORD said to Moses, "Depart
and go up from here, you [a]and the
people whom you have brought out of the
land of Egypt, to the land of which I swore
to Abraham, Isaac, and Jacob, saying, [b]'To
your descendants I will give it.' 2 [a]And I will
send *My* Angel before you, [b]and I will drive
out the Canaanite and the Amorite and the

32:10 [c] Num. 14:12 **32:11** [a] Deut. 9:18, 26–29 **32:12** [a] Num. 14:13–19 [b] Ex. 32:14 **32:13** [a] [Heb. 6:13] [b] Gen. 12:7; 13:15; 15:7, 18; 22:17; 26:4; 35:11, 12 [1] Genesis 13:15 and 22:17 **32:14** [a] 2 Sam. 24:16 **32:15** [a] Deut. 9:15 **32:16** [a] Ex. 31:18 **32:19** [a] Deut. 9:16, 17 **32:20** [a] Deut. 9:21 **32:21** [a] Gen. 26:10 **32:22** [a] Deut. 9:24 **32:25** [a] Ex. 33:4, 5 [b] 2 Chr. 28:19 **32:27** [a] Num. 25:5–13 **32:29** [a] Ex. 28:41 **32:30** [a] 1 Sam. 12:20, 23 [b] 2 Sam. 16:12 [c] Num. 25:13 **32:31** [a] Deut. 9:18 [b] Ex. 20:23 **32:32** [a] Ps. 69:28 [b] Dan. 12:1 **32:33** [a] [Ezek. 18:4; 33:2, 14, 15] [b] Ex. 17:14 **32:34** [a] Ex. 3:17 [b] Ex. 23:20 [c] Deut. 32:35 [d] Ps. 89:32 **32:35** [a] Neh. 9:18 **33:1** [a] Ex. 32:1, 7, 13 [b] Gen. 12:7 **33:2** [a] Ex. 32:34 [b] Josh. 24:11

Hittite and the Perizzite and the Hivite and
the Jebusite. 3 *Go up* [a]to a land flowing with
milk and honey; for I will not go up in your
midst, lest [b]I consume you on the way, for
you *are* a [c]stiff-necked people."
4 And when the people heard this bad
news, [a]they mourned, [b]and no one put on
his ornaments. 5 For the LORD had said to
Moses, "Say to the children of Israel, 'You *are*
a stiff-necked people. I could come up into
your midst in one moment and consume
you. Now therefore, take off your ornaments,
that I may [a]know what to do to you.' " 6 So
the children of Israel stripped themselves
of their ornaments by Mount Horeb.

Moses Meets with the LORD

7 Moses took his tent and pitched it outside
the camp, far from the camp, and [a]called it the
tabernacle of meeting. And it came to pass *that*
everyone who [b]sought the LORD went out to
the tabernacle of meeting which *was* outside
the camp. 8 So it was, whenever Moses went out
to the tabernacle, *that* all the people rose, and
each man stood [a]*at* his tent door and watched
Moses until he had gone into the tabernacle.
9 And it came to pass, when Moses entered the
tabernacle, that the pillar of cloud descended
and stood *at* the door of the tabernacle, and *the*
LORD [a]talked with Moses. 10 All the people saw
the pillar of cloud standing *at* the tabernacle
door, and all the people rose and [a]worshiped,
each man *in* his tent door. 11 So [a]the LORD spoke
to Moses face to face, as a man speaks to his
friend. And he would return to the camp, but
[b]his servant Joshua the son of Nun, a young
man, did not depart from the tabernacle.

The Promise of God's Presence

12 Then Moses said to the LORD, "See, [a]You
say to me, 'Bring up this people.' But You have
not let me know whom You will send with me.
Yet You have said, [b]'I know you by name, and
you have also found grace in My sight.' 13 Now
therefore, I pray, [a]if I have found grace in Your
sight, [b]show me now Your way, that I may know
You and that I may find grace in Your sight.
And consider that this nation *is* [c]Your people."
14 And He said, [a]"My Presence will go *with*
you, and I will give you [b]rest."
15 Then he said to Him, [a]"If Your Presence
does not go *with us,* do not bring us up from
here. 16 For how then will it be known that
Your people and I have found grace in Your
sight, [a]except You go with us? So we [b]shall
be separate, Your people and I, from all the
people who *are* upon the face of the earth."
17 So the LORD said to Moses, [a]"I will also
do this thing that you have spoken; for you
have found grace in My sight, and I know
you by name."
18 And he said, "Please, show me [a]Your glory."
19 Then He said, "I will make all My [a]good-
ness pass before you, and I will proclaim
the name of the LORD before you. [b]I will be
gracious to whom I will be [c]gracious, and I
will have compassion on whom I will have
compassion." 20 But He said, "You cannot see
My face; for [a]no man shall see Me, and live."
21 And the LORD said, "Here is a place by Me,
and you shall stand on the rock. 22 So it shall
be, while My glory passes by, that I will put
you [a]in the cleft of the rock, and will [b]cover
you with My hand while I pass by. 23 Then I
will take away My hand, and you shall see My
back; but My face shall [a]not be seen."

Moses Makes New Tablets

34 And the LORD said to Moses, [a]"Cut two
tablets of stone like the first *ones,* and
[b]I will write on *these* tablets the words that
were on the first tablets which you broke.
2 So be ready in the morning, and come up
in the morning to Mount Sinai, and present
yourself to Me there [a]on the top of the mountain. 3 And no man shall [a]come up with you,
and let no man be seen throughout all the
mountain; let neither flocks nor herds feed
before that mountain."
4 So he cut two tablets of stone like the first
ones. Then Moses rose early in the morning
and went up Mount Sinai, as the LORD had
commanded him; and he took in his hand
the two tablets of stone.
5 Now the LORD descended in the [a]cloud
and stood with him there, and [b]proclaimed
the name of the LORD. 6 And the LORD passed
before him and proclaimed, "The LORD, the
LORD [a]God, merciful and gracious, longsuffering, and abounding in [b]goodness and
[c]truth, 7 [a]keeping mercy for thousands, [b]for-
giving iniquity and transgression and sin,
[c]by no means clearing *the guilty,* visiting the
iniquity of the fathers upon the children and
the children's children to the third and the
fourth generation."

33:3 [a] Ex. 3:8 [b] Num. 16:21, 45 [c] Ex. 32:9; 33:5 **33:4** [a] Num. 14:1, 39 [b] Ezra 9:3 **33:5** [a] [Ps. 139:23] **33:7** [a] Ex. 29:42, 43 [b] Deut. 4:29 **33:8** [a] Num. 16:27 **33:9** [a] Ps. 99:7 **33:10** [a] Ex. 4:31 **33:11** [a] Num. 12:8 [b] Ex. 24:13 **33:12** [a] Ex. 3:10; 32:34 [b] Ex. 33:17 **33:13** [a] Ex. 34:9 [b] Ps. 25:4; 27:11; 86:11; 119:33 [c] Deut. 9:26, 29 **33:14** [a] Is. 63:9 [b] Josh. 21:44; 22:4 **33:15** [a] Ex. 33:3 **33:16** [a] Num. 14:14 [b] Ex. 34:10 **33:17** [a] [James 5:16] **33:18** [a] [1 Tim. 6:16] **33:19** [a] Ex. 34:6, 7 [b] [Rom. 9:15, 16, 18] [c] [Rom. 4:4, 16] **33:20** [a] [Gen. 32:30] **33:22** [a] Is. 2:21 [b] Ps. 91:1, 4 **33:23** [a] [John 1:18] **34:1** [a] [Ex. 24:12; 31:18; 32:15, 16, 19] [b] Deut. 10:2, 4 **34:2** [a] Ex. 19:11, 18, 20 **34:3** [a] Ex. 19:12, 13; 24:9–11 **34:5** [a] Ex. 19:9 [b] Ex. 33:19 **34:6** [a] Neh. 9:17 [b] Rom. 2:4 [c] Ps. 108:4 **34:7** [a] Ex. 20:6 [b] Ps. 103:3, 4 [c] Job 10:14

8 So Moses made haste and [a]bowed his head toward the earth, and worshiped. 9 Then he said, "If now I have found grace in Your sight, O Lord, [a]let my Lord, I pray, go among us, even though we *are* a [b]stiff-necked people; and pardon our iniquity and our sin, and take us as [c]Your inheritance."

The Covenant Renewed

10 And He said: "Behold, [a]I make a covenant. Before all your people I will [b]do marvels such as have not been done in all the earth, nor in any nation; and all the people among whom you *are* shall see the work of the LORD. For it *is* [c]an awesome thing that I will do with you. 11 [a]Observe what I command you this day. Behold, [b]I am driving out from before you the Amorite and the Canaanite and the Hittite and the Perizzite and the Hivite and the Jebusite. 12 [a]Take heed to yourself, lest you make a covenant with the inhabitants of the land where you are going, lest it be a snare in your midst. 13 But you shall [a]destroy their altars, break their *sacred* pillars, and [b]cut down their wooden images 14 (for you shall worship [a]no other god, for the LORD, whose [b]name *is* Jealous, *is* a [c]jealous God), 15 lest you make a covenant with the inhabitants of the land, and they [a]play the harlot with their gods and make sacrifice to their gods, and *one of them* [b]invites you and you [c]eat of his sacrifice, 16 and you take of [a]his daughters for your sons, and his daughters [b]play the harlot with their gods and make your sons play the harlot with their gods.

17 [a]"You shall make no molded gods for yourselves.

18 "The Feast of [a]Unleavened Bread you shall keep. Seven days you shall eat unleavened bread, as I commanded you, in the appointed time of the month of Abib; for in the [b]month of Abib you came out from Egypt.

19 [a]"All that open the womb *are* Mine, and every male firstborn among your livestock, *whether* ox or sheep. 20 But [a]the firstborn of a donkey you shall redeem with a lamb. And if you will not redeem *him,* then you shall break his neck. All the firstborn of your sons you shall redeem.

"And none shall appear before Me [b]empty-handed.

21 [a]"Six days you shall work, but on the seventh day you shall rest; in plowing time and in harvest you shall rest.

22 "And you shall observe the Feast of Weeks, of the firstfruits of wheat harvest, and the Feast of Ingathering at the year's end. 23 [a]"Three times in the year all your men shall appear before the Lord, the LORD God of Israel. 24 For I will [a]cast out the nations before you and enlarge your borders; neither will any man covet your land when you go up to appear before the LORD your God three times in the year.

25 "You shall not offer the blood of My sacrifice with leaven, [a]nor shall the sacrifice of the Feast of the Passover be left until morning.

26 [a]"The first of the firstfruits of your land you shall bring to the house of the LORD your God. You shall not boil a young goat in its mother's milk."

27 Then the LORD said to Moses, "Write [a]these words, for according to the tenor of these words I have made a covenant with you and with Israel." 28 [a]So he was there with the LORD forty days and forty nights; he neither ate bread nor drank water. And [b]He wrote on the tablets the words of the covenant, the Ten Commandments.[1]

The Shining Face of Moses

29 Now it was so, when Moses came down from Mount Sinai (and the [a]two tablets of the Testimony *were* in Moses' hand when he came down from the mountain), that Moses did not know that [b]the skin of his face shone while he talked with Him. 30 So when Aaron and all the children of Israel saw Moses, behold, the skin of his face shone, and they were afraid to come near him. 31 Then Moses called to them, and Aaron and all the rulers of the congregation returned to him; and Moses talked with them. 32 Afterward all the children of Israel came near, [a]and he gave them as commandments all that the LORD had spoken with him on Mount Sinai. 33 And when Moses had finished speaking with them, he put [a]a veil on his face. 34 But [a]whenever Moses went in before the LORD to speak with Him, he would take the veil off until he came out; and he would come out and speak to the children of Israel whatever he had been commanded. 35 And whenever the children of Israel saw the face of Moses, that the skin of Moses' face shone, then Moses would put the veil on his face again, until he went in to speak with Him.

34:8 [a] Ex. 4:31 **34:9** [a] Ex. 33:12–16 [b] Ex. 33:3 [c] Ps. 33:12; 94:14 **34:10** [a] Deut. 5:2 [b] Ps. 77:14 [c] Ps. 145:6 **34:11** [a] Deut. 6:25 [b] Ex. 23:20–33; 33:2 **34:12** [a] Ex. 23:32, 33 **34:13** [a] Deut. 12:3 [b] 2 Kin. 18:4 **34:14** [a] [Ex. 20:3–5] [b] [Is. 9:6; 57:15] [c] [Deut. 4:24] **34:15** [a] Judg. 2:17 [b] Num. 25:1, 2 [c] 1 Cor. 8:4, 7, 10 **34:16** [a] Gen. 28:1 [b] Num. 25:1, 2 **34:17** [a] Ex. 20:4, 23; 32:8 **34:18** [a] Ex. 12:15, 16 [b] Ex. 12:2; 13:4 **34:19** [a] Ex. 13:2; 22:29 **34:20** [a] Ex. 13:13 [b] Ex. 22:29; 23:15 **34:21** [a] Ex. 20:9; 23:12; 31:15; 35:2 **34:23** [a] Ex. 23:14–17 **34:24** [a] [Ex. 33:2] **34:25** [a] Ex. 12:10 **34:26** [a] Ex. 23:19 **34:27** [a] Deut. 31:9 **34:28** [a] Ex. 24:18 [b] Ex. 34:1, 4 [1] Literally *Ten Words* **34:29** [a] Ex. 32:15 [b] 2 Cor. 3:7 **34:32** [a] Ex. 24:3 **34:33** [a] [2 Cor. 3:13, 14] **34:34** [a] [2 Cor. 3:13–16]

Sabbath Regulations

35 Then Moses gathered all the congregation of the children of Israel together,
and said to them, [a]"These *are* the words which
the LORD has commanded *you* to do: 2 Work
shall be done for [a]six days, but the seventh
day shall be a holy day for you, a Sabbath of
rest to the LORD. Whoever does any work on
it shall be put to [b]death. 3 [a]You shall kindle
no fire throughout your dwellings on the
Sabbath day."

Offerings for the Tabernacle

4 And Moses spoke to all the congregation
of the children of Israel, saying, [a]"This *is* the
thing which the LORD commanded, saying:
5 'Take from among you an offering to the
LORD. [a]Whoever *is* of a willing heart, let him
bring it as an offering to the LORD: [b]gold, silver,
and bronze; 6 [a]blue, purple, and scarlet *thread,*
fine linen, and [b]goats' *hair;* 7 ram skins dyed
red, badger skins, and acacia wood; 8 oil for the
light, [a]and spices for the anointing oil and for
the sweet incense; 9 onyx stones, and stones
to be set in the ephod and in the breastplate.

Articles of the Tabernacle

10 [a]'All *who are* gifted artisans among you
shall come and make all that the LORD has
commanded: 11 [a]the tabernacle, its tent, its
covering, its clasps, its boards, its bars, its pillars, and its sockets; 12 [a]the ark and its poles,
with the mercy seat, and the veil of the covering; 13 the [a]table and its poles, all its utensils,
[b]and the showbread; 14 also [a]the lampstand
for the light, its utensils, its lamps, and the
oil for the light; 15 [a]the incense altar, its poles,
[b]the anointing oil, [c]the sweet incense, and
the screen for the door at the entrance of the
tabernacle; 16 [a]the altar of burnt offering with
its bronze grating, its poles, all its utensils,
and the laver and its base; 17 [a]the hangings of
the court, its pillars, their sockets, and the
screen for the gate of the court; 18 the pegs
of the tabernacle, the pegs of the court, and
their cords; 19 [a]the garments of ministry,[1] for
ministering in the holy *place*—the holy garments for Aaron the priest and the garments
of his sons, to minister as priests.' "

The Tabernacle Offerings Presented

20 And all the congregation of the children of Israel departed from the presence of
Moses. 21 Then everyone came [a]whose heart
was stirred, and everyone whose spirit was
willing, *and* they [b]brought the LORD's offering
for the work of the tabernacle of meeting,
for all its service, and for the holy garments.
22 They came, both men and women, as many
as had a willing heart, *and* brought [a]earrings
and nose rings, rings and necklaces, all [b]jew-
elry of gold, that is, every man who *made* an
offering of gold to the LORD. 23 And [a]every
man, with whom was found blue, purple,
and scarlet *thread,* fine linen, and goats' *hair,*
red skins of rams, and badger skins, brought
them. 24 Everyone who offered an offering of
silver or bronze brought the LORD's offering.
And everyone with whom was found acacia
wood for any work of the service, brought *it.*
25 All the women *who were* [a]gifted artisans
spun yarn with their hands, and brought
what they had spun, of blue, purple, *and*
scarlet, and fine linen. 26 And all the women
whose hearts stirred with wisdom spun yarn
of goats' *hair.* 27 [a]The rulers brought onyx
stones, and the stones to be set in the ephod
and in the breastplate, 28 and [a]spices and oil
for the light, for the anointing oil, and for
the sweet incense. 29 The children of Israel
brought a [a]freewill offering to the LORD,
all the men and women whose hearts were
willing to bring *material* for all kinds of work
which the LORD, by the hand of Moses, had
commanded to be done.

The Artisans Called by God

30 And Moses said to the children of Israel,
"See, [a]the LORD has called by name Bezalel

> **PEACE NOTE**
>
> The peace of God rules our finances when we put the Lord first by honoring Him with our tithes and offerings.
>
> EXODUS 35:21

35:1 [a] Ex. 34:32 **35:2** [a] Lev. 23:3 [b] Num. 15:32–36 **35:3** [a] Ex. 12:16; 16:23 **35:4** [a] Ex. 25:1, 2 **35:5** [a] Ex. 25:2 [b] Ex. 38:24 **35:6** [a] Ex. 36:8 [b] Ex. 36:14 **35:8** [a] Ex. 25:6; 30:23–25 **35:10** [a] Ex. 31:2–6; 36:1, 2 **35:11** [a] Ex. 26:1, 2; 36:14 **35:12** [a] Ex. 25:10–22 **35:13** [a] Ex. 25:23 [b] Ex. 25:30 **35:14** [a] Ex. 25:31 **35:15** [a] Ex. 30:1 [b] Ex. 30:25 [c] Ex. 30:34–38 **35:16** [a] Ex. 27:1–8 **35:17** [a] Ex. 27:9–18 **35:19** [a] Ex. 31:10; 39:1, 41 [1] Or *woven garments* **35:21** [a] Ex. 25:2; 35:5, 22, 26, 29; 36:2 [b] Ex. 35:24 **35:22** [a] Ex. 32:2, 3 [b] Ex. 11:2 **35:23** [a] 1 Chr. 29:8 **35:25** [a] Ex. 28:3; 31:6; 36:1 **35:27** [a] Ezra 2:68 **35:28** [a] Ex. 30:23 **35:29** [a] 1 Chr. 29:9 **35:30** [a] Ex. 31:1–6

the son of Uri, the son of Hur, of the tribe of
Judah; 31 and He has filled him with the Spirit
of God, in wisdom and understanding, in
knowledge and all manner of workmanship,
32 to design artistic works, to work in gold
and silver and bronze, 33 in cutting jewels for
setting, in carving wood, and to work in all
manner of artistic workmanship.

34 "And He has put in his heart the ability to
teach, *in* him and [a]Aholiab the son of Ahisamach, of the tribe of Dan. 35 He has [a]filled
them with skill to do all manner of work
of the engraver and the designer and the
tapestry maker, in blue, purple, and scarlet
thread, and fine linen, and of the weaver—
those who do every work and those who
design artistic works.

36 "And Bezalel and Aholiab, and every
[a]gifted artisan in whom the LORD has
put wisdom and understanding, to know how
to do all manner of work for the service of
the [b]sanctuary, shall do according to all that
the LORD has commanded."

The People Give More than Enough

2 Then Moses called Bezalel and Aholiab,
and every gifted artisan in whose heart the
LORD had put wisdom, everyone [a]whose
heart was stirred, to come and do the work.
3 And they received from Moses all the [a]offer-
ing which the children of Israel [b]had brought
for the work of the service of making the
sanctuary. So they continued bringing to him
freewill offerings every morning. 4 Then all
the craftsmen who were doing all the work of
the sanctuary came, each from the work he
was doing, 5 and they spoke to Moses, saying,
[a]"The people bring much more than enough
for the service of the work which the LORD
commanded *us* to do."

6 So Moses gave a commandment, and they
caused it to be proclaimed throughout the
camp, saying, "Let neither man nor woman
do any more work for the offering of the
sanctuary." And the people were restrained
from bringing, 7 for the material they had
was sufficient for all the work to be done—
indeed too [a]much.

Building the Tabernacle

8 [a]Then all the gifted artisans among them
who worked on the tabernacle made ten
curtains woven of fine linen, and of blue,
purple, and scarlet *thread; with* artistic designs of cherubim they made them. 9 The
length of each curtain *was* twenty-eight
cubits, and the width of each curtain four
cubits; the curtains *were* all the same size.
10 And he coupled five curtains to one another, and *the other* five curtains he coupled to
one another. 11 He made loops of blue *yarn*
on the edge of the curtain on the selvedge
of one set; likewise he did on the outer edge
of *the other* curtain of the second set. 12 [a]Fifty
loops he made on one curtain, and fifty
loops he made on the edge of the curtain
on the end of the second set; the loops held
one *curtain* to another. 13 And he made fifty
clasps of gold, and coupled the curtains to
one another with the clasps, that it might
be one tabernacle.

14 [a]He made curtains of goats' *hair* for the
tent over the tabernacle; he made eleven
curtains. 15 The length of each curtain *was*
thirty cubits, and the width of each curtain
four cubits; the eleven curtains *were* the
same size. 16 He coupled five curtains by
themselves and six curtains by themselves.
17 And he made fifty loops on the edge of the
curtain that is outermost in one set, and fifty
loops he made on the edge of the curtain of
the second set. 18 He also made fifty bronze
clasps to couple the tent together, that it
might be one. 19 [a]Then he made a covering for
the tent of ram skins dyed red, and a covering
of badger skins above *that.*

20 For the tabernacle [a]he made boards of
acacia wood, standing upright. 21 The length
of each board *was* ten cubits, and the width
of each board a cubit and a half. 22 Each board
had two tenons [a]for binding one to another. Thus he made for all the boards of the
tabernacle. 23 And he made boards for the
tabernacle, twenty boards for the south side.
24 Forty sockets of silver he made to go under
the twenty boards: two sockets under each of
the boards for its two tenons. 25 And for the
other side of the tabernacle, the north side,
he made twenty boards 26 and their forty
sockets of silver: two sockets under each of
the boards. 27 For the west side of the tabernacle he made six boards. 28 He also made
two boards for the two back corners of the
tabernacle. 29 And they were coupled at the
bottom and coupled together at the top by
one ring. Thus he made both of them for the
two corners. 30 So there were eight boards and
their sockets—sixteen sockets of silver—two
sockets under each of the boards.

31 And he made [a]bars of acacia wood: five
for the boards on one side of the tabernacle, 32 five bars for the boards on the other
side of the tabernacle, and five bars for the
boards of the tabernacle on the far side

35:34 [a] Ex. 31:6 **35:35** [a] 1 Kin. 7:14 **36:1** [a] Ex. 28:3; 31:6; 35:10, 35 [b] Ex. 25:8 **36:2** [a] 1 Chr. 29:5, 9, 17 **36:3** [a] Ex. 35:5
[b] Ex. 35:27 **36:5** [a] [2 Cor. 8:2, 3] **36:7** [a] 1 Kin. 8:64 **36:8** [a] Ex. 26:1–14 **36:12** [a] Ex. 26:5 **36:14** [a] Ex. 26:7 **36:19** [a] Ex.
26:14 **36:20** [a] Ex. 26:15–29 **36:22** [a] Ex. 26:17 **36:31** [a] Ex. 26:26–29

westward. 33 And he made the middle bar
to pass through the boards from one end
to the other. 34 He overlaid the boards with
gold, made their rings of gold *to be* holders
for the bars, and overlaid the bars with gold.
35 And he made [a]a veil of blue, purple, and
scarlet *thread,* and fine woven linen; it was
worked *with* an artistic design of cherubim.
36 He made for it four pillars of acacia *wood,*
and overlaid them with gold, with their hooks
of gold; and he cast four sockets of silver
for them.
37 He also made a [a]screen for the tabernacle
door, of blue, purple, and scarlet *thread,* and
fine woven linen, made by a weaver, 38 and its
five pillars with their hooks. And he overlaid
their capitals and their rings with gold, but
their five sockets *were* bronze.

Making the Ark of the Testimony

37 Then [a]Bezalel made [b]the ark of acacia wood; two and a half cubits *was*
its length, a cubit and a half its width, and
a cubit and a half its height. 2 He overlaid
it with pure gold inside and outside, and
made a molding of gold all around it. 3 And
he cast for it four rings of gold *to be set* in
its four corners: two rings on one side, and
two rings on the other side of it. 4 He made
poles of acacia wood, and overlaid them with
gold. 5 And he put the poles into the rings at
the sides of the ark, to bear the ark. 6 He also
made the [a]mercy seat of pure gold; two and
a half cubits *was* its length and a cubit and
a half its width. 7 He made two cherubim of
beaten gold; he made them of one piece at
the two ends of the mercy seat: 8 one cherub
at one end on this side, and the other cherub
at the *other* end on that side. He made the
cherubim at the two ends *of one piece* with
the mercy seat. 9 The cherubim spread out
their wings above, *and* covered the [a]mercy
seat with their wings. They faced one another;
the faces of the cherubim were toward the
mercy seat.

Making the Table for the Showbread

10 He made [a]the table of acacia wood; two
cubits *was* its length, a cubit its width, and a
cubit and a half its height. 11 And he overlaid
it with pure gold, and made a molding of
gold all around it. 12 Also he made a frame
of a handbreadth all around it, and made a
molding of gold for the frame all around it.
13 And he cast for it four rings of gold, and put
the rings on the four corners that *were* at its
four legs. 14 The rings were close to the frame,
as holders for the poles to bear the table.

> PEACE NOTE
>
> It is costly to listen to anxious people without judging and to minister to their needs. We have to guide them to the truth of God and the presence of Jesus.

15 And he made the poles of acacia wood to
bear the table, and overlaid them with gold.
16 He made of pure gold the utensils which
were on the table: its [a]dishes, its cups, its
bowls, and its pitchers for pouring.

Making the Gold Lampstand

17 He also made the [a]lampstand of pure
gold; of hammered work he made the lampstand. Its shaft, its branches, its bowls, its
ornamental knobs, and its flowers were of
the same piece. 18 And six branches came out
of its sides: three branches of the lampstand
out of one side, and three branches of the
lampstand out of the other side. 19 There were
three bowls made like almond *blossoms* on
one branch, with an *ornamental* knob and a
flower, and three bowls made like almond
blossoms on the other branch, with an *ornamental* knob and a flower—and so for the
six branches coming out of the lampstand.
20 And on the lampstand itself *were* four
bowls made like almond *blossoms, each with*
its *ornamental* knob and flower. 21 *There was*
a knob under the *first* two branches of the
same, a knob under the *second* two branches
of the same, and a knob under the *third* two
branches of the same, according to the six
branches extending from it. 22 Their knobs
and their branches were of one piece; all of it
was one hammered piece of pure gold. 23 And
he made its seven lamps, its [a]wick-trimmers,
and its trays of pure gold. 24 Of a talent of pure
gold he made it, with all its utensils.

Making the Altar of Incense

25 [a]He made the incense altar of acacia
wood. Its length *was* a cubit and its width a
cubit—*it was* square—and two cubits *was*

36:35 [a] Ex. 26:31–37 36:37 [a] Ex. 26:36 37:1 [a] Ex. 35:30; 36:1 [b] Ex. 25:10–20 37:6 [a] Ex. 25:17 37:9 [a] Ex. 25:20
37:10 [a] Ex. 25:23–29 37:16 [a] Ex. 25:29 37:17 [a] Ex. 25:31–39 37:23 [a] Num. 4:9 37:25 [a] Ex. 30:1–5

its height. Its horns were *of one piece* with it. 26 And he overlaid it with pure gold: its top, its sides all around, and its horns. He also made for it a molding of gold all around it. 27 He made two rings of gold for it under its molding, by its two corners on both sides, as holders for the poles with which to bear it. 28 And he [a]made the poles of acacia wood, and overlaid them with gold.

Making the Anointing Oil and the Incense

29 He also made [a]the holy anointing oil and the pure incense of sweet spices, according to the work of the perfumer.

Making the Altar of Burnt Offering

38 He made [a]the altar of burnt offering of acacia wood; five cubits *was* its length and five cubits its width—*it was* square—and its height *was* three cubits. 2 He made its horns on its four corners; the horns were *of one piece* with it. And he overlaid it with bronze. 3 He made all the utensils for the altar: the pans, the shovels, the basins, the forks, and the firepans; all its utensils he made of bronze. 4 And he made a grate of bronze network for the altar, under its rim, midway from the bottom. 5 He cast four rings for the four corners of the bronze grating, *as* holders for the poles. 6 And he made the poles of acacia wood, and overlaid them with bronze. 7 Then he put the poles into the rings on the sides of the altar, with which to bear it. He made the altar hollow with boards.

Making the Bronze Laver

8 He made [a]the laver of bronze and its base of bronze, from the bronze mirrors of the serving women who assembled at the door of the tabernacle of meeting.

Making the Court of the Tabernacle

9 Then he made [a]the court on the south side; the hangings of the court *were of* fine woven linen, one hundred cubits long. 10 There *were* twenty pillars for them, with twenty bronze sockets. The hooks of the pillars and their bands *were* silver. 11 On the north side *the hangings were* one hundred cubits *long,* with twenty pillars and their twenty bronze sockets. The hooks of the pillars and their bands *were* silver. 12 And on the west side *there were* hangings of fifty cubits, with ten pillars and their ten sockets. The hooks of the pillars and their bands *were* silver. 13 For the east side *the hangings were* fifty cubits. 14 The hangings of one side *of the gate were* fifteen cubits *long, with* their three pillars and their three sockets, 15 and the same for the other side of the court gate; on this side and that *were* hangings of fifteen cubits, *with* their three pillars and their three sockets. 16 All the hangings of the court all around *were of* fine woven linen. 17 The sockets for the pillars *were* bronze, the hooks of the pillars and their bands *were* silver, and the overlay of their capitals *was* silver; and all the pillars of the court had bands of silver. 18 The screen for the gate of the court *was* woven of blue, purple, and scarlet *thread,* and of fine woven linen. The length *was* twenty cubits, and the height along its width *was* five cubits, corresponding to the hangings of the court. 19 And *there were* four pillars *with* their four sockets of bronze; their hooks *were* silver, and the overlay of their capitals and their bands *was* silver. 20 All the [a]pegs of the tabernacle, and of the court all around, *were* bronze.

Materials of the Tabernacle

21 This is the inventory of the tabernacle, [a]the tabernacle of the Testimony, which was counted according to the commandment of Moses, for the service of the Levites, [b]by the hand of [c]Ithamar, son of Aaron the priest.

22 [a]Bezalel the son of Uri, the son of Hur, of the tribe of Judah, made all that the LORD had commanded Moses. 23 And with him *was* [a]Aholiab the son of Ahisamach, of the tribe of Dan, an engraver and designer, a weaver of blue, purple, and scarlet *thread,* and of fine linen.

24 All the gold that was used in all the work of the holy *place,* that is, the gold of the [a]offering, was twenty-nine talents and seven hundred and thirty shekels, according to [b]the shekel of the sanctuary. 25 And the silver from those who were [a]numbered of the congregation *was* one hundred talents and one thousand seven hundred and seventy-five shekels, according to the shekel of the sanctuary: 26 [a]a bekah for each man (*that is,* half a shekel, according to the shekel of the sanctuary), for everyone included in the numbering from twenty years old and above, for [b]six hundred and three thousand, five hundred and fifty *men.* 27 And from the hundred talents of silver were cast [a]the sockets of the sanctuary and the bases of the veil: one hundred sockets from the hundred talents, one talent for each socket. 28 Then from the one thousand seven hundred and seventy-five *shekels* he made hooks for the pillars, overlaid their capitals, and [a]made bands for them.

37:28 [a] Ex. 30:5 37:29 [a] Ex. 30:23–25 38:1 [a] Ex. 27:1–8 38:8 [a] Ex. 30:18 38:9 [a] Ex. 27:9–19 38:20 [a] Ex. 27:19 38:21 [a] Acts 7:44 [b] Num. 4:28, 33 [c] Lev. 10:6, 16 38:22 [a] Ex. 31:2, 6 38:23 [a] Ex. 31:6; 36:1 38:24 [a] Ex. 35:5, 22 [b] Ex. 30:13, 24 38:25 [a] Ex. 30:11–16 38:26 [a] Ex. 30:13, 15 [b] Num. 1:46; 26:51 38:27 [a] Ex. 26:19, 21, 25, 32 38:28 [a] Ex. 27:17

29 The offering of bronze *was* seventy talents and two thousand four hundred shekels. 30 And with it he made the sockets for
the door of the tabernacle of meeting, the
bronze altar, the bronze grating for it, and
all the utensils for the altar, 31 the sockets for
the court all around, the bases for the court
gate, all the pegs for the tabernacle, and all
the pegs for the court all around.

Making the Garments of the Priesthood

39 Of the [a]blue, purple, and scarlet *thread*
they made [b]garments of ministry,[1] for
ministering in the holy *place,* and made the
holy garments for Aaron, [c]as the LORD had
commanded Moses.

Making the Ephod

2 [a]He made the [b]ephod of gold, blue, purple, and scarlet *thread,* and of fine woven
linen. 3 And they beat the gold into thin sheets
and cut *it into* threads, to work *it* in *with*
the blue, purple, and scarlet *thread,* and the
fine linen, *into* artistic designs. 4 They made
shoulder straps for it to couple *it* together; it
was coupled together at its two edges. 5 And
the intricately woven band of his ephod that
was on it *was* of the same workmanship, *woven of* gold, blue, purple, and scarlet *thread,*
and *of* fine woven linen, as the LORD had
commanded Moses.

6 [a]And they set onyx stones, enclosed in
settings of gold; they were engraved, as signets are engraved, with the names of the sons
of Israel. 7 He put them on the shoulders of
the ephod *as* [a]memorial stones for the sons of
Israel, as the LORD had commanded Moses.

Making the Breastplate

8 [a]And he made the breastplate, artistically
woven like the workmanship of the ephod, of
gold, blue, purple, and scarlet *thread,* and of
fine woven linen. 9 They made the breastplate
square by doubling it; a span *was* its length
and a span its width when doubled. 10 [a]And
they set in it four rows of stones: a row with
a sardius, a topaz, and an emerald was the
first row; 11 the second row, a turquoise, a
sapphire, and a diamond; 12 the third row,
a jacinth, an agate, and an amethyst; 13 the
fourth row, a beryl, an onyx, and a jasper.
They were enclosed in settings of gold in
their mountings. 14 *There were* [a]twelve stones
according to the names of the sons of Israel:
according to their names, *engraved like* a signet, each one with its own name according to
the twelve tribes. 15 And they made chains for
the breastplate at the ends, like braided cords
of pure gold. 16 They also made two settings
of gold and two gold rings, and put the two
rings on the two ends of the breastplate. 17 And
they put the two braided *chains* of gold in
the two rings on the ends of the breastplate.
18 The two ends of the two braided *chains* they
fastened in the two settings, and put them
on the shoulder straps of the ephod in the
front. 19 And they made two rings of gold and
put *them* on the two ends of the breastplate,
on the edge of it, which *was* on the inward
side of the ephod. 20 They made two *other*
gold rings and put them on the two shoulder straps, underneath the ephod toward its
front, right at the seam above the intricately
woven band of the ephod. 21 And they bound
the breastplate by means of its rings to the
rings of the ephod with a blue cord, so that
it would be above the intricately woven band
of the ephod, and that the breastplate would
not come loose from the ephod, as the LORD
had commanded Moses.

Making the Other Priestly Garments

22 [a]He made the [b]robe of the ephod of
woven work, all of blue. 23 And *there was* an
opening in the middle of the robe, like the
opening in a coat of mail, *with* a woven binding all around the opening, so that it would
not tear. 24 They made on the hem of the robe
pomegranates of blue, purple, and scarlet,
and of fine woven *linen.* 25 And they made
[a]bells of pure gold, and put the bells between
the pomegranates on the hem of the robe all
around between the pomegranates: 26 a bell
and a pomegranate, a bell and a pomegranate,
all around the hem of the robe to minister in,
as the LORD had commanded Moses.

27 [a]They made tunics, artistically woven
of fine linen, for Aaron and his sons, 28 [a]a
turban of fine linen, exquisite hats of fine
linen, [b]short trousers of fine woven linen,
29 [a]and a sash of fine woven linen with blue,
purple, and scarlet *thread,* made by a weaver,
as the LORD had commanded Moses.

30 [a]Then they made the plate of the holy
crown of pure gold, and wrote on it an inscription *like* the engraving of a signet:

[b]HOLINESS TO THE LORD.

31 And they tied to it a blue cord, to fasten *it*
above on the turban, as the LORD had commanded Moses.

39:1 [a] Ex. 25:4; 35:23 [b] Ex. 31:10; 35:19 [c] Ex. 28:4 [1] Or *woven garments* **39:2** [a] Ex. 28:6–14 [b] Lev. 8:7 **39:6** [a] Ex. 28:9–11 **39:7** [a] Ex. 28:12, 29 **39:8** [a] Ex. 28:15–30 **39:10** [a] Ex. 28:17 **39:14** [a] Rev. 21:12 **39:22** [a] Ex. 28:31–35 [b] Ex. 29:5 **39:25** [a] Ex. 28:33 **39:27** [a] Ex. 28:39, 40 **39:28** [a] Ex. 28:4, 39 [b] Ex. 28:42 **39:29** [a] Ex. 28:39 **39:30** [a] Ex. 28:36, 37 [b] Zech. 14:20

The Work Completed

32 Thus all the work of the tabernacle of
the tent of meeting was [a]finished. And the
children of Israel did [b]according to all that
the LORD had commanded Moses; so they
did. 33 And they brought the tabernacle to
Moses, the tent and all its furnishings: its
clasps, its boards, its bars, its pillars, and
its sockets; 34 the covering of ram skins
dyed red, the covering of badger skins, and
the veil of the covering; 35 the ark of the
Testimony with its poles, and the mercy
seat; 36 the table, all its utensils, and the
[a]showbread; 37 the pure *gold* lampstand
with its lamps (the lamps set in order), all
its utensils, and the oil for light; 38 the gold
altar, the anointing oil, and the sweet incense; the screen for the tabernacle door;
39 the bronze altar, its grate of bronze, its
poles, and all its utensils; the laver with
its base; 40 the hangings of the court, its
pillars and its sockets, the screen for the
court gate, its cords, and its pegs; all the
utensils for the service of the tabernacle,
for the tent of meeting; 41 and the garments
of ministry,[1] to minister in the holy *place:*
the holy garments for Aaron the priest, and
his sons' garments, to minister as priests.

42 According to all that the LORD had commanded Moses, so the children of Israel [a]did
all the work. 43 Then Moses looked over all
the work, and indeed they had done it; as
the LORD had commanded, just so they had
done it. And Moses [a]blessed them.

The Tabernacle Erected and Arranged

40 Then the LORD [a]spoke to Moses,
saying: 2 "On the first day of the [a]first
month you shall set up [b]the tabernacle of
the tent of meeting. 3 [a]You shall put in it the
ark of the Testimony, and partition off the
ark with the veil. 4 [a]You shall bring in the
table and [b]arrange the things that are to
be set in order on it; [c]and you shall bring
in the lampstand and light its lamps. 5 [a]You
shall also set the altar of gold for the incense
before the ark of the Testimony, and put up
the screen for the door of the tabernacle.
6 Then you shall set the [a]altar of the burnt
offering before the door of the tabernacle
of the tent of meeting. 7 And [a]you shall set
the laver between the tabernacle of meeting
and the altar, and put water in it. 8 You shall
set up the court all around, and hang up the
screen at the court gate.

9 "And you shall take the anointing oil, and
[a]anoint the tabernacle and all that *is* in it;
and you shall hallow it and all its utensils,
and it shall be holy. 10 You shall [a]anoint the
altar of the burnt offering and all its utensils,
and consecrate the altar. [b]The altar shall be
most holy. 11 And you shall anoint the laver
and its base, and consecrate it.

12 [a]"Then you shall bring Aaron and his
sons to the door of the tabernacle of meeting
and wash them with water. 13 You shall put the
holy [a]garments on Aaron, [b]and anoint him
and consecrate him, that he may minister
to Me as priest. 14 And you shall bring his

39:32 [a] Ex. 40:17 [b] Ex. 25:40; 39:42, 43 **39:36** [a] Ex. 23—30 **39:41** [1] Or *woven garments* **39:42** [a] Ex. 35:10 **39:43** [a] Lev. 9:22, 23 **40:1** [a] Ex. 25:1—31:18 **40:2** [a] Ex. 12:2; 13:4 [b] Ex. 26:1, 30; 40:17 **40:3** [a] Num. 4:5 **40:4** [a] Ex. 26:35; 40:22 [b] Ex. 25:30; 40:23 [c] Ex. 40:24, 25 **40:5** [a] Ex. 40:26 **40:6** [a] Ex. 39:39 **40:7** [a] Ex. 30:18; 40:30 **40:9** [a] Ex. 30:26 **40:10** [a] Ex. 30:26–30 [b] Ex. 29:36, 37 **40:12** [a] Lev. 8:1–13 **40:13** [a] Ex. 29:5; 39:1, 41 [b] [Ex. 28:41]

GOD'S GLORIOUS PEACE

The glory of the LORD filled the tabernacle.

EXODUS 40:34

Constructing the tabernacle of meeting exactly as God directed, the people erected the tent and saw "the glory of the LORD" filling it. In filling it with His glory, God brought the throne room of heaven into our world and, along with it, His goodness and peace. This was a major step toward redeeming Adam's sin and ending humanity's estrangement from God. It is this estrangement that broke the peace between us and God, something God has been actively restoring since. In the tabernacle (and later the grand temple that Solomon would build), God would ramp up His peace mission of reconciling sinful humanity to Himself.

In the Person and presence of Jesus, we have the new Temple. Heaven and earth came together in Christ to each of us. You don't have to go to Jerusalem or a tabernacle to find the peace of God today because the full peace of God is found in Jesus. And He is available to you right now, wherever you are.

THE THIRD BOOK OF MOSES CALLED

LEVITICUS

AUTHOR

Moses is declared to be the author of Leviticus fifty-six times within the book. External evidence supporting the authorship of Moses includes (1) a uniform ancient testimony, (2) parallels found in the Ras Shamra Tablets dating from 1400 BC, and (3) the testimony of Christ (cf. Matt. 8:2–4 and Lev. 14:1–4; cf. Matt. 12:4 and Lev. 24:9; Luke 2:22).

TIME

c. 1405 BC

KEY VERSE

Leviticus 20:7–8

THEME

Leviticus is God's guidebook for His newly redeemed people. It shows them how to worship and live holy lives. The instructions for the sacrificial system point to a holy God and what He requires from people who would serve Him. The laws of holiness and sanctification provide basic instructions for living in a community. Together the two groups of laws are a framework for relationship between God and humanity. Blessings result from obedience to these laws, and discipline is the result of disobedience.

Peace (or more specifically *shalom*) appears more in Leviticus than any other book in the Torah (i.e., The Book of the Law or Pentateuch). The God of the Bible is regularly identified as *Yahweh* as though it were a proper name. In the Greek, this name is regularly translated as *kyrios*, which means "lord." In fact, because *Yahweh* is so sacred, devout Jews are reluctant to speak it and the Hebrew word *adonai*, which also means "lord," is often used in its place. But the important thing to remember is that the God of the Bible, the God of the patriarchs Abraham, Isaac, and Jacob, has a name unlike those of the other gods of great antiquity. He is simply the "one who is," the ground of all being, the Creator and Sustainer of all life and the Giver of all peace.

sons and clothe them with tunics. 15 You shall
anoint them, as you anointed their father,
that they may minister to Me as priests; for
their anointing shall surely be [a]an everlasting
priesthood throughout their generations."
16 Thus Moses did; according to all that
the LORD had commanded him, so he did.
17 And it came to pass in the first month of
the second year, on the first *day* of the month,
that the [a]tabernacle was raised up. 18 So Moses
raised up the tabernacle, fastened its sockets,
set up its boards, put in its bars, and raised up
its pillars. 19 And he spread out the tent over
the tabernacle and put the covering of the
tent on top of it, as the LORD had commanded
Moses. 20 He took [a]the Testimony and put *it*
into the ark, inserted the poles through the
rings of the ark, and put the mercy seat on top
of the ark. 21 And he brought the ark into the
tabernacle, [a]hung up the veil of the covering,
and partitioned off the ark of the Testimony,
as the LORD had commanded Moses.
22 [a]He put the table in the tabernacle of
meeting, on the north side of the tabernacle,
outside the veil; 23 [a]and he set the bread in order upon it before the LORD, as the LORD had
commanded Moses. 24 [a]He put the lampstand
in the tabernacle of meeting, across from the
table, on the south side of the tabernacle;
25 and [a]he lit the lamps before the LORD, as
the LORD had commanded Moses. 26 [a]He put
the gold altar in the tabernacle of meeting
in front of the veil; 27 [a]and he burned sweet
incense on it, as the LORD had commanded
Moses. 28 [a]He hung up the screen *at* the door
of the tabernacle. 29 [a]And he put the altar of
burnt offering *before* the door of the tabernacle of the tent of meeting, and [b]offered
upon it the burnt offering and the grain offering, as the LORD had commanded Moses.
30 [a]He set the laver between the tabernacle of
meeting and the altar, and put water there for
washing; 31 and Moses, Aaron, and his sons
would [a]wash their hands and their feet *with
water* from it. 32 Whenever they went into the
tabernacle of meeting, and when they came
near the altar, they washed, [a]as the LORD had
commanded Moses. 33 [a]And he raised up the
court all around the tabernacle and the altar,
and hung up the screen of the court gate. So
Moses [b]finished the work.

The Cloud and the Glory

34 [a]Then the [b]cloud covered the tabernacle
of meeting, and the [c]glory of the LORD filled
the tabernacle. 35 And Moses [a]was not able
to enter the tabernacle of meeting, because
the cloud rested above it, and the glory of the
LORD filled the tabernacle. 36 [a]Whenever the
cloud was taken up from above the tabernacle, the children of Israel would go onward
in all their journeys. 37 But [a]if the cloud was
not taken up, then they did not journey till
the day that it was taken up. 38 For [a]the cloud
of the LORD *was* above the tabernacle by day,
and fire was over it by night, in the sight of
all the house of Israel, throughout all their
journeys.

40:15 [a] Num. 25:13 **40:17** [a] Ex. 40:2 **40:20** [a] Ex. 25:16 **40:21** [a] Ex. 26:33 **40:22** [a] Ex. 26:35 **40:23** [a] Ex. 40:4 **40:24** [a] Ex. 26:35 **40:25** [a] Ex. 25:37; 30:7, 8; 40:4 **40:26** [a] Ex. 30:1, 6; 40:5 **40:27** [a] Ex. 30:7 **40:28** [a] Ex. 26:36; 40:5 **40:29** [a] Ex. 40:6 [b] Ex. 29:38–42 **40:30** [a] Ex. 30:18; 40:7 **40:31** [a] Ex. 30:19, 20 **40:32** [a] Ex. 30:19 **40:33** [a] Ex. 27:9–18; 40:8 [b] [Heb. 3:2–5] **40:34** [a] Num. 9:15 [b] 1 Kin. 8:10, 11 [c] Lev. 9:6, 23 **40:35** [a] 1 Kin. 8:11 **40:36** [a] Num. 9:17 **40:37** [a] Num. 9:19–22 **40:38** [a] Ex. 13:21

The Burnt Offering

1 Now the LORD [a]called to Moses, and spoke
to him [b]from the tabernacle of meeting,
saying, 2"Speak to the children of Israel, and
say to them: [a]'When any one of you brings
an offering to the LORD, you shall bring your
offering of the livestock—of the herd and of
the flock.
3'If his offering *is* a burnt sacrifice of the
herd, let him offer a male [a]without blemish;
he shall offer it of his own free will at the door
of the tabernacle of meeting before the LORD.
4[a]Then he shall put his hand on the head of
the burnt offering, and it will be [b]accepted on
his behalf [c]to make atonement for him. 5He
shall kill the [a]bull before the LORD; [b]and the
priests, Aaron's sons, shall bring the blood [c]and
sprinkle the blood all around on the altar that
is by the door of the tabernacle of meeting.
6And he shall [a]skin the burnt offering and cut
it into its pieces. 7The sons of Aaron the priest
shall put [a]fire on the altar, and [b]lay the wood
in order on the fire. 8Then the priests, Aaron's
sons, shall lay the parts, the head, and the fat
in order on the wood that *is* on the fire upon
the altar; 9but he shall wash its entrails and its
legs with water. And the priest shall burn all on
the altar as a burnt sacrifice, an offering made
by fire, a [a]sweet aroma to the LORD.
10'If his offering *is* of the flocks—of the
sheep or of the goats—as a burnt sacrifice,
he shall bring a male [a]without blemish. 11[a]He
shall kill it on the north side of the altar before the LORD; and the priests, Aaron's sons,
shall sprinkle its blood all around on the
altar. 12And he shall cut it into its pieces,
with its head and its fat; and the priest shall
lay them in order on the wood that *is* on the
fire upon the altar; 13but he shall wash the
entrails and the legs with water. Then the
priest shall bring *it* all and burn *it* on the altar;
it *is* a burnt sacrifice, an [a]offering made by
fire, a sweet aroma to the LORD.
14'And if the burnt sacrifice of his offering
to the LORD *is* of birds, then he shall bring
his offering of [a]turtledoves or young pigeons.
15The priest shall bring it to the altar, wring
off its head, and burn *it* on the altar; its blood
shall be drained out at the side of the altar. 16And he shall remove its crop with its
feathers and cast it [a]beside the altar on the
east side, into the place for ashes. 17Then he
shall split it at its wings, *but* [a]shall not divide
it completely; and the priest shall burn it on
the altar, on the wood that *is* on the fire. [b]It
is a burnt sacrifice, an offering made by fire,
a sweet aroma to the LORD.

> **PEACE NOTE**
>
> Rigid legalism and man-made religion will never bring God's peace. God's peace comes to us through His grace.

The Grain Offering

2 'When anyone offers [a]a grain offering
to the LORD, his offering shall be *of* fine
flour. And he shall pour oil on it, and put
[b]frankincense on it. 2He shall bring it to
Aaron's sons, the priests, one of whom shall
take from it his handful of fine flour and oil
with all the frankincense. And the priest
shall burn [a]*it as* a memorial on the altar, an
offering made by fire, a sweet aroma to the
LORD. 3[a]The rest of the grain offering *shall be*
Aaron's and his [b]sons'. [c]*It is* most holy of the
offerings to the LORD made by fire.
4'And if you bring as an offering a grain
offering baked in the oven, *it shall be* unleavened cakes of fine flour mixed with oil, or
unleavened wafers [a]anointed with oil. 5But
if your offering *is* a grain offering *baked* in
a pan, *it shall be of* fine flour, unleavened,
mixed with oil. 6You shall break it in pieces
and pour oil on it; it *is* a grain offering.
7'If your offering *is* a grain offering *baked*
in a [a]covered pan, it shall be made *of* fine
flour with oil. 8You shall bring the grain offering that is made of these things to the
LORD. And when it is presented to the priest,
he shall bring it to the altar. 9Then the priest
shall take from the grain offering [a]a memorial portion, and burn *it* on the altar. *It is* an
[b]offering made by fire, a sweet aroma to the
LORD. 10And [a]what is left of the grain offering
shall be Aaron's and his sons'. *It is* most holy
of the offerings to the LORD made by fire.

1:1 [a] Ex. 19:3; 25:22 [b] Ex. 40:34 **1:2** [a] Lev. 22:18, 19 **1:3** [a] Eph. 5:27 **1:4** [a] Lev. 3:2, 8, 13; 4:15 [b] [Rom. 12:1] [c] 2 Chr. 29:23, 24 **1:5** [a] Mic. 6:6 [b] 2 Chr. 35:11 [c] [Heb. 12:24] **1:6** [a] Lev. 7:8 **1:7** [a] Mal. 1:10 [b] Gen. 22:9 **1:9** [a] Gen. 8:21 **1:10** [a] Lev. 1:3 **1:11** [a] Lev. 1:5 **1:13** [a] Num. 15:4–7; 28:12–14 **1:14** [a] Lev. 5:7, 11; 12:8 **1:16** [a] Lev. 6:10 **1:17** [a] Gen. 15:10 [b] Lev. 1:9, 13 **2:1** [a] Num. 15:4 [b] Lev. 5:11 **2:2** [a] Lev. 2:9; 5:12; 6:15; 24:7 **2:3** [a] Lev. 7:9 [b] Lev. 6:6; 10:12, 13 [c] Num. 18:9 **2:4** [a] Ex. 29:2 **2:7** [a] Lev. 7:9 **2:9** [a] Lev. 2:2, 16; 5:12; 6:15 [b] Ex. 29:18 **2:10** [a] Lev. 2:3; 6:16

11'No grain offering which you bring to the
LORD shall be made with [a]leaven, for you shall
burn no leaven nor any honey in any offering
to the LORD made by fire. 12[a]As for the offering
of the firstfruits, you shall offer them to the
LORD, but they shall not be burned on the altar
for a sweet aroma. 13And every offering of your
grain offering [a]you shall season with salt; you
shall not allow [b]the salt of the covenant of your
God to be lacking from your grain offering.
[c]With all your offerings you shall offer salt.

14'If you offer a grain offering of your firstfruits to the LORD, [a]you shall offer for the
grain offering of your firstfruits green heads
of grain roasted on the fire, grain beaten from
[b]full heads. 15And [a]you shall put oil on it, and
lay frankincense on it. It *is* a grain offering.
16Then the priest shall burn [a]the memorial
portion: *part* of its beaten grain and *part* of its
oil, with all the frankincense, as an offering
made by fire to the LORD.

The Peace Offering

3 'When his offering *is* a [a]sacrifice of a peace
offering, if he offers *it* of the herd, whether male or female, he shall offer it [b]without
blemish before the LORD. 2And [a]he shall lay
his hand on the head of his offering, and kill it
at the door of the tabernacle of meeting; and
Aaron's sons, the priests, shall [b]sprinkle the
blood all around on the altar. 3Then he shall
offer from the sacrifice of the peace offering
an offering made by fire to the LORD. [a]The fat
that covers the entrails and all the fat that *is*
on the entrails, 4the two kidneys and the fat
that *is* on them by the flanks, and the fatty
lobe *attached* to the liver above the kidneys, he
shall remove; 5and Aaron's sons [a]shall burn it
on the altar upon the [b]burnt sacrifice, which *is*
on the wood that *is* on the fire, *as* an [c]offering
made by fire, a [d]sweet aroma to the LORD.

6'If his offering as a sacrifice of a peace
offering to the LORD *is* of the flock, *whether*
male or female, [a]he shall offer it without
blemish. 7If he offers a [a]lamb as his offering, then he shall [b]offer it [c]before the LORD.
8And he shall lay his hand on the head of his
offering, and kill it before the tabernacle of
meeting; and Aaron's sons shall sprinkle its
blood all around on the altar.

9'Then he shall offer from the sacrifice of
the peace offering, as an offering made by
fire to the LORD, its fat *and* the whole fat tail
which he shall remove close to the backbone.
And the fat that covers the entrails and all the
fat that *is* on the entrails, 10the two kidneys
and the fat that *is* on them by the flanks, and
the fatty lobe *attached* to the liver above the
kidneys, he shall remove; 11and the priest
shall burn *them* on the altar *as* [a]food, an
offering made by fire to the LORD.

12'And if his [a]offering *is* a goat, then [b]he
shall offer it before the LORD. 13He shall lay
his hand on its head and kill it before the
tabernacle of meeting; and the sons of Aaron
shall sprinkle its blood all around on the altar.
14Then he shall offer from it his offering, as
an offering made by fire to the LORD. The fat
that covers the entrails and all the fat that *is*
on the entrails, 15the two kidneys and the fat
that *is* on them by the flanks, and the fatty
lobe *attached* to the liver above the kidneys,
he shall remove; 16and the priest shall burn
them on the altar *as* food, an offering made by
fire for a sweet aroma; [a]all the fat *is* the LORD's.

17'*This shall be* a [a]perpetual statute throughout your generations in all your dwellings:
you shall eat neither fat nor [b]blood.' "

The Sin Offering

4 Now the LORD spoke to Moses, saying,
2"Speak to the children of Israel, saying:
[a]'If a person sins unintentionally against any
of the commandments of the LORD *in anything*
which ought not to be done, and does any of
them, 3[a]if the anointed priest sins, bringing
guilt on the people, then let him offer to the
LORD for his sin which he has sinned [b]a young
bull without blemish as a [c]sin offering. 4He
shall bring the bull [a]to the door of the tabernacle of meeting before the LORD, lay his hand
on the bull's head, and kill the bull before the
LORD. 5Then the anointed priest [a]shall take
some of the bull's blood and bring it to the
tabernacle of meeting. 6The priest shall dip his
finger in the blood and sprinkle some of the
blood seven times before the LORD, in front of
the [a]veil of the sanctuary. 7And the priest shall
[a]put some of the blood on the horns of the altar
of sweet incense before the LORD, which is in
the tabernacle of meeting; and he shall pour
[b]the remaining blood of the bull at the base
of the altar of the burnt offering, which is at
the door of the tabernacle of meeting. 8He
shall take from it all the fat of the bull as the
sin offering. The fat that covers the entrails
and all the fat which *is* on the entrails, 9the
two kidneys and the fat that *is* on them by

2:11 [a] Lev. 6:16, 17 **2:12** [a] Lev. 23:10, 11, 17, 18 **2:13** [a] [Col. 4:6] [b] Num. 18:19 [c] Ezek. 43:24 **2:14** [a] Lev. 23:10, 14 [b] 2 Kin. 4:42 **2:15** [a] Lev. 2:1 **2:16** [a] Lev. 2:2 **3:1** [a] Lev. 7:11, 29 [b] Lev. 1:3; 22:20–24 **3:2** [a] Lev. 1:4, 5; 16:21 [b] Lev. 1:5 **3:3** [a] Lev. 1:8; 3:16; 4:8, 9 **3:5** [a] Ex. 29:13 [b] 2 Chr. 35:14 [c] Num. 28:3–10 [d] Num. 15:8–10 **3:6** [a] Lev. 3:1; 22:20–24 **3:7** [a] Num. 15:4, 5 [b] 1 Kin. 8:62 [c] Lev. 17:8, 9 **3:11** [a] Num. 28:2 **3:12** [a] Num. 15:6–11 [b] Lev. 3:1, 7 **3:16** [a] Lev. 7:23–25 **3:17** [a] Lev. 6:18; 7:36; 17:7; 23:14 [b] Lev. 7:23, 26; 17:10, 14 **4:2** [a] Lev. 5:15–18 **4:3** [a] Lev. 8:12 [b] Lev. 3:1; 9:2 [c] Lev. 9:7 **4:4** [a] Lev. 1:3, 4; 4:15 **4:5** [a] Lev. 16:14 **4:6** [a] Ex. 40:21, 26 **4:7** [a] Lev. 4:18, 25, 30, 34; 8:15; 9:9; 16:18 [b] Ex. 40:5, 6; Lev. 5:9

the flanks, and the fatty lobe *attached* to the liver above the kidneys, he shall remove, 10 [a]as it was taken from the bull of the sacrifice of the peace offering; and the priest shall burn them on the altar of the burnt offering. 11 [a]But the bull's hide and all its flesh, with its head and legs, its entrails and offal— 12 the whole bull he shall carry outside the camp to a clean place, [a]where the ashes are poured out, and [b]burn it on wood with fire; where the ashes are poured out it shall be burned.

13 'Now [a]if the whole congregation of Israel sins unintentionally, [b]and the thing is hidden from the eyes of the assembly, and they have done *something against* any of the commandments of the LORD *in anything* which should not be done, and are guilty; 14 when the sin which they have committed becomes known, then the assembly shall offer a young bull for the sin, and bring it before the tabernacle of meeting. 15 And the elders of the congregation [a]shall lay their hands on the head of the bull before the LORD. Then the bull shall be killed before the LORD. 16 [a]The anointed priest shall bring some of the bull's blood to the tabernacle of meeting. 17 Then the priest shall dip his finger in the blood and sprinkle *it* seven times before the LORD, in front of the veil. 18 And he shall put *some* of the blood on the horns of the altar which *is* before the LORD, which *is* in the tabernacle of meeting; and he shall pour the remaining blood at the base of the altar of burnt offering, which is at the door of the tabernacle of meeting. 19 He shall take all the fat from it and burn *it* on the altar. 20 And he shall do [a]with the bull as he did with the bull as a sin offering; thus he shall do with it. [b]So the priest shall make atonement for them, and it shall be forgiven them. 21 Then he shall carry the bull outside the camp, and burn it as he burned the first bull. It *is* a sin offering for the assembly.

22 'When a ruler has sinned, and [a]done *something* unintentionally *against* any of the commandments of the LORD his God *in anything* which should not be done, and is guilty, 23 or [a]if his sin which he has committed comes to his knowledge, he shall bring as his offering a kid of the goats, a male without blemish. 24 And [a]he shall lay his hand on the head of the goat, and kill it at the place where they kill the burnt offering before the LORD. It *is* a sin offering. 25 [a]The priest shall take some of the blood of the sin offering with his finger, put *it* on the horns of the altar of burnt offering, and pour its blood at the base of the altar of burnt offering. 26 And he shall burn all its fat on the altar, like [a]the fat of the sacrifice of the peace offering. [b]So the priest shall make atonement for him concerning his sin, and it shall be forgiven him.

27 [a]'If anyone of the common people sins unintentionally by doing *something against* any of the commandments of the LORD *in anything* which ought not to be done, and is guilty, 28 or [a]if his sin which he has committed comes to his knowledge, then he shall bring as his offering a kid of the goats, a female

4:10 [a] Lev. 3:3–5 **4:11** [a] Ex. 29:14 **4:12** [a] Lev. 4:21; 6:10, 11; 16:27 [b] [Heb. 13:11, 12] **4:13** [a] Num. 15:24–26 [b] Lev. 5:2–4, 17 **4:15** [a] Lev. 1:3, 4 **4:16** [a] Lev. 4:5 **4:20** [a] Lev. 4:3 [b] Num. 15:25 **4:22** [a] Lev. 4:2, 13, 27 **4:23** [a] Lev. 4:14; 5:4 **4:24** [a] [Is. 53:6] **4:25** [a] Lev. 4:7, 18, 30, 34 **4:26** [a] Lev. 3:3–5 [b] Lev. 4:20 **4:27** [a] Num. 15:27 **4:28** [a] Lev. 4:23

THE CYCLE OF PEACE

"So the priest shall make atonement for him concerning his sin, and it shall be forgiven him."

LEVITICUS 4:26

There is no peace with God without forgiveness. So God makes it easy for us to receive forgiveness. The sin offering is mentioned several times in the Bible (see Ex. 20:24; 24:5; 29:28; 32:6; Lev. 3:1; 4:35). Here in Leviticus 4:26, the sin offering is linked to atonement, which formalizes forgiveness. Sin has been atoned for, therefore one is forgiven. When one is forgiven, peace is restored. It doesn't stop there. The forgiven human being can then forgive others. And that's a very good thing!

What we have here is a wonderful, circular cycle of forgiveness and peace, each one leading to the other. God knows us—He knows we are sinful and often mess things up. He lovingly reaches out and makes it easy for us to come to Him, honestly confess our sin, and find peace restored. What's beautiful is that we, in turn, offer the same forgiveness to those who have wronged us. Our relationship with God and our relationship with our fellows is renewed. And peace reigns!

without blemish, for his sin which he has
committed. 29[a]And he shall lay his hand on
the head of the sin offering, and kill the sin
offering at the place of the burnt offering.
30Then the priest shall take *some* of its blood
with his finger, put *it* on the horns of the altar
of burnt offering, and pour all *the remaining*
blood at the base of the altar. 31[a]He shall remove all its fat, [b]as fat is removed from the
sacrifice of the peace offering; and the priest
shall burn it on the altar for a [c]sweet aroma
to the LORD. [d]So the priest shall make atonement for him, and it shall be forgiven him.

32'If he brings a lamb as his sin offering, [a]he
shall bring a female without blemish. 33Then
he shall [a]lay his hand on the head of the sin
offering, and kill it as a sin offering at the place
where they kill the burnt offering. 34The priest
shall take *some* of the blood of the sin offering
with his finger, put *it* on the horns of the altar
of burnt offering, and pour all *the remaining*
blood at the base of the altar. 35He shall remove
all its fat, as the fat of the lamb is removed from
the sacrifice of the peace offering. Then the
priest shall burn it on the altar, [a]according to
the offerings made by fire to the LORD. [b]So the
priest shall make atonement for his sin that he
has committed, and it shall be forgiven him.

The Trespass Offering

5 'If a person sins in [a]hearing the utterance
of an oath, and *is* a witness, whether he
has seen or known *of the matter*—if he does
not tell *it*, he [b]bears guilt.

2'Or [a]if a person touches any unclean thing,
whether *it is* the carcass of an unclean beast, or
the carcass of unclean livestock, or the carcass
of unclean creeping things, and he is unaware
of it, he also shall be unclean and [b]guilty. 3Or
if he touches [a]human uncleanness—whatever
uncleanness with which a man may be defiled,
and he is unaware of it—when he realizes *it*,
then he shall be guilty.

4'Or if a person swears, speaking thought-
lessly with *his* lips [a]to do evil or [b]to do good,
whatever *it is* that a man may pronounce by
an oath, and he is unaware of it—when he
realizes *it*, then he shall be guilty in any of
these *matters*.

5'And it shall be, when he is guilty in any of
these *matters*, that he shall [a]confess that he
has sinned in that *thing;* 6and he shall bring
his trespass offering to the LORD for his sin
which he has committed, a female from the
flock, a lamb or a kid of the goats as a sin
offering. So the priest shall make atonement
for him concerning his sin.

7[a]'If he is not able to bring a lamb, then
he shall bring to the LORD, for his trespass
which he has committed, two [b]turtledoves or
two young pigeons: one as a sin offering and
the other as a burnt offering. 8And he shall
bring them to the priest, who shall offer *that*
which *is* for the sin offering first, and [a]wring
off its head from its neck, but shall not divide
it completely. 9Then he shall sprinkle *some*
of the blood of the sin offering on the side of
the altar, and the [a]rest of the blood shall be
drained out at the base of the altar. It *is* a sin
offering. 10And he shall offer the second *as* a
burnt offering according to the [a]prescribed
manner. So [b]the priest shall make atonement
on his behalf for his sin which he has committed, and it shall be forgiven him.

11'But if he is [a]not able to bring two turtledoves or two young pigeons, then he who
sinned shall bring for his offering one-tenth of
an ephah of fine flour as a sin offering. [b]He shall
put no oil on it, nor shall he put frankincense
on it, for it *is* a sin offering. 12Then he shall
bring it to the priest, and the priest shall take
his handful of it [a]as a memorial portion, and
burn *it* on the altar [b]according to the offerings
made by fire to the LORD. It *is* a sin offering.
13[a]The priest shall make atonement for him, for
his sin that he has committed in any of these
matters; and it shall be forgiven him. [b]*The rest*
shall be the priest's as a grain offering.' "

Offerings with Restitution

14Then the LORD spoke to Moses, saying:
15[a]"If a person commits a trespass, and sins
unintentionally in regard to the holy things
of the LORD, then [b]he shall bring to the LORD
as his trespass offering a ram without blemish from the flocks, with your valuation in
shekels of silver according to [c]the shekel of
the sanctuary, as a trespass offering. 16And
he shall make restitution for the harm that
he has done in regard to the holy thing, [a]and
shall add one-fifth to it and give it to the
priest. [b]So the priest shall make atonement
for him with the ram of the trespass offering,
and it shall be forgiven him.

17"If a person sins, and commits any of
these things which are forbidden to be done
by the commandments of the LORD, [a]though
he does not know *it*, yet he is [b]guilty and

4:29 [a] Lev. 1:4; 4:4, 24 **4:31** [a] Lev. 3:14 [b] Lev. 3:3, 4 [c] Ex. 29:18 [d] Lev. 4:26 **4:32** [a] Lev. 4:28 **4:33** [a] Num. 8:12 **4:35** [a] Lev. 3:5 [b] Lev. 4:26, 31 **5:1** [a] Prov. 29:24 [b] Num. 9:13 **5:2** [a] Num. 19:11–16 [b] Lev. 5:17 **5:3** [a] Lev. 5:12, 13, 15 **5:4** [a] Acts 23:12 [b] [James 5:12] **5:5** [a] Prov. 28:13 **5:7** [a] Lev. 12:6, 8; 14:21 [b] Lev. 1:14 **5:8** [a] Lev. 1:15–17 **5:9** [a] Lev. 4:7, 18, 30, 34 **5:10** [a] Lev. 1:14–17 [b] Lev. 4:20, 26; 5:13, 16 **5:11** [a] Lev. 14:21–32 [b] Num. 5:15 **5:12** [a] Lev. 2:2 [b] Lev. 4:35 **5:13** [a] Lev. 4:26 [b] Lev. 2:3; 6:17, 26 **5:15** [a] Lev. 4:2; 22:14 [b] Ezra 10:19 [c] Ex. 30:13 **5:16** [a] Num. 5:7 [b] Lev. 4:26 **5:17** [a] Lev. 4:2, 13, 22, 27 [b] Lev. 5:1, 2

shall bear his iniquity. 18[a]And he shall bring
to the priest a ram without blemish from
the flock, with your valuation, as a trespass
offering. So the priest shall make atonement
for him regarding his ignorance in which
he erred and did not know *it*, and it shall be
forgiven him. 19 It is a trespass offering; [a]he
has certainly trespassed against the LORD."

6 And the LORD spoke to Moses, saying: 2"If
a person sins and [a]commits a trespass
against the LORD by [b]lying to his neighbor
about [c]what was delivered to him for safekeeping, or about a pledge, or about a robbery, or if he has [d]extorted from his neighbor,
3 or if he [a]has found what was lost and lies
concerning it, and [b]swears falsely—in any
one of these things that a man may do in
which he sins: 4 then it shall be, because he
has sinned and is guilty, that he shall restore
[a]what he has stolen, or the thing which he
has extorted, or what was delivered to him
for safekeeping, or the lost thing which he
found, 5 or all that about which he has sworn
falsely. He shall [a]restore its full value, add
one-fifth more to it, *and* give it to whomever
it belongs, on the day of his trespass offering.
6 And he shall bring his trespass offering
to the LORD, [a]a ram without blemish from
the flock, with your valuation, as a trespass
offering, to the priest. 7[a]So the priest shall
make atonement for him before the LORD,
and he shall be forgiven for any one of these
things that he may have done in which he
trespasses."

The Law of the Burnt Offering

8 Then the LORD spoke to Moses, saying,
9"Command Aaron and his sons, saying, 'This
is the [a]law of the burnt offering: The burnt
offering *shall be* on the hearth upon the altar
all night until morning, and the fire of the
altar shall be kept burning on it. 10[a]And the
priest shall put on his linen garment, and
his linen trousers he shall put on his body,
and take up the ashes of the burnt offering
which the fire has consumed on the altar, and
he shall put them [b]beside the altar. 11 Then
[a]he shall take off his garments, put on other
garments, and carry the ashes outside the
camp [b]to a clean place. 12 And the fire on the
altar shall be kept burning on it; it shall not
be put out. And the priest shall burn wood on
it every morning, and lay the burnt offering
in order on it; and he shall burn on it [a]the fat
of the peace offerings. 13 A fire shall always be
burning on the [a]altar; it shall never go out.

The Law of the Grain Offering

14"This *is* the law of the grain offering: The
sons of Aaron shall offer it on the altar before
the LORD. 15 He shall take from it his handful
of the fine flour of the grain offering, with
its oil, and all the frankincense which *is* on
the grain offering, and shall burn *it* on the
altar *for* a sweet aroma, as a memorial to the
LORD. 16 And the remainder of it Aaron and
his sons shall eat; with unleavened bread it
shall be eaten in a holy place; in the court of
the tabernacle of meeting they shall eat it. 17 It
shall not be baked with leaven. I have given
it *as* their portion of My offerings made by
fire; it *is* most holy, like the sin offering and
the [a]trespass offering. 18[a]All the males among
the children of Aaron may eat it. [b]*It shall be* a
statute forever in your generations concerning the offerings made by fire to the LORD.
[c]Everyone who touches them must be holy.' "[1]

19 And the LORD spoke to Moses, saying,
20[a]"This *is* the offering of Aaron and his sons,
which they shall offer to the LORD, *beginning*
on the day when he is anointed: one-tenth
of an [b]ephah of fine flour as a daily grain
offering, half of it in the morning and half of
it at night. 21 It shall be made in a [a]pan with
oil. *When it is* mixed, you shall bring it in. The
baked pieces of the grain offering you shall
offer *for* a sweet aroma to the LORD. 22 The
priest from among his sons, [a]who is anointed
in his place, shall offer it. *It is* a statute forever
to the LORD. [b]It shall be wholly burned. 23 For
every grain offering for the priest shall be
wholly burned. It shall not be eaten."

The Law of the Sin Offering

24 Also the LORD spoke to Moses, saying,
25"Speak to Aaron and to his sons, saying,
'This *is* the law of the sin offering: [a]In the place
where the burnt offering is killed, the sin offering shall be killed before the LORD. It *is* most
holy. 26[a]The priest who offers it for sin shall
eat it. In a holy place it shall be eaten, in the
court of the tabernacle of meeting. 27[a]Every-
one who touches its flesh must be holy.[1] And
when its blood is sprinkled on any garment,
you shall wash that on which it was sprinkled,
in a holy place. 28 But the earthen vessel in
which it is boiled [a]shall be broken. And if it is
boiled in a bronze pot, it shall be both scoured

5:18 [a] Lev. 5:15 5:19 [a] Ezra 10:2 6:2 [a] Num. 5:6 [b] Lev. 19:11 [c] Ex. 22:7, 10 [d] Prov. 24:28 6:3 [a] Deut. 22:1–4 [b] Ex. 22:11 6:4 [a] Lev. 24:18, 21 6:5 [a] Lev. 5:16 6:6 [a] Lev. 1:3; 5:15 6:7 [a] Lev. 4:26 6:9 [a] Ex. 29:38–42 6:10 [a] Ex. 28:39–43 [b] Lev. 1:16 6:11 [a] Ezek. 44:19 [b] Lev. 4:12 6:12 [a] Lev. 3:3, 5, 9, 14 6:13 [a] Lev. 1:7 6:17 [a] Lev. 7:7 6:18 [a] Lev. 6:29; 7:6 [b] Lev. 3:17 [c] Ex. 29:37; Num. 4:15; Hag. 2:11–13 [1] Compare Numbers 4:15 and Haggai 2:11–13 6:20 [a] Ex. 29:2 [b] Ex. 16:36 6:21 [a] Lev. 2:5; 7:9 6:22 [a] Lev. 4:3 [b] Ex. 29:25 6:25 [a] Lev. 1:1, 3, 5, 11 6:26 [a] [Ezek. 44:28, 29] 6:27 [a] Ex. 29:37; Num. 4:15; Hag. 2:11–13 [1] Compare Numbers 4:15 and Haggai 2:11–13 6:28 [a] Lev. 11:33; 15:12

and rinsed in water. 29 All the males among
the priests may eat it. It *is* most holy. 30 [a]But
no sin offering from which *any* of the blood
is brought into the tabernacle of meeting, to
make atonement in the holy [b]*place*,[1] shall be
[c]eaten. It shall be [d]burned in the fire.

The Law of the Trespass Offering

7 'Likewise [a]this *is* the law of the trespass
offering (it *is* most holy): 2 In the place
where they kill the burnt offering they shall
kill the trespass offering. And its blood he
shall sprinkle all around on the altar. 3 And he
shall offer from it all its fat. The fat tail and the
fat that covers the entrails, 4 the two kidneys
and the fat that *is* on them by the flanks, and
the fatty lobe *attached* to the liver above the
kidneys, he shall remove; 5 and the priest shall
burn them on the altar *as* an offering made
by fire to the LORD. It *is* a trespass offering.
6 [a]Every male among the priests may eat it. It
shall be eaten in a holy place. [b]It *is* most holy.
7 [a]The trespass offering *is* like the sin offering;
there is one law for them both: the priest who
makes atonement with it shall have *it*. 8 And
the priest who offers anyone's burnt offering,
that priest shall have for himself the skin of
the burnt offering which he has offered. 9 Also
[a]every grain offering that is baked in the oven
and all that is prepared in the covered pan,
or in a pan, shall be the priest's who offers it.
10 Every grain offering, *whether* mixed with oil
or dry, shall belong to all the sons of Aaron,
to one *as much* as the other.

The Law of Peace Offerings

11 [a]'This *is* the law of the sacrifice of peace
offerings which he shall offer to the LORD:
12 If he offers it for a thanksgiving, then he
shall offer, with the sacrifice of thanksgiving,
unleavened cakes mixed with oil, unleavened
wafers [a]anointed with oil, or cakes of blended
flour mixed with oil. 13 Besides the cakes, *as*
his offering he shall offer [a]leavened bread
with the sacrifice of thanksgiving of his peace
offering. 14 And from it he shall offer one cake
from each offering *as* a heave offering to
the LORD. [a]It shall belong to the priest who
sprinkles the blood of the peace offering.
15 [a]'The flesh of the sacrifice of his peace
offering for thanksgiving shall be eaten the
same day it is offered. He shall not leave any
of it until morning. 16 But [a]if the sacrifice of
his offering *is* a vow or a voluntary offering, it

PEACE NOTE

Jesus has saved me. He's forgiven me of my sins, and He loves me. I know it's true, and that fact alone brings me eternal peace.

shall be eaten the same day that he offers his
sacrifice; but on the next day the remainder
of it also may be eaten; 17 the remainder of the
flesh of the sacrifice on the third day must be
burned with fire. 18 And if *any* of the flesh of
the sacrifice of his peace offering is eaten at
all on the third day, it shall not be accepted,
nor shall it be [a]imputed to him; it shall be an
[b]abomination *to* him who offers it, and the
person who eats of it shall bear guilt.
19 'The flesh that touches any unclean thing
shall not be eaten. It shall be burned with fire.
And as for the *clean* flesh, all who are clean
may eat of it. 20 But the person who eats the
flesh of the sacrifice of the peace offering that
belongs to the [a]LORD, [b]while he is unclean,
that person [c]shall be cut off from his people.
21 Moreover the person who touches any unclean thing, *such as* [a]human uncleanness, *an*
[b]unclean animal, or any [c]abominable unclean
thing,[1] and who eats the flesh of the sacrifice
of the peace offering that *belongs* to the LORD,
that person [d]shall be cut off from his people.' "

Fat and Blood May Not Be Eaten

22 And the LORD spoke to Moses, saying,
23 "Speak to the children of Israel, saying:
[a]'You shall not eat any fat, of ox or sheep or
goat. 24 And the fat of an animal that dies
naturally, and the fat of what is torn by wild
beasts, may be used in any other way; but you
shall by no means eat it. 25 For whoever eats
the fat of the animal of which men offer an
offering made by fire to the LORD, the person
who eats *it* shall be cut off from his people.

6:30 [a] Lev. 4:7, 11, 12, 18, 21; 10:18; 16:27 [b] Ex. 26:33 [c] Lev. 6:16, 23, 26 [d] Lev. 16:27 [1] The Most Holy Place when capitalized **7:1** [a] Lev. 5:14—6:7 **7:6** [a] Lev. 6:16–18, 29 [b] Lev. 2:3 **7:7** [a] Lev. 6:24–30; 14:13 **7:9** [a] Lev. 2:3, 10 **7:11** [a] Lev. 3:1; 22:18, 21 **7:12** [a] Num. 6:15 **7:13** [a] Amos 4:5 **7:14** [a] Num. 18:8, 11, 19 **7:15** [a] Lev. 22:29, 30 **7:16** [a] Lev. 19:5–8 **7:18** [a] Num. 18:27 [b] Lev. 11:10, 11, 41; 19:7 **7:20** [a] [Heb. 2:17] [b] Num. 19:13 [c] Gen. 17:14 **7:21** [a] Lev. 5:2, 3, 5 [b] Lev. 11:24, 28 [c] Ezek. 4:14 [d] Lev. 7:20 [1] Following Masoretic Text, Septuagint, and Vulgate; Samaritan Pentateuch, Syriac, and Targum read *swarming thing* (compare 5:2). **7:23** [a] Lev. 3:17; 17:10–15

26 [a]Moreover you shall not eat any blood in
any of your dwellings, *whether* of bird or
beast. 27 Whoever eats any blood, that person
shall be cut off from his people.' "

The Portion of Aaron and His Sons

28 Then the LORD spoke to Moses, saying,
29 "Speak to the children of Israel, saying:
[a]'He who offers the sacrifice of his peace
offering to the LORD shall bring his offering
to the LORD from the sacrifice of his peace
offering. 30 [a]His own hands shall bring the
offerings made by fire to the LORD. The fat
with the breast he shall bring, that the [b]breast
may be waved *as* a wave offering before the
LORD. 31 [a]And the priest shall burn the fat
on the altar, but the [b]breast shall be Aaron's
and his sons'. 32 [a]Also the right thigh you
shall give to the priest *as* a heave offering
from the sacrifices of your peace offerings.
33 He among the sons of Aaron, who offers
the blood of the peace offering and the fat,
shall have the right thigh for *his* part. 34 For
[a]the breast of the wave offering and the thigh
of the heave offering I have taken from the
children of Israel, from the sacrifices of their
peace offerings, and I have given them to
Aaron the priest and to his sons from the
children of Israel by a statute forever.' "

35 This *is* the consecrated portion for Aaron
and his sons, from the offerings made by fire
to the LORD, on the day when *Moses* presented them to minister to the LORD as priests.
36 The LORD commanded this to be given to
them by the children of Israel, [a]on the day
that He anointed them, *by* a statute forever
throughout their generations.

37 This *is* the law [a]of the burnt offering,
[b]the grain offering, [c]the sin offering, [d]the
trespass offering, [e]the consecrations, and
[f]the sacrifice of the peace offering, 38 which
the LORD commanded Moses on Mount Sinai,
on the day when He commanded the children
of Israel [a]to offer their offerings to the LORD
in the Wilderness of Sinai.

Aaron and His Sons Consecrated

8 And the LORD spoke to Moses, saying:
2 [a]"Take Aaron and his sons with him,
and [b]the garments, [c]the anointing oil, a [d]bull
as the sin offering, two [e]rams, and a basket
of unleavened bread; 3 and gather all the
congregation together at the door of the
tabernacle of meeting."

4 So Moses did as the LORD commanded
him. And the congregation was gathered
together at the door of the tabernacle of
meeting. 5 And Moses said to the congregation, "This *is* what the LORD commanded to
be done."

6 Then Moses brought Aaron and his sons
and [a]washed them with water. 7 And he [a]put
the tunic on him, girded him with the sash,
clothed him with the robe, and put the ephod
on him; and he girded him with the intricately woven band of the ephod, and with it tied
the ephod on him. 8 Then he put the breastplate on him, and he [a]put the Urim and the
Thummim[1] in the breastplate. 9 [a]And he put
the turban on his head. Also on the turban,
on its front, he put the golden plate, the holy
crown, as the LORD had commanded Moses.

10 [a]Also Moses took the anointing oil, and
anointed the tabernacle and all that *was* in it,
and consecrated them. 11 He sprinkled some
of it on the altar seven times, anointed the
altar and all its utensils, and the laver and its
base, to consecrate them. 12 And he [a]poured
some of the anointing oil on Aaron's head
and anointed him, to consecrate him.

13 [a]Then Moses brought Aaron's sons and
put tunics on them, girded them with sashes, and put hats on them, as the LORD had
commanded Moses.

14 [a]And he brought the bull for the sin offering. Then Aaron and his sons [b]laid their
hands on the head of the bull for the sin
offering, 15 and Moses killed *it*. [a]Then he took
the blood, and put *some* on the horns of the
altar all around with his finger, and purified the altar. And he poured the blood at
the base of the altar, and consecrated it, to
make atonement for it. 16 [a]Then he took all
the fat that *was* on the entrails, the fatty lobe
attached to the liver, and the two kidneys with
their fat, and Moses burned *them* on the altar.
17 But the bull, its hide, its flesh, and its offal,
he burned with fire outside the camp, as the
LORD [a]had commanded Moses.

18 [a]Then he brought the ram as the burnt
offering. And Aaron and his sons laid their
hands on the head of the ram, 19 and Moses
killed *it*. Then he sprinkled the blood all
around on the altar. 20 And he cut the ram
into pieces; and Moses [a]burned the head,
the pieces, and the fat. 21 Then he washed
the entrails and the legs in water. And Moses
burned the whole ram on the altar. It *was* a

7:26 [a] Acts 15:20, 29 **7:29** [a] Lev. 3:1; 22:21 **7:30** [a] Lev. 3:3, 4, 9, 14 [b] Ex. 29:24, 27 **7:31** [a] Lev. 3:5, 11, 16 [b] Deut. 18:3 **7:32** [a] Num. 6:20 **7:34** [a] Lev. 10:14, 15 **7:36** [a] Lev. 8:12, 30 **7:37** [a] Lev. 6:9 [b] Lev. 6:14 [c] Lev. 6:25 [d] Lev. 7:1 [e] Ex. 29:1 [f] Lev. 7:11 **7:38** [a] Lev. 1:1, 2 **8:2** [a] Ex. 29:1–3 [b] Ex. 28:2, 4 [c] Ex. 30:24, 25 [d] Ex. 29:10 [e] Ex. 29:15, 19 **8:6** [a] Heb. 10:22 **8:7** [a] Ex. 39:1–31 **8:8** [a] Ex. 28:30 [1]Literally *the Lights and the Perfections* (compare Exodus 28:30) **8:9** [a] Ex. 28:36, 37; 29:6 **8:10** [a] Ex. 30:26–29; 40:10, 11 **8:12** [a] Ps. 133:2 **8:13** [a] Ex. 29:8, 9 **8:14** [a] Ezek. 43:19 [b] Lev. 4:4 **8:15** [a] Lev. 4:7 **8:16** [a] Ex. 29:13 **8:17** [a] Lev. 4:11, 12 **8:18** [a] Ex. 29:15 **8:20** [a] Lev. 1:8

burnt sacrifice for a sweet aroma, an offering
made by fire to the LORD, [a]as the LORD had
commanded Moses.

22 And [a]he brought the second ram, the
ram of consecration. Then Aaron and his
sons laid their hands on the head of the ram,
23 and Moses killed *it*. Also he took *some* of [a]its
blood and put it on the tip of Aaron's right ear,
on the thumb of his right hand, and on the
big toe of his right foot. 24 Then he brought
Aaron's sons. And Moses put *some* of the
[a]blood on the tips of their right ears, on the
thumbs of their right hands, and on the big
toes of their right feet. And Moses sprinkled
the blood all around on the altar. 25 [a]Then he
took the fat and the fat tail, all the fat that
was on the entrails, the fatty lobe *attached to*
the liver, the two kidneys and their fat, and
the right thigh; 26 [a]and from the basket of
unleavened bread that was before the LORD
he took one unleavened cake, a cake of bread
anointed with oil, and one wafer, and put *them*
on the fat and on the right thigh; 27 and he put
all *these* [a]in Aaron's hands and in his sons'
hands, and waved them *as* a wave offering
before the LORD. 28 [a]Then Moses took them
from their hands and burned *them* on the
altar, on the burnt offering. They *were* consecration offerings for a sweet aroma. That
was an offering made by fire to the LORD.
29 And [a]Moses took the [b]breast and waved
it *as* a wave offering before the LORD. It was
Moses' [c]part of the ram of consecration, as
the LORD had commanded Moses.

30 Then [a]Moses took some of the anointing
oil and some of the blood which *was* on the
altar, and sprinkled *it* on Aaron, on his garments, on his sons, and on the garments of
his sons with him; and he consecrated Aaron,
his garments, his sons, and the garments of
his sons with him.

31 And Moses said to Aaron and his sons,
[a]"Boil the flesh *at* the door of the tabernacle
of meeting, and eat it there with the bread
that *is* in the basket of consecration offerings, as I commanded, saying, 'Aaron and
his sons shall eat it.' 32 [a]What remains of the
flesh and of the bread you shall burn with
fire. 33 And you shall not go outside the door
of the tabernacle of meeting *for* seven days,
until the days of your consecration are ended. For [a]seven days he shall consecrate you.
34 [a]As he has done this day, *so* the LORD has
commanded to do, to make atonement for
you. 35 Therefore you shall stay *at* the door of
the tabernacle of meeting day and night for
seven days, and [a]keep the charge of the LORD,
so that you may not die; for so I have been
commanded." 36 So Aaron and his sons did
all the things that the LORD had commanded
by the hand of Moses.

The Priestly Ministry Begins

9 It came to pass on the [a]eighth day that
Moses called Aaron and his sons and the
elders of Israel. 2 And he said to Aaron, "Take
for yourself a young [a]bull as a sin offering and
a ram as a burnt offering, without blemish,
and offer *them* before the LORD. 3 And to the
children of Israel you shall speak, saying,
[a]'Take a kid of the goats as a sin offering, and a
calf and a lamb, *both* of the first year, without
blemish, as a burnt offering, 4 also a bull and
a ram as peace offerings, to sacrifice before
the LORD, and [a]a grain offering mixed with
oil; for [b]today the LORD will appear to you.' "

5 So they brought what Moses commanded
before the tabernacle of meeting. And all the
congregation drew near and stood before
the LORD. 6 Then Moses said, "This *is* the
thing which the LORD commanded you to
do, and the glory of the LORD will appear to
you." 7 And Moses said to Aaron, "Go to the
altar, [a]offer your sin offering and your burnt
offering, and make atonement for yourself
and for the people. [b]Offer the offering of the
people, and make atonement for them, as
the LORD commanded."

8 Aaron therefore went to the altar and
killed the calf of the sin offering, which *was*
for himself. 9 Then the sons of Aaron brought
the blood to him. And he dipped his finger
in the blood, put *it* on the horns of the altar,
and poured the blood at the base of the altar.
10 [a]But the fat, the kidneys, and the fatty lobe
from the liver of the sin offering he burned
on the altar, as the LORD had commanded
Moses. 11 [a]The flesh and the hide he burned
with fire outside the camp.

12 And he killed the burnt offering; and
Aaron's sons presented to him the blood,
[a]which he sprinkled all around on the altar.
13 [a]Then they presented the burnt offering to
him, with its pieces and head, and he burned
them on the altar. 14 [a]And he washed the entrails and the legs, and burned *them* with the
burnt offering on the altar.

15 [a]Then he brought the people's offering, and
took the goat, which *was* the sin offering for the
people, and killed it and offered it for sin, like

8:21 [a] Ex. 29:18 **8:22** [a] Ex. 29:19, 31 **8:23** [a] Lev. 14:14 **8:24** [a] [Heb. 9:13, 14, 18–23] **8:25** [a] Ex. 29:22 **8:26** [a] Ex. 29:23 **8:27** [a] Ex. 29:24 **8:28** [a] Ex. 29:25 **8:29** [a] Ps. 99:6 [b] Ex. 29:27 [c] Ex. 29:26 **8:30** [a] Ex. 29:21; 30:30 **8:31** [a] Ex. 29:31, 32 **8:32** [a] Ex. 29:34 **8:33** [a] Ex. 29:30, 35 **8:34** [a] [Heb. 7:16] **8:35** [a] Deut. 11:1 **9:1** [a] Ezek. 43:27 **9:2** [a] Lev. 4:1–12 **9:3** [a] Lev. 4:23, 28 **9:4** [a] Lev. 2:4 [b] Ex. 29:43 **9:7** [a] [Heb. 5:3–5; 7:27] [b] Lev. 4:16, 20 **9:10** [a] Lev. 8:16 **9:11** [a] Lev. 4:11, 12; 8:17 **9:12** [a] Lev. 1:5; 8:19 **9:13** [a] Lev. 8:20 **9:14** [a] Lev. 8:21 **9:15** [a] [Is. 53:10]

the first one. 16 And he brought the burnt offering and offered it [a]according to the prescribed
manner. 17 Then he brought the grain offering,
took a handful of it, and burned *it* on the altar,
[a]besides the burnt sacrifice of the morning.
18 He also killed the bull and the ram *as*
[a]sacrifices of peace offerings, which *were*
for the people. And Aaron's sons presented to him the blood, which he sprinkled all
around on the altar, 19 and the fat from the
bull and the ram—the fatty tail, what covers
the entrails and the kidneys, and the fatty lobe
attached to the liver; 20 and they put the fat
on the breasts. [a]Then he burned the fat on
the altar; 21 but the breasts and the right thigh
Aaron waved [a]*as* a wave offering before the
LORD, as Moses had commanded.
22 Then Aaron lifted his hand toward the
people, [a]blessed them, and came down from
offering the sin offering, the burnt offering,
and peace offerings. 23 And Moses and Aaron
went into the tabernacle of meeting, and
came out and blessed the people. Then the
glory of the LORD appeared to all the people,
24 and [a]fire came out from before the LORD
and consumed the burnt offering and the fat
on the altar. When all the people saw *it*, they
[b]shouted and fell on their [c]faces.

The Profane Fire of Nadab and Abihu

10 Then [a]Nadab and Abihu, the sons of
Aaron, [b]each took his censer and put
fire in it, put incense on it, and offered [c]pro-
fane fire before the LORD, which He had not
commanded them. 2 So [a]fire went out from
the LORD and devoured them, and they died
before the LORD. 3 And Moses said to Aaron,
"This is what the LORD spoke, saying:

'By those [a]who come near Me
I must be regarded as holy;
And before all the people
I must be glorified.' "

So Aaron held his peace.
4 Then Moses called Mishael and Elzaphan,
the sons of Uzziel the uncle of Aaron, and said
to them, "Come near, [a]carry your brethren
from before the sanctuary out of the camp."
5 So they went near and carried them by their
tunics out of the camp, as Moses had said.
6 And Moses said to Aaron, and to Eleazar
and Ithamar, his sons, "Do not uncover your
heads nor tear your clothes, lest you die, and
[a]wrath come upon all the people. But let your
brethren, the whole house of Israel, bewail
the burning which the LORD has kindled.
7 [a]You shall not go out from the door of the
tabernacle of meeting, lest you die, [b]for the
anointing oil of the LORD *is* upon you." And
they did according to the word of Moses.

Conduct Prescribed for Priests

8 Then the LORD spoke to Aaron, saying:
9 [a]"Do not drink wine or intoxicating drink,
you, nor your sons with you, when you go into
the tabernacle of meeting, lest you die. *It shall
be* a statute forever throughout your generations, 10 that you may [a]distinguish between
holy and unholy, and between unclean and
clean, 11 [a]and that you may teach the children
of Israel all the statutes which the LORD has
spoken to them by the hand of Moses."
12 And Moses spoke to Aaron, and to Eleazar
and Ithamar, his sons who were left: [a]"Take the
grain offering that remains of the offerings
made by fire to the LORD, and eat it without
leaven beside the altar; [b]for it *is* most holy.
13 You shall eat it in a [a]holy place, because it *is*
your due and your sons' due, of the sacrifices
made by fire to the LORD; for [b]so I have been
commanded. 14 [a]The breast of the wave offering
and the thigh of the heave offering you shall
eat in a clean place, you, your sons, and your
[b]daughters with you; for *they are* your due
and your sons' [c]due, *which* are given from the
sacrifices of peace offerings of the children
of Israel. 15 [a]The thigh of the heave offering
and the breast of the wave offering they shall
bring with the offerings of fat made by fire, to
offer *as* a wave offering before the LORD. And
it shall be yours and your sons' with you, by a
statute forever, as the LORD has commanded."
16 Then Moses made careful inquiry about
[a]the goat of the sin offering, and there it
was—burned up. And he was angry with
Eleazar and Ithamar, the sons of Aaron *who
were* left, saying, 17 [a]"Why have you not eat-
en the sin offering in a holy place, since it
is most holy, and *God* has given it to you to
bear [b]the guilt of the congregation, to make
atonement for them before the LORD? 18 See!
[a]Its blood was not brought inside the holy
place;[1] indeed you should have eaten it in a
holy *place*, [b]as I commanded."
19 And Aaron said to Moses, "Look, [a]this
day they have offered their sin offering and
their burnt offering before the LORD, and

9:16 [a] Lev. 1:1–13 **9:17** [a] Ex. 29:38, 39 **9:18** [a] Lev. 3:1–11 **9:20** [a] Lev. 3:5, 16 **9:21** [a] Lev. 7:30–34 **9:22** [a] Luke 24:50 **9:24** [a] Judg. 6:21 [b] Ezra 3:11 [c] 1 Kin. 18:38, 39 **10:1** [a] Num. 3:2–4 [b] Lev. 16:12 [c] Ex. 30:9 **10:2** [a] Num. 11:1; 16:35 **10:3** [a] Ex. 19:22 **10:4** [a] Acts 5:6, 10 **10:6** [a] 2 Sam. 24:1 **10:7** [a] Lev. 8:33; 21:12 [b] Lev. 8:30 **10:9** [a] Ezek. 44:21 **10:10** [a] Ezek. 22:26; 44:23 **10:11** [a] Deut. 24:8 **10:12** [a] Num. 18:9 [b] Lev. 21:22 **10:13** [a] Num. 18:10 [b] Lev. 2:3; 6:16 **10:14** [a] Num. 18:11 [b] Lev. 22:13 [c] Num. 18:10 **10:15** [a] Lev. 7:29, 30, 34 **10:16** [a] Lev. 9:3, 15 **10:17** [a] Lev. 6:24–30 [b] Ex. 28:38 **10:18** [a] Lev. 6:30 [b] Lev. 6:26, 30 [1] The Most Holy Place when capitalized **10:19** [a] Lev. 9:8, 12

such things have befallen me! *If* I had eaten the sin offering today, [b]would it have been accepted in the sight of the LORD?" 20 So when Moses heard *that*, he was content.

Foods Permitted and Forbidden

11 Now the LORD spoke to Moses and Aaron, saying to them, 2 "Speak to the children of Israel, saying, [a]'These *are* the animals which you may eat among all the animals that *are* on the earth: 3 Among the animals, whatever divides the hoof, having cloven hooves *and* chewing the cud—that you may eat. 4 Nevertheless these you shall [a]not eat among those that chew the cud or those that have cloven hooves: the camel, because it chews the cud but does not have cloven hooves, is unclean to you; 5 the rock hyrax, because it chews the cud but does not have cloven hooves, *is* unclean to you; 6 the hare, because it chews the cud but does not have cloven hooves, *is* unclean to you; 7 and the swine, though it divides the hoof, having cloven hooves, yet does not chew the cud, [a]*is* unclean to you. 8 Their flesh you shall not eat, and their carcasses you shall not touch. [a]They *are* unclean to you.

9 [a]'These you may eat of all that *are* in the water: whatever in the water has fins and scales, whether in the seas or in the rivers—that you may eat. 10 But all in the seas or in the rivers that do not have fins and scales, all that move in the water or any living thing which *is* in the water, they *are* an [a]abomination to you. 11 They shall be an abomination to you; you shall not eat their flesh, but you shall regard their carcasses as an abomination. 12 Whatever in the water does not have fins or scales—that *shall be* an abomination to you.

13 [a]'And these you shall regard as an abomination among the birds; they shall not be eaten, they *are* an abomination: the eagle, the vulture, the buzzard, 14 the kite, and the falcon after its kind; 15 every raven after its kind, 16 the ostrich, the short-eared owl, the sea gull, and the hawk after its kind; 17 the little owl, the fisher owl, and the screech owl; 18 the white owl, the jackdaw, and the carrion vulture; 19 the stork, the heron after its kind, the hoopoe, and the bat.

20 'All flying insects that creep on *all* fours *shall be* an abomination to you. 21 Yet these you may eat of every flying insect that creeps on *all* fours: those which have jointed legs above their feet with which to leap on the earth. 22 These you may eat: [a]the locust after its kind, the destroying locust after its kind, the cricket after its kind, and the grasshopper after its kind. 23 But all *other* flying insects which have four feet *shall be* an abomination to you.

Unclean Animals

24 'By these you shall become unclean; whoever touches the carcass of any of them shall be unclean until evening; 25 whoever carries part of the carcass of any of them [a]shall wash his clothes and be unclean until evening: 26 *The carcass* of any animal which divides the foot, but is not cloven-hoofed or does not chew the cud, *is* unclean to you. Everyone who touches it shall be unclean. 27 And whatever goes on its paws, among all kinds of animals that go on *all* fours, those *are* unclean to you. Whoever touches any such carcass shall be unclean until evening. 28 Whoever carries *any such* carcass shall wash his clothes and be unclean until evening. It *is* unclean to you.

29 'These also *shall be* unclean to you among the creeping things that creep on the earth: the mole, [a]the mouse, and the large lizard after its kind; 30 the gecko, the monitor lizard, the sand reptile, the sand lizard, and the chameleon. 31 These *are* unclean to you among all that creep. Whoever [a]touches them when they are dead shall be unclean until evening. 32 Anything on which *any* of them falls, when they are dead shall be unclean, whether *it is* any item of wood or clothing or skin or sack, whatever item *it is*, in which *any* work is done, [a]it must be put in water. And it shall be unclean until evening; then it shall be clean. 33 Any [a]earthen vessel into which *any* of them falls [b]you shall break; and whatever *is* in it shall be unclean: 34 in such a vessel, any edible food upon which water falls becomes unclean, and any drink that may be drunk from it becomes unclean. 35 And everything on which *a part* of *any such* carcass falls shall be unclean; *whether it is* an oven or cooking stove, it shall be broken down; *for* they *are* unclean, and shall be unclean to you. 36 Nevertheless a spring or a cistern, *in which there is* plenty of water, shall be clean, but whatever touches any such carcass becomes unclean. 37 And if a part of *any such* carcass falls on any planting seed which is to be sown, it *remains* clean. 38 But if water is put on the seed, and if *a part* of *any such* carcass falls on it, it *becomes* unclean to you.

39 'And if any animal which you may eat dies, he who touches its carcass shall be [a]unclean until evening. 40 [a]He who eats of its carcass

10:19 [b] [Is. 1:11–15] **11:2** [a] Deut. 14:4 **11:4** [a] Acts 10:14 **11:7** [a] Is. 65:4; 66:3, 17 **11:8** [a] Is. 52:11 **11:9** [a] Deut. 14:9 **11:10** [a] Lev. 7:18, 21 **11:13** [a] Is. 66:17 **11:22** [a] Matt. 3:4 **11:25** [a] Num. 19:10, 21, 22; 31:24 **11:29** [a] Is. 66:17 **11:31** [a] Hag. 2:13 **11:32** [a] Lev. 15:12 **11:33** [a] Lev. 6:28 [b] Lev. 15:12 **11:39** [a] Hag. 2:11–13 **11:40** [a] Lev. 17:15; 22:8

shall wash his clothes and be unclean until
evening. He also who carries its carcass shall
wash his clothes and be unclean until evening.
41 'And every creeping thing that creeps on
the earth *shall be* an abomination. It shall
not be eaten. 42 Whatever crawls on its belly,
whatever goes on *all* fours, or whatever has
many feet among all creeping things that
creep on the earth—these you shall not eat,
for they *are* an abomination. 43 [a]You shall
not make yourselves abominable with any
creeping thing that creeps; nor shall you
make yourselves unclean with them, lest
you be defiled by them. 44 For I *am* the LORD
your [a]God. You shall therefore consecrate
yourselves, and [b]you shall be holy; for I *am*
holy. Neither shall you defile yourselves with
any creeping thing that creeps on the earth.
45 [a]For I *am* the LORD who brings you up out
of the land of Egypt, to be your God. [b]You
shall therefore be holy, for I *am* holy.

PEACE NOTE

We consecrate or set apart to God every area of our lives—even our diet. Our ambition to completely please the Lord always brings peace.

LEVITICUS 11:44

46 'This *is* the law of the animals and the
birds and every living creature that moves in
the waters, and of every creature that creeps
on the earth, 47 [a]to distinguish between the
unclean and the clean, and between the animal that may be eaten and the animal that
may not be eaten.' "

The Ritual After Childbirth

12 Then the LORD spoke to Moses, saying,
2 "Speak to the children of Israel, saying: 'If a [a]woman has conceived, and borne
a male child, then [b]she shall be unclean sev-
en days; [c]as in the days of her customary
impurity she shall be unclean. 3 And on the
[a]eighth day the flesh of his foreskin shall be
circumcised. 4 She shall then continue in the
blood of *her* purification thirty-three days.
She shall not touch any hallowed thing, nor
come into the sanctuary until the days of her
purification are fulfilled.
5 'But if she bears a female child, then she
shall be unclean two weeks, as in her customary impurity, and she shall continue in
the blood of *her* purification sixty-six days.
6 [a]'When the days of her purification are
fulfilled, whether for a son or a daughter, she
shall bring to the priest a [b]lamb of the first
year as a burnt offering, and a young pigeon
or a turtledove as a [c]sin offering, to the door
of the tabernacle of meeting. 7 Then he shall
offer it before the LORD, and make atonement
for her. And she shall be clean from the flow
of her blood. This *is* the law for her who has
borne a male or a female.
8 [a]'And if she is not able to bring a lamb,
then she may bring two turtledoves or two
young pigeons—one as a burnt offering and
the other as a sin offering. [b]So the priest
shall make atonement for her, and she will
be clean.' "

The Law Concerning Leprosy

13 And the LORD spoke to Moses and
Aaron, saying: 2 "When a man has on
the skin of his body a swelling, [a]a scab, or a
bright spot, and it becomes on the skin of his
body *like* a leprous[1] sore, [b]then he shall be
brought to Aaron the priest or to one of his
sons the priests. 3 The priest shall examine
the sore on the skin of the body; and if the
hair on the sore has turned white, and the
sore appears *to be* deeper than the skin of his
body, it *is* a leprous sore. Then the priest shall
examine him, and pronounce him unclean.
4 But if the bright spot *is* white on the skin of
his body, and does not appear *to be* deeper
than the skin, and its hair has not turned
white, then the priest shall isolate *the one
who has* the sore [a]seven days. 5 And the priest
shall examine him on the seventh day; and
indeed *if* the sore appears to be as it was, *and*
the sore has not spread on the skin, then the
priest shall isolate him another seven days.
6 Then the priest shall examine him again on
the seventh day; and indeed *if* the sore has
faded, *and* the sore has not spread on the
skin, then the priest shall pronounce him
clean; it *is only* a scab, and he [a]shall wash his
clothes and be clean. 7 But if the scab should
at all spread over the skin, after he has been

11:43 [a] Lev. 20:25 **11:44** [a] Ex. 6:7 [b] 1 Pet. 1:15, 16 **11:45** [a] Ex. 6:7; 20:2 [b] Lev. 11:44 **11:47** [a] Ezek. 44:23 **12:2** [a] Lev. 15:19 [b] Luke 2:22 [c] Lev. 18:19 **12:3** [a] Gen. 17:12 **12:6** [a] Luke 2:22 [b] [John 1:29] [c] Lev. 5:7 **12:8** [a] Lev. 5:7 [b] Lev. 4:26 **13:2** [a] Is. 3:17 [b] Mal. 2:7 [1] Hebrew *saraath,* disfiguring skin diseases, including leprosy, and so in verses 2–46 and 14:2–32 **13:4** [a] Lev. 14:8 **13:6** [a] Lev. 11:25; 14:8

seen by the priest for his cleansing, he shall
be seen by the priest again. 8 And *if* the priest
sees that the scab has indeed spread on the
skin, then the priest shall pronounce him
unclean. It *is* leprosy.

9"When the leprous sore is on a person,
then he shall be brought to the priest. 10 [a]And
the priest shall examine *him;* and indeed *if*
the swelling on the skin *is* white, and it has
turned the hair white, and *there is* a spot of
raw flesh in the swelling, 11 it *is* an old leprosy
on the skin of his body. The priest shall pronounce him unclean, and shall not isolate
him, for he *is* unclean.

12"And if leprosy breaks out all over the
skin, and the leprosy covers all the skin of
the one who has the sore, from his head to
his foot, wherever the priest looks, 13 then
the priest shall consider; and indeed *if* the
leprosy has covered all his body, he shall
pronounce *him* clean *who has* the sore. It has
all turned [a]white. He *is* clean. 14 But when raw
flesh appears on him, he shall be unclean.
15 And the priest shall examine the raw flesh
and pronounce him to be unclean; *for* the
raw flesh *is* unclean. It *is* leprosy. 16 Or if the
raw flesh changes and turns white again,
he shall come to the priest. 17 And the priest
shall examine him; and indeed *if* the sore has
turned white, then the priest shall pronounce
him clean *who has* the sore. He *is* clean.

18"If the body develops a [a]boil in the skin,
and it is healed, 19 and in the place of the
boil there comes a white swelling or a bright
spot, reddish-white, then it shall be shown
to the priest; 20 and *if,* when the priest sees
it, it indeed appears deeper than the skin,
and its hair has turned white, the priest shall
pronounce him unclean. It *is* a leprous sore
which has broken out of the boil. 21 But if the
priest examines it, and indeed *there are* no
white hairs in it, and it *is* not deeper than
the skin, but has faded, then the priest shall
isolate him seven days; 22 and if it should at
all spread over the skin, then the priest shall
pronounce him unclean. It *is* a leprous sore.
23 But if the bright spot stays in one place,
and has not spread, it *is* the scar of the boil;
and the priest shall pronounce him clean.

24"Or if the body receives a [a]burn on its skin
by fire, and the raw *flesh* of the burn becomes
a bright spot, reddish-white or white, 25 then
the priest shall examine it; and indeed *if* the
hair of the bright spot has turned white, and it
appears deeper than the skin, it *is* leprosy broken out in the burn. Therefore the priest shall
pronounce him unclean. It *is* a leprous sore.
26 But if the priest examines it, and indeed
there are no white hairs in the bright spot, and
it *is* not deeper than the skin, but has faded,
then the priest shall isolate him seven days.
27 And the priest shall examine him on the
seventh day. If it has at all spread over the skin,
then the priest shall pronounce him unclean.
It *is* a leprous sore. 28 But if the bright spot
stays in one place, *and* has not spread on the
skin, but has faded, it *is* a swelling from the
burn. The priest shall pronounce him clean,
for it *is* the scar from the burn.

29"If a man or woman has a sore on the
head or the beard, 30 then the priest shall
examine the sore; and indeed if it appears
deeper than the skin, *and there is* in it thin
yellow hair, then the priest shall pronounce
him unclean. It *is* a scaly leprosy of the head
or beard. 31 But if the priest examines the
scaly sore, and indeed it does not appear
deeper than the skin, and *there is* no black
hair in it, then the priest shall isolate *the one*
who has the scale seven days. 32 And on the
seventh day the priest shall examine the
sore; and indeed *if* the scale has not spread,
and there is no yellow hair in it, and the scale
does not appear deeper than the skin, 33 he
shall shave himself, but the scale he shall
not shave. And the priest shall isolate *the one*
who has the scale another seven days. 34 On
the seventh day the priest shall examine the
scale; and indeed *if* the scale has not spread
over the skin, and does not appear deeper
than the skin, then the priest shall pronounce
him clean. He shall wash his clothes and be
clean. 35 But if the scale should at all spread
over the skin after his cleansing, 36 then the
priest shall examine him; and indeed *if* the
scale has spread over the skin, the priest need
not seek for yellow hair. He *is* unclean. 37 But
if the scale appears to be at a standstill, and
there is black hair grown up in it, the scale
has healed. He *is* clean, and the priest shall
pronounce him clean.

38"If a man or a woman has bright spots
on the skin of the body, *specifically* white
bright spots, 39 then the priest shall look;
and indeed *if* the bright spots on the skin of
the body *are* dull white, it *is* a white spot *that*
grows on the skin. He *is* clean.

40"As for the man whose hair has fallen
from his head, he *is* bald, *but* he *is* clean. 41 He
whose hair has fallen from his forehead, he *is*
bald on the forehead, *but* he *is* clean. 42 And if
there is on the bald head or bald [a]forehead a
reddish-white sore, it *is* leprosy breaking out
on his bald head or his bald forehead. 43 Then
the priest shall examine it; and indeed *if* the
swelling of the sore *is* reddish-white on his

13:10 [a] Num. 12:10, 12 **13:13** [a] Ex. 4:6 **13:18** [a] Ex. 9:9; 15:26 **13:24** [a] Is. 3:24 **13:42** [a] 2 Chr. 26:19

bald head or on his bald forehead, as the appearance of leprosy on the skin of the body,
44 he is a leprous man. He *is* unclean. The
priest shall surely pronounce him unclean;
his sore *is* on his [a]head.
45 "Now the leper on whom the sore *is*, his
clothes shall be torn and his head [a]bare; and
he shall [b]cover his mustache, and cry, [c]'Unclean! Unclean!' 46 He shall be unclean. All
the days he has the sore he shall be unclean.
He *is* unclean, and he shall dwell alone; his
dwelling *shall be* [a]outside the camp.

The Law Concerning Leprous Garments

47 "Also, if a garment has a leprous plague[1]
in it, *whether it is* a woolen garment or a
linen garment, 48 whether *it is* in the warp
or woof of linen or wool, whether in leather
or in anything made of leather, 49 and if the
plague is greenish or reddish in the garment
or in the leather, whether in the warp or in
the woof, or in anything made of leather, it
is a leprous plague and shall be shown to the
priest. 50 The priest shall examine the plague
and isolate *that which has* the plague seven
days. 51 And he shall examine the plague on
the seventh day. If the plague has spread in
the garment, either in the warp or in the woof,
in the leather *or* in anything made of leather,
the plague *is* [a]an active leprosy. It *is* unclean.
52 He shall therefore burn that garment in
which is the plague, whether warp or woof,
in wool or in linen, or anything of leather,
for it *is* an active leprosy; *the garment* shall
be burned in the fire.
53 "But if the priest examines *it*, and indeed the plague has not spread in the garment, either in the warp or in the woof, or in
anything made of leather, 54 then the priest
shall command that they wash *the thing* in
which *is* the plague; and he shall isolate it
another seven days. 55 Then the priest shall
examine the plague after it has been washed;
and indeed *if* the plague has not changed
its color, though the plague has not spread,
it *is* unclean, and you shall burn it in the
fire; it continues eating away, *whether* the
damage *is* outside or inside. 56 If the priest
examines *it*, and indeed the plague has faded
after washing it, then he shall tear it out of
the garment, whether out of the warp or out
of the woof, or out of the leather. 57 But if it
appears again in the garment, either in the
warp or in the woof, or in anything made of
leather, it *is* a spreading *plague*; you shall
burn with fire that in which is the plague.
58 And if you wash the garment, either warp

PEACE NOTE

Our lives should be defined by gratitude that confirms we do not accomplish anything on our own. Gratitude reveals a humble and dependent heart.

or woof, or whatever is made of leather, if the
plague has disappeared from it, then it shall
be washed a second time, and shall be clean.
59 "This *is* the law of the leprous plague
in a garment of wool or linen, either in the
warp or woof, or in anything made of leather, to pronounce it clean or to pronounce it
unclean."

The Ritual for Cleansing Healed Lepers

14 Then the LORD spoke to Moses, saying,
2 "This shall be the law of the leper for the
day of his cleansing: He [a]shall be brought to the
priest. 3 And the priest shall go out of the camp,
and the priest shall examine *him*; and indeed,
if the leprosy is healed in the leper, 4 then the
priest shall command to take for him who is to
be cleansed two living *and* clean birds, [a]cedar
wood, [b]scarlet, and [c]hyssop. 5 And the priest
shall command that one of the birds be killed
in an earthen vessel over running water. 6 As
for the living bird, he shall take it, the cedar
wood and the scarlet and the hyssop, and dip
them and the living bird in the blood of the
bird *that was* killed over the running water.
7 And he shall [a]sprinkle it [b]seven times on him
who is to be cleansed from the leprosy, and
shall pronounce him clean, and shall let the
living bird loose in the open field. 8 He who is
to be cleansed [a]shall wash his clothes, shave
off all his hair, and [b]wash himself in water, that
he may be clean. After that he shall come into
the camp, and [c]shall stay outside his tent seven
days. 9 But on the [a]seventh day he shall shave
all the hair off his head and his beard and his
eyebrows—all his hair he shall shave off. He
shall wash his clothes and wash his body in
water, and he shall be clean.

13:44 [a] Is. 1:5 13:45 [a] Lev. 10:6; 21:10 [b] Ezek. 24:17, 22 [c] Lam. 4:15 13:46 [a] Num. 5:1–4; 12:14 13:47 [1] A mold, fungus, or similar infestation, and so in verses 47–59 13:51 [a] Lev. 14:44 14:2 [a] Matt. 8:2, 4 14:4 [a] Num. 19:6 [b] Ex. 25:4 [c] Ps. 51:7 14:7 [a] Num. 19:18, 19 [b] Ps. 51:2 14:8 [a] Num. 8:7 [b] [Heb. 10:22] [c] Num. 5:2, 3; 12:14, 15 14:9 [a] Num. 19:19

10"And on the eighth day [a]he shall take two male lambs without blemish, one ewe lamb of the first year without blemish, three-tenths *of an ephah* of fine flour mixed with oil as [b]a grain offering, and one log of oil. 11Then the priest who makes *him* clean shall present the man who is to be made clean, and those things, before the LORD, *at* the door of the tabernacle of meeting. 12And the priest shall take one male lamb and [a]offer it as a trespass offering, and the log of oil, and [b]wave them *as* a wave offering before the LORD. 13Then he shall kill the lamb [a]in the place where he kills the sin offering and the burnt offering, in a holy place; for [b]as the sin offering *is* the priest's, so *is* the trespass offering. [c]It *is* most holy. 14The priest shall take *some* of the blood of the trespass offering, and the priest shall put *it* [a]on the tip of the right ear of him who is to be cleansed, on the thumb of his right hand, and on the big toe of his right foot. 15And the priest shall take *some* of the log of oil, and pour *it* into the palm of his own left hand. 16Then the priest shall dip his right finger in the oil that *is* in his left hand, and shall [a]sprinkle some of the oil with his finger seven times before the LORD. 17And of the rest of the oil in his hand, the priest shall put *some* on the tip of the right ear of him who is to be cleansed, on the thumb of his right hand, and on the big toe of his right foot, on the blood of the trespass offering. 18The rest of the oil that *is* in the priest's hand he shall put on the head of him who is to be cleansed. [a]So the priest shall make atonement for him before the LORD.

19"Then the priest shall offer [a]the sin offering, and make atonement for him who is to be cleansed from his uncleanness. Afterward he shall kill the burnt offering. 20And the priest shall offer the burnt offering and the grain offering on the altar. So the priest shall make atonement for him, and he shall be [a]clean.

21"But [a]if he *is* poor and cannot afford it, then he shall take one male lamb *as* a trespass offering to be waved, to make atonement for him, one-tenth *of an ephah* of fine flour mixed with oil as a grain offering, a log of oil, 22[a]and two turtledoves or two young pigeons, such as he is able to afford: one shall be a sin offering and the other a burnt offering. 23[a]He shall bring them to the priest on the eighth day for his cleansing, to the door of the tabernacle of meeting, before the LORD. 24[a]And the priest shall take the lamb of the trespass offering and the log of oil, and the priest shall wave them *as* a wave offering before the LORD. 25Then he shall kill the lamb of the trespass offering, [a]and the priest shall take *some* of the blood of the trespass offering and put *it* on the tip of the right ear of him who is to be cleansed, on the thumb of his right hand, and on the big toe of his right foot. 26And the priest shall pour some of the oil into the palm of his own left hand. 27Then the priest shall sprinkle with his right finger *some* of the oil that *is* in his left hand seven times before the LORD. 28And the priest shall put *some* of the oil that *is* in his hand on the tip of the right ear of him who is to be cleansed, on the thumb of the right hand, and on the big toe of his right foot, on the place of the blood of the trespass offering. 29The rest of the oil that *is* in the priest's hand he shall put on the head of him who is to be cleansed, to make atonement for him before the LORD. 30And he shall offer one of [a]the turtledoves or young pigeons, such as he can afford— 31such as he is able to afford, the one *as* a sin offering and the other *as* a burnt offering, with the grain offering. So the priest shall make atonement for him who is to be cleansed before the LORD. 32This *is* the law *for one* who had a leprous sore, who cannot afford [a]the usual cleansing."

The Law Concerning Leprous Houses

33And the LORD spoke to Moses and Aaron, saying: 34[a]"When you have come into the land of Canaan, which I give you as a possession, and [b]I put the leprous plague[1] in a house in the land of your possession, 35and he who owns the house comes and tells the priest, saying, 'It seems to me that *there is* [a]some plague in the house,' 36then the priest shall command that they empty the house, before the priest goes *into it* to examine the plague, that all that *is* in the house may not be made unclean; and afterward the priest shall go in to examine the house. 37And he shall examine the plague; and indeed *if* the plague *is* on the walls of the house with ingrained streaks, greenish or reddish, which appear to be deep in the wall, 38then the priest shall go out of the house, to the door of the house, and shut up the house seven days. 39And the priest shall come again on the seventh day and look; and indeed *if* the plague has spread on the walls of the house, 40then the priest shall command that they take away the stones in which *is* the plague, and they

14:10 [a] Matt. 8:4 [b] Lev. 2:1 **14:12** [a] Lev. 5:6, 18; 6:6; 14:19 [b] Ex. 29:22–24, 26 **14:13** [a] Ex. 29:11 [b] Lev. 6:24–30; 7:7 [c] Lev. 2:3; 7:6; 21:22 **14:14** [a] Lev. 8:23, 24 **14:16** [a] Lev. 4:6 **14:18** [a] Lev. 4:26; 5:6 **14:19** [a] Lev. 5:1, 6; 12:7 **14:20** [a] Lev. 14:8, 9 **14:21** [a] Lev. 5:7, 11; 12:8; 27:8 **14:22** [a] Lev. 12:8; 15:14, 15 **14:23** [a] Lev. 14:10, 11 **14:24** [a] Lev. 14:12 **14:25** [a] Lev. 14:14, 17 **14:30** [a] Lev. 14:22; 15:14, 15 **14:32** [a] Lev. 14:10 **14:34** [a] Deut. 7:1; 32:49 [b] [Prov. 3:33] [1] Decomposition by mildew, mold, dry rot, etc., and so in verses 34–53 **14:35** [a] [Ps. 91:9, 10]

shall cast them into an unclean place outside the city. 41 And he shall cause the house to be scraped inside, all around, and the dust that they scrape off they shall pour out in an unclean place outside the city. 42 Then they shall take other stones and put *them* in the place of *those* stones, and he shall take other mortar and plaster the house.

43 "Now if the plague comes back and breaks out in the house, after he has taken away the stones, after he has scraped the house, and after it is plastered, 44 then the priest shall come and look; and indeed *if* the plague has spread in the house, it *is* [a]an active leprosy in the house. It *is* unclean. 45 And he shall break down the house, its stones, its timber, and all the plaster of the house, and he shall carry *them* outside the city to an unclean place. 46 Moreover he who goes into the house at all while it is shut up shall be unclean [a]until evening. 47 And he who lies down in the house shall [a]wash his clothes, and he who eats in the house shall wash his clothes.

48 "But if the priest comes in and examines *it,* and indeed the plague has not spread in the house after the house was plastered, then the priest shall pronounce the house clean, because the plague is healed. 49 And [a]he shall take, to cleanse the house, two birds, cedar wood, scarlet, and hyssop. 50 Then he shall kill one of the birds in an earthen vessel over running water; 51 and he shall take the cedar wood, the hyssop, the scarlet, and the living bird, and dip them in the blood of the slain bird and in the running water, and sprinkle the house seven times. 52 And he shall cleanse the house with the blood of the bird and the running water and the living bird, with the cedar wood, the hyssop, and the scarlet. 53 Then he shall let the living bird loose outside the city in the open field, and [a]make atonement for the house, and it shall be clean.

54 "This *is* the law for any [a]leprous sore and scale, 55 for the [a]leprosy of a garment [b]and of a house, 56 [a]for a swelling and a scab and a bright spot, 57 to [a]teach when *it is* unclean and when *it is* clean. This *is* the law of leprosy."

The Law Concerning Bodily Discharges

15 And the LORD spoke to Moses and Aaron, saying, 2 "Speak to the children of Israel, and say to them: [a]'When any man has a discharge from his body, his discharge *is* unclean. 3 And this shall be his uncleanness in regard to his discharge—whether his body runs with his discharge, or his body is stopped up by his discharge, it *is* his uncleanness. 4 Every bed is unclean on which he who has the discharge lies, and everything on which he sits shall be unclean. 5 And whoever [a]touches his bed shall [b]wash his clothes and [c]bathe in water, and be unclean until evening. 6 He who sits on anything on which he who has the [a]discharge sat shall wash his clothes and bathe in water, and be unclean until evening. 7 And he who touches the body of him who has the discharge shall wash his clothes and bathe in water, and be unclean until evening. 8 If he who has the discharge [a]spits on him who is clean, then he shall wash his clothes and bathe in water, and be unclean until evening. 9 Any saddle on which he who has the discharge rides shall be unclean. 10 Whoever touches anything that was under him shall be unclean until evening. He who carries *any of* those things shall wash his clothes and bathe in water, and be unclean until evening. 11 And whomever the one who has the discharge touches, and has not rinsed his hands in water, he shall wash his clothes and bathe in water, and be unclean until evening. 12 The [a]vessel of earth that he who has the discharge touches shall be broken, and every vessel of wood shall be rinsed in water.

13 'And when he who has a discharge is cleansed of his discharge, then [a]he shall count for himself seven days for his cleansing, wash his clothes, and bathe his body in running water; then he shall be clean. 14 On the eighth day he shall take for himself [a]two turtledoves or two young pigeons, and come before the LORD, to the door of the tabernacle of meeting, and give them to the priest. 15 Then the priest shall offer them, [a]the one *as* a sin offering and the other *as* a burnt offering. [b]So the priest shall make atonement for him before the LORD because of his discharge.

16 [a]'If any man has an emission of semen, then he shall wash all his body in water, and be unclean until evening. 17 And any garment and any leather on which there is semen, it shall be washed with water, and be unclean until evening. 18 Also, when a woman lies with a man, and *there is* an emission of semen, they shall bathe in water, and [a]be unclean until evening.

19 [a]'If a woman has a discharge, *and* the discharge from her body is blood, she shall be set apart seven days; and whoever touches her shall be unclean until evening. 20 Everything

14:44 [a] Lev. 13:51 **14:46** [a] Lev. 11:24; 15:5 **14:47** [a] Lev. 14:8 **14:49** [a] Lev. 14:4 **14:53** [a] Lev. 14:20 **14:54** [a] Lev. 13:30; 26:21 **14:55** [a] Lev. 13:47–52 [b] Lev. 14:34 **14:56** [a] Lev. 13:2 **14:57** [a] Deut. 24:8 **15:2** [a] Num. 5:2 **15:5** [a] Lev. 5:2; 14:46 [b] Lev. 14:8, 47 [c] Lev. 11:25; 17:15 **15:6** [a] Deut. 23:10 **15:8** [a] Num. 12:14 **15:12** [a] Lev. 6:28; 11:32, 33 **15:13** [a] Lev. 14:8; 15:28 **15:14** [a] Lev. 14:22, 23, 30, 31 **15:15** [a] Lev. 14:30, 31 [b] Lev. 14:19, 31 **15:16** [a] Lev. 22:4 **15:18** [a] [1 Sam. 21:4] **15:19** [a] Lev. 12:2

that she lies on during her impurity shall be
unclean; also everything that she sits on shall
be unclean. 21 Whoever touches her bed shall
wash his clothes and bathe in water, and be
unclean until evening. 22 And whoever touches
anything that she sat on shall wash his clothes
and bathe in water, and be unclean until evening. 23 If *anything* is on *her* bed or on anything
on which she sits, when he touches it, he shall
be unclean until evening. 24 And [a]if any man
lies with her at all, so that her impurity is on
him, he shall be unclean seven days; and every
bed on which he lies shall be unclean.

25 'If [a]a woman has a discharge of blood
for many days, other than at the time of her
customary impurity, or if it runs beyond
her *usual time of* impurity, all the days of her
unclean discharge shall be as the days of her
customary impurity. She *shall be* unclean.
26 Every bed on which she lies all the days of
her discharge shall be to her as the bed of her
impurity; and whatever she sits on shall be
unclean, as the uncleanness of her impurity.
27 Whoever touches those things shall be unclean; he shall wash his clothes and bathe in
water, and be unclean until evening.

28 'But [a]if she is cleansed of her discharge,
then she shall count for herself seven days,
and after that she shall be clean. 29 And on
the eighth day she shall take for herself two
turtledoves or two young pigeons, and bring
them to the priest, to the door of the tabernacle of meeting. 30 Then the priest shall offer
the one *as* a sin offering and the other *as* a
[a]burnt offering, and the priest shall make
atonement for her before the LORD for the
discharge of her uncleanness.

31 'Thus you shall [a]separate the children of
Israel from their uncleanness, lest they die
in their uncleanness when they [b]defile My
tabernacle that *is* among them. 32 [a]This *is* the
law for one who has a discharge, [b]and *for him*
who emits semen and is unclean thereby,
33 [a]and for her who is indisposed because
of her *customary* impurity, and for one who
has a discharge, either man [b]or woman, [c]and
for him who lies with her who is unclean.' "

The Day of Atonement

16 Now the LORD spoke to Moses after
[a]the death of the two sons of Aaron,
when they offered *profane fire* before the
LORD, and died; 2 and the LORD said to Moses:
"Tell Aaron your brother [a]not to come at *just*
any time into the Holy *Place* inside the veil,
before the mercy seat which *is* on the ark, lest
he die; for [b]I will appear in the cloud above
the mercy seat.

3 "Thus Aaron shall [a]come into the Holy
Place: [b]with *the blood of* a young bull as a sin
offering, and *of* a ram as a burnt offering. 4 He
shall put the [a]holy linen tunic and the linen
trousers on his body; he shall be girded with a
linen sash, and with the linen turban he shall
be attired. These *are* holy garments. Therefore
[b]he shall wash his body in water, and put them
on. 5 And he shall take from [a]the congregation
of the children of Israel two kids of the goats as
a sin offering, and one ram as a burnt offering.

6 "Aaron shall offer the bull as a sin offering, which *is* for himself, and [a]make atonement for himself and for his house. 7 He shall
take the two goats and present them before
the LORD *at* the door of the tabernacle of
meeting. 8 Then Aaron shall cast lots for the
two goats: one lot for the LORD and the other
lot for the scapegoat. 9 And Aaron shall bring
the goat on which the LORD's lot fell, and
offer it *as* a sin offering. 10 But the goat on
which the lot fell to be the scapegoat shall
be presented alive before the LORD, to make
[a]atonement upon it, *and* to let it go as the
scapegoat into the wilderness.

11 "And Aaron shall bring the bull of the
sin offering, which is for [a]himself, and make
atonement for himself and for his house, and
shall kill the bull as the sin offering which *is*
for himself. 12 Then he shall take [a]a censer
full of burning coals of fire from the altar
before the LORD, with his hands full of [b]sweet
incense beaten fine, and bring *it* inside the
veil. 13 [a]And he shall put the incense on the
fire before the LORD, that the cloud of incense
may cover the [b]mercy seat that *is* on the Testimony, lest he [c]die. 14 [a]He shall take some of
the blood of the bull and [b]sprinkle *it* with his
finger on the mercy seat on the east *side;* and
before the mercy seat he shall sprinkle some
of the blood with his finger seven times.

15 [a]"Then he shall kill the goat of the sin offering, which *is* for the people, bring its blood
[b]inside the veil, do with that blood as he did
with the blood of the bull, and sprinkle it on
the mercy seat and before the mercy seat. 16 So
he shall [a]make atonement for the Holy *Place*,
because of the uncleanness of the children of
Israel, and because of their transgressions,
for all their sins; and so he shall do for the

15:24 [a] Lev. 18:19; 20:18 **15:25** [a] Matt. 9:20 **15:28** [a] Lev. 15:13–15 **15:30** [a] Lev. 5:7 **15:31** [a] Deut. 24:8 [b] Num. 5:3; 19:13, 20 **15:32** [a] Lev. 15:2 [b] Lev. 15:16 **15:33** [a] Lev. 15:19 [b] Lev. 15:25 [c] Lev. 15:24 **16:1** [a] Lev. 10:1, 2 **16:2** [a] Ex. 30:10 [b] Ex. 25:21, 22; 40:34 **16:3** [a] [Heb. 9:7, 12, 24, 25] [b] Lev. 4:3 **16:4** [a] Ex. 28:39, 42, 43 [b] Ex. 30:20 **16:5** [a] Lev. 4:14 **16:6** [a] [Heb. 5:3; 7:27, 28; 9:7] **16:10** [a] [1 John 2:2] **16:11** [a] [Heb. 7:27; 9:7] **16:12** [a] Lev. 10:1 [b] Ex. 30:34–38 **16:13** [a] Ex. 30:7, 8 [b] Ex. 25:21 [c] Ex. 28:43 **16:14** [a] [Heb. 9:25; 10:4] [b] Lev. 4:6, 17 **16:15** [a] [Heb. 2:17] [b] [Heb. 6:19; 7:27; 9:3, 7, 12] **16:16** [a] Ex. 29:36; 30:10

tabernacle of meeting which remains among them in the midst of their uncleanness. 17 There shall be [a]no man in the tabernacle of meeting when he goes in to make atonement in the Holy *Place*, until he comes out, that he may make atonement for himself, for his household, and for all the assembly of Israel. 18 And he shall go out to the altar that *is* before the LORD, and make atonement for [a]it, and shall take some of the blood of the bull and some of the blood of the goat, and put it on the horns of the altar all around. 19 Then he shall sprinkle some of the blood on it with his finger seven times, cleanse it, and [a]consecrate it from the uncleanness of the children of Israel.

20 "And when he has made an end of atoning for the Holy *Place*, the tabernacle of meeting, and the altar, he shall bring the live goat. 21 Aaron shall lay both his hands on the head of the live goat, [a]confess over it all the iniquities of the children of Israel, and all their transgressions, concerning all their sins, [b]putting them on the head of the goat, and shall send *it* away into the wilderness by the hand of a suitable man. 22 The goat shall [a]bear on itself all their iniquities to an uninhabited land; and he shall [b]release the goat in the wilderness.

23 "Then Aaron shall come into the tabernacle of meeting, [a]shall take off the linen garments which he put on when he went into the Holy *Place*, and shall leave them there. 24 And he shall wash his body with water in a holy place, put on his garments, come out and offer his burnt offering and the burnt offering of the people, and make atonement for himself and for the people. 25 [a]The fat of the sin offering he shall burn on the altar. 26 And he who released the goat as the scapegoat shall wash his clothes [a]and bathe his body in water, and afterward he may come into the camp. 27 [a]The bull *for* the sin offering and the goat *for* the sin offering, whose blood was brought in to make atonement in the Holy *Place*, shall be carried outside the camp. And they shall burn in the fire their skins, their flesh, and their offal. 28 Then he who burns them shall wash his clothes and bathe his body in water, and afterward he may come into the camp.

29 "*This* shall be a statute forever for you: [a]In the seventh month, on the tenth *day* of the month, you shall afflict your souls, and do no work at all, *whether* a native of your own country or a stranger who dwells among you. 30 For on that day *the priest* shall make atonement for you, to [a]cleanse you, *that* you may be clean from all your sins before the LORD. 31 [a]It *is* a sabbath of solemn rest for you, and you shall afflict your souls. *It is* a statute forever. 32 [a]And the priest, who is anointed and [b]consecrated to minister as priest in his father's place, shall make atonement, and put on the linen clothes, the holy garments; 33 then he shall make atonement for the Holy Sanctuary,[1] and he shall make atonement for the tabernacle of meeting and for the altar, and he shall make atonement for the priests and for all the people of the assembly. 34 [a]This shall be an everlasting statute for you, to make atonement for the children of Israel, for all their sins, [b]once a year." And he did as the LORD commanded Moses.

The Sanctity of Blood

17 And the LORD spoke to Moses, saying, 2 "Speak to Aaron, to his sons, and to all the children of Israel, and say to them, 'This *is* the thing which the LORD has commanded, saying: 3 "Whatever man of the house of Israel who [a]kills an ox or lamb or goat in the camp, or who kills *it* outside the camp, 4 and does not bring it to the door of the tabernacle of meeting to offer an offering to the LORD before the tabernacle of the LORD, the guilt of bloodshed shall be [a]imputed to that man. He has shed blood; and that man shall be cut off from among his people, 5 to the end that the children of Israel may bring their sacrifices [a]which they offer in the open field, that they may bring them to the LORD at the door of the tabernacle of meeting, to the priest, and offer them *as* peace offerings to the LORD. 6 And the priest [a]shall sprinkle the blood on the altar

PEACE NOTE

We usually read the word "blessed," but *happy* is the better word. *Happiness* describes what it means to live in the peace of God.

16:17 [a] Luke 1:10 **16:18** [a] Ex. 29:36 **16:19** [a] Ezek. 43:20 **16:21** [a] Lev. 5:5; 26:40 [b] [Is. 53:6] **16:22** [a] [Is. 53:6, 11, 12] [b] Lev. 14:7 **16:23** [a] Ezek. 42:14; 44:19 **16:25** [a] Lev. 1:8; 4:10 **16:26** [a] Lev. 15:5 **16:27** [a] Heb. 13:11 **16:29** [a] Lev. 23:27–32 **16:30** [a] Jer. 33:8 **16:31** [a] Lev. 23:27, 32 **16:32** [a] Lev. 4:3, 5, 16; 21:10 [b] Ex. 29:29, 30 **16:33** [1] That is, *the Most Holy Place* **16:34** [a] Lev. 23:31 [b] [Heb. 9:7, 25, 28] **17:3** [a] Deut. 12:5, 15, 21 **17:4** [a] Rom. 5:13 **17:5** [a] Deut. 12:1–27 **17:6** [a] Lev. 3:2

of the LORD *at* the door of the tabernacle of
meeting, and [b]burn the fat for a sweet aroma
to the LORD. 7 They shall no more offer their
sacrifices [a]to demons, after whom they [b]have
played the harlot. This shall be a statute forever for them throughout their generations." '
8 "Also you shall say to them: 'Whatever
man of the house of Israel, or of the strangers
who dwell among you, [a]who offers a burnt
offering or sacrifice, 9 and does not [a]bring it
to the door of the tabernacle of meeting, to
offer it to the LORD, that man shall be cut off
from among his people.
10 [a]'And whatever man of the house of Israel, or of the strangers who dwell among you,
who eats any blood, [b]I will set My face against
that person who eats blood, and will cut him
off from among his people. 11 For the [a]life of
the flesh *is* in the blood, and I have given it
to you upon the altar [b]to make atonement
for your souls; for [c]it *is* the blood *that* makes
atonement for the soul.' 12 Therefore I said to
the children of Israel, 'No one among you
shall eat blood, nor shall any stranger who
dwells among you eat blood.'
13 "Whatever man of the children of Israel,
or of the strangers who dwell among you, who
[a]hunts and catches any animal or bird that
may be eaten, he shall [b]pour out its blood
and [c]cover it with dust; 14 [a]for *it is* the life of
all flesh. Its blood sustains its life. Therefore I
said to the children of Israel, 'You shall not eat
the blood of any flesh, for the life of all flesh
is its blood. Whoever eats it shall be cut off.'
15 [a]"And every person who eats what died
naturally or what was torn *by beasts, whether
he is* a native of your own country or a stranger,
[b]he shall both wash his clothes and [c]bathe in
water, and be unclean until evening. Then he
shall be clean. 16 But if he does not wash *them*
or bathe his body, then [a]he shall bear his guilt."

Laws of Sexual Morality

18 Then the LORD spoke to Moses, saying, 2 "Speak to the children of Israel, and say to them: [a]'I am the LORD your
God. 3 [a]According to the doings of the land
of Egypt, where you dwelt, you shall not do;
and [b]according to the doings of the land of
Canaan, where I am bringing you, you shall
not do; nor shall you walk in their ordinances.
4 [a]You shall observe My judgments and keep
My ordinances, to walk in them: I *am* the
LORD your God. 5 You shall therefore keep My
statutes and My judgments, which if a man
does, he shall live by them: I *am* the LORD.
6 'None of you shall approach anyone who is
near of kin to him, to uncover his nakedness:
I *am* the LORD. 7 The nakedness of your father
or the nakedness of your mother you shall
not uncover. She *is* your mother; you shall
not uncover her nakedness. 8 The nakedness
of your [a]father's wife you shall not uncover; it
is your father's nakedness. 9 [a]The nakedness
of your sister, the daughter of your father, or
the daughter of your mother, *whether* born at
home or elsewhere, their nakedness you shall
not uncover. 10 The nakedness of your son's
daughter or your daughter's daughter, their
nakedness you shall not uncover; for theirs
is your own nakedness. 11 The nakedness of
your father's wife's daughter, begotten by
your father—she *is* your sister—you shall
not uncover her nakedness. 12 [a]You shall not
uncover the nakedness of your father's sister;
she *is* near of kin to your father. 13 You shall
not uncover the nakedness of your mother's
sister, for she *is* near of kin to your mother.
14 [a]You shall not uncover the nakedness of
your father's brother. You shall not approach
his wife; she *is* your aunt. 15 You shall not
uncover the nakedness of your daughter-
in-law—she *is* your son's wife—you shall
not uncover her nakedness. 16 You shall not
uncover the nakedness of your brother's
wife; it *is* your brother's nakedness. 17 You
shall not uncover the nakedness of a woman
and her [a]daughter, nor shall you take her
son's daughter or her daughter's daughter, to
uncover her nakedness. They *are* near of kin
to her. It *is* wickedness. 18 Nor shall you take
a woman [a]as a rival to her sister, to uncover
her nakedness while the other is alive.
19 'Also you shall not approach a woman
to uncover her nakedness as [a]long as she
is in her [b]*customary* impurity. 20 [a]Moreover
you shall not lie carnally with your [b]neigh-
bor's wife, to defile yourself with her. 21 And
you shall not let any of your descendants
[a]pass through [b]*the fire* to [c]Molech, nor shall
you profane the name of your God: I *am* the
LORD. 22 You shall not lie with [a]a male as with
a woman. It *is* an abomination. 23 Nor shall
you mate with any [a]animal, to defile yourself
with it. Nor shall any woman stand before
an animal to mate with it. It *is* perversion.
24 [a]'Do not defile yourselves with any of
these things; [b]for by all these the nations

17:6 [b] Num. 18:17 **17:7** [a] Deut. 32:17 [b] Ezek. 23:8 **17:8** [a] Lev. 1:2, 3; 18:26 **17:9** [a] Lev. 14:23 **17:10** [a] Gen. 9:4 [b] Lev. 20:3, 5, 6 **17:11** [a] Gen. 9:4 [b] [Matt. 26:28] [c] [Heb. 9:22] **17:13** [a] Lev. 7:26 [b] Deut. 12:16, 24 [c] Ezek. 24:7 **17:14** [a] Gen. 9:4 **17:15** [a] Ex. 22:31 [b] Lev. 11:25 [c] Lev. 15:5 **17:16** [a] Lev. 5:1 **18:2** [a] Ex. 6:7 **18:3** [a] Ezek. 20:7, 8 [b] Lev. 18:24–30; 20:23 **18:4** [a] Ezek. 20:19 **18:8** [a] Gen. 35:22 **18:9** [a] Deut. 27:22 **18:12** [a] Lev. 20:19 **18:14** [a] Lev. 20:20 **18:17** [a] Lev. 20:14 **18:18** [a] 1 Sam. 1:6, 8 **18:19** [a] Ezek. 18:6 [b] Lev. 15:24; 20:18 **18:20** [a] [Prov. 6:25–33] [b] Lev. 20:10 **18:21** [a] Lev. 20:2–5 [b] 2 Kin. 16:3 [c] 1 Kin. 11:7, 33 **18:22** [a] Lev. 20:13 **18:23** [a] Ex. 22:19 **18:24** [a] Matt. 15:18–20 [b] Deut. 18:12

are defiled, which I am casting out before you. 25 For [a]the land is defiled; therefore I [b]visit the punishment of its iniquity upon it, and the land [c]vomits out its inhabitants. 26 [a]You shall therefore keep My statutes and My judgments, and shall not commit *any* of these abominations, *either* any of your own nation or any stranger who dwells among you 27 (for all these abominations the men of the land have done, who *were* before you, and thus the land is defiled), 28 lest [a]the land vomit you out also when you defile it, as it vomited out the nations that *were* before you. 29 For whoever commits any of these abominations, the persons who commit *them* shall be cut off from among their people.

30 'Therefore you shall keep My ordinance, so [a]that *you* do not commit *any* of these abominable customs which were committed before you, and that you do not defile yourselves by them: [b]I *am* the LORD your God.' "

Moral and Ceremonial Laws

19 And the LORD spoke to Moses, saying, 2 "Speak to all the congregation of the children of Israel, and say to them: [a]'You shall be holy, for I the LORD your God *am* holy.

3 [a]'Every one of you shall revere his mother and his father, and [b]keep My Sabbaths: I *am* the LORD your God.

4 [a]'Do not turn to idols, [b]nor make for yourselves molded gods: I *am* the LORD your God.

5 'And [a]if you offer a sacrifice of a peace offering to the LORD, you shall offer it of your own free will. 6 It shall be eaten the same day you offer *it*, and on the next day. And if any remains until the third day, it shall be burned in the fire. 7 And if it is eaten at all on the third day, it *is* an abomination. It shall not be accepted. 8 Therefore *everyone* who eats it shall bear his iniquity, because he has profaned the hallowed *offering* of the LORD; and that person shall be cut off from his people.

9 [a]'When you reap the harvest of your land, you shall not wholly reap the corners of your field, nor shall you gather the gleanings of your harvest. 10 And you shall not glean your vineyard, nor shall you gather *every* grape of your vineyard; you shall leave them for the poor and the stranger: I *am* the LORD your God.

11 [a]'You shall not steal, nor deal falsely, [b]nor lie to one another. 12 And you shall not [a]swear by My name falsely, [b]nor shall you profane the name of your God: I *am* the LORD.

13 [a]'You shall not cheat your neighbor, nor rob *him*. [b]The wages of him who is hired shall not remain with you all night until morning. 14 You shall not curse the deaf, [a]nor put a stumbling block before the blind, but shall fear your God: I *am* the LORD.

15 'You shall do no injustice in [a]judgment. You shall not [b]be partial to the poor, nor honor the person of the mighty. In righteousness you shall judge your neighbor. 16 You shall not go about *as* a [a]talebearer among your people; nor shall you [b]take a stand against the life of your neighbor: I *am* the LORD.

17 [a]'You shall not hate your brother in your heart. [b]You shall surely rebuke your neighbor, and not bear sin because of him. 18 [a]You shall not take vengeance, nor bear any grudge against the children of your people, [b]but you shall love your neighbor as yourself: I *am* the LORD.

19 'You shall keep My statutes. You shall not let your livestock breed with another kind. You shall not sow your field with mixed seed. Nor shall a garment of mixed linen and wool come upon you.

20 'Whoever lies carnally with a woman who *is* [a]betrothed to a man as a concubine, and who has not at all been redeemed nor given her freedom, for this there shall be scourging; *but* they shall not be put to death, because she was not free. 21 And he shall bring his trespass offering to the LORD, to the door of the tabernacle of meeting, a ram as a trespass offering. 22 The priest shall make atonement for him with the ram of the trespass offering before the LORD for his sin which he has committed. And the sin which he has committed shall be forgiven him.

23 'When you come into the land, and have planted all kinds of trees for food, then you shall count their fruit as uncircumcised. Three years it shall be as uncircumcised to you. *It* shall not be eaten. 24 But in the fourth year all its fruit shall be holy, a praise to the LORD. 25 And in the fifth year you may eat its fruit, that it may yield to you its increase: I *am* the LORD your God.

26 'You shall not eat *anything* with the blood, nor shall you practice divination or soothsaying. 27 You shall not shave around the sides of your head, nor shall you disfigure the edges of your beard. 28 You shall not [a]make any cuttings in your flesh for the dead, nor tattoo any marks on you: I *am* the LORD.

29 [a]'Do not prostitute your daughter, to

18:25 [a] Num. 35:33, 34 [b] Jer. 5:9 [c] Lev. 18:28; 20:22 **18:26** [a] Lev. 18:5, 30 **18:28** [a] Jer. 9:19 **18:30** [a] Lev. 18:3; 22:9 [b] Lev. 18:2 **19:2** [a] Lev. 11:44; 20:7, 26 **19:3** [a] Ex. 20:12 [b] Ex. 16:23; 20:8; 31:13 **19:4** [a] Ex. 20:4 [b] Ex. 34:17 **19:5** [a] Lev. 7:16 **19:9** [a] Deut. 24:19–22 **19:11** [a] Ex. 20:15, 16 [b] Eph. 4:25 **19:12** [a] Deut. 5:11 [b] Lev. 18:21 **19:13** [a] Ex. 22:7–15, 21–27 [b] Deut. 24:15 **19:14** [a] Deut. 27:18 **19:15** [a] Deut. 16:19 [b] Ex. 23:3, 6 **19:16** [a] Prov. 11:13; 18:8; 20:19 [b] 1 Kin. 21:7–19 **19:17** [a] [1 John 2:9, 11; 3:15] [b] Matt. 18:15 **19:18** [a] [Deut. 32:35] [b] Mark 12:31 **19:20** [a] Deut. 22:23–27 **19:28** [a] Jer. 16:6 **19:29** [a] Deut. 22:21; 23:17, 18

cause her to be a harlot, lest the land fall into harlotry, and the land become full of wickedness.

30 'You shall keep My Sabbaths and [a]reverence My sanctuary: I *am* the LORD.

31 'Give no regard to mediums and familiar spirits; do not seek after [a]them, to be defiled by them: I *am* the LORD your God.

32 [a]'You shall rise before the gray headed and honor the presence of an old man, and [b]fear your God: I *am* the LORD.

33 'And [a]if a stranger dwells with you in your land, you shall not mistreat him. 34 [a]The stranger who dwells among you shall be to you as one born among you, and [b]you shall love him as yourself; for you were strangers in the land of Egypt: I *am* the LORD your God.

> PEACE NOTE
>
> Allow God to change your heart to be more compassionate so you will care for helpless people. His grace can shine through you.
>
> LEVITICUS 19:33

35 'You shall do no injustice in judgment, in measurement of length, weight, or volume. 36 You shall have [a]honest scales, honest weights, an honest ephah, and an honest hin: I *am* the LORD your God, who brought you out of the land of Egypt.

37 [a]'Therefore you shall observe all My statutes and all My judgments, and perform them: I *am* the LORD.' "

Penalties for Breaking the Law

20 Then the LORD spoke to Moses, saying, 2 [a]"Again, you shall say to the children of Israel: [b]'Whoever of the children of Israel, or of the strangers who dwell in Israel, who gives *any* of his descendants to Molech, he shall surely be put to death. The people of the land shall [c]stone him with stones. 3 [a]I will set My face against that man, and will cut him off from his people, because he has given *some* of his descendants to Molech, to defile My sanctuary and profane My holy name. 4 And if the people of the land should in any way hide their eyes from the man, when he gives *some* of his descendants to Molech, and they do not kill him, 5 then I will set My face against that man and against his family; and I will cut him off from his people, and all who prostitute themselves with him to commit harlotry with Molech.

6 'And [a]the person who turns to mediums and familiar spirits, to prostitute himself with them, I will set My face against that person and cut him off from his people. 7 [a]Consecrate yourselves therefore, and be holy, for I *am* the LORD your God. 8 And you shall keep [a]My statutes, and perform them: [b]I *am* the LORD who sanctifies you.

9 'For [a]everyone who curses his father or his mother shall surely be put to death. He has cursed his father or his mother. [b]His blood *shall be* upon him.

10 [a]'The man who commits adultery with *another* man's wife, *he* who commits adultery with his neighbor's wife, the adulterer and the adulteress, shall surely be put to death. 11 The man who lies with his [a]father's wife has uncovered his father's nakedness; both of them shall surely be put to death. Their blood *shall be* upon them. 12 If a man lies with his [a]daughter-in-law, both of them shall surely be put to death. They have committed perversion. Their blood *shall be* upon them. 13 [a]If a man lies with a male as he lies with a woman, both of them have committed an abomination. They shall surely be put to death. Their blood *shall be* upon them. 14 If a man marries a woman and her [a]mother, it *is* wickedness. They shall be burned with fire, both he and they, that there may be no wickedness among you. 15 If a man mates with an [a]animal, he shall surely be put to death, and you shall kill the animal. 16 If a woman approaches any animal and mates with it, you shall kill the woman and the animal. They shall surely be put to death. Their blood *is* upon them.

17 'If a man takes his [a]sister, his father's daughter or his mother's daughter, and sees her nakedness and she sees his nakedness, it *is* a wicked thing. And they shall be cut off in the sight of their people. He has uncovered his sister's nakedness. He shall bear his guilt. 18 [a]If a man lies with a woman during her

19:30 [a] Lev. 26:2 **19:31** [a] Lev. 20:6, 27 **19:32** [a] 1 Tim. 5:1 [b] Lev. 19:14 **19:33** [a] Ex. 22:21 **19:34** [a] Ex. 12:48 [b] Deut. 10:19 **19:36** [a] Deut. 25:13–15 **19:37** [a] Lev. 18:4, 5 **20:2** [a] Lev. 18:2 [b] Lev. 18:21 [c] Deut. 17:2–5 **20:3** [a] Lev. 17:10 **20:6** [a] Lev. 19:31 **20:7** [a] Lev. 19:2 **20:8** [a] Lev. 19:19, 37 [b] Ex. 31:13 **20:9** [a] Ex. 21:17 [b] 2 Sam. 1:16 **20:10** [a] Ex. 20:14 **20:11** [a] Lev. 18:7, 8 **20:12** [a] Lev. 18:15 **20:13** [a] Lev. 18:22 **20:14** [a] Lev. 18:17 **20:15** [a] Lev. 18:23 **20:17** [a] Lev. 18:9 **20:18** [a] Lev. 15:24; 18:19

sickness and uncovers her nakedness, he has
exposed her flow, and she has uncovered the
flow of her blood. Both of them shall be cut
off from their people.
19‘You shall not uncover the nakedness of
your [a]mother’s sister nor of your [b]father’s
sister, for that would uncover his near of
kin. They shall bear their guilt. 20If a man
lies with his [a]uncle’s wife, he has uncovered
his uncle’s nakedness. They shall bear their
sin; they shall die childless. 21If a man takes
his [a]brother’s wife, it *is* an unclean thing. He
has uncovered his brother’s nakedness. They
shall be childless.
22‘You shall therefore keep all My [a]statutes
and all My judgments, and perform them,
that the land where I am bringing you to
dwell [b]may not vomit you out. 23[a]And you
shall not walk in the statutes of the nation
which I am casting out before you; for they
commit all these things, and [b]therefore I
abhor them. 24But [a]I have said to you, “You
shall inherit their land, and I will give it to
you to possess, a land flowing with milk and
honey.” I *am* the LORD your God, [b]who has
separated you from the peoples. 25[a]You shall
therefore distinguish between clean animals
and unclean, between unclean birds and
clean, [b]and you shall not make yourselves
abominable by beast or by bird, or by any kind
of living thing that creeps on the ground,
which I have separated from you as unclean.
26And you shall be holy to Me, [a]for I the LORD
am holy, and have separated you from the
peoples, that you should be Mine.
27[a]‘A man or a woman who is a medium, or
who has familiar spirits, shall surely be put
to death; they shall stone them with stones.
Their blood *shall be* upon them.’ ”

Regulations for Conduct of Priests

21 And the LORD said to Moses, “Speak to
the priests, the sons of Aaron, and say
to them: [a]‘None shall defile himself for the
dead among his people, 2except for his relatives who are nearest to him: his mother, his
father, his son, his daughter, and his brother;
3also his virgin sister who is near to him, who
has had no husband, for her he may defile
himself. 4*Otherwise* he shall not defile himself, *being* a chief man among his people, to
profane himself.
5[a]‘They shall not make any bald *place* on
their heads, nor shall they shave the edges of
their beards nor make any cuttings in their
flesh. 6They shall be [a]holy to their God and
not profane the name of their God, for they
offer the offerings of the LORD made by fire,
and the [b]bread of their God; [c]therefore they
shall be holy. 7[a]They shall not take a wife *who*
is a harlot or a defiled woman, nor shall they
take a woman [b]divorced from her husband;
for *the priest*[1] is holy to his God. 8Therefore
you shall consecrate him, for he offers the
bread of your God. He shall be holy to you,
for [a]I the LORD, who [b]sanctify you, *am* holy.
9The daughter of any priest, if she profanes
herself by playing the harlot, she profanes
her father. She shall be [a]burned with fire.
10‘*He who is* the high priest among his
brethren, on whose head the anointing oil
was [a]poured and who is consecrated to wear
the garments, shall not [b]uncover his head nor
tear his clothes; 11nor shall he go [a]near any
dead body, nor defile himself for his father
or his mother; 12[a]nor shall he go out of the
sanctuary, nor profane the sanctuary of his
God; for the [b]consecration of the anointing
oil of his God *is* upon him: I *am* the LORD.
13And he shall take a wife in her virginity.
14A widow or a divorced woman or a defiled
woman *or* a harlot—these he shall not marry;
but he shall take a virgin of his own people
as wife. 15Nor shall he profane his posterity
among his people, for I the LORD sanctify
him.’ ”
16And the LORD spoke to Moses, saying,
17“Speak to Aaron, saying: ‘No man of your
descendants in *succeeding* generations, who
has *any* defect, may approach to offer the
bread of his God. 18For any man who has
a [a]defect shall not approach: a man blind
or lame, who has a marred *face* or any *limb*
[b]too long, 19a man who has a broken foot or
broken hand, 20or is a hunchback or a dwarf,
or *a man* who has a defect in his eye, or eczema or scab, or is a eunuch. 21No man of the
descendants of Aaron the priest, who has a
defect, shall come near to offer the offerings
made by fire to the LORD. He has a defect; he
shall not come near to offer the bread of his
God. 22He may eat the bread of his God, *both*
the most holy and the holy; 23only he shall
not go near the [a]veil or approach the altar,
because he has a defect, lest [b]he profane My
sanctuaries; for I the LORD sanctify them.’ ”
24And Moses told *it* to Aaron and his sons,
and to all the children of Israel.

20:19 [a] Lev. 18:13 [b] Lev. 18:12 **20:20** [a] Lev. 18:14 **20:21** [a] Lev. 18:16 **20:22** [a] Lev. 18:26; 19:37 [b] Lev. 18:25, 28 **20:23** [a] Lev. 18:3, 24 [b] Deut. 9:5 **20:24** [a] Ex. 3:17; 6:8; 13:5; 33:1–3 [b] Ex. 19:5; 33:16 **20:25** [a] Lev. 10:10; 11:1–47 [b] Lev. 11:43 **20:26** [a] Lev. 19:2 **20:27** [a] Lev. 19:31 **21:1** [a] Ezek. 44:25 **21:5** [a] Deut. 14:1 **21:6** [a] Ex. 22:31 [b] Lev. 3:11 [c] Is. 52:11 **21:7** [a] Ezek. 44:22 [b] Deut. 24:1, 2 [1] Literally *he* **21:8** [a] Lev. 11:44, 45 [b] Lev. 8:12, 30 **21:9** [a] Deut. 22:21 **21:10** [a] Lev. 8:12 [b] Lev. 10:6, 7 **21:11** [a] Num. 19:14 **21:12** [a] Lev. 10:7 [b] Ex. 29:6, 7 **21:18** [a] Lev. 22:19–25 [b] Lev. 22:23 **21:23** [a] Lev. 16:2 [b] Lev. 21:12

22 Then the LORD spoke to Moses, saying,
2"Speak to Aaron and his sons, that they
[a]separate themselves from the holy things of
the children of Israel, and that they [b]do not
profane My holy name *by* what they [c]dedicate
to Me: I *am* the LORD. 3Say to them: 'Whoever of
all your descendants throughout your generations, who goes near the holy things which the
children of Israel dedicate to the LORD, [a]while
he has uncleanness upon him, that person shall
be cut off from My presence: I *am* the LORD.

4'Whatever man of the descendants of Aaron,
who *is* a [a]leper or has [b]a discharge, shall not
eat the holy offerings [c]until he is clean. And
[d]whoever touches anything made unclean *by*
a corpse, or [e]a man who has had an emission
of semen, 5or [a]whoever touches any creeping
thing by which he would be made unclean, or
[b]any person by whom he would become unclean, whatever his uncleanness may be— 6the
person who has touched any such thing shall
be unclean until evening, and shall not eat the
holy *offerings* unless he [a]washes his body with
water. 7And when the sun goes down he shall
be clean; and afterward he may eat the holy
offerings, because [a]it *is* his food. 8[a]Whatever
dies *naturally* or is torn *by beasts* he shall not
eat, to defile himself with it: I *am* the LORD.

9'They shall therefore keep [a]My ordinance,
[b]lest they bear sin for it and die thereby, if
they profane it: I the LORD sanctify them.

10[a]'No outsider shall eat the holy *offering;* one
who dwells with the priest, or a hired servant,
shall not eat the holy thing. 11But if the priest
[a]buys a person with his money, he may eat it;
and one who is born in his house may eat his
food. 12If the priest's daughter is married to an
outsider, she may not eat of the holy offerings.
13But if the priest's daughter is a widow or divorced, and has no child, and has returned to
her father's house as in her youth, she may eat
her father's food; but no outsider shall eat it.

14'And if a man eats the holy *offering* unintentionally, then he shall restore a holy
offering to the priest, and add one-fifth to it.
15They shall not profane the [a]holy *offerings*
of the children of Israel, which they offer to
the LORD, 16or allow them to bear the guilt of
trespass when they eat their holy *offerings;*
for I the LORD sanctify them.' "

Offerings Accepted and Not Accepted

17And the LORD spoke to Moses, saying,
18"Speak to Aaron and his sons, and to all the
children of Israel, and say to them: [a]'Whatever man of the house of Israel, or of the
strangers in Israel, who offers his sacrifice
for any of his vows or for any of his freewill
offerings, which they offer to the LORD as
a burnt offering— 19[a]*you shall offer* of your
own free will a male without blemish from
the cattle, from the sheep, or from the goats.
20[a]Whatever has a defect, you shall not offer,
for it shall not be acceptable on your behalf.
21And [a]whoever offers a sacrifice of a peace
offering to the LORD, [b]to fulfill *his* vow, or a
freewill offering from the cattle or the sheep,
it must be perfect to be accepted; there shall
be no defect in it. 22[a]Those *that are* blind
or broken or maimed, or have an ulcer or
eczema or scabs, you shall not offer to the
LORD, nor make [b]an offering by fire of them
on the altar to the LORD. 23Either a bull or a
lamb that has any limb [a]too long or too short
you may offer *as* a freewill offering, but for
a vow it shall not be accepted.

24'You shall not offer to the LORD what is
bruised or crushed, or torn or cut; nor shall you
make *any offering of them* in your land. 25Nor
[a]from a foreigner's hand shall you offer any of
these as [b]the bread of your God, because their
[c]corruption *is* in them, *and* defects *are* in them.
They shall not be accepted on your behalf.' "

26And the LORD spoke to Moses, saying:
27[a]"When a bull or a sheep or a goat is born, it
shall be seven days with its mother; and from
the eighth day and thereafter it shall be accepted as an offering made by fire to the LORD.
28*Whether it is* a cow or ewe, do not kill both
her [a]and her young on the same day. 29And
when you [a]offer a sacrifice of thanksgiving to
the LORD, offer *it* of your own free will. 30On
the same day it shall be eaten; you shall leave
[a]none of it until morning: I *am* the LORD.

31[a]"Therefore you shall keep My commandments, and perform them: I *am* the LORD.
32[a]You shall not profane My holy name, but
[b]I will be hallowed among the children of
Israel. I *am* the LORD who [c]sanctifies you,
33[a]who brought you out of the land of Egypt,
to be your God: I *am* the LORD."

Feasts of the LORD

23 And the LORD spoke to Moses, saying,
2"Speak to the children of Israel, and
say to them: 'The feasts of the LORD, which
you shall proclaim *to be* [a]holy convocations,
these *are* My feasts.

22:2 [a] Num. 6:3 [b] Lev. 18:21 [c] Ex. 28:38 **22:3** [a] Lev. 7:20, 21 **22:4** [a] Num. 5:2 [b] Lev. 15:2 [c] Lev. 14:2; 15:13 [d] Num. 19:11 [e] Lev. 15:16, 17 **22:5** [a] Lev. 11:23–28 [b] Lev. 15:7, 19 **22:6** [a] Lev. 15:5 **22:7** [a] Num. 18:11, 13 **22:8** [a] Lev. 7:24; 11:39, 40; 17:15 **22:9** [a] Lev. 18:30 [b] Ex. 28:43 **22:10** [a] Ex. 29:33 **22:11** [a] Ex. 12:44 **22:15** [a] Num. 18:32 **22:18** [a] Lev. 1:2, 3, 10 **22:19** [a] Lev. 1:3 **22:20** [a] Deut. 15:21; 17:1 **22:21** [a] Lev. 3:1, 6 [b] Num. 15:3, 8 **22:22** [a] Mal. 1:8 [b] Lev. 1:9, 13; 3:3, 5 **22:23** [a] Lev. 21:18 **22:25** [a] Num. 15:15, 16 [b] Lev. 21:6, 17 [c] Mal. 1:14 **22:27** [a] Ex. 22:30 **22:28** [a] Deut. 22:6, 7 **22:29** [a] Lev. 7:12 **22:30** [a] Lev. 7:15 **22:31** [a] Deut. 4:40 **22:32** [a] Lev. 18:21 [b] Lev. 10:3 [c] Lev. 20:8 **22:33** [a] Lev. 19:36, 37 **23:2** [a] Ex. 12:16

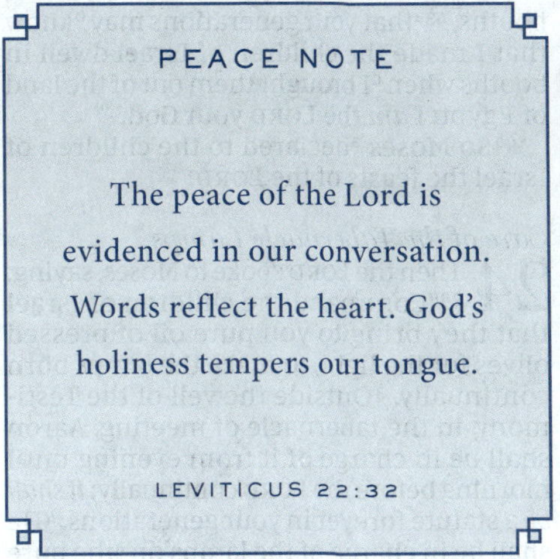

The Sabbath

3[a]'Six days shall work be done, but the seventh day *is* a Sabbath of solemn rest, a holy
convocation. You shall do no work *on it;* it *is*
the Sabbath of the LORD in all your dwellings.

The Passover and Unleavened Bread

4[a]'These *are* the feasts of the LORD, holy
convocations which you shall proclaim at
their appointed times. 5[a]On the fourteenth
day of the first month at twilight *is* the LORD's
Passover. 6And on the fifteenth day of the
same month *is* the Feast of Unleavened Bread
to the LORD; seven days you must eat unleavened bread. 7[a]On the first day you shall have a
holy convocation; you shall do no customary
work on it. 8But you shall offer an offering
made by fire to the LORD for seven days. The
seventh day *shall be* a holy convocation; you
shall do no customary work *on it.*' "

The Feast of Firstfruits

9And the LORD spoke to Moses, saying,
10"Speak to the children of Israel, and say to
them: [a]'When you come into the land which
I give to you, and reap its harvest, then you
shall bring a sheaf of [b]the firstfruits of your
harvest to the priest. 11He shall [a]wave the
sheaf before the LORD, to be accepted on your
behalf; on the day after the Sabbath the priest
shall wave it. 12And you shall offer on that
day, when you wave the sheaf, a male lamb
of the first year, without blemish, as a burnt
offering to the LORD. 13Its grain offering
shall be two-tenths *of an ephah* of fine flour
mixed with oil, an offering made by fire to
the LORD, for a sweet aroma; and its drink
offering *shall be* of wine, one-fourth of a hin.
14You shall eat neither bread nor parched
grain nor fresh grain until the same day that
you have brought an offering to your God;
it shall be a statute forever throughout your
generations in all your dwellings.

The Feast of Weeks

15'And you shall count for yourselves from
the day after the Sabbath, from the day that
you brought the sheaf of the wave offering:
seven Sabbaths shall be completed. 16Count
[a]fifty days to the day after the seventh Sabbath; then you shall offer [b]a new grain offering to the LORD. 17You shall bring from your
dwellings two wave *loaves* of two-tenths *of an
ephah.* They shall be of fine flour; they shall
be baked with leaven. *They are* [a]the firstfruits
to the LORD. 18And you shall offer with the
bread seven lambs of the first year, without
blemish, one young bull, and two rams. They
shall be *as* a burnt offering to the LORD, with
their grain offering and their drink offerings,
an offering made by fire for a sweet aroma
to the LORD. 19Then you shall sacrifice [a]one
kid of the goats as a sin offering, and two
male lambs of the first year as a sacrifice of
a [b]peace offering. 20The priest shall wave
them with the bread of the firstfruits *as* a
wave offering before the LORD, with the two
lambs. [a]They shall be holy to the LORD for
the priest. 21And you shall proclaim on the
same day *that* it is a holy convocation to
you. You shall do no customary work *on it. It
shall be* a statute forever in all your dwellings
throughout your generations.

22[a]'When you reap the harvest of your land,
you shall not wholly reap the corners of your
field when you reap, nor shall you gather any
gleaning from your harvest. You shall leave
them for the poor and for the stranger: I *am*
the LORD your God.' "

The Feast of Trumpets

23Then the LORD spoke to Moses, saying,
24"Speak to the children of Israel, saying:
'In the [a]seventh month, on the first *day* of
the month, you shall have a sabbath-*rest,*
[b]a memorial of blowing of trumpets, a holy
convocation. 25You shall do no customary
work *on it;* and you shall offer an offering
made by fire to the LORD.' "

The Day of Atonement

26And the LORD spoke to Moses, saying:
27[a]"Also the tenth *day* of this seventh month
shall be the Day of Atonement. It shall be a
holy convocation for you; you shall afflict your

23:3 [a] Luke 13:14 23:4 [a] Ex. 23:14–16 23:5 [a] Ex. 12:1–28 23:7 [a] Ex. 12:16 23:10 [a] Ex. 23:19; 34:26 [b] [Rom. 11:16] 23:11 [a] Ex. 29:24 23:16 [a] Acts 2:1 [b] Num. 28:26 23:17 [a] Num. 15:17–21 23:19 [a] Num. 28:30 [b] Lev. 3:1 23:20 [a] Deut. 18:4 23:22 [a] Lev. 19:9, 10 23:24 [a] Num. 29:1 [b] Lev. 25:9 23:27 [a] Num. 29:7

souls, and offer an offering made by fire to the LORD. 28 And you shall do no work on that same day, for it *is* the Day of Atonement, [a]to make atonement for you before the LORD your God. 29 For any person who is not [a]afflicted *in soul* on that same day [b]shall be cut off from his people. 30 And any person who does any work on that same day, [a]that person I will destroy from among his people. 31 You shall do no manner of work; *it shall be* a statute forever throughout your generations in all your dwellings. 32 It *shall be* to you a sabbath of *solemn* rest, and you shall afflict your souls; on the ninth *day* of the month at evening, from evening to evening, you shall celebrate your sabbath."

The Feast of Tabernacles

33 Then the LORD spoke to Moses, saying, 34 "Speak to the children of Israel, saying: [a]'The fifteenth day of this seventh month *shall be* the Feast of Tabernacles *for* seven days to the LORD. 35 On the first day *there shall be* a holy convocation. You shall do no customary work *on it*. 36 *For* seven days you shall offer an [a]offering made by fire to the LORD. [b]On the eighth day you shall have a holy convocation, and you shall offer an offering made by fire to the LORD. It *is* a [c]sacred assembly, *and* you shall do no customary work *on it*.

37 [a]'These *are* the feasts of the LORD which you shall proclaim *to be* holy convocations, to offer an offering made by fire to the LORD, a burnt offering and a grain offering, a sacrifice and drink offerings, everything on its day— 38 [a]besides the Sabbaths of the LORD, besides your gifts, besides all your vows, and besides all your freewill offerings which you give to the LORD.

39 'Also on the fifteenth day of the seventh month, when you have [a]gathered in the fruit of the land, you shall keep the feast of the LORD *for* seven days; on the first day *there shall be* a sabbath-*rest*, and on the eighth day a sabbath-*rest*. 40 And [a]you shall take for yourselves on the first day the fruit of beautiful trees, branches of palm trees, the boughs of leafy trees, and willows of the brook; [b]and you shall rejoice before the LORD your God for seven days. 41 [a]You shall keep it as a feast to the LORD for seven days in the year. *It shall be* a statute forever in your generations. You shall celebrate it in the seventh month. 42 [a]You shall dwell in booths for seven days. [b]All who are native Israelites shall dwell in booths, 43 [a]that your generations may [b]know that I made the children of Israel dwell in booths when [c]I brought them out of the land of Egypt: I *am* the LORD your God.' "

44 So Moses [a]declared to the children of Israel the feasts of the LORD.

Care of the Tabernacle Lamps

24 Then the LORD spoke to Moses, saying: 2 [a]"Command the children of Israel that they bring to you pure oil of pressed olives for the light, to make the lamps burn continually. 3 Outside the veil of the Testimony, in the tabernacle of meeting, Aaron shall be in charge of it from evening until morning before the LORD continually; *it shall be* a statute forever in your generations. 4 He shall be in charge of the lamps on [a]the pure *gold* lampstand before the LORD continually.

The Bread of the Tabernacle

5 "And you shall take fine flour and bake twelve [a]cakes with it. Two-tenths *of an ephah* shall be in each cake. 6 You shall set them in two rows, six in a row, [a]on the pure *gold* table before the LORD. 7 And you shall put pure frankincense on *each* row, that it may be on the bread for a [a]memorial, an offering made by fire to the LORD. 8 [a]Every Sabbath he shall set it in order before the LORD continually, *being taken* from the children of Israel by an everlasting covenant. 9 And [a]it shall be for Aaron and his sons, [b]and they shall eat it in a holy place; for it *is* most holy to him from the offerings of the LORD made by fire, by a perpetual statute."

The Penalty for Blasphemy

10 Now the son of an Israelite woman, whose father *was* an Egyptian, went out among the children of Israel; and this Israelite *woman's* son and a man of Israel fought each other in the camp. 11 And the Israelite woman's son [a]blasphemed the name *of the LORD* and [b]cursed; and so they [c]brought him to Moses. (His mother's name *was* Shelomith the daughter of Dibri, of the tribe of Dan.) 12 Then they [a]put him in custody, [b]that the mind of the LORD might be shown to them.

13 And the LORD spoke to Moses, saying, 14 "Take outside the camp him who has cursed; then let all who heard *him* [a]lay their hands on his head, and let all the congregation stone him.

23:28 [a] Lev. 16:34 **23:29** [a] Jer. 31:9 [b] Num. 5:2 **23:30** [a] Lev. 20:3–6 **23:34** [a] Num. 29:12 **23:36** [a] Num. 29:12–34 [b] Num. 29:35–38 [c] Deut. 16:8 **23:37** [a] Lev. 23:2, 4 **23:38** [a] Num. 29:39 **23:39** [a] Ex. 23:16 **23:40** [a] Neh. 8:15 [b] Deut. 12:7; 16:14, 15 **23:41** [a] Num. 29:12 **23:42** [a] [Is. 4:6] [b] Neh. 8:14–16 **23:43** [a] Deut. 31:13 [b] Ex. 10:2 [c] Lev. 22:33 **23:44** [a] Lev. 23:2 **24:2** [a] Ex. 27:20, 21 **24:4** [a] Ex. 25:31; 31:8; 37:17 **24:5** [a] Ex. 25:30; 39:36; 40:23 **24:6** [a] 1 Kin. 7:48 **24:7** [a] Lev. 2:2, 9, 16 **24:8** [a] 1 Chr. 9:32 **24:9** [a] Matt. 12:4 [b] Ex. 29:33 **24:11** [a] Ex. 22:28 [b] Is. 8:21 [c] Ex. 18:22, 26 **24:12** [a] Num. 15:34 [b] Num. 27:5 **24:14** [a] Deut. 13:9; 17:7

15 "Then you shall speak to the children of
Israel, saying: 'Whoever curses his God [a]shall
bear his sin. 16 And whoever [a]blasphemes
the name of the LORD shall surely be put to
death. All the congregation shall certainly
stone him, the stranger as well as him who
is born in the land. When he blasphemes the
name *of the LORD*, he shall be put to death.

17 [a]'Whoever kills any man shall surely be
put to death. 18 [a]Whoever kills an animal shall
make it good, animal for animal.

19 'If a man causes disfigurement of his
neighbor, as [a]he has done, so shall it be done
to him— 20 fracture for [a]fracture, [b]eye for eye,
tooth for tooth; as he has caused disfigurement of a man, so shall it be done to him.
21 And whoever kills an animal shall restore
it; but whoever kills a man shall be put to
death. 22 You shall have [a]the same law for the
stranger and for one from your own country;
for I *am* the LORD your God.' "

23 Then Moses spoke to the children of
Israel; and they took outside the camp him
who had cursed, and stoned him with stones.
So the children of Israel did as the LORD
commanded Moses.

The Sabbath of the Seventh Year

25 And the LORD spoke to Moses on
Mount [a]Sinai, saying, 2 "Speak to the
children of Israel, and say to them: 'When you
come into the land which I give you, then the
land shall [a]keep a sabbath to the LORD. 3 Six
years you shall sow your field, and six years
you shall prune your vineyard, and gather
its fruit; 4 but in the [a]seventh year there shall
be a sabbath of solemn [b]rest for the land, a
sabbath to the LORD. You shall neither sow
your field nor prune your vineyard. 5 [a]What
grows of its own accord of your harvest you
shall not reap, nor gather the grapes of your
untended vine, *for* it is a year of rest for the
land. 6 And the sabbath *produce* of the land
shall be food for you: for you, your male and
female servants, your hired man, and the
stranger who dwells with you, 7 for your livestock and the beasts that *are* in your land—all
its produce shall be for food.

The Year of Jubilee

8 'And you shall count seven sabbaths
of years for yourself, seven times seven
years; and the time of the seven sabbaths of
years shall be to you forty-nine years. 9 Then
you shall cause the trumpet of the Jubilee
to sound on the tenth *day* of the seventh
month; [a]on the Day of Atonement you shall
make the trumpet to sound throughout all
your land. 10 And you shall consecrate the
fiftieth year, and [a]proclaim liberty throughout *all* the land to all its inhabitants. It shall
be a Jubilee for you; [b]and each of you shall
return to his possession, and each of you
shall return to his family. 11 That fiftieth
year shall be a Jubilee to you; in it [a]you
shall neither sow nor reap what grows of its
own accord, nor gather *the grapes* of your
untended vine. 12 For it *is* the Jubilee; it shall
be holy to you; [a]you shall eat its produce
from the field.

13 [a]'In this Year of Jubilee, each of you shall
return to his possession. 14 And if you sell
anything to your neighbor or buy from your
neighbor's hand, you shall not [a]oppress one
another. 15 [a]According to the number of years
after the Jubilee you shall buy from your
neighbor, and according to the number of
years of crops he shall sell to you. 16 According
to the multitude of years you shall increase
its price, and according to the fewer number
of years you shall diminish its price; for he
sells to you *according* to the number *of the
years* of the crops. 17 Therefore [a]you shall not
oppress one another, [b]but you shall fear your
God; for I *am* the LORD your God.

Provisions for the Seventh Year

18 [a]'So you shall observe My statutes and
keep My judgments, and perform them; [b]and
you will dwell in the land in safety. 19 Then
the land will yield its fruit, and [a]you will eat
your fill, and dwell there in safety.

20 'And if you say, [a]"What shall we eat in
the seventh year, since [b]we shall not sow
nor gather in our produce?" 21 Then I will
[a]command My blessing on you in the [b]sixth
year, and it will bring forth produce enough
for three years. 22 [a]And you shall sow in the
eighth year, and eat [b]old produce until the
ninth year; until its produce comes in, you
shall eat *of* the old *harvest*.

Redemption of Property

23 'The land shall not be sold permanently,
for [a]the land *is* Mine; for you *are* [b]strangers
and sojourners with Me. 24 And in all the land
of your possession you shall grant redemption of the land.

24:15 [a] Lev. 20:17 **24:16** [a] [Mark 3:28, 29] **24:17** [a] Ex. 21:12 **24:18** [a] Lev. 24:21 **24:19** [a] Ex. 21:24 **24:20** [a] Ex. 21:23 [b] [Matt. 5:38, 39] **24:22** [a] Ex. 12:49 **25:1** [a] Lev. 26:46 **25:2** [a] Lev. 26:34, 35 **25:4** [a] Deut. 15:1 [b] [Heb. 4:9] **25:5** [a] 2 Kin. 19:29 **25:9** [a] Lev. 23:24, 27 **25:10** [a] Jer. 34:8, 15, 17 [b] Num. 36:4 **25:11** [a] Lev. 25:5 **25:12** [a] Lev. 25:6, 7 **25:13** [a] Lev. 25:10; 27:24 **25:14** [a] Lev. 19:13 **25:15** [a] Lev. 27:18, 23 **25:17** [a] Lev. 25:14 [b] Lev. 19:14, 32; 25:43 **25:18** [a] Lev. 19:37 [b] Deut. 12:10 **25:19** [a] Lev. 26:5 **25:20** [a] Matt. 6:25, 31 [b] Lev. 25:4, 5 **25:21** [a] Deut. 28:8 [b] Ex. 16:29 **25:22** [a] 2 Kin. 19:29 [b] Josh. 5:11 **25:23** [a] Ex. 19:5 [b] Ps. 39:12

25[a]‘If one of your brethren becomes poor,
and has sold *some* of his possession, and if
[b]his redeeming relative comes to redeem it,
then he may redeem what his brother sold.
26 Or if the man has no one to redeem it, but he
himself becomes able to redeem it, 27 then [a]let
him count the years since its sale, and restore
the remainder to the man to whom he sold it,
that he may return to his possession. 28 But if
he is not able to have *it* restored to himself,
then what was sold shall remain in the hand
of him who bought it until the Year of Jubilee;
[a]and in the Jubilee it shall be released, and
he shall return to his possession.

29‘If a man sells a house in a walled city,
then he may redeem it within a whole year after it is sold; *within* a full year he may redeem
it. 30 But if it is not redeemed within the space
of a full year, then the house in the walled city
shall belong permanently to him who bought
it, throughout his generations. It shall not be
released in the Jubilee. 31 However the houses
of villages which have no wall around them
shall be counted as the fields of the country.
They may be redeemed, and they shall be
released in the Jubilee. 32 Nevertheless [a]the
cities of the Levites, *and* the houses in the
cities of their possession, the Levites may
redeem at any time. 33 And if a man purchases
a house from the Levites, then the house that
was sold in the city of his possession shall
be released in the Jubilee; for the houses in
the cities of the Levites *are* their possession
among the children of Israel. 34 But [a]the field
of the common-land of their cities may not
be [b]sold, for it *is* their perpetual possession.

Lending to the Poor

35‘If one of your brethren becomes poor,
and falls into poverty among you, then you
shall [a]help him, like a stranger or a sojourner,
that he may live with you. 36[a]Take no usury or
interest from him; but [b]fear your God, that your
brother may live with you. 37 You shall not lend
him your money for usury, nor lend him your
food at a profit. 38[a]I *am* the LORD your God, who
brought you out of the land of Egypt, to give
you the land of Canaan *and* to be your God.

The Law Concerning Slavery

39‘And if *one of* your brethren *who dwells* by
you becomes poor, and sells himself to you, you
shall not compel him to serve as a slave. 40 As a
hired servant *and* a sojourner he shall be with
you, *and* shall serve you until the Year of Jubilee. 41 And *then* he shall depart from you—he
and his children [a]with him—and shall return
to his own family. He shall return to the possession of his fathers. 42 For they *are* [a]My servants,
whom I brought out of the land of Egypt; they
shall not be sold as slaves. 43[a]You shall not
rule over him [b]with rigor, but you [c]shall fear
your God. 44 And as for your male and female
slaves whom you may have—from the nations
that are around you, from them you may buy
male and female slaves. 45 Moreover you may
buy [a]the children of the strangers who dwell
among you, and their families who are with
you, which they beget in your land; and they
shall become your property. 46 And [a]you may
take them as an inheritance for your children
after you, to inherit *them as* a possession; they
shall be your permanent slaves. But regarding
your brethren, the children of Israel, you shall
not rule over one another with rigor.

47‘Now if a sojourner or stranger close to
you becomes rich, and *one of* your brethren
who dwells by him becomes poor, and sells
himself to the stranger *or* sojourner close to
you, or to a member of the stranger's family,
48 after he is sold he may be redeemed again.
One of his brothers may redeem him; 49 or his
uncle or his uncle's son may redeem him; or
anyone who is near of kin to him in his family may redeem him; or if he is able he may
redeem himself. 50 Thus he shall reckon with
him who bought him: The price of his release
shall be according to the number of years,
from the year that he was sold to him until the
Year of Jubilee; *it shall be* [a]according to the
time of a hired servant for him. 51 If *there are*
still many years *remaining*, according to them
he shall repay the price of his redemption
from the money with which he was bought.
52 And if there remain but a few years until
the Year of Jubilee, then he shall reckon with
him, *and* according to his years he shall repay
him the price of his redemption. 53 He shall
be with him as a yearly hired servant, and
he shall not rule with rigor over him in your
sight. 54 And if he is not redeemed in these
years, then he shall be released in the Year
of Jubilee—he and his children with him.
55 For the children of Israel *are* servants to
Me; they *are* My servants whom I brought out
of the land of Egypt: I *am* the LORD your God.

Promise of Blessing and Retribution

26 ‘You shall [a]not make idols for yourselves;
neither a carved image nor a *sacred* pillar
shall you rear up for yourselves;

25:25 [a] Ruth 2:20; 4:4, 6 [b] Ruth 3:2, 9, 12 **25:27** [a] Lev. 25:50–52 **25:28** [a] Lev. 25:10, 13 **25:32** [a] Num. 35:1–8 **25:34** [a] Num. 35:2–5 [b] Acts 4:36, 37 **25:35** [a] Deut. 15:7–11; 24:14, 15 **25:36** [a] Ex. 22:25 [b] Neh. 5:9 **25:38** [a] Lev. 11:45; 22:32, 33 **25:41** [a] Ex. 21:3 **25:42** [a] [Rom. 6:22] **25:43** [a] Eph. 6:9 [b] Ex. 1:13, 14 [c] Mal. 3:5 **25:45** [a] [Is. 56:3, 6, 7] **25:46** [a] Is. 14:2 **25:50** [a] Job 7:1 **26:1** [a] Ex. 20:4, 5

nor shall you set up an engraved stone
in your land, to bow down to it;
for I *am* the LORD your God.
2 [a]You shall keep My Sabbaths and reverence My sanctuary:
I *am* the LORD.

3 [a]'If you walk in My statutes and keep My
commandments, and perform them,
4 [a]then I will give you rain in its season,
[b]the land shall yield its produce, and
the trees of the field shall yield their
fruit.
5 [a]Your threshing shall last till the time of
vintage, and the vintage shall last till
the time of sowing;
you shall eat your bread to the full, and
[b]dwell in your land safely.
6 [a]I will give peace in the land, and [b]you
shall lie down, and none will make *you*
afraid;
I will rid the land of [c]evil beasts,
and [d]the sword will not go through your
land.

PEACE NOTE

Each time you experience anxiety rather than peace, try to identify the lies you are thinking and focus instead on the truth.

LEVITICUS 26:6

7 You will chase your enemies, and they
shall fall by the sword before you.
8 [a]Five of you shall chase a hundred, and a
hundred of you shall put ten thousand
to flight;
your enemies shall fall by the sword before you.

9 'For I will [a]look on you favorably and
[b]make you fruitful, multiply you and
confirm My [c]covenant with you.

PEACE NOTE

God's being and bringing peace is not just a New Testament idea. *Yahweh* was identified with peace (Judg. 6:24) and promised peace to His people for obedience.

LEVITICUS 26:6

10 You shall eat the [a]old harvest, and clear
out the old because of the new.
11 [a]I will set My tabernacle among you, and
My soul shall not abhor you.
12 [a]I will walk among you and be your God,
and you shall be My people.
13 I *am* the LORD your God, who brought
you out of the land of Egypt, that *you*
should not be their slaves;
I have broken the bands of your [a]yoke
and made you walk upright.

14 'But if you do not obey Me, and do not
observe all these commandments,
15 and if you despise My statutes, or if your
soul abhors My judgments, so that
you do not perform all My commandments, *but* break My covenant,
16 I also will do this to you:
I will even appoint terror over you, [a]wasting
disease and fever which shall [b]consume
the eyes and [c]cause sorrow of heart.
And [d]you shall sow your seed in vain, for
your enemies shall eat it.
17 I will set [a]My face against you, and [b]you
shall be defeated by your enemies.
[c]Those who hate you shall reign over you,
and you shall [d]flee when no one pursues you.

18 'And after all this, if you do not obey Me,
then I will punish you [a]seven times
more for your sins.
19 I will [a]break the pride of your power;
I [b]will make your heavens like iron and
your earth like bronze.

26:2 [a] Lev. 19:30 **26:3** [a] Deut. 28:1–14 **26:4** [a] Is. 30:23 [b] Ps. 67:6 **26:5** [a] Amos 9:13 [b] Lev. 25:18, 19 **26:6** [a] Is. 45:7 [b] Job 11:19 [c] 2 Kin. 17:25 [d] Ezek. 14:17 **26:8** [a] Deut. 32:30 **26:9** [a] Ex. 2:25 [b] Gen. 17:6, 7 [c] Gen. 17:1–7 **26:10** [a] Lev. 25:22 **26:11** [a] Ex. 25:8; 29:45, 46 **26:12** [a] [2 Cor. 6:16] **26:13** [a] Gen. 27:40 **26:16** [a] Deut. 28:22 [b] 1 Sam. 2:33 [c] Ezek. 24:23; 33:10 [d] Judg. 6:3–6 **26:17** [a] Ps. 34:16 [b] Deut. 28:25 [c] Ps. 106:41 [d] Prov. 28:1 **26:18** [a] 1 Sam. 2:5 **26:19** [a] Is. 25:11 [b] Deut. 28:23

20 And your [a]strength shall be spent in vain;
for your [b]land shall not yield its produce,
nor shall the trees of the land yield
their fruit.

21 'Then, if you walk contrary to Me, and are
not willing to obey Me, I will bring on
you seven times more plagues, according to your sins.
22 [a]I will also send wild beasts among you,
which shall rob you of your children,
destroy your livestock, and make you
few in number;
and [b]your highways shall be desolate.

23 'And if [a]by these things you are not re-
formed by Me, but walk contrary to Me,
24 [a]then I also will walk contrary to you, and
I will punish you yet seven times for
your sins.
25 And [a]I will bring a sword against you
that will execute the vengeance of the
covenant;
when you are gathered together within your cities [b]I will send pestilence
among you;
and you shall be delivered into the hand
of the enemy.
26 [a]When I have cut off your supply of bread,
ten women shall bake your bread in
one oven, and they shall bring back
your bread by weight, [b]and you shall
eat and not be satisfied.

27 'And after all this, if you do not obey Me,
but walk contrary to Me,
28 then I also will walk contrary to you in
fury;
and I, even I, will chastise you seven times
for your sins.
29 [a]You shall eat the flesh of your sons, and
you shall eat the flesh of your daughters.
30 [a]I will destroy your high places, cut down
your incense altars, and cast your carcasses on the lifeless forms of your
idols;
and My soul shall abhor you.
31 I will lay your [a]cities waste and [b]bring
your sanctuaries to desolation, and I
will not [c]smell the fragrance of your
sweet aromas.
32 [a]I will bring the land to desolation, and
your enemies who dwell in it shall be
astonished at it.
33 [a]I will scatter you among the nations and
draw out a sword after you;
your land shall be desolate and your cities
waste.
34 [a]Then the land shall enjoy its sabbaths as
long as it lies desolate and you *are* in
your enemies' land;
then the land shall rest and enjoy its
sabbaths.
35 As long as *it* lies desolate it shall rest—
for the time it did not rest on your [a]sab-
baths when you dwelt in it.

36 'And as for those of you who are left, I will
send [a]faintness into their hearts in the
lands of their enemies;
the sound of a shaken leaf shall cause
them to flee;
they shall flee as though fleeing from a
sword, and they shall fall when no one
pursues.
37 [a]They shall stumble over one another, as
it were before a sword, when no one
pursues;
and [b]you shall have no *power* to stand
before your enemies.
38 You shall [a]perish among the nations, and
the land of your enemies shall eat you up.
39 And those of you who are left [a]shall waste
away in their iniquity in your enemies'
lands;
also in their [b]fathers' iniquities, which
are with them, they shall waste away.

40 '*But* [a]if they confess their iniquity and
the iniquity of their fathers, with their
unfaithfulness in which they were unfaithful to Me, and that they also have
walked contrary to Me,
41 and *that* I also have walked contrary to
them and have brought them into the
land of their enemies;
if their [a]uncircumcised hearts are [b]hum-
bled, and they [c]accept their guilt—
42 then I will [a]remember My covenant with
Jacob, and My covenant with Isaac
and My covenant with Abraham I will
remember;
I will [b]remember the land.
43 [a]The land also shall be left empty by them,
and will enjoy its sabbaths while it lies
desolate without them;
they will accept their guilt, because they
[b]despised My judgments and because
their soul abhorred My statutes.

26:20 [a] Ps. 127:1 [b] Gen. 4:12 **26:22** [a] Deut. 32:24 [b] Judg. 5:6 **26:23** [a] Amos 4:6–12 **26:24** [a] Lev. 26:28, 41 **26:25** [a] Ezek. 5:17 [b] Deut. 28:21 **26:26** [a] Ps. 105:16 [b] Mic. 6:14 **26:29** [a] 2 Kin. 6:28, 29 **26:30** [a] 2 Chr. 34:3 **26:31** [a] 2 Kin. 25:4, 10 [b] Ps. 74:7 [c] Is. 1:11–15 **26:32** [a] Jer. 9:11; 18:16 **26:33** [a] Deut. 4:27 **26:34** [a] 2 Chr. 36:21 **26:35** [a] Lev. 25:2 **26:36** [a] Ezek. 21:7, 12, 15 **26:37** [a] 1 Sam. 14:15, 16 [b] Josh. 7:12, 13 **26:38** [a] Deut. 4:26 **26:39** [a] Ezek. 4:17; 33:10 [b] Ex. 34:7 **26:40** [a] Neh. 9:2 **26:41** [a] Acts 7:51 [b] 2 Chr. 12:6, 7, 12 [c] Dan. 9:7 **26:42** [a] Ex. 2:24; 6:5 [b] Ps. 136:23 **26:43** [a] Lev. 26:34, 35 [b] Lev. 26:15

44 Yet for all that, when they are in the land
of their enemies, [a]I will not cast them
away, nor shall I abhor them, to utterly
destroy them and break My covenant
with them;
for I *am* the LORD their God.
45 But [a]for their sake I will remember the
covenant of their ancestors, [b]whom I
brought out of the land of Egypt [c]in
the sight of the nations, that I might
be their God:
I *am* the LORD.' "

46 [a]These *are* the statutes and judgments
and laws which the LORD made between
Himself and the children of Israel [b]on Mount
Sinai by the hand of Moses.

Redeeming Persons and Property Dedicated to God

27 Now the LORD spoke to Moses, saying,
2 "Speak to the children of Israel, and
say to them: [a]'When a man consecrates by a
vow certain persons to the LORD, according
to your valuation, 3 if your valuation is of a
male from twenty years old up to sixty years
old, then your valuation shall be fifty shekels of silver, [a]according to the shekel of the
sanctuary. 4 If it *is* a female, then your valuation shall be thirty shekels; 5 and if from five
years old up to twenty years old, then your
valuation for a male shall be twenty shekels,
and for a female ten shekels; 6 and if from
a month old up to five years old, then your
valuation for a male shall be five shekels of
silver, and for a female your valuation shall
be three shekels of silver; 7 and if from sixty
years old and above, if *it is* a male, then your
valuation shall be fifteen shekels, and for a
female ten shekels.

8 'But if he is too poor to pay your valuation, then he shall present himself before
the priest, and the priest shall set a value
for [a]him; according to the ability of him who
vowed, the priest shall value him.

9 'If *it is* an animal that men may bring
as an offering to the LORD, all that *anyone*
gives to the LORD shall be holy. 10 He shall
not substitute it or exchange it, good for bad
or bad for good; and if he at all exchanges
animal for animal, then both it and the one
exchanged for it shall be [a]holy. 11 If *it is* an
unclean animal which they do not offer as a
sacrifice to the LORD, then he shall present
the animal before the priest; 12 and the priest
shall set a value for it, whether it is good or
bad; as you, the priest, value it, so it shall be.
13 [a]But if he *wants* at all *to* redeem it, then he
must add one-fifth to your valuation.

14 'And when a man dedicates his house *to
be* holy to the LORD, then the priest shall set
a value for it, whether it is good or bad; as the
priest values it, so it shall stand. 15 If he who
dedicated it *wants to* redeem his house, then
he must add one-fifth of the money of your
valuation to it, and it shall be his.

16 'If a man dedicates to the LORD *part* of a
field of his possession, then your valuation
shall be according to the seed for it. A homer
of barley seed *shall be valued* at fifty shekels
of silver. 17 If he dedicates his field from the
Year of Jubilee, according to your valuation
it shall stand. 18 But if he dedicates his field
after the Jubilee, then the priest shall [a]reckon
to him the money due according to the years
that remain till the Year of Jubilee, and it
shall be deducted from your valuation. 19 And
if he who dedicates the field ever wishes to
redeem it, then he must add one-fifth of the
money of your valuation to it, and it shall
belong to him. 20 But if he does not want to
redeem the field, or if he has sold the field
to another man, it shall not be redeemed
anymore; 21 but the field, [a]when it is released
in the Jubilee, shall be holy to the LORD, as
a [b]devoted field; it shall be [c]the possession
of the priest.

22 'And if a man dedicates to the LORD a
field which he has bought, which is not the
field of [a]his possession, 23 then the priest shall
reckon to him the worth of your valuation,
up to the Year of Jubilee, and he shall give
your valuation on that day *as* a holy *offering*
to the LORD. 24 [a]In the Year of Jubilee the
field shall return to him from whom it was
bought, to the one who *owned* the land as a
possession. 25 And all your valuations shall
be according to the shekel of the sanctuary:
[a]twenty gerahs to the shekel.

26 'But the [a]firstborn of the animals, which
should be the LORD's firstborn, no man shall
dedicate; whether *it is* an ox or sheep, it *is*
the LORD's. 27 And if *it is* an unclean animal,
then he shall redeem *it* according to your
valuation, and [a]shall add one-fifth to it; or
if it is not redeemed, then it shall be sold
according to your valuation.

28 [a]'Nevertheless no devoted *offering* that
a man may devote to the LORD of all that
he has, *both* man and beast, or the field of
his possession, shall be sold or redeemed;
every devoted *offering is* most holy to the

26:44 [a] Deut. 4:31 **26:45** [a] [Rom. 11:28] [b] Lev. 22:33; 25:38 [c] Ps. 98:2 **26:46** [a] [John 1:17] [b] Lev. 25:1 **27:2** [a] Num. 6:2 **27:3** [a] Ex. 30:13 **27:8** [a] Lev. 5:11; 14:21–24 **27:10** [a] Lev. 27:33 **27:13** [a] Lev. 6:5; 22:14; 27:15, 19 **27:18** [a] Lev. 25:15, 16, 28 **27:21** [a] Lev. 25:10, 28, 31 [b] Lev. 27:28 [c] Num. 18:14 **27:22** [a] Lev. 25:10, 25 **27:24** [a] Lev. 25:10–13, 28 **27:25** [a] Ex. 30:13 **27:26** [a] Ex. 13:2, 12; 22:30 **27:27** [a] Lev. 27:11, 12 **27:28** [a] Josh. 6:17–19

LORD. 29[a]No person under the ban, who may
become doomed to destruction among men,
shall be redeemed, *but* shall surely be put to
death. 30 And [a]all the tithe of the land, *whether*
of the seed of the land *or* of the fruit of the
tree, *is* the LORD's. It *is* holy to the LORD.
31[a]If a man wants at all to redeem *any* of
his tithes, he shall add one-fifth to it. 32 And
concerning the tithe of the herd or the flock,
of whatever [a]passes under the rod, the tenth
one shall be holy to the LORD. 33 He shall not
inquire whether it is good or bad, [a]nor shall
he exchange it; and if he exchanges it at all,
then both it and the one exchanged for it shall
be holy; it shall not be redeemed.' "
34[a]These *are* the commandments which
the LORD commanded Moses for the children
of Israel on Mount [b]Sinai.

27:29 [a] Num. 21:2 27:30 [a] Gen. 28:22 27:31 [a] Lev. 27:13 27:32 [a] Jer. 33:13 27:33 [a] Lev. 27:10 27:34 [a] Lev. 26:46 [b] [Heb. 12:18–29]

THE FOURTH BOOK OF MOSES CALLED

NUMBERS

AUTHOR

Jews, Samaritans, and the early church testify to Moses' authorship. Several New Testament passages attribute events cited from Numbers to Moses (John 3:14; Acts 7; 13; 1 Cor. 10:1–11; Heb. 3–4), and there are more than eighty claims within Numbers that state that the Lord spoke to Moses (e.g., Num. 1:1). Numbers 33:2 says that Moses recorded their journeys at the Lord's command. As an eyewitness who kept detailed records, and the central character of the events in the book, no one was better qualified to write this book than Moses.

TIME

c. 1444–1405 BC

KEY VERSE

Numbers 14:22–23

THEME

At Sinai, this newly resurrected nation of Israel receives its laws, its system of sacrifices, and its national charter. The people should be ready to take the next step into the Promised Land, but they aren't. Numbers largely has Israel in a holding pattern. While the book records further steps taken in organizing the nation, its central narrative is that of the refusal of the people to go into Canaan. But God still doesn't give up on His people. He continues to discipline them in an effort to have a new generation ready to fulfill His plan. In this context Numbers points to God's sovereignty, His patience, and His desire to bless His people.

Nearly one hundred times we hear "the Lord spoke to Moses" (in the original Hebrew) even though His people were "in the Wilderness" (3:14) because the peace of God led the people of God. The name of the book, Numbers, was taken from the Greek Septuagint primarily because of the two great censuses (chs. 1; 26). Numbers confirms God's peaceful care over seemingly the smallest details of our lives. The great and timeless Aaronic Blessing pronounced God's peace over His people (6:26), including us.

The First Census of Israel

1 Now the LORD spoke to Moses [a]in the
Wilderness of Sinai, [b]in the tabernacle
of meeting, on the [c]first *day* of the second
month, in the second year after they had
come out of the land of Egypt, saying: 2 [a]"Take
a census of all the congregation of the children of Israel, by their families, by their
fathers' houses, according to the number
of names, every male [b]individually, 3 from
[a]twenty years old and above—all who *are*
able to go to war in Israel. You and Aaron shall
number them by their armies. 4 And with you
there shall be a man from every tribe, each
one the head of his father's house.
5 "These are the names of the men who
shall stand with you: from Reuben, Elizur the
son of Shedeur; 6 from Simeon, Shelumiel
the son of Zurishaddai; 7 from Judah, Nahshon the son of Amminadab; 8 from Issachar,
Nethanel the son of Zuar; 9 from Zebulun,
Eliab the son of Helon; 10 from the sons of
Joseph: from Ephraim, Elishama the son
of Ammihud; from Manasseh, Gamaliel the
son of Pedahzur; 11 from Benjamin, Abidan
the son of Gideoni; 12 from Dan, Ahiezer the
son of Ammishaddai; 13 from Asher, Pagiel
the son of Ocran; 14 from Gad, Eliasaph the
son of [a]Deuel;[1] 15 from Naphtali, Ahira the
son of Enan." 16 [a]These *were* [b]chosen from the
congregation, leaders of their fathers' tribes,
[c]heads of the divisions in Israel.
17 Then Moses and Aaron took these men
who had been mentioned [a]by name, 18 and
they assembled all the congregation together
on the first *day* of the second month; and
they recited their [a]ancestry by families, by
their fathers' houses, according to the number of names, from twenty years old and
above, each one individually. 19 As the LORD
commanded Moses, so he numbered them
in the Wilderness of Sinai.
20 Now the [a]children of Reuben, Israel's
oldest son, their genealogies by their families, by their fathers' house, according to the
number of names, every male individually,
from twenty years old and above, all who
were able to go to war: 21 those who were numbered of the tribe of Reuben *were* forty-six
thousand five hundred.
22 From the [a]children of Simeon, their genealogies by their families, by their fathers'
house, of those who were numbered, according to the number of names, every male individually, from twenty years old and above,
all who *were able to* go to war: 23 those who
were numbered of the tribe of Simeon *were*
fifty-nine thousand three hundred.
24 From the [a]children of Gad, their genealogies by their families, by their fathers' house,
according to the number of names, from
twenty years old and above, all who *were able*
to go to war: 25 those who were numbered of
the tribe of Gad *were* forty-five thousand six
hundred and fifty.
26 From the [a]children of Judah, their genealogies by their families, by their fathers'
house, according to the number of names,
from twenty years old and above, all who *were*
able to go to war: 27 those who were numbered
of the tribe of Judah *were* [a]seventy-four thousand six hundred.
28 From the [a]children of Issachar, their genealogies by their families, by their fathers'
house, according to the number of names,
from twenty years old and above, all who
were able to go to war: 29 those who were
numbered of the tribe of Issachar *were* fifty-
four thousand four hundred.
30 From the [a]children of Zebulun, their
genealogies by their families, by their fathers' house, according to the number of
names, from twenty years old and above,
all who *were able to* go to war: 31 those who
were numbered of the tribe of Zebulun *were*
fifty-seven thousand four hundred.
32 From the sons of Joseph, the [a]children
of Ephraim, their genealogies by their families, by their fathers' house, according to the
number of names, from twenty years old and
above, all who *were able to* go to war: 33 those
who were numbered of the tribe of Ephraim
were forty thousand five hundred.
34 From the [a]children of Manasseh, their
genealogies by their families, by their fathers'
house, according to the number of names,
from twenty years old and above, all who
were able to go to war: 35 those who were
numbered of the tribe of Manasseh *were*
thirty-two thousand two hundred.
36 From the [a]children of Benjamin, their
genealogies by their families, by their fathers' house, according to the number of
names, from twenty years old and above,
all who *were able to* go to war: 37 those who
were numbered of the tribe of Benjamin *were*
thirty-five thousand four hundred.
38 From the [a]children of Dan, their genealogies by their families, by their fathers'
house, according to the number of names,

1:1 [a] Ex. 19:1 [b] Ex. 25:22 [c] Num. 9:1; 10:11 **1:2** [a] Num. 26:2, 63, 64 [b] Ex. 30:12, 13; 38:26 **1:3** [a] Ex. 30:14; 38:26 **1:14** [a] Num. 7:42 [1] Spelled *Reuel* in 2:14 **1:16** [a] Num. 7:2 [b] Num. 16:2 [c] Ex. 18:21, 25 **1:17** [a] Is. 43:1 **1:18** [a] Ezra 2:59 **1:20** [a] Num. 2:10, 11; 26:5–11; 32:6, 15, 21, 29 **1:22** [a] Num. 2:12, 13; 26:12–14 **1:24** [a] Num. 26:15–18 **1:26** [a] 2 Sam. 24:9 **1:27** [a] 2 Chr. 17:14 **1:28** [a] Num. 2:5, 6 **1:30** [a] Num. 2:7, 8; 26:26, 27 **1:32** [a] Num. 26:28–37 **1:34** [a] Num. 2:20, 21; 26:28–34 **1:36** [a] Num. 26:38–41 **1:38** [a] Gen. 30:6; 46:23

from twenty years old and above, all who *were able to* go to war: 39 those who were numbered of the tribe of Dan *were* sixty-two thousand seven hundred.

40 From the [a]children of Asher, their genealogies by their families, by their fathers' house, according to the number of names, from twenty years old and above, all who *were able to* go to war: 41 those who were numbered of the tribe of Asher *were* forty-one thousand five hundred.

42 From the children of Naphtali, their genealogies by their families, by their fathers' house, according to the number of names, from twenty years old and above, all who *were able to* go to war: 43 those who were numbered of the tribe of Naphtali *were* fifty-three thousand four hundred.

44 [a]These are the ones who were numbered, whom Moses and Aaron numbered, with the leaders of Israel, twelve men, each one representing his father's house. 45 So all who were numbered of the children of Israel, by their fathers' houses, from twenty years old and above, all who *were able to* go to war in Israel— 46 all who were numbered were [a]six hundred and three thousand five hundred and fifty.

47 But [a]the Levites were not numbered among them by their fathers' tribe; 48 for the LORD had spoken to Moses, saying: 49 [a]"Only the tribe of Levi you shall not number, nor take a census of them among the children of Israel; 50 [a]but you shall appoint the Levites over the tabernacle of the Testimony, over all its furnishings, and over all things that belong to it; they shall carry the tabernacle and all its furnishings; they shall attend to it [b]and camp around the tabernacle. 51 [a]And when the tabernacle is to go forward, the Levites shall take it down; and when the tabernacle is to be set up, the Levites shall set it [b]up. [c]The outsider who comes near shall be put to death. 52 The children of Israel shall pitch their tents, [a]everyone by his own camp, everyone by his own standard, according to their armies; 53 [a]but the Levites shall camp around the tabernacle of the Testimony, that there may be no [b]wrath on the congregation of the children of Israel; and the Levites shall [c]keep charge of the tabernacle of the Testimony."

54 Thus the children of Israel did; according to all that the LORD commanded Moses, so they did.

The Tribes and Leaders by Armies

2 And the LORD spoke to Moses and Aaron, saying: 2 [a]"Everyone of the children of Israel shall camp by his own standard, beside the emblems of his father's house; they shall camp [b]some distance from the tabernacle of meeting. 3 On the [a]east side, toward the rising of the sun, those of the standard of the forces with Judah shall camp according to their armies; and [b]Nahshon the son of Amminadab *shall be* the leader of the children of Judah." 4 And his army was numbered at seventy-four thousand six hundred.

5 "Those who camp next to him *shall be* the tribe of Issachar, and Nethanel the son of Zuar *shall be* the leader of the children of Issachar." 6 And his army was numbered at fifty-four thousand four hundred.

7 "Then *comes* the tribe of Zebulun, and Eliab the son of Helon *shall be* the leader of the children of Zebulun." 8 And his army was numbered at fifty-seven thousand four hundred. 9 "All who were numbered according to their armies of the forces with Judah, one hundred and eighty-six thousand four hundred—[a]these shall break camp first.

10 "On the [a]south side *shall be* the standard of the forces with Reuben according to their armies, and the leader of the children of Reuben *shall be* Elizur the son of Shedeur." 11 And his army was numbered at forty-six thousand five hundred.

12 "Those who camp next to him *shall be* the tribe of Simeon, and the leader of the children of Simeon *shall be* Shelumiel the son of Zurishaddai." 13 And his army was numbered at fifty-nine thousand three hundred.

PEACE NOTE

One of the key characteristics of Jesus' earthly ministry was presence, that is, showing up when someone least expected it and at the point of greatest need.

1:40 [a] Num. 2:27, 28; 26:44–47 **1:44** [a] Num. 26:64 **1:46** [a] Ex. 12:37; 38:26 **1:47** [a] Num. 2:33; 3:14–22; 26:57–62 **1:49** [a] Num. 2:33; 26:62 **1:50** [a] Ex. 38:21 [b] Num. 3:23, 29, 35, 38 **1:51** [a] Num. 4:5–15; 10:17, 21 [b] Num. 10:21 [c] Num. 3:10, 38; 4:15, 19, 20; 18:22 **1:52** [a] Num. 2:2, 34; 24:2 **1:53** [a] Num. 1:50 [b] Lev. 10:6 [c] 1 Chr. 23:32 **2:2** [a] Num. 1:52; 24:2 [b] Josh. 3:4 **2:3** [a] Num. 10:5 [b] 1 Chr. 2:10 **2:9** [a] Num. 10:14 **2:10** [a] Num. 10:6

14 "Then *comes* the tribe of Gad, and the leader of the children of Gad *shall be* Eliasaph the son of Reuel."[1] 15 And his army was numbered at forty-five thousand six hundred and fifty. 16 "All who were numbered according to their armies of the forces with Reuben, one hundred and fifty-one thousand four hundred and fifty—[a]they shall be the second to break camp.

17 [a]"And the tabernacle of meeting shall move out with the camp of the Levites [b]in the middle of the camps; as they camp, so they shall move out, everyone in his place, by their standards.

18 "On the west side *shall be* the standard of the forces with Ephraim according to their armies, and the leader of the children of Ephraim *shall be* Elishama the son of Ammihud." 19 And his army was numbered at forty thousand five hundred.

20 "Next to him *comes* the tribe of Manasseh, and the leader of the children of Manasseh *shall be* Gamaliel the son of Pedahzur." 21 And his army was numbered at thirty-two thousand two hundred.

22 "Then *comes* the tribe of Benjamin, and the leader of the children of Benjamin *shall be* Abidan the son of Gideoni." 23 And his army was numbered at thirty-five thousand four hundred. 24 "All who were numbered according to their armies of the forces with Ephraim, one hundred and eight thousand one hundred—[a]they shall be the third to break camp.

25 "The standard of the forces with Dan *shall be* on the north side according to their armies, and the leader of the children of Dan *shall be* Ahiezer the son of Ammishaddai." 26 And his army was numbered at sixty-two thousand seven hundred.

27 "Those who camp next to him *shall be* the tribe of Asher, and the leader of the children of Asher *shall be* Pagiel the son of Ocran." 28 And his army was numbered at forty-one thousand five hundred.

29 "Then *comes* the tribe of Naphtali, and the leader of the children of Naphtali *shall be* Ahira the son of Enan." 30 And his army was numbered at fifty-three thousand four hundred. 31 "All who were numbered of the forces with Dan, one hundred and fifty-seven thousand six hundred—[a]they shall break camp last, with their standards."

32 These *are* the ones who were numbered of the children of Israel by their fathers' houses. [a]All who were numbered according to their armies of the forces *were* six hundred and three thousand five hundred and fifty. 33 But [a]the Levites were not numbered among the children of Israel, just as the LORD commanded Moses.

34 Thus the children of Israel [a]did according to all that the LORD commanded Moses; [b]so they camped by their standards and so they broke camp, each one by his family, according to their fathers' houses.

The Sons of Aaron

3 Now these *are* the [a]records of Aaron and Moses when the LORD spoke with Moses on Mount Sinai. 2 And these *are* the names of the sons of Aaron: Nadab, the [a]firstborn, and [b]Abihu, Eleazar, and Ithamar. 3 These *are* the names of the sons of Aaron, [a]the anointed priests, whom he consecrated to minister as priests. 4 [a]Nadab and Abihu had died before the LORD when they offered profane fire before the LORD in the Wilderness of Sinai; and they had no children. So Eleazar and Ithamar ministered as priests in the presence of Aaron their father.

The Levites Serve in the Tabernacle

5 And the LORD spoke to Moses, saying: 6 [a]"Bring the tribe of Levi near, and present them before Aaron the priest, that they may serve him. 7 And they shall attend to his needs and the needs of the whole congregation before the tabernacle of meeting, to do [a]the work of the tabernacle. 8 Also they shall attend to all the furnishings of the tabernacle of meeting, and to the needs of the children of Israel, to do the work of the tabernacle. 9 And [a]you shall give the Levites to Aaron and his sons; they *are* given entirely to him[1] from among the children of Israel. 10 So you shall appoint Aaron and his sons, [a]and they shall attend to their priesthood; [b]but the outsider who comes near shall be put to death."

11 Then the LORD spoke to Moses, saying: 12 "Now behold, [a]I Myself have taken the Levites from among the children of Israel instead of every firstborn who opens the womb among the children of Israel. Therefore the Levites shall be [b]Mine, 13 because [a]all the firstborn *are* Mine. [b]On the day that I struck all the firstborn in the land of Egypt, I sanctified to Myself all the firstborn in Israel, both man and beast. They shall be Mine: I *am* the LORD."

2:14 [1] Spelled *Deuel* in 1:14 and 7:42 **2:16** [a] Num. 10:18 **2:17** [a] Num. 10:17, 21 [b] Num. 1:53 **2:24** [a] Num. 10:22 **2:31** [a] Num. 10:25 **2:32** [a] Ex. 38:26 **2:33** [a] Num. 1:47; 26:57–62 **2:34** [a] Num. 1:54 [b] Num. 24:2, 5, 6 **3:1** [a] Ex. 6:16–27 **3:2** [a] Ex. 6:23 [b] Num. 26:60, 61 **3:3** [a] Ex. 28:41 **3:4** [a] 1 Chr. 24:2 **3:6** [a] Num. 8:6–22; 18:1–7 **3:7** [a] Num. 1:50; 8:11, 15, 24, 26 **3:9** [a] Num. 8:19; 18:6, 7 [1] Samaritan Pentateuch and Septuagint read *Me.* **3:10** [a] Ex. 29:9 [b] Num. 1:51; 3:38; 16:40 **3:12** [a] Num. 3:41; 8:16; 18:6 [b] Num. 3:45; 8:14 **3:13** [a] Ex. 13:2 [b] Num. 8:17

Census of the Levites Commanded

14 Then the LORD spoke to Moses in the Wilderness of Sinai, saying: 15 "Number the children of Levi by their fathers' houses, by their families; you shall number [a]every male from a month old and above."

16 So Moses numbered them according to the word of the LORD, as he was commanded. 17 [a]These were the sons of Levi by their names: Gershon, Kohath, and Merari. 18 And these *are* the names of the sons of [a]Gershon by their families: [b]Libni and Shimei. 19 And the sons of [a]Kohath by their families: [b]Amram, Izehar, Hebron, and Uzziel. 20 [a]And the sons of Merari by their families: Mahli and Mushi. These *are* the families of the Levites by their fathers' houses.

21 From Gershon *came* the family of the Libnites and the family of the Shimites; these *were* the families of the Gershonites. 22 Those who were numbered, according to the number of all the males from a month old and above—of those who were numbered *there were* seven thousand five hundred. 23 [a]The families of the Gershonites were to camp behind the tabernacle westward. 24 And the leader of the father's house of the Gershonites *was* Eliasaph the son of Lael. 25 [a]The duties of the children of Gershon in the tabernacle of meeting *included* [b]the tabernacle, [c]the tent with [d]its covering, [e]the screen for the door of the tabernacle of meeting, 26 [a]the screen for the door of the court, [b]the hangings of the court which *are* around the tabernacle and the altar, and [c]their cords, according to all the work relating to them.

27 [a]From Kohath *came* the family of the Amramites, the family of the Izharites, the family of the Hebronites, and the family of the Uzzielites; these *were* the families of the Kohathites. 28 According to the number of all the males, from a month old and above, *there were* eight thousand six[1] hundred keeping charge of the sanctuary. 29 [a]The families of the children of Kohath were to camp on the south side of the tabernacle. 30 And the leader of the fathers' house of the families of the Kohathites *was* Elizaphan the son of [a]Uzziel. 31 [a]Their duty *included* [b]the ark, [c]the table, [d]the lampstand, [e]the altars, the utensils of the sanctuary with which they ministered, [f]the screen, and all the work relating to them.

32 And Eleazar the son of Aaron the priest *was to be* chief over the leaders of the Levites, *with* oversight of those who kept charge of the sanctuary.

33 From Merari *came* the family of the Mahlites and the family of the Mushites; these *were* the families of Merari. 34 And those who were numbered, according to the number of all the males from a month old and above, *were* six thousand two hundred. 35 The leader of the fathers' house of the families of Merari *was* Zuriel the son of Abihail. [a]These *were* to camp on the north side of the tabernacle. 36 And [a]the appointed duty of the children of Merari *included* the boards of the tabernacle, its bars, its pillars, its sockets, its utensils, all the work relating to them, 37 and the pillars of the court all around, with their sockets, their pegs, and their cords.

38 [a]Moreover those who were to camp before the tabernacle on the east, before the tabernacle of meeting, *were* Moses, Aaron, and his sons, [b]keeping charge of the sanctuary, [c]to meet the needs of the children of Israel; but [d]the outsider who came near was to be put to death. 39 [a]All who were numbered of the Levites, whom Moses and Aaron numbered at the commandment of the LORD, by their families, all the males from a month old and above, *were* twenty-two thousand.

Levites Dedicated Instead of the Firstborn

40 Then the LORD said to Moses: [a]"Number all the firstborn males of the children of Israel from a month old and above, and take the number of their names. 41 [a]And you shall take the Levites for Me—I *am* the LORD—instead of all the firstborn among the children of Israel, and the livestock of the Levites instead of all the firstborn among the livestock of the children of Israel." 42 So Moses numbered all the firstborn among the children of Israel, as the LORD commanded him. 43 And all the firstborn males, according to the number of names from a month old and above, of those who were numbered of them, were twenty-two thousand two hundred and seventy-three.

44 Then the LORD spoke to Moses, saying: 45 [a]"Take the Levites instead of all the firstborn among the children of Israel, and the livestock of the Levites instead of their livestock. The Levites shall be Mine: I *am* the LORD. 46 And for [a]the redemption of the two hundred and seventy-three of the firstborn of the children of Israel, [b]who are more than

3:15 [a] Num. 3:39; 26:62 **3:17** [a] Ex. 6:16–22 **3:18** [a] Num. 4:38–41 [b] Ex. 6:17 **3:19** [a] Num. 4:34–37 [b] Ex. 6:18 **3:20** [a] Ex. 6:19 **3:23** [a] Num. 1:53 **3:25** [a] Num. 4:24–26 [b] Ex. 25:9 [c] Ex. 26:1 [d] Ex. 26:7, 14 [e] Ex. 26:36 **3:26** [a] Ex. 27:9, 12, 14, 15 [b] Ex. 27:16 [c] Ex. 35:18 **3:27** [a] 1 Chr. 26:23 **3:28** [1] Some manuscripts of the Septuagint read *three*. **3:29** [a] Num. 1:53 **3:30** [a] Lev. 10:4 **3:31** [a] Num. 4:15 [b] Ex. 25:10 [c] Ex. 25:23 [d] Ex. 25:31 [e] Ex. 27:1; 30:1 [f] Ex. 26:31–33 **3:35** [a] Num. 1:53; 2:25 **3:36** [a] Num. 4:31, 32 **3:38** [a] Num. 1:53 [b] Num. 18:5 [c] Num. 3:7, 8 [d] Num. 3:10 **3:39** [a] Num. 3:43; 4:48; 26:62 **3:40** [a] Num. 3:15 **3:41** [a] Num. 3:12, 45 **3:45** [a] Num. 3:12, 41 **3:46** [a] Ex. 13:13, 15 [b] Num. 3:39, 43

the number of the Levites, 47 you shall take [a]five shekels for each one [b]individually; you shall take *them* in the currency of the shekel of the sanctuary, [c]the shekel of twenty gerahs. 48 And you shall give the money, with which the excess number of them is redeemed, to Aaron and his sons."

49 So Moses took the redemption money from those who were over and above those who were redeemed by the Levites. 50 From the firstborn of the children of Israel he took the money, [a]one thousand three hundred and sixty-five *shekels,* according to the shekel of the sanctuary. 51 And Moses [a]gave their redemption money to Aaron and his sons, according to the word of the LORD, as the LORD commanded Moses.

> **PEACE NOTE**
>
> Uncertainty is not dangerous. I can be full of faith and peace and still not have everything figured out.

Duties of the Sons of Kohath

4 Then the LORD spoke to Moses and Aaron, saying: 2 "Take a census of the sons of [a]Kohath from among the children of Levi, by their families, by their fathers' house, 3 [a]from thirty years old and above, even to fifty years old, all who enter the service to do the work in the tabernacle of meeting.

4 [a]"This *is* the service of the sons of Kohath in the tabernacle of meeting, *relating to* [b]the most holy things: 5 When the camp prepares to journey, Aaron and his sons shall come, and they shall take down [a]the covering veil and cover the [b]ark of the Testimony with it. 6 Then they shall put on it a covering of badger skins, and spread over *that* a cloth entirely of [a]blue; and they shall insert [b]its poles.

7 "On the [a]table of showbread they shall spread a blue cloth, and put on it the dishes, the pans, the bowls, and the pitchers for pouring; and the [b]showbread[1] shall be on it. 8 They shall spread over them a scarlet cloth, and cover the same with a covering of badger skins; and they shall insert its poles. 9 And they shall take a blue cloth and cover the [a]lampstand of the light, [b]with its lamps, its wick-trimmers, its trays, and all its oil vessels, with which they service it. 10 Then they shall put it with all its utensils in a covering of badger skins, and put *it* on a carrying beam.

11 "Over [a]the golden altar they shall spread a blue cloth, and cover it with a covering of badger skins; and they shall insert its poles. 12 Then they shall take all the [a]utensils of service with which they minister in the sanctuary, put *them* in a blue cloth, cover them with a covering of badger skins, and put *them* on a carrying beam. 13 Also they shall take away the ashes from the altar, and spread a purple cloth over it. 14 They shall put on it all its implements with which they minister there—the firepans, the forks, the shovels, the basins, and all the utensils of the altar—and they shall spread on it a covering of badger skins, and insert its poles. 15 And when Aaron and his sons have finished covering the sanctuary and all the furnishings of the sanctuary, when the camp is set to go, then [a]the sons of Kohath shall come to carry *them;* [b]but they shall not touch any holy thing, lest they die.

"[c]These *are* the things in the tabernacle of meeting which the sons of Kohath are to carry.

16 "The appointed duty of Eleazar the son of Aaron the priest *is* [a]the oil for the light, the [b]sweet incense, [c]the daily grain offering, the [d]anointing oil, the oversight of all the tabernacle, of all that *is* in it, with the sanctuary and its furnishings."

17 Then the LORD spoke to Moses and Aaron, saying: 18 "Do not cut off the tribe of the families of the Kohathites from among the Levites; 19 but do this in regard to them, that they may live and not die when they approach [a]the most holy things: Aaron and his sons shall go in and appoint each of them to his service and his task. 20 [a]But they shall not go in to watch while the holy things are being covered, lest they die."

Duties of the Sons of Gershon

21 Then the LORD spoke to Moses, saying: 22 "Also take a census of the sons of [a]Gershon,

3:47 [a] Lev. 27:6 [b] Num. 1:2, 18, 20 [c] Ex. 30:13 **3:50** [a] Num. 3:46, 47 **3:51** [a] Num. 3:48 **4:2** [a] Num. 3:27–32 **4:3** [a] Num. 4:23, 30, 35; 8:24 **4:4** [a] Num. 4:15 [b] Num. 4:19 **4:5** [a] Ex. 26:31 [b] Ex. 25:10, 16 **4:6** [a] Ex. 39:1 [b] Ex. 25:13 **4:7** [a] Ex. 25:23, 29, 30 [b] Lev. 24:5–9 [1] Literally *the continual bread* **4:9** [a] Ex. 25:31 [b] Ex. 25:37, 38 **4:11** [a] Ex. 30:1–5 **4:12** [a] Ex. 25:9 **4:15** [a] Deut. 31:9 [b] 2 Sam. 6:6, 7 [c] Num. 3:31 **4:16** [a] Lev. 24:2 [b] Ex. 30:34 [c] Ex. 29:38 [d] Ex. 30:23–25 **4:19** [a] Num. 4:4 **4:20** [a] Ex. 19:21 **4:22** [a] Num. 3:22

by their fathers' house, by their families.
23 [a]From thirty years old and above, even to
fifty years old, you shall number them, all who
enter to perform the service, to do the work
in the tabernacle of meeting. 24 This *is* the
[a]service of the families of the Gershonites, in
serving and carrying: 25 [a]They shall carry the
[b]curtains of the tabernacle and the tabernacle
of meeting *with* its covering, the covering
of [c]badger skins that *is* on it, the screen for
the door of the tabernacle of meeting, 26 the
screen for the door of the gate of the court,
the hangings of the court which *are* around
the tabernacle and altar, and their cords, all
the furnishings for their service and all that
is made for these things: so shall they serve.
27 "Aaron and his sons shall assign all the
service of the sons of the Gershonites, all
their tasks and all their service. And you shall
appoint to them all their tasks as their duty.
28 This *is* the service of the families of the sons
of Gershon in the tabernacle of meeting. And
their duties *shall be* [a]under the authority[1] of
Ithamar the son of Aaron the priest.

Duties of the Sons of Merari

29 "*As for* the sons of [a]Merari, you shall number them by their families and by their fathers'
house. 30 [a]From thirty years old and above,
even to fifty years old, you shall number them,
everyone who enters the service to do the work
of the tabernacle of meeting. 31 And [a]this *is*
[b]what they must carry as all their service for
the tabernacle of meeting: [c]the boards of the
tabernacle, its bars, its pillars, its sockets, 32 and
the pillars around the court with their sockets,
pegs, and cords, with all their furnishings and
all their service; and you shall [a]assign *to each*
man by name the items he must carry. 33 This
is the service of the families of the sons of
Merari, as all their service for the tabernacle
of meeting, under the authority[1] of Ithamar
the son of Aaron the priest."

Census of the Levites

34 [a]And Moses, Aaron, and the leaders of
the congregation numbered the sons of the
Kohathites by their families and by their
fathers' house, 35 from thirty [a]years old and
above, even to fifty years old, everyone who
entered the service for work in the tabernacle
of meeting; 36 and those who were numbered
by their families were two thousand seven
hundred and fifty. 37 These *were* the ones
who were numbered of the families of the
Kohathites, all who might serve in the tabernacle of meeting, whom Moses and Aaron
numbered according to the commandment
of the LORD by the hand of Moses.
38 And those who were numbered of the
sons of Gershon, by their families and by
their fathers' house, 39 from thirty years old
and above, even to fifty years old, everyone who entered the service for work in the
tabernacle of meeting— 40 those who were
numbered by their families, by their fathers'
house, were two thousand six hundred and
thirty. 41 [a]These *are* the ones who were numbered of the families of the sons of Gershon,
of all who might serve in the tabernacle of
meeting, whom Moses and Aaron numbered
according to the commandment of the LORD.
42 Those of the families of the sons of Merari who were numbered, by their families, by
their fathers' house, 43 from thirty years old and
above, even to fifty years old, everyone who
entered the service for work in the tabernacle
of meeting— 44 those who were numbered by
their families were three thousand two hundred. 45 These *are* the ones who were numbered
of the families of the sons of Merari, whom
Moses and Aaron numbered [a]according to
the word of the LORD by the hand of Moses.
46 All who were [a]numbered of the Levites,
whom Moses, Aaron, and the leaders of Israel numbered, by their families and by their
fathers' houses, 47 [a]from thirty years old and
above, even to fifty years old, everyone who
came to do the work of service and the work
of bearing burdens in the tabernacle of meeting— 48 those who were numbered were eight
thousand five hundred and eighty.
49 According to the commandment of the
LORD they were numbered by the hand of
Moses, [a]each according to his service and according to his task; thus were they numbered
by him, [b]as the LORD commanded Moses.

Ceremonially Unclean Persons Isolated

5 And the LORD spoke to Moses, saying:
2 "Command the children of Israel that
they put out of the camp every [a]leper, everyone who has a [b]discharge, and whoever becomes [c]defiled by a corpse. 3 You shall put out
both male and female; you shall put them
outside the camp, that they may not defile
their camps [a]in the midst of which I dwell."
4 And the children of Israel did so, and put
them outside the camp; as the LORD spoke
to Moses, so the children of Israel did.

4:23 [a] Num. 4:3 **4:24** [a] Num. 7:7 **4:25** [a] Num. 3:25, 26 [b] Ex. 36:8 [c] Ex. 26:14 **4:28** [a] Num. 4:33 [1] Literally *hand*
4:29 [a] Num. 3:33–37 **4:30** [a] Num. 4:3; 8:24–26 **4:31** [a] Num. 3:36, 37 [b] Num. 7:8 [c] Ex. 26:15 **4:32** [a] Ex. 25:9; 38:21
4:33 [1] Literally *hand* **4:34** [a] Num. 4:2 **4:35** [a] Num. 4:47 **4:41** [a] Num. 4:22 **4:45** [a] Num. 4:29 **4:46** [a] 1 Chr. 23:3–23
4:47 [a] Num. 4:3, 23, 30 **4:49** [a] Num. 4:15, 24, 31 [b] Num. 4:1, 21 **5:2** [a] Lev. 13:3, 8, 46 [b] Lev. 15:2 [c] Lev. 21:1 **5:3** [a] Lev. 26:11, 12

Confession and Restitution

5 Then the LORD spoke to Moses, saying, 6 "Speak to the children of Israel: [a]'When a man or woman commits any sin that men commit in unfaithfulness against the LORD, and that person is guilty, 7 [a]then he shall confess the sin which he has committed. He shall make restitution for his trespass [b]in full, plus one-fifth of it, and give *it* to the one he has wronged. 8 But if the man has no relative to whom restitution may be made for the wrong, the restitution for the wrong *must go* to the LORD for the priest, in addition to [a]the ram of the atonement with which atonement is made for him. 9 Every [a]offering of all the holy things of the children of Israel, which they bring to the priest, shall be [b]his. 10 And every man's holy things shall be his; whatever any man gives the priest shall be [a]his.' "

Concerning Unfaithful Wives

11 And the LORD spoke to Moses, saying, 12 "Speak to the children of Israel, and say to them: 'If any man's wife goes astray and behaves unfaithfully toward him, 13 and a man [a]lies with her carnally, and it is hidden from the eyes of her husband, and it is concealed that she has defiled herself, and *there was* no witness against her, nor was she [b]caught— 14 if the spirit of jealousy comes upon him and he becomes [a]jealous of his wife, who has defiled herself; or if the spirit of jealousy comes upon him and he becomes jealous of his wife, although she has not defiled herself— 15 then the man shall bring his wife to the priest. He shall [a]bring the offering required for her, one-tenth of an ephah of barley meal; he shall pour no oil on it and put no frankincense on it, because it *is* a grain offering of jealousy, an offering for remembering, for [b]bringing iniquity to remembrance.

16 'And the priest shall bring her near, and set her before the LORD. 17 The priest shall take holy water in an earthen vessel, and take some of the dust that is on the floor of the tabernacle and put *it* into the water. 18 Then the priest shall stand the woman before the [a]LORD, uncover the woman's head, and put the offering for remembering in her hands, which *is* the grain offering of jealousy. And the priest shall have in his hand the bitter water that brings a curse. 19 And the priest shall put her under oath, and say to the woman, "If no man has lain with you, and if you have not gone astray to uncleanness *while* under your husband's *authority,* be free from this bitter water that brings a curse. 20 But if you have gone astray *while* under your husband's *authority,* and if you have defiled yourself and some man other than your husband has lain with you"— 21 then the priest shall [a]put the woman under the oath of the curse, and he shall say to the woman—[b]"the LORD make you a curse and an oath among your people, when the LORD makes your thigh rot and your belly swell; 22 and may this water that causes the curse [a]go into your stomach, and make *your* belly swell and *your* thigh rot."

'[b]Then the woman shall say, "Amen, so be it."

23 'Then the priest shall write these curses in a book, and he shall scrape *them* off into the bitter water. 24 And he shall make the woman drink the bitter water that brings a curse, and the water that brings the curse shall enter her *to become* bitter. 25 [a]Then the priest shall take the grain offering of jealousy from the woman's hand, shall [b]wave the offering before the LORD, and bring it to the altar; 26 and the priest shall take a handful of the offering, [a]as its memorial portion, burn *it* on the altar, and afterward make the woman drink the water. 27 When he has made her drink the water, then it shall be, if she has defiled herself and behaved unfaithfully toward her husband, that the water that brings a [a]curse will enter her *and become* bitter, and her belly will swell, her thigh will rot, and the woman [b]will become a curse among her people. 28 But if the woman has not defiled herself, and is clean, then she shall be free and may conceive children.

29 'This *is* the law of jealousy, when a wife, *while* under her husband's *authority,* [a]goes astray and defiles herself, 30 or when the spirit of jealousy comes upon a man, and he becomes jealous of his wife; then he shall stand the woman before the LORD, and the priest shall execute all this law upon her. 31 Then the man shall be free from iniquity, but that woman [a]shall bear her guilt.' "

The Law of the Nazirite

6 Then the LORD spoke to Moses, saying, 2 "Speak to the children of Israel, and say to them: 'When either a man or woman consecrates an offering to take the vow of a Nazirite, [a]to separate himself to the LORD, 3 [a]he shall separate himself from wine and *similar* drink; he shall drink neither vinegar made from wine nor vinegar made from *similar* drink; neither shall he drink any grape juice,

5:6 [a] Lev. 5:14—6:7 5:7 [a] Lev. 5:5; 26:40, 41 [b] Lev. 6:4, 5 5:8 [a] Lev. 5:15; 6:6, 7; 7:7 5:9 [a] Ex. 29:28 [b] Lev. 7:32–34; 10:14, 15 5:10 [a] Lev. 10:13 5:13 [a] Lev. 18:20; 20:10 [b] John 8:4 5:14 [a] Prov. 6:34 5:15 [a] Lev. 5:11 [b] 1 Kin. 17:18 5:18 [a] Heb. 13:4 5:21 [a] Josh. 6:26 [b] Jer. 29:22 5:22 [a] Ps. 109:18 [b] Deut. 27:15–26 5:25 [a] Lev. 8:27 [b] Lev. 2:2, 9 5:26 [a] Lev. 2:2, 9 5:27 [a] Jer. 24:9; 29:18, 22; 42:18 [b] Num. 5:21 5:29 [a] Num. 5:19 5:31 [a] Lev. 20:17, 19, 20 6:2 [a] Judg. 13:5 6:3 [a] Luke 1:15

nor eat fresh grapes or raisins. 4 All the days of his separation he shall eat nothing that is produced by the grapevine, from seed to skin.

5 'All the days of the vow of his separation no [a]razor shall come upon his head; until the days are fulfilled for which he separated himself to the LORD, he shall be holy. *Then* he shall let the locks of the hair of his head grow. 6 All the days that he separates himself to the LORD [a]he shall not go near a dead body. 7 [a]He shall not make himself unclean even for his father or his mother, for his brother or his sister, when they die, because his separation to God *is* on his head. 8 [a]All the days of his separation he shall be holy to the LORD.

9 'And if anyone dies very suddenly beside him, and he defiles his consecrated head, then he shall [a]shave his head on the day of his cleansing; on the seventh day he shall shave it. 10 Then [a]on the eighth day he shall bring two turtledoves or two young pigeons to the priest, to the door of the tabernacle of meeting; 11 and the priest shall offer one as a sin offering and *the* other as a burnt offering, and make atonement for him, because he sinned in regard to the corpse; and he shall sanctify his head that same day. 12 He shall consecrate to the LORD the days of his separation, and bring a male lamb in its first year [a]as a trespass offering; but the former days shall be lost, because his separation was defiled.

13 'Now this *is* the law of the Nazirite: [a]When the days of his separation are fulfilled, he shall be brought to the door of the tabernacle of meeting. 14 And he shall present his offering to the LORD: one male lamb in its first year without blemish as a burnt offering, one ewe lamb in its first year without blemish [a]as a sin offering, one ram without blemish [b]as a peace offering, 15 a basket of unleavened bread, [a]cakes of fine flour mixed with oil, unleavened wafers [b]anointed with oil, and their grain offering with their [c]drink offerings.

16 'Then the priest shall bring *them* before the LORD and offer his sin offering and his burnt offering; 17 and he shall offer the ram as a sacrifice of a peace offering to the LORD, with the basket of unleavened bread; the priest shall also offer its grain offering and its drink offering. 18 [a]Then the Nazirite shall shave his consecrated head *at* the door of the tabernacle of meeting, and shall take the hair from his consecrated head and put *it* on the fire which is under the sacrifice of the peace offering.

19 'And the priest shall take the [a]boiled shoulder of the ram, one [b]unleavened cake from the basket, and one unleavened wafer, and [c]put *them* upon the hands of the Nazirite after he has shaved his consecrated *hair,* 20 and the priest shall wave them as a wave offering before the LORD; [a]they *are* holy for the priest, together with the breast of the wave offering and the thigh of the heave offering. After that the Nazirite may drink wine.'

21 "This is the law of the Nazirite who vows to the LORD the offering for his separation, and besides that, whatever else his hand is able to provide; according to the vow which he takes, so he must do according to the law of his separation."

The Priestly Blessing

22 And the LORD spoke to Moses, saying: 23 "Speak to Aaron and his sons, saying, 'This is the way you shall bless the children of Israel. Say to them:

24 "The LORD [a]bless you and [b]keep you;
25 The LORD [a]make His face shine upon you,
And [b]be gracious to you;
26 [a]The LORD lift up His countenance upon you,
And [b]give you peace."'

27 [a]"So they shall put My name on the children of Israel, and [b]I will bless them."

> **PEACE NOTE**
>
> In the ministry of Jesus, we often find the word *peace* used in its Old Testament sense of completion and wholeness. Jesus taught us that peace *with* God will result in the peace *of* God.
>
> NUMBERS 6:26

Offerings of the Leaders

7 Now it came to pass, when Moses had finished [a]setting up the tabernacle, that he [b]anointed it and consecrated it and all its furnishings, and the altar and all its utensils;

6:5 [a] 1 Sam. 1:11 **6:6** [a] Num. 19:11–22 **6:7** [a] Num. 9:6 **6:8** [a] [2 Cor. 6:17, 18] **6:9** [a] Lev. 14:8, 9 **6:10** [a] Lev. 5:7; 14:22; 15:14, 29 **6:12** [a] Lev. 5:6 **6:13** [a] Acts 21:26 **6:14** [a] Lev. 4:2, 27, 32 [b] Lev. 3:6 **6:15** [a] Lev. 2:4 [b] Ex. 29:2 [c] Num. 15:5, 7, 10 **6:18** [a] Acts 21:23, 24 **6:19** [a] 1 Sam. 2:15 [b] Ex. 29:23, 24 [c] Lev. 7:30 **6:20** [a] Ex. 29:27, 28 **6:24** [a] Deut. 28:3–6 [b] John 7:11 **6:25** [a] Dan. 9:17 [b] Mal. 1:9 **6:26** [a] Ps. 4:6; 89:15 [b] Lev. 26:6 **6:27** [a] Is. 43:7 [b] Num. 23:20 **7:1** [a] Ex. 40:17–33 [b] Lev. 8:10, 11

so he anointed them and consecrated them.
2 Then [a]the leaders of Israel, the heads of their
fathers' houses, who *were* the leaders of the
tribes and over those who were numbered,
made an offering. 3 And they brought their
offering before the LORD, six covered carts
and twelve oxen, a cart for *every* two of the
leaders, and for each one an ox; and they
presented them before the tabernacle.

4 Then the LORD spoke to Moses, saying,
5 "Accept *these* from them, that they may be
used in doing the work of the tabernacle of
meeting; and you shall give them to the Levites, *to* every man according to his service."
6 So Moses took the carts and the oxen, and
gave them to the Levites. 7 Two carts and four
oxen [a]he gave to the sons of Gershon, according to their service; 8 [a]and four carts and eight
oxen he gave to the sons of Merari, according
to their service, under the authority[1] of Ithamar the son of Aaron the priest. 9 But to the
sons of Kohath he gave none, because theirs
was [a]the service of the holy things, [b]*which*
they carried on their shoulders.

10 Now the leaders offered [a]the dedication
offering for the altar when it was anointed;
so the leaders offered their offering before
the altar. 11 For the LORD said to Moses, "They
shall offer their offering, one leader each day,
for the dedication of the altar."

12 And the one who offered his offering on
the first day *was* [a]Nahshon the son of Amminadab, from the tribe of Judah. 13 His offering
was one silver platter, the weight of which
was one hundred and thirty *shekels,* and one
silver bowl of seventy shekels, according to
[a]the shekel of the sanctuary, both of them
full of fine flour mixed with oil as a [b]grain
offering; 14 one gold pan of ten *shekels,* full of
[a]incense; 15 [a]one young bull, one ram, and one
male lamb [b]in its first year, as a burnt offering; 16 one kid of the goats as a [a]sin offering;
17 and for [a]the sacrifice of peace offerings:
two oxen, five rams, five male goats, and five
male lambs in their first year. This *was* the
offering of Nahshon the son of Amminadab.

18 On the second day Nethanel the son of
Zuar, leader of Issachar, presented *an offering.* 19 *For* his offering he offered one silver
platter, the weight of which *was* one hundred
and thirty *shekels,* and one silver bowl of
seventy shekels, according to the shekel of
the sanctuary, both of them full of fine flour
mixed with oil as a grain offering; 20 one
gold pan of ten *shekels,* full of incense; 21 one
young bull, one ram, and one male lamb in
its first year, as a burnt offering; 22 one kid
of the goats as a sin offering; 23 and as the
sacrifice of peace offerings: two oxen, five
rams, five male goats, and five male lambs
in their first year. This *was* the offering of
Nethanel the son of Zuar.

24 On the third day Eliab the son of Helon,
leader of the children of Zebulun, *presented an
offering.* 25 His offering *was* one silver platter,
the weight of which *was* one hundred and
thirty *shekels,* and one silver bowl of seventy
shekels, according to the shekel of the sanctuary, both of them full of fine flour mixed
with oil as a grain offering; 26 one gold pan of
ten *shekels,* full of incense; 27 one young bull,
one ram, and one male lamb in its first year,
as a burnt offering; 28 one kid of the goats as
a sin offering; 29 and for the sacrifice of peace
offerings: two oxen, five rams, five male goats,
and five male lambs in their first year. This
was the offering of Eliab the son of Helon.

30 On the fourth day [a]Elizur the son of
Shedeur, leader of the children of Reuben,
presented an offering. 31 His offering *was* one
silver platter, the weight of which *was* one
hundred and thirty *shekels,* and one silver
bowl of seventy shekels, according to the
shekel of the sanctuary, both of them full of
fine flour mixed with oil as a grain offering;
32 one gold pan of ten *shekels,* full of incense;
33 one young bull, one ram, and one male
lamb in its first year, as a burnt offering;
34 one kid of the goats as a sin offering; 35 and
as the sacrifice of peace offerings: two oxen,
five rams, five male goats, and five male
lambs in their first year. This *was* the offering
of Elizur the son of Shedeur.

36 On the fifth day [a]Shelumiel the son of
Zurishaddai, leader of the children of Simeon, *presented an offering.* 37 His offering *was*
one silver platter, the weight of which *was*
one hundred and thirty *shekels,* and one
silver bowl of seventy shekels, according to
the shekel of the sanctuary, both of them
full of fine flour mixed with oil as a grain
offering; 38 one gold pan of ten *shekels,* full
of incense; 39 one young bull, one ram, and
one male lamb in its first year, as a burnt
offering; 40 one kid of the goats as a sin offering; 41 and as the sacrifice of peace offerings:
two oxen, five rams, five male goats, and five
male lambs in their first year. This *was* the
offering of Shelumiel the son of Zurishaddai.

42 On the sixth day [a]Eliasaph the son of
Deuel,[1] leader of the children of Gad, *presented
an offering.* 43 His offering *was* one silver platter, the weight of which *was* one hundred and
thirty *shekels,* and one silver bowl of seventy

7:2 [a] Num. 1:4 **7:7** [a] Num. 4:24–28 **7:8** [a] Num. 4:29–33 [1] Literally *hand* **7:9** [a] Num. 4:15 [b] Num. 4:6–14 **7:10** [a] 2 Chr. 7:5, 9 **7:12** [a] Num. 2:3 **7:13** [a] Ex. 30:13 [b] Lev. 2:1 **7:14** [a] Ex. 30:34, 35 **7:15** [a] Lev. 1:2 [b] Ex. 12:5 **7:16** [a] Lev. 4:23 **7:17** [a] Lev. 3:1 **7:30** [a] Num. 1:5; 2:10 **7:36** [a] Num. 1:6; 2:12; 7:41 **7:42** [a] Num. 1:14; 2:14; 10:20 [1] Spelled *Reuel* in 2:14

shekels, according to the shekel of the sanctuary, both of them full of fine flour mixed
with oil as a grain offering; 44 one gold pan of
ten *shekels,* full of incense; 45 one young bull,
one ram, and one male lamb in its first year,
as [a]a burnt offering; 46 one kid of the goats as
a sin offering; 47 and as the sacrifice of peace
offerings: two oxen, five rams, five male goats,
and five male lambs in their first year. This
was the offering of Eliasaph the son of Deuel.
48 On the seventh day [a]Elishama the son of
Ammihud, leader of the children of Ephraim,
presented an offering. 49 His offering *was* one
silver platter, the weight of which *was* one
hundred and thirty *shekels,* and one silver
bowl of seventy shekels, according to the
shekel of the sanctuary, both of them full of
fine flour mixed with oil as a grain offering;
50 one gold pan of ten *shekels,* full of incense;
51 one young bull, one ram, and one male
lamb in its first year, as a burnt offering;
52 one kid of the goats as a sin offering; 53 and
as the sacrifice of peace offerings: two oxen,
five rams, five male goats, and five male
lambs in their first year. This *was* the offering
of Elishama the son of Ammihud.
54 On the eighth day [a]Gamaliel the son of
Pedahzur, leader of the children of Manasseh,
presented an offering. 55 His offering *was* one
silver platter, the weight of which *was* one
hundred and thirty *shekels,* and one silver
bowl of seventy shekels, according to the
shekel of the sanctuary, both of them full of
fine flour mixed with oil as a grain offering;
56 one gold pan of ten *shekels,* full of incense;
57 one young bull, one ram, and one male
lamb in its first year, as a burnt offering;
58 one kid of the goats as a sin offering; 59 and
as the sacrifice of peace offerings: two oxen,
five rams, five male goats, and five male
lambs in their first year. This *was* the offering
of Gamaliel the son of Pedahzur.
60 On the ninth day [a]Abidan the son of
Gideoni, leader of the children of Benjamin,
presented an offering. 61 His offering *was* one
silver platter, the weight of which *was* one
hundred and thirty *shekels,* and one silver
bowl of seventy shekels, according to the
shekel of the sanctuary, both of them full of
fine flour mixed with oil as a grain offering;
62 one gold pan of ten *shekels,* full of incense;
63 one young bull, one ram, and one male
lamb in its first year, as a burnt offering;
64 one kid of the goats as a sin offering; 65 and
as the sacrifice of peace offerings: two oxen,
five rams, five male goats, and five male
lambs in their first year. This *was* the offering
of Abidan the son of Gideoni.
66 On the tenth day [a]Ahiezer the son of
Ammishaddai, leader of the children of Dan,
presented an offering. 67 His offering *was* one
silver platter, the weight of which *was* one
hundred and thirty *shekels,* and one silver
bowl of seventy shekels, according to the
shekel of the sanctuary, both of them full of
fine flour mixed with oil as a grain offering;
68 one gold pan of ten *shekels,* full of incense;
69 one young bull, one ram, and one male
lamb in its first year, as a burnt offering;
70 one kid of the goats as a sin offering; 71 and
as the sacrifice of peace offerings: two oxen,
five rams, five male goats, and five male
lambs in their first year. This *was* the offering
of Ahiezer the son of Ammishaddai.
72 On the eleventh day [a]Pagiel the son of
Ocran, leader of the children of Asher, *presented an offering.* 73 His offering *was* one
silver platter, the weight of which *was* one
hundred and thirty *shekels,* and one silver
bowl of seventy shekels, according to the
shekel of the sanctuary, both of them full of
fine flour mixed with oil as a grain offering;
74 one gold pan of ten *shekels,* full of incense;
75 one young bull, one ram, and one male
lamb in its first year, as a burnt offering;
76 one kid of the goats as a sin offering; 77 and
as the sacrifice of peace offerings: two oxen,
five rams, five male goats, and five male
lambs in their first year. This *was* the offering
of Pagiel the son of Ocran.
78 On the twelfth day [a]Ahira the son of
Enan, leader of the children of Naphtali,
presented an offering. 79 His offering *was* one
silver platter, the weight of which *was* one
hundred and thirty *shekels,* and one silver
bowl of seventy shekels, according to the
shekel of the sanctuary, both of them full of
fine flour mixed with oil as a grain offering;
80 one gold pan of ten *shekels,* full of incense;
81 one young bull, one ram, and one male
lamb in its first year, as a burnt offering;
82 one kid of the goats as a sin offering; 83 and
as the sacrifice of peace offerings: two oxen,
five rams, five male goats, and five male
lambs in their first year. This *was* the offering
of Ahira the son of Enan.
84 This *was* [a]the dedication *offering* for
the altar from the leaders of Israel, when it
was anointed: twelve silver platters, twelve
silver bowls, and twelve gold pans. 85 Each
silver platter *weighed* one hundred and thirty
shekels and each bowl seventy *shekels.* All the
silver of the vessels *weighed* two thousand
four hundred *shekels,* according to the shekel of the sanctuary. 86 The twelve gold pans
full of incense *weighed* ten *shekels* apiece,

7:45 [a] Ps. 40:6 **7:48** [a] Num. 1:10; 2:18 **7:54** [a] Num. 1:10; 2:20 **7:60** [a] Num. 1:11; 2:22 **7:66** [a] Num. 1:12; 2:25
7:72 [a] Num. 1:13; 2:27 **7:78** [a] Num. 1:15; 2:29 **7:84** [a] Num. 7:10

according to the shekel of the sanctuary; all the gold of the pans *weighed* one hundred and twenty *shekels.* 87 All the oxen for the burnt offering *were* twelve young bulls, the rams twelve, the male lambs in their first year twelve, with their grain offering, and the kids of the goats as a sin offering twelve. 88 And all the oxen for the sacrifice of peace offerings were twenty-four bulls, the rams sixty, the male goats sixty, and the lambs in their first year sixty. This *was* the dedication *offering* for the altar after it was [a]anointed.

89 Now when Moses went into the tabernacle of meeting [a]to speak with Him, he heard [b]the voice of One speaking to him from above the mercy seat that *was* on the ark of the Testimony, from [c]between the two cherubim; thus He spoke to him.

PEACE NOTE

The church must spread a theology of *shalom.*

Arrangement of the Lamps

8 And the LORD spoke to Moses, saying: 2 "Speak to Aaron, and say to him, 'When you [a]arrange the lamps, the seven [b]lamps shall give light in front of the lampstand.' " 3 And Aaron did so; he arranged the lamps to face toward the front of the lampstand, as the LORD commanded Moses. 4 [a]Now this workmanship of the lampstand *was* hammered gold; from its shaft to its flowers it *was* [b]hammered work. [c]According to the pattern which the LORD had shown Moses, so he made the lampstand.

Cleansing and Dedication of the Levites

5 Then the LORD spoke to Moses, saying: 6 "Take the Levites from among the children of Israel and cleanse them *ceremonially.* 7 Thus you shall do to them to cleanse them: Sprinkle [a]water of purification on them, and [b]let them shave all their body, and let them wash their clothes, and *so* make themselves clean. 8 Then let them take a young bull with [a]its grain offering of fine flour mixed with oil, and you shall take another young bull as a sin offering. 9 [a]And you shall bring the Levites before the tabernacle of meeting, [b]and you shall gather together the whole congregation of the children of Israel. 10 So you shall bring the Levites before the LORD, and the children of Israel [a]shall lay their hands on the Levites; 11 and Aaron shall offer the Levites before the LORD *like* a [a]wave offering from the children of Israel, that they may perform the work of the LORD. 12 [a]Then the Levites shall lay their hands on the heads of the young bulls, and you shall offer one as a sin offering and the other as a burnt offering to the LORD, to make atonement for the Levites.

13 "And you shall stand the Levites before Aaron and his sons, and then offer them *like* a wave offering to the LORD. 14 Thus you shall [a]separate the Levites from among the children of Israel, and the Levites shall be [b]Mine. 15 After that the Levites shall go in to service the tabernacle of meeting. So you shall cleanse them and [a]offer them *like* a wave offering. 16 For they *are* [a]wholly given to Me from among the children of Israel; I have taken them for Myself [b]instead of all who open the womb, the firstborn of all the children of Israel. 17 [a]For all the firstborn among the children of Israel *are* Mine, *both* man and beast; on the day that I struck all the firstborn in the land of Egypt I sanctified them to Myself. 18 I have taken the Levites instead of all the firstborn of the children of Israel. 19 And [a]I have given the Levites as a gift to Aaron and his sons from among the children of Israel, to do the work for the children of Israel in the tabernacle of meeting, and to make atonement for the children of Israel, [b]that there be no plague among the children of Israel when the children of Israel come near the sanctuary."

20 Thus Moses and Aaron and all the congregation of the children of Israel did to the Levites; according to all that the LORD commanded Moses concerning the Levites, so the children of Israel did to them. 21 [a]And the Levites purified themselves and washed their clothes; then Aaron presented them *like* a wave offering before the LORD, and Aaron made atonement for them to cleanse

7:88 [a] Num. 7:1, 10 **7:89** [a] [Ex. 33:9, 11] [b] Ex. 25:21, 22 [c] Ps. 80:1; 99:1 **8:2** [a] Lev. 24:2–4 [b] Ex. 25:37; 40:25 **8:4** [a] Ex. 25:31 [b] Ex. 25:18 [c] Ex. 25:40 **8:7** [a] Num. 19:9, 13, 17, 20 [b] Lev. 14:8, 9 **8:8** [a] Lev. 2:1 **8:9** [a] Ex. 29:4; 40:12 [b] Lev. 8:3 **8:10** [a] Lev. 1:4 **8:11** [a] Num. 18:6 **8:12** [a] Ex. 29:10 **8:14** [a] Num. 16:9 [b] Num. 3:12, 45; 16:9 **8:15** [a] Num. 8:11, 13 **8:16** [a] Num. 3:9 [b] Num. 3:12, 45 **8:17** [a] Ex. 12:2, 12, 13, 15 **8:19** [a] Num. 3:9 [b] Num. 1:53; 16:46; 18:5 **8:21** [a] Num. 8:7

them. 22 [a]After that the Levites went in to
do their work in the tabernacle of meeting
before Aaron and his sons; [b]as the LORD
commanded Moses concerning the Levites,
so they did to them.
23 Then the LORD spoke to Moses, saying,
24 "This *is* what *pertains* to the Levites: [a]From
twenty-five years old and above one may
enter to perform service in the work of the
tabernacle of meeting; 25 and at the age of
fifty years they must cease performing this
work, and shall work no more. 26 They may
minister with their brethren in the tabernacle of meeting, [a]to attend to needs, but they
themselves shall do no work. Thus you shall
do to the Levites regarding their duties."

The Second Passover

9 Now the LORD spoke to Moses in the Wilderness of Sinai, in the first month of the
second year after they had come out of the land
of Egypt, saying: 2 "Let the children of Israel
keep [a]the Passover at its appointed [b]time. 3 On
the fourteenth day of this month, at twilight,
you shall keep it at its appointed time. According to all its rites and ceremonies you shall
keep it." 4 So Moses told the children of Israel
that they should keep the Passover. 5 And [a]they
kept the Passover on the fourteenth day of
the first month, at twilight, in the Wilderness
of Sinai; according to all that the LORD commanded Moses, so the children of Israel did.
6 Now there were *certain* men who were
[a]defiled by a human corpse, so that they
could not keep the Passover on that day;
[b]and they came before Moses and Aaron
that day. 7 And those men said to him, "We
became defiled by a human corpse. Why
are we kept from presenting the offering of
the LORD at its appointed time among the
children of Israel?"
8 And Moses said to them, "Stand still, that
[a]I may hear what the LORD will command
concerning you."
9 Then the LORD spoke to Moses, saying,
10 "Speak to the children of Israel, saying: 'If
anyone of you or your posterity is unclean because of a corpse, or *is* far away on a journey,
he may still keep the LORD's Passover. 11 On
[a]the fourteenth day of the second month,
at twilight, they may keep it. They shall [b]eat
it with unleavened bread and bitter herbs.
12 [a]They shall leave none of it until morning,
[b]nor break one of its bones. [c]According to
all the ordinances of the Passover they shall
keep it. 13 But the man who *is* clean and is not
on a journey, and ceases to keep the Passover, that same person [a]shall be cut off from
among his people, because he [b]did not bring
the offering of the LORD at its appointed
time; that man shall [c]bear his sin.
14 'And if a stranger dwells among you, and
would keep the LORD's Passover, he must do
so according to the rite of the Passover and
according to its ceremony; [a]you shall have
one ordinance, both for the stranger and the
native of the land.' "

The Cloud and the Fire

15 Now [a]on the day that the tabernacle was
raised up, the cloud [b]covered the tabernacle,
the tent of the Testimony; [c]from evening until
morning it was above the tabernacle like the
appearance of fire. 16 So it was always: the cloud
covered it *by day,* and the appearance of fire
by night. 17 Whenever the cloud [a]was taken
up from above the tabernacle, after that the
children of Israel would journey; and in the
place where the cloud settled, there the children of Israel would pitch their tents. 18 At the
command of the LORD the children of Israel
would journey, and at the command of the
LORD they would camp; [a]as long as the cloud
stayed above the tabernacle they remained
encamped. 19 Even when the cloud continued
long, many days above the tabernacle, the children of Israel [a]kept the charge of the LORD and
did not journey. 20 So it was, when the cloud was
above the tabernacle a few days: according to
the command of the LORD they would remain
encamped, and according to the command of
the LORD they would journey. 21 So it was, when
the cloud remained only from evening until
morning: when the cloud was taken up in the
morning, then they would journey; whether
by day or by night, whenever the cloud was
taken up, they would journey. 22 *Whether it
was* two days, a month, or a year that the cloud
remained above the tabernacle, the children
of Israel [a]would remain encamped and not
journey; but when it was taken up, they would
journey. 23 At the command of the LORD they
remained encamped, and at the command of
the LORD they journeyed; they [a]kept the charge
of the LORD, at the command of the LORD by
the hand of Moses.

Two Silver Trumpets

10 And the LORD spoke to Moses, saying: 2 "Make two silver trumpets for
yourself; you shall make them of hammered
work; you shall use them for [a]calling the

8:22 [a] Num. 8:15 [b] Num. 8:5 **8:24** [a] Num. 4:3 **8:26** [a] Num. 1:53 **9:2** [a] Lev. 23:5 [b] 2 Chr. 30:1–15 **9:5** [a] Josh. 5:10 **9:6** [a] Num. 5:2; 19:11–22 [b] Num. 27:2 **9:8** [a] Num. 27:5 **9:11** [a] 2 Chr. 30:2, 15 [b] Ex. 12:8 **9:12** [a] Ex. 12:10 [b] Ex. 12:46 [c] Ex. 12:43 **9:13** [a] Ex. 12:15, 47 [b] Num. 9:7 [c] Num. 5:31 **9:14** [a] Ex. 12:49 **9:15** [a] Ex. 40:33, 34 [b] Is. 4:5 [c] Ex. 13:21, 22; 40:38 **9:17** [a] Ex. 40:36–38 **9:18** [a] 1 Cor. 10:1 **9:19** [a] Num. 1:53; 3:8 **9:22** [a] Ex. 40:36, 37 **9:23** [a] Num. 9:19 **10:2** [a] Is. 1:13

congregation and for directing the movement of the camps. 3 When [a]they blow both
of them, all the congregation shall gather
before you at the door of the tabernacle of
meeting. 4 But if they blow *only* one, then
the leaders, the [a]heads of the divisions of
Israel, shall gather to you. 5 When you sound
the [a]advance, [b]the camps that lie on the east
side shall then begin their journey. 6 When
you sound the advance the second time,
then the camps that lie [a]on the south side
shall begin their journey; they shall sound
the call for them to begin their journeys.
7 And when the assembly is to be gathered
together, [a]you shall blow, but not [b]sound the
advance. 8 [a]The sons of Aaron, the priests,
shall blow the trumpets; and these shall be
to you as an ordinance forever throughout
your generations.

9 [a]"When you go to war in your land against
the enemy who [b]oppresses you, then you
shall sound an alarm with the trumpets, and
you will be [c]remembered before the LORD
your God, and you will be saved from your
enemies. 10 Also [a]in the day of your gladness, in your appointed feasts, and at the
beginning of your months, you shall blow
the trumpets over your burnt offerings and
over the sacrifices of your peace offerings;
and they shall be [b]a memorial for you before
your God: I *am* the LORD your God."

Departure from Sinai

11 Now it came to pass on the twentieth *day*
of the second month, in the second year, that
the cloud [a]was taken up from above the tabernacle of the Testimony. 12 And the children
of Israel set out from the [a]Wilderness of Sinai
on [b]their journeys; then the cloud settled
down in the [c]Wilderness of Paran. 13 So they
started out for the first time [a]according to the
command of the LORD by the hand of Moses.

14 The standard of the camp of the children of Judah [a]set out first according to their
armies; over their army was [b]Nahshon the
son of Amminadab. 15 Over the army of the
tribe of the children of Issachar *was* Nethanel
the son of Zuar. 16 And over the army of the
tribe of the children of Zebulun *was* Eliab
the son of Helon.

17 Then [a]the tabernacle was taken down;
and the sons of Gershon and the sons of Merari set out, [b]carrying the tabernacle.

18 And [a]the standard of the camp of Reuben set out according to their armies; over
their army *was* Elizur the son of Shedeur.
19 Over the army of the tribe of the children
of Simeon *was* Shelumiel the son of Zurishaddai. 20 And over the army of the tribe
of the children of Gad *was* Eliasaph the son
of Deuel.

21 Then the Kohathites set out, carrying
the [a]holy things. (The tabernacle would be
prepared for their arrival.)

22 And [a]the standard of the camp of the
children of Ephraim set out according to
their armies; over their army *was* Elishama
the son of Ammihud. 23 Over the army of the
tribe of the children of Manasseh *was* Gamaliel the son of Pedahzur. 24 And over the army
of the tribe of the children of Benjamin *was*
Abidan the son of Gideoni.

25 Then [a]the standard of the camp of the
children of Dan (the rear guard of all the
camps) set out according to their armies;
over their army *was* Ahiezer the son of Ammishaddai. 26 Over the army of the tribe of
the children of Asher *was* Pagiel the son of
Ocran. 27 And over the army of the tribe of
the children of Naphtali *was* Ahira the son
of Enan.

28 [a]Thus *was* the order of march of the
children of Israel, according to their armies,
when they began their journey.

29 Now Moses said to [a]Hobab the son of
[b]Reuel[1] the Midianite, Moses' father-in-law,
"We are setting out for the place of which the
LORD said, [c]'I will give it to you.' Come with
us, and [d]we will treat you well; for [e]the LORD
has promised good things to Israel."

30 And he said to him, "I will not go, but
I will depart to my *own* land and to my relatives."

31 So *Moses* said, "Please do not leave, inasmuch as you know how we are to camp in the
wilderness, and you can be our [a]eyes. 32 And
it shall be, if you go with us—indeed it shall
be—that [a]whatever good the LORD will do to
us, the same we will do to you."

33 So they departed from [a]the mountain
of the LORD on a journey of three days; and
the ark of the covenant of the LORD [b]went
before them for the three days' journey, to
search out a resting place for them. 34 And
[a]the cloud of the LORD *was* above them by
day when they went out from the camp.

10:3 [a] Jer. 4:5 **10:4** [a] Ex. 18:21 **10:5** [a] Joel 2:1 [b] Num. 2:3 **10:6** [a] Num. 2:10 **10:7** [a] Num. 10:3 [b] Joel 2:1
10:8 [a] Num. 31:6 **10:9** [a] Josh. 6:5 [b] Judg. 2:18; 4:3; 6:9; 10:8, 12 [c] Gen. 8:1 **10:10** [a] Lev. 23:24 [b] Num. 10:9
10:11 [a] Num. 9:17 **10:12** [a] Ex. 19:1 [b] Ex. 40:36 [c] Gen. 21:21 **10:13** [a] Num. 10:5, 6 **10:14** [a] Num. 2:3–9 [b] Num. 1:7
10:17 [a] Num. 1:51 [b] Num. 4:21–32; 7:7–9 **10:18** [a] Num. 2:10–16 **10:21** [a] Num. 4:4–20; 7:9 **10:22** [a] Num. 2:18–24
10:25 [a] Num. 2:25–31 **10:28** [a] Num. 2:34 **10:29** [a] Judg. 4:11 [b] Ex. 2:18; 3:1; 18:12 [c] Gen. 12:7 [d] Judg. 1:16 [e] Ex. 3:8
[1] Septuagint reads *Raguel* (compare Exodus 2:18). **10:31** [a] Job 29:15 **10:32** [a] Judg. 1:16 **10:33** [a] Ex. 3:1 [b] Deut. 1:33
10:34 [a] Ex. 13:21

[35]So it was, whenever the ark set out, that
Moses said:

[a]"Rise up, O LORD!
Let Your enemies be scattered,
And let those who hate You flee before
You."

[36]And when it rested, he said:

"Return, O LORD,
To the many thousands of Israel."

The People Complain

11 Now [a]*when* the people complained,
it displeased the LORD; [b]for the LORD
heard *it,* and His anger was aroused. So the
[c]fire of the LORD burned among them, and
consumed *some* in the outskirts of the camp.
[2]Then the people [a]cried out to Moses, and
when Moses [b]prayed to the LORD, the fire
was quenched. [3]So he called the name of the
place Taberah,[1] because the fire of the LORD
had burned among them.
[4]Now the [a]mixed multitude who were
among them yielded to [b]intense craving;
so the children of Israel also wept again and
said: [c]"Who will give us meat to eat? [5][a]We
remember the fish which we ate freely in
Egypt, the cucumbers, the melons, the leeks,
the onions, and the garlic; [6]but now [a]our
whole being *is* dried up; *there is* nothing at
all except this manna *before* our eyes!"
[7]Now [a]the manna *was* like coriander seed,
and its color like the color of bdellium. [8]The
people went about and gathered *it,* ground *it*
on millstones or beat *it* in the mortar, cooked
it in pans, and made cakes of it; and [a]its taste
was like the taste of pastry prepared with oil.
[9]And [a]when the dew fell on the camp in the
night, the manna fell on it.
[10]Then Moses heard the people weeping
throughout their families, everyone at the
door of his tent; and [a]the anger of the LORD
was greatly aroused; Moses also was displeased. [11][a]So Moses said to the LORD, "Why
have You afflicted Your servant? And why
have I not found favor in Your sight, that You
have laid the burden of all these people on
me? [12]Did I conceive all these people? Did I
beget them, that You should say to me, [a]'Carry
them in your bosom, as a [b]guardian carries a
nursing child,' to the land which You [c]swore
to their fathers? [13][a]Where am I to get meat to
give to all these people? For they weep all over

PEACE NOTE

The blessings of peace with God, including forgiveness, assurance, and perhaps even physical health, will rest on the person who embraces Jesus' message.

me, saying, 'Give us meat, that we may eat.'
[14][a]I am not able to bear all these people alone,
because the burden *is* too heavy for me. [15]If
You treat me like this, please kill me here and
now—if I have found favor in Your sight—and
[a]do not let me see my wretchedness!"

The Seventy Elders

[16]So the LORD said to Moses: "Gather to Me
[a]seventy men of the elders of Israel, whom
you know to be the elders of the people and
[b]officers over them; bring them to the tabernacle of meeting, that they may stand there
with you. [17]Then I will come down and talk
with you there. [a]I will take of the Spirit that *is*
upon you and will put *the same* upon them;
and they shall bear the burden of the people
with you, that you may not bear *it* yourself
alone. [18]Then you shall say to the people,
'Consecrate yourselves for tomorrow, and
you shall eat meat; for you have wept [a]in
the hearing of the LORD, saying, "Who will
give us meat to eat? For *it was* well with us
in Egypt." Therefore the LORD will give you
meat, and you shall eat. [19]You shall eat, not
one day, nor two days, nor five days, nor ten
days, nor twenty days, [20][a]but *for* a whole
month, until it comes out of your nostrils
and becomes loathsome to you, because you
have [b]despised the LORD who is among you,
and have wept before Him, saying, [c]"Why did
we ever come up out of Egypt?" ' "
[21]And Moses said, [a]"The people whom I
am among *are* six hundred thousand men
on foot; yet You have said, 'I will give them
meat, that they may eat *for* a whole month.'

10:35 [a] Ps. 68:1, 2; 132:8 **11:1** [a] Num. 14:2; 16:11; 17:5 [b] Ps. 78:21 [c] Lev. 10:2 **11:2** [a] Num. 12:11, 13; 21:7 [b] [James 5:16] **11:3** [1] Literally *Burning* **11:4** [a] Ex. 12:38 [b] 1 Cor. 10:6 [c] [Ps. 78:18] **11:5** [a] Ex. 16:3 **11:6** [a] Num. 21:5 **11:7** [a] Ex. 16:14, 31 **11:8** [a] Ex. 16:31 **11:9** [a] Ex. 16:13, 14 **11:10** [a] Ps. 78:21 **11:11** [a] Deut. 1:12 **11:12** [a] Is. 40:11 [b] Is. 49:23 [c] Gen. 26:3 **11:13** [a] Mark 8:4 **11:14** [a] Ex. 18:18 **11:15** [a] Rev. 3:17 **11:16** [a] Ex. 18:25; 24:1, 9 [b] Deut. 16:18 **11:17** [a] 1 Sam. 10:6 **11:18** [a] Ex. 16:7 **11:20** [a] Ps. 78:29; 106:15 [b] 1 Sam. 10:19 [c] Num. 21:5 **11:21** [a] Gen. 12:2

22[a]Shall flocks and herds be slaughtered for
them, to provide enough for them? Or shall
all the fish of the sea be gathered together for
them, to provide enough for them?"
23 And the LORD said to Moses, [a]"Has the
LORD's arm been shortened? Now you shall see
whether [b]what I say will happen to you or not."
24 So Moses went out and told the people the
words of the LORD, and he [a]gathered the seventy
men of the elders of the people and placed them
around the tabernacle. 25 Then the LORD came
down in the cloud, and spoke to him, and took
of the Spirit that *was* upon him, and placed *the
same* upon the seventy elders; and it happened,
[a]when the Spirit rested upon them, that [b]they
prophesied, although they never did *so* again.[1]
26 But two men had remained in the camp:
the name of one *was* Eldad, and the name of
the other Medad. And the Spirit rested upon
them. Now they *were* among those listed, but
who [a]had not gone out to the tabernacle; yet
they prophesied in the camp. 27 And a young
man ran and told Moses, and said, "Eldad
and Medad are prophesying in the camp."
28 So Joshua the son of Nun, Moses' assistant, *one* of his choice men, answered and
said, "Moses my lord, [a]forbid them!"
29 Then Moses said to him, "Are you zealous
for my sake? [a]Oh, that all the LORD's people
were prophets *and* that the LORD would put
His Spirit upon them!" 30 And Moses returned
to the camp, he and the elders of Israel.

The LORD Sends Quail

31 Now a [a]wind went out from the LORD, and
it brought quail from the sea and left *them*
fluttering near the camp, about a day's journey
on this side and about a day's journey on the
other side, all around the camp, and about two
cubits above the surface of the ground. 32 And
the people stayed up all that day, all night, and
all the next day, and gathered the quail (he who
gathered least gathered ten [a]homers); and they
spread *them* out for themselves all around the
camp. 33 But while the [a]meat *was* still between
their teeth, before it was chewed, the wrath of
the LORD was aroused against the people, and
the LORD struck the people with a very great
plague. 34 So he called the name of that place
Kibroth Hattaavah,[1] because there they buried
the people who had yielded to craving.
35[a]From Kibroth Hattaavah the people
moved to Hazeroth, and camped at Hazeroth.

Dissension of Aaron and Miriam

12 Then [a]Miriam and Aaron spoke [b]against
Moses because of the Ethiopian woman
whom he had married; for [c]he had married
an Ethiopian woman. 2 So they said, "Has the
LORD indeed spoken only through [a]Moses?
[b]Has He not spoken through us also?" And
the LORD [c]heard *it*. 3(Now the man Moses *was*
very humble, more than all men who *were*
on the face of the earth.)
4[a]Suddenly the LORD said to Moses, Aaron,
and Miriam, "Come out, you three, to the tabernacle of meeting!" So the three came out.
5[a]Then the LORD came down in the pillar of
cloud and stood *in* the door of the tabernacle,
and called Aaron and Miriam. And they both
went forward. 6 Then He said,

"Hear now My words:
If there is a prophet among you,
I, the LORD, make Myself known to him
[a]in a vision;
I speak to him [b]in a dream.
7 Not so with [a]My servant Moses;
[b]He *is* faithful in all [c]My house.
8 I speak with him [a]face to face,
Even [b]plainly, and not in dark sayings;
And he sees [c]the form of the LORD.
Why then [d]were you not afraid
To speak against My servant Moses?"

9 So the anger of the LORD was aroused
against them, and He departed. 10 And when
the cloud departed from above the tabernacle,
[a]suddenly Miriam *became* [b]leprous, as *white
as* snow. Then Aaron turned toward Miriam,
and there she was, a leper. 11 So Aaron said to
Moses, "Oh, my lord! Please [a]do not lay *this* sin
on us, in which we have done foolishly and in
which we have sinned. 12 Please [a]do not let her
be as one dead, whose flesh is half consumed
when he comes out of his mother's womb!"
13 So Moses cried out to the LORD, saying,
"Please [a]heal her, O God, I pray!"
14 Then the LORD said to Moses, "If her father
had but [a]spit in her face, would she not be
shamed seven days? Let her be [b]shut out of
the camp seven days, and afterward she may
be received *again*." 15[a]So Miriam was shut out
of the camp seven days, and the people did
not journey till Miriam was brought in *again*.
16 And afterward the people moved from [a]Ha-
zeroth and camped in the Wilderness of Paran.

11:22 [a] 2 Kin. 7:2 **11:23** [a] Is. 50:2; 59:1 [b] Num. 23:19 **11:24** [a] Num. 11:16 **11:25** [a] 2 Kin. 2:15 [b] Joel 2:28 [1] Targum and Vulgate read *did not cease.* **11:26** [a] Jer. 36:5 **11:28** [a] [Mark 9:38–40] **11:29** [a] 1 Cor. 14:5 **11:31** [a] Ex. 16:13 **11:32** [a] Ezek. 45:11 **11:33** [a] Ps. 78:29–31; 106:15 **11:34** [1] Literally *Graves of Craving* **11:35** [a] Num. 33:17 **12:1** [a] Num. 20:1 [b] Num. 11:1 [c] Ex. 2:21 **12:2** [a] Num. 16:3 [b] Mic. 6:4 [c] Ezek. 35:12, 13 **12:4** [a] [Ps. 76:9] **12:5** [a] Ex. 19:9; 34:5 **12:6** [a] Gen. 46:2 [b] Gen. 31:10 **12:7** [a] Josh. 1:1 [b] Heb. 3:2, 5 [c] 1 Tim. 1:12 **12:8** [a] Deut. 34:10 [b] [1 Cor. 13:12] [c] Ex. 33:19–23 [d] 2 Pet. 2:10 **12:10** [a] Deut. 24:9 [b] 2 Kin. 5:27; 15:5 **12:11** [a] 2 Sam. 19:19; 24:10 **12:12** [a] Ps. 88:4 **12:13** [a] Ps. 103:3 **12:14** [a] Deut. 25:9 [b] Lev. 13:46 **12:15** [a] Deut. 24:9 **12:16** [a] Num. 11:35; 33:17, 18

Spies Sent into Canaan

13 And the LORD spoke to Moses, saying, 2 [a]"Send men to spy out the land of Canaan, which I am giving to the children of Israel; from each tribe of their fathers you shall send a man, every one a leader among them."

3 So Moses sent them [a]from the Wilderness of Paran according to the command of the LORD, all of them men who *were* heads of the children of Israel. 4 Now these *were* their names: from the tribe of Reuben, Shammua the son of Zaccur; 5 from the tribe of Simeon, Shaphat the son of Hori; 6 [a]from the tribe of Judah, [b]Caleb the son of Jephunneh; 7 from the tribe of Issachar, Igal the son of Joseph; 8 from the tribe of Ephraim, Hoshea[1] the son of Nun; 9 from the tribe of Benjamin, Palti the son of Raphu; 10 from the tribe of Zebulun, Gaddiel the son of Sodi; 11 from the tribe of Joseph, *that is,* from the tribe of Manasseh, Gaddi the son of Susi; 12 from the tribe of Dan, Ammiel the son of Gemalli; 13 from the tribe of Asher, Sethur the son of Michael; 14 from the tribe of Naphtali, Nahbi the son of Vophsi; 15 from the tribe of Gad, Geuel the son of Machi.

16 These *are* the names of the men whom Moses sent to spy out the land. And Moses called [a]Hoshea[1] the son of Nun, Joshua.

17 Then Moses sent them to spy out the land of Canaan, and said to them, "Go up this *way* into the South, and go up to [a]the mountains, 18 and see what the land is like: whether the people who dwell in it *are* strong or weak, few or many; 19 whether the land they dwell in *is* good or bad; whether the cities they inhabit *are* like camps or strongholds; 20 whether the land *is* rich or poor; and whether there are forests there or not. [a]Be of good courage. And bring some of the fruit of the land." Now the time *was* the season of the first ripe grapes.

21 So they went up and spied out the land [a]from the Wilderness of Zin as far as [b]Rehob, near the entrance of [c]Hamath. 22 And they went up through the South and came to [a]Hebron; Ahiman, Sheshai, and Talmai, the descendants of [b]Anak, *were* there. (Now Hebron was built seven years before Zoan in Egypt.) 23 [a]Then they came to the Valley of Eshcol, and there cut down a branch with one cluster of grapes; they carried it between two of them on a pole. *They* also *brought* some of the pomegranates and figs. 24 The place was called the Valley of Eshcol,[1] because of the cluster which the men of Israel cut down there. 25 And they returned from spying out the land after forty days.

26 Now they departed and came back to Moses and Aaron and all the congregation of the children of Israel in the Wilderness of Paran, at [a]Kadesh; they brought back word to them and to all the congregation, and showed them the fruit of the land. 27 Then they told him, and said: "We went to the land where you sent us. It truly flows with [a]milk and honey, [b]and this *is* its fruit. 28 Nevertheless the [a]people who dwell in the land *are* strong; the cities *are* fortified *and* very large; moreover we saw the descendants of [b]Anak there. 29 [a]The Amalekites dwell in the land of the South; the Hittites, the Jebusites, and the Amorites dwell in the mountains; and the Canaanites dwell by the sea and along the banks of the Jordan."

30 Then [a]Caleb quieted the people before Moses, and said, "Let us go up at once and take possession, for we are well able to overcome it."

31 [a]But the men who had gone up with him said, "We are not able to go up against the people, for they *are* stronger than we." 32 And they [a]gave the children of Israel a bad report of the land which they had spied out, saying, "The land through which we have gone as spies *is* a land that devours its inhabitants, and [b]all the people whom we saw in it *are* men of *great* stature. 33 There we saw the giants[1] ([a]the descendants of Anak came from the giants); and we were [b]like grasshoppers in our own sight, and so we were [c]in their sight."

Israel Refuses to Enter Canaan

14 So all the congregation lifted up their voices and cried, and the people [a]wept that night. 2 [a]And all the children of Israel complained against Moses and Aaron, and the whole congregation said to them, "If only we had died in the land of Egypt! Or if only we had died in this wilderness! 3 Why has the LORD brought us to this land to fall by the sword, that our wives and [a]children should become victims? Would it not be better for us to return to Egypt?" 4 So they said to one another, [a]"Let us select a leader and [b]return to Egypt."

5 Then Moses and Aaron fell on their faces before all the assembly of the congregation of the children of Israel.

13:2 [a]Deut. 1:22; 9:23 **13:3** [a]Num. 12:16; 32:8 **13:6** [a]Num. 34:19 [b]Josh. 14:6, 7 **13:8** [1]Septuagint and Vulgate read *Oshea.* **13:16** [a]Ex. 17:9 [1]Septuagint and Vulgate read *Oshea.* **13:17** [a]Judg. 1:9 **13:20** [a]Deut. 31:6, 7, 23 **13:21** [a]Num. 20:1; 27:14; 33:36 [b]Josh. 19:28 [c]Josh. 13:5 **13:22** [a]Josh. 15:13, 14 [b]Josh. 11:21, 22 **13:23** [a]Deut. 1:24, 25 **13:24** [1]Literally *Cluster* **13:26** [a]Deut. 1:19 **13:27** [a]Ex. 3:8, 17; 13:5; 33:3 [b]Deut. 1:25 **13:28** [a]Deut. 1:28; 9:1, 2 [b]Josh. 11:21, 22 **13:29** [a]Judg. 6:3 **13:30** [a]Num. 14:6, 24 **13:31** [a]Deut. 1:28; 9:1–3 **13:32** [a]Num. 14:36, 37 [b]Amos 2:9 **13:33** [a]Deut. 1:28; 9:2 [b]Is. 40:22 [c]1 Sam. 17:42 [1]Hebrew *nephilim* **14:1** [a]Deut. 1:45 **14:2** [a]Ex. 16:2; 17:3 **14:3** [a]Deut. 1:39 **14:4** [a]Neh. 9:17 [b]Acts 7:39

PANIC OR PEACE

Caleb . . . said, "Let us go up at once and take possession, for we are well able to overcome it."

NUMBERS 13:30

Have you ever stepped into a room—in which you needed to give a speech, mend a relationship, start some herculean task—looked around, and thought, *I can't do this*? Something tells you that you are not up to the task. Most of the spies who snuck into the Promised Land, took a look around, and then returned told Moses there was no way the people of Israel could secure their new homeland.

Well, Caleb thought otherwise. He gave what we might call a minority report: "Let us go up at once and take possession, for we are well able to overcome it." Would that the people of Israel had listened to him! Instead of wandering about in the wilderness for forty years, the Israelites could have entered the Promised Land immediately. But no, the other spies could see only "giants" (v. 33) they were sure would conquer them. Panic chased away their faith in God.

Every time you want to say, "I can't do this!" God responds, "But I can!" If we obey God, we'll find peace.

6 But Joshua the son of Nun and Caleb the
son of Jephunneh, *who were* among those
who had spied out the land, tore their clothes;
7 and they spoke to all the congregation of
the children of Israel, saying: [a]"The land we
passed through to spy out *is* an exceedingly
good land. 8 If the LORD [a]delights in us, then
He will bring us into this land and give it to
us, [b]'a land which flows with milk and honey.'[1]
9 Only [a]do not rebel against the LORD, [b]nor
fear the people of the land, for [c]they *are* our
bread; their protection has departed from
them, [d]and the LORD *is* with us. Do not fear
them."
10 [a]And all the congregation said to stone
them with stones. Now [b]the glory of the LORD
appeared in the tabernacle of meeting before
all the children of Israel.

Moses Intercedes for the People

11 Then the LORD said to Moses: "How long
will these people [a]reject Me? And how long
will they not [b]believe Me, with all the signs
which I have performed among them? 12 I will
strike them with the pestilence and disinherit
them, and I will [a]make of you a nation greater
and mightier than they."
13 And [a]Moses said to the LORD: [b]"Then the
Egyptians will hear *it,* for by Your might You
brought these people up from among them,
14 and they will tell *it* to the inhabitants of
this land. They have [a]heard that You, LORD,
are among these people; that You, LORD, are
seen face to face and Your cloud stands above
them, and You go before them in a pillar of
cloud by day and in a pillar of fire by night.
15 Now *if* You kill these people as one man,
then the nations which have heard of Your
fame will speak, saying, 16 'Because the LORD
was not [a]able to bring this people to the land
which He swore to give them, therefore He
killed them in the wilderness.' 17 And now, I
pray, let the power of my Lord be great, just
as You have spoken, saying, 18 [a]'The LORD is
longsuffering and abundant in mercy, forgiving iniquity and transgression; but He by no
means clears *the guilty,* [b]visiting the iniquity
of the fathers on the children to the third and
fourth *generation.*'[1] 19 [a]Pardon the iniquity of
this people, I pray, [b]according to the greatness
of Your mercy, just [c]as You have forgiven this
people, from Egypt even until now."
20 Then the LORD said: "I have pardoned,
[a]according to your word; 21 but truly, as I live,
[a]all the earth shall be filled with the glory of
the LORD— 22 [a]because all these men who
have seen My glory and the signs which I did
in Egypt and in the wilderness, and have put
Me to the test now [b]these ten times, and have
not heeded My voice, 23 they certainly shall
not [a]see the land of which I swore to their
fathers, nor shall any of those who rejected Me

14:7 [a] Num. 13:27 **14:8** [a] Deut. 10:15 [b] Num. 13:27 [1] Exodus 3:8 **14:9** [a] Deut. 1:26; 9:7, 23, 24 [b] Deut. 7:18 [c] Num. 24:8 [d] Deut. 20:1, 3, 4; 31:6–8 **14:10** [a] Ex. 17:4 [b] Ex. 16:10 **14:11** [a] Heb. 3:8 [b] Deut. 9:23 **14:12** [a] Ex. 32:10 **14:13** [a] Ps. 106:23 [b] Ex. 32:12 **14:14** [a] Deut. 2:25 **14:16** [a] Deut. 9:28 **14:18** [a] Ex. 34:6, 7 [b] Ex. 20:5 [1] Exodus 34:6, 7 **14:19** [a] Ex. 32:32; 34:9 [b] Ps. 51:1; 106:45 [c] Ps. 78:38 **14:20** [a] Mic. 7:18–20 **14:21** [a] Ps. 72:19 **14:22** [a] Deut. 1:35 [b] Gen. 31:7 **14:23** [a] Num. 26:65; 32:11

see it. 24 But My servant [a]Caleb, because he has a different spirit in him and [b]has followed Me fully, I will bring into the land where he went, and his descendants shall inherit it. 25 Now the Amalekites and the Canaanites dwell in the valley; tomorrow turn and [a]move out into the wilderness by the Way of the Red Sea."

Death Sentence on the Rebels

26 And the LORD spoke to Moses and Aaron, saying, 27 [a]"How long *shall I bear with* this evil congregation who complain against Me? [b]I have heard the complaints which the children of Israel make against Me. 28 Say to them, [a]'As I live,' says the LORD, 'just as you have spoken in My hearing, so I will do to you: 29 The carcasses of you who have complained against Me shall fall in this wilderness, [a]all of you who were numbered, according to your entire number, from twenty years old and above. 30 [a]Except for Caleb the son of Jephunneh and Joshua the son of Nun, you shall by no means enter the land which I swore I would make you dwell in. 31 [a]But your little ones, whom you said would be victims, I will bring in, and they shall know the land which [b]you have despised. 32 But *as for* you, [a]your carcasses shall fall in this wilderness. 33 And your sons shall [a]be shepherds in the wilderness [b]forty years, and [c]bear the brunt of your infidelity, until your carcasses are consumed in the wilderness. 34 [a]According to the number of the days in which you spied out the land, [b]forty days, for each day you shall bear your guilt one year, *namely* forty years, [c]and you shall know My rejection. 35 [a]I the LORD have spoken this. I will surely do so to all [b]this evil congregation who are gathered together against Me. In this wilderness they shall be consumed, and there they shall die.'"

36 Now the men whom Moses sent to spy out the land, who returned and made all the congregation complain against him by bringing a bad report of the land, 37 those very men who brought the evil report about the land, [a]died by the plague before the LORD. 38 [a]But Joshua the son of Nun and Caleb the son of Jephunneh remained alive, of the men who went to spy out the land.

A Futile Invasion Attempt

39 Then Moses told these words to all the children of Israel, [a]and the people mourned greatly. 40 And they rose early in the morning and went up to the top of the mountain, saying, [a]"Here we are, and we will go up to the place which the LORD has promised, for we have sinned!"

41 And Moses said, "Now why do you transgress the command of the LORD? For this will not succeed. 42 [a]Do not go up, lest you be defeated by your enemies, for the LORD *is* not among you. 43 For the Amalekites and the Canaanites *are* there before you, and you shall fall by the sword; [a]because you have turned away from the LORD, the LORD will not be with you."

44 [a]But they presumed to go up to the mountaintop. Nevertheless, neither the ark of the covenant of the LORD nor Moses departed from the camp. 45 Then the Amalekites and the Canaanites who dwelt in that mountain came down and attacked them, and drove them back as far as [a]Hormah.

Laws of Grain and Drink Offerings

15 And the LORD spoke to Moses, saying, 2 [a]"Speak to the children of Israel, and say to them: 'When you have come into the land you are to inhabit, which I am giving to you, 3 and you [a]make an offering by fire to the LORD, a burnt offering or a sacrifice, [b]to fulfill a vow or as a freewill offering or [c]in your appointed feasts, to make a [d]sweet aroma to the LORD, from the herd or the flock, 4 then [a]he who presents his offering to the LORD shall bring [b]a grain offering of one-tenth *of an ephah* of fine flour mixed [c]with one-fourth of a hin of oil; 5 [a]and one-fourth of a hin of wine as a drink offering you shall prepare with the burnt offering or the sacrifice, for each [b]lamb. 6 [a]Or for a ram you shall prepare as a grain offering two-tenths *of an ephah* of fine flour mixed with one-third of a hin of oil; 7 and as a drink offering you shall offer one-third of a hin of wine as a sweet aroma to the LORD. 8 And when you prepare a young bull as a burnt offering, or as a sacrifice to fulfill a vow, or as a [a]peace offering to the LORD, 9 then shall be offered [a]with the young bull a grain offering of three-tenths *of an ephah* of fine flour mixed with half a hin of oil; 10 and you shall bring as the drink offering half a hin of wine as an offering made by fire, a sweet aroma to the LORD.

14:24 [a] Josh. 14:6, 8, 9 [b] Num. 32:12 **14:25** [a] Deut. 1:40 **14:27** [a] Ex. 16:28 [b] Ex. 16:12 **14:28** [a] Heb. 3:16–19 **14:29** [a] Num. 1:45, 46; 26:64 **14:30** [a] Deut. 1:36–38 **14:31** [a] Deut. 1:39 [b] Ps. 106:24 **14:32** [a] Num. 26:64, 65; 32:13 **14:33** [a] Ps. 107:40 [b] Deut. 2:14 [c] Ezek. 23:35 **14:34** [a] Num. 13:25 [b] Ezek. 4:6 [c] [Heb. 4:1] **14:35** [a] Num. 23:19 [b] 1 Cor. 10:5 **14:37** [a] [1 Cor. 10:10] **14:38** [a] Josh. 14:6, 10 **14:39** [a] Ex. 33:4 **14:40** [a] Deut. 1:41–44 **14:42** [a] Deut. 1:42; 31:17 **14:43** [a] 2 Chr. 15:2 **14:44** [a] Deut. 1:43 **14:45** [a] Num. 21:3 **15:2** [a] Lev. 23:10 **15:3** [a] Lev. 1:2, 3 [b] Lev. 7:16; 22:18, 21 [c] Lev. 23:2, 8, 12, 38 [d] Ex. 29:18 **15:4** [a] Lev. 2:1; 6:14 [b] Ex. 29:40 [c] Num. 28:5 **15:5** [a] Num. 28:7, 14 [b] Lev. 1:10; 3:6 **15:6** [a] Num. 28:12, 14 **15:8** [a] Lev. 7:11 **15:9** [a] Num. 28:12, 14

11[a]'Thus it shall be done for each young bull,
for each ram, or for each lamb or young goat.
12 According to the number that you prepare,
so you shall do with everyone according to
their number. 13 All who are native-born shall
do these things in this manner, in presenting
an offering made by fire, a sweet aroma to
the LORD. 14 And if a stranger dwells with you,
or whoever *is* among you throughout your
generations, and would present an offering
made by fire, a sweet aroma to the LORD, just
as you do, so shall he do. 15[a]One ordinance
shall be for you of the assembly and for the
stranger who dwells *with you,* an ordinance
forever throughout your generations; as you
are, so shall the stranger be before the LORD.
16 One law and one custom shall be for you
and for the stranger who dwells with you.' "[1]
17 Again the LORD spoke to Moses, saying,
18[a]"Speak to the children of Israel, and say
to them: 'When you come into the land to
which I bring you, 19 then it will be, when
you eat of [a]the bread of the land, that you
shall offer up a heave offering to the LORD.
20[a]You shall offer up a cake of the first of your
ground meal *as* a heave offering; as [b]a heave
offering of the threshing floor, so shall you
offer it up. 21 Of the first of your ground meal
you shall give to the LORD a heave offering
throughout your generations.

Laws Concerning Unintentional Sin

22[a]'If you sin unintentionally, and do not
observe all these commandments which the
LORD has spoken to Moses— 23 all that the
LORD has commanded you by the hand of
Moses, from the day the LORD gave commandment and onward throughout your genera-
tions— 24 then it will be, [a]if it is unintentionally
committed, without the knowledge of the
congregation, that the whole congregation
shall offer one young bull as a burnt offering,
as a sweet aroma to the LORD, [b]with its grain
offering and its drink offering, according to
the ordinance, and [c]one kid of the goats as
a sin offering. 25[a]So the priest shall make
atonement for the whole congregation of
the children of Israel, and it shall be forgiven
them, for it was unintentional; they shall bring
their offering, an offering made by fire to the
LORD, and their sin offering before the LORD,
for their unintended sin. 26 It shall be forgiven
the whole congregation of the children of Israel and the stranger who dwells among them,
because all the people *did it* unintentionally.
27'And [a]if a person sins unintentionally,
then he shall bring a female goat in its first
year as a sin offering. 28[a]So the priest shall
make atonement for the person who sins
unintentionally, when he sins unintentionally before the LORD, to make atonement for
him; and it shall be forgiven him. 29[a]You shall
have one law for him who sins unintentionally, *for* him who is native-born among the
children of Israel and for the stranger who
dwells among them.

Law Concerning Presumptuous Sin

30[a]'But the person who does *anything* presumptuously, *whether he is* native-born or
a stranger, that one brings reproach on the
LORD, and he shall be cut off from among
his people. 31 Because he has [a]despised the
word of the LORD, and has broken His commandment, that person shall be completely
cut off; his guilt *shall be* upon him.' "

Penalty for Violating the Sabbath

32 Now while the children of Israel were in
the wilderness, [a]they found a man gathering
sticks on the Sabbath day. 33 And those who
found him gathering sticks brought him to
Moses and Aaron, and to all the congregation. 34 They put him [a]under guard, because
it had not been explained what should be
done to him.
35 Then the LORD said to Moses, [a]"The man
must surely be put to death; all the congregation shall [b]stone him with stones outside
the camp." 36 So, as the LORD commanded
Moses, all the congregation brought him outside the camp and stoned him with stones,
and he died.

Tassels on Garments

37 Again the LORD spoke to Moses, saying,
38"Speak to the children of Israel: Tell [a]them
to make tassels on the corners of their garments throughout their generations, and to
put a blue thread in the tassels of the corners.
39 And you shall have the tassel, that you
may look upon it and [a]remember all the
commandments of the LORD and do them,
and that you [b]*may* not [c]follow the harlotry
to which your own heart and your own eyes
are inclined, 40 and that you may remember
and do all My commandments, and be [a]holy
for your God. 41 I *am* the LORD your God, who
brought you out of the land of Egypt, to be
your God: I *am* the LORD your God."

15:11 [a] Num. 28 **15:15** [a] Num. 9:14; 15:29 **15:16** [1] Compare Exodus 12:49 **15:18** [a] Deut. 26:1 **15:19** [a] Josh. 5:11, 12 **15:20** [a] Lev. 23:10, 14, 17 [b] Lev. 2:14; 23:10, 16 **15:22** [a] Lev. 4:2 **15:24** [a] Lev. 4:13 [b] Num. 15:8–10 [c] Lev. 4:23 **15:25** [a] [Heb. 2:17] **15:27** [a] Lev. 4:27–31 **15:28** [a] Lev. 4:35 **15:29** [a] Num. 15:15 **15:30** [a] Deut. 1:43; 17:12 **15:31** [a] Prov. 13:13 **15:32** [a] Ex. 31:14, 15; 35:2, 3 **15:34** [a] Lev. 24:12 **15:35** [a] Ex. 31:14, 15 [b] Lev. 24:14 **15:38** [a] Matt. 23:5 **15:39** [a] Ps. 103:18 [b] Deut. 29:19 [c] James 4:4 **15:40** [a] [Lev. 11:44, 45]

Rebellion Against Moses and Aaron

16 Now [a]Korah the son of Izhar, the son
of Kohath, the son of Levi, with [b]Da-
than and Abiram the sons of Eliab, and On
the son of Peleth, sons of Reuben, took *men;*
2 and they rose up before Moses with some of
the children of Israel, two hundred and fifty
leaders of the congregation, [a]representatives
of the congregation, men of renown. 3 [a]They
gathered together against Moses and Aaron,
and said to them, "*You take* too much upon
yourselves, for [b]all the congregation *is* holy,
every one of them, [c]and the LORD *is* among
them. Why then do you exalt yourselves
above the assembly of the LORD?"

> PEACE NOTE
>
> In rebellion, Korah, Dathan, and Abiram offended God's holiness and inherited the dire consequences. Be watchful of friendships that rob you of God's peace.
>
> NUMBERS 16:3

4 So when Moses heard *it,* he [a]fell on his
face; 5 and he spoke to Korah and all his company, saying, "Tomorrow morning the LORD
will show who *is* [a]His and *who is* [b]holy, and
will cause *him* to come near to Him. That one
whom He chooses He will cause to [c]come
near to Him. 6 Do this: Take censers, Korah
and all your company; 7 put fire in them and
put incense in them before the LORD tomorrow, and it shall be *that* the man whom the
LORD chooses *is* the holy one. *You take* too
much upon yourselves, you sons of Levi!"
8 Then Moses said to Korah, "Hear now, you
sons of Levi: 9 *Is it* [a]a small thing to you that
the God of Israel has [b]separated you from
the congregation of Israel, to bring you near
to Himself, to do the work of the tabernacle
of the LORD, and to stand before the congregation to serve them; 10 and that He has
brought you near *to Himself,* you and all your
brethren, the sons of Levi, with you? And are
you seeking the priesthood also? 11 Therefore
you and all your company *are* gathered together against the LORD. [a]And what *is* Aaron
that you complain against him?"
12 And Moses sent to call Dathan and Abiram the sons of Eliab, but they said, "We will
not come up! 13 *Is it* a small thing that you
have brought us up out of [a]a land flowing
with milk and honey, to kill us in the wilderness, that you should [b]keep acting like
a prince over us? 14 Moreover [a]you have not
brought us into [b]a land flowing with milk and
honey, nor given us inheritance of fields and
vineyards. Will you put out the eyes of these
men? We will not come up!"
15 Then Moses was very angry, and said to
the LORD, [a]"Do not respect their offering. [b]I
have not taken one donkey from them, nor
have I hurt one of them."
16 And Moses said to Korah, "Tomorrow,
you and all your company be present [a]before
the LORD—you and they, as well as Aaron.
17 Let each take his censer and put incense
in it, and each of you bring his censer before
the LORD, two hundred and fifty censers;
both you and Aaron, each *with* his censer."
18 So every man took his censer, put fire in
it, laid incense on it, and stood at the door
of the tabernacle of meeting with Moses
and Aaron. 19 And Korah gathered all the
congregation against them at the door of
the tabernacle of meeting. Then [a]the glory of
the LORD appeared to all the congregation.
20 And the LORD spoke to Moses and Aaron,
saying, 21 [a]"Separate yourselves from among
this congregation, that I may [b]consume them
in a moment."
22 Then they [a]fell on their faces, and said,
"O God, [b]the God of the spirits of all flesh,
shall one man sin, and You be angry with all
the [c]congregation?"
23 So the LORD spoke to Moses, saying,
24 "Speak to the congregation, saying, 'Get away
from the tents of Korah, Dathan, and Abiram.'"
25 Then Moses rose and went to Dathan and
Abiram, and the elders of Israel followed him.
26 And he spoke to the congregation, saying,
[a]"Depart now from the tents of these wicked
men! Touch nothing of theirs, lest you be
consumed in all their sins." 27 So they got away
from around the tents of Korah, Dathan, and
Abiram; and Dathan and Abiram came out
and stood at the door of their tents, with their
wives, their sons, and their little [a]children.

16:1 [a] Ex. 6:21 [b] Num. 26:9 **16:2** [a] Num. 1:16; 26:9 **16:3** [a] Ps. 106:16 [b] Ex. 19:6 [c] Ex. 29:45 **16:4** [a] Num. 14:5; 20:6
16:5 [a] [2 Tim. 2:19] [b] Lev. 21:6–8, 12 [c] Ezek. 40:46; 44:15, 16 **16:9** [a] Is. 7:13 [b] Deut. 10:8 **16:11** [a] Ex. 16:7, 8
16:13 [a] Num. 11:4–6 [b] Ex. 2:14 **16:14** [a] Num. 14:1–4 [b] Ex. 3:8 **16:15** [a] Gen. 4:4, 5 [b] 1 Sam. 12:3 **16:16** [a] 1 Sam. 12:3, 7
16:19 [a] Num. 14:10 **16:21** [a] Gen. 19:17 [b] Ex. 32:10; 33:5 **16:22** [a] Num. 14:5 [b] Num. 27:16 [c] Gen. 18:23–32; 20:4
16:26 [a] Gen. 19:12, 14, 15, 17 **16:27** [a] Num. 26:11

28 And Moses said: [a]"By this you shall know
that the LORD has sent me to do all these
works, for *I have* not *done them* [b]of my own
will. 29 If these men die naturally like all men,
or if they are [a]visited by the common fate
of all men, *then* the LORD has not sent me.
30 But if the LORD creates [a]a new thing, and
the earth opens its mouth and swallows them
up with all that belongs to them, and they [b]go
down alive into the pit, then you will understand that these men have rejected the LORD."
31 [a]Now it came to pass, as he finished
speaking all these words, that the ground
split apart under them, 32 and the earth
opened its mouth and swallowed them up,
with their households and [a]all the men with
Korah, with all *their* goods. 33 So they and all
those with them went down alive into the pit;
the earth closed over them, and they perished
from among the assembly. 34 Then all Israel
who *were* around them fled at their cry, for
they said, "Lest the earth swallow us up *also!*"
35 And [a]a fire came out from the LORD and
consumed the two hundred and fifty men
who were offering incense.
36 Then the LORD spoke to Moses, saying:
37 "Tell Eleazar, the son of Aaron the priest, to
pick up the censers out of the blaze, for [a]they
are holy, and scatter the fire some distance
away. 38 The censers of [a]these men who sinned
against their own souls, let them be made
into hammered plates as a covering for the
altar. Because they presented them before the
LORD, therefore they are holy; [b]and they shall
be a sign to the children of Israel." 39 So Eleazar the priest took the bronze censers, which
those who were burned up had presented, and
they were hammered out as a covering on
the altar, 40 *to be* a memorial to the children
of Israel [a]that no outsider, who *is* not a descendant of Aaron, should come near to offer
incense before the LORD, that he might not
become like Korah and his companions, just
as the LORD had said to him through Moses.

Complaints of the People

41 On the next day [a]all the congregation of
the children of Israel complained against
Moses and Aaron, saying, "You have killed
the people of the LORD." 42 Now it happened,
when the congregation had gathered against
Moses and Aaron, that they turned toward
the tabernacle of meeting; and suddenly [a]the
cloud covered it, and the glory of the LORD
appeared. 43 Then Moses and Aaron came
before the tabernacle of meeting.
44 And the LORD spoke to Moses, saying,
45 "Get away from among this congregation,
that I may consume them in a moment."
And they fell on their faces.
46 So Moses said to Aaron, "Take a censer
and put fire in it from the altar, put incense
on it, and take it quickly to the congregation
and make atonement for them; [a]for wrath
has gone out from the LORD. The plague
has begun." 47 Then Aaron took *it* as Moses
commanded, and ran into the midst of the
assembly; and already the plague had begun
among the people. So he put in the incense
and made atonement for the people. 48 And
he stood between the dead and the living; so
[a]the plague was stopped. 49 Now those who
died in the plague were fourteen thousand
seven hundred, besides those who died in
the Korah incident. 50 So Aaron returned to
Moses at the door of the tabernacle of meeting, for the plague had stopped.

The Budding of Aaron's Rod

17 And the LORD spoke to Moses, saying:
2 "Speak to the children of Israel, and
get from them a rod from each father's house,
all their leaders according to their fathers'
houses—twelve rods. Write each man's name
on his rod. 3 And you shall write Aaron's name
on the rod of Levi. For there shall be one rod
for the head of *each* father's house. 4 Then you
shall place them in the tabernacle of meeting
before [a]the Testimony, [b]where I meet with
you. 5 And it shall be *that* the rod of the man
[a]whom I choose will blossom; thus I will rid
Myself of the complaints of the children of
Israel, [b]which they make against you."
6 So Moses spoke to the children of Israel, and each of their leaders gave him a rod
apiece, for each leader according to their
fathers' houses, twelve rods; and the rod of
Aaron *was* among their rods. 7 And Moses
placed the rods before the LORD in [a]the tabernacle of witness.
8 Now it came to pass on the next day that
Moses went into the tabernacle of witness,
and behold, the [a]rod of Aaron, of the house
of Levi, had sprouted and put forth buds, had
produced blossoms and yielded ripe almonds.
9 Then Moses brought out all the rods from
before the LORD to all the children of Israel;
and they looked, and each man took his rod.
10 And the LORD said to Moses, "Bring [a]Aar-
on's rod back before the Testimony, to be kept
[b]as a sign against the rebels, [c]that you may
put their complaints away from Me, lest they

16:28 [a] John 5:36 [b] John 5:30 **16:29** [a] Ex. 20:5 **16:30** [a] Job 31:3 [b] [Ps. 55:15] **16:31** [a] Num. 26:10 **16:32** [a] Num. 26:11 **16:35** [a] Num. 11:1–3; 26:10 **16:37** [a] Lev. 27:28 **16:38** [a] Hab. 2:10 [b] Num. 17:10 **16:40** [a] Num. 3:10 **16:41** [a] Num. 14:2 **16:42** [a] Ex. 40:34 **16:46** [a] Num. 18:5 **16:48** [a] Num. 25:8 **17:4** [a] Ex. 25:16 [b] Ex. 25:22; 29:42, 43; 30:36 **17:5** [a] Num. 16:5 [b] Num. 16:11 **17:7** [a] Ex. 38:21 **17:8** [a] [Ezek. 17:24] **17:10** [a] Heb. 9:4 [b] Deut. 9:7, 24 [c] Num. 17:5

die." 11 Thus did Moses; just as the LORD had commanded him, so he did.

12 So the children of Israel spoke to Moses, saying, "Surely we die, we perish, we all perish! 13 [a]Whoever even comes near the tabernacle of the LORD must die. Shall we all utterly die?"

Duties of Priests and Levites

18 Then the LORD said to Aaron: [a]"You and your sons and your father's house with you shall [b]bear the iniquity *related to* the sanctuary, and you and your sons with you shall bear the iniquity *associated with* your priesthood. 2 Also bring with you your brethren of the [a]tribe of Levi, the tribe of your father, that they may be [b]joined with you and serve you while you and your sons *are* with you before the tabernacle of witness. 3 They shall attend to your needs and [a]all the needs of the tabernacle; [b]but they shall not come near the articles of the sanctuary and the altar, [c]lest they die—they and you also. 4 They shall be joined with you and attend to the needs of the tabernacle of meeting, for all the work of the tabernacle; [a]but an outsider shall not come near you. 5 And you shall attend to [a]the duties of the sanctuary and the duties of the altar, [b]that there *may* be no more wrath on the children of Israel. 6 Behold, I Myself have [a]taken your brethren the Levites from among the children of Israel; [b]*they are* a gift to you, given by the LORD, to do the work of the tabernacle of meeting. 7 Therefore [a]you and your sons with you shall attend to your priesthood for everything at the altar and [b]behind the veil; and you shall serve. I give your priesthood *to you* as a [c]gift for service, but the outsider who comes near shall be put to death."

Offerings for Support of the Priests

8 And the LORD spoke to Aaron: "Here, [a]I Myself have also given you charge of My heave offerings, all the holy gifts of the children of Israel; I have given them [b]as a portion to you and your sons, as an ordinance forever. 9 This shall be yours of the most holy things *reserved* from the fire: every offering of theirs, every [a]grain offering and every [b]sin offering and every [c]trespass offering which they render to Me, *shall be* most holy for you and your sons. 10 [a]In a most holy *place* you shall eat it; every male shall eat it. It shall be holy to you.

11 "This also *is* yours: [a]the heave offering of their gift, with all the wave offerings of the children of Israel; I have given them to you, and your sons and daughters with you, as an ordinance forever. [b]Everyone who is clean in your house may eat it.

12 [a]"All the best of the oil, all the best of the new wine and the grain, [b]their firstfruits which they offer to the LORD, I have given them to you. 13 Whatever first ripe fruit is in their land, [a]which they bring to the LORD, shall be yours. Everyone who is clean in your house may eat it.

14 [a]"Every devoted thing in Israel shall be yours.

15 "Everything that first opens [a]the womb of all flesh, which they bring to the LORD, whether man or beast, shall be yours; nevertheless [b]the firstborn of man you shall surely redeem, and the firstborn of unclean animals you shall redeem. 16 And those redeemed of the devoted things you shall redeem when one month old, [a]according to your valuation, for five shekels of silver, according to the shekel of the sanctuary, which *is* [b]twenty gerahs. 17 [a]But the firstborn of a cow, the firstborn of a sheep, or the firstborn of a goat you shall not redeem; they *are* holy. [b]You shall sprinkle their blood on the altar, and burn their fat *as* an offering made by fire for a sweet aroma to the LORD. 18 And their flesh shall be yours, just as the [a]wave breast and the right thigh are yours.

19 "All the heave offerings of the holy things, which the children of Israel offer to the LORD, I have given to you and your sons and daughters with you as an ordinance forever; [a]it *is* a covenant of salt forever before the LORD with you and your descendants with you."

20 Then the LORD said to Aaron: "You shall have [a]no inheritance in their land, nor shall you have any portion among them; [b]I *am* your portion and your inheritance among the children of Israel.

Tithes for Support of the Levites

21 "Behold, [a]I have given the children of Levi all the tithes in Israel as an inheritance in return for the work which they perform, [b]the work of the tabernacle of meeting. 22 [a]Hereafter the children of Israel shall not come near the tabernacle of meeting, [b]lest they bear sin and die. 23 But the Levites shall

17:13 [a] Num. 1:51, 53; 18:4, 7 **18:1** [a] Num. 17:13 [b] Ex. 28:38 **18:2** [a] Num. 1:47 [b] Num. 3:5–10 **18:3** [a] Num. 3:25, 31, 36 [b] Num. 16:40 [c] Num. 4:15 **18:4** [a] Num. 3:10 **18:5** [a] Lev. 24:3 [b] Num. 8:19; 16:46 **18:6** [a] Num. 3:12, 45 [b] Num. 3:9 **18:7** [a] Num. 3:10; 18:5 [b] Heb. 9:3, 6 [c] 1 Pet. 5:2, 3 **18:8** [a] Lev. 6:16, 18; 7:28–34 [b] Ex. 29:29; 40:13, 15 **18:9** [a] Lev. 2:2, 3; 10:12, 13 [b] Lev. 6:25, 26 [c] Lev. 7:7 **18:10** [a] Lev. 6:16, 26 **18:11** [a] Deut. 18:3–5 [b] Lev. 22:1–16 **18:12** [a] Ex. 23:19 [b] Ex. 22:29 **18:13** [a] Ex. 22:29; 23:19; 34:26 **18:14** [a] Lev. 27:1–33 **18:15** [a] Ex. 13:2 [b] Ex. 13:12–15 **18:16** [a] Lev. 27:6 [b] Ex. 30:13 **18:17** [a] Deut. 15:19 [b] Lev. 3:2, 5 **18:18** [a] Ex. 29:26–28 **18:19** [a] 2 Chr. 13:5 **18:20** [a] Josh. 13:14, 33 [b] Ezek. 44:28 **18:21** [a] Lev. 27:30–33 [b] Num. 3:7, 8 **18:22** [a] Num. 1:51 [b] Lev. 22:9

perform the work of the tabernacle of meeting, and they shall bear their iniquity; *it shall*
be a statute forever, throughout your generations, that among the children of Israel they
shall have no inheritance. 24 For the tithes of
the children of Israel, which they offer up *as*
a heave offering to the LORD, I have given to
the Levites as an inheritance; therefore I have
said to them, 'Among the children of Israel
they shall have no inheritance.' "

The Tithe of the Levites

25 Then the LORD spoke to Moses, saying,
26 "Speak thus to the Levites, and say to them:
'When you take from the children of Israel
the tithes which I have given you from them
as your inheritance, then you shall offer up
a heave offering of it to the LORD, [a]a tenth of
the tithe. 27 And your heave offering shall be
reckoned to you as though *it were* the grain of
the [a]threshing floor and as the fullness of the
winepress. 28 Thus you shall also offer a heave
offering to the LORD from all your tithes which
you receive from the children of Israel, and
you shall give the LORD's heave offering from it
to Aaron the priest. 29 Of all your gifts you shall
offer up every heave offering due to the LORD,
from all the best of them, the consecrated part
of them.' 30 Therefore you shall say to them:
'When you have lifted up the best of it, then
the rest shall be accounted to the Levites as
the produce of the threshing floor and as the
produce of the winepress. 31 You may eat it in
any place, you and your households, for it *is*
[a]your reward for your work in the tabernacle
of meeting. 32 And you shall [a]bear no sin because of it, when you have lifted up the best
of it. But you shall not [b]profane the holy gifts
of the children of Israel, lest you die.' "

Laws of Purification

19 Now the LORD spoke to Moses and
Aaron, saying, 2 "This *is* the ordinance
of the law which the LORD has commanded,
saying: 'Speak to the children of Israel, that
they bring you a red heifer without blemish,
in which there *is* no [a]defect [b]*and* on which a
yoke has never come. 3 You shall give it to Eleazar the priest, that he may take it [a]outside the
camp, and it shall be slaughtered before him;
4 and Eleazar the priest shall take some of its
blood with his finger, and [a]sprinkle some of
its blood seven times directly in front of the
tabernacle of meeting. 5 Then the heifer shall
be burned in his sight: [a]its hide, its flesh, its
blood, and its offal shall be burned. 6 And the
priest shall take [a]cedar wood and [b]hyssop and
scarlet, and cast *them* into the midst of the
fire burning the heifer. 7 [a]Then the priest shall
wash his clothes, he shall bathe in water, and
afterward he shall come into the camp; the
priest shall be unclean until evening. 8 And
the one who burns it shall wash his clothes
in water, bathe in water, and shall be unclean
until evening. 9 Then a man *who is* clean shall
gather up [a]the ashes of the heifer, and store
them outside the camp in a clean place; and
they shall be kept for the congregation of the
children of Israel [b]for the water of purification;[1] it *is* for purifying from sin. 10 And the one
who gathers the ashes of the heifer shall wash
his clothes, and be unclean until evening. It
shall be a statute forever to the children of Israel and to the stranger who dwells among them.

11 [a]'He who touches the dead body of anyone
shall be unclean seven days. 12 [a]He shall purify
himself with the water on the third day and
on the seventh day; *then* he will be clean. But
if he does not purify himself on the third day
and on the seventh day, he will not be clean.
13 Whoever touches the body of anyone who has
died, and [a]does not purify himself, [b]defiles the
tabernacle of the LORD. That person shall be cut
off from Israel. He shall be unclean, because
[c]the water of purification was not sprinkled on
him; [d]his uncleanness *is* still on him.

14 'This *is* the law when a man dies in a tent:
All who come into the tent and all who *are* in
the tent shall be unclean seven days; 15 and every [a]open vessel, which has no cover fastened
on it, *is* unclean. 16 [a]Whoever in the open field
touches one who is slain by a sword or who
has died, or a bone of a man, or a grave, shall
be unclean seven days.

17 'And for an unclean *person* they shall take
some of the [a]ashes of the heifer burnt for purification from sin, and running water shall
be put on them in a vessel. 18 A clean person
shall take [a]hyssop and dip *it* in the water,
sprinkle *it* on the tent, on all the vessels, on
the persons who were there, or on the one
who touched a bone, the slain, the dead, or
a grave. 19 The clean *person* shall sprinkle the
unclean on the third day and on the seventh
day; [a]and on the seventh day he shall purify
himself, wash his clothes, and bathe in water;
and at evening he shall be clean.

20 'But the man who is unclean and does
not purify himself, that person shall be cut
off from among the assembly, because he

18:26 [a] Neh. 10:38 **18:27** [a] Num. 15:20 **18:31** [a] [Luke 10:7] **18:32** [a] Lev. 19:8; 22:16 [b] Lev. 22:2, 15 **19:2** [a] Lev. 22:20–25 [b] Deut. 21:3 **19:3** [a] Lev. 4:12, 21 **19:4** [a] Lev. 4:6 **19:5** [a] Ex. 29:14 **19:6** [a] Lev. 14:4, 6, 49 [b] Ex. 12:22 **19:7** [a] Lev. 11:25; 15:5; 16:26, 28 **19:9** [a] [Heb. 9:13, 14] [b] Num. 19:13, 20, 21 [1] Literally *impurity* **19:11** [a] Lev. 21:1, 11 **19:12** [a] Num. 19:19; 31:19 **19:13** [a] Lev. 22:3–7 [b] Lev. 15:31 [c] Num. 8:7; 19:9 [d] Lev. 7:20; 22:3 **19:15** [a] Num. 31:20 **19:16** [a] Num. 19:11; 31:19 **19:17** [a] Num. 19:9 **19:18** [a] Ps. 51:7 **19:19** [a] Lev. 14:9

has [a]defiled the sanctuary of the LORD. The
water of purification has not been sprinkled
on him; he *is* unclean. 21 It shall be a perpetual
statute for them. He who sprinkles the water
of purification shall wash his clothes; and he
who touches the water of purification shall
be unclean until evening. 22 [a]Whatever the
unclean *person* touches shall be unclean; and
[b]the person who touches *it* shall be unclean
until evening.' "

Moses' Error at Kadesh

20 Then[a] the children of Israel, the whole
congregation, came into the Wilderness of Zin in the first month, and the people
stayed in [b]Kadesh; and [c]Miriam died there
and was buried there.
2 [a]Now there was no water for the congregation; [b]so they gathered together against
Moses and Aaron. 3 And the people [a]contend-
ed with Moses and spoke, saying: "If only we
had died [b]when our brethren died before the
LORD! 4 [a]Why have you brought up the assembly of the LORD into this wilderness, that we
and our animals should die here? 5 And why
have you made us come up out of Egypt, to
bring us to this evil place? It *is* not a place of
grain or figs or vines or pomegranates; nor
is there any water to drink." 6 So Moses and
Aaron went from the presence of the assembly to the door of the tabernacle of meeting,
and [a]they fell on their faces. And [b]the glory
of the LORD appeared to them.
7 Then the LORD spoke to Moses, saying,
8 [a]"Take the rod; you and your brother Aaron
gather the congregation together. Speak to
the rock before their eyes, and it will yield
its water; thus [b]you shall bring water for
them out of the rock, and give drink to the
congregation and their animals." 9 So Moses
took the rod [a]from before the LORD as He
commanded him.
10 And Moses and Aaron gathered the assembly together before the rock; and he said
to them, [a]"Hear now, you rebels! Must we bring
water for you out of this rock?" 11 Then Moses
lifted his hand and struck the rock twice with
his rod; [a]and water came out abundantly, and
the congregation and their animals drank.
12 Then the LORD spoke to Moses and
Aaron, "Because [a]you did not believe Me, to
[b]hallow Me in the eyes of the children of Israel, therefore you shall not bring this assembly
into the land which I have given them."

> PEACE NOTE
>
> Moses' striking the rock robbed him of entering the Promised Land. Seemingly small acts of disobedience can have devastating consequences in our lives.
>
> NUMBERS 20:11

13 [a]This *was* the water of Meribah,[1] because
the children of Israel contended with the
LORD, and He was hallowed among them.

Passage Through Edom Refused

14 [a]Now Moses sent messengers from Kadesh to the king of [b]Edom. [c]"Thus says your
brother Israel: 'You know all the hardship
that has befallen us, 15 [a]how our fathers went
down to Egypt, [b]and we dwelt in Egypt a
long time, [c]and the Egyptians afflicted us
and our fathers. 16 [a]When we cried out to
the LORD, He heard our voice and [b]sent the
Angel and brought us up out of Egypt; now
here we are in Kadesh, a city on the edge of
your border. 17 Please [a]let us pass through
your country. We will not pass through fields
or vineyards, nor will we drink water from
wells; we will go along the King's Highway;
we will not turn aside to the right hand or
to the left until we have passed through
your territory.' "
18 Then [a]Edom said to him, "You shall not
pass through my *land,* lest I come out against
you with the sword."
19 So the children of Israel said to him,
"We will go by the Highway, and if I or my
livestock drink any of your water, [a]then I will
pay for it; let me only pass through on foot,
nothing *more.*"
20 Then he said, [a]"You shall not pass through."
So Edom came out against them with many
men and with a strong hand. 21 Thus Edom
[a]refused to give Israel passage through his
territory; so Israel [b]turned away from him.

19:20 [a] Num. 19:13 **19:22** [a] Hag. 2:11–13 [b] Lev. 15:5 **20:1** [a] Num. 13:21; 33:36 [b] Num. 13:26 [c] Ex. 15:20 **20:2** [a] Ex. 17:1 [b] Num. 16:19, 42 **20:3** [a] Ex. 17:2 [b] Num. 11:1, 33; 14:37; 16:31–35, 49 **20:4** [a] Ex. 17:3 **20:6** [a] Num. 14:5; 16:4, 22, 45 [b] Num. 14:10 **20:8** [a] Ex. 4:17, 20; 17:5, 6 [b] Neh. 9:15 **20:9** [a] Num. 17:10 **20:10** [a] Ps. 106:33 **20:11** [a] [1 Cor. 10:4] **20:12** [a] Deut. 1:37; 3:26, 27; 34:5 [b] Lev. 10:3 **20:13** [a] Deut. 33:8 [1] Literally *Contention* **20:14** [a] Judg. 11:16, 17 [b] Gen. 36:31–39 [c] Deut. 2:4 **20:15** [a] Gen. 46:6 [b] Ex. 12:40 [c] Deut. 26:6 **20:16** [a] Ex. 2:23; 3:7 [b] Ex. 3:2; 14:19 **20:17** [a] Num. 21:22 **20:18** [a] Num. 24:18 **20:19** [a] Deut. 2:6, 28 **20:20** [a] Judg. 11:17 **20:21** [a] Deut. 2:27, 30 [b] Judg. 11:18

Death of Aaron

22 Now the children of Israel, the whole
congregation, journeyed from [a]Kadesh [b]and
came to Mount Hor. 23 And the LORD spoke to
Moses and Aaron in Mount Hor by the border
of the land of Edom, saying: 24 "Aaron shall be
[a]gathered to his people, for he shall not enter
the land which I have given to the children of
Israel, because you rebelled against My word
at the water of Meribah. 25 [a]Take Aaron and
Eleazar his son, and bring them up to Mount
Hor; 26 and strip Aaron of his garments and
put them on Eleazar his son; for Aaron shall
be gathered *to his people* and die there." 27 So
Moses did just as the LORD commanded, and
they went up to Mount Hor in the sight of all
the congregation. 28 [a]Moses stripped Aaron
of his garments and put them on Eleazar his
son; and [b]Aaron died there on the top of the
mountain. Then Moses and Eleazar came
down from the mountain. 29 Now when all
the congregation saw that Aaron was dead,
all the house of Israel mourned for Aaron
[a]thirty days.

Canaanites Defeated at Hormah

21 The [a]king of Arad, the Canaanite, who
dwelt in the South, heard that Israel
was coming on the road to Atharim. Then
he fought against Israel and took *some* of
them prisoners. 2 [a]So Israel made a vow to
the LORD, and said, "If You will indeed deliver
this people into my hand, then [b]I will utterly
destroy their cities." 3 And the LORD listened
to the voice of Israel and delivered up the
Canaanites, and they utterly destroyed them
and their cities. So the name of that place
was called Hormah.[1]

The Bronze Serpent

4 Then they journeyed from Mount Hor
by the Way of the Red Sea, to [a]go around the
land of Edom; and the soul of the people
became very discouraged on the way. 5 And
the people [a]spoke against God and against
Moses: "Why have you brought us up out of
Egypt to die in the wilderness? For *there is* no
food and no water, and our soul loathes this
worthless bread." 6 So [a]the LORD sent [b]fiery
serpents among the people, and they bit the
people; and many of the people of Israel died.

7 [a]Therefore the people came to Moses, and
said, "We have [b]sinned, for we have spoken
against the LORD and against you; [c]pray to
the LORD that He take away the serpents from
us." So Moses prayed for the people.

8 Then the LORD said to Moses, [a]"Make
a [b]fiery *serpent,* and set it on a pole; and it
shall be that everyone who is bitten, when
he looks at it, shall live." 9 So [a]Moses made a
bronze serpent, and put it on a pole; and so
it was, if a serpent had bitten anyone, when
he looked at the bronze serpent, he lived.

From Mount Hor to Moab

10 Now the children of Israel moved on
and [a]camped in Oboth. 11 And they journeyed
from Oboth and camped at Ije Abarim, in
the wilderness which *is* east of Moab, toward
the sunrise. 12 [a]From there they moved and
camped in the Valley of Zered. 13 From there
they moved and camped on the other side
of the Arnon, which *is* in the wilderness that
extends from the border of the Amorites; for
[a]the Arnon *is* the border of Moab, between
Moab and the Amorites. 14 Therefore it is said
in the Book of the Wars of the LORD:

"Waheb in Suphah,[1]
The brooks of the Arnon,
15 And the slope of the brooks
That reaches to the dwelling of [a]Ar,
And lies on the border of Moab."

16 From there *they went* [a]to Beer, which
is the well where the LORD said to Moses,
"Gather the people together, and I will give
them water." 17 [a]Then Israel sang this song:

"Spring up, O well!
All of you sing to it—
18 The well the leaders sank,
Dug by the nation's nobles,
By the [a]lawgiver, with their staves."

And from the wilderness *they went* to Mattanah, 19 from Mattanah to Nahaliel, from
Nahaliel to Bamoth, 20 and from Bamoth, *in*
the valley that *is* in the country of Moab, to
the top of Pisgah which looks [a]down on the
wasteland.[1]

King Sihon Defeated

21 Then [a]Israel sent messengers to Sihon
king of the Amorites, saying, 22 [a]"Let me pass
through your land. We will not turn aside
into fields or vineyards; we will not drink
water from wells. We will go by the King's

20:22 [a] Num. 33:37 [b] Num. 21:4 **20:24** [a] Gen. 25:8 **20:25** [a] Num. 33:38 **20:28** [a] Ex. 29:29, 30 [b] Num. 33:38 **20:29** [a] Deut. 34:8 **21:1** [a] Judg. 1:16 **21:2** [a] Gen. 28:20 [b] Deut. 2:34 **21:3** [1] Literally *Utter Destruction* **21:4** [a] Judg. 11:18 **21:5** [a] Num. 20:4, 5 **21:6** [a] 1 Cor. 10:9 [b] Deut. 8:15 **21:7** [a] Num. 11:2 [b] Lev. 26:40 [c] Ex. 8:8 **21:8** [a] [John 3:14, 15] [b] Is. 14:29; 30:6 **21:9** [a] John 3:14, 15 **21:10** [a] Num. 33:43, 44 **21:12** [a] Deut. 2:13 **21:13** [a] Num. 22:36 **21:14** [1] Ancient unknown places; Vulgate reads *What He did in the Red Sea.* **21:15** [a] Deut. 2:9, 18, 29 **21:16** [a] Judg. 9:21 **21:17** [a] Ex. 15:1 **21:18** [a] Is. 33:22 **21:20** [a] Num. 23:28 [1] Hebrew *Jeshimon* **21:21** [a] Deut. 2:26–37 **21:22** [a] Num. 20:16, 17

Highway until we have passed through your
territory." 23[a]But Sihon would not allow Israel to pass through his territory. So Sihon
gathered all his people together and went
out against Israel in the wilderness, [b]and
he came to Jahaz and fought against Israel.
24Then [a]Israel defeated him with the edge
of the sword, and took possession of his
land from the Arnon to the Jabbok, as far as
the people of Ammon; for the border of the
people of Ammon *was* fortified. 25So Israel
took all these cities, and Israel [a]dwelt in all
the cities of the Amorites, in Heshbon and
in all its villages. 26For Heshbon *was* the
city of Sihon king of the Amorites, who had
fought against the former king of Moab, and
had taken all his land from his hand as far
as the Arnon. 27Therefore those who speak
in proverbs say:

"Come to Heshbon, let it be built;
Let the city of Sihon be repaired.

28 "For [a]fire went out from Heshbon,
A flame from the city of Sihon;
It consumed [b]Ar of Moab,
The lords of the [c]heights of the Arnon.
29 Woe to you, [a]Moab!
You have perished, O people of
[b]Chemosh!
He has given his [c]sons as fugitives,
And his [d]daughters into captivity,
To Sihon king of the Amorites.

30 "But we have shot at them;
Heshbon has perished [a]as far as Dibon.
Then we laid waste as far as Nophah,
Which *reaches* to [b]Medeba."

31Thus Israel dwelt in the land of the Amorites. 32Then Moses sent to spy out [a]Jazer;
and they took its villages and drove out the
Amorites who *were* there.

King Og Defeated

33[a]And they turned and went up by the way
to [b]Bashan. So Og king of Bashan went out
against them, he and all his people, to battle
[c]at Edrei. 34Then the LORD said to Moses, [a]"Do
not fear him, for I have delivered him into
your hand, with all his people and his land;
and [b]you shall do to him as you did to Sihon
king of the Amorites, who dwelt at Heshbon."
35[a]So they defeated him, his sons, and all his
people, until there was no survivor left him;
and they took possession of his land.

Balak Sends for Balaam

22 Then [a]the children of Israel moved,
and camped in the plains of Moab on
the side of the Jordan *across from* Jericho.
2Now [a]Balak the son of Zippor saw all that
Israel had done to the Amorites. 3And [a]Moab
was exceedingly afraid of the people because
they *were* many, and Moab was sick with
dread because of the children of Israel. 4So
Moab said to [a]the elders of Midian, "Now this
company will lick up everything around us,
as an ox licks up the grass of the field." And
Balak the son of Zippor *was* king of the Moabites at that time. 5Then [a]he sent messengers
to Balaam the son of Beor at [b]Pethor, which *is*
near the River[1] in the land of the sons of his
people,[2] to call him, saying: "Look, a people
has come from Egypt. See, they cover the
face of the earth, and are settling next to me!
6[a]Therefore please come at once, [b]curse this
people for me, for they *are* too mighty for me.
Perhaps I shall be able to defeat them and
drive them out of the land, for I know that
he whom you bless *is* blessed, and he whom
you curse is cursed."
7So the elders of Moab and the elders of
Midian departed with [a]the diviner's fee in
their hand, and they came to Balaam and
spoke to him the words of Balak. 8And he said
to them, [a]"Lodge here tonight, and I will bring
back word to you, as the LORD speaks to me."
So the princes of Moab stayed with Balaam.

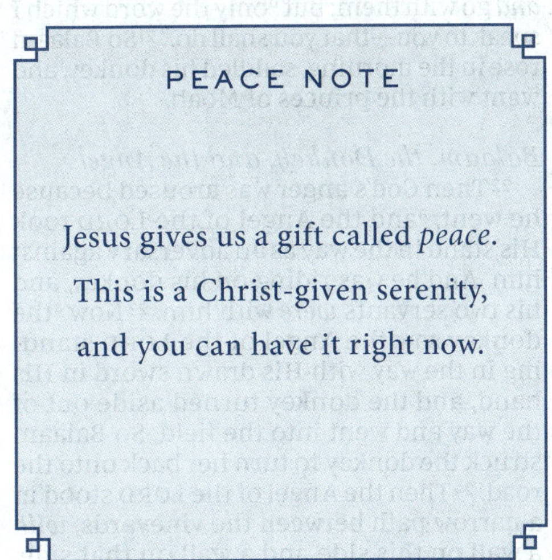

21:23 [a] Deut. 29:7 [b] Judg. 11:20 21:24 [a] Amos 2:9 21:25 [a] Amos 2:10 21:28 [a] Jer. 48:45, 46 [b] Is. 15:1 [c] Num. 22:41; 33:52 21:29 [a] Jer. 48:46 [b] Judg. 11:24 [c] Is. 15:2, 5 [d] Is. 16:2 21:30 [a] Num. 32:3, 34 [b] Is. 15:2 21:32 [a] Jer. 48:32 21:33 [a] Deut. 29:7 [b] Deut. 3:1 [c] Josh. 13:12 21:34 [a] Deut. 3:2 [b] Num. 21:24 21:35 [a] Deut. 3:3, 4; 29:7 22:1 [a] Num. 33:48, 49 22:2 [a] Judg. 11:25 22:3 [a] Ex. 15:15 22:4 [a] Num. 25:15–18; 31:1–3 22:5 [a] 2 Pet. 2:15 [b] Deut. 23:4 [1] That is, the Euphrates [2] Or *the people of Amau* 22:6 [a] Num. 22:17; 23:7, 8 [b] Num. 22:12; 24:9 22:7 [a] 1 Sam. 9:7, 8 22:8 [a] Num. 22:19

9 [a]Then God came to Balaam and said,
"Who *are* these men with you?"
10 So Balaam said to God, "Balak the son of
Zippor, king of Moab, has sent to me, *saying,*
11 'Look, a people has come out of Egypt, and
they cover the face of the earth. Come now,
curse them for me; perhaps I shall be able
to overpower them and drive them out.' "
12 And God said to Balaam, "You shall not
go with them; you shall not curse the people,
for [a]they *are* blessed."
13 So Balaam rose in the morning and said
to the princes of Balak, "Go back to your
land, for the LORD has refused to give me
permission to go with you."
14 And the princes of Moab rose and went
to Balak, and said, "Balaam refuses to come
with us."
15 Then Balak again sent princes, more
numerous and more honorable than they.
16 And they came to Balaam and said to him,
"Thus says Balak the son of Zippor: 'Please
let nothing hinder you from coming to me;
17 for I will certainly [a]honor you greatly, and
I will do whatever you say to me. [b]Therefore
please come, curse this people for me.' "
18 Then Balaam answered and said to the
servants of Balak, [a]"Though Balak were to
give me his house full of silver and gold, [b]I
could not go beyond the word of the LORD
my God, to do less or more. 19 Now therefore,
please, you also [a]stay here tonight, that I may
know what more the LORD will say to me."
20 [a]And God came to Balaam at night and
said to him, "If the men come to call you, rise
and go with them; but [b]only the word which I
speak to you—that you shall do." 21 So Balaam
rose in the morning, saddled his donkey, and
went with the princes of Moab.

Balaam, the Donkey, and the Angel

22 Then God's anger was aroused because
he went, [a]and the Angel of the LORD took
His stand in the way as an adversary against
him. And he was riding on his donkey, and
his two servants *were* with him. 23 Now [a]the
donkey saw the Angel of the LORD standing in the way with His drawn sword in His
hand, and the donkey turned aside out of
the way and went into the field. So Balaam
struck the donkey to turn her back onto the
road. 24 Then the Angel of the LORD stood in
a narrow path between the vineyards, *with*
a wall on this side and a wall on that side.
25 And when the donkey saw the Angel of the
LORD, she pushed herself against the wall
and crushed Balaam's foot against the wall;
so he struck her again. 26 Then the Angel of
the LORD went further, and stood in a narrow
place where there *was* no way to turn either
to the right hand or to the left. 27 And when
the donkey saw the Angel of the LORD, she
lay down under Balaam; so Balaam's anger
was aroused, and he struck the donkey with
his staff.
28 Then the LORD [a]opened the mouth of
the donkey, and she said to Balaam, "What
have I done to you, that you have struck me
these three times?"
29 And Balaam said to the donkey, "Because
you have abused me. I wish there were a
sword in my hand, [a]for now I would kill you!"
30 [a]So the donkey said to Balaam, "*Am* I
not your donkey on which you have ridden,
ever since *I became* yours, to this day? Was I
ever disposed to do this to you?"
And he said, "No."
31 Then the LORD [a]opened Balaam's eyes,
and he saw the Angel of the LORD standing
in the way with His drawn sword in His hand;
and he bowed his head and fell flat on his
face. 32 And the Angel of the LORD said to
him, "Why have you struck your donkey these
three times? Behold, I have come out to stand
against you, because *your* way is [a]perverse
before Me. 33 The donkey saw Me and turned
aside from Me these three times. If she had
not turned aside from Me, surely I would
also have killed you by now, and let her live."
34 And Balaam said to the Angel of the
LORD, [a]"I have sinned, for I did not know You
stood in the way against me. Now therefore,
if it displeases You, I will turn back."
35 Then the Angel of the LORD said to Balaam, "Go with the men, [a]but only the word
that I speak to you, that you shall speak." So
Balaam went with the princes of Balak.
36 Now when Balak heard that Balaam was
coming, [a]he went out to meet him at the city
of Moab, [b]which *is* on the border at the Arnon,
the boundary of the territory. 37 Then Balak
said to Balaam, "Did I not earnestly send to
you, calling for you? Why did you not come
to me? Am I not able [a]to honor you?"
38 And Balaam said to Balak, "Look, I have
come to you! Now, have I any power at all to
say anything? [a]The word that God puts in my
mouth, that I must speak." 39 So Balaam went
with Balak, and they came to Kirjath Huzoth.
40 Then Balak offered oxen and sheep, and
he sent *some* to Balaam and to the princes
who *were* with him.

22:9 [a] Gen. 20:3 **22:12** [a] [Rom. 11:28] **22:17** [a] Num. 24:11 [b] Num. 22:6 **22:18** [a] Num. 22:38; 24:13 [b] 1 Kin. 22:14 **22:19** [a] Num. 22:8 **22:20** [a] Num. 22:9 [b] Num. 22:35; 23:5, 12, 16, 26; 24:13 **22:22** [a] Ex. 4:24 **22:23** [a] Josh. 5:13 **22:28** [a] 2 Pet. 2:16 **22:29** [a] [Prov. 12:10] **22:30** [a] 2 Pet. 2:16 **22:31** [a] Gen. 21:19 **22:32** [a] [2 Pet. 2:14, 15] **22:34** [a] 2 Sam. 12:13 **22:35** [a] Num. 22:20 **22:36** [a] Gen. 14:17 [b] Num. 21:13 **22:37** [a] Num. 22:17; 24:11 **22:38** [a] 1 Kin. 22:14

Balaam's First Prophecy
41 So it was, the next day, that Balak took Balaam and brought him up to the [a]high places
of Baal, that from there he might observe the
extent of the people.

23 Then Balaam said to Balak, [a]"Build
seven altars for me here, and prepare
for me here seven bulls and seven rams."
2 And Balak did just as Balaam had spoken,
and Balak and Balaam [a]offered a bull and
a ram on *each* altar. 3 Then Balaam said to
Balak, [a]"Stand by your burnt offering, and I
will go; perhaps the LORD will come [b]to meet
me, and whatever He shows me I will tell
you." So he went to a desolate height. 4 [a]And
God met Balaam, and he said to Him, "I have
prepared the seven altars, and I have offered
on *each* altar a bull and a ram."
5 Then the LORD [a]put a word in Balaam's
mouth, and said, "Return to Balak, and thus
you shall speak." 6 So he returned to him, and
there he was, standing by his burnt offering,
he and all the princes of Moab.
7 And he [a]took up his oracle and said:

"Balak the king of Moab has brought me
from Aram,
From the mountains of the east.
[b]'Come, curse Jacob for me,
And come, [c]denounce Israel!'

8 "How[a] shall I curse whom God has not
cursed?
And how shall I denounce *whom* the
LORD has not denounced?
9 For from the top of the rocks I see
him,
And from the hills I behold him;
There! [a]A people dwelling alone,
[b]Not reckoning itself among the
nations.

10 "Who[a] can count the dust[1] of Jacob,
Or number one-fourth of Israel?
Let me die [b]the death of the righteous,
And let my end be like his!"

11 Then Balak said to Balaam, "What have
you done to me? [a]I took you to curse my
enemies, and look, you have blessed *them*
bountifully!"
12 So he answered and said, [a]"Must I not
take heed to speak what the LORD has put
in my mouth?"

Balaam's Second Prophecy
13 Then Balak said to him, "Please come
with me to another place from which you
may see them; you shall see only the outer
part of them, and shall not see them all; curse
them for me from there." 14 So he brought him
to the field of Zophim, to the top of Pisgah,
[a]and built seven altars, and offered a bull
and a ram on *each* altar.
15 And he said to Balak, "Stand here by
your burnt offering while I meet[1] *the LORD*
over there."
16 Then the LORD met Balaam, and [a]put a
word in his mouth, and said, "Go back to Balak,
and thus you shall speak." 17 So he came to him,
and there he was, standing by his burnt offering,
and the princes of Moab were with him. And
Balak said to him, "What has the LORD spoken?"
18 Then he took up his oracle and said:

[a]"Rise up, Balak, and hear!
Listen to me, son of Zippor!

19 "God[a] *is* not a man, that He should lie,
Nor a son of man, that He should repent.
Has He [b]said, and will He not do?
Or has He spoken, and will He not
make it good?
20 Behold, I have received *a command* to
bless;
[a]He has blessed, and I cannot reverse it.

21 "He[a] has not observed iniquity in Jacob,
Nor has He seen wickedness in Israel.
The LORD his God *is* with him,
[b]And the shout of a King *is* among them.
22 [a]God brings them out of Egypt;
He has [b]strength like a wild ox.

23 "For *there is* no sorcery against Jacob,
Nor any divination against Israel.
It now must be said of Jacob
And of Israel, 'Oh, [a]what God has done!'
24 Look, a people rises [a]like a lioness,
And lifts itself up like a lion;
[b]It shall not lie down until it devours
the prey,
And drinks the blood of the slain."

25 Then Balak said to Balaam, "Neither
curse them at all, nor bless them at all!"
26 So Balaam answered and said to Balak,
"Did I not tell you, saying, [a]'All that the LORD
speaks, that I must do'?"

23:41 [a] Num. 21:28 **23:1** [a] Num. 23:29 **23:2** [a] Num. 23:14, 30 **23:3** [a] Num. 23:15 [b] Num. 23:4, 16 **23:4** [a] Num. 23:16 **23:5** [a] Deut. 18:18 **23:7** [a] Deut. 23:4 [b] Num. 22:6, 11, 17 [c] 1 Sam. 17:10 **23:8** [a] Num. 22:12 **23:9** [a] Deut. 32:8; 33:28 [b] Ex. 33:16 **23:10** [a] Gen. 13:16; 22:17; 28:14 [b] Ps. 116:15 [1] Or *dust cloud* **23:11** [a] Num. 22:11 **23:12** [a] Num. 22:38 **23:14** [a] Num. 23:1, 2 **23:15** [1] Following Masoretic Text, Targum, and Vulgate; Syriac reads *call;* Septuagint reads *go and ask God.* **23:16** [a] Num. 22:35; 23:5 **23:18** [a] Judg. 3:20 **23:19** [a] Mal. 3:6 [b] 1 Kin. 8:56 **23:20** [a] Num. 22:12 **23:21** [a] [Rom. 4:7, 8] [b] Ps. 89:15–18 **23:22** [a] Num. 24:8 [b] Deut. 33:17 **23:23** [a] Ps. 31:19; 44:1 **23:24** [a] Gen. 49:9 [b] Gen. 49:27 **23:26** [a] Num. 22:38

Balaam's Third Prophecy

27 Then Balak said to Balaam, "Please come,
I will take you to another place; perhaps it will
please God that you may curse them for me
from there." 28 So Balak took Balaam to the
top of Peor, that [a]overlooks the wasteland.[1]
29 Then Balaam said to Balak, "Build for me
here seven altars, and prepare for me here
seven bulls and seven rams." 30 And Balak
did as Balaam had said, and offered a bull
and a ram on *every* altar.

24 Now when Balaam saw that it pleased
the LORD to bless Israel, he did not go
as at [a]other times, to seek to use sorcery, but
he set his face toward the wilderness. 2 And
Balaam raised his eyes, and saw Israel [a]en-
camped according to their tribes; and [b]the
Spirit of God came upon him.

3 [a]Then he took up his oracle and said:

"The utterance of Balaam the son of Beor,
The utterance of the man whose eyes
are opened,
4 The utterance of him who hears the
words of God,
Who sees the vision of the Almighty,
Who [a]falls down, with eyes wide open:

5 "How lovely are your tents, O Jacob!
Your dwellings, O Israel!
6 Like valleys that stretch out,
Like gardens by the riverside,
[a]Like aloes [b]planted by the LORD,
Like cedars beside the waters.
7 He shall pour water from his buckets,
And his seed *shall be* [a]in many waters.

"His king shall be higher than [b]Agag,
And his [c]kingdom shall be exalted.

8 "God[a] brings him out of Egypt;
He has strength like a wild ox;
He shall [b]consume the nations, his
enemies;
He shall [c]break their bones
And [d]pierce *them* with his arrows.
9 'He[a] bows down, he lies down as a lion;
And as a lion, who shall rouse him?'[1]

[b]"Blessed *is* he who blesses you,
And cursed *is* he who curses you."

10 Then Balak's anger was aroused against
Balaam, and he [a]struck his hands together;
and Balak said to Balaam, [b]"I called you to
curse my enemies, and look, you have bountifully blessed *them* these three times! 11 Now
therefore, flee to your place. [a]I said I would
greatly honor you, but in fact, the LORD has
kept you back from honor."

12 So Balaam said to Balak, "Did I not also
speak to your messengers whom you sent
to me, saying, 13 'If Balak were to give me his
house full of silver and gold, I could not go
beyond the word of the LORD, to do good
or bad of my own will. What the LORD says,
that I must speak'? 14 And now, indeed, I am
going to my people. Come, [a]I will advise you
what this people will do to your people in
the [b]latter days."

Balaam's Fourth Prophecy

15 So he took up his oracle and said:

"The utterance of Balaam the son of
Beor,
And the utterance of the man whose
eyes are opened;
16 The utterance of him who hears the
words of God,
And has the knowledge of the Most
High,
Who sees the vision of the Almighty,
Who falls down, with eyes wide open:

17 "I[a] see Him, but not now;
I behold Him, but not near;
[b]A Star shall come out of Jacob;
[c]A Scepter shall rise out of Israel,
And batter the brow of Moab,
And destroy all the sons of tumult.[1]

18 "And [a]Edom shall be a possession;
Seir also, his enemies, shall be a
possession,
While Israel does valiantly.
19 [a]Out of Jacob One shall have dominion,
And destroy the remains of the city."

20 Then he looked on Amalek, and he took
up his oracle and said:

"Amalek *was* first among the nations,
But *shall be* last until he perishes."

21 Then he looked on the Kenites, and he
took up his oracle and said:

"Firm is your dwelling place,
And your nest is set in the rock;

23:28 [a] Num. 21:20 [1] Hebrew *Jeshimon* 24:1 [a] Num. 23:3, 15 24:2 [a] Num. 2:2, 34 [b] Num. 11:25 24:3 [a] Num. 23:7, 18 24:4 [a] Ezek. 1:28 24:6 [a] Jer. 17:8 [b] Ps. 104:16 24:7 [a] Jer. 51:13 [b] 1 Sam. 15:8, 9 [c] 2 Sam. 5:12 24:8 [a] Num. 23:22 [b] Num. 14:9; 23:24 [c] Ps. 2:9 [d] Ps. 45:5 24:9 [a] Gen. 49:9 [b] Gen. 12:3; 27:29 [1] Genesis 49:9 24:10 [a] Ezek. 21:14, 17 [b] Num. 23:11 24:11 [a] Num. 22:17, 37 24:14 [a] [Mic. 6:5] [b] Gen. 49:1 24:17 [a] Rev. 1:7 [b] Matt. 2:2 [c] Gen. 49:10 [1] Hebrew *Sheth* (compare Jeremiah 48:45) 24:18 [a] 2 Sam. 8:14 24:19 [a] Amos 9:11, 12

UNEXPECTED BLESSINGS

A Star shall come out of Jacob; a Scepter shall rise out of Israel.

NUMBERS 24:17

God never made a more unusual promise than the one here in verse 17. Balak, king of Moab, feared the approaching people of Israel, so he hired the well-known prophet and magician Balaam to curse Israel. Only the words that came out of Balaam's mouth were blessings!

In all, Balaam gave utterance to four oracles (see 23:7–10, 18–24; 24:3–9, 15–24). In the fourth, Balaam says, "A Star shall come out of Jacob; a Scepter shall rise out of Israel" (v. 17). Interpreters ancient and modern believe this is a prophecy of Israel's Messiah. The "Scepter" probably alludes to Jacob's blessing pronounced on Judah (see Gen. 49:8–12), which also was understood as a messianic prophecy.

Poor old Balak; he didn't get what he thought he paid for. Not only were the approaching people of Israel blessed instead of cursed, they were given a prophecy of their coming Savior!

When we see what God has done in history and what He has promised through His prophets—we see that nothing that comes from Him is too good to be true. And that should give us hope and peace.

22 Nevertheless Kain shall be burned.
How long until Asshur carries you
away captive?"

23 Then he took up his oracle and said:

"Alas! Who shall live when God does this?
24 But ships *shall come* from the coasts of
[a]Cyprus,[1]
And they shall afflict Asshur and afflict
[b]Eber,
And so shall *Amalek*,[2] until he perishes."

25 So Balaam rose and departed and [a]re-
turned to his place; Balak also went his way.

Israel's Harlotry in Moab

25 Now Israel remained in [a]Acacia Grove,[1]
and the [b]people began to commit harlotry with the women of Moab. 2 [a]They invited
the people to [b]the sacrifices of their gods, and
the people ate and [c]bowed down to their gods.
3 So Israel was joined to Baal of Peor, and [a]the
anger of the LORD was aroused against Israel.
4 Then the LORD said to Moses, [a]"Take all
the leaders of the people and hang the offenders before the LORD, out in the sun, [b]that
the fierce anger of the LORD may turn away
from Israel."
5 So Moses said to [a]the judges of Israel,
[b]"Every one of you kill his men who were
joined to Baal of Peor."
6 And indeed, one of the children of Israel
came and presented to his brethren a Midianite woman in the sight of Moses and in the
sight of all the congregation of the children
of Israel, [a]who *were* weeping at the door of
the tabernacle of meeting. 7 Now [a]when Phinehas [b]the son of Eleazar, the son of Aaron
the priest, saw *it*, he rose from among the
congregation and took a javelin in his hand;
8 and he went after the man of Israel into the
tent and thrust both of them through, the
man of Israel, and the woman through her
body. So [a]the plague was [b]stopped among
the children of Israel. 9 And [a]those who died
in the plague were twenty-four thousand.
10 Then the LORD spoke to Moses, saying:
11 [a]"Phinehas the son of Eleazar, the son of Aaron
the priest, has turned back My wrath from the
children of Israel, because he was zealous with
My zeal among them, so that I did not consume
the children of Israel in [b]My zeal. 12 Therefore say,
[a]'Behold, I give to him My [b]covenant of peace;
13 and it shall be to him and [a]his descendants
after him a covenant of [b]an everlasting priesthood, because he was [c]zealous for his God, and
[d]made atonement for the children of Israel.' "

24:24 [a] Gen. 10:4 [b] Gen. 10:21, 25 [1] Hebrew *Kittim* [2] Literally *he* or *that one* **24:25** [a] Num. 22:5; 31:8 **25:1** [a] Josh. 2:1 [b] Rev. 2:14 [1] Hebrew *Shittim* **25:2** [a] Hos. 9:10 [b] Ex. 34:15 [c] Ex. 20:5 **25:3** [a] Ps. 106:28, 29 **25:4** [a] Deut. 4:3 [b] Num. 25:11 **25:5** [a] Ex. 18:21 [b] Deut. 13:6, 9 **25:6** [a] Joel 2:17 **25:7** [a] Ps. 106:30 [b] Ex. 6:25 **25:8** [a] Ps. 106:30 [b] Num. 16:46–48 **25:9** [a] Deut. 4:3 **25:11** [a] Ps. 106:30 [b] [Ex. 20:5] **25:12** [a] [Mal. 2:4, 5; 3:1] [b] Is. 54:10 **25:13** [a] 1 Chr. 6:4–15 [b] Ex. 40:15 [c] Acts 22:3 [d] [Heb. 2:17]

THE BOND OF PEACE

"Behold, I give to [Phinehas] My covenant of peace."

NUMBERS 25:12

In the wilderness, Israel encountered pagan peoples who were eager to introduce Israel to their gods and practices. Moses exhorted the people to remain faithful, but some Israelites saw no harm in friendly compromise. Would it hurt to show a little respect to their neighbors' gods?

The sin was so outrageous it brought judgment on the entire camp. But Phinehas's zeal brought it to an end, and God gave him a "covenant of peace" (v. 12; see Ps. 106:30–31). Sometimes taking firm, perhaps unpopular, action is necessary to keep the peace. This is God's covenant, "My covenant" (v. 12), which means that the promise of God's peace is based on God's unchanging nature and immutable character. A covenant is a bond or promise of obligation. God's peace is absolute and dependable because God cannot fail. God has obligated Himself to bringing us peace if we act in faith and trust Him—as Phinehas did.

Does a situation in your life call for a peacemaker? Could you make a difference?

PEACE NOTE

The peace that Jesus gives heals, restores, and makes complete.

NUMBERS 25:12

14 Now the name of the Israelite who was
killed, who was killed with the Midianite
woman, *was* Zimri the son of Salu, a leader
of a father's house among the Simeonites.
15 And the name of the Midianite woman
who was killed *was* Cozbi the daughter of
[a]Zur; he *was* head of the people of a father's
house in Midian.

16 Then the LORD spoke to Moses, saying:
17 [a]"Harass the Midianites, and attack them;
18 for they harassed you with their [a]schemes by
which they seduced you in the matter of Peor
and in the matter of Cozbi, the daughter of a
leader of Midian, their sister, who was killed
in the day of the plague because of Peor."

The Second Census of Israel

26 And it came to pass, after the [a]plague,
that the LORD spoke to Moses and
Eleazar the son of Aaron the priest, saying:
2 [a]"Take a census of all the congregation of
the children of Israel [b]from twenty years old
and above, by their fathers' houses, all who
are able to go to war in Israel." 3 So Moses
and Eleazar the priest spoke with them [a]in
the plains of Moab by the Jordan, *across
from* Jericho, saying: 4 "*Take a census of the
people* from twenty years old and above,
just as the LORD [a]commanded Moses and
the children of Israel who came out of the
land of Egypt."

5 [a]Reuben *was* the firstborn of Israel. The
children of Reuben *were: of* Hanoch, the
family of the Hanochites; *of* Pallu, the family of the Palluites; 6 *of* Hezron, the family
of the Hezronites; *of* Carmi, the family of
the Carmites. 7 These *are* the families of
the Reubenites: those who were numbered
of them were forty-three thousand seven
hundred and thirty. 8 And the son of Pallu
was Eliab. 9 The sons of Eliab *were* Nemuel,
Dathan, and Abiram. These *are* the Dathan
and Abiram, [a]representatives of the congregation, who contended against Moses
and Aaron in the company of Korah, when
they contended against the LORD; 10 [a]and
the earth opened its mouth and swallowed
them up together with Korah when that
company died, when the fire devoured two
hundred and fifty men; [b]and they became a

25:15 [a] Num. 31:8 **25:17** [a] Num. 31:1–3 **25:18** [a] Rev. 2:14 **26:1** [a] Num. 25:9 **26:2** [a] Num. 1:2; 14:29 [b] Num. 1:3 **26:3** [a] Num. 22:1; 31:12; 33:48; 35:1 **26:4** [a] Num. 1:1 **26:5** [a] Ex. 6:14 **26:9** [a] Num. 1:16; 16:1, 2 **26:10** [a] Num. 16:32–35 [b] Num. 16:38–40

sign. 11 Nevertheless [a]the children of Korah
did not die.

12 The sons of Simeon according to
their families *were: of* Nemuel,[1] the family of the Nemuelites; *of* Jamin, the family
of the Jaminites; *of* Jachin,[2] the family of
the Jachinites; 13 *of* Zerah,[1] the family of the
Zarhites; *of* Shaul, the family of the Shaulites.
14 These *are* the families of the Simeonites:
twenty-two thousand two hundred.

15 The sons of Gad according to their families *were: of* Zephon,[1] the family of the Ze-
phonites; *of* Haggi, the family of the Haggites;
of Shuni, the family of the Shunites; 16 *of* Ozni,[1]
the family of the Oznites; *of* Eri, the family
of the Erites; 17 *of* Arod,[1] the family of the
Arodites; *of* Areli, the family of the Arelites.
18 These *are* the families of the sons of Gad
according to those who were numbered of
them: forty thousand five hundred.

19 [a]The sons of Judah *were* Er and Onan;
and Er and Onan died in the land of Canaan.
20 And [a]the sons of Judah according to their
families were: *of* Shelah, the family of the
Shelanites; *of* Perez, the family of the Parzites;
of Zerah, the family of the Zarhites. 21 And the
sons of Perez were: *of* Hezron, the family of
the Hezronites; *of* Hamul, the family of the
Hamulites. 22 These *are* the families of Judah
according to those who were numbered of
them: seventy-six thousand five hundred.

23 The sons of Issachar according to their
families *were: of* Tola, the family of the To-
laites; of Puah,[1] the family of the Punites;[2]
24 of Jashub, the family of the Jashubites;
of Shimron, the family of the Shimronites.
25 These *are* the families of Issachar according to those who were numbered of them:
sixty-four thousand three hundred.

26 [a]The sons of Zebulun according to their
families *were:* of Sered, the family of the Sar-
dites; of Elon, the family of the Elonites; of
Jahleel, the family of the Jahleelites. 27 These
are the families of the Zebulunites according
to those who were numbered of them: sixty
thousand five hundred.

28 [a]The sons of Joseph according to their
families, by Manasseh and Ephraim, *were:*
29 The sons of [a]Manasseh: of [b]Machir, the
family of the Machirites; and Machir begot
Gilead; of Gilead, the family of the Gileadites.
30 These *are* the sons of Gilead: *of* Jeezer,[1] the
family of the Jeezerites; of Helek, the family
of the Helekites; 31 *of* Asriel, the family of
the Asrielites; *of* Shechem, the family of the
Shechemites; 32 *of* Shemida, the family of
the Shemidaites; *of* Hepher, the family of
the Hepherites. 33 Now [a]Zelophehad the son
of Hepher had no sons, but daughters; and
the names of the daughters of Zelophehad
were Mahlah, Noah, Hoglah, Milcah, and Tirzah. 34 These *are* the families of Manasseh;
and those who were numbered of them *were*
fifty-two thousand seven hundred.

35 These *are* the sons of Ephraim according
to their families: of Shuthelah, the family of
the Shuthalhites; of Becher,[1] the family of the
Bachrites; of Tahan, the family of the Tahan-
ites. 36 And these *are* the sons of Shuthelah: of
Eran, the family of the Eranites. 37 These *are*
the families of the sons of Ephraim according
to those who were numbered of them: thirty-
two thousand five hundred.

These *are* the sons of Joseph according to
their families.

38 [a]The sons of Benjamin according to their
families were: of Bela, the family of the Bela-
ites; of Ashbel, the family of the Ashbelites; of
[b]Ahiram, the family of the Ahiramites; 39 of
[a]Shupham,[1] the family of the Shuphamites;
of Hupham,[2] the family of the Huphamites.
40 And the sons of Bela were Ard[1] and Naaman: [a]*of Ard,* the family of the Ardites; of
Naaman, the family of the Naamites. 41 These
are the sons of Benjamin according to their
families; and those who were numbered of
them *were* forty-five thousand six hundred.

42 These *are* the sons of Dan according to
their families: of Shuham,[1] the family of the
Shuhamites. These *are* the families of Dan
according to their families. 43 All the families
of the Shuhamites, according to those who
were numbered of them, *were* sixty-four
thousand four hundred.

44 [a]The sons of Asher according to their
families *were:* of Jimna, the family of the
Jimnites; of Jesui, the family of the Jesuites;
of Beriah, the family of the Beriites. 45 Of
the sons of Beriah: of Heber, the family of
the Heberites; of Malchiel, the family of the
Malchielites. 46 And the name of the daughter
of Asher *was* Serah. 47 These *are* the families

26:11 [a] Ex. 6:24 **26:12** [1] Spelled *Jemuel* in Genesis 46:10 and Exodus 6:15 [2] Called *Jarib* in 1 Chronicles 4:24 **26:13** [1] Called *Zohar* in Genesis 46:10 **26:15** [1] Called *Ziphion* in Genesis 46:16 **26:16** [1] Called *Ezbon* in Genesis 46:16 **26:17** [1] Spelled *Arodi* in Samaritan Pentateuch, Syriac, and Genesis 46:16 **26:19** [a] Gen. 38:2; 46:12 **26:20** [a] 1 Chr. 2:3 **26:23** [1] Hebrew *Puvah* (compare Genesis 46:13 and 1 Chronicles 7:1); Samaritan Pentateuch, Septuagint, Syriac, and Vulgate read *Puah.* [2] Samaritan Pentateuch, Septuagint, Syriac, and Vulgate read *Puaites.* **26:26** [a] Gen. 46:14 **26:28** [a] Gen. 46:20 **26:29** [a] Josh. 17:1 [b] 1 Chr. 7:14, 15 **26:30** [1] Called *Abiezer* in Joshua 17:2 **26:33** [a] Num. 27:1; 36:11 **26:35** [1] Called *Bered* in 1 Chronicles 7:20 **26:38** [a] Gen. 46:21 [b] 1 Chr. 8:1, 2 **26:39** [a] 1 Chr. 7:12 [1] Masoretic Text reads *Shephupham,* spelled *Shephuphan* in 1 Chronicles 8:5. [2] Called *Huppim* in Genesis 46:21 **26:40** [a] 1 Chr. 8:3 [1] Called *Addar* in 1 Chronicles 8:3 **26:42** [1] Called *Hushim* in Genesis 46:23 **26:44** [a] Gen. 46:17

of the sons of Asher according to those who
were numbered of them: fifty-three thousand
four hundred.
48 [a]The sons of Naphtali according to their
families *were:* of Jahzeel,[1] the family of the
Jahzeelites; of Guni, the family of the Gunites;
49 of Jezer, the family of the Jezerites; of [a]Shil-
lem, the family of the Shillemites. 50 These
are the families of Naphtali according to their
families; and those who were numbered of
them *were* forty-five thousand four hundred.
51 [a]These *are* those who were numbered of
the children of Israel: six hundred and one
thousand seven hundred and thirty.
52 Then the LORD spoke to Moses, saying:
53 [a]"To these the land shall be [b]divided as an inheritance, according to the number of names.
54 [a]To a large *tribe* you shall give a larger inheritance, and to a small *tribe* you shall give
a smaller inheritance. Each shall be given
its inheritance according to those who were
numbered of them. 55 But the land shall be
[a]divided by lot; they shall inherit according to
the names of the tribes of their fathers. 56 According to the lot their inheritance shall be
divided between the larger and the smaller."
57 [a]And these *are* those who were numbered
of the Levites according to their families: of
Gershon, the family of the Gershonites; of Kohath, the family of the Kohathites; of Merari,
the family of the Merarites. 58 These *are* the
families of the Levites: the family of the Libnites, the family of the Hebronites, the family
of the Mahlites, the family of the Mushites,
and the family of the Korathites. And Kohath
begot Amram. 59 The name of Amram's wife
was [a]Jochebed the daughter of Levi, who was
born to Levi in Egypt; and to Amram she bore
Aaron and Moses and their sister Miriam. 60 [a]To
Aaron were born Nadab and Abihu, Eleazar and
Ithamar. 61 And [a]Nadab and Abihu died when
they offered profane fire before the LORD.
62 [a]Now those who were numbered of them
were twenty-three thousand, every male
from a month old and above; [b]for they were
not numbered among the other children of
Israel, because there was [c]no inheritance
given to them among the children of Israel.
63 These *are* those who were numbered by
Moses and Eleazar the priest, who numbered
the children of Israel [a]in the plains of Moab
by the Jordan, *across from* Jericho. 64 [a]But
among these there was not a man of those
who were numbered by Moses and Aaron the
priest when they numbered the children of

PEACE NOTE

The peace of God, which includes happiness and joy, is a discipline we learn, not an automatic skill or natural Christian ability.

Israel in the [b]Wilderness of Sinai. 65 For the
LORD had said of them, "They [a]shall surely
die in the wilderness." So there was not left
a man of them, [b]except Caleb the son of Jephunneh and Joshua the son of Nun.

Inheritance Laws

27 Then came the daughters of [a]Zelophe-
had the son of Hepher, the son of Gilead,
the son of Machir, the son of Manasseh, from
the families of Manasseh the son of Joseph;
and these *were* the names of his daughters:
Mahlah, Noah, Hoglah, Milcah, and Tirzah.
2 And they stood before Moses, before Eleazar
the priest, and before the leaders and all the
congregation, *by* the doorway of the tabernacle
of meeting, saying: 3 "Our father [a]died in the
wilderness; but he was not in the company of
those who gathered together against the LORD,
[b]in company with Korah, but he died in his
own sin; and he had no sons. 4 Why should the
name of our father be [a]removed from among
his family because he had no son? [b]Give us
a possession among our father's brothers."
5 So Moses [a]brought their case before the
LORD.
6 And the LORD spoke to Moses, saying: 7 "The
daughters of Zelophehad speak *what is* right;
[a]you shall surely give them a possession of
inheritance among their father's brothers, and
cause the inheritance of their father to pass to
them. 8 And you shall speak to the children of
Israel, saying: 'If a man dies and has no son,
then you shall cause his inheritance to pass
to his daughter. 9 If he has no daughter, then
you shall give his inheritance to his brothers.

26:48 [a] 1 Chr. 7:13 [1] Spelled *Jahziel* in 1 Chronicles 7:13 **26:49** [a] 1 Chr. 7:13 **26:51** [a] Num. 1:46; 11:21 **26:53** [a] Josh. 11:23; 14:1 [b] Num. 33:54 **26:54** [a] Num. 33:54 **26:55** [a] Num. 33:54; 34:13 **26:57** [a] Gen. 46:11 **26:59** [a] Ex. 2:1, 2; 6:20 **26:60** [a] Num. 3:2 **26:61** [a] Lev. 10:1, 2 **26:62** [a] Num. 3:39 [b] Num. 1:49 [c] Num. 18:20, 23, 24 **26:63** [a] Num. 26:3 **26:64** [a] Num. 14:29–35 [b] Num. 1:1–46 **26:65** [a] Num. 14:26–35 [b] Num. 14:30 **27:1** [a] Num. 26:33; 36:1, 11 **27:3** [a] Num. 14:35; 26:64, 65 [b] Num. 16:1, 2 **27:4** [a] Deut. 25:6 [b] Josh. 17:4 **27:5** [a] Ex. 18:13–26 **27:7** [a] Num. 36:2

10 If he has no brothers, then you shall give his
inheritance to his father's brothers. 11 And if
his father has no brothers, then you shall give
his inheritance to the relative closest to him
in his family, and he shall possess it.' " And it
shall be to the children of Israel [a]a statute of
judgment, just as the LORD commanded Moses.

Joshua the Next Leader of Israel

12 Now the LORD said to Moses: [a]"Go up
into this Mount Abarim, and see the land
which I have given to the children of Israel.
13 And when you have seen it, you also [a]shall
be gathered to your people, as Aaron your
brother was gathered. 14 For in the Wilderness
of Zin, during the strife of the congregation,
you [a]rebelled against My command to hallow
Me at the waters before their eyes." (These
are the [b]waters of Meribah, at Kadesh in the
Wilderness of Zin.)
15 Then Moses spoke to the LORD, saying:
16 "Let the LORD, [a]the God of the spirits of all
flesh, set a man over the congregation, 17 [a]who
may go out before them and go in before
them, who may lead them out and bring them
in, that the congregation of the LORD may
not be [b]like sheep which have no shepherd."
18 And the LORD said to Moses: "Take Joshua the son of Nun with you, a man [a]in whom
is the Spirit, and [b]lay your hand on him; 19 set
him before Eleazar the priest and before all
the congregation, and [a]inaugurate him in
their sight. 20 And [a]you shall give *some* of your
authority to him, that all the congregation
of the children of Israel [b]may be obedient.
21 [a]He shall stand before Eleazar the priest,
who shall inquire before the LORD for him
[b]by the judgment of the Urim. [c]At his word
they shall go out, and at his word they shall
come in, he and all the children of Israel with
him—all the congregation."
22 So Moses did as the LORD commanded
him. He took Joshua and set him before Eleazar the priest and before all the congregation.
23 And he laid his hands on him [a]and inaugurated him, just as the LORD commanded
by the hand of Moses.

Daily Offerings

28 Now the LORD spoke to Moses, saying,
2 "Command the children of Israel,
and say to them, 'My offering, [a]My food for
My offerings made by fire as a sweet aroma
to Me, you shall be careful to offer to Me at
their appointed time.'
3 "And you shall say to them, [a]'This *is* the
offering made by fire which you shall offer
to the LORD: two male lambs in their first
year without blemish, day by day, as a regular
burnt offering. 4 The one lamb you shall offer
in the morning, the other lamb you shall offer
in the evening, 5 and [a]one-tenth of an ephah
of fine flour as a [b]grain offering mixed with
one-fourth of a hin of pressed oil. 6 *It is* [a]a
regular burnt offering which was ordained
at Mount Sinai for a sweet aroma, an offering made by fire to the LORD. 7 And its drink
offering *shall be* one-fourth of a hin for each
lamb; [a]in a holy *place* you shall pour out the
drink to the LORD as an offering. 8 The other
lamb you shall offer in the evening; as the
morning grain offering and its drink offering,
you shall offer *it* as an offering made by fire,
a sweet aroma to the LORD.

Sabbath Offerings

9 'And on the Sabbath day two lambs in
their first year, without blemish, and two-
tenths *of an ephah* of fine flour as a grain
offering, mixed with oil, with its drink offering— 10 *this is* [a]the burnt offering for every
Sabbath, besides the regular burnt offering
with its drink offering.

Monthly Offerings

11 [a]'At the beginnings of your months you
shall present a burnt offering to the LORD: two
young bulls, one ram, and seven lambs in their
first year, without blemish; 12 [a]three-tenths
of an ephah of fine flour as a grain offering,
mixed with oil, for each bull; two-tenths *of an
ephah* of fine flour as a grain offering, mixed
with oil, for the one ram; 13 and one-tenth *of an
ephah* of fine flour, mixed with oil, as a grain
offering for each lamb, as a burnt offering of
sweet aroma, an offering made by fire to the
LORD. 14 Their drink offering shall be half a hin
of wine for a bull, one-third of a hin for a ram,
and one-fourth of a hin for a lamb; this *is* the
burnt offering for each month throughout
the months of the year. 15 Also [a]one kid of
the goats as a sin offering to the LORD shall
be offered, besides the regular burnt offering
and its drink offering.

Offerings at Passover

16 [a]'On the fourteenth day of the first month
is the Passover of the LORD. 17 [a]And on the
fifteenth day of this month *is* the feast; unleavened bread shall be eaten for seven days.

27:11 [a] Num. 35:29 **27:12** [a] Num. 33:47 **27:13** [a] Deut. 10:6; 34:5, 6 **27:14** [a] Ps. 106:32, 33 [b] Ex. 17:7 **27:16** [a] Num. 16:22 **27:17** [a] Deut. 31:2 [b] Zech. 10:2 **27:18** [a] Gen. 41:38 [b] Deut. 34:9 **27:19** [a] Deut. 3:28; 31:3, 7, 8, 23 **27:20** [a] Num. 11:17 [b] Josh. 1:16–18 **27:21** [a] 1 Sam. 23:9; 30:7 [b] Ex. 28:30 [c] 1 Sam. 22:10 **27:23** [a] Deut. 3:28; 31:7, 8 **28:2** [a] Lev. 3:11; 21:6, 8 **28:3** [a] Ex. 29:38–42 **28:5** [a] Ex. 16:36 [b] Lev. 2:1 **28:6** [a] Ex. 29:42 **28:7** [a] Ex. 29:42 **28:10** [a] Ezek. 46:4 **28:11** [a] Num. 10:10 **28:12** [a] Num. 15:4–12 **28:15** [a] Num. 15:24; 28:3, 22 **28:16** [a] Lev. 23:5–8 **28:17** [a] Lev. 23:6

18 On the [a]first day *you shall have* a holy convocation. You shall do no customary work.
19 And you shall present an offering made
by fire as a burnt offering to the LORD: two
young bulls, one ram, and seven lambs in
their first year. [a]Be sure they are without
blemish. 20 Their grain offering shall be of
fine flour mixed with oil: three-tenths *of
an ephah* you shall offer for a bull, and two-
tenths for a ram; 21 you shall offer one-tenth *of
an ephah* for each of the seven lambs; 22 also
[a]one goat *as* a sin offering, to make atonement for you. 23 You shall offer these besides
the burnt offering of the morning, which *is*
for a regular burnt offering. 24 In this manner
you shall offer the food of the offering made
by fire daily for seven days, as a sweet aroma
to the LORD; it shall be offered besides the
regular burnt offering and its drink offering.
25 And [a]on the seventh day you shall have a
holy convocation. You shall do no customary work.

Offerings at the Feast of Weeks

26 'Also [a]on the day of the firstfruits, when
you bring a new grain offering to the LORD
at your *Feast of* Weeks, you shall have a holy
convocation. You shall do no customary
work. 27 You shall present a burnt offering
as a sweet aroma to the LORD: [a]two young
bulls, one ram, and seven lambs in their first
year, 28 with their grain offering of fine flour
mixed with oil: three-tenths *of an ephah* for
each bull, two-tenths for the one ram, 29 and
one-tenth for each of the seven lambs; 30 *also*
one kid of the goats, to make atonement for
you. 31 [a]Be sure they are without blemish. You
shall present *them* with their drink offerings,
besides the regular burnt offering with its
grain offering.

Offerings at the Feast of Trumpets

29 'And in the seventh month, on the
first *day* of the month, you shall have
a holy convocation. You shall do no customary work. For you [a]it is a day of blowing the
trumpets. 2 You shall offer a burnt offering as
a sweet aroma to the LORD: one young bull,
one ram, *and* seven lambs in their first year,
without blemish. 3 Their grain offering *shall
be* fine flour mixed with oil: three-tenths *of
an ephah* for the bull, two-tenths for the ram,
4 and one-tenth for each of the seven lambs;
5 also one kid of the goats *as* a sin offering,
to make atonement for you; 6 besides [a]the
burnt offering with its grain offering for the
New Moon, [b]the regular burnt offering with
its grain offering, and their drink offerings,
[c]according to their ordinance, as a sweet
aroma, an offering made by fire to the LORD.

Offerings on the Day of Atonement

7 [a]'On the tenth *day* of this seventh month
you shall have a holy convocation. You shall
[b]afflict your souls; you shall not do any work.
8 You shall present a burnt offering to the
LORD *as* a sweet aroma: one young bull, one
ram, *and* seven lambs in their first year. [a]Be
sure they are without blemish. 9 Their grain
offering *shall be of* fine flour mixed with oil:
three-tenths *of an ephah* for the bull, two-
tenths for the one ram, 10 and one-tenth for
each of the seven lambs; 11 also one kid of
the goats *as* a sin offering, besides [a]the sin
offering for atonement, the regular burnt
offering with its grain offering, and their
drink offerings.

Offerings at the Feast of Tabernacles

12 [a]'On the fifteenth day of the seventh
month you shall have a holy convocation.
You shall do no customary work, and you
shall keep a feast to the LORD seven days.
13 [a]You shall present a burnt offering, an
offering made by fire as a sweet aroma to
the LORD: thirteen young bulls, two rams,
and fourteen lambs in their first year. They
shall be without blemish. 14 Their grain
offering *shall be of* fine flour mixed with
oil: three-tenths *of an ephah* for each of
the thirteen bulls, two-tenths for each of
the two rams, 15 and one-tenth for each of
the fourteen lambs; 16 also one kid of the
goats *as* a sin offering, besides the regular
burnt offering, its grain offering, and its
drink offering.

17 'On the [a]second day *present* twelve young
bulls, two rams, fourteen lambs in their first
year without blemish, 18 and their grain offering and their drink offerings for the bulls, for
the rams, and for the lambs, by their number,
[a]according to the ordinance; 19 also one kid
of the goats *as* a sin offering, besides the
regular burnt offering with its grain offering,
and their drink offerings.

20 'On the third day *present* eleven bulls,
two rams, fourteen lambs in their first year
without blemish, 21 and their grain offering
and their drink offerings for the bulls, for
the rams, and for the lambs, by their number, [a]according to the ordinance; 22 also one
goat *as* a sin offering, besides the regular

28:18 [a] Lev. 23:7 **28:19** [a] Deut. 15:21 **28:22** [a] Num. 28:15 **28:25** [a] Lev. 23:8 **28:26** [a] Deut. 16:9–12 **28:27** [a] Lev. 23:18, 19 **28:31** [a] Num. 28:3, 19 **29:1** [a] Lev. 23:23–25 **29:6** [a] Num. 28:11–15 [b] Num. 28:3 [c] Num. 15:11, 12 **29:7** [a] Lev. 16:29–34; 23:26–32 [b] Is. 58:5 **29:8** [a] Num. 28:19 **29:11** [a] Lev. 16:3, 5 **29:12** [a] Deut. 16:13–15 **29:13** [a] Ezra 3:4 **29:17** [a] Lev. 23:36 **29:18** [a] Num. 15:12; 28:7, 14; 29:3, 4, 9, 10 **29:21** [a] Num. 29:18

burnt offering, its grain offering, and its drink offering.

23'On the fourth day *present* ten bulls, two rams, *and* fourteen lambs in their first year, without blemish, 24and their grain offering and their drink offerings for the bulls, for the rams, and for the lambs, by their number, according to the ordinance; 25also one kid of the goats *as* a sin offering, besides the regular burnt offering, its grain offering, and its drink offering.

26'On the fifth day *present* nine bulls, two rams, *and* fourteen lambs in their first year without blemish, 27and their grain offering and their drink offerings for the bulls, for the rams, and for the lambs, by their number, according to the ordinance; 28also one goat *as* a sin offering, besides the regular burnt offering, its grain offering, and its drink offering.

29'On the sixth day *present* eight bulls, two rams, *and* fourteen lambs in their first year without blemish, 30and their grain offering and their drink offerings for the bulls, for the rams, and for the lambs, by their number, according to the ordinance; 31also one goat *as* a sin offering, besides the regular burnt offering, its grain offering, and its drink offering.

32'On the seventh day *present* seven bulls, two rams, *and* fourteen lambs in their first year without blemish, 33and their grain offering and their drink offerings for the bulls, for the rams, and for the lambs, by their number, according to the ordinance; 34also one goat *as* a sin offering, besides the regular burnt offering, its grain offering, and its drink offering.

35'On the eighth day you shall have a [a]sacred assembly. You shall do no customary work. 36You shall present a burnt offering, an offering made by fire as a sweet aroma to the LORD: one bull, one ram, seven lambs in their first year without blemish, 37and their grain offering and their drink offerings for the bull, for the ram, and for the lambs, by their number, according to the ordinance; 38also one goat *as* a sin offering, besides the regular burnt offering, its grain offering, and its drink offering.

39'These you shall present to the LORD at your [a]appointed feasts (besides your [b]vowed offerings and your freewill offerings) as your burnt offerings and your grain offerings, as your drink offerings and your peace offerings.' "

40So Moses told the children of Israel everything, just as the LORD commanded Moses.

The Law Concerning Vows

30 Then Moses spoke to [a]the heads of the tribes concerning the children of Israel, saying, "This *is* the thing which the LORD has commanded: 2[a]If a man makes a vow to the LORD, or [b]swears an oath to bind himself by some agreement, he shall not break his word; he shall [c]do according to all that proceeds out of his mouth.

PEACE NOTE

To maintain the peace of the Lord in our lives, we must be exceedingly careful of the commitments we make. Always meditate before the Lord prior to making any pledge.

NUMBERS 30:2

3"Or if a woman makes a vow to the LORD, and binds *herself* by some agreement while in her father's house in her youth, 4and her father hears her vow and the agreement by which she has bound herself, and her father holds his peace, then all her vows shall stand, and every agreement with which she has bound herself shall stand. 5But if her father overrules her on the day that he hears, then none of her vows nor her agreements by which she has bound herself shall stand; and the LORD will release her, because her father overruled her.

6"If indeed she takes a husband, while bound by her vows or by a rash utterance from her lips by which she bound herself, 7and her husband hears *it,* and makes no response to her on the day that he hears, then her vows shall stand, and her agreements by which she bound herself shall stand. 8But if her husband [a]overrules her on the day that he hears *it,* he shall make void her vow which she took and what she uttered with her lips, by which she bound herself, and the LORD will release her.

9"Also any vow of a widow or a divorced woman, by which she has bound herself, shall stand against her.

10"If she vowed in her husband's house, or bound herself by an agreement with an oath,

29:35 [a] Lev. 23:36 **29:39** [a] Lev. 23:1–44 [b] Lev. 7:16; 22:18, 21, 23; 23:38 **30:1** [a] Num. 1:4, 16; 7:2 **30:2** [a] Lev. 27:2 [b] Matt. 14:9 [c] Job 22:27 **30:8** [a] [Gen. 3:16]

11 and her husband heard *it,* and made no response to her *and* did not overrule her, then
all her vows shall stand, and every agreement
by which she bound herself shall stand. 12 But if
her husband truly made them void on the day
he heard *them,* then whatever proceeded from
her lips concerning her vows or concerning
the agreement binding her, it shall not stand;
her husband has made them void, and the
LORD will release her. 13 Every vow and every
binding oath to afflict her soul, her husband
may confirm it, or her husband may make it
void. 14 Now if her husband makes no response
whatever to her from day to day, then he confirms all her vows or all the agreements that
bind her; he confirms them, because he made
no response to her on the day that he heard
them. 15 But if he does make them void after he
has heard *them,* then he shall bear her guilt."
16 These *are* the statutes which the LORD
commanded Moses, between a man and his
wife, and between a father and his daughter
in her youth in her father's house.

Vengeance on the Midianites

31 And the LORD spoke to Moses, saying:
2 [a]"Take vengeance on the Midianites
for the children of Israel. Afterward you shall
[b]be gathered to your people."
3 So Moses spoke to the people, saying,
"Arm some of yourselves for war, and let
them go against the Midianites to take vengeance for the LORD on [a]Midian. 4 A thousand
from each tribe of all the tribes of Israel you
shall send to the war."
5 So there were recruited from the divisions
of Israel one thousand from *each* tribe, twelve
thousand armed for war. 6 Then Moses sent
them to the war, one thousand from *each*
tribe; he sent them to the war with Phinehas
the son of Eleazar the priest, with the holy
articles and [a]the signal trumpets in his hand.
7 And they warred against the Midianites, just
as the LORD commanded Moses, and [a]they
killed all the [b]males. 8 They killed the kings
of Midian with *the rest of* those who were
killed—[a]Evi, Rekem, [b]Zur, Hur, and Reba,
the five kings of Midian. [c]Balaam the son of
Beor they also killed with the sword.
9 And the children of Israel took the women
of Midian captive, with their little ones, and
took as spoil all their cattle, all their flocks,
and all their goods. 10 They also burned with
fire all the cities where they dwelt, and all
their forts. 11 And [a]they took all the spoil and
all the booty—of man and beast.

Return from the War

12 Then they brought the captives, the
booty, and the spoil to Moses, to Eleazar
the priest, and to the congregation of the
children of Israel, to the camp in the plains
of Moab by the Jordan, *across from* Jericho.
13 And Moses, Eleazar the priest, and all the
leaders of the congregation, went to meet
them outside the camp. 14 But Moses was
angry with the officers of the army, *with* the
captains over thousands and captains over
hundreds, who had come from the battle.
15 And Moses said to them: "Have you kept
[a]all the women alive? 16 Look, [a]these *women*
caused the children of Israel, through the
[b]counsel of Balaam, to trespass against the
LORD in the incident of Peor, and [c]there was a
plague among the congregation of the LORD.
17 Now therefore, [a]kill every male among the
little ones, and kill every woman who has
known a man intimately. 18 But keep alive
[a]for yourselves all the young girls who have
not known a man intimately. 19 And as for
you, [a]remain outside the camp seven days;
whoever has killed any person, and [b]whoever
has touched any slain, purify yourselves and
your captives on the third day and on the
seventh day. 20 Purify every garment, everything made of leather, everything woven of
goats' *hair,* and everything made of wood."
21 Then Eleazar the priest said to the men
of war who had gone to the battle, "This *is*
the ordinance of the law which the LORD
commanded Moses: 22 Only the gold, the
silver, the bronze, the iron, the tin, and the
lead, 23 everything that can endure fire, you
shall put through the fire, and it shall be
clean; and it shall be purified [a]with the water
of purification. But all that cannot endure
fire you shall put through water. 24 [a]And you
shall wash your clothes on the seventh day
and be clean, and afterward you may come
into the camp."

Division of the Plunder

25 Now the LORD spoke to Moses, saying:
26 "Count up the plunder that was taken—of
man and beast—you and Eleazar the priest
and the chief fathers of the congregation;
27 and [a]divide the plunder into two parts,
between those who took part in the war, who
went out to battle, and all the congregation.
28 And levy a tribute for the LORD on the men
of war who went out to battle: [a]one of every
five hundred of the persons, the cattle, the
donkeys, and the sheep; 29 take *it* from their

31:2 [a] Num. 25:17 [b] Num. 27:12, 13 **31:3** [a] Josh. 13:21 **31:6** [a] Num. 10:9 **31:7** [a] Deut. 20:13 [b] Gen. 34:25 **31:8** [a] Josh. 13:21 [b] Num. 25:15 [c] Josh. 13:22 **31:11** [a] Deut. 20:14 **31:15** [a] Deut. 20:14 **31:16** [a] Num. 25:2 [b] Rev. 2:14 [c] Num. 25:9 **31:17** [a] Deut. 7:2; 20:16–18 **31:18** [a] Deut. 21:10–14 **31:19** [a] Num. 5:2 [b] Num. 19:11–22 **31:23** [a] Num. 19:9, 17 **31:24** [a] Lev. 11:25 **31:27** [a] Josh. 22:8 **31:28** [a] Num. 31:30, 47

half, and [a]give *it* to Eleazar the priest as a
heave offering to the LORD. 30 And from the
children of Israel's half you shall take [a]one
of every fifty, drawn from the persons, the
cattle, the donkeys, and the sheep, from all
the livestock, and give them to the Levites
[b]who keep charge of the tabernacle of the
LORD." 31 So Moses and Eleazar the priest did
as the LORD commanded Moses.

32 The booty remaining from the plunder,
which the men of war had taken, was six
hundred and seventy-five thousand sheep,
33 seventy-two thousand cattle, 34 sixty-one
thousand donkeys, 35 and thirty-two thousand persons in all, of women who had not
known a man intimately. 36 And the half,
the portion for those who had gone out
to war, was in number three hundred and
thirty-seven thousand five hundred sheep;
37 and the LORD's tribute of the sheep was
six hundred and seventy-five. 38 The cattle
were thirty-six thousand, of which the LORD's
tribute *was* seventy-two. 39 The donkeys *were*
thirty thousand five hundred, of which the
LORD's tribute *was* sixty-one. 40 The persons
were sixteen thousand, of which the LORD's
tribute *was* thirty-two persons. 41 So Moses
gave the tribute *which was* the LORD's heave
offering to Eleazar the priest, [a]as the LORD
commanded Moses.

42 And from the children of Israel's half,
which Moses separated from the men who
fought— 43 now the half belonging to the
congregation was three hundred and thirty-
seven thousand five hundred sheep, 44 thirty-
six thousand cattle, 45 thirty thousand five
hundred donkeys, 46 and sixteen thousand
persons— 47 and [a]from the children of Israel's half Moses took one of every fifty, drawn
from man and beast, and gave them to the
Levites, who kept charge of the tabernacle of
the LORD, as the LORD commanded Moses.

48 Then the officers who *were* over thousands of the army, the captains of thousands and captains of hundreds, came near
to Moses; 49 and they said to Moses, "Your
servants have taken a count of the men of
war who *are* under our command, and not
a man of us is missing. 50 Therefore we have
brought an offering for the LORD, what every
man found of ornaments of gold: armlets and
bracelets and signet rings and earrings and
necklaces, [a]to make atonement for ourselves
before the LORD." 51 So Moses and Eleazar the
priest received the gold from them, all the
fashioned ornaments. 52 And all the gold of
the offering that they offered to the LORD,
from the captains of thousands and captains
of hundreds, was sixteen thousand seven
hundred and fifty shekels. 53 [a](The men of
war had taken spoil, every man for himself.)
54 And Moses and Eleazar the priest received
the gold from the captains of thousands
and of hundreds, and brought it into the
tabernacle of meeting [a]as a memorial for the
children of Israel before the LORD.

The Tribes Settling East of the Jordan

32 Now the children of Reuben and the
children of Gad had a very great multitude of livestock; and when they saw the
land of [a]Jazer and the land of [b]Gilead, that
indeed the region *was* a place for livestock,
2 the children of Gad and the children of
Reuben came and spoke to Moses, to Eleazar the priest, and to the leaders of the
congregation, saying, 3 "Ataroth, Dibon, Jazer,
[a]Nimrah, [b]Heshbon, Elealeh, [c]Shebam, Nebo,
and [d]Beon, 4 the country [a]which the LORD
defeated before the congregation of Israel, *is*
a land for livestock, and your servants have
livestock." 5 Therefore they said, "If we have
found favor in your sight, let this land be
given to your servants as a possession. Do
not take us over the Jordan."

6 And Moses said to the children of Gad
and to the children of Reuben: "Shall your
brethren go to war while you sit here? 7 Now
why will you [a]discourage the heart of the
children of Israel from going over into the
land which the LORD has given them? 8 Thus
your fathers did [a]when I sent them away from
Kadesh Barnea [b]to see the land. 9 For [a]when

PEACE NOTE

When you're going through hard times and God seems distant, keep "abounding in the work of the Lord, knowing that your labor is not in vain in the Lord" (1 Cor. 15:58).

31:29 [a] Deut. 18:1–5 **31:30** [a] Num. 31:42–47 [b] Num. 3:7, 8, 25, 31, 36; 18:3, 4 **31:41** [a] Num. 5:9, 10; 18:8, 19
31:47 [a] Num. 31:30 **31:50** [a] Ex. 30:12–16 **31:53** [a] Deut. 20:14 **31:54** [a] Ex. 30:16 **32:1** [a] Num. 21:32 [b] Deut. 3:13
32:3 [a] Num. 32:36 [b] Josh. 13:17, 26 [c] Num. 32:38 [d] Num. 32:38 **32:4** [a] Num. 21:24, 34, 35 **32:7** [a] Num. 13:27—14:4
32:8 [a] Num. 13:3, 26 [b] Deut. 1:19–25 **32:9** [a] Deut. 1:24, 28

they went up to the Valley of Eshcol and saw the land, they discouraged the heart of the children of Israel, so that they did not go into the land which the LORD had given them. 10 [a]So the LORD's anger was aroused on that day, and He swore an oath, saying, 11 'Surely none of the men who came up from Egypt, [a]from twenty years old and above, shall see the land of which I swore to Abraham, Isaac, and Jacob, because [b]they have not wholly followed Me, 12 except Caleb the son of Jephunneh, the Kenizzite, and Joshua the son of Nun, [a]for they have wholly followed the LORD.' 13 So the LORD's anger was aroused against Israel, and He made them [a]wander in the wilderness forty years, until [b]all the generation that had done evil in the sight of the LORD was gone. 14 And look! You have risen in your fathers' place, a brood of sinful men, to increase still more the [a]fierce anger of the LORD against Israel. 15 For if you [a]turn away from following Him, He will once again leave them in the wilderness, and you will destroy all these people."

16 Then they came near to him and said: "We will build sheepfolds here for our livestock, and cities for our little ones, 17 but [a]we ourselves will be armed, ready *to go* before the children of Israel until we have brought them to their place; and our little ones will dwell in the fortified cities because of the inhabitants of the land. 18 [a]We will not return to our homes until every one of the children of Israel has received his inheritance. 19 For we will not inherit with them on the other side of the Jordan and beyond, [a]because our inheritance has fallen to us on this eastern side of the Jordan."

20 Then [a]Moses said to them: "If you do this thing, if you arm yourselves before the LORD for the war, 21 and all your armed men cross over the Jordan before the LORD until He has driven out His enemies from before Him, 22 and [a]the land is subdued before the LORD, then afterward [b]you may return and be blameless before the LORD and before Israel; and [c]this land shall be your possession before the LORD. 23 But if you do not do so, then take note, you have sinned against the LORD; and be sure [a]your sin will find you out. 24 [a]Build cities for your little ones and folds for your sheep, and do what has proceeded out of your mouth."

25 And the children of Gad and the children of Reuben spoke to Moses, saying: "Your servants will do as my lord commands. 26 [a]Our little ones, our wives, our flocks, and all our livestock will be there in the cities of Gilead; 27 [a]but your servants will cross over, every man armed for war, before the LORD to battle, just as my lord says."

28 So Moses gave command [a]concerning them to Eleazar the priest, to Joshua the son of Nun, and to the chief fathers of the tribes of the children of Israel. 29 And Moses said to them: "If the children of Gad and the children of Reuben cross over the Jordan with you, every man armed for battle before the LORD, and the land is subdued before you, then you shall give them the land of Gilead as a possession. 30 But if they do not cross over armed with you, they shall have possessions among you in the land of Canaan."

31 Then the children of Gad and the children of Reuben answered, saying: "As the LORD has said to your servants, so we will do. 32 We will cross over armed before the LORD into the land of Canaan, but the possession of our inheritance *shall remain* with us on this side of the Jordan."

33 So [a]Moses gave to the children of Gad, to the children of Reuben, and to half the tribe of Manasseh the son of Joseph, [b]the kingdom of Sihon king of the Amorites and the kingdom of Og king of Bashan, the land with its cities within the borders, the cities of the surrounding country. 34 And the children of Gad built [a]Dibon and Ataroth and [b]Aroer, 35 Atroth and Shophan and [a]Jazer and Jogbehah, 36 [a]Beth Nimrah and Beth Haran, [b]fortified cities, and folds for sheep. 37 And the children of Reuben built [a]Heshbon and Elealeh and Kirjathaim, 38 [a]Nebo and [b]Baal Meon [c](*their* names being changed) and Shibmah; and they gave *other* names to the cities which they built.

39 And the children of [a]Machir the son of Manasseh went to Gilead and took it, and dispossessed the Amorites who *were* in it. 40 So Moses [a]gave Gilead to Machir the son of Manasseh, and he dwelt in it. 41 Also [a]Jair the son of Manasseh went and took its small towns, and called them [b]Havoth Jair.[1] 42 Then Nobah went and took Kenath and its villages, and he called it Nobah, after his own name.

32:10 [a] Deut. 1:34–36 **32:11** [a] Num. 14:28, 29; 26:63–65 [b] Num. 14:24, 30 **32:12** [a] Deut. 1:36 **32:13** [a] Num. 14:33–35 [b] Num. 26:64, 65 **32:14** [a] Deut. 1:34 **32:15** [a] Deut. 30:17, 18 **32:17** [a] Josh. 4:12, 13 **32:18** [a] Josh. 22:1–4 **32:19** [a] Josh. 12:1; 13:8 **32:20** [a] Deut. 3:18 **32:22** [a] Deut. 3:20 [b] Josh. 22:4 [c] Deut. 3:12, 15, 16, 18 **32:23** [a] Is. 59:12 **32:24** [a] Num. 32:16 **32:26** [a] Josh. 1:14 **32:27** [a] Josh. 4:12 **32:28** [a] Josh. 1:13 **32:33** [a] Deut. 3:8–17; 29:8 [b] Num. 21:24, 33, 35 **32:34** [a] Num. 33:45, 46 [b] Deut. 2:36 **32:35** [a] Num. 32:1, 3 **32:36** [a] Num. 32:3 [b] Num. 32:24 **32:37** [a] Num. 21:27 **32:38** [a] Is. 46:1 [b] Ezek. 25:9 [c] Ex. 23:13 **32:39** [a] Gen. 50:23 **32:40** [a] Deut. 3:12, 13, 15 **32:41** [a] Deut. 3:14 [b] Judg. 10:4 [1] Literally *Towns of Jair*

Israel's Journey from Egypt Reviewed

33 These *are* the journeys of the children of Israel, who went out of the land of Egypt by their armies under the [a]hand of Moses and Aaron. 2 Now Moses wrote down the starting points of their journeys at the command of the LORD. And these *are* their journeys according to their starting points:

3 They [a]departed from Rameses in [b]the first month, on the fifteenth day of the first month; on the day after the Passover the children of Israel went out [c]with boldness in the sight of all the Egyptians. 4 For the Egyptians were burying all *their* firstborn, [a]whom the LORD had killed among them. Also [b]on their gods the LORD had executed judgments.

5 [a]Then the children of Israel moved from Rameses and camped at Succoth. 6 They departed from [a]Succoth and camped at Etham, which *is* on the edge of the wilderness. 7 [a]They moved from Etham and turned back to Pi Hahiroth, which *is* east of Baal Zephon; and they camped near Migdol. 8 They departed from before Hahiroth[1] and [a]passed through the midst of the sea into the wilderness, went three days' journey in the Wilderness of Etham, and camped at Marah. 9 They moved from Marah and [a]came to Elim. At Elim *were* twelve springs of water and seventy palm trees; so they camped there.

10 They moved from Elim and camped by the Red Sea. 11 They moved from the Red Sea and camped in the [a]Wilderness of Sin. 12 They journeyed from the Wilderness of Sin and camped at Dophkah. 13 They departed from Dophkah and camped at Alush. 14 They moved from Alush and camped at [a]Rephidim, where there was no water for the people to drink.

15 They departed from Rephidim and camped in the [a]Wilderness of Sinai. 16 They moved from the Wilderness of Sinai and camped [a]at Kibroth Hattaavah. 17 They departed from Kibroth Hattaavah and [a]camped at Hazeroth. 18 They departed from Hazeroth and camped at [a]Rithmah. 19 They departed from Rithmah and camped at Rimmon Perez. 20 They departed from Rimmon Perez and camped at Libnah. 21 They moved from Libnah and camped at Rissah. 22 They journeyed from Rissah and camped at Kehelathah. 23 They went from Kehelathah and camped at Mount Shepher. 24 They moved from Mount Shepher and camped at Haradah. 25 They moved from Haradah and camped at Makheloth. 26 They moved from Makheloth and camped at Tahath. 27 They departed from Tahath and camped at Terah. 28 They moved from Terah and camped at Mithkah. 29 They went from Mithkah and camped at Hashmonah. 30 They departed from Hashmonah and [a]camped at Moseroth. 31 They departed from Moseroth and camped at Bene Jaakan. 32 They moved from [a]Bene Jaakan and [b]camped at Hor Hagidgad. 33 They went from Hor Hagidgad and camped at Jotbathah. 34 They moved from Jotbathah and camped at Abronah. 35 They departed from Abronah [a]and camped at Ezion Geber. 36 They moved from Ezion Geber and camped in the [a]Wilderness of Zin, which *is* Kadesh. 37 They moved from [a]Kadesh and camped at Mount Hor, on the boundary of the land of Edom.

38 Then [a]Aaron the priest went up to Mount Hor at the command of the LORD, and died there in the fortieth year after the children of Israel had come out of the land of Egypt, on the first *day* of the fifth month. 39 Aaron *was* one hundred and twenty-three years old when he died on Mount Hor.

40 Now [a]the king of Arad, the Canaanite, who dwelt in the South in the land of Canaan, heard of the coming of the children of Israel.

41 So they departed from Mount Hor and camped at Zalmonah. 42 They departed from Zalmonah and camped at Punon. 43 They departed from Punon and [a]camped at Oboth. 44 [a]They departed from Oboth and camped at Ije Abarim, at the border of Moab. 45 They departed from Ijim[1] and camped [a]at Dibon Gad. 46 They moved from Dibon Gad and camped at [a]Almon Diblathaim. 47 They moved from Almon Diblathaim [a]and camped in the mountains of Abarim, before Nebo. 48 They departed from the mountains of Abarim and [a]camped in the plains of Moab by the Jordan, *across from* Jericho. 49 They camped by the Jordan, from Beth Jesimoth as far as the [a]Abel Acacia Grove[1] in the plains of Moab.

Instructions for the Conquest of Canaan

50 Now the LORD spoke to Moses in the plains of Moab by the Jordan, *across from* Jericho, saying, 51 "Speak to the children of Israel, and say to them: [a]'When you have

33:1 [a] Ps. 77:20 **33:3** [a] Ex. 12:37 [b] Ex. 12:2; 13:4 [c] Ex. 14:8 **33:4** [a] Ex. 12:29 [b] Is. 19:1 **33:5** [a] Ex. 12:37 **33:6** [a] Ex. 13:20 **33:7** [a] Ex. 14:1, 2, 9 **33:8** [a] Ex. 14:22; 15:22, 23 [1] Many Hebrew manuscripts, Samaritan Pentateuch, Syriac, Targum, and Vulgate read *from Pi Hahiroth* (compare verse 7). **33:9** [a] Ex. 15:27 **33:11** [a] Ex. 16:1 **33:14** [a] Ex. 17:1; 19:2 **33:15** [a] Ex. 16:1; 19:1, 2 **33:16** [a] Num. 11:34 **33:17** [a] Num. 11:35 **33:18** [a] Num. 12:16 **33:30** [a] Deut. 10:6 **33:32** [a] Deut. 10:6 [b] Deut. 10:7 **33:35** [a] Deut. 2:8 **33:36** [a] Num. 20:1; 27:14 **33:37** [a] Num. 20:22, 23; 21:4 **33:38** [a] Num. 20:25, 28 **33:40** [a] Num. 21:1 **33:43** [a] Num. 21:10 **33:44** [a] Num. 21:11 **33:45** [a] Num. 32:34 [1] Same as *Ije Abarim*, verse 44 **33:46** [a] Jer. 48:22 **33:47** [a] Deut. 32:49 **33:48** [a] Num. 22:1; 31:12; 35:1 **33:49** [a] Num. 25:1 [1] Hebrew *Abel Shittim* **33:51** [a] Josh. 3:17

crossed the Jordan into the land of Canaan, 52 [a]then you shall drive out all the inhabitants of the land from before you, destroy all their engraved stones, destroy all their molded images, and demolish all their high places; 53 you shall dispossess *the inhabitants of* the land and dwell in it, for I have given you the land to [a]possess. 54 And [a]you shall divide the land by lot as an inheritance among your families; to the larger you shall give a larger inheritance, and to the smaller you shall give a smaller inheritance; there everyone's *inheritance* shall be whatever falls to him by lot. You shall inherit according to the tribes of your fathers. 55 But if you do not drive out the inhabitants of the land from before you, then it shall be that those whom you let remain *shall be* [a]irritants in your eyes and thorns in your sides, and they shall harass you in the land where you dwell. 56 Moreover it shall be *that* I will do to you as I thought to do to them.' "

The Appointed Boundaries of Canaan

34 Then the LORD spoke to Moses, saying, 2 "Command the children of Israel, and say to them: 'When you come into [a]the land of Canaan, this *is* the land that shall fall to you as an inheritance—the land of Canaan to its boundaries. 3 [a]Your southern border shall be from the Wilderness of Zin along the border of Edom; then your southern border shall extend eastward to the end of [b]the Salt Sea; 4 your border shall turn from the southern side of [a]the Ascent of Akrabbim, continue to Zin, and be on the south of [b]Kadesh Barnea; then it shall go on to [c]Hazar Addar, and continue to Azmon; 5 the border shall turn from Azmon [a]to the Brook of Egypt, and it shall end at the Sea.

6 'As for the [a]western border, you shall have the Great Sea for a border; this shall be your western border.

7 'And this shall be your northern border: From the Great Sea you shall mark out your *border* line to [a]Mount Hor; 8 from Mount Hor you shall mark out *your border* [a]to the entrance of Hamath; then the direction of the border shall be toward [b]Zedad; 9 the border shall proceed to Ziphron, and it shall end at [a]Hazar Enan. This shall be your northern border.

10 'You shall mark out your eastern border from Hazar Enan to Shepham; 11 the border shall go down from Shepham [a]to Riblah on the east side of Ain; the border shall go down and reach to the eastern side of the Sea [b]of Chinnereth; 12 the border shall go down along the Jordan, and it shall end at [a]the Salt Sea. This shall be your land with its surrounding boundaries.' "

13 Then Moses commanded the children of Israel, saying: [a]"This *is* the land which you shall inherit by lot, which the LORD has commanded to give to the nine tribes and to the half-tribe. 14 [a]For the tribe of the children of Reuben according to the house of their fathers, and the tribe of the children of Gad according to the house of their fathers, have received *their inheritance;* and the half-tribe of Manasseh has received its inheritance. 15 The two tribes and the half-tribe have received their inheritance on this side of the Jordan, *across from* Jericho eastward, toward the sunrise."

The Leaders Appointed to Divide the Land

16 And the LORD spoke to Moses, saying, 17 "These *are* the names of the men who shall divide the land among you as an inheritance: [a]Eleazar the priest and Joshua the son of Nun. 18 And you shall take one [a]leader of every tribe to divide the land for the inheritance. 19 These *are* the names of the men: from the tribe of Judah, Caleb the son of Jephunneh; 20 from the tribe of the children of Simeon, Shemuel the son of Ammihud; 21 from the tribe of Benjamin, Elidad the son of Chislon; 22 a leader from the tribe of the children of Dan, Bukki the son of Jogli; 23 from the sons of Joseph: a leader from the tribe of the children of Manasseh, Hanniel the son of Ephod, 24 and a leader from the tribe of the children of Ephraim, Kemuel the son of Shiphtan;

PEACE NOTE

The Israelites inherited the covenant and the land God promised them. By obeying the Lord, you too will receive His promises—and His peace.

NUMBERS 34:2

33:52 [a] Deut. 7:2, 5; 12:3 33:53 [a] Deut. 11:31 33:54 [a] Num. 26:53–56 33:55 [a] Josh. 23:13 34:2 [a] Gen. 17:8 34:3 [a] Josh. 15:1–3 [b] Gen. 14:3 34:4 [a] Josh. 15:3 [b] Num. 13:26; 32:8 [c] Josh. 15:3, 4 34:5 [a] Josh. 15:4, 47 34:6 [a] Ezek. 47:20 34:7 [a] Num. 33:37 34:8 [a] Num. 13:21 [b] Ezek. 47:15 34:9 [a] Ezek. 47:17 34:11 [a] 2 Kin. 23:33 [b] Deut. 3:17 34:12 [a] Num. 34:3 34:13 [a] Josh. 14:1–5 34:14 [a] Num. 32:33 34:17 [a] Josh. 14:1, 2; 19:51 34:18 [a] Num. 1:4, 16

25 a leader from the tribe of the children of
Zebulun, Elizaphan the son of Parnach; 26 a
leader from the tribe of the children of Issachar, Paltiel the son of Azzan; 27 a leader from
the tribe of the children of Asher, Ahihud the
son of Shelomi; 28 and a leader from the tribe
of the children of Naphtali, Pedahel the son
of Ammihud."
29 These *are* the ones the LORD commanded to divide the inheritance among the children of Israel in the land of Canaan.

Cities for the Levites

35 And the LORD spoke to Moses in [a]the
plains of Moab by the Jordan *across
from* Jericho, saying: 2 [a]"Command the children of Israel that they give the Levites cities to dwell in from the inheritance of their
possession, and you shall *also* give the Levites [b]common-land around the cities. 3 They
shall have the cities to dwell in; and their
common-land shall be for their cattle, for
their herds, and for all their animals. 4 The
common-land of the cities which you will give
the Levites *shall extend* from the wall of the
city outward a thousand cubits all around.
5 And you shall measure outside the city on
the east side two thousand cubits, on the
south side two thousand cubits, on the west
side two thousand cubits, and on the north
side two thousand cubits. The city *shall be*
in the middle. This shall belong to them as
common-land for the cities.
6 "Now among the cities which you will give
to the Levites *you shall appoint* [a]six cities of
refuge, to which a manslayer may flee. And
to these you shall add forty-two cities. 7 So all
the cities you will give to the Levites *shall be*
[a]forty-eight; these *you shall give* with their
common-land. 8 And the cities which you
will give *shall be* [a]from the possession of the
children of Israel; [b]from the larger *tribe* you
shall give many, from the smaller you shall
give few. Each shall give some of its cities to
the Levites, in proportion to the inheritance
that each receives."

Cities of Refuge

9 Then the LORD spoke to Moses, saying,
10 "Speak to the children of Israel, and say to
them: [a]'When you cross the Jordan into the
land of Canaan, 11 then [a]you shall appoint
cities to be cities of refuge for you, that the
manslayer who kills any person accidentally may flee there. 12 [a]They shall be cities of
refuge for you from the avenger, that the
manslayer may not die until he stands before
the congregation in judgment. 13 And of the
cities which you give, you shall have [a]six cities
of refuge. 14 [a]You shall appoint three cities on
this side of the Jordan, and three cities you
shall appoint in the land of Canaan, *which* will
be cities of refuge. 15 These six cities shall be
for refuge for the children of Israel, [a]for the
stranger, and for the sojourner among them,
that anyone who kills a person accidentally
may flee there.
16 [a]'But if he strikes him with an iron implement, so that he dies, he *is* a murderer; the
murderer shall surely be put to death. 17 And
if he strikes him with a stone in the hand, by
which one could die, and he does die, he *is* a
murderer; the murderer shall surely be put
to death. 18 Or *if* he strikes him with a wooden
hand weapon, by which one could die, and
he does die, he *is* a murderer; the murderer
shall surely be put to death. 19 [a]The avenger
of blood himself shall put the murderer to
death; when he meets him, he shall put him
to death. 20 [a]If he pushes him out of hatred or,
[b]while lying in wait, hurls something at him
so that he dies, 21 or in enmity he strikes him
with his hand so that he dies, the one who
struck *him* shall surely be put to death. He *is*
a murderer. The avenger of blood shall put
the murderer to death when he meets him.
22 'However, if he pushes him suddenly
[a]without enmity, or throws anything at him
without lying in wait, 23 or uses a stone, by
which a man could die, throwing *it* at him
without seeing *him*, so that he dies, while
he was not his enemy or seeking his harm,
24 then [a]the congregation shall judge between the manslayer and the avenger of
blood according to these judgments. 25 So
the congregation shall deliver the manslayer
from the hand of the avenger of blood, and
the congregation shall return him to the
city of refuge where he had fled, and [a]he
shall remain there until the death of the
high priest [b]who was anointed with the holy
oil. 26 But if the manslayer at any time goes
outside the limits of the city of refuge where
he fled, 27 and the avenger of blood finds him
outside the limits of his city of refuge, and the
avenger of blood kills the manslayer, he shall
not be guilty of blood, 28 because he should
have remained in his city of refuge until the
death of the high priest. But after the death
of the high priest the manslayer may return
to the land of his possession.
29 'And these *things* shall be [a]a statute of

35:1 [a] Num. 33:50 **35:2** [a] Josh. 14:3, 4; 21:2, 3 [b] Lev. 25:32–34 **35:6** [a] Josh. 20:2, 7, 8; 21:3, 13 **35:7** [a] Josh. 21:41
35:8 [a] Josh. 21:3 [b] Num. 26:54; 33:54 **35:10** [a] Josh. 20:1–9 **35:11** [a] Ex. 21:13 **35:12** [a] Deut. 19:6 **35:13** [a] Num. 35:6
35:14 [a] Deut. 4:41 **35:15** [a] Num. 15:16 **35:16** [a] Lev. 24:17 **35:19** [a] Num. 35:21, 24, 27 **35:20** [a] Gen. 4:8 [b] Ex. 21:14
35:22 [a] Ex. 21:13 **35:24** [a] Josh. 20:6 **35:25** [a] Josh. 20:6 [b] Ex. 29:7 **35:29** [a] Num. 27:11

judgment to you throughout your generations in all your dwellings. 30 Whoever kills a
person, the murderer shall be put to death on
the [a]testimony of witnesses; but one witness
is not *sufficient* testimony against a person
for the death *penalty.* 31 Moreover you shall
take no ransom for the life of a murderer who
is guilty of death, but he shall surely be put
to death. 32 And you shall take no ransom for
him who has fled to his city of refuge, that
he may return to dwell in the land before the
death of the priest. 33 So you shall not pollute
the land where you *are;* for blood [a]defiles the
land, and no atonement can be made for the
land, for the blood that is shed on it, except
[b]by the blood of him who shed it. 34 Therefore
[a]do not defile the land which you inhabit, in
the midst of which I dwell; for [b]I the LORD
dwell among the children of Israel.' "

Marriage of Female Heirs

36 Now the chief fathers of the families
of the [a]children of Gilead the son of
Machir, the son of Manasseh, of the families
of the sons of Joseph, came near and [b]spoke
before Moses and before the leaders, the
chief fathers of the children of Israel. 2 And
they said: [a]"The LORD commanded my lord
Moses to give the land as an inheritance by
lot to the children of Israel, and [b]my lord
was commanded by the LORD to give the
inheritance of our brother Zelophehad to his
daughters. 3 Now if they are married to any of
the sons of the *other* tribes of the children of
Israel, then their inheritance will be [a]taken
from the inheritance of our fathers, and it
will be added to the inheritance of the tribe
into which they marry; so it will be taken
from the lot of our inheritance. 4 And when
[a]the Jubilee of the children of Israel comes,
then their inheritance will be added to the inheritance of the tribe into which they marry;
so their inheritance will be taken away from
the inheritance of the tribe of our fathers."

5 Then Moses commanded the children
of Israel according to the word of the LORD,
saying: [a]"What the tribe of the sons of Joseph speaks is right. 6 This *is* what the LORD
commands concerning the daughters of Zelophehad, saying, 'Let them marry whom
they think best, [a]but they may marry only
within the family of their father's tribe.' 7 So
the inheritance of the children of Israel shall
not change hands from tribe to tribe, for every
one of the children of Israel shall [a]keep the
inheritance of the tribe of his fathers. 8 And
[a]every daughter who possesses an inheritance
in any tribe of the children of Israel shall be
the wife of one of the family of her father's
tribe, so that the children of Israel each may
possess the inheritance of his fathers. 9 Thus
no inheritance shall change hands from *one*
tribe to another, but every tribe of the children
of Israel shall keep its own inheritance."

10 Just as the LORD commanded Moses,
so did the daughters of Zelophehad; 11 [a]for
Mahlah, Tirzah, Hoglah, Milcah, and Noah,
the daughters of Zelophehad, were married
to the sons of their father's brothers. 12 They
were married into the families of the children
of Manasseh the son of Joseph, and their
inheritance remained in the tribe of their
father's family.

13 These *are* the commandments and the
judgments which the LORD commanded
the children of Israel by the hand of Moses
[a]in the plains of Moab by the Jordan, *across
from* Jericho.

35:30 [a] Deut. 17:6; 19:15 **35:33** [a] Ps. 106:38 [b] Gen. 9:6 **35:34** [a] Lev. 18:24, 25 [b] Ex. 29:45, 46 **36:1** [a] Num. 26:29 [b] Num. 27:1–11 **36:2** [a] Josh. 17:4 [b] Num. 27:1, 5–7 **36:3** [a] Num. 27:4 **36:4** [a] Lev. 25:10 **36:5** [a] Num. 27:7 **36:6** [a] Num. 36:11, 12 **36:7** [a] 1 Kin. 21:3 **36:8** [a] 1 Chr. 23:22 **36:11** [a] Num. 26:33; 27:1 **36:13** [a] Num. 26:3; 33:50

THE FIFTH BOOK OF MOSES CALLED

DEUTERONOMY

AUTHOR

Numerous external and internal evidences support this book's authorship by Moses. The Old Testament attributes Deuteronomy to Moses (Josh. 1:7; Judg. 3:4; 1 Kin. 2:3; 2 Kin. 14:6; Ezra 3:2; Neh. 1:7; Ps. 103:7; Dan. 9:11; Mal. 4:4), and there is evidence from Joshua and 1 Samuel to indicate that these laws existed in the form of codified written statutes that influenced the Israelites in Canaan. Christ quoted Deuteronomy when He was being tempted (Matt. 4:4, 7, 10) and attributed it to Moses (Matt. 19:7–9; Mark 7:10; Luke 20:28; John 5:45–47), as do the more than eighty citations of Deuteronomy in the New Testament. Internally, the book includes about forty claims to Moses as the author (Deut. 1:1–5; 4:44–46; 29:1; 31:9, 24–26). The political and geographic details of Deuteronomy indicate a firsthand knowledge of the events.

TIME

c. 1405 BC

KEY VERSE

Deuteronomy 30:19–20

THEME

Deuteronomy is a series of addresses that Moses gives to the nation of Israel just before the people enter the Promised Land. In many ways it can be seen as the coach's speech given to a team just before it takes the field. The book reviews and reiterates what has been taught in the previous books of Moses in the same way that a coach's last instructions contain a review of the basic game plan and what has been covered in practice. The purpose of that speech is to focus on what to do and then motivate the people to carry it out. For the Israelites much of the previous instruction was somewhat hypothetical. Many of the laws assumed the occupation of the land. Now, as they stand looking over the Jordan River, they're within reach of moving from the hypothetical to the real and practical. God has renewed His marvelous covenant with them. Now is the time to live up to its requirements.

In this final book of the Law, we learn the guardrails to living in the peace of God. Indeed, the hard lesson is that the path to peace is *not* following one's heart. Deuteronomy 29:19 warns of the futility of saying, "I shall have peace, even though I follow the dictates of my heart"—Moses noted, "as though the drunkard could be included with the sober." Jesus, the Prince of Peace, alluded to or quoted from Deuteronomy seventeen times, and seventeen of the twenty-seven New Testament books quote Deuteronomy. In fact, when Jesus was tempted by the devil, He was at His strongest spiritually by quoting from the words of this book. The closing description of Moses, who spoke to God "face to face" (Num. 12:8; Deut. 34:10), is a messianic reminder of the promised "prophet like Moses" (34:10; see 18:15–22) ultimately fulfilled by Jesus Christ.

The Previous Command to Enter Canaan

1 These *are* the words which Moses spoke to all Israel [a]on this side of the Jordan in the wilderness, in the plain[1] opposite Suph,[2] between Paran, Tophel, Laban, Hazeroth, and Dizahab. 2 *It is* eleven days' *journey* from Horeb by way of Mount Seir [a]to Kadesh Barnea. 3 Now it came to pass [a]in the fortieth year, in the eleventh month, on the first *day* of the month, *that* Moses spoke to the children of Israel according to all that the LORD had given him as commandments to them, 4 [a]after he had killed Sihon king of the Amorites, who dwelt in Heshbon, and Og king of Bashan, who dwelt at Ashtaroth [b]in[1] Edrei.

5 On this side of the Jordan in the land of Moab, Moses began to explain this law, saying, 6 "The LORD our God spoke to us [a]in Horeb, saying: 'You have dwelt long [b]enough at this mountain. 7 Turn and take your journey, and go to the mountains of the Amorites, to all the neighboring *places* in the plain,[1] in the mountains and in the lowland, in the South and on the seacoast, to the land of the Canaanites and to Lebanon, as far as the great river, the River Euphrates. 8 See, I have set the land before you; go in and possess the land which the LORD swore to your fathers—to [a]Abraham, Isaac, and Jacob—to give to them and their descendants after them.'

Tribal Leaders Appointed

9 "And [a]I spoke to you at that time, saying: 'I alone am not able to bear you. 10 The LORD your God has multiplied you, [a]and here you *are* today, as the stars of heaven in multitude. 11 [a]May the LORD God of your fathers make you a thousand times more numerous than you are, and bless you [b]as He has promised you! 12 [a]How can I alone bear your problems and your burdens and your complaints? 13 Choose wise, understanding, and knowledgeable men from among your tribes, and I will make them heads over you.' 14 And you answered me and said, 'The thing which you have told *us* to do *is* good.' 15 So I took [a]the heads of your tribes, wise and knowledgeable men, and made them heads over you, leaders of thousands, leaders of hundreds, leaders of fifties, leaders of tens, and officers for your tribes.

16 "Then I commanded your judges at that time, saying, 'Hear *the cases* between your brethren, and [a]judge righteously between a man and his [b]brother or the stranger who is with him. 17 [a]You shall not show partiality in judgment; you shall hear the small as well as the great; you shall not be afraid in any man's presence, for [b]the judgment *is* God's. The case that is too hard for you, [c]bring to me, and I will hear it.' 18 And I commanded you at that time all the things which you should do.

PEACE NOTE

The basis of our peace, happiness, and gratitude is the fact of our redemption. The strength of our peace and happiness in Christ is based on God's promises.

DEUTERONOMY 1:11

Israel's Refusal to Enter the Land

19 "So we departed from Horeb, [a]and went through all that great and terrible wilderness which you saw on the way to the mountains of the Amorites, as the LORD our God had commanded us. Then [b]we came to Kadesh Barnea. 20 And I said to you, 'You have come to the mountains of the Amorites, which the LORD our God is giving us. 21 Look, the LORD your God has set the land before you; go up *and* possess *it,* as the LORD God of your fathers has spoken to you; [a]do not fear or be discouraged.'

22 "And every one of you came near to me and said, 'Let us send men before us, and let them search out the land for us, and bring back word to us of the way by which we should go up, and of the cities into which we shall come.'

23 "The plan pleased me well; so [a]I took twelve of your men, one man from *each* tribe. 24 [a]And they departed and went up into the mountains, and came to the Valley of Eshcol, and spied it out. 25 They also took *some* of the fruit of the land in their hands and brought *it* down to us; and they brought back word to us, saying, '*It is* a [a]good land which the LORD our God is giving us.'

1:1 [a] Deut. 4:44–46 [1] Hebrew *arabah* [2] One manuscript of the Septuagint, also Targum and Vulgate, read *Red Sea.* **1:2** [a] Num. 13:26; 32:8 **1:3** [a] Num. 33:38 **1:4** [a] Num. 21:23, 24, 33–35 [b] Josh. 13:12 [1] Septuagint, Syriac, and Vulgate read *and* (compare Joshua 12:4). **1:6** [a] Ex. 3:1, 12 [b] Ex. 19:1, 2 **1:7** [1] Hebrew *arabah* **1:8** [a] Gen. 12:7; 15:5; 22:17; 26:3; 28:13 **1:9** [a] Ex. 18:18, 24 **1:10** [a] Gen. 15:5; 22:17 **1:11** [a] 2 Sam. 24:3 [b] Gen. 15:5 **1:12** [a] 1 Kin. 3:8, 9 **1:15** [a] Ex. 18:25 **1:16** [a] Deut. 16:18 [b] Lev. 24:22 **1:17** [a] Prov. 24:23–26 [b] 2 Chr. 19:6 [c] Ex. 18:22, 26 **1:19** [a] Deut. 2:7; 8:15; 32:10 [b] Num. 13:26 **1:21** [a] Josh. 1:6, 9 **1:23** [a] Num. 13:2, 3 **1:24** [a] Num. 13:21–25 **1:25** [a] Num. 13:27

26[a]"Nevertheless you would not go up, but rebelled against the command of the LORD your God; 27 and you [a]complained in your tents, and said, 'Because the LORD [b]hates us, He has brought us out of the land of Egypt to deliver us into the hand of the Amorites, to destroy us. 28 Where can we go up? Our brethren have discouraged our hearts, saying, [a]"The people *are* greater and taller than we; the cities *are* great and fortified up to heaven; moreover we have seen the sons of the [b]Anakim there." '

29"Then I said to you, 'Do not be terrified, [a]or afraid of them. 30[a]The LORD your God, who goes before you, He will fight for you, according to all He did for you in Egypt before your eyes, 31 and in the wilderness where you saw how the LORD your God carried you, as a [a]man carries his son, in all the way that you went until you came to this place.' 32 Yet, for all that, [a]you did not believe the LORD your God, 33[a]who went in the way before you [b]to search out a place for you to pitch your tents, to show you the way you should go, in the fire by night and in the cloud by day.

The Penalty for Israel's Rebellion

34"And the LORD heard the sound of your words, and was angry, [a]and took an oath, saying, 35[a]'Surely not one of these men of this evil generation shall see that good land of which I swore to give to your fathers, 36[a]except Caleb the son of Jephunneh; he shall see it, and to him and his children I am giving the land on which he walked, because [b]he wholly followed the LORD.' 37[a]The LORD was also angry with me for your sakes, saying, 'Even you shall not go in there. 38[a]Joshua the son of Nun, [b]who stands before you, he shall go in there. [c]Encourage him, for he shall cause Israel to inherit it.

39[a]'Moreover your little ones and your children, who [b]you say will be victims, who today [c]have no knowledge of good and evil, they shall go in there; to them I will give it, and they shall possess it. 40[a]But *as for* you, turn and take your journey into the wilderness by the Way of the Red Sea.'

41"Then you answered and said to me, [a]'We have sinned against the LORD; we will go up and fight, just as the LORD our God commanded us.' And when everyone of you had girded on his weapons of war, you were ready to go up into the mountain.

42"And the LORD said to me, 'Tell them, [a]"Do not go up nor fight, for I *am* not among you; lest you be defeated before your enemies." ' 43 So I spoke to you; yet you would not listen, but [a]rebelled against the command of the LORD, and [b]presumptuously went up into the mountain. 44 And the Amorites who dwelt in that mountain came out against you and chased you [a]as bees do, and drove you back from Seir to Hormah. 45 Then you returned and wept before the LORD, but the LORD would not listen to your voice nor give ear to you.

46[a]"So you remained in Kadesh many days, according to the days that you spent *there.*

The Desert Years

2 "Then we turned and [a]journeyed into the wilderness of the Way of the Red Sea, [b]as the LORD spoke to me, and we skirted Mount Seir for many days.

2"And the LORD spoke to me, saying: 3'You have skirted this mountain [a]long enough; turn northward. 4 And command the people, saying, [a]"You *are about to* pass through the territory of [b]your brethren, the descendants of Esau, who live in Seir; and they will be afraid of you. Therefore watch yourselves carefully. 5 Do not meddle with them, for I will not give you *any* of their land, no, not so much as one footstep, [a]because I have given Mount Seir to Esau *as* a possession. 6 You shall buy food from them with money, that you may eat; and you shall also buy water from them with money, that you may drink.

7"For the LORD your God has blessed you in all the work of your hand. He knows your trudging through this great wilderness. [a]These forty years the LORD your God *has been* with you; you have lacked nothing." '

8"And when we passed beyond our brethren, the descendants of Esau who dwell in Seir, away from the road of the plain, away from [a]Elath and Ezion Geber, we [b]turned and passed by way of the Wilderness of Moab. 9 Then the LORD said to me, 'Do not harass Moab, nor contend with them in battle, for I will not give you *any* of their land *as* a possession, because I have given [a]Ar to [b]the descendants of Lot *as* a possession.' "

10[a](The Emim had dwelt there in times past, a people as great and numerous and tall as [b]the Anakim. 11 They were also regarded as giants,[1] like the Anakim, but the Moabites

1:26 [a] Num. 14:1–4 **1:27** [a] Ps. 106:25 [b] Deut. 9:28 **1:28** [a] Deut. 9:1, 2 [b] Num. 13:28 **1:29** [a] Num. 14:9 **1:30** [a] Ex. 14:14 **1:31** [a] Is. 46:3, 4; 63:9 **1:32** [a] Jude 5 **1:33** [a] Ex. 13:21 [b] Num. 10:33 **1:34** [a] Deut. 2:14, 15 **1:35** [a] Num. 14:22, 23 **1:36** [a] [Josh. 14:9] [b] Num. 32:11, 12 **1:37** [a] Deut. 3:26; 4:21; 34:4 **1:38** [a] Num. 14:30 [b] 1 Sam. 16:22 [c] Deut. 31:7, 23 **1:39** [a] Num. 14:31 [b] Num. 14:3 [c] Is. 7:15, 16 **1:40** [a] Num. 14:25 **1:41** [a] Num. 14:40 **1:42** [a] Num. 14:41–43 **1:43** [a] Num. 14:44 [b] Deut. 17:12, 13 **1:44** [a] Ps. 118:12 **1:46** [a] Deut. 2:7, 14 **2:1** [a] Deut. 1:40 [b] Num. 14:25 **2:3** [a] Deut. 2:7, 14 **2:4** [a] Num. 20:14–21 [b] Deut. 23:7 **2:5** [a] Gen. 36:8 **2:7** [a] Deut. 8:2–4 **2:8** [a] Judg. 11:18 [b] Num. 21:4 **2:9** [a] Deut. 2:18, 29 [b] Gen. 19:36–38 **2:10** [a] Gen. 14:5 [b] Deut. 9:2 **2:11** [1] Hebrew *rephaim*

call them Emim. 12[a]The Horites formerly dwelt in Seir, but the descendants of Esau dispossessed them and destroyed them from before them, and dwelt in their place, just as Israel did to the land of their possession which the LORD gave them.)

13" 'Now rise and cross over [a]the Valley of the Zered.' So we crossed over the Valley of the Zered. 14And the time we took to come [a]from Kadesh Barnea until we crossed over the Valley of the Zered *was* thirty-eight years, [b]until all the generation of the men of war was consumed from the midst of the camp, [c]just as the LORD had sworn to them. 15For indeed the hand of the LORD was against them, to destroy them from the midst of the camp until they were consumed.

16"So it was, when all the men of war had finally perished from among the people, 17that the LORD spoke to me, saying: 18'This day you are to cross over at Ar, the boundary of Moab. 19And *when* you come near the people of Ammon, do not harass them or meddle with them, for I will not give you *any* of the land of the people of Ammon *as* a possession, because I have given it to [a]the descendants of Lot *as* a possession.' "

20(That was also regarded as a land of giants;[1] giants formerly dwelt there. But the Ammonites call them [a]Zamzummim, 21[a]a people as great and numerous and tall as the Anakim. But the LORD destroyed them before them, and they dispossessed them and dwelt in their place, 22just as He had done for the descendants of Esau, [a]who dwelt in Seir, when He destroyed [b]the Horites from before them. They dispossessed them and dwelt in their place, even to this day. 23And [a]the Avim, who dwelt in villages as far as Gaza—[b]the Caphtorim, who came from Caphtor, destroyed them and dwelt in their place.)

24" 'Rise, take your journey, and [a]cross over the River Arnon. Look, I have given into your hand [b]Sihon the Amorite, king of Heshbon, and his land. Begin to possess *it,* and engage him in battle. 25[a]This day I will begin to put the dread and fear of you upon the nations under the whole heaven, who shall hear the report of you, and shall [b]tremble and be in anguish because of you.'

King Sihon Defeated

26"And I [a]sent messengers from the Wilderness of Kedemoth to Sihon king of Heshbon, [b]with words of peace, saying, 27[a]'Let me pass through your land; I will keep strictly to the road, and I will turn neither to the right nor to the left. 28You shall sell me food for money, that I may eat, and give me water for money, that I may drink; [a]only let me pass through on foot, 29[a]just as the descendants of Esau who dwell in Seir and the Moabites who dwell in Ar did for me, until I cross the Jordan to the land which the LORD our God is giving us.'

30[a]"But Sihon king of Heshbon would not let us pass through, for [b]the LORD your God [c]hardened his spirit and made his heart obstinate, that He might deliver him into your hand, as *it is* this day.

31"And the LORD said to me, 'See, I have begun to [a]give Sihon and his land over to you. Begin to possess *it,* that you may inherit his land.' 32[a]Then Sihon and all his people came out against us to fight at Jahaz. 33And [a]the LORD our God delivered him over to us; so [b]we defeated him, his sons, and all his people. 34We took all his cities at that time, and we [a]utterly destroyed the men, women, and little ones of every city; we left none remaining. 35We took only the livestock as plunder for ourselves, with the spoil of the cities which we took. 36[a]From Aroer, which *is* on the bank of the River Arnon, and *from* [b]the city that *is* in the ravine, as far as Gilead, there was not one city too strong for us; [c]the LORD our God delivered all to us. 37Only you did not go near the land of the people of Ammon—anywhere along the River [a]Jabbok, or to the cities of the mountains, or [b]wherever the LORD our God had forbidden us.

King Og Defeated

3 "Then we turned and went up the road to Bashan; and [a]Og king of Bashan came out against us, he and all his people, to battle [b]at Edrei. 2And the LORD said to me, 'Do not fear him, for I have delivered him and all his people and his land into your hand; you shall do to him as you did to [a]Sihon king of the Amorites, who dwelt at Heshbon.'

3"So the LORD our God also delivered into our hands Og king of Bashan, with all his people, and we attacked him until he had no survivors remaining. 4And we took all his cities at that time; there was not a city which we did not take from them: sixty cities, [a]all the region of Argob, the kingdom of Og in Bashan. 5All these cities *were* fortified with high walls, gates, and bars, besides a great

2:12 [a] Deut. 2:22 **2:13** [a] Num. 21:12 **2:14** [a] Num. 13:26 [b] Deut. 1:34, 35 [c] Num. 14:35 **2:19** [a] Gen. 19:38 **2:20** [a] Gen. 14:5 [1] Hebrew *rephaim* **2:21** [a] Deut. 2:10 **2:22** [a] Gen. 36:8 [b] Gen. 14:6; 36:20–30 **2:23** [a] Josh. 13:3 [b] Gen. 10:14 **2:24** [a] Judg. 11:18 [b] Deut. 1:4 **2:25** [a] Ex. 23:27 [b] Ex. 15:14–16 **2:26** [a] Num. 21:21–32 [b] Deut. 20:10 **2:27** [a] Judg. 11:19 **2:28** [a] Num. 20:19 **2:29** [a] Deut. 23:3, 4 **2:30** [a] Num. 21:23 [b] Josh. 11:20 [c] Ex. 4:21 **2:31** [a] Deut. 1:3, 8 **2:32** [a] Num. 21:23 **2:33** [a] Deut. 7:2 [b] Num. 21:24 **2:34** [a] Lev. 27:28 **2:36** [a] Deut. 3:12; 4:48 [b] Josh. 13:9, 16 [c] Ps. 44:3 **2:37** [a] Gen. 32:22 [b] Deut. 2:5, 9, 19 **3:1** [a] Num. 21:33–35 [b] Deut. 1:4 **3:2** [a] Num. 21:34 **3:4** [a] Deut. 3:13, 14

many rural towns. 6 And we utterly destroyed them, as we did to Sihon king [a]of Heshbon, utterly destroying the men, women, and children of every city. 7 But all the livestock and the spoil of the cities we took as booty for ourselves.

8 "And at that time we took the [a]land from the hand of the two kings of the Amorites who *were* on this side of the Jordan, from the River Arnon to Mount [b]Hermon 9 (the Sidonians call [a]Hermon Sirion, and the Amorites call it Senir), 10 [a]all the cities of the plain, all Gilead, and [b]all Bashan, as far as Salcah and Edrei, cities of the kingdom of Og in Bashan.

11 [a]"For only Og king of Bashan remained of the remnant of [b]the giants.[1] Indeed his bedstead *was* an iron bedstead. (*Is* it not in [c]Rabbah of the people of Ammon?) Nine cubits *is* its length and four cubits its width, according to the standard cubit.

The Land East of the Jordan Divided

12 "And this [a]land, *which* we possessed at that time, [b]from Aroer, which *is* by the River Arnon, and half the mountains of Gilead and [c]its cities, I gave to the Reubenites and the Gadites. 13 [a]The rest of Gilead, and all Bashan, the kingdom of Og, I gave to half the tribe of Manasseh. (All the region of Argob, with all Bashan, was called the land of the giants.[1] 14 [a]Jair the son of Manasseh took all the region of Argob, [b]as far as the border of the Geshurites and the Maachathites, and [c]called Bashan after his own name, Havoth Jair,[1] to this day.)

15 "Also I gave [a]Gilead to Machir. 16 And to the Reubenites [a]and the Gadites I gave from Gilead as far as the River Arnon, the middle of the river as *the* border, as far as the River Jabbok, [b]the border of the people of Ammon; 17 the plain also, with the Jordan as *the* border, from Chinnereth [a]as far as the east side of the Sea of the Arabah [b](the Salt Sea), below the slopes of Pisgah.

18 "Then I commanded you at that time, saying: 'The LORD your God has given you this land to possess. [a]All you men of valor shall cross over armed before your brethren, the children of Israel. 19 But your wives, your little ones, and your livestock (I know that you have much livestock) shall stay in your cities which I have given you, 20 until the LORD has given [a]rest to your brethren as to you, and they also possess the land which the LORD your God is giving them beyond the Jordan. Then each of you may [b]return to his possession which I have given you.'

21 "And [a]I commanded Joshua at that time, saying, 'Your eyes have seen all that the LORD your God has done to these two kings; so will the LORD do to all the kingdoms through which you pass. 22 You must not fear them, for [a]the LORD your God Himself fights for you.'

Moses Forbidden to Enter the Land

23 "Then [a]I pleaded with the LORD at that time, saying: 24 'O Lord GOD, You have begun to show Your servant [a]Your greatness and Your mighty hand, for [b]what god *is there* in heaven or on earth who can do *anything* like Your works and Your mighty *deeds?* 25 I pray, let me cross over and see [a]the good land beyond the Jordan, those pleasant mountains, and Lebanon.'

26 "But the LORD [a]was angry with me on your account, and would not listen to me. So the LORD said to me: 'Enough of that! Speak no more to Me of this matter. 27 [a]Go up to the top of Pisgah, and lift your eyes toward the west, the north, the south, and the east; behold *it* with your eyes, for you shall not cross over this Jordan. 28 But [a]command Joshua, and encourage him and strengthen him; for he shall go over before this people, and he shall cause them to inherit the land which you will see.'

29 "So we stayed in [a]the valley opposite Beth Peor.

Moses Commands Obedience

4 "Now, O Israel, listen to [a]the statutes and the judgments which I teach you to observe, that you may live, and go in and possess the land which the LORD God of your fathers is giving you. 2 [a]You shall not add to the word which I command you, nor take from it, that you may keep the commandments of the LORD your God which I command you. 3 Your eyes have seen what the LORD did at [a]Baal Peor; for the LORD your God has destroyed from among you all the men who followed Baal of Peor. 4 But you who held fast to the LORD your God *are* alive today, every one of you.

5 "Surely I have taught you statutes and judgments, just as the LORD my God commanded me, that you should act according *to them* in the land which you go to possess.

3:6 [a] Deut. 2:24, 34, 35 **3:8** [a] Josh. 12:6; 13:8–12 [b] 1 Chr. 5:23 **3:9** [a] 1 Chr. 5:23 **3:10** [a] Deut. 4:49 [b] Josh. 12:5; 13:11 **3:11** [a] Amos 2:9 [b] Deut. 2:11, 20 [c] Jer. 49:2 [1] Hebrew *rephaim* **3:12** [a] Num. 32:33 [b] Deut. 2:36 [c] Num. 34:14 **3:13** [a] Josh. 13:29–31; 17:1 [1] Hebrew *rephaim* **3:14** [a] 1 Chr. 2:22 [b] Josh. 13:13 [c] Num. 32:41 [1] Literally *Towns of Jair* **3:15** [a] Num. 32:39, 40 **3:16** [a] 2 Sam. 24:5 [b] Num. 21:24 **3:17** [a] Num. 34:11, 12 [b] Gen. 14:3 **3:18** [a] Num. 32:20 **3:20** [a] Deut. 12:9, 10 [b] Josh. 22:4 **3:21** [a] [Num. 27:22, 23] **3:22** [a] Ex. 14:14 **3:23** [a] [2 Cor. 12:8, 9] **3:24** [a] Deut. 5:24; 11:2 [b] 2 Sam. 7:22 **3:25** [a] Deut. 4:22 **3:26** [a] Num. 20:12; 27:14 **3:27** [a] Num. 23:14; 27:12 **3:28** [a] Num. 27:18, 23 **3:29** [a] Deut. 4:46; 34:6 **4:1** [a] [Rom. 10:5] **4:2** [a] Prov. 30:6 **4:3** [a] Num. 25:1–9

A LIVING WITNESS TO PEACE

Now, O Israel, listen to the statutes and the judgments which I teach you to observe, that you may live.

DEUTERONOMY 4:1

The way to peace is through the Word of God. God's Word is complete. God's Word is perfect. God's Word is the source of ultimate truth. We live in a time of confusion, just like Israel, and we live among so many competing voices. We must listen to the voice of truth to find peace. For Israel, the danger was similar because the Gentiles would pressure God's people to adopt their gods and pagan ways. But God's people were to model for their neighbors what true faith and righteousness were and how they adhered to God's law. Moses would have said, *Your lives as faithful Israelites should make pagans question their lack of belief in the Lord. Therefore heed the statutes and the judgments that I teach you so that you may live.*

True believers cause others to reflect on their own beliefs. How can you use the Word to seek and obey God's ultimate truth? How can you use truth to sort through the competing voices in society so you follow just the voice of the Lord? In surrender and obedience to the Lord you can find peace.

6 Therefore be careful to observe *them;* for this *is* [a]your wisdom and your understanding in the sight of the peoples who will hear all these statutes, and say, 'Surely this great nation *is* a wise and understanding people.'

7 "For [a]what great nation *is there* that has [b]God *so* near to it, as the LORD our God *is* to us, for whatever *reason* we may call upon Him? 8 And what great nation *is there* that has *such* statutes and righteous judgments as are in all this law which I set before you this day? 9 Only take heed to yourself, and diligently [a]keep yourself, lest you [b]forget the things your eyes have seen, and lest they depart from your heart all the days of your life. And [c]teach them to your children and your grandchildren, 10 *especially concerning* [a]the day you stood before the LORD your God in Horeb, when the LORD said to me, 'Gather the people to Me, and I will let them hear My words, that they may learn to fear Me all the days they live on the earth, and *that* they may teach their children.'

11 "Then you came near and stood at the foot of the mountain, and the mountain burned with fire to the midst of heaven, with darkness, cloud, and thick darkness. 12 [a]And the LORD spoke to you out of the midst of the fire. You heard the sound of the words, but saw no form; [b]*you* only *heard* a voice. 13 [a]So He declared to you His covenant which He commanded you to perform, [b]the Ten Commandments; and [c]He wrote them on two tablets of stone. 14 And [a]the LORD commanded me at that time to teach you statutes and judgments, that you might observe them in the land which you cross over to possess.

Beware of Idolatry

15 [a]"Take careful heed to yourselves, for you saw no [b]form when the LORD spoke to you at Horeb out of the midst of the fire, 16 lest you [a]act corruptly and [b]make for yourselves a carved image in the form of any figure: [c]the likeness of male or female, 17 the likeness of any animal that *is* on the earth or the likeness of any winged bird that flies in the air, 18 the likeness of anything that creeps on the ground or the likeness of any fish that *is* in the water beneath the earth. 19 And *take heed,* lest you [a]lift your eyes to heaven, and *when* you see the sun, the moon, and the stars, [b]all the host of heaven, you feel driven to [c]worship them and serve them, which the LORD your God has given to all the peoples under the whole heaven as a heritage. 20 But the LORD has taken you and [a]brought you out of the iron furnace, out of Egypt, to be [b]His people, an inheritance, as you are this day. 21 Furthermore [a]the LORD was angry with me for your sakes, and swore that [b]I would not cross over the Jordan, and that I would not

4:6 [a] [2 Tim. 3:15] **4:7** [a] [2 Sam. 7:23] [b] [Is. 55:6] **4:9** [a] Prov. 4:23 [b] Deut. 29:2–8 [c] Gen. 18:19 **4:10** [a] Ex. 19:9, 16, 17 **4:12** [a] Deut. 5:4, 22 [b] 1 Kin. 19:11–18 **4:13** [a] Deut. 9:9, 11 [b] Ex. 34:28 [c] Ex. 24:12 **4:14** [a] Ex. 21:1 **4:15** [a] Josh. 23:11 [b] Is. 40:18 **4:16** [a] Deut. 9:12; 31:29 [b] Ex. 20:4, 5 [c] Rom. 1:23 **4:19** [a] Deut. 17:3 [b] 2 Kin. 21:3 [c] [Rom. 1:25] **4:20** [a] Jer. 11:4 [b] Deut. 7:6; 27:9 **4:21** [a] Num. 20:12 [b] Num. 27:13, 14

enter the good land which the LORD your God is giving you as an inheritance. 22 But [a]I must die in this land, [b]I must not cross over the Jordan; but you shall cross over and possess [c]that good land. 23 Take heed to yourselves, lest you forget the covenant of the LORD your God which He made with you, [a]and make for yourselves a carved image in the form of anything which the LORD your God has forbidden you. 24 For [a]the LORD your God *is* a consuming fire, [b]a jealous God.

25 "When you beget children and grandchildren and have grown old in the land, and act corruptly and make a carved image in the form of anything, and [a]do evil in the sight of the LORD your God to provoke Him to anger, 26 [a]I call heaven and earth to witness against you this day, that you will soon utterly perish from the land which you cross over the Jordan to possess; you will not prolong *your* days in it, but will be utterly destroyed. 27 And the LORD [a]will scatter you among the peoples, and you will be left few in number among the nations where the LORD will drive you. 28 And [a]there you will serve gods, the work of men's hands, wood and stone, [b]which neither see nor hear nor eat nor smell. 29 [a]But from there you will seek the LORD your God, and you will find *Him* if you seek Him with all your heart and with all your soul. 30 When you are in distress, and all these things come upon you in the [a]latter days, when you [b]turn to the LORD your God and obey His voice 31 (for the LORD your God *is* a merciful God), He will not forsake you nor [a]destroy you, nor forget the covenant of your fathers which He swore to them.

32 "For [a]ask now concerning the days that are past, which were before you, since the day that God created man on the earth, and *ask* [b]from one end of heaven to the other, whether *any* great *thing* like this has happened, or *anything* like it has been heard. 33 [a]Did *any* people *ever* hear the voice of God speaking out of the midst of the fire, as you have heard, and live? 34 Or did God *ever* try to go *and* take for Himself a nation from the midst of *another* nation, [a]by trials, [b]by signs, by wonders, by war, [c]by a mighty hand and [d]an outstretched arm, [e]and by great terrors, according to all that the LORD your God did for you in Egypt before your eyes? 35 To you it was shown, that you might know that the LORD Himself *is* God; [a]*there is* none other besides Him. 36 [a]Out of heaven He let you hear His voice, that He might instruct you; on earth He showed you His great fire, and you heard His words out of the midst of the fire. 37 And because [a]He loved your fathers, therefore He chose their descendants after them; and [b]He brought you out of Egypt with His Presence, with His mighty power, 38 [a]driving out from before you nations greater and mightier than you, to bring you in, to give you their land *as* an inheritance, as *it is* this day. 39 Therefore know this day, and consider *it* in your heart, that [a]the LORD Himself *is* God in heaven above and on the earth beneath; *there is* no other. 40 [a]You shall therefore keep His statutes and His commandments which I command you today, that it may go well with you and with your children after you, and that you may prolong *your* days in the land which the LORD your God is giving you for all time."

Cities of Refuge East of the Jordan

41 Then Moses [a]set apart three cities on this side of the Jordan, toward the rising of the sun, 42 [a]that the manslayer might flee there, who kills his neighbor unintentionally, without having hated him in time past, and that by fleeing to one of these cities he might live: 43 [a]Bezer in the wilderness on the plateau for the Reubenites, Ramoth in Gilead for the Gadites, and Golan in Bashan for the Manassites.

Introduction to God's Law

44 Now this *is* the law which Moses set before the children of Israel. 45 These *are* the testimonies, the statutes, and the judgments which Moses spoke to the children of Israel after they came out of Egypt, 46 on this side of the Jordan, [a]in the valley opposite Beth Peor, in the land of Sihon king of the Amorites, who dwelt at Heshbon, whom Moses and the children of Israel [b]defeated after they came out of Egypt. 47 And they took possession of his land and the land [a]of Og king of Bashan, two kings of the Amorites, who *were* on this side of the Jordan, toward the rising of the sun, 48 [a]from Aroer, which *is* on the bank of the River Arnon, even to Mount Sion[1] (that is, [b]Hermon), 49 and all the plain on the east side of the Jordan as far as the Sea of the Arabah, below the [a]slopes of Pisgah.

4:22 [a] 2 Pet. 1:13–15 [b] Deut. 3:27 [c] Deut. 3:25 **4:23** [a] Deut. 4:16 **4:24** [a] Deut. 9:3 [b] Ex. 20:5; 34:14 **4:25** [a] 2 Kin. 17:17 **4:26** [a] Deut. 30:18, 19 **4:27** [a] Deut. 28:62 **4:28** [a] Jer. 16:13 [b] Ps. 115:4–7; 135:15–17 **4:29** [a] [2 Chr. 15:4] **4:30** [a] Hos. 3:5 [b] Joel 2:12 **4:31** [a] Jer. 30:11 **4:32** [a] Job 8:8 [b] Matt. 24:31 **4:33** [a] Deut. 5:24–26 **4:34** [a] Deut. 7:19 [b] Ex. 7:3 [c] Ex. 13:3 [d] Ex. 6:6 [e] Deut. 26:8 **4:35** [a] Mark 12:32 **4:36** [a] Heb. 12:19, 25 **4:37** [a] Deut. 7:7, 8; 10:15; 33:3 [b] Ex. 13:3, 9, 14 **4:38** [a] Deut. 7:1 **4:39** [a] Josh. 2:11 **4:40** [a] Lev. 22:31 **4:41** [a] Num. 35:6 **4:42** [a] Deut. 19:4 **4:43** [a] Josh. 20:8 **4:46** [a] Deut. 3:29 [b] Num. 21:24 **4:47** [a] Num. 21:33–35 **4:48** [a] Deut. 2:36; 3:12 [b] Deut. 3:9 [1] Syriac reads *Sirion* (compare 3:9). **4:49** [a] Deut. 3:17

The Ten Commandments Reviewed

5 And Moses called all Israel, and said to
them: "Hear, O Israel, the statutes and
judgments which I speak in your hearing
today, that you may learn them and be careful
to observe them. 2 [a]The LORD our God made
a covenant with us in Horeb. 3 The LORD [a]did
not make this covenant with our fathers, but
with us, those who *are* here today, all of us
who *are* alive. 4 [a]The LORD talked with you
face to face on the mountain from the midst
of the fire. 5 [a]I stood between the LORD and
you at that time, to declare to you the word
of the LORD; for [b]you were afraid because of
the fire, and you did not go up the mountain.
He said:

6 [a]'I *am* the LORD your God who brought
you out of the land of Egypt, out of the
house of bondage.

7 [a]'You shall have no other gods before Me.

8 [a]'You shall not make for yourself a carved
image—any likeness *of anything* that *is*
in heaven above, or that *is* in the earth
beneath, or that *is* in the water under
the earth; 9 you shall not [a]bow down to
them nor serve them. For I, the LORD
your God, *am* a jealous God, visiting
the iniquity of the fathers upon the
children to the third and fourth *generations* of those who hate Me, 10 [a]but
showing mercy to thousands, to those
who love Me and keep My commandments.

11 [a]'You shall not take the name of the LORD
your God in vain, for the LORD will not
hold *him* guiltless who takes His name
in vain.

12 [a]'Observe the Sabbath day, to keep it holy,
as the LORD your God commanded
you. 13 [a]Six days you shall labor and do
all your work, 14 but the seventh day *is*
the [a]Sabbath of the LORD your God. *In
it* you shall do no work: you, nor your
son, nor your daughter, nor your male
servant, nor your female servant, nor
your ox, nor your donkey, nor any of
your cattle, nor your stranger who *is*
within your gates, that your male servant and your female servant may rest
as well as you. 15 [a]And remember that
you were a slave in the land of Egypt,
and the LORD your God brought you
out from there [b]by a mighty hand and
by an outstretched arm; therefore the
LORD your God commanded you to
keep the Sabbath day.

16 [a]'Honor your father and your mother, as
the LORD your God has commanded
you, [b]that your days may be long, and
that it may be well with [c]you in the land
which the LORD your God is giving you.

17 [a]'You shall not murder.

18 [a]'You shall not commit adultery.

19 [a]'You shall not steal.

20 [a]'You shall not bear false witness against
your neighbor.

5:2 [a] Ex. 19:5 5:3 [a] Heb. 8:9 5:4 [a] Ex. 19:9 5:5 [a] Gal. 3:19 [b] Ex. 19:16 5:6 [a] Ex. 20:2–17 5:7 [a] Hos. 13:4 5:8 [a] Ex. 20:4 5:9 [a] Ex. 34:7, 14–16 5:10 [a] Dan. 9:4 5:11 [a] Ex. 20:7 5:12 [a] Ex. 20:8 5:13 [a] Ex. 23:12; 35:2 5:14 [a] [Heb. 4:4] 5:15 [a] Deut. 15:15 [b] Deut. 4:34, 37 5:16 [a] Lev. 19:3 [b] Deut. 6:2 [c] Deut. 4:40 5:17 [a] Matt. 5:21 5:18 [a] Ex. 20:14 5:19 [a] [Rom. 13:9] 5:20 [a] Ex. 20:16; 23:1

THE PATH TO WALK

Hear, O Israel, the statutes and judgments which I speak in your hearing today, that you may learn them and be careful to observe them.

DEUTERONOMY 5:1

Peace will elude us if we are not careful to follow Christ's teaching. When God speaks to us, convicts us, leads us, or reveals application of His Word, we must be responsive! We cannot be flat-footed and find peace. We have to walk forward, following the Lord, and God's peace will be ours. Receiving it presupposes obedience.

Before Israel could enter the Promised Land, the people had to plant in their hearts God's "statutes and judgments" and "be careful to observe them." If they did that, they would enter the land promised to the patriarchs long before, and they would live there in peace.

That's how it works for us today. God's peace is at hand, but we can't receive it if we ignore His righteous commands and ways. If we live according to God's truth and take Him at His word, we will find ourselves living lives of peace.

21 [a]'You shall not covet your neighbor's wife;
and you shall not desire your neigh-
bor's house, his field, his male servant,
his female servant, his ox, his donkey,
or anything that *is* your neighbor's.'
22"These words the LORD spoke to all your
assembly, in the mountain from the midst
of the fire, the cloud, and the thick darkness,
with a loud voice; and He added no more.
And [a]He wrote them on two tablets of stone
and gave them to me.

The People Afraid of God's Presence

23[a]"So it was, when you heard the voice
from the midst of the darkness, while the
mountain was burning with fire, that you
came near to me, all the heads of your tribes
and your elders. 24 And you said: 'Surely the
LORD our God has shown us His glory and
His greatness, and [a]we have heard His voice
from the midst of the fire. We have seen this
day that God speaks with man; yet he [b]*still*
lives. 25 Now therefore, why should we die?
For this great fire will consume us; [a]if we
hear the voice of the LORD our God anymore,
then we shall die. 26[a]For who *is there* of all
flesh who has heard the voice of the living
God speaking from the midst of the fire, as
we *have*, and lived? 27 You go near and hear
all that the LORD our God may say, and [a]tell
us all that the LORD our God says to you, and
we will hear and do *it*.'
28"Then the LORD heard the voice of your
words when you spoke to me, and the LORD
said to me: 'I have heard the voice of the
words of this people which they have spoken
to you. [a]They are right *in* all that they have
spoken. 29[a]Oh, that they had such a heart in
them that they would fear Me and [b]always
keep all My commandments, [c]that it might
be well with them and with their children
forever! 30 Go and say to them, "Return to your
tents." 31 But as for you, stand here by Me, [a]and
I will speak to you all the commandments, the
statutes, and the judgments which you shall
teach them, that they may observe *them* in
the land which I am giving them to possess.'
32"Therefore you shall be careful to do as
the LORD your God has commanded you;
[a]you shall not turn aside to the right hand
or to the left. 33 You shall walk in [a]all the ways
which the LORD your God has commanded
you, that you may live [b]and *that it may be* well
with you, and *that* you may prolong *your* days
in the land which you shall possess.

The Greatest Commandment

6 "Now this *is* [a]the commandment, *and
these are* the statutes and judgments
which the LORD your God has commanded
to teach you, that you may observe *them* in
the land which you are crossing over to possess, 2[a]that you may fear the LORD your God,
to keep all His statutes and His commandments which I command you, you and your
son and your grandson, all the days of your
life, [b]and that your days may be prolonged.
3 Therefore hear, O Israel, and be careful to
observe *it*, that it may be well with you, and
that you may [a]multiply greatly [b]as the LORD
God of your fathers has promised you—[c]'a
land flowing with milk and honey.'[1]
4[a]"Hear, O Israel: The LORD our God, the
LORD *is* one![1] 5[a]You shall love the LORD your
God with all your heart, [b]with all your soul,
and with all your strength.

> **PEACE NOTE**
>
> In the Hebrew language, the words for "heart" (*lebav*) and "soul" (*nephesh*) imply thought and will, not emotion only. We must love God with all we are to experience His peace.
>
> DEUTERONOMY 6:4-5

6"And [a]these words which I command
you today shall be in your heart. 7[a]You shall
teach them diligently to your children, and
shall talk of them when you sit in your house,
when you walk by the way, when you lie down,
and when you rise up. 8[a]You shall bind them
as a sign on your hand, and they shall be
as frontlets between your eyes. 9[a]You shall
write them on the doorposts of your house
and on your gates.

Caution Against Disobedience

10"So it shall be, when the LORD your God
brings you into the land of which He swore to
your fathers, to Abraham, Isaac, and Jacob, to

5:21 [a] Ex. 20:17 **5:22** [a] Deut. 4:13 **5:23** [a] Ex. 20:18, 19 **5:24** [a] Ex. 19:19 [b] Deut. 4:33 **5:25** [a] Deut. 18:16 **5:26** [a] Deut. 4:33 **5:27** [a] Ex. 20:19 **5:28** [a] Deut. 18:17 **5:29** [a] Ps. 81:13 [b] Deut. 11:1 [c] Deut. 4:40 **5:31** [a] [Gal. 3:19] **5:32** [a] Deut. 17:20; 28:14 **5:33** [a] Deut. 10:12 [b] Deut. 4:40 **6:1** [a] Deut. 12:1 **6:2** [a] [Eccl. 12:13] [b] Deut. 4:40 **6:3** [a] Deut. 7:13 [b] Gen. 22:17 [c] Ex. 3:8, 17 [1] Exodus 3:8 **6:4** [a] [1 Cor. 8:4, 6] [1] Or *The LORD is our God, the LORD alone* (that is, the only one) **6:5** [a] Matt. 22:37 [b] 2 Kin. 23:25 **6:6** [a] Deut. 11:18–20 **6:7** [a] Deut. 4:9; 11:19 **6:8** [a] Prov. 3:3; 6:21; 7:3 **6:9** [a] Deut. 11:20

TRUSTING THE ONE TRUE GOD

Hear, O Israel: The LORD our God, the LORD is one! You shall love the LORD your God with all your heart, with all your soul, and with all your strength.

DEUTERONOMY 6:4-5

Because God is *one*, that is, *not many*, our loyalty to Him must be undivided. We are to love this one God with all our hearts, souls, and strength. For ancient Israel this was a challenging command, for the world they lived in was a culture of polytheism and idolatry. People made their gods and then begged them for blessings. Treating the Lord this way was as insulting as it was foolish.

Peace will never be found if one embraces the "gods" of this world. You may wonder if you love God enough. Listen, either you are in or you are out. It's like getting on an airplane. You either board the plane or stay on the Jetway.

By putting our trust in and loving Him, we are saying no to the idols and false gods that the world offers. The world may speak of peace, may even promise it, but it cannot provide it. You and I will find that true peace only in loving Him who gives it.

give you large and beautiful cities [a]which you
did not build, 11 houses full of all good things,
which you did not fill, hewn-out wells which
you did not dig, vineyards and olive trees which
you did not plant—[a]when you have eaten and
are full— 12 *then* beware, lest you forget the
[a]LORD who brought you out of the land of
Egypt, from the house of bondage. 13 You shall
[a]fear the LORD your God and serve Him, and
[b]shall take oaths in His name. 14 You shall not
go after other gods, [a]the gods of the peoples
who *are* all around you 15 (for [a]the LORD your
God *is* a jealous God [b]among you), lest the anger
of the LORD your God be aroused against you
and destroy you from the face of the earth.
16 [a]"You shall not tempt the LORD your
God [b]as you tempted *Him* in Massah. 17 You
shall [a]diligently keep the commandments
of the LORD your God, His testimonies, and
His statutes which He has commanded you.
18 And you [a]shall do *what is* right and good in
the sight of the LORD, that it may be well with
you, and that you may go in and possess the
good land of which the LORD swore to your
fathers, 19 [a]to cast out all your enemies from
before you, as the LORD has spoken.
20 [a]"When your son asks you in time to come,
saying, 'What *is the meaning of* the testimonies,
the statutes, and the judgments which the
LORD our God has commanded you?' 21 then
you shall say to your son: 'We were slaves of
Pharaoh in Egypt, and the LORD brought us
out of Egypt [a]with a mighty hand; 22 and the
LORD showed signs and wonders before our
eyes, great and severe, against Egypt, Pharaoh,
and all his household. 23 Then He brought us
out from there, that He might bring us in,
to give us the land of which He swore to our
fathers. 24 And the LORD commanded us to
observe all these statutes, [a]to fear the LORD
our God, [b]for our good always, that [c]He might
preserve us alive, as *it is* this day. 25 Then [a]it
will be righteousness for us, if we are careful
to observe all these commandments before
the LORD our God, as He has commanded us.'

A Chosen People

7 "When the LORD your God brings you
into the land which you go to [a]possess,
and has cast out many [b]nations before you,
[c]the Hittites and the Girgashites and the
Amorites and the Canaanites and the Perizzites and the Hivites and the Jebusites,
seven nations greater and mightier than
you, 2 and when the LORD your God delivers
[a]them over to you, you shall conquer them
and utterly destroy them. [b]You shall make
no covenant with them nor show mercy to
them. 3 [a]Nor shall you make marriages with
them. You shall not give your daughter to
their son, nor take their daughter for your
son. 4 For they will turn your sons away from
following Me, to serve other gods; [a]so the
anger of the LORD will be aroused against

6:10 [a] Josh. 24:13 **6:11** [a] Deut. 8:10; 11:15; 14:29 **6:12** [a] Deut. 8:11–18 **6:13** [a] Matt. 4:10 [b] Deut. 5:11 **6:14** [a] Deut. 13:7 **6:15** [a] Ex. 20:5 [b] Ex. 33:3 **6:16** [a] Luke 4:12 [b] [1 Cor. 10:9] **6:17** [a] Deut. 11:22 **6:18** [a] Ex. 15:26 **6:19** [a] Num. 33:52, 53 **6:20** [a] Ex. 13:8, 14 **6:21** [a] Ex. 13:3 **6:24** [a] Deut. 6:2 [b] Jer. 32:39 [c] Deut. 4:1 **6:25** [a] [Rom. 10:3, 5] **7:1** [a] Deut. 6:10 [b] Gen. 15:19–21 [c] Ex. 33:2 **7:2** [a] Num. 31:17 [b] Josh. 2:14 **7:3** [a] 1 Kin. 11:2 **7:4** [a] Deut. 6:15

you and destroy you suddenly. 5 But thus you
shall deal with them: you shall [a]destroy their
altars, and break down their *sacred* pillars,
and cut down their wooden images,[1] and burn
their carved images with fire.
6 "For you *are* a holy people to the LORD
your God; [a]the LORD your God has chosen you
to be a people for Himself, a special treasure
above all the peoples on the face of the earth.
7 The LORD did not set His [a]love on you nor
choose you because you were more in number
than any other people, for you were [b]the least
of all peoples; 8 but [a]because the LORD loves
you, and because He would keep [b]the oath
which He swore to your fathers, [c]the LORD
has brought you out with a mighty hand, and
redeemed you from the house of bondage,
from the hand of Pharaoh king of Egypt.
9 "Therefore know that the LORD your God,
He *is* God, [a]the faithful God [b]who keeps covenant and mercy for a thousand generations
with those who love Him and keep His commandments; 10 and He repays those who hate
Him to their face, to destroy them. He will
not be [a]slack with him who hates Him; He
will repay him to his face. 11 Therefore you
shall keep the commandment, the statutes,
and the judgments which I command you
today, to observe them.

Blessings of Obedience

12 "Then it shall come to pass, because you
listen to these judgments, and keep and do
them, that the LORD your God will keep with
you the covenant and the mercy which He
swore to your fathers. 13 And He will [a]love you
and bless you and multiply you; [b]He will also
bless the fruit of your womb and the fruit of
your land, your grain and your new wine and
your oil, the increase of your cattle and the
offspring of your flock, in the land of which
He swore to your fathers to give you. 14 You
shall be blessed above all peoples; there shall
not be a male or female [a]barren among you
or among your livestock. 15 And the LORD
will take away from you all sickness, and will
afflict you with none of the [a]terrible diseases
of Egypt which you have known, but will lay
them on all those who hate you. 16 Also you
shall destroy all the peoples whom the LORD
your God delivers over to you; your eye shall
have no pity on them; nor shall you serve
their gods, for that *will* [a]*be* a snare to you.
17 "If you should say in your heart, 'These
nations are greater than I; how can I dispossess
them?'— 18 you shall not be afraid of them, *but*
you shall [a]remember well what the LORD your
God did to Pharaoh and to all Egypt: 19 [a]the
great trials which your eyes saw, the signs and
the wonders, the mighty hand and the outstretched arm, by which the LORD your God
brought you out. So shall the LORD your God
do to all the peoples of whom you are afraid.
20 [a]Moreover the LORD your God will send the
hornet among them until those who are left,
who hide themselves from you, are destroyed.
21 You shall not be terrified of them; for the
LORD your God, the great and awesome God, *is*
among you. 22 And the LORD your God will drive
out those nations before you [a]little by little;
you will be unable to destroy them at once, lest
the beasts of the field become *too* numerous
for you. 23 But the LORD your God will deliver
them over to you, and will inflict defeat upon
them until they are destroyed. 24 And [a]He will
deliver their kings into your hand, and you
will destroy their name from under heaven;
[b]no one shall be able to stand against you until
you have destroyed them. 25 You shall burn the
carved images of their gods with fire; you shall
not [a]covet the silver or gold *that is* on them, nor
take *it* for yourselves, lest you be snared by it;
for it *is* an abomination to the LORD your God.
26 Nor shall you bring an abomination into your
house, lest you be doomed to destruction like
it. You shall utterly detest it and utterly abhor
it, [a]for it *is* an accursed thing.

Remember the LORD Your God

8 "Every commandment which I command
you today [a]you must be careful to observe,
that you may live and [b]multiply, and go in and
possess the land of which the LORD swore to
your fathers. 2 And you shall remember that the
LORD your God [a]led you all the way these forty
years in the wilderness, to humble you *and* [b]test
you, [c]to know what *was* in your heart, whether
you would keep His commandments or not.
3 So He humbled you, [a]allowed you to hunger,
and [b]fed you with manna which you did not
know nor did your fathers know, that He might
make you know that man shall [c]not live by
bread alone; but man lives by every *word* that
proceeds from the mouth of the LORD. 4 [a]Your
garments did not wear out on you, nor did your
foot swell these forty years. 5 [a]You should know
in your heart that as a man chastens his son,
so the LORD your God chastens you.

7:5 [a] Ex. 23:24; 34:13 [1] Hebrew *Asherim,* Canaanite deities **7:6** [a] Ex. 19:5, 6 **7:7** [a] Deut. 4:37 [b] Deut. 10:22 **7:8** [a] Deut. 10:15 [b] Luke 1:55, 72, 73 [c] Ex. 13:3, 14 **7:9** [a] 1 Cor. 1:9 [b] Neh. 1:5 **7:10** [a] [2 Pet. 3:9, 10] **7:13** [a] John 14:21 [b] Deut. 28:4 **7:14** [a] Ex. 23:26 **7:15** [a] Ex. 9:14; 15:26 **7:16** [a] Judg. 8:27 **7:18** [a] Ps. 105:5 **7:19** [a] Deut. 4:34; 29:3 **7:20** [a] Josh. 24:12 **7:22** [a] Ex. 23:29, 30 **7:24** [a] Josh. 10:24, 42; 12:1–24 [b] Josh. 23:9 **7:25** [a] Prov. 23:6 **7:26** [a] Deut. 13:17 **8:1** [a] Deut. 4:1; 6:24 [b] Deut. 30:16 **8:2** [a] Amos 2:10 [b] Ex. 16:4 [c] [John 2:25] **8:3** [a] Ex. 16:2, 3 [b] Ex. 16:12, 14, 35 [c] Matt. 4:4 **8:4** [a] Neh. 9:21 **8:5** [a] 2 Sam. 7:14

PEACE NOTE

Our thinking determines our anxiety. Ask yourself: *Am I trusting what I know is true in my life through Christ, or am I focused on the problem, having factored God out of the situation?*

6 "Therefore you shall keep the commandments of the LORD your God, [a]to walk in His ways and to fear Him. 7 For the LORD your God is bringing you into a good land, [a]a land of brooks of water, of fountains and springs, that flow out of valleys and hills; 8 a land of wheat and barley, of vines and fig trees and pomegranates, a land of olive oil and honey; 9 a land in which you will eat bread without scarcity, in which you will lack nothing; a land whose stones *are* iron and out of whose hills you can dig copper. 10 [a]When you have eaten and are full, then you shall bless the LORD your God for the good land which He has given you.

11 "Beware that you do not forget the LORD your God by not keeping His commandments, His judgments, and His statutes which I command you today, 12 [a]lest—*when* you have eaten and are full, and have built beautiful houses and dwell *in them;* 13 and *when* your herds and your flocks multiply, and your silver and your gold are multiplied, and all that you have is multiplied; 14 [a]when your heart is lifted up, and you [b]forget the LORD your God who brought you out of the land of Egypt, from the house of bondage; 15 who [a]led you through that great and terrible wilderness, [b]*in which were* fiery serpents and scorpions and thirsty land where there was no water; [c]who brought water for you out of the flinty rock; 16 who fed you in the wilderness with [a]manna, which your fathers did not know, that He might humble you and that He might test you, [b]to do you good in the end— 17 then you say in your heart, 'My power and the might of my hand have gained me this wealth.'

18 "And you shall remember the LORD your God, [a]for *it is* He who gives you power to get wealth, [b]that He may establish His covenant which He swore to your fathers, as *it is* this day. 19 Then it shall be, if you by any means forget the LORD your God, and follow other gods, and serve them and worship them, [a]I testify against you this day that you shall surely perish. 20 As the nations which the LORD destroys before you, [a]so you shall perish, because you would not be obedient to the voice of the LORD your God.

Israel's Rebellions Reviewed

9 "Hear, O Israel: You *are* to cross over the Jordan today, and go in to dispossess nations greater and mightier than yourself, cities great and fortified up to heaven, 2 a people great and tall, the [a]descendants of the Anakim, whom you know, and *of whom* you heard *it said,* 'Who can stand before the descendants of Anak?' 3 Therefore understand today that the LORD your God *is* He who [a]goes over before you *as* a [b]consuming fire. [c]He will destroy them and bring them down before you; [d]so you shall drive them out and destroy them quickly, as the LORD has said to you.

4 [a]"Do not think in your heart, after the LORD your God has cast them out before you, saying, 'Because of my righteousness the LORD has brought me in to possess this land'; but *it is* [b]because of the wickedness of these nations *that* the LORD is driving them out from before you. 5 [a]*It is* not because of your righteousness or the uprightness of your heart *that* you go in to possess their land, but because of the wickedness of these nations *that* the LORD your God drives them out from before you, and that He may fulfill the [b]word which the LORD swore to your fathers, to Abraham, Isaac, and Jacob. 6 Therefore understand that the LORD your God is not giving you this good land to possess because of your righteousness, for you *are* a [a]stiff-necked people.

7 "Remember! Do not forget how you [a]provoked the LORD your God to wrath in the wilderness. [b]From the day that you departed from the land of Egypt until you came to this place, you have been rebellious against the LORD. 8 Also [a]in Horeb you provoked the LORD to wrath, so that the LORD was angry *enough* with you to have destroyed you. 9 [a]When I

8:6 [a] [Deut. 5:33] 8:7 [a] Deut. 11:9–12 8:10 [a] Deut. 6:11, 12 8:12 [a] Hos. 13:6 8:14 [a] 1 Cor. 4:7 [b] Ps. 106:21 8:15 [a] Is. 63:12–14 [b] Num. 21:6 [c] Num. 20:11 8:16 [a] Ex. 16:15 [b] [Heb. 12:11] 8:18 [a] Hos. 2:8 [b] Deut. 7:8, 12 8:19 [a] Deut. 4:26; 30:18 8:20 [a] [Dan. 9:11, 12] 9:2 [a] Num. 13:22, 28, 33 9:3 [a] Josh. 3:11; 5:14 [b] Deut. 4:24 [c] Deut. 7:24 [d] Ex. 23:31 9:4 [a] Deut. 8:17 [b] Lev. 18:3, 24–30 9:5 [a] [Titus 3:5] [b] Gen. 50:24 9:6 [a] Deut. 31:27 9:7 [a] Num. 14:22 [b] Ex. 14:11 9:8 [a] Ex. 32:1–8 9:9 [a] Deut. 5:2–22

went up into the mountain to receive the
tablets of stone, the tablets of the covenant
which the LORD made with you, then I stayed
on the mountain forty days and [b]forty nights.
I neither ate bread nor drank water. 10 [a]Then
the LORD delivered to me two tablets of stone
written with the finger of God, and on them
were all the words which the LORD had spoken to you on the mountain from the midst
of the fire [b]in the day of the assembly. 11 And
it came to pass, at the end of forty days and
forty nights, *that* the LORD gave me the two
tablets of stone, the tablets of the covenant.

12 "Then the LORD said to me, [a]'Arise, go
down quickly from here, for your people
whom you brought out of Egypt have acted
corruptly; they have [b]quickly turned aside
from the way which I commanded them;
they have made themselves a molded image.'

13 "Furthermore [a]the LORD spoke to me,
saying, 'I have seen this people, and indeed
[b]they are a stiff-necked people. 14 [a]Let Me
alone, that I may destroy them and [b]blot out
their name from under heaven; [c]and I will
make of you a nation mightier and greater
than they.'

15 [a]"So I turned and came down from the
mountain, and [b]the mountain burned with
fire; and the two tablets of the covenant *were*
in my two hands. 16 And [a]I looked, and behold, you had sinned against the LORD your
God—had made for yourselves a molded calf!
You had turned aside quickly from the way
which the LORD had commanded you. 17 Then
I took the two tablets and threw them out of
my two hands and [a]broke them before your
eyes. 18 And I [a]fell down before the LORD,
as at the first, forty days and forty nights; I
neither ate bread nor drank water, because
of all your sin which you committed in doing
wickedly in the sight of the LORD, to provoke
Him to anger. 19 [a]For I was afraid of the anger
and hot displeasure with which the LORD was
angry with you, to destroy you. [b]But the LORD
listened to me at that time also. 20 And the
LORD was very angry with Aaron *and* would
have destroyed him; so I prayed for Aaron
also at the same time. 21 Then I took your sin,
the calf which you had made, and burned it
with fire and crushed it *and* ground *it* very
small, until it was as fine as dust; and I [a]threw
its dust into the brook that descended from
the mountain.

22 "Also at [a]Taberah and [b]Massah and [c]Kib-
roth Hattaavah you provoked the LORD to
wrath. 23 Likewise, [a]when the LORD sent you
from Kadesh Barnea, saying, 'Go up and possess the land which I have given you,' then
you rebelled against the commandment of
the LORD your God, and [b]you did not believe
Him nor obey His voice. 24 [a]You have been
rebellious against the LORD from the day
that I knew you.

25 [a]"Thus I prostrated myself before the
LORD; forty days and forty nights I kept pros-
trating myself, because the LORD had said
He would destroy you. 26 Therefore I prayed
to the LORD, and said: 'O Lord GOD, do not
destroy Your people and [a]Your inheritance
whom You have redeemed through Your
greatness, whom You have brought out of
Egypt with a mighty hand. 27 Remember Your
servants, Abraham, Isaac, and Jacob; do not
look on the stubbornness of this people, or
on their wickedness or their sin, 28 lest the
land from which You brought us should say,
"Because the LORD was not able to bring
them to the land which He promised them,
and because He hated them, He has brought
them out to kill them in the wilderness." 29 Yet
they *are* Your people and Your inheritance,
whom You brought out by Your mighty power
and by Your outstretched arm.'

The Second Pair of Tablets

10 "At that time the LORD said to me, 'Hew
for yourself two tablets of stone like the
first, and come up to Me on the mountain and
make yourself an [a]ark of wood. 2 And I will
write on the tablets the words that were on
the first tablets, which you broke; and [a]you
shall put them in the ark.'

3 "So I made an ark of acacia wood, hewed
two tablets of stone like the first, and went up
the mountain, having the two tablets in my
hand. 4 And He wrote on the tablets according
to the first writing, the Ten Commandments,
[a]which the LORD had spoken to you in the
mountain from the midst of the fire in the
day of the assembly; and the LORD gave them
to me. 5 Then I turned and [a]came down from
the mountain, and [b]put the tablets in the ark
which I had made; [c]and there they are, just
as the LORD commanded me."

6 (Now the children of Israel journeyed
from the wells of Bene Jaakan to Moserah,
where Aaron [a]died, and where he was buried;
and Eleazar his son ministered as priest in
his stead. 7 [a]From there they journeyed to
Gudgodah, and from Gudgodah to Jotbathah,

9:9 [b] Ex. 24:18 **9:10** [a] Deut. 4:13 [b] Ex. 19:17 **9:12** [a] Ex. 32:7, 8 [b] Deut. 31:29 **9:13** [a] Ex. 32:9 [b] Deut. 9:6 **9:14** [a] Ex. 32:10 [b] Deut. 29:20 [c] Num. 14:12 **9:15** [a] Ex. 32:15–19 [b] Ex. 19:18 **9:16** [a] Ex. 32:19 **9:17** [a] Ex. 32:19 **9:18** [a] Ex. 34:28 **9:19** [a] Ex. 32:10, 11 [b] Ex. 32:14 **9:21** [a] Ex. 32:20 **9:22** [a] Num. 11:1, 3 [b] Ex. 17:7 [c] Num. 11:4, 34 **9:23** [a] Num. 13:3 [b] Ps. 106:24, 25 **9:24** [a] Deut. 9:7; 31:27 **9:25** [a] Deut. 9:18 **9:26** [a] Deut. 32:9 **10:1** [a] Ex. 25:10 **10:2** [a] Ex. 25:16, 21 **10:4** [a] Ex. 20:1; 34:28 **10:5** [a] Ex. 34:29 [b] Ex. 40:20 [c] 1 Kin. 8:9 **10:6** [a] Num. 20:25–28; 33:38 **10:7** [a] Num. 33:32–34

a land of rivers of water. 8 At that time [a]the
LORD separated the tribe of Levi [b]to bear the
ark of the covenant of the LORD, [c]to stand
before the LORD to minister to Him and [d]to
bless in His name, to this day. 9 [a]Therefore
Levi has no portion nor inheritance with his
brethren; the LORD *is* his inheritance, just as
the LORD your God promised him.)
10 "As at the first time, [a]I stayed in the mountain forty days and forty nights; [b]the LORD also
heard me at that time, *and* the LORD chose not
to destroy you. 11 [a]Then the LORD said to me,
'Arise, begin *your* journey before the people,
that they may go in and possess the land which
I swore to their fathers to give them.'

The Essence of the Law

12 "And now, Israel, [a]what does the LORD
your God require of you, but to fear the LORD
your God, to walk in all His ways and to [b]love
Him, to serve the LORD your God with all
your heart and with all your soul, 13 *and* to
keep the commandments of the LORD and
His statutes which I command you today
[a]for your good? 14 Indeed heaven and the
highest heavens belong to the [a]LORD your
God, *also* the earth with all that *is* in it. 15 The
LORD delighted only in your fathers, to love
them; and He chose their descendants after
them, you above all peoples, as *it is* this day.
16 Therefore circumcise the foreskin of your
[a]heart, and be [b]stiff-necked no longer. 17 For
the LORD your God *is* [a]God of gods and [b]Lord
of lords, the great God, [c]mighty and awesome,
who [d]shows no partiality nor takes a bribe.
18 [a]He administers justice for the fatherless
and the widow, and loves the stranger, giving
him food and clothing. 19 Therefore love the
stranger, for you were strangers in the land of
Egypt. 20 [a]You shall fear the LORD your God;
you shall serve Him, and to Him you shall
hold fast, and take oaths in His name. 21 He
is your praise, and He *is* your God, who has
done for you these great and awesome things
which your eyes have seen. 22 Your fathers
went down to Egypt with seventy persons,
and now the LORD your God has made you
as the stars of heaven in multitude.

Love and Obedience Rewarded

11 "Therefore you shall love the LORD your
God, and keep His charge, His statutes,
His judgments, and His commandments always. 2 Know today that *I do* not *speak* with
your children, who have not known and who

PEACE NOTE

If you don't take captive your thoughts (2 Cor 10:5), they will take you captive. You don't have to do this alone, though. God will freely make His Spirit available to you.

have not seen the chastening of the LORD
your God, His greatness and His mighty hand
and His outstretched arm— 3 His signs and
His acts which He did in the midst of Egypt,
to Pharaoh king of Egypt, and to all his land;
4 what He did to the army of Egypt, to their
horses and their chariots: [a]how He made the
waters of the Red Sea overflow them as they
pursued you, and *how* the LORD has destroyed
them to this day; 5 what He did for you in
the wilderness until you came to this place;
6 and [a]what He did to Dathan and Abiram
the sons of Eliab, the son of Reuben: how the
earth opened its mouth and swallowed them
up, their households, their tents, and all the
substance that *was* in their possession, in the
midst of all Israel— 7 but your eyes have [a]seen
every great act of the LORD which He did.
8 "Therefore you shall keep every commandment which I command you today, that
you may [a]be strong, and go in and possess
the land which you cross over to possess,
9 and [a]that you may prolong *your* days in
the land [b]which the LORD swore to give your
fathers, to them and their descendants, [c]'a
land flowing with milk and honey.'[1] 10 For the
land which you go to possess *is* not like the
land of Egypt from which you have come,
where you sowed your seed and watered *it*
by foot, as a vegetable garden; 11 [a]but the land
which you cross over to possess *is* a land of
hills and valleys, which drinks water from the
rain of heaven, 12 a land for which the LORD
your God cares; [a]the eyes of the LORD your
God *are* always on it, from the beginning of
the year to the very end of the year.

10:8 [a] Num. 3:6 [b] Num. 4:5, 15; 10:21 [c] Deut. 18:5 [d] Num. 6:23 **10:9** [a] Deut. 18:1, 2 **10:10** [a] Deut. 9:18 [b] Ex. 32:14 **10:11** [a] Ex. 33:1 **10:12** [a] Mic. 6:8 [b] Deut. 6:5 **10:13** [a] Deut. 6:24 **10:14** [a] [Neh. 9:6] **10:16** [a] Jer. 4:4 [b] Deut. 9:6, 13 **10:17** [a] Dan. 2:47 [b] Rev. 19:16 [c] Deut. 7:21 [d] Acts 10:34 **10:18** [a] Ps. 68:5; 146:9 **10:20** [a] Matt. 4:10 **11:4** [a] Ps. 106:11 **11:6** [a] Ps. 106:16–18 **11:7** [a] Deut. 10:21; 29:2 **11:8** [a] Josh. 1:6, 7 **11:9** [a] Deut. 4:40; 5:16, 33; 6:2 [b] Deut. 9:5 [c] Ex. 3:8 [1] Exodus 3:8 **11:11** [a] Deut. 8:7 **11:12** [a] 1 Kin. 9:3

13 'And it shall be that if you earnestly obey
My commandments which I command you
today, to love the LORD your God and serve
Him with all your heart and with all your soul,
14 then [a]I[1] will give *you* the rain for your land in
its season, [b]the early rain and the latter rain,
that you may gather in your grain, your new
wine, and your oil. 15 [a]And I will send grass in
your fields for your livestock, that you may
[b]eat and be filled.' 16 Take heed to yourselves,
[a]lest your heart be deceived, and you turn
aside and [b]serve other gods and worship
them, 17 lest [a]the LORD's anger be aroused
against you, and He [b]shut up the heavens
so that there be no rain, and the land yield
no produce, and [c]you perish quickly from
the good land which the LORD is giving you.

18 "Therefore [a]you shall lay up these words
of mine in your heart and in your [b]soul, and
[c]bind them as a sign on your hand, and they
shall be as frontlets between your eyes. 19 [a]You
shall teach them to your children, speaking
of them when you sit in your house, when
you walk by the way, when you lie down, and
when you rise up. 20 [a]And you shall write
them on the doorposts of your house and on
your gates, 21 that [a]your days and the days of
your children may be multiplied in the land
of which the LORD swore to your fathers
to give them, like [b]the days of the heavens
above the earth.

22 "For if [a]you carefully keep all these commandments which I command you to do—to
love the LORD your God, to walk in all His
ways, and [b]to hold fast to Him— 23 then the
LORD will [a]drive out all these nations from
before you, and you will [b]dispossess greater
and mightier nations than yourselves. 24 [a]Ev-
ery place on which the sole of your foot treads
shall be yours: [b]from the wilderness and Lebanon, from the river, the River Euphrates,
even to the Western Sea,[1] shall be your territory. 25 No man shall be able to [a]stand against
you; the LORD your God will put the [b]dread
of you and the fear of you upon all the land
where you tread, just as He has said to you.

26 [a]"Behold, I set before you today a blessing and a curse: 27 [a]the blessing, if you obey
the commandments of the LORD your God
which I command you today; 28 and the
[a]curse, if you do not obey the commandments of the LORD your God, but turn aside
from the way which I command you today,
to go after other gods which you have not
known. 29 Now it shall be, when the LORD your
God has brought you into the land which you
go to possess, that you shall put the [a]blessing
on Mount Gerizim and the [b]curse on Mount
Ebal. 30 *Are* they not on the other side of the
Jordan, toward the setting sun, in the land
of the Canaanites who dwell in the plain opposite Gilgal, [a]beside the terebinth trees of
Moreh? 31 For you will cross over the Jordan
and go in to possess the land which the LORD
your God is giving you, and you will possess
it and dwell in it. 32 And you shall be careful
to observe all the statutes and judgments
which I set before you today.

A Prescribed Place of Worship

12 "These [a]*are* the statutes and judgments
which you shall be careful to observe in
the land which the LORD God of your fathers
is giving you to possess, [b]all the days that you
live on the earth. 2 [a]You shall utterly destroy
all the places where the nations which you
shall dispossess served their gods, [b]on the
high mountains and on the hills and under
every green tree. 3 And [a]you shall destroy
their altars, break their *sacred* pillars, and
burn their wooden images with fire; you shall
cut down the carved images of their gods
and destroy their names from that place.
4 You shall not [a]worship the LORD your God
with such *things*.

5 "But you shall seek the [a]place where the
LORD your God chooses, out of all your tribes,
to put His name for His [b]dwelling place;
and there you shall go. 6 [a]There you shall
take your burnt offerings, your sacrifices,
your tithes, the heave offerings of your hand,
your vowed offerings, your freewill offerings,
and the [b]firstborn of your herds and flocks.
7 And [a]there you shall eat before the LORD
your God, and [b]you shall rejoice in all to
which you have put your hand, you and your
households, in which the LORD your God has
blessed you.

8 "You shall not at all do as we are doing
here today—[a]every man doing whatever *is*
right in his own eyes— 9 for as yet you have
not come to the [a]rest and the inheritance
which the LORD your God is giving you. 10 But
when you cross over the Jordan and dwell in

11:14 [a] Deut. 28:12 [b] Joel 2:23 [1] Following Masoretic Text and Targum; Samaritan Pentateuch, Septuagint, and Vulgate read *He*. **11:15** [a] Ps. 104:14 [b] Deut. 6:11 **11:16** [a] Job 31:27 [b] Deut. 8:19 **11:17** [a] Deut. 6:15; 9:19 [b] 2 Chr. 6:26; 7:13 [c] Deut. 4:26 **11:18** [a] Deut. 6:6–9 [b] Ps. 119:2, 34 [c] Deut. 6:8 **11:19** [a] Deut. 4:9, 10; 6:7 **11:20** [a] Deut. 6:9 **11:21** [a] Deut. 4:40 [b] Ps. 72:5; 89:29 **11:22** [a] Deut. 11:1 [b] Deut. 10:20 **11:23** [a] Deut. 4:38 [b] Deut. 9:1 **11:24** [a] Josh. 1:3; 14:9 [b] Gen. 15:18 [1] That is, the Mediterranean **11:25** [a] Deut. 7:24 [b] Deut. 2:25 **11:26** [a] Deut. 30:1, 15, 19 **11:27** [a] Deut. 28:1–14 **11:28** [a] Deut. 28:15–68 **11:29** [a] Josh. 8:33 [b] Deut. 27:13–26 **11:30** [a] Gen. 12:6 **12:1** [a] Deut. 6:1 [b] Deut. 4:9, 10 **12:2** [a] Ex. 34:13 [b] 2 Kin. 16:4; 17:10, 11 **12:3** [a] Num. 33:52 **12:4** [a] Deut. 12:31 **12:5** [a] Ex. 20:24 [b] Ex. 15:13 **12:6** [a] Lev. 17:3, 4 [b] Deut. 14:23 **12:7** [a] Deut. 14:26 [b] Deut. 12:12, 18 **12:8** [a] Judg. 17:6; 21:25 **12:9** [a] Deut. 3:20; 25:19

the land which the LORD your God is giving you to inherit, and He gives you [a]rest from all your enemies round about, so that you dwell in safety, 11 then there will be the place where the LORD your God chooses to make His name abide. There you shall bring all that I command you: your burnt offerings, your sacrifices, your tithes, the heave offerings of your hand, and all your choice offerings which you vow to the LORD. 12 And [a]you shall rejoice before the LORD your God, you and your sons and your daughters, your male and female servants, and the [b]Levite who *is* within your gates, since he has no portion nor inheritance with you. 13 Take heed to yourself that you do not offer your burnt offerings in every place that you see; 14 but in the place which the LORD chooses, in one of your tribes, there you shall offer your burnt offerings, and there you shall do all that I command you.

15 "However, [a]you may slaughter and eat meat within all your gates, whatever your heart desires, according to the blessing of the LORD your God which He has given you; [b]the unclean and the clean may eat of it, [c]of the gazelle and the deer alike. 16 [a]Only you shall not eat the blood; you shall pour it on the earth like water. 17 You may not eat within your gates the tithe of your grain or your new wine or your oil, of the firstborn of your herd or your flock, of any of your offerings which you vow, of your freewill offerings, or of the heave offering of your hand. 18 But you must eat them before the LORD your God in the place which the LORD your God chooses, you and your son and your daughter, your male servant and your female servant, and the Levite who *is* within your gates; and you shall rejoice before the LORD your God in all to which you put your hands. 19 Take heed to yourself that you do not forsake the Levite as long as you live in your land.

20 "When the LORD your God [a]enlarges your border as He has promised you, and you say, 'Let me eat meat,' because you long to eat meat, you may eat as much meat as your heart desires. 21 If the place where the LORD your God chooses to put His name is too far from [a]you, then you may slaughter from your herd and from your flock which the LORD has given you, just as I have commanded you, and you may eat within your gates as much as your heart desires. 22 Just as the gazelle and the deer are eaten, so you may eat them; the unclean and the clean alike may eat them. 23 Only be sure that you do not eat the blood, [a]for the blood *is* the life; you may not eat the life with the meat. 24 You shall not eat it; you shall pour it on the earth like water. 25 You shall not eat it, [a]that it may go well with you and your children after you, [b]when you do *what is* right in the sight of the LORD. 26 Only the [a]holy things which you have, and your vowed offerings, you shall take and go to the place which the LORD chooses. 27 And [a]you shall offer your burnt offerings, the meat and the blood, on the altar of the LORD your God; and the blood of your sacrifices shall be poured out on the altar of the LORD your God, and you shall eat the meat. 28 Observe and obey all these words which I command you, [a]that it may go well with you and your children after you forever, when you do *what is* good and right in the sight of the LORD your God.

Beware of False Gods

29 "When [a]the LORD your God cuts off from before you the nations which you go to dispossess, and you displace them and dwell in their land, 30 take heed to yourself that you are not ensnared to follow them, after they are destroyed from before you, and that you do not inquire after their gods, saying, 'How did these nations serve their gods? I also will do likewise.' 31 [a]You shall not worship the LORD your God in that way; for every abomination to the LORD which He hates they have done to their gods; for [b]they burn even their sons and daughters in the fire to their gods.

32 "Whatever I command you, be careful to observe it; [a]you shall not add to it nor take away from it.

Punishment of Apostates

13 "If there arises among you a prophet or a [a]dreamer of dreams, [b]and he gives you a sign or a wonder, 2 and [a]the sign or the wonder comes to pass, of which he spoke to you, saying, 'Let us go after other gods'—which you have not known—'and let us serve them,' 3 you shall not listen to the words of that prophet or that dreamer of dreams, for the LORD your God [a]is testing you to know whether you love the LORD your God with all your heart and with all your soul. 4 You shall [a]walk after the LORD your God and fear Him, and keep His commandments and obey His voice; you shall serve Him and [b]hold fast to Him. 5 But [a]that

12:10 [a] Josh. 11:23 **12:12** [a] Deut. 12:18; 26:11 [b] Deut. 10:9; 14:29 **12:15** [a] Deut. 12:21 [b] Deut. 12:22 [c] Deut. 14:5 **12:16** [a] Gen. 9:4 **12:20** [a] Ex. 34:24 **12:21** [a] Deut. 14:24 **12:23** [a] Gen. 9:4 **12:25** [a] Deut. 4:40; 6:18 [b] Ex. 15:26 **12:26** [a] Num. 5:9, 10; 18:19 **12:27** [a] Lev. 1:5, 9, 13, 17 **12:28** [a] Deut. 12:25 **12:29** [a] Ex. 23:23 **12:31** [a] Lev. 18:3, 26, 30; 20:1, 2 [b] Deut. 18:10 **12:32** [a] Rev. 22:18, 19 **13:1** [a] Zech. 10:2 [b] Matt. 24:24 **13:2** [a] Deut. 18:22 **13:3** [a] Deut. 8:2, 16 **13:4** [a] 2 Kin. 23:3 [b] Deut. 30:20 **13:5** [a] Jer. 14:15

DISMISS THE IMPOSTERS OF PEACE

If there arises among you a prophet or a dreamer of dreams, and he [says], "Let us go after other gods" . . . you shall not listen.

DEUTERONOMY 13:1–3

Often, what prevents us from finding God's peace are the many offers and assurances of false peace we hear all day long. In the days of the early church, the Roman emperor promised serenity: "peace" and "safety" were key words in the imperial propaganda (see 1 Thess. 5:3). Placing one's faith in the emperor and the gods of the Greeks and Romans was expected. In the Jewish world, men came forward claiming to be prophets and offering signs of salvation (see Matt. 24:24; Mark 13:22).

Speaking through Moses, the Lord warned Israel of the dangers of these false prophets and dreamers. Such people try to steer us in novel and dubious directions. These pernicious false teachings often promise things that people are desperate to find. But there are no shortcuts to finding peace. Everything outside God's truth is a lie.

Have you tried shortcuts in pursuit of peace? How can you lean on the Lord instead?

prophet or that dreamer of dreams shall be put to death, because he has spoken in order to turn *you* away from the LORD your God, who brought you out of the land of Egypt and redeemed you from the house of bondage, to entice you from the way in which the LORD your God commanded you to walk. [b]So you shall put away the evil from your midst.

6 [a]"If your brother, the son of your mother, your son or your daughter, [b]the wife of your bosom, or your friend [c]who is as your own soul, secretly entices you, saying, 'Let us go and serve other gods,' which you have not known, neither you nor your fathers, 7 of the gods of the people which *are* all around you, near to you or far off from you, from *one* end of the earth to the *other* end of the earth, 8 you shall [a]not consent to him or listen to him, nor shall your eye pity him, nor shall you spare him or conceal him; 9 but you shall surely kill him; your hand shall be first against him to put him to [a]death, and afterward the hand of all the people. 10 And you shall stone him with stones until he dies, because he sought to entice you away from the LORD your God, who brought you out of the land of Egypt, from the house of bondage. 11 So all Israel shall hear and [a]fear, and not again do such wickedness as this among you.

12 [a]"If you hear someone in one of your cities, which the LORD your God gives you to dwell in, saying, 13 'Corrupt men have gone out from among you and enticed the inhabitants of their city, saying, "Let us go and serve other gods" '—which you have not known— 14 then you shall inquire, search out, and ask diligently. And *if it is* indeed true *and* certain *that* such an abomination was committed among you, 15 you shall surely strike the inhabitants of that city with the edge of the sword, utterly destroying it, all that is in it and its livestock—with the edge of the sword. 16 And you shall gather all its plunder into the middle of the street, and completely [a]burn with fire the city and all its plunder, for the LORD your God. It shall be [b]a heap forever; it shall not be built again. 17 [a]So none of the accursed things shall remain in your hand, that the LORD may [b]turn from the fierceness of His anger and show you mercy, have compassion on you and multiply you, just as He swore to your fathers, 18 because you have listened to the voice of the LORD your God, [a]to keep all His commandments which I command you today, to do *what is* right in the eyes of the LORD your God.

Improper Mourning

14 "You *are* [a]the children of the LORD your God; [b]you shall not cut yourselves nor shave the front of your head for the dead. 2 [a]For you *are* a holy people to the LORD your God, and the LORD has chosen you to be a people for Himself, a special treasure above all the peoples who *are* on the face of the earth.

13:5 [b] Deut. 17:5, 7 13:6 [a] Deut. 17:2 [b] Gen. 16:5 [c] 1 Sam. 18:1, 3 13:8 [a] Prov. 1:10 13:9 [a] Deut. 17:7 13:11 [a] Deut. 17:13 13:12 [a] Judg. 20:1–48 13:16 [a] Josh. 6:24 [b] Josh. 8:28 13:17 [a] Josh. 6:18 [b] Josh. 7:26 13:18 [a] Deut. 12:25, 28, 32 14:1 [a] [Rom. 8:16] [b] Lev. 19:28; 21:1–5 14:2 [a] Lev. 20:26

Clean and Unclean Meat

3 [a]“You shall not eat any detestable thing.
4 [a]These *are* the animals which you may eat:
the ox, the sheep, the goat, 5 the deer, the
gazelle, the roe deer, the wild goat, the mountain goat,[1] the antelope, and the mountain
sheep. 6 And you may eat every animal with
cloven hooves, having the hoof split into two
parts, *and that* chews the cud, among the
animals. 7 Nevertheless, of those that chew
the cud or have cloven hooves, you shall not
eat, *such as* these: the camel, the hare, and
the rock hyrax; for they chew the cud but do
not have cloven hooves; they *are* unclean
for you. 8 Also the swine is unclean for you,
because it has cloven hooves, yet *does* not
chew the cud; you shall not eat their flesh
[a]or touch their dead carcasses.

9 [a]“These you may eat of all that *are* in the
waters: you may eat all that have fins and
scales. 10 And whatever does not have fins and
scales you shall not eat; it *is* unclean for you.

11 “All clean birds you may eat. 12 [a]But these
you shall not eat: the eagle, the vulture, the
buzzard, 13 the red kite, the falcon, and the
kite after their kinds; 14 every raven after its
kind; 15 the ostrich, the short-eared owl, the
sea gull, and the hawk after their kinds; 16 the
little owl, the screech owl, the white owl, 17 the
jackdaw, the carrion vulture, the fisher owl,
18 the stork, the heron after its kind, and the
hoopoe and the bat.

19 “Also [a]every creeping thing that flies is
unclean for you; [b]they shall not be eaten.

20 “You may eat all clean birds.

21 [a]“You shall not eat anything that dies
of itself; you may give it to the alien who *is*
within your gates, that he may eat it, or you
may sell it to a foreigner; [b]for you *are* a holy
people to the LORD your God.

“[c]You shall not boil a young goat in its
mother’s milk.

Tithing Principles

22 [a]“You shall truly tithe all the increase of
your grain that the field produces year by year.
23 [a]And you shall eat before the LORD your God,
in the place where He chooses to make His
name abide, the tithe of your grain and your
new wine and your oil, of [b]the firstborn of your
herds and your flocks, that you may learn to
fear the LORD your God always. 24 But if the
journey is too long for you, so that you are not
able to carry *the tithe, or* [a]if the place where
the LORD your God chooses to put His name
is too far from you, when the LORD your God
has blessed you, 25 then you shall exchange
it for money, take the money in your hand,
and go to the place which the LORD your God
chooses. 26 And you shall spend that money
for whatever your heart desires: for oxen or
sheep, for wine or similar drink, for whatever
your heart desires; you shall eat there before
the LORD your God, and you shall [a]rejoice, you
and your household. 27 You shall not forsake
the [a]Levite who *is* within your gates, for he has
no part nor inheritance with you.

28 [a]“At the end of *every* third year you shall
bring out the [b]tithe of your produce of that
year and store *it* up within your gates. 29 And
the Levite, because he has no portion nor
inheritance with you, and the stranger and
the fatherless and the widow who *are* within
your gates, may come and eat and be satisfied, that the LORD your God may bless you
in all the work of your hand which you do.

Debts Canceled Every Seven Years

15 “At the end of [a]*every* seven years you
shall grant a release *of debts.* 2 And this
is the form of the release: Every creditor who
has lent *anything* to his neighbor shall release
it; he shall not require *it* of his neighbor or
his brother, because it is called the LORD’s
release. 3 Of a foreigner you may require *it;*
but you shall give up your claim to what is
owed by your brother, 4 except when there
may be no poor among you; for the LORD
will greatly [a]bless you in the land which the
LORD your God is giving you to possess *as*
an inheritance— 5 only if you carefully obey
the voice of the LORD your God, to observe
with care all these commandments which I

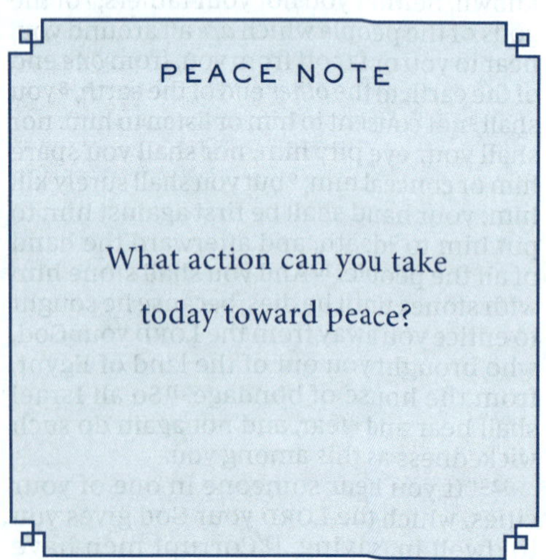

14:3 [a] Ezek. 4:14 **14:4** [a] Lev. 11:2–45 **14:5** [1] Or *addax* **14:8** [a] Lev. 11:26, 27 **14:9** [a] Lev. 11:9 **14:12** [a] Lev. 11:13 **14:19** [a] Lev. 11:20 [b] Lev. 11:23 **14:21** [a] Lev. 17:15; 22:8 [b] Deut. 14:2 [c] Ex. 23:19; 34:26 **14:22** [a] Lev. 27:30 **14:23** [a] Deut. 12:5–7 [b] Deut. 15:19, 20 **14:24** [a] Deut. 12:5, 21 **14:26** [a] Deut. 12:7 **14:27** [a] Deut. 12:12 **14:28** [a] Deut. 26:12 [b] Num. 18:21–24 **15:1** [a] Ex. 21:2; 23:10, 11 **15:4** [a] Deut. 7:13

command you today. 6 For the LORD your God will bless you just as He promised you; [a]you shall lend to many nations, but you shall not borrow; you shall reign over many nations, but they shall not reign over you.

Generosity to the Poor

7 "If there is among you a poor man of your brethren, within any of the gates in your land which the LORD your God is giving you, [a]you shall not harden your heart nor shut your hand from your poor brother, 8 but [a]you shall open your hand wide to him and willingly lend him sufficient for his need, whatever he needs. 9 Beware lest there be a wicked thought in your heart, saying, 'The seventh year, the year of release, is at hand,' and your [a]eye be evil against your poor brother and you give him nothing, and [b]he cry out to the LORD against you, and [c]it become sin among you. 10 You shall surely give to him, and [a]your heart should not be grieved when you give to him, because [b]for this thing the LORD your God will bless you in all your works and in all to which you put your hand. 11 For [a]the poor will never cease from the land; therefore I command you, saying, 'You shall open your hand wide to your brother, to your poor and your needy, in your land.'

The Law Concerning Bondservants

12 [a]"If your brother, a Hebrew man, or a Hebrew woman, is [b]sold to you and serves you six years, then in the seventh year you shall let him go free from you. 13 And when you send him away free from you, you shall not let him go away empty-handed; 14 you shall supply him liberally from your flock, from your threshing floor, and from your winepress. *From what* the LORD your God has [a]blessed you with, you shall give to him. 15 [a]You shall remember that you were a slave in the land of Egypt, and the LORD your God redeemed you; therefore I command you this thing today. 16 And [a]if it happens that he says to you, 'I will not go away from you,' because he loves you and your house, since he prospers with you, 17 then you shall take an awl and thrust *it* through his ear to the door, and he shall be your servant forever. Also to your female servant you shall do likewise. 18 It shall not seem hard to you when you send him away free from you; for he has been worth [a]a double hired servant in serving you six years. Then the LORD your God will bless you in all that you do.

The Law Concerning Firstborn Animals

19 [a]"All the firstborn males that come from your herd and your flock you shall sanctify to the LORD your God; you shall do no work with the firstborn of your herd, nor shear the firstborn of your flock. 20 [a]You and your household shall eat *it* before the LORD your God year by year in the place which the LORD chooses. 21 [a]But if there is a defect in it, *if it is* lame or blind *or has* any serious defect, you shall not sacrifice it to the LORD your God. 22 You may eat it within your gates; [a]the unclean and the clean *person* alike *may eat it,* as *if it were* a gazelle or a deer. 23 Only you shall not eat its blood; you shall pour it on the ground like water.

The Passover Reviewed

16 "Observe the [a]month of Abib, and keep the Passover to the LORD your God, for [b]in the month of Abib the LORD your God brought you out of Egypt by night. 2 Therefore you shall sacrifice the Passover to the LORD your God, from the flock and [a]the herd, in the [b]place where the LORD chooses to put His name. 3 You shall eat no leavened bread with it; [a]seven days you shall eat unleavened bread with it, *that is,* the bread of affliction (for you came out of the land of Egypt in haste), that you may [b]remember the day in which you came out of the land of Egypt all the days of your life. 4 [a]And no leaven shall be seen among you in all your territory for seven days, nor shall *any* of the meat which you sacrifice the first day at twilight remain overnight until [b]morning.

5 "You may not sacrifice the Passover within any of your gates which the LORD your God gives you; 6 but at the place where the LORD your God chooses to make His name abide, there you shall sacrifice the Passover [a]at twilight, at the going down of the sun, at the time you came out of Egypt. 7 And you shall roast and eat *it* [a]in the place which the LORD your God chooses, and in the morning you shall turn and go to your tents. 8 Six days you shall eat unleavened bread, and [a]on the seventh day there *shall be* a sacred assembly to the LORD your God. You shall do no work *on it.*

The Feast of Weeks Reviewed

9 "You shall count seven weeks for yourself; begin to count the seven weeks from *the time* you begin *to put* the sickle to the grain. 10 Then you shall keep the [a]Feast of Weeks to the LORD

15:6 [a] Deut. 28:12, 44 **15:7** [a] Lev. 25:35–37 **15:8** [a] Matt. 5:42 **15:9** [a] Deut. 28:54, 56 [b] Deut. 24:15 [c] [Matt. 25:41, 42] **15:10** [a] 2 Cor. 9:5, 7 [b] Deut. 14:29 **15:11** [a] Matt. 26:11 **15:12** [a] Ex. 21:2–6 [b] Lev. 25:39–46 **15:14** [a] Prov. 10:22 **15:15** [a] Deut. 5:15 **15:16** [a] Ex. 21:5, 6 **15:18** [a] Is. 16:14 **15:19** [a] Ex. 13:2, 12 **15:20** [a] Deut. 12:5; 14:23 **15:21** [a] Lev. 22:19–25 **15:22** [a] Deut. 12:15, 16, 22 **16:1** [a] Ex. 12:2 [b] Ex. 13:4 **16:2** [a] Num. 28:19 [b] Deut. 12:5, 26; 15:20 **16:3** [a] Num. 29:12 [b] Ex. 13:3 **16:4** [a] Ex. 13:7 [b] Num. 9:12 **16:6** [a] Ex. 12:7–10 **16:7** [a] 2 Kin. 23:23 **16:8** [a] Lev. 23:8, 36 **16:10** [a] Ex. 34:22

your God with the tribute of a freewill offering
from your hand, which you shall give [b]as the
LORD your God blesses you. 11[a]You shall rejoice
before the LORD your God, you and your son
and your daughter, your male servant and
your female servant, the Levite who *is* within
your gates, the stranger and the fatherless and
the widow who *are* among you, at the place
where the LORD your God chooses to make
His name abide. 12[a]And you shall remember
that you were a slave in Egypt, and you shall
be careful to observe these statutes.

The Feast of Tabernacles Reviewed

13[a]"You shall observe the Feast of Tabernacles seven days, when you have gathered
from your threshing floor and from your
winepress. 14 And [a]you shall rejoice in your
feast, you and your son and your daughter,
your male servant and your female servant
and the Levite, the stranger and the fatherless
and the widow, who *are* within your gates.
15[a]Seven days you shall keep a sacred feast
to the LORD your God in the place which the
LORD chooses, because the LORD your God
will bless you in all your produce and in all the
work of your hands, so that you surely rejoice.
16[a]"Three times a year all your males shall
appear before the LORD your God in the place
which He chooses: at the Feast of Unleavened
Bread, at the Feast of Weeks, and at the Feast
of Tabernacles; and [b]they shall not appear
before the LORD empty-handed. 17 Every
man *shall give* as he is able, [a]according to
the blessing of the LORD your God which He
has given you.

Justice Must Be Administered

18"You shall appoint [a]judges and officers
in all your gates, which the LORD your God
gives you, according to your tribes, and they
shall judge the people with just judgment.
19[a]You shall not pervert justice; [b]you shall
not show partiality, [c]nor take a bribe, for a
bribe blinds the eyes of the wise and twists
the words of the righteous. 20 You shall follow
what is altogether just, that you may [a]live
and inherit the land which the LORD your
God is giving you.
21[a]"You shall not plant for yourself any
tree, as a wooden image, near the altar which
you build for yourself to the LORD your God.
22[a]You shall not set up a *sacred* pillar, which
the LORD your God hates.

17 "You [a]shall not sacrifice to the LORD
your God a bull or sheep which has any
blemish *or* defect, for that *is* an abomination
to the LORD your God.
2[a]"If there is found among you, within
any of your gates which the LORD your God
gives you, a man or a woman who has been
wicked in the sight of the LORD your God, [b]in
transgressing His covenant, 3 who has gone
and served other gods and worshiped them,
either [a]the sun or moon or any of the host of
heaven, [b]which I have not commanded, 4[a]and
it is told you, and you hear *of it,* then you shall
inquire diligently. And if *it is* indeed true *and*
certain that such an abomination has been
committed in Israel, 5 then you shall bring
out to your gates that man or woman who
has committed that wicked thing, and [a]shall
stone [b]to death that man or woman with
stones. 6 Whoever is deserving of death shall
be put to death on the testimony of two or
three [a]witnesses; he shall not be put to death
on the testimony of one witness. 7 The hands
of the witnesses shall be the first against him
to put him to death, and afterward the hands
of all the people. So you shall put away the
evil from among [a]you.
8[a]"If a matter arises which is too hard for
you to judge, between degrees of guilt for
bloodshed, between one judgment or another, or between one punishment or another,
matters of controversy within your gates,
then you shall arise and go up to the [b]place
which the LORD your God chooses. 9 And
[a]you shall come to the priests, the Levites,
and [b]to the judge *there* in those days, and
inquire *of them;* [c]they shall pronounce upon
you the sentence of judgment. 10 You shall
do according to the sentence which they
pronounce upon you in that place which
the LORD chooses. And you shall be careful
to do according to all that they order you.
11 According to the sentence of the law in
which they instruct you, according to the
judgment which they tell you, you shall do;
you shall not turn aside *to* the right hand
or *to* the left from the sentence which they
pronounce upon you. 12 Now [a]the man who
acts presumptuously and will not heed the
priest who stands to minister there before
the LORD your God, or the judge, that man
shall die. So you shall put away the evil from
Israel. 13[a]And all the people shall hear and
fear, and no longer act presumptuously.

16:10 [b] 1 Cor. 16:2 **16:11** [a] Deut. 16:14 **16:12** [a] Deut. 15:15 **16:13** [a] Ex. 23:16 **16:14** [a] Neh. 8:9 **16:15** [a] Lev. 23:39–41 **16:16** [a] Ex. 23:14–17; 34:22–24 [b] Ex. 23:15 **16:17** [a] Deut. 16:10 **16:18** [a] Deut. 1:16, 17 **16:19** [a] Ex. 23:2, 6 [b] Deut. 1:17 [c] Ex. 23:8 **16:20** [a] Ezek. 18:5–9 **16:21** [a] Ex. 34:13 **16:22** [a] Lev. 26:1 **17:1** [a] Deut. 15:21 **17:2** [a] Deut. 13:6 [b] Josh. 7:11 **17:3** [a] Deut. 4:19 [b] Jer. 7:22 **17:4** [a] Deut. 13:12, 14 **17:5** [a] Lev. 24:14–16 [b] Deut. 13:6–18 **17:6** [a] Num. 35:30 **17:7** [a] Deut. 13:5; 19:19 **17:8** [a] Deut. 1:17 [b] Deut. 12:5; 16:2 **17:9** [a] Jer. 18:18 [b] Deut. 19:17–19 [c] Ezek. 44:24 **17:12** [a] Num. 15:30 **17:13** [a] Deut. 13:11

Principles Governing Kings

14 "When you come to the land which the
LORD your God is giving you, and possess
it and dwell in it, and say, [a]'I will set a king
over me like all the nations that *are* around
me,' 15 you shall surely set a king over you
[a]whom the LORD your God chooses; *one*
[b]from among your brethren you shall set
as king over you; you may not set a foreigner over you, who *is* not your brother. 16 But
he shall not multiply [a]horses for himself,
nor cause the people [b]to return to Egypt to
multiply horses, for [c]the LORD has said to
you, [d]'You shall not return that way again.'
17 Neither shall he multiply wives for himself,
lest his heart turn away; nor shall he greatly
multiply silver and [a]gold for himself.
18 "Also it shall be, when he sits on the
throne of his kingdom, that he shall write
for himself a copy of this law in a book, from
the one [a]before the priests, the Levites. 19 And
[a]it shall be with him, and he shall read it all
the days of his life, that he may learn to fear
the LORD his God and be careful to observe
all the words of this law and these statutes,
20 that his heart may not be lifted above his
brethren, that he [a]may not turn aside from
the commandment *to* the right hand or *to*
the left, and that he may prolong *his* days
in his kingdom, he and his children in the
midst of Israel.

The Portion of the Priests and Levites

18 "The priests, the Levites—all the tribe
of Levi—shall have no part nor [a]inher-
itance with Israel; they shall eat the offerings
of the LORD made by fire, and His portion.
2 Therefore they shall have no inheritance
among their brethren; the LORD is their inheritance, as He said to them.
3 "And this shall be the priest's [a]due from
the people, from those who offer a sacrifice,
whether *it is* bull or sheep: they shall give to
the priest the shoulder, the cheeks, and the
stomach. 4 [a]The firstfruits of your grain and
your new wine and your oil, and the first of
the fleece of your sheep, you shall give him.
5 For [a]the LORD your God has chosen him out
of all your tribes [b]to stand to minister in the
name of the LORD, him and his sons forever.
6 "So if a Levite comes from any of your
gates, from where he [a]dwells among all Israel,
and comes with all the desire of his mind [b]to
the place which the LORD chooses, 7 then he
may serve in the name of the LORD his God
[a]as all his brethren the Levites *do,* who stand
there before the LORD. 8 They shall have equal
[a]portions to eat, besides what comes from
the sale of his inheritance.

Avoid Wicked Customs

9 "When you come into the land which the
LORD your God is giving you, [a]you shall not
learn to follow the abominations of those nations. 10 There shall not be found among you
anyone who makes his son or his daughter
[a]pass through the fire, [b]*or one* who practices
witchcraft, *or* a soothsayer, or one who interprets omens, or a sorcerer, 11 [a]or one who
conjures spells, or a medium, or a spiritist,
or [b]one who calls up the dead. 12 For all who
do these things *are* an abomination to the
LORD, and [a]because of these abominations
the LORD your God drives them out from
before you. 13 You shall be blameless before
the LORD your God. 14 For these nations which
you will dispossess listened to soothsayers
and diviners; but as for you, the LORD your
God has not appointed such for you.

A New Prophet Like Moses

15 [a]"The LORD your God will raise up for you
a Prophet like me from your midst, from your
brethren. Him you shall hear, 16 according to
all you desired of the LORD your God in Horeb
[a]in the day of the assembly, saying, [b]'Let me
not hear again the voice of the LORD my
God, nor let me see this great fire anymore,
lest I die.'

PEACE NOTE

As new covenant believers, we fear (or revere) God as our heavenly Father but are not afraid of Him because in His presence is joy and peace.

17:14 [a] 1 Sam. 8:5, 19, 20; 10:19 17:15 [a] 1 Sam. 9:15, 16; 10:24; 16:12, 13 [b] Jer. 30:21 17:16 [a] 1 Kin. 4:26; 10:26–29 [b] Ezek. 17:15 [c] Ex. 13:17, 18 [d] Deut. 28:68 17:17 [a] 1 Kin. 10:14 17:18 [a] Deut. 31:24–26 17:19 [a] Ps. 119:97, 98 17:20 [a] Deut. 5:32 18:1 [a] Deut. 10:9 18:3 [a] Lev. 7:32–34; 1 Sam. 2:13–16, 29 18:4 [a] Ex. 22:29 18:5 [a] Ex. 28:1 [b] Deut. 10:8 18:6 [a] Num. 35:2 [b] Deut. 12:5; 14:23 18:7 [a] 2 Chr. 31:2 18:8 [a] 2 Chr. 31:4 18:9 [a] Deut. 12:29, 30; 20:16–18 18:10 [a] Deut. 12:31 [b] Is. 8:19 18:11 [a] Lev. 20:27 [b] 1 Sam. 28:7 18:12 [a] Lev. 18:24 18:15 [a] Matt. 21:11; Luke 1:76; 2:25–34; 7:16; 24:19; John 1:45; Acts 3:22 18:16 [a] Deut. 5:23–27 [b] Ex. 20:18, 19

17“And the LORD said to me: [a]‘What they
have spoken is good. 18[a]I will raise up for
them a Prophet like you from among their
brethren, and [b]will put My words in His
mouth, [c]and He shall speak to them all that
I command Him. 19[a]And it shall be *that* whoever will not hear My words, which He speaks
in My name, I will require *it* of him. 20But
[a]the prophet who presumes to speak a word
in My name, which I have not commanded
him to speak, or [b]who speaks in the name
of other gods, that prophet shall die.’ 21And
if you say in your heart, ‘How shall we know
the word which the LORD has not spoken?’—
22[a]when a prophet speaks in the name of the
LORD, [b]if the thing does not happen or come
to pass, that *is* the thing which the LORD has
not spoken; the prophet has spoken it [c]pre-
sumptuously; you shall not be afraid of him.

Three Cities of Refuge

19 “When the LORD your God [a]has cut off
the nations whose land the LORD your
God is giving you, and you dispossess them
and dwell in their cities and in their houses,
2[a]you shall separate three cities for yourself
in the midst of your land which the LORD
your God is giving you to possess. 3You shall
prepare roads for yourself, and divide into
three parts the territory of your land which
the LORD your God is giving you to inherit,
that any manslayer may flee there.

4“And [a]this *is* the case of the manslayer
who flees there, that he may live: Whoever
kills his neighbor unintentionally, not having
hated him in time past— 5as when *a man*
goes to the woods with his neighbor to cut
timber, and his hand swings a stroke with the
ax to cut down the tree, and the head slips
from the handle and strikes his neighbor so
that he dies—he shall flee to one of these
cities and live; 6[a]lest the avenger of blood,
while his anger is hot, pursue the manslayer
and overtake him, because the way is long,
and kill him, though he *was* not deserving of
death, since he had not hated the victim in
time past. 7Therefore I command you, saying,
‘You shall separate three cities for yourself.’

8“Now if the LORD your God [a]enlarges
your territory, as He swore to [b]your fathers,
and gives you the land which He promised
to give to your fathers, 9and if you keep all
these commandments and do them, which
I command you today, to love the LORD your
God and to walk always in His ways, [a]then
you shall add three more cities for yourself
besides these three, 10[a]lest innocent blood be
shed in the midst of your land which the LORD
your God is giving you *as* an inheritance, and
thus guilt of bloodshed be upon you.

11“But [a]if anyone hates his neighbor, lies
in wait for him, rises against him and strikes
him mortally, so that he dies, and he flees to
one of these cities, 12then the elders of his
city shall send and bring him from there, and
deliver him over to the hand of the avenger
of blood, that he may die. 13[a]Your eye shall
not pity him, [b]but you shall put away *the guilt
of* innocent blood from Israel, that it may go
well with you.

Property Boundaries

14[a]“You shall not remove your neighbor’s
landmark, which the men of old have set,
in your inheritance which you will inherit
in the land that the LORD your God is giving
you to possess.

The Law Concerning Witnesses

15[a]“One witness shall not rise against a
man concerning any iniquity or any sin that
he commits; by the mouth of two or three
witnesses the matter shall be established.
16If a false witness [a]rises against any man to
testify against him of wrongdoing, 17then both
men in the controversy shall stand before
the LORD, [a]before the priests and the judges
who serve in those days. 18And the judges
shall make careful inquiry, and indeed, *if* the
witness *is* a false witness, who has testified
falsely against his brother, 19[a]then you shall
do to him as he thought to have done to his
brother; so [b]you shall put away the evil from
among you. 20[a]And those who remain shall
hear and fear, and hereafter they shall not
again commit such evil among you. 21[a]Your
eye shall not pity: [b]life *shall be* for life, eye
for eye, tooth for tooth, hand for hand, foot
for foot.

Principles Governing Warfare

20 “When you go out to battle against
your enemies, and see [a]horses and
chariots *and* people more numerous than
you, do not be [b]afraid of them; for the LORD
your God *is* [c]with you, who brought you up
from the land of Egypt. 2So it shall be, when
you are on the verge of battle, that the priest

18:17 [a] Deut. 5:28 **18:18** [a] John 1:45; 6:14; Acts 3:22 [b] Is. 49:2; 51:16; John 17:8 [c] [John 4:25; 8:28] **18:19** [a] Acts 3:23; [Heb. 12:25] **18:20** [a] Jer. 14:14, 15 [b] Jer. 2:8 **18:22** [a] Jer. 28:9 [b] Deut. 13:2 [c] Deut. 18:20 **19:1** [a] Deut. 12:29 **19:2** [a] Num. 35:10–15 **19:4** [a] Num. 35:9–34 **19:6** [a] Num. 35:12 **19:8** [a] Deut. 12:20 [b] Gen. 15:18–21 **19:9** [a] Josh. 20:7–9 **19:10** [a] Deut. 21:1–9 **19:11** [a] Num. 35:16, 24 **19:13** [a] Deut. 13:8 [b] 1 Kin. 2:31 **19:14** [a] Prov. 22:28 **19:15** [a] Num. 35:30 **19:16** [a] Ex. 23:1 **19:17** [a] Deut. 17:8–11; 21:5 **19:19** [a] Prov. 19:5 [b] Deut. 13:5; 17:7; 21:21; 22:21 **19:20** [a] Deut. 17:13; 21:21 **19:21** [a] Deut. 19:13 [b] Ex. 21:23, 24 **20:1** [a] Ps. 20:7 [b] Deut. 7:18 [c] 2 Chr. 13:12; 32:7, 8

shall approach and speak to the people. 3 And
he shall say to them, 'Hear, O Israel: Today
you are on the verge of battle with your enemies. Do not let your heart faint, do not be
afraid, and do not tremble or be terrified
because of them; 4 for the LORD your God
is He who goes with you, [a]to fight for you
against your enemies, to save you.'

5 "Then the officers shall speak to the people, saying: 'What man *is there* who has built
a new house and has not [a]dedicated it? Let
him go and return to his house, lest he die
in the battle and another man dedicate it.
6 Also what man *is there* who has planted a
vineyard and has not eaten of it? Let him go
and return to his house, lest he die in the
battle and another man eat of it. 7 [a]And what
man *is there* who is betrothed to a woman
and has not married her? Let him go and
return to his house, lest he die in the battle
and another man marry her.'

8 "The officers shall speak further to the
people, and say, [a]'What man *is there who is*
fearful and fainthearted? Let him go and
return to his house, lest the heart of his brethren faint[1] like his heart.' 9 And so it shall be,
when the officers have finished speaking to
the people, that they shall make captains of
the armies to lead the people.

10 "When you go near a city to fight against it,
[a]then proclaim an offer of peace to it. 11 And it
shall be that if they accept your offer of peace,
and open to you, then all the people *who are*
found in it shall be placed under tribute to you,
and serve you. 12 Now if *the city* will not make
peace with you, but war against you, then you
shall besiege it. 13 And when the LORD your God
delivers it into your hands, [a]you shall strike
every male in it with the edge of the sword.
14 But the women, the little ones, [a]the livestock,
and all that is in the city, all its spoil, you shall
plunder for yourself; and [b]you shall eat the
enemies' plunder which the LORD your God
gives you. 15 Thus you shall do to all the cities
which are very far from you, which *are* not of
the cities of these nations.

16 "But [a]of the cities of these peoples which
the LORD your God gives you *as* an inheritance, you shall let nothing that breathes
remain alive, 17 but you shall utterly destroy
them: the Hittite and the Amorite and the
Canaanite and the Perizzite and the Hivite
and the Jebusite, just as the LORD your God
has commanded you, 18 lest [a]they teach you
to do according to all their abominations
which they have done for their gods, and you
[b]sin against the LORD your God.

19 "When you besiege a city for a long time,
while making war against it to take it, you shall
not destroy its trees by wielding an ax against
them; if you can eat of them, do not cut them
down to use in the siege, for the tree of the field
is man's *food*. 20 Only the trees which you know
are not trees for food you may destroy and
cut down, to build siegeworks against the city
that makes war with you, until it is subdued.

20:4 [a] Josh. 23:10 **20:5** [a] Neh. 12:27 **20:7** [a] Deut. 24:5 **20:8** [a] Judg. 7:3 [1] Following Masoretic Text and Targum; Samaritan Pentateuch, Septuagint, Syriac, and Vulgate read *lest he make his brother's heart faint.* **20:10** [a] 2 Sam. 10:19 **20:13** [a] Num. 31:7 **20:14** [a] Josh. 8:2 [b] 1 Sam. 14:30 **20:16** [a] Deut. 7:1–5 **20:18** [a] Deut. 7:4; 12:30; 18:9 [b] Ex. 23:33

THE PRAYER THAT BRINGS PEACE

When you go near a city to fight against it, then proclaim an offer of peace to it.

DEUTERONOMY 20:10

God gave the land of Canaan, better known as the Promised Land, to the great patriarch Abraham and his descendants. When He led the people of Israel out of Egypt and guided them toward this land, they encountered peoples who chose either to oppose or befriend them. Some of these peoples were more discerning than others, and they recognized that God was with Israel. Others, however, chose to fight.

Those who recognized and respected the God of Israel were offered peace. Battle was only the last resort. This is true for us—but in reverse! As we wend our way to the kingdom of God, we will encounter conflict. As strange as it may sound, sometimes we have to fight for peace. In our personal relationships, conflict will arise. We have to fight in prayer for peace in our families, with our spouses, and within our communities. We see a mandate in Scripture time and again to humble ourselves to pray—this is how we fight for peace.

You can change your life today by God's grace if you seek His peace.

The Law Concerning Unsolved Murder

21 "If *anyone* is found slain, lying in the
field in the land which the LORD your
God is giving you to possess, *and* it is not
known who killed him, 2 then your elders and
your judges shall go out and measure *the distance* from the slain man to the surrounding
cities. 3 And it shall be *that* the elders of the
city nearest to the slain man will take a heifer
which has not been worked *and* which has not
pulled with a [a]yoke. 4 The elders of that city
shall bring the heifer down to a valley with
flowing water, which is neither plowed nor
sown, and they shall break the heifer's neck
there in the valley. 5 Then the priests, the sons
of Levi, shall come near, for [a]the LORD your
God has chosen them to minister to Him and
to bless in the name of the LORD; [b]by their
word every controversy and every assault shall
be *settled.* 6 And all the elders of that city nearest to the slain *man* [a]shall wash their hands
over the heifer whose neck was broken in the
valley. 7 Then they shall answer and say, 'Our
hands have not shed this blood, nor have our
eyes seen *it.* 8 Provide atonement, O LORD, for
Your people Israel, whom You have redeemed,
[a]and do not lay innocent blood to the charge
of Your people Israel.' And atonement shall
be provided on their behalf for the blood.
9 So [a]you shall put away the *guilt of* innocent
blood from among you when you do *what is*
right in the sight of the LORD.

Female Captives

10 "When you go out to war against your
enemies, and the LORD your God delivers
them into your hand, and you take them
captive, 11 and you see among the captives a
beautiful woman, and desire her and would
take her for your [a]wife, 12 then you shall bring
her home to your house, and she shall [a]shave
her head and trim her nails. 13 She shall put
off the clothes of her captivity, remain in
your house, and [a]mourn her father and her
mother a full month; after that you may go
in to her and be her husband, and she shall
be your wife. 14 And it shall be, if you have no
delight in her, then you shall set her free, but
you certainly shall not sell her for money;
you shall not treat her brutally, because you
have [a]humbled her.

Firstborn Inheritance Rights

15 "If a man has two wives, one loved [a]and
the other unloved, and they have borne him
children, *both* the loved and the unloved, and
if the firstborn son is of her who is unloved,
16 then it shall be, [a]on the day he bequeaths
his possessions to his sons, *that* he must
not bestow firstborn status on the son of
the loved wife in preference to the son of
the unloved, the *true* firstborn. 17 But he shall
acknowledge the son of the unloved wife *as*
the firstborn [a]by giving him a double portion
of all that he has, for he [b]*is* the beginning of
his strength; [c]the right of the firstborn *is* his.

The Rebellious Son

18 "If a man has a stubborn and rebellious son
who will not obey the voice of his father or the
voice of his mother, and *who,* when they have
chastened him, will not heed them, 19 then his
father and his mother shall take hold of him
and bring him out to the elders of his city, to
the gate of his city. 20 And they shall say to the
elders of his city, 'This son of ours is stubborn
and rebellious; he will not obey our voice; he
is a glutton and a drunkard.' 21 Then all the
men of his city shall stone him to death with
stones; [a]so you shall put away the evil from
among you, [b]and all Israel shall hear and fear.

Miscellaneous Laws

22 "If a man has committed a sin [a]deserving
of death, and he is put to death, and you hang
him on a tree, 23 [a]his body shall not remain
overnight on the tree, but you shall surely
bury him that day, so that [b]you do not defile
the land which the LORD your God is giving
you *as* an inheritance; for [c]he who is hanged
is accursed of God.

22 "You [a]shall not see your brother's ox
or his sheep going astray, and hide
yourself from them; you shall certainly
bring them back to your brother. 2 And if
your brother *is* not near you, or if you do not
know him, then you shall bring it to your own
house, and it shall remain with you until your
brother seeks it; then you shall restore it to
him. 3 You shall do the same with his donkey,
and so shall you do with his garment; with
any lost thing of your brother's, which he
has lost and you have found, you shall do
likewise; you must not hide yourself.

4 [a]"You shall not see your brother's donkey
or his ox fall down along the road, and hide
yourself from them; you shall surely help
him lift *them* up again.

5 "A woman shall not wear anything that
pertains to a man, nor shall a man put on a
woman's garment, for all who do so *are* an
abomination to the LORD your God.

21:3 [a] Num. 19:2 **21:5** [a] 1 Chr. 23:13 [b] Deut. 17:8, 9 **21:6** [a] Matt. 27:24 **21:8** [a] Jon. 1:14 **21:9** [a] Deut. 19:13 **21:11** [a] Num. 31:18 **21:12** [a] Lev. 14:8, 9 **21:13** [a] Ps. 45:10 **21:14** [a] Judg. 19:24 **21:15** [a] Gen. 29:33 **21:16** [a] 1 Chr. 5:2; 26:10 **21:17** [a] 2 Kin. 2:9 [b] Gen. 49:3 [c] Gen. 25:31, 33 **21:21** [a] Deut. 13:5; 19:19, 20; 22:21, 24 [b] Deut. 13:11 **21:22** [a] Acts 23:29 **21:23** [a] John 19:31 [b] Lev. 18:25 [c] Gal. 3:13 **22:1** [a] Ex. 23:4 **22:4** [a] Ex. 23:5

6 “If a bird’s nest happens to be before you
along the way, in any tree or on the ground,
with young ones or eggs, with the mother
sitting on the young or on the eggs, [a]you shall
not take the mother with the young; 7 you
shall surely let the mother go, and take the
young for yourself, [a]that it may be well with
you and *that* you may prolong *your* days.

8 “When you build a new house, then you
shall make a parapet for your roof, that you
may not bring guilt of bloodshed on your
household if anyone falls from it.

9 [a]“You shall not sow your vineyard with
different kinds of seed, lest the yield of the
seed which you have sown and the fruit of
your vineyard be defiled.

10 [a]“You shall not plow with an ox and a
donkey together.

11 [a]“You shall not wear a garment of different sorts, *such as* wool and linen mixed
together.

12 “You shall make [a]tassels on the four corners of the clothing with which you cover
yourself.

Laws of Sexual Morality

13 “If any man takes a wife, and goes in to
her, and [a]detests her, 14 and charges her with
shameful conduct, and brings a bad name
on her, and says, ‘I took this woman, and
when I came to her I found she *was* not a
virgin,’ 15 then the father and mother of the
young woman shall take and bring out *the
evidence of* the young woman’s virginity to
the elders of the city at the gate. 16 And the
young woman’s father shall say to the elders,
‘I gave my daughter to this man as wife, and
he detests her. 17 Now he has charged her with
shameful conduct, saying, “I found your
daughter *was* not a virgin,” and yet these
are the evidences of my daughter’s virginity.’
And they shall spread the cloth before the
elders of the city. 18 Then the elders of that
city shall take that man and punish him;
19 and they shall fine him one hundred *shekels*
of silver and give *them* to the father of the
young woman, because he has brought a bad
name on a virgin of Israel. And she shall be
his wife; he cannot divorce her all his days.

20 “But if the thing is true, *and evidences of*
virginity are not found for the young woman,
21 then they shall bring out the young woman
to the door of her father’s house, and the
men of her city shall stone her to death with
[a]stones, because she has [b]done a disgraceful thing in Israel, to play the harlot in her
father’s house. [c]So you shall put away the
evil from among you.

22 [a]“If a man is found lying with a woman
married to a husband, then both of them
shall die—the man that lay with the woman,
and the woman; so you shall put away the
evil from Israel.

23 “If a young woman *who is* a virgin is
[a]betrothed to a husband, and a man finds
her in the city and lies with her, 24 then you
shall bring them both out to the gate of that
city, and you shall stone them to death with
stones, the young woman because she did not
cry out in the city, and the man because he
[a]humbled his neighbor’s wife; [b]so you shall
put away the evil from among you.

25 “But if a man finds a betrothed young
woman in the countryside, and the man
forces her and lies with her, then only the
man who lay with her shall die. 26 But you
shall do nothing to the young woman; *there
is* in the young woman no sin *deserving* of
death, for just as when a man rises against
his neighbor and kills him, even so *is* this
matter. 27 For he found her in the countryside,
and the betrothed young woman cried out,
but *there was* no one to save her.

28 [a]“If a man finds a young woman *who is*
a virgin, who is not betrothed, and he seizes
her and lies with her, and they are found out,
29 then the man who lay with her shall give
to the young woman’s father [a]fifty *shekels* of
silver, and she shall be his wife [b]because he
has humbled her; he shall not be permitted
to divorce her all his days.

30 [a]“A man shall not take his father’s wife,
nor [b]uncover his father’s bed.

PEACE NOTE

Ask the most mature Christian, “Hey, do you ever struggle to read your Bible?” and he or she may say, “Of course” or share other ways he or she struggles.

22:6 [a] Lev. 22:28 **22:7** [a] Deut. 4:40 **22:9** [a] Lev. 19:19 **22:10** [a] [2 Cor. 6:14–16] **22:11** [a] Lev. 19:19 **22:12** [a] Num. 15:37–41 **22:13** [a] Deut. 21:15; 24:3 **22:21** [a] Deut. 21:21 [b] Gen. 34:7 [c] Deut. 13:5 **22:22** [a] Lev. 20:10 **22:23** [a] Matt. 1:18, 19 **22:24** [a] Deut. 21:14 [b] Deut. 22:21, 22 **22:28** [a] Ex. 22:16, 17 **22:29** [a] Ex. 22:16, 17 [b] Deut. 22:24 **22:30** [a] Deut. 27:20 [b] Ezek. 16:8

Those Excluded from the Congregation

23 “He who is emasculated by crushing
or mutilation shall [a]not enter the assembly of the LORD.
2 “One of illegitimate birth shall not enter
the assembly of the LORD; even to the tenth
generation none of his *descendants* shall
enter the assembly of the LORD.
3 [a]“An Ammonite or Moabite shall not enter the assembly of the LORD; even to the
tenth generation none of his *descendants*
shall enter the assembly of the LORD forever,
4 [a]because they did not meet you with bread
and water on the road when you came out of
Egypt, and [b]because they hired against you
Balaam the son of Beor from Pethor of Mesopotamia,[1] to curse you. 5 Nevertheless the
LORD your God would not listen to Balaam,
but the LORD your God turned the curse into
a blessing for you, because the LORD your God
[a]loves you. 6 [a]You shall not seek their peace
nor their prosperity all your days forever.
7 “You shall not abhor an Edomite, [a]for he
is your brother. You shall not abhor an Egyptian, because [b]you were an alien in his land.
8 The children of the third generation born
to them may enter the assembly of the LORD.

Cleanliness of the Campsite

9 “When the army goes out against your enemies, then keep yourself from every wicked
thing. 10 [a]If there is any man among you who
becomes unclean by some occurrence in the
night, then he shall go outside the camp; he
shall not come inside the camp. 11 But it shall
be, when evening comes, that [a]he shall wash
with water; and when the sun sets, he may
come into the camp.
12 “Also you shall have a place outside the
camp, where you may go out; 13 and you shall
have an implement among your equipment,
and when you sit down outside, you shall
dig with it and turn and cover your refuse.
14 For the LORD your God [a]walks in the midst
of your camp, to deliver you and give your
enemies over to you; therefore your camp
shall be holy, that He may see no unclean
thing among you, and turn away from you.

Miscellaneous Laws

15 [a]“You shall not give back to his master
the slave who has escaped from his master to
you. 16 He may dwell with you in your midst,
in the place which he chooses within one of
your gates, where it seems best to him; [a]you
shall not oppress him.
17 “There shall be no *ritual* harlot[1] [a]of the
daughters of Israel, or a [b]perverted[2] one of
the sons of Israel. 18 You shall not bring the
wages of a harlot or the price of a dog to the
house of the LORD your God for any vowed
offering, for both of these *are* an abomination
to the LORD your God.
19 [a]“You shall not charge interest to your
brother—interest on money *or* food *or* anything that is lent out at interest. 20 [a]To a foreigner you may charge interest, but to your
brother you shall not charge interest, [b]that
the LORD your God may bless you in all to
which you set your hand in the land which
you are entering to possess.
21 [a]“When you make a vow to the LORD
your God, you shall not delay to pay it; for
the LORD your God will surely require it of
you, and it would be sin to you. 22 But if you
abstain from vowing, it shall not be sin to you.
23 [a]That which has gone from your lips you
shall keep and perform, for you voluntarily
vowed to the LORD your God what you have
promised with your mouth.
24 “When you come into your neighbor’s
vineyard, you may eat your fill of grapes at
your pleasure, but you shall not put *any* in
your container. 25 When you come into your
neighbor’s standing grain, [a]you may pluck
the heads with your hand, but you shall not
use a sickle on your neighbor’s standing
grain.

Law Concerning Divorce

24 “When a [a]man takes a wife and marries her, and it happens that she finds
no favor in his eyes because he has found
some uncleanness in her, and he writes her
a [b]certificate of divorce, puts *it* in her hand,
and sends her out of his house, 2 when she
has departed from his house, and goes and
becomes another man’s *wife,* 3 *if* the latter
husband detests her and writes her a certificate of divorce, puts *it* in her hand, and
sends her out of his house, or if the latter
husband dies who took her as his wife, 4 [a]*then*
her former husband who divorced her must
not take her back to be his wife after she has
been defiled; for that *is* an abomination before the LORD, and you shall not bring sin on
the land which the LORD your God is giving
you *as* an inheritance.

23:1 [a] Lev. 21:20; 22:24 **23:3** [a] Neh. 13:1, 2 **23:4** [a] Deut. 2:27–30 [b] Num. 22:5, 6; 23:7 [1] Hebrew *Aram Naharaim* **23:5** [a] Deut. 4:37 **23:6** [a] Ezra 9:12 **23:7** [a] Obad. 10, 12 [b] Deut. 10:19 **23:10** [a] Lev. 15:16 **23:11** [a] Lev. 15:5 **23:14** [a] Lev. 26:12 **23:15** [a] 1 Sam. 30:15 **23:16** [a] Ex. 22:21 **23:17** [a] Lev. 19:29 [b] 2 Kin. 23:7 [1] Hebrew *qedeshah,* feminine of *qadesh* (see next note) [2] Hebrew *qadesh,* that is, one practicing sodomy and prostitution in religious rituals **23:19** [a] Ex. 22:25 **23:20** [a] Deut. 15:3 [b] Deut. 15:10 **23:21** [a] Eccl. 5:4, 5 **23:23** [a] Ps. 66:13, 14 **23:25** [a] Luke 6:1 **24:1** [a] [Matt. 5:31; 19:7] [b] [Jer. 3:8] **24:4** [a] [Jer. 3:1]

Miscellaneous Laws

5[a]“When a man has taken a new wife, he
shall not go out to war or be charged with any
business; he shall be free at home one year, and
[b]bring happiness to his wife whom he has taken.

6“No man shall take the lower or the upper
millstone in pledge, for he takes *one's* living
in pledge.

7“If a man is [a]found kidnapping any of his
brethren of the children of Israel, and mistreats him or sells him, then that kidnapper
shall die; [b]and you shall put away the evil
from among you.

8“Take heed in [a]an outbreak of leprosy,
that you carefully observe and do according
to all that the priests, the Levites, shall teach
you; just as I commanded them, *so* you shall
be careful to do. 9[a]Remember what the LORD
your God did [b]to Miriam on the way when
you came out of Egypt!

10“When you [a]lend your brother anything,
you shall not go into his house to get his
pledge. 11You shall stand outside, and the man
to whom you lend shall bring the pledge out
to you. 12And if the man *is* poor, you shall not
keep his pledge overnight. 13[a]You shall in any
case return the pledge to him again when the
sun goes down, that he may sleep in his own
garment and [b]bless you; and [c]it shall be righteousness to you before the LORD your God.

14“You shall not [a]oppress a hired servant
who is poor and needy, *whether* one of your
brethren or one of the aliens who *is* in your
land within your gates. 15Each day [a]you shall
give *him* his wages, and not let the sun go
down on it, for he *is* poor and has set his
heart on it; [b]lest he cry out against you to
the LORD, and it be sin to you.

16[a]“Fathers shall not be put to death for
their children, nor shall children be put to
death for *their* fathers; a person shall be put
to death for his own sin.

17[a]“You shall not pervert justice due the
stranger or the fatherless, [b]nor take a widow's
garment as a pledge. 18But [a]you shall remember that you were a slave in Egypt, and the
LORD your God redeemed you from there;
therefore I command you to do this thing.

19[a]“When you reap your harvest in your
field, and forget a sheaf in the field, you shall
not go back to get it; it shall be for the stranger,
the fatherless, and the widow, that the LORD
your God may [b]bless you in all the work of
your hands. 20When you beat your olive trees,
you shall not go over the boughs again; it shall
be for the stranger, the fatherless, and the
widow. 21When you gather the grapes of your
vineyard, you shall not glean *it* afterward; it
shall be for the stranger, the fatherless, and
the widow. 22And you shall remember that you
were a slave in the land of Egypt; therefore I
command you to do this thing.

25 “If there is a [a]dispute between men,
and they come to court, that *the judges*
may judge them, and they [b]justify the righteous and condemn the wicked, 2then it shall
be, if the wicked man [a]deserves to be beaten,
that the judge will cause him to lie down
[b]and be beaten in his presence, according
to his guilt, with a certain number of blows.
3[a]Forty blows he may give him *and* no more,
lest he should exceed this and beat him with
many blows above these, and your brother
[b]be humiliated in your sight.

4[a]“You shall not muzzle an ox while it
treads out *the grain*.

Marriage Duty of the Surviving Brother

5[a]“If brothers dwell together, and one of
them dies and has no son, the widow of the
dead man shall not be *married* to a stranger
outside *the family;* her husband's brother shall
go in to her, take her as his wife, and perform
the duty of a husband's brother to her. 6And it
shall be *that* the firstborn son which she bears
[a]will succeed to the name of his dead brother,
that [b]his name may not be blotted out of Israel. 7But if the man does not want to take his
brother's wife, then let his brother's wife go
up to the [a]gate to the elders, and say, ‘My husband's brother refuses to raise up a name to his
brother in Israel; he will not perform the duty
of my husband's brother.’ 8Then the elders of
his city shall call him and speak to him. But
if he stands firm and says, [a]‘I do not want to
take her,’ 9then his brother's wife shall come
to him in the presence of the elders, [a]remove
his sandal from his foot, spit in his face, and
answer and say, ‘So shall it be done to the man
who will not [b]build up his brother's house.’
10And his name shall be called in Israel, ‘The
house of him who had his sandal removed.’

Miscellaneous Laws

11“If *two* men fight together, and the wife of
one draws near to rescue her husband from
the hand of the one attacking him, and puts
out her hand and seizes him by the genitals,
12then you shall cut off her hand; [a]your eye
shall not pity *her*.

24:5 [a] Deut. 20:7 [b] Prov. 5:18 **24:7** [a] Ex. 21:16 [b] Deut. 19:19 **24:8** [a] Lev. 13:2; 14:2 **24:9** [a] [1 Cor. 10:6] [b] Num. 12:10 **24:10** [a] Matt. 5:42 **24:13** [a] Ex. 22:26 [b] 2 Tim. 1:18 [c] Deut. 6:25 **24:14** [a] [Mal. 3:5] **24:15** [a] Lev. 19:13 [b] James 5:4 **24:16** [a] Ezek. 18:20 **24:17** [a] Ex. 23:6 [b] Ex. 22:26 **24:18** [a] Deut. 24:22 **24:19** [a] Lev. 19:9, 10 [b] Ps. 41:1 **25:1** [a] Deut. 17:8–13; 19:17 [b] Prov. 17:15 **25:2** [a] Prov. 19:29 [b] Matt. 10:17 **25:3** [a] 2 Cor. 11:24 [b] Job 18:3 **25:4** [a] [Prov. 12:10] **25:5** [a] Matt. 22:24 **25:6** [a] Gen. 38:9 [b] Ruth 4:5, 10 **25:7** [a] Ruth 4:1, 2 **25:8** [a] Ruth 4:6 **25:9** [a] Ruth 4:7, 8 [b] Ruth 4:11 **25:12** [a] Deut. 7:2; 19:13

13[a]"You shall not have in your bag differing
weights, a heavy and a light. 14You shall not
have in your house differing measures, a large
and a small. 15You shall have a perfect and just
weight, a perfect and just measure, [a]that your
days may be lengthened in the land which the
LORD your God is giving you. 16For [a]all who
do such things, all who behave unrighteously,
are an abomination to the LORD your God.

Destroy the Amalekites

17[a]"Remember what Amalek did to you on
the way as you were coming out of Egypt, 18how
he met you on the way and attacked your rear
ranks, all the stragglers at your rear, when you
were tired and weary; and he [a]did not fear God.
19Therefore it shall be, [a]when the LORD your
God has given you rest from your enemies all
around, in the land which the LORD your God
is giving you to possess *as* an inheritance, *that*
you will [b]blot out the remembrance of Amalek from under heaven. You shall not forget.

Offerings of Firstfruits and Tithes

26 "And it shall be, when you come into the
land which the LORD your God is giving
you *as* an inheritance, and you possess it and
dwell in it, 2[a]that you shall take some of the
first of all the produce of the ground, which
you shall bring from your land that the LORD
your God is giving you, and put *it* in a basket
and [b]go to the place where the LORD your God
chooses to make His name abide. 3And you
shall go to the one who is priest in those days,
and say to him, 'I declare today to the LORD
your[1] God that I have come to the country
which the LORD swore to our fathers to give us.'

4"Then the priest shall take the basket
out of your hand and set it down before the
altar of the LORD your God. 5And you shall
answer and say before the LORD your God:
'My father *was* [a]a Syrian,[1] [b]about to perish,
and [c]he went down to Egypt and dwelt there,
[d]few in number; and there he became a nation, [e]great, mighty, and populous. 6But the
[a]Egyptians mistreated us, afflicted us, and
laid hard bondage on us. 7[a]Then we cried out
to the LORD God of our fathers, and the LORD
heard our voice and looked on our affliction
and our labor and our oppression. 8So [a]the
LORD brought us out of Egypt with a mighty
hand and with an outstretched arm, [b]with
great terror and with signs and wonders. 9He
has brought us to this place and has given
us this land, [a]"a land flowing with milk and
honey";[1] 10and now, behold, I have brought
the firstfruits of the land which you, O LORD,
have given me.'

"Then you shall set it before the LORD your
God, and worship before the LORD your God.
11So [a]you shall rejoice in every good *thing*
which the LORD your God has given to you
and your house, you and the Levite and the
stranger who *is* among you.

25:13 [a] Mic. 6:11 **25:15** [a] Ex. 20:12 **25:16** [a] Prov. 11:1 **25:17** [a] Ex. 17:8–16 **25:18** [a] Rom. 3:18 **25:19** [a] 1 Sam. 15:3 [b] Ex. 17:14 **26:2** [a] Ex. 22:29; 23:16, 19 [b] Deut. 12:5 **26:3** [1] Septuagint reads *my*. **26:5** [a] Hos. 12:12 [b] Gen. 43:1, 2; 45:7, 11 [c] Acts 7:15 [d] Deut. 10:22 [e] Deut. 1:10 [1] Or *Aramean* **26:6** [a] Ex. 1:8–11, 14 **26:7** [a] Ex. 2:23–25; 3:9; 4:31 **26:8** [a] Deut. 5:15 [b] Deut. 4:34; 34:11, 12 **26:9** [a] Ex. 3:8, 17 [1] Exodus 3:8 **26:11** [a] Deut. 12:7; 16:11

GIVE IT AWAY

He has brought us to this place and has given us this land.

DEUTERONOMY 26:9

Moses gave the new generation of Israel the law a second time, which is where Deuteronomy, "second law," gets its name. The final part of this restatement is in chapter 26, in which Moses instructs the Israelites to bring the firstfruits of their harvest to the tabernacle (later the temple) and declare, "My father was a Syrian . . . The LORD brought us out of Egypt . . . He has brought us to this place and has given us this land . . . behold, I have brought the firstfruits of the land which You, O LORD, have given me" (vv. 5, 8–10).

I have quoted only a small part of this confession. I love it because God's people acknowledged what He had done and in response, they swore to keep God's statutes, which included caring for the poor and showing mercy to orphans and widows. Peace is a gift from God and at the same time, it is an assignment. God's peace is to be shared, not hoarded.

Is there any way in which you have hoarded rather than shared God's peace? How can you correct that?

12 "When you have finished laying aside all the [a]tithe of your increase in the third year—[b]the year of tithing—and have given *it* to the Levite, the stranger, the fatherless, and the widow, so that they may eat within your gates and be filled, 13 then you shall say before the LORD your God: 'I have removed the holy *tithe* from *my* house, and also have given them to the Levite, the stranger, the fatherless, and the widow, according to all Your commandments which You have commanded me; I have not transgressed Your commandments, [a]nor have I forgotten *them*. 14 [a]I have not eaten any of it when in mourning, nor have I removed *any* of it for an unclean *use*, nor given *any* of it for the dead. I have obeyed the voice of the LORD my God, and have done according to all that You have commanded me. 15 [a]Look down from Your holy habitation, from heaven, and bless Your people Israel and the land which You have given us, just as You swore to our fathers, [b]"a land flowing with milk and honey." '[1]

A Special People of God

16 "This day the LORD your God commands you to observe these statutes and judgments; therefore you shall be careful to observe them with all your heart and with all your soul. 17 Today you have [a]proclaimed the LORD to be your God, and that you will walk in His ways and keep His statutes, His commandments, and His judgments, and that you will [b]obey His voice. 18 Also today [a]the LORD has proclaimed you to be His special people, just as He promised you, that *you* should keep all His commandments, 19 and that He will set you [a]high above all nations which He has made, in praise, in name, and in honor, and that you may be [b]a holy people to the LORD your God, just as He has spoken."

The Law Inscribed on Stones

27 Now Moses, with the elders of Israel, commanded the people, saying: "Keep all the commandments which I command you today. 2 And it shall be, on the day [a]when you cross over the Jordan to the land which the LORD your God is giving you, that [b]you shall set up for yourselves large stones, and whitewash them with lime. 3 You shall write on them all the words of this law, when you have crossed over, that you may enter the land which the LORD your God is giving you, [a]'a land flowing with milk and honey,'[1] just as the LORD God of your fathers promised you. 4 Therefore it shall be, when you have crossed over the Jordan, *that* [a]on Mount Ebal you shall set up these stones, which I command you today, and you shall whitewash them with lime. 5 And there you shall build an altar to the LORD your God, an altar of stones; [a]you shall not use an iron *tool* on them. 6 You shall build with whole stones the altar of the LORD your God, and offer burnt offerings on it to the LORD your God. 7 You shall offer peace offerings, and shall eat there, and [a]rejoice before the LORD

26:12 [a] Lev. 27:30 [b] Deut. 14:28, 29 **26:13** [a] Ps. 119:141, 153, 176 **26:14** [a] Hos. 9:4 **26:15** [a] Is. 63:15 [b] Ex. 3:8 [1] Exodus 3:8 **26:17** [a] Ex. 20:19 [b] Deut. 15:5 **26:18** [a] Ex. 6:7; 19:5 **26:19** [a] Deut. 4:7, 8; 28:1 [b] [1 Pet. 2:9] **27:2** [a] Josh. 4:1 [b] Josh. 8:32 **27:3** [a] Ex. 3:8 [1] Exodus 3:8 **27:4** [a] Deut. 11:29 **27:5** [a] Ex. 20:25 **27:7** [a] Deut. 26:11

INVITING OTHERS

You shall offer peace offerings, and shall eat there, and rejoice before the LORD your God.

DEUTERONOMY 27:7

If God invited you to dinner, would you accept? Among the thousands of ancient papyri discovered in Egypt more than a century ago, several "invitations" to dinner from various gods were found. Some were invitations from pagan gods that invited followers to a banquet. We may assume that these invitations were not declined!

In the Books of Moses, the peace offering is a wonderful tradition and conjures up a beautiful picture of the believer and family sharing a meal with God. In biblical times eating a meal together was a sign of fellowship and friendship. In the early church, proof that all peoples were united as one in Christ was seen in their sharing of meals. Eating together is a joyful experience.

This is one of the most appealing aspects of God's peace—that of fellowship and even rejoicing before the Lord. Knowing God and walking according to His ways is not onerous and life-negating (as some think). It is positive and life-fulfilling.

your God. 8 And you shall [a]write very plainly on the stones all the words of this law."

9 Then Moses and the priests, the Levites, spoke to all Israel, saying, "Take heed and listen, O Israel: [a]This day you have become the people of the LORD your God. 10 Therefore you shall obey the voice of the LORD your God, and observe His commandments and His statutes which I command you today."

Curses Pronounced from Mount Ebal

11 And Moses commanded the people on the same day, saying, 12 "These shall stand [a]on Mount Gerizim to bless the people, when you have crossed over the Jordan: Simeon, Levi, Judah, Issachar, Joseph, and Benjamin; 13 and [a]these shall stand on Mount Ebal to curse: Reuben, Gad, Asher, Zebulun, Dan, and Naphtali.

14 "And [a]the Levites shall speak with a loud voice and say to all the men of Israel: 15 [a]'Cursed *is* the one who makes a carved or molded image, an abomination to the LORD, the work of the hands of the craftsman, and sets *it* up in secret.'

[b]"And all the people shall answer and say, 'Amen!'

16 [a]'Cursed *is* the one who treats his father or his mother with contempt.'

"And all the people shall say, 'Amen!'

17 [a]'Cursed *is* the one who moves his neighbor's landmark.'

"And all the people shall say, 'Amen!'

18 [a]'Cursed *is* the one who makes the blind to wander off the road.'

"And all the people shall say, 'Amen!'

19 [a]'Cursed *is* the one who perverts the justice due the stranger, the fatherless, and widow.'

"And all the people shall say, 'Amen!'

20 [a]'Cursed *is* the one who lies with his father's wife, because he has uncovered his father's bed.'

"And all the people shall say, 'Amen!'

21 [a]'Cursed *is* the one who lies with any kind of animal.'

"And all the people shall say, 'Amen!'

22 [a]'Cursed *is* the one who lies with his sister, the daughter of his father or the daughter of his mother.'

"And all the people shall say, 'Amen!'

23 [a]'Cursed *is* the one who lies with his mother-in-law.'

"And all the people shall say, 'Amen!'

24 [a]'Cursed *is* the one who attacks his neighbor secretly.'

"And all the people shall say, 'Amen!'

25 [a]'Cursed *is* the one who takes a bribe to slay an innocent person.'

"And all the people shall say, 'Amen!'

26 [a]'Cursed *is* the one who does not confirm *all* the words of this law by observing them.'

"And all the people shall say, 'Amen!' "

Blessings on Obedience

28 "Now it shall come to pass, [a]if you diligently obey the voice of the LORD your God, to observe carefully all His commandments which I command you today, that the LORD your God [b]will set you high above all nations of the earth. 2 And all these blessings shall come upon you and [a]overtake you, because you obey the voice of the LORD your God:

3 [a]"Blessed *shall* you *be* in the city, and blessed *shall* you *be* [b]in the country.

4 "Blessed *shall be* [a]the fruit of your body, the produce of your ground and the increase of your herds, the increase of your cattle and the offspring of your flocks.

5 "Blessed *shall be* your basket and your kneading bowl.

6 [a]"Blessed *shall* you *be* when you come in, and blessed *shall* you *be* when you go out.

7 "The LORD [a]will cause your enemies who rise against you to be defeated before your face; they shall come out against you one way and flee before you seven ways.

8 "The LORD will [a]command the blessing on you in your storehouses and in all to which you [b]set your hand, and He will bless you in the land which the LORD your God is giving you.

9 [a]"The LORD will establish you as a holy people to Himself, just as He has sworn to you, if you keep the commandments of the LORD your God and walk in His ways. 10 Then all peoples of the earth shall see that you are [a]called by the name of the LORD, and they shall be [b]afraid of you. 11 And [a]the LORD will grant you plenty of goods, in the fruit of your body, in the increase of your livestock, and in the produce of your ground, in the land of which the LORD swore to your fathers to give you. 12 The LORD will open to you His good treasure, the heavens, [a]to give the rain to your land in its season, and [b]to bless all the work of your hand. [c]You shall lend to many nations,

27:8 [a] Josh. 8:32 **27:9** [a] Deut. 26:18 **27:12** [a] Josh. 8:33 **27:13** [a] Deut. 11:29 **27:14** [a] Deut. 33:10 **27:15** [a] Ex. 20:4, 23; 34:17 [b] Num. 5:22 **27:16** [a] Ezek. 22:7 **27:17** [a] Deut. 19:14 **27:18** [a] Lev. 19:14 **27:19** [a] Ex. 22:21, 22; 23:9 **27:20** [a] Deut. 22:30 **27:21** [a] Lev. 18:23; 20:15, 16 **27:22** [a] Lev. 18:9 **27:23** [a] Lev. 18:17; 20:14 **27:24** [a] Ex. 20:13; 21:12 **27:25** [a] Ex. 23:7 **27:26** [a] Gal. 3:10 **28:1** [a] Ex. 15:26 [b] Deut. 26:19 **28:2** [a] Deut. 28:15 **28:3** [a] Ps. 128:1, 4 [b] Gen. 39:5 **28:4** [a] Gen. 22:17 **28:6** [a] Ps. 121:8 **28:7** [a] Lev. 26:7, 8 **28:8** [a] Lev. 25:21 [b] Deut. 15:10 **28:9** [a] Ex. 19:5, 6 **28:10** [a] Num. 6:27 [b] Deut. 11:25 **28:11** [a] Deut. 30:9 **28:12** [a] Lev. 26:4 [b] Deut. 14:29 [c] Deut. 15:6

but you shall not borrow. 13And the LORD will make [a]you the head and not the tail; you shall be above only, and not be beneath, if you heed the commandments of the LORD your God, which I command you today, and are careful to observe *them.* 14[a]So you shall not turn aside from any of the words which I command you this day, *to* the right or the left, to go after other gods to serve them.

Curses on Disobedience

15"But it shall come to pass, [a]if you do not obey the voice of the LORD your God, to observe carefully all His commandments and His statutes which I command you today, that all these curses will come upon you and overtake you:

16"Cursed *shall* you *be* in the city, and cursed *shall* you *be* in the country.

17"Cursed *shall be* your basket and your kneading bowl.

18"Cursed *shall be* the fruit of your body and the produce of your land, the increase of your cattle and the offspring of your flocks.

19"Cursed *shall* you *be* when you come in, and cursed *shall* you *be* when you go out.

20"The LORD will send on you [a]cursing, [b]confusion, and [c]rebuke in all that you set your hand to do, until you are destroyed and until you perish quickly, because of the wickedness of your doings in which you have forsaken Me. 21The LORD will make the plague cling to you until He has consumed you from the land which you are going to possess. 22[a]The LORD will strike you with consumption, with fever, with inflammation, with severe burning fever, with the sword, with [b]scorching, and with mildew; they shall pursue you until you perish. 23And [a]your heavens which *are* over your head shall be bronze, and the earth which is under you *shall be* iron. 24The LORD will change the rain of your land to powder and dust; from the heaven it shall come down on you until you are destroyed.

25[a]"The LORD will cause you to be defeated before your enemies; you shall go out one way against them and flee seven ways before them; and you shall become troublesome to all the kingdoms of the earth. 26[a]Your carcasses shall be food for all the birds of the air and the beasts of the earth, and no one shall frighten *them* away. 27The LORD will strike you with [a]the boils of Egypt, with [b]tumors, with the scab, and with the itch, from which you cannot be healed. 28The LORD will strike you with madness and blindness and [a]confusion of heart. 29And you shall [a]grope at noonday, as a blind man gropes in darkness; you shall not prosper in your ways; you shall be only oppressed and plundered continually, and no one shall save *you.*

30[a]"You shall betroth a wife, but another man shall lie with her; [b]you shall build a house, but you shall not dwell in it; [c]you shall plant a vineyard, but shall not gather its grapes. 31Your ox *shall be* slaughtered before your eyes, but you shall not eat of it; your donkey *shall be* violently taken away from before you, and shall not be restored to you; your sheep *shall be* given to your enemies, and you shall have no one to rescue *them.* 32Your sons and your daughters *shall be* given to [a]another people, and your eyes shall look and [b]fail *with longing* for them all day long; and *there shall be* no strength in your [c]hand. 33A nation whom you have not known shall eat [a]the fruit of your land and the produce of your labor, and you shall be only oppressed and crushed continually. 34So you shall be driven mad because of the sight which your eyes see. 35The LORD will strike you in the knees and on the legs with severe boils which cannot be healed, and from the sole of your foot to the top of your head.

36"The LORD will [a]bring you and the king whom you set over you to a nation which neither you nor your fathers have known, and [b]there you shall serve other gods—wood and stone. 37And you shall become [a]an astonishment, a proverb, [b]and a byword among all nations where the LORD will drive you.

38[a]"You shall carry much seed out to the field but gather little in, for [b]the locust shall consume it. 39You shall plant vineyards and tend *them,* but you shall neither drink *of* the [a]wine nor gather the *grapes;* for the worms shall eat them. 40You shall have olive trees throughout all your territory, but you shall not anoint *yourself* with the oil; for your olives shall drop off. 41You shall beget sons and daughters, but they shall not be yours; for [a]they shall go into captivity. 42Locusts shall consume all your trees and the produce of your land.

43"The alien who *is* among you shall rise higher and higher above you, and you shall come down lower and lower. 44He shall lend to you, but you shall not lend to him; he shall be the head, and you shall be the tail.

45"Moreover all these curses shall come upon you and pursue and overtake you, until

28:13 [a] [Is. 9:14, 15] **28:14** [a] Deut. 5:32 **28:15** [a] Lev. 26:14–39 **28:20** [a] Mal. 2:2 [b] Is. 65:14 [c] Is. 30:17 **28:22** [a] Lev. 26:16 [b] Amos 4:9 **28:23** [a] Lev. 26:19 **28:25** [a] Deut. 32:30 **28:26** [a] 1 Sam. 17:44 **28:27** [a] Ex. 15:26 [b] 1 Sam. 5:6 **28:28** [a] Jer. 4:9 **28:29** [a] Job 5:14 **28:30** [a] Jer. 8:10 [b] Amos 5:11 [c] Deut. 20:6 **28:32** [a] 2 Chr. 29:9 [b] Ps. 119:82 [c] Neh. 5:5 **28:33** [a] Jer. 5:15, 17 **28:36** [a] Jer. 39:1–9 [b] Deut. 4:28 **28:37** [a] 1 Kin. 9:7, 8 [b] Ps. 44:14 **28:38** [a] Mic. 6:15 [b] Joel 1:4 **28:39** [a] Zeph. 1:13 **28:41** [a] Lam. 1:5

you are destroyed, because you did not obey the voice of the LORD your God, to keep His commandments and His statutes which He commanded you. 46 And they shall be upon [a]you for a sign and a wonder, and on your descendants forever.

47 [a]"Because you did not serve the LORD your God with joy and gladness of heart, [b]for the abundance of everything, 48 therefore you shall serve your enemies, whom the LORD will send against you, in [a]hunger, in thirst, in nakedness, and in need of everything; and He [b]will put a yoke of iron on your neck until He has destroyed you. 49 [a]The LORD will bring a nation against you from afar, from the end of the earth, [b]*as swift* as the eagle flies, a nation whose language you will not understand, 50 a nation of fierce countenance, [a]which does not respect the elderly nor show favor to the young. 51 And they shall eat the increase of your livestock and the produce of your land, until you are destroyed; they shall not leave you grain or new wine or oil, *or* the increase of your cattle or the offspring of your flocks, until they have destroyed you.

52 "They shall [a]besiege you at all your gates until your high and fortified walls, in which you trust, come down throughout all your land; and they shall besiege you at all your gates throughout all your land which the LORD your God has given you. 53 [a]You shall eat the fruit of your own body, the flesh of your sons and your daughters whom the LORD your God has given you, in the siege and desperate straits in which your enemy shall distress you. 54 The sensitive and very refined man among you [a]will be hostile toward his brother, toward [b]the wife of his bosom, and toward the rest of his children whom he leaves behind, 55 so that he will not give any of them the flesh of his children whom he will eat, because he has nothing left in the siege and desperate straits in which your enemy shall distress you at all your gates. 56 The tender and delicate woman among you, who would not venture to set the sole of her foot on the ground because of her delicateness and sensitivity, will refuse[1] to the husband of her bosom, and to her son and her daughter, 57 her placenta which comes out [a]from between her feet and her children whom she bears; for she will eat them secretly for lack of everything in the siege and desperate straits in which your enemy shall distress you at all your gates.

58 "If you do not carefully observe all the words of this law that are written in this book, that you may fear [a]this glorious and awesome name, THE LORD YOUR GOD, 59 then the LORD will bring upon you and your descendants [a]extraordinary plagues—great and prolonged plagues—and serious and prolonged sicknesses. 60 Moreover He will bring back on you all [a]the diseases of Egypt, of which you were afraid, and they shall cling to you. 61 Also every sickness and every plague, which *is* not written in this Book of the Law, will the LORD bring upon you until you are destroyed. 62 You [a]shall be left few in number, whereas you were [b]as the stars of heaven in multitude, because you would not obey the voice of the LORD your God. 63 And it shall be, *that* just as the LORD [a]rejoiced over you to do you good and multiply you, so the LORD [b]will rejoice over you to destroy you and bring you to nothing; and you shall be [c]plucked from off the land which you go to possess.

64 "Then the LORD [a]will scatter you among all peoples, from one end of the earth to the other, and [b]there you shall serve other gods, which neither you nor your fathers have known—wood and stone. 65 And [a]among those nations you shall find no rest, nor shall the sole of your foot have a resting place; [b]but there the LORD will give you a trembling heart, failing eyes, and [c]anguish of soul. 66 Your life shall hang in doubt before you; you shall fear day and night, and have no assurance of life. 67 [a]In the morning you shall say, 'Oh, that it were evening!' And at evening you shall say, 'Oh, that it were morning!' because of the fear which terrifies your heart, and [b]because of the sight which your eyes see.

68 "And the LORD [a]will take you back to Egypt in ships, by the way of which I said to you, [b]'You shall never see it again.' And there you shall be offered for sale to your enemies as male and female slaves, but no one will buy *you*."

The Covenant Renewed in Moab

29 These *are* the words of the covenant which the LORD commanded Moses to make with the children of Israel in the land of Moab, besides the [a]covenant which He made with them in Horeb.

2 Now Moses called all Israel and said to them: [a]"You have seen all that the LORD did before your eyes in the land of Egypt, to Pharaoh and to all his servants and to

28:46 [a] Is. 8:18 **28:47** [a] Neh. 9:35–37 [b] Deut. 32:15 **28:48** [a] Lam. 4:4–6 [b] Jer. 28:13, 14 **28:49** [a] Jer. 5:15 [b] Jer. 48:40; 49:22 **28:50** [a] 2 Chr. 36:17 **28:52** [a] 2 Kin. 25:1, 2, 4 **28:53** [a] Lev. 26:29 **28:54** [a] Deut. 15:9 [b] Deut. 13:6 **28:56** [1] Literally *her eye shall be evil toward* **28:57** [a] Gen. 49:10 **28:58** [a] Ex. 6:3 **28:59** [a] Dan. 9:12 **28:60** [a] Deut. 7:15 **28:62** [a] Deut. 4:27 [b] Neh. 9:23 **28:63** [a] Jer. 32:41 [b] Prov. 1:26 [c] Jer. 12:14; 45:4 **28:64** [a] Jer. 16:13 [b] Deut. 28:36 **28:65** [a] Amos 9:4 [b] Lev. 26:36 [c] Lev. 26:16 **28:67** [a] Job 7:4 [b] Deut. 28:34 **28:68** [a] Hos. 8:13 [b] Deut. 17:16 **29:1** [a] Deut. 5:2, 3 **29:2** [a] Ex. 19:4

all his land— 3 [a]the great trials which your eyes have seen, the signs, and those great wonders. 4 Yet [a]the LORD has not given you a heart to perceive and eyes to see and ears to hear, to this *very* day. 5 [a]And I have led you forty years in the wilderness. [b]Your clothes have not worn out on you, and your sandals have not worn out on your feet. 6 [a]You have not eaten bread, nor have you drunk wine or *similar* drink, that you may know that I *am* the LORD your God. 7 And when you came to this place, [a]Sihon king of Heshbon and Og king of Bashan came out against us to battle, and we conquered them. 8 We took their land and [a]gave it as an inheritance to the Reubenites, to the Gadites, and to half the tribe of Manasseh. 9 Therefore [a]keep the words of this covenant, and do them, that you may [b]prosper in all that you do.

10 "All of you stand today before the LORD your God: your leaders and your tribes and your elders and your officers, all the men of Israel, 11 your little ones and your wives—also the stranger who *is* in your camp, from [a]the one who cuts your wood to the one who draws your water— 12 that you may enter into covenant with the LORD your God, and [a]into His oath, which the LORD your God makes with you today, 13 that He may [a]establish you today as a people for Himself, and *that* He may be God to you, [b]just as He has spoken to you, and [c]just as He has sworn to your fathers, to Abraham, Isaac, and Jacob.

14 "I make this covenant and this oath, [a]not with you alone, 15 but with *him* who stands here with us today before the LORD our God, [a]as well as with *him* who *is* not here with us today 16 (for you know that we dwelt in the land of Egypt and that we came through the nations which you passed by, 17 and you saw their abominations and their idols which *were* among them—wood and stone and silver and gold); 18 so that there may not be among you man or woman or family or tribe, [a]whose heart turns away today from the LORD our God, to go *and* serve the gods of these nations, [b]and that there may not be among you a root bearing [c]bitterness or wormwood; 19 and so it may not happen, when he hears the words of this curse, that he blesses himself in his heart, saying, 'I shall have peace, even though I follow the [a]dictates[1] of my heart'—[b]as though the drunkard could be included with the sober.

20 [a]"The LORD would not spare him; for then [b]the anger of the LORD and [c]His jealousy would burn against that man, and every curse that is written in this book would settle on him, and the LORD [d]would blot out his name from under heaven. 21 And the LORD [a]would separate him from all the tribes of Israel for adversity, according to all the curses of the covenant that are written in this Book of the [b]Law, 22 so that the coming generation of your children who rise up after you, and the foreigner who comes from a far land, would say, when they [a]see the plagues of that land and the sicknesses which the LORD has laid on it:

23 'The whole land *is* brimstone, [a]salt, and burning; it is not sown, nor does it bear, nor does any grass grow there, [b]like the overthrow of Sodom and Gomorrah, Admah, and Zeboiim, which the LORD overthrew in His anger and His wrath.' 24 All nations would say, [a]'Why has the LORD done so to this land? What does the heat of this great anger mean?' 25 Then *people* would say: 'Because they have forsaken the covenant of the LORD God of their fathers, which He made with them when He brought them out of the land of Egypt; 26 for they went and served other gods and worshiped them, gods that they did not know and that He had not given to them. 27 Then the anger of the LORD was aroused against this land, [a]to bring on it every curse that is written in this book. 28 And the LORD [a]uprooted them from their land in anger, in wrath, and in great indignation, and cast them into another land, as *it is* this day.'

29 "The secret *things belong* to the LORD our God, but those *things which are* revealed *belong* to us and to our children forever, that *we* may do all the words of this law.

The Blessing of Returning to God

30 "Now [a]it shall come to pass, when [b]all these things come upon you, the blessing and the [c]curse which I have set before you, and [d]you call *them* to mind among all the nations where the LORD your God drives you, 2 and you [a]return to the LORD your God and obey His voice, according to all that I command you today, you and your children, with all your heart and with all your soul, 3 [a]that the LORD your God will bring you back from captivity, and have compassion on you, and [b]gather you again from all the nations where

29:3 [a] Deut. 4:34; 7:19 **29:4** [a] [Acts 28:26, 27] **29:5** [a] Deut. 1:3; 8:2 [b] Deut. 8:4 **29:6** [a] Deut. 8:3 **29:7** [a] Num. 21:23, 24 **29:8** [a] Deut. 3:12, 13 **29:9** [a] Deut. 4:6 [b] Josh. 1:7 **29:11** [a] Josh. 9:21, 23, 27 **29:12** [a] Neh. 10:29 **29:13** [a] Deut. 28:9 [b] Ex. 6:7 [c] Gen. 17:7, 8 **29:14** [a] [Jer. 31:31] **29:15** [a] Acts 2:39 **29:18** [a] Deut. 11:16 [b] Heb. 12:15 [c] Deut. 32:32 **29:19** [a] Jer. 3:17; 7:24 [b] Is. 30:1 [1] Or *stubbornness* **29:20** [a] Ezek. 14:7 [b] Ps. 74:1 [c] Ps. 79:5 [d] Deut. 9:14 **29:21** [a] [Matt. 24:51] [b] Deut. 30:10 **29:22** [a] Jer. 19:8; 49:17; 50:13 **29:23** [a] Zeph. 2:9 [b] Gen. 19:24, 25 **29:24** [a] 1 Kin. 9:8 **29:27** [a] Dan. 9:11 **29:28** [a] 1 Kin. 14:15 **30:1** [a] Lev. 26:40 [b] Deut. 28:2 [c] Deut. 28:15–45 [d] Deut. 4:29, 30 **30:2** [a] Neh. 1:9 **30:3** [a] Jer. 29:14 [b] Ezek. 34:13

PEACE NOTE

Jesus described a state of blessedness that includes laughing and giggling. Where did we get the idea that being a Christian means being a killjoy?

the LORD your God has scattered you. [4][a]If *any* of you are driven out to the farthest *parts* under heaven, from there the LORD your God will gather you, and from there He will bring you. [5]Then the LORD your God will bring you to the land which your fathers possessed, and you shall possess it. He will prosper you and multiply you more than your fathers. [6]And [a]the LORD your God will circumcise your heart and the heart of your descendants, to love the LORD your God with all your heart and with all your soul, that you may live.

[7]"Also the LORD your God will put all these [a]curses on your enemies and on those who hate you, who persecuted you. [8]And you will [a]again obey the voice of the LORD and do all His commandments which I command you today. [9][a]The LORD your God will make you abound in all the work of your hand, in the fruit of your body, in the increase of your livestock, and in the produce of your land for good. For the LORD will again [b]rejoice over you for good as He rejoiced over your fathers, [10]if you obey the voice of the LORD your God, to keep His commandments and His statutes which are written in this Book of the Law, *and* if you turn to the LORD your God with all your heart and with all your soul.

The Choice of Life or Death

[11]"For this commandment which I command you today [a]*is* not *too* mysterious for you, nor *is* it far off. [12][a]It *is* not in heaven, that you should say, 'Who will ascend into heaven for us and bring it to us, that we may hear it and do it?' [13]Nor *is* it beyond the sea, that you should say, 'Who will go over the sea for us and bring it to us, that we may hear it and do it?' [14]But the word *is* very near you, [a]in your mouth and in your heart, that you may do it.

[15]"See, [a]I have set before you today life and good, death and evil, [16]in that I command you today to love the LORD your God, to walk in His ways, and to keep His commandments, His statutes, and His judgments, that you may live and multiply; and the LORD your God will bless you in the land which you go to possess. [17]But if your heart turns away so that you do not hear, and are drawn away, and worship other gods and serve them, [18][a]I announce to you today that you shall surely perish; you shall not prolong *your* days in the land which you cross over the Jordan to go in and possess. [19][a]I call heaven and earth as witnesses today against you, *that* [b]I have set before you life and death, blessing and cursing; therefore choose life, that both you and your descendants may live; [20]that you may love the LORD your God, that you may obey His voice, and that you may cling to Him, for He *is* your [a]life and the length of your days; and that you may dwell in the land which the LORD swore to your fathers, to Abraham, Isaac, and Jacob, to give them."

Joshua the New Leader of Israel

31 Then Moses went and spoke these words to all Israel. [2]And he said to them: "I [a]*am* one hundred and twenty years old today. I can no longer [b]go out and come in. Also the LORD has said to me, [c]'You shall not cross over this Jordan.' [3]The LORD your God [a]Himself crosses over before you; He will destroy these nations from before you, and you shall dispossess them. [b]Joshua himself crosses over before you, just [c]as the LORD has said. [4][a]And the LORD will do to them [b]as He did to Sihon and Og, the kings of the Amorites and their land, when He destroyed them. [5][a]The LORD will give them over to you, that you may do to them according to every commandment which I have commanded you. [6][a]Be strong and of good courage, [b]do not fear nor be afraid of them; for the LORD your God, [c]He *is* the One who goes with you. [d]He will not leave you nor forsake you."

[7]Then Moses called Joshua and said to him in the sight of all Israel, [a]"Be strong and of good courage, for you must go with this people to the land which the LORD has sworn to their fathers to give them, and you shall cause them to inherit it. [8]And the LORD, [a]He

30:4 [a] Neh. 1:9 **30:6** [a] Deut. 10:16 **30:7** [a] Jer. 30:16, 20 **30:8** [a] Zeph. 3:20 **30:9** [a] Deut. 28:11 [b] Jer. 32:41 **30:11** [a] Is. 45:19 **30:12** [a] Rom. 10:6–8 **30:14** [a] Rom. 10:8 **30:15** [a] Deut. 30:1, 19 **30:18** [a] Deut. 4:26; 8:19 **30:19** [a] Deut. 4:26 [b] Deut. 30:15 **30:20** [a] [John 11:25; 14:6] **31:2** [a] Deut. 34:7 [b] 1 Kin. 3:7 [c] Num. 20:12 **31:3** [a] Deut. 9:3 [b] Num. 27:18 [c] Num. 27:21 **31:4** [a] Deut. 3:21 [b] Num. 21:24, 33 **31:5** [a] Deut. 7:2; 20:10–20 **31:6** [a] Josh. 10:25 [b] Deut. 1:29 [c] Deut. 20:4 [d] Heb. 13:5 **31:7** [a] Deut. 31:23 **31:8** [a] Ex. 13:21

is the One who goes before you. [b]He will be with you, He will not leave you nor forsake you; do not fear nor be dismayed."

The Law to Be Read Every Seven Years

9 So Moses wrote this law [a]and delivered it to the priests, the sons of Levi, [b]who bore the ark of the covenant of the LORD, and to all the elders of Israel. 10 And Moses commanded them, saying: "At the end of *every* seven years, at the appointed time in the [a]year of release, [b]at the Feast of Tabernacles, 11 when all Israel comes to [a]appear before the LORD your God in the [b]place which He chooses, [c]you shall read this law before all Israel in their hearing. 12 [a]Gather the people together, men and women and little ones, and the stranger who *is* within your gates, that they may hear and that they may learn to fear the LORD your God and carefully observe all the words of this law, 13 and *that* their children, [a]who have not known it, [b]may hear and learn to fear the LORD your God as long as you live in the land which you cross the Jordan to possess."

Prediction of Israel's Rebellion

14 Then the LORD said to Moses, [a]"Behold, the days approach when you must die; call Joshua, and present yourselves in the tabernacle of meeting, that [b]I may inaugurate him."

So Moses and Joshua went and presented themselves in the tabernacle of meeting. 15 Now [a]the LORD appeared at the tabernacle in a pillar of cloud, and the pillar of cloud stood above the door of the tabernacle.

16 And the LORD said to Moses: "Behold, you will rest with your fathers; and this people will [a]rise and [b]play the harlot with the gods of the foreigners of the land, where they go *to be* among them, and they will [c]forsake Me and [d]break My covenant which I have made with them. 17 Then My anger shall be [a]aroused against them in that day, and [b]I will forsake them, and I will [c]hide My face from them, and they shall be devoured. And many evils and troubles shall befall them, so that they will say in that day, [d]'Have not these evils come upon us because our God *is* [e]not among us?' 18 And [a]I will surely hide My face in that day because of all the evil which they have done, in that they have turned to other gods.

19 "Now therefore, write down this song for yourselves, and teach it to the children of Israel; put it in their mouths, that this song may be [a]a witness for Me against the children of Israel. 20 When I have brought them to the land flowing with milk and honey, of which I swore to their fathers, and they have eaten and filled themselves [a]and grown fat, [b]then they will turn to other gods and serve them; and they will provoke Me and break My covenant. 21 Then it shall be, [a]when many evils and troubles have come upon them, that this song will testify against them as a witness; for it will not be forgotten in the mouths of their descendants, for [b]I know the inclination [c]of their behavior today, even before I have brought them to the land of which I swore *to give them.*"

22 Therefore Moses wrote this song the same day, and taught it to the children of Israel. 23 [a]Then He inaugurated Joshua the son of Nun, and said, [b]"Be strong and of good courage; for you shall bring the children of Israel into the land of which I swore to them, and I will be with you."

24 So it was, when Moses had completed writing the words of this law in a book, when they were finished, 25 that Moses commanded the Levites, who bore the ark of the covenant of the LORD, saying: 26 "Take this Book of the Law, [a]and put it beside the ark of the covenant of the LORD your God, that it may be there [b]as a witness against you; 27 [a]for I know your rebellion and your [b]stiff neck. *If* today, while I am yet alive with you, you have been rebellious against the LORD, then how much more after my death? 28 Gather to me all the elders of your tribes, and your officers, that I may speak these words in their hearing [a]and call heaven and earth to witness against them. 29 For I know that after my death you will [a]become utterly corrupt, and turn aside from the way which I have commanded you. And [b]evil will befall you [c]in the latter days, because you will do evil in the sight of the LORD, to provoke Him to anger through the work of your hands."

The Song of Moses

30 Then Moses spoke in the hearing of all the assembly of Israel the words of this song until they were ended:

32 "Give [a]ear, O heavens, and I will speak;
And hear, O [b]earth, the words of my mouth.
2 Let [a]my teaching drop as the rain,
My speech distill as the dew,

31:8 [b] Josh. 1:5 **31:9** [a] Deut. 17:18; 31:25, 26 [b] Josh. 3:3 **31:10** [a] Deut. 15:1, 2 [b] Lev. 23:34 **31:11** [a] Deut. 16:16 [b] Deut. 12:5 [c] Josh. 8:34 **31:12** [a] Deut. 4:10 **31:13** [a] Deut. 11:2 [b] Ps. 78:6, 7 **31:14** [a] Num. 27:13 [b] Deut. 3:28 **31:15** [a] Ex. 33:9 **31:16** [a] Deut. 29:22 [b] Ex. 34:15 [c] Deut. 32:15 [d] Judg. 2:20 **31:17** [a] Judg. 2:14; 6:13 [b] 2 Chr. 15:2 [c] Deut. 32:20 [d] Judg. 6:13 [e] Num. 14:42 **31:18** [a] Deut. 31:17 **31:19** [a] Deut. 31:22, 26 **31:20** [a] Deut. 32:15–17 [b] Deut. 31:16 **31:21** [a] Deut. 31:17 [b] Hos. 5:3 [c] Amos 5:25, 26 **31:23** [a] Num. 27:23 [b] Deut. 31:7 **31:26** [a] 2 Kin. 22:8 [b] Deut. 31:19 **31:27** [a] Deut. 9:7, 24 [b] Ex. 32:9 **31:28** [a] Deut. 30:19 **31:29** [a] Judg. 2:19 [b] Deut. 28:15 [c] Gen. 49:1 **32:1** [a] Deut. 4:26 [b] Jer. 6:19 **32:2** [a] Is. 55:10, 11

[b]As raindrops on the tender herb,
And as showers on the grass.
3 For I proclaim the [a]name of the LORD:
[b]Ascribe greatness to our God.
4 *He is* [a]the Rock, [b]His work *is* perfect;
For all His ways *are* justice,
[c]A God of truth and [d]without injustice;
Righteous and upright *is* He.

5 "They[a] have corrupted themselves;
They are not His children,
Because of their blemish:
A [b]perverse and crooked generation.
6 Do you thus [a]deal with the LORD,
O foolish and unwise people?
Is He not [b]your Father, *who* [c]bought you?
Has He not [d]made you and established you?

7 "Remember[a] the days of old,
Consider the years of many generations.
[b]Ask your father, and he will show you;
Your elders, and they will tell you:
8 When the Most High [a]divided their inheritance to the nations,
When He [b]separated the sons of Adam,
He set the boundaries of the peoples
According to the number of the children of Israel.
9 For [a]the LORD's portion *is* His people;
Jacob *is* the place of His inheritance.

10 "He found him [a]in a desert land
And in the wasteland, a howling wilderness;
He encircled him, He instructed him,
He [b]kept him as the apple of His eye.
11 [a]As an eagle stirs up its nest,
Hovers over its young,
Spreading out its wings, taking them up,
Carrying them on its wings,
12 *So* the LORD alone led him,
And *there was* no foreign god with him.

13 "He[a] made him ride in the heights of the earth,
That he might eat the produce of the fields;
He made him draw honey from the rock,
And oil from the flinty rock;
14 Curds from the cattle, and milk of the flock,
[a]With fat of lambs;
And rams of the breed of Bashan, and goats,
With the choicest wheat;
And you drank wine, the [b]blood of the grapes.

15 "But Jeshurun grew fat and kicked;
[a]You grew fat, you grew thick,
You are obese!
Then he [b]forsook God *who* [c]made him,
And scornfully esteemed the [d]Rock of his salvation.
16 [a]They provoked Him to jealousy with foreign *gods;*
With abominations they provoked Him to anger.
17 [a]They sacrificed to demons, not to God,
To gods they did not know,
To new *gods,* new arrivals
That your fathers did not fear.
18 [a]Of the Rock *who* begot you, you are unmindful,
And have [b]forgotten the God who fathered you.

19 "And[a] when the LORD saw *it,* He spurned *them,*
Because of the provocation of His sons and His daughters.
20 And He said: 'I will hide My face from them,
I will see what their end *will be,*
For they *are* a perverse generation,
[a]Children in whom *is* no faith.
21 [a]They have provoked Me to jealousy by *what* is not God;
They have moved Me to anger [b]by their foolish idols.
But [c]I will provoke them to jealousy by *those who are* not a nation;
I will move them to anger by a foolish nation.
22 For [a]a fire is kindled in My anger,
And shall burn to the lowest hell;
It shall consume the earth with her increase,
And set on fire the foundations of the mountains.

23 'I will [a]heap disasters on them;
[b]I will spend My arrows on them.
24 *They shall be* wasted with hunger,
Devoured by pestilence and bitter destruction;
I will also send against them the [a]teeth of beasts,
With the poison of serpents of the dust.

32:2 [b]Ps. 72:6 **32:3** [a]Deut. 28:58 [b]1 Chr. 29:11 **32:4** [a]Ps. 18:2 [b]2 Sam. 22:31 [c]Is. 65:16 [d]Job 34:10 **32:5** [a]Deut. 4:25; 31:29 [b]Phil. 2:15 **32:6** [a]Ps. 116:12 [b]Is. 63:16 [c]Ps. 74:2 [d]Deut. 32:15 **32:7** [a]Ps. 44:1 [b]Ps. 78:5–8 **32:8** [a]Acts 17:26 [b]Gen. 11:8 **32:9** [a]Ex. 19:5 **32:10** [a]Jer. 2:6 [b]Ps. 17:8 **32:11** [a]Is. 31:5 **32:13** [a]Is. 58:14 **32:14** [a]Ps. 81:16 [b]Gen. 49:11 **32:15** [a]Deut. 31:20 [b]Is. 1:4 [c]Is. 51:13 [d]Ps. 95:1 **32:16** [a]1 Cor. 10:22 **32:17** [a]Rev. 9:20 **32:18** [a]Is. 17:10 [b]Jer. 2:32 **32:19** [a]Judg. 2:14 **32:20** [a]Matt. 17:17 **32:21** [a]Ps. 78:58 [b]Ps. 31:6 [c]Rom. 10:19 **32:22** [a]Lam. 4:11 **32:23** [a]Ex. 32:12 [b]Ps. 7:12, 13 **32:24** [a]Lev. 26:22

25 The sword shall destroy outside;
There shall be terror within
For the young man and virgin,
The nursing child with the man of gray hairs.
26 [a]I would have said, "I will dash them in pieces,
I will make the memory of them to cease from among men,"
27 Had I not feared the wrath of the enemy,
Lest their adversaries should misunderstand,
Lest they should say, [a]"Our hand *is* high;
And it is not the LORD who has done all this." '

28 "For they *are* a nation void of counsel,
Nor *is there any* understanding in them.
29 [a]Oh, that they were wise, *that* they understood this,
That they would consider their [b]latter end!
30 How could one chase a thousand,
And two put ten thousand to flight,
Unless their Rock [a]had sold them,
And the LORD had surrendered them?
31 For their rock *is* not like our Rock,
[a]Even our enemies themselves *being* judges.
32 For [a]their vine *is* of the vine of Sodom
And of the fields of Gomorrah;
Their grapes *are* grapes of gall,
Their clusters *are* bitter.
33 Their wine *is* [a]the poison of serpents,
And the cruel [b]venom of cobras.

34 '*Is* this not [a]laid up in store with Me,
Sealed up among My treasures?
35 [a]Vengeance is Mine, and recompense;
Their foot shall slip in *due* time;
[b]For the day of their calamity *is* at hand,
And the things to come hasten upon them.'

36 "For[a] the LORD will judge His people
[b]And have compassion on His servants,
When He sees that *their* power is gone,
And [c]*there is* no one *remaining,* bond or free.
37 He will say: [a]'Where *are* their gods,
The rock in which they sought refuge?
38 Who ate the fat of their sacrifices,
And drank the wine of their drink offering?
Let them rise and help you,
And be your refuge.

39 'Now see that [a]I, *even* I, *am* He,
And [b]*there is* no God besides Me;
[c]I kill and I make alive;
I wound and I heal;
Nor *is there any* who can deliver from My hand.
40 For I raise My hand to heaven,
And say, "As I live forever,
41 [a]If I whet My glittering sword,
And My hand takes hold on judgment,
I will render vengeance to My enemies,
And repay those who hate Me.
42 I will make My arrows drunk with blood,
And My sword shall devour flesh,
With the blood of the slain and the captives,
From the heads of the leaders of the enemy." '

43 "Rejoice,[a] O Gentiles, *with* His people;[1]
For He will [b]avenge the blood of His servants,
And render vengeance to His adversaries;
He [c]will provide atonement for His land *and* His people."

44 So Moses came with Joshua[1] the son of
Nun and spoke all the words of this song in
the hearing of the people. 45 Moses finished
speaking all these words to all Israel, 46 and
he said to them: [a]"Set your hearts on all the
words which I testify among you today, which
you shall command your [b]children to be
careful to observe—all the words of this law.
47 For it *is* not a futile thing for you, because
it *is* your [a]life, and by this word you shall
prolong *your* days in the land which you
cross over the Jordan to possess."

Moses to Die on Mount Nebo

48 Then the LORD spoke to Moses that very
same day, saying: 49 [a]"Go up this mountain of
the Abarim, Mount Nebo, which *is* in the land
of Moab, across from Jericho; view the land of
Canaan, which I give to the children of Israel as
a possession; 50 and die on the mountain which

32:26 [a] Ezek. 20:23 **32:27** [a] Is. 10:12–15 **32:29** [a] [Luke 19:42] [b] Deut. 31:29 **32:30** [a] Judg. 2:14 **32:31** [a] [1 Sam. 4:7, 8] **32:32** [a] Is. 1:8–10 **32:33** [a] Ps. 58:4 [b] Rom. 3:13 **32:34** [a] [Jer. 2:22] **32:35** [a] Heb. 10:30 [b] 2 Pet. 2:3 **32:36** [a] Ps. 135:14 [b] Jer. 31:20 [c] 2 Kin. 14:26 **32:37** [a] Judg. 10:14 **32:39** [a] Is. 41:4; 43:10 [b] Is. 45:5 [c] 1 Sam. 2:6 **32:41** [a] Is. 1:24; 66:16 **32:43** [a] Rom. 15:10 [b] Rev. 6:10; 19:2 [c] Ps. 65:3; 79:9; 85:1 [1] A Dead Sea Scroll fragment adds *And let all the gods (angels) worship Him* (compare Septuagint and Hebrews 1:6). **32:44** [1] Hebrew *Hoshea* (compare Numbers 13:8, 16) **32:46** [a] Ezek. 40:4; 44:5 [b] Deut. 11:19 **32:47** [a] Deut. 8:3; 30:15–20 **32:49** [a] Num. 27:12–14

you ascend, and be gathered to your people,
just as [a]Aaron your brother died on Mount Hor
and was gathered to his people; 51 because [a]you
trespassed against Me among the children of
Israel at the waters of Meribah Kadesh, in the
Wilderness of Zin, because you [b]did not hallow
Me in the midst of the children of Israel. 52 [a]Yet
you shall see the land before *you,* though you
shall not go there, into the land which I am
giving to the children of Israel."

Moses' Final Blessing on Israel

33 Now this *is* [a]the blessing with which
Moses [b]the man of God blessed the
children of Israel before his death. 2 And
he said:

[a]"The LORD came from Sinai,
And dawned on them from [b]Seir;
He shone forth from [c]Mount Paran,
And He came with [d]ten thousands of
saints;
From His right hand
Came a fiery law for them.
3 Yes, [a]He loves the people;
[b]All His saints *are* in Your hand;
They [c]sit down at Your feet;
Everyone [d]receives Your words.
4 [a]Moses commanded a law for us,
[b]A heritage of the congregation of Jacob.
5 And He was [a]King in [b]Jeshurun,
When the leaders of the people were
gathered,
All the tribes of Israel together.

6 "Let [a]Reuben live, and not die,
Nor let his men be few."

7 And this he said of [a]Judah:

"Hear, LORD, the voice of Judah,
And bring him to his people;
[b]Let his hands be sufficient for him,
And may You be [c]a help against his
enemies."

8 And of [a]Levi he said:

[b]"*Let* Your Thummim and Your Urim *be*
with Your holy one,
[c]Whom You tested at Massah,
And with whom You contended at the
waters of Meribah,
9 [a]Who says of his father and mother,
'I have not [b]seen them';
[c]Nor did he acknowledge his brothers,
Or know his own children;
For [d]they have observed Your word
And kept Your covenant.
10 [a]They shall teach Jacob Your judgments,
And Israel Your law.
They shall put incense before You,
[b]And a whole burnt sacrifice on Your
altar.
11 Bless his substance, LORD,
And [a]accept the work of his hands;
Strike the loins of those who rise
against him,
And of those who hate him, that they
rise not again."

12 Of Benjamin he said:

"The beloved of the LORD shall dwell in
safety by Him,
Who shelters him all the day long;
And he shall dwell between His
shoulders."

13 And of Joseph he said:

[a]"Blessed of the LORD *is* his land,
With the precious things of heaven,
with the [b]dew,
And the deep lying beneath,
14 With the precious fruits of the sun,
With the precious produce of the months,
15 With the best things of [a]the ancient
mountains,
With the precious things [b]of the
everlasting hills,
16 With the precious things of the earth
and its fullness,
And the favor of [a]Him who dwelt in the
bush.
Let *the blessing* come [b]'on the head of
Joseph,
And on the crown of the head of him
who was separate from his brothers.'[1]
17 His glory *is like* a [a]firstborn bull,
And his horns *like* the [b]horns of the
wild ox;
Together with them
[c]He shall push the peoples
To the ends of the earth;
[d]They *are* the ten thousands of Ephraim,
And they *are* the thousands of
Manasseh."

32:50 [a] Num. 20:25, 28; 33:38 32:51 [a] Num. 20:11–13 [b] Lev. 10:3 32:52 [a] Deut. 34:1–5 33:1 [a] Gen. 49:28 [b] Ps. 90
33:2 [a] Ps. 68:8, 17 [b] Deut. 2:1, 4 [c] Num. 10:12 [d] Dan. 7:10 33:3 [a] Hos. 11:1 [b] 1 Sam. 2:9 [c] [Luke 10:39] [d] Prov. 2:1
33:4 [a] John 1:17; 7:19 [b] Ps. 119:111 33:5 [a] Ex. 15:18 [b] Deut. 32:15 33:6 [a] Gen. 49:3, 4 33:7 [a] Gen. 49:8–12 [b] Gen. 49:8
[c] Ps. 146:5 33:8 [a] Gen. 49:5 [b] Ex. 28:30 [c] Ps. 81:7 33:9 [a] [Num. 25:5–8] [b] [Gen. 29:32] [c] Ex. 32:26–28 [d] Mal. 2:5, 6
33:10 [a] Lev. 10:11 [b] Ps. 51:19 33:11 [a] 2 Sam. 24:23 33:13 [a] Gen. 49:22–26 [b] Gen. 27:28 33:15 [a] Gen. 49:26 [b] Hab. 3:6
33:16 [a] Ex. 3:2–4 [b] Gen. 49:26 [1] Genesis 49:26 33:17 [a] 1 Chr. 5:1 [b] Num. 23:22 [c] Ps. 44:5 [d] Gen. 48:19

18 And of Zebulun he said:

[a]"Rejoice, Zebulun, in your going out,
And Issachar in your tents!
19 They shall [a]call the peoples *to* the
mountain;
There [b]they shall offer sacrifices of
righteousness;
For they shall partake *of* the abundance
of the seas
And *of* treasures hidden in the sand."

20 And of Gad he said:

"Blessed *is* he who [a]enlarges Gad;
He dwells as a lion,
And tears the arm and the crown of his
head.
21 [a]He provided the first *part* for himself,
Because a lawgiver's portion was
reserved there.
[b]He came *with* the heads of the people;
He administered the justice of the
LORD,
And His judgments with Israel."

22 And of Dan he said:

"Dan *is* a lion's whelp;
[a]He shall leap from Bashan."

23 And of Naphtali he said:

"O Naphtali, [a]satisfied with favor,
And full of the blessing of the LORD,
[b]Possess the west and the south."

24 And of Asher he said:

[a]"Asher *is* most blessed of sons;
Let him be favored by his brothers,
And let him [b]dip his foot in oil.
25 Your sandals *shall be* [a]iron and bronze;
As your days, *so shall* your strength *be*.

26 "*There is* [a]no one like the God of
[b]Jeshurun,
[c]*Who* rides the heavens to help you,
And in His excellency on the
clouds.
27 The eternal God *is your* [a]refuge,
And underneath *are* the everlasting
arms;
[b]He will thrust out the enemy from
before you,
And will say, 'Destroy!'
28 Then [a]Israel shall dwell in safety,
[b]The fountain of Jacob [c]alone,
In a land of grain and new wine;
His [d]heavens shall also drop dew.
29 [a]Happy *are* you, O Israel!

33:18 [a] Gen. 49:13–15 **33:19** [a] Is. 2:3 [b] Ps. 4:5; 51:19 **33:20** [a] 1 Chr. 12:8 **33:21** [a] Num. 32:16, 17 [b] Josh. 4:12 **33:22** [a] Josh. 19:47 **33:23** [a] Gen. 49:21 [b] Josh. 19:32 **33:24** [a] Gen. 49:20 [b] Job 29:6 **33:25** [a] Deut. 8:9 **33:26** [a] Ex. 15:11 [b] Deut. 32:15 [c] Ps. 68:3, 33, 34; 104:3 **33:27** [a] [Ps. 90:1; 91:2, 9] [b] Deut. 9:3–5 **33:28** [a] Jer. 23:6; 33:16 [b] Deut. 8:7, 8 [c] Num. 23:9 [d] Gen. 27:28 **33:29** [a] Ps. 144:15

A DAY FOR DECLARATIONS

Happy are you, O Israel! Who is like you, a people saved by the LORD,
the shield of your help and the sword of your majesty!

DEUTERONOMY 33:29

Merriam-Webster's says a beatitude is a state of bliss, of blessedness. The first beatitude came from Moses shortly before his death: "Happy are you, O Israel!" he exclaimed, reminding his people that the Lord was "the shield of your help and the sword of your majesty!" Centuries later the queen of Sheba pronounced beatitudes on King Solomon: "Happy are these your servants, who stand continually before you and hear your wisdom!" (1 Kin. 10:8). Job, the righteous sufferer, pronounced a beatitude on the person whom God loves enough to discipline (Job 5:17).

Most of the beatitudes appear in the Psalms: "Oh, taste and see that the LORD is good" (34:8). "Happy is he . . . whose hope is in the LORD his God" (146:5). It's clear from Scripture that a state of bliss is the result of delighting in the Lord.

Can you think of anyone you can bless with a beatitude today? Take these beatitudes as your own and declare them in faith over your life. Beatitudes can bring peace to the giver and the receiver.

THE EXAMPLE OF MOSES

His eyes were not dim nor his natural vigor diminished.

DEUTERONOMY 34:7

The life of Moses was extraordinary. In the last chapter of Deuteronomy, the fifth and final Book of Moses, God wrote the great lawgiver's obituary. After being given a glimpse of the Promised Land from atop Mount Nebo, Moses died at the age of 120, but "his eyes were not dim nor his natural vigor diminished."

Although Moses the man was not perfect—he was, at first, timid and reluctant to do what God commanded—God was nevertheless able to achieve great things through him. Not only did Moses lead Israel out of Egypt; through him God gave His covenant and law to Israel. Moses' work protecting and preparing the people to enter the Promised Land, along with delivering the law that God had given him, changed the world.

Moses' hesitance to follow God's call on his life did not stop God from knowing him "face to face" (v. 10) and letting him see the Promised Land before he died. Ask the Lord to show you the land of peace today. Ask the Lord to know you face-to-face as He did Moses. Therein lies peace.

[b]Who *is* like you, a people saved by the
LORD,
[c]The shield of your help
And the sword of your majesty!
Your enemies [d]shall submit to you,
And [e]you shall tread down their high
places."

PEACE NOTE

Almost all occurrences of *asher* ("blessed" or "happy") in the Hebrew Scriptures are examples of beatitudes. Being focused on God's peace makes us all "ashers" because we are happy living for the Lord.

DEUTERONOMY 33:29

Moses Dies on Mount Nebo

34 Then Moses went up from the plains
of Moab [a]to Mount Nebo, to the top of
Pisgah, which is across from Jericho. And the
LORD showed him all the land of Gilead as far
as Dan, 2 all Naphtali and the land of Ephraim
and Manasseh, all the land of Judah as far as
the Western Sea,[1] 3 the South, and the plain of
the Valley of Jericho, [a]the city of palm trees, as
far as Zoar. 4 Then the LORD said to him, [a]"This
is the land of which I swore to give Abraham,
Isaac, and Jacob, saying, 'I will give it to your
descendants.' [b]I have caused you to see *it* with
your eyes, but you shall not cross over there."
5 [a]So Moses the servant of the LORD died
there in the land of Moab, according to the
word of the LORD. 6 And He buried him in
a valley in the land of Moab, opposite Beth
Peor; but [a]no one knows his grave to this
day. 7 [a]Moses *was* one hundred and twenty
years old when he died. [b]His eyes were not
dim nor his natural vigor diminished. 8 And
the children of Israel wept for Moses in the
plains of Moab [a]thirty days. So the days of
weeping *and* mourning for Moses ended.
9 Now Joshua the son of Nun was full of
the [a]spirit of wisdom, for [b]Moses had laid
his hands on him; so the children of Israel
heeded him, and did as the LORD had commanded Moses.
10 But since then there [a]has not arisen in
Israel a prophet like Moses, [b]whom the LORD
knew face to face, 11 in all [a]the signs and wonders which the LORD sent him to do in the
land of Egypt, before Pharaoh, before all his
servants, and in all his land, 12 and by all that
mighty power and all the great terror which
Moses performed in the sight of all Israel.

33:29 [b] 2 Sam. 7:23 [c] Ps. 115:9 [d] Ps. 18:44; 66:3 [e] Num. 33:52 **34:1** [a] Deut. 32:49 **34:2** [1] That is, the Mediterranean **34:3** [a] 2 Chr. 28:15 **34:4** [a] Gen. 12:7 [b] Deut. 3:27 **34:5** [a] Deut. 32:50; Josh. 1:1, 2 **34:6** [a] Jude 9 **34:7** [a] Deut. 31:2 [b] Gen. 27:1; 48:10 **34:8** [a] Gen. 50:3, 10 **34:9** [a] Is. 11:2 [b] Num. 27:18, 23 **34:10** [a] Deut. 18:15, 18 [b] Ex. 33:11 **34:11** [a] Deut. 7:19

THE BOOK OF

JOSHUA

AUTHOR

Jewish tradition seems correct in assigning the authorship of this book to Joshua himself. The unity of style and organization suggests a single authorship for the majority of the book, with the exception of three small portions that may have been added after Joshua's death: Othniel's capture of Kirjath Sepher (Josh. 15:13–19); Dan's migration to the north (19:47); and Joshua's death and burial (24:29–33). However, Joshua 24:26 makes this clear statement: "Then Joshua wrote these words in the Book of the Law of God."

TIME

c. 1405–1398 BC

KEY VERSE

Joshua 11:23

THEME

In the Book of Joshua, the Israelites are commanded to destroy everything and everybody so that they can take full possession of the land. The transition of leadership is from Moses to Joshua. A nomadic people attach themselves to given tracts of land, and a nation is formed from a wandering tribe as the conquest is completed in 21:43–45. We also see how a failure to carry out God's plan completely lays a foundation for future problems.

This book of conquest highlighting the leadership of General Joshua is bookended by a Hebrew descriptor for peace: rest. Joshua helps us understand how biblical rest is ceasing activity and trusting in the Lord. Through Moses, the Lord promised to give the people of God a peace-filled rest as they entered the Promised Land; this is why Joshua opens and closes with the fulfillment of *shalom* in the Promised Land (1:13; 23:1). Beginning with Jericho and concluding at the stronghold of Hazor (ch. 11), a number of major battles are featured in Joshua, and one includes his short, powerful prayer: "Sun, stand still" (10:12). Neither cosmic influence nor the mightiest forces opposing Israel could stop the people of God from experiencing God's rest—which is also true for the people of God today.

God’s Commission to Joshua

1 After the death of Moses the servant of the
LORD, it came to pass that the LORD spoke
to Joshua the son of Nun, Moses’ [a]assistant,
saying: 2[a]“Moses My servant is dead. Now
therefore, arise, go over this Jordan, you and
all this people, to the land which I am giving
to them—the children of Israel. 3[a]Every place
that the sole of your foot will tread upon I
have given you, as I said to Moses. 4[a]From
the wilderness and this Lebanon as far as the
great river, the River Euphrates, all the land
of the Hittites, and to the Great Sea toward
the going down of the sun, shall be your territory. 5[a]No man shall *be able to* stand before
you all the days of your life; [b]as I was with
Moses, *so* [c]I will be with you. [d]I will not leave
you nor forsake you. 6[a]Be strong and of good
courage, for to this people you shall divide
as an inheritance the land which I swore to
their fathers to give them. 7Only be strong
and very courageous, that you may observe
to do according to all the law [a]which Moses
My servant commanded you; [b]do not turn
from it to the right hand or to the left, that
you may prosper wherever you go. 8[a]This
Book of the Law shall not depart from your
mouth, but [b]you shall meditate in it day and
night, that you may observe to do according
to all that is written in it. For then you will
make your way prosperous, and then you will
have good success. 9[a]Have I not commanded
you? Be strong and of good courage; [b]do not
be afraid, nor be dismayed, for the LORD your
God *is* with you wherever you go.”

The Order to Cross the Jordan

10Then Joshua commanded the officers of
the people, saying, 11“Pass through the camp
and command the people, saying, ‘Prepare
provisions for yourselves, for [a]within three
days you will cross over this Jordan, to go in
to possess the land which the LORD your God
is giving you to possess.’ ”
12And to the Reubenites, the Gadites, and

1:1 [a] Ex. 24:13 1:2 [a] Deut. 34:5 1:3 [a] Deut. 11:24 1:4 [a] Gen. 15:18 1:5 [a] Deut. 7:24 [b] Ex. 3:12 [c] Deut. 31:8, 23 [d] Deut. 31:6, 7 1:6 [a] Deut. 31:7, 23 1:7 [a] Deut. 31:7 [b] Deut. 5:32 1:8 [a] Josh. 8:34 [b] Ps. 1:1–3 1:9 [a] Deut. 31:7 [b] Ps. 27:1 1:11 [a] Deut. 9:1

PEACE NOTE

Christian happiness, anchored to the eternal truths of God’s Word and character, dispels fear. In fact, it causes us to be bold in our witness for Jesus Christ because we are not ashamed but peaceful.

JOSHUA 1:9

BE STRONG AND COURAGEOUS

“Have I not commanded you? Be strong and of good courage; do not be afraid.”

JOSHUA 1:9

One of the greatest enemies of peace is fear. Of course, in our uncertain world there is much to fear. Paul the apostle may have used thoughts from this Joshua 1 command in his letters to Timothy, writing, “For God has not given us a spirit of fear” (2 Tim. 1:7). Recalling Joshua’s character, Paul urged his protégé to be strong and bold because God would be present with him.

The great test for Joshua came when Moses died. Can you imagine stepping into the shoes of a man like that? Moses survived a precarious infancy, fled from the court of Pharaoh, years later confronted Pharaoh, led the people out of Egypt, met God on Mount Sinai, and received the covenant and law. That was a tough act to follow! And now it was Joshua’s turn. But God didn’t ask Joshua to work alone—He promised to be with His servant: “Be strong and of good courage; do not be afraid, nor be dismayed, for the LORD your God is with you wherever you go” (Josh. 1:9). Believing that God is with us replaces fear with peace.

How can you erase worry and fear in order to embrace confidence and peace?

half the tribe of Manasseh Joshua spoke, saying, 13 "Remember [a]the word which Moses the servant of the LORD commanded you, saying, 'The LORD your God is giving you rest and is giving you this land.' 14 Your wives, your little ones, and your livestock shall remain in the land which Moses gave you on this side of the Jordan. But you shall pass before your brethren armed, all your mighty men of valor, and help them, 15 until the LORD has given your brethren rest, as He *gave* you, and they also have taken possession of the land which the LORD your God is giving them. [a]Then you shall return to the land of your possession and enjoy it, which Moses the LORD's servant gave you on this side of the Jordan toward the sunrise."

16 So they answered Joshua, saying, "All that you command us we will do, and wherever you send us we will go. 17 Just as we heeded Moses in all things, so we will heed you. Only the LORD your God [a]be with you, as He was with Moses. 18 Whoever rebels against your command and does not heed your words, in all that you command him, shall be put to death. Only be strong and of good courage."

Rahab Hides the Spies

2 Now Joshua the son of Nun sent out two men [a]from Acacia Grove[1] to spy secretly, saying, "Go, view the land, especially Jericho."

So they went, and [b]came to the house of a harlot named [c]Rahab, and lodged there. 2 And [a]it was told the king of Jericho, saying, "Behold, men have come here tonight from the children of Israel to search out the country."

3 So the king of Jericho sent to Rahab, saying, "Bring out the men who have come to you, who have entered your house, for they have come to search out all the country."

4 [a]Then the woman took the two men and hid them. So she said, "Yes, the men came to me, but I did not know where they *were* from. 5 And it happened as the gate was being shut, when it was dark, that the men went out. Where the men went I do not know; pursue them quickly, for you may overtake them." 6 (But [a]she had brought them up to the roof and hidden them with the stalks of flax, which she had laid in order on the roof.) 7 Then the men pursued them by the road to the Jordan, to the fords. And as soon as those who pursued them had gone out, they shut the gate.

8 Now before they lay down, she came up to them on the roof, 9 and said to the men: [a]"I know that the LORD has given you the land, that [b]the terror of you has fallen on us, and that all the inhabitants of the land [c]are fainthearted because of you. 10 For we have heard how the LORD [a]dried up the water of the Red Sea for you when you came out of Egypt, and [b]what you did to the two kings of the Amorites who *were* on the other side of the Jordan, Sihon and Og, whom you [c]utterly destroyed. 11 And as soon as we [a]heard *these things,* [b]our hearts melted; neither did there remain any more courage in anyone because of you, for [c]the LORD your God, He *is* God in heaven above and on earth beneath. 12 Now therefore, I beg you, [a]swear to me by the LORD, since I have shown you kindness, that you also will show kindness to [b]my father's house, and [c]give me a true token, 13 and [a]spare my father, my mother, my brothers, my sisters, and all that they have, and deliver our lives from death."

14 So the men answered her, "Our lives for yours, if none of you tell this business of ours. And it shall be, when the LORD has given us the land, that [a]we will deal kindly and truly with you."

15 Then she [a]let them down by a rope through the window, for her house *was* on the city wall; she dwelt on the wall. 16 And she said to them, "Get to the mountain, lest the pursuers meet you. Hide there three days, until the pursuers have returned. Afterward you may go your way."

17 So the men said to her: "We *will be* [a]blameless of this oath of yours which you have made us swear, 18 [a]unless, *when* we come into the land, you bind this line of scarlet cord in the window through which you let us down, [b]and unless you bring your father, your mother, your brothers, and all your father's household to your own home. 19 So it shall be *that* whoever goes outside the doors of your house into the street, his blood *shall be* on his own head, and we *will be* guiltless. And whoever is with you in the house, [a]his blood *shall be* on our head if a hand is laid on him. 20 And if you tell this business of ours, then we will be free from your oath which you made us swear."

21 Then she said, "According to your words, so *be* it." And she sent them away, and they departed. And she bound the scarlet cord in the window.

22 They departed and went to the mountain, and stayed there three days until the pursuers returned. The pursuers sought *them* all along the way, but did not find *them.* 23 So the two men returned, descended from the mountain,

1:13 [a] Num. 32:20–28 **1:15** [a] Josh. 22:1–4 **1:17** [a] 1 Sam. 20:13 **2:1** [a] Num. 25:1 [b] James 2:25 [c] Matt. 1:5 [1] Hebrew *Shittim* **2:2** [a] Josh. 2:22 **2:4** [a] 2 Sam. 17:19, 20 **2:6** [a] Ex. 1:17 **2:9** [a] Deut. 1:8 [b] Deut. 2:25; 11:25 [c] Josh. 5:1 **2:10** [a] Ex. 14:21 [b] Num. 21:21–35 [c] Josh. 6:21 **2:11** [a] Ex. 15:14, 15 [b] Josh. 5:1; 7:5 [c] Deut. 4:39 **2:12** [a] 1 Sam. 20:14, 15, 17 [b] 1 Tim. 5:8 [c] Josh. 2:18 **2:13** [a] Josh. 6:23–25 **2:14** [a] Judg. 1:24 **2:15** [a] Acts 9:25 **2:17** [a] Ex. 20:7 **2:18** [a] Josh. 2:12 [b] Josh. 6:23 **2:19** [a] 1 Kin. 2:32

and crossed over; and they came to Joshua the son of Nun, and told him all that had befallen them. 24 And they said to Joshua, "Truly [a]the LORD has delivered all the land into our hands, for indeed all the inhabitants of the country are fainthearted because of us."

Israel Crosses the Jordan

3 Then Joshua rose early in the morning; and they set out [a]from Acacia Grove[1] and came to the Jordan, he and all the children of Israel, and lodged there before they crossed over. 2 So it was, [a]after three days, that the officers went through the camp; 3 and they commanded the people, saying, [a]"When you see the ark of the covenant of the LORD your God, [b]and the priests, the Levites, bearing it, then you shall set out from your place and go after it. 4 [a]Yet there shall be a space between you and it, about two thousand cubits by measure. Do not come near it, that you may know the way by which you must go, for you have not passed *this* way before."

5 And Joshua said to the people, [a]"Sanctify yourselves, for tomorrow the LORD will do wonders among you." 6 Then Joshua spoke to the priests, saying, [a]"Take up the ark of the covenant and cross over before the people."

So they took up the ark of the covenant and went before the people.

7 And the LORD said to Joshua, "This day I will begin to [a]exalt you in the sight of all Israel, that they may know that, [b]as I was with Moses, *so* I will be with you. 8 You shall command [a]the priests who bear the ark of the covenant, saying, 'When you have come to the edge of the water of the Jordan, [b]you shall stand in the Jordan.' "

9 So Joshua said to the children of Israel, "Come here, and hear the words of the LORD your God." 10 And Joshua said, "By this you shall know that [a]the living God *is* among you, and *that* He will without fail [b]drive out from before you the [c]Canaanites and the Hittites and the Hivites and the Perizzites and the Girgashites and the Amorites and the Jebusites: 11 Behold, the ark of the covenant of [a]the Lord of all the earth is crossing over before you into the Jordan. 12 Now therefore, [a]take for yourselves twelve men from the tribes of Israel, one man from every tribe. 13 And it shall come to pass, [a]as soon as the soles of the feet of the priests who bear the ark of the LORD, [b]the Lord of all the earth, shall rest in the waters of the Jordan, *that* the waters of the Jordan shall be cut off, the waters that come down from upstream, and they [c]shall stand as a heap."

> **PEACE NOTE**
>
> The Lord is the Author of our happiness, hope, and peace. He is the Source of our wholeness and well-being.

14 So it was, when the people set out from their camp to cross over the Jordan, with the priests bearing the [a]ark of the covenant before the people, 15 and as those who bore the ark came to the Jordan, and [a]the feet of the priests who bore the ark dipped in the edge of the water (for the [b]Jordan overflows all its banks [c]during the whole time of harvest), 16 that the waters which came down from upstream stood *still, and* rose in a heap very far away at Adam, the city that *is* beside [a]Zaretan. So the waters that went down [b]into the Sea of the Arabah, [c]the Salt Sea, failed, *and* were cut off; and the people crossed over opposite Jericho. 17 Then the priests who bore the ark of the covenant of the LORD stood firm on dry ground in the midst of the Jordan; [a]and all Israel crossed over on dry ground, until all the people had crossed completely over the Jordan.

The Memorial Stones

4 And it came to pass, when all the people had completely crossed [a]over the Jordan, that the LORD spoke to Joshua, saying: 2 [a]"Take for yourselves twelve men from the people, one man from every tribe, 3 and command them, saying, 'Take for yourselves twelve stones from here, out of the midst of the Jordan, from the place where [a]the priests' feet stood firm. You shall carry them over with you and leave them in [b]the lodging place where you lodge tonight.' "

2:24 [a] Ex. 23:31 **3:1** [a] Josh. 2:1 [1] Hebrew *Shittim* **3:2** [a] Josh. 1:10, 11 **3:3** [a] Num. 10:33 [b] Deut. 31:9, 25 **3:4** [a] Ex. 19:12 **3:5** [a] Josh. 7:13 **3:6** [a] Num. 4:15 **3:7** [a] Josh. 4:14 [b] Josh. 1:5, 9 **3:8** [a] Josh. 3:3 [b] Josh. 3:17 **3:10** [a] 1 Thess. 1:9 [b] Ex. 33:2 [c] Acts 13:19 **3:11** [a] Zech. 4:14; 6:5 **3:12** [a] Josh. 4:2, 4 **3:13** [a] Josh. 3:15, 16 [b] Josh. 3:11 [c] Ps. 78:13; 114:3 **3:14** [a] Acts 7:44, 45 **3:15** [a] Josh. 3:13 [b] 1 Chr. 12:15 [c] Josh. 4:18; 5:10, 12 **3:16** [a] 1 Kin. 4:12; 7:46 [b] Deut. 3:17 [c] Gen. 14:3 **3:17** [a] Ex. 3:8; 6:1–8; 14:21, 22, 29; 33:1 **4:1** [a] Deut. 27:2 **4:2** [a] Josh. 3:12 **4:3** [a] Josh. 3:13 [b] Josh. 4:19, 20

4 Then Joshua called the twelve men whom
he had appointed from the children of Israel,
one man from every tribe; 5 and Joshua said to
them: "Cross over before the ark of the LORD
your God into the midst of the Jordan, and
each one of you take up a stone on his shoulder, according to the number of the tribes of
the children of Israel, 6 that this may be [a]a sign
among you [b]when your children ask in time
to come, saying, 'What do these stones *mean*
to you?' 7 Then you shall answer them that
[a]the waters of the Jordan were cut off before
the ark of the covenant of the LORD; when it
crossed over the Jordan, the waters of the Jordan were cut off. And these stones shall be for
[b]a memorial to the children of Israel forever."
8 And the children of Israel did so, just
as Joshua commanded, and took up twelve
stones from the midst of the Jordan, as the
LORD had spoken to Joshua, according to the
number of the tribes of the children of Israel, and carried them over with them to the
place where they lodged, and laid them down
there. 9 Then Joshua set up twelve stones in
the midst of the Jordan, in the place where
the feet of the priests who bore the ark of the
covenant stood; and they are there to this day.
10 So the priests who bore the ark stood
in the midst of the Jordan until everything
was finished that the LORD had commanded
Joshua to speak to the people, according
to all that Moses had commanded Joshua;
and the people hurried and crossed over.
11 Then it came to pass, when all the people
had completely crossed over, that the [a]ark
of the LORD and the priests crossed over in
the presence of the people. 12 And [a]the men
of Reuben, the men of Gad, and half the tribe
of Manasseh crossed over armed before the
children of Israel, as Moses had spoken to
them. 13 About forty thousand prepared for
war crossed over before the LORD for battle,
to the plains of Jericho. 14 On that day the
LORD [a]exalted Joshua in the sight of all Israel; and they feared him, as they had feared
Moses, all the days of his life.
15 Then the LORD spoke to Joshua, saying,
16 "Command the priests who bear [a]the ark of
the Testimony to come up from the Jordan."
17 Joshua therefore commanded the priests,
saying, "Come up from the Jordan." 18 And it
came to pass, when the priests who bore the
ark of the covenant of the LORD had come
from the midst of the Jordan, *and* the soles
of the priests' feet touched the dry land, that
the waters of the Jordan returned to their
place [a]and overflowed all its banks as before.
19 Now the people came up from the Jordan on the tenth *day* of the first month, and
they camped [a]in Gilgal on the east border of
Jericho. 20 And [a]those twelve stones which
they took out of the Jordan, Joshua set up
in Gilgal. 21 Then he spoke to the children
of Israel, saying: [a]"When your children ask
their fathers in time to come, saying, 'What
are these stones?' 22 then you shall let your
children know, saying, [a]'Israel crossed over
this Jordan on [b]dry land'; 23 for the LORD
your God dried up the waters of the Jordan
before you until you had crossed over, as the
LORD your God did to the Red Sea, [a]which He
dried up before us until we had crossed over,
24 [a]that all the peoples of the earth may know
the hand of the LORD, that it *is* [b]mighty, that
you may [c]fear the LORD your God forever."

The Second Generation Circumcised

5 So it was, when all the kings of the Amorites who *were* on the west side of the
Jordan, and all the kings of the Canaanites
[a]who *were* by the sea, [b]heard that the LORD
had dried up the waters of the Jordan from
before the children of Israel until we[1] had
crossed over, that their heart melted; [c]and
there was no spirit in them any longer because of the children of Israel.
2 At that time the LORD said to Joshua,
"Make [a]flint knives for yourself, and circumcise the sons of Israel again the second time."
3 So Joshua made flint knives for himself, and
circumcised the sons of Israel at the hill of
the foreskins.[1] 4 And this *is* the reason why
Joshua circumcised them: [a]All the people
who came out of Egypt *who were* males, all
the men of war, had died in the wilderness
on the way, after they had come out of Egypt.
5 For all the people who came out had been
circumcised, but all the people born in the
wilderness, on the way as they came out of
Egypt, had not been circumcised. 6 For the
children of Israel walked [a]forty years in the
wilderness, till all the people *who were* men
of war, who came out of Egypt, were consumed, because they did not obey the voice
of the LORD—to whom the LORD swore that
[b]He would not show them the land which
the LORD had sworn to their fathers that He
would give us, [c]"a land flowing with milk and
honey."[1] 7 Then Joshua circumcised [a]their
sons *whom* He raised up in their place; for

4:6 [a] Deut. 27:2 [b] Deut. 6:20 **4:7** [a] Josh. 3:13, 16 [b] Num. 16:40 **4:11** [a] Josh. 3:11; 6:11 **4:12** [a] Num. 32:17, 20, 27, 28 **4:14** [a] Josh. 3:7 **4:16** [a] Ex. 25:16, 22 **4:18** [a] Josh. 3:15 **4:19** [a] Josh. 5:9 **4:20** [a] Josh. 4:3; 5:9, 10 **4:21** [a] Josh. 4:6 **4:22** [a] Deut. 26:5–9 [b] Josh. 3:17 **4:23** [a] Ex. 14:21 **4:24** [a] 1 Kin. 8:42 [b] 1 Chr. 29:12 [c] Jer. 10:7 **5:1** [a] Num. 13:29 [b] Ex. 15:14, 15 [c] Josh. 2:10, 11; 9:9 [1] Following Kethib; Qere, some Hebrew manuscripts and editions, Septuagint, Syriac, Targum, and Vulgate read *they.* **5:2** [a] Ex. 4:25 **5:3** [1] Hebrew *Gibeath Haaraloth* **5:4** [a] Deut. 2:14–16 **5:6** [a] Num. 14:33 [b] Heb. 3:11 [c] Ex. 3:8 [1] Exodus 3:8 **5:7** [a] Deut. 1:39

they were uncircumcised, because they had
not been circumcised on the way.
8 So it was, when they had finished circum-
cising all the people, that they stayed in their
places in the camp [a]till they were healed.
9 Then the LORD said to Joshua, "This day
I have rolled away [a]the reproach of Egypt
from you." Therefore the name of the place
is called [b]Gilgal[1] to this day.
10 Now the children of Israel camped in Gilgal, and kept the Passover [a]on the fourteenth
day of the month at twilight on the plains of
Jericho. 11 And they ate of the produce of the
land on the day after the Passover, unleavened bread and parched grain, on the very
same day. 12 Then [a]the manna ceased on the
day after they had eaten the produce of the
land; and the children of Israel no longer had
manna, but they ate the food of the land of
Canaan that year.

The Commander of the Army of the LORD

13 And it came to pass, when Joshua was by
Jericho, that he lifted his eyes and looked,
and behold, [a]a Man stood opposite him [b]with
His sword drawn in His hand. And Joshua
went to Him and said to Him, "*Are* You for
us or for our adversaries?"
14 So He said, "No, but *as* Commander of the
army of the LORD I have now come."

And Joshua [a]fell on his face to the earth
and [b]worshiped, and said to Him, "What does
my Lord say to His servant?"
15 Then the Commander of the LORD's army
said to Joshua, [a]"Take your sandal off your
foot, for the place where you stand *is* holy."
And Joshua did so.

The Destruction of Jericho

6 Now [a]Jericho was securely shut up because of the children of Israel; none went
out, and none came in. 2 And the LORD said to
Joshua: "See! [a]I have given Jericho into your
hand, its [b]king, *and* the mighty men of valor.
3 You shall march around the city, all *you*
men of war; you shall go all around the city
once. This you shall do six days. 4 And seven
priests shall bear seven [a]trumpets of rams'
horns before the ark. But the seventh day you
shall march around the city [b]seven times,
and [c]the priests shall blow the trumpets. 5 It
shall come to pass, when they make a long
blast with the ram's horn, *and* when you hear
the sound of the trumpet, that all the people
shall shout with a great shout; then the wall
of the city will fall down flat. And the people
shall go up every man straight before him."
6 Then Joshua the son of Nun called the
priests and said to them, "Take up the ark of
the covenant, and let seven priests bear seven
trumpets of rams' horns before the ark of the
LORD." 7 And he said to the people, "Proceed,
and march around the city, and let him who
is armed advance before the ark of the LORD."
8 So it was, when Joshua had spoken to the
people, that the seven priests bearing the sev-
en trumpets of rams' horns before the LORD
advanced and blew the trumpets, and the ark
of the covenant of the LORD followed them.
9 The armed men went before the priests
who blew the trumpets, [a]and the rear guard
came after the ark, while *the priests* continued
blowing the trumpets. 10 Now Joshua had
commanded the people, saying, "You shall
not shout or make any noise with your voice,
nor shall a word proceed out of your mouth,
until the day I say to you, 'Shout!' Then you
shall shout." 11 So he had [a]the ark of the LORD
circle the city, going around *it* once. Then they
came into the camp and lodged in the camp.
12 And Joshua rose early in the morning,
[a]and the priests took up the ark of the LORD.
13 Then seven priests bearing seven trumpets
of rams' horns before the ark of the LORD
went on continually and blew with the trumpets. And the armed men went before them.
But the rear guard came after the ark of the
LORD, while *the priests* continued blowing
the trumpets. 14 And the second day they
marched around the city once and returned
to the camp. So they did six days.
15 But it came to pass on the seventh day
that they rose early, about the dawning of
the day, and marched around the city seven
times in the same manner. On that day only
they marched around the city seven times.
16 And the seventh time it happened, when the
priests blew the trumpets, that Joshua said to
the people: "Shout, for the LORD has given you
the city! 17 Now the city shall be [a]doomed by
the LORD to destruction, it and all who *are* in
it. Only [b]Rahab the harlot shall live, she and
all who *are* with her in the house, because
[c]she hid the messengers that we sent. 18 And
you, [a]by all means abstain from the accursed
things, lest you become accursed when you
take of the accursed things, and make the
camp of Israel a curse, [b]and trouble it. 19 But
all the silver and gold, and vessels of bronze
and iron, *are* consecrated to the LORD; they
shall come into the treasury of the LORD."

5:8 [a] Gen. 34:25 **5:9** [a] Gen. 34:14 [b] Josh. 4:19 [1] Literally *Rolling* **5:10** [a] Ex. 12:6 **5:12** [a] Ex. 16:35 **5:13** [a] Gen. 18:1, 2; 32:24, 30 [b] Num. 22:23 **5:14** [a] Gen. 17:3 [b] Ex. 34:8 **5:15** [a] Ex. 3:5 **6:1** [a] Josh. 2:1 **6:2** [a] Josh. 2:9, 24; 8:1 [b] Deut. 7:24 **6:4** [a] Lev. 25:9 [b] 1 Kin. 18:43 [c] Num. 10:8 **6:9** [a] Num. 10:25 **6:11** [a] Josh. 4:11 **6:12** [a] Deut. 31:25 **6:17** [a] Deut. 13:17 [b] Matt. 1:5 [c] Josh. 2:4, 6 **6:18** [a] Deut. 7:26 [b] Josh. 7:1, 12, 25

20 So the people shouted when *the priests* blew the trumpets. And it happened when the people heard the sound of the trumpet, and the people shouted with a great shout, that [a]the wall fell down flat. Then the people went up into the city, every man straight before him, and they took the city. 21 And they [a]utterly destroyed all that *was* in the city, both man and woman, young and old, ox and sheep and donkey, with the edge of the sword.

22 But Joshua had said to the two men who had spied out the country, "Go into the harlot's house, and from there bring out the woman and all that she has, [a]as you swore to her." 23 And the young men who had been spies went in and brought out Rahab, [a]her father, her mother, her brothers, and all that she had. So they brought out all her relatives and left them outside the camp of Israel. 24 But they burned the city and all that *was* in it with fire. Only the silver and gold, and the vessels of bronze and iron, they put into the treasury of the house of the LORD. 25 And Joshua spared Rahab the harlot, her father's household, and all that she had. So [a]she dwells in Israel to this day, because she hid the messengers whom Joshua sent to spy out Jericho.

26 Then Joshua charged *them* at that time, saying, [a]"Cursed *be* the man before the LORD who rises up and builds this city Jericho; he shall lay its foundation with his firstborn, and with his youngest he shall set up its gates."

27 So the LORD was with Joshua, and his fame spread throughout all the country.

Defeat at Ai

7 But the children of Israel committed a [a]trespass regarding the [b]accursed things, for [c]Achan the son of Carmi, the son of Zabdi,[1] the son of Zerah, of the tribe of Judah, took of the accursed things; so the anger of the LORD burned against the children of Israel.

2 Now Joshua sent men from Jericho to Ai, which *is* beside Beth Aven, on the east side of Bethel, and spoke to them, saying, "Go up and spy out the country." So the men went up and spied out Ai. 3 And they returned to Joshua and said to him, "Do not let all the people go up, but let about two or three thousand men go up and attack Ai. Do not weary all the people there, for *the people of Ai are* few." 4 So about three thousand men went up there from the people, [a]but they fled before the men of Ai. 5 And the men of Ai struck down about thirty-six men, for they chased them *from* before the gate as far as Shebarim, and struck them down on the descent; therefore [a]the hearts of the people melted and became like water.

6 Then Joshua [a]tore his clothes, and fell to the earth on his face before the ark of the LORD until evening, he and the elders of Israel; and they [b]put dust on their heads. 7 And Joshua said, "Alas, Lord GOD, [a]why have You brought this people over the Jordan at all—to deliver us into the hand of the Amorites, to destroy us? Oh, that we had been content, and dwelt on the other side of the Jordan! 8 O Lord, what shall I say when Israel turns its back before its enemies? 9 For the Canaanites and all the inhabitants of the land will hear *it,* and surround us, and [a]cut off our name from the earth. Then [b]what will You do for Your great name?"

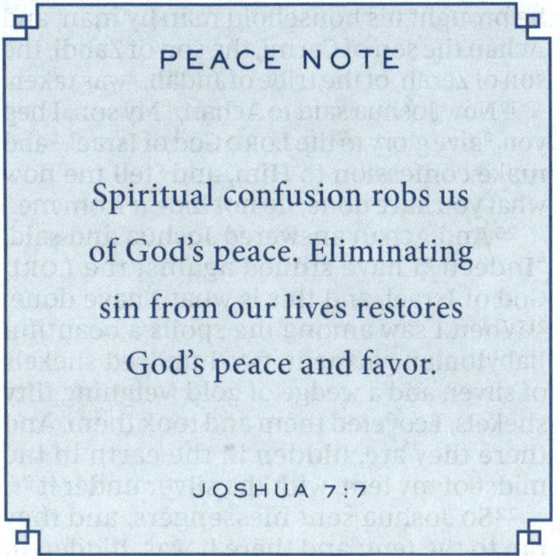

The Sin of Achan

10 So the LORD said to Joshua: "Get up! Why do you lie thus on your face? 11 Israel has sinned, and they have also transgressed My covenant which I commanded them. [a]For they have even taken some of the accursed things, and have both stolen and [b]deceived; and they have also put *it* among their own stuff. 12 [a]Therefore the children of Israel could not stand before their enemies, *but* turned *their* backs before their enemies, because [b]they have become doomed to destruction. Neither will I be with you anymore, unless you destroy the accursed from among you. 13 Get up, [a]sanctify the people, and say, [b]'Sanctify yourselves for tomorrow, because thus says the LORD God of Israel: *"There is* an accursed thing in your midst, O Israel; you cannot stand before your enemies

6:20 [a] Heb. 11:30 **6:21** [a] Deut. 7:2; 20:16, 17 **6:22** [a] Josh. 2:12–19 **6:23** [a] Josh. 2:13 **6:25** [a] [Matt. 1:5] **6:26** [a] 1 Kin. 16:34 **7:1** [a] Josh. 7:20, 21 [b] Josh. 6:17–19 [c] Josh. 22:20 [1] Called *Zimri* in 1 Chronicles 2:6 **7:4** [a] Lev. 26:17 **7:5** [a] Lev. 26:36 **7:6** [a] Gen. 37:29, 34 [b] 1 Sam. 4:12 **7:7** [a] Ex. 17:3 **7:9** [a] Deut. 32:26 [b] Ex. 32:12 **7:11** [a] Josh. 6:17–19 [b] Acts 5:1, 2 **7:12** [a] Judg. 2:14 [b] [Hag. 2:13, 14] **7:13** [a] Ex. 19:10 [b] Josh. 3:5

until you take away the accursed thing from
among you." 14 In the morning therefore you
shall be brought according to your tribes.
And it shall be *that* the tribe which [a]the LORD
takes shall come according to families; and
the family which the LORD takes shall come
by households; and the household which the
LORD takes shall come man by man. 15 [a]Then it
shall be *that* he who is taken with the accursed
thing shall be burned with fire, he and all that
he has, because he has [b]transgressed the covenant of the LORD, and because he [c]has done
a disgraceful thing in Israel.' "
16 So Joshua rose early in the morning and
brought Israel by their tribes, and the tribe
of Judah was taken. 17 He brought the clan of
Judah, and he took the family of the Zarhites;
and he brought the family of the Zarhites
man by man, and Zabdi was taken. 18 Then
he brought his household man by man, and
Achan the son of Carmi, the son of Zabdi, the
son of Zerah, of the tribe of Judah, [a]was taken.
19 Now Joshua said to Achan, "My son, I beg
you, [a]give glory to the LORD God of Israel, [b]and
make confession to Him, and [c]tell me now
what you have done; do not hide *it* from me."
20 And Achan answered Joshua and said,
"Indeed [a]I have sinned against the LORD
God of Israel, and this is what I have done:
21 When I saw among the spoils a beautiful
Babylonian garment, two hundred shekels
of silver, and a wedge of gold weighing fifty
shekels, I coveted them and took them. And
there they are, hidden in the earth in the
midst of my tent, with the silver under it."
22 So Joshua sent messengers, and they
ran to the tent; and there it was, hidden in
his tent, with the silver under it. 23 And they
took them from the midst of the tent, brought
them to Joshua and to all the children of Israel, and laid them out before the LORD. 24 Then
Joshua, and all Israel with him, took Achan
the son of Zerah, the silver, the garment, the
wedge of gold, his sons, his daughters, his
oxen, his donkeys, his sheep, his tent, and [a]all
that he had, and they brought them to [b]the
Valley of Achor. 25 And Joshua said, [a]"Why
have you troubled us? The LORD will trouble
you this day." [b]So all Israel stoned him with
stones; and they burned them with fire after
they had stoned them with stones.
26 Then they [a]raised over him a great heap
of stones, still there to this day. So [b]the LORD
turned from the fierceness of His anger.
Therefore the name of that place has been
called [c]the Valley of Achor[1] to this day.

The Fall of Ai

8 Now the LORD said to Joshua: [a]"Do not
be afraid, nor be dismayed; take all the
people of war with you, and arise, go up to
Ai. See, [b]I have given into your hand the king
of Ai, his people, his city, and his land. 2 And
you shall do to Ai and its king as you did to
[a]Jericho and its king. Only [b]its spoil and its
cattle you shall take as booty for yourselves.
Lay an ambush for the city behind it."
3 So Joshua arose, and all the people of war,
to go up against Ai; and Joshua chose thirty
thousand mighty men of valor and sent them
away by night. 4 And he commanded them,
saying: "Behold, [a]you shall lie in ambush
against the city, behind the city. Do not go
very far from the city, but all of you be ready.
5 Then I and all the people who *are* with me
will approach the city; and it will come about,
when they come out against us as at the first,
that [a]we shall flee before them. 6 For they will
come out after us till we have drawn them
from the city, for they will say, '*They are* fleeing before us as at the first.' Therefore we will
flee before them. 7 Then you shall rise from
the ambush and seize the city, for the LORD
your God will deliver it into your hand. 8 And
it will be, when you have taken the city, *that*
you shall set the city on fire. According to
the commandment of the LORD you shall
do. [a]See, I have commanded you."
9 Joshua therefore sent them out; and they
went to lie in ambush, and stayed between
Bethel and Ai, on the west side of Ai; but
Joshua lodged that night among the people.
10 Then Joshua rose up early in the morning
and mustered the people, and went up, he
and the elders of Israel, before the people to
Ai. 11 [a]And all the people of war who *were* with
him went up and drew near; and they came
before the city and camped on the north side
of Ai. Now a valley *lay* between them and Ai.
12 So he took about five thousand men and
set them in ambush between Bethel and Ai,
on the west side of the city. 13 And when they
had set the people, all the army that *was* on
the north of the city, and its rear guard on
the west of the city, Joshua went that night
into the midst of the valley.
14 Now it happened, when the king of Ai saw
it, that the men of the city hurried and rose
early and went out against Israel to battle,
he and all his people, at an appointed place
before the plain. But he [a]did not know that
there was an ambush against him behind
the city. 15 And Joshua and all Israel [a]made

7:14 [a] [Prov. 16:33] **7:15** [a] 1 Sam. 14:38, 39 [b] Josh. 7:11 [c] Gen. 34:7 **7:18** [a] 1 Sam. 14:42 **7:19** [a] Jer. 13:16 [b] Num. 5:6, 7 [c] 1 Sam. 14:43 **7:20** [a] Num. 22:34 **7:24** [a] Num. 16:32, 33 [b] Josh. 7:26; 15:7 **7:25** [a] Josh. 6:18 [b] Deut. 17:5 **7:26** [a] 2 Sam. 18:17 [b] Deut. 13:17 [c] Is. 65:10 [1] Literally *Trouble* **8:1** [a] Josh. 1:9; 10:8 [b] Josh. 6:2 **8:2** [a] Josh. 6:21 [b] Deut. 20:14 **8:4** [a] Judg. 20:29 **8:5** [a] Judg. 20:32 **8:8** [a] 2 Sam. 13:28 **8:11** [a] Josh. 8:5 **8:14** [a] Judg. 20:34 **8:15** [a] Judg. 20:36

as if they were beaten before them, and fled by the way of the wilderness. 16 So all the people who *were* in Ai were called together to pursue them. And they pursued Joshua and were drawn away from the city. 17 There was not a man left in Ai or Bethel who did not go out after Israel. So they left the city open and pursued Israel.

18 Then the LORD said to Joshua, "Stretch out the spear that *is* in your hand toward Ai, for I will give it into your hand." And Joshua stretched out the spear that *was* in his hand toward the city. 19 So *those in* ambush arose quickly out of their place; they ran as soon as he had stretched out his hand, and they entered the city and took it, and hurried to set the city on fire. 20 And when the men of Ai looked behind them, they saw, and behold, the smoke of the city ascended to heaven. So they had no power to flee this way or that way, and the people who had fled to the wilderness turned back on the pursuers.

21 Now when Joshua and all Israel saw that the ambush had taken the city and that the smoke of the city ascended, they turned back and struck down the men of Ai. 22 Then the others came out of the city against them; so they were *caught* in the midst of Israel, some on this side and some on that side. And they struck them down, so that they [a]let none of them remain or escape. 23 But the king of Ai they took alive, and brought him to Joshua.

24 And it came to pass when Israel had made an end of slaying all the inhabitants of Ai in the field, in the wilderness where they pursued them, and when they all had fallen by the edge of the sword until they were consumed, that all the Israelites returned to Ai and struck it with the edge of the sword. 25 So it was *that* all who fell that day, both men and women, *were* twelve thousand—all the people of Ai. 26 For Joshua did not draw back his hand, with which he stretched out the spear, until he had [a]utterly destroyed all the inhabitants of Ai. 27 [a]Only the livestock and the spoil of that city Israel took as booty for themselves, according to the word of the LORD which He had [b]commanded Joshua. 28 So Joshua burned Ai and made it [a]a heap forever, a desolation to this day. 29 [a]And the king of Ai he hanged on a tree until evening. [b]And as soon as the sun was down, Joshua commanded that they should take his corpse down from the tree, cast it at the entrance of the gate of the city, and [c]raise over it a great heap of stones *that remains* to this day.

Joshua Renews the Covenant

30 Now Joshua built an altar to the LORD God of Israel [a]in Mount Ebal, 31 as Moses the servant of the LORD had commanded the children of Israel, as it is written in the Book of the Law of Moses: [a]"an altar of whole stones over which no man has wielded an iron *tool.*"[1] And [b]they offered on it burnt offerings to the LORD, and sacrificed peace offerings. 32 And there, in the presence of the children of Israel, [a]he wrote on the stones a copy of the law of Moses, which he had written. 33 Then all Israel, with their elders and officers and judges, stood on either side of the ark before the priests, the Levites, [a]who bore the ark of the covenant of the LORD, [b]the stranger as well as he who was born among them. Half of them *were* in front of Mount Gerizim and half of them in front of Mount Ebal, [c]as Moses the servant of the LORD had commanded before, that they should bless the people of Israel. 34 And afterward [a]he read all the words of the law, [b]the blessings and the cursings, according to all that is written in the [c]Book of the Law. 35 There was not a word of all that Moses had commanded which Joshua did not read before all the assembly of Israel, [a]with the women, the little ones, [b]and the strangers who were living among them.

The Treaty with the Gibeonites

9 And it came to pass when [a]all the kings who *were* on this side of the Jordan, in the hills and in the lowland and in all the coasts of [b]the Great Sea toward Lebanon—[c]the Hittite, the Amorite, the Canaanite, the Perizzite, the Hivite, and the Jebusite—heard *about it,* 2 that they [a]gathered together to fight with Joshua and Israel with one accord.

3 But when the inhabitants of [a]Gibeon [b]heard what Joshua had done to Jericho and Ai, 4 they worked craftily, and went and pretended to be ambassadors. And they took old sacks on their donkeys, old wineskins torn and mended, 5 old and patched sandals on their feet, and old garments on themselves; and all the bread of their provision was dry *and* moldy. 6 And they went to Joshua, [a]to the camp at Gilgal, and said to him and to the men of Israel, "We have come from a far country; now therefore, make a covenant with us."

7 Then the men of Israel said to the [a]Hivites, "Perhaps you dwell among us; so [b]how can we make a covenant with you?"

8:22 [a] Deut. 7:2 **8:26** [a] Josh. 6:21 **8:27** [a] Num. 31:22, 26 [b] Josh. 8:2 **8:28** [a] Deut. 13:16 **8:29** [a] Josh. 10:26 [b] Deut. 21:22, 23 [c] Josh. 7:26; 10:27 **8:30** [a] Deut. 27:4–8 **8:31** [a] Ex. 20:25 [b] Ex. 20:24 [1] Deuteronomy 27:5, 6 **8:32** [a] Deut. 27:2, 3, 8 **8:33** [a] Deut. 31:9, 25 [b] Deut. 31:12 [c] Deut. 11:29; 27:12 **8:34** [a] Neh. 8:3 [b] Deut. 28:2, 15, 45; 29:20, 21; 30:19 [c] Josh. 1:8 **8:35** [a] Deut. 31:12 [b] Josh. 8:33 **9:1** [a] Josh. 3:10 [b] Num. 34:6 [c] Ex. 3:17; 23:23 **9:2** [a] Ps. 83:3, 5 **9:3** [a] Josh. 9:17, 22; 10:2; 21:17 [b] Josh. 6:27 **9:6** [a] Josh. 5:10 **9:7** [a] Josh. 9:1; 11:19 [b] Ex. 23:32

8 But they said to Joshua, [a]"We *are* your servants."

And Joshua said to them, "Who *are* you, and where do you come from?"

9 So they said to him: [a]"From a very far country your servants have come, because of the name of the LORD your God; for we have [b]heard of His fame, and all that He did in Egypt, 10 and [a]all that He did to the two kings of the Amorites who *were* beyond the Jordan—to Sihon king of Heshbon, and Og king of Bashan, who was at Ashtaroth. 11 Therefore our elders and all the inhabitants of our country spoke to us, saying, 'Take provisions with you for the journey, and go to meet them, and say to them, "We *are* your servants; now therefore, make a covenant with us." ' 12 This bread of ours we took hot *for* our provision from our houses on the day we departed to come to you. But now look, it is dry and moldy. 13 And these wineskins which we filled *were* new, and see, they are torn; and these our garments and our sandals have become old because of the very long journey."

14 Then the men of Israel took some of their provisions; [a]but they did not ask counsel of the LORD. 15 So Joshua [a]made peace with them, and made a covenant with them to let them live; and the rulers of the congregation swore to them.

16 And it happened at the end of three days, after they had made a covenant with them, that they heard that they *were* their neighbors who dwelt near them. 17 Then the children of Israel journeyed and came to their cities on the third day. Now their cities *were* [a]Gibeon, Chephirah, Beeroth, and Kirjath Jearim. 18 But the children of Israel did not attack them, [a]because the rulers of the congregation had sworn to them by the LORD God of Israel. And all the congregation complained against the rulers.

19 Then all the rulers said to all the congregation, "We have sworn to them by the LORD God of Israel; now therefore, we may not touch them. 20 This we will do to them: We will let them live, lest [a]wrath be upon us because of the oath which we swore to them." 21 And the rulers said to them, "Let them live, but let them be [a]woodcutters and water carriers for all the congregation, as the rulers had [b]promised them."

22 Then Joshua called for them, and he spoke to them, saying, "Why have you deceived us, saying, [a]'We *are* very far from you,' when [b]you dwell near us? 23 Now therefore, you *are* [a]cursed, and none of you shall be freed from being slaves—woodcutters and water carriers for the house of my God."

24 So they answered Joshua and said, "Because your servants were clearly told that the LORD your God [a]commanded His servant Moses to give you all the land, and to destroy all the inhabitants of the land from before you; therefore [b]we were very much afraid for our lives because of you, and have done this thing. 25 And now, here we are, [a]in your hands; do with us as it seems good and right to do to us." 26 So he did to them, and delivered them out of the hand of the children of Israel, so that they did not kill them. 27 And that day Joshua made them [a]woodcutters and water carriers for the congregation and for the altar of the LORD, [b]in the place which He would choose, even to this day.

The Sun Stands Still

10 Now it came to pass when Adoni-Zedek king of Jerusalem [a]heard how Joshua had taken [b]Ai and had utterly destroyed it—[c]as he had done to Jericho and its king, so he had done to [d]Ai and its king—and [e]how the inhabitants of Gibeon had made peace with Israel and were among them, 2 that they [a]feared greatly, because Gibeon *was* a great city, like one of the royal cities, and because it *was* greater than Ai, and all its men *were* mighty. 3 Therefore Adoni-Zedek king of Jerusalem sent to Hoham king of Hebron, Piram king of Jarmuth, Japhia king of Lachish, and Debir king of Eglon, saying, 4 "Come up to me and help me, that we may attack Gibeon, for [a]it has made peace with Joshua and with the children of Israel." 5 Therefore the five kings of the [a]Amorites, the king of Jerusalem, the king of Hebron, the king of Jarmuth, the king of Lachish, *and* the king of Eglon, [b]gathered together and went up, they and all their armies, and camped before Gibeon and made war against it.

6 And the men of Gibeon sent to Joshua at the camp [a]at Gilgal, saying, "Do not forsake your servants; come up to us quickly, save us and help us, for all the kings of the Amorites who dwell in the mountains have gathered together against us."

7 So Joshua ascended from Gilgal, he and [a]all the people of war with him, and all the mighty men of valor. 8 And the LORD said to

9:8 [a] Deut. 20:11 **9:9** [a] Deut. 20:15 [b] Josh. 2:9, 10; 5:1 **9:10** [a] Num. 21:24, 33 **9:14** [a] Num. 27:21 **9:15** [a] 2 Sam. 21:2 **9:17** [a] Josh. 18:25 **9:18** [a] Ps. 15:4 **9:20** [a] 2 Sam. 21:1, 2, 6 **9:21** [a] Deut. 29:11 [b] Josh. 9:15 **9:22** [a] Josh. 9:6, 9 [b] Josh. 9:16 **9:23** [a] Gen. 9:25 **9:24** [a] Deut. 7:1, 2 [b] Ex. 15:14 **9:25** [a] Gen. 16:6 **9:27** [a] Josh. 9:21, 23 [b] Deut. 12:5 **10:1** [a] Josh. 9:1 [b] Josh. 8:1 [c] Josh. 6:21 [d] Josh. 8:22, 26, 28 [e] Josh. 9:15 **10:2** [a] Ex. 15:14–16 **10:4** [a] Josh. 9:15; 10:1 **10:5** [a] Num. 13:29 [b] Josh. 9:2 **10:6** [a] Josh. 5:10; 9:6 **10:7** [a] Josh. 8:1

Joshua, [a]"Do not fear them, for I have delivered them into your hand; [b]not a man of them shall [c]stand before you." 9 Joshua therefore came upon them suddenly, having marched all night from Gilgal. 10 So the LORD [a]routed them before Israel, killed them with a great slaughter at Gibeon, chased them along the road that goes [b]to Beth Horon, and struck them down as far as [c]Azekah and Makkedah. 11 And it happened, as they fled before Israel *and* were on the descent of Beth Horon, [a]that the LORD cast down large hailstones from heaven on them as far as Azekah, and they died. *There were* more who died from the hailstones than the children of Israel killed with the sword.

12 Then Joshua spoke to the LORD in the day when the LORD delivered up the Amorites before the children of Israel, and he said in the sight of Israel:

[a]"Sun, stand still over Gibeon;
And Moon, in the Valley of [b]Aijalon."
13 So the sun stood still,
And the moon stopped,
Till the people had revenge
Upon their enemies.

[a]*Is* this not written in the Book of Jasher? So the sun stood still in the midst of heaven, and did not hasten to go *down* for about a whole day. 14 And there has been [a]no day like that, before it or after it, that the LORD heeded the voice of a man; for [b]the LORD fought for Israel.

15 [a]Then Joshua returned, and all Israel with him, to the camp at Gilgal.

The Amorite Kings Executed

16 But these five kings had fled and hidden themselves in a cave at Makkedah. 17 And it was told Joshua, saying, "The five kings have been found hidden in the cave at Makkedah."

18 So Joshua said, "Roll large stones against the mouth of the cave, and set men by it to guard them. 19 And do not stay *there* yourselves, *but* pursue your enemies, and attack their rear *guard.* Do not allow them to enter their cities, for the LORD your God has delivered them into your hand." 20 Then it happened, while Joshua and the children of Israel made an end of slaying them with a very great slaughter, till they had finished, that those who escaped entered fortified cities. 21 And all the people returned to the camp, to Joshua at Makkedah, in peace. [a]No one moved his tongue against any of the children of Israel.

22 Then Joshua said, "Open the mouth of the cave, and bring out those five kings to me from the cave." 23 And they did so, and brought out those five kings to him from the cave: the king of Jerusalem, the king of Hebron, the king of Jarmuth, the king of Lachish, *and* the king of Eglon.

24 So it was, when they brought out those kings to Joshua, that Joshua called for all the men of Israel, and said to the captains of the men of war who went with him, "Come near, put your feet on the necks of these kings." And they drew near and [a]put their feet on their necks. 25 Then Joshua said to them, [a]"Do not be afraid, nor be dismayed; be strong and of good courage, for [b]thus the LORD will do to all your enemies against whom you fight." 26 And afterward Joshua struck them and killed them, and hanged them on five trees; and they [a]were hanging on the trees until evening. 27 So it was at the time of the going down of the sun *that* Joshua commanded, and they [a]took them down from the trees, cast them into the cave where they had been hidden, and laid large stones against the cave's mouth, *which remain* until this very day.

PEACE NOTE

You will experience peace as you learn how God will protect you from your enemies and detractors, as He did Israel, when you are obedient to Him.

JOSHUA 10:25

Conquest of the Southland

28 On that day Joshua took Makkedah, and struck it and its king with the edge of the sword. He utterly [a]destroyed them[1]—all the people who *were* in it. He let none remain. He also did to the king of Makkedah [b]as he had done to the king of Jericho.

10:8 [a] Josh. 11:6 [b] Josh. 1:5, 9 [c] Josh. 21:44 **10:10** [a] Is. 28:21 [b] Josh. 16:3, 5 [c] Josh. 15:35 **10:11** [a] Is. 30:30 **10:12** [a] Hab. 3:11 [b] Judg. 12:12 **10:13** [a] 2 Sam. 1:18 **10:14** [a] Is. 38:7, 8 [b] Deut. 1:30; 20:4 **10:15** [a] Josh. 10:43 **10:21** [a] Ex. 11:7 **10:24** [a] Mal. 4:3 **10:25** [a] Deut. 31:6–8 [b] Deut. 3:21; 7:19 **10:26** [a] Josh. 8:29 **10:27** [a] Deut. 21:22, 23 **10:28** [a] Deut. 7:2, 16 [b] Josh. 6:21 [1] Following Masoretic Text and most authorities; many Hebrew manuscripts, some manuscripts of the Septuagint, and some manuscripts of the Targum read *it*.

29 Then Joshua passed from Makkedah,
and all Israel with him, to [a]Libnah; and they
fought against Libnah. 30 And the LORD also
delivered it and its king into the hand of
Israel; he struck it and all the people who
were in it with the edge of the sword. He let
none remain in it, but did to its king as he
had done to the king of Jericho.
31 Then Joshua passed from Libnah, and all
Israel with him, to Lachish; and they encamped
against it and fought against it. 32 And the LORD
delivered Lachish into the hand of Israel, who
took it on the second day, and struck it and
all the people who *were* in it with the edge of
the sword, according to all that he had done
to Libnah. 33 Then Horam king of Gezer came
up to help Lachish; and Joshua struck him and
his people, until he left him none remaining.
34 From Lachish Joshua passed to Eglon,
and all Israel with him; and they encamped
against it and fought against it. 35 They took
it on that day and struck it with the edge of
the sword; all the people who *were* in it he
utterly destroyed that day, according to all
that he had done to Lachish.
36 So Joshua went up from Eglon, and all
Israel with him, to [a]Hebron; and they fought
against it. 37 And they took it and struck it
with the edge of the sword—its king, all its
cities, and all the people who *were* in it; he
left none remaining, according to all that he
had done to Eglon, but utterly destroyed it
and all the people who *were* in it.
38 Then Joshua returned, and all Israel with
him, to [a]Debir; and they fought against it.
39 And he took it and its king and all its cities;
they struck them with the edge of the sword
and utterly destroyed all the people who *were*
in it. He left none remaining; as he had done
to Hebron, so he did to Debir and its king,
as he had done also to Libnah and its king.
40 So Joshua conquered all the land: the
[a]mountain country and the South[1] and the
lowland and the wilderness slopes, and [b]all
their kings; he left none remaining, but [c]ut-
terly destroyed all that breathed, as the LORD
God of Israel had commanded. 41 And Joshua
conquered them from [a]Kadesh Barnea as far
as [b]Gaza, [c]and all the country of Goshen, even
as far as Gibeon. 42 All these kings and their
land Joshua took at one time, [a]because the
LORD God of Israel fought for Israel. 43 Then
Joshua returned, and all Israel with him, to
the camp at Gilgal.

The Northern Conquest

11 And it came to pass, when Jabin king
of Hazor heard *these things,* that he
[a]sent to Jobab king of Madon, to the king
[b]of Shimron, to the king of Achshaph, 2 and
to the kings who *were* from the north, in the
mountains, in the plain south of [a]Chinneroth,
in the lowland, and in the heights [b]of Dor
on the west, 3 to the Canaanites in the east
and in the west, the [a]Amorite, the Hittite,
the Perizzite, the Jebusite in the mountains,
[b]and the Hivite below [c]Hermon [d]in the land
of Mizpah. 4 So they went out, they and all
their armies with them, *as* many people [a]*as*
the sand that *is* on the seashore in multitude,
with very many horses and chariots. 5 And
when all these kings had met together, they
came and camped together at the waters of
Merom to fight against Israel.
6 But the LORD said to Joshua, [a]"Do not be
afraid because of them, for tomorrow about
this time I will deliver all of them slain before
Israel. You shall [b]hamstring their horses and
burn their chariots with fire." 7 So Joshua and
all the people of war with him came against
them suddenly by the waters of Merom, and
they attacked them. 8 And the LORD delivered
them into the hand of Israel, who defeated
them and chased them to Greater [a]Sidon, to
the Brook [b]Misrephoth,[1] and to the Valley of
Mizpah eastward; they attacked them until
they left none of them remaining. 9 So Joshua did to them as the LORD had told him: he
hamstrung their horses and burned their
chariots with fire.
10 Joshua turned back at that time and took
Hazor, and struck its king with the sword;
for Hazor was formerly the head of all those
kingdoms. 11 And they struck all the people
who *were* in it with the edge of the sword,
[a]utterly destroying *them.* There was none left
[b]breathing. Then he burned Hazor with fire.
12 So all the cities of those kings, and all
their kings, Joshua took and struck with the
edge of the sword. He utterly destroyed them,
[a]as Moses the servant of the LORD had commanded. 13 But *as for* the cities that stood on
their mounds,[1] Israel burned none of them,
except Hazor only, *which* Joshua burned.
14 And all the [a]spoil of these cities and the
livestock, the children of Israel took as booty
for themselves; but they struck every man
with the edge of the sword until they had destroyed them, and they left none breathing.

10:29 [a] Josh. 15:42; 21:13 **10:36** [a] Josh. 14:13–15; 15:13 **10:38** [a] Josh. 15:15 **10:40** [a] Deut. 1:7 [b] Deut. 7:24 [c] Deut. 20:16, 17 [1] Hebrew *Negev,* and so throughout this book **10:41** [a] Deut. 9:23 [b] Gen. 10:19 [c] Josh. 11:16; 15:51 **10:42** [a] Josh. 10:14 **11:1** [a] Josh. 10:3 [b] Josh. 19:15 **11:2** [a] Num. 34:11 [b] Josh. 17:11 **11:3** [a] Josh. 9:1 [b] Judg. 3:3, 5 [c] Josh. 11:17; 13:5, 11 [d] Gen. 31:49 **11:4** [a] Judg. 7:12 **11:6** [a] Josh. 10:8 [b] 2 Sam. 8:4 **11:8** [a] Gen. 49:13 [b] Josh. 13:6 [1] Hebrew *Misrephoth Maim* **11:11** [a] Deut. 20:16 [b] Josh. 10:40 **11:12** [a] Num. 33:50–56 **11:13** [1] Hebrew *tel,* a heap of successive city ruins **11:14** [a] Deut. 20:14–18

15[a]As the LORD had commanded Moses His
servant, so [b]Moses commanded Joshua, and
[c]so Joshua did. He left nothing undone of
all that the LORD had commanded Moses.

Summary of Joshua's Conquests

16 Thus Joshua took all this land: [a]the
mountain country, all the South, [b]all the
land of Goshen, the lowland, and the Jordan
plain[1]—the mountains of Israel and its lowlands, 17[a]from Mount Halak and the ascent to
Seir, even as far as Baal Gad in the Valley of
Lebanon below Mount Hermon. He captured
[b]all their kings, and struck them down and
killed them. 18 Joshua made war a long time
with all those kings. 19 There was not a city
that made peace with the children of Israel,
except [a]the Hivites, the inhabitants of Gibeon. All *the others* they took in battle. 20 For
[a]it was of the LORD to harden their hearts,
that they should come against Israel in battle, that He might utterly destroy them, *and*
that they might receive no mercy, but that
He might destroy them, [b]as the LORD had
commanded Moses.

21 And at that time Joshua came and cut
off [a]the Anakim from the mountains: from
Hebron, from Debir, from Anab, from all
the mountains of Judah, and from all the
mountains of Israel; Joshua utterly destroyed
them with their cities. 22 None of the Anakim
were left in the land of the children of Israel;
they remained only [a]in Gaza, in Gath, [b]and
in Ashdod.

23 So Joshua took the whole land, [a]accord-
ing to all that the LORD had said to Moses;
and Joshua gave it as an inheritance to Israel
[b]according to their divisions by their tribes.
Then the land [c]rested from war.

The Kings Conquered by Moses

12 These *are* the kings of the land whom
the children of Israel defeated, and
whose land they possessed on the other side
of the Jordan toward the rising of the sun,
[a]from the River Arnon [b]to Mount Hermon,
and all the eastern Jordan plain: 2 *One king
was* [a]Sihon king of the Amorites, who dwelt in
Heshbon *and* ruled half of Gilead, from Aroer,
which is on the bank of the River Arnon,
from the middle of that river, even as far as
the River Jabbok, *which is* the border of the
Ammonites, 3 and [a]the eastern Jordan plain
from the Sea of Chinneroth as far as the Sea
of the Arabah (the Salt Sea), [b]the road to Beth
Jeshimoth, and southward below [c]the slopes
of Pisgah. 4 *The other king was* [a]Og king of
Bashan and his territory, *who was* of [b]the
remnant of the giants, [c]who dwelt at Ashtaroth and at Edrei, 5 and reigned over [a]Mount
Hermon, [b]over Salcah, over all Bashan, [c]as
far as the border of the Geshurites and the
Maachathites, and over half of Gilead *to* the
border of Sihon king of Heshbon.

6[a]These Moses the servant of the LORD
and the children of Israel had conquered;
and [b]Moses the servant of the LORD had
given it *as* a possession to the Reubenites,
the Gadites, and half the tribe of Manasseh.

The Kings Conquered by Joshua

7 And these *are* the kings of the country
[a]which Joshua and the children of Israel
conquered on this side of the Jordan, on the
west, from Baal Gad in the Valley of Lebanon
as far as Mount Halak and the ascent to [b]Seir,
which Joshua [c]gave to the tribes of Israel *as*
a possession according to their divisions,
8[a]in the mountain country, in the lowlands,
in the *Jordan* plain, in the slopes, in the
wilderness, and in the South—[b]the Hittites,
the Amorites, the Canaanites, the Perizzites,
the Hivites, and the Jebusites: 9[a]the king of
Jericho, one; [b]the king of Ai, which *is* beside
Bethel, one; 10[a]the king of Jerusalem, one;
the king of Hebron, one; 11 the king of Jarmuth, one; the king of Lachish, one; 12 the
king of Eglon, one; [a]the king of Gezer, one;
13[a]the king of Debir, one; the king of Geder,
one; 14 the king of Hormah, one; the king of
Arad, one; 15[a]the king of Libnah, one; the
king of Adullam, one; 16[a]the king of Makkedah, one; [b]the king of Bethel, one; 17 the
king of Tappuah, one; [a]the king of Hepher,
one; 18 the king of Aphek, one; the king of La-
sharon, one; 19 the king of Madon, one; [a]the
king of Hazor, one; 20 the king of [a]Shimron
Meron, one; the king of Achshaph, one; 21 the
king of Taanach, one; the king of Megiddo,
one; 22[a]the king of Kedesh, one; the king of
Jokneam in Carmel, one; 23 the king of Dor
in the [a]heights of Dor, one; the king of [b]the
people of Gilgal, one; 24 the king of Tirzah,
one—[a]all the kings, thirty-one.

11:15 [a] Ex. 34:10–17 [b] Deut. 31:7, 8 [c] Josh. 1:7 **11:16** [a] Josh. 12:8 [b] Josh. 10:40, 41 [1] Hebrew *arabah* **11:17** [a] Josh. 12:7 [b] Deut. 7:24 **11:19** [a] Josh. 9:3–7 **11:20** [a] Deut. 2:30 [b] Deut. 20:16, 17 **11:21** [a] Num. 13:22, 33 **11:22** [a] 1 Sam. 17:4 [b] Josh. 15:46 **11:23** [a] Num. 34:2–15 [b] Num. 26:53 [c] Deut. 12:9, 10; 25:19 **12:1** [a] Num. 21:24 [b] Deut. 3:8 **12:2** [a] Deut. 2:24–27 **12:3** [a] Deut. 3:17 [b] Josh. 13:20 [c] Deut. 3:17; 4:49 **12:4** [a] Num. 21:33 [b] Deut. 3:11 [c] Deut. 1:4 **12:5** [a] Deut. 3:8 [b] Deut. 3:10 [c] Deut. 3:14 **12:6** [a] Num. 21:24, 35 [b] Num. 32:29–33 **12:7** [a] Josh. 11:17 [b] Gen. 14:6; 32:3 [c] Josh. 11:23 **12:8** [a] Josh. 10:40; 11:16 [b] Ex. 3:8; 23:23 **12:9** [a] Josh. 6:2 [b] Josh. 8:29 **12:10** [a] Josh. 10:23 **12:12** [a] Josh. 10:33 **12:13** [a] Josh. 10:38, 39 **12:15** [a] Josh. 10:29, 30 **12:16** [a] Josh. 10:28 [b] Judg. 1:22 **12:17** [a] 1 Kin. 4:10 **12:19** [a] Josh. 11:10 **12:20** [a] Josh. 11:1; 19:15 **12:22** [a] Josh. 19:37; 20:7; 21:32 **12:23** [a] Josh. 11:2 [b] Is. 9:1 **12:24** [a] Deut. 7:24

Remaining Land to Be Conquered

13 Now Joshua [a]was old, advanced in years. And the LORD said to him: "You are old, advanced in years, and there remains very much land yet to be possessed. 2[a]This is the land that yet remains: [b]all the territory of the Philistines and all [c]*that of* the Geshurites, 3[a]from Sihor, which *is* east of Egypt, as far as the border of Ekron northward (*which* is counted as Canaanite); the [b]five lords of the Philistines—the Gazites, the Ashdodites, the Ashkelonites, the Gittites, and the Ekronites; also [c]the Avites; 4from the south, all the land of the Canaanites, and Mearah that belongs to the Sidonians [a]as far as Aphek, to the border of [b]the Amorites; 5the land of [a]the Gebalites,[1] and all Lebanon, toward the sunrise, [b]from Baal Gad below Mount Hermon as far as the entrance to Hamath; 6all the inhabitants of the mountains from Lebanon as far as [a]the Brook Misrephoth,[1] *and* all the Sidonians—them [b]I will drive out from before the children of Israel; only [c]divide it by lot to Israel as an inheritance, as I have commanded you. 7Now therefore, divide this land as an inheritance to the nine tribes and half the tribe of Manasseh."

The Land Divided East of the Jordan

8With the other half-tribe the Reubenites and the Gadites received their inheritance, [a]which Moses had given them, [b]beyond the Jordan eastward, as Moses the servant of the LORD had given them: 9from Aroer which *is* on the bank of the River Arnon, and the town that *is* in the midst of the ravine, [a]and all the plain of Medeba as far as Dibon; 10[a]all the cities of Sihon king of the Amorites, who reigned in Heshbon, as far as the border of the children of Ammon; 11[a]Gilead, and the border of the Geshurites and Maachathites, all Mount Hermon, and all Bashan as far as Salcah; 12all the kingdom of Og in Bashan, who reigned in Ashtaroth and Edrei, who remained of [a]the remnant of the giants; [b]for Moses had defeated and cast out these.

13Nevertheless the children of Israel [a]did not drive out the Geshurites or the Maachathites, but the Geshurites and the Maachathites dwell among the Israelites until this day.

14[a]Only to the tribe of Levi he had given no inheritance; the sacrifices of the LORD God of Israel made by fire *are* their inheritance, [b]as He said to them.

The Land of Reuben

15[a]And Moses had given to the tribe of the children of Reuben *an inheritance* according to their families. 16Their territory was [a]from Aroer, which *is* on the bank of the River Arnon, [b]and the city that *is* in the midst of the ravine, [c]and all the plain by Medeba; 17[a]Heshbon and all its cities that *are* in the plain: Dibon, Bamoth Baal, Beth Baal Meon, 18[a]Jahaza, Kedemoth, Mephaath, 19[a]Kirjathaim, [b]Sibmah, Zereth Shahar on the mountain of the valley, 20Beth Peor, [a]the slopes of Pisgah, and Beth Jeshimoth— 21[a]all the cities of the plain and all the kingdom of Sihon king of the Amorites, who reigned in Heshbon, [b]whom Moses had struck [c]with the princes of Midian: Evi, Rekem, Zur, Hur, and Reba, who *were* princes of Sihon dwelling in the country. 22The children of Israel also killed with the sword [a]Balaam the son of Beor, the soothsayer, among those who were killed by them. 23And the border of the children of Reuben was the bank of the Jordan. This *was* the inheritance of the children of Reuben according to their families, the cities and their villages.

The Land of Gad

24[a]Moses also had given *an inheritance* to the tribe of Gad, to the children of Gad according to their families. 25[a]Their territory was Jazer, and all the cities of Gilead, [b]and half the land of the Ammonites as far as Aroer, which *is* before [c]Rabbah, 26and from Heshbon to Ramath Mizpah and Betonim, and from Mahanaim to the border of Debir, 27and in the valley [a]Beth Haram, Beth Nimrah, [b]Succoth, and Zaphon, the rest of the kingdom of Sihon king of Heshbon, with the Jordan as *its* border, as far as the edge [c]of the Sea of Chinnereth, on the other side of the Jordan eastward. 28This *is* the inheritance of the children of Gad according to their families, the cities and their villages.

Half the Tribe of Manasseh (East)

29[a]Moses also had given *an inheritance* to half the tribe of Manasseh; it was for half the tribe of the children of Manasseh according to their families: 30Their territory was from Mahanaim, all Bashan, all the kingdom of Og king of Bashan, and [a]all the towns of Jair which are in Bashan, sixty cities; 31half of Gilead, and

13:1 [a] Josh. 14:10; 23:1, 2 **13:2** [a] Judg. 3:1–3 [b] Joel 3:4 [c] 2 Sam. 3:3 **13:3** [a] Jer. 2:18 [b] Judg. 3:3 [c] Deut. 2:23 **13:4** [a] Josh. 12:18; 19:30 [b] Judg. 1:34 **13:5** [a] 1 Kin. 5:18; Ezek. 27:9 [b] Josh. 12:7 [1] Or *Giblites* **13:6** [a] Josh. 11:8 [b] Josh. 23:13 [c] Josh. 14:1, 2 [1] Hebrew *Misrephoth Maim* **13:8** [a] Num. 32:33 [b] Josh. 12:1–6 **13:9** [a] Num. 21:30 **13:10** [a] Num. 21:24, 25 **13:11** [a] Josh. 12:5 **13:12** [a] Deut. 3:11 [b] Num. 21:24, 34, 35 **13:13** [a] Josh. 13:11 **13:14** [a] Josh. 14:3, 4 [b] Josh. 13:33 **13:15** [a] Num. 34:14 **13:16** [a] Josh. 12:2 [b] Num. 21:28 [c] Num. 21:30 **13:17** [a] Num. 21:28, 30 **13:18** [a] Num. 21:23 **13:19** [a] Num. 32:37 [b] Num. 32:38 **13:20** [a] Deut. 3:17 **13:21** [a] Deut. 3:10 [b] Num. 21:24 [c] Num. 31:8 **13:22** [a] Num. 22:5; 31:8 **13:24** [a] Num. 34:14 **13:25** [a] Num. 32:1, 35 [b] Judg. 11:13, 15 [c] Deut. 3:11 **13:27** [a] Num. 32:36 [b] Gen. 33:17 [c] Num. 34:11 **13:29** [a] Num. 34:14 **13:30** [a] Num. 32:41

[a]Ashtaroth and Edrei, cities of the kingdom of Og in Bashan, *were* for the [b]children of Machir the son of Manasseh, for half of the children of Machir according to their families.

32 These *are the areas* which Moses had distributed as an inheritance in the plains of Moab on the other side of the Jordan, by Jericho eastward. 33 [a]But to the tribe of Levi Moses had given no inheritance; the LORD God of Israel *was* their inheritance, [b]as He had said to them.

The Land Divided West of the Jordan

14 These *are the areas* which the children of Israel inherited in the land of Canaan, [a]which Eleazar the priest, Joshua the son of Nun, and the heads of the fathers of the tribes of the children of Israel distributed as an inheritance to them. 2 Their inheritance *was* [a]by lot, as the LORD had commanded by the hand of Moses, for the nine tribes and the half-tribe. 3 [a]For Moses had given the inheritance of the two tribes and the half-tribe on the other side of the Jordan; but to the Levites he had given no inheritance among them. 4 For [a]the children of Joseph were two tribes: Manasseh and Ephraim. And they gave no part to the Levites in the land, except [b]cities to dwell *in*, with their common-lands for their livestock and their property. 5 [a]As the LORD had commanded Moses, so the children of Israel did; and they divided the land.

Caleb Inherits Hebron

6 Then the children of Judah came to Joshua in Gilgal. And Caleb the son of Jephunneh the [a]Kenizzite said to him: "You know [b]the word which the LORD said to Moses the man of God concerning [c]you and me in Kadesh Barnea. 7 I *was* forty years old when Moses the servant of the LORD [a]sent me from Kadesh Barnea to spy out the land, and I brought back word to him as *it was* in my heart. 8 Nevertheless [a]my brethren who went up with me made the heart of the people melt, but I wholly [b]followed the LORD my God. 9 So Moses swore on that day, saying, [a]'Surely the land [b]where your foot has trodden shall be your inheritance and your children's forever, because you have wholly followed the LORD my God.' 10 And now, behold, the LORD has kept me [a]alive, [b]as He said, these forty-five years, ever since the LORD spoke this word to Moses while Israel wandered

> **PEACE NOTE**
>
> The peace of the Lord in the believer induces strength! Joshua illustrated this by his enduring strength throughout a lifetime of battles as he led Israel.
>
> JOSHUA 14:11

in the wilderness; and now, here I am this day, eighty-five years old. 11 [a]As yet I *am as* strong this day as on the day that Moses sent me; just as my strength *was* then, so now *is* my strength for war, both [b]for going out and for coming in. 12 Now therefore, give me this mountain of which the LORD spoke in that day; for you heard in that day how [a]the Anakim *were* there, and *that* the cities *were* great *and* fortified. [b]It may be that the LORD *will be* with me, and [c]I shall be able to drive them out as the LORD said."

13 And Joshua [a]blessed him, [b]and gave Hebron to Caleb the son of Jephunneh as an inheritance. 14 [a]Hebron therefore became the inheritance of Caleb the son of Jephunneh the Kenizzite to this day, because he [b]wholly followed the LORD God of Israel. 15 And [a]the name of Hebron formerly was Kirjath Arba (*Arba was* the greatest man among the Anakim).

[b]Then the land had rest from war.

The Land of Judah

15 So *this* was the lot of the tribe of the children of Judah according to their families:

[a]The border of Edom at the [b]Wilderness of Zin southward *was* the extreme southern boundary. 2 And their [a]southern border began at the shore of the Salt Sea, from the bay that faces southward. 3 Then it went out to the southern side of [a]the Ascent of Akrabbim, passed along to Zin, ascended on the south side of Kadesh Barnea, passed along to

13:31 [a] Josh. 9:10; 12:4; 13:12 [b] Num. 32:39, 40 **13:33** [a] Josh. 13:14; 18:7 [b] Num. 18:20 **14:1** [a] Num. 34:16–29 **14:2** [a] Num. 26:55; 33:54; 34:13 **14:3** [a] Josh. 13:8, 32, 33 **14:4** [a] 2 Chr. 30:1 [b] Num. 35:2–8 **14:5** [a] Josh. 21:2 **14:6** [a] Num. 32:11, 12 [b] Num. 14:24, 30 [c] Num. 13:26 **14:7** [a] Num. 13:6, 17; 14:6 **14:8** [a] Num. 13:31, 32 [b] Num. 14:24 **14:9** [a] Num. 14:23, 24 [b] Deut. 1:36 **14:10** [a] Num. 14:24, 30, 38 [b] Josh. 5:6 **14:11** [a] Deut. 34:7 [b] Deut. 31:2 **14:12** [a] Num. 13:28, 33 [b] Rom. 8:31 [c] Josh. 15:14 **14:13** [a] Josh. 22:6 [b] Josh. 10:37; 15:13 **14:14** [a] Josh. 21:12 [b] Josh. 14:8, 9 **14:15** [a] Gen. 23:2 [b] Josh. 11:23 **15:1** [a] Num. 34:3 [b] Num. 33:36 **15:2** [a] Num. 34:3, 4 **15:3** [a] Num. 34:4

Hezron, went up to Adar, and went around to Karkaa. 4 *From there* it passed [a]toward Azmon and went out to the Brook of Egypt; and the border ended at the sea. This shall be your southern border.

5 The east border *was* the Salt Sea as far as the mouth of the Jordan.

And the [a]border on the northern quarter *began* at the bay of the sea at the mouth of the Jordan. 6 The border went up to [a]Beth Hoglah and passed north of Beth Arabah; and the border went up [b]to the stone of Bohan the son of Reuben. 7 Then the border went up toward [a]Debir from [b]the Valley of Achor, and it turned northward toward Gilgal, which *is* before the Ascent of Adummim, which *is* on the south side of the valley. The border continued toward the waters of En Shemesh and ended at [c]En Rogel. 8 And the border went up [a]by the Valley of the Son of Hinnom to the southern slope of the [b]Jebusite *city* (which *is* Jerusalem). The border went up to the top of the mountain that *lies* before the Valley of Hinnom westward, which *is* at the end of the Valley [c]of Rephaim[1] northward. 9 Then the border went around from the top of the hill to [a]the fountain of the water of Nephtoah, and extended to the cities of Mount Ephron. And the border went around [b]to Baalah (which *is* [c]Kirjath Jearim). 10 Then the border turned westward from Baalah to Mount Seir, passed along to the side of Mount Jearim on the north (which *is* Chesalon), went down to Beth Shemesh, and passed on to [a]Timnah. 11 And the border went out to the side of [a]Ekron northward. Then the border went around to Shicron, passed along to Mount Baalah, and extended to Jabneel; and the border ended at the sea.

12 The west border *was* [a]the coastline of the Great Sea. This *is* the boundary of the children of Judah all around according to their families.

Caleb Occupies Hebron and Debir

13 [a]Now to Caleb the son of Jephunneh he gave a share among the children of [b]Judah, according to the commandment of the LORD to Joshua, *namely,* [c]Kirjath Arba, which *is* Hebron (*Arba was* the father of Anak). 14 Caleb drove out [a]the three sons of Anak from there: [b]Sheshai, Ahiman, and Talmai, the children of Anak. 15 Then [a]he went up from there to the inhabitants of Debir (formerly the name of Debir *was* Kirjath Sepher).

16 [a]And Caleb said, "He who attacks Kirjath Sepher and takes it, to him I will give Achsah my daughter as wife." 17 So [a]Othniel the [b]son of Kenaz, the brother of Caleb, took it; and he gave him [c]Achsah his daughter as wife. 18 [a]Now it was so, when she came *to him,* that she persuaded him to ask her father for a field. So [b]she dismounted from *her* donkey, and Caleb said to her, "What do you wish?" 19 She answered, "Give me a [a]blessing; since you have given me land in the South, give me also springs of water." So he gave her the upper springs and the lower springs.

The Cities of Judah

20 This *was* the inheritance of the tribe of the children of Judah according to their families:

21 The cities at the limits of the tribe of the children of Judah, toward the border of Edom in the South, were Kabzeel, [a]Eder, Jagur, 22 Kinah, Dimonah, Adadah, 23 Kedesh, Hazor, Ithnan, 24 [a]Ziph, Telem, Bealoth, 25 Hazor, Hadattah, Kerioth, Hezron (which *is* Hazor), 26 Amam, Shema, Moladah, 27 Hazar Gaddah, Heshmon, Beth Pelet, 28 Hazar Shual, [a]Beersheba, Bizjothjah, 29 Baalah, Ijim, Ezem, 30 Eltolad, Chesil, [a]Hormah, 31 [a]Ziklag, Madmannah, Sansannah, 32 Lebaoth, Shilhim, Ain, and [a]Rimmon: all the cities *are* twenty-nine, with their villages.

33 In the lowland: [a]Eshtaol, Zorah, Ashnah, 34 Zanoah, En Gannim, Tappuah, Enam, 35 Jarmuth, [a]Adullam, Socoh, Azekah, 36 Sharaim, Adithaim, Gederah, and Gederothaim: fourteen cities with their villages; 37 Zenan, Hadashah, Migdal Gad, 38 Dilean, Mizpah, [a]Joktheel, 39 [a]Lachish, Bozkath, [b]Eglon, 40 Cabbon, Lahmas,[1] Kithlish, 41 Gederoth, Beth Dagon, Naamah, and Makkedah: sixteen cities with their villages; 42 [a]Libnah, Ether, Ashan, 43 Jiphtah, Ashnah, Nezib, 44 Keilah, Achzib, and Mareshah: nine cities with their villages; 45 Ekron, with its towns and villages; 46 from Ekron to the sea, all that *lay* near [a]Ashdod, with their villages; 47 Ashdod with its towns and villages, Gaza with its towns and villages—as far as [a]the Brook of Egypt and [b]the Great Sea with *its* coastline.

15:4 [a] Num. 34:5 **15:5** [a] Josh. 18:15–19 **15:6** [a] Josh. 18:19, 21 [b] Josh. 18:17 **15:7** [a] Josh. 13:26 [b] Josh. 7:26 [c] 2 Sam. 17:17 **15:8** [a] Josh. 18:16 [b] Judg. 1:21; 19:10 [c] Josh. 18:16 [1] Literally *Giants* **15:9** [a] Josh. 18:15 [b] 1 Chr. 13:6 [c] Judg. 18:12 **15:10** [a] Gen. 38:13 **15:11** [a] Josh. 19:43 **15:12** [a] Num. 34:6, 7 **15:13** [a] Josh. 14:13 [b] Num. 13:6 [c] Josh. 14:15 **15:14** [a] Judg. 1:10, 20 [b] Num. 13:22 **15:15** [a] Judg. 1:11 **15:16** [a] Judg. 1:12 **15:17** [a] Judg. 1:13; 3:9 [b] Num. 32:12 [c] Judg. 1:12 **15:18** [a] Judg. 1:14 [b] Gen. 24:64 **15:19** [a] Gen. 33:11 **15:21** [a] Gen. 35:21 **15:24** [a] 1 Sam. 23:14 **15:28** [a] Gen. 21:31 **15:30** [a] Josh. 19:4 **15:31** [a] 1 Sam. 27:6; 30:1 **15:32** [a] Judg. 20:45, 47 **15:33** [a] Judg. 13:25; 16:31 **15:35** [a] 1 Sam. 22:1 **15:38** [a] 2 Kin. 14:7 **15:39** [a] 2 Kin. 14:19 [b] Josh. 10:3 **15:40** [1] Or *Lahmam* **15:42** [a] Josh. 21:13 **15:46** [a] Josh. 11:22 **15:47** [a] Josh. 15:4 [b] Num. 34:6

48 And in the mountain country: Shamir, Jattir, Sochoh, 49 Dannah, Kirjath Sannah (which *is* Debir), 50 Anab, Eshtemoh, Anim, 51 [a]Goshen, Holon, and Giloh: eleven cities with their villages; 52 Arab, Dumah, Eshean, 53 Janum, Beth Tappuah, Aphekah, 54 Humtah, [a]Kirjath Arba (which *is* Hebron), and Zior: nine cities with their villages; 55 [a]Maon, Carmel, Ziph, Juttah, 56 Jezreel, Jokdeam, Zanoah, 57 Kain, Gibeah, and Timnah: ten cities with their villages; 58 Halhul, Beth Zur, Gedor, 59 Maarath, Beth Anoth, and Eltekon: six cities with their villages; 60 [a]Kirjath Baal (which *is* Kirjath Jearim) and Rabbah: two cities with their villages.

61 In the wilderness: Beth Arabah, Middin, Secacah, 62 Nibshan, the City of Salt, and [a]En Gedi: six cities with their villages.

63 As for the Jebusites, the inhabitants of Jerusalem, [a]the children of Judah could not drive them out; [b]but the Jebusites dwell with the children of Judah at Jerusalem to this day.

Ephraim and West Manasseh

16 The lot fell to the children of Joseph from the Jordan, by Jericho, to the waters of Jericho on the east, to the [a]wilderness that goes up from Jericho through the mountains to Bethel, 2 then went out from [a]Bethel to Luz,[1] passed along to the border of the Archites at Ataroth, 3 and went down westward to the boundary of the Japhletites, [a]as far as the boundary of Lower Beth Horon to [b]Gezer; and it ended at the sea.

4 [a]So the children of Joseph, Manasseh and Ephraim, took their inheritance.

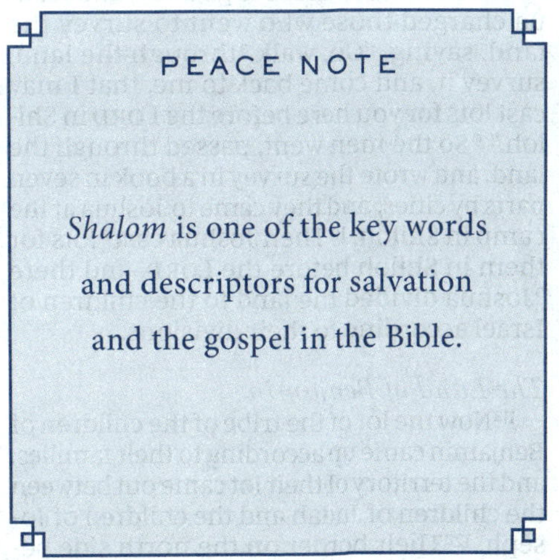

The Land of Ephraim

5 [a]The border of the children of Ephraim, according to their families, was *thus:* The border of their inheritance on the east side was [b]Ataroth Addar [c]as far as Upper Beth Horon.

6 And the border went out toward the sea on the north side of [a]Michmethath; then the border went around eastward to Taanath Shiloh, and passed by it on the east of Janohah. 7 Then it went down from Janohah to Ataroth and Naarah,[1] reached to Jericho, and came out at the Jordan.

8 The border went out from [a]Tappuah westward to the [b]Brook Kanah, and it ended at the sea. This *was* the inheritance of the tribe of the children of Ephraim according to their families. 9 [a]The separate cities for the children of Ephraim *were* among the inheritance of the children of Manasseh, all the cities with their villages.

10 [a]And they did not drive out the Canaanites who dwelt in Gezer; but the Canaanites dwell among the Ephraimites to this day and have become forced laborers.

The Other Half-Tribe of Manasseh (West)

17 There was also a lot for the tribe of Manasseh, for he *was* the [a]firstborn of Joseph: *namely* for [b]Machir the firstborn of Manasseh, the father of Gilead, because he was a man of war; therefore he was given [c]Gilead and Bashan. 2 And there was *a lot* for [a]the rest of the children of Manasseh according to their families: [b]for the children of Abiezer,[1] the children of Helek, [c]the children of Asriel, the children of Shechem, [d]the children of Hepher, and the children of Shemida; these *were* the male children of Manasseh the son of Joseph according to their families.

3 But [a]Zelophehad the son of Hepher, the son of Gilead, the son of Machir, the son of Manasseh, had no sons, but only daughters. And these *are* the names of his daughters: Mahlah, Noah, Hoglah, Milcah, and Tirzah. 4 And they came near before [a]Eleazar the priest, before Joshua the son of Nun, and before the rulers, saying, [b]"The LORD commanded Moses to give us an inheritance among our brothers." Therefore, according to the commandment of the LORD, he gave them an inheritance among their father's brothers. 5 Ten shares fell to [a]Manasseh, besides the land of Gilead and Bashan, which

15:51 [a] Josh. 10:41; 11:16 **15:54** [a] Josh. 14:15 **15:55** [a] 1 Sam. 23:24, 25 **15:60** [a] Josh. 18:14 **15:62** [a] 1 Sam. 23:29 **15:63** [a] 2 Sam. 5:6 [b] Judg. 1:21 **16:1** [a] Josh. 8:15; 18:12 **16:2** [a] Josh. 18:13 [1] Septuagint reads *Bethel* (that is, Luz). **16:3** [a] 2 Chr. 8:5 [b] 1 Kin. 9:15 **16:4** [a] Josh. 17:14 **16:5** [a] Judg. 1:29 [b] Josh. 18:13 [c] 2 Chr. 8:5 **16:6** [a] Josh. 17:7 **16:7** [1] Or *Naaran* (compare 1 Chronicles 7:28) **16:8** [a] Josh. 17:8 [b] Josh. 17:9 **16:9** [a] Josh. 17:9 **16:10** [a] Judg. 1:29 **17:1** [a] Gen. 41:51; 46:20; 48:18 [b] Gen. 50:23 [c] Deut. 3:15 **17:2** [a] Num. 26:29–33 [b] 1 Chr. 7:18 [c] Num. 26:31 [d] Num. 26:32 [1] Called *Jeezer* in Numbers 26:30 **17:3** [a] Num. 26:33; 27:1; 36:2 **17:4** [a] Josh. 14:1 [b] Num. 27:2–11 **17:5** [a] Josh. 22:7

were on the other side of the Jordan, 6 because the daughters of Manasseh received an inheritance among his sons; and the rest of Manasseh's sons had the land of Gilead.

7 And the territory of Manasseh was from Asher to [a]Michmethath, that *lies* east of Shechem; and the border went along south to the inhabitants of En Tappuah. 8 Manasseh had the land of Tappuah, but [a]Tappuah on the border of Manasseh *belonged* to the children of Ephraim. 9 And the border descended to the Brook Kanah, southward to the brook. [a]These cities of Ephraim *are* among the cities of Manasseh. The border of Manasseh *was* on the north side of the brook; and it ended at the sea.

10 Southward *it was* Ephraim's, northward *it was* Manasseh's, and the sea was its border. Manasseh's territory was adjoining Asher on the north and Issachar on the east. 11 And in Issachar and in Asher, [a]Manasseh had [b]Beth Shean and its towns, Ibleam and its towns, the inhabitants of Dor and its towns, the inhabitants of En Dor and its towns, the inhabitants of Taanach and its towns, and the inhabitants of Megiddo and its towns—three hilly regions. 12 Yet [a]the children of Manasseh could not drive out *the inhabitants of* those cities, but the Canaanites were determined to dwell in that land. 13 And it happened, when the children of Israel grew strong, that they put the Canaanites to [a]forced labor, but did not utterly drive them out.

More Land for Ephraim and Manasseh

14 [a]Then the children of Joseph spoke to Joshua, saying, "Why have you given us *only* [b]one lot and one share to inherit, since we *are* [c]a great people, inasmuch as the LORD has blessed us until now?"

15 So Joshua answered them, "If you *are* a great people, *then* go up to the forest *country* and clear a place for yourself there in the land of the Perizzites and the giants, since the mountains of Ephraim are too confined for you."

16 But the children of Joseph said, "The mountain country is not enough for us; and all the Canaanites who dwell in the land of the valley have [a]chariots of iron, *both those* who *are* of Beth Shean and its towns and *those* who *are* [b]of the Valley of Jezreel."

17 And Joshua spoke to the house of Joseph—to Ephraim and Manasseh—saying, "You *are* a great people and have great power; you shall not have *only* one lot, 18 but the mountain country shall be yours. Although it *is* wooded, you shall cut it down, and its farthest extent shall be yours; for you shall drive out the Canaanites, [a]though they have iron chariots *and* are strong."

The Remainder of the Land Divided

18 Now the whole congregation of the children of Israel assembled together [a]at Shiloh, and [b]set up the tabernacle of meeting there. And the land was subdued before them. 2 But there remained among the children of Israel seven tribes which had not yet received their inheritance.

3 Then Joshua said to the children of Israel: [a]"How long will you neglect to go and possess the land which the LORD God of your fathers has given you? 4 Pick out from among you three men for *each* tribe, and I will send them; they shall rise and go through the land, survey it according to their inheritance, and come *back* to me. 5 And they shall divide it into seven parts. [a]Judah shall remain in their territory on the south, and the [b]house of Joseph shall remain in their territory on the north. 6 You shall therefore survey the land in seven parts and bring *the survey* here to me, [a]that I may cast lots for you here before the LORD our God. 7 [a]But the Levites have no part among you, for the priesthood of the LORD *is* their inheritance. [b]And Gad, Reuben, and half the tribe of Manasseh have received their inheritance beyond the Jordan on the east, which Moses the servant of the LORD gave them."

8 Then the men arose to go away; and Joshua charged those who went to survey the land, saying, "Go, walk [a]through the land, survey it, and come back to me, that I may cast lots for you here before the LORD in Shiloh." 9 So the men went, passed through the land, and wrote the survey in a book in seven parts by cities; and they came to Joshua at the camp in Shiloh. 10 Then Joshua cast [a]lots for them in Shiloh before the LORD, and there [b]Joshua divided the land to the children of Israel according to their divisions.

The Land of Benjamin

11 [a]Now the lot of the tribe of the children of Benjamin came up according to their families, and the territory of their lot came out between the children of Judah and the children of Joseph. 12 [a]Their border on the north side began at the Jordan, and the border went up to

17:7 [a] Josh. 16:6 **17:8** [a] Josh. 16:8 **17:9** [a] Josh. 16:9 **17:11** [a] 1 Chr. 7:29 [b] 1 Kin. 4:12 **17:12** [a] Judg. 1:19, 27, 28 **17:13** [a] Josh. 16:10 **17:14** [a] Josh. 16:4 [b] Gen. 48:22 [c] Gen. 48:19 **17:16** [a] Judg. 1:19; 4:3 [b] 1 Kin. 4:12 **17:18** [a] Deut. 20:1 **18:1** [a] Jer. 7:12 [b] Judg. 18:31 **18:3** [a] Judg. 18:9 **18:5** [a] Josh. 15:1 [b] Josh. 16:1—17:18 **18:6** [a] Josh. 14:2; 18:10 **18:7** [a] Josh. 13:33 [b] Josh. 13:8 **18:8** [a] Gen. 13:17 **18:10** [a] Acts 13:19 [b] Num. 34:16–29 **18:11** [a] Judg. 1:21 **18:12** [a] Josh. 16:1

the side of Jericho on the north, and went up through the mountains westward; it ended at the Wilderness of Beth Aven. 13 The border went over from there toward Luz, to the side of Luz [a](which *is* Bethel) southward; and the border descended to Ataroth Addar, near the hill that *lies* on the south side [b]of Lower Beth Horon.

14 Then the border extended around the west side to the south, from the hill that *lies* before Beth Horon southward; and it ended at [a]Kirjath Baal (which *is* Kirjath Jearim), a city of the children of Judah. This *was* the west side.
15 The south side *began* at the end of Kirjath Jearim, and the border extended on the west and went out to [a]the spring of the waters of Nephtoah. 16 Then the border came down to the end of the mountain that *lies* before [a]the Valley of the Son of Hinnom, which *is* in the Valley of the Rephaim[1] on the north, descended to the Valley of Hinnom, to the side of the Jebusite *city* on the south, and descended to [b]En Rogel. 17 And it went around from the north, went out to En Shemesh, and extended toward Geliloth, which is before the Ascent of Adummim, and descended to [a]the stone of Bohan the son of Reuben.
18 Then it passed along toward the north side of Arabah,[1] and went down to Arabah. 19 And the border passed along to the north side of Beth Hoglah; then the border ended at the north bay at the [a]Salt Sea, at the south end of the Jordan. This *was* the southern boundary.
20 The Jordan was its border on the east side. This *was* the inheritance of the children of Benjamin, according to its boundaries all around, according to their families.

21 Now the cities of the tribe of the children of Benjamin, according to their families, were Jericho, Beth Hoglah, Emek Keziz, 22 Beth Arabah, Zemaraim, Bethel, 23 Avim, Parah, Ophrah, 24 Chephar Haammoni, Ophni, and Gaba: twelve cities with their villages; 25 [a]Gibeon, [b]Ramah, Beeroth, 26 Mizpah, Chephirah, Mozah, 27 Rekem, Irpeel, Taralah, 28 Zelah, Eleph, [a]Jebus (which *is* Jerusalem), Gibeath, *and* Kirjath: fourteen cities with their villages. This was the inheritance of the children of Benjamin according to their families.

Simeon's Inheritance with Judah

19 The [a]second lot came out for Simeon, for the tribe of the children of Simeon according to their families. [b]And their inheritance was within the inheritance of the children of Judah. 2 [a]They had in their inheritance Beersheba (Sheba), Moladah, 3 Hazar Shual, Balah, Ezem, 4 Eltolad, Bethul, Hormah, 5 Ziklag, Beth Marcaboth, Hazar Susah, 6 Beth Lebaoth, and Sharuhen: thirteen cities and their villages; 7 Ain, Rimmon, Ether, and Ashan: four cities and their villages; 8 and all the villages that *were* all around these cities as far as Baalath Beer, [a]Ramah of the South. This *was* the inheritance of the tribe of the children of Simeon according to their families.
9 The inheritance of the children of Simeon *was included* in the share of the children of Judah, for the share of the children of Judah was too much for them. [a]Therefore the children of Simeon had *their* inheritance within the inheritance of that people.

> **PEACE NOTE**
>
> Only God, through His unique Son, Jesus, can offer genuine peace and security. The peace that God offers is a healing wholeness.

The Land of Zebulun

10 The third lot came out for the children of Zebulun according to their families, and the border of their inheritance was as far as Sarid. 11 [a]Their border went toward the west and to Maralah, went to Dabbasheth, and extended along the brook that is [b]east of Jokneam. 12 Then from Sarid it went eastward toward the sunrise along the border of Chisloth Tabor, and went out toward [a]Daberath, bypassing Japhia. 13 And from there it passed along on the east of [a]Gath Hepher, toward Eth Kazin, and extended to Rimmon, which borders on Neah. 14 Then the border went around it on the north side of Hannathon, and it ended in the Valley of Jiphthah El. 15 Included were Kattath, Nahallal, Shimron, Idalah, and Bethlehem: twelve cities with their villages. 16 This *was* the inheritance of the children of Zebulun according to their families, these cities with their villages.

18:13 [a] Gen. 28:19 [b] Josh. 16:3 **18:14** [a] Josh. 15:9 **18:15** [a] Josh. 15:9 **18:16** [a] Josh. 15:8 [b] Josh. 15:7 [1] Literally *Giants* **18:17** [a] Josh. 15:6 **18:18** [1] Or *Beth Arabah* (compare 15:6 and 18:22) **18:19** [a] Josh. 15:2, 5 **18:25** [a] 1 Kin. 3:4, 5 [b] Jer. 31:15 **18:28** [a] Josh. 15:8, 63 **19:1** [a] Judg. 1:3 [b] Josh. 19:9 **19:2** [a] 1 Chr. 4:28 **19:8** [a] 1 Sam. 30:27 **19:9** [a] Josh. 19:1 **19:11** [a] Gen. 49:13 [b] Josh. 12:22 **19:12** [a] 1 Chr. 6:72 **19:13** [a] 2 Kin. 14:25

The Land of Issachar

17 The fourth lot came out to Issachar, for the children of Issachar according to their families. 18 And their territory went to Jezreel, and *included* Chesulloth, Shunem, 19 Haphraim, Shion, Anaharath, 20 Rabbith, Kishion, Abez, 21 Remeth, En Gannim, En Haddah, and Beth Pazzez. 22 And the border reached to Tabor, Shahazimah, and [a]Beth Shemesh; their border ended at the Jordan: sixteen cities with their villages. 23 This *was* the inheritance of the tribe of the children of Issachar according to their families, the cities and their villages.

The Land of Asher

24 [a]The fifth lot came out for the tribe of the children of Asher according to their families. 25 And their territory included Helkath, Hali, Beten, Achshaph, 26 Alammelech, Amad, and Mishal; it reached to [a]Mount Carmel westward, along *the Brook* Shihor Libnath. 27 It turned toward the sunrise to Beth Dagon; and it reached to Zebulun and to the Valley of Jiphthah El, then northward beyond Beth Emek and Neiel, bypassing [a]Cabul *which was* on the left, 28 including Ebron,[1] Rehob, Hammon, and Kanah, [a]as far as Greater Sidon. 29 And the border turned to Ramah and to the fortified city of Tyre; then the border turned to Hosah, and ended at the sea by the region of [a]Achzib. 30 Also Ummah, Aphek, and Rehob *were included:* twenty-two cities with their villages. 31 This *was* the inheritance of the tribe of the children of Asher according to their families, these cities with their villages.

The Land of Naphtali

32 [a]The sixth lot came out to the children of Naphtali, for the children of Naphtali according to their families. 33 And their border began at Heleph, enclosing the territory from the terebinth tree in Zaanannim, Adami Nekeb, and Jabneel, as far as Lakkum; it ended at the Jordan. 34 [a]From Heleph the border extended westward to Aznoth Tabor, and went out from there toward Hukkok; it adjoined Zebulun on the south side and Asher on the west side, and ended at Judah by the Jordan toward the sunrise. 35 And the fortified cities *are* Ziddim, Zer, Hammath, Rakkath, Chinnereth, 36 Adamah, Ramah, Hazor, 37 [a]Kedesh, Edrei, En Hazor, 38 Iron, Migdal El, Horem, Beth Anath, and Beth Shemesh: nineteen cities with their villages. 39 This *was* the inheritance of the tribe of the children of Naphtali according to their families, the cities and their villages.

The Land of Dan

40 [a]The seventh lot came out for the tribe of the children of Dan according to their families. 41 And the territory of their inheritance was Zorah, [a]Eshtaol, Ir Shemesh, 42 [a]Shaalabbin, [b]Aijalon, Jethlah, 43 Elon, Timnah, [a]Ekron, 44 Eltekeh, Gibbethon, Baalath, 45 Jehud, Bene Berak, Gath Rimmon, 46 Me Jarkon, and Rakkon, with the region near Joppa. 47 And the [a]border of the children of Dan went beyond these, because the children of Dan went up to fight against Leshem and took it; and they struck it with the edge of the sword, took possession of it, and dwelt in it. They called Leshem, [b]Dan, after the name of Dan their father. 48 This *is* the inheritance of the tribe of the children of Dan according to their families, these cities with their villages.

Joshua's Inheritance

49 When they had made an end of dividing the land as an inheritance according to their borders, the children of Israel gave an inheritance among them to Joshua the son of Nun. 50 According to the word of the LORD they gave him the city which he asked for, [a]Timnath [b]Serah in the mountains of Ephraim; and he built the city and dwelt in it.

51 [a]These *were* the inheritances which Eleazar the priest, Joshua the son of Nun, and the heads of the fathers of the tribes of the children of Israel divided as an inheritance by lot [b]in Shiloh before the LORD, at the door of the tabernacle of meeting. So they made an end of dividing the country.

The Cities of Refuge

20 The LORD also spoke to Joshua, saying, 2 "Speak to the children of Israel, saying: [a]'Appoint for yourselves cities of refuge, of which I spoke to you through Moses, 3 that the slayer who kills a person accidentally *or* unintentionally may flee there; and they shall be your refuge from the avenger of blood. 4 And when he flees to one of those cities, and stands at the entrance of the gate of the city, and declares his case in the hearing of the elders of that city, they shall take him into the city as one of them, and give him a place, that he may dwell among them. 5 [a]Then if the avenger of blood pursues him, they shall

19:22 [a] Josh. 15:10 **19:24** [a] Judg. 1:31, 32 **19:26** [a] Jer. 46:18 **19:27** [a] 1 Kin. 9:13 **19:28** [a] Judg. 1:31 [1] Following Masoretic Text, Targum, and Vulgate; a few Hebrew manuscripts read *Abdon* (compare 21:30 and 1 Chronicles 6:74). **19:29** [a] Judg. 1:31 **19:32** [a] Judg. 1:33 **19:34** [a] Deut. 33:23 **19:37** [a] Josh. 20:7 **19:40** [a] Judg. 1:34–36 **19:41** [a] Josh. 15:33 **19:42** [a] Judg. 1:35 [b] Josh. 10:12; 21:24 **19:43** [a] Judg. 1:18 **19:47** [a] Judg. 18 [b] Judg. 18:29 **19:50** [a] Josh. 24:30 [b] 1 Chr. 7:24 **19:51** [a] Num. 34:17 [b] Josh. 18:1, 10 **20:2** [a] Num. 35:6–34 **20:5** [a] Num. 35:12

not deliver the slayer into his hand, because he struck his neighbor unintentionally, but did not hate him beforehand. 6 And he shall dwell in that city [a]until he stands before the congregation for judgment, *and* until the death of the one who is high priest in those days. Then the slayer may return and come to his own city and his own house, to the city from which he fled.' "

7 So they appointed [a]Kedesh in Galilee, in the mountains of Naphtali, [b]Shechem in the mountains of Ephraim, and [c]Kirjath Arba (which *is* Hebron) in [d]the mountains of Judah. 8 And on the other side of the Jordan, by Jericho eastward, they assigned [a]Bezer in the wilderness on the plain, from the tribe of Reuben, [b]Ramoth in Gilead, from the tribe of Gad, and [c]Golan in Bashan, from the tribe of Manasseh. 9 [a]These were the cities appointed for all the children of Israel and for the stranger who dwelt among them, that whoever killed a person accidentally might flee there, and not die by the hand of the avenger of blood [b]until he stood before the congregation.

Cities of the Levites

21 Then the heads of the fathers' *houses* of the [a]Levites came near to [b]Eleazar the priest, to Joshua the son of Nun, and to the heads of the fathers' *houses* of the tribes of the children of Israel. 2 And they spoke to them at [a]Shiloh in the land of Canaan, saying, [b]"The LORD commanded through Moses to give us cities to dwell in, with their common-lands for our livestock." 3 So the children of Israel gave to the Levites from their inheritance, at the commandment of the LORD, these cities and their common-lands:

4 Now the lot came out for the families of the Kohathites. And [a]the children of Aaron the priest, *who were* of the Levites, [b]had thirteen cities by lot from the tribe of Judah, from the tribe of Simeon, and from the tribe of Benjamin. 5 [a]The rest of the children of Kohath had ten cities by lot from the families of the tribe of Ephraim, from the tribe of Dan, and from the half-tribe of Manasseh.

6 And [a]the children of Gershon had thirteen cities by lot from the families of the tribe of Issachar, from the tribe of Asher, from the tribe of Naphtali, and from the half-tribe of Manasseh in Bashan.

7 [a]The children of Merari according to their families had twelve cities from the tribe of Reuben, from the tribe of Gad, and from the tribe of Zebulun.

8 [a]And the children of Israel gave these cities with their common-lands by lot to the Levites, [b]as the LORD had commanded by the hand of Moses.

9 So they gave from the tribe of the children of Judah and from the tribe of the children of Simeon these cities which are designated by name, 10 which were for the children of Aaron, one of the families of the Kohathites, *who were* of the children of Levi; for the lot was theirs first. 11 [a]And they gave them Kirjath Arba (*Arba was* the father of [b]Anak), [c]which *is* Hebron, in the mountains of Judah, with the common-land surrounding it. 12 But [a]the fields of the city and its villages they gave to Caleb the son of Jephunneh as his possession.

13 Thus [a]to the children of Aaron the priest they gave [b]Hebron with its common-land (a city of refuge for the slayer), [c]Libnah with its common-land, 14 [a]Jattir with its common-land, [b]Eshtemoa with its common-land, 15 [a]Holon with its common-land, [b]Debir with its common-land, 16 [a]Ain with its common-land, [b]Juttah with its common-land, and [c]Beth Shemesh with its common-land: nine cities from those two tribes; 17 and from the tribe of Benjamin, [a]Gibeon with its common-land, [b]Geba with its common-land, 18 Anathoth with its common-land, and [a]Almon with its common-land: four cities. 19 All the cities of the children of Aaron, the priests, *were* thirteen cities with their common-lands.

20 [a]And the families of the children of Kohath, the Levites, the rest of the children of Kohath, even they had the cities of their lot from the tribe of Ephraim. 21 For they gave them [a]Shechem with its common-land in the mountains of Ephraim (a city of refuge for the slayer), [b]Gezer with its common-land, 22 Kibzaim with its common-land, and Beth Horon with its common-land: four cities; 23 and from the tribe of Dan, Eltekeh with its common-land, Gibbethon with its common-land, 24 [a]Aijalon with its common-land, *and* Gath Rimmon with its common-land: four cities; 25 and from the half-tribe of Manasseh, Tanach with its common-land and Gath Rimmon with its common-land: two cities. 26 All the ten cities with their common-lands were for the rest of the families of the children of Kohath.

20:6 [a] Num. 35:12, 24, 25 **20:7** [a] 1 Chr. 6:76 [b] Josh. 21:21 [c] Josh. 14:15; 21:11, 13 [d] Luke 1:39 **20:8** [a] Deut. 4:43 [b] Josh. 21:38 [c] Josh. 21:27 **20:9** [a] Num. 35:15 [b] Josh. 20:6 **21:1** [a] Num. 35:1–8 [b] Josh. 14:1; 17:4 **21:2** [a] Josh. 18:1 [b] Num. 35:2 **21:4** [a] Josh. 21:8, 19 [b] Josh. 19:51 **21:5** [a] Josh. 21:20 **21:6** [a] Josh. 21:27 **21:7** [a] Josh. 21:34 **21:8** [a] Josh. 21:3 [b] Num. 35:2 **21:11** [a] 1 Chr. 6:55 [b] Josh. 14:15; 15:13, 14 [c] Josh. 20:7 **21:12** [a] Josh. 14:14 **21:13** [a] 1 Chr. 6:57 [b] Josh. 15:54; 20:2, 7 [c] Josh. 15:42 **21:14** [a] Josh. 15:48 [b] Josh. 15:50 **21:15** [a] 1 Chr. 6:58 [b] Josh. 15:49 **21:16** [a] 1 Chr. 6:59 [b] Josh. 15:55 [c] Josh. 15:10 **21:17** [a] Josh. 18:25 [b] Josh. 18:24 **21:18** [a] 1 Chr. 6:60 **21:20** [a] 1 Chr. 6:66 **21:21** [a] Josh. 20:7 [b] Judg. 1:29 **21:24** [a] Josh. 10:12

27 [a]Also to the children of Gershon, of the families of the Levites, from the *other* half-tribe of Manasseh, *they gave* [b]Golan in Bashan with its common-land (a city of refuge for the slayer), and Be Eshterah with its common-land: two cities; 28 and from the tribe of Issachar, Kishion with its common-land, Daberath with its common-land, 29 Jarmuth with its common-land, *and* En Gannim with its common-land: four cities; 30 and from the tribe of Asher, Mishal with its common-land, Abdon with its common-land, 31 Helkath with its common-land, and Rehob with its common-land: four cities; 32 and from the tribe of Naphtali, [a]Kedesh in Galilee with its common-land (a city of refuge for the slayer), Hammoth Dor with its common-land, and Kartan with its common-land: three cities. 33 All the cities of the Gershonites according to their families *were* thirteen cities with their common-lands.

34 [a]And to the families of the children of Merari, the rest of the Levites, from the tribe of Zebulun, Jokneam with its common-land, Kartah with its common-land, 35 Dimnah with its common-land, *and* Nahalal with its common-land: four cities; 36 and from the tribe of Reuben, [a]Bezer with its common-land, Jahaz with its common-land, 37 Kedemoth with its common-land, and Mephaath with its common-land: four cities;[1] 38 and from the tribe of Gad, [a]Ramoth in Gilead with its common-land (a city of refuge for the slayer), Mahanaim with its common-land, 39 Heshbon with its common-land, *and* Jazer with its common-land: four cities in all. 40 So all the cities for the children of Merari according to their families, the rest of the families of the Levites, were *by* their lot twelve cities.

41 [a]All the cities of the Levites within the possession of the children of Israel *were* forty-eight cities with their common-lands. 42 Every one of these cities had its common-land surrounding it; thus *were* all these cities.

The Promise Fulfilled

43 So the LORD gave to Israel [a]all the land of which He had sworn to give to their fathers, and they [b]took possession of it and dwelt in it. 44 [a]The LORD gave them [b]rest all around, according to all that He had sworn to their fathers. And [c]not a man of all their enemies stood against them; the LORD delivered all their enemies into their hand. 45 [a]Not a word failed of any good thing which the LORD had spoken to the house of Israel. All came to pass.

PEACE NOTE

The Lord gives His people rest not just in the future, eternal world but also in the here and now. Rest is peace. Be careful to listen to and obey the Lord.

JOSHUA 21:44

Eastern Tribes Return to Their Lands

22 Then Joshua called the Reubenites, the Gadites, and half the tribe of Manasseh, 2 and said to them: "You have kept [a]all that Moses the servant of the LORD commanded you, [b]and have obeyed my voice in all that I commanded you. 3 You have not left your brethren these many days, up to this day, but have kept the charge of the commandment of the LORD your God. 4 And now the LORD your God has given [a]rest to your brethren, as He promised them; now therefore, return and go to your tents *and* to the land of your possession, [b]which Moses the servant of the LORD gave you on the other side of the Jordan. 5 But [a]take careful heed to do the commandment and the law which Moses the servant of the LORD commanded you, [b]to love the LORD your God, to walk in all His ways, to keep His commandments, to hold fast to Him, and to serve Him with all your heart and with all your soul." 6 So Joshua [a]blessed them and sent them away, and they went to their tents.

7 Now to half the tribe of Manasseh Moses had given a possession in Bashan, [a]but to the *other* half of it Joshua gave *a possession* among their brethren on this side of the Jordan, westward. And indeed, when Joshua sent them away to their tents, he blessed them, 8 and spoke to them, saying, "Return with much riches to your tents, with very much livestock, with silver, with gold, with bronze, with iron, and with very much clothing. [a]Divide the spoil of your enemies with your brethren."

21:27 [a] 1 Chr. 6:71 [b] Josh. 20:8 **21:32** [a] Josh. 20:7 **21:34** [a] 1 Chr. 6:77–81 **21:36** [a] Josh. 20:8 **21:37** [1] Following Septuagint and Vulgate (compare 1 Chronicles 6:78, 79); Masoretic Text, Bomberg, and Targum omit verses 36 and 37. **21:38** [a] Josh. 20:8 **21:41** [a] Num. 35:7 **21:43** [a] Gen. 12:7; 26:3, 4; 28:4, 13, 14 [b] Num. 33:53 **21:44** [a] Deut. 7:23, 24 [b] Josh. 1:13, 15; 11:23 [c] Deut. 7:24 **21:45** [a] Josh. 23:14 **22:2** [a] Num. 32:20–22 [b] Josh. 1:12–18 **22:4** [a] Josh. 21:44 [b] Num. 32:33 **22:5** [a] Deut. 6:6, 17; 11:22 [b] Deut. 10:12; 11:13, 22 **22:6** [a] 2 Sam. 6:18 **22:7** [a] Josh. 17:1–13 **22:8** [a] 1 Sam. 30:24

9 So the children of Reuben, the children of
Gad, and half the tribe of Manasseh returned,
and departed from the children of Israel at
Shiloh, which *is* in the land of Canaan, to
go to [a]the country of Gilead, to the land of
their possession, which they had obtained
according to the word of the LORD by the
hand of Moses.

An Altar by the Jordan

10 And when they came to the region of
the Jordan which *is* in the land of Canaan,
the children of Reuben, the children of Gad,
and half the tribe of Manasseh built an altar
there by the Jordan—a great, impressive
altar. 11 Now the children of Israel [a]heard
someone say, "Behold, the children of Reuben, the children of Gad, and half the tribe of
Manasseh have built an altar on the frontier
of the land of Canaan, in the region of the
Jordan—on the children of Israel's side."
12 And when the children of Israel heard *of
it,* [a]the whole congregation of the children
of Israel gathered together at Shiloh to go to
war against them.

13 Then the children of Israel [a]sent [b]Phin-
ehas the son of Eleazar the priest to the children of Reuben, to the children of Gad, and
to half the tribe of Manasseh, into the land of
Gilead, 14 and with him ten rulers, one ruler
each from the chief house of every tribe of
Israel; and [a]each one *was* the head of the
house of his father among the divisions[1] of
Israel. 15 Then they came to the children of
Reuben, to the children of Gad, and to half the
tribe of Manasseh, to the land of Gilead, and
they spoke with them, saying, 16 "Thus says
the whole congregation of the LORD: 'What
[a]treachery *is* this that you have committed
against the God of Israel, to turn away this
day from following the LORD, in that you have
built for yourselves an altar, [b]that you might
rebel this day against the LORD? 17 *Is* the iniquity [a]of Peor not enough for us, from which
we are not cleansed till this day, although
there was a plague in the congregation of
the LORD, 18 but that you must turn away this
day from following the LORD? And it shall
be, if you rebel today against the LORD, that
tomorrow [a]He will be angry with the whole
congregation of Israel. 19 Nevertheless, if
the land of your possession *is* unclean, *then*
cross over to the land of the possession of the
LORD, [a]where the LORD's tabernacle stands,
and take possession among us; but do not
rebel against the LORD, nor rebel against
us, by building yourselves an altar besides
the altar of the LORD our God. 20 [a]Did not
Achan the son of Zerah commit a trespass
in the accursed thing, and wrath fell on all
the congregation of Israel? And that man did
not perish alone in his iniquity.' "

21 Then the children of Reuben, the children
of Gad, and half the tribe of Manasseh answered and said to the heads of the divisions[1]
of Israel: 22 "The LORD [a]God of gods, the LORD
God of gods, He [b]knows, and let Israel itself
know—if *it is* in rebellion, or if in treachery
against the LORD, do not save us this day. 23 If
we have built ourselves an altar to turn from
following the LORD, or if to offer on it burnt
offerings or grain offerings, or if to offer peace
offerings on it, let the LORD Himself [a]require
an account. 24 But in fact we have done it for
fear, for a reason, saying, 'In time to come your
descendants may speak to our descendants,
saying, "What have you to do with the LORD
God of Israel? 25 For the LORD has made the
Jordan a border between you and us, *you* children of Reuben and children of Gad. You have
no part in the LORD." So your descendants
would make our descendants cease fearing
the LORD.' 26 Therefore we said, 'Let us now
prepare to build ourselves an altar, not for
burnt offering nor for sacrifice, 27 but *that* it
may be [a]a witness between you and us and our
generations after us, that we may [b]perform the
service of the LORD before Him with our burnt
offerings, with our sacrifices, and with our
peace offerings; that your descendants may
not say to our descendants in time to come,
"You have no part in the LORD." ' 28 Therefore
we said that it will be, when they say *this* to us
or to our generations in time to come, that
we may say, 'Here is the replica of the altar
of the LORD which our fathers made, though
not for burnt offerings nor for sacrifices; but
it *is* a witness between you and us.' 29 Far be
it from us that we should rebel against the
LORD, and turn from following the LORD this
day, [a]to build an altar for burnt offerings, for
grain offerings, or for sacrifices, besides the
altar of the LORD our God which *is* before His
tabernacle."

30 Now when Phinehas the priest and the
rulers of the congregation, the heads of the
divisions[1] of Israel who *were* with him, heard
the words that the children of Reuben, the
children of Gad, and the children of Manasseh spoke, it pleased them. 31 Then Phinehas
the son of Eleazar the priest said to the children of Reuben, the children of Gad, and the

22:9 [a] Num. 32:1, 26, 29 **22:11** [a] Judg. 20:12, 13 **22:12** [a] Josh. 18:1 **22:13** [a] Deut. 13:14 [b] Ex. 6:25 **22:14** [a] Num. 1:4 [1] Literally *thousands* **22:16** [a] Deut. 12:5–14 [b] Lev. 17:8, 9 **22:17** [a] Num. 25:1–9 **22:18** [a] Num. 16:22 **22:19** [a] Josh. 18:1 **22:20** [a] Josh. 7:1–26 **22:21** [1] Literally *thousands* **22:22** [a] Deut. 4:35; 10:17 [b] [Jer. 12:3] **22:23** [a] 1 Sam. 20:16 **22:27** [a] Gen. 31:48 [b] Deut. 12:5, 14 **22:29** [a] Deut. 12:13, 14 **22:30** [1] Literally *thousands*

children of Manasseh, "This day we perceive that the LORD *is* [a]among us, because you have not committed this treachery against the LORD. Now you have delivered the children of Israel out of the hand of the LORD."

32 And Phinehas the son of Eleazar the priest, and the rulers, returned from the children of Reuben and the children of Gad, from the land of Gilead to the land of Canaan, to the children of Israel, and brought back word to them. 33 So the thing pleased the children of Israel, and the children of Israel [a]blessed God; they spoke no more of going against them in battle, to destroy the land where the children of Reuben and Gad dwelt.

34 The children of Reuben and the children of Gad[1] called the altar, *Witness,* "For *it is* a witness between us that the LORD *is* God."

Joshua's Farewell Address

23 Now it came to pass, a long time after the LORD [a]had given rest to Israel from all their enemies round about, that Joshua [b]was old, advanced in age. 2 And Joshua [a]called for all Israel, for their elders, for their heads, for their judges, and for their officers, and said to them:

"I am old, advanced in age. 3 You have seen all that the [a]LORD your God has done to all these nations because of you, for the [b]LORD your God *is* He who has fought for you. 4 See, [a]I have divided to you by lot these nations that remain, to be an inheritance for your tribes, from the Jordan, with all the nations that I have cut off, as far as the Great Sea westward. 5 And the LORD your God [a]will expel them from before you and drive them out of your sight. So you shall possess their land, [b]as the LORD your God promised you. 6 [a]Therefore be very courageous to keep and to do all that is written in the Book of the Law of Moses, [b]lest you turn aside from it to the right hand or to the left, 7 *and* lest you [a]go among these nations, these who remain among you. You shall not [b]make mention of the name of their gods, nor cause *anyone* to [c]swear *by them;* you shall not [d]serve them nor bow down to them, 8 but you shall [a]hold fast to the LORD your God, as you have done to this day. 9 [a]For the LORD has driven out from before you great and strong nations; but *as for* you, no one has been able to stand against you to this day. 10 [a]One man of you shall chase a thousand, for the LORD your God *is* He who fights for you, [b]as He promised you. 11 [a]Therefore take careful heed to yourselves, that you love the LORD your God. 12 Or else, if indeed you do [a]go back, and cling to the remnant of these nations—these that remain among you—and [b]make marriages with them, and go in to them and they to you, 13 know for certain that [a]the LORD your God will no longer drive out these nations from before you. [b]But they shall be snares and traps to you, and scourges on your sides and thorns in your eyes, until you perish from this good land which the LORD your God has given you.

14 "Behold, this day [a]I *am* going the way of all the earth. And you know in all your hearts and in all your souls that [b]not one thing has failed of all the good things which the LORD your God spoke concerning you. All have come to pass for you; not one word of them has failed. 15 [a]Therefore it shall come to pass, that as all the good things have come upon you which the LORD your God promised you, so the LORD will bring upon you [b]all harmful things, until He has destroyed you from this good land which the LORD your God has given you. 16 When you have transgressed the covenant of the LORD your God, which He commanded you, and have gone and served other gods, and bowed down to them, then the [a]anger of the LORD will burn against you, and you shall perish quickly from the good land which He has given you."

The Covenant at Shechem

24 Then Joshua gathered all the tribes of Israel to [a]Shechem and [b]called for the elders of Israel, for their heads, for their judges, and for their officers; and they [c]presented themselves before God. 2 And Joshua said to all the people, "Thus says the LORD God of Israel: [a]'Your fathers, *including* Terah, the father of Abraham and the father of Nahor, dwelt on the other side of the River[1] in old times; and [b]they served other gods. 3 [a]Then I took your father Abraham from the other side of the River, led him throughout all the land of Canaan, and multiplied his descendants and [b]gave him Isaac. 4 To Isaac I gave [a]Jacob and Esau. To [b]Esau I gave the mountains of Seir to possess, [c]but Jacob and his children went

22:31 [a] Lev. 26:11, 12 **22:33** [a] 1 Chr. 29:20 **22:34** [1] Septuagint adds *and half the tribe of Manasseh.* **23:1** [a] Josh. 21:44; 22:4 [b] Josh. 13:1; 24:29 **23:2** [a] Deut. 31:28 **23:3** [a] Ps. 44:3 [b] Deut. 1:30 **23:4** [a] Josh. 13:2, 6; 18:10 **23:5** [a] Ex. 23:30; 33:2 [b] Num. 33:53 **23:6** [a] Josh. 1:7 [b] Deut. 5:32 **23:7** [a] Deut. 7:2, 3 [b] Ex. 23:13 [c] Deut. 6:13; 10:20 [d] Ex. 20:5 **23:8** [a] Deut. 10:20 **23:9** [a] Deut. 7:24; 11:23 **23:10** [a] Lev. 26:8 [b] Ex. 14:14 **23:11** [a] Josh. 22:5 **23:12** [a] [2 Pet. 2:20, 21] [b] Deut. 7:3, 4 **23:13** [a] Judg. 2:3 [b] Ex. 23:33; 34:12 **23:14** [a] 1 Kin. 2:2 [b] Josh. 21:45 **23:15** [a] Deut. 28:63 [b] Deut. 28:15–68 **23:16** [a] Deut. 4:24–28 **24:1** [a] Gen. 35:4 [b] Josh. 23:2 [c] 1 Sam. 10:19 **24:2** [a] Gen. 11:7–32 [b] Josh. 24:14 [1] Hebrew *Nahar,* the Euphrates, and so in verses 3, 14, and 15 **24:3** [a] Gen. 12:1; Acts 7:2, 3 [b] [Ps. 127:3] **24:4** [a] Gen. 25:24–26 [b] Deut. 2:5 [c] Gen. 46:1, 3, 6

down to Egypt. 5 [a]Also I sent Moses and Aaron,
and [b]I plagued Egypt, according to what I did
among them. Afterward I brought you out.
6 'Then I [a]brought your fathers out of
Egypt, and you came to the sea; and the Egyptians pursued your fathers with chariots and
horsemen to the Red Sea. 7 So they cried out
to the LORD; and He put [a]darkness between
you and the Egyptians, brought the sea upon
them, and covered them. And [b]your eyes saw
what I did in Egypt. Then you dwelt in the
wilderness [c]a long time. 8 And I brought you
into the land of the Amorites, who dwelt on
the other side of the Jordan, [a]and they fought
with you. But I gave them into your hand, that
you might possess their land, and I destroyed
them from before you. 9 Then [a]Balak the son
of Zippor, king of Moab, arose to make war
against Israel, and [b]sent and called Balaam
the son of Beor to curse you. 10 [a]But I would
not listen to Balaam; [b]therefore he continued
to bless you. So I delivered you out of his
hand. 11 Then [a]you went over the Jordan and
came to Jericho. And [b]the men of Jericho
fought against you—*also* the Amorites, the
Perizzites, the Canaanites, the Hittites, the
Girgashites, the Hivites, and the Jebusites.
But I delivered them into your hand. 12 [a]I sent
the hornet before you which drove them out
from before you, *also* the two kings of the
Amorites, *but* [b]not with your sword or with
your bow. 13 I have given you a land for which
you did not labor, and [a]cities which you did
not build, and you dwell in them; you eat of
the vineyards and olive groves which you
did not plant.'
14 [a]"Now therefore, fear the LORD, serve
Him in [b]sincerity and in truth, and [c]put away
the gods which your fathers served on the
other side of the River and [d]in Egypt. Serve
the LORD! 15 And if it seems evil to you to
serve the LORD, [a]choose for yourselves this
day whom you will serve, whether [b]the gods
which your fathers served that *were* on the
other side of the River, or [c]the gods of the
Amorites, in whose land you dwell. [d]But as
for me and my house, we will serve the LORD."
16 So the people answered and said: "Far be
it from us that we should forsake the LORD
to serve other gods; 17 for the LORD our God
is He who brought us and our fathers up
out of the land of Egypt, from the house of
bondage, who did those great signs in our
sight, and preserved us in all the way that
we went and among all the people through
whom we passed. 18 And the LORD drove out
from before us all the people, including the
Amorites who dwelt in the land. [a]We also will
serve the LORD, for He *is* our God."
19 But Joshua said to the people, [a]"You
cannot serve the LORD, for He *is* a [b]holy God.
He *is* [c]a jealous God; [d]He will not forgive your

24:5 [a] Ex. 3:10 [b] Ex. 7—10 **24:6** [a] Ex. 12:37, 51; 14:2–31 **24:7** [a] Ex. 14:20 [b] Deut. 4:34 [c] Josh. 5:6 **24:8** [a] Num. 21:21–35 **24:9** [a] Judg. 11:25 [b] Num. 22:2–14 **24:10** [a] Deut. 23:5 [b] Num. 23:11, 20; 24:10 **24:11** [a] Josh. 3:14, 17 [b] Josh. 6:1; 10:1 **24:12** [a] Ex. 23:28 [b] Ps. 44:3 **24:13** [a] Deut. 6:10, 11 **24:14** [a] 1 Sam. 12:24 [b] 2 Cor. 1:12 [c] Ezek. 20:18 [d] Ezek. 20:7, 8 **24:15** [a] 1 Kin. 18:21 [b] Josh. 24:2 [c] Ex. 23:24, 32 [d] Gen. 18:19 **24:18** [a] Ps. 116:16 **24:19** [a] Matt. 6:24 [b] 1 Sam. 6:20 [c] Ex. 20:5 [d] Ex. 23:21

THE EVERYDAY CHOICE TO MAKE

Now therefore, fear the LORD, serve Him in sincerity and in truth . . .
As for me and my house, we will serve the LORD.

JOSHUA 24:14-15

Under Joshua's leadership, the people of Israel possessed much of the land that God had promised Abraham centuries earlier. But here Joshua was nearing the end of his life. I'm sure he worried about the strength of Israel's commitment to God. Although the original generation had passed on, the new generation of Israelites who had entered the Promised Land could still succumb to the temptation to follow pagan gods. Polytheism in those days was hard to avoid.

In life we worry at the beginning of things—of family, of career, of a big move. But we also worry as we approach the end of life. Above all we worry about our children and grandchildren. So Joshua exhorted Israel to "fear the LORD" and to "serve Him in sincerity and in truth." *Would they?* he wondered. Joshua had always led by example, so he assured the people that he and his family would continue to "serve the LORD."

It is in faithfulness to the Lord that we will find peace.

transgressions nor your sins. 20 [a]If you forsake the LORD and serve foreign gods, [b]then
He will turn and do you harm and consume
you, after He has done you good."
21 And the people said to Joshua, "No, but
we will serve the LORD!"
22 So Joshua said to the people, "You *are*
witnesses against yourselves that [a]you have
chosen the LORD for yourselves, to serve
Him."
And they said, "*We are* witnesses!"
23 "Now therefore," *he said,* [a]"put away the
foreign gods which *are* among you, and [b]in-
cline your heart to the LORD God of Israel."
24 And the people [a]said to Joshua, "The
LORD our God we will serve, and His voice
we will obey!"
25 So Joshua [a]made a covenant with the
people that day, and made for them a statute
and an ordinance [b]in Shechem.
26 Then Joshua [a]wrote these words in the
Book of the Law of God. And he took [b]a large
stone, and [c]set it up there [d]under the oak that
was by the sanctuary of the LORD. 27 And Joshua said to all the people, "Behold, this stone
shall be [a]a witness to us, for [b]it has heard all
the words of the LORD which He spoke to us.
It shall therefore be a witness to you, lest you
deny your God." 28 So [a]Joshua let the people
depart, each to his own inheritance.

Death of Joshua and Eleazar

29 [a]Now it came to pass after these things
that Joshua the son of Nun, the servant of
the LORD, died, *being* one hundred and ten
years old. 30 And they buried him within the
border of his inheritance at [a]Timnath Serah,
which *is* in the mountains of Ephraim, on the
north side of Mount Gaash.
31 [a]Israel served the LORD all the days of
Joshua, and all the days of the elders who
outlived Joshua, who had [b]known all the
works of the LORD which He had done for
Israel.
32 [a]The bones of Joseph, which the children of Israel had brought up out of Egypt,
they buried at Shechem, in the plot of
ground [b]which Jacob had bought from the
sons of Hamor the father of Shechem for
one hundred pieces of silver, and which
had become an inheritance of the children
of Joseph.
33 And [a]Eleazar the son of Aaron died. They
buried him in a hill *belonging to* [b]Phinehas
his son, which was given to him in the mountains of Ephraim.

24:20 [a] Ezra 8:22 [b] Deut. 4:24–26 **24:22** [a] Ps. 119:173 **24:23** [a] Gen. 35:2 [b] 1 Kin. 8:57, 58 **24:24** [a] Deut. 5:24–27 **24:25** [a] Ex. 15:25 [b] Josh. 24:1 **24:26** [a] Deut. 31:24 [b] Judg. 9:6 [c] Gen. 28:18 [d] Gen. 35:4 **24:27** [a] Gen. 31:48 [b] Deut. 32:1 **24:28** [a] Judg. 2:6, 7 **24:29** [a] Judg. 2:8 **24:30** [a] Josh. 19:50 **24:31** [a] Judg. 2:7 [b] Deut. 11:2 **24:32** [a] Gen. 50:25 [b] Gen. 33:19 **24:33** [a] Ex. 28:1 [b] Ex. 6:25

THE BOOK OF JUDGES

AUTHOR

Although the author of Judges is anonymous, Jewish tradition contained in the Talmud attributes Judges to Samuel. Samuel lived during the time the book could have been written, and he was a principal character in the transition to the next phase. He would have been aware of the events that occur in the book. Samuel certainly was the crucial link between the period of the judges and the period of the kings. His prophetic ministry clearly fits the moral commentary of Judges, and the consistent style and orderly scheme of the book points to a single compiler.

TIME

c. 1380–1045 BC

KEY VERSE

Judges 2:20–21

THEME

The Book of Judges describes a time in which the land wasn't fully conquered and there was political chaos. The Israelites appeared to live mostly in the land between the cities of the Philistines, who dominated them much of the time. Two common phrases occur in the book: the Israelites "did evil in the sight of the LORD" (e.g., 2:11); and "everyone did what was right in his own eyes" (17:6; 21:25). In the midst of this situation, God raises up judges who, in addition to playing the role of adjudicators, also provide leadership in pulling the tribes together to fight the unconquered nations. Most are reluctant. Nevertheless, God is able to use them and demonstrate His power through these individuals.

Judges and Ruth were probably one book originally in the Hebrew Bible and served as a bridge from Joshua's death to the first mention of David (Ruth 4:17). These were some of the darkest days of Israel's history, yet they produced the most visual depiction of *shalom* in all the Old Testament. In Gideon, a fearful man with a history of messy obedience to God and a huge reluctance to lead, let alone be the hero of Israel, we find the best portrayal of God's peace. It is reflected in Gideon's altar, which he calls "The-LORD-Is-Peace" (Judg. 6:24), and this gives us a new name for God: *Jehovah-Shalom*.

The Continuing Conquest of Canaan

1 Now after the [a]death of Joshua it came
to pass that the children of Israel [b]asked
the LORD, saying, "Who shall be first to go
up for us against the [c]Canaanites to fight
against them?"
2 And the LORD said, [a]"Judah shall go up. Indeed I have delivered the land into his hand."
3 So Judah said to [a]Simeon his brother,
"Come up with me to my allotted territory,
that we may fight against the Canaanites;
and [b]I will likewise go with you to your allotted territory." And Simeon went with him.
4 Then Judah went up, and the LORD delivered
the Canaanites and the Perizzites into their
hand; and they killed ten thousand men at
[a]Bezek. 5 And they found Adoni-Bezek in
Bezek, and fought against him; and they
defeated the Canaanites and the Perizzites.
6 Then Adoni-Bezek fled, and they pursued
him and caught him and cut off his thumbs
and big toes. 7 And Adoni-Bezek said, "Seventy kings with their thumbs and big toes cut
off used to gather *scraps* under my table; [a]as I
have done, so God has repaid me." Then they
brought him to Jerusalem, and there he died.
8 Now [a]the children of Judah fought against
Jerusalem and took it; they struck it with the
edge of the sword and set the city on fire.
9 [a]And afterward the children of Judah went
down to fight against the Canaanites who
dwelt in the mountains, in the South,[1] and in
the lowland. 10 Then Judah went against the
Canaanites who dwelt in [a]Hebron. (Now the
name of Hebron *was* formerly [b]Kirjath Arba.)
And they killed Sheshai, Ahiman, and Talmai.
11 [a]From there they went against the inhabitants of Debir. (The name of Debir *was* formerly Kirjath Sepher.)
12 [a]Then Caleb said, "Whoever attacks Kirjath Sepher and takes it, to him I will give my
daughter Achsah as wife." 13 And Othniel the
son of Kenaz, [a]Caleb's younger brother, took
it; so he gave him his daughter Achsah as
wife. 14 [a]Now it happened, when she came *to*
him, that she urged him[1] to ask her father for
a field. And she dismounted from *her* donkey,
and Caleb said to her, "What do you wish?"
15 So she said to him, [a]"Give me a blessing;
since you have given me land in the South,
give me also springs of water."
And Caleb gave her the upper springs and
the lower springs.
16 [a]Now the children of the Kenite, Moses'
father-in-law, went up [b]from the City of Palms
with the children of Judah into the Wilderness
of Judah, which *lies* in the South *near* [c]Arad;
[d]and they went and dwelt among the people.
17 [a]And Judah went with his brother Simeon,
and they attacked the Canaanites who inhabited Zephath, and utterly destroyed it. So the
name of the city was called [b]Hormah. 18 Also
Judah took [a]Gaza with its territory, Ashkelon
with its territory, and Ekron with its territory. 19 So the LORD was with Judah. And they
drove out the mountaineers, but they could
not drive out the inhabitants of the lowland,
because they had [a]chariots of iron. 20 [a]And
they gave Hebron to Caleb, as Moses had said.
Then he expelled from there the [b]three sons
of Anak. 21 [a]But the children of Benjamin did
not drive out the Jebusites who inhabited
Jerusalem; so the Jebusites dwell with the
children of Benjamin in Jerusalem to this day.
22 And the house of Joseph also went up
against Bethel, [a]and the LORD *was* with them.
23 So the house of Joseph [a]sent men to spy out
Bethel. (The name of the city *was* formerly
[b]Luz.) 24 And when the spies saw a man coming
out of the city, they said to him, "Please show
us the entrance to the city, and [a]we will show
you mercy." 25 So he showed them the entrance
to the city, and they struck the city with the
edge of the sword; but they let the man and
all his family go. 26 And the man went to the
land of the Hittites, built a city, and called its
name Luz, which *is* its name to this day.

Incomplete Conquest of the Land

27 [a]However, Manasseh did not drive out *the*
inhabitants of Beth Shean and its villages, or
[b]Taanach and its villages, or the inhabitants
of [c]Dor and its villages, or the inhabitants of
Ibleam and its villages, or the inhabitants of
Megiddo and its villages; for the Canaanites
were determined to dwell in that land. 28 And
it came to pass, when Israel was strong, that
they put the Canaanites under tribute, but
did not completely drive them out.
29 [a]Nor did Ephraim drive out the Canaanites who dwelt in Gezer; so the Canaanites
dwelt in Gezer among them.
30 Nor did [a]Zebulun drive out the inhabitants of Kitron or the inhabitants of Nahalol;
so the Canaanites dwelt among them, and
were put under tribute.

1:1 [a] Josh. 24:29 [b] Num. 27:21 [c] Josh. 17:12, 13 **1:2** [a] Gen. 49:8, 9 **1:3** [a] Josh. 19:1 [b] Judg. 1:17 **1:4** [a] 1 Sam. 11:8 **1:7** [a] Lev. 24:19 **1:8** [a] Josh. 15:63 **1:9** [a] Josh. 10:36; 11:21; 15:13 [1] Hebrew *Negev,* and so throughout this book **1:10** [a] Josh. 15:13–19 [b] Josh. 14:15 **1:11** [a] Josh. 15:15 **1:12** [a] Josh. 15:16, 17 **1:13** [a] Judg. 3:9 **1:14** [a] Josh. 15:18, 19 [1] Septuagint and Vulgate read *he urged her.* **1:15** [a] Gen. 33:11 **1:16** [a] Num. 10:29–32 [b] Deut. 34:3 [c] Josh. 12:14 [d] 1 Sam. 15:6 **1:17** [a] Judg. 1:3 [b] Num. 21:3 **1:18** [a] Josh. 11:22 **1:19** [a] Josh. 17:16, 18 **1:20** [a] Josh. 14:9, 14 [b] Josh. 15:14 **1:21** [a] Josh. 15:63 **1:22** [a] Judg. 1:19 **1:23** [a] Josh. 2:1; 7:2 [b] Gen. 28:19 **1:24** [a] Josh. 2:12, 14 **1:27** [a] Josh. 17:11–13 [b] Josh. 21:25 [c] Josh. 17:11 **1:29** [a] Josh. 16:10 **1:30** [a] Josh. 19:10–16

31 [a]Nor did Asher drive out the inhabitants
of Acco or the inhabitants of Sidon, or of
Ahlab, Achzib, Helbah, Aphik, or Rehob. 32 So
the Asherites [a]dwelt among the Canaanites,
the inhabitants of the land; for they did not
drive them out.

33 [a]Nor did Naphtali drive out the inhabitants of Beth Shemesh or the inhabitants of
Beth Anath; but they dwelt among the Canaanites, the inhabitants of the land. Nevertheless the inhabitants of Beth Shemesh and
Beth Anath were put under tribute to them.

34 And the Amorites forced the children of
Dan into the mountains, for they would not
allow them to come down to the valley; 35 and
the Amorites were determined to dwell in
Mount Heres, [a]in Aijalon, and in Shaalbim;[1]
yet when the strength of the house of Joseph
became greater, they were put under tribute.

36 Now the boundary of the Amorites *was*
[a]from the Ascent of Akrabbim, from Sela,
and upward.

Israel's Disobedience

2 Then the Angel of the LORD came up from
Gilgal to Bochim, and said: [a]"I led you up
from Egypt and [b]brought you to the land of
which I swore to your fathers; and [c]I said, 'I
will never break My covenant with you. 2 And
[a]you shall make no covenant with the inhabitants of this land; [b]you shall tear down their
altars.' [c]But you have not obeyed My voice.
Why have you done this? 3 Therefore I also
said, 'I will not drive them out before you;
but they shall be [a]*thorns* in your side,[1] and

> **PEACE NOTE**
>
> Remember that you don't have to generate peace. Paul said, "May the Lord of peace Himself give you peace always in every way" (2 Thess. 3:16).

[b]their gods shall be a [c]snare to you.' " 4 So it
was, when the Angel of the LORD spoke these
words to all the children of Israel, that the
people lifted up their voices and wept.

5 Then they called the name of that place
Bochim;[1] and they sacrificed there to the
LORD. 6 And when [a]Joshua had dismissed
the people, the children of Israel went each
to his own inheritance to possess the land.

Death of Joshua

7 [a]So the people served the LORD all the
days of Joshua, and all the days of the elders
who outlived Joshua, who had seen all the
great works of the LORD which He had done
for Israel. 8 Now [a]Joshua the son of Nun, the
servant of the LORD, died *when he was* one
hundred and ten years old. 9 [a]And they buried
him within the border of his inheritance at
[b]Timnath Heres, in the mountains of Ephraim, on the north side of Mount Gaash. 10 When
all that generation had been gathered to their
fathers, another generation arose after them
who [a]did not know the LORD nor the work
which He had done for Israel.

Israel's Unfaithfulness

11 Then the children of Israel did [a]evil in
the sight of the LORD, and served the Baals;
12 and they [a]forsook the LORD God of their
fathers, who had brought them out of the
land of Egypt; and they followed [b]other gods
from *among* the gods of the people who *were*
all around them, and they [c]bowed down to
them; and they provoked the LORD to anger.
13 They forsook the LORD [a]and served Baal and
the Ashtoreths.[1] 14 [a]And the anger of the LORD
was hot against Israel. So He [b]delivered them
into the hands of plunderers who despoiled
them; and [c]He sold them into the hands of
their enemies all around, so that they [d]could
no longer stand before their enemies. 15 Wherever they went out, the hand of the LORD was
against them for calamity, as the LORD had
said, and as the LORD had [a]sworn to them.
And they were greatly distressed.

16 Nevertheless, [a]the LORD raised up judges
who delivered them out of the hand of those
who plundered them. 17 Yet they would not
listen to their judges, but they [a]played the
harlot with other gods, and bowed down to
them. They turned quickly from the way in
which their fathers walked, in obeying the
commandments of the LORD; they did not

1:31 [a] Josh. 19:24–31 **1:32** [a] Ps. 106:34, 35 **1:33** [a] Josh. 19:32–39 **1:35** [a] Josh. 19:42 [1] Spelled *Shaalabbin* in Joshua 19:42 **1:36** [a] Josh. 15:3 **2:1** [a] Ex. 20:2 [b] Deut. 1:8 [c] Gen. 17:7, 8 **2:2** [a] Deut. 7:2 [b] Deut. 12:3 [c] Ps. 106:34 **2:3** [a] Josh. 23:13 [b] Judg. 3:6 [c] Ps. 106:36 [1] Septuagint, Targum, and Vulgate read *enemies to you.* **2:5** [1] Literally *Weeping* **2:6** [a] Josh. 22:6; 24:28–31 **2:7** [a] Josh. 24:31 **2:8** [a] Josh. 24:29 **2:9** [a] Josh. 24:30 [b] Josh. 19:49, 50 **2:10** [a] 1 Sam. 2:12 **2:11** [a] Judg. 3:7, 12; 4:1; 6:1 **2:12** [a] Deut. 31:16 [b] Deut. 6:14 [c] Ex. 20:5 **2:13** [a] Judg. 10:6 [1] Canaanite goddesses **2:14** [a] Deut. 31:17 [b] 2 Kin. 17:20 [c] Is. 50:1 [d] Lev. 26:37 **2:15** [a] Lev. 26:14–26 **2:16** [a] Ps. 106:43–45 **2:17** [a] Ex. 34:15

do so. 18 And when the LORD raised up judges for them, [a]the LORD was with the judge and delivered them out of the hand of their enemies all the days of the judge; [b]for the LORD was moved to pity by their groaning because of those who oppressed them and harassed them. 19 And it came to pass, [a]when the judge was dead, that they reverted and behaved more corruptly than their fathers, by following other gods, to serve them and bow down to them. They did not cease from their own doings nor from their stubborn way.

20 Then the anger of the LORD was hot against Israel; and He said, "Because this nation has [a]transgressed My covenant which I commanded their fathers, and has not heeded My voice, 21 I also will no longer drive out before them any of the nations which Joshua [a]left when he died, 22 so [a]that through them I may [b]test Israel, whether they will keep the ways of the LORD, to walk in them as their fathers kept *them,* or not." 23 Therefore the LORD left those nations, without driving them out immediately; nor did He deliver them into the hand of Joshua.

The Nations Remaining in the Land

3 Now these *are* [a]the nations which the LORD left, that He might test Israel by them, *that is,* all who had not known any of the wars in Canaan 2 (*this was* only so that the generations of the children of Israel might be taught to know war, at least those who had not formerly known it), 3 *namely,* [a]five lords of the Philistines, all the Canaanites, the Sidonians, and the Hivites who dwelt in Mount Lebanon, from Mount Baal Hermon to the entrance of Hamath. 4 And they were *left, that He might* test Israel by them, to know whether they would obey the commandments of the LORD, which He had commanded their fathers by the hand of Moses.

5 [a]Thus the children of Israel dwelt among the Canaanites, the Hittites, the Amorites, the Perizzites, the Hivites, and the Jebusites. 6 And [a]they took their daughters to be their wives, and gave their daughters to their sons; and they served their gods.

Othniel

7 So the children of Israel did [a]evil in the sight of the LORD. They [b]forgot the LORD their God, and served the Baals and Asherahs.[1] 8 Therefore the anger of the LORD was hot against Israel, and He [a]sold them into the hand of [b]Cushan-Rishathaim king of Mesopotamia; and the children of Israel served Cushan-Rishathaim eight years. 9 When the children of Israel [a]cried out to the LORD, the LORD [b]raised up a deliverer for the children of Israel, who delivered them: [c]Othniel the son of Kenaz, Caleb's younger brother. 10 [a]The Spirit of the LORD came upon him, and he judged Israel. He went out to war, and the LORD delivered Cushan-Rishathaim king of Mesopotamia into his hand; and his hand prevailed over Cushan-Rishathaim. 11 So the land had rest for forty years. Then Othniel the son of Kenaz died.

Ehud

12 [a]And the children of Israel again did evil in the sight of the LORD. So the LORD strengthened [b]Eglon king of Moab against Israel, because they had done evil in the sight of the LORD. 13 Then he gathered to himself the people of Ammon and [a]Amalek, went and defeated Israel, and took possession of [b]the City of Palms. 14 So the children of Israel [a]served Eglon king of Moab eighteen years.

15 But when the children of Israel [a]cried out to the LORD, the LORD raised up a deliverer for them: Ehud the son of Gera, the Benjamite, a [b]left-handed man. By him the children of Israel sent tribute to Eglon king of Moab. 16 Now Ehud made himself a dagger (it was double-edged and a cubit in length) and fastened it under his clothes on his right thigh. 17 So he brought the tribute to Eglon king of Moab. (Now Eglon *was* a very fat man.) 18 And when he had finished presenting the tribute, he sent away the people who had carried the tribute. 19 But he himself turned back [a]from the stone images that *were* at Gilgal, and said, "I have a secret message for you, O king."

He said, "Keep silence!" And all who attended him went out from him.

20 So Ehud came to him (now he was sitting upstairs in his cool private chamber). Then Ehud said, "I have a message from God for you." So he arose from *his* seat. 21 Then Ehud reached with his left hand, took the dagger from his right thigh, and thrust it into his belly. 22 Even the hilt went in after the blade, and the fat closed over the blade, for he did not draw the dagger out of his belly; and his entrails came out. 23 Then Ehud went out through the porch and shut the doors of the upper room behind him and locked them.

2:18 [a] Josh. 1:5 [b] Gen. 6:6 **2:19** [a] Judg. 3:12 **2:20** [a] [Josh. 23:16] **2:21** [a] Josh. 23:4, 5, 13 **2:22** [a] Judg. 3:1, 4 [b] Deut. 8:2, 16; 13:3 **3:1** [a] Judg. 1:1; 2:21, 22 **3:3** [a] Josh. 13:3 **3:5** [a] Ps. 106:35 **3:6** [a] Ex. 34:15, 16 **3:7** [a] Judg. 2:11 [b] Deut. 32:18 [1] Name or symbol for Canaanite goddesses **3:8** [a] Judg. 2:14 [b] Hab. 3:7 **3:9** [a] Judg. 3:15 [b] Judg. 2:16 [c] Judg. 1:13 **3:10** [a] Num. 27:18 **3:12** [a] Judg. 2:19 [b] 1 Sam. 12:9 **3:13** [a] Judg. 5:14 [b] Judg. 1:16 **3:14** [a] Deut. 28:48 **3:15** [a] Ps. 78:34 [b] Judg. 20:16 **3:19** [a] Josh. 4:20

24 When he had gone out, *Eglon's*[1] servants
came to look, and *to their* surprise, the doors
of the upper room were locked. So they said,
"He is probably [a]attending to his needs in the
cool chamber." 25 So they waited till they were
[a]embarrassed, and still he had not opened
the doors of the upper room. Therefore they
took the key and opened *them.* And there was
their master, fallen dead on the floor.
26 But Ehud had escaped while they delayed, and passed beyond the stone images
and escaped to Seirah. 27 And it happened,
when he arrived, that [a]he blew the trumpet
in the [b]mountains of Ephraim, and the children of Israel went down with him from the
mountains; and he led them. 28 Then he said
to them, "Follow *me,* for [a]the LORD has delivered your enemies the Moabites into your
hand." So they went down after him, seized
the [b]fords of the Jordan leading to Moab, and
did not allow anyone to cross over. 29 And
at that time they killed about ten thousand
men of Moab, all stout men of valor; not a
man escaped. 30 So Moab was subdued that
day under the hand of Israel. And [a]the land
had rest for eighty years.

Shamgar

31 After him was [a]Shamgar the son of Anath,
who killed six hundred men of the Philistines
[b]with an ox goad; [c]and he also delivered
[d]Israel.

Deborah

4 When Ehud was dead, [a]the children of
Israel again did [b]evil in the sight of the
LORD. 2 So the LORD [a]sold them into the
hand of Jabin king of Canaan, who reigned
in [b]Hazor. The commander of his army *was*
[c]Sisera, who dwelt in [d]Harosheth Hagoyim.
3 And the children of Israel cried out to the
LORD; for Jabin had nine hundred [a]chariots
of iron, and for twenty years [b]he had harshly
oppressed the children of Israel.
4 Now Deborah, a prophetess, the wife of
Lapidoth, was judging Israel at that time.
5 [a]And she would sit under the palm tree of
Deborah between Ramah and Bethel in the
mountains of Ephraim. And the children of
Israel came up to her for judgment. 6 Then
she sent and called for [a]Barak the son of
Abinoam from [b]Kedesh in Naphtali, and
said to him, "Has not the LORD God of Israel
commanded, 'Go and deploy *troops* at Mount
[c]Tabor; take with you ten thousand men of

PEACE NOTE

Christians aren't gullible. They are careful and critical thinkers who focus on God's peace in their families, friends, and community.

the sons of Naphtali and of the sons of Zebulun; 7 and against you [a]I will deploy Sisera, the
commander of Jabin's army, with his chariots
and his multitude at the [b]River Kishon; and
I will deliver him into your hand'?"
8 And Barak said to her, "If you will go with
me, then I will go; but if you will not go with
me, I will not go!"
9 So she said, "I will surely go with you; nevertheless there will be no glory for you in the
journey you are taking, for the LORD will [a]sell
Sisera into the hand of a woman." Then Deborah arose and went with Barak to Kedesh.
10 And Barak called [a]Zebulun and Naphtali to
Kedesh; he went up with ten thousand men
[b]under his command,[1] and Deborah went
up with him.
11 Now Heber [a]the Kenite, of the children of
[b]Hobab the father-in-law of Moses, had separated himself from the Kenites and pitched
his tent near the terebinth tree at Zaanaim,
[c]which *is* beside Kedesh.
12 And they reported to Sisera that Barak
the son of Abinoam had gone up to Mount
Tabor. 13 So Sisera gathered together all his
chariots, nine hundred chariots of iron, and
all the people who *were* with him, from Harosheth Hagoyim to the River Kishon.
14 Then Deborah said to Barak, "Up! For this
is the day in which the LORD has delivered
Sisera into your hand. [a]Has not the LORD
gone out before you?" So Barak went down
from Mount Tabor with ten thousand men
following him. 15 And the LORD routed Sisera
and all *his* chariots and all *his* army with the
edge of the sword before Barak; and Sisera

3:24 [a] 1 Sam. 24:3 [1] Literally *his* **3:25** [a] 2 Kin. 2:17; 8:11 **3:27** [a] 1 Sam. 13:3 [b] Josh. 17:15 **3:28** [a] Judg. 7:9, 15 [b] Josh. 2:7 **3:30** [a] Judg. 3:11 **3:31** [a] Judg. 5:6 [b] 1 Sam. 17:47 [c] Judg. 2:16 [d] 1 Sam. 4:1 **4:1** [a] Judg. 2:19 [b] Judg. 2:11 **4:2** [a] Judg. 2:14 [b] Josh. 11:1, 10 [c] 1 Sam. 12:9 [d] Judg. 4:13, 16 **4:3** [a] Judg. 1:19 [b] Ps. 106:42 **4:5** [a] Gen. 35:8 **4:6** [a] Heb. 11:32 [b] Josh. 19:37; 21:32 [c] Judg. 8:18 **4:7** [a] Ex. 14:4 [b] Ps. 83:9, 10 **4:9** [a] Judg. 2:14 **4:10** [a] Judg. 5:18 [b] 1 Kin. 20:10 [1] Literally *at his feet* **4:11** [a] Judg. 1:16 [b] Num. 10:29 [c] Judg. 4:6 **4:14** [a] Deut. 9:3; 31:3

alighted from *his* chariot and fled away on
foot. 16 But Barak pursued the chariots and
the army as far as Harosheth Hagoyim, and
all the army of Sisera fell by the edge of the
sword; not a man was [a]left.
17 However, Sisera had fled away on foot
to the tent of [a]Jael, the wife of Heber the Kenite; for *there was* peace between Jabin king of
Hazor and the house of Heber the Kenite. 18 And
Jael went out to meet Sisera, and said to him,
"Turn aside, my lord, turn aside to me; do not
fear." And when he had turned aside with her
into the tent, she covered him with a blanket.
19 Then he said to her, "Please give me a
little water to drink, for I am thirsty." So she
opened [a]a jug of milk, gave him a drink, and
covered him. 20 And he said to her, "Stand at
the door of the tent, and if any man comes
and inquires of you, and says, 'Is there any
man here?' you shall say, 'No.' "
21 Then Jael, Heber's wife, [a]took a tent peg
and took a hammer in her hand, and went
softly to him and drove the peg into his temple, and it went down into the ground; for he
was fast asleep and weary. So he died. 22 And
then, as Barak pursued Sisera, Jael came out
to meet him, and said to him, "Come, I will
show you the man whom you seek." And
when he went into her *tent*, there lay Sisera,
dead with the peg in his temple.
23 So on that day God subdued Jabin king
of Canaan in the presence of the children of
Israel. 24 And the hand of the children of Israel grew stronger and stronger against Jabin
king of Canaan, until they had destroyed
Jabin king of Canaan.

The Song of Deborah

5 Then Deborah and Barak the son of Abinoam [a]sang on that day, saying:

2 "When leaders [a]lead in Israel,
[b]When the people willingly offer
themselves,
Bless the LORD!

3 "Hear,[a] O kings! Give ear, O princes!
I, *even* [b]I, will sing to the LORD;
I will sing praise to the LORD God of
Israel.

4 "LORD, [a]when You went out from Seir,
When You marched from [b]the field of
Edom,
The earth trembled and the heavens
poured,
The clouds also poured water;
5 [a]The mountains gushed before the
LORD,
[b]This Sinai, before the LORD God of Israel.

6 "In the days of [a]Shamgar, son of Anath,
In the days of [b]Jael,
[c]The highways were deserted,
And the travelers walked along the
byways.
7 Village life ceased, it ceased in Israel,
Until I, Deborah, arose,
Arose a mother in Israel.
8 They chose [a]new gods;
Then *there was* war in the gates;
Not a shield or spear was seen among
forty thousand in Israel.
9 My heart *is* with the rulers of Israel
Who offered themselves willingly with
the people.
Bless the LORD!

10 "Speak, you who ride on white [a]donkeys,
Who sit in judges' attire,
And who walk along the road.
11 Far from the noise of the archers,
among the watering places,
There they shall recount the righteous
acts of the LORD,
The righteous acts *for* His villagers in
Israel;
Then the people of the LORD shall go
down to the gates.

12 "Awake,[a] awake, Deborah!
Awake, awake, sing a song!
Arise, Barak, and lead your captives
away,
O son of Abinoam!

13 "Then the survivors came down, the
people against the nobles;
The LORD came down for me against
the mighty.
14 From Ephraim *were* those whose roots
were in [a]Amalek.
After you, Benjamin, with your peoples,
From Machir rulers came down,
And from Zebulun those who bear the
recruiter's staff.
15 And the princes of Issachar[1] *were* with
Deborah;
As Issachar, so *was* Barak
Sent into the valley under his command;[2]
Among the divisions of Reuben
There were great resolves of heart.

4:16 [a] Ex. 14:28 4:17 [a] Judg. 5:6 4:19 [a] Judg. 5:24–27 4:21 [a] Judg. 5:24–27 5:1 [a] Judg. 4:4 5:2 [a] Ps. 18:47 [b] 2 Chr. 17:16 5:3 [a] Deut. 32:1, 3 [b] Ps. 27:6 5:4 [a] Deut. 33:2 [b] Ps. 68:8 5:5 [a] Ps. 97:5 [b] Ex. 19:18 5:6 [a] Judg. 3:31 [b] Judg. 4:17 [c] Is. 33:8 5:8 [a] Deut. 32:17 5:10 [a] Judg. 10:4; 12:14 5:12 [a] Ps. 57:8 5:14 [a] Judg. 3:13 5:15 [1] Following Septuagint, Syriac, Targum, and Vulgate; Masoretic Text reads *And my princes in Issachar.* [2] Literally *at his feet*

16 Why did you sit among the sheepfolds,
To hear the pipings for the flocks?
The divisions of Reuben have great
searchings of heart.
17 [a]Gilead stayed beyond the Jordan,
And why did Dan remain on ships?[1]
[b]Asher continued at the seashore,
And stayed by his inlets.
18 [a]Zebulun *is* a people *who* jeopardized
their lives to the point of death,
Naphtali also, on the heights of the
battlefield.

19 "The kings came *and* fought,
Then the kings of Canaan fought
In [a]Taanach, by the waters of Megiddo;
They took no spoils of silver.
20 They fought from the heavens;
The stars from their courses fought
against Sisera.
21 [a]The torrent of Kishon swept them away,
That ancient torrent, the torrent of
Kishon.
O my soul, march on in strength!
22 Then the horses' hooves pounded,
The galloping, galloping of his steeds.
23 'Curse Meroz,' said the angel[1] of the LORD,
'Curse its inhabitants bitterly,
Because they did not come to the help
of the LORD,
To the help of the LORD against the
mighty.'

24 "Most blessed among women is Jael,
The wife of Heber the Kenite;
[a]Blessed is she among women in tents.
25 He asked for water, she gave milk;
She brought out cream in a lordly bowl.
26 She stretched her hand to the tent peg,
Her right hand to the workmen's
hammer;
She pounded Sisera, she pierced his head,
She split and struck through his temple.
27 At her feet he sank, he fell, he lay still;
At her feet he sank, he fell;
Where he sank, there he fell [a]dead.

28 "The mother of Sisera looked through
the window,
And cried out through the lattice,
'Why is his chariot *so* long in coming?
Why tarries the clatter of his chariots?'
29 Her wisest ladies answered her,
Yes, she answered herself,
30 'Are they not finding and dividing the
spoil:
To every man a girl *or* two;
For Sisera, plunder of dyed garments,
Plunder of garments embroidered and
dyed,
Two pieces of dyed embroidery for the
neck of the looter?'

31 "Thus let all Your enemies [a]perish, O LORD!
But *let* those who love Him *be* [b]like the
[c]sun
When it comes out in full [d]strength."

So the land had rest for forty years.

Midianites Oppress Israel

6 Then the children of Israel did [a]evil in the
sight of the LORD. So the LORD delivered
them into the hand of [b]Midian for seven years,
2 and the hand of Midian prevailed against Israel. Because of the Midianites, the children
of Israel made for themselves the dens, [a]the
caves, and the strongholds which *are* in the
mountains. 3 So it was, whenever Israel had
sown, Midianites would come up; also Amalekites and the [a]people of the East would come
up against them. 4 Then they would encamp
against them and [a]destroy the produce of the
earth as far as Gaza, and leave no sustenance
for Israel, neither sheep nor ox nor [b]donkey.
5 For they would come up with their livestock
and their tents, coming in as numerous as
locusts; both they and their camels were without number; and they would enter the land to
destroy it. 6 So Israel was greatly impoverished
because of the Midianites, and the children
of Israel [a]cried out to the LORD.
7 And it came to pass, when the children of
Israel cried out to the LORD because of the
Midianites, 8 that the LORD sent a prophet to
the children of Israel, who said to them, "Thus
says the LORD God of Israel: 'I brought you up
from Egypt and brought you out of the [a]house
of bondage; 9 and I delivered you out of the
hand of the Egyptians and out of the hand of
all who oppressed you, and [a]drove them out
before you and gave you their land. 10 Also I said
to you, "I *am* the LORD your God; [a]do not fear
the gods of the Amorites, in whose land you
dwell." But you have not obeyed My [b]voice.' "

Gideon

11 Now the Angel of the LORD came and sat
under the terebinth tree which *was* in Ophrah, which *belonged* to Joash [a]the Abiezrite,
while his son [b]Gideon threshed wheat in
the winepress, in order to hide *it* from the

5:17 [a] Josh. 22:9 [b] Josh. 19:29, 31 [1] Or *at ease* **5:18** [a] Judg. 4:6, 10 **5:19** [a] Judg. 1:27 **5:21** [a] Judg. 4:7 **5:23** [1] Or *Angel* **5:24** [a] [Luke 1:28] **5:27** [a] Judg. 4:18–21 **5:31** [a] Ps. 92:9 [b] 2 Sam. 23:4 [c] Ps. 37:6; 89:36, 37 [d] Ps. 19:5 **6:1** [a] Judg. 2:11 [b] Num. 22:4; 31:1–3 **6:2** [a] 1 Sam. 13:6 **6:3** [a] Judg. 7:12 **6:4** [a] Lev. 26:16 [b] Deut. 28:31 **6:6** [a] Hos. 5:15 **6:8** [a] Josh. 24:17 **6:9** [a] Ps. 44:2, 3 **6:10** [a] 2 Kin. 17:35, 37, 38 [b] Judg. 2:1, 2 **6:11** [a] Josh. 17:2 [b] Heb. 11:32

Midianites. 12 And the [a]Angel of the LORD appeared to him, and said to him, "The LORD *is* [b]with you, you mighty man of valor!"

13 Gideon said to Him, "O my lord,[1] if the LORD is with us, why then has all this happened to us? And [a]where *are* all His miracles [b]which our fathers told us about, saying, 'Did not the LORD bring us up from Egypt?' But now the LORD has [c]forsaken us and delivered us into the hands of the Midianites."

14 Then the LORD turned to him and said, [a]"Go in this might of yours, and you shall save Israel from the hand of the Midianites. [b]Have I not sent you?"

15 So he said to Him, "O my Lord,[1] how can I save Israel? Indeed [a]my clan *is* the weakest in Manasseh, and I *am* the least in my father's house."

16 And the LORD said to him, [a]"Surely I will be with you, and you shall defeat the Midianites as one man."

17 Then he said to Him, "If now I have found favor in Your sight, then [a]show me a sign that it is You who talk with me. 18 [a]Do not depart from here, I pray, until I come to You and bring out my offering and set *it* before You."

And He said, "I will wait until you come back."

19 [a]So Gideon went in and prepared a young goat, and unleavened bread from an ephah of flour. The meat he put in a basket, and he put the broth in a pot; and he brought *them* out to Him under the terebinth tree and presented *them.* 20 The Angel of God said to him, "Take the meat and the unleavened bread and [a]lay *them* on this rock, and [b]pour out the broth." And he did so.

21 Then the Angel of the LORD put out the end of the staff that *was* in His hand, and touched the meat and the unleavened bread; and [a]fire rose out of the rock and consumed the meat and the unleavened bread. And the Angel of the LORD departed out of his sight.

22 Now Gideon [a]perceived that He *was* the Angel of the LORD. So Gideon said, "Alas, O Lord GOD! [b]For I have seen the Angel of the LORD face to face."

23 Then the LORD said to him, [a]"Peace *be* with you; do not fear, you shall not die." 24 So Gideon built an altar there to the LORD, and called it The-LORD-*Is*-Peace.[1] To this day it *is* still [a]in Ophrah of the Abiezrites.

25 Now it came to pass the same night that the LORD said to him, "Take your father's young bull, the second bull of seven years old, and [a]tear down the altar of [b]Baal that your father has, and [c]cut down the wooden image[1] that *is* beside it; 26 and build an altar to the LORD your God on top of this rock in the proper arrangement, and take the second bull and offer a burnt sacrifice with the wood of the image which you shall cut down." 27 So Gideon took ten men from among his servants and did as the LORD had said to him. But because he feared his father's household and the men of the city too much to do *it* by day, he did *it* by night.

PEACE NOTE

Absolute biblical truths—*There is a God who loves me; I am made in His image; my value is unchanging in His eyes*—inspire peace.

JUDGES 6:23

Gideon Destroys the Altar of Baal

28 And when the men of the city arose early in the morning, there was the altar of Baal, torn down; and the wooden image that *was*

PEACE NOTE

We all have battles to fight and adversity to overcome, but we can face each challenge living in the same peace Gideon experienced because our God is *shalom.*

JUDGES 6:24

6:12 [a] Judg. 13:3 [b] Josh. 1:5 6:13 [a] [Is. 59:1] [b] Ps. 44:1 [c] Ps. 44:9–16 [1] Hebrew *adoni,* used of man 6:14 [a] 1 Sam. 12:11 [b] Josh. 1:9 6:15 [a] 1 Sam. 9:21 [1] Hebrew *Adonai,* used of God 6:16 [a] Ex. 3:12 6:17 [a] Judg. 6:36, 37 6:18 [a] Gen. 18:3, 5 6:19 [a] Gen. 18:6–8 6:20 [a] Judg. 13:19 [b] 1 Kin. 18:33, 34 6:21 [a] Lev. 9:24 6:22 [a] Judg. 13:21, 22 [b] Gen. 16:13 6:23 [a] Dan. 10:19 6:24 [a] Judg. 8:32 [1] Hebrew *YHWH Shalom* 6:25 [a] Judg. 2:2 [b] Judg. 3:7 [c] Ex. 34:13 [1] Hebrew *Asherah,* a Canaanite goddess

WHEN ALL SEEMS LOST

The LORD said to [Gideon], "Peace be with you; do not fear, you shall not die."

JUDGES 6:23

Exhausted? Considering giving up on God? Like Gideon, are you wondering where God's miracles are—the ones you've heard about from others but haven't seen yourself?

Gideon considered himself the weakest, least qualified servant to obey God. He even charged God with forsaking him. A moment after the Lord promised His presence and described Gideon as a "mighty man of valor" (v. 12), Gideon flinched and accused God of abandoning him to Israel's enemies. The Angel of the Lord promised His presence with Gideon four times, and the reluctant warrior still didn't trust.

Often our trials obscure God's promises. But Moses heard "I will certainly be with you" once and led Israel out of bondage (Ex. 3:12). Joshua relied on the promise of God's peaceful presence (Josh. 1:5), and the sun stood still. The *shalom* peace of God meets us at our greatest point of need, bringing the same power Gideon experienced to move forward in faith when everything inside pressed him to retreat.

Will you join me in praying Gideon's prayer over your life? "The-LORD-Is-Peace" (Judg. 6:24) is not just the name of Gideon's altar—it is a prayer and a praise.

beside it was cut down, and the second bull
was being offered on the altar *which had*
been built. 29 So they said to one another,
"Who has done this thing?" And when they
had inquired and asked, they said, "Gideon
the son of Joash has done this thing." 30 Then
the men of the city said to Joash, "Bring out
your son, that he may die, because he has
torn down the altar of Baal, and because he
has cut down the wooden image that *was*
beside it."
31 But Joash said to all who stood against
him, "Would you plead for Baal? Would you
save him? Let the one who would plead for
him be put to death by morning! If he *is* a
god, let him plead for himself, because his
altar has been torn down!" 32 Therefore on
that day he called him [a]Jerubbaal,[1] saying,
"Let Baal plead against him, because he has
torn down his altar."
33 Then all [a]the Midianites and Amalekites,
the people of the East, gathered together;
and they crossed over and encamped in [b]the
Valley of Jezreel. 34 But [a]the Spirit of the LORD
came upon Gideon; then he [b]blew the trumpet, and the Abiezrites gathered behind him.
35 And he sent messengers throughout all
Manasseh, who also gathered behind him.
He also sent messengers to [a]Asher, [b]Zeb-
ulun, and Naphtali; and they came up to
meet them.

The Sign of the Fleece

36 So Gideon said to God, "If You will save
Israel by my hand as You have said— 37 [a]look,
I shall put a fleece of wool on the threshing
floor; if there is dew on the fleece only, and
it is dry on all the ground, then I shall know
that You will save Israel by my hand, as You
have said." 38 And it was so. When he rose
early the next morning and squeezed the
fleece together, he wrung the dew out of the
fleece, a bowlful of water. 39 Then Gideon said
to God, [a]"Do not be angry with me, but let me
speak just once more: Let me test, I pray, just
once more with the fleece; let it now be dry
only on the fleece, but on all the ground let
there be dew." 40 And God did so that night.
It was dry on the fleece only, but there was
dew on all the ground.

Gideon's Valiant Three Hundred

7 Then [a]Jerubbaal (that *is,* Gideon) and all
the people who *were* with him rose early
and encamped beside the well of Harod, so
that the camp of the Midianites was on the
north side of them by the hill of Moreh in
the valley.
2 And the LORD said to Gideon, "The people
who *are* with you *are* too many for Me to give
the Midianites into their hands, lest Israel
[a]claim glory for itself against Me, saying, 'My
own hand has saved me.' 3 Now therefore,

6:32 [a] 1 Sam. 12:11 [1] Literally *Let Baal Plead* 6:33 [a] Judg. 6:3 [b] Josh. 17:16 6:34 [a] Judg. 3:10 [b] Judg. 3:27 6:35 [a] Judg. 5:17; 7:23 [b] Judg. 4:6, 10; 5:18 6:37 [a] [Ex. 4:3–7] 6:39 [a] Gen. 18:32 7:1 [a] Judg. 6:32 7:2 [a] Deut. 8:17

proclaim in the hearing of the people, saying,
[a]'Whoever *is* fearful and afraid, let him turn
and depart at once from Mount Gilead.' " And
twenty-two thousand of the people returned,
and ten thousand remained.
4 But the LORD said to Gideon, "The people
are still *too* many; bring them down to the
water, and I will test them for you there. Then
it will be, *that* of whom I say to you, 'This one
shall go with you,' the same shall go with you;
and of whomever I say to you, 'This one shall
not go with you,' the same shall not go." 5 So
he brought the people down to the water. And
the LORD said to Gideon, "Everyone who laps
from the water with his tongue, as a dog laps,
you shall set apart by himself; likewise everyone who gets down on his knees to drink."
6 And the number of those who lapped, *putting*
their hand to their mouth, was three hundred
men; but all the rest of the people got down
on their knees to drink water. 7 Then the LORD
said to Gideon, [a]"By the three hundred men
who lapped I will save you, and deliver the
Midianites into your hand. Let all the *other*
people go, every man to his place." 8 So the
people took provisions and their trumpets
in their hands. And he sent away all *the rest
of* Israel, every man to his tent, and retained
those three hundred men. Now the camp of
Midian was below him in the valley.
9 It happened on the same [a]night that the
LORD said to him, "Arise, go down against
the camp, for I have delivered it into your
hand. 10 But if you are afraid to go down, go
down to the camp with Purah your servant,
11 and you shall [a]hear what they say; and afterward your hands shall be strengthened
to go down against the camp." Then he went
down with Purah his servant to the outpost
of the armed men who *were* in the camp.
12 Now the Midianites and Amalekites, [a]all the
people of the East, were lying in the valley
[b]as numerous as locusts; and their camels
were without number, as the sand by the
seashore in multitude.
13 And when Gideon had come, there was
a man telling a dream to his companion. He
said, "I have had a dream: *To my* surprise, a
loaf of barley bread tumbled into the camp of
Midian; it came to a tent and struck it so that
it fell and overturned, and the tent collapsed."
14 Then his companion answered and said,
"This *is* nothing else but the sword of Gideon the son of Joash, a man of Israel! Into
his hand [a]God has delivered Midian and the
whole camp."
15 And so it was, when Gideon heard the
telling of the dream and its interpretation,
that he worshiped. He returned to the camp
of Israel, and said, "Arise, for the LORD has
delivered the camp of Midian into your hand."
16 Then he divided the three hundred men *into*
three companies, and he put a trumpet into
every man's hand, with empty pitchers, and
torches inside the pitchers. 17 And he said to
them, "Look at me and do likewise; watch, and
when I come to the edge of the camp you shall
do as I do: 18 When I blow the trumpet, I and
all who *are* with me, then you also blow the
trumpets on every side of the whole camp, and
say, '*The sword of* the LORD and of Gideon!' "
19 So Gideon and the hundred men who
were with him came to the outpost of the
camp at the beginning of the middle watch,
just as they had posted the watch; and they
blew the trumpets and broke the pitchers
that *were* in their hands. 20 Then the three
companies blew the trumpets and broke
the pitchers—they held the torches in their
left hands and the trumpets in their right
hands for blowing—and they cried, "The
sword of the LORD and of Gideon!" 21 And
[a]every man stood in his place all around the
camp; [b]and the whole army ran and cried out
and fled. 22 When the three hundred [a]blew
the trumpets, [b]the LORD set [c]every man's
sword against his companion throughout
the whole camp; and the army fled to Beth
Acacia,[1] toward Zererah, as far as the border
of [d]Abel Meholah, by Tabbath.
23 And the men of Israel gathered together
from [a]Naphtali, Asher, and all Manasseh, and
pursued the Midianites.
24 Then Gideon sent messengers throughout all the [a]mountains of Ephraim, saying,
"Come down against the Midianites, and seize
from them the watering places as far as Beth
Barah and the Jordan." Then all the men of
Ephraim gathered together and [b]seized the
watering places as far as [c]Beth Barah and the
Jordan. 25 And they captured [a]two princes of
the Midianites, [b]Oreb and Zeeb. They killed
Oreb at the rock of Oreb, and Zeeb they killed
at the winepress of Zeeb. They pursued Midian and brought the heads of Oreb and Zeeb
to Gideon on the [c]other side of the Jordan.

Gideon Subdues the Midianites

8 Now [a]the men of Ephraim said to him,
"Why have you done this to us by not calling us when you went to fight with the Midianites?" And they reprimanded him sharply.

7:3 [a] Deut. 20:8 **7:7** [a] 1 Sam. 14:6 **7:9** [a] Judg. 6:25 **7:11** [a] 1 Sam. 14:9, 10 **7:12** [a] Judg. 6:3, 33; 8:10 [b] Judg. 6:5 **7:14** [a] Judg. 6:14, 16 **7:21** [a] 2 Chr. 20:17 [b] 2 Kin. 7:7 **7:22** [a] Josh. 6:4, 16, 20 [b] Is. 9:4 [c] 1 Sam. 14:20 [d] 1 Kin. 4:12 [1] Hebrew *Beth Shittah* **7:23** [a] Judg. 6:35 **7:24** [a] Judg. 3:27 [b] Judg. 3:28 [c] John 1:28 **7:25** [a] Judg. 8:3 [b] Ps. 83:11 [c] Judg. 8:4 **8:1** [a] Judg. 12:1

2 So he said to them, "What have I done now in comparison with you? *Is* not the gleaning *of the grapes* of Ephraim better than the vintage of [a]Abiezer? 3 [a]God has delivered into your hands the princes of Midian, Oreb and Zeeb. And what was I able to do in comparison with you?" Then their [b]anger toward him subsided when he said that.

4 When Gideon came [a]to the Jordan, he and [b]the three hundred men who *were* with him crossed over, exhausted but still in pursuit. 5 Then he said to the men of [a]Succoth, "Please give loaves of bread to the people who follow me, for they are exhausted, and I am pursuing Zebah and Zalmunna, kings of Midian."

6 And the leaders of Succoth said, [a]"*Are* the hands of Zebah and Zalmunna now in your hand, that [b]we should give bread to your army?"

7 So Gideon said, "For this cause, when the LORD has delivered Zebah and Zalmunna into my hand, [a]then I will tear your flesh with the thorns of the wilderness and with briers!" 8 Then he went up from there [a]to Penuel and spoke to them in the same way. And the men of Penuel answered him as the men of Succoth had answered. 9 So he also spoke to the men of Penuel, saying, "When I [a]come back in peace, [b]I will tear down this tower!"

10 Now Zebah and Zalmunna *were* at Karkor, and their armies with them, about fifteen thousand, all who were left of [a]all the army of the people of the East; for [b]one hundred and twenty thousand men who drew the sword had fallen. 11 Then Gideon went up by the road of those who dwell in tents on the east of [a]Nobah and Jogbehah; and he attacked the army while the camp felt [b]secure. 12 When Zebah and Zalmunna fled, he pursued them; and he [a]took the two kings of Midian, Zebah and Zalmunna, and routed the whole army.

13 Then Gideon the son of Joash returned from battle, from the Ascent of Heres. 14 And he caught a young man of the men of Succoth and interrogated him; and he wrote down for him the leaders of Succoth and its elders, seventy-seven men. 15 Then he came to the men of Succoth and said, "Here are Zebah and Zalmunna, about whom you [a]ridiculed me, saying, '*Are* the hands of Zebah and Zalmunna now in your hand, that we should give bread to your weary men?' " 16 [a]And he took the elders of the city, and thorns of the wilderness and briers, and with them he taught the men of Succoth. 17 [a]Then he tore down the tower of [b]Penuel and killed the men of the city.

18 And he said to Zebah and Zalmunna, "What kind of men *were they* whom you killed at [a]Tabor?"

So they answered, "As you *are,* so *were* they; each one resembled the son of a king."

19 Then he said, "They *were* my brothers, the sons of my mother. *As* the LORD lives, if you had let them live, I would not kill you." 20 And he said to Jether his firstborn, "Rise, kill them!" But the youth would not draw his sword; for he was afraid, because he *was* still a youth.

21 So Zebah and Zalmunna said, "Rise yourself, and kill us; for as a man *is, so is* his strength." So Gideon arose and [a]killed Zebah and Zalmunna, and took the crescent ornaments that *were* on their camels' necks.

Gideon's Ephod

22 Then the men of Israel said to Gideon, [a]"Rule over us, both you and your son, and your grandson also; for you have [b]delivered us from the hand of Midian."

23 But Gideon said to them, "I will not rule over you, nor shall my son rule over you; [a]the LORD shall rule over you." 24 Then Gideon said to them, "I would like to make a request of you, that each of you would give me the earrings from his plunder." For they had golden earrings, [a]because they *were* Ishmaelites.

25 So they answered, "We will gladly give *them.*" And they spread out a garment, and each man threw into it the earrings from his plunder. 26 Now the weight of the gold earrings that he requested was one thousand seven hundred *shekels* of gold, besides the crescent ornaments, pendants, and purple robes which *were* on the kings of Midian, and besides the chains that *were* around their camels' necks. 27 Then Gideon [a]made it into an ephod and set it up in his city, [b]Ophrah. And all Israel [c]played the harlot with it there. It became [d]a snare to Gideon and to his house. 28 Thus Midian was subdued before the children of Israel, so that they lifted their heads no more. [a]And the country was quiet for forty years in the days of Gideon.

Death of Gideon

29 Then [a]Jerubbaal the son of Joash went and dwelt in his own house. 30 Gideon had [a]seventy sons who were his own offspring, for he had many wives. 31 [a]And his concubine

8:2 [a] Judg. 6:11 **8:3** [a] Judg. 7:24, 25 [b] Prov. 15:1 **8:4** [a] Judg. 7:25 [b] Judg. 7:6 **8:5** [a] Gen. 33:17 **8:6** [a] Judg. 8:15 [b] 1 Sam. 25:11 **8:7** [a] Judg. 8:16 **8:8** [a] Gen. 32:30, 31 **8:9** [a] 1 Kin. 22:27 [b] Judg. 8:17 **8:10** [a] Judg. 7:12 [b] Judg. 6:5 **8:11** [a] Num. 32:35, 42 [b] Judg. 18:27 **8:12** [a] Ps. 83:11 **8:15** [a] Judg. 8:6 **8:16** [a] Judg. 8:7 **8:17** [a] Judg. 8:9 [b] 1 Kin. 12:25 **8:18** [a] Judg. 4:6 **8:21** [a] Ps. 83:11 **8:22** [a] [Judg. 9:8] [b] Judg. 3:9; 9:17 **8:23** [a] 1 Sam. 8:7; 10:19; 12:12 **8:24** [a] Gen. 37:25, 28 **8:27** [a] Judg. 17:5 [b] Judg. 6:11, 24 [c] [Ps. 106:39] [d] Deut. 7:16 **8:28** [a] Judg. 5:31 **8:29** [a] Judg. 6:32; 7:1 **8:30** [a] Judg. 9:2, 5 **8:31** [a] Judg. 9:1

who *was* in Shechem also bore him a son,
whose name he called Abimelech. 32 Now
Gideon the son of Joash died [a]at a good old
age, and was buried in the tomb of Joash his
father, [b]in Ophrah of the Abiezrites.
33 So it was, [a]as soon as Gideon was dead,
that the children of Israel again [b]played the
harlot with the Baals, [c]and made Baal-Berith
their god. 34 Thus the children of Israel [a]did not
remember the LORD their God, who had delivered them from the hands of all their enemies
on every side; 35 [a]nor did they show kindness to
the house of Jerubbaal (Gideon) in accordance
with the good he had done for Israel.

Abimelech's Conspiracy

9 Then Abimelech the son of Jerubbaal went
to Shechem, to [a]his mother's brothers,
and spoke with them and with all the family
of the house of his mother's father, saying,
2 "Please speak in the hearing of all the men
of Shechem: 'Which is better for you, that all
[a]seventy of the sons of Jerubbaal reign over
you, or that one reign over you?' Remember
that I *am* your own flesh and [b]bone."
3 And his mother's brothers spoke all
these words concerning him in the hearing
of all the men of Shechem; and their heart
was inclined to follow Abimelech, for they
said, "He is our [a]brother." 4 So they gave him
seventy *shekels* of silver from the temple of
[a]Baal-Berith, with which Abimelech hired
[b]worthless and reckless men; and they followed him. 5 Then he went to his father's
house [a]at Ophrah and [b]killed his brothers,
the seventy sons of Jerubbaal, on one stone.
But Jotham the youngest son of Jerubbaal
was left, because he hid himself. 6 And all the
men of Shechem gathered together, all of
Beth Millo, and they went and made Abimelech king beside the terebinth tree at the
pillar that *was* in Shechem.

The Parable of the Trees

7 Now when they told Jotham, he went and
stood on top of [a]Mount Gerizim, and lifted
his voice and cried out. And he said to them:

"Listen to me, you men of Shechem,
That God may listen to you!

8 "The[a] trees once went forth to anoint a
king over them.
And they said to the olive tree,
[b]'Reign over us!'
9 But the olive tree said to them,
'Should I cease giving my oil,
[a]With which they honor God and men,
And go to sway over trees?'
10 "Then the trees said to the fig tree,
'You come *and* reign over us!'
11 But the fig tree said to them,
'Should I cease my sweetness and my
good fruit,
And go to sway over trees?'
12 "Then the trees said to the vine,
'You come *and* reign over us!'
13 But the vine said to them,
'Should I cease my new wine,
[a]Which cheers *both* God and men,
And go to sway over trees?'

14 "Then all the trees said to the bramble,
'You come *and* reign over us!'
15 And the bramble said to the trees,
'If in truth you anoint me as king over
you,
Then come *and* take shelter in my
[a]shade;
But if not, [b]let fire come out of the
bramble
And devour the [c]cedars of Lebanon!'

16 "Now therefore, if you have acted in truth
and sincerity in making Abimelech king, and
if you have dealt well with Jerubbaal and
his house, and have done to him [a]as he deserves— 17 for my [a]father fought for you, risked
his life, and [b]delivered you out of the hand of
Midian; 18 [a]but you have risen up against my
father's house this day, and killed his seventy
sons on one stone, and made Abimelech, the
son of his [b]female servant, king over the men
of Shechem, because he is your brother— 19 if
then you have acted in truth and sincerity
with Jerubbaal and with his house this day,
then [a]rejoice in Abimelech, and let him also
rejoice in you. 20 But if not, [a]let fire come from
Abimelech and devour the men of Shechem
and Beth Millo; and let fire come from the
men of Shechem and from Beth Millo and
devour Abimelech!" 21 And Jotham ran away
and fled; and he went to [a]Beer and dwelt there,
for fear of Abimelech his brother.

Downfall of Abimelech

22 After Abimelech had reigned over Israel three years, 23 [a]God sent a [b]spirit of ill

8:32 [a] Gen. 25:8 [b] Judg. 6:24; 8:27 8:33 [a] Judg. 2:19 [b] Judg. 2:17 [c] Judg. 9:4, 46 8:34 [a] Deut. 4:9 8:35 [a] Judg. 9:16–18
9:1 [a] Judg. 8:31, 35 9:2 [a] Judg. 8:30; 9:5, 18 [b] Gen. 29:14 9:3 [a] Gen. 29:15 9:4 [a] Judg. 8:33 [b] Judg. 11:3 9:5 [a] Judg. 6:24 [b] 2 Kin. 11:1, 2 9:7 [a] Deut. 11:29; 27:12 9:8 [a] 2 Kin. 14:9 [b] Judg. 8:22, 23 9:9 [a] [John 5:23] 9:13 [a] Ps. 104:15
9:15 [a] Is. 30:2 [b] Num. 21:28 [c] 2 Kin. 14:9 9:16 [a] Judg. 8:35 9:17 [a] Judg. 7 [b] Judg. 8:22 9:18 [a] Judg. 8:30, 35; 9:2, 5, 6 [b] Judg. 8:31 9:19 [a] Is. 8:6 9:20 [a] Judg. 9:15, 45, 56, 57 9:21 [a] Num. 21:16 9:23 [a] Is. 19:14 [b] 1 Sam. 16:14; 18:9, 10

will between Abimelech and the men of Shechem; and the men of Shechem [c]dealt treacherously with Abimelech, 24 [a]that the crime *done* to the seventy sons of Jerubbaal might be settled and their [b]blood be laid on Abimelech their brother, who killed them, and on the men of Shechem, who aided him in the killing of his brothers. 25 And the men of Shechem set men in ambush against him on the tops of the mountains, and they robbed all who passed by them along that way; and it was told Abimelech.

26 Now Gaal the son of Ebed came with his brothers and went over to Shechem; and the men of Shechem put their confidence in him. 27 So they went out into the fields, and gathered *grapes* from their vineyards and trod *them,* and made merry. And they went into [a]the house of their god, and ate and drank, and cursed Abimelech. 28 Then Gaal the son of Ebed said, [a]"Who *is* Abimelech, and who *is* Shechem, that we should serve him? *Is he* not the son of Jerubbaal, and *is not* Zebul his officer? Serve the men of [b]Hamor the father of Shechem; but why should we serve him? 29 [a]If only this people were under my authority![1] Then I would remove Abimelech." So he[2] said to Abimelech, "Increase your army and come out!"

30 When Zebul, the ruler of the city, heard the words of Gaal the son of Ebed, his anger was aroused. 31 And he sent messengers to Abimelech secretly, saying, "Take note! Gaal the son of Ebed and his brothers have come to Shechem; and here they are, fortifying the city against you. 32 Now therefore, get up by night, you and the people who *are* with you, and lie in wait in the field. 33 And it shall be, as soon as the sun is up in the morning, *that* you shall rise early and rush upon the city; and *when* he and the people who are with him come out against you, you may then do to them as you find opportunity."

34 So Abimelech and all the people who *were* with him rose by night, and lay in wait against Shechem in four companies. 35 When Gaal the son of Ebed went out and stood in the entrance to the city gate, Abimelech and the people who *were* with him rose from lying in wait. 36 And when Gaal saw the people, he said to Zebul, "Look, people are coming down from the tops of the mountains!"

But Zebul said to him, "You see the shadows of the mountains as *if they were* men."

37 So Gaal spoke again and said, "See, people are coming down from the center of the land, and another company is coming from the Diviners'[1] Terebinth Tree."

38 Then Zebul said to him, "Where indeed *is* your mouth now, with which you [a]said, 'Who is Abimelech, that we should serve him?' *Are* not these the people whom you despised? Go out, if you will, and fight with them now."

39 So Gaal went out, leading the men of Shechem, and fought with Abimelech. 40 And Abimelech chased him, and he fled from him; and many fell wounded, to the *very* entrance of the gate. 41 Then Abimelech dwelt at Arumah, and Zebul drove out Gaal and his brothers, so that they would not dwell in Shechem.

42 And it came about on the next day that the people went out into the field, and they told Abimelech. 43 So he took his people, divided them into three companies, and lay in wait in the field. And he looked, and there were the people, coming out of the city; and he rose against them and attacked them. 44 Then Abimelech and the company that *was* with him rushed forward and stood at the entrance of the gate of the city; and the *other* two companies rushed upon all who *were* in the fields and killed them. 45 So Abimelech fought against the city all that day; [a]he took the city and killed the people who *were* in it; and he [b]demolished the city and sowed it with salt.

46 Now when all the men of the tower of Shechem had heard *that,* they entered the stronghold of the temple [a]of the god Berith. 47 And it was told Abimelech that all the men of the tower of Shechem were gathered together. 48 Then Abimelech went up to Mount [a]Zalmon, he and all the people who *were* with him. And Abimelech took an ax in his hand and cut down a bough from the trees, and took it and laid *it* on his shoulder; then he said to the people who were with him, "What you have seen me do, make haste *and* do as I *have done.*" 49 So each of the people likewise cut down his own bough and followed Abimelech, put *them* against the stronghold, and set the stronghold on fire above them, so that all the people of the tower of Shechem died, about a thousand men and women.

50 Then Abimelech went to Thebez, and he encamped against Thebez and took it. 51 But there was a strong tower in the city, and all the men and women—all the people of the city—fled there and shut themselves in; then they went up to the top of the tower. 52 So Abimelech came as far as the tower and fought against it; and he drew near the door of the tower to burn it with fire. 53 But a certain woman [a]dropped an upper millstone

9:23 [c] Is. 33:1 **9:24** [a] 1 Kin. 2:32 [b] Num. 35:33 **9:27** [a] Judg. 9:4 **9:28** [a] 1 Sam. 25:10 [b] Gen. 34:2, 6 **9:29** [a] 2 Sam. 15:4
[1] Literally *hand* [2] Following Masoretic Text and Targum; Dead Sea Scrolls read *they;* Septuagint reads *I.* **9:37** [1] Hebrew *Meonenim* **9:38** [a] Judg. 9:28, 29 **9:45** [a] Judg. 9:20 [b] 2 Kin. 3:25 **9:46** [a] Judg. 8:33 **9:48** [a] Ps. 68:14 **9:53** [a] 2 Sam. 11:21

on Abimelech's head and crushed his skull.
54 Then [a]he called quickly to the young man,
his armorbearer, and said to him, "Draw
your sword and kill me, lest men say of me,
'A woman killed him.' " So his young man
thrust him through, and he died. 55 And when
the men of Israel saw that Abimelech was
dead, they departed, every man to his place.
56 [a]Thus God repaid the wickedness of
Abimelech, which he had done to his father
by killing his seventy brothers. 57 And all the
evil of the men of Shechem God returned
on their own heads, and on them came [a]the
curse of Jotham the son of Jerubbaal.

> PEACE NOTE
>
> Abimelech is a stark reminder of the chaos that results when we live in disobedience to God. Remember: obedience = peace; disobedience = turmoil.
>
> JUDGES 9:56

Tola

10 After Abimelech there [a]arose to save
Israel Tola the son of Puah, the son
of Dodo, a man of Issachar; and he dwelt in
Shamir in the mountains of Ephraim. 2 He
judged Israel twenty-three years; and he died
and was buried in Shamir.

Jair

3 After him arose Jair, a Gileadite; and he
judged Israel twenty-two years. 4 Now he had
thirty sons who [a]rode on thirty donkeys;
they also had thirty towns, [b]which are called
"Havoth Jair"[1] to this day, which *are* in the
land of Gilead. 5 And Jair died and was buried
in Camon.

Israel Oppressed Again

6 Then [a]the children of Israel again did evil
in the sight of the LORD, and [b]served the Baals
and the Ashtoreths, [c]the gods of Syria, the
gods of [d]Sidon, the gods of Moab, the gods
of the people of Ammon, and the gods of the
Philistines; and they forsook the LORD and did
not serve Him. 7 So the anger of the LORD was
hot against Israel; and He [a]sold them into the
hands of the [b]Philistines and into the hands
of the people of [c]Ammon. 8 From that year
they harassed and oppressed the children of
Israel for eighteen years—all the children of
Israel who *were* on the other side of the Jordan in the [a]land of the Amorites, in Gilead.
9 Moreover the people of Ammon crossed over
the Jordan to fight against Judah also, against
Benjamin, and against the house of Ephraim,
so that Israel was severely distressed.
10 [a]And the children of Israel cried out to
the LORD, saying, "We have [b]sinned against
You, because we have both forsaken our God
and served the Baals!"
11 So the LORD said to the children of Israel,
"*Did I* not *deliver you* [a]from the Egyptians and
[b]from the Amorites and [c]from the people of
Ammon and [d]from the Philistines? 12 Also
[a]the Sidonians [b]and Amalekites and Maon-
ites[1] [c]oppressed you; and you cried out to Me,
and I delivered you from their hand. 13 [a]Yet
you have forsaken Me and served other gods.
Therefore I will deliver you no more. 14 Go and
[a]cry out to the gods which you have chosen;
let them deliver you in your time of distress."
15 And the children of Israel said to the LORD,
"We have sinned! [a]Do to us whatever seems best
to You; only deliver us this day, we pray." 16 [a]So
they put away the foreign gods from among
them and served the LORD. And [b]His soul could
no longer endure the misery of Israel.
17 Then the people of Ammon gathered
together and encamped in Gilead. And the
children of Israel assembled together and
encamped in [a]Mizpah. 18 And the people, the
leaders of Gilead, said to one another, "Who
is the man who will begin the fight against
the people of Ammon? He shall [a]be head over
all the inhabitants of Gilead."

Jephthah

11 Now [a]Jephthah the Gileadite was [b]a
mighty man of valor, but he *was* the
son of a harlot; and Gilead begot Jephthah.
2 Gilead's wife bore sons; and when his wife's
sons grew up, they drove Jephthah out, and
said to him, "You shall have [a]no inheritance
in our father's house, for you *are* the son of

9:54 [a] 1 Sam. 31:4 **9:56** [a] Job 31:3 **9:57** [a] Judg. 9:20 **10:1** [a] Judg. 2:16 **10:4** [a] Judg. 5:10; 12:14 [b] Deut. 3:14 [1] Literally *Towns of Jair* (compare Numbers 32:41 and Deuteronomy 3:14) **10:6** [a] Judg. 2:11; 3:7; 6:1; 13:1 [b] Judg. 2:13 [c] Judg. 2:12 [d] 1 Kin. 11:33 **10:7** [a] 1 Sam. 12:9 [b] Judg. 13:1 [c] Judg. 3:13 **10:8** [a] Num. 32:33 **10:10** [a] 1 Sam. 12:10 [b] Deut. 1:41 **10:11** [a] Ex. 14:30 [b] Num. 21:21, 24, 25 [c] Judg. 3:12, 13 [d] Judg. 3:31 **10:12** [a] Judg. 1:31; 5:19 [b] Judg. 6:3; 7:12 [c] Ps. 106:42, 43 [1] Some Septuagint manuscripts read *Midianites.* **10:13** [a] [Jer. 2:13] **10:14** [a] Deut. 32:37, 38 **10:15** [a] 1 Sam. 3:18 **10:16** [a] Jer. 18:7, 8 [b] Is. 63:9 **10:17** [a] Judg. 11:11, 29 **10:18** [a] Judg. 11:8, 11 **11:1** [a] Heb. 11:32 [b] 2 Kin. 5:1 **11:2** [a] Gen. 21:10

PEACE NOTE

We all skate on emotional thin ice at times. But that doesn't change the objective truth of God's Word. To find peace, change your focus from fear to faith.

another woman." 3 Then Jephthah fled from
his brothers and dwelt in the land of [a]Tob;
and [b]worthless men banded together with
Jephthah and went out *raiding* with him.
4 It came to pass after a time that the [a]people
of Ammon made war against Israel. 5 And so
it was, when the people of Ammon made war
against Israel, that the elders of Gilead went to
get Jephthah from the land of Tob. 6 Then they
said to Jephthah, "Come and be our commander,
that we may fight against the people of Ammon."
7 So Jephthah said to the elders of Gilead,
[a]"Did you not hate me, and expel me from
my father's house? Why have you come to
me now when you are in distress?"
8 [a]And the elders of Gilead said to Jephthah, "That is why we have [b]turned again to
you now, that you may go with us and fight
against the people of Ammon, and be [c]our
head over all the inhabitants of Gilead."
9 So Jephthah said to the elders of Gilead,
"If you take me back home to fight against
the people of Ammon, and the LORD delivers
them to me, shall I be your head?"
10 And the elders of Gilead said to Jephthah,
[a]"The LORD will be a witness between us, if we
do not do according to your words." 11 Then
Jephthah went with the elders of Gilead, and
the people made him [a]head and commander
over them; and Jephthah spoke all his words
[b]before the LORD in Mizpah.
12 Now Jephthah sent messengers to the
king of the people of Ammon, saying, [a]"What
do you have against me, that you have come
to fight against me in my land?"
13 And the king of the people of Ammon
answered the messengers of Jephthah, [a]"Because Israel took away my land when they
came up out of Egypt, from [b]the Arnon as
far as [c]the Jabbok, and to the Jordan. Now
therefore, restore those *lands* peaceably."
14 So Jephthah again sent messengers to
the king of the people of Ammon, 15 and said
to him, "Thus says Jephthah: [a]'Israel did not
take away the land of Moab, nor the land
of the people of Ammon; 16 for when Israel
came up from Egypt, they walked through the
wilderness as far as the Red Sea and [a]came
to Kadesh. 17 Then [a]Israel sent messengers
to the king of Edom, saying, "Please let me
pass through your land." [b]But the king of
Edom would not heed. And in like manner
they sent to the [c]king of Moab, but he would
not *consent*. So Israel [d]remained in Kadesh.
18 And they [a]went along through the wilderness and [b]bypassed the land of Edom and
the land of Moab, came to the east side of the
land of Moab, and encamped on the other
side of the Arnon. But they did not enter the
border of Moab, for the Arnon *was* the border
of Moab. 19 Then [a]Israel sent messengers to
Sihon king of the Amorites, king of Heshbon;
and Israel said to him, "Please [b]let us pass
through your land into our place." 20 [a]But
Sihon did not trust Israel to pass through
his territory. So Sihon gathered all his people
together, encamped in Jahaz, and fought
against Israel. 21 And the LORD God of Israel
[a]delivered Sihon and all his people into the
hand of Israel, and they [b]defeated them. Thus
Israel gained possession of all the land of
the Amorites, who inhabited that country.
22 They took possession of [a]all the territory
of the Amorites, from the Arnon to the Jabbok and from the wilderness to the Jordan.
23 'And now the LORD God of Israel has
dispossessed the Amorites from before His
people Israel; should you then possess it?
24 Will you not possess whatever [a]Chemosh
your god gives you to possess? So whatever
[b]the LORD our God takes possession of before
us, we will possess. 25 And now, *are* you any
better than [a]Balak the son of Zippor, king of
Moab? Did he ever strive against Israel? Did
he ever fight against them? 26 While Israel
dwelt in [a]Heshbon and its villages, in [b]Aroer
and its villages, and in all the cities along the
banks of the Arnon, for three hundred years,
why did you not recover *them* within that

11:3 [a] 2 Sam. 10:6, 8 [b] 1 Sam. 22:2 **11:4** [a] Judg. 10:9, 17 **11:7** [a] Gen. 26:27 **11:8** [a] Judg. 10:18 [b] [Luke 17:4] [c] Judg. 10:18 **11:10** [a] Jer. 29:23; 42:5 **11:11** [a] Judg. 11:8 [b] Judg. 10:17; 20:1 **11:12** [a] 2 Sam. 16:10 **11:13** [a] Num. 21:24–26 [b] Josh. 13:9 [c] Gen. 32:22 **11:15** [a] Deut. 2:9, 19 **11:16** [a] Num. 13:26; 20:1 **11:17** [a] Num. 20:14 [b] Num. 20:14–21 [c] Josh. 24:9 [d] Num. 20:1 **11:18** [a] Deut. 2:9, 18, 19 [b] Num. 21:4 **11:19** [a] Num. 21:21 [b] Deut. 2:27 **11:20** [a] Deut. 2:27 **11:21** [a] Josh. 24:8 [b] Num. 21:24, 25 **11:22** [a] Deut. 2:36, 37 **11:24** [a] Num. 21:29 [b] [Deut. 9:4, 5] **11:25** [a] Num. 22:2 **11:26** [a] Num. 21:25, 26 [b] Deut. 2:36

time? 27 Therefore I have not sinned against you, but you wronged me by fighting against me. May the LORD, [a]the Judge, [b]render judgment this day between the children of Israel and the people of Ammon.' " 28 However, the king of the people of Ammon did not heed the words which Jephthah sent him.

Jephthah's Vow and Victory

29 Then [a]the Spirit of the LORD came upon Jephthah, and he passed through Gilead and Manasseh, and passed through Mizpah of Gilead; and from Mizpah of Gilead he advanced *toward* the people of Ammon. 30 And Jephthah [a]made a vow to the LORD, and said, "If You will indeed deliver the people of Ammon into my hands, 31 then it will be that whatever comes out of the doors of my house to meet me, when I return in peace from the people of Ammon, [a]shall surely be the LORD's, [b]and I will offer it up as a burnt offering."

32 So Jephthah advanced toward the people of Ammon to fight against them, and the LORD delivered them into his hands. 33 And he defeated them from Aroer as far as [a]Minnith—twenty cities—and to Abel Keramim,[1] with a very great slaughter. Thus the people of Ammon were subdued before the children of Israel.

Jephthah's Daughter

34 When Jephthah came to his house at [a]Mizpah, there was [b]his daughter, coming out to meet him with timbrels and dancing; and she *was his* only child. Besides her he had neither son nor daughter. 35 And it came to pass, when he saw her, that he [a]tore his clothes, and said, "Alas, my daughter! You have brought me very low! You are among those who trouble me! For I [b]have given my word to the LORD, and [c]I cannot go back on it."

36 So she said to him, "My father, *if* you have given your word to the LORD, [a]do to me according to what has gone out of your mouth, because [b]the LORD has avenged you of your enemies, the people of Ammon." 37 Then she said to her father, "Let this thing be done for me: let me alone for two months, that I may go and wander on the mountains and bewail my virginity, my friends and I."

38 So he said, "Go." And he sent her away *for* two months; and she went with her friends, and bewailed her virginity on the mountains. 39 And it was so at the end of two months that she returned to her father, and he [a]carried out his vow with her which he had vowed. She knew no man.

And it became a custom in Israel 40 *that* the daughters of Israel went four days each year to lament the daughter of Jephthah the Gileadite.

Jephthah's Conflict with Ephraim

12 Then [a]the men of Ephraim gathered together, crossed over toward Zaphon, and said to Jephthah, "Why did you cross over to fight against the people of Ammon, and did not call us to go with you? We will burn your house down on you with fire!"

2 And Jephthah said to them, "My people and I were in a great struggle with the people of Ammon; and when I called you, you did not deliver me out of their hands. 3 So when I saw that you would not deliver *me,* I [a]took my life in my hands and crossed over against the people of Ammon; and the LORD delivered them into my hand. Why then have you come up to me this day to fight against me?" 4 Now Jephthah gathered together all the men of Gilead and fought against Ephraim. And the men of Gilead defeated Ephraim, because they said, "You Gileadites [a]*are* fugitives of Ephraim among the Ephraimites *and* among the Manassites." 5 The Gileadites seized the [a]fords of the Jordan before the Ephraimites *arrived.* And when *any* Ephraimite who escaped said, "Let me cross over," the men of Gilead would say to him, "*Are* you an Ephraimite?" If he said, "No," 6 then they would say to him, "Then say, [a]'Shibboleth'!" And he would say, "Sibboleth," for he could not pronounce *it* right. Then they would take him and kill him at the fords of the Jordan. There fell at that time forty-two thousand Ephraimites.

7 And Jephthah judged Israel six years. Then Jephthah the Gileadite died and was buried among the cities of Gilead.

Ibzan, Elon, and Abdon

8 After him, Ibzan of Bethlehem judged Israel. 9 He had thirty sons. And he gave away thirty daughters in marriage, and brought in thirty daughters from elsewhere for his sons. He judged Israel seven years. 10 Then Ibzan died and was buried at Bethlehem.

11 After him, Elon the Zebulunite judged Israel. He judged Israel ten years. 12 And Elon the Zebulunite died and was buried at Aijalon in the country of Zebulun.

13 After him, Abdon the son of Hillel the Pirathonite judged Israel. 14 He had forty sons and thirty grandsons, who [a]rode on seventy young donkeys. He judged Israel eight years.

11:27 [a] Gen. 18:25 [b] Gen. 16:5; 31:53 **11:29** [a] Judg. 3:10 **11:30** [a] Gen. 28:20 **11:31** [a] Lev. 27:2, 3, 28 [b] Ps. 66:13 **11:33** [a] Ezek. 27:17 [1] Literally *Plain of Vineyards* **11:34** [a] Judg. 10:17; 11:11 [b] Ex. 15:20 **11:35** [a] Gen. 37:29, 34 [b] Eccl. 5:2, 4, 5 [c] Num. 30:2 **11:36** [a] Num. 30:2 [b] 2 Sam. 18:19, 31 **11:39** [a] Judg. 11:31 **12:1** [a] Judg. 8:1 **12:3** [a] 1 Sam. 19:5; 28:21 **12:4** [a] 1 Sam. 25:10 **12:5** [a] Josh. 22:11 **12:6** [a] Ps. 69:2, 15 **12:14** [a] Judg. 5:10; 10:4

15 Then Abdon the son of Hillel the Pirathonite died and was buried in Pirathon in the
land of Ephraim, [a]in the mountains of the
Amalekites.

The Birth of Samson

13 Again the children of Israel [a]did evil
in the sight of the LORD, and the LORD
delivered them [b]into the hand of the Philistines for forty years.
2 Now there was a certain man from [a]Zorah,
of the family of the Danites, whose name *was*
Manoah; and his wife *was* barren and had
no children. 3 And the [a]Angel of the LORD
appeared to the woman and said to her, "Indeed now, you are barren and have borne no
children, but you shall conceive and bear a
son. 4 Now therefore, please be careful [a]not
to drink wine or *similar* drink, and not to
eat anything unclean. 5 For behold, you shall
conceive and bear a son. And no [a]razor shall
come upon his head, for the child shall be
[b]a Nazirite to God from the womb; and he
shall [c]begin to deliver Israel out of the hand
of the Philistines."
6 So the woman came and told her husband, saying, [a]"A Man of God came to me, and
His [b]countenance *was* like the countenance
of the Angel of God, very awesome; but I [c]did
not ask Him where He *was* from, and He did
not tell me His name. 7 And He said to me,
'Behold, you shall conceive and bear a son.
Now drink no wine or *similar* drink, nor eat
anything unclean, for the child shall be a
Nazirite to God from the womb to the day
of his death.' "
8 Then Manoah prayed to the LORD, and
said, "O my Lord, please let the Man of God
whom You sent come to us again and teach us
what we shall do for the child who will be born."
9 And God listened to the voice of Manoah,
and the Angel of God came to the woman
again as she was sitting in the field; but Manoah her husband *was* not with her. 10 Then
the woman ran in haste and told her husband, and said to him, "Look, the Man who
came to me the *other* day has just now appeared to me!"
11 So Manoah arose and followed his wife.
When he came to the Man, he said to Him,
"Are You the Man who spoke to this woman?"
And He said, "I *am*."
12 Manoah said, "Now let Your words come
to pass! What will be the boy's rule of life,
and his work?"
13 So the Angel of the LORD said to Manoah, "Of all that I said to the woman let her
be careful. 14 She may not eat anything that
comes from the vine, [a]nor may she drink
wine or *similar* drink, nor eat anything
unclean. All that I commanded her let her
observe."
15 Then Manoah said to the Angel of the
LORD, "Please [a]let us detain You, and we will
prepare a young goat for You."
16 And the Angel of the LORD said to Manoah, "Though you detain Me, I will not eat
your food. But if you offer a burnt offering,
you must offer it to the LORD." (For Manoah
did not know He *was* the Angel of the LORD.)
17 Then Manoah said to the Angel of the
LORD, "What *is* Your name, that when Your
words come *to pass* we may honor You?"
18 And the Angel of the LORD said to him,
[a]"Why do you ask My name, seeing it *is* wonderful?"
19 So Manoah took the young goat with the
grain offering, [a]and offered it upon the rock
to the LORD. And He did a wondrous thing
while Manoah and his wife looked on— 20 it
happened as the flame went up toward heav-
en from the altar—the Angel of the LORD
ascended in the flame of the altar! When
Manoah and his wife *saw this,* they [a]fell on
their faces to the ground. 21 When the Angel
of the LORD appeared no more to Manoah
and his wife, [a]then Manoah knew that He
was the Angel of the LORD.
22 And Manoah said to his wife, [a]"We shall
surely die, because we have seen God!"
23 But his wife said to him, "If the LORD had
desired to kill us, He would not have accepted
a burnt offering and a grain offering from
our hands, nor would He have shown us all
these *things,* nor would He have told us *such
things* as these at this time."
24 So the woman bore a son and called his
name [a]Samson; and [b]the child grew, and the
LORD blessed him. 25 [a]And the Spirit of the
LORD began to move upon him at Mahaneh
Dan[1] [b]between Zorah and [c]Eshtaol.

Samson's Philistine Wife

14 Now Samson went down [a]to Timnah,
and [b]saw a woman in Timnah of the
daughters of the Philistines. 2 So he went up
and told his father and mother, saying, "I
have seen a woman in Timnah of the daughters of the Philistines; now therefore, [a]get her
for me as a wife."

12:15 [a] Judg. 3:13, 27; 5:14 13:1 [a] Judg. 2:11 [b] 1 Sam. 12:9 13:2 [a] Josh. 19:41 13:3 [a] Judg. 6:12 13:4 [a] Num. 6:2, 3, 20
13:5 [a] Num. 6:5 [b] Num. 6:2 [c] 1 Sam. 7:13 13:6 [a] Gen. 32:24–30 [b] Matt. 28:3 [c] Judg. 13:17, 18 13:14 [a] Num. 6:3, 4
13:15 [a] Gen. 18:5 13:18 [a] Gen. 32:29 13:19 [a] Judg. 6:19–21 13:20 [a] Ezek. 1:28 13:21 [a] Judg. 6:22 13:22 [a] Deut.
5:26 13:24 [a] Heb. 11:32 [b] 1 Sam. 3:19 13:25 [a] Judg. 3:10 [b] Judg. 18:11 [c] Judg. 16:31 [1] Literally *Camp of Dan* (compare
18:12) 14:1 [a] Josh. 15:10, 57 [b] Gen. 34:2 14:2 [a] Gen. 21:21

PEACE NOTE

The peace of the Lord is a prerequisite for making every decision. Ask the Lord, "What would You have me do or say?" Samson didn't, and he suffered.

JUDGES 14:3

3 Then his father and mother said to him,
"*Is there* no woman among the daughters
of [a]your brethren, or among all my people,
that you must go and get a wife from the
[b]uncircumcised Philistines?"
And Samson said to his father, "Get her
for me, for she pleases me well."
4 But his father and mother did not know that
it was [a]of the LORD—that He was seeking an occasion to move against the Philistines. For at that
time [b]the Philistines had dominion over Israel.
5 So Samson went down to Timnah with his
father and mother, and came to the vineyards
of Timnah.
Now *to his* surprise, a young lion *came*
roaring against him. 6 And [a]the Spirit of the
LORD came mightily upon him, and he tore
the lion apart as one would have torn apart
a young goat, though *he had* nothing in his
hand. But he did not tell his father or his
mother what he had done.
7 Then he went down and talked with the
woman; and she pleased Samson well. 8 After
some time, when he returned to get her, he
turned aside to see the carcass of the lion.
And behold, a swarm of bees and honey *were*
in the carcass of the lion. 9 He took some of it
in his hands and went along, eating. When he
came to his father and mother, he gave *some*
to them, and they also ate. But he did not tell
them that he had taken the honey out of the
[a]carcass of the lion.
10 So his father went down to the woman.
And Samson gave a feast there, for young
men used to do so. 11 And it happened, when
they saw him, that they brought thirty companions to be with him.
12 Then Samson said to them, "Let me [a]pose
a riddle to you. If you can correctly solve
and explain it to me [b]within the seven days
of the feast, then I will give you thirty linen
garments and thirty [c]changes of clothing.
13 But if you cannot explain *it* to me, then
you shall give me thirty linen garments and
thirty changes of clothing."
And they said to him, [a]"Pose your riddle,
that we may hear it."
14 So he said to them:

"Out of the eater came something to eat,
And out of the strong came something
sweet."

Now for three days they could not explain
the riddle.
15 But it came to pass on the seventh[1] day
that they said to Samson's wife, [a]"Entice your
husband, that he may explain the riddle to
us, [b]or else we will burn you and your father's
house with fire. Have you invited us in order
to take what is ours? *Is that* not *so?*"
16 Then Samson's wife wept on him, and
said, [a]"You only hate me! You do not love me!
You have posed a riddle to the sons of my
people, but you have not explained *it* to me."
And he said to her, "Look, I have not explained *it* to my father or my mother; so
should I explain *it* to you?" 17 Now she had
wept on him the seven days while their feast
lasted. And it happened on the seventh day
that he told her, because she pressed him so
much. Then she explained the riddle to the
sons of her people. 18 So the men of the city
said to him on the seventh day before the
sun went down:

"What *is* sweeter than honey?
And what *is* stronger than a lion?"

And he said to them:

"If you had not plowed with my heifer,
You would not have solved my riddle!"

19 Then [a]the Spirit of the LORD came upon
him mightily, and he went down to Ashkelon and killed thirty of their men, took their
apparel, and gave the changes *of clothing* to
those who had explained the riddle. So his
anger was aroused, and he went back up to
his father's house. 20 And Samson's wife [a]was
given to his companion, who had been [b]his
best man.

14:3 [a] Gen. 24:3, 4 [b] Gen. 34:14 **14:4** [a] Josh. 11:20 [b] Deut. 28:48 **14:6** [a] Judg. 3:10 **14:9** [a] Lev. 11:27 **14:12** [a] Ezek. 17:2 [b] Gen. 29:27 [c] 2 Kin. 5:22 **14:13** [a] Ezek. 17:2 **14:15** [a] Judg. 16:5 [b] Judg. 15:6 [1] Following Masoretic Text, Targum, and Vulgate; Septuagint and Syriac read *fourth.* **14:16** [a] Judg. 16:15 **14:19** [a] Judg. 3:10; 13:25 **14:20** [a] Judg. 15:2 [b] John 3:29

Samson Defeats the Philistines

15 After a while, in the time of wheat harvest, it happened that Samson visited his wife with a [a]young goat. And he said, "Let me go in to my wife, into *her* room." But her father would not permit him to go in.

2 Her father said, "I really thought that you thoroughly [a]hated her; therefore I gave her to your companion. *Is* not her younger sister better than she? Please, take her instead."

3 And Samson said to them, "This time I shall be blameless regarding the Philistines if I harm them!" 4 Then Samson went and caught three hundred foxes; and he took torches, turned *the foxes* tail to tail, and put a torch between each pair of tails. 5 When he had set the torches on fire, he let *the foxes* go into the standing grain of the Philistines, and burned up both the shocks and the standing grain, as well as the vineyards *and* olive groves.

6 Then the Philistines said, "Who has done this?"

And they answered, "Samson, the son-in-law of the Timnite, because he has taken his wife and given her to his companion." [a]So the Philistines came up and burned her and her father with fire.

7 Samson said to them, "Since you would do a thing like this, I will surely take revenge on you, and after that I will cease." 8 So he attacked them hip and thigh with a great slaughter; then he went down and dwelt in the cleft of the rock of [a]Etam.

9 Now the Philistines went up, encamped in Judah, and deployed themselves [a]against Lehi. 10 And the men of Judah said, "Why have you come up against us?"

So they answered, "We have come up to arrest Samson, to do to him as he has done to us."

11 Then three thousand men of Judah went down to the cleft of the rock of Etam, and said to Samson, "Do you not know that the Philistines [a]rule over us? What *is* this you have done to us?"

And he said to them, "As they did to me, so I have done to them."

12 But they said to him, "We have come down to arrest you, that we may deliver you into the hand of the Philistines."

Then Samson said to them, "Swear to me that you will not kill me yourselves."

13 So they spoke to him, saying, "No, but we will tie you securely and deliver you into their hand; but we will surely not kill you." And they bound him with two [a]new ropes and brought him up from the rock.

14 When he came to Lehi, the Philistines came shouting against him. Then [a]the Spirit of the LORD came mightily upon him; and the ropes that *were* on his arms became like flax that is burned with fire, and his bonds broke loose from his hands. 15 He found a fresh jawbone of a donkey, reached out his hand and took it, and [a]killed a thousand men with it. 16 Then Samson said:

"With the jawbone of a donkey,
Heaps upon heaps,
With the jawbone of a donkey
I have slain a thousand men!"

17 And so it was, when he had finished speaking, that he threw the jawbone from his hand, and called that place Ramath Lehi.[1]

18 Then he became very thirsty; so he cried out to the LORD and said, [a]"You have given this great deliverance by the hand of Your servant; and now shall I die of thirst and fall into the hand of the uncircumcised?" 19 So God split the hollow place that *is* in Lehi,[1] and water came out, and he drank; and [a]his spirit returned, and he revived. Therefore he called its name En Hakkore,[2] which is in Lehi to this day. 20 And [a]he judged Israel [b]twenty years [c]in the days of the Philistines.

Samson and Delilah

16 Now Samson went to [a]Gaza and saw a harlot there, and went in to her. 2 *When* the Gazites *were told,* "Samson has come here!" they [a]surrounded *the place* and lay in wait for him all night at the gate of the city. They were quiet all night, saying, "In the morning, when it is daylight, we will kill him." 3 And Samson lay *low* till midnight; then he arose at midnight, took hold of the doors of the gate of the city and the two gateposts, pulled them up, bar and all, put *them* on his shoulders, and carried them to the top of the hill that faces Hebron.

4 Afterward it happened that he loved a woman in the Valley of Sorek, whose name *was* Delilah. 5 And the [a]lords of the Philistines came up to her and said to her, [b]"Entice him, and find out where his great strength *lies,* and by what *means* we may overpower him, that we may bind him to afflict him; and every one of us will give you eleven hundred *pieces* of silver."

6 So Delilah said to Samson, "Please tell me where your great strength *lies,* and with what you may be bound to afflict you."

7 And Samson said to her, "If they bind me

15:1 [a] Gen. 38:17 **15:2** [a] Judg. 14:20 **15:6** [a] Judg. 14:15 **15:8** [a] 2 Chr. 11:6 **15:9** [a] Judg. 15:19 **15:11** [a] Judg. 13:1; 14:4 **15:13** [a] Judg. 16:11, 12 **15:14** [a] Judg. 3:10; 14:6 **15:15** [a] Lev. 26:8 **15:17** [1] Literally *Jawbone Height* **15:18** [a] Ps. 3:7 **15:19** [a] Is. 40:29 [1] Literally *Jawbone* (compare verse 14) [2] Literally *Spring of the Caller* **15:20** [a] Judg. 10:2; 12:7–14 [b] Judg. 16:31 [c] Judg. 13:1 **16:1** [a] Josh. 15:47 **16:2** [a] 1 Sam. 23:26 **16:5** [a] Josh. 13:3 [b] Judg. 14:15

with seven fresh bowstrings, not yet dried,
then I shall become weak, and be like any
other man."
8 So the lords of the Philistines brought up
to her seven fresh bowstrings, not yet dried,
and she bound him with them. 9 Now *men*
were lying in wait, staying with her in the
room. And she said to him, "The Philistines
are upon you, Samson!" But he broke the
bowstrings as a strand of yarn breaks when
it touches fire. So the secret of his strength
was not known.
10 Then Delilah said to Samson, "Look,
you have mocked me and told me lies. Now,
please tell me what you may be bound with."
11 So he said to her, "If they bind me securely with [a]new ropes that have never been
used, then I shall become weak, and be like
any *other* man."
12 Therefore Delilah took new ropes and
bound him with them, and said to him, "The
Philistines *are* upon you, Samson!" And *men*
were lying in wait, staying in the room. But
he broke them off his arms like a thread.
13 Delilah said to Samson, "Until now you
have mocked me and told me lies. Tell me
what you may be bound with."
And he said to her, "If you weave the seven
locks of my head into the web of the loom"—
14 So she wove *it* tightly with the batten of
the loom, and said to him, "The Philistines
are upon you, Samson!" But he awoke from
his sleep, and pulled out the batten and the
web from the loom.
15 Then she said to him, [a]"How can you say,
'I love you,' when your heart *is* not with me?
You have mocked me these three times, and
have not told me where your great strength
lies." 16 And it came to pass, when she pestered
him daily with her words and pressed him,
so that his soul was vexed to death, 17 that he
[a]told her all his heart, and said to her, [b]"No
razor has ever come upon my head, for I
have been a Nazirite to God from my mother's
womb. If I am shaven, then my strength will
leave me, and I shall become weak, and be
like any *other* man."
18 When Delilah saw that he had told her all
his heart, she sent and called for the lords of
the Philistines, saying, "Come up once more,
for he has told me all his heart." So the lords
of the Philistines came up to her and brought
the money in their hand. 19 [a]Then she lulled
him to sleep on her knees, and called for a
man and had him shave off the seven locks
of his head. Then she began to torment him,[1]
and his strength left him. 20 And she said,
"The Philistines *are* upon you, Samson!" So
he awoke from his sleep, and said, "I will
go out as before, at other times, and shake
myself free!" But he did not know that the
LORD [a]had departed from him.
21 Then the Philistines took him and put
out his [a]eyes, and brought him down to Gaza.
They bound him with bronze fetters, and he
became a grinder in the prison. 22 However,
the hair of his head began to grow again after
it had been shaven.

Samson Dies with the Philistines

23 Now the lords of the Philistines gathered
together to offer a great sacrifice to [a]Dagon
their god, and to rejoice. And they said:

"Our god has delivered into our hands
Samson our enemy!"

24 When the people saw him, they [a]praised
their god; for they said:

"Our god has delivered into our hands
our enemy,
The destroyer of our land,
And the one who multiplied our dead."

25 So it happened, when their hearts were
[a]merry, that they said, "Call for Samson, that
he may perform for us." So they called for
Samson from the prison, and he performed
for them. And they stationed him between
the pillars. 26 Then Samson said to the lad
who held him by the hand, "Let me feel the
pillars which support the temple, so that I
can lean on them." 27 Now the temple was
full of men and women. All the lords of the
Philistines *were* there—about three thousand men and women on the [a]roof watching
while Samson performed.
28 Then Samson called to the LORD, saying, "O Lord GOD, [a]remember me, I pray!
Strengthen me, I pray, just this once, O God,
that I may with one *blow* take vengeance on
the Philistines for my two eyes!" 29 And Samson took hold of the two middle pillars which
supported the temple, and he braced himself
against them, one on his right and the other
on his left. 30 Then Samson said, "Let me die
with the Philistines!" And he pushed with *all*
his might, and the temple fell on the lords
and all the people who *were* in it. So the dead
that he killed at his death were more than he
had killed in his life.
31 And his brothers and all his father's
household came down and took him, and

16:11 [a] Judg. 15:13 **16:15** [a] Judg. 14:16 **16:17** [a] [Mic. 7:5] [b] Judg. 13:5 **16:19** [a] Prov. 7:26, 27 [1] Following Masoretic Text, Targum, and Vulgate; Septuagint reads *he began to be weak*. **16:20** [a] [Josh. 7:12] **16:21** [a] 2 Kin. 25:7 **16:23** [a] 1 Sam. 5:2 **16:24** [a] Dan. 5:4 **16:25** [a] Judg. 9:27 **16:27** [a] Deut. 22:8 **16:28** [a] Jer. 15:15

brought *him* up and [a]buried him between
Zorah and Eshtaol in the tomb of his father
Manoah. He had judged Israel [b]twenty years.

Micah's Idolatry

17 Now there was a man from the mountains of Ephraim, whose name *was*
[a]Micah. 2 And he said to his mother, "The
eleven hundred *shekels* of silver that were
taken from you, and on which you [a]put a
curse, even saying it in my ears—here *is* the
silver with me; I took it."

And his mother said, [b]"*May you be* blessed
by the LORD, my son!" 3 So when he had returned the eleven hundred *shekels* of silver
to his mother, his mother said, "I had wholly
dedicated the silver from my hand to the
LORD for my son, to [a]make a carved image
and a molded image; now therefore, I will
return it to you." 4 Thus he returned the silver
to his mother. Then his mother [a]took two
hundred *shekels* of silver and gave them to
the silversmith, and he made it into a carved
image and a molded image; and they were
in the house of Micah.

5 The man Micah had a [a]shrine, and made
an [b]ephod and [c]household idols;[1] and he
consecrated one of his sons, who became
his priest. 6 [a]In those days *there was* no king
in Israel; [b]everyone did *what was* right in
his own eyes.

7 Now there was a young man from [a]Bethle-
hem in Judah, of the family of Judah; he *was*
a Levite, and [b]was staying there. 8 The man
departed from the city of Bethlehem in Judah
to stay wherever he could find *a place*. Then
he came to the mountains of Ephraim, to the
house of Micah, as he journeyed. 9 And Micah
said to him, "Where do you come from?"

So he said to him, "I *am* a Levite from
Bethlehem in Judah, and I am on my way
to find *a place* to stay."

10 Micah said to him, "Dwell with me, [a]and
be a [b]father and a priest to me, and I will
give you ten *shekels* of silver per year, a suit
of clothes, and your sustenance." So the Levite went in. 11 Then the Levite was content to
dwell with the man; and the young man became like one of his sons to him. 12 So Micah
[a]consecrated the Levite, and the young man
[b]became his priest, and lived in the house of
Micah. 13 Then Micah said, "Now I know that
the LORD will be good to me, since I have a
Levite as [a]priest!"

The Danites Adopt Micah's Idolatry

18 In [a]those days *there was* no king in
Israel. And in those days [b]the tribe of
the Danites was seeking an inheritance for
itself to dwell in; for until that day *their* inheritance among the tribes of Israel had not
fallen to them. 2 So the children of Dan sent
five men of their family from their territory,
men of valor from [a]Zorah and Eshtaol, [b]to
spy out the land and search it. They said to
them, "Go, search the land." So they went to
the mountains of Ephraim, to the [c]house of
Micah, and lodged there. 3 While they *were*
at the house of Micah, they recognized the
voice of the young Levite. They turned aside
and said to him, "Who brought you here?
What are you doing in this *place?* What do
you have here?"

4 He said to them, "Thus and so Micah did
for me. He has [a]hired me, and I have become
his priest."

5 So they said to him, "Please [a]inquire [b]of
God, that we may know whether the journey
on which we go will be prosperous."

6 And the priest said to them, [a]"Go in peace.
The presence of the LORD *be* with you on
your way."

PEACE NOTE

How do you discover the will of God for your life? Perhaps you have prayed, "Lord, which opportunity shall I pursue?" A clear determiner is the peace of God.

JUDGES 18:6

7 So the five men departed and went to
[a]Laish. They saw the people who *were* there,
[b]how they dwelt safely, in the manner of the
Sidonians, quiet and secure. *There were* no
rulers in the land who might put *them* to
shame for anything. They *were* far from the
[c]Sidonians, and they had no ties with anyone.[1]

16:31 [a] Judg. 13:25 [b] Judg. 15:20 **17:1** [a] Judg. 18:2 **17:2** [a] Lev. 5:1 [b] Gen. 14:19 **17:3** [a] Ex. 20:4, 23; 34:17 **17:4** [a] Is. 46:6 **17:5** [a] Judg. 18:24 [b] Judg. 8:27; 18:14 [c] Gen. 31:19, 30 [1] Hebrew *teraphim* **17:6** [a] Judg. 18:1; 19:1 [b] Deut. 12:8 **17:7** [a] Matt. 2:1, 5, 6 [b] Deut. 18:6 **17:10** [a] Judg. 18:19 [b] Gen. 45:8 **17:12** [a] Judg. 17:5 [b] Judg. 18:30 **17:13** [a] Judg. 18:4 **18:1** [a] Judg. 17:6; 19:1; 21:25 [b] Josh. 19:40–48 **18:2** [a] Judg. 13:25 [b] Num. 13:17 [c] Judg. 17:1 **18:4** [a] Judg. 17:10, 12 **18:5** [a] Hos. 4:12 [b] Judg. 1:1; 17:5; 18:14 **18:6** [a] 1 Kin. 22:6 **18:7** [a] Josh. 19:47 [b] Judg. 18:27–29 [c] Judg. 10:12 [1] Following Masoretic Text, Targum, and Vulgate; Septuagint reads *with Syria*.

8 Then *the spies* came back to their brethren
at [a]Zorah and Eshtaol, and their brethren said
to them, "What *is* your *report?*"
9 So they said, [a]"Arise, let us go up against
them. For we have seen the land, and indeed
it *is* very good. *Would* you [b]*do* nothing? Do not
hesitate to go, *and* enter to possess the land.
10 When you go, you will come to a [a]secure
people and a large land. For God has given
it into your hands, [b]a place where *there is* no
lack of anything that *is* on the earth."
11 And six hundred men of the family of
the Danites went from there, from Zorah and
Eshtaol, armed with weapons of war. 12 Then
they went up and encamped in [a]Kirjath Jearim in Judah. (Therefore they call that place
[b]Mahaneh Dan[1] to this day. There *it is,* west of
Kirjath Jearim.) 13 And they passed from there
to the mountains of Ephraim, and came to
[a]the house of Micah.
14 [a]Then the five men who had gone to spy
out the country of Laish answered and said
to their brethren, "Do you know that [b]there
are in these houses an ephod, household
idols, a carved image, and a molded image?
Now therefore, consider what you should
do." 15 So they turned aside there, and came
to the house of the young Levite man—to the
house of Micah—and greeted him. 16 The [a]six
hundred men armed with their weapons of
war, who *were* of the children of Dan, stood
by the entrance of the gate. 17 Then [a]the five
men who had gone to spy out the land went
up. Entering there, they took [b]the carved
image, the ephod, the household idols, and
the molded image. The priest stood at the
entrance of the gate with the six hundred
men *who were* armed with weapons of war.
18 When these went into Micah's house
and took the carved image, the ephod, the
household idols, and the molded image, the
priest said to them, "What are you doing?"
19 And they said to him, "Be quiet, [a]put
your hand over your mouth, and come with
us; [b]be a father and a priest to us. *Is it* better
for you to be a priest to the household of one
man, or that you be a priest to a tribe and a
family in Israel?" 20 So the priest's heart was
glad; and he took the ephod, the household
idols, and the carved image, and took his
place among the people.
21 Then they turned and departed, and put
the little ones, the livestock, and the goods in
front of them. 22 When they were a good way
from the house of Micah, the men who *were*
in the houses near Micah's house gathered together and overtook the children of Dan. 23 And
they called out to the children of Dan. So they
turned around and said to Micah, [a]"What ails
you, that you have gathered such a company?"
24 So he said, "You have [a]taken away my
gods which I made, and the priest, and you
have gone away. Now what more do I have?
How can you say to me, 'What ails you?' "
25 And the children of Dan said to him, "Do
not let your voice be heard among us, lest
angry men fall upon you, and you lose your
life, with the lives of your household!" 26 Then
the children of Dan went their way. And when
Micah saw that they *were* too strong for him,
he turned and went back to his house.

Danites Settle in Laish

27 So they took *the things* Micah had made,
and the priest who had belonged to him, and
went to Laish, to a people quiet and secure;
[a]and they struck them with the edge of the
sword and burned the city with fire. 28 *There
was* no deliverer, because it *was* [a]far from
Sidon, and they had no ties with anyone. It
was in the valley that belongs [b]to Beth Rehob.
So they rebuilt the city and dwelt there. 29 And
[a]they called the name of the city [b]Dan, after
the name of Dan their father, who was born
to Israel. However, the name of the city formerly *was* Laish.
30 Then the children of Dan set up for
themselves the carved image; and Jonathan
the son of Gershom, the son of Manasseh,[1]
and his sons were priests to the tribe of Dan
[a]until the day of the captivity of the land. 31 So
they set up for themselves Micah's carved
image which he made, [a]all the time that the
house of God was in Shiloh.

The Levite's Concubine

19 And it came to pass in those days,
[a]when *there was* no king in Israel,
that there was a certain Levite staying in
the remote mountains of Ephraim. He took
for himself a concubine from [b]Bethlehem in
Judah. 2 But his concubine played the harlot
against him, and went away from him to her
father's house at Bethlehem in Judah, and
was there four whole months. 3 Then her
husband arose and went after her, to [a]speak
kindly to her *and* bring her back, having his
servant and a couple of donkeys with him.
So she brought him into her father's house;
and when the father of the young woman

18:8 [a] Judg. 18:2 **18:9** [a] Num. 13:30 [b] 1 Kin. 22:3 **18:10** [a] Judg. 18:7, 27 [b] Deut. 8:9 **18:12** [a] Josh. 15:60 [b] Judg. 13:25 [1] Literally *Camp of Dan* **18:13** [a] Judg. 18:2 **18:14** [a] 1 Sam. 14:28 [b] Judg. 17:5 **18:16** [a] Judg. 18:11 **18:17** [a] Judg. 18:2, 14 [b] Judg. 17:4, 5 **18:19** [a] Job 21:5; 29:9; 40:4 [b] Judg. 17:10 **18:23** [a] 2 Kin. 6:28 **18:24** [a] Gen. 31:30 **18:27** [a] Josh. 19:47 **18:28** [a] Judg. 18:7 [b] 2 Sam. 10:6 **18:29** [a] Josh. 19:47 [b] Judg. 20:1 **18:30** [a] 2 Kin. 15:29 [1] Septuagint and Vulgate read *Moses.* **18:31** [a] Josh. 18:1, 8 **19:1** [a] Judg. 17:6; 18:1; 21:25 [b] Judg. 17:7 **19:3** [a] Gen. 34:3; 50:21

saw him, he was glad to meet him. 4 Now
his father-in-law, the young woman's father,
detained him; and he stayed with him three
days. So they ate and drank and lodged there.
5 Then it came to pass on the fourth day
that they arose early in the morning, and
he stood to depart; but the young woman's
father said to his son-in-law, [a]"Refresh your
heart with a morsel of bread, and afterward
go your way."
6 So they sat down, and the two of them ate
and drank together. Then the young woman's
father said to the man, "Please be content
to stay all night, and let your heart be merry." 7 And when the man stood to depart, his
father-in-law urged him; so he lodged there
again. 8 Then he arose early in the morning
on the fifth day to depart, but the young
woman's father said, "Please refresh your
heart." So they delayed until afternoon; and
both of them ate.
9 And when the man stood to depart—
he and his concubine and his servant—his
father-in-law, the young woman's father, said
to him, "Look, the day is now drawing toward
evening; please spend the night. See, the day
is coming to an end; lodge here, that your
heart may be merry. Tomorrow go your way
early, so that you may get home."
10 However, the man was not willing to
spend that night; so he rose and departed,
and came opposite [a]Jebus (that *is,* Jerusalem). With him were the two saddled donkeys; his concubine *was* also with him. 11 They
were near Jebus, and the day was far spent;
and the servant said to his master, "Come,
please, and let us turn aside into this city [a]of
the Jebusites and lodge in it."
12 But his master said to him, "We will not
turn aside here into a city of foreigners, who
are not of the children of Israel; we will go
on [a]to Gibeah." 13 So he said to his servant,
"Come, let us draw near to one of these places,
and spend the night in Gibeah or in [a]Ramah."
14 And they passed by and went their way; and
the sun went down on them near Gibeah,
which belongs to Benjamin. 15 They turned
aside there to go in to lodge in Gibeah. And
when he went in, he sat down in the open
square of the city, for no one would [a]take
them into *his* house to spend the night.
16 Just then an old man came in from [a]his
work in the field at evening, who also *was*
from the mountains of Ephraim; he was staying in Gibeah, whereas the men of the place
were Benjamites. 17 And when he raised his
eyes, he saw the traveler in the open square
of the city; and the old man said, "Where are
you going, and where do you come from?"
18 So he said to him, "We *are* passing from
Bethlehem in Judah toward the remote
mountains of Ephraim; I *am* from there.
I went to Bethlehem in Judah; *now* I am
going to [a]the house of the LORD. But there
is no one who will take me into his house,
19 although we have both straw and fodder
for our donkeys, and bread and wine for
myself, for your female servant, and for the
young man *who is* with your servant; *there*
is no lack of anything."
20 And the old man said, [a]"Peace *be* with
you! However, *let* all your needs *be* my responsibility; [b]only do not spend the night
in the open square." 21 [a]So he brought him
into his house, and gave fodder to the donkeys. [b]And they washed their feet, and ate
and drank.

Gibeah's Crime

22 As they were [a]enjoying themselves, suddenly [b]certain men of the city, [c]perverted
men,[1] surrounded the house *and* beat on
the door. They spoke to the master of the
house, the old man, saying, [d]"Bring out the
man who came to your house, that we may
know him *carnally!*"
23 But [a]the man, the master of the house,
went out to them and said to them, "No, my
brethren! I beg you, do not act *so* wickedly!
Seeing this man has come into my house, [b]do
not commit this outrage. 24 [a]Look, *here is* my
virgin daughter and *the man's*[1] concubine;
let me bring them out now. [b]Humble them,
and do with them as you please; but to this
man do not do such a vile thing!" 25 But the
men would not heed him. So the man took
his concubine and brought *her* out to them.
And they [a]knew her and abused her all night
until morning; and when the day began to
break, they let her go.
26 Then the woman came as the day was
dawning, and fell down at the door of the
man's house where her master *was,* till it
was light.
27 When her master arose in the morning,
and opened the doors of the house and went
out to go his way, there was his concubine,
fallen *at* the door of the house with her hands
on the threshold. 28 And he said to her, "Get
up and let us be going." But [a]there was no answer. So the man lifted her onto the donkey;
and the man got up and went to his place.

19:5 [a] Gen. 18:5 **19:10** [a] 1 Chr. 11:4, 5 **19:11** [a] Josh. 15:8, 63 **19:12** [a] Josh. 18:28 **19:13** [a] Josh. 18:25 **19:15** [a] Matt. 25:43 **19:16** [a] Ps. 104:23 **19:18** [a] Josh. 18:1 **19:20** [a] Gen. 43:23 [b] Gen. 19:2 **19:21** [a] Gen. 24:32; 43:24 [b] John 13:5 **19:22** [a] Judg. 16:25; 19:6, 9 [b] Hos. 9:9; 10:9 [c] Deut. 13:13 [d] [Rom. 1:26, 27] [1] Literally *sons of Belial* **19:23** [a] Gen. 19:6, 7 [b] 2 Sam. 13:12 **19:24** [a] Gen. 19:8 [b] Gen. 34:2 [1] Literally *his* **19:25** [a] Gen. 4:1 **19:28** [a] Judg. 20:5

29 When he entered his house he took a
knife, laid hold of his concubine, and [a]divided
her into twelve pieces, limb by limb,[1] and sent
her throughout all the territory of Israel.
30 And so it was that all who saw it said, "No
such deed has been done or seen from the
day that the children of Israel came up from
the land of Egypt until this day. Consider it,
[a]confer, and speak up!"

Israel's War with the Benjamites

20 So [a]all the children of Israel came out,
from [b]Dan to [c]Beersheba, as well as
from the land of Gilead, and the congregation gathered together as one man before
the LORD [d]at Mizpah. 2 And the leaders of all
the people, all the tribes of Israel, presented
themselves in the assembly of the people of
God, four hundred thousand foot soldiers
[a]who drew the sword. 3 (Now the children of
Benjamin heard that the children of Israel
had gone up to Mizpah.)

Then the children of Israel said, "Tell *us*,
how did this wicked deed happen?"

4 So the Levite, the husband of the woman
who was murdered, answered and said, "My
concubine and [a]I went into Gibeah, which
belongs to Benjamin, to spend the night.
5 [a]And the men of Gibeah rose against me,
and surrounded the house at night because
of me. They intended to kill me, [b]but instead
they ravished my concubine so that she died.
6 So [a]I took hold of my concubine, cut her in
pieces, and sent her throughout all the territory of the inheritance of Israel, because they
[b]committed lewdness and outrage in Israel.
7 Look! All of you *are* children of Israel; [a]give
your advice and counsel here and now!"

8 So all the people arose as one man, saying,
"None *of us* will go to his tent, nor will any
turn back to his house; 9 but now this *is* the
thing which we will do to Gibeah: *We will go
up* [a]against it by lot. 10 We will take ten men
out of *every* hundred throughout all the tribes
of Israel, a hundred out of *every* thousand,
and a thousand out of *every* ten thousand, to
make provisions for the people, that when
they come to Gibeah in Benjamin, they may
repay all the vileness that they have done in
Israel." 11 So all the men of Israel were gathered
against the city, united together as one man.

12 [a]Then the tribes of Israel sent men through
all the tribe of Benjamin, saying, "What *is* this
wickedness that has occurred among you?
13 Now therefore, deliver up the men, [a]the

PEACE NOTE

God wants us to experience joy and peace, and that's what we feel when our faith in God is guided by the facts of Scripture.

perverted men[1] who *are* in Gibeah, that we
may put them to death and [b]remove the evil
from Israel!" But the children of Benjamin
would not listen to the voice of their brethren,
the children of Israel. 14 Instead, the children of
Benjamin gathered together from their cities
to Gibeah, to go to battle against the children of
Israel. 15 And from their cities at that time [a]the
children of Benjamin numbered twenty-six
thousand men who drew the sword, besides
the inhabitants of Gibeah, who numbered
seven hundred select men. 16 Among all this
people *were* seven hundred select men *who
were* [a]left-handed; every one could sling a
stone at a hair's *breadth* and not miss. 17 Now
besides Benjamin, the men of Israel numbered
four hundred thousand men who drew the
sword; all of these *were* men of war.

18 Then the children of Israel arose and
[a]went up to the house of God[1] to [b]inquire of
God. They said, "Which of us shall go up first
to battle against the children of Benjamin?"

The LORD said, [c]"Judah first!"

19 So the children of Israel rose in the
morning and encamped against Gibeah.
20 And the men of Israel went out to battle
against Benjamin, and the men of Israel put
themselves in battle array to fight against
them at Gibeah. 21 Then [a]the children of Benjamin came out of Gibeah, and on that day
cut down to the ground twenty-two thousand
men of the Israelites. 22 And the people, that
is, the men of Israel, encouraged themselves
and again formed the battle line at the place
where they had put themselves in array on
the first day. 23 [a]Then the children of Israel

19:29 [a] 1 Sam. 11:7 [1] Literally *with her bones* **19:30** [a] Judg. 20:7 **20:1** [a] Josh. 22:12 [b] 2 Sam. 3:10; 24:2 [c] Josh. 19:2 [d] 1 Sam. 7:5 **20:2** [a] Judg. 8:10 **20:4** [a] Judg. 19:15 **20:5** [a] Judg. 19:22 [b] Judg. 19:25, 26 **20:6** [a] Judg. 19:29 [b] Josh. 7:15 **20:7** [a] Judg. 19:30 **20:9** [a] Judg. 1:3 **20:12** [a] Deut. 13:14 **20:13** [a] Deut. 13:13 [b] Deut. 17:12 [1] Literally *sons of Belial* **20:15** [a] Num. 1:36, 37; 2:23; 26:41 **20:16** [a] 1 Chr. 12:2 **20:18** [a] Judg. 20:23, 26 [b] Num. 27:21 [c] Judg. 1:1, 2 [1] Or *Bethel* **20:21** [a] [Gen. 49:27] **20:23** [a] Judg. 20:26, 27

went up and wept before the LORD until evening, and asked counsel of the LORD, saying, "Shall I again draw near for battle against the children of my brother Benjamin?"

And the LORD said, "Go up against him."

24 So the children of Israel approached the children of Benjamin on the second day. 25 And [a]Benjamin went out against them from Gibeah on the second day, and cut down to the ground eighteen thousand more of the children of Israel; all these drew the sword.

26 Then all the children of Israel, that is, all the people, [a]went up and came to the house of God[1] and wept. They sat there before the LORD and fasted that day until evening; and they offered burnt offerings and peace offerings before the LORD. 27 So the children of Israel inquired of the LORD ([a]the ark of the covenant of God *was* there in those days, 28 [a]and Phinehas the son of Eleazar, the son of Aaron, [b]stood before it in those days), saying, "Shall I yet again go out to battle against the children of my brother Benjamin, or shall I cease?"

And the LORD said, "Go up, for tomorrow I will deliver them into your hand."

29 Then Israel [a]set men in ambush all around Gibeah. 30 And the children of Israel went up against the children of Benjamin on the third day, and put themselves in battle array against Gibeah as at the other times. 31 So the children of Benjamin went out against the people, *and* were drawn away from the city. They began to strike down *and* kill some of the people, as at the other times, in the highways [a](one of which goes up to Bethel and the other to Gibeah) and in the field, about thirty men of Israel. 32 And the children of Benjamin said, "They *are* defeated before us, as at first."

But the children of Israel said, "Let us flee and draw them away from the city to the highways." 33 So all the men of Israel rose from their place and put themselves in battle array at Baal Tamar. Then Israel's men in ambush burst forth from their position in the plain of Geba. 34 And ten thousand select men from all Israel came against Gibeah, and the battle was fierce. [a]But *the Benjamites*[1] did not know that disaster *was* upon them. 35 The LORD defeated Benjamin before Israel. And the children of Israel destroyed that day twenty-five thousand one hundred Benjamites; all these drew the sword.

36 So the children of Benjamin saw that they were defeated. [a]The men of Israel had given ground to the Benjamites, because they relied on the men in ambush whom they had set against Gibeah. 37 [a]And the men in ambush quickly rushed upon Gibeah; the men in ambush spread out and struck the whole city with the edge of the sword. 38 Now the appointed signal between the men of Israel and the men in ambush was that they would make a great cloud of [a]smoke rise up from the city, 39 whereupon the men of Israel would turn in battle. Now Benjamin had begun to strike *and* kill about thirty of the men of Israel. For they said, "Surely they are defeated before us, as *in* the first battle." 40 But when the cloud began to rise from the city in a column of smoke, the Benjamites [a]looked behind them, and there was the whole city going up *in smoke* to heaven. 41 And when the men of Israel turned back, the men of Benjamin panicked, for they saw that disaster had come upon them. 42 Therefore they turned *their backs* before the men of Israel in the direction of the wilderness; but the battle overtook them, and whoever *came* out of the cities they destroyed in their midst. 43 They surrounded the Benjamites, chased them, *and* easily trampled them down as far as the front of Gibeah toward the east. 44 And eighteen thousand men of Benjamin fell; all these *were* men of valor. 45 Then they[1] turned and fled toward the wilderness to the rock of [a]Rimmon; and they cut down five thousand of them on the highways. Then they pursued them relentlessly up to Gidom, and killed two thousand of them. 46 So all who fell of Benjamin that day were twenty-five thousand men who drew the sword; all these *were* men of valor.

47 [a]But six hundred men turned and fled toward the wilderness to the rock of Rimmon, and they stayed at the rock of Rimmon for four months. 48 And the men of Israel turned back against the children of Benjamin, and struck them down with the edge of the sword—from *every* city, men and beasts, all who were found. They also set fire to all the cities they came to.

Wives Provided for the Benjamites

21 Now [a]the men of Israel had sworn an oath at Mizpah, saying, "None of us shall give his daughter to Benjamin as a wife." 2 Then the people came [a]to the house of God,[1] and remained there before God till evening. They lifted up their voices and wept bitterly, 3 and said, "O LORD God of Israel, why has this come to pass in Israel, that today there should be one tribe *missing* in Israel?"

20:25 [a] Judg. 20:21 **20:26** [a] Judg. 20:18, 23; 21:2 [1] Or *Bethel* **20:27** [a] Josh. 18:1 **20:28** [a] Josh. 24:33 [b] Deut. 10:8; 18:5 **20:29** [a] Josh. 8:4 **20:31** [a] Judg. 21:19 **20:34** [a] Josh. 8:14 [1] Literally *they* **20:36** [a] Josh. 8:15 **20:37** [a] Josh. 8:19 **20:38** [a] Josh. 8:20 **20:40** [a] Josh. 8:20 **20:45** [a] Josh. 15:32 [1] Septuagint reads *the rest.* **20:47** [a] Judg. 21:13 **21:1** [a] Judg. 20:1 **21:2** [a] Judg. 20:18, 26 [1] Or *Bethel*

4 So it was, on the next morning, that the people rose early and [a]built an altar there, and offered burnt offerings and peace offerings. 5 The children of Israel said, "Who *is there* among all the tribes of Israel who did not come up with the assembly to the LORD?" [a]For they had made a great oath concerning anyone who had not come up to the LORD at Mizpah, saying, "He shall surely be put to death." 6 And the children of Israel grieved for Benjamin their brother, and said, "One tribe is cut off from Israel today. 7 What shall we do for wives for those who remain, seeing we have sworn by the LORD that we will not give them our daughters as wives?"

8 And they said, "What one *is there* from the tribes of Israel who did not come up to Mizpah to the LORD?" And, in fact, no one had come to the camp from [a]Jabesh Gilead to the assembly. 9 For when the people were counted, indeed, not one of the inhabitants of Jabesh Gilead *was* there. 10 So the congregation sent out there twelve thousand of their most valiant men, and commanded them, saying, [a]"Go and strike the inhabitants of Jabesh Gilead with the edge of the sword, including the women and children. 11 And this *is* the thing that you shall do: [a]You shall utterly destroy every male, and every woman who has known a man intimately." 12 So they found among the inhabitants of Jabesh Gilead four hundred young virgins who had not known a man intimately; and they brought them to the camp at [a]Shiloh, which is in the land of Canaan.

13 Then the whole congregation sent *word* to the children of Benjamin [a]who *were* at the rock of Rimmon, and announced peace to them. 14 So Benjamin came back at that time, and they gave them the women whom they had saved alive of the women of Jabesh Gilead; and yet they had not found enough for them.

15 And the people [a]grieved for Benjamin, because the LORD had made a void in the tribes of Israel.

16 Then the elders of the congregation said, "What shall we do for wives for those who remain, since the women of Benjamin have been destroyed?" 17 And they said, "*There must be* an inheritance for the survivors of Benjamin, that a tribe may not be destroyed from Israel. 18 However, we cannot give them wives from our daughters, [a]for the children of Israel have sworn an oath, saying, 'Cursed *be* the one who gives a wife to Benjamin.' " 19 Then they said, "In fact, *there is* a yearly [a]feast of the LORD in [b]Shiloh, which *is* north of Bethel, on the east side of the [c]highway that goes up from Bethel to Shechem, and south of Lebonah."

20 Therefore they instructed the children of Benjamin, saying, "Go, lie in wait in the vineyards, 21 and watch; and just when the daughters of Shiloh come out [a]to perform their dances, then come out from the vineyards, and every man catch a wife for himself from the daughters of Shiloh; then go to the land of Benjamin. 22 Then it shall be, when their fathers or their brothers come to us to complain, that we will say to them, 'Be kind to them for our sakes, because we did not take a wife for any of them in the war; for *it is* not *as though* you have given the *women* to them at this time, making yourselves guilty of your oath.' "

23 And the children of Benjamin did so; they took enough wives for their number from those who danced, whom they caught. Then they went and returned to their inheritance, and they [a]rebuilt the cities and dwelt in them. 24 So the children of Israel departed from there at that time, every man to his tribe and family; they went out from there, every man to his inheritance.

25 [a]In those days *there was* no king in Israel; [b]everyone did *what was* right in his own eyes.

21:4 [a] 2 Sam. 24:25 21:5 [a] Judg. 20:1–3 21:8 [a] 1 Sam. 11:1; 31:11 21:10 [a] Num. 31:17 21:11 [a] Num. 31:17 21:12 [a] Josh. 18:1 21:13 [a] Judg. 20:47 21:15 [a] Judg. 21:6 21:18 [a] Judg. 11:35; 21:1 21:19 [a] Lev. 23:2 [b] 1 Sam. 1:3 [c] Judg. 20:31 21:21 [a] Judg. 11:34 21:23 [a] Judg. 20:48 21:25 [a] Judg. 17:6; 18:1; 19:1 [b] Judg. 17:6

THE BOOK OF RUTH

AUTHOR

The Book of Ruth provides a cameo of the other side of the biblical story—the godly remnant who remained true to the laws of God. Although the author of Ruth is not given anywhere in the book, the anonymity should not detract from its spiritual value or literary beauty. Tradition has attributed the writing of Ruth to Samuel, but this is difficult to reconcile with the mention of David when Samuel died before David was installed as king.

TIME

During the time of the judges

KEY VERSE

Ruth 1:16

THEME

Ruth is a simple yet intriguing short story. Throughout the story, the characters develop and eventually exhibit wisdom, loyalty, and obedience to God and the customs of the day. We see an interesting romance bloom out of most unusual circumstances. It provides a platform for some profound understanding of God's covenant plans with His people, Israel. We see the details of His plan unfold in the lives of a widow, her foreign-born daughter-in-law, and a distant relative. We also see the lineage of David and Christ established and blessed.

Ruth's name in Hebrew means "friendship," and in God's providential protection she was the great-grandmother of King David. She is included in Matthew's messianic genealogy of Jesus (Matt. 1:5). Though the Hebrew verb for "bring peace" occurs only once in this short book (it's translated "repay" in Ruth 2:12), the verse is powerful, and Ruth's life is emblematic of living in the peace of God amid great adversity. Her heroic, all-encompassing compassion for her mother-in-law, Naomi, is summed up in one statement: "Your people shall be my people, and your God, my God" (1:16). Of Moabite origin yet having embraced the Hebrew God, Ruth lived in a way that was reflective of God's love, peace, and protection.

Elimelech's Family Goes to Moab

1 Now it came to pass, in the days when [a]the
judges ruled, that there was [b]a famine in
the land. And a certain man of [c]Bethlehem,
Judah, went to dwell in the country of [d]Moab,
he and his wife and his two sons. 2 The name
of the man *was* Elimelech, the name of his
wife *was* Naomi, and the names of his two
sons *were* Mahlon and Chilion—[a]Ephrathites
of Bethlehem, Judah. And they went [b]to the
country of Moab and remained there. 3 Then
Elimelech, Naomi's husband, died; and she was
left, and her two sons. 4 Now they took wives of
the women of Moab: the name of the one *was*
Orpah, and the name of the other Ruth. And
they dwelt there about ten years. 5 Then both
Mahlon and Chilion also died; so the woman
survived her two sons and her husband.

Naomi Returns with Ruth

6 Then she arose with her daughters-in-law
that she might return from the country of
Moab, for she had heard in the country of Moab
that the LORD had [a]visited His people by [b]giving
them bread. 7 Therefore she went out from the
place where she was, and her two daughters-
in-law with her; and they went on the way to
return to the land of Judah. 8 And Naomi said
to her two daughters-in-law, [a]"Go, return each
to her mother's house. [b]The LORD deal kindly
with you, as you have dealt [c]with the dead and
with me. 9 The LORD grant that you may find
[a]rest, each in the house of her husband."

So she kissed them, and they lifted up their
voices and wept. 10 And they said to her, "Surely we will return with you to your people."

11 But Naomi said, "Turn back, my daughters; why will you go with me? *Are* there still
sons in my womb, [a]that they may be your
husbands? 12 Turn back, my daughters, go—
for I am too old to have a husband. If I should
say I have hope, *if* I should have a husband
tonight and should also bear sons, 13 would
you wait for them till they were grown? Would
you restrain yourselves from having husbands? No, my daughters; for it grieves me
very much for your sakes that [a]the hand of
the LORD has gone out against me!"

14 Then they lifted up their voices and wept
again; and Orpah kissed her mother-in-law,
but Ruth [a]clung to her.

15 And she said, "Look, your sister-in-law
has gone back to [a]her people and to her gods;
[b]return after your sister-in-law."

16 But Ruth said:

[a]"Entreat me not to leave you,
Or to turn back from following after you;
For wherever you go, I will go;
And wherever you lodge, I will lodge;
[b]Your people *shall be* my people,
And your God, my God.

1:1 [a] Judg. 2:16–18 [b] Gen. 12:10; 26:1 [c] Judg. 17:8 [d] Gen. 19:37 1:2 [a] Gen. 35:19 [b] Judg. 3:30 1:6 [a] Ex. 3:16; 4:31 [b] Matt. 6:11 1:8 [a] Josh. 24:15 [b] 2 Tim. 1:16–18 [c] Ruth 2:20 1:9 [a] Ruth 3:1 1:11 [a] Deut. 25:5 1:13 [a] Judg. 2:15 1:14 [a] [Prov. 17:17] 1:15 [a] Judg. 11:24 [b] Josh. 1:15 1:16 [a] 2 Kin. 2:2, 4, 6 [b] Ruth 2:11, 12

THE FAITH OF A WIDOW

Your people shall be my people, and your God, my God.

RUTH 1:16

Over time, the rabbis came to regard Ruth, the Moabite widow who clung to her Israelite mother-in-law, Naomi, as the model proselyte or convert. I completely agree. The story of Ruth is one of the most inspirational and endearing stories in the Old Testament. For reasons we will never know, Ruth chose to accompany Naomi back to Bethlehem. This meant leaving behind her own family along with their gods. She declared, "Your people shall be my people, and your God, my God."

Perhaps Ruth had come to believe that the God of the people of Israel was real and that the gods of Moab were nothing more than lifeless idols. The irony here is that Ruth's faith in God was greater than Naomi's: bereft of husband and sons, the older woman had become bitter. Ruth's trust—and therefore her peace—in the God of Israel was not crushed by circumstances.

Ruth is included in the messianic line, with King David being her direct descendant. God can use the most unexpected people to bring about His will and His peace. Pray for the faith of Ruth today; pray that you will trust God no matter what and be a conduit of His peace.

17 Where you die, I will die,
And there will I be buried.
[a]The LORD do so to me, and more also,
If *anything but* death parts you and me."
18 [a]When she saw that she was determined
to go with her, she stopped speaking to her.
19 Now the two of them went until they
came to Bethlehem. And it happened, when
they had come to Bethlehem, that [a]all the
city was excited because of them; and the
women said, [b]"*Is* this Naomi?"
20 But she said to them, "Do not call me
Naomi;[1] call me Mara,[2] for the Almighty has
dealt very bitterly with me. 21 I went out full,
[a]and the LORD has brought me home again
empty. Why do you call me Naomi, since
the LORD has testified against me, and the
Almighty has afflicted me?"
22 So Naomi returned, and Ruth the Moabitess her daughter-in-law with her, who
returned from the country of Moab. Now
they came to Bethlehem [a]at the beginning
of barley harvest.

Ruth Meets Boaz

2 There was a [a]relative of Naomi's husband,
a man of great wealth, of the family of
[b]Elimelech. His name *was* [c]Boaz. 2 So Ruth
the Moabitess said to Naomi, "Please let me
go to the [a]field, and glean heads of grain after
him in whose sight I may find favor."
And she said to her, "Go, my daughter."
3 Then she left, and went and gleaned in
the field after the reapers. And she happened
to come to the part of the field *belonging* to
Boaz, who *was* of the family of Elimelech.
4 Now behold, Boaz came from [a]Bethle-
hem, and said to the reapers, [b]"The LORD
be with you!"
And they answered him, "The LORD bless
you!"
5 Then Boaz said to his servant who was in
charge of the reapers, "Whose young woman
is this?"
6 So the servant who was in charge of the
reapers answered and said, "It *is* the young
Moabite woman [a]who came back with Naomi
from the country of Moab. 7 And she said,
'Please let me glean and gather after the
reapers among the sheaves.' So she came
and has continued from morning until now,
though she rested a little in the house."
8 Then Boaz said to Ruth, "You will listen, my
daughter, will you not? Do not go to glean in
another field, nor go from here, but stay close by
my young women. 9 *Let* your eyes *be* on the field
which they reap, and go after them. Have I not
commanded the young men not to touch you?
And when you are thirsty, go to the vessels and
drink from what the young men have drawn."
10 So she [a]fell on her face, bowed down to
the ground, and said to him, "Why have I
found [b]favor in your eyes, that you should
take notice of me, since I *am* a foreigner?"
11 And Boaz answered and said to her, "It has
been fully reported to me, [a]all that you have
done for your mother-in-law since the death
of your husband, and *how* you have left your
father and your mother and the land of your
birth, and have come to a people whom you
did not know before. 12 [a]The LORD repay your
work, and a full reward be given you by the
LORD God of Israel, [b]under whose wings you
have come for refuge."
13 Then she said, [a]"Let me find favor in
your sight, my lord; for you have comforted
me, and have spoken kindly to your maidservant, [b]though I am not like one of your
maidservants."
14 Now Boaz said to her at mealtime, "Come
here, and eat of the bread, and dip your piece
of bread in the vinegar." So she sat beside
the reapers, and he passed parched *grain* to
her; and she ate and [a]was satisfied, and kept
some back. 15 And when she rose up to glean,
Boaz commanded his young men, saying,
"Let her glean even among the sheaves, and
do not reproach her. 16 Also let *grain* from
the bundles fall purposely for her; leave *it*
that she may glean, and do not rebuke her."
17 So she gleaned in the field until evening,
and beat out what she had gleaned, and it
was about an ephah of [a]barley. 18 Then she
took *it* up and went into the city, and her
mother-in-law saw what she had gleaned. So
she brought out and gave to her [a]what she
had kept back after she had been satisfied.
19 And her mother-in-law said to her,
"Where have you gleaned today? And where
did you work? Blessed be the one who [a]took
notice of you."
So she told her mother-in-law with whom
she had worked, and said, "The man's name
with whom I worked today *is* Boaz."
20 Then Naomi said to her daughter-in-law,
[a]"Blessed *be* he of the LORD, who [b]has not
forsaken His kindness to the living and the
dead!" And Naomi said to her, "This man *is* a
relation of ours, [c]one of our close relatives."

1:17 [a] 1 Sam. 3:17 **1:18** [a] Acts 21:14 **1:19** [a] Matt. 21:10 [b] Lam. 2:15 **1:20** [1] Literally *Pleasant* [2] Literally *Bitter*
1:21 [a] Job 1:21 **1:22** [a] 2 Sam. 21:9 **2:1** [a] Ruth 3:2, 12 [b] Ruth 1:2 [c] Ruth 4:21 **2:2** [a] Lev. 19:9, 10; 23:22 **2:4** [a] Ruth 1:1
[b] Ps. 129:7, 8 **2:6** [a] Ruth 1:22 **2:10** [a] 1 Sam. 25:23 [b] 1 Sam. 1:18 **2:11** [a] Ruth 1:14–18 **2:12** [a] 1 Sam. 24:19 [b] Ruth 1:16
2:13 [a] Gen. 33:15 [b] 1 Sam. 25:41 **2:14** [a] Ruth 2:18 **2:17** [a] Ruth 1:22 **2:18** [a] Ruth 2:14 **2:19** [a] [Ps. 41:1] **2:20** [a] 2 Sam.
2:5 [b] Prov. 17:17 [c] Ruth 3:9; 4:4, 6

21 Ruth the Moabitess said, "He also said to
me, 'You shall stay close by my young men
until they have finished all my harvest.' "
22 And Naomi said to Ruth her daughter-
in-law, "*It is* good, my daughter, that you go
out with his young women, and that people
do not meet you in any other field." 23 So
she stayed close by the young women of
Boaz, to glean until the end of barley harvest
and wheat harvest; and she dwelt with her
mother-in-law.

Ruth's Redemption Assured

3 Then Naomi her mother-in-law said
to her, "My daughter, [a]shall I not seek
[b]security for you, that it may be well with
you? 2 Now Boaz, [a]whose young women you
were with, *is he* not our relative? In fact, he
is winnowing barley tonight at the threshing
floor. 3 Therefore wash yourself and [a]anoint
yourself, put on your *best* garment and go
down to the threshing floor; *but* do not make
yourself known to the man until he has finished eating and drinking. 4 Then it shall
be, when he lies down, that you shall notice
the place where he lies; and you shall go in,
uncover his feet, and lie down; and he will
tell you what you should do."
5 And she said to her, "All that you say to
me I will do."
6 So she went down to the threshing
floor and did according to all that her
mother-in-law instructed her. 7 And after
Boaz had eaten and drunk, and [a]his heart
was cheerful, he went to lie down at the end
of the heap of grain; and she came softly,
uncovered his feet, and lay down.
8 Now it happened at midnight that the
man was startled, and turned himself; and
there, a woman was lying at his feet. 9 And
he said, "Who *are* you?"
So she answered, "I *am* Ruth, your maidservant. [a]Take your maidservant under your
wing,[1] for you are [b]a close relative."
10 Then he said, [a]"Blessed *are* you of the
LORD, my daughter! For you have shown
more kindness at the end than [b]at the beginning, in that you did not go after young
men, whether poor or rich. 11 And now, my
daughter, do not fear. I will do for you all that
you request, for all the people of my town
know that you *are* a [a]virtuous woman. 12 Now
it is true that I *am* a [a]close relative; however,
[b]there is a relative closer than I. 13 Stay this
night, and in the morning it shall be *that* if
he will [a]perform the duty of a close relative
for you—good; let him do it. But if he does
not want to perform the duty for you, then I
will perform the duty for you, [b]*as* the LORD
lives! Lie down until morning."

3:1 [a] 1 Tim. 5:8 [b] Ruth 1:9 3:2 [a] Ruth 2:3, 8 3:3 [a] 2 Sam. 14:2 3:7 [a] Judg. 19:6, 9, 22 3:9 [a] Ezek. 16:8 [b] Ruth 2:20; 3:12 [1] Or *Spread the corner of your garment over your maidservant* 3:10 [a] Ruth 2:20 [b] Ruth 1:8 3:11 [a] Prov. 12:4; 31:10–31 3:12 [a] Ruth 3:9 [b] Ruth 4:1 3:13 [a] Deut. 25:5–10 [b] Jer. 4:2; 12:16

FROM KINDNESS SPRINGS PEACE

The LORD repay your work, and a full reward be given you by the LORD God of Israel, under whose wings you have come for refuge.

RUTH 2:12

The root meaning of the Hebrew word *shalom*, "peace," is "fullness" or "completeness." The root of this wonderful word occurs twice in the story of Ruth when Boaz, who had heard of Ruth's faithfulness, said to her, "The LORD repay [*shalem*] your work, and a full [*shallun*] reward be given you by the LORD God of Israel, under whose wings you have come for refuge." I like this guy.

Ruth's faithfulness to her mother-in-law, Naomi, stood out in the ancient world primarily because Ruth was not an Israelite; she was a woman from Moab, an ethnic group that sometimes warred with Israel. From the Israelite point of view, Ruth was a Gentile, and few saw much worth in her. But Boaz did. He saw in Ruth kindness and goodness. He also believed that the God of Israel rewarded those who took shelter under His wings. He prayed that Ruth be given a full reward for her surprising heart, and a full reward would bring with it peace.

Can you bless someone today with your faithfulness, kindness, and goodness? Peace follows that kind of gift!

14 So she lay at his feet until morning, and
she arose before one could recognize another. Then he said, [a]"Do not let it be known
that the woman came to the threshing floor."
15 Also he said, "Bring the shawl that *is* on
you and hold it." And when she held it, he
measured six *ephahs* of barley, and laid *it* on
her. Then she[1] went into the city.
16 When she came to her mother-in-law,
she said, "*Is* that you, my daughter?"
Then she told her all that the man had
done for her. 17 And she said, "These six
ephahs of barley he gave me; for he said
to me, 'Do not go empty-handed to your
mother-in-law.' "
18 Then she said, [a]"Sit still, my daughter,
until you know how the matter will turn out;
for the man will not rest until he has concluded the matter this day."

Boaz Redeems Ruth

4 Now Boaz went up to the gate and sat
down there; and behold, [a]the close relative of whom Boaz had spoken came by.
So Boaz said, "Come aside, friend,[1] sit down
here." So he came aside and sat down. 2 And
he took ten men of [a]the elders of the city, and
said, "Sit down here." So they sat down. 3 Then
he said to the close relative, "Naomi, who has
come back from the country of Moab, sold the
piece of land [a]which *belonged* to our brother
Elimelech. 4 And I thought to inform you,
saying, [a]'Buy *it* back [b]in the presence of the
inhabitants and the elders of my people. If
you will redeem *it,* redeem *it;* but if you[1] will
not redeem *it, then* tell me, that I may know;
[c]for *there is* no one but you to redeem *it,* and
I *am* next after you.' "
And he said, "I will redeem *it.*"
5 Then Boaz said, "On the day you buy the
field from the hand of Naomi, you must also
buy *it* from Ruth the Moabitess, the wife of
the dead, [a]to perpetuate[1] the name of the
dead through his inheritance."
6 [a]And the close relative said, "I cannot redeem *it* for myself, lest I ruin my own inheritance. You redeem my right of redemption
for yourself, for I cannot redeem *it.*"
7 [a]Now this *was the custom* in former
times in Israel concerning redeeming and
exchanging, to confirm anything: one man
took off his sandal and gave *it* to the other,
and this *was* a confirmation in Israel.
8 Therefore the close relative said to Boaz,
"Buy *it* for yourself." So he took off his sandal.
9 And Boaz said to the elders and all the people, "You *are* witnesses this day that I have
bought all that was Elimelech's, and all that

3:14 [a] [1 Cor. 10:32] **3:15** [1] Many Hebrew manuscripts, Syriac, and Vulgate read *she;* Masoretic Text, Septuagint, and Targum read *he.* **3:18** [a] [Ps. 37:3, 5] **4:1** [a] Ruth 3:12 [1] Hebrew *peloni almoni;* literally *so and so* **4:2** [a] 1 Kin. 21:8 **4:3** [a] Lev. 25:25 **4:4** [a] Jer. 32:7, 8 [b] Gen. 23:18 [c] Lev. 25:25 [1] Following many Hebrew manuscripts, Septuagint, Syriac, Targum, and Vulgate; Masoretic Text reads *he.* **4:5** [a] Matt. 22:24 [1] Literally *raise up* **4:6** [a] Ruth 3:12, 13 **4:7** [a] Deut. 25:7–10

LEANING ON ONE ANOTHER

May he be to you a restorer of life . . . for your daughter-in-law, who loves you . . . has borne him.

RUTH 4:15

Ruth's fidelity to her mother-in-law, Naomi, resulted in blessings for all concerned. Because she stayed with Naomi, Ruth, the Moabite widow, found a new husband in Boaz the Israelite. This resulted in the birth of a son, which guaranteed Ruth and Naomi's place in the family of Naomi's new son-in-law.

How can we explain Ruth's loyalty? She must have come to recognize that the God of Elimelech, Naomi, and their two sons was the living God, not one of the idols of the Moabites or other peoples. Somehow she sensed that in the God of Israel she would find salvation. Perhaps she sensed God's peace and so was determined to enter that kingdom in which God ruled. The circumstances were bleak and the future uncertain, but Ruth had made up her mind that the God of Naomi would be her God.

Sometimes we spot peace in someone and are drawn to it. For Ruth, this meant redemption in this life and salvation in the next. Have you ever felt pulled by the peace you see in someone? Why?

was Chilion's and Mahlon's, from the hand
of Naomi. 10 Moreover, Ruth the Moabitess,
the widow of Mahlon, I have acquired as my
wife, to perpetuate the name of the dead
through his inheritance, [a]that the name of
the dead may not be cut off from among his
brethren and from his position at the gate.[1]
You *are* witnesses this day."

11 And all the people who *were* at the gate,
and the elders, said, "*We are* witnesses. [a]The
LORD make the woman who is coming to
your house like Rachel and Leah, the two
who [b]built the house of Israel; and may you
prosper in [c]Ephrathah and be famous in
[d]Bethlehem. 12 May your house be like the
house of [a]Perez, [b]whom Tamar bore to Judah,
because of [c]the offspring which the LORD will
give you from this young woman."

Descendants of Boaz and Ruth

13 So Boaz [a]took Ruth and she became
his wife; and when he went in to her, [b]the
LORD gave her conception, and she bore
a son. 14 Then [a]the women said to Naomi,
"Blessed *be* the LORD, who has not left you
this day without a close relative; and may his
name be famous in Israel! 15 And may he be
to you a restorer of life and a nourisher of
your old age; for your daughter-in-law, who
loves you, who is [a]better to you than seven
sons, has borne him." 16 Then Naomi took
the child and laid him on her bosom, and
became a nurse to him. 17 [a]Also the neighbor
women gave him a name, saying, "There is
a son born to Naomi." And they called his
name Obed. He *is* the father of Jesse, the
father of David.

18 [a]Now this *is* the genealogy of Perez:
[b]Perez begot Hezron; 19 Hezron begot Ram,
and Ram begot Amminadab; 20 Amminadab begot [a]Nahshon, and Nahshon begot
[b]Salmon;[1] 21 Salmon begot Boaz, and Boaz
begot Obed; 22 Obed begot Jesse, and Jesse
begot [a]David.

4:10 [a] Deut. 25:6 [1] Probably his civic office **4:11** [a] Ps. 127:3; 128:3 [b] Gen. 29:25–30 [c] Gen. 35:16–18 [d] Mic. 5:2
4:12 [a] Matt. 1:3 [b] Gen. 38:6–29 [c] 1 Sam. 2:20 **4:13** [a] Ruth 3:11 [b] Gen. 29:31; 33:5 **4:14** [a] Luke 1:58 **4:15** [a] 1 Sam. 1:8
4:17 [a] Luke 1:58 **4:18** [a] 1 Chr. 2:4, 5 [b] Num. 26:20, 21 **4:20** [a] Num. 1:7 [b] Matt. 1:4 [1] Hebrew *Salmah* **4:22** [a] Matt. 1:6

THE FIRST BOOK OF

SAMUEL

AUTHOR

The author of 1 and 2 Samuel is anonymous. Samuel may have written the first portion of the book, but his death recorded in 1 Samuel 25:1 makes it clear that he did not write all of 1 or 2 Samuel. It is very possible that a single compiler, perhaps a member of a prophetic school or group, used the various writings referenced in 1 Chronicles 29:29, including the chronicles of "Nathan the prophet," "Gad the seer," and "Samuel the seer."

TIME

1105–1011 BC

KEY VERSE

1 Samuel 13:14

THEME

First Samuel tells the story of three characters: Samuel, Saul, and David. Saul's story includes being the first in the line of Israel's monarchy. His story ends with the end of 1 Samuel. David's starts in 1 Samuel, goes through 2 Samuel and ends in the first few chapters of 1 Kings. All three of the main characters in this book make mistakes that cost them dearly. Samuel has problems with his own sons. The result is the end of the rule of judges. Saul's life seems to be a classic study in what a poor self-image can do to a person. David's early violence prevents him from being able to build the temple later on when he is king. The far-reaching truth of *shalom* illustrated in 1 Samuel is that God knows each human heart. In fact, God knows us better than we know ourselves: "Man looks at the outward appearance, but the LORD looks at the heart" (16:7). We see how compromise and disobedience stole peace from God's people as illustrated in Saul's disobedience to God's command to destroy the Amalekites (chs. 12–15). The peace of God and obedience to God go hand in hand.

The Family of Elkanah

1 Now there was a certain man of Ramathaim
Zophim, of the [a]mountains of Ephraim, and
his name *was* [b]Elkanah the son of Jeroham, the
son of Elihu,[1] the son of Tohu,[2] the son of Zuph,
[c]an Ephraimite. 2 And he had [a]two wives: the
name of one *was* Hannah, and the name of the
other Peninnah. Peninnah had children, but
Hannah had no children. 3 This man went up
from his city [a]yearly [b]to worship and sacrifice
to the LORD of hosts in [c]Shiloh. Also the two
sons of Eli, Hophni and Phinehas, the priests
of the LORD, *were* there. 4 And whenever the
time came for Elkanah to make an [a]offering,
he would give portions to Peninnah his wife
and to all her sons and daughters. 5 But to
Hannah he would give a double portion, for he
loved Hannah, [a]although the LORD had closed
her womb. 6 And her rival also [a]provoked her
severely, to make her miserable, because the
LORD had closed her womb. 7 So it was, year
by year, when she went up to the house of the
LORD, that she provoked her; therefore she
wept and did not eat.

Hannah's Vow

8 Then Elkanah her husband said to her,
"Hannah, why do you weep? Why do you not
eat? And why is your heart grieved? *Am* I not
[a]better to you than ten sons?"

9 So Hannah arose after they had finished
eating and drinking in Shiloh. Now Eli the
priest was sitting on the seat by the doorpost
of [a]the tabernacle[1] of the LORD. 10 [a]And she
was in bitterness of soul, and prayed to the
LORD and wept in anguish. 11 Then she [a]made
a vow and said, "O LORD of hosts, if You will
indeed [b]look on the affliction of Your maidservant and [c]remember me, and not forget
Your maidservant, but will give Your maidservant a male child, then I will give him to
the LORD all the days of his life, and [d]no razor
shall come upon his head."

12 And it happened, as she continued praying before the LORD, that Eli watched her
mouth. 13 Now Hannah spoke in her heart;
only her lips moved, but her voice was not
heard. Therefore Eli thought she was drunk.
14 So Eli said to her, "How long will you be
drunk? Put your wine away from you!"

15 But Hannah answered and said, "No, my
lord, I *am* a woman of sorrowful spirit. I have
drunk neither wine nor intoxicating drink, but
have [a]poured out my soul before the LORD.
16 Do not consider your maidservant a [a]wick-
ed woman,[1] for out of the abundance of my
complaint and grief I have spoken until now."

17 Then Eli answered and said, [a]"Go in
peace, and [b]the God of Israel grant your petition which you have asked of Him."

1:1 [a] Josh. 17:17, 18; 24:33 [b] 1 Chr. 6:27, 33–38 [c] Ruth 1:2 [1] Spelled *Eliel* in 1 Chronicles 6:34 [2] Spelled *Toah* in 1 Chronicles 6:34 **1:2** [a] Deut. 21:15–17 **1:3** [a] Luke 2:41 [b] Deut. 12:5–7; 16:16 [c] Josh. 18:1 **1:4** [a] Deut. 12:17, 18 **1:5** [a] Gen. 16:1; 30:1, 2 **1:6** [a] Job 24:21 **1:8** [a] Ruth 4:15 **1:9** [a] 1 Sam. 3:3 [1] Hebrew *heykal,* palace or temple **1:10** [a] Job 7:11 **1:11** [a] Num. 30:6–11 [b] Ps. 25:18 [c] Gen. 8:1 [d] Num. 6:5 **1:15** [a] Ps. 42:4; 62:8 **1:16** [a] Deut. 13:13 [1] Literally *daughter of Belial* **1:17** [a] Mark 5:34 [b] Ps. 20:3–5

EVEN BY MUMBLED PRAYERS

Go in peace, and the God of Israel grant your petition which you have asked of Him.

1 SAMUEL 1:17

Hannah was a troubled woman. She had no peace, only sorrow. Unlike her husband's other wife, Hannah had no children. In the culture of the ancient Near East, this failure raised doubts about her worth. Nevertheless her husband treated her with kindness and provided for her. But that was no consolation.

Not knowing what else to do, Hannah went to the house of God and mumbled a prayer. The kindly old priest Eli assured Hannah that "the God of Israel" would grant her request (v. 17). She gave her biggest care to God and "her face was no longer sad" (v. 18). God answered Hannah's prayer and gave her Samuel.

How often do you speak words of peace and faith to others when they are struggling? Peace-filled believers constantly find ways to speak peace to others. Never underestimate how far a prayer, a word of encouragement, or sharing a Bible verse with someone hurting can go. Eli spoke words of faith for Hannah, and she went in peace. We can do the same.

What can you release to God today? How valuable is peace to you right now?

18 And she said, [a]"Let your maidservant
find favor in your sight." So the woman [b]went
her way and ate, and her face was no longer
sad.

Samuel Is Born and Dedicated

19 Then they rose early in the morning and
worshiped before the LORD, and returned
and came to their house at Ramah. And Elkanah [a]knew Hannah his wife, and the LORD
[b]remembered her. 20 So it came to pass in
the process of time that Hannah conceived
and bore a son, and called his name Samuel,[1]
saying, "Because I have asked for him from
the LORD."

21 Now the man Elkanah and all his house
[a]went up to offer to the LORD the yearly sacrifice and his vow. 22 But Hannah did not go
up, for she said to her husband, "*Not* until the
child is weaned; then I will [a]take him, that
he may appear before the LORD and [b]remain
there [c]forever."

23 So [a]Elkanah her husband said to her, "Do
what seems best to you; wait until you have
weaned him. Only let the LORD establish His[1]
word." Then the woman stayed and nursed
her son until she had weaned him.

24 Now when she had weaned him, she
[a]took him up with her, with three bulls,[1]
one ephah of flour, and a skin of wine, and
brought him to [b]the house of the LORD in
Shiloh. And the child *was* young. 25 Then
they slaughtered a bull, and [a]brought the
child to Eli. 26 And she said, "O my lord! [a]As
your soul lives, my lord, I *am* the woman
who stood by you here, praying to the LORD.
27 [a]For this child I prayed, and the LORD
has granted me my petition which I asked
of Him. 28 Therefore I also have lent him
to the LORD; as long as he lives he shall be
lent to the LORD." So they [a]worshiped the
LORD there.

Hannah's Prayer

2 And Hannah [a]prayed and said:

[b]"My heart rejoices in the LORD;
[c]My horn[1] is exalted in the LORD.
I smile at my enemies,
Because I [d]rejoice in Your salvation.

2 "No[a] one is holy like the LORD,
For *there is* [b]none besides You,
Nor *is there* any [c]rock like our God.

3 "Talk no more so very proudly;
[a]Let no arrogance come from your
mouth,
For the LORD *is* the God of [b]knowledge;
And by Him actions are weighed.

1:18 [a] Ruth 2:13 [b] Rom. 15:13 **1:19** [a] Gen. 4:1 [b] Gen. 21:1; 30:22 **1:20** [1] Literally *Heard by God* **1:21** [a] 1 Sam. 1:3 **1:22** [a] Luke 2:22 [b] 1 Sam. 1:11, 28 [c] Ex. 21:6 **1:23** [a] Num. 30:7, 10, 11 [1] Following Masoretic Text, Targum, and Vulgate; Dead Sea Scrolls, Septuagint, and Syriac read *your.* **1:24** [a] Num. 15:9, 10 [b] Josh. 18:1 [1] Dead Sea Scrolls, Septuagint, and Syriac read *a three-year-old bull.* **1:25** [a] Luke 2:22 **1:26** [a] 2 Kin. 2:2, 4, 6; 4:30 **1:27** [a] [Matt. 7:7] **1:28** [a] Gen. 24:26, 52 **2:1** [a] Phil. 4:6 [b] Luke 1:46–55 [c] Ps. 75:10; 89:17, 24; 92:10; 112:9 [d] Ps. 9:14; 13:5; 35:9 [1] That is, strength **2:2** [a] Ex. 15:11 [b] Deut. 4:35 [c] Deut. 32:4, 30, 31 **2:3** [a] Ps. 94:4 [b] 1 Sam. 16:7

PEACE SINGS

My heart rejoices in the LORD.

I SAMUEL 2:1

Hannah, wife of Elkanah, gave birth to a healthy baby boy. She named him Samuel, which means "Heard by God," that is, God had heard her prayer and answered it. When the lad was weaned, she took him to the house of God where, as she had promised, he would live and serve the Lord. Little did Hannah know that she had brought into the world one of the most important figures in the history of Israel, the very man who someday would anoint David as Israel's king.

God had answered her prayer by giving her a son, and she had fulfilled her vow to the Lord by giving her son to the Lord's work. She was so moved by it all that she sang a beautiful song of exaltation (vv. 1–10). Take time like Hannah to artistically memorialize the times in your life God comes through. Hannah sang a lovely hymn to the Lord and lived in the peace of God. Sing about the peace of God in your life. It works!

Prayer for help and mercy + obedience = peace.

4 "The[a] bows of the mighty men *are* broken,
And those who stumbled are girded with strength.
5 *Those who were* full have hired themselves out for bread,
And the hungry have ceased *to hunger.*
Even [a]the barren has borne seven,
And [b]she who has many children has become feeble.

6 "The[a] LORD kills and makes alive;
He brings down to the grave and brings up.
7 The LORD [a]makes poor and makes rich;
[b]He brings low and lifts up.
8 [a]He raises the poor from the dust
And lifts the beggar from the ash heap,
[b]To set *them* among princes
And make them inherit the throne of glory.

[c]"For the pillars of the earth *are* the LORD's,
And He has set the world upon them.
9 [a]He will guard the feet of His saints,
But the [b]wicked shall be silent in darkness.

"For by strength no man shall prevail.
10 The adversaries of the LORD shall be [a]broken in pieces;
[b]From heaven He will thunder against them.
[c]The LORD will judge the ends of the earth.

[d]"He will give [e]strength to His king,
And [f]exalt the horn of His anointed."

11 Then Elkanah went to his house at Ramah.
But the child ministered to the LORD before
Eli the priest.

The Wicked Sons of Eli

12 Now the sons of Eli *were* [a]corrupt;[1] [b]they
did not know the LORD. 13 And the priests' custom with the people *was that* when any man
offered a sacrifice, the priest's servant would
come with a three-pronged fleshhook in his
hand while the meat was boiling. 14 Then he
would thrust *it* into the pan, or kettle, or
caldron, or pot; and the priest would take for
himself all that the fleshhook brought up. So
they did in [a]Shiloh to all the Israelites who
came there. 15 Also, before they [a]burned the
fat, the priest's servant would come and say
to the man who sacrificed, "Give meat for
roasting to the priest, for he will not take
boiled meat from you, but raw."
16 And *if* the man said to him, "They should
really burn the fat first; *then* you may take *as
much* as your heart desires," he would then
answer him, "*No,* but you must give *it* now;
and if not, I will take *it* by force."
17 Therefore the sin of the young men was
very great [a]before the LORD, for men [b]ab-
horred the offering of the LORD.

Samuel's Childhood Ministry

18 [a]But Samuel ministered before the LORD,
even as a child, [b]wearing a linen ephod.
19 Moreover his mother used to make him a
little robe, and bring *it* to him year by year
when she [a]came up with her husband to offer
the yearly sacrifice. 20 And Eli [a]would bless
Elkanah and his wife, and say, "The LORD
give you descendants from this woman for
the loan that was [b]given to the LORD." Then
they would go to their own home.
21 And the LORD [a]visited Hannah, so that
she conceived and bore three sons and two
daughters. Meanwhile the child Samuel
[b]grew before the LORD.

Prophecy Against Eli's Household

22 Now Eli was very old; and he heard everything his sons did to all Israel,[1] and how they
lay with [a]the women who assembled at the
door of the tabernacle of meeting. 23 So he
said to them, "Why do you do such things?
For I hear of your evil dealings from all the
people. 24 No, my sons! For *it is* not a good
report that I hear. You make the LORD's people transgress. 25 If one man sins against
another, [a]God will judge him. But if a man
[b]sins against the LORD, who will intercede
for him?" Nevertheless they did not heed
the voice of their father, [c]because the LORD
desired to kill them.
26 And the child Samuel [a]grew in stature,
and [b]in favor both with the LORD and men.
27 Then a [a]man of God came to Eli and
said to him, "Thus says the LORD: [b]'Did I not
clearly reveal Myself to the house of your
father when they were in Egypt in Pharaoh's

2:4 [a] Ps. 37:15; 46:9 **2:5** [a] Ps. 113:9 [b] Is. 54:1 **2:6** [a] Deut. 32:39 **2:7** [a] Deut. 8:17, 18 [b] Ps. 75:7 **2:8** [a] Luke 1:52 [b] Job 36:7 [c] Job 38:4–6 **2:9** [a] [1 Pet. 1:5] [b] [Rom. 3:19] **2:10** [a] Ps. 2:9 [b] Ps. 18:13, 14 [c] Ps. 96:13; 98:9 [d] [Matt. 28:18] [e] Ps. 21:1, 7 [f] Ps. 89:24 **2:12** [a] Deut. 13:13 [b] Judg. 2:10 [1] Literally *sons of Belial* **2:14** [a] 1 Sam. 1:3 **2:15** [a] Lev. 3:3–5, 16 **2:17** [a] Gen. 6:11 [b] [Mal. 2:7–9] **2:18** [a] 1 Sam. 2:11; 3:1 [b] Ex. 28:4 **2:19** [a] 1 Sam. 1:3, 21 **2:20** [a] Gen. 14:19 [b] 1 Sam. 1:11, 27, 28 **2:21** [a] Gen. 21:1 [b] 1 Sam. 2:26; 3:19–21 **2:22** [a] Ex. 38:8 [1] Following Masoretic Text, Targum, and Vulgate; Dead Sea Scrolls and Septuagint omit the rest of this verse. **2:25** [a] Deut. 1:17; 25:1, 2 [b] Num. 15:30 [c] Josh. 11:20 **2:26** [a] 1 Sam. 2:21 [b] Prov. 3:4 **2:27** [a] 1 Kin. 13:1 [b] Ex. 4:14–16; 12:1

house? 28 Did I not [a]choose him out of all
the tribes of Israel *to be* My priest, to offer
upon My altar, to burn incense, and to wear
an ephod before Me? And [b]did I not give to
the house of your father all the offerings of
the children of Israel made by fire? 29 Why
do you [a]kick at My sacrifice and My offering
which I have commanded *in My* [b]dwelling
place, and honor your sons more than [c]Me,
to make yourselves fat with the best of all the
offerings of Israel My people?' 30 Therefore
the LORD God of Israel says: [a]'I said indeed
that your house and the house of your father
would walk before Me forever.' But now the
LORD says: [b]'Far be it from Me; for those
who honor Me I will honor, and [c]those who
despise Me shall be lightly esteemed. 31 Behold, [a]the days are coming that I will cut off
your arm and the arm of your father's house,
so that there will not be an old man in your
house. 32 And you will see an enemy *in My*
dwelling place, *despite* all the good which
God does for Israel. And there shall not be
[a]an old man in your house forever. 33 But
any of your men *whom* I do not cut off from
My altar shall consume your eyes and grieve
your heart. And all the descendants of your
house shall die in the flower of their age.
34 Now this *shall be* [a]a sign to you that will
come upon your two sons, on Hophni and
Phinehas: [b]in one day they shall die, both
of them. 35 Then [a]I will raise up for Myself a
faithful priest *who* shall do according to what
is in My heart and in My mind. [b]I will build
him a sure house, and he shall walk before
[c]My anointed forever. 36 [a]And it shall come to
pass that everyone who is left in your house
will come *and* bow down to him for a piece of
silver and a morsel of bread, and say, "Please,
put me in one of the priestly positions, that
I may eat a piece of bread." ' "

Samuel's First Prophecy

3 Now [a]the boy Samuel ministered to the
LORD before Eli. And [b]the word of the
LORD was rare in those days; *there was* no
widespread revelation. 2 And it came to pass
at that time, while Eli *was* lying down in his
place, and when his eyes had begun to grow
[a]so dim that he could not see, 3 and before
[a]the lamp of God went out in the tabernacle[1]
of the LORD where the ark of God *was*, and
while Samuel was lying down, 4 that the LORD
called Samuel. And he answered, "Here I
am!" 5 So he ran to Eli and said, "Here I am,
for you called me."

And he said, "I did not call; lie down again."
And he went and lay down.

6 Then the LORD called yet again, "Samuel!"
So Samuel arose and went to Eli, and said,
"Here I am, for you called me." He answered,
"I did not call, my son; lie down again." 7 (Now
Samuel [a]did not yet know the LORD, nor was
the word of the LORD yet revealed to him.)

8 And the LORD called Samuel again the
third time. So he arose and went to Eli, and
said, "Here I am, for you did call me."

Then Eli perceived that the LORD had
called the boy. 9 Therefore Eli said to Samuel, "Go, lie down; and it shall be, if He calls
you, that you must say, [a]'Speak, LORD, for
Your servant hears.' " So Samuel went and
lay down in his place.

10 Now the LORD came and stood and called
as at other times, "Samuel! Samuel!"

And Samuel answered, "Speak, for Your
servant hears."

11 Then the LORD said to Samuel: "Behold,
I will do something in Israel [a]at which both
ears of everyone who hears it will tingle.
12 In that day I will perform against Eli [a]all
that I have spoken concerning his house,
from beginning to end. 13 [a]For I have told
him that I will [b]judge his house forever for
the iniquity which he knows, because [c]his
sons made themselves vile, and he [d]did not
restrain them. 14 And therefore I have sworn
to the house of Eli that the iniquity of Eli's
house [a]shall not be atoned for by sacrifice
or offering forever."

15 So Samuel lay down until morning,[1] and
opened the doors of the house of the LORD.
And Samuel was afraid to tell Eli the vision.
16 Then Eli called Samuel and said, "Samuel,
my son!"

He answered, "Here I am."

17 And he said, "What *is* the word that *the
LORD* spoke to you? Please do not hide *it*
from me. [a]God do so to you, and more also,
if you hide anything from me of all the things
that He said to you." 18 Then Samuel told him
everything, and hid nothing from him. And
he said, [a]"It *is* the LORD. Let Him do what
seems good to Him."

19 So Samuel [a]grew, and [b]the LORD was
with him [c]and let none of his words fall to

2:28 [a] Ex. 28:1, 4 [b] Num. 5:9 **2:29** [a] Deut. 32:15 [b] Deut. 12:5 [c] Matt. 10:37 **2:30** [a] Ex. 29:9 [b] Jer. 18:9, 10 [c] Mal. 2:9–12 **2:31** [a] 1 Kin. 2:27, 35 **2:32** [a] Zech. 8:4 **2:34** [a] 1 Kin. 13:3 [b] 1 Sam. 4:11, 17 **2:35** [a] 1 Kin. 2:35 [b] 1 Kin. 11:38 [c] Ps. 18:50 **2:36** [a] 1 Kin. 2:27 **3:1** [a] 1 Sam. 2:11, 18 [b] Ps. 74:9 **3:2** [a] 1 Sam. 4:15 **3:3** [a] Ex. 27:20, 21 [1] Hebrew *heykal,* palace or temple **3:7** [a] 1 Sam. 2:12 **3:9** [a] 1 Kin. 2:17 **3:11** [a] 2 Kin. 21:12 **3:12** [a] 1 Sam. 2:27–36 **3:13** [a] 1 Sam. 2:29–31 [b] 1 Sam. 2:22 [c] 1 Sam. 2:12, 17, 22 [d] 1 Sam. 2:23, 25 **3:14** [a] Num. 15:30, 31 **3:15** [1] Following Masoretic Text, Targum, and Vulgate; Septuagint adds *and he arose in the morning.* **3:17** [a] Ruth 1:17 **3:18** [a] Is. 39:8 **3:19** [a] 1 Sam. 2:21 [b] Gen. 21:22; 28:15; 39:2, 21, 23 [c] 1 Sam. 9:6

the ground. 20 And all Israel [a]from Dan to Beersheba knew that Samuel *had been* established as a prophet of the LORD. 21 Then the LORD appeared again in Shiloh. For the LORD revealed Himself to Samuel in Shiloh by [a]the word of the LORD.

4 And the word of Samuel came to all Israel.[1]

The Ark of God Captured

Now Israel went out to battle against the Philistines, and encamped beside [a]Ebenezer; and the Philistines encamped in Aphek. 2 Then the [a]Philistines put themselves in battle array against Israel. And when they joined battle, Israel was defeated by the Philistines, who killed about four thousand men of the army in the field. 3 And when the people had come into the camp, the elders of Israel said, "Why has the LORD defeated us today before the Philistines? [a]Let us bring the ark of the covenant of the LORD from Shiloh to us, that when it comes among us it may save us from the hand of our enemies." 4 So the people sent to Shiloh, that they might bring from there the ark of the covenant of the LORD of hosts, [a]who dwells *between* [b]the cherubim. And the [c]two sons of Eli, Hophni and Phinehas, *were* there with the ark of the covenant of God.

5 And when the ark of the covenant of the LORD came into the camp, all Israel shouted so loudly that the earth shook. 6 Now when the Philistines heard the noise of the shout, they said, "What *does* the sound of this great shout in the camp of the Hebrews *mean?*" Then they understood that the ark of the LORD had come into the camp. 7 So the Philistines were afraid, for they said, "God has come into the camp!" And they said, [a]"Woe to us! For such a thing has never happened before. 8 Woe to us! Who will deliver us from the hand of these mighty gods? These *are* the gods who struck the Egyptians with all the plagues in the wilderness. 9 [a]Be strong and conduct yourselves like men, you Philistines, that you do not become servants of the Hebrews, [b]as they have been to you. Conduct yourselves like men, and fight!"

10 So the Philistines fought, and [a]Israel was defeated, and every man fled to his tent. There was a very great slaughter, and there fell of Israel thirty thousand foot soldiers. 11 Also [a]the ark of God was captured; and [b]the two sons of Eli, Hophni and Phinehas, died.

Death of Eli

12 Then a man of Benjamin ran from the battle line the same day, and [a]came to Shiloh with his clothes torn and [b]dirt on his head. 13 Now when he came, there was Eli, sitting on [a]a seat by the wayside watching,[1] for his heart trembled for the ark of God. And when the man came into the city and told *it,* all the city cried out. 14 When Eli heard the noise of the outcry, he said, "What *does* the sound of this tumult *mean?*" And the man came quickly and told Eli. 15 Eli was ninety-eight years old, and [a]his eyes were so dim that he could not see.

16 Then the man said to Eli, "I *am* he who came from the battle. And I fled today from the battle line."

And he said, [a]"What happened, my son?"

17 So the messenger answered and said, "Israel has fled before the Philistines, and there has been a great slaughter among the people. Also your two sons, Hophni and Phinehas, are dead; and the ark of God has been captured."

18 Then it happened, when he made mention of the ark of God, that Eli fell off the seat backward by the side of the gate; and his neck was broken and he died, for the man was old and heavy. And he had judged Israel forty years.

Ichabod

19 Now his daughter-in-law, Phinehas' wife, was with child, *due* to be delivered; and when she heard the news that the ark of God was captured, and that her father-in-law and her husband were dead, she bowed herself and gave birth, for her labor pains came upon her. 20 And about the time of her death [a]the women who stood by her said to her, "Do not fear, for you have borne a son." But she did not answer, nor did she regard *it.* 21 Then she named the child [a]Ichabod,[1] saying, [b]"The glory has departed from Israel!" because the ark of God had been captured and because of her father-in-law and her husband. 22 And she said, "The glory has departed from Israel, for the ark of God has been captured."

The Philistines and the Ark

5 Then the Philistines took the ark of God and brought it [a]from Ebenezer to Ashdod. 2 When the Philistines took the ark of God, they brought it into the house of [a]Dagon[1]

3:20 [a] Judg. 20:1 **3:21** [a] 1 Sam. 3:1, 4 **4:1** [a] 1 Sam. 7:12 [1] Following Masoretic Text and Targum; Septuagint and Vulgate add *And it came to pass in those days that the Philistines gathered themselves together to fight;* Septuagint adds further *against Israel.* **4:2** [a] 1 Sam. 12:9 **4:3** [a] Josh. 6:6–21 **4:4** [a] 1 Sam. 6:2 [b] Num. 7:89 [c] 1 Sam. 2:12 **4:7** [a] Ex. 15:14 **4:9** [a] 1 Cor. 16:13 [b] Judg. 13:1 **4:10** [a] Deut. 28:15, 25 **4:11** [a] Ps. 78:60, 61 [b] 1 Sam. 2:34 **4:12** [a] 2 Sam. 1:2 [b] Josh. 7:6 **4:13** [a] 1 Sam. 1:9; 4:18 [1] Following Masoretic Text and Vulgate; Septuagint reads *beside the gate watching the road.* **4:15** [a] 1 Sam. 3:2 **4:16** [a] 2 Sam. 1:4 **4:20** [a] Gen. 35:16–19 **4:21** [a] 1 Sam. 14:3 [b] Ps. 26:8; 78:61 [1] Literally *Inglorious* **5:1** [a] 1 Sam. 4:1; 7:12 **5:2** [a] 1 Chr. 10:8–10 [1] A Philistine idol

and set it by Dagon. 3 And when the people of Ashdod arose early in the morning, there was Dagon, [a]fallen on its face to the earth before the ark of the LORD. So they took Dagon and [b]set it in its place again. 4 And when they arose early the next morning, there was Dagon, fallen on its face to the ground before the ark of the LORD. [a]The head of Dagon and both the palms of its hands *were* broken off on the threshold; only Dagon's *torso*[1] was left of it. 5 Therefore neither the priests of Dagon nor any who come into Dagon's house [a]tread on the threshold of Dagon in Ashdod to this day.

6 But the [a]hand of the LORD was heavy on the people of Ashdod, and He [b]ravaged them and struck them with [c]tumors,[1] *both* Ashdod and its [d]territory. 7 And when the men of Ashdod saw how *it was,* they said, "The ark of the [a]God of Israel must not remain with us, for His hand is harsh toward us and Dagon our god." 8 Therefore they sent and gathered to themselves all the [a]lords of the Philistines, and said, "What shall we do with the ark of the God of Israel?"

And they answered, "Let the ark of the God of Israel be carried away to [b]Gath." So they carried the ark of the God of Israel away. 9 So it was, after they had carried it away, that [a]the hand of the LORD was against the city with a very great destruction; and He struck the men of the city, both small and great, and tumors broke out on them.

10 Therefore they sent the ark of God to Ekron. So it was, as the ark of God came to Ekron, that the Ekronites cried out, saying, "They have brought the ark of the God of Israel to us, to kill us and our people!" 11 So they sent and gathered together all the lords of the Philistines, and said, "Send away the ark of the God of Israel, and let it go back to its own place, so that it does not kill us and our people." For there was a deadly destruction throughout all the city; the hand of God was very heavy there. 12 And the men who did not die were stricken with the tumors, and the [a]cry of the city went up to heaven.

The Ark Returned to Israel

6 Now the ark of the LORD was in the country of the Philistines seven months. 2 And the Philistines [a]called for the priests and the diviners, saying, "What shall we do with the ark of the LORD? Tell us how we should send it to its place."

3 So they said, "If you send away the ark of the God of Israel, do not send it [a]empty; but by all means return *it* to Him *with* [b]a trespass offering. Then you will be healed, and it will be known to you why His hand is not removed from you."

4 Then they said, "What *is* the trespass offering which we shall return to Him?"

They answered, [a]"Five golden tumors and five golden rats, *according to* the number of the lords of the Philistines. For the same plague *was* on all of you and on your lords. 5 Therefore you shall make images of your tumors and images of your rats that [a]ravage the land, and you shall [b]give glory to the God of Israel; perhaps He will [c]lighten His hand from you, from [d]your gods, and from your land. 6 Why then do you harden your hearts [a]as the Egyptians and Pharaoh hardened their hearts? When He did mighty things among them, [b]did they not let the people go, that they might depart? 7 Now therefore, make [a]a new cart, take two milk cows [b]which have never been yoked, and hitch the cows to the cart; and take their calves home, away from them. 8 Then take the ark of the LORD and set it on the cart; and put [a]the articles of gold which you are returning to Him *as* a trespass offering in a chest by its side. Then send it away, and let it go. 9 And watch: if it goes up the road to its own territory, to [a]Beth Shemesh, *then* He has done us this great evil. But if not, then [b]we shall know that *it is* not His hand *that* struck us—it happened to us by chance."

10 Then the men did so; they took two milk cows and hitched them to the cart, and shut up their calves at home. 11 And they set the ark of the LORD on the cart, and the chest with the gold rats and the images of their tumors. 12 Then the cows headed straight for the road to Beth Shemesh, *and* went along the [a]highway, lowing as they went, and did not turn aside to the right hand or the left. And the lords of the Philistines went after them to the border of Beth Shemesh.

13 Now *the people of* Beth Shemesh *were* reaping their [a]wheat harvest in the valley; and they lifted their eyes and saw the ark, and rejoiced to see *it.* 14 Then the cart came into the field of Joshua of Beth Shemesh, and stood

5:3 [a] Is. 19:1; 46:1, 2 [b] Is. 46:7 **5:4** [a] Mic. 1:7 [1] Following Septuagint, Syriac, Targum, and Vulgate; Masoretic Text reads *Dagon.* **5:5** [a] Zeph. 1:9 **5:6** [a] Ex. 9:3 [b] 1 Sam. 6:5 [c] Deut. 28:27; Ps. 78:66 [d] Josh. 15:46, 47 [1] Probably bubonic plague. Septuagint and Vulgate add here *And in the midst of their land rats sprang up, and there was a great death panic in the city.* **5:7** [a] 1 Sam. 6:5 **5:8** [a] 1 Sam. 6:4 [b] Josh. 11:22 **5:9** [a] Deut. 2:15 **5:12** [a] Jer. 14:2 **6:2** [a] Gen. 41:8 **6:3** [a] Deut. 16:16 [b] Lev. 5:15, 16 **6:4** [a] 1 Sam. 5:6, 9, 12; 6:17 **6:5** [a] 1 Sam. 5:6 [b] Josh. 7:19 [c] 1 Sam. 5:6, 11 [d] 1 Sam. 5:3, 4, 7 **6:6** [a] Ex. 7:13; 8:15; 9:34; 14:17 [b] Ex. 12:31 **6:7** [a] 2 Sam. 6:3 [b] Num. 19:2 **6:8** [a] 1 Sam. 6:4, 5 **6:9** [a] Josh. 15:10; 21:16 [b] 1 Sam. 6:3 **6:12** [a] Num. 20:19 **6:13** [a] 1 Sam. 12:17

there; a large stone *was* there. So they split the wood of the cart and offered the cows as a burnt offering to the LORD. 15 The Levites took down the ark of the LORD and the chest that *was* with it, in which *were* the articles of gold, and put *them* on the large stone. Then the men of Beth Shemesh offered burnt offerings and made sacrifices the same day to the LORD. 16 So when [a]the five lords of the Philistines had seen *it,* they returned to Ekron the same day.

17 [a]These *are* the golden tumors which the Philistines returned *as* a trespass offering to the LORD: one for Ashdod, one for Gaza, one for Ashkelon, one for [b]Gath, one for Ekron; 18 and the golden rats, *according to* the number of all the cities of the Philistines *belonging* to the five lords, *both* fortified cities and country villages, even as far as the large *stone of* Abel on which they set the ark of the LORD, *which stone remains* to this day in the field of Joshua of Beth Shemesh.

19 Then [a]He struck the men of Beth Shemesh, because they had looked into the ark of the LORD. He [b]struck fifty thousand and seventy men[1] of the people, and the people lamented because the LORD had struck the people with a great slaughter.

The Ark at Kirjath Jearim

20 And the men of Beth Shemesh said, [a]"Who is able to stand before this holy LORD God? And to whom shall it go up from us?" 21 So they sent messengers to the inhabitants of [a]Kirjath Jearim, saying, "The Philistines have brought back the ark of the LORD; come down *and* take it up with you."

PEACE NOTE

The men of Beth Shemesh asked, "Who is able to stand before this holy LORD God?" Only Christians can say, "We can because we have peace with God through our Lord Jesus Christ."

1 SAMUEL 6:20

7 Then the men of [a]Kirjath Jearim came and took the ark of the LORD, and brought it into the house of [b]Abinadab on the hill, and [c]consecrated Eleazar his son to keep the ark of the LORD.

Samuel Judges Israel

2 So it was that the ark remained in Kirjath Jearim a long time; it was there twenty years. And all the house of Israel lamented after the LORD.

3 Then Samuel spoke to all the house of Israel, saying, "If you [a]return to the LORD with all your hearts, *then* [b]put away the foreign gods and the [c]Ashtoreths[1] from among you, and [d]prepare your hearts for the LORD, and [e]serve Him only; and He will deliver you from the hand of the Philistines." 4 So the children of Israel put away the [a]Baals and the Ashtoreths,[1] and served the LORD only.

5 And Samuel said, [a]"Gather all Israel to Mizpah, and [b]I will pray to the LORD for you." 6 So they gathered together at Mizpah, [a]drew water, and poured *it* out before the LORD. And they [b]fasted that day, and said there, [c]"We have sinned against the LORD." And Samuel judged the children of Israel at Mizpah.

7 Now when the Philistines heard that the children of Israel had gathered together at Mizpah, the lords of the Philistines went up against Israel. And when the children of Israel heard *of it,* they were afraid of the Philistines. 8 So the children of Israel said to Samuel, [a]"Do not cease to cry out to the LORD our God for us, that He may save us from the hand of the Philistines."

9 And Samuel took a [a]suckling lamb and offered *it as* a whole burnt offering to the LORD. Then [b]Samuel cried out to the LORD for Israel, and the LORD answered him. 10 Now as Samuel was offering up the burnt offering, the Philistines drew near to battle against Israel. [a]But the LORD thundered with a loud thunder upon the Philistines that day, and so confused them that they were overcome before Israel. 11 And the men of Israel went out of Mizpah and pursued the Philistines, and drove them back as far as below Beth Car. 12 Then Samuel [a]took a stone and set *it* up between Mizpah and Shen, and called its name Ebenezer,[1] saying, "Thus far the LORD has helped us."

13 [a]So the Philistines were subdued, and they [b]did not come anymore into the territory of Israel. And the hand of the LORD was

6:16 [a] Josh. 13:3 **6:17** [a] 1 Sam. 6:4 [b] 1 Sam. 5:8 **6:19** [a] Ex. 19:21 [b] 2 Sam. 6:7 [1] Or *He struck seventy men of the people and fifty oxen of a man* **6:20** [a] Mal. 3:2 **6:21** [a] 1 Chr. 13:5, 6 **7:1** [a] 1 Sam. 6:21 [b] 2 Sam. 6:3, 4 [c] Lev. 21:8 **7:3** [a] Deut. 30:2–10 [b] Gen. 35:2 [c] Judg. 2:13 [d] Job 11:13 [e] Luke 4:8 [1] Canaanite goddesses **7:4** [a] Judg. 2:11; 10:16 [1] Canaanite goddesses **7:5** [a] Judg. 10:17; 20:1 [b] 1 Sam. 12:17–19 **7:6** [a] 2 Sam. 14:14 [b] Neh. 9:1, 2 [c] 1 Sam. 12:10 **7:8** [a] Is. 37:4 **7:9** [a] Lev. 22:27 [b] 1 Sam. 12:18 **7:10** [a] 2 Sam. 22:14, 15 **7:12** [a] Josh. 4:9; 24:26 [1] Literally *Stone of Help* **7:13** [a] Judg. 13:1 [b] 1 Sam. 13:5

against the Philistines all the days of Samuel.
14 Then the cities which the Philistines had
taken from Israel were restored to Israel,
from Ekron to Gath; and Israel recovered its
territory from the hands of the Philistines.
Also there was peace between Israel and the
Amorites.
15 And Samuel [a]judged Israel all the days
of his life. 16 He went from year to year on
a circuit to Bethel, Gilgal, and Mizpah, and
judged Israel in all those places. 17 But [a]he
always returned to Ramah, for his home *was*
there. There he judged Israel, and there he
[b]built an altar to the LORD.

Israel Demands a King

8 Now it came to pass when Samuel was [a]old
that he [b]made his [c]sons judges over Israel.
2 The name of his firstborn was Joel, and the
name of his second, Abijah; *they were* judges
in Beersheba. 3 But his sons [a]did not walk in
his ways; they turned aside [b]after dishonest
gain, [c]took bribes, and perverted justice.
4 Then all the elders of Israel gathered together and came to Samuel at Ramah, 5 and
said to him, "Look, you are old, and your sons
do not walk in your ways. Now [a]make us a
king to judge us like all the nations."
6 But the thing [a]displeased Samuel when they
said, "Give us a king to judge us." So Samuel
[b]prayed to the LORD. 7 And the LORD said to Samuel, "Heed the voice of the people in all that they
say to you; for [a]they have not rejected you, but
[b]they have rejected Me, that I should not reign
over them. 8 According to all the works which
they have done since the day that I brought them
up out of Egypt, even to this day—with which
they have forsaken Me and served other gods—
so they are doing to you also. 9 Now therefore,
heed their voice. However, you shall solemnly
forewarn them, and [a]show them the behavior
of the king who will reign over them."
10 So Samuel told all the words of the LORD
to the people who asked him for a king. 11 And
he said, [a]"This will be the behavior of the king
who will reign over you: He will take your
[b]sons and appoint *them* for his own [c]chariots
and *to be* his horsemen, and *some* will run
before his chariots. 12 He will [a]appoint captains over his thousands and captains over
his fifties, *will set some* to plow his ground
and reap his harvest, and *some* to make
his weapons of war and equipment for his
chariots. 13 He will take your daughters *to be*
perfumers, cooks, and bakers. 14 And [a]he will
take the best of your fields, your vineyards,
and your olive groves, and give *them* to his
servants. 15 He will take a tenth of your grain
and your vintage, and give it to his officers
and servants. 16 And he will take your male
servants, your female servants, your finest
young men,[1] and your donkeys, and put *them*
to his work. 17 He will take a tenth of your
sheep. And you will be his servants. 18 And
you will cry out in that day because of your
king whom you have chosen for yourselves,
and the LORD [a]will not hear you in that day."
19 Nevertheless the people [a]refused to obey
the voice of Samuel; and they said, "No, but
we will have a king over us, 20 that we also
may be [a]like all the nations, and that our
king may judge us and go out before us and
fight our battles."
21 And Samuel heard all the words of the
people, and he repeated them in the hearing
of the LORD. 22 So the LORD said to Samuel,
[a]"Heed their voice, and make them a king."
And Samuel said to the men of Israel, "Every man go to his city."

Saul Chosen to Be King

9 There was a man of Benjamin whose
name *was* [a]Kish the son of Abiel, the
son of Zeror, the son of Bechorath, the son
of Aphiah, a Benjamite, a mighty man of
power. 2 And he had a choice and handsome
son whose name *was* Saul. *There was* not
a more handsome person than he among
the children of Israel. [a]From his shoulders
upward *he was* taller than any of the people.
3 Now the donkeys of Kish, Saul's father,
were lost. And Kish said to his son Saul,
"Please take one of the servants with you,
and arise, go and look for the donkeys." 4 So
he passed through the mountains of Ephraim
and through the land of [a]Shalisha, but they
did not find *them*. Then they passed through
the land of Shaalim, and *they were* not *there*.
Then he passed through the land of the Benjamites, but they did not find *them*.
5 When they had come to the land of [a]Zuph,
Saul said to his servant who *was* with him,
"Come, let [b]us return, lest my father cease
caring about the donkeys and become worried about us."
6 And he said to him, "Look now, *there is* in
this city [a]a man of God, and *he is* an honorable
man; [b]all that he says surely comes to pass.
So let us go there; perhaps he can show us
the way that we should go."

7:15 [a] 1 Sam. 12:11 **7:17** [a] 1 Sam. 8:4 [b] Judg. 21:4 **8:1** [a] 1 Sam. 12:2 [b] Deut. 16:18, 19 [c] Judg. 10:4 **8:3** [a] Jer. 22:15–17 [b] Ex. 18:21 [c] Ex. 23:6–8 **8:5** [a] Deut. 17:14, 15 **8:6** [a] 1 Sam. 12:17 [b] 1 Sam. 7:9 **8:7** [a] Ex. 16:8 [b] 1 Sam. 10:19 **8:9** [a] 1 Sam. 8:11–18 **8:11** [a] Deut. 17:14–20 [b] 1 Sam. 14:52 [c] 2 Sam. 15:1 **8:12** [a] 1 Sam. 22:7 **8:14** [a] 1 Kin. 21:7 **8:16** [1] Septuagint reads *cattle*. **8:18** [a] Is. 1:15 **8:19** [a] Jer. 44:16 **8:20** [a] 1 Sam. 8:5 **8:22** [a] Hos. 13:11 **9:1** [a] 1 Chr. 8:33; 9:36–39 **9:2** [a] 1 Sam. 10:23 **9:4** [a] 2 Kin. 4:42 **9:5** [a] 1 Sam. 1:1 [b] 1 Sam. 10:2 **9:6** [a] Deut. 33:1 [b] 1 Sam. 3:19

7 Then Saul said to his servant, "But look, *if* we go, [a]what shall we bring the man? For the bread in our vessels is all gone, and *there is* no present to bring to the man of God. What do we have?"

8 And the servant answered Saul again and said, "Look, I have here at hand one-fourth of a shekel of silver. I will give *that* to the man of God, to tell us our way." 9 (Formerly in Israel, when a man [a]went to inquire of God, he spoke thus: "Come, let us go to the seer"; for *he who is* now *called* a prophet was formerly called [b]a seer.)

10 Then Saul said to his servant, "Well said; come, let us go." So they went to the city where the man of God *was.*

11 As they went up the hill to the city, [a]they met some young women going out to draw water, and said to them, "Is the seer here?"

12 And they answered them and said, "Yes, there he is, just ahead of you. Hurry now; for today he came to this city, because [a]there is a sacrifice of the people today [b]on the high place. 13 As soon as you come into the city, you will surely find him before he goes up to the high place to eat. For the people will not eat until he comes, because he must bless the sacrifice; afterward those who are invited will eat. Now therefore, go up, for about this time you will find him." 14 So they went up to the city. As they were coming into the city, there was Samuel, coming out toward them on his way up to the high place.

15 [a]Now the LORD had told Samuel in his ear the day before Saul came, saying, 16 "Tomorrow about this time [a]I will send you a man from the land of Benjamin, [b]and you shall anoint him commander over My people Israel, that he may save My people from the hand of the Philistines; for I have [c]looked upon My people, because their cry has come to Me."

17 So when Samuel saw Saul, the LORD said to him, [a]"There he is, the man of whom I spoke to you. This one shall reign over My people." 18 Then Saul drew near to Samuel in the gate, and said, "Please tell me, where *is* the seer's house?"

19 Samuel answered Saul and said, "I *am* the seer. Go up before me to the high place, for you shall eat with me today; and tomorrow I will let you go and will tell you all that *is* in your heart. 20 But as for [a]your donkeys that were lost three days ago, do not be anxious about them, for they have been found. And on whom [b]*is* all the desire of Israel? *Is it* not on you and on all your father's house?"

21 And Saul answered and said, [a]"*Am* I not a Benjamite, of the [b]smallest of the tribes of Israel, and [c]my family the least of all the families of the tribe[1] of Benjamin? Why then do you speak like this to me?"

22 Now Samuel took Saul and his servant and brought them into the hall, and had them sit in the place of honor among those who were invited; there *were* about thirty persons. 23 And Samuel said to the cook, "Bring the portion which I gave you, of which I said to you, 'Set it apart.'" 24 So the cook took up [a]the thigh with its upper part and set *it* before Saul. And *Samuel* said, "Here it is, what was kept back. *It* was set apart for you. Eat; for until this time it has been kept for you, since I said I invited the people." So Saul ate with Samuel that day.

25 When they had come down from the high place into the city, *Samuel* spoke with Saul on [a]the top of the house.[1] 26 They arose early; and it was about the dawning of the day that Samuel called to Saul on the top of the house, saying, "Get up, that I may send you on your way." And Saul arose, and both of them went outside, he and Samuel.

Saul Anointed King

27 As they were going down to the outskirts of the city, Samuel said to Saul, "Tell the servant to go on ahead of us." And he went on. "But you stand here awhile, that I may announce to you the word of God."

10 Then [a]Samuel took a flask of oil and poured *it* on his head, [b]and kissed him and said: "*Is it* not because [c]the LORD has anointed you commander over [d]His inheritance?[1] 2 When you have departed from me today, you will find two men by [a]Rachel's tomb in the territory of Benjamin [b]at Zelzah; and they will say to you, 'The donkeys which you went to look for have been found. And now your father has ceased caring about the donkeys and is worrying about [c]you, saying, "What shall I do about my son?"' 3 Then you shall go on forward from there and come to the terebinth tree of Tabor. There three men going up [a]to God at Bethel will meet

9:7 [a] Judg. 6:18; 13:17 **9:9** [a] Gen. 25:22 [b] 2 Kin. 17:13 **9:11** [a] Ex. 2:16 **9:12** [a] Gen. 31:54 [b] 1 Kin. 3:2 **9:15** [a] 1 Sam. 15:1 **9:16** [a] Deut. 17:15 [b] 1 Sam. 10:1 [c] Ex. 2:23–25; 3:7, 9 **9:17** [a] 1 Sam. 16:12 **9:20** [a] 1 Sam. 9:3 [b] 1 Sam. 8:5, 19; 12:13 **9:21** [a] 1 Sam. 15:17 [b] Judg. 20:46–48 [c] Judg. 6:15 [1] Literally *tribes* **9:24** [a] Lev. 7:32, 33 **9:25** [a] Deut. 22:8 [1] Following Masoretic Text and Targum; Septuagint omits *He spoke with Saul on the top of the house;* Septuagint and Vulgate add *And he prepared a bed for Saul on the top of the house, and he slept.* **10:1** [a] 2 Kin. 9:3, 6 [b] Ps. 2:12 [c] Acts 13:21 [d] Deut. 32:9 [1] Following Masoretic Text, Targum, and Vulgate; Septuagint reads *His people Israel; and you shall rule the people of the Lord;* Septuagint and Vulgate add *And you shall deliver His people from the hands of their enemies all around them. And this shall be a sign to you, that God has anointed you to be a prince.* **10:2** [a] Gen. 35:16–20; 48:7 [b] Josh. 18:28 [c] 1 Sam. 9:3–5 **10:3** [a] Gen. 28:22; 35:1, 3, 7

you, one carrying three young goats, another
carrying three loaves of bread, and another
carrying a skin of wine. 4 And they will greet
you and give you two *loaves* of bread, which
you shall receive from their hands. 5 After
that you shall come to the hill of God [a]where
the Philistine garrison *is*. And it will happen,
when you have come there to the city, that
you will meet a group of prophets coming
down [b]from the high place with a stringed
instrument, a tambourine, a flute, and a harp
before them; [c]and they will be prophesying.
6 Then [a]the Spirit of the LORD will come upon
you, and [b]you will prophesy with them and
be turned into another man. 7 And let it be,
when these [a]signs come to you, *that* you do as
the occasion demands; for [b]God *is* with you.
8 You shall go down before me [a]to Gilgal; and
surely I will come down to you to offer burnt
offerings *and* make sacrifices of peace offerings. [b]Seven days you shall wait, till I come
to you and show you what you should do."

PEACE NOTE

Little is much when God is in it! Let the refrain of the passage linger in your mind every night and day: "God is with you." Peace becomes greater with closer proximity to God!

I SAMUEL 10:7

9 So it was, when he had turned his back to
go from Samuel, that God gave him another
heart; and all those signs came to pass that
day. 10 [a]When they came there to the hill, there
was [b]a group of prophets to meet him; then
the Spirit of God came upon him, and he
prophesied among them. 11 And it happened,
when all who knew him formerly saw that
he indeed prophesied among the prophets,
that the people said to one another, "What
is this *that* has come upon the son of Kish?
[a]*Is* Saul also among the prophets?" 12 Then
a man from there answered and said, "But
[a]who *is* their father?" Therefore it became a
proverb: "*Is* Saul also among the prophets?"
13 And when he had finished prophesying, he
went to the high place.
14 Then Saul's [a]uncle said to him and his
servant, "Where did you go?"
So he said, "To look for the donkeys. When
we saw that *they were* nowhere *to be found*,
we went to Samuel."
15 And Saul's uncle said, "Tell me, please,
what Samuel said to you."
16 So Saul said to his uncle, "He told us
plainly that the donkeys had been [a]found."
But about the matter of the kingdom, he did
not tell him what Samuel had said.

Saul Proclaimed King

17 Then Samuel called the people together [a]to
the LORD [b]at Mizpah, 18 and said to the children
of Israel, [a]"Thus says the LORD God of Israel: 'I
brought up Israel out of Egypt, and delivered
you from the hand of the Egyptians *and* from
the hand of all kingdoms and from those who
oppressed you.' 19 [a]But you have today rejected
your God, who Himself saved you from all
your adversities and your tribulations; and
you have said to Him, 'No, set a king over us!'
Now therefore, present yourselves before the
LORD by your tribes and by your clans."[1]
20 And when Samuel had [a]caused all the
tribes of Israel to come near, the tribe of
Benjamin was chosen. 21 When he had caused
the tribe of Benjamin to come near by their
families, the family of Matri was chosen. And
Saul the son of Kish was chosen. But when
they sought him, he could not be found.
22 Therefore they [a]inquired of the LORD further, "Has the man come here yet?"
And the LORD answered, "There he is, hidden among the equipment."
23 So they ran and brought him from there;
and when he stood among the people, [a]he
was taller than any of the people from his
shoulders upward. 24 And Samuel said to
all the people, "Do you see him [a]whom the
LORD has chosen, that *there is* no one like
him among all the people?"
So all the people shouted and said, [b]"Long
live the king!"
25 Then Samuel explained to the people
[a]the behavior of royalty, and wrote *it* in a
book and laid *it* up before the LORD. And
Samuel sent all the people away, every man
to his house. 26 And Saul also went home
[a]to Gibeah; and valiant *men* went with him,

10:5 [a] 1 Sam. 13:2, 3 [b] 1 Sam. 19:12, 20 [c] 2 Kin. 3:15 **10:6** [a] Num. 11:25, 29 [b] 1 Sam. 10:10; 19:23, 24 **10:7** [a] Ex. 4:8 [b] Judg. 6:12 **10:8** [a] 1 Sam. 11:14, 15; 13:8 [b] 1 Sam. 13:8–10 **10:10** [a] 1 Sam. 10:5 [b] 1 Sam. 19:20 **10:11** [a] Matt. 13:54–57 **10:12** [a] John 5:30, 36 **10:14** [a] 1 Sam. 14:50 **10:16** [a] 1 Sam. 9:20 **10:17** [a] Judg. 20:1 [b] 1 Sam. 7:5, 6 **10:18** [a] Judg. 6:8, 9 **10:19** [a] 1 Sam. 8:7, 19; 12:12 [1] Literally *thousands* **10:20** [a] Acts 1:24, 26 **10:22** [a] 1 Sam. 23:2, 4, 10, 11 **10:23** [a] 1 Sam. 9:2 **10:24** [a] 2 Sam. 21:6 [b] 1 Kin. 1:25, 39 **10:25** [a] 1 Sam. 8:11–18 **10:26** [a] Judg. 20:14

whose hearts God had touched. 27 [a]But some
[b]rebels said, "How can this man save us?"
So they despised him, [c]and brought him no
presents. But he held his peace.

Saul Saves Jabesh Gilead

11 Then [a]Nahash the Ammonite came up
and encamped against [b]Jabesh Gilead;
and all the men of Jabesh said to Nahash,
[c]"Make a covenant with us, and we will serve
you."
2 And Nahash the Ammonite answered
them, "On this *condition* I will make *a covenant* with you, that I may put out all your
right eyes, and bring [a]reproach on all Israel."
3 Then the elders of Jabesh said to him,
"Hold off for seven days, that we may send
messengers to all the territory of Israel. And
then, if *there is* no one to save us, we will
come out to you."
4 So the messengers came [a]to Gibeah of
Saul and told the news in the hearing of the
people. And [b]all the people lifted up their
voices and wept. 5 Now there was Saul, coming behind the herd from the field; and Saul
said, "What *troubles* the people, that they
weep?" And they told him the words of the
men of Jabesh. 6 [a]Then the Spirit of God came
upon Saul when he heard this news, and his
anger was greatly aroused. 7 So he took a yoke
of oxen and [a]cut them in pieces, and sent
them throughout all the territory of Israel by
the hands of messengers, saying, [b]"Whoever
does not go out with Saul and Samuel to
battle, so it shall be done to his oxen."
And the fear of the LORD fell on the people,
and they came out with one consent. 8 When
he numbered them in [a]Bezek, the children
[b]of Israel were three hundred thousand, and
the men of Judah thirty thousand. 9 And they
said to the messengers who came, "Thus
you shall say to the men of Jabesh Gilead:
'Tomorrow, by *the time* the sun is hot, you
shall have help.' " Then the messengers came
and reported *it* to the men of Jabesh, and
they were glad. 10 Therefore the men of Jabesh said, "Tomorrow we will come out to
you, and you may do with us whatever seems
good to you."
11 So it was, on the next day, that [a]Saul
put the people [b]in three companies; and
they came into the midst of the camp in the
morning watch, and killed Ammonites until
the heat of the day. And it happened that
those who survived were scattered, so that
no two of them were left together.
12 Then the people said to Samuel, [a]"Who *is*
he who said, 'Shall Saul reign over us?' [b]Bring
the men, that we may put them to death."
13 But Saul said, [a]"Not a man shall be put
to death this day, for today [b]the LORD has
accomplished salvation in Israel."
14 Then Samuel said to the people, "Come,
let us go [a]to Gilgal and renew the kingdom
there." 15 So all the people went to Gilgal, and
there they made Saul king [a]before the LORD
in Gilgal. [b]There they made sacrifices of peace
offerings before the LORD, and there Saul and
all the men of Israel rejoiced greatly.

Samuel's Address at Saul's Coronation

12 Now Samuel said to all Israel: "Indeed I
have heeded [a]your voice in all that you
said to me, and [b]have made a king over you.
2 And now here is the king, [a]walking before
you; [b]and I am old and grayheaded, and look,
my sons *are* with you. I have walked before
you from my childhood to this day. 3 Here I
am. Witness against me before the LORD and
before [a]His anointed: [b]Whose ox have I taken,
or whose donkey have I taken, or whom have
I cheated? Whom have I oppressed, or from
whose hand have I received *any* [c]bribe with
which to [d]blind my eyes? I will restore *it* to you."
4 And they said, [a]"You have not cheated us
or oppressed us, nor have you taken anything
from any man's hand."
5 Then he said to them, "The LORD *is* witness against you, and His anointed *is* witness
this day, [a]that you have not found anything
[b]in my hand."
And they answered, "*He is* witness."
6 Then Samuel said to the people, [a]"*It is* the
LORD who raised up Moses and Aaron, and
who brought your fathers up from the land of
Egypt. 7 Now therefore, stand still, that I may
[a]reason with you before the LORD concerning
all the [b]righteous acts of the LORD which He
did to you and your fathers: 8 [a]When Jacob
had gone into Egypt,[1] and your fathers [b]cried
out to the LORD, then the LORD [c]sent Moses
and Aaron, who brought your fathers out of
Egypt and made them dwell in this place.
9 And when they [a]forgot the LORD their God,

10:27 [a] 1 Sam. 11:12 [b] Deut. 13:13 [c] 1 Kin. 4:21; 10:25 **11:1** [a] 1 Sam. 12:12 [b] Judg. 21:8 [c] Gen. 26:28 **11:2** [a] Gen. 34:14 **11:4** [a] 1 Sam. 10:26; 15:34 [b] Judg. 2:4; 20:23, 26; 21:2 **11:6** [a] Judg. 3:10; 6:34; 11:29; 13:25; 14:6 **11:7** [a] Judg. 19:29 [b] Judg. 21:5, 8, 10 **11:8** [a] Judg. 1:5 [b] 2 Sam. 24:9 **11:11** [a] 1 Sam. 31:11 [b] Judg. 7:16, 20 **11:12** [a] 1 Sam. 10:27 [b] Luke 19:27 **11:13** [a] 2 Sam. 19:22 [b] Ex. 14:13, 30 **11:14** [a] 1 Sam. 7:16; 10:8 **11:15** [a] 1 Sam. 10:17 [b] 1 Sam. 10:8 **12:1** [a] 1 Sam. 8:5, 7, 9, 20, 22 [b] 1 Sam. 10:24; 11:14, 15 **12:2** [a] Num. 27:17 [b] 1 Sam. 8:1, 5 **12:3** [a] 1 Sam. 10:1; 24:6 [b] Num. 16:15 [c] Ex. 23:8 [d] Deut. 16:19 **12:4** [a] Lev. 19:13 **12:5** [a] Acts 23:9; 24:20 [b] Ex. 22:4 **12:6** [a] Mic. 6:4 **12:7** [a] Is. 1:18 [b] Judg. 5:11 **12:8** [a] Gen. 46:5, 6 [b] Ex. 2:23–25 [c] Ex. 3:10; 4:14–16 [1] Following Masoretic Text, Targum, and Vulgate; Septuagint adds *and the Egyptians afflicted them.* **12:9** [a] Judg. 3:7

He sold them into the hand of [b]Sisera, commander of the army of Hazor, into the hand
of the [c]Philistines, and into the hand of the
king of [d]Moab; and they fought against them.
10 Then they cried out to the LORD, and said,
[a]'We have sinned, because we have forsaken
the LORD [b]and served the Baals and Ashtoreths;[1] but now deliver us from the hand of
our enemies, and we will serve You.' 11 And the
LORD sent Jerubbaal,[1] Bedan,[2] [a]Jephthah, and
[b]Samuel,[3] and delivered you out of the hand
of your enemies on every side; and you dwelt
in safety. 12 And when you saw that [a]Nahash
king of the Ammonites came against you, [b]you
said to me, 'No, but a king shall reign over
us,' when [c]the LORD your God *was* your king.
13 "Now therefore, [a]here is the king [b]whom
you have chosen *and* whom you have desired. And take note, [c]the LORD has set a king
over you. 14 If you [a]fear the LORD and serve
Him and obey His voice, and do not rebel
against the commandment of the LORD, then
both you and the king who reigns over you
will continue following the LORD your God.
15 However, if you do [a]not obey the voice of the
LORD, but [b]rebel against the commandment
of the LORD, then the hand of the LORD will
be against you, as *it was* against your fathers.
16 "Now therefore, [a]stand and see this great
thing which the LORD will do before your
eyes: 17 *Is* today not the [a]wheat harvest? [b]I will
call to the LORD, and He will send thunder
and [c]rain, that you may perceive and see that
[d]your wickedness *is* great, which you have
done in the sight of the LORD, in asking a
king for yourselves."
18 So Samuel called to the LORD, and the
LORD sent thunder and rain that day; and
[a]all the people greatly feared the LORD and
Samuel.
19 And all the people said to Samuel, [a]"Pray
for your servants to the LORD your God, that
we may not die; for we have added to all our
sins the evil of asking a king for ourselves."
20 Then Samuel said to the people, "Do not
fear. You have done all this wickedness; [a]yet
do not turn aside from following the LORD,
but serve the LORD with all your heart. 21 And
[a]do not turn aside; [b]for *then you would go* after
empty things which cannot profit or deliver,
for they *are* nothing. 22 For [a]the LORD will not

PEACE NOTE

Paul met Jesus. For the first time in his troubled life, he was enveloped by the peace of God—a peace so transforming and overwhelming it surpassed his ability to understand it.

forsake [b]His people, [c]for His great name's sake,
because [d]it has pleased the LORD to make you
His people. 23 Moreover, as for me, far be it
from me that I should sin against the LORD
[a]in ceasing to pray for you; but [b]I will teach
you the [c]good and the right way. 24 [a]Only fear
the LORD, and serve Him in truth with all your
heart; for [b]consider what [c]great things He has
done for you. 25 But if you still do wickedly, [a]you
shall be swept away, [b]both you and your king."

Saul's Unlawful Sacrifice

13 Saul reigned one year; and when he had
reigned two years over Israel,[1] 2 Saul
chose for himself three thousand *men* of
Israel. Two thousand were with Saul in [a]Mich-
mash and in the mountains of Bethel, and
a thousand were with [b]Jonathan in [c]Gibeah
of Benjamin. The rest of the people he sent
away, every man to his tent.
3 And Jonathan attacked [a]the garrison of
the Philistines that *was* in [b]Geba, and the
Philistines heard *of it*. Then Saul blew the
trumpet throughout all the land, saying, "Let
the Hebrews hear!" 4 Now all Israel heard it
said *that* Saul had attacked a garrison of the
Philistines, and *that* Israel had also become
an abomination to the Philistines. And the
people were called together to Saul at Gilgal.
5 Then the Philistines gathered together to
fight with Israel, thirty[1] thousand chariots and
six thousand horsemen, and people [a]as the

12:9 [b] Judg. 4:2 [c] Judg. 3:31; 10:7; 13:1 [d] Judg. 3:12–30 **12:10** [a] Judg. 10:10 [b] Judg. 2:13; 3:7 [1] Canaanite goddesses **12:11** [a] Judg. 11:1 [b] 1 Sam. 7:13 [1] Syriac reads *Deborah;* Targum reads *Gideon.* [2] Septuagint and Syriac read *Barak;* Targum reads *Simson.* [3] Syriac reads *Simson.* **12:12** [a] 1 Sam. 11:1, 2 [b] 1 Sam. 8:5, 19, 20 [c] Judg. 8:23 **12:13** [a] 1 Sam. 10:24 [b] 1 Sam. 8:5; 12:17, 19 [c] Hos. 13:11 **12:14** [a] Josh. 24:14 **12:15** [a] Deut. 28:15 [b] Is. 1:20 **12:16** [a] Ex. 14:13, 31 **12:17** [a] Gen. 30:14 [b] [James 5:16–18] [c] Ezra 10:9 [d] 1 Sam. 8:7 **12:18** [a] Ex. 14:31 **12:19** [a] Ex. 9:28 **12:20** [a] Deut. 11:16 **12:21** [a] 2 Chr. 25:15 [b] Is. 41:29 **12:22** [a] Deut. 31:6 [b] Is. 43:21 [c] Jer. 14:21 [d] Deut. 7:6–11 **12:23** [a] Rom. 1:9 [b] Ps. 34:11 [c] 1 Kin. 8:36 **12:24** [a] Eccl. 12:13 [b] Is. 5:12 [c] Deut. 10:21 **12:25** [a] Josh. 24:20 [b] Deut. 28:36 **13:1** [1] The Hebrew is difficult (compare 2 Samuel 5:4; 2 Kings 14:2; see also 2 Samuel 2:10; Acts 13:21). **13:2** [a] 1 Sam. 14:5, 31 [b] 1 Sam. 14:1 [c] 1 Sam. 10:26 **13:3** [a] 1 Sam. 10:5 [b] 2 Sam. 5:25 **13:5** [a] Judg. 7:12 [1] Following Masoretic Text, Septuagint, Targum, and Vulgate; Syriac and some manuscripts of the Septuagint read *three.*

sand which *is* on the seashore in multitude.
And they came up and encamped in Michmash, to the east of [b]Beth Aven. 6 When the
men of Israel saw that they were in danger (for
the people were distressed), then the people
[a]hid in caves, in thickets, in rocks, in holes,
and in pits. 7 And *some of* the Hebrews crossed
over the Jordan to the [a]land of Gad and Gilead.
As for Saul, he *was* still in Gilgal, and all the
people followed him trembling. 8 [a]Then he
waited seven days, according to the time set
by Samuel. But Samuel did not come to Gilgal; and the people were scattered from him.
9 So Saul said, "Bring a burnt offering and
peace offerings here to me." And he offered
the burnt offering. 10 Now it happened, as
soon as he had finished presenting the burnt
offering, that Samuel came; and Saul went
out to meet him, that he might greet him.
11 And Samuel said, "What have you done?"
Saul said, "When I saw that the people
were scattered from me, and *that* you did not
come within the days appointed, and *that* the
Philistines gathered together at Michmash,
12 then I said, 'The Philistines will now come
down on me at Gilgal, and I have not made
supplication to the LORD.' Therefore I felt
compelled, and offered a burnt offering."
13 And Samuel said to Saul, [a]"You have
done foolishly. [b]You have not kept the commandment of the LORD your God, which He
commanded you. For now the LORD would
have established your kingdom over Israel
forever. 14 [a]But now your kingdom shall not
continue. [b]The LORD has sought for Himself
a man [c]after His own heart, and the LORD has
commanded him *to be* commander over His
people, because you have [d]not kept what the
LORD commanded you."
15 Then Samuel arose and went up from
Gilgal to Gibeah of Benjamin.[1] And Saul numbered the people present with him, [a]about
six hundred men.

No Weapons for the Army

16 Saul, Jonathan his son, and the people
present with them remained in Gibeah of
Benjamin. But the Philistines encamped in
Michmash. 17 Then raiders came out of the
camp of the Philistines in three companies.
One company turned onto the road to [a]Oph-
rah, to the land of Shual, 18 another company turned to the road *to* [a]Beth Horon, and
another company turned *to* the road of the
border that overlooks the Valley of [b]Zeboim
toward the wilderness.
19 Now [a]there was no blacksmith to be found
throughout all the land of Israel, for the Philistines said, "Lest the Hebrews make swords
or spears." 20 But all the Israelites would go
down to the Philistines to sharpen each man's
plowshare, his mattock, his ax, and his sickle; 21 and the charge for a sharpening was a
pim[1] for the plowshares, the mattocks, the
forks, and the axes, and to set the points of
the goads. 22 So it came about, on the day
of battle, that [a]there was neither sword nor
spear found in the hand of any of the people
who *were* with Saul and Jonathan. But they
were found with Saul and Jonathan his son.
23 [a]And the garrison of the Philistines went
out to the pass of Michmash.

Jonathan Defeats the Philistines

14 Now it happened one day that Jonathan
the son of Saul said to the young man
who bore his armor, "Come, let us go over to
the Philistines' garrison that *is* on the other
side." But he did not tell his father. 2 And Saul
was sitting in the outskirts of [a]Gibeah under
a pomegranate tree which *is* in Migron. The
people who *were* with him *were* about six
hundred men. 3 [a]Ahijah the son of Ahitub,
[b]Ichabod's brother, the son of Phinehas, the
son of Eli, the LORD's priest in Shiloh, was
[c]wearing an ephod. But the people did not
know that Jonathan had gone.
4 Between the passes, by which Jonathan
sought to go over [a]to the Philistines' garrison, *there was* a sharp rock on one side and
a sharp rock on the other side. And the name
of one *was* Bozez, and the name of the other
Seneh. 5 The front of one faced northward
opposite Michmash, and the other southward
opposite Gibeah.
6 Then Jonathan said to the young man
who bore his armor, "Come, let us go over
to the garrison of these [a]uncircumcised; it
may be that the LORD will work for us. For
nothing restrains the LORD [b]from saving by
many or by few."
7 So his armorbearer said to him, "Do all
that is in your heart. Go then; here I am with
you, according to your heart."
8 Then Jonathan said, "Very well, let us
cross over to *these* men, and we will show
ourselves to them. 9 If they say thus to us,
'Wait until we come to you,' then we will stand

13:5 [b] Josh. 7:2 **13:6** [a] Judg. 6:2 **13:7** [a] Num. 32:1–42 **13:8** [a] 1 Sam. 10:8 **13:13** [a] 2 Chr. 16:9 [b] 1 Sam. 15:11, 22, 28 **13:14** [a] 1 Sam. 15:28; 31:6 [b] 1 Sam. 16:1 [c] Acts 7:46; 13:22 [d] 1 Sam. 15:11, 19 **13:15** [a] 1 Sam. 13:2, 6, 7; 14:2 [1] Following Masoretic Text and Targum; Septuagint and Vulgate add *And the rest of the people went up after Saul to meet the people who fought against them, going from Gilgal to Gibeah in the hill of Benjamin.* **13:17** [a] Josh. 18:23 **13:18** [a] Josh. 16:3; 18:13, 14 [b] Neh. 11:34 **13:19** [a] Judg. 5:8 **13:21** [1] About two-thirds shekel weight **13:22** [a] Judg. 5:8 **13:23** [a] 1 Sam. 14:1, 4 **14:2** [a] 1 Sam. 13:15, 16 **14:3** [a] 1 Sam. 22:9, 11, 20 [b] 1 Sam. 4:21 [c] 1 Sam. 2:28 **14:4** [a] 1 Sam. 13:23 **14:6** [a] 1 Sam. 17:26, 36 [b] Judg. 7:4, 7

still in our place and not go up to them. 10 But
if they say thus, 'Come up to us,' then we will
go up. For the LORD has delivered them into
our hand, and [a]this *will be* a sign to us."
11 So both of them showed themselves to
the garrison of the Philistines. And the Philistines said, "Look, the Hebrews are coming
out of the holes where they have [a]hidden."
12 Then the men of the garrison called to Jonathan and his armorbearer, and said, "Come
up to us, and we will show you something."
Jonathan said to his armorbearer, "Come
up after me, for the LORD has delivered them
into the hand of Israel." 13 And Jonathan
climbed up on his hands and knees with
his armorbearer after him; and they [a]fell
before Jonathan. And as he came after him,
his armorbearer killed them. 14 That first
slaughter which Jonathan and his armorbearer made was about twenty men within
about half an acre of land.[1]
15 And [a]there was trembling in the camp,
in the field, and among all the people. The
garrison and [b]the raiders also trembled;
and the earth quaked, so that it was [c]a very
great trembling. 16 Now the watchmen of
Saul in Gibeah of Benjamin looked, and *there*
was the multitude, melting away; and they
[a]went here and there. 17 Then Saul said to the
people who *were* with him, "Now call the roll
and see who has gone from us." And when
they had called the roll, surprisingly, Jonathan and his armorbearer *were* not *there.*
18 And Saul said to Ahijah, "Bring the ark[1] of
God here" (for at that time the ark[2] of God
was with the children of Israel). 19 Now it
happened, while Saul [a]talked to the priest,
that the noise which *was* in the camp of the
Philistines continued to increase; so Saul
said to the priest, "Withdraw your hand."
20 Then Saul and all the people who *were* with
him assembled, and they went to the battle;
and indeed [a]every man's sword was against
his neighbor, *and there was* very great confusion. 21 Moreover the Hebrews *who* were
with the Philistines before that time, who
went up with them into the camp *from the*
surrounding *country,* they also joined the
Israelites who *were* with Saul and Jonathan.
22 Likewise all the men of Israel who [a]had
hidden in the mountains of Ephraim, *when*
they heard that the Philistines fled, they also
followed hard after them in the battle. 23 [a]So
the LORD saved Israel that day, and the battle
shifted [b]to Beth Aven.

Saul's Rash Oath

24 And the men of Israel were distressed
that day, for Saul had [a]placed the people under oath, saying, "Cursed *is* the man who eats
any food until evening, before I have taken
vengeance on my enemies." So none of the
people tasted food. 25 [a]Now all *the people* of
the land came to a forest; and there was [b]hon-
ey on the ground. 26 And when the people had
come into the woods, there was the honey,
dripping; but no one put his hand to his
mouth, for the people feared the oath. 27 But
Jonathan had not heard his father charge the
people with the oath; therefore he stretched
out the end of the rod that *was* in his hand
and dipped it in a honeycomb, and put his
hand to his mouth; and his countenance
brightened. 28 Then one of the people said,
"Your father strictly charged the people with
an oath, saying, 'Cursed *is* the man who eats
food this day.'" And the people were faint.
29 But Jonathan said, "My father has troubled the land. Look now, how my countenance has brightened because I tasted a
little of this honey. 30 How much better if the
people had eaten freely today of the spoil
of their enemies which they found! For now
would there not have been a much greater
slaughter among the Philistines?"
31 Now they had driven back the Philistines
that day from Michmash to Aijalon. So the
people were very faint. 32 And the people
rushed on the spoil, and took sheep, oxen,
and calves, and slaughtered *them* on the
ground; and the people ate *them* [a]with the
blood. 33 Then they told Saul, saying, "Look,
the people are sinning against the LORD by
eating with the blood!"
So he said, "You have dealt treacherously;
roll a large stone to me this day." 34 Then Saul
said, "Disperse yourselves among the people,
and say to them, 'Bring me here every man's
ox and every man's sheep, slaughter *them*
here, and eat; and do not sin against the
LORD by eating with the blood.'" So every
one of the people brought his ox with him
that night, and slaughtered *it* there. 35 Then
Saul [a]built an altar to the LORD. This was the
first altar that he built to the LORD.
36 Now Saul said, "Let us go down after
the Philistines by night, and plunder them
until the morning light; and let us not leave
a man of them."
And they said, "Do whatever seems good
to you."

14:10 [a] Gen. 24:14 **14:11** [a] 1 Sam. 13:6; 14:22 **14:13** [a] Lev. 26:8 **14:14** [1] Literally *half the area plowed by a yoke* (of oxen in a day) **14:15** [a] Job 18:11 [b] 1 Sam. 13:17 [c] Gen. 35:5 **14:16** [a] 1 Sam. 14:20 **14:18** [1] Following Masoretic Text, Targum, and Vulgate; Septuagint reads *ephod.* [2] Following Masoretic Text, Targum, and Vulgate; Septuagint reads *ephod.* **14:19** [a] Num. 27:21 **14:20** [a] Judg. 7:22 **14:22** [a] 1 Sam. 13:6 **14:23** [a] Ex. 14:30 [b] 1 Sam. 13:5 **14:24** [a] Josh. 6:26 **14:25** [a] Deut. 9:28 [b] Ex. 3:8 **14:32** [a] Deut. 12:16, 23, 24 **14:35** [a] 1 Sam. 7:12, 17

Then the priest said, "Let us draw near to
God here."
37 So Saul [a]asked counsel of God, "Shall I go
down after the Philistines? Will You deliver them
into the hand of Israel?" But [b]He did not answer
him that day. 38 And Saul said, [a]"Come over here,
all you chiefs of the people, and know and see
what this sin was today. 39 For [a]*as* the LORD lives,
who saves Israel, though it be in Jonathan my
son, he shall surely die." But not a man among
all the people answered him. 40 Then he said to
all Israel, "You be on one side, and my son Jonathan and I will be on the other side."
And the people said to Saul, "Do what
seems good to you."
41 Therefore Saul said to the LORD God
of Israel, [a]"Give a perfect *lot*."[1] [b]So Saul and
Jonathan were taken, but the people escaped.
42 And Saul said, "Cast *lots* between my son
Jonathan and me." So Jonathan was taken.
43 Then Saul said to Jonathan, [a]"Tell me what
you have done."
And Jonathan told him, and said, [b]"I only
tasted a little honey with the end of the rod
that *was* in my hand. So now I must die!"
44 Saul answered, [a]"God do so and more
also; [b]for you shall surely die, Jonathan."
45 But the people said to Saul, "Shall Jonathan die, who has accomplished this great
deliverance in Israel? Certainly not! [a]*As* the
LORD lives, not one hair of his head shall fall
to the ground, for he has worked [b]with God
this day." So the people rescued Jonathan,
and he did not die.
46 Then Saul returned from pursuing the
Philistines, and the Philistines went to their
own place.

Saul's Continuing Wars

47 So Saul established his sovereignty over
Israel, and fought against all his enemies on
every side, against Moab, against the people
of [a]Ammon, against Edom, against the kings
of [b]Zobah, and against the Philistines. Wherever he turned, he harassed *them*.[1] 48 And he
gathered an army and [a]attacked the Amalekites, and delivered Israel from the hands of
those who plundered them.
49 [a]The sons of Saul were Jonathan, Jishui,[1] and Malchishua. And the names of
his two daughters *were these*: the name of
the firstborn Merab, and the name of the
younger [b]Michal. 50 The name of Saul's wife
was Ahinoam the daughter of Ahimaaz. And
the name of the commander of his army *was*
Abner the son of Ner, Saul's [a]uncle. 51 [a]Kish
was the father of Saul, and Ner the father of
Abner *was* the son of Abiel.
52 Now there was fierce war with the Philistines all the days of Saul. And when Saul
saw any strong man or any valiant man, [a]he
took him for himself.

Saul Spares King Agag

15 Samuel also said to Saul, [a]"The LORD
sent me to anoint you king over His
people, over Israel. Now therefore, heed the
voice of the words of the LORD. 2 Thus says the
LORD of hosts: 'I will punish Amalek *for* what
he did to Israel, [a]how he ambushed him on
the way when he came up from Egypt. 3 Now
go and [a]attack Amalek, and [b]utterly destroy
all that they have, and do not spare them. But
kill both man and woman, infant and nursing
child, ox and sheep, camel and donkey.' "
4 So Saul gathered the people together
and numbered them in Telaim, two hundred
thousand foot soldiers and ten thousand
men of Judah. 5 And Saul came to a city of
Amalek, and lay in wait in the valley.
6 Then Saul said to [a]the Kenites, [b]"Go, depart, get down from among the Amalekites,
lest I destroy you with them. For [c]you showed
kindness to all the children of Israel when
they came up out of Egypt." So the Kenites
departed from among the Amalekites. 7 [a]And
Saul attacked the Amalekites, from [b]Havilah
all the way to [c]Shur, which is east of Egypt.
8 [a]He also took Agag king of the Amalekites
alive, and [b]utterly destroyed all the people
with the edge of the sword. 9 But Saul and
the people [a]spared Agag and the best of the
sheep, the oxen, the fatlings, the lambs, and
all *that was* good, and were unwilling to utterly destroy them. But everything despised
and worthless, that they utterly destroyed.

Saul Rejected as King

10 Now the word of the LORD came to Samuel, saying, 11 [a]"I greatly regret that I have set
up Saul *as* king, for he has [b]turned back from
following Me, [c]and has not performed My

14:37 [a] Judg. 20:18 [b] 1 Sam. 28:6 **14:38** [a] Josh. 7:14 **14:39** [a] 2 Sam. 12:5 **14:41** [a] Acts 1:24–26 [b] 1 Sam. 10:20, 21 [1] Following Masoretic Text and Targum; Septuagint and Vulgate read *Why do You not answer Your servant today? If the injustice is with me or Jonathan my son, O LORD God of Israel, give proof; and if You say it is with Your people Israel, give holiness.* **14:43** [a] Josh. 7:19 [b] 1 Sam. 14:27 **14:44** [a] Ruth 1:17 [b] 1 Sam. 14:39 **14:45** [a] 1 Kin. 1:52 [b] [2 Cor. 6:1] **14:47** [a] 1 Sam. 11:1–13 [b] 2 Sam. 10:6 [1] Septuagint and Vulgate read *prospered*. **14:48** [a] 1 Sam. 15:3–7 **14:49** [a] 1 Sam. 31:2 [b] 1 Sam. 18:17–20, 27; 19:12 [1] Called *Abinadab* in 1 Chronicles 8:33 and 9:39 **14:50** [a] 1 Sam. 10:14 **14:51** [a] 1 Sam. 9:1, 21 **14:52** [a] 1 Sam. 8:11 **15:1** [a] 1 Sam. 9:16; 10:1 **15:2** [a] Deut. 25:17–19 **15:3** [a] Deut. 25:19 [b] Num. 24:20 **15:6** [a] Num. 24:21 [b] Gen. 18:25; 19:12, 14 [c] Ex. 18:10, 19 **15:7** [a] 1 Sam. 14:48 [b] Gen. 2:11; 25:17, 18 [c] Gen. 16:7 **15:8** [a] 1 Sam. 15:32, 33 [b] 1 Sam. 27:8, 9 **15:9** [a] 1 Sam. 15:3, 15, 19 **15:11** [a] Gen. 6:6, 7 [b] 1 Kin. 9:6 [c] 1 Sam. 13:13; 15:3, 9

commandments." And it [d]grieved Samuel,
and he cried out to the LORD all night. 12 So
when Samuel rose early in the morning to
meet Saul, it was told Samuel, saying, "Saul
went to [a]Carmel, and indeed, he set up a
monument for himself; and he has gone on
around, passed by, and gone down to Gilgal."
13 Then Samuel went to Saul, and Saul said to
him, [a]"Blessed *are* you of the LORD! I have
performed the commandment of the LORD."
14 But Samuel said, "What then *is* this bleating of the sheep in my ears, and the lowing
of the oxen which I hear?"
15 And Saul said, "They have brought them
from the Amalekites; [a]for the people spared
the best of the sheep and the oxen, to sacrifice
to the LORD your God; and the rest we have
utterly destroyed."
16 Then Samuel said to Saul, "Be quiet!
And I will tell you what the LORD said to me
last night."

And he said to him, "Speak on."
17 So Samuel said, [a]"When you *were* little
in your own eyes, *were* you not head of
the tribes of Israel? And did not the LORD
anoint you king over Israel? 18 Now the
LORD sent you on a mission, and said, 'Go,
and utterly destroy the sinners, the Amalekites, and fight against them until they
are consumed.' 19 Why then did you not obey
the voice of the LORD? Why did you swoop
down on the spoil, and do evil in the sight
of the LORD?"
20 And Saul said to Samuel, [a]"But I have
obeyed the voice of the LORD, and gone on
the mission on which the LORD sent me, and
brought back Agag king of Amalek; I have
utterly destroyed the Amalekites. 21 [a]But the
people took of the plunder, sheep and oxen,
the best of the things which should have been
utterly destroyed, to sacrifice to the LORD
your God in Gilgal."
22 So Samuel said:

[a]"Has the LORD *as great* delight in burnt
offerings and sacrifices,
As in obeying the voice of the LORD?
Behold, [b]to obey is better than
sacrifice,
And to heed than the fat of rams.
23 For rebellion *is as* the sin of witchcraft,
And stubbornness *is as* iniquity and
idolatry.
Because you have rejected the word of
the LORD,
[a]He also has rejected you from *being*
king."

24 [a]Then Saul said to Samuel, "I have
sinned, for I have transgressed the commandment of the LORD and your words,
because I [b]feared the people and obeyed
their voice. 25 Now therefore, please pardon
my sin, and return with me, that I may worship the LORD."
26 But Samuel said to Saul, "I will not return

15:11 [d] 1 Sam. 15:35; 16:1 **15:12** [a] Josh. 15:55 **15:13** [a] Judg. 17:2 **15:15** [a] [Gen. 3:12, 13]; 1 Sam. 15:9, 21 **15:17** [a] 1 Sam. 9:21; 10:22 **15:20** [a] 1 Sam. 15:13 **15:21** [a] 1 Sam. 15:15 **15:22** [a] [Is. 1:11–17] [b] [Hos. 6:6] **15:23** [a] 1 Sam. 13:14; 16:1 **15:24** [a] Josh. 7:20 [b] [Is. 51:12, 13]

TRUST AND OBEY

Behold, to obey is better than sacrifice.

I SAMUEL 15:22

People around the world try to find peace with God through religious activities, which isn't necessarily bad—they may be very good things—but doing things that God didn't command is not the same thing as obeying God. Without obedience there can be no peace.

Israel's first king, Saul, was a tragic example of this truth. He tried to compensate for his lack of obedience by doing "religious" things. When he had been instructed not to seize the spoil of the Amalekites, he did it anyway. When Samuel the priest confronted him, he said he had done so in order to offer sacrifice to the Lord. To offer sacrifice, Saul thought, made everything okay. But it did not. "To obey," said Samuel, "is better than sacrifice" (v. 22). After all, in Saul's day sinners offered sacrifices to atone for their sin of disobeying the Lord.

Throughout his rule Saul struggled to obey the Lord, and so the Lord removed the crown from him and gave it to another. Saul proved to be a tragic example of a man who could not find peace because he could not, as the great hymn says, "trust and obey."

with you, [a]for you have rejected the word of
the LORD, and the LORD has rejected you
from being king over Israel."
27 And as Samuel turned around to go away,
[a]*Saul* seized the edge of his robe, and it tore.
28 So Samuel said to him, [a]"The LORD has
torn the kingdom of Israel from you today,
and has given it to a neighbor of yours, *who*
is better than you. 29 And also the Strength
of Israel [a]will not lie nor relent. For He *is* not
a man, that He should relent."
30 Then he said, "I have sinned; *yet* [a]hon-
or me now, please, before the elders of my
people and before Israel, and return with
me, that I may worship the LORD your God."
31 So Samuel turned back after Saul, and Saul
worshiped the LORD.
32 Then Samuel said, "Bring Agag king of
the Amalekites here to me." So Agag came
to him cautiously.

And Agag said, "Surely the bitterness of
death is past."
33 But Samuel said, [a]"As your sword has
made women childless, so shall your mother
be childless among women." And Samuel
hacked Agag in pieces before the LORD in
Gilgal.
34 Then Samuel went to [a]Ramah, and Saul
went up to his house at [b]Gibeah of Saul. 35 And
[a]Samuel went no more to see Saul until
the day of his death. Nevertheless Samuel
mourned for Saul, and the LORD regretted
that He had made Saul king over Israel.

David Anointed King

16 Now the LORD said to Samuel, [a]"How
long will you mourn for Saul, seeing I
have rejected him from reigning over Israel?
[b]Fill your horn with oil, and go; I am sending
you to [c]Jesse the Bethlehemite. For [d]I have
provided Myself a king among his sons."
2 And Samuel said, "How can I go? If Saul
hears *it*, he will kill me."

But the LORD said, "Take a heifer with
you, and say, [a]'I have come to sacrifice to
the LORD.' 3 Then invite Jesse to the sacrifice,
and I will show you what you shall do; you
shall anoint for Me the one I name to you."
4 So Samuel did what the LORD said, and
went to Bethlehem. And the elders of the
town [a]trembled at his coming, and said, [b]"Do
you come peaceably?"
5 And he said, "Peaceably; I have come to
sacrifice to the LORD. [a]Sanctify yourselves,
and come with me to the sacrifice." Then he
consecrated Jesse and his sons, and invited
them to the sacrifice.
6 So it was, when they came, that he looked
at [a]Eliab and [b]said, "Surely the LORD's anointed *is* before Him!"
7 But the LORD said to Samuel, [a]"Do not
look at his appearance or at his physical
stature, because I have refused him. [b]For
the LORD does not *see* as man sees;[1] for man
[c]looks at the outward appearance, but the
LORD looks at the [d]heart."
8 So Jesse called Abinadab, and made him
pass before Samuel. And he said, "Neither has
the LORD chosen this one." 9 Then Jesse made
Shammah pass by. And he said, "Neither
has the LORD chosen this one." 10 Thus Jesse
made seven of his sons pass before Samuel.
And Samuel said to Jesse, "The LORD has not
chosen these." 11 And Samuel said to Jesse,
"Are all the young men here?" Then he said,
"There remains yet the youngest, and there
he is, keeping the [a]sheep."

And Samuel said to Jesse, "Send and bring
him. For we will not sit down[1] till he comes
here." 12 So he sent and brought him in. Now
he *was* [a]ruddy, [b]with bright eyes, and good-
looking. [c]And the LORD said, "Arise, anoint
him; for this *is* the one!" 13 Then Samuel took
the horn of oil and anointed him in the midst
of his brothers; and [a]the Spirit of the LORD
came upon David from that day forward. So
Samuel arose and went to Ramah.

A Distressing Spirit Troubles Saul

14 [a]But the Spirit of the LORD departed from
Saul, and [b]a distressing spirit from the LORD
troubled him. 15 And Saul's servants said to
him, "Surely, a distressing spirit from God
is troubling you. 16 Let our master now command your servants, *who are* before you, to
seek out a man *who is* a skillful player on the
harp. And it shall be that he will [a]play it with
his hand when the distressing spirit from God
is upon you, and you shall be well."
17 So Saul said to his servants, "Provide
me now a man who can play well, and bring
him to me."
18 Then one of the servants answered and
said, "Look, I have seen a son of Jesse the

15:26 [a] 1 Sam. 2:30 **15:27** [a] 1 Kin. 11:30, 31 **15:28** [a] 1 Kin. 11:31 **15:29** [a] Num. 23:19 **15:30** [a] [John 5:44; 12:43] **15:33** [a] [Gen. 9:6] **15:34** [a] 1 Sam. 7:17 [b] 1 Sam. 11:4 **15:35** [a] 1 Sam. 19:24 **16:1** [a] 1 Sam. 15:23, 35 [b] 1 Sam. 9:16; 10:1 [c] Ruth 4:18–22 [d] Acts 13:22 **16:2** [a] 1 Sam. 9:12 **16:4** [a] 1 Sam. 21:1 [b] 1 Kin. 2:13 **16:5** [a] Ex. 19:10 **16:6** [a] 1 Sam. 17:13, 28 [b] 1 Kin. 12:26 **16:7** [a] Ps. 147:10 [b] Is. 55:8, 9 [c] 2 Cor. 10:7 [d] 1 Kin. 8:39 [1] Septuagint reads *For God does not see as man sees;* Targum reads *It is not by the appearance of a man;* Vulgate reads *Nor do I judge according to the looks of a man.* **16:11** [a] 2 Sam. 7:8 [1] Following Septuagint and Vulgate; Masoretic Text reads *turn around;* Targum and Syriac read *turn away.* **16:12** [a] 1 Sam. 17:42 [b] Gen. 39:6 [c] 1 Sam. 9:17 **16:13** [a] Num. 27:18 **16:14** [a] Judg. 16:20 [b] Judg. 9:23 **16:16** [a] 1 Sam. 18:10; 19:9

ANOINTED WITH THE SPIRIT OF PEACE

Then Samuel took the horn of oil and anointed him in the midst of his brothers; and the Spirit of the LORD came upon David from that day forward.

1 SAMUEL 16:13

In the hands of God, little can be much. We see this great principle at work in the selection of David, son of Jesse, to be Israel's new king. God had directed Samuel to Jesse. Beginning with the oldest son, each passed before the priest. All were strong and promising, yet none was the right man. Was there another? There was—young David tending the sheep.

Given the values and assumptions of the ancient Near Eastern culture, David hardly seemed the right choice. Most would have assumed that Jesse's oldest son—said to be tall and handsome—would have been first pick. But the obvious is not always the way God works.

What impresses me about Samuel's anointing of David is how "the Spirit of the LORD came upon David from that day forward" (v. 13). God didn't just call David to be king; He *empowered* him to be king. We find peace when we trust God to enable. And that's what David did; he relied on the Lord and accomplished amazing things.

Bethlehemite, *who is* skillful in playing, a
mighty man of valor, a man of war, prudent
in speech, and a handsome person; and [a]the
LORD *is* with him."
19 Therefore Saul sent messengers to Jesse,
and said, "Send me your son David, who *is*
with the sheep." 20 And Jesse [a]took a donkey *loaded with* bread, a skin of wine, and a
young goat, and sent *them* by his son David
to Saul. 21 So David came to Saul and [a]stood
before him. And he loved him greatly, and he
became his armorbearer. 22 Then Saul sent
to Jesse, saying, "Please let David stand before me, for he has found favor in my sight."
23 And so it was, whenever the spirit from
God was upon Saul, that David would take
a harp and play *it* with his hand. Then Saul
would become refreshed and well, and the
distressing spirit would depart from him.

David and Goliath

17 Now the Philistines gathered their
armies together to battle, and were
gathered at [a]Sochoh, which *belongs* to Judah;
they encamped between Sochoh and Azekah,
in Ephes Dammim. 2 And Saul and the men
of Israel were gathered together, and they
encamped in the Valley of Elah, and drew up
in battle array against the Philistines. 3 The
Philistines stood on a mountain on one side,
and Israel stood on a mountain on the other
side, with a valley between them.
4 And a champion went out from the camp
of the Philistines, named [a]Goliath, from
[b]Gath, whose height *was* six cubits and a
span. 5 *He had* a bronze helmet on his head,
and he *was* armed with a coat of mail, and
the weight of the coat *was* five thousand
shekels of bronze. 6 And *he had* bronze armor
on his legs and a bronze javelin between his
shoulders. 7 Now the staff of his spear *was*
like a weaver's beam, and his iron spearhead
weighed six hundred shekels; and a shield-
bearer went before him. 8 Then he stood and
cried out to the armies of Israel, and said to
them, "Why have you come out to line up for
battle? *Am* I not a Philistine, and you the [a]ser-
vants of Saul? Choose a man for yourselves,
and let him come down to me. 9 If he is able
to fight with me and kill me, then we will be
your servants. But if I prevail against him and
kill him, then you shall be our servants and
[a]serve us." 10 And the Philistine said, "I [a]defy
the armies of Israel this day; give me a man,
that we may fight together." 11 When Saul and
all Israel heard these words of the Philistine,
they were dismayed and greatly afraid.
12 Now David *was* [a]the son of that [b]Ephrath-
ite of Bethlehem Judah, whose name *was*
Jesse, and who had [c]eight sons. And the man
was old, advanced *in years,* in the days of Saul.
13 The three oldest sons of Jesse had gone to
follow Saul to the battle. The [a]names of his
three sons who went to the battle *were* Eliab

16:18 [a] 1 Sam. 3:19; 18:12, 14 **16:20** [a] 1 Sam. 10:4, 27 **16:21** [a] Gen. 41:46 **17:1** [a] Josh. 15:35 **17:4** [a] 2 Sam. 21:19 [b] Josh. 11:21, 22 **17:8** [a] 1 Sam. 8:17 **17:9** [a] 1 Sam. 11:1 **17:10** [a] 1 Sam. 17:26, 36, 45 **17:12** [a] Ruth 4:22 [b] Gen. 35:19 [c] 1 Sam. 16:10, 11 **17:13** [a] 1 Sam. 16:6, 8, 9

the firstborn, next to him Abinadab, and the third Shammah. 14 David *was* the youngest. And the three oldest followed Saul. 15 But David occasionally went and returned from Saul [a]to feed his father's sheep at Bethlehem.

16 And the Philistine drew near and presented himself forty days, morning and evening.

17 Then Jesse said to his son David, "Take now for your brothers an ephah of this dried *grain* and these ten loaves, and run to your brothers at the camp. 18 And carry these ten cheeses to the captain of *their* thousand, and [a]see how your brothers fare, and bring back news of them." 19 Now Saul and they and all the men of Israel *were* in the Valley of Elah, fighting with the Philistines.

20 So David rose early in the morning, left the sheep with a keeper, and took *the things* and went as Jesse had commanded him. And he came to the camp as the army was going out to the fight and shouting for the battle. 21 For Israel and the Philistines had drawn up in battle array, army against army. 22 And David left his supplies in the hand of the supply keeper, ran to the army, and came and greeted his brothers. 23 Then as he talked with them, there was the champion, the Philistine of Gath, Goliath by name, coming up from the armies of the Philistines; and he spoke [a]according to the same words. So David heard *them.* 24 And all the men of Israel, when they saw the man, fled from him and were dreadfully afraid. 25 So the men of Israel said, "Have you seen this man who has come up? Surely he has come up to defy Israel; and it shall be *that* the man who kills him the king will enrich with great riches, [a]will give him his daughter, and give his father's house exemption *from taxes* in Israel."

26 Then David spoke to the men who stood by him, saying, "What shall be done for the man who kills this Philistine and takes away [a]the reproach from Israel? For who *is* this [b]uncircumcised Philistine, that he should [c]defy the armies of [d]the living God?"

27 And the people answered him in this manner, saying, [a]"So shall it be done for the man who kills him."

28 Now Eliab his oldest brother heard when he spoke to the men; and Eliab's [a]anger was aroused against David, and he said, "Why did you come down here? And with whom have you left those few sheep in the wilderness? I know your pride and the insolence of your heart, for you have come down to see the battle."

29 And David said, "What have I done now? [a]*Is there* not a cause?" 30 Then he turned from him toward another and [a]said the same thing; and these people answered him as the first ones *did.*

31 Now when the words which David spoke were heard, they reported *them* to Saul; and he sent for him. 32 Then David said to Saul, [a]"Let no man's heart fail because of him; [b]your servant will go and fight with this Philistine."

33 And Saul said to David, [a]"You are not able to go against this Philistine to fight with him; for you *are* a youth, and he a man of war from his youth."

34 But David said to Saul, "Your servant used to keep his father's sheep, and when a [a]lion or a bear came and took a lamb out of the flock, 35 I went out after it and struck it, and delivered *the lamb* from its mouth; and when it arose against me, I caught *it* by its beard, and struck and killed it. 36 Your servant has killed both lion and bear; and this uncircumcised Philistine will be like one of them, seeing he has defied the armies of the living God." 37 Moreover David said, [a]"The LORD, who delivered me from the paw of the lion and from the paw of the bear, He will deliver me from the hand of this Philistine."

And Saul said to David, [b]"Go, and the LORD be with you!"

38 So Saul clothed David with his armor, and he put a bronze helmet on his head; he also clothed him with a coat of mail. 39 David fastened his sword to his armor and tried to walk, for he had not tested *them.* And David said to Saul, "I cannot walk with these, for I have not tested *them.*" So David took them off.

40 Then he took his staff in his hand; and he chose for himself five smooth stones from the brook, and put them in a shepherd's bag, in a pouch which he had, and his sling was in his hand. And he drew near to the Philistine. 41 So the Philistine came, and began drawing near to David, and the man who bore the shield *went* before him. 42 And when the Philistine looked about and saw David, he [a]disdained him; for he was *only* a youth, [b]ruddy and good-looking. 43 So the Philistine [a]said to David, "*Am* I a dog, that you come to me with sticks?" And the Philistine cursed David by his gods. 44 And the Philistine [a]said to David, "Come to me, and I will give your flesh to the birds of the air and the beasts of the field!"

45 Then David said to the Philistine, "You

17:15 [a] 1 Sam. 16:11, 19 **17:18** [a] Gen. 37:13, 14 **17:23** [a] 1 Sam. 17:8–10 **17:25** [a] Josh. 15:16 **17:26** [a] 1 Sam. 11:2 [b] 1 Sam. 14:6; 17:36 [c] 1 Sam. 17:10 [d] Deut. 5:26 **17:27** [a] 1 Sam. 17:25 **17:28** [a] [Matt. 10:36] **17:29** [a] 1 Sam. 17:17 **17:30** [a] 1 Sam. 17:26, 27 **17:32** [a] Deut. 20:1–4 [b] 1 Sam. 16:18 **17:33** [a] Num. 13:31 **17:34** [a] Judg. 14:5 **17:37** [a] [2 Cor. 1:10] [b] 1 Chr. 22:11, 16 **17:42** [a] [Ps. 123:4] [b] 1 Sam. 16:12 **17:43** [a] 2 Kin. 8:13 **17:44** [a] 1 Kin. 20:10, 11

NEITHER LION NOR BEAR

The LORD, who delivered me from the paw of the lion and from the paw of the bear, He will deliver me from the hand of this Philistine.

I SAMUEL 17:37

Knowing what God has done builds faith and gives peace. David was a warrior—but above all, he was a prayer warrior. He wrote many of the Psalms, and most of the ones he wrote are prayers.

When David faced the giant, Goliath, I have no doubt he prayed. Perhaps he prayed the words of his best-known psalm: "The LORD is my shepherd; I shall not want . . . Yea, though I walk through the valley of the shadow of death, I will fear no evil; for You are with me; Your rod and Your staff, they comfort me" (Ps. 23:1, 4). David reasoned that, if God had delivered him "from the paw of the lion and from the paw of the bear," then He would deliver him "from the hand of [the] Philistine" (1 Sam. 17:37).

This is the logic of peace: if God has delivered us in the past, He will be by our side today and every day when we face challenges and dangers. To access His peace, we pray. David showed us how. It is also important that we remember to speak words of faith and peace over our circumstance: *I will make it. I will get through this mess. God will lead me, by His grace. He's done it before, and He will do it again.*

come to me with a sword, with a spear, and
with a javelin. [a]But I come to you in the name
of the LORD of hosts, the God of the armies
of Israel, whom you have [b]defied. 46 This day
the LORD will deliver you into my hand, and I
will strike you and take your head from you.
And this day I will give [a]the carcasses of the
camp of the Philistines to the birds of the air
and the wild beasts of the earth, [b]that all the
earth may know that there is a God in Israel.
47 Then all this assembly shall know that the
LORD [a]does not save with sword and spear;
for [b]the battle *is* the LORD's, and He will give
you into our hands."

48 So it was, when the Philistine arose and
came and drew near to meet David, that David
hurried and [a]ran toward the army to meet the
Philistine. 49 Then David put his hand in his
bag and took out a stone; and he slung *it* and
struck the Philistine in his forehead, so that
the stone sank into his forehead, and he fell on
his face to the earth. 50 So David prevailed over
the Philistine with a [a]sling and a stone, and
struck the Philistine and killed him. But *there*
was no sword in the hand of David. 51 Therefore
David ran and stood over the Philistine, took
his [a]sword and drew it out of its sheath and
killed him, and cut off his head with it.

And when the Philistines saw that their
champion was dead, [b]they fled. 52 Now the
men of Israel and Judah arose and shouted,
and pursued the Philistines as far as the
entrance of the valley[1] and to the gates of
Ekron. And the wounded of the Philistines
fell along the road to [a]Shaaraim, even as
far as Gath and Ekron. 53 Then the children
of Israel returned from chasing the Philistines, and they plundered their tents.
54 And David took the head of the Philistine
and brought it to Jerusalem, but he put his
armor in his tent.

55 When Saul saw David going out against
the Philistine, he said to [a]Abner, the commander of the army, "Abner, [b]whose son *is*
this youth?"

And Abner said, "As your soul lives, O king,
I do not know."

56 So the king said, "Inquire whose son this
young man *is*."

57 Then, as David returned from the slaughter of the Philistine, Abner took him and
brought him before Saul [a]with the head of
the Philistine in his hand. 58 And Saul said
to him, "Whose son *are* you, young man?"

So David answered, [a]"*I am* the son of your
servant Jesse the Bethlehemite."

17:45 [a] Heb. 11:33, 34 [b] 1 Sam. 17:10 **17:46** [a] Deut. 28:26 [b] Josh. 4:24 **17:47** [a] Hos. 1:7 [b] 2 Chr. 20:15 **17:48** [a] Ps. 27:3 **17:50** [a] Judg. 3:31; 15:15; 20:16 **17:51** [a] 1 Sam. 21:9 [b] Heb. 11:34 **17:52** [a] Josh. 15:36 [1] Following Masoretic Text, Syriac, Targum, and Vulgate; Septuagint reads *Gath*. **17:55** [a] 1 Sam. 14:50 [b] 1 Sam. 16:21, 22 **17:57** [a] 1 Sam. 17:54 **17:58** [a] 1 Sam. 17:12

Saul Resents David

18 Now when he had finished speaking to Saul, [a]the soul of Jonathan was knit to the soul of David, [b]and Jonathan loved him as his own soul. 2 Saul took him that day, [a]and would not let him go home to his father's house anymore. 3 Then Jonathan and David made a [a]covenant, because he loved him as his own soul. 4 And Jonathan took off the robe that *was* on him and gave it to David, with his armor, even to his sword and his bow and his belt.

5 So David went out wherever Saul sent him, *and* behaved wisely. And Saul set him over the men of war, and he was accepted in the sight of all the people and also in the sight of Saul's servants. 6 Now it had happened as they were coming *home,* when David was returning from the slaughter of the Philistine, that [a]the women had come out of all the cities of Israel, singing and dancing, to meet King Saul, with tambourines, with joy, and with musical instruments. 7 So the women [a]sang as they danced, and said:

> [b]"Saul has slain his thousands,
> And David his ten thousands."

8 Then Saul was very angry, and the saying [a]displeased him; and he said, "They have ascribed to David ten thousands, and to me they have ascribed *only* thousands. Now *what* more can he have but [b]the kingdom?" 9 So Saul eyed David from that day forward.

10 And it happened on the next day that [a]the distressing spirit from God came upon Saul, [b]and he prophesied inside the house. So David [c]played *music* with his hand, as at other times; [d]but *there was* a spear in Saul's hand. 11 And Saul [a]cast the spear, for he said, "I will pin David to the wall!" But David escaped his presence twice.

12 Now Saul was [a]afraid of David, because [b]the LORD was with him, but had [c]departed from Saul. 13 Therefore Saul removed him from his presence, and made him his captain over a thousand; and [a]he went out and came in before the people. 14 And David behaved wisely in all his ways, and [a]the LORD *was* with him. 15 Therefore, when Saul saw that he behaved very wisely, he was afraid of him. 16 But [a]all Israel and Judah loved David, because he went out and came in before them.

David Marries Michal

17 Then Saul said to David, "Here is my older daughter Merab; [a]I will give her to you as a wife. Only be valiant for me, and fight [b]the LORD's battles." For Saul thought, [c]"Let my hand not be against him, but let the hand of the Philistines be against him."

18 So David said to Saul, [a]"Who *am* I, and what *is* my life *or* my father's family in Israel, that I should be son-in-law to the king?" 19 But it happened at the time when Merab, Saul's daughter, should have been given to David, that she was given to [a]Adriel the [b]Meholathite as a wife.

20 [a]Now Michal, Saul's daughter, loved David. And they told Saul, and the thing pleased him. 21 So Saul said, "I will give her to him, that she may be a snare to him, and that [a]the hand of the Philistines may be against him." Therefore Saul said to David a second time, [b]"You shall be my son-in-law today."

22 And Saul commanded his servants, "Communicate with David secretly, and say, 'Look, the king has delight in you, and all his servants love you. Now therefore, become the king's son-in-law.' "

23 So Saul's servants spoke those words in the hearing of David. And David said, "Does it seem to you *a* light *thing* to be a king's son-in-law, seeing I *am* a poor and lightly esteemed man?" 24 And the servants of Saul told him, saying, "In this manner David spoke."

25 Then Saul said, "Thus you shall say to David: 'The king does not desire any [a]dowry but one hundred foreskins of the Philistines, to take [b]vengeance on the king's enemies.' " But Saul [c]thought to make David fall by the hand of the Philistines. 26 So when his servants told David these words, it pleased David well to become the king's son-in-law. Now [a]the days had not expired; 27 therefore David arose and went, he and [a]his men, and killed two hundred men of the Philistines. And [b]David brought their foreskins, and they gave them in full count to the king, that he might become the king's son-in-law. Then Saul gave him Michal his daughter as a wife.

28 Thus Saul saw and knew that the LORD *was* with David, and *that* Michal, Saul's daughter, loved him; 29 and Saul was still more afraid of David. So Saul became David's enemy continually. 30 Then the princes of the Philistines [a]went out *to war.* And so it was,

18:1 [a] Gen. 44:30 [b] 1 Sam. 20:17 **18:2** [a] 1 Sam. 17:15 **18:3** [a] 1 Sam. 20:8–17 **18:6** [a] Ex. 15:20, 21 **18:7** [a] Ex. 15:21 [b] 1 Sam. 21:11; 29:5 **18:8** [a] Eccl. 4:4 [b] 1 Sam. 15:28 **18:10** [a] 1 Sam. 16:14 [b] 1 Sam. 19:24 [c] 1 Sam. 16:23 [d] 1 Sam. 19:9, 10 **18:11** [a] 1 Sam. 19:10; 20:33 **18:12** [a] 1 Sam. 18:15, 29 [b] 1 Sam. 16:13, 18 [c] 1 Sam. 16:14; 28:15 **18:13** [a] Num. 27:17 **18:14** [a] Josh. 6:27 **18:16** [a] 1 Sam. 18:5 **18:17** [a] 1 Sam. 14:49; 17:25 [b] Num. 32:20, 27, 29 [c] 1 Sam. 18:21, 25 **18:18** [a] 2 Sam. 7:18 **18:19** [a] 2 Sam. 21:8 [b] Judg. 7:22 **18:20** [a] 1 Sam. 18:28 **18:21** [a] 1 Sam. 18:17 [b] 1 Sam. 18:26 **18:25** [a] Ex. 22:17 [b] 1 Sam. 14:24 [c] 1 Sam. 18:17 **18:26** [a] 1 Sam. 18:21 **18:27** [a] 1 Sam. 18:13 [b] 2 Sam. 3:14 **18:30** [a] 2 Sam. 11:1

whenever they went out, *that* David [b]behaved
more wisely than all the servants of Saul,
so that his name became highly esteemed.

Saul Persecutes David

19 Now Saul spoke to Jonathan his son
and to all his servants, that they should
kill [a]David; but Jonathan, Saul's son, [b]de-
lighted greatly in David. 2 So Jonathan told
David, saying, "My father Saul seeks to kill
you. Therefore please be on your guard until morning, and stay in a secret *place* and
hide. 3 And I will go out and stand beside my
father in the field where you *are*, and I will
speak with my father about you. Then what
I observe, I will tell [a]you."

4 Thus Jonathan [a]spoke well of David to Saul
his father, and said to him, "Let not the king
[b]sin against his servant, against David, because
he has not sinned against you, and because
his works *have been* very good toward you.
5 For he took his [a]life in his hands and [b]killed
the Philistine, and [c]the LORD brought about
a great deliverance for all Israel. You saw *it*
and rejoiced. [d]Why then will you [e]sin against
innocent blood, to kill David without a cause?"

6 So Saul heeded the voice of Jonathan,
and Saul swore, "*As* the LORD lives, he shall
not be killed." 7 Then Jonathan called David,
and Jonathan told him all these things. So
Jonathan brought David to Saul, and he was
in his presence [a]as in times past.

8 And there was war again; and David went
out and fought with the Philistines, [a]and
struck them with a mighty blow, and they
fled from him.

9 Now [a]the distressing spirit from the LORD
came upon Saul as he sat in his house with
his spear in his hand. And David was playing
music with *his* hand. 10 Then Saul sought to
pin David to the wall with the spear, but he
slipped away from Saul's presence; and he
drove the spear into the wall. So David fled
and escaped that night.

11 [a]Saul also sent messengers to David's
house to watch him and to kill him in the
morning. And Michal, David's wife, told him,
saying, "If you do not save your life tonight,
tomorrow you will be killed." 12 So Michal [a]let
David down through a window. And he went
and fled and escaped. 13 And Michal took an
image and laid *it* in the bed, put a cover of
goats' *hair* for his head, and covered *it* with
clothes. 14 So when Saul sent messengers to
take David, she said, "He *is* sick."

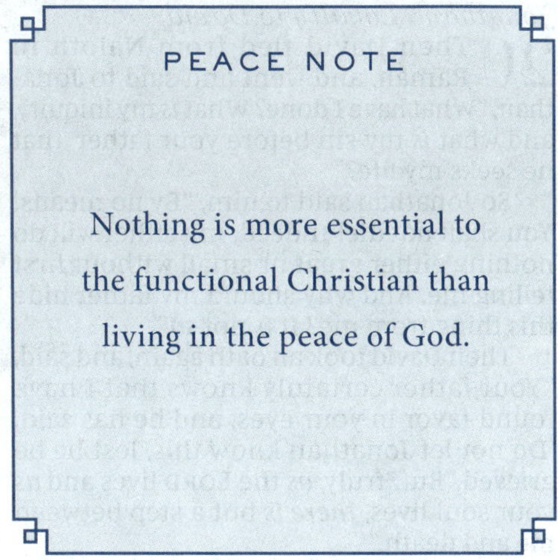
PEACE NOTE

Nothing is more essential to the functional Christian than living in the peace of God.

15 Then Saul sent the messengers *back* to
see David, saying, "Bring him up to me in
the bed, that I may kill him." 16 And when
the messengers had come in, there was the
image in the bed, with a cover of goats' *hair*
for his head. 17 Then Saul said to Michal, "Why
have you deceived me like this, and sent my
enemy away, so that he has escaped?"

And Michal answered Saul, "He said to me,
'Let me go! [a]Why should I kill you?' "

18 So David fled and escaped, and went to
[a]Samuel at [b]Ramah, and told him all that
Saul had done to him. And he and Samuel
went and stayed in Naioth. 19 Now it was told
Saul, saying, "Take note, David *is* at Naioth
in Ramah!" 20 Then [a]Saul sent messengers to
take David. [b]And when they saw the group of
prophets prophesying, and Samuel standing
as leader over them, the Spirit of God came
upon the messengers of Saul, and they also
[c]prophesied. 21 And when Saul was told, he
sent other messengers, and they prophesied
likewise. Then Saul sent messengers again
the third time, and they prophesied also.
22 Then he also went to Ramah, and came to
the great well that *is* at Sechu. So he asked,
and said, "Where *are* Samuel and David?"

And *someone* said, "Indeed *they are* at Naioth in Ramah." 23 So he went there to Naioth
in Ramah. Then [a]the Spirit of God was upon
him also, and he went on and prophesied until
he came to Naioth in Ramah. 24 [a]And he also
stripped off his clothes and prophesied before
Samuel in like manner, and lay down [b]naked
all that day and all that night. Therefore they
say, [c]"*Is* Saul also among the prophets?"[1]

18:30 [b] 1 Sam. 18:5 **19:1** [a] 1 Sam. 8:8, 9 [b] 1 Sam. 18:1 **19:3** [a] 1 Sam. 20:8–13 **19:4** [a] [Prov. 31:8, 9] [b] [Prov. 17:13] **19:5** [a] Judg. 9:17; 12:3 [b] 1 Sam. 17:49, 50 [c] 1 Sam. 11:13 [d] 1 Sam. 20:32 [e] [Deut. 19:10–13] **19:7** [a] 1 Sam. 16:21; 18:2, 10, 13 **19:8** [a] 1 Sam. 18:27; 23:5 **19:9** [a] 1 Sam. 16:14; 18:10, 11 **19:11** [a] Ps. 59:title **19:12** [a] Josh. 2:15 **19:17** [a] 2 Sam. 2:22 **19:18** [a] 1 Sam. 16:13 [b] 1 Sam. 7:17 **19:20** [a] John 7:32 [b] 1 Sam. 10:5, 6, 10 [c] Joel 2:28 **19:23** [a] 1 Sam. 10:10 **19:24** [a] Is. 20:2 [b] Mic. 1:8 [c] 1 Sam. 10:10–12 [1] Compare 1 Samuel 10:12

Jonathan's Loyalty to David

20 Then David fled from Naioth in
Ramah, and went and said to Jona-
than, "What have I done? What *is* my iniquity,
and what *is* my sin before your father, that
he seeks my life?"
2 So Jonathan said to him, "By no means!
You shall not die! Indeed, my father will do
nothing either great or small without first
telling me. And why should my father hide
this thing from me? It *is* not *so!*"
3 Then David took an oath again, and said,
"Your father certainly knows that I have
found favor in your eyes, and he has said,
'Do not let Jonathan know this, lest he be
grieved.' But [a]truly, *as* the LORD lives and *as*
your soul lives, *there is* but a step between
me and death."
4 So Jonathan said to David, "Whatever you
yourself desire, I will do *it* for you."
5 And David said to Jonathan, "Indeed tomorrow *is* the [a]New Moon, and I should not
fail to sit with the king to eat. But let me go,
that I may [b]hide in the field until the third
day at evening. 6 If your father misses me at
all, then say, 'David earnestly asked *permission* of me that he might run over [a]to Bethlehem, his city, for *there is* a yearly sacrifice
there for all the family.' 7 [a]If he says thus: '*It
is* well,' your servant will be safe. But if he is
very angry, be sure that [b]evil is determined
by him. 8 Therefore you shall [a]deal kindly
with your servant, for [b]you have brought
your servant into a covenant of the LORD
with you. Nevertheless, [c]if there is iniquity
in me, kill me yourself, for why should you
bring me to your father?"
9 But Jonathan said, "Far be it from you! For
if I knew certainly that evil was determined
by my father to come upon you, then would
I not tell you?"
10 Then David said to Jonathan, "Who will
tell me, or what *if* your father answers you
roughly?"
11 And Jonathan said to David, "Come, let us
go out into the field." So both of them went
out into the field. 12 Then Jonathan said to
David: "The LORD God of Israel *is witness!*
When I have sounded out my father sometime tomorrow, *or* the third *day,* and indeed
there is good toward David, and I do not send
to you and tell you, 13 may [a]the LORD do so
and much more to Jonathan. But if it pleases
my father *to do* you evil, then I will report it
to you and send you away, that you may go in
safety. And [b]the LORD be with you as He has
[c]been with my father. 14 And you shall not only
show me the kindness of the LORD while I still
live, that I may not die; 15 but [a]you shall not
cut off your kindness from my house forever,
no, not when the LORD has cut off every one
of the enemies of David from the face of the
earth." 16 So Jonathan made *a covenant* with
the house of David, *saying,* [a]"Let the LORD
require *it* at the hand of David's enemies."
17 Now Jonathan again caused David to vow,
because he loved him; [a]for he loved him as
he loved his own soul. 18 Then Jonathan said
to David, [a]"Tomorrow *is* the New Moon; and
you will be missed, because your seat will be
empty. 19 And *when* you have stayed three
days, go down quickly and come to [a]the place
where you hid on the day of the deed; and
remain by the stone Ezel. 20 Then I will shoot
three arrows to the side, as though I shot at
a target; 21 and there I will send a lad, *saying,*
'Go, find the arrows.' If I expressly say to the
lad, 'Look, the arrows *are* on this side of you;
get them and come'—then, [a]as the LORD lives,
there is safety for you and no harm. 22 But if I
say thus to the young man, 'Look, the arrows
are beyond you'—go your way, for the LORD
has sent you away. 23 And as for [a]the matter
which you and I have spoken of, indeed the
LORD *be* between you and me forever."
24 Then David hid in the field. And when the
New Moon had come, the king sat down to eat
the feast. 25 Now the king sat on his seat, as at
other times, on a seat by the wall. And Jonathan arose,[1] and Abner sat by Saul's side, but
David's place was empty. 26 Nevertheless Saul
did not say anything that day, for he thought,
"Something has happened to him; he *is* unclean, surely he *is* [a]unclean." 27 And it happened
the next day, the second *day* of the month,
that David's place was empty. And Saul said to
Jonathan his son, "Why has the son of Jesse
not come to eat, either yesterday or today?"
28 So Jonathan [a]answered Saul, "David
earnestly asked *permission* of me *to go* to
Bethlehem. 29 And he said, 'Please let me go,
for our family has a sacrifice in the city, and
my brother has commanded me *to be there.*
And now, if I have found favor in your eyes,
please let me get away and see my brothers.'
Therefore he has not come to the king's table."
30 Then Saul's anger was aroused against
Jonathan, and he said to him, "You son of a
perverse, rebellious *woman!* Do I not know
that you have chosen the son of Jesse to your

20:3 [a] 1 Sam. 27:1 **20:5** [a] Num. 10:10; 28:11–15 [b] 1 Sam. 19:2, 3 **20:6** [a] 1 Sam. 16:4; 17:12 **20:7** [a] 2 Sam. 17:4 [b] 1 Sam. 25:17 **20:8** [a] Josh. 2:14 [b] 1 Sam. 18:3; 20:16; 23:18 [c] 2 Sam. 14:32 **20:13** [a] Ruth 1:17 [b] Josh. 1:5 [c] 1 Sam. 10:7 **20:15** [a] 2 Sam. 9:1, 3, 7; 21:7 **20:16** [a] 1 Sam. 25:22; 31:2 **20:17** [a] 1 Sam. 18:1 **20:18** [a] 1 Sam. 20:5, 24 **20:19** [a] 1 Sam. 19:2 **20:21** [a] Jer. 4:2 **20:23** [a] 1 Sam. 20:14, 15 **20:25** [1] Following Masoretic Text, Syriac, Targum, and Vulgate; Septuagint reads *he sat across from Jonathan.* **20:26** [a] Lev. 7:20, 21; 15:5 **20:28** [a] 1 Sam. 20:6

own shame and to the shame of your mother's
nakedness? 31 For as long as the son of Jesse
lives on the earth, you shall not be established,
nor your kingdom. Now therefore, send and
bring him to me, for he shall surely die."
32 And Jonathan answered Saul his father,
and said to him, [a]"Why should he be killed?
What has he done?" 33 Then Saul [a]cast a spear at
him to kill him, [b]by which Jonathan knew that
it was determined by his father to kill David.
34 So Jonathan arose from the table in fierce
anger, and ate no food the second day of the
month, for he was grieved for David, because
his father had treated him shamefully.
35 And so it was, in the morning, that Jonathan went out into the field at the time appointed with David, and a little lad *was* with
him. 36 Then he said to his lad, "Now run, find
the arrows which I shoot." As the lad ran, he
shot an arrow beyond him. 37 When the lad had
come to the place where the arrow was which
Jonathan had shot, Jonathan cried out after
the lad and said, "*Is* not the arrow beyond you?"
38 And Jonathan cried out after the lad, "Make
haste, hurry, do not delay!" So Jonathan's lad
gathered up the arrows and came back to his
master. 39 But the lad did not know anything.
Only Jonathan and David knew of the matter.
40 Then Jonathan gave his weapons to his lad,
and said to him, "Go, carry *them* to the city."
41 As soon as the lad had gone, David arose
from *a place* toward the south, fell on his face
to the ground, and bowed down three times.
And they kissed one another; and they wept
together, but David more so. 42 Then Jonathan said to David, [a]"Go in peace, since we
have both sworn in the name of the LORD,
saying, 'May the LORD be between you and
me, and between your descendants and my
descendants, forever.'" So he arose and departed, and Jonathan went into the city.

David and the Holy Bread

21 Now David came to Nob, to Ahimelech
the priest. And [a]Ahimelech was [b]afraid
when he met David, and said to him, "Why
are you alone, and no one is with you?"
2 So David said to Ahimelech the priest,
"The king has ordered me on some business,
and said to me, 'Do not let anyone know
anything about the business on which I send
you, or what I have commanded you.' And
I have directed *my* young men to such and
such a place. 3 Now therefore, what have you
on hand? Give *me* five *loaves of* bread in my
hand, or whatever can be found."
4 And the priest answered David and said,
"*There is* no common bread on hand; but
there is [a]holy bread, [b]if the young men have
at least kept themselves from women."
5 Then David answered the priest, and said
to him, "Truly, women *have been* kept from
us about three days since I came out. And
the [a]vessels of the young men are holy, and
the bread is in effect common, even though
it was consecrated [b]in the vessel this day."
6 So the priest [a]gave him holy *bread;* for
there was no bread there but the showbread
[b]which had been taken from before the LORD,
in order to put hot bread *in its place* on the
day when it was taken away.
7 Now a certain man of the servants of
Saul *was* there that day, detained before the
LORD. And his name *was* [a]Doeg, an Edomite, the chief of the herdsmen who *belonged*
to Saul.
8 And David said to Ahimelech, "Is there
not here on hand a spear or a sword? For
I have brought neither my sword nor my
weapons with me, because the king's business required haste."
9 So the priest said, "The sword of Goliath
the Philistine, whom you killed in [a]the Valley
of Elah, [b]there it is, wrapped in a cloth behind
the ephod. If you will take that, take *it.* For
there is no other except that one here."
And David said, "*There is* none like it; give
it to me."

David Flees to Gath

10 Then David arose and fled that day from
before Saul, and went to Achish the king of
Gath. 11 And [a]the servants of Achish said to
him, "*Is* this not David the king of the land?
Did they not sing of him to one another in
dances, saying:

[b]'Saul has slain his thousands,
And David his ten thousands'?"[1]

12 Now David [a]took these words to heart,
and was very much afraid of Achish the king
of Gath. 13 So [a]he changed his behavior before
them, pretended madness in their hands,
scratched on the doors of the gate, and let his
saliva fall down on his beard. 14 Then Achish
said to his servants, "Look, you see the man
is insane. Why have you brought him to me?
15 Have I need of madmen, that you have
brought this *fellow* to play the madman in
my presence? Shall this *fellow* come into
my house?"

20:32 [a] Gen. 31:36 **20:33** [a] 1 Sam. 18:11; 19:10 [b] 1 Sam. 20:7 **20:42** [a] 1 Sam. 1:17 **21:1** [a] 1 Sam. 14:3 [b] 1 Sam. 16:4 **21:4** [a] Lev. 24:5–9 [b] Ex. 19:15 **21:5** [a] 1 Thess. 4:4 [b] Lev. 8:26 **21:6** [a] Luke 6:3, 4 [b] Lev. 24:8, 9 **21:7** [a] 1 Sam. 14:47; 22:9 **21:9** [a] 1 Sam. 17:2, 50 [b] 1 Sam. 31:10 **21:11** [a] Ps. 56:title [b] 1 Sam. 18:6–8; 29:5 [1] Compare 1 Samuel 18:7 **21:12** [a] Luke 2:19 **21:13** [a] Ps. 34:title

David's Four Hundred Men

22 David therefore departed from there and [a]escaped [b]to the cave of Adullam. So when his brothers and all his father's house heard *it,* they went down there to him. 2 [a]And everyone *who was* in distress, everyone who *was* in debt, and everyone *who was* discontented gathered to him. So he became captain over them. And there were about [b]four hundred men with him.

3 Then David went from there to Mizpah of [a]Moab; and he said to the king of Moab, "Please let my father and mother come here with you, till I know what God will do for me." 4 So he brought them before the king of Moab, and they dwelt with him all the time that David was in the stronghold.

5 Now the prophet [a]Gad said to David, "Do not stay in the stronghold; depart, and go to the land of Judah." So David departed and went into the forest of Hereth.

> **PEACE NOTE**
>
> Listen carefully to the voice of the Lord. The Bible is God's Word to you. As quickly as David heard the prophet Gad, you too can follow the Lord's prompting (and peace) in your life.
>
> 1 SAMUEL 22:5

Saul Murders the Priests

6 When Saul heard that David and the men who *were* with him had been discovered—now Saul was staying in [a]Gibeah under a tamarisk tree in Ramah, with his spear in his hand, and all his servants standing about him— 7 then Saul said to his servants who stood about him, "Hear now, you Benjamites! Will the son of Jesse [a]give every one of you fields and vineyards, *and* make you all captains of thousands and captains of hundreds? 8 All of you have conspired against me, and *there is* no one who reveals to me that [a]my son has made a covenant with the son of Jesse; and *there is* not one of you who is sorry for me or reveals to me that my son has stirred up my servant against me, to lie in wait, as *it is* this day."

9 Then answered [a]Doeg the Edomite, who was set over the servants of Saul, and said, "I saw the son of Jesse going to Nob, to [b]Ahimelech the son of [c]Ahitub. 10 [a]And he inquired of the LORD for him, [b]gave him provisions, and gave him the sword of Goliath the Philistine."

11 So the king sent to call Ahimelech the priest, the son of Ahitub, and all his father's house, the priests who *were* in Nob. And they all came to the king. 12 And Saul said, "Hear now, son of Ahitub!"

He answered, "Here I am, my lord."

13 Then Saul said to him, "Why have you conspired against me, you and the son of Jesse, in that you have given him bread and a sword, and have inquired of God for him, that he should rise against me, to lie in wait, as it is this day?"

14 So Ahimelech answered the king and said, "And who among all your servants *is as* [a]faithful as David, who is the king's son-in-law, who goes at your bidding, and is honorable in your house? 15 Did I then begin to inquire of God for him? Far be it from me! Let not the king impute anything to his servant, *or* to any in the house of my father. For your servant knew nothing of all this, little or much."

16 And the king said, "You shall surely die, Ahimelech, you and all [a]your father's house!" 17 Then the king said to the guards who stood about him, "Turn and kill the priests of the LORD, because their hand also *is* with David, and because they knew when he fled and did not tell it to me." But the servants of the king [a]would not lift their hands to strike the priests of the LORD. 18 And the king said to Doeg, "You turn and kill the priests!" So Doeg the Edomite turned and struck the priests, and [a]killed on that day eighty-five men who wore a linen ephod. 19 [a]Also Nob, the city of the priests, he struck with the edge of the sword, both men and women, children and nursing infants, oxen and donkeys and sheep—with the edge of the sword.

20 [a]Now one of the sons of Ahimelech the son of Ahitub, named Abiathar, [b]escaped and fled after David. 21 And Abiathar told David that Saul had killed the LORD's priests. 22 So David said to Abiathar, "I knew that day, when Doeg the Edomite *was* there, that he would surely tell Saul. I have caused *the death* of all the persons of your father's house. 23 Stay with me; do not fear. [a]For he who seeks my life seeks your life, but with me you *shall be* safe."

22:1 [a] Ps. 57:title; 142:title [b] 2 Sam. 23:13 **22:2** [a] Judg. 11:3 [b] 1 Sam. 25:13 **22:3** [a] 2 Sam. 8:2 **22:5** [a] 2 Sam. 24:11 **22:6** [a] 1 Sam. 15:34 **22:7** [a] 1 Sam. 8:14 **22:8** [a] 1 Sam. 18:3; 20:16, 30 **22:9** [a] 1 Sam. 21:7; 22:22 [b] 1 Sam. 21:1 [c] 1 Sam. 14:3 **22:10** [a] Num. 27:21 [b] 1 Sam. 21:6, 9 **22:14** [a] 1 Sam. 19:4, 5; 20:32; 24:11 **22:16** [a] Deut. 24:16 **22:17** [a] Ex. 1:17 **22:18** [a] 1 Sam. 2:31 **22:19** [a] 1 Sam. 22:9, 11 **22:20** [a] 1 Sam. 23:6, 9; 30:7 [b] 1 Sam. 2:33 **22:23** [a] 1 Kin. 2:26

David Saves the City of Keilah

23 Then they told David, saying, "Look,
the Philistines are fighting against
[a]Keilah, and they are robbing the threshing
floors."
2 Therefore David [a]inquired of the LORD,
saying, "Shall I go and attack these Philistines?"
And the LORD said to David, "Go and attack
the Philistines, and save Keilah."
3 But David's men said to him, "Look, we
are afraid here in Judah. How much more
then if we go to Keilah against the armies
of the Philistines?" 4 Then David inquired of
the LORD once again.
And the LORD answered him and said,
"Arise, go down to Keilah. For I will deliver
the Philistines into your hand." 5 And David
and his men went to Keilah and [a]fought with
the Philistines, struck them with a mighty
blow, and took away their livestock. So David
saved the inhabitants of Keilah.
6 Now it happened, when Abiathar the son
of Ahimelech [a]fled to David at Keilah, *that*
he went down *with* an ephod in his hand.
7 And Saul was told that David had gone
to Keilah. So Saul said, "God has delivered
him into my hand, for he has shut himself in
by entering a town that has gates and bars."
8 Then Saul called all the people together for
war, to go down to Keilah to besiege David
and his men.
9 When David knew that Saul plotted evil
against him, [a]he said to Abiathar the priest,
"Bring the ephod here." 10 Then David said,
"O LORD God of Israel, Your servant has certainly heard that Saul seeks to come to Keilah
[a]to destroy the city for my sake. 11 Will the
men of Keilah deliver me into his hand? Will
Saul come down, as Your servant has heard?
O LORD God of Israel, I pray, tell Your servant."
And the LORD said, "He will come down."
12 Then David said, "Will the men of Keilah deliver me and my men into the hand
of Saul?"
And the LORD said, "They will deliver *you*."
13 So David and his men, [a]about six hundred, arose and departed from Keilah and
went wherever they could go. Then it was told
Saul that David had escaped from Keilah; so
he halted the expedition.

David in Wilderness Strongholds

14 And David stayed in strongholds in the
wilderness, and remained in [a]the mountains
in the Wilderness of [b]Ziph. Saul [c]sought him
every day, but God did not deliver him into
his hand. 15 So David saw that Saul had come
out to seek his life. And David *was* in the
Wilderness of Ziph in a forest.[1] 16 Then Jonathan, Saul's son, arose and went to David
in the woods and strengthened his hand in
God. 17 And he said to him, [a]"Do not fear,
for the hand of Saul my father shall not
find you. You shall be king over Israel, and
I shall be next to you. [b]Even my father Saul
knows that." 18 So the two of them [a]made
a covenant before the LORD. And David
stayed in the woods, and Jonathan went to
his own house.
19 Then the Ziphites [a]came up to Saul at
Gibeah, saying, "Is David not hiding with
us in strongholds in the woods, in the hill
of Hachilah, which *is* on the south of Jeshimon? 20 Now therefore, O king, come down
according to all the desire of your soul to
come down; and [a]our part *shall be* to deliver
him into the king's hand."
21 And Saul said, "Blessed *are* you of the
LORD, for you have compassion on me.
22 Please go and find out for sure, and see
the place where his hideout is, *and* who has
seen him there. For I am told he is very crafty.
23 See therefore, and take knowledge of all
the lurking places where he hides; and come
back to me with certainty, and I will go with
you. And it shall be, if he is in the land, that I
will search for him throughout all the clans[1]
of Judah."
24 So they arose and went to Ziph before
Saul. But David and his men *were* in the Wilderness [a]of Maon, in the plain on the south
of Jeshimon. 25 When Saul and his men went
to seek *him*, they told David. Therefore he
went down to the rock, and stayed in the
Wilderness of Maon. And when Saul heard
that, he pursued David in the Wilderness of
Maon. 26 Then Saul went on one side of the
mountain, and David and his men on the
other side of the mountain. [a]So David made
haste to get away from Saul, for Saul and his
men [b]were encircling David and his men to
take them.
27 [a]But a messenger came to Saul, saying,
"Hurry and come, for the Philistines have
invaded the land!" 28 Therefore Saul returned
from pursuing David, and went against the
Philistines; so they called that place the Rock
of Escape.[1] 29 Then David went up from there
and dwelt in strongholds at [a]En Gedi.

23:1 [a] Josh. 15:44 **23:2** [a] 2 Sam. 5:19, 23 **23:5** [a] 1 Sam. 19:8 **23:6** [a] 1 Sam. 22:20 **23:9** [a] 1 Sam. 23:6; 30:7 **23:10** [a] 1 Sam. 22:19 **23:13** [a] 1 Sam. 22:2; 25:13 **23:14** [a] Ps. 11:1 [b] Josh. 15:55 [c] Ps. 32:7; 54:3, 4 **23:15** [1] Or *in Horesh* **23:17** [a] [Heb. 13:6] [b] 1 Sam. 20:31; 24:20 **23:18** [a] 2 Sam. 9:1; 21:7 **23:19** [a] 1 Sam. 26:1 **23:20** [a] Ps. 54:3 **23:23** [1] Literally *thousands* **23:24** [a] 1 Sam. 25:2 **23:26** [a] Ps. 31:22 [b] Ps. 17:9 **23:27** [a] 2 Kin. 19:9 **23:28** [1] Hebrew *Sela Hammahlekoth* **23:29** [a] 2 Chr. 20:2

David Spares Saul

24 Now it happened, [a]when Saul had returned from following the Philistines,
that it was told him, saying, “Take note! David
is in the Wilderness of En Gedi.” 2 Then Saul
took three thousand chosen men from all
Israel, and [a]went to seek David and his men
on the Rocks of the Wild Goats. 3 So he came
to the sheepfolds by the road, where there
was a cave; and [a]Saul went in to [b]attend to his
needs. ([c]David and his men were staying in
the recesses of the cave.) 4 [a]Then the men of
David said to him, “This is the day of which
the LORD said to you, ‘Behold, I will deliver
your enemy into your hand, that you may do
to him as it seems good to you.’ ” And David
arose and secretly cut off a corner of Saul’s
robe. 5 Now it happened afterward that [a]Da-
vid’s heart troubled him because he had cut
Saul’s robe. 6 And he said to his men, [a]“The
LORD forbid that I should do this thing to
my master, the LORD’s anointed, to stretch
out my hand against him, seeing he *is* the
anointed of the LORD.” 7 So David [a]restrained
his servants with *these* words, and did not
allow them to rise against Saul. And Saul
got up from the cave and went on *his* way.
8 David also arose afterward, went out of
the cave, and called out to Saul, saying, “My
lord the king!” And when Saul looked behind
him, David stooped with his face to the earth,
and bowed down. 9 And David said to Saul:
[a]“Why do you listen to the words of men who
say, ‘Indeed David seeks your harm’? 10 Look,
this day your eyes have seen that the LORD
delivered you today into my hand in the cave,
and *someone* urged *me* to kill you. But *my eye*
spared you, and I said, ‘I will not stretch out
my hand against my lord, for he *is* the LORD’s
anointed.’ 11 Moreover, my father, see! Yes, see
the corner of your robe in my hand! For in that
I cut off the corner of your robe, and did not
kill you, know and see that *there is* [a]neither
evil nor rebellion in my hand, and I have not
sinned against you. Yet you [b]hunt my life to
take it. 12 [a]Let the LORD judge between you and
me, and let the LORD avenge me on you. But
my hand shall not be against you. 13 As the
proverb of the ancients says, [a]‘Wickedness
proceeds from the wicked.’ But my hand shall
not be against you. 14 After whom has the king
of Israel come out? Whom do you pursue? [a]A
dead dog? [b]A flea? 15 [a]Therefore let the LORD
be judge, and judge between you and me, and
[b]see and [c]plead my case, and deliver me out
of your hand.”
16 So it was, when David had finished speaking these words to Saul, that Saul said, [a]“*Is* this
your voice, my son David?” And Saul lifted up
his voice and wept. 17 [a]Then he said to David:
“You *are* [b]more righteous than I; for [c]you
have rewarded me with good, whereas I have
rewarded you with evil. 18 And you have shown
this day how you have dealt well with me; for
when [a]the LORD delivered me into your hand,
you did not kill me. 19 For if a man finds his
enemy, will he let him get away safely? Therefore may the LORD reward you with good for
what you have done to me this day. 20 And
now [a]I know indeed that you shall surely be
king, and that the kingdom of Israel shall be
established in your hand. 21 [a]Therefore swear
now to me by the LORD [b]that you will not cut
off my descendants after me, and that you will
not destroy my name from my father’s house.”
22 So David swore to Saul. And Saul went
home, but David and his men went up to
[a]the stronghold.

Death of Samuel

25 Then [a]Samuel died; and the Israelites
gathered together and [b]lamented for
him, and buried him at his home in Ramah.
And David arose and went down [c]to the Wilderness of Paran.[1]

David and the Wife of Nabal

2 Now *there was* a man [a]in Maon whose
business *was* in [b]Carmel, and the man *was*

PEACE NOTE

The first step in spreading the gospel of peace is practicing the ministry of presence in someone’s life. Show up. Be present.

24:1 [a] 1 Sam. 23:19, 28, 29 **24:2** [a] 1 Sam. 26:2 **24:3** [a] 1 Sam. 24:10 [b] Judg. 3:24 [c] Ps. 57:title; 142:title **24:4** [a] 1 Sam. 26:8–11 **24:5** [a] 2 Sam. 24:10 **24:6** [a] 1 Sam. 26:11 **24:7** [a] [Matt. 5:44] **24:9** [a] Ps. 141:6 **24:11** [a] Ps. 7:3; 35:7 [b] 1 Sam. 26:20 **24:12** [a] 1 Sam. 26:10–23 **24:13** [a] [Matt. 7:16–20] **24:14** [a] 2 Sam. 9:8 [b] 1 Sam. 26:20 **24:15** [a] 1 Sam. 24:12 [b] 2 Chr. 24:22 [c] Ps. 35:1; 43:1; 119:154 **24:16** [a] 1 Sam. 26:17 **24:17** [a] 1 Sam. 26:21 [b] Gen. 38:26 [c] [Matt. 5:44] **24:18** [a] 1 Sam. 26:23 **24:20** [a] 1 Sam. 23:17 **24:21** [a] Gen. 21:23 [b] 2 Sam. 21:6–8 **24:22** [a] 1 Sam. 23:29 **25:1** [a] 1 Sam. 28:3 [b] Deut. 34:8 [c] Gen. 21:21 [1] Following Masoretic Text, Syriac, Targum, and Vulgate; Septuagint reads *Maon.* **25:2** [a] 1 Sam. 23:24 [b] Josh. 15:55

very rich. He had three thousand sheep and a
thousand goats. And he was shearing his sheep
in Carmel. 3 The name of the man *was* Nabal,
and the name of his wife Abigail. And *she was*
a woman of good understanding and beautiful
appearance; but the man *was* harsh and evil
in *his* doings. He *was of the house of* [a]Caleb.
4 When David heard in the wilderness that
Nabal was [a]shearing his sheep, 5 David sent
ten young men; and David said to the young
men, "Go up to Carmel, go to Nabal, and greet
him in my name. 6 And thus you shall say to
him who lives *in prosperity:* [a]'Peace *be* to you,
peace to your house, and peace to all that
you have! 7 Now I have heard that you have
shearers. Your shepherds were with us, and
we did not hurt them, [a]nor was there anything
missing from them all the while they were in
Carmel. 8 Ask your young men, and they will
tell you. Therefore let *my* young men find
favor in your eyes, for we come on [a]a feast
day. Please give whatever comes to your hand
to your servants and to your son David.' "
9 So when David's young men came, they
spoke to Nabal according to all these words
in the name of David, and waited.
10 Then Nabal answered David's servants,
and said, [a]"Who *is* David, and who *is* the son
of Jesse? There are many servants nowadays
who break away each one from his master.
11 [a]Shall I then take my bread and my water
and my meat that I have killed for my shearers, and give *it* to men when I do not know
where they *are* from?"
12 So David's young men turned on their
heels and went back; and they came and
told him all these words. 13 Then David said
to his men, "Every man gird on his sword."
So every man girded on his sword, and David
also girded on his sword. And about four hundred men went with David, and two hundred
[a]stayed with the supplies.
14 Now one of the young men told Abigail, Nabal's wife, saying, "Look, David sent
messengers from the wilderness to greet
our master; and he reviled them. 15 But the
men *were* very good to us, and [a]we were not
hurt, nor did we miss anything as long as
we accompanied them, when we were in
the fields. 16 They were [a]a wall to us both by
night and day, all the time we were with them
keeping the sheep. 17 Now therefore, know
and consider what you will do, for [a]harm is
determined against our master and against
all his household. For he *is such* a [b]scoundrel[1]
that *one* cannot speak to him."
18 Then Abigail made haste and [a]took two
hundred *loaves* of bread, two skins of wine,
five sheep already dressed, five seahs of roasted *grain,* one hundred clusters of raisins, and
two hundred cakes of figs, and loaded *them*
on donkeys. 19 And she said to her servants,
[a]"Go on before me; see, I am coming after
you." But she did not tell her husband Nabal.
20 So it was, *as* she rode on the donkey, that
she went down under cover of the hill; and
there were David and his men, coming down
toward her, and she met them. 21 Now David
had said, "Surely in vain I have protected all
that this *fellow* has in the wilderness, so that
nothing was missed of all that *belongs* to him.
And he has [a]repaid me evil for good. 22 [a]May
God do so, and more also, to the enemies of
David, if I [b]leave [c]one male of all who *belong*
to him by morning light."
23 Now when Abigail saw David, she [a]dis-
mounted quickly from the donkey, fell on
her face before David, and bowed down to
the ground. 24 So she fell at his feet and said:
"On me, my lord, *on* me *let* this iniquity *be!*
And please let your maidservant speak in
your ears, and hear the words of your maidservant. 25 Please, let not my lord regard this
scoundrel Nabal. For as his name *is,* so *is* he:
Nabal[1] *is* his name, and folly *is* with him! But I,
your maidservant, did not see the young men
of my lord whom you sent. 26 Now therefore,
my lord, [a]*as* the LORD lives and *as* your soul
lives, since the LORD has [b]held you back from
coming to bloodshed and from [c]avenging
yourself with your own hand, now then, [d]let
your enemies and those who seek harm for
my lord be as Nabal. 27 And now [a]this present which your maidservant has brought
to my lord, let it be given to the young men
who follow my lord. 28 Please forgive the
trespass of your maidservant. For [a]the LORD
will certainly make for my lord an enduring
house, because my lord [b]fights the battles
of the LORD, [c]and evil is not found in you
throughout your days. 29 Yet a man has risen
to pursue you and seek your life, but the life
of my lord shall be [a]bound in the bundle of
the living with the LORD your God; and the
lives of your enemies He shall [b]sling out, *as*
from the pocket of a sling. 30 And it shall come
to pass, when the LORD has done for my lord
according to all the good that He has spoken

25:3 [a] Josh. 15:13 **25:4** [a] Gen. 38:13 **25:6** [a] 1 Chr. 12:18 **25:7** [a] 1 Sam. 25:15, 21 **25:8** [a] Esth. 8:17; 9:19, 22 **25:10** [a] Judg. 9:28 **25:11** [a] Judg. 8:6, 15 **25:13** [a] 1 Sam. 30:24 **25:15** [a] 1 Sam. 25:7, 21 **25:16** [a] Ex. 14:22 **25:17** [a] 1 Sam. 20:7 [b] Deut. 13:13 [1] Literally *son of Belial* **25:18** [a] Gen. 32:13 **25:19** [a] Gen. 32:16, 20 **25:21** [a] Ps. 109:5 **25:22** [a] 1 Sam. 3:17; 20:13, 16 [b] 1 Sam. 25:34 [c] 1 Kin. 14:10; 21:21 **25:23** [a] Judg. 1:14 **25:25** [1] Literally *Fool* **25:26** [a] 2 Kin. 2:2 [b] Gen. 20:6 [c] [Rom. 12:19] [d] 2 Sam. 18:32 **25:27** [a] Gen. 33:11 **25:28** [a] 2 Sam. 7:11–16, 27 [b] 1 Sam. 18:17 [c] 1 Sam. 24:11 **25:29** [a] [Col. 3:3] [b] Jer. 10:18

concerning you, and has appointed you [a]ruler over Israel, 31 that this will be no grief to you, nor offense of heart to my lord, either that you have shed blood without cause, or that my lord has avenged himself. But when the LORD has dealt well with my lord, then remember your maidservant."

32 Then David said to Abigail: [a]"Blessed *is* the LORD God of Israel, who sent you this day to meet me! 33 And blessed *is* your advice and blessed *are* you, because you have [a]kept me this day from coming to bloodshed and from avenging myself with my own hand. 34 For indeed, *as* the LORD God of Israel lives, who has [a]kept me back from hurting you, unless you had hurried and come to meet me, surely [b]by morning light no males would have been left to Nabal!" 35 So David received from her hand what she had brought him, and said to her, [a]"Go up in peace to your house. See, I have heeded your voice and [b]respected your person."

36 Now Abigail went to Nabal, and there he was, [a]holding a feast in his house, like the feast of a king. And Nabal's heart *was* merry within him, for he *was* very drunk; therefore she told him nothing, little or much, until morning light. 37 So it was, in the morning, when the wine had gone from Nabal, and his wife had told him these things, that his heart died within him, and he became *like* a stone. 38 Then it happened, *after* about ten days, that the LORD [a]struck Nabal, and he died.

39 So when David heard that Nabal was dead, he said, [a]"Blessed *be* the LORD, who has [b]pleaded the cause of my reproach from the hand of Nabal, and has [c]kept His servant from evil! For the LORD has [d]returned the wickedness of Nabal on his own head."

And David sent and proposed to Abigail, to take her as his wife. 40 When the servants of David had come to Abigail at Carmel, they spoke to her saying, "David sent us to you, to ask you to become his wife."

41 Then she arose, bowed her face to the earth, and said, "Here is your maidservant, a servant to [a]wash the feet of the servants of my lord." 42 So Abigail rose in haste and rode on a donkey, attended by five of her maidens; and she followed the messengers of David, and became his wife. 43 David also took Ahinoam [a]of Jezreel, [b]and so both of them were his wives.

44 But Saul had given [a]Michal his daughter, David's wife, to Palti[1] the son of Laish, who *was* from [b]Gallim.

David Spares Saul a Second Time

26 Now the Ziphites came to Saul at Gibeah, saying, [a]"Is David not hiding in the hill of Hachilah, opposite Jeshimon?" 2 Then Saul arose and went down to the Wilderness of Ziph, having [a]three thousand chosen men of Israel with him, to seek David in the Wilderness of Ziph. 3 And Saul encamped in the hill of Hachilah, which *is* opposite Jeshimon, by the road. But David stayed in the wilderness, and he saw that Saul came after him into the wilderness. 4 David therefore sent out spies, and understood that Saul had indeed come.

5 So David arose and came to the place where Saul had encamped. And David saw the place where Saul lay, and [a]Abner the son of Ner, the commander of his army. Now Saul lay within the camp, with the people encamped all around him. 6 Then David answered, and said to Ahimelech the Hittite and to Abishai [a]the son of Zeruiah, brother of [b]Joab, saying, "Who will [c]go down with me to Saul in the camp?"

And [d]Abishai said, "I will go down with you."

7 So David and Abishai came to the people by night; and there Saul lay sleeping within the camp, with his spear stuck in the ground by his head. And Abner and the people lay all around him. 8 Then Abishai said to David, [a]"God has delivered your enemy into your hand this day. Now therefore, please, let me strike him at once with the spear, right to the earth; and I will not *have to strike* him a second time!"

9 But David said to Abishai, "Do not destroy him; [a]for who can stretch out his hand against the LORD's anointed, and be guiltless?" 10 David said furthermore, "*As* the LORD lives, [a]the LORD shall strike him, or [b]his day shall come to die, or he shall [c]go out to battle and perish. 11 [a]The LORD forbid that I should stretch out my hand against the LORD's anointed. But please, take now the spear and the jug of water that *are* by his head, and let us go." 12 So David took the spear and the jug of water *by* Saul's head, and they got away; and no man saw or knew *it* or awoke. For they *were* all asleep, because [a]a deep sleep from the LORD had fallen on them.

13 Now David went over to the other side, and stood on the top of a hill afar off, a great distance *being* between them. 14 And David called out to the people and to Abner the son of Ner, saying, "Do you not answer, Abner?"

Then Abner answered and said, "Who *are* you, calling out to the king?"

25:30 [a] 1 Sam. 13:14; 15:28 **25:32** [a] Luke 1:68 **25:33** [a] 1 Sam. 25:26 **25:34** [a] 1 Sam. 25:26 [b] 1 Sam. 25:22 **25:35** [a] 2 Kin. 5:19 [b] Gen. 19:21 **25:36** [a] 2 Sam. 13:28 **25:38** [a] 1 Sam. 26:10 **25:39** [a] 1 Sam. 25:32 [b] Prov. 22:23 [c] 1 Sam. 25:26, 34 [d] 1 Kin. 2:44 **25:41** [a] Luke 7:38, 44 **25:43** [a] Josh. 15:56 [b] 1 Sam. 27:3; 30:5 **25:44** [a] 2 Sam. 3:14 [b] Is. 10:30 [1] Spelled *Paltiel* in 2 Samuel 3:15 **26:1** [a] 1 Sam. 23:19 **26:2** [a] 1 Sam. 13:2; 24:2 **26:5** [a] 1 Sam. 14:50, 51; 17:55 **26:6** [a] 1 Chr. 2:16 [b] 2 Sam. 2:13 [c] Judg. 7:10, 11 [d] 2 Sam. 2:18, 24 **26:8** [a] 1 Sam. 24:4 **26:9** [a] 1 Sam. 24:6, 7 **26:10** [a] 1 Sam. 25:26, 38 [b] [Job 7:1; 14:5] [c] 1 Sam. 31:6 **26:11** [a] 1 Sam. 24:6–12 **26:12** [a] Gen. 2:21; 15:12

15 So David said to Abner, "*Are* you not a
man? And who *is* like you in Israel? Why then
have you not guarded your lord the king? For
one of the people came in to destroy your
lord the king. 16 This thing that you have done
is not good. As the LORD lives, you deserve
to die, because you have not guarded your
master, the LORD's anointed. And now see
where the king's spear *is,* and the jug of water
that *was* by his head."
17 Then Saul knew David's voice, and said,
[a]"*Is* that your voice, my son David?"
David said, "*It is* my voice, my lord, O king."
18 And he said, [a]"Why does my lord thus pursue his servant? For what have I done, or what
evil *is* in my hand? 19 Now therefore, please,
let my lord the king hear the words of his servant: If the LORD has [a]stirred you up against
me, let Him accept an offering. But if *it is* the
children of men, *may* they *be* cursed before
the LORD, [b]for they have driven me out this
day from sharing in the [c]inheritance of the
LORD, saying, 'Go, serve other gods.' 20 So now,
do not let my blood fall to the earth before
the face of the LORD. For the king of Israel has
come out to seek [a]a flea, as when one hunts
a partridge in the mountains."
21 Then Saul said, [a]"I have sinned. Return,
my son David. For I will harm you no more,
because my life was precious in your eyes
this day. Indeed I have played the fool and
erred exceedingly."
22 And David answered and said, "Here is
the king's spear. Let one of the young men
come over and get it. 23 [a]May the LORD [b]re-
pay every man *for* his righteousness and
his faithfulness; for the LORD delivered you
into *my* hand today, but I would not stretch
out my hand against the LORD's anointed.
24 And indeed, as your life was valued much
this day in my eyes, so let my life be valued
much in the eyes of the LORD, and let Him
deliver me out of all tribulation."
25 Then Saul said to David, "*May* you *be*
blessed, my son David! You shall both do
great things and also still [a]prevail."
So David went on his way, and Saul returned to his place.

David Allied with the Philistines

27 And David said in his heart, "Now I
shall perish someday by the hand of
Saul. *There is* nothing better for me than that
I should speedily escape to the land of the Philistines; and Saul will despair of me, to seek me
anymore in any part of Israel. So I shall escape
out of his hand." 2 Then David arose [a]and went
over with the six hundred men who *were* with
him [b]to Achish the son of Maoch, king of Gath.
3 So David dwelt with Achish at Gath, he and his
men, each man with his household, *and* David
[a]with his two wives, Ahinoam the Jezreelitess,
and Abigail the Carmelitess, Nabal's widow.
4 And it was told Saul that David had fled to
Gath; so he sought him no more.
5 Then David said to Achish, "If I have now
found favor in your eyes, let them give me a
place in some town in the country, that I may
dwell there. For why should your servant dwell
in the royal city with you?" 6 So Achish gave him
Ziklag that day. Therefore [a]Ziklag has belonged
to the kings of Judah to this day. 7 Now the
time that David [a]dwelt in the country of the
Philistines was one full year and four months.
8 And David and his men went up and
raided [a]the Geshurites, [b]the Girzites,[1] and
the [c]Amalekites. For those *nations* were the
inhabitants of the land from of old, [d]as you
go to Shur, even as far as the land of Egypt.
9 Whenever David attacked the land, he left
neither man nor woman alive, but took away
the sheep, the oxen, the donkeys, the camels,
and the apparel, and returned and came to
Achish. 10 Then Achish would say, "Where have
you made a raid today?" And David would
say, "Against the southern *area* of Judah, or
against the southern *area* of [a]the Jerahmeelites, or against the southern *area* of [b]the
Kenites." 11 David would save neither man nor
woman alive, to bring *news* to Gath, saying,
"Lest they should inform on us, saying, 'Thus
David did.'" And thus *was* his behavior all the
time he dwelt in the country of the Philistines.

PEACE NOTE

In His masterful way, Jesus expressed the idea that to know God is to know peace. The mind focused on the Spirit of God is a calm, reassured mind.

26:17 [a] 1 Sam. 24:16 **26:18** [a] 1 Sam. 24:9, 11–14 **26:19** [a] 2 Sam. 16:11; 24:1 [b] Deut. 4:27, 28 [c] 2 Sam. 14:16; 20:19 **26:20** [a] 1 Sam. 24:14 **26:21** [a] 1 Sam. 15:24, 30; 24:17 **26:23** [a] Ps. 7:8; 18:20; 62:12 [b] 2 Sam. 22:21 **26:25** [a] Gen. 32:28 **27:2** [a] 1 Sam. 25:13 [b] 1 Sam. 21:10 **27:3** [a] 1 Sam. 25:42, 43 **27:6** [a] Josh. 15:31; 19:5 **27:7** [a] 1 Sam. 29:3 **27:8** [a] Josh. 13:2, 13 [b] Judg. 1:29 [c] Ex. 17:8, 16 [d] Gen. 25:18 [1] Or *Gezrites* **27:10** [a] 1 Chr. 2:9, 25 [b] Judg. 1:16

12 So Achish believed David, saying, "He has
made his people Israel utterly abhor him;
therefore he will be my servant forever."

28 Now [a]it happened in those days that
the Philistines gathered their armies
together for war, to fight with Israel. And
Achish said to David, "You assuredly know
that you will go out with me to battle, you
and your men."

2 So David said to Achish, "Surely you know
what your servant can do."

And Achish said to David, "Therefore I will
make you one of my chief guardians forever."

Saul Consults a Medium

3 Now [a]Samuel had died, and all Israel had
lamented for him and buried him in [b]Ramah,
in his own city. And Saul had put [c]the mediums and the spiritists out of the land.

4 Then the Philistines gathered together,
and came and encamped at [a]Shunem. So
Saul gathered all Israel together, and they
encamped at [b]Gilboa. 5 When Saul saw the
army of the Philistines, he was [a]afraid, and
his heart trembled greatly. 6 And when Saul
inquired of the LORD, [a]the LORD did not answer him, either by [b]dreams or [c]by Urim or
by the prophets.

7 Then Saul said to his servants, "Find me
a woman who is a medium, [a]that I may go
to her and inquire of her."

And his servants said to him, "In fact, *there
is* a woman who is a medium at En Dor."

8 So Saul disguised himself and put on
other clothes, and he went, and two men
with him; and they came to the woman by
night. And [a]he said, "Please conduct a séance
for me, and bring up for me the one I shall
name to you."

9 Then the woman said to him, "Look, you
know what Saul has done, how he has [a]cut
off the mediums and the spiritists from the
land. Why then do you lay a snare for my life,
to cause me to die?"

10 And Saul swore to her by the LORD, saying, "*As* the LORD lives, no punishment shall
come upon you for this thing."

11 Then the woman said, "Whom shall I
bring up for you?"

And he said, "Bring up Samuel for me."

12 When the woman saw Samuel, she cried
out with a loud voice. And the woman spoke
to Saul, saying, "Why have you deceived me?
For you *are* Saul!"

13 And the king said to her, "Do not be
afraid. What did you see?"

And the woman said to Saul, "I saw [a]a spirit[1] ascending out of the earth."

14 So he said to her, "What *is* his form?"

And she said, "An old man is coming up,
and he *is* covered with [a]a mantle." And Saul
perceived that it *was* Samuel, and he stooped
with *his* face to the ground and bowed down.

15 Now Samuel said to Saul, "Why have you
[a]disturbed me by bringing me up?"

And Saul answered, "I am deeply distressed; for the Philistines make war against
me, and [b]God has departed from me and
[c]does not answer me anymore, neither by
prophets nor by dreams. Therefore I have
called you, that you may reveal to me what
I should do."

16 Then Samuel said: "So why do you ask
me, seeing the LORD has departed from you
and has become your enemy? 17 And the LORD
has done for Himself[1] [a]as He spoke by me. For
the LORD has torn the kingdom out of your
hand and given it to your neighbor, David.
18 [a]Because you did not obey the voice of the
LORD nor execute His fierce wrath upon
[b]Amalek, therefore the LORD has done this
thing to you this day. 19 Moreover the LORD
will also deliver Israel with you into the hand
of the Philistines. And tomorrow you and
your sons *will be* with [a]me. The LORD will
also deliver the army of Israel into the hand
of the Philistines."

20 Immediately Saul fell full length on the
ground, and was dreadfully afraid because
of the words of Samuel. And there was no
strength in him, for he had eaten no food
all day or all night.

21 And the woman came to Saul and saw
that he was severely troubled, and said to
him, "Look, your maidservant has obeyed
your voice, and I have [a]put my life in my
hands and heeded the words which you
spoke to me. 22 Now therefore, please, heed
also the voice of your maidservant, and let
me set a piece of bread before you; and eat,
that you may have strength when you go
on *your* way."

23 But he refused and said, "I will not eat."

So his servants, together with the woman,
urged him; and he heeded their voice. Then
he arose from the ground and sat on the
bed. 24 Now the woman had a fatted calf in
the house, and she hastened to kill it. And
she took flour and kneaded *it,* and baked
unleavened bread from it. 25 So she brought
it before Saul and his servants, and they ate.
Then they rose and went away that night.

28:1 [a] 1 Sam. 29:1, 2 **28:3** [a] 1 Sam. 25:1 [b] 1 Sam. 1:19 [c] Deut. 18:10, 11 **28:4** [a] Josh. 19:18 [b] 1 Sam. 31:1 **28:5** [a] Job 18:11 **28:6** [a] 1 Sam. 14:37 [b] Num. 12:6 [c] Ex. 28:30 **28:7** [a] 1 Chr. 10:13 **28:8** [a] Deut. 18:10, 11 **28:9** [a] 1 Sam. 28:3 **28:13** [a] Ex. 22:28 [1] Hebrew *elohim* **28:14** [a] 1 Sam. 15:27 **28:15** [a] Is. 14:9 [b] 1 Sam. 16:14; 18:12 [c] 1 Sam. 28:6 **28:17** [a] 1 Sam. 15:28 [1] Or *him,* that is, David **28:18** [a] 1 Chr. 10:13 [b] 1 Sam. 15:3–9 **28:19** [a] Job 3:17–19 **28:21** [a] Job 13:14

The Philistines Reject David

29 Then [a]the Philistines gathered together all their armies [b]at Aphek, and the Israelites encamped by a fountain which *is* in Jezreel. 2 And the [a]lords of the Philistines passed in review by hundreds and by thousands, but [b]David and his men passed in review at the rear with Achish. 3 Then the princes of the Philistines said, "What *are* these Hebrews *doing here?*"

And Achish said to the princes of the Philistines, "*Is* this not David, the servant of Saul king of Israel, who has been with me [a]these days, or these years? And to this day I have [b]found no fault in him since he defected *to me.*"

4 But the princes of the Philistines were angry with him; so the princes of the Philistines said to him, [a]"Make this fellow return, that he may go back to the place which you have appointed for him, and do not let him go down with us to [b]battle, lest [c]in the battle he become our adversary. For with what could he reconcile himself to his master, if not with the heads of these [d]men? 5 *Is* this not David, [a]of whom they sang to one another in dances, saying:

> [b]'Saul has slain his thousands,
> And David his ten thousands'?"[1]

6 Then Achish called David and said to him, "Surely, *as* the LORD lives, you have been upright, and [a]your going out and your coming in with me in the army *is* good in my sight. For to this day [b]I have not found evil in you since the day of your coming to me. Nevertheless the lords do not favor you. 7 Therefore return now, and go in peace, that you may not displease the lords of the Philistines."

8 So David said to Achish, "But what have I done? And to this day what have you found in your servant as long as I have been with you, that I may not go and fight against the enemies of my lord the king?"

9 Then Achish answered and said to David, "I know that you *are* as good in my sight [a]as an angel of God; nevertheless [b]the princes of the Philistines have said, 'He shall not go up with us to the battle.' 10 Now therefore, rise early in the morning with your master's servants [a]who have come with you.[1] And as soon as you are up early in the morning and have light, depart."

11 So David and his men rose early to depart in the morning, to return to the land of the Philistines. [a]And the Philistines went up to Jezreel.

David's Conflict with the Amalekites

30 Now it happened, when David and his men came to [a]Ziklag, on the third day, that the [b]Amalekites had invaded the South and Ziklag, attacked Ziklag and burned it with fire, 2 and had taken captive the [a]women and those who *were* there, from small to great; they did not kill anyone, but carried *them* away and went their way. 3 So David and his men came to the city, and there it was, burned with fire; and their wives, their sons, and their daughters had been taken captive. 4 Then David and the people who *were* with him lifted up their voices and wept, until they had no more power to weep. 5 And David's two [a]wives, Ahinoam the Jezreelitess, and Abigail the widow of Nabal the Carmelite, had been taken captive. 6 Now David was greatly distressed, for [a]the people spoke of stoning him, because the soul of all the people was grieved, every man for his sons and his daughters. [b]But David strengthened himself in the LORD his God.

PEACE NOTE

Every time we rely on our strength, we will fail. We cannot create our own peace. We must rely on God for strength and peace.

1 SAMUEL 30:6

7 [a]Then David said to Abiathar the priest, Ahimelech's son, "Please bring the ephod here to me." And [b]Abiathar brought the ephod to David. 8 [a]So David inquired of the LORD, saying, "Shall I pursue this troop? Shall I overtake them?"

29:1 [a] 1 Sam. 28:1 [b] 1 Sam. 4:1 **29:2** [a] 1 Sam. 6:4; 7:7 [b] 1 Sam. 28:1, 2 **29:3** [a] 1 Sam. 27:7 [b] Dan. 6:5 **29:4** [a] 1 Sam. 27:6 [b] 1 Sam. 14:21 [c] 1 Sam. 29:9 [d] 1 Chr. 12:19, 20 **29:5** [a] 1 Sam. 21:11 [b] 1 Sam. 18:7 [1] Compare 1 Samuel 18:7 **29:6** [a] 2 Sam. 3:25 [b] 1 Sam. 29:3 **29:9** [a] 2 Sam. 14:17, 20; 19:27 [b] 1 Sam. 29:4 **29:10** [a] 1 Chr. 12:19, 22 [1] Following Masoretic Text, Targum, and Vulgate; Septuagint adds *and go to the place which I have selected for you there; and set no bothersome word in your heart, for you are good before me. And rise on your way.* **29:11** [a] 2 Sam. 4:4 **30:1** [a] 1 Sam. 27:6 [b] 1 Sam. 15:7; 27:8 **30:2** [a] 1 Sam. 27:2, 3 **30:5** [a] 1 Sam. 25:42, 43 **30:6** [a] Ex. 17:4 [b] Hab. 3:17–19 **30:7** [a] 1 Sam. 23:2–9 [b] 1 Sam. 23:6 **30:8** [a] 1 Sam. 23:2, 4

And He answered him, "Pursue, for you shall surely overtake *them* and without fail recover *all.*"

9 So David went, he and the six hundred men who *were* with him, and came to the Brook Besor, where those stayed who were left behind. 10 But David pursued, he and four hundred men; [a]for two hundred stayed *behind,* who were so weary that they could not cross the Brook Besor.

11 Then they found an Egyptian in the field, and brought him to David; and they gave him bread and he ate, and they let him drink water. 12 And they gave him a piece of [a]a cake of figs and two clusters of raisins. So [b]when he had eaten, his strength came back to him; for he had eaten no bread nor drunk water for three days and three nights. 13 Then David said to him, "To whom do you *belong,* and where *are* you from?"

And he said, "I *am* a young man from Egypt, servant of an Amalekite; and my master left me behind, because three days ago I fell sick. 14 We made an invasion of the southern *area* of [a]the Cherethites, in the *territory* which *belongs* to Judah, and of the southern *area* [b]of Caleb; and we burned Ziklag with fire."

15 And David said to him, "Can you take me down to this troop?"

So he said, "Swear to me by God that you will neither kill me nor deliver me into the hands of my [a]master, and I will take you down to this troop."

16 And when he had brought him down, there they were, spread out over all the land, [a]eating and drinking and dancing, because of all the great spoil which they had taken from the land of the Philistines and from the land of Judah. 17 Then David attacked them from twilight until the evening of the next day. Not a man of them escaped, except four hundred young men who rode on camels and fled. 18 So David recovered all that the Amalekites had carried away, and David rescued his two wives. 19 And nothing of theirs was lacking, either small or great, sons or daughters, spoil or anything which they had taken from them; [a]David recovered all. 20 Then David took all the flocks and herds they had driven before those *other* livestock, and said, "This *is* David's spoil."

21 Now David came to the [a]two hundred men who had been so weary that they could not follow David, whom they also had made to stay at the Brook Besor. So they went out to meet David and to meet the people who *were* with him. And when David came near the people, he greeted them. 22 Then all the wicked and [a]worthless men[1] of those who went with David answered and said, "Because they did not go with us, we will not give them *any* of the spoil that we have recovered, except for every man's wife and children, that they may lead *them* away and depart."

23 But David said, "My brethren, you shall not do so with what the LORD has given us, who has preserved us and delivered into our hand the troop that came against us. 24 For who will heed you in this matter? But [a]as his part *is* who goes down to the battle, so *shall* his part *be* who stays by the supplies; they shall share alike." 25 So it was, from that day forward; he made it a statute and an ordinance for Israel to this day.

26 Now when David came to Ziklag, he sent *some* of the spoil to the elders of Judah, to his friends, saying, "Here is a present for you from the spoil of the enemies of the LORD"— 27 to *those* who *were* in Bethel, *those* who *were* in [a]Ramoth of the South, *those* who *were* in [b]Jattir, 28 *those* who *were* in [a]Aroer, *those* who *were* in [b]Siphmoth, *those* who *were* in [c]Eshtemoa, 29 *those* who *were* in Rachal, *those* who *were* in the cities of [a]the Jerahmeelites, *those* who *were* in the cities of the [b]Kenites, 30 *those* who *were* in [a]Hormah, *those* who *were* in Chorashan,[1] *those* who *were* in Athach, 31 *those* who *were* in [a]Hebron, and to all the places where David himself and his men were accustomed to [b]rove.

The Tragic End of Saul and His Sons

31 Now [a]the Philistines fought against Israel; and the men of Israel fled from before the Philistines, and fell slain on Mount [b]Gilboa. 2 Then the Philistines followed hard after Saul and his sons. And the Philistines killed [a]Jonathan, Abinadab, and Malchishua, Saul's sons. 3 [a]The battle became fierce against Saul. The archers hit him, and he was severely wounded by the archers.

4 [a]Then Saul said to his armorbearer, "Draw your sword, and thrust me through with it, lest [b]these uncircumcised men come and thrust me through and abuse me."

But his armorbearer would not, [c]for he was greatly afraid. Therefore Saul took a sword and [d]fell on it. 5 And when his armorbearer

30:10 [a] 1 Sam. 30:9, 21 **30:12** [a] 1 Sam. 25:18 [b] Judg. 15:19 **30:14** [a] 2 Sam. 8:18 [b] Josh. 14:13; 15:13 **30:15** [a] Deut. 23:15 **30:16** [a] 1 Thess. 5:3 **30:19** [a] 1 Sam. 30:8 **30:21** [a] 1 Sam. 30:10 **30:22** [a] Deut. 13:13 [1] Literally *men of Belial* **30:24** [a] Josh. 22:8 **30:27** [a] Josh. 19:8 [b] Josh. 15:48; 21:14 **30:28** [a] Josh. 13:16 [b] 1 Chr. 27:27 [c] Josh. 15:50 **30:29** [a] 1 Sam. 27:10 [b] Judg. 1:16 **30:30** [a] Judg. 1:17 [1] Or *Borashan* **30:31** [a] 2 Sam. 2:1 [b] 1 Sam. 23:22 **31:1** [a] 1 Chr. 10:1–12 [b] 1 Sam. 28:4 **31:2** [a] 1 Sam. 14:49 **31:3** [a] 2 Sam. 1:6 **31:4** [a] Judg. 9:54 [b] 1 Sam. 14:6; 17:26, 36 [c] 2 Sam. 1:14 [d] 2 Sam. 1:6, 10

THE SECOND BOOK OF

SAMUEL

AUTHOR

No author is mentioned anywhere in this book. Although the traditional view is that Samuel wrote 2 Samuel, it was probably compiled by one man who combined the written chronicles of "Nathan the prophet" and "Gad the seer" (1 Chr. 29:29). In addition to these written sources, the compiler evidently used another source called the "Book of Jasher" (2 Sam. 1:18).

TIME

c. 1011–971 BC

KEY VERSE

2 Samuel 7:12–13

THEME

Second Samuel begins with Saul's death and David's ascension to the throne of Judah. A few years later David becomes the king of all Israel. During his reign there were many problems, most of which can be traced back to David's own behavior. He abuses power and plays favorites with his sons. The result is much personal sorrow and the seeds of discord that follow in succeeding generations. Second Samuel gives us a full picture of a king, a poet, a soldier, and a sinner who yearns after God's own heart and follows where He leads.

The prerequisite for peace in 2 Samuel is wisdom. David shows compassionate wisdom to Mephibosheth, the son of his late best friend, Jonathan, of the house of Saul. The peace Mephibosheth received from David is illustrative of the unearned favor, grace, and peace we receive from Jesus Christ. We also meet the wise woman of 2 Samuel, who said, "I am among the peaceable and faithful in Israel" (20:19), and through savvy and quick action she preserved her community's peace. In fact, her actions are a descriptor for her intervention: "Then the woman in her wisdom went to all the people" (20:22). We also learn how foolishness and deceit rob communities and families of God's peace.

saw that Saul was dead, he also fell on his
sword, and died with him. 6 So Saul, his three
sons, his armorbearer, and all his men died
together that same day.

7 And when the men of Israel who *were*
on the other side of the valley, and *those*
who *were* on the other side of the Jordan,
saw that the men of Israel had fled and that
Saul and his sons were dead, they forsook
the cities and fled; and the Philistines came
and dwelt in them. 8 So it happened the next
day, when the Philistines came to strip the
slain, that they found Saul and his three sons
fallen on Mount Gilboa. 9 And they cut off his
head and stripped off his armor, and sent
word throughout the land of the Philistines,
to [a]proclaim *it in* the temple of their idols
and among the people. 10 [a]Then they put
his armor in the temple of the [b]Ashtoreths,
and [c]they fastened his body to the wall of
[d]Beth Shan.[1]

11 [a]Now when the inhabitants of Jabesh
Gilead heard what the Philistines had done
to Saul, 12 [a]all the valiant men arose and traveled all night, and took the body of Saul and
the bodies of his sons from the wall of Beth
Shan; and they came to Jabesh and [b]burned
them there. 13 Then they took their bones
and [a]buried *them* under the tamarisk tree
at Jabesh, [b]and fasted seven days.

31:9 [a] 2 Sam. 1:20 **31:10** [a] 1 Sam. 21:9 [b] Judg. 2:13 [c] 2 Sam. 21:12 [d] Judg. 1:27 [1] Spelled *Beth Shean* in Joshua 17:11 and elsewhere **31:11** [a] 1 Sam. 11:1–13 **31:12** [a] 2 Sam. 2:4–7 [b] 2 Chr. 16:14 **31:13** [a] 2 Sam. 2:4, 5; 21:12–14 [b] Gen. 50:10

The Report of Saul's Death

1 Now it came to pass after the [a]death of
Saul, when David had returned from [b]the
slaughter of the Amalekites, and David had
stayed two days in Ziklag, 2 on the third day,
behold, it happened that [a]a man came from
Saul's camp [b]with his clothes torn and dust
on his head. So it was, when he came to David,
that he [c]fell to the ground and prostrated
himself.

3 And David said to him, "Where have you
come from?"

So he said to him, "I have escaped from
the camp of Israel."

4 Then David said to him, [a]"How did the
matter go? Please tell me."

And he answered, "The people have fled
from the battle, many of the people are fallen
and dead, and Saul and [b]Jonathan his son
are dead also."

5 So David said to the young man who told
him, "How do you know that Saul and Jonathan his son are dead?"

6 Then the young man who told him said,
"As I happened by chance *to be* on [a]Mount
Gilboa, there was [b]Saul, leaning on his spear;
and indeed the chariots and horsemen followed hard after him. 7 Now when he looked
behind him, he saw me and called to me. And
I answered, 'Here I am.' 8 And he said to me,
'Who *are* you?' So I answered him, 'I *am* an
Amalekite.' 9 He said to me again, 'Please
stand over me and kill me, for anguish has
come upon me, but my life still *remains* in
me.' 10 So I stood over him and [a]killed him,
because I was sure that he could not live after
he had fallen. And I took the crown that *was*
on his head and the bracelet that *was* on his
arm, and have brought them here to my lord."

11 Therefore David took hold of his own
clothes and [a]tore them, and *so did* all the men
who *were* with him. 12 And they [a]mourned
and wept and [b]fasted until evening for Saul
and for Jonathan his son, for the [c]people of
the LORD and for the house of Israel, because
they had fallen by the sword.

13 Then David said to the young man who
told him, "Where *are* you from?"

And he answered, "I *am* the son of an alien,
an Amalekite."

14 So David said to him, "How [a]was it you
were not [b]afraid to [c]put forth your hand to
destroy the LORD's anointed?" 15 Then [a]David
called one of the young men and said, "Go
near, *and* execute him!" And he struck him
so that he died. 16 So David said to him, [a]"Your
blood *is* on your own head, for [b]your own
mouth has testified against you, saying, 'I
have killed the LORD's anointed.'"

The Song of the Bow

17 Then David lamented with this lamentation over Saul and over Jonathan his son,
18 [a]and he told *them* to teach the children of
Judah *the Song of* the Bow; indeed *it is* written
[b]in the Book of Jasher:

19 "The beauty of Israel is slain on your
high places!
[a]How the mighty have fallen!
20 [a]Tell *it* not in Gath,
Proclaim *it* not in the streets of
[b]Ashkelon—
Lest [c]the daughters of the Philistines
rejoice,
Lest the daughters of [d]the
uncircumcised triumph.

21 "O [a]mountains of Gilboa,
[b]*Let there be* no dew nor rain upon you,
Nor fields of offerings.
For the shield of the mighty is cast
away there!
The shield of Saul, not [c]anointed with oil.
22 From the blood of the slain,
From the fat of the mighty,
[a]The bow of Jonathan did not turn back,
And the sword of Saul did not return
empty.

23 "Saul and Jonathan *were* beloved and
pleasant in their lives,
And in their [a]death they were not
divided;
They were swifter than eagles,
They were [b]stronger than lions.

24 "O daughters of Israel, weep over Saul,
Who clothed you in scarlet, with luxury;
Who put ornaments of gold on your
apparel.

25 "How the mighty have fallen in the
midst of the battle!
Jonathan *was* slain in your high places.
26 I am distressed for you, my brother
Jonathan;
You have been very pleasant to me;
[a]Your love to me was wonderful,
Surpassing the love of women.

1:1 [a] 1 Sam. 31:6 [b] 1 Sam. 30:1, 17, 26 **1:2** [a] 2 Sam. 4:10 [b] 1 Sam. 4:12 [c] 1 Sam. 25:23 **1:4** [a] 1 Sam. 4:16; 31:3 [b] 1 Sam. 31:2 **1:6** [a] 1 Sam. 31:1 [b] 1 Sam. 31:2–4 **1:10** [a] Judg. 9:54 **1:11** [a] 2 Sam. 3:31; 13:31 **1:12** [a] 2 Sam. 3:31 [b] 1 Sam. 31:13 [c] 2 Sam. 6:21 **1:14** [a] Num. 12:8 [b] 1 Sam. 31:4 [c] 1 Sam. 24:6; 26:9 **1:15** [a] 2 Sam. 4:10, 12 **1:16** [a] 1 Kin. 2:32–37 [b] Luke 19:22 **1:18** [a] 1 Sam. 31:3 [b] Josh. 10:13 **1:19** [a] 2 Sam. 1:27 **1:20** [a] Mic. 1:10 [b] Jer. 25:20 [c] Ex. 15:20 [d] 1 Sam. 31:4 **1:21** [a] 1 Sam. 31:1 [b] Ezek. 31:15 [c] 1 Sam. 10:1 **1:22** [a] 1 Sam. 18:4 **1:23** [a] 1 Sam. 31:2–4 [b] Judg. 14:18 **1:26** [a] 1 Sam. 18:1–4; 19:2; 20:17

FRIENDS AND ENEMIES

How the mighty have fallen!

2 SAMUEL 1:19

Grace is not listed among the "fruit of the Spirit" (Gal. 5:22–23); grace is the condition from which the fruit of the Spirit can grow and become a blessing. Among the fruit of the Spirit listed by the apostle Paul is peace. Grace and peace go hand in hand. The man or woman of peace has experienced God's grace and is happy to extend it to others, even when others do not deserve it.

David exhibited extraordinary grace in his difficult, contentious, and at times dangerous relationship with King Saul. Several times Saul tried to kill David. On two occasions David could have killed Saul but spared his life. When Saul and his sons died in battle, David did not rejoice. He didn't even express relief that his enemy was no more. Rather, he wrote and sang one of the most beautiful elegies in Scripture: "The beauty of Israel is slain on your high places! How the mighty have fallen! . . . Saul and Jonathan were beloved and pleasant in their lives, and in their death they were not divided" (2 Sam. 1:19, 23).

Honoring a sometimes-enemy is an act of grace that brings peace. Is there someone at odds with you whom you could honor in some way?

27 "How[a] the mighty have fallen,
And the weapons of war perished!"

David Anointed King of Judah

2 It happened after this that David [a]in-
quired of the LORD, saying, "Shall I go
up to any of the cities of Judah?"
And the LORD said to him, "Go up."
David said, "Where shall I go up?"
And He said, "To [b]Hebron."
2 So David went up there, and his [a]two
wives also, Ahinoam the Jezreelitess, and
Abigail the widow of Nabal the Carmelite.
3 And David brought up [a]the men who *were*
with him, every man with his household. So
they dwelt in the cities of Hebron.
4 [a]Then the men of Judah came, and there
they [b]anointed David king over the house of
Judah. And they told David, saying, [c]"The
men of Jabesh Gilead *were the ones* who buried Saul." 5 So David sent messengers to the
men of Jabesh Gilead, and said to them, [a]"You
are blessed of the LORD, for you have shown
this kindness to your lord, to Saul, and have
buried him. 6 And now may [a]the LORD show
kindness and truth to you. I also will repay
you this kindness, because you have done
this thing. 7 Now therefore, let your hands be
strengthened, and be valiant; for your master
Saul is dead, and also the house of Judah has
anointed me king over them."

Ishbosheth Made King of Israel

8 But [a]Abner the son of Ner, commander
of Saul's army, took Ishbosheth[1] the son of
Saul and brought him over to [b]Mahanaim;
9 and he made him king over [a]Gilead, over
the [b]Ashurites, over [c]Jezreel, over Ephraim,
over Benjamin, and over all Israel. 10 Ishbosheth, Saul's son, *was* forty years old when
he began to reign over Israel, and he reigned
two years. Only the house of Judah followed
David. 11 And [a]the time that David was king in
Hebron over the house of Judah was seven
years and six months.

Israel and Judah at War

12 Now Abner the son of Ner, and the servants of Ishbosheth the son of Saul, went
out from Mahanaim to [a]Gibeon. 13 And [a]Joab
the son of Zeruiah, and the servants of David, went out and met them by [b]the pool
of Gibeon. So they sat down, one on one
side of the pool and the other on the other
side of the pool. 14 Then Abner said to Joab,
"Let the young men now arise and compete
before us."
And Joab said, "Let them arise."

1:27 [a] 2 Sam. 1:19, 25 **2:1** [a] Judg. 1:1 [b] 1 Sam. 30:31 **2:2** [a] 1 Sam. 25:42, 43; 30:5 **2:3** [a] 1 Chr. 12:1 **2:4** [a] 1 Sam. 30:26 [b] 1 Sam. 16:13 [c] 1 Sam. 31:11–13 **2:5** [a] Ruth 2:20; 3:10 **2:6** [a] 2 Tim. 1:16, 18 **2:8** [a] 1 Sam. 14:50 [b] 2 Sam. 17:24 [1] Called *Esh-Baal* in 1 Chronicles 8:33 and 9:39 **2:9** [a] Josh. 22:9 [b] Judg. 1:32 [c] 1 Sam. 29:1 **2:11** [a] 2 Sam. 5:5 **2:12** [a] Josh. 10:2–12; 18:25 **2:13** [a] 1 Chr. 2:16; 11:6 [b] Jer. 41:12

15 So they arose and went over by number, twelve from Benjamin, *followers* of Ishbosheth the son of Saul, and twelve from the servants of David. 16 And each one grasped his opponent by the head and *thrust* his sword in his opponent's side; so they fell down together. Therefore that place was called the Field of Sharp Swords,[1] which *is* in Gibeon. 17 So there was a very fierce battle that day, and Abner and the men of Israel were beaten before the servants of David.

18 Now the [a]three sons of Zeruiah were there: Joab and Abishai and Asahel. And Asahel *was* [b]*as* fleet of foot [c]as a wild gazelle. 19 So Asahel pursued Abner, and in going he did not turn to the right hand or to the left from following Abner.

20 Then Abner looked behind him and said, "*Are* you Asahel?"

He answered, "I *am.*"

21 And Abner said to him, "Turn aside to your right hand or to your left, and lay hold on one of the young men and take his armor for yourself." But Asahel would not turn aside from following him. 22 So Abner said again to Asahel, "Turn aside from following me. Why should I strike you to the ground? How then could I face your brother Joab?" 23 However, he refused to turn aside. Therefore Abner struck him [a]in the stomach with the blunt end of the spear, so that the spear came out of his back; and he fell down there and died on the spot. So it was *that* as many as came to the place where Asahel fell down and died, stood [b]still.

24 Joab and Abishai also pursued Abner. And the sun was going down when they came to the hill of Ammah, which *is* before Giah by the road to the Wilderness of Gibeon. 25 Now the children of Benjamin gathered together behind Abner and became a unit, and took their stand on top of a hill. 26 Then Abner called to Joab and said, "Shall the sword devour forever? Do you not know that it will be bitter in the latter end? How long will it be then until you tell the people to return from pursuing their brethren?"

27 And Joab said, "*As* God lives, unless [a]you had spoken, surely then by morning all the people would have given up pursuing their brethren." 28 So Joab blew a trumpet; and all the people stood still and did not pursue Israel anymore, nor did they fight anymore. 29 Then Abner and his men went on all that night through the plain, crossed over the Jordan, and went through all Bithron; and they came to Mahanaim.

PEACE NOTE

Don't let doubt become a toxic experience.

30 So Joab returned from pursuing Abner. And when he had gathered all the people together, there were missing of David's servants nineteen men and Asahel. 31 But the servants of David had struck down, of Benjamin and Abner's men, three hundred and sixty men who died. 32 Then they took up Asahel and buried him in his father's tomb, which *was in* [a]Bethlehem. And Joab and his men went all night, and they came to Hebron at daybreak.

3 Now there was a long [a]war between the house of Saul and the house of David. But David grew stronger and stronger, and the house of Saul grew weaker and weaker.

Sons of David

2 Sons were born [a]to David in Hebron: His firstborn was Amnon [b]by Ahinoam the Jezreelitess; 3 his second, Chileab, by Abigail the widow of Nabal the Carmelite; the third, [a]Absalom the son of Maacah, the daughter of Talmai, king [b]of Geshur; 4 the fourth, [a]Adonijah the son of Haggith; the fifth, Shephatiah the son of Abital; 5 and the sixth, Ithream, by David's wife Eglah. These were born to David in Hebron.

Abner Joins Forces with David

6 Now it was so, while there was war between the house of Saul and the house of David, that Abner was strengthening *his hold* on the house of Saul.

7 And Saul had a concubine, whose name *was* [a]Rizpah, the daughter of Aiah. So *Ishbosheth* said to Abner, "Why have you [b]gone in to my father's concubine?"

8 Then Abner became very angry at the words of Ishbosheth, and said, "*Am* I [a]a dog's

2:16 [1] Hebrew *Helkath Hazzurim* 2:18 [a] 1 Chr. 2:16 [b] 1 Chr. 12:8 [c] Ps. 18:33 2:23 [a] 2 Sam. 3:27; 4:6; 20:10 [b] 2 Sam. 20:12 2:27 [a] 2 Sam. 2:14 2:32 [a] 1 Sam. 20:6 3:1 [a] 1 Kin. 14:30 3:2 [a] 1 Chr. 3:1–4 [b] 1 Sam. 25:42, 43 3:3 [a] 2 Sam. 15:1–10 [b] Josh. 13:13 3:4 [a] 1 Kin. 1:5 3:7 [a] 2 Sam. 21:8–11 [b] 2 Sam. 16:21 3:8 [a] 1 Sam. 24:14

head that belongs to Judah? Today I show loyalty to the house of Saul your father, to his brothers, and to his friends, and have not delivered you into the hand of David; and you charge me today with a fault concerning this woman? 9 [a]May God do so to Abner, and more also, if I do not do for David [b]as the LORD has sworn to him— 10 to transfer the kingdom from the house of Saul, and set up the throne of David over Israel and over Judah, [a]from Dan to Beersheba." 11 And he could not answer Abner another word, because he feared him.

12 Then Abner sent messengers on his behalf to David, saying, "Whose *is* the land?" saying *also,* "Make your covenant with me, and indeed my hand *shall be* with you to bring all Israel to you."

13 And *David* said, "Good, I will make a covenant with you. But one thing I require of you: [a]you shall not see my face unless you first bring [b]Michal, Saul's daughter, when you come to see my face." 14 So David sent messengers to [a]Ishbosheth, Saul's son, saying, "Give *me* my wife Michal, whom I betrothed to myself [b]for a hundred foreskins of the Philistines." 15 And Ishbosheth sent and took her from *her* husband, from Paltiel[1] the son of Laish. 16 Then her husband went along with her to [a]Bahurim, weeping behind her. So Abner said to him, "Go, return!" And he returned.

17 Now Abner had communicated with the elders of Israel, saying, "In time past you were seeking for David *to be* king over you. 18 Now then, do *it!* [a]For the LORD has spoken of David, saying, 'By the hand of My servant David, I[1] will save My people Israel from the hand of the Philistines and the hand of all their enemies.' " 19 And Abner also spoke in the hearing of [a]Benjamin. Then Abner also went to speak in the hearing of David in Hebron all that seemed good to Israel and the whole house of Benjamin.

20 So Abner and twenty men with him came to David at Hebron. And David made a feast for Abner and the men who *were* with him. 21 Then Abner said to David, "I will arise and go, and [a]gather all Israel to my lord the king, that they may make a covenant with you, and that you may [b]reign over all that your heart desires." So David sent Abner away, and he went in peace.

Joab Murders Abner

22 At that moment the servants of David and Joab came from a raid and brought much spoil with them. But Abner *was* not with David in Hebron, for he had sent him away, and he had gone in peace. 23 When Joab and all the troops that *were* with him had come, they told Joab, saying, "Abner the son of Ner came to the king, and he sent him away, and he has gone in peace." 24 Then Joab came to the king and said, "What have you done? Look, Abner came to you; why *is it that* you sent him away, and he has already gone? 25 Surely you realize that Abner the son of Ner came to deceive you, to know [a]your going out and your coming in, and to know all that you are doing."

26 And when Joab had gone from David's presence, he sent messengers after Abner, who brought him back from the well of Sirah. But David did not know *it.* 27 Now when Abner had returned to Hebron, Joab [a]took him aside in the gate to speak with him privately, and there stabbed him [b]in the stomach, so that he died for the blood of [c]Asahel his brother.

28 Afterward, when David heard *it,* he said, "My kingdom and I *are* guiltless before the LORD forever of the blood of Abner the son of Ner. 29 [a]Let it rest on the head of Joab and on all his father's house; and let there never fail to be in the house of Joab one [b]who has a discharge or is a leper, who leans on a staff or falls by the sword, or who lacks bread." 30 So Joab and Abishai his brother killed Abner, because he had killed their brother [a]Asahel at Gibeon in the battle.

David's Mourning for Abner

31 Then David said to Joab and to all the people who were with him, [a]"Tear your clothes, [b]gird yourselves with sackcloth, and mourn for Abner." And King David followed the coffin. 32 So they buried Abner in Hebron; and the king lifted up his voice and wept at the grave of Abner, and all the people wept. 33 And the king sang *a lament* over Abner and said:

"Should Abner die as a [a]fool dies?
34 Your hands were not bound
Nor your feet put into fetters;
As a man falls before wicked men, *so* you fell."

Then all the people wept over him again.

35 And when all the people came [a]to persuade David to eat food while it was still day, David took an oath, saying, [b]"God do so to me, and more also, if I taste bread or anything else [c]till the sun goes down!" 36 Now all the

3:9 [a] 1 Kin. 19:2 [b] 1 Chr. 12:23 **3:10** [a] 1 Sam. 3:20 **3:13** [a] Gen. 43:3 [b] 1 Sam. 18:20; 19:11; 25:44 **3:14** [a] 2 Sam. 2:10 [b] 1 Sam. 18:25–27 **3:15** [1] Spelled *Palti* in 1 Samuel 25:44 **3:16** [a] 2 Sam. 16:5; 19:16 **3:18** [a] 2 Sam. 3:9 [1] Following many Hebrew manuscripts, Septuagint, Syriac, and Targum; Masoretic Text reads *he.* **3:19** [a] 1 Chr. 12:29 **3:21** [a] 2 Sam. 3:10, 12 [b] 1 Kin. 11:37 **3:25** [a] 1 Sam. 29:6 **3:27** [a] 1 Kin. 2:5 [b] 2 Sam. 4:6 [c] 2 Sam. 2:23 **3:29** [a] 1 Kin. 2:32, 33 [b] Lev. 15:2 **3:30** [a] 2 Sam. 2:23 **3:31** [a] Josh. 7:6 [b] Gen. 37:34 **3:33** [a] 2 Sam. 13:12, 13 **3:35** [a] 2 Sam. 12:17 [b] Ruth 1:17 [c] 2 Sam. 1:12

people took note *of it,* and it pleased them,
since whatever the king did pleased all the
people. 37 For all the people and all Israel
understood that day that it had not been
the king's *intent* to kill Abner the son of Ner.
38 Then the king said to his servants, "Do you
not know that a prince and a great man has
fallen this day in Israel? 39 And I *am* weak
today, though anointed king; and these men,
the sons of Zeruiah, [a]*are* too harsh for me.
[b]The LORD shall repay the evildoer according
to his wickedness."

Ishbosheth Is Murdered

4 When Saul's son[1] heard that Abner had
died in Hebron, [a]he lost heart, and all
Israel was [b]troubled. 2 Now Saul's son *had*
two men *who were* captains of troops. The
name of one *was* Baanah and the name of
the other Rechab, the sons of Rimmon the
Beerothite, of the children of Benjamin. (For
[a]Beeroth also was *part* of Benjamin, 3 because
the Beerothites fled to [a]Gittaim and have
been sojourners there until this day.)
4 [a]Jonathan, Saul's son, had a son *who was*
lame in *his* feet. He was five years old when
the news about Saul and Jonathan came
[b]from Jezreel; and his nurse took him up and
fled. And it happened, as she made haste to
flee, that he fell and became lame. His name
was [c]Mephibosheth.[1]
5 Then the sons of Rimmon the Beerothite,
Rechab and Baanah, set out and came at
about the heat of the day to the [a]house of
Ishbosheth, who was lying on his bed at
noon. 6 And they came there, all the way into
the house, *as though* to get wheat, and they
stabbed him [a]in the stomach. Then Rechab
and Baanah his brother escaped. 7 For when
they came into the house, he was lying on
his bed in his bedroom; then they struck him
and killed him, beheaded him and took his
head, and were all night escaping through
the plain. 8 And they brought the head of
Ishbosheth to David at Hebron, and said to
the king, "Here is the head of Ishbosheth, the
son of Saul your enemy, [a]who sought your
life; and the LORD has avenged my lord the
king this day of Saul and his descendants."
9 But David answered Rechab and Baanah his
brother, the sons of Rimmon the Beerothite,
and said to them, "*As* the LORD lives, [a]who has
redeemed my life from all adversity, 10 when
[a]someone told me, saying, 'Look, Saul is dead,'
thinking to have brought good news, I arrested
him and had him executed in Ziklag—the one
who *thought* I would give him a reward for *his*
news. 11 How much more, when wicked men
have killed a righteous person in his own house
on his bed? Therefore, shall I not now [a]require
his blood at your hand and remove you from
the earth?" 12 So David [a]commanded his young
men, and they executed them, cut off their
hands and feet, and hanged *them* by the pool in
Hebron. But they took the head of Ishbosheth
and buried *it* in the [b]tomb of Abner in Hebron.

David Reigns over All Israel

5 Then all the tribes of Israel [a]came to David at Hebron and spoke, saying, "Indeed
[b]we *are* your bone and your flesh. 2 Also, in
time past, when Saul was king over us, [a]you
were the one who led Israel out and brought
them in; and the LORD said to you, [b]'You shall
shepherd My people Israel, and be ruler over
Israel.' " 3 [a]Therefore all the elders of Israel
came to the king at Hebron, [b]and King David
made a covenant with them at Hebron [c]before
the LORD. And they anointed David king over
Israel. 4 David *was* [a]thirty years old when he
began to reign, *and* [b]he reigned forty years. 5 In
Hebron he reigned over Judah [a]seven years
and six months, and in Jerusalem he reigned
thirty-three years over all Israel and Judah.

The Conquest of Jerusalem

6 [a]And the king and his men went to Jerusalem against [b]the Jebusites, the inhabitants
of the land, who spoke to David, saying, "You

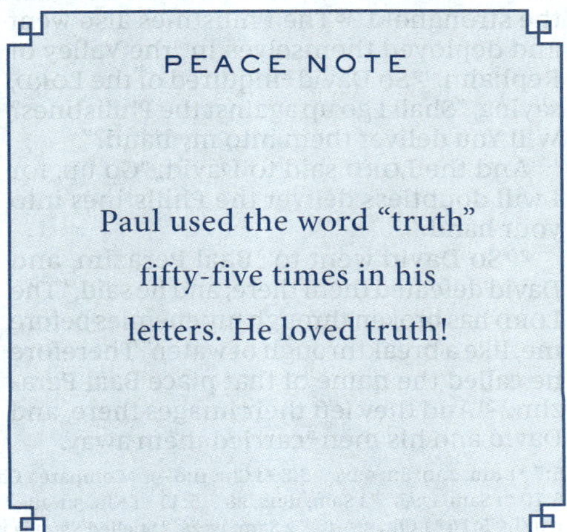

3:39 [a] 2 Sam. 19:5–7 [b] 1 Kin. 2:5, 6, 32–34 **4:1** [a] Ezra 4:4 [b] Matt. 2:3 [1] That is, Ishbosheth **4:2** [a] Josh. 18:25 **4:3** [a] Neh. 11:33 **4:4** [a] 2 Sam. 9:3 [b] 1 Sam. 29:1, 11 [c] 2 Sam. 9:6 [1] Called *Merib-Baal* in 1 Chronicles 8:34 and 9:40 **4:5** [a] 2 Sam. 2:8, 9 **4:6** [a] 2 Sam. 2:23; 20:10 **4:8** [a] 1 Sam. 19:2, 10, 11; 23:15; 25:29 **4:9** [a] Gen. 48:16 **4:10** [a] 2 Sam. 1:2–16 **4:11** [a] [Gen. 9:5, 6] **4:12** [a] 2 Sam. 1:15 [b] 2 Sam. 3:32 **5:1** [a] 1 Chr. 11:1–3 [b] 2 Sam. 19:12, 13 **5:2** [a] 1 Sam. 18:5, 13, 16 [b] 1 Sam. 16:1 **5:3** [a] 2 Sam. 3:17 [b] 2 Kin. 11:17 [c] 1 Sam. 23:18 **5:4** [a] Gen. 41:46 [b] 1 Chr. 26:31; 29:27 **5:5** [a] 2 Sam. 2:11 **5:6** [a] Judg. 1:21 [b] Josh. 15:63

shall not come in here; but the blind and the
lame will repel you," thinking, "David cannot
come in here." 7 Nevertheless David took the
stronghold of Zion [a](that *is,* the City of David).
8 Now David said on that day, "Whoever
climbs up by way of the water shaft and defeats
the Jebusites (the lame and the blind, *who
are* hated by David's soul), [a]*he shall be chief
and captain.*"[1] Therefore they say, "The blind
and the lame shall not come into the house."
9 Then David dwelt in the stronghold, and
called it [a]the City of David. And David built
all around from the Millo[1] and inward. 10 So
David went on and became great, and [a]the
LORD God of hosts *was* with [b]him.
11 Then [a]Hiram [b]king of Tyre sent messengers to David, and cedar trees, and carpenters
and masons. And they built David a house.
12 So David knew that the LORD had established him as king over Israel, and that He
had [a]exalted His kingdom [b]for the sake of
His people Israel.
13 And [a]David took more concubines and
wives from Jerusalem, after he had come
from Hebron. Also more sons and daughters were born to David. 14 Now [a]these *are*
the names of those who were born to him
in Jerusalem: Shammua,[1] Shobab, Nathan,
[b]Solomon, 15 Ibhar, Elishua,[1] Nepheg, Japhia,
16 Elishama, Eliada, and Eliphelet.

The Philistines Defeated

17 [a]Now when the Philistines heard that
they had anointed David king over Israel, all
the Philistines went up to search for David.
And David heard *of it* [b]and went down to
the stronghold. 18 The Philistines also went
and deployed themselves in [a]the Valley of
Rephaim. 19 So David [a]inquired of the LORD,
saying, "Shall I go up against the Philistines?
Will You deliver them into my hand?"

And the LORD said to David, "Go up, for
I will doubtless deliver the Philistines into
your hand."

20 So David went to [a]Baal Perazim, and
David defeated them there; and he said, "The
LORD has broken through my enemies before
me, like a breakthrough of water." Therefore
he called the name of that place Baal Perazim.[1] 21 And they left their images there, and
David and his men [a]carried them away.

22 [a]Then the Philistines went up once again
and deployed themselves in the Valley of
Rephaim. 23 Therefore [a]David inquired of the
LORD, and He said, "You shall not go up; circle
around behind them, and come upon them
in front of the mulberry trees. 24 And it shall
be, when you [a]hear the sound of marching
in the tops of the mulberry trees, then you
shall advance quickly. For then [b]the LORD
will go out before you to strike the camp of
the Philistines." 25 And David did so, as the
LORD commanded him; and he drove back
the Philistines from [a]Geba[1] as far as [b]Gezer.

The Ark Brought to Jerusalem

6 Again David gathered all *the* choice *men*
of Israel, thirty thousand. 2 And [a]David
arose and went with all the people who *were*
with him from Baale Judah to bring up from
there the ark of God, whose name is called by
the Name,[1] the LORD of Hosts, [b]who dwells
between the cherubim. 3 So they set the ark of
God on a new cart, and brought it out of the
house of Abinadab, which *was* on [a]the hill;
and Uzzah and Ahio, the sons of Abinadab,
drove the new cart.[1] 4 And they brought it
out of [a]the house of Abinadab, which *was* on
the hill, accompanying the ark of God; and
Ahio went before the ark. 5 Then David and
all the house of Israel [a]played *music* before
the LORD on all kinds of *instruments of* fir
wood, on harps, on stringed instruments, on
tambourines, on sistrums, and on cymbals.
6 And when they came to [a]Nachon's threshing floor, Uzzah put out *his* [b]*hand* to the ark of
God and took hold of it, for the oxen stumbled.
7 Then the anger of the LORD was aroused
against Uzzah, and God struck him there for
his error; and he died there by the ark of God.
8 And David became angry because of the
LORD's outbreak against Uzzah; and he called
the name of the place Perez Uzzah[1] to this day.
9 [a]David was afraid of the LORD that day;
and he said, "How can the ark of the LORD
come to me?" 10 So David would not move
the ark of the LORD with him into the [a]City
of David; but David took it aside into the
house of Obed-Edom the [b]Gittite. 11 [a]The ark
of the LORD remained in the house of Obed-
Edom the Gittite three months. And the LORD
[b]blessed Obed-Edom and all his household.

5:7 [a] 1 Kin. 2:10; 8:1; 9:24 **5:8** [a] 1 Chr. 11:6–9 [1] Compare 1 Chronicles 11:6 **5:9** [a] 2 Sam. 5:7 [1] Literally *The Landfill* **5:10** [a] 1 Sam. 17:45 [b] 1 Sam. 18:12, 28 **5:11** [a] 1 Kin. 5:1–18 [b] 1 Chr. 14:1 **5:12** [a] Num. 24:7 [b] Is. 45:4 **5:13** [a] [Deut. 17:17] **5:14** [a] 1 Chr. 3:5–8 [b] 2 Sam. 12:24 [1] Spelled *Shimea* in 1 Chronicles 3:5 **5:15** [1] Spelled *Elishama* in 1 Chronicles 3:6 **5:17** [a] 1 Chr. 11:16 [b] 2 Sam. 23:14 **5:18** [a] 1 Chr. 11:15 **5:19** [a] 1 Sam. 23:2 **5:20** [a] Is. 28:21 [1] Literally *Master of Breakthroughs* **5:21** [a] Deut. 7:5, 25 **5:22** [a] 1 Chr. 14:13 **5:23** [a] 2 Sam. 5:19 **5:24** [a] 1 Chr. 14:15 [b] Judg. 4:14 **5:25** [a] 1 Chr. 14:16 [b] Josh. 16:10 [1] Following Masoretic Text, Targum, and Vulgate; Septuagint reads *Gibeon.* **6:2** [a] 1 Chr. 13:5, 6 [b] Ps. 80:1 [1] Septuagint, Targum, and Vulgate omit *by the Name;* many Hebrew manuscripts and Syriac read *there.* **6:3** [a] 1 Sam. 26:1 [1] Septuagint adds *with the ark.* **6:4** [a] 1 Sam. 7:1 **6:5** [a] 1 Sam. 18:6, 7 **6:6** [a] 1 Chr. 13:9 [b] Num. 4:15, 19, 20 **6:8** [1] Literally *Outburst Against Uzzah* **6:9** [a] Ps. 119:120 **6:10** [a] 2 Sam. 5:7 [b] 1 Chr. 13:13; 26:4–8 **6:11** [a] 1 Chr. 13:14 [b] Gen. 30:27; 39:5

12 Now it was told King David, saying, "The LORD has blessed the house of Obed-Edom and all that *belongs* to him, because of the ark of God." [a]So David went and brought up the ark of God from the house of Obed-Edom to the City of David with gladness. 13 And so it was, when [a]those bearing the ark of the LORD had gone six paces, that he sacrificed [b]oxen and fatted sheep. 14 Then David [a]danced before the LORD with all *his* might; and David *was* wearing [b]a linen ephod. 15 [a]So David and all the house of Israel brought up the ark of the LORD with shouting and with the sound of the trumpet.

16 Now as the ark of the LORD came into the City of David, [a]Michal, Saul's daughter, looked through a window and saw King David leaping and whirling before the LORD; and she despised him in her heart. 17 So [a]they brought the ark of the LORD, and set it in [b]its place in the midst of the tabernacle that David had erected for it. Then David [c]offered burnt offerings and peace offerings before the LORD. 18 And when David had finished offering burnt offerings and peace offerings, [a]he blessed the people in the name of the LORD of hosts. 19 [a]Then he distributed among all the people, among the whole multitude of Israel, both the women and the men, to everyone a loaf of bread, a piece *of meat,* and a cake of raisins. So all the people departed, everyone to his house.

20 [a]Then David returned to bless his household. And Michal the daughter of Saul came out to meet David, and said, "How glorious was the king of Israel today, [b]uncovering himself today in the eyes of the maids of his servants, as one of the [c]base fellows shamelessly uncovers himself!"

21 So David said to Michal, "*It was* before the LORD, [a]who chose me instead of your father and all his house, to appoint me ruler over the [b]people of the LORD, over Israel. Therefore I will play *music* before the LORD. 22 And I will be even more undignified than this, and will be humble in my own sight. But as for the maidservants of whom you have spoken, by them I will be held in honor."

23 Therefore Michal the daughter of Saul had no children [a]to the day of her death.

God's Covenant with David

7 Now it came to pass [a]when the king was dwelling in his house, and the LORD had given him rest from all his enemies all around, 2 that the king said to Nathan the prophet, "See now, I dwell in [a]a house of cedar, [b]but the ark of God dwells inside tent [c]curtains."

3 Then Nathan said to the king, "Go, do all that *is* in your [a]heart, for the LORD *is* with you."

4 But it happened that night that the word of the LORD came to Nathan, saying, 5 "Go and

6:12 [a] 1 Chr. 15:25—16:3 **6:13** [a] Josh. 3:3 [b] 1 Kin. 8:5 **6:14** [a] Ps. 30:11; 149:3 [b] 1 Sam. 2:18, 28 **6:15** [a] 1 Chr. 15:28 **6:16** [a] 2 Sam. 3:14 **6:17** [a] 1 Chr. 16:1 [b] 1 Chr. 15:1 [c] 1 Kin. 8:5, 62, 63 **6:18** [a] 1 Kin. 8:14, 15, 55 **6:19** [a] 1 Chr. 16:3 **6:20** [a] Ps. 30:title [b] 2 Sam. 6:14, 16 [c] Judg. 9:4 **6:21** [a] 1 Sam. 13:14; 15:28 [b] 2 Kin. 11:17 **6:23** [a] Is. 22:14 **7:1** [a] 1 Chr. 17:1–27 **7:2** [a] 2 Sam. 5:11 [b] Acts 7:46 [c] Ex. 26:1 **7:3** [a] 1 Kin. 8:17, 18

BUILDING A LEGACY

I dwell in a house of cedar, but the ark of God dwells inside tent curtains.

2 SAMUEL 7:2

After years of civil war, the Lord, the Bible says, had given David "rest from all his enemies" (v. 1). With the kingdom at peace, David was determined to do something for the Lord.

To his credit David desired to build a house for God. After all, he himself lived in a palace and the house of God was nothing more than a tent. But God made His thinking and will clear through Nathan the prophet: no one outgives or outbuilds God. David wanted to build God a house. As it turns out, God wanted to build David a house! The house that God had in mind for David was not a literal one; it was a dynasty, a succession of kings that would someday reach its climax in the enthronement of the Messiah, Jesus of Nazareth, God's Son.

David's peace and desire to bless God in the midst of it set the stage for the coming of the Prince of Peace. The most important thing on David's mind in his last days was planning the construction of a new, ornate temple worthy of the glory of God. This reminds me that I need to make plans to have the peace of God and pass a legacy of peace to my family when I go to heaven.

tell My servant David, 'Thus says the LORD:
[a]"Would you build a house for Me to dwell in?
6 For I have not dwelt in a house [a]since the time
that I brought the children of Israel up from
Egypt, even to this day, but have moved about
in [b]a tent and in a tabernacle. 7 Wherever I have
[a]moved about with all the children of Israel,
have I ever spoken a word to anyone from
the tribes of Israel, whom I commanded [b]to
shepherd My people Israel, saying, 'Why have
you not built Me a house of cedar?' " ' 8 Now
therefore, thus shall you say to My servant
David, 'Thus says the LORD of hosts: [a]"I took
you from the sheepfold, from following the
sheep, to be ruler over My people, over Israel.
9 And [a]I have been with you wherever you have
gone, [b]and have cut off all your enemies from
before you, and have made you a great name,
like the name of the great men who *are* on the
earth. 10 Moreover I will appoint a place for My
people Israel, and will [a]plant them, that they
may dwell in a place of their own and move
no more; [b]nor shall the sons of wickedness
oppress them anymore, as previously, 11 [a]since
the time that I commanded judges *to be* over
My people Israel, and have caused you to rest
from all your enemies. Also the LORD tells you
[b]that He will make you a house.[1]

12 [a]"When your days are fulfilled and you
[b]rest with your fathers, [c]I will set up your
seed after you, who will come from your
body, and I will establish his kingdom. 13 [a]He
shall build a house for My name, and I will
[b]establish the throne of his kingdom forever.
14 [a]I will be his Father, and he shall be [b]My son.
If he commits iniquity, I will chasten him with
the rod of men and with the blows of the sons of
men. 15 But My mercy shall not depart from him,
[a]as I took *it* from Saul, whom I removed from
before you. 16 And [a]your house and your kingdom shall be established forever before you.[1]
Your throne shall be established forever." ' "

17 According to all these words and according to all this vision, so Nathan spoke
to David.

David's Thanksgiving to God

18 Then King David went in and sat before
the LORD; and he said: [a]"Who *am* I, O Lord
GOD? And what is my house, that You have
brought me this far? 19 And yet this was a small
thing in Your sight, O Lord GOD; and You have
also spoken of Your servant's house for a great
while to come. [a]*Is* this the manner of man,
O Lord GOD? 20 Now what more can David
say to You? For You, Lord GOD, [a]know Your
servant. 21 For Your word's sake, and according
to Your own heart, You have done all these
great things, to make Your servant know *them*.
22 Therefore [a]You are great, O Lord GOD.[1] For
[b]*there is* none like You, nor *is there any* God
besides You, according to all that we have
heard with our [c]ears. 23 And who *is* like Your
people, like Israel, [a]the one nation on the earth
whom God went to redeem for Himself as a
people, to make for Himself a name—and to
do for Yourself great and awesome deeds for
Your land—before [b]Your people whom You redeemed for Yourself from Egypt, the nations,
and their gods? 24 For [a]You have made Your
people Israel Your very own people forever;
[b]and You, LORD, have become their God.

25 "Now, O LORD God, the word which You
have spoken concerning Your servant and
concerning his house, establish *it* forever and
do as You have said. 26 So let Your name be
magnified forever, saying, 'The LORD of hosts
is the God over Israel.' And let the house of
Your servant David be established before You.
27 For You, O LORD of hosts, God of Israel, have
revealed *this* to Your servant, saying, 'I will
build you a house.' Therefore Your servant has
found it in his heart to pray this prayer to You.

28 "And now, O Lord GOD, You are God, and
[a]Your words are true, and You have promised
this goodness to Your servant. 29 Now therefore, let it please You to bless the house of
Your servant, that it may continue before You
forever; for You, O Lord GOD, have spoken *it*,
and with Your blessing let the house of Your
servant be blessed [a]forever."

David's Further Conquests

8 After this it came to pass that David attacked the Philistines and subdued them.
And David took Metheg Ammah from the
hand of the Philistines.

2 Then [a]he defeated Moab. Forcing them
down to the ground, he measured them off
with a line. With two lines he measured off
those to be put to death, and with one full line
those to be kept alive. So the Moabites became David's [b]servants, *and* [c]brought tribute.

3 David also defeated Hadadezer the son of
Rehob, king of [a]Zobah, as he went to recover
[b]his territory at the River Euphrates. 4 David

7:5 [a] 1 Kin. 5:3, 4; 8:19 **7:6** [a] 1 Kin. 8:16 [b] Ex. 40:18, 34 **7:7** [a] Lev. 26:11, 12 [b] 2 Sam. 5:2 **7:8** [a] 1 Sam. 16:11, 12 **7:9** [a] 2 Sam. 5:10 [b] 1 Sam. 31:6 **7:10** [a] Ps. 44:2; 80:8 [b] Ps. 89:22, 23 **7:11** [a] Judg. 2:14–16 [b] 2 Sam. 7:27 [1] That is, a royal dynasty **7:12** [a] 1 Kin. 2:1 [b] Deut. 31:16 [c] Ps. 132:11 **7:13** [a] 1 Kin. 5:5; 8:19 [b] [Is. 9:7; 49:8] **7:14** [a] [Heb. 1:5] [b] [Ps. 2:7; 89:26, 27, 30] **7:15** [a] 1 Sam. 15:23, 28; 16:14 **7:16** [a] 2 Sam. 7:13 [1] Septuagint reads *Me*. **7:18** [a] Ex. 3:11 **7:19** [a] [Is. 55:8, 9] **7:20** [a] John 21:17 **7:22** [a] Deut. 10:17 [b] Ex. 15:11 [c] Ex. 10:2 [1] Targum and Syriac read *O LORD God*. **7:23** [a] Ps. 147:20 [b] Deut. 9:26; 33:29 **7:24** [a] [Deut. 26:18] [b] Ps. 48:14 **7:28** [a] John 17:17 **7:29** [a] 2 Sam. 22:51 **8:2** [a] Num. 24:17 [b] 2 Sam. 12:31 [c] 1 Kin. 4:21 **8:3** [a] 1 Sam. 14:47 [b] 2 Sam. 10:15–19

took from him one thousand *chariots,* seven
hundred[1] horsemen, and twenty thousand
foot soldiers. Also David [a]hamstrung all the
chariot *horses*, except that he spared *enough*
of them for one hundred chariots.
5[a]When the Syrians of Damascus came to
help Hadadezer king of Zobah, David killed
twenty-two thousand of the Syrians. 6Then
David put garrisons in Syria of Damascus;
and the Syrians became David's servants,
and brought tribute. So [a]the LORD preserved
David wherever he went. 7And David took
[a]the shields of gold that had belonged to the
servants of Hadadezer, and brought them
to Jerusalem. 8Also from Betah[1] and from
[a]Berothai, cities of Hadadezer, King David
took a large amount of bronze.
9When Toi[1] king of [a]Hamath heard that
David had defeated all the army of Hadadezer, 10then Toi sent Joram[1] his son to King
David, to greet him and bless him, because he
had fought against Hadadezer and defeated
him (for Hadadezer had been at war with Toi);
and *Joram* brought with him articles of silver,
articles of gold, and articles of bronze. 11King
David also [a]dedicated these to the LORD,
along with the silver and gold that he had
dedicated from all the nations which he had
subdued— 12from Syria,[1] from Moab, from
the people of Ammon, from the [a]Philistines,
from Amalek, and from the spoil of Hadadezer the son of Rehob, king of Zobah.
13And David made *himself* a [a]name when
he returned from killing [b]eighteen thousand
Syrians[1] in [c]the Valley of Salt. 14He also put
garrisons in Edom; throughout all Edom he
put garrisons, and [a]all the Edomites became
David's servants. And the LORD preserved
David wherever he went.

David's Administration

15So David reigned over all Israel; and
David administered judgment and justice
to all his people. 16[a]Joab the son of Zeruiah
was over the army; [b]Jehoshaphat the son
of Ahilud *was* recorder; 17[a]Zadok the son of
Ahitub and Ahimelech the son of Abiathar
were the priests; Seraiah[1] *was* the scribe;
18[a]Benaiah the son of Jehoiada *was over* both
the [b]Cherethites and the Pelethites; and David's sons were chief ministers.

David's Kindness to Mephibosheth

9 Now David said, "Is there still anyone
who is left of the house of Saul, that I may
[a]show him kindness for Jonathan's sake?"
2And *there was* a servant of the house of
Saul whose name *was* [a]Ziba. So when they
had called him to David, the king said to him,
"*Are* you Ziba?"
He said, "At your service!"
3Then the king said, "*Is* there not still
someone of the house of Saul, to whom I
may show [a]the kindness of God?"
And Ziba said to the king, "There is still
a son of Jonathan *who is* [b]lame in *his* feet."
4So the king said to him, "Where *is* he?"
And Ziba said to the king, "Indeed he *is*
in the house of [a]Machir the son of Ammiel,
in Lo Debar."
5Then King David sent and brought him
out of the house of Machir the son of Ammiel, from Lo Debar.
6Now when [a]Mephibosheth the son of Jonathan, the son of Saul, had come to David, he
fell on his face and prostrated himself. Then
David said, "Mephibosheth?"
And he answered, "Here is your servant!"
7So David said to him, "Do not fear, for I
will surely show you kindness for Jonathan
your father's sake, and will restore to you
all the land of Saul your grandfather; and
you shall eat bread at my table continually."
8Then he bowed himself, and said, "What
is your servant, that you should look upon
such [a]a dead dog as I?"
9And the king called to Ziba, Saul's servant, and said to him, [a]"I have given to your
master's son all that belonged to Saul and
to all his house. 10You therefore, and your
sons and your servants, shall work the land
for him, and you shall bring in *the harvest,*
that your master's son may have food to eat.
But Mephibosheth your master's son [a]shall
eat bread at my table always." Now Ziba had
[b]fifteen sons and twenty servants.
11Then Ziba said to the king, "According to
all that my lord the king has commanded his
servant, so will your servant do."
"As for Mephibosheth," *said the king,* "he
shall eat at my table[1] like one of the king's
sons." 12Mephibosheth had a young son
[a]whose name *was* Micha. And all who dwelt

8:4 [a] Josh. 11:6, 9 [1] Or *seven thousand* (compare 1 Chronicles 18:4) **8:5** [a] 1 Kin. 11:23–25 **8:6** [a] 2 Sam. 7:9; 8:14 **8:7** [a] 1 Kin. 10:16 **8:8** [a] Ezek. 47:16 [1] Spelled *Tibhath* in 1 Chronicles 18:8 **8:9** [a] 1 Kin. 8:65 [1] Spelled *Tou* in 1 Chronicles 18:9 **8:10** [1] Spelled *Hadoram* in 1 Chronicles 18:10 **8:11** [a] 1 Kin. 7:51 **8:12** [a] 2 Sam. 5:17–25 [1] Septuagint, Syriac, and some Hebrew manuscripts read *Edom.* **8:13** [a] 2 Sam. 7:9 [b] 2 Kin. 14:7 [c] 1 Chr. 18:12 [1] Septuagint, Syriac, and some Hebrew manuscripts read *Edomites* (compare 1 Chronicles 18:12). **8:14** [a] Gen. 27:29, 37–40 **8:16** [a] 2 Sam. 19:13; 20:23 [b] 1 Kin. 4:3 **8:17** [a] 1 Chr. 6:4–8; 24:3 [1] Spelled *Shavsha* in 1 Chronicles 18:16 **8:18** [a] 1 Chr. 18:17 [b] 1 Sam. 30:14 **9:1** [a] 1 Sam. 18:3; 20:14–16 **9:2** [a] 2 Sam. 16:1–4; 19:17, 29 **9:3** [a] 1 Sam. 20:14 [b] 2 Sam. 4:4 **9:4** [a] 2 Sam. 17:27–29 **9:6** [a] 2 Sam. 16:4; 19:24–30 **9:8** [a] 2 Sam. 16:9 **9:9** [a] 2 Sam. 16:4; 19:29 **9:10** [a] 2 Sam. 9:7, 11, 13; 19:28 [b] 2 Sam. 19:17 **9:11** [1] Septuagint reads *David's table.* **9:12** [a] 1 Chr. 8:34

HONOR THAT GIVES REST

I will surely show you kindness for Jonathan your father's sake . . . and you shall eat bread at my table continually.

2 SAMUEL 9:7

After David became king, Saul and his sons died, but one of Jonathan's sons—Mephibosheth—survived. Arguably he could have claimed his grandfather's throne. In ancient times it was common to eliminate a defeated king's family members. But David not only allowed Mephibosheth to live, he protected and provided for him: "So Mephibosheth dwelt in Jerusalem, for he ate continually at the king's table" (v. 13).

Here we catch a glimpse of David's heart. No doubt some of his counselors encouraged him either to kill or banish Mephibosheth. But David was a man of mercy as well as justice. And it is justice—treating others fairly and honorably—that nurtures true peace, God's authentic *shalom*. From David's peace he enacted justice; from David's justice he created peace.

If it is within your influence today to bring someone peace, don't hesitate. Take David's example as your own. The Lord will honor your gesture of peace because it reflects His character and heart to bring peace to others.

in the house of Ziba *were* servants of Mephibosheth. 13 So Mephibosheth dwelt in Jerusalem, [a]for he ate continually at the king's table. And he [b]was lame in both his feet.

The Ammonites and Syrians Defeated

10 It happened after this that the [a]king of the people of Ammon died, and Hanun his son reigned in his place. 2 Then David said, "I will show [a]kindness to Hanun the son of [b]Nahash, as his father showed kindness to me."

So David sent by the hand of his servants to comfort him concerning his father. And David's servants came into the land of the people of Ammon. 3 And the princes of the people of Ammon said to Hanun their lord, "Do you think that David really honors your father because he has sent comforters to you? Has David not *rather* sent his servants to you to search the city, to spy it out, and to overthrow it?"

4 Therefore Hanun took David's servants, shaved off half of their beards, cut off their garments in the middle, [a]at their buttocks, and sent them away. 5 When they told David, he sent to meet them, because the men were greatly ashamed. And the king said, "Wait at Jericho until your beards have grown, and *then* return."

6 When the people of Ammon saw that they [a]had made themselves repulsive to David, the people of Ammon sent and hired [b]the Syrians of [c]Beth Rehob and the Syrians of Zoba, twenty thousand foot soldiers; and from the king of [d]Maacah one thousand men, and from [e]Ish-Tob twelve thousand men. 7 Now when David heard *of it,* he sent Joab and all the army of [a]the mighty men. 8 Then the people of Ammon came out and put themselves in battle array at the entrance of the gate. And [a]the Syrians of Zoba, Beth Rehob, Ish-Tob, and Maacah *were* by themselves in the field.

9 When Joab saw that the battle line was against him before and behind, he chose some of Israel's best and put *them* in battle array against the Syrians. 10 And the rest of the people he put under the command of [a]Abishai his brother, that he might set *them* in battle array against the people of Ammon. 11 Then he said, "If the Syrians are too strong for me, then you shall help me; but if the people of Ammon are too strong for you, then I will come and help you. 12 [a]Be of good courage, and let us [b]be strong for our people and for the cities of our God. And may [c]the LORD do *what is* good in His sight."

13 So Joab and the people who *were* with him drew near for the battle against the Syrians, and they fled before him. 14 When the people of Ammon saw that the Syrians were fleeing, they also fled before Abishai, and entered the city. So Joab returned from the people of Ammon and went to [a]Jerusalem.

9:13 [a] 2 Sam. 9:7, 10, 11 [b] 2 Sam. 9:3 **10:1** [a] 1 Chr. 19:1 **10:2** [a] 2 Sam. 9:1 [b] 1 Sam. 11:1 **10:4** [a] Is. 20:4; 47:2 **10:6** [a] Gen. 34:30 [b] 2 Sam. 8:3, 5 [c] Judg. 18:28 [d] Deut. 3:14 [e] Judg. 11:3, 5 **10:7** [a] 2 Sam. 23:8 **10:8** [a] 2 Sam. 10:6 **10:10** [a] 2 Sam. 3:30 **10:12** [a] Deut. 31:6 [b] 1 Cor. 16:13 [c] 1 Sam. 3:18 **10:14** [a] 2 Sam. 11:1

15 When the Syrians saw that they had been
defeated by Israel, they gathered together.
16 Then Hadadezer[1] sent and brought out the
Syrians who *were* beyond the River,[2] and they
came to Helam. And Shobach the commander of Hadadezer's army *went* before them.
17 When it was told David, he gathered all Israel,
crossed over the Jordan, and came to Helam.
And the Syrians set themselves in battle array
against David and fought with him. 18 Then the
Syrians fled before Israel; and David killed
seven hundred charioteers and forty thousand
[a]horsemen of the Syrians, and struck Shobach
the commander of their army, who died there.
19 And when all the kings *who were* servants
to Hadadezer[1] saw that they were defeated by
Israel, they made peace with Israel and [a]served
them. So the Syrians were afraid to help the
people of Ammon anymore.

David, Bathsheba, and Uriah

11 It happened in the spring of the year,
at the [a]time when kings go out *to battle,*
that [b]David sent Joab and his servants with
him, and all Israel; and they destroyed the
people of Ammon and besieged [c]Rabbah.
But David remained at Jerusalem.

2 Then it happened one evening that David
arose from his bed [a]and walked on the roof of
the king's house. And from the roof he [b]saw
a woman bathing, and the woman *was* very
beautiful to behold. 3 So David sent and inquired about the woman. And *someone* said,
"*Is* this not Bathsheba, the daughter of Eliam,
the wife [a]of Uriah the [b]Hittite?" 4 Then David
sent messengers, and took her; and she came to
him, and [a]he lay with her, for she was [b]cleansed
from her impurity; and she returned to her
house. 5 And the woman conceived; so she
sent and told David, and said, "I *am* with child."

6 Then David sent to Joab, *saying,* "Send
me Uriah the Hittite." And Joab sent Uriah to
David. 7 When Uriah had come to him, David
asked how Joab was doing, and how the people were doing, and how the war prospered.
8 And David said to Uriah, "Go down to your
house and [a]wash your feet." So Uriah departed
from the king's house, and a gift *of food* from
the king followed him. 9 But Uriah slept at the
[a]door of the king's house with all the servants
of his lord, and did not go down to his house.
10 So when they told David, saying, "Uriah
did not go down to his house," David said to
Uriah, "Did you not come from a journey?
Why did you not go down to your house?"

11 And Uriah said to David, [a]"The ark and
Israel and Judah are dwelling in tents, and
[b]my lord Joab and the servants of my lord
are encamped in the open fields. Shall I then
go to my house to eat and drink, and to lie
with my wife? *As* you live, and *as* your soul
lives, I will not do this thing."

12 Then David said to Uriah, "Wait here today also, and tomorrow I will let you depart."
So Uriah remained in Jerusalem that day and
the next. 13 Now when David called him, he
ate and drank before him; and he made him
[a]drunk. And at evening he went out to lie on
his bed [b]with the servants of his lord, but he
did not go down to his house.

14 In the morning it happened that David
[a]wrote a letter to Joab and sent *it* by the hand
of Uriah. 15 And he wrote in the letter, saying,
"Set Uriah in the forefront of the hottest
battle, and retreat from him, that he may [a]be
struck down and die." 16 So it was, while Joab
besieged the city, that he assigned Uriah to
a place where he knew there *were* valiant
men. 17 Then the men of the city came out
and fought with Joab. And *some* of the people
of the servants of David fell; and Uriah the
Hittite died also.

18 Then Joab sent and told David all the
things concerning the war, 19 and charged the
messenger, saying, "When you have finished
telling the matters of the war to the king,
20 if it happens that the king's wrath rises,
and he says to you: 'Why did you approach
so near to the city when you fought? Did
you not know that they would shoot from
the wall? 21 Who struck [a]Abimelech the son
of Jerubbesheth?[1] Was it not a woman who
cast a piece of a millstone on him from the
wall, so that he died in Thebez? Why did you
go near the wall?'—then you shall say, 'Your
servant Uriah the Hittite is dead also.' "

22 So the messenger went, and came and
told David all that Joab had sent by him.
23 And the messenger said to David, "Surely
the men prevailed against us and came out
to us in the field; then we drove them back
as far as the entrance of the gate. 24 The archers shot from the wall at your servants;
and *some* of the king's servants are dead, and
your servant Uriah the Hittite is dead also."

25 Then David said to the messenger, "Thus
you shall say to Joab: 'Do not let this thing displease you, for the sword devours one as well
as another. Strengthen your attack against the
city, and overthrow it.' So encourage him."

10:16 [1] Hebrew *Hadarezer* [2] That is, the Euphrates **10:18** [a] 1 Chr. 19:18 **10:19** [a] 2 Sam. 8:6 [1] Hebrew *Hadarezer*
11:1 [a] 1 Kin. 20:22–26 [b] 1 Chr. 20:1 [c] 2 Sam. 12:26 **11:2** [a] Deut. 22:8 [b] Gen. 34:2 **11:3** [a] 2 Sam. 23:39 [b] 1 Sam. 26:6
11:4 [a] [James 1:14, 15] [b] Lev. 15:19, 28 **11:8** [a] Gen. 18:4; 19:2 **11:9** [a] 1 Kin. 14:27, 28 **11:11** [a] 2 Sam. 7:2, 6 [b] 2 Sam. 20:6–22 **11:13** [a] Gen. 19:33, 35 [b] 2 Sam. 11:9 **11:14** [a] 1 Kin. 21:8, 9 **11:15** [a] 2 Sam. 12:9 **11:21** [a] Judg. 9:50–54
[1] Same as *Jerubbaal* (Gideon), Judges 6:32ff

26 When the wife of Uriah heard that Uriah her husband was dead, she mourned for her husband. 27 And when her mourning was over, David sent and brought her to his house, and she [a]became his wife and bore him a son. But the thing that David had done [b]displeased the LORD.

Nathan's Parable and David's Confession

12 Then the LORD sent Nathan to David. And [a]he came to him, and [b]said to him: "There were two men in one city, one rich and the other poor. 2 The rich *man* had exceedingly many flocks and herds. 3 But the poor *man* had nothing, except one little ewe lamb which he had bought and nourished; and it grew up together with him and with his children. It ate of his own food and drank from his own cup and lay in his bosom; and it was like a daughter to him. 4 And a traveler came to the rich man, who refused to take from his own flock and from his own herd to prepare one for the wayfaring man who had come to him; but he took the poor man's lamb and prepared it for the man who had come to him."

5 So David's anger was greatly aroused against the man, and he said to Nathan, "*As* the LORD lives, the man who has done this shall surely die! 6 And he shall restore [a]fourfold for the lamb, because he did this thing and because he had no pity."

7 Then Nathan said to David, "You *are* the man! Thus says the LORD God of Israel: 'I [a]anointed you king over Israel, and I delivered you from the hand of Saul. 8 I gave you your master's house and your master's wives into your keeping, and gave you the house of Israel and Judah. And if *that had been* too little, I also would have given you much more! 9 [a]Why have you [b]despised the commandment of the LORD, to do evil in His sight? [c]You have killed Uriah the Hittite with the sword; you have taken his wife *to be* your wife, and have killed him with the sword of the people of Ammon. 10 Now therefore, [a]the sword shall never depart from your house, because you have despised Me, and have taken the wife of Uriah the Hittite to be your wife.' 11 Thus says the LORD: 'Behold, I will raise up adversity against you from your own house; and I will [a]take your wives before your eyes and give *them* to your neighbor, and he shall lie with your wives in the sight of this sun. 12 For you did *it* secretly, [a]but I will do this thing before all Israel, before the sun.' "

13 [a]So David said to Nathan, [b]"I have sinned against the LORD."

And Nathan said to David, "The LORD also has [c]put away your sin; you shall not die.

11:27 [a] 2 Sam. 12:9 [b] 1 Chr. 21:7 **12:1** [a] Ps. 51:title [b] 1 Kin. 20:35–41 **12:6** [a] [Ex. 22:1] **12:7** [a] 1 Sam. 16:13 **12:9** [a] 1 Sam. 15:19 [b] Num. 15:31 [c] 2 Sam. 11:14–17, 27 **12:10** [a] [Amos 7:9] **12:11** [a] 2 Sam. 16:21, 22 **12:12** [a] 2 Sam. 16:22 **12:13** [a] 1 Sam. 15:24 [b] 2 Sam. 24:10 [c] [Mic. 7:18]

FINDING FORGIVENESS

Why have you despised the commandment of the LORD, to do evil in His sight?

2 SAMUEL 12:9

It is hard to believe that the David upon whom the Spirit of God rested, the David who defeated Goliath, who survived countless dangers, who became the king of Israel, and who received God's promise of an everlasting dynasty was the David who committed adultery and murder. Yet he was. The man God described as "a man after His own heart" (1 Sam. 13:14) sinned grievously.

When Nathan the prophet confronted the king, David confessed, "I have sinned against the LORD" (2 Sam. 12:13). David offered no excuse; he acknowledged his guilt. And then came the word of grace: "The LORD also has put away your sin; you shall not die" (v. 13).

Reconciliation with God restores peace. See Psalm 51:3, 10: "I acknowledge my transgressions . . . Create in me a clean heart, O God, and renew a steadfast spirit within me." Although David's sin led to tragedy, he was reconciled with God and his peace was renewed.

Is there a relationship in your life in which reconciliation could create peace? Will you act on that?

14 However, because by this deed you have given great occasion to the enemies of the LORD [a]to blaspheme, the child also *who is* born to you shall surely die." 15 Then Nathan departed to his house.

The Death of David's Son

And the [a]LORD struck the child that Uriah's wife bore to David, and it became ill. 16 David therefore pleaded with God for the child, and David fasted and went in and [a]lay all night on the ground. 17 So the elders of his house arose *and went* to him, to raise him up from the ground. But he would not, nor did he eat food with them. 18 Then on the seventh day it came to pass that the child died. And the servants of David were afraid to tell him that the child was dead. For they said, "Indeed, while the child was alive, we spoke to him, and he would not heed our voice. How can we tell him that the child is dead? He may do some harm!"

19 When David saw that his servants were whispering, David perceived that the child was dead. Therefore David said to his servants, "Is the child dead?"

And they said, "He is dead."

20 So David arose from the ground, washed and [a]anointed himself, and changed his clothes; and he went into the house of the LORD and [b]worshiped. Then he went to his own house; and when he requested, they set food before him, and he ate. 21 Then his servants said to him, "What *is* this that you have done? You fasted and wept for the child *while he was* alive, but when the child died, you arose and ate food."

22 And he said, "While the child was alive, I fasted and wept; [a]for I said, 'Who can tell *whether* the LORD[1] will be gracious to me, that the child may live?' 23 But now he is dead; why should I fast? Can I bring him back again? I shall go [a]to him, but [b]he shall not return to me."

Solomon Is Born

24 Then David comforted Bathsheba his wife, and went in to her and lay with her. So [a]she bore a son, and [b]he[1] called his name Solomon. Now the LORD loved him, 25 and He sent *word* by the hand of Nathan the prophet: So he[1] called his name Jedidiah,[2] because of the LORD.

Rabbah Is Captured

26 Now [a]Joab fought against [b]Rabbah of the people of Ammon, and took the royal city. 27 And Joab sent messengers to David, and said, "I have fought against Rabbah, and I have taken the city's water *supply.* 28 Now therefore, gather the rest of the people together and encamp against the city and take it, lest I take the city and it be called after my name." 29 So David gathered all the people together and went to Rabbah, fought against it, and took it. 30 [a]Then he took their king's crown from his head. Its weight *was* a talent of gold, with precious stones. And it was *set* on David's head. Also he brought out the spoil of the city in great abundance. 31 And he brought out the people who *were* in it, and put *them to work* with saws and iron picks and iron axes, and made them cross over to the brick works. So he did to all the cities of the people of Ammon. Then David and all the people returned to Jerusalem.

Amnon and Tamar

13 After this [a]Absalom the son of David had a lovely sister, whose name *was* [b]Tamar; and [c]Amnon the son of David loved her. 2 Amnon was so distressed over his sister Tamar that he became sick; for she *was* a virgin. And it was improper for Amnon to do anything to her. 3 But Amnon had a friend whose name *was* Jonadab [a]the son of Shimeah, David's brother. Now Jonadab *was* a very crafty man. 4 And he said to him, "Why *are* you, the king's son, becoming thinner day after day? Will you not tell me?"

Amnon said to him, "I love Tamar, my brother Absalom's sister."

5 So Jonadab said to him, "Lie down on your bed and pretend to be ill. And when your father comes to see you, say to him, 'Please let my sister Tamar come and give me food, and prepare the food in my sight, that I may see *it* and eat it from her hand.' " 6 Then Amnon lay down and pretended to be ill; and when the king came to see him, Amnon said to the king, "Please let Tamar my sister come and [a]make a couple of cakes for me in my sight, that I may eat from her hand."

7 And David sent home to Tamar, saying, "Now go to your brother Amnon's house, and prepare food for him." 8 So Tamar went to her brother Amnon's house; and he was lying down. Then she took flour and kneaded *it,* made cakes in his sight, and baked the cakes. 9 And she took the pan and placed *them* out before him, but he refused to eat. Then Amnon said, [a]"Have everyone go out from me." And they all went out from him. 10 Then

12:14 [a] Is. 52:5 **12:15** [a] 1 Sam. 25:38 **12:16** [a] 2 Sam. 13:31 **12:20** [a] Ruth 3:3 [b] Job 1:20 **12:22** [a] Jon. 3:9 [1] A few Hebrew manuscripts and Syriac read *God.* **12:23** [a] Gen. 37:35 [b] Job 7:8–10 **12:24** [a] Matt. 1:6 [b] 1 Chr. 22:9 [1] Following Kethib, Septuagint, and Vulgate; Qere, a few Hebrew manuscripts, Syriac, and Targum read *she.* **12:25** [1] Qere, some Hebrew manuscripts, Syriac, and Targum read *she.* [2] Literally *Beloved of the LORD* **12:26** [a] 1 Chr. 20:1 [b] Deut. 3:11 **12:30** [a] 1 Chr. 20:2 **13:1** [a] 2 Sam. 3:2, 3 [b] 1 Chr. 3:9 [c] 2 Sam. 3:2 **13:3** [a] 1 Sam. 16:9 **13:6** [a] Gen. 18:6 **13:9** [a] Gen. 45:1

Amnon said to Tamar, "Bring the food into the bedroom, that I may eat from your hand." And Tamar took the cakes which she had made, and brought *them* to Amnon her brother in the bedroom. 11 Now when she had brought *them* to him to eat, [a]he took hold of her and said to her, "Come, lie with me, my sister."

12 But she answered him, "No, my brother, do not force me, for [a]no such thing should be done in Israel. Do not do this [b]disgraceful thing! 13 And I, where could I take my shame? And as for you, you would be like one of the fools in Israel. Now therefore, please speak to the king; [a]for he will not withhold me from you." 14 However, he would not heed her voice; and being stronger than she, he [a]forced her and lay with her.

15 Then Amnon hated her exceedingly, so that the hatred with which he hated her *was* greater than the love with which he had loved her. And Amnon said to her, "Arise, be gone!"

16 So she said to him, "No, indeed! This evil of sending me away *is* worse than the other that you did to me."

But he would not listen to her. 17 Then he called his servant who attended him, and said, "Here! Put this *woman* out, away from me, and bolt the door behind her." 18 Now she had on [a]a robe of many colors, for the king's virgin daughters wore such apparel. And his servant put her out and bolted the door behind her.

19 Then Tamar put [a]ashes on her head, and tore her robe of many colors that *was* on her, and [b]laid her hand on her head and went away crying bitterly. 20 And Absalom her brother said to her, "Has Amnon your brother been with you? But now hold your peace, my sister. He *is* your brother; do not take this thing to heart." So Tamar remained desolate in her brother Absalom's house.

21 But when King David heard of all these things, he was very angry. 22 And Absalom spoke to his brother Amnon [a]neither good nor bad. For Absalom [b]hated Amnon, because he had forced his sister Tamar.

Absalom Murders Amnon

23 And it came to pass, after two full years, that Absalom [a]had sheepshearers in Baal Hazor, which *is* near Ephraim; so Absalom invited all the king's sons. 24 Then Absalom came to the king and said, "Kindly note, your servant has sheepshearers; please, let the king and his servants go with your servant."

25 But the king said to Absalom, "No, my son, let us not all go now, lest we be a burden to you." Then he urged him, but he would not go; and he blessed him.

26 Then Absalom said, "If not, please let my brother Amnon go with us."

And the king said to him, "Why should he go with you?" 27 But Absalom urged him; so he let Amnon and all the king's sons go with him.

28 Now Absalom had commanded his servants, saying, "Watch now, when Amnon's [a]heart is merry with wine, and when I say to you, 'Strike Amnon!' then kill him. Do not be afraid. Have I not commanded you? Be courageous and valiant." 29 So the servants of Absalom [a]did to Amnon as Absalom had commanded. Then all the king's sons arose, and each one got on [b]his mule and fled.

30 And it came to pass, while they were on the way, that news came to David, saying, "Absalom has killed all the king's sons, and not one of them is left!" 31 So the king arose and [a]tore his garments and [b]lay on the ground, and all his servants stood by with their clothes torn. 32 Then [a]Jonadab the son of Shimeah, David's brother, answered and said, "Let not my lord suppose they have killed all the young men, the king's sons, for only Amnon is dead. For by the command of Absalom this has been determined from the day that he forced his sister Tamar. 33 Now therefore, [a]let not my lord the king take the thing to his heart, to think that all the king's sons are dead. For only Amnon is dead."

Absalom Flees to Geshur

34 [a]Then Absalom fled. And the young man who was keeping watch lifted his eyes and looked, and there, many people were coming from the road on the hillside behind him.[1] 35 And Jonadab said to the king, "Look, the king's sons are coming; as your servant said, so it is." 36 So it was, as soon as he had finished speaking, that the king's sons indeed came, and they lifted up their voice and wept. Also the king and all his servants wept very bitterly.

37 But Absalom fled and went to [a]Talmai the son of Ammihud, king of Geshur. And *David* mourned for his son every day. 38 So Absalom fled and went to [a]Geshur, and was there three years. 39 And King David[1] longed to go to[2] Absalom. For he had been [a]comforted concerning Amnon, because he was dead.

13:11 [a] Gen. 39:12 *13:12* [a] [Lev. 18:9–11; 20:17] [b] Judg. 19:23; 20:6 **13:13** [a] Gen. 20:12 **13:14** [a] 2 Sam. 12:11 **13:18** [a] Gen. 37:3 **13:19** [a] Josh. 7:6 [b] Jer. 2:37 **13:22** [a] Gen. 24:50; 31:24 [b] [Lev. 19:17, 18] **13:23** [a] 1 Sam. 25:4 **13:28** [a] 1 Sam. 25:36 **13:29** [a] 2 Sam. 12:10 [b] 2 Sam. 18:9 **13:31** [a] 2 Sam. 1:11 [b] 2 Sam. 12:16 **13:32** [a] 2 Sam. 13:3–5 **13:33** [a] 2 Sam. 19:19 **13:34** [a] 2 Sam. 13:37, 38 [1] Septuagint adds *And the watchman went and told the king, and said, "I see men from the way of Horonaim, from the regions of the mountains."* **13:37** [a] 2 Sam. 3:3 **13:38** [a] 2 Sam. 14:23, 32; 15:8 **13:39** [a] 2 Sam. 12:19, 23 [1] Following Masoretic Text, Syriac, and Vulgate; Septuagint reads *the spirit of the king;* Targum reads *the soul of King David.* [2] Following Masoretic Text and Targum; Septuagint and Vulgate read *ceased to pursue after.*

Absalom Returns to Jerusalem

14 So Joab the son of Zeruiah perceived that the king's heart *was* concerned [a]about Absalom. 2 And Joab sent to [a]Tekoa and brought from there a wise woman, and said to her, "Please pretend to be a mourner, [b]and put on mourning apparel; do not anoint yourself with oil, but act like a woman who has been mourning a long time for the dead. 3 Go to the king and speak to him in this manner." So Joab [a]put the words in her mouth.

4 And when the woman of Tekoa spoke[1] to the king, she [a]fell on her face to the ground and prostrated herself, and said, [b]"Help, O king!"

5 Then the king said to her, "What troubles you?"

And she answered, [a]"Indeed I *am* a widow, my husband is dead. 6 Now your maidservant had two sons; and the two fought with each other in the field, and *there was* no one to part them, but the one struck the other and killed him. 7 And now the whole family has risen up against your maidservant, and they said, 'Deliver him who struck his brother, that we may execute him [a]for the life of his brother whom he killed; and we will destroy the heir also.' So they would extinguish my ember that is left, and leave to my husband *neither* name nor remnant on the earth."

8 Then the king said to the woman, "Go to your house, and I will give orders concerning you."

9 And the woman of Tekoa said to the king, "My lord, O king, *let* [a]the iniquity *be* on me and on my father's house, [b]and the king and his throne *be* guiltless."

10 So the king said, "Whoever says *anything* to you, bring him to me, and he shall not touch you anymore."

11 Then she said, "Please let the king remember the LORD your God, and do not permit [a]the avenger of blood to destroy anymore, lest they destroy my son."

And he said, [b]"*As* the LORD lives, not one hair of your son shall fall to the ground."

12 Therefore the woman said, "Please, let your maidservant speak *another* word to my lord the king."

And he said, "Say on."

13 So the woman said: "Why then have you schemed such a thing against [a]the people of God? For the king speaks this thing as one who is guilty, *in that* the king does not bring [b]his banished one home again. 14 For we [a]will surely die and *become* like water spilled on the ground, which cannot be gathered up again. Yet God does not [b]take away a life; but He [c]devises means, so that His banished ones are not expelled from Him. 15 Now therefore, I have come to speak of this thing to my lord the king because the people have made me afraid. And your maidservant said, 'I will now speak to the king; it may be that the king will perform the request of his maidservant. 16 For the king will hear and deliver his maidservant from the hand of the man *who would* destroy me and my son together from the [a]inheritance of God.' 17 Your maidservant said, 'The word of my lord the king will now be comforting; for [a]as the angel of God, so *is* my lord the king in [b]discerning good and evil. And may the LORD your God be with you.'"

18 Then the king answered and said to the woman, "Please do not hide from me anything that I ask you."

And the woman said, "Please, let my lord the king speak."

19 So the king said, "*Is* the hand of Joab with you in all this?" And the woman answered and said, "*As* you live, my lord the king, no one can turn to the right hand or to the left from anything that my lord the king has spoken. For your servant Joab commanded me, and [a]he put all these words in the mouth of your maidservant. 20 To bring about this change of affairs your servant Joab has done this thing; but my lord *is* wise, [a]according to the wisdom of the angel of God, to know everything that *is* in the earth."

21 And the king said to Joab, "All right, I have granted this thing. Go therefore, bring back the young man Absalom."

PEACE NOTE

Learn from every situation, but don't ever allow anyone else to think for you. Own your faith. Think through your faith. Then you will be on the path to God's peace.

14:1 [a] 2 Sam. 13:39 **14:2** [a] 2 Chr. 11:6 [b] Ruth 3:3 **14:3** [a] 2 Sam. 14:19 **14:4** [a] 1 Sam. 20:41; 25:23 [b] 2 Kin. 6:26, 28
[1] Many Hebrew manuscripts, Septuagint, Syriac, and Vulgate read *came.* **14:5** [a] [Zech. 7:10] **14:7** [a] Deut. 19:12, 13
14:9 [a] 1 Sam. 25:24 [b] 1 Kin. 2:33 **14:11** [a] Num. 35:19, 21 [b] 1 Sam. 14:45 **14:13** [a] Judg. 20:2 [b] 2 Sam. 13:37, 38
14:14 [a] [Heb. 9:27] [b] Job 34:19 [c] Num. 35:15 **14:16** [a] Deut. 32:9 **14:17** [a] 2 Sam. 19:27 [b] 1 Kin. 3:9 **14:19** [a] 2 Sam. 14:3
14:20 [a] 2 Sam. 14:17; 19:27

22 Then Joab fell to the ground on his face
and bowed himself, and thanked the king.
And Joab said, "Today your servant knows
that I have found favor in your sight, my
lord, O king, in that the king has fulfilled
the request of his servant." 23 So Joab arose
[a]and went to Geshur, and brought Absalom
to Jerusalem. 24 And the king said, "Let him
return to his own house, but [a]do not let him
see my face." So Absalom returned to his own
house, but did not see the king's face.

David Forgives Absalom

25 Now in all Israel there was no one who was
praised as much as Absalom for his good looks.
[a]From the sole of his foot to the crown of his
head there was no blemish in him. 26 And when
he cut the hair of his head—at the end of every
year he cut *it* because it was heavy on him—
when he cut it, he weighed the hair of his head
at two hundred shekels according to the king's
standard. 27 [a]To Absalom were born three sons,
and one daughter whose name *was* Tamar. She
was a woman of beautiful appearance.
28 And Absalom dwelt two full years in
Jerusalem, [a]but did not see the king's face.
29 Therefore Absalom sent for Joab, to send
him to the king, but he would not come to
him. And when he sent again the second
time, he would not come. 30 So he said to
his servants, "See, Joab's field is near mine,
and he has barley there; go and set it on fire."
And Absalom's servants set the field on fire.
31 Then Joab arose and came to Absalom's
house, and said to him, "Why have your servants set my field on fire?"
32 And Absalom answered Joab, "Look,
I sent to you, saying, 'Come here, so that I
may send you to the king, to say, "Why have
I come from Geshur? *It would be* better for
me *to be* there still." ' Now therefore, let me
see the king's face; but [a]if there is iniquity in
me, let him execute me."
33 So Joab went to the king and told him.
And when he had called for Absalom, he
came to the king and bowed himself on his
face to the ground before the king. Then the
king [a]kissed Absalom.

Absalom's Treason

15 After this [a]it happened that Absalom
[b]provided himself with chariots and
horses, and fifty men to run before him. 2 Now
Absalom would rise early and stand beside the
way to the gate. So it was, whenever anyone who
had a [a]lawsuit came to the king for a decision,
that Absalom would call to him and say, "What
city *are* you from?" And he would say, "Your
servant *is* from such and such a tribe of Israel."
3 Then Absalom would say to him, "Look, your
case *is* good and right; but *there is* no deputy
of the king to hear you." 4 Moreover Absalom
would say, [a]"Oh, that I were made judge in the
land, and everyone who has any suit or cause
would come to me; then I would give him justice." 5 And *so* it was, whenever anyone came
near to bow down to him, that he would put out
his hand and take him and [a]kiss him. 6 In this
manner Absalom acted toward all Israel who
came to the king for judgment. [a]So Absalom
stole the hearts of the men of Israel.
7 Now it came to pass [a]after forty[1] years that
Absalom said to the king, "Please, let me go
to [b]Hebron and pay the vow which I made
to the LORD. 8 [a]For your servant [b]took a vow
[c]while I dwelt at Geshur in Syria, saying, 'If
the LORD indeed brings me back to Jerusalem, then I will serve the LORD.' "
9 And the king said to him, "Go in peace."
So he arose and went to Hebron.
10 Then Absalom sent spies throughout
all the tribes of Israel, saying, "As soon as
you hear the sound of the trumpet, then
you shall say, 'Absalom [a]reigns in Hebron!' "
11 And with Absalom went two hundred men
[a]invited from Jerusalem, and they [b]went
along innocently and did not know anything.
12 Then Absalom sent for Ahithophel the Gilonite, [a]David's counselor, from his city—from
[b]Giloh—while he offered sacrifices. And the
conspiracy grew strong, for the people with
Absalom [c]continually increased in number.

David Escapes from Jerusalem

13 Now a messenger came to David, saying,
[a]"The hearts of the men of Israel are with
Absalom."
14 So David said to all his servants who *were*
with him at Jerusalem, "Arise, and let us [a]flee,
or we shall not escape from Absalom. Make
haste to depart, lest he overtake us suddenly
and bring disaster upon us, and strike the
city with the edge of the sword."
15 And the king's servants said to the king,
"We *are* your servants, *ready to do* whatever
my lord the king commands." 16 Then [a]the king
went out with all his household after him. But
the king left [b]ten women, concubines, to keep
the house. 17 And the king went out with all the
people after him, and stopped at the outskirts.

14:23 [a] 2 Sam. 13:37, 38 **14:24** [a] 2 Sam. 3:13 **14:25** [a] Is. 1:6 **14:27** [a] 2 Sam. 13:1; 18:18 **14:28** [a] 2 Sam. 14:24 **14:32** [a] 1 Sam. 20:8 **14:33** [a] Luke 15:20 **15:1** [a] 2 Sam. 12:11 [b] 1 Kin. 1:5 **15:2** [a] Deut. 19:17 **15:4** [a] Judg. 9:29 **15:5** [a] 2 Sam. 14:33; 20:9 **15:6** [a] [Rom. 16:18] **15:7** [a] [Deut. 23:21] [b] 2 Sam. 3:2, 3 [1] Septuagint manuscripts, Syriac, and Josephus read *four.* **15:8** [a] 1 Sam. 16:2 [b] Gen. 28:20, 21 [c] 2 Sam. 13:38 **15:10** [a] 1 Kin. 1:34 **15:11** [a] 1 Sam. 16:3, 5 [b] Gen. 20:5 **15:12** [a] 1 Chr. 27:33 [b] Josh. 15:51 [c] Ps. 3:1 **15:13** [a] Judg. 9:3 **15:14** [a] Ps. 3:title **15:16** [a] Ps. 3:title [b] 2 Sam. 12:11; 16:21, 22

18 Then all his servants passed before him; [a]and
all the Cherethites, all the Pelethites, and all the
Gittites, [b]six hundred men who had followed
him from Gath, passed before the king.
19 Then the king said to [a]Ittai the Gittite,
"Why are you also going with us? Return and
remain with the king. For you *are* a foreigner
and also an exile from your own place. 20 In
fact, you came *only* yesterday. Should I make
you wander up and down with us today, since
I go [a]I know not where? Return, and take your
brethren back. Mercy and truth *be* with you."
21 But Ittai answered the king and said,
[a]"*As* the LORD lives, and *as* my lord the king
lives, surely in whatever place my lord the
king shall be, whether in death or life, even
there also your servant will be."
22 So David said to Ittai, "Go, and cross
over." Then Ittai the Gittite and all his men
and all the little ones who *were* with him
crossed over. 23 And all the country wept
with a loud voice, and all the people crossed
over. The king himself also crossed over the
Brook Kidron, and all the people crossed over
toward the way of the [a]wilderness.
24 There was [a]Zadok also, and all the Levites
with him, bearing the [b]ark of the covenant of
God. And they set down the ark of God, and
[c]Abiathar went up until all the people had
finished crossing over from the city. 25 Then
the king said to Zadok, "Carry the ark of God
back into the city. If I find favor in the eyes of
the LORD, He [a]will bring me back and show me
both it and [b]His dwelling place. 26 But if He says
thus: 'I have no [a]delight in you,' here I am, [b]let
Him do to me as seems good to Him." 27 The
king also said to Zadok the priest, "*Are* you
not a [a]seer? Return to the city in peace, and
[b]your two sons with you, Ahimaaz your son,
and Jonathan the son of Abiathar. 28 See, [a]I will
wait in the plains of the wilderness until word
comes from you to inform me." 29 Therefore
Zadok and Abiathar carried the ark of God
back to Jerusalem. And they remained there.
30 So David went up by the Ascent of the
Mount of Olives, and wept as he went up; and
he [a]had his head covered and went [b]barefoot.
And all the people who *were* with him [c]covered
their heads and went up, [d]weeping as they went
up. 31 Then *someone* told David, saying, [a]"Ahithophel *is* among the conspirators with Absalom." And David said, "O LORD, I pray, [b]turn
the counsel of Ahithophel into foolishness!"
32 Now it happened when David had come
to the top *of the mountain,* where he worshiped God—there was Hushai the [a]Archite
coming to meet him [b]with his robe torn and
dust on his head. 33 David said to him, "If
you go on with me, then you will become [a]a
burden to me. 34 But if you return to the city,
and say to Absalom, [a]'I will be your servant,
O king; *as* I *was* your father's servant previously, so I *will* now also *be* your servant,' then
you may defeat the counsel of Ahithophel for
me. 35 And *do* you not *have* Zadok and Abiathar the priests with you there? Therefore it
will be *that* whatever you hear from the king's
house, you shall tell to [a]Zadok and Abiathar
the priests. 36 Indeed *they have* there [a]with
them their two sons, Ahimaaz, Zadok's *son,*
and Jonathan, Abiathar's *son;* and by them
you shall send me everything you hear."
37 So Hushai, [a]David's friend, went into the
city. [b]And Absalom came into Jerusalem.

Mephibosheth's Servant

16 When[a] David was a little past the top
of the mountain, there was [b]Ziba the
servant of Mephibosheth, who met him with
a couple of saddled donkeys, and on them
two hundred *loaves* of bread, one hundred
clusters of raisins, one hundred summer
fruits, and a skin of wine. 2 And the king said
to Ziba, "What do you mean to do with these?"
So Ziba said, "The donkeys *are* for the
king's household to ride on, the bread and
summer fruit for the young men to eat, and
the wine for [a]those who are faint in the wilderness to drink."
3 Then the king said, "And where *is* your
[a]master's son?"
[b]And Ziba said to the king, "Indeed he is
staying in Jerusalem, for he said, 'Today the
house of Israel will restore the kingdom of
my father to me.' "
4 So the king said to Ziba, "Here, all that
belongs to Mephibosheth *is* yours."
And Ziba said, "I humbly bow before you,
that I may find favor in your sight, my lord,
O king!"

Shimei Curses David

5 Now when King David came to [a]Bahu-
rim, there was a man from the family of
the house of Saul, whose name *was* [b]Shim-
ei the son of Gera, coming from there. He

15:18 [a] 2 Sam. 8:18 [b] 1 Sam. 23:13; 25:13; 30:1, 9 **15:19** [a] 2 Sam. 18:2 **15:20** [a] 1 Sam. 23:13 **15:21** [a] Ruth 1:16, 17 **15:23** [a] 2 Sam. 15:28; 16:2 **15:24** [a] 2 Sam. 8:17 [b] Num. 4:15 [c] 1 Sam. 22:20 **15:25** [a] [Ps. 43:3] [b] Ex. 15:13 **15:26** [a] Num. 14:8 [b] 1 Sam. 3:18 **15:27** [a] 1 Sam. 9:6–9 [b] 2 Sam. 17:17–20 **15:28** [a] 2 Sam. 17:16 **15:30** [a] Esth. 6:12 [b] Is. 20:2–4 [c] Jer. 14:3, 4 [d] [Ps. 126:6] **15:31** [a] Ps. 3:1, 2; 55:12 [b] 2 Sam. 16:23; 17:14, 23 **15:32** [a] Josh. 16:2 [b] 2 Sam. 1:2 **15:33** [a] 2 Sam. 19:35 **15:34** [a] 2 Sam. 16:19 **15:35** [a] 2 Sam. 17:15, 16 **15:36** [a] 2 Sam. 15:27 **15:37** [a] 1 Chr. 27:33 [b] 2 Sam. 16:15 **16:1** [a] 2 Sam. 15:30, 32 [b] 2 Sam. 9:2; 19:17, 29 **16:2** [a] 2 Sam. 15:23; 17:29 **16:3** [a] 2 Sam. 9:9, 10 [b] 2 Sam. 19:27 **16:5** [a] 2 Sam. 3:16 [b] 2 Sam. 19:21

came out, cursing continuously as he came.
6 And he threw stones at David and at all the
servants of King David. And all the people
and all the mighty men *were* on his right
hand and on his left. 7 Also Shimei said thus
when he cursed: "Come out! Come out! You
bloodthirsty man, [a]you rogue! 8 The LORD has
[a]brought upon you all [b]the blood of the house
of Saul, in whose place you have reigned; and
the LORD has delivered the kingdom into the
hand of Absalom your son. So now you *are
caught* in your own evil, because you are a
bloodthirsty man!"

9 Then Abishai the son of Zeruiah said to
the king, "Why should this [a]dead dog [b]curse
my lord the king? Please, let me go over and
take off his head!"

10 But the king said, [a]"What have I to do
with you, you sons of Zeruiah? So let him
curse, because [b]the LORD has said to him,
'Curse David.' [c]Who then shall say, 'Why have
you done so?' "

11 And David said to Abishai and all his
servants, "See how [a]my son who [b]came from
my own body seeks my life. How much more
now *may this* Benjamite? Let him alone, and
let him curse; for so the LORD has ordered
him. 12 It may be that the LORD will look on
my affliction,[1] and that the LORD will [a]repay
me with [b]good for his cursing this day." 13 And
as David and his men went along the road,
Shimei went along the hillside opposite him
and cursed as he went, threw stones at him
and kicked up dust. 14 Now the king and all
the people who *were* with him became weary;
so they refreshed themselves there.

The Advice of Ahithophel

15 Meanwhile [a]Absalom and all the people,
the men of Israel, came to Jerusalem; and
Ahithophel *was* with him. 16 And so it was,
when Hushai the Archite, [a]David's friend,
came to Absalom, that [b]Hushai said to Absalom, "*Long* live the king! *Long* live the king!"

17 So Absalom said to Hushai, "*Is* this your
loyalty to your friend? [a]Why did you not go
with your friend?"

18 And Hushai said to Absalom, "No, but
whom the LORD and this people and all the
men of Israel choose, his I will be, and with
him I will remain. 19 Furthermore, [a]whom
should I serve? *Should I* not *serve* in the presence of his son? As I have served in your father's presence, so will I be in your presence."

20 Then Absalom said to [a]Ahithophel, "Give
advice as to what we should do."

21 And Ahithophel said to Absalom, "Go
in to your father's [a]concubines, whom he
has left to keep the house; and all Israel will
hear that you [b]are abhorred by your father.
Then [c]the hands of all who are with you will
be strong." 22 So they pitched a tent for Absalom on the top of the house, and Absalom
went in to his father's concubines [a]in the
sight of all Israel.

23 Now the advice of Ahithophel, which
he gave in those days, *was* as if one had inquired at the oracle of God. So *was* all the
advice of Ahithophel [a]both with David and
with Absalom.

17 Moreover Ahithophel said to Absalom,
"Now let me choose twelve thousand
men, and I will arise and pursue David tonight. 2 I will come upon him while he *is*
[a]weary and weak, and make him afraid. And
all the people who *are* with him will flee, and
I will [b]strike only the king. 3 Then I will bring
back all the people to you. When all return
except the man whom you seek, all the people
will be at peace." 4 And the saying pleased
Absalom and all the [a]elders of Israel.

The Advice of Hushai

5 Then Absalom said, "Now call Hushai the
Archite also, and let us hear what he [a]says
too." 6 And when Hushai came to Absalom,
Absalom spoke to him, saying, "Ahithophel
has spoken in this manner. Shall we do as he
says? If not, speak up."

PEACE NOTE

Paul said, "I have learned" (Phil. 4:12). Peace and happiness happen through learning in the Christian life.

16:7 [a] Deut. 13:13 16:8 [a] Judg. 9:24, 56, 57 [b] 2 Sam. 1:16; 3:28, 29; 4:11, 12 16:9 [a] 2 Sam. 9:8 [b] Ex. 22:28
16:10 [a] 2 Sam. 3:39; 19:22 [b] [Lam. 3:38] [c] [Rom. 9:20] 16:11 [a] 2 Sam. 12:11 [b] Gen. 15:4 16:12 [a] Prov. 20:22
[b] [Rom. 8:28] [1] Following Kethib, Septuagint, Syriac, and Vulgate; Qere reads *my eyes;* Targum reads *tears of my eyes.* 16:15 [a] 2 Sam. 15:12, 37 16:16 [a] 2 Sam. 15:37 [b] 2 Sam. 15:34 16:17 [a] 2 Sam. 19:25 16:19 [a] 2 Sam. 15:34
16:20 [a] 2 Sam. 15:12 16:21 [a] 2 Sam. 15:16; 20:3 [b] Gen. 34:30 [c] 2 Sam. 2:7 16:22 [a] 2 Sam. 12:11, 12 16:23 [a] 2 Sam. 15:12
17:2 [a] 2 Sam. 16:14 [b] Zech. 13:7 17:4 [a] 2 Sam. 5:3; 19:11 17:5 [a] 2 Sam. 15:32–34

7 So Hushai said to Absalom: "The advice that
Ahithophel has given *is* not good at this time.
8 For," said Hushai, "you know your father and
his men, that they *are* mighty men, and they *are*
enraged in their minds, like [a]a bear robbed of
her cubs in the field; and your father *is* a man of
war, and will not camp with the people. 9 Surely
by now he is hidden in some pit, or in some
other place. And it will be, when some of them
are overthrown at the first, that whoever hears
it will say, 'There is a slaughter among the people who follow Absalom.' 10 And even he *who is*
valiant, whose heart *is* like the heart of a lion,
will [a]melt completely. For all Israel knows that
your father *is* a mighty man, and *those* who *are*
with him *are* valiant men. 11 Therefore I advise
that all Israel be fully gathered to you, [a]from
Dan to Beersheba, [b]like the sand that *is* by the
sea for multitude, and that you go to battle in
person. 12 So we will come upon him in some
place where he may be found, and we will fall
on him as the dew falls on the ground. And of
him and all the men who *are* with him there
shall not be left so much as one. 13 Moreover,
if he has withdrawn into a city, then all Israel
shall bring ropes to that city; and we will [a]pull
it into the river, until there is not one small
stone found there."

14 So Absalom and all the men of Israel
said, "The advice of Hushai the Archite *is*
better than the advice of Ahithophel." For
[a]the LORD had purposed to defeat the good
advice of Ahithophel, to the intent that the
LORD might bring disaster on Absalom.

Hushai Warns David to Escape

15 [a]Then Hushai said to Zadok and Abiathar
the priests, "Thus and so Ahithophel advised
Absalom and the elders of Israel, and thus
and so I have advised. 16 Now therefore, send
quickly and tell David, saying, 'Do not spend
this night [a]in the plains of the wilderness, but
speedily cross over, lest the king and all the
people who *are* with him be swallowed up.' "
17 [a]Now Jonathan and Ahimaaz [b]stayed at [c]En
Rogel, for they dared not be seen coming into
the city; so a female servant would come and
tell them, and they would go and tell King
David. 18 Nevertheless a lad saw them, and
told Absalom. But both of them went away
quickly and came to a man's house [a]in Bahurim, who had a well in his court; and they
went down into it. 19 [a]Then the woman took
and spread a covering over the well's mouth,
and spread ground grain on it; and the thing
was not known. 20 And when Absalom's servants came to the woman at the house, they
said, "Where *are* Ahimaaz and Jonathan?"

So [a]the woman said to them, "They have
gone over the water brook."

And when they had searched and could not
find *them,* they returned to Jerusalem. 21 Now it
came to pass, after they had departed, that they
came up out of the well and went and told King
David, and said to David, [a]"Arise and cross over
the water quickly. For thus has Ahithophel advised against you." 22 So David and all the people
who *were* with him arose and crossed over the
Jordan. By morning light not one of them was
left who had not gone over the Jordan.

23 Now when Ahithophel saw that his advice was not followed, he saddled a donkey,
and arose and went home to [a]his house, to
his city. Then he put his [b]household in order,
and [c]hanged himself, and died; and he was
buried in his father's tomb.

24 Then David went to [a]Mahanaim. And
Absalom crossed over the Jordan, he and all
the men of Israel with him. 25 And Absalom
made [a]Amasa captain of the army instead of
Joab. This Amasa *was* the son of a man whose
name *was* Jithra,[1] an Israelite,[2] who had gone
in to [b]Abigail the daughter of Nahash, sister
of Zeruiah, Joab's mother. 26 So Israel and
Absalom encamped in the land of Gilead.

27 Now it happened, when David had come
to Mahanaim, that [a]Shobi the son of Nahash from Rabbah of the people of Ammon,
[b]Machir the son of Ammiel from Lo Debar,
and [c]Barzillai the Gileadite from Rogelim,
28 brought beds and basins, earthen vessels
and wheat, barley and flour, parched *grain*
and beans, lentils and parched *seeds,* 29 honey
and curds, sheep and cheese of the herd, for
David and the people who *were* with him to
eat. For they said, "The people are hungry
and weary and thirsty [a]in the wilderness."

Absalom's Defeat and Death

18 And David numbered the people who
were with him, and [a]set captains of thousands and captains of hundreds over them.
2 Then David sent out one third of the people
under the hand of Joab, [a]one third under the
hand of Abishai the son of Zeruiah, Joab's
brother, and one third under the hand of [b]Ittai

17:8 [a] Hos. 13:8 **17:10** [a] Josh. 2:11 **17:11** [a] 2 Sam. 3:10 [b] Gen. 22:17 **17:13** [a] Mic. 1:6 **17:14** [a] 2 Sam. 15:31, 34 **17:15** [a] 2 Sam. 15:35, 36 **17:16** [a] 2 Sam. 15:28 **17:17** [a] 2 Sam. 15:27, 36 [b] Josh. 2:4–6 [c] Josh. 15:7; 18:16 **17:18** [a] 2 Sam. 3:16; 16:5 **17:19** [a] Josh. 2:4–6 **17:20** [a] Josh. 2:3–5 **17:21** [a] 2 Sam. 17:15, 16 **17:23** [a] 2 Sam. 15:12 [b] 2 Kin. 20:1 [c] Matt. 27:5 **17:24** [a] 2 Sam. 2:8; 19:32 **17:25** [a] 1 Kin. 2:5, 32 [b] 1 Chr. 2:16 [1] Spelled *Jether* in 1 Chronicles 2:17 and elsewhere [2] Following Masoretic Text, some manuscripts of the Septuagint, and Targum; some manuscripts of the Septuagint read *Ishmaelite* (compare 1 Chronicles 2:17); Vulgate reads *of Jezrael.* **17:27** [a] 2 Sam. 10:1; 12:29 [b] 2 Sam. 9:4 [c] 2 Sam. 19:31, 32 **17:29** [a] 2 Sam. 16:2, 14 **18:1** [a] Ex. 18:25 **18:2** [a] Judg. 7:16 [b] 2 Sam. 15:19–22

the Gittite. And the king said to the people, "I
also will surely go out with you myself."

3 [a]But the people answered, "You shall not go
out! For if we flee away, they will not care about
us; nor if half of us die, will they care about
us. But *you are* worth ten thousand of us now.
For you are now more help to us in the city."

4 Then the king said to them, "Whatever
seems best to you I will do." So the king stood
beside the gate, and all the people went out
by hundreds and by thousands. 5 Now the
king had commanded Joab, Abishai, and
Ittai, saying, "*Deal* gently for my sake with
the young man Absalom." [a]And all the people
heard when the king gave all the captains
orders concerning Absalom.

6 So the people went out into the field of
battle against Israel. And the battle was in
the [a]woods of Ephraim. 7 The people of Israel
were overthrown there before the servants of
David, and a great slaughter of twenty thousand took place there that day. 8 For the battle
there was scattered over the face of the whole
countryside, and the woods devoured more
people that day than the sword devoured.

9 Then Absalom met the servants of David.
Absalom rode on a mule. The mule went
under the thick boughs of a great terebinth
tree, and [a]his head caught in the terebinth;
so he was left hanging between heaven and
earth. And the mule which *was* under him
went on. 10 Now a certain man saw *it* and told
Joab, and said, "I just saw Absalom hanging
in a terebinth tree!"

11 So Joab said to the man who told him,
"You just saw *him!* And why did you not strike
him there to the ground? I would have given
you ten *shekels* of silver and a belt."

12 But the man said to Joab, "Though I were
to receive a thousand *shekels* of silver in my
hand, I would not raise my hand against
the king's son. [a]For in our hearing the king
commanded you and Abishai and Ittai, saying, 'Beware lest anyone *touch* the young
man Absalom!'[1] 13 Otherwise I would have
dealt falsely against my own life. For there
is nothing hidden from the king, and you
yourself would have set yourself against *me.*"

14 Then Joab said, "I cannot linger with
you." And he took three spears in his hand
and thrust them through Absalom's heart,
while he was *still* alive in the midst of the
terebinth tree. 15 And ten young men who
bore Joab's armor surrounded Absalom, and
struck and killed him.

16 So Joab blew the trumpet, and the people
returned from pursuing Israel. For Joab held
back the people. 17 And they took Absalom
and cast him into a large pit in the woods,
and [a]laid a very large heap of stones over him.
Then all Israel [b]fled, everyone to his tent.

18 Now Absalom in his lifetime had taken
and set up a pillar for himself, which *is* in
[a]the King's Valley. For he said, [b]"I have no
son to keep my name in remembrance." He
called the pillar after his own name. And to
this day it is called Absalom's Monument.

David Hears of Absalom's Death

19 Then [a]Ahimaaz the son of Zadok said, "Let
me run now and take the news to the king, how
the LORD has avenged him of his enemies."

20 And Joab said to him, "You shall not
take the news this day, for you shall take the
news another day. But today you shall take
no news, because the king's son is dead."
21 Then Joab said to the Cushite, "Go, tell the
king what you have seen." So the Cushite
bowed himself to Joab and ran.

22 And Ahimaaz the son of Zadok said again
to Joab, "But whatever happens, please let
me also run after the Cushite."

So Joab said, "Why will you run, my son,
since you have no news ready?"

23 "But whatever happens," *he said,* "let me
run."

So he said to him, "Run." Then Ahimaaz ran
by way of the plain, and outran the Cushite.
24 Now David was sitting between the [a]two
gates. And the watchman went up to the roof
over the gate, to the wall, lifted his eyes and
looked, and there was a man, running alone.
25 Then the watchman cried out and told the
king. And the king said, "If he *is* alone, *there
is* news in his mouth." And he came rapidly
and drew near.

26 Then the watchman saw *another* man
running, and the watchman called to the
gatekeeper and said, "There is *another* man,
running alone!"

And the king said, "He also brings news."

27 So the watchman said, "I think the running of the first is like the running of Ahimaaz the son of Zadok."

And the king said, "He *is* a good man, and
comes with [a]good news."

28 So Ahimaaz called out and said to the
king, "All is well!" Then he bowed down with
his face to the earth before the king, and
said, [a]"Blessed *be* the LORD your God, who
has delivered up the men who raised their
hand against my lord the king!"

29 The king said, "Is the young man Absalom safe?"

18:3 [a] 2 Sam. 21:17 **18:5** [a] 2 Sam. 18:12 **18:6** [a] Josh. 17:15, 18 **18:9** [a] 2 Sam. 14:26 **18:12** [a] 2 Sam. 18:5 [1] The ancient versions read *'Protect the young man Absalom for me!'* **18:17** [a] Josh. 7:26; 8:29 [b] 2 Sam. 19:8; 20:1, 22 **18:18** [a] Gen. 14:17 [b] 2 Sam. 14:27 **18:19** [a] 2 Sam. 15:36; 17:17 **18:24** [a] 2 Kin. 9:17 **18:27** [a] 1 Kin. 1:42 **18:28** [a] 2 Sam. 16:12

Ahimaaz answered, "When Joab sent the
king's servant and *me* your servant, I saw
a great tumult, but I did not know what *it*
was about."
30 And the king said, "Turn aside *and* stand
here." So he turned aside and stood still.
31 Just then the Cushite came, and the
Cushite said, "There is good news, my lord
the king! For the LORD has avenged you this
day of all those who rose against you."
32 And the king said to the Cushite, "Is the
young man Absalom safe?"

So the Cushite answered, "May the enemies
of my lord the king, and all who rise against
you to do harm, be like *that* young man!"

David's Mourning for Absalom

33 Then the king was deeply moved, and went
up to the chamber over the gate, and wept. And
as he went, he said thus: [a]"O my son Absalom—
my son, my son Absalom—if only I had died
in your place! O Absalom my son, [b]my son!"

19 And Joab was told, "Behold, the king
is weeping and [a]mourning for Absa-
lom." 2 So the victory that day was *turned* into
[a]mourning for all the people. For the people
heard it said that day, "The king is grieved
for his son." 3 And the people stole back [a]into
the city that day, as people who are ashamed
steal away when they flee in battle. 4 But the
king [a]covered his face, and the king cried
out with a loud voice, [b]"O my son Absalom!
O Absalom, my son, my son!"
5 Then [a]Joab came into the house to the
king, and said, "Today you have disgraced all
your servants who today have saved your life,
the lives of your sons and daughters, the lives
of your wives and the lives of your concubines,
6 in that you love your enemies and hate your
friends. For you have declared today that you
regard neither princes nor servants; for today
I perceive that if Absalom had lived and all of
us had died today, then it would have pleased
you well. 7 Now therefore, arise, go out and
speak comfort to your servants. For I swear
by the LORD, if you do not go out, not one will
stay with you this night. And that will be worse
for you than all the evil that has befallen you
from your youth until now." 8 Then the king
arose and sat in the [a]gate. And they told all the
people, saying, "There is the king, sitting in the
gate." So all the people came before the king.

For everyone of Israel had [b]fled to his tent.

David Returns to Jerusalem

9 Now all the people were in a dispute
throughout all the tribes of Israel, saying,
"The king saved us from the hand of our
[a]enemies, he delivered us from the hand of
the [b]Philistines, and now he has [c]fled from
the land because of Absalom. 10 But Absalom,
whom we anointed over us, has died in battle.
Now therefore, why do you say nothing about
bringing back the king?"
11 So King David sent to [a]Zadok and Abiathar
the priests, saying, "Speak to the elders of
Judah, saying, 'Why are you the last to bring
the king back to his house, since the words
of all Israel have come to the king, to his *very*
house? 12 You *are* my brethren, you *are* [a]my
bone and my flesh. Why then are you the last
to bring back the king?' 13 [a]And say to Amasa,
'*Are* you not my bone and my flesh? [b]God do
so to me, and more also, if you are not commander of the army before me continually
in place of Joab.' " 14 So he swayed the hearts
of all the men of Judah, [a]just as *the heart of*
one man, so that they sent *this word* to the
king: "Return, you and all your servants!"
15 Then the king returned and came to the
Jordan. And Judah came to [a]Gilgal, to go to
meet the king, to escort the king [b]across the
Jordan. 16 And [a]Shimei the son of Gera, a
Benjamite, who *was* from Bahurim, hurried
and came down with the men of Judah to
meet King David. 17 *There were* a thousand
men of [a]Benjamin with him, and [b]Ziba the
servant of the house of Saul, and his fifteen
sons and his twenty servants with him; and
they went over the Jordan before the king.
18 Then a ferryboat went across to carry over
the king's household, and to do what he
thought good.

PEACE NOTE

We are to be generous and open-minded. But we are not to be credulous and naïve. We have to use wisdom from God to live in God's peace.

18:33 [a] 2 Sam. 12:10 [b] 2 Sam. 19:4 **19:1** [a] Jer. 14:2 **19:2** [a] Esth. 4:3 **19:3** [a] 2 Sam. 17:24, 27; 19:32 **19:4** [a] 2 Sam. 15:30 [b] 2 Sam. 18:33 **19:5** [a] 2 Sam. 18:14 **19:8** [a] 2 Sam. 15:2; 18:24 [b] 2 Sam. 18:17 **19:9** [a] 2 Sam. 8:1–14 [b] 2 Sam. 3:18 [c] 2 Sam. 15:14 **19:11** [a] 2 Sam. 15:24 **19:12** [a] 2 Sam. 5:1 **19:13** [a] 2 Sam. 17:25 [b] Ruth 1:17 **19:14** [a] Judg. 20:1 **19:15** [a] Josh. 5:9 [b] 2 Sam. 17:22 **19:16** [a] 2 Sam. 16:5 **19:17** [a] 1 Kin. 12:21 [b] 2 Sam. 9:2, 10; 16:1, 2

David's Mercy to Shimei

Now Shimei the son of Gera fell down before the king when he had crossed the Jordan.
19 Then he said to the king, [a]"Do not let my
lord impute iniquity to me, or remember
what [b]wrong your servant did on the day that
my lord the king left Jerusalem, that the king
should [c]take *it* to heart. 20 For I, your servant,
know that I have sinned. Therefore here I am,
the first to come today of all [a]the house of
Joseph to go down to meet my lord the king."

21 But Abishai the son of Zeruiah answered
and said, "Shall not Shimei be put to death
for this, [a]because he [b]cursed the LORD's
anointed?"

22 And David said, [a]"What have I to do with
you, you sons of Zeruiah, that you should be
adversaries to me today? [b]Shall any man be
put to death today in Israel? For do I not know
that today I *am* king over Israel?" 23 Therefore
[a]the king said to Shimei, "You shall not die."
And the king swore to him.

David and Mephibosheth Meet

24 Now [a]Mephibosheth the son of Saul came
down to meet the king. And he had not cared
for his feet, nor trimmed his mustache, nor
washed his clothes, from the day the king
departed until the day he returned in peace.
25 So it was, when he had come to Jerusalem to
meet the king, that the king said to him, [a]"Why
did you not go with me, Mephibosheth?"

26 And he answered, "My lord, O king, my
servant deceived me. For your servant said, 'I
will saddle a donkey for myself, that I may ride
on it and go to the king,' because your servant
is lame. 27 And [a]he has slandered your servant
to my lord the king, [b]but my lord the king *is*
like the angel of God. Therefore do *what is*
good in your eyes. 28 For all my father's house
were but dead men before my lord the king.
[a]Yet you set your servant among those who
eat at your own table. Therefore what right
have I still to cry out anymore to the king?"

29 So the king said to him, "Why do you
speak anymore of your matters? I have said,
'You and Ziba divide the land.' "

30 Then Mephibosheth said to the king,
"Rather, let him take it all, inasmuch as my
lord the king has come back in peace to his
own house."

David's Kindness to Barzillai

31 And [a]Barzillai the Gileadite came down
from Rogelim and went across the Jordan
with the king, to escort him across the Jordan.
32 Now Barzillai was a very aged man, eighty
years old. And [a]he had provided the king with
supplies while he stayed at Mahanaim, for he
was a very rich man. 33 And the king said to Barzillai, "Come across with me, and I will provide
for you while you are with me in Jerusalem."

34 But Barzillai said to the king, "How long
have I to live, that I should go up with the king
to Jerusalem? 35 I *am* today [a]eighty years old.
Can I discern between the good and bad? Can
your servant taste what I eat or what I drink?
Can I hear any longer the voice of singing men
and singing women? Why then should your
servant be a further burden to my lord the
king? 36 Your servant will go a little way across
the Jordan with the king. And why should the
king repay me *with* such a reward? 37 Please let
your servant turn back again, that I may die in
my own city, near the grave of my father and
mother. But here is your servant [a]Chimham;
let him cross over with my lord the king, and
do for him what seems good to you."

38 And the king answered, "Chimham shall
cross over with me, and I will do for him
what seems good to you. Now whatever you
request of me, I will do for you." 39 Then all
the people went over the Jordan. And when
the king had crossed over, the king [a]kissed
Barzillai and blessed him, and he returned
to his own place.

The Quarrel About the King

40 Now the king went on to Gilgal, and
Chimham[1] went on with him. And all the
people of Judah escorted the king, and also
half the people of Israel. 41 Just then all the
men of Israel came to the king, and said to
the king, "Why have our brethren, the men
of Judah, stolen you away and [a]brought the
king, his household, and all David's men with
him across the Jordan?"

42 So all the men of Judah answered the
men of Israel, "Because the king *is* [a]a close
relative of ours. Why then are you angry over
this matter? Have we ever eaten at the king's
expense? Or has he given us any gift?"

43 And the men of Israel answered the men
of Judah, and said, "We have [a]ten shares in
the king; therefore we also have more *right*
to David than you. Why then do you despise
us—were we not the first to advise bringing
back our king?"

Yet [b]the words of the men of Judah were
fiercer than the words of the men of Israel.

19:19 [a] 1 Sam. 22:15 [b] 2 Sam. 16:5, 6 [c] 2 Sam. 13:33 **19:20** [a] Judg. 1:22 **19:21** [a] [Ex. 22:28] [b] [1 Sam. 26:9] **19:22** [a] 2 Sam. 3:39; 16:10 [b] 1 Sam. 11:13 **19:23** [a] 1 Kin. 2:8, 9, 37, 46 **19:24** [a] 2 Sam. 9:6; 21:7 **19:25** [a] 2 Sam. 16:17 **19:27** [a] 2 Sam. 16:3, 4 [b] 2 Sam. 14:17, 20 **19:28** [a] 2 Sam. 9:7–13 **19:31** [a] 1 Kin. 2:7 **19:32** [a] 2 Sam. 17:27–29 **19:35** [a] Ps. 90:10 **19:37** [a] Jer. 41:17 **19:39** [a] Gen. 31:55 **19:40** [1] Masoretic Text reads *Chimhan.* **19:41** [a] 2 Sam. 19:15 **19:42** [a] 2 Sam. 19:12 **19:43** [a] 1 Kin. 11:30, 31 [b] Judg. 8:1; 12:1

The Rebellion of Sheba

20 And there happened to be there a
rebel,[1] whose name *was* Sheba the
son of Bichri, a Benjamite. And he blew a
trumpet, and said:

[a]"We have no share in David,
Nor do we have inheritance in the son
of Jesse;
[b]Every man to his tents, O Israel!"

2 So every man of Israel deserted David, *and*
followed Sheba the son of Bichri. But the
[a]men of Judah, from the Jordan as far as Jerusalem, remained loyal to their king.
3 Now David came to his house at Jerusalem. And the king took the ten women, [a]his
concubines whom he had left to keep the
house, and put them in seclusion and supported them, but did not go in to them. So
they were shut up to the day of their death,
living in widowhood.
4 And the king said to Amasa, [a]"Assemble
the men of Judah for me within three days,
and be present here yourself." 5 So Amasa
went to assemble *the men of* Judah. But he
delayed longer than the set time which David had appointed him. 6 And David said to
[a]Abishai, "Now Sheba the son of Bichri will
do us more harm than Absalom. Take [b]your
lord's servants and pursue him, lest he find
for himself fortified cities, and escape us."
7 So Joab's men, with the [a]Cherethites, the
Pelethites, and [b]all the mighty men, went
out after him. And they went out of Jerusalem to pursue Sheba the son of Bichri.
8 When they *were* at the large stone which *is*
in Gibeon, Amasa came before them. Now
Joab was dressed in battle armor; on it was
a belt *with* a sword fastened in its sheath at
his hips; and as he was going forward, it fell
out. 9 Then Joab said to Amasa, "*Are* you in
health, my brother?" [a]And Joab took Amasa
by the beard with his right hand to kiss him.
10 But Amasa did not notice the sword that
was in Joab's hand. And [a]he struck him with
it [b]in the stomach, and his entrails poured
out on the ground; and he did not *strike* him
again. Thus he died.
Then Joab and Abishai his brother pursued Sheba the son of Bichri. 11 Meanwhile
one of Joab's men stood near Amasa, and
said, "Whoever favors Joab and whoever
is for David—follow Joab!" 12 But Amasa
wallowed in *his* blood in the middle of the
highway. And when the man saw that all the
people stood still, he moved Amasa from
the highway to the field and threw a garment over him, when he saw that everyone
who came upon him halted. 13 When he was
removed from the highway, all the people
went on after Joab to pursue Sheba the son
of Bichri.
14 And he went through all the tribes of Israel
to [a]Abel and Beth Maachah and all the Berites.
So they were gathered together and also went
after *Sheba*.[1] 15 Then they came and besieged
him in Abel of Beth Maachah; and they [a]cast
up a siege mound against the city, and it stood
by the rampart. And all the people who *were*
with Joab battered the wall to throw it down.
16 Then a wise woman cried out from the
city, "Hear, hear! Please say to Joab, 'Come
nearby, that I may speak with you.'" 17 When
he had come near to her, the woman said,
"*Are* you Joab?"
He answered, "I *am*."
Then she said to him, "Hear the words of
your maidservant."
And he answered, "I am listening."
18 So she spoke, saying, "They used to talk
in former times, saying, 'They shall surely
seek *guidance* at Abel,' and so they would
end *disputes*. 19 I *am among the* peaceable
and faithful in Israel. You seek to destroy a
city and a mother in Israel. Why would you
swallow up [a]the inheritance of the LORD?"
20 And Joab answered and said, "Far be it,
far be it from me, that I should swallow up
or destroy! 21 That *is* not so. But a man from
the mountains of Ephraim, Sheba the son of
Bichri by name, has raised his hand against
the king, against David. Deliver him only,
and I will depart from the city."
So the woman said to Joab, "Watch, his
head will be thrown to you over the wall."
22 Then the woman [a]in her wisdom went to all
the people. And they cut off the head of Sheba
the son of Bichri, and threw *it* out to Joab.
Then he blew a trumpet, and they withdrew
from the city, every man to his tent. So Joab
returned to the king at Jerusalem.

David's Government Officers

23 And [a]Joab *was* over all the army of Israel; Benaiah the son of Jehoiada *was* over
the Cherethites and the Pelethites; 24 Adoram
was [a]in charge of revenue; [b]Jehoshaphat the
son of Ahilud *was* recorder; 25 Sheva *was*
scribe; [a]Zadok and Abiathar *were* the priests;
26 [a]and Ira the Jairite was a chief minister
under David.

20:1 [a] 1 Kin. 12:16 [b] 2 Sam. 18:17 [1] Literally *man of Belial* **20:2** [a] 2 Sam. 19:14 **20:3** [a] 2 Sam. 15:16; 16:21, 22
20:4 [a] 2 Sam. 17:25; 19:13 **20:6** [a] 2 Sam. 21:17 [b] 2 Sam. 11:11 **20:7** [a] 1 Kin. 1:38, 44 [b] 2 Sam. 15:18 **20:9** [a] Matt. 26:49
20:10 [a] 1 Kin. 2:5 [b] 2 Sam. 2:23 **20:14** [a] 2 Kin. 15:29 [1] Literally *him* **20:15** [a] 2 Kin. 19:32 **20:19** [a] 1 Sam. 26:19
20:22 [a] [Eccl. 9:13–16] **20:23** [a] 2 Sam. 8:16–18 **20:24** [a] 1 Kin. 4:6 [b] 2 Sam. 8:16 **20:25** [a] 1 Kin. 4:4 **20:26** [a] 2 Sam. 8:18

David Avenges the Gibeonites

21 Now there was a famine in the days of
David for three years, year after year;
and David [a]inquired of the LORD. And the
LORD answered, "*It is* because of Saul and
his bloodthirsty house, because he killed the
Gibeonites." 2 So the king called the Gibeonites and spoke to them. Now the Gibeonites
were not of the children of Israel, but [a]of
the remnant of the Amorites; the children
of Israel had sworn protection to them, but
Saul had sought to kill them [b]in his zeal for
the children of Israel and Judah.

3 Therefore David said to the Gibeonites,
"What shall I do for you? And with what shall
I make atonement, that you may bless [a]the
inheritance of the LORD?"

4 And the Gibeonites said to him, "We will
have no silver or gold from Saul or from his
house, nor shall you kill any man in Israel
for us."

So he said, "Whatever you say, I will do
for you."

5 Then they answered the king, "As for the
man who consumed us and plotted against
us, *that* we should be destroyed from remaining in any of the territories of Israel, 6 let
seven men of his descendants be delivered
[a]to us, and we will hang them before the LORD
[b]in Gibeah of Saul, [c]*whom* the LORD chose."

And the king said, "I will give *them*."

7 But the king spared [a]Mephibosheth the
son of Jonathan, the son of Saul, because
of [b]the LORD's oath that *was* between them,
between David and Jonathan the son of Saul.
8 So the king took Armoni and Mephibosheth, the two sons of [a]Rizpah the daughter
of Aiah, whom she bore to Saul, and the five
sons of Michal[1] the daughter of Saul, whom
she brought up for Adriel the son of Barzillai
the Meholathite; 9 and he delivered them into
the hands of the Gibeonites, and they hanged
them on the hill [a]before the LORD. So they
fell, *all* seven together, and were put to death
in the days of harvest, in the first *days*, in the
beginning of barley harvest.

10 Now [a]Rizpah the daughter of Aiah took
sackcloth and spread it for herself on the
rock, [b]from the beginning of harvest until
the late rains poured on them from heaven.
And she did not allow the birds of the air to
rest on them by day nor the beasts of the
field by night.

11 And David was told what Rizpah the
daughter of Aiah, the concubine of Saul,
had done. 12 Then David went and took the
bones of Saul, and the bones of Jonathan
his son, from the men of [a]Jabesh Gilead
who had stolen them from the street of
Beth Shan,[1] where the [b]Philistines had hung
them up, after the Philistines had struck
down Saul in Gilboa. 13 So he brought up
the bones of Saul and the bones of Jonathan his son from there; and they gathered
the bones of those who had been hanged.
14 They buried the bones of Saul and Jonathan his son in the country of Benjamin
in [a]Zelah, in the tomb of Kish his father.
So they performed all that the king commanded. And after that [b]God heeded the
prayer for the land.

Philistine Giants Destroyed

15 When the Philistines were at war again
with Israel, David and his servants with
him went down and fought against the
Philistines; and David grew faint. 16 Then
Ishbi-Benob, who *was* one of the sons of
the [a]giant, the weight of whose bronze spear
was three hundred *shekels*, who was bearing
a new *sword*, thought he could kill David.
17 But [a]Abishai the son of Zeruiah came to
his aid, and struck the Philistine and killed
him. Then the men of David swore to him,
saying, [b]"You shall go out no more with
us to battle, lest you quench the [c]lamp of
Israel."

18 [a]Now it happened afterward that there
was again a battle with the Philistines at Gob.
Then [b]Sibbechai the Hushathite killed Saph,[1]
who *was* one of the sons of the giant. 19 Again
there was war at Gob with the Philistines,
where [a]Elhanan the son of Jaare-Oregim[1] the
Bethlehemite killed [b]*the brother of* Goliath
the Gittite, the shaft of whose spear *was* like
a weaver's beam.

20 Yet again [a]there was war at Gath, where
there was a man of *great* stature, who had six
fingers on each hand and six toes on each
foot, twenty-four in number; and he also
was born to the giant. 21 So when he [a]defied
Israel, Jonathan the son of Shimea,[1] David's
brother, killed him.

22 [a]These four were born to the giant in
Gath, and fell by the hand of David and by
the hand of his servants.

21:1 [a] Num. 27:21 ***21:2*** [a] Josh. 9:3, 15–20 [b] [Ex. 34:11–16] **21:3** [a] 2 Sam. 20:19 **21:6** [a] Num. 25:4 [b] 1 Sam. 10:26 [c] 1 Sam. 10:24 **21:7** [a] 2 Sam. 4:4; 9:10 [b] 2 Sam. 9:1–7 **21:8** [a] 2 Sam. 3:7 [1] Or *Merab* (compare 1 Samuel 18:19 and 25:44; 2 Samuel 3:14 and 6:23) **21:9** [a] 2 Sam. 6:17 **21:10** [a] 2 Sam. 3:7; 21:8 [b] Deut. 21:23 **21:12** [a] 1 Sam. 31:11–13 [b] 1 Sam. 31:8 [1] Spelled *Beth Shean* in Joshua 17:11 and elsewhere **21:14** [a] Josh. 18:28 [b] 2 Sam. 24:25 **21:16** [a] 2 Sam. 21:18–22 **21:17** [a] 2 Sam. 20:6–10 [b] 2 Sam. 18:3 [c] 1 Kin. 11:36 **21:18** [a] 1 Chr. 20:4–8 [b] 1 Chr. 11:29; 27:11 [1] Spelled *Sippai* in 1 Chronicles 20:4 **21:19** [a] 2 Sam. 23:24 [b] 1 Chr. 20:5 [1] Spelled *Jair* in 1 Chronicles 20:5 **21:20** [a] 1 Chr. 20:6 **21:21** [a] 1 Sam. 17:10 [1] Spelled *Shammah* in 1 Samuel 16:9 and elsewhere **21:22** [a] 1 Chr. 20:8

Praise for God's Deliverance

22 Then David [a]spoke to the LORD the words of this song, on the day when the LORD had [b]delivered him from the hand of all his enemies, and from the hand of Saul.
2 And he [a]said:[1]

[b]"The LORD *is* my rock and my [c]fortress
and my deliverer;
3 The God of my strength, [a]in whom I
will trust;
My [b]shield and the [c]horn of my salvation,
My [d]stronghold and my [e]refuge;
My Savior, You save me from violence.
4 I will call upon the LORD, *who is worthy*
to be praised;
So shall I be saved from my enemies.

5 "When the waves of death
surrounded me,
The floods of ungodliness made me
afraid.
6 The [a]sorrows of Sheol surrounded me;
The snares of death confronted me.
7 In my distress [a]I called upon the LORD,
And cried out to my God;
He [b]heard my voice from His temple,
And my cry *entered* His ears.

8 "Then [a]the earth shook and trembled;
[b]The foundations of heaven[1] quaked
and were shaken,
Because He was angry.
9 Smoke went up from His nostrils,
And devouring [a]fire from His mouth;
Coals were kindled by it.
10 He [a]bowed the heavens also, and came
down
With [b]darkness under His feet.
11 He rode upon a cherub, and flew;
And He was seen[1] [a]upon the wings of
the wind.
12 He made [a]darkness canopies around
Him,
Dark waters *and* thick clouds of the
skies.
13 From the brightness before Him
Coals of fire were kindled.

14 "The LORD [a]thundered from heaven,
And the Most High uttered His voice.
15 He sent out [a]arrows and scattered
them;
Lightning bolts, and He vanquished
them.
16 Then the channels of the sea [a]were seen,
The foundations of the world were
uncovered,
At the [b]rebuke of the LORD,
At the blast of the breath of His nostrils.

17 "He[a] sent from above, He took me,
He drew me out of many waters.
18 He delivered me from my strong
enemy,
From those who hated me;
For they were too strong for me.
19 They confronted me in the day of my
calamity,
But the LORD was my [a]support.
20 [a]He also brought me out into a broad
place;
He delivered me because He [b]delighted
in me.

21 "The[a] LORD rewarded me according to
my righteousness;
According to the [b]cleanness of my hands
He has recompensed me.
22 For I have [a]kept the ways of the LORD,
And have not wickedly departed from
my God.
23 For all His [a]judgments *were* before me;
And *as for* His statutes, I did not depart
from them.
24 I was also [a]blameless before Him,
And I kept myself from my iniquity.
25 Therefore [a]the LORD has recompensed
me according to my righteousness,
According to my cleanness in His eyes.[1]

26 "With [a]the merciful You will show
Yourself merciful;
With a blameless man You will show
Yourself blameless;
27 With the pure You will show Yourself
pure;
And [a]with the devious You will show
Yourself shrewd.
28 You will save the [a]humble people;
But Your eyes *are* on [b]the haughty, *that*
You may bring *them* down.

22:1 [a] Ex. 15:1 [b] Ps. 18:title; 34:19 **22:2** [a] Ps. 18 [b] Deut. 32:4 [c] Ps. 91:2 [1] Compare Psalm 18 **22:3** [a] Heb. 2:13 [b] Gen. 15:1 [c] Luke 1:69 [d] Prov. 18:10 [e] Ps. 9:9; 46:1, 7, 11 **22:6** [a] Ps. 116:3 **22:7** [a] Ps. 116:4; 120:1 [b] Ex. 3:7 **22:8** [a] Judg. 5:4 [b] Job 26:11 [1] Following Masoretic Text, Septuagint, and Targum; Syriac and Vulgate read *hills* (compare Psalm 18:7). **22:9** [a] Heb. 12:29 **22:10** [a] Is. 64:1 [b] Ex. 20:21 **22:11** [a] Ps. 104:3 [1] Following Masoretic Text and Septuagint; many Hebrew manuscripts, Syriac, and Vulgate read *He flew* (compare Psalm 18:10); Targum reads *He spoke with power.* **22:12** [a] Job 36:29 **22:14** [a] Job 37:2–5 **22:15** [a] Deut. 32:23 **22:16** [a] Nah. 1:4 [b] Ex. 15:8 **22:17** [a] Ps. 144:7 **22:19** [a] Is. 10:20 **22:20** [a] Ps. 31:8; 118:5 [b] 2 Sam. 15:26 **22:21** [a] 1 Sam. 26:23 [b] Ps. 24:4 **22:22** [a] Ps. 119:3 **22:23** [a] [Deut. 6:6–9; 7:12] **22:24** [a] [Eph. 1:4] **22:25** [a] 2 Sam. 22:21 [1] Septuagint, Syriac, and Vulgate read *the cleanness of my hands in His sight* (compare Psalm 18:24); Targum reads *my cleanness before His word.* **22:26** [a] [Matt. 5:7] **22:27** [a] [Lev. 26:23, 24] **22:28** [a] Ps. 72:12 [b] Job 40:11

29 "For You *are* my [a]lamp, O LORD;
The LORD shall enlighten my darkness.
30 For by You I can run against a troop;
By my God I can leap over a [a]wall.
31 *As for* God, [a]His way *is* perfect;
[b]The word of the LORD *is* proven;
He *is* a shield to all who trust in Him.

PEACE NOTE

David gave the greatest expression of the protective presence and power of God: "His way is perfect; the word of the LORD is proven; He is a shield to all who trust in Him."

2 SAMUEL 22:31

32 "For [a]who *is* God, except the LORD?
And who *is* a rock, except our God?
33 God *is* my [a]strength *and* power,[1]
And He [b]makes my[2] way [c]perfect.
34 He makes my[1] feet [a]like the *feet* of deer,
And [b]sets me on my high places.
35 He teaches my hands to make war,
So that my arms can bend a bow of bronze.

36 "You have also given me the shield of Your salvation;
Your gentleness has made me great.
37 You [a]enlarged my path under me;
So my feet did not slip.

38 "I have pursued my enemies and destroyed them;
Neither did I turn back again till they were destroyed.
39 And I have destroyed them and wounded them,
So that they could not rise;
They have fallen [a]under my feet.
40 For You have [a]armed me with strength for the battle;
You have subdued under me [b]those who rose against me.
41 You have also given me the [a]necks of my enemies,
So that I destroyed those who hated me.
42 They looked, but *there was* none to save;
Even [a]to the LORD, but He did not answer them.
43 Then I beat them as fine [a]as the dust of the earth;
I trod them [b]like dirt in the streets,
And I spread them out.

44 "You[a] have also delivered me from the strivings of my people;
You have kept me as the [b]head of the nations.
[c]A people I have not known shall serve me.
45 The foreigners submit to me;
As soon as they hear, they obey me.
46 The foreigners fade away,
And come frightened[1] [a]from their hideouts.

47 "The LORD lives!
Blessed *be* my Rock!
Let God be exalted,
The [a]Rock of my salvation!
48 *It is* God who avenges me,
And [a]subdues the peoples under me;
49 He delivers me from my enemies.
You also lift me up above those who rise against me;
You have delivered me from the [a]violent man.
50 Therefore I will give thanks to You,
O LORD, among [a]the Gentiles,
And sing praises to Your [b]name.

51 "*He*[a] *is* the tower of salvation to His king,
And shows mercy to His [b]anointed,
To David and [c]his descendants forevermore."

22:29 [a] Ps. 119:105; 132:17 **22:30** [a] 2 Sam. 5:6–8 **22:31** [a] [Matt. 5:48] [b] Ps. 12:6 **22:32** [a] Is. 45:5, 6 **22:33** [a] Ps. 27:1 [b] [Heb. 13:21] [c] Ps. 101:2, 6 [1] Dead Sea Scrolls, Septuagint, Syriac, and Vulgate read *It is God who arms me with strength (compare Psalm 18:32); Targum reads It is God who sustains me with strength.* [2] Following Qere, Septuagint, Syriac, Targum, and Vulgate (compare Psalm 18:32); Kethib reads *His.* **22:34** [a] 2 Sam. 2:18 [b] Is. 33:16 [1] Following Qere, Septuagint, Syriac, Targum, and Vulgate (compare Psalm 18:33); Kethib reads *His.* **22:37** [a] Prov. 4:12 **22:39** [a] Mal. 4:3 **22:40** [a] [Ps. 18:32] [b] [Ps. 44:5] **22:41** [a] Gen. 49:8 **22:42** [a] 1 Sam. 28:6 **22:43** [a] Ps. 18:42 [b] Is. 10:6 **22:44** [a] 2 Sam. 3:1 [b] Deut. 28:13 [c] [Is. 55:5] **22:46** [a] [Mic. 7:17] [1] Following Septuagint, Targum, and Vulgate (compare Psalm 18:45); Masoretic Text reads *gird themselves.* **22:47** [a] Ps. 89:26 **22:48** [a] Ps. 144:2 **22:49** [a] Ps. 140:1, 4, 11 **22:50** [a] 2 Sam. 8:1–14 [b] Rom. 15:9 **22:51** [a] Ps. 144:10 [b] Ps. 89:20 [c] 2 Sam. 7:12–16

David's Last Words

23 Now these *are* the last words of David.

Thus says David the son of Jesse;
Thus says [a]the man raised up on
high,
[b]The anointed of the God of Jacob,
And the sweet psalmist of Israel:

2 "The[a] Spirit of the LORD spoke by me,
And His word *was* on my tongue.
3 The God of Israel said,
[a]The Rock of Israel spoke to me:
'He who rules over men *must be* just,
Ruling [b]in the fear of God.
4 And [a]*he shall be* like the light of the
morning *when* the sun rises,
A morning without clouds,
Like the tender grass *springing* out of
the earth,
By clear shining after rain.'

5 "Although my house *is* not so with God,
[a]Yet He has made with me an
everlasting covenant,
Ordered in all *things* and secure.
For *this is* all my salvation and all *my*
desire;
Will He not make *it* increase?
6 But *the sons* of rebellion *shall* all *be* as
thorns thrust away,
Because they cannot be taken with
hands.
7 But the man *who* touches them
Must be armed with iron and the shaft
of a spear,
And they shall be utterly burned with
fire in *their* place."

David's Mighty Men

8 These *are* the names of the mighty men
whom David had: Josheb-Basshebeth[1] the
Tachmonite, chief among the captains.[2] He
was called Adino the Eznite, because he had
killed eight hundred men at one time. 9 And
after him *was* [a]Eleazar the son of Dodo,[1] the
Ahohite, *one* of the three mighty men with
David when they defied the Philistines *who*
were gathered there for battle, and the men of
Israel had retreated. 10 He arose and attacked
the Philistines until his hand was [a]weary,
and his hand stuck to the sword. The LORD
brought about a great victory that day; and
the people returned after him only to [b]plun-
der. 11 And after him *was* [a]Shammah the son
of Agee the Hararite. [b]The Philistines had
gathered together into a troop where there
was a piece of ground full of lentils. So the
people fled from the Philistines. 12 But he
stationed himself in the middle of the field,
defended it, and killed the Philistines. So the
LORD brought about a great victory.

23:1 [a] 2 Sam. 7:8, 9 [b] 1 Sam. 16:12, 13 23:2 [a] [2 Pet. 1:21] 23:3 [a] [Deut. 32:4] [b] Ex. 18:21 23:4 [a] Ps. 89:36 23:5 [a] Ps. 89:29 23:8 [1] Literally *One Who Sits in the Seat* (compare 1 Chronicles 11:11) [2] Following Masoretic Text and Targum; Septuagint and Vulgate read *the three.* 23:9 [a] 1 Chr. 11:12; 27:4 [1] Spelled *Dodai* in 1 Chronicles 27:4 23:10 [a] Judg. 8:4 [b] 1 Sam. 30:24, 25 23:11 [a] 1 Chr. 11:27 [b] 1 Chr. 11:13, 14

THE TRUE SOURCE

Yet He has made with me an everlasting covenant, ordered in all things and secure.

2 SAMUEL 23:5

Near the end of his life, David related what God said to him: "He who rules over men must be just, ruling in the fear of God" (v. 3). He then acknowledged that he and his house had fallen short of some of God's principles, saying, "Although my house is not so with God, yet He has made with me an everlasting covenant" (v. 5).

We should take comfort in David's story. Few of us will rule as kings, but all of us will at times *fall far short of* God's standards. The good news is that even in the face of our unfaithfulness, God's love and grace hold steady. Therefore when we, like David, acknowledge our failings, peace is again available to us. If we confess when we fall, God will raise us up.

David could have listed all his accomplishments at the end of his life; he didn't. David's peace was found in God, not in his influence or achievements. David's story makes it clear: even when we sin, even when we fall short of God's righteousness, we can be restored and enjoy His rich, restorative peace. Day by day, like David, allow God's peace to renew you because of His faithfulness.

13 Then [a]three of the thirty chief men went down at harvest time and came to David at [b]the cave of Adullam. And the troop of Philistines encamped in [c]the Valley of Rephaim. 14 David *was* then in [a]the stronghold, and the garrison of the Philistines *was* then *in* Bethlehem. 15 And David said with longing, "Oh, that someone would give me a drink of the water from the well of Bethlehem, which *is* by the gate!" 16 So the three mighty men broke through the camp of the Philistines, drew water from the well of Bethlehem that *was* by the gate, and took it and brought *it* to David. Nevertheless he would not drink it, but poured it out to the LORD. 17 And he said, "Far be it from me, O LORD, that I should do this! Is *this not* [a]the blood of the men who went in *jeopardy of* their lives?" Therefore he would not drink it.

These things were done by the three mighty men.

18 Now [a]Abishai the brother of Joab, the son of Zeruiah, was chief of *another* three.[1] He lifted his spear against three hundred *men,* killed *them,* and won a name among *these* three. 19 Was he not the most honored of three? Therefore he became their captain. However, he did not attain to the *first* three.

20 Benaiah *was* the son of Jehoiada, the son of a valiant man from [a]Kabzeel, who had done many deeds. [b]He had killed two lion-like heroes of Moab. He also had gone down and killed a lion in the midst of a pit on a snowy day. 21 And he killed an Egyptian, a spectacular man. The Egyptian *had* a spear in his hand; so he went down to him with a staff, wrested the spear out of the Egyptian's hand, and killed him with his own spear. 22 These *things* Benaiah the son of Jehoiada did, and won a name among three mighty men. 23 He was more honored than the thirty, but he did not attain to the *first* three. And David appointed him [a]over his guard.

24 [a]Asahel the brother of Joab *was* one of the thirty; Elhanan the son of Dodo of Bethlehem, 25 [a]Shammah the Harodite, Elika the Harodite, 26 Helez the Paltite, Ira the son of Ikkesh the Tekoite, 27 Abiezer the Anathothite, Mebunnai the Hushathite, 28 Zalmon the Ahohite, Maharai the Netophathite, 29 Heleb the son of Baanah (the Netophathite), Ittai the son of Ribai from Gibeah of the children of Benjamin, 30 Benaiah a Pirathonite, Hiddai from the brooks of [a]Gaash, 31 Abi-Albon the Arbathite, Azmaveth the Barhumite, 32 Eliahba the Shaalbonite (of the sons of Jashen), Jonathan, 33 [a]Shammah the Hararite, Ahiam the son of Sharar the Hararite, 34 Eliphelet the son of Ahasbai, the son of the Maachathite, Eliam the son of [a]Ahithophel the Gilonite, 35 Hezrai[1] the Carmelite, Paarai the Arbite, 36 Igal the son of Nathan of [a]Zobah, Bani the Gadite, 37 Zelek the Ammonite, Naharai the Beerothite (armorbearer of Joab the son of Zeruiah), 38 [a]Ira the Ithrite, Gareb the Ithrite, 39 *and* [a]Uriah the Hittite: thirty-seven in all.

David's Census of Israel and Judah

24 Again [a]the anger of the LORD was aroused against Israel, and He moved David against them to say, [b]"Go, number Israel and Judah."

2 So the king said to Joab the commander of the army who *was* with him, "Now go throughout all the tribes of Israel, [a]from Dan to Beersheba, and count the people, that [b]I may know the number of the people."

3 And Joab said to the king, "Now may the LORD your God [a]add to the people a hundred times more than there are, and may the eyes of my lord the king see *it.* But why does my lord the king desire this thing?" 4 Nevertheless the king's word prevailed against Joab and against the captains of the army. Therefore Joab and the captains of the army went out from the presence of the king to count the people of Israel.

5 And they crossed over the Jordan and camped in [a]Aroer, on the right side of the town which *is* in the midst of the ravine of Gad, and toward [b]Jazer. 6 Then they came to Gilead and to the land of Tahtim Hodshi; they came to [a]Dan Jaan and around to [b]Sidon; 7 and they came to the stronghold of [a]Tyre and to all the cities of the [b]Hivites and the Canaanites. Then they went out to South Judah *as far as* Beersheba. 8 So when they had gone through all the land, they came to Jerusalem at the end of nine months and twenty days. 9 Then Joab gave the sum of the number of the people to the king. [a]And there were in Israel eight hundred thousand valiant men who drew the sword, and the men of Judah were five hundred thousand men.

23:13 [a] *1 Chr. 11:15* [b] *1 Sam. 22:1* [c] 2 Sam. 5:18 **23:14** [a] 1 Sam. 22:4, 5 **23:17** [a] [Lev. 17:10] **23:18** [a] 1 Chr. 11:20 [1] Following Masoretic Text, Septuagint, and Vulgate; some Hebrew manuscripts and Syriac read *thirty;* Targum reads *the mighty men.* **23:20** [a] Josh. 15:21 [b] Ex. 15:15 **23:23** [a] 2 Sam. 8:18; 20:23 **23:24** [a] 2 Sam. 2:18 **23:25** [a] 1 Chr. 11:27 **23:30** [a] Judg. 2:9 **23:33** [a] 2 Sam. 23:11 **23:34** [a] 2 Sam. 15:12 **23:35** [1] Spelled *Hezro* in 1 Chronicles 11:37 **23:36** [a] 2 Sam. 8:3 **23:38** [a] 1 Chr. 2:53 **23:39** [a] 2 Sam. 11:3, 6 **24:1** [a] 2 Sam. 21:1, 2 [b] 1 Chr. 27:23, 24 **24:2** [a] Judg. 20:1 [b] [Jer. 17:5] **24:3** [a] Deut. 1:11 **24:5** [a] Deut. 2:36 [b] Num. 32:1, 3 **24:6** [a] Judg. 18:29 [b] Josh. 19:28 **24:7** [a] Josh. 19:29 [b] Josh. 11:3 **24:9** [a] 1 Chr. 21:5

The Judgment on David's Sin

10 And [a]David's heart condemned him after
he had numbered the people. So [b]David said
to the LORD, [c]"I have sinned greatly in what
I have done; but now, I pray, O LORD, take
away the iniquity of Your servant, for I have
[d]done very foolishly."

11 Now when David arose in the morning,
the word of the LORD came to the prophet
[a]Gad, David's [b]seer, saying, 12 "Go and tell
David, 'Thus says the LORD: "I offer you three
things; choose one of them for yourself, that
I may do *it* to you." ' " 13 So Gad came to David and told him; and he said to him, "Shall
[a]seven[1] years of famine come to you in your
land? Or shall you flee three months before
your enemies, while they pursue you? Or
shall there be three days' plague in your land?
Now consider and see what answer I should
take back to Him who sent me."

14 And David said to Gad, "I am in great
distress. Please let us fall into the hand of the
LORD, [a]for His mercies *are* great; but [b]do not
let me fall into the hand of man."

15 So [a]the LORD sent a plague upon Israel
from the morning till the appointed time.
From Dan to Beersheba seventy thousand
men of the people died. 16 [a]And when the angel[1] stretched out His hand over Jerusalem
to destroy it, [b]the LORD relented from the
destruction, and said to the angel who was destroying the people, "It is enough; now restrain
your hand." And the angel of the LORD was by
the threshing floor of Araunah[2] the Jebusite.

17 Then David spoke to the LORD when he
saw the angel who was striking the people,
and said, "Surely [a]I have sinned, and I have
done wickedly; but these sheep, what have
they done? Let Your hand, I pray, be against
me and against my father's house."

The Altar on the Threshing Floor

18 And Gad came that day to David and said to
him, [a]"Go up, erect an altar to the LORD on the
threshing floor of Araunah the Jebusite." 19 So
David, according to the word of Gad, went up as
the LORD commanded. 20 Now Araunah looked,
and saw the king and his servants coming
toward him. So Araunah went out and bowed
before the king with his face to the ground.

21 Then Araunah said, "Why has my lord
the king come to his servant?"

[a]And David said, "To buy the threshing
floor from you, to build an altar to the LORD,
that [b]the plague may be withdrawn from
the people."

22 Now Araunah said to David, "Let my lord
the king take and offer up whatever *seems*
good to him. [a]Look, *here are* oxen for burnt
sacrifice, and threshing implements and
the yokes of the oxen for wood. 23 All these,
O king, Araunah has given to the king."

And Araunah said to the king, "May the
LORD your God [a]accept you."

24 Then the king said to Araunah, "No, but
I will surely buy *it* from you for a price; nor
will I offer burnt offerings to the LORD my
God with that which costs me nothing." So
[a]David bought the threshing floor and the
oxen for fifty shekels of silver. 25 And David
built there an altar to the LORD, and offered
burnt offerings and peace offerings. [a]So the
LORD heeded the prayers for the land, and
[b]the plague was withdrawn from Israel.

24:10 [a] 1 Sam. 24:5 [b] 2 Sam. 23:1 [c] 2 Sam. 12:13 [d] 1 Sam. 13:13 **24:11** [a] 1 Sam. 22:5 [b] 1 Sam. 9:9 **24:13** [a] Ezek. 14:21 [1] Following Masoretic Text, Syriac, Targum, and Vulgate; Septuagint reads *three* (compare 1 Chronicles 21:12). **24:14** [a] [Ps. 51:1; 103:8, 13, 14; 119:156; 130:4, 7] [b] [Is. 47:6] **24:15** [a] 1 Chr. 21:14 **24:16** [a] Ex. 12:23 [b] Gen. 6:6 [1] Or *Angel* [2] Spelled *Ornan* in 1 Chronicles 21:15 **24:17** [a] Ps. 74:1 **24:18** [a] 1 Chr. 21:18 **24:21** [a] Gen. 23:8–16 [b] Num. 16:48, 50 **24:22** [a] 1 Kin. 19:21 **24:23** [a] [Ezek. 20:40, 41] **24:24** [a] 1 Chr. 21:24, 25 **24:25** [a] 2 Sam. 21:14 [b] 2 Sam. 24:21

THE FIRST BOOK OF THE

KINGS

AUTHOR

Both 1 and 2 Kings emphasize God's righteous judgment on idolatry and immorality. The style of these books is similar to that found in Jeremiah. The author of 1 Kings is unknown, but evidence supports the Talmudic tradition that Kings was written by Jeremiah. Clearly, the author was a prophet/historian as evidenced in the prophetic exposé of apostasy.

TIME

c. 971–851 BC

KEY VERSE

1 Kings 9:4–5

THEME

First Kings continues the saga of the kings of Israel after David. Solomon's reign and the details of the building of the temple take up a major portion of the book. After Solomon, the kingdom divides, and we have parallel narratives of the northern kingdom, Israel, and the southern kingdom, Judah. The book covers a span of about 120 years. During these years, idolatry becomes the norm, and God is largely forgotten. After Solomon, the main character of the book is Elijah the prophet.

The prophet Jeremiah authored what was once a single book, 1–2 Kings. No Old Testament prophet used the term *shalom* (in Hebrew) more than Jeremiah did. The great contribution of Jeremiah's description of Israel's kings is the combination of humility, wise leadership, and the peace of God. God gave Solomon wisdom, which brought peace "as He had promised" (1 Kin. 5:12). A lifestyle of peace occurs when Christians are "loyal to the Lord [their] God" (8:61). "Loyalty" here is from the same root word as *shalom* (*shalem*) and means "full or complete" loyalty. One of the most consequential requests a believer can make is described in 4:24: "He had peace on every side all around him."

Adonijah Presumes to Be King

1 Now King David was [a]old, advanced in years; and they put covers on him, but he could not get warm. 2 Therefore his servants said to him, "Let a young woman, a virgin, be sought for our lord the king, and let her stand before the king, and let her care for him; and let her lie in your bosom, that our lord the king may be warm." 3 So they sought for a lovely young woman throughout all the territory of Israel, and found [a]Abishag the [b]Shunammite, and brought her to the king. 4 The young woman *was* very lovely; and she cared for the king, and served him; but the king did not know her.

5 Then [a]Adonijah the son of Haggith exalted himself, saying, "I will be king"; and [b]he prepared for himself chariots and horsemen, and fifty men to run before him. 6 (And his father had not rebuked him at any time by saying, "Why have you done so?" He *was* also very good-looking. [a]*His mother* had borne him after Absalom.) 7 Then he conferred with [a]Joab the son of Zeruiah and with [b]Abiathar the priest, and [c]they followed and helped Adonijah. 8 But [a]Zadok the priest, [b]Benaiah the son of Jehoiada, [c]Nathan the prophet, [d]Shimei, Rei, and [e]the mighty men who *belonged* to David were not with Adonijah.

9 And Adonijah sacrificed sheep and oxen and fattened cattle by the stone of Zoheleth, which *is* by [a]En Rogel; he also invited all his brothers, the king's sons, and all the men of Judah, the king's servants. 10 But he did not invite Nathan the prophet, Benaiah, the mighty men, or [a]Solomon his brother.

11 So Nathan spoke to Bathsheba the mother of Solomon, saying, "Have you not heard that Adonijah the son of [a]Haggith has become king, and David our lord does not know *it?* 12 Come, please, let me now give you advice, that you may save your own life and the life of your son Solomon. 13 Go immediately to King David and say to him, 'Did you not, my lord, O king, swear to your maidservant, saying, [a]"Assuredly your son Solomon shall reign after me, and he shall sit on my throne"? Why then has Adonijah become king?' 14 Then, while you are still talking there with the king, I also will come in after you and confirm your words."

15 So Bathsheba went into the chamber to the king. (Now the king was very old, and Abishag the Shunammite was serving the king.) 16 And Bathsheba bowed and did homage to the king. Then the king said, "What is your wish?"

17 Then she said to him, "My lord, [a]you swore by the LORD your God to your maidservant, *saying,* 'Assuredly Solomon your son shall reign after me, and he shall sit on my throne.' 18 So now, look! Adonijah has become king; and now, my lord the king, you do not know about *it.* 19 [a]He has sacrificed oxen and fattened cattle and sheep in abundance, and has invited all the sons of the king, Abiathar the priest, and Joab the commander of the army; but Solomon your servant he has not invited. 20 And as for you, my lord, O king, the eyes of all Israel *are* on you, that you should tell them who will sit on the throne of my lord the king after him. 21 Otherwise it will happen, when my lord the king [a]rests with his fathers, that I and my son Solomon will be counted as offenders."

22 And just then, while she was still talking with the king, Nathan the prophet also came in. 23 So they told the king, saying, "Here is Nathan the prophet." And when he came in before the king, he bowed down before the king with his face to the ground. 24 And Nathan said, "My lord, O king, have you said, 'Adonijah shall reign after me, and he shall sit on my throne'? 25 [a]For he has gone down today, and has sacrificed oxen and fattened cattle and sheep in abundance, and has invited all the king's sons, and the commanders of the army, and Abiathar the priest; and look! They are eating and drinking before him; and they say, [b]'*Long* live King Adonijah!' 26 But he has not invited me—me your servant—nor Zadok the priest, nor Benaiah the son of Jehoiada, nor your servant Solomon. 27 Has this thing been done by my lord the king, and you have not told your servant who should sit on the throne of my lord the king after him?"

David Proclaims Solomon King

28 Then King David answered and said, "Call Bathsheba to me." So she came into the king's presence and stood before the king. 29 And the king took an oath and said, [a]"*As* the LORD lives, who has redeemed my life from every distress, 30 [a]just as I swore to you by the LORD God of Israel, saying, 'Assuredly Solomon your son shall be king after me, and he shall sit on my throne in my place,' so I certainly will do this day."

31 Then Bathsheba bowed with *her* face to the earth, and paid homage to the king, and said, [a]"Let my lord King David live forever!"

32 And King David said, "Call to me Zadok the priest, Nathan the prophet, and Benaiah

1:1 [a] 1 Chr. 23:1 **1:3** [a] 1 Kin. 2:17 [b] Josh. 19:18 **1:5** [a] 2 Sam. 3:4 [b] 2 Sam. 15:1 **1:6** [a] 2 Sam. 3:3, 4 **1:7** [a] 1 Chr. 11:6 [b] 2 Sam. 20:25 [c] 1 Kin. 2:22, 28 **1:8** [a] 1 Kin. 2:35 [b] 1 Kin. 2:25 [c] 2 Sam. 12:1 [d] 1 Kin. 4:18 [e] 2 Sam. 23:8 **1:9** [a] Josh. 15:7; 18:16 **1:10** [a] 2 Sam. 12:24 **1:11** [a] 2 Sam. 3:4 **1:13** [a] 1 Chr. 22:9–13 **1:17** [a] 1 Kin. 1:13, 30 **1:19** [a] 1 Kin. 1:7–9, 25 **1:21** [a] Deut. 31:16 **1:25** [a] 1 Kin. 1:9, 19 [b] 1 Sam. 10:24 **1:29** [a] 2 Sam. 4:9; 12:5 **1:30** [a] 1 Kin. 1:13, 17 **1:31** [a] Dan. 2:4; 3:9

the son of Jehoiada." So they came before the king. 33 The king also said to them, [a]"Take with you the servants of your lord, and have Solomon my son ride on my own [b]mule, and take him down to [c]Gihon. 34 There let Zadok the priest and Nathan the prophet [a]anoint him king over Israel; and [b]blow the horn, and say, '*Long* live King Solomon!' 35 Then you shall come up after him, and he shall come and sit on my throne, and he shall be king in my place. For I have appointed him to be ruler over Israel and Judah."

36 Benaiah the son of Jehoiada answered the king and said, [a]"Amen! May the LORD God of my lord the king say so *too.* 37 [a]As the LORD has been with my lord the king, even so may He be with Solomon, and [b]make his throne greater than the throne of my lord King David."

38 So Zadok the priest, Nathan the prophet, [a]Benaiah the son of Jehoiada, the [b]Cherethites, and the Pelethites went down and had Solomon ride on King David's mule, and took him to Gihon. 39 Then Zadok the priest took a horn of [a]oil from the tabernacle and [b]anointed Solomon. And they blew the horn, [c]and all the people said, "*Long* live King Solomon!" 40 And all the people went up after him; and the people played the flutes and rejoiced with great joy, so that the earth *seemed to* split with their sound.

41 Now Adonijah and all the guests who *were* with him heard *it* as they finished eating. And when Joab heard the sound of the horn, he said, "Why *is* the city in such a noisy uproar?" 42 While he was still speaking, there came [a]Jonathan, the son of Abiathar the priest. And Adonijah said to him, "Come in, for [b]you *are* a prominent man, and bring good news."

43 Then Jonathan answered and said to Adonijah, "No! Our lord King David has made Solomon king. 44 The king has sent with him Zadok the priest, Nathan the prophet, Benaiah the son of Jehoiada, the Cherethites, and the Pelethites; and they have made him ride on the king's mule. 45 So Zadok the priest and Nathan the prophet have anointed him king at Gihon; and they have gone up from there rejoicing, so that the city is in an uproar. This *is* the noise that you have heard. 46 Also Solomon [a]sits on the throne of the kingdom. 47 And moreover the king's servants have gone to bless our lord King David, saying, [a]'May God make the name of Solomon better than your name, and may He make his throne greater than your throne.' [b]Then the king bowed himself on the bed. 48 Also the king said thus, 'Blessed *be* the LORD God of Israel, who has [a]given *one* to sit on my throne this day, while my eyes see [b]*it!*' "

49 So all the guests who were with Adonijah were afraid, and arose, and each one went his way.

50 Now Adonijah was afraid of Solomon; so he arose, and went and [a]took hold of the horns of the altar. 51 And it was told Solomon, saying, "Indeed Adonijah is afraid of King Solomon; for look, he has taken hold of the horns of the altar, saying, 'Let King Solomon swear to me today that he will not put his servant to death with the sword.' "

52 Then Solomon said, "If he proves himself a worthy man, [a]not one hair of him shall fall to the earth; but if wickedness is found in him, he shall die." 53 So King Solomon sent them to bring him down from the altar. And he came and fell down before King Solomon; and Solomon said to him, "Go to your house."

David's Instructions to Solomon

2 Now [a]the days of David drew near that he should die, and he charged Solomon his son, saying: 2 [a]"I go the way of all the earth; [b]be strong, therefore, and prove yourself a man. 3 And keep the charge of the LORD your God: to walk in His ways, to keep His statutes, His commandments, His judgments, and His testimonies, as it is written in the Law of Moses, that you may [a]prosper in all that you do and wherever you turn; 4 that the LORD may [a]fulfill His word which He spoke concerning me, saying, [b]'If your sons take heed to their way, to [c]walk before Me in truth with all their heart and with all their soul,' He said, [d]'you shall not lack a man on the throne of Israel.'

5 "Moreover you know also what Joab the son of Zeruiah [a]did to me, *and* what he did to the two commanders of the armies of Israel, to [b]Abner the son of Ner and [c]Amasa the son of Jether, whom he killed. And he shed the blood of war in peacetime, and put the blood of war on his belt that *was* around his waist, and on his sandals that *were* on his feet. 6 Therefore do [a]according to your wisdom, and do not let his gray hair go down to the grave in peace.

1:33 [a] 2 Sam. 20:6 [b] Esth. 6:8 [c] 2 Chr. 32:30; 33:14 **1:34** [a] 1 Sam. 10:1; 16:3, 12 [b] 2 Sam. 15:10 **1:36** [a] Jer. 28:6 **1:37** [a] 1 Sam. 20:13 [b] 1 Kin. 1:47 **1:38** [a] 2 Sam. 8:18; 23:20–23 [b] 2 Sam. 20:7 **1:39** [a] Ps. 89:20 [b] 1 Chr. 29:22 [c] 1 Sam. 10:24 **1:42** [a] 2 Sam. 17:17, 20 [b] 2 Sam. 18:27 **1:46** [a] 1 Chr. 29:23 **1:47** [a] 1 Kin. 1:37 [b] Gen. 47:31 **1:48** [a] 1 Kin. 3:6 [b] 2 Sam. 7:12 **1:50** [a] 1 Kin. 2:28 **1:52** [a] 1 Sam. 14:45 **2:1** [a] Gen. 47:29 **2:2** [a] Josh. 23:14 [b] Deut. 31:7, 23 **2:3** [a] [Deut. 29:9] **2:4** [a] 2 Sam. 7:25 [b] [Ps. 132:12] [c] 2 Kin. 20:3 [d] 2 Sam. 7:12, 13 **2:5** [a] 2 Sam. 3:39; 18:5, 12, 14 [b] 2 Sam. 3:27 [c] 2 Sam. 20:10 **2:6** [a] 1 Kin. 2:9

7 "But show kindness to the sons of [a]Barzillai the Gileadite, and let them be among those who [b]eat at your table, for so [c]they came to me when I fled from Absalom your brother.

8 "And see, *you have* with you [a]Shimei the son of Gera, a Benjamite from Bahurim, who cursed me with a malicious curse in the day when I went to Mahanaim. But [b]he came down to meet me at the Jordan, and [c]I swore to him by the LORD, saying, 'I will not put you to death with the sword.' 9 Now therefore, [a]do not hold him guiltless, for you *are* a wise man and know what you ought to do to him; but [b]bring his gray hair down to the grave with blood."

Death of David

10 So [a]David rested with his fathers, and was buried in [b]the City of David. 11 The period that David [a]reigned over Israel *was* forty years; seven years he reigned in Hebron, and in Jerusalem he reigned thirty-three years. 12 [a]Then Solomon sat on the throne of his father David; and his kingdom was [b]firmly established.

> PEACE NOTE
>
> *Rest* is almost a synonym for *peace* in our text. David had followed God and passed the baton to his son Solomon to finish God's work. Then we read, "David rested with his fathers."
>
> 1 KINGS 2:10

Solomon Executes Adonijah

13 Now Adonijah the son of Haggith came to Bathsheba the mother of Solomon. So she said, [a]"Do you come peaceably?"

And he said, "Peaceably." 14 Moreover he said, "I have something *to say* to you."

And she said, "Say it."

15 Then he said, "You know that the kingdom was [a]mine, and all Israel had set their expectations on me, that I should reign. However, the kingdom has been turned over, and has become my brother's; for [b]it was his from the LORD. 16 Now I ask one petition of you; do not deny me."

And she said to him, "Say it."

17 Then he said, "Please speak to King Solomon, for he will not refuse you, that he may give me [a]Abishag the Shunammite as wife."

18 So Bathsheba said, "Very well, I will speak for you to the king."

19 Bathsheba therefore went to King Solomon, to speak to him for Adonijah. And the king rose up to meet her and [a]bowed down to her, and sat down on his throne and had a throne set for the king's mother; [b]so she sat at his right hand. 20 Then she said, "I desire one small petition of you; do not refuse me."

And the king said to her, "Ask it, my mother, for I will not refuse you."

21 So she said, "Let Abishag the Shunammite be given to Adonijah your brother as wife."

22 And King Solomon answered and said to his mother, "Now why do you ask Abishag the Shunammite for Adonijah? Ask for him the kingdom also—for he *is* my [a]older brother—for him, and for [b]Abiathar the priest, and for Joab the son of Zeruiah." 23 Then King Solomon swore by the LORD, saying, [a]"May God do so to me, and more also, if Adonijah has not spoken this word against his own life! 24 Now therefore, *as* the LORD lives, who has confirmed me and set me on the throne of David my father, and who has established a house[1] for me, as He [a]promised, Adonijah shall be put to death today!"

25 So King Solomon sent by the hand of [a]Benaiah the son of Jehoiada; and he struck him down, and he died.

Abiathar Exiled, Joab Executed

26 And to Abiathar the priest the king said, "Go to [a]Anathoth, to your own fields, for you *are* deserving of death; but I will not put you to death at this time, [b]because you carried the ark of the Lord GOD before my father David, and because you were afflicted every time my father was afflicted." 27 So Solomon removed Abiathar from being priest to the LORD, that he might [a]fulfill the word of the LORD which He spoke concerning the house of Eli at Shiloh.

28 Then news came to Joab, for Joab [a]had defected to Adonijah, though he had not defected to Absalom. So Joab fled to the

2:7 [a] 2 Sam. 19:31–39 [b] 2 Sam. 9:7, 10; 19:28 [c] 2 Sam. 17:17–29 **2:8** [a] 2 Sam. 16:5–13 [b] 2 Sam. 19:18 [c] 2 Sam. 19:23 **2:9** [a] Ex. 20:7 [b] Gen. 42:38; 44:31 **2:10** [a] Acts 2:29; 13:36 [b] 2 Sam. 5:7 **2:11** [a] 2 Sam. 5:4, 5 **2:12** [a] 1 Chr. 29:23 [b] 2 Chr. 1:1 **2:13** [a] 1 Sam. 16:4, 5 **2:15** [a] 1 Kin. 1:11, 18 [b] [Dan. 2:21] **2:17** [a] 1 Kin. 1:3, 4 **2:19** [a] [Ex. 20:12] [b] Ps. 45:9 **2:22** [a] 1 Chr. 3:2, 5 [b] 1 Kin. 1:7 **2:23** [a] Ruth 1:17 **2:24** [a] 2 Sam. 7:11, 13 [1] That is, a royal dynasty **2:25** [a] 2 Sam. 8:18 **2:26** [a] Josh. 21:18 [b] 2 Sam. 15:14, 29 **2:27** [a] 1 Sam. 2:31–35 **2:28** [a] 1 Kin. 1:7

tabernacle of the LORD, and [b]took hold of
the horns of the altar. 29 And King Solomon
was told, "Joab has fled to the tabernacle
of the LORD; there *he is,* by the altar." Then
Solomon sent Benaiah the son of Jehoiada,
saying, "Go, [a]strike him down." 30 So Benaiah
went to the tabernacle of the LORD, and said
to him, "Thus says the king, [a]'Come out!' "

And he said, "No, but I will die here." And
Benaiah brought back word to the king, saying,
"Thus said Joab, and thus he answered me."

31 Then the king said to him, [a]"Do as he has
said, and strike him down and bury him, [b]that
you may take away from me and from the
house of my father the innocent blood which
Joab shed. 32 So the LORD [a]will return his
blood on his head, because he struck down
two men more righteous [b]and better than he,
and killed them with the sword—[c]Abner the
son of Ner, the commander of the army of
Israel, and [d]Amasa the son of Jether, the commander of the army of Judah—though my
father David did not know *it.* 33 Their blood
shall therefore return upon the head of Joab
and [a]upon the head of his descendants forever. [b]But upon David and his descendants,
upon his house and his throne, there shall
be peace forever from the LORD."

34 So Benaiah the son of Jehoiada went
up and struck and killed him; and he was
buried in his own house in the wilderness.
35 The king put Benaiah the son of Jehoiada
in his place over the army, and the king put
[a]Zadok the priest in the place of [b]Abiathar.

Shimei Executed

36 Then the king sent and called for [a]Shim-
ei, and said to him, "Build yourself a house
in Jerusalem and dwell there, and do not go
out from there anywhere. 37 For it shall be,
on the day you go out and cross [a]the Brook
Kidron, know for certain you shall surely
die; [b]your blood shall be on your own head."

38 And Shimei said to the king, "The saying
is good. As my lord the king has said, so your
servant will do." So Shimei dwelt in Jerusalem many days.

39 Now it happened at the end of three years,
that two slaves of Shimei ran away to [a]Achish
the son of Maachah, king of Gath. And they
told Shimei, saying, "Look, your slaves *are* in
Gath!" 40 So Shimei arose, saddled his donkey,
and went to Achish at Gath to seek his slaves.
And Shimei went and brought his slaves from
Gath. 41 And Solomon was told that Shimei had
gone from Jerusalem to Gath and had come
back. 42 Then the king sent and called for Shimei, and said to him, "Did I not make you swear
by the LORD, and warn you, saying, 'Know for
certain that on the day you go out and travel
anywhere, you shall surely die'? And you said
to me, 'The word I have heard *is* good.' 43 Why
then have you not kept the oath of the LORD
and the commandment that I gave you?" 44 The
king said moreover to Shimei, "You know, as
your heart acknowledges, [a]all the wickedness
that you did to my father David; therefore
the LORD will [b]return your wickedness on
your own head. 45 But King Solomon *shall
be* blessed, and [a]the throne of David shall be
established before the LORD forever."

46 So the king commanded Benaiah the son
of Jehoiada; and he went out and struck him
down, and he died. Thus the [a]kingdom was
established in the hand of Solomon.

Solomon Requests Wisdom

3 Now [a]Solomon made a treaty with Pharaoh king of Egypt, and married Pharaoh's
daughter; then he brought her [b]to the City of
David until he had finished building his [c]own
house, and [d]the house of the LORD, and [e]the
wall all around Jerusalem. 2 [a]Meanwhile the
people sacrificed at the high places, because
there was no house built for the name of
the LORD until those days. 3 And Solomon
[a]loved the LORD, [b]walking in the statutes of
his father David, except that he sacrificed and
burned incense at the high places.

4 Now [a]the king went to Gibeon to sacrifice
there, [b]for that *was* the great high place: Solomon offered a thousand burnt offerings on
that altar. 5 [a]At Gibeon the LORD appeared to
Solomon [b]in a dream by night; and God said,
"Ask! What shall I give you?"

6 [a]And Solomon said: "You have shown
great mercy to Your servant David my father,
because he [b]walked before You in truth, in
righteousness, and in uprightness of heart
with You; You have continued this great kindness for him, and You [c]have given him a son
to sit on his throne, as *it is* this day. 7 Now,
O LORD my God, You have made Your servant
king instead of my father David, but I *am* a
[a]little child; I do not know *how* [b]to go out or
come in. 8 And Your servant *is* in the midst of
Your people whom You [a]have chosen, a great
people, [b]too numerous to be numbered or

2:28 [b] 1 Kin. 1:50 **2:29** [a] 1 Kin. 2:5, 6 **2:30** [a] [Ex. 21:14] **2:31** [a] [Ex. 21:14] [b] [Num. 35:33] **2:32** [a] Judg. 9:24, 57 [b] 2 Chr. 21:13, 14 [c] 2 Sam. 3:27 [d] 2 Sam. 20:9, 10 **2:33** [a] 2 Sam. 3:29 [b] [Prov. 25:5] **2:35** [a] 1 Sam. 2:35 [b] 1 Kin. 2:27 **2:36** [a] 1 Kin. 2:8 **2:37** [a] 2 Sam. 15:23 [b] Josh. 2:19 **2:39** [a] 1 Sam. 27:2 **2:44** [a] 2 Sam. 16:5–13 [b] 1 Sam. 25:39 **2:45** [a] [Prov. 25:5] **2:46** [a] 2 Chr. 1:1 **3:1** [a] 1 Kin. 7:8; 9:24 [b] 2 Sam. 5:7 [c] 1 Kin. 7:1 [d] 1 Kin. 6 [e] 1 Kin. 9:15, 19 **3:2** [a] [Deut. 12:2–5, 13, 14] **3:3** [a] [Rom. 8:28] [b] [1 Kin. 3:6, 14] **3:4** [a] 2 Chr. 1:3 [b] 1 Chr. 16:39; 21:29 **3:5** [a] 1 Kin. 9:2; 11:9 [b] Num. 12:6 **3:6** [a] 2 Chr. 1:8 [b] 1 Kin. 2:4; 9:4 [c] 1 Kin. 1:48 **3:7** [a] Jer. 1:6, 7 [b] Num. 27:17 **3:8** [a] [Deut. 7:6] [b] Gen. 13:6; 15:5; 22:17

counted. 9 [a]Therefore give to Your servant an
understanding heart [b]to judge Your people,
that I may [c]discern between good and evil.
For who is able to judge this great people
of Yours?"
10 The speech pleased the Lord, that Solomon had asked this thing. 11 Then God said
to him: "Because you have asked this thing,
and have [a]not asked long life for yourself,
nor have asked riches for yourself, nor have
asked the life of your enemies, but have asked
for yourself understanding to discern justice, 12 [a]behold, I have done according to your
words; [b]see, I have given you a wise and understanding heart, so that there has not been
anyone like you before you, nor shall any like
you arise after you. 13 And I have also [a]given
you what you have not asked: both [b]riches
and honor, so that there shall not be anyone
like you among the kings all your days. 14 So
[a]if you walk in My ways, to keep My statutes
and My commandments, [b]as your father David walked, then I will [c]lengthen your days."
15 Then Solomon [a]awoke; and indeed it had
been a dream. And he came to Jerusalem and
stood before the ark of the covenant of the
LORD, offered up burnt offerings, offered peace
offerings, and [b]made a feast for all his servants.

Solomon's Wise Judgment

16 Now two women *who were* harlots came
to the king, and [a]stood before him. 17 And one
woman said, "O my lord, this woman and I dwell
in the same house; and I gave birth while she
was in the house. 18 Then it happened, the third
day after I had given birth, that this woman also
gave birth. And we *were* together; no one *was*
with us in the house, except the two of us in
the house. 19 And this woman's son died in the
night, because she lay on him. 20 So she arose
in the middle of the night and took my son
from my side, while your maidservant slept,
and laid him in her bosom, and laid her dead
child in my bosom. 21 And when I rose in the
morning to nurse my son, there he was, dead.
But when I had examined him in the morning,
indeed, he was not my son whom I had borne."
22 Then the other woman said, "No! But
the living one *is* my son, and the dead one
is your son."
And the first woman said, "No! But the
dead one *is* your son, and the living one *is*
my son."
Thus they spoke before the king.
23 And the king said, "The one says, 'This *is*
my son, who lives, and your son *is* the dead
one'; and the other says, 'No! But your son *is*
the dead one, and my son *is* the living one.' "
24 Then the king said, "Bring me a sword." So
they brought a sword before the king. 25 And
the king said, "Divide the living child in two,
and give half to one, and half to the other."
26 Then the woman whose son *was* living
spoke to the king, for [a]she yearned with compassion for her son; and she said, "O my lord,
give her the living child, and by no means
kill him!"
But the other said, "Let him be neither
mine nor yours, *but* divide *him*."
27 So the king answered and said, "Give
the first woman the living child, and by no
means kill him; she *is* his mother."
28 And all Israel heard of the judgment
which the king had rendered; and they feared
the king, for they saw that the [a]wisdom of God
was in him to administer justice.

Solomon's Administration

4 So King Solomon was king over all Israel.
2 And these *were* his officials: Azariah the
son of Zadok, the priest; 3 Elihoreph and Ahijah, the sons of Shisha, scribes; [a]Jehoshaphat
the son of Ahilud, the recorder; 4 [a]Benaiah
the son of Jehoiada, over the army; Zadok
and [b]Abiathar, the priests; 5 Azariah the son
of Nathan, over [a]the officers; Zabud the son
of Nathan, [b]a priest *and* [c]the king's friend;
6 Ahishar, over the household; and [a]Adoni-
ram the son of Abda, over the labor force.
7 And Solomon had twelve governors over
all Israel, who provided food for the king and
his household; each one made provision for
one month of the year. 8 These *are* their names:
Ben-Hur,[1] in the mountains of Ephraim; 9 Ben-
Deker,[1] in Makaz, Shaalbim, Beth Shemesh,
and Elon Beth Hanan; 10 Ben-Hesed,[1] in Arub-
both; to him *belonged* Sochoh and all the land
of Hepher; 11 Ben-Abinadab,[1] *in* all the regions
of Dor; he had Taphath the daughter of Solomon as wife; 12 Baana the son of Ahilud, *in*
Taanach, Megiddo, and all Beth Shean, which
is beside Zaretan below Jezreel, from Beth
Shean to Abel Meholah, as far as the other side
of Jokneam; 13 Ben-Geber,[1] in Ramoth Gilead;
to him *belonged* [a]the towns of Jair the son of
Manasseh, in Gilead; to him *also belonged* [b]the
region of Argob in Bashan—sixty large cities
with walls and bronze gate-bars; 14 Ahinadab
the son of Iddo, *in* Mahanaim; 15 [a]Ahimaaz, in
Naphtali; he also took Basemath the daughter

3:9 [a] 2 Chr. 1:10 [b] Ps. 72:1, 2 [c] [Heb. 5:14] **3:11** [a] [James 4:3] **3:12** [a] [1 John 5:14, 15] [b] Eccl. 1:16 **3:13** [a] [Matt. 6:33] [b] 1 Kin. 4:21, 24; 10:23 **3:14** [a] [1 Kin. 6:12] [b] 1 Kin. 15:5 [c] Ps. 91:16 **3:15** [a] Gen. 41:7 [b] 1 Kin. 8:65 **3:16** [a] Num. 27:2 **3:26** [a] Jer. 31:20 **3:28** [a] 1 Kin. 3:9, 11, 12 **4:3** [a] 2 Sam. 8:16; 20:24 **4:4** [a] 1 Kin. 2:35 [b] 1 Kin. 2:27 **4:5** [a] 1 Kin. 4:7 [b] 2 Sam. 8:18; 20:26 [c] 2 Sam. 15:37; 16:16 **4:6** [a] 1 Kin. 5:14 **4:8** [1] Literally *Son of Hur* **4:9** [1] Literally *Son of Deker* **4:10** [1] Literally *Son of Hesed* **4:11** [1] Literally *Son of Abinadab* **4:13** [a] Num. 32:41 [b] Deut. 3:4 [1] Literally *Son of Geber* **4:15** [a] 2 Sam. 15:27

of Solomon as wife; 16 Baanah the son of [a]Hu-
shai, in Asher and Aloth; 17 Jehoshaphat the
son of Paruah, in Issachar; 18 [a]Shimei the son
of Elah, in Benjamin; 19 Geber the son of Uri,
in the land of Gilead, *in* [a]the country of Sihon
king of the Amorites, and of Og king of Bashan.
He was the only governor who *was* in the land.

Prosperity and Wisdom of Solomon's Reign

20 Judah and Israel *were* as numerous [a]as
the sand by the sea in multitude, [b]eating
and drinking and rejoicing. 21 So [a]Solomon
reigned over all kingdoms from [b]the River[1]
to the land of the Philistines, as far as the
border of Egypt. [c]*They* brought tribute and
served Solomon all the days of his life.

22 [a]Now Solomon's provision for one day
was thirty kors of fine flour, sixty kors of
meal, 23 ten fatted oxen, twenty oxen from
the pastures, and one hundred sheep, besides
deer, gazelles, roebucks, and fatted fowl.

24 For he had dominion over all *the region*
on this side of the River[1] from Tiphsah even
to Gaza, namely over [a]all the kings on this
side of the River; and [b]he had peace on every
side all around him. 25 And Judah and Israel
[a]dwelt safely, [b]each man under his vine and
his fig tree, [c]from Dan as far as Beersheba,
all the days of Solomon.

26 [a]Solomon had forty[1] thousand stalls of
[b]horses for his chariots, and twelve thousand horsemen. 27 And [a]these governors,
each man in his month, provided food for
King Solomon and for all who came to King
Solomon's table. There was no lack in their
supply. 28 They also brought barley and straw
to the proper place, for the horses and steeds,
each man according to his charge.

29 And [a]God gave Solomon wisdom and exceedingly great understanding, and largeness
of heart like the sand on the seashore. 30 Thus
Solomon's wisdom excelled the wisdom of all
the men [a]of the East and all [b]the wisdom of
Egypt. 31 For he was [a]wiser than all men—[b]than
Ethan the Ezrahite, [c]and Heman, Chalcol, and
Darda, the sons of Mahol; and his fame was in
all the surrounding nations. 32 [a]He spoke three
thousand proverbs, and his [b]songs were one
thousand and five. 33 Also he spoke of trees,
from the cedar tree of Lebanon even to the
hyssop that springs out of the wall; he spoke
also of animals, of birds, of creeping things,
and of fish. 34 And men of all nations, from all
the kings of the earth who had heard of his wisdom, [a]came to hear the wisdom of Solomon.

Solomon Prepares to Build the Temple

5 Now [a]Hiram king of Tyre sent his servants
to Solomon, because he heard that they
had anointed him king in place of his father,
[b]for Hiram had always loved David. 2 Then
[a]Solomon sent to Hiram, saying:

3 [a]You know how my father David could
not build a house for the name of the
LORD his God [b]because of the wars
which were fought against him on
every side, until the LORD put *his foes*[1]
under the soles of his feet.
4 But now the LORD my God has given
me [a]rest on every side; *there is* neither
adversary nor evil occurrence.
5 [a]And behold, I propose to build a
house for the name of the LORD my
God, [b]as the LORD spoke to my father
David, saying, "Your son, whom I will
set on your throne in your place, he
shall build the house for My name."
6 Now therefore, command that they cut
down [a]cedars for me from Lebanon; and
my servants will be with your servants,
and I will pay you wages for your servants
according to whatever you say. For you
know *there is* none among us who has
skill to cut timber like the Sidonians.

7 So it was, when Hiram heard the words of
Solomon, that he rejoiced greatly and said,

Blessed *be* the LORD this day, for He
has given David a wise son over this
great people!

8 Then Hiram sent to Solomon, saying:

I have considered *the message* which
you sent me, *and* I will do all you desire
concerning the cedar and cypress logs.
9 My servants shall bring *them* down
[a]from Lebanon to the sea; I will float
them in rafts by sea to the place you
indicate to me, and will have them
broken apart there; then you can take
them away. And you shall fulfill my
desire [b]by giving food for my household.

4:16 [a] *1 Chr. 27:33* **4:18** [a] *1 Kin. 1:8* **4:19** [a] Deut. 3:8–10 **4:20** [a] Gen. 22:17; 32:12 [b] Mic. 4:4 **4:21** [a] Ps. 72:8 [b] Gen. 15:18 [c] Ps. 68:29 [1] That is, the Euphrates **4:22** [a] Neh. 5:18 **4:24** [a] Ps. 72:11 [b] 1 Chr. 22:9 [1] That is, the Euphrates **4:25** [a] [Jer. 23:6] [b] [Mic. 4:4] [c] Judg. 20:1 **4:26** [a] 1 Kin. 10:26 [b] [Deut. 17:16] [1] Following Masoretic Text and most other authorities; some manuscripts of the Septuagint read *four* (compare 2 Chronicles 9:25). **4:27** [a] 1 Kin. 4:7 **4:29** [a] 1 Kin. 3:12 **4:30** [a] Gen. 25:6 [b] Is. 19:11, 12 **4:31** [a] 1 Kin. 3:12 [b] 1 Chr. 15:19 [c] 1 Chr. 2:6 **4:32** [a] Eccl. 12:9 [b] Song 1:1 **4:34** [a] 1 Kin. 10:1 **5:1** [a] 2 Chr. 2:3 [b] 2 Sam. 5:11 **5:2** [a] 2 Chr. 2:3 **5:3** [a] 1 Chr. 28:2, 3 [b] 1 Chr. 22:8; 28:3 [1] Literally *them* **5:4** [a] 1 Kin. 4:24 **5:5** [a] 2 Chr. 2:4 [b] 2 Sam. 7:12, 13 **5:6** [a] 2 Chr. 2:8, 10 **5:9** [a] Ezra 3:7 [b] Ezek. 27:17

10 Then Hiram gave Solomon cedar and
cypress logs *according to* all his desire. 11 [a]And
Solomon gave Hiram twenty thousand kors
of wheat *as* food for his household, and twenty[1] kors of pressed oil. Thus Solomon gave to
Hiram year by year.
12 So the LORD gave Solomon wisdom, [a]as
He had promised him; and there was peace
between Hiram and Solomon, and the two
of them made a treaty together.
13 Then King Solomon raised up a labor
force out of all Israel; and the labor force was
thirty thousand men. 14 And he sent them to
Lebanon, ten thousand a month in shifts: they
were one month in Lebanon *and* two months
at home; [a]Adoniram *was* in charge of the labor force. 15 [a]Solomon had seventy thousand
who carried burdens, and eighty thousand
who quarried *stone* in the mountains, 16 besides three thousand three hundred[1] from the
[a]chiefs of Solomon's deputies, who supervised
the people who labored in the work. 17 And
the king commanded them to quarry large
stones, costly stones, *and* [a]hewn stones, to lay
the foundation of the temple.[1] 18 So Solomon's
builders, Hiram's builders, and the Gebalites
quarried *them;* and they prepared timber and
stones to build the temple.

Solomon Builds the Temple

6 And [a]it came to pass in the four hundred
and eightieth[1] year after the children of
Israel had come out of the land of Egypt, in
the fourth year of Solomon's reign over Israel, in the month of Ziv, which *is* the second
month, [b]that he began to build the house
of the LORD. 2 Now [a]the house which King
Solomon built for the LORD, its length *was*
sixty cubits, its width twenty, and its height
thirty cubits. 3 The vestibule in front of the
sanctuary[1] of the house *was* twenty cubits
long across the width of the house, *and* the
width of *the vestibule*[2] *extended* ten cubits
from the front of the house. 4 And he made
for the house [a]windows with beveled frames.
5 Against the wall of the temple he built
[a]chambers all around, *against* the walls of the
temple, all around the sanctuary [b]and the inner sanctuary.[1] Thus he made side chambers
all around it. 6 The lowest chamber *was* five
cubits wide, the middle *was* six cubits wide,

PEACE NOTE

The peace of the Lord leads to precision in planning and action. In obedience to God, young Solomon marshaled a workforce of thirty thousand men to build the Lord's temple.

1 KINGS 5:13

and the third *was* seven cubits wide; for he
made narrow ledges around the outside of
the temple, so that *the support beams* would
not be fastened into the walls of the temple.
7 And [a]the temple, when it was being built,
was built with stone finished at the quarry,
so that no hammer or chisel *or* any iron tool
was heard in the temple while it was being
built. 8 The doorway for the middle story[1] *was*
on the right side of the temple. They went up
by stairs to the middle *story,* and from the
middle to the third.
9 [a]So he built the temple and finished it,
and he paneled the temple with beams and
boards of cedar. 10 And he built side chambers
against the entire temple, each five cubits
high; they were attached to the temple with
cedar beams.
11 Then the word of the LORD came to Solomon, saying: 12 "*Concerning* this temple
which you are building, [a]if you walk in My
statutes, execute My judgments, keep all
My commandments, and walk in them, then
I will perform My word with you, [b]which
I spoke to your father David. 13 And [a]I will
dwell among the children of Israel, and will
not [b]forsake My people Israel."
14 So Solomon built the temple and finished it. 15 And he built the inside walls of
the temple with cedar boards; from the floor
of the temple to the ceiling he paneled the
inside with wood; and he covered the floor

5:11 [a] 2 Chr. 2:10 [1] Following Masoretic Text, Targum, and Vulgate; Septuagint and Syriac read *twenty thousand.* **5:12** [a] 1 Kin. 3:12 **5:14** [a] 1 Kin. 12:18 **5:15** [a] 2 Chr. 2:17, 18 **5:16** [a] 1 Kin. 9:23 [1] Following Masoretic Text, Targum, and Vulgate; Septuagint reads *three thousand six hundred.* **5:17** [a] 1 Kin. 6:7 [1] Literally *house,* and so frequently throughout this book **6:1** [a] 2 Chr. 3:1, 2 [b] Acts 7:47 [1] Following Masoretic Text, Targum, and Vulgate; Septuagint reads *fortieth.* **6:2** [a] Ezek. 41:1 **6:3** [1] Hebrew *heykal;* here the main room of the temple, elsewhere called the holy place (compare Exodus 26:33 and Ezekiel 41:1) [2] Literally *it* **6:4** [a] Ezek. 40:16; 41:16 **6:5** [a] Ezek. 41:6 [b] 1 Kin. 6:16, 19–21, 31 [1] Hebrew *debir;* here the inner room of the temple, elsewhere called the Most Holy Place (compare verse 16) **6:7** [a] Deut. 27:5, 6 **6:8** [1] Following Masoretic Text and Vulgate; Septuagint reads *upper story;* Targum reads *ground story.* **6:9** [a] 1 Kin. 6:14, 38 **6:12** [a] 1 Kin. 2:4; 9:4 [b] [2 Sam. 7:13] **6:13** [a] Ex. 25:8 [b] [Deut. 31:6]

of the temple with planks of cypress. 16 Then he built the twenty-cubit room at the rear of the temple, from floor to ceiling, with cedar boards; he built *it* inside as the inner sanctuary, as the [a]Most Holy *Place.* 17 And in front of it the temple sanctuary was forty cubits *long.* 18 The inside of the temple was cedar, carved with ornamental buds and open flowers. All *was* cedar; there was no stone *to be* seen.

19 And he prepared the inner sanctuary inside the temple, to set the ark of the covenant of the LORD there. 20 The inner sanctuary *was* twenty cubits long, twenty cubits wide, and twenty cubits high. He overlaid it with pure gold, and overlaid the altar of cedar. 21 So Solomon overlaid the inside of the temple with pure gold. He stretched gold chains across the front of the inner sanctuary, and overlaid it with gold. 22 The whole temple he overlaid with gold, until he had finished all the temple; also he overlaid with gold [a]the entire altar that *was* by the inner sanctuary.

23 Inside the inner sanctuary [a]he made two cherubim *of* olive wood, *each* ten cubits high. 24 One wing of the cherub *was* five cubits, and the other wing of the cherub five cubits: ten cubits from the tip of one wing to the tip of the other. 25 And the other cherub *was* ten cubits; both cherubim *were* of the same size and shape. 26 The height of one cherub *was* ten cubits, and so *was* the other cherub. 27 Then he set the cherubim inside the inner room;[1] and [a]they stretched out the wings of the cherubim so that the wing of the one touched *one* wall, and the wing of the other cherub touched the other wall. And their wings touched each other in the middle of the room. 28 Also he overlaid the cherubim with gold.

29 Then he carved all the walls of the temple all around, both the inner and outer *sanctuaries,* with carved [a]figures of cherubim, palm trees, and open flowers. 30 And the floor of the temple he overlaid with gold, both the inner and outer *sanctuaries.*

31 For the entrance of the inner sanctuary he made doors *of* olive wood; the lintel *and* doorposts *were* one-fifth *of the wall.* 32 The two doors *were of* olive wood; and he carved on them figures of cherubim, palm trees, and open flowers, and overlaid *them* with gold; and he spread gold on the cherubim and on the palm trees. 33 So for the door of the sanctuary he also made doorposts *of* olive wood, one-fourth *of the wall.* 34 And the *two doors were of* cypress wood; [a]two panels *comprised* one folding door, and two panels *comprised* the other folding door. 35 Then he carved cherubim, palm trees, and open flowers *on them,* and overlaid *them* with gold applied evenly on the carved work.

36 And he built the [a]inner court with three rows of hewn stone and a row of cedar beams.

37 [a]In the fourth year the foundation of the house of the LORD was laid, in the month of Ziv. 38 And in the eleventh year, in the month of Bul, which is the eighth month, the house was finished in all its details and according to all its plans. So he was [a]seven years in building it.

Solomon's Other Buildings

7 But Solomon took [a]thirteen years to build his own house; so he finished all his house.

2 He also built the [a]House of the Forest of Lebanon; its length *was* one hundred cubits, its width fifty cubits, and its height thirty cubits, with four rows of cedar pillars, and cedar beams on the pillars. 3 And *it was* paneled with cedar above the beams that *were* on forty-five pillars, fifteen *to* a row. 4 *There were* windows *with beveled frames in* three rows, and window *was* opposite window *in* three tiers. 5 And all the doorways and doorposts *had* rectangular frames; and window *was* opposite window *in* three tiers.

6 He also made the Hall of Pillars: its length *was* fifty cubits, and its width thirty cubits; and in front of them *was* a portico with pillars, and a canopy *was* in front of them.

7 Then he made a hall for the throne, the Hall of Judgment, where he might judge; and *it was* paneled with cedar from floor to ceiling.[1]

8 And the house where he dwelt *had* another court inside the hall, of like workmanship. Solomon also made a house like this hall for Pharaoh's daughter, [a]whom he had taken *as wife.*

9 All these *were of* costly stones cut to size, trimmed with saws, inside and out, from the foundation to the eaves, and also on the outside to the great court. 10 The foundation *was of* costly stones, large stones, some ten cubits and some eight cubits. 11 And above *were* costly stones, hewn to size, and cedar wood. 12 The great court *was* enclosed with three rows of hewn stones and a row of cedar beams. So were the [a]inner court of the house of the LORD [b]and the vestibule of the temple.

Hiram the Craftsman

13 Now King Solomon sent and brought Huram[1] from Tyre. 14 [a]He *was* the son of a widow from the tribe of Naphtali, and [b]his

6:16 [a] Ex. 26:33 **6:22** [a] Ex. 30:1, 3, 6 **6:23** [a] 2 Chr. 3:10–12 **6:27** [a] 2 Chr. 5:8 [1] Literally *house* **6:29** [a] Ex. 36:8, 35 **6:34** [a] Ezek. 41:23–25 **6:36** [a] 1 Kin. 7:12 **6:37** [a] 1 Kin. 6:1 **6:38** [a] 1 Kin. 5:5; 6:1; 8:19 **7:1** [a] 2 Chr. 8:1 **7:2** [a] 2 Chr. 9:16 **7:7** [1] Literally *floor,* that is, of the upper level **7:8** [a] 2 Chr. 8:11 **7:12** [a] 1 Kin. 6:36 [b] John 10:23 **7:13** [1] Hebrew *Hiram* (compare 2 Chronicles 2:13, 14) **7:14** [a] 2 Chr. 2:14 [b] 2 Chr. 4:16

father *was* a man of Tyre, a bronze worker; [c]he was filled with wisdom and understanding and skill in working with all kinds of bronze work. So he came to King Solomon and did all his work.

The Bronze Pillars for the Temple

15 And he cast [a]two pillars of bronze, each one eighteen cubits high, and a line of twelve cubits measured the circumference of each. 16 Then he made two capitals *of* cast bronze, to set on the tops of the pillars. The height of one capital *was* five cubits, and the height of the other capital *was* five cubits. 17 *He made* a lattice network, with wreaths of chainwork, for the capitals which *were* on top of the pillars: seven chains for one capital and seven for the other capital. 18 So he made the pillars, and two rows of pomegranates above the network all around to cover the capitals that *were* on top; and thus he did for the other capital.

19 The capitals which *were* on top of the pillars in the hall *were* in the shape of lilies, four cubits. 20 The capitals on the two pillars also *had pomegranates* above, by the convex surface which *was* next to the network; and there *were* [a]two hundred such pomegranates in rows on each of the capitals all around.

21 [a]Then he set up the pillars by the vestibule of the temple; he set up the pillar on the right and called its name Jachin, and he set up the pillar on the left and called its name Boaz. 22 The tops of the pillars were in the shape of lilies. So the work of the pillars was finished.

The Sea and the Oxen

23 And he made [a]the Sea of cast bronze, ten cubits from one brim to the other; *it was* completely round. Its height *was* five cubits, and a line of thirty cubits measured its circumference.

24 Below its brim *were* ornamental buds encircling it all around, ten to a cubit, [a]all the way around the Sea. The ornamental buds *were* cast in two rows when it was cast. 25 It stood on [a]twelve oxen: three looking toward the north, three looking toward the west, three looking toward the south, and three looking toward the east; the Sea *was set* upon them, and all their back parts *pointed* inward. 26 It *was* a handbreadth thick; and its brim was shaped like the brim of a cup, *like* a lily blossom. It contained two thousand[1] baths.

The Carts and the Lavers

27 He also made ten carts of bronze; four cubits *was* the length of each cart, four cubits its width, and three cubits its height. 28 And this *was* the design of the carts: They had panels, and the panels *were* between frames; 29 on the panels that *were* between the frames *were* lions, oxen, and cherubim. And on the frames *was* a pedestal on top. Below the lions and oxen *were* wreaths of plaited work. 30 Every cart had four bronze wheels and axles of bronze, and its four feet had supports. Under the laver *were* supports of cast *bronze* beside each wreath. 31 Its opening inside the crown at the top *was* one cubit in diameter; and the opening *was* round, shaped *like* a pedestal, one and a half cubits in outside diameter; and also on the opening *were* engravings, but the panels were square, not round. 32 Under the panels *were* the four wheels, and the axles of the wheels *were joined* to the cart. The height of a wheel *was* one and a half cubits. 33 The workmanship of the wheels *was* like the workmanship of a chariot wheel; their axle pins, their rims, their spokes, and their hubs *were* all of cast *bronze.* 34 And *there were* four supports at the four corners of each cart; its supports *were* part of the cart itself. 35 On the top of the cart, at the height of half a cubit, *it was* perfectly round. And on the top of the cart, its flanges and its panels *were* of the same casting. 36 On the plates of its flanges and on its panels he engraved cherubim, lions, and palm trees, wherever there was a clear space on each, with wreaths all around. 37 Thus he made the ten carts. All of them were of the same mold, one measure, *and* one shape.

38 Then [a]he made ten lavers of bronze; each laver contained forty baths, *and* each laver *was* four cubits. On each of the ten carts *was* a laver. 39 And he put five carts on the right side of the house, and five on the left side of the house. He set the Sea on the right side of the house, toward the southeast.

Furnishings of the Temple

40 [a]Huram[1] made the lavers and the shovels and the bowls. So Huram finished doing all the work that he was to do for King Solomon *for* the house of the LORD: 41 the two pillars, the *two* bowl-shaped capitals that *were* on top of the two pillars; the two [a]networks covering the two bowl-shaped capitals which *were* on top of the pillars; 42 [a]four hundred pomegranates for the two networks (two rows of pomegranates for each network, to cover the two bowl-shaped capitals that *were* on top of the pillars); 43 the ten carts, and ten lavers on the carts; 44 one Sea, and

7:14 [c] Ex. 31:3; 36:1 **7:15** [a] Jer. 52:21 **7:20** [a] Jer. 52:23 **7:21** [a] 2 Chr. 3:17 **7:23** [a] 2 Chr. 4:2 **7:24** [a] 2 Chr. 4:3 **7:25** [a] Jer. 52:20 **7:26** [1] Or *three thousand* (compare 2 Chronicles 4:5) **7:38** [a] 2 Chr. 4:6 **7:40** [a] 2 Chr. 4:11—5:1 [1] Hebrew *Hiram* (compare 2 Chronicles 2:13, 14) **7:41** [a] 1 Kin. 7:17, 18 **7:42** [a] 1 Kin. 7:20

twelve oxen under the Sea; 45 [a]the pots, the shovels, and the bowls.

All these articles which Huram[1] made for King Solomon *for* the house of the LORD *were of* burnished bronze. 46 [a]In the plain of Jordan the king had them cast in clay molds, between [b]Succoth and [c]Zaretan. 47 And Solomon did not weigh all the articles, because *there were* so many; the weight of the bronze was not [a]determined.

48 Thus Solomon had all the furnishings made for the house of the LORD: [a]the altar of gold, and [b]the table of gold on which *was* [c]the showbread; 49 the lampstands of pure gold, five on the right *side* and five on the left in front of the inner sanctuary, with the flowers and the lamps and the wick-trimmers of gold; 50 the basins, the trimmers, the bowls, the ladles, and the censers of pure gold; and the hinges of gold, *both* for the doors of the inner room (the Most Holy *Place*) *and* for the doors of the main hall of the temple.

51 So all the work that King Solomon had done for the house of the LORD was finished; and Solomon brought in the things [a]which his father David had dedicated: the silver and the gold and the furnishings. He put them in the treasuries of the house of the LORD.

The Ark Brought into the Temple

8 Now [a]Solomon assembled the elders of Israel and all the heads of the tribes, the chief fathers of the children of Israel, to King Solomon in Jerusalem, [b]that they might bring [c]up the ark of the covenant of the LORD from the City of David, which *is* Zion. 2 Therefore all the men of Israel assembled with King Solomon at the [a]feast in the month of Ethanim, which *is* the seventh month. 3 So all the elders of Israel came, [a]and the priests took up the ark. 4 Then they brought up the ark of the LORD, [a]the tabernacle of meeting, and all the holy furnishings that *were* in the tabernacle. The priests and the Levites brought them up. 5 Also King Solomon, and all the congregation of Israel who were assembled with him, *were* with him before the ark, [a]sacrificing sheep and oxen that could not be counted or numbered for multitude. 6 Then the priests [a]brought in the ark of the covenant of the LORD to [b]its place, into the inner sanctuary of the temple, to the Most Holy *Place,* [c]under the wings of the cherubim. 7 For the cherubim spread *their* two wings over the place of the ark, and the cherubim overshadowed the ark and its poles. 8 The poles [a]extended so that the ends of the poles could be seen from the holy *place,* in front of the inner sanctuary; but they could not be seen from outside. And they are there to this day. 9 [a]Nothing *was* in the ark [b]except the two tablets of stone which Moses [c]put there at Horeb, [d]when the LORD made *a covenant* with the children of Israel, when they came out of the land of Egypt.

10 And it came to pass, when the priests came out of the holy *place,* that the cloud [a]filled the house of the LORD, 11 so that the priests could not continue ministering because of the cloud; for the [a]glory of the LORD filled the house of the LORD.

12 [a]Then Solomon spoke:

"The LORD said He would dwell [b]in the
 dark cloud.
13 [a]I have surely built You an exalted house,
 [b]And a place for You to dwell in forever."

Solomon's Speech at Completion of the Work

14 Then the king turned around and [a]blessed the whole assembly of Israel, while all the assembly of Israel was standing. 15 And he said: [a]"Blessed *be* the LORD God of Israel, who [b]spoke with His mouth to my father David, and with His hand has fulfilled *it,* saying, 16 'Since the day that I brought My people Israel out of Egypt, I have chosen no city from any tribe of Israel *in which* to build a house, that [a]My name might be there; but I chose [b]David to be over My people Israel.' 17 Now [a]it was in the heart of my father David to build a temple[1] for the name of the LORD God of Israel. 18 [a]But the LORD said to my father David, 'Whereas it was in your heart to build a temple for My name, you did well that it was in your heart. 19 Nevertheless [a]you shall not build the temple, but your son who will come from your body, he shall build the temple for My name.' 20 So the LORD has fulfilled His word which He spoke; and I have filled the position of my father David, and sit on the throne of Israel, [a]as the LORD promised; and I have built a temple for the name of the LORD God of Israel. 21 And there I have made a place for the ark, in which *is* [a]the covenant of the LORD which He made with our fathers, when He brought them out of the land of Egypt."

7:45 [a] *Ex. 27:3* [1] *Hebrew Hiram* (compare 2 Chronicles 2:13, 14) **7:46** [a] 2 Chr. 4:17 [b] Gen. 33:17 [c] Josh. 3:16 **7:47** [a] 1 Chr. 22:3, 14 **7:48** [a] Ex. 37:25, 26; 2 Chr. 4:8 [b] Ex. 37:10, 11 [c] Lev. 24:5–8 **7:51** [a] 2 Sam. 8:11 **8:1** [a] 2 Chr. 5:2–14 [b] 2 Sam. 6:12–17 [c] 2 Sam. 5:7; 6:12, 16 **8:2** [a] Lev. 23:34 **8:3** [a] Num. 4:15; 7:9 **8:4** [a] 2 Chr. 1:3 **8:5** [a] 2 Sam. 6:13 **8:6** [a] 2 Sam. 6:17 [b] 1 Kin. 6:19 [c] 1 Kin. 6:27 **8:8** [a] Ex. 25:13–15; 37:4, 5 **8:9** [a] Ex. 25:21 [b] Deut. 10:5 [c] Ex. 24:7, 8; 40:20 [d] Ex. 34:27, 28 **8:10** [a] Ex. 40:34, 35 **8:11** [a] 2 Chr. 7:1, 2 **8:12** [a] 2 Chr. 6:1 [b] Ps. 18:11; 97:2 **8:13** [a] 2 Sam. 7:13 [b] Ps. 132:14 **8:14** [a] 2 Sam. 6:18 **8:15** [a] Luke 1:68 [b] 2 Sam. 7:2, 12, 13, 25 **8:16** [a] 1 Kin. 8:29 [b] 2 Sam. 7:8 **8:17** [a] 2 Sam. 7:2, 3 [1] Literally *house,* and so in verses 18–20 **8:18** [a] 2 Chr. 6:8, 9 **8:19** [a] 2 Sam. 7:5, 12, 13 **8:20** [a] 1 Chr. 28:5, 6 **8:21** [a] Deut. 31:26

Solomon's Prayer of Dedication

22 Then Solomon stood before [a]the altar of the LORD in the presence of all the assembly of Israel, and [b]spread out his hands toward heaven; 23 and he said: "LORD God of Israel, [a]*there is* no God in heaven above or on earth below like You, [b]who keep *Your* covenant and mercy with Your servants who [c]walk before You with all their hearts. 24 You have kept what You promised Your servant David my father; You have both spoken with Your mouth and fulfilled *it* with Your hand, as *it is* this day. 25 Therefore, LORD God of Israel, now keep what You promised Your servant David my father, saying, [a]'You shall not fail to have a man sit before Me on the throne of Israel, only if your sons take heed to their way, that they walk before Me as you have walked before Me.' 26 [a]And now I pray, O God of Israel, let Your word come true, which You have spoken to Your servant David my father.

27 "But [a]will God indeed dwell on the earth? Behold, heaven and the [b]heaven of heavens cannot contain You. How much less this temple which I have built! 28 Yet regard the prayer of Your servant and his supplication, O LORD my God, and listen to the cry and the prayer which Your servant is praying before You today: 29 that Your eyes may be open toward this temple night and day, toward the place of which You said, [a]'My name shall be [b]there,' that You may hear the prayer which Your servant makes [c]toward this place. 30 [a]And may You hear the supplication of Your servant and of Your people Israel, when they pray toward this place. Hear in heaven Your dwelling place; and when You hear, forgive.

31 "When anyone sins against his neighbor, and is forced to take [a]an oath, and comes *and* takes an oath before Your altar in this temple, 32 then hear in heaven, and act, and judge Your servants, [a]condemning the wicked, bringing his way on his head, and justifying the righteous by giving him according to his righteousness.

33 [a]"When Your people Israel are defeated before an enemy because they have sinned against You, and [b]when they turn back to You and confess Your name, and pray and make supplication to You in this temple, 34 then hear in heaven, and forgive the sin of Your people Israel, and bring them back to the land which You gave to their [a]fathers.

35 [a]"When the heavens are shut up and there is no rain because they have sinned against You, when they pray toward this place and confess Your name, and turn from their sin because You afflict them, 36 then hear in heaven, and forgive the sin of Your servants, Your people Israel, that You may [a]teach them [b]the good way in which they should walk; and send rain on Your land which You have given to Your people as an inheritance.

37 [a]"When there is famine in the land, pestilence *or* blight *or* mildew, locusts *or* grasshoppers; when their enemy besieges them in the land of their cities; whatever plague or whatever sickness *there is;* 38 whatever prayer, whatever supplication is made by anyone, *or* by all Your people Israel, when each one knows the plague of his own heart, and spreads out his hands toward this temple: 39 then hear in heaven Your dwelling place, and forgive, and act, and give to everyone according to all his ways, whose heart You know (for You alone [a]know the hearts of all the sons of men), 40 [a]that they may fear You all the days that they live in the land which You gave to our fathers.

41 "Moreover, concerning a foreigner, who *is* not of Your people Israel, but has come from a far country for Your name's sake 42 (for they will hear of Your great name and Your [a]strong hand and Your outstretched arm), when he comes and prays toward this temple, 43 hear in heaven Your dwelling place, and do according to all for which the foreigner calls to You, [a]that all peoples of the earth may know Your name and [b]fear You, as *do* Your people Israel, and that they may know that this temple which I have built is called by Your name.

44 "When Your people go out to battle against their enemy, wherever You send them, and when they pray to the LORD toward the city which You have chosen and the temple which I have built for Your name, 45 then hear in heaven their prayer and their supplication, and maintain their cause.

46 "When they sin against You [a](for *there is* no one who does not sin), and You become angry with them and deliver them to the enemy, and they take them captive [b]to the land of the enemy, far or near; 47 [a]*yet* when they come to themselves in the land where they were carried captive, and repent, and make supplication to You in the land of those who took them captive, [b]saying, 'We have sinned and done wrong, we have committed

8:22 [a] 2 Chr. 6:12 [b] Ezra 9:5 **8:23** [a] Ex. 15:11 [b] [Neh. 1:5] [c] [Gen. 17:1] **8:25** [a] 1 Kin. 2:4; 9:5 **8:26** [a] 2 Sam. 7:25 **8:27** [a] [Acts 7:49; 17:24] [b] 2 Cor. 12:2 **8:29** [a] Deut. 12:11 [b] 1 Kin. 9:3 [c] Dan. 6:10 **8:30** [a] Neh. 1:6 **8:31** [a] Ex. 22:8–11 **8:32** [a] Deut. 25:1 **8:33** [a] Deut. 28:25 [b] Lev. 26:39, 40 **8:34** [a] [Lev. 26:40–42] **8:35** [a] Deut. 28:23 **8:36** [a] Ps. 25:4; 27:11; 94:12 [b] 1 Sam. 12:23 **8:37** [a] Lev. 26:16, 25, 26 **8:39** [a] [1 Sam. 16:7] **8:40** [a] [Ps. 130:4] **8:42** [a] Deut. 3:24 **8:43** [a] [1 Sam. 17:46] [b] Ps. 102:15 **8:46** [a] Ps. 130:3 [b] Lev. 26:34, 44 **8:47** [a] [Lev. 26:40–42] [b] Dan. 9:5

SO OTHERS WILL KNOW PEACE

Concerning a foreigner . . . do according to all for which the foreigner calls to You, that all peoples of the earth may know Your name.

1 KINGS 8:41, 43

As a people, the Israelites knew they were special and that they were not to follow Gentile customs. God wanted them to avoid idolatry and polytheism. The Gentiles worshiped many gods.

One of the most astounding passages in the Old Testament is found in King Solomon's dedication of the temple. Solomon asked that when the foreigner "comes and prays toward this temple, hear in heaven Your dwelling place" (vv. 42–43). Solomon, whose name meant "Peaceful," recognized that God is the God of all people and that He will respond to everyone who calls on His name. God wishes to be at peace with all people—and Solomon, Israel's peaceful king, was willing to share Him.

Solomon's universal perspective anticipates the risen Jesus' commission that His followers make disciples of "all the nations" (Matt. 28:19). Beyond that, Solomon's request reflects God's heart.

Is there someone with whom you would like to share the God of Peace? What will you do about it today?

wickedness'; 48 and *when* they [a]return to You with all their heart and with all their soul in the land of their enemies who led them away captive, and [b]pray to You toward their land which You gave to their fathers, the city which You have chosen and the temple which I have built for Your name: 49 then hear in heaven Your dwelling place their prayer and their supplication, and maintain their cause, 50 and forgive Your people who have sinned against You, and all their transgressions which they have transgressed against You; and [a]grant them compassion before those who took them captive, that they may have compassion on them 51 (for [a]they *are* Your people and Your inheritance, whom You brought out of Egypt, [b]out of the iron furnace), 52 [a]that Your eyes may be open to the supplication of Your servant and the supplication of Your people Israel, to listen to them whenever they call to You. 53 For You separated them from among all the peoples of the earth *to be* Your inheritance, [a]as You spoke by Your servant Moses, when You brought our fathers out of Egypt, O Lord GOD."

Solomon Blesses the Assembly

54 [a]And so it was, when Solomon had finished praying all this prayer and supplication to the LORD, that he arose from before the altar of the LORD, from kneeling on his knees with his hands spread up to heaven. 55 Then he stood [a]and blessed all the assembly of Israel with a loud voice, saying: 56 "Blessed *be* the LORD, who has given [a]rest to His people Israel, according to all that He promised. [b]There has not failed one word of all His good promise, which He promised through His servant Moses. 57 May the LORD our God be with us, as He was with our fathers. [a]May He not leave us nor forsake us, 58 that He may [a]incline our hearts to Himself, to walk in all His ways, and to keep His commandments and His statutes and His judgments, which He commanded our fathers. 59 And may these words of mine, with which I have made supplication before the LORD, be near the LORD our God day and night, that He may maintain the cause of His servant and the cause of His people Israel, as each day may require, 60 [a]that all the peoples of the earth may know that [b]the LORD *is* God; *there is* no other. 61 Let your [a]heart therefore be loyal to the LORD our God, to walk in His statutes and keep His commandments, as at this day."

Solomon Dedicates the Temple

62 Then [a]the king and all Israel with him offered sacrifices before the LORD. 63 And

8:48 [a] Jer. 29:12–14 [b] Dan. 6:10 **8:50** [a] Ps. 106:46 **8:51** [a] Deut. 9:26–29 [b] Jer. 11:4 **8:52** [a] 1 Kin. 8:29 **8:53** [a] Ex. 19:5, 6 **8:54** [a] 2 Chr. 7:1 **8:55** [a] 2 Sam. 6:18 **8:56** [a] 1 Chr. 22:18 [b] Deut. 12:10 **8:57** [a] Deut. 31:6 **8:58** [a] Ps. 119:36 **8:60** [a] 1 Sam. 17:46 [b] Deut. 4:35, 39 **8:61** [a] Deut. 18:13 **8:62** [a] 2 Chr. 7:4–10

Solomon offered a sacrifice of peace offerings,
which he offered to the LORD, twenty-two
thousand bulls and one hundred and twenty
thousand sheep. So the king and all the children of Israel dedicated the house of the LORD.
64 On [a]the same day the king consecrated the
middle of the court that *was* in front of the
house of the LORD; for there he offered burnt
offerings, grain offerings, and the fat of the
peace offerings, because the [b]bronze altar that
was before the LORD *was* too small to receive
the burnt offerings, the grain offerings, and
the fat of the peace offerings.
65 At that time Solomon held [a]a feast, and
all Israel with him, a great assembly from
[b]the entrance of Hamath to [c]the Brook of
Egypt, before the LORD our God, [d]seven days
and seven *more* days—fourteen days. 66 [a]On
the eighth day he sent the people away; and
they blessed the king, and went to their tents
joyful and glad of heart for all the good that
the LORD had done for His servant David,
and for Israel His people.

God's Second Appearance to Solomon

9 And [a]it came to pass, when Solomon had
finished building the house of the LORD
[b]and the king's house, and [c]all Solomon's
desire which he wanted to do, 2 that the LORD
appeared to Solomon the second time, [a]as
He had appeared to him at Gibeon. 3 And the
LORD said to him: [a]"I have heard your prayer
and your supplication that you have made
before Me; I have consecrated this house
which you have built [b]to put My name there
forever, [c]and My eyes and My heart will be
there perpetually. 4 Now if you [a]walk before
Me [b]as your father David walked, in integrity
of heart and in uprightness, to do according
to all that I have commanded you, *and* if you
[c]keep My statutes and My judgments, 5 then
I will establish the throne of your kingdom
over Israel forever, [a]as I promised David your
father, saying, 'You shall not fail to have a man
on the throne of Israel.' 6 [a]*But* if you or your
sons at all turn from following Me, and do
not keep My commandments *and* My statutes
which I have set before you, but go and serve
other gods and worship them, 7 [a]then I will cut
off Israel from the land which I have given
them; and this house which I have consecrated [b]for My name I will cast out of My sight.
[c]Israel will be a proverb and a byword among
all peoples. 8 And *as for* [a]this house, *which* is
exalted, everyone who passes by it will be astonished and will hiss, and say, [b]'Why has the
LORD done thus to this land and to this house?'
9 Then they will answer, 'Because they forsook
the LORD their God, who brought their fathers
out of the land of Egypt, and have embraced
other gods, and worshiped them and served
them; therefore the LORD has brought all this
[a]calamity on them.' "

Solomon and Hiram Exchange Gifts

10 Now [a]it happened at the end of twenty
years, when Solomon had built the two houses,
the house of the LORD and the king's house
11 [a](Hiram the king of Tyre had supplied Solomon with cedar and cypress and gold, as
much as he desired), *that* King Solomon then
gave Hiram twenty cities in the land of Galilee.
12 Then Hiram went from Tyre to see the cities
which Solomon had given him, but they did not
please him. 13 So he said, "What *kind of* cities *are*
these which you have given me, my brother?"
[a]And he called them the land of Cabul,[1] as they
are to this day. 14 Then Hiram sent the king one
hundred and twenty talents of gold.

Solomon's Additional Achievements

15 And this *is* the reason for [a]the labor force
which King Solomon raised: to build the house
of the LORD, his own house, the [b]Millo,[1] the wall
of Jerusalem, [c]Hazor, [d]Megiddo, and [e]Gezer.
16 (Pharaoh king of Egypt had gone up and
taken Gezer and burned it with fire, [a]had killed
the Canaanites who dwelt in the city, and had
given it *as* a dowry to his daughter, Solomon's
wife.) 17 And Solomon built Gezer, Lower [a]Beth
Horon, 18 [a]Baalath, and Tadmor in the wilderness, in the land *of Judah,* 19 all the storage cities
that Solomon had, cities for [a]his chariots and
cities for his [b]cavalry, and whatever Solomon
[c]desired to build in Jerusalem, in Lebanon,
and in all the land of his dominion.
20 [a]All the people *who were* left of the Amorites, Hittites, Perizzites, Hivites, and Jebusites, who *were* not of the children of Israel— 21 that is, their descendants [a]who were
left in the land after them, [b]whom the children of Israel had not been able to destroy
completely—[c]from these Solomon raised
[d]forced labor, as it is to this day. 22 But of the
children of Israel Solomon [a]made no forced
laborers, because they *were* men of war and

8:64 [a] 2 Chr. 7:7 [b] 2 Chr. 4:1 **8:65** [a] Lev. 23:34 [b] Num. 34:8 [c] Gen. 15:18 [d] 2 Chr. 7:8 **8:66** [a] 2 Chr. 7:9 **9:1** [a] 2 Chr. 7:11 [b] 1 Kin. 7:1 [c] 2 Chr. 8:6 **9:2** [a] 1 Kin. 3:5; 11:9 **9:3** [a] Ps. 10:17 [b] 1 Kin. 8:29 [c] Deut. 11:12 **9:4** [a] Gen. 17:1 [b] 1 Kin. 11:4, 6; 15:5 [c] 1 Kin. 8:61 **9:5** [a] 2 Sam. 7:12, 16 **9:6** [a] 2 Sam. 7:14–16 **9:7** [a] [Lev. 18:24–29] [b] [Jer. 7:4–14] [c] Ps. 44:14 **9:8** [a] 2 Chr. 7:21 [b] [Deut. 29:24–26] **9:9** [a] [Deut. 29:25–28] **9:10** [a] 2 Chr. 8:1 **9:11** [a] 1 Kin. 5:1 **9:13** [a] Josh. 19:27 [1] Literally *Good for Nothing* **9:15** [a] 1 Kin. 5:13 [b] 2 Sam. 5:9 [c] Josh. 11:1; 19:36 [d] Josh. 17:11 [e] Josh. 16:10 [1] Literally *The Landfill* **9:16** [a] Josh. 16:10 **9:17** [a] 2 Chr. 8:5 **9:18** [a] Josh. 19:44 **9:19** [a] 1 Kin. 10:26 [b] 1 Kin. 4:26 [c] 1 Kin. 9:1 **9:20** [a] 2 Chr. 8:7 **9:21** [a] Judg. 1:21–36; 3:1 [b] Josh. 15:63; 17:12, 13 [c] Judg. 1:28, 35 [d] Ezra 2:55, 58 **9:22** [a] [Lev. 25:39]

his servants: his officers, his captains, commanders of his chariots, and his cavalry.
23 Others *were* chiefs of the officials who
were over Solomon's work: [a]five hundred
and fifty, who ruled over the people who
did the work.
24 But [a]Pharaoh's daughter came up from
the City of David to [b]her house which *Solomon*[1]
had built for her. [c]Then he built the Millo.
25 [a]Now three times a year Solomon offered
burnt offerings and peace offerings on the
altar which he had built for the LORD, and
he burned incense with them *on the altar*
that *was* before the LORD. So he finished
the temple.
26 [a]King Solomon also built a fleet of ships
at [b]Ezion Geber, which *is* near Elath[1] on the
shore of the Red Sea, in the land of Edom.
27 [a]Then Hiram sent his servants with the
fleet, seamen who knew the sea, to work
with the servants of Solomon. 28 And they
went to [a]Ophir, and acquired four hundred
and twenty talents of gold from there, and
brought *it* to King Solomon.

The Queen of Sheba's Praise of Solomon

10 Now when the [a]queen of Sheba heard
of the fame of Solomon concerning the
name of the LORD, she came [b]to test him with
hard questions. 2 She came to Jerusalem with
a very great retinue, with camels that bore
spices, very much gold, and precious stones;
and when she came to Solomon, she spoke
with him about all that was in her heart. 3 So
Solomon answered all her questions; there
was nothing so difficult for the king that he
could not explain *it* to her. 4 And when the
queen of Sheba had seen all the wisdom of
Solomon, the house that he had built, 5 the
food on his table, the seating of his servants,
the service of his waiters and their apparel,
his cupbearers, [a]and his entryway by which he
went up to the house of the LORD, there was
no more spirit in her. 6 Then she said to the
king: "It was a true report which I heard in my
own land about your words and your wisdom.
7 However I did not believe the words until I
came and saw with my own eyes; and indeed
the half was not told me. Your wisdom and
prosperity exceed the fame of which I heard.
8 [a]Happy *are* your men and happy *are* these
your servants, who stand continually before
you *and* hear your wisdom! 9 [a]Blessed be the
LORD your God, who [b]delighted in you, setting
you on the throne of Israel! Because the LORD
has loved Israel forever, therefore He made
you king, [c]to do justice and righteousness."
10 Then she [a]gave the king one hundred and
twenty talents of gold, spices in great quantity,
and precious stones. There never again came
such abundance of spices as the queen of
Sheba gave to King Solomon. 11 [a]Also, the ships
of Hiram, which brought gold from Ophir,
brought great quantities of almug[1] wood and
precious stones from Ophir. 12 [a]And the king
made steps of the almug wood for the house
of the LORD and for the king's house, also
harps and stringed instruments for singers.
There never again came such [b]almug wood,
nor has the like been seen to this day.
13 Now King Solomon gave the queen of
Sheba all she desired, whatever she asked,
besides what Solomon had given her according to the royal generosity. So she turned
and went to her own country, she and her
servants.

Solomon's Great Wealth

14 The weight of gold that came to Solomon
yearly was six hundred and sixty-six talents
of gold, 15 besides *that* from the [a]traveling
merchants, from the income of traders,
[b]from all the kings of Arabia, and from the
governors of the country.
16 And King Solomon made two hundred
large shields *of* hammered gold; six hundred
shekels of gold went into each shield. 17 He also
made [a]three hundred shields *of* hammered
gold; three minas of gold went into each
shield. The king put them in the [b]House of
the Forest of Lebanon.
18 [a]Moreover the king made a great throne
of ivory, and overlaid it with pure gold. 19 The
throne had six steps, and the top of the
throne *was* round at the back; *there were*
armrests on either side of the place of the
seat, and two lions stood beside the armrests.
20 Twelve lions stood there, one on each side
of the six steps; nothing like *this* had been
made for any *other* kingdom.
21 [a]All King Solomon's drinking vessels
were gold, and all the vessels of the House
of the Forest of Lebanon *were* pure gold.
Not *one was* silver, for this was accounted
as nothing in the days of Solomon. 22 For
the king had [a]merchant ships[1] at sea with
the fleet of Hiram. Once every three years
the merchant [b]ships came bringing gold,

9:23 [a] 2 Chr. 8:10 **9:24** [a] 1 Kin. 3:1 [b] 1 Kin. 7:8 [c] 2 Sam. 5:9 [1] Literally *he* (compare 2 Chronicles 8:11) **9:25** [a] Ex. 23:14–17
9:26 [a] 2 Chr. 8:17, 18 [b] Num. 33:35 [1] Hebrew *Eloth* (compare 2 Kings 14:22) **9:27** [a] 1 Kin. 5:6, 9; 10:11 **9:28** [a] Job 22:24
10:1 [a] Matt. 12:42 [b] Judg. 14:12 **10:5** [a] 1 Chr. 26:16 **10:8** [a] Prov. 8:34 **10:9** [a] 1 Kin. 5:7 [b] 2 Sam. 22:20 [c] Ps. 72:2
10:10 [a] Ps. 72:10, 15 **10:11** [a] 1 Kin. 9:27, 28 [1] Or *algum* (compare 2 Chronicles 9:10, 11) **10:12** [a] 2 Chr. 9:11 [b] 2 Chr. 9:10
10:15 [a] 2 Chr. 1:16 [b] Ps. 72:10 **10:17** [a] 1 Kin. 14:26 [b] 1 Kin. 7:2 **10:18** [a] 2 Chr. 9:17 **10:21** [a] 2 Chr. 9:20 **10:22** [a] Gen.
10:4 [b] 1 Kin. 9:26–28; 22:48 [1] Literally *ships of Tarshish,* deep-sea vessels

silver, ivory, apes, and monkeys.[2] 23 So [a]King Solomon surpassed all the kings of the earth in riches and wisdom.

24 Now all the earth sought the presence of Solomon to hear his wisdom, which God had put in his heart. 25 Each man brought his present: articles of silver and gold, garments, armor, spices, horses, and mules, at a set rate year by year.

26 [a]And Solomon [b]gathered chariots and horsemen; he had one thousand four hundred chariots and twelve thousand horsemen, whom he stationed[1] in the chariot cities and with the king at Jerusalem. 27 [a]The king made silver *as common* in Jerusalem as stones, and he made cedar trees as abundant as the sycamores which *are* in the lowland.

28 [a]Also Solomon had horses imported from Egypt and Keveh; the king's merchants bought them in Keveh at the *current* price. 29 Now a chariot that was imported from Egypt cost six hundred *shekels* of silver, and a horse one hundred and fifty; [a]and thus, through their agents,[1] they exported *them* to all the kings of the Hittites and the kings of Syria.

Solomon's Heart Turns from the LORD

11 But [a]King Solomon loved [b]many foreign women, as well as the daughter of Pharaoh: women of the Moabites, Ammonites, Edomites, Sidonians, *and* Hittites— 2 from the nations of whom the LORD had said to the children of Israel, [a]"You shall not intermarry with them, nor they with you. Surely they will turn away your hearts after their gods." Solomon clung to these in love. 3 And he had seven hundred wives, princesses, and three hundred concubines; and his wives turned away his heart. 4 For it was so, when Solomon was old, [a]that his wives turned his heart after other gods; and his [b]heart was not loyal to the LORD his God, [c]as *was* the heart of his father David. 5 For Solomon went after [a]Ashtoreth the goddess of the Sidonians, and after [b]Milcom the abomination of the [c]Ammonites. 6 Solomon did evil in the sight of the LORD, and did not fully follow the LORD, as *did* his father David. 7 [a]Then Solomon built a high place for [b]Chemosh the abomination of Moab, on [c]the hill that *is* east of Jerusalem, and for Molech the abomination of the people of Ammon. 8 And he did likewise for all his foreign wives, who burned incense and sacrificed to their gods.

PEACE NOTE

As Jesus' hands and feet on earth, we have the privilege to help people who are dealing with sin. We guide them to repent and experience God's peace.

9 So the LORD became angry with Solomon, because his heart had turned from the LORD God of Israel, [a]who had appeared to him twice, 10 and [a]had commanded him concerning this thing, that he should not go after other gods; but he did not keep what the LORD had commanded. 11 Therefore the LORD said to Solomon, "Because you have done this, and have not kept My covenant and My statutes, which I have commanded you, [a]I will surely tear the kingdom away from you and give it to your [b]servant. 12 Nevertheless I will not do it in your days, for the sake of your father David; I will tear it out of the hand of your son. 13 [a]However I will not tear away the whole kingdom; I will give [b]one tribe to your son [c]for the sake of My servant David, and for the sake of Jerusalem [d]which I have chosen."

Adversaries of Solomon

14 Now the LORD [a]raised up an adversary against Solomon, Hadad the Edomite; he *was* a descendant of the king in Edom. 15 [a]For it happened, when David was in Edom, and Joab the commander of the army had gone up to bury the slain, [b]after he had killed every male in Edom 16 (because for six months Joab remained there with all Israel, until he had cut down every male in Edom), 17 that Hadad fled to go to Egypt, he and certain Edomites of his father's servants with him. Hadad *was* still a little child. 18 Then they arose from Midian and came to Paran; and they took men with them from Paran and came to Egypt, to Pharaoh king of Egypt, who gave him a house,

10:22 [2] Or *peacocks* **10:23** [a] 1 Kin. 3:12, 13; 4:30 **10:26** [a] 1 Kin. 4:26 [b] 1 Kin. 9:19 [1] Following Septuagint, Syriac, Targum, and Vulgate (compare 2 Chronicles 9:25); Masoretic Text reads *led.* **10:27** [a] 2 Chr. 1:15–17 **10:28** [a] [Deut. 17:16] **10:29** [a] 2 Kin. 7:6, 7 [1] Literally *by their hands* **11:1** [a] [Neh. 13:26] [b] [Deut. 17:17] **11:2** [a] [Deut. 7:3, 4] **11:4** [a] [Deut. 17:17] [b] 1 Kin. 8:61 [c] 1 Kin. 9:4 **11:5** [a] Judg. 2:13 [b] [Lev. 20:2–5] [c] 2 Kin. 23:13 **11:7** [a] Num. 33:52 [b] Judg. 11:24 [c] 2 Kin. 23:13 **11:9** [a] 1 Kin. 3:5; 9:2 **11:10** [a] 1 Kin. 6:12; 9:6, 7 **11:11** [a] 1 Kin. 11:31; 12:15, 16 [b] 1 Kin. 11:31, 37 **11:13** [a] 2 Sam. 7:15 [b] 1 Kin. 12:20 [c] 2 Sam. 7:15, 16 [d] Deut. 12:11 **11:14** [a] 1 Chr. 5:26 **11:15** [a] 2 Sam. 8:14 [b] Num. 24:18, 19

apportioned food for him, and gave him land.
19 And Hadad found great favor in the sight of
Pharaoh, so that he gave him as wife the sister
of his own wife, that is, the sister of Queen Tahpenes. 20 Then the sister of Tahpenes bore him
Genubath his son, whom Tahpenes weaned in
Pharaoh's house. And Genubath was in Pharaoh's household among the sons of Pharaoh.
21 [a]So when Hadad heard in Egypt that
David rested with his fathers, and that Joab
the commander of the army was dead, Hadad
said to Pharaoh, "Let me depart, that I may
go to my own country."
22 Then Pharaoh said to him, "But what
have you lacked with me, that suddenly you
seek to go to your own country?"
So he answered, "Nothing, but do let me
go anyway."
23 And God raised up *another* adversary
against him, Rezon the son of Eliadah, who
had fled from his lord, [a]Hadadezer king of
Zobah. 24 So he gathered men to him and
became captain over a band *of raiders,* [a]when
David killed those *of Zobah.* And they went to
Damascus and dwelt there, and reigned in
Damascus. 25 He was an adversary of Israel
all the days of Solomon (besides the trouble
that Hadad *caused*); and he abhorred Israel,
and reigned over Syria.

Jeroboam's Rebellion

26 Then Solomon's servant, [a]Jeroboam the
son of Nebat, an Ephraimite from Zereda,
whose mother's name *was* Zeruah, a widow,
[b]also [c]rebelled against the king.
27 And this *is* what caused him to rebel
against the king: [a]Solomon had built the
Millo *and* repaired the damages to the City
of David his father. 28 The man Jeroboam *was*
a mighty man of valor; and Solomon, seeing
that the young man was [a]industrious, made
him the officer over all the labor force of the
house of Joseph.
29 Now it happened at that time, when Jeroboam went out of Jerusalem, that the prophet
[a]Ahijah the Shilonite met him on the way; and
he had clothed himself with a new garment,
and the two *were* alone in the field. 30 Then
Ahijah took hold of the new garment that *was*
on him, and [a]tore it *into* twelve pieces. 31 And
he said to Jeroboam, "Take for yourself ten
pieces, for [a]thus says the LORD, the God of
Israel: 'Behold, I will tear the kingdom out of
the hand of Solomon and will give ten tribes
to you 32 *(but he shall* have one tribe for the
sake of My servant David, and for the sake of
Jerusalem, the city which I have chosen out of
all the tribes of Israel), 33 [a]because they have[1]
forsaken Me, and worshiped Ashtoreth the
goddess of the Sidonians, Chemosh the god
of the Moabites, and Milcom the god of the
people of Ammon, and have not walked in My
ways to do *what is* right in My eyes and *keep* My
statutes and My judgments, as *did* his father
David. 34 However I will not take the whole
kingdom out of his hand, because I have made
him ruler all the days of his life for the sake
of My servant David, whom I chose because
he kept My commandments and My statutes.
35 But [a]I will take the kingdom out of his son's
hand and give it to you—ten tribes. 36 And to his
son I will give one tribe, that [a]My servant David
may always have a lamp before Me in Jerusalem, the city which I have chosen for Myself,
to put My name there. 37 So I will take you, and
you shall reign over all your heart desires, and
you shall be king over Israel. 38 Then it shall
be, if you heed all that I command you, walk
in My ways, and do *what is* right in My sight,
to keep My statutes and My commandments,
as My servant David did, then [a]I will be with
you and [b]build for you an enduring house, as
I built for David, and will give Israel to you.
39 And I will afflict the descendants of David
because of this, but not forever.' "
40 Solomon therefore sought to kill Jeroboam. But Jeroboam arose and fled to Egypt,
to [a]Shishak king of Egypt, and was in Egypt
until the death of Solomon.

Death of Solomon

41 Now [a]the rest of the acts of Solomon,
all that he did, and his wisdom, *are* they not
written in the book of the acts of Solomon?
42 [a]And the period that Solomon reigned in
Jerusalem over all Israel *was* forty years.
43 [a]Then Solomon rested with his fathers, and
was buried in the City of David his father.
And Rehoboam his son reigned in his [b]place.

The Revolt Against Rehoboam

12 And [a]Rehoboam went to [b]Shechem,
for all Israel had gone to Shechem to
make him king. 2 So it happened, when [a]Jer-
oboam the son of Nebat heard *it* (he was still
in [b]Egypt, for he had fled from the presence
of King Solomon and had been dwelling in
Egypt), 3 that they sent and called him. Then
Jeroboam and the whole assembly of Israel came and spoke to Rehoboam, saying,

11:21 [a] 1 Kin. 2:10, 34 **11:23** [a] 2 Sam. 8:3; 10:16 **11:24** [a] 2 Sam. 8:3; 10:8, 18 **11:26** [a] 1 Kin. 12:2 [b] 2 Chr. 13:6 [c] 2 Sam. 20:21 **11:27** [a] 1 Kin. 9:15, 24 **11:28** [a] [Prov. 22:29] **11:29** [a] 2 Chr. 9:29 **11:30** [a] 1 Sam. 15:27, 28; 24:5 **11:31** [a] 1 Kin. 11:11, 13 **11:33** [a] 1 Kin. 11:5–8 [1] Following Masoretic Text and Targum; Septuagint, Syriac, and Vulgate read *he has.*
11:35 [a] 1 Kin. 12:16, 17 **11:36** [a] [1 Kin. 15:4] **11:38** [a] Josh. 1:5 [b] 2 Sam. 7:11, 27 **11:40** [a] 2 Chr. 12:2–9 **11:41** [a] 2 Chr. 9:29
11:42 [a] 2 Chr. 9:30 **11:43** [a] 2 Chr. 9:31 [b] 2 Chr. 10:1 **12:1** [a] 2 Chr. 10:1 [b] Judg. 9:6 **12:2** [a] 1 Kin. 11:26 [b] 1 Kin. 11:40

4 "Your father made our [a]yoke heavy; now
therefore, lighten the burdensome service
of your father, and his heavy yoke which he
put on us, and we will serve you."

5 So he said to them, "Depart *for* three days,
then come back to me." And the people departed.

6 Then King Rehoboam consulted the elders who stood before his father Solomon
while he still lived, and he said, "How do you
advise *me* to answer these people?"

7 And they spoke to him, saying, [a]"If you
will be a servant to these people today, and
serve them, and answer them, and speak
good words to them, then they will be your
servants forever."

8 But he rejected the advice which the elders
had given him, and consulted the young men
who had grown up with him, who stood before
him. 9 And he said to them, "What advice do
you give? How should we answer this people
who have spoken to me, saying, 'Lighten the
yoke which your father put on us'?"

10 Then the young men who had grown up
with him spoke to him, saying, "Thus you
should speak to this people who have spoken to
you, saying, 'Your father made our yoke heavy,
but you make *it* lighter on us'—thus you shall
say to them: 'My little *finger* shall be thicker than
my father's waist! 11 And now, whereas my father
put a heavy yoke on you, I will add to your yoke;
my father chastised you with whips, but I will
chastise you with scourges!' "[1]

12 So Jeroboam and all the people came to
Rehoboam the third day, as the king had directed, saying, "Come back to me the third day."
13 Then the king answered the people roughly,
and rejected the advice which the elders had
given him; 14 and he spoke to them according
to the advice of the young men, saying, "My
father made your yoke heavy, but I will add to
your yoke; my father chastised you with whips,
but I will chastise you with scourges!"[1] 15 So the
king did not listen to the people; for [a]the turn *of
events* was from the LORD, that He might fulfill
His word, which the LORD had [b]spoken by Ahijah the Shilonite to Jeroboam the son of Nebat.

16 Now when all Israel saw that the king
did not listen to them, the people answered
the king, saying:

[a]"What share have we in David?
We have no inheritance in the son of
Jesse.
To your tents, O Israel!
Now, see to your own house, O David!"

So Israel departed to their tents. 17 But Rehoboam reigned over [a]the children of Israel
who dwelt in the cities of Judah.

18 Then King Rehoboam [a]sent Adoram, who
was in charge of the revenue; but all Israel
stoned him with stones, and he died. Therefore King Rehoboam mounted his chariot
in haste to flee to Jerusalem. 19 So [a]Israel
has been in rebellion against the house of
David to this day.

20 Now it came to pass when all Israel heard
that Jeroboam had come back, they sent for
him and called him to the congregation, and
made him king over all [a]Israel. There was
none who followed the house of David, but
the tribe of Judah [b]only.

21 And when [a]Rehoboam came to Jerusalem,
he assembled all the house of Judah with the
tribe of [b]Benjamin, one hundred and eighty
thousand chosen *men* who were warriors,
to fight against the house of Israel, that he
might restore the kingdom to Rehoboam
the son of Solomon. 22 But [a]the word of God
came to Shemaiah the man of God, saying,
23 "Speak to Rehoboam the son of Solomon,
king of Judah, to all the house of Judah and
Benjamin, and to the rest of the people, saying,
24 'Thus says the LORD: "You shall not go up
nor fight against your brethren the children
of Israel. Let every man return to his house,
[a]for this thing is from Me." ' " Therefore they
obeyed the word of the LORD, and turned back,
according to the word of the LORD.

Jeroboam's Gold Calves

25 Then Jeroboam [a]built Shechem in the
mountains of Ephraim, and dwelt there. Also
he went out from there and built [b]Penuel.
26 And Jeroboam said in his heart, "Now the
kingdom may return to the house of David:
27 If these people [a]go up to offer sacrifices
in the house of the LORD at Jerusalem, then
the heart of this people will turn back to
their lord, Rehoboam king of Judah, and
they will kill me and go back to Rehoboam
king of Judah."

28 Therefore the king asked advice, [a]made
two calves of gold, and said to the people, "It
is too much for you to go up to Jerusalem.
[b]Here are your gods, O Israel, which brought
you up from the land of Egypt!" 29 And he
set up one in [a]Bethel, and the other he put
in [b]Dan. 30 Now this thing became [a]a sin, for
the people went *to worship* before the one as
far as Dan. 31 He made shrines[1] on the high

12:4 [a] 1 Sam. 8:11–18 **12:7** [a] 2 Chr. 10:7 **12:11** [1] Literally *scorpions* **12:14** [1] Literally *scorpions* **12:15** [a] Judg. 14:4 [b] 1 Kin. 11:11, 29, 31 **12:16** [a] 2 Sam. 20:1 **12:17** [a] 1 Kin. 11:13, 36 **12:18** [a] 1 Kin. 4:6; 5:14 **12:19** [a] 2 Kin. 17:21 **12:20** [a] 2 Kin. 17:21 [b] 1 Kin. 11:13, 32, 36 **12:21** [a] 2 Chr. 11:1–4 [b] 2 Sam. 19:17 **12:22** [a] 2 Chr. 11:2; 12:5–7 **12:24** [a] 1 Kin. 12:15 **12:25** [a] Judg. 9:45–49 [b] Judg. 8:8, 17 **12:27** [a] [Deut. 12:5–7, 14] **12:28** [a] 2 Kin. 10:29; 17:16 [b] Ex. 32:4, 8 **12:29** [a] Gen. 28:19 [b] Judg. 18:26–31 **12:30** [a] 1 Kin. 13:34 **12:31** [1] Literally *a house*

places, [a]and made priests from every class
of people, who were not of the sons of Levi.
32 Jeroboam ordained a feast on the fifteenth day of the eighth month, like [a]the feast
that *was* in Judah, and offered sacrifices on
the altar. So he did at Bethel, sacrificing to
the calves that he had made. [b]And at Bethel
he installed the priests of the high places
which he had made. 33 So he made offerings
on the altar which he had made at Bethel
on the fifteenth day of the eighth month,
in the month which he had [a]devised in his
own heart. And he ordained a feast for the
children of Israel, and offered sacrifices on
the altar and [b]burned incense.

The Message of the Man of God

13 And behold, [a]a man of God went from
Judah to Bethel by the word of the
LORD, [b]and Jeroboam stood by the altar to
burn incense. 2 Then he cried out against the
altar by the word of the LORD, and said, "O altar, altar! Thus says the LORD: 'Behold, a child,
[a]Josiah by name, shall be born to the house
of David; and on you he shall sacrifice the
priests of the high places who burn incense
on you, and men's bones shall be [b]burned
on you.' " 3 And he gave [a]a sign the same day,
saying, "This *is* the sign which the LORD has
spoken: Surely the altar shall split apart, and
the ashes on it shall be poured out."
4 So it came to pass when King Jeroboam
heard the saying of the man of God, who
cried out against the altar in Bethel, that he
stretched out his hand from the altar, saying, "Arrest him!" Then his hand, which he
stretched out toward him, withered, so that
he could not pull it back to himself. 5 The altar
also was split apart, and the ashes poured out
from the altar, according to the sign which
the man of God had given by the word of the
LORD. 6 Then the king answered and said to
the man of God, "Please [a]entreat the favor
of the LORD your God, and pray for me, that
my hand may be restored to me."
So the man of God entreated the LORD,
and the king's hand was restored to him, and
became as before. 7 Then the king said to the
man of God, "Come home with me and refresh yourself, and [a]I will give you a reward."
8 But the man of God said to the king, [a]"If
you were to give me half your house, I would
not go in with you; nor would I eat bread nor
drink water in this place. 9 For so it was com-
manded me by the word of the LORD, saying,
[a]'You shall not eat bread, nor drink water, nor
return by the same way you came.' " 10 So he
went another way and did not return by the
way he came to Bethel.

Death of the Man of God

11 Now an [a]old prophet dwelt in Bethel, and
his sons came and told him all the works
that the man of God had done that day in
Bethel; they also told their father the words
which he had spoken to the king. 12 And their
father said to them, "Which way did he go?"
For his sons had seen[1] which way the man of
God went who came from Judah. 13 Then he
said to his sons, "Saddle the donkey for me."
So they saddled the donkey for him; and he
rode on it, 14 and went after the man of God,
and found him sitting under an oak. Then
he said to him, "*Are* you the man of God who
came from Judah?"
And he said, "I *am.*"
15 Then he said to him, "Come home with
me and eat bread."
16 And he said, [a]"I cannot return with you
nor go in with you; neither can I eat bread
nor drink water with you in this place. 17 For I
have been told [a]by the word of the LORD, 'You
shall not eat bread nor drink water there, nor
return by going the way you came.' "
18 He said to him, "I too *am* a prophet as you
are, and an angel spoke to me by the word of
the LORD, saying, 'Bring him back with you to
your house, that he may eat bread and drink
water.' " (He was lying to him.)
19 So he went back with him, and ate bread
in his house, and drank water.
20 Now it happened, as they sat at the table,
that the word of the LORD came to the prophet
who had brought him back; 21 and he cried
out to the man of God who came from Judah,
saying, "Thus says the LORD: 'Because you
have disobeyed the word of the LORD, and
have not kept the commandment which the
LORD your God commanded you, 22 but you
came back, ate bread, and drank water in the
[a]place of which *the LORD* said to you, "Eat no
bread and drink no water," your corpse shall
not come to the tomb of your fathers.' "
23 So it was, after he had eaten bread and after he had drunk, that he saddled the donkey
for him, the prophet whom he had brought
back. 24 When he was gone, [a]a lion met him on
the road and killed him. And his corpse was
thrown on the road, and the donkey stood by
it. The lion also stood by the corpse. 25 And
there, men passed by and saw the corpse
thrown on the road, and the lion standing

12:31 [a] 2 Kin. 17:32 **12:32** [a] Lev. 23:33, 34 [b] Amos 7:10–13 **12:33** [a] Num. 15:39 [b] 1 Kin. 13:1 **13:1** [a] 2 Kin. 23:17 [b] 1 Kin. 12:32, 33 **13:2** [a] 2 Kin. 23:15, 16 [b] [Lev. 26:30] **13:3** [a] Is. 7:14; 38:7 **13:6** [a] [James 5:16] **13:7** [a] 1 Sam. 9:7 **13:8** [a] Num. 22:18; 24:13 **13:9** [a] [1 Cor. 5:11] **13:11** [a] 1 Kin. 13:25 **13:12** [1] Septuagint, Syriac, Targum, and Vulgate read *showed him.* **13:16** [a] 1 Kin. 13:8, 9 **13:17** [a] 1 Kin. 20:35 **13:22** [a] 1 Kin. 13:9 **13:24** [a] 1 Kin. 20:36

by the corpse. Then they went and told *it* in the city where the old prophet dwelt.

26 Now when the prophet who had brought him back from the way heard *it,* he said, "It *is* the man of God who was disobedient to the word of the LORD. Therefore the LORD has delivered him to the lion, which has torn him and killed him, according to the word of the LORD which He spoke to him." 27 And he spoke to his sons, saying, "Saddle the donkey for me." So they saddled *it.* 28 Then he went and found his corpse thrown on the road, and the donkey and the lion standing by the corpse. The lion had not eaten the corpse nor torn the donkey. 29 And the prophet took up the corpse of the man of God, laid it on the donkey, and brought it back. So the old prophet came to the city to mourn, and to bury him. 30 Then he laid the corpse in his own tomb; and they mourned over him, *saying,* [a]"Alas, my brother!" 31 So it was, after he had buried him, that he spoke to his sons, saying, "When I am dead, then bury me in the tomb where the man of God *is* buried; [a]lay my bones beside his bones. 32 [a]For the saying which he cried out by the word of the LORD against the altar in Bethel, and against all the shrines[1] on the high places which *are* in the cities of [b]Samaria, will surely come to pass."

33 [a]After this event Jeroboam did not turn from his evil way, but again he made priests from every class of people for the high places; whoever wished, he consecrated him, and he became *one* of the priests of the high places. 34 [a]And this thing was the sin of the house of Jeroboam, so as [b]to exterminate and destroy *it* from the face of the earth.

Judgment on the House of Jeroboam

14 At that time Abijah the son of Jeroboam became sick. 2 And Jeroboam said to his wife, "Please arise, and disguise yourself, that they may not recognize you as the wife of Jeroboam, and go to Shiloh. Indeed, Ahijah the prophet *is* there, who told me that [a]*I would be* king over this people. 3 [a]Also take with you ten loaves, *some* cakes, and a jar of honey, and go to him; he will tell you what will become of the child." 4 And Jeroboam's wife did so; she arose [a]and went to Shiloh, and came to the house of Ahijah. But Ahijah could not see, for his eyes were glazed by reason of his age.

5 Now the LORD had said to Ahijah, "Here is the wife of Jeroboam, coming to ask you something about her son, for he *is* sick. Thus and thus you shall say to her; for it will be, when she comes in, that she will pretend *to be* another *woman.*"

> PEACE NOTE
>
> The Lord's message regarding Jeroboam's wife allowed Ahijah the prophet to see with spiritual eyes. Living in the peace of God gives us discernment.
>
> 1 KINGS 14:5

6 And so it was, when Ahijah heard the sound of her footsteps as she came through the door, he said, "Come in, wife of Jeroboam. Why do you pretend *to be* another *person?* For I *have been* sent to you *with* bad *news.* 7 Go, tell Jeroboam, 'Thus says the LORD God of Israel: [a]"Because I exalted you from among the people, and made you ruler over My people Israel, 8 and [a]tore the kingdom away from the house of David, and gave it to you; and *yet* you have not been as My servant David, [b]who kept My commandments and who followed Me with all his heart, to do only *what was* right in My eyes; 9 but you have done more evil than all who were before you, [a]for you have gone and made for yourself other gods and molded images to provoke Me to anger, and [b]have cast Me behind your back— 10 therefore behold! [a]I will bring disaster on the house of Jeroboam, and [b]will cut off from Jeroboam every male in Israel, [c]bond and free; I will take away the remnant of the house of Jeroboam, as one takes away refuse until it is all gone. 11 The dogs shall eat [a]whoever belongs to Jeroboam and dies in the city, and the birds of the air shall eat whoever dies in the field; for the LORD has spoken!"' 12 Arise therefore, go to your own house. [a]When your feet enter the city, the child shall die. 13 And all Israel shall mourn for him and bury him, for he is the only one of Jeroboam who shall come to the grave, because in him [a]there is found something good toward the LORD God of Israel in the house of Jeroboam.

13:30 [a] Jer. 22:18 **13:31** [a] 2 Kin. 23:17, 18 **13:32** [a] 2 Kin. 23:16, 19 [b] 1 Kin. 16:24 [1] Literally *houses* **13:33** [a] 1 Kin. 12:31, 32 **13:34** [a] 1 Kin. 12:30 [b] [1 Kin. 14:10; 15:29, 30] **14:2** [a] 1 Kin. 11:29–31 **14:3** [a] 1 Sam. 9:7, 8 **14:4** [a] 1 Kin. 11:29 **14:7** [a] 1 Kin. 16:2 **14:8** [a] 1 Kin. 11:31 [b] 1 Kin. 11:33, 38; 15:5 **14:9** [a] 1 Kin. 12:28 [b] Ps. 50:17 **14:10** [a] 1 Kin. 15:29 [b] 1 Kin. 21:21 [c] Deut. 32:36 **14:11** [a] 1 Kin. 16:4; 21:24 **14:12** [a] 1 Kin. 14:17 **14:13** [a] 2 Chr. 12:12; 19:3

14[a]"Moreover the LORD will raise up for Himself a king over Israel who shall cut off the house of Jeroboam; this is the day. What? Even now! 15 For the LORD will strike Israel, as a reed is shaken in the water. He will [a]uproot Israel from this [b]good land which He gave to their fathers, and will scatter them [c]beyond the River,[1] [d]because they have made their wooden images,[2] provoking the LORD to anger. 16 And He will give Israel up because of the sins of Jeroboam, [a]who sinned and who made Israel sin."

17 Then Jeroboam's wife arose and departed, and came to [a]Tirzah. [b]When she came to the threshold of the house, the child died. 18 And they buried him; and all Israel mourned for him, [a]according to the word of the LORD which He spoke through His servant Ahijah the prophet.

Death of Jeroboam

19 Now the rest of the acts of Jeroboam, how he [a]made war and how he reigned, indeed they *are* written in the book of the chronicles of the kings of Israel. 20 The period that Jeroboam reigned *was* twenty-two years. So he rested with his fathers. Then [a]Nadab his son reigned in his place.

Rehoboam Reigns in Judah

21 And Rehoboam the son of Solomon reigned in Judah. [a]Rehoboam *was* forty-one years old when he became king. He reigned seventeen years in Jerusalem, the city [b]which the LORD had chosen out of all the tribes of Israel, to put His name there. [c]His mother's name *was* Naamah, an Ammonitess. 22[a]Now Judah did evil in the sight of the LORD, and they [b]provoked Him to jealousy with their sins which they committed, more than all that their fathers had done. 23 For they also built for themselves [a]high places, [b]*sacred* pillars, and [c]wooden images on every high hill and [d]under every green tree. 24[a]And there were also perverted persons[1] in the land. They did according to all the [b]abominations of the nations which the LORD had cast out before the children of [c]Israel.

25[a]It happened in the fifth year of King Rehoboam *that* Shishak king of Egypt came up against Jerusalem. 26[a]And he took away the treasures of the house of the LORD and the treasures of the king's house; he took away everything. He also took away all the gold shields [b]which Solomon had made. 27 Then King Rehoboam made bronze shields in their place, and committed *them* to the hands of the captains of the guard, who guarded the doorway of the king's house. 28 And whenever the king entered the house of the LORD, the guards carried them, then brought them back into the guardroom.

29[a]Now the rest of the acts of Rehoboam, and all that he did, *are* they not written in the book of the chronicles of the kings of Judah? 30 And there was [a]war between Rehoboam and Jeroboam all *their* days. 31[a]So Rehoboam rested with his fathers, and was buried with his fathers in the City of David. [b]His mother's name *was* Naamah, an Ammonitess. Then [c]Abijam[1] his son reigned in his place.

Abijam Reigns in Judah

15 [a]In the eighteenth year of King Jeroboam the son of Nebat, Abijam became king over Judah. 2 He reigned three years in Jerusalem. [a]His mother's name *was* [b]Maachah the granddaughter of [c]Abishalom. 3 And he walked in all the sins of his father, which he had done before him; [a]his heart was not loyal to the LORD his God, as was the heart of his father David. 4 Nevertheless [a]for David's sake the LORD his God gave him a lamp in Jerusalem, by setting up his son after him and by establishing Jerusalem; 5 because David [a]did *what was* right in the eyes of the LORD, and had not turned aside from anything that He commanded him all the days of his life, [b]except in the matter of Uriah the Hittite. 6[a]And there was war between Rehoboam[1] and Jeroboam all the days of his life. 7[a]Now the rest of the acts of Abijam, and all that he did, *are* they not written in the book of the chronicles of the kings of Judah? And there was war between Abijam and Jeroboam.

8[a]So Abijam rested with his fathers, and they buried him in the City of David. Then Asa his son reigned in his place.

Asa Reigns in Judah

9 In the twentieth year of Jeroboam king of Israel, Asa became king over Judah. 10 And he reigned forty-one years in Jerusalem. His grandmother's name *was* Maachah the

14:14 [a] 1 Kin. 15:27–29 **14:15** [a] 2 Kin. 17:6 [b] [Josh. 23:15, 16] [c] 2 Kin. 15:29 [d] [Ex. 34:13, 14] [1] That is, the Euphrates [2] Hebrew *Asherim*, Canaanite deities **14:16** [a] 1 Kin. 12:30; 13:34; 15:30, 34; 16:2 **14:17** [a] Song 6:4 [b] 1 Kin. 14:12 **14:18** [a] 1 Kin. 14:13 **14:19** [a] 2 Chr. 13:2–20 **14:20** [a] 1 Kin. 15:25 **14:21** [a] 2 Chr. 12:13 [b] 1 Kin. 11:32, 36 [c] 1 Kin. 14:31 ***14:22*** *[a] 2 Chr. 12:1, 14* *[b] Deut. 32:21* **14:23** [a] Deut. 12:2 [b] [Deut. 16:22] [c] [2 Kin. 17:9, 10] [d] Is. 57:5 **14:24** [a] Deut. 23:17 [b] Deut. 20:18 [c] [Deut. 9:4, 5] [1] Hebrew *qadesh*, that is, one practicing sodomy and prostitution in religious rituals **14:25** [a] 1 Kin. 11:40 **14:26** [a] 2 Chr. 12:9–11 [b] 1 Kin. 10:17 **14:29** [a] 2 Chr. 12:15, 16 **14:30** [a] 1 Kin. 12:21–24; 15:6 **14:31** [a] 2 Chr. 12:16 [b] 1 Kin. 14:21 [c] 2 Chr. 12:16 [1] Spelled *Abijah* in 2 Chronicles 12:16ff **15:1** [a] 2 Chr. 13:1 **15:2** [a] 2 Chr. 11:20–22 [b] 2 Chr. 13:2 [c] 2 Chr. 11:21 **15:3** [a] Ps. 119:80 **15:4** [a] 2 Sam. 21:17 **15:5** [a] 1 Kin. 9:4; 14:8 [b] 2 Sam. 11:3, 15–17; 12:9, 10 **15:6** [a] 1 Kin. 14:30 [1] Following Masoretic Text, Septuagint, Targum, and Vulgate; some Hebrew manuscripts and Syriac read *Abijam.* **15:7** [a] 2 Chr. 13:2–22 **15:8** [a] 2 Chr. 14:1

granddaughter of Abishalom. 11 [a]Asa did *what*
was right in the eyes of the LORD, as *did* his
father David. 12 [a]And he banished the perverted persons[1] from the land, and removed all
the idols that his fathers had made. 13 Also he
removed [a]Maachah his grandmother from
being queen mother, because she had made
an obscene image of Asherah.[1] And Asa cut
down her obscene image and [b]burned *it*
by the Brook Kidron. 14 [a]But the high places were not removed. Nevertheless Asa's
[b]heart was loyal to the LORD all his days. 15 He
also brought into the house of the LORD the
things which his father [a]had dedicated, and
the things which he himself had dedicated:
silver and gold and utensils.

16 Now there was war between Asa and Baasha king of Israel all their days. 17 And [a]Ba-
asha king of Israel came up against Judah,
and built [b]Ramah, [c]that he might let none go
out or come in to Asa king of Judah. 18 Then
Asa took all the silver and gold *that was* left
in the treasuries of the house of the LORD
and the treasuries of the king's house, and
delivered them into the hand of his servants.
And King Asa sent them to [a]Ben-Hadad the
son of Tabrimmon, the son of Hezion, king of
Syria, who dwelt in [b]Damascus, saying, 19 "*Let*
there be a treaty between you and me, as there
was between my father and your father. See,
I have sent you a present of silver and gold.
Come and break your treaty with Baasha king
of Israel, so that he will withdraw from me."

20 So Ben-Hadad heeded King Asa, and
[a]sent the captains of his armies against the
cities of Israel. He attacked [b]Ijon, [c]Dan, [d]Abel
Beth Maachah, and all Chinneroth, with all
the land of Naphtali. 21 Now it happened,
when Baasha heard *it*, that he stopped building Ramah, and remained in [a]Tirzah.

22 [a]Then King Asa made a proclamation
throughout all Judah; none *was* exempted.
And they took away the stones and timber of
Ramah, which Baasha had used for building;
and with them King Asa built [b]Geba of Benjamin, and [c]Mizpah.

23 The rest of all the acts of Asa, all his
might, all that he did, and the cities which
he built, *are* they not written in the book of
the chronicles of the kings of Judah? But
[a]in the time of his old age he was diseased
in his feet. 24 So Asa rested with his fathers,
and was buried with his fathers in the City
of David his father. [a]Then [b]Jehoshaphat his
son reigned in his place.

Nadab Reigns in Israel

25 Now [a]Nadab the son of Jeroboam became king over Israel in the second year of
Asa king of Judah, and he reigned over Israel
two years. 26 And he did evil in the sight of the
LORD, and walked in the way of his father, and
in [a]his sin by which he had made Israel sin.

27 [a]Then Baasha the son of Ahijah, of the
house of Issachar, conspired against him. And
Baasha killed him at [b]Gibbethon, which *be-*
longed to the Philistines, while Nadab and all
Israel laid siege to Gibbethon. 28 Baasha killed
him in the third year of Asa king of Judah, and
reigned in his place. 29 And it was so, when he
became king, *that* he killed all the house of Jeroboam. He did not leave to Jeroboam anyone
that breathed, until he had destroyed him,
according to [a]the word of the LORD which He
had spoken by His servant Ahijah the Shilonite,
30 [a]because of the sins of Jeroboam, which he
had sinned and by which he had made Israel
sin, because of his provocation with which he
had provoked the LORD God of Israel to anger.

31 Now the rest of the acts of Nadab, and all
that he did, *are* they not written in the book of
the chronicles of the kings of Israel? 32 [a]And
there was war between Asa and Baasha king
of Israel all their days.

Baasha Reigns in Israel

33 In the third year of Asa king of Judah,
Baasha the son of Ahijah became king over
all Israel in Tirzah, and *reigned* twenty-four
years. 34 He did evil in the sight of the LORD,
and walked in [a]the way of Jeroboam, and
in his sin by which he had made Israel sin.

16 Then the word of the LORD came to
[a]Jehu the son of [b]Hanani, against [c]Ba-
asha, saying: 2 [a]"Inasmuch as I lifted you
out of the dust and made you ruler over My
people Israel, and [b]you have walked in the
way of Jeroboam, and have made My people
Israel sin, to provoke Me to anger with their
sins, 3 surely I will [a]take away the posterity of
Baasha and the posterity of his house, and I
will make your house like [b]the house of Jeroboam the son of Nebat. 4 The dogs shall eat
[a]whoever belongs to Baasha and dies in the

15:11 [a] 2 Chr. 14:2 **15:12** [a] 1 Kin. 14:24; 22:46 [1] Hebrew *qedeshim,* that is, those practicing sodomy and prostitution in religious rituals **15:13** [a] 2 Chr. 15:16–18 [b] Ex. 32:20 [1] A Canaanite goddess **15:14** [a] 1 Kin. 3:2; 22:43 [b] 1 Kin. 8:61; 15:3 **15:15** [a] 1 Kin. 7:51 **15:17** [a] 2 Chr. 16:1–6 [b] Josh. 18:25 [c] 1 Kin. 12:26–29 **15:18** [a] 2 Chr. 16:2 [b] 1 Kin. 11:23, 24 **15:20** [a] 1 Kin. 20:1 [b] 2 Kin. 15:29 [c] Judg. 18:29 [d] 2 Sam. 20:14, 15 **15:21** [a] 1 Kin. 14:17; 16:15–18 **15:22** [a] 2 Chr. 16:6 [b] Josh. 21:17 [c] Josh. 18:26 **15:23** [a] 2 Chr. 16:11–14 **15:24** [a] 2 Chr. 17:1 [b] Matt. 1:8 **15:25** [a] 1 Kin. 14:20 **15:26** [a] 1 Kin. 12:28–33; 14:16 **15:27** [a] 1 Kin. 14:14 [b] Josh. 19:44; 21:23 **15:29** [a] 1 Kin. 14:10–14 **15:30** [a] 1 Kin. 14:9, 16 **15:32** [a] 1 Kin. 15:16 **15:34** [a] 1 Kin. 13:33; 14:16 **16:1** [a] 2 Chr. 19:2; 20:34 [b] 2 Chr. 16:7–10 [c] 1 Kin. 15:27 **16:2** [a] 1 Kin. 14:7 [b] 1 Kin. 12:25–33; 15:34 **16:3** [a] 1 Kin. 16:11; 21:21 [b] 1 Kin. 14:10; 15:29 **16:4** [a] 1 Kin. 14:11; 21:24

city, and the birds of the air shall eat whoever
dies in the fields."

5 Now the rest of the acts of Baasha, what
he did, and his might, [a]*are* they not written
in the book of the chronicles of the kings of
Israel? 6 So Baasha rested with his fathers
and was buried in [a]Tirzah. Then Elah his son
reigned in his place.

7 And also the word of the LORD came by
the prophet [a]Jehu the son of Hanani against
Baasha and his house, because of all the
evil that he did in the sight of the LORD in
provoking Him to anger with the work of his
hands, in being like the house of Jeroboam,
and because [b]he killed them.

Elah Reigns in Israel

8 In the twenty-sixth year of Asa king of
Judah, Elah the son of Baasha became king
over Israel, *and reigned* two years in Tirzah. 9 [a]Now his servant Zimri, commander
of half *his* chariots, conspired against him
as he was in Tirzah drinking himself drunk
in the house of Arza, [b]steward of *his* house in
Tirzah. 10 And Zimri went in and struck him
and killed him in the twenty-seventh year of
Asa king of Judah, and reigned in his place.

11 Then it came to pass, when he began to
reign, as soon as he was seated on his throne,
that he killed all the household of Baasha; he
[a]did not leave him one male, neither of his
relatives nor of his friends. 12 Thus Zimri destroyed all the household of Baasha, [a]accord-
ing to the word of the LORD, which He spoke
against Baasha by Jehu the prophet, 13 for all
the sins of Baasha and the sins of Elah his
son, by which they had sinned and by which
they had made Israel sin, in provoking the
LORD God of Israel to anger [a]with their idols.

14 Now the rest of the acts of Elah, and all
that he did, *are* they not written in the book
of the chronicles of the kings of Israel?

Zimri Reigns in Israel

15 In the twenty-seventh year of Asa king
of Judah, Zimri had reigned in Tirzah seven
days. And the people *were* encamped [a]against
Gibbethon, which *belonged* to the Philistines.
16 Now the people *who were* encamped heard
it said, "Zimri has conspired and also has
killed the king." So all Israel made Omri, the
commander of the army, king over Israel
that day in the camp. 17 Then Omri and all
Israel with him went up from Gibbethon,
and they besieged Tirzah. 18 And it happened,
when Zimri saw that the city was taken, that
he went into the citadel of the king's house
and burned the king's house down upon
himself with fire, and died, 19 because of the
sins which he had committed in doing evil
in the sight of the LORD, [a]in walking in the
[b]way of Jeroboam, and in his sin which he
had committed to make Israel sin.

20 Now the rest of the acts of Zimri, and the
treason he committed, *are* they not written
in the book of the chronicles of the kings
of Israel?

Omri Reigns in Israel

21 Then the people of Israel were divided
into two parts: half of the people followed
Tibni the son of Ginath, to make him king,
and half followed Omri. 22 But the people who
followed Omri prevailed over the people who
followed Tibni the son of Ginath. So Tibni
died and Omri reigned. 23 In the thirty-first
year of Asa king of Judah, Omri became king
over Israel, *and reigned* twelve years. Six years
he reigned in [a]Tirzah. 24 And he bought the
hill of Samaria from Shemer for two talents
of silver; then he built on the hill, and called
the name of the city which he built, [a]Samaria,
after the name of Shemer, owner of the hill.
25 [a]Omri did evil in the eyes of the LORD, and
did worse than all who *were* before him. 26 For
he [a]walked in all the ways of Jeroboam the
son of Nebat, and in his sin by which he had
made Israel sin, provoking the LORD God of
Israel to anger with their [b]idols.

27 Now the rest of the acts of Omri which he
did, and the might that he showed, *are* they
not written in the book of the chronicles of
the kings of Israel?

28 So Omri rested with his fathers and was
buried in Samaria. Then Ahab his son reigned
in his place.

Ahab Reigns in Israel

29 In the thirty-eighth year of Asa king of
Judah, Ahab the son of Omri became king over
Israel; and Ahab the son of Omri reigned over
Israel in Samaria twenty-two years. 30 Now Ahab
the son of Omri did evil in the sight of the LORD,
more than all who *were* before him. 31 And it
came to pass, as though it had been a trivial
thing for him to walk in the sins of Jeroboam
the son of Nebat, [a]that he took as wife Jezebel
the daughter of Ethbaal, king of the [b]Sidonians;
[c]and he went and served Baal and worshiped
him. 32 Then he set up an altar for Baal in [a]the
temple of Baal, which he had built in Samaria.
33 [a]And Ahab made a wooden image.[1] Ahab

16:5 [a] 2 Chr. 16:11 **16:6** [a] 1 Kin. 14:17; 15:21 **16:7** [a] 1 Kin. 16:1 [b] 1 Kin. 15:27, 29 **16:9** [a] 2 Kin. 9:30–33 [b] 1 Kin. 18:3 **16:11** [a] 1 Sam. 25:22 **16:12** [a] 1 Kin. 16:3 **16:13** [a] Deut. 32:21 **16:15** [a] 1 Kin. 15:27 **16:19** [a] 1 Kin. 15:26, 34 [b] 1 Kin. 12:25–33 **16:23** [a] 1 Kin. 15:21 **16:24** [a] 1 Kin. 13:32 **16:25** [a] Mic. 6:16 **16:26** [a] 1 Kin. 16:19 [b] 1 Kin. 16:13 **16:31** [a] Deut. 7:3 [b] Judg. 18:7 [c] 1 Kin. 21:25, 26 **16:32** [a] 2 Kin. 10:21, 26, 27 **16:33** [a] 2 Kin. 13:6 [1] Hebrew *Asherah,* a Canaanite goddess

[b]did more to provoke the LORD God of Israel
to anger than all the kings of Israel who were
before him. 34 In his days Hiel of Bethel built
Jericho. He laid its foundation with Abiram his
firstborn, and with his youngest *son* Segub he
set up its gates, [a]according to the word of the
LORD, which He had spoken through Joshua
the son of Nun.[1]

Elijah Proclaims a Drought

17 And Elijah the Tishbite, of the [a]inhab-
itants of Gilead, said to Ahab, [b]"As the
LORD God of Israel lives, [c]before whom I
stand, [d]there shall not be dew nor rain [e]these
years, except at my word."
2 Then the word of the LORD came to him,
saying, 3 "Get away from here and turn eastward, and hide by the Brook Cherith, which
flows into the Jordan. 4 And it will be *that*
you shall drink from the brook, and I have
commanded the [a]ravens to feed you there."
5 So he went and did according to the word
of the LORD, for he went and stayed by the
Brook Cherith, which flows into the Jordan.
6 The ravens brought him bread and meat
in the morning, and bread and meat in the
evening; and he drank from the brook. 7 And
it happened after a while that the brook dried
up, because there had been no rain in the land.

Elijah and the Widow

8 Then the word of the LORD came to him,
saying, 9 "Arise, go to [a]Zarephath, which *belongs*
to [b]Sidon, and dwell there. See, I have commanded a widow there to provide for you." 10 So
he arose and went to Zarephath. And when he
came to the gate of the city, indeed a widow
was there gathering sticks. And he called to
her and said, "Please bring me a little water in
a cup, that I may drink." 11 And as she was going
to get *it*, he called to her and said, "Please bring
me a morsel of bread in your hand."
12 So she said, "As the LORD your God lives,
I do not have bread, only a handful of flour
in a bin, and a little oil in a jar; and see, I *am*
gathering a couple of sticks that I may go in
and prepare it for myself and my son, that
we may eat it, and [a]die."
13 And Elijah said to her, "Do not fear; go *and*
do as you have said, but make me a small cake
from it first, and bring *it* to me; and afterward
make *some* for yourself and your son. 14 For thus
says the LORD God of Israel: 'The bin of flour
shall not be used up, nor shall the jar of oil run
dry, until the day the LORD sends rain on the
earth.'"
15 So she went away and did according to
the word of Elijah; and she and he and her
household ate for *many* days. 16 The bin of
flour was not used up, nor did the jar of oil
run dry, according to the word of the LORD
which He spoke by Elijah.

Elijah Revives the Widow's Son

17 Now it happened after these things *that*
the son of the woman who owned the house
became sick. And his sickness was so serious
that there was no breath left in him. 18 So
she said to Elijah, [a]"What have I to do with
you, O man of God? Have you come to me to
bring my sin to remembrance, and to kill my
son?"
19 And he said to her, "Give me your son."
So he took him out of her arms and carried
him to the upper room where he was staying,
and laid him on his own bed. 20 Then he cried
out to the LORD and said, "O LORD my God,
have You also brought tragedy on the widow
with whom I lodge, by killing her son?" 21 [a]And
he stretched himself out on the child three
times, and cried out to the LORD and said,
"O LORD my God, I pray, let this child's soul
come back to him." 22 Then the LORD heard
the voice of Elijah; and the soul of the child
came back to him, and he [a]revived.
23 And Elijah took the child and brought
him down from the upper room into the
house, and gave him to his mother. And Elijah said, "See, your son lives!"
24 Then the woman said to Elijah, "Now by
this [a]I know that you *are* a man of God, *and*
that the word of the LORD in your mouth *is*
the truth."

PEACE NOTE

At times I may not *feel* peaceful, but I can trust God to bring me His peace in the midst of adversity. The Lord is faithful to meet us with His peace—and sometimes we even feel it.

1 KINGS 17:24

16:33 [b] 1 Kin. 14:9; 16:29, 30; 21:25 **16:34** [a] Josh. 6:26 [1] Compare Joshua 6:26 **17:1** [a] Judg. 12:4 [b] 2 Kin. 3:14; 5:20 [c] Deut. 10:8 [d] James 5:17 [e] Luke 4:25 **17:4** [a] Job 38:41 **17:9** [a] Obad. 20 [b] 2 Sam. 24:6 **17:12** [a] Deut. 28:23, 24 **17:18** [a] Luke 5:8 **17:21** [a] 2 Kin. 4:34, 35 **17:22** [a] Heb. 11:35 **17:24** [a] John 2:11; 3:2; 16:30

Elijah's Message to Ahab

18 And it came to pass *after* [a]many days that the word of the LORD came to Elijah, in the third year, saying, "Go, present yourself to Ahab, and [b]I will send rain on the earth."

2 So Elijah went to present himself to Ahab; and *there was* a severe famine in Samaria. 3 And Ahab had called Obadiah, who *was* in charge of *his* house. (Now Obadiah feared the LORD greatly. 4 For so it was, while Jezebel massacred the prophets of the LORD, that Obadiah had taken one hundred prophets and hidden them, fifty to a cave, and had fed them with bread and water.) 5 And Ahab had said to Obadiah, "Go into the land to all the springs of water and to all the brooks; perhaps we may find grass to keep the horses and mules alive, so that we will not have to kill any livestock." 6 So they divided the land between them to explore it; Ahab went one way by himself, and Obadiah went another way by himself.

7 Now as Obadiah was on his way, suddenly Elijah met him; and he [a]recognized him, and fell on his face, and said, "*Is* that you, my lord Elijah?"

8 And he answered him, "*It is* I. Go, tell your master, 'Elijah *is here.*' "

9 So he said, "How have I sinned, that you are delivering your servant into the hand of Ahab, to kill me? 10 *As* the LORD your God lives, there is no nation or kingdom where my master has not sent someone to hunt for you; and when they said, '*He is* not *here,*' he took an oath from the kingdom or nation that they could not find you. 11 And now you say, 'Go, tell your master, "Elijah *is here*" '! 12 And it shall come to pass, *as soon as* I am gone from you, that [a]the Spirit of the LORD will carry you to a place I do not know; so when I go and tell Ahab, and he cannot find you, he will kill me. But I your servant have feared the LORD from my youth. 13 Was it not reported to my lord what I did when Jezebel killed the prophets of the LORD, how I hid one hundred men of the LORD's prophets, fifty to a cave, and fed them with bread and water? 14 And now you say, 'Go, tell your master, "Elijah *is here.*" ' He will kill me!"

15 Then Elijah said, "*As* the LORD of hosts lives, before whom I stand, I will surely present myself to him today."

16 So Obadiah went to meet Ahab, and told *him; and Ahab* went to meet Elijah.

17 Then it happened, when Ahab saw Elijah, that Ahab said to him, [a]"*Is that* you, O [b]troubler of Israel?"

18 And he answered, "I have not troubled Israel, but you and your father's house *have,* [a]in that you have forsaken the commandments of the LORD and have followed the Baals. 19 Now therefore, send *and* gather all Israel to me on [a]Mount Carmel, the four hundred and fifty prophets of Baal, [b]and the four hundred prophets of Asherah,[1] who eat at Jezebel's table."

Elijah's Mount Carmel Victory

20 So Ahab sent for all the children of Israel, and [a]gathered the prophets together on Mount Carmel. 21 And Elijah came to all the people, and said, [a]"How long will you falter between two opinions? If the LORD *is* God, follow Him; but if Baal, [b]follow him." But the people answered him not a word. 22 Then Elijah said to the people, [a]"I alone am left a prophet of the LORD; [b]but Baal's prophets *are* four hundred and fifty men. 23 Therefore let them give us two bulls; and let them choose one bull for themselves, cut it in pieces, and lay *it* on the wood, but put no fire *under it;* and I will prepare the other bull, and lay *it* on the wood, but put no fire *under it.* 24 Then you call on the name of your gods, and I will call on the name of the LORD; and the God who [a]answers by fire, He is God."

So all the people answered and said, "It is well spoken."

25 Now Elijah said to the prophets of Baal, "Choose one bull for yourselves and prepare *it* first, for you *are* many; and call on the name of your god, but put no fire *under it.*"

26 So they took the bull which was given them, and they prepared *it,* and called on the name of Baal from morning even till noon, saying, "O Baal, hear us!" But *there was* [a]no voice; no one answered. Then they leaped about the altar which they had made.

27 And so it was, at noon, that Elijah mocked them and said, "Cry aloud, for he *is* a god; either he is meditating, or he is busy, or he is on a journey, *or* perhaps he is sleeping and must be awakened." 28 So they cried aloud, and [a]cut themselves, as was their custom, with knives and lances, until the blood gushed out on them. 29 And when midday was past, [a]they prophesied until the *time* of the offering of the *evening* sacrifice. But *there was* [b]no voice; no one answered, no one paid attention.

30 Then Elijah said to all the people, "Come near to me." So all the people came near to him. [a]And he repaired the altar of the LORD

18:1 [a] Luke 4:25 [b] Deut. 28:12 18:7 [a] 2 Kin. 1:6–8 18:12 [a] Acts 8:39 18:17 [a] 1 Kin. 21:20 [b] Josh. 7:25 18:18 [a] [2 Chr. 15:2] 18:19 [a] Josh. 19:26 [b] 1 Kin. 16:33 [1] A Canaanite goddess 18:20 [a] 1 Kin. 22:6 18:21 [a] [Matt. 6:24] [b] Josh. 24:15 18:22 [a] 1 Kin. 19:10, 14 [b] 1 Kin. 18:19 18:24 [a] 1 Chr. 21:26 18:26 [a] Jer. 10:5 18:28 [a] [Deut. 14:1] 18:29 [a] Ex. 29:39, 41 [b] 1 Kin. 18:26 18:30 [a] 2 Chr. 33:16

that was broken down. 31 And Elijah took
twelve stones, according to the number of
the tribes of the sons of Jacob, to whom the
word of the LORD had come, saying, [a]"Israel
shall be your name."[1] 32 Then with the stones
he built an altar [a]in the name of the LORD;
and he made a trench around the altar large
enough to hold two seahs of seed. 33 And he
[a]put the wood in order, cut the bull in pieces,
and laid *it* on the wood, and said, "Fill four
waterpots with water, and [b]pour *it* on the
burnt sacrifice and on the wood." 34 Then
he said, "Do *it* a second time," and they did
it a second time; and he said, "Do *it* a third
time," and they did *it* a third time. 35 So the
water ran all around the altar; and he also
filled [a]the trench with water.

36 And it came to pass, at *the time of* the
offering of the *evening* sacrifice, that Elijah
the prophet came near and said, "LORD [a]God
of Abraham, Isaac, and Israel, [b]let it be known
this day that You *are* God in Israel and I *am*
Your servant, and *that* [c]I have done all these
things at Your word. 37 Hear me, O LORD, hear
me, that this people may know that You *are*
the LORD God, and *that* You have turned their
hearts back *to You* again."

38 Then [a]the fire of the LORD fell and consumed the burnt sacrifice, and the wood and
the stones and the dust, and it licked up the
water that *was* in the trench. 39 Now when all
the people saw *it*, they fell on their faces; and
they said, [a]"The LORD, He *is* God! The LORD,
He *is* God!"

40 And Elijah said to them, [a]"Seize the
prophets of Baal! Do not let one of them
escape!" So they seized them; and Elijah
brought them down to the Brook [b]Kishon
and [c]executed them there.

The Drought Ends

41 Then Elijah said to Ahab, "Go up, eat and
drink; for *there is* the sound of abundance of
rain." 42 So Ahab went up to eat and drink.
And Elijah went up to the top of Carmel;
[a]then he bowed down on the ground, and put
his face between his knees, 43 and said to his
servant, "Go up now, look toward the sea."

So he went up and looked, and said, "*There is*
nothing." And seven times he said, "Go again."

44 Then it came to pass the seventh *time*,
that he said, "There is a cloud, as small as a
man's hand, rising out of the sea!" So he said,
"Go up, say to Ahab, 'Prepare *your chariot*, and
go down before the rain stops you.' "

45 Now it happened in the meantime that
the sky became black with clouds and wind,
and there was a heavy rain. So Ahab rode
away and went to Jezreel. 46 Then the [a]hand
of the LORD came upon Elijah; and he [b]girded
up his loins and ran ahead of Ahab to the
entrance of Jezreel.

18:31 [a] Gen. 32:28; 35:10 [1] Genesis 32:28 **18:32** [a] [Col. 3:17] **18:33** [a] Lev. 1:6–8 [b] Judg. 6:20 **18:35** [a] 1 Kin. 18:32, 38 **18:36** [a] Ex. 3:6; 4:5 [b] 1 Kin. 8:43 [c] Num. 16:28 **18:38** [a] 1 Chr. 21:26 **18:39** [a] 1 Kin. 18:21, 24 **18:40** [a] 2 Kin. 10:25 [b] Judg. 4:7; 5:21 [c] [Deut. 13:5; 18:20] **18:42** [a] James 5:17, 18 **18:46** [a] 2 Kin. 3:15 [b] 2 Kin. 4:29; 9:1

TAKE A STAND

Hear me, O LORD, hear me, that this people may know that You are the LORD God.

1 KINGS 18:37

Have you felt alone, like the odd one out? At work, at school, or among your friends, you might be lonely when standing up for what is right. The great prophet Elijah found himself in that situation. Much of Israel was apostate thanks to King Ahab's weak leadership and the influence of his pagan wife, Jezebel, who surrounded herself with the priests and prophets of Baal, her god.

Elijah confronted Ahab and challenged him to bring the prophets of Baal to Mount Carmel and find out who really was God. The prophets of Baal built their altar and called on Baal to send fire. They prayed, they yelled, and they mocked. Nothing happened. Then Elijah repaired the altar of the Lord, drenched it with water, and prayed, "LORD God of Abraham, Isaac, and Israel, let it be known this day that You are God in Israel" (v. 36). God answered him "by fire" (v. 24).

To live a holy life filled with peace, we have to be willing, like Elijah, to confront the godless culture around us. When you take opportunities to stand for your faith, you may be ridiculed, but you can be assured of the peaceful presence of Almighty God in your life.

Elijah Escapes from Jezebel

19 And Ahab told Jezebel all that Elijah had done, also how he had [a]executed all the prophets with the sword. 2 Then Jezebel sent a messenger to Elijah, saying, [a]"So let the gods do *to me,* and more also, if I do not make your life as the life of one of them by tomorrow about this time." 3 And when he saw *that,* he arose and ran for his life, and went to Beersheba, which *belongs* to Judah, and left his servant there.

4 But he himself went a day's journey into the wilderness, and came and sat down under a broom tree. And he [a]prayed that he might die, and said, "It is enough! Now, LORD, take my life, for I *am* no better than my fathers!"

5 Then as he lay and slept under a broom tree, suddenly an angel[1] touched him, and said to him, "Arise *and* eat." 6 Then he looked, and there by his head *was* a cake baked on coals, and a jar of water. So he ate and drank, and lay down again. 7 And the angel[1] of the LORD came back the second time, and touched him, and said, "Arise *and* eat, because the journey *is* too great for you." 8 So he arose, and ate and drank; and he went in the strength of that food forty days and [a]forty nights as far as [b]Horeb, the mountain of God.

9 And there he went into a cave, and spent the night in that place; and behold, the word of the LORD *came* to him, and He said to him, "What are you doing here, Elijah?"

10 So he said, [a]"I have been very [b]zealous for the LORD God of hosts; for the children of Israel have forsaken Your covenant, torn down Your altars, and [c]killed Your prophets with the sword. [d]I alone am left; and they seek to take my life."

God's Revelation to Elijah

11 Then He said, "Go out, and stand [a]on the mountain before the LORD." And behold, the LORD [b]passed by, and [c]a great and strong wind tore into the mountains and broke the rocks in pieces before the LORD, *but* the LORD *was* not in the wind; and after the wind an earthquake, *but* the LORD *was* not in the earthquake; 12 and after the earthquake a fire, *but* the LORD *was* not in the fire; and after the fire a still small voice.

13 So it was, when Elijah heard *it,* that [a]he wrapped his face in his mantle and went out and stood in the entrance of the cave. [b]Suddenly a voice *came* to him, and said, "What are you doing here, Elijah?"

14 [a]And he said, "I have been very zealous for the LORD God of hosts; because the children of Israel have forsaken Your covenant, torn down Your altars, and killed Your prophets with the sword. I alone am left; and they seek to take my life."

15 Then the LORD said to him: "Go, return on your way to the Wilderness of Damascus; [a]and when you arrive, anoint Hazael *as* king

19:1 [a] 1 Kin. 18:40 **19:2** [a] Ruth 1:17 **19:4** [a] Num. 11:15 **19:5** [1] Or *Angel* **19:7** [1] Or *Angel* **19:8** [a] Matt. 4:2 [b] Ex. 3:1; 4:27 **19:10** [a] Rom. 11:3 [b] Ps. 69:9 [c] 1 Kin. 18:4 [d] 1 Kin. 18:22 **19:11** [a] Ex. 19:20; 24:12, 18 [b] Ex. 33:21, 22 [c] Ezek. 1:4; 37:7 **19:13** [a] Ex. 3:6 [b] 1 Kin. 19:9 **19:14** [a] 1 Kin. 19:10 **19:15** [a] 2 Kin. 8:8–15

THE STILL, SMALL VOICE

The LORD was not in the fire; and after the fire a still small voice.

I KINGS 19:12

Isolation is the enemy of God's peace. The great prophet Elijah, who ministered in Israel in the ninth century BC, felt the fear of being alone. Have you ever been so discouraged and so ready to give up that you wanted to die? There was a brief time in Elijah's ministry when he was so discouraged that he asked God to remove him from the earth. He saw no point in continuing his ministry or his life. Almost all Israel had fallen into idolatry. Elijah had given up hope.

As it turned out, Elijah's ministry was far from finished. What jump-started Elijah's work was the provision of a meal and God's quiet voice. Renewed in mission and purpose, the prophet anointed two kings and Elisha, his great successor. Listen for the voice of the Lord to find His peace and presence. Often the Lord answers our prayers in small, grace-filled ways, and His peace shines forth in our lives.

Often it is that moment of ultimate discouragement that sets the stage for renewal. When we admit to God that we can't go on in our own strength, that is when God steps up.

over Syria. 16 Also you shall anoint [a]Jehu the
son of Nimshi *as* king over Israel. And [b]Eli-
sha the son of Shaphat of Abel Meholah you
shall anoint *as* prophet in your place. 17 [a]It
shall be *that* whoever escapes the sword of
Hazael, Jehu will [b]kill; and whoever escapes
the sword of Jehu, [c]Elisha will kill. 18 [a]Yet I
have reserved seven thousand in Israel, all
whose knees have not bowed to Baal, [b]and
every mouth that has not kissed him."

Elisha Follows Elijah

19 So he departed from there, and found
Elisha the son of Shaphat, who *was* plowing
with twelve yoke *of oxen* before him, and he
was with the twelfth. Then Elijah passed by
him and threw his [a]mantle on him. 20 And
he left the oxen and ran after Elijah, and
said, [a]"Please let me kiss my father and my
mother, and *then* I will follow you."

And he said to him, "Go back again, for
what have I done to you?"

21 So *Elisha* turned back from him, and took
a yoke of oxen and slaughtered them and
[a]boiled their flesh, using the oxen's equipment, and gave it to the people, and they
ate. Then he arose and followed Elijah, and
became his servant.

Ahab Defeats the Syrians

20 Now [a]Ben-Hadad the king of Syria
gathered all his forces together; thirty-
two kings *were* with him, with horses and
chariots. And he went up and besieged [b]Sa-
maria, and made war against it. 2 Then he sent
messengers into the city to Ahab king of Israel, and said to him, "Thus says Ben-Hadad:
3 'Your silver and your gold *are* mine; your
loveliest wives and children are mine.' "

4 And the king of Israel answered and said,
"My lord, O king, just as you say, I and all that
I have *are* yours."

5 Then the messengers came back and said,
"Thus speaks Ben-Hadad, saying, 'Indeed I
have sent to you, saying, "You shall deliver to
me your silver and your gold, your wives and
your children"; 6 but I will send my servants
to you tomorrow about this time, and they
shall search your house and the houses of
your servants. And *it shall be, that* whatever
is pleasant in your eyes, they will put *it* in
their hands and take *it.*' "

7 So the king of Israel called all the elders
of the land, and said, "Notice, please, and see
how this *man* seeks trouble, for he sent to me
for my wives, my children, my silver, and my
gold; and I did not deny him."

8 And all the elders and all the people said
to him, "Do not listen or consent."

9 Therefore he said to the messengers of
Ben-Hadad, "Tell my lord the king, 'All that
you sent for to your servant the first time I
will do, but this thing I cannot do.' "

And the messengers departed and brought
back word to him.

10 Then Ben-Hadad sent to him and said,
[a]"The gods do so to me, and more also, if
enough dust is left of Samaria for a handful
for each of the people who follow me."

11 So the king of Israel answered and said,
"Tell *him,* 'Let not the one who puts on *his
armor* [a]boast like the one who takes *it off.*' "

12 And it happened when *Ben-Hadad* heard
this message, as he and the kings *were* [a]drink-
ing at the command post, that he said to his
servants, "Get ready." And they got ready to
attack the city.

13 Suddenly a prophet approached Ahab
king of Israel, saying, "Thus says the LORD:
'Have you seen all this great multitude? Behold, [a]I will deliver it into your hand today,
and you shall know that I *am* the LORD.' "

14 So Ahab said, "By whom?"

And he said, "Thus says the LORD: 'By the
young leaders of the provinces.' "

Then he said, "Who will set the battle in order?"

And he answered, "You."

15 Then he mustered the young leaders of
the provinces, and there were two hundred
and thirty-two; and after them he mustered
all the people, all the children of Israel—
seven thousand.

16 So they went out at noon. Meanwhile
Ben-Hadad and the thirty-two kings helping
him were [a]getting drunk at the command
post. 17 The young leaders of the provinces
went out first. And Ben-Hadad sent out *a
patrol,* and they told him, saying, "Men are
coming out of Samaria!" 18 So he said, "If they
have come out for peace, take them alive; and
if they have come out for war, take them alive."

19 Then these young leaders of the provinces
went out of the city with the army which followed them. 20 And each one killed his man;
so the Syrians fled, and Israel pursued them;
and Ben-Hadad the king of Syria escaped on a
horse with the cavalry. 21 Then the king of Israel
went out and attacked the horses and chariots,
and killed the Syrians with a great slaughter.

22 And the prophet came to the king of Israel and said to him, "Go, strengthen yourself;
take note, and see what you should do, [a]for
in the spring of the year the king of Syria will
come up against you."

19:16 [a] 2 Kin. 9:1–10 [b] 2 Kin. 2:9–15 **19:17** [a] 2 Kin. 8:12; 13:3, 22 [b] 2 Kin. 9:14—10:28 [c] [Hos. 6:5] **19:18** [a] Rom. 11:4 [b] Hos. 13:2
19:19 [a] 2 Kin. 2:8, 13, 14 **19:20** [a] [Matt. 8:21, 22] **19:21** [a] 2 Sam. 24:22 **20:1** [a] 2 Kin. 6:24 [b] 1 Kin. 16:24 **20:10** [a] 1 Kin. 19:2
20:11 [a] Prov. 27:1 **20:12** [a] 1 Kin. 20:16 **20:13** [a] 1 Kin. 20:28 **20:16** [a] 1 Kin. 16:9; 20:12 **20:22** [a] 2 Sam. 11:1

The Syrians Again Defeated

23 Then the servants of the king of Syria
said to him, "Their gods *are* gods of the hills.
Therefore they were stronger than we; but if
we fight against them in the plain, surely we
will be stronger than they. 24 So do this thing:
Dismiss the kings, each from his position,
and put captains in their places; 25 and you
shall muster an army like the army that you
have lost, horse for horse and chariot for
chariot. Then we will fight against them in the
plain; surely we will be stronger than they."

And he listened to their voice and did so.
26 So it was, in the spring of the year, that
Ben-Hadad mustered the Syrians and went
up to [a]Aphek to fight against Israel. 27 And the
children of Israel were mustered and given
provisions, and they went against them. Now
the children of Israel encamped before them
like two little flocks of goats, while the Syrians filled the [a]countryside.

28 Then a [a]man of God came and spoke
to the king of Israel, and said, "Thus says
the LORD: 'Because the Syrians have said,
"The LORD *is* God of the hills, but He *is* not
God of the valleys," therefore [b]I will deliver
all this great multitude into your hand, and
you shall know that I *am* the LORD.' " 29 And
they encamped opposite each other for seven
days. So it was that on the seventh day the
battle was joined; and the children of Israel
killed one hundred thousand foot soldiers *of*
the Syrians in one day. 30 But the rest fled to
Aphek, into the city; then a wall fell on twenty-
seven thousand of the men *who were* left.

And Ben-Hadad fled and went into the city,
into an inner chamber.

Ahab's Treaty with Ben-Hadad

31 Then his servants said to him, "Look now,
we have heard that the kings of the house
of Israel *are* merciful kings. Please, let us
[a]put sackcloth around our waists and ropes
around our heads, and go out to the king of
Israel; perhaps he will spare your life." 32 So
they wore sackcloth around their waists and
put ropes around their heads, and came to
the king of Israel and said, "Your servant
Ben-Hadad says, 'Please let me live.' "

And he said, "*Is* he still alive? He *is* my brother."
33 Now the men were watching closely to
see whether *any sign of mercy would come*
from him; and they quickly grasped *at this
word* and said, "Your brother Ben-Hadad."

So he said, "Go, bring him." Then
Ben-Hadad came out to him; and he had
him come up into the chariot.

34 So *Ben-Hadad* said to him, [a]"The cities
which my father took from your father I will
restore; and you may set up marketplaces
for yourself in Damascus, as my father did
in Samaria."

Then *Ahab said,* "I will send you away with
this treaty." So he made a treaty with him and
sent him away.

Ahab Condemned

35 Now a certain man of [a]the sons of the
prophets said to his neighbor [b]by the word
of the LORD, "Strike me, please." And the man
refused to strike him. 36 Then he said to him,
"Because you have not obeyed the voice of
the LORD, surely, as soon as you depart from
me, a lion shall kill you." And as soon as he
left him, [a]a lion found him and killed him.

37 And he found another man, and said,
"Strike me, please." So the man struck him,
inflicting a wound. 38 Then the prophet departed and waited for the king by the road,
and disguised himself with a bandage over
his eyes. 39 Now [a]as the king passed by, he
cried out to the king and said, "Your servant went out into the midst of the battle;
and there, a man came over and brought a
man to me, and said, 'Guard this man; if by
any means he is missing, [b]your life shall be
for his life, or else you shall pay a talent of
silver.' 40 While your servant was busy here
and there, he was gone."

Then the king of Israel said to him, "So
shall your judgment *be;* you yourself have
decided *it.*"

41 And he hastened to take the bandage
away from his eyes; and the king of Israel recognized him as one of the prophets.
42 Then he said to him, "Thus says the LORD:
[a]'Because you have let slip out of *your* hand a
man whom I appointed to utter destruction,
therefore your life shall go for his life, and
your people for his people.' "

43 So the king of Israel [a]went to his house
sullen and displeased, and came to Samaria.

Naboth Is Murdered for His Vineyard

21 And it came to pass after these things
that Naboth the Jezreelite had a vineyard which *was* in [a]Jezreel, next to the palace
of Ahab king of Samaria. 2 So Ahab spoke to
Naboth, saying, "Give me your [a]vineyard,
that I may have it for a vegetable garden,
because it *is* near, next to my house; and for
it I will give you a vineyard better than it.
Or, if it seems good to you, I will give you its
worth in money."

20:26 [a] Josh. 13:4 20:27 [a] Judg. 6:3–5 20:28 [a] 1 Kin. 17:18 [b] 1 Kin. 20:13 20:31 [a] Gen. 37:34 20:34 [a] 1 Kin. 15:20
20:35 [a] 2 Kin. 2:3, 5, 7, 15 [b] 1 Kin. 13:17, 18 20:36 [a] 1 Kin. 13:24 20:39 [a] 2 Sam. 12:1 [b] 2 Kin. 10:24
20:42 [a] 1 Kin. 22:31–37 20:43 [a] 1 Kin. 21:4 21:1 [a] 1 Kin. 18:45, 46 21:2 [a] 1 Sam. 8:14

PEACE NOTE

You practice the ministry of presence when you help someone at a time of great need or affliction. Then you are truly an ambassador of God's peace.

3 But Naboth said to Ahab, "The LORD forbid [a]that I should give the inheritance of my fathers to you!"

4 So Ahab went into his house sullen and displeased because of the word which Naboth the Jezreelite had spoken to him; for he had said, "I will not give you the inheritance of my fathers." And he lay down on his bed, and turned away his face, and would eat no food.
5 But [a]Jezebel his wife came to him, and said to him, "Why is your spirit so sullen that you eat no food?"

6 He said to her, "Because I spoke to Naboth the Jezreelite, and said to him, 'Give me your vineyard for money; or else, if it pleases you, I will give you *another* vineyard for it.' And he answered, 'I will not give you my vineyard.'"
7 Then Jezebel his wife said to him, "You now exercise authority over Israel! Arise, eat food, and let your heart be cheerful; I will give you the vineyard of Naboth the Jezreelite."
8 And she wrote letters in Ahab's name, sealed *them* with his seal, and sent the letters to the elders and the nobles who *were* dwelling in the city with Naboth.
9 She wrote in the letters, saying,

> Proclaim a fast, and seat Naboth with high honor among the people;
> 10 and seat two men, scoundrels, before him to bear witness against him, saying, "You have [a]blasphemed God and the king." *Then* take him out, and [b]stone him, that he may die.

11 So the men of his city, the elders and nobles who were inhabitants of his city, did as Jezebel had sent to them, as it *was* written in the letters which she had sent to them.
12 [a]They proclaimed a fast, and seated Naboth with high honor among the people.
13 And two men, scoundrels, came in and sat before him; and the scoundrels [a]witnessed against him, against Naboth, in the presence of the people, saying, "Naboth has blasphemed God and the king!" [b]Then they took him outside the city and stoned him with stones, so that he died.
14 Then they sent to Jezebel, saying, "Naboth has been stoned and is dead."
15 And it came to pass, when Jezebel heard that Naboth had been stoned and was dead, that Jezebel said to Ahab, "Arise, take possession of the vineyard of Naboth the Jezreelite, which he refused to give you for money; for Naboth is not alive, but dead."
16 So it was, when Ahab heard that Naboth was dead, that Ahab got up and went down to take possession of the vineyard of Naboth the Jezreelite.

The LORD Condemns Ahab

17 [a]Then the word of the LORD came to [b]Elijah the Tishbite, saying,
18 "Arise, go down to meet Ahab king of Israel, [a]who *lives* in Samaria. There *he is,* in the vineyard of Naboth, where he has gone down to take possession of it.
19 You shall speak to him, saying, 'Thus says the LORD: "Have you murdered and also taken possession?"' And you shall speak to him, saying, 'Thus says the LORD: [a]"In the place where dogs licked the blood of Naboth, dogs shall lick your blood, even yours."'"

20 So Ahab said to Elijah, [a]"Have you found me, O my enemy?"

And he answered, "I have found *you,* because [b]you have sold yourself to do evil in the sight of the LORD:
21 'Behold, [a]I will bring calamity on you. I will take away your [b]posterity, and will cut off from Ahab [c]every male in Israel, both [d]bond and free.
22 I will make your house like the house of [a]Jeroboam the son of Nebat, and like the house of [b]Baasha the son of Ahijah, because of the provocation with which you have provoked *Me* to anger, and made Israel sin.'
23 And [a]concerning Jezebel the LORD also spoke, saying, 'The dogs shall eat Jezebel by the wall[1] of Jezreel.'
24 The dogs shall eat [a]whoever belongs to Ahab and dies in the city, and the birds of the air shall eat whoever dies in the field."
25 But [a]there was no one like Ahab who sold himself to do wickedness in the sight of the LORD, [b]because Jezebel his wife stirred

21:3 [a] [Num. 36:7] **21:5** [a] 1 Kin. 19:1, 2 **21:10** [a] [Ex. 22:28] [b] [Lev. 24:14] **21:12** [a] Is. 58:4 **21:13** [a] [Ex. 20:16; 23:1, 7] [b] 2 Kin. 9:26 **21:17** [a] [Ps. 9:12] [b] 1 Kin. 19:1 **21:18** [a] 2 Chr. 22:9 **21:19** [a] 1 Kin. 22:38 **21:20** [a] 1 Kin. 18:17 [b] [Rom. 7:14] **21:21** [a] 1 Kin. 14:10 [b] 2 Kin. 10:10 [c] 1 Sam. 25:22 [d] 1 Kin. 14:10 **21:22** [a] 1 Kin. 15:29 [b] 1 Kin. 16:3, 11 **21:23** [a] 2 Kin. 9:10, 30–37 [1] Following Masoretic Text and Septuagint; some Hebrew manuscripts, Syriac, Targum, and Vulgate read *plot of ground* (compare 2 Kings 9:36). **21:24** [a] 1 Kin. 14:11; 16:4 **21:25** [a] 1 Kin. 16:30–33; 21:20 [b] 1 Kin. 16:31

him up. 26 And he behaved very abominably
in following idols, according to all [a]*that* the
Amorites had done, whom the LORD had cast
out before the children of Israel.
27 So it was, when Ahab heard those words,
that he tore his clothes and [a]put sackcloth
on his body, and fasted and lay in sackcloth,
and went about mourning.
28 And the word of the LORD came to Elijah
the Tishbite, saying, 29 "See how Ahab has
humbled himself before Me? Because he [a]has
humbled himself before Me, I will not bring
the calamity in his days. [b]In the days of his
son I will bring the calamity on his house."

Micaiah Warns Ahab

22 Now three years passed without war
between Syria and Israel. 2 Then it
came to pass, in the third year, that [a]Jehosh-
aphat the king of Judah went down to *visit*
the king of Israel.
3 And the king of Israel said to his servants, "Do you know that [a]Ramoth in Gilead
is ours, but we hesitate to take it out of the
hand of the king of Syria?" 4 So he said to
Jehoshaphat, "Will you go with me to fight
at Ramoth Gilead?"
Jehoshaphat said to the king of Israel, [a]"I
am as you *are,* my people as your people, my
horses as your horses." 5 Also Jehoshaphat
said to the king of Israel, [a]"Please inquire
for the word of the LORD today."
6 Then the king of Israel [a]gathered the
prophets together, about four hundred men,
and said to them, "Shall I go against Ramoth
Gilead to fight, or shall I refrain?"
So they said, "Go up, for the Lord will deliver *it* into the hand of the king."
7 And [a]Jehoshaphat said, "*Is there* not still
a prophet of the LORD here, that we may
inquire of Him?"[1]
8 So the king of Israel said to Jehoshaphat,
"*There is* still one man, Micaiah the son of
Imlah, by whom we may inquire of the LORD;
but I hate him, because he does not prophesy
good concerning me, but evil."
And Jehoshaphat said, "Let not the king
say such things!"
9 Then the king of Israel called an officer
and said, "Bring Micaiah the son of Imlah
quickly!"
10 The king of Israel and Jehoshaphat the
king of Judah, having put on *their* robes, sat
each on his throne, at a threshing floor at
the entrance of the gate of Samaria; and all
the prophets prophesied before them. 11 Now
Zedekiah the son of Chenaanah had made
[a]horns of iron for himself; and he said, "Thus
says the LORD: 'With these you shall [b]gore the
Syrians until they are destroyed.' " 12 And all
the prophets prophesied so, saying, "Go up
to Ramoth Gilead and prosper, for the LORD
will deliver *it* into the king's hand."
13 Then the messenger who had gone to call
Micaiah spoke to him, saying, "Now listen,
the words of the prophets with one accord
encourage the king. Please, let your word
be like the word of one of them, and speak
encouragement."
14 And Micaiah said, "*As* the LORD lives, [a]what-
ever the LORD says to me, that I will speak."
15 Then he came to the king; and the king
said to him, "Micaiah, shall we go to war
against Ramoth Gilead, or shall we refrain?"
And he answered him, "Go and prosper,
for the LORD will deliver *it* into the hand of
the king!"
16 So the king said to him, "How many times
shall I make you swear that you tell me nothing but the truth in the name of the LORD?"
17 Then he said, "I saw all Israel [a]scattered
on the mountains, as sheep that have no
shepherd. And the LORD said, 'These have
no master. Let each return to his house in
peace.' "
18 And the king of Israel said to Jehoshaphat, "Did I not tell you he would not prophesy good concerning me, but evil?"
19 Then *Micaiah* said, "Therefore hear the
word of the LORD: [a]I saw the LORD sitting on
His throne, [b]and all the host of heaven standing by, on His right hand and on His left. 20 And
the LORD said, 'Who will persuade Ahab to go
up, that he may fall at Ramoth Gilead?' So one
spoke in this manner, and another spoke in
that manner. 21 Then a spirit came forward
and stood before the LORD, and said, 'I will
persuade him.' 22 The LORD said to him, 'In
what way?' So he said, 'I will go out and be a
lying spirit in the mouth of all his prophets.'
And the LORD said, [a]'You shall persuade *him,*
and also prevail. Go out and do so.' 23 [a]There-
fore look! The LORD has put a lying spirit in
the mouth of all these prophets of yours, and
the LORD has declared disaster against you."
24 Now Zedekiah the son of Chenaanah
went near and [a]struck Micaiah on the cheek,
and said, [b]"Which way did the spirit from the
LORD go from me to speak to you?"
25 And Micaiah said, "Indeed, you shall
see on that day when you go into an [a]inner
chamber to hide!"

21:26 [a] 2 Kin. 21:11 **21:27** [a] Gen. 37:34 **21:29** [a] [2 Kin. 22:19] [b] 2 Kin. 9:25; 10:11, 17 **22:2** [a] 2 Chr. 18:2 **22:3** [a] Deut. 4:43 **22:4** [a] 2 Kin. 3:7 **22:5** [a] 2 Kin. 3:11 **22:6** [a] 1 Kin. 18:19 **22:7** [a] 2 Kin. 3:11 [1] Or *him* **22:11** [a] Zech. 1:18–21 [b] Deut. 33:17 **22:14** [a] Num. 22:38; 24:13 **22:17** [a] Matt. 9:36 **22:19** [a] Is. 6:1 [b] Dan. 7:10 **22:22** [a] Judg. 9:23 **22:23** [a] [Ezek. 14:9] **22:24** [a] Jer. 20:2 [b] 2 Chr. 18:23 **22:25** [a] 1 Kin. 20:30

26 So the king of Israel said, "Take Micaiah, and return him to Amon the governor of the city and to Joash the king's son; 27 and say, 'Thus says the king: "Put this *fellow* in [a]prison, and feed him with bread of affliction and water of affliction, until I come in peace." ' "

28 But Micaiah said, "If you ever return in peace, [a]the LORD has not spoken by me." And he said, "Take heed, all you people!"

Ahab Dies in Battle

29 So the king of Israel and Jehoshaphat the king of Judah went up to Ramoth Gilead. 30 And the king of Israel said to Jehoshaphat, "I will disguise myself and go into battle; but you put on your robes." So the king of Israel [a]disguised himself and went into battle.

31 Now the [a]king of Syria had commanded the thirty-two [b]captains of his chariots, saying, "Fight with no one small or great, but only with the king of Israel." 32 So it was, when the captains of the chariots saw Jehoshaphat, that they said, "Surely it *is* the king of Israel!" Therefore they turned aside to fight against him, and Jehoshaphat [a]cried out. 33 And it happened, when the captains of the chariots saw that it *was* not the king of Israel, that they turned back from pursuing him. 34 Now a *certain* man drew a bow at random, and struck the king of Israel between the joints of his armor. So he said to the driver of his chariot, "Turn around and take me out of the battle, for I am wounded."

35 The battle increased that day; and the king was propped up in his chariot, facing the Syrians, and died at evening. The blood ran out from the wound onto the floor of the chariot. 36 Then, as the sun was going down, a shout went throughout the army, saying, "Every man to his city, and every man to his own country!"

37 So the king died, and was brought to Samaria. And they buried the king in Samaria. 38 Then *someone* washed the chariot at a pool in Samaria, and the dogs licked up his blood while the harlots bathed,[1] according [a]to the word of the LORD which He had spoken.

39 Now the rest of the acts of Ahab, and all that he did, [a]the ivory house which he built and all the cities that he built, *are* they not written in the book of the chronicles of the kings of Israel? 40 So Ahab rested with his fathers. Then [a]Ahaziah his son reigned in his place.

Jehoshaphat Reigns in Judah

41 [a]Jehoshaphat the son of Asa had become king over Judah in the fourth year of Ahab king of Israel. 42 Jehoshaphat *was* thirty-five years old when he became king, and he reigned twenty-five years in Jerusalem. His mother's name *was* Azubah the daughter of Shilhi. 43 And [a]he walked in all the ways of his father Asa. He did not turn aside from them, doing *what was* right in the eyes of the LORD. Nevertheless [b]the high places were not taken away, *for* the people offered sacrifices and burned incense on the high places. 44 Also [a]Jehoshaphat made [b]peace with the king of Israel.

45 Now the rest of the acts of Jehoshaphat, the might that he showed, and how he made war, *are* they not written [a]in the book of the chronicles of the kings of Judah? 46 [a]And the rest of the perverted persons,[1] who remained in the days of his father Asa, he banished from the land. 47 [a]*There was* then no king in Edom, only a deputy of the king.

48 [a]Jehoshaphat [b]made merchant ships[1] to go to [c]Ophir for gold; [d]but they never sailed, for the ships were wrecked at [e]Ezion Geber. 49 Then Ahaziah the son of Ahab said to Jehoshaphat, "Let my servants go with your servants in the ships." But Jehoshaphat would not.

50 And [a]Jehoshaphat rested with his fathers, and was buried with his fathers in the City of David his father. Then Jehoram his son reigned in his place.

Ahaziah Reigns in Israel

51 [a]Ahaziah the son of Ahab became king over Israel in Samaria in the seventeenth year of Jehoshaphat king of Judah, and reigned two years over Israel. 52 He did evil in the sight of the LORD, and [a]walked in the way of his father and in the way of his mother and in the way of Jeroboam the son of Nebat, who had made Israel sin; 53 for [a]he served Baal and worshiped him, and provoked the LORD God of Israel to anger, [b]according to all that his father had done.

22:27 [a] 2 Chr. 16:10; 18:25–27 **22:28** [a] Num. 16:29 **22:30** [a] 2 Chr. 35:22 **22:31** [a] 1 Kin. 20:1 [b] 1 Kin. 20:24 **22:32** [a] 2 Chr. 18:31 **22:38** [a] 1 Kin. 21:19 [1] Syriac and Targum read *they washed his armor.* **22:39** [a] Amos 3:15 **22:40** [a] 2 Kin. 1:2, 18 **22:41** [a] 2 Chr. 20:31 **22:43** [a] 2 Chr. 17:3; 20:32, 33 [b] 2 Kin. 12:3 **22:44** [a] 2 Chr. 19:2 [b] 2 Chr. 18:1 **22:45** [a] 2 Chr. 20:34 **22:46** [a] 1 Kin. 14:24; 15:12 [1] Hebrew *qadesh,* that is, one practicing sodomy and prostitution in religious rituals **22:47** [a] 2 Sam. 8:14 **22:48** [a] 2 Chr. 20:35–37 [b] 1 Kin. 10:22 [c] 1 Kin. 9:28 [d] 2 Chr. 20:37 [e] 1 Kin. 9:26 [1] Or *ships of Tarshish* **22:50** [a] 2 Chr. 21:1 **22:51** [a] 1 Kin. 22:40 **22:52** [a] 1 Kin. 15:26; 21:25 **22:53** [a] Judg. 2:11 [b] 1 Kin. 16:30–32

THE SECOND BOOK OF THE

KINGS

AUTHOR

This book, thought to originally be part of 1 Kings, is similar to the Book of Jeremiah. It has been observed that the omission of Jeremiah's ministry in the account of King Josiah and his successors may indicate that Jeremiah himself was the recorder of the events. The last two chapters were evidently added to the book after the Babylonian captivity and written by someone other than Jeremiah.

TIME

853–560 BC

KEY VERSE

2 Kings 17:22–23

THEME

Both Elijah in 1 Kings and Elisha in 2 Kings are prime examples of how prophets functioned in Israel. They fearlessly confronted kings. They were involved in miracles. Both seemed always to be involved in some political controversy. Most important, they called on God and got results. In 2 Kings, Israel's story begins with the reign of Ahab's son, Ahaziah, continues with the capture and deportation of Israel to Assyria in 722 BC, and ends with Judah's fall in 586 BC, when Nebuchadnezzar burns the temple and palace in Jerusalem and deports many people to Babylon.

A powerful question evokes emotion and prayerful contemplation: "Will there not be peace and truth at least in my days?" (2 Kin. 20:19). How we find peace and truth in our times is the overarching theme of 2 Kings. Judges of Israel often spoke as prophets on behalf of the Lord to Israel, and chapter 9 is a fascinating indictment against finding peace without seeking the Lord according to Jehu: "What have you to do with peace? Turn around and follow me" (9:19). In a moment of absolute desperation, Hezekiah throws himself on God's mercy, counting on Him to know his heart and his steadfast love and faithfulness: "I have walked before You in truth and with a loyal [*shalem*] heart" (20:3). Later God raised up a woman, Huldah, to bring a revival of the Bible and repentance through godly King Josiah, and God's peace was restored to the kingdom (22:14–20).

God Judges Ahaziah

1 Moab [a]rebelled against Israel [b]after the
death of Ahab.
2 Now [a]Ahaziah fell through the lattice of
his upper room in Samaria, and was injured;
so he sent messengers and said to them, "Go,
inquire of [b]Baal-Zebub, the god of [c]Ekron,
whether I shall recover from this injury." 3 But
the angel[1] of the LORD said to Elijah the Tishbite, "Arise, go up to meet the messengers
of the king of Samaria, and say to them, '*Is*
it because *there is* no God in Israel *that* you
are going to inquire of Baal-Zebub, the god of
Ekron?' 4 Now therefore, thus says the LORD:
'You shall not come down from the bed to
which you have gone up, but you shall surely
die.' " So Elijah departed.
5 And when the messengers returned to
him, he said to them, "Why have you come
back?"
6 So they said to him, "A man came up to
meet us, and said to us, 'Go, return to the king
who sent you, and say to him, "Thus says the
LORD: '*Is it* because *there is* no God in Israel
that you are sending to inquire of Baal-Zebub,
the god of Ekron? Therefore you shall not
come down from the bed to which you have
gone up, but you shall surely die.' " ' "
7 Then he said to them, "What kind of man
was it who came up to meet you and told you
these words?"
8 So they answered him, [a]"A hairy man
wearing a leather belt around his waist."
And he said, [b]"It *is* Elijah the Tishbite."
9 Then the king sent to him a captain of
fifty with his fifty men. So he went up to him;
and there he was, sitting on the top of a hill.
And he spoke to him: "Man of God, the king
has said, 'Come down!' "
10 So Elijah answered and said to the captain of fifty, "If I *am* a man of God, then [a]let
fire come down from heaven and consume
you and your fifty men." And fire came down
from heaven and consumed him and his fifty.
11 Then he sent to him another captain of fifty
with his fifty men.
And he answered and said to him: "Man
of God, thus has the king said, 'Come down
quickly!' "
12 So Elijah answered and said to them,
"If I *am* a man of God, let fire come down
from heaven and consume you and your
fifty men." And the fire of God came down
from heaven and consumed him and his fifty.
13 Again, he sent a third captain of fifty
with his fifty men. And the third captain of
fifty went up, and came and fell on his knees
before Elijah, and pleaded with him, and said
to him: "Man of God, please let my life and
the life of these fifty servants of yours [a]be
precious in your sight. 14 Look, fire has come
down from heaven and burned up the first
two captains of fifties with their fifties. But
let my life now be precious in your sight."
15 And the angel[1] of the LORD said to Elijah,
"Go down with him; do not be afraid of him."
So he arose and went down with him to the
king. 16 Then he said to him, "Thus says the
LORD: 'Because you have sent messengers to
inquire of Baal-Zebub, the god of Ekron, *is it*
because *there is* no God in Israel to inquire
of His word? Therefore you shall not come
down from the bed to which you have gone
up, but you shall surely die.' "
17 So *Ahaziah* died according to the word of
the LORD which Elijah had spoken. Because
he had no son, [a]Jehoram[1] became king in his
place, in the second year of Jehoram the son
of Jehoshaphat, king of Judah.
18 Now the rest of the acts of Ahaziah which
he did, *are* they not written in the book of the
chronicles of the kings of Israel?

Elijah Ascends to Heaven

2 And it came to pass, when the LORD was
about to [a]take up Elijah into heaven by
a whirlwind, that Elijah went with [b]Elisha
from Gilgal. 2 Then Elijah said to Elisha, [a]"Stay
here, please, for the LORD has sent me on
to Bethel."
But Elisha said, "*As* the LORD lives, and [b]*as*
your soul lives, I will not leave you!" So they
went down to Bethel.
3 Now [a]the sons of the prophets who *were*
at Bethel came out to Elisha, and said to him,
"Do you know that the LORD will take away
your master from over you today?"
And he said, "Yes, I know; keep silent!"
4 Then Elijah said to him, "Elisha, stay
here, please, for the LORD has sent me on
to Jericho."
But he said, "*As* the LORD lives, and *as*
your soul lives, I will not leave you!" So they
came to Jericho.
5 Now the sons of the prophets who *were* at
Jericho came to Elisha and said to him, "Do
you know that the LORD will take away your
master from over you today?"
So he answered, "Yes, I know; keep silent!"
6 Then Elijah said to him, "Stay here, please,
for the LORD has sent me on to the Jordan."
But he said, "*As* the LORD lives, and *as* your
soul lives, I will not leave you!" So the two
of them went on. 7 And fifty men of the sons

1:1 [a] 2 Sam. 8:2 [b] 2 Kin. 3:5 **1:2** [a] 1 Kin. 22:40 [b] Matt. 10:25 [c] 1 Sam. 5:10 **1:3** [1] Or *Angel* **1:8** [a] Zech. 13:4 [b] 1 Kin. 18:7 **1:10** [a] Luke 9:54 **1:13** [a] 1 Sam. 26:21 **1:15** [1] Or *Angel* **1:17** [a] 1 Kin. 22:50 [1] The son of Ahab king of Israel (compare 3:1) **2:1** [a] Gen. 5:24 [b] 1 Kin. 19:16–21 **2:2** [a] Ruth 1:15, 16 [b] 1 Sam. 1:26 **2:3** [a] 1 Kin. 20:35

of the prophets went and stood facing *them*
at a distance, while the two of them stood
by the Jordan. 8 Now Elijah took his mantle,
rolled *it* up, and struck the water; and [a]it was
divided this way and that, so that the two of
them crossed over on dry [b]ground.
9 And so it was, when they had crossed over,
that Elijah said to Elisha, "Ask! What may I do
for you, before I am taken away from you?"
Elisha said, "Please let a double portion
of your spirit be upon me."
10 So he said, "You have asked a hard thing.
Nevertheless, if you see me *when I am* taken
from you, it shall be so for you; but if not, it
shall not be *so.*" 11 Then it happened, as they
continued on and talked, that suddenly [a]a
chariot of fire *appeared* with horses of fire,
and separated the two of them; and Elijah
[b]went up by a whirlwind into heaven.
12 And Elisha saw *it,* and he cried out, [a]"My
father, my father, the chariot of Israel and
its horsemen!" So he saw him no more. And
he took hold of his own clothes and tore
them into two pieces. 13 He also took up the
mantle of Elijah that had fallen from him,
and went back and stood by the bank of the
Jordan. 14 Then he took the mantle of Elijah
that had fallen from him, and struck the
water, and said, "Where *is* the LORD God of
Elijah?" And when he also had struck the
water, [a]it was divided this way and that; and
Elisha crossed over.
15 Now when the sons of the prophets who
were [a]from Jericho saw him, they said, "The
spirit of Elijah rests on Elisha." And they
came to meet him, and bowed to the ground
before him. 16 Then they said to him, "Look
now, there are fifty strong men with your
servants. Please let them go and search for
your master, [a]lest perhaps the Spirit of the
LORD has taken him up and cast him upon
some mountain or into some valley."
And he said, "You shall not send anyone."
17 But when they urged him till he was
[a]ashamed, he said, "Send *them!*" Therefore they
sent fifty men, and they searched for three days
but did not find him. 18 And when they came
back to him, for he had stayed in Jericho, he
said to them, "Did I not say to you, 'Do not go'?"

Elisha Performs Miracles

19 Then the men of the city said to Elisha,
"Please notice, the situation of this city *is*
pleasant, as my lord sees; but the water *is*
bad, and the ground barren."
20 And he said, "Bring me a new bowl,
and put salt in it." So they brought *it* to him.
21 Then he went out to the source of the water,
and [a]cast in the salt there, and said, "Thus
says the LORD: 'I have healed this water;
from it there shall be no more death or barrenness.' " 22 So the water remains [a]healed
to this day, according to the word of Elisha
which he spoke.

2:8 [a] Ex. 14:21, 22 [b] Josh. 3:17 **2:11** [a] 2 Kin. 6:17 [b] Heb. 11:5 **2:12** [a] 2 Kin. 13:14 **2:14** [a] 2 Kin. 2:8 **2:15** [a] 2 Kin. 2:7 **2:16** [a] 1 Kin. 18:12 **2:17** [a] 2 Kin. 8:11 **2:21** [a] Ex. 15:25, 26 **2:22** [a] Ezek. 47:8, 9

ASK FOR MORE

Suddenly a chariot of fire appeared with horses of fire . . .
and Elijah went up by a whirlwind into heaven.

2 KINGS 2:11

I have no doubt that Elijah found heaven a peaceful place after a turbulent and, at times, dangerous ministry on earth. But what a way to go! At the beginning of his ministry to an obdurate, faithless Israel, Elijah called down fire as a demonstration of God's reality and power (1 Kin. 18:36–38), and then at the end of his ministry the prophet was taken up into heaven in "a chariot of fire" (2 Kin. 2:11) as a demonstration of God's power for Elisha's benefit. Elisha had requested "a double portion" (v. 9) of Elijah's spirit. Here he "took up the mantle of Elijah that had fallen from him" (v. 13).

Few of us experience such dramatic demonstrations of divine power. But all of us can experience the peace of God. How we get there may vary, but arrive there we will if we ask for a portion of God's Spirit.

Have you asked for His Spirit for peace? The first step is accepting Jesus as your personal Lord and Savior (see "How to Find God and His Peace"). We can pray bold prayers like Elisha and ask the Lord to bless us with a double portion of His peace.

23 Then he went up from there to Bethel;
and as he was going up the road, some youths
came from the city and mocked him, and
said to him, "Go up, you baldhead! Go up,
you baldhead!"
24 So he turned around and looked at them,
and [a]pronounced a curse on them in the
name of the LORD. And two female bears
came out of the woods and mauled forty-two
of the youths.
25 Then he went from there to [a]Mount Carmel, and from there he returned to Samaria.

Moab Rebels Against Israel

3 Now [a]Jehoram the son of Ahab became
king over Israel at Samaria in the eighteenth year of Jehoshaphat king of Judah,
and reigned twelve years. 2 And he did evil in
the sight of the LORD, but not like his father
and mother; for he put away the *sacred* pillar
of Baal [a]that his father had made. 3 Nevertheless he persisted in [a]the sins of Jeroboam
the son of Nebat, who had made Israel sin;
he did not depart from them.
4 Now Mesha king of Moab was a sheepbreeder, and he [a]regularly paid the king of
Israel one hundred thousand [b]lambs and the
wool of one hundred thousand rams. 5 But
it happened, when [a]Ahab died, that the king
of Moab rebelled against the king of Israel.
6 So King Jehoram went out of Samaria
at that time and mustered all Israel. 7 Then
he went and sent to Jehoshaphat king of
Judah, saying, "The king of Moab has rebelled against me. Will you go with me to
fight against Moab?"
And he said, "I will go up; [a]I *am* as you *are,* my
people as your people, my horses as your horses." 8 Then he said, "Which way shall we go up?"
And he answered, "By way of the Wilderness of Edom."
9 So the king of Israel went with the king
of Judah and the king of Edom, and they
marched on that roundabout route seven
days; and there was no water for the army,
nor for the animals that followed them. 10 And
the king of Israel said, "Alas! For the LORD has
called these three kings together to deliver
them into the hand of Moab."
11 But [a]Jehoshaphat said, "*Is there* no
prophet of the LORD here, that we may inquire of the LORD by him?"
So one of the servants of the king of Israel answered and said, "Elisha the son of
Shaphat *is* here, who [b]poured water on the
hands of Elijah."
12 And Jehoshaphat said, "The word of the
LORD is with him." So the king of Israel and
Jehoshaphat and the king of Edom [a]went
down to him.
13 Then Elisha said to the king of Israel,
[a]"What have I to do with you? [b]Go to [c]the
prophets of your father and the [d]prophets
of your mother."
But the king of Israel said to him, "No, for
the LORD has called these three kings *together*
to deliver them into the hand of Moab."
14 And Elisha said, [a]"*As* the LORD of hosts
lives, before whom I stand, surely were it not
that I regard the presence of Jehoshaphat
king of Judah, I would not look at you, nor
see you. 15 But now bring me [a]a musician."
Then it happened, when the musician
[b]played, that [c]the hand of the LORD came
upon him. 16 And he said, "Thus says the
LORD: [a]'Make this valley full of ditches.' 17 For
thus says the LORD: 'You shall not see wind,
nor shall you see rain; yet that valley shall
be filled with water, so that you, your cattle,
and your animals may drink.' 18 And this is
a simple matter in the sight of the LORD;
He will also deliver the Moabites into your
hand. 19 Also you shall attack every fortified
city and every choice city, and shall cut down
every good tree, and stop up every spring
of water, and ruin every good piece of land
with stones."
20 Now it happened in the morning, when
[a]the grain offering was offered, that suddenly
water came by way of Edom, and the land
was filled with water.
21 And when all the Moabites heard that
the kings had come up to fight against them,
all who were able to bear arms and older
were gathered; and they stood at the border.
22 Then they rose up early in the morning,
and the sun was shining on the water; and
the Moabites saw the water on the other side
as red as blood. 23 And they said, "This is
blood; the kings have surely struck swords
and have killed one another; now therefore,
Moab, to the spoil!"
24 So when they came to the camp of Israel,
Israel rose up and attacked the Moabites, so
that they fled before them; and they entered
their land, killing the Moabites. 25 Then they
destroyed the cities, and each man threw a
stone on every good piece of land and filled it;
and they stopped up all the springs of water
and cut down all the good trees. But they left
the stones of [a]Kir Haraseth *intact.* However
the slingers surrounded and attacked it.

2:24 [a] Deut. 27:13–26 **2:25** [a] 2 Kin. 4:25 **3:1** [a] 2 Kin. 1:17 **3:2** [a] 1 Kin. 16:31, 32 **3:3** [a] 1 Kin. 12:28–32 **3:4** [a] 2 Sam. 8:2 [b] Is. 16:1, 2 **3:5** [a] 2 Kin. 1:1 **3:7** [a] 1 Kin. 22:4 **3:11** [a] 1 Kin. 22:7 [b] 1 Kin. 19:21 **3:12** [a] 2 Kin. 2:25 **3:13** [a] [Ezek. 14:3] [b] Judg. 10:14 [c] 1 Kin. 22:6–11 [d] 1 Kin. 18:19 **3:14** [a] 1 Kin. 17:1 **3:15** [a] 1 Sam. 10:5 [b] 1 Sam. 16:16, 23 [c] Ezek. 1:3; 3:14, 22; 8:1 **3:16** [a] Jer. 14:3 **3:20** [a] Ex. 29:39, 40 **3:25** [a] Is. 16:7, 11

26 And when the king of Moab saw that the battle was too fierce for him, he took with him seven hundred men who drew swords, to break through to the king of Edom, but they could not. 27 Then [a]he took his eldest son who would have reigned in his place, and offered him *as* a burnt offering upon the wall; and there was great indignation against Israel. [b]So they departed from him and returned to *their own* land.

Elisha and the Widow's Oil

4 A certain woman of the wives of [a]the sons of the prophets cried out to Elisha, saying, "Your servant my husband is dead, and you know that your servant feared the LORD. And the creditor is coming [b]to take my two sons to be his slaves."

2 So Elisha said to her, "What shall I do for you? Tell me, what do you have in the house?" And she said, "Your maidservant has nothing in the house but a jar of oil."

3 Then he said, "Go, borrow vessels from everywhere, from all your neighbors—empty vessels; [a]do not gather just a few. 4 And when you have come in, you shall shut the door behind you and your sons; then pour it into all those vessels, and set aside the full ones."

5 So she went from him and shut the door behind her and her sons, who brought *the vessels* to her; and she poured *it* out. 6 Now it came to pass, when the vessels were full, that she said to her son, "Bring me another vessel."

And he said to her, "*There is* not another vessel." So the oil ceased. 7 Then she came and told the man of God. And he said, "Go, sell the oil and pay your debt; and you *and* your sons live on the rest."

Elisha Raises the Shunammite's Son

8 Now it happened one day that Elisha went to [a]Shunem, where there *was* a notable woman, and she persuaded him to eat some food. So it was, as often as he passed by, he would turn in there to eat some food. 9 And she said to her husband, "Look now, I know that this *is* a holy man of God, who passes by us regularly. 10 Please, let us make a small upper room on the wall; and let us put a bed for him there, and a table and a chair and a lampstand; so it will be, whenever he comes to us, he can turn in there."

11 And it happened one day that he came there, and he turned in to the upper room and lay down there. 12 Then he said to [a]Gehazi his servant, "Call this Shunammite woman." When he had called her, she stood before him. 13 And he said to him, "Say now to her, 'Look, you have been concerned for us with all this care. What *can I* do for you? Do you want me to speak on your behalf to the king or to the commander of the army?' "

She answered, "I dwell among my own people."

14 So he said, "What then *is* to be done for her?"

And Gehazi answered, "Actually, she has no son, and her husband is old."

15 So he said, "Call her." When he had called her, she stood in the doorway. 16 Then he said, "About this time next year you shall embrace a son."

And she said, "No, my lord. Man of God, [a]do not lie to your maidservant!"

17 But the woman conceived, and bore a son when the appointed time had come, of which Elisha had told her.

18 And the child grew. Now it happened one day that he went out to his father, to the reapers. 19 And he said to his father, "My head, my head!"

So he said to a servant, "Carry him to his mother." 20 When he had taken him and brought him to his mother, he sat on her knees till noon, and *then* died. 21 And she went up and laid him on the bed of the man of God, shut *the door* upon him, and went out. 22 Then she called to her husband, and said, "Please send me one of the young men and one of the donkeys, that I may run to the man of God and come back."

23 So he said, "Why are you going to him today? *It is* neither the [a]New Moon nor the Sabbath."

And she said, "*It is* well." 24 Then she saddled a donkey, and said to her servant, "Drive, and go forward; do not slacken the pace for me unless I tell you." 25 And so she departed, and went to the man of God [a]at Mount Carmel.

So it was, when the man of God saw her afar off, that he said to his servant Gehazi, "Look, the Shunammite woman! 26 Please run now to meet her, and say to her, '*Is it* well with you? *Is it* well with your husband? *Is it* well with the child?' "

And she answered, "*It is* well." 27 Now when she came to the man of God at the hill, she caught him by the feet, but Gehazi came near to push her away. But the man of God said, "Let her alone; for her soul *is* in deep distress, and the LORD has hidden *it* from me, and has not told me."

28 So she said, "Did I ask a son of my lord? [a]Did I not say, 'Do not deceive me'?"

3:27 [a] [Amos 2:1] [b] 2 Kin. 8:20 4:1 [a] 1 Kin. 20:35 [b] [Lev. 25:39–41, 48] 4:3 [a] 2 Kin. 3:16 4:8 [a] Josh. 19:18 4:12 [a] 2 Kin. 4:29–31; 5:20–27; 8:4, 5 4:16 [a] 2 Kin. 4:28 4:23 [a] 1 Chr. 23:31 4:25 [a] 2 Kin. 2:25 4:28 [a] 2 Kin. 4:16

29 Then he said to Gehazi, [a]"Get yourself
ready, and take my staff in your hand, and be
on your way. If you meet anyone, [b]do not greet
him; and if anyone greets you, do not answer
him; but [c]lay my staff on the face of the child."
30 And the mother of the child said, [a]"*As*
the LORD lives, and *as* your soul lives, I will
not [b]leave you." So he arose and followed her.
31 Now Gehazi went on ahead of them, and laid
the staff on the face of the child; but *there*
was neither voice nor hearing. Therefore he
went back to meet him, and told him, saying,
"The child has [a]not awakened."
32 When Elisha came into the house, there
was the child, lying dead on his bed. 33 He
[a]went in therefore, shut the door behind
the two of them, [b]and prayed to the LORD.
34 And he went up and lay on the child, and
put his mouth on his mouth, his eyes on
his eyes, and his hands on his hands; and
[a]he stretched himself out on the child, and
the flesh of the child became warm. 35 He
returned and walked back and forth in the
house, and again went up [a]and stretched
himself out on him; then [b]the child sneezed
seven times, and the child opened his eyes.
36 And he called Gehazi and said, "Call this
Shunammite woman." So he called her. And
when she came in to him, he said, "Pick up
your son." 37 So she went in, fell at his feet,
and bowed to the ground; then she [a]picked
up her son and went out.

Elisha Purifies the Pot of Stew

38 And Elisha returned to [a]Gilgal, and *there*
was a [b]famine in the land. Now the sons of the
prophets *were* [c]sitting before him; and he said
to his servant, "Put on the large pot, and boil
stew for the sons of the prophets." 39 So one went
out into the field to gather herbs, and found a
wild vine, and gathered from it a lapful of wild
gourds, and came and sliced *them* into the pot
of stew, though they did not know *what they*
were. 40 Then they served it to the men to eat.
Now it happened, as they were eating the stew,
that they cried out and said, "Man of God, *there*
is [a]death in the pot!" And they could not eat *it.*
41 So he said, "Then bring some flour." And
[a]he put *it* into the pot, and said, "Serve *it* to
the people, that they may eat." And there was
nothing harmful in the pot.

Elisha Feeds One Hundred Men

42 Then a man came from [a]Baal Shalisha,
[b]and brought the man of God bread of the
firstfruits, twenty loaves of barley bread, and
newly ripened grain in his knapsack. And he
said, "Give *it* to the people, that they may eat."
43 But his servant said, [a]"What? Shall I set
this before one hundred men?"
He said again, "Give it to the people, that
they may eat; for thus says the LORD: [b]'They
shall eat and have *some* left over.'" 44 So he set
it before them; and they ate [a]and had *some*
left over, according to the word of the LORD.

4:29 [a] 1 Kin. 18:46 [b] Luke 10:4 [c] Ex. 7:19; 14:16 **4:30** [a] 2 Kin. 2:2 [b] 2 Kin. 2:4 **4:31** [a] John 11:11 **4:33** [a] [Matt. 6:6] [b] 1 Kin. 17:20 **4:34** [a] 1 Kin. 17:21–23 **4:35** [a] 1 Kin. 17:21 [b] 2 Kin. 8:1, 5 **4:37** [a] [Heb. 11:35] **4:38** [a] 2 Kin. 2:1 [b] 2 Kin. 8:1 [c] Acts 22:3 **4:40** [a] Ex. 10:17 **4:41** [a] Ex. 15:25 **4:42** [a] 1 Sam. 9:4 [b] [1 Cor. 9:11] **4:43** [a] John 6:9 [b] Luke 9:17 **4:44** [a] John 6:13

EVEN WHEN WE NEED A MIRACLE

So she went in, fell at his feet, and bowed to the ground;
then she picked up her son and went out.

2 KINGS 4:37

One of the most astounding works that God did through Elijah was restore the life of a widow's young son (1 Kin. 17:17–24). Because Elisha possessed a double portion of that same spiritual power, he was able to raise the Shunammite's son from death (2 Kin. 4:18–37). In both of these amazing events, the mothers recognized God's presence in those remarkable prophets. The widowed woman proclaimed to Elijah, "Now by this I know that you are a man of God, and that the word of the LORD in your mouth is the truth" (1 Kin. 17:24), whereas the Shunammite woman fell at Elisha's feet. In doing so she acknowledged that God had worked through the prophet.

Recognizing God's power and authority provides the foundation on which a life of peace may be built. Knowing that even in challenging times God is present makes peace possible. God has the power to bring good out of the impossible circumstances of our lives. You may need a miracle today the way the Shunammite woman did. Fall at the feet of Jesus and ask Him to act powerfully on your behalf and fill you with His peace.

Naaman's Leprosy Healed

5 Now [a]Naaman, commander of the army of the king of Syria, was [b]a great and honorable man in the eyes of his master, because by him the LORD had given victory to Syria. He was also a mighty man of valor, *but* a leper. 2 And the Syrians had gone out [a]on raids, and had brought back captive a young girl from the land of Israel. She waited on Naaman's wife. 3 Then she said to her mistress, "If only my master *were* with the prophet who *is* in Samaria! For he would heal him of his leprosy." 4 And *Naaman* went in and told his master, saying, "Thus and thus said the girl who *is* from the land of Israel."

5 Then the king of Syria said, "Go now, and I will send a letter to the king of Israel."

So he departed and [a]took with him ten talents of silver, six thousand *shekels* of gold, and ten changes of clothing. 6 Then he brought the letter to the king of Israel, which said,

> Now be advised, when this letter comes to you, that I have sent Naaman my servant to you, that you may heal him of his leprosy.

7 And it happened, when the king of Israel read the letter, that he tore his clothes and said, "*Am* I [a]God, to kill and make alive, that this man sends a man to me to heal him of his leprosy? Therefore please consider, and see how he seeks a quarrel with me."

8 So it was, when Elisha the man of God heard that the king of Israel had torn his clothes, that he sent to the king, saying, "Why have you torn your clothes? Please let him come to me, and he shall know that there is a prophet in Israel."

9 Then Naaman went with his horses and chariot, and he stood at the door of Elisha's house. 10 And Elisha sent a messenger to him, saying, "Go and [a]wash in the Jordan seven times, and your flesh shall be restored to you, and *you shall* be clean." 11 But Naaman became furious, and went away and said, "Indeed, I said to myself, 'He will surely come out *to me,* and stand and call on the name of the LORD his God, and wave his hand over the place, and heal the leprosy.' 12 *Are* not the Abanah[1] and the Pharpar, the rivers of Damascus, better than all the waters of Israel? Could I not wash in them and be clean?" So he turned and went away in a rage. 13 And his [a]servants came near and spoke to him, and said, "My father, *if* the prophet had told you *to do* something great, would you not have done *it?* How much more then, when he says to you, 'Wash, and be clean'?" 14 So he went down and dipped seven times in the Jordan, according to the saying of the man of God; and his [a]flesh was restored like the flesh of a little child, and [b]he was clean.

15 And he returned to the man of God, he and all his aides, and came and stood before him; and he said, "Indeed, now I know that

5:1 [a] Luke 4:27 [b] Ex. 11:3 5:2 [a] 2 Kin. 6:23; 13:20 5:5 [a] 1 Sam. 9:8 5:7 [a] [Gen. 30:2] 5:10 [a] John 9:7
5:12 [1] Following Kethib, Septuagint, and Vulgate; Qere, Syriac, and Targum read *Amanah.* 5:13 [a] 1 Sam. 28:23
5:14 [a] Job 33:25 [b] Luke 4:27; 5:13

NO MATTER WHAT, OBEY

Now I know that there is no God in all the earth, except in Israel.

2 KINGS 5:15

One of the most extraordinary stories in the Bible concerns a man who found himself in a hopeless situation. Naaman was a commander in the Syrian army. He had wealth, position and power, and access to the king—a pretty good life, all in all. But he faced a serious problem: he suffered from leprosy. And in ancient times that meant a slow, disfiguring death.

Naaman had prayed to his gods and visited his country's physicians, but he found no cure. No one and nothing could help him. Then an Israelite servant girl told him of the great prophet Elisha. Naaman traveled to Israel and, as the prophet instructed, reluctantly dipped himself three times in the Jordan River. To his astonishment he was healed! Naaman confessed to his companions, "Now I know that there is no God in all the earth, except in Israel." What Naaman discovered—and this is why Jesus Himself later referred to this great story (see Luke 4:27)—is that God responds to all who seek Him.

In what area do you need healing? Do you believe it is possible for you? Has anyone ever given you strange-sounding advice that worked?

there is [a]no God in all the earth, except in Israel; now therefore, please take [b]a gift from
your servant."
16 But he said, [a]"*As* the LORD lives, before
whom I stand, [b]I will receive nothing." And
he urged him to take *it,* but he refused.
17 So Naaman said, "Then, if not, please
let your servant be given two mule-loads of
earth; for your servant will no longer offer
either burnt offering or sacrifice to other
gods, but to the LORD. 18 Yet in this thing
may the LORD pardon your servant: when
my master goes into the temple of Rimmon
to worship there, and [a]he leans on my hand,
and I bow down in the temple of Rimmon—
when I bow down in the temple of Rimmon,
may the LORD please pardon your servant
in this thing."
19 Then he said to him, "Go in peace." So he
departed from him a short distance.

Gehazi's Greed

20 But [a]Gehazi, the servant of Elisha the
man of God, said, "Look, my master has
spared Naaman this Syrian, while not receiving from his hands what he brought; but *as*
the LORD lives, I will run after him and take
something from him." 21 So Gehazi pursued
Naaman. When Naaman saw *him* running
after him, he got down from the chariot to
meet him, and said, "*Is* all well?"
22 And he said, "All *is* [a]well. My master has
sent me, saying, 'Indeed, just now two young
men of the sons of the prophets have come to
me from the mountains of Ephraim. Please
give them a talent of silver and two changes
of garments.'"
23 So Naaman said, "Please, take two talents." And he urged him, and bound two
talents of silver in two bags, with two changes
of garments, and handed *them* to two of his
servants; and they carried *them* on ahead of
him. 24 When he came to the citadel, he took
them from their hand, and stored *them* away
in the house; then he let the men go, and
they departed. 25 Now he went in and stood
before his master. Elisha said to him, "Where
did you go, Gehazi?"
And he said, "Your servant did not go anywhere."
26 Then he said to him, "Did not my heart
go *with you* when the man turned back from
his chariot to meet you? *Is it* [a]time to receive money and to receive clothing, olive
groves and vineyards, sheep and oxen, male
and female servants? 27 Therefore the leprosy of Naaman [a]shall cling to you and your
descendants forever." And he went out from
his presence [b]leprous, *as white* as snow.

The Floating Ax Head

6 And [a]the sons of the prophets said to Elisha, "See now, the place where we dwell
with you is too small for us. 2 Please, let us
go to the Jordan, and let every man take a
beam from there, and let us make there a
place where we may dwell."
So he answered, "Go."
3 Then one said, [a]"Please consent to go
with your servants."
And he answered, "I will go." 4 So he went
with them. And when they came to the Jordan, they cut down trees. 5 But as one was
cutting down a tree, the iron *ax head* fell into
the water; and he cried out and said, "Alas,
master! For it was [a]borrowed."
6 So the man of God said, "Where did it fall?"
And he showed him the place. So [a]he cut off a
stick, and threw *it* in there; and he made the iron
float. 7 Therefore he said, "Pick *it* up for yourself." So he reached out his hand and took it.

The Blinded Syrians Captured

8 Now the [a]king of Syria was making war
against Israel; and he consulted with his servants, saying, "My camp *will be* in such and
such a place." 9 And the man of God sent to
the king of Israel, saying, "Beware that you do
not pass this place, for the Syrians are coming
down there." 10 Then the king of Israel sent
someone to the place of which the man of God
had told him. Thus he warned him, and he
was watchful there, not just once or twice.
11 Therefore the heart of the king of Syria was
greatly troubled by this thing; and he called
his servants and said to them, "Will you not
show me which of us *is* for the king of Israel?"
12 And one of his servants said, "None, my
lord, O king; but Elisha, the prophet who *is* in
Israel, tells the king of Israel the words that
you speak in your bedroom."
13 So he said, "Go and see where he *is,* that
I may send and get him."
And it was told him, saying, "Surely *he is*
in [a]Dothan."
14 Therefore he sent horses and chariots and
a great army there, and they came by night and
surrounded the city. 15 And when the servant
of the man of God arose early and went out,
there was an army, surrounding the city with
horses and chariots. And his servant said to
him, "Alas, my master! What shall we do?"
16 So he answered, [a]"Do not fear, for [b]those
who *are* with us *are* more than those who

5:15 [a] Dan. 2:47; 3:29; 6:26, 27 [b] Gen. 33:11 **5:16** [a] 2 Kin. 3:14 [b] Gen. 14:22, 23 **5:18** [a] 2 Kin. 7:2, 17 **5:20** [a] 2 Kin. 4:12; 8:4, 5 **5:22** [a] 2 Kin. 4:26 **5:26** [a] [Eccl. 3:1, 6] **5:27** [a] [1 Tim. 6:10] [b] Ex. 4:6 **6:1** [a] 2 Kin. 4:38 **6:3** [a] 2 Kin. 5:23 **6:5** [a] [Ex. 22:14] **6:6** [a] 2 Kin. 2:21; 4:41 **6:8** [a] 2 Kin. 8:28, 29 **6:13** [a] Gen. 37:17 **6:16** [a] Ex. 14:13 [b] [Rom. 8:31]

SURROUNDED

Do not fear, for those who are with us are more than those who are with them.

2 KINGS 6:16

Peace results when God's mercy is expressed. Sometimes His mercy is reflected in His people. When the king of Syria learned that Elisha informed the king of Israel of all that Syria was planning, he sent his army to capture the great prophet. Elisha's servant was terrified, but the prophet reassured him: "Do not fear, for those who are with us are more than those who are with them." The Lord intervened and the Syrian army found itself trapped in the midst of Israel. The king of Israel asked Elisha if he should kill the Syrians, but the prophet replied, "You shall not kill them. Would you kill those whom you have taken captive with your sword and your bow? Set food and water before them, that they may eat and drink and go to their master" (v. 22).

In this story, as in the story of the healing of Naaman, the Syrian commander, we see an amazing example of God's mercy and peace. Syria and Israel were mortal enemies, frequently at war. Yet when threatened by assassins, Elisha, Israel's great prophet, extended mercy. Mercy and peace go hand in hand.

When have you seen peace result from a merciful act?

are with them." 17 And Elisha prayed, and
said, "LORD, I pray, open his eyes that he
may see." Then the LORD [a]opened the eyes
of the young man, and he saw. And behold,
the mountain *was* full of [b]horses and chariots
of fire all around Elisha. 18 So when *the Syrians* came down to him, Elisha prayed to the
LORD, and said, "Strike this people, I pray,
with blindness." And [a]He struck them with
blindness according to the word of Elisha.
19 Now Elisha said to them, "This *is* not the
way, nor *is* this the city. Follow me, and I will
bring you to the man whom you seek." But
he led them to Samaria.
20 So it was, when they had come to Samaria, that Elisha said, "LORD, open the eyes of
these *men,* that they may see." And the LORD
opened their eyes, and they saw; and there
they were, inside Samaria!
21 Now when the king of Israel saw them, he
said to Elisha, "My [a]father, shall I kill *them?*
Shall I kill *them?*"
22 But he answered, "You shall not kill *them.*
Would you kill those whom you have taken
captive with your sword and your bow? [a]Set
food and water before them, that they may eat
and drink and go to their master." 23 Then he
prepared a great feast for them; and after they
ate and drank, he sent them away and they
went to their master. So [a]the bands of Syrian
raiders came no more into the land of Israel.

Syria Besieges Samaria in Famine

24 And it happened after this that
[a]Ben-Hadad king of Syria gathered all his
army, and went up and besieged Samaria.
25 And there was a great [a]famine in Samaria;
and indeed they besieged it until a donkey's
head was *sold* for eighty *shekels* of silver, and
one-fourth of a kab of dove droppings for
five *shekels* of silver.
26 Then, as the king of Israel was passing
by on the wall, a woman cried out to him,
saying, "Help, my lord, O king!"
27 And he said, "If the LORD does not help
you, where can I find help for you? From the
threshing floor or from the winepress?" 28 Then
the king said to her, "What is troubling you?"
And she answered, "This woman said to
me, 'Give your son, that we may eat him today,
and we will eat my son tomorrow.' 29 So [a]we
boiled my son, and ate him. And I said to
her on the next day, 'Give your son, that we
may eat him'; but she has hidden her son."
30 Now it happened, when the king heard
the words of the woman, that he [a]tore his
clothes; and as he passed by on the wall, the
people looked, and there underneath *he had*
sackcloth on his body. 31 Then he said, [a]"God do
so to me and more also, if the head of Elisha
the son of Shaphat remains on him today!"
32 But Elisha was sitting in his house, and
[a]the elders were sitting with him. And *the king*

6:17 [a] Num. 22:31 [b] 2 Kin. 2:11 **6:18** [a] Gen. 19:11 **6:21** [a] 2 Kin. 2:12; 5:13; 8:9 **6:22** [a] [Rom. 12:20] **6:23** [a] 2 Kin. 5:2; 6:8, 9 **6:24** [a] 1 Kin. 20:1 **6:25** [a] 2 Kin. 4:38; 8:1 **6:29** [a] Lev. 26:27–29 **6:30** [a] 1 Kin. 21:27 **6:31** [a] Ruth 1:17 **6:32** [a] Ezek. 8:1; 14:1; 20:1

sent a man ahead of him, but before the messenger came to him, he said to the elders, [b]"Do
you see how this son of [c]a murderer has sent
someone to take away my head? Look, when
the messenger comes, shut the door, and hold
him fast at the door. *Is* not the sound of his
master's feet behind him?" 33 And while he was
still talking with them, there was the messenger, coming down to him; and then *the king*
said, "Surely this calamity *is* from the LORD;
[a]why should I wait for the LORD any longer?"

7 Then Elisha said, "Hear the word of the
LORD. Thus says the LORD: [a]'Tomorrow
about this time a seah of fine flour *shall be*
sold for a shekel, and two seahs of barley for
a shekel, at the gate of Samaria.' "

2 [a]So an officer on whose hand the king
leaned answered the man of God and said,
"Look, [b]*if* the LORD would make windows in
heaven, could this thing be?"

And he said, "In fact, you shall see *it* with
your eyes, but you shall not eat of it."

The Syrians Flee

3 Now there were four leprous men [a]at the
entrance of the gate; and they said to one another, "Why are we sitting here until we die?
4 If we say, 'We will enter the city,' the famine *is*
in the city, and we shall die there. And if we sit
here, we die also. Now therefore, come, let us
surrender to the [a]army of the Syrians. If they
keep us alive, we shall live; and if they kill us,
we shall only die." 5 And they rose at twilight
to go to the camp of the Syrians; and when
they had come to the outskirts of the Syrian
camp, to their surprise no one *was* there. 6 For
the Lord had caused the army of the Syrians
[a]to hear the noise of chariots and the noise
of horses—the noise of a great army; so they
said to one another, "Look, the king of Israel
has hired against us [b]the kings of the Hittites
and the kings of the Egyptians to attack us!"
7 Therefore they [a]arose and fled at twilight, and
left the camp intact—their tents, their horses,
and their donkeys—and they fled for their lives.
8 And when these lepers came to the outskirts
of the camp, they went into one tent and ate
and drank, and carried from it silver and gold
and clothing, and went and hid *them;* then they
came back and entered another tent, and carried *some* from there *also,* and went and hid *it.*

9 Then they said to one another, "We are not
doing right. This day *is* a day of good news,
and we remain silent. If we wait until morning
light, some punishment will come upon us.
Now therefore, come, let us go and tell the
king's household." 10 So they went and called
to the gatekeepers of the city, and told them,
saying, "We went to the Syrian camp, and
surprisingly no one *was* there, not a human
sound—only horses and donkeys tied, and the
tents intact." 11 And the gatekeepers called out,
and they told *it* to the king's household inside.

12 So the king arose in the night and said to
his servants, "Let me now tell you what the
Syrians have done to us. They know that we

6:32 [b] Luke 13:32 [c] 1 Kin. 18:4, 13, 14; 21:10, 13 **6:33** [a] Job 2:9 **7:1** [a] 2 Kin. 7:18, 19 **7:2** [a] 2 Kin. 5:18; 7:17, 19, 20 [b] Mal. 3:10 **7:3** [a] [Num. 5:2–4; 12:10–14] **7:4** [a] 2 Kin. 6:24 **7:6** [a] 2 Sam. 5:24 [b] 1 Kin. 10:29 **7:7** [a] Ps. 48:4–6

DISCOURAGED BUT READY

The king said, "Surely this calamity is from the LORD; why should I wait for the LORD any longer?"

2 KINGS 6:33

Syria couldn't seem to learn its lesson. Time and again Syrian aggression against Israel failed, and in some instances, Israel even responded with kindness and mercy. In chapter 6 Ben-Hadad, king of Syria, had invaded Israel and besieged Samaria, the capital city. The siege resulted in food shortages. The king of Israel foolishly blamed Elisha for this state of affairs and sent an assassin, but the prophet assured the king's agent that the next day, *food would be cheap* and abundant. And so it happened: the Syrians fled in panic, leaving behind all their provisions. The prophet's word was fulfilled.

The king's agent found it impossible to imagine how food so scarce one day could become abundant the next. The peace of God can be that way. The troubles of today seem beyond solution, so we cannot imagine rescue. Yet peace is at hand if we ask God for it! Will we? God can dramatically change our circumstances. One way to live in the peace of God is never to make a decision when you are discouraged. Wait for the Lord to work, and He will give you His peace along the way.

are [a]hungry; therefore they have gone out of the camp to hide themselves in the field, saying, 'When they come out of the city, we shall catch them alive, and get into the city.' "

13 And one of his servants answered and said, "Please, let several *men* take five of the remaining horses which are left in the city. Look, they *may either become* like all the multitude of Israel that are left in it; or indeed, *I say,* they *may become* like all the multitude of Israel left from those who are consumed; so let us send them and see." 14 Therefore they took two chariots with horses; and the king sent them in the direction of the Syrian army, saying, "Go and see." 15 And they went after them to the Jordan; and indeed all the road *was* full of garments and weapons which the Syrians had thrown away in their haste. So the messengers returned and told the king. 16 Then the people went out and plundered the tents of the Syrians. So a seah of fine flour was *sold* for a shekel, and two seahs of barley for a shekel, [a]according to the word of the LORD.

17 Now the king had appointed the officer on whose hand he leaned to have charge of the gate. But the people trampled him in the gate, and he died, just [a]as the man of God had said, who spoke when the king came down to him. 18 So it happened just as the man of God had spoken to the king, saying, [a]"Two seahs of barley for a shekel, and a seah of fine flour for a shekel, shall be *sold* tomorrow about this time in the gate of Samaria."

19 Then that officer had answered the man of God, and said, "Now look, *if* the LORD would make windows in heaven, could such a thing be?"

And he had said, "In fact, you shall see *it* with your eyes, but you shall not eat of it." 20 And so it happened to him, for the people trampled him in the gate, and he died.

The King Restores the Shunammite's Land

8 Then Elisha spoke to the woman [a]whose son he had restored to life, saying, "Arise and go, you and your household, and stay wherever you can; for the LORD [b]has called for a [c]famine, and furthermore, it will come upon the land for seven years." 2 So the woman arose and did according to the saying of the man of God, and she went with her household and dwelt in the land of the Philistines seven years.

3 *It came to pass, at the* end of seven years, that the woman returned from the land of the Philistines; and she went to make an appeal to the king for her house and for her land. 4 Then the king talked with [a]Gehazi, the servant of the man of God, saying, "Tell me, please, all the great things Elisha has done." 5 Now it happened, as he was telling the king how he had restored the dead to life, that there was the woman whose son he had [a]restored to life, appealing to the king for her house and for her land. And Gehazi said, "My lord, O king, this *is* the woman, and this *is* her son whom Elisha restored to life." 6 And when the king asked the woman, she told him.

So the king appointed a certain officer for her, saying, "Restore all that *was* hers, and all the proceeds of the field from the day that she left the land until now."

Death of Ben-Hadad

7 Then Elisha went to Damascus, and [a]Ben-Hadad king of Syria was sick; and it was told him, saying, "The man of God has come here." 8 And the king said to [a]Hazael, [b]"Take a present in your hand, and go to meet the man of God, and [c]inquire of the LORD by him, saying, 'Shall I recover from this disease?' " 9 So [a]Hazael went to meet him and took a present with him, of every good thing of Damascus, forty camel-loads; and he came and stood before him, and said, "Your son Ben-Hadad king of Syria has sent me to you, saying, 'Shall I recover from this disease?' "

10 And Elisha said to him, "Go, say to him, 'You shall certainly recover.' However the LORD has shown me that [a]he will really die." 11 Then he set his countenance in a stare until he was ashamed; and the man of God [a]wept. 12 And Hazael said, "Why is my lord weeping?"

He answered, "Because I know [a]the evil that you will do to the children of Israel: Their strongholds you will set on fire, and their young men you will kill with the sword; and you [b]will dash their children, and rip open their women with child."

13 So Hazael said, "But what [a]*is* your servant—a dog, that he should do this gross thing?"

And Elisha answered, [b]"The LORD has shown me that you *will become* king over Syria."

14 Then he departed from Elisha, and came to his master, who said to him, "What did Elisha say to you?" And he answered, "He told me you would surely recover." 15 But it happened on the next day that he took a thick cloth and dipped *it* in water, and spread *it* over his face so that he died; and Hazael reigned in his place.

7:12 [a] 2 Kin. 6:24–29 **7:16** [a] 2 Kin. 7:1 **7:17** [a] 2 Kin. 6:32; 7:2 **7:18** [a] 2 Kin. 7:1 **8:1** [a] 2 Kin. 4:18, 31–35 [b] Hag. 1:11 [c] 2 Sam. 21:1 **8:4** [a] 2 Kin. 4:12; 5:20–27 **8:5** [a] 2 Kin. 4:35 **8:7** [a] 2 Kin. 6:24 **8:8** [a] 1 Kin. 19:15 [b] 1 Sam. 9:7 [c] 2 Kin. 1:2 **8:9** [a] 1 Kin. 19:15 **8:10** [a] 2 Kin. 8:15 **8:11** [a] Luke 19:41 **8:12** [a] Amos 1:3, 4 [b] Hos. 13:16 **8:13** [a] 1 Sam. 17:43 [b] 1 Kin. 19:15

PEACE NOTE

The world praises success at
all costs. Jesus tells us that the
ministry of presence is about
not missing the opportunities in
the mundane to pass the peace.

Jehoram Reigns in Judah

16 Now [a]in the fifth year of Joram the son of
Ahab, king of Israel, Jehoshaphat *having been*
king of Judah, [b]Jehoram the son of Jehoshaphat began to reign as king of Judah. 17 He
was [a]thirty-two years old when he became
king, and he reigned eight years in Jerusalem. 18 And he walked in the way of the kings
of Israel, just as the house of Ahab had done,
for [a]the daughter of Ahab was his wife; and
he did evil in the sight of the LORD. 19 Yet the
LORD would not destroy Judah, for the sake
of His servant David, [a]as He promised him
to give a lamp to him *and* his sons forever.
20 In his days [a]Edom revolted against Judah's authority, [b]and made a king over themselves. 21 So Joram[1] went to Zair, and all his
chariots with him. Then he rose by night and
attacked the Edomites who had surrounded
him and the captains of the chariots; and the
troops fled to their tents. 22 Thus Edom has
been in revolt against Judah's authority to
this day. [a]And Libnah revolted at that time.
23 Now the rest of the acts of Joram, and
all that he did, *are* they not written in the
book of the chronicles of the kings of Judah?
24 So Joram rested with his fathers, and was
buried with his fathers in the City of David.
Then [a]Ahaziah his son reigned in his place.

Ahaziah Reigns in Judah

25 In the twelfth year of Joram the son of
Ahab, king of Israel, Ahaziah the son of Jehoram, king of Judah, began to reign. 26 Ahaziah
was [a]twenty-two years old when he became
king, and he reigned one year in Jerusalem.
His mother's name *was* Athaliah the granddaughter of Omri, king of Israel. 27 [a]And he
walked in the way of the house of Ahab, and
did evil in the sight of the LORD, like the
house of Ahab, for he *was* the son-in-law of
the house of Ahab.
28 Now he went [a]with Joram the son of
Ahab to war against Hazael king of Syria at
[b]Ramoth Gilead; and the Syrians wounded
Joram. 29 Then [a]King Joram went back to Jezreel to recover from the wounds which the
Syrians had inflicted on him at Ramah, when
he fought against Hazael king of Syria. [b]And
Ahaziah the son of Jehoram, king of Judah,
went down to see Joram the son of Ahab in
Jezreel, because he was sick.

Jehu Anointed King of Israel

9 And Elisha the prophet called one of [a]the
sons of the prophets, and said to him, [b]"Get
yourself ready, take this flask of oil in your
hand, [c]and go to Ramoth Gilead. 2 Now when
you arrive at that place, look there for Jehu
the son of Jehoshaphat, the son of Nimshi,
and go in and make him rise up from among
[a]his associates, and take him to an inner room.
3 Then [a]take the flask of oil, and pour *it* on his
head, and say, 'Thus says the LORD: "I have
anointed you king over Israel." ' Then open
the door and flee, and do not delay."
4 So the young man, the servant of the
prophet, went to Ramoth Gilead. 5 And when
he arrived, there *were* the captains of the
army sitting; and he said, "I have a message
for you, Commander."
Jehu said, "For which *one* of us?"
And he said, "For you, Commander." 6 Then
he arose and went into the house. And he
poured the oil on his head, and said to him,
[a]"Thus says the LORD God of Israel: 'I have
anointed you king over the people of the
LORD, over Israel. 7 You shall strike down
the house of Ahab your master, that I may
[a]avenge the blood of My servants the prophets, and the blood of all the servants of the
LORD, [b]at the hand of Jezebel. 8 For the whole
house of Ahab shall perish; and [a]I will cut
off from Ahab all [b]the males in Israel, both
[c]bond and free. 9 So I will make the house of
Ahab like the house of [a]Jeroboam the son
of Nebat, and like the house of [b]Baasha the
son of Ahijah. 10 [a]The dogs shall eat Jezebel
on the plot *of ground* at Jezreel, and *there
shall be* none to bury *her*.' " And he opened
the door and fled.

8:16 [a] 2 Kin. 1:17; 3:1 [b] 2 Chr. 21:3 **8:17** [a] 2 Chr. 21:5–10 **8:18** [a] 2 Kin. 8:26, 27 **8:19** [a] 2 Sam. 7:13 **8:20** [a] Gen. 27:40 [b] 1 Kin. 22:47 **8:21** [1] Spelled *Jehoram* in verse 16 **8:22** [a] Josh. 21:13 **8:24** [a] 2 Chr. 22:1, 7 **8:26** [a] 2 Chr. 22:2 **8:27** [a] 2 Chr. 22:3, 4 **8:28** [a] 2 Chr. 22:5 [b] 1 Kin. 22:3, 29 **8:29** [a] 2 Kin. 9:15 [b] 2 Chr. 22:6, 7 **9:1** [a] 1 Kin. 20:35 [b] 2 Kin. 4:29 [c] 2 Kin. 8:28, 29 **9:2** [a] 2 Kin. 9:5, 11 **9:3** [a] 1 Kin. 19:16 **9:6** [a] 2 Chr. 22:7 **9:7** [a] [Deut. 32:35, 41] [b] 1 Kin. 18:4; 21:15 **9:8** [a] 2 Kin. 10:17 [b] 1 Sam. 25:22 [c] Deut. 32:36 **9:9** [a] 1 Kin. 14:10; 15:29; 21:22 [b] 1 Kin. 16:3, 11 **9:10** [a] 1 Kin. 21:23

11 Then Jehu came out to the servants of
his master, and *one* said to him, "*Is* all well?
Why did [a]this madman come to you?"
And he said to them, "You know the man
and his babble."
12 And they said, "A lie! Tell us now."
So he said, "Thus and thus he spoke to me,
saying, 'Thus says the LORD: "I have anointed
you king over Israel." ' "
13 Then each man hastened [a]to take his
garment and put *it* under him on the top of
the steps; and they blew trumpets, saying,
"Jehu is king!"

Joram of Israel Killed

14 So Jehu the son of Jehoshaphat, the son
of Nimshi, conspired against [a]Joram. (Now
Joram had been defending Ramoth Gilead,
he and all Israel, against Hazael king of Syria.
15 But [a]King Joram had returned to Jezreel to
recover from the wounds which the Syrians
had inflicted on him when he fought with
Hazael king of Syria.) And Jehu said, "If you
are so minded, let no one leave *or* escape
from the city to go and tell *it* in Jezreel." 16 So
Jehu rode in a chariot and went to Jezreel,
for Joram was laid up there; [a]and Ahaziah
king of Judah had come down to see Joram.
17 Now a watchman stood on the tower in
Jezreel, and he saw the company of Jehu as
he came, and said, "I see a company of men."
And Joram said, "Get a horseman and
send him to meet them, and let him say, '*Is
it* peace?' "
18 So the horseman went to meet him, and
said, "Thus says the king: '*Is it* peace?' "
And Jehu said, "What have you to do with
peace? Turn around and follow me."
So the watchman reported, saying, "The messenger went to them, but is not coming back."
19 Then he sent out a second horseman
who came to them, and said, "Thus says the
king: '*Is it* peace?' "
And Jehu answered, "What have you to
do with peace? Turn around and follow me."
20 So the watchman reported, saying, "He
went up to them and is not coming back; and
the driving *is* like the driving of Jehu the son
of Nimshi, for he drives furiously!"
21 Then Joram said, "Make ready." And his
chariot was made ready. Then [a]Joram king of
Israel and Ahaziah king of Judah went out,
each in his chariot; and they went out to meet
Jehu, and met him [b]on the property of Naboth
the Jezreelite. 22 Now it happened, when Joram
saw Jehu, that he said, "*Is it* peace, Jehu?"
So he answered, "What peace, as long as
the harlotries of your mother Jezebel and
her witchcraft *are so* many?"
23 Then Joram turned around and fled, and
said to Ahaziah, "Treachery, Ahaziah!" 24 Now
Jehu drew his bow with full strength and shot
Jehoram between his arms; and the arrow
came out at his heart, and he sank down in
his chariot. 25 Then *Jehu* said to Bidkar his
captain, "Pick *him* up, *and* throw him into
the tract of the field of Naboth the Jezreelite;
for remember, when you and I were riding
together behind Ahab his father, that [a]the
LORD laid this [b]burden upon him: 26 'Surely
I saw yesterday the blood of Naboth and the
blood of his sons,' says the LORD, [a]'and I will
repay you in this plot,' says the LORD. Now
therefore, take *and* throw him on the plot *of
ground,* according to the word of the LORD."

Ahaziah of Judah Killed

27 But when Ahaziah king of Judah saw *this,*
he fled by the road to Beth Haggan.[1] So Jehu
pursued him, and said, "Shoot him also in the
chariot." *And they shot him* at the Ascent of Gur,
which is by Ibleam. Then he fled to [a]Megiddo,
and died there. 28 And his servants carried him
in the chariot to Jerusalem, and buried him in
his tomb with his fathers in the City of David.
29 In the eleventh year of Joram the son of
Ahab, Ahaziah had become king over Judah.

Jezebel's Violent Death

30 Now when Jehu had come to Jezreel,
Jezebel heard *of it;* [a]and she put paint on
her eyes and adorned her head, and looked
through a window. 31 Then, as Jehu entered
at the gate, she said, [a]"*Is it* peace, Zimri, murderer of your master?"
32 And he looked up at the window, and said,
"Who *is* on my side? Who?" So two *or* three eunuchs looked out at him. 33 Then he said, "Throw
her down." So they threw her down, and *some*
of her blood spattered on the wall and on the
horses; and he trampled her underfoot. 34 And
when he had gone in, he ate and drank. Then
he said, "Go now, see to this accursed *woman,*
and bury her, for [a]she was a king's daughter."
35 So they went to bury her, but they found no
more of her than the skull and the feet and the
palms of *her* hands. 36 Therefore they came back
and told him. And he said, "This *is* the word of
the LORD, which He spoke by His servant Elijah
the Tishbite, saying, [a]'On the plot *of ground* at
Jezreel dogs shall eat the flesh of Jezebel;[1] 37 and
the corpse of Jezebel shall be [a]as refuse on the
surface of the field, in the plot at Jezreel, so that
they shall not say, "Here *lies* Jezebel." ' "

9:11 [a] Jer. 29:26 **9:13** [a] Matt. 21:7, 8 **9:14** [a] 2 Kin. 8:28 **9:15** [a] 2 Kin. 8:29 **9:16** [a] 2 Kin. 8:29 **9:21** [a] 1 Kin. 19:17 [b] 1 Kin. 21:1–14 **9:25** [a] 1 Kin. 21:19, 24–29 [b] Is. 13:1 **9:26** [a] 1 Kin. 21:13, 19 **9:27** [a] 2 Chr. 22:7, 9 [1] Literally *The Garden House* **9:30** [a] Ezek. 23:40 **9:31** [a] 1 Kin. 16:9–20 **9:34** [a] 1 Kin. 16:31 **9:36** [a] 1 Kin. 21:23 [1] 1 Kings 21:23 **9:37** [a] Ps. 83:10

Ahab's Seventy Sons Killed

10 Now Ahab had seventy sons in Samaria.
And Jehu wrote and sent letters to Samaria, to the rulers of Jezreel,[1] to the elders,
and to those who reared Ahab's *sons,* saying:

2 Now as soon as this letter comes to
you, since your master's sons *are* with
you, and you have chariots and horses,
a fortified city also, and weapons,
3 choose the best qualified of your
master's sons, set *him* on his father's
throne, and fight for your master's
house.

4 But they were exceedingly afraid, and
said, "Look, [a]two kings could not stand up to
him; how then can we stand?" 5 And he who
was in charge of the house, and he who *was*
in charge of the city, the elders also, and those
who reared *the sons,* sent to Jehu, saying, "We
are your servants, we will do all you tell us;
but we will not make anyone king. Do *what is*
good in your sight." 6 Then he wrote a second
letter to them, saying:

If you *are* for me and will obey my
voice, take the heads of the men, your
master's sons, and come to me at
Jezreel by this time tomorrow.

Now the king's sons, seventy persons, *were*
with the great men of the city, *who* were rear-
ing them. 7 So it was, when the letter came
to them, that they took the king's sons and
[a]slaughtered seventy persons, put their heads
in baskets and sent *them* to him at Jezreel.
8 Then a messenger came and told him,
saying, "They have brought the heads of the
king's sons."
And he said, "Lay them in two heaps at the
entrance of the gate until morning."
9 So it was, in the morning, that he went
out and stood, and said to all the people, "You
are righteous. Indeed [a]I conspired against
my master and killed him; but who killed all
these? 10 Know now that nothing shall [a]fall to
the earth of the word of the LORD which the
LORD spoke concerning the house of Ahab;
for the LORD *has done what He spoke* [b]by
His servant Elijah." 11 So Jehu killed all who
remained of the house of Ahab in Jezreel,
and all his great men and his close acquaintances and his priests, until he left him none
remaining.

Ahaziah's Forty-two Brothers Killed

12 And he arose and departed and went
to Samaria. On the way, at Beth Eked[1] of the
Shepherds, 13 [a]Jehu met with the brothers
of Ahaziah king of Judah, and said, "Who
are you?"
So they answered, "We *are* the brothers
of Ahaziah; we have come down to greet the
sons of the king and the sons of the queen
mother."
14 And he said, "Take them alive!" So they
took them alive, and [a]killed them at the well
of Beth Eked, forty-two men; and he left none
of them.

The Rest of Ahab's Family Killed

15 Now when he departed from there, he
met [a]Jehonadab the son of [b]Rechab, *coming*
to meet him; and he greeted him and said
to him, "Is your heart right, as my heart *is*
toward your heart?"
And Jehonadab answered, "It is."
Jehu said, "If it is, [c]give *me* your hand."
So he gave *him* his hand, and he took him
up to him into the chariot. 16 Then he said,
"Come with me, and see my [a]zeal for the
LORD." So they had him ride in his chariot.
17 And when he came to Samaria, [a]he killed
all who remained to Ahab in Samaria, till he
had destroyed them, according to the word
of the LORD [b]which He spoke to Elijah.

Worshipers of Baal Killed

18 Then Jehu gathered all the people together, and said to them, [a]"Ahab served Baal
a little, Jehu will serve him much. 19 Now
therefore, call to me all the [a]prophets of
Baal, all his servants, and all his priests. Let
no one be missing, for I have a great sacrifice
for Baal. Whoever is missing shall not live."
But Jehu acted deceptively, with the intent
of destroying the worshipers of Baal. 20 And
Jehu said, "Proclaim a solemn assembly for
Baal." So they proclaimed *it.* 21 Then Jehu sent
throughout all Israel; and all the worshipers
of Baal came, so that there was not a man
left who did not come. So they came into
the temple[1] of Baal, and the [a]temple of Baal
was full from one end to the other. 22 And he
said to the one in charge of the wardrobe,
"Bring out vestments for all the worshipers
of Baal." So he brought out vestments for
them. 23 Then Jehu and Jehonadab the son
of Rechab went into the temple of Baal, and
said to the worshipers of Baal, "Search and

10:1 [1] Following Masoretic Text, Syriac, and Targum; Septuagint reads *Samaria;* Vulgate reads *city.* 10:4 [a] 2 Kin. 9:24, 27 10:7 [a] 1 Kin. 21:21 10:9 [a] 2 Kin. 9:14–24 10:10 [a] 1 Sam. 3:19 [b] 1 Kin. 21:17–24, 29 10:12 [1] Or *The Shearing House* 10:13 [a] 2 Chr. 22:8 10:14 [a] 2 Chr. 22:8 10:15 [a] Jer. 35:6 [b] 1 Chr. 2:55 [c] Ezra 10:19 10:16 [a] 1 Kin. 19:10 10:17 [a] 2 Kin. 9:8 [b] 1 Kin. 21:21, 29 10:18 [a] 1 Kin. 16:31, 32 10:19 [a] 1 Kin. 18:19; 22:6 10:21 [a] 1 Kin. 16:32 [1] Literally *house,* and so elsewhere in this chapter

see that no servants of the LORD are here with you, but only the worshipers of Baal." 24 So they went in to offer sacrifices and burnt offerings. Now Jehu had appointed for himself eighty men on the outside, and had said, "*If* any of the men whom I have brought into your hands escapes, *whoever lets him escape, it shall be* [a]his life for the life of the other."

25 Now it happened, as soon as he had made an end of offering the burnt offering, that Jehu said to the guard and to the captains, "Go in *and* kill them; let no one come out!" And they killed them with the edge of the sword; then the guards and the officers threw *them* out, and went into the inner room of the temple of Baal. 26 And they brought the [a]*sacred* pillars out of the temple of Baal and burned them. 27 Then they broke down the *sacred* pillar of Baal, and tore down the temple of Baal and [a]made it a refuse dump to this day. 28 Thus Jehu destroyed Baal from Israel.

29 However Jehu did not turn away from the sins of Jeroboam the son of Nebat, who had made Israel sin, *that is,* from [a]the golden calves that *were* at Bethel and Dan. 30 And the LORD [a]said to Jehu, "Because you have done well in doing *what is* right in My sight, *and* have done to the house of Ahab all that *was* in My heart, [b]your sons shall sit on the throne of Israel to the fourth *generation.*" 31 But Jehu took no heed to walk in the law of the LORD God of Israel with all his heart; for he did not depart from [a]the sins of Jeroboam, who had made Israel sin.

Death of Jehu

32 In those days the LORD began to cut off *parts* of Israel; and [a]Hazael conquered them in all the territory of Israel 33 from the Jordan eastward: all the land of Gilead—Gad, Reuben, and Manasseh—from [a]Aroer, which *is* by the River Arnon, including [b]Gilead and Bashan.

34 Now the rest of the acts of Jehu, all that he did, and all his might, *are* they not written in the book of the chronicles of the kings of Israel? 35 So Jehu rested with his fathers, and they buried him in Samaria. Then [a]Jehoahaz his son reigned in his place. 36 And the period that Jehu reigned over Israel in Samaria *was* twenty-eight years.

Athaliah Reigns in Judah

11 When [a]Athaliah [b]the mother of Ahaziah saw that her son was [c]dead, she arose and destroyed all the royal heirs. 2 But Jehosheba, the daughter of King Joram, sister of [a]Ahaziah, took Joash the son of Ahaziah, and stole him away from among the king's sons *who were* being murdered; and they hid him and his nurse in the bedroom, from Athaliah, so that he was not killed. 3 So he was hidden with her in the house of the LORD for six years, while Athaliah reigned over the land.

Joash Crowned King of Judah

4 In [a]the seventh year Jehoiada sent and brought the captains of hundreds—of the bodyguards and the escorts—and brought them into the house of the LORD to him. And he made a covenant with them and took an oath from them in the house of the LORD, and showed them the king's son. 5 Then he commanded them, saying, "This *is* what you shall do: One-third of you who come on duty [a]on the Sabbath shall be keeping watch over the king's house, 6 one-third *shall be* at the gate of Sur, and one-third at the gate behind the escorts. You shall keep the watch of the house, lest it be broken down. 7 The two contingents of you who go off duty on the Sabbath shall keep the watch of the house of the LORD for the king. 8 But you shall surround the king on all sides, every man with his weapons in his hand; and whoever comes within range, let him be put to death. You are to be with the king as he goes out and as he comes in."

9 [a]So the captains of the hundreds did according to all that Jehoiada the priest commanded. Each of them took his men who were to be on duty on the Sabbath, with those who were going off duty on the Sabbath, and came to Jehoiada the priest. 10 And the priest gave the captains of hundreds the spears and shields which *had belonged* to King David, [a]that were in the temple of the LORD. 11 Then the escorts stood, every man with his weapons in his hand, all around the king, from the right side of the temple to the left side of the temple, by the altar and the house. 12 And he brought out the king's son, put the crown on him, and *gave him* the [a]Testimony;[1] they made him king and anointed him, and they clapped their hands and said, [b]"Long live the king!"

Death of Athaliah

13 [a]Now when Athaliah heard the noise of the escorts *and* the people, she came to the people *in* the temple of the LORD. 14 When she looked, there was the king standing by [a]a pillar according to custom; and the leaders

10:24 [a] 1 Kin. 20:39 **10:26** [a] [Deut. 7:5, 25] **10:27** [a] Ezra 6:11 **10:29** [a] 1 Kin. 12:28–30; 13:33, 34 **10:30** [a] 2 Kin. 9:6, 7 [b] 2 Kin. 13:1, 10; 14:23; 15:8, 12 **10:31** [a] 1 Kin. 14:16 **10:32** [a] 2 Kin. 8:12; 13:22 **10:33** [a] Deut. 2:36 [b] Amos 1:3–5 **10:35** [a] 2 Kin. 13:1 **11:1** [a] 2 Chr. 22:10 [b] 2 Kin. 8:26 [c] 2 Kin. 9:27 **11:2** [a] 2 Kin. 8:25 **11:4** [a] 2 Chr. 23:1 **11:5** [a] 1 Chr. 9:25 **11:9** [a] 2 Chr. 23:8 **11:10** [a] 2 Sam. 8:7 **11:12** [a] Ex. 25:16; 31:18 [b] 1 Sam. 10:24 [1] That is, the Law (compare Exodus 25:16, 21 and Deuteronomy 31:9) **11:13** [a] 2 Chr. 23:12 **11:14** [a] 2 Chr. 34:31

and the trumpeters were by the king. All the
people of the land were rejoicing and blowing
trumpets. So Athaliah tore her clothes and
cried out, "Treason! Treason!"
15 And Jehoiada the priest commanded the
captains of the hundreds, the officers of the
army, and said to them, "Take her outside under guard, and slay with the sword whoever
follows her." For the priest had said, "Do not
let her be killed in the house of the LORD."
16 So they seized her; and she went by way of
the horses' entrance *into* the king's house,
and there she was killed.
17 [a]Then Jehoiada [b]made a covenant between
the LORD, the king, and the people, that they
should be the LORD's people, and *also* [c]between
the king and the people. 18 And all the people
of the land went to the [a]temple of Baal, and
tore it down. They thoroughly [b]broke in pieces
its altars and images, and [c]killed Mattan the
priest of Baal before the altars. And [d]the priest
appointed officers over the house of the LORD.
19 Then he took the captains of hundreds, the
bodyguards, the escorts, and all the people
of the land; and they brought the king down
from the house of the LORD, and went by way
of the gate of the escorts to the king's house.
Then he sat on the throne of the kings. 20 So
all the people of the land rejoiced; and the
city was quiet, for they had slain Athaliah with
the sword *in* the king's house. 21 Jehoash *was*
[a]seven years old when he became king.

Jehoash Repairs the Temple

12 In the seventh year of Jehu, [a]Jeho-
ash[1] became king, and he reigned forty
years in Jerusalem. His mother's name *was*
Zibiah of Beersheba. 2 Jehoash did *what was*
right in the sight of the LORD all the days in
which [a]Jehoiada the priest instructed him.
3 But [a]the high places were not taken away;
the people still sacrificed and burned incense
on the high places.
4 And Jehoash said to the priests, [a]"All the
money of the dedicated gifts that are brought
into the house of the LORD—each man's
[b]census money, each man's [c]assessment
money[1]—*and* all the money that a man [d]pur-
poses in his heart to bring into the house of
the LORD, 5 let the priests take *it* themselves,
each from his constituency; and let them
repair the damages of the temple, wherever
any dilapidation is found."
6 Now it was so, by the twenty-third year of
King Jehoash, [a]*that* the priests had not repaired
the damages of the temple. 7 [a]So King Jehoash
called Jehoiada the priest and the *other* priests,
and said to them, "Why have you not repaired
the damages of the temple? Now therefore, do
not take *more* money from your constituency,
but deliver it for repairing the damages of the
temple." 8 And the priests agreed that they
would neither receive *more* money from the
people, nor repair the damages of the temple.
9 Then Jehoiada the priest took [a]a chest,

11:17 [a] 2 Chr. 23:16 [b] Josh. 24:24, 25 [c] 2 Sam. 5:3 **11:18** [a] 2 Kin. 10:26, 27 [b] [Deut. 12:3] [c] 1 Kin. 18:40 [d] 2 Chr. 23:18 **11:21** [a] 2 Chr. 24:1–14 **12:1** [a] 2 Chr. 24:1 [1] Spelled *Joash* in 11:2ff **12:2** [a] 2 Kin. 11:4 **12:3** [a] 2 Kin. 14:4; 15:35 **12:4** [a] 2 Kin. 22:4 [b] Ex. 30:13–16 [c] Lev. 27:2–28 [d] Ex. 35:5 [1] Compare Leviticus 27:2ff **12:6** [a] 2 Chr. 24:5 **12:7** [a] 2 Chr. 24:6 **12:9** [a] 2 Chr. 23:1; 24:8

PERSIST TOWARD PEACE

Jehoash said to the priests, "All the money of the dedicated gifts . . . let the priests take it themselves, each from his constituency; and let them repair the damages of the temple."

2 KINGS 12:4-5

Jehoash became king of Judah at the age of seven (ninth century BC). He ordered the priests to collect money to repair Solomon's famous temple that in recent years had suffered neglect. The priests were reluctant to comply (and perhaps embezzling some of the funds), but the young king was persistent and in time the temple was repaired.

One has to admire the young king's tenacity as well as his devotion to God. The biblical narrative doesn't say so explicitly, but we should assume that there was some tension, perhaps even conflict, between the king and the priests. Nevertheless the king persisted and succeeded. Only doing right, in spite of conflict, will result in peace.

Where has conflict in your life kept peace at bay? Sometimes we must act boldly to live in the peace of God. Would some persistence on your part change the trajectory and give God glory?

bored a hole in its lid, and set it beside the
altar, on the right side as one comes into the
house of the LORD; and the priests who kept
the door put [b]there all the money brought
into the house of the LORD. 10 So it was, whenever they saw that *there was* much money
in the chest, that the king's [a]scribe and the
high priest came up and put it in bags, and
counted the money that was found in the
house of the LORD. 11 Then they gave the
money, which had been apportioned, into
the hands of those who did the work, who
had the oversight of the house of the LORD;
and they paid it out to the carpenters and
builders who worked on the house of the
LORD, 12 and to masons and stonecutters,
and for buying timber and hewn stone, to
[a]repair the damage of the house of the LORD,
and for all that was paid out to repair the
temple. 13 However [a]there were not made
for the house of the LORD basins of silver,
trimmers, sprinkling-bowls, trumpets, any
articles of gold or articles of silver, from the
money brought into the house of the LORD.
14 But they gave that to the workmen, and
they repaired the house of the LORD with it.
15 Moreover [a]they did not require an account
from the men into whose hand they delivered the money to be paid to workmen, for
they dealt faithfully. 16 [a]The money from the
trespass offerings and the money from the
sin offerings was not brought into the house
of the LORD. [b]It belonged to the priests.

Hazael Threatens Jerusalem

17 [a]Hazael king of Syria went up and fought
against Gath, and took it; then [b]Hazael set
his face to go up to Jerusalem. 18 And Jehoash king of Judah [a]took all the sacred things
that his fathers, Jehoshaphat and Jehoram
and Ahaziah, kings of Judah, had dedicated,
and his own sacred things, and all the gold
found in the treasuries of the house of the
LORD and in the king's house, and sent *them*
to Hazael king of Syria. Then he went away
from Jerusalem.

Death of Joash

19 Now the rest of the acts of Joash,[1] and all
that he did, *are* they not written in the book
of the chronicles of the kings of Judah?
20 And [a]his servants arose and formed a
conspiracy, and killed Joash in the house
of the Millo,[1] which goes down to Silla. 21 For
Jozachar[1] the son of Shimeath and Jehozabad the son of Shomer,[2] his servants, struck
him. So he died, and they buried him with his
fathers in the City of David. Then [a]Amaziah
his son reigned in his place.

Jehoahaz Reigns in Israel

13 In the twenty-third year of [a]Joash[1] the
son of Ahaziah, king of Judah, [b]Jehoa-
haz the son of Jehu became king over Israel
in Samaria, *and reigned* seventeen years.
2 And he did evil in the sight of the LORD,
and followed the [a]sins of Jeroboam the son
of Nebat, who had made Israel sin. He did
not depart from them.
3 Then [a]the anger of the LORD was aroused
against Israel, and He delivered them into the
hand of [b]Hazael king of Syria, and into the
hand of [c]Ben-Hadad the son of Hazael, all *their*
days. 4 So Jehoahaz [a]pleaded with the LORD,
and the LORD listened to him; for [b]He saw the
oppression of Israel, because the king of Syria
oppressed them. 5 [a]Then the LORD gave Israel
a deliverer, so that they escaped from under
the hand of the Syrians; and the children of
Israel dwelt in their tents as before. 6 Nevertheless they did not depart from the sins of the
house of Jeroboam, who had made Israel sin,
but walked in them; [a]and the wooden image[1]
also remained in Samaria. 7 For He left of the
army of Jehoahaz only fifty horsemen, ten
chariots, and ten thousand foot soldiers; for
the king of Syria had destroyed them [a]and
made them [b]like the dust at threshing.
8 Now the rest of the acts of Jehoahaz, all
that he did, and his might, *are* they not written
in the book of the chronicles of the kings of
Israel? 9 So Jehoahaz rested with his fathers,
and they buried him in Samaria. Then Joash
his son reigned in his place.

Jehoash Reigns in Israel

10 In the thirty-seventh year of Joash king
of Judah, Jehoash[1] the son of Jehoahaz became king over Israel in Samaria, *and reigned*
sixteen years. 11 And he did evil in the sight
of the LORD. He did not depart from all the
sins of Jeroboam the son of Nebat, who made
Israel sin, *but* walked in them.
12 [a]Now the rest of the acts of Joash, [b]all that
he did, and [c]his might with which he fought
against Amaziah king of Judah, *are* they not

12:9 [b] Mark 12:41 **12:10** [a] 2 Sam. 8:17 **12:12** [a] 2 Kin. 22:5, 6 **12:13** [a] 2 Chr. 24:14 **12:15** [a] 2 Kin. 22:7 **12:16** [a] [Lev. 5:15, 18] [b] [Num. 18:9] **12:17** [a] 2 Kin. 8:12 [b] 2 Chr. 24:23 **12:18** [a] 1 Kin. 15:18 **12:19** [1] Spelled *Jehoash* in 12:1ff **12:20** [a] 2 Kin. 14:5 [1] Literally *The Landfill* **12:21** [a] 2 Chr. 24:27 [1] Called *Zabad* in 2 Chronicles 24:26 [2] Called *Shimrith* in 2 Chronicles 24:26 **13:1** [a] 2 Kin. 12:1 [b] 2 Kin. 10:35 [1] Spelled *Jehoash* in 12:1ff **13:2** [a] 1 Kin. 12:26–33 **13:3** [a] Judg. 2:14 [b] 2 Kin. 8:12 [c] Amos 1:4 **13:4** [a] [Ps. 78:34] [b] [Ex. 3:7, 9] **13:5** [a] 2 Kin. 13:25; 14:25, 27 **13:6** [a] 1 Kin. 16:33 [1] Hebrew *Asherah,* a Canaanite goddess **13:7** [a] 2 Kin. 10:32 [b] [Amos 1:3] **13:10** [1] Spelled *Joash* in verse 9 **13:12** [a] 2 Kin. 14:8–15 [b] 2 Kin. 13:14–19, 25 [c] 2 Kin. 14:9

written in the book of the chronicles of the kings of Israel? 13 So Joash [a]rested with his fathers. Then Jeroboam sat on his throne. And Joash was buried in Samaria with the kings of Israel.

Death of Elisha

14 Elisha had become sick with the illness of which he would die. Then Joash the king of Israel came down to him, and wept over his face, and said, "O my father, my father, [a]the chariots of Israel and their horsemen!"

15 And Elisha said to him, "Take a bow and some arrows." So he took himself a bow and some arrows. 16 Then he said to the king of Israel, "Put your hand on the bow." So he put his hand *on it,* and Elisha put his hands on the king's hands. 17 And he said, "Open the east window"; and he opened *it.* Then Elisha said, "Shoot"; and he shot. And he said, "The arrow of the LORD's deliverance and the arrow of deliverance from Syria; for you must strike the Syrians at [a]Aphek till you have destroyed *them.*" 18 Then he said, "Take the arrows"; so he took *them.* And he said to the king of Israel, "Strike the ground"; so he struck three times, and stopped. 19 And the man of God was angry with him, and said, "You should have struck five or six times; then you would have struck Syria till you had destroyed *it!* [a]But now you will strike Syria *only* three times."

20 Then Elisha died, and they buried him. And the [a]*raiding* bands from Moab invaded the land in the spring of the year. 21 So it was, as they were burying a man, that suddenly they spied a band *of raiders;* and they put the man in the tomb of Elisha; and when the man was let down and touched the bones of Elisha, he revived and stood on his feet.

Israel Recaptures Cities from Syria

22 And [a]Hazael king of Syria oppressed Israel all the days of Jehoahaz. 23 But the LORD was [a]gracious to them, had compassion on them, and [b]regarded them, [c]because of His covenant with Abraham, Isaac, and Jacob, and would not yet destroy them or cast them from His presence.

24 Now Hazael king of Syria died. Then Ben-Hadad his son reigned in his place. 25 And Jehoash[1] the son of Jehoahaz recaptured from the hand of Ben-Hadad, the son of Hazael, the cities which he had taken out of the hand of Jehoahaz his father by war. [a]Three times Joash defeated him and recaptured the cities of Israel.

Amaziah Reigns in Judah

14 In [a]the second year of Joash the son of Jehoahaz, king of Israel, [b]Amaziah the son of Joash, king of Judah, became king. 2 He was twenty-five years old when he became king, and he reigned twenty-nine years in Jerusalem. His mother's name was Jehoaddan of Jerusalem. 3 And he did *what was* right in the sight of the LORD, yet not like his father David; he did everything [a]as his father Joash had done. 4 [a]However the high places were not taken away, and the people still sacrificed and burned incense on the high places.

5 Now it happened, as soon as the kingdom was established in his hand, that he executed his servants [a]who had murdered his father the king. 6 But the children of the murderers he did not execute, according to what is written in the Book of the Law of Moses, in which the LORD commanded, saying, [a]"Fathers shall not be put to death for their children, nor shall children be put to death for their fathers; but a person shall be put to death for his own sin."[1]

7 [a]He killed ten thousand Edomites in [b]the Valley of Salt, and took Sela by war, [c]and called its name Joktheel to this day.

8 [a]Then Amaziah sent messengers to Jehoash[1] the son of Jehoahaz, the son of Jehu, king of Israel, saying, "Come, let us face one another *in battle.*" 9 And Jehoash king of Israel sent to Amaziah king of Judah, saying, [a]"The thistle that *was* in Lebanon sent to the [b]cedar that *was* in Lebanon, saying, 'Give your daughter to my son as wife'; and a wild beast that *was* in Lebanon passed by and trampled

PEACE NOTE

We have to resist the busyness that pulls us from the unscheduled moments to be the presence of Jesus for others. And then we'll experience His peace and power in fresh ways.

13:13 [a] 2 Kin. 14:16 **13:14** [a] 2 Kin. 2:12 **13:17** [a] 1 Kin. 20:26 **13:19** [a] 2 Kin. 13:25 **13:20** [a] 2 Kin. 3:5; 24:2 **13:22** [a] 2 Kin. 8:12, 13 **13:23** [a] 2 Kin. 14:27 [b] [Ex. 2:24, 25] [c] Ex. 32:13 **13:25** [a] 2 Kin. 13:18, 19 [1] Spelled *Joash* in verses 12–14, 25 **14:1** [a] 2 Kin. 13:10 [b] 2 Chr. 25:1, 2 **14:3** [a] 2 Kin. 12:2 **14:4** [a] 2 Kin. 12:3 **14:5** [a] 2 Kin. 12:20 **14:6** [a] [Ezek. 18:4, 20] [1] Deuteronomy 24:16 **14:7** [a] 2 Chr. 25:5–16 [b] 2 Sam. 8:13 [c] Josh. 15:38 **14:8** [a] 2 Chr. 25:17, 18 [1] Spelled *Joash* in 13:12ff and 2 Chronicles 25:17ff **14:9** [a] Judg. 9:8–15 [b] 1 Kin. 4:33

the thistle. 10 You have indeed defeated Edom,
and [a]your heart has lifted you up. Glory *in
that,* and stay at home; for why should you
meddle with trouble so that you fall—you
and Judah with you?"

11 But Amaziah would not heed. Therefore
Jehoash king of Israel went out; so he and
Amaziah king of Judah faced one another at
[a]Beth Shemesh, which *belongs* to Judah. 12 And
Judah was defeated by Israel, and every man
fled to his tent. 13 Then Jehoash king of Israel
captured Amaziah king of Judah, the son of
Jehoash, the son of Ahaziah, at Beth Shemesh;
and he went to Jerusalem, and broke
down the wall of Jerusalem from [a]the Gate of
Ephraim to [b]the Corner Gate—four hundred
cubits. 14 And he took all [a]the gold and silver,
all the articles that were found in the house
of the LORD and in the treasuries of the king's
house, and hostages, and returned to Samaria.

15 [a]Now the rest of the acts of Jehoash which
he did—his might, and how he fought with
Amaziah king of Judah—*are* they not written
in the book of the chronicles of the kings of Israel?
16 So Jehoash rested with his fathers, and
was buried in Samaria with the kings of Israel.
Then Jeroboam his son reigned in his place.

17 [a]Amaziah the son of Joash, king of Judah,
lived fifteen years after the death of Jehoash
the son of Jehoahaz, king of Israel. 18 Now the
rest of the acts of Amaziah, *are* they not written
in the book of the chronicles of the kings
of Judah? 19 And [a]they formed a conspiracy
against him in Jerusalem, and he fled to [b]Lachish;
but they sent after him to Lachish and
killed him there. 20 Then they brought him
on horses, and he was buried at Jerusalem
with his fathers in the City of David.

21 And all the people of Judah took [a]Azariah,[1]
who *was* sixteen years old, and made
him king instead of his father Amaziah. 22 He
built [a]Elath and restored it to Judah, after the
king rested with his fathers.

Jeroboam II Reigns in Israel

23 In the fifteenth year of Amaziah the son
of Joash, king of Judah, Jeroboam the son
of Joash, king of Israel, became king in Samaria,
and reigned forty-one years. 24 And
he did evil in the sight of the LORD; he did
not depart from all the [a]sins of Jeroboam
the son of Nebat, who had made Israel sin.
25 He [a]restored the territory of Israel [b]from
the entrance of Hamath to [c]the Sea of the
Arabah, according to the word of the LORD
God of Israel, which He had spoken through
His servant [d]Jonah the son of Amittai, the
prophet who *was* from [e]Gath Hepher. 26 For
the LORD [a]saw *that* the affliction of Israel *was*
very bitter; and whether bond or free, [b]there
was no helper for Israel. 27 [a]And the LORD did
not say that He would blot out the name of
Israel from under heaven; but He saved them
by the hand of Jeroboam the son of Joash.

28 Now the rest of the acts of Jeroboam, and
all that he did—his might, how he made war,
and how he recaptured for Israel, from [a]Damascus
and Hamath, [b]*what had belonged* to
Judah—*are* they not written in the book of the
chronicles of the kings of Israel? 29 So Jeroboam
rested with his fathers, the kings of Israel.
Then [a]Zechariah his son reigned in his place.

Azariah Reigns in Judah

15 In the twenty-seventh year of Jeroboam
king of Israel, [a]Azariah the son of Amaziah,
king of Judah, [b]became king. 2 He was
sixteen years old when he became king, and
he reigned fifty-two years in Jerusalem. His
mother's name *was* Jecholiah of Jerusalem.
3 And he did *what was* right in the sight of the
LORD, according to all that his father Amaziah
had done, 4 [a]except that the high places were
not removed; the people still sacrificed and
burned incense on the high places. 5 Then
the LORD [a]struck the king, so that he was a
leper until the day of his [b]death; so he [c]dwelt
in an isolated house. And Jotham the king's
son *was* over the *royal* house, judging the
people of the land.

6 Now the rest of the acts of Azariah, and all
that he did, *are* they not written in the book
of the chronicles of the kings of Judah? 7 So
Azariah rested with his fathers, and [a]they
buried him with his fathers in the City of David.
Then Jotham his son reigned in his place.

Zechariah Reigns in Israel

8 In the thirty-eighth year of Azariah king
of Judah, [a]Zechariah the son of Jeroboam
reigned over Israel in Samaria six months.
9 And he did evil in the sight of the LORD, [a]as
his fathers had done; he did not depart from
the sins of Jeroboam the son of Nebat, who
had made Israel sin. 10 Then Shallum the son
of Jabesh conspired against him, and [a]struck
and killed him in front of the people; and he
reigned in his place.

14:10 [a] Deut. 8:14 **14:11** [a] Josh. 19:38; 21:16 **14:13** [a] Neh. 8:16; 12:39 [b] Jer. 31:38 **14:14** [a] 1 Kin. 7:51 **14:15** [a] 2 Kin. 13:12, 13 **14:17** [a] 2 Chr. 25:25–28 **14:19** [a] 2 Chr. 25:27 [b] Josh. 10:31 **14:21** [a] 2 Kin. 15:13 [1] Called *Uzziah* in 2 Chronicles 26:1ff, Isaiah 6:1, and elsewhere **14:22** [a] 2 Kin. 16:6 **14:24** [a] 1 Kin. 12:26–33 **14:25** [a] 2 Kin. 10:32; 13:5, 25 [b] 1 Kin. 8:65 [c] Deut. 3:17 [d] Jon. 1:1 [e] Josh. 19:13 **14:26** [a] 2 Kin. 13:4 [b] Deut. 32:36 **14:27** [a] [2 Kin. 13:5, 23] **14:28** [a] 1 Kin. 11:24 [b] 2 Chr. 8:3 **14:29** [a] 2 Kin. 15:8 **15:1** [a] 2 Kin. 15:13, 30 [b] 2 Kin. 14:21 **15:4** [a] 2 Kin. 12:3; 14:4; 15:35 **15:5** [a] 2 Chr. 26:19–23 [b] Is. 6:1 [c] [Lev. 13:46] **15:7** [a] 2 Chr. 26:23 **15:8** [a] 2 Kin. 14:29 **15:9** [a] 2 Kin. 14:24 **15:10** [a] Amos 7:9

11 Now the rest of the acts of Zechariah,
indeed they *are* written in the book of the
chronicles of the kings of Israel.
12 This *was* the word of the LORD which He
spoke to Jehu, saying, [a]"Your sons shall sit on
the throne of Israel to the fourth *generation*."[1]
And so it was.

Shallum Reigns in Israel

13 Shallum the son of Jabesh became king
in the thirty-ninth year of Uzziah[1] king of
Judah; and he reigned a full month in Samaria. 14 For Menahem the son of Gadi went
up from [a]Tirzah, came to Samaria, and struck
Shallum the son of Jabesh in Samaria and
killed him; and he reigned in his place.
15 Now the rest of the acts of Shallum, and
the conspiracy which he led, indeed they *are*
written in the book of the chronicles of the
kings of Israel. 16 Then from Tirzah, Menahem
attacked [a]Tiphsah, all who *were* there, and
its territory. Because they did not surrender,
therefore he attacked *it*. All [b]the women there
who were with child he ripped open.

Menahem Reigns in Israel

17 In the thirty-ninth year of Azariah king
of Judah, Menahem the son of Gadi became
king over Israel, *and reigned* ten years in Samaria. 18 And he did evil in the sight of the
LORD; he did not depart all his days from
the sins of Jeroboam the son of Nebat, who
had made Israel sin. 19 [a]Pul[1] king of Assyria
came against the land; and Menahem gave
Pul a thousand talents of silver, that his hand
might be with him to [b]strengthen the kingdom under his control. 20 And Menahem
[a]exacted the money from Israel, from all the
very wealthy, from each man fifty shekels of
silver, to give to the king of Assyria. So the
king of Assyria turned back, and did not stay
there in the land.
21 Now the rest of the acts of Menahem,
and all that he did, *are* they not written in the
book of the chronicles of the kings of Israel?
22 So Menahem rested with his fathers. Then
Pekahiah his son reigned in his place.

Pekahiah Reigns in Israel

23 In the fiftieth year of Azariah king
of Judah, Pekahiah the son of Menahem
became king over Israel in Samaria, *and
reigned* two years. 24 And he did evil in the
sight of the LORD; he did not depart from
the sins of Jeroboam the son of Nebat, who
had made Israel sin. 25 Then Pekah the son
of Remaliah, an officer of his, conspired
against him and killed him in Samaria, in
the [a]citadel of the king's house, along with
Argob and Arieh; and with him were fifty
men of Gilead. He killed him and reigned
in his place.
26 Now the rest of the acts of Pekahiah, and
all that he did, indeed they *are* written in the
book of the chronicles of the kings of Israel.

Pekah Reigns in Israel

27 In the fifty-second year of Azariah king
of Judah, [a]Pekah the son of Remaliah became king over Israel in Samaria, *and reigned*
twenty years. 28 And he did evil in the sight of
the LORD; he did not depart from the sins of
Jeroboam the son of Nebat, who had made
Israel sin. 29 In the days of Pekah king of Israel, Tiglath-Pileser king of Assyria [a]came
and took [b]Ijon, Abel Beth Maachah, Jano-
ah, Kedesh, Hazor, Gilead, and Galilee, all
the land of Naphtali; and he [c]carried them
captive to Assyria. 30 Then Hoshea the son
of Elah led a conspiracy against Pekah the
son of Remaliah, and struck and killed him;
so he [a]reigned in his place in the twentieth
year of Jotham the son of Uzziah.
31 Now the rest of the acts of Pekah, and all
that he did, indeed they *are* written in the
book of the chronicles of the kings of Israel.

Jotham Reigns in Judah

32 In the second year of Pekah the son of
Remaliah, king of Israel, [a]Jotham the son
of Uzziah, king of Judah, began to reign.
33 He was twenty-five years old when he became king, and he reigned sixteen years in
Jerusalem. His mother's name *was* Jerusha[1] the daughter of Zadok. 34 And he did
what was right in the sight of the LORD; he
did [a]according to all that his father Uzziah
had done. 35 [a]However the high places were
not removed; the people still sacrificed and
burned incense on the high places. [b]He built
the Upper Gate of the house of the LORD.
36 Now the rest of the acts of Jotham, and all
that he did, *are* they not written in the book
of the chronicles of the kings of Judah? 37 In
those days the LORD began to send [a]Rezin
king of Syria and [b]Pekah the son of Remaliah against Judah. 38 So Jotham rested with
his fathers, and was buried with his fathers
in the City of David his father. Then Ahaz his
son reigned in his place.

15:12 [a] 2 Kin. 10:30 [1] 2 Kings 10:30 **15:13** [1] Called *Azariah* in 14:21ff and 15:1ff **15:14** [a] 1 Kin. 14:17 **15:16** [a] 1 Kin. 4:24 [b] 2 Kin. 8:12 **15:19** [a] Hos. 8:9 [b] 2 Kin. 14:5 [1] That is, Tiglath-Pileser III (compare verse 29) **15:20** [a] 2 Kin. 23:35 **15:25** [a] 1 Kin. 16:18 **15:27** [a] Is. 7:1 **15:29** [a] 1 Chr. 5:26 [b] 1 Kin. 15:20 [c] 2 Kin. 17:6 **15:30** [a] [Hos. 10:3, 7, 15] **15:32** [a] 2 Chr. 27:1 **15:33** [1] Spelled *Jerushah* in 2 Chronicles 27:1 **15:34** [a] 2 Kin. 15:3, 4 **15:35** [a] 2 Kin. 15:4 [b] 2 Chr. 23:20; 27:3 **15:37** [a] 2 Kin. 16:5–9 [b] 2 Kin. 15:26, 27

Ahaz Reigns in Judah

16 In the seventeenth year of Pekah the
son of Remaliah, Ahaz the son of Jotham, king of Judah, began to reign. 2 Ahaz
was twenty years old when he became king,
and he reigned sixteen years in Jerusalem;
and he did not do *what was* right in the sight
of the LORD his God, as his father David *had*
done. 3 But he walked in the way of the kings of
Israel; indeed [a]he made his son pass through
the fire, according to the [b]abominations of the
nations whom the LORD had cast out from before the children of Israel. 4 And he sacrificed
and burned incense on the [a]high places, [b]on
the hills, and under every green tree.
5 [a]Then Rezin king of Syria and Pekah the
son of Remaliah, king of Israel, came up to
Jerusalem to *make* war; and they besieged
Ahaz but could not overcome *him.* 6 At that
time Rezin king of Syria [a]captured Elath
for Syria, and drove the men of Judah from
Elath. Then the Edomites[1] went to Elath, and
dwell there to this day.
7 So Ahaz sent messengers to [a]Tiglath-
Pileser king of Assyria, saying, "I *am* your servant and your son. Come up and save me from
the hand of the king of Syria and from the hand
of the king of Israel, who rise up against me."
8 And Ahaz [a]took the silver and gold that was
found in the house of the LORD, and in the
treasuries of the king's house, and sent *it as*
a present to the king of Assyria. 9 So the king
of Assyria heeded him; for the king of Assyria
went up against [a]Damascus and [b]took it, carried
its people captive to [c]Kir, and killed Rezin.
10 Now King Ahaz went to Damascus to
meet Tiglath-Pileser king of Assyria, and
saw an altar that *was* at Damascus; and King
Ahaz sent to Urijah the priest the design of
the altar and its pattern, according to all its
workmanship. 11 Then [a]Urijah the priest built
an altar according to all that King Ahaz had
sent from Damascus. So Urijah the priest
made *it* before King Ahaz came back from
Damascus. 12 And when the king came back
from Damascus, the king saw the altar; and
[a]the king approached the altar and made
offerings on it. 13 So he burned his burnt offering and his grain offering; and he poured
his drink offering and sprinkled the blood
of his peace offerings on the altar. 14 He also
brought [a]the bronze altar which *was* before
the LORD, from the front of the temple—from
between the *new* altar and the house of the
LORD—*and put it on the north* side of the
new altar. 15 Then King Ahaz commanded
Urijah the priest, saying, "On the great *new*
altar burn [a]the morning burnt offering, the
evening grain offering, the king's burnt sacrifice, and his grain offering, with the burnt
offering of all the people of the land, their
grain offering, and their drink offerings;
and sprinkle on it all the blood of the burnt
offering and all the blood of the sacrifice. And
the bronze altar shall be for me to inquire
by." 16 Thus did Urijah the priest, according
to all that King Ahaz commanded.
17 [a]And King Ahaz cut off [b]the panels of the
carts, and removed the lavers from them; and
he took down [c]the Sea from the bronze oxen
that *were* under it, and put it on a pavement
of stones. 18 Also he removed the Sabbath
pavilion which they had built in the temple,
and he removed the king's outer entrance
from the house of the LORD, on account of
the king of Assyria.
19 Now the rest of the acts of Ahaz which he
did, *are* they not written in the book of the
chronicles of the kings of Judah? 20 So Ahaz
rested with his fathers, and [a]was buried with
his fathers in the City of David. Then Hezekiah his son reigned in his place.

Hoshea Reigns in Israel

17 In the twelfth year of Ahaz king of
Judah, [a]Hoshea the son of Elah became
king of Israel in Samaria, *and he reigned* nine
years. 2 And he did evil in the sight of the
LORD, but not as the kings of Israel who were
before him. 3 [a]Shalmaneser king of Assyria
came up against him; and Hoshea [b]became
his vassal, and paid him tribute money. 4 And
the king of Assyria uncovered a conspiracy

PEACE NOTE

The most courageous step on your journey into God's peace is to ask for help. God wants to help you, and so do His people.

16:3 [a] [Lev. 18:21] [b] [Deut. 12:31] 16:4 [a] 2 Kin. 15:34, 35 [b] [Deut. 12:2] 16:5 [a] Is. 7:1, 4 16:6 [a] 2 Kin. 14:22 [1] Some ancient authorities read *Syrians.* 16:7 [a] 1 Chr. 5:26 16:8 [a] 2 Kin. 12:17, 18 16:9 [a] 2 Kin. 14:28 [b] Amos 1:5 [c] Amos 9:7 16:11 [a] Is. 8:2 16:12 [a] 2 Chr. 26:16, 19 16:14 [a] 2 Chr. 4:1 16:15 [a] Ex. 29:39–41 16:17 [a] 2 Chr. 28:24 [b] 1 Kin. 7:27–29 [c] 1 Kin. 7:23–25 16:20 [a] 2 Chr. 28:27 17:1 [a] 2 Kin. 15:30 17:3 [a] 2 Kin. 18:9–12 [b] 2 Kin. 24:1

by Hoshea; for he had sent messengers to So,
king of Egypt, and brought no tribute to the
king of Assyria, as *he had done* year by year.
Therefore the king of Assyria shut him up,
and bound him in prison.

Israel Carried Captive to Assyria

5 Now [a]the king of Assyria went throughout
all the land, and went up to Samaria and besieged it for three years. 6 [a]In the ninth year
of Hoshea, the king of Assyria took Samaria and [b]carried Israel away to Assyria, [c]and
placed them in Halah and by the Habor, the
River of Gozan, and in the cities of the Medes.
7 For [a]so it was that the children of Israel had sinned against the LORD their God,
who had brought them up out of the land of
Egypt, from under the hand of Pharaoh king
of Egypt; and they had [b]feared other gods,
8 and [a]had walked in the statutes of the nations
whom the LORD had cast out from before the
children of Israel, and of the kings of Israel,
which they had made. 9 Also the children of
Israel secretly did against the LORD their God
things that *were* not right, and they built for
themselves high places in all their cities, [a]from
watchtower to fortified city. 10 [a]They set up for
themselves *sacred* pillars and [b]wooden images[1] [c]on every high hill and under every green
tree. 11 There they burned incense on all the
high places, like the nations whom the LORD
had carried away before them; and they did
wicked things to provoke the LORD to anger,
12 for they served idols, [a]of which the LORD had
said to them, [b]"You shall not do this thing."
13 Yet the LORD testified against Israel and
against Judah, by all of His [a]prophets, [b]every
seer, saying, [c]"Turn from your evil ways, and
keep My commandments *and* My statutes,
according to all the law which I commanded
your fathers, and which I sent to you by My
servants the prophets." 14 Nevertheless they
would not hear, but [a]stiffened their necks, like
the necks of their fathers, who [b]did not believe
in the LORD their God. 15 And they [a]rejected His
statutes [b]and His covenant that He had made
with their fathers, and His testimonies which
He had testified against them; they followed
[c]idols, [d]became idolaters, and *went* after the
nations who *were* all around them, *concerning*
whom the LORD had charged them that they
should [e]not do like them. 16 So they left all the
commandments of the LORD their God, [a]made
for themselves a molded image *and* two calves,
[b]made a wooden image and worshiped all
the [c]host of heaven, [d]and served Baal. 17 [a]And
they caused their sons and daughters to pass
through the fire, [b]practiced witchcraft and
soothsaying, and [c]sold themselves to do evil in
the sight of the LORD, to provoke Him to anger.
18 Therefore the LORD was very angry with Israel, and removed them from His sight; there
was none left [a]but the tribe of Judah alone.
19 Also [a]Judah did not keep the commandments of the LORD their God, but walked in the
statutes of Israel which they made. 20 And the
LORD rejected all the descendants of Israel,
afflicted them, and [a]delivered them into the
hand of plunderers, until He had cast them
from His [b]sight. 21 For [a]He tore Israel from the
house of David, and [b]they made Jeroboam
the son of Nebat king. Then Jeroboam drove
Israel from following the LORD, and made
them commit a great sin. 22 For the children
of Israel walked in all the sins of Jeroboam
which he did; they did not depart from them,
23 until the LORD removed Israel out of His
sight, [a]as He had said by all His servants the
prophets. [b]So Israel was carried away from
their own land to Assyria, *as it is* to this day.

Assyria Resettles Samaria

24 [a]Then the king of Assyria brought *people*
from Babylon, Cuthah, [b]Ava, Hamath, and
from Sepharvaim, and placed *them* in the
cities of Samaria instead of the children of
Israel; and they took possession of Samaria
and dwelt in its cities. 25 And it was so, at the
beginning of their dwelling there, *that* they
did not fear the LORD; therefore the LORD
sent lions among them, which killed *some*
of them. 26 So they spoke to the king of Assyria, saying, "The nations whom you have
removed and placed in the cities of Samaria
do not know the rituals of the God of the land;
therefore He has sent lions among them, and
indeed, they are killing them because they
do not know the rituals of the God of the
land." 27 Then the king of Assyria commanded, saying, "Send there one of the priests
whom you brought from there; let him go
and dwell there, and let him teach them the
rituals of the God of the land." 28 Then one
of the priests whom they had carried away
from Samaria came and dwelt in Bethel, and
taught them how they should fear the LORD.

17:5 [a] Hos. 13:16 **17:6** [a] Hos. 1:4; 13:16 [b] [Deut. 28:36, 64; 29:27, 28] [c] 1 Chr. 5:26 **17:7** [a] [Josh. 23:16] [b] Judg. 6:10 **17:8** [a] [Lev. 18:3] **17:9** [a] 2 Kin. 18:8 **17:10** [a] Is. 57:5 [b] [Ex. 34:12–14] [c] [Deut. 12:2] [1] Hebrew *Asherim*, Canaanite deities **17:12** [a] [Ex. 20:3–5] [b] [Deut. 4:19] **17:13** [a] Neh. 9:29, 30 [b] 1 Sam. 9:9 [c] [Jer. 18:11; 25:5; 35:15] **17:14** [a] [Acts 7:51] [b] Deut. 9:23 **17:15** [a] Jer. 44:3 [b] Deut. 29:25 [c] Deut. 32:21 [d] [Rom. 1:21–23] [e] [Deut. 12:30, 31] **17:16** [a] 1 Kin. 12:28 [b] [1 Kin. 14:15] [c] [Deut. 4:19] [d] 1 Kin. 16:31; 22:53 **17:17** [a] 2 Kin. 16:3 [b] [Deut. 18:10–12] [c] 1 Kin. 21:20 **17:18** [a] 1 Kin. 11:13, 32 **17:19** [a] Jer. 3:8 **17:20** [a] 2 Kin. 13:3; 15:29 [b] 2 Kin. 24:20 **17:21** [a] 1 Kin. 11:11, 31 [b] 1 Kin. 12:20, 28 **17:23** [a] 1 Kin. 14:16 [b] 2 Kin. 17:6 **17:24** [a] Ezra 4:2, 10 [b] 2 Kin. 18:34

29 However every nation continued to make gods of its own, and put *them* [a]in the shrines on the high places which the Samaritans had made, *every* nation in the cities where they dwelt. 30 The men of [a]Babylon made Succoth Benoth, the men of Cuth made Nergal, the men of Hamath made Ashima, 31 [a]and the Avites made Nibhaz and Tartak; and the Sepharvites [b]burned their children in fire to Adrammelech and Anammelech, the gods of Sepharvaim. 32 So they feared the LORD, [a]and from every class they appointed for themselves priests of the high places, who sacrificed for them in the shrines of the high places. 33 [a]They feared the LORD, yet served their own gods—according to the rituals of the nations from among whom they were carried away.

34 To this day they continue practicing the former rituals; they do not fear the LORD, nor do they follow their statutes or their ordinances, or the law and commandment which the LORD had commanded the children of Jacob, [a]whom He named Israel, 35 with whom the LORD had made a covenant and charged them, saying: [a]"You shall not fear other gods, nor [b]bow down to them nor serve them nor sacrifice to them; 36 but the LORD, who [a]brought you up from the land of Egypt with great power and [b]an outstretched arm, [c]Him you shall fear, Him you shall worship, and to Him you shall offer sacrifice. 37 And the statutes, the ordinances, the law, and the commandment which He wrote for you, [a]you shall be careful to observe forever; you shall not fear other gods. 38 And the covenant that I have made with you, [a]you shall not forget, nor shall you fear other gods. 39 But the LORD your God you shall fear; and He will deliver you from the hand of all your enemies." 40 However they did not obey, but they followed their former rituals. 41 [a]So these nations feared the LORD, yet served their carved images; also their children and their children's children have continued doing as their fathers did, even to this day.

Hezekiah Reigns in Judah

18 Now it came to pass in the third year of [a]Hoshea the son of Elah, king of Israel, *that* [b]Hezekiah the son of Ahaz, king of Judah, began to reign. 2 He was twenty-five years old when he became king, and he reigned twenty-nine years in Jerusalem. His mother's name *was* [a]Abi[1] the daughter of Zechariah. 3 And he did *what was* right in the sight of the LORD, according to all that his father David had done.

4 [a]He removed the high places and broke the *sacred* pillars, cut down the wooden image[1] and broke in pieces the [b]bronze serpent that Moses had made; for until those days the children of Israel burned incense to it, and called it Nehushtan.[2] 5 He [a]trusted in the LORD God of Israel, [b]so that after him was none like him among all the kings of Judah, nor who were before him. 6 For he [a]held fast to the LORD; he did not depart from following Him, but kept His commandments, which the LORD had commanded Moses. 7 The LORD [a]was with him; he [b]prospered wherever he went. And he [c]rebelled against the king of Assyria and did not serve him. 8 [a]He subdued the Philistines, as far as Gaza and its territory, [b]from watchtower to fortified city.

9 Now [a]it came to pass in the fourth year of King Hezekiah, which *was* the seventh year of Hoshea the son of Elah, king of Israel, *that* Shalmaneser king of Assyria came up against Samaria and besieged it. 10 And at the end of three years they took it. In the sixth year of Hezekiah, that *is*, [a]the ninth year of Hoshea king of Israel, Samaria was taken. 11 [a]Then the king of Assyria carried Israel away captive to Assyria, and put them [b]in Halah and by the Habor, the River of Gozan, and in the cities of the Medes, 12 because they [a]did not obey the voice of the LORD their God, but transgressed His covenant *and* all that Moses the servant of the LORD had commanded; and they would neither hear nor do *them.*

13 And [a]in the fourteenth year of King Hezekiah, Sennacherib king of Assyria came up against all the fortified cities of Judah and took them. 14 Then Hezekiah king of Judah sent to the king of Assyria at Lachish, saying, "I have done wrong; turn away from me; whatever you impose on me I will pay." And the king of Assyria assessed Hezekiah king of Judah three hundred talents of silver and thirty talents of gold. 15 So Hezekiah [a]gave *him* all the silver that was found in the house of the LORD and in the treasuries of the king's house. 16 At that time Hezekiah stripped *the gold from* the doors of the temple of the LORD, and *from* the pillars which Hezekiah king of Judah had overlaid, and gave it to the king of Assyria.

17:29 [a] *1 Kin. 12:31; 13:32* **17:30** [a] 2 Kin. 17:24 **17:31** [a] Ezra 4:9 [b] [Deut. 12:31] **17:32** [a] 1 Kin. 12:31; 13:33 **17:33** [a] Zeph. 1:5 **17:34** [a] Gen. 32:28; 35:10 **17:35** [a] Judg. 6:10 [b] [Ex. 20:5] **17:36** [a] Ex. 14:15–30 [b] Ex. 6:6; 9:15 [c] [Deut. 10:20] **17:37** [a] Deut. 5:32 **17:38** [a] Deut. 4:23; 6:12 **17:41** [a] 2 Kin. 17:32, 33 **18:1** [a] 2 Kin. 17:1 [b] 2 Chr. 28:27; 29:1 **18:2** [a] Is. 38:5 [1] Called *Abijah* in 2 Chronicles 29:1ff **18:4** [a] 2 Chr. 31:1 [b] Num. 21:5–9 [1] Hebrew *Asherah*, a Canaanite goddess [2] Literally *Bronze Thing* **18:5** [a] 2 Kin. 19:10 [b] 2 Kin. 23:25 **18:6** [a] Deut. 10:20 **18:7** [a] [2 Chr. 15:2] [b] 1 Sam. 18:5, 14 [c] 2 Kin. 16:7 **18:8** [a] Is. 14:29 [b] 2 Kin. 17:9 **18:9** [a] 2 Kin. 17:3 **18:10** [a] 2 Kin. 17:6 **18:11** [a] 2 Kin. 17:6 [b] 1 Chr. 5:26 **18:12** [a] 2 Kin. 17:7–18 **18:13** [a] 2 Chr. 32:1 **18:15** [a] 2 Kin. 12:18; 16:8

Sennacherib Boasts Against the L*ORD*

17 Then the king of Assyria sent *the* Tartan,[1]
the Rabsaris,[2] *and the* Rabshakeh[3] from Lachish, with a great army against Jerusalem, to
King Hezekiah. And they went up and came to
Jerusalem. When they had come up, they went
and stood by the [a]aqueduct from the upper
pool, [b]which *was* on the highway to the Fuller's
Field. 18 And when they had called to the king,
[a]Eliakim the son of Hilkiah, who *was* over the
household, Shebna the scribe, and Joah the
son of Asaph, the recorder, came out to them.
19 Then *the* Rabshakeh said to them, "Say now
to Hezekiah, 'Thus says the great king, the king
of Assyria: [a]"What confidence *is* this in which
you trust? 20 You speak of *having* plans and
power for war; but *they are* mere words. And
in whom do you trust, that you rebel against
me? 21 [a]Now look! You are trusting in the staff
of this broken reed, Egypt, on which if a man
leans, it will go into his hand and pierce it.
So *is* Pharaoh king of Egypt to all who trust
in him. 22 But if you say to me, 'We trust in
the LORD our God,' *is* it not He [a]whose high
places and whose altars Hezekiah has taken
away, and said to Judah and Jerusalem, 'You
shall worship before this altar in Jerusalem'?" '
23 Now therefore, I urge you, give a pledge to
my master the king of Assyria, and I will give
you two thousand horses—if you are able
on your part to put riders on them! 24 How
then will you repel one captain of the least
of my master's servants, and put your trust
in Egypt for chariots and horsemen? 25 Have
I now come up without the LORD against this
place to destroy it? The LORD said to me, 'Go
up against this land, and destroy it.' "

26 [a]Then Eliakim the son of Hilkiah, Shebna,
and Joah said to *the* Rabshakeh, "Please speak
to your servants in [b]Aramaic, for we understand *it;* and do not speak to us in Hebrew[1] in
the hearing of the people who *are* on the wall."

27 But *the* Rabshakeh said to them, "Has my
master sent me to your master and to you to
speak these words, and not to the men who
sit on the wall, who will eat and drink their
own waste with you?"

28 Then *the* Rabshakeh stood and called
out with a loud voice in Hebrew, and spoke,
saying, "Hear the word of the great king, the
king of Assyria! 29 Thus says the king: [a]'Do not
let Hezekiah deceive you, for he shall not be
able to deliver you from his hand; 30 nor let
Hezekiah make you trust in the LORD, saying,
"The LORD will surely deliver us; this city shall
not be given into the hand of the king of Assyria." ' 31 Do not listen to Hezekiah; for thus
says the king of Assyria: 'Make *peace* with me
by a present and come out to me; and every
one of you eat from his own [a]vine and every
one from his own fig tree, and every one of
you drink the waters of his own cistern; 32 until
I come and take you away to a land like your
own land, [a]a land of grain and new wine, a land
of bread and vineyards, a land of olive groves
and honey, that you may live and not die. But
do not listen to Hezekiah, lest he persuade
you, saying, "The LORD will deliver us." 33 [a]Has
any of the gods of the nations at all delivered
its land from the hand of the king of Assyria?
34 Where *are* the gods of [a]Hamath and Arpad?
Where *are* the gods of Sepharvaim and Hena
and [b]Ivah? Indeed, have they delivered Samaria from my hand? 35 Who among all the gods
of the lands have delivered their countries
from my hand, [a]that the LORD should deliver
Jerusalem from my hand?' "

36 But the people held their peace and answered him not a word; for the king's commandment was, "Do not answer him." 37 Then
Eliakim the son of Hilkiah, who *was* over the
household, Shebna the scribe, and Joah the
son of Asaph, the recorder, came to Hezekiah [a]with *their* clothes torn, and told him the
words of *the* Rabshakeh.

Isaiah Assures Deliverance

19 And [a]so it was, when King Hezekiah
heard *it,* that he tore his clothes, covered himself with [b]sackcloth, and went into
the house of the LORD. 2 Then he sent Eliakim,
who *was* over the household, Shebna the
scribe, and the elders of the priests, covered
with sackcloth, to Isaiah the prophet, the
son of Amoz. 3 And they said to him, "Thus
says Hezekiah: 'This day *is* a day of trouble,
and rebuke, and blasphemy; for the children
have come to birth, but *there is* no strength
to bring them forth. 4 [a]It may be that the
LORD your God will hear all the words of *the*
Rabshakeh, whom his master the king of
Assyria has sent to [b]reproach the living God,
and will [c]rebuke the words which the LORD
your God has heard. Therefore lift up *your*
prayer for the remnant that is left.' "

5 So the servants of King Hezekiah came
to Isaiah. 6 [a]And Isaiah said to them, "Thus
you shall say to your master, 'Thus says the
LORD: "Do not be [b]afraid of the words which
you have heard, with which the [c]servants of

18:17 [a] 2 Kin. 20:20 [b] Is. 7:3 [1] A title, probably *Commander in Chief* [2] A title, probably *Chief Officer* [3] A title, probably *Chief of Staff* or *Governor* **18:18** [a] Is. 22:20 **18:19** [a] 2 Chr. 32:10 **18:21** [a] Ezek. 29:6, 7 **18:22** [a] 2 Kin. 18:4 **18:26** [a] Is. 36:11—39:8 [b] Ezra 4:7 [1] Literally *Judean* **18:29** [a] 2 Chr. 32:15 **18:31** [a] 1 Kin. 4:20, 25 **18:32** [a] Deut. 8:7–9; 11:12 **18:33** [a] 2 Kin. 19:12 **18:34** [a] 2 Kin. 19:13 [b] 2 Kin. 17:24 **18:35** [a] Dan. 3:15 **18:37** [a] Is. 33:7 **19:1** [a] Is. 37:1 [b] Ps. 69:11 **19:4** [a] 2 Sam. 16:12 [b] 2 Kin. 18:35 [c] Ps. 50:21 **19:6** [a] Is. 37:6 [b] [Ps. 112:7] [c] 2 Kin. 18:17

the king of Assyria have blasphemed Me. 7 Surely I will send [a]a spirit upon him, and he shall hear a rumor and return to his own land; and I will cause him to fall by the sword in his own land." ' "

Sennacherib's Threat and Hezekiah's Prayer

8 Then *the* Rabshakeh returned and found the king of Assyria warring against Libnah, for he heard that he had departed [a]from Lachish. 9 And [a]the king heard concerning Tirhakah king of Ethiopia, "Look, he has come out to make war with you." So he again sent messengers to Hezekiah, saying, 10 "Thus you shall speak to Hezekiah king of Judah, saying: 'Do not let your God [a]in whom you trust deceive you, saying, "Jerusalem shall not be given into the hand of the king of Assyria." 11 Look! You have heard what the kings of Assyria have done to all lands by utterly destroying them; and shall you be delivered? 12 [a]Have the gods of the nations delivered those whom my fathers have destroyed, Gozan and Haran and Rezeph, and the people of [b]Eden who *were* in Telassar? 13 [a]Where *is* the king of Hamath, the king of Arpad, and the king of the city of Sepharvaim, Hena, and Ivah?' "

14 [a]And Hezekiah received the letter from the hand of the messengers, and read it; and Hezekiah went up to the house of the LORD, and spread it before the LORD. 15 Then Hezekiah prayed before the LORD, and said: "O LORD God of Israel, *the One* [a]who dwells *between* the cherubim, [b]You are God, You alone, of all the kingdoms of the earth. You have made heaven and earth. 16 [a]Incline Your ear, O LORD, and hear; [b]open Your eyes, O LORD, and see; and hear the words of Sennacherib, [c]which he has sent to reproach the living God. 17 Truly, LORD, the kings of Assyria have laid waste the nations and their lands, 18 and have cast their gods into the fire; for they *were* [a]not gods, but [b]the work of men's hands—wood and stone. Therefore they destroyed them. 19 Now therefore, O LORD our God, I pray, save us from his hand, [a]that all the kingdoms of the earth may [b]know that You *are* the LORD God, You alone."

The Word of the LORD Concerning Sennacherib

20 Then Isaiah the son of Amoz sent to Hezekiah, saying, "Thus says the LORD God of Israel: [a]'Because you have prayed to Me against Sennacherib king of Assyria, [b]I have heard.' 21 This *is* the word which the LORD has spoken concerning him:

'The virgin, [a]the daughter of Zion,
Has despised you, laughed you to scorn;
The daughter of Jerusalem
[b]Has shaken *her* head behind your back!

19:7 [a] 2 Kin. 19:35–37 **19:8** [a] 2 Kin. 18:14, 17 **19:9** [a] 1 Sam. 23:27 **19:10** [a] 2 Kin. 18:5 **19:12** [a] 2 Kin. 18:33, 34 [b] Ezek. 27:23 **19:13** [a] 2 Kin. 18:34 **19:14** [a] Is. 37:14 **19:15** [a] Ex. 25:22 [b] [Is. 44:6] **19:16** [a] Ps. 31:2 [b] 2 Chr. 6:40 [c] 2 Kin. 19:4 **19:18** [a] [Jer. 10:3–5] [b] [Acts 17:29] **19:19** [a] Ps. 83:18 [b] 1 Kin. 8:42, 43 **19:20** [a] Is. 37:21 [b] 2 Kin. 20:5 **19:21** [a] Lam. 2:13 [b] Ps. 22:7, 8

HOPE-FILLED HEZEKIAH

Save us from his hand, that all the kingdoms of the earth may know that You are the LORD God, You alone.

2 KINGS 19:19

One of the greatest stories in Israel's history is the miraculous deliverance of Jerusalem in the eighth century BC. Had Sennacherib, king of Assyria, not been turned back, Israel's story would have ended. The Assyrian tyrant invaded Judah (the southern kingdom) and then laid siege to Jerusalem itself.

Standing before the walls of Jerusalem, the tyrant's messenger mocked Hezekiah and God. The messenger boasted that Sennacherib had conquered all who opposed him and captured every city; Jerusalem would be no exception. Hezekiah was given a letter demanding his surrender. So "Hezekiah went up to the house of the LORD, and spread it before the LORD. Then Hezekiah prayed before the LORD" (vv. 14–15).

From a human point of view, Hezekiah's situation was hopeless. But God heard Hezekiah's prayer. The Assyrian army was stricken and Sennacherib returned to Assyria where he was assassinated. We can have peace when we remember God's saving power.

22 'Whom have you reproached and
blasphemed?
Against whom have you raised *your*
voice,
And lifted up your eyes on high?
Against [a]the Holy *One* of Israel.
23 [a]By your messengers you have
reproached the Lord,
And said: [b]"By the multitude of my
chariots
I have come up to the height of the
mountains,
To the limits of Lebanon;
I will cut down its tall cedars
And its choice cypress trees;
I will enter the extremity of its borders,
To its fruitful forest.
24 I have dug and drunk strange water,
And with the soles of my feet I have
[a]dried up
All the brooks of defense."

25 'Did you not hear long ago
How [a]I made it,
From ancient times that I formed it?
Now I have brought it to pass,
That [b]you should be
For crushing fortified cities *into* heaps
of ruins.
26 Therefore their inhabitants had little
power;
They were dismayed and confounded;
They were *as* the grass of the field
And the green herb,
As [a]the grass on the housetops
And *grain* blighted before it is grown.

27 'But [a]I know your dwelling place,
Your going out and your coming in,
And your rage against Me.
28 Because your rage against Me and your
tumult
Have come up to My ears,
Therefore [a]I will put My hook in your nose
And My bridle in your lips,
And I will turn you back
[b]By the way which you came.

29"This *shall be* a [a]sign to you:

'You shall eat this year such as grows of
itself,
And in the second year what springs
from the same;
Also in the third year sow and reap,
Plant vineyards and eat the fruit of
them.
30 [a]And the remnant who have escaped of
the house of Judah
Shall again take root downward,
And bear fruit upward.
31 For out of Jerusalem shall go a
remnant,
And those who escape from Mount
Zion.
[a]The zeal of the LORD of hosts[1] will do
this.'

32"Therefore thus says the LORD concerning the king of Assyria:

'He shall [a]not come into this city,
Nor shoot an arrow there,
Nor come before it with shield,
Nor build a siege mound against it.
33 By the way that he came,
By the same shall he return;
And he shall not come into this city,'
Says the LORD.
34 'For [a]I will [b]defend this city, to save it
For My own sake and [c]for My servant
David's sake.' "

Sennacherib's Defeat and Death

35And [a]it came to pass on a certain night
that the angel[1] of the LORD went out, and killed
in the camp of the Assyrians one hundred and
eighty-five thousand; and when *people* arose
early in the morning, there were the corpses—
all dead. 36So Sennacherib king of Assyria
departed and went away, returned *home,* and
remained at [a]Nineveh. 37Now it came to pass,
as he was worshiping in the temple of Nisroch
his god, that his sons [a]Adrammelech and Sharezer [b]struck him down with the sword; and
they escaped into the land of Ararat. Then
[c]Esarhaddon his son reigned in his place.

Hezekiah's Life Extended

20 In [a]those days Hezekiah was sick and
near death. And Isaiah the prophet,
the son of Amoz, went to him and said to
him, "Thus says the LORD: 'Set your house in
order, for you shall die, and not live.' "
2Then he turned his face toward the wall,
and prayed to the LORD, saying, 3[a]"Remember now, O LORD, I pray, how I have walked
before You in truth and with a loyal heart,
and have done *what was* good in Your sight."
And Hezekiah wept bitterly.

19:22 [a] Jer. 51:5 **19:23** [a] 2 Kin. 18:17 [b] Ps. 20:7 **19:24** [a] Is. 19:6 **19:25** [a] [Is. 45:7] [b] Is. 10:5, 6 **19:26** [a] Ps. 129:6 **19:27** [a] Ps. 139:1–3 **19:28** [a] Ezek. 29:4; 38:4 [b] 2 Kin. 19:33, 36 **19:29** [a] 2 Kin. 20:8, 9 **19:30** [a] 2 Chr. 32:22, 23 **19:31** [a] Is. 9:7 [1] Following many Hebrew manuscripts and ancient versions (compare Isaiah 37:32); Masoretic Text omits *of hosts.* **19:32** [a] Is. 8:7–10 **19:34** [a] 2 Kin. 20:6 [b] Is. 31:5 [c] 1 Kin. 11:12, 13 **19:35** [a] Is. 10:12–19; 37:36 [1] Or *Angel* **19:36** [a] Gen. 10:11 **19:37** [a] 2 Kin. 17:31 [b] 2 Kin. 19:7 [c] Ezra 4:2 **20:1** [a] Is. 38:1–22 **20:3** [a] Neh. 13:22

4 And it happened, before Isaiah had gone
out into the middle court, that the word of the
LORD came to him, saying, 5 "Return and tell
Hezekiah [a]the leader of My people, 'Thus says
the LORD, the God of David your father: [b]"I
have heard your prayer, I have seen [c]your tears;
surely I will heal you. On the third day you
shall go up to the house of the LORD. 6 And I
will add to your days fifteen years. I will deliver
you and this city from the hand of the king of
Assyria; and [a]I will defend this city for My own
sake, and for the sake of My servant David." ' "
7 Then [a]Isaiah said, "Take a lump of figs."
So they took and laid *it* on the boil, and he
recovered.
8 And Hezekiah said to Isaiah, [a]"What *is*
the sign that the LORD will heal me, and that
I shall go up to the house of the LORD the
third day?"
9 Then Isaiah said, [a]"This is the sign to you
from the LORD, that the LORD will do the thing
which He has spoken: *shall* the shadow go forward ten degrees or go backward ten degrees?"
10 And Hezekiah answered, "It is an easy
thing for the shadow to go down ten degrees; no, but let the shadow go backward
ten degrees."
11 So Isaiah the prophet cried out to the
LORD, and [a]He brought the shadow ten degrees backward, by which it had gone down
on the sundial of Ahaz.

The Babylonian Envoys

12 [a]At that time Berodach-Baladan[1] the son
of Baladan, king of Babylon, sent letters and a
present to Hezekiah, for he heard that Hezekiah had been sick. 13 And [a]Hezekiah was attentive
to them, and showed them all the house of his
treasures—the silver and gold, the spices and
precious ointment, and all[1] his armory—all
that was found among his treasures. There
was nothing in his house or in all his dominion
that Hezekiah did not show them.
14 Then Isaiah the prophet went to King Hezekiah, and said to him, "What did these men
say, and from where did they come to you?"
So Hezekiah said, "They came from a far
country, from Babylon."
15 And he said, "What have they seen in
your house?"
So Hezekiah answered, [a]"They have seen all
that *is* in my house; there is nothing among
my treasures that I have not shown them."
16 Then Isaiah said to Hezekiah, "Hear the
word of the LORD: 17 'Behold, the days are
coming when all that *is* in your house, and
what your fathers have accumulated until
this day, [a]shall be carried to Babylon; nothing shall be left,' says the LORD. 18 'And [a]they
shall take away some of your sons who will
descend from you, whom you will beget; [b]and
they shall be [c]eunuchs in the palace of the
king of Babylon.' "

20:5 [a] 1 Sam. 9:16; 10:1 [b] Ps. 65:2 [c] Ps. 39:12; 56:8 **20:6** [a] 2 Kin. 19:34 **20:7** [a] Is. 38:21 **20:8** [a] Judg. 6:17, 37, 39 **20:9** [a] Is. 38:7, 8 **20:11** [a] Is. 38:8 **20:12** [a] Is. 39:1–8 [1] Spelled *Merodach-Baladan* in Isaiah 39:1 **20:13** [a] 2 Chr. 32:27, 31 [1] Following many Hebrew manuscripts, Syriac, and Targum; Masoretic Text omits *all.* **20:15** [a] 2 Kin. 20:13 **20:17** [a] Jer. 27:21, 22; 52:17 **20:18** [a] 2 Kin. 24:12 [b] Dan. 1:3–7 [c] Dan. 1:11, 18

FROM TEARS TO HEALING

"I have heard your prayer, I have seen your tears; surely I will heal you."

2 KINGS 20:5

God delivered Hezekiah from the Assyrian tyrant, Sennacherib. The king then contracted a serious illness. Told by the prophet to put his house in order, for he was about to die, Hezekiah prayed. It's interesting that he refused to accept the first word from the Lord—that he would die—and asked for a different answer! That was gutsy. He really fought for his peace. The Lord answered through Isaiah the prophet: "I have heard your prayer, I have seen your tears; surely I will heal you."

What impresses me about Hezekiah is that in his distress he immediately, without reluctance, turned to the Lord—and only to the Lord. Unlike so many of the kings of Israel, Hezekiah did not run to the idols and gods of the nations. He remained faithful to the Lord God of the patriarchs, the God who revealed Himself to Moses on Mount Sinai. Hezekiah's prayer *was answered, and he lived his remaining years in peace* (see v. 19).

A God who hears our prayers and acknowledges our tears—truly He is a God of love and peace. What can you take to Him today?

19 So Hezekiah said to Isaiah, [a]"The word of the LORD which you have spoken *is* good!" For he said, "Will there not be peace and truth at least in my days?"

Death of Hezekiah

20 [a]Now the rest of the acts of Hezekiah—all his might, and how he [b]made a [c]pool and a tunnel and [d]brought water into the city—*are* they not written in the book of the chronicles of the kings of Judah? 21 So [a]Hezekiah rested with his fathers. Then Manasseh his son reigned in his place.

Manasseh Reigns in Judah

21 Manasseh [a]*was* twelve years old when he became king, and he reigned fifty-five years in Jerusalem. His mother's name *was* Hephzibah. 2 And he did evil in the sight of the LORD, [a]according to the abominations of the nations whom the LORD had cast out before the children of Israel. 3 For he rebuilt the high places [a]which Hezekiah his father had destroyed; he raised up altars for Baal, and made a wooden image,[1] [b]as Ahab king of Israel had done; and he [c]worshiped all the host of heaven[2] and served them. 4 [a]He also built altars in the house of the LORD, of which the LORD had said, [b]"In Jerusalem I will put My name." 5 And he built altars for all the host of heaven in the [a]two courts of the house of the LORD. 6 [a]Also he made his son pass through the fire, practiced [b]soothsaying, used witchcraft, and consulted spiritists and mediums. He did much evil in the sight of the LORD, to provoke *Him* to anger. 7 He even set a carved image of Asherah[1] that he had made, in the house of which the LORD had said to David and to Solomon his son, [a]"In this house and in Jerusalem, which I have chosen out of all the tribes of Israel, I will put My name forever; 8 [a]and I will not make the feet of Israel wander anymore from the land which I gave their fathers—only if they are careful to do according to all that I have commanded them, and according to all the law that My servant Moses commanded them." 9 But they paid no attention, and Manasseh [a]seduced them to do more evil than the nations whom the LORD had destroyed before the children of Israel.

10 And the LORD spoke [a]by His servants the prophets, saying, 11 [a]"Because Manasseh king of Judah has done these abominations ([b]he has acted more wickedly than all the [c]Amorites who *were* before him, and [d]has also made Judah sin with his idols), 12 therefore thus says the LORD God of Israel: 'Behold, *I* am bringing *such* calamity upon Jerusalem and Judah, that whoever hears of it, both [a]his ears will tingle. 13 And I will stretch over Jerusalem [a]the measuring line of Samaria and the plummet of the house of Ahab; [b]I will wipe Jerusalem as *one* wipes a dish, wiping *it* and turning *it* upside down. 14 So I will forsake the [a]remnant of My inheritance and deliver them into the hand of their enemies; and they shall become victims of plunder to all their enemies, 15 because they have done evil in My sight, and have provoked Me to anger since the day their fathers came out of Egypt, even to this day.' "

16 [a]Moreover Manasseh shed very much innocent blood, till he had filled Jerusalem from one end to another, besides his sin by which he made Judah sin, in doing evil in the sight of the LORD.

17 Now [a]the rest of the acts of [b]Manasseh—all that he did, and the sin that he committed—*are* they not written in the book of the chronicles of the kings of Judah? 18 So [a]Manasseh rested with his fathers, and was buried in the garden of his own house, in the garden of Uzza. Then his son Amon reigned in his place.

Amon's Reign and Death

19 [a]Amon *was* twenty-two years old when he became king, and he reigned two years in Jerusalem. His mother's name *was* Meshullemeth the daughter of Haruz of Jotbah. 20 And he did evil in the sight of the LORD, [a]as his father Manasseh had done. 21 So he walked in all the ways that his father had walked; and he served the idols that his father had served, and worshiped them. 22 He [a]forsook the LORD God of his fathers, and did not walk in the way of the LORD.

23 [a]Then the servants of Amon [b]conspired against him, and killed the king in his own house. 24 But the people of the land [a]executed all those who had conspired against King Amon. Then the people of the land made his son Josiah king in his place.

20:19 [a] 1 Sam. 3:18 **20:20** [a] 2 Chr. 32:32 [b] Neh. 3:16 [c] Is. 7:3 [d] 2 Chr. 32:3, 30 **20:21** [a] 2 Chr. 32:33 **21:1** [a] 2 Chr. 33:1–9 **21:2** [a] 2 Kin. 16:3 **21:3** [a] 2 Kin. 18:4, 22 [b] 1 Kin. 16:31–33 [c] [Deut. 4:19; 17:2–5] [1] Hebrew *Asherah*, a Canaanite goddess [2] The gods of the Assyrians **21:4** [a] Jer. 7:30; 32:34 [b] 1 Kin. 11:13 **21:5** [a] 1 Kin. 6:36; 7:12 **21:6** [a] [Lev. 18:21; 20:2] [b] [Deut. 18:10–14] **21:7** [a] 1 Kin. 8:29; 9:3 [1] A Canaanite goddess **21:8** [a] 2 Sam. 7:10 **21:9** [a] [Prov. 29:12] **21:10** [a] 2 Kin. 17:13 **21:11** [a] 2 Kin. 23:26, 27; 24:3, 4 [b] 1 Kin. 21:26 [c] Gen. 15:16 [d] 2 Kin. 21:9 **21:12** [a] Jer. 19:3 **21:13** [a] Amos 7:7, 8 [b] 2 Kin. 22:16–19; 25:4–11 **21:14** [a] Jer. 6:9 **21:16** [a] 2 Kin. 24:4 **21:17** [a] 2 Chr. 33:11–19 [b] 2 Kin. 20:21 **21:18** [a] 2 Chr. 33:20 **21:19** [a] 2 Chr. 33:21–23 **21:20** [a] 2 Kin. 21:2–6, 11, 16 **21:22** [a] 1 Kin. 11:33 **21:23** [a] 2 Chr. 33:24, 25 [b] 2 Kin. 12:20; 14:19 **21:24** [a] 2 Kin. 14:5

25 Now the rest of the acts of Amon which he did, *are* they not written in the book of the chronicles of the kings of Judah? 26 And he was buried in his tomb in the garden of Uzza. Then Josiah his son reigned in his place.

Josiah Reigns in Judah

22 Josiah [a]*was* eight years old when he became king, and he reigned thirty-one years in Jerusalem. His mother's name *was* Jedidah the daughter of Adaiah of [b]Bozkath. 2 And he did *what was* right in the sight of the LORD, and walked in all the ways of his father David; he [a]did not turn aside to the right hand or to the left.

Hilkiah Finds the Book of the Law

3 [a]Now it came to pass, in the eighteenth year of King Josiah, *that* the king sent Shaphan the scribe, the son of Azaliah, the son of Meshullam, to the house of the LORD, saying: 4 "Go up to Hilkiah the high priest, that he may count the money which has been [a]brought into the house of the LORD, which [b]the doorkeepers have gathered from the people. 5 And let them [a]deliver it into the hand of those doing the work, who are the overseers in the house of the LORD; let them give it to those who *are* in the house of the LORD doing the work, to repair the damages of the house— 6 to carpenters and builders and masons—and to buy timber and hewn stone to repair the house. 7 However [a]there need be no accounting made with them of the money delivered into their hand, because they deal faithfully."

8 Then Hilkiah the high priest said to Shaphan the scribe, [a]"I have found the Book of the Law in the house of the LORD." And Hilkiah gave the book to Shaphan, and he read it. 9 So Shaphan the scribe went to the king, bringing the king word, saying, "Your servants have gathered the money that was found in the house, and have delivered it into the hand of those who do the work, who oversee the house of the LORD." 10 Then Shaphan the scribe showed the king, saying, "Hilkiah the priest has given me a book." And Shaphan read it before the king.

11 Now it happened, when the king heard the words of the Book of the Law, that he tore his clothes. 12 Then the king commanded Hilkiah the priest, [a]Ahikam the son of Shaphan, Achbor[1] the son of Michaiah, Shaphan the scribe, and Asaiah a servant of the king, saying, 13 "Go, inquire of the LORD for me, *for the people and for all Judah, concerning* the words of this book that has been found; for great *is* [a]the wrath of the LORD that is aroused against us, because our fathers have not obeyed the words of this book, to do according to all that is written concerning us."

14 So Hilkiah the priest, Ahikam, Achbor, Shaphan, and Asaiah went to Huldah the prophetess, the wife of Shallum the son of [a]Tikvah, the son of Harhas, keeper of the wardrobe. (She dwelt in Jerusalem in the Second Quarter.) And they spoke with her. 15 Then she said to them, "Thus says the LORD God of Israel, 'Tell the man who sent you to Me, 16 "Thus says the LORD: 'Behold, [a]I will bring calamity on this place and on its inhabitants—all the words of the book which the king of Judah has read— 17 [a]because they have forsaken Me and burned incense to other gods, that they might provoke Me to anger with all the works of their hands. Therefore My wrath shall be aroused against this place and shall not be quenched.' " ' 18 But as for [a]the king of Judah, who sent you to inquire of the LORD, in this manner you shall speak to him, 'Thus says the LORD God of Israel: "*Concerning* the words which you have heard— 19 because your [a]heart was tender, and you [b]humbled yourself before the LORD when you heard what I spoke against this place and against its inhabitants, that they would become [c]a desolation and [d]a curse, and you tore your clothes and wept before Me, I also have heard *you*," says the LORD. 20 "Surely, therefore, I will gather you to your fathers, and you [a]shall be gathered to your grave in peace; and your eyes shall not see all the calamity which I will bring on this place." ' " So they brought back word to the king.

Josiah Restores True Worship

23 Now [a]the king sent them to gather all the elders of Judah and Jerusalem to him. 2 The king went up to the house of the LORD with all the men of Judah, and with him all the inhabitants of Jerusalem—the priests and the prophets and all the people, both small and great. And he [a]read in their hearing all the words of the Book of the Covenant [b]which had been found in the house of the LORD.

3 Then the king [a]stood by a pillar and made a [b]covenant before the LORD, to follow the LORD and to keep His commandments and His testimonies and His statutes, with all *his* heart and all *his* soul, to perform the words of this covenant that were written in this book. And all the people took a stand for the covenant.

22:1 [a] 2 Chr. 34:1 [b] Josh. 15:39 **22:2** [a] Deut. 5:32 **22:3** [a] 2 Chr. 34:8 **22:4** [a] 2 Kin. 12:4 [b] 2 Kin. 12:9, 10 **22:5** [a] 2 Kin. 12:11–14 **22:7** [a] 2 Kin. 12:15 **22:8** [a] Deut. 31:24–26 **22:12** [a] Jer. 26:24 [1] *Abdon the son of Micah* in 2 Chronicles 34:20 **22:13** [a] [Deut. 29:23–28; 31:17, 18] **22:14** [a] 2 Chr. 34:22 **22:16** [a] Deut. 29:27 **22:17** [a] Deut. 29:25–27 **22:18** [a] 2 Chr. 34:26 **22:19** [a] [Ps. 51:17] [b] 1 Kin. 21:29 [c] Lev. 26:31, 32 [d] Jer. 26:6; 44:22 **22:20** [a] [Is. 57:1, 2] **23:1** [a] 2 Chr. 34:29, 30 **23:2** [a] Deut. 31:10–13 [b] 2 Kin. 22:8 **23:3** [a] 2 Kin. 11:14 [b] 2 Kin. 11:17

PEACE IN LIFE AND DEATH

"I will gather you to your fathers, and you shall be gathered to your grave in peace."

2 KINGS 22:20

In repairing the temple, which included cleaning up and removing debris, workers discovered an old scroll. When a scribe read the scroll to King Josiah, his reaction was instant repentance. The king's response and other references in chapters 22–23 make it clear that the scroll was the Book of Deuteronomy. This may seem strange to us, but in those ancient times there was no Bible as we have today. An ancient scroll like Deuteronomy could rest on a shelf collecting dust for centuries.

The reading of the scroll provoked reform and spiritual renewal. Pagan altars were torn down, the temple was purified, and the Passover was celebrated. We can learn something from King Josiah. His response to God's holiness—his varied expressions of humility—so moved God that He promised Josiah *peace*. In other words, repentance, meekness, initiative, and turning quickly to the Lord are all paths to peace from His hand. And make no mistake, without the Word of God, we are wrecked. We have to travel the ancient paths in the Word (Jer. 6:16) to find God's ever-present peace.

How can you seek it today?

4 And the king commanded Hilkiah the high
priest, the [a]priests of the second order, and the
doorkeepers, to bring [b]out of the temple of the
LORD all the articles that were made for Baal,
for Asherah,[1] and for all the host of heaven;[2]
and he burned them outside Jerusalem in
the fields of Kidron, and carried their ashes
to Bethel. 5 Then he removed the idolatrous
priests whom the kings of Judah had ordained
to burn incense on the high places in the cities
of Judah and in the places all around Jerusalem, and those who burned incense to Baal,
to the sun, to the moon, to the constellations,
and to [a]all the host of heaven. 6 And he brought
out the [a]wooden image[1] from the house of the
LORD, to the Brook Kidron outside Jerusalem,
burned it at the Brook Kidron and ground *it*
to [b]ashes, and threw its ashes on [c]the graves
of the common people. 7 Then he tore down
the *ritual* booths [a]of the perverted persons[1]
that *were* in the house of the LORD, [b]where the
[c]women wove hangings for the wooden image.
8 And he brought all the priests from the cities
of Judah, and defiled the high places where
the priests had burned incense, from [a]Geba to
Beersheba; also he broke down the high places
at the gates which *were* at the entrance of the
Gate of Joshua the governor of the city, which
were to the left of the city gate. 9 [a]Nevertheless
the priests of the high places did not come up
to the altar of the LORD in Jerusalem, [b]but they
ate unleavened bread among their brethren.
10 And he defiled [a]Topheth, which *is* in
[b]the Valley of the Son[1] of Hinnom, [c]that no
man might make his son or his daughter
[d]pass through the fire to Molech. 11 Then he
removed the horses that the kings of Judah
had dedicated to the sun, at the entrance to
the house of the LORD, by the chamber of
Nathan-Melech, the officer who *was* in the
court; and he burned the chariots of the sun
with fire. 12 The altars that *were* [a]on the roof,
the upper chamber of Ahaz, which the kings
of Judah had made, and the altars which
[b]Manasseh had made in the two courts of the
house of the LORD, the king broke down and
pulverized there, and threw their dust into
the Brook Kidron. 13 Then the king defiled
the high places that *were* east of Jerusalem,
which *were* on the south of the Mount of
Corruption, which [a]Solomon king of Israel
had built for Ashtoreth the abomination of
the Sidonians, for Chemosh the abomination
of the Moabites, and for Milcom the abomination of the people of Ammon. 14 And he
[a]broke in pieces the *sacred* pillars and cut

23:4 [a] 2 Kin. 25:18 [b] 2 Kin. 21:3–7 [1] A Canaanite goddess [2] The gods of the Assyrians **23:5** [a] 2 Kin. 21:3 **23:6** [a] 2 Kin. 21:7 [b] Ex. 32:20 [c] 2 Chr. 34:4 [1] Hebrew *Asherah,* a Canaanite goddess **23:7** [a] 1 Kin. 14:24; 15:12 [b] Ezek. 16:16 [c] Ex. 38:8 [1] Hebrew *qedeshim,* that is, those practicing sodomy and prostitution in religious rituals **23:8** [a] Josh. 21:17 **23:9** [a] [Ezek. 44:10–14] [b] 1 Sam. 2:36 **23:10** [a] Is. 30:33 [b] Josh. 15:8 [c] [Lev. 18:21] [d] 2 Kin. 21:6 [1] Kethib reads *Sons.* **23:12** [a] Jer. 19:13 [b] 2 Kin. 21:5 **23:13** [a] 1 Kin. 11:5–7 **23:14** [a] [Ex. 23:24]

down the wooden images, and filled their places with the bones of men.

15 Moreover the altar that *was* at Bethel, *and* the high place [a]which Jeroboam the son of Nebat, who made Israel sin, had made, both that altar and the high place he broke down; and he burned the high place *and* crushed *it* to powder, and burned the wooden image. 16 As Josiah turned, he saw the tombs that *were* there on the mountain. And he sent and took the bones out of the tombs and burned *them* on the altar, and defiled it according to the [a]word of the LORD which the man of God proclaimed, who proclaimed these words. 17 Then he said, "What gravestone *is* this that I see?"

So the men of the city told him, "*It is* [a]the tomb of the man of God who came from Judah and proclaimed these things which you have done against the altar of Bethel."

18 And he said, "Let him alone; let no one move his bones." So they let his bones alone, with the bones of [a]the prophet who came from Samaria.

19 Now Josiah also took away all the shrines of the high places that *were* [a]in the cities of Samaria, which the kings of Israel had made to provoke the LORD[1] to anger; and he did to them according to all the deeds he had done in Bethel. 20 [a]He [b]executed all the priests of the high places who *were* there, on the altars, and [c]burned men's bones on them; and he returned to Jerusalem.

21 Then the king commanded all the people, saying, [a]"Keep the Passover to the LORD your God, [b]as *it is* written in this Book of the Covenant." 22 [a]Such a Passover surely had never been held since the days of the judges who judged Israel, nor in all the days of the kings of Israel and the kings of Judah. 23 But in the eighteenth year of King Josiah this Passover was held before the LORD in Jerusalem. 24 Moreover Josiah put away those who consulted mediums and spiritists, the household gods and idols, all the abominations that were seen in the land of Judah and in Jerusalem, that he might perform the words of [a]the law which were written in the book [b]that Hilkiah the priest found in the house of the LORD. 25 [a]Now before him there was no king like him, who turned to the LORD with all his heart, with all his soul, and with all his might, according to all the Law of Moses; nor after him did *any* arise like him.

Impending Judgment on Judah

26 Nevertheless the LORD did not turn from the fierceness of His great wrath, with which His anger was aroused against Judah, [a]because of all the provocations with which Manasseh had provoked Him. 27 And the LORD said, "I will also remove Judah from My sight, as [a]I have removed Israel, and will cast off this city Jerusalem which I have chosen, and the house of which I said, [b]'My name shall be there.' "[1]

23:15 [a] 1 Kin. 12:28–33 **23:16** [a] 1 Kin. 13:2 **23:17** [a] 1 Kin. 13:1, 30, 31 **23:18** [a] 1 Kin. 13:11, 31 **23:19** [a] 2 Chr. 34:6, 7 [1] Following Septuagint, Syriac, and Vulgate; Masoretic Text and Targum omit *the LORD.* **23:20** [a] 1 Kin. 13:2 [b] 2 Kin. 10:25; 11:18 [c] 2 Chr. 34:5 **23:21** [a] 2 Chr. 35:1 [b] Deut. 16:2–8 **23:22** [a] 2 Chr. 35:18, 19 **23:24** [a] [Lev. 19:31; 20:27] [b] 2 Kin. 22:8 **23:25** [a] 2 Kin. 18:5 **23:26** [a] Jer. 15:4 **23:27** [a] 2 Kin. 17:18, 20; 18:11; 21:13 [b] 1 Kin. 8:29; 9:3 [1] 1 Kings 8:29

LEAD OTHERS TO PEACE

Now before him there was no king like him, who turned to the LORD with all his heart, with all his soul, and with all his might.

2 KINGS 23:25

As did King Jehoash years before, King Josiah collected money and repaired the temple. It is not surprising that the Book of Kings says of Josiah, "He did what was right in the sight of the LORD, and walked in all the ways of his father David; he did not turn aside to the right hand or to the left" (22:2). Righteous King Josiah's commitment to Israel's ancient faith extended the life of the Davidic dynasty and the life of the kingdom of Israel.

The faithfulness of God's people creates a context in which joy, hope, and peace flourish and become the dominant characteristics of our lives. Undergirding all of this is our faith in God. We should ask ourselves, *What kind of context is my life creating? Am I creating a context of peace in my community?* Make a list of what activates more of God's peace in your community. Do those things.

If we hold nothing back but give all to God, we will find the peace that the world craves.

Josiah Dies in Battle

28 Now the rest of the acts of Josiah, and all that he did, *are* they not written in the book of the chronicles of the kings of Judah? 29 [a]In his days Pharaoh Necho king of Egypt went to the aid of the king of Assyria, to the River Euphrates; and King Josiah went against him. And *Pharaoh Necho* killed him at [b]Megiddo when he [c]confronted him. 30 [a]Then his servants moved his body in a chariot from Megiddo, brought him to Jerusalem, and buried him in his own tomb. And [b]the people of the land took Jehoahaz the son of Josiah, anointed him, and made him king in his father's place.

The Reign and Captivity of Jehoahaz

31 [a]Jehoahaz *was* twenty-three years old when he became king, and he reigned three months in Jerusalem. His mother's name *was* [b]Hamutal the daughter of Jeremiah of Libnah. 32 And he did evil in the sight of the LORD, according to all that his fathers had done. 33 Now Pharaoh Necho put him in prison [a]at Riblah in the land of Hamath, that he might not reign in Jerusalem; and he imposed on the land a tribute of one hundred talents of silver and a talent of gold. 34 Then [a]Pharaoh Necho made Eliakim the son of Josiah king in place of his father Josiah, and [b]changed his name to [c]Jehoiakim. And *Pharaoh* took Jehoahaz [d]and went to Egypt, and he[1] died there.

Jehoiakim Reigns in Judah

35 So Jehoiakim gave [a]the silver and gold to Pharaoh; but he taxed the land to give money according to the command of Pharaoh; he exacted the silver and gold from the people of the land, from every one according to his assessment, to give *it* to Pharaoh Necho. 36 [a]Jehoiakim *was* twenty-five years old when he became king, and he reigned eleven years in Jerusalem. His mother's name *was* Zebudah the daughter of Pedaiah of Rumah. 37 And he did evil in the sight of the LORD, according to all that his fathers had done.

Judah Overrun by Enemies

24 *In* [a]*his days Nebuchadnezzar* king of [b]Babylon came up, and Jehoiakim became his vassal *for* three years. Then he turned and rebelled against him. 2 [a]And the LORD sent against him *raiding* bands of Chaldeans, bands of Syrians, bands of Moabites, and bands of the people of Ammon; He sent them against Judah to destroy it, [b]according to the word of the LORD which He had spoken by His servants the prophets. 3 Surely at the commandment of the LORD *this* came upon Judah, to remove *them* from His sight [a]because of the sins of Manasseh, according to all that he had done, 4 [a]and also because of the innocent blood that he had shed; for he had filled Jerusalem with innocent blood, which the LORD would not pardon.

5 Now the rest of the acts of Jehoiakim, and all that he did, *are* they not written in the book of the chronicles of the kings of Judah? 6 [a]So Jehoiakim rested with his fathers. Then Jehoiachin his son reigned in his place.

7 And [a]the king of Egypt did not come out of his land anymore, for [b]the king of Babylon had taken all that belonged to the king of Egypt from the Brook of Egypt to the River Euphrates.

The Reign and Captivity of Jehoiachin

8 [a]Jehoiachin *was* eighteen years old when he became king, and he reigned in Jerusalem three months. His mother's name *was* Nehushta the daughter of Elnathan of Jerusalem. 9 And he did evil in the sight of the LORD, according to all that his father had done.

10 [a]At that time the servants of Nebuchadnezzar king of Babylon came up against Jerusalem, and the city was besieged. 11 And Nebuchadnezzar king of Babylon came against the city, as his servants were besieging it. 12 [a]Then Jehoiachin king of Judah, his mother, his servants, his princes, and his officers went out to the king of Babylon; and the king of Babylon, [b]in the eighth year of his reign, took him prisoner.

The Captivity of Jerusalem

13 [a]And he carried out from there all the treasures of the house of the LORD and the treasures of the king's house, and he [b]cut in pieces all the articles of gold which Solomon king of Israel had made in the temple of the LORD, [c]as the LORD had said. 14 Also [a]he carried into captivity all Jerusalem: all the captains and all the mighty men of valor, [b]ten thousand captives, and [c]all the craftsmen and smiths. None remained except [d]the poorest people of the land. 15 And [a]he carried Jehoiachin captive to Babylon. The king's mother,

23:29 [a] Jer. 2:16; 46:2 [b] Zech. 12:11 [c] 2 Kin. 14:8 **23:30** [a] 2 Chr. 35:24 [b] 2 Chr. 36:1–4 **23:31** [a] Jer. 22:11 [b] 2 Kin. 24:18 **23:33** [a] 2 Kin. 25:6 **23:34** [a] 2 Chr. 36:4 [b] Dan. 1:7 [c] Matt. 1:11 [d] Ezek. 19:3, 4 [1] That is, Jehoahaz **23:35** [a] 2 Kin. 23:33 **23:36** [a] 2 Chr. 36:5 **24:1** [a] Dan. 1:1 [b] 2 Kin. 20:14 **24:2** [a] Jer. 25:9; 32:28; 35:11 [b] 2 Kin. 20:17; 21:12–14; 23:27 **24:3** [a] 2 Kin. 21:2, 11; 23:26 **24:4** [a] 2 Kin. 21:16 **24:6** [a] Jer. 22:18, 19 **24:7** [a] Jer. 37:5–7 [b] Jer. 46:2 **24:8** [a] 2 Chr. 36:9 **24:10** [a] Dan. 1:1 **24:12** [a] Jer. 22:24–30; 24:1; 29:1, 2 [b] 2 Chr. 36:10 **24:13** [a] Is. 39:6 [b] Dan. 5:2, 3 [c] Jer. 20:5 **24:14** [a] Jer. 24:1 [b] 2 Kin. 24:16 [c] 1 Sam. 13:19 [d] 2 Kin. 25:12 **24:15** [a] Jer. 22:24–28

the king's wives, his officers, and the mighty
of the land he carried into captivity from Jerusalem to Babylon. 16 [a]All the valiant men,
seven thousand, and craftsmen and smiths,
one thousand, all *who were* strong *and* fit
for war, these the king of Babylon brought
captive to Babylon.

Zedekiah Reigns in Judah

17 Then [a]the king of Babylon made Mattaniah, [b]*Jehoiachin's*[1] uncle, king in his place,
and [c]changed his name to Zedekiah.
18 [a]Zedekiah *was* twenty-one years old
when he became king, and he reigned elev-
en years in Jerusalem. His mother's name
was [b]Hamutal the daughter of Jeremiah of
Libnah. 19 [a]He also did evil in the sight of the
LORD, according to all that Jehoiakim had
done. 20 For because of the anger of the LORD
this happened in Jerusalem and Judah, that
He finally cast them out from His presence.
[a]Then Zedekiah rebelled against the king
of Babylon.

The Fall and Captivity of Judah

25 Now it came to pass [a]in the ninth year
of his reign, in the tenth month, on the
tenth *day* of the month, *that* Nebuchadnezzar
king of Babylon and all his army came against
Jerusalem and encamped against it; and
they built a siege wall against it all around.
2 So the city was besieged until the eleventh
year of King Zedekiah. 3 By the ninth *day* of
the [a]*fourth* month the famine had become
so severe in the city that there was no food
for the people of the land.
4 Then [a]the city wall was broken through,
and all the men of war *fled* at night by way
of the gate between two walls, which was by
the king's garden, even though the Chaldeans
were still encamped all around against the
city. And [b]*the king*[1] went by way of the plain.[2]
5 But the army of the Chaldeans pursued the
king, and they overtook him in the plains of
Jericho. All his army was scattered from him.
6 So they took the king and brought him up
to the king of Babylon [a]at Riblah, and they
pronounced judgment on him. 7 Then they
killed the sons of Zedekiah before his eyes,
[a]put out the eyes of Zedekiah, bound him
with bronze fetters, and took him to Babylon.
8 And in the fifth month, [a]on the seventh
day of the month (which *was* [b]the nineteenth
year of King Nebuchadnezzar king of Babylon), [c]Nebuzaradan the captain of the guard,
a servant of the king of Babylon, came to
Jerusalem. 9 [a]He burned the house of the
LORD [b]and the king's house; all the houses of
Jerusalem, that is, all the houses of the great,
[c]he burned with fire. 10 And all the army of
the Chaldeans who *were with* the captain of
the guard [a]broke down the walls of Jerusalem all around.
11 Then Nebuzaradan the captain of the
guard carried away captive [a]the rest of the
people *who* remained in the city and the
defectors who had deserted to the king of
Babylon, with the rest of the multitude.
12 But the captain of the guard [a]left *some*
of the poor of the land as vinedressers and
farmers. 13 [a]The bronze [b]pillars that *were* in
the house of the LORD, and [c]the carts and
[d]the bronze Sea that *were* in the house of
the LORD, the Chaldeans broke in pieces,
and [e]carried their bronze to Babylon. 14 They
also took away [a]the pots, the shovels, the
trimmers, the spoons, and all the bronze
utensils with which the priests ministered.
15 The firepans and the basins, the things of
solid gold and solid silver, the captain of the
guard took away. 16 The two pillars, one Sea,
and the carts, which Solomon had made for
the house of the LORD, [a]the bronze of all
these articles was beyond measure. 17 [a]The
height of one pillar *was* eighteen cubits,
and the capital on it *was* of bronze. The
height of the capital was three cubits, and
the network and pomegranates all around
the capital were all of bronze. The second
pillar was the same, with a network.
18 [a]And the captain of the guard took [b]Se-
raiah the chief priest, [c]Zephaniah the second priest, and the three doorkeepers. 19 He
also took out of the city an officer who had
charge of the men of war, [a]five men of the
king's close associates who were found in the
city, the chief recruiting officer of the army,
who mustered the people of the land, and
sixty men of the people of the land *who were*
found in the city. 20 So Nebuzaradan, captain
of the guard, took these and brought them
to the king of Babylon at Riblah. 21 Then the
king of Babylon struck them and put them
to death at Riblah in the land of Hamath.
[a]Thus Judah was carried away captive from
its own land.

24:16 [a] *Jer. 52:28* ***24:17*** [a] *Jer. 37:1* [b] *2 Chr. 36:10* [c] 2 Chr. 36:4 [1] Literally *his* **24:18** [a] Jer. 52:1 [b] 2 Kin. 23:31 **24:19** [a] 2 Chr. 36:12 **24:20** [a] Ezek. 17:15 **25:1** [a] Jer. 6:6; 34:2 **25:3** [a] Lam. 4:9, 10 **25:4** [a] Jer. 39:2 [b] Ezek. 12:12 [1] Literally *he* [2] Or *Arabah,* that is, the Jordan Valley **25:6** [a] Jer. 52:9 **25:7** [a] Jer. 39:7 **25:8** [a] Jer. 52:12 [b] 2 Kin. 24:12 [c] Jer. 39:9 **25:9** [a] 2 Chr. 36:19 [b] Jer. 39:8 [c] Jer. 17:27 **25:10** [a] Neh. 1:3 **25:11** [a] Jer. 5:19; 39:9 **25:12** [a] Jer. 39:10; 40:7; 52:16 **25:13** [a] Jer. 52:17 [b] 1 Kin. 7:15 [c] 1 Kin. 7:27 [d] 1 Kin. 7:23 [e] Jer. 27:19–22 **25:14** [a] Ex. 27:3 **25:16** [a] 1 Kin. 7:47 **25:17** [a] 1 Kin. 7:15–22 **25:18** [a] Jer. 39:9–13; 52:12–16, 24 [b] Ezra 7:1 [c] Jer. 21:1; 29:25, 29 **25:19** [a] Jer. 52:25 **25:21** [a] Deut. 28:36, 64

LEAVE YOUR PRISON WITH PEACE

Jehoiachin changed from his prison garments, and he ate bread regularly before the king all the days of his life.

2 KINGS 25:29

Even in the context of disaster and destruction, the peace of God has a way of working itself into our lives. Jehoiachin's tragic story is a case in point. The young prince succeeded his father, Jehoiakim, whose rebellion brought the Babylonian army against Jerusalem. Jehoiachin gave himself up to bring peace, but it didn't last. His uncle Zedekiah, Israel's new king, was corrupt and incompetent. His rule led to a return of the Babylonian army, the capture of Jerusalem, the destruction of the temple, and the exile of most of the Jewish people.

As tragic as all of this is, the Book of Kings ends on a hopeful note. The Babylonian king released Jehoiachin from prison and invited him to sit at the royal table. No one would ever want to go through what Jehoiachin endured, but his experience once again reveals our sovereign God at work. He was never forgotten. He was never abandoned to his fate. He was never without hope of deliverance.

Neither are you. We can have peace when we remember that no matter how discouraging life may be, God is still there and He is more than able to deliver.

Gedaliah Made Governor of Judah

22 Then he made Gedaliah the son of [a]Ahi-
kam, the son of Shaphan, governor over [b]the
people who remained in the land of Judah,
whom Nebuchadnezzar king of Babylon
had left. 23 Now when all the [a]captains of the
armies, they and *their* men, heard that the
king of Babylon had made Gedaliah governor,
they came to Gedaliah at Mizpah—Ishmael the son of Nethaniah, Johanan the son
of Careah, Seraiah the son of Tanhumeth
the Netophathite, and Jaazaniah[1] the son of
a Maachathite, they and their men. 24 And
Gedaliah took an oath before them and their
men, and said to them, "Do not be afraid of
the servants of the Chaldeans. Dwell in the
land and serve the king of Babylon, and it
shall be well with you."
25 But [a]it happened in the seventh month
that Ishmael the son of Nethaniah, the son of
Elishama, of the royal family, came with ten
men and struck and killed Gedaliah, the Jews,
as well as the Chaldeans who were with him
at Mizpah. 26 And all the people, small and
great, and the captains of the armies, arose
[a]and went to Egypt; for they were afraid of
the Chaldeans.

Jehoiachin Released from Prison

27 [a]Now it came to pass in the thirty-
seventh year of the captivity of Jehoiachin
king of Judah, in the twelfth month, on the
twenty-seventh *day* of the month, *that* Evil-
Merodach[1] king of Babylon, in the year that
he began to reign, [b]released Jehoiachin king
of Judah from prison. 28 He spoke kindly to
him, and gave him a more prominent seat
than those of the kings who *were* with him in
Babylon. 29 So Jehoiachin changed from his
prison garments, and he [a]ate bread regularly
before the king all the days of his life. 30 And
as for his provisions, *there was* a regular
ration given him by the king, a portion for
each day, all the days of his life.

25:22 [a] 2 Kin. 22:12 [b] Is. 1:9; Jer. 40:5 **25:23** [a] Jer. 40:7–9 [1] Spelled *Jezaniah* in Jeremiah 40:8 **25:25** [a] Jer. 41:1–3 **25:26** [a] Jer. 43:4–7 **25:27** [a] Jer. 52:31–34 [b] Gen. 40:13, 20 [1] Literally *Man of Marduk* **25:29** [a] 2 Sam. 9:7

THE FIRST BOOK OF THE

CHRONICLES

AUTHOR

Tradition in the Jewish Talmud supports Ezra the priest as the author of 1 Chronicles. The content points to priestly authorship because of the emphasis on the temple, the priesthood, and the theocratic line of David in the southern kingdom of Judah. Ezra was an educated scribe (Ezra 7:6), and according to the apocryphal book of 2 Maccabees (2:13–15), Nehemiah collected an extensive library, which was available to Ezra for his use in compiling Chronicles.

TIME

c. 1004–971 BC

KEY VERSE

1 Chronicles 17:11–14

THEME

First Chronicles is largely a retelling of the texts of 1 and 2 Samuel with administrative details and the roles that the various tribes and alliances played in the events of the nation. We don't see the family conflict with Michal when the ark is brought to Jerusalem or the affair with Bathsheba and its fallout. When it comes to succession, all we are told is that David chose Solomon to succeed him. This is a primary document of the history of Israel.

The role of the Holy Spirit in peace is emphasized in a powerful way through Amasai, chief of the captains: "Then the Spirit came upon Amasai . . . 'Peace, peace to you, and peace to your helpers! For your God helps you'" (1 Chr. 12:18). The last words of David to his son Solomon are a blessing for all parents to speak over their children for a life of peace: "Know the God of your father, and serve Him with a loyal [*shalom*—'complete'] heart and with a willing mind; for the LORD searches all hearts and understands all the intent of the thoughts" (28:9). While the focus of 1 Chronicles is the importance of the Davidic line and David himself, Ezra (the author) goes to great lengths to establish David's kingship through the most exhaustive Old Testament genealogy. The reader will grasp how vital God's peace was in the life and times of David and how desperately David desired peace for his son and family. First Chronicles reminds us that though we may be separated from David by time and history, we share in his concern that God would establish us in His peace and use us to bring peace to our families.

The Family of Adam—Seth to Abraham

1 Adam,[a] [b]Seth, Enosh, 2 Cainan,[1] Mahalalel, Jared, 3 Enoch, Methuselah, Lamech,
4 [a]Noah,[1] Shem, Ham, and Japheth.
5 [a]The sons of Japheth *were* Gomer, Magog,
Madai, Javan, Tubal, Meshech, and Tiras.
6 The sons of Gomer *were* Ashkenaz, Diphath,[1]
and Togarmah. 7 The sons of Javan *were* Elishah, Tarshishah,[1] Kittim, and Rodanim.[2]
8 [a]The sons of Ham *were* Cush, Mizraim, Put,
and Canaan. 9 The sons of Cush *were* Seba, Havilah, Sabta,[1] Raama,[2] and Sabtecha. The sons of
Raama *were* Sheba and Dedan. 10 Cush [a]begot
Nimrod; he began to be a mighty one on the
earth. 11 Mizraim begot Ludim, Anamim, Lehabim, Naphtuhim, 12 Pathrusim, Casluhim (from
whom came the Philistines and the [a]Caph-
torim). 13 [a]Canaan begot Sidon, his firstborn, and
Heth; 14 the Jebusite, the Amorite, and the Girgashite; 15 the Hivite, the Arkite, and the Sinite;
16 the Arvadite, the Zemarite, and the Hamathite.
17 The sons of [a]Shem *were* Elam, Asshur,
[b]Arphaxad, Lud, Aram, Uz, Hul, Gether, and
Meshech.[1] 18 Arphaxad begot Shelah, and Shelah begot Eber. 19 To Eber were born two sons:
the name of one *was* Peleg,[1] for in his days the
earth was divided; and his brother's name *was*
Joktan. 20 [a]Joktan begot Almodad, Sheleph,
Hazarmaveth, Jerah, 21 Hadoram, Uzal, Diklah, 22 Ebal,[1] Abimael, Sheba, 23 Ophir, Havilah,
and Jobab. All these *were* the sons of Joktan.
24 [a]Shem, Arphaxad, Shelah, 25 [a]Eber, Peleg,
Reu, 26 Serug, Nahor, Terah, 27 and [a]Abram,
who *is* Abraham. 28 [a]The sons of Abraham
were [b]Isaac and [c]Ishmael.

The Family of Ishmael

29 These *are* their genealogies: The [a]first-
born of Ishmael *was* Nebajoth; then Kedar,
Adbeel, Mibsam, 30 Mishma, Dumah, Massa,
Hadad,[1] Tema, 31 Jetur, Naphish, and Kedemah. These *were* the sons of Ishmael.

The Family of Keturah

32 Now [a]the sons born to Keturah, Abraham's
concubine, *were* Zimran, Jokshan, Medan,
Midian, Ishbak, and Shuah. The sons of Jok-
shan *were* Sheba and Dedan. 33 The sons of
Midian *were* Ephah, Epher, Hanoch, Abida, and
Eldaah. All these were the children of Keturah.

The Family of Isaac

34 And [a]Abraham begot Isaac. [b]The sons
of Isaac *were* Esau and Israel. 35 The sons of
[a]Esau *were* Eliphaz, Reuel, Jeush, Jaalam,
and Korah. 36 And the sons of Eliphaz *were*
Teman, Omar, Zephi,[1] Gatam, *and* Kenaz;
and *by* [a]Timna,[2] Amalek. 37 The sons of Reuel
were Nahath, Zerah, Shammah, and Mizzah.

The Family of Seir

38 [a]The sons of Seir *were* Lotan, Shobal, Zibeon, Anah, Dishon, Ezer, and Dishan. 39 And
the sons of Lotan *were* Hori and Homam;
Lotan's sister *was* Timna. 40 The sons of Shobal *were* Alian,[1] Manahath, Ebal, Shephi,[2]
and Onam. The sons of Zibeon *were* Ajah
and Anah. 41 The son of Anah *was* [a]Dishon.
The sons of Dishon *were* Hamran,[1] Eshban,
Ithran, and Cheran. 42 The sons of Ezer *were*
Bilhan, Zaavan, *and* Jaakan.[1] The sons of Dishan *were* Uz and Aran.

The Kings of Edom

43 Now these *were* the [a]kings who reigned
in the land of Edom before a king reigned
over the children of Israel: Bela the son of
Beor, and the name of his city was Dinhabah. 44 And when Bela died, Jobab the son
of Zerah of Bozrah reigned in his place.
45 When Jobab died, Husham of the land of
the Temanites reigned in his place. 46 And
when Husham died, Hadad the son of
Bedad, who attacked Midian in the field of
Moab, reigned in his place. The name of his
city *was* Avith. 47 When Hadad died, Samlah
of Masrekah reigned in his place. 48 [a]And
when Samlah died, Saul of Rehoboth-by-
the-River reigned in his place. 49 When Saul
died, Baal-Hanan the son of Achbor reigned
in his place. 50 And when Baal-Hanan died,
Hadad[1] reigned in his place; and the name
of his city was Pai.[2] His wife's name was
Mehetabel the daughter of Matred, the
daughter of Mezahab. 51 Hadad died also.
And the chiefs of Edom were Chief Timnah,
Chief Aliah,[1] Chief Jetheth, 52 Chief Aholibamah, Chief Elah, Chief Pinon, 53 Chief
Kenaz, Chief Teman, Chief Mibzar, 54 Chief
Magdiel, and Chief Iram. These *were* the
chiefs of Edom.

1:1 [a] Gen. 1:27; 2:7; 5:1, 2, 5 [b] Gen. 4:25, 26; 5:3–9 **1:2** [1] Hebrew *Qenan* **1:4** [a] Gen. 5:28—10:1 [1] Following Masoretic Text and Vulgate; Septuagint adds *the sons of Noah.* **1:5** [a] Gen. 10:2–4 **1:6** [1] Spelled *Riphath* in Genesis 10:3 **1:7** [1] Spelled *Tarshish* in Genesis 10:4 [2] Spelled *Dodanim* in Genesis 10:4 **1:8** [a] Gen. 10:6 **1:9** [1] Spelled *Sabtah* in Genesis 10:7 [2] Spelled *Raamah* in Genesis 10:7 **1:10** [a] Gen. 10:8–10, 13 **1:12** [a] Deut. 2:23 **1:13** [a] Gen. 9:18, 25–27; 10:15 **1:17** [a] Gen. 10:22–29; 11:10 [b] Luke 3:36 [1] Spelled *Mash* in Genesis 10:23 **1:19** [1] Literally *Division* **1:20** [a] Gen. 10:26 **1:22** [1] Spelled *Obal* in Genesis 10:28 **1:24** [a] Luke 3:34–36 **1:25** [a] Gen. 11:15 **1:27** [a] Gen. 17:5 **1:28** [a] Gen. 21:2, 3 [b] Gen. 21:2 [c] Gen. 16:11, 15 **1:29** [a] Gen. 25:13–16 **1:30** [1] Spelled *Hadar* in Genesis 25:15 **1:32** [a] Gen. 25:1–4 **1:34** [a] Gen. 21:2 [b] Gen. 25:9, 25, 26, 29; 32:28 **1:35** [a] Gen. 36:10–19 **1:36** [a] Gen. 36:12 [1] Spelled *Zepho* in Genesis 36:11 [2] Compare Genesis 36:12 **1:38** [a] Gen. 36:20–28 **1:40** [1] Spelled *Alvan* in Genesis 36:23 [2] Spelled *Shepho* in Genesis 36:23 **1:41** [a] Gen. 36:25 [1] Spelled *Hemdan* in Genesis 36:26 **1:42** [1] Spelled *Akan* in Genesis 36:27 **1:43** [a] Gen. 36:31–43 **1:48** [a] Gen. 36:37 **1:50** [1] Spelled *Hadar* in Genesis 36:39 [2] Spelled *Pau* in Genesis 36:39 **1:51** [1] Spelled *Alvah* in Genesis 36:40

The Family of Israel

2 These *were* the [a]sons of Israel: [b]Reuben, Simeon, Levi, Judah, Issachar, Zebulun, 2 Dan, Joseph, Benjamin, Naphtali, Gad, and Asher.

From Judah to David

3 The sons of [a]Judah *were* Er, Onan, and Shelah. *These* three were born to him by the daughter of [b]Shua, the Canaanitess. [c]Er, the firstborn of Judah, was wicked in the sight of the LORD; so He killed him. 4 And [a]Tamar, his daughter-in-law, [b]bore him Perez and Zerah. All the sons of Judah *were* five.

5 The sons of [a]Perez *were* Hezron and Hamul. 6 The sons of Zerah *were* Zimri, [a]Ethan, Heman, Calcol, and Dara—five of them in all.

7 The son of [a]Carmi *was* Achar,[1] the troubler of Israel, who transgressed in the [b]accursed thing.

8 The son of Ethan *was* Azariah.

9 Also the sons of Hezron who were born to him *were* Jerahmeel, Ram, and Chelubai.[1] 10 Ram [a]begot Amminadab, and Amminadab begot Nahshon, [b]leader of the children of Judah; 11 Nahshon begot Salma,[1] and Salma begot Boaz; 12 Boaz begot Obed, and Obed begot Jesse; 13 [a]Jesse begot Eliab his firstborn, Abinadab the second, Shimea[1] the third, 14 Nethanel the fourth, Raddai the fifth, 15 Ozem the sixth, *and* David the [a]seventh.

16 Now their sisters *were* Zeruiah and Abigail. [a]And the sons of Zeruiah *were* Abishai, Joab, and Asahel—three. 17 Abigail bore Amasa; and the father of Amasa *was* Jether the Ishmaelite.[1]

The Family of Hezron

18 Caleb the son of Hezron had children by Azubah, *his* wife, and by Jerioth. Now these were her sons: Jesher, Shobab, and Ardon. 19 When Azubah died, Caleb took [a]Ephrath[1] as his wife, who bore him Hur. 20 And Hur begot Uri, and Uri begot [a]Bezalel.

21 Now afterward Hezron went in to the daughter of [a]Machir the father of Gilead, whom he married when he *was* sixty years old; and she bore him Segub. 22 Segub begot [a]Jair, who had twenty-three cities in the land of Gilead. 23 [a](Geshur and Syria took from them the towns of Jair, with Kenath and its towns—sixty towns.) All these *belonged to* the sons of Machir the father of Gilead. 24 After Hezron died in Caleb Ephrathah, Hezron's wife Abijah bore him [a]Ashhur the father of Tekoa.

> **PEACE NOTE**
>
> Even when we experience grief and deep loss, the *shalom* of God—the peace and presence of Christ—is real and steadfast.

The Family of Jerahmeel

25 The sons of Jerahmeel, the firstborn of Hezron, *were* Ram, the firstborn, and Bunah, Oren, Ozem, *and* Ahijah. 26 Jerahmeel had another wife, whose name was Atarah; she was the mother of Onam. 27 The sons of Ram, the firstborn of Jerahmeel, were Maaz, Jamin, and Eker. 28 The sons of Onam were Shammai and Jada. The sons of Shammai *were* Nadab and Abishur.

29 And the name of the wife of Abishur *was* Abihail, and she bore him Ahban and Molid. 30 The sons of Nadab *were* Seled and Appaim; Seled died without children. 31 The son of Appaim *was* Ishi, the son of Ishi *was* Sheshan, and [a]Sheshan's son *was* Ahlai. 32 The sons of Jada, the brother of Shammai, *were* Jether and Jonathan; Jether died without children. 33 The sons of Jonathan *were* Peleth and Zaza. These were the sons of Jerahmeel.

34 Now Sheshan had no sons, only daughters. And Sheshan had an Egyptian servant whose name *was* Jarha. 35 Sheshan gave his daughter to Jarha his servant as wife, and she bore him Attai. 36 Attai begot Nathan, and Nathan begot [a]Zabad; 37 Zabad begot Ephlal, and Ephlal begot [a]Obed; 38 Obed begot Jehu, and Jehu begot Azariah; 39 Azariah begot Helez, and Helez begot Eleasah; 40 Eleasah begot Sismai, and Sismai begot Shallum; 41 Shallum begot Jekamiah, and Jekamiah begot Elishama.

2:1 [a] Gen. 29:32–35; 35:23, 26; 46:8–27 [b] Gen. 29:32; 35:22 **2:3** [a] Num. 26:19 [b] Gen. 38:2 [c] Gen. 38:7 **2:4** [a] Gen. 38:6 [b] Matt. 1:3 **2:5** [a] Ruth 4:18 **2:6** [a] 1 Kin. 4:31 **2:7** [a] 1 Chr. 4:1 [b] Josh. 6:18 [1] Spelled *Achan* in Joshua 7:1 and elsewhere **2:9** [1] Spelled *Caleb* in 2:18, 42 **2:10** [a] Matt. 1:4 [b] Num. 1:7; 2:3 **2:11** [1] Spelled *Salmon* in Ruth 4:21 and Luke 3:32 **2:13** [a] 1 Sam. 16:6 [1] Spelled *Shammah* in 1 Samuel 16:9 and elsewhere **2:15** [a] 1 Sam. 16:10, 11; 17:12 **2:16** [a] 2 Sam. 2:18 **2:17** [1] Compare 2 Samuel 17:25 **2:19** [a] 1 Chr. 2:50 [1] Spelled *Ephrathah* elsewhere **2:20** [a] Ex. 31:2; 38:22 **2:21** [a] Num. 27:1 **2:22** [a] Judg. 10:3 **2:23** [a] Deut. 3:14 **2:24** [a] 1 Chr. 4:5 **2:31** [a] 1 Chr. 2:34, 35 **2:36** [a] 1 Chr. 11:41 **2:37** [a] 2 Chr. 23:1

The Family of Caleb

42 The descendants of Caleb the brother of
Jerahmeel *were* Mesha, his firstborn, who was
the father of Ziph, and the sons of Mareshah
the father of Hebron. 43 The sons of Hebron
were Korah, Tappuah, Rekem, and Shema.
44 Shema begot Raham the father of Jorkoam,
and Rekem begot Shammai. 45 And the son
of Shammai *was* Maon, and Maon *was* the
father of Beth Zur.

46 Ephah, Caleb's concubine, bore Haran,
Moza, and Gazez; and Haran begot Gazez.
47 And the sons of Jahdai *were* Regem, Jotham, Geshan, Pelet, Ephah, and Shaaph.

48 Maachah, Caleb's concubine, bore She-
ber and Tirhanah. 49 She also bore Shaaph
the father of Madmannah, Sheva the father
of Machbenah and the father of Gibea. And
the daughter of Caleb *was* [a]Achsah.

50 These were the descendants of Caleb:
The sons of [a]Hur, the firstborn of Ephrathah,
were Shobal the father of [b]Kirjath Jearim,
51 Salma the father of Bethlehem, *and* Hareph
the father of Beth Gader.

52 And Shobal the father of Kirjath Jearim
had descendants: Haroeh, *and* half of the
families of Manuhoth.[1] 53 The families of Kirjath Jearim *were* the Ithrites, the Puthites, the
Shumathites, and the Mishraites. From these
came the Zorathites and the Eshtaolites.

54 The sons of Salma *were* Bethlehem, the
Netophathites, Atroth Beth Joab, half of the
Manahethites, and the Zorites.

55 And the families of the scribes who dwelt
at Jabez *were* the Tirathites, the Shimeathites,
and the Suchathites. These *were* the [a]Kenites
who came from Hammath, the father of the
house of [b]Rechab.

The Family of David

3 Now these were the sons of David who
were born to him in Hebron: The firstborn *was* [a]Amnon, by [b]Ahinoam the [c]Jez-
reelitess; the second, Daniel,[1] by [d]Abigail
the Carmelitess; 2 the third, [a]Absalom the
son of Maacah, the daughter of Talmai, king
of Geshur; the fourth, [b]Adonijah the son of
Haggith; 3 the fifth, Shephatiah, by Abital; the
sixth, Ithream, by his wife [a]Eglah.

4 *These* six were born to him in Hebron.
[a]There he reigned seven years and six months,
and [b]in Jerusalem he reigned thirty-three
years. 5 [a]And these were born to him in Jerusalem: Shimea,[1] Shobab, Nathan, and [b]Sol-
omon—four by Bathshua[2] the daughter of
Ammiel.[3] 6 Also *there* were Ibhar, Elishama,[1]
Eliphelet,[2] 7 Nogah, Nepheg, Japhia, 8 Elishama, Eliada,[1] and Eliphelet—[a]nine *in all.* 9 *These*
were all the sons of David, besides the sons
of the concubines, and [a]Tamar their sister.

The Family of Solomon

10 Solomon's son *was* [a]Rehoboam; Abijah[1]
was his son, Asa his son, Jehoshaphat his
son, 11 Joram[1] his son, Ahaziah his son, Joash[2]
his son, 12 Amaziah his son, Azariah[1] his son,
Jotham his son, 13 Ahaz his son, Hezekiah his
son, Manasseh his son, 14 Amon his son, *and*
Josiah his son. 15 The sons of Josiah *were* Johanan the firstborn, the second Jehoiakim,
the third Zedekiah, and the fourth Shallum.[1]
16 The sons of [a]Jehoiakim *were* Jeconiah his
son *and* Zedekiah[1] his son.

The Family of Jeconiah

17 And the sons of Jeconiah[1] *were* Assir,[2]
Shealtiel [a]his son, 18 *and* Malchiram, Pedaiah,
Shenazzar, Jecamiah, Hoshama, and Neda-
biah. 19 The sons of Pedaiah *were* Zerubbabel
and Shimei. The sons of Zerubbabel *were*
Meshullam, Hananiah, Shelomith their sister,
20 and Hashubah, Ohel, Berechiah, Hasadiah,
and Jushab-Hesed—five *in all.*

21 The sons of Hananiah *were* Pelatiah and
Jeshaiah, the sons of Rephaiah, the sons of
Arnan, the sons of Obadiah, and the sons
of Shechaniah. 22 The son of Shechaniah
was Shemaiah. The sons of Shemaiah *were*
[a]Hattush, Igal, Bariah, Neariah, and Shaphat—six *in all.* 23 The sons of Neariah *were*
Elioenai, Hezekiah, and Azrikam—three *in*
all. 24 The sons of Elioenai *were* Hodaviah,
Eliashib, Pelaiah, Akkub, Johanan, Delaiah,
and Anani—seven *in all.*

The Family of Judah

4 The sons of Judah *were* [a]Perez, Hezron,
Carmi, Hur, and Shobal. 2 And Reaiah the
son of Shobal begot Jahath, and Jahath begot
Ahumai and Lahad. These *were* the families
of the Zorathites. 3 These *were the sons of* the
father of Etam: Jezreel, Ishma, and Idbash;

2:49 [a] Josh. 15:17 **2:50** [a] 1 Chr. 4:4 [b] Josh. 9:17; 18:14 **2:52** [1] Same as *the Manahethites,* verse 54 **2:55** [a] Judg. 1:16 [b] Jer. 35:2 **3:1** [a] 2 Sam. 3:2–5 [b] 1 Sam. 25:43 [c] Josh. 15:56 [d] 1 Sam. 25:39–42 [1] Called *Chileab* in 2 Samuel 3:3 **3:2** [a] 2 Sam. 13:37; 15:1 [b] 1 Kin. 1:5 **3:3** [a] 2 Sam. 3:5 **3:4** [a] 2 Sam. 2:11 [b] 2 Sam. 5:5 **3:5** [a] 1 Chr. 14:4–7 [b] 2 Sam. 12:24, 25 [1] Spelled *Shammua* in 14:4 and 2 Samuel 5:14 [2] Spelled *Bathsheba* in 2 Samuel 11:3 [3] Called *Eliam* in 2 Samuel 11:3 **3:6** [1] Spelled *Elishua* in 14:5 and 2 Samuel 5:15 [2] Spelled *Elpelet* in 14:5 **3:8** [a] 2 Sam. 5:14–16 [1] Spelled *Beeliada* in 14:7 **3:9** [a] 2 Sam. 13:1 **3:10** [a] 1 Kin. 11:43 [1] Spelled *Abijam* in 1 Kings 15:1 **3:11** [1] Spelled *Jehoram* in 2 Kings 1:17 and 8:16 [2] Spelled *Jehoash* in 2 Kings 12:1 **3:12** [1] Called *Uzziah* in Isaiah 6:1 **3:15** [1] Called *Jehoahaz* in 2 Kings 23:31 **3:16** [a] Matt. 1:11 [1] Compare 2 Kings 24:17 **3:17** [a] Matt. 1:12 [1] Also called *Coniah* in Jeremiah 22:24 and *Jehoiachin* in 2 Kings 24:8 [2] Or *Jeconiah the captive were* **3:22** [a] Ezra 8:2 **4:1** [a] Gen. 38:29; 46:12

and the name of their sister *was* Hazelelpo-
ni; 4 and Penuel *was* the father of Gedor, and
Ezer *was the* father of Hushah.
These *were* the sons of [a]Hur, the firstborn
of Ephrathah the father of Bethlehem.
5 And [a]Ashhur the father of Tekoa had two
wives, Helah and Naarah. 6 Naarah bore him
Ahuzzam, Hepher, Temeni, and Haahashtari.
These *were* the sons of Naarah. 7 The sons of
Helah *were* Zereth, Zohar, and Ethnan; 8 and
Koz begot Anub, Zobebah, and the families
of Aharhel the son of Harum.
9 Now Jabez was [a]more honorable than his
brothers, and his mother called his name
Jabez,[1] saying, "Because I bore *him* in pain."
10 And Jabez called on the God of Israel saying, "Oh, that You would bless me indeed,
and enlarge my territory, that Your hand
would be with me, and that You would keep
me from evil, that I may not cause pain!" So
God granted him what he requested.

PEACE NOTE

The peace of the Lord leads to the provision of the Lord—God's blessings! Be bold enough to pay Jabez's prayer!

1 CHRONICLES 4:10

11 Chelub the brother of [a]Shuhah begot
Mehir, who *was* the father of Eshton. 12 And
Eshton begot Beth-Rapha, Paseah, and Te-
hinnah the father of Ir-Nahash. These *were*
the men of Rechah.
13 The sons of Kenaz *were* [a]Othniel and
Seraiah. The sons of Othniel *were* Hathath,[1]
14 and Meonothai *who* begot Ophrah. Seraiah
begot Joab the father of [a]Ge Harashim,[1] for
they were craftsmen. 15 The sons of [a]Caleb
the son of Jephunneh *were* Iru, Elah, and
Naam. The son of Elah *was* Kenaz. 16 The
sons of Jehallelel *were* Ziph, Ziphah, Tiria,
and Asarel. 17 *The sons of Ezrah were* Jether,
Mered, Epher, and Jalon. And *Mered's wife*[1]
bore Miriam, Shammai, and Ishbah the father of Eshtemoa. 18 (His wife Jehudijah[1] bore
Jered the father of Gedor, Heber the father
of Sochoh, and Jekuthiel the father of Zanoah.) And these were the sons of Bithiah
the daughter of Pharaoh, whom Mered took.
19 The sons of Hodiah's wife, the sister of
Naham, *were* the fathers of Keilah the Gar-
mite and of Eshtemoa the [a]Maachathite.
20 And the sons of Shimon *were* Amnon,
Rinnah, Ben-Hanan, and Tilon. And the sons
of Ishi *were* Zoheth and Ben-Zoheth.
21 The sons of [a]Shelah [b]the son of Judah
were Er the father of Lecah, Laadah the father of Mareshah, and the families of the
house of the linen workers of the house of
Ashbea; 22 also Jokim, the men of Chozeba,
and Joash; Saraph, who ruled in Moab, and
Jashubi-Lehem. Now the records are ancient.
23 These *were* the potters and those who dwell
at Netaim[1] and Gederah;[2] there they dwelt
with the king for his work.

The Family of Simeon

24 The [a]sons of Simeon *were* Nemuel,
Jamin, Jarib,[1] Zerah,[2] *and* Shaul, 25 Shallum
his son, Mibsam his son, and Mishma his
son. 26 And the sons of Mishma *were* Hamuel
his son, Zacchur his son, and Shimei his son.
27 Shimei had sixteen sons and six daughters;
but his brothers did not have many children,
[a]nor did any of their families multiply as
much as the children of Judah.
28 They dwelt at Beersheba, Moladah, Hazar
Shual, 29 Bilhah, Ezem, Tolad, 30 Bethuel, Hormah, Ziklag, 31 Beth Marcaboth, Hazar Susim,
Beth Biri, and at Shaaraim. These *were* their
cities until the reign of David. 32 And their
villages *were* Etam, Ain, Rimmon, Tochen,
and Ashan—five cities— 33 and all the villages
that *were* around these cities as far as Baal.[1]
These *were* their dwelling places, and they
maintained their genealogy: 34 Meshobab,
Jamlech, and Joshah the son of Amaziah;
35 Joel, and Jehu the son of Joshibiah, the son
of Seraiah, the son of Asiel; 36 Elioenai, Jaako-
bah, Jeshohaiah, Asaiah, Adiel, Jesimiel, and
Benaiah; 37 Ziza the son of Shiphi, the son of
Allon, the son of Jedaiah, the son of Shimri,
the son of Shemaiah— 38 these mentioned
by name *were* leaders in their families, and
their father's house increased greatly.
39 So they went to the entrance of Gedor,
as far as the east side of the valley, to seek

4:4 [a] 1 Chr. 2:50 **4:5** [a] 1 Chr. 2:24 **4:9** [a] Gen. 34:19 [1] Literally *He Will Cause Pain* **4:11** [a] Job 8:1 **4:13** [a] Josh. 15:17 [1] Septuagint and Vulgate add *and Meonothai.* **4:14** [a] Neh. 11:35 [1] Literally *Valley of Craftsmen* **4:15** [a] 1 Chr. 6:56 **4:17** [1] Literally *she* **4:18** [1] Or *His Judean wife* **4:19** [a] 2 Kin. 25:23 **4:21** [a] Gen. 38:11, 14 [b] Gen. 38:1–5; 46:12 **4:23** [1] Literally *Plants* [2] Literally *Hedges* **4:24** [a] Num. 26:12–14 [1] Called *Jachin* in Genesis 46:10 [2] Called *Zohar* in Genesis 46:10 **4:27** [a] Num. 2:9 **4:33** [1] Or *Baalath Beer* (compare Joshua 19:8)

pasture for their flocks. 40 And they found
rich, good pasture, and the land *was* broad,
quiet, and peaceful; for some Hamites formerly lived there.

41 These recorded by name came in the
days of Hezekiah king of Judah; and they
[a]attacked their tents and the Meunites who
were found there, and [b]utterly destroyed
them, as it is to this day. So they dwelt in
their place, because *there was* pasture for
their flocks there. 42 Now *some* of them, five
hundred men of the sons of Simeon, went to
Mount Seir, having as their captains Pelatiah, Neariah, Rephaiah, and Uzziel, the sons
of Ishi. 43 And they defeated [a]the rest of the
Amalekites who had escaped. They have
dwelt there to this day.

The Family of Reuben

5 Now the sons of Reuben the firstborn
of Israel—[a]he *was* indeed the firstborn,
but because he [b]defiled his father's bed, [c]his
birthright was given to the sons of Joseph,
the son of Israel, so that the genealogy is
not listed according to the birthright; 2 yet
[a]Judah prevailed over his brothers, and from
him *came* a [b]ruler, although the birthright
was Joseph's— 3 the sons of [a]Reuben the
firstborn of Israel were Hanoch, Pallu, Hezron, and Carmi.

4 The sons of Joel *were* Shemaiah his son,
Gog his son, Shimei his son, 5 Micah his son,
Reaiah his son, Baal his son, 6 and Beerah
his son, whom Tiglath-Pileser[1] king of Assyria [a]carried into captivity. He *was* leader
of the Reubenites. 7 And his brethren by
their families, [a]when the genealogy of their
generations was registered: the chief, Jeiel,
and Zechariah, 8 and Bela the son of Azaz,
the son of Shema, the son of Joel, who dwelt
in [a]Aroer, as far as Nebo and Baal Meon.
9 Eastward they settled as far as the entrance
of the wilderness this side of the River Euphrates, because their cattle had multiplied
[a]in the land of Gilead.

10 Now in the days of Saul they made war
[a]with the Hagrites, who fell by their hand;
and they dwelt in their tents throughout the
entire *area* east of Gilead.

The Family of Gad

11 And the [a]children of Gad dwelt next to
them in the land of [b]Bashan as far as [c]Salcah:
12 Joel *was* the chief, Shapham the next, then
Jaanai and Shaphat in Bashan, 13 and their
brethren of their father's house: Michael,
Meshullam, Sheba, Jorai, Jachan, Zia, and
Eber—seven *in all.* 14 These *were* the children
of Abihail the son of Huri, the son of Jaroah,
the son of Gilead, the son of Michael, the
son of Jeshishai, the son of Jahdo, the son
of Buz; 15 Ahi the son of Abdiel, the son of
Guni, *was* chief of their father's house. 16 And
the Gadites dwelt in Gilead, in Bashan and
in its villages, and in all the common-lands
of [a]Sharon within their borders. 17 All these
were registered by genealogies in the days
of [a]Jotham king of Judah, and in the days of
[b]Jeroboam king of Israel.

18 The sons of Reuben, the Gadites, and
half the tribe of Manasseh *had* forty-four
thousand seven hundred and sixty valiant
men, men able to bear shield and sword, to
shoot with the bow, and skillful in war, who
went to war. 19 They made war with the Hagrites, [a]Jetur, Naphish, and Nodab. 20 And [a]they
were helped against them, and the Hagrites
were delivered into their hand, and all who
were with them, for they [b]cried out to God in
the battle. He heeded their prayer, because
they [c]put their trust in Him. 21 Then they took
away their livestock—fifty thousand of their
camels, two hundred and fifty thousand
of their sheep, and two thousand of their
donkeys—also one hundred thousand of
their men; 22 for many fell dead, because the
war [a]*was* God's. And they dwelt in their place
until [b]the captivity.

The Family of Manasseh (East)

23 So the children of the half-tribe of Manasseh dwelt in the land. Their *numbers* increased from Bashan to Baal Hermon, that
is, to [a]Senir, or Mount Hermon. 24 These *were*
the heads of their fathers' houses: Epher, Ishi,
Eliel, Azriel, Jeremiah, Hodaviah, and Jahdi-
el. They were mighty men of valor, famous
men, *and* heads of their fathers' houses.

25 And they were unfaithful to the God of
their fathers, and [a]played the harlot after the
gods of the peoples of the land, whom God
had destroyed before them. 26 So the God of
Israel stirred up the spirit of [a]Pul king of Assyria, that is, [b]Tiglath-Pileser[1] king of Assyria.
He carried the Reubenites, the Gadites, and
the half-tribe of Manasseh into captivity. He
took them to [c]Halah, Habor, Hara, and the
river of Gozan to this day.

4:41 [a] 2 Kin. 18:8 [b] 2 Kin. 19:11 **4:43** [a] 1 Sam. 15:8; 30:17 **5:1** [a] Gen. 29:32; 49:3 [b] Gen. 35:22; 49:4 [c] Gen. 48:15, 22 **5:2** [a] Gen. 49:8, 10 [b] Mic. 5:2 **5:3** [a] Ex. 6:14 **5:6** [a] 2 Kin. 18:11 [1] Hebrew *Tilgath-Pilneser* **5:7** [a] 1 Chr. 5:17 **5:8** [a] Josh. 12:2; 13:15, 16 **5:9** [a] Josh. 22:8, 9 **5:10** [a] Gen. 25:12 **5:11** [a] Num. 26:15–18 [b] Josh. 13:11, 24–28 [c] Deut. 3:10 **5:16** [a] 1 Chr. 27:29 **5:17** [a] 2 Kin. 15:5, 32 [b] 2 Kin. 14:16, 28 **5:19** [a] Gen. 25:15 **5:20** [a] [1 Chr. 5:22] [b] 2 Chr. 14:11–13 [c] Ps. 9:10; 20:7, 8; 22:4, 5 **5:22** [a] [Josh. 23:10] [b] 2 Kin. 15:29; 17:6 **5:23** [a] Deut. 3:9 **5:25** [a] 2 Kin. 17:7 **5:26** [a] 2 Kin. 15:19 [b] 2 Kin. 15:29 [c] 2 Kin. 17:6; 18:11 [1] Hebrew *Tilgath-Pilneser*

The Family of Levi

6 The sons of Levi *were* [a]Gershon, Kohath, and Merari. 2 The sons of Kohath *were* Amram, [a]Izhar, Hebron, and Uzziel. 3 The children of Amram *were* Aaron, Moses, and Miriam. And the sons of Aaron *were* [a]Nadab, Abihu, Eleazar, and Ithamar. 4 Eleazar begot Phinehas, *and* Phinehas begot Abishua; 5 Abishua begot Bukki, and Bukki begot Uzzi; 6 Uzzi begot Zerahiah, and Zerahiah begot Meraioth; 7 Meraioth begot Amariah, and Amariah begot Ahitub; 8 [a]Ahitub begot [b]Zadok, and Zadok begot Ahimaaz; 9 Ahimaaz begot Azariah, and Azariah begot Johanan; 10 Johanan begot Azariah (it was he [a]who ministered as priest in the [b]temple that Solomon built in Jerusalem); 11 [a]Azariah begot [b]Amariah, and Amariah begot Ahitub; 12 Ahitub begot Zadok, and Zadok begot Shallum; 13 Shallum begot Hilkiah, and Hilkiah begot Azariah; 14 Azariah begot [a]Seraiah, and Seraiah begot Jehozadak. 15 Jehozadak went *into captivity* [a]when the LORD carried Judah and Jerusalem into captivity by the hand of Nebuchadnezzar.

16 The sons of Levi *were* [a]Gershon,[1] Kohath, and Merari. 17 These are the names of the sons of Gershon: Libni and Shimei. 18 The sons of Kohath *were* Amram, Izhar, Hebron, and Uzziel. 19 The sons of Merari *were* Mahli and Mushi. Now these *are* the families of the Levites according to their fathers: 20 Of Gershon *were* Libni his son, Jahath his son, [a]Zimmah his son, 21 Joah his son, Iddo his son, Zerah his son, *and* Jeatherai his son. 22 The sons of Kohath *were* Amminadab his son, [a]Korah his son, Assir his son, 23 Elkanah his son, Ebiasaph his son, Assir his son, 24 Tahath his son, Uriel his son, Uzziah his son, and Shaul his son. 25 The sons of Elkanah *were* [a]Amasai and Ahimoth. 26 *As for* Elkanah,[1] the sons of Elkanah *were* Zophai[2] his son, Nahath[3] his son, 27 Eliab[1] his son, Jeroham his son, *and* Elkanah his son. 28 The sons of Samuel *were* *Joel*[1] the firstborn, and Abijah the second.[2] 29 The sons of Merari *were* Mahli, Libni his son, Shimei his son, Uzzah his son, 30 Shimea his son, Haggiah his son, *and* Asaiah his son.

Musicians in the House of the LORD

31 Now these are [a]the men whom David appointed over the service of song in the house of the LORD, after the [b]ark came to rest. 32 They were ministering with music before the dwelling place of the tabernacle of meeting, until Solomon had built the house of the LORD in Jerusalem, and they served in their office according to their order.

33 And these *are* the ones who ministered with their sons: Of the sons of the [a]Kohathites *were* Heman the singer, the son of Joel, the son of Samuel, 34 the son of Elkanah, the son of Jeroham, the son of Eliel,[1] the son of Toah,[2] 35 the son of Zuph, the son of Elkanah, the son of Mahath, the son of Amasai, 36 the son of Elkanah, the son of Joel, the son of Azariah, the son of Zephaniah, 37 the son of Tahath, the son of Assir, the son of [a]Ebiasaph, the son of Korah, 38 the son of Izhar, the son of Kohath, the son of Levi, the son of Israel. 39 And his brother [a]Asaph, who stood at his right hand, *was* Asaph the son of Berachiah, the son of Shimea, 40 the son of Michael, the son of Baaseiah, the son of Malchijah, 41 the son of [a]Ethni, the son of Zerah, the son of Adaiah, 42 the son of Ethan, the son of Zimmah, the son of Shimei, 43 the son of Jahath, the son of Gershon, the son of Levi.

44 Their brethren, the sons of Merari, on the left hand, *were* Ethan the son of Kishi, the son of Abdi, the son of Malluch, 45 the son of Hashabiah, the son of Amaziah, the son of Hilkiah, 46 the son of Amzi, the son of Bani, the son of Shamer, 47 the son of Mahli, the son of Mushi, the son of Merari, the son of Levi.

48 And their brethren, the Levites, *were* appointed to every [a]kind of service of the tabernacle of the house of God.

The Family of Aaron

49 [a]But Aaron and his sons offered sacrifices [b]on the altar of burnt offering and [c]on the altar of incense, for all the work of the Most Holy *Place,* and to make atonement for Israel, according to all that Moses the servant of God had commanded. 50 Now these *are* the [a]sons of Aaron: Eleazar his son, Phinehas his son, Abishua his son, 51 Bukki his son, Uzzi his son, Zerahiah his son, 52 Meraioth his son, Amariah his son, Ahitub his son, 53 Zadok his son, *and* Ahimaaz his son.

Dwelling Places of the Levites

54 [a]Now these *are* their dwelling places throughout their settlements in their territory, for they were *given* by lot to the sons

6:1 [a] Ex. 6:16 **6:2** [a] 1 Chr. 6:18, 22 **6:3** [a] Lev. 10:1, 2 **6:8** [a] 2 Sam. 8:17 [b] 2 Sam. 15:27 **6:10** [a] 2 Chr. 26:17, 18 [b] 1 Kin. 6:1 ***6:11*** [a] *Ezra 7:3* [b] *2 Chr. 19:11* **6:14** [a] Neh. 11:11 **6:15** [a] 2 Kin. 25:21 **6:16** [a] Ex. 6:16 [1] Hebrew Gershom (alternate spelling of *Gershon,* as in verses 1, 17, 20, 43, 62, and 71) **6:20** [a] 1 Chr. 6:42 **6:22** [a] Num. 16:1 **6:25** [a] 1 Chr. 6:35, 36 **6:26** [1] Compare verse 35 [2] Spelled *Zuph* in verse 35 and 1 Samuel 1:1 [3] Compare verse 34 **6:27** [1] Compare verse 34 **6:28** [1] Following Septuagint, Syriac, and Arabic (compare verse 33 and 1 Samuel 8:2) [2] Hebrew *Vasheni* **6:31** [a] 1 Chr. 15:16–22, 27; 16:4–6 [b] 1 Chr. 15:25—16:1 **6:33** [a] Num. 26:57 **6:34** [1] Spelled *Elihu* in 1 Samuel 1:1 [2] Spelled *Tohu* in 1 Samuel 1:1 **6:37** [a] Ex. 6:24 **6:39** [a] 2 Chr. 5:12 **6:41** [a] 1 Chr. 6:21 **6:48** [a] 1 Chr. 9:14–34 **6:49** [a] [Num. 18:1–8] [b] Lev. 1:8, 9 [c] Ex. 30:7 **6:50** [a] 1 Chr. 6:4–8 **6:54** [a] Josh. 21

of Aaron, of the family of the Kohathites:
55 [a]They gave them Hebron in the land of
Judah, with its surrounding common-lands.
56 [a]But the fields of the city and its villages
they gave to Caleb the son of Jephunneh.
57 And [a]to the sons of Aaron they gave *one of*
the cities of refuge, Hebron; also Libnah with
its common-lands, Jattir, Eshtemoa with its
common-lands, 58 Hilen[1] with its common-
lands, Debir with its common-lands, 59 Ashan[1]
with its common-lands, and Beth Shemesh
with its common-lands. 60 And from the tribe
of Benjamin: Geba with its common-lands,
Alemeth[1] with its common-lands, and Anathoth with its common-lands. All their cities
among their families *were* thirteen.

61 [a]To the rest of the family of the tribe of
the Kohathites *they gave* [b]by lot ten cities
from half the tribe of Manasseh. 62 And to the
sons of Gershon, throughout their families,
they gave thirteen cities from the tribe of
Issachar, from the tribe of Asher, from the
tribe of Naphtali, and from the tribe of Manasseh in Bashan. 63 To the sons of Merari,
throughout their families, *they gave* [a]twelve
cities from the tribe of Reuben, from the tribe
of Gad, and from the tribe of Zebulun. 64 So
the children of Israel gave *these* cities with
their common-lands to the Levites. 65 And
they gave by lot from the tribe of the children
of Judah, from the tribe of the children of
Simeon, and from the tribe of the children
of Benjamin these cities which are called by
their names.

66 Now [a]some of the families of the sons
of Kohath *were given* cities as their territory
from the tribe of Ephraim. 67 [a]And they gave
them *one of* the cities of refuge, Shechem
with its common-lands, in the mountains of
Ephraim, also Gezer with its common-lands,
68 [a]Jokmeam with its common-lands, Beth
Horon with its common-lands, 69 Aijalon with
its common-lands, and Gath Rimmon with its
common-lands. 70 And from the half-tribe of
Manasseh: Aner with its common-lands and
Bileam with its common-lands, for the rest
of the family of the sons of Kohath.

71 From the family of the half-tribe of Manasseh the sons of Gershon *were given* Golan
in Bashan *with its* common-lands and Ashtaroth with its common-lands. 72 And from the
tribe of Issachar: Kedesh with its common-
lands, Daberath with its common-lands,
73 Ramoth with its common-lands, and Anem
with its common-lands. 74 And from the tribe
of Asher: Mashal with its common-lands,
Abdon with its common-lands, 75 Hukok
with its common-lands, and Rehob with
its common-lands. 76 And from the tribe of
Naphtali: Kedesh in Galilee with its common-
lands, Hammon with its common-lands, and
Kirjathaim with its common-lands.

77 From the tribe of Zebulun the rest of
the children of Merari *were given* Rimmon[1]
with its common-lands and Tabor with its
common-lands. 78 And on the other side of
the Jordan, across from Jericho, on the east
side of the Jordan, *they were given* from the
tribe of Reuben: Bezer in the wilderness with
its common-lands, Jahzah with its common-
lands, 79 Kedemoth with its common-lands,
and Mephaath with its common-lands.
80 And from the tribe of Gad: Ramoth in
Gilead with its common-lands, Mahanaim
with its common-lands, 81 Heshbon with its
common-lands, and Jazer with its common-
lands.

The Family of Issachar

7 The sons of Issachar *were* [a]Tola, Puah,[1] Jashub, and Shimron—four *in all.* 2 The sons
of Tola *were* Uzzi, Rephaiah, Jeriel, Jahmai,
Jibsam, and Shemuel, heads of their father's
house. *The sons* of Tola *were* mighty men of
valor in their generations; [a]their number in
the days of David *was* twenty-two thousand
six hundred. 3 The son of Uzzi *was* Izrahiah,
and the sons of Izrahiah *were* Michael, Obadiah, Joel, and Ishiah. All five of them *were*
chief men. 4 And with them, by their generations, according to their fathers' houses, *were*
thirty-six thousand troops ready for war; for
they had many wives and sons.

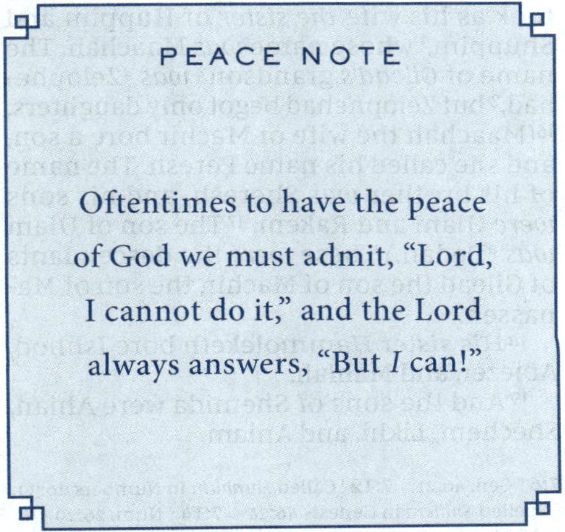

6:55 [a] Josh. 14:13; 21:11, 12 6:56 [a] Josh. 14:13; 15:13 6:57 [a] Josh. 21:13, 19 6:58 [1] Spelled *Holon* in Joshua 21:15 6:59 [1] Spelled *Ain* in Joshua 21:16 6:60 [1] Spelled *Almon* in Joshua 21:18 6:61 [a] 1 Chr. 6:66–70 [b] Josh. 21:5 6:63 [a] Josh. 21:7, 34–40 6:66 [a] 1 Chr. 6:61 6:67 [a] Josh. 21:21 6:68 [a] Josh. 21:22 6:77 [1] Hebrew *Rimmono,* alternate spelling of *Rimmon;* see 4:32 7:1 [a] Num. 26:23–25 [1] Spelled *Puvah* in Genesis 46:13 7:2 [a] 2 Sam. 24:1–9

5 Now their brethren among all the families of Issachar *were* mighty men of valor, listed by their genealogies, eighty-seven thousand in all.

The Family of Benjamin

6 *The sons* of [a]Benjamin *were* Bela, Becher, and Jediael—three *in all.* 7 The sons of Bela were Ezbon, Uzzi, Uzziel, Jerimoth, and Iri—five *in all.* They *were* heads of *their* fathers' houses, and they were listed by their genealogies, twenty-two thousand and thirty-four mighty men of valor.

8 The sons of Becher *were* Zemirah, Joash, Eliezer, Elioenai, Omri, Jerimoth, Abijah, Anathoth, and Alemeth. All these *are* the sons of Becher. 9 And they were recorded by genealogy according to their generations, heads of their fathers' houses, twenty thousand two hundred mighty men of valor. 10 The son of Jediael *was* Bilhan, and the sons of Bilhan *were* Jeush, Benjamin, Ehud, Chenaanah, Zethan, Tharshish, and Ahishahar.

11 All these sons of Jediael *were* heads of their fathers' houses; *there were* seventeen thousand two hundred mighty men of valor fit to go out for war *and* battle. 12 Shuppim and Huppim[1] *were* the sons of Ir, *and* Hushim *was* the son of Aher.

The Family of Naphtali

13 The [a]sons of Naphtali *were* Jahziel,[1] Guni, Jezer, and Shallum,[2] the sons of Bilhah.

The Family of Manasseh (West)

14 The [a]descendants of Manasseh: his Syrian concubine bore him [b]Machir the father of Gilead, the father of Asriel.[1] 15 Machir took as his wife *the sister* of Huppim and Shuppim,[1] whose name *was* Maachah. The name of *Gilead's* grandson[2] *was* [a]Zelophehad,[3] but Zelophehad begot only daughters. 16 (Maachah the wife of Machir bore a son, and she called his name Peresh. The name of his brother *was* Sheresh, and his sons *were* Ulam and Rakem. 17 The son of Ulam *was* [a]Bedan.) These *were* the descendants of Gilead the son of Machir, the son of Manasseh.

18 His sister Hammoleketh bore Ishhod, Abiezer, and Mahlah.

19 And the sons of Shemida were Ahian, Shechem, Likhi, and Aniam.

The Family of Ephraim

20 [a]The sons of Ephraim *were* Shuthelah, Bered his son, Tahath his son, Eladah his son, Tahath his son, 21 Zabad his son, Shuthelah his son, and Ezer and Elead. The men of Gath who were born in *that* land killed *them* because they came down to take away their cattle. 22 Then Ephraim their father mourned many days, and his brethren came to comfort him.

23 And when he went in to his wife, she conceived and bore a son; and he called his name Beriah,[1] because tragedy had come upon his house. 24 Now his daughter *was* Sheerah, who built Lower and Upper [a]Beth Horon and Uzzen Sheerah; 25 and Rephah *was* his son, *as well* as Resheph, and Telah his son, Tahan his son, 26 Laadan his son, Ammihud his son, [a]Elishama his son, 27 Nun[1] his son, and [a]Joshua his son.

28 Now their [a]possessions and dwelling places *were* Bethel and its towns: to the east Naaran, to the west Gezer and its towns, and Shechem and its towns, as far as Ayyah[1] and its towns; 29 and by the borders of the children of [a]Manasseh *were* Beth Shean and its towns, Taanach and its towns, [b]Megiddo and its towns, Dor and its towns. In these dwelt the children of Joseph, the son of Israel.

The Family of Asher

30 [a]The sons of Asher *were* Imnah, Ishvah, Ishvi, Beriah, and their sister Serah. 31 The sons of Beriah *were* Heber and Malchiel, who was the father of Birzaith.[1] 32 And Heber begot Japhlet, Shomer,[1] Hotham,[2] and their sister Shua. 33 The sons of Japhlet *were* Pasach, Bimhal, and Ashvath. These *were* the children of Japhlet. 34 The sons of [a]Shemer *were* Ahi, Rohgah, Jehubbah, and Aram. 35 And the sons of his brother Helem *were* Zophah, Imna, Shelesh, and Amal. 36 The sons of Zophah *were* Suah, Harnepher, Shual, Beri, Imrah, 37 Bezer, Hod, Shamma, Shilshah, Jithran,[1] and Beera. 38 The sons of Jether *were* Jephunneh, Pispah, and Ara. 39 The sons of Ulla *were* Arah, Haniel, and Rizia.

40 All these *were* the children of Asher, heads of *their* fathers' houses, choice men, mighty men of valor, chief leaders. And they were recorded by genealogies among the army fit for battle; their number *was* twenty-six thousand.

7:6 [a] Gen. 46:21 **7:12** [1] Called *Hupham* in Numbers 26:39 **7:13** [a] Num. 26:48–50 [1] Spelled *Jahzeel* in Genesis 46:24 [2] Spelled *Shillem* in Genesis 46:24 **7:14** [a] Num. 26:29–34 [b] 1 Chr. 2:21 [1] The son of Gilead (compare Numbers 26:30, 31) **7:15** [a] Num. 26:30–33; 27:1 [1] Compare verse 12 [2] Literally *the second* [3] Compare Numbers 26:30–33 **7:17** [a] 1 Sam. 12:11 **7:20** [a] Num. 26:35–37 **7:23** [1] Literally *In Tragedy* **7:24** [a] Josh. 16:3, 5 **7:26** [a] Num. 10:22 **7:27** [a] Ex. 17:9, 14; 24:13; 33:11 [1] Hebrew *Non* **7:28** [a] Josh. 16:1–10 [1] Many Hebrew manuscripts, Bomberg, Septuagint, Targum, and Vulgate read *Gazza.* **7:29** [a] Josh. 17:7 [b] Josh. 17:11 **7:30** [a] Num. 26:44–47 **7:31** [1] Or *Birzavith* or *Birzoth* **7:32** [1] Spelled *Shemer* in verse 34 [2] Spelled *Helem* in verse 35 **7:34** [a] 1 Chr. 7:32 **7:37** [1] Spelled *Jether* in verse 38

The Family Tree of King Saul of Benjamin

8 Now Benjamin begot [a]Bela his firstborn, Ashbel the second, Aharah[1] the third, 2 Nohah the fourth, and Rapha the fifth. 3 The sons of Bela *were* Addar,[1] Gera, Abihud, 4 Abishua, Naaman, Ahoah, 5 Gera, Shephuphan, and Huram.

6 These *are* the sons of Ehud, who were the heads of the fathers' *houses* of the inhabitants of [a]Geba, and who forced them to move to [b]Manahath: 7 Naaman, Ahijah, and Gera who forced them to move. He begot Uzza and Ahihud.

8 Also Shaharaim had children in the country of Moab, after he had sent away Hushim and Baara his wives. 9 By Hodesh his wife he begot Jobab, Zibia, Mesha, Malcam, 10 Jeuz, Sachiah, and Mirmah. These *were* his sons, heads of their fathers' *houses.*

11 And by Hushim he begot Abitub and Elpaal. 12 The sons of Elpaal *were* Eber, Misham, and Shemed, who built Ono and Lod with its towns; 13 and Beriah and [a]Shema, who *were* heads of their fathers' *houses* of the inhabitants of Aijalon, who drove out the inhabitants of Gath. 14 Ahio, Shashak, Jeremoth, 15 Zebadiah, Arad, Eder, 16 Michael, Ispah, and Joha *were* the sons of Beriah. 17 Zebadiah, Meshullam, Hizki, Heber, 18 Ishmerai, Jizliah, and Jobab *were* the sons of Elpaal. 19 Jakim, Zichri, Zabdi, 20 Elienai, Zillethai, Eliel, 21 Adaiah, Beraiah, and Shimrath *were* the sons of Shimei. 22 Ishpan, Eber, Eliel, 23 Abdon, Zichri, Hanan, 24 Hananiah, Elam, Antothijah, 25 Iphdeiah, and Penuel *were* the sons of Shashak. 26 Shamsherai, Shehariah, Athaliah, 27 Jaareshiah, Elijah, and Zichri *were* the sons of Jeroham.

28 These *were* heads of the fathers' *houses* by their generations, chief men. These dwelt in Jerusalem.

29 Now the father of Gibeon, whose [a]wife's name *was* Maacah, dwelt at Gibeon. 30 And his firstborn son *was* Abdon, then Zur, Kish, Baal, Nadab, 31 Gedor, Ahio, Zecher, 32 and Mikloth, *who* begot Shimeah.[1] They also dwelt alongside their relatives in Jerusalem, with their brethren. 33 [a]Ner[1] begot Kish, Kish begot Saul, and Saul begot Jonathan, Malchishua, *Abinadab,*[2] *and Esh-Baal.*[3] 34 The son of Jonathan *was* Merib-Baal,[1] and Merib-Baal begot [a]Micah. 35 The sons of Micah *were* Pithon, Melech, Tarea, and Ahaz. 36 And Ahaz begot Jehoaddah;[1] Jehoaddah begot Alemeth, Azmaveth, and Zimri; and Zimri begot Moza. 37 Moza begot Binea, Raphah[1] his son, Eleasah his son, *and* Azel his son.

38 Azel had six sons whose names *were* these: Azrikam, Bocheru, Ishmael, Sheariah, Obadiah, and Hanan. All these *were* the sons of Azel. 39 And the sons of Eshek his brother *were* Ulam his firstborn, Jeush the second, and Eliphelet the third.

40 The sons of Ulam were mighty men of valor—archers. *They* had many sons and grandsons, one hundred and fifty *in all.* These *were* all sons of Benjamin.

9 So [a]all Israel was recorded by genealogies, and indeed, they *were* inscribed in the book of the kings of Israel. But Judah was carried away captive to Babylon because of their unfaithfulness. 2 [a]And the first inhabitants who *dwelt* in their possessions in their cities *were* Israelites, priests, Levites, and [b]the Nethinim.

PEACE NOTE

The people of Judah lost God's peace as they were taken captive to Babylon. Avoid anything or anyone who leads you away from the peace and presence of God.

1 CHRONICLES 9:1

Dwellers in Jerusalem

3 Now in [a]Jerusalem the children of Judah dwelt, and some of the children of Benjamin, and of the children of Ephraim and Manasseh: 4 Uthai the son of Ammihud, the son of Omri, the son of Imri, the son of Bani, of the descendants of Perez, the son of Judah. 5 Of the Shilonites: Asaiah the firstborn and his sons. 6 Of the sons of Zerah: Jeuel, and their brethren—six hundred and ninety. 7 Of the sons of Benjamin: Sallu the son of Meshullam, the son of Hodaviah, the son of Hassenuah; 8 Ibneiah the son of Jeroham; Elah the son of Uzzi, the son of Michri; Meshullam the son of Shephatiah, the son of Reuel, the son of Ibnijah; 9 and their brethren, according to

8:1 [a] Gen. 46:21 [1] Spelled *Ahiram* in Numbers 26:38 **8:3** [1] Called *Ard* in Numbers 26:40 **8:6** [a] 1 Chr. 6:60 [b] 1 Chr. 2:52 **8:13** [a] 1 Chr. 8:21 **8:29** [a] 1 Chr. 9:35–38 **8:32** [1] Spelled *Shimeam* in 9:38 **8:33** [a] 1 Sam. 14:51 [1] Also the son of Gibeon (compare 9:36, 39) [2] Called *Jishui* in 1 Samuel 14:49 [3] Called *Ishbosheth* in 2 Samuel 2:8 and elsewhere **8:34** [a] 2 Sam. 9:12 [1] Called *Mephibosheth* in 2 Samuel 4:4 **8:36** [1] Spelled *Jarah* in 9:42 **8:37** [1] Spelled *Rephaiah* in 9:43 **9:1** [a] Ezra 2:59 **9:2** [a] Neh. 7:73 [b] Ezra 2:43; 8:20 **9:3** [a] Neh. 11:1, 2

their generations—nine hundred and fifty-six. All these men *were* heads of a father's *house* in their fathers' houses.

The Priests at Jerusalem

10 [a]Of the priests: Jedaiah, Jehoiarib, and Jachin; 11 Azariah the son of Hilkiah, the son of Meshullam, the son of Zadok, the son of Meraioth, the son of Ahitub, the [a]officer over the house of God; 12 Adaiah the son of Jeroham, the son of Pashur, the son of Malchijah; Maasai the son of Adiel, the son of Jahzerah, the son of Meshullam, the son of Meshillemith, the son of Immer; 13 and their brethren, heads of their fathers' houses—one thousand seven hundred and sixty. *They were* very able men for the work of the service of the house of God.

The Levites at Jerusalem

14 Of the Levites: Shemaiah the son of Hasshub, the son of Azrikam, the son of Hashabiah, of the sons of Merari; 15 Bakbakkar, Heresh, Galal, and Mattaniah the son of Micah, the son of [a]Zichri, the son of Asaph; 16 [a]Obadiah the son of [b]Shemaiah, the son of Galal, the son of Jeduthun; and Berechiah the son of Asa, the son of Elkanah, who lived in the villages of the Netophathites.

The Levite Gatekeepers

17 And the gatekeepers *were* Shallum, Akkub, Talmon, Ahiman, and their brethren. Shallum *was* the chief. 18 Until then *they had been* gatekeepers for the camps of the children of Levi at the King's Gate on the east.

19 Shallum the son of Kore, the son of Ebiasaph, the son of Korah, and his brethren, from his father's house, the Korahites, *were* in charge of the work of the service, gatekeepers of the tabernacle. Their fathers had been keepers of the entrance to the camp of the LORD. 20 And [a]Phinehas the son of Eleazar had been the officer over them in time past; the LORD *was* with him. 21 [a]Zechariah the son of Meshelemiah *was* keeper of the door of the tabernacle of meeting.

22 All those chosen as gatekeepers *were* two hundred and twelve. [a]They were recorded by their genealogy, in their villages. David and Samuel [b]the seer had appointed them to their trusted office. 23 So they and their children *were* in charge of the gates of the house of the LORD, the house of the tabernacle, by assignment. 24 The gatekeepers were assigned to the four directions: the east, west, north, and south. 25 And their brethren in their villages *had* to come with them from time to time [a]for seven days. 26 For in this trusted office *were* four chief gatekeepers; they were Levites. And they had charge over the chambers and treasuries of the house of God. 27 And they lodged *all* around the house of God because they *had* the [a]responsibility, and they *were* in charge of opening *it* every morning.

Other Levite Responsibilities

28 Now *some* of them were in charge of the serving vessels, for they brought them in and took them out by count. 29 *Some* of them *were* appointed over the furnishings and over all the implements of the sanctuary, and over the [a]fine flour and the wine and the oil and the incense and the spices. 30 And *some* of the sons of the priests made [a]the ointment of the spices.

31 Mattithiah of the Levites, the firstborn of Shallum the Korahite, had the trusted office [a]over the things that were baked in the pans. 32 And some of their brethren of the sons of the Kohathites [a]*were* in charge of preparing the showbread for every Sabbath.

33 These are [a]the singers, heads of the fathers' *houses* of the Levites, *who lodged* in the chambers, *and were* free *from other duties;* for they were employed in *that* work day and night. 34 These heads of the fathers' *houses* of the Levites *were* heads throughout their generations. They dwelt at Jerusalem.

The Family of King Saul

35 Jeiel the father of Gibeon, whose wife's name *was* [a]Maacah, dwelt at Gibeon. 36 His firstborn son *was* Abdon, then Zur, Kish, Baal, Ner, Nadab, 37 Gedor, Ahio, Zechariah,[1] and Mikloth. 38 And Mikloth begot Shimeam.[1] They also dwelt alongside their relatives in Jerusalem, with their brethren. 39 [a]Ner begot Kish, Kish begot Saul, and Saul begot Jonathan, Malchishua, Abinadab, and Esh-Baal. 40 The son of Jonathan *was* Merib-Baal, and Merib-Baal begot Micah. 41 The sons of Micah *were* Pithon, Melech, Tahrea,[1] [a]and Ahaz.[2] 42 And Ahaz begot Jarah;[1] Jarah begot Alemeth, Azmaveth, and Zimri; and Zimri begot Moza; 43 Moza begot Binea, Rephaiah[1] his son, Eleasah his son, and Azel his son.

44 And Azel had six sons whose names *were* these: Azrikam, Bocheru, Ishmael, Sheariah, Obadiah, and Hanan; these *were* the sons of Azel.

9:10 [a] Neh. 11:10–14 **9:11** [a] Jer. 20:1 **9:15** [a] Neh. 11:17 **9:16** [a] Neh. 11:17 [b] Neh. 11:17 **9:20** [a] Num. 25:6–13; 31:6 **9:21** [a] 1 Chr. 26:2, 14 **9:22** [a] 1 Chr. 26:1, 2 [b] 1 Sam. 9:9 **9:25** [a] 2 Kin. 11:4–7 **9:27** [a] 1 Chr. 23:30–32 **9:29** [a] 1 Chr. 23:29 **9:30** [a] Ex. 30:22–25 **9:31** [a] Lev. 2:5; 6:21 **9:32** [a] Lev. 24:5–8 **9:33** [a] 1 Chr. 6:31; 25:1 **9:35** [a] 1 Chr. 8:29–32 **9:37** [1] Called *Zecher* in 8:31 **9:38** [1] Spelled *Shimeah* in 8:32 **9:39** [a] 1 Chr. 8:33–38 **9:41** [a] 1 Chr. 8:35 [1] Spelled *Tarea* in 8:35 [2] Following Arabic, Syriac, Targum, and Vulgate (compare 8:35); Masoretic Text and Septuagint omit *and Ahaz.* **9:42** [1] Spelled *Jehoaddah* in 8:36 **9:43** [1] Spelled *Raphah* in 8:37

Tragic End of Saul and His Sons

10 Now [a]the Philistines fought against Israel; and the men of Israel fled from before the Philistines, and fell slain on Mount Gilboa. 2 Then the Philistines followed hard after Saul and his sons. And the Philistines killed Jonathan, Abinadab, and Malchishua, Saul's sons. 3 The battle became fierce against Saul. The archers hit him, and he was wounded by the archers. 4 Then Saul said to his armorbearer, "Draw your sword, and thrust me through with it, lest these uncircumcised men come and abuse me." But his armorbearer would not, for he was greatly afraid. Therefore Saul took a sword and fell on it. 5 And when his armorbearer saw that Saul was dead, he also fell on his sword and died. 6 So Saul and his three sons died, and all his house died together. 7 And when all the men of Israel who *were* in the valley saw that they had fled and that Saul and his sons were dead, they forsook their cities and fled; then the Philistines came and dwelt in them.

8 So it happened the next day, when the Philistines came to strip the slain, that they found Saul and his sons fallen on Mount Gilboa. 9 And they stripped him and took his head and his armor, and sent word throughout the land of the Philistines to proclaim the news *in the temple* of their idols and among the people. 10 [a]Then they put his armor in the temple of their gods, and fastened his head in the temple of Dagon.

11 And when all Jabesh Gilead heard all that the Philistines had done to Saul, 12 all the [a]valiant men arose and took the body of Saul and the bodies of his sons; and they brought them to [b]Jabesh, and buried their bones under the tamarisk tree at Jabesh, and fasted seven days.

13 So Saul died for his unfaithfulness which he had committed against the LORD, [a]because he did not keep the word of the LORD, and also because [b]he consulted a medium for guidance. 14 But *he* did not inquire of the LORD; therefore He killed him, and [a]turned the kingdom over to David the son of Jesse.

David Made King over All Israel

11 Then [a]all Israel came together to David at Hebron, saying, "Indeed we *are* your bone and your flesh. 2 Also, in time past, even when Saul was king, you *were* the one who led Israel out and brought them in; and the LORD your [a]God said to you, 'You shall [b]shepherd My people Israel, and be ruler over My people Israel.' " 3 Therefore all the elders of Israel came to the king at Hebron, and David made a covenant with them at Hebron before the LORD. And [a]they anointed David king over Israel, according to the word of the LORD by [b]Samuel.

The City of David

4 And David and all Israel [a]went to Jerusalem, which is Jebus, [b]where the Jebusites *were,* the inhabitants of the land. 5 But the inhabitants of Jebus said to David, "You shall not come in here!" Nevertheless David took the stronghold of Zion (that is, the City of David). 6 Now David said, "Whoever attacks the Jebusites first shall be chief and captain." And Joab the son of Zeruiah went up first, and became chief. 7 Then David dwelt in the stronghold; therefore they called it the City of David. 8 And he built the city around it, from the Millo[1] to the surrounding area. Joab repaired the rest of the city. 9 So David [a]went on and became great, and the LORD of hosts *was* with [b]him.

The Mighty Men of David

10 Now [a]these *were* the heads of the mighty men whom David had, who strengthened themselves with him in his kingdom, with all Israel, to make him king, according to [b]the word of the LORD concerning Israel.

11 And this *is* the number of the mighty men whom David had: [a]Jashobeam the son of a Hachmonite, [b]chief of the captains;[1] he had lifted up his spear against three hundred, killed *by him* at one time.

12 After him *was* Eleazar the son of [a]Dodo, the Ahohite, who *was one* of the three mighty men. 13 He was with David at Pasdammim. Now there the Philistines were gathered for battle, and there was a piece of ground full of barley. So the people fled from the Philistines. 14 But they stationed themselves in the middle of *that* field, defended it, and killed the Philistines. So the LORD brought about a great victory.

15 Now three of the thirty chief men [a]went down to the rock to David, into the cave of Adullam; and the army of the Philistines encamped [b]in the Valley of Rephaim. 16 David *was* then in the stronghold, and the garrison of the Philistines *was* then in Bethlehem. 17 And David said with longing, "Oh, that someone would give me a drink of water

10:1 [a] 1 Sam. 31:1, 2 **10:10** [a] 1 Sam. 31:10 **10:12** [a] 1 Sam. 14:52 [b] 2 Sam. 21:12 **10:13** [a] 1 Sam. 13:13, 14; 15:22–26 [b] 1 Sam. 28:7 **10:14** [a] 1 Sam. 15:28 **11:1** [a] 2 Sam. 5:1 **11:2** [a] Ps. 78:70–72 [b] 2 Sam. 7:7 **11:3** [a] 2 Sam. 5:3 [b] 1 Sam. 16:1, 4, 12, 13 **11:4** [a] 2 Sam. 5:6 [b] Judg. 1:21; 19:10, 11 **11:8** [1] Literally *The Landfill* **11:9** [a] 2 Sam. 3:1 [b] 1 Sam. 16:18 **11:10** [a] 2 Sam. 23:8 [b] 1 Sam. 16:1, 12 **11:11** [a] 1 Chr. 27:2 [b] 1 Chr. 12:18 [1] Following Qere; Kethib, Septuagint, and Vulgate read *the thirty* (compare 2 Samuel 23:8). **11:12** [a] 1 Chr. 27:4 **11:15** [a] 2 Sam. 23:13 [b] 2 Sam. 5:18

from the well of Bethlehem, which is by the
gate!" 18 So the three broke through the camp
of the Philistines, drew water from the well of
Bethlehem that *was* by the gate, and took *it*
and brought *it* to David. Nevertheless David
would not drink it, but poured it out to the
LORD. 19 And he said, "Far be it from me, O my
God, that I should do this! Shall I drink the
blood of these men *who have put* their lives
in jeopardy? For at the risk of their lives they
brought it." Therefore he would not drink it.
These things were done by the three mighty
men.

20 [a]Abishai the brother of Joab was chief
of *another* three.[1] He had lifted up his spear
against three hundred *men,* killed *them,* and
won a name among *these* three. 21 [a]Of the
three he was more honored than the other
two men. Therefore he became their captain.
However he did not attain to the *first* three.

22 Benaiah was the son of Jehoiada, the
son of a valiant man from Kabzeel, who had
done many deeds. [a]He had killed two lion-like
heroes of Moab. He also had gone down and
killed a lion in the midst of a pit on a snowy
day. 23 And he killed an Egyptian, a man of
great height, five cubits tall. In the Egyptian's
hand *there was* a spear like a weaver's beam;
and he went down to him with a staff, wrested
the spear out of the Egyptian's hand, and
killed him with his own spear. 24 These *things*
Benaiah the son of Jehoiada did, and won a
name among three mighty men. 25 Indeed
he was more honored than the thirty, but he
did not attain to the *first* three. And David
appointed him over his guard.

26 Also the mighty warriors *were* [a]Asahel
the brother of Joab, Elhanan the son of Dodo
of Bethlehem, 27 Shammoth the Harorite,[1]
[a]Helez the Pelonite,[2] 28 [a]Ira the son of Ikkesh the Tekoite, [b]Abiezer the Anathothite,
29 Sibbechai the Hushathite, Ilai the Ahohite,
30 [a]Maharai the Netophathite, Heled[1] the son
of Baanah the Netophathite, 31 Ithai[1] the son of
Ribai of Gibeah, of the sons of Benjamin, [a]Be-
naiah the Pirathonite, 32 Hurai[1] of the brooks
of Gaash, Abiel[2] the Arbathite, 33 Azmaveth
the Baharumite,[1] Eliahba the Shaalbonite,
34 the sons of Hashem the Gizonite, Jonathan
the son of Shageh the Hararite, 35 Ahiam the
son of Sacar the Hararite, Eliphal the son of
Ur, 36 Hepher the Mecherathite, Ahijah the
Pelonite, 37 Hezro the Carmelite, Naarai the
son of Ezbai, 38 Joel the brother of Nathan,
Mibhar the son of Hagri, 39 Zelek the Ammonite, Naharai the Berothite[1] (the armorbearer
of Joab the son of Zeruiah), 40 Ira the Ithrite,
Gareb the Ithrite, 41 [a]Uriah the Hittite, Zabad
the son of Ahlai, 42 Adina the son of Shiza the
Reubenite (a chief of the Reubenites) and
thirty with him, 43 Hanan the son of Maachah,
Joshaphat the Mithnite, 44 Uzzia the Ashte-
rathite, Shama and Jeiel the sons of Hotham
the Aroerite, 45 Jediael the son of Shimri,
and Joha his brother, the Tizite, 46 Eliel the
Mahavite, Jeribai and Joshaviah the sons of
Elnaam, Ithmah the Moabite, 47 Eliel, Obed,
and Jaasiel the Mezobaite.

The Growth of David's Army

12 Now [a]these *were* the men who came
to David at [b]Ziklag while he was still a
fugitive from Saul the son of Kish; and they
were among the mighty men, helpers in
the war, 2 armed with bows, using both the
right hand and [a]the left in *hurling* stones and
shooting arrows with the bow. *They were* of
Benjamin, Saul's brethren.

3 The chief *was* Ahiezer, then Joash, the
sons of Shemaah the Gibeathite; Jeziel and
Pelet the sons of Azmaveth; Berachah, and
Jehu the Anathothite; 4 Ishmaiah the Gibeonite, a mighty man among the thirty, and over
the thirty; Jeremiah, Jahaziel, Johanan, and
Jozabad the Gederathite; 5 Eluzai, Jerimoth,
Bealiah, Shemariah, and Shephatiah the Ha-
ruphite; 6 Elkanah, Jisshiah, Azarel, Joezer,
and Jashobeam, the Korahites; 7 and Joelah
and Zebadiah the sons of Jeroham of Gedor.

8 *Some* Gadites joined David at the stronghold in the wilderness, mighty men of valor,
men trained for battle, who could handle shield
and spear, whose faces *were like* the faces of
lions, and *were* [a]as swift as gazelles on the
mountains: 9 Ezer the first, Obadiah the second,
Eliab the third, 10 Mishmannah the fourth,
Jeremiah the fifth, 11 Attai the sixth, Eliel the
seventh, 12 Johanan the eighth, Elzabad the
ninth, 13 Jeremiah the tenth, and Machbanai the
eleventh. 14 These *were* from the sons of Gad,
captains of the army; the least was over a hundred, and the greatest was over a [a]thousand.
15 These *are* the ones who crossed the Jordan
in the first month, when it had overflowed all
its [a]banks; and they put to flight all *those* in the
valleys, to the east and to the west.

11:20 [a] 2 Sam. 23:18 [1] *Following Masoretic* Text, Septuagint, and Vulgate; Syriac reads thirty. **11:21** [a] 2 Sam. 23:19 **11:22** [a] 2 Sam. 23:20 **11:26** [a] 2 Sam. 23:24 **11:27** [a] 1 Chr. 27:10 [1] Spelled *Harodite* in 2 Samuel 23:25 [2] Called *Paltite* in 2 Samuel 23:26 **11:28** [a] 1 Chr. 27:9 [b] 1 Chr. 27:12 **11:30** [a] 1 Chr. 27:13 [1] Spelled *Heleb* in 2 Samuel 23:29 and *Heldai* in 1 Chronicles 27:15 **11:31** [a] 1 Chr. 27:14 [1] Spelled *Ittai* in 2 Samuel 23:29 **11:32** [1] Spelled *Hiddai* in 2 Samuel 23:30 [2] Spelled *Abi-Albon* in 2 Samuel 23:31 **11:33** [1] Spelled *Barhumite* in 2 Samuel 23:31 **11:39** [1] Spelled *Beerothite* in 2 Samuel 23:37 **11:41** [a] 2 Sam. 11 **12:1** [a] 1 Sam. 27:2 [b] 1 Sam. 27:6 **12:2** [a] Judg. 3:15; 20:16 **12:8** [a] 2 Sam. 2:18 **12:14** [a] 1 Sam. 18:13 **12:15** [a] Josh. 3:15; 4:18, 19

16 Then some of the sons of Benjamin and Judah came to David at the stronghold. 17 And David went out to meet them, and answered and said to them, "If you have come peaceably to me to help me, my heart will be united with you; but if to betray me to my enemies, since *there is* no wrong in my hands, may the God of our fathers look and bring judgment." 18 Then the Spirit came upon [a]Amasai, chief of the captains, *and he said:*

"*We are* yours, O David;
We *are* on your side, O son of Jesse!
Peace, peace to you,
And peace to your helpers!
For your God helps you."

So David received them, and made them captains of the troop.

19 And *some* from Manasseh defected to David [a]when he was going with the Philistines to battle against Saul; but they did not help them, for the lords of the Philistines sent him away by agreement, saying, [b]"He may defect to his master Saul *and endanger* our heads." 20 When he went to Ziklag, those of Manasseh who defected to him were Adnah, Jozabad, Jediael, Michael, Jozabad, Elihu, and Zillethai, captains of the thousands who *were* from Manasseh. 21 And they helped David against [a]the bands *of raiders,* for they *were* all mighty men of valor, and they were captains in the army. 22 For at *that* time they came to David day by day to help him, until *it was* a great army, [a]like the army of God.

David's Army at Hebron

23 Now these *were* the numbers of the divisions *that were* equipped for war, *and* [a]came to David at [b]Hebron to [c]turn *over* the kingdom of Saul to him, [d]according to the word of the LORD: 24 of the sons of Judah bearing shield and spear, six thousand eight hundred armed for war; 25 of the sons of Simeon, mighty men of valor fit for war, seven thousand one hundred; 26 of the sons of Levi four thousand six hundred; 27 Jehoiada, the leader of the Aaronites, and with him three thousand seven hundred; 28 [a]Zadok, a young man, a valiant warrior, and from his father's house twenty-two captains; 29 of the sons of Benjamin, relatives of Saul, three thousand (until then [a]the greatest part of them had remained loyal to the house of Saul); 30 of the sons of Ephraim twenty thousand eight hundred, mighty men of valor, famous men throughout their father's house; 31 of the half-tribe of Manasseh eighteen thousand, who were designated by name to come and make David king; 32 of the sons of Issachar [a]who had understanding of the times, to know what Israel ought to do, their chiefs were two hundred; and all their brethren were at their command; 33 of Zebulun there were fifty thousand who went out to battle, expert in war with

12:18 [a] 2 Sam. 17:25 12:19 [a] 1 Sam. 29:2 [b] 1 Sam. 29:4 12:21 [a] 1 Sam. 30:1, 9, 10 12:22 [a] Josh. 5:13–15
12:23 [a] 2 Sam. 2:1–4 [b] 1 Chr. 11:1 [c] 1 Chr. 10:14 [d] 1 Sam. 16:1–4 12:28 [a] 2 Sam. 8:17 12:29 [a] 2 Sam. 2:8, 9
12:32 [a] Esth. 1:13

PEACE IS SO MUCH MORE

O David . . . Peace, peace to you, and peace to your helpers! For your God helps you.

I CHRONICLES 12:18

The author of the Book of Chronicles retells the stories of the Books of Samuel and Kings. He also draws out their theological and spiritual implications. What is stated matter-of-factly in Samuel and Kings is presented in Chronicles with deep insight for faith and living.

In Samuel we hear of David gathering his forces in preparation for unifying the kingdom of Israel and bringing the ark of the covenant to Jerusalem. In Chronicles, though, we are *told of the Holy Spirit coming* upon Amasai, one of David's military leaders, prompting him to burst forth in song: "We are yours, O David; we are on your side, O son of Jesse! Peace, peace to you, and peace to your helpers! For your God helps you" (v. 18).

The peace (*shalom*) that Amasai called for is not simply cessation of war but the fullness and wholeness that God gives to those who rely on Him. David was a man of war, but he was also a man of peace. Only God could provide the peace that David longed for above all.

Have you found peace anywhere but in the Lord? No! So, trust Him for today's needs.

> **PEACE NOTE**
>
> The peace of the Lord gives us the Lord's perspective in our spiritual lives. The sons of Issachar had an "understanding of the times" to know how to advise Israel.
>
> 1 CHRONICLES 12:32

all weapons of war, [a]stouthearted men who
could keep ranks; 34 of Naphtali one thousand
captains, and with them thirty-seven thousand with shield and spear; 35 of the Danites
who could keep battle formation, twenty-eight
thousand six hundred; 36 of Asher, those who
could go out to war, able to keep battle formation, forty thousand; 37 of the Reubenites and
the Gadites and the half-tribe of Manasseh,
from the other side of the Jordan, one hundred
and twenty thousand armed for battle with
every *kind* of weapon of war.
38 All these men of war, who could keep
ranks, came to Hebron with a loyal heart,
to make David king over all Israel; and all
the rest of Israel *were* of [a]one mind to make
David king. 39 And they were there with David
three days, eating and drinking, for their
brethren had prepared for them. 40 Moreover
those who were near to them, from as far
away as Issachar and Zebulun and Naphtali,
were bringing food on donkeys and camels,
on mules and oxen—provisions of flour and
cakes of figs and cakes of raisins, wine and
oil and oxen and sheep abundantly, for *there*
was joy in Israel.

The Ark Brought from Kirjath Jearim

13 Then David consulted with the [a]cap-
tains of thousands and hundreds, *and*
with every leader. 2 And David said to all the
assembly of Israel, "If *it seems* good to you,
and if it is of the LORD our God, let us send
out to our brethren everywhere *who are* [a]left
in all the land of Israel, and with them to the
priests and Levites who are in their cities *and*
their common-lands, that they may gather
together to us; 3 and let us bring the ark of
our God back to us, [a]for we have not inquired
at it since the days of Saul." 4 Then all the
assembly said that they would do so, for the
thing was right in the eyes of all the people.
5 So [a]David gathered all Israel together,
from [b]Shihor in Egypt to as far as the entrance of Hamath, to bring the ark of God
[c]from Kirjath Jearim. 6 And David and all
Israel went up to [a]Baalah,[1] to Kirjath Jearim,
which belonged to Judah, to bring up from
there the ark of God the LORD, [b]who dwells
between the cherubim, where *His* name is
proclaimed. 7 So they carried the ark of God
[a]on a new cart [b]from the house of Abinadab,
and Uzza and Ahio drove the cart. 8 Then
[a]David and all Israel played *music* before God
with all *their* might, with singing, on harps,
on stringed instruments, on tambourines,
on cymbals, and with trumpets.
9 And when they came to Chidon's[1] threshing floor, Uzza put out his hand to hold the
ark, for the oxen stumbled. 10 Then the anger
of the LORD was aroused against Uzza, and
He struck him [a]because he put his hand to
the ark; and he [b]died there before God. 11 And
David became angry because of the LORD's
outbreak against Uzza; therefore that place
is called Perez Uzza[1] to this day. 12 David was
afraid of God that day, saying, "How can I
bring the ark of God to me?"
13 So David would not move the ark with
him into the City of David, but took it aside
into the house of Obed-Edom the Gittite.
14 [a]The ark of God remained with the family of
Obed-Edom in his house three months. And
the LORD blessed [b]the house of Obed-Edom
and all that he had.

David Established at Jerusalem

14 Now [a]Hiram king of Tyre sent messengers to David, and cedar trees,
with masons and carpenters, to build him
a house. 2 So David knew that the LORD had
established him as king over Israel, for his
kingdom was [a]highly exalted for the sake of
His people Israel.
3 Then David took more wives in Jerusalem, and David begot more sons and daughters. 4 And [a]these are the names of his children whom he had in Jerusalem: Shammua,[1]
Shobab, Nathan, Solomon, 5 Ibhar, Elishua,[1]
Elpelet,[2] 6 Nogah, Nepheg, Japhia, 7 Elishama,
Beeliada,[1] and Eliphelet.

12:33 [a] Ps. 12:2 **12:38** [a] 2 Chr. 30:12 **13:1** [a] 1 Chr. 11:15; 12:34 **13:2** [a] Is. 37:4 **13:3** [a] 1 Sam. 7:1, 2 **13:5** [a] 1 Sam. 7:5 [b] Josh. 13:3 [c] 1 Sam. 6:21; 7:1, 2 **13:6** [a] Josh. 15:9, 60 [b] Ex. 25:22 [1] Called *Baale Judah* in 2 Samuel 6:2 **13:7** [a] 1 Sam. 6:7 [b] 1 Sam. 7:1 **13:8** [a] 2 Sam. 6:5 **13:9** [1] Called *Nachon* in 2 Samuel 6:6 **13:10** [a] [Num. 4:15] [b] Lev. 10:2 **13:11** [1] Literally *Outburst Against Uzza* **13:14** [a] 2 Sam. 6:11 [b] 1 Chr. 26:4–8 **14:1** [a] 2 Sam. 5:11 **14:2** [a] Num. 24:7 **14:4** [a] 1 Chr. 3:5–8 [1] Spelled *Shimea* in 3:5 **14:5** [1] Spelled *Elishama* in 3:6 [2] Spelled *Eliphelet* in 3:6 **14:7** [1] Spelled *Eliada* in 3:8

The Philistines Defeated

8 Now when the Philistines heard that [a]David had been anointed king over all Israel, all the Philistines went up to search for David. And David heard *of it* and went out against them. 9 Then the Philistines went and made a raid [a]on the Valley of Rephaim. 10 And David [a]inquired of God, saying, "Shall I go up against the Philistines? Will You deliver them into my hand?"

The LORD said to him, "Go up, for I will deliver them into your hand."

11 So they went up to Baal Perazim, and David defeated them there. Then David said, "God has broken through my enemies by my hand like a breakthrough of water." Therefore they called the name of that place Baal Perazim.[1] 12 And when they left their gods there, David gave a commandment, and they were burned with fire.

13 [a]Then the Philistines once again made a raid on the valley. 14 Therefore David inquired again of God, and God said to him, "You shall not go up after them; circle around them, [a]and come upon them in front of the mulberry trees. 15 And it shall be, when you hear a sound of marching in the tops of the mulberry trees, then you shall go out to battle, for God has gone out before you to strike the camp of the Philistines." 16 So David did as God commanded him, and they drove back the army of the Philistines from Gibeon as far as Gezer. 17 Then [a]the fame of David went out into all lands, and the LORD [b]brought the fear of him upon all nations.

The Ark Brought to Jerusalem

15 *David* built houses for himself in the City of David; and he prepared a place for the ark of God, [a]and pitched a tent for it. 2 Then David said, "No one may carry the [a]ark of God but the Levites, for [b]the LORD has chosen them to carry the ark of God and to minister before Him forever." 3 And David [a]gathered all Israel together at Jerusalem, to bring up the ark of the LORD to its place, which he had prepared for it. 4 Then David assembled the children of Aaron and the Levites: 5 of the sons of Kohath, Uriel the chief, *and one hundred and twenty of his* brethren; 6 of the sons of Merari, Asaiah the chief, and two hundred and twenty of his brethren; 7 of the sons of Gershom, Joel the chief, and one hundred and thirty of his brethren; 8 of the sons of [a]Elizaphan, Shemaiah the chief, and two hundred of his brethren; 9 of the sons of [a]Hebron, Eliel the chief, and eighty of his brethren; 10 of the sons of Uzziel, Amminadab the chief, and one hundred and twelve of his brethren.

11 And David called for [a]Zadok and [b]Abiathar the priests, and for the Levites: for Uriel, Asaiah, Joel, Shemaiah, Eliel, and Amminadab. 12 He said to them, "You *are* the heads of the fathers' *houses* of the Levites; sanctify yourselves, you and your brethren, that you may bring up the ark of the LORD God of Israel to *the place* I have prepared for it. 13 For [a]because you *did* not *do it* the first *time,* [b]the LORD our God broke out against us, because we did not consult Him about the proper order."

14 So the priests and the Levites sanctified themselves to bring up the ark of the LORD God of Israel. 15 And the children of the Levites bore the ark of God on their shoulders, by its poles, as [a]Moses had commanded according to the word of the LORD.

16 Then David spoke to the leaders of the Levites to appoint their brethren *to be* the singers accompanied by instruments of music, stringed instruments, harps, and cymbals, by raising the voice with resounding joy. 17 So the Levites appointed [a]Heman the son of Joel; and of his brethren, [b]Asaph the son of Berechiah; and of their brethren, the sons of Merari, [c]Ethan the son of Kushaiah; 18 and with them their brethren of the second *rank:* Zechariah, Ben,[1] Jaaziel, Shemiramoth, Jehiel, Unni, Eliab, Benaiah, Maaseiah, Mattithiah, Elipheleh, Mikneiah, Obed-Edom, and Jeiel, the gatekeepers; 19 the singers, Heman, Asaph, and Ethan, *were* to sound the cymbals of bronze; 20 Zechariah, Aziel, Shemiramoth, Jehiel, Unni, Eliab, Maaseiah, and Benaiah, with strings according to [a]Alamoth; 21 Mattithiah, Elipheleh, Mikneiah, Obed-Edom, Jeiel, and Azaziah, to direct with harps on the [a]Sheminith; 22 Chenaniah, leader of the Levites, was instructor *in charge of* the music, because he *was* skillful; 23 Berechiah and Elkanah *were* doorkeepers for the ark; 24 Shebaniah, Joshaphat, Nethanel, Amasai, Zechariah, Benaiah, and Eliezer, the priests, [a]were to blow the trumpets before the ark of God; and [b]Obed-Edom and Jehiah, doorkeepers for the ark.

25 So [a]David, the elders of Israel, and the captains over thousands went to bring up the ark of the covenant of the LORD from

14:8 [a] 2 Sam. 5:17–21 **14:9** [a] 1 Chr. 11:15; 14:13 **14:10** [a] 1 Sam. 23:2, 4; 30:8 **14:11** [1] Literally *Master of Breakthroughs* **14:13** [a] 2 Sam. 5:22–25 **14:14** [a] 2 Sam. 5:23 **14:17** [a] Josh. 6:27 [b] [Deut. 2:25; 11:25] **15:1** [a] 1 Chr. 16:1 **15:2** [a] [Num. 4:15] [b] Deut. 10:8; 31:9 **15:3** [a] 1 Kin. 8:1 **15:8** [a] Ex. 6:22 **15:9** [a] Ex. 6:18 **15:11** [a] 1 Chr. 12:28 [b] 1 Kin. 2:22, 26, 27 **15:13** [a] 2 Sam. 6:3 [b] 1 Chr. 13:7–11 **15:15** [a] Ex. 25:14 **15:17** [a] 1 Chr. 6:33; 25:1 [b] 1 Chr. 6:39 [c] 1 Chr. 6:44 **15:18** [1] Following Masoretic Text and Vulgate; Septuagint omits *Ben.* **15:20** [a] Ps. 46:title **15:21** [a] Ps. 6:title **15:24** [a] [Num. 10:8] [b] 1 Chr. 13:13, 14 **15:25** [a] 1 Kin. 8:1

WALK IT OUT

David, the elders of Israel, and the captains . . . went to bring up the ark of the covenant of the LORD from the house of Obed-Edom with joy.

I CHRONICLES 15:25

What would you say is the greatest accomplishment of your life? What have you done that has defined you? I'm not sure I can answer these questions. It's hard to single out one thing, and if I did, tomorrow I might decide differently. But I suspect if David was asked this question, his answer would be prompt: bringing the ark of the covenant to Jerusalem, the holy city, the capital of the kingdom of Israel.

The priests offered up sacrifices and "all Israel brought up the ark of the covenant of the LORD with shouting and with the sound of the horn, with trumpets and with cymbals, making music with stringed instruments and harps" (v. 28). For David this was the greatest moment in Israel's history: God's people possessed Jerusalem and Jerusalem now possessed the ark, the symbol of God's presence and covenant.

Peace was now Israel's, but peace is something that must be maintained—and Israel did not always maintain it. Peace is not a once-for-all experience but a daily walk.

the house of Obed-Edom with joy. 26 And so
it was, when God helped the Levites who bore
the ark of the covenant of the LORD, that they
offered seven bulls and seven rams. 27 David
was clothed with a robe of fine [a]linen, as were
all the Levites who bore the ark, the singers, and Chenaniah the music master *with*
the singers. David also wore a linen ephod.
28 [a]Thus all Israel brought up the ark of the
covenant of the LORD with shouting and with
the sound of the horn, with trumpets and
with cymbals, making music with stringed
instruments and harps.
29 And it happened, [a]*as* the ark of the covenant of the LORD came to the City of David,
that Michal, Saul's daughter, looked through
a window and saw King David whirling and
playing music; and she despised him in her
heart.

The Ark Placed in the Tabernacle

16 So [a]they brought the ark of God, and set
it in the midst of the tabernacle that David had erected for it. Then they offered burnt
offerings and peace offerings before God.
2 And when David had finished offering the
burnt offerings and the peace offerings, [a]he
blessed the people in the name of the LORD.
3 Then he distributed to everyone of Israel,
both man *and* woman, *to* everyone a loaf of
bread, a piece *of meat*, and a cake of raisins.
4 And he appointed some of the Levites
to minister before the ark of the LORD, to
[a]commemorate, to thank, and to praise the
LORD God of Israel: 5 Asaph the chief, and
next to him Zechariah, *then* [a]Jeiel, Shemiramoth, Jehiel, Mattithiah, Eliab, Benaiah,
and Obed-Edom: Jeiel with stringed instruments and harps, but Asaph made music with
cymbals; 6 Benaiah and Jahaziel the priests
regularly *blew* the trumpets before the ark
of the covenant of God.

David's Song of Thanksgiving

7 On that day [a]David [b]first delivered *this*
psalm into the hand of Asaph and his brethren, to thank the LORD:

8 [a]Oh, give thanks to the LORD!
Call upon His name;
Make known His deeds among the
peoples!
9 Sing to Him, sing psalms to Him;
Talk of all His wondrous works!
10 Glory in His holy name;
Let the hearts of those rejoice who seek
the LORD!
11 Seek the LORD and His strength;
Seek His face evermore!
12 Remember His marvelous works which
He has done,
His wonders, and the judgments of His
mouth,
13 O seed of Israel His servant,
You children of Jacob, His chosen
ones!

15:27 [a] 1 Sam. 2:18, 28 **15:28** [a] 1 Chr. 13:8 **15:29** [a] 2 Sam. 3:13, 14; 6:16, 20–23 **16:1** [a] 2 Sam. 6:17 **16:2** [a] 1 Kin. 8:14 **16:4** [a] Ps. 38:title; 70:title **16:5** [a] 1 Chr. 15:18 **16:7** [a] 2 Sam. 22:1; 23:1 [b] Ps. 105:1–15 **16:8** [a] Ps. 105:1–15

14 He *is* the LORD our God;
His [a]judgments *are* in all the earth.
15 Remember His covenant forever,
The word which He commanded, for a
thousand generations,
16 *The* [a]*covenant which* He made with
Abraham,
And His oath to Isaac,
17 And [a]confirmed it to [b]Jacob for a
statute,
To Israel *for* an everlasting covenant,
18 Saying, "To you I will give the land of
Canaan
As the allotment of your inheritance,"
19 When you were [a]few in number,
Indeed very few, and strangers in it.

20 When they went from one nation to
another,
And from *one* kingdom to another
people,
21 He permitted no man to do them wrong;
Yes, He [a]rebuked kings for their sakes,
22 *Saying,* [a]"Do not touch My anointed
ones,
And do My prophets no harm."[1]

23 [a]Sing to the LORD, all the earth;
Proclaim the good news of His
salvation from day to day.
24 Declare His glory among the nations,
His wonders among all peoples.

25 For the LORD *is* great and greatly to be
praised;
He *is* also to be feared above all gods.
26 For all the gods [a]of the peoples *are*
idols,
But the LORD made the heavens.
27 Honor and majesty *are* before Him;
Strength and gladness are in His place.

28 Give to the LORD, O families of the
peoples,
Give to the LORD glory and strength.
29 Give to the LORD the glory *due* His
name;
Bring an offering, and come before
Him.
Oh, worship the LORD in the beauty of
holiness!
30 Tremble before Him, all the earth.
The world also is firmly established,
It shall not be moved.

31 Let the heavens rejoice, and let the
earth be glad;
And let them say among the nations,
"The LORD reigns."
32 Let the sea roar, and all its fullness;
Let the field rejoice, and all that *is*
in it.
33 Then the [a]trees of the woods shall
rejoice before the LORD,
For He is [b]coming to judge the
earth.[1]

34 [a]Oh, give thanks to the LORD, for *He is*
good!
For His mercy *endures* forever.[1]
35 [a]And say, "Save us, O God of our
salvation;
Gather us together, and deliver us from
the Gentiles,
To give thanks to Your holy name,
To triumph in Your praise."

36 [a]Blessed *be* the LORD God of Israel
From everlasting to everlasting![1]

And all [b]the people said, "Amen!" and praised
the LORD.

Regular Worship Maintained

37 So he left [a]Asaph and his brothers there
before the ark of the covenant of the LORD
to minister before the ark regularly, as every
day's work [b]required; 38 and [a]Obed-Edom with
his sixty-eight brethren, including Obed-
Edom the son of Jeduthun, and Hosah, *to
be* gatekeepers; 39 and Zadok the priest and
his brethren the priests, [a]before the tabernacle of the LORD [b]at the high place that *was*
at Gibeon, 40 to offer burnt offerings to the
LORD on the altar of burnt offering regularly
[a]morning and evening, and *to do* according
to all that is written in the Law of the LORD
which He commanded Israel; 41 and with
them Heman and Jeduthun and the rest
who were chosen, who were designated by
name, to give thanks to the LORD, [a]because
His mercy *endures* forever; 42 and with them
Heman and Jeduthun, to sound aloud with
trumpets and cymbals and the musical instruments of God. Now the sons of Jeduthun
were gatekeepers.
43 [a]Then all the people departed, every
man to his house; and David returned to
bless his house.

16:14 [a] [Is. 26:9] **16:16** [a] Gen. 17:2; 26:3; 28:13; 35:11 **16:17** [a] Gen. 35:11, 12 [b] Gen. 28:10–15 **16:19** [a] Gen. 34:30 **16:21** [a] Gen. 12:17; 20:3 **16:22** [a] Gen. 20:7 [1] Compare verses 8–22 with Psalm 105:1–15 **16:23** [a] Ps. 96:1–13 **16:26** [a] Lev. 19:4 **16:33** [a] Is. 55:12, 13 [b] [Matt. 25:31–46] [1] Compare verses 23–33 with Psalm 96:1–13 **16:34** [a] Ps. 106:1; 107:1; 118:1; 136:1 [1] Compare verse 34 with Psalm 106:1 **16:35** [a] Ps. 106:47, 48 **16:36** [a] 1 Kin. 8:15, 56 [b] Deut. 27:15 [1] Compare verses 35, 36 with Psalm 106:47, 48 **16:37** [a] 1 Chr. 16:4, 5 [b] Ezra 3:4 **16:38** [a] 1 Chr. 13:14 **16:39** [a] 2 Chr. 1:3 [b] 1 Kin. 3:4 **16:40** [a] [Ex. 29:38–42] **16:41** [a] 2 Chr. 5:13; 7:3 **16:43** [a] 2 Sam. 6:18–20

PEACE NOTE

Even when I feel emotionally out of sorts, the truth of the Scripture is that because of Christ, God's got me.

God's Covenant with David

17 Now [a]it came to pass, when David was dwelling in his house, that David said to Nathan the prophet, "See now, I dwell in a house of cedar, but the ark of the covenant of the LORD *is* under tent curtains."

2 Then Nathan said to David, "Do all that *is* in your heart, for God *is* with you."

3 But it happened that night that the word of God came to Nathan, saying, 4 "Go and tell My servant David, 'Thus says the LORD: "You shall [a]not build Me a house to dwell in. 5 For I have not dwelt in a house since the time that I brought up Israel, even to this day, but have gone from tent to tent, and from *one* tabernacle *to another.* 6 Wherever I have moved about with all Israel, have I ever spoken a word to any of the judges of Israel, whom I commanded to shepherd My people, saying, 'Why have you not built Me a house of cedar?' " ' 7 Now therefore, thus shall you say to My servant David, 'Thus says the LORD of hosts: "I took you [a]from the sheepfold, from following the sheep, to be ruler over My people Israel. 8 And I have been with you wherever you have gone, and have cut off all your enemies from before you, and have made you a name like the name of the great men who *are* on the earth. 9 Moreover I will appoint a place for My people Israel, and will [a]plant them, that they may dwell in a place of their own and move no more; nor shall the sons of wickedness oppress them anymore, as previously, 10 since the time that I commanded judges *to be* over My people Israel. Also I will subdue all your enemies. Furthermore I tell you that the LORD will build you a house.[1] 11 And it shall be, when your days are [a]fulfilled, when you must go *to be* with your fathers, that I will set up your [b]seed after you, who will be of your sons; and I will establish his kingdom. 12 [a]He shall build Me a house, and I will establish his throne forever. 13 [a]I will be his Father, and he shall be My son; and I will not take My mercy away from him, [b]as I took *it* from *him* who was before you. 14 And [a]I will establish him in My house and in My kingdom forever; and his throne shall be established forever." ' "

15 According to all these words and according to all this vision, so Nathan spoke to David.

16 [a]Then King David went in and sat before the LORD; and he said: "Who *am* I, O LORD God? And what is my house, that You have brought me this far? 17 And *yet* this was a small thing in Your sight, O God; and You have *also* spoken of Your servant's house for a great while to come, and have regarded me according to the rank of a man of high degree, O LORD God. 18 What more can David *say* to You for the honor of Your servant? For You know Your servant. 19 O LORD, for Your servant's sake, and according to Your own heart, You have done all this greatness, in making known all these great things. 20 O LORD, *there is* none like You, nor *is there any* God besides You, according to all that we have heard with our ears. 21 [a]And who *is* like Your people Israel, the one nation on the earth whom God went to redeem for Himself *as* a people—to make for Yourself a name by great and awesome deeds, by driving out nations from before Your people whom You redeemed from Egypt? 22 For You have made Your people Israel Your very own people forever; and You, LORD, have become their God.

23 "And now, O LORD, the word which You have spoken concerning Your servant and concerning his house, *let it* be established forever, and do as You have said. 24 So let it be established, that Your name may be magnified forever, saying, 'The LORD of hosts, the God of Israel, *is* Israel's God.' And let the house of Your servant David be established before You. 25 For You, O my God, have revealed to Your servant that You will build him a house. Therefore Your servant has found it *in his heart* to pray before You. 26 And now, LORD, You are God, and have promised this goodness to Your servant. 27 Now You have been pleased to bless the house of Your servant, that it may continue before You forever; for You have blessed it, O LORD, and *it shall be* blessed forever."

17:1 [a] 2 Sam. 7:1 17:4 [a] [1 Chr. 28:2, 3] 17:7 [a] 1 Sam. 16:11–13 17:9 [a] Amos 9:14 17:10 [1] That is, a royal dynasty 17:11 [a] 1 Kin. 2:10 [b] [1 Chr. 22:9–13; 28:20]; Matt. 1:6; Luke 3:31 17:12 [a] [Ps. 89:20–37; Luke 1:33] 17:13 [a] Heb. 1:5 [b] [1 Sam. 15:23–28] 17:14 [a] Matt. 19:28; 25:31; [Luke 1:31–33]; Acts 2:30 17:16 [a] 2 Sam. 7:18 17:21 [a] Ps. 147:20

David's Further Conquests

18 After this [a]it came to pass that David attacked the Philistines, subdued them, and took Gath and its towns from the hand of the Philistines. 2 Then he defeated [a]Moab, and the Moabites became David's [b]servants, *and* brought tribute.

3 And [a]David defeated Hadadezer[1] king of Zobah *as far as* Hamath, as he went to establish his power by the River Euphrates. 4 David took from him one thousand chariots, seven thousand[1] horsemen, and twenty thousand foot soldiers. Also David hamstrung all the chariot *horses,* except that he spared enough of them for one hundred chariots.

5 When the [a]Syrians of Damascus came to help Hadadezer king of Zobah, David killed twenty-two thousand of the Syrians. 6 Then David put *garrisons* in Syria of Damascus; and the Syrians became David's servants, *and* brought tribute. So the LORD preserved David wherever he went. 7 And David took the shields of gold that were on the servants of Hadadezer, and brought them to Jerusalem. 8 Also from Tibhath[1] and from Chun, cities of Hadadezer, David brought a large amount of [a]bronze, with which [b]Solomon made the bronze Sea, the pillars, and the articles of bronze.

9 Now when Tou[1] king of Hamath heard that David had defeated all the army of Hadadezer king of Zobah, 10 he sent Hadoram[1] his son to King David, to greet him and bless him, because he had fought against Hadadezer and defeated him (for Hadadezer had been at war with Tou); and *Hadoram brought with him* all kinds of [a]articles of gold, silver, and bronze. 11 King David also dedicated these to the LORD, along with the silver and gold that he had brought from all *these* nations—from Edom, from Moab, from the [a]people of Ammon, from the [b]Philistines, and from [c]Amalek.

12 Moreover [a]Abishai the son of Zeruiah killed [b]eighteen thousand Edomites[1] in the Valley of Salt. 13 [a]He also put garrisons in Edom, and all the Edomites became David's servants. And the LORD preserved David wherever he went.

David's Administration

14 So David reigned over all Israel, and administered judgment and justice to all his people. 15 Joab the son of Zeruiah *was* over the army; Jehoshaphat the son of Ahilud *was* recorder; 16 Zadok the son of Ahitub and Abimelech the son of Abiathar *were* the priests; Shavsha[1] *was* the scribe; 17 [a]Benaiah the son of Jehoiada *was* over the Cherethites and the Pelethites; and David's sons *were* chief ministers at the king's side.

The Ammonites and Syrians Defeated

19 It[a] happened after this that Nahash the king of the people of Ammon died, and his son reigned in his place. 2 Then David said, "I will show kindness to Hanun the son of Nahash, because his father showed kindness to me." So David sent messengers to comfort him concerning his father. And David's servants came to Hanun in the land of the people of Ammon to comfort him.

3 And the princes of the people of Ammon said to Hanun, "Do you think that David really honors your father because he has sent comforters to you? Did his servants not come to you to search and to overthrow and to spy out the land?"

4 Therefore Hanun took David's servants, shaved them, and cut off their garments in the middle, at their [a]buttocks, and sent them away. 5 Then *some* went and told David about the men; and he sent to meet them, because the men were greatly ashamed. And the king said, "Wait at Jericho until your beards have grown, and *then* return."

6 When the people of Ammon saw that they had made themselves repulsive to David, Hanun and the people of Ammon sent a thousand talents of silver to hire for themselves chariots and horsemen from Mesopotamia,[1] from Syrian Maacah, [a]and from Zobah.[2] 7 So they hired for themselves thirty-two thousand chariots, with the king of Maacah and his people, who came and encamped before Medeba. Also the people of Ammon gathered together from their cities, and came to battle.

8 Now when David heard *of it,* he sent Joab and all the army of the mighty men. 9 Then the people of Ammon came out and put themselves in battle array before the gate of the city, and the kings who had come *were* by themselves in the field.

10 When Joab saw that the battle line was against him before and behind, he chose some of Israel's best and put *them* in battle array against the Syrians. 11 And the rest of the people he put under the command of Abishai his brother, and they set *themselves*

18:1 [a] 2 Sam. 8:1–18 **18:2** [a] 2 Sam. 8:2 [b] Ps. 60:8 **18:3** [a] 2 Sam. 8:3 [1] Hebrew *Hadarezer,* and so throughout chapters 18 and 19 **18:4** [1] Or *seven hundred* (compare 2 Samuel 8:4) **18:5** [a] 2 Sam. 8:5, 6 **18:8** [a] 2 Sam. 8:8 [b] 1 Kin. 7:15, 23 [1] Spelled *Betah* in 2 Samuel 8:8 **18:9** [1] Spelled *Toi* in 2 Samuel 8:9, 10 **18:10** [a] 2 Sam. 8:10–12 [1] Spelled *Joram* in 2 Samuel 8:10 **18:11** [a] 2 Sam. 10:14 [b] 2 Sam. 5:17–25 [c] 2 Sam. 1:1 **18:12** [a] 2 Sam. 23:18 [b] 2 Sam. 8:13 [1] Or *Syrians* (compare 2 Samuel 8:13) **18:13** [a] 2 Sam. 8:14 **18:16** [1] Spelled *Seraiah* in 2 Samuel 8:17 **18:17** [a] 2 Sam. 8:18 **19:1** [a] 2 Sam. 10:1–19 **19:4** [a] Is. 20:4 **19:6** [a] 1 Chr. 18:5, 9 [1] Hebrew *Aram Naharaim* [2] Spelled *Zoba* in 2 Samuel 10:6

in battle array against the people of Ammon. 12 Then he said, "If the Syrians are too strong for me, then you shall help me; but if the people of Ammon are too strong for you, then I will help you. 13 Be of good courage, and let us be strong for our people and for the cities of our God. And may the LORD do *what is* good in His sight."

14 So Joab and the people who *were* with him drew near for the battle against the Syrians, and they fled before him. 15 When the people of Ammon saw that the Syrians were fleeing, they also fled before Abishai his brother, and entered the city. So Joab went to Jerusalem.

16 Now when the Syrians saw that they had been defeated by Israel, they sent messengers and brought the Syrians who were beyond the River,[1] and Shophach[2] the commander of Hadadezer's army *went* before them. 17 When it was told David, he gathered all Israel, crossed over the Jordan and came upon them, and set up in battle array against them. So when David had set up in battle array against the Syrians, they fought with him. 18 Then the Syrians fled before Israel; and David killed seven thousand[1] charioteers and forty thousand foot soldiers[2] of the Syrians, and killed Shophach the commander of the army. 19 And when the servants of Hadadezer saw that they were defeated by Israel, they made peace with David and became his servants. So the Syrians were not willing to help the people of Ammon anymore.

Rabbah Is Conquered

20 It[a] happened in the spring of the year, at the time kings go out *to battle,* that Joab led out the armed forces and ravaged the country of the people of Ammon, and came and besieged Rabbah. But [b]David stayed at Jerusalem. And [c]Joab defeated Rabbah and overthrew it. 2 Then David [a]took their king's crown from his head, and found it to weigh a talent of gold, and *there were* precious stones in it. And it was set on David's head. Also he brought out the spoil of the city in great abundance. 3 And he brought out the people who *were* in it, and put *them* to work[1] with saws, with iron picks, and with axes. So David did to all the cities of the people of Ammon. Then David and all the people returned *to* Jerusalem.

Philistine Giants Destroyed

4 Now it happened afterward [a]that war broke out at Gezer with the Philistines, at

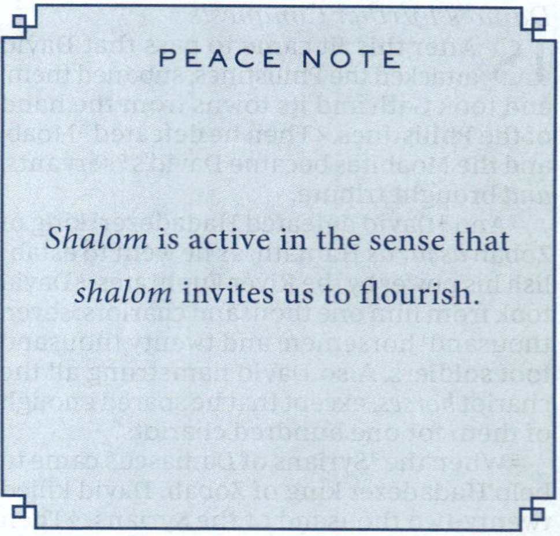

which time [b]Sibbechai the Hushathite killed Sippai,[1] *who was one* of the sons of the giant. And they were subdued.

5 Again there was war with the Philistines, and Elhanan the son of Jair[1] killed Lahmi the brother of Goliath the Gittite, the shaft of whose spear *was* like a weaver's [a]beam.

6 Yet again [a]there was war at Gath, where there was a man of *great* stature, with twenty-four fingers and toes, six *on each hand* and six *on each foot;* and he also was born to the giant. 7 So when he defied Israel, Jonathan the son of Shimea,[1] David's brother, killed him.

8 These were born to the giant in Gath, and they fell by the hand of David and by the hand of his servants.

The Census of Israel and Judah

21 Now [a]Satan stood up against Israel, and moved David to number Israel. 2 So David said to Joab and to the leaders of the people, "Go, number Israel from Beersheba to Dan, [a]and bring the number of them to me that I may know *it.*"

3 And Joab answered, "May the LORD make His people a hundred times more than they are. But, my lord the king, *are* they not all my lord's servants? Why then does my lord require this thing? Why should he be a cause of guilt in Israel?"

4 Nevertheless the king's word prevailed against Joab. Therefore Joab departed and went throughout all Israel and came to Jerusalem. 5 Then Joab gave the sum of the number of the people to David. All Israel *had* one million one hundred thousand men

19:16 [1] That is, the Euphrates [2] Spelled *Shobach* in 2 Samuel 10:16 **19:18** [1] Or *seven hundred* (compare 2 Samuel 10:18) [2] Or *horsemen* (compare 2 Samuel 10:18) **20:1** [a] 2 Sam. 11:1 [b] 2 Sam. 11:2—12:25 [c] 2 Sam. 12:26 **20:2** [a] 2 Sam. 12:30, 31 **20:3** [1] Septuagint reads *cut them.* **20:4** [a] 2 Sam. 21:18 [b] 1 Chr. 11:29 [1] Spelled *Saph* in 2 Samuel 21:18 **20:5** [a] 1 Sam. 17:7 [1] Spelled *Jaare-Oregim* in 2 Samuel 21:19 **20:6** [a] 2 Sam. 21:20 **20:7** [1] Spelled *Shimeah* in 2 Samuel 21:21 and *Shammah* in 1 Samuel 16:9 **21:1** [a] 2 Sam. 24:1–25 **21:2** [a] 1 Chr. 27:23, 24

who drew the sword, and Judah *had* four
hundred and seventy thousand men who
drew the sword. 6 [a]But he did not count Levi
and Benjamin among them, for the king's
word was abominable to Joab.
7 And God was displeased with this thing;
therefore He struck Israel. 8 So David said to
God, [a]"I have sinned greatly, because I have
done this thing; [b]but now, I pray, take away
the iniquity of Your servant, for I have done
very foolishly."
9 Then the LORD spoke to Gad, David's
[a]seer, saying, 10 "Go and tell David, [a]saying,
'Thus says the LORD: "I offer you three *things;*
choose one of them for yourself, that I may
do *it* to you." ' "
11 So Gad came to David and said to him,
"Thus says the LORD: 'Choose for yourself,
12 [a]either three[1] years of famine, or three
months to be defeated by your foes with
the sword of your enemies overtaking *you,* or
else for three days the sword of the LORD—
the plague in the land, with the angel[2] of the
LORD destroying throughout all the territory
of Israel.' Now consider what answer I should
take back to Him who sent me."
13 And David said to Gad, "I am in great
distress. Please let me fall into the hand of
the LORD, for His [a]mercies *are* very great;
but do not let me fall into the hand of man."
14 So the LORD sent a [a]plague upon Israel,
and seventy thousand men of Israel fell.
15 And God sent an [a]angel to Jerusalem to
destroy it. As he[1] was destroying, the LORD
looked and [b]relented of the disaster, and
said to the angel who was destroying, "It is
enough; now restrain your[2] hand." And the
angel of the LORD stood by the [c]threshing
floor of Ornan[3] the Jebusite.
16 Then David lifted his eyes and [a]saw the
angel of the LORD standing between earth
and heaven, having in his hand a drawn
sword stretched out over Jerusalem. So David and the elders, clothed in sackcloth, fell
on their faces. 17 And David said to God, "Was
it not I who commanded the people to be
numbered? I am the one who has sinned and
done evil indeed; but these [a]sheep, what have
they done? Let Your hand, I pray, O LORD my
God, be against me and my father's house,
but not against Your people that they should
be plagued."
18 Therefore, the [a]angel of the LORD commanded Gad to say to David that David should
go and erect an altar to the LORD on the
threshing floor of Ornan the Jebusite. 19 So
David went up at the word of Gad, which he
had spoken in the name of the LORD. 20 Now
Ornan turned and saw the angel; and his four
sons *who were* with him hid themselves, but
Ornan continued threshing wheat. 21 So David
came to Ornan, and Ornan looked and saw
David. And he went out from the threshing
floor, and bowed before David with *his* face
to the ground. 22 Then David said to Ornan,
"Grant me the place of *this* threshing floor,
that I may build an altar on it to the LORD. You
shall grant it to me at the full price, that the
plague may be withdrawn from the people."
23 But Ornan said to David, "Take *it* to yourself, and let my lord the king do *what is* good
in his eyes. Look, I *also* give *you* the oxen for
burnt offerings, the threshing implements
for wood, and the wheat for the grain offering; I give *it* all."
24 Then King David said to Ornan, "No, but I
will surely buy *it* for the full price, for I will not
take what is yours for the LORD, nor offer burnt
offerings with *that which* costs *me* nothing."
25 So [a]David gave Ornan six hundred shekels of
gold by weight for the place. 26 And David built
there an altar to the LORD, and offered burnt
offerings and peace offerings, and called on
the LORD; and [a]He answered him from heaven
by fire on the altar of burnt offering.
27 So the LORD commanded the angel, and
he returned his sword to its sheath.
28 At that time, when David saw that the
LORD had answered him on the threshing
floor of Ornan the Jebusite, he sacrificed
there. 29 [a]For the tabernacle of the LORD and
the altar of the burnt offering, which Moses
had made in the wilderness, *were* at that time
at the high place in [b]Gibeon. 30 But David could
not go before it to inquire of God, for he was
afraid of the sword of the angel of the LORD.

David Prepares to Build the Temple

22 Then David said, [a]"This *is* the house
of the LORD God, and this *is* the altar
of burnt offering for Israel." 2 So David commanded to gather the [a]aliens who *were* in the
land of Israel; and he appointed masons to
[b]cut hewn stones to build the house of God.
3 And David prepared iron in abundance for
the nails of the doors of the gates and for the
joints, and bronze in abundance [a]beyond
measure, 4 and cedar trees in abundance; for
the [a]Sidonians and those from Tyre brought
much cedar wood to David.

21:6 [a] 1 Chr. 27:24 **21:8** [a] 2 Sam. 24:10 [b] 2 Sam. 12:13 **21:9** [a] 1 Sam. 9:9 **21:10** [a] 2 Sam. 24:12–14 **21:12** [a] 2 Sam. 24:13 [1] Or *seven* (compare 2 Samuel 24:13) [2] Or *Angel,* and so elsewhere in this chapter **21:13** [a] Ps. 51:1; 130:4, 7 **21:14** [a] 1 Chr. 27:24 **21:15** [a] 2 Sam. 24:16 [b] Gen. 6:6 [c] 2 Chr. 3:1 [1] Or *He* [2] Or *Your* [3] Spelled *Araunah* in 2 Samuel 24:16 **21:16** [a] 2 Chr. 3:1 **21:17** [a] 2 Sam. 7:8 **21:18** [a] 2 Chr. 3:1 **21:25** [a] 2 Sam. 24:24 **21:26** [a] Lev. 9:24 **21:29** [a] 1 Kin. 3:4 [b] 1 Chr. 16:39 **22:1** [a] Deut. 12:5 **22:2** [a] 1 Kin. 9:20, 21 [b] 1 Kin. 5:17, 18 **22:3** [a] 1 Kin. 7:47 **22:4** [a] 1 Kin. 5:6–10

5 Now David said, [a]"Solomon my son *is* young and inexperienced, and the house to be built for the LORD *must be* exceedingly magnificent, famous and glorious throughout all countries. I will now make preparation for it." So David made abundant preparations before his death.

6 Then he called for his son Solomon, and charged him to build a house for the LORD God of Israel. 7 And David said to Solomon: "My son, as for me, [a]it was in my mind to build a house [b]to the name of the LORD my God; 8 but the word of the LORD came to me, saying, [a]'You have shed much blood and have made great wars; you shall not build a house for My name, because you have shed much blood on the earth in My sight. 9 [a]Behold, a son shall be born to you, who shall be a man of rest; and I will give him [b]rest from all his enemies all around. His name shall be Solomon,[1] for I will give peace and quietness to Israel in his days. 10 [a]He shall build a house for My name, and [b]he shall be My son, and I *will be* his Father; and I will establish the throne of his kingdom over Israel forever.' 11 Now, my son, may [a]the LORD be with you; and may you prosper, and build the house of the LORD your God, as He has said to you. 12 Only may the LORD [a]give you wisdom and understanding, and give you charge concerning Israel, that you may keep the law of the LORD your God. 13 [a]Then you will prosper, if you take care to fulfill the statutes and judgments with which the LORD charged Moses concerning Israel. [b]Be strong and of good courage; do not fear nor be dismayed. 14 Indeed I have taken much trouble to prepare for the house of the LORD one hundred thousand talents of gold and one million talents of silver, and bronze and iron [a]beyond measure, for it is so abundant. I have prepared timber and stone also, and you may add to them. 15 Moreover *there are* workmen with you in abundance: woodsmen and stonecutters, and all types of skillful men for every kind of work. 16 Of gold and silver and bronze and iron *there is* no limit. Arise and begin working, and [a]the LORD be with you."

17 David also commanded all the [a]leaders of Israel to help Solomon his son, *saying,* 18 "*Is* not the LORD your God with you? [a]And has He *not* given you rest on every side? For He has given the inhabitants of the land into my hand, and the land is subdued before the LORD and before His people. 19 Now set your heart and your soul to seek the LORD your God. Therefore arise and build the sanctuary of the LORD God, to [a]bring the ark of the covenant of the LORD and the holy articles of God into the house that is to be built [b]for the name of the LORD."

22:5 [a] 1 Chr. 29:1, 2 **22:7** [a] 2 Sam. 7:1, 2 [b] Deut. 12:5, 11 **22:8** [a] 1 Chr. 28:3 **22:9** [a] 1 Chr. 28:5 [b] 1 Kin. 4:20, 25; 5:4 [1] Literally *Peaceful* **22:10** [a] 1 Chr. 17:12, 13; 28:6 [b] Matt. 1:6; Heb. 1:5 **22:11** [a] 1 Chr. 22:16 **22:12** [a] 1 Kin. 3:9–12 **22:13** [a] 1 Chr. 28:7 [b] [Josh. 1:6, 7, 9] **22:14** [a] 1 Chr. 22:3 **22:16** [a] 1 Chr. 22:11 **22:17** [a] 1 Chr. 28:1–6 **22:18** [a] Josh. 22:4 **22:19** [a] 2 Chr. 5:2–14 [b] 1 Kin. 5:3

OUR GIFT OF PEACE TO OTHERS

"Behold, a son shall be born to you, who shall be a man of rest; and I will give him rest from all his enemies all around. His name shall be Solomon, for I will give peace and quietness to Israel in his days."

1 CHRONICLES 22:9

Our world is full of noise, ads, clicks, pings, and interruptions. Everything about our normal day is abnormal for a life intentionally lived in the *shalom*-peace of God. In this passage from Chronicles, we learn that the catalyst for a life marked by wisdom, rest, freedom, and peace is *quietness* and *tranquility*.

Consider David's life. All he and Israel had known was bloodshed and conflict. David was promised that his son Solomon would rule a kingdom known for its peace. In verse 9, a triple promise appears: Solomon would be a man and leader of rest, not conflict. Furthermore, peace and quietness (*shalom* and *shaqat*) would be the experience of all Israel under his leadership.

Ask yourself: *Like Solomon, do I bring peace, rest, and security to those around me? Or am I an agent of conflict?* May we seek quietness and tranquility with the Lord moment by moment and then share it with those around us.

The Divisions of the Levites

23 So when David was old and full of
days, he made his son [a]Solomon king
over Israel.
2 And he gathered together all the leaders of
Israel, with the priests and the Levites. 3 Now
the Levites were numbered from the age of
[a]thirty years and above; and the number
of individual males was thirty-eight thousand. 4 Of these, twenty-four thousand *were*
to [a]look after the work of the house of the
LORD, six thousand *were* [b]officers and judges,
5 four thousand *were* gatekeepers, and four
thousand [a]praised the LORD with *musical*
instruments, [b]"which I made," *said David,*
"for giving praise."
6 Also [a]David separated them into divisions among the sons of Levi: Gershon, Kohath, and Merari.
7 Of the [a]Gershonites: Laadan[1] and Shimei.
8 The sons of Laadan: the first Jehiel, then
Zetham and Joel—three *in all.* 9 The sons of
Shimei: Shelomith, Haziel, and Haran—three
in all. These were the heads of the fathers'
houses of Laadan. 10 And the sons of Shimei:
Jahath, Zina,[1] Jeush, and Beriah. These *were*
the four sons of Shimei. 11 Jahath was the first
and Zizah the second. But Jeush and Beriah
did not have many sons; therefore they were
assigned as one father's house.
12 [a]The sons of Kohath: Amram, Izhar, Hebron, and Uzziel—four *in all.* 13 The sons of
[a]Amram: Aaron and Moses; and [b]Aaron was
set apart, he and his sons forever, that he
should sanctify the most holy things, [c]to
burn incense before the LORD, [d]to minister
to Him, and [e]to give the blessing in His name
forever. 14 Now [a]the sons of Moses the man of
God were reckoned to the tribe of Levi. 15 [a]The
sons of Moses *were* Gershon[1] and Eliezer. 16 Of
the sons of Gershon, [a]Shebuel[1] *was* the first.
17 Of the descendants of Eliezer, [a]Rehabiah was
the first. And Eliezer had no other sons, but
the sons of Rehabiah were very many. 18 Of
the sons of Izhar, [a]Shelomith *was* the first.
19 [a]Of the sons of Hebron, Jeriah *was* the first,
Amariah the second, Jahaziel the third, and
Jekameam the fourth. 20 Of the sons of Uzziel,
Michah *was* the first and Jesshiah the second.
21 [a]The sons of Merari *were* Mahli and
Mushi. The sons of Mahli *were* Eleazar and
[b]Kish. 22 And Eleazar died, and [a]had no sons,
but only daughters; and their brethren, the
sons of Kish, [b]took them *as wives.* 23 [a]The
sons of Mushi *were* Mahli, Eder, and Jeremoth—three *in all.*
24 These *were* the sons of [a]Levi by their
fathers' houses—the heads of the fathers'
houses as they were counted individually by
the number of their names, who did the work
for the service of the house of the LORD, from
the age of [b]twenty years and above.
25 For David said, "The LORD God of Israel
[a]has given rest to His people, that they may
dwell in Jerusalem forever"; 26 and also to
the Levites, "They shall no longer [a]carry
the tabernacle, or any of the articles for its
service." 27 For by the [a]last words of David
the Levites *were* numbered from twenty
years old and above; 28 because their duty
was to help the sons of Aaron in the service
of the house of the LORD, in the courts and
in the chambers, in the purifying of all holy
things and the work of the service of the
house of God, 29 both with [a]the showbread
and [b]the fine flour for the grain offering,
with [c]the unleavened cakes and [d]*what is
baked in* the pan, with what is mixed and
with all kinds of [e]measures and sizes; 30 to
stand every morning to thank and praise
the LORD, and likewise at evening; 31 and
at every presentation of a burnt offering
to the LORD [a]on the Sabbaths and on the
New Moons and on the [b]set feasts, by number according to the ordinance governing
them, regularly before the LORD; 32 and
that they should [a]attend to the [b]needs of
the tabernacle of meeting, the needs of
the holy *place,* and the [c]needs of the sons
of Aaron their brethren in the work of the
house of the LORD.

The Divisions of the Priests

24 Now *these are* the divisions of the sons
of Aaron. [a]The sons of Aaron *were*
Nadab, Abihu, Eleazar, and Ithamar. 2 And
[a]Nadab and Abihu died before their father,
and had no children; therefore Eleazar and
Ithamar ministered as priests. 3 Then David
with Zadok of the sons of Eleazar, and [a]Ahim-
elech of the sons of Ithamar, divided them
according to the schedule of their service.

23:1 [a] 1 Kin. 1:33–40 **23:3** [a] Num. 4:1–3 **23:4** [a] Ezra 3:8, 9 [b] Deut. 16:18–20 **23:5** [a] 1 Chr. 15:16 [b] 2 Chr. 29:25–27 **23:6** [a] Ex. 6:16 **23:7** [a] 1 Chr. 26:21 [1] Spelled *Libni* in Exodus 6:17 **23:10** [1] Septuagint and Vulgate read *Zizah* (compare verse 11). **23:12** [a] Ex. 6:18 **23:13** [a] Ex. 6:20 [b] Heb. 5:4 [c] 1 Sam. 2:28 [d] [Deut. 21:5] [e] Num. 6:23 **23:14** [a] 1 Chr. 26:20–24 **23:15** [a] Ex. 18:3, 4 [1] Hebrew *Gershom* (compare 6:16) **23:16** [a] 1 Chr. 26:24 [1] Spelled *Shubael* in 24:20 **23:17** [a] 1 Chr. 26:25 **23:18** [a] 1 Chr. 24:22 **23:19** [a] 1 Chr. 24:23 **23:21** [a] 1 Chr. 24:26 [b] 1 Chr. 24:29 **23:22** [a] 1 Chr. 24:28 [b] Num. 36:6 **23:23** [a] 1 Chr. 24:30 **23:24** [a] Num. 10:17, 21 [b] Ezra 3:8 **23:25** [a] 1 Chr. 22:18 **23:26** [a] Num. 4:5, 15; 7:9 **23:27** [a] 2 Sam. 23:1 **23:29** [a] Ex. 25:30 [b] Lev. 6:20 [c] Lev. 2:1, 4 [d] Lev. 2:5, 7 [e] Lev. 19:35 **23:31** [a] Num. 10:10 [b] Lev. 23:2–4 **23:32** [a] 2 Chr. 13:10, 11 [b] [Num. 1:53] [c] Num. 3:6–9, 38 **24:1** [a] Lev. 10:1–6 **24:2** [a] Num. 3:1–4; 26:61 **24:3** [a] 1 Chr. 18:16

GOD'S WILL IS YOUR REST

The LORD God of Israel has given rest to His people.

I CHRONICLES 23:25

David had consolidated his rule, the ark was now in Jerusalem, and Israel was at rest and enjoyed peace. The people of Israel were enjoying that state of spiritual stability and well-being that God intends for all of us. David proclaimed, "The LORD God of Israel has given rest to His people, that they may dwell in Jerusalem forever" (v. 25). The word *heniach* literally means "rest," but in this context it is not wrong to translate it as "peace."

One of the important lessons we learn from David's struggles and accomplishments is how he was able to find peace despite many dangers and setbacks. Peace did not come easily or quickly. David determined throughout his life to pursue the will of God, and in due course he found rest and experienced the peace that God had promised him.

Rest is an integral aspect of God's peace, yet we seem more hurried than ever in our fast-paced society. This is where observing the Sabbath is an immediate, practical way of reminding ourselves that God is in control, and we can have peaceful rest today in the Lord.

4 There were more leaders found of the
sons of Eleazar than of the sons of Ithamar,
and *thus* they were divided. Among the sons
of Eleazar *were* sixteen heads of *their* fathers'
houses, and eight heads of their fathers'
houses among the sons of Ithamar. 5 Thus
they were divided by lot, one group as another, for there were officials of the sanctuary
and officials *of the house* of God, from the
sons of Eleazar and from the sons of Ithamar. 6 And the scribe, Shemaiah the son
of Nethanel, *one of* the Levites, wrote them
down before the king, the leaders, Zadok
the priest, Ahimelech the son of Abiathar,
and the heads of the fathers' *houses* of the
priests and Levites, one father's house taken
for Eleazar and *one* for Ithamar.
7 Now the first lot fell to Jehoiarib, the
second to Jedaiah, 8 the third to Harim, the
fourth to Seorim, 9 the fifth to Malchijah, the
sixth to Mijamin, 10 the seventh to Hakkoz,
the eighth to [a]Abijah, 11 the ninth to Jeshua,
the tenth to Shecaniah, 12 the eleventh to Eliashib, the twelfth to Jakim, 13 the thirteenth to
Huppah, the fourteenth to Jeshebeab, 14 the
fifteenth to Bilgah, the sixteenth to Immer,
15 the seventeenth to Hezir, the eighteenth to
Happizzez,[1] 16 the nineteenth to Pethahiah,
the twentieth to Jehezekel,[1] 17 the twenty-first
to Jachin, the twenty-second to Gamul, 18 the
*twenty-third to Delaiah, the twenty-*fourth
to Maaziah.
19 This *was* the schedule of their service [a]for
coming into the house of the LORD according to their ordinance by the hand of Aaron
their father, as the LORD God of Israel had
commanded him.

Other Levites

20 And the rest of the sons of Levi: of the
sons of Amram, Shubael;[1] of the sons of Shubael, Jehdeiah. 21 Concerning [a]Rehabiah, of
the sons of Rehabiah, the first *was* Isshiah.
22 Of the Izharites, Shelomoth;[1] of the sons of
Shelomoth, Jahath. 23 Of the sons *of* [a]*Hebron*,[1]
Jeriah *was the first*,[2] Amariah the second, Jahaziel the third, *and* Jekameam the fourth.
24 *Of* the sons of Uzziel, Michah; of the sons
of Michah, Shamir. 25 The brother of Michah,
Isshiah; of the sons of Isshiah, Zechariah.
26 [a]The sons of Merari *were* Mahli and Mushi;
the son of Jaaziah, Beno. 27 The sons of Merari by Jaaziah *were* Beno, Shoham, Zaccur,
and Ibri. 28 Of Mahli: Eleazar, [a]who had no
sons. 29 Of Kish: the son of Kish, Jerahmeel.
30 Also [a]the sons of Mushi *were* Mahli, Eder,
and Jerimoth. These *were* the sons of the
Levites according to their fathers' houses.
31 These also cast lots just as their brothers
the sons of Aaron did, in the presence of King
David, Zadok, Ahimelech, and the heads of
the fathers' *houses* of the priests and Levites.
The chief fathers did just as their younger
brethren.

24:10 [a] Luke 1:5 **24:15** [1] Septuagint and Vulgate read *Aphses*. **24:16** [1] Masoretic Text reads *Jehezkel*. **24:19** [a] 1 Chr. 9:25 **24:20** [1] Spelled *Shebuel* in 23:16 **24:21** [a] 1 Chr. 23:17 **24:22** [1] Spelled *Shelomith* in 23:18 **24:23** [a] 1 Chr. 23:19; 26:31 [1] Supplied from 23:19 (following some Hebrew manuscripts and Septuagint manuscripts) [2] Supplied from 23:19 (following some Hebrew manuscripts and Septuagint manuscripts) **24:26** [a] Ex. 6:19 **24:28** [a] 1 Chr. 23:22 **24:30** [a] 1 Chr. 23:23

The Musicians

25 Moreover David and the captains of the army separated for the service *some* of the sons of [a]Asaph, of Heman, and of Jeduthun, who *should* prophesy with harps, stringed instruments, and cymbals. And the number of the skilled men performing their service was: 2 Of the sons of Asaph: Zaccur, Joseph, Nethaniah, and Asharelah;[1] the sons of Asaph *were* under the direction of Asaph, who prophesied according to the order of the king. 3 Of [a]Jeduthun, the sons of Jeduthun: Gedaliah, Zeri,[1] Jeshaiah, *Shimei,* Hashabiah, and Mattithiah, six,[2] under the direction of their father Jeduthun, who prophesied with a harp to give thanks and to praise the LORD. 4 Of Heman, the sons of Heman: Bukkiah, Mattaniah, Uzziel,[1] Shebuel,[2] Jerimoth,[3] Hananiah, Hanani, Eliathah, Giddalti, Romamti-Ezer, Joshbekashah, Mallothi, Hothir, *and* Mahazioth. 5 All these *were* the sons of Heman the king's seer in the words of God, to exalt his [a]horn.[1] For God gave Heman fourteen sons and three daughters.

6 All these *were* under the direction of their father for the music *in* the house of the LORD, with cymbals, stringed instruments, and [a]harps, for the service of the house of God. Asaph, Jeduthun, and Heman *were* [b]under the authority of the king. 7 So the [a]number of them, with their brethren who were instructed in the songs of the LORD, all who were skillful, *was* two hundred and eighty-eight.

8 And they cast lots for their duty, the small as well as the great, [a]the teacher with the student.

9 Now the first lot for Asaph came out for Joseph; the second for Gedaliah, him with his brethren and sons, twelve; 10 the third for Zaccur, his sons and his brethren, twelve; 11 the fourth for Jizri,[1] his sons and his brethren, twelve; 12 the fifth for Nethaniah, his sons and his brethren, twelve; 13 the sixth for Bukkiah, his sons and his brethren, twelve; 14 the seventh for Jesharelah,[1] his sons and his brethren, twelve; 15 the eighth for Jeshaiah, his sons and his brethren, twelve; 16 the ninth for Mattaniah, his sons and his brethren, twelve; 17 the tenth for Shimei, his sons and his brethren, twelve; 18 the eleventh for Azarel,[1] his sons and his brethren, twelve; 19 the twelfth for Hashabiah, his sons and his brethren, twelve; 20 the thirteenth for Shubael,[1] his sons and his brethren, twelve; 21 the fourteenth for Mattithiah, his sons and his brethren, twelve; 22 the fifteenth for Jeremoth,[1] his sons and his brethren, twelve; 23 the sixteenth for Hananiah, his sons and his brethren, twelve; 24 the seventeenth for Joshbekashah, his sons and his brethren, twelve; 25 the eighteenth for Hanani, his sons and his brethren, twelve; 26 the nineteenth for Mallothi, his sons and his brethren, twelve; 27 the twentieth for Eliathah, his sons and his brethren, twelve; 28 the twenty-first for Hothir, his sons and his brethren, twelve; 29 the twenty-second for Giddalti, his sons and his brethren, twelve; 30 the twenty-third for Mahazioth, his sons and his brethren, twelve; 31 the twenty-fourth for Romamti-Ezer, his sons and his brethren, twelve.

PEACE NOTE

The Hebrew word *shalom*, which is normally translated "peace," occurs more than two hundred times in the Hebrew Bible (the Old Testament).

The Gatekeepers

26 Concerning the divisions of the gatekeepers: of the Korahites, Meshelemiah the son of [a]Kore, of the sons of Asaph. 2 And the sons of Meshelemiah *were* [a]Zechariah the firstborn, Jediael the second, Zebadiah the third, Jathniel the fourth, 3 Elam the fifth, Jehohanan the sixth, Eliehoenai the seventh.

4 Moreover the sons of [a]Obed-Edom *were* Shemaiah the firstborn, Jehozabad the second, Joah the third, Sacar the fourth, Nethanel the fifth, 5 Ammiel the sixth, Issachar the seventh, Peulthai the eighth; for God blessed him.

6 Also to Shemaiah his son were sons born who governed their fathers' houses, because they *were* men of great ability. 7 The sons of Shemaiah *were* Othni, Rephael, Obed, and Elzabad, whose brothers Elihu and Semachiah *were* able men.

25:1 [a] 1 Chr. 6:30, 33, 39, 44 **25:2** [1] Spelled *Jesharelah* in verse 14 **25:3** [a] 1 Chr. 16:41, 42 [1] Spelled *Jizri* in verse 11 [2] *Shimei,* appearing in one Hebrew and several Septuagint manuscripts, completes the total of six sons (compare verse 17). **25:4** [1] Spelled *Azarel* in verse 18 [2] Spelled *Shubael* in verse 20 [3] Spelled *Jeremoth* in verse 22 **25:5** [a] 1 Chr. 16:42 [1] That is, to increase his power or influence **25:6** [a] 1 Chr. 15:16 [b] 1 Chr. 15:19; 25:2 **25:7** [a] 1 Chr. 23:5 **25:8** [a] 2 Chr. 23:13 **25:11** [1] Spelled *Zeri* in verse 3 **25:14** [1] Spelled *Asharelah* in verse 2 **25:18** [1] Spelled *Uzziel* in verse 4 **25:20** [1] Spelled *Shebuel* in verse 4 **25:22** [1] Spelled *Jerimoth* in verse 4 **26:1** [a] Ps. 42:title **26:2** [a] 1 Chr. 9:21 **26:4** [a] 1 Chr. 15:18, 21

PEACE NOTE

All the folks mentioned in the Hall of Faith (Heb. 11) endured uncertainty, challenge, transition, or temptation. Always base your peace not on your performance but on God's promises and faithfulness.

8 All these *were* of the sons of Obed-Edom,
they and their sons and their brethren, [a]able
men with strength for the work: sixty-two of
Obed-Edom.
9 And Meshelemiah had sons and brethren,
eighteen able men.
10 Also [a]Hosah, of the children of Merari, had sons: Shimri the first (for *though* he
was not the firstborn, his father made him
the first), 11 Hilkiah the second, Tebaliah the
third, Zechariah the fourth; all the sons and
brethren of Hosah *were* thirteen.
12 Among these *were* the divisions of the
gatekeepers, among the chief men, *having*
duties just like their brethren, to serve in the
house of the LORD. 13 And they [a]cast lots for
each gate, the small as well as the great, according to their father's house. 14 The lot for the East
Gate fell to Shelemiah. Then they cast lots *for*
his son Zechariah, a wise counselor, and his lot
came out for the North Gate; 15 to Obed-Edom
the South Gate, and to his sons the storehouse.[1]
16 To Shuppim and Hosah *the lot came out* for
the West Gate, with the Shallecheth Gate on
the [a]ascending highway—watchman opposite
watchman. 17 On the east *were* six Levites, on
the north four each day, on the south four each
day, and for the storehouse[1] two by two. 18 As for
the Parbar[1] on the west, *there were* four on the
highway *and* two at the Parbar. 19 These were
the divisions of the gatekeepers among the
sons of Korah and among the sons of Merari.

The Treasuries and Other Duties

20 Of the Levites, Ahijah *was* [a]over the
treasuries of the house of God and over the
treasuries of the [b]dedicated things. 21 The
sons of Laadan, the descendants of the Gershonites of Laadan, heads of their fathers'
houses, of Laadan the Gershonite: Jehieli.
22 The sons of Jehieli, Zetham and Joel his
brother, *were* over the treasuries of the house
of the LORD. 23 Of the [a]Amramites, the Izharites, the Hebronites, and the Uzzielites:
24 [a]Shebuel the son of Gershom, the son of
Moses, *was* overseer of the treasuries. 25 And
his brethren by Eliezer *were* Rehabiah his
son, Jeshaiah his son, Joram his son, Zichri
his son, and [a]Shelomith his son.
26 This Shelomith and his brethren *were* over
all the treasuries of the dedicated things [a]which
King David and the heads of fathers' *houses,* the
captains over thousands and hundreds, and the
captains of the army, had dedicated. 27 Some
of the spoils won in battles they dedicated to
maintain the house of the LORD. 28 And all that
Samuel [a]the seer, Saul the son of Kish, Abner
the son of Ner, and Joab the son of Zeruiah had
dedicated, every dedicated *thing,* was under the
hand of Shelomith and his brethren.
29 Of the Izharites, Chenaniah and his sons
[a]*performed* duties as [b]officials and judges
over Israel outside Jerusalem.
30 Of the Hebronites, [a]Hashabiah and his
brethren, one thousand seven hundred able
men, had the oversight of Israel on the west
side of the Jordan for all the business of the
LORD, and in the service of the king. 31 Among
the Hebronites, [a]Jerijah *was* head of the Hebronites according to his genealogy of the
fathers. In the fortieth year of the reign of David they were sought, and there were found
among them capable men [b]at Jazer of Gilead.
32 And his brethren *were* two thousand seven
hundred able men, heads of fathers' *houses,*
whom King David made officials over the
Reubenites, the Gadites, and the half-tribe
of Manasseh, for every matter pertaining to
God and the [a]affairs of the king.

The Military Divisions

27 And the children of Israel, according
to their number, the heads of fathers'
houses, the captains of thousands and hundreds and their officers, served the king in
every matter of the *military* divisions. *These
divisions* came in and went out month by
month throughout all the months of the year,
each division *having* twenty-four thousand.
2 Over the first division for the first month
was [a]Jashobeam the son of Zabdiel, and in his

26:8 [a] 1 Chr. 9:13 **26:10** [a] 1 Chr. 16:38 **26:13** [a] 1 Chr. 24:5, 31; 25:8 **26:15** [1] Hebrew *asuppim* **26:16** [a] 1 Kin. 10:5 **26:17** [1] Hebrew *asuppim* **26:18** [1] Probably a court or colonnade extending west of the temple **26:20** [a] 1 Chr. 9:26 [b] 1 Chr. 26:22, 24, 26; 28:12 **26:23** [a] Ex. 6:18 **26:24** [a] 1 Chr. 23:16 **26:25** [a] 1 Chr. 23:18 **26:26** [a] 2 Sam. 8:11 **26:28** [a] 1 Sam. 9:9 **26:29** [a] Neh. 11:16 [b] 1 Chr. 23:4 **26:30** [a] 1 Chr. 27:17 **26:31** [a] 1 Chr. 23:19 [b] Josh. 21:39 **26:32** [a] 2 Chr. 19:11 **27:2** [a] 1 Chr. 11:11

division *were* twenty-four thousand; 3 *he was* of the children of Perez, and the chief of all the captains of the army for the first month. 4 Over the division of the second month *was* Dodai[1] an Ahohite, and of his division Mikloth also *was* the leader; in his division *were* twenty-four thousand. 5 The third captain of the army for the third month *was* [a]Benaiah, the son of Jehoiada the priest, who was chief; in his division *were* twenty-four thousand. 6 This was the Benaiah *who was* [a]mighty *among* the thirty, and was over the thirty; in his division *was* Ammizabad his son. 7 The fourth *captain* for the fourth month *was* [a]Asahel the brother of Joab, and Zebadiah his son after him; in his division *were* twenty-four thousand. 8 The fifth captain for the fifth month *was* Shamhuth[1] the Izrahite; in his division were twenty-four thousand. 9 The sixth *captain* for the sixth month *was* [a]Ira the son of Ikkesh the Tekoite; in his division *were* twenty-four thousand. 10 The seventh *captain* for the seventh month *was* [a]Helez the Pelonite, of the children of Ephraim; in his division *were* twenty-four thousand. 11 The eighth *captain* for the eighth month *was* [a]Sibbechai the Hushathite, of the Zarhites; in his division *were* twenty-four thousand. 12 The ninth *captain* for the ninth month *was* [a]Abiezer the Anathothite, of the Benjamites; in his division *were* twenty-four thousand. 13 The tenth *captain* for the tenth month *was* [a]Maharai the Netophathite, of the Zarhites; in his division *were* twenty-four thousand. 14 The eleventh *captain* for the eleventh month *was* [a]Benaiah the Pirathonite, of the children of Ephraim; in his division *were* twenty-four thousand. 15 The twelfth *captain* for the twelfth month *was* Heldai[1] the Netophathite, of Othniel; in his division *were* twenty-four thousand.

Leaders of Tribes

16 Furthermore, over the tribes of Israel: the officer over the Reubenites *was* Eliezer the son of Zichri; over the Simeonites, Shephatiah the son of Maachah; 17 *over* the Levites, [a]Hashabiah the son of Kemuel; over the Aaronites, Zadok; 18 *over* Judah, [a]Elihu, *one* of David's brothers; *over* Issachar, Omri the son of Michael; 19 *over* Zebulun, Ishmaiah the son of Obadiah; *over* Naphtali, Jerimoth the son of Azriel; 20 *over* the children of Ephraim, Hoshea the son of Azaziah; *over* the half-tribe of Manasseh, Joel the son of Pedaiah; 21 *over* the half-*tribe* of Manasseh in Gilead, Iddo the son of Zechariah; *over* Benjamin, Jaasiel the son of Abner; 22 *over* Dan, Azarel the son of Jeroham. These *were* the leaders of the tribes of Israel.

23 But David did not take the number of those twenty years old and under, because [a]the LORD had said He would multiply Israel like the [b]stars of the heavens. 24 Joab the son of Zeruiah began a census, but he did not finish, for [a]wrath came upon Israel because of this census; nor was the number recorded in the account of the chronicles of King David.

Other State Officials

25 And Azmaveth the son of Adiel *was* over the king's treasuries; and Jehonathan the son of Uzziah was over the storehouses in the field, in the cities, in the villages, and in the fortresses. 26 Ezri the son of Chelub was over those who did the work of the field for tilling the ground. 27 And Shimei the Ramathite *was* over the vineyards, and Zabdi the Shiphmite was over the produce of the vineyards for the supply of wine. 28 Baal-Hanan the Gederite was over the olive trees and the sycamore trees that *were* in the lowlands, and Joash *was* over the store of oil. 29 And Shitrai the Sharonite *was* over the herds that fed in Sharon, and Shaphat the son of Adlai was over the herds *that were* in the valleys. 30 Obil the Ishmaelite *was* over the camels, Jehdeiah the Meronothite *was* over the donkeys, 31 and Jaziz the [a]Hagrite *was* over the flocks. All these *were* the officials over King David's property.

32 Also Jehonathan, David's uncle, *was* a counselor, a wise man, and a scribe; and Jehiel the son of Hachmoni *was* with the king's sons. 33 [a]Ahithophel *was* the king's counselor, and [b]Hushai the Archite *was* the king's companion. 34 After Ahithophel *was* Jehoiada the son of Benaiah, then [a]Abiathar. And the general of the king's army *was* [b]Joab.

Solomon Instructed to Build the Temple

28 Now David assembled at Jerusalem all [a]the leaders of Israel: the officers of the tribes and [b]the captains of the divisions who served the king, the captains over thousands and captains over hundreds, and [c]the stewards over all the substance and possessions of the king and of his sons, with the officials, the valiant men, and all [d]the mighty men of valor.

27:4 [1] Hebrew *Dodai,* usually spelled *Dodo* (compare 2 Samuel 23:9) **27:5** [a] 1 Chr. 18:17 **27:6** [a] 2 Sam. 23:20–23 **27:7** [a] 1 Chr. 11:26 **27:8** [1] Spelled *Shammoth* in 11:27 and *Shammah* in 2 Samuel 23:11 **27:9** [a] 1 Chr. 11:28 **27:10** [a] 1 Chr. 11:27 **27:11** [a] 2 Sam. 21:18 **27:12** [a] 1 Chr. 11:28 **27:13** [a] 1 Chr. 11:30 **27:14** [a] 1 Chr. 11:31 **27:15** [1] Spelled *Heled* in 11:30 and *Heleb* in 2 Samuel 23:29 **27:17** [a] 1 Chr. 26:30 **27:18** [a] 1 Sam. 16:6 **27:23** [a] [Deut. 6:3] [b] Gen. 15:5; 22:17; 26:4 **27:24** [a] 1 Chr. 21:1–7 **27:31** [a] 1 Chr. 5:10 **27:33** [a] 2 Sam. 15:12 [b] 2 Sam. 15:32–37 **27:34** [a] 1 Kin. 1:7 [b] 1 Chr. 11:6 **28:1** [a] 1 Chr. 27:16 [b] 1 Chr. 27:1, 2 [c] 1 Chr. 27:25 [d] 1 Chr. 11:10–47

2 Then King David rose to his feet and said, "Hear me, my brethren and my people: [a]I *had* it in my heart to build a house of rest for the ark of the covenant of the LORD, and for [b]the footstool of our God, and had made preparations to build it. 3 But God said to me, [a]'You shall not build a house for My name, because you *have been* a man of war and have shed [b]blood.' 4 However the LORD God of Israel [a]chose me above all the house of my father to be king over Israel forever, for He has chosen [b]Judah *to be* the ruler. And of the house of Judah, [c]the house of my father, and [d]among the sons of my father, He was pleased with me to make *me* king over all Israel. 5 [a]And of all my sons (for the LORD has given me many sons) [b]He has chosen my son Solomon to sit on the throne of the kingdom of the LORD over Israel. 6 Now He said to me, 'It is [a]your son Solomon *who* shall build My house and My courts; for I have chosen him *to be* My son, and I will be his Father. 7 Moreover I will establish his kingdom forever, [a]if he is steadfast to observe My commandments and My judgments, as it is this day.' 8 Now therefore, in the sight of all Israel, the assembly of the LORD, and in the hearing of our God, be careful to seek out all the commandments of the LORD your God, that you may possess this good land, and leave *it* as an inheritance for your children after you forever.

9 "As for you, my son Solomon, [a]know the God of your father, and serve Him [b]with a loyal heart and with a willing mind; for [c]the LORD searches all hearts and understands all the intent of the thoughts. [d]If you seek Him, He will be found by you; but if you forsake Him, He will [e]cast you off forever. 10 Consider now, [a]for the LORD has chosen you to build a house for the sanctuary; be strong, and do it."

11 Then David gave his son Solomon [a]the plans for the vestibule, its houses, its treasuries, its upper chambers, its inner chambers, and the place of the mercy seat; 12 and the [a]plans for all that he had by the Spirit, of the courts of the house of the LORD, of all the chambers all around, [b]of the treasuries of the house of God, and of the treasuries for the dedicated things; 13 also for the division of the priests and the [a]Levites, for all the work of the service of the house of the LORD, and for all the articles of service in the house of the LORD. 14 *He gave* gold by weight for *things* of gold, for all articles used in every kind of service; also *silver* for all articles of silver by weight, for all articles used in every kind of service; 15 the weight for the [a]lampstands of gold, and their lamps of gold, by weight for each lampstand and its lamps; for the lampstands of silver by weight, for the lampstand and its lamps, according to the use of each lampstand. 16 And by weight *he gave* gold for the tables of the showbread, for each [a]table, and silver for the tables of silver; 17 also pure gold for the forks, the basins, the pitchers of pure gold, and the golden bowls—*he gave gold* by weight for every bowl; and for the silver bowls, *silver* by weight for every bowl; 18 and refined gold by weight for the [a]altar of incense, and for the construction of the chariot, that is, the gold [b]cherubim that spread *their wings* and overshadowed the ark of the covenant of the LORD. 19 "All *this," said David,* [a]"the LORD made me understand in writing, by *His* hand upon me, all the works of these plans."

20 And David said to his son Solomon, [a]"Be strong and of good courage, and do *it;* do not fear nor be dismayed, for the LORD God—my God—*will be* with you. [b]He will not leave you nor forsake you, until you have finished all the work for the service of the house of the LORD. 21 *Here are* [a]the divisions of the priests and the Levites for all the service of the house of God; and [b]every willing craftsman *will be* with you for all manner of workmanship, for every kind of service; also the leaders and all the people *will be* completely at your command."

Offerings for Building the Temple

29 Furthermore King David said to all the assembly: "My son Solomon, whom alone God has [a]chosen, *is* [b]young and inexperienced; and the work *is* great, because the temple[1] *is* not for man but for the LORD God. 2 Now for the house of my God I have prepared with all my might: gold for *things to be made of* gold, silver for *things of* silver, bronze for *things of* bronze, iron for *things of* iron, wood for *things of* wood, [a]onyx stones, *stones* to be set, glistening stones of various colors, all kinds of precious stones, and marble slabs in abundance. 3 Moreover, because I have set my affection on the house of my God, I have given to the house of my God, over and above all that I have prepared for the holy house, my own special treasure of gold and silver: 4 three thousand talents of gold, of the gold of [a]Ophir, and seven thousand talents of refined silver, to overlay the walls of the houses; 5 the gold

28:2 [a] 2 Sam. 7:2 [b] Ps. 99:5; 132:7 **28:3** [a] 2 Sam. 7:5, 13 [b] [1 Chr. 17:4; 22:8] **28:4** [a] 1 Sam. 16:6–13 [b] Gen. 49:8–10 [c] 1 Sam. 16:1 [d] 1 Sam. 13:14; 16:12, 13 **28:5** [a] 1 Chr. 3:1–9; 14:3–7; 23:1 [b] 1 Chr. 22:9; 29:1 **28:6** [a] 2 Sam. 7:13, 14 **28:7** [a] 1 Chr. 22:13 **28:9** [a] [John 17:3] [b] 2 Kin. 20:3 [c] [1 Sam. 16:7] [d] 2 Chr. 15:2 [e] Deut. 31:17 **28:10** [a] 1 Chr. 22:13; 28:6 **28:11** [a] 1 Chr. 28:19 **28:12** [a] Heb. 8:5 [b] 1 Chr. 26:20, 28 **28:13** [a] 1 Chr. 23:6 **28:15** [a] Ex. 25:31–39 **28:16** [a] 1 Kin. 7:48 **28:18** [a] Ex. 30:1–10 [b] Ex. 25:18–22 **28:19** [a] Ex. 25:40 **28:20** [a] 1 Chr. 22:13 [b] Josh. 1:5 **28:21** [a] 1 Chr. 24—26 [b] Ex. 35:25–35; 36:1, 2 **29:1** [a] 1 Chr. 28:5 [b] 1 Kin. 3:7 [1] Literally *palace* **29:2** [a] Is. 54:11, 12 **29:4** [a] 1 Kin. 9:28

WHEN GOD DOES THE WORK

The work is great, because the temple is not for man but for the LORD God.

1 CHRONICLES 29:1

David made provision for the temple that Solomon would build. David knew that Solomon was "young and inexperienced; and the work is great" (v. 1), so the king gathered gold and silver as well as building materials.

After the collection of these things David offered a beautiful prayer, part of which reads: "Yours, O LORD, is the greatness, the power and the glory . . . Yours is the kingdom, O LORD, and You are exalted as head over all" (v. 11). Does this remind you of the Lord's Prayer? "For Yours is the kingdom and the power and the glory forever" (Matt. 6:13).

David recognized that his kingdom really wasn't his; it was *God's*. This is why the Chronicler said, "Then Solomon sat on the throne of the LORD as king instead of David his father" (1 Chr. 29:23). The throne wasn't Solomon's; it was God's. Peace comes when we recognize what belongs to God. We should acknowledge to the Lord that all we are and all we have are from Him. With that spirit, we find a greater reliance on the Lord's presence and His peace.

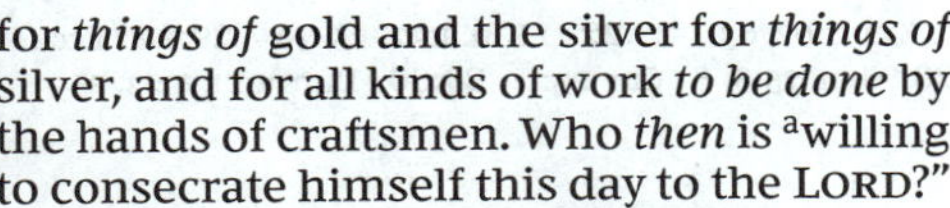

for *things of* gold and the silver for *things of*
silver, and for all kinds of work *to be done* by
the hands of craftsmen. Who *then* is [a]willing
to consecrate himself this day to the LORD?"
6 Then [a]the leaders of the fathers' *houses,*
leaders of the tribes of Israel, the captains
of thousands and of hundreds, with [b]the
officers over the king's work, [c]offered willingly. 7 They gave for the work of the house of
God five thousand talents and ten thousand
darics of gold, ten thousand talents of silver,
eighteen thousand talents of bronze, and
one hundred thousand talents of iron. 8 And
whoever had *precious* stones gave *them* to
the treasury of the house of the LORD, into
the hand of [a]Jehiel[1] the Gershonite. 9 Then
the people rejoiced, for they had offered
willingly, because with a loyal heart they
had [a]offered willingly to the LORD; and King
David also rejoiced greatly.

David's Praise to God

10 Therefore David blessed the LORD before
all the assembly; and David said:

"Blessed are You, LORD God of Israel,
our Father, forever and ever.
11 [a]Yours, O LORD, *is* the greatness,
The power and the glory,
The victory and the majesty;
For all *that is* in heaven and in earth *is*
Yours;
Yours *is* the kingdom, O LORD,
And You are exalted as head over all.
12 [a]Both riches and honor *come* from You,
And You reign over all.
In Your hand *is* power and might;
In Your hand *it is* to make great
And to give strength to all.

13 "Now therefore, our God,
We thank You
And praise Your glorious name.
14 But who *am* I, and who *are* my people,
That we should be able to offer so
willingly as this?
For all things *come* from You,
And of Your own we have given You.
15 For [a]we *are* aliens and pilgrims before
You,
As *were* all our fathers;
[b]Our days on earth *are* as a shadow,
And without hope.

16 "O LORD our God, all this abundance that
we have prepared to build You a house for
Your holy name is from Your hand, and *is* all
Your own. 17 I know also, my God, that You [a]test
the heart and [b]have pleasure in uprightness.
As for me, in the uprightness of my heart I
have willingly offered all these *things;* and
now with joy I have seen Your people, who are
present here to offer willingly to You. 18 O LORD
God of Abraham, Isaac, and Israel, our fathers,

29:5 [a] [2 Cor. 8:5, 12] **29:6** [a] 1 Chr. 27:1; 28:1 [b] 1 Chr. 27:25–31 [c] Ex. 35:21–35 **29:8** [a] 1 Chr. 23:8 [1] Possibly the same as *Jehieli* (compare 26:21, 22) **29:9** [a] 2 Cor. 9:7 **29:11** [a] 1 Tim. 1:17 **29:12** [a] Rom. 11:36 **29:15** [a] Heb. 11:13, 14 [b] Job 14:2 **29:17** [a] [1 Chr. 28:9] [b] Prov. 11:20

keep this forever in the intent of the thoughts
of the heart of Your people, and fix their heart
toward You. 19 And [a]give my son Solomon a
loyal heart to keep Your commandments and
Your testimonies and Your statutes, to do all
these things, and to build the temple[1] for which
[b]I have made provision."

20 Then David said to all the assembly,
"Now bless the LORD your God." So all the
assembly blessed the LORD God of their fathers, and bowed their heads and prostrated
themselves before the LORD and the king.

Solomon Anointed King

21 And they made sacrifices to the LORD
and offered burnt offerings to the LORD on
the next day: a thousand bulls, a thousand
rams, a thousand lambs, with their drink
offerings, and [a]sacrifices in abundance for
all Israel. 22 So they ate and drank before the
LORD with great gladness on that day. And
they made Solomon the son of David king
the second time, and [a]anointed *him* before
the LORD *to be* the leader, and Zadok *to be*
priest. 23 Then Solomon sat on the throne of
the LORD as king instead of David his father,
and prospered; and all Israel obeyed him.
24 All the leaders and the mighty men, and
also all the sons of King David, [a]submitted
themselves to King Solomon. 25 So the LORD
exalted Solomon exceedingly in the sight of
all Israel, and [a]bestowed on him *such* royal
majesty as had not been on any king before
him in Israel.

The Close of David's Reign

26 Thus David the son of Jesse reigned over
all Israel. 27 [a]And the period that he reigned
over Israel *was* forty years; [b]seven years he
reigned in Hebron, and thirty-three *years*
he reigned in Jerusalem. 28 So he [a]died in
a good old age, [b]full of days and riches and
honor; and Solomon his son reigned in his
place. 29 Now the acts of King David, first and
last, indeed they *are* written in the book of
Samuel the seer, in the book of Nathan the
prophet, and in the book of Gad the seer,
30 with all his reign and his might, [a]and the
events that happened to him, to Israel, and
to all the kingdoms of the lands.

29:19 [a] [1 Chr. 28:9] [b] 1 Chr. 29:1, 2 [1] Literally *palace* **29:21** [a] 1 Kin. 8:62, 63 **29:22** [a] 1 Kin. 1:32–35, 39 **29:24** [a] Eccl. 8:2 **29:25** [a] 1 Kin. 3:13 **29:27** [a] 1 Kin. 2:11 [b] 2 Sam. 5:5 **29:28** [a] Gen. 25:8 [b] 1 Chr. 23:1 **29:30** [a] Dan. 2:21; 4:23, 25

THE SECOND BOOK OF THE

CHRONICLES

AUTHOR

The sources of 1 and 2 Chronicles include multiple official and prophetic records. In addition to these, the author-compiler had access to genealogical lists and documents, such as the message and letters of Sennacherib (2 Chr. 32:10–17). It seems likely that Ezra was the author, as Jewish tradition suggests.

TIME

c. 991–538 BC

KEY VERSE

2 Chronicles 7:14

THEME

Second Chronicles begins with Solomon's reign and ends with the fall of Jerusalem. It covers more extensively the details involved in the building and dedication of the temple. The kings of Judah are detailed down through the last king, Zedekiah, who is exiled to Babylon in 597 BC. It largely ignores what happens in the northern kingdom after the split into two nations.

The Scriptures do not hide from us the embarrassing details of what happens when people turn away from God. The Bible teaches us about real people, real places, and real events. Here we learn what happens when societies and cultures refuse to follow the Lord: "And in those times there was no peace to the one who went out, nor to the one who came in, but great turmoil was on all the inhabitants of the lands" (15:5). In a shocking and descriptive narrative, we see how quickly peace is lost and how elusive it can be to restore. We also see that obedience to the Lord without a loyal (*shalem*) heart is empty obedience (19:9).

Solomon Requests Wisdom

1 Now [a]Solomon the son of David was strengthened in his kingdom, and [b]the LORD his God *was* with him and [c]exalted him exceedingly.

2 And Solomon spoke to all Israel, to [a]the captains of thousands and of hundreds, to the judges, and to every leader in all Israel, the heads of the fathers' *houses.* 3 Then Solomon, and all the assembly with him, went to the high place that *was* at [a]Gibeon; for the tabernacle of meeting with God was there, which Moses the servant of the LORD had [b]made in the wilderness. 4 [a]But David had brought up the ark of God from Kirjath Jearim to *the place* David had prepared for it, for he had pitched a tent for it at Jerusalem. 5 Now [a]the bronze altar that [b]Bezalel the son of Uri, the son of Hur, had made, he put[1] before the tabernacle of the LORD; Solomon and the assembly sought Him *there.* 6 And Solomon went up there to the bronze altar before the LORD, which *was* at the tabernacle of meeting, and [a]offered a thousand burnt offerings on it.

7 [a]On that night God appeared to Solomon, and said to him, "Ask! What shall I give you?"

8 And Solomon said to God: "You have shown great [a]mercy to David my father, and have made me [b]king in his place. 9 Now, O LORD God, let Your promise to David my father be established, [a]for You have made me king over a people like the [b]dust of the earth in multitude. 10 [a]Now give me wisdom and knowledge, that I may [b]go out and come in before this people; for who can judge this great people of Yours?"

11 [a]Then God said to Solomon: "Because this was in your heart, and you have not asked riches or wealth or honor or the life of your enemies, nor have you asked long life—but have asked wisdom and knowledge for yourself, that you may judge My people over whom I have made you king— 12 wisdom and knowledge *are* granted to you; and I will give you riches and wealth and honor, such as [a]none of the kings have had who *were* before you, nor shall any after you have the like."

Solomon's Military and Economic Power

13 So Solomon came to Jerusalem from the high place that *was* at Gibeon, from before the tabernacle of meeting, and reigned over Israel. 14 [a]And Solomon gathered chariots and horsemen; he had one thousand four hundred chariots and twelve thousand horsemen, whom he stationed in the chariot cities and with the king in Jerusalem. 15 [a]Also the king made silver and gold as common in Jerusalem as stones, and he made cedars as abundant as the sycamores which *are* in the lowland. 16 [a]And Solomon had horses imported from

1:1 [a] 1 Kin. 2:46 [b] Gen. 39:2 [c] 1 Chr. 29:25 **1:2** [a] 1 Chr. 27:1–34 **1:3** [a] 1 Kin. 3:4 [b] Ex. 25—27; 35:4—36:38 **1:4** [a] 2 Sam. 6:2–17 **1:5** [a] Ex. 27:1, 2; 38:1, 2 [b] Ex. 31:2 [1] Some authorities read *it was there.* **1:6** [a] 1 Kin. 3:4 **1:7** [a] 1 Kin. 3:5–14; 9:2 **1:8** [a] Ps. 18:50 [b] 1 Chr. 28:5 **1:9** [a] 2 Sam. 7:8–16 [b] Gen. 13:16 **1:10** [a] 1 Kin. 3:9 [b] Deut. 31:2 **1:11** [a] 1 Kin. 3:11–13 **1:12** [a] 2 Chr. 9:22 **1:14** [a] 1 Kin. 10:26 **1:15** [a] 2 Chr. 9:27 **1:16** [a] 1 Kin. 10:28; 22:36

WISDOM AND PEACE

Now give me wisdom and knowledge.

2 CHRONICLES 1:10

Many a joke is told about what people might wish for if they found a magic lamp. There are no magic lamps, of course, but we do make wishes and decisions—and they are not always wise. Even in prayer we often make requests that are shortsighted and selfish.

God appeared to Solomon early in his reign and invited him to request what he wanted. The king did not ask for wealth or fame but for wisdom that he might fulfill God's promises made to David: "Now give me wisdom and knowledge, that I may go out and come in before this people; for who can judge this great people of Yours?" (v. 10). The words "go out and come in" remind us of Moses' leadership; nearing the end of his life he said to the Lord, "I can no longer go out and come in" (Deut. 31:2). Solomon asked God for the wisdom to lead the people of Israel even as Moses had led them centuries ago.

Solomon asked God for wisdom to know the Lord better and the by-product was a life and reign that can be described as "flourishing" (*shalom*). Ask the Lord for wisdom today in your life to know Him better so you can flourish in His peace.

Egypt and Keveh; the king's merchants bought
them in Keveh at the *current* price. 17 They also
acquired and imported from Egypt a chariot
for six hundred *shekels* of silver, and a horse
for one hundred and fifty; thus, through their
agents,[1] they exported them to all the kings of
the Hittites and the kings of Syria.

Solomon Prepares to Build the Temple

2 Then Solomon [a]determined to build a
temple for the name of the LORD, and a
royal house for himself. 2 [a]Solomon selected
seventy thousand men to bear burdens, eighty
thousand to quarry *stone* in the mountains, and
three thousand six hundred to oversee them.
3 Then Solomon sent to Hiram[1] king of
Tyre, saying:

[a]As you have dealt with David my
father, and sent him cedars to build
himself a house to dwell in, *so deal
with me.* 4 Behold, [a]I am building a
temple for the name of the LORD my
God, to dedicate *it* to Him, [b]to burn
before Him sweet incense, for [c]the
continual showbread, for [d]the burnt
offerings morning and evening, on the
[e]Sabbaths, on the New Moons, and on
the set feasts of the LORD our God. This
is an ordinance forever to Israel.

5 And the temple which I build *will be*
great, for [a]our God is greater than all
gods. 6 [a]But who is able to build Him a
temple, since heaven and the heaven of
heavens cannot contain Him? Who *am* I
then, that I should build Him a temple,
except to burn sacrifice before Him?

7 Therefore send me at once a man
skillful to work in gold and silver, in
bronze and iron, in purple and crimson
and blue, who has skill to engrave with
the skillful men who are with me in
Judah and Jerusalem, [a]whom David
my father provided. 8 [a]Also send me
cedar and cypress and algum logs from
Lebanon, for I know that your servants
have skill to cut timber in Lebanon;
and indeed my servants *will be* with
your servants, 9 to prepare timber for
me in abundance, for the temple which
I am about to build *shall be* great and
wonderful.

10 [a]And indeed I will give to your
servants, the woodsmen who cut
timber, twenty thousand kors of
ground wheat, twenty thousand kors of
barley, twenty thousand baths of wine,
and twenty thousand baths of oil.

1:17 [1] Literally *by their hands* 2:1 [a] 1 Kin. 5:5 2:2 [a] 2 Chr. 2:18 2:3 [a] 1 Chr. 14:1 [1] Hebrew *Huram* (compare 1 Kings 5:1) 2:4 [a] 2 Chr. 2:1 [b] Ex. 30:7 [c] Ex. 25:30 [d] Ex. 29:38–42 [e] Num. 28:3, 9–11 2:5 [a] Ps. 135:5 2:6 [a] 1 Kin. 8:27 2:7 [a] 1 Chr. 22:15 2:8 [a] 1 Kin. 5:6 2:10 [a] 1 Kin. 5:11

HOW GREAT IS OUR GOD

Who is able to build Him a temple, since heaven and the heaven of heavens cannot contain Him?

2 CHRONICLES 2:6

Pagan polytheism (the belief in many gods) suffers because of its failure to understand the sovereignty of God. God is not small and localized. He does not live in a shrine. He has no needs that humans can meet.

Solomon understood this so he said, "Who am I then that I should build Him a temple?" (v. 6). He recognized that God, whom the very heavens cannot contain, does not literally live in a house. Rather, said Solomon, the temple will be a place where people may offer *up sacrifice and worship God.* This great truth is repeated by the prophet Isaiah (see Is. 66:1–2) and the early Christians (see Acts 7:47–50).

Solomon's confession reflects the wisdom that God gave him. Recognizing the uniqueness, majesty, and power of God provides the foundation on which our faith may rest, and with that faith comes God's peace. We need a reminder of the "bigness" of God in our lives. Sometimes we allow our problems to appear larger than life and God Himself. They are not. When I remind myself of our unlimited God, of who He is, I have His peace, knowing that He is in total control.

11 Then Hiram king of Tyre answered in
writing, which he sent to Solomon:

[a]Because the LORD loves His people,
He has made you king over them.

12 Hiram[1] also said:

[a]Blessed *be* the LORD God of Israel, [b]who
made heaven and earth, for He has
given King David a wise son, endowed
with prudence and understanding, who
will build a temple for the LORD and a
royal house for himself!

13 And now I have sent a skillful man,
endowed with understanding, Huram[1]
my master[2] *craftsman* 14 [a](the son of a
woman of the daughters of Dan, and
his father was a man of Tyre), skilled
to work in gold and silver, bronze and
iron, stone and wood, purple and blue,
fine linen and crimson, and to make
any engraving and to accomplish any
plan which may be given to him, with
your skillful men and with the skillful
men of my lord David your father.

15 Now therefore, the wheat, the barley,
the oil, and the wine which [a]my lord
has spoken of, let him send to his
servants. 16 [a]And we will cut wood from
Lebanon, as much as you need; we will
bring it to you in rafts by sea to Joppa,
and you will carry it up to Jerusalem.

17 [a]Then Solomon numbered all the aliens
who *were* in the land of Israel, after the census
in which [b]David his father had numbered
them; and there were found to be one hundred
and fifty-three thousand six hundred. 18 And
he made [a]seventy thousand of them bearers of
burdens, eighty thousand stonecutters in the
mountain, and three thousand six hundred
overseers to make the people work.

Solomon Builds the Temple

3 Now [a]Solomon began to build the house of
the LORD at [b]Jerusalem on Mount Moriah,
where *the LORD*[1] had appeared to his father David, at the place that David had prepared on the
threshing floor of [c]Ornan[2] the Jebusite. 2 And
he began to build on the second *day* of the
second month in the fourth year of his reign.
3 This is the foundation [a]which Solomon laid
for building the house of God: The length *was*
sixty cubits (by cubits according to the former
measure) and the width twenty cubits. 4 And
the [a]vestibule that *was* in front *of the sanctuary*[1]
was twenty cubits long across the width of the
house, and the height *was* one hundred and[2]
twenty. He overlaid the inside with pure gold.
5 [a]The larger room[1] he [b]paneled with cypress
which he overlaid with fine gold, and he carved
palm trees and chainwork on it. 6 And he dec-
orated the house with precious stones for
beauty, and the gold *was* gold from Parvaim.
7 He also overlaid the house—the beams and
doorposts, its walls and doors—with gold; and
he carved cherubim on the walls.
8 And he made the [a]Most Holy Place. Its
length was according to the width of the
house, twenty cubits, and its width twenty
cubits. He overlaid it with six hundred talents
of fine gold. 9 The weight of the nails *was* fifty
shekels of gold; and he overlaid the upper
[a]area with gold. 10 [a]In the Most Holy Place he
made two cherubim, fashioned by carving,
and overlaid them with gold. 11 The wings of
the cherubim *were* twenty cubits in *overall*
length: one wing *of the one cherub was* five
cubits, touching the wall of the room, and
the other wing *was* five cubits, touching the
wing of the other cherub; 12 *one* wing of the
other cherub *was* five cubits, touching the
wall of the room, and the other wing *also*
was five cubits, touching the wing of the
other cherub. 13 The wings of these cherubim
spanned twenty cubits overall. They stood
on their feet, and they faced inward. 14 And
he made the [a]veil of blue, purple, crimson,
and fine linen, and wove cherubim into it.
15 Also he made in front of the temple[1] [a]two
pillars thirty-five[2] cubits high, and the capital
that *was* on the top of each of *them* was five
cubits. 16 He made wreaths of chainwork, as
in the inner sanctuary, and put *them* on top
of the pillars; and he made [a]one hundred
pomegranates, and put *them* on the wreaths
of chainwork. 17 Then he [a]set up the pillars
before the temple, one on the right hand
and the other on the left; he called the name

2:11 [a] 2 Chr. 9:8 **2:12** [a] 1 Kin. 5:7 [b] Rev. 10:6 [1] Hebrew *Huram* (compare 1 Kings 5:1) **2:13** [1] Spelled *Hiram* in 1 Kings 7:13 [2] Literally *father* (compare 1 Kings 7:13, 14) **2:14** [a] 1 Kin. 7:13, 14 **2:15** [a] 2 Chr. 2:10 **2:16** [a] 1 Kin. 5:8, 9 **2:17** [a] 1 Kin. 5:13; 2 Chr. 8:7, 8 [b] 1 Chr. 22:2 **2:18** [a] 2 Chr. 2:2 **3:1** [a] 1 Kin. 6:1 [b] Gen. 22:2–14 [c] 1 Chr. 21:18; 22:1 [1] Literally *He,* following Masoretic Text and Vulgate; Septuagint reads *the LORD;* Targum reads *the Angel of the LORD.* [2] Spelled *Araunah* in 2 Samuel 24:16ff **3:3** [a] 1 Kin. 6:2 **3:4** [a] 1 Kin. 6:3 [1] The main room of the temple; elsewhere called the holy place (compare 1 Kings 6:3) [2] Following Masoretic Text, Septuagint, and Vulgate; Arabic, some manuscripts of the Septuagint, and Syriac omit *one hundred and.* **3:5** [a] 1 Kin. 6:17 [b] 1 Kin. 6:15 [1] Literally *house* **3:8** [a] Ex. 26:33 **3:9** [a] 1 Chr. 28:11 **3:10** [a] 1 Kin. 6:23–28 **3:14** [a] Ex. 26:31 **3:15** [a] 1 Kin. 7:15–20 [1] Literally *house* [2] Or *eighteen* (compare 1 Kings 7:15; 2 Kings 25:17; and Jeremiah 52:21) **3:16** [a] 1 Kin. 7:20 **3:17** [a] 1 Kin. 7:21

of the one on the right hand Jachin, and the name of the one on the left Boaz.

Furnishings of the Temple

4 Moreover he made [a]a bronze altar: twenty cubits was its length, twenty cubits its width, and ten cubits its height.

2 [a]Then he made the Sea of cast *bronze,* ten cubits from one brim to the other; *it was* completely round. Its height *was* five cubits, and a line of thirty cubits measured its circumference. 3 [a]And under it *was* the likeness of oxen encircling it all around, ten to a cubit, all the way around the Sea. The oxen *were* cast in two rows, when it was cast. 4 It stood on twelve [a]oxen: three looking toward the north, three looking toward the west, three looking toward the south, and three looking toward the east; the Sea *was set* upon them, and all their back parts *pointed* inward. 5 It *was* a handbreadth thick; and its brim was shaped like the brim of a cup, *like* a lily blossom. It contained three thousand[1] baths.

6 He also made [a]ten lavers, and put five on the right side and five on the left, to wash in them; such things as they offered for the burnt offering they would wash in them, but the Sea *was* for the [b]priests to wash in. 7 [a]And he made ten lampstands of gold [b]according to their design, and set *them* in the temple, five on the right side and five on the left. 8 [a]He also made ten tables, and placed *them* in the temple, five on the right side and five on the left. And he made one hundred [b]bowls of gold.

9 Furthermore [a]he made the court of the priests, and the [b]great court and doors for the court; and he overlaid these doors with bronze. 10 [a]He set the Sea on the right side, toward the southeast.

11 Then [a]Huram made the pots and the shovels and the bowls. So Huram finished doing the work that he was to do for King Solomon for the house of God: 12 the two pillars and [a]the bowl-shaped capitals *that were* on top of the two pillars; the two networks covering the two bowl-shaped capitals which *were* on top of the pillars; 13 [a]four hundred pomegranates for the two networks (two rows of pomegranates for each network, to cover the two bowl-shaped capitals that *were* on the pillars); 14 he also made [a]carts and the lavers on the carts; 15 one Sea and twelve oxen under it; 16 also the pots, the shovels, the forks—and all their articles [a]Huram his master[1] *craftsman* made of burnished bronze for King Solomon for the house of the LORD.

PEACE NOTE

Recognizing who Jesus really was gave Peter a happiness that he had never experienced. We too should proclaim Christ's lordship over our lives and invite others to peace.

17 In the plain of Jordan the king had them cast in clay molds, between Succoth and Zeredah.[1] 18 [a]And Solomon had all these articles made in such great abundance that the weight of the bronze was not determined.

19 Thus [a]Solomon had all the furnishings made for the house of God: the altar of gold and the tables on which *was* [b]the showbread; 20 the lampstands with their lamps of pure gold, to burn [a]in the prescribed manner in front of the inner sanctuary, 21 with [a]the flowers and the lamps and the wick-trimmers of gold, of purest gold; 22 the trimmers, the bowls, the ladles, and the censers of pure gold. As for the entry of the sanctuary, its inner doors to the Most Holy *Place,* and the doors of the main hall of the temple, *were* gold.

5 So [a]all the work that Solomon had done for the house of the LORD was finished; and Solomon brought in the things which his father David had dedicated: the silver and the gold and all the furnishings. And he put *them* in the treasuries of the house of God.

The Ark Brought into the Temple

2 [a]Now Solomon assembled the elders of Israel and all the heads of the tribes, the chief fathers of the children of Israel, in Jerusalem, that they might bring the ark of the covenant of the LORD up [b]from the City of David, which *is* Zion. 3 [a]Therefore all the men of Israel assembled with the king [b]at the feast, which *was* in the seventh month. 4 So all the elders of Israel came, and the [a]Levites took up the ark. 5 Then they brought up the ark, the tabernacle of meeting, and all the holy furnishings

4:1 [a] Ex. 27:1, 2 **4:2** [a] 1 Kin. 7:23–26 **4:3** [a] 1 Kin. 7:24–26 **4:4** [a] 1 Kin. 7:25 **4:5** [1] Or *two thousand* (compare 1 Kings 7:26)
4:6 [a] 1 Kin. 7:38, 40 [b] Ex. 30:19–21 **4:7** [a] 1 Kin. 7:49 [b] Ex. 25:31 **4:8** [a] 1 Kin. 7:48 [b] 1 Chr. 28:17 **4:9** [a] 1 Kin. 6:36 [b] 2 Kin. 21:5
4:10 [a] 1 Kin. 7:39 **4:11** [a] 1 Kin. 7:40–51 **4:12** [a] 1 Kin. 7:41 **4:13** [a] 1 Kin. 7:20 **4:14** [a] 1 Kin. 7:27, 43 **4:16** [a] 1 Kin. 7:45
[1] Literally *father* **4:17** [1] Spelled *Zaretan* in 1 Kings 7:46 **4:18** [a] 1 Kin. 7:47 **4:19** [a] 1 Kin. 7:48–50 [b] Ex. 25:30 **4:20** [a] Ex. 27:20, 21
4:21 [a] Ex. 25:31 **5:1** [a] 1 Kin. 7:51 **5:2** [a] 1 Kin. 8:1–9 [b] 2 Sam. 6:12 **5:3** [a] 1 Kin. 8:2 [b] 2 Chr. 7:8–10 **5:4** [a] 1 Chr. 15:2, 15

that *were* in the tabernacle. The priests and
the Levites brought them up. 6 Also King
Solomon, and all the congregation of Israel
who were assembled with him before the ark,
were sacrificing sheep and oxen that could
not be counted or numbered for multitude.
7 Then the priests brought in the ark of the
covenant of the LORD to its place, into the
[a]inner sanctuary of the temple,[1] to the Most
Holy *Place,* under the wings of the cherubim.
8 For the cherubim spread *their* wings over
the place of the ark, and the cherubim overshadowed the ark and its poles. 9 The poles
extended so that the ends of the [a]poles of the
ark could be seen from *the holy place,* in front
of the inner sanctuary; but they could not be
seen from outside. And they are there to this
day. 10 Nothing was in the ark except the two
tablets which Moses [a]put *there* at Horeb, when
the LORD made *a covenant* with the children
of Israel, when they had come out of Egypt.
11 And it came to pass when the priests came
out of the *Most* Holy *Place* (for all the priests
who *were* present had sanctified themselves,
without keeping to their [a]divisions), 12 [a]and
the Levites *who were* the singers, all those of
Asaph and Heman and Jeduthun, with their
sons and their brethren, stood at the east end
of the altar, clothed in white linen, having
cymbals, stringed instruments and harps,
[b]and with them one hundred and twenty
priests sounding with trumpets— 13 indeed
it came to pass, when the trumpeters and
singers *were* as one, to make one sound to
be heard in praising and thanking the LORD,
and when they lifted up their voice with the
trumpets and cymbals and instruments of
music, and praised the LORD, *saying:*

[a]"*For He is* good,
For His mercy *endures* forever,"[1]

that the house, the house of the LORD, was
filled with a cloud, 14 so that the priests could
not continue ministering because of the
cloud; [a]for the glory of the LORD filled the
house of God.

6 Then [a]Solomon spoke:

"The LORD said He would dwell in the
[b]dark cloud.
2 I have surely built You an exalted house,
And [a]a place for You to dwell in
forever."

Solomon's Speech upon Completion of the Work

3 Then the king turned around and [a]blessed
the whole assembly of Israel, while all the assembly of Israel was standing. 4 And he said:
"Blessed *be* the LORD God of Israel, who has
fulfilled with His hands *what* He spoke with
His mouth to my father David, [a]saying, 5 'Since
the day that I brought My people out of the
land of Egypt, I have chosen no city from any
tribe of Israel *in which* to build a house, that
My name might be there, nor did I choose any
man to be a ruler over My people Israel. 6 [a]Yet I
have chosen Jerusalem, that My name may be
there, and I [b]have chosen David to be over My
people Israel.' 7 Now [a]it was in the heart of my
father David to build a temple[1] for the name
of the LORD God of Israel. 8 But the LORD said
to my father David, 'Whereas it was in your
heart to build a temple for My name, you did
well in that it was in your heart. 9 Nevertheless
you shall not build the temple, but your son
who will come from your body, he shall build
the temple for My [a]name.' 10 So the LORD has
fulfilled His word which He spoke, and I have
filled the position of my father David, and [a]sit
on the throne of Israel, as the LORD promised;
and I have built the temple for the name of
the LORD God of Israel. 11 And there I have put
the ark, [a]in which *is* the covenant of the LORD
which He made with the children of Israel."

Solomon's Prayer of Dedication

12 [a]Then *Solomon*[1] stood before the altar of
the LORD in the presence of all the assembly
of Israel, and spread out his hands 13 (for Solomon had made a bronze platform five cubits
long, five cubits wide, and three cubits high,
and had set it in the midst of the court; and
he stood on it, knelt down on his knees before
all the assembly of Israel, and spread out his
hands toward heaven); 14 and he said: "LORD
God of Israel, [a]*there is* no God in heaven or
on earth like You, who keep *Your* [b]covenant
and mercy with Your servants who walk before You with all their hearts. 15 [a]You have
kept what You promised Your servant David
my father; You have both spoken with Your
mouth and fulfilled *it* with Your hand, as *it*
is this day. 16 Therefore, LORD God of Israel,
now keep what You promised Your servant
David my father, saying, [a]'You shall not fail
to have a man sit before Me on the throne of
Israel, [b]only if your sons take heed to their

5:7 [a] 2 Chr. 4:20 [1] Literally *house* **5:9** [a] Ex. 25:13–15 **5:10** [a] Deut. 10:2, 5 **5:11** [a] 1 Chr. 24:1–5 **5:12** [a] 1 Chr. 25:1–7 [b] 1 Chr. 13:8; 15:16, 24 **5:13** [a] 1 Chr. 16:34, 41; Ps. 100:5; 106:1; 136 [1] Compare Psalm 106:1 **5:14** [a] Ex. 40:35
6:1 [a] 1 Kin. 8:12–21 [b] [Lev. 16:2] **6:2** [a] 2 Chr. 7:12 **6:3** [a] 2 Sam. 6:18 **6:4** [a] 1 Chr. 17:5 **6:6** [a] Deut. 12:5–7 [b] 1 Chr. 28:4
6:7 [a] 2 Sam. 7:2 [1] Literally *house,* and so in verses 8–10 **6:9** [a] 1 Chr. 28:3–6 **6:10** [a] 1 Kin. 2:12; 10:9 **6:11** [a] 2 Chr. 5:7–10 **6:12** [a] 1 Kin. 8:22 [1] Literally *he* (compare 1 Kings 8:22) **6:14** [a] [Ex. 15:11] [b] [Deut. 7:9] **6:15** [a] 1 Chr. 22:9, 10
6:16 [a] 2 Chr. 7:18 [b] Ps. 132:12

way, that they walk in My law as you have
walked before Me.' 17 And now, O LORD God
of Israel, let Your word come true, which You
have spoken to Your servant David.
18 "But will God indeed dwell with men on
the earth? [a]Behold, heaven and the heaven
of heavens cannot contain You. How much
less this temple[1] which I have built! 19 Yet
regard the prayer of Your servant and his
supplication, O LORD my God, and listen to
the cry and the prayer which Your servant
is praying before You: 20 that Your eyes may
be [a]open toward this temple day and night,
toward the place where *You* said *You would*
put Your name, that You may hear the prayer
which Your servant makes [b]toward this place.
21 And may You hear the supplications of Your
servant and of Your people Israel, when they
pray toward this place. Hear from heaven Your
dwelling place, and when You hear, [a]forgive.
22 "If anyone sins against his neighbor, and
is forced to take an [a]oath, and comes *and*
takes an oath before Your altar in this temple,
23 then hear from heaven, and act, and judge
Your servants, bringing retribution on the
wicked by bringing his way on his own head,
and justifying the righteous by giving him
according to his [a]righteousness.
24 "Or if Your people Israel are defeated
before an [a]enemy because they have sinned
against You, and return and confess Your
name, and pray and make supplication before You in this temple, 25 then hear from
heaven and forgive the sin of Your people
Israel, and bring them back to the land which
You gave to them and their fathers.
26 "When the [a]heavens are shut up and
there is no rain because they have sinned
against You, when they pray toward this place
and confess Your name, and turn from their
sin because You afflict them, 27 then hear *in*
heaven, and forgive the sin of Your servants,
Your people Israel, that You may teach them
the good way in which they should walk; and
send rain on Your land which You have given
to Your people as an inheritance.
28 "When there [a]is famine in the land, pestilence or blight or mildew, locusts or grasshoppers; when their enemies besiege them
in the land of their cities; whatever plague
or whatever [b]sickness *there is;* 29 whatever
prayer, whatever supplication is *made* by
anyone, or by all Your people Israel, when
each one knows his own burden and his own
grief, and spreads out his hands to this temple: 30 then hear from heaven Your dwelling
place, and forgive, and give to everyone according to all his ways, whose heart You know
(for You alone [a]know the [b]hearts of the sons
of men), 31 that they may fear You, to walk in
Your ways as long as they live in the land
which You gave to our fathers.
32 "Moreover, concerning a foreigner, [a]who
is not of Your people Israel, but has come
from a far country for the sake of Your great
name and Your mighty hand and Your outstretched arm, when they come and pray in
this temple; 33 then hear from heaven Your
dwelling place, and do according to all for
which the foreigner calls to You, that all peoples of the earth may know Your name and
fear You, as *do* Your people Israel, and that
they may know that this temple which I have
built is called by Your name.
34 "When Your people go out to battle
against their enemies, wherever You send
them, and when they pray to You toward this
city which You have chosen and the temple
which I have built for Your name, 35 then hear
from heaven their prayer and their supplication, and maintain their cause.
36 "When they sin against You (for *there is*
[a]no one who does not sin), and You become
angry with them and deliver them to the enemy, and they take them [b]captive to a land far
or near; 37 *yet* when they come to themselves
in the land where they were carried captive,
and repent, and make supplication to You in
the land of their captivity, saying, 'We have
sinned, we have done wrong, and have committed wickedness'; 38 and *when* they return
to You with all their heart and with all their
soul in the land of their captivity, where they
have been carried captive, and pray toward
their land which You gave to their fathers,
the [a]city which You have chosen, and toward
the temple which I have built for Your name:
39 then hear from heaven Your dwelling place
their prayer and their supplications, and
maintain their cause, and forgive Your people
who have sinned against You. 40 Now, my God,
I pray, let Your eyes be [a]open and *let* Your ears
be attentive to the prayer *made* in this place.

41 "Now[a] therefore,
Arise, O LORD God, to Your [b]resting
place,
You and the ark of Your strength.
Let Your priests, O LORD God, be
clothed with salvation,
And let Your saints [c]rejoice in
goodness.

6:18 [a] [2 Chr. 2:6] [1] Literally *house* 6:20 [a] 2 Chr. 7:15 [b] Dan. 6:10 6:21 [a] [Mic. 7:18] 6:22 [a] Ex. 22:8–11 6:23 [a] [Job 34:11] 6:24 [a] 2 Kin. 21:14, 15 6:26 [a] 1 Kin. 17:1 6:28 [a] 2 Chr. 20:9 [b] [Mic. 6:13] 6:30 [a] [1 Chr. 28:9] [b] [1 Sam. 16:7] 6:32 [a] John 12:20 6:36 [a] [Rom. 3:9, 19; 5:12] [b] Deut. 28:63–68 6:38 [a] Dan. 6:10 6:40 [a] 2 Chr. 6:20 6:41 [a] Ps. 132:8–10, 16 [b] 1 Chr. 28:2 [c] Neh. 9:25

PEACE IN REPENTANCE

Forgive Your people who have sinned against You.

2 CHRONICLES 6:39

We have already looked at Solomon's prayer of dedication (1 Kin. 8), in which he asked God to hear the prayers of all who went to the temple. Here the Chronicler repeats this wonderful prayer, but what I find especially moving is what the king says about repentance and forgiveness: "When they return to You with all their heart and with all their soul . . . then hear from heaven Your dwelling place their prayer and their supplications, and maintain their cause, and forgive Your people who have sinned against You" (2 Chr. 6:38–39). What is important here is that the Book of Chronicles was written *after* Israel's return from captivity. The people did indeed repent, and God made it possible for them to go home.

If you have lost peace, you can get it back. Solomon's prayer and Israel's actual experience in history show us that regaining a right standing with God and recovering His peace are possible. We must never despair. There is a God in heaven, as Solomon says, who hears prayer and answers it. Our peace rests upon that wonderful truth.

42 "O LORD God, do not turn away the face
of Your Anointed;
[a]Remember the mercies of Your servant
David."[1]

Solomon Dedicates the Temple

7 When [a]Solomon had finished praying,
[b]fire came down from heaven and consumed the burnt offering and the sacrifices;
and [c]the glory of the LORD filled the temple.[1]
2 [a]And the priests could not enter the house of
the LORD, because the glory of the LORD had
filled the LORD's house. 3 When all the children of Israel saw how the fire came down,
and the glory of the LORD on the temple,
they bowed their faces to the ground on the
pavement, and worshiped and praised the
LORD, *saying:*

[a]"For *He is* good,
[b]For His mercy *endures* forever."[1]

4 [a]Then the king and all the people offered
sacrifices before the LORD. 5 King Solomon
offered a sacrifice of twenty-two thousand
bulls and one hundred and twenty thousand
sheep. So the king and all the people dedicated the house of God. 6 [a]And the priests
attended to their services; the Levites also
with instruments of the music of the LORD,
which King David had made to praise the
LORD, saying, "For His mercy *endures* forever,"[1] whenever David offered praise by their
ministry. [b]The priests sounded trumpets
opposite them, while all Israel stood.
7 Furthermore [a]Solomon consecrated the
middle of the court that *was* in front of the
house of the LORD; for there he offered burnt
offerings and the fat of the peace offerings,
because the bronze altar which Solomon
had made was not able to receive the burnt
offerings, the grain offerings, and the fat.
8 [a]At that time Solomon kept the feast seven
days, and all Israel with him, a very great assembly [b]from the entrance of Hamath to [c]the
Brook of Egypt.[1] 9 And on the eighth day they
held a [a]sacred assembly, for they observed the
dedication of the altar seven days, and the feast
seven days. 10 [a]On the twenty-third day of the
seventh month he sent the people away to their
tents, joyful and glad of heart for the good that
the LORD had done for David, for Solomon, and
for His people Israel. 11 Thus [a]Solomon finished
the house of the LORD and the king's house;
and Solomon successfully accomplished all
that came into his heart to make in the house
of the LORD and in his own house.

God's Second Appearance to Solomon

12 Then the LORD [a]appeared to Solomon
by night, and said to him: "I have heard your
prayer, [b]and have chosen this [c]place for Myself

6:42 [a] Ps. 89:49; 132:1, 8–10 [1] Compare Psalm 132:8–10 **7:1** [a] 1 Kin. 8:54 [b] Lev. 9:24 [c] 1 Kin. 8:10, 11 [1] Literally *house* **7:2** [a] 2 Chr. 5:14 **7:3** [a] Ps. 106:1; 136:1 [b] 2 Chr. 20:21 [1] Compare Psalm 106:1 **7:4** [a] 1 Kin. 8:62, 63 **7:6** [a] 1 Chr. 15:16 [b] 2 Chr. 5:12 [1] Compare Psalm 106:1 **7:7** [a] 1 Kin. 8:64–66; 9:3 **7:8** [a] 1 Kin. 8:65 [b] 1 Kin. 4:21, 24 [c] Josh. 13:3 [1] That is, the Shihor (compare 1 Chronicles 13:5) **7:9** [a] Lev. 23:36 **7:10** [a] 1 Kin. 8:66 **7:11** [a] 1 Kin. 9:1 **7:12** [a] 1 Kin. 3:5; 11:9 [b] Deut. 12:5, 11 [c] 2 Chr. 6:20

LOOK FOR GOD'S GLORY

And the glory of the LORD filled the temple.

2 CHRONICLES 7:1

Many people have experienced dramatic events that clearly point to God's presence or action. These moments open our eyes and increase faith. This is what happened when Solomon concluded his prayer of dedication for the newly built temple: "Fire came down from heaven and consumed the burnt offering and the sacrifices; and the glory of the LORD filled the temple" (v. 1). This dramatic event reminds me of what happened after Aaron and his sons were consecrated as priests (Lev. 9:24), and it anticipates what will happen when Elijah confronts the prophets of Baal (1 Kin. 18:36–39).

On that day with Solomon, the people of Israel witnessed God's tangible presence. You'd think that God's people would have had unwavering faith and would never stray from God's law, but they did. We, too, can wander away from God. We should instead take God at His word. Keep seeking, keep asking.

as a house of sacrifice. 13[a]When I shut up heav-
en and there is no rain, or command the locusts to devour the land, or send pestilence
among My people, 14if My people who are
[a]called by My name will [b]humble themselves,
and pray and seek My face, and turn from their
wicked ways, [c]then I will hear from heaven,
and will forgive their sin and heal their land.
15Now [a]My eyes will be open and My ears attentive to prayer *made* in this place. 16For
now [a]I have chosen and sanctified this house,
that My name may be there forever; and My
eyes and My heart will be there perpetually.
17[a]As for you, if you walk before Me as your
father David walked, and do according to all
that I have commanded you, and if you keep
My statutes and My judgments, 18then I will
establish the throne of your kingdom, as I covenanted with David your father, saying, [a]'You
shall not fail *to have* a man as ruler in Israel.'
19[a]"But if you turn away and forsake My
statutes and My commandments which I
have set before you, and go and serve other
gods, and worship them, 20[a]then I will uproot
them from My land which I have given them;
and this house which I have sanctified for My
name I will cast out of My sight, and will make
it a proverb and a [b]byword among all peoples.
21"And *as for* [a]this house, which is exalted,
everyone who passes by it will be [b]astonished
and say, [c]'Why has the LORD done thus to
this land and this house?' 22Then they will
answer, 'Because they forsook the LORD God
of their fathers, who brought them out of the
land of Egypt, and embraced other gods, and
worshiped them and served them; therefore
He has brought all this calamity on them.' "

Solomon's Additional Achievements

8 It [a]came to pass at the end of [b]twenty
years, when Solomon had built the house
of the LORD and his own house, 2that the
cities which Hiram[1] had given to Solomon,
Solomon built them; and he settled the children of Israel there. 3And Solomon went to
Hamath Zobah and seized it. 4[a]He also built
Tadmor in the wilderness, and all the storage
cities which he built in [b]Hamath. 5He built
Upper Beth Horon and [a]Lower Beth Horon,
fortified cities *with* walls, gates, and bars,
6also Baalath and all the storage cities that
Solomon had, and all the chariot cities and
the cities of the cavalry, and all that Solomon
[a]desired to build in Jerusalem, in Lebanon,
and in all the land of his dominion.
7[a]All the people *who were* left of the Hittites, Amorites, Perizzites, Hivites, and Jebusites, who *were* not of Israel— 8that is, their
descendants who were left in the land after
them, whom the children of Israel did not
destroy—from these Solomon raised forced
labor, as it is to this day. 9But Solomon did
not make the children of Israel servants for
his work. Some *were* men of war, captains
of his officers, captains of his chariots, and
his cavalry. 10And others *were* chiefs of the
officials of King Solomon: [a]two hundred and
fifty, who ruled over the people.

7:13 [a] 2 Chr. 6:26–28 **7:14** [a] [Is. 43:7] [b] [James 4:10] [c] 2 Chr. 6:27, 30 **7:15** [a] 2 Chr. 6:20, 40 **7:16** [a] 2 Chr. 6:6 **7:17** [a] 1 Kin. 9:4 **7:18** [a] 2 Chr. 6:16 **7:19** [a] Lev. 26:14, 33 **7:20** [a] Deut. 28:63–68 [b] Ps. 44:14 **7:21** [a] 2 Kin. 25:9 [b] 2 Chr. 29:8 [c] [Deut. 29:24, 25] **8:1** [a] 1 Kin. 9:10–14 [b] 1 Kin. 6:38—7:1 **8:2** [1] Hebrew *Huram* (compare 2 Chronicles 2:3) **8:4** [a] 1 Kin. 9:17, 18 [b] 1 Chr. 18:3, 9 **8:5** [a] 1 Chr. 7:24 **8:6** [a] 2 Chr. 7:11 **8:7** [a] 1 Kin. 9:20 **8:10** [a] 1 Kin. 9:23

11 Now Solomon [a]brought the daughter of
Pharaoh up from the City of David to the
house he had built for her, for he said, "My
wife shall not dwell in the house of David king
of Israel, because *the places* to which the ark
of the LORD has come are holy."
12 Then Solomon offered burnt offerings
to the LORD on the altar of the LORD which
he had built before the vestibule, 13 according
to the [a]daily rate, offering according to the
commandment of Moses, for the Sabbaths, the
New Moons, and the [b]three appointed yearly
[c]feasts—the Feast of Unleavened Bread, the
Feast of Weeks, and the Feast of Tabernacles.
14 And, according to the order of David his
father, he appointed the [a]divisions of the
priests for their service, [b]the Levites for their
duties (to praise and serve before the priests)
as the duty of each day required, and the [c]gate-
keepers by their divisions at each gate; for
so David the man of God had commanded.
15 They did not depart from the command of
the king to the priests and Levites concerning
any matter or concerning the [a]treasuries.
16 Now all the work of Solomon was well-
ordered from[1] the day of the foundation of
the house of the LORD until it was finished.
So the house of the LORD was completed.
17 Then Solomon went to [a]Ezion Geber and
Elath[1] on the seacoast, in the land of Edom.
18 [a]And Hiram sent him ships by the hand of
his servants, and servants who knew the sea.
They went with the servants of Solomon to
[b]Ophir, and acquired four hundred and fifty
talents of gold from there, and brought it to
King Solomon.

The Queen of Sheba's Praise of Solomon

9 Now [a]when the queen of Sheba heard of
the fame of Solomon, she came to Jerusalem to test Solomon with hard questions,
having a very great retinue, camels that bore
spices, gold in abundance, and precious
stones; and when she came to Solomon, she
spoke with him about all that was in her heart.
2 So Solomon answered all her questions;
there was nothing so difficult for Solomon
that he could not explain it to her. 3 And when
the queen of Sheba had seen the wisdom of
Solomon, the house that he had built, 4 the
food on his table, the seating of his servants,
the service of his waiters and their apparel,
his [a]cupbearers and their apparel, and his
entryway by which he went up to the house
of the LORD, there was no more spirit in her.
5 Then she said to the king: "*It was* a true
report which I heard in my own land about
your words and your wisdom. 6 However I did
not believe their words until I came and saw
with my own eyes; and indeed the half of the
greatness of your wisdom was not told me.
You exceed the fame of which I heard. 7 Happy
are your men and happy *are* these your servants, who stand continually before you and
hear your wisdom! 8 Blessed be the LORD your
God, who delighted in you, setting you on His

8:11 [a] 1 Kin. 3:1; 7:8; 9:24; 11:1 **8:13** [a] Num. 28:3, 9, 11, 26; 29:1 [b] Ex. 23:14–17; 34:22, 23 [c] Lev. 23:1–44 **8:14** [a] 1 Chr. 24:3 [b] 1 Chr. 25:1 [c] 1 Chr. 9:17; 26:1 **8:15** [a] 1 Chr. 26:20–28 **8:16** [1] Following Septuagint, Syriac, and Vulgate; Masoretic Text reads *as far as*. **8:17** [a] 1 Kin. 9:26 [1] Hebrew *Eloth* (compare 2 Kings 14:22) **8:18** [a] 2 Chr. 9:10, 13 [b] 1 Chr. 29:4 **9:1** [a] [Matt. 12:42] **9:4** [a] Neh. 1:11

BEAR WITNESS

The queen of Sheba . . . came to Jerusalem to test Solomon with hard questions.

2 CHRONICLES 9:1

In his prayer of dedication for the temple, Solomon confessed that foreigners would pray before God's house. The queen of Sheba is a dramatic example of that expectation. She "heard of the fame of Solomon," so she traveled to Jerusalem to see him for herself (v. 1).

After the queen saw Solomon's abilities and his kingdom, verse 4 says, "There was no more spirit in her." Here the meaning is "took her breath away." The queen of Sheba was so impressed by what she saw in Jerusalem, she was left speechless.

The queen's reaction to her encounter with Solomon testifies to the work that God was doing through David's son. She saw in Solomon what she had seen in no one else. This is often the reaction people have when they meet people who are possessed by the peace of God.

When have you encountered someone glowing with God's peace? What was your reaction?

throne *to be* king for the LORD your God! Because your God has [a]loved Israel, to establish
them forever, therefore He made you king
over them, to do justice and righteousness."
9 And she gave the king one hundred and
twenty talents of gold, spices in great abundance, and precious stones; there never were
any spices such as those the queen of Sheba
gave to King Solomon.
10 Also, the servants of Hiram and the servants of Solomon, [a]who brought gold from
Ophir, brought algum[1] wood and precious
stones. 11 And the king made walkways *of* the
algum[1] wood for the house of the LORD and
for the king's house, also harps and stringed
instruments for singers; and there were none
such *as these* seen before in the land of Judah.
12 Now King Solomon gave to the queen of
Sheba all she desired, whatever she asked,
much more than she had brought to the king.
So she turned and went to her own country,
she and her servants.

Solomon's Great Wealth

13 [a]The weight of gold that came to Solomon yearly was six hundred and sixty-six
talents of gold, 14 besides *what* the traveling merchants and traders brought. And
all the kings of Arabia and governors of the
country brought gold and silver to Solomon.
15 And King Solomon made two hundred
large shields of hammered gold; six hundred
shekels of hammered gold went into each
shield. 16 *He* also *made* three hundred shields
of hammered gold; three hundred *shekels*[1]
of gold went into each shield. The king put
them in the [a]House of the Forest of Lebanon.
17 Moreover the king made a great throne
of ivory, and overlaid it with pure gold. 18 The
throne *had* six steps, with a footstool of gold,
which were fastened to the throne; there were
armrests on either side of the place of the
seat, and two lions stood beside the armrests.
19 Twelve lions stood there, one on each side
of the six steps; nothing like *this* had been
made for any *other* kingdom.
20 All King Solomon's drinking vessels *were*
gold, and all the vessels of the House of the
Forest of Lebanon *were* pure gold. Not *one was*
silver, for this was accounted as nothing in the
days of Solomon. 21 For the king's ships went
to [a]Tarshish with the servants of Hiram.[1] Once
every three years the merchant ships[2] came,
bringing gold, silver, ivory, apes, and monkeys.[3]
22 So King Solomon surpassed all the kings
of the earth in riches and wisdom. 23 And all
the kings of the earth sought the presence
of Solomon to hear his wisdom, which God
had put in his heart. 24 Each man brought his
present: articles of silver and gold, garments,
[a]armor, spices, horses, and mules, at a set
rate year by year.
25 Solomon [a]had four thousand stalls for
horses and chariots, and twelve thousand
horsemen whom he stationed in the chariot
cities and with the king at Jerusalem.
26 [a]So he reigned over all the kings [b]from
the River[1] to the land of the Philistines, as
far as the border of Egypt. 27 [a]The king made
silver *as common* in Jerusalem as stones,
and he made cedar trees [b]as abundant as the
sycamores which *are* in the lowland. 28 [a]And
they brought horses to Solomon from Egypt
and from all lands.

Death of Solomon

29 [a]Now the rest of the acts of Solomon,
first and last, *are* they not written in the book
of Nathan the prophet, in the prophecy of
[b]Ahijah the Shilonite, and in the visions of
[c]Iddo the seer concerning Jeroboam the son
of Nebat? 30 [a]Solomon reigned in Jerusalem
over all Israel forty years. 31 Then Solomon
rested with his fathers, and was buried in the
City of David his father. And Rehoboam his
son reigned in his place.

The Revolt Against Rehoboam

10 And [a]Rehoboam went to Shechem, for
all Israel had gone to Shechem to make
him king. 2 So it happened, when Jeroboam the
son of Nebat heard *it* (he was in Egypt, [a]where
he had fled from the presence of King Solomon), that Jeroboam returned from Egypt.
3 Then they sent for him and called him. And
Jeroboam and all Israel came and spoke to Rehoboam, saying, 4 "Your father made our yoke
heavy; now therefore, lighten the burdensome
service of your father and his heavy yoke which
he put on us, and we will serve you."
5 So he said to them, "Come back to me
after three days." And the people departed.
6 Then King Rehoboam consulted the elders who stood before his father Solomon
while he still lived, saying, "How do you advise *me* to answer these people?"
7 And they spoke to him, saying, "If you
are kind to these people, and please them,

9:8 [a] Deut. 7:8 **9:10** [a] 2 Chr. 8:18 [1] Or *almug* (compare 1 Kings 10:11, 12) **9:11** [1] Or *almug* (compare 1 Kings 10:11, 12) **9:13** [a] 1 Kin. 10:14–29 **9:16** [a] 1 Kin. 7:2 [1] Or *three minas* (compare 1 Kings 10:17) **9:21** [a] 2 Chr. 20:36, 37 [1] Hebrew *Huram* (compare 1 Kings 10:22) [2] Literally *ships of Tarshish* (deep-sea vessels) [3] Or *peacocks* **9:24** [a] 1 Kin. 20:11 **9:25** [a] 1 Kin. 4:26; 10:26 **9:26** [a] 1 Kin. 4:21 [b] Gen. 15:18 [1] That is, the Euphrates **9:27** [a] 1 Kin. 10:27 [b] 2 Chr. 1:15–17 **9:28** [a] 2 Chr. 1:16 **9:29** [a] 1 Kin. 11:41 [b] 1 Kin. 11:29 [c] 2 Chr. 12:15; 13:22 **9:30** [a] 1 Kin. 4:21; 11:42, 43 **10:1** [a] 1 Kin. 12:1–20 **10:2** [a] 1 Kin. 11:40

and speak good words to them, they will be
your servants forever."
8 [a]But he rejected the advice which the
elders had given him, and consulted the
young men who had grown up with him,
who stood before him. 9 And he said to them,
"What advice do you give? How should we
answer this people who have spoken to me,
saying, 'Lighten the yoke which your father
put on us'?"
10 Then the young men who had grown up
with him spoke to him, saying, "Thus you
should speak to the people who have spoken
to you, saying, 'Your father made our yoke
heavy, but you make *it* lighter on us'—thus
you shall say to them: 'My little *finger* shall
be thicker than my father's waist! 11 And now,
whereas my father put a heavy yoke on you,
I will add to your yoke; my father chastised
you with whips, but I *will chastise you* with
scourges!' "[1]
12 So [a]Jeroboam and all the people came to
Rehoboam on the third day, as the king had
directed, saying, "Come back to me the third
day." 13 Then the king answered them roughly.
King Rehoboam rejected the advice of the
elders, 14 and he spoke to them according
to the advice of the young men, saying, "My
father[1] made your yoke heavy, but I will add
to it; my father chastised you with whips, but
I *will chastise you* with scourges!"[2] 15 So the
king did not listen to the people; [a]for the turn
of events was from God, that the LORD might
fulfill His [b]word, which He had spoken by the
hand of Ahijah the Shilonite to Jeroboam
the son of Nebat.
16 Now when all Israel *saw* that the king
did not listen to them, the people answered
the king, saying:

"What share have we in David?
We have no inheritance in the son of
Jesse.
Every man to your tents, O Israel!
Now see to your own house, O David!"

So all Israel departed to their tents. 17 But
Rehoboam reigned over the children of Israel
who dwelt in the cities of Judah.
18 Then King Rehoboam sent Hadoram,
who *was* in charge of revenue; but the children of Israel stoned him with stones, and
he died. Therefore King Rehoboam mounted
his chariot in haste to flee to Jerusalem. 19 [a]So
Israel has been in rebellion against the house
of David to this day.

PEACE NOTE

I need to focus on how the Bible says I should be living. And you know what? When I do that, my life is full and peaceful.

11 Now [a]when Rehoboam came to Jerusalem, he assembled from the house of
Judah and Benjamin one hundred and eighty
thousand chosen *men* who were warriors, to
fight against Israel, that he might restore the
kingdom to Rehoboam.
2 But the word of the LORD came [a]to Shemaiah the man of God, saying, 3 "Speak to Rehoboam the son of Solomon, king of Judah, and
to all Israel in Judah and Benjamin, saying,
4 'Thus says the LORD: "You shall not go up or
fight against your brethren! Let every man return to his house, for this thing is from Me." ' "
Therefore they obeyed the words of the LORD,
and turned back from attacking Jeroboam.

Rehoboam Fortifies the Cities

5 So Rehoboam dwelt in Jerusalem, and
built cities for defense in Judah. 6 And he
built Bethlehem, Etam, Tekoa, 7 Beth Zur,
Sochoh, Adullam, 8 Gath, Mareshah, Ziph,
9 Adoraim, Lachish, Azekah, 10 Zorah, Aijalon, and Hebron, which are in Judah and
Benjamin, fortified cities. 11 And he fortified
the strongholds, and put captains in them,
and stores of food, oil, and wine. 12 Also in
every city *he put* shields and spears, and
made them very strong, having Judah and
Benjamin on his side.

Priests and Levites Move to Judah

13 And from all their territories the priests
and the Levites who *were* in all Israel took
their stand with him. 14 For the Levites left
[a]their common-lands and their possessions
and came to Judah and Jerusalem, for [b]Jer-
oboam and his sons had rejected them from

10:8 [a] 1 Kin. 12:8–11 **10:11** [1] Literally *scorpions* **10:12** [a] 1 Kin. 12:12–14 **10:14** [1] Following many Hebrew manuscripts, Septuagint, Syriac, and Vulgate (compare verse 10 and 1 Kings 12:14); Masoretic Text reads *I*. [2] Literally *scorpions* **10:15** [a] 1 Chr. 5:22 [b] 1 Kin. 11:29–39 **10:19** [a] 1 Kin. 12:19 **11:1** [a] 1 Kin. 12:21–24 **11:2** [a] 1 Chr. 12:5 **11:14** [a] Num. 35:2–5 [b] 2 Chr. 13:9

serving as priests to the LORD. 15 [a]Then he appointed for himself priests for the high places, for [b]the demons, and [c]the calf idols which he had made. 16 [a]And after *the* Levites *left,*[1] those from all the tribes of Israel, such as set their heart to seek the LORD God of Israel, [b]came to Jerusalem to sacrifice to the LORD God of their fathers. 17 So they [a]strengthened the kingdom of Judah, and made Rehoboam the son of Solomon strong for three years, because they walked in the way of David and Solomon for three years.

The Family of Rehoboam

18 Then Rehoboam took for himself as wife Mahalath the daughter of Jerimoth the son of David, *and of* Abihail the daughter of [a]Eliah the son of Jesse. 19 And she bore him children: Jeush, Shamariah, and Zaham. 20 After her he took [a]Maachah the granddaughter[1] of [b]Absalom; and she bore him [c]Abijah, Attai, Ziza, and Shelomith. 21 Now Rehoboam loved Maachah the granddaughter of Absalom more than all his [a]wives and his concubines; for he took eighteen wives and sixty concubines, and begot twenty-eight sons and sixty daughters. 22 And Rehoboam [a]appointed [b]Abijah the son of Maachah as chief, *to be* leader among his brothers; for he *intended* to make him king. 23 He dealt wisely, and dispersed some of his sons throughout all the territories of Judah and Benjamin, to every [a]fortified city; and he gave them provisions in abundance. He also sought many wives *for them.*

Egypt Attacks Judah

12 Now [a]it came to pass, when Rehoboam had established the kingdom and had strengthened himself, that [b]he forsook the law of the LORD, and all Israel along with him. 2 [a]And it happened in the fifth year of King Rehoboam *that* Shishak king of Egypt came up against Jerusalem, because they had transgressed against the LORD, 3 with twelve hundred chariots, sixty thousand horsemen, and people without number who came with him out of Egypt—[a]the Lubim and the Sukkiim and the Ethiopians. 4 And he took the fortified cities of Judah and came to Jerusalem.

5 Then [a]Shemaiah the prophet came to Rehoboam and the leaders of Judah, who were gathered together in Jerusalem because of Shishak, and said to them, "Thus says the LORD: 'You have forsaken Me, and therefore I also have left you in the hand of Shishak.' "

6 So the leaders of Israel and the king [a]humbled themselves; and they said, [b]"The LORD *is* righteous."

7 Now when the LORD saw that they humbled themselves, [a]the word of the LORD came to Shemaiah, saying, "They have humbled themselves; *therefore* I will not destroy them, but I will grant them some deliverance. My wrath shall not be poured out on Jerusalem by the hand of Shishak. 8 Nevertheless [a]they will be his servants, that they may distinguish [b]My service from the service of the kingdoms of the nations."

9 [a]So Shishak king of Egypt came up against Jerusalem, and took away the treasures of the house of the LORD and the treasures of the king's house; he took everything. He also carried away the gold shields which Solomon had [b]made. 10 Then King Rehoboam made bronze shields in their place, and committed *them* [a]to the hands of the captains of the guard, who guarded the doorway of the king's house. 11 And whenever the king entered the house of the LORD, the guard would go and bring them out; then they would take them back into the guardroom. 12 When he humbled himself, the wrath of the LORD turned from him, so as not to destroy *him* completely; and things also went well in Judah.

The End of Rehoboam's Reign

13 Thus King Rehoboam strengthened himself in Jerusalem and reigned. Now [a]Rehoboam *was* forty-one years old when he became king; and he reigned seventeen years in Jerusalem, [b]the city which the LORD had chosen out of all the tribes of Israel, to put His name there. His mother's name *was* Naamah, an [c]Ammonitess. 14 And he did evil, because he did not prepare his heart to seek the LORD.

15 The acts of Rehoboam, first and last, *are* they not written in the book of Shemaiah the prophet, [a]and of Iddo the seer concerning genealogies? [b]And *there were* wars between Rehoboam and Jeroboam all their days. 16 So Rehoboam rested with his fathers, and was buried in the City of David. Then [a]Abijah[1] his son reigned in his place.

11:15 [a] 1 Kin. 12:31; 13:33; 14:9 [b] [Lev. 17:7] [c] 1 Kin. 12:28 **11:16** [a] 2 Chr. 14:7 [b] 2 Chr. 15:9, 10; 30:11, 18 [1] Literally *after them* **11:17** [a] 2 Chr. 12:1, 13 **11:18** [a] 1 Sam. 16:6 **11:20** [a] 2 Chr. 13:2 [b] 1 Kin. 15:2 [c] 1 Kin. 14:31 [1] Literally *daughter,* but in the broader sense of granddaughter (compare 2 Chronicles 13:2) **11:21** [a] Deut. 17:17 **11:22** [a] Deut. 21:15–17 [b] 2 Chr. 13:1 **11:23** [a] 2 Chr. 11:5 **12:1** [a] 2 Chr. 11:17 [b] 1 Kin. 14:22–24 **12:2** [a] 1 Kin. 11:40; 14:25 **12:3** [a] 2 Chr. 16:8 **12:5** [a] 2 Chr. 11:2 **12:6** [a] [James 4:10] [b] Ex. 9:27 **12:7** [a] 1 Kin. 21:28, 29 **12:8** [a] Is. 26:13 [b] [Deut. 28:47, 48] **12:9** [a] 1 Kin. 14:25, 26 [b] 2 Chr. 9:15, 16 **12:10** [a] 1 Kin. 14:27 **12:13** [a] 1 Kin. 14:21 [b] 2 Chr. 6:6 [c] 1 Kin. 11:1, 5 **12:15** [a] 2 Chr. 9:29; 13:22 [b] 1 Kin. 14:30 **12:16** [a] 2 Chr. 11:20–22 [1] Spelled *Abijam* in 1 Kings 14:31

PEACE NOTE

Was Jesus a happy Person? I should think so! It is the will of the Lord for you to be a happy person.

Abijah Reigns in Judah

13 In [a]the eighteenth year of King Jeroboam, Abijah became king over [b]Judah. 2 He reigned three years in Jerusalem. His mother's name *was* Michaiah[1] the daughter of Uriel of Gibeah.

And there was war between Abijah and Jeroboam. 3 Abijah set the battle in order with an army of valiant warriors, four hundred thousand choice men. Jeroboam also drew up in battle formation against him with eight hundred thousand choice men, mighty men of valor.

4 Then Abijah stood on Mount [a]Zemaraim, which *is* in the mountains of Ephraim, and said, "Hear me, Jeroboam and all Israel: 5 Should you not know that the LORD God of Israel [a]gave the dominion over Israel to David forever, to him and his sons, [b]by a covenant of salt? 6 Yet Jeroboam the son of Nebat, the servant of Solomon the son of David, rose up and [a]rebelled against his lord. 7 Then [a]worthless rogues gathered to him, and strengthened themselves against Rehoboam the son of Solomon, when Rehoboam was [b]young and inexperienced and could not withstand them. 8 And now you think to withstand the kingdom of the LORD, which is in the hand of the sons of David; and you *are* a great multitude, and with you are the gold calves which Jeroboam [a]made for you as gods. 9 [a]Have you not cast out the priests of the LORD, the sons of Aaron, and the Levites, and made for yourselves priests, like the peoples of *other* lands, [b]so that whoever comes to consecrate himself *with* a young *bull* and seven rams may be a priest of [c]*things that are* not gods? 10 But as for us, the LORD *is* our [a]God, and we have not forsaken Him; and the priests who minister to the LORD *are* the sons of Aaron, and the Levites *attend* to *their* duties. 11 [a]And they burn to the LORD every morning and every evening burnt sacrifices and sweet incense; *they* also *set* the [b]showbread *in order on* the pure *gold* table, and the lampstand of gold with its lamps [c]to burn every evening; for we keep the command of the LORD our God, but you have forsaken Him. 12 Now look, God Himself is with us as *our* [a]head, [b]and His priests with sounding trumpets to sound the alarm against you. O children of Israel, do not fight against the LORD God of your fathers, for you shall not prosper!"

13 But Jeroboam caused an ambush to go around behind them; so they were in front of Judah, and the ambush *was* behind them. 14 And when Judah looked around, to their surprise the battle line *was* at both front and rear; and they [a]cried out to the LORD, and the priests sounded the trumpets. 15 Then the men of Judah gave a shout; and as the men of Judah shouted, it happened that God [a]struck Jeroboam and all Israel before Abijah and Judah. 16 And the children of Israel fled before Judah, and God delivered them into their hand. 17 Then Abijah and his people struck them with a great slaughter; so five hundred thousand choice men of Israel fell slain. 18 Thus the children of Israel were subdued at that time; and the children of Judah prevailed, [a]because they relied on the LORD God of their fathers.

19 And Abijah pursued Jeroboam and took cities from him: Bethel with its villages, Jeshanah with its villages, and [a]Ephrain[1] with its villages. 20 So Jeroboam did not recover strength again in the days of Abijah; and the LORD [a]struck him, and [b]he died.

21 But Abijah grew mighty, married fourteen wives, and begot twenty-two sons and sixteen daughters. 22 Now the rest of the acts of Abijah, his ways, and his sayings *are* written in [a]the annals of the prophet Iddo.

14 So Abijah rested with his fathers, and they buried him in the City of David. Then [a]Asa his son reigned in his place. In his days the land was quiet for ten years.

Asa Reigns in Judah

2 Asa did *what was* good and right in the eyes of the LORD his God, 3 for he removed the

13:1 [a] 1 Kin. 15:1 [b] 1 Kin. 12:17 **13:2** [1] Spelled *Maachah* in 11:20, 21 and 1 Kings 15:2 **13:4** [a] Josh. 18:22 **13:5** [a] 2 Sam. 7:8–16 [b] Num. 18:19 **13:6** [a] 1 Kin. 11:28; 12:20 **13:7** [a] Judg. 9:4 [b] 2 Chr. 12:13 **13:8** [a] 1 Kin. 12:28; 14:9 **13:9** [a] 2 Chr. 11:13–15 [b] Ex. 29:29–33 [c] Jer. 2:11; 5:7 **13:10** [a] Josh. 24:15 **13:11** [a] 2 Chr. 2:4 [b] Lev. 24:5–9 [c] Ex. 27:20, 21 **13:12** [a] [Heb. 2:10] [b] [Num. 10:8–10] **13:14** [a] 2 Chr. 6:34, 35; 14:11 **13:15** [a] 2 Chr. 14:12 **13:18** [a] 2 Chr. 14:11 **13:19** [a] Josh. 15:9 [1] Or *Ephron* **13:20** [a] 1 Sam. 2:6; 25:38 [b] 1 Kin. 14:20 **13:22** [a] 2 Chr. 9:29 **14:1** [a] 1 Kin. 15:8

altars of the foreign *gods* and [a]the high places,
and [b]broke down the *sacred* pillars [c]and cut
down the wooden images. 4 He commanded
Judah to [a]seek the LORD God of their fathers,
and to observe the law and the commandment. 5 He also removed the high places and
the incense altars from all the cities of Judah,
and the kingdom was quiet under him. 6 And
he built fortified cities in Judah, for the land
had rest; he had no war in those years, because
the LORD had given him [a]rest. 7 Therefore he
said to Judah, "Let us build these cities and
make walls around *them,* and towers, gates,
and bars, *while* the land *is* yet before us, because we have sought the LORD our God; we
have sought *Him,* and He has given us rest on
every side." So they built and prospered. 8 And
Asa had an army of three hundred thousand
from Judah who carried shields and spears,
and from Benjamin two hundred and eighty
thousand men who carried shields and drew
[a]bows; all these *were* mighty men of [b]valor.
9 [a]Then Zerah the Ethiopian came out
against them with an army of a million men
and three hundred chariots, and he came to
[b]Mareshah. 10 So Asa went out against him, and
they set the troops in battle array in the Valley
of Zephathah at Mareshah. 11 And Asa [a]cried
out to the LORD his God, and said, "LORD, *it is*
[b]nothing for You to help, whether with many or
with those who have no power; help us, O LORD
our God, for we rest on You, and [c]in Your name
we go against this multitude. O LORD, You *are*
our God; do not let man prevail against You!"
12 So the LORD [a]struck the Ethiopians before Asa and Judah, and the Ethiopians fled.
13 And Asa and the people who *were* with
him pursued them to [a]Gerar. So the Ethiopians were overthrown, and they could not
recover, for they were broken before the
LORD and His army. And they carried away
very much spoil. 14 Then they defeated all the
cities around Gerar, for [a]the fear of the LORD
came upon them; and they plundered all the
cities, for there was exceedingly much spoil
in them. 15 They also attacked the livestock
enclosures, and carried off sheep and camels
in abundance, and returned to Jerusalem.

The Reforms of Asa

15 Now [a]the Spirit of God came upon Azariah the son of Oded. 2 And he went
out to meet Asa, and said to him: "Hear me,
Asa, and all Judah and Benjamin. [a]The LORD

> **PEACE NOTE**
>
> Azariah challenged Asa to seek God. Although he had a massive army, Asa found true strength and protection in the Lord. Peace comes from seeking the Lord.
>
> 2 CHRONICLES 15:2

is with you while you are with Him. [b]If you
seek Him, He will be found by you; but [c]if
you forsake Him, He will forsake you. 3 [a]For
a long time Israel *has been* without the true
God, without a [b]teaching priest, and without
[c]law; 4 but [a]when in their trouble they turned
to the LORD God of Israel, and sought Him,
He was found by them. 5 And in those times
there was no peace to the one who went out,
nor to the one who came in, but great turmoil
was on all the inhabitants of the lands. 6 [a]So
nation was destroyed by nation, and city
by city, for God troubled them with every
adversity. 7 But you, be strong and do not
let your hands be weak, for your work shall
be rewarded!"
8 And when Asa heard these words and
the prophecy of Oded[1] the prophet, he took
courage, and removed the abominable idols
from all the land of Judah and Benjamin
and from the cities [a]which he had taken in
the mountains of Ephraim; and he restored
the altar of the LORD that *was* before the
vestibule of the LORD. 9 Then he gathered all
Judah and Benjamin, and [a]those who dwelt
with them from Ephraim, Manasseh, and
Simeon, for they came over to him in great
numbers from Israel when they saw that the
LORD his God was with him.
10 So they gathered together at Jerusalem
in the third month, in the fifteenth year of
the reign of Asa. 11 [a]And they offered to the
LORD at that time seven hundred bulls and
seven thousand sheep from the spoil they
had brought. 12 Then they [a]entered into a

14:3 [a] 1 Kin. 15:14 [b] [Ex. 34:13] [c] 1 Kin. 11:7 **14:4** [a] [2 Chr. 7:14] **14:6** [a] 2 Chr. 15:15 **14:8** [a] 1 Chr. 12:2 [b] 2 Chr. 13:3 **14:9** [a] 2 Chr. 12:2, 3; 16:8 [b] Josh. 15:44 **14:11** [a] Ex. 14:10 [b] [1 Sam. 14:6] [c] 1 Sam. 17:45 **14:12** [a] 2 Chr. 13:15 **14:13** [a] Gen. 10:19; 20:1 **14:14** [a] 2 Chr. 17:10 **15:1** [a] 2 Chr. 20:14; 24:20 **15:2** [a] [James 4:8] [b] [1 Chr. 28:9] [c] 2 Chr. 24:20 **15:3** [a] Hos. 3:4 [b] 2 Kin. 12:2 [c] Lev. 10:11 **15:4** [a] [Deut. 4:29] **15:6** [a] Matt. 24:7 **15:8** [a] 2 Chr. 13:19 [1] Following Masoretic Text and Septuagint; Syriac and Vulgate read *Azariah the son of Oded* (compare verse 1). **15:9** [a] 2 Chr. 11:16 **15:11** [a] 2 Chr. 14:13–15 **15:12** [a] 2 Kin. 23:3

covenant to seek the LORD God of their fathers with all their heart and with all their soul; 13 [a]and whoever would not seek the LORD God of Israel [b]was to be put to death, whether small or great, whether man or woman. 14 Then they took an oath before the LORD with a loud voice, with shouting and trumpets and rams' horns. 15 And all Judah rejoiced at the oath, for they had sworn with all their heart and [a]sought Him with all their soul; and He was found by them, and the LORD gave them [b]rest all around.

16 Also he removed [a]Maachah, the mother of Asa the king, from *being* queen mother, because she had made an obscene image of Asherah;[1] and Asa cut down her obscene image, then crushed and burned *it* by the Brook Kidron. 17 But [a]the high places were not removed from Israel. Nevertheless the heart of Asa was loyal all his days.

18 He also brought into the house of God the things that his father had dedicated and that he himself had dedicated: silver and gold and utensils. 19 And there was no war until the thirty-fifth year of the reign of Asa.

Asa's Treaty with Syria

16 In the thirty-sixth year of the reign of Asa, [a]Baasha king of Israel came up against Judah and built Ramah, [b]that he might let none go out or come in to Asa king of Judah. 2 Then Asa brought silver and gold from the treasuries of the house of the LORD and of the king's house, and sent to Ben-Hadad king of Syria, who dwelt in Damascus, saying, 3 "*Let there be* a treaty between you and me, as there was between my father and your father. See, I have sent you silver and gold; come, break your treaty with Baasha king of Israel, so that he will withdraw from me."

4 So Ben-Hadad heeded King Asa, and sent the captains of his armies against the cities of Israel. They attacked Ijon, Dan, Abel Maim, and all the storage cities of Naphtali. 5 Now it happened, when Baasha heard *it,* that he stopped building Ramah and ceased his work. 6 Then King Asa took all Judah, and they carried away the stones and timber of Ramah, which Baasha had used for building; and with them he built Geba and Mizpah.

Hanani's Message to Asa

7 And at that time [a]Hanani the seer came to Asa king of Judah, and said to him: [b]"Because you have relied on the king of Syria, and have not relied on the LORD your God, therefore the army of the king of Syria has escaped from your hand. 8 Were [a]the Ethiopians and [b]the Lubim not a huge army with very many chariots and horsemen? Yet, because you relied on the LORD, He delivered them into your [c]hand. 9 [a]For the eyes of the LORD run to and fro throughout the whole earth, to show Himself strong on behalf of *those* whose heart *is* loyal to Him. In this [b]you have done foolishly; therefore from now on [c]you shall have wars." 10 Then Asa was angry with the seer, and [a]put him in prison, for *he was* enraged at him because of this. And Asa oppressed *some* of the people at that time.

Illness and Death of Asa

11 [a]Note that the acts of Asa, first and last, are indeed written in the book of the kings of Judah and Israel. 12 And in the thirty-ninth year of his reign, Asa became diseased in his feet, and his malady was severe; yet in his disease he [a]did not seek the LORD, but the physicians.

13 [a]So Asa rested with his fathers; he died in the forty-first year of his reign. 14 They buried him in his own tomb, which he had made for himself in the City of David; and they laid him in the bed which was filled [a]with spices and various ingredients prepared in a mixture of ointments. They made [b]a very great burning for him.

Jehoshaphat Reigns in Judah

17 Then [a]Jehoshaphat his son reigned in his place, and strengthened himself against Israel. 2 And he placed troops in all the fortified cities of Judah, and set garrisons in the land of [a]Judah and in the cities of Ephraim [b]which Asa his father had taken. 3 Now the LORD was with Jehoshaphat, because he walked in the former ways of his father David; he did not seek the Baals, 4 but sought the God[1] of his father, and walked in His commandments and not according to [a]the acts of Israel. 5 Therefore the LORD established the kingdom in his hand; and all Judah [a]gave presents to Jehoshaphat, [b]and he had riches and honor in abundance. 6 And his heart took delight in the ways of the LORD; moreover [a]he removed the high places and wooden images from Judah.

7 Also in the third year of his reign he sent his leaders, Ben-Hail, Obadiah, Zechariah,

15:13 [a] Ex. 22:20 [b] Deut. 13:5–15 **15:15** [a] 2 Chr. 15:2 [b] 2 Chr. 14:7 **15:16** [a] 1 Kin. 15:2, 10, 13 [1] A Canaanite deity **15:17** [a] 1 Kin. 15:14 **16:1** [a] 1 Kin. 15:17–22 [b] 2 Chr. 15:9 **16:7** [a] 2 Chr. 19:2 [b] [Jer. 17:5] **16:8** [a] 2 Chr. 14:9 [b] 2 Chr. 12:3 [c] 2 Chr. 13:16, 18 **16:9** [a] Zech. 4:10 [b] 1 Sam. 13:13 [c] 1 Kin. 15:32 **16:10** [a] Jer. 20:2 **16:11** [a] 1 Kin. 15:23, 24 **16:12** [a] [Jer. 17:5] **16:13** [a] 1 Kin. 15:24 **16:14** [a] John 19:39, 40 [b] 2 Chr. 21:19 **17:1** [a] 1 Kin. 15:24 **17:2** [a] 2 Chr. 11:5 [b] 2 Chr. 15:8 **17:4** [a] 1 Kin. 12:28 [1] Septuagint reads *LORD God.* **17:5** [a] 1 Kin. 10:25 [b] 2 Chr. 18:1 **17:6** [a] 1 Kin. 22:43

PEACE NOTE

Imitate Jehoshaphat, whose heart delighted in the ways of the Lord. Remove what hinders and replace it with what enhances Christ in your life.

2 CHRONICLES 17:6

Nethanel, and Michaiah, [a]to teach in the cities
of Judah. 8 And with them *he sent* Levites:
Shemaiah, Nethaniah, Zebadiah, Asahel,
Shemiramoth, Jehonathan, Adonijah, Tobijah, and Tobadonijah—the Levites; and with
them Elishama and Jehoram, the priests.
9 [a]So they taught in Judah, and *had* the Book
of the Law of the LORD with them; they went
throughout all the cities of Judah and taught
the people.

10 And [a]the fear of the LORD fell on all the
kingdoms of the lands that *were* around
Judah, so that they did not make war against
Jehoshaphat. 11 Also *some* of the Philistines
[a]brought Jehoshaphat presents and silver as
tribute; and the Arabians brought him flocks,
seven thousand seven hundred rams and
seven thousand seven hundred male goats.

12 So Jehoshaphat became increasingly
powerful, and he built fortresses and storage cities in Judah. 13 He had much property
in the cities of Judah; and the men of war,
mighty men of valor, *were* in Jerusalem.

14 These *are* their numbers, according to
their fathers' houses. Of Judah, the captains
of thousands: Adnah the captain, and with
him three hundred thousand mighty men
of valor; 15 and next to him *was* Jehohanan
the captain, and with him two hundred and
eighty thousand; 16 and next to him *was* Am-
asiah the son of Zichri, [a]who willingly offered
himself to the LORD, and with him two hundred thousand mighty men of valor. 17 Of
Benjamin: Eliada a mighty man of valor, and
with him two hundred thousand men armed
with bow and shield; 18 and next to him *was*
Jehozabad, and with him one hundred and
eighty thousand prepared for war. 19 These
served the king, besides [a]those the king put
in the fortified cities throughout all Judah.

Micaiah Warns Ahab

18 Jehoshaphat [a]had riches and honor in
abundance; and by marriage he [b]allied
himself with [c]Ahab. 2 [a]After some years he
went down to *visit* Ahab in Samaria; and
Ahab killed sheep and oxen in abundance
for him and the people who were with him,
and persuaded him to go up *with him* to Ramoth Gilead. 3 So Ahab king of Israel said to
Jehoshaphat king of Judah, "Will you go with
me *against* Ramoth Gilead?"

And he answered him, "I *am* as you *are,*
and my people as your people; *we will be*
with you in the war."

4 Also Jehoshaphat said to the king of Israel, [a]"Please inquire for the word of the LORD
today."

5 Then the king of Israel gathered the
prophets together, four hundred men, and
said to them, "Shall we go to war against Ramoth Gilead, or shall I refrain?"

So they said, "Go up, for God will deliver it
into the king's hand."

6 But Jehoshaphat said, *"Is there* not still
a prophet of the LORD here, that we may
inquire of [a]Him?"[1]

7 So the king of Israel said to Jehoshaphat,
"There is still one man by whom we may inquire of the LORD; but I hate him, because he
never prophesies good concerning me, but
always evil. He *is* Micaiah the son of Imla."

And Jehoshaphat said, "Let not the king
say such things!"

8 Then the king of Israel called one *of his*
officers and said, "Bring Micaiah the son of
Imla quickly!"

9 The king of Israel and Jehoshaphat king
of Judah, clothed in *their* robes, sat each on
his throne; and they sat at a threshing floor
at the entrance of the gate of Samaria; and
all the prophets prophesied before them.
10 Now Zedekiah the son of Chenaanah had
made [a]horns of iron for himself; and he said,
"Thus says the LORD: 'With these you shall
gore the Syrians until they are destroyed.' "

11 And all the prophets prophesied so, saying, "Go up to Ramoth Gilead and prosper, for
the LORD will deliver *it* into the king's hand."

12 Then the messenger who had gone to call
Micaiah spoke to him, saying, "Now listen,
the words of the prophets with one accord
encourage the king. Therefore please let
your word be like *the word of* one of them,
and speak encouragement."

17:7 [a] 2 Chr. 15:3; 35:3 **17:9** [a] Neh. 8:3, 7 **17:10** [a] 2 Chr. 14:14 **17:11** [a] 2 Chr. 9:14; 26:8 **17:16** [a] Judg. 5:2, 9 **17:19** [a] 2 Chr. 17:2 **18:1** [a] 2 Chr. 17:5 [b] 2 Kin. 8:18 [c] 1 Kin. 22:40 **18:2** [a] 1 Kin. 22:2 **18:4** [a] 2 Sam. 2:1 **18:6** [a] 2 Kin. 3:11
[1] Or *him* **18:10** [a] Zech. 1:18–21

13 And Micaiah said, "*As* the LORD lives,
[a]whatever my God says, that I will speak."
14 Then he came to the king; and the king
said to him, "Micaiah, shall we go to war
against Ramoth Gilead, or shall I refrain?"
And he said, "Go and prosper, and they
shall be delivered into your hand!"
15 So the king said to him, "How many times
shall I make you swear that you tell me nothing but the truth in the name of the LORD?"
16 Then he said, "I saw all Israel [a]scattered on
the mountains, as sheep that have no [b]shep-
herd. And the LORD said, 'These have no master. Let each return to his house in peace.' "
17 And the king of Israel said to Jehoshaphat, "Did I not tell you he would not prophesy good concerning me, but evil?"
18 Then *Micaiah* said, "Therefore hear the
word of the LORD: I saw the LORD sitting on His
[a]throne, and all the host of heaven standing
on His right hand and His left. 19 And the LORD
said, 'Who will persuade Ahab king of Israel to
go up, that he may fall at Ramoth Gilead?' So
one spoke in this manner, and another spoke
in that manner. 20 Then a [a]spirit came forward
and stood before the LORD, and said, 'I will
persuade him.' The LORD said to him, 'In what
way?' 21 So he said, 'I will go out and be a lying
spirit in the mouth of all his prophets.' And *the*
LORD said, 'You shall persuade *him* and also
prevail; go out and do so.' 22 Therefore look!
[a]The LORD has put a lying spirit in the mouth
of these prophets of yours, and the LORD has
declared disaster against you."
23 Then Zedekiah the son of Chenaanah
went near and [a]struck Micaiah on the cheek,
and said, "Which way did the spirit from the
LORD go from me to speak to you?"
24 And Micaiah said, "Indeed you shall
see on that day when you go into an inner
chamber to hide!"
25 Then the king of Israel said, "Take Micaiah, and return him to Amon the governor of
the city and to Joash the king's son; 26 and say,
'Thus says the king: [a]"Put this *fellow* in prison,
and feed him with bread of affliction and
water of affliction, until I return in peace." ' "
27 But Micaiah said, "If you ever return in
peace, the LORD has not spoken by [a]me." And
he said, "Take heed, all you people!"

Ahab Dies in Battle

28 So the king of Israel and Jehoshaphat
the king of Judah went up to Ramoth Gilead.
29 *And the king of Israel said to* Jehoshaphat,
"I will [a]disguise myself and go into battle; but
you put on your robes." So the king of Israel
disguised himself, and they went into battle.
30 Now the king of Syria had commanded
the captains of the chariots who *were* with
him, saying, "Fight with no one small or great,
but only with the king of Israel."
31 So it was, when the captains of the chariots
saw Jehoshaphat, that they said, "It *is* the king
of Israel!" Therefore they surrounded him to
attack; but Jehoshaphat [a]cried out, and the
LORD helped him, and God diverted them from
him. 32 For so it was, when the captains of the
chariots saw that it was not the king of Israel,
that they turned back from pursuing him.
33 Now a certain man drew a bow at random,
and struck the king of Israel between the joints
of his armor. So he said to the driver of his chariot, "Turn around and take me out of the battle,
for I am wounded." 34 The battle increased that
day, and the king of Israel propped *himself* up
in *his* chariot facing the Syrians until evening;
and about the time of sunset he died.

19 Then Jehoshaphat the king of Judah
returned safely to his house in Jerusalem. 2 And Jehu the son of Hanani [a]the seer
went out to meet him, and said to King Jehoshaphat, "Should you help the wicked and
[b]love those who hate the LORD? Therefore the
[c]wrath of the LORD *is* upon you. 3 Nevertheless
[a]good things are found in you, in that you have
removed the wooden images from the land,
and have [b]prepared your heart to seek God."

The Reforms of Jehoshaphat

4 So Jehoshaphat dwelt at Jerusalem; and
he went out again among the people from
Beersheba to the mountains of Ephraim, and
brought them back to the LORD God of their
[a]fathers. 5 Then he set [a]judges in the land
throughout all the fortified cities of Judah,
city by city, 6 and said to the judges, "Take
heed to what you are doing, for [a]you do not
judge for man but for the LORD, [b]who *is* with
you in the judgment. 7 Now therefore, let the
fear of the LORD be upon you; take care and
do *it*, for [a]*there is* no iniquity with the LORD
our God, no [b]partiality, nor taking of bribes."
8 Moreover in Jerusalem, for the judgment
of the LORD and for controversies, Jehoshaphat [a]appointed some of the Levites and
priests, and some of the chief fathers of Israel, when they returned to Jerusalem.[1] 9 And
he commanded them, saying, "Thus you shall
act [a]in the fear of the LORD, faithfully and

18:13 [a] Num. 22:18–20, 35; 23:12, 26 **18:16** [a] [Jer. 23:1–8; 31:10] [b] Matt. 9:36 **18:18** [a] Is. 6:1–5 **18:20** [a] Job 1:6 **18:22** [a] Ezek. 14:9 **18:23** [a] Jer. 20:2 **18:26** [a] 2 Chr. 16:10 **18:27** [a] Deut. 18:22 **18:29** [a] 2 Chr. 35:22 **18:31** [a] 2 Chr. 13:14, 15 **19:2** [a] 1 Kin. 16:1 [b] Ps. 139:21 [c] 2 Chr. 32:25 **19:3** [a] 2 Chr. 17:4, 6 [b] 2 Chr. 30:19 **19:4** [a] 2 Chr. 15:8–13 **19:5** [a] [Deut. 16:18–20] **19:6** [a] [Deut. 1:17] [b] Ps. 82:1 **19:7** [a] [Deut. 32:4] [b] [Deut. 10:17, 18] **19:8** [a] 2 Chr. 17:8

[1] Septuagint and Vulgate read *for the inhabitants of Jerusalem.* **19:9** [a] [2 Sam. 23:3]

with a loyal heart: 10 [a]Whatever case comes
to you from your brethren who dwell in their
cities, whether of bloodshed or offenses
against law or commandment, against statutes or ordinances, you shall warn them, lest
they trespass against the LORD and [b]wrath
come upon [c]you and your brethren. Do this,
and you will not be guilty. 11 And take notice:
[a]Amariah the chief priest *is* over you [b]in all
matters of the LORD; and Zebadiah the son
of Ishmael, the ruler of the house of Judah,
for all the king's matters; also the Levites *will*
be officials before you. Behave courageously,
and the LORD will be [c]with the good."

Ammon, Moab, and Mount Seir Defeated

20 It happened after this *that* the people
of [a]Moab with the people of [b]Ammon,
and *others* with them besides the [c]Ammon-
ites,[1] came to battle against Jehoshaphat.
2 Then some came and told Jehoshaphat, saying, "A great multitude is coming against you
from beyond the sea, from Syria;[1] and they are
[a]in Hazazon Tamar" (which *is* [b]En Gedi). 3 And
Jehoshaphat feared, and set himself to [a]seek
the LORD, and [b]proclaimed a fast throughout
all Judah. 4 So Judah gathered together to ask
[a]*help* from the LORD; and from all the cities
of Judah they came to seek the LORD.

5 Then Jehoshaphat stood in the assembly of Judah and Jerusalem, in the house of
the LORD, before the new court, 6 and said:
"O LORD God of our fathers, *are* You not [a]God
in heaven, and [b]do You *not* rule over all the
kingdoms of the nations, and [c]in Your hand
is there not power and might, so that no one is
able to withstand You? 7 *Are* You not [a]our God,
who [b]drove out the inhabitants of this land
before Your people Israel, and gave it to the
descendants of Abraham [c]Your friend forever? 8 And they dwell in it, and have built You
a sanctuary in it for Your name, saying, 9 [a]'If
disaster comes upon us—sword, judgment,
pestilence, or famine—we will stand before
this temple and in Your presence (for Your
[b]name *is* in this temple), and cry out to You
in our affliction, and You will hear and save.'
10 And now, here are the people of Ammon,
Moab, and Mount Seir—whom You [a]would
not let Israel invade when they came out of
the land of Egypt, but [b]they turned from them
and did not destroy them— 11 here they are,
rewarding us [a]by coming to throw us out of
Your possession which You have given us to
inherit. 12 O our God, will You not [a]judge them?
For we have no power against this great multitude that is coming against us; nor do we
know what to do, but [b]our eyes *are* upon You."

13 Now all Judah, with their little ones, their
wives, and their children, stood before the
LORD.

14 Then [a]the Spirit of the LORD came upon
Jahaziel the son of Zechariah, the son of Benaiah, the son of Jeiel, the son of Mattaniah,
a Levite of the sons of Asaph, in the midst of
the assembly. 15 And he said, "Listen, all you of
Judah and you inhabitants of Jerusalem, and
you, King Jehoshaphat! Thus says the LORD to
you: [a]'Do not be afraid nor dismayed because
of this great multitude, [b]for the battle *is* not
yours, but God's. 16 Tomorrow go down against
them. They will surely come up by the Ascent
of Ziz, and you will find them at the end of the
brook before the Wilderness of Jeruel. 17 [a]You
will not *need* to fight in this *battle*. Position
yourselves, stand still and see the salvation of
the LORD, who is with you, O Judah and Jerusalem!' Do not fear or be dismayed; tomorrow
go out against them, [b]for the LORD *is* with you."

18 And Jehoshaphat [a]bowed his head with
his face to the ground, and all Judah and the
inhabitants of Jerusalem bowed before the
LORD, worshiping the LORD. 19 Then the Levites of the children of the Kohathites and
of the children of the Korahites stood up to
praise the LORD God of Israel with voices
loud and high.

20 So they rose early in the morning and
went out into the Wilderness of Tekoa; and as
they went out, Jehoshaphat stood and said,
"Hear me, O Judah and you inhabitants of Jerusalem: [a]Believe in the LORD your God, and
you shall be established; believe His prophets, and you shall prosper." 21 And when he
had consulted with the people, he appointed
those who should sing to the LORD, [a]and who
should praise the beauty of holiness, as they
went out before the army and were saying:

[b]"Praise the LORD,
[c]For His mercy *endures* forever."[1]

22 Now when they began to sing and to
praise, [a]the LORD set ambushes against the

19:10 [a] Deut. 17:8 [b] Num. 16:46 [c] [Ezek. 3:18] **19:11** [a] Ezra 7:3 [b] 1 Chr. 26:30 [c] [2 Chr. 15:2; 20:17] **20:1** [a] 1 Chr. 18:2 [b] 1 Chr. 19:15 [c] 2 Chr. 26:7 [1] Following Masoretic Text and Vulgate; Septuagint reads *Meunites* (compare 26:7). **20:2** [a] Gen. 14:7 [b] Josh. 15:62 [1] Following Masoretic Text, Septuagint, and Vulgate; some Hebrew manuscripts and Old Latin read *Edom*. **20:3** [a] 2 Chr. 19:3 [b] Ezra 8:21 **20:4** [a] 2 Chr. 14:11 **20:6** [a] Deut. 4:39 [b] Dan. 4:17, 25, 32 [c] 1 Chr. 29:12 **20:7** [a] Ex. 6:7 [b] Ps. 44:2 [c] Is. 41:8 **20:9** [a] 2 Chr. 6:28–30 [b] 2 Chr. 6:20 **20:10** [a] Deut. 2:4, 9, 19 [b] Num. 20:21 **20:11** [a] Ps. 83:1–18 **20:12** [a] Judg. 11:27 [b] Ps. 25:15; 121:1, 2; 123:1, 2; 141:8 **20:14** [a] 2 Chr. 15:1; 24:20 **20:15** [a] [Deut. 1:29, 30; 31:6, 8] [b] 1 Sam. 17:47 **20:17** [a] Ex. 14:13, 14 [b] Num. 14:9 **20:18** [a] Ex. 4:31 **20:20** [a] Is. 7:9 **20:21** [a] 1 Chr. 16:29 [b] Ps. 106:1; 136:1 [c] 2 Chr. 5:13 [1] Compare Psalm 106:1 **20:22** [a] Judg. 7:22

ESTABLISHING PEACE

Believe in the LORD your God, and you shall be established.

2 CHRONICLES 20:20

Belief is a powerful force in our lives. Faced with threatening armies from Ammon, Moab, and Mount Seir, the righteous king Jehoshaphat called on the priests and the people of Jerusalem to fall on their faces and worship the Lord. After that, they stood up and sang praises to God. Jehoshaphat did not issue a call to arms but a call to prayer and praise, exhorting the people, "Hear me, O Judah and you inhabitants of Jerusalem: Believe in the LORD your God, and you shall be established" (v. 20).

Careful readers of Scripture will hear an echo in the king's words. It was the king's ancestor David who was told by the prophet Nathan, "Your house and your kingdom shall be established forever before you" (2 Sam. 7:16). Alluding to this very promise, Isaiah warned the fearful and wavering King Ahaz, "If you will not believe, surely you shall not be established" (Is. 7:9). What most readers probably don't know is that the words "establish" and "believe" are from the word that gives us "amen." If the king and the people did not believe in God, they could hardly expect to be established. Faith keeps us close to God. The peace of God will not be present in our lives if we do not rest in the promises of God. I believe and stand on the promises of God day by day to maintain the peace of the Lord in my life.

people of Ammon, Moab, and Mount Seir, who
had come against Judah; and they were defeated. 23 For the people of Ammon and Moab
stood up against the inhabitants of Mount
Seir to utterly kill and destroy *them*. And when
they had made an end of the inhabitants of
Seir, [a]they helped to destroy one another.
24 So when Judah came to a place overlook-
ing the wilderness, they looked toward the
multitude; and there *were* their dead bodies,
fallen on the earth. No one had escaped.
25 When Jehoshaphat and his people came
to take away their spoil, they found among
them an abundance of valuables on the dead
bodies,[1] and precious jewelry, which they
stripped off for themselves, more than they
could carry away; and they were three days
gathering the spoil because there was so
much. 26 And on the fourth day they assembled in the Valley of Berachah, for there they
blessed the LORD; therefore the name of that
place was called The Valley of Berachah[1] until
this day. 27 Then they returned, every man of
Judah and Jerusalem, with Jehoshaphat in
front of them, to go back to Jerusalem with
joy, for the LORD had [a]made them rejoice over
their enemies. 28 So they came to Jerusalem,
with stringed instruments and harps and
trumpets, to the house of the LORD. 29 And
[a]the fear of God was on all the kingdoms of
those countries when they heard that the
LORD had fought against the enemies of Israel. 30 Then the realm of Jehoshaphat was
quiet, for his [a]God gave him rest all around.

The End of Jehoshaphat's Reign

31 [a]So Jehoshaphat was king over Judah.
He was thirty-five years old when he became
king, and he reigned twenty-five years in
Jerusalem. His mother's name *was* Azubah
the daughter of Shilhi. 32 And he walked in
the way of his father [a]Asa, and did not turn
aside from it, doing *what was* right in the
sight of the LORD. 33 Nevertheless [a]the high
places were not taken away, for as yet the
people had not [b]directed their hearts to the
God of their fathers.
34 Now the rest of the acts of Jehoshaphat,
first and last, indeed they *are* written in the
book of Jehu the son of Hanani, [a]which *is*
mentioned in the book of the kings of Israel.
35 After this [a]Jehoshaphat king of Judah
allied himself with Ahaziah king of Israel,
[b]who acted very [c]wickedly. 36 And he allied
himself with him [a]to make ships to go to
Tarshish, and they made the ships in Ezion
Geber. 37 But Eliezer the son of Dodavah of
Mareshah prophesied against Jehoshaphat,

20:23 [a] 1 Sam. 14:20 **20:25** [1] A few Hebrew manuscripts, Old Latin, and Vulgate read *garments;* Septuagint reads *armor.* **20:26** [1] Literally *Blessing* **20:27** [a] Neh. 12:43 **20:29** [a] 2 Chr. 14:14; 17:10 **20:30** [a] Job 34:29 **20:31** [a] [1 Kin. 22:41–43] **20:32** [a] 2 Chr. 14:2 **20:33** [a] 2 Chr. 15:17; 17:6 [b] 2 Chr. 12:14; 19:3 **20:34** [a] 1 Kin. 16:1, 7 **20:35** [a] 2 Chr. 18:1 [b] 1 Kin. 22:48–53 [c] [2 Chr. 19:2] **20:36** [a] 1 Kin. 9:26; 10:22

saying, "Because you have allied yourself
with Ahaziah, the LORD has destroyed your
works." [a]Then the ships were wrecked, so
that they were not able to go [b]to Tarshish.

Jehoram Reigns in Judah

21 And [a]Jehoshaphat rested with his fathers, and was buried with his fathers
in the City of David. Then Jehoram his son
reigned in his place. 2 He had brothers, the
sons of Jehoshaphat: Azariah, Jehiel, Zechariah, Azaryahu, Michael, and Shephatiah; all
these *were* the sons of Jehoshaphat king of
Israel. 3 Their father gave them great gifts of
silver and gold and precious things, with fortified cities in Judah; but he gave the kingdom
to Jehoram, because he *was* the firstborn.
4 Now when Jehoram was established over
the kingdom of his father, he strengthened
himself and killed all his brothers with the
sword, and also *others* of the princes of Israel.
5 [a]Jehoram *was* thirty-two years old when
he became king, and he reigned eight years
in Jerusalem. 6 And he walked in the way of
the kings of Israel, just as the house of Ahab
had done, for he had the daughter of [a]Ahab
as a wife; and he did evil in the sight of the
LORD. 7 Yet the LORD would not destroy the
house of David, because of the [a]covenant
that He had made with David, and since He
had promised to give a lamp to him and to
his [b]sons forever.
8 [a]In his days Edom revolted against Judah's authority, and made a king over themselves. 9 So Jehoram went out with his officers, and all his chariots with him. And he
rose by night and attacked the Edomites
who had surrounded him and the captains
of the chariots. 10 Thus Edom has been in
revolt against Judah's authority to this day.
At that time Libnah revolted against his rule,
because he had forsaken the LORD God of
his fathers. 11 Moreover he made high places
in the mountains of Judah, and caused the
inhabitants of Jerusalem to [a]commit harlotry, and led Judah astray.
12 And a letter came to him from Elijah the
prophet, saying,

> *Thus says the* LORD *God* of your father
> David:
> Because you have not walked in the
> ways of Jehoshaphat your father, or
> in the ways of Asa king of Judah, 13 but
> have walked in the way of the kings
> of Israel, and have [a]made Judah and
> the inhabitants of Jerusalem to [b]play
> the harlot like the [c]harlotry of the
> house of Ahab, and also have [d]killed
> your brothers, those of your father's
> household, *who were* better than
> yourself, 14 behold, the LORD will strike
> your people with a serious affliction—
> your children, your wives, and all your
> possessions; 15 and you *will become* very
> sick with a [a]disease of your intestines,
> until your intestines come out by
> reason of the sickness, day by day.

16 Moreover the [a]LORD [b]stirred up against
Jehoram the spirit of the Philistines and the
[c]Arabians who *were* near the Ethiopians.
17 And they came up into Judah and invaded
it, and carried away all the possessions that
were found in the king's house, and also [a]his
sons and his wives, so that there was not a
son left to him except Jehoahaz,[1] the youngest of his sons.
18 After all this the LORD struck him [a]in his
intestines with an incurable disease. 19 Then
it happened in the course of time, after the
end of two years, that his intestines came out
because of his sickness; so he died in severe
pain. And his people made no burning for
him, like [a]the burning for his fathers.
20 He was thirty-two years old when he
became king. He reigned in Jerusalem eight
years and, to no one's sorrow, departed. However they buried him in the City of David, but
not in the tombs of the kings.

Ahaziah Reigns in Judah

22 Then the inhabitants of Jerusalem
made [a]Ahaziah his youngest son king
in his place, for the raiders who came with
the [b]Arabians into the camp had killed all the
[c]older *sons.* So Ahaziah the son of Jehoram,
king of Judah, reigned. 2 Ahaziah *was* forty-
two[1] years old when he became king, and he
reigned one year in Jerusalem. His mother's
name *was* [a]Athaliah the granddaughter of
Omri. 3 He also walked in the ways of the house
of Ahab, for his mother advised him to do
wickedly. 4 Therefore he did evil in the sight of
the LORD, like the house of Ahab; for they were
his counselors after the death of his father, to
his destruction. 5 He also followed their advice,
and went with Jehoram[1] the son of Ahab king

20:37 [a] 1 Kin. 22:48 [b] 2 Chr. 9:21 **21:1** [a] 1 Kin. 22:50 **21:5** [a] 2 Kin. 8:17–22 **21:6** [a] 2 Chr. 18:1 **21:7** [a] 2 Sam. 7:8–17 [b] 1 Kin. 11:36 **21:8** [a] 2 Kin. 8:20; 14:7, 10 **21:11** [a] [Lev. 20:5] **21:13** [a] 2 Chr. 21:11 [b] Deut. 31:16 [c] 2 Kin. 9:22 [d] 2 Chr. 21:4 **21:15** [a] 2 Chr. 21:18, 19 **21:16** [a] 2 Chr. 33:11 [b] 1 Kin. 11:14, 23 [c] 2 Chr. 17:11 **21:17** [a] 2 Chr. 24:7 [1] Elsewhere called *Ahaziah* (compare 2 Chronicles 22:1) **21:18** [a] 2 Chr. 13:20; 21:15 **21:19** [a] 2 Chr. 16:14 **22:1** [a] 2 Chr. 21:17; 22:6 [b] 2 Chr. 21:16 [c] 2 Chr. 21:17 **22:2** [a] 2 Chr. 21:6 [1] Or *twenty-two* (compare 2 Kings 8:26) **22:5** [1] Also spelled *Joram* (compare verses 5 and 7; 2 Kings 8:28; and elsewhere)

PEACE NOTE

Too many Christians are racked with shame and doubt, wrongly thinking that they should never feel uncertain or anxious. Doubt is a normal part of belief.

of Israel to war against Hazael king of Syria at Ramoth Gilead; and the Syrians wounded Joram. 6[a]Then he returned to Jezreel to recover from the wounds which he had received at Ramah, when he fought against Hazael king of Syria. And Azariah[1] the son of Jehoram, king of Judah, went down to see Jehoram the son of Ahab in Jezreel, because he was sick.

7 His going to Joram [a]was God's occasion for Ahaziah's downfall; for when he arrived, [b]he went out with Jehoram against Jehu the son of Nimshi, [c]whom the LORD had anointed to cut off the house of Ahab. 8 And it happened, when Jehu was [a]executing judgment on the house of Ahab, and [b]found the princes of Judah and the sons of Ahaziah's brothers who served Ahaziah, that he killed them. 9[a]Then he searched for Ahaziah; and they caught him (he was hiding in Samaria), and brought him to Jehu. When they had killed him, they buried him, "because," they said, "he is the son of [b]Jehoshaphat, who [c]sought the LORD with all his heart."

So the house of Ahaziah had no one to assume power over the kingdom.

Athaliah Reigns in Judah

10[a]Now when Athaliah the mother of Ahaziah saw that her son was dead, she arose and destroyed all the royal heirs of the house of Judah. 11 But Jehoshabeath,[1] the daughter of the king, took [a]Joash the son of Ahaziah, and stole him away from among the king's sons who were being murdered, and put him and his nurse in a bedroom. So Jehoshabeath, the daughter of King Jehoram, the wife of Jehoiada the priest (for she was the sister of Ahaziah), hid him from Athaliah so that she did not kill him. 12 And he was hidden with them in the house of God for six years, while Athaliah reigned over the land.

Joash Crowned King of Judah

23 In [a]the seventh year [b]Jehoiada strengthened himself, *and made a* covenant with the captains of hundreds: Azariah the son of Jeroham, Ishmael the son of Jehohanan, Azariah the son of [c]Obed, Maaseiah the son of Adaiah, and Elishaphat the son of Zichri. 2 And they went throughout Judah and gathered the Levites from all the cities of Judah, and the [a]chief fathers of Israel, and they came to Jerusalem.

3 Then all the assembly made a covenant with the king in the house of God. And he said to them, "Behold, the king's son shall reign, as the LORD has [a]said of the sons of David. 4 This *is* what you shall do: One-third of you [a]entering on the Sabbath, of the priests and the Levites, *shall be* keeping watch over the doors; 5 one-third *shall be* at the king's house; and one-third at the Gate of the Foundation. All the people *shall be* in the courts of the house of the LORD. 6 But let no one come into the house of the LORD except the priests and [a]those of the Levites who serve. They may go in, for they *are* holy; but all the people shall keep the watch of the LORD. 7 And the Levites shall surround the king on all sides, every man with his weapons in his hand; and whoever comes into the house, let him be put to death. You are to be with the king when he comes in and when he goes out."

8 So the Levites and all Judah did according to all that Jehoiada the priest commanded. And each man took his men who were to be on duty on the Sabbath, with those who were going *off duty* on the Sabbath; for Jehoiada the priest had not dismissed [a]the divisions. 9 And Jehoiada the priest gave to the captains of hundreds the spears and the large and small [a]shields which *had belonged* to King David, that *were* in the temple of God. 10 Then he set all the people, every man with his weapon in his hand, from the right side of the temple to the left side of the temple, along by the altar and by the temple, all around the king. 11 And they brought out the king's son, put the crown on him, [a]*gave him* the Testimony,[1] and made him king. Then Jehoiada and his sons anointed him, and said, "*Long* live the king!"

22:6 [a] 2 Kin. 9:15 [1] Some Hebrew manuscripts, Septuagint, Syriac, Vulgate, and 2 Kings 8:29 read *Ahaziah.*
22:7 [a] 2 Chr. 10:15 [b] 2 Kin. 9:21–24 [c] 2 Kin. 9:6, 7 **22:8** [a] 2 Kin. 9:22–24 [b] 2 Kin. 10:10–14 **22:9** [a] [2 Kin. 9:27] [b] 1 Kin. 15:24 [c] 2 Chr. 17:4; 20:3, 4 **22:10** [a] 2 Kin. 11:1–3 **22:11** [a] 2 Kin. 12:18 [1] Spelled *Jehosheba* in 2 Kings 11:2 **23:1** [a] 2 Kin. 11:4 [b] 2 Kin. 12:2 [c] 1 Chr. 2:37, 38 **23:2** [a] Ezra 1:5 **23:3** [a] 2 Sam. 7:12 **23:4** [a] 1 Chr. 9:25 **23:6** [a] 1 Chr. 23:28–32 **23:8** [a] 1 Chr. 24:1–31 **23:9** [a] 2 Sam. 8:7 **23:11** [a] Deut. 17:18 [1] That is, the Law (compare Exodus 25:16, 21; 31:18)

Death of Athaliah
12 Now when [a]Athaliah heard the noise of
the people running and praising the king,
she came to the people *in* the temple of the
LORD. 13 *When* she looked, there was the king
standing by his pillar at the entrance; and
the leaders and the trumpeters *were* by the
king. All the people of the land were rejoicing
and blowing trumpets, also the singers with
musical instruments, and [a]those who led in
praise. So Athaliah tore her clothes and said,
[b]"Treason! Treason!"
14 And Jehoiada the priest brought out the
captains of hundreds who were set over the
army, and said to them, "Take her outside under guard, and slay with the sword whoever
follows her." For the priest had said, "Do not
kill her in the house of the LORD."
15 So they seized her; and she went by way
of the entrance [a]of the Horse Gate *into* the
king's house, and they killed her there.
16 Then Jehoiada made a [a]covenant between himself, the people, and the king, that
they should be the LORD's people. 17 And all
the people went to the temple[1] of Baal, and
tore it down. They broke in pieces its altars
and images, and [a]killed Mattan the priest
of Baal before the altars. 18 Also Jehoiada
appointed the oversight of the house of the
LORD to the hand of the priests, the Levites,
whom David had [a]assigned in the house of
the LORD, to offer the burnt offerings of the
LORD, as *it is* written in the [b]Law of Moses,
with rejoicing and with singing, *as it was
established* by David. 19 And he set the [a]gate-
keepers at the gates of the house of the LORD,
so that no one *who was* in any way unclean
should enter.
20 [a]Then he took the captains of hundreds,
the nobles, the governors of the people, and
all the people of the land, and brought the
king down from the house of the LORD; and
they went through the Upper Gate to the
king's house, and set the king on the throne
of the kingdom. 21 So all the people of the land
rejoiced; and the city was quiet, for they had
slain Athaliah with the sword.

Joash Repairs the Temple
24 *Joash [a]was seven years old* when he
became king, and he reigned forty
years in Jerusalem. His mother's name *was*
Zibiah of Beersheba. 2 Joash [a]did *what was*
right in the sight of the LORD all the days of
Jehoiada the priest. 3 And Jehoiada took two
wives for him, and he had sons and daughters.
4 Now it happened after this *that* Joash
set his heart on repairing the house of the
LORD. 5 Then he gathered the priests and the
Levites, and said to them, "Go out to the cities
of Judah, and [a]gather from all Israel money
to repair the house of your God from year to
year, and see that you do it quickly."
However the Levites did not do it quickly.
6 [a]So the king called Jehoiada the chief *priest,*
and said to him, "Why have you not required
the Levites to bring in from Judah and from
Jerusalem the collection, *according to the
commandment* of [b]Moses the servant of the
LORD and of the assembly of Israel, for the
[c]tabernacle of witness?" 7 For [a]the sons of
Athaliah, that wicked woman, had broken
into the house of God, and had also presented
all the [b]dedicated things of the house of the
LORD to the Baals.
8 Then at the king's command [a]they made
a chest, and set it outside at the gate of the
house of the LORD. 9 And they made a proclamation throughout Judah and Jerusalem to
bring to the LORD [a]the collection *that* Moses
the servant of God *had imposed* on Israel in
the wilderness. 10 Then all the leaders and all
the people rejoiced, brought their contribu-
tions, and put *them* into the chest until all
had given. 11 So it was, at that time, when the
chest was brought to the king's official by
the hand of the Levites, and [a]when they saw
that *there was* much money, that the king's
scribe and the high priest's officer came and
emptied the chest, and took it and returned
it to its place. Thus they did day by day, and
gathered money in abundance.
12 The king and Jehoiada gave it to those
who did the work of the service of the house
of the LORD; and they hired masons and carpenters to [a]repair the house of the LORD, and
also those who worked in iron and bronze
to restore the house of the LORD. 13 So the
workmen labored, and the work was completed by them; they restored the house of
God to its original condition and reinforced
it. 14 When they had finished, they brought
the rest of the money before the king and
Jehoiada; [a]they made from it articles for
the house of the LORD, articles for serving
and offering, spoons and vessels of gold and
silver. And they offered burnt offerings in
the house of the LORD continually all the
days of Jehoiada.

23:12 [a] 2 Chr. 22:10 **23:13** [a] 1 Chr. 25:6–8 [b] 2 Kin. 9:23 **23:15** [a] Neh. 3:28 **23:16** [a] Josh. 24:24, 25 **23:17** [a] Deut. 13:6–9 [1] Literally *house* **23:18** [a] 1 Chr. 23:6, 30, 31; 24:1 [b] Num. 28:2 **23:19** [a] 1 Chr. 26:1–19 **23:20** [a] 2 Kin. 11:19 **24:1** [a] 2 Kin. 11:21; 12:1–15 **24:2** [a] 2 Chr. 26:4, 5 **24:5** [a] 2 Kin. 12:4 **24:6** [a] 2 Kin. 12:7 [b] Ex. 30:12–16 [c] Num. 1:50 **24:7** [a] 2 Chr. 21:17 [b] 2 Kin. 12:4 **24:8** [a] 2 Kin. 12:9 **24:9** [a] 2 Chr. 24:6 **24:11** [a] 2 Kin. 12:10 **24:12** [a] 2 Chr. 30:12 **24:14** [a] 2 Kin. 12:13

Apostasy of Joash

15 But Jehoiada grew old and was full of days, and he died; *he was* one hundred and thirty years old when he died. 16 And they buried him in the City of David among the kings, because he had done good in Israel, both toward God and His house.

17 Now after the death of Jehoiada the leaders of Judah came and bowed down to the king. And the king listened to them. 18 Therefore they left the house of the LORD God of their fathers, and served [a]wooden images and idols; and [b]wrath came upon Judah and Jerusalem because of their trespass. 19 Yet He [a]sent prophets to them, to bring them back to the LORD; and they testified against them, but they would not listen.

20 Then the Spirit of God came upon [a]Zechariah the son of Jehoiada the priest, who stood above the people, and said to them, "Thus says God: [b]'Why do you transgress the commandments of the LORD, so that you cannot prosper? [c]Because you have forsaken the LORD, He also has forsaken you.' " 21 So they conspired against him, and at the command of the king they [a]stoned him with stones in the court of the house of the LORD. 22 Thus Joash the king did not remember the kindness which Jehoiada his father had done to him, but killed his son; and as he died, he said, "The LORD look on *it,* and [a]repay!"

Death of Joash

23 So it happened in the spring of the year *that* [a]the army of Syria came up against him; and they came to Judah and Jerusalem, and destroyed all the leaders of the people from among the people, and sent all their spoil to the king of Damascus. 24 For the army of the Syrians [a]came with a small company of men; but the LORD [b]delivered a very great army into their hand, because they had forsaken the LORD God of their fathers. So they [c]executed judgment against Joash. 25 And when they had withdrawn from him (for they left him severely wounded), [a]his own servants conspired against him because of the blood of the sons[1] of Jehoiada the priest, and killed him on his bed. So he died. And they buried him in the City of David, but they did not bury him in the tombs of the kings.

26 These are the ones who conspired against him: Zabad[1] the son of Shimeath the Ammonitess, and Jehozabad the son of Shimrith[2] the Moabitess. 27 Now *concerning* his sons, and [a]the many oracles about him, and the repairing of the house of God, indeed they *are* written in the annals of the book of the kings. [b]Then Amaziah his son reigned in his place.

Amaziah Reigns in Judah

25 Amaziah [a]*was* twenty-five years old *when* he became king, and he reigned twenty-nine years in Jerusalem. His mother's name *was* Jehoaddan of Jerusalem. 2 And he did *what was* right in the sight of the LORD, [a]but not with a loyal heart.

3 [a]Now it happened, as soon as the kingdom was established for him, that he executed his servants who had murdered his father the king. 4 However he did not execute their children, but *did* as *it is* written in the Law in the Book of Moses, where the LORD commanded, saying, [a]"The fathers shall not be put to death for their children, nor shall the children be put to death for their fathers; but a person shall die for his own sin."[1]

The War Against Edom

5 Moreover Amaziah gathered Judah together and set over them captains of thousands and captains of hundreds, according to *their* fathers' houses, throughout all Judah and Benjamin; and he numbered them [a]from twenty years old and above, and found them to be three hundred thousand choice *men, able* to go to war, who could handle spear and shield. 6 He also hired one hundred thousand mighty men of valor from Israel for one hundred talents of silver. 7 But a [a]man of God came to him, saying, "O king, do not let the army of Israel go with you, for the LORD *is* not with Israel—*not with* any of the children of Ephraim. 8 But if you go, be gone! Be strong in battle! *Even so,* God shall make you fall before the enemy; for God has [a]power to help and to overthrow."

9 Then Amaziah said to the man of God, "But what *shall we* do about the hundred talents which I have given to the troops of Israel?"

And the man of God answered, [a]"The LORD is able to give you much more than this." 10 So Amaziah discharged the troops that had come to him from Ephraim, to go back home. Therefore their anger was greatly aroused against Judah, and they returned home in great anger.

11 Then Amaziah strengthened himself, and leading his people, he went to [a]the Valley of Salt and killed ten thousand of the people of

24:18 [a] 1 Kin. 14:23 [b] [Ex. 34:12–14] **24:19** [a] 2 Chr. 36:15, 16 **24:20** [a] Matt. 23:35 [b] Num. 14:41 [c] [2 Chr. 15:2] **24:21** [a] [Neh. 9:26] **24:22** [a] [Gen. 9:5] **24:23** [a] 2 Kin. 12:17 **24:24** [a] Lev. 26:8; Is. 30:17 [b] Lev. 26:25 [c] 2 Chr. 22:8 **24:25** [a] 2 Kin. 12:20, 21 [1] Septuagint and Vulgate read *son* (compare verses 20–22). **24:26** [1] Or *Jozachar* (compare 2 Kings 12:21) [2] Or *Shomer* (compare 2 Kings 12:21) **24:27** [a] 2 Kin. 12:18 [b] 2 Kin. 12:21 **25:1** [a] 2 Kin. 14:1–6 **25:2** [a] 2 Chr. 25:14 **25:3** [a] 2 Kin. 14:5 **25:4** [a] Deut. 24:16 [1] Deuteronomy 24:16 **25:5** [a] Num. 1:3 **25:7** [a] 2 Chr. 11:2 **25:8** [a] 2 Chr. 14:11; 20:6 **25:9** [a] [Deut. 8:18] **25:11** [a] 2 Kin. 14:7

Seir. 12 Also the children of Judah took captive
ten thousand alive, brought them to the top of
the rock, and cast them down from the top of
the rock, so that they all were dashed in pieces.
13 But as for the soldiers of the army which
Amaziah had discharged, so that they would
not go with him to battle, they raided the cities
of Judah from Samaria to Beth Horon, killed
three thousand in them, and took much spoil.
14 Now it was so, after Amaziah came from
the slaughter of the Edomites, that [a]he
brought the gods of the people of Seir, set
them up *to be* [b]his gods, and bowed down
before them and burned incense to them.
15 Therefore the anger of the LORD was
aroused against Amaziah, and He sent him
a prophet who said to him, "Why have you
sought [a]the gods of the people, which [b]could
not rescue their own people from your hand?"
16 So it was, as he talked with him, that *the
king* said to him, "Have we made you the king's
counselor? Cease! Why should you be killed?"
Then the prophet ceased, and said, "I know
that God has [a]determined to destroy you,
because you have done this and have not
heeded my advice."

Israel Defeats Judah

17 Now [a]Amaziah king of Judah asked advice and sent to Joash[1] the son of Jehoahaz,
the son of Jehu, king of Israel, saying, "Come,
let us face one another *in battle.*"
18 And Joash king of Israel sent to Amaziah
king of Judah, saying, "The thistle that *was* in
Lebanon sent to the cedar that was in Lebanon,
saying, 'Give your daughter to my son as wife';
and a wild beast that *was* in Lebanon passed
by and trampled the thistle. 19 Indeed you say
that you have defeated the Edomites, and your
heart is lifted up to [a]boast. Stay at home now;
why should you meddle with trouble, that you
should fall—you and Judah with you?"
20 But Amaziah would not heed, for [a]it *came*
from God, that He might give them into the
hand *of their enemies,* because they [b]sought
the gods of Edom. 21 So Joash king of Israel
went out; and he and Amaziah king of Judah
faced one another at [a]Beth Shemesh, which
belongs to Judah. 22 And Judah was defeated by Israel, and every man fled to his tent.
23 Then Joash the king of Israel captured Amaziah king of Judah, the son of Joash, the son of
[a]Jehoahaz, at Beth Shemesh; and he brought
him to Jerusalem, and broke down the wall of
Jerusalem from the Gate of Ephraim to the
Corner Gate—four hundred cubits. 24 And *he
took* all the gold and silver, all the articles that
were found in the house of God with [a]Obed-
Edom, the treasures of the king's house, and
hostages, and returned to Samaria.

Death of Amaziah

25 [a]Amaziah the son of Joash, king of
Judah, lived fifteen years after the death of
Joash the son of Jehoahaz, king of Israel.
26 Now the rest of the acts of Amaziah, from
first to last, indeed *are* they not written in
the book of the kings of Judah and Israel?
27 After the time that Amaziah turned away
from following the LORD, they made a conspiracy against him in Jerusalem, and he
fled to Lachish; but they sent after him to
Lachish and killed him there. 28 Then they
brought him on horses and buried him with
his fathers in the City of Judah.

Uzziah Reigns in Judah

26 Now all the people of Judah took Uzziah,[1] who *was* sixteen years old, and
made him king instead of his father Amaziah.
2 He built Elath[1] and restored it to Judah, after
the king rested with his fathers.
3 Uzziah *was* sixteen years old when he became king, and he reigned fifty-two years in
Jerusalem. His mother's name was Jecholiah
of Jerusalem. 4 And he did *what was* [a]right in
the sight of the LORD, according to all that his
father Amaziah had done. 5 [a]He sought God in
the days of Zechariah, who [b]had understanding in the visions[1] of God; and as long as he
sought the LORD, God made him [c]prosper.

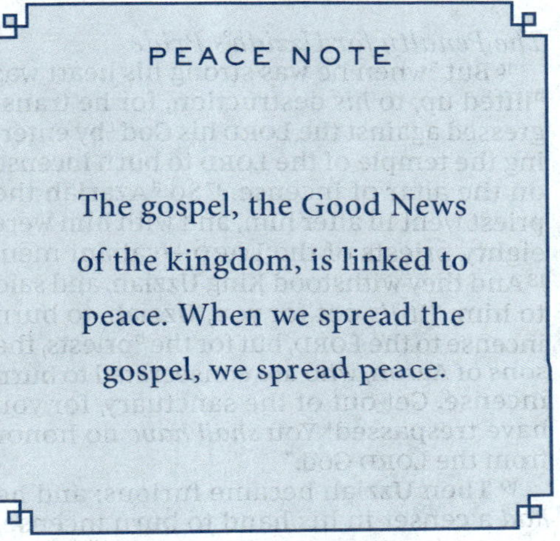

25:14 [a] 2 Chr. 28:23 [b] [Ex. 20:3, 5] **25:15** [a] [Ps. 96:5] [b] 2 Chr. 25:11 **25:16** [a] [1 Sam. 2:25] **25:17** [a] 2 Kin. 14:8–14 [1] Spelled *Jehoash* in 2 Kings 14:8ff **25:19** [a] 2 Chr. 26:16; 32:25 **25:20** [a] 1 Kin. 12:15 [b] 2 Chr. 25:14 **25:21** [a] Josh. 19:38 **25:23** [a] 2 Chr. 21:17; 22:1, 6 **25:24** [a] 1 Chr. 26:15 **25:25** [a] 2 Kin. 14:17–22 **26:1** [1] Called *Azariah* in 2 Kings 14:21ff **26:2** [1] Hebrew *Eloth* **26:4** [a] 2 Chr. 24:2 **26:5** [a] 2 Chr. 24:2 [b] Dan. 1:17; 10:1 [c] [2 Chr. 15:2; 20:20; 31:21] [1] Several Hebrew manuscripts, Septuagint, Syriac, Targum, and Arabic read *fear.*

6 Now he went out and [a]made war against the
Philistines, and broke down the wall of Gath,
the wall of Jabneh, and the wall of Ashdod;
and he built cities *around* Ashdod and among
the Philistines. 7 God helped him against [a]the
Philistines, against the Arabians who lived in
Gur Baal, and against the Meunites. 8 Also the
Ammonites [a]brought tribute to Uzziah. His
fame spread as far as the entrance of Egypt,
for he became exceedingly strong.
9 And Uzziah built towers in Jerusalem at
the [a]Corner Gate, at the Valley Gate, and at the
corner buttress of the wall; then he fortified
them. 10 Also he built towers in the desert. He
dug many wells, for he had much livestock,
both in the lowlands and in the plains; *he also
had* farmers and vinedressers in the mountains and in Carmel, for he loved the soil.
11 Moreover Uzziah had an army of fighting
men who went out to war by companies,
according to the number on their roll as
prepared by Jeiel the scribe and Maaseiah
the officer, under the hand of Hananiah, *one*
of the king's captains. 12 The total number of
chief officers[1] of the mighty men of valor *was*
two thousand six hundred. 13 And under their
authority *was* an army of three hundred and
seven thousand five hundred, that made war
with mighty power, to help the king against
the enemy. 14 Then Uzziah prepared for them,
for the entire army, shields, spears, helmets,
body armor, bows, and slings *to cast* stones.
15 And he made devices in Jerusalem, invent-
ed by [a]skillful men, to be on the towers and
the corners, to shoot arrows and large stones.
So his fame spread far and wide, for he was
marvelously helped till he became strong.

The Penalty for Uzziah's Pride

16 But [a]when he was strong his heart was
[b]lifted up, to *his* destruction, for he transgressed against the LORD his God [c]by entering the temple of the LORD to burn incense
on the altar of incense. 17 So [a]Azariah the
priest went in after him, and with him were
eighty priests of the LORD—valiant men.
18 And they withstood King Uzziah, and said
to him, "*It* [a]*is* not for you, Uzziah, to burn
incense to the LORD, but for the [b]priests, the
sons of Aaron, who are consecrated to burn
incense. Get out of the sanctuary, for you
have trespassed! You *shall have* no honor
from the LORD God."
19 Then Uzziah became furious; and he
had a censer in *his* hand to burn incense.
And while he was angry with the priests,
[a]leprosy broke out on his forehead, before
the priests in the house of the LORD, beside
the incense altar. 20 And Azariah the chief
priest and all the priests looked at him, and
there, on his forehead, he *was* leprous; so
they thrust him out of that place. Indeed he
also [b]hurried to get out, because the LORD
had struck him.
21 [a]King Uzziah was a leper until the day
of his death. He dwelt in an [b]isolated house,
because he was a leper; for he was cut off
from the house of the LORD. Then Jotham
his son *was* over the king's house, judging
the people of the land.
22 Now the rest of the acts of Uzziah, from
first to last, the prophet [a]Isaiah the son of
Amoz wrote. 23 [a]So Uzziah rested with his
fathers, and they buried him with his fathers
in the field of burial which *belonged* to the
kings, for they said, "He is a leper." Then Jotham his son reigned in his place.

Jotham Reigns in Judah

27 Jotham [a]*was* twenty-five years old
when he became king, and he reigned
sixteen years in Jerusalem. His mother's
name *was* Jerushah[1] the daughter of Zadok.
2 And he did *what was* right in the sight of
the LORD, according to all that his father
Uzziah had done (although he did not enter
the temple of the LORD). But still [a]the people
acted corruptly.
3 He built the Upper Gate of the house of
the LORD, and he built extensively on the
wall of [a]Ophel. 4 Moreover he built cities in
the mountains of Judah, and in the forests he
built fortresses and towers. 5 He also fought
with the king of the [a]Ammonites and defeated them. And the people of Ammon gave him
in that year one hundred talents of silver, ten
thousand kors of wheat, and ten thousand
of barley. The people of Ammon paid this
to him in the second and third years also.
6 So Jotham became mighty, [a]because he
prepared his ways before the LORD his God.
7 Now the rest of the acts of Jotham, and
all his wars and his ways, indeed they *are*
written in the book of the kings of Israel
and Judah. 8 He was twenty-five years old
when he became king, and he reigned sixteen years in Jerusalem. 9 [a]So Jotham rested
with his fathers, and they buried him in the
City of David. Then [b]Ahaz his son reigned
in his place.

26:6 [a] Is. 14:29 **26:7** [a] 2 Chr. 21:16 **26:8** [a] 2 Chr. 17:11 **26:9** [a] Neh. 3:13, 19, 32 **26:12** [1] Literally *chief fathers* **26:15** [a] Ex. 39:3, 8 **26:16** [a] [Deut. 32:15] [b] 2 Chr. 25:19 [c] 2 Kin. 16:12, 13 **26:17** [a] 1 Chr. 6:10 **26:18** [a] [Num. 3:10; 16:39, 40; 18:7] [b] Ex. 30:7, 8 **26:19** [a] 2 Kin. 5:25–27 **26:20** [a] Esth. 6:12 **26:21** [a] 2 Kin. 15:5 [b] [Lev. 13:46] **26:22** [a] Is. 1:1 **26:23** [a] Is. 6:1 **27:1** [a] 2 Kin. 15:32–35 [1] Spelled *Jerusha* in 2 Kings 15:33 **27:2** [a] 2 Kin. 15:35 **27:3** [a] 2 Chr. 33:14 **27:5** [a] 2 Chr. 26:8 **27:6** [a] 2 Chr. 26:5 **27:9** [a] 2 Kin. 15:38 [b] Is. 1:1

Ahaz Reigns in Judah

28 Ahaz [a]*was* twenty years old when he
became king, and he reigned sixteen
years in Jerusalem; and he did not do *what*
was right in the sight of the LORD, as his father
David *had done.* 2 For he walked in the ways of
the kings of Israel, and made [a]molded images
for [b]the Baals. 3 He burned incense in [a]the
Valley of the Son of Hinnom, and burned [b]his
children in the [c]fire, according to the abominations of the nations whom the LORD had
[d]cast out before the children of Israel. 4 And
he sacrificed and burned incense on the high
places, on the hills, and under every green tree.

Syria and Israel Defeat Judah

5 Therefore [a]the LORD his God delivered
him into the hand of the king of Syria. They
[b]defeated him, and carried away a great multitude of them as captives, and brought *them* to
Damascus. Then he was also delivered into the
hand of the king of Israel, who defeated him
with a great slaughter. 6 For [a]Pekah the son
of Remaliah killed one hundred and twenty
thousand in Judah in one day, all valiant men,
[b]because they had forsaken the LORD God of
their fathers. 7 Zichri, a mighty man of Ephraim, killed Maaseiah the king's son, Azrikam
the officer over the house, and Elkanah *who*
was second to the king. 8 And the children of
Israel carried away captive of their [a]brethren
two hundred thousand women, sons, and
daughters; and they also took away much spoil
from them, and brought the spoil to Samaria.

Israel Returns the Captives

9 But a [a]prophet of the LORD was there,
whose name *was* Oded; and he went out before the army that came to Samaria, and
said to them: "Look, [b]because the LORD God
of your fathers was angry with Judah, He
has delivered them into your hand; but you
have killed them in a rage *that* [c]reaches up to
heaven. 10 And now you propose to force the
children of Judah and Jerusalem to be your
[a]male and female slaves; *but are* you not also
guilty before the LORD your God? 11 Now hear
me, therefore, and return the captives, whom
you have taken captive from your brethren,
[a]for the fierce wrath of the LORD *is* upon you."
12 Then some of the heads of the children
of Ephraim, Azariah the son of Johanan,
Berechiah the son of Meshillemoth, Jehiz-
kiah the son of Shallum, and Amasa the son
of Hadlai, stood up against those who came
from the war, 13 and said to them, "You shall
not bring the captives here, for we *already*
have offended the LORD. You intend to add

28:1 [a] 2 Kin. 16:2–4 **28:2** [a] Ex. 34:17 [b] Judg. 2:11 **28:3** [a] Josh. 15:8 [b] 2 Kin. 23:10 [c] [Lev. 18:21] [d] [Lev. 18:24–30] **28:5** [a] [Is. 10:5] [b] Is. 7:1, 17 **28:6** [a] 2 Kin. 15:27 [b] [2 Chr. 29:8] **28:8** [a] Deut. 28:25, 41 **28:9** [a] 2 Chr. 25:15 [b] [Is. 10:5; 47:6] [c] Rev. 18:5 **28:10** [a] [Lev. 25:39, 42, 43, 46] **28:11** [a] James 2:13

BE THE BLESSING OF PEACE

Then the men . . . rose up and took the captives, and from
the spoil they clothed all who were naked.

2 CHRONICLES 28:15

People around the world refer to the "good Samaritan" who renders aid to someone in need. A good Samaritan does this often anonymously and with no expectation of reward—as it is in the parable in Luke 10. It was the man from Samaria who tended the wounded Jewish man lying beside the road, not the priest or Levite who had previously passed by.

The parable had a much earlier precedent found in 2 Chronicles 28. The chapter describes a battle between Judah and Israel in which God had brought defeat on Judah because of its idolatry. But Israel had been overzealous and cruel to its prisoners, so God sent the prophet Oded to rebuke them. Afterward, the Samaritans "took the captives, and . . . clothed all who were naked . . . and anointed them; and they let all the feeble ones ride on donkeys. So they brought them to their brethren at Jericho . . . Then they returned to Samaria" (v. 15).

Nothing generates peace faster than mercy. One of the strongest means of living in the peace of God is to focus on others. Often, when we face anxiety, we fixate on ourselves and exclude others. One of the most dramatic ways you can reset the peace of God in your life is by spreading mercy to others in their time of need. The intensity of our problems starts to diminish when we focus on meeting others' needs, and we mysteriously live more at peace in the Lord.

to our sins and to our guilt; for our guilt is
great, and *there is* fierce wrath against Israel."
14 So the armed men left the captives and the
spoil before the leaders and all the assembly.
15 Then the men [a]who were designated by
name rose up and took the captives, and from
the spoil they clothed all who were naked
among them, dressed them and gave them
sandals, [b]gave them food and drink, and
anointed them; and they let all the feeble
ones ride on donkeys. So they brought them
to their brethren at Jericho, [c]the city of palm
trees. Then they returned to Samaria.

Assyria Refuses to Help Judah

16 [a]At the same time King Ahaz sent to the
kings[1] of Assyria to help him. 17 For again the
[a]Edomites had come, attacked Judah, and
carried away captives. 18 [a]The Philistines also
had invaded the cities of the lowland and
of the South of Judah, and had taken Beth
Shemesh, Aijalon, Gederoth, Sochoh with
its villages, Timnah with its villages, and
Gimzo with its villages; and they dwelt there.
19 For the LORD brought Judah low because
of Ahaz king of [a]Israel, for he had [b]encour-
aged moral decline in Judah and had been
continually unfaithful to the LORD. 20 Also
[a]Tiglath-Pileser[1] king of Assyria came to him
and distressed him, and did not assist him.
21 For Ahaz took part *of the treasures* from the
house of the LORD, from the house of the
king, and from the leaders, and he gave *it* to
the king of Assyria; but he did not help him.

Apostasy and Death of Ahaz

22 Now in the time of his distress King Ahaz
became increasingly unfaithful to the LORD.
This *is that* King Ahaz. 23 For [a]he sacrificed to
the gods of Damascus which had defeated
him, saying, "Because the gods of the kings of
Syria help them, I will sacrifice to them [b]that
they may help me." But they were the ruin
of him and of all Israel. 24 So Ahaz gathered
the articles of the house of God, cut in pieces
the articles of the house of God, [a]shut up the
doors of the house of the LORD, and made for
himself altars in every corner of Jerusalem.
25 And in every single city of Judah he made
high places to burn incense to other gods, and
provoked to anger the LORD God of his fathers.

26 [a]Now the rest of his acts and all his ways,
from first to last, indeed they *are* written in
the book of the kings of Judah and Israel.
27 So Ahaz rested with his fathers, and they
buried him in the city, in Jerusalem; but
they [a]did not bring him into the tombs of
the kings of Israel. Then Hezekiah his son
reigned in his place.

Hezekiah Reigns in Judah

29 Hezekiah [a]became king *when he was*
twenty-five years old, and he reigned
twenty-nine years in Jerusalem. His mother's
name *was* Abijah[1] the daughter of Zechariah. 2 And he did *what was* right in the sight
of the LORD, according to all that his father
David had done.

Hezekiah Cleanses the Temple

3 In the first year of his reign, in the first
month, he [a]opened the doors of the house
of the LORD and repaired them. 4 Then he
brought in the priests and the Levites, and
gathered them in the East Square, 5 and said
to them: "Hear me, Levites! Now sanctify
yourselves, [a]sanctify the house of the LORD
God of your fathers, and carry out the rubbish
from the holy *place*. 6 For our fathers have
trespassed and done evil in the eyes of the
LORD our God; they have forsaken Him, have
[a]turned their faces away from the dwelling
place of the LORD, and turned *their* backs *on*
Him. 7 [a]They have also shut up the doors of
the vestibule, put out the lamps, and have not
burned incense or offered burnt offerings in
the holy *place* to the God of Israel. 8 Therefore
the [a]wrath of the LORD fell upon Judah and
Jerusalem, and He has [b]given them up to
trouble, to desolation, and to [c]jeering, as you
see with your [d]eyes. 9 For indeed, because of
this [a]our fathers have fallen by the sword;
and our sons, our daughters, and our wives
are in captivity.

10 "Now *it is* in my heart to make [a]a covenant with the LORD God of Israel, that His
fierce wrath may turn away from us. 11 My
sons, do not be negligent now, for the LORD
has [a]chosen you to stand before Him, to serve
Him, and that you should minister to Him
and burn incense."

12 Then these Levites arose: [a]Mahath the
son of Amasai and Joel the son of Azariah,
of the sons of the [b]Kohathites; of the sons of
Merari, Kish the son of Abdi and Azariah the
son of Jehallelel; of the Gershonites, Joah the
son of Zimmah and Eden the son of Joah; 13 of
the sons of Elizaphan, Shimri and Jeiel; of the

28:15 [a] 2 Chr. 28:12 [b] [Prov. 25:21, 22] [c] Deut. 34:3 **28:16** [a] 2 Kin. 16:7 [1] Septuagint, Syriac, and Vulgate read *king* (compare verse 20). **28:17** [a] Obad. 10–14 **28:18** [a] Ezek. 16:27, 57 **28:19** [a] 2 Chr. 21:2 [b] Ex. 32:25 **28:20** [a] 1 Chr. 5:26 [1] Hebrew *Tilgath-Pilneser* **28:23** [a] 2 Chr. 25:14 [b] Jer. 44:17, 18 **28:24** [a] 2 Chr. 29:3, 7 **28:26** [a] 2 Kin. 16:19, 20 **28:27** [a] 2 Chr. 21:20; 24:25 **29:1** [a] 2 Kin. 18:1 [1] Spelled *Abi* in 2 Kings 18:2 **29:3** [a] 2 Chr. 28:24; 29:7 **29:5** [a] 2 Chr. 29:15, 34; 35:6 **29:6** [a] Ezek. 8:16 **29:7** [a] 2 Chr. 28:24 **29:8** [a] 2 Chr. 24:18 [b] 2 Chr. 28:5 [c] 1 Kin. 9:8 [d] Deut. 28:32 **29:9** [a] 2 Chr. 28:5–8, 17 **29:10** [a] 2 Chr. 15:12; 23:16 **29:11** [a] Num. 3:6; 8:14; 18:2, 6 **29:12** [a] 2 Chr. 31:13 [b] Num. 3:19, 20

sons of Asaph, Zechariah and Mattaniah; 14 of
the sons of Heman, Jehiel and Shimei; and of
the sons of Jeduthun, Shemaiah and Uzziel.
15 And they gathered their brethren, [a]sanc-
tified themselves, and went according to the
commandment of the king, at the words of
the LORD, [b]to cleanse the house of the LORD.
16 Then the priests went into the inner part
of the house of the LORD to cleanse *it,* and
brought out all the debris that they found in
the temple of the LORD to the court of the
house of the LORD. And the Levites took *it*
out and carried *it* to the Brook [a]Kidron.
17 Now they began to sanctify on the first
day of the first month, and on the eighth day
of the month they came to the vestibule of
the LORD. So they sanctified the house of the
LORD in eight days, and on the sixteenth day
of the first month they finished.
18 Then they went in to King Hezekiah and
said, "We have cleansed all the house of the
LORD, the altar of burnt offerings with all
its articles, and the table of the showbread
with all its articles. 19 Moreover all the articles
which King Ahaz in his reign had [a]cast aside
in his transgression we have prepared and
sanctified; and there they *are,* before the
altar of the LORD."

Hezekiah Restores Temple Worship

20 Then King Hezekiah rose early, gathered
the rulers of the city, and went up to the house
of the LORD. 21 And they brought seven bulls,
seven rams, seven lambs, and seven male
goats for a [a]sin offering for the kingdom,
for the sanctuary, and for Judah. Then he
commanded the priests, the sons of Aaron,
to offer *them* on the altar of the LORD. 22 So
they killed the bulls, and the priests received
the blood and [a]sprinkled *it* on the altar. Likewise they killed the rams and sprinkled the
blood on the altar. They also killed the lambs
and sprinkled the blood on the altar. 23 Then
they brought out the male goats *for* the sin
offering before the king and the assembly,
and they laid their [a]hands on them. 24 And
the priests killed them; and they presented
their blood on the altar as a sin offering [a]to
make an atonement for all Israel, for the king
commanded that the burnt offering and the
sin offering *be made* for all Israel.
25 [a]And he stationed the Levites in the
house of the LORD with cymbals, with
stringed instruments, and with harps, [b]ac-
cording to the commandment of David,
of [c]Gad the king's seer, and of Nathan the
prophet; [d]for thus *was* the commandment
of the LORD by His prophets. 26 The Levites
stood with the instruments [a]of David, and
the priests with [b]the trumpets. 27 Then Hezekiah commanded *them* to offer the burnt
offering on the altar. And when the burnt
offering began, [a]the song of the LORD *also*
began, with the trumpets and with the instruments of David king of Israel. 28 So all the
assembly worshiped, the singers sang, and
the trumpeters sounded; all *this continued*
until the burnt offering was finished. 29 And
when they had finished offering, [a]the king
and all who were present with him bowed and
worshiped. 30 Moreover King Hezekiah and
the leaders commanded the Levites to sing
praise to the LORD with the words of David
and of Asaph the seer. So they sang praises
with gladness, and they bowed their heads
and worshiped.
31 Then Hezekiah answered and said, "Now
that you have consecrated yourselves to the
LORD, come near, and bring sacrifices and
[a]thank offerings into the house of the LORD."
So the assembly brought in sacrifices and
thank offerings, and as many as were of a
[b]willing heart *brought* burnt offerings. 32 And
the number of the burnt offerings which the
assembly brought was seventy bulls, one
hundred rams, *and* two hundred lambs; all
these *were* for a burnt offering to the LORD.
33 The consecrated things *were* six hundred
bulls and three thousand sheep. 34 But the
priests were too few, so that they could not
skin all the burnt offerings; therefore [a]their
brethren the Levites helped them until the
work was ended and until the *other* priests
had sanctified themselves, [b]for the Levites
were [c]more diligent in [d]sanctifying themselves than the priests. 35 Also the burnt
offerings *were* in abundance, with [a]the fat
of the peace offerings and *with* [b]the drink
offerings for *every* burnt offering.
So the service of the house of the LORD
was set in order. 36 Then Hezekiah and all
the people rejoiced that God had prepared
the people, since the events took place so
suddenly.

Hezekiah Keeps the Passover

30 And Hezekiah sent to all Israel and
Judah, and also wrote letters to Ephraim and Manasseh, that they should come
to the house of the LORD at Jerusalem, to
keep the Passover to the LORD God of Israel. 2 For the king and his leaders and all the

29:15 [a] 2 Chr. 29:5 [b] 1 Chr. 23:28 **29:16** [a] 2 Chr. 15:16; 30:14 **29:19** [a] 2 Chr. 28:24 **29:21** [a] Lev. 4:3–14 **29:22** [a] Lev. 8:14, 15, 19, 24 **29:23** [a] Lev. 4:15, 24; 8:14 **29:24** [a] Lev. 14:20 **29:25** [a] 1 Chr. 16:4; 25:6 [b] 2 Chr. 8:14 [c] 2 Sam. 24:11 [d] 2 Chr. 30:12 **29:26** [a] 1 Chr. 23:5 [b] 2 Chr. 5:12 **29:27** [a] 2 Chr. 23:18 **29:29** [a] 2 Chr. 20:18 **29:31** [a] Lev. 7:12 [b] Ex. 35:5, 22 **29:34** [a] 2 Chr. 35:11 [b] 2 Chr. 30:3 [c] Ps. 7:10 [d] 2 Chr. 29:5 **29:35** [a] Lev. 3:15, 16 [b] Num. 15:5–10

assembly in Jerusalem had agreed to keep
the Passover in the second [a]month. 3 For they
could not keep it [a]at the regular time,[1] [b]be-
cause a sufficient number of priests had not
consecrated themselves, nor had the people
gathered together at Jerusalem. 4 And the
matter pleased the king and all the assembly.
5 So they resolved to make a proclamation
throughout all Israel, from Beersheba to Dan,
that they should come to keep the Passover
to the LORD God of Israel at Jerusalem, since
they had not done *it* for a long *time* in the
prescribed manner.
6 Then the [a]runners went throughout all Israel and Judah with the letters from the king
and his leaders, and spoke according to the
command of the king: "Children of Israel, [b]re-
turn to the LORD God of Abraham, Isaac, and
Israel; then He will return to the remnant of
you who have escaped from the hand of [c]the
kings of [d]Assyria. 7 And do not be [a]like your
fathers and your brethren, who trespassed
against the LORD God of their fathers, so that
He [b]gave them up to [c]desolation, as you see.
8 Now do not be [a]stiff-necked, as your fathers
were, but yield yourselves to the LORD; and
enter His sanctuary, which He has sanctified
forever, and serve the LORD your God, [b]that
the fierceness of His wrath may turn away
from you. 9 For if you return to the LORD, your
brethren and your children *will be treated*
with [a]compassion by those who lead them
captive, so that they may come back to this
land; for the LORD your God *is* [b]gracious and
merciful, and will not turn *His* face from you
if you [c]return to Him."
10 So the runners passed from city to city
through the country of Ephraim and Manasseh, as far as Zebulun; but [a]they laughed
at them and mocked them. 11 Nevertheless
[a]some from Asher, Manasseh, and Zebulun
humbled themselves and came to Jerusalem. 12 Also [a]the hand of God was on Judah
to give them singleness of heart to obey the
command of the king and the leaders, [b]at
the word of the LORD.
13 Now many people, a very great assembly,
gathered at Jerusalem to keep the Feast of
[a]Unleavened Bread in the second month.
14 They arose and took away the [a]altars that
were in Jerusalem, and they took away all the
incense altars and cast *them* into the Brook
[b]Kidron. 15 Then they slaughtered the Passover *lambs* on the fourteenth *day* of the second month. The priests and the Levites were
[a]ashamed, and sanctified themselves, and
brought the burnt offerings to the house of
the LORD. 16 They stood in their [a]place according to their custom, according to the Law of
Moses the man of God; the priests sprinkled

30:2 [a] Num. 9:10, 11 **30:3** [a] Ex. 12:6, 18 [b] 2 Chr. 29:17, 34 [1] That is, the first month (compare Leviticus 23:5); literally *at that time* **30:6** [a] Esth. 8:14 [b] [Jer. 4:1] [c] 2 Kin. 15:19, 29 [d] 2 Chr. 28:20 **30:7** [a] Ezek. 20:18 [b] Is. 1:9 [c] 2 Chr. 29:8 **30:8** [a] Ex. 32:9 [b] 2 Chr. 29:10 **30:9** [a] Ps. 106:46 [b] [Ex. 34:6] [c] [Is. 55:7] **30:10** [a] 2 Chr. 36:16 **30:11** [a] 2 Chr. 11:16; 30:18, 21 **30:12** [a] [Phil. 2:13] [b] 2 Chr. 29:25 **30:13** [a] Lev. 23:6 **30:14** [a] 2 Chr. 28:24 [b] 2 Chr. 29:16 **30:15** [a] 2 Chr. 29:34 **30:16** [a] 2 Chr. 35:10, 15

CLEANING HOUSE

May the good LORD provide atonement for everyone who prepares his heart to seek God.

2 CHRONICLES 30:18-19

When faced with threats, we often retreat and retrench. That is understandable. King Hezekiah found himself in that predicament. He inherited a political mess from his father, King Ahaz, whose dubious political alliances threatened his son's rule. An aggressive Assyria had crushed Syria and was threatening Israel's northern kingdom.

In the midst of all this negativity, Hezekiah purified the temple and then made preparation for a great celebration of Passover. This was no ordinary celebration. Hezekiah sent invitations to the tribes of Israel in the north, bidding them to come to Jerusalem and take part in the festival. Commentators see in Hezekiah's action the hope of the future reunification of the divided kingdoms of Israel and Judah. The celebration was a huge success, leading to further purification of the land.

Developing a life of peace requires cleaning house, as it were. We can't expect to enjoy God's peace when our lives are cluttered with sinful baggage and habits that distract us from living in the will of God. If you feel static instead of peace, maybe it's time to do some spring cleaning.

the blood *received* from the hand of the Levites. 17 For *there were* many in the assembly who had not sanctified themselves; [a]therefore the Levites had charge of the slaughter of the Passover *lambs* for everyone *who was* not clean, to sanctify *them* to the LORD. 18 For a multitude of the people, [a]many from Ephraim, Manasseh, Issachar, and Zebulun, had not cleansed themselves, [b]yet they ate the Passover contrary to what was written. But Hezekiah prayed for them, saying, "May the good LORD provide atonement for everyone 19 *who* [a]prepares his heart to seek God, the LORD God of his fathers, though *he is* not *cleansed* according to the purification of the sanctuary." 20 And the LORD listened to Hezekiah and healed the people.

21 So the children of Israel who were present at Jerusalem kept [a]the Feast of Unleavened Bread seven days with great gladness; and the Levites and the priests praised the LORD day by day, *singing* to the LORD, accompanied by loud instruments. 22 And Hezekiah gave encouragement to all the Levites [a]who taught the good knowledge of the LORD; and they ate throughout the feast seven days, offering peace offerings and [b]making confession to the LORD God of their fathers.

23 Then the whole assembly agreed to keep *the feast* [a]another seven days, and they kept it *another* seven days with gladness. 24 For Hezekiah king of Judah [a]gave to the assembly a thousand bulls and seven thousand sheep, and the leaders gave to the assembly a thousand bulls and ten thousand sheep; and a great number of priests [b]sanctified themselves. 25 The whole assembly of Judah rejoiced, also the priests and Levites, all the assembly that came from Israel, the sojourners [a]who came from the land of Israel, and those who dwelt in Judah. 26 So there was great joy in Jerusalem, for since the time of [a]Solomon the son of David, king of Israel, *there had* been nothing like this in Jerusalem. 27 Then the priests, the Levites, arose and [a]blessed the people, and their voice was heard; and their prayer came *up* to [b]His holy dwelling place, to heaven.

The Reforms of Hezekiah

31 Now when all this was finished, all Israel who were present went out to the cities of Judah and [a]broke the *sacred* pillars in pieces, cut down the wooden images, and threw down the high places and the altars—from all Judah, Benjamin, Ephraim, and Manasseh—until they had utterly destroyed them all. Then all the children of Israel returned to their own cities, every man to his possession.

2 And Hezekiah appointed [a]the divisions of the priests and the Levites according to their divisions, each man according to his service, the priests and Levites [b]for burnt offerings and peace offerings, to serve, to give thanks, and to praise in the gates of the camp[1] of the LORD. 3 The king also *appointed* a portion of his [a]possessions for the burnt offerings: for the morning and evening burnt offerings, the burnt offerings for the Sabbaths and the New Moons and the set feasts, as *it is* written in the [b]Law of the LORD.

4 Moreover he commanded the people who dwelt in Jerusalem to contribute [a]support for the priests and the Levites, that they might devote themselves to [b]the Law of the LORD.

5 As soon as the commandment was circulated, the children of Israel brought in abundance [a]the firstfruits of grain and wine, oil and honey, and of all the produce of the field; and they brought in abundantly the [b]tithe of everything. 6 And the children of Israel and Judah, who dwelt in the cities of Judah, brought the tithe of oxen and sheep; also the [a]tithe of holy things which were consecrated to the LORD their God they laid in heaps.

7 In the third month they began laying them in heaps, and they finished in the seventh month. 8 And when Hezekiah and the leaders came and saw the heaps, they blessed the LORD and His people Israel. 9 Then Hezekiah questioned the priests and the Levites concerning the heaps. 10 And Azariah the chief priest, from the [a]house of Zadok, answered him and said, [b]"Since *the people* began to bring the offerings into the house of the LORD, we have had enough to eat and have plenty left, for the LORD has blessed His people; and what is left *is* this great [c]abundance."

11 Now Hezekiah commanded *them* to prepare [a]rooms in the house of the LORD, and they prepared them. 12 Then they faithfully brought in the offerings, the tithes, and the dedicated things; [a]Cononiah the Levite had charge of them, and Shimei his brother *was* the next. 13 Jehiel, Azaziah, Nahath, Asahel, Jerimoth, Jozabad, Eliel, Ismachiah, Mahath, and Benaiah *were* overseers under the hand of Cononiah and Shimei his brother, at the commandment of Hezekiah the king and Azariah the [a]ruler of the house of God. 14 Kore

30:17 [a] 2 Chr. 29:34 **30:18** [a] 2 Chr. 30:1, 11, 25 [b] [Num. 9:10] **30:19** [a] 2 Chr. 19:3 **30:21** [a] Ex. 12:15; 13:6 **30:22** [a] 2 Chr. 17:9; 35:3 [b] Ezra 10:11 **30:23** [a] 1 Kin. 8:65 **30:24** [a] 2 Chr. 35:7, 8 [b] 2 Chr. 29:34 **30:25** [a] 2 Chr. 30:11, 18 **30:26** [a] 2 Chr. 7:8–10 **30:27** [a] Num. 6:23 [b] Deut. 26:15 **31:1** [a] 2 Kin. 18:4 **31:2** [a] 1 Chr. 23:6; 24:1 [b] 1 Chr. 23:30, 31 [1] That is, the temple **31:3** [a] 2 Chr. 35:7 [b] Num. 28:1—29:40 **31:4** [a] Num. 18:8 [b] Mal. 2:7 **31:5** [a] Ex. 22:29 [b] [Lev. 27:30] **31:6** [a] Deut. 14:28 **31:10** [a] 1 Chr. 6:8, 9 [b] [Mal. 3:10] [c] Ex. 36:5 **31:11** [a] 1 Kin. 6:5–8 **31:12** [a] 2 Chr. 35:9 **31:13** [a] Jer. 20:1

the son of Imnah the Levite, the keeper of the
East Gate, *was* over the [a]freewill offerings to
God, to distribute the offerings of the LORD
and the most holy things. 15 And under him
were [a]Eden, Miniamin, Jeshua, Shemaiah,
Amariah, and Shecaniah, *his* faithful assis-
tants in [b]the cities of the priests, to distribute
[c]allotments to their brethren by divisions, to
the great as well as the small.

16 Besides those males from three years old
and up who were written in the genealogy,
they distributed to everyone who entered the
house of the LORD his daily portion for the
work of his service, by his division, 17 and to
the priests who were written in the genealogy
according to their father's house, and to the
Levites [a]from twenty years old and up according to their work, by their divisions, 18 and to
all who were written in the genealogy—their
little ones and their wives, their sons and
daughters, the whole company of them—for
in their faithfulness they sanctified themselves in holiness.

19 Also for the sons of Aaron the priests,
who were in [a]the fields of the common-lands
of their cities, in every single city, *there were*
men who were [b]designated by name to distribute portions to all the males among the
priests and to all who were listed by genealogies among the Levites.

20 Thus Hezekiah did throughout all Judah,
and he [a]did what *was* good and right and true
before the LORD his God. 21 And in every work
that he began in the service of the house of
God, in the law and in the commandment,
to seek his God, he did *it* with all his heart.
So he [a]prospered.

PEACE NOTE

Am I missing peace because
I've missed Jesus? Many
"religious" people miss Jesus.

Sennacherib Boasts Against the LORD

32 After [a]these deeds of faithfulness, Sennacherib king of Assyria came and
entered Judah; he encamped against the
fortified cities, thinking to win them over to
himself. 2 And when Hezekiah saw that Sennacherib had come, and that his purpose was
to make war against Jerusalem, 3 he consulted
with his leaders and commanders[1] to stop the
water from the springs which *were* outside
the city; and they helped him. 4 Thus many
people gathered together who stopped all the
[a]springs and the brook that ran through the
land, saying, "Why should the kings[1] of Assyria come and find much water?" 5 And [a]he
strengthened himself, [b]built up all the wall
that was broken, raised *it* up to the towers, and
built another wall outside; also he repaired the
[c]Millo[1] *in* the City of David, and made weapons and shields in abundance. 6 Then he set
military captains over the people, gathered
them together to him in the open square of
the city gate, and [a]gave them encouragement,
saying, 7 [a]"Be strong and courageous; [b]do not
be afraid nor dismayed before the king of Assyria, nor before all the multitude that *is* with
him; for [c]*there are* more with us than with him.
8 With him *is* an [a]arm of flesh; but [b]with us *is*
the LORD our God, to help us and to fight our
battles." And the people were strengthened by
the words of Hezekiah king of Judah.

9 [a]After this Sennacherib king of Assyria
sent his servants to Jerusalem (but he and all
the forces with him *laid siege* against Lachish),
to Hezekiah king of Judah, and to all Judah
who *were* in Jerusalem, saying, 10 [a]"Thus says
Sennacherib king of Assyria: 'In what do you
trust, that you remain under siege in Jerusalem? 11 Does not Hezekiah persuade you to
give yourselves over to die by famine and by
thirst, saying, [a]"The LORD our God will deliver
us from the hand of the king of Assyria"? 12 [a]Has
not the same Hezekiah taken away His high
places and His altars, and commanded Judah
and Jerusalem, saying, "You shall worship
before one altar and burn incense on [b]it"? 13 Do
you not know what I and my fathers have done
to all the peoples of *other* lands? [a]Were the gods
of the nations of those lands in any way able
to deliver their lands out of my hand? 14 Who
was there among all the gods of those nations

31:14 [a] Deut. 23:23 31:15 [a] 2 Chr. 29:12 [b] Josh. 21:1–3, 9 [c] 1 Chr. 9:26 31:17 [a] 1 Chr. 23:24, 27 31:19 [a] Lev. 25:34
[b] 2 Chr. 31:12–15 31:20 [a] 2 Kin. 20:3; 22:2 31:21 [a] Ps. 1:3 32:1 [a] 2 Kin. 18:13—19:37 32:3 [1] Literally *mighty men*
32:4 [a] 2 Kin. 20:20 [1] Following Masoretic Text and Vulgate; Arabic, Septuagint, and Syriac read *king*. 32:5 [a] Is. 22:9, 10
[b] 2 Chr. 25:23 [c] 2 Sam. 5:9 [1] Literally *The Landfill* 32:6 [a] 2 Chr. 30:22 32:7 [a] [Deut. 31:6] [b] 2 Chr. 20:15 [c] 2 Kin. 6:16
32:8 [a] [Jer. 17:5] [b] [Rom. 8:31] 32:9 [a] 2 Kin. 18:17 32:10 [a] 2 Kin. 18:19 32:11 [a] 2 Kin. 18:30 32:12 [a] 2 Kin. 18:22
[b] 2 Chr. 31:1, 2 32:13 [a] 2 Kin. 18:33–35

that my fathers utterly destroyed that could deliver his people from my hand, that your God should be able to deliver you from my [a]hand? 15 Now therefore, [a]do not let Hezekiah deceive you or persuade you like this, and do not believe him; for no god of any nation or kingdom was able to deliver his people from my hand or the hand of my fathers. How much less will your God deliver you from my hand?'"

16 Furthermore, his servants spoke against the LORD God and against His servant Hezekiah.

17 He also wrote letters to revile the LORD God of Israel, and to speak against Him, saying, [a]"As the gods of the nations of *other* lands have not delivered their people from my hand, so the God of Hezekiah will not deliver His people from my [b]hand." 18 [a]Then they called out with a loud voice in Hebrew[1] to the people of Jerusalem who *were* on the wall, to frighten them and trouble them, that they might take the city. 19 And they spoke against the God of Jerusalem, as against the gods of the people of the earth—[a]the work of men's hands.

Sennacherib's Defeat and Death

20 [a]Now because of this King Hezekiah and [b]the prophet Isaiah, the son of Amoz, prayed and cried out to heaven. 21 [a]Then the LORD sent an angel who cut down every mighty man of valor, leader, and captain in the camp of the king of Assyria. So he returned [b]shamefaced to his own land. And when he had gone into the temple of his god, some of his own offspring struck him down with the sword there.

22 Thus the LORD saved Hezekiah and the inhabitants of Jerusalem from the hand of Sennacherib the king of Assyria, and from the hand of all *others,* and guided them[1] on every side. 23 And many brought gifts to the LORD at Jerusalem, and [a]presents to Hezekiah king of Judah, so that he was [b]exalted in the sight of all nations thereafter.

Hezekiah Humbles Himself

24 [a]In those days Hezekiah was sick and near death, and he prayed to the LORD; and He spoke to him and gave him a sign. 25 But Hezekiah [a]did not repay according to the favor *shown* him, for [b]his heart was lifted up; [c]therefore wrath was looming over him and over Judah and Jerusalem. 26 [a]Then Hezekiah humbled himself for the pride of his heart, he and the inhabitants of Jerusalem, so that the wrath of the LORD did not come upon them [b]in the days of Hezekiah.

Hezekiah's Wealth and Honor

27 Hezekiah had very great riches and honor. And he made himself treasuries for silver, for gold, for precious stones, for spices, for shields, and for all kinds of desirable items; 28 storehouses for the harvest of grain, wine, and oil; and stalls for all kinds of livestock, and folds for flocks.[1] 29 Moreover he provided cities for himself, and possessions of flocks and herds in abundance; for [a]God had given him very much property. 30 [a]This same Hezekiah also stopped the water outlet of Upper Gihon, and brought the water by tunnel[1] to the west side of the City of David. Hezekiah [b]prospered in all his works.

31 However, *regarding* the ambassadors of the princes of Babylon, whom they [a]sent to him to inquire about the wonder that was *done* in the land, God withdrew from him, in order to [b]test him, that He might know all *that was* in his heart.

Death of Hezekiah

32 Now the rest of the acts of Hezekiah, and his goodness, indeed they *are* written in [a]the vision of Isaiah the prophet, the son of Amoz, *and* in the [b]book of the kings of Judah and Israel. 33 [a]So Hezekiah rested with his fathers, and they buried him in the upper tombs of the sons of David; and all Judah and the inhabitants of Jerusalem [b]honored him at his death. Then Manasseh his son reigned in his place.

Manasseh Reigns in Judah

33 Manasseh [a]*was* twelve years old when he became king, and he reigned fifty-five years in Jerusalem. 2 But he did evil in the sight of the LORD, according to the [a]abominations of the nations whom the LORD had cast out before the children of Israel. 3 For he rebuilt the high places which Hezekiah his father had [a]broken down; he raised up altars for the Baals, and [b]made wooden images; and he worshiped [c]all the host of heaven[1] and served them. 4 He also built altars in the house of the LORD, of which the LORD had said, [a]"In Jerusalem shall My name be

32:14 [a] [Is. 10:5–12] **32:15** [a] 2 Kin. 18:29 **32:17** [a] 2 Kin. 19:9 **32:17** [b] 2 Kin. 19:12 **32:18** [a] 2 Kin. 18:28 [1] Literally *Judean* **32:19** [a] [Ps. 96:5; 115:4–8] **32:20** [a] 2 Kin. 19:15 [b] 2 Kin. 19:2 **32:21** [a] Zech. 14:3 [b] Ps. 44:7 **32:22** [1] Septuagint reads *gave them rest;* Vulgate reads *gave them treasures.* **32:23** [a] 2 Sam. 8:10 [b] 2 Chr. 1:1 **32:24** [a] Is. 38:1–8 **32:25** [a] Ps. 116:12 [b] [Hab. 2:4] [c] 2 Chr. 24:18 **32:26** [a] Jer. 26:18, 19 [b] 2 Kin. 20:19 **32:28** [1] Following Septuagint and Vulgate; Arabic and Syriac omit *folds for flocks;* Masoretic Text reads *flocks for sheepfolds.* **32:29** [a] 1 Chr. 29:12 **32:30** [a] Is. 22:9–11 [b] 2 Chr. 31:21 [1] Literally *brought it straight* (compare 2 Kings 20:20) **32:31** [a] Is. 39:1 [b] [Deut. 8:2, 16] **32:32** [a] Is. 36—39 [b] 2 Kin. 18—20 **32:33** [a] 2 Kin. 20:21 [b] Prov. 10:7 **33:1** [a] 2 Kin. 21:1–9 **33:2** [a] 2 Chr. 28:3 **33:3** [a] 2 Kin. 18:4 [b] Deut. 16:21 [c] Deut. 17:3 [1] The gods of the Assyrians **33:4** [a] 2 Chr. 6:6; 7:16

forever." 5 And he built altars for all the host
of heaven [a]in the two courts of the house of
the LORD. 6 [a]Also he caused his sons to pass
through the fire in the Valley of the Son of
Hinnom; he practiced [b]soothsaying, used
witchcraft and sorcery, and [c]consulted mediums and spiritists. He did much evil in the
sight of the LORD, to provoke Him to anger.
7 [a]He even set a carved image, the idol which
he had made, in the house of God, of which
God had said to David and to Solomon his
son, [b]"In this house and in Jerusalem, which
I have chosen out of all the tribes of Israel,
I will put My name forever; 8 [a]and I will not
again remove the foot of Israel from the land
which I have appointed for your fathers—
only if they are careful to do all that I have
commanded them, according to the whole
law and the statutes and the ordinances by
the hand of Moses." 9 So Manasseh seduced
Judah and the inhabitants of Jerusalem to do
more evil than the nations whom the LORD
had destroyed before the children of Israel.

Manasseh Restored After Repentance

10 And the LORD spoke to Manasseh and his
people, but they would not listen. 11 [a]Therefore
the LORD brought upon them the captains of
the army of the king of Assyria, who took Manasseh with hooks,[1] [b]bound him with bronze
fetters, and carried him off to Babylon. 12 Now
when he was in affliction, he implored the
LORD his God, and [a]humbled himself greatly
before the God of his fathers, 13 and prayed
to Him; and He [a]received his entreaty, heard
his supplication, and brought him back to
Jerusalem into his kingdom. Then Manasseh
[b]knew that the LORD *was* God.

14 After this he built a wall outside the City
of David on the west side of [a]Gihon, in the
valley, as far as the entrance of the Fish Gate;
and *it* [b]enclosed Ophel, and he raised it to a
very great height. Then he put military captains in all the fortified cities of Judah. 15 He
took away [a]the foreign gods and the idol from
the house of the LORD, and all the altars that
he had built in the mount of the house of the
LORD and in Jerusalem; and he cast *them* out
of the city. 16 He also repaired the altar of the
LORD, sacrificed peace offerings and [a]thank
offerings on it, and commanded Judah to
serve the LORD God of Israel. 17 [a]Nevertheless
the people still sacrificed on the high places,
but only to the LORD their God.

Death of Manasseh

18 Now the rest of the acts of Manasseh, his
prayer to his God, and the words of [a]the seers
who spoke to him in the name of the LORD
God of Israel, indeed they *are written* in the
book[1] of the kings of Israel. 19 Also his prayer
and *how God* received his entreaty, and all
his sin and trespass, and the sites where he
built high places and set up wooden images
and carved images, before he was humbled,
indeed they *are* written among the sayings
of Hozai.[1] 20 [a]So Manasseh rested with his fathers, and they buried him in his own house.
Then his son Amon reigned in his place.

Amon's Reign and Death

21 [a]Amon *was* twenty-two years old when
he became king, and he reigned two years in
Jerusalem. 22 But he did evil in the sight of
the LORD, as his father Manasseh had done;
for Amon sacrificed to all the carved images
which his father Manasseh had made, and
served them. 23 And he did not humble himself before the LORD, [a]as his father Manasseh
had humbled himself; but Amon trespassed
more and more.

24 [a]Then his servants conspired against
him, and [b]killed him in his own house. 25 But
the people of the land executed all those who
had conspired against King Amon. Then the
people of the land made his son Josiah king
in his place.

Josiah Reigns in Judah

34 Josiah [a]*was* eight years old when he
became king, and he reigned thirty-
one years in Jerusalem. 2 And he did *what was*
right in the sight of the LORD, and walked in
the ways of his father David; *he* did *not* turn
aside to the right hand or to the left.

3 For in the eighth year of his reign, while
he was still [a]young, he began to [b]seek the God
of his father David; and in the twelfth year he
began [c]to purge Judah and Jerusalem [d]of the
high places, the wooden images, the carved
images, and the molded images. 4 [a]They broke
down the altars of the Baals in his presence,
and the incense altars which *were* above
them he cut down; and the wooden images,
the carved images, and the molded images
he broke in pieces, and made dust of them
[b]and scattered *it* on the graves of those who
had sacrificed to them. 5 He also [a]burned
the bones of the priests on their [b]altars, and

33:5 [a] 2 Chr. 4:9 **33:6** [a] [Lev. 18:21] [b] Deut. 18:11 [c] 2 Kin. 21:6 **33:7** [a] 2 Chr. 25:14 [b] Ps. 132:14 **33:8** [a] 2 Sam. 7:10 **33:11** [a] Deut. 28:36 [b] 2 Chr. 36:6 [1] That is, nose hooks (compare 2 Kings 19:28) **33:12** [a] 2 Chr. 7:14; 32:26 **33:13** [a] Ezra 8:23 [b] Dan. 4:25 **33:14** [a] 1 Kin. 1:33 [b] 2 Chr. 27:3 **33:15** [a] 2 Chr. 33:3, 5, 7 **33:16** [a] Lev. 7:12 **33:17** [a] 2 Chr. 32:12 **33:18** [a] 1 Sam. 9:9 [1] Literally *words* **33:19** [1] Septuagint reads *the seers.* **33:20** [a] 2 Kin. 21:18 **33:21** [a] 2 Kin. 21:19–24 **33:23** [a] 2 Chr. 33:12, 19 **33:24** [a] 2 Chr. 24:25 [b] 2 Chr. 25:27 **34:1** [a] 2 Kin. 22:1, 2 **34:3** [a] Eccl. 12:1 [b] 2 Chr. 15:2 [c] 1 Kin. 13:2 [d] 2 Chr. 33:17–19, 22 **34:4** [a] Lev. 26:30 [b] 2 Kin. 23:6 **34:5** [a] 1 Kin. 13:2 [b] 2 Kin. 23:20

cleansed Judah and Jerusalem. 6 And *so he did* in the cities of Manasseh, Ephraim, and Simeon, as far as Naphtali and all around, with axes.[1] 7 When he had broken down the altars and the wooden images, had [a]beaten the carved images into powder, and cut down all the incense altars throughout all the land of Israel, he returned to Jerusalem.

Hilkiah Finds the Book of the Law

8 [a]In the eighteenth year of his reign, when he had purged the land and the temple,[1] he sent [b]Shaphan the son of Azaliah, Maaseiah the [c]governor of the city, and Joah the son of Joahaz the recorder, to repair the house of the LORD his God. 9 When they came to Hilkiah the high priest, they delivered [a]the money that was brought into the house of God, which the Levites who kept the doors had gathered from the hand of Manasseh and Ephraim, from all the [b]remnant of Israel, from all Judah and Benjamin, and *which* they had brought back to Jerusalem. 10 Then they put *it* in the hand of the foremen who had the oversight of the house of the LORD; and they gave it to the workmen who worked in the house of the LORD, to repair and restore the house. 11 They gave *it* to the craftsmen and builders to buy hewn stone and timber for beams, and to floor the houses which the kings of Judah had destroyed. 12 And the men did the work faithfully. Their overseers *were* Jahath and Obadiah the Levites, of the sons of Merari, and Zechariah and Meshullam, of the sons of the Kohathites, to supervise. *Others of* the Levites, all of whom were skillful with instruments of music, 13 *were* [a]over the burden bearers and *were* overseers of all who did work in any kind of service. [b]And *some* of the Levites *were* scribes, officers, and gatekeepers.

14 Now when they brought out the money that was brought into the house of the LORD, Hilkiah the priest [a]found the Book of the Law of the LORD *given* by Moses. 15 Then Hilkiah answered and said to Shaphan the scribe, "I have found the Book of the Law in the house of the LORD." And Hilkiah gave the [a]book to Shaphan. 16 So Shaphan carried the book to the king, bringing the king word, saying, "All *that was committed to your servants* they are doing. 17 And they have gathered the money that was found in the house of the LORD, and have delivered it into the hand of the overseers and the workmen." 18 Then Shaphan the scribe told the king, saying, "Hilkiah the priest has given me a book." And Shaphan read it before the king.

19 Thus it happened, when the king heard the words of the Law, that he tore his clothes. 20 Then the king commanded Hilkiah, [a]Ahikam the son of Shaphan, Abdon[1] the son of Micah, Shaphan the scribe, and Asaiah a servant of the king, saying, 21 "Go, inquire of the LORD for me, and for those who are left in Israel and Judah, concerning the words of the book that is found; for great *is* the wrath of the LORD that is poured out on us, because our fathers have not [a]kept the word of the LORD, to do according to all that is written in this book."

22 So Hilkiah and those the king *had appointed* went to Huldah the prophetess, the wife of Shallum the son of Tokhath,[1] the son of Hasrah,[2] keeper of the wardrobe. (She dwelt in Jerusalem in the Second Quarter.) And they spoke to her to that *effect.*

23 Then she answered them, "Thus says the LORD God of Israel, 'Tell the man who sent you to Me, 24 "Thus says the LORD: 'Behold, I will [a]bring calamity on this place and on its inhabitants, all the curses that are written in the [b]book which they have read before the king of Judah, 25 because they have forsaken Me and burned incense to other gods, that they might provoke Me to anger with all the works of their hands. Therefore My wrath will be poured out on this place, and not be quenched.' " ' 26 But as for the king of Judah, who sent you to inquire of the LORD, in this manner you shall speak to him, 'Thus says the LORD God of Israel: "*Concerning* the words which you have heard— 27 because your heart was tender, and you humbled yourself before God when you heard His words against this place and against its inhabitants, and you humbled yourself before Me, and you tore your clothes and wept before Me, I also have heard *you,*" says the [a]LORD. 28 "Surely I will gather you to your fathers, and you shall be gathered to your grave in peace; and your eyes shall not see all the calamity which I will bring on this place and its inhabitants." ' " So they brought back word to the king.

Josiah Restores True Worship

29 [a]Then the king sent and gathered all the elders of Judah and Jerusalem. 30 The king went up to the house of the LORD, with all the men of Judah and the inhabitants of Jerusalem—the priests and the Levites, and all the people, great and small. And he [a]read in their hearing all the words of the Book of the

34:6 [1] Literally *swords* **34:7** [a] Deut. 9:21 **34:8** [a] 2 Kin. 22:3–20 [b] 2 Kin. 25:22 [c] 2 Chr. 18:25 [1] Literally *house* **34:9** [a] 2 Kin. 12:4 [b] 2 Chr. 30:6 **34:13** [a] 2 Chr. 8:10 [b] 1 Chr. 23:4, 5 **34:14** [a] 2 Kin. 22:8 **34:15** [a] Deut. 31:24, 26 **34:20** [a] Jer. 26:24 [1] *Achbor the son of Michaiah* in 2 Kings 22:12 **34:21** [a] 2 Kin. 17:15–19 **34:22** [1] Spelled *Tikvah* in 2 Kings 22:14 [2] Spelled *Harhas* in 2 Kings 22:14 **34:24** [a] 2 Chr. 36:14–20 [b] Deut. 28:15–68 **34:27** [a] 2 Chr. 12:7; 30:6; 33:12, 13 **34:29** [a] 2 Kin. 23:1–3 **34:30** [a] Neh. 8:1–3

Covenant which had been found in the house
of the LORD. 31 Then the king [a]stood in [b]his
place and made a [c]covenant before the LORD,
to follow the LORD, and to keep His commandments and His testimonies and His statutes
with all his heart and all his soul, to perform
the words of the covenant that were written in
this book. 32 And he made all who were present
in Jerusalem and Benjamin take a stand. So
the inhabitants of Jerusalem did according to
the covenant of God, the God of their fathers.
33 Thus Josiah removed all the [a]abominations
from all the country that *belonged* to the children of Israel, and made all who were present
in Israel diligently serve the LORD their God.
[b]All his days they did not depart from following
the LORD God of their fathers.

Josiah Keeps the Passover

35 Now [a]Josiah kept a Passover to the
LORD in Jerusalem, and they slaughtered the Passover *lambs* on the [b]fourteenth
day of the first month. 2 And he set the priests
in their [a]duties and [b]encouraged them for
the service of the house of the LORD. 3 Then
he said to the Levites [a]who taught all Israel,
who were holy to the LORD: [b]"Put the holy
ark [c]in the house which Solomon the son of
David, king of Israel, built. [d]*It shall* no longer
be a burden on *your* shoulders. Now serve
the LORD your God and His people Israel.
4 Prepare *yourselves* [a]according to your fathers' houses, according to your divisions,
following the [b]written instruction of David
king of Israel and the [c]written instruction
of Solomon his son. 5 And [a]stand in the holy
place according to the divisions of the fathers'
houses of your brethren the *lay* people, and
according to the division of the father's house
of the Levites. 6 So slaughter the Passover
offerings, [a]consecrate yourselves, and prepare *them* for your brethren, that *they* may
do according to the word of the LORD by the
hand of Moses."
7 Then Josiah [a]gave the *lay* people lambs
and young goats from the flock, all for Passover *offerings* for all who were present, to
the number of thirty thousand, as well as
three thousand cattle; these *were* from the
king's [b]possessions. 8 And his [a]leaders gave
willingly to the people, to the priests, and to
the Levites. Hilkiah, Zechariah, and Jehiel,
rulers of the house of God, gave to the priests
for the Passover *offerings* two thousand six
hundred *from the flock,* and three hundred
cattle. 9 Also [a]Conaniah, his brothers Shemaiah and Nethanel, and Hashabiah and Jeiel
and Jozabad, chief of the Levites, gave to the
Levites for Passover *offerings* five thousand
from the flock and five hundred cattle.
10 So the service was prepared, and the
priests [a]stood in their places, and the [b]Levites

34:31 [a] 2 Chr. 6:13 [b] 2 Kin. 11:14; 23:3 [c] 2 Chr. 23:16; 29:10 **34:33** [a] 1 Kin. 11:5 [b] Jer. 3:10 **35:1** [a] 2 Kin. 23:21, 22 [b] Ex. 12:6 **35:2** [a] 2 Chr. 23:18 [b] 2 Chr. 29:5–15 **35:3** [a] Deut. 33:10 [b] 2 Chr. 34:14 [c] 2 Chr. 5:7 [d] 1 Chr. 23:26 **35:4** [a] 1 Chr. 9:10–13 [b] 1 Chr. 23—26 [c] 2 Chr. 8:14 **35:5** [a] Ps. 134:1 **35:6** [a] 2 Chr. 29:5, 15 **35:7** [a] 2 Chr. 30:24 [b] 2 Chr. 31:3 **35:8** [a] Num. 7:2 **35:9** [a] 2 Chr. 31:12 **35:10** [a] Ezra 6:18 [b] 2 Chr. 5:12; 7:6; 8:14, 15; 13:10; 29:25–34

NO MATTER THE COST

Then Josiah gave the lay people lambs and young goats from the flock, all for Passover offerings . . . to the number of thirty thousand.

2 CHRONICLES 35:7

King Josiah kept the Passover in Jerusalem in a big way. What made this Passover celebration so special was that Josiah made generous provision for the common people, many of whom we should assume would not have been able to present lambs for sacrifice. This Passover was the last great spiritual moment in the history of Israel's kingdom. Soon after, Josiah was killed and Egypt began to exert political and military pressure on God's people. Israel's power dwindled, and eventually Jerusalem itself was snuffed out by the Babylonians (ch. 36).

Josiah showed himself to be a righteous man, and God was able to bless one more generation of His people before their tragic destruction and captivity. The king played the role of a *shepherd protecting* his flock. Sometimes promoting peace has a high cost. Josiah promoted peace by offering lambs to all the people to help them live lives that were at peace with God. We should follow Josiah's righteous example and bring peace, no matter the cost, to our loved ones and community.

in their divisions, according to the king's command. 11 And they slaughtered the Passover
offerings; and the priests [a]sprinkled *the blood*
with their hands, while the Levites [b]skinned
the animals. 12 Then they removed the burnt
offerings that *they* might give them to the divisions of the fathers' houses of the *lay* people,
to offer to the LORD, as *it is* written [a]in the Book
of Moses. And so *they did* with the cattle. 13 Also
they [a]roasted the Passover *offerings* with fire
according to the ordinance; but the *other* holy
offerings they [b]boiled in pots, in caldrons, and
in pans, and divided *them* quickly among all
the *lay* people. 14 Then afterward they prepared
portions for themselves and for the priests,
because the priests, the sons of Aaron, *were*
busy in offering burnt offerings and fat until
night; therefore the Levites prepared portions
for themselves and for the priests, the sons of
Aaron. 15 And the singers, the sons of Asaph,
were in their places, according to the [a]com-
mand of David, Asaph, Heman, and Jeduthun
the king's seer. Also the gatekeepers [b]were
at each gate; they did not have to leave their
position, because their brethren the Levites
prepared portions for them.

16 So all the service of the LORD was prepared the same day, to keep the Passover and
to offer burnt offerings on the altar of the
LORD, according to the command of King
Josiah. 17 And the children of Israel who were
present kept the Passover at that time, and
the Feast of [a]Unleavened Bread for seven
days. 18 [a]There had been no Passover kept in
Israel like that since the days of Samuel the
prophet; and none of the kings of Israel had
kept such a Passover as Josiah kept, with the
priests and the Levites, all Judah and Israel
who were present, and the inhabitants of
Jerusalem. 19 In the eighteenth year of the
reign of Josiah this Passover was kept.

Josiah Dies in Battle

20 [a]After all this, when Josiah had prepared
the temple, Necho king of Egypt came up to
fight against [b]Carchemish by the Euphrates;
and Josiah went out against him. 21 But he
sent messengers to him, saying, "What have I
to do with you, king of Judah? *I have* not *come*
against you *this* day, but against the house
with which I have war; for God commanded
me to make haste. Refrain *from meddling with*
God, who *is* with me, lest He destroy you."
22 Nevertheless Josiah would not turn his face
from him, but [a]disguised himself so that he
might fight with him, and did not heed the
words of Necho from the mouth of God. So
he came to fight in the Valley of Megiddo.
23 And the archers shot King Josiah; and
the king said to his servants, "Take me away,
for I am severely wounded." 24 [a]His servants
therefore took him out of that chariot and
put him in the second chariot that he had,
and they brought him to Jerusalem. So he
died, and was buried in *one of* the tombs of
his fathers. And [b]all Judah and Jerusalem
mourned for Josiah.

25 Jeremiah also [a]lamented for [b]Josiah.
And to this day [c]all the singing men and the
singing women speak of Josiah in their lamentations. [d]They made it a custom in Israel;
and indeed they *are* written in the Laments.
26 Now the rest of the acts of Josiah and his
goodness, according to *what was* written in
the Law of the LORD, 27 and his deeds from
first to last, indeed they *are* written in the
book of the kings of Israel and Judah.

The Reign and Captivity of Jehoahaz

36 Then [a]the people of the land took
Jehoahaz the son of Josiah, and
made him king in his father's place in Jerusalem. 2 Jehoahaz[1] *was* twenty-three years
old when he became king, and he reigned
three months in Jerusalem. 3 Now the king
of Egypt deposed him at Jerusalem; and he
imposed on the land a tribute of one hundred
talents of silver and a talent of gold. 4 Then
the king of Egypt made *Jehoahaz's*[1] brother
Eliakim king over Judah and Jerusalem, and
changed his name to Jehoiakim. And Necho
took Jehoahaz[2] his brother and carried him
off to Egypt.

The Reign and Captivity of Jehoiakim

5 [a]Jehoiakim *was* twenty-five years old
when he became king, and he reigned eleven
years in Jerusalem. And he did [b]evil in the
sight of the LORD his God. 6 [a]Nebuchadnezzar
king of Babylon came up against him, and
bound him in bronze *fetters* to [b]carry him off
to Babylon. 7 [a]Nebuchadnezzar also carried
off *some* of the articles from the house of
the LORD to Babylon, and put them in his
temple at Babylon. 8 Now the rest of the acts
of Jehoiakim, the abominations which he
did, and what was found against him, indeed
they *are* written in the book of the kings of
Israel and Judah. Then Jehoiachin his son
reigned in his place.

35:11 [a] 2 Chr. 29:22 [b] 2 Chr. 29:34 **35:12** [a] Ezra 6:18 **35:13** [a] Ex. 12:8, 9 [b] 1 Sam. 2:13–15 **35:15** [a] 1 Chr. 25:1–6 [b] 1 Chr. 9:17, 18 **35:17** [a] Ex. 12:15; 13:6 **35:18** [a] 2 Kin. 23:22, 23 **35:20** [a] 2 Kin. 23:29 [b] Jer. 46:2 **35:22** [a] 2 Chr. 18:29 **35:24** [a] 2 Kin. 23:30 [b] Zech. 12:11 **35:25** [a] Lam. 4:20 [b] Jer. 22:10, 11 [c] Matt. 9:23 [d] Jer. 22:20 **36:1** [a] 2 Kin. 23:30–34 **36:2** [1] Masoretic Text reads *Joahaz.* **36:4** [1] Literally *his* [2] Masoretic Text reads *Joahaz.* **36:5** [a] 2 Kin. 23:36, 37 [b] [Jer. 22:13–19] **36:6** [a] 2 Kin. 24:1 [b] Jer. 36:30 **36:7** [a] Dan. 1:1, 2

The Reign and Captivity of Jehoiachin

9 [a]Jehoiachin *was* eight[1] years old when he
became king, and he reigned in Jerusalem
three months and ten days. And he did evil
in the sight of the LORD. 10 At the turn of the
year [a]King Nebuchadnezzar summoned *him*
and took him to Babylon, [b]with the costly
articles from the house of the LORD, and
made [c]Zedekiah, *Jehoiakim's*[1] brother, king
over Judah and Jerusalem.

Zedekiah Reigns in Judah

11 [a]Zedekiah *was* twenty-one years old when
he became king, and he reigned eleven years
in Jerusalem. 12 He did evil in the sight of the
LORD his God, *and* [a]did not humble himself
before Jeremiah the prophet, *who spoke* from
the mouth of the LORD. 13 And he also [a]re-
belled against King Nebuchadnezzar, who
had made him swear *an oath* by God; but he
[b]stiffened his neck and hardened his heart
against turning to the LORD God of Israel.
14 Moreover all the leaders of the priests and
the people transgressed more and more,
according to all the abominations of the
nations, and defiled the house of the LORD
which He had consecrated in Jerusalem.

The Fall of Jerusalem

15 [a]And the LORD God of their fathers sent
warnings to them by His messengers, rising up
early and sending *them,* because He had compassion on His people and on His dwelling
place. 16 But [a]they mocked the messengers of
God, [b]despised His words, and [c]scoffed at His
prophets, until the [d]wrath of the LORD arose
against His people, till *there was* no remedy.
17 [a]Therefore He brought against them
the king of the Chaldeans, who [b]killed their
young men with the sword in the house of
their sanctuary, and had no compassion
on young man or virgin, on the aged or the
weak; He gave *them* all into his hand. 18 [a]And
all the articles from the house of God, great
and small, the treasures of the house of the
LORD, and the treasures of the king and of his
leaders, all *these* he took to Babylon. 19 [a]Then
they burned the house of God, broke down
the wall of Jerusalem, burned all its palaces
with fire, and destroyed all its precious possessions. 20 And [a]those who escaped from the
sword he carried away to Babylon, [b]where
they became servants to him and his sons
until the rule of the kingdom of Persia, 21 to
fulfill the word of the LORD by the mouth of
[a]Jeremiah, until the land [b]had enjoyed her
Sabbaths. As long as she lay desolate [c]she
kept Sabbath, to fulfill seventy years.

The Proclamation of Cyrus

22 [a]Now in the first year of Cyrus king of
Persia, that the word of the LORD by the
mouth of [b]Jeremiah might be fulfilled, the
LORD stirred up the spirit of [c]Cyrus king
of Persia, so that he made a proclamation
throughout all his kingdom, and also *put it*
in writing, saying,

23 [a]Thus says Cyrus king of Persia:
All the kingdoms of the earth the LORD
God of heaven has given me. And He
has commanded me to build Him a
house at Jerusalem which is in Judah.
Who *is* among you of all His people?
May the LORD his God *be* with him, and
let him go up!

36:9 [a] 2 Kin. 24:8–17 [1] Some Hebrew manuscripts, Septuagint, Syriac, and 2 Kings 24:8 read *eighteen.* **36:10** [a] 2 Kin. 24:10–17 [b] Dan. 1:1, 2 [c] Jer. 37:1 [1] Literally *his* (compare 2 Kings 24:17) **36:11** [a] Jer. 52:1 **36:12** [a] Jer. 21:3–7; 44:10 **36:13** [a] Ezek. 17:15 [b] 2 Kin. 17:14 **36:15** [a] Jer. 7:13; 25:3, 4 **36:16** [a] Jer. 5:12, 13 [b] [Prov. 1:24–32] [c] Jer. 38:6 [d] Ps. 79:5 **36:17** [a] 2 Kin. 25:1 [b] Ps. 74:20 **36:18** [a] 2 Kin. 25:13–15 **36:19** [a] 2 Kin. 25:9 **36:20** [a] 2 Kin. 25:11 [b] Jer. 17:4; 27:7 **36:21** [a] Jer. 25:9–12; 27:6–8; 29:10 [b] Lev. 26:34–43 [c] Lev. 25:4, 5 **36:22** [a] Ezra 1:1–3 [b] Jer. 29:10 [c] Is. 44:28; 45:1 **36:23** [a] Ezra 1:2, 3

THE BOOK OF

EZRA

AUTHOR

Although Ezra is not specifically named as the author, Jewish tradition attributes the book to him. This seems appropriate, as portions of the book are written in the first person, from Ezra's point of view (Ezra 7:28—9:15). Similar to Chronicles, this book has a strong priestly emphasis. Ezra was a direct descendant of Aaron through Eleazar, Phinehas, and Zadok, and so came from a long and illustrious priestly line. It is believed that Ezra had access to the extensive library of written documents gathered by Nehemiah and that this was one of the sources used in writing this book as well as Chronicles.

TIME

c. 538–457 BC

KEY VERSE

Ezra 1:3

THEME

Many scholars think Ezra and Nehemiah belong together as one book. Together they tell parts of the same story. The exile is over, and the temple is to be rebuilt along with the wall of Jerusalem despite considerable opposition. While Nehemiah's perspective is that of a civil servant and building contractor, Ezra is a teacher of the law and a priest and as such, he provides leadership by bringing God's Word to the people and by restoring proper worship. When the people respond to the Word and reestablish their relationship with God through worship, the building process is renewed and completed.

Ezra is the great reminder that God keeps His promises even when we find ourselves in captivity. From this writer we learn the powerful peace formula: the promises of God mixed with faith bring peace (7:6). Through the prophet Jeremiah, God promised that Israel would be in captivity for seventy years (Jer. 25:12). Ezra knew the time of captivity had ended, and it was time to return the people of God to the Promised Land. He reminds us of the guaranteed success of the person who "prepared his heart to seek the Law of the LORD, and to do it" (Ezra 7:10). This book shows the power of prayer, peace, and the protection from God we glean by remaining undefiled through affiliations with people who do not love Him (9:12).

End of the Babylonian Captivity

1 Now in the first year of Cyrus king of
Persia, that the word of the LORD [a]by the
mouth of Jeremiah might be fulfilled, the
LORD stirred up the spirit of Cyrus king of
Persia, [b]so that he made a proclamation
throughout all his kingdom, and also *put it*
in writing, saying,

2 Thus says Cyrus king of Persia:
All the kingdoms of the earth the
LORD God of heaven has given me.
And He has [a]commanded me to build
Him a house at Jerusalem which
is in Judah. 3 Who *is* among you of
all His people? May his God be with
him, and let him go up to Jerusalem
which *is* in Judah, and build the
house of the LORD God of Israel [a](He
is God), which *is* in Jerusalem. 4 And
whoever is left in any place where he
dwells, let the men of his place help
him with silver and gold, with goods
and livestock, besides the freewill
offerings for the house of God which
is in Jerusalem.

5 Then the heads of the fathers' *houses*
of Judah and Benjamin, and the priests
and the Levites, with all whose spirits [a]God
had moved, arose to go up and build the
house of the LORD which *is* in Jerusalem.
6 And all those who *were* around them encouraged them with articles of silver and
gold, with goods and livestock, and with
precious things, besides all *that* was [a]will-
ingly offered.
7 [a]King Cyrus also brought out the articles
of the house of the LORD, [b]which Nebuchadnezzar had taken from Jerusalem and put in
the temple of his gods; 8 and Cyrus king of
Persia brought them out by the hand of Mithredath the treasurer, and counted them out
to [a]Sheshbazzar the prince of Judah. 9 This
is the number of them: thirty gold platters,
one thousand silver platters, twenty-nine
knives, 10 thirty gold basins, four hundred
and ten silver basins of a similar *kind, and*
one thousand other articles. 11 All the articles
of gold and silver *were* five thousand four
hundred. All *these* Sheshbazzar took with the
captives who were brought from Babylon to
Jerusalem.

The Captives Who Returned to Jerusalem

2 Now[1] [a]these *are* the people of the province who came back from the captivity,
of those who had been carried away, [b]whom
Nebuchadnezzar the king of Babylon had
carried away to Babylon, and who returned
to Jerusalem and Judah, everyone to his
own city.
2 *Those* who came with Zerubbabel *were*
Jeshua, Nehemiah, Seraiah, Reelaiah, Mordecai, Bilshan, Mispar,[1] Bigvai, Rehum,[2] *and*
Baanah. The number of the men of the people
of Israel: 3 the people of Parosh, two thousand
one hundred and seventy-two; 4 the people of
Shephatiah, three hundred and seventy-two;
5 the people of Arah, [a]seven hundred and
seventy-five; 6 the people of [a]Pahath-Moab,
of the people of Jeshua *and* Joab, two thousand eight hundred and twelve; 7 the people
of Elam, one thousand two hundred and
fifty-four; 8 the people of Zattu, nine hundred
and forty-five; 9 the people of Zaccai, seven
hundred and sixty; 10 the people of Bani,[1] six
hundred and forty-two; 11 the people of Bebai,
six hundred and twenty-three; 12 the people
of Azgad, one thousand two hundred and
twenty-two; 13 the people of Adonikam, six
hundred and sixty-six; 14 the people of Bigvai, two thousand and fifty-six; 15 the people
of Adin, four hundred and fifty-four; 16 the
people of Ater of Hezekiah, ninety-eight; 17 the
people of Bezai, three hundred and twenty-
three; 18 the people of Jorah,[1] one hundred
and twelve; 19 the people of Hashum, two
hundred and twenty-three; 20 the people of
Gibbar,[1] ninety-five; 21 the people of Bethlehem, one hundred and twenty-three; 22 the
men of Netophah, fifty-six; 23 the men of Anathoth, one hundred and twenty-eight; 24 the
people of Azmaveth,[1] forty-two; 25 the people
of Kirjath Arim,[1] Chephirah, and Beeroth,
seven hundred and forty-three; 26 the people
of Ramah and Geba, six hundred and twenty-
one; 27 the men of Michmas, one hundred
and twenty-two; 28 the men of Bethel and Ai,
two hundred and twenty-three; 29 the people
of Nebo, fifty-two; 30 the people of Magbish,
one hundred and fifty-six; 31 the people of
the other [a]Elam, one thousand two hundred
and fifty-four; 32 the people of Harim, three
hundred and twenty; 33 the people of Lod,
Hadid, and Ono, seven hundred and twenty-
five; 34 the people of Jericho, three hundred

1:1 [a] 2 Chr. 36:22, 23 [b] Ezra 5:13, 14 **1:2** [a] Is. 44:28; 45:1, 13 **1:3** [a] Dan. 6:26 **1:5** [a] [Phil. 2:13] **1:6** [a] Ezra 2:68 **1:7** [a] Ezra 5:14; 6:5 [b] 2 Kin. 24:13 **1:8** [a] Ezra 5:14, 16 **2:1** [a] Neh. 7:6–73 [b] 2 Kin. 24:14–16; 25:11 [1] Compare this chapter with Nehemiah 7:6–73. **2:2** [1] Spelled *Mispereth* in Nehemiah 7:7 [2] Spelled *Nehum* in Nehemiah 7:7 **2:5** [a] Neh. 7:10 **2:6** [a] Neh. 7:11 **2:10** [1] Spelled *Binnui* in Nehemiah 7:15 **2:18** [1] Called *Hariph* in Nehemiah 7:24 **2:20** [1] Called *Gibeon* in Nehemiah 7:25 **2:24** [1] Called *Beth Azmaveth* in Nehemiah 7:28 **2:25** [1] Called *Kirjath Jearim* in Nehemiah 7:29 **2:31** [a] Ezra 2:7

and forty-five; 35 the people of Senaah, three
thousand six hundred and thirty.
36 The priests: the sons of [a]Jedaiah, of the
house of Jeshua, nine hundred and seventy-
three; 37 the sons of [a]Immer, one thousand
and fifty-two; 38 the sons of [a]Pashhur, one
thousand two hundred and forty-seven; 39 the
sons of [a]Harim, one thousand and seventeen.
40 The Levites: the sons of Jeshua and Kadmiel, of the sons of Hodaviah,[1] seventy-four.
41 The singers: the sons of Asaph, one hundred and twenty-eight.
42 The sons of the gatekeepers: the sons
of Shallum, the sons of Ater, the sons of Talmon, the sons of Akkub, the sons of Hatita,
and the sons of Shobai, one hundred and
thirty-nine *in* all.
43 [a]The Nethinim: the sons of Ziha, the sons
of Hasupha, the sons of Tabbaoth, 44 the sons
of Keros, the sons of Siaha,[1] the sons of Padon,
45 the sons of Lebanah, the sons of Hagabah,
the sons of Akkub, 46 the sons of Hagab, the
sons of Shalmai, the sons of Hanan, 47 the
sons of Giddel, the sons of Gahar, the sons
of Reaiah, 48 the sons of Rezin, the sons of
Nekoda, the sons of Gazzam, 49 the sons of
Uzza, the sons of Paseah, the sons of Besai,
50 the sons of Asnah, the sons of Meunim, the
sons of Nephusim,[1] 51 the sons of Bakbuk, the
sons of Hakupha, the sons of Harhur, 52 the
sons of Bazluth,[1] the sons of Mehida, the sons
of Harsha, 53 the sons of Barkos, the sons of
Sisera, the sons of Tamah, 54 the sons of Neziah, and the sons of Hatipha.
55 The sons of [a]Solomon's servants: the sons
of Sotai, the sons of [b]Sophereth, the sons of
Peruda,[1] 56 the sons of Jaala, the sons of Darkon, the sons of Giddel, 57 the sons of Shephatiah, the sons of Hattil, the sons of Pochereth
of Zebaim, and the sons of Ami.[1] 58 All the
[a]Nethinim and the children of [b]Solomon's
servants were three hundred and ninety-two.
59 And these *were* the ones who came up
from Tel Melah, Tel Harsha, Cherub, Addan,[1]
and Immer; but they could not identify their
father's house or their genealogy,[2] whether
they *were* of Israel: 60 the sons of Delaiah,
the sons of Tobiah, and the sons of Nekoda, six hundred and fifty-two; 61 and of the
sons of the priests: the sons of [a]Habaiah,
the sons of Koz,[1] and the sons of [b]Barzillai,
who took a wife of the daughters of Barzillai
the Gileadite, and was called by their name.
62 These sought their listing *among* those
who were registered by genealogy, but they
were not found; [a]therefore they *were excluded*
from the priesthood as defiled. 63 And the
governor[1] said to them that they [a]should not
eat of the most holy things till a priest could
consult with the [b]Urim and Thummim.
64 [a]The whole assembly together *was*
forty-two thousand three hundred *and* sixty, 65 besides their male and female servants,
of whom *there were* seven thousand three
hundred and thirty-seven; and they had two
hundred men and women singers. 66 Their
horses *were* seven hundred and thirty-six,
their mules two hundred and forty-five,
67 their camels four hundred and thirty-five,
and *their* donkeys six thousand seven hundred and twenty.
68 [a]*Some* of the heads of the fathers' *houses,*
when they came to the house of the LORD
which *is* in Jerusalem, offered freely for the
house of God, to erect it in its place: 69 According to their ability, they gave to the [a]treasury
for the work sixty-one thousand gold drachmas, five thousand minas of silver, and one
hundred priestly garments.
70 [a]So the priests and the Levites, *some*
of the people, the singers, the gatekeepers,
and the Nethinim, dwelt in their cities, and
all Israel in their cities.

Worship Restored at Jerusalem

3 And when the [a]seventh month had come,
and the children of Israel *were* in the
cities, the people gathered together as one
man to Jerusalem. 2 Then Jeshua the son
of [a]Jozadak[1] and his brethren the priests,
[b]and Zerubbabel the son of [c]Shealtiel and
his brethren, arose and built the altar of the
God of Israel, to offer burnt offerings on it,
as *it is* [d]written in the Law of Moses the man
of God. 3 Though fear *had come* upon them
because of the people of those countries, they
set the altar on its bases; and they offered
[a]burnt offerings on it to the LORD, *both* the
morning and evening burnt offerings. 4 [a]They
also kept the Feast of Tabernacles, [b]as *it is*
written, and [c]*offered* the daily burnt offerings in the number required by ordinance
for each day. 5 Afterwards *they offered* the
[a]regular burnt offering, and *those* for New

2:36 [a] 1 Chr. 24:7–18 **2:37** [a] 1 Chr. 24:14 **2:38** [a] 1 Chr. 9:12 **2:39** [a] 1 Chr. 24:8 **2:40** [1] Spelled *Hodevah* in Nehemiah 7:43 **2:43** [a] 1 Chr. 9:2 **2:44** [1] Spelled *Sia* in Nehemiah 7:47 **2:50** [1] Spelled *Nephishesim* in Nehemiah 7:52 **2:52** [1] Spelled *Bazlith* in Nehemiah 7:54 **2:55** [a] 1 Kin. 9:21 [b] Neh. 7:57–60 [1] Spelled *Perida* in Nehemiah 7:57 **2:57** [1] Spelled *Amon* in Nehemiah 7:59 **2:58** [a] 1 Chr. 9:2 [b] 1 Kin. 9:21 **2:59** [1] Spelled *Addon* in Nehemiah 7:61 [2] Literally *seed* **2:61** [a] Neh. 7:63 [b] 2 Sam. 17:27 [1] Or *Hakkoz* **2:62** [a] Num. 3:10 **2:63** [a] Lev. 22:2, 10, 15, 16 [b] Ex. 28:30 [1] Hebrew *Tirshatha* **2:64** [a] Neh. 7:66 **2:68** [a] Neh. 7:70 **2:69** [a] Ezra 8:25–35 **2:70** [a] Neh. 7:73 **3:1** [a] Neh. 7:73; 8:1, 2 **3:2** [a] Neh. 12:1, 8 [b] Ezra 2:2; 4:2, 3; 5:2 [c] 1 Chr. 3:17 [d] Deut. 12:5, 6 [1] Spelled *Jehozadak* in 1 Chronicles 6:14 **3:3** [a] Num. 28:3 **3:4** [a] Neh. 8:14–18 [b] Ex. 23:16 [c] Num. 29:12, 13 **3:5** [a] Ex. 29:38

Moons and for all the appointed feasts of the LORD that were consecrated, and *those* of everyone who willingly offered a freewill offering to the LORD.
6 From the first day of the seventh month they began to offer burnt offerings to the LORD, although the foundation of the temple of the LORD had not been laid.
7 They also gave money to the masons and the carpenters, and [a]food, drink, and oil to the people of Sidon and Tyre to bring cedar logs from Lebanon to the sea, to [b]Joppa, [c]according to the permission which they had from Cyrus king of Persia.

Restoration of the Temple Begins

8 Now in the second month of the second year of their coming to the house of God at Jerusalem, [a]Zerubbabel the son of Shealtiel, Jeshua the son of Jozadak,[1] and the rest of their brethren the priests and the Levites, and all those who had come out of the captivity to Jerusalem, began *work* [b]and appointed the Levites from twenty years old and above to oversee the work of the house of the LORD.
9 Then Jeshua *with* his sons and brothers, Kadmiel *with* his sons, and the sons of Judah,[1] arose as one to oversee those working on the house of God: the sons of Henadad *with* their sons and their brethren the Levites.
10 When the builders laid the foundation of the temple of the LORD, [a]the priests stood[1] in their apparel with trumpets, and the Levites, the sons of Asaph, with cymbals, to praise the LORD, according to the [b]ordinance of David king of Israel.
11 [a]And they sang responsively, praising and giving thanks to the LORD:

> [b]"For *He is* good,
> [c]For His mercy *endures* forever toward
> Israel."[1]

Then all the people shouted with a great shout, when they praised the LORD, because the foundation of the house of the LORD was laid.
12 But many of the priests and Levites and [a]heads of the fathers' *houses,* old men who had seen the first temple, wept with a loud voice when the foundation of this temple was laid before their eyes. Yet many shouted aloud for joy,
13 so that the people could not discern the noise of the shout of joy from the noise of the weeping of the people, for the people shouted with a loud shout, and the sound was heard afar off.

Resistance to Rebuilding the Temple

4 Now when [a]the adversaries of Judah and Benjamin heard that the descendants of the captivity were building the temple of the LORD God of Israel,
2 they came to Zerubbabel

3:7 [a] Acts 12:20 [b] 2 Chr. 2:16 [c] Ezra 1:2; 6:3 **3:8** [a] Ezra 3:2; 4:3 [b] 1 Chr. 23:4, 24 [1] Spelled *Jehozadak* in 1 Chronicles 6:14 **3:9** [1] Or *Hodaviah* (compare 2:40) **3:10** [a] 1 Chr. 16:5, 6 [b] 1 Chr. 6:31; 16:4; 25:1 [1] Following Septuagint, Syriac, and Vulgate; Masoretic Text reads *they stationed the priests.* **3:11** [a] Neh. 12:24 [b] Ps. 136:1 [c] Jer. 33:11 [1] Compare Psalm 136:1 **3:12** [a] Ezra 2:68 **4:1** [a] Ezra 4:7–9

DO HARD THINGS

All the people shouted with a great shout, when they praised the LORD, because the foundation of the house of the LORD was laid.

EZRA 3:11

The gift of God's peace leads us to attempt great tasks. With that peace we can do things that may seem undoable. God's peace gives us courage.

After the Babylonian exile, Israelites found it hard to go home and restart as free people. Even harder was the rebuilding of the temple. Not only were the materials expensive and the laborers few, but local Gentiles tried hard to prevent it. On top of that, when the foundation was laid, the old people—who remembered Solomon's temple in all its glory—wept knowing it could never be re-created.

Nevertheless, the people who had returned to Israel kept at it and finally rebuilt the temple. In time, the walls of Jerusalem were reinstated, and the grand old city began to come back *to life. It had been a long road to renewal*, and it was time to do difficult things to bring the peace of God back to the people. No matter where you find yourself today (captivity, on the road to renewal, starting a new project in faith), be reminded from verse 11 that you can do hard things in the peace of God.

and the heads of the fathers' *houses,* and said
to them, "Let us build with you, for we seek
your God as you *do;* and we have sacrificed
to Him [a]since the days of Esarhaddon king of
Assyria, who brought us here." 3 But Zerubbabel and Jeshua and the rest of the heads of the
fathers' *houses* of Israel said to them, [a]"You
may do nothing with us to build a house for
our God; but we alone will build to the LORD
God of Israel, as [b]King Cyrus the king of Persia
has commanded us." 4 Then [a]the people of the
land tried to discourage the people of Judah.
They troubled them in building, 5 and hired
counselors against them to frustrate their
purpose all the days of Cyrus king of Persia,
even until the reign of [a]Darius king of Persia.

Rebuilding of Jerusalem Opposed

6 In the reign of Ahasuerus, in the beginning of his reign, they wrote an accusation
against the inhabitants of Judah and Jerusalem.

7 In the days of [a]Artaxerxes also, Bishlam,
Mithredath, Tabel, and the rest of their companions wrote to Artaxerxes king of Persia;
and the letter *was* written in [b]Aramaic script,
and translated into the Aramaic language.
8 Rehum[1] the commander and Shimshai the
scribe wrote a letter against Jerusalem to
King Artaxerxes in this fashion:

9 From[1] Rehum the commander,
Shimshai the scribe, and the rest of
their companions—*representatives* of
[a]the Dinaites, the Apharsathchites, the
Tarpelites, the people of Persia and
Erech and Babylon and Shushan,[2] the
Dehavites, the Elamites, 10 [a]and the rest
of the nations whom the great and noble
Osnapper took captive and settled in
the cities of Samaria and the remainder
beyond the River[1]—[b]and so forth.[2]

11 (This *is* a copy of the letter that they sent
him.)

To King Artaxerxes from your servants,
the men *of the region* beyond the River,
and so forth:[1]

12 Let it be known to the king that the
Jews who came up from you have
come to us at Jerusalem, and are
building the [a]rebellious and evil
city, and are finishing *its* [b]walls and
repairing the foundations. 13 Let it now
be known to the king that, if this city is
built and the walls completed, they will
not pay [a]tax, tribute, or custom, and
the king's treasury will be diminished.
14 Now because we receive support
from the palace, it was not proper for
us to see the king's dishonor; therefore
we have sent and informed the king,
15 that search may be made in the book
of the records of your fathers. And you
will find in the book of the records and
know that this city *is* a rebellious city,
harmful to kings and provinces, and
that they have incited sedition within
the city in former times, for which
cause this city was destroyed.

16 We inform the king that if this city is
rebuilt and its walls are completed,
the result will be that you will have no
dominion beyond the River.

17 The king sent an answer:

To Rehum the commander, *to*
Shimshai the scribe, *to* the rest of their
companions who dwell in Samaria, and
to the remainder beyond the River:

Peace, and so forth.[1]

18 The letter which you sent to us has
been clearly read before me. 19 And
I gave the command, and a search
has been made, and it was found
that this city in former times has
revolted against kings, and rebellion
and sedition have been fostered in it.
20 There have also been mighty kings
over Jerusalem, who have [a]ruled over
all *the region* [b]beyond the River; and
tax, tribute, and custom were paid to
them. 21 Now give the command to
make these men cease, that this city
may not be built until the command is
given by me.

22 Take heed now that you do not fail to
do this. Why should damage increase
to the hurt of the kings?

23 Now when the copy of King Artaxerxes'
letter *was* read before Rehum, Shimshai the
scribe, and their companions, they went up
in haste to Jerusalem against the Jews, and
by force of arms made them cease. 24 Thus

4:2 [a] 2 Kin. 17:24; 19:37 **4:3** [a] Neh. 2:20 [b] Ezra 1:1–4 **4:4** [a] Ezra 3:3 **4:5** [a] Ezra 5:5; 6:1 **4:7** [a] Ezra 7:1, 7, 21 [b] 2 Kin. 18:26 **4:8** [1] The original language of Ezra 4:8 through 6:18 is Aramaic. **4:9** [a] 2 Kin. 17:30, 31 [1] Literally *Then* [2] Or *Susa* **4:10** [a] 2 Kin. 17:24 [b] Ezra 4:11, 17; 7:12 [1] That is, the Euphrates [2] Literally *and now* **4:11** [1] Literally *and now* **4:12** [a] 2 Chr. 36:13 [b] Ezra 5:3, 9 **4:13** [a] Ezra 4:20; 7:24 **4:17** [1] Literally *and now* **4:20** [a] Ps. 72:8 [b] Gen. 15:18

the work of the house of God which *is* at Jerusalem ceased, and it was discontinued
until the second year of the reign of Darius
king of Persia.

Restoration of the Temple Resumed

5 Then the prophet [a]Haggai and [b]Zechariah
the son of Iddo, prophets, prophesied to
the Jews who *were* in Judah and Jerusalem, in
the name of the God of Israel, *who was* over
them. 2 So [a]Zerubbabel the son of Shealtiel
and Jeshua the son of Jozadak[1] rose up and
began to build the house of God which *is* in
Jerusalem; and [b]the prophets of God *were*
with them, helping them.
3 At the same time [a]Tattenai the governor
of *the region* beyond the River[1] and Shethar-
Boznai and their companions came to them
and spoke thus to them: [b]"Who has commanded you to build this temple and finish
this wall?" 4 [a]Then, accordingly, we told them
the names of the men who were constructing
this building. 5 But [a]the eye of their God was
upon the elders of the Jews, so that they could
not make them cease till a report could go to
Darius. Then a [b]written answer was returned
concerning this *matter.* 6 This is a copy of the
letter that Tattenai sent:

> The governor of *the region* beyond the
> River, and Shethar-Boznai, [a]and his
> companions, the Persians who *were in
> the region* beyond the River, to Darius
> the king.

7 (They sent a letter to him, in which was written thus.)

> To Darius the king:
>
> All peace.
>
> 8 Let it be known to the king that we
> went into the province of Judea, to the
> temple of the great God, which is being
> built with heavy stones, and timber is
> being laid in the walls; and this work
> goes on diligently and prospers in their
> hands.
>
> 9 Then we asked those elders, *and* spoke
> thus to them: [a]"Who commanded you
> to build this temple and to finish these
> walls?" 10 We also asked them their
> names to inform you, that we might
> write the names of the men who *were*
> chief among them.
>
> 11 And thus they returned us an answer,
> saying: "We are the servants of the
> God of heaven and earth, and we are
> rebuilding the temple that was built
> many years ago, which a great king
> of Israel built [a]and completed. 12 But
> [a]because our fathers provoked the God
> of heaven to wrath, He gave them into
> the hand of [b]Nebuchadnezzar king of
> Babylon, the Chaldean, *who* destroyed
> this temple and [c]carried the people
> away to Babylon. 13 However, in the
> first year of [a]Cyrus king of Babylon,
> King Cyrus issued a decree to build
> this house of God. 14 Also, [a]the gold
> and silver articles of the house of God,
> which Nebuchadnezzar had taken from
> the temple that *was* in Jerusalem and
> carried into the temple of Babylon—
> those King Cyrus took from the temple
> of Babylon, and they were given to
> [b]one named Sheshbazzar, whom he
> had made governor. 15 And he said
> to him, 'Take these articles; go, carry
> them to the temple *site* that *is* in
> Jerusalem, and let the house of God
> be rebuilt on its former site.' 16 Then
> the same Sheshbazzar came *and* [a]laid
> the foundation of the house of God
> which *is* in Jerusalem; but from that
> time even until now it has been under
> construction, and [b]it is not finished."
>
> 17 Now therefore, if *it seems* good to
> the king, [a]let a search be made in the
> king's treasure house, which *is* there in
> Babylon, whether it is *so* that a decree
> was issued by King Cyrus to build this
> house of God at Jerusalem, and let the
> king send us his pleasure concerning
> this *matter.*

The Decree of Darius

6 Then King Darius issued a decree, [a]and a
search was made in the archives,[1] where
the treasures were stored in Babylon. 2 And
at Achmetha,[1] in the palace that *is* in the
province of [a]Media, a scroll was found, and
in it a record *was* written thus:

> 3 In the first year of King Cyrus, King
> Cyrus issued a [a]decree *concerning*

5:1 [a] Hag. 1:1 [b] Zech. 1:1 **5:2** [a] Ezra 3:2 [b] Hag. 2:4 [1] Spelled *Jehozadak* in 1 Chronicles 6:14 **5:3** [a] Ezra 5:6; 6:6 [b] Ezra 1:3; 5:9 [1] That is, the Euphrates **5:4** [a] Ezra 5:10 **5:5** [a] Ps. 33:18 [b] Ezra 6:6 **5:6** [a] Ezra 4:7–10 **5:9** [a] Ezra 5:3, 4 **5:11** [a] 1 Kin. 6:1, 38 **5:12** [a] 2 Chr. 34:25; 36:16, 17 [b] 2 Kin. 24:2; 25:8–11 [c] Jer. 13:19 **5:13** [a] Ezra 1:1 **5:14** [a] Ezra 1:7, 8; 6:5 [b] Hag. 1:14; 2:2, 21 **5:16** [a] Ezra 3:8–10 [b] Ezra 6:15 **5:17** [a] Ezra 6:1, 2 **6:1** [a] Ezra 5:17 [1] Literally *house of the scrolls* **6:2** [a] 2 Kin. 17:6 [1] Probably *Ecbatana,* the ancient capital of Media **6:3** [a] Ezra 1:1; 5:13

PEACE NOTE

We find peace in knowing that the king's heart is in the hand of the Lord! King Darius's search revealed King Cyrus's provision for the Jews to return to Jerusalem to rebuild.

EZRA 6:1

the house of God at Jerusalem: "Let
the house be rebuilt, the place where
they offered sacrifices; and let the
foundations of it be firmly laid, its
height sixty cubits *and* its width sixty
cubits, [4][a]*with* three rows of heavy
stones and one row of new timber. Let
the [b]expenses be paid from the king's
treasury. [5]Also let [a]the gold and silver
articles of the house of God, which
Nebuchadnezzar took from the temple
which *is* in Jerusalem and brought to
Babylon, be restored and taken back to
the temple which *is* in Jerusalem, *each*
to its place; and deposit *them* in the
house of God"—

6 [a]Now *therefore,* Tattenai, governor
of *the region* beyond the River, and
Shethar-Boznai, and your companions
the Persians who *are* beyond the River,
keep yourselves far from there. [7]Let
the work of this house of God alone; let
the governor of the Jews and the elders
of the Jews build this house of God on
its site.

8 Moreover I issue a decree *as to* what
you shall do for the elders of these
Jews, for the building of this house of
God: Let the cost be paid at the king's
expense from taxes *on the region*
beyond the River; this is to be given
immediately to these men, so that they
are not hindered. [9]And whatever they
need—young bulls, rams, and lambs
for the burnt offerings of the God
of heaven, wheat, salt, wine, and oil,
according to the request of the priests
who *are* in Jerusalem—let it be given
them day by day without fail, [10][a]that
they may offer sacrifices of sweet
aroma to the God of heaven, and pray
for the life of the king and his sons.

11 Also I issue a decree that whoever
alters this edict, let a timber be pulled
from his house and erected, and let
him be hanged on it; [a]and let his house
be made a refuse heap because of this.
[12]And may the God who causes His
[a]name to dwell there destroy any king
or people who put their hand to alter it,
or to destroy this house of God which
is in Jerusalem. I Darius issue a decree;
let it be done diligently.

The Temple Completed and Dedicated

[13]Then Tattenai, governor of *the region*
beyond the River, Shethar-Boznai, and their
companions diligently did according to what
King Darius had sent. [14][a]So the elders of the
Jews built, and they prospered through the
prophesying of Haggai the prophet and Zechariah the son of Iddo. And they built and
finished *it,* according to the commandment
of the God of Israel, and according to the
command of [b]Cyrus, [c]Darius, and [d]Arta-
xerxes king of Persia. [15]Now the temple was
finished on the third day of the month of
Adar, which was in the sixth year of the reign
of King Darius. [16]Then the children of Israel,
the priests and the Levites and the rest of
the descendants of the captivity, celebrated
[a]the dedication of this house of God with joy.
[17]And they [a]offered sacrifices at the dedication of this house of God, one hundred bulls,
two hundred rams, four hundred lambs, and
as a sin offering for all Israel twelve male
goats, according to the number of the tribes
of Israel. [18]They assigned the priests to their
[a]divisions and the Levites to their [b]divisions,
over the service of God in Jerusalem, [c]as it
is written in the Book of Moses.

The Passover Celebrated

[19]And the descendants of the captivity
kept the Passover [a]on the fourteenth *day*
of the first month. [20]For the priests and the
Levites had [a]purified themselves; all of them
were ritually clean. And they [b]slaughtered the
Passover *lambs* for all the descendants of the
captivity, for their brethren the priests, and
for themselves. [21]Then the children of Israel who had returned from the captivity ate

6:4 [a] 1 Kin. 6:36 [b] Ezra 3:7 **6:5** [a] Ezra 1:7, 8; 5:14 **6:6** [a] Ezra 5:3, 6 **6:10** [a] Ezra 7:23 **6:11** [a] Dan. 2:5; 3:29 **6:12** [a] 1 Kin. 9:3 **6:14** [a] Ezra 5:1, 2 [b] Ezra 1:1; 5:13; 6:3 [c] Ezra 4:24; 6:12 [d] Ezra 7:1, 11 **6:16** [a] 1 Kin. 8:63 **6:17** [a] Ezra 8:35 **6:18** [a] 1 Chr. 24:1 [b] 1 Chr. 23:6 [c] Num. 3:6; 8:9 **6:19** [a] Ex. 12:6 **6:20** [a] 2 Chr. 29:34; 30:15 [b] 2 Chr. 35:11

together with all who had separated themselves from the [a]filth of the nations of the
land in order to seek the LORD God of Israel.
22 And they kept the [a]Feast of Unleavened
Bread seven days with joy; for the LORD made
them joyful, and [b]turned the heart [c]of the
king of Assyria toward them, to strengthen
their hands in the work of the house of God,
the God of Israel.

The Arrival of Ezra

7 Now after these things, in the reign of
[a]Artaxerxes king of Persia, Ezra the [b]son
of Seraiah, [c]the son of Azariah, the son of
[d]Hilkiah, 2 the son of Shallum, the son of
Zadok, the son of Ahitub, 3 the son of Amariah, the son of Azariah, the son of Meraioth,
4 the son of Zerahiah, the son of Uzzi, the
son of Bukki, 5 the son of Abishua, the son
of Phinehas, the son of Eleazar, the son of
Aaron the chief priest— 6 this Ezra came up
from Babylon; and he *was* [a]a skilled scribe
in the Law of Moses, which the LORD God of
Israel had given. The king granted him all his
request, [b]according to the hand of the LORD
his God upon him. 7 [a]*Some* of the children of
Israel, the priests, [b]the Levites, the singers,
the gatekeepers, and [c]the Nethinim came
up to Jerusalem in the seventh year of King
Artaxerxes. 8 And Ezra came to Jerusalem
in the fifth month, which *was* in the seventh
year of the king. 9 On the first *day* of the first
month he began *his* journey from Babylon,
and on the first *day* of the fifth month he
came to Jerusalem, [a]according to the good
hand of his God upon him. 10 For Ezra had
prepared his heart to [a]seek the Law of the
LORD, and to do *it,* and to [b]teach statutes and
ordinances in Israel.

The Letter of Artaxerxes to Ezra

11 This *is* a copy of the letter that King Artaxerxes gave Ezra the priest, the scribe, expert
in the words of the commandments of the
LORD, and of His statutes to Israel:

12 Artaxerxes,[1] [a]king of kings,

To Ezra the priest, a scribe of the Law
of the God of heaven:

Perfect *peace,* [b]and so forth.[2]

13 I issue a decree that all those of the
people of Israel and the priests and
Levites in my realm, who volunteer to
go up to Jerusalem, may go with you.
14 And whereas you are being sent by
the king and his [a]seven counselors
to inquire concerning Judah and
Jerusalem, with regard to the Law of
your God which *is* in your hand; 15 and
whereas you are to carry the silver and
gold which the king and his counselors
have freely offered to the God of Israel,
[a]whose dwelling *is* in Jerusalem; 16 [a]and
whereas all the silver and gold that you
may find in all the province of Babylon,
along with the freewill offering of the
people and the priests, *are to be* [b]freely
offered for the house of their God
in Jerusalem— 17 now therefore, be
careful to buy with this money bulls,
rams, and lambs, with their [a]grain
offerings and their drink offerings, and
[b]offer them on the altar of the house of
your God in Jerusalem.

18 And whatever seems good to you and
your brethren to do with the rest of the
silver and the gold, do it according to
the will of your God. 19 Also the articles
that are given to you for the service of
the house of your God, deliver in full
before the God of Jerusalem. 20 And
whatever more may be needed for the
house of your God, which you may
have occasion to provide, pay *for it*
from the king's treasury.

21 And I, *even* I, Artaxerxes the king, issue
a decree to all the treasurers who *are*
in the region beyond the River, that
whatever Ezra the priest, the scribe
of the Law of the God of heaven, may
require of you, let it be done diligently,
22 up to one hundred talents of silver,
one hundred kors of wheat, one
hundred baths of wine, one hundred
baths of oil, and salt without prescribed
limit. 23 Whatever is commanded by the
God of heaven, let it diligently be done
for the house of the God of heaven. For
why should there be wrath against the
realm of the king and his sons?

24 Also we inform you that it shall not be
lawful to impose tax, tribute, or custom
on any of the priests, Levites, singers,
gatekeepers, Nethinim, or servants
of this house of God. 25 And you, Ezra,
according to your God-given wisdom,

6:21 [a] Ezra 9:11 **6:22** [a] Ex. 12:15; 13:6, 7 [b] [Prov. 21:1] [c] Ezra 1:1; 6:1 **7:1** [a] Neh. 2:1 [b] 1 Chr. 6:14 [c] Jer. 52:24 [d] 2 Chr. 35:8 **7:6** [a] Ezra 7:11, 12, 21 [b] Ezra 7:9, 28; 8:22 **7:7** [a] Ezra 8:1–14 [b] Ezra 8:15 [c] Ezra 2:43; 8:20 **7:9** [a] Neh. 2:8, 18 **7:10** [a] Ps. 119:45 [b] Deut. 33:10 **7:12** [a] Dan. 2:37 [b] Ezra 4:10 [1] The original language of Ezra 7:12–26 is Aramaic. [2] Literally *and now* **7:14** [a] Esth. 1:14 **7:15** [a] Ezra 6:12 **7:16** [a] Ezra 8:25 [b] 1 Chr. 29:6, 9 **7:17** [a] Num. 15:4–13 [b] Deut. 12:5–11

[a]set magistrates and judges who may
judge all the people who *are in the region*
beyond the River, all such as know the
laws of your God; and [b]teach those who
do not know *them.* 26 Whoever will not
observe the law of your God and the law
of the king, let judgment be executed
speedily on him, whether *it be* death, or
banishment, or confiscation of goods, or
imprisonment.

27 [a]Blessed *be* the LORD God of our fathers,
[b]who has put *such a thing* as this in the king's
heart, to beautify the house of the LORD
which *is* in Jerusalem, 28 and [a]has extended
mercy to me before the king and his counselors, and before all the king's mighty princes.

So I was encouraged, as [b]the hand of the
LORD my God *was* upon me; and I gathered
leading men of Israel to go up with me.

Heads of Families Who Returned with Ezra

8 These *are* the heads of their fathers' *houses,* and *this is* the genealogy of those who
went up with me from Babylon, in the reign
of King Artaxerxes: 2 of the sons of Phinehas,
Gershom; of the sons of Ithamar, Daniel; of
the sons of David, [a]Hattush; 3 of the sons of
Shecaniah, of the sons of [a]Parosh, Zechariah;
and registered with him *were* one hundred and
fifty males; 4 of the sons of [a]Pahath-Moab, Eliehoenai the son of Zerahiah, and with him two
hundred males; 5 of the sons of Shechaniah,[1]
Ben-Jahaziel, and with him three hundred
males; 6 of the sons of Adin, Ebed the son of
Jonathan, and with him fifty males; 7 of the
sons of Elam, Jeshaiah the son of Athaliah,
and with him seventy males; 8 of the sons of
Shephatiah, Zebadiah the son of Michael, and
with him eighty males; 9 of the sons of Joab,
Obadiah the son of Jehiel, and with him two
hundred and eighteen males; 10 of the sons
of Shelomith,[1] Ben-Josiphiah, and with him
one hundred and sixty males; 11 of the sons of
[a]Bebai, Zechariah the son of Bebai, and with
him twenty-eight males; 12 of the sons of Azgad,
Johanan the son of Hakkatan, and with him
one hundred and ten males; 13 of the last sons
of Adonikam, whose names *are* these—Eliphelet, Jeiel, and Shemaiah—and with them sixty
males; 14 also of the sons of Bigvai, Uthai and
Zabbud, and with them seventy males.

Servants for the Temple

15 Now I gathered them by the river that
flows to Ahava, and we camped there three
days. And I looked among the people and the
priests, and found none of the [a]sons of Levi
there. 16 Then I sent for Eliezer, Ariel, Shemaiah, Elnathan, Jarib, Elnathan, Nathan, Zechariah, and [a]Meshullam, leaders; also for Joiarib
and Elnathan, men of understanding. 17 And I
gave them a command for Iddo the chief man
at the place Casiphia, and I told them what
they should say to Iddo *and* his brethren[1] the
Nethinim at the place Casiphia—that they
should bring us servants for the house of our
God. 18 Then, by the good hand of our God upon
us, they [a]brought us a man of understanding,
of the sons of Mahli the son of Levi, the son
of Israel, namely Sherebiah, with his sons and
brothers, eighteen men; 19 and [a]Hashabiah,
and with him Jeshaiah of the sons of Merari, his brothers and their sons, twenty men;
20 [a]also of the Nethinim, whom David and the
leaders had appointed for the service of the
Levites, two hundred and twenty Nethinim.
All of them were designated by name.

Fasting and Prayer for Protection

21 Then I [a]proclaimed a fast there at the river of Ahava, that we might [b]humble ourselves
before our God, to seek from Him the [c]right
way for us and our little ones and all our possessions. 22 For [a]I was ashamed to request of
the king an escort of soldiers and horsemen
to help us against the enemy on the road,
because we had spoken to the king, saying,
[b]"The hand of our God *is* upon all those for
[c]good who seek Him, but His power and His
wrath *are* [d]against all those who [e]forsake
Him." 23 So we fasted and entreated our God
for this, and He [a]answered our prayer.

Gifts for the Temple

24 And I separated twelve of the leaders of
the priests—Sherebiah, Hashabiah, and ten
of their brethren with them— 25 and weighed
out to them [a]the silver, the gold, and the articles, the offering for the house of our God
which the king and his counselors and his
princes, and all Israel *who were* present, had
offered. 26 I weighed into their hand six hundred and fifty talents of silver, silver articles
weighing one hundred talents, one hundred
talents of gold, 27 twenty gold basins *worth* a

7:25 [a] Ex. 18:21, 22 [b] [Mal. 2:7] **7:27** [a] 1 Chr. 29:10 [b] Ezra 6:22 **7:28** [a] Ezra 9:9 [b] Ezra 5:5; 7:6, 9; 8:18 **8:2** [a] 1 Chr. 3:22 **8:3** [a] Ezra 2:3 **8:4** [a] Ezra 10:30 **8:5** [1] Following Masoretic Text and Vulgate; Septuagint reads *the sons of Zatho, Shechaniah.* **8:10** [1] Following Masoretic Text and Vulgate; Septuagint reads *the sons of Banni, Shelomith.* **8:11** [a] Ezra 10:28 **8:15** [a] Ezra 7:7; 8:2 **8:16** [a] Ezra 10:15 **8:17** [1] Following Vulgate; Masoretic Text reads *to Iddo his brother;* Septuagint reads *to their brethren.* **8:18** [a] Neh. 8:7 **8:19** [a] Neh. 12:24 **8:20** [a] Ezra 2:43; 7:7 **8:21** [a] 1 Sam. 7:6 [b] Is. 58:3, 5 [c] Ps. 5:8 **8:22** [a] 1 Cor. 9:15 [b] Ezra 7:6, 9, 28 [c] [Rom. 8:28] [d] [Ps. 34:16] [e] [2 Chr. 15:2] **8:23** [a] 2 Chr. 33:13 **8:25** [a] Ezra 7:15, 16

thousand drachmas, and two vessels of fine
polished bronze, precious as gold. 28 And I
said to them, "You *are* [a]holy to the LORD;
the articles *are* [b]holy also; and the silver and
the gold *are* a freewill offering to the LORD
God of your fathers. 29 Watch and keep *them*
until you weigh *them* before the leaders of
the priests and the Levites and [a]heads of the
fathers' *houses* of Israel in Jerusalem, *in* the
chambers of the house of the LORD." 30 So the
priests and the Levites received the silver and
the gold and the articles by weight, to bring
them to Jerusalem to the house of our God.

The Return to Jerusalem

31 Then we departed from the river of Ahava
on the twelfth *day* of the first month, to go
to Jerusalem. And [a]the hand of our God was
upon us, and He delivered us from the hand
of the enemy and from ambush along the
road. 32 So we [a]came to Jerusalem, and stayed
there three days.

33 Now on the fourth day the silver and the
gold and the articles were [a]weighed in the
house of our God by the hand of Meremoth
the son of Uriah the priest, and with him *was*
Eleazar the son of Phinehas; with them *were*
the Levites, [b]Jozabad the son of Jeshua and
Noadiah the son of Binnui, 34 with the number *and* weight of everything. All the weight
was written down at that time.

35 The children of those who had been [a]car-
ried away captive, who had come from the
captivity, [b]offered burnt offerings to the God
of Israel: twelve bulls for all Israel, ninety-six
rams, seventy-seven lambs, and twelve male
goats *as* a sin offering. All *this was* a burnt
offering to the LORD.

36 And they delivered the king's [a]orders to
the king's satraps and the governors *in the
region* beyond the River. So they gave support
to the people and the house of God.

Intermarriage with Pagans

9 When these things were done, the leaders
came to me, saying, "The people of Israel and the priests and the Levites have not
[a]separated themselves from the peoples of
the lands, [b]with respect to the abominations
of the Canaanites, the Hittites, the Perizzites,
the Jebusites, the Ammonites, the Moabites,
the Egyptians, and the Amorites. 2 For they
have [a]taken some of their daughters *as wives*
for themselves and their sons, so that the
[b]holy seed *is* [c]mixed *with* the peoples of *those*
lands. Indeed, the hand of the leaders and
rulers has been foremost in this trespass."
3 So when I heard this thing, [a]I tore my garment and my robe, and plucked out some of
the hair of my head and beard, and sat down
[b]astonished. 4 Then everyone who [a]trembled
at the words of the God of Israel assembled
to me, because of the transgression of those
who had been carried away captive, and I
sat astonished until the [b]evening sacrifice.

5 At the evening sacrifice I arose from my
fasting; and having torn my garment and
my robe, I fell on my knees and [a]spread out my
hands to the LORD my God. 6 And I said: "O my
God, I am too [a]ashamed and humiliated to lift
up my face to You, my God; for [b]our iniquities
have risen higher than *our* heads, and our guilt
has [c]grown up to the heavens. 7 Since the days
of our fathers to this day [a]we *have been* very
guilty, and for our iniquities [b]we, our kings,
and our priests have been delivered into the
hand of the kings of the lands, to the [c]sword,
to captivity, to plunder, and to [d]humiliation,
as *it is* this day. 8 And now for a little while
grace has been *shown* from the LORD our God,
to leave us a remnant to escape, and to give
us a peg in His holy place, that our God may
[a]enlighten our eyes and give us a measure of
revival in our bondage. 9 [a]For we *were* slaves.
[b]Yet our God did not forsake us in our bondage;
but [c]He extended mercy to us in the sight of
the kings of Persia, to revive us, to repair the
house of our God, to rebuild its ruins, and to
give us [d]a wall in Judah and Jerusalem. 10 And
now, O our God, what shall we say after this?
For we have forsaken Your commandments,
11 which You commanded by Your servants
the prophets, saying, 'The land which you are
entering to possess is an unclean land, with the
[a]uncleanness of the peoples of the lands, with
their abominations which have filled it from
one end to another with their impurity. 12 Now
therefore, [a]do not give your daughters as wives
for their sons, nor take their daughters to your
sons; and [b]never seek their peace or prosperity, that you may be strong and eat the good
of the land, and [c]leave *it* as an inheritance to
your children forever.' 13 And after all that has
come upon us for our evil deeds and for our
great guilt, since You our God [a]have punished
us less than our iniquities *deserve,* and have
given us *such* deliverance as this, 14 should we
[a]again break Your commandments, and [b]join
in marriage with the people *committing* these
abominations? Would You not be [c]angry with

8:28 [a] Lev. 21:6–9 [b] Lev. 22:2, 3 **8:29** [a] Ezra 4:3 **8:31** [a] Ezra 7:6, 9, 28 **8:32** [a] Neh. 2:11 **8:33** [a] Ezra 8:26, 30 [b] Neh. 11:16 **8:35** [a] Ezra 2:1 [b] Ezra 6:17 **8:36** [a] Ezra 7:21–24 **9:1** [a] Neh. 9:2 [b] Deut. 12:30, 31 **9:2** [a] [Deut. 7:3] [b] Ex. 22:31 [c] [2 Cor. 6:14] **9:3** [a] Job 1:20 [b] Ps. 143:4 **9:4** [a] Ezra 10:3 [b] Ex. 29:39 **9:5** [a] Ex. 9:29 **9:6** [a] Dan. 9:7, 8 [b] Ps. 38:4 [c] Rev. 18:5 **9:7** [a] Dan. 9:5, 6 [b] Deut. 28:36 [c] Deut. 32:25 [d] Dan. 9:7, 8 **9:8** [a] Ps. 34:5 **9:9** [a] Neh. 9:36 [b] Ps. 136:23 [c] Ezra 7:28 [d] Is. 5:2 **9:11** [a] Ezra 6:21 **9:12** [a] [Deut. 7:3, 4] [b] Deut. 23:6 [c] [Prov. 13:22; 20:7] **9:13** [a] [Ps. 103:10] **9:14** [a] [John 5:14] [b] Neh. 13:23 [c] Deut. 9:8

us until You had consumed *us,* so that *there would be* no remnant or survivor? 15 O LORD God of Israel, [a]You *are* righteous, for we are left as a remnant, as *it is* this day. [b]Here we *are* before You, [c]in our guilt, though no one can stand before You because of this!"

Confession of Improper Marriages

10 Now [a]while Ezra was praying, and while he was confessing, weeping, and bowing down [b]before the house of God, a very large assembly of men, women, and children gathered to him from Israel; for the people wept very [c]bitterly. 2 And Shechaniah the son of Jehiel, *one* of the sons of Elam, spoke up and said to Ezra, "We have [a]trespassed against our God, and have taken pagan wives from the peoples of the land; yet now there is hope in Israel in spite of this. 3 Now therefore, let us make [a]a covenant with our God to put away all these wives and those who have been born to them, according to the advice of my master and of those who [b]tremble at [c]the commandment of our God; and let it be done according to the [d]law. 4 Arise, for *this* matter *is* your *responsibility.* We also *are* with you. [a]Be of good courage, and do *it.*"

> **PEACE NOTE**
>
> Ezra made peace with God on behalf of the Lord's people. Notice the elements of his prayer: confession, weeping, and bowing down. Pray like this!
>
> EZRA 10:1

5 Then Ezra arose, and made the leaders of the priests, the Levites, and all Israel [a]swear an oath that they would do according to this word. So they swore an oath. 6 Then Ezra rose up from before the house of God, and went into the chamber of Jehohanan the son of Eliashib; and *when* he came there, he [a]ate no bread and drank no water, for he mourned because of the guilt of those from the captivity.

7 And they issued a proclamation throughout Judah and Jerusalem to all the descendants of the captivity, that they must gather at Jerusalem, 8 and that whoever would not come within three days, according to the instructions of the leaders and elders, all his property would be confiscated, and he himself would be separated from the assembly of those from the captivity.

9 So all the men of Judah and Benjamin gathered at Jerusalem within three days. It *was* the ninth month, on the twentieth of the month; and [a]all the people sat in the open square of the house of God, trembling because of *this* matter and because of heavy rain. 10 Then Ezra the priest stood up and said to them, "You have transgressed and have taken pagan wives, adding to the guilt of Israel. 11 Now therefore, [a]make confession to the LORD God of your fathers, and do His will; [b]separate yourselves from the peoples of the land, and from the pagan wives."

12 Then all the assembly answered and said with a loud voice, "Yes! As you have said, so we must do. 13 But *there are* many people; *it is* the season for heavy rain, and we are not able to stand outside. Nor *is this* the work of one or two days, for *there are* many of us who have transgressed in this matter. 14 Please, let the leaders of our entire assembly stand; and let all those in our cities who have taken pagan wives come at appointed times, together with the elders and judges of their cities, until [a]the fierce wrath of our God is turned away from us in this matter." 15 Only Jonathan the son of Asahel and Jahaziah the son of Tikvah opposed this, and [a]Meshullam and Shabbethai the Levite gave them support.

16 Then the descendants of the captivity did so. And Ezra the priest, *with* certain [a]heads of the fathers' *households,* were set apart by the fathers' households, each of them by name; and they sat down on the first day of the tenth month to examine the matter. 17 By the first day of the first month they finished *questioning* all the men who had taken pagan wives.

Pagan Wives Put Away

18 And among the sons of the priests who had taken pagan wives *the following* were found of the sons of [a]Jeshua the son of Jozadak,[1] and his brothers: Maaseiah, Eliezer, Jarib, and Gedaliah. 19 And they [a]gave their promise that they would put away their wives; and *being* [b]guilty, *they presented* a ram of the flock as their [c]trespass offering.

9:15 [a] Dan. 9:14 [b] [Rom. 3:19] [c] 1 Cor. 15:17 **10:1** [a] Dan. 9:4, 20 [b] 2 Chr. 20:9 [c] Neh. 8:1–9 **10:2** [a] Neh. 13:23–27 **10:3** [a] 2 Chr. 34:31 [b] Ezra 9:4 [c] Deut. 7:2, 3 [d] Deut. 24:1, 2 **10:4** [a] 1 Chr. 28:10 **10:5** [a] Neh. 5:12; 13:25 **10:6** [a] Deut. 9:18 **10:9** [a] 1 Sam. 12:18 **10:11** [a] [Prov. 28:13] [b] Ezra 10:3 **10:14** [a] 2 Chr. 28:11–13; 29:10; 30:8 **10:15** [a] Neh. 3:4 **10:16** [a] Ezra 4:3 **10:18** [a] Ezra 5:2 [1] Spelled *Jehozadak* in 1 Chronicles 6:14 **10:19** [a] 2 Kin. 10:15 [b] Lev. 6:4, 6 [c] Lev. 5:6, 15

20 Also of the sons of Immer: Hanani and
Zebadiah; 21 of the sons of Harim: Maaseiah,
Elijah, Shemaiah, Jehiel, and Uzziah; 22 of the
sons of Pashhur: Elioenai, Maaseiah, Ishmael, Nethanel, Jozabad, and Elasah.

23 Also of the Levites: Jozabad, Shimei, Kelaiah (the same *is* Kelita), Pethahiah, Judah, and Eliezer.

24 Also of the singers: Eliashib; and of the gatekeepers: Shallum, Telem, and Uri.

25 And others of Israel: of the [a]sons of Parosh: Ramiah, Jeziah, Malchiah, Mijamin, Eleazar, Malchijah, and Benaiah; 26 of
the sons of Elam: Mattaniah, Zechariah,
Jehiel, Abdi, Jeremoth, and Eliah; 27 of the
sons of Zattu: Elioenai, Eliashib, Mattaniah,
Jeremoth, Zabad, and Aziza; 28 of the [a]sons
of Bebai: Jehohanan, Hananiah, Zabbai,
and Athlai; 29 of the sons of Bani: Meshullam, Malluch, Adaiah, Jashub, Sheal, *and*
Ramoth;[1] 30 of the [a]sons of Pahath-Moab:
Adna, Chelal, Benaiah, Maaseiah, Mattaniah, Bezalel, Binnui, and Manasseh; 31 *of* the
sons of Harim: Eliezer, Ishijah, Malchijah,
Shemaiah, Shimeon, 32 Benjamin, Malluch,
and Shemariah; 33 of the sons of Hashum:
Mattenai, Mattattah, Zabad, Eliphelet, Jeremai, Manasseh, *and* Shimei; 34 of the sons of
Bani: Maadai, Amram, Uel, 35 Benaiah, Bedeiah, Cheluh,[1] 36 Vaniah, Meremoth, Eliashib,
37 Mattaniah, Mattenai, Jaasai,[1] 38 Bani, Binnui, Shimei, 39 Shelemiah, Nathan, Adaiah,
40 Machnadebai, Shashai, Sharai, 41 Azarel,
Shelemiah, Shemariah, 42 Shallum, Amariah, *and* Joseph; 43 of the sons of Nebo:
Jeiel, Mattithiah, Zabad, Zebina, Jaddai,[1]
Joel, *and* Benaiah.

44 All these had taken pagan wives, and *some* of them had wives *by whom* they had children.

10:25 [a] Ezra 2:3; 8:3 10:28 [a] Ezra 8:11 10:29 [1] Or *Jeremoth* 10:30 [a] Ezra 8:4 10:35 [1] Or *Cheluhi*, or *Cheluhu*
10:37 [1] Or *Jaasu* 10:43 [1] Or *Jaddu*

THE BOOK OF

NEHEMIAH

AUTHOR

It is apparent that much of this book came from Nehemiah's personal memoirs. The account is extremely vivid and frank. Obviously, Nehemiah 1:1—7:5; 12:27–43; and 13:4–31 are the "words of Nehemiah" (1:1). Some scholars state that Nehemiah composed the above portions and compiled the rest. Others feel that Ezra wrote 7:6—12:26 and 12:44—13:3, then put together the rest using Nehemiah's diary. Nehemiah 7:5–73 and Ezra 2:1–70 are almost identical, but both lists may have been pulled from an existing record of the same period.

TIME

444–425 BC

KEY VERSE

Nehemiah 6:15

THEME

Nehemiah's role in rebuilding the temple and the walls of Jerusalem is more political than physical as he deals with the new political situation arising in Persia and in Jerusalem. He also serves as the general contractor who pulls together the raw materials and the workers while orchestrating the rebuilding process. Within all his work there is an underlying understanding that God has called him to do this work, and he is fulfilling God's purposes. When the people don't follow through with adhering to the law, Nehemiah is just as forceful as Ezra in calling the people back to repentance and obedience.

Although the word "peace" appears only one time in the original language in this book, the entire volume is emblematic of seeking the safety of God's peace and putting up walls against those who would steal it: "So the wall was finished [*shalom*] on the twenty-fifth day" (Neh. 6:15). Nehemiah also reveals the importance of short, powerful prayers, especially when one needs wisdom in difficult decisions (2:4). So often we miss the peace of God by not seeking the Lord before making choices! Nehemiah had a singular focus on building the walls of Jerusalem. He refused to come off the wall, saying, "I am doing a great work, so that I cannot come down" (6:3), which reminds us to resist distractions when we are pursuing the peace of God.

Nehemiah Prays for His People

1 The words of [a]Nehemiah the son of
Hachaliah.
It came to pass in the month of Chislev, *in*
the [b]twentieth year, as I was in [c]Shushan[1] the
citadel, 2 that [a]Hanani one of my brethren
came with men from Judah; and I asked
them concerning the Jews who had escaped,
who had survived the captivity, and concerning Jerusalem. 3 And they said to me, "The
survivors who are left from the captivity
in the [a]province *are* there in great distress
and [b]reproach. [c]The wall of Jerusalem [d]*is*
also broken down, and its gates are burned
with fire."
4 So it was, when I heard these words, that
I sat down and wept, and mourned *for many*
days; I was fasting and praying before the
God of heaven.
5 And I said: "I pray, [a]LORD God of heav-
en, O great and [b]awesome God, [c]*You* who
keep *Your* covenant and mercy with those
who love You[1] and observe Your[2] commandments, 6 please let Your ear be attentive and
[a]Your eyes open, that You may hear the
prayer of Your servant which I pray before
You now, day and night, for the children
of Israel Your servants, and [b]confess the
sins of the children of Israel which we have
sinned against You. Both my father's house
and I have sinned. 7 [a]We have acted very
corruptly against You, and have [b]not kept
the commandments, the statutes, nor the
ordinances which You commanded Your
servant Moses. 8 Remember, I pray, the word
that You commanded Your servant Moses,
saying, [a]'*If* you are unfaithful, I will scatter
you among the nations;[1] 9 [a]but *if* you return
to Me, and keep My commandments and
do them, [b]though some of you were cast
out to the farthest part of the heavens, *yet*
I will gather them from there, and bring
them to the place which I have chosen as
a dwelling for My name.'[1] 10 [a]Now these *are*
Your servants and Your people, whom You
have redeemed by Your great power, and by
Your strong hand. 11 O Lord, I pray, please [a]let
Your ear be attentive to the prayer of Your
servant, and to the prayer of Your servants
who [b]desire to fear Your name; and let Your
servant prosper this day, I pray, and grant
him mercy in the sight of this man."
For I was the king's [c]cupbearer.

Nehemiah Sent to Judah

2 And it came to pass in the month of Nisan,
in the twentieth year of [a]King Artaxerxes,
when wine *was* before him, that [b]I took the wine
and gave it to the king. Now I had never been
sad in his presence before. 2 Therefore the king
said to me, "Why *is* your face sad, since you *are*
not sick? This *is* nothing but [a]sorrow of heart."
So I became dreadfully afraid, 3 and said
to the king, [a]"May the king live forever! Why
should my face not be sad, when [b]the city, the
place of my fathers' tombs, *lies* waste, and its
gates are burned with [c]fire?"
4 Then the king said to me, "What do you
request?"
So I [a]prayed to the God of heaven. 5 And I
said to the king, "If it pleases the king, and if
your servant has found favor in your sight,
I ask that you send me to Judah, to the city
of my fathers' tombs, that I may rebuild it."
6 Then the king said to me (the queen also
sitting beside him), "How long will your journey
be? And when will you return?" So it pleased
the king to send me; and I set him [a]a time.
7 Furthermore I said to the king, "If it pleases the king, let letters be given to me for the
[a]governors *of the region* beyond the River,[1]
that they must permit me to pass through till
I come to Judah, 8 and a letter to Asaph the
keeper of the king's forest, that he must give
me timber to make beams for the gates of the
citadel which *pertains* [a]to the temple,[1] for the
city wall, and for the house that I will occupy."
And the king granted *them* to me [b]according
to the good hand of my God upon me.

PEACE NOTE

After the name of Jesus, there is no finer word or concept than *shalom* (peace). *Shalom* and its variations appear more than 575 times in Scripture.

1:1 [a] Neh. 10:1 [b] Neh. 2:1 [c] Esth. 1:1, 2, 5 [1] Or *Susa* **1:2** [a] Neh. 7:2 **1:3** [a] Neh. 7:6 [b] Neh. 2:17 [c] Neh. 2:17 [d] 2 Kin. 25:10 **1:5** [a] Dan. 9:4 [b] Neh. 4:14 [c] [Ex. 20:6; 34:6, 7] [1] Literally *Him* [2] Literally *His* **1:6** [a] 2 Chr. 6:40 [b] Dan. 9:20 **1:7** [a] Dan. 9:5 [b] Deut. 28:15 **1:8** [a] Lev. 26:33 [1] Leviticus 26:33 **1:9** [a] [Deut. 4:29–31; 30:2–5] [b] Deut. 30:4 [1] Deuteronomy 30:2–5 **1:10** [a] Deut. 9:29 **1:11** [a] Neh. 1:6 [b] Is. 26:8 [c] Neh. 2:1 **2:1** [a] Ezra 7:1 [b] Neh. 1:11 **2:2** [a] Prov. 15:13 **2:3** [a] Dan. 2:4; 5:10; 6:6, 21 [b] 2 Chr. 36:19 [c] Neh. 1:3 **2:4** [a] Neh. 1:4 **2:6** [a] Neh. 5:14; 13:6 **2:7** [a] Ezra 7:21; 8:36 [1] That is, the Euphrates, and so elsewhere in this book **2:8** [a] Neh. 3:7 [b] Ezra 5:5; 7:6, 9, 28 [1] Literally *house*

9 Then I went to the governors *in the region*
beyond the River, and gave them the king's
letters. Now the king had sent captains of
the army and horsemen with me. 10 When
[a]Sanballat the Horonite and Tobiah the Ammonite official[1] heard *of it,* they were deeply
disturbed that a man had come to seek the
well-being of the children of Israel.

Nehemiah Views the Wall of Jerusalem

11 So I [a]came to Jerusalem and was there three
days. 12 Then I arose in the night, I and a few men
with me; I told no one what my God had put in
my heart to do at Jerusalem; nor was there any
animal with me, except the one on which I rode.
13 And I went out by night [a]through the Valley
Gate to the Serpent Well and the Refuse Gate,
and viewed the walls of Jerusalem which were
[b]broken down and its gates which were burned
with fire. 14 Then I went on to the [a]Fountain Gate
and to the [b]King's Pool, but *there was* no room
for the animal under me to pass. 15 So I went up
in the night by the [a]valley, and viewed the wall;
then I turned back and entered by the Valley
Gate, and so returned. 16 And the officials did not
know where I had gone or what I had done; I
had not yet told the Jews, the priests, the nobles,
the officials, or the others who did the work.

17 Then I said to them, "You see the distress
that we *are* in, how Jerusalem *lies* waste, and its
gates are burned with fire. Come and let us build
the wall of Jerusalem, that we may no longer be
[a]a reproach." 18 And I told them of [a]the hand of
my God which had been good upon me, and also
of the king's words that he had spoken to me.

So they said, "Let us rise up and build."
Then they [b]set their hands to *this* good *work.*
19 But when Sanballat the Horonite, Tobiah
the Ammonite official, and Geshem the Arab
heard *of it,* they laughed at us and despised
us, and said, "What *is* this thing that you are
doing? [a]Will you rebel against the king?"

20 So I answered them, and said to them,
"The God of heaven Himself will prosper
us; therefore we His servants will arise and
build, [a]but you have no heritage or right or
memorial in Jerusalem."

Rebuilding the Wall

3 Then [a]*Eliashib the high* priest rose up
with his brethren the priests [b]and built
the Sheep Gate; they consecrated it and hung
its doors. They built [c]as far as the Tower of
the Hundred,[1] *and* consecrated it, then as far
as the Tower of [d]Hananel. 2 Next to *Eliashib*[1]
[a]the men of Jericho built. And next to them
Zaccur the son of Imri built.

3 Also the sons of Hassenaah built [a]the
Fish Gate; they laid its beams and [b]hung its
doors with its bolts and bars. 4 And next to
them [a]Meremoth the son of Urijah, the son of
Koz,[1] made repairs. Next to them [b]Meshullam
the son of Berechiah, the son of Meshezabel, made repairs. Next to them Zadok the
son of Baana made repairs. 5 Next to them
the Tekoites made repairs; but their nobles
did not put their shoulders[1] to [a]the work of
their Lord.

6 Moreover Jehoiada the son of Paseah and
Meshullam the son of Besodeiah repaired
[a]the Old Gate; they laid its beams and hung
its doors, with its bolts and bars. 7 And next
to them Melatiah the Gibeonite, Jadon the
Meronothite, the [a]men of Gibeon and Mizpah,
repaired the [b]residence[1] of the governor *of the*
region beyond the River. 8 Next to him Uzziel
the son of Harhaiah, one of the goldsmiths,
made repairs. Also next to him Hananiah,
one[1] of the perfumers, made repairs; and
they fortified Jerusalem as far as the [a]Broad
Wall. 9 And next to them Rephaiah the son of
Hur, leader of half the district of Jerusalem,
made repairs. 10 Next to them Jedaiah the
son of Harumaph made repairs in front of
his house. And next to him Hattush the son
of Hashabniah made repairs.

11 Malchijah the son of Harim and Hashub
the son of Pahath-Moab repaired another
section, [a]as well as the Tower of the Ovens.
12 And next to him was Shallum the son of
Hallohesh, leader of half the district of Jerusalem; he and his daughters made repairs.

13 Hanun and the inhabitants of Zanoah
repaired [a]the Valley Gate. They built it, hung
its doors with its bolts and bars, and *repaired*
a thousand cubits of the wall as far as [b]the
Refuse Gate.

14 Malchijah the son of Rechab, leader of
the district of [a]Beth Haccerem, repaired the
Refuse Gate; he built it and hung its doors
with its bolts and bars.

15 Shallun the son of Col-Hozeh, leader of
the district of Mizpah, repaired [a]the Fountain
Gate; he built it, covered it, hung its doors
with its bolts and bars, and repaired the wall
of the Pool of [b]Shelah by the [c]King's Garden,
as far as the stairs that go down from the City
of David. 16 After him Nehemiah the son of

2:10 [a] Neh. 2:19; 4:1 [1] Literally *servant,* and so elsewhere in this book **2:11** [a] Ezra 8:32 **2:13** [a] Neh. 3:13 [b] Neh. 1:3; 2:17 **2:14** [a] Neh. 3:15 [b] 2 Kin. 20:20 **2:15** [a] 2 Sam. 15:23 **2:17** [a] Neh. 1:3 **2:18** [a] Neh. 2:8 [b] 2 Sam. 2:7 **2:19** [a] Neh. 6:6 **2:20** [a] Ezra 4:3 **3:1** [a] Neh. 3:20; 12:10; 13:4, 7, 28 [b] John 5:2 [c] Neh. 12:39 [d] Jer. 31:38 [1] Hebrew *Hammeah,* also at 12:39 **3:2** [a] Neh. 7:36 [1] Literally *On his hand* **3:3** [a] Zeph. 1:10 [b] Neh. 6:1; 7:1 **3:4** [a] Ezra 8:33 [b] Ezra 10:15 [1] Or *Hakkoz* **3:5** [a] [Judg. 5:23] [1] Literally *necks* **3:6** [a] Neh. 12:39 **3:7** [a] Neh. 7:25 [b] Neh. 2:7–9 [1] Literally *throne* **3:8** [a] Neh. 12:38 [1] Literally *the son* **3:11** [a] Neh. 12:38 **3:13** [a] Neh. 2:13, 15 [b] Neh. 2:13 **3:14** [a] Jer. 6:1 **3:15** [a] Neh. 2:14 [b] Is. 8:6 [c] 2 Kin. 25:4

Azbuk, leader of half the district of Beth Zur,
made repairs as far as *the place* in front of the
tombs[1] of David, to the [a]man-made pool, and
as far as the House of the Mighty.
17 After him the Levites, *under* Rehum the
son of Bani, made repairs. Next to him Hashabiah, leader of half the district of Keilah,
made repairs for his district. 18 After him their
brethren, *under* Bavai[1] the son of Henadad,
leader of the *other* half of the district of Keilah, made repairs. 19 And next to him Ezer the
son of Jeshua, the leader of Mizpah, repaired
another section in front of the Ascent to the
Armory at the [a]buttress. 20 After him Baruch
the son of Zabbai[1] carefully repaired the other
section, from the buttress to the door of the
house of Eliashib the high priest. 21 After him
Meremoth the son of Urijah, the son of Koz,[1]
repaired another section, from the door of
the house of Eliashib to the end of the house
of Eliashib.
22 And after him the priests, the men of
the plain, made repairs. 23 After him Benjamin and Hasshub made repairs opposite
their house. After them Azariah the son of
Maaseiah, the son of Ananiah, made repairs
by his house. 24 After him [a]Binnui the son of
Henadad repaired another section, from the
house of Azariah to [b]the buttress, even as far
as the corner. 25 Palal the son of Uzai *made repairs* opposite the buttress, and on the tower
which projects from the king's upper house
that *was* by the [a]court of the prison. After
him Pedaiah the son of Parosh *made repairs.*
26 Moreover [a]the Nethinim who dwelt in
[b]Ophel *made repairs* as far as *the place* in
front of [c]the Water Gate toward the east, and
on the projecting tower. 27 After them the
Tekoites repaired another section, next to
the great projecting tower, and as far as the
wall of Ophel.
28 Beyond the [a]Horse Gate the priests made
repairs, each in front of his *own* house. 29 After them Zadok the son of Immer made repairs in front of his *own* house. After him
Shemaiah the son of Shechaniah, the keeper
of the East Gate, made repairs. 30 After him
Hananiah the son of Shelemiah, and Hanun,
the sixth son of Zalaph, repaired another section. After him Meshullam the son of Berechiah made repairs in front of his dwelling.
31 After him Malchijah, one of the goldsmiths,
made repairs as far as the house of the Nethinim and of the merchants, in front of the
Miphkad[1] Gate, and as far as the upper room
at the corner. 32 And between the upper room
at the corner, as far as the [a]Sheep Gate, the
goldsmiths and the merchants made repairs.

The Wall Defended Against Enemies

4 But it so happened, [a]when Sanballat
heard that we were rebuilding the wall,
that he was furious and very indignant, and
mocked the Jews. 2 And he spoke before his
brethren and the army of Samaria, and said,
"What are these feeble Jews doing? Will they
fortify themselves? Will they offer sacrifices?
Will they complete it in a day? Will they revive
the stones from the heaps of rubbish—*stones*
that are burned?"
3 Now [a]Tobiah the Ammonite *was* beside
him, and he said, "Whatever they build, if
even a fox goes up *on it,* he will break down
their stone wall."
4 [a]Hear, O our God, for we are despised;
[b]turn their reproach on their own heads, and
give them as plunder to a land of captivity!
5 [a]Do not cover their iniquity, and do not let
their sin be blotted out from before You;
for they have provoked *You* to anger before
the builders.
6 So we built the wall, and the entire wall
was joined together up to half its *height,* for
the people had a mind to work.
7 Now it happened, [a]when Sanballat, Tobiah, [b]the Arabs, the Ammonites, and the
Ashdodites heard that the walls of Jerusalem were being restored and the gaps were
beginning to be closed, that they became
very angry, 8 and all of them [a]conspired together to come *and* attack Jerusalem and
create confusion. 9 Nevertheless [a]we made
our prayer to our God, and because of them
we set a watch against them day and night.
10 Then Judah said, "The strength of the
laborers is failing, and *there is* so much rubbish that we are not able to build the wall."
11 And our adversaries said, "They will neither know nor see anything, till we come
into their midst and kill them and cause the
work to cease."
12 So it was, when the Jews who dwelt near
them came, that they told us ten times, "From
whatever place you turn, *they will be* upon us."
13 Therefore I positioned *men* behind the
lower parts of the wall, at the openings; and
I set the people according to their families,
with their swords, their spears, and their

3:16 [a] 2 Kin. 20:20 [1] Septuagint, Syriac, and Vulgate read *tomb.* **3:18** [1] Following Masoretic Text and Vulgate; some Hebrew manuscripts, Septuagint, and Syriac read *Binnui* (compare verse 24). **3:19** [a] 2 Chr. 26:9 **3:20** [1] A few Hebrew manuscripts, Syriac, and Vulgate read *Zaccai.* **3:21** [1] Or *Hakkoz* **3:24** [a] Ezra 8:33 [b] Neh. 3:19 **3:25** [a] Jer. 32:2; 33:1; 37:21 **3:26** [a] Neh. 11:21 [b] 2 Chr. 27:3 [c] Neh. 8:1, 3; 12:37 **3:28** [a] 2 Chr. 23:15 **3:31** [1] Literally *Inspection* or *Recruiting* **3:32** [a] Neh. 3:1; 12:39 **4:1** [a] Neh. 2:10, 19 **4:3** [a] Neh. 2:10, 19 **4:4** [a] Ps. 123:3, 4 [b] Ps. 79:12 **4:5** [a] Jer. 18:23 **4:7** [a] Neh. 4:1 [b] Neh. 2:19 **4:8** [a] Ps. 83:3–5 **4:9** [a] [Ps. 50:15]

bows. 14 And I looked, and arose and said
to the nobles, to the leaders, and to the rest
of the people, [a]"Do not be afraid of them.
Remember the Lord, [b]great and awesome,
and [c]fight for your brethren, your sons, your
daughters, your wives, and your houses."
15 And it happened, when our enemies
heard that it was known to us, and [a]*that* God
had brought their plot to nothing, that all of
us returned to the wall, everyone to his work.
16 So it was, from that time on, *that* half of
my servants worked at construction, while
the other half held the spears, the shields,
the bows, and *wore* armor; and the leaders
were behind all the house of Judah. 17 Those
who built on the wall, and those who carried
burdens, loaded themselves so that with one
hand they worked at construction, and with
the other held a weapon. 18 Every one of the
builders had his sword girded at his side as he
built. And the one who sounded the trumpet
was beside me.
19 Then I said to the nobles, the rulers, and
the rest of the people, "The work *is* great and
extensive, and we are separated far from one
another on the wall. 20 Wherever you hear the
sound of the trumpet, rally to us there. [a]Our
God will fight for us."
21 So we labored in the work, and half of
the men[1] held the spears from daybreak until
the stars appeared. 22 At the same time I also
said to the people, "Let each man and his
servant stay at night in Jerusalem, that they
may be our guard by night and a working
party by day." 23 So neither I, my brethren,
my servants, nor the men of the guard who
followed me took off our clothes, *except* that
everyone took them off for washing.

Nehemiah Deals with Oppression

5 And there was a great [a]outcry of the people and their wives against their [b]Jewish
brethren. 2 For there were those who said,
"We, our sons, and our daughters *are* many;
therefore let us get grain, that we may eat
and live."
3 There were also *some* who said, "We have
mortgaged our lands and vineyards and
houses, that we might buy grain because of
the famine."
4 There were also those who said, "We have
borrowed money for the king's tax *on* our
lands and vineyards. 5 Yet now [a]our flesh *is*
as the flesh of our brethren, our children as
their children; and indeed we [b]are forcing our
sons and our daughters to be slaves, and *some*
of our daughters have been brought into

> **PEACE NOTE**
>
> Doubt is not disbelief.
> Eliminating doubt from life
> is impossible. Live your faith
> as a discipline in belief for
> increasing peace in your life.

slavery. *It is* not in our power *to redeem them,*
for other men have our lands and vineyards."
6 And I became very angry when I heard
their outcry and these words. 7 After serious
thought, I rebuked the nobles and rulers,
and said to them, [a]"Each of you is exacting
usury from his brother." So I called a great
assembly against them. 8 And I said to them,
"According to our ability we have [a]redeemed
our Jewish brethren who were sold to the
nations. Now indeed, will you even sell your
brethren? Or should they be sold to us?"
Then they were silenced and found nothing *to say.* 9 Then I said, "What you are doing *is* not good. Should you not walk [a]in the
fear of our God [b]because of the reproach
of the nations, our enemies? 10 I also, *with*
my brethren and my servants, am lending
them money and grain. Please, let us stop
this usury! 11 Restore now to them, even this
day, their lands, their vineyards, their olive
groves, and their houses, also a hundredth of
the money and the grain, the new wine and
the oil, that you have charged them."
12 So they said, "We will restore *it,* and will
require nothing from them; we will do as
you say."
Then I called the priests, [a]and required an
oath from them that they would do according to this promise. 13 Then [a]I shook out the
fold of my garment[1] and said, "So may God
shake out each man from his house, and
from his property, who does not perform
this promise. Even thus may he be shaken
out and emptied."
And all the assembly said, "Amen!" and
praised the LORD. [b]Then the people did according to this promise.

4:14 [a] Deut. 1:29 [b] [Deut. 10:17] [c] 2 Sam. 10:12 **4:15** [a] Job 5:12 **4:20** [a] Ex. 14:14, 25 **4:21** [1] Literally *them* **5:1** [a] Neh. 5:7, 8 [b] Deut. 15:7 **5:5** [a] Is. 58:7 [b] Ex. 21:7 **5:7** [a] [Ex. 22:25] **5:8** [a] Lev. 25:48 **5:9** [a] Lev. 25:36 [b] 2 Sam. 12:14 **5:12** [a] Ezra 10:5 **5:13** [a] Acts 13:51; 18:6 [b] 2 Kin. 23:3 [1] Literally *my lap*

The Generosity of Nehemiah

14 Moreover, from the time that I was appointed to be their governor in the land of Judah, from the twentieth year [a]until the thirty-second year of King Artaxerxes, twelve years, neither I nor my brothers [b]ate the governor's provisions. 15 But the former governors who *were* before me laid burdens on the people, and took from them bread and wine, besides forty shekels of silver. Yes, even their servants bore rule over the people, but [a]I did not do so, because of the [b]fear of God. 16 Indeed, I also continued the [a]work on this wall, and we[1] did not buy any land. All my servants *were* gathered there for the work.

17 And [a]at my table *were* one hundred and fifty Jews and rulers, besides those who came to us from the nations around us. 18 Now *that* [a]which was prepared daily *was* one ox *and* six choice sheep. Also fowl were prepared for me, and once every ten days an abundance of all kinds of wine. Yet in spite of this [b]I did not demand the governor's provisions, because the bondage was heavy on this people.

19 [a]Remember me, my God, for good, *according to* all that I have done for this people.

Conspiracy Against Nehemiah

6 Now it happened [a]when Sanballat, Tobiah, Geshem the Arab, and the rest of our enemies heard that I had rebuilt the wall, and *that* there were no breaks left in it [b](though at that time I had not hung the doors in the gates), 2 that Sanballat and Geshem [a]sent to me, saying, "Come, let us meet together among the villages in the plain of [b]Ono." But they [c]thought to do me harm.

3 So I sent messengers to them, saying, "I *am* doing a great work, so that I cannot come down. Why should the work cease while I leave it and go down to you?"

4 But they sent me this message four times, and I answered them in the same manner.

5 Then Sanballat sent his servant to me as before, the fifth time, with an open letter in his hand. 6 In it *was* written:

> It is reported among the nations, and Geshem[1] says, *that* you and the Jews plan to rebel; therefore, according to these rumors, you are rebuilding the wall, [a]that you may be their king. 7 And you have also appointed prophets to proclaim concerning you at Jerusalem, saying, *"There is* a king in Judah!" Now these matters will be reported to the king. So come, therefore, and let us consult together.

8 Then I sent to him, saying, "No such things as you say are being done, but you invent them in your own heart."

9 For they all *were trying to* make us afraid, saying, "Their hands will be weakened in the work, and it will not be done."

Now therefore, *O God,* strengthen my hands.

10 Afterward I came to the house of Shemaiah the son of Delaiah, the son of Mehetabel, who *was* a secret informer; and he said, "Let us meet together in the house of God, within the temple, and let us close the doors of the temple, for they are coming to kill you; indeed, at night they will come to kill you."

11 And I said, "Should such a man as I flee? And who *is there* such as I who would go into the temple to save his life? I will not go in!" 12 Then I perceived that God had not sent him at all, but that [a]he pronounced *this* prophecy against me because Tobiah and Sanballat had hired him. 13 For this reason he *was* hired, that I should be afraid and act that way and sin, so *that* they might have *cause* for an evil report, that they might reproach me.

14 [a]My God, remember Tobiah and Sanballat, according to these their works, and the [b]prophetess Noadiah and the rest of the prophets who would have made me afraid.

The Wall Completed

15 So the wall was finished on the twenty-fifth *day* of Elul, in fifty-two days. 16 And it happened, [a]when all our enemies heard *of it,* and all the nations around us saw *these things,* that they were very disheartened in their own eyes; for [b]they perceived that this work was done by our God.

17 Also in those days the nobles of Judah sent many letters to Tobiah, and *the letters of* Tobiah came to them. 18 For many in Judah were pledged to him, because he was the [a]son-in-law of Shechaniah the son of Arah, and his son Jehohanan had married the daughter of [b]Meshullam the son of Berechiah. 19 Also they reported his good deeds before me, and reported my words to him. Tobiah sent letters to frighten me.

7 Then it was, when the wall was built and I had [a]hung the doors, when the gatekeepers, the singers, and the Levites had been appointed, 2 that I gave the charge of Jerusalem to my brother [a]Hanani, and Hananiah the

5:14 [a] Neh. 2:1; 13:6 [b] [1 Cor. 9:4–15] **5:15** [a] 2 Cor. 11:9; 12:13 [b] Neh. 5:9 **5:16** [a] Neh. 4:1; 6:1 [1] Following Masoretic Text; Septuagint, Syriac, and Vulgate read *I*. **5:17** [a] 1 Kin. 18:19 **5:18** [a] 1 Kin. 4:22 [b] Neh. 5:14, 15 **5:19** [a] Neh. 13:14, 22, 31 **6:1** [a] Neh. 2:10, 19; 4:1, 7; 13:28 [b] Neh. 3:1, 3 **6:2** [a] Prov. 26:24, 25 [b] 1 Chr. 8:12 [c] Ps. 37:12, 32 **6:6** [a] Neh. 2:19 [1] Hebrew *Gashmu* **6:12** [a] Ezek. 13:22 **6:14** [a] Neh. 13:29 [b] Ezek. 13:17 **6:16** [a] Neh. 2:10, 20; 4:1, 7; 6:1 [b] Ps. 126:2 **6:18** [a] Neh. 13:4, 28 [b] Ezra 10:15 **7:1** [a] Neh. 6:1, 15 **7:2** [a] Neh. 1:2

leader [b]of the citadel, for he *was* a faithful man and [c]feared God more than many.
3 And I said to them, "Do not let the gates of Jerusalem be opened until the sun is hot; and while they stand *guard,* let them shut and bar the doors; and appoint guards from among the inhabitants of Jerusalem, one at his watch station and another in front of his own house."

The Captives Who Returned to Jerusalem

4 Now the city *was* large and spacious, but the people in it *were* [a]few, and the houses *were* not rebuilt. 5 Then my God put it into my heart to gather the nobles, the rulers, and the people, that they might be registered by genealogy. And I found a register of the genealogy of those who had come up in the first *return,* and found written in it:

6 [a]These[1] *are* the people of the province who came back from the captivity, of those who had been carried away, whom Nebuchadnezzar the king of Babylon had carried away, and who returned to Jerusalem and Judah, everyone to his city.

7 Those who came with [a]Zerubbabel *were* Jeshua, Nehemiah, Azariah, Raamiah, Nahamani, Mordecai, Bilshan, Mispereth,[1] Bigvai, Nehum, and Baanah.

The number of the men of the people of Israel: 8 the sons of Parosh, two thousand one hundred and seventy-two;
9 the sons of Shephatiah, three hundred and seventy-two;
10 the sons of Arah, six hundred and fifty-two;
11 the sons of Pahath-Moab, of the sons of Jeshua and Joab, two thousand eight hundred and eighteen;
12 the sons of Elam, one thousand two hundred and fifty-four;
13 the sons of Zattu, eight hundred and forty-five;
14 the sons of Zaccai, seven hundred and sixty;
15 the sons of Binnui,[1] six hundred and forty-eight;
16 the sons of Bebai, six hundred and twenty-eight;
17 the sons of Azgad, two thousand three hundred and twenty-two;
18 the sons of Adonikam, six hundred and sixty-seven;
19 the sons of Bigvai, two thousand and sixty-seven;
20 the sons of Adin, six hundred and fifty-five;
21 the sons of Ater of Hezekiah, ninety-eight;
22 the sons of Hashum, three hundred and twenty-eight;
23 the sons of Bezai, three hundred and twenty-four;
24 the sons of Hariph,[1] one hundred and twelve;
25 the sons of Gibeon,[1] ninety-five;
26 the men of Bethlehem and Netophah, one hundred and eighty-eight;
27 the men of Anathoth, one hundred and twenty-eight;
28 the men of Beth Azmaveth,[1] forty-two;
29 the men of Kirjath Jearim, Chephirah, and Beeroth, seven hundred and forty-three;
30 the men of Ramah and Geba, six hundred and twenty-one;
31 the men of Michmas, one hundred and twenty-two;
32 the men of Bethel and Ai, one hundred and twenty-three;
33 the men of the other Nebo, fifty-two;
34 the sons of the other [a]Elam, one thousand two hundred and fifty-four;
35 the sons of Harim, three hundred and twenty;
36 the sons of Jericho, three hundred and forty-five;
37 the sons of Lod, Hadid, and Ono, seven hundred and twenty-one;
38 the sons of Senaah, three thousand nine hundred and thirty.

39 The priests: the sons of [a]Jedaiah, of the house of Jeshua, nine hundred and seventy-three;
40 the sons of [a]Immer, one thousand and fifty-two;
41 the sons of [a]Pashhur, one thousand two hundred and forty-seven;
42 the sons of [a]Harim, one thousand and seventeen.

43 The Levites: the sons of Jeshua, of Kadmiel,
and of the sons of Hodevah,[1] seventy-four.

44 The singers: the sons of Asaph, one hundred and forty-eight.

7:2 [b] Neh. 2:8; 10:23 [c] Ex. 18:21 **7:4** [a] Deut. 4:27 **7:6** [a] Ezra 2:1–70 [1] Compare verses 6–72 with Ezra 2:1–70 **7:7** [a] Ezra 5:2 [1] Spelled *Mispar* in Ezra 2:2 **7:15** [1] Spelled *Bani* in Ezra 2:10 **7:24** [1] Called *Jorah* in Ezra 2:18 **7:25** [1] Called *Gibbar* in Ezra 2:20 **7:28** [1] Called *Azmaveth* in Ezra 2:24 **7:34** [a] Neh. 7:12 **7:39** [a] 1 Chr. 24:7 **7:40** [a] 1 Chr. 9:12 **7:41** [a] Ezra 2:38; 10:22 **7:42** [a] 1 Chr. 24:8 **7:43** [1] Spelled *Hodaviah* in Ezra 2:40

45 The gatekeepers: the sons of Shallum,
the sons of Ater,
the sons of Talmon,
the sons of Akkub,
the sons of Hatita,
the sons of Shobai, one hundred and
thirty-eight.

46 The Nethinim: the sons of Ziha,
the sons of Hasupha,
the sons of Tabbaoth,
47 the sons of Keros,
the sons of Sia,[1]
the sons of Padon,
48 the sons of Lebana,[1]
the sons of Hagaba,[2]
the sons of Salmai,[3]
49 the sons of Hanan,
the sons of Giddel,
the sons of Gahar,
50 the sons of Reaiah,
the sons of Rezin,
the sons of Nekoda,
51 the sons of Gazzam,
the sons of Uzza,
the sons of Paseah,
52 the sons of Besai,
the sons of Meunim,
the sons of Nephishesim,[1]
53 the sons of Bakbuk,
the sons of Hakupha,
the sons of Harhur,
54 the sons of Bazlith,[1]
the sons of Mehida,
the sons of Harsha,
55 the sons of Barkos,
the sons of Sisera,
the sons of Tamah,
56 the sons of Neziah,
and the sons of Hatipha.

57 The sons of Solomon's servants: the
sons of Sotai,
the sons of Sophereth,
the sons of Perida,[1]
58 the sons of Jaala,
the sons of Darkon,
the sons of Giddel,
59 the sons of Shephatiah,
the sons of Hattil,
the sons of Pochereth of Zebaim,
and the sons of Amon.[1]
60 All the Nethinim, and the sons
of Solomon's servants, *were* three
hundred and ninety-two.

61 And these *were* the ones who came up
from Tel Melah, Tel Harsha, Cherub,
Addon,[1] and Immer, but they could not
identify their father's house nor their
lineage, whether they *were* of Israel:
62 the sons of Delaiah,
the sons of Tobiah,
the sons of Nekoda, six hundred and
forty-two;
63 and of the priests: the sons of
Habaiah,
the sons of Koz,[1]
the sons of Barzillai, who took a wife of
the daughters of Barzillai the Gileadite,
and was called by their name.
64 These sought their listing *among*
those who were registered by
genealogy, but it was not found;
therefore they were excluded from
the priesthood as defiled. 65 And the
governor[1] said to them that they
should not eat of the most holy things
till a priest could consult with the Urim
and Thummim.

66 Altogether the whole assembly *was*
forty-two thousand three hundred and
sixty, 67 besides their male and female
servants, of whom *there were* seven
thousand three hundred and thirty-
seven; and they had two hundred and
forty-five men and women singers.
68 Their horses were seven hundred and
thirty-six, their mules two hundred and
forty-five, 69 *their* camels four hundred
and thirty-five, *and* donkeys six
thousand seven hundred and twenty.

70 And some of the heads of the fathers'
houses gave to the work. [a]The governor[1]
gave to the treasury one thousand
gold drachmas, fifty basins, and five
hundred and thirty priestly garments.
71 Some of the heads of the fathers'
houses gave to the treasury of the work
[a]twenty thousand gold drachmas,
and two thousand two hundred silver
minas. 72 And that which the rest of the
people gave *was* twenty thousand gold
drachmas, two thousand silver minas,
and sixty-seven priestly garments.

73 So the priests, the Levites, the gatekeepers, the singers, *some* of the people, the
Nethinim, and all Israel dwelt in their cities.

7:47 [1] Spelled *Siaha* in Ezra 2:44 **7:48** [1] Masoretic Text reads *Lebanah.* [2] Masoretic Text reads *Hogabah.* [3] Or *Shalmai,* or *Shamlai* **7:52** [1] Spelled *Nephusim* in Ezra 2:50 **7:54** [1] Spelled *Bazluth* in Ezra 2:52 **7:57** [1] Spelled *Peruda* in Ezra 2:55 **7:59** [1] Spelled *Ami* in Ezra 2:57 **7:61** [1] Spelled *Addan* in Ezra 2:59 **7:63** [1] Or *Hakkoz* **7:65** [1] Hebrew *Tirshatha* **7:70** [a] Neh. 8:9 [1] Hebrew *Tirshatha* **7:71** [a] Ezra 2:69

Ezra Reads the Law
[a]When the seventh month came, the children of Israel *were* in their cities.

8 Now all [a]the people gathered together as
one man in the open square that *was* [b]in
front of the Water Gate; and they told Ezra
the [c]scribe to bring the Book of the Law of
Moses, which the LORD had commanded
Israel. 2 So Ezra the priest brought [a]the Law
before the assembly of men and women and
all who *could* hear with understanding [b]on
the first day of the seventh month. 3 Then he
[a]read from it in the open square that *was* in
front of the Water Gate from morning until
midday, before the men and women and
those who could understand; and the ears
of all the people *were attentive* to the Book
of the Law.
4 So Ezra the scribe stood on a platform of
wood which they had made for the purpose;
and beside him, at his right hand, stood Mattithiah, Shema, Anaiah, Urijah, Hilkiah, and
Maaseiah; and at his left hand Pedaiah, Mishael, Malchijah, Hashum, Hashbadana, Zechariah, *and* Meshullam. 5 And Ezra opened the
book in the sight of all the people, for he was
standing above all the people; and when he
opened it, all the people [a]stood up. 6 And Ezra
blessed the LORD, the great God.
Then all the people [a]answered, "Amen,
Amen!" while [b]lifting up their hands. And
they [c]bowed their heads and worshiped the
LORD with *their* faces to the ground.
7 Also Jeshua, Bani, Sherebiah, Jamin,
Akkub, Shabbethai, Hodijah, Maaseiah, Kelita, Azariah, Jozabad, Hanan, Pelaiah, and the
Levites, [a]helped the people to understand the
Law; and the people [b]*stood* in their place. 8 So
they read distinctly from the book, in the Law
of God; and they gave the sense, and helped
them to understand the reading.
9 [a]And Nehemiah, who *was* the governor,[1]
Ezra the priest *and* scribe, and the Levites

PEACE NOTE

The true God of the Bible is a happy God who wants us to be happy too. Happiness is God's will! A life lived in the peace of God is a joyous life—like Nehemiah's.

NEHEMIAH 8:10

7:73 [a] Ezra 3:1 8:1 [a] Ezra 3:1 [b] Neh. 3:26 [c] Ezra 7:6 8:2 [a] [Deut. 31:11, 12] [b] Lev. 23:24 8:3 [a] 2 Kin. 23:2 8:5 [a] Judg. 3:20 8:6 [a] Neh. 5:13 [b] Ps. 28:2 [c] 2 Chr. 20:18 8:7 [a] [Mal. 2:7] [b] Neh. 9:3 8:9 [a] Neh. 7:65, 70; 10:1 [1] Hebrew *Tirshatha*

FAITHFUL TO THE WORD

So they read distinctly from the book, in the Law of God; and they gave the sense, and helped them to understand the reading.

NEHEMIAH 8:8

True restoration of Israel required not only the rebuilding of the altar and temple but also a renewed commitment to the Law of Moses. To that end, Ezra the scribe assembled the people and read from the Book of the Law. Servants explained the meaning of the Hebrew text to people who, since the days of captivity, spoke Aramaic. Here we have the beginning of the tradition of reading the biblical text in its original language and then explaining it to folks in their native tongue. This tradition eventually developed into the practice in synagogue and church of reading Scripture and then preaching a sermon.

The people of Israel, having experienced defeat and exile, had learned their lesson. No more idolatry; no more flirting with the gods of the pagans. To acquire and maintain peace requires knowing God's Word, and knowing God's Word means hearing it read and explained regularly. The destruction of Jerusalem's first temple and horror of exile were tragic, but what came out of these experiences was a wholly new appreciation of Scripture's centrality for a life of faith and peace.

How important is Scripture to you? How is your peace?

PEACE NOTE

The words "joy" and "rejoice" appear almost three hundred times in the original languages of Scripture. Rejoicing is a simple path to peace.

NEHEMIAH 8:10

who taught the people said to all the people,
[b]"This day *is* holy to the LORD your God; [c]do
not mourn nor weep." For all the people wept,
when they heard the words of the Law.
10 Then he said to them, "Go your way, eat
the fat, drink the sweet, [a]and send portions
to those for whom nothing is prepared; for
this day *is* holy to our Lord. Do not sorrow, for
the joy of the LORD is your strength."
11 So the Levites quieted all the people,
saying, "Be still, for the day *is* holy; do not
be grieved." 12 And all the people went their
way to eat and drink, to [a]send portions and
rejoice greatly, because they [b]understood the
words that were declared to them.

The Feast of Tabernacles

13 Now on the second day the heads of the
fathers' *houses* of all the people, with the
priests and Levites, were gathered to Ezra
the scribe, in order to understand the words
of the Law. 14 And they found written in the
Law, which the LORD had commanded by
Moses, that the children of Israel should dwell
in [a]booths during the feast of the seventh
month, 15 and [a]that they should announce and
proclaim in all their cities and [b]in Jerusalem,
saying, "Go out to the mountain, and [c]bring
olive branches, branches of oil trees, myrtle
branches, palm branches, and branches of
leafy trees, to make booths, as *it is* written."
16 Then the people went out and brought
them and made themselves booths, each one
on the [a]roof of his house, or in their courtyards
or the courts of the house of God, and in the
open square of the [b]Water Gate [c]and in the
open square of the Gate of Ephraim. 17 So the
whole assembly of those who had returned
from the captivity made booths and sat under
the booths; for since the days of Joshua the
son of Nun until that day the children of Israel had not done so. And there was very [a]great
gladness. 18 Also [a]day by day, from the first day
until the last day, he read from the Book of the
Law of God. And they kept the feast [b]seven
days; and on the [c]eighth day *there was* a sacred
assembly, according to the *prescribed* manner.

The People Confess Their Sins

9 Now on the twenty-fourth day of [a]this
month the children of Israel were assembled with fasting, in sackcloth, [b]and with
dust on their heads.[1] 2 Then [a]those of Israelite lineage separated themselves from all
foreigners; and they stood and [b]confessed
their sins and the iniquities of their fathers.
3 And they stood up in their place and [a]read
from the Book of the Law of the LORD their
God *for one*-fourth of the day; and *for another*
fourth they confessed and worshiped the
LORD their God.
4 Then Jeshua, Bani, Kadmiel, Shebaniah,
Bunni, Sherebiah, Bani, *and* Chenani stood
on the stairs of the Levites and cried out with
a loud voice to the LORD their God. 5 And the
Levites, Jeshua, Kadmiel, Bani, Hashabniah,
Sherebiah, Hodijah, Shebaniah, *and* Pethahiah, said:

"Stand up *and* bless the LORD your God
Forever and ever!

"Blessed be [a]Your glorious name,
Which is exalted above all blessing and
praise!
6 [a]You alone *are* the LORD;
[b]You have made heaven,
[c]The heaven of heavens, with [d]all their
host,
The earth and everything on it,
The seas and all that is in them,
And You [e]preserve them all.
The host of heaven worships You.

7 "You *are* the LORD God,
Who chose [a]Abram,
And brought him out of Ur of the
Chaldeans,
And gave him the name [b]Abraham;
8 You found his heart [a]faithful before You,
And made a [b]covenant with him

8:9 [b] Num. 29:1 [c] Deut. 16:14 8:10 [a] Rev. 11:10 8:12 [a] Neh. 8:10 [b] Neh. 8:7, 8 8:14 [a] Lev. 23:34, 40, 42 8:15 [a] Lev. 23:4 [b] Deut. 16:16 [c] Lev. 23:40 8:16 [a] Deut. 22:8 [b] Neh. 12:37 [c] 2 Kin. 14:13 8:17 [a] 2 Chr. 30:21 8:18 [a] Deut. 31:11 [b] Lev. 23:36 [c] Num. 29:35 9:1 [a] Neh. 8:2 [b] 1 Sam. 4:12 [1] Literally *earth on them* 9:2 [a] Neh. 13:3, 30 [b] Neh. 1:6 9:3 [a] Neh. 8:7, 8 9:5 [a] 1 Chr. 29:13 9:6 [a] 2 Kin. 19:15, 19 [b] Rev. 14:7 [c] [Deut. 10:14] [d] Gen. 2:1 [e] [Ps. 36:6] 9:7 [a] Gen. 11:31 [b] Gen. 17:5 9:8 [a] Gen. 15:6; 22:1–3 [b] Gen. 15:18

To give the land of the Canaanites,
The Hittites, the Amorites,
The Perizzites, the Jebusites,
And the Girgashites—
To give *it* to his descendants.
You [c]have performed Your words,
For You *are* righteous.

9 "You[a] saw the affliction of our fathers in Egypt,
And [b]heard their cry by the Red Sea.
10 You [a]showed signs and wonders against Pharaoh,
Against all his servants,
And against all the people of his land.
For You knew that they [b]acted proudly against them.
So You [c]made a name for Yourself, as *it is* this day.
11 [a]And You divided the sea before them,
So that they went through the midst of the sea on the dry land;
And their persecutors You threw into the deep,
[b]As a stone into the mighty waters.
12 Moreover You [a]led them by day with a cloudy pillar,
And by night with a pillar of fire,
To give them light on the road
Which they should travel.

13 "You[a] came down also on Mount Sinai,
And spoke with them from heaven,
And gave them [b]just ordinances and true laws,
Good statutes and commandments.
14 You made known to them Your [a]holy Sabbath,
And commanded them precepts, statutes and laws,
By the hand of Moses Your servant.
15 You [a]gave them bread from heaven for their hunger,
And [b]brought them water out of the rock for their thirst,
And told them to [c]go in to possess the land
Which You had sworn to give them.

16 "But[a] *they and our fathers acted* proudly,
[b]Hardened their necks,
And did not heed Your commandments.
17 They refused to obey,
And [a]they were not mindful of Your wonders
That You did among them.
But they hardened their necks,
And in their rebellion[1]
They appointed [b]a leader
To return to their bondage.
But You *are* God,
Ready to pardon,
[c]Gracious and merciful,
Slow to anger,
Abundant in kindness,
And did not forsake them.

18 "Even [a]when they made a molded calf for themselves,
And said, 'This *is* your god
That brought you up out of Egypt,'
And worked great provocations,
19 Yet in Your [a]manifold mercies
You did not forsake them in the wilderness.
The [b]pillar of the cloud did not depart from them by day,
To lead them on the road;
Nor the pillar of fire by night,
To show them light,
And the way they should go.
20 You also gave Your [a]good Spirit to instruct them,
And did not withhold Your [b]manna from their mouth,
And gave them [c]water for their thirst.
21 [a]Forty years You sustained them in the wilderness;
They lacked nothing;
Their [b]clothes did not wear out[1]
And their feet did not swell.

22 "Moreover You gave them kingdoms and nations,
And divided them into districts.[1]
So they took possession of the land of [a]Sihon,
The land of[2] the king of Heshbon,
And the land of Og king of Bashan.
23 You also multiplied [a]their children as the stars of heaven,
And brought them into the land
Which You had told their fathers
To go in and possess.
24 So [a]the people went in
And possessed the land;

9:8 [c] Josh. 23:14 **9:9** [a] Ex. 2:25; 3:7 [b] Ex. 14:10 **9:10** [a] Ex. 7—14 [b] Ex. 18:11 [c] Jer. 32:20 **9:11** [a] Ex. 14:20–28 [b] Ex. 15:1, 5 **9:12** [a] Ex. 13:21, 22 **9:13** [a] Ex. 20:1–18 [b] [Rom. 7:12] **9:14** [a] Gen. 2:3 **9:15** [a] Ex. 16:14–17 [b] Ex. 17:6 [c] Deut. 1:8 **9:16** [a] Ps. 106:6 [b] Deut. 1:26–33; 31:27 **9:17** [a] Ps. 78:11, 42–45 [b] Num. 14:4 [c] Joel 2:13 [1] Following Masoretic Text and Vulgate; Septuagint reads *in Egypt*. **9:18** [a] Ex. 32:4–8, 31 **9:19** [a] Ps. 106:45 [b] 1 Cor. 10:1 **9:20** [a] Num. 11:17 [b] Ex. 16:14–16 [c] Ex. 17:6 **9:21** [a] Deut. 2:7 [b] Deut. 8:4; 29:5 [1] Compare Deuteronomy 29:5 **9:22** [a] Num. 21:21–35 [1] Literally *corners* [2] Following Masoretic Text and Vulgate; Septuagint omits *The land of*. **9:23** [a] Gen. 15:5; 22:17 **9:24** [a] Josh. 1:2–4

[b]You subdued before them the
inhabitants of the land,
The Canaanites,
And gave them into their hands,
With their kings
And the people of the land,
That they might do with them as they
wished.
25 And they took strong cities and a [a]rich
land,
And possessed [b]houses full of all goods,
Cisterns *already* dug, vineyards, olive
groves,
And fruit trees in abundance.
So they ate and were filled and [c]grew fat,
And delighted themselves in Your
great [d]goodness.

26 "Nevertheless they [a]were disobedient
And rebelled against You,
[b]Cast Your law behind their backs
And killed Your [c]prophets, who
testified against them
To turn them to Yourself;
And they worked great provocations.
27 [a]Therefore You delivered them into the
hand of their enemies,
Who oppressed them;
And in the time of their trouble,
When they cried to You,
You [b]heard from heaven;
And according to Your abundant mercies
[c]You gave them deliverers who saved
them
From the hand of their enemies.

28 "But after they had rest,
[a]They again did evil before You.
Therefore You left them in the hand of
their enemies,
So that they had dominion over them;
Yet when they returned and cried out
to You,
You heard from heaven;
And [b]many times You delivered them
according to Your mercies,
29 And testified against them,
That You might bring them back to
Your law.
Yet they acted proudly,
And did not heed Your commandments,
But sinned against Your judgments,
[a]'Which if a man does, he shall live by
them.'[1]
And they shrugged their shoulders,
Stiffened their necks,
And would not hear.
30 Yet for many years You had patience
with them,
And testified [a]against them by Your
Spirit [b]in Your prophets.
Yet they would not listen;
[c]Therefore You gave them into the hand
of the peoples of the lands.

9:24 [b] [Ps. 44:2, 3] 9:25 [a] Num. 13:27 [b] Deut. 6:11 [c] [Deut. 32:15] [d] Hos. 3:5 9:26 [a] Judg. 2:11 [b] 1 Kin. 14:9 [c] 1 Kin. 18:4; 19:10 9:27 [a] Judg. 2:14 [b] Ps. 106:44 [c] Judg. 2:18 9:28 [a] Judg. 3:12 [b] Ps. 106:43 9:29 [a] Lev. 18:5 [1] Leviticus 18:5 9:30 [a] Jer. 7:25 [b] [Acts 7:51] [c] Is. 5:5

RETURN TO YOUR ROOTS

We make a sure covenant and write it; our leaders, our Levites, and our priests seal it.

NEHEMIAH 9:38

Sometimes we have to battle our way back to peace with God and with ourselves. No matter how hard the road is and how seemingly impossible recovery looks, we can get back on the right road with God's help. This was Israel's experience.

When Ezra finished reading the Law of Moses, the people celebrated the feast of tabernacles. Later the people fasted and confessed their sins. The celebration of confession and worship concluded with Ezra's prayer that rehearsed the history of God's redemption of Israel, of Israel's sin, punishment, and restoration. God's people were ready to begin a new chapter of their history. A nation crushed and scattered had been reassembled and renewed.

Have you lost your way? Has peace vanished? Do you know how to get it back? Israel lost its way and suffered greatly, but through repentance and forgiveness that wayward nation found the path that took it home. This can be true for us, too. Even if lost, even if far from home, through repentance and God's mercy we can come back to our heavenly Father and find peace. Share this word of hope with someone you know who is in need.

31 Nevertheless in Your great mercy
[a]You did not utterly consume them nor forsake them;
For You *are* God, gracious and merciful.

32 "Now therefore, our God,
The great, the [a]mighty, and awesome God,
Who keeps covenant and mercy:
Do not let all the trouble seem small before You
That has come upon us,
Our kings and our princes,
Our priests and our prophets,
Our fathers and on all Your people,
[b]From the days of the kings of Assyria until this day.
33 However [a]You *are* just in all that has befallen us;
For You have dealt faithfully,
But [b]we have done wickedly.
34 Neither our kings nor our princes,
Our priests nor our fathers,
Have kept Your law,
Nor heeded Your commandments and Your testimonies,
With which You testified against them.
35 For they have [a]not served You in their kingdom,
Or in the many good *things* that You gave them,
Or in the large and rich land which You set before them;
Nor did they turn from their wicked works.

36 "Here [a]we *are*, servants today!
And the land that You gave to our fathers,
To eat its fruit and its bounty,
Here we *are*, servants in it!
37 And [a]it yields much increase to the kings
You have set over us,
Because of our sins;
Also they have [b]dominion over our bodies and our cattle
At their pleasure;
And we *are* in great distress.

38 "And because of all this,
We [a]make a sure *covenant* and write *it;*
Our leaders, our Levites, *and* our priests [b]seal *it.*"

The People Who Sealed the Covenant

10 Now those who placed *their* seal on *the document were:*
Nehemiah the governor, [a]the son of
Hacaliah, and Zedekiah, 2 [a]Seraiah, Azariah,
Jeremiah, 3 Pashhur, Amariah, Malchijah,
4 Hattush, Shebaniah, Malluch, 5 Harim, Meremoth, Obadiah, 6 Daniel, Ginnethon, Baruch,
7 Meshullam, Abijah, Mijamin, 8 Maaziah,
Bilgai, *and* Shemaiah. These *were* the priests.
9 The Levites: Jeshua the son of Azaniah,
Binnui of the sons of Henadad, *and* Kadmiel.
10 Their brethren: Shebaniah, Hodijah, Kelita, Pelaiah, Hanan, 11 Micha, Rehob, Hashabiah, 12 Zaccur, Sherebiah, Shebaniah, 13 Hodijah, Bani, *and* Beninu.
14 The leaders of the people: [a]Parosh,
Pahath-Moab, Elam, Zattu, Bani, 15 Bunni,
Azgad, Bebai, 16 Adonijah, Bigvai, Adin, 17 Ater,
Hezekiah, Azzur, 18 Hodijah, Hashum, Bezai,
19 Hariph, Anathoth, Nebai, 20 Magpiash, Meshullam, Hezir, 21 Meshezabel, Zadok, Jaddua,
22 Pelatiah, Hanan, Anaiah, 23 Hoshea, Hananiah, Hasshub, 24 Hallohesh, Pilha, Shobek,
25 Rehum, Hashabnah, Maaseiah, 26 Ahijah,
Hanan, Anan, 27 Malluch, Harim, *and* Baanah.

The Covenant That Was Sealed

28 [a]Now the rest of the people—the priests,
the Levites, the gatekeepers, the singers, the
Nethinim, [b]and all those who had separated
themselves from the peoples of the lands to
the Law of God, their wives, their sons, and
their daughters, everyone who had knowledge and understanding— 29 these joined
with their brethren, their nobles, [a]and entered
into a curse and an oath [b]to walk in God's Law,
which was given by Moses the servant of God,
and to observe and do all the commandments
of the LORD our Lord, and His ordinances
and His statutes: 30 We would not give [a]our
daughters as wives to the peoples of the land,
nor take their daughters for our sons; 31 [a]*if*
the peoples of the land brought wares or any
grain to sell on the Sabbath day, we would not
buy it from them on the Sabbath, or on a holy
day; and we would forego the [b]seventh year's
produce and the [c]exacting of every debt.
32 Also we made ordinances for ourselves,
to exact from ourselves yearly [a]one-third of
a shekel for the service of the house of our
God: 33 for [a]the showbread, for the regular
grain offering, for the [b]regular burnt offering
of the Sabbaths, the New Moons, and the
set feasts; for the holy things, for the sin
offerings to make atonement for Israel, and
all the work of the house of our God. 34 We
cast lots among the priests, the Levites, and
the people, [a]for bringing the wood offering
into the house of our God, according to our

9:31 [a] Jer. 4:27 **9:32** [a] [Ex. 34:6, 7] [b] 2 Kin. 15:19; 17:3–6 **9:33** [a] [Dan. 9:14] [b] [Dan. 9:5, 6, 8] **9:35** [a] Deut. 28:47 **9:36** [a] Deut. 28:48 **9:37** [a] Deut. 28:33, 51 [b] Deut. 28:48 **9:38** [a] 2 Kin. 23:3 [b] Neh. 10:1 **10:1** [a] Neh. 1:1 **10:2** [a] Neh. 12:1–21 **10:14** [a] Ezra 2:3 **10:28** [a] Ezra 2:36–43 [b] Neh. 13:3 **10:29** [a] Deut. 29:12 [b] 2 Kin. 23:3 **10:30** [a] Ex. 34:16 **10:31** [a] Ex. 20:10 [b] Lev. 25:4 [c] [Deut. 15:1, 2] **10:32** [a] Matt. 17:24 **10:33** [a] Lev. 24:5 [b] Num. 28; 29 **10:34** [a] Neh. 13:31

[a]purified themselves, and purified the people, the gates, and the wall.
31 So I brought the leaders of Judah up on
the wall, and appointed two large thanksgiving choirs. [a]*One* went to the right hand
on the wall [b]toward the Refuse Gate. 32 After
them went Hoshaiah and half of the leaders of Judah, 33 and Azariah, Ezra, Meshullam, 34 Judah, Benjamin, Shemaiah, Jeremiah, 35 and some of the priests' sons [a]with
trumpets—Zechariah the son of Jonathan,
the son of Shemaiah, the son of Mattaniah,
the son of Michaiah, the son of Zaccur, the
son of Asaph, 36 and his brethren, Shemaiah,
Azarel, Milalai, Gilalai, Maai, Nethanel, Judah,
and Hanani, with [a]the musical [b]instruments
of David the man of God. And Ezra the scribe
went before them. 37 [a]By the Fountain Gate,
in front of them, they went up [b]the stairs
of the [c]City of David, on the stairway of the
wall, beyond the house of David, as far as
[d]the Water Gate eastward.
38 [a]The other thanksgiving choir went the
opposite *way,* and I *was* behind them with
half of the people on the wall, going past the
[b]Tower of the Ovens as far as [c]the Broad Wall,
39 [a]and above the Gate of Ephraim, above [b]the
Old Gate, above [c]the Fish Gate, [d]the Tower of
Hananel, the Tower of the Hundred, as far as
[e]the Sheep Gate; and they stopped by [f]the
Gate of the Prison.
40 So the two thanksgiving choirs stood in
the house of God, likewise I and the half of
the rulers with me; 41 and the priests, Eliakim,
Maaseiah, Minjamin,[1] Michaiah, Elioenai,
Zechariah, *and* Hananiah, with trumpets;
42 also Maaseiah, Shemaiah, Eleazar, Uzzi,
Jehohanan, Malchijah, Elam, and Ezer. The
singers sang loudly with Jezrahiah the di-
rector.
43 Also that day they offered great sacrifices, and rejoiced, for God had made them
rejoice with great joy; the women and the
children also rejoiced, so that the joy of Jerusalem was heard [a]afar off.

Temple Responsibilities

44 [a]And at the same time some were appointed over the rooms of the storehouse for
the offerings, the firstfruits, and the [b]tithes,
to gather into them from the fields of the
cities the portions specified by the Law for
the priests and Levites; for Judah rejoiced
over the priests and Levites who ministered.
45 Both the singers and the gatekeepers kept
the charge of their God and the charge of the
purification, [a]according to the command
of David *and* Solomon his son. 46 For in the
days of David [a]and Asaph of old *there were*
chiefs of the singers, and songs of praise and
thanksgiving to God. 47 In the days of Zerubbabel and in the days of Nehemiah all Israel
gave the portions for the singers and the
gatekeepers, a portion for [a]each day. [b]They
also consecrated *holy things* for the Levites,
[c]and the Levites consecrated *them* for the
children of Aaron.

Principles of Separation

13 On that day [a]they read from the Book
of Moses in the hearing of the people,
and in it was found written [b]that no Ammonite or Moabite should ever come into
the assembly of God, 2 because they had not
met the children of Israel with bread and
water, but [a]hired Balaam against them to
curse them. [b]However, our God turned the
curse into a blessing. 3 So it was, when they
had heard the Law, [a]that they separated all
the mixed multitude from Israel.

The Reforms of Nehemiah

4 Now before this, [a]Eliashib the priest, having authority over the storerooms of the
house of our God, *was* allied with [b]Tobiah.
5 And he had prepared for him a large room,
[a]where previously they had stored the grain
offerings, the frankincense, the articles, the
tithes of grain, the new wine and oil, [b]which
were commanded *to be given* to the Levites
and singers and gatekeepers, and the offerings for the priests. 6 But during all this I was
not in Jerusalem, [a]for in the thirty-second
year of Artaxerxes king of Babylon I had
returned to the king. Then after certain days
I obtained leave from the king, 7 and I came
to Jerusalem and discovered the evil that
Eliashib had done for Tobiah, in [a]preparing
a room for him in the courts of the house of
God. 8 And it grieved me bitterly; therefore
I threw all the household goods of Tobiah
out of the room. 9 Then I commanded them
to [a]cleanse the rooms; and I brought back
into them the articles of the house of God,
with the grain offering and the frankincense.
10 I also realized that the portions for the

12:30 [a] Neh. 13:22, 30 **12:31** [a] Neh. 12:38 [b] Neh. 2:13; 3:13 **12:35** [a] Num. 10:2, 8 **12:36** [a] 1 Chr. 23:5 [b] 2 Chr. 29:26, 27 **12:37** [a] Neh. 2:14; 3:15 [b] Neh. 3:15 [c] 2 Sam. 5:7–9 [d] Neh. 3:26; 8:1, 3, 16 **12:38** [a] Neh. 12:31 [b] Neh. 3:11 [c] Neh. 3:8 **12:39** [a] 2 Kin. 14:13 [b] Neh. 3:6 [c] Neh. 3:3 [d] Neh. 3:1 [e] Neh. 3:32 [f] Jer. 32:2 **12:41** [1] Or *Mijamin* (compare verse 5) **12:43** [a] Ezra 3:13 **12:44** [a] Neh. 13:5, 12, 13 [b] Neh. 10:37–39 **12:45** [a] 1 Chr. 25; 26 **12:46** [a] 2 Chr. 29:30 **12:47** [a] Neh. 11:23 [b] Num. 18:21, 24 [c] Num. 18:26 **13:1** [a] Neh. 8:3, 8; 9:3 [b] Deut. 23:3, 4 **13:2** [a] Num. 22:5 [b] Num. 23:1; 24:10 **13:3** [a] Neh. 9:2; 10:28 **13:4** [a] Neh. 12:10 [b] Neh. 2:10; 4:3; 6:1 **13:5** [a] Neh. 12:44 [b] Num. 18:21, 24 **13:6** [a] Neh. 5:14–16 **13:7** [a] Neh. 13:1, 5 **13:9** [a] 2 Chr. 29:5, 15, 16

Levites had [a]not been given *them;* for each of
the Levites and the singers who did the work
had gone back to [b]his field. 11So [a]I contended
with the rulers, and said, [b]"Why is the house
of God forsaken?" And I gathered them together and set them in their place. 12[a]Then
all Judah brought the tithe of the grain and
the new wine and the oil to the storehouse.
13[a]And I appointed as treasurers over the
storehouse Shelemiah the priest and Zadok
the scribe, and of the Levites, Pedaiah; and
next to them *was* Hanan the son of Zaccur,
the son of Mattaniah; for they were considered [b]faithful, and their task *was* to distribute
to their brethren.

14[a]Remember me, O my God, concerning
this, and do not wipe out my good deeds that
I have done for the house of my God, and for
its services!

15In those days I saw *people* in Judah treading winepresses [a]on the Sabbath, and bringing
in sheaves, and loading donkeys with wine,
grapes, figs, and all *kinds of* burdens, [b]which
they brought into Jerusalem on the Sabbath
day. And I warned *them* about the day on which
they were selling provisions. 16Men of Tyre
dwelt there also, who brought in fish and all
kinds of goods, and sold *them* on the Sabbath
to the children of Judah, and in Jerusalem.

17Then I contended with the nobles of
Judah, and said to them, "What evil thing *is*
this that you do, by which you profane the
Sabbath day? 18[a]Did not your fathers do thus,
and did not our God bring all this disaster
on us and on this city? Yet you bring added
wrath on Israel by profaning the Sabbath."

19So it was, at the gates of Jerusalem, as it
[a]began to be dark before the Sabbath, that I
commanded the gates to be shut, and charged
that they must not be opened till after the
Sabbath. [b]Then I posted *some* of my servants
at the gates, *so that* no burdens would be
brought in on the Sabbath day. 20Now the
merchants and sellers of all kinds of wares
lodged outside Jerusalem once or twice.

21Then I warned them, and said to them,
"Why do you spend the night around the
wall? If you do *so* again, I will lay hands on
you!" From that time on they came no *more*
on the Sabbath. 22And I commanded the Levites that [a]they should cleanse themselves,
and that they should go and guard the gates,
to sanctify the Sabbath day.

Remember me, O my God, *concerning* this
also, and spare me according to the greatness
of Your mercy!

23In those days I also saw Jews *who* [a]had
married women of [b]Ashdod, Ammon, *and*
Moab. 24And half of their children spoke
the language of Ashdod, and could not
speak the language of Judah, but spoke according to the language of one or the other
people.

25So I [a]contended with them and cursed
them, struck some of them and pulled out
their hair, and made them [b]swear by God,
saying, "You shall not give your daughters as
wives to their sons, nor take their daughters
for your sons or yourselves. 26[a]Did not Solomon king of Israel sin by these things? Yet
among many nations there was no king like
him, [b]who was beloved of his God; and God
made him king over all Israel. [c]Neverthe-
less pagan women caused even him to sin.
27Should we then hear of your doing all this
great evil, [a]transgressing against our God by
marrying pagan women?"

28And *one* of the sons [a]of Joiada, the son
of Eliashib the high priest, *was* a son-in-law
of [b]Sanballat the Horonite; therefore I drove
him from me.

29[a]Remember them, O my God, because
they have defiled the priesthood and [b]the
covenant of the priesthood and the Levites.

30[a]Thus I cleansed them of everything
pagan. I also [b]assigned duties to the priests
and the Levites, each to his service, 31and *to
bringing* [a]the wood offering and the firstfruits
at appointed times.

[b]Remember me, O my God, for good!

13:10 [a] Neh. 10:37 [b] Num. 35:2 **13:11** [a] Neh. 13:17, 25 [b] Neh. 10:39 **13:12** [a] Neh. 10:38; 12:44 **13:13** [a] 2 Chr. 31:12 [b] 1 Cor. 4:2 **13:14** [a] Neh. 5:19; 13:22, 31 **13:15** [a] [Ex. 20:10] [b] [Jer. 17:21] **13:18** [a] [Jer. 17:21] **13:19** [a] Lev. 23:32 [b] Jer. 17:21, 22 **13:22** [a] Neh. 12:30 **13:23** [a] Ezra 9:2 [b] Neh. 4:7 **13:25** [a] Prov. 28:4 [b] Neh. 10:29, 30 **13:26** [a] 1 Kin. 11:1, 2 [b] 2 Sam. 12:24, 25 [c] 1 Kin. 11:4–8 **13:27** [a] [Ezra 10:2] **13:28** [a] Neh. 12:10, 12 [b] Neh. 4:1, 7; 6:1, 2 **13:29** [a] Neh. 6:14 [b] Mal. 2:4, 11, 12 **13:30** [a] Neh. 10:30 [b] Neh. 12:1 **13:31** [a] Neh. 10:34 [b] Neh. 13:14, 22

THE BOOK OF ESTHER

AUTHOR

Even though the author's identity is not given in the text, it is obvious from the intimate knowledge of Persian customs and etiquette, the palace in Shushan (or Susa), and the details of the reign of King Ahasuerus, that the author lived in Persia during this period. The love expressed here for the Jewish people and the author's knowledge of Jewish customs further suggest Jewish authorship. It is also thought that this Persian Jew was either an eyewitness to the events or knew an eyewitness. It may be that this author had access to the detailed records kept by Mordecai.

TIME

c. 483–473 BC

KEY VERSE

Esther 4:14

THEME

The Book of Esther is unique in the Scriptures for two reasons: God is never mentioned by name, and the heroine is a woman from the harem of a foreign king. The events of the book take place about thirty years before Nehemiah, after the temple in Jerusalem was rebuilt but before the walls were refinished. Esther probably helped pave the way for Nehemiah's work. The book fits well within the tapestry of the Old Testament. Just as in so many other Old Testament narratives, God provides the means to preserve His people in the face of a severe crisis. It is still read aloud as part of the Jewish people's Purim celebration.

Esther shows us the importance of protection and peace. God's providential protection is evident throughout the book. Ever since Amalek fought with the children of Israel leaving Egypt (Ex. 17:14–16), a spirit of Amalek has been attacking the Jews and attempting their genocide. Haman from Persia (modern-day Iran) wanted to wipe out the Jews. God raised up Esther "for such a time as this" (Esth. 4:14) to fulfill His promise to always protect the chosen people. We also see the word *peace* as a descriptor of the relationship between Mordecai and Esther: thank God for the older, wiser, faithful friends and relatives God brings into our lives, who seek to "learn of [our] welfare" (2:11). Furthermore, Mordecai brought peace by constantly speaking words of *shalom* (9:30; 10:3).

The King Dethrones Queen Vashti

1 Now it came to pass in the days of [a]Ahasuerus[1] (this *was* the Ahasuerus who reigned [b]over one hundred and twenty-seven provinces, [c]from India to Ethiopia), 2 in those days when King Ahasuerus [a]sat on the throne of his kingdom, which *was* in [b]Shushan[1] the citadel, 3 *that* in the third year of his reign he [a]made a feast for all his officials and servants—the powers of Persia and Media, the nobles, and the princes of the provinces *being* before him— 4 when he showed the riches of his glorious kingdom and the splendor of his excellent majesty for many days, one hundred and eighty days *in all.*

5 And when these days were completed, the king made a feast lasting seven days for all the people who were present in Shushan the citadel, from great to small, in the court of the garden of the king's palace. 6 *There were* white and blue linen *curtains* fastened with cords of fine linen and purple on silver rods and marble pillars; *and the* [a]couches *were* of gold and silver on a *mosaic* pavement of alabaster, turquoise, and white and black marble. 7 And they served drinks in golden vessels, each vessel being different from the other, with royal wine in abundance, [a]according to the generosity of the king. 8 In accordance with the law, the drinking was not compulsory; for so the king had ordered all the officers of his household, that they should do according to each man's pleasure.

9 Queen Vashti also made a feast for the women *in* the royal palace which *belonged* to King Ahasuerus.

10 On the seventh day, when the heart of the king was merry with wine, he commanded Mehuman, Biztha, [a]Harbona, Bigtha, Abagtha, Zethar, and Carcas, seven eunuchs who served in the presence of King Ahasuerus, 11 to bring Queen Vashti before the king, *wearing* her royal crown, in order to show her beauty to the people and the officials, for she *was* beautiful to behold. 12 But Queen Vashti refused to come at the king's command *brought* by *his* eunuchs; therefore the king was furious, and his anger burned within him.

13 Then the king said to the [a]wise men [b]who *understood the times* (for this *was* the king's manner toward all who knew law and justice, 14 those closest to him *being* Carshena, Shethar, Admatha, Tarshish, Meres, Marsena, and Memucan, the [a]seven princes of Persia and Media, [b]who had access to the king's presence, *and* who ranked highest in the kingdom): 15 "What *shall we* do to Queen Vashti, according to law, because she did not obey the command of King Ahasuerus *brought to her* by the eunuchs?"

16 And Memucan answered before the king and the princes: "Queen Vashti has not only wronged the king, but also all the princes, and all the people who *are* in all the provinces of King Ahasuerus. 17 For the queen's behavior will become known to all women, so that they will [a]despise their husbands in their eyes, when they report, 'King Ahasuerus commanded Queen Vashti to be brought in before him, but she did not come.' 18 This very day the *noble* ladies of Persia and Media will say to all the king's officials that they have heard of the behavior of the queen. Thus *there will be* excessive contempt and wrath. 19 If it pleases the king, let a royal decree go out from him, and let it be recorded in the laws of the Persians and the Medes, so that it will [a]not be altered, that Vashti shall come no more before King Ahasuerus; and let the king give her royal position to another who is better than she. 20 When the king's decree which he will make is proclaimed throughout all his empire (for it is great), all wives will [a]honor their husbands, both great and small."

21 And the reply pleased the king and the princes, and the king did according to the word of Memucan. 22 Then he sent letters to all the king's provinces, [a]to each province in its own script, and to every people in their own language, that each man should [b]be master in his own house, and speak in the language of his own people.

Esther Becomes Queen

2 After these things, when the wrath of King Ahasuerus subsided, he remembered Vashti, [a]what she had done, and what had been decreed against her. 2 Then the king's servants who attended him said: "Let beautiful young virgins be sought for the king; 3 and let the king appoint officers in all the provinces of his kingdom, that they may gather all the beautiful young virgins to Shushan the citadel, into the women's quarters, under the custody of Hegai[1] the king's eunuch, custodian of the women. And let beauty preparations be given *them.* 4 Then let the young woman who pleases the king be queen instead of Vashti."

This thing pleased the king, and he did so.

5 In Shushan the citadel there was a certain Jew whose name *was* Mordecai the son of Jair, the son of Shimei, the son of [a]Kish,

1:1 [a] Ezra 4:6 [b] Esth. 8:9 [c] Dan. 6:1 [1] Generally identified with Xerxes I (485–464 BC) **1:2** [a] 1 Kin. 1:46 [b] Neh. 1:1 [1] Or *Susa,* and so throughout this book **1:3** [a] Gen. 40:20 **1:6** [a] Amos 2:8; 6:4 **1:7** [a] Esth. 2:18 **1:10** [a] Esth. 7:9 **1:13** [a] Dan. 2:12 [b] 1 Chr. 12:32 **1:14** [a] Ezra 7:14 [b] 2 Kin. 25:19 **1:17** [a] [Eph. 5:33] **1:19** [a] Esth. 8:8 **1:20** [a] [Col. 3:18] **1:22** [a] Esth. 3:12; 8:9 [b] [Eph. 5:22–24] **2:1** [a] Esth. 1:19, 20 **2:3** [1] Hebrew *Hege* **2:5** [a] 1 Sam. 9:1

a Benjamite. 6 [a]*Kish*[1] had been carried away
from Jerusalem with the captives who had
been captured with Jeconiah[2] king of Judah,
whom Nebuchadnezzar the king of Babylon had carried away. 7 And *Mordecai* had
brought up Hadassah, that *is,* Esther, [a]his
uncle's daughter, for she had neither father
nor mother. The young woman *was* lovely
and beautiful. When her father and mother
died, Mordecai took her as his own daughter.
8 So it was, when the king's command and
decree were heard, and when many young
women were [a]gathered at Shushan the citadel, *under* the custody of Hegai, that Esther
also was taken to the king's palace, into the
care of Hegai the custodian of the women.
9 Now the young woman pleased him, and she
obtained his favor; so he readily gave [a]beauty
preparations to her, besides her allowance.
Then seven choice maidservants were provided for her from the king's palace, and he
moved her and her maidservants to the best
place in the house of the women.
10 [a]Esther had not revealed her people or
family, for Mordecai had charged her not to
reveal *it.* 11 And every day Mordecai paced in
front of the court of the women's quarters,
to learn of Esther's welfare and what was
happening to her.
12 Each young woman's turn came to go in
to King Ahasuerus after she had completed twelve months' preparation, according
to the regulations for the women, for thus
were the days of their preparation apportioned: six months with oil of myrrh, and six
months with perfumes and preparations for
beautifying women. 13 Thus *prepared, each*
young woman went to the king, and she was
given whatever she desired to take with her
from the women's quarters to the king's palace. 14 In the evening she went, and in the
morning she returned to the second house
of the women, to the custody of Shaashgaz,
the king's eunuch who kept the concubines.
She would not go in to the king again unless
the king delighted in her and called for her
by name.
15 Now when the turn came for Esther [a]the
daughter of Abihail the uncle of Mordecai,
who had taken her as his daughter, to go in
to the king, she requested nothing but what
Hegai the king's eunuch, the custodian of
the women, advised. And Esther [b]obtained
favor in the sight of all who saw her. 16 So
Esther was taken to King Ahasuerus, into his
royal palace, in the tenth month, which *is* the
month of Tebeth, in the seventh year of his
reign. 17 The king loved Esther more than all
the *other* women, and she obtained grace and
favor in his sight more than all the virgins;
so he set the royal [a]crown upon her head and
made her queen instead of Vashti. 18 Then the
king [a]made a great feast, the Feast of Esther,
for all his officials and servants; and he proclaimed a holiday in the provinces and gave
gifts according to the generosity of a king.

Mordecai Discovers a Plot

19 When virgins were gathered together a
second time, Mordecai sat within the king's
gate. 20 [a]*Now* Esther had not revealed her
family and her people, just as Mordecai had

2:6 [a] 2 Kin. 24:14, 15 [1] Literally *Who* [2] Same as *Jehoiachin,* 2 Kings 24:6 and elsewhere **2:7** [a] Esth. 2:15 **2:8** [a] Esth. 2:3 **2:9** [a] Esth. 2:3, 12 **2:10** [a] Esth. 2:20 **2:15** [a] Esth. 2:7; 9:29 [b] Esth. 5:2, 8 **2:17** [a] Esth. 1:11 **2:18** [a] Esth. 1:3 **2:20** [a] Esth. 2:10

A PEACE THAT IS SEEN

The king loved Esther more than all the other women . . .
so he set the royal crown upon her head.

ESTHER 2:17

I wonder what the Persian king appreciated in Esther, the Jewish woman, besides her appearance. The Babylonians had conquered the Jewish people a generation earlier. The Israelites were a defeated nation living in captivity in a foreign land. Yet Scripture says, "Esther obtained favor in the sight of all who saw her. So Esther was taken to King Ahasuerus, into his royal palace" (vv. 15–16). The king was so favorably impressed by the young woman that he made her his new queen and gave a lavish banquet in her honor.

The man or woman of peace *will* find favor. Our peace will be noticed. The peace you have is a gift from God, and other people want it. The Persian king saw something in Esther that he hadn't seen in the other women in his court. May God see in us that something special, that peace that people crave, and may we pass it along freely.

charged her, for Esther obeyed the command
of Mordecai as when she was brought up
by him.
21 In those days, while Mordecai sat within
the king's gate, two of the king's eunuchs,
Bigthan and Teresh, doorkeepers, became
furious and sought to lay hands on King
Ahasuerus. 22 So the matter became known
to Mordecai, [a]who told Queen Esther, and Esther informed the king in Mordecai's name.
23 And when an inquiry was made into the
matter, it was confirmed, and both were
hanged on a gallows; and it was written in
[a]the book of the chronicles in the presence
of the king.

Haman's Conspiracy Against the Jews

3 After these things King Ahasuerus promoted Haman, the son of Hammedatha
the [a]Agagite, and [b]advanced him and set his
seat above all the princes who *were* with him.
2 And all the king's servants who *were* [a]within
the king's gate bowed and paid homage to
Haman, for so the king had commanded
concerning him. But Mordecai [b]would not
bow or pay homage. 3 Then the king's servants who *were* within the king's gate said to
Mordecai, "Why do you transgress the [a]king's
command?" 4 Now it happened, when they
spoke to him daily and he would not listen
to them, that they told *it* to Haman, to see
whether Mordecai's words would stand; for
Mordecai had told them that he *was* a Jew.
5 When Haman saw that Mordecai [a]did not
bow or pay him homage, Haman was [b]filled
with wrath. 6 But he disdained to lay hands
on Mordecai alone, for they had told him
of the people of Mordecai. Instead, Haman
[a]sought to destroy all the Jews who *were*
throughout the whole kingdom of Ahasuerus—the people of Mordecai.
7 In the first month, which is the month
of Nisan, in the twelfth year of King Ahasuerus, [a]they cast Pur (that *is,* the lot), before
Haman to determine the day and the month,[1]
until *it fell on the* twelfth *month,*[2] which *is* the
month of Adar.
8 Then Haman said to King Ahasuerus,
"There is a certain people scattered and dispersed among the people in all the provinces
of your kingdom; [a]their laws *are* different
from all *other* people's, and they do not keep
the king's laws. Therefore it *is* not fitting for
the king to let them remain. 9 If it pleases
the king, let *a decree* be written that they be
destroyed, and I will pay ten thousand talents
of silver into the hands of those who do the
work, to bring *it* into the king's treasuries."
10 So the king [a]took [b]his signet ring from
his hand and gave it to Haman, the son of
Hammedatha the Agagite, the [c]enemy of the
Jews. 11 And the king said to Haman, "The
money and the people *are* given to you, to
do with them as seems good to you."
12 [a]Then the king's scribes were called on
the thirteenth day of the first month, and
a decree was written according to all that
Haman commanded—to the king's satraps,
to the governors who *were* over each province, to the officials of all people, to every
province [b]according to its script, and to every
people in their language. [c]In the name of
King Ahasuerus it was written, and sealed
with the king's signet ring. 13 And the letters
were [a]sent by couriers into all the king's provinces, to destroy, to kill, and to annihilate all
the Jews, both young and old, little children
and women, [b]in one day, on the thirteenth
day of the twelfth month, which *is* the month
of Adar, and [c]to plunder their possessions.[1]
14 [a]A copy of the document was to be issued
as law in every province, being published
for all people, that they should be ready for
that day. 15 The couriers went out, hastened
by the king's command; and the decree was
proclaimed in Shushan the citadel. So the
king and Haman sat down to drink, but [a]the
city of Shushan was perplexed.

Esther Agrees to Help the Jews

4 When Mordecai learned all that had happened, he [a]tore his clothes and put on
sackcloth [b]and ashes, and went out into the
midst of the city. He [c]cried out with a loud
and bitter cry. 2 He went as far as the front of
the king's gate, for no one *might* enter the
king's gate clothed with sackcloth. 3 And in
every province where the king's command
and decree arrived, *there was* great mourning
among the Jews, with fasting, weeping, and
wailing; and many lay in sackcloth and ashes.
4 So Esther's maids and eunuchs came and
told her, and the queen was deeply distressed.
Then she sent garments to clothe Mordecai
and take his sackcloth away from him, but he
would not accept *them.* 5 Then Esther called
Hathach, *one* of the king's eunuchs whom he
had appointed to attend her, and she gave him

2:22 [a] Esth. 6:1, 2 **2:23** [a] Esth. 6:1 **3:1** [a] Num. 24:7 [b] Esth. 5:11 **3:2** [a] Esth. 2:19, 21; 5:9 [b] Ps. 15:4 **3:3** [a] Esth. 3:2 **3:5** [a] Esth. 3:2; 5:9 [b] Dan. 3:19 **3:6** [a] Ps. 83:4 **3:7** [a] Esth. 9:24–26 [1] Septuagint adds *to destroy the people of Mordecai in one day;* Vulgate adds *the nation of the Jews should be destroyed.* [2] Following Masoretic Text and Vulgate; Septuagint reads *and the lot fell on the fourteenth of the month.* **3:8** [a] Acts 16:20, 21 **3:10** [a] Gen. 41:42 [b] Esth. 8:2, 8 [c] Esth. 7:6 **3:12** [a] Esth. 8:9 [b] Esth. 1:22 [c] Esth. 8:8–10 **3:13** [a] Esth. 8:10, 14 [b] Esth. 8:12 [c] Esth. 8:11; 9:10 [1] Septuagint adds the text of the letter here. **3:14** [a] Esth. 8:13, 14 **3:15** [a] Esth. 8:15 **4:1** [a] 2 Sam. 1:11 [b] Josh. 7:6 [c] Gen. 27:34

a command concerning Mordecai, to learn what and why this *was.* 6 So Hathach went out to Mordecai in the city square that *was* in front of the king's gate. 7 And Mordecai told him all that had happened to him, and [a]the sum of money that Haman had promised to pay into the king's treasuries to destroy the Jews. 8 He also gave him [a]a copy of the written decree for their destruction, which was given at Shushan, that he might show it to Esther and explain it to her, and that he might command her to go in to the king to make supplication to him and plead before him for her people. 9 So Hathach returned and told Esther the words of Mordecai.

10 Then Esther spoke to Hathach, and gave him a command for Mordecai: 11 "All the king's servants and the people of the king's provinces know that any man or woman who goes into [a]the inner court to the king, who has not been called, [b]*he has* but one law: put *all* to death, except the one [c]to whom the king holds out the golden scepter, that he may live. Yet I myself have not been [d]called to go in to the king these thirty days." 12 So they told Mordecai Esther's words.

13 And Mordecai told *them* to answer Esther: "Do not think in your heart that you will escape in the king's palace any more than all the other Jews. 14 For if you remain completely silent at this time, relief and deliverance will arise for the Jews from another place, but you and your father's house will perish. Yet who knows whether you have come to the kingdom for *such* a time as this?"

15 Then Esther told *them* to reply to Mordecai: 16 "Go, gather all the Jews who are present in Shushan, and fast for me; neither eat nor drink for [a]three days, night or day. My maids and I will fast likewise. And so I will go to the king, which *is* against the law; [b]and if I perish, I perish!"

17 So Mordecai went his way and did according to all that Esther commanded him.[1]

Esther's Banquet

5 Now it happened [a]on the third day that Esther put on *her* royal *robes* and stood in [b]the inner court of the king's palace, across from the king's house, while the king sat on his royal throne in the royal house, facing the entrance of the house.[1] 2 So it was, when the king saw Queen Esther standing in the court, *that* [a]she found favor in his sight, and [b]the king held out to Esther the golden scepter that *was* in his hand. Then Esther went near and touched the top of the scepter.

3 And the king said to her, "What do you wish, Queen Esther? What *is* your request? [a]It shall be given to you—up to half the kingdom!"

4 So Esther answered, "If it pleases the king, let the king and Haman come today to the banquet that I have prepared for him."

5 Then the king said, "Bring Haman quickly, that he may do as Esther has said." So the king and Haman went to the banquet that Esther had prepared.

6 At the banquet of wine [a]the king said to Esther, [b]"What *is* your petition? It shall be granted you. What *is* your request, up to half the kingdom? It shall be done!"

7 Then Esther answered and said, "My petition and request *is this:* 8 If I have found favor in the sight of the king, and if it pleases the king to grant my petition and fulfill my request, then let the king and Haman come to the [a]banquet which I will prepare for them, and tomorrow I will do as the king has said."

Haman's Plot Against Mordecai

9 So Haman went out that day [a]joyful and with a glad heart; but when Haman saw Mordecai in the king's gate, and [b]that he did not stand or tremble before him, he was filled with indignation against Mordecai. 10 Nevertheless Haman [a]restrained himself and went home, and he sent and called for his friends and his wife Zeresh. 11 Then Haman told them of his great riches, [a]the multitude of his children, everything in which the king had promoted him, and how he had [b]advanced him above the officials and servants of the king.

PEACE NOTE

Esther's life was emblematic of peace. No one expected that she could stand up for her people. But she did and the Lord used her to preserve the messianic line. What is God calling you to stand for?

ESTHER 4:14

4:7 [a] Esth. 3:9 **4:8** [a] Esth. 3:14, 15 **4:11** [a] Esth. 5:1; 6:4 [b] Dan. 2:9 [c] Esth. 5:2; 8:4 [d] Esth. 2:14 **4:16** [a] Esth. 5:1 [b] Gen. 43:14 **4:17** [1] Septuagint adds a prayer of Mordecai here. **5:1** [a] Esth. 4:16 [b] Esth. 4:11; 6:4 [1] Septuagint adds many extra details in verses 1 and 2. **5:2** [a] [Prov. 21:1] [b] Esth. 4:11; 8:4 **5:3** [a] Mark 6:23 **5:6** [a] Esth. 7:2 [b] Esth. 9:12 **5:8** [a] Esth. 6:14 **5:9** [a] [Job 20:5] [b] Esth. 3:5 **5:10** [a] 2 Sam. 13:22 **5:11** [a] Esth. 9:7–10 [b] Esth. 3:1

12 Moreover Haman said, "Besides, Queen Esther invited no one but me to come in with the king to the banquet that she prepared; and tomorrow I am again invited by her, along with the king. 13 Yet all this avails me nothing, so long as I see Mordecai the Jew sitting at the king's gate."

14 Then his wife Zeresh and all his friends said to him, "Let a [a]gallows be made, fifty cubits high, and in the morning [b]suggest to the king that Mordecai be hanged on it; then go merrily with the king to the banquet."

And the thing pleased Haman; so he had [c]the gallows made.

The King Honors Mordecai

6 That night the king could not sleep. So one was commanded to bring [a]the book of the records of the chronicles; and they were read before the king. 2 And it was found written that Mordecai had told of Bigthana and Teresh, two of the king's eunuchs, the doorkeepers who had sought to lay hands on King Ahasuerus. 3 Then the king said, "What honor or dignity has been bestowed on Mordecai for this?"

And the king's servants who attended him said, "Nothing has been done for him."

4 So the king said, "Who *is* in the court?" Now Haman had *just* entered [a]the outer court of the king's palace [b]to suggest that the king hang Mordecai on the gallows that he had prepared for him.

5 The king's servants said to him, "Haman is there, standing in the court."

And the king said, "Let him come in."

6 So Haman came in, and the king asked him, "What shall be done for the man whom the king delights to honor?"

Now Haman thought in his heart, "Whom would the king delight to honor more than [a]me?" 7 And Haman answered the king, "*For* the man whom the king delights to honor, 8 let a royal robe be brought which the king has worn, and [a]a horse on which the king has ridden, which has a royal crest placed on its head. 9 Then let this robe and horse be delivered to the hand of one of the king's most noble princes, that he may array the *man whom the king delights* to honor. Then parade him on horseback through the city square, [a]and proclaim before him: 'Thus shall it be done to the man whom the king delights to honor!' "

10 Then the king said to Haman, "Hurry, take the robe and the horse, as you have suggested, and do so for Mordecai the Jew who sits within the king's gate! Leave nothing undone of all that you have spoken."

> **PEACE NOTE**
>
> There's not a drop of peace apart from God in this whole world.

11 So Haman took the robe and the horse, arrayed Mordecai and led him on horseback through the city square, and proclaimed before him, "Thus shall it be done to the man whom the king delights to honor!"

12 Afterward Mordecai went back to the king's gate. But Haman [a]hurried to his house, mourning [b]and with his head covered. 13 When Haman told his wife Zeresh and all his friends everything that had happened to him, his wise men and his wife Zeresh said to him, "If Mordecai, before whom you have begun to fall, is of Jewish descent, you will not prevail against [a]him but will surely fall before him."

14 While they *were* still talking with him, the king's eunuchs came, and hastened to bring Haman to [a]the banquet which Esther had prepared.

Haman Hanged Instead of Mordecai

7 So the king and Haman went to dine with Queen Esther. 2 And on the second day, [a]at the banquet of wine, the king again said to Esther, "What *is* your petition, Queen Esther? It shall be granted you. And what *is* your request, up to half the kingdom? It shall be done!"

3 Then Queen Esther answered and said, "If I have found favor in your sight, O king, and if it pleases the king, let my life be given me at my petition, and my people at my request. 4 For we have been [a]sold, my people and I, to be destroyed, to be killed, and to be annihilated. Had we been sold as [b]male and female slaves, I would have held my tongue, although the enemy could never compensate for the king's loss."

5:14 [a] Esth. 7:9 [b] Esth. 6:4 [c] Esth. 7:10 **6:1** [a] Esth. 2:23; 10:2 **6:4** [a] Esth. 5:1 [b] Esth. 5:14 **6:6** [a] [Prov. 16:18; 18:12] **6:8** [a] 1 Kin. 1:33 **6:9** [a] Gen. 41:43 **6:12** [a] 2 Chr. 26:20 [b] 2 Sam. 15:30 **6:13** [a] Zech. 2:8 **6:14** [a] Esth. 5:8 **7:2** [a] Esth. 5:6 **7:4** [a] Esth. 3:9; 4:7 [b] Deut. 28:68

5So King Ahasuerus answered and said to
Queen Esther, "Who is he, and where is he,
who would dare presume in his heart to do
such a thing?"
6And Esther said, "The adversary and [a]en-
emy *is* this wicked Haman!"
So Haman was terrified before the king
and queen.
7Then the king arose in his wrath from the
banquet of wine *and went* into the palace garden; but Haman stood before Queen Esther,
pleading for his life, for he saw that evil was
determined against him by the king. 8When
the king returned from the palace garden to
the place of the banquet of wine, Haman had
fallen across [a]the couch where Esther *was*.
Then the king said, "Will he also assault the
queen while I *am* in the house?"
As the word left the king's mouth, they
[b]covered Haman's face. 9Now [a]Harbonah,
one of the eunuchs, said to the king, "Look!
[b]The gallows, fifty cubits high, which Haman
made for Mordecai, who spoke [c]good on
the king's behalf, is standing at the house
of Haman."
Then the king said, "Hang him on it!"
10So [a]they [b]hanged Haman on the gallows
that he had prepared for Mordecai. Then the
king's wrath subsided.

Esther Saves the Jews

8 On that day King Ahasuerus gave Queen
Esther the house of Haman, the [a]enemy
of the Jews. And Mordecai came before the
king, for Esther had told [b]how he *was related*
to her. 2So the king took off [a]his signet ring,
which he had taken from Haman, and gave it
to Mordecai; and Esther appointed Mordecai
over the house of Haman.
3Now Esther spoke again to the king, fell
down at his feet, and implored him with tears to
counteract the evil of Haman the Agagite, and
the scheme which he had devised against the
Jews. 4And [a]the king held out the golden scepter
toward Esther. So Esther arose and stood before
the king, 5and said, "If it pleases the king, and
if I have found favor in his sight and the thing
seems right to the king and I am pleasing in
his eyes, let it be written to revoke the [a]letters
devised by Haman, the son of Hammedatha
the Agagite, which he wrote to annihilate the
Jews who *are* in all the king's provinces. 6For
how can I endure to see [a]the evil that will come
to my people? Or how can I endure to see the
destruction of my countrymen?"

PEACE NOTE

Jesus established peace for us! His peace is an objective reality, and the subjective feeling of tranquility will come as we allow Christ to be established in our hearts.

7Then King Ahasuerus said to Queen Esther and Mordecai the Jew, "Indeed, [a]I have
given Esther the house of Haman, and they
have hanged him on the gallows because he
tried to lay his hand on the Jews. 8You yourselves write *a decree* concerning the Jews,
as you please, in the king's name, and seal
it with the king's signet ring; for whatever is
written in the king's name and sealed with
the king's signet ring [a]no one can revoke."
9[a]So the king's scribes were called at that
time, in the third month, which *is* the month
of Sivan, on the twenty-third *day;* and it was
written, according to all that Mordecai commanded, to the Jews, the satraps, the governors, and the princes of the provinces [b]from
India to Ethiopia, one hundred and twenty-
seven provinces *in all,* to every province [c]in
its own script, to every people in their own
language, and to the Jews in their own script
and language. 10[a]And he wrote in the name of
King Ahasuerus, sealed *it* with the king's signet
ring, and sent letters by couriers on horseback,
riding on royal horses bred from swift steeds.[1]
11By these letters the king permitted the
Jews who *were* in every city to [a]gather together and protect their lives—to [b]destroy, kill,
and annihilate all the forces of any people or
province that would assault them, *both* little
children and women, and to plunder their
possessions, 12[a]on one day in all the provinces of King Ahasuerus, on the thirteenth *day*
of the twelfth month, which *is* the month of
Adar.[1] 13[a]A copy of the document was to be
issued as a decree in every province and published for all people, so that the Jews would

7:6 [a] Esth. 3:10 **7:8** [a] Esth. 1:6 [b] Job 9:24 **7:9** [a] Esth. 1:10 [b] Esth. 5:14 [c] Esth. 6:2 **7:10** [a] [Ps. 7:16; 94:23] [b] Dan. 6:24
8:1 [a] Esth. 7:6 [b] Esth. 2:7, 15 **8:2** [a] Esth. 3:10 **8:4** [a] Esth. 4:11; 5:2 **8:5** [a] Esth. 3:13 **8:6** [a] Neh. 2:3 **8:7** [a] Prov. 13:22
8:8 [a] Dan. 6:8, 12, 15 **8:9** [a] Esth. 3:12 [b] Esth. 1:1 [c] Esth. 1:22; 3:12 **8:10** [a] 1 Kin. 21:8 [1] Literally *sons of the swift horses*
8:11 [a] Esth. 9:2 [b] Esth. 9:10, 15, 16 **8:12** [a] Esth. 3:13; 9:1 [1] Septuagint adds the text of the letter here.
8:13 [a] Esth. 3:14, 15

be ready on that day to avenge themselves
on their enemies. 14 The couriers who rode on
royal horses went out, hastened and pressed
on by the king's command. And the decree
was issued in Shushan the citadel.
15 So Mordecai went out from the presence
of the king in royal apparel of blue and white,
with a great crown of gold and a garment
of fine linen and purple; and [a]the city of
Shushan rejoiced and was glad. 16 The Jews
had [a]light and gladness, joy and honor. 17 And
in every province and city, wherever the king's
command and decree came, the Jews had joy
and gladness, a feast [a]and a holiday. Then
many of the people of the land [b]became Jews,
because [c]fear of the Jews fell upon them.

The Jews Destroy Their Tormentors

9 Now [a]in the twelfth month, that *is*, the
month of Adar, on the thirteenth day, [b]*the
time* came for the king's command and his
decree to be executed. On the day that the
enemies of the Jews had hoped to overpower
them, the opposite occurred, in that the Jews
themselves [c]overpowered those who hated
them. 2 The Jews [a]gathered together in their
cities throughout all the provinces of King
Ahasuerus to lay hands on those who [b]sought
their harm. And no one could withstand
them, [c]because fear of them fell upon all people. 3 And all the officials of the provinces, the
satraps, the governors, and all those doing
the king's work, helped the Jews, because the
fear of Mordecai fell upon them. 4 For Mordecai *was* great in the king's palace, and his
fame spread throughout all the provinces;
for this man Mordecai [a]became increasingly
prominent. 5 Thus the Jews defeated all their
enemies with the stroke of the sword, with
slaughter and destruction, and did what they
pleased with those who hated them.
6 And in [a]Shushan the citadel the Jews
killed and destroyed five hundred men. 7 Also
Parshandatha, Dalphon, Aspatha, 8 Poratha,
Adalia, Aridatha, 9 Parmashta, Arisai, Aridai,
and Vajezatha— 10 [a]the ten sons of Haman
the son of Hammedatha, the enemy of the
Jews—they killed; [b]but they did not lay a
hand on the plunder.
11 On that day the number of those who were
killed in Shushan the citadel was brought to
the king. 12 And the king said to Queen Esther,
"The Jews have killed and destroyed five
hundred men in Shushan the citadel, and the
ten sons of Haman. What have they done in
the rest of the king's provinces? Now [a]what
is your petition? It shall be granted to you. Or
what *is* your further request? It shall be done."
13 Then Esther said, "If it pleases the king,
let it be granted to the Jews who *are* in
Shushan to do again tomorrow [a]according
to today's decree, and let Haman's ten sons
[b]be hanged on the gallows."
14 So the king commanded this to be done;
the decree was issued in Shushan, and they
hanged Haman's ten sons.
15 And the Jews who *were* in Shushan [a]gath-
ered together again on the fourteenth day of
the month of Adar and killed three hundred
men at Shushan; [b]but they did not lay a hand
on the plunder.
16 The remainder of the Jews in the king's
provinces [a]gathered together and protected their lives, had rest from their enemies,
and killed seventy-five thousand of their
enemies; [b]but they did not lay a hand on the
plunder. 17 *This was* on the thirteenth day of
the month of Adar. And on the fourteenth
of *the month*[1] they rested and made it a day
of feasting and gladness.

The Feast of Purim

18 But the Jews who *were* at Shushan assembled together [a]on the thirteenth *day*, as well
as on the fourteenth; and on the fifteenth of
the month[1] they rested, and made it a day of
feasting and gladness. 19 Therefore the Jews of
the villages who dwelt in the unwalled towns
celebrated the fourteenth day of the month of
Adar [a]*with* gladness and feasting, [b]as a holiday,
and for [c]sending presents to one another.
20 And Mordecai wrote these things and
sent letters to all the Jews, near and far, who
were in all the provinces of King Ahasuerus, 21 to establish among them that they
should celebrate yearly the fourteenth
and fifteenth days of the month of Adar,
22 as the days on which the Jews had rest
from their enemies, as the month which
was turned from sorrow to joy for them,
and from mourning to a holiday; that they
should make them days of feasting and joy,
of [a]sending presents to one another and
gifts to the [b]poor. 23 So the Jews accepted the
custom which they had begun, as Mordecai
had written to them, 24 because Haman,
the son of Hammedatha the Agagite, the
enemy of all the Jews, [a]had plotted against
the Jews to annihilate them, and had cast
Pur (that *is*, the lot), to consume them and

8:15 [a] Prov. 29:2 **8:16** [a] Ps. 97:11; 112:4 **8:17** [a] Esth. 9:19 [b] Ps. 18:43 [c] Gen. 35:5 **9:1** [a] Esth. 8:12 [b] Esth. 3:13 [c] 2 Sam. 22:41 **9:2** [a] Esth. 8:11; 9:15–18 [b] Ps. 71:13, 14 [c] Esth. 8:17 **9:4** [a] 2 Sam. 3:1 **9:6** [a] Esth. 1:2; 3:15; 4:16 **9:10** [a] Esth. 5:11; 9:7–10 [b] Esth. 8:11 **9:12** [a] Esth. 5:6; 7:2 **9:13** [a] Esth. 8:11; 9:15 [b] 2 Sam. 21:6, 9 **9:15** [a] Esth. 8:11; 9:2 [b] Esth. 9:10 **9:16** [a] Esth. 9:2 [b] Esth. 8:11 **9:17** [1] Literally *it* **9:18** [a] Esth. 9:11, 15 [1] Literally *it* **9:19** [a] Deut. 16:11, 14 [b] Esth. 8:16, 17 [c] Neh. 8:10, 12 **9:22** [a] Neh. 8:10 [b] [Deut. 15:7–11] **9:24** [a] Esth. 3:6, 7; 9:26

THE GREAT INTERVENTION

Mordecai the Jew was second to King Ahasuerus, and was great among the Jews.

ESTHER 10:3

One of the scariest moments in Israel's history was the near annihilation of God's people at the hands of the wicked Haman, a man intensely jealous of Mordecai and his beautiful niece Esther, who, through God's sovereign work, had become the queen of Persia. Haman deceived the Persian king and almost succeeded. But then Esther intervened, Haman's plot unraveled, and the Jewish people were spared. Mordecai was vindicated, and at the end of the biblical story we are told that the faithful man became second in rank to the king "and was great among the Jews and well received by the multitude of his brethren, seeking the good of his people and speaking peace to all his countrymen" (v. 3).

Mordecai's experience makes me think of Barnabas in the New Testament because he celebrated the work and peace of God in others' lives. We should do the same. The Lord God is very much alive, and He intervenes so the universe's destiny is redemption and new life. Let that great truth give you lasting peace.

destroy them; 25 but [a]when *Esther*[1] came before the king, he commanded by letter that this[2] wicked plot which *Haman* had devised against the Jews should [b]return on his own head, and that he and his sons should be hanged on the gallows.

26 So they called these days Purim, after the name Pur. Therefore, because of all the words of [a]this letter, what they had seen concerning this matter, and what had happened to them, 27 the Jews established and imposed it upon themselves and their descendants and all who would [a]join them, that without fail they should celebrate these two days every year, according to the written *instructions* and according to the *prescribed* time, 28 *that* these days *should be* remembered and kept throughout every generation, every family, every province, and every city, that these days of Purim should not fail *to be observed* among the Jews, and *that* the memory of them should not perish among their descendants.

29 Then Queen Esther, [a]the daughter of Abihail, with Mordecai the Jew, wrote with full authority to confirm this [b]second letter about Purim. 30 And *Mordecai* sent letters to all the Jews, to [a]the one hundred and twenty-seven provinces of the kingdom of Ahasuerus, *with* words of peace and truth, 31 to confirm these days of Purim at their *appointed* time, as Mordecai the Jew and Queen Esther had prescribed for them, and as they had decreed for themselves and their descendants concerning matters of their [a]fasting and lamenting. 32 So the decree of Esther confirmed these matters of Purim, and it was written in the book.

Mordecai's Advancement

10 And King Ahasuerus imposed tribute on the land and *on* [a]the islands of the sea. 2 Now all the acts of his power and his might, and the account of the greatness of Mordecai, [a]to which the king advanced him, *are* they not written in the book of the [b]chronicles of the kings of Media and Persia? 3 For Mordecai the Jew *was* [a]second to King Ahasuerus, and was great among the Jews and well received by the multitude of his brethren, [b]seeking the good of his people and speaking peace to all his countrymen.[1]

9:25 [a] Esth. 7:4–10; 8:3; 9:13, 14 [b] Esth. 7:10 [1] Literally *she* or *it* [2] Literally *his* **9:26** [a] Esth. 9:20 **9:27** [a] Esth. 8:17 **9:29** [a] Esth. 2:15 [b] Esth. 8:10; 9:20, 21 **9:30** [a] Esth. 1:1 **9:31** [a] Esth. 4:3, 16 **10:1** [a] Is. 11:11; 24:15 **10:2** [a] Esth. 8:15; 9:4 [b] Esth. 6:1 **10:3** [a] Gen. 41:40, 43, 44 [b] Neh. 2:10 [1] Literally *seed*. Septuagint and Vulgate add a dream of Mordecai here; Vulgate adds six more chapters.

THE BOOK OF JOB

AUTHOR

The author of Job is unknown and there are no textual hints as to his identity. The non-Hebraic cultural background may point to a Gentile authorship, but an interesting school of thought maintains that Moses may have written this book. The "land of Uz" (Job 1:1) is directly adjacent to Midian, where Moses lived for forty years. Perhaps the oldest book of the Bible, Job is set in the time of the patriarchs (Abraham, Isaac, Jacob, and Joseph), and it is conceivable that Moses obtained a record of the dialogue left by Job or Elihu.

TIME

Unknown

KEY VERSE

Job 13:15

THEME

There are many things that set Job apart from the rest of Scripture. Its dramatic format is unique. Its story is not part of the flow of the history of Israel. And the thematic focus is narrower than in other books of its size. A classic work of literature, its primary subject matter is the most basic question humanity has of God: Why do we suffer? The Book of Job is the biblical text that addresses this issue head-on, and the dramatic nature of the story intensifies the conflict of ideas and understanding between God and humanity.

Our response to the adversities of life will determine whether we have God's peace. Job and his wife experienced the same losses, but they responded in far different ways. Job ultimately reacted in faith, saying, "The LORD gave, and the LORD has taken away; blessed be the name of the LORD" (1:21). Job's wife, however, encouraged him to "curse God and die!" (2:9). From Job's example, which helpfully shows the pains he endured and his many emotional ups and downs, we learn the invaluable definition of God's peace: confidence and trust in God's wise control of our lives no matter what.

Job and His Family in Uz

1 There was a man [a]in the land of Uz, whose
name *was* [b]Job; and that man was [c]blame-
less and upright, and one who [d]feared God
and shunned evil. 2 And seven sons and three
daughters were born to him. 3 Also, his possessions were seven thousand sheep, three
thousand camels, five hundred yoke of oxen,
five hundred female donkeys, and a very
large household, so that this man was the
greatest of all the people of the East.
4 And his sons would go and feast *in their*
houses, each on his *appointed* day, and would
send and invite their three sisters to eat and
drink with them. 5 So it was, when the days
of feasting had run their course, that Job
would send and sanctify them, and he would
rise early in the morning [a]and offer burnt
offerings *according to* the number of them
all. For Job said, "It may be that my sons have
sinned and [b]cursed[1] God in their hearts." Thus
Job did regularly.

Satan Attacks Job's Character

6 Now [a]there was a day when the sons of God
came to present themselves before the LORD,
and Satan[1] also came among them. 7 And the
LORD said to Satan, "From where do you come?"
So Satan answered the LORD and said,
"From [a]going to and fro on the earth, and
from walking back and forth on it."
8 Then the LORD said to Satan, "Have you
considered My servant Job, that *there is* none
like him on the earth, a blameless and upright
man, one who fears God and shuns evil?"
9 So Satan answered the LORD and said,
"Does Job fear God for nothing? 10 [a]Have You
not made a hedge around him, around his
household, and around all that he has on
every side? [b]You have blessed the work of his
hands, and his possessions have increased
in the land. 11 [a]But now, stretch out Your hand
and touch all that he has, and he will surely
[b]curse You to Your face!"
12 And the LORD said to Satan, "Behold, all
that he has *is* in your power; only do not lay
a hand on his *person*."
So Satan went out from the presence of
the LORD.

Job Loses His Property and Children

13 Now there was a day [a]when his sons and
daughters *were* eating and drinking wine in
their oldest brother's house; 14 and a messenger came to Job and said, "The oxen were
plowing and the donkeys feeding beside
them, 15 when the Sabeans[1] raided *them* and
took them away—indeed they have killed
the servants with the edge of the sword; and
I alone have escaped to tell you!"
16 While he *was* still speaking, another also
came and said, "The fire of God fell from

1:1 [a] 1 Chr. 1:17 [b] Ezek. 14:14, 20 [c] Gen. 6:9; 17:1 [d] [Prov. 16:6] **1:5** [a] [Job 42:8] [b] 1 Kin. 21:10, 13 [1] Literally *blessed*, but used here in the evil sense, and so in verse 11 and 2:5, 9 **1:6** [a] Job 2:1 [1] Literally *the Adversary*, and so throughout this book **1:7** [a] [1 Pet. 5:8] **1:10** [a] Ps. 34:7 [b] [Prov. 10:22] **1:11** [a] Job 2:5; 19:21 [b] Is. 8:21 **1:13** [a] [Eccl. 9:12] **1:15** [1] Literally *Sheba* (compare 6:19)

FAITHFUL JOB

Job . . . [was] one who feared God and shunned evil.

JOB 1:1

With prosperity comes a sense of security, and with security comes a sense of peace. We all think this way, at least to a degree, and it is natural. I think this is why Job's story bothers us. Job was a "blameless and upright" man (v. 1). He worshiped God, he offered up sacrifices for himself and for his children. From an Old Testament point of view, Job was every bit as righteous and deserving as any of the great men and women in the Bible, such as Abraham or Moses. Ancient readers were hardly surprised to hear of his great wealth. If anyone had a sense of security and peace, it was Job. But not for long.

God was willing to allow Job to fall on hard times, to be sorely tested, to find out if his faith existed only because he was prosperous or because he truly was a righteous man. Job lost his wealth, his children, and his health. What's worse, his friends and neighbors assumed that because of some unconfessed sin, Job had brought this calamity upon himself. Circumstances like these severely threaten peace.

What brings or breaks your peace? Faith in God will sustain it when calamity tries to break it.

heaven and burned up the sheep and the
servants, and consumed them; and I alone
have escaped to tell you!"
17 While he *was* still speaking, another also
came and said, "The Chaldeans formed three
bands, raided the camels and took them away,
yes, and killed the servants with the edge of the
sword; and I alone have escaped to tell you!"
18 While he *was* still speaking, another also
came and said, [a]"Your sons and daughters
were eating and drinking wine in their oldest
brother's house, 19 and suddenly a great wind
came from across[1] the wilderness and struck
the four corners of the house, and it fell on
the young people, and they are dead; and I
alone have escaped to tell you!"
20 Then Job arose, [a]tore his robe, and
shaved his head; and he [b]fell to the ground
and worshiped. 21 And he said:

[a]"Naked I came from my mother's womb,
And naked shall I return there.
The LORD [b]gave, and the LORD has
[c]taken away;
[d]Blessed be the name of the LORD."

22 [a]In all this Job did not sin nor charge
God with wrong.

Satan Attacks Job's Health

2 Again [a]there was a day when the sons
of God came to present themselves before the LORD, and Satan came also among
them to present himself before the LORD.

PEACE NOTE

Living by faith and in peace means obeying God's Word despite feelings and circumstances. No matter how dark the day seems, we can know that He is working out His perfect plan.

JOB 1:21

2 And the LORD said to Satan, "From where
do you come?"
[a]Satan answered the LORD and said, "From
going to and fro on the earth, and from walking back and forth on it."
3 Then the LORD said to Satan, "Have you
considered My servant Job, that *there is* none
like him on the earth, [a]a blameless and upright man, one who fears God and shuns
evil? And still he [b]holds fast to his integrity,
although you incited Me against him, [c]to
destroy him without cause."
4 So Satan answered the LORD and said,
"Skin for skin! Yes, all that a man has he will
give for his life. 5 [a]But stretch out Your hand

1:18 [a] Job 1:4, 13 1:19 [1] Septuagint omits *across.* 1:20 [a] Gen. 37:29, 34 [b] [1 Pet. 5:6] 1:21 [a] [Eccl. 5:15] [b] [James 1:17] [c] Gen. 31:16 [d] Eph. 5:20 1:22 [a] Job 2:10 2:1 [a] Job 1:6–8 2:2 [a] Job 1:7 2:3 [a] Job 1:1, 8 [b] Job 27:5, 6 [c] Job 9:17 2:5 [a] Job 1:11

WHEN ALL IS LOST

The LORD gave, and the LORD has taken away.

JOB 1:21

My heart goes out to Job. All his property had been destroyed; his wealth had vanished; his children were no more. When he learned what had happened, Job "fell to the ground and worshiped" (v. 20). He confessed that all he had God had given him and God had taken it away: "Blessed be the name of the LORD" (v. 21). But Job's trials were not over. God permitted Satan to afflict Job with ill health. This was too much for his wife, who bitterly told him, "Curse God and die!" (2:9). Job rebuked his wife, confessing that from God we receive both good and evil. The author of the book says, "In all this Job did not sin with his lips" (2:10).

What sustained Job? How could he refuse to curse God? Job was dismayed, he was grieved, and he was confused, but he said instead, "Blessed be the name of the LORD" (1:21)! How was that possible? I believe Job trusted God in thick and thin. Ultimately his peace came from God, *not from his possessions*. This is a huge, important truth. Peace attached to things is a peace that can vanish overnight. To what is your peace attached?

now, and touch his [b]bone and his flesh, and
he will surely curse You to Your face!"
6 [a]And the LORD said to Satan, "Behold, he
is in your hand, but spare his life."
7 So Satan went out from the presence of
the LORD, and struck Job with painful boils
[a]from the sole of his foot to the crown of his
head. 8 And he took for himself a potsherd
with which to scrape himself [a]while he sat
in the midst of the ashes.
9 Then his wife said to him, "Do you still
hold fast to your integrity? Curse God and die!"
10 But he said to her, "You speak as one of
the foolish women speaks. [a]Shall we indeed
accept good from God, and shall we not accept adversity?" [b]In all this Job did not [c]sin
with his lips.

Job's Three Friends

11 Now when Job's three friends heard of
all this adversity that had come upon him,
each one came from his own place—Eliphaz the [a]Temanite, Bildad the [b]Shuhite,
and Zophar the Naamathite. For they had
made an appointment together to come [c]and
mourn with him, and to comfort him. 12 And
when they raised their eyes from afar, and
did not recognize him, they lifted their voices
and wept; and each one tore his robe and
[a]sprinkled dust on his head toward heaven.
13 So they sat down with him on the ground
[a]seven days and seven nights, and no one
spoke a word to him, for they saw that *his*
grief was very great.

Job Deplores His Birth

3 After this Job opened his mouth and
cursed the day of his *birth*. 2 And Job
spoke, and said:

3 "May[a] the day perish on which I was born,
And the night *in which* it was said,
'A male child is conceived.'
4 May that day be darkness;
May God above not seek it,
Nor the light shine upon it.
5 May darkness and [a]the shadow of
death claim it;
May a cloud settle on it;
May the blackness of the day terrify it.
6 *As for* that night, may darkness seize it;
May it not rejoice[1] among the days of
the year,
May it not come into the number of the
months.
7 Oh, may that night be barren!
May no joyful shout come into it!
8 May those curse it who curse the day,
Those [a]who are ready to arouse
Leviathan.
9 May the stars of its morning be dark;
May it look for light, but *have* none,
And not see the dawning of the day;
10 Because it did not shut up the doors of
my *mother's* womb,
Nor hide sorrow from my eyes.

11 "Why[a] did I not die at birth?
Why did I *not* perish when I came from
the womb?
12 [a]Why did the knees receive me?
Or why the breasts, that I should nurse?
13 For now I would have lain still and
been quiet,
I would have been asleep;
Then I would have been at rest
14 With kings and counselors of the earth,
Who [a]built ruins for themselves,
15 Or with princes who had gold,
Who filled their houses *with* silver;
16 Or *why* was I not hidden [a]like a
stillborn child,
Like infants who never saw light?
17 There the wicked cease *from* troubling,
And there the weary are at [a]rest.
18 *There* the prisoners rest together;
[a]They do not hear the voice of the
oppressor.
19 The small and great are there,
And the servant *is* free from his master.

20 "Why[a] is light given to him who is in
misery,
And life to the [b]bitter of soul,
21 Who [a]long for death, but it does not *come*,
And search for it more than [b]hidden
treasures;
22 Who rejoice exceedingly,
And are glad when they can find the
[a]grave?
23 *Why is light given* to a man whose way
is hidden,
[a]And whom God has hedged in?
24 For my sighing comes before I eat,[1]
And my groanings pour out like water.
25 For the thing I greatly [a]feared has
come upon me,
And what I dreaded has happened to me.
26 I am not at ease, nor am I quiet;
I have no rest, for trouble comes."

2:5 [b] Job 19:20 2:6 [a] Job 1:12 2:7 [a] Is. 1:6 2:8 [a] Ezek. 27:30 2:10 [a] Job 1:21, 22 [b] Job 1:22 [c] Ps. 39:1 2:11 [a] Gen. 36:11 [b] Gen. 25:2 [c] Rom. 12:15 2:12 [a] Neh. 9:1 2:13 [a] Gen. 50:10 3:3 [a] Jer. 20:14–18 3:5 [a] Jer. 13:16
3:6 [1] Septuagint, Syriac, Targum, and Vulgate read *be joined*. 3:8 [a] Jer. 9:17 3:11 [a] Job 10:18, 19 3:12 [a] Gen. 30:3 3:14 [a] Job 15:28 3:16 [a] Ps. 58:8 3:17 [a] Job 17:16 3:18 [a] Job 39:7 3:20 [a] Jer. 20:18 [b] 2 Kin. 4:27 3:21 [a] Rev. 9:6 [b] Prov. 2:4 3:22 [a] Job 7:15, 16 3:23 [a] Job 19:8 3:24 [1] Literally *my bread* 3:25 [a] [Job 9:28; 30:15]

CONFESS YOUR TROUBLED SOUL

I have no rest, for trouble comes.

JOB 3:26

Faith in God that He can be trusted provides the context for hope that He will fulfill all that He promised, which in turn makes a deep and genuine peace possible.

Though bewildered by what had happened, Job would not curse God. But his sorrows were so great that he "cursed the day of his birth" (v. 1). He told his companions, "I am not at ease . . . I have no rest" (v. 26). I appreciate Job's honesty. He hadn't rejected God; he knew God had been good to him. Job was sure he hadn't failed God, but his companions thought differently. God can handle your realities and difficulties. There is no need to sugarcoat your situation because God sees you. He knows. He is there. Job models authentic Christian living for us while attempting to seek and apply the peace of God in our lives.

Peace is restored when we confess the truth, when we approach God with no deceit, and when we place our faith in Him, not in our own righteousness. In the end, Job will do just that, and God will restore him (see 42:7–17). What do you need to confess to restore your peace?

Eliphaz: Job Has Sinned

4 Then Eliphaz the Temanite answered
and said:

2 "*If* one attempts a word with you, will
you become weary?
But who can withhold himself from
speaking?
3 Surely you have instructed many,
And you [a]have strengthened weak hands.
4 Your words have upheld him who was
stumbling,
And you [a]have strengthened the feeble
knees;
5 But now it comes upon you, and you
are weary;
It touches you, and you are troubled.
6 *Is* not [a]your reverence [b]your confidence?
And the integrity of your ways your hope?

7 "Remember now, [a]who *ever* perished
being innocent?
Or where were the upright *ever* cut off?
8 Even as I have seen,
[a]Those who plow iniquity
And sow trouble reap the same.
9 By the blast of God they perish,
And by the breath of His anger they are
consumed.
10 The roaring of the lion,
The voice of the fierce lion,
And [a]the teeth of the young lions are
broken.
11 [a]The old lion perishes for lack of prey,
And the cubs of the lioness are
scattered.

12 "Now a word was secretly brought to me,
And my ear received a whisper of it.
13 [a]In disquieting thoughts from the
visions of the night,
When deep sleep falls on men,
14 Fear came upon me, and [a]trembling,
Which made all my bones shake.
15 Then a spirit passed before my face;
The hair on my body stood up.
16 It stood still,
But I could not discern its appearance.
A form *was* before my eyes;
There was silence;
Then I heard a voice *saying:*
17 'Can a mortal be more righteous than
God?
Can a man be more pure than his Maker?
18 If He [a]puts no trust in His servants,
If He charges His angels with error,
19 How much more those who dwell in
houses of clay,
Whose foundation is in the dust,
Who are crushed before a moth?
20 [a]They are broken in pieces from
morning till evening;
They perish forever, with no one
regarding.
21 Does not their own excellence go away?
They die, even without wisdom.'

4:3 [a] Is. 35:3 **4:4** [a] Is. 35:3 **4:6** [a] Job 1:1 [b] Prov. 3:26 **4:7** [a] [Ps. 37:25] **4:8** [a] [Prov. 22:8] **4:10** [a] Ps. 58:6 **4:11** [a] Ps. 34:10 **4:13** [a] Job 33:15 **4:14** [a] Hab. 3:16 **4:18** [a] Job 15:15 **4:20** [a] Ps. 90:5, 6

Eliphaz: Job Is Chastened by God

5 "Call out now;
Is there anyone who will answer you?
And to which of the holy ones will you turn?
2 For wrath kills a foolish man,
And envy slays a simple one.
3 [a]I have seen the foolish taking root,
But suddenly I cursed his dwelling place.
4 His sons are [a]far from safety,
They are crushed in the gate,
And [b]*there is* no deliverer.
5 Because the hungry eat up his harvest,
Taking it even from the thorns,[1]
And a snare snatches their substance.[2]
6 For affliction does not come from the dust,
Nor does trouble spring from the ground;
7 Yet man is [a]born to trouble,
As the sparks fly upward.

8 "But as for me, I would seek God,
And to God I would commit my cause—
9 Who does great things, and unsearchable,
Marvelous things without number.
10 [a]He gives rain on the earth,
And sends waters on the fields.
11 [a]He sets on high those who are lowly,
And those who mourn are lifted to safety.
12 [a]He frustrates the devices of the crafty,
So that their hands cannot carry out their plans.
13 He catches the [a]wise in their own craftiness,
And the counsel of the cunning comes quickly upon them.
14 They meet with darkness in the daytime,
And grope at noontime as in the night.
15 But [a]He saves the needy from the sword,
From the mouth of the mighty,
And from their hand.
16 [a]So the poor have hope,
And injustice shuts her mouth.

17 "Behold,[a] happy *is* the man whom God corrects;
Therefore do not despise the chastening of the Almighty.
18 [a]For He bruises, but He binds up;
He wounds, but His hands make whole.
19 [a]He shall deliver you in six troubles,
Yes, in seven [b]no evil shall touch you.
20 [a]In famine He shall redeem you from death,
And in war from the power of the sword.
21 [a]You shall be hidden from the scourge of the tongue,
And you shall not be afraid of destruction when it comes.
22 You shall laugh at destruction and famine,
And [a]you shall not be afraid of the [b]beasts of the earth.
23 [a]For you shall have a covenant with the stones of the field,
And the beasts of the field shall be at peace with you.
24 You shall know that your tent *is* in peace;
You shall visit your dwelling and find nothing amiss.
25 You shall also know that [a]your descendants *shall be* many,
And your offspring [b]like the grass of the earth.
26 [a]You shall come to the grave at a full age,
As a sheaf of grain ripens in its season.
27 Behold, this we have [a]searched out;
It *is* true.
Hear it, and know for yourself."

Job: My Complaint Is Just

6 Then Job answered and said:
2 "Oh, that my grief were fully weighed,
And my calamity laid with it on the scales!
3 For then it would be heavier than the sand of the sea—
Therefore my words have been rash.
4 [a]For the arrows of the Almighty *are* within me;
My spirit drinks in their poison;
[b]The terrors of God are arrayed [c]against me.
5 Does the [a]wild donkey bray when it has grass,
Or does the ox low over its fodder?
6 Can flavorless food be eaten without salt?
Or is there *any* taste in the white of an egg?
7 My soul refuses to touch them;
They *are* as loathsome food to me.

5:3 [a] Jer. 12:1–3 **5:4** [a] Ps. 119:155 [b] Ps. 109:12 **5:5** [1] Septuagint reads *They shall not be taken from evil men;* Vulgate reads *And the armed man shall take him by violence.* [2] Septuagint reads *The might shall draw them off;* Vulgate reads *And the thirsty shall drink up their riches.* **5:7** [a] Job 14:1 **5:10** [a] [Job 36:27–29; 37:6–11; 38:26] **5:11** [a] Ps. 113:7 **5:12** [a] Neh. 4:15 **5:13** [a] [1 Cor. 3:19] **5:15** [a] Ps. 35:10 **5:16** [a] 1 Sam. 2:8 **5:17** [a] Ps. 94:12 **5:18** [a] [1 Sam. 2:6, 7] **5:19** [a] Ps. 34:19; 91:3 [b] Ps. 91:10 **5:20** [a] Ps. 33:19, 20; 37:19 **5:21** [a] Ps. 31:20 **5:22** [a] Ezek. 34:25 [b] Hos. 2:18 **5:23** [a] Ps. 91:12 **5:25** [a] Ps. 112:2 [b] Ps. 72:16 **5:26** [a] [Prov. 9:11; 10:27] **5:27** [a] Ps. 111:2 **6:4** [a] Ps. 38:2 [b] Ps. 88:15, 16 [c] Job 30:15 **6:5** [a] Job 39:5–8

PEACE NOTE

When has a believer shown up in your life at just the right moment? When have you shown up for someone else at a critical moment? Was peace the result?

JOB 6:1

8 "Oh, that I might have my request,
That God would grant *me* the thing that
I long for!
9 That it would please God to crush me,
That He would loose His hand and [a]cut
me off!
10 Then I would still have comfort;
Though in anguish I would exult,
He will not spare;
For [a]I have not concealed the words of
[b]the Holy One.

11 "What strength do I have, that I should
hope?
And what *is* my end, that I should
prolong my life?
12 *Is* my strength the strength of stones?
Or is my flesh bronze?
13 *Is* my help not within me?
And is success driven from me?

14 "To[a] him who is afflicted, kindness
should be shown by his friend,
Even though he forsakes the fear of the
Almighty.
15 [a]My brothers have dealt deceitfully like
a brook,
[b]Like the streams of the brooks that
pass away,
16 Which are dark because of the ice,
And into which the snow vanishes.
17 When it is warm, they cease to flow;
When it is hot, they vanish from their
place.
18 The paths of their way turn aside,
They go nowhere and perish.
19 The caravans of [a]Tema look,
The travelers of [b]Sheba hope for them.
20 They are [a]disappointed because they
were confident;
They come there and are confused.
21 For now [a]you are nothing,
You see terror and [b]are afraid.
22 Did I ever say, 'Bring *something* to me'?
Or, 'Offer a bribe for me from your
wealth'?
23 Or, 'Deliver me from the enemy's hand'?
Or, 'Redeem me from the hand of
oppressors'?

24 "Teach me, and I will hold my tongue;
Cause me to understand wherein I
have erred.
25 How forceful are right words!
But what does your arguing prove?
26 Do you intend to rebuke *my* words,
And the speeches of a desperate one,
which are as wind?
27 Yes, you overwhelm the fatherless,
And you [a]undermine your friend.
28 Now therefore, be pleased to look at
me;
For I would never lie to your face.
29 [a]Yield now, let there be no injustice!
Yes, concede, my [b]righteousness still
stands!
30 Is there injustice on my tongue?
Cannot my taste discern the
unsavory?

Job: My Suffering Is Comfortless

7 "*Is there* not [a]a time of hard service for
man on earth?
Are not his days also like the days of a
hired man?
2 Like a servant who earnestly desires
the shade,
And like a hired man who eagerly looks
for his wages,
3 So I have been allotted [a]months of
futility,
And wearisome nights have been
appointed to me.
4 [a]When I lie down, I say, 'When shall I
arise,
And the night be ended?'
For I have had my fill of tossing till
dawn.
5 My flesh is [a]caked with worms and dust,
My skin is cracked and breaks out
afresh.

6 "My[a] days are swifter than a weaver's
shuttle,
And are spent without hope.

6:9 [a] Job 7:16; 9:21; 10:1 **6:10** [a] Acts 20:20 [b] [Is. 57:15] **6:14** [a] [Prov. 17:17] **6:15** [a] Ps. 38:11 [b] Jer. 15:18 **6:19** [a] Gen. 25:15 [b] 1 Kin. 10:1 **6:20** [a] Jer. 14:3 **6:21** [a] Job 13:4 [b] Ps. 38:11 **6:27** [a] Ps. 57:6 **6:29** [a] Job 17:10 [b] Job 27:5, 6; 34:5 **7:1** [a] [Job 14:5, 13, 14] **7:3** [a] [Job 15:31] **7:4** [a] Deut. 28:67 **7:5** [a] Is. 14:11 **7:6** [a] Job 9:25; 16:22; 17:11

7 Oh, remember that [a]my life *is* a breath!
My eye will never again see good.
8 [a]The eye of him who sees me will see
me no *more;*
While your eyes *are* upon me, I shall no
longer *be.*
9 *As* the cloud disappears and vanishes
away,
So [a]he who goes down to the grave
does not come up.
10 He shall never return to his house,
[a]Nor shall his place know him
anymore.

11 "Therefore I will [a]not restrain my
mouth;
I will speak in the anguish of my
spirit;
I will [b]complain in the bitterness of my
soul.
12 *Am* I a sea, or a sea serpent,
That You set a guard over me?
13 [a]When I say, 'My bed will comfort me,
My couch will ease my complaint,'
14 Then You scare me with dreams
And terrify me with visions,
15 So that my soul chooses strangling
And death rather than my body.[1]
16 [a]I loathe *my life;*
I would not live forever.
[b]Let me alone,
For [c]my days *are but* a breath.

17 "What[a] *is* man, that You should exalt
him,
That You should set Your heart
on him,
18 That You should visit him every
morning,
And test him every moment?
19 How long?
Will You not look away from me,
And let me alone till I swallow my
saliva?
20 Have I sinned?
What have I done to You, [a]O watcher of
men?
Why [b]have You set me as Your target,
So that I am a burden to myself?[1]
21 Why then do You not pardon my
transgression,
And take away my iniquity?
For now I will lie down in the dust,
And You will seek me diligently,
But I *will* no longer *be.*"

Bildad: Job Should Repent

8 Then Bildad the Shuhite answered and
said:

2 "How long will you speak these *things,*
And the words of your mouth *be like* a
strong wind?
3 [a]Does God subvert judgment?
Or does the Almighty pervert justice?
4 If [a]your sons have sinned against Him,
He has cast them away for their
transgression.
5 [a]If you would earnestly seek God
And make your supplication to the
Almighty,
6 If you *were* pure and upright,
Surely now He would awake for you,
And prosper your rightful dwelling
place.
7 Though your beginning was small,
Yet your latter end would [a]increase
abundantly.

8 "For[a] inquire, please, of the former age,
And consider the things discovered by
their fathers;
9 For [a]we *were born* yesterday, and know
nothing,
Because our days on earth *are* a shadow.
10 Will they not teach you and tell you,
And utter words from their heart?

11 "Can the papyrus grow up without a
marsh?
Can the reeds flourish without
water?
12 [a]While it *is* yet green *and* not cut down,
It withers before any *other* plant.
13 So *are* the paths of all who [a]forget God;
And the hope of the [b]hypocrite shall
perish,
14 Whose confidence shall be cut off,
And whose trust *is* a spider's web.
15 [a]He leans on his house, but it does not
stand.
He holds it fast, but it does not
endure.
16 He grows green in the sun,
And his branches spread out in his
garden.
17 His roots wrap around the rock heap,
And look for a place in the stones.
18 [a]If he is destroyed from his place,
Then *it* will deny him, *saying,* 'I have
not seen you.'

7:7 [a] Ps. 78:39; 89:47 **7:8** [a] Job 8:18; 20:9 **7:9** [a] 2 Sam. 12:23 **7:10** [a] Ps. 103:16 **7:11** [a] Ps. 39:1, 9 [b] 1 Sam. 1:10 **7:13** [a] Job 9:27 **7:15** [1] Literally *my bones* **7:16** [a] Job 10:1 [b] Job 14:6 [c] Ps. 62:9 **7:17** [a] Ps. 8:4; 144:3 **7:20** [a] Ps. 36:6 [b] Ps. 21:12 [1] Following Masoretic Text, Targum, and Vulgate; Septuagint and Jewish tradition read *to You.* **8:3** [a] [Deut. 32:4] **8:4** [a] Job 1:5, 18, 19 **8:5** [a] [Job 5:17–27; 11:13] **8:7** [a] Job 42:12 **8:8** [a] Deut. 4:32; 32:7 **8:9** [a] Gen. 47:9 **8:12** [a] Ps. 129:6 **8:13** [a] Ps. 9:17 [b] Job 11:20; 18:14; 27:8 **8:15** [a] Job 8:22; 27:18 **8:18** [a] Job 7:10

19 "Behold, this is the joy of His way,
And [a]out of the earth others will grow.
20 Behold, [a]God will not cast away the blameless,
Nor will He uphold the evildoers.
21 He will yet fill your mouth with laughing,
And your lips with rejoicing.
22 Those who hate you will be [a]clothed with shame,
And the dwelling place of the wicked will come to nothing."[1]

Job: There Is No Mediator

9 Then Job answered and said:

2 "Truly I know *it is* so,
But how can a [a]man be [b]righteous before God?
3 If one wished to contend with Him,
He could not answer Him one time out of a thousand.
4 [a]*God is* wise in heart and mighty in strength.
Who has hardened *himself* against Him and prospered?
5 He removes the mountains, and they do not know
When He overturns them in His anger;
6 He [a]shakes the earth out of its place,
And its [b]pillars tremble;
7 He commands the sun, and it does not rise;
He seals off the stars;
8 [a]He alone spreads out the heavens,
And treads on the waves of the sea;
9 [a]He made the Bear, Orion, and the Pleiades,
And the chambers of the south;
10 [a]He does great things past finding out,
Yes, wonders without number.
11 [a]If He goes by me, I do not see *Him;*
If He moves past, I do not perceive Him;
12 [a]If He takes away, who can hinder Him?
Who can say to Him, 'What are You doing?'
13 God will not withdraw His anger,
[a]The allies of the proud[1] lie prostrate *beneath Him.*

14 "How then can I answer Him,
And choose my words *to reason* with Him?
15 [a]For though I were righteous, I could not answer Him;
I would beg mercy of my Judge.
16 If I called and He answered me,
I would not believe that He was listening to my voice.
17 For He crushes me with a tempest,
And multiplies my wounds [a]without cause.
18 He will not allow me to catch my breath,
But fills me with bitterness.
19 If *it is a matter* of strength, indeed *He is* strong;
And if of justice, who will appoint my day *in court?*
20 Though I were righteous, my own mouth would condemn me;
Though I *were* blameless, it would prove me perverse.

21 "I am blameless, yet I do not know myself;
I despise my life.
22 It *is* all one *thing;*
Therefore I say, [a]'He destroys the blameless and the wicked.'
23 If the scourge slays suddenly,
He laughs at the plight of the innocent.
24 The earth is given into the hand of the wicked.
He covers the faces of its judges.
If it is not *He,* who else could it be?

25 "Now [a]my days are swifter than a runner;
They flee away, they see no good.
26 They pass by like swift ships,
[a]Like an eagle swooping on its prey.

PEACE NOTE

What today's confused folks cannot find is peace and the assurance that all is right between them and God.

8:19 [a] Ps. 113:7 **8:20** [a] Job 4:7 **8:22** [a] Ps. 35:26; 109:29 [1] Literally *will not be* **9:2** [a] [Job 4:17; 15:14–16] [b] [Hab. 2:4] **9:4** [a] Job 36:5 **9:6** [a] Heb. 12:26 [b] Job 26:11 **9:8** [a] Ps. 104:2, 3 **9:9** [a] Amos 5:8 **9:10** [a] Job 5:9 **9:11** [a] [Job 23:8, 9; 35:14] **9:12** [a] [Is. 45:9] **9:13** [a] Job 26:12 [1] Hebrew *rahab* **9:15** [a] Job 10:15; 23:1–7 **9:17** [a] Job 2:3 **9:22** [a] Ezek. 21:3 **9:25** [a] Job 7:6, 7 **9:26** [a] Hab. 1:8

27 [a]If I say, 'I will forget my complaint,
I will put off my sad face and wear a smile,'
28 [a]I am afraid of all my sufferings;
I know that You [b]will not hold me innocent.
29 *If* I am condemned,
Why then do I labor in vain?
30 [a]If I wash myself with snow water,
And cleanse my hands with soap,
31 Yet You will plunge me into the pit,
And my own clothes will abhor me.

32 "For [a]*He is* not a man, as I *am,*
That I may answer Him,
And that we should go to court together.
33 [a]Nor is there any mediator between us,
Who may lay his hand on us both.
34 [a]Let Him take His rod away from me,
And do not let dread of Him terrify me.
35 *Then* I would speak and not fear Him,
But it is not so with me.

Job: I Would Plead with God

10 "My [a]soul loathes my life;
I will give free course to my complaint,
[b]I will speak in the bitterness of my soul.
2 I will say to God, 'Do not condemn me;
Show me why You contend with me.
3 *Does it* seem good to You that You should oppress,
That You should despise the work of Your hands,
And smile on the counsel of the wicked?
4 Do You have eyes of flesh?
Or [a]do You see as man sees?
5 *Are* Your days like the days of a mortal man?
Are Your years like the days of a mighty man,
6 That You should seek for my iniquity
And search out my sin,
7 Although You know that I am not wicked,
And *there is* no one who can deliver from Your hand?

8 'Your[a] hands have made me and fashioned me,
An intricate unity;
Yet You would [b]destroy me.
9 *Remember, I pray,* [a]*that* You have made me like clay.
And will You turn me into dust again?
10 [a]Did You not pour me out like milk,
And curdle me like cheese,
11 Clothe me with skin and flesh,
And knit me together with bones and sinews?
12 You have granted me life and favor,
And Your care has preserved my spirit.

13 'And these *things* You have hidden in Your heart;
I know that this *was* with You:
14 If I sin, then [a]You mark me,
And will not acquit me of my iniquity.
15 If I am wicked, [a]woe to me;
[b]Even *if* I am righteous, I cannot lift up my head.
I am full of disgrace;
[c]See my misery!
16 If *my head* is exalted,
[a]You hunt me like a fierce lion,
And again You show Yourself awesome against me.
17 You renew Your witnesses against me,
And increase Your indignation toward me;
Changes and war are *ever* with me.
18 'Why[a] then have You brought me out of the womb?
Oh, that I had perished and no eye had seen me!
19 I would have been as though I had not been.
I would have been carried from the womb to the grave.
20 [a]Are not my days few?
Cease! [b]Leave me alone, that I may take a little comfort,
21 Before I go *to the place from which* I shall not return,
[a]To the land of darkness [b]and the shadow of death,
22 A land as dark as darkness *itself,*
As the shadow of death, without any order,
Where even the light *is* like darkness.' "

Zophar Urges Job to Repent

11 Then Zophar the Naamathite answered and said:

2 "Should not the multitude of words be answered?
And should a man full of talk be vindicated?

9:27 [a] Job 7:13 **9:28** [a] Ps. 119:120 [b] Ex. 20:7 **9:30** [a] [Jer. 2:22] **9:32** [a] [Is. 45:9] **9:33** [a] [1 Sam. 2:25] **9:34** [a] Job 13:20, 21 **10:1** [a] Job 7:16 [b] Job 7:11 **10:4** [a] [1 Sam. 16:7] **10:8** [a] Ps. 119:73 [b] [Job 9:22] **10:9** [a] Gen. 2:7 **10:10** [a] [Ps. 139:14–16] **10:14** [a] Ps. 139:1 **10:15** [a] Is. 3:11 [b] [Job 9:12, 15] [c] Ps. 25:18 **10:16** [a] Is. 38:13 **10:18** [a] Job 3:11–13 **10:20** [a] Ps. 39:5 [b] Job 7:16, 19 **10:21** [a] Ps. 88:12 [b] Ps. 23:4

3 Should your empty talk make men
hold their peace?
And when you mock, should no one
rebuke you?
4 For you have said,
[a]'My doctrine *is* pure,
And I am clean in your eyes.'
5 But oh, that God would speak,
And open His lips against you,
6 That He would show you the secrets of
wisdom!
For *they would* double *your* prudence.
Know therefore that [a]God exacts from
you
Less than your iniquity *deserves.*

7 "Can[a] you search out the deep things of
God?
Can you find out the limits of the
Almighty?
8 *They are* higher than heaven—what
can you do?
Deeper than Sheol—what can you know?
9 Their measure *is* longer than the earth
And broader than the sea.

10 "If[a] He passes by, imprisons, and
gathers *to judgment,*
Then who can hinder Him?
11 For [a]He knows deceitful men;
He sees wickedness also.
Will He not then consider *it?*
12 For an [a]empty-headed man will be wise,
When a wild donkey's colt is born a
man.

13 "If you would [a]prepare your heart,
And [b]stretch out your hands toward
Him;
14 If iniquity *were* in your hand, *and you*
put it far away,
And [a]would not let wickedness dwell in
your tents;
15 [a]Then surely you could lift up your face
without spot;
Yes, you could be steadfast, and not
fear;
16 Because you would [a]forget *your* misery,
And remember *it* as waters *that have*
passed away,
17 And *your* life [a]would be brighter than
noonday.
Though you were dark, you would be
like the morning.
18 And you would be secure, because
there is hope;

PEACE NOTE

Shalom looks forward through the eyes of faith to the resurrected and re-created cosmos where everything and everyone will have *shalom.*

Yes, you would dig *around you, and*
[a]take your rest in safety.
19 You would also lie down, and no one
would make *you* afraid;
Yes, many would court your favor.
20 But [a]the eyes of the wicked will fail,
And they shall not escape,
And [b]their hope—loss of life!"

Job Answers His Critics

12 Then Job answered and said:
2 "No doubt you *are* the people,
And wisdom will die with you!
3 But I have understanding as well as
you;
I *am* not [a]inferior to you.
Indeed, who does not *know* such things
as these?

4 "I[a] am one mocked by his friends,
Who [b]called on God, and He answered
him,
The just and blameless *who is* ridiculed.
5 A lamp[1] is despised in the thought of
one who is at ease;
It is made ready for [a]those whose feet
slip.
6 [a]The tents of robbers prosper,
And those who provoke God are
secure—
In what God provides by His hand.

7 "But now ask the beasts, and they will
teach you;
And the birds of the air, and they will
tell you;

11:4 [a] Job 6:30 11:6 [a] [Ezra 9:13] 11:7 [a] [Eccl. 3:11] 11:10 [a] [Rev. 3:7] 11:11 [a] [Ps. 10:14] 11:12 [a] Rom. 1:22 11:13 [a] [1 Sam. 7:3] [b] Ps. 88:9 11:14 [a] Ps. 101:3 11:15 [a] Ps. 119:6 11:16 [a] Is. 65:16 11:17 [a] Is. 58:8, 10 11:18 [a] Lev. 26:5, 6 11:20 [a] Deut. 28:65 [b] [Prov. 11:7] 12:3 [a] Job 13:2 12:4 [a] Job 21:3 [b] Ps. 91:15 12:5 [a] Prov. 14:2 [1] Or *disaster* 12:6 [a] [Job 9:24; 21:6–16]

8 Or speak to the earth, and it will teach you;
And the fish of the sea will explain to you.
9 Who among all these does not know
That the hand of the LORD has done this,
10 [a]In whose hand *is* the life of every living thing,
And the [b]breath of all mankind?
11 Does not the ear test words
And the mouth taste its food?
12 Wisdom *is* with aged men,
And with length of days, understanding.

13 "With Him *are* [a]wisdom and strength,
He has counsel and understanding.
14 If [a]He breaks *a thing* down, it cannot be rebuilt;
If He imprisons a man, there can be no release.
15 If He [a]withholds the waters, they dry up;
If He [b]sends them out, they overwhelm the earth.
16 With Him *are* strength and prudence.
The deceived and the deceiver *are* His.
17 He leads counselors away plundered,
And makes fools of the judges.
18 He loosens the bonds of kings,
And binds their waist with a belt.
19 He leads princes[1] away plundered,
And overthrows the mighty.
20 [a]He deprives the trusted ones of speech,
And takes away the discernment of the elders.
21 [a]He pours contempt on princes,
And disarms the mighty.
22 He [a]uncovers deep things out of darkness,
And brings the shadow of death to light.
23 [a]He makes nations great, and destroys them;
He enlarges nations, and guides them.
24 He takes away the understanding[1] of the chiefs of the people of the earth,
And [a]makes them wander in a pathless wilderness.
25 [a]They grope in the dark without light,
And He makes them [b]stagger like a drunken *man*.

13 "Behold, my eye has seen all *this*,
My ear has heard and understood it.
2 [a]What you know, I also know;
I *am* not inferior to you.
3 [a]But I would speak to the Almighty,
And I desire to reason with God.
4 But you forgers of lies,
[a]You *are* all worthless physicians.
5 Oh, that you would be silent,
And [a]it would be your wisdom!
6 Now hear my reasoning,
And heed the pleadings of my lips.
7 [a]Will you speak wickedly for God,
And talk deceitfully for Him?
8 Will you show partiality for Him?
Will you contend for God?
9 Will it be well when He searches you out?
Or can you mock Him as one mocks a man?
10 He will surely rebuke you
If you secretly show partiality.
11 Will not His excellence make you afraid,
And the dread of Him fall upon you?
12 Your platitudes *are* proverbs of ashes,
Your defenses are defenses of clay.

13 "Hold your peace with me, and let me speak,
Then let come on me what *may!*
14 Why [a]do I take my flesh in my teeth,
And put my life in my hands?
15 [a]Though He slay me, yet will I trust Him.
[b]Even so, I will defend my own ways before Him.
16 He also *shall* be my salvation,
For a [a]hypocrite could not come before Him.
17 Listen carefully to my speech,
And to my declaration with your ears.
18 See now, I have prepared *my* case,
I know that I shall be [a]vindicated.
19 [a]Who *is* he *who* will contend with me?
If now I hold my tongue, I perish.

Job's Despondent Prayer

20 "Only[a] two *things* do not do to me,
Then I will not hide myself from You:
21 [a]Withdraw Your hand far from me,
And let not the dread of You make me afraid.
22 Then call, and I will [a]answer;
Or let me speak, then You respond to me.

12:10 [a] [Acts 17:28] [b] Job 27:3; 33:4 **12:13** [a] Job 9:4; 36:5 **12:14** [a] Job 11:10 **12:15** [a] [1 Kin. 8:35, 36] [b] Gen. 7:11–24 **12:19** [1] Literally *priests*, but not in a technical sense **12:20** [a] Job 32:9 **12:21** [a] Ps. 107:40 **12:22** [a] [1 Cor. 4:5] **12:23** [a] Is. 9:3; 26:15 **12:24** [a] Ps. 107:4 [1] Literally *heart* **12:25** [a] Job 5:14; 15:30; 18:18 [b] Ps. 107:27 **13:2** [a] Job 12:3 **13:3** [a] Job 23:3; 31:35 **13:4** [a] Job 6:21 **13:5** [a] Prov. 17:28 **13:7** [a] Job 27:4; 36:4 **13:14** [a] Job 18:4 **13:15** [a] Ps. 23:4 [b] Job 27:5 **13:16** [a] Job 8:13 **13:18** [a] [Rom. 8:34] **13:19** [a] Is. 50:8 **13:20** [a] Job 9:34 **13:21** [a] Ps. 39:10 **13:22** [a] Job 9:16; 14:15

23 How many *are* my iniquities and sins?
Make me know my transgression and my sin.
24 [a]Why do You hide Your face,
And [b]regard me as Your enemy?
25 [a]Will You frighten a leaf driven to and fro?
And will You pursue dry stubble?
26 For You write bitter things against me,
And [a]make me inherit the iniquities of my youth.
27 [a]You put my feet in the stocks,
And watch closely all my paths.
You set a limit[1] for the soles of my feet.

28 "*Man*[1] decays like a rotten thing,
Like a garment that is moth-eaten.

14 "Man *who is* born of woman
Is of few days and [a]full of trouble.
2 [a]He comes forth like a flower and fades away;
He flees like a shadow and does not continue.
3 And [a]do You open Your eyes on such a one,
And [b]bring me[1] to judgment with Yourself?
4 Who [a]can bring a clean *thing* out of an unclean?
No one!
5 [a]Since his days *are* determined,
The number of his months *is* with You;
You have appointed his limits, so that he cannot pass.
6 [a]Look away from him that he may rest,
Till [b]like a hired man he finishes his day.

7 "For there is hope for a tree,
If it is cut down, that it will sprout again,
And that its tender shoots will not cease.
8 Though its root may grow old in the earth,
And its stump may die in the ground,
9 *Yet* at the scent of water it will bud
And bring forth branches like a plant.
10 But man dies and is laid away;
Indeed he breathes his last
And where *is* [a]he?
11 *As* water disappears from the sea,
And a river becomes parched and dries up,
12 So man lies down and does not rise.
[a]Till the heavens *are* no more,
They will not awake
Nor be roused from their sleep.

13 "Oh, that You would hide me in the grave,
That You would conceal me until Your wrath is past,
That You would appoint me a set time, and remember me!
14 If a man dies, shall he live *again?*
All the days of my hard service [a]I will wait,
Till my change comes.
15 [a]You shall call, and I will answer You;
You shall desire the work of Your hands.
16 For now [a]You number my steps,
But do not watch over my sin.
17 [a]My transgression *is* sealed up in a bag,
And You cover[1] my iniquity.

18 "But *as* a mountain falls *and* crumbles away,
And *as* a rock is moved from its place;
19 *As* water wears away stones,
And as torrents wash away the soil of the earth;
So You destroy the hope of man.
20 You prevail forever against him, and he passes on;
You change his countenance and send him away.
21 His sons come to honor, and [a]he does not know *it;*
They are brought low, and he does not perceive *it.*
22 But his flesh will be in pain over it,
And his soul will mourn over it."

Eliphaz Accuses Job of Folly

15 Then [a]Eliphaz the Temanite answered and said:

2 "Should a wise man answer with empty knowledge,
And fill himself with the east wind?
3 Should he reason with unprofitable talk,
Or by speeches with which he can do no good?
4 Yes, you cast off fear,
And restrain prayer before God.
5 For your iniquity teaches your mouth,
And you choose the tongue of the crafty.
6 [a]Your own mouth condemns you, and not I;
Yes, your own lips testify against you.

13:24 [a] [Deut. 32:20] [b] Lam. 2:5 **13:25** [a] Is. 42:3 **13:26** [a] Job 20:11 **13:27** [a] Job 33:11 [1] Literally *inscribe a print* **13:28** [1] Literally *He* **14:1** [a] Eccl. 2:23 **14:2** [a] Job 8:9 **14:3** [a] Ps. 8:4; 144:3 [b] [Ps. 143:2] [1] Septuagint, Syriac, and Vulgate read *him.* **14:4** [a] [Ps. 51:2, 5, 10] **14:5** [a] Job 7:1; 21:21 **14:6** [a] Ps. 39:13 [b] Job 7:1 **14:10** [a] Job 10:21, 22 **14:12** [a] [Is. 51:6; 65:17; 66:22] **14:14** [a] Job 13:15 **14:15** [a] Job 13:22 **14:16** [a] Prov. 5:21 **14:17** [a] Deut. 32:32–34 [1] Literally *plaster over* **14:21** [a] Eccl. 9:5 **15:1** [a] Job 4:1 **15:6** [a] [Luke 19:22]

PEACE NOTE

If you set your mind on living according to the Spirit, you will find "life and peace" (Rom. 8:6).

7 "*Are* you the first man *who* was born?
[a]Or were you made before the hills?
8 [a]Have you heard the counsel of God?
Do you limit wisdom to yourself?
9 [a]What do you know that we do not know?
What do you understand that *is* not in us?
10 [a]Both the gray-haired and the aged *are* among us,
Much older than your father.
11 *Are* the consolations of God too small for you,
And the word *spoken* gently[1] with you?
12 Why does your heart carry you away,
And what do your eyes wink at,
13 That you turn your spirit against God,
And let *such* words go out of your mouth?

14 "What[a] *is* man, that he could be pure?
And *he who is* born of a woman, that he could be righteous?
15 [a]If *God* puts no trust in His saints,
And the heavens are not pure in His sight,
16 [a]How much less man, *who is* abominable and filthy,
[b]Who drinks iniquity like water!

17 "I will tell you, hear me;
What I have seen I will declare,
18 What wise men have told,
Not hiding *anything received* [a]from their fathers,
19 *To whom alone the land* was given,
And [a]no alien passed among them:
20 The wicked man writhes with pain all *his* days,
[a]And the number of years is hidden from the oppressor.
21 Dreadful sounds *are* in his ears;
[a]In prosperity the destroyer comes upon him.
22 He does not believe that he will [a]return from darkness,
For a sword is waiting for him.
23 He [a]wanders about for bread, *saying*, 'Where *is it?*'
He knows [b]that a day of darkness is ready at his hand.
24 Trouble and anguish make him afraid;
They overpower him, like a king ready for battle.
25 For he stretches out his hand against God,
And acts defiantly against the Almighty,
26 Running stubbornly against Him
With his strong, embossed shield.

27 "Though[a] he has covered his face with his fatness,
And made *his* waist heavy with fat,
28 He dwells in desolate cities,
In houses which no one inhabits,
Which are destined to become ruins.
29 He will not be rich,
Nor will his wealth [a]continue,
Nor will his possessions overspread the earth.
30 He will not depart from darkness;
The flame will dry out his branches,
And [a]by the breath of His mouth he will go away.
31 Let him not [a]trust in futile *things*, deceiving himself,
For futility will be his reward.
32 It will be accomplished [a]before his time,
And his branch will not be green.
33 He will shake off his unripe grape like a vine,
And cast off his blossom like an olive tree.
34 For the company of hypocrites *will be* barren,
And fire will consume the tents of bribery.
35 [a]They conceive trouble and bring forth futility;
Their womb prepares deceit."

15:7 [a] Prov. 8:25 **15:8** [a] Rom. 11:34 **15:9** [a] Job 12:3; 13:2 **15:10** [a] Job 8:8–10; 12:12; 32:6, 7 **15:11** [1] Septuagint reads *a secret thing.* **15:14** [a] Prov. 20:9 **15:15** [a] Job 4:18; 25:5 **15:16** [a] Ps. 14:3; 53:3 [b] Prov. 19:28 **15:18** [a] Job 8:8; 20:4 **15:19** [a] Joel 3:17 **15:20** [a] Ps. 90:12 **15:21** [a] 1 Thess. 5:3 **15:22** [a] Job 14:10–12 **15:23** [a] Ps. 59:15; 109:10 [b] Job 18:12 **15:27** [a] Ps. 17:10; 73:7; 119:70 **15:29** [a] Job 20:28; 27:16, 17 **15:30** [a] Job 4:9 **15:31** [a] Is. 59:4 **15:32** [a] Job 22:16 **15:35** [a] Is. 59:4

Job Reproaches His Pitiless Friends

16 Then Job answered and said:
2 "I have heard many such things;
[a]Miserable comforters *are* you all!
3 Shall words of wind have an end?
Or what provokes you that you answer?
4 I also could speak as you *do,*
If your soul were in my soul's place.
I could heap up words against you,
And [a]shake my head at you;
5 *But* I would strengthen you with my mouth,
And the comfort of my lips would relieve *your grief.*

6 "Though I speak, my grief is not relieved;
And *if* I remain silent, how am I eased?
7 But now He has [a]worn me out;
You [b]have made desolate all my company.
8 You have shriveled me up,
And it is a [a]witness *against me;*
My leanness rises up against me
And bears witness to my face.
9 [a]He tears *me* in His wrath, and hates me;
He gnashes at me with His teeth;
[b]My adversary sharpens His gaze on me.
10 They [a]gape at me with their mouth,
They [b]strike me reproachfully on the cheek,
They gather together against me.
11 God [a]has delivered me to the ungodly,
And turned me over to the hands of the wicked.
12 I was at ease, but He has [a]shattered me;
He also has taken *me* by my neck, and shaken me to pieces;
He has [b]set me up for His target,
13 His archers surround me.
He pierces my heart[1] and does not pity;
He pours out my gall on the ground.
14 He breaks me with wound upon wound;
He runs at me like a warrior.[1]

15 "I have sewn sackcloth over my skin,
And [a]laid my head[1] in the dust.
16 *My face is flushed from* weeping,
And on my eyelids *is* the shadow of death;
17 Although no violence *is* in my hands,
And my prayer *is* pure.

18 "O earth, do not cover my blood,
And [a]let my cry have no *resting* place!
19 Surely even now [a]my witness *is* in heaven,
And my evidence *is* on high.
20 My friends scorn me;
My eyes pour out *tears* to God.
21 [a]Oh, that one might plead for a man with God,
As a man *pleads* for his neighbor!
22 For when a few years are finished,
I shall [a]go the way of no return.

Job Prays for Relief

17 "My spirit is broken,
My days are extinguished,
[a]The grave *is ready* for me.
2 *Are* not mockers with me?
And does not my eye dwell on their [a]provocation?

3 "Now put down a pledge for me with Yourself.
Who *is* he *who* [a]will shake hands with me?
4 For You have hidden their heart from [a]understanding;
Therefore You will not exalt *them.*
5 He who speaks flattery to *his* friends,
Even the eyes of his children will [a]fail.

6 "But He has made me [a]a byword of the people,
And I have become one in whose face men spit.
7 [a]My eye has also grown dim because of sorrow,
And all my members *are* like shadows.
8 Upright *men* are astonished at this,
And the innocent stirs himself up against the hypocrite.
9 Yet the righteous will hold to his [a]way,
And he who has [b]clean hands will be stronger and stronger.

10 "But please, [a]come back again, all of you,[1]
For I shall not find *one* wise *man* among you.
11 [a]My days are past,
My purposes are broken off,
Even the thoughts of my heart.
12 They change the night into day;
'The light *is* near,' *they say,* in the face of darkness.

16:2 [a] Job 13:4; 21:34 **16:4** [a] Ps. 22:7; 109:25 **16:7** [a] Job 7:3 [b] Job 16:20; 19:13–15 **16:8** [a] Job 10:17 **16:9** [a] Hos. 6:1 [b] Job 13:24; 33:10 **16:10** [a] Ps. 22:13; 35:21 [b] Lam. 3:30 **16:11** [a] Job 1:15, 17 **16:12** [a] Job 9:17 [b] Job 7:20 **16:13** [1] Literally *kidneys* **16:14** [1] Vulgate reads *giant.* **16:15** [a] Ps. 7:5 [1] Literally *horn* **16:18** [a] [Ps. 66:18] **16:19** [a] Rom. 1:9 **16:21** [a] Job 31:35 **16:22** [a] Eccl. 12:5 **17:1** [a] Ps. 88:3, 4 **17:2** [a] Job 12:4; 17:6; 30:1, 9; 34:7 **17:3** [a] Prov. 6:1; 17:18; 22:26 **17:4** [a] Job 12:20; 32:9 **17:5** [a] Job 11:20 **17:6** [a] Job 30:9 **17:7** [a] Ps. 6:7; 31:9 **17:9** [a] Prov. 4:18 [b] Ps. 24:4 **17:10** [a] Job 6:29 [1] Following some Hebrew manuscripts, Septuagint, Syriac, and Vulgate; Masoretic Text and Targum read *all of them.* **17:11** [a] Job 7:6

13 If I wait *for* the grave *as* my house,
If I make my bed in the darkness,
14 If I say to corruption, 'You *are* my father,'
And to the worm, 'You *are* my mother and my sister,'
15 Where then *is* my [a]hope?
As for my hope, who can see it?
16 *Will* they go down [a]to the gates of Sheol?
Shall *we have* [b]rest together in the dust?"

Bildad: The Wicked Are Punished

18 Then [a]Bildad the Shuhite answered and said:

2 "How long *till* you put an end to words?
Gain understanding, and afterward we will speak.
3 Why are we counted [a]as beasts,
And regarded as stupid in your sight?
4 [a]You who tear yourself in anger,
Shall the earth be forsaken for you?
Or shall the rock be removed from its place?

5 "The[a] light of the wicked indeed goes out,
And the flame of his fire does not shine.
6 The light is dark in his tent,
[a]And his lamp beside him is put out.
7 The steps of his strength are shortened,
And [a]his own counsel casts him down.
8 For [a]he is cast into a net by his own feet,
And he walks into a snare.
9 The net takes *him* by the heel,
And [a]a snare lays hold of him.
10 A noose *is* hidden for him on the ground,
And a trap for him in the road.
11 [a]Terrors frighten him on every side,
And drive him to his feet.
12 His strength is starved,
And [a]destruction *is* ready at his side.
13 It devours patches of his skin;
The firstborn of death devours his limbs.
14 He is uprooted from [a]the shelter of his tent,
And they parade him before the king of terrors.
15 They dwell in his tent *who are* none of his;
Brimstone is scattered on his dwelling.
16 [a]His roots are dried out below,
And his branch withers above.
17 [a]The memory of him perishes from the earth,
And he has no name among the renowned.[1]
18 He is driven from light into darkness,
And chased out of the world.
19 [a]He has neither son nor posterity among his people,
Nor any remaining in his dwellings.
20 Those in the west are astonished [a]at his day,
As those in the east are frightened.
21 Surely such *are* the dwellings of the wicked,
And this *is* the place *of him who* [a]does not know God."

Job Trusts in His Redeemer

19 Then Job answered and said:

2 "How long will you torment my soul,
And break me in pieces with words?
3 These ten times you have reproached me;
You are not ashamed *that* you have wronged me.[1]
4 And if indeed I have erred,
My error remains with me.
5 If indeed you [a]exalt *yourselves* against me,
And plead my disgrace against me,
6 Know then that [a]God has wronged me,
And has surrounded me with His net.

7 "If I cry out concerning wrong, I am not heard.
If I cry aloud, *there is* no justice.
8 [a]He has fenced up my way, so that I cannot pass;
And He has set darkness in my paths.
9 [a]He has stripped me of my glory,
And taken the crown *from* my head.
10 He breaks me down on every side,
And I am gone;
My [a]hope He has uprooted like a tree.
11 He has also kindled His wrath against me,
And [a]He counts me as *one of* His enemies.
12 His troops come together
And build up their road against me;
They encamp all around my tent.

17:15 [a] Job 7:6; 13:15; 14:19; 19:10 17:16 [a] Jon. 2:6 [b] Job 3:17–19; 21:33 18:1 [a] Job 8:1 18:3 [a] Ps. 73:22 18:4 [a] Job 13:14 18:5 [a] Prov. 13:9; 20:20; 24:20 18:6 [a] Job 21:17 18:7 [a] Job 5:12, 13; 15:6 18:8 [a] Job 22:10 18:9 [a] Job 5:5 18:11 [a] Jer. 6:25 18:12 [a] Job 15:23 18:14 [a] Job 11:20 18:16 [a] Job 29:19 18:17 [a] [Ps. 34:16] [1] Literally *before the outside,* meaning distinguished, famous 18:19 [a] Is. 14:22 18:20 [a] Ps. 37:13 18:21 [a] Jer. 9:3 19:3 [1] A Jewish tradition reads *make yourselves strange to me.* 19:5 [a] Ps. 35:26; 38:16; 55:12, 13 19:6 [a] Job 16:11 19:8 [a] Job 3:23 19:9 [a] Ps. 89:44 19:10 [a] Job 17:14–16 19:11 [a] Job 13:24; 33:10

13 "He[a] has removed my brothers far
from me,
And my acquaintances are completely
estranged from me.
14 My relatives have failed,
And my close friends have forgotten me.
15 Those who dwell in my house, and my
maidservants,
Count me as a stranger;
I am an alien in their sight.
16 I call my servant, but he gives no answer;
I beg him with my mouth.
17 My breath is offensive to my wife,
And I am repulsive to the children of
my own body.
18 Even [a]young children despise me;
I arise, and they speak against me.
19 [a]All my close friends abhor me,
And those whom I love have turned
against me.
20 [a]My bone clings to my skin and to my
flesh,
And I have escaped by the skin of my
teeth.

21 "Have pity on me, have pity on me,
O you my friends,
For the hand of God has struck me!
22 Why do you [a]persecute me as God *does*,
And are not satisfied with my flesh?

23 "Oh, that my words were written!
Oh, that they were inscribed in a book!
24 That they were engraved on a rock
With an iron pen and lead, forever!
25 For I know *that* my Redeemer lives,
And He shall stand at last on the
earth;

PEACE NOTE

You can't feel your way out of the crisis you face today. You have to think and believe your way through it. Apply the truth of God's Word to your life to experience His peace.

JOB 19:25

26 And after my skin is destroyed, this *I
know*,
That [a]in my flesh I shall see God,
27 Whom I shall see for myself,
And my eyes shall behold, and not
another.
How my heart yearns within me!
28 If you should say, 'How shall we
persecute him?'—
Since the root of the matter is found
in me,
29 Be afraid of the sword for yourselves;
For wrath *brings* the punishment of the
sword,
That you may know *there is* a
judgment."

Zophar's Sermon on the Wicked Man

20 Then [a]Zophar the Naamathite answered and said:

2 "Therefore my anxious thoughts make
me answer,
Because of the turmoil within me.
3 I have heard the rebuke that
reproaches me,
And the spirit of my understanding
causes me to answer.

4 "Do you *not* know this of [a]old,
Since man was placed on earth,
5 [a]That the triumphing of the wicked is
short,
And the joy of the hypocrite is *but* for a
[b]moment?
6 [a]Though his haughtiness mounts up to
the heavens,
And his head reaches to the clouds,
7 *Yet* he will perish forever like his own
refuse;
Those who have seen him will say,
'Where is he?'
8 He will fly away [a]like a dream, and not
be found;
Yes, he [b]will be chased away like a
vision of the night.
9 The eye *that* saw him will *see him* no
more,
Nor will his place behold him
anymore.
10 His children will seek the favor of the
poor,
And his hands will restore his wealth.
11 His bones are full of [a]his youthful
vigor,
[b]But it will lie down with him in the
dust.

19:13 [a] Ps. 31:11; 38:11; 69:8; 88:8, 18 **19:18** [a] 2 Kin. 2:23 **19:19** [a] Ps. 38:11; 55:12, 13 **19:20** [a] Ps. 102:5 **19:22** [a] Ps. 69:26 **19:26** [a] [Ps. 17:15] **20:1** [a] Job 11:1 **20:4** [a] Job 8:8; 15:10 **20:5** [a] Ps. 37:35, 36 [b] [Job 8:13; 13:16; 15:34; 27:8] **20:6** [a] Is. 14:13, 14 **20:8** [a] Ps. 73:20; 90:5 [b] Job 18:18; 27:21–23 **20:11** [a] Job 13:26 [b] Job 21:26

12 "Though evil is sweet in his mouth,
And he hides it under his tongue,
13 *Though* he spares it and does not forsake it,
But still keeps it in his mouth,
14 *Yet* his food in his stomach turns sour;
It becomes cobra venom within him.
15 He swallows down riches
And vomits them up again;
God casts them out of his belly.
16 He will suck the poison of cobras;
The viper's tongue will slay him.
17 He will not see [a]the streams,
The rivers flowing with honey and cream.
18 He will restore that for which he labored,
And will not swallow *it* down;
From the proceeds of business
He will get no enjoyment.
19 For he has oppressed *and* forsaken the poor,
He has violently seized a house which he did not build.

20 "Because[a] he knows no quietness in his heart,[1]
He will not save anything he desires.
21 Nothing is left for him to eat;
Therefore his well-being will not last.
22 In his self-sufficiency he will be in distress;
Every hand of misery will come against him.
23 *When* he is about to fill his stomach,
God will cast on him the fury of His wrath,
And will rain *it* on him while he is eating.
24 [a]He will flee from the iron weapon;
A bronze bow will pierce him through.
25 It is drawn, and comes out of the body;
Yes, [a]the glittering *point comes* out of his gall.
[b]Terrors *come* upon him;
26 Total darkness *is* reserved for his treasures.
[a]An unfanned fire will consume him;
It shall go ill with him who is left in his tent.
27 The heavens will reveal his iniquity,
And the earth will rise up against him.
28 The increase of his house will depart,
And his goods will flow away in the day of His [a]wrath.
29 [a]This *is* the portion from God for a wicked man,
The heritage appointed to him by God."

Job's Discourse on the Wicked

21 Then Job answered and said:

2 "Listen carefully to my speech,
And let this be your consolation.
3 Bear with me that I may speak,
And after I have spoken, keep [a]mocking.

4 "As for me, *is* my complaint against man?
And if *it were,* why should I not be impatient?
5 Look at me and be astonished;
[a]Put *your* hand over *your* mouth.
6 Even when I remember I am terrified,
And trembling takes hold of my flesh.
7 [a]Why do the wicked live *and* become old,
Yes, become mighty in power?
8 Their descendants are established with them in their sight,
And their offspring before their eyes.
9 Their houses *are* safe from fear,
[a]Neither *is* the rod of God upon them.
10 Their bull breeds without failure;
Their cow calves [a]without miscarriage.
11 They send forth their little ones like a flock,
And their children dance.
12 They sing to the tambourine and harp,
And rejoice to the sound of the flute.
13 They [a]spend their days in wealth,
And in a moment go down to the grave.[1]
14 [a]Yet they say to God, 'Depart from us,
For we do not desire the knowledge of Your ways.
15 [a]Who *is* the Almighty, that we should serve Him?
And [b]what profit do we have if we pray to Him?'
16 Indeed their prosperity *is* not in their hand;
[a]The counsel of the wicked is far from me.

17 "How often is the lamp of the wicked put out?
How often does their destruction come upon them,
The sorrows *God* [a]distributes in His anger?
18 [a]They are like straw before the wind,
And like chaff that a storm carries away.
19 *They say,* 'God lays up one's[1] iniquity [a]for his children';
Let Him recompense him, that he may know *it.*

20:17 [a] Jer. 17:8 **20:20** [a] Eccl. 5:13–15 [1] Literally *belly* **20:24** [a] Amos 5:19 **20:25** [a] Job 16:13 [b] Job 18:11, 14 **20:26** [a] Ps. 21:9 **20:28** [a] Job 20:15; 21:30 **20:29** [a] Job 27:13; 31:2, 3 **21:3** [a] Job 16:10 **21:5** [a] Judg. 18:19 **21:7** [a] [Jer. 12:1] **21:9** [a] Ps. 73:5 **21:10** [a] Ex. 23:26 **21:13** [a] Job 21:23; 36:11 [1] Or *Sheol* **21:14** [a] Job 22:17 **21:15** [a] Ex. 5:2 [b] Mal. 3:14 **21:16** [a] Prov. 1:10 **21:17** [a] [Luke 12:46] **21:18** [a] Ps. 1:4; 35:5 **21:19** [a] [Ex. 20:5] [1] Literally *his*

20 Let his eyes see his destruction,
And [a]let him drink of the wrath of the Almighty.
21 For what does he care about his household after him,
When the number of his months is cut in half?

22 "Can[a] *anyone* teach God knowledge,
Since He judges those on high?
23 One dies in his full strength,
Being wholly at ease and secure;
24 His pails[1] are full of milk,
And the marrow of his bones is moist.
25 Another man dies in the bitterness of his soul,
Never having eaten with pleasure.
26 They [a]lie down alike in the dust,
And worms cover them.

27 "Look, I know your thoughts,
And the schemes *with which* you would wrong me.
28 For you say,
'Where *is* the house of the prince?
And where *is* the tent,[1]
The dwelling place of the wicked?'
29 Have you not asked those who travel the road?
And do you not know their signs?
30 [a]For the wicked are reserved for the day of doom;
They shall be brought out on the day of wrath.
31 Who condemns his way to his face?
And who repays him *for what* he has done?
32 Yet he shall be brought to the grave,
And a vigil kept over the tomb.
33 The clods of the valley shall be sweet to him;
[a]Everyone shall follow him,
As countless *have gone* before him.
34 How then can you comfort me with empty words,
Since falsehood remains in your answers?"

Eliphaz Accuses Job of Wickedness

22 Then [a]Eliphaz the Temanite answered and said:

2 "Can[a] a man be profitable to God,
Though he who is wise may be profitable to himself?
3 *Is it* any pleasure to the Almighty that you are righteous?
Or *is it* gain *to Him* that you make your ways blameless?

4 "Is it because of your fear of Him that He corrects you,
And enters into judgment with you?
5 *Is* not your wickedness great,
And your iniquity without end?
6 For you have [a]taken pledges from your brother for no reason,
And stripped the naked of their clothing.
7 You have not given the weary water to drink,
And you [a]have withheld bread from the hungry.
8 But the mighty man possessed the land,
And the honorable man dwelt in it.
9 You have sent widows away empty,
And the strength of the fatherless was crushed.
10 Therefore snares *are* all around you,
And sudden fear troubles you,
11 Or darkness *so that* you cannot see;
And an abundance of [a]water covers you.

12 "Is not God in the height of heaven?
And see the highest stars, how lofty they are!
13 And you say, [a]'What does God know?
Can He judge through the deep darkness?
14 [a]Thick clouds cover Him, so that He cannot see,
And He walks above the circle of heaven.'
15 Will you keep to the old way
Which wicked men have trod,
16 Who [a]were cut down before their time,
Whose foundations were swept away by a flood?
17 [a]They said to God, 'Depart from us!
What can the Almighty do to them?'[1]
18 Yet He filled their houses with good *things;*
But the counsel of the wicked is far from me.

19 "The[a] righteous see *it* and are glad,
And the innocent laugh at them:
20 'Surely our adversaries[1] are cut down,
And the fire consumes their remnant.'

21:20 [a] Is. 51:17 **21:22** [a] [Is. 40:13; 45:9] **21:24** [1] Septuagint and Vulgate read *bowels;* Syriac reads *sides;* Targum reads *breasts.* **21:26** [a] Eccl. 9:2 **21:28** [1] Vulgate omits *the tent.* **21:30** [a] [Prov. 16:4] **21:33** [a] Heb. 9:27 **22:1** [a] Job 4:1; 15:1; 42:9 **22:2** [a] [Luke 17:10] **22:6** [a] [Ex. 22:26, 27] **22:7** [a] Deut. 15:7 **22:11** [a] Ps. 69:1, 2; 124:5 **22:13** [a] Ps. 73:11 **22:14** [a] Ps. 139:11, 12 **22:16** [a] Job 14:19; 15:32 **22:17** [a] Job 21:14, 15 [1] Septuagint and Syriac read *us.* **22:19** [a] Ps. 52:6; 58:10; 107:42 **22:20** [1] Septuagint reads *substance.*

PEACE NOTE

Where God is, there is peace. Frequent contemplation of Scriptures related to God's peace helps heal our minds and eliminate anxiety.

JOB 22:21

21 "Now acquaint yourself with Him, and [a]be at peace;
Thereby good will come to you.
22 Receive, please, [a]instruction from His mouth,
And [b]lay up His words in your heart.
23 If you return to the Almighty, you will be built up;
You will remove iniquity far from your tents.
24 Then you will [a]lay your gold in the dust,
And the *gold* of Ophir among the stones of the brooks.
25 Yes, the Almighty will be your gold[1]
And your precious silver;
26 For then you will have your [a]delight in the Almighty,
And lift up your face to God.
27 [a]You will make your prayer to Him,
He will hear you,
And you will pay your vows.
28 You will also declare a thing,
And it will be established for you;
So light will shine on your ways.
29 When they cast *you* down, and you say, 'Exaltation *will come!*'
Then [a]He will save the humble *person.*
30 He will *even* deliver one who is not innocent;
Yes, he will be delivered by the purity *of your hands.*"

Job Proclaims God's Righteous Judgments

23 Then Job answered and said:
2 "Even today my [a]complaint is bitter;
My[1] hand is listless because of my groaning.
3 [a]Oh, that I knew where I might find Him,
That I might come to His seat!
4 I would present *my* case before Him,
And fill my mouth with arguments.
5 I would know the words *which* He would answer me,
And understand what He would say to me.
6 [a]Would He contend with me in His great power?
No! But He would take *note* of me.
7 There the upright could reason with Him,
And I would be delivered forever from my Judge.

8 "Look,[a] I go forward, but He is not *there,*
And backward, but I cannot perceive Him;
9 When He works on the left hand, I cannot behold *Him;*
When He turns to the right hand, I cannot see *Him.*
10 But [a]He knows the way that I take;
When [b]He has tested me, I shall come forth as gold.
11 [a]My foot has held fast to His steps;
I have kept His way and not turned aside.

PEACE NOTE

Often the tests or trials the Lord lovingly sends to us leave us confused and uncertain. We must remember that God is arranging everything for our good. Then peace comes.

JOB 23:10

22:21 [a] Is. 27:5 22:22 [a] Prov. 2:6 [b] [Ps. 119:11] 22:24 [a] 2 Chr. 1:15 22:25 [1] The ancient versions suggest *defense;* Hebrew reads *gold* as in verse 24. 22:26 [a] Job 27:10; Ps. 37:4; Is. 58:14 22:27 [a] [Is. 58:9–11] 22:29 [a] [1 Pet. 5:5]
23:2 [a] Job 7:11 [1] Following Masoretic Text, Targum, and Vulgate; Septuagint and Syriac read *His.* 23:3 [a] Job 13:3, 18; 16:21; 31:35 23:6 [a] Is. 57:16 23:8 [a] Job 9:11; 35:14 23:10 [a] [Ps. 1:6; 139:1–3] [b] [James 1:12] 23:11 [a] Ps. 17:5

12 I have not departed from the
[a]commandment of His lips;
[b]I have treasured the words of His mouth
More than my necessary *food.*

13 "But He *is* unique, and who can make
Him change?
And *whatever* [a]His soul desires, *that* He
does.
14 For He performs *what is* [a]appointed
for me,
And many such *things are* with Him.
15 Therefore I am terrified at His presence;
When I consider *this,* I am afraid of
Him.
16 For God [a]made my heart weak,
And the Almighty terrifies me;
17 Because I was not [a]cut off from the
presence of darkness,
And He did *not* hide deep darkness
from my face.

Job Complains of Violence on the Earth

24 "*Since* [a]times are not hidden from
the Almighty,
Why do those who know Him see not
His [b]days?

2 "*Some* remove [a]landmarks;
They seize flocks violently and feed *on
them;*
3 They drive away the donkey of the
fatherless;
They [a]take the widow's ox as a pledge.
4 They push the needy off the road;
All the [a]poor of the land are forced to
hide.
5 Indeed, *like* wild donkeys in the desert,
They go out to their work, searching for
food.
The wilderness *yields* food for them
and for *their* children.
6 They gather their fodder in the field
And glean in the vineyard of the
wicked.
7 They [a]spend the night naked, without
clothing,
And have no covering in the cold.
8 They are wet with the showers of the
mountains,
And [a]huddle around the rock for want
of shelter.

9 "*Some* snatch the fatherless from the
breast,
And take a pledge from the poor.
10 They cause *the poor* to go naked,
without [a]clothing;
And they take away the sheaves from
the hungry.
11 They press out oil within their walls,
And tread winepresses, yet suffer
thirst.
12 The dying groan in the city,
And the souls of the wounded cry out;
Yet God does not charge *them* with
wrong.

13 "There are those who rebel against the
light;
They do not know its ways
Nor abide in its paths.
14 [a]The murderer rises with the light;
He kills the poor and needy;
And in the night he is like a thief.
15 [a]The eye of the adulterer waits for the
twilight,
[b]Saying, 'No eye will see me';
And he disguises *his* face.
16 In the dark they break into houses
Which they marked for themselves in
the daytime;
[a]They do not know the light.
17 For the morning is the same to them as
the shadow of death;
If *someone* recognizes *them,*
They are in the terrors of the shadow of
death.

18 "They *should be* swift on the face of the
waters,
Their portion *should be* cursed in the
earth,
So that no *one would* turn into the way
of their vineyards.
19 As drought and heat consume the
snow waters,
So the grave[1] *consumes those who* have
sinned.
20 The womb *should* forget him,
The worm *should* feed sweetly on him;
[a]He *should* be remembered no more,
And wickedness *should* be broken like a
tree.
21 For he preys on the barren *who* do not
bear,
And does no good for the widow.

22 "But *God* draws the mighty away with
His power;
He rises up, but no *man* is sure of
life.

23:12 [a] Job 6:10; 22:22 [b] Ps. 44:18 **23:13** [a] [Ps. 115:3] **23:14** [a] [1 Thess. 3:2–4] **23:16** [a] Ps. 22:14 **23:17** [a] Job 10:18, 19 **24:1** [a] [Acts 1:7] [b] [Is. 2:12] **24:2** [a] [Deut. 19:14; 27:17] **24:3** [a] [Deut. 24:6, 10, 12, 17] **24:4** [a] Prov. 28:28 **24:7** [a] Ex. 22:26, 27 **24:8** [a] Lam. 4:5 **24:10** [a] Job 31:19 **24:14** [a] Ps. 10:8 **24:15** [a] Prov. 7:7–10 [b] Ps. 10:11 **24:16** [a] [John 3:20] **24:19** [1] Or *Sheol* **24:20** [a] Prov. 10:7

PEACE NOTE

Never forget that salvation happens in a moment, but transformation is a process.

Let the peace of God do its work in your life.

23 He gives them security, and they rely
on it;
Yet [a]His eyes *are* on their ways.
24 They are exalted for a little while,
Then they are gone.
They are brought low;
They are taken out of the way like all
others;
They dry out like the heads of grain.

25 "Now if *it is* not *so,* who will prove me a
liar,
And make my speech worth nothing?"

Bildad: How Can Man Be Righteous?

25 Then [a]Bildad the Shuhite answered
and said:

2 "Dominion and fear *belong* to Him;
He makes peace in His high places.
3 Is there any number to His armies?
Upon whom does [a]His light not rise?
4 [a]How then can man be righteous before
God?
Or how can he be [b]pure *who is* born of a
woman?
5 If even the moon does not shine,
And the stars are not pure in His [a]sight,
6 How much less man, *who is* [a]a maggot,
And a son of man, *who is* a worm?"

Job: Man's Frailty and God's Majesty

26 But Job answered and said:

2 "How have you helped *him who is*
without power?
How have you saved the arm *that has*
no strength?
3 How have you counseled *one who has*
no wisdom?
And *how* have you declared sound
advice to many?
4 To whom have you uttered words?
And whose spirit came from you?

5 "The dead tremble,
Those under the waters and those
inhabiting them.
6 [a]Sheol *is* naked before Him,
And Destruction has no covering.
7 [a]He stretches out the north over empty
space;
He hangs the earth on nothing.
8 [a]He binds up the water in His thick
clouds,
Yet the clouds are not broken under it.
9 He covers the face of *His* throne,
And spreads His cloud over it.
10 [a]He drew a circular horizon on the face
of the waters,
At the boundary of light and darkness.
11 The pillars of heaven tremble,
And are astonished at His rebuke.
12 [a]He stirs up the sea with His power,
And by His understanding He breaks
up the storm.
13 [a]By His Spirit He adorned the heavens;
His hand pierced [b]the fleeing serpent.
14 Indeed these *are* the mere edges of His
ways,
And how small a whisper we hear of
Him!
But the thunder of His power who can
understand?"

Job Maintains His Integrity

27 Moreover Job continued his discourse,
and said:

2 "*As* God lives, [a]*who* has taken away my
justice,
And the Almighty, *who* has made my
soul bitter,
3 As long as my breath *is* in me,
And the breath of God in my nostrils,
4 My lips will not speak wickedness,
Nor my tongue utter deceit.
5 Far be it from me
That I should say you are right;
Till I die [a]I will not put away my
integrity from me.
6 My righteousness I [a]hold fast, and will
not let it go;
[b]My heart shall not reproach *me* as long
as I live.

24:23 [a] [Prov. 15:3] **25:1** [a] Job 8:1; 18:1 **25:3** [a] James 1:17 **25:4** [a] Job 4:17; 15:14 [b] [Job 14:4] **25:5** [a] Job 15:15 **25:6** [a] Ps. 22:6 **26:6** [a] Prov. 15:11 **26:7** [a] Job 9:8 **26:8** [a] Prov. 30:4 **26:10** [a] Prov. 8:29 **26:12** [a] Is. 51:15 **26:13** [a] Ps. 33:6 [b] Is. 27:1 **27:2** [a] Job 34:5 **27:5** [a] Job 2:9; 13:15 **27:6** [a] Job 2:3; 33:9 [b] Acts 24:16

7 "May my enemy be like the wicked,
And he who rises up against me like the unrighteous.
8 [a]For what is the hope of the hypocrite,
Though he may gain *much,*
If God takes away his life?
9 [a]Will God hear his cry
When trouble comes upon him?
10 [a]Will he delight himself in the Almighty?
Will he always call on God?

11 "I will teach you about the hand of God;
What *is* with the Almighty I will not conceal.
12 Surely all of you have seen *it;*
Why then do you behave with complete nonsense?

13 "This[a] is the portion of a wicked man with God,
And the heritage of oppressors, received from the Almighty:
14 [a]If his children are multiplied, *it is* for the sword;
And his offspring shall not be satisfied with bread.
15 Those who survive him shall be buried in death,
And [a]their[1] widows shall not weep,
16 Though he heaps up silver like dust,
And piles up clothing like clay—
17 He may pile *it* up, but [a]the just will wear *it,*
And the innocent will divide the silver.
18 He builds his house like a moth,[1]
[a]Like a booth *which* a watchman makes.
19 The rich man will lie down,
But not be gathered *up;*[1]
He opens his eyes,
And he *is* [a]no more.
20 [a]Terrors overtake him like a flood;
A tempest steals him away in the night.
21 The east wind carries him away, and he is gone;
It sweeps him out of his place.
22 *It hurls against him* and does not [a]spare;
He flees desperately from its power.
23 *Men* shall clap their hands at him,
And shall hiss him out of his place.

Job's Discourse on Wisdom

28 "Surely there is a mine for silver,
And a place *where* gold is refined.
2 Iron is taken from the earth,
And copper *is* smelted *from* ore.
3 *Man* puts an end to darkness,
And searches every recess
For ore in the darkness and the shadow of death.
4 He breaks open a shaft away from people;
In places forgotten by feet
They hang far away from men;
They swing to and fro.
5 *As for* the earth, from it comes bread,
But underneath it is turned up as by fire;
6 Its stones *are* the source of sapphires,
And it contains gold dust.
7 *That* path no bird knows,
Nor has the falcon's eye seen it.
8 The proud lions[1] have not trodden it,
Nor has the fierce lion passed over it.
9 He puts his hand on the flint;
He overturns the mountains at the roots.
10 He cuts out channels in the rocks,
And his eye sees every precious thing.
11 He dams up the streams from trickling;
What is hidden he brings forth to light.

12 "But[a] where can wisdom be found?
And where *is* the place of understanding?
13 Man does not know its [a]value,
Nor is it found in the land of the living.

PEACE NOTE

Did you know there are 7,487 promises in the Scriptures from God to us? When anxiety and uncertainty attack your peace, do you have a promise to cling to?

27:8 [a] Matt. 16:26 **27:9** [a] Jer. 14:12 **27:10** [a] Job 22:26, 27 **27:13** [a] Job 20:29 **27:14** [a] Deut. 28:41 **27:15** [a] Ps. 78:64 [1] Literally *his* **27:17** [a] Prov. 28:8 **27:18** [a] Is. 1:8 [1] Following Masoretic Text and Vulgate; Septuagint and Syriac read *spider* (compare 8:14); Targum reads *decay.* **27:19** [a] Job 7:8, 21; 20:7 [1] Following Masoretic Text and Targum; Septuagint and Syriac read *But shall not add* (that is, do it again); Vulgate reads *But take away nothing.* **27:20** [a] Job 18:11 **27:22** [a] Jer. 13:14 **28:8** [1] Literally *sons of pride,* figurative of the great lions **28:12** [a] Eccl. 7:24 **28:13** [a] Prov. 3:15

14 [a]The deep says, '*It is* not in me';
And the sea says, '*It is* not with me.'
15 It [a]cannot be purchased for gold,
Nor can silver be weighed *for* its price.
16 It cannot be valued in the gold of Ophir,
In precious onyx or sapphire.
17 Neither [a]gold nor crystal can equal it,
Nor can it be exchanged for jewelry of fine gold.
18 No mention shall be made of coral or quartz,
For the price of wisdom *is* above [a]rubies.
19 The topaz of Ethiopia cannot equal it,
Nor can it be valued in pure [a]gold.

20 "From[a] where then does wisdom come?
And where *is* the place of understanding?
21 It is hidden from the eyes of all living,
And concealed from the birds of the air.
22 [a]Destruction and Death say,
'We have heard a report about it with our ears.'
23 God understands its way,
And He knows its place.
24 For He looks to the ends of the earth,
And [a]sees under the whole heavens,
25 [a]To establish a weight for the wind,
And apportion the waters by measure.
26 When He [a]made a law for the rain,
And a path for the thunderbolt,
27 Then He saw *wisdom*[1] and declared it;
He prepared it, indeed, He searched it out.
28 And to man He said,
'Behold, [a]the fear of the Lord, that *is* wisdom,
And to depart from evil *is* understanding.' "

Job's Summary Defense

29 Job further continued his discourse, and said:

2 "Oh, that I were as *in* months [a]past,
As *in* the days *when* God [b]watched over me;
3 [a]When His lamp shone upon my head,
And when by His light I walked *through* darkness;
4 Just as I was in the days of my prime,
When [a]the friendly counsel of God *was* over my tent;
5 When the Almighty *was* yet with me,
When my children *were* around me;
6 When [a]my steps were bathed with cream,[1]
And [b]the rock poured out rivers of oil for me!

7 "When I went out to the gate by the city,
When I took my seat in the open square,
8 The young men saw me and hid,
And the aged arose *and* stood;
9 The princes refrained from talking,
And [a]put *their* hand on their mouth;
10 The voice of nobles was hushed,
And their [a]tongue stuck to the roof of their mouth.
11 When the ear heard, then it blessed me,
And when the eye saw, then it approved me;
12 Because [a]I delivered the poor who cried out,
The fatherless and *the one who* had no helper.
13 The blessing of a perishing *man* came upon me,
And I caused the widow's heart to sing for joy.
14 [a]I put on righteousness, and it clothed me;
My justice *was* like a robe and a turban.
15 I *was* [a]eyes to the blind,
And I *was* feet to the lame.
16 I *was* a father to the poor,
And [a]I searched out the case *that* I did not know.
17 I broke [a]the fangs of the wicked,
And plucked the victim from his teeth.

18 "Then I said, [a]'I shall die in my nest,
And multiply *my* days as the sand.
19 [a]My root *is* spread out [b]to the waters,
And the dew lies all night on my branch.
20 My glory *is* fresh within me,
And my [a]bow is renewed in my hand.'

21 "*Men* listened to me and waited,
And kept silence for my counsel.
22 After my words they did not speak again,
And my speech settled on them *as dew*.
23 They waited for me *as* for the rain,
And they opened their mouth wide *as* for [a]the spring rain.

28:14 [a] *Job 28:22* *28:15* [a] Prov. 3:13–15; 8:10, 11, 19 **28:17** [a] Prov. 8:10; 16:16 **28:18** [a] Prov. 3:15; 8:11 **28:19** [a] Prov. 8:19 **28:20** [a] Job 28:12 **28:22** [a] Job 28:14 **28:24** [a] [Prov. 15:3] **28:25** [a] Ps. 135:7 **28:26** [a] Job 37:3; 38:25 **28:27** [1] Literally *it* **28:28** [a] [Prov. 1:7; 9:10] **29:2** [a] Job 1:1–5 [b] Job 1:10 **29:3** [a] Job 18:6 **29:4** [a] [Ps. 25:14] **29:6** [a] Deut. 32:14; Job 20:17 [b] Ps. 81:16 [1] Masoretic Text reads *wrath;* ancient versions and some Hebrew manuscripts read *cream* (compare 20:17). **29:9** [a] Job 21:5 **29:10** [a] Ps. 137:6 **29:12** [a] [Ps. 72:12] **29:14** [a] [Is. 59:17; 61:10] **29:15** [a] Num. 10:31 **29:16** [a] Prov. 29:7 **29:17** [a] Prov. 30:14 **29:18** [a] Ps. 30:6 **29:19** [a] Job 18:16 [b] Ps. 1:3 **29:20** [a] Gen. 49:24 **29:23** [a] [Zech. 10:1]

24 *If* I mocked at them, they did not
believe *it*,
And the light of my countenance they
did not cast down.
25 I chose the way for them, and sat as
chief;
So I dwelt as a king in the army,
As one *who* comforts mourners.

30 "But now they mock at me, *men*
younger than I,
Whose fathers I disdained to put with
the dogs of my flock.
2 Indeed, what *profit* is the strength of
their hands to me?
Their vigor has perished.
3 *They are* gaunt from want and famine,
Fleeing late to the wilderness, desolate
and waste,
4 Who pluck mallow by the bushes,
And broom tree roots *for* their food.
5 They were driven out from among *men*,
They shouted at them as *at* a thief.
6 *They had* to live in the clefts of the
valleys,
In caves of the earth and the rocks.
7 Among the bushes they brayed,
Under the nettles they nestled.
8 *They were* sons of fools,
Yes, sons of vile men;
They were scourged from the land.

9 "And[a] now I am their taunting song;
Yes, I am their byword.
10 They abhor me, they keep far from me;
They do not hesitate [a]to spit in my face.
11 Because [a]He has loosed my[1] bowstring
and afflicted me,
They have cast off restraint before me.
12 At *my* right *hand* the rabble arises;
They push away my feet,
And [a]they raise against me their ways
of destruction.
13 They break up my path,
They promote my calamity;
They have no helper.
14 They come as broad breakers;
Under the ruinous storm they roll along.
15 Terrors are turned upon me;
They pursue my honor as the wind,
And my prosperity has passed like a
cloud.

16 "And[a] now my soul is [b]poured out
because of my *plight;*
The days of affliction take hold of me.
17 My bones are pierced in me at night,
And my gnawing pains take no rest.
18 By great force my garment is disfigured;
It binds me about as the collar of my
coat.
19 He has cast me into the mire,
And I have become like dust and ashes.

20 "I [a]cry out to You, but You do not
answer me;
I stand up, and You regard me.
21 *But* You have become cruel to me;
With the strength of Your hand You
[a]oppose me.
22 You lift me up to the wind and cause
me to ride *on it;*
You spoil my success.
23 For I know *that* You will bring me *to*
death,
And *to* the house [a]appointed for all
living.

24 "Surely He would not stretch out *His*
hand against a heap of ruins,
If they cry out when He destroys *it*.
25 [a]Have I not wept for him who was in
trouble?
Has *not* my soul grieved for the poor?
26 [a]But when I looked for good, evil came
to me;
And when I waited for light, then came
darkness.
27 My heart is in turmoil and cannot rest;
Days of affliction confront me.
28 [a]I go about mourning, but not in the sun;
I stand up in the assembly *and* cry out
for help.
29 [a]I am a brother of jackals,
And a companion of ostriches.
30 [a]My skin grows black and falls from me;
[b]My bones burn with fever.
31 My harp is *turned* to mourning,
And my flute to the voice of those who
weep.

31 "I have made a covenant with my
eyes;
Why then should I look upon a [a]young
woman?
2 For what *is* the [a]allotment of God from
above,
And the inheritance of the Almighty
from on high?
3 *Is* it not destruction for the wicked,
And disaster for the workers of
iniquity?

30:9 [a] Job 17:6 **30:10** [a] Is. 50:6 **30:11** [a] Job 12:18 [1] Following Masoretic Text, Syriac, and Targum; Septuagint and Vulgate read *His*. **30:12** [a] Job 19:12 **30:16** [a] Ps. 42:4 [b] Ps. 22:14 **30:20** [a] Job 19:7 **30:21** [a] Job 10:3; 16:9, 14; 19:6, 22 **30:23** [a] [Heb. 9:27] **30:25** [a] Ps. 35:13, 14 **30:26** [a] Jer. 8:15 **30:28** [a] Ps. 38:6; 42:9; 43:2 **30:29** [a] Mic. 1:8 **30:30** [a] Ps. 119:83 [b] Ps. 102:3 **31:1** [a] [Matt. 5:28] **31:2** [a] Job 20:29

PEACE NOTE

The Christian's unwavering commitment to spiritual purity like Job's is central to the peace of God. We have no peace when we allow impurity into our lives.

JOB 31:1

4 [a]Does He not see my ways,
And count all my steps?

5 "If I have walked with falsehood,
Or if my foot has hastened to deceit,
6 Let me be weighed on honest scales,
That God may know my [a]integrity.
7 If my step has turned from the way,
Or [a]my heart walked after my eyes,
Or if any spot adheres to my hands,
8 *Then* [a]let me sow, and another eat;
Yes, let my harvest be rooted out.

9 "If my heart has been enticed by a woman,
Or *if* I have lurked at my neighbor's door,
10 *Then* let my wife grind for [a]another,
And let others bow down over her.
11 For that *would be* wickedness;
Yes, [a]it *would be* iniquity *deserving of* judgment.
12 For that *would be* a fire *that* consumes to destruction,
And would root out all my increase.

13 "If I have [a]despised the cause of my male or female servant
When they complained against me,
14 What then shall I do when [a]God rises up?
When He punishes, how shall I answer Him?
15 [a]Did not He who made me in the womb make them?
Did not the same One fashion us in the *womb?*

16 "If I have kept the poor from *their* desire,
Or caused the eyes of the widow to [a]fail,
17 Or eaten my morsel by myself,
So that the fatherless could not eat of it
18 (But from my youth I reared him as a father,
And from my mother's womb I guided *the widow*[1]);
19 If I have seen anyone perish for lack of clothing,
Or any poor *man* without covering;
20 If his heart[1] has not [a]blessed me,
And *if* he was *not* warmed with the fleece of my sheep;
21 If I have raised my hand [a]against the fatherless,
When I saw I had help in the gate;
22 *Then* let my arm fall from my shoulder,
Let my arm be torn from the socket.
23 For [a]destruction *from* God *is* a terror to me,
And because of His magnificence I cannot endure.

24 "If[a] I have made gold my hope,
Or said to fine gold, '*You are* my confidence';
25 [a]If I have rejoiced because my wealth *was* great,
And because my hand had gained much;
26 [a]If I have observed the sun[1] when it shines,
Or the moon moving *in* brightness,
27 So that my heart has been secretly enticed,
And my mouth has kissed my hand;
28 This also *would be* an iniquity *deserving of* judgment,
For I would have denied God *who is* above.

29 "If[a] I have rejoiced at the destruction of him who hated me,
Or lifted myself up when evil found him
30 [a](Indeed I have not allowed my mouth to sin
By asking for a curse on his soul);
31 If the men of my tent have not said,
'Who is there that has not been satisfied with his meat?'
32 [a](*But* no sojourner had to lodge in the street,
For I have opened my doors to the traveler[1]);

31:4 [a] [2 Chr. 16:9] **31:6** [a] Job 23:10; 27:5, 6 **31:7** [a] Ezek. 6:9 **31:8** [a] Lev. 26:16 **31:10** [a] Jer. 8:10 **31:11** [a] Gen. 38:24 **31:13** [a] [Deut. 24:14, 15] **31:14** [a] [Ps. 44:21] **31:15** [a] Job 34:19 **31:16** [a] Job 29:12 **31:18** [1] Literally *her* (compare verse 16) **31:20** [a] [Deut. 24:13] [1] Literally *loins* **31:21** [a] Job 22:9 **31:23** [a] Is. 13:6 **31:24** [a] [Mark 10:23–25] **31:25** [a] Ps. 62:10 **31:26** [a] Ezek. 8:16 [1] Literally *light* **31:29** [a] [Prov. 17:5; 24:17] **31:30** [a] [Matt. 5:44] **31:32** [a] Gen. 19:2, 3
[1] Following Septuagint, Syriac, Targum, and Vulgate; Masoretic Text reads *road*.

33 If I have covered my transgressions [a]as
Adam,
By hiding my iniquity in my bosom,
34 Because I feared the great [a]multitude,
And dreaded the contempt of families,
So that I kept silence
And did not go out of the door—
35 [a]Oh, that I had one to hear me!
Here is my mark.
Oh, [b]*that* the Almighty would answer me,
That my Prosecutor had written a book!
36 Surely I would carry it on my shoulder,
And bind it on me *like* a crown;
37 I would declare to Him the number of
my steps;
Like a prince I would approach Him.

38 "If my land cries out against me,
And its furrows weep together;
39 If [a]I have eaten its fruit[1] without
money,
Or [b]caused its owners to lose their
lives;
40 *Then* let [a]thistles grow instead of wheat,
And weeds instead of barley."

The words of Job are ended.

Elihu Contradicts Job's Friends

32 So these three men ceased answering Job, because he *was* [a]righteous in
his own eyes. 2 Then the wrath of Elihu, the
son of Barachel the [a]Buzite, of the family of
Ram, was aroused against Job; his wrath was
aroused because he [b]justified himself rather
than God. 3 Also against his three friends his
wrath was aroused, because they had found
no answer, and *yet* had condemned Job.
4 Now because they *were* years older than he,
Elihu had waited to speak to Job.[1] 5 When Elihu
saw that *there was* no answer in the mouth of
these three men, his wrath was aroused.
6 So Elihu, the son of Barachel the Buzite,
answered and said:

"I *am* [a]young in years, and you *are* very
old;
Therefore I was afraid,
And dared not declare my opinion to
you.
7 I said, 'Age[1] should speak,
And multitude of years should teach
wisdom.'
8 But *there is* a spirit in man,
And [a]the breath of the Almighty gives
him understanding.
9 [a]Great men[1] are not *always* wise,
Nor do the aged *always* understand
justice.

10 "Therefore I say, 'Listen to me,
I also will declare my opinion.'
11 Indeed I waited for your words,
I listened to your reasonings, while you
searched out what to say.
12 I paid close attention to you;
And surely not one of you convinced
Job,
Or answered his words—
13 [a]Lest you say,
'We have found wisdom';
God will vanquish him, not man.
14 Now he has not directed *his* words
against me;
So I will not answer him with your
words.

15 "They are dismayed and answer no more;
Words escape them.
16 And I have waited, because they did
not speak,
Because they stood still *and* answered
no more.
17 I also will answer my part,
I too will declare my opinion.
18 For I am full of words;
The spirit within me compels me.
19 Indeed my belly *is* like wine *that* has no
vent;
It is ready to burst like new wineskins.
20 I will speak, that I may find relief;
I must open my lips and answer.
21 Let me not, I pray, show partiality to
anyone;
Nor let me flatter any man.
22 For I do not know how to flatter,
Else my Maker would soon take me
[a]away.

Elihu Contradicts Job

33 "But please, Job, hear my speech,
And listen to all my words.
2 Now, I open my mouth;
My tongue speaks in my mouth.
3 My words *come* from my upright heart;
My lips utter pure knowledge.
4 [a]The Spirit of God has made me,
And the breath of the Almighty gives
me life.
5 If you can answer me,
Set *your words* in order before me;
Take your stand.

31:33 [a] [Prov. 28:13] **31:34** [a] Ex. 23:2 **31:35** [a] Job 19:7; 30:20, 24, 28 [b] Job 13:22, 24; 33:10 **31:39** [a] Job 24:6, 10–12 [b] 1 Kin. 21:19 [1] Literally *its strength* **31:40** [a] Gen. 3:18 **32:1** [a] Job 6:29; 31:6; 33:9 **32:2** [a] Gen. 22:21 [b] Job 27:5, 6 **32:4** [1] Vulgate reads *till Job had spoken.* **32:6** [a] Lev. 19:32 **32:7** [1] Literally *Days,* that is, years **32:8** [a] [Prov. 2:6] **32:9** [a] [1 Cor. 1:26] [1] Or *Men of many years* **32:13** [a] [Jer. 9:23] **32:22** [a] Job 27:8 **33:4** [a] [Gen. 2:7]

6 [a]Truly I *am* as your spokesman[1] before
God;
I also have been formed out of clay.
7 [a]Surely no fear of me will terrify you,
Nor will my hand be heavy on you.

8 "Surely you have spoken in my hearing,
And I have heard the sound of *your*
words, *saying,*
9 'I[a] *am* pure, without transgression;
I *am* innocent, and *there is* no iniquity
in me.
10 Yet He finds occasions against me,
[a]He counts me as His enemy;
11 [a]He puts my feet in the stocks,
He watches all my paths.'

12 "Look, *in* this you are not righteous.
I will answer you,
For God is greater than man.
13 Why do you [a]contend with Him?
For He does not give an accounting of
any of His words.
14 [a]For God may speak in one way, or in
another,
Yet man does not perceive it.
15 [a]In a dream, in a vision of the night,
When deep sleep falls upon men,
While slumbering on their beds,
16 [a]Then He opens the ears of men,
And seals their instruction.
17 In order to turn man *from his* deed,
And conceal pride from man,
18 He keeps back his soul from the Pit,
And his life from perishing by the sword.

19 "*Man* is also chastened with pain on his
[a]bed,
And with strong *pain* in many of his
bones,
20 [a]So that his life abhors [b]bread,
And his soul succulent food.
21 His flesh wastes away from sight,
And his bones stick out *which once*
were not seen.
22 Yes, his soul draws near the Pit,
And his life to the executioners.

23 "If there is a messenger for him,
A mediator, one among a thousand,
To show man His uprightness,
24 Then He is gracious to him, and says,
'Deliver him from going down to the
Pit;
I have found a ransom';
25 His flesh shall be young like a child's,
He shall return to the days of his
youth.
26 He shall pray to God, and He will
delight in him,
He shall see His face with joy,
For He restores to man His
righteousness.
27 Then he looks at men and [a]says,
'I have sinned, and perverted *what was*
right,
And it [b]did not profit me.'
28 He will [a]redeem his[1] soul from going
down to the Pit,
And his[2] life shall see the light.

29 "Behold, God works all these *things,*
Twice, *in fact,* three *times* with a man,
30 [a]To bring back his soul from the Pit,
That he may be enlightened with the
light of life.

31 "Give ear, Job, listen to me;
Hold your peace, and I will speak.
32 If you have anything to say, answer me;
Speak, for I desire to justify you.
33 If not, [a]listen to me;
Hold your peace, and I will teach you
wisdom."

Elihu Proclaims God's Justice

34 Elihu further answered and said:

2 "Hear my words, you wise *men;*
Give ear to me, you who have
knowledge.
3 [a]For the ear tests words
As the palate tastes food.
4 Let us choose justice for ourselves;
Let us know among ourselves what *is*
good.

5 "For Job has said, [a]'I am righteous,
But [b]God has taken away my justice;
6 [a]Should I lie concerning my right?
My wound *is* incurable, *though I am*
without transgression.'
7 What man *is* like Job,
[a]*Who* drinks scorn like water,
8 Who goes in company with the workers
of iniquity,
And walks with wicked men?
9 For [a]he has said, 'It profits a man
nothing
That he should delight in God.'

33:6 [a] Job 4:19 [1] Literally *as your mouth* **33:7** [a] Job 9:34 **33:9** [a] Job 10:7 **33:10** [a] Job 13:24; 16:9 **33:11** [a] Job 13:27; 19:8 **33:13** [a] [Is. 45:9] **33:14** [a] Ps. 62:11 **33:15** [a] [Num. 12:6] **33:16** [a] [Job 36:10, 15] **33:19** [a] Job 30:17 **33:20** [a] Ps. 107:18 [b] Job 3:24; 6:7 **33:27** [a] [Luke 15:21] [b] [Rom. 6:21] **33:28** [a] Is. 38:17 [1] Or *my* (Kethib) [2] Or *my* (Kethib) **33:30** [a] Ps. 56:13 **33:33** [a] Ps. 34:11 **34:3** [a] Job 6:30; 12:11 **34:5** [a] Job 13:18; 33:9 [b] Job 27:2 **34:6** [a] Job 6:4; 9:17 **34:7** [a] Job 15:16 **34:9** [a] Mal. 3:14

10 "Therefore listen to me, you men of
understanding:
[a]Far be it from God *to do* wickedness,
And *from* the Almighty to *commit*
iniquity.
11 [a]For He repays man *according to* his
work,
And makes man to find a reward
according to *his* way.
12 Surely God will never do wickedly,
Nor will the Almighty [a]pervert justice.
13 Who gave Him charge over the earth?
Or who appointed *Him over* the whole
world?
14 If He should set His heart on it,
If He should [a]gather to Himself His
Spirit and His breath,
15 [a]All flesh would perish together,
And man would return to dust.

16 "If *you have* understanding, hear this;
Listen to the sound of my words:
17 [a]Should one who hates justice govern?
Will you [b]condemn *Him who is* most
just?
18 [a]*Is it fitting* to say to a king, '*You are*
worthless,'
And to nobles, '*You are* wicked'?
19 Yet He [a]is not partial to princes,
Nor does He regard the rich more than
the poor;
For [b]they *are* all the work of His hands.
20 In a moment they die, [a]in the middle of
the night;
The people are shaken and pass away;
The mighty are taken away without a
hand.

21 "For[a] His eyes *are* on the ways of man,
And He sees all his steps.
22 [a]There is no darkness nor shadow of
death
Where the workers of iniquity may
hide themselves.
23 For He need not further consider a
man,
That he should go before God in
judgment.
24 [a]He breaks in pieces mighty men
without inquiry,
And sets others in their place.
25 Therefore He knows their works;
He overthrows *them* in the night,
And they are crushed.
26 He strikes them as wicked *men*
In the open sight of others,
27 Because they [a]turned back from Him,
And [b]would not consider any of His
ways,
28 So that they [a]caused the cry of the poor
to come to Him;
For He [b]hears the cry of the afflicted.
29 When He gives quietness, who then
can make trouble?
And when He hides *His* face, who then
can see Him,
Whether *it is* against a nation or a man
alone?—
30 That the hypocrite should not reign,
Lest the people be ensnared.

31 "For has *anyone* said to God,
'I have borne *chastening;*
I will offend no more;
32 Teach me *what* I do not see;
If I have done iniquity, I will do no
more'?
33 Should He repay *it* according to your
terms,
Just because you disavow it?
You must choose, and not I;
Therefore speak what you know.

34 "Men of understanding say to me,
Wise men who listen to me:
35 'Job[a] speaks without knowledge,
His words *are* without wisdom.'
36 Oh, that Job were tried to the utmost,
Because *his* answers *are like* those of
wicked men!
37 For he adds [a]rebellion to his sin;
He claps *his hands* among us,
And multiplies his words against God."

Elihu Condemns Self-Righteousness

35 Moreover Elihu answered and said:
2 "Do you think this is right?
Do you say,
'My righteousness is more than God's'?
3 For [a]you say,
'What advantage will it be to You?
What profit shall I have, more than *if* I
had sinned?'

4 "I will answer you,
And [a]your companions with you.
5 [a]Look to the heavens and see;
And behold the clouds—
They are higher than you.
6 If you sin, what do you accomplish
[a]against Him?

34:10 [a] Job 8:3; 36:23 **34:11** [a] Ps. 62:12 **34:12** [a] Job 8:3 **34:14** [a] Ps. 104:29 **34:15** [a] [Gen. 3:19] **34:17** [a] 2 Sam. 23:3 [b] Job 40:8 **34:18** [a] Ex. 22:28 **34:19** [a] [Deut. 10:17] [b] Job 31:15 **34:20** [a] Ex. 12:29 **34:21** [a] Job 31:4 **34:22** [a] [Amos 9:2, 3] **34:24** [a] [Dan. 2:21] **34:27** [a] 1 Sam. 15:11 [b] Is. 5:12 **34:28** [a] Job 35:9 [b] [Ex. 22:23] **34:35** [a] Job 35:16; 38:2 **34:37** [a] Job 7:11; 10:1 **35:3** [a] Job 21:15; 34:9 **35:4** [a] Job 34:8 **35:5** [a] [Job 22:12] **35:6** [a] [Jer. 7:19]

PEACE NOTE

Expect commentary from friends and family when you endure trials. Filter everything you hear through the Word of God, the character of God, and the peace of God.

JOB 35:1

Or, *if* your transgressions are
multiplied, what do you do to Him?
7 [a]If you are righteous, what do you give
Him?
Or what does He receive from your
hand?
8 Your wickedness affects a man such as
you,
And your righteousness a son of man.

9 "Because[a] of the multitude of
oppressions they cry out;
They cry out for help because of the
arm of the mighty.
10 But no one says, [a]'Where *is* God my
Maker,
[b]Who gives songs in the night,
11 Who [a]teaches us more than the beasts
of the earth,
And makes us wiser than the birds of
heaven?'
12 [a]There they cry out, but He does not
answer,
Because of the pride of evil men.
13 [a]Surely God will not listen to empty *talk*,
Nor will the Almighty regard it.
14 [a]Although you say you do not see Him,
Yet justice *is* before Him, and [b]you
must wait for Him.
15 And now, because He has not
[a]punished in His anger,
Nor taken much notice of folly,
16 [a]Therefore Job opens his mouth in
vain;
He multiplies words without
knowledge."

Elihu Proclaims God's Goodness

36 Elihu also proceeded and said:
2 "Bear with me a little, and I will show you
That *there are* yet words to speak on
God's behalf.
3 I will fetch my knowledge from afar;
I will ascribe righteousness to my Maker.
4 For truly my words *are* not false;
One who is perfect in knowledge *is* with
you.

5 "Behold, God *is* mighty, but despises *no
one;*
[a]*He is* mighty in strength of
understanding.
6 He does not preserve the life of the
wicked,
But gives justice to the [a]oppressed.
7 [a]He does not withdraw His eyes from
the righteous;
But [b]*they are* on the throne with kings,
For He has seated them forever,
And they are exalted.
8 And [a]if *they are* bound in fetters,
Held in the cords of affliction,
9 Then He tells them their work and
their transgressions—
That they have acted defiantly.
10 [a]He also opens their ear to instruction,
And commands that they turn from
iniquity.
11 If they obey and serve *Him,*
They shall [a]spend their days in prosperity,
And their years in pleasures.
12 But if they do not obey,
They shall perish by the sword,
And they shall die without [a]knowledge.[1]

13 "But the hypocrites in heart [a]store up
wrath;
They do not cry for help when He binds
them.
14 [a]They die in youth,
And their life *ends* among the
perverted persons.[1]
15 He delivers the poor in their affliction,
And opens their ears in oppression.

16 "Indeed He would have brought you out
of dire distress,
[a]*Into* a broad place where *there is* no
restraint;
And [b]what is set on your table *would be*
full of [c]richness.

35:7 [a] Prov. 9:12 35:9 [a] Job 34:28 35:10 [a] Is. 51:13 [b] Acts 16:25 35:11 [a] Ps. 94:12 35:12 [a] Prov. 1:28 35:13 [a] [Is. 1:15] 35:14 [a] Job 9:11 [b] [Ps. 37:5, 6] 35:15 [a] Ps. 89:32 35:16 [a] Job 34:35; 38:2 36:5 [a] Job 12:13, 16; 37:23 36:6 [a] Job 5:15 36:7 [a] [Ps. 33:18; 34:15] [b] Ps. 113:8 36:8 [a] Ps. 107:10 36:10 [a] Job 33:16; 36:15 36:11 [a] [Is. 1:19, 20] 36:12 [a] Job 4:21 [1] Masoretic Text reads *as one without knowledge.* 36:13 [a] [Rom. 2:5] 36:14 [a] Ps. 55:23 [1] Hebrew *qedeshim,* that is, those practicing sodomy and prostitution in religious rituals 36:16 [a] Ps. 18:19; 31:8; 118:5 [b] Ps. 23:5 [c] Ps. 36:8

17 But you are filled with the judgment
due the [a]wicked;
Judgment and justice take hold *of you.*
18 Because *there is* wrath, *beware* lest He
take you away with *one* blow;
For [a]a large ransom would not help you
avoid *it.*
19 [a]Will your riches,
Or all the mighty forces,
Keep you from distress?
20 Do not desire the night,
When people are cut off in their place.
21 Take heed, [a]do not turn to iniquity,
For [b]you have chosen this rather than
affliction.

22 "Behold, God is exalted by His power;
Who teaches like Him?
23 [a]Who has assigned Him His way,
Or who has said, 'You have done [b]wrong'?

Elihu Proclaims God's Majesty

24 "Remember to [a]magnify His work,
Of which men have sung.
25 Everyone has seen it;
Man looks on *it* from afar.

26 "Behold, God *is* great, and we [a]do not
know *Him;*
[b]Nor can the number of His years *be*
discovered.
27 For He [a]draws up drops of water,
Which distill as rain from the mist,
28 [a]Which the clouds drop down
And pour abundantly on man.
29 Indeed, can *anyone* understand the
spreading of clouds,
The thunder from His canopy?
30 Look, He [a]scatters His light upon it,
And covers the depths of the sea.
31 For [a]by these He judges the peoples;
He [b]gives food in abundance.
32 [a]He covers *His* hands with lightning,
And commands it to strike.
33 [a]His thunder declares it,
The cattle also, concerning the rising
storm.

37 "At this also my heart trembles,
And leaps from its place.
2 Hear attentively the thunder of His voice,
And the rumbling *that* comes from His
mouth.
3 He sends it forth under the whole heaven,
His lightning to the ends of the earth.
4 After it [a]a voice roars;
He thunders with His majestic voice,
And He does not restrain them when
His voice is heard.
5 God thunders marvelously with His voice;
[a]He does great things which we cannot
comprehend.
6 For [a]He says to the snow, 'Fall *on* the earth';
Likewise to the gentle rain and the
heavy rain of His strength.
7 He seals the hand of every man,
[a]That [b]all men may know His work.
8 The beasts [a]go into dens,
And remain in their lairs.
9 From the chamber *of the south* comes
the whirlwind,
And cold from the scattering winds *of
the north.*
10 [a]By the breath of God ice is given,
And the broad waters are frozen.
11 Also with moisture He saturates the
thick clouds;
He scatters His bright clouds.
12 And they swirl about, being turned by
His guidance,
That they may [a]do whatever He
commands them
On the face of the whole earth.[1]
13 [a]He causes it to come,
Whether for correction,
Or [b]for His land,
Or [c]for mercy.

14 "Listen to this, O Job;
Stand still and [a]consider the wondrous
works of God.

PEACE NOTE

Thanks to amazing instruments, we can see faraway galaxies and the tiniest atoms. And to think, all this was created for our enjoyment in fellowship with God marked by His peace. Wow.

JOB 37:14

36:17 [a] Job 22:5, 10, 11 **36:18** [a] Ps. 49:7 **36:19** [a] [Prov. 11:4] **36:21** [a] [Ps. 31:6; 66:18] [b] [Heb. 11:25] **36:23** [a] Job 34:13; [Is. 40:13, 14] [b] Job 8:3 **36:24** [a] [Rev. 15:3] **36:26** [a] [1 Cor. 13:12] [b] Heb. 1:12 **36:27** [a] Ps. 147:8 **36:28** [a] [Prov. 3:20] **36:30** [a] Job 37:3 **36:31** [a] [Acts 14:17] [b] Ps. 104:14, 15 **36:32** [a] Ps. 147:8 **36:33** [a] 1 Kin. 18:41 **37:4** [a] Ps. 29:3 **37:5** [a] Job 5:9; 9:10; 36:26 **37:6** [a] Ps. 147:16, 17 **37:7** [a] Ps. 109:27 [b] Ps. 19:3, 4 **37:8** [a] Ps. 104:21, 22 **37:10** [a] Ps. 147:17, 18 **37:12** [a] Job 36:32 [1] Literally *the world of the earth* **37:13** [a] Ex. 9:18, 23 [b] Job 38:26, 27 [c] 1 Kin. 18:41–46 **37:14** [a] Ps. 111:2

15 Do you know when God dispatches them,
And causes the light of His cloud to shine?
16 [a]Do you know how the clouds are balanced,
Those wondrous works of [b]Him who is perfect in knowledge?
17 Why *are* your garments hot,
When He quiets the earth by the south *wind?*
18 With Him, have you [a]spread out the [b]skies,
Strong as a cast metal mirror?

19 "Teach us what we should say to Him,
For we can prepare nothing because of the darkness.
20 Should He be told that I *wish to* speak?
If a man were to speak, surely he would be swallowed up.
21 Even now *men* cannot look at the light *when it is* bright in the skies,
When the wind has passed and cleared them.
22 He comes from the north *as* golden *splendor;*
With God *is* awesome majesty.
23 *As for* the Almighty, [a]we cannot find Him;
[b]*He is* excellent in power,
In judgment and abundant justice;
He does not oppress.
24 Therefore men [a]fear Him;
He shows no partiality to any *who are* [b]wise of heart."

The LORD Reveals His Omnipotence to Job

38 Then the LORD answered Job [a]out of the whirlwind, and said:

2 "Who[a] *is* this who darkens counsel
By [b]words without knowledge?
3 [a]Now prepare yourself like a man;
I will question you, and you shall answer Me.

4 "Where[a] were you when I laid the foundations of the earth?
Tell *Me,* if you have understanding.
5 Who determined its measurements?
Surely you know!
Or who stretched the line upon it?
6 To what were its foundations fastened?
Or who laid its cornerstone,
7 When the morning stars sang together,
And all [a]the sons of God shouted for joy?

8 "Or[a] *who* shut in the sea with doors,
When it burst forth *and* issued from the womb;
9 When I made the clouds its garment,
And thick darkness its swaddling band;

37:16 [a] Job 36:29 [b] Job 36:4 **37:18** [a] [Is. 44:24] [b] Ps. 104:2 **37:23** [a] [1 Tim. 6:16] [b] [Job 9:4; 36:5] **37:24** [a] [Matt. 10:28] [b] [Matt. 11:25] **38:1** [a] Ex. 19:16 **38:2** [a] Job 34:35; 42:3 [b] 1 Tim. 1:7 **38:3** [a] Job 40:7 **38:4** [a] Ps. 104:5 **38:7** [a] Job 1:6 **38:8** [a] Gen. 1:9

GOD, OUR ETERNAL KING

"Where were you when I laid the foundations of the earth?"

JOB 38:4

At the lowest point in his life Job lost all hope. He still had some faith in God, but not much. His counselors gave their opinions, sometimes voicing typical human ideas that missed the mark. They provided no comfort to Job. Then God spoke. "Where were you when I laid the foundations of the earth?" He asked. God was not belittling Job; rather, He was reminding Job that He is the Creator and the Sustainer of all. God's speech was not intended to mock Job but to reassure him, restore his faith, and give him a renewed sense of peace.

When God created the world, He informed Job, "all the sons of God shouted for joy" (v. 7). Creation is a good thing, and the host of heaven recognized that and rejoiced. Our Creator's goodness tells us that God cares for His creation, above all, the humans He made in His image. From this great truth Job could once again find peace, knowing that God *has everything in control.*

What feels out of control in your life right now? How do you feel knowing that nothing, including you, slips from God's hands?

10 When [a]I fixed My limit for it,
And set bars and doors;
11 When I said,
'This far you may come, but no farther,
And here your proud waves [a]must stop!'

12 "Have you [a]commanded the morning since your days *began*,
And caused the dawn to know its place,
13 That it might take hold of the ends of the earth,
And [a]the wicked be shaken out of it?
14 It takes on form like clay *under* a seal,
And stands out like a garment.
15 From the wicked their [a]light is withheld,
And [b]the upraised arm is broken.

16 "Have you [a]entered the springs of the sea?
Or have you walked in search of the depths?
17 Have [a]the gates of death been revealed to you?
Or have you seen the doors of the shadow of death?
18 Have you comprehended the breadth of the earth?
Tell *Me*, if you know all this.

19 "Where *is* the way *to* the dwelling of light?
And darkness, where *is* its place,
20 That you may take it to its territory,
That you may know the paths *to* its home?
21 Do you know *it*, because you were born then,
Or *because* the number of your days *is* great?

22 "Have you entered [a]the treasury of snow,
Or have you seen the treasury of hail,
23 [a]Which I have reserved for the time of trouble,
For the day of battle and war?
24 By what way is light diffused,
Or the east wind scattered over the earth?

25 "Who [a]has divided a channel for the overflowing *water*,
Or a path for the thunderbolt,
26 To cause it to rain on a land *where there is* no one,
A wilderness in which *there is* no man;
27 [a]To satisfy the desolate waste,
And cause to spring forth the growth of tender grass?
28 [a]Has the rain a father?
Or who has begotten the drops of dew?
29 From whose womb comes the ice?
And the [a]frost of heaven, who gives it birth?
30 The waters harden like stone,
And the surface of the deep is [a]frozen.

31 "Can you bind the cluster of the [a]Pleiades,
Or loose the belt of Orion?
32 Can you bring out Mazzaroth[1] in its season?
Or can you guide the Great Bear with its cubs?
33 Do you know [a]the ordinances of the heavens?
Can you set their dominion over the earth?

34 "Can you lift up your voice to the clouds,
That an abundance of water may cover you?
35 Can you send out lightnings, that they may go,
And say to you, 'Here we *are!*'?
36 [a]Who has put wisdom in the mind?[1]
Or who has given understanding to the heart?
37 Who can number the clouds by wisdom?
Or who can pour out the bottles of heaven,
38 When the dust hardens in clumps,
And the clods cling together?

39 "Can[a] you hunt the prey for the lion,
Or satisfy the appetite of the young lions,
40 When they crouch in *their* dens,
Or lurk in their lairs to lie in wait?
41 [a]Who provides food for the raven,
When its young ones cry to God,
And wander about for lack of food?

39 "Do you know the time when the wild [a]mountain goats bear young?
Or can you mark when [b]the deer gives birth?

38:10 [a] Job 26:10 **38:11** [a] [Ps. 89:9; 93:4] **38:12** [a] [Ps. 74:16; 148:5] **38:13** [a] Ps. 104:35 **38:15** [a] Job 18:5 [b] Ps. 10:15; 37:17 **38:16** [a] [Ps. 77:19] **38:17** [a] Ps. 9:13 **38:22** [a] Ps. 135:7 **38:23** [a] Is. 30:30 **38:25** [a] Job 28:26 **38:27** [a] Ps. 104:13, 14; 107:35 **38:28** [a] Job 36:27, 28 **38:29** [a] Ps. 147:16, 17 **38:30** [a] [Job 37:10] **38:31** [a] Amos 5:8 **38:32** [1] Literally *Constellations* **38:33** [a] Jer. 31:35, 36 **38:36** [a] [Ps. 51:6] [1] Literally *inward parts* **38:39** [a] Ps. 104:21 **38:41** [a] [Matt. 6:26] **39:1** [a] Ps. 104:18 [b] Ps. 29:9

2 Can you number the months *that* they fulfill?
Or do you know the time when they bear young?
3 They bow down,
They bring forth their young,
They deliver their offspring.[1]
4 Their young ones are healthy,
They grow strong with grain;
They depart and do not return to them.

5 "Who set the wild donkey free?
Who loosed the bonds of the onager,
6 [a]Whose home I have made the wilderness,
And the barren land his dwelling?
7 He scorns the tumult of the city;
He does not heed the shouts of the driver.
8 The range of the mountains *is* his pasture,
And he searches after [a]every green thing.

9 "Will the [a]wild ox be willing to serve you?
Will he bed by your manger?
10 Can you bind the wild ox in the furrow with ropes?
Or will he plow the valleys behind you?
11 Will you trust him because his strength *is* great?
Or will you leave your labor to him?
12 Will you trust him to bring home your grain,
And gather it to your threshing floor?

13 "The wings of the ostrich wave proudly,
But are her wings and pinions *like the* kindly stork's?
14 For she leaves her eggs on the ground,
And warms them in the dust;
15 She forgets that a foot may crush them,
Or that a wild beast may break them.
16 She [a]treats her young harshly, as though *they were* not hers;
Her labor is in vain, without concern,
17 Because God deprived her of wisdom,
And did not [a]endow her with understanding.
18 When she lifts herself on high,
She scorns the horse and its rider.

19 "Have you given the horse strength?
Have you clothed his neck with *thunder?*[1]
20 Can you frighten him like a locust?
His majestic snorting strikes terror.
21 He paws in the valley, and rejoices in *his* strength;
[a]He gallops into the clash of arms.
22 He mocks at fear, and is not frightened;
Nor does he turn back from the sword.
23 The quiver rattles against him,
The glittering spear and javelin.
24 He devours the distance with fierceness and rage;
Nor does he come to a halt because the trumpet *has* sounded.
25 At *the blast of* the trumpet he says, 'Aha!'
He smells the battle from afar,
The thunder of captains and shouting.

26 "Does the hawk fly by your wisdom,
And spread its wings toward the south?
27 Does the [a]eagle mount up at your command,
And [b]make its nest on high?
28 On the rock it dwells and resides,
On the crag of the rock and the stronghold.
29 From there it spies out the prey;
Its eyes observe from afar.
30 Its young ones suck up blood;
And [a]where the slain *are,* there it *is.*"

40

Moreover the LORD [a]answered Job, and said:

2 "Shall [a]the one who contends with the Almighty correct *Him?*
He who [b]rebukes God, let him answer it."

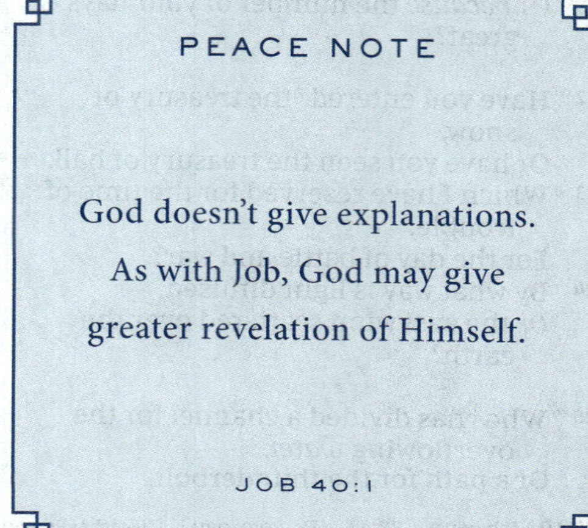
PEACE NOTE

God doesn't give explanations. As with Job, God may give greater revelation of Himself.

JOB 40:1

39:3 [1] Literally *pangs,* figurative of offspring 39:6 [a] Jer. 2:24 39:8 [a] Gen. 1:29 39:9 [a] Num. 23:22 39:16 [a] Lam. 4:3 39:17 [a] Job 35:11 39:19 [1] Or *a mane* 39:21 [a] Jer. 8:6 39:27 [a] Prov. 30:18, 19 [b] Jer. 49:16 39:30 [a] Matt. 24:28 40:1 [a] Job 38:1 40:2 [a] Job 9:3; 10:2; 33:13 [b] Job 13:3; 23:4

Job's Response to God

3 Then Job answered the LORD and said:

4 "Behold,[a] I am vile;
What shall I answer You?
[b]I lay my hand over my mouth.
5 Once I have spoken, but I will not answer;
Yes, twice, but I will proceed no further."

God's Challenge to Job

6 [a]Then the LORD answered Job out of the whirlwind, and said:

7 "Now[a] prepare yourself like a man;
[b]I will question you, and you shall answer Me:

8 "Would[a] you indeed annul My judgment?
Would you condemn Me that you may be justified?
9 Have you an arm like God?
Or can you thunder with [a]a voice like His?
10 [a]Then adorn yourself *with* majesty and splendor,
And array yourself with glory and beauty.
11 Disperse the rage of your wrath;
Look on everyone *who is* proud, and humble him.
12 Look on everyone *who is* [a]proud, *and* bring him low;
Tread down the wicked in their place.
13 Hide them in the dust together,
Bind their faces in hidden *darkness.*
14 Then I will also confess to you
That your own right hand can save you.

15 "Look now at the behemoth,[1] which I made *along* with you;
He eats grass like an ox.
16 See now, his strength *is* in his hips,
And his power *is* in his stomach muscles.
17 He moves his tail like a cedar;
The sinews of his thighs are tightly knit.
18 His bones *are like* beams of bronze,
His ribs like bars of iron.
19 He *is* the first of the [a]ways of God;
Only He who made him can bring near His sword.
20 Surely the mountains [a]yield food for him,
And all the beasts of the field play there.
21 He lies under the lotus trees,
In a covert of reeds and marsh.
22 The lotus trees cover him *with* their shade;
The willows by the brook surround him.
23 Indeed the river may rage,
Yet he is not disturbed;
He is confident, though the Jordan gushes into his mouth,
24 *Though* he takes it in his eyes,
Or one pierces *his* nose with a snare.

41 "Can you draw out [a]Leviathan[1] with a hook,
Or *snare* his tongue with a line *which* you lower?
2 Can you [a]put a reed through his nose,
Or pierce his jaw with a hook?
3 Will he make many supplications to you?
Will he speak softly to you?
4 Will he make a covenant with you?
Will you take him as a servant forever?
5 Will you play with him as *with* a bird,
Or will you leash him for your maidens?
6 Will *your* companions make a banquet[1] of him?
Will they apportion him among the merchants?
7 Can you fill his skin with harpoons,
Or his head with fishing spears?
8 Lay your hand on him;
Remember the battle—
Never do it again!
9 Indeed, *any* hope of *overcoming* him is false;
Shall *one not* be overwhelmed at the sight of him?
10 No one *is so* fierce that he would dare stir him up.
Who then is able to stand against Me?
11 [a]Who has preceded Me, that I should pay *him?*
[b]Everything under heaven is Mine.

12 "I will not conceal[1] his limbs,
His mighty power, or his graceful proportions.
13 Who can remove his outer coat?
Who can approach *him* with a double bridle?

40:4 [a] Ezra 9:6 [b] Job 29:9 **40:6** [a] Job 38:1 **40:7** [a] Job 38:3 [b] Job 42:4 **40:8** [a] [Rom. 3:4] **40:9** [a] [Ps. 29:3, 4] **40:10** [a] Ps. 93:1; 104:1 **40:12** [a] Dan. 4:37 **40:15** [1] A large animal, exact identity unknown **40:19** [a] Job 26:14 **40:20** [a] Ps. 104:14 **41:1** [a] Is. 27:1 [1] A large sea creature, exact identity unknown **41:2** [a] Is. 37:29 **41:6** [1] Or *bargain over him* **41:11** [a] [Rom. 11:35] [b] Ps. 24:1; 50:12 **41:12** [1] Literally *keep silent about*

14 Who can open the doors of his face,
With his terrible teeth all around?
15 *His* rows of scales are *his* pride,
Shut up tightly *as with* a seal;
16 One is so near another
That no air can come between them;
17 They are joined one to another,
They stick together and cannot be parted.
18 His sneezings flash forth light,
And his eyes *are* like the eyelids of the morning.
19 Out of his mouth go burning lights;
Sparks of fire shoot out.
20 Smoke goes out of his nostrils,
As *from* a boiling pot and burning rushes.
21 His breath kindles coals,
And a flame goes out of his mouth.
22 Strength dwells in his neck,
And sorrow dances before him.
23 The folds of his flesh are joined together;
They are firm on him and cannot be moved.
24 His heart is as hard as stone,
Even as hard as the lower *millstone.*
25 When he raises himself up, the mighty are afraid;
Because of his crashings they are beside[1] themselves.
26 *Though* the sword reaches him, it cannot avail;
Nor does spear, dart, or javelin.
27 He regards iron as straw,
And bronze as rotten wood.
28 The arrow cannot make him flee;
Slingstones become like stubble to him.
29 Darts are regarded as straw;
He laughs at the threat of javelins.
30 His undersides *are* like sharp potsherds;
He spreads pointed *marks* in the mire.
31 He makes the deep boil like a pot;
He makes the sea like a pot of ointment.
32 He leaves a shining wake behind him;
One would think the deep had white hair.
33 On earth there is nothing like him,
Which is made without fear.
34 He beholds every high *thing;*
He *is* king over all the children of pride."

Job's Repentance and Restoration

42 Then Job answered the LORD and said:
2 "I know that You [a]can do everything,
And that no purpose *of Yours* can be withheld from You.

41:25 [1] Or *purify themselves* 42:2 [a] [Matt. 19:26]

THE GOD WHO RESTORES

And the LORD restored Job's losses . . . Indeed the LORD gave Job twice as much as he had before.

JOB 42:10

Life can be tough. Not everything works out. We are sometimes compensated for losses, but not always. And it is this lack of compensation, this lack of justice and fairness, that can lead to despair and loss of peace.

The story of Job is troubling and reassuring at the same time. It is troubling because of the extent of the losses and suffering that this good man experienced. It is reassuring because we learn that God is still very much in control and, in the end, Job is greatly rewarded: "Indeed the LORD gave Job twice as much as he had before." Wouldn't it be nice if that is how it always turned out? But it doesn't. Sometimes we experience loss, and nothing good seems to arise from it.

What do we learn from the story of Job? We learn that God is faithful, that He cares, and *that in the end, He will make all things right.* It may not all happen in this life, but it will in eternity. Life is filled with problems, but you and I don't need to understand them to be at peace. God understands them, and we can have confidence in His character that everything will be just after all.

3 *You asked,* [a]'Who *is* this who hides
counsel without knowledge?'
Therefore I have uttered what I did not
understand,
[b]Things too wonderful for me, which I
did not know.
4 Listen, please, and let me speak;
You said, [a]'I will question you, and you
shall answer Me.'

5 "I have [a]heard of You by the hearing of
the ear,
But now my eye sees You.
6 Therefore I [a]abhor *myself,*
And repent in dust and ashes."

7 And so it was, after the LORD had spoken
these words to Job, that the LORD said to
Eliphaz the Temanite, "My wrath is aroused
against you and your two friends, for you
have not spoken of Me *what is* right, as My
servant Job *has.* 8 Now therefore, take for
yourselves [a]seven bulls and seven rams, [b]go
to My servant Job, and offer up for yourselves
a burnt offering; and My servant Job shall
[c]pray for you. For I will accept him, lest I deal
with you *according to your* folly; because you
have not spoken of Me *what is* right, as My
servant Job *has.*"
9 So Eliphaz the Temanite and Bildad the
Shuhite *and* Zophar the Naamathite went
and did as the LORD commanded them; for
the LORD had accepted Job.
10 [a]And the LORD
restored Job's losses[1] when he prayed for his
friends. Indeed the LORD gave Job [b]twice
as much as he had before.
11 Then [a]all his
brothers, all his sisters, and all those who had
been his acquaintances before, came to him
and ate food with him in his house; and they
consoled him and comforted him for all the
adversity that the LORD had brought upon
him. Each one gave him a piece of silver and
each a ring of gold.
12 Now the LORD blessed [a]the latter *days*
of Job more than his beginning; for he had
[b]fourteen thousand sheep, six thousand
camels, one thousand yoke of oxen, and
one thousand female donkeys.
13 [a]He also
had seven sons and three daughters.
14 And
he called the name of the first Jemimah,
the name of the second Keziah, and the
name of the third Keren-Happuch.
15 In all
the land were found no women *so* beautiful
as the daughters of Job; and their father
gave them an inheritance among their
brothers.
16 After this Job [a]lived one hundred and
forty years, and saw his children and grandchildren *for* four generations.
17 So Job died,
old and [a]full of days.

42:3 [a] Job 38:2 [b] Ps. 40:5; 131:1; 139:6 **42:4** [a] Job 38:3; 40:7 **42:5** [a] Job 26:14 **42:6** [a] Ezra 9:6 **42:8** [a] Num. 23:1 [b] [Matt. 5:24] [c] Gen. 20:17 **42:10** [a] Deut. 30:3 [b] Is. 40:2 [1] Literally *Job's captivity,* that is, what was captured from Job **42:11** [a] Job 19:13 **42:12** [a] James 5:11 [b] Job 1:3 **42:13** [a] Job 1:2 **42:16** [a] Job 5:26; Prov. 3:16 **42:17** [a] Gen. 15:15; 25:8

THE BOOK OF

PSALMS

AUTHOR

Seventy-five of the psalms in this book are designated as Davidic: Psalms 3–9; 11–32; 34–41; 51–65; 68–70; 86; 101; 103; 108–110; 122; 124; 131; 133; and 138–145. The New Testament tells us that the "anonymous" Psalms 2 and 95 were also written by David. In addition to these, twelve are by Asaph, a priest who headed the service of music; ten are by the sons of Korah, a guild of singers and composers; two are by Solomon, Israel's most powerful king; one is by Moses; one is by Heman the Ezrahite, a wise man; and one is by Ethan the Ezrahite, another wise man. The remaining fifty psalms are anonymous, but tradition attributes them to Ezra.

TIME

c. 1410–430 BC

KEY VERSE

Psalm 19:14

THEME

A collection of songs that literally covers hundreds of years of Jewish history from the patriarchs down through the postexilic period, the Book of Psalms is practical and personal as well as scenic and magnificently beautiful. The Psalms teach us how to pray, how to grieve, how to rejoice, and how to worship. Any Christian who makes building a relationship with God a priority in his or her life will find great spiritual nourishment in the Psalms. It is the prayer book for all who believe in the God of the universe. Jesus used it as such, and so should we.

The Psalms' message is a warning not to pray too religiously. Life is messy, grace is essential, and we often do not see God's faithfulness until we look in life's rearview mirror. We need to wrap ourselves in the truth of God's peace in our lives daily. Did you know that Jesus of Nazareth quoted from Psalms more than from any other Old Testament book except Isaiah? Nearly all the 2,461 verses comprising the 150 chapters of the Psalms are promises from God. No other book of the Bible is studied, memorized, quoted, prayed through, sung, or appealed to more than the Psalms. In it we find pathways to the peace of God.

BOOK ONE

Psalms 1–41

PSALM 1

The Way of the Righteous and the End of the Ungodly

1 Blessed [a]*is* the man
Who walks not in the counsel of the ungodly,
Nor stands in the path of sinners,
[b]Nor sits in the seat of the scornful;
2 But [a]his delight *is* in the law of the LORD,
[b]And in His law he meditates day and night.
3 He shall be like a tree
[a]Planted by the rivers of water,
That brings forth its fruit in its season,
Whose leaf also shall not wither;
And whatever he does shall [b]prosper.

4 The ungodly *are* not so,
But *are* [a]like the chaff which the wind drives away.
5 Therefore the ungodly shall not stand in the judgment,
Nor sinners in the congregation of the righteous.

6 For [a]the LORD knows the way of the righteous,
But the way of the ungodly shall perish.

PSALM 2

The Messiah's Triumph and Kingdom

1 Why [a]do the nations rage,
And the people plot a vain thing?
2 The kings of the earth set themselves,
And the [a]rulers take counsel together,
Against the LORD and against His [b]Anointed, *saying,*
3 "Let [a]us break Their bonds in pieces
And cast away Their cords from us."

4 He who sits in the heavens [a]shall laugh;
The Lord shall hold them in derision.
5 Then He shall speak to them in His wrath,
And distress them in His deep displeasure:
6 "Yet I have set My King
On My holy hill of Zion."

7 "I will declare the decree:
The LORD has said to Me,
[a]'You *are* My Son,
Today I have begotten You.
8 Ask of Me, and I will give *You*
The nations *for* Your inheritance,
And the ends of the earth *for* Your possession.
9 [a]You shall break[1] them with a rod of iron;
You shall dash them to pieces like a potter's vessel.' "

10 Now therefore, be wise, O kings;
Be instructed, you judges of the earth.

1:1 [a] Prov. 4:14 [b] Jer. 15:17 **1:2** [a] Ps. 119:14, 16, 35 [b] [Josh. 1:8] **1:3** [a] Jer. 17:8 [b] Gen. 39:2, 3, 23 **1:4** [a] Job 21:18 **1:6** [a] Ps. 37:18 **2:1** [a] Acts 4:25, 26 **2:2** [a] [Matt. 12:14; 26:3, 4, 59–66; 27:1, 2; Mark 3:6; 11:18]; Acts 4:25–28 [b] [John 1:41] **2:3** [a] Luke 19:14 **2:4** [a] Ps. 37:13 **2:7** [a] [Heb. 1:5; 5:5] **2:9** [a] Ps. 89:23; 110:5, 6 [1] Following Masoretic Text and Targum; Septuagint, Syriac, and Vulgate read *rule* (compare Revelation 2:27).

DELIGHT IN GOD

Blessed is the man who walks not in the counsel of the ungodly . . . his delight is in the law of the LORD, and in His law he meditates day and night.

PSALM 1:1-2

God's peace and utter happiness remain on the person who "meditates day and night" on *the truth of God and His Word.* To open the Psalms, written over a millennium, the writer began by illustrating that true happiness and peace result from avoiding anti-God counsel, moving out of the everyone-is-doing-it mentality, and staying away from the lifestyle of those who boast against the way of peace. The first phrase of the Psalms is a promise: "Blessed is."

Blessed could be translated "Oh how happy," and by no means does this describe a momentary happiness that melts away. God's Word declares you utterly happy and characterized by peace because God knows that your heart seeks Him. You delight in what delights God. You love all He loves. By faith, claim this Old Testament promise of peace and happiness for your life.

11 Serve the LORD with fear,
And rejoice with trembling.
12 Kiss the Son,[1] lest He[2] be angry,
And you perish *in* the way,
When [a]His wrath is kindled but a little.
[b]Blessed *are* all those who put their trust in Him.

PSALM 3

The LORD Helps His Troubled People

A Psalm of David [a]when he fled from Absalom his son.

1 LORD, how they have increased who trouble me!
Many *are* they who rise up against me.
2 Many *are* they who say of me,
"*There is* no help for him in God." *Selah*

3 But You, O LORD, *are* [a]a shield for me,
My glory and [b]the One who lifts up my head.
4 I cried to the LORD with my voice,
And [a]He heard me from His [b]holy hill. *Selah*

5 [a]I lay down and slept;
I awoke, for the LORD sustained me.
6 [a]I will not be afraid of ten thousands of people
Who have set *themselves* against me all around.

7 Arise, O LORD;
Save me, O my God!
[a]For You have struck all my enemies on the cheekbone;
You have broken the teeth of the ungodly.
8 [a]Salvation *belongs* to the LORD.
Your blessing *is* upon Your people. *Selah*

PSALM 4

The Safety of the Faithful

To the Chief Musician. With stringed instruments. A Psalm of David.

1 Hear me when I call, O God of my righteousness!
You have relieved me in *my* distress;
Have mercy on me, and hear my prayer.

2 How long, O you sons of men,
Will you turn my glory to shame?
How long will you love worthlessness
And seek falsehood? *Selah*
3 But know that [a]the LORD has set apart[1] for Himself him who is godly;
The LORD will hear when I call to Him.

2:12 [a] [Rev. 6:16, 17] [b] [Ps. 5:11; 34:22] [1] Septuagint and Vulgate read *Embrace discipline;* Targum reads *Receive instruction.* [2] Septuagint reads *the LORD.* **3:title** [a] 2 Sam. 15:13–17 **3:3** [a] Ps. 5:12; 28:7 [b] Ps. 9:13; 27:6 **3:4** [a] Ps. 4:3; 34:4 [b] Ps. 2:6; 15:1; 43:3 **3:5** [a] Lev. 26:6 **3:6** [a] Ps. 23:4; 27:3 **3:7** [a] Job 16:10 **3:8** [a] [Is. 43:11] **4:3** [a] [2 Tim. 2:19]
[1] Many Hebrew manuscripts, Septuagint, Targum, and Vulgate read *made wonderful.*

THE GOD WHO HEARS OUR CRIES

But You, O LORD, are a shield for me . . . I cried to the LORD with my voice, and He heard me from His holy hill.

PSALM 3:3-4

King David wrote many of the Psalms, and they reflect events in his tumultuous life. When David sang praises to God, usually they concerned matters of life and death. When he called God a "shield," he was not exaggerating. On more than one occasion David was just able to dodge a spear! The man was opposed by people inside and outside Israel who desired to kill him. Yet God protected David.

David's peace was very real, almost tangible. It was a peace experienced in the trials of life, which included political intrigue, domestic tragedies, and the battlefield. Through all these dangers and difficulties David had learned to trust God and find peace. I am not surprised that the word "peace" and related words occur almost fifty times in the original language of the king's psalms. I have known godly people who have endured many and extreme hardships, and they are blessed with a deep sense of peace. They are not delusional; they are not in denial. They know that God is with them, and that assurance gives them peace.

If David, in the midst of the trials he faced, found peace, so can we.

4 [a]Be angry, and do not sin.
[b]Meditate within your heart on your bed, and be still. *Selah*
5 Offer [a]the sacrifices of righteousness,
And [b]put your trust in the LORD.

6 *There are* many who say,
"Who will show us *any* good?"
[a]LORD, lift up the light of Your countenance upon us.
7 You have put [a]gladness in my heart,
More than in the season that their grain and wine increased.
8 [a]I will both lie down in peace, and sleep;
[b]For You alone, O LORD, make me dwell in safety.

PSALM 5

A Prayer for Guidance

To the Chief Musician. With flutes.[1] A Psalm of David.

1 Give [a]ear to my words, O LORD,
Consider my meditation.
2 Give heed to the voice of my cry,
My King and my God,
For to You I will pray.
3 My voice You shall hear in the morning, O LORD;
[a]In the morning I will direct *it* to You,
And I will look up.
4 For You *are* not a God who takes pleasure in wickedness,
Nor shall evil dwell with You.
5 The [a]boastful shall not [b]stand in Your sight;
You hate all workers of iniquity.
6 You shall destroy those who speak falsehood;
The LORD abhors the [a]bloodthirsty and deceitful man.

7 But as for me, I will come into Your house in the multitude of Your mercy;
In fear of You I will worship toward Your holy temple.
8 [a]Lead me, O LORD, in Your righteousness because of my enemies;
Make Your way straight before my face.

9 For *there is* no faithfulness in their mouth;
Their inward part *is* destruction;
[a]Their throat *is* an open tomb;
They flatter with their tongue.
10 Pronounce them guilty, O God!
Let them fall by their own counsels;
Cast them out in the multitude of their transgressions,
For they have rebelled against You.

11 But let all those rejoice who put their trust in You;

4:4 [a] [Eph. 4:26] [b] Ps. 77:6 **4:5** [a] Deut. 33:19 [b] Ps. 37:3, 5; 62:8 **4:6** [a] Num. 6:26 **4:7** [a] Is. 9:3 **4:8** [a] Ps. 3:5 [b] [Lev. 25:18] **5:title** [1] Hebrew *nehiloth* **5:1** [a] Ps. 4:1 **5:3** [a] Ps. 55:17; 88:13 **5:5** [a] [Hab. 1:13] [b] Ps. 1:5 **5:6** [a] Ps. 55:23 **5:8** [a] Ps. 25:4, 5; 27:11; 31:3 **5:9** [a] Rom. 3:13

HOW DID YOU SLEEP?

I will both lie down in peace, and sleep; for You alone, O LORD, make me dwell in safety.

PSALM 4:8

It has been said that the path to peace is paved with prayer. I agree. When we pray, things happen and the peace of God guards our hearts. We see this truth put into practice several times in the Psalms. Here in Psalm 4 David had been accused and his honor called into question. He called out to God for help and urged his friends to put their trust in the Lord. After his prayers and exhortations, the godly man was ready for bed: "I will both lie down in peace, and sleep; for You alone, O LORD, make me dwell in safety." David could lie down "in peace" and sleep because he knew that God was with him and would protect him.

This may sound almost childish, but there is nothing like going to sleep in the confidence that God is there, watching over us. I have made it my practice never to make a tough decision before prayer and a night's sleep. To lie down "in peace" and awaken the following morning refreshed keeps one's spirit healthy and ready for the challenges that lie ahead.

Do you go to sleep with trepidation or peace? If the former, how can you change that?

TALK TO THE LORD

Give ear to my words, O LORD, consider my meditation. Give heed to the voice of my cry.

PSALM 5:1-2

It may not be a coincidence that Psalm 5 follows Psalm 4. Psalm 4 ends with the psalmist (probably David) praying and lying down "in peace" (4:8), while Psalm 5 says the psalmist prays and offers sacrifice "in the morning" (5:3). What a great example for all of us! To go to bed with prayer on our lips and hours later to awaken also with prayer! Perhaps we have here a secret to peace. Perhaps this is why the apostle Paul, who also experienced many trials and challenges, urged believers to "pray without ceasing" (1 Thess. 5:17).

Because the meaning of the *shalom*-peace is wholeness, it implies that nothing is missing, no essential element is lost. Peace with God is not an abstract idea or feeling but a relationship. What relationship can survive if there is no communication? If we never talk to God, how can we expect our relationship with Him to remain strong? That relationship creates peace and a sense of well-being. Let us pray at the end of day, and let us pray when we awaken.

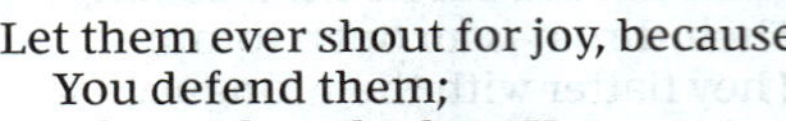

Let them ever shout for joy, because
You defend them;
Let those also who love Your name
Be joyful in You.
12 For You, O LORD, will bless the
righteous;
With favor You will surround him as
with a shield.

PSALM 6

A Prayer of Faith in Time of Distress

To the Chief Musician. With stringed instruments. [a]On an eight-stringed harp.[1] A Psalm of David.

1 O LORD, [a]do not rebuke me in Your
anger,
Nor chasten me in Your hot displeasure.
2 Have mercy on me, O LORD, for I *am*
weak;
O LORD, [a]heal me, for my bones are
troubled.
3 My soul also is greatly [a]troubled;
But You, O LORD—how long?

4 Return, O LORD, deliver me!
Oh, save me for Your mercies' sake!
5 [a]For in death *there is* no remembrance
of You;
In the grave who will give You thanks?

6 I am weary with my groaning;
All night I make my bed swim;
I drench my couch with my tears.
7 [a]My eye wastes away because of grief;
It grows old because of all my enemies.

8 [a]Depart from me, all you workers of
iniquity;
For the LORD has [b]heard the voice of
my weeping.
9 The LORD has heard my supplication;
The LORD will receive my prayer.
10 Let all my enemies be ashamed and
greatly troubled;
Let them turn back *and* be ashamed
suddenly.

PSALM 7

Prayer and Praise for Deliverance from Enemies

A [a]Meditation[1] of David, which he sang to the LORD [b]concerning the words of Cush, a Benjamite.

1 O LORD my God, in You I put my trust;
[a]Save me from all those who persecute me;
And deliver me,
2 [a]Lest they tear me like a lion,
[b]Rending *me* in pieces, while *there is*
none to deliver.

3 O LORD my God, [a]if I have done this:
If there is [b]iniquity in my hands,
4 If I have repaid evil to him who was at
peace with me,
Or [a]have plundered my enemy without
cause,

6:title [a] Ps. 12:title [1] Hebrew *Sheminith* **6:1** [a] Ps. 38:1; 118:18 **6:2** [a] [Hos. 6:1] **6:3** [a] Ps. 88:3 **6:5** [a] [Eccl. 9:10] **6:7** [a] Job 17:7 **6:8** [a] [Matt. 25:41] [b] Ps. 3:4; 28:6 **7:title** [a] Hab. 3:1 [b] 2 Sam. 16 [1] Hebrew *Shiggaion* **7:1** [a] Ps. 31:15 **7:2** [a] Is. 38:13 [b] Ps. 50:22 **7:3** [a] 2 Sam. 16:7 [b] 1 Sam. 24:11 **7:4** [a] 1 Sam. 24:7; 26:9

5 Let the enemy pursue me and
overtake *me;*
Yes, let him trample my life to the earth,
And lay my honor in the dust. *Selah*

6 Arise, O LORD, in Your anger;
[a]Lift Yourself up because of the rage of
my enemies;
[b]Rise up for me[1] *to* the judgment You
have commanded!
7 So the congregation of the peoples
shall surround You;
For their sakes, therefore, return on
high.
8 The LORD shall judge the peoples;
[a]Judge me, O LORD, [b]according to my
righteousness,
And according to my integrity
within me.

9 Oh, let the wickedness of the wicked
come to an end,
But establish the just;
[a]For the righteous God tests the hearts
and minds.
10 My defense *is* of God,
Who saves the [a]upright in heart.

11 God *is* a just judge,
And God is angry *with the wicked* every
day.
12 If he does not turn back,
He will [a]sharpen His sword;
He bends His bow and makes it ready.
13 He also prepares for Himself
instruments of death;
He makes His arrows into fiery shafts.

14 [a]Behold, *the wicked* brings forth
iniquity;
Yes, he conceives trouble and brings
forth falsehood.
15 He made a pit and dug it out,
[a]And has fallen into the ditch *which* he
made.
16 [a]His trouble shall return upon his own
head,
And his violent dealing shall come
down on his own crown.

17 I will praise the LORD according to His
righteousness,
And will sing praise to the name of the
LORD Most High.

PSALM 8

The Glory of the LORD in Creation

To the Chief Musician. On the instrument of Gath.[1] A Psalm of David.

1 O LORD, our Lord,
How [a]excellent *is* Your name in all the
earth,
Who have [b]set Your glory above the
heavens!

2 [a]Out of the mouth of babes and nursing
infants
You have ordained strength,
Because of Your enemies,
That You may silence [b]the enemy and
the avenger.

3 When I [a]consider Your heavens, the
work of Your fingers,
The moon and the stars, which You
have ordained,
4 [a]What is man that You are mindful of
him,
And the son of man that You [b]visit
him?
5 For You have made him a little lower
than the angels,[1]
And You have crowned him with glory
and honor.

6 [a]You have made him to have dominion
over the works of Your hands;
[b]You have put all *things* under his feet,
7 All sheep and oxen—
Even the beasts of the field,
8 The birds of the air,
And the fish of the sea
That pass through the paths of the
seas.

9 [a]O LORD, our Lord,
How excellent *is* Your name in all the
earth!

PSALM 9

Prayer and Thanksgiving for the LORD's Righteous Judgments

To the Chief Musician. To *the tune of* "Death of the Son."[1] A Psalm of David.

1 I will praise *You,* O LORD, with my
whole heart;
I will tell of all Your marvelous works.

7:6 [a] Ps. 94:2 [b] Ps. 35:23; 44:23 [1] Following Masoretic Text, Targum, and Vulgate; Septuagint reads *O LORD my God.* **7:8** [a] Ps. 26:1; 35:24; 43:1 [b] Ps. 18:20; 35:24 **7:9** [a] [1 Sam. 16:7] **7:10** [a] Ps. 97:10, 11; 125:4 **7:12** [a] Deut. 32:41 **7:14** [a] Is. 59:4 **7:15** [a] [Job 4:8] **7:16** [a] Esth. 9:25 **8:title** [1] Hebrew *Al Gittith* **8:1** [a] Ps. 148:13 [b] Ps. 113:4 **8:2** [a] [1 Cor. 1:27] [b] Ps. 44:16 **8:3** [a] Ps. 111:2 **8:4** [a] Job 7:17, 18 [b] [Job 10:12] **8:5** [1] Hebrew *Elohim, God;* Septuagint, Syriac, Targum, and Jewish tradition translate as *angels.* **8:6** [a] [Gen. 1:26, 28] [b] [Heb. 2:8] **8:9** [a] Ps. 8:1 **9:title** [1] Hebrew *Muth Labben*

YOUR GREAT VALUE

You have made him a little lower than the angels, and You have crowned him with glory and honor.

PSALM 8:5

The opening line of Psalm 8 is classic: "O LORD, our Lord, how excellent is Your name in all the earth!" (vv. 1, 9). The psalm celebrates God's glory seen throughout the universe. The reference to humanity is especially interesting: "What is man that You are mindful of him? . . . For You have made him a little lower than the angels, and You have crowned him with glory and honor" (vv. 4–5).

God's excellence is seen in the earth and—what is especially astounding—in humanity, the pinnacle of God's creation. Considering how humans behave, the psalmist comparing us to heavenly beings and describing us as "crowned" is a generous assessment! But God means what He says. We are the highest on earth, only a bit lower than the angels of heaven. God has bestowed on us glory and honor. Knowing that God values us so highly should build our faith and give us peace.

Perhaps you've fallen into a sin pattern yet again. Take a moment and return to the Lord in repentance and renewal of faith. All He wants is for you to turn to Him and live in His peace.

2 I will be glad and [a]rejoice in You;
I will sing praise to Your name,
[b]O Most High.

3 When my enemies turn back,
They shall fall and perish at Your presence.
4 For You have maintained my right and my cause;
You sat on the throne judging in righteousness.
5 You have rebuked the nations,
You have destroyed the wicked;
You have [a]blotted out their name forever and ever.

6 O enemy, destructions are finished forever!
And you have destroyed cities;
Even their memory has [a]perished.
7 [a]But the LORD shall endure forever;
He has prepared His throne for judgment.
8 [a]He shall judge the world in righteousness,
And He shall administer judgment for the peoples in uprightness.

9 The LORD also will be a [a]refuge for the oppressed,
A refuge in times of trouble.
10 And those who [a]know Your name will put their trust in You;
For You, LORD, have not forsaken those who seek You.

11 Sing praises to the LORD, who dwells in Zion!
[a]Declare His deeds among the people.
12 [a]When He avenges blood, He remembers them;
He does not forget the cry of the humble.

PEACE NOTE

Faith says, "Lord, even though I feel lost from Your sight, I still trust."

PSALM 9:10

9:2 [a] Ps. 5:11; 104:34 [b] [Ps. 83:18; 92:1] 9:5 [a] Prov. 10:7 9:6 [a] [Ps. 34:16] 9:7 [a] Heb. 1:11 9:8 [a] [Ps. 96:13; 98:9]
9:9 [a] Ps. 32:7; 46:1; 91:2 9:10 [a] Ps. 91:14 9:11 [a] Ps. 66:16; 107:22 9:12 [a] [Ps. 72:14]

FROM JUDGMENT, PEACE

He shall judge the world in righteousness.

PSALM 9:8

One of the things that really gets under my skin is injustice—whether it's in my neighborhood or anywhere in the world. We hear of corrupt politicians in our own country and brutal dictators in countries overseas. Of course this isn't only a modern problem; people experienced these things (and probably worse) in the time of King David. And yet David gave thanks to the Lord, spoke of His "marvelous works" (v. 1), and looked forward to the day when God would "judge the world in righteousness" (v. 8).

What David longed for is a big part of the Bible's message: the day will come when God will rule the earth. It will be a day when injustice and immorality are no more. This great hope gives us peace. The imperfect rule of humans will be replaced with the just and holy rule of the Almighty and His Son, King Jesus. It will not just be peace for us; it will be peace for all creation. The true meaning of *shalom*, "wholeness," will become a reality. The peace we experience now is but a foretaste of that coming fullness. We should be full of hope today because we know a greater day is coming when the Prince of Peace returns to rule forever! How does this truth affect you and your concerns right now?

13 Have mercy on me, O LORD!
Consider my trouble from those who hate me,
You who lift me up from the gates of death,
14 That I may tell of all Your praise
In the gates of the daughter of Zion.
I will [a]rejoice in Your salvation.

15 [a]The nations have sunk down in the pit *which* they made;
In the net which they hid, their own foot is caught.
16 The LORD is [a]known *by* the judgment He executes;
The wicked is snared in the work of his own hands.
[b]Meditation.[1] *Selah*

17 The wicked shall be turned into hell,
And all the nations [a]that forget God.
18 [a]For the needy shall not always be forgotten;
[b]The expectation of the poor shall *not* perish forever.

19 Arise, O LORD,
Do not let man prevail;
Let the nations be judged in Your sight.
20 Put them in fear, O LORD,
That the nations may know themselves *to be but* men. *Selah*

PSALM 10

A Song of Confidence in God's Triumph over Evil

1 Why do You stand afar off, O LORD?
Why do You hide in times of trouble?
2 The wicked in *his* pride persecutes the poor;
[a]Let them be caught in the plots which they have devised.

3 For the wicked [a]boasts of his heart's desire;
He [b]blesses the greedy *and* renounces the LORD.
4 The wicked in his proud countenance does not seek *God;*
God *is* in none of his [a]thoughts.

5 His ways are always prospering;
Your judgments *are* far above, out of his sight;
As for all his enemies, he sneers at them.
6 [a]He has said in his heart, "I shall not be moved;
[b]I shall never be in adversity."
7 [a]His mouth is full of cursing and [b]deceit and oppression;
Under his tongue *is* trouble and iniquity.

9:14 [a] Ps. 13:5; 20:5; 35:9 9:15 [a] Ps. 7:15, 16 9:16 [a] Ex. 7:5 [b] Ps. 92:3 [1] Hebrew *Higgaion* 9:17 [a] Job 8:13 9:18 [a] Ps. 9:12; 12:5 [b] Prov. 23:18 10:2 [a] Ps. 7:16; 9:16 10:3 [a] Ps. 49:6; 94:3, 4 [b] Prov. 28:4 10:4 [a] Ps. 14:1; 36:1 10:6 [a] [Eccl. 8:11] [b] Rev. 18:7 10:7 [a] [Rom. 3:14] [b] Ps. 55:10, 11

8 He sits in the lurking places of the villages;
In the secret places he murders the innocent;
His eyes are secretly fixed on the helpless.
9 He lies in wait secretly, as a lion in his den;
He lies in wait to catch the poor;
He catches the poor when he draws him into his net.
10 So he crouches, he lies low,
That the helpless may fall by his strength.
11 He has said in his heart,
"God has forgotten;
He hides His face;
He will never see."

12 Arise, O LORD!
O God, [a]lift up Your hand!
Do not forget the [b]humble.
13 Why do the wicked renounce God?
He has said in his heart,
"You will not require *an account.*"

14 But You have [a]seen, for You observe trouble and grief,
To repay *it* by Your hand.
The helpless [b]commits himself to You;
[c]You are the helper of the fatherless.
15 Break the arm of the wicked and the evil *man;*
Seek out his wickedness *until* You find none.

16 [a]The LORD *is* King forever and ever;
The nations have perished out of His land.
17 LORD, You have heard the desire of the humble;
You will prepare their heart;
You will cause Your ear to hear,
18 To do justice to the fatherless and the oppressed,
That the man of the earth may oppress no more.

PSALM 11

Faith in the LORD's Righteousness

To the Chief Musician. *A Psalm* of David.

1 In [a]the LORD I put my trust;
How can you say to my soul,
"Flee *as* a bird to your mountain"?
2 For look! [a]The wicked bend *their* bow,
They make ready their arrow on the string,
That they may shoot secretly at the upright in heart.
3 [a]If the foundations are destroyed,
What can the righteous do?

4 The LORD *is* in His holy temple,
The LORD's [a]throne *is* in heaven;
[b]His eyes behold,
His eyelids test the sons of men.
5 The LORD [a]tests the righteous,
But the wicked and the one who loves violence His soul hates.
6 Upon the wicked He will rain coals;
Fire and brimstone and a burning wind
[a]*Shall be* the portion of their cup.

7 For the LORD *is* righteous,
He [a]loves righteousness;
His countenance beholds the upright.[1]

PSALM 12

Man's Treachery and God's Constancy

To the Chief Musician. [a]On an eight-stringed harp.[1] A Psalm of David.

1 Help, LORD, for the godly man [a]ceases!
For the faithful disappear from among the sons of men.
2 [a]They speak idly everyone with his neighbor;
With flattering lips *and* a double heart they speak.

PEACE NOTE

Cultivating healthy emotions such as joy, contentment, and peace is the fruit of living in line with biblical values.

10:12 [a] Mic. 5:9 [b] Ps. 9:12 **10:14** [a] [Ps. 11:4] [b] [2 Tim. 1:12] [c] Ps. 68:5 **10:16** [a] Ps. 29:10 **11:1** [a] Ps. 56:11 **11:2** [a] Ps. 64:3, 4 **11:3** [a] Ps. 82:5; 87:1; 119:152 **11:4** [a] [Is. 66:1] [b] [Ps. 33:18; 34:15, 16] **11:5** [a] Gen. 22:1 **11:6** [a] Ps. 75:8 **11:7** [a] Ps. 33:5; 45:7 [1] Or *The upright beholds His countenance* **12:title** [a] Ps. 6:title [1] Hebrew *Sheminith* **12:1** [a] [Is. 57:1] **12:2** [a] Ps. 10:7; 41:6

3 May the LORD cut off all flattering lips,
And the tongue that speaks proud things,
4 Who have said,
"With our tongue we will prevail;
Our lips *are* our own;
Who *is* lord over us?"

5 "For the oppression of the poor, for the sighing of the needy,
Now I will arise," says the LORD;
"I will set *him* in the safety for which he yearns."

6 The words of the LORD *are* [a]pure words,
Like silver tried in a furnace of earth,
Purified seven times.
7 You shall keep them, O LORD,
You shall preserve them from this generation forever.

8 The wicked prowl on every side,
When vileness is exalted among the sons of men.

PSALM 13

Trust in the Salvation of the LORD

To the Chief Musician. A Psalm of David.

1 How long, O LORD? Will You forget me forever?
[a]How long will You hide Your face from me?
2 How long shall I take counsel in my soul,
Having sorrow in my heart daily?
How long will my enemy be exalted over me?

3 Consider *and* hear me, O LORD my God;
[a]Enlighten my eyes,
[b]Lest I sleep the *sleep of* death;
4 Lest my enemy say,
"I have prevailed against him";
Lest those who trouble me rejoice when I am moved.

5 But I have trusted in Your mercy;
My heart shall rejoice in Your salvation.
6 I will sing to the LORD,
Because He has dealt bountifully with me.

PSALM 14

Folly of the Godless, and God's Final Triumph

To the Chief Musician. *A Psalm* of David.

1 The [a]fool has said in his heart,
"*There is* no God."
They are corrupt,
They have done abominable works,
There is none who does good.

2 [a]The LORD looks down from heaven upon the children of men,
To see if there are any who understand, who seek God.
3 [a]They have all turned aside,
They have together become corrupt;
There is none who does good,
No, not one.

4 Have all the workers of iniquity no knowledge,
Who eat up my people *as* they eat bread,
And [a]do not call on the LORD?
5 There they are in great fear,
For God *is* with the generation of the righteous.
6 You shame the counsel of the poor,
But the LORD *is* his [a]refuge.

7 [a]Oh, that the salvation of Israel *would come* out of Zion!
[b]When the LORD brings back the captivity of His people,
Let Jacob rejoice *and* Israel be glad.

PSALM 15

The Character of Those Who May Dwell with the LORD

A Psalm of David.

1 LORD, [a]who may abide in Your tabernacle?
Who may dwell in Your holy hill?

2 He who walks uprightly,
And works righteousness,
And speaks the [a]truth in his heart;
3 He *who* [a]does not backbite with his tongue,
Nor does evil to his neighbor,
[b]Nor does he take up a reproach against his friend;
4 [a]In whose eyes a vile person is despised,
But he honors those who fear the LORD;
He *who* [b]swears to his own hurt and does not change;

12:6 [a] 2 Sam. 22:31; Ps. 18:30; 119:140 **13:1** [a] Job 13:24 **13:3** [a] Ezra 9:8 [b] Jer. 51:39 **14:1** [a] Ps. 10:4; 53:1 **14:2** [a] Ps. 33:13, 14; 102:19 **14:3** [a] Rom. 3:12 **14:4** [a] Is. 64:7 **14:6** [a] Ps. 9:9; 40:17; 46:1; 142:5 **14:7** [a] Ps. 53:6 [b] Job 42:10 **15:1** [a] Ps. 24:3–5 **15:2** [a] [Eph. 4:25] **15:3** [a] [Lev. 19:16–18] [b] Ex. 23:1 **15:4** [a] Esth. 3:2 [b] Lev. 5:4

NUMBERED AMONG GOD'S PEOPLE

LORD, who may abide in Your tabernacle? Who may dwell in Your holy hill?

PSALM 15:1

Have you wondered what it would be like to live in God's house? In ancient Israel the leather tent, or tabernacle, housed the ark of the covenant and other sacred furniture and utensils. Just to be in the tabernacle was a great honor. The people knew that God did not literally live in this tent, but there His presence was felt. It was the place where His people offered sacrifices and prayers to Him and where, through His priests and prophets, He spoke to His people.

Commentators think David was asking here who could be part of God's congregation (not who could literally spend the night in the tabernacle). David answered this question by saying it is the one who "walks uprightly, and works righteousness, and speaks the truth in his heart" (v. 2). The people who belong to God demonstrate it by how they live. "There is no peace . . . for the wicked" (Is. 48:22; 57:21). But there is peace for the righteous, for those who do justice (Ps. 15:3–5). They will dwell in the house of God. They will be numbered among God's people. And they will enjoy His peace.

Do you dwell in the house of God? Why or why not?

5 He *who* does not put out his money at usury,
Nor does he take a bribe against the innocent.

He who does these *things* [a]shall never be moved.

PSALM 16

The Hope of the Faithful, and the Messiah's Victory

A [a]Michtam of David.

1 Preserve me, O God, for in You I put my trust.

2 *O my soul,* you have said to the LORD,
"You *are* my Lord,
[a]My goodness is nothing apart from You."
3 As for the saints who *are* on the earth,
"They are the excellent ones, in [a]whom is all my delight."

4 Their sorrows shall be multiplied who hasten *after* another *god;*
Their drink offerings of [a]blood I will not offer,
[b]*Nor take up their names on my lips.*

5 O LORD, *You are* the portion of my inheritance and my cup;
You maintain my lot.
6 The lines have fallen to me in pleasant *places;*
Yes, I have a good inheritance.

7 I will bless the LORD who has given me counsel;
My heart also instructs me in the night seasons.
8 [a]I have set the LORD always before me;
Because *He is* at my right hand I shall not be moved.

9 Therefore my heart is glad, and my glory rejoices;
My flesh also will rest in hope.
10 [a]For You will not leave my soul in Sheol,
Nor will You allow Your Holy One to see corruption.
11 You will show me the [a]path of life;
In Your presence *is* fullness of joy;
At Your right hand *are* pleasures forevermore.

PSALM 17

Prayer with Confidence in Final Salvation

A Prayer of David.

1 Hear a just cause, O LORD,
Attend to my cry;

15:5 [a] 2 Pet. 1:10 16:title [a] Ps. 56—60 16:2 [a] Job 35:7 16:3 [a] Ps. 119:63 16:4 [a] Ps. 106:37, 38 [b] [Ex. 23:13]
16:8 [a] [Acts 2:25–28] 16:10 [a] Ps. 49:15; 86:13 16:11 [a] [Matt. 7:14]

HE IS MY ONLY SUPPLY

You are my Lord, my goodness is nothing apart from You.

PSALM 16:2

Psalm 16 is a song of trust, an expression of faith in God. David said, "You are my Lord, my goodness is nothing apart from You." Israel's famous king went on to say, "O LORD, You are the portion of my inheritance and my cup . . . I will bless the LORD who has given me counsel" (vv. 5, 7). Note the reference to "counsel." David blessed God for giving him advice. Implicit in that idea is that David accepted God's counsel and *acted on it*. People wonder why they have no peace; they ask how to find it. But have they asked for God's counsel? Have they *obeyed* God's commands? Good advice isn't worth much if it is ignored!

David added, "I have set the LORD always before me; because He is at my right hand I shall not be moved" (v. 8). David held steady in his faith in God because he had "set the LORD always before" him and kept the Lord at his "right hand." We enjoy God's peace if we keep Him near and do what He tells us to do.

Give ear to my prayer *which is* not from
deceitful lips.
2 Let my vindication come from Your
presence;
Let Your eyes look on the things that
are upright.

3 You have tested my heart;
You have visited *me* in the night;
[a]You have tried me and have found
nothing;
I have purposed that my mouth shall
not [b]transgress.
4 Concerning the works of men,
By the word of Your lips,
I have kept away from the paths of the
destroyer.
5 [a]Uphold my steps in Your
paths,
That my footsteps may not
slip.

6 [a]I have called upon You, for You will
hear me, O God;
Incline Your ear to me, *and* hear my
speech.
7 Show Your marvelous lovingkindness
by Your right hand,
O You who save those who trust *in
You*
From those who rise up *against
them.*
8 Keep me as the apple of Your eye;
Hide me under the shadow of Your
wings,
9 From the wicked who oppress me,
From my deadly enemies who
surround me.

10 They have closed up their [a]fat
hearts;
With their mouths they [b]speak
proudly.
11 They have now surrounded us in our
steps;
They have set their eyes, crouching
down to the earth,
12 As a lion is eager to tear his
prey,
And like a young lion lurking in secret
places.

13 Arise, O LORD,
Confront him, cast him down;
Deliver my life from the wicked with
Your sword,
14 With Your hand from men,
O LORD,
From men of the world *who have* their
portion in *this* life,
And whose belly You fill with Your
hidden treasure.
They are satisfied with children,
And leave the rest of their *possession*
for their babes.

15 As for me, [a]I will see Your face in
righteousness;
[b]I shall be satisfied when I [c]awake in
Your likeness.

17:3 [a] Job 23:10 [b] Ps. 39:1 **17:5** [a] Ps. 44:18; 119:133 **17:6** [a] Ps. 86:7; 116:2 **17:10** [a] Ezek. 16:49 [b] [1 Sam. 2:3]
17:15 [a] [1 John 3:2] [b] Ps. 4:6, 7; 16:11 [c] [Is. 26:19]

PSALM 18

God the Sovereign Savior

To the Chief Musician. *A Psalm* of David
[a]the servant of the LORD, who spoke
to the LORD the words of [b]this song on the day
that the LORD delivered him from the hand
of all his enemies and from the hand of Saul.
And he said:

1 I [a]will love You, O LORD, my strength.
2 The LORD is my rock and my fortress
and my deliverer;
My God, my strength, [a]in whom I will
trust;
My shield and the horn of my
salvation, my stronghold.
3 I will call upon the LORD, [a]*who is
worthy* to be praised;
So shall I be saved from my
enemies.

4 [a]The pangs of death surrounded me,
And the floods of ungodliness made
me afraid.
5 The sorrows of Sheol surrounded me;
The snares of death confronted me.
6 In my distress I called upon the
LORD,
And cried out to my God;
He heard my voice from His temple,
And my cry came before Him, *even* to
His ears.
7 [a]Then the earth shook and trembled;
The foundations of the hills also
quaked and were shaken,
Because He was angry.
8 Smoke went up from His nostrils,
And devouring fire from His mouth;
Coals were kindled by it.
9 [a]He bowed the heavens also, and came
down
With darkness under His feet.
10 [a]And He rode upon a cherub, and flew;
[b]He flew upon the wings of the wind.
11 He made darkness His secret place;
[a]His canopy around Him *was* dark waters
And thick clouds of the skies.
12 [a]From the brightness before Him,
His thick clouds passed with hailstones
and coals of fire.

13 The LORD thundered from heaven,
And the Most High uttered [a]His voice,
Hailstones and coals of fire.[1]
14 [a]He sent out His arrows and scattered
the foe,
Lightnings in abundance, and He
vanquished them.
15 Then the channels of the sea were seen,
The foundations of the world were
uncovered
At Your rebuke, O LORD,
At the blast of the breath of Your
nostrils.

18:title [a] Ps. 36:title [b] 2 Sam. 22 **18:1** [a] Ps. 144:1 **18:2** [a] Heb. 2:13 **18:3** [a] Rev. 5:12 **18:4** [a] Ps. 116:3 **18:7** [a] Acts 4:31 **18:9** [a] Ps. 144:5 **18:10** [a] Ps. 80:1; 99:1 [b] [Ps. 104:3] **18:11** [a] Ps. 97:2 **18:12** [a] Ps. 97:3; 140:10 **18:13** [a] [Ps. 29:3–9; 104:7] [1] Following Masoretic Text, Targum, and Vulgate; a few Hebrew manuscripts and Septuagint omit *Hailstones and coals of fire.* **18:14** [a] Ps. 144:6

PEACE OR VENGEANCE

I will love You, O LORD, my strength . . . My God, my strength, in whom I will trust.

PSALM 18:1-2

David wrote this song when he was hiding from a paranoid, wrathful King Saul. Many times David's life was threatened, and every time, he escaped. What impresses me about this psalm is what David said in verses 21–22: "I have kept the ways of the LORD, and have not wickedly departed from my God. For all His judgments were before me." How had David "not wickedly departed" from God? We are not certain, but I believe David was referring to his opportunities to murder King Saul (in self-defense!) that he didn't take.

David took the moral high ground that a shamed and remorseful Saul acknowledged. There is a great lesson here for us. Most of us will never be in a life-and-death struggle for a throne, but we will face the temptation to strike out against someone who threatens to harm us in one way or another. People of peace are peacemakers (see Matt. 5:9), not seekers of vengeance.

Where can you wage peace over war?

16 [a]He sent from above, He took me;
He drew me out of many waters.
17 He delivered me from my strong enemy,
From those who hated me,
For they were too strong for me.
18 They confronted me in the day of my calamity,
But the LORD was my support.
19 [a]He also brought me out into a broad place;
He delivered me because He delighted in me.

20 [a]The LORD rewarded me according to my righteousness;
According to the cleanness of my hands
He has recompensed me.
21 For I have kept the ways of the LORD,
And have not wickedly departed from my God.
22 For all His judgments *were* before me,
And I did not put away His statutes from me.
23 I was also blameless before Him,
And I kept myself from my iniquity.
24 [a]Therefore the LORD has recompensed me according to my righteousness,
According to the cleanness of my hands in His sight.

25 [a]With the merciful You will show Yourself merciful;
With a blameless man You will show Yourself blameless;
26 With the pure You will show Yourself pure;
And [a]with the devious You will show Yourself shrewd.
27 For You will save the humble people,
But will bring down [a]haughty looks.

28 [a]For You will light my lamp;
The LORD my God will enlighten my darkness.
29 For by You I can run against a troop,
By my God I can leap over a wall.
30 *As for* God, [a]His way *is* perfect;
[b]The word of the LORD is proven;
He *is* a shield [c]to all who trust in Him.

31 [a]For who *is* God, except the LORD?
And who *is* a rock, except our God?
32 *It is* God who [a]arms me with strength,
And makes my way perfect.
33 [a]He makes my feet like the *feet of* deer,
And [b]sets me on my high places.
34 [a]He teaches my hands to make war,
So that my arms can bend a bow of bronze.

35 You have also given me the shield of Your salvation;
Your right hand has held me up,
Your gentleness has made me great.
36 You enlarged my path under me,
[a]So my feet did not slip.

18:16 [a] Ps. 144:7 **18:19** [a] Ps. 4:1; 31:8; 118:5 **18:20** [a] 1 Sam. 24:19 **18:24** [a] 1 Sam. 26:23 **18:25** [a] [1 Kin. 8:32] **18:26** [a] [Lev. 26:23–28] **18:27** [a] [Ps. 101:5] **18:28** [a] Job 18:6 **18:30** [a] Rev. 15:3 [b] Ps. 12:6; 119:140 [c] [Ps. 17:7] **18:31** [a] [1 Sam. 2:2] **18:32** [a] [Ps. 91:2] **18:33** [a] Hab. 3:19 [b] Deut. 32:13; 33:29 **18:34** [a] Ps. 144:1 **18:36** [a] Prov. 4:12

BOWING INTO PEACE

With the merciful You will show Yourself merciful . . . You will save the humble.

PSALM 18:25, 27

Peace is nourished by mercy and humility. We see this in the second half of Psalm 18. David had reflected on the strife between himself and King Saul. Whereas most in his time would have seen no sin in killing the king, David chose not to harm the "LORD's anointed" (1 Sam. 24:6, 10; 26:11); rather, he left everything in God's hands. This is why David could *say with integrity,* "With the merciful You will show Yourself merciful; with a blameless man You will show Yourself blameless; with the pure You will show Yourself pure . . . For You will save the humble" (Ps. 18:25–27).

How can we expect mercy from God if we do not show it to others? How can we claim God's peace when we are in conflict with those around us? The arrogant person is seldom at peace. He grasps at power; she looks for praise. In contrast, the person blessed with the peace that comes only from God shows mercy, is willing to assist those in need, and is ready to share God's love with those who have not experienced it. What kind of person are you?

37 I have pursued my enemies and
overtaken them;
Neither did I turn back again till they
were destroyed.
38 I have wounded them,
So that they could not rise;
They have fallen under my feet.
39 For You have armed me with strength
for the battle;
You have subdued under me those who
rose up against me.
40 You have also given me the necks of
my enemies,
So that I destroyed those who
hated me.
41 They cried out, but *there was* none to
save;
[a]*Even* to the LORD, but He did not
answer them.
42 Then I beat them as fine as the dust
before the wind;
I [a]cast them out like dirt in the streets.

43 You have delivered me from the
strivings of the people;
[a]You have made me the head of the
nations;
[b]A people I have not known shall serve me.
44 As soon as they hear of me they obey me;
The foreigners submit to me.
45 [a]The foreigners fade away,
And come frightened from their
hideouts.

46 The LORD lives!
Blessed *be* my Rock!
Let the God of my salvation be exalted.
47 *It is* God who avenges me,
[a]And subdues the peoples under me;
48 He delivers me from my enemies.
[a]You also lift me up above those who
rise against me;
You have delivered me from the
violent man.
49 [a]Therefore I will give thanks to You,
O LORD, among the Gentiles,
And sing praises to Your name.
50 [a]Great deliverance He gives to His
king,
And shows mercy to His anointed,
To David and his descendants
forevermore.

PSALM 19

The Perfect Revelation of the LORD

To the Chief Musician. A Psalm of David.

1 The [a]heavens declare the glory of
God;
And the [b]firmament shows His
handiwork.
2 Day unto day utters speech,
And night unto night reveals
knowledge.
3 *There is* no speech nor language
Where their voice is not heard.

18:41 [a] Job 27:9 18:42 [a] Zech. 10:5 18:43 [a] 2 Sam. 8 [b] Is. 52:15 18:45 [a] Mic. 7:17 18:47 [a] Ps. 47:3 18:48 [a] Ps. 27:6; 59:1 18:49 [a] Rom. 15:9 18:50 [a] Ps. 21:1; 144:10 19:1 [a] Is. 40:22 [b] Gen. 1:6, 7

A GALACTIC VIEW OF PEACE

The heavens declare the glory of God; and the firmament shows His handiwork.

PSALM 19:1

Psalm 19 celebrates creation. Creation reveals much about God, but His Word reveals even more: "The law of the LORD is perfect, converting the soul; the testimony of the LORD is sure . . . The statutes of the LORD are right, rejoicing the heart" (vv. 7–8). Creation illustrates God's goodness and brilliance; His Word exposes His moral perfection and redemptive work.

People who experience the peace of God are aware of God's goodness and His purposes for creation—including us. Knowing that God has made the world, that it is good (see Gen. 1), and that we have a purpose is very reassuring, and with that reassurance comes peace. The person gripped with anxiety is uncertain of the future and is unsure whether life has any meaning. David, Israel's great king and founder of the dynasty that realized its fulfillment in the birth of Jesus, had experienced God's goodness in his life. Now he could see it everywhere.

Have you discovered your purpose? To help, can you ask friends and family what skills and talents they see in you?

4 [a]Their line[1] has gone out through all the
earth,
And their words to the end of the world.

In them He has set a tabernacle for the
sun,
5 Which *is* like a bridegroom coming out
of his chamber,
[a]*And* rejoices like a strong man to run
its race.
6 Its rising *is* from one end of heaven,
And its circuit to the other end;
And there is nothing hidden from its
heat.

7 [a]The law of the LORD *is* perfect,
converting the soul;
The testimony of the LORD *is* sure,
making [b]wise the simple;
8 The statutes of the LORD *are* right,
rejoicing the heart;
The commandment of the LORD *is*
pure, enlightening the eyes;
9 The fear of the LORD *is* clean, enduring
forever;
The judgments of the LORD *are* true
and righteous altogether.
10 More to be desired *are they* than [a]gold,
Yea, than much fine gold;
Sweeter also than honey and the
honeycomb.
11 Moreover by them Your servant is
warned,
And in keeping them *there is* great
reward.

12 Who can understand *his* errors?
[a]Cleanse me from secret *faults.*
13 Keep back Your servant also from
[a]presumptuous *sins;*
Let them not have [b]dominion over me.
Then I shall be blameless,
And I shall be innocent of great
transgression.

14 [a]Let the words of my mouth and the
meditation of my heart
Be acceptable in Your sight,
O LORD, my strength and my
[b]Redeemer.

PSALM 20

The Assurance of God's Saving Work

To the Chief Musician. A Psalm of David.

1 May the LORD answer you in the day of
trouble;
May the name of the God of Jacob
defend you;
2 May He send you help from the
sanctuary,
And strengthen you out of Zion;
3 May He remember all your offerings,
And accept your burnt sacrifice. *Selah*

4 May He grant you according to your
heart's *desire,*
And [a]fulfill all your purpose.
5 We will rejoice in your salvation,
And in the name of our God we will set
up *our* banners!
May the LORD fulfill all your petitions.

6 Now I know that the LORD saves His
anointed;
He will answer him from His holy
heaven
With the saving strength of His right
hand.

7 Some *trust* in chariots, and some in
[a]horses;
But we will remember the name of the
LORD our God.
8 They have bowed down and fallen;
But we have risen and stand upright.

9 Save, LORD!
May the King answer us when we call.

PSALM 21

Joy in the Salvation of the LORD

To the Chief Musician.
A Psalm of David.

1 The king shall have joy in Your
strength, O LORD;
And in Your salvation how greatly shall
he rejoice!
2 You have given him his heart's
desire,
And have not withheld the [a]request of
his lips. *Selah*

3 For You meet him with the blessings of
goodness;
You set a crown of pure gold upon his
head.
4 [a]He asked life from You, *and* You gave *it*
to him—
Length of days forever and ever.
5 His glory *is* great in Your salvation;
Honor and majesty You have placed
upon him.

19:4 [a] Rom. 10:18 [1] Septuagint, Syriac, and Vulgate read *sound;* Targum reads *business.* **19:5** [a] Eccl. 1:5 **19:7** [a] Ps. 111:7 [b] Ps. 119:130 **19:10** [a] Ps. 119:72, 127 **19:12** [a] [Ps. 51:1, 2] **19:13** [a] Num. 15:30 [b] Ps. 119:133 **19:14** [a] Ps. 51:15 [b] Is. 47:4 **20:4** [a] Ps. 21:2 **20:7** [a] Ps. 33:16, 17 **21:2** [a] 2 Sam. 7:26–29 **21:4** [a] Ps. 61:5, 6; 133:3

6 For You have made him most blessed
forever;
[a]You have made him exceedingly glad
with Your presence.
7 For the king trusts in the LORD,
And through the mercy of the Most
High he shall not be moved.

8 Your hand will find all Your
enemies;
Your right hand will find those who
hate You.
9 You shall make them as a fiery oven in
the time of Your anger;
The LORD shall swallow them up in His
wrath,
And the fire shall devour them.
10 Their offspring You shall destroy from
the earth,
And their descendants from among
the sons of men.
11 For they intended evil against
You;
They devised a plot *which* they are not
able *to* [a]*perform.*
12 Therefore You will make them turn
their back;
You will make ready *Your arrows* on
Your string toward their faces.

13 Be exalted, O LORD, in Your own
strength!
We will sing and praise Your
power.

PSALM 22

The Suffering, Praise, and Posterity of the Messiah

To the Chief Musician. Set to "The Deer
of the Dawn."[1] A Psalm of David.

1 My [a]God, My God, why have You
forsaken Me?
Why are You so far from helping Me,
And from the words of My groaning?
2 O My God, I cry in the daytime, but You
do not hear;
And in the night season, and am not
silent.

3 But You *are* holy,
Enthroned in the [a]praises of Israel.
4 Our fathers trusted in You;
They trusted, and You delivered them.
5 They cried to You, and were delivered;
[a]They trusted in You, and were not
ashamed.

6 But I *am* [a]a worm, and no man;
[b]A reproach of men, and despised by
the people.
7 [a]All those who see Me ridicule Me;
They shoot out the lip, they shake the
head, *saying,*
8 "He[a] trusted[1] in the LORD, let Him
rescue Him;
[b]Let Him deliver Him, since He delights
in Him!"

9 [a]But You *are* He who took Me out of the
womb;
You made Me trust *while* on My
mother's breasts.
10 I was cast upon You from birth.
From My mother's womb
[a]You *have been* My God.
11 Be not far from Me,
For trouble *is* near;
For *there is* none to help.

12 [a]Many bulls have surrounded Me;
Strong *bulls* of [b]Bashan have
encircled Me.
13 [a]They gape at Me *with* their mouths,
Like a raging and roaring lion.

14 I am poured out like water,
[a]And all My bones are out of joint;
My heart is like wax;
It has melted within Me.
15 [a]My strength is dried up like a potsherd,
And [b]My tongue clings to My jaws;
You have brought Me to the dust of death.

16 For dogs have surrounded Me;
The congregation of the wicked has
enclosed Me.
[a]They pierced[1] My hands and My feet;
17 I can count all My bones.
[a]They look *and* stare at Me.
18 [a]They divide My garments among them,
And for My clothing they cast lots.

19 But You, O LORD, do not be far from Me;
O My Strength, hasten to help Me!
20 Deliver Me from the sword,
[a]My precious *life* from the power of the
dog.

21:6 [a] Ps. 16:11; 45:7 21:11 [a] Ps. 2:1–4 22:title [1] Hebrew *Aijeleth Hashahar* 22:1 [a] [Mark 15:34] 22:3 [a] Deut. 10:21 22:5 [a] Is. 49:23 22:6 [a] Is. 41:14 [b] [Is. 53:3] 22:7 [a] Matt. 27:39 22:8 [a] Matt. 27:43 [b] Ps. 91:14 [1] Septuagint, Syriac, and Vulgate read *hoped;* Targum reads *praised.* 22:9 [a] [Ps. 71:5, 6] 22:10 [a] [Is. 46:3; 49:1] 22:12 [a] Ps. 22:21; 68:30 [b] Deut. 32:14 22:13 [a] Job 16:10 22:14 [a] Dan. 5:6 22:15 [a] Prov. 17:22 [b] John 19:28 22:16 [a] Matt. 27:35 [1] Following some Hebrew manuscripts, Septuagint, Syriac, Vulgate; Masoretic Text reads *Like a lion.* 22:17 [a] Luke 23:27, 35 22:18 [a] Matt. 27:35 22:20 [a] Ps. 35:17

21 [a]Save Me from the lion's mouth
And from the horns of the wild oxen!

[b]You have answered Me.

22 [a]I will declare Your name to [b]My brethren;
In the midst of the assembly I will
praise You.
23 [a]You who fear the LORD, praise Him!
All you descendants of Jacob, glorify
Him,
And fear Him, all you offspring of Israel!
24 For He has not despised nor abhorred
the affliction of the afflicted;
Nor has He hidden His face from Him;
But [a]when He cried to Him, He heard.

25 [a]My praise *shall be* of You in the great
assembly;
[b]I will pay My vows before those who
fear Him.
26 The poor shall eat and be satisfied;
Those who seek Him will praise the
LORD.
Let your heart live forever!
27 All the ends of the world
Shall remember and turn to the LORD,
And all the families of the nations
Shall worship before You.[1]
28 [a]For the kingdom *is* the LORD's,
And He rules over the nations.

29 [a]All the prosperous of the earth
Shall eat and worship;
[b]All those who go down to the dust
Shall bow before Him,
Even he who cannot keep himself alive.

30 A posterity shall serve Him.
It will be recounted of the Lord to the
next generation,
31 They will come and declare His
righteousness to a people who will
be born,
That He has done *this*.

PSALM 23

The Lord the Shepherd of His People

A Psalm of David.

1 The LORD *is* [a]my shepherd;
[b]I shall not want.
2 [a]He makes me to lie down in green
pastures;
[b]He leads me beside the still waters.
3 He restores my soul;
[a]He leads me in the paths of
righteousness
For His name's sake.

22:21 [a] 2 Tim. 4:17 [b] Is. 34:7 **22:22** [a] Heb. 2:12 [b] [Rom. 8:29] **22:23** [a] Ps. 135:19, 20 **22:24** [a] Heb. 5:7 **22:25** [a] Ps. 35:18; 40:9, 10 [b] Eccl. 5:4 **22:27** [1] Following Masoretic Text, Septuagint, and Targum; Arabic, Syriac, and Vulgate read *Him*. **22:28** [a] Matt. 6:13 **22:29** [a] Ps. 17:10; 45:12 [b] [Is. 26:19] **23:1** [a] [Is. 40:11] [b] [Phil. 4:19] **23:2** [a] Ezek. 34:14 [b] [Rev. 7:17] **23:3** [a] Ps. 5:8; 31:3

OUR GOOD SHEPHERD OF PEACE

The LORD is my shepherd.

PSALM 23:1

So begins what is probably the best-known psalm in all the Psalter. David likened God and His care for His people to a faithful shepherd who tended his flock. A shepherd found green pastures and still waters where his sheep could feed and drink. A shepherd protected his sheep—he used his rod and staff to drive off the predator that attacked. But for David, depicting God as a Shepherd points to a far deeper reality. God's leading results in restoration of the soul while treading the paths of righteousness (v. 3). It means protection, provision, and vindication (vv. 4–5). God's work as Shepherd means "goodness and mercy" follow those who cling to Him (v. 6). Jesus is our Great Shepherd, and He works good in us so we may find peace: "Now may the God of peace who brought up our Lord Jesus from the dead, that great Shepherd of the sheep . . . [work] in you what is well pleasing in His sight" (Heb. 13:20–21).

Since God is our Shepherd, our needs will be met—especially our spiritual needs. God does not promise wealth. He does not say challenges will be rare. He promises He will not abandon us. Psalm 23:1 and Hebrews 13:20–21 form a peace promise we can claim today to find the deep tranquility we crave.

PEACE NOTE

To grow in God's peace: (1) Focus on the truth of Scripture; (2) gather good community around you; and (3) seek some daily time for being quiet (restored) before Him.

PSALM 23:3

4 Yea, though I walk through the valley
of [a]the shadow of death,
[b]I will fear no evil;
[c]For You *are* with me;
Your rod and Your staff, they comfort me.

5 You [a]prepare a table before me in the
presence of my enemies;
You [b]anoint my head with oil;
My cup runs over.
6 Surely goodness and mercy shall
follow me
All the days of my life;
And I will dwell[1] in the house of the
LORD
Forever.

PSALM 24

The King of Glory and His Kingdom

A Psalm of David.

1 The [a]earth *is* the LORD's, and all its
fullness,
The world and those who dwell therein.
2 For He has [a]founded it upon the seas,
And established it upon the waters.

3 [a]Who may ascend into the hill of the
LORD?
Or who may stand in His holy place?
4 He who has [a]clean hands and [b]a pure
heart,
Who has not lifted up his soul to an idol,
Nor [c]sworn deceitfully.
5 He shall receive blessing from the LORD,
And righteousness from the God of his
salvation.
6 This *is* Jacob, the generation of those
who [a]seek Him,
Who seek Your face. *Selah*

7 [a]Lift up your heads, O you gates!
And be lifted up, you everlasting doors!
[b]And the King of glory shall come in.
8 Who *is* this King of glory?
The LORD strong and mighty,
The LORD mighty in [a]battle.
9 Lift up your heads, O you gates!
Lift up, you everlasting doors!
And the King of glory shall come in.
10 Who is this King of glory?
The LORD of hosts,
He *is* the King of glory. *Selah*

PSALM 25

A Plea for Deliverance and Forgiveness

A *Psalm* of David.

1 To [a]You, O LORD, I lift up my soul.
2 O my God, I [a]trust in You;
Let me not be ashamed;
[b]Let not my enemies triumph over me.
3 Indeed, let no one who waits on You be
ashamed;
Let those be ashamed who deal
treacherously without cause.

4 [a]Show me Your ways, O LORD;
Teach me Your paths.
5 Lead me in Your truth and
teach me,
For You *are* the God of my salvation;
On You I wait all the day.

6 Remember, O LORD, [a]Your tender
mercies and Your lovingkindnesses,
For they *are* from of old.
7 Do not remember [a]the sins of my
youth, nor my transgressions;
[b]According to Your mercy remember
me,
For Your goodness' sake, O LORD.

8 Good and upright *is* the LORD;
Therefore He teaches sinners in the
way.
9 The humble He guides in justice,
And the humble He teaches
His way.
10 All the paths of the LORD *are* mercy
and truth,
To such as keep His covenant and His
testimonies.

23:4 [a] Job 3:5; 10:21, 22; 24:17 [b] [Ps. 3:6; 27:1] [c] [Is. 43:2] **23:5** [a] Ps. 104:15 [b] Ps. 92:10 **23:6** [1] Following Septuagint, Syriac, Targum, and Vulgate; Masoretic Text reads *return.* **24:1** [a] 1 Cor. 10:26, 28 **24:2** [a] Ps. 89:11 **24:3** [a] Ps. 15:1–5 **24:4** [a] [Job 17:9] [b] [Matt. 5:8] [c] Ps. 15:4 **24:6** [a] Ps. 27:4, 8 **24:7** [a] Is. 26:2 [b] Ps. 29:2, 9; 97:6 **24:8** [a] Rev. 19:13–16 **25:1** [a] Ps. 86:4; 143:8 **25:2** [a] Ps. 34:8 [b] Ps. 13:4; 41:11 **25:4** [a] Ex. 33:13 **25:6** [a] Ps. 103:17; 106:1 **25:7** [a] [Jer. 3:25] [b] Ps. 51:1

FROM HEAVEN'S THRONE

Who is this King of glory?

PSALM 24:8

When David asked this question, the answer was already given. The King of glory is He who made the earth "and all its fullness . . . and those who dwell therein" (v. 1). God may be called "King of glory" (v. 8) not only because He is the Creator but because His ways are righteous and good. Those who approach Him must have "clean hands" and pure hearts (v. 4). The righteous person "shall receive blessing from the LORD" (v. 5). Implicit in these affirmations are contrasts with pagan worship of the gods and idols of the ancient Near East. Pagan gods accepted bribes, and the gods of the nations warped the morality of their followers. Not so the God of David.

Truth, justice, and moral integrity are vital to mental health and a sense of well-being. In short, peace is the fruit of faith and righteousness—in God and in ourselves. The righteousness and faithfulness of God provide for us our life's paradigm and at the same time motivate us to put it into practice.

If you lack peace, is it possible you are neglecting truth, justice, and/or moral integrity in some way?

11 [a]For Your name's sake, O LORD,
Pardon my iniquity, for it *is* great.

12 Who *is* the man that fears the LORD?
[a]Him shall He[1] teach in the way He[2] chooses.
13 [a]He himself shall dwell in prosperity,
And [b]his descendants shall inherit the earth.
14 [a]The secret of the LORD *is* with those who fear Him,
And He will show them His covenant.
15 [a]My eyes *are* ever toward the LORD,
For He shall pluck my feet out of the net.

16 [a]Turn Yourself to me, and have mercy on me,
For I *am* desolate and afflicted.
17 The troubles of my heart have enlarged;
Bring me out of my distresses!
18 [a]Look on my affliction and my pain,
And forgive all my sins.
19 Consider my enemies, for they are many;
And they hate me with cruel hatred.
20 Keep my soul, and deliver me;
Let me not be ashamed, for I put my trust in You.
21 Let integrity and uprightness preserve me,
For I wait for You.

22 [a]Redeem Israel, O God,
Out of all their troubles!

PSALM 26

A Prayer for Divine Scrutiny and Redemption

A Psalm of David.

1 Vindicate [a]me, O LORD,
For I have [b]walked in my integrity.
[c]I have also trusted in the LORD;
I shall not slip.
2 [a]Examine me, O LORD, and prove me;
Try my mind and my heart.
3 For Your lovingkindness *is* before my eyes,
And [a]I have walked in Your truth.
4 I have not [a]sat with idolatrous mortals,
Nor will I go in with hypocrites.
5 I have [a]hated the assembly of evildoers,
And will not sit with the wicked.

6 I will wash my hands in innocence;
So I will go about Your altar, O LORD,
7 That I may proclaim with the voice of thanksgiving,
And tell of all Your wondrous works.

25:11 [a] Ps. 31:3; 79:9; 109:21; 143:11 **25:12** [a] [Ps. 25:8; 37:23] [1] Or *he* [2] Or *he* **25:13** [a] [Prov. 19:23] [b] Matt. 5:5 **25:14** [a] [John 7:17] **25:15** [a] [Ps. 123:2; 141:8] **25:16** [a] Ps. 69:16 **25:18** [a] 2 Sam. 16:12 **25:22** [a] [Ps. 130:8] **26:1** [a] Ps. 7:8 [b] 2 Kin. 20:3 [c] [Ps. 13:5; 28:7] **26:2** [a] Ps. 17:3; 139:23 **26:3** [a] 2 Kin. 20:3 **26:4** [a] Ps. 1:1 **26:5** [a] Ps. 31:6; 139:21

THE GOD WHO FORGETS

Do not remember the sins of my youth.

PSALM 25:7

Most of us have done things that we are not proud of, things we wish we could undo, spoken words we'd love to take back. What sins of his youth David had in mind are unknown—the sin he committed with Bathsheba took place much later in his life (2 Sam. 11; Ps. 51). The sins of our youth can haunt us and create guilt that robs us of peace. Even after we confess and make things right, negative memories linger.

David desired God but worried that his sins had alienated Him. "To you, O LORD, I lift up my soul," the king wrote. "I trust in You; let me not be ashamed" (25:1–2). David petitioned God, "Show me Your ways, O LORD; teach me Your paths" (v. 4). The king didn't ask for blessings with no strings attached; he asked God to teach him. David reminded God of his "tender mercies" and "lovingkindnesses, for they are from of old" (v. 6), that is, God had always treated Israel with mercy. It is then that David pleaded, "Do not remember the sins of my youth" (v. 7). He won't, because He is a God of mercy. Doesn't that give you peace?

8 LORD, [a]I have loved the habitation of
Your house,
And the place where Your glory dwells.

9 [a]Do not gather my soul with sinners,
Nor my life with bloodthirsty men,
10 In whose hands *is* a sinister scheme,
And whose right hand is full of [a]bribes.

11 But as for me, I will walk in my
integrity;
Redeem me and be merciful to me.
12 [a]My foot stands in an even place;
In the congregations I will bless the
LORD.

PEACE NOTE

To have the peace of God, we must saturate our minds in truth. Let's make sure we're not following every new psychological fad.

PSALM 26:3

PSALM 27

An Exuberant Declaration of Faith

A Psalm of David.

1 The LORD *is* my [a]light and my
salvation;
Whom shall I fear?
The [b]LORD *is* the strength of my life;
Of whom shall I be afraid?
2 When the wicked came against me
To [a]eat up my flesh,
My enemies and foes,
They stumbled and fell.
3 [a]Though an army may encamp against
me,
My heart shall not fear;
Though war may rise against me,
In this I *will be* confident.

4 [a]One *thing* I have desired of the LORD,
That will I seek:
That I may [b]dwell in the house of the
LORD
All the days of my life,
To behold the beauty of the LORD,
And to inquire in His temple.
5 For [a]in the time of trouble
He shall hide me in His pavilion;
In the secret place of His tabernacle
He shall hide me;
He shall [b]set me high upon a rock.

6 And now [a]my head shall be lifted up
above my enemies all around me;

26:8 [a] Ps. 27:4; 84:1–4, 10 **26:9** [a] Ps. 28:3 **26:10** [a] 1 Sam. 8:3 **26:12** [a] Ps. 40:2 **27:1** [a] [Mic. 7:8] [b] Ps. 62:7; 118:14
27:2 [a] Ps. 14:4 **27:3** [a] Ps. 3:6 **27:4** [a] Ps. 26:8; 65:4 [b] Luke 2:37 **27:5** [a] Ps. 31:20; 91:1 [b] Ps. 40:2 **27:6** [a] Ps. 3:3

ROBBING THE THIEF OF PEACE

Whom shall I fear?

PSALM 27:1

Fear is a thief of peace. We fear many things: failure in marriage, in other relationships, at work. We fear the future, we worry about our finances, and we obsess about our health. It is nearly impossible to experience peace when we are beset by fears and worries.

David's fears were well grounded; many plotted against him and he was sometimes attacked. The one thing that he sought: "that I may dwell in the house of the LORD all the days of my life, to behold the beauty of the LORD" (v. 4). David's request was extraordinary. One would have expected him to say his desire was to defeat his enemies or to remain safe. He wanted those things to be sure, but what David yearned for *above all* was to gaze upon God's beauty. Through his eventful life David learned that walking closely with his Creator was what truly mattered.

With God is true security. David asked, "Whom shall I fear?" (v. 1). His answer: no one. This is because David lived the theological truth that the presence of God brings the peace of God. When we are in the presence of God, we do not fear.

Therefore I will offer sacrifices of joy in
His tabernacle;
I will sing, yes, I will sing praises to the
LORD.

7 Hear, O LORD, *when* I cry with my voice!
Have mercy also upon me, and
answer me.
8 *When You said,* "Seek My face,"
My heart said to You, "Your face, LORD,
I will seek."
9 [a]Do not hide Your face from me;
Do not turn Your servant away in
anger;
You have been my help;
Do not leave me nor forsake me,
O God of my salvation.
10 [a]When my father and my mother
forsake me,
Then the LORD will take care of me.

11 [a]Teach me Your way, O LORD,
And lead me in a smooth path, because
of my enemies.
12 Do not deliver me to the will of my
adversaries;
For [a]false witnesses have risen against
me,
And such as breathe out violence.
13 *I would have lost heart,* unless I had
believed
That I would see the goodness of the
LORD
[a]In the land of the living.

14 [a]Wait on the LORD;
Be of good courage,
And He shall strengthen your
heart;
Wait, I say, on the LORD!

PSALM 28

Rejoicing in Answered Prayer

A Psalm of David.

1 To You I will cry, O LORD my Rock:
[a]Do not be silent to me,
[b]Lest, if You *are* silent to me,
I become like those who go down to
the pit.
2 Hear the voice of my supplications
When I cry to You,
[a]When I lift up my hands [b]toward Your
holy sanctuary.

3 Do not take me away with the wicked
And with the workers of iniquity,
[a]Who speak peace to their neighbors,
But evil *is* in their hearts.
4 [a]Give them according to their deeds,
And according to the wickedness of
their endeavors;

27:9 [a] Ps. 69:17; 143:7 **27:10** [a] Is. 49:15 **27:11** [a] Ps. 25:4; 86:11; 119:33 **27:12** [a] Ps. 35:11 **27:13** [a] Ezek. 26:20 **27:14** [a] Is. 25:9 **28:1** [a] Ps. 35:22; 39:12; 83:1 [b] Ps. 88:4; 143:7 **28:2** [a] Ps. 5:7 [b] Ps. 138:2 **28:3** [a] Ps. 12:2; 55:21; 62:4 **28:4** [a] [Rev. 18:6; 22:12]

Give them according to the work of
their hands;
Render to them what they deserve.
5 Because [a]they do not regard the works
of the LORD,
Nor the operation of His hands,
He shall destroy them
And not build them up.

6 Blessed *be* the LORD,
Because He has heard the voice of my
supplications!
7 The LORD *is* [a]my strength and my shield;
My heart [b]trusted in Him, and I am
helped;
Therefore my heart greatly rejoices,
And with my song I will praise Him.

8 The LORD *is* their strength,[1]
And He *is* the [a]saving refuge of His
anointed.
9 Save Your people,
And bless [a]Your inheritance;
Shepherd them also,
[b]And bear them up forever.

PSALM 29

Praise to God in His Holiness and Majesty

A Psalm of David.

1 Give [a]unto the LORD, O you mighty
ones,
Give unto the LORD glory and strength.
2 Give unto the LORD the glory due to
His name;
Worship the LORD in [a]the beauty of
holiness.

3 The voice of the LORD *is* over the waters;
[a]The God of glory thunders;
The LORD *is* over many waters.
4 The voice of the LORD *is* powerful;
The voice of the LORD *is* full of majesty.

5 The voice of the LORD breaks [a]the
cedars,
Yes, the LORD splinters the cedars of
Lebanon.
6 [a]He makes them also skip like a calf,
Lebanon and [b]Sirion like a young
wild ox.
7 The voice of the LORD divides the
flames of fire.
8 The voice of the LORD shakes the
wilderness;
The LORD shakes the Wilderness of
[a]Kadesh.
9 The voice of the LORD makes the [a]deer
give birth,
And strips the forests bare;
And in His temple everyone says, "Glory!"

10 The [a]LORD sat *enthroned* at the Flood,
And [b]the LORD sits as King forever.
11 [a]The LORD will give strength to His
people;
The LORD will bless His people with
peace.

PEACE NOTE

God wants your lifestyle to be peace. He wants you to live in peace continually!

PSALM 29:11

PSALM 30

The Blessedness of Answered Prayer

A Psalm. A Song [a]at the dedication of the house of David.

1 I will extol You, O LORD, for You have
[a]lifted me up,
And have not let my foes [b]rejoice over me.
2 O LORD my God, I cried out to You,
And You [a]healed me.
3 O LORD, [a]You brought my soul up from
the grave;
You have kept me alive, that I should
not go down to the pit.[1]

4 [a]Sing praise to the LORD, you saints of
His,
And give thanks at the remembrance
of His holy name.[1]

28:5 [a] Is. 5:12 28:7 [a] Ps. 18:2; 59:17 [b] Ps. 13:5; 112:7 28:8 [a] Ps. 20:6 [1] Following Masoretic Text and Targum; Septuagint, Syriac, and Vulgate read *the strength of His people.* 28:9 [a] [Deut. 9:29; 32:9] [b] Deut. 1:31 29:1 [a] 1 Chr. 16:28, 29 29:2 [a] 2 Chr. 20:21 29:3 [a] [Job 37:4, 5] 29:5 [a] Is. 2:13; 14:8 29:6 [a] Ps. 114:4 [b] Deut. 3:9 29:8 [a] Num. 13:26 29:9 [a] Job 39:1 29:10 [a] Gen. 6:17 [b] Ps. 10:16 29:11 [a] Ps. 28:8; 68:35 30:title [a] Deut. 20:5 30:1 [a] Ps. 28:9 [b] Ps. 25:2 30:2 [a] Ps. 6:2; 103:3 30:3 [a] Ps. 86:13 [1] Following Qere and Targum; Kethib, Septuagint, Syriac, and Vulgate read *from those who descend to the pit.* 30:4 [a] Ps. 97:12 [1] Or *His holiness*

WRAPPED IN GOD'S PEACE

The LORD will give strength to His people; the LORD will bless His people with peace.

PSALM 29:11

What has been your experience with peace? Is it a lasting release from daily cares, a momentary escape from a dreaded situation, an elusive but longed-for quality you want to mark your life?

In Scripture peace is tied to strength. The experiential peace God offers you is very different from the temporal kind found apart from Him. Within this prayer of praise, David reminded himself that true peace came only from the Lord Himself. Who receives the peace and strength of the Lord? Those who are His. The people of God are blessed with a strength that stabilizes them in the *shalom* of God.

Living in the peace of God is not automatic. Like David, we must remind ourselves of the truth in which we stand. Today, wrap yourself in the presence of God's strength within you. There is no peace without proximity to the Lord. Let us allow the Holy Spirit to move in our hearts to feel the strength and peace He promised to provide.

5 For [a]His anger *is but for* a
moment,
[b]His favor *is for* life;
Weeping may endure for a night,
But joy *comes* in the morning.

6 Now in my prosperity I said,
"I shall never be moved."
7 LORD, by Your favor You have made my
mountain stand strong;
[a]You hid Your face, *and* I was
troubled.

8 I cried out to You, O LORD;
And to the LORD I made
supplication:
9 "What profit *is there* in my blood,
When I go down to the pit?
[a]Will the dust praise You?
Will it declare Your truth?
10 Hear, O LORD, and have mercy
on me;
LORD, be my helper!"

11 [a]*You have turned for me my mourning*
into dancing;
You have put off my sackcloth and
clothed me with gladness,
12 To the end that *my* glory may sing
praise to You and not be silent.
O LORD my God, I will give thanks to
You forever.

PSALM 31

The LORD a Fortress in Adversity

To the Chief Musician. A Psalm of David.

1 In [a]You, O LORD, I put my trust;
Let me never be ashamed;
Deliver me in Your righteousness.
2 [a]Bow down Your ear to me,
Deliver me speedily;
Be my rock of refuge,
A fortress of defense to save me.

3 [a]For You *are* my rock and my fortress;
Therefore, [b]for Your name's sake,
Lead me and guide me.
4 Pull me out of the net which they have
secretly laid for me,
For You *are* my strength.
5 [a]Into Your hand I commit my spirit;
You have redeemed me, O LORD God of
[b]truth.

6 I have hated those [a]who regard useless
idols;
But I trust in the LORD.
7 I will be glad and rejoice in Your mercy,
For You have considered my trouble;
You have [a]known my soul in
adversities,
8 And have not [a]shut me up into the
hand of the enemy;
[b]You have set my feet in a wide place.

30:5 [a] Ps. 103:9 [b] Ps. 63:3 30:7 [a] [Ps. 104:29; 143:7] 30:9 [a] [Ps. 6:5] 30:11 [a] Jer. 31:4 31:1 [a] Ps. 22:5 31:2 [a] Ps. 17:6; 71:2; 86:1; 102:2 31:3 [a] [Ps. 18:2] [b] Ps. 23:3; 25:11 31:5 [a] Luke 23:46 [b] [Deut. 32:4] 31:6 [a] Jon. 2:8 31:7 [a] [John 10:27] 31:8 [a] [Deut. 32:30] [b] [Ps. 4:1; 18:19]

9 Have mercy on me, O LORD, for I am in
trouble;
[a]My eye wastes away with grief,
Yes, my soul and my body!
10 For my life is spent with grief,
And my years with sighing;
My strength fails because of my
iniquity,
And my bones waste away.
11 [a]I am a reproach among all my
enemies,
But [b]especially among my neighbors,
And *am* repulsive to my acquaintances;
[c]Those who see me outside flee from me.
12 [a]I am forgotten like a dead man, out of
mind;
I am like a broken vessel.
13 [a]For I hear the slander of many;
[b]Fear *is* on every side;
While they [c]take counsel together
against me,
They scheme to take away my life.

14 But as for me, I trust in You, O LORD;
I say, "You *are* my God."
15 My times *are* in Your [a]hand;
Deliver me from the hand of my enemies,
And from those who persecute me.
16 [a]Make Your face shine upon Your
servant;
Save me for Your mercies' sake.
17 [a]Do not let me be ashamed, O LORD, for
I have called upon You;
Let the wicked be ashamed;
[b]Let them be silent in the grave.
18 [a]Let the lying lips be put to silence,
Which [b]speak insolent things proudly
and contemptuously against the
righteous.

19 [a]Oh, how great *is* Your goodness,
Which You have laid up for those who
fear You,
Which You have prepared for those
who trust in You
In the presence of the sons of men!
20 [a]You shall hide them in the secret place
of Your presence
From the plots of man;
[b]You shall keep them secretly in a
pavilion
From the strife of tongues.

21 Blessed *be* the LORD,
For [a]He has shown me His marvelous
kindness in a strong city!
22 For I said in my haste,
"I am cut off from before Your eyes";
Nevertheless You heard the voice of my
supplications
When I cried out to You.

23 Oh, love the LORD, all you His saints!
For the LORD preserves the faithful,
And fully repays the proud person.
24 [a]Be of good courage,
And He shall strengthen your heart,
All you who hope in the LORD.

PSALM 32

The Joy of Forgiveness

A Psalm of David. A Contemplation.[1]

1 Blessed *is he whose* [a]transgression *is*
forgiven,
Whose sin *is* covered.
2 Blessed *is* the man to whom the LORD
[a]does not impute iniquity,
And [b]in whose spirit *there is* no deceit.

PEACE NOTE

The peace of God results in a state of genuine, meaningful happiness. Having met and embraced the risen Christ, believers know that they are forgiven and can affirm the psalmist's words.

PSALM 32:1-2

3 When I kept silent, my bones grew old
Through my groaning all the day
long.
4 For day and night Your [a]hand was
heavy upon me;
My vitality was turned into the drought
of summer. *Selah*
5 I acknowledged my sin to You,
And my iniquity I have not hidden.
[a]I said, "I will confess my transgressions
to the LORD,"
And You forgave the iniquity of my sin. *Selah*

31:9 [a] Ps. 6:7 31:11 [a] [Is. 53:4] [b] Job 19:13 [c] Ps. 64:8 31:12 [a] Ps. 88:4, 5 31:13 [a] Jer. 20:10 [b] Lam. 2:22 [c] Matt. 27:1 31:15 [a] [Job 14:5; 24:1] 31:16 [a] Ps. 4:6; 80:3 31:17 [a] Ps. 25:2, 20 [b] Ps. 94:17; 115:17 31:18 [a] Ps. 109:2; 120:2 [b] Ps. 94:4 31:19 [a] [Rom. 2:4; 11:22] 31:20 [a] [Ps. 27:5; 32:7] [b] Job 5:21 31:21 [a] [Ps. 17:7] 31:24 [a] [Ps. 27:14] 32:title [1] Hebrew *Maschil* 32:1 [a] [Ps. 85:2; 103:3] 32:2 [a] [2 Cor. 5:19] [b] John 1:47 32:4 [a] 1 Sam. 5:6 32:5 [a] [Prov. 28:13]

6 [a]For this cause everyone who is godly
shall [b]pray to You
In a time when You may be found;
Surely in a flood of great waters
They shall not come near him.
7 [a]You *are* my hiding place;
You shall preserve me from trouble;
You shall surround me with [b]songs of
deliverance. *Selah*

8 I will instruct you and teach you in the
way you should go;
I will guide you with My eye.
9 Do not be like the [a]horse *or* like the mule,
Which have no understanding,
Which must be harnessed with bit and
bridle,
Else they will not come near you.
10 [a]Many sorrows *shall be* to the wicked;
But [b]he who trusts in the LORD, mercy
shall surround him.
11 [a]Be glad in the LORD and rejoice, you
righteous;
And shout for joy, all *you* upright in
heart!

PSALM 33

The Sovereignty of the LORD in Creation and History

1 Rejoice [a]in the LORD, O you righteous!
For praise from the upright is beautiful.
2 Praise the LORD with the harp;
Make melody to Him with an
instrument of ten strings.
3 Sing to Him a new song;
Play skillfully with a shout of joy.

4 For the word of the LORD *is* right,
And all His work *is done* in truth.
5 He loves righteousness and justice;
The earth is full of the goodness of the
LORD.

6 [a]By the word of the LORD the heavens
were made,
And all the [b]host of them [c]by the
breath of His mouth.
7 [a]*He gathers the waters of the sea*
together as a heap;[1]
He lays up the deep in storehouses.

8 Let all the earth fear the LORD;
Let all the inhabitants of the world
stand in awe of Him.
9 For [a]He spoke, and it was *done;*
He commanded, and it stood fast.

10 [a]The LORD brings the counsel of the
nations to nothing;
He makes the plans of the peoples of
no effect.
11 [a]The counsel of the LORD stands forever,
The plans of His heart to all generations.
12 Blessed *is* the nation whose God *is* the
LORD,
The people He has [a]chosen as His own
inheritance.

13 [a]The LORD looks from heaven;
He sees all the sons of men.
14 From the place of His dwelling He looks
On all the inhabitants of the earth;
15 He fashions their hearts individually;
[a]He considers all their works.

16 [a]No king *is* saved by the multitude of an
army;
A mighty man is not delivered by great
strength.
17 [a]A horse *is* a vain hope for safety;
Neither shall it deliver *any* by its great
strength.

18 [a]Behold, the eye of the LORD *is* on those
who fear Him,
On those who hope in His mercy,
19 To deliver their soul from death,
And [a]to keep them alive in famine.

20 Our soul waits for the LORD;
He *is* our help and our shield.

PEACE NOTE

There's nothing passive about waiting on God—to wait is the strongest expression of faith in all the Bible. Only when I wait on God will I experience the power of God's peace in my life.

PSALM 33:20

32:6 [a] [1 Tim. 1:16] [b] Is. 55:6 32:7 [a] Ps. 9:9 [b] Ex. 15:1 32:9 [a] Prov. 26:3 32:10 [a] [Rom. 2:9] [b] Prov. 16:20 32:11 [a] Ps. 64:10; 68:3; 97:12 33:1 [a] Ps. 32:11; 97:12 33:6 [a] [Heb. 11:3] [b] Gen. 2:1 [c] [Job 26:13] 33:7 [a] Job 26:10; 38:8 [1] Septuagint, Targum, and Vulgate read *in a vessel.* 33:9 [a] Gen. 1:3 33:10 [a] Is. 8:10; 19:3 33:11 [a] [Job 23:13] 33:12 [a] [Ex. 19:5] 33:13 [a] Job 28:24 33:15 [a] [Jer. 32:19] 33:16 [a] Ps. 44:6; 60:11 33:17 [a] [Prov. 21:31] 33:18 [a] [Job 36:7] 33:19 [a] Job 5:20

21 For our heart shall rejoice in Him,
Because we have trusted in His holy name.
22 Let Your mercy, O LORD, be upon us,
Just as we hope in You.

PSALM 34

The Happiness of Those Who Trust in God

A Psalm of David [a]when he pretended madness before Abimelech, who drove him away, and he departed.

1 I will [a]bless the LORD at all times;
His praise *shall* continually *be* in my mouth.
2 My soul shall make its boast in the LORD;
The humble shall hear *of it* and be glad.
3 Oh, magnify the LORD with me,
And let us exalt His name together.

PEACE NOTE

When we boast only in Jesus Christ and His redeeming work in our lives, the Bible promises that we will live by God's peace.

PSALM 34:2

4 I [a]sought the LORD, and He heard me,
And delivered me from all my fears.
5 They looked to Him and were radiant,
And their faces were not ashamed.
6 This poor man cried out, and the LORD heard *him*,
And saved him out of all his troubles.
7 [a]The angel[1] of the LORD [b]encamps all around those who fear Him,
And delivers them.

8 Oh, [a]taste and see that the LORD *is* good;
[b]Blessed *is* the man *who* trusts in Him!
9 Oh, fear the LORD, you His saints!
There is no want to those who fear Him.
10 The young lions lack and suffer hunger;
[a]But those who seek the LORD shall not lack any good *thing*.

11 Come, you children, listen to me;
[a]I will teach you the fear of the LORD.
12 [a]Who *is* the man *who* desires life,
And loves *many* days, that he may see good?
13 Keep your tongue from evil,
And your lips from speaking [a]deceit.
14 [a]Depart from evil and do good;
[b]Seek peace and pursue it.

15 [a]The eyes of the LORD *are* on the righteous,
And His ears *are open* to their cry.
16 [a]The face of the LORD *is* against those who do evil,
[b]To cut off the remembrance of them from the earth.

17 *The righteous* cry out, and [a]the LORD hears,
And delivers them out of all their troubles.
18 [a]The LORD *is* near [b]to those who have a broken heart,
And saves such as have a contrite spirit.

19 [a]Many *are* the afflictions of the righteous,
[b]But the LORD delivers him out of them all.
20 He guards all his bones;
[a]Not one of them is broken.
21 [a]Evil shall slay the wicked,
And those who hate the righteous shall be condemned.
22 The LORD [a]redeems the soul of His servants,
And none of those who trust in Him shall be condemned.

PSALM 35

The LORD the Avenger of His People

A Psalm of David.

1 Plead *my cause,* O LORD, with those who strive with me;
Fight against those who fight against me.
2 Take hold of shield and buckler,
And stand up for my help.
3 Also draw out the spear,
And stop those who pursue me.
Say to my soul,
"I *am* your salvation."

34:title [a] 1 Sam. 21:10–15 34:1 [a] [Eph. 5:20] 34:4 [a] [Matt. 7:7] 34:7 [a] Dan. 6:22 [b] 2 Kin. 6:17 [1] Or *Angel* 34:8 [a] 1 Pet. 2:3 [b] Ps. 2:12 34:10 [a] [Ps. 84:11] 34:11 [a] Ps. 32:8 34:12 [a] [1 Pet. 3:10–12] 34:13 [a] [Eph. 4:25] 34:14 [a] Ps. 37:27 [b] [Rom. 14:19] 34:15 [a] Job 36:7 34:16 [a] Lev. 17:10 [b] [Prov. 10:7] 34:17 [a] Ps. 34:6; 145:19 34:18 [a] [Ps. 145:18] [b] [Is. 57:15] 34:19 [a] Prov. 24:16 [b] Ps. 34:4, 6, 17 34:20 [a] John 19:33, 36 34:21 [a] Ps. 94:23; 140:11 34:22 [a] 1 Kin. 1:29

PURSUING PEACE

Depart from evil and do good; seek peace and pursue it.

PSALM 34:14

David asked, "Who is the man who desires life, and loves many days, that he may see good?" (v. 12). Surely that applies to everyone. But we do not always ask what is required to achieve this. According to David, if you want to live long and see good, then "keep your tongue from evil, and your lips from speaking deceit. Depart from evil and do good; seek peace and pursue it" (vv. 13–14).

Seeking peace does not guarantee a healthy, prosperous life (as preachers sometimes teach), for even righteous people suffer. But in many cases a life marked by the pursuit of peace, a life characterized by truth and integrity, has a much better chance of great happiness. A person known for his or her goodness experiences peace. David had learned that from experience and so proclaimed it here in Psalm 34. His world-changing Descendant, Jesus, taught, "Blessed are the peacemakers" (Matt. 5:9).

Far too many believers are not seeking peace and wondering why they live in anxiety and hopelessness. David reminds us of the truth—wow, what a reminder for me today! Instead of seeking fleeting pleasure or entertainment, let's pursue the peace of God every day.

4 [a]Let those be put to shame and brought
to dishonor
Who seek after my life;
Let those be [b]turned back and brought
to confusion
Who plot my hurt.
5 [a]Let them be like chaff before the wind,
And let the angel[1] of the LORD chase
them.
6 Let their way be [a]dark and slippery,
And let the angel of the LORD pursue
them.
7 For without cause they have [a]hidden
their net for me *in* a pit,
Which they have dug without cause for
my life.
8 Let [a]destruction come upon him
unexpectedly,
And let his net that he has hidden
catch himself;
Into that very destruction let him fall.

9 And my soul *shall* be joyful in the
LORD;
It shall rejoice in His salvation.
10 [a]All my bones shall say,
"LORD, [b]who *is* like You,
Delivering the poor from him who is
too strong for him,
Yes, the poor and the needy from him
who plunders him?"

11 Fierce witnesses rise up;
They ask me *things* that I do not
know.
12 [a]They reward me evil for good,
To the sorrow of my soul.
13 But as for me, [a]when they were sick,
My clothing *was* sackcloth;
I humbled myself with fasting;
And my prayer would return to my
own heart.
14 I paced about as though *he were* my
friend *or* brother;
I bowed down heavily, as one who
mourns *for his* mother.

15 But in my adversity they rejoiced
And gathered together;
Attackers gathered against me,
And I did not know *it;*
They tore *at me* and did not cease;
16 With ungodly mockers at feasts
They gnashed at me with their
teeth.

17 Lord, how long will You [a]look on?
Rescue me from their destructions,
My precious *life* from the lions.
18 I will give You thanks in the great
assembly;
I will praise You among many
people.

35:4 [a] Ps. 40:14, 15; 70:2, 3 [b] Ps. 129:5 **35:5** [a] Job 21:18 [1] Or *Angel* **35:6** [a] Ps. 73:18 **35:7** [a] Ps. 9:15 **35:8** [a] [1 Thess. 5:3] **35:10** [a] Ps. 51:8 [b] [Ex. 15:11] **35:12** [a] John 10:32 **35:13** [a] Job 30:25 **35:17** [a] [Hab. 1:13]

19 [a]Let them not rejoice over me who are
wrongfully my enemies;
Nor let them wink with the eye who
hate me without a cause.
20 For they do not speak peace,
But they devise deceitful matters
Against *the* quiet ones in the
land.
21 They also opened their mouth wide
against me,
And said, "Aha, aha!
Our eyes have seen *it.*"

22 *This* You have seen, O LORD;
Do not keep silence.
O Lord, do not be far from me.
23 Stir up Yourself, and awake to my
vindication,
To my cause, my God and my Lord.
24 Vindicate me, O LORD my God,
according to Your righteousness;
And let them not rejoice over me.
25 Let them not say in their hearts, "Ah, so
we would have it!"
Let them not say, "We have swallowed
him up."

26 Let them be ashamed and brought to
mutual confusion
Who rejoice at my hurt;
Let them be [a]clothed with shame and
dishonor
Who exalt themselves against me.
27 [a]Let them shout for joy and be glad,
Who favor my righteous cause;
And let them say continually,
"Let the LORD be magnified,
Who has pleasure in the prosperity of
His servant."
28 And my tongue shall speak of Your
righteousness
And of Your praise all the day long.

PSALM 36

Man's Wickedness and God's Perfections

To the Chief Musician. *A Psalm* of David
the servant of the LORD.

1 An oracle within my heart concerning
the transgression of the wicked:
[a]*There is* no fear of God before his eyes.
2 For he flatters himself in his own eyes,
When he finds out his iniquity *and*
when he hates.
3 The words of his mouth *are* wickedness
and deceit;
[a]He has ceased to be wise *and* to do good.
4 [a]He devises wickedness on his bed;
He sets himself [b]in a way *that is* not
good;
He does not abhor [c]evil.

5 Your mercy, O LORD, *is* in the heavens;
Your faithfulness *reaches* to the clouds.
6 Your righteousness *is* like the great
mountains;

35:19 [a] Ps. 69:4; 109:3 35:26 [a] Ps. 109:29 35:27 [a] Rom. 12:15 36:1 [a] Rom. 3:18 36:3 [a] Jer. 4:22 36:4 [a] Prov. 4:16 [b] Is. 65:2 [c] [Rom. 12:9]

GOD DELIGHTS IN YOUR PEACE

Let the LORD be magnified, who has pleasure in the prosperity of His servant.

PSALM 35:27

Psalm 35 reflects a period of David's life when he was on the run, probably pursued by King Saul who was unreasonably convinced that David plotted against him. David cried out to God to protect him.

Few of us can identify with the treachery and excitement that David experienced. But we do sometimes experience unsettling troubles, including false accusations and unfair criticism that can be very hurtful. The natural impulse is to respond in anger, perhaps even retaliate. But David did not do that. In his psalm he asked God to vindicate him, to protect him from those who wished him harm. This is the response of a person of peace. David invited his friends and supporters to sing, "Let the LORD be magnified, who has pleasure in the prosperity of His servant" (v. 27). What the New King James Version translates as "prosperity" in both the Hebrew original and the Greek translation is actually "peace." God takes pleasure in our peace. It is His will that we pursue and experience His peace.

How can you follow David's example of pursuing peace right now?

PEACE NOTE

Faith is not what I feel; faith is what I believe because of my faithful God!

PSALM 36:5

[a]Your judgments *are* a great deep;
O LORD, You preserve man and beast.

7 How precious *is* Your lovingkindness,
O God!
Therefore the children of men [a]put
their trust under the shadow of Your
wings.
8 [a]They are abundantly satisfied with the
fullness of Your house,
And You give them drink from [b]the
river of Your pleasures.
9 [a]For with You *is* the fountain of life;
[b]In Your light we see light.

10 Oh, continue Your lovingkindness to
those who know You,
And Your righteousness to the upright
in heart.
11 Let not the foot of pride come against me,
And let not the hand of the wicked
drive me away.
12 There the workers of iniquity have fallen;
They have been cast down and are not
able to rise.

PSALM 37

The Heritage of the Righteous and the Calamity of the Wicked

A Psalm of David.

1 Do[a] not fret because of evildoers,
Nor be envious of the workers of
iniquity.
2 For they shall soon be cut down [a]like
the grass,
And wither as the green herb.

3 Trust in the LORD, and do good;
Dwell in the land, and feed on His
faithfulness.
4 [a]Delight yourself also in the LORD,
And He shall give you the desires of
your [b]heart.

5 [a]Commit your way to the LORD,
Trust also in Him,
And He shall bring *it* to pass.
6 [a]He shall bring forth your righteousness
as the light,
And your justice as the noonday.

7 Rest in the LORD, [a]and wait patiently
for Him;
Do not fret because of him who
[b]prospers in his way,
Because of the man who brings wicked
schemes to pass.
8 [a]Cease from anger, and forsake wrath;
[b]Do not fret—*it* only *causes* harm.

9 For evildoers shall be cut off;
But those who wait on the LORD,
They shall [a]inherit the earth.
10 For [a]yet a little while and the wicked
shall be no *more;*
Indeed, [b]you will look carefully for his
place,
But it *shall be* no *more.*
11 [a]But the meek shall inherit the earth,
And shall delight themselves in the
abundance of peace.

12 The wicked plots against the just,
[a]And gnashes at him with his teeth.

PEACE NOTE

Waiting on God is not just about what you get at the end but about what you become as you wait. Waiting changes you when you understand that there is no peace apart from God.

PSALM 37:7

36:6 [a] [Rom. 11:33] **36:7** [a] Ps. 17:8; 57:1; 91:4 **36:8** [a] Ps. 63:5; 65:4 [b] Rev. 22:1 **36:9** [a] [Jer. 2:13] [b] [1 Pet. 2:9] **37:1** [a] Ps. 73:3 **37:2** [a] Ps. 90:5, 6; 92:7 **37:4** [a] Is. 58:14 [b] Ps. 21:2; 145:19 **37:5** [a] [Ps. 55:22] **37:6** [a] Job 11:17 **37:7** [a] [Lam. 3:26] [b] [Ps. 73:3–12] **37:8** [a] [Eph. 4:26] [b] Ps. 73:3 **37:9** [a] [Is. 57:13; 60:21] **37:10** [a] [Heb. 10:37] [b] Job 7:10 **37:11** [a] [Matt. 5:5] **37:12** [a] Ps. 35:16

PEACE NOTE

Meekness, or humility, is a path to the Lord and "the abundance of peace."

PSALM 37:11

13 [a]The Lord laughs at him,
For He sees that [b]his day is coming.
14 The wicked have drawn the sword
And have bent their bow,
To cast down the poor and needy,
To slay those who are of upright
conduct.
15 Their sword shall enter their own
heart,
And their bows shall be broken.

16 [a]A little that a righteous man has
Is better than the riches of many
wicked.
17 For the arms of the wicked shall be
broken,
But the LORD upholds the righteous.

18 The LORD knows the days of the
upright,
And their inheritance shall be
forever.
19 They shall not be ashamed in the evil
time,
And in the days of famine they shall be
satisfied.
20 But the wicked shall perish;
And the enemies of the LORD,
Like the splendor of the meadows,
shall vanish.
Into smoke they shall vanish
away.

21 The wicked borrows and does not
repay,
But [a]the righteous shows mercy and
gives.
22 [a]For *those* blessed by Him shall inherit
the earth,
But *those* cursed by Him shall be cut off.

23 [a]The steps of a *good* man are ordered by
the LORD,
And He delights in his way.
24 [a]Though he fall, he shall not be utterly
cast down;
For the LORD upholds *him with* His hand.

25 I have been young, and *now* am old;
Yet I have not seen the righteous
forsaken,
Nor his descendants begging bread.
26 [a]*He is* ever merciful, and lends;
And his descendants *are* blessed.

27 Depart from evil, and do good;
And dwell forevermore.
28 For the LORD loves justice,
And does not forsake His saints;
They are preserved forever,
But the descendants of the wicked shall
be cut off.
29 [a]The righteous shall inherit the land,
And dwell in it forever.

30 [a]The mouth of the righteous speaks
wisdom,
And his tongue talks of justice.
31 The law of his God *is* in his heart;
None of his steps shall slide.

32 The wicked [a]watches the righteous,
And seeks to slay him.
33 The LORD [a]will not leave him in his hand,
Nor condemn him when he is judged.

34 [a]Wait on the LORD,
And keep His way,
And He shall exalt you to inherit the
land;
When the wicked are cut off, you shall
see *it*.
35 I have seen the wicked in great power,
And spreading himself like a native
green tree.
36 Yet he passed away,[1] and behold, he
was no *more;*
Indeed I sought him, but he could not
be found.

37 Mark the blameless *man*, and observe
the upright;
For the future of *that* man *is* peace.

37:13 [a] Ps. 2:4; 59:8 [b] 1 Sam. 26:10 **37:16** [a] Prov. 15:16; 16:8 **37:21** [a] Ps. 112:5, 9 **37:22** [a] [Prov. 3:33] **37:23** [a] [1 Sam. 2:9] **37:24** [a] Prov. 24:16 **37:26** [a] [Deut. 15:8] **37:29** [a] Prov. 2:21 **37:30** [a] [Matt. 12:35] **37:32** [a] Ps. 10:8; 17:11 **37:33** [a] [2 Pet. 2:9] **37:34** [a] Ps. 27:14; 37:9 **37:36** [1] Following Masoretic Text, Septuagint, and Targum; Syriac and Vulgate read *I passed by.*

BE HOLY

Mark the blameless man, and observe the upright; for the future of that man is peace.

PSALM 37:37

When I was young, wondering what career path to follow, I took great comfort in Psalm 37, especially verse 4, where David wrote, "Delight yourself also in the LORD, and He shall give you the desires of your heart." I did that and (after a few false starts!) I found that God did give me the desires of my heart. Many years later, I now have a deeper appreciation for this psalm, having given the rest of it greater attention. For example, the psalm exhorts, "Commit your way to the LORD, trust also in Him" (v. 5) and "Rest in the LORD, and wait patiently for Him" (v. 7). These verbs—"commit," "trust," "rest," and "wait"—spell out what it means to "delight" (v. 4) oneself in the Lord. God will indeed give you the desires of your heart if you do these things.

In the latter part of the psalm David advised that we "mark the blameless man, and observe the upright; for the future of that man is peace" (v. 37). Such men and women serve as our models. Theirs will be a future of peace. Ours can be too.

What blameless person can you emulate as you seek a life of peace?

38 [a]But the transgressors shall be
destroyed together;
The future of the wicked shall be cut off.

39 But the salvation of the righteous *is*
from the LORD;
He is their strength [a]in the time of
trouble.
40 And [a]the LORD shall help them and
deliver them;
He shall deliver them from the wicked,
And save them,
[b]Because they trust in Him.

PSALM 38

Prayer in Time of Chastening

A Psalm of David. [a]To bring to remembrance.

1 O LORD, do not [a]rebuke me in Your wrath,
Nor chasten me in Your hot
displeasure!
2 For Your arrows pierce me deeply,
And Your hand presses me down.

3 *There is* no soundness in my flesh
Because of Your anger,
Nor *any* health in my bones
Because of my sin.
4 For my iniquities have gone over my
head;
Like a heavy burden they are too heavy
for me.
5 My wounds are foul *and* festering
Because of my foolishness.

6 I am troubled, I am bowed down
greatly;
I go mourning all the day long.
7 For my loins are full of inflammation,
And *there is* no soundness in my
flesh.
8 I am feeble and severely broken;
I groan because of the turmoil of my
heart.

9 Lord, all my desire *is* before You;
And my sighing is not hidden from
You.
10 My heart pants, my strength fails me;
As for the light of my eyes, it also has
gone from me.

11 My loved ones and my friends [a]stand
aloof from my plague,
And my relatives stand afar off.
12 Those also who seek my life lay snares
for me;
Those who seek my hurt speak of
destruction,
And plan deception all the day long.

13 But I, like a deaf *man,* do not hear;
And *I am* like a mute *who* does not
open his mouth.

37:38 [a] [Ps. 1:4–6; 37:20, 28] 37:39 [a] Ps. 9:9; 37:19 37:40 [a] Is. 31:5 [b] 1 Chr. 5:20 38:title [a] Ps. 70:title 38:1 [a] Ps. 6:1
38:11 [a] Ps. 31:11; 88:18

PEACE NOTE

Make no mistake: the trials and adversity you overcome by God's grace will become the source of your greatest future ministry and spiritual impact. What you learn will help others.

14 Thus I am like a man who does not
hear,
And in whose mouth *is* no response.

15 For in You, O LORD, [a]I hope;
You will hear, O Lord my God.
16 For I said, "*Hear me,* lest they rejoice
over me,
Lest, when my foot slips, they exalt
themselves against me."

17 [a]For I *am* ready to fall,
And my sorrow *is* continually before me.
18 For I will [a]declare my iniquity;
I will be [b]in anguish over my sin.
19 But my enemies *are* vigorous, *and* they
are strong;
And those who hate me wrongfully
have multiplied.
20 Those also [a]who render evil for good,
They are my adversaries, because I
follow *what is* good.

21 Do not forsake me, O LORD;
O my God, [a]be not far from me!
22 Make haste to help me,
O Lord, my salvation!

PSALM 39

Prayer for Wisdom and Forgiveness

To the Chief Musician. To Jeduthun. A Psalm of David.

1 I said, "I will guard my ways,
Lest I sin with my [a]tongue;
I will restrain my mouth with a muzzle,
While the wicked are before me."
2 [a]I was mute with silence,
I held my peace *even* from good;
And my sorrow was stirred up.
3 My heart was hot within me;
While I was musing, the fire burned.
Then I spoke with my tongue:

4 "LORD, [a]make me to know my end,
And what *is* the measure of my days,
That I may know how frail I *am.*
5 Indeed, You have made my days *as*
handbreadths,
And my age *is* as nothing before You;
Certainly every man at his best state *is*
but [a]vapor. *Selah*
6 Surely every man walks about like a
shadow;
Surely they busy themselves in vain;
He heaps up *riches,*
And does not know who will gather them.

7 "And now, Lord, what do I wait for?
My [a]hope *is* in You.
8 Deliver me from all my transgressions;
Do not make me [a]the reproach of the
foolish.
9 [a]I was mute, I did not open my mouth,
Because it was [b]You who did *it.*
10 [a]Remove Your plague from me;
I am consumed by the blow of Your
hand.
11 When with rebukes You correct man
for iniquity,
You make his beauty [a]melt away like a
moth;
Surely every man *is* vapor. *Selah*
12 "Hear my prayer, O LORD,
And give ear to my cry;
Do not be silent at my tears;
For I *am* a stranger with You,
A sojourner, [a]as all my fathers *were.*
13 [a]Remove Your gaze from me, that I may
regain strength,
Before I go away and [b]am no more."

PSALM 40

Faith Persevering in Trial

To the Chief Musician. A Psalm of David.

1 I [a]waited patiently for the LORD;
And He inclined to me,
And heard my cry.
2 He also brought me up out of a
horrible pit,
Out of [a]the miry clay,

38:15 [a] [Ps. 39:7] 38:17 [a] Ps. 51:3 38:18 [a] Ps. 32:5 [b] [2 Cor. 7:9, 10] 38:20 [a] Ps. 35:12 38:21 [a] Ps. 22:19; 35:22 39:1 [a] [James 3:5–12] 39:2 [a] Ps. 38:13 39:4 [a] Ps. 90:12; 119:84 39:5 [a] Ps. 62:9 39:7 [a] Ps. 38:15 39:8 [a] Ps. 44:13; 79:4; 119:22 39:9 [a] Ps. 39:2 [b] Job 2:10 39:10 [a] Job 9:34; 13:21 39:11 [a] Job 13:28 39:12 [a] Gen. 47:9 39:13 [a] Job 7:19; 10:20, 21; 14:6 [b] [Job 14:10] 40:1 [a] Ps. 25:5; 27:14; 37:7 40:2 [a] Ps. 69:2, 14

And [b]set my feet upon a rock,
And established my steps.
3 [a]He has put a new song in my mouth—
Praise to our God;
Many will see *it* and fear,
And will trust in the LORD.

4 [a]Blessed *is* that man who makes the LORD his trust,
And does not respect the proud, nor such as turn aside to lies.
5 [a]Many, O LORD my God, *are* Your wonderful works
Which You have done;
[b]And Your thoughts toward us
Cannot be recounted to You in order;
If I would declare and speak *of them,*
They are more than can be numbered.

6 [a]Sacrifice and offering You did not desire;
My ears You have opened.
Burnt offering and sin offering You did not require.
7 Then I said, "Behold, I come;
In the scroll of the book *it is* written of me.
8 [a]I delight to do Your will, O my God,
And Your law *is* [b]within my heart."

9 [a]I have proclaimed the good news of righteousness
In the great assembly;
Indeed, [b]I do not restrain my lips,
O LORD, You Yourself know.
10 [a]I have not hidden Your righteousness within my heart;
I have declared Your faithfulness and Your salvation;
I have not concealed Your lovingkindness and Your truth
From the great assembly.

11 Do not withhold Your tender mercies from me, O LORD;
[a]Let Your lovingkindness and Your truth continually preserve me.
12 For innumerable evils have surrounded me;
[a]My iniquities have overtaken me, so that I am not able to look up;
They are more than the hairs of my head;
Therefore my heart fails me.

13 [a]Be pleased, O LORD, to deliver me;
O LORD, make haste to help me!
14 [a]Let them be ashamed and brought to mutual confusion
Who seek to destroy my life;
Let them be driven backward and brought to dishonor
Who wish me evil.
15 Let them be [a]confounded because of their shame,
Who say to me, "Aha, aha!"

16 [a]Let all those who seek You rejoice and be glad in You;
Let such as love Your salvation [b]say continually,
"The LORD be magnified!"
17 [a]But I *am* poor and needy;
[b]*Yet* the LORD thinks upon me.
You *are* my help and my deliverer;
Do not delay, O my God.

PSALM 41

The Blessing and Suffering of the Godly

To the Chief Musician. A Psalm of David.

1 Blessed *is* he who considers the poor;
The LORD will deliver him in time of trouble.
2 The LORD will preserve him and keep him alive,
And he will be blessed on the earth;
[a]You will not deliver him to the will of his enemies.
3 The LORD will strengthen him on his bed of illness;
You will sustain him on his sickbed.

4 I said, "LORD, be merciful to me;
[a]Heal my soul, for I have sinned against You."
5 My enemies speak evil of me:
"When will he die, and his name perish?"
6 And if he comes to see *me,* he speaks lies;
His heart gathers iniquity to itself;
When he goes out, he tells *it.*

7 All who hate me whisper together against me;
Against me they devise my hurt.
8 "An evil disease," *they say,* "clings to him.
And *now* that he lies down, he will rise up no more."
9 [a]Even my own familiar friend in whom I trusted,
[b]Who ate my bread,
Has lifted up *his* heel against me.

40:2 [b] Ps. 27:5 **40:3** [a] Ps. 32:7; 33:3 **40:4** [a] Ps. 34:8; 84:12 **40:5** [a] Job 9:10 [b] [Is. 55:8] **40:6** [a] [Heb. 10:5–9] **40:8** [a] [John 4:34; 6:38] [b] [Jer. 31:33] **40:9** [a] Ps. 22:22, 25 [b] Ps. 119:13 **40:10** [a] Acts 20:20, 27 **40:11** [a] Ps. 61:7 **40:12** [a] Ps. 38:4; 65:3 **40:13** [a] Ps. 70:1 **40:14** [a] Ps. 35:4, 26; 70:2; 71:13 **40:15** [a] Ps. 73:19 **40:16** [a] Ps. 70:4 [b] Ps. 35:27 **40:17** [a] Ps. 70:5; 86:1; 109:22 [b] 1 Pet. 5:7 **41:2** [a] Ps. 27:12 **41:4** [a] Ps. 6:2; 103:3; 147:3 **41:9** [a] 2 Sam. 15:12 [b] John 13:18, 21–30

10 But You, O LORD, be merciful to me,
And raise me up,
That I may repay them.
11 By this I know that You are well pleased with me,
Because my enemy does not triumph over me.
12 As for me, You uphold me in my integrity,
And [a]set me before Your face forever.

13 [a]Blessed *be* the LORD God of Israel
From everlasting to everlasting!
Amen and Amen.

BOOK TWO

Psalms 42–72

PSALM 42

Yearning for God in the Midst of Distresses

To the Chief Musician. A Contemplation[1] of the sons of Korah.

1 As the deer pants for the water brooks,
So pants my soul for You, O God.
2 [a]My soul thirsts for God, for the [b]living God.
When shall I come and appear before God?[1]
3 [a]My tears have been my food day and night,
While they continually say to me,
[b]"Where *is* your God?"

PEACE NOTE

Stop believing in a made-up and distorted God. The only God who will bring you peace is the Lord as revealed in Scripture.

PSALM 42:1

PEACE NOTE

People's threats cannot stop the flow of God's peace. Many a martyr has sung, praised, and prayed his or her way through hardship.

PSALM 42:8

4 When I remember these *things,*
[a]I pour out my soul within me.
For I used to go with the multitude;
[b]I went with them to the house of God,
With the voice of joy and praise,
With a multitude that kept a pilgrim feast.

5 [a]Why are you cast down, O my soul?
And *why* are you disquieted within me?
[b]Hope in God, for I shall yet praise Him
For the help of His countenance.[1]

6 O my God,[1] my soul is cast down within me;
Therefore I will remember You from the land of the Jordan,
And from the heights of Hermon,
From the Hill Mizar.
7 Deep calls unto deep at the noise of Your waterfalls;
[a]All Your waves and billows have gone over me.
8 The LORD will [a]command His lovingkindness in the daytime,
And [b]in the night His song *shall be* with me—
A prayer to the God of my life.

9 I will say to God my Rock,
[a]"Why have You forgotten me?
Why do I go mourning because of the oppression of the enemy?"

41:12 [a] [Job 36:7] 41:13 [a] Ps. 72:18, 19; 89:52; 106:48; 150:6 42:title [1] Hebrew *Maschil* 42:2 [a] Ps. 63:1; 84:2; 143:6 [b] 1 Thess. 1:9 [1] Following Masoretic Text and Vulgate; some Hebrew manuscripts, Septuagint, Syriac, and Targum read *I see the face of God.* 42:3 [a] Ps. 80:5; 102:9 [b] Ps. 79:10; 115:2 42:4 [a] Job 30:16 [b] Is. 30:29 42:5 [a] Ps. 42:11; 43:5 [b] Lam. 3:24 [1] Following Masoretic Text and Targum; a few Hebrew manuscripts, Septuagint, Syriac, and Vulgate read *The help of my countenance, my God.* 42:6 [1] Following Masoretic Text and Targum; a few Hebrew manuscripts, Septuagint, Syriac, and Vulgate put *my God* at the end of verse 5. 42:7 [a] Ps. 69:1, 2; 88:7 42:8 [a] Deut. 28:8 [b] Job 35:10 42:9 [a] Ps. 38:6

10 *As* with a breaking of my bones,
My enemies reproach me,
[a]While they say to me all day long,
"Where *is* your God?"

11 [a]Why are you cast down, O my soul?
And why are you disquieted within me?
Hope in God;
For I shall yet praise Him,
The help of my countenance and my God.

PSALM 43

Prayer to God in Time of Trouble

1 Vindicate [a]me, O God,
And [b]plead my cause against an ungodly nation;
Oh, deliver me from the deceitful and unjust man!
2 For You *are* the God of my strength;
Why do You cast me off?
[a]Why do I go mourning because of the oppression of the enemy?

3 [a]Oh, send out Your light and Your truth!
Let them lead me;
Let them bring me to [b]Your holy hill
And to Your tabernacle.
4 Then I will go to the altar of God,
To God my exceeding joy;
And on the harp I will praise You,
O God, my God.

5 [a]Why are you cast down, O my soul?
And why are you disquieted within me?
Hope in God;
For I shall yet praise Him,
The help of my countenance and my God.

PSALM 44

Redemption Remembered in Present Dishonor

To the Chief Musician. A [a]Contemplation[1] of the sons of Korah.

1 We have heard with our ears, O God,
[a]Our fathers have told us,
The deeds You did in their days,
In days of old:
2 [a]You drove out the nations with Your hand,
But them You planted;
You afflicted the peoples, and cast them out.
3 For [a]they did not gain possession of the land by their own sword,
Nor did their own arm save them;
But it was Your right hand, Your arm, and the light of Your countenance,
[b]Because You favored them.

4 [a]You are my King, O God;[1]
Command[2] victories for Jacob.
5 Through You [a]we will push down our enemies;
Through Your name we will trample those who rise up against us.
6 For [a]I will not trust in my bow,
Nor shall my sword save me.
7 But You have saved us from our enemies,
And have put to shame those who hated us.
8 [a]In God we boast all day long,
And praise Your name forever. *Selah*

9 But [a]You have cast *us* off and put us to shame,
And You do not go out with our armies.
10 You make us [a]turn back from the enemy,
And those who hate us have taken spoil for themselves.
11 [a]You have given us up like sheep *intended* for food,
And have [b]scattered us among the nations.
12 [a]You sell Your people for *next to* nothing,
And are not enriched by selling them.

13 [a]You make us a reproach to our neighbors,
A scorn and a derision to those all around us.
14 [a]You make us a byword among the nations,
[b]A shaking of the head among the peoples.
15 My dishonor *is* continually before me,
And the shame of my face has covered me,
16 Because of the voice of him who reproaches and reviles,
[a]Because of the enemy and the avenger.

42:10 [a] Joel 2:17 **42:11** [a] Ps. 43:5 **43:1** [a] [Ps. 26:1; 35:24] [b] Ps. 35:1 **43:2** [a] Ps. 42:9 **43:3** [a] [Ps. 40:11] [b] Ps. 3:4 **43:5** [a] Ps. 42:5, 11 **44:title** [a] Ps. 42:title [1] Hebrew *Maschil* **44:1** [a] [Ex. 12:26, 27] **44:2** [a] Ex. 15:17 **44:3** [a] [Deut. 8:17, 18] [b] [Deut. 4:37; 7:7, 8] **44:4** [a] [Ps. 74:12] [1] Following Masoretic Text and Targum; Septuagint and Vulgate read *and my God.* [2] Following Masoretic Text and Targum; Septuagint, Syriac, and Vulgate read *Who commands.* **44:5** [a] [Dan. 8:4] **44:6** [a] Ps. 33:16 **44:8** [a] Ps. 34:2 **44:9** [a] Ps. 60:1 **44:10** [a] Lev. 26:17 **44:11** [a] Rom. 8:36 [b] Deut. 4:27; 28:64 **44:12** [a] Is. 52:3, 4 **44:13** [a] Jer. 24:9 **44:14** [a] Deut. 28:37 [b] Job 16:4 **44:16** [a] Ps. 8:2

17 [a]All this has come upon us;
But we have not forgotten You,
Nor have we dealt falsely with Your covenant.
18 Our heart has not turned back,
[a]Nor have our steps departed from Your way;
19 But You have severely broken us in [a]the place of jackals,
And covered us [b]with the shadow of death.

20 If we had forgotten the name of our God,
Or [a]stretched out our hands to a foreign god,
21 [a]Would not God search this out?
For He knows the secrets of the heart.
22 [a]Yet for Your sake we are killed all day long;
We are accounted as sheep for the slaughter.

23 [a]Awake! Why do You sleep, O Lord?
Arise! Do not cast *us* off forever.
24 [a]Why do You hide Your face,
And forget our affliction and our oppression?
25 For [a]our soul is bowed down to the dust;
Our body clings to the ground.
26 Arise for our help,
And redeem us for Your mercies' sake.

PSALM 45

The Glories of the Messiah and His Bride

To the Chief Musician. [a]Set to "The Lilies."[1] A Contemplation[2] of the sons of Korah. A Song of Love.

1 My heart is overflowing with a good theme;
I recite my composition concerning the King;
My tongue *is* the pen of a ready writer.

2 You are fairer than the sons of men;
[a]Grace is poured upon Your lips;
Therefore God has blessed You forever.
3 Gird Your [a]sword upon *Your* thigh,
[b]O Mighty One,
With Your [c]glory and Your majesty.
4 [a]And in Your majesty ride prosperously because of truth, humility, *and* righteousness;
And Your right hand shall teach You awesome things.
5 Your arrows *are* sharp in the heart of the King's enemies;
The peoples fall under You.

6 [a]Your throne, O God, *is* forever and ever;
A [b]scepter of righteousness *is* the scepter of Your kingdom.
7 You love righteousness and hate wickedness;
Therefore God, Your God, has [a]anointed You
With the oil of [b]gladness more than Your companions.
8 All Your garments *are* [a]*scented* with myrrh and aloes *and* cassia,
Out of the ivory palaces, by which they have made You glad.
9 [a]Kings' daughters *are* among Your honorable women;
[b]At Your right hand stands the queen in gold from Ophir.

10 Listen, O daughter,
Consider and incline your ear;
[a]Forget your own people also, and your father's house;
11 So the King will greatly desire your beauty;
[a]Because He *is* your Lord, worship Him.
12 And the daughter of Tyre *will come* with a gift;
[a]The rich among the people will seek your favor.

13 The royal daughter *is* all glorious within *the palace;*
Her clothing *is* woven with gold.
14 [a]She shall be brought to the King in robes of many colors;
The virgins, her companions who follow her, shall be brought to You.
15 With gladness and rejoicing they shall be brought;
They shall enter the King's palace.

16 Instead of Your fathers shall be Your sons,
[a]Whom You shall make princes in all the earth.
17 [a]I will make Your name to be remembered in all generations;
Therefore the people shall praise You forever and ever.

44:17 [a] Dan. 9:13 **44:18** [a] Job 23:11 **44:19** [a] Is. 34:13 [b] [Ps. 23:4] **44:20** [a] [Deut. 6:14] **44:21** [a] [Ps. 139:1, 2] **44:22** [a] Rom. 8:36 **44:23** [a] Ps. 7:6 **44:24** [a] Job 13:24 **44:25** [a] Ps. 119:25 **45:title** [a] Ps. 69:title [1] Hebrew *Shoshannim* [2] Hebrew *Maschil* **45:2** [a] Luke 4:22 **45:3** [a] [Heb. 4:12] [b] [Is. 9:6] [c] Jude 25 **45:4** [a] Rev. 6:2 **45:6** [a] [Ps. 93:2] [b] [Num. 24:17] **45:7** [a] Ps. 2:2 [b] Ps. 21:6 **45:8** [a] Song 1:12, 13 **45:9** [a] Song 6:8 [b] 1 Kin. 2:19 **45:10** [a] Deut. 21:13 **45:11** [a] [Is. 54:5] **45:12** [a] Is. 49:23 **45:14** [a] Song 1:4 **45:16** [a] [1 Pet. 2:9] **45:17** [a] Mal. 1:11

PSALM 46

God the Refuge of His People and Conqueror of the Nations

To the Chief Musician. *A Psalm* of the sons of Korah. A Song [a]for Alamoth.

1 God *is* our [a]refuge and strength,
[b]A very present help in trouble.
2 Therefore we will not fear,
Even though the earth be removed,
And though the mountains be carried into the midst of the sea;
3 [a]*Though* its waters roar *and* be troubled,
Though the mountains shake with its swelling. *Selah*

4 *There is* a [a]river whose streams shall make glad the [b]city of God,
The holy *place* of the tabernacle of the Most High.
5 God *is* [a]in the midst of her, she shall not be moved;
God shall help her, just at the break of dawn.
6 [a]The nations raged, the kingdoms were moved;
He uttered His voice, the earth melted.

7 The [a]LORD of hosts *is* with us;
The God of Jacob *is* our refuge. *Selah*

8 Come, behold the works of the LORD,
Who has made desolations in the earth.
9 [a]He makes wars cease to the end of the earth;
[b]He breaks the bow and cuts the spear in two;
[c]He burns the chariot in the fire.

10 Be still, and know that I *am* God;
[a]I will be exalted among the nations,
I will be exalted in the earth!

11 The LORD of hosts *is* with us;
The God of Jacob *is* our refuge. *Selah*

PSALM 47

Praise to God, the Ruler of the Earth

To the Chief Musician. A Psalm of the sons of Korah.

1 Oh, clap your hands, all you peoples!
Shout to God with the voice of triumph!
2 For the LORD Most High *is* awesome;
He is a great [a]King over all the earth.

PEACE NOTE

It has been said that busyness is the greatest enemy of good thinking. It is also an enemy of mental health and living in *shalom*. Take time to "be still, and know that [He] is God."

PSALM 46:10

3 [a]He will subdue the peoples under us,
And the nations under our feet.
4 He will choose our [a]inheritance for us,
The excellence of Jacob whom He loves. *Selah*

5 [a]God has gone up with a shout,
The LORD with the sound of a trumpet.
6 Sing praises to God, sing praises!
Sing praises to our King, sing praises!
7 [a]For God *is* the King of all the earth;
[b]Sing praises with understanding.

8 [a]God reigns over the nations;
God [b]sits on His [c]holy throne.
9 The princes of the people have gathered together,
[a]The people of the God of Abraham.
[b]For the shields of the earth *belong* to God;
He is greatly exalted.

PSALM 48

The Glory of God in Zion

A Song. A Psalm of the sons of Korah.

1 Great *is* the LORD, and greatly to be praised
In the [a]city of our God,
In His holy mountain.
2 [a]Beautiful in elevation,
The joy of the whole earth,
Is Mount Zion *on* the sides of the north,
The city of the great King.
3 God *is* in her palaces;
He is known as her refuge.

46:title [a] 1 Chr. 15:20 **46:1** [a] Ps. 62:7, 8 [b] [Deut. 4:7] **46:3** [a] [Ps. 93:3, 4] **46:4** [a] [Ezek. 47:1–12] [b] Is. 60:14 **46:5** [a] [Zeph. 3:15] **46:6** [a] Ps. 2:1, 2 **46:7** [a] Num. 14:9 **46:9** [a] Is. 2:4 [b] Ps. 76:3 [c] Ezek. 39:9 **46:10** [a] [Is. 2:11, 17] **47:2** [a] Neh. 1:5 **47:3** [a] Ps. 18:47 **47:4** [a] [1 Pet. 1:4] **47:5** [a] Ps. 68:24, 25 **47:7** [a] Zech. 14:9 [b] 1 Cor. 14:15 **47:8** [a] 1 Chr. 16:31 [b] Ps. 97:2 [c] Ps. 48:1 **47:9** [a] [Rom. 4:11, 12] [b] [Ps. 89:18] **48:1** [a] Ps. 46:4; 87:3 **48:2** [a] Ps. 50:2

PEACE NOTE

I believe it is God's will for me to live in His peace, so I will.

4 For behold, [a]the kings assembled,
They passed by together.
5 They saw *it, and* so they marveled;
They were troubled, they hastened away.
6 Fear [a]took hold of them there,
And pain, as of a woman in birth pangs,
7 *As when* You break the [a]ships of Tarshish
With an east wind.

8 As we have heard,
So we have seen
In the city of the LORD of hosts,
In the city of our God:
God will [a]establish it forever. *Selah*

9 We have thought, O God, on [a]Your lovingkindness,
In the midst of Your temple.
10 According to [a]Your name, O God,
So *is* Your praise to the ends of the earth;
Your right hand is full of righteousness.
11 Let Mount Zion rejoice,
Let the daughters of Judah be glad,
Because of Your judgments.

12 Walk about Zion,
And go all around her.
Count her towers;
13 Mark well her bulwarks;
Consider her palaces;
That you may [a]tell *it* to the generation *following.*
14 For this *is* God,
Our God forever and ever;
[a]He will be our guide
Even to death.[1]

PSALM 49

The Confidence of the Foolish

To the Chief Musician. A Psalm of the sons of Korah.

1 Hear this, all peoples;
Give ear, all inhabitants of the world,
2 Both low and high,
Rich and poor together.
3 My mouth shall speak wisdom,
And the meditation of my heart *shall give* understanding.
4 I will incline my ear to a proverb;
I will disclose my dark saying on the harp.

5 Why should I fear in the days of evil,
When the iniquity at my heels surrounds me?
6 Those who [a]trust in their wealth
And boast in the multitude of their riches,
7 None *of them* can by any means redeem *his* brother,
Nor [a]give to God a ransom for him—
8 For [a]the redemption of their souls *is* costly,
And it shall cease forever—
9 That he should continue to live eternally,
And [a]not see the Pit.

10 For he sees wise men die;
Likewise the fool and the senseless person perish,
And leave their wealth to others.
11 Their inner thought *is that* their houses *will last* forever,[1]
Their dwelling places to all generations;
They [a]call *their* lands after their own names.
12 Nevertheless man, *though* in honor, does not remain;[1]
He is like the beasts *that* perish.

13 This is the way of those who *are* [a]foolish,
And of their posterity who approve their sayings. *Selah*

48:4 [a] 2 Sam. 10:6, 14 **48:6** [a] Ex. 15:15 **48:7** [a] Ezek. 27:25 **48:8** [a] [Ps. 87:5] **48:9** [a] Ps. 26:3 **48:10** [a] Mal. 1:11 **48:13** [a] [Ps. 78:5–7] **48:14** [a] Is. 58:11 [1] Following Masoretic Text and Syriac; Septuagint and Vulgate read *Forever.* **49:6** [a] [Mark 10:23, 24] **49:7** [a] Job 36:18, 19 **49:8** [a] [Matt. 16:26] **49:9** [a] Ps. 89:48 **49:11** [a] Gen. 4:17 [1] Septuagint, Syriac, Targum, and Vulgate read *Their graves shall be their houses forever.* **49:12** [1] Following Masoretic Text and Targum; Septuagint, Syriac, and Vulgate read *understand* (compare verse 20). **49:13** [a] [Luke 12:20]

14 Like sheep they are laid in the grave;
Death shall feed on them;
[a]The upright shall have dominion over them in the morning;
[b]And their beauty shall be consumed in the grave, far from their dwelling.
15 But God [a]will redeem my soul from the power of the grave,
For He shall [b]receive me. *Selah*

16 Do not be afraid when one becomes rich,
When the glory of his house is increased;
17 For when he dies he shall carry nothing away;
His glory shall not descend after him.
18 Though while he lives [a]he blesses himself
(For *men* will praise you when you do well for yourself),
19 He shall go to the generation of his fathers;
They shall never see [a]light.
20 A man *who is* in honor, yet does not understand,
[a]Is like the beasts *that* perish.

PSALM 50

God the Righteous Judge

A Psalm of Asaph.

1 The [a]Mighty One, God the LORD,
Has spoken and called the earth
From the rising of the sun to its going down.
2 Out of Zion, the perfection of beauty,
[a]God will shine forth.
3 Our God shall come, and shall not keep silent;
[a]A fire shall devour before Him,
And it shall be very tempestuous all around Him.

4 [a]He shall call to the heavens from above,
And to the earth, that He may judge His people:
5 "Gather [a]My saints together to Me,
[b]Those who have made a covenant with Me by sacrifice."
6 Let the [a]heavens declare His righteousness,
For [b]God Himself *is* Judge. *Selah*

7 "Hear, O My people, and I will speak,
O Israel, and I will testify against you;
[a]I *am* God, your God!
8 [a]I will not rebuke you [b]for your sacrifices
Or your burnt offerings,
Which are continually before Me.
9 [a]I will not take a bull from your house,
Nor goats out of your folds.
10 For every beast of the forest *is* Mine,
And the cattle on a thousand hills.
11 I know all the birds of the mountains,
And the wild beasts of the field *are* Mine.

12 "If I were hungry, I would not tell you;
[a]For the world *is* Mine, and all its fullness.
13 [a]Will I eat the flesh of bulls,
Or drink the blood of goats?
14 [a]Offer to God thanksgiving,
And [b]pay your vows to the Most High.
15 [a]Call upon Me in the day of trouble;
I will deliver you, and you shall glorify Me."

16 But to the wicked God says:
"What *right* have you to declare My statutes,
Or take My covenant in your mouth,
17 [a]Seeing you hate instruction
And cast My words behind you?
18 When you saw a thief, you [a]consented[1] with him,
And have been a [b]partaker with adulterers.
19 You give your mouth to evil,
And [a]your tongue frames deceit.
20 You sit *and* speak against your brother;
You slander your own mother's son.
21 These *things* you have done, and I kept silent;
[a]You thought that I was altogether like you;
But I will rebuke you,
And [b]set *them* in order before your eyes.

22 "Now consider this, you who [a]forget God,
Lest I tear *you* in pieces,
And *there be* none to deliver:
23 Whoever offers praise glorifies Me;
And [a]to him who orders *his* conduct *aright*
I will show the salvation of God."

49:14 [a] [Dan. 7:18] [b] Job 4:21 **49:15** [a] [Hos. 13:4] [b] Ps. 73:24 **49:18** [a] Deut. 29:19 **49:19** [a] Job 33:30 **49:20** [a] Eccl. 3:19 **50:1** [a] Is. 9:6 **50:2** [a] Ps. 80:1 **50:3** [a] [Ps. 97:3] **50:4** [a] Is. 1:2 **50:5** [a] Deut. 33:3 [b] Ex. 24:7 **50:6** [a] [Ps. 97:6] [b] Ps. 75:7 **50:7** [a] Ex. 20:2 **50:8** [a] Jer. 7:22 [b] [Hos. 6:6] **50:9** [a] Ps. 69:31 **50:12** [a] Ex. 19:5 **50:13** [a] [Ps. 51:15–17] **50:14** [a] Heb. 13:15 [b] Deut. 23:21 **50:15** [a] [Zech. 13:9] **50:17** [a] Rom. 2:21 **50:18** [a] [Rom. 1:32] [b] 1 Tim. 5:22
[1] Septuagint, Syriac, Targum, and Vulgate read *ran.* **50:19** [a] Ps. 52:2 **50:21** [a] [Rom. 2:4] [b] [Ps. 90:8] **50:22** [a] [Job 8:13] **50:23** [a] Gal. 6:16

PSALM 51

A Prayer of Repentance

To the Chief Musician. A Psalm of David [a]when Nathan the prophet went to him, after he had gone in to Bathsheba.

1 Have mercy upon me, O God,
According to Your lovingkindness;
According to the multitude of Your tender mercies,
[a]Blot out my transgressions.
2 [a]Wash me thoroughly from my iniquity,
And cleanse me from my sin.

3 For I acknowledge my transgressions,
And my sin *is* always before me.
4 [a]Against You, You only, have I sinned,
And done *this* evil [b]in Your sight—
[c]That You may be found just when You speak,[1]
And blameless when You judge.

5 [a]Behold, I was brought forth in iniquity,
And in sin my mother conceived me.
6 Behold, You desire truth in the inward parts,
And in the hidden *part* You will make me to know wisdom.

7 [a]Purge me with hyssop, and I shall be clean;
Wash me, and I shall be [b]whiter than snow.
8 Make me hear joy and gladness,
That the bones You have broken [a]may rejoice.
9 Hide Your face from my sins,
And blot out all my iniquities.

10 [a]Create in me a clean heart, O God,
And renew a steadfast spirit within me.
11 Do not cast me away from Your presence,
And do not take Your [a]Holy Spirit from me.

PEACE NOTE

When sin moves in, peace moves out. Confess your sin to renew your peace.

PSALM 51:8

51:title [a] 2 Sam. 12:1 51:1 [a] [Is. 43:25; 44:22] 51:2 [a] [Heb. 9:14] 51:4 [a] 2 Sam. 12:13 [b] [Luke 5:21] [c] Rom. 3:4
[1] Septuagint, Targum, and Vulgate read *in Your words*. 51:5 [a] [Job 14:4] 51:7 [a] Heb. 9:19 [b] [Is. 1:18] 51:8 [a] [Matt. 5:4]
51:10 [a] [Ezek. 18:31] 51:11 [a] [Luke 11:13]

LET GOD PURIFY YOU

Create in me a clean heart, O God.

PSALM 51:10

David made many mistakes in his long and adventurous life, but his sin with Bathsheba and murder of her husband were by far his most egregious. When confronted by Nathan the prophet, David unwittingly pronounced judgment upon himself: "As the LORD lives, the man who has done this shall surely die!" (2 Sam. 12:5). Of course, what David heard was a parable (we refer to it as *the parable of the ewe lamb*). In fact, it described his own sin. "You are the man!" Nathan said (2 Sam. 12:7). David confessed and he was forgiven, but his sin led to heartache and tragedy in the years ahead.

It was likely in response to his sin that David wrote Psalm 51: "Have mercy upon me, O God, according to Your lovingkindness" (v. 1). David didn't simply beg forgiveness; he pleaded with God to give him a fresh start: "Create in me a clean heart, O God, and renew a steadfast spirit within me. Do not cast me away from Your presence . . . Restore to me the joy of Your salvation" (vv. 10–12). From these verses we have a beautiful song of repentance and renewal—two things that lead to peace. Let these verses be your prayer as well.

12 Restore to me the joy of Your salvation,
And uphold me *by Your* [a]generous
Spirit.
13 *Then* I will teach transgressors Your
ways,
And sinners shall be converted to You.

14 Deliver me from the guilt of bloodshed,
O God,
The God of my salvation,
And my tongue shall sing aloud of Your
righteousness.
15 O Lord, open my lips,
And my mouth shall show forth Your
praise.
16 For [a]You do not desire sacrifice, or else
I would give *it;*
You do not delight in burnt offering.
17 [a]The sacrifices of God *are* a broken
spirit,
A broken and a contrite heart—
These, O God, You will not despise.

18 Do good in Your good pleasure to Zion;
Build the walls of Jerusalem.
19 Then You shall be pleased with [a]the
sacrifices of righteousness,
With burnt offering and whole burnt
offering;
Then they shall offer bulls on Your
altar.

PSALM 52

The End of the Wicked and the Peace of the Godly

To the Chief Musician. A Contemplation[1] of David [a]when Doeg the Edomite went and [b]told Saul, and said to him, "David has gone to the house of Ahimelech."

1 Why do you boast in evil, O mighty
man?
The goodness of God *endures*
continually.
2 Your tongue devises destruction,
Like a sharp razor, working deceitfully.
3 You love evil more than good,
Lying rather than speaking
righteousness. *Selah*
4 You love all devouring words,
You deceitful tongue.

5 God shall likewise destroy you
forever;
He shall take you away, and pluck you
out of *your* dwelling place,
And uproot you from the land of the
living. *Selah*
6 The righteous also shall see and fear,
And shall laugh at him, *saying,*
7 "Here is the man *who* did not make God
his strength,
But trusted in the abundance of his
riches,
And strengthened himself in his
wickedness."

8 But I *am* [a]like a green olive tree in the
house of God;
I trust in the mercy of God forever and
ever.
9 I will praise You forever,
Because You have done *it;*
And in the presence of Your saints
I will wait on Your name, for *it is*
good.

PSALM 53

Folly of the Godless, and the Restoration of Israel

To the Chief Musician. Set to "Mahalath." A Contemplation[1] of David.

1 The [a]fool has said in his heart,
"*There is* no God."
They are corrupt, and have done
abominable iniquity;
[b]*There is* none who does good.

2 God looks down from heaven upon the
children of men,
To see if there are *any* who understand,
who [a]seek God.
3 Every one of them has turned aside;
They have together become corrupt;
There is none who does good,
No, not one.

PEACE NOTE

God wants you to live in His peace right now. Focus on God's grace. It is the manna that He provides us each day.

51:12 [a] [2 Cor. 3:17] 51:16 [a] [1 Sam. 15:22] 51:17 [a] Ps. 34:18 51:19 [a] Ps. 4:5 52:title [a] 1 Sam. 22:9 [b] Ezek. 22:9
[1] Hebrew *Maschil* 52:8 [a] Jer. 11:16 53:title [1] Hebrew *Maschil* 53:1 [a] Ps. 10:4 [b] Rom. 3:10–12 53:2 [a] [2 Chr. 15:2]

4 Have the workers of iniquity [a]no
knowledge,
Who eat up my people *as* they eat bread,
And do not call upon God?
5 [a]There they are in great fear
Where no fear was,
For God has scattered the bones of him
who encamps against you;
You have put *them* to shame,
Because God has despised them.

6 [a]Oh, that the salvation of Israel would
come out of Zion!
When God brings back the captivity of
His people,
Let Jacob rejoice *and* Israel be glad.

PSALM 54

Answered Prayer for Deliverance from Adversaries

To the Chief Musician. With stringed instruments.[1] A Contemplation[2] of David [a]when the Ziphites went and said to Saul, "Is David not hiding with us?"

1 Save me, O God, by Your name,
And vindicate me by Your strength.
2 Hear my prayer, O God;
Give ear to the words of my mouth.
3 For strangers have risen up against me,
And oppressors have sought after my life;
They have not set God before them.
Selah

4 Behold, God *is* my helper;
The Lord *is* with those who uphold my life.
5 He will repay my enemies for their evil.
Cut them off in Your truth.

6 I will freely sacrifice to You;
I will praise Your name, O LORD, for *it*
is good.
7 For He has delivered me out of all
trouble;
[a]And my eye has seen *its desire* upon
my enemies.

PSALM 55

Trust in God Concerning the Treachery of Friends

To the Chief Musician. With stringed instruments.[1] A Contemplation[2] of David.

1 Give ear to my prayer, O God,
And do not hide Yourself from my
supplication.
2 Attend to me, and hear me;
I [a]am restless in my complaint, and
moan noisily,
3 Because of the voice of the enemy,
Because of the oppression of the
wicked;
[a]For they bring down trouble upon me,
And in wrath they hate me.

4 [a]My heart is severely pained within me,
And the terrors of death have fallen
upon me.
5 Fearfulness and trembling have come
upon me,
And horror has overwhelmed me.
6 So I said, "Oh, that I had wings like a
dove!
I would fly away and be at rest.
7 Indeed, I would wander far off,
And remain in the wilderness. *Selah*
8 I would hasten my escape
From the windy storm *and* tempest."

9 Destroy, O Lord, *and* divide their tongues,
For I have seen [a]violence and strife in
the city.
10 Day and night they go around it on its
walls;
[a]Iniquity and trouble *are* also in the
midst of it.
11 Destruction *is* in its midst;
[a]Oppression and deceit do not depart
from its streets.

12 [a]For *it is* not an enemy *who*
reproaches me;
Then I could bear *it*.
Nor *is it* one *who* hates me who has
[b]exalted *himself* against me;
Then I could hide from him.
13 But *it was* you, a man my equal,
[a]My companion and my acquaintance.
14 We took sweet counsel together,
And [a]walked to the house of God in the
throng.

15 Let death seize them;
Let them [a]go down alive into hell,
For wickedness *is* in their dwellings
and among them.

16 As for me, I will call upon God,
And the LORD shall save me.
17 [a]Evening and morning and at noon
I will pray, and cry aloud,
And He shall hear my voice.

53:4 [a] Jer. 4:22 **53:5** [a] Prov. 28:1 **53:6** [a] Ps. 14:7 **54:title** [a] 1 Sam. 23:19 [1] Hebrew *neginoth* [2] Hebrew *Maschil* **54:7** [a] Ps. 59:10 **55:title** [1] Hebrew *neginoth* [2] Hebrew *Maschil* **55:2** [a] Is. 38:14; 59:11 **55:3** [a] 2 Sam. 16:7, 8 **55:4** [a] Ps. 116:3 **55:9** [a] Jer. 6:7 **55:10** [a] Ps. 10:7 **55:11** [a] Ps. 10:7 **55:12** [a] Ps. 41:9 [b] Ps. 35:26; 38:16 **55:13** [a] 2 Sam. 15:12 **55:14** [a] Ps. 42:4 **55:15** [a] Num. 16:30, 33 **55:17** [a] Dan. 6:10

18 He has redeemed my soul in peace
from the battle *that was*
against me,
For [a]there were many against me.
19 God will hear, and afflict them,
[a]Even He who abides from of
old. *Selah*
Because they do not change,
Therefore they do not fear God.

20 He has [a]put forth his hands against
those who [b]were at peace
with him;
He has broken his covenant.
21 [a]*The words* of his mouth were smoother
than butter,
But war *was* in his heart;
His words were softer than oil,
Yet they *were* drawn swords.

22 [a]Cast your burden on the LORD,
And [b]He shall sustain you;
He shall never permit the righteous to
be moved.

23 But You, O God, shall bring them down
to the pit of destruction;
[a]Bloodthirsty and deceitful men [b]shall
not live out half their days;
But I will trust in You.

PSALM 56

Prayer for Relief from Tormentors

To the Chief Musician. Set to "The Silent Dove in Distant Lands."[1] A Michtam of David when the [a]Philistines captured him in Gath.

1 Be [a]merciful to me, O God, for man
would swallow me up;
Fighting all day he oppresses me.
2 My enemies would [a]hound *me*
all day,
For *there are* many who fight against
me, O Most High.

3 Whenever I am afraid,
I will trust in You.
4 In God (I will praise His word),
In God I have put my trust;
[a]I will not fear.
What can flesh do to me?

5 All day they twist my words;
All their thoughts *are* against me for
evil.
6 They gather together,
They hide, they mark my steps,
When they lie in wait for my life.
7 Shall they escape by iniquity?
In anger cast down the peoples,
O God!

55:18 [a] 2 Chr. 32:7, 8 **55:19** [a] [Deut. 33:27] **55:20** [a] Acts 12:1 [b] Ps. 7:4 **55:21** [a] Ps. 28:3; 57:4 **55:22** [a] [Ps. 37:5] [b] Ps. 37:24 **55:23** [a] Ps. 5:6 [b] Prov. 10:27 **56:title** [a] 1 Sam. 21:11 [1] Hebrew *Jonath Elem Rechokim* **56:1** [a] Ps. 57:1 **56:2** [a] Ps. 57:3 **56:4** [a] Ps. 118:6

PRESERVED IN PEACE

He has redeemed my soul in peace from the battle that was against me, for there were many against me.

PSALM 55:18

We once again encounter a psalm in which David complained of enemies. He pleaded with God, "Give ear to my prayer, O God, and do not hide Yourself from my supplication" (v. 1). He continued, "Attend to me, and hear me; I am restless in my complaint, and moan noisily" (v. 2). Psalm 55 is one of several Lament Psalms in which David asked God to change his circumstances. These psalms refreshingly remind us that it is okay to be open with God, to express our true feelings even if they are negative. We sometimes think God wants to hear only positive comments and words of praise. God wants to hear those expressions, to be sure, but He also wants to hear our cries for help.

Although David described his unhappiness through most of the psalm, near the middle he expressed gratitude: "He has redeemed my soul in peace from the battle that was against me, for there were many against me" (v. 18). Here "peace," *shalom*, once again refers to the state of well-being. Despite David's facing battles, God preserved him in peace.

What do you think it means to be *preserved in peace*? How do you need to experience this today?

8 You number my wanderings;
Put my tears into Your bottle;
[a]*Are they* not in Your book?
9 When I cry out *to You,*
Then my enemies will turn back;
This I know, because [a]God *is* for me.
10 In God (I will praise *His* word),
In the LORD (I will praise *His* word),
11 In God I have put my trust;
I will not be afraid.
What can man do to me?

12 Vows *made* to You *are binding* upon me, O God;
I will render praises to You,
13 [a]For You have delivered my soul from death.
Have You not *kept* my feet from falling,
That I may walk before God
In the [b]light of the living?

PSALM 57

Prayer for Safety from Enemies

To the Chief Musician. Set to "Do Not Destroy."[1] A Michtam of David [a]when he fled from Saul into the cave.

1 Be merciful to me, O God, be merciful to me!
For my soul trusts in You;
[a]And in the shadow of Your wings I will make my refuge,
[b]Until *these* calamities have passed by.

2 I will cry out to God Most High,
To God [a]who performs *all things* for me.
3 [a]He shall send from heaven and save me;
He reproaches the one who would swallow me up. *Selah*
God [b]shall send forth His mercy and His truth.

4 My soul *is* among lions;
I lie *among* the sons of men
Who are set on fire,
[a]Whose teeth *are* spears and arrows,
And their tongue a sharp sword.
5 [a]Be exalted, O God, above the heavens;
Let Your glory *be* above all the earth.

6 [a]They have prepared a net for my steps;
My soul is bowed down;
They have dug a pit before me;
Into the midst of it they themselves have fallen. *Selah*

7 [a]My heart is steadfast, O God, my heart is steadfast;
I will sing and give praise.
8 Awake, [a]my glory!
Awake, lute and harp!
I will awaken the dawn.

9 [a]I will praise You, O Lord, among the peoples;
I will sing to You among the nations.
10 [a]For Your mercy reaches unto the heavens,
And Your truth unto the clouds.

11 [a]Be exalted, O God, above the heavens;
Let Your glory *be* above all the earth.

PSALM 58

The Just Judgment of the Wicked

To the Chief Musician. Set to "Do Not Destroy."[1] A Michtam of David.

1 Do you indeed speak righteousness, you silent ones?
Do you judge uprightly, you sons of men?
2 No, in heart you work wickedness;
You weigh out the violence of your hands in the earth.

3 [a]The wicked are estranged from the womb;
They go astray as soon as they are born, speaking lies.
4 [a]Their poison *is* like the poison of a serpent;
They are like the deaf cobra *that* stops its ear,
5 Which will not [a]heed the voice of charmers,
Charming ever so skillfully.

6 [a]Break their teeth in their mouth, O God!
Break out the fangs of the young lions, O LORD!
7 [a]Let them flow away as waters *which* run continually;
When he bends *his bow,*
Let his arrows be as if cut in pieces.
8 *Let them be* like a snail which melts away as it goes,
[a]*Like* a stillborn child of a woman, that they may not see the sun.

56:8 [a][Mal. 3:16] 56:9 [a][Rom. 8:31] 56:13 [a]Ps. 116:8, 9 [b]Job 33:30 57:title [a]1 Sam. 22:1 [1]Hebrew *Al Tashcheth* 57:1 [a]Ps. 17:8; 63:7 [b]Is. 26:20 57:2 [a][Ps. 138:8] 57:3 [a]Ps. 144:5, 7 [b]Ps. 43:3 57:4 [a]Prov. 30:14 57:5 [a]Ps. 108:5 57:6 [a]Ps. 9:15 57:7 [a]Ps. 108:1–5 57:8 [a]Ps. 16:9 57:9 [a]Ps. 108:3 57:10 [a]Ps. 103:11 57:11 [a]Ps. 57:5 58:title [1]Hebrew *Al Tashcheth* 58:3 [a][Is. 48:8] 58:4 [a]Eccl. 10:11 58:5 [a]Jer. 8:17 58:6 [a]Job 4:10 58:7 [a]Josh. 2:11; 7:5 58:8 [a]Job 3:16

9 Before your [a]pots can feel *the burning* thorns,
He shall take them away [b]as with a whirlwind,
As in His living and burning wrath.
10 The righteous shall rejoice when he sees the [a]vengeance;
[b]He shall wash his feet in the blood of the wicked,
11 [a]So that men will say,
"Surely *there is* a reward for the righteous;
Surely He is God who [b]judges in the earth."

PSALM 59

The Assured Judgment of the Wicked

To the Chief Musician. Set to "Do Not Destroy."[1] A Michtam of David [a]when Saul sent men, and they watched the house in order to kill him.

1 Deliver me from my enemies, O my God;
Defend me from those who rise up against me.
2 Deliver me from the workers of iniquity,
And save me from bloodthirsty men.

3 For look, they lie in wait for my life;
[a]The mighty gather against me,
Not *for* my transgression nor *for* my sin, O LORD.
4 They run and prepare themselves through no fault *of mine.*

[a]Awake to help me, and behold!
5 You therefore, O LORD God of hosts, the God of Israel,
Awake to punish all the nations;
Do not be merciful to any wicked transgressors. *Selah*

6 [a]At evening they return,
They growl like a dog,
And go all around the city.
7 Indeed, they belch with their mouth;
[a]Swords *are* in their lips;
For *they say,* [b]"Who hears?"

8 But [a]You, O LORD, shall laugh at them;
You shall have all the nations in derision.
9 I will wait for You, O You his Strength;[1]
[a]For God *is* my defense.
10 My God of mercy[1] shall [a]come to meet me;
God shall let [b]me see *my desire* on my enemies.

11 Do not slay them, lest my people forget;
Scatter them by Your power,
And bring them down,
O Lord our shield.
12 [a]*For* the sin of their mouth *and* the words of their lips,
Let them even be taken in their pride,
And for the cursing and lying *which* they speak.
13 [a]Consume *them* in wrath, consume *them,*
That they *may* not *be;*
And [b]let them know that God rules in Jacob
To the ends of the earth. *Selah*

14 And [a]at evening they return,
They growl like a dog,
And go all around the city.
15 They [a]wander up and down for food,
And howl[1] if they are not satisfied.

16 But I will sing of Your power;
Yes, I will sing aloud of Your mercy in the morning;
For You have been my defense
And refuge in the day of my trouble.
17 To You, [a]O my Strength, I will sing praises;
For God *is* my defense,
My God of mercy.

PEACE NOTE

Following Jesus doesn't lead to a carefree existence (see John 16:33). Problems offer opportunities to truly understand the power of God's peace in our lives.

PSALM 59:16

58:9 [a] Eccl. 7:6 [b] Prov. 10:25 **58:10** [a] Jer. 11:20 [b] Ps. 68:23 **58:11** [a] Ps. 92:15 [b] Ps. 50:6; 75:7 **59:title** [a] 1 Sam. 19:11 [1] Hebrew *Al Tashcheth* **59:3** [a] Ps. 56:6 **59:4** [a] Ps. 35:23 **59:6** [a] Ps. 59:14 **59:7** [a] Prov. 12:18 [b] Ps. 10:11 **59:8** [a] Prov. 1:26 **59:9** [a] [Ps. 62:2] [1] Following Masoretic Text and Syriac; some Hebrew manuscripts, Septuagint, Targum, and Vulgate read *my Strength.* **59:10** [a] Ps. 21:3 [b] Ps. 54:7 [1] Following Qere; some Hebrew manuscripts, Septuagint, and Vulgate read *My God, His mercy;* Kethib, some Hebrew manuscripts and Targum read *O God, my mercy;* Syriac reads *O God, Your mercy.* **59:12** [a] Prov. 12:13 **59:13** [a] Ps. 104:35 [b] Ps. 83:18 **59:14** [a] Ps. 59:6 **59:15** [a] Job 15:23 [1] Following Septuagint and Vulgate; Masoretic Text, Syriac, and Targum read *spend the night.* **59:17** [a] Ps. 18:1

PSALM 60

Urgent Prayer for the Restored Favor of God

To the Chief Musician. [a]Set to "Lily of the Testimony."[1] A Michtam of David. For teaching. [b]When he fought against Mesopotamia and Syria of Zobah, and Joab returned and killed twelve thousand Edomites in the Valley of Salt.

1 O God, [a]You have cast us off;
You have broken us down;
You have been displeased;
Oh, restore us again!
2 You have made the earth tremble;
You have broken it;
[a]Heal its breaches, for it is shaking.
3 [a]You have shown Your people hard things;
[b]You have made us drink the wine of confusion.

4 [a]You have given a banner to those who fear You,
That it may be displayed because of the truth. *Selah*
5 [a]That Your beloved may be delivered,
Save *with* Your right hand, and hear me.

6 God has [a]spoken in His holiness:
"I will rejoice;
I will [b]divide [c]Shechem
And measure out [d]the Valley of Succoth.
7 Gilead *is* Mine, and Manasseh *is* Mine;
[a]Ephraim also *is* the helmet for My head;
[b]Judah *is* My lawgiver.
8 [a]Moab *is* My washpot;
[b]Over Edom I will cast My shoe;
[c]Philistia, shout in triumph because of Me."

9 Who will bring me *to* the strong city?
Who will lead me to Edom?
10 *Is it* not You, O God, [a]*who* cast us off?
And You, O God, *who* did [b]not go out with our armies?
11 Give us help from trouble,
[a]For the help of man *is* useless.
12 Through God [a]we will do valiantly,
For *it is* He *who* shall tread down our enemies.[1]

PSALM 61

Assurance of God's Eternal Protection

To the Chief Musician. On a stringed instrument.[1] A *Psalm* of David.

1 Hear my cry, O God;
Attend to my prayer.
2 From the end of the earth I will cry to You,
When my heart is overwhelmed;
Lead me to the rock that is higher than I.

3 For You have been a shelter for me,
[a]A strong tower from the enemy.
4 I will abide in Your tabernacle forever;
[a]I will trust in the shelter of Your wings. *Selah*

5 For You, O God, have heard my vows;
You have given *me* the heritage of those who fear Your name.
6 You will prolong the king's life,
His years as many generations.
7 He shall abide before God forever.
Oh, prepare mercy [a]and truth, *which* may preserve him!

8 So I will sing praise to Your name forever,
That I may daily perform my vows.

PSALM 62

A Calm Resolve to Wait for the Salvation of God

To the Chief Musician. To [a]Jeduthun. A Psalm of David.

1 Truly [a]my soul silently *waits* for God;
From Him *comes* my salvation.
2 He only *is* my rock and my salvation;
He is my defense;
I shall not be greatly [a]moved.

3 How long will you attack a man?
You shall be slain, all of you,
[a]Like a leaning wall and a tottering fence.
4 They only consult to cast *him* down from his high position;
They [a]delight in lies;
They bless with their mouth,
But they curse inwardly. *Selah*

5 My soul, wait silently for God alone,
For my expectation *is* from Him.

60:title [a] Ps. 80 [b] 2 Sam. 8:3, 13 [1] Hebrew *Shushan Eduth* **60:1** [a] Ps. 44:9 **60:2** [a] [2 Chr. 7:14] **60:3** [a] Ps. 71:20 [b] Jer. 25:15 **60:4** [a] Ps. 20:5 **60:5** [a] Ps. 108:6–13 **60:6** [a] Ps. 89:35 [b] Josh. 1:6 [c] Gen. 12:6 [d] Josh. 13:27 **60:7** [a] Deut. 33:17 [b] [Gen. 49:10] **60:8** [a] 2 Sam. 8:2 [b] 2 Sam. 8:14 [c] 2 Sam. 8:1 **60:10** [a] Ps. 108:11 [b] Josh. 7:12 **60:11** [a] Ps. 118:8; 146:3 **60:12** [a] Num. 24:18 [1] Compare verses 5–12 with 108:6–13 **61:title** [1] Hebrew *neginah* **61:3** [a] Prov. 18:10 **61:4** [a] Ps. 91:4 **61:7** [a] Ps. 40:11 **62:title** [a] 1 Chr. 25:1 **62:1** [a] Ps. 33:20 **62:2** [a] Ps. 55:22 **62:3** [a] Is. 30:13 **62:4** [a] Ps. 28:3

6 He only *is* my rock and my salvation;
He is my defense;
I shall not be moved.
7 [a]In God *is* my salvation and my glory;
The rock of my strength,
And my refuge, *is* in God.

8 Trust in Him at all times, you people;
[a]Pour out your heart before Him;
God *is* a refuge for us. *Selah*

PEACE NOTE

God already knows everything about you! He knows you are struggling. He knows exactly where your pressure points are right now. Why don't you take them to the Lord?

PSALM 62:8

9 [a]Surely men of low degree *are* a vapor,
Men of high degree *are* a lie;
If they are weighed on the scales,
They *are* altogether *lighter* than vapor.
10 Do not trust in oppression,
Nor vainly hope in robbery;
[a]If riches increase,
Do not set *your* heart *on them.*

11 God has spoken once,
Twice I have heard this:
That power *belongs* to God.
12 Also to You, O Lord, *belongs* mercy;
For [a]You render to each one according to his work.

PSALM 63

Joy in the Fellowship of God

A Psalm of David [a]when he was in the wilderness of Judah.

1 O God, You *are* my God;
Early will I seek You;
[a]My soul thirsts for You;
My flesh longs for You
In a dry and thirsty land
Where there is no water.
2 So I have looked for You in the sanctuary,
To see [a]Your power and Your glory.

3 [a]Because Your lovingkindness *is* better than life,
My lips shall praise You.
4 Thus I will bless You while I live;
I will [a]lift up my hands in Your name.
5 My soul shall be satisfied as with marrow and fatness,
And my mouth shall praise *You* with joyful lips.

6 When [a]I remember You on my bed,
I meditate on You in the *night* watches.
7 Because You have been my help,
Therefore in the shadow of Your wings I will rejoice.
8 My soul follows close behind You;
Your right hand upholds me.

9 But those *who* seek my life, to destroy *it,*
Shall go into the lower parts of the earth.
10 They shall fall by the sword;
They shall be a portion for jackals.

11 But the king shall rejoice in God;
[a]Everyone who swears by Him shall glory;
But the mouth of those who speak lies shall be stopped.

PEACE NOTE

Instead of focusing on what you can't resolve, concentrate on what you know for certain.

PSALM 62:11

62:7 [a] [Jer. 3:23] 62:8 [a] 1 Sam. 1:15 62:9 [a] Is. 40:17 62:10 [a] [Luke 12:15] 62:12 [a] [Matt. 16:27] 63:title [a] 1 Sam. 22:5
63:1 [a] Ps. 42:2 63:2 [a] Ps. 27:4 63:3 [a] Ps. 138:2 63:4 [a] Ps. 28:2; 143:6 63:6 [a] Ps. 42:8 63:11 [a] Deut. 6:13

PEACE NOTE

Shalom is such a pregnant word. The whole Bible is about God's replacing chaos with *shalom* through Jesus.

PSALM 64

Oppressed by the Wicked but Rejoicing in the Lord

To the Chief Musician. A Psalm of David.

1 Hear my voice, O God, in my meditation;
Preserve my life from fear of the enemy.
2 Hide me from the secret plots of the wicked,
From the rebellion of the workers of iniquity,
3 Who sharpen their tongue like a sword,
[a]And bend *their bows to shoot* their arrows—bitter words,
4 That they may shoot in secret at the blameless;
Suddenly they shoot at him and do not fear.

5 They encourage themselves *in* an evil matter;
They talk of laying snares secretly;
[a]They say, "Who will see them?"
6 They devise iniquities:
"We have perfected a shrewd scheme."
Both the inward thought and the heart of man are deep.

7 But God shall shoot at them *with* an arrow;
Suddenly they shall be wounded.
8 So He will make them stumble over their own tongue;
[a]All who see them shall flee away.
9 All men *shall fear,*
And shall [a]declare the work of God;
For they shall wisely consider His doing.

10 [a]The righteous shall be glad in the Lord, and trust in Him.
And all the upright in heart shall glory.

PSALM 65

Praise to God for His Salvation and Providence

To the Chief Musician. A Psalm of David. A Song.

1 Praise is awaiting You, O God, in Zion;
And to You the vow shall be performed.
2 O You who hear prayer,
[a]To You all flesh will come.
3 Iniquities prevail against me;
As for our transgressions,
You will [a]provide atonement for them.

4 [a]Blessed *is the man* You [b]choose,
And cause to approach *You,*
That he may dwell in Your courts.
[c]We shall be satisfied with the goodness of Your house,
Of Your holy temple.

5 *By* awesome deeds in righteousness You will answer us,
O God of our salvation,
You who are the confidence of all the ends of the earth,
And of the far-off seas;
6 Who established the mountains by His strength,
[a]*Being* clothed with power;
7 [a]You who still the noise of the seas,
The noise of their waves,
[b]And the tumult of the peoples.
8 They also who dwell in the farthest parts are afraid of Your signs;
You make the outgoings of the morning and evening rejoice.

9 You visit the earth and [a]water it,
You greatly enrich it;
[b]The river of God is full of water;
You provide their grain,
For so You have prepared it.
10 You water its ridges abundantly,
You settle its furrows;
You make it soft with showers,
You bless its growth.

11 You crown the year with Your goodness,
And Your paths drip *with* abundance.
12 They drop *on* the pastures of the wilderness,

64:3 [a] Ps. 58:7 **64:5** [a] Ps. 10:11; 59:7 **64:8** [a] Ps. 31:11 **64:9** [a] Jer. 50:28; 51:10 **64:10** [a] Ps. 32:11 **65:2** [a] [Is. 66:23] **65:3** [a] [Heb. 9:14] **65:4** [a] Ps. 33:12 [b] Ps. 4:3 [c] Ps. 36:8 **65:6** [a] Ps. 93:1 **65:7** [a] Matt. 8:26 [b] Is. 17:12, 13 **65:9** [a] Jer. 5:24 [b] Ps. 46:4; 104:13; 147:8

And the little hills rejoice on every side.
13 The pastures are clothed with flocks;
[a]The valleys also are covered with grain;
They shout for joy, they also sing.

PSALM 66

Praise to God for His Awesome Works

To the Chief Musician. A Song. A Psalm.

1 Make [a]a joyful shout to God, all the earth!
2 Sing out the honor of His name;
Make His praise glorious.
3 Say to God,
"How [a]awesome are Your works!
[b]Through the greatness of Your power
Your enemies shall submit themselves to You.
4 [a]All the earth shall worship You
And sing praises to You;
They shall sing praises *to* Your name." *Selah*

5 Come and see the works of God;
He is awesome *in His* doing toward the sons of men.
6 [a]He turned the sea into dry *land;*
[b]They went through the river on foot.
There we will rejoice in Him.
7 He rules by His power forever;
His eyes observe the nations;
Do not let the rebellious exalt themselves. *Selah*

8 Oh, bless our God, you peoples!
And make the voice of His praise to be heard,
9 Who keeps our soul among the living,
And does not allow our feet to be moved.
10 For [a]You, O God, have tested us;
[b]You have refined us as silver is refined.
11 [a]You brought us into the net;
You laid affliction on our backs.
12 [a]You have caused men to ride over our heads;
[b]We went through fire and through water;
But You brought us out to rich *fulfillment.*

13 [a]I will go into Your house with burnt offerings;
[b]I will pay You my vows,
14 Which my lips have uttered
And my mouth has spoken when I was in trouble.

PEACE NOTE

One of the greatest prayers you can pray over yourself, your family, and your friends is this: "The God of peace be with you all. Amen" (Rom. 15:33).

15 I will offer You burnt sacrifices of fat animals,
With the sweet aroma of rams;
I will offer bulls with goats. *Selah*

16 Come *and* hear, all you who fear God,
And I will declare what He has done for my soul.
17 I cried to Him with my mouth,
And He was extolled with my tongue.
18 [a]If I regard iniquity in my heart,
The Lord will not hear.
19 *But* certainly God [a]has heard *me;*
He has attended to the voice of my prayer.

20 Blessed *be* God,
Who has not turned away my prayer,
Nor His mercy from me!

PSALM 67

An Invocation and a Doxology

To the Chief Musician. On stringed instruments.[1] A Psalm. A Song.

1 God be merciful to us and bless us,
And [a]cause His face to shine upon us, *Selah*
2 That [a]Your way may be known on earth,
[b]Your salvation among all nations.

3 Let the peoples praise You, O God;
Let all the peoples praise You.
4 Oh, let the nations be glad and sing for joy!
For [a]You shall judge the people righteously,
And govern the nations on earth. *Selah*

65:13 [a] Is. 44:23; 55:12 **66:1** [a] Ps. 100:1 **66:3** [a] Ps. 65:5 [b] Ps. 18:44 **66:4** [a] Ps. 117:1 **66:6** [a] Ex. 14:21 [b] Josh. 3:14–16 **66:10** [a] Ps. 17:3 [b] [1 Pet. 1:7] **66:11** [a] Lam. 1:13 **66:12** [a] Is. 51:23 [b] Is. 43:2 **66:13** [a] Ps. 100:4; 116:14, 17–19 [b] [Eccl. 5:4] **66:18** [a] Is. 1:15 **66:19** [a] Ps. 116:1, 2 **67:title** [1] Hebrew *neginoth* **67:1** [a] Num. 6:25 **67:2** [a] Acts 18:25 [b] Titus 2:11 **67:4** [a] [Ps. 96:10, 13; 98:9]

5 Let the peoples praise You, O God;
Let all the peoples praise You.
6 [a]*Then* the earth shall yield her increase;
God, our own God, shall bless us.
7 God shall bless us,
And all the ends of the earth shall fear
Him.

PSALM 68

The Glory of God in His Goodness to Israel

To the Chief Musician. A Psalm of David. A Song.

1 Let [a]God arise,
Let His enemies be scattered;
Let those also who hate Him flee
before Him.
2 [a]As smoke is driven away,
So drive *them* away;
[b]As wax melts before the fire,
So let the wicked perish at the presence
of God.
3 But [a]let the righteous be glad;
Let them rejoice before God;
Yes, let them rejoice exceedingly.

4 Sing to God, sing praises to His name;
[a]Extol Him who rides on the clouds,[1]
[b]By His name YAH,
And rejoice before Him.

5 [a]A father of the fatherless, a defender of
widows,
Is God in His holy habitation.
6 [a]God sets the solitary in families;
[b]He brings out those who are bound
into prosperity;
But [c]the rebellious dwell in a dry *land.*

7 O God, [a]when You went out before Your
people,
When You marched through the
wilderness, *Selah*
8 The earth shook;
The heavens also dropped *rain* at the
presence of God;
Sinai itself *was moved* at the presence
of God, the God of Israel.
9 [a]You, O God, sent a plentiful rain,
Whereby You confirmed Your
inheritance,
When it was weary.
10 Your congregation dwelt in it;
[a]You, O God, provided from Your
goodness for the poor.

11 The Lord gave the word;
Great *was* the company of those who
proclaimed *it:*
12 "Kings[a] of armies flee, they flee,
And she who remains at home divides
the spoil.
13 [a]Though you lie down among the
sheepfolds,
[b]*You will be* like the wings of a dove
covered with silver,
And her feathers with yellow gold."
14 [a]When the Almighty scattered kings in
it,
It was *white* as snow in Zalmon.

15 A mountain of God *is* the mountain of
Bashan;
A mountain *of many* peaks *is* the
mountain of Bashan.
16 Why do you fume with envy, you
mountains of *many* peaks?
[a]*This is* the mountain *which* God desires
to dwell in;
Yes, the LORD will dwell *in it* forever.

17 [a]The chariots of God *are* twenty
thousand,
Even thousands of thousands;
The Lord is among them *as in* Sinai, in
the Holy *Place.*
18 [a]You have ascended on high,
[b]You have led captivity captive;
[c]You have received gifts among men,
Even *from* [d]the rebellious,
[e]That the LORD God might dwell *there.*

19 Blessed *be* the Lord,
Who daily loads us *with benefits,*
The God of our salvation! *Selah*
20 Our God *is* the God of salvation;
And [a]to GOD the Lord *belong* escapes
from death.

21 But [a]God will wound the head of His
enemies,
[b]The hairy scalp of the one who still
goes on in his trespasses.
22 The Lord said, "I will bring [a]back from
Bashan,
I will bring *them* back [b]from the depths
of the sea,

67:6 [a] Lev. 26:4 68:1 [a] Num. 10:35 68:2 [a] [Is. 9:18] [b] Mic. 1:4 68:3 [a] Ps. 32:11 68:4 [a] Deut. 33:26 [b] [Ex. 6:3]
[1] Masoretic Text reads *deserts;* Targum reads *heavens* (compare verse 34 and Isaiah 19:1). 68:5 [a] [Ps. 10:14, 18; 146:9]
68:6 [a] Ps. 107:4–7 [b] Acts 12:6–11 [c] Ps. 107:34 68:7 [a] Ex. 13:21 68:9 [a] Deut. 11:11 68:10 [a] Deut. 26:5 68:12 [a] Josh. 10:16 68:13 [a] Ps. 81:6 [b] Ps. 105:37 68:14 [a] Josh. 10:10 68:16 [a] [Deut. 12:5] 68:17 [a] Deut. 33:2 68:18 [a] Eph. 4:8
[b] Judg. 5:12 [c] Acts 2:4, 33; 10:44–46 [d] [1 Tim. 1:13] [e] Ps. 78:60 68:20 [a] [Deut. 32:39] 68:21 [a] Hab. 3:13 [b] Ps. 55:23
68:22 [a] Num. 21:33 [b] Ex. 14:22

23 [a]That your foot may crush *them*[1] in
blood,
[b]And the tongues of your dogs *may
have* their portion from *your*
enemies."
24 They have seen Your procession,
O God,
The procession of my God, my King,
into the sanctuary.
25 [a]The singers went before, the players on
instruments *followed* after;
Among *them were* the maidens playing
timbrels.
26 Bless God in the congregations,
The Lord, from [a]the fountain of Israel.
27 [a]There *is* little Benjamin, their leader,
The princes of Judah *and* their
company,
The princes of Zebulun *and* the princes
of Naphtali.
28 Your God has [a]commanded[1] your
strength;
Strengthen, O God, what You have done
for us.
29 Because of Your temple at Jerusalem,
[a]Kings will bring presents to You.
30 Rebuke the beasts of the reeds,
[a]The herd of bulls with the calves of the
peoples,
Till everyone [b]submits himself with
pieces of silver.
Scatter the peoples *who* delight in war.
31 [a]Envoys will come out of Egypt;
[b]Ethiopia will quickly [c]stretch out her
hands to God.
32 Sing to God, you [a]kingdoms of the
earth;
Oh, sing praises to the Lord, *Selah*
33 To Him [a]who rides on the heaven of
heavens, *which were* of old!
Indeed, He sends out His voice, a
[b]mighty voice.
34 [a]Ascribe strength to God;
His excellence *is* over Israel,
And His strength *is* in the clouds.
35 O God, [a]*You are* more awesome than
Your holy places.
The God of Israel *is* He who gives
strength and power to *His* people.

Blessed *be* God!

PSALM 69

An Urgent Plea for Help in Trouble

To the Chief Musician. Set to "The Lilies."[1]
A Psalm of David.

1 Save me, O God!
For [a]the waters have come up to *my*
neck.
2 [a]I sink in deep mire,
Where *there is* no standing;
I have come into deep waters,
Where the floods overflow me.
3 [a]I am weary with my crying;
My throat is dry;
[b]My eyes fail while I wait for my God.

4 Those who [a]hate me without a cause
Are more than the hairs of my head;
They are mighty who would destroy me,
Being my enemies wrongfully;
Though I have stolen nothing,
I *still* must restore *it*.

5 O God, You know my foolishness;
And my sins are not hidden from You.
6 Let not those who wait for You, O Lord
GOD of hosts, be ashamed because
of me;
Let not those who seek You be
confounded because of me, O God of
Israel.
7 Because for Your sake I have borne
reproach;
Shame has covered my face.
8 [a]I have become a stranger to my
brothers,
And an alien to my mother's children;
9 [a]Because zeal for Your house has eaten
me up,
[b]And the reproaches of those who
reproach You have fallen on me.
10 When I wept *and chastened* my soul
with fasting,
That became my reproach.
11 I also made sackcloth my garment;
I became a byword to them.
12 Those who sit in the gate speak
against me,
And I *am* the song of the [a]drunkards.

13 But as for me, my prayer *is* to You,
O LORD, *in* the acceptable time;
O God, in the multitude of Your mercy,
Hear me in the truth of Your salvation.

68:23 [a] Ps. 58:10 [b] 1 Kin. 21:19 [1] Septuagint, Syriac, Targum, and Vulgate read *you may dip your foot.* **68:25** [a] 1 Chr. 13:8 **68:26** [a] Deut. 33:28 **68:27** [a] 1 Sam. 9:21 **68:28** [a] Is. 26:12 [1] Septuagint, Syriac, Targum, and Vulgate read *Command, O God.* **68:29** [a] Ps. 45:12; 72:10 **68:30** [a] Ps. 22:12 [b] 2 Sam. 8:2 **68:31** [a] Is. 19:19–23 [b] Is. 45:14 [c] Ps. 44:20 **68:32** [a] [Ps. 67:3, 4] **68:33** [a] Ps. 18:10 [b] Ps. 46:6 **68:34** [a] Ps. 29:1 **68:35** [a] Ps. 76:12 **69:title** [1] Hebrew *Shoshannim* **69:1** [a] Jon. 2:5 **69:2** [a] Ps. 40:2 **69:3** [a] Ps. 6:6 [b] Ps. 119:82, 123 **69:4** [a] John 15:25 **69:8** [a] Is. 53:3 **69:9** [a] John 2:17 [b] Rom. 15:3 **69:12** [a] Job 30:9

PEACE NOTE

We find that happiness is one of the natural outcomes of following Christ!

14 Deliver me out of the mire,
And let me not sink;
Let me be delivered from those who
hate me,
And out of the deep waters.
15 Let not the floodwater overflow me,
Nor let the deep swallow me up;
And let not the pit shut its mouth
on me.

16 Hear me, O LORD, for Your
lovingkindness *is* good;
Turn to me according to the multitude
of Your tender mercies.
17 And do not hide Your face from Your
servant,
For I am in trouble;
Hear me speedily.
18 Draw near to my soul, *and* redeem it;
Deliver me because of my enemies.

19 You know [a]my reproach, my shame,
and my dishonor;
My adversaries *are* all before You.
20 Reproach has broken my heart,
And I am full of heaviness;
[a]I looked *for someone* to take pity, but
there was none;
And for [b]comforters, but I found
none.
21 They also gave me gall for my food,
[a]And for my thirst they gave me vinegar
to drink.

22 [a]Let their table become a snare before
them,
And their well-being a trap.
23 [a]Let their eyes be darkened, so that they
do not see;
And make their loins shake
continually.
24 [a]Pour out Your indignation upon them,
And let Your wrathful anger take hold
of them.
25 [a]Let their dwelling place be desolate;
Let no one live in their tents.
26 For they persecute the *ones* [a]You have
struck,
And talk of the grief of those You have
wounded.
27 [a]Add iniquity to their iniquity,
[b]And let them not come into Your
righteousness.
28 Let them [a]be blotted out of the book of
the living,
[b]And not be written with the righteous.

29 But I *am* poor and sorrowful;
Let Your salvation, O God, set me up on
high.
30 [a]I will praise the name of God with a
song,
And will magnify Him with
thanksgiving.
31 [a]*This* also shall please the LORD better
than an ox *or* bull,
Which has horns and hooves.
32 [a]The humble shall see *this and* be
glad;
And you who seek God, [b]your hearts
shall live.
33 For the LORD hears the poor,
And does not despise [a]His prisoners.

34 [a]Let heaven and earth praise Him,
The seas [b]and everything that moves in
them.
35 [a]For God will save Zion
And build the cities of Judah,
That they may dwell there and
possess it.
36 Also, [a]the descendants of His servants
shall inherit it,
And those who love His name shall
dwell in it.

PSALM 70

Prayer for Relief from Adversaries

To the Chief Musician. *A Psalm* of David.
[a]To bring to remembrance.

1 *Make haste,* [a]O God, to deliver me!
Make haste to help me, O LORD!

69:19 [a] Ps. 22:6, 7 **69:20** [a] Is. 63:5 [b] Job 16:2 **69:21** [a] Matt. 27:34, 48 **69:22** [a] Rom. 11:9, 10 **69:23** [a] Is. 6:9, 10 **69:24** [a] [1 Thess. 2:16] **69:25** [a] Matt. 23:38 **69:26** [a] [Is. 53:4] **69:27** [a] [Rom. 1:28] [b] [Is. 26:10] **69:28** [a] [Ex. 32:32] [b] Ezek. 13:9 **69:30** [a] [Ps. 28:7] **69:31** [a] Ps. 50:13, 14, 23; 51:16 **69:32** [a] Ps. 34:2 [b] Ps. 22:26 **69:33** [a] Eph. 3:1 **69:34** [a] Ps. 96:11 [b] Is. 55:12 **69:35** [a] Is. 44:26 **69:36** [a] Ps. 102:28 **70:title** [a] Ps. 38:title **70:1** [a] Ps. 40:13–17

2 [a]Let them be ashamed and confounded
Who seek my life;
Let them be turned back[1] and confused
Who desire my hurt.
3 [a]Let them be turned back because of
their shame,
Who say, "Aha, aha!"

4 Let all those who seek You rejoice and
be glad in You;
And let those who love Your salvation
say continually,
"Let God be magnified!"

5 [a]But I *am* poor and needy;
[b]Make haste to me, O God!
You *are* my help and my deliverer;
O LORD, do not delay.

PSALM 71

God the Rock of Salvation

1 In [a]You, O LORD, I put my trust;
Let me never be put to shame.
2 [a]Deliver me in Your righteousness, and
cause me to escape;
[b]Incline Your ear to me, and save me.
3 [a]Be my strong refuge,
To which I may resort continually;
You have given the [b]commandment to
save me,
For You *are* my rock and my fortress.

4 [a]Deliver me, O my God, out of the hand
of the wicked,
Out of the hand of the unrighteous and
cruel man.
5 For You are [a]my hope, O Lord GOD;
You are my trust from my youth.
6 [a]By You I have been upheld from birth;
You are He who took me out of my
mother's womb.
My praise *shall be* continually of You.

7 [a]I have become as a wonder to many,
But You *are* my strong refuge.
8 Let [a]my mouth be filled *with* Your praise
And with Your glory all the day.

9 Do not cast me off in the time of old age;
Do not forsake me when my strength
fails.
10 For my enemies speak against me;
And those who lie in wait for my life
[a]take counsel together,
11 Saying, "God has forsaken him;
Pursue and take him, for *there is* none
to deliver *him*."

12 [a]O God, do not be far from me;
O my God, [b]make haste to help me!
13 Let them be confounded *and* consumed
Who are adversaries of my life;
Let them be covered *with* reproach and
dishonor
Who seek my hurt.

14 But I will hope continually,
And will praise You yet more and more.
15 My mouth shall tell of Your righteousness
And Your salvation all the day,
For I do not know *their* limits.
16 I will go in the strength of the Lord GOD;
I will make mention of Your
righteousness, of Yours only.

17 O God, You have taught me from my
[a]youth;
And to this *day* I declare Your
wondrous works.
18 Now also [a]when *I am* old and grayheaded,
O God, do not forsake me,
Until I declare Your strength to *this*
generation,
Your power to everyone *who* is to come.

19 Also [a]Your righteousness, O God, *is*
very high,
You who have done great things;
[b]O God, who *is* like You?
20 [a]*You,* who have shown me great and
severe troubles,
[b]Shall revive me again,
And bring me up again from the
depths of the earth.
21 You shall increase my greatness,
And comfort me on every side.

22 Also [a]with the lute I will praise You—
And Your faithfulness, O my God!
To You I will sing with the harp,
O [b]Holy One of Israel.
23 My lips shall greatly rejoice when I sing
to You,
And [a]my soul, which You have redeemed.
24 My tongue also shall talk of Your
righteousness all the day long;
For they are confounded,
For they are brought to shame
Who seek my hurt.

70:2 [a] Ps. 35:4, 26 [1] Following Masoretic Text, Septuagint, Targum, and Vulgate; some Hebrew manuscripts and Syriac read *be appalled* (compare 40:15). **70:3** [a] Ps. 40:15 **70:5** [a] Ps. 72:12, 13 [b] Ps. 141:1 **71:1** [a] Ps. 25:2, 3 **71:2** [a] Ps. 31:1 [b] Ps. 17:6 **71:3** [a] Ps. 31:2, 3 [b] Ps. 44:4 **71:4** [a] Ps. 140:1, 3 **71:5** [a] Jer. 14:8; 17:7, 13, 17; 50:7 **71:6** [a] Ps. 22:9, 10 **71:7** [a] Is. 8:18 **71:8** [a] Ps. 35:28 **71:10** [a] 2 Sam. 17:1 **71:12** [a] Ps. 35:22 [b] Ps. 70:1 **71:17** [a] Deut. 4:5; 6:7 **71:18** [a] [Is. 46:4] **71:19** [a] Ps. 57:10 [b] Ps. 35:10 **71:20** [a] Ps. 60:3 [b] Hos. 6:1, 2 **71:22** [a] Ps. 92:1–3 [b] 2 Kin. 19:22 **71:23** [a] Ps. 103:4

PSALM 72

Glory and Universality of the Messiah's Reign

A Psalm [a]of Solomon.

1 Give the king Your judgments, O God,
And Your righteousness to the king's Son.
2 [a]He will judge Your people with righteousness,
And Your poor with justice.
3 [a]The mountains will bring peace to the people,
And the little hills, by righteousness.
4 [a]He will bring justice to the poor of the people;
He will save the children of the needy,
And will break in pieces the oppressor.

5 They shall fear You[1]
[a]As long as the sun and moon endure,
Throughout all generations.
6 [a]He shall come down like rain upon the grass before mowing,
Like showers *that* water the earth.
7 In His days the righteous shall flourish,
[a]And abundance of peace,
Until the moon is no more.

8 [a]He shall have dominion also from sea to sea,
And from the River to the ends of the earth.
9 [a]Those who dwell in the wilderness will bow before Him,
[b]And His enemies will lick the dust.
10 [a]The kings of Tarshish and of the isles
Will bring presents;
The kings of Sheba and Seba
Will offer gifts.
11 [a]Yes, all kings shall fall down before Him;
All nations shall serve Him.

12 For He [a]will deliver the needy when he cries,
The poor also, and *him* who has no helper.
13 He will spare the poor and needy,
And will save the souls of the needy.
14 He will redeem their life from oppression and violence;
And [a]precious shall be their blood in His sight.
15 And He shall live;
And the gold of [a]Sheba will be given to Him;
Prayer also will be made for Him continually,
And daily He shall be praised.

72:title [a] Ps. 127:title **72:2** [a] [Is. 9:7; 11:2–5; 32:1] **72:3** [a] Ps. 85:10 **72:4** [a] Is. 11:4 **72:5** [a] Ps. 72:7, 17; 89:36 [1] Following Masoretic Text and Targum; Septuagint and Vulgate read *They shall continue.* **72:6** [a] Hos. 6:3 **72:7** [a] Is. 2:4 **72:8** [a] Ex. 23:31 **72:9** [a] Is. 23:13 [b] Is. 49:23 **72:10** [a] 2 Chr. 9:21 **72:11** [a] Is. 49:23 **72:12** [a] Job 29:12 **72:14** [a] [Ps. 116:15] **72:15** [a] Is. 60:6

NO MATTER THE TERRAIN

The mountains will bring peace to the people, and the little hills, by righteousness.

PSALM 72:3

King Solomon, David's son, wrote this psalm. Although Solomon is famous for his collection of sayings in the Book of Proverbs, the great monarch was also a writer of psalms and songs. In the first verse of Psalm 72, Solomon asked for God's "judgments" and "righteousness." He wanted wisdom in order to govern the people of Israel wisely and justly. This is the very request Solomon made when God spoke to him in a dream and invited him to ask for anything he desired. Solomon chose wisdom. God was pleased with the king's request and gave him "a wise and understanding heart" (1 Kin. 3:12).

Throughout Psalm 72, Solomon related God's care for the land (rainfall, sunshine, abundant grain) to His care for His people. "The mountains will bring peace to the people" (v. 3), "the righteous shall flourish," and there shall be "abundance of peace" (v. 7). All these things God will provide His people, but the psalmist stated that these things would come "by righteousness" (v. 3). God is generous, providing what we need, so that we may enjoy His peace, but this generosity presupposes righteous living.

16 There will be an abundance of grain in
the earth,
On the top of the mountains;
Its fruit shall wave like Lebanon;
[a]And *those* of the city shall flourish like
grass of the earth.

17 [a]His name shall endure forever;
His name shall continue as long as
the sun.
And [b]*men* shall be blessed in Him;
[c]All nations shall call Him blessed.

18 [a]Blessed *be* the LORD God, the God of
Israel,
[b]Who only does wondrous things!
19 And [a]blessed *be* His glorious name
forever!
[b]And let the whole earth be filled *with*
His glory.
Amen and Amen.

20 The prayers of David the son of Jesse
are ended.

BOOK THREE

Psalms 73–89

PSALM 73

The Tragedy of the Wicked,
and the Blessedness of Trust in God

A Psalm of [a]Asaph.

1 Truly God *is* good to Israel,
To such as are pure in heart.
2 But as for me, my feet had almost
stumbled;
My steps had nearly [a]slipped.
3 [a]For I *was* envious of the boastful,
When I saw the prosperity of the
[b]wicked.

4 For *there are* no pangs in their
death,
But their strength *is* firm.
5 [a]They *are* not in trouble *as other* men,
Nor are they plagued like *other* men.
6 Therefore pride serves as their
necklace;
Violence covers them [a]*like* a garment.
7 [a]Their eyes bulge[1] with abundance;
They have more than heart could
wish.
8 [a]They scoff and speak wickedly
concerning oppression;
They [b]speak loftily.
9 They set their mouth [a]against the
heavens,
And their tongue walks through the
earth.

10 Therefore his people return here,
[a]And waters of a full *cup* are drained by
them.
11 And they say, [a]"How does God know?
And is there knowledge in the Most
High?"
12 Behold, these *are* the ungodly,
Who are always at ease;
They increase *in* riches.
13 Surely I have cleansed my heart *in*
[a]vain,
And washed my hands in innocence.
14 For all day long I have been plagued,
And chastened every morning.

15 If I had said, "I will speak thus,"
Behold, I would have been untrue to
the generation of Your children.
16 When I thought *how* to understand
this,
It *was* too painful for me—
17 Until I went into the sanctuary of God;
Then I understood their [a]end.

18 Surely [a]You set them in slippery places;
You cast them down to destruction.
19 Oh, how they are *brought* to desolation,
as in a moment!
They are utterly consumed with
terrors.
20 As a dream when *one* awakes,
So, Lord, when You awake,
You shall despise their image.

21 Thus my heart was grieved,
And I was vexed in my mind.
22 [a]I *was* so foolish and ignorant;
I was *like* a beast before You.
23 Nevertheless I *am* continually with
You;
You hold *me* by my right hand.
24 [a]You will guide me with Your counsel,
And afterward receive me *to* glory.

25 [a]Whom have I in heaven *but You?*
And *there is* none upon earth *that* I
desire besides You.

72:16 [a] 1 Kin. 4:20 **72:17** [a] [Ps. 89:36] [b] [Gen. 12:3] [c] Luke 1:48 **72:18** [a] 1 Chr. 29:10 [b] Ex. 15:11 **72:19** [a] [Neh. 9:5] [b] Num. 14:21 **73:title** [a] Ps. 50:title **73:2** [a] Job 12:5 **73:3** [a] Ps. 37:1, 7 [b] Job 21:5–16 **73:5** [a] Job 21:9 **73:6** [a] Ps. 109:18 **73:7** [a] Jer. 5:28 [1] Targum reads *face bulges;* Septuagint, Syriac, and Vulgate read *iniquity bulges.* **73:8** [a] Ps. 53:1 [b] 2 Pet. 2:18 **73:9** [a] Rev. 13:6 **73:10** [a] [Ps. 75:8] **73:11** [a] Job 22:13 **73:13** [a] Job 21:15; 35:3 **73:17** [a] [Ps. 37:38; 55:23] **73:18** [a] Ps. 35:6 **73:22** [a] Ps. 92:6 **73:24** [a] Ps. 32:8; 48:14 **73:25** [a] [Phil. 3:8]

26 [a]My flesh and my heart fail;
But God *is* the strength of my heart and my [b]portion forever.
27 For indeed, [a]those who are far from You shall perish;
You have destroyed all those who desert You for harlotry.
28 But *it is* good for me to [a]draw near to God;
I have put my trust in the Lord GOD,
That I may [b]declare all Your works.

PEACE NOTE

Instead of waiting to feel perfectly close to God, start moving toward Him and believe that He is doing the same.

PSALM 73:28

PSALM 74

A Plea for Relief from Oppressors

A Contemplation[1] of Asaph.

1 O God, why have You cast *us* off forever?
Why does Your anger smoke against the sheep of Your pasture?
2 Remember Your congregation, *which* You have purchased of old,
The tribe of Your inheritance, *which* You have redeemed—
This Mount Zion where You have dwelt.
3 Lift up Your feet to the perpetual desolations.
The enemy has damaged everything in the sanctuary.
4 [a]Your enemies roar in the midst of Your meeting place;
[b]They set up their banners *for* signs.
5 *They seem like men who lift up*
Axes among the thick trees.
6 And now they break down its carved work, all at once,
With axes and hammers.
7 They have set fire to Your sanctuary;
They have defiled the dwelling place of Your name to the ground.
8 [a]They said in their hearts,
"Let us destroy them altogether."
They have burned up all the meeting places of God in the land.

9 We do not see our signs;
[a]*There is* no longer any prophet;
Nor *is there* any among us who knows how long.
10 O God, how long will the adversary reproach?
Will the enemy blaspheme Your name forever?
11 [a]Why do You withdraw Your hand, even Your right hand?
Take it out of Your bosom and destroy *them*.
12 For [a]God *is* my King from of old,
Working salvation in the midst of the earth.
13 [a]You divided the sea by Your strength;
You broke the heads of the sea serpents in the waters.
14 You broke the heads of Leviathan in pieces,
And gave him *as* food to the people inhabiting the wilderness.
15 [a]You broke open the fountain and the flood;
[b]You dried up mighty rivers.
16 The day *is* Yours, the night also *is* [a]Yours;
[b]You have prepared the light and the sun.
17 You have [a]set all the borders of the earth;
[b]You have made summer and winter.

18 Remember this, *that* the enemy has reproached, O LORD,
And *that* a foolish people has blasphemed Your name.
19 Oh, do not deliver the life of Your turtledove to the wild beast!
Do not forget the life of Your poor forever.
20 [a]Have respect to the covenant;
For the dark places of the earth are full of the haunts of cruelty.
21 Oh, do not let the oppressed return ashamed!
Let the poor and needy praise Your name.

73:26 [a] Ps. 84:2 [b] Ps. 16:5 73:27 [a] [Ps. 119:155] 73:28 [a] [Heb. 10:22] [b] 2 Cor. 4:13 74:title [1] Hebrew *Maschil* 74:4 [a] Lam. 2:7 [b] Num. 2:2 74:8 [a] Ps. 83:4 74:9 [a] Amos 8:11 74:11 [a] Lam. 2:3 74:12 [a] Ps. 44:4 74:13 [a] Ex. 14:21 74:15 [a] Ex. 17:5, 6 [b] Josh. 2:10; 3:13 74:16 [a] Job 38:12 [b] Gen. 1:14–18 74:17 [a] Acts 17:26 [b] Gen. 8:22 74:20 [a] Lev. 26:44, 45

22 Arise, O God, plead Your own cause;
Remember how the foolish man
reproaches You daily.
23 Do not forget the voice of Your
enemies;
The tumult of those who rise up
against You increases continually.

PSALM 75

Thanksgiving for God's Righteous Judgment

To the Chief Musician. Set to [a]"Do Not Destroy."[1] A Psalm of Asaph. A Song.

1 We give thanks to You, O God, we give
thanks!
For Your wondrous works declare *that*
Your name is near.

2 "When I choose the proper time,
I will judge uprightly.
3 The earth and all its inhabitants are
dissolved;
I set up its pillars firmly. *Selah*

4 "I said to the boastful, 'Do not deal
boastfully,'
And to the wicked, [a]'Do not lift up the
horn.
5 Do not lift up your horn on high;
Do *not* speak with a stiff neck.' "

6 For exaltation *comes* neither from the
east
Nor from the west nor from the south.
7 But [a]God *is* the Judge:
[b]He puts down one,
And exalts another.
8 For [a]in the hand of the LORD *there is* a
cup,
And the wine is red;
It is fully mixed, and He pours
it out;
Surely its dregs shall all the wicked of
the earth
Drain *and* drink down.

9 But I will declare forever,
I will sing praises to the God of
Jacob.

10 "All[a] the horns of the wicked I will also
cut off,
But [b]the horns of the righteous shall be
[c]exalted."

PSALM 76

The Majesty of God in Judgment

To the Chief Musician. On stringed instruments.[1] A Psalm of Asaph. A Song.

1 In [a]Judah God *is* known;
His name *is* great in Israel.
2 In Salem[1] also is His tabernacle,
And His dwelling place in Zion.
3 There He broke the arrows of the bow,
The shield and sword of battle. *Selah*

4 You *are* more glorious and excellent
[a]*Than* the mountains of prey.
5 [a]The stouthearted were plundered;
[b]They have sunk into their sleep;
And none of the mighty men have
found the use of their hands.
6 [a]At Your rebuke, O God of Jacob,
Both the chariot and horse were cast
into a dead sleep.

7 You, Yourself, *are* to be feared;
And [a]who may stand in Your presence
When once You are angry?
8 [a]You caused judgment to be heard from
heaven;
[b]The earth feared and was still,
9 When God [a]arose to judgment,
To deliver all the oppressed of the
earth. *Selah*

10 [a]Surely the wrath of man shall praise
You;
With the remainder of wrath You shall
gird Yourself.

11 [a]Make vows to the LORD your God, and
pay *them;*
[b]Let all who are around Him bring
presents to Him who ought to be
feared.
12 He shall cut off the spirit of princes;
[a]*He is* awesome to the kings of the
earth.

PSALM 77

The Consoling Memory of God's Redemptive Works

To the Chief Musician. [a]To Jeduthun. A Psalm of Asaph.

1 I cried out to God with my voice—
To God with my voice;
And He gave ear to me.

75:title [a] Ps. 57:title [1] Hebrew *Al Tashcheth* **75:4** [a] [1 Sam. 2:3] **75:7** [a] Ps. 50:6 [b] 1 Sam. 2:7 **75:8** [a] Jer. 25:15 **75:10** [a] Jer. 48:25 [b] Ps. 89:17; 148:14 [c] 1 Sam. 2:1 **76:title** [1] Hebrew *neginoth* **76:1** [a] Ps. 48:1, 3 **76:2** [1] That is, Jerusalem **76:4** [a] Ezek. 38:12 **76:5** [a] Is. 10:12; 46:12 [b] Ps. 13:3 **76:6** [a] Ex. 15:1–21 **76:7** [a] [Nah. 1:6] **76:8** [a] Ex. 19:9 [b] 2 Chr. 20:29 **76:9** [a] [Ps. 9:7–9] **76:10** [a] Rom. 9:17 **76:11** [a] [Eccl. 5:4–6] [b] 2 Chr. 32:22, 23 **76:12** [a] Ps. 68:35 **77:title** [a] Ps. 39:title

PEACE NOTE

We sound like Asaph with all our whys. Put an exclamation mark next to a Bible promise in your mind when questions arise.

PSALM 77:1

2 In the day of my trouble I sought the Lord;
My hand was stretched out in the night without ceasing;
My soul refused to be comforted.
3 I remembered God, and was troubled;
I complained, and my spirit was overwhelmed. *Selah*

4 You hold my eyelids *open;*
I am so troubled that I cannot speak.
5 I have considered the days of old,
The years of ancient times.
6 I call to remembrance my song in the night;
I meditate within my heart,
And my spirit makes diligent search.

7 Will the Lord cast off forever?
And will He be favorable no more?
8 Has His mercy ceased forever?
Has *His* [a]promise failed forevermore?
9 Has God forgotten to be gracious?
Has He in anger shut up His tender mercies? *Selah*

10 And I said, "This *is* my anguish;
But I will remember the years of the right hand of the Most High."
11 I will remember the works of the LORD;
Surely I will remember Your wonders of old.
12 I will also meditate on all Your work,
And talk of Your deeds.
13 Your way, O God, *is in the* [a]*sanctuary;*
Who *is* so great a God as *our* God?
14 You *are* the God who does wonders;
You have declared Your strength among the peoples.
15 You have with *Your* arm redeemed Your people,
The sons of Jacob and Joseph. *Selah*

16 The waters saw You, O God;
The waters saw You, they were [a]afraid;
The depths also trembled.
17 The clouds poured out water;
The skies sent out a sound;
Your arrows also flashed about.
18 The voice of Your thunder *was* in the whirlwind;
The lightnings lit up the world;
The earth trembled and shook.
19 Your way *was* in the sea,
Your path in the great waters,
And Your footsteps were not known.
20 You led Your people like a flock
By the hand of Moses and Aaron.

PSALM 78

God's Kindness to Rebellious Israel

A [a]Contemplation[1] of Asaph.

1 Give ear, O my people, *to* my law;
Incline your ears to the words of my mouth.
2 I will open my mouth in a [a]parable;
I will utter dark sayings of old,
3 Which we have heard and known,
And our fathers have told us.
4 [a]We will not hide *them* from their children,
[b]Telling to the generation to come the praises of the LORD,
And His strength and His wonderful works that He has done.

5 For [a]He established a testimony in Jacob,
And appointed a law in Israel,
Which He commanded our fathers,
That [b]they should make them known to their children;
6 [a]That the generation to come might know *them,*
The children *who* would be born,
That they may arise and declare *them* to their children,
7 That they may set their hope in God,
And not forget the works of God,
But keep His commandments;
8 And [a]may not be like their fathers,
[b]A stubborn and rebellious generation,

77:8 [a] [2 Pet. 3:8, 9] 77:13 [a] Ps. 73:17 77:16 [a] Ex. 14:21 78:title [a] Ps. 74:title [1] Hebrew *Maschil* 78:2 [a] Matt. 13:34, 35
78:4 [a] Deut. 4:9; 6:7 [b] Ex. 13:8, 14 78:5 [a] Ps. 147:19 [b] Deut. 4:9; 11:19 78:6 [a] Ps. 102:18 78:8 [a] 2 Kin. 17:14
[b] Ex. 32:9

A generation [c]*that* did not set its heart
aright,
And whose spirit was not faithful to God.
9 The children of Ephraim, *being* armed
and carrying bows,
Turned back in the day of battle.
10 [a]They did not keep the covenant of God;
They refused to walk in His law,
11 And [a]forgot His works
And His wonders that He had shown
them.

12 [a]Marvelous things He did in the sight of
their fathers,
In the land of Egypt, [b]*in* the field of
Zoan.
13 [a]He divided the sea and caused them to
pass through;
And [b]He made the waters stand up like
a heap.
14 [a]In the daytime also He led them with
the cloud,
And all the night with a light of fire.
15 [a]He split the rocks in the wilderness,
And gave *them* drink in abundance like
the depths.
16 He also brought [a]streams out of the
rock,
And caused waters to run down like
rivers.

17 But they sinned even more against Him
By [a]rebelling against the Most High in
the wilderness.
18 And [a]they tested God in their heart
By asking for the food of their fancy.
19 [a]Yes, they spoke against God:
They said, "Can God prepare a table in
the wilderness?
20 [a]Behold, He struck the rock,
So that the waters gushed out,
And the streams overflowed.
Can He give bread also?
Can He provide meat for His people?"

21 Therefore the LORD heard *this* and
[a]was furious;
So a fire was kindled against Jacob,
And anger also came up against Israel,
22 Because they [a]did not believe in God,
And did not trust in His salvation.
23 Yet He had commanded the clouds above,
[a]And opened the doors of heaven,
24 [a]Had rained down manna on them to
eat,
And given them of the bread of [b]heaven.
25 Men ate angels' food;
He sent them food to the full.

26 [a]He caused an east wind to blow in the
heavens;
And by His power He brought in the
south wind.
27 He also rained meat on them like the
dust,
Feathered fowl like the sand of the
seas;
28 And He let *them* fall in the midst of
their camp,
All around their dwellings.
29 [a]So they ate and were well filled,
For He gave them their own desire.
30 They were not deprived of their
craving;
But [a]while their food *was* still in their
mouths,
31 The wrath of God came against them,
And slew the stoutest of them,
And struck down the choice *men* of
Israel.

32 In spite of this [a]they still sinned,
And [b]did not believe in His wondrous
works.
33 [a]Therefore their days He consumed in
futility,
And their years in fear.

34 [a]When He slew them, then they sought
Him;
And they returned and sought
earnestly for God.
35 Then they remembered that [a]God *was*
their rock,
And the Most High God [b]their
Redeemer.
36 Nevertheless they [a]flattered Him with
their mouth,
And they lied to Him with their tongue;
37 For their heart was not steadfast with
Him,
Nor were they faithful in His covenant.
38 [a]But He, *being* full of [b]compassion,
forgave *their* iniquity,
And did not destroy *them.*
Yes, many a time [c]He turned His anger
away,

78:8 [c] Ps. 78:37 **78:10** [a] 2 Kin. 17:15 **78:11** [a] Ps. 106:13 **78:12** [a] Ex. 7—12 [b] Num. 13:22 **78:13** [a] Ex. 14:21 [b] Ex. 15:8 **78:14** [a] Ex. 13:21 **78:15** [a] Num. 20:11 **78:16** [a] Num. 20:8, 10, 11 **78:17** [a] Heb. 3:16 **78:18** [a] Ex. 16:2 **78:19** [a] Num. 11:4; 20:3; 21:5 **78:20** [a] Num. 20:11 **78:21** [a] Num. 11:1 **78:22** [a] [Heb. 3:18] **78:23** [a] [Mal. 3:10] **78:24** [a] Ex. 16:4 [b] John 6:31 **78:26** [a] Num. 11:31 **78:29** [a] Num. 11:19, 20 **78:30** [a] Num. 11:33 **78:32** [a] Num. 14:16, 17 [b] Num. 14:11 **78:33** [a] Num. 14:29, 35 **78:34** [a] [Hos. 5:15] **78:35** [a] [Deut. 32:4, 15] [b] Is. 41:14; 44:6; 63:9 **78:36** [a] Ezek. 33:31 **78:38** [a] [Num. 14:18–20] [b] Ex. 34:6 [c] [Is. 48:9]

And [d]did not stir up all His wrath;
39 For [a]He remembered [b]that they *were* *but* flesh,
[c]A breath that passes away and does not come again.

40 How often they [a]provoked Him in the wilderness,
And grieved Him in the desert!
41 Yes, [a]again and again they tempted God,
And limited the Holy One of Israel.
42 They did not remember His power:
The day when He redeemed them from the enemy,
43 When He worked His signs in Egypt,
And His wonders in the field of Zoan;
44 [a]Turned their rivers into blood,
And their streams, that they could not drink.
45 [a]He sent swarms of flies among them, which devoured them,
And [b]frogs, which destroyed them.
46 He also gave their crops to the caterpillar,
And their labor to the [a]locust.
47 [a]He destroyed their vines with hail,
And their sycamore trees with frost.
48 He also gave up their [a]cattle to the hail,
And their flocks to fiery lightning.
49 He cast on them the fierceness of His anger,
Wrath, indignation, and trouble,
By sending angels of destruction *among them.*
50 He made a path for His anger;
He did not spare their soul from death,
But gave their life over to the plague,
51 And destroyed all the [a]firstborn in Egypt,
The first of *their* strength in the tents of Ham.
52 But He [a]made His own people go forth like sheep,
And guided them in the wilderness like a flock;
53 And He [a]led them on safely, so that they did not fear;
But the sea [b]overwhelmed their enemies.
54 And He brought them to His [a]holy border,
This mountain [b]*which* His right hand had acquired.
55 [a]He also drove out the nations before them,
[b]Allotted them an inheritance by survey,
And made the tribes of Israel dwell in their tents.

56 [a]Yet they tested and provoked the Most High God,
And did not keep His testimonies,
57 But [a]turned back and acted unfaithfully like their fathers;
They were turned aside [b]like a deceitful bow.
58 [a]For they provoked Him to anger with their [b]high places,
And moved Him to jealousy with their carved images.
59 When God heard *this,* He was furious,
And greatly abhorred Israel,
60 [a]So that He forsook the tabernacle of Shiloh,
The tent He had placed among men,
61 [a]And delivered His strength into captivity,
And His glory into the enemy's hand.
62 [a]He also gave His people over to the sword,
And was furious with His inheritance.
63 The fire consumed their young men,
And [a]their maidens were not given in marriage.
64 [a]Their priests fell by the sword,
And [b]their widows made no lamentation.

65 Then the Lord awoke as *from* sleep,
[a]Like a mighty man who shouts because of wine.
66 And [a]He beat back His enemies;
He put them to a perpetual reproach.

67 Moreover He rejected the tent of Joseph,
And did not choose the tribe of Ephraim,
68 But chose the tribe of Judah,
Mount Zion [a]which He loved.
69 And He built His [a]sanctuary like the heights,
Like the earth which He has established forever.
70 [a]He also chose David His servant,
And took him from the sheepfolds;
71 From following [a]the ewes that had young He brought him,
[b]To shepherd Jacob His people,
And Israel His inheritance.

78:38 [d]1 Kin. 21:29 **78:39** [a]Job 10:9 [b]John 3:6 [c][Job 7:7, 16] **78:40** [a]Heb. 3:16 **78:41** [a]Num. 14:22 **78:44** [a]Ex. 7:20 **78:45** [a]Ex. 8:24 [b]Ex. 8:6 **78:46** [a]Ex. 10:14 **78:47** [a]Ex. 9:23–25 **78:48** [a]Ex. 9:19 **78:51** [a]Ex. 12:29, 30 **78:52** [a]Ps. 77:20 **78:53** [a]Ex. 14:19, 20 [b]Ex. 14:27, 28 **78:54** [a]Ex. 15:17 [b]Ps. 44:3 **78:55** [a]Ps. 44:2 [b]Josh. 13:7; 19:51; 23:4 **78:56** [a]Judg. 2:11–13 **78:57** [a]Ezek. 20:27, 28 [b]Hos. 7:16 **78:58** [a]Judg. 2:12 [b]Deut. 12:2 **78:60** [a]1 Sam. 4:11 **78:61** [a]Judg. 18:30 **78:62** [a]1 Sam. 4:10 **78:63** [a]Jer. 7:34; 16:9; 25:10 **78:64** [a]1 Sam. 4:17; 22:18 [b]Job 27:15; Ezek. 24:23 **78:65** [a]Is. 42:13 **78:66** [a]1 Sam. 5:6 **78:68** [a][Ps. 87:2] **78:69** [a]1 Kin. 6:1–38 **78:70** [a]1 Sam. 16:11, 12 **78:71** [a][Is. 40:11] [b]2 Sam. 5:2

72 So he shepherded them according to
the [a]integrity of his heart,
And guided them by the skillfulness of
his hands.

PSALM 79

A Dirge and a Prayer for Israel, Destroyed by Enemies

A Psalm of Asaph.

1 O God, the nations have come into
[a]Your inheritance;
Your holy temple they have defiled;
[b]They have laid Jerusalem in
heaps.
2 [a]The dead bodies of Your servants
They have given *as* food for the birds of
the heavens,
The flesh of Your saints to the beasts of
the earth.
3 Their blood they have shed like water
all around Jerusalem,
And *there was* no one to bury *them.*
4 We have become a reproach to our
[a]neighbors,
A scorn and derision to those who are
around us.

5 [a]How long, LORD?
Will You be angry forever?
Will Your [b]jealousy burn like fire?
6 [a]Pour out Your wrath on the nations
that [b]do not know You,
And on the kingdoms that [c]do not call
on Your name.
7 For they have devoured Jacob,
And laid waste his dwelling place.

8 [a]Oh, do not remember former iniquities
against us!
Let Your tender mercies come speedily
to meet us,
For we have been brought very
low.
9 Help us, O God of our salvation,
For the glory of Your name;
And deliver us, and provide atonement
for our sins,
[a]For Your name's sake!
10 [a]Why *should* the nations say,
"Where *is* their God?"
Let there be known among the nations
in our sight
The avenging of the blood of Your
servants *which has been* shed.

PEACE NOTE

When an anxiety attack hits, too many Christians go to Google instead of God's Word. No lasting peace will be found there.

11 Let [a]the groaning of the prisoner come
before You;
According to the greatness of Your power
Preserve those who are appointed to die;
12 And return to our neighbors
[a]sevenfold into their bosom
[b]Their reproach with which they have
reproached You, O Lord.

13 So [a]we, Your people and sheep of Your
pasture,
Will give You thanks forever;
[b]We will show forth Your praise to all
generations.

PSALM 80

Prayer for Israel's Restoration

To the Chief Musician. [a]Set to "The Lilies."[1]
A Testimony[2] of Asaph. A Psalm.

1 Give ear, O Shepherd of Israel,
[a]You who lead Joseph [b]like a flock;
You who dwell *between* the cherubim,
[c]shine forth!
2 Before [a]Ephraim, Benjamin, and
Manasseh,
Stir up Your strength,
And come *and* save us!

3 [a]Restore us, O God;
[b]Cause Your face to shine,
And we shall be saved!

4 O LORD God of hosts,
[a]How long will You be angry
Against the prayer of Your people?

78:72 [a] 1 Kin. 9:4 **79:1** [a] Ps. 74:2 [b] Mic. 3:12 **79:2** [a] Jer. 7:33; 19:7; 34:20 **79:4** [a] Ps. 44:13 **79:5** [a] Ps. 74:1, 9 [b] [Zeph. 3:8] **79:6** [a] Jer. 10:25 [b] Is. 45:4, 5 [c] Ps. 53:4 **79:8** [a] Is. 64:9 **79:9** [a] Jer. 14:7, 21 **79:10** [a] Ps. 42:10 **79:11** [a] Ps. 102:20 **79:12** [a] Gen. 4:15 [b] Ps. 74:10, 18, 22 **79:13** [a] Ps. 74:1; 95:7 [b] Is. 43:21 **80:title** [a] Ps. 45:title [1] Hebrew *Shoshannim* [2] Hebrew *Eduth* **80:1** [a] [Ex. 25:20–22] [b] Ps. 77:20 [c] Deut. 33:2 **80:2** [a] Ps. 78:9, 67 **80:3** [a] Lam. 5:21 [b] Num. 6:25 **80:4** [a] Ps. 79:5

5 [a]You have fed them with the bread of tears,
And given them tears to drink in great measure.
6 You have made us a strife to our neighbors,
And our enemies laugh among themselves.

7 Restore us, O God of hosts;
Cause Your face to shine,
And we shall be saved!

8 You have brought [a]a vine out of Egypt;
[b]You have cast out the nations, and planted it.
9 You prepared *room* for it,
And caused it to take deep root,
And it filled the land.
10 The hills were covered with its shadow,
And the mighty cedars with its [a]boughs.
11 She sent out her boughs to the Sea,[1]
And her branches to the River.[2]

12 Why have You [a]broken down her hedges,
So that all who pass by the way pluck her *fruit?*
13 The boar out of the woods uproots it,
And the wild beast of the field devours it.

14 Return, we beseech You, O God of hosts;
[a]Look down from heaven and see,
And visit this vine
15 And the vineyard which Your right hand has planted,
And the branch *that* You made strong [a]for Yourself.
16 *It is* burned with fire, *it is* cut down;
[a]They perish at the rebuke of Your countenance.
17 [a]Let Your hand be upon the man of Your right hand,
Upon the son of man *whom* You made strong for Yourself.
18 Then we will not turn back from You;
Revive us, and we will call upon Your name.

19 Restore us, O LORD God of hosts;
Cause Your face to shine,
And we shall be saved!

PSALM 81

An Appeal for Israel's Repentance

To the Chief Musician. [a]On an instrument of Gath.[1] *A Psalm* of Asaph.

1 Sing aloud to God our strength;
Make a joyful shout to the God of Jacob.
2 Raise a song and strike the timbrel,
The pleasant harp with the lute.

3 Blow the trumpet at the time of the New Moon,
At the full moon, on our solemn feast day.
4 For [a]this *is* a statute for Israel,
A law of the God of Jacob.
5 This He established in Joseph *as* a testimony,
When He went throughout the land of Egypt,
[a]*Where* I heard a language I did not understand.

6 "I removed his shoulder from the burden;
His hands were freed from the baskets.
7 [a]You called in trouble, and I delivered you;
[b]I answered you in the secret place of thunder;
I [c]tested you at the waters of Meribah. *Selah*

8 "Hear,[a] O My people, and I will admonish you!
O Israel, if you will listen to Me!
9 There shall be no [a]foreign god among you;
Nor shall you worship any foreign god.
10 [a]I *am* the LORD your God,
Who brought you out of the land of Egypt;
[b]Open your mouth wide, and I will fill it.

11 "But My people would not heed My voice,
And Israel would *have* [a]none of Me.
12 [a]So I gave them over to their own stubborn heart,
To walk in their own counsels.

13 "Oh,[a] that My people would listen to Me,
That Israel would walk in My ways!
14 I would soon subdue their enemies,
And turn My hand against their adversaries.
15 [a]The haters of the LORD would pretend submission to Him,
But their fate would endure forever.

80:5 [a] Is. 30:20 **80:8** [a] [Is. 5:1, 7] [b] Ps. 44:2 **80:10** [a] Lev. 23:40 **80:11** [1] That is, the Mediterranean [2] That is, the Euphrates **80:12** [a] Is. 5:5 **80:14** [a] Is. 63:15 **80:15** [a] [Is. 49:5] **80:16** [a] [Ps. 39:11] **80:17** [a] Ps. 89:21 **81:title** [a] Ps. 8:title [1] Hebrew *Al Gittith* **81:4** [a] Num. 10:10 **81:5** [a] Ps. 114:1 **81:7** [a] Ex. 2:23; 14:10 [b] Ex. 19:19; 20:18 [c] Ex. 17:6, 7 **81:8** [a] [Ps. 50:7] **81:9** [a] [Is. 43:12] **81:10** [a] Ex. 20:2 [b] Ps. 103:5 **81:11** [a] Deut. 32:15 **81:12** [a] [Acts 7:42] **81:13** [a] [Is. 48:18] **81:15** [a] Rom. 1:30

16 He would [a]have fed them also with the
finest of wheat;
And with honey [b]from the rock I would
have satisfied you."

PSALM 82

A Plea for Justice

A Psalm of Asaph.

1 God [a]stands in the congregation of the
mighty;
He judges among [b]the gods.[1]
2 How long will you judge unjustly,
And [a]show partiality to the wicked?
Selah
3 Defend the poor and fatherless;
Do justice to the afflicted and [a]needy.
4 Deliver the poor and needy;
Free *them* from the hand of the wicked.

5 They do not know, nor do they
understand;
They walk about in darkness;
All the [a]foundations of the earth are
unstable.

6 I said, [a]"You *are* gods,'
And all of you *are* children of the Most
High.
7 But you shall die like men,
And fall like one of the princes."

8 Arise, O God, judge the earth;
[a]For You shall inherit all nations.

PSALM 83

Prayer to Frustrate Conspiracy Against Israel

A Song. A Psalm of Asaph.

1 Do[a] not keep silent, O God!
Do not hold Your peace,
And do not be still, O God!
2 For behold, [a]Your enemies make a
tumult;
And those who hate You have lifted up
their head.
3 They have taken crafty counsel against
Your people,
And consulted together [a]against Your
sheltered ones.
4 They have said, "Come, and [a]let us cut
them off from *being* a nation,
That the name of Israel may be
remembered no more."

PEACE NOTE

The church is central in the healing equation for the multitudes who are seeking peace and joy but struggling with anxiety.

5 For they have consulted together with
one consent;
They form a confederacy against You:
6 [a]The tents of Edom and the
Ishmaelites;
Moab and the Hagrites;
7 Gebal, Ammon, and Amalek;
Philistia with the inhabitants of Tyre;
8 Assyria also has joined with them;
They have helped the children of Lot.
Selah

9 Deal with them as *with* [a]Midian,
As *with* [b]Sisera,
As *with* Jabin at the Brook Kishon,
10 Who perished at En Dor,
[a]*Who* became *as* refuse on the earth.
11 Make their nobles like [a]Oreb and like
Zeeb,
Yes, all their princes like [b]Zebah and
Zalmunna,
12 Who said, "Let us take for ourselves
The pastures of God for a possession."

13 [a]O my God, make them like the whirling
dust,
[b]Like the chaff before the wind!
14 As the fire burns the woods,
And as the flame [a]sets the mountains
on fire,
15 So pursue them with Your tempest,
And frighten them with Your storm.
16 Fill their faces with shame,
That they may seek Your name, O LORD.
17 Let them be confounded and dismayed
forever;

81:16 [a] Deut. 32:14 [b] Job 29:6 **82:1** [a] [2 Chr. 19:6] [b] Ps. 82:6 [1] Hebrew *elohim, mighty ones;* that is, the judges **82:2** [a] [Deut. 1:17] **82:3** [a] [Deut. 24:17] **82:5** [a] Ps. 11:3 **82:6** [a] John 10:34 [1] Hebrew *elohim, mighty ones;* that is, the judges **82:8** [a] [Rev. 11:15] **83:1** [a] Ps. 28:1 **83:2** [a] Ps. 81:15 **83:3** [a] [Ps. 27:5] **83:4** [a] Jer. 11:19; 31:36 **83:6** [a] 2 Chr. 20:1, 10, 11 **83:9** [a] Judg. 7:22 [b] Judg. 4:15–24; 5:20, 21 **83:10** [a] Zeph. 1:17 **83:11** [a] Judg. 7:25 [b] Judg. 8:12–21 **83:13** [a] Is. 17:13 [b] Ps. 35:5 **83:14** [a] Deut. 32:22

Yes, let them be put to shame and
perish,
18 [a]That they may know that You, whose
[b]name alone *is* the LORD,
Are [c]the Most High over all the earth.

PSALM 84

The Blessedness of Dwelling in the House of God

To the Chief Musician. [a]On an instrument of Gath.[1] A Psalm of the sons of Korah.

1 How [a]lovely *is* Your tabernacle,
O LORD of hosts!
2 [a]My soul longs, yes, even faints
For the courts of the LORD;
My heart and my flesh cry out for the
living God.

3 Even the sparrow has found a home,
And the swallow a nest for herself,
Where she may lay her young—
Even Your altars, O LORD of hosts,
My King and my God.
4 Blessed *are* those who dwell in Your
[a]house;
They will still be praising You. *Selah*

5 Blessed *is* the man whose strength *is* in
You,
Whose heart *is* set on pilgrimage.
6 *As they* pass through the Valley [a]of Baca,
They make it a spring;
The rain also covers it with pools.
7 They go [a]from strength to strength;
Each one [b]appears before God in Zion.[1]

8 O LORD God of hosts, hear my prayer;
Give ear, O God of Jacob! *Selah*
9 [a]O God, behold our shield,
And look upon the face of Your
anointed.

10 For a day in Your courts *is* better than a
thousand.
I would rather be a doorkeeper in the
house of my God
Than dwell in the tents of wickedness.
11 For the LORD God *is* [a]a sun and
[b]shield;
The LORD will give grace and glory;
[c]No good *thing* will He withhold
From those who walk uprightly.

12 *O LORD of hosts,*
[a]Blessed *is* the man who trusts in You!

PSALM 85

Prayer that the LORD Will Restore Favor to the Land

To the Chief Musician. A Psalm [a]of the sons of Korah.

1 LORD, You have been favorable to Your
land;
You have [a]brought back the captivity of
Jacob.
2 You have forgiven the iniquity of Your
people;
You have covered all their sin. *Selah*
3 You have taken away all Your wrath;
You have turned from the fierceness of
Your anger.

4 [a]Restore us, O God of our salvation,
And cause Your anger toward us to
cease.
5 [a]Will You be angry with us forever?
Will You prolong Your anger to all
generations?
6 Will You not [a]revive us again,
That Your people may rejoice in
You?
7 Show us Your mercy, LORD,
And grant us Your salvation.

8 I will hear what God the LORD will
speak,
For He will speak peace
To His people and to His saints;
But let them not turn back to folly.
9 Surely [a]His salvation *is* near to those
who fear Him,
[b]That glory may dwell in our land.

PEACE NOTE

The peace of God comes from obedience to God even when the storms of life hit us. The Bible promises, "No good thing will He withhold from those who walk uprightly."

PSALM 84:11

83:18 [a] Ps. 59:13 [b] Ex. 6:3 [c] [Ps. 92:8] **84:title** [a] Ps. 8:title [1] Hebrew *Al Gittith* **84:1** [a] Ps. 27:4; 46:4, 5 **84:2** [a] Ps. 42:1, 2 **84:4** [a] [Ps. 65:4] **84:6** [a] 2 Sam. 5:22–25 **84:7** [a] Prov. 4:18 [b] Deut. 16:16 [1] Septuagint, Syriac, and Vulgate read *The God of gods shall be seen.* **84:9** [a] Gen. 15:1 **84:11** [a] Is. 60:19, 20 [b] Gen. 15:1 [c] Ps. 34:9, 10 **84:12** [a] [Ps. 2:12; 40:4] **85:title** [a] Ps. 42:title **85:1** [a] Joel 3:1 **85:4** [a] Ps. 80:3, 7 **85:5** [a] Ps. 79:5 **85:6** [a] Hab. 3:2 **85:9** [a] Is. 46:13 [b] Zech. 2:5

MERCY AND TRUTH MEET

I will hear what God the LORD will speak, for He will speak peace to His people and to His saints.

PSALM 85:8

This psalm is credited to the "sons of Korah," descendants of the family of Aaron, brother of Moses (see Ex. 6:24). These sons produced several psalms, some dating to the preexilic period, some to the postexilic period when the Jewish people were allowed to return to Jerusalem. Psalm 85 probably alludes to the return: "You have brought back the captivity of Jacob" (v. 1). The psalmists pleaded, "Restore us . . . Show us your mercy, LORD, and grant us Your salvation" (vv. 4, 7).

The writers were confident that God would do as they asked, for they anticipated that He would "speak peace to His people" (v. 8). But this mercy and salvation presuppose a people "who fear Him" (v. 9), that is, a people who respect God and obey Him. "Yes, the LORD will give what is good; and our land will yield its increase" (v. 12), but the giving of good presumes righteousness. As the writers put it, "Mercy and truth have met together; righteousness and peace have kissed" (v. 10). God's mercy is granted to those who live by His truth; God's peace will "kiss" those who are righteous.

On the path to peace, how can you pursue righteousness today?

10 Mercy and truth have met together;
[a]Righteousness and peace have kissed.
11 Truth shall spring out of the earth,
And righteousness shall look down from heaven.
12 [a]Yes, the LORD will give *what is* good;
And our land will yield its increase.
13 Righteousness will go before Him,
And shall make His footsteps *our* pathway.

PSALM 86

Prayer for Mercy, with Meditation on the Excellencies of the LORD

A Prayer of David.

1 Bow down Your ear, O LORD, hear me;
For I *am* poor and needy.
2 Preserve my life, for I *am* holy;
You are my God;
Save Your servant who trusts in You!
3 Be merciful to me, O Lord,
For I cry to You all day long.
4 Rejoice the soul of Your servant,
[a]For to You, O Lord, I lift up my soul.
5 For [a]You, Lord, *are* good, and ready to forgive,
And abundant in mercy to all those who call upon You.
6 Give ear, O LORD, to my prayer;
And attend to the voice of my supplications.
7 In the day of my trouble I will call upon You,
For You will answer me.

8 [a]Among the gods *there is* none like You, O Lord;
Nor *are there any works* like Your works.
9 All nations whom You have made
Shall come and worship before You, O Lord,
And shall glorify Your name.
10 For You *are* great, and [a]do wondrous things;
[b]You alone *are* God.

11 [a]Teach me Your way, O LORD;
I will walk in Your truth;
Unite my heart to fear Your name.
12 I will praise You, O Lord my God, with all my heart,
And I will glorify Your name forevermore.
13 For great *is* Your mercy toward me,
And You have delivered my soul from the depths of Sheol.

85:10 [a] Ps. 72:3 85:12 [a] [Ps. 84:11] 86:4 [a] Ps. 25:1; 143:8 86:5 [a] [Joel 2:13] 86:8 [a] [Ex. 15:11] 86:10 [a] [Ex. 15:11] [b] Deut. 6:4 86:11 [a] Ps. 27:11; 143:8

GIVE YOUR COMPLAINT TO GOD

Bow down Your ear, O LORD, hear me; for I am poor and needy.

PSALM 86:1

In this psalm David begged God to hear him. How could David be "poor and needy" (v. 1)? Although we cannot be certain what David was referring to in this psalm, he was probably writing about his spiritual walk. If it was when Saul was pursuing him, then David may have experienced literal need (see 1 Sam. 21:1–9), but much of the psalm suggests that his concern was spiritual in nature. Whatever his circumstances, David petitioned God: "Teach me Your way, O LORD; I will walk in Your truth; unite my heart to fear Your name"; he promised, "I will praise You, O Lord my God, with all my heart" (Ps. 86:11–12).

We can learn from David's response to hardship and uncertainty: he prayed. He expressed faith in God. He described his situation, knowing God would listen and respond. In the end, God gave him assurance and peace. We find this theme in the Psalms many times, probably because David had discovered that it worked. We can go to God in prayer—complaints and all—and experience His joy and peace.

Will you describe your troubling situation to God today in pursuit of His joy and peace?

PEACE NOTE

Anything that costs you your peace is too expensive. But how do you find peace? Truth is the first step. Think about it; walk in it.

PSALM 86:11

14 O God, the proud have risen against me,
And a mob of violent *men* have sought
my life,
And have not set You before them.
15 But [a]You, O Lord, *are* a God full of
compassion, and gracious,
Longsuffering and abundant in mercy
and truth.

16 *Oh, turn to me, and have mercy on me!*
Give Your strength to Your servant,
And save the son of Your maidservant.
17 Show me a sign for good,
That those who hate me may see *it* and
be ashamed,
Because You, LORD, have helped me
and comforted me.

PSALM 87

The Glories of the City of God

A Psalm of the sons of Korah. A Song.

1 His foundation *is* in the holy mountains.
2 [a]The LORD loves the gates of Zion
More than all the dwellings of Jacob.
3 [a]Glorious things are spoken of you,
O city of God! *Selah*

4 "I will make mention of Rahab and
Babylon to those who know Me;
Behold, O Philistia and Tyre, with
Ethiopia:
'This *one* was born there.' "

5 And of Zion it will be said,
"This *one* and that *one* were born in her;
And the Most High Himself shall
establish her."
6 The LORD will record,
When He [a]registers the peoples:
"This *one* was born there." *Selah*

7 Both the singers and the players on
instruments *say,*
"All my springs *are* in you."

86:15 [a] Ex. 34:6 87:2 [a] Ps. 78:67, 68 87:3 [a] Is. 60:1 87:6 [a] Is. 4:3

PSALM 88

A Prayer for Help in Despondency

A Song. A Psalm of the sons of Korah. To the Chief Musician. Set to "Mahalath Leannoth." A Contemplation[1] of [a]Heman the Ezrahite.

1 O LORD, [a]God of my salvation,
I have cried out day and night before You.
2 Let my prayer come before You;
Incline Your ear to my cry.

3 For my soul is full of troubles,
And my life [a]draws near to the grave.
4 I am counted with those who [a]go down to the pit;
[b]I am like a man *who has* no strength,
5 Adrift among the dead,
Like the slain who lie in the grave,
Whom You remember no more,
And who are cut off from Your hand.

6 You have laid me in the lowest pit,
In darkness, in the depths.
7 Your wrath lies heavy upon me,
And You have afflicted *me* with all [a]Your waves. *Selah*
8 [a]You have put away my acquaintances far from me;
You have made me an abomination to them;
[b]*I am* shut up, and I cannot get out;
9 My eye wastes away because of affliction.

[a]LORD, I have called daily upon You;
I have stretched out my hands to You.
10 Will You work wonders for the dead?
Shall the dead arise *and* praise You? *Selah*
11 Shall Your lovingkindness be declared in the grave?
Or Your faithfulness in the place of destruction?
12 Shall Your wonders be known in the dark?
And Your righteousness in the land of forgetfulness?

13 But to You I have cried out, O LORD,
And in the morning my prayer comes before You.
14 LORD, why do You cast off my soul?
Why do You hide Your face from me?
15 I *have been* afflicted and ready to die from *my* youth;
I suffer Your terrors;
I am distraught.
16 Your fierce wrath has gone over me;
Your terrors have cut me off.
17 They came around me all day long like water;
They engulfed me altogether.
18 [a]Loved one and friend You have put far from me,
And my acquaintances into darkness.

PSALM 89

Remembering the Covenant with David, and Sorrow for Lost Blessings

A Contemplation[1] of [a]Ethan the Ezrahite.

1 I will sing of the mercies of the LORD forever;
With my mouth will I make known
Your faithfulness to all generations.
2 For I have said, "Mercy shall be built up forever;
[a]Your faithfulness You shall establish in the very heavens."

3 "I[a] have made a covenant with My chosen,
I have [b]sworn to My servant David:
4 'Your seed I will establish forever,
And build up your throne [a]to all generations.'" *Selah*

5 And [a]the heavens will praise Your wonders, O LORD;
Your faithfulness also in the assembly of the saints.
6 [a]For who in the heavens can be compared to the LORD?
Who among the sons of the mighty can be likened to the LORD?
7 [a]God is greatly to be feared in the assembly of the saints,
And to be held in reverence by all *those* around Him.
8 O LORD God of hosts,
Who *is* mighty like You, O LORD?
Your faithfulness also surrounds You.
9 [a]You rule the raging of the sea;
When its waves rise, You still them.
10 [a]You have broken Rahab in pieces, as one who is slain;
You have scattered Your enemies with Your mighty arm.

11 [a]The heavens *are* Yours, the earth also *is* Yours;
The world and all its fullness, You have founded them.

88:title [a] 1 Kin. 4:31 [1] Hebrew *Maschil* **88:1** [a] Ps. 27:9 **88:3** [a] Ps. 107:18 **88:4** [a] [Ps. 28:1] [b] Ps. 31:12 **88:7** [a] Ps. 42:7 **88:8** [a] Job 19:13, 19 [b] Lam. 3:7 **88:9** [a] Ps. 86:3 **88:18** [a] Ps. 31:11; 38:11 **89:title** [a] 1 Kin. 4:31 [1] Hebrew *Maschil* **89:2** [a] [Ps. 119:89, 90] **89:3** [a] 1 Kin. 8:16 [b] 2 Sam. 7:11 **89:4** [a] [Luke 1:33] **89:5** [a] [Ps. 19:1] **89:6** [a] Ps. 86:8; 113:5 **89:7** [a] Ps. 76:7, 11 **89:9** [a] Ps. 65:7; 93:3, 4; 107:29 **89:10** [a] Ps. 87:4 **89:11** [a] [Gen. 1:1]

12 The north and the south, You have created them;
[a]Tabor and [b]Hermon rejoice in Your name.
13 You have a mighty arm;
Strong is Your hand, *and* high is Your right hand.
14 Righteousness and justice *are* the foundation of Your throne;
Mercy and truth go before Your face.
15 Blessed *are* the people who know the [a]joyful sound!
They walk, O LORD, in the light of Your countenance.
16 In Your name they rejoice all day long,
And in Your righteousness they are exalted.
17 For You *are* the glory of their strength,
And in Your favor our horn is [a]exalted.
18 For our shield *belongs* to the LORD,
And our king to the Holy One of Israel.

19 Then You spoke in a vision to Your holy one,[1]
And said: "I have given help to *one who is* mighty;
I have exalted one [a]chosen from the people.
20 [a]I have found My servant David;
With My holy oil I have anointed him,
21 [a]With whom My hand shall be established;
Also My arm shall strengthen him.
22 The enemy shall not outwit him,
Nor the son of wickedness afflict him.
23 I will beat down his foes before his face,
And plague those who hate him.

24 "But My faithfulness and My mercy *shall be* with him,
And in My name his horn shall be exalted.
25 Also I will [a]set his hand over the sea,
And his right hand over the rivers.
26 He shall cry to Me, 'You *are* [a]my Father,
My God, and [b]the rock of my salvation.'
27 Also I will make him [a]*My* firstborn,
[b]The highest of the kings of the earth.
28 [a]My mercy I will keep for him forever,
And My covenant shall stand firm with him.
29 His seed also I will make *to endure* forever,
[a]And his throne [b]as the days of heaven.

30 "If[a] his sons [b]forsake My law
And do not walk in My judgments,
31 If they break My statutes
And do not keep My commandments,
32 Then I will punish their transgression with the rod,
And their iniquity with stripes.
33 [a]Nevertheless My lovingkindness I will not utterly take from him,
Nor allow My faithfulness to fail.
34 My covenant I will not break,
Nor [a]alter the word that has gone out of My lips.
35 Once I have sworn [a]by My holiness;
I will not lie to David:
36 [a]His seed shall endure forever,
And his throne [b]as the sun before Me;
37 It shall be established forever like the moon,
Even *like* the faithful witness in the sky." *Selah*

38 But You have [a]cast off and [b]abhorred,
You have been furious with Your anointed.
39 You have renounced the covenant of Your servant;
[a]You have profaned his crown *by casting it* to the ground.
40 You have broken down all his hedges;
You have brought his strongholds to ruin.
41 All who pass by the way [a]plunder him;
He is a reproach to his neighbors.
42 You have exalted the right hand of his adversaries;
You have made all his enemies rejoice.
43 You have also turned back the edge of his sword,
And have not sustained him in the battle.
44 You have made his glory cease,
And cast his throne down to the ground.
45 The days of his youth You have shortened;
You have covered him with shame. *Selah*

46 How long, LORD?
Will You hide Yourself forever?
Will Your wrath burn like fire?

89:12 [a] Josh. 19:22 [b] Josh. 11:17; 12:1 **89:15** [a] Ps. 98:6 **89:17** [a] Ps. 75:10; 92:10; 132:17 **89:19** [a] 1 Kin. 11:34 [1] Following many Hebrew manuscripts; Masoretic Text, Septuagint, Targum, and Vulgate read *holy ones.* **89:20** [a] 1 Sam. 13:14; 16:1–12 **89:21** [a] Ps. 80:17 **89:25** [a] Ps. 72:8 **89:26** [a] [1 Chr. 22:10] [b] 2 Sam. 22:47 **89:27** [a] [Col. 1:15, 18] [b] Rev. 19:16 **89:28** [a] Is. 55:3 **89:29** [a] Jer. 33:17 [b] Deut. 11:21 **89:30** [a] [2 Sam. 7:14] [b] Ps. 119:53 **89:33** [a] 2 Sam. 7:14, 15 **89:34** [a] Jer. 33:20–22 **89:35** [a] Amos 4:2 **89:36** [a] [Luke 1:33] [b] Ps. 72:17 **89:38** [a] [1 Chr. 28:9] [b] Deut. 32:19 **89:39** [a] Lam. 5:16 **89:41** [a] Ps. 80:12

47 Remember how short my time [a]is;
For what [b]futility have You created all the children of men?
48 What man can live and not see [a]death?
Can he deliver his life from the power of the grave? *Selah*

49 Lord, where *are* Your former lovingkindnesses,
Which You [a]swore to David [b]in Your truth?
50 Remember, Lord, the reproach of Your servants—
[a]*How* I bear in my bosom *the reproach of* all the many peoples,
51 [a]With which Your enemies have reproached, O LORD,
With which they have reproached the footsteps of Your anointed.

52 [a]Blessed *be* the LORD forevermore!
Amen and Amen.

BOOK FOUR

Psalms 90–106

PSALM 90

The Eternity of God, and Man's Frailty

A Prayer [a]of Moses the man of God.

1 Lord, [a]You have been our dwelling place[1] in all generations.
2 [a]Before the mountains were brought forth,
Or ever You had formed the earth and the world,
Even from everlasting to everlasting, You *are* God.

3 You turn man to destruction,
And say, [a]"Return, O children of men."
4 [a]For a thousand years in Your sight
Are like yesterday when it is past,
And *like* a watch in the night.
5 You carry them away *like* a flood;
[a]*They are* like a sleep.
In the morning [b]they are like grass *which* grows up:
6 In the morning it flourishes and grows up;
In the evening it is cut down and withers.

7 For we have been consumed by Your anger,
And by Your wrath we are terrified.
8 [a]You have set our iniquities before You,
Our [b]secret *sins* in the light of Your countenance.
9 For all our days have passed away in Your wrath;
We finish our years like a sigh.
10 The days of our lives *are* seventy years;
And if by reason of strength *they are* eighty years,
Yet their boast *is* only labor and sorrow;
For it is soon cut off, and we fly away.
11 Who knows the power of Your anger?
For as the fear of You, *so is* Your wrath.
12 [a]So teach *us* to number our days,
That we may gain a heart of wisdom.

13 Return, O LORD!
How long?
And [a]have compassion on Your servants.
14 Oh, satisfy us early with Your mercy,
[a]That we may rejoice and be glad all our days!
15 Make us glad according to the days *in which* You have afflicted us,
The years *in which* we have seen evil.
16 Let [a]Your work appear to Your servants,
And Your glory to their children.
17 [a]And let the beauty of the LORD our God be upon us,
And [b]establish the work of our hands for us;
Yes, establish the work of our hands.

PSALM 91

Safety of Abiding in the Presence of God

1 He [a]who dwells in the secret place of the Most High
Shall abide [b]under the shadow of the Almighty.
2 [a]I will say of the LORD, "*He is* my refuge and my fortress;
My God, in Him I will trust."

3 Surely [a]He shall deliver you from the snare of the fowler[1]
And from the perilous pestilence.
4 [a]He shall cover you with His feathers,
And under His wings you shall take refuge;
His truth *shall be your* shield and buckler.

89:47 [a] Ps. 90:9 [b] Ps. 62:9 **89:48** [a] [Eccl. 3:19] **89:49** [a] [2 Sam. 7:15] [b] Ps. 54:5 **89:50** [a] Ps. 69:9, 19 **89:51** [a] Ps. 74:10, 18, 22 **89:52** [a] Ps. 41:13 **90:title** [a] Deut. 33:1 **90:1** [a] [Ezek. 11:16] [1] Septuagint, Targum, and Vulgate read *refuge*. **90:2** [a] [Prov. 8:25, 26] **90:3** [a] Gen. 3:19 **90:4** [a] 2 Pet. 3:8 **90:5** [a] Ps. 73:20 [b] Is. 40:6 **90:8** [a] Ps. 50:21 [b] Ps. 19:12 **90:12** [a] Ps. 39:4 **90:13** [a] Deut. 32:36 **90:14** [a] Ps. 85:6 **90:16** [a] Hab. 3:2 **90:17** [a] Ps. 27:4 [b] Is. 26:12 **91:1** [a] Ps. 27:5; 31:20; 32:7 [b] Ps. 17:8 **91:2** [a] Ps. 142:5 **91:3** [a] Ps. 124:7 [1] That is, one who catches birds in a trap or snare **91:4** [a] Ps. 17:8

PEACE NOTE

The peaceful dwell "in the secret place of the Most High" and they "abide under the shadow of the Almighty."

PSALM 91:1

5 [a]You shall not be afraid of the terror by
night,
Nor of the arrow *that* flies by day,
6 *Nor* of the pestilence *that* walks in
darkness,
Nor of the destruction *that* lays waste
at noonday.

7 A thousand may fall at your side,
And ten thousand at your right hand;
But it shall not come near you.
8 Only [a]with your eyes shall you look,
And see the reward of the wicked.

9 Because you have made the LORD, *who
is* [a]my refuge,
Even the Most High, [b]your dwelling
place,
10 [a]No evil shall befall you,
Nor shall any plague come near your
dwelling;
11 [a]For He shall give His angels charge
over you,
To keep you in all your ways.
12 In *their* hands they shall bear you up,
[a]Lest you dash your foot against a stone.
13 You shall tread upon the lion and the
cobra,
The young lion and the serpent you
shall trample underfoot.

14 "Because he has set his love upon Me,
therefore I will deliver him;
I will set him on high, because he has
[a]known My name.
15 *He shall [a]call upon Me, and I will*
answer him;
I *will be* [b]with him in trouble;
I will deliver him and honor him.
16 With long life I will satisfy him,
And show him My salvation."

PSALM 92

Praise to the LORD for His Love and Faithfulness

A Psalm. A Song for the Sabbath day.

1 *It is* [a]good to give thanks to the LORD,
And to sing praises to Your name,
O Most High;
2 To [a]declare Your lovingkindness in the
morning,
And Your faithfulness every night,
3 [a]On an instrument of ten strings,
On the lute,
And on the harp,
With harmonious sound.
4 For You, LORD, have made me glad
through Your work;
I will triumph in the works of Your
hands.

5 [a]O LORD, how great are Your works!
[b]Your thoughts are very deep.
6 [a]A senseless man does not know,
Nor does a fool understand this.
7 When [a]the wicked spring up like grass,
And when all the workers of iniquity
flourish,
It is that they may be destroyed forever.

8 [a]But You, LORD, *are* on high
forevermore.
9 For behold, Your enemies, O LORD,
For behold, Your enemies shall perish;
All the workers of iniquity shall [a]be
scattered.

10 But [a]my horn You have exalted like a
wild ox;
I have been [b]anointed with fresh oil.
11 [a]My eye also has seen *my desire* on my
enemies;
My ears hear *my desire* on the wicked
Who rise up against me.

12 [a]The righteous shall flourish like a palm
tree,
He shall grow like a cedar in
Lebanon.
13 Those who are planted in the house of
the LORD
Shall flourish in the courts of our God.

91:5 [a] [Job 5:19] 91:8 [a] Mal. 1:5 91:9 [a] Ps. 91:2 [b] Ps. 90:1 91:10 [a] [Prov. 12:21] 91:11 [a] [Heb. 1:14] 91:12 [a] Matt. 4:6 91:14 [a] [Ps. 9:10] 91:15 [a] Ps. 50:15 [b] Is. 43:2 92:1 [a] Ps. 147:1 92:2 [a] Ps. 89:1 92:3 [a] 1 Chr. 23:5 92:5 [a] Ps. 40:5 [b] [Is. 28:29] 92:6 [a] Ps. 73:22 92:7 [a] Job 12:6 92:8 [a] [Ps. 83:18] 92:9 [a] Ps. 68:1 92:10 [a] Ps. 89:17 [b] Ps. 23:5 92:11 [a] Ps. 54:7 92:12 [a] Ps. 52:8

14 They shall still bear fruit in old age;
They shall be fresh and flourishing,
15 To declare that the LORD is upright;
[a]*He is* my rock, and [b]*there is* no
unrighteousness in Him.

PSALM 93

The Eternal Reign of the LORD

1 The [a]LORD reigns, He is clothed with
majesty;
The LORD is clothed,
[b]He has girded Himself with strength.
Surely the world is established, so that
it cannot be moved.
2 [a]Your throne *is* established from
of old;
You *are* from everlasting.

3 The floods have lifted up, O LORD,
The floods have lifted up their voice;
The floods lift up their waves.
4 [a]The LORD on high *is* mightier
Than the noise of many waters,
Than the mighty waves of the sea.

5 Your testimonies are very sure;
Holiness adorns Your house,
O LORD, forever.

PSALM 94

God the Refuge of the Righteous

1 O LORD God, [a]to whom vengeance
belongs—
O God, to whom vengeance belongs,
shine forth!
2 Rise up, O [a]Judge of the earth;
Render punishment to the proud.
3 LORD, [a]how long will the wicked,
How long will the wicked triumph?

4 They [a]utter speech, *and* speak insolent
things;
All the workers of iniquity boast in
themselves.
5 They break in pieces Your people,
O LORD,
And afflict Your heritage.
6 They slay the widow and the stranger,
And murder the fatherless.
7 [a]Yet they say, "The LORD does not see,
Nor does the God of Jacob
understand."

8 Understand, you senseless among the
people;
And *you* fools, when will you be
wise?
9 [a]He who planted the ear, shall He not
hear?
He who formed the eye, shall He not
see?
10 He who instructs the nations, shall He
not correct,
He who teaches man knowledge?
11 The LORD [a]knows the thoughts
of man,
That they *are* futile.

12 Blessed *is* the man whom You [a]instruct,
O LORD,
And teach out of Your law,
13 That You may give him rest from the
days of adversity,
Until the pit is dug for the wicked.
14 For the LORD will not cast off His
people,
Nor will He forsake His inheritance.
15 But judgment will return to
righteousness,
And all the upright in heart will
follow it.

16 Who will rise up for me against the
evildoers?
Who will stand up for me against the
workers of iniquity?
17 Unless the LORD *had been* my help,
My soul would soon have settled in
silence.
18 If I say, "My foot slips,"
Your mercy, O LORD, will hold
me up.
19 In the multitude of my anxieties
within me,
Your comforts delight my soul.

20 Shall [a]the throne of iniquity, which
devises evil by law,
Have fellowship with You?
21 They gather together against the life of
the righteous,
And condemn [a]innocent blood.
22 But the LORD has been my
defense,
And my God the rock of my
refuge.
23 He has brought on them their own
iniquity,
And shall cut them off in their own
wickedness;
The LORD our God shall cut them
off.

92:15 [a] [Deut. 32:4] [b] [Rom. 9:14] **93:1** [a] Ps. 96:10 [b] Ps. 65:6 **93:2** [a] Ps. 45:6 **93:4** [a] Ps. 65:7 **94:1** [a] [Nah. 1:2] **94:2** [a] [Gen. 18:25] **94:3** [a] [Job 20:5] **94:4** [a] Ps. 31:18 **94:7** [a] Ps. 10:11 **94:9** [a] [Ex. 4:11] **94:11** [a] 1 Cor. 3:20 **94:12** [a] [Heb. 12:5, 6] **94:20** [a] Amos 6:3 **94:21** [a] [Ex. 23:7]

PEACE NOTE

What is the outward manifestation of God's peace in your life? Singing, shouting joyfully, and thanksgiving are all wonderful ways of expressing your peace.

PSALM 95:1

PSALM 95

A Call to Worship and Obedience

1 Oh come, let us sing to the LORD!
Let us shout joyfully to the Rock of our salvation.
2 Let us come before His presence with thanksgiving;
Let us shout joyfully to Him with [a]psalms.
3 For [a]the LORD *is* the great God,
And the great King above all gods.
4 In His hand *are* the deep places of the earth;
The heights of the hills *are* His also.
5 [a]The sea *is* His, for He made it;
And His hands formed the dry *land.*

6 Oh come, let us worship and bow down;
Let [a]us kneel before the LORD our Maker.
7 For He *is* our God,
And [a]we *are* the people of His pasture,
And the sheep of His hand.

[b]Today, if you will hear His voice:
8 "Do not harden your hearts, as in the rebellion,[1]
[a]As *in* the day of trial[2] in the wilderness,
9 When [a]your fathers tested Me;
They tried Me, though they [b]saw My work.
10 For [a]forty years I was grieved with *that* generation,
And said, 'It is a people who go astray in their hearts,
And they do not know My ways.'
11 So [a]I swore in My wrath,
'They shall not enter My rest.' "

PSALM 96

A Song of Praise to God Coming in Judgment

1 Oh, [a]sing to the LORD a new song!
Sing to the LORD, all the earth.
2 Sing to the LORD, bless His name;
Proclaim the good news of His salvation from day to day.
3 Declare His glory among the nations,
His wonders among all peoples.

4 For [a]the LORD *is* great and [b]greatly to be praised;
[c]He *is* to be feared above all gods.
5 For [a]all the gods of the peoples *are* idols,
[b]But the LORD made the heavens.
6 Honor and majesty *are* before Him;
Strength and [a]beauty *are* in His sanctuary.

7 [a]Give to the LORD, O families of the peoples,
Give to the LORD glory and strength.
8 Give to the LORD the glory *due* His name;
Bring an offering, and come into His courts.
9 Oh, worship the LORD [a]in the beauty of holiness!
Tremble before Him, all the earth.

10 Say among the nations, [a]"The LORD reigns;
The world also is firmly established,
It shall not be moved;
[b]He shall judge the peoples righteously."
11 [a]Let the heavens rejoice, and let the earth be glad;
[b]Let the sea roar, and all its fullness;
12 Let the field be joyful, and all that *is* in it.
Then all the trees of the woods will rejoice
13 before the LORD.
For He is coming, for He is coming to judge the earth.
[a]He shall judge the world with righteousness,
And the peoples with His truth.

95:2 [a] James 5:13 95:3 [a] [Ps. 96:4] 95:5 [a] Gen. 1:9, 10 95:6 [a] [Phil. 2:10] 95:7 [a] Ps. 79:13 [b] Heb. 3:7–11, 15; 4:7 95:8 [a] Ex. 17:2–7 [1] Or *Meribah* [2] Or *Massah* 95:9 [a] Ps. 78:18 [b] Num. 14:22 95:10 [a] Heb. 3:10, 17 95:11 [a] Heb. 4:3, 5 96:1 [a] 1 Chr. 16:23–33 96:4 [a] Ps. 145:3 [b] Ps. 18:3 [c] Ps. 95:3 96:5 [a] [Jer. 10:11] [b] Is. 42:5 96:6 [a] Ps. 29:2 96:7 [a] Ps. 29:1, 2 96:9 [a] Ps. 29:2 96:10 [a] Ps. 93:1; 97:1 [b] Ps. 67:4 96:11 [a] Ps. 69:34 [b] Ps. 98:7 96:13 [a] [Rev. 19:11]

PSALM 97

A Song of Praise to the Sovereign LORD

1 The LORD [a]reigns;
Let the earth rejoice;
Let the multitude of isles be glad!

2 [a]Clouds and darkness surround Him;
[b]Righteousness and justice *are* the foundation of His throne.
3 [a]A fire goes before Him,
And burns up His enemies round about.
4 [a]His lightnings light the world;
The earth sees and trembles.
5 [a]The mountains melt like wax at the presence of the LORD,
At the presence of the Lord of the whole earth.
6 [a]The heavens declare His righteousness,
And all the peoples see His glory.

7 [a]Let all be put to shame who serve carved images,
Who boast of idols.
[b]Worship Him, all *you* gods.
8 Zion hears and is glad,
And the daughters of Judah rejoice
Because of Your judgments, O LORD.
9 For You, LORD, *are* [a]most high above all the earth;
[b]You are exalted far above all gods.

10 You who love the LORD, [a]hate evil!
[b]He preserves the souls of His saints;
[c]He delivers them out of the hand of the wicked.
11 [a]Light is sown for the righteous,
And gladness for the upright in heart.
12 [a]Rejoice in the LORD, you righteous,
[b]And give thanks at the remembrance of His holy name.[1]

PSALM 98

A Song of Praise to the LORD for His Salvation and Judgment

A Psalm.

1 Oh, [a]sing to the LORD a new song!
For He has [b]done marvelous things;
His right hand and His holy arm have gained Him the victory.
2 [a]The LORD has made known His salvation;
[b]His righteousness He has revealed in the sight of the nations.

PEACE NOTE

Is my life currently defined by living in peace, a truce, or conflict? Do I bring peace, or am I an agent of conflict in my home and community?

3 He has remembered His mercy and His faithfulness to the house of Israel;
[a]All the ends of the earth have seen the salvation of our God.

4 Shout joyfully to the LORD, all the earth;
Break forth in song, rejoice, and sing praises.
5 Sing to the LORD with the harp,
With the harp and the sound of a psalm,
6 With trumpets and the sound of a horn;
Shout joyfully before the LORD, the King.

7 Let the sea roar, and all its fullness,
The world and those who dwell in it;
8 Let the rivers clap *their* hands;
Let the hills be joyful together
9 before the LORD,
[a]For He is coming to judge the earth.
With righteousness He shall judge the world,
And the peoples with equity.

PSALM 99

Praise to the LORD for His Holiness

1 The LORD reigns;
Let the peoples tremble!
[a]He dwells *between* the cherubim;
Let the earth be moved!
2 The LORD *is* great in Zion,
And He *is* high above all the peoples.
3 Let them praise Your great and awesome name—
He *is* holy.

97:1 [a] [Ps. 96:10] 97:2 [a] Ps. 18:11 [b] [Ps. 89:14] 97:3 [a] Ps. 18:8 97:4 [a] Ex. 19:18 97:5 [a] Mic. 1:4 97:6 [a] Ps. 19:1 97:7 [a] [Ex. 20:4] [b] [Heb. 1:6] 97:9 [a] Ps. 83:18 [b] Ex. 18:11 97:10 [a] [Ps. 34:14] [b] Prov. 2:8 [c] Ps. 37:40 97:11 [a] Job 22:28 97:12 [a] Ps. 33:1 [b] Ps. 30:4 [1] Or *His holiness* 98:1 [a] Is. 42:10 [b] Ex. 15:11 98:2 [a] Is. 52:10 [b] Is. 62:2 98:3 [a] Luke 3:6 98:9 [a] [Ps. 96:10, 13] 99:1 [a] Ex. 25:22

4 The King's strength also loves justice;
You have established equity;
You have executed justice and
righteousness in Jacob.
5 Exalt the LORD our God,
And worship at His footstool—
He *is* holy.

6 Moses and Aaron were among His
priests,
And Samuel was among those who
[a]called upon His name;
They called upon the LORD, and He
answered them.
7 He spoke to them in the cloudy pillar;
They kept His testimonies and the
ordinance He gave them.

8 You answered them, O LORD our God;
You were to them God-Who-Forgives,
Though You took vengeance on their
deeds.
9 Exalt the LORD our God,
And worship at His holy hill;
For the LORD our God *is* holy.

PSALM 100

A Song of Praise for the LORD's Faithfulness to His People

[a]A Psalm of Thanksgiving.

1 Make [a]a joyful shout to the LORD, all
you lands!
2 Serve the LORD with gladness;
Come before His presence with
singing.
3 Know that the LORD, He *is* God;
[a]*It is* He *who* has made us, and not we
ourselves;[1]
[b]*We are* His people and the sheep of His
pasture.

4 [a]Enter into His gates with thanksgiving,
And into His courts with praise.
Be thankful to Him, *and* bless His name.
5 For the LORD *is* good;
[a]His mercy *is* everlasting,
And His truth *endures* to all
generations.

PSALM 101

Promised Faithfulness to the LORD

A Psalm of David.

1 *I will sing of mercy and justice;*
To You, O LORD, I will sing praises.

PEACE NOTE

Gratitude emanates from the peaceful knowledge that God is always in control, even when things seem out of control!

PSALM 100:4

2 I will behave wisely in a perfect way.
Oh, when will You come to me?
I will [a]walk within my house with a
perfect heart.

3 I will set nothing wicked before my eyes;
[a]I hate the work of those [b]who fall away;
It shall not cling to me.
4 A perverse heart shall depart from me;
I will not [a]know wickedness.

5 Whoever secretly slanders his neighbor,
Him I will destroy;
[a]The one who has a haughty look and a
proud heart,
Him I will not endure.

6 My eyes *shall be* on the faithful of the land,
That they may dwell with me;
He who walks in a perfect way,
He shall serve me.
7 He who works deceit shall not dwell
within my house;
He who tells lies shall not continue in
my presence.
8 [a]Early I will destroy all the wicked of the
land,
That I may cut off all the evildoers
[b]from the city of the LORD.

PSALM 102

The LORD's Eternal Love

A Prayer of the afflicted, [a]when he is overwhelmed and pours out his complaint before the LORD.

1 Hear my prayer, O LORD,
And let my cry come to You.

99:6 [a] 1 Sam. 7:9; 12:18 **100:title** [a] Ps. 145:title **100:1** [a] Ps. 95:1 **100:3** [a] [Eph. 2:10] [b] Ezek. 34:30, 31 [1] Following Kethib, Septuagint, and Vulgate; Qere, many Hebrew manuscripts, and Targum read *we are His.* **100:4** [a] Ps. 66:13; 116:17–19 **100:5** [a] Ps. 136:1 **101:2** [a] 1 Kin. 11:4 **101:3** [a] Ps. 97:10 [b] Josh. 23:6 **101:4** [a] [Ps. 119:115] **101:5** [a] Prov. 6:17 **101:8** [a] Jer. 21:12 [b] Ps. 48:2, 8 **102:title** [a] Ps. 61:2

7 And He led them forth by the [a]right way,
That they might go to a city for a dwelling place.
8 [a]Oh, that *men* would give thanks to the LORD *for* His goodness,
And *for* His wonderful works to the children of men!
9 For [a]He satisfies the longing soul,
And fills the hungry soul with goodness.

10 Those who [a]sat in darkness and in the shadow of death,
[b]Bound in affliction and irons—
11 Because they [a]rebelled against the words of God,
And despised [b]the counsel of the Most High,
12 Therefore He brought down their heart with labor;
They fell down, and *there was* [a]none to help.
13 Then they cried out to the LORD in their trouble,
And He saved them out of their distresses.
14 [a]He brought them out of darkness and the shadow of death,
And broke their chains in pieces.
15 Oh, that *men* would give thanks to the LORD *for* His goodness,
And *for* His wonderful works to the children of men!
16 For He has [a]broken the gates of bronze,
And cut the bars of iron in two.

17 Fools, [a]because of their transgression,
And because of their iniquities, were afflicted.
18 [a]Their soul abhorred all manner of food,
And they [b]drew near to the gates of death.
19 Then they cried out to the LORD in their trouble,
And He saved them out of their distresses.
20 [a]He sent His word and [b]healed them,
And [c]delivered *them* from their destructions.
21 Oh, that *men* would give thanks to the LORD *for* His goodness,
And *for* His wonderful works to the children of men!
22 [a]Let them sacrifice the sacrifices of thanksgiving,
And [b]declare His works with rejoicing.

23 Those who go down to the sea in ships,
Who do business on great waters,
24 They see the works of the LORD,
And His wonders in the deep.
25 For He commands and [a]raises the stormy wind,
Which lifts up the waves of the sea.
26 They mount up to the heavens,
They go down again to the depths;
[a]Their soul melts because of trouble.
27 They reel to and fro, and stagger like a drunken man,
And are at their wits' end.
28 Then they cry out to the LORD in their trouble,
And He brings them out of their distresses.
29 [a]He calms the storm,
So that its waves are still.
30 Then they are glad because they are quiet;
So He guides them to their desired haven.
31 [a]Oh, that *men* would give thanks to the LORD *for* His goodness,
And *for* His wonderful works to the children of men!
32 Let them exalt Him also [a]in the assembly of the people,
And praise Him in the company of the elders.

33 He [a]turns rivers into a wilderness,
And the watersprings into dry ground;
34 A [a]fruitful land into barrenness,
For the wickedness of those who dwell in it.
35 [a]He turns a wilderness into pools of water,
And dry land into watersprings.
36 There He makes the hungry dwell,
That they may establish a city for a dwelling place,
37 And sow fields and plant vineyards,
That they may yield a fruitful harvest.
38 [a]He also blesses them, and they multiply greatly;
And He does not let their cattle [b]decrease.

39 When they are [a]diminished and brought low
Through oppression, affliction, and sorrow,

107:7 [a] Ezra 8:21 **107:8** [a] Ps. 107:15, 21 **107:9** [a] [Ps. 34:10] **107:10** [a] [Luke 1:79] [b] Job 36:8 **107:11** [a] Lam. 3:42 [b] [Ps. 73:24] **107:12** [a] Ps. 22:11 **107:14** [a] Ps. 68:6 **107:16** [a] Is. 45:1, 2 **107:17** [a] Lam. 3:39 **107:18** [a] Job 33:20 [b] Job 33:22 **107:20** [a] Matt. 8:8 [b] Ps. 30:2 [c] Job 33:28, 30 **107:22** [a] Lev. 7:12 [b] Ps. 9:11 **107:25** [a] Jon. 1:4 **107:26** [a] Ps. 22:14 **107:29** [a] Ps. 89:9 **107:31** [a] Ps. 107:8, 15, 21 **107:32** [a] Ps. 22:22, 25 **107:33** [a] 1 Kin. 17:1, 7 **107:34** [a] Gen. 13:10 **107:35** [a] Ps. 114:8 **107:38** [a] Gen. 12:2; 17:16, 20 [b] [Deut. 7:14] **107:39** [a] 2 Kin. 10:32

40 [a]He pours contempt on princes,
And causes them to wander in the wilderness *where there is* no way;
41 [a]Yet He sets the poor on high, far from affliction,
And [b]makes *their* families like a flock.
42 [a]The righteous see *it* and rejoice,
And all [b]iniquity stops its mouth.

43 [a]Whoever *is* wise will observe these *things,*
And they will understand the lovingkindness of the LORD.

PSALM 108

Assurance of God's Victory over Enemies

A Song. A Psalm of David.

1 O [a]God, my heart is steadfast;
I will sing and give praise, even with my glory.
2 [a]Awake, lute and harp!
I will awaken the dawn.
3 I will praise You, O LORD, among the peoples,
And I will sing praises to You among the nations.
4 For Your mercy *is* great above the heavens,
And Your truth *reaches* to the clouds.

5 [a]Be exalted, O God, above the heavens,
And Your glory above all the earth;
6 [a]That Your beloved may be delivered,
Save *with* Your right hand, and hear me.

7 God has spoken in His holiness:
"I will rejoice;
I will divide Shechem
And measure out the Valley of Succoth.
8 Gilead *is* Mine; Manasseh *is* Mine;
Ephraim also *is* the helmet for My head;
[a]Judah *is* My lawgiver.
9 Moab *is* My washpot;
Over Edom I will cast My shoe;
Over Philistia I will triumph."

10 [a]Who will bring me *into* the strong city?
Who will lead me to Edom?
11 *Is it* not *You,* O God, *who* cast us off?
And *You,* O God, *who* did not go out with our armies?
12 Give us help from trouble,
For the help of man is useless.
13 [a]Through God we will do valiantly,
For *it is* He *who* shall tread down our enemies.[1]

PSALM 109

Plea for Judgment of False Accusers

To the Chief Musician. A Psalm of David.

1 Do[a] not keep silent,
O God of my praise!
2 For the mouth of the wicked and the mouth of the deceitful
Have opened against me;
They have spoken against me with a [a]lying tongue.
3 They have also surrounded me with words of hatred,
And fought against me [a]without a cause.
4 In return for my love they are my accusers,
But I *give myself to* prayer.
5 Thus [a]they have rewarded me evil for good,
And hatred for my love.

6 Set a wicked man over him,
And let [a]an accuser[1] stand at his right hand.
7 When he is judged, let him be found guilty,
And [a]let his prayer become sin.
8 Let his days be [a]few,
And [b]let another take his office.
9 [a]Let his children be fatherless,
And his wife a widow.
10 Let his children continually be vagabonds, and beg;
Let them seek *their bread*[1] also from their desolate places.
11 [a]Let the creditor seize all that he has,
And let strangers plunder his labor.
12 Let there be none to extend mercy to him,
Nor let there be any to favor his fatherless children.
13 [a]Let his posterity be cut off,
And in the generation following let their [b]name be blotted out.

14 [a]Let the iniquity of his fathers be remembered before the LORD,

107:40 [a] Job 12:21, 24 **107:41** [a] 1 Sam. 2:8 [b] Ps. 78:52 **107:42** [a] Job 5:15, 16 [b] [Rom. 3:19] **107:43** [a] Jer. 9:12 **108:1** [a] Ps. 57:7–11 **108:2** [a] Ps. 57:8–11 **108:5** [a] Ps. 57:5, 11 **108:6** [a] Ps. 60:5–12 **108:8** [a] [Gen. 49:10] **108:10** [a] Ps. 60:9 **108:13** [a] Ps. 60:12 [1] Compare verses 6–13 with 60:5–12 **109:1** [a] Ps. 83:1 **109:2** [a] Ps. 27:12 **109:3** [a] John 15:25 **109:5** [a] Ps. 35:7, 12; 38:20 **109:6** [a] Zech. 3:1 [1] Hebrew *satan* **109:7** [a] [Prov. 28:9] **109:8** [a] [Ps. 55:23] [b] Acts 1:20 **109:9** [a] Ex. 22:24 **109:10** [1] Following Masoretic Text and Targum; Septuagint and Vulgate read *be cast out.* **109:11** [a] Job 5:5; 18:9 **109:13** [a] Job 18:19 [b] Prov. 10:7 **109:14** [a] [Ex. 20:5]

And let not the sin of his mother [b]be blotted out.
15 Let them be continually before the LORD,
That He may [a]cut off the memory of them from the earth;
16 Because he did not remember to show mercy,
But persecuted the poor and needy man,
That he might even slay the [a]broken in heart.
17 [a]As he loved cursing, so let it come to him;
As he did not delight in blessing, so let it be far from him.
18 As he clothed himself with cursing as with his garment,
So let it [a]enter his body like water,
And like oil into his bones.
19 Let it be to him like the garment which covers him,
And for a belt with which he girds himself continually.
20 *Let* this *be* the LORD's reward to my accusers,
And to those who speak evil against my person.

21 But You, O GOD the Lord,
Deal with me for Your name's sake;
Because Your mercy *is* good, deliver me.
22 For I *am* poor and needy,
And my heart is wounded within me.
23 I am gone [a]like a shadow when it lengthens;
I am shaken off like a locust.
24 My [a]knees are weak through fasting,
And my flesh is feeble from lack of fatness.
25 I also have become [a]a reproach to them;
When they look at me, [b]they shake their heads.

26 Help me, O LORD my God!
Oh, save me according to Your mercy,
27 [a]That they may know that this *is* Your hand—
That You, LORD, have done it!
28 [a]*Let them curse, but You bless;*
When they arise, let them be ashamed,
But let [b]Your servant rejoice.
29 [a]Let my accusers be clothed with shame,
And let them cover themselves with their own disgrace as with a mantle.
30 I will greatly praise the LORD with my mouth;
Yes, [a]I will praise Him among the multitude.
31 For [a]He shall stand at the right hand of the poor,
To save *him* from those who condemn him.

PSALM 110

Announcement of the Messiah's Reign

A Psalm of David.

1 The [a]LORD said to my Lord,
"Sit at My right hand,
Till I make Your enemies Your [b]footstool."
2 The LORD shall send the rod of Your strength [a]out of Zion.
[b]Rule in the midst of Your enemies!

3 [a]Your people *shall be* volunteers
In the day of Your power;
[b]In the beauties of holiness, from the womb of the morning,
You have the dew of Your youth.
4 The LORD has sworn
And [a]will not relent,
"You *are* a [b]priest forever
According to the order of [c]Melchizedek."

5 The Lord *is* [a]at Your right hand;
He shall execute kings [b]in the day of His wrath.
6 He shall judge among the nations,
He shall fill *the places* with dead bodies,
[a]He shall execute the heads of many countries.
7 He shall drink of the brook by the wayside;
[a]Therefore He shall lift up the head.

PSALM 111

Praise to God for His Faithfulness and Justice

1 Praise the LORD!

[a]I will praise the LORD with *my* whole heart,
In the assembly of the upright and *in* the congregation.

109:14 [b] Neh. 4:5 **109:15** [a] Job 18:17 **109:16** [a] [Ps. 34:18] **109:17** [a] Prov. 14:14 **109:18** [a] Num. 5:22 **109:23** [a] Ps. 102:11 **109:24** [a] Heb. 12:12 **109:25** [a] Ps. 22:7 [b] Matt. 27:39 **109:27** [a] Job 37:7 **109:28** [a] 2 Sam. 6:11, 12 [b] Is. 65:14 **109:29** [a] Ps. 35:26 **109:30** [a] Ps. 35:18; 111:1 **109:31** [a] [Ps. 16:8] **110:1** [a] Matt. 22:44 [b] [1 Cor. 15:25] **110:2** [a] [Rom. 11:26, 27] [b] [Dan. 7:13, 14] **110:3** [a] Judg. 5:2 [b] Ps. 96:9 **110:4** [a] [Num. 23:19] [b] [Zech. 6:13] [c] [Heb. 5:6, 10; 6:20] **110:5** [a] [Ps. 16:8] [b] Ps. 2:5, 12 **110:6** [a] Ps. 68:21 **110:7** [a] [Is. 53:12] **111:1** [a] Ps. 35:18

2 [a]The works of the LORD *are* great,
[b]Studied by all who have pleasure in them.
3 His work *is* [a]honorable and glorious,
And His righteousness endures forever.
4 He has made His wonderful works to be remembered;
[a]The LORD *is* gracious and full of compassion.
5 He has given food to those who fear Him;
He will ever be mindful of His covenant.
6 He has declared to His people the power of His works,
In giving them the heritage of the nations.

7 The works of His hands *are* [a]verity and justice;
All His precepts *are* sure.
8 [a]They stand fast forever and ever,
And are [b]done in truth and uprightness.
9 [a]He has sent redemption to His people;
He has commanded His covenant forever:
[b]Holy and awesome *is* His name.

10 [a]The fear of the LORD *is* the beginning of wisdom;
A good understanding have all those who do *His commandments.*
His praise endures forever.

PEACE NOTE

To have the peace of the Lord in our hearts, each day we must live in the conscious, constant awareness of God, who is always at work.

PSALM 111:10

PSALM 112

The Blessed State of the Righteous

1 Praise the LORD!

Blessed *is* the man *who* fears the LORD,
Who [a]delights greatly in His commandments.

2 [a]His descendants will be mighty on earth;
The generation of the upright will be blessed.
3 [a]Wealth and riches *will be* in his house,
And his righteousness endures forever.
4 [a]Unto the upright there arises light in the darkness;
He is gracious, and full of compassion, and righteous.
5 [a]A good man deals graciously and lends;
He will guide his affairs [b]with discretion.
6 Surely he will never be shaken;
[a]The righteous will be in everlasting remembrance.
7 [a]He will not be afraid of evil tidings;
His heart is steadfast, trusting in the LORD.
8 His [a]heart *is* established;
[b]He will not be afraid,
Until he [c]sees *his desire* upon his enemies.

9 He has dispersed abroad,
He has given to the poor;
His righteousness endures forever;
His horn will be exalted with honor.
10 The wicked will see *it* and be grieved;
He will gnash his teeth and melt away;
The desire of the wicked shall perish.

PSALM 113

The Majesty and Condescension of God

1 Praise the LORD!

[a]Praise, O servants of the LORD,
Praise the name of the LORD!
2 [a]Blessed be the name of the LORD
From this time forth and forevermore!
3 [a]From the rising of the sun to its going down
The LORD's name *is* to be praised.

4 The LORD *is* [a]high above all nations,
[b]His glory above the heavens.

111:2 [a] Ps. 92:5 [b] Ps. 143:5 111:3 [a] Ps. 145:4, 5 111:4 [a] [Ps. 86:5] 111:7 [a] [Rev. 15:3] 111:8 [a] Is. 40:8 [b] [Rev. 15:3] 111:9 [a] Luke 1:68 [b] Luke 1:49 111:10 [a] Eccl. 12:13 112:1 [a] Ps. 128:1 112:2 [a] [Ps. 102:28] 112:3 [a] [Matt. 6:33] 112:4 [a] Job 11:17 112:5 [a] [Luke 6:35] [b] [Eph. 5:15] 112:6 [a] Prov. 10:7 112:7 [a] [Prov. 1:33] 112:8 [a] Heb. 13:9 [b] Prov. 1:33; 3:24 [c] Ps. 59:10 113:1 [a] Ps. 135:1 113:2 [a] [Dan. 2:20] 113:3 [a] Is. 59:19 113:4 [a] Ps. 97:9; 99:2 [b] [Ps. 8:1]

5 [a]Who *is* like the LORD our God,
Who dwells on high,
6 [a]Who humbles Himself to behold
The things that are in the heavens and in the earth?

7 [a]He raises the poor out of the dust,
And lifts the [b]needy out of the ash heap,
8 That He may [a]seat *him* with princes—
With the princes of His people.
9 [a]He grants the barren woman a home,
Like a joyful mother of children.

Praise the LORD!

PSALM 114

The Power of God in His Deliverance of Israel

1 When [a]Israel went out of Egypt,
The house of Jacob [b]from a people of strange language,
2 [a]Judah became His sanctuary,
And Israel His dominion.

3 [a]The sea saw *it* and fled;
[b]Jordan turned back.
4 [a]The mountains skipped like rams,
The little hills like lambs.
5 [a]What ails you, O sea, that you fled?
O Jordan, *that* you turned back?
6 O mountains, *that* you skipped like rams?
O little hills, like lambs?

7 Tremble, O earth, at the presence of the Lord,
At the presence of the God of Jacob,
8 [a]Who turned the rock *into* a pool of water,
The flint into a fountain of waters.

PSALM 115

The Futility of Idols and the Trustworthiness of God

1 Not [a]unto us, O LORD, not unto us,
But to Your name give glory,
Because of Your mercy,
Because of Your truth.
2 Why should the Gentiles say,
[a]"So where *is* their God?"

3 [a]But our God *is* in heaven;
He does whatever He pleases.
4 [a]Their idols *are* silver and gold,
The work of men's hands.

PEACE NOTE

When we walk in the peace of the Lord, we always give God all the credit. Only God can imbue us with His tranquil calm as we navigate life's challenges.

PSALM 115:1

5 They have mouths, but they do not speak;
Eyes they have, but they do not see;
6 They have ears, but they do not hear;
Noses they have, but they do not smell;
7 They have hands, but they do not handle;
Feet they have, but they do not walk;
Nor do they mutter through their throat.
8 [a]Those who make them are like them;
So is everyone who trusts in them.

9 [a]O Israel, trust in the LORD;
[b]He *is* their help and their shield.
10 O house of Aaron, trust in the LORD;
He *is* their help and their shield.
11 You who fear the LORD, trust in the LORD;
He *is* their help and their shield.

12 The LORD has been mindful of *us;*
He will bless us;
He will bless the house of Israel;
He will bless the house of Aaron.
13 [a]He will bless those who fear the LORD,
Both small and great.

14 May the LORD give you increase more and more,
You and your children.
15 *May* you *be* [a]blessed by the LORD,
[b]Who made heaven and earth.

16 The heaven, *even* the heavens, *are* the LORD's;
But the earth He has given to the children of men.

113:5 [a] [Is. 57:15] 113:6 [a] [Ps. 11:4] 113:7 [a] 1 Sam. 2:8 [b] Ps. 72:12 113:8 [a] [Job 36:7] 113:9 [a] 1 Sam. 2:5
114:1 [a] Ex. 12:51; 13:3 [b] Ps. 81:5 114:2 [a] Ex. 6:7; 19:6; 25:8; 29:45, 46 114:3 [a] Ex. 14:21 [b] Josh. 3:13–16 114:4 [a] Ps. 29:6
114:5 [a] Hab. 3:8 114:8 [a] Ex. 17:6 115:1 [a] [Is. 48:11] 115:2 [a] Ps. 42:3, 10 115:3 [a] [1 Chr. 16:26] 115:4 [a] Jer. 10:3
115:8 [a] Is. 44:9–11 115:9 [a] Ps. 118:2, 3 [b] Ps. 33:20 115:13 [a] Ps. 128:1, 4 115:15 [a] [Gen. 14:19] [b] Gen. 1:1

17 [a]The dead do not praise the LORD,
Nor any who go down into silence.
18 [a]But we will bless the LORD
From this time forth and forevermore.

Praise the LORD!

PSALM 116

Thanksgiving for Deliverance from Death

1 I [a]love the LORD, because He has heard
My voice *and* my supplications.
2 Because He has inclined His ear to me,
Therefore I will call *upon Him* as long as I live.

3 [a]The pains of death surrounded me,
And the pangs of Sheol laid hold of me;
I found trouble and sorrow.
4 Then I called upon the name of the LORD:
"O LORD, I implore You, deliver my soul!"

5 [a]Gracious *is* the LORD, and [b]righteous;
Yes, our God *is* merciful.
6 The LORD preserves the simple;
I was brought low, and He saved me.
7 Return to your [a]rest, O my soul,
For [b]the LORD has dealt bountifully with you.

8 [a]For You have delivered my soul from death,
My eyes from tears,
And my feet from falling.
9 I will walk before the LORD
[a]In the land of the living.
10 [a]I believed, therefore I spoke,
"I am greatly afflicted."
11 [a]I said in my haste,
[b]"All men *are* liars."

12 What shall I render to the LORD
For all His benefits toward me?
13 I will take up the cup of salvation,
And call upon the name of the LORD.
14 [a]I will pay my vows to the LORD
Now in the presence of all His people.

15 [a]Precious in the sight of the LORD
Is the death of His saints.
16 O LORD, truly [a]I *am* Your servant;
I *am* Your servant, [b]the son of Your maidservant;
You have loosed my bonds.
17 I will offer to You [a]the sacrifice of thanksgiving,
And will call upon the name of the LORD.
18 I will pay my vows to the LORD
Now in the presence of all His people,
19 In the [a]courts of the LORD's house,
In the midst of you, O Jerusalem.

Praise the LORD!

PSALM 117

Let All Peoples Praise the LORD

1 Praise [a]the LORD, all you Gentiles!
Laud Him, all you peoples!
2 For His merciful kindness is great toward us,
And [a]the truth of the LORD *endures* forever.

Praise the LORD!

PSALM 118

Praise to God for His Everlasting Mercy

1 Oh, [a]give thanks to the LORD, for *He is* good!
[b]For His mercy *endures* forever.

2 [a]Let Israel now say,
"His mercy *endures* forever."
3 Let the house of Aaron now say,
"His mercy *endures* forever."
4 Let those who fear the LORD now say,
"His mercy *endures* forever."

5 [a]I called on the LORD in distress;
The LORD answered me *and* [b]*set me* in a broad place.
6 [a]The LORD *is* on my side;
I will not fear.
What can man do to me?
7 [a]The LORD is for me among those who help me;
Therefore [b]I shall see *my desire* on those who hate me.
8 [a]*It is* better to trust in the LORD
Than to put confidence in man.
9 [a]*It is* better to trust in the LORD
Than to put confidence in princes.

115:17 [a] [Is. 38:18] **115:18** [a] Dan. 2:20 **116:1** [a] Ps. 18:1 **116:3** [a] Ps. 18:4–6 **116:5** [a] [Ps. 103:8] [b] [Ezra 9:15] **116:7** [a] [Jer. 6:16] [b] Ps. 13:6 **116:8** [a] Ps. 56:13 **116:9** [a] Ps. 27:13 **116:10** [a] 2 Cor. 4:13 **116:11** [a] Ps. 31:22 [b] Rom. 3:4 **116:14** [a] Ps. 116:18 **116:15** [a] Ps. 72:14 **116:16** [a] Ps. 119:125; 143:12 [b] Ps. 86:16 **116:17** [a] Lev. 7:12 **116:19** [a] Ps. 96:8 **117:1** [a] Rom. 15:11 **117:2** [a] [Ps. 100:5] **118:1** [a] 1 Chr. 16:8, 34 [b] [Ps. 136:1–26] **118:2** [a] [Ps. 115:9] **118:5** [a] Ps. 120:1 [b] Ps. 18:19 **118:6** [a] Ps. 27:1; 56:9 **118:7** [a] Ps. 54:4 [b] Ps. 59:10 **118:8** [a] Ps. 40:4 **118:9** [a] Ps. 146:3

PEACE NOTE

The Bible says peace is confidence and trust in God's wise control of our lives. The opposite of peace is anxiety.

PSALM 118:6

10 All nations surrounded me,
But in the name of the LORD I will
destroy them.
11 They [a]surrounded me,
Yes, they surrounded me;
But in the name of the LORD I will
destroy them.
12 They surrounded me [a]like bees;
They were quenched [b]like a fire of
thorns;
For in the name of the LORD I will
destroy them.
13 You pushed me violently, that I might
fall,
But the LORD helped me.
14 [a]The LORD *is* my strength and song,
And He has become my salvation.[1]
15 The voice of rejoicing and salvation
Is in the tents of the righteous;
The right hand of the LORD does
valiantly.
16 [a]The right hand of the LORD is exalted;
The right hand of the LORD does
valiantly.
17 [a]I shall not die, but live,
And [b]declare the works of the LORD.
18 The LORD has [a]chastened me severely,
But He has not given me over to death.

19 [a]Open to me the gates of righteousness;
I will go through them,
And I will praise the LORD.
20 [a]This is the gate of the LORD,
[b]Through which the righteous shall enter.

21 I will praise You,
For You have [a]answered me,
And have become my salvation.

22 [a]The stone *which* the builders rejected
Has become the chief cornerstone.
23 This was the LORD's doing;
It *is* marvelous in our eyes.
24 This *is* the day the LORD has made;
We will rejoice and be glad in it.

25 Save now, I pray, O LORD;
O LORD, I pray, send now prosperity.
26 [a]Blessed *is* he who comes in the name
of the LORD!
We have blessed you from the house of
the LORD.
27 God *is* the LORD,
And He has given us [a]light;
Bind the sacrifice with cords to the
horns of the altar.
28 You *are* my God, and I will praise You;
[a]*You are* my God, I will exalt You.

29 Oh, give thanks to the LORD, for *He is*
good!
For His mercy *endures* forever.

PSALM 119

Meditations on the Excellencies of the Word of God

א ALEPH

1 Blessed *are* the undefiled in the way,
[a]Who walk in the law of the LORD!
2 Blessed *are* those who keep His
testimonies,
Who seek Him with the [a]whole heart!
3 [a]They also do no iniquity;
They walk in His ways.
4 You have commanded *us*
To keep Your precepts diligently.
5 Oh, that my ways were directed
To keep Your statutes!
6 [a]Then I would not be ashamed,
When I look into all Your
commandments.
7 I will praise You with uprightness of
heart,
When I learn Your righteous
judgments.
8 I will keep Your statutes;
Oh, do not forsake me utterly!

ב BETH

9 How can a young man cleanse his way?
By taking heed according to Your word.

118:11 [a] Ps. 88:17 118:12 [a] Deut. 1:44 [b] Nah. 1:10 118:14 [a] Is. 12:2 [1] Compare Exodus 15:2 118:16 [a] Ex. 15:6 118:17 [a] Hab. 1:12 [b] Ps. 73:28 118:18 [a] 2 Cor. 6:9 118:19 [a] Is. 26:2 118:20 [a] Ps. 24:7 [b] Is. 35:8 118:21 [a] Ps. 116:1 118:22 [a] Matt. 21:42 118:26 [a] Mark 11:9 118:27 [a] [1 Pet. 2:9] 118:28 [a] Is. 25:1 119:1 [a] Ps. 128:1 119:2 [a] Deut. 6:5; 10:12; 11:13; 13:3 119:3 [a] [1 John 3:9; 5:18] 119:6 [a] Job 22:26

PEACE NOTE

Sometimes we will not immediately "feel" peaceful when we claim a promise of God's Word, but our feelings will eventually fall in line with the facts of our faith.

PSALM 119:10

10 With my whole heart I have [a]sought
You;
Oh, let me not wander from Your
commandments!
11 [a]Your word I have hidden in my heart,
That I might not sin against You.
12 Blessed *are* You, O LORD!
Teach me Your statutes.
13 With my lips I have [a]declared
All the judgments of Your mouth.
14 I have rejoiced in the way of Your
testimonies,
As *much as* in all riches.
15 I will meditate on Your precepts,
And contemplate Your ways.
16 I will [a]delight myself in Your statutes;
I will not forget Your word.

ג GIMEL

17 [a]Deal bountifully with Your servant,
That I may live and keep Your word.
18 Open my eyes, that I may see
Wondrous things from Your law.
19 [a]I *am* a stranger in the earth;
Do not hide Your commandments
from me.
20 [a]My soul breaks with longing
For Your judgments at all times.
21 You rebuke the proud—the cursed,
Who stray from Your commandments.
22 [a]Remove from me reproach and contempt,
For I have kept Your testimonies.
23 Princes also sit *and* speak against me,
But Your servant meditates on Your
statutes.
24 Your testimonies also *are* my delight
And my counselors.

ד DALETH

25 [a]My soul clings to the dust;
[b]Revive me according to Your word.
26 I have declared my ways, and You
answered me;
[a]Teach me Your statutes.
27 Make me understand the way of Your
precepts;
So [a]shall I meditate on Your wonderful
works.
28 [a]My soul melts from heaviness;
Strengthen me according to Your
word.
29 Remove from me the way of lying,
And grant me Your law graciously.
30 I have chosen the way of truth;
Your judgments I have laid
before me.
31 I cling to Your testimonies;
O LORD, do not put me to shame!
32 I will run the course of Your
commandments,
For You shall [a]enlarge my heart.

ה HE

33 [a]Teach me, O LORD, the way of Your
statutes,
And I shall keep it *to* the end.
34 [a]Give me understanding, and I shall
keep Your law;
Indeed, I shall observe it with *my*
whole heart.
35 Make me walk in the path of Your
commandments,
For I delight in it.
36 Incline my heart to Your testimonies,
And not to [a]covetousness.

PEACE NOTE

We have to wrap our feelings in the truth of God's Word. It is a lifelong journey to align our thinking with God's truth; peace will follow.

PSALM 119:10

119:10 [a] 2 Chr. 15:15 119:11 [a] Luke 2:19 119:13 [a] Ps. 34:11 119:16 [a] Ps. 1:2 119:17 [a] Ps. 116:7 119:19 [a] Heb. 11:13 119:20 [a] Ps. 42:1, 2; 63:1; 84:2 119:22 [a] Ps. 39:8 119:25 [a] Ps. 44:25 [b] Ps. 143:11 119:26 [a] Ps. 25:4; 27:11; 86:11 119:27 [a] Ps. 145:5, 6 119:28 [a] Ps. 107:26 119:32 [a] Is. 60:5 119:33 [a] [Rev. 2:26] 119:34 [a] [Prov. 2:6] 119:36 [a] Ezek. 33:31

PEACE NOTE

One of the most important ways to experience God's peace is to identify a group of Scriptures that really speak to you. Memorize them and keep them in front of you.

PSALM 119:11

37 [a]Turn away my eyes from [b]looking at
worthless things,
And revive me in Your way.[1]
38 [a]Establish Your word to Your servant,
Who *is devoted* to fearing You.
39 Turn away my reproach which I
dread,
For Your judgments *are* good.
40 Behold, I long for Your precepts;
Revive me in Your righteousness.

ו WAW

41 Let Your mercies come also to me,
O LORD—
Your salvation according to Your word.
42 So shall I have an answer for him who
reproaches me,
For I trust in Your word.
43 And take not the word of truth utterly
out of my mouth,
For I have hoped in Your
ordinances.
44 So shall I keep Your law continually,
Forever and ever.
45 And I will walk at [a]liberty,
For I seek Your precepts.
46 [a]I will speak of Your testimonies also
before kings,
And will not be ashamed.
47 And I will delight myself in Your
commandments,
Which I love.
48 My hands also I will lift up to Your
commandments,
Which I love,
And I will meditate on Your
statutes.

ז ZAYIN

49 Remember the word to Your servant,
Upon which You have caused me to
hope.
50 This *is* my [a]comfort in my affliction,
For Your word has given me life.
51 The proud have me in great derision,
Yet I do not turn aside from Your law.
52 I remembered Your judgments of old,
O LORD,
And have comforted myself.
53 [a]Indignation has taken hold of me
Because of the wicked, who forsake
Your law.
54 Your statutes have been my songs
In the house of my pilgrimage.
55 [a]I remember Your name in the night,
O LORD,
And I keep Your law.
56 This has become mine,
Because I kept Your precepts.

ח HETH

57 [a]*You are* my portion, O LORD;
I have said that I would keep Your words.
58 I entreated Your favor with *my* whole
heart;
Be merciful to me according to Your
word.
59 I [a]thought about my ways,
And turned my feet to Your testimonies.
60 I made haste, and did not delay
To keep Your commandments.
61 The cords of the wicked have bound me,
But I have not forgotten Your law.
62 [a]At midnight I will rise to give thanks to
You,
Because of Your righteous judgments.
63 I *am* a companion of all who fear You,
And of those who keep Your precepts.
64 [a]The earth, O LORD, is full of Your mercy;
Teach me Your statutes.

ט TETH

65 You have dealt well with Your servant,
O LORD, according to Your word.
66 Teach me good judgment and
[a]knowledge,
For I believe Your commandments.
67 Before I was [a]afflicted I went astray,
But now I keep Your word.
68 You *are* [a]good, and do good;
Teach me Your statutes.
69 The proud have [a]forged a lie against me,
But I will keep Your precepts with *my*
whole heart.

119:37 [a] Is. 33:15 [b] Prov. 23:5 [1] Following Masoretic Text, Septuagint, and Vulgate; Targum reads *Your words.*
119:38 [a] 2 Sam. 7:25 **119:45** [a] Prov. 4:12 **119:46** [a] Matt. 10:18 **119:50** [a] [Rom. 15:4] **119:53** [a] Ezra 9:3 **119:55** [a] Ps. 63:6
119:57 [a] Jer. 10:16 **119:59** [a] Luke 15:17 **119:62** [a] Acts 16:25 **119:64** [a] Ps. 33:5 **119:66** [a] Phil. 1:9 **119:67** [a] [Heb. 12:5–11]
119:68 [a] [Matt. 19:17] **119:69** [a] Job 13:4

70 [a]Their heart is as fat as grease,
But I delight in Your law.
71 *It is* good for me that I have been
afflicted,
That I may learn Your statutes.
72 [a]The law of Your mouth *is* better to me
Than thousands of *coins of* gold and
silver.

י YOD

73 [a]Your hands have made me and
fashioned me;
Give me understanding, that I may
learn Your commandments.
74 [a]Those who fear You will be glad when
they see me,
Because I have hoped in Your word.
75 I know, O LORD, [a]that Your judgments
are right,
And *that* in faithfulness You have
afflicted me.
76 Let, I pray, Your merciful kindness be
for my comfort,
According to Your word to Your
servant.
77 Let Your tender mercies come to me,
that I may live;
For Your law *is* my delight.
78 Let the proud [a]be ashamed,
For they treated me wrongfully with
falsehood;
But I will meditate on Your precepts.
79 Let those who fear You turn to me,
Those who know Your testimonies.
80 Let my heart be blameless regarding
Your statutes,
That I may not be ashamed.

כ KAPH

81 [a]My soul faints for Your salvation,
But I hope in Your word.
82 My eyes fail *from searching* Your
word,
Saying, "When will You comfort me?"
83 For [a]I have become like a wineskin in
smoke,
Yet I do not forget Your statutes.
84 [a]How many *are* the days of Your
servant?
[b]When will You execute judgment on
those who persecute me?
85 [a]The proud have dug pits for me,
Which *is* not according to Your law.
86 All Your commandments *are* faithful;
They persecute me [a]wrongfully;
Help me!
87 They almost made an end of me on
earth,
But I did not forsake Your precepts.
88 Revive me according to Your
lovingkindness,
So that I may keep the testimony of
Your mouth.

ל LAMED

89 [a]Forever, O LORD,
Your word is settled in heaven.
90 Your faithfulness *endures* to all
generations;
You established the earth, and it
abides.
91 They continue this day according to
[a]Your ordinances,
For all *are* Your servants.
92 Unless Your law *had been* my delight,
I would then have perished in my
affliction.
93 I will never forget Your precepts,
For by them You have given me life.
94 I *am* Yours, save me;
For I have sought Your precepts.
95 The wicked wait for me to
destroy me,
But I will consider Your testimonies.
96 [a]I have seen the consummation of all
perfection,
But Your commandment *is* exceedingly
broad.

מ MEM

97 Oh, how I love Your law!
[a]It *is* my meditation all the day.
98 You, through Your commandments,
make me [a]wiser than my enemies;
For they *are* ever with me.
99 I have more understanding than all my
teachers,
[a]For Your testimonies *are* my
meditation.
100 [a]I understand more than the ancients,
Because I keep Your precepts.
101 I have restrained my feet from every
evil way,
That I may keep Your word.
102 I have not departed from Your
judgments,
For You Yourself have taught me.
103 [a]How sweet are Your words to my taste,
Sweeter than honey to my mouth!
104 Through Your precepts I get
understanding;
Therefore I hate every false way.

119:70 [a] Acts 28:27 119:72 [a] Ps. 19:10 119:73 [a] Job 10:8; 31:15 119:74 [a] Ps. 34:2 119:75 [a] [Heb. 12:10]
119:78 [a] Ps. 25:3 119:81 [a] Ps. 73:26; 84:2 119:83 [a] Job 30:30 119:84 [a] Ps. 39:4 [b] Rev. 6:10 119:85 [a] Ps. 35:7
119:86 [a] Ps. 35:19 119:89 [a] Matt. 24:35 119:91 [a] Jer. 33:25 119:96 [a] Matt. 5:18 119:97 [a] Ps. 1:2 119:98 [a] Deut. 4:6
119:99 [a] [2 Tim. 3:15] 119:100 [a] [Job 32:7–9] 119:103 [a] Prov. 8:11

PEACE NOTE

We have to meditate on God's promises if we are to live in peace and happiness and unleash His reality in our lives.

PSALM 119:105

נ NUN

105 [a]Your word *is* a lamp to my feet
And a light to my path.
106 [a]I have sworn and confirmed
That I will keep Your righteous
judgments.
107 I am afflicted very much;
Revive me, O LORD, according to Your
word.
108 Accept, I pray, [a]the freewill offerings of
my mouth, O LORD,
And teach me Your judgments.
109 [a]My life *is* continually in my hand,
Yet I do not forget Your law.
110 [a]The wicked have laid a snare for me,
Yet I have not strayed from Your
precepts.
111 [a]Your testimonies I have taken as a
heritage forever,
For they *are* the rejoicing of my heart.
112 I have inclined my heart to perform
Your statutes
Forever, to the very end.

ס SAMEK

113 I hate the double-minded,
But I love Your law.
114 [a]You *are* my hiding place and my shield;
I hope in Your word.
115 [a]Depart from me, you evildoers,
For I will keep the commandments of
my God!
116 Uphold me according to Your word,
that I may live;
And do not let me [a]be ashamed of my
hope.
117 Hold me up, and I shall be safe,
And I shall observe Your statutes
continually.
118 You reject all those who stray from
Your statutes,
For their deceit *is* falsehood.
119 You put away all the wicked of the
earth [a]*like* dross;
Therefore I love Your testimonies.
120 [a]My flesh trembles for fear of You,
And I am afraid of Your judgments.

ע AYIN

121 I have done justice and righteousness;
Do not leave me to my oppressors.
122 Be [a]surety for Your servant for good;
Do not let the proud oppress me.
123 My eyes fail *from seeking* Your salvation
And Your righteous word.
124 Deal with Your servant according to
Your mercy,
And teach me Your statutes.
125 [a]I *am* Your servant;
Give me understanding,
That I may know Your testimonies.
126 *It is* time for *You* to act, O LORD,
For they have regarded Your law as
void.
127 [a]Therefore I love Your commandments
More than gold, yes, than fine gold!
128 Therefore all *Your* precepts *concerning*
all *things*
I consider *to be* right;
I hate every false way.

פ PE

129 Your testimonies are wonderful;
Therefore my soul keeps them.
130 The entrance of Your words gives
light;
[a]It gives understanding to the [b]simple.
131 I opened my mouth and [a]panted,
For I longed for Your commandments.
132 [a]Look upon me and be merciful to me,
[b]As Your custom *is* toward those who
love Your name.
133 [a]Direct my steps by Your word,
And [b]let no iniquity have dominion
over me.
134 [a]Redeem me from the oppression of
man,
That I may keep Your precepts.
135 [a]Make Your face shine upon Your
servant,
And teach me Your statutes.

119:105 [a] Prov. 6:23 **119:106** [a] Neh. 10:29 **119:108** [a] Hos. 14:2 **119:109** [a] Job 13:14 **119:110** [a] Ps. 140:5 **119:111** [a] Deut. 33:4 **119:114** [a] [Ps. 32:7] **119:115** [a] Matt. 7:23 **119:116** [a] [Rom. 5:5; 9:33; 10:11] **119:119** [a] Ezek. 22:18, 19 **119:120** [a] Hab. 3:16 **119:122** [a] Heb. 7:22 **119:125** [a] Ps. 116:16 **119:127** [a] Ps. 19:10 **119:130** [a] Prov. 6:23 [b] [Ps. 19:7] **119:131** [a] Ps. 42:1 **119:132** [a] Ps. 106:4 [b] [2 Thess. 1:6] **119:133** [a] Ps. 17:5 [b] [Rom. 6:12] **119:134** [a] Luke 1:74 **119:135** [a] Ps. 4:6

PEACE NOTE

One of the worst things a believer can do is listen to his or her heart. You have to speak truth to your heart *every day*. That's the only way to peace.

PSALM 119:133

136 [a]Rivers of water run down from my eyes,
Because *men* do not keep Your law.

צ TSADDE

137 [a]Righteous *are* You, O LORD,
And upright *are* Your judgments.
138 [a]Your testimonies, *which* You have commanded,
Are righteous and very faithful.
139 [a]My zeal has consumed me,
Because my enemies have forgotten Your words.
140 [a]Your word *is* very pure;
Therefore Your servant loves it.
141 I *am* small and despised,
Yet I do not forget Your precepts.
142 Your righteousness *is* an everlasting righteousness,
And Your law *is* [a]truth.
143 Trouble and anguish have overtaken me,
Yet Your commandments *are* my delights.
144 The righteousness of Your testimonies *is* everlasting;
Give me understanding, and I shall live.

ק QOPH

145 I cry out with *my* whole heart;
Hear me, O LORD!
I will keep Your statutes.
146 I cry out to You;
Save me, and I will keep Your testimonies.
147 [a]I rise before the dawning of the morning,
And cry for help;
I hope in Your word.
148 [a]My eyes are awake through the *night* watches,
That I may meditate on Your word.
149 Hear my voice according to Your lovingkindness;
O LORD, revive me according to Your justice.
150 They draw near who follow after wickedness;
They are far from Your law.
151 You *are* [a]near, O LORD,
And all Your commandments *are* truth.
152 Concerning Your testimonies,
I have known of old that You have founded them [a]forever.

ר RESH

153 [a]Consider my affliction and deliver me,
For I do not forget Your law.
154 [a]Plead my cause and redeem me;
Revive me according to Your word.
155 Salvation *is* far from the wicked,
For they do not seek Your statutes.
156 Great *are* Your tender mercies, O LORD;
Revive me according to Your judgments.
157 Many *are* my persecutors and my enemies,
Yet I do not [a]turn from Your testimonies.
158 I see the treacherous, and [a]am disgusted,
Because they do not keep Your word.
159 Consider how I love Your precepts;
Revive me, O LORD, according to Your lovingkindness.
160 The entirety of Your word *is* truth,
And every one of Your righteous judgments *endures* forever.

ש SHIN

161 [a]Princes persecute me without a cause,
But my heart stands in awe of Your word.
162 I rejoice at Your word
As one who finds great treasure.
163 I hate and abhor lying,
But I love Your law.
164 Seven times a day I praise You,
Because of Your righteous judgments.
165 [a]Great peace have those who love Your law,
And nothing causes them to stumble.
166 [a]LORD, I hope for Your salvation,
And I do Your commandments.

119:136 [a] Jer. 9:1, 18; 14:17 **119:137** [a] Neh. 9:33 **119:138** [a] [Ps. 19:7–9] **119:139** [a] John 2:17 **119:140** [a] Ps. 12:6 **119:142** [a] [John 17:17] **119:147** [a] Ps. 5:3 **119:148** [a] Ps. 63:1, 6 **119:151** [a] [Ps. 145:18] **119:152** [a] Luke 21:33 **119:153** [a] Lam. 5:1 **119:154** [a] 1 Sam. 24:15 **119:157** [a] Ps. 44:18 **119:158** [a] Ezek. 9:4 **119:161** [a] 1 Sam. 24:11; 26:18 **119:165** [a] Prov. 3:2 **119:166** [a] Gen. 49:18

167 My soul keeps Your testimonies,
And I love them exceedingly.
168 I keep Your precepts and Your testimonies,
[a]For all my ways *are* before You.

ת TAU
169 Let my cry come before You, O LORD;
[a]Give me understanding according to Your word.
170 Let my supplication come before You;
Deliver me according to Your word.
171 [a]My lips shall utter praise,
For You teach me Your statutes.
172 My tongue shall speak of Your word,
For all Your commandments *are* righteousness.
173 Let Your hand become my help,
For [a]I have chosen Your precepts.
174 [a]I long for Your salvation, O LORD,
And [b]Your law *is* my delight.
175 Let my soul live, and it shall praise You;
And let Your judgments help me.
176 [a]I have gone astray like a lost sheep;
Seek Your servant,
For I do not forget Your commandments.

PSALM 120

Plea for Relief from Bitter Foes

A Song of Ascents.

1 In [a]my distress I cried to the LORD,
And He heard me.
2 Deliver my soul, O LORD, from lying lips
And from a deceitful tongue.

3 What shall be given to you,
Or what shall be done to you,
You false tongue?
4 Sharp arrows of the warrior,
With coals of the broom tree!

5 Woe is me, that I dwell in [a]Meshech,
[b]*That* I dwell among the tents of Kedar!
6 My soul has dwelt too long
With one who hates peace.
7 I *am for* peace;
But when I speak, they *are* for war.

PSALM 121

God the Help of Those Who Seek Him

A Song of Ascents.

1 I [a]will lift up my eyes to the hills—
From whence comes my help?
2 [a]My help *comes* from the LORD,
Who made heaven and earth.

3 [a]He will not allow your foot to be moved;
[b]He who keeps you will not slumber.
4 Behold, He who keeps Israel
Shall neither slumber nor sleep.

5 The LORD *is* your keeper;
The LORD *is* [a]your shade [b]at your right hand.
6 [a]The sun shall not strike you by day,
Nor the moon by night.

7 The LORD shall preserve you from all evil;
He shall [a]preserve your soul.
8 The LORD shall [a]preserve your going out and your coming in
From this time forth, and even forevermore.

PSALM 122

The Joy of Going to the House of the LORD

A Song of Ascents. Of David.

1 I was glad when they said to me,
[a]"Let us go into the house of the LORD."
2 Our feet have been standing
Within your gates, O Jerusalem!

3 Jerusalem is built
As a city that is [a]compact together,
4 [a]Where the tribes go up,
The tribes of the LORD,
To [b]the Testimony of Israel,
To give thanks to the name of the LORD.
5 [a]For thrones are set there for judgment,
The thrones of the house of David.

6 [a]Pray for the peace of Jerusalem:
"May they prosper who love you.
7 Peace be within your walls,
Prosperity within your palaces."

119:168 [a] Prov. 5:21 119:169 [a] Ps. 119:27, 144 119:171 [a] Ps. 119:7 119:173 [a] Josh. 24:22 119:174 [a] Ps. 119:166 [b] Ps. 119:16, 24 119:176 [a] [Is. 53:6] 120:1 [a] Jon. 2:2 120:5 [a] Gen. 10:2 [b] Gen. 25:13 121:1 [a] [Jer. 3:23] 121:2 [a] [Ps. 124:8] 121:3 [a] 1 Sam. 2:9 [b] Is. 27:3 121:5 [a] Is. 25:4 [b] Ps. 16:8 121:6 [a] Is. 49:10 121:7 [a] Ps. 41:2 121:8 [a] Deut. 28:6 122:1 [a] [Is. 2:3] 122:3 [a] 2 Sam. 5:9 122:4 [a] Deut. 16:16 [b] Ex. 16:34 122:5 [a] Deut. 17:8 122:6 [a] Ps. 51:18

8 For the sake of my brethren and
companions,
I will now say, "Peace *be* within
you."
9 Because of the house of the LORD our
God
I will [a]seek your good.

PSALM 123

Prayer for Relief from Contempt

A Song of Ascents.

1 Unto You [a]I lift up my eyes,
O You [b]who dwell in the
heavens.
2 Behold, as the eyes of servants *look* to
the hand of their masters,
As the eyes of a maid to the hand of her
mistress,
[a]So our eyes *look* to the LORD our
God,
Until He has mercy on us.

3 Have mercy on us, O LORD, have mercy
on us!
For we are exceedingly filled with
contempt.
4 Our soul is exceedingly filled
With the scorn of those who are at
ease,
With the contempt of the proud.

PSALM 124

The LORD the Defense of His People

A Song of Ascents. Of David.

1 "If it had not been the LORD who was on
our [a]side,"
[b]Let Israel now say—
2 "If it had not been the LORD who was on
our side,
When men rose up against us,
3 Then they would have [a]swallowed us
alive,
When their wrath was kindled against
us;
4 Then the waters would have
overwhelmed us,
The stream would have gone over our
soul;
5 Then the swollen waters
Would have gone over our soul."

6 Blessed *be* the LORD,
Who has not given us *as* prey to their
teeth.
7 [a]Our soul has escaped [b]as a bird from
the snare of the fowlers;[1]
The snare is broken, and we have
escaped.
8 [a]Our help *is* in the name of the LORD,
[b]Who made heaven and
earth.

122:9 [a] Neh. 2:10 **123:1** [a] Ps. 121:1; 141:8 [b] Ps. 2:4; 11:4; 115:3 **123:2** [a] Ps. 25:15 **124:1** [a] [Rom. 8:31] [b] Ps. 129:1 **124:3** [a] Prov. 1:12 **124:7** [a] Ps. 91:3 [b] Prov. 6:5 [1] That is, persons who catch birds in a trap or snare **124:8** [a] [Ps. 121:2] [b] Gen. 1:1

PEACE WITHIN AND WITHOUT

Pray for the peace of Jerusalem . . . Peace be within your walls . . . I will now say, "Peace be within you."

PSALM 122:6-8

Psalm 122 is a Song of Ascents. Locals and pilgrims from afar sang this song as they ascended the hills that led to Jerusalem and the holy mount on which the temple of the Lord stood. David began his psalm by declaring, "I was glad when they said to me, 'Let us go into the house of the LORD'" (v. 1). The focus of the psalm seems to be on the unity of the people of Israel who traveled to Jerusalem and the house of the Lord "to give thanks to the name of the LORD" (v. 4). What brings about this unity and what results from it is peace, a word that appears three times in as many verses: "Pray for the peace of Jerusalem . . . Peace be within your walls . . . I will now say, 'Peace be within you'" (vv. 6–8).

This is an important but sometimes overlooked aspect of peace—it cultivates harmony and unity. Individual peace is good, but community peace is special, whether in the family, the church, or a city. When people of peace assemble, the goodness and wholeness of peace are multiplied.

Are you aware of disharmony in your family, your church, your friends? How can you bring peace to the points of conflict in order to restore unity?

PSALM 125

The LORD the Strength of His People

A Song of Ascents.

1 Those who trust in the LORD
Are like Mount Zion,
Which cannot be moved, *but* abides
forever.
2 As the mountains surround Jerusalem,
So the LORD surrounds His people
From this time forth and forever.

3 For [a]the scepter of wickedness shall
not rest
On the land allotted to the righteous,
Lest the righteous reach out their
hands to iniquity.

4 Do good, O LORD, to *those who are*
good,
And to *those who are* upright in their
hearts.

5 As for such as turn aside to their
[a]crooked ways,
The LORD shall lead them away
With the workers of iniquity.

[b]Peace *be* upon Israel!

PSALM 126

A Joyful Return to Zion

A Song of Ascents.

1 When [a]the LORD brought back the
captivity of Zion,
[b]We were like those who dream.
2 Then [a]our mouth was filled with
laughter,
And our tongue with singing.
Then they said among the nations,
"The LORD has done great things for
them."
3 The LORD has done great things for us,
And we are glad.

4 Bring back our captivity, O LORD,
As the streams in the South.

5 [a]Those who sow in tears
Shall reap in joy.
6 He who continually goes forth
weeping,
Bearing seed for sowing,
Shall doubtless come again with
[a]rejoicing,
Bringing his sheaves *with him.*

PEACE NOTE

The peace of God comes from our trust in God. Scripture compares those who trust in the Lord to a mountain that "cannot be moved."

PSALM 125:1

PSALM 127

Laboring and Prospering with the LORD

A Song of Ascents. Of Solomon.

1 Unless the LORD builds the house,
They labor in vain who build it;
Unless [a]the LORD guards the city,
The watchman stays awake in vain.
2 *It is* vain for you to rise up early,
To sit up late,
To [a]eat the bread of sorrows;
For so He gives His beloved sleep.

3 Behold, [a]children *are* a heritage from
the LORD,
[b]The fruit of the womb *is* a [c]reward.
4 Like arrows in the hand of a warrior,
So *are* the children of one's youth.
5 [a]Happy *is* the man who has his quiver
full of them;
[b]They shall not be ashamed,
But shall speak with their enemies in
the gate.

PSALM 128

Blessings of Those Who Fear the LORD

A Song of Ascents.

1 Blessed [a]*is* every one who fears the LORD,
Who walks in His ways.

2 [a]When you eat the labor of your hands,
You *shall be* happy, and *it shall be* [b]well
with you.
3 Your wife *shall be* [a]like a fruitful vine
In the very heart of your house,
Your [b]children [c]like olive plants
All around your table.

125:3 [a] Prov. 22:8 125:5 [a] Prov. 2:15 [b] [Gal. 6:16] 126:1 [a] Hos. 6:11 [b] Acts 12:9 126:2 [a] Job 8:21 126:5 [a] Jer. 31:9 126:6 [a] Is. 61:3 127:1 [a] [Ps. 121:3–5] 127:2 [a] [Gen. 3:17, 19] 127:3 [a] [Josh. 24:3, 4] [b] Deut. 7:13; 28:4 [c] [Ps. 113:9] 127:5 [a] Ps. 128:2, 3 [b] Prov. 27:11 128:1 [a] Ps. 119:1 128:2 [a] Is. 3:10 [b] Deut. 4:40 128:3 [a] Ezek. 19:10 [b] Ps. 127:3–5 [c] Ps. 52:8; 144:12

PEACE NOTE

The devil will do everything he can to isolate us. Let's be present for others when they hurt and vice versa; we can share the richness of God's peace.

4 Behold, thus shall the man be blessed
Who fears the LORD.

5 [a]The LORD bless you out of Zion,
And may you see the good of Jerusalem
All the days of your life.
6 Yes, may you [a]see your children's
children.

[b]Peace *be* upon Israel!

PSALM 129

Song of Victory over Zion's Enemies

A Song of Ascents.

1 "Many a time they have [a]afflicted me
from [b]my youth,"
[c]Let Israel now say—
2 "Many a time they have afflicted me
from my youth;
Yet they have not prevailed against me.
3 The plowers plowed on my back;
They made their furrows long."
4 The LORD *is* righteous;
He has cut in pieces the cords of the
wicked.

5 Let all those who hate Zion
Be put to shame and turned back.
6 Let them be as the [a]grass *on* the housetops,
Which withers before it grows up,
7 With which the reaper does not fill his
hand,
Nor he who binds sheaves, his arms.
8 Neither let those who pass by them say,
[a]"The blessing of the LORD *be* upon you;
We bless you in the name of the LORD!"

PSALM 130

Waiting for the Redemption of the LORD

A Song of Ascents.

1 Out [a]of the depths I have cried to You,
O LORD;
2 Lord, hear my voice!
Let Your ears be attentive
To the voice of my supplications.

3 [a]If You, LORD, should mark iniquities,
O Lord, who could [b]stand?
4 But *there is* [a]forgiveness with You,
That [b]You may be feared.

5 [a]I wait for the LORD, my soul waits,
And [b]in His word I do hope.
6 [a]My soul *waits* for the Lord
More than those who watch for the
morning—
Yes, more than those who watch for the
morning.

7 [a]O Israel, hope in the LORD;
For [b]with the LORD *there is* mercy,
And with Him *is* abundant redemption.
8 And [a]He shall redeem Israel
From all his iniquities.

PSALM 131

Simple Trust in the LORD

A Song of Ascents. Of David.

1 LORD, my heart is not haughty,
Nor my eyes lofty.
[a]Neither do I concern myself with great
matters,
Nor with things too profound for me.

2 Surely I have calmed and quieted my
soul,
[a]Like a weaned child with his mother;
Like a weaned child *is* my soul
within me.

3 [a]O Israel, hope in the LORD
From this time forth and forever.

PSALM 132

The Eternal Dwelling of God in Zion

A Song of Ascents.

1 LORD, remember David
And all his afflictions;
2 How he swore to the LORD,
[a]*And* vowed to [b]the Mighty One of Jacob:

128:5 [a] Ps. 134:3 128:6 [a] Job 42:16 [b] Ps. 125:5 129:1 [a] [Jer. 1:19; 15:20] [b] Ezek. 23:3 [c] Ps. 124:1 129:6 [a] Ps. 37:2 129:8 [a] Ruth 2:4 130:1 [a] Lam. 3:55 130:3 [a] [Ps. 143:2] [b] [Nah. 1:6] 130:4 [a] [Ex. 34:7] [b] [1 Kin. 8:39, 40] 130:5 [a] [Ps. 27:14] [b] Ps. 119:81 130:6 [a] Ps. 119:147 130:7 [a] Ps. 131:3 [b] [Is. 55:7] 130:8 [a] [Ps. 103:3, 4] 131:1 [a] [Rom. 12:16] 131:2 [a] [Matt. 18:3] 131:3 [a] [Ps. 130:7] 132:2 [a] Ps. 65:1 [b] Gen. 49:24

3 "Surely I will not go into the chamber of
my house,
Or go up to the comfort of my bed;
4 I will [a]not give sleep to my eyes
Or slumber to my eyelids,
5 Until I [a]find a place for the LORD,
A dwelling place for the Mighty One of
Jacob."

6 Behold, we heard of it [a]in Ephrathah;
[b]We found it [c]in the fields of the woods.[1]
7 Let us go into His tabernacle;
[a]Let us worship at His footstool.
8 [a]Arise, O LORD, to Your resting place,
You and [b]the ark of Your strength.
9 Let Your priests [a]be clothed with
righteousness,
And let Your saints shout for joy.

10 For Your servant David's sake,
Do not turn away the face of Your
Anointed.

11 [a]The LORD has sworn *in* truth to David;
He will not turn from it:
"I will set upon your throne [b]the fruit of
your body.
12 If your sons will keep My covenant
And My testimony which I shall teach
them,
Their sons also shall sit upon your
throne forevermore."

13 [a]For the LORD has chosen Zion;
He has desired *it* for His dwelling place:
14 "This[a] *is* My resting place forever;
Here I will dwell, for I have desired it.
15 [a]I will abundantly bless her provision;
I will satisfy her poor with bread.
16 [a]I will also clothe her priests with
salvation,
[b]And her saints shall shout aloud for joy.
17 [a]There I will make the horn of David
grow;
[b]I will prepare a lamp for My Anointed.
18 His enemies I will [a]clothe with shame,
But upon Himself His crown shall
flourish."

PSALM 133

Blessed Unity of the People of God

A Song of Ascents. Of David.

1 Behold, how good and how pleasant *it is*
For [a]brethren to dwell together in unity!

PEACE NOTE

Jesus manifests His powerful presence through our lives to others! You can be like Jesus today when you practice the ministry of presence in His name.

2 *It is* like the precious oil upon the head,
Running down on the beard,
The beard of Aaron,
Running down on the edge of his
garments.
3 *It is* like the dew of [a]Hermon,
Descending upon the mountains of Zion;
For [b]there the LORD commanded the
blessing—
Life forevermore.

PSALM 134

Praising the LORD in His House at Night

A Song of Ascents.

1 Behold, bless the LORD,
All *you* servants of the LORD,
Who by night stand in the house of the
LORD!
2 [a]Lift up your hands *in* the sanctuary,
And bless the LORD.

3 The LORD who made heaven and earth
Bless you from Zion!

PSALM 135

Praise to God in Creation and Redemption

1 Praise the LORD!

Praise the name of the LORD;
[a]Praise *Him,* O you servants of the LORD!
2 [a]You who stand in the house of the LORD,
In [b]the courts of the house of our God,

132:4 [a] Prov. 6:4 **132:5** [a] Acts 7:46 **132:6** [a] 1 Sam. 17:12 [b] 1 Sam. 7:1 [c] 1 Chr. 13:5 [1] Hebrew *Jaar* **132:7** [a] Ps. 5:7; 99:5 **132:8** [a] Num. 10:35 [b] Ps. 78:61 **132:9** [a] Job 29:14 **132:11** [a] [Ps. 89:3, 4, 33; 110:4] [b] 2 Sam. 7:12 **132:13** [a] [Ps. 48:1, 2] **132:14** [a] Ps. 68:16 **132:15** [a] Ps. 147:14 **132:16** [a] 2 Chr. 6:41 [b] 1 Sam. 4:5 **132:17** [a] Ezek. 29:21 [b] 1 Kin. 11:36; 15:4 **132:18** [a] Ps. 35:26 **133:1** [a] Gen. 13:8 **133:3** [a] Deut. 4:48 [b] Lev. 25:21 **134:2** [a] [1 Tim. 2:8] **135:1** [a] Ps. 113:1 **135:2** [a] Luke 2:37 [b] Ps. 116:19

3 Praise the LORD, for [a]the LORD *is* good;
Sing praises to His name, [b]for *it is* pleasant.
4 For [a]the LORD has chosen Jacob for Himself,
Israel for His special treasure.

5 For I know that [a]the LORD *is* great,
And our Lord *is* above all gods.
6 [a]Whatever the LORD pleases He does,
In heaven and in earth,
In the seas and in all deep places.
7 [a]He causes the vapors to ascend from the ends of the earth;
[b]He makes lightning for the rain;
He brings the wind out of His [c]treasuries.

PEACE NOTE

Because the Lord is so great,
He can carry you, calm you,
and lead you to victory!

PSALM 135:5

8 [a]He destroyed the firstborn of Egypt,
Both of man and beast.
9 [a]He sent signs and wonders into the midst of you, O Egypt,
[b]Upon Pharaoh and all his servants.
10 [a]He defeated many nations
And slew mighty kings—
11 Sihon king of the Amorites,
Og king of Bashan,
And [a]all the kingdoms of Canaan—
12 [a]And gave their land *as* a heritage,
A heritage to Israel His people.

13 [a]Your name, O LORD, *endures* forever,
Your fame, O LORD, throughout all generations.
14 [a]For the LORD will judge His people,
And He will have compassion on His *servants*.

15 [a]The idols of the nations *are* silver and gold,
The work of men's hands.
16 They have mouths, but they do not speak;
Eyes they have, but they do not see;
17 They have ears, but they do not hear;
Nor is there *any* breath in their mouths.
18 Those who make them are like them;
So is everyone who trusts in them.

19 [a]Bless the LORD, O house of Israel!
Bless the LORD, O house of Aaron!
20 Bless the LORD, O house of Levi!
You who fear the LORD, bless the LORD!
21 Blessed be the LORD [a]out of Zion,
Who dwells in Jerusalem!

Praise the LORD!

PSALM 136

Thanksgiving to God for His Enduring Mercy

1 Oh, [a]give thanks to the LORD, for *He is* good!
[b]For His mercy *endures* forever.
2 Oh, give thanks to [a]the God of gods!
For His mercy *endures* forever.
3 Oh, give thanks to the Lord of lords!
For His mercy *endures* forever:

4 To Him [a]who alone does great wonders,
For His mercy *endures* forever;
5 [a]To Him who by wisdom made the heavens,
For His mercy *endures* forever;
6 [a]To Him who laid out the earth above the waters,
For His mercy *endures* forever;
7 [a]To Him who made great lights,
For His mercy *endures* forever—
8 [a]The sun to rule by day,
For His mercy *endures* forever;
9 The moon and stars to rule by night,
For His mercy *endures* forever.

10 [a]To Him who struck Egypt in their firstborn,
For His mercy *endures* forever;
11 [a]And brought out Israel from among them,
For His mercy *endures* forever;

135:3 [a] [Ps. 119:68] [b] Ps. 147:1 135:4 [a] [Ex. 19:5] 135:5 [a] Ps. 95:3; 97:9 135:6 [a] Ps. 115:3 135:7 [a] Jer. 10:13 [b] Job 28:25, 26; 38:24–28 [c] Jer. 51:16 135:8 [a] Ex. 12:12 135:9 [a] Ex. 7:10 [b] Ps. 136:15 135:10 [a] Num. 21:24 135:11 [a] Josh. 12:7–24 135:12 [a] Ps. 78:55; 136:21, 22 135:13 [a] [Ex. 3:15] 135:14 [a] Deut. 32:36 135:15 [a] [Ps. 115:4–8] 135:19 [a] [Ps. 115:9] 135:21 [a] Ps. 134:3 136:1 [a] Ps. 106:1 [b] 1 Chr. 16:34 136:2 [a] [Deut. 10:17] 136:4 [a] Ps. 72:18 136:5 [a] Jer. 51:15 136:6 [a] Jer. 10:12 136:7 [a] Gen. 1:14–18 136:8 [a] Gen. 1:16 136:10 [a] Ex. 12:29 136:11 [a] Ex. 12:51; 13:3, 16

12 [a]With a strong hand, and with an outstretched arm,
For His mercy *endures* forever;
13 [a]To Him who divided the Red Sea in two,
For His mercy *endures* forever;
14 And made Israel pass through the midst of it,
For His mercy *endures* forever;
15 [a]But overthrew Pharaoh and his army in the Red Sea,
For His mercy *endures* forever;
16 [a]To Him who led His people through the wilderness,
For His mercy *endures* forever;
17 [a]To Him who struck down great kings,
For His mercy *endures* forever;
18 [a]And slew famous kings,
For His mercy *endures* forever—
19 [a]Sihon king of the Amorites,
For His mercy *endures* forever;
20 [a]And Og king of Bashan,
For His mercy *endures* forever—
21 [a]And gave their land as a heritage,
For His mercy *endures* forever;
22 A heritage to Israel His servant,
For His mercy *endures* forever.

23 Who [a]remembered us in our lowly state,
For His mercy *endures* forever;
24 And [a]rescued us from our enemies,
For His mercy *endures* forever;
25 [a]Who gives food to all flesh,
For His mercy *endures* forever.

26 Oh, give thanks to the God of heaven!
For His mercy *endures* forever.

PSALM 137

Longing for Zion in a Foreign Land

1 By the rivers of Babylon,
There we sat down, yea, we wept
When we remembered Zion.
2 We hung our harps
Upon the willows in the midst of it.
3 For there those who carried us away captive asked of us a song,
And those who [a]plundered us *requested* mirth,
Saying, "Sing us *one* of the songs of Zion!"

4 How shall we sing the LORD's song
In a foreign land?
5 If I forget you, O Jerusalem,
Let my right hand forget *its skill!*
6 If I do not remember you,
Let my [a]tongue cling to the roof of my mouth—
If I do not exalt Jerusalem
Above my chief joy.

7 Remember, O LORD, against [a]the sons of Edom
The day of Jerusalem,
Who said, "Raze *it,* raze *it,*
To its very foundation!"

8 O daughter of Babylon, [a]who are to be destroyed,
Happy the one [b]who repays you as you have served us!
9 Happy the one who takes and [a]dashes
Your little ones against the rock!

PSALM 138

The LORD's Goodness to the Faithful

A Psalm of David.

1 I will praise You with my whole heart;
[a]Before the gods I will sing praises to You.
2 [a]I will worship [b]toward Your holy temple,
And praise Your name
For Your lovingkindness and Your truth;
For You have [c]magnified Your word above all Your name.
3 In the day when I cried out, You answered me,
And made me bold *with* strength in my soul.

4 [a]All the kings of the earth shall praise You, O LORD,
When they hear the words of Your mouth.
5 Yes, they shall sing of the ways of the LORD,
For great *is* the glory of the LORD.
6 [a]Though the LORD *is* on high,
Yet [b]He regards the lowly;
But the proud He knows from afar.

7 [a]Though I walk in the midst of trouble, You will revive me;
You will stretch out Your hand
Against the wrath of my enemies,
And Your right hand will save me.
8 [a]The LORD will perfect *that which* concerns me;
Your mercy, O LORD, *endures* forever;
[b]Do not forsake the works of Your hands.

136:12 [a] Ex. 6:6 **136:13** [a] Ex. 14:21 **136:15** [a] Ex. 14:27 **136:16** [a] Ex. 13:18; 15:22 **136:17** [a] Ps. 135:10–12 **136:18** [a] Deut. 29:7 **136:19** [a] Num. 21:21 **136:20** [a] Num. 21:33 **136:21** [a] Josh. 12:1 **136:23** [a] Gen. 8:1 **136:24** [a] Ps. 44:7 **136:25** [a] Ps. 104:27; 145:15 **137:3** [a] Ps. 79:1 **137:6** [a] Ezek. 3:26 **137:7** [a] Jer. 49:7–22 **137:8** [a] Is. 13:1–6; 47:1 [b] Jer. 50:15 **137:9** [a] Is. 13:16 **138:1** [a] Ps. 119:46 **138:2** [a] Ps. 28:2 [b] 1 Kin. 8:29 [c] Is. 42:21 **138:4** [a] Ps. 102:15 **138:6** [a] [Ps. 113:4–7] [b] [James 4:6] **138:7** [a] [Ps. 23:3, 4] **138:8** [a] Ps. 57:2 [b] Job 10:3, 8

PSALM 139

God's Perfect Knowledge of Man

For the Chief Musician. A Psalm of David.

1 O LORD, [a]You have searched me and
known *me.*
2 [a]You know my sitting down and my
rising up;
You [b]understand my thought afar off.
3 [a]You comprehend my path and my
lying down,
And are acquainted with all my ways.
4 For *there is* not a word on my tongue,
But behold, O LORD, [a]You know it
altogether.
5 You have hedged me behind and before,
And laid Your hand upon me.
6 [a]*Such* knowledge *is* too wonderful for me;
It is high, I cannot *attain* it.

7 [a]Where can I go from Your Spirit?
Or where can I flee from Your presence?
8 [a]If I ascend into heaven, You *are* there;
[b]If I make my bed in hell, behold, You
are there.
9 *If* I take the wings of the morning,
And dwell in the uttermost parts of the
sea,
10 Even there Your hand shall lead me,
And Your right hand shall hold me.
11 If I say, "Surely the darkness shall fall[1]
on me,"
Even the night shall be light about me;
12 Indeed, [a]the darkness shall not hide
from You,
But the night shines as the day;
The darkness and the light *are* both
alike *to You.*

13 For You formed my inward parts;
You covered me in my mother's
womb.
14 I will praise You, for I am fearfully *and*
wonderfully made;[1]
Marvelous are Your works,
And *that* my soul knows very well.
15 [a]My frame was not hidden from You,
When I was made in secret,
And skillfully wrought in the lowest
parts of the earth.
16 Your eyes saw my substance, being yet
unformed.
And in Your book they all were written,
The days fashioned for me,
When *as yet there were* none of them.

PEACE NOTE

Step back and humbly say, "God, I don't understand, but I will trust You with this mystery and praise You because You do understand."

PSALM 139:6

17 [a]How precious also are Your thoughts to
me, O God!
How great is the sum of them!
18 *If* I should count them, they would be
more in number than the sand;
When I awake, I am still with You.

19 Oh, that You would [a]slay the wicked,
O God!
[b]Depart from me, therefore, you
bloodthirsty men.
20 For they [a]speak against You
wickedly;
Your enemies take *Your name* in vain.[1]
21 [a]Do I not hate them, O LORD, who hate
You?
And do I not loathe those who rise up
against You?
22 I hate them with perfect hatred;
I count them my enemies.

23 [a]Search me, O God, and know my heart;
Try me, and know my anxieties;
24 And see if *there is any* wicked way
in me,
And [a]lead me in the way everlasting.

PSALM 140

Prayer for Deliverance from Evil Men

To the Chief Musician. A Psalm of David.

1 Deliver me, O LORD, from evil men;
Preserve me from violent men,
2 Who plan evil things in *their* hearts;
[a]They continually gather together *for*
war.

139:1 [a] Ps. 17:3 **139:2** [a] 2 Kin. 19:27 [b] Matt. 9:4 **139:3** [a] Job 14:16; 31:4 **139:4** [a] [Heb. 4:13] **139:6** [a] Job 42:3 **139:7** [a] [Jer. 23:24] **139:8** [a] [Amos 9:2–4] [b] [Job 26:6] **139:11** [1] Vulgate and Symmachus read *cover.* **139:12** [a] Job 26:6; 34:22 **139:14** [1] Following Masoretic Text and Targum; Septuagint, Syriac, and Vulgate read *You are fearfully wonderful.* **139:15** [a] Job 10:8, 9 **139:17** [a] [Ps. 40:5] **139:19** [a] [Is. 11:4] [b] Ps. 119:115 **139:20** [a] Jude 15 [1] Septuagint and Vulgate read *They take Your cities in vain.* **139:21** [a] 2 Chr. 19:2 **139:23** [a] Job 31:6 **139:24** [a] Ps. 5:8; 143:10 **140:2** [a] Ps. 56:6

GOD SEES ALL OF YOU

Search me, O God, and know my heart . . . see if there is any wicked way in me.

PSALM 139:23-24

Psalm 139 is one of the most powerful, emotional psalms in the Psalter. The psalm may have resulted from years of reflection long after David's sin with Bathsheba as the king began to understand humans' moral weakness on the one hand and the power and grace of God on the other. What strikes me about this psalm is David's desire that God know him well, that no corrupt part of himself should escape God's gaze. Our natural inclination is to hide our sin (as did Adam and Eve). But David had learned that confession and transparency are essential if recovery, forgiveness, and redemption are to take place.

"Search me, O God, and know my heart . . . see if there is any wicked way in me," David petitioned. He longed for this spiritual and moral cleansing to create a closer relationship. Peace cannot be built on a façade; it will not flourish in dishonesty. Peace grows in a context of transparency with God, in the person who seeks His will.

Is there anything you've been hiding from God? How does that affect your peace?

3 They sharpen their tongues like a
serpent;
The [a]poison of asps *is* under their lips. *Selah*

4 [a]Keep me, O LORD, from the hands of
the wicked;
Preserve me from violent men,
Who have purposed to make my steps
stumble.
5 The proud have hidden a [a]snare for
me, and cords;
They have spread a net by the wayside;
They have set traps for me. *Selah*

6 I said to the LORD: "You *are* my God;
Hear the voice of my supplications,
O LORD.
7 O GOD the Lord, the strength of my
salvation,
You have covered my head in the day
of battle.
8 Do not grant, O LORD, the desires of the
wicked;
Do not further his *wicked* scheme,
[a]*Lest* they be exalted. *Selah*

9 "*As for* the head of those who surround me,
Let the evil of their lips cover them;
10 [a]Let burning coals fall upon them;
Let them be cast into the fire,
Into deep pits, that they rise not up
again.
11 Let not a slanderer be established in
the earth;
Let evil hunt the violent man to
overthrow *him*."

12 I know that the LORD will [a]maintain
The cause of the afflicted,
And justice for the poor.
13 Surely the righteous shall give thanks
to Your name;
The upright shall dwell in Your presence.

PSALM 141

Prayer for Safekeeping from Wickedness

A Psalm of David.

1 LORD, I cry out to You;
Make haste to me!
Give ear to my voice when I cry out to You.
2 Let my prayer be set before You [a]*as*
incense,
[b]The lifting up of my hands *as* [c]the
evening sacrifice.

3 Set a guard, O LORD, over my [a]mouth;
Keep watch over the door of my lips.
4 Do not incline my heart to any evil thing,
To practice wicked works
With men who work iniquity;
[a]And do not let me eat of their delicacies.

5 [a]Let the righteous strike me;
It shall be a kindness.

140:3 [a] Ps. 58:4 **140:4** [a] Ps. 71:4 **140:5** [a] Jer. 18:22 **140:8** [a] Deut. 32:27 **140:10** [a] Ps. 11:6 **140:12** [a] 1 Kin. 8:45
141:2 [a] [Rev. 5:8; 8:3, 4] [b] [1 Tim. 2:8] [c] Ex. 29:39, 41 **141:3** [a] [Prov. 13:3; 21:23] **141:4** [a] Prov. 23:6 **141:5** [a] [Prov. 9:8]

And let him rebuke me;
It shall be as excellent oil;
Let my head not refuse it.

For still my prayer *is* against the deeds of the wicked.
6 Their judges are overthrown by the sides of the cliff,
And they hear my words, for they are sweet.
7 Our bones are scattered at the mouth of the grave,
As when one plows and breaks up the earth.

8 But [a]my eyes *are* upon You, O GOD the Lord;
In You I take refuge;
Do not leave my soul destitute.
9 Keep me from [a]the snares they have laid for me,
And from the traps of the workers of iniquity.
10 [a]Let the wicked fall into their own nets,
While I escape safely.

PSALM 142

A Plea for Relief from Persecutors

A [a]Contemplation[1] of David. A Prayer [b]when he was in the cave.

1 I cry out to the LORD with my voice;
With my voice to the LORD I make my supplication.
2 I pour out my complaint before Him;
I declare before Him my trouble.

3 When my spirit was [a]overwhelmed within me,
Then You knew my path.
In the way in which I walk
They have secretly [b]set a snare for me.
4 Look on *my* right hand and see,
For *there is* no one who acknowledges me;
Refuge has failed me;
No one cares for my soul.

5 I cried out to You, O LORD:
I said, "You *are* my refuge,
My portion in the land of the living.
6 Attend to my cry,
For I am brought very low;
Deliver me from my persecutors,
For they are stronger than I.
7 Bring my soul out of prison,
That I may [a]praise Your name;
The righteous shall surround me,
For You shall deal bountifully with me."

PSALM 143

An Earnest Appeal for Guidance and Deliverance

A Psalm of David.

1 Hear my prayer, O LORD,
Give ear to my supplications!
In Your faithfulness answer me,
And in Your righteousness.
2 Do not enter into judgment with Your servant,
[a]For in Your sight no one living is righteous.

3 For the enemy has persecuted my soul;
He has crushed my life to the ground;
He has made me dwell in darkness,
Like those who have long been dead.
4 [a]Therefore my spirit is overwhelmed within me;
My heart within me is distressed.

5 [a]I remember the days of old;
I meditate on all Your works;
I muse on the work of Your hands.
6 I spread out my hands to You;
[a]My soul *longs* for You like a thirsty land. *Selah*

7 Answer me speedily, O LORD;
My spirit fails!
Do not hide Your face from me,
[a]Lest I be like those who go down into the pit.
8 Cause me to hear Your lovingkindness [a]in the morning,
For in You do I trust;
[b]Cause me to know the way in which I should walk,
For [c]I lift up my soul to You.

9 Deliver me, O LORD, from my enemies;
In You I take shelter.[1]
10 [a]Teach me to do Your will,
For You *are* my God;
[b]Your Spirit *is* good.
Lead me in [c]the land of uprightness.

11 [a]Revive me, O LORD, for Your name's sake!
For Your righteousness' sake bring my soul out of trouble.
12 In Your mercy [a]cut off my enemies,
And destroy all those who afflict my soul;
For I *am* Your servant.

141:8 [a] Ps. 25:15 141:9 [a] Ps. 119:110 141:10 [a] Ps. 35:8 142:title [a] Ps. 32:title [b] 1 Sam. 22:1 [1] Hebrew *Maschil* 142:3 [a] Ps. 77:3 [b] Ps. 141:9 142:7 [a] Ps. 34:1, 2 143:2 [a] [Gal. 2:16] 143:4 [a] Ps. 77:3 143:5 [a] Ps. 77:5, 10, 11 143:6 [a] Ps. 63:1 143:7 [a] Ps. 28:1 143:8 [a] Ps. 46:5 [b] Ps. 5:8 [c] Ps. 25:1 143:9 [1] Septuagint and Vulgate read *To You I flee.* 143:10 [a] Ps. 25:4, 5 [b] Neh. 9:20 [c] Is. 26:10 143:11 [a] Ps. 119:25 143:12 [a] Ps. 54:5

PSALM 144

A Song to the LORD Who Preserves and Prospers His People

A *Psalm* of David.

1 Blessed *be* the LORD my Rock,
[a]Who trains my hands for war,
And my fingers for battle—
2 My lovingkindness and my fortress,
My high tower and my deliverer,
My shield and *the One* in whom I take refuge,
Who subdues my people[1] under me.

3 [a]LORD, what *is* man, that You take knowledge of him?
Or the son of man, that You are mindful of him?
4 [a]Man is like a breath;
[b]His days *are* like a passing shadow.
5 [a]Bow down Your heavens, O LORD, and come down;
[b]Touch the mountains, and they shall smoke.
6 [a]Flash forth lightning and scatter them;
Shoot out Your arrows and destroy them.
7 Stretch out Your hand from above;
Rescue me and deliver me out of great waters,
From the hand of foreigners,
8 Whose mouth [a]speaks lying words,
And whose right hand *is* a right hand of falsehood.

9 I will [a]sing a new song to You, O God;
On a harp of ten strings I will sing praises to You,
10 *The One* who gives salvation to kings,
[a]Who delivers David His servant
From the deadly sword.

11 Rescue me and deliver me from the hand of foreigners,
Whose mouth speaks lying words,
And whose right hand *is* a right hand of falsehood—
12 That our sons *may be* [a]as plants grown up in their youth;
That our daughters *may be* as pillars,
Sculptured in palace style;
13 *That* our barns *may be* full,
Supplying all kinds of produce;
That our sheep may bring forth thousands
And ten thousands in our fields;
14 *That* our oxen *may be* well laden;
That there be no breaking in or going out;
That there be no outcry in our streets.
15 [a]Happy *are* the people who are in such a state;
Happy *are* the people whose God *is* the LORD!

144:1 [a] 2 Sam. 22:35 **144:2** [1] Following Masoretic Text, Septuagint, and Vulgate; Syriac and Targum read *the peoples* (compare 18:47). **144:3** [a] Heb. 2:6 **144:4** [a] Ps. 39:11 [b] Job 8:9; 14:2 **144:5** [a] Ps. 18:9 [b] Ps. 104:32 **144:6** [a] Ps. 18:13, 14 **144:8** [a] Ps. 12:2 **144:9** [a] Ps. 33:2, 3; 40:3 **144:10** [a] Ps. 18:50 **144:12** [a] Ps. 128:3 **144:15** [a] [Ps. 33:12]

BE HAPPY!

Happy are the people whose God is the LORD!

PSALM 144:15

The peace of God results in a state of genuine, meaningful happiness. Peace and happiness are not one and the same. But no one can be happy in a deep and meaningful way if one does not also possess peace. In Hebrew the word translated "blessed" or "happy" first appears in reference to the birth of Asher, one of Jacob's sons. Upon his birth, his mother said, "I am happy, for the daughters will call me blessed" (Gen. 30:13).

The apostle Paul experienced peaceful happiness as well. Having met and embraced the risen Christ, Paul knew that he was forgiven and so could affirm the words of the psalmist: "[Happy] are those whose lawless deeds are forgiven, and whose sins are covered; [happy] is the man to whom the LORD shall not impute sin" (Rom. 4:7–8).

Does God desire for us to be happy? Absolutely. But the happiness we experience derives from the unshakable truth that we have been forgiven and live in a state of peace with God through Jesus. Biblical happiness comes from being in right relationship and fellowship with our God.

PSALM 145

A Song of God's Majesty and Love

[a]A Praise of David.

1 I will extol You, my God, O King;
And I will bless Your name forever and ever.
2 Every day I will bless You,
And I will praise Your name forever and ever.
3 [a]Great *is* the LORD, and greatly to be praised;
And [b]His greatness *is* unsearchable.

4 [a]One generation shall praise Your works to another,
And shall declare Your mighty acts.
5 I[1] will meditate on the glorious splendor of Your majesty,
And on Your wondrous works.[2]
6 *Men* shall speak of the might of Your awesome acts,
And I will declare Your greatness.
7 They shall utter the memory of Your great goodness,
And shall sing of Your righteousness.

8 [a]The LORD *is* gracious and full of compassion,
Slow to anger and great in mercy.
9 [a]The LORD *is* good to all,
And His tender mercies *are* over all His works.

10 [a]All Your works shall praise You, O LORD,
And Your saints shall bless You.
11 They shall speak of the glory of Your kingdom,
And talk of Your power,
12 To make known to the sons of men His mighty acts,
And the glorious majesty of His kingdom.
13 [a]Your kingdom *is* an everlasting kingdom,
And Your dominion *endures* throughout all generations.[1]

14 The LORD upholds all who fall,
And [a]raises up all *who are* bowed down.
15 [a]The eyes of all look expectantly to You,
And [b]You give them their food in due season.
16 You open Your hand
[a]And satisfy the desire of every living thing.

17 The LORD *is* righteous in all His ways,
Gracious in all His works.
18 [a]The LORD *is* near to all who call upon Him,
To all who call upon Him [b]in truth.
19 He will fulfill the desire of those who fear Him;
He also will hear their cry and save them.
20 [a]The LORD preserves all who love Him,
But all the wicked He will destroy.
21 My mouth shall speak the praise of the LORD,
And all flesh shall bless His holy name
Forever and ever.

PSALM 146

The Happiness of Those Whose Help Is the LORD

1 Praise the LORD!

[a]Praise the LORD, O my soul!
2 [a]While I live I will praise the LORD;
I will sing praises to my God while I have my being.

3 [a]Do not put your trust in princes,
Nor in a son of man, in whom *there is* no help.
4 [a]His spirit departs, he returns to his earth;
In that very day [b]his plans perish.

5 [a]Happy *is he* who *has* the God of Jacob for his help,
Whose hope *is* in the LORD his God,
6 [a]Who made heaven and earth,
The sea, and all that *is* in them;
Who keeps truth forever,
7 [a]Who executes justice for the oppressed,
[b]Who gives food to the hungry.
[c]The LORD gives freedom to the prisoners.

145:title [a] *Ps. 100:title* **145:3** [a] [Ps. 147:5] [b] [Rom. 11:33] **145:4** [a] Is. 38:19 **145:5** [1] Following Masoretic Text and Targum; Dead Sea Scrolls, Septuagint, Syriac, and Vulgate read *They*. [2] Literally *on the words of Your wondrous works* **145:8** [a] [Num. 14:18] **145:9** [a] Nah. 1:7 **145:10** [a] Ps. 19:1 **145:13** [a] [1 Tim. 1:17] [1] Following Masoretic Text and Targum; Dead Sea Scrolls, Septuagint, Syriac, and Vulgate add *The LORD is faithful in all His words, And holy in all His works.* **145:14** [a] Ps. 146:8 **145:15** [a] Ps. 104:27 [b] Ps. 136:25 **145:16** [a] Ps. 104:21, 28 **145:18** [a] [Deut. 4:7] [b] [John 4:24] **145:20** [a] [Ps. 31:23] **146:1** [a] Ps. 103:1 **146:2** [a] Ps. 104:33 **146:3** [a] [Is. 2:22] **146:4** [a] [Eccl. 12:7] [b] [1 Cor. 2:6] **146:5** [a] Jer. 17:7 **146:6** [a] Rev. 14:7 **146:7** [a] Ps. 103:6 [b] Ps. 107:9 [c] Ps. 107:10

8 [a]The LORD opens *the eyes of* the blind;
[b]The LORD raises those who are bowed down;
The LORD loves the righteous.
9 [a]The LORD watches over the strangers;
He relieves the fatherless and widow;
[b]But the way of the wicked He turns upside down.

10 [a]The LORD shall reign forever—
Your God, O Zion, to all generations.

Praise the LORD!

PSALM 147

Praise to God for His Word and Providence

1 Praise the LORD!
For [a]*it is* good to sing praises to our God;
[b]For *it is* pleasant, *and* [c]praise is beautiful.

2 The LORD [a]builds up Jerusalem;
[b]He gathers together the outcasts of Israel.
3 [a]He heals the brokenhearted
And binds up their wounds.
4 [a]He counts the number of the stars;
He calls them all by name.
5 [a]Great *is* our Lord, and [b]mighty in power;
[c]His understanding *is* infinite.
6 [a]The LORD lifts up the humble;
He casts the wicked down to the ground.

7 Sing to the LORD with thanksgiving;
Sing praises on the harp to our God,
8 [a]Who covers the heavens with clouds,
Who prepares rain for the earth,
Who makes grass to grow on the mountains.
9 [a]He gives to the beast its food,
And [b]to the young ravens that cry.

10 [a]He does not delight in the strength of the horse;
He takes no pleasure in the legs of a man.
11 The LORD takes pleasure in those who fear Him,
In those who hope in His mercy.

12 Praise the LORD, O Jerusalem!
Praise your God, O Zion!
13 For He has strengthened the bars of your gates;
He has blessed your children within you.
14 [a]He makes peace *in* your borders,
And [b]fills you with the finest wheat.

146:8 [a]Matt. 9:30 [b]Luke 13:13 146:9 [a]Deut. 10:18 [b]Ps. 147:6 146:10 [a]Ex. 15:18 147:1 [a]Ps. 92:1 [b]Ps. 135:3 [c]Ps. 33:1 147:2 [a]Ps. 102:16 [b]Deut. 30:3 147:3 [a][Ps. 51:17] 147:4 [a]Is. 40:26 147:5 [a]Ps. 48:1 [b]Nah. 1:3 [c]Is. 40:28 147:6 [a]Ps. 146:8, 9 147:8 [a]Job 38:26 147:9 [a]Job 38:41 [b][Matt. 6:26] 147:10 [a]Ps. 33:16, 17 147:14 [a]Is. 54:13; 60:17, 18 [b]Ps. 132:15

WHEN GOD PROVIDES

He makes peace in your borders, and fills you with the finest wheat.

PSALM 147:14

Psalm 147 was composed after Israel's exile to Babylon and the people's return to their land. The psalm enjoins the faithful to "praise the LORD! For it is good to sing praises to our God" (v. 1). Israel had a reason to sing praises to God, for He "builds up Jerusalem; He gathers together the outcasts of Israel. He heals the brokenhearted and binds up their wounds" (vv. 2–3). Israel was a broken nation, a people who had sinned grievously, but God in His mercy had brought them back to their land. "He makes peace in your borders," the psalmist noted, "and fills you with the finest wheat" (v. 14).

When they were a broken nation, the Israelites were not secure: raiders plundered their struggling farms, burning and stealing crops. But God had begun to repair the borders, making peace and providing the people with abundant food. God began His redemptive work in response to His people's newfound respect for Him and hope in His mercy (v. 11). Again and again we find in Scripture faithfulness rewarded with a peace that is sometimes very tangible.

When have you experienced an almost touchable peace when walking faithfully with God?

15 [a]He sends out His command *to the*
earth;
His word runs very swiftly.
16 [a]He gives snow like wool;
He scatters the frost like ashes;
17 He casts out His hail like morsels;
Who can stand before His cold?
18 [a]He sends out His word and melts them;
He causes His wind to blow, *and* the
waters flow.

19 [a]He declares His word to Jacob,
[b]His statutes and His judgments to
Israel.
20 [a]He has not dealt thus with any nation;
And *as for His* judgments, they have
not known them.

Praise the LORD!

PSALM 148

Praise to the LORD from Creation

1 Praise the LORD!

Praise the LORD from the heavens;
Praise Him in the heights!
2 Praise Him, all His angels;
Praise Him, all His hosts!
3 Praise Him, sun and moon;
Praise Him, all you stars of light!
4 Praise Him, [a]you heavens of
heavens,
And [b]you waters above the heavens!

5 Let them praise the name of the LORD,
For [a]He commanded and they were
created.
6 [a]He also established them forever and
ever;
He made a decree which shall not pass
away.

7 Praise the LORD from the earth,
[a]You great sea creatures and all the
depths;
8 Fire and hail, snow and clouds;
Stormy wind, fulfilling His word;
9 [a]Mountains and all hills;
Fruitful trees and all cedars;
10 Beasts and all cattle;
Creeping things and flying fowl;
11 Kings of the earth and all peoples;
Princes and all judges of the earth;
12 Both young men and maidens;
Old men and children.

13 Let them praise the name of the LORD,
For His [a]name alone is exalted;
His glory *is* above the earth and
heaven.
14 And He [a]has exalted the horn of His
people,
The praise of [b]all His saints—
Of the children of Israel,
[c]A people near to Him.

Praise the LORD!

PSALM 149

Praise to God for His Salvation and Judgment

1 Praise the LORD!

[a]Sing to the LORD a new song,
And His praise in the assembly of
saints.

2 Let Israel rejoice in their Maker;
Let the children of Zion be joyful in
their [a]King.
3 [a]Let them praise His name with the
dance;
Let them sing praises to Him with the
timbrel and harp.
4 For [a]the LORD takes pleasure in His
people;
[b]He will beautify the humble with
salvation.

5 Let the saints be joyful in glory;
Let them [a]sing aloud on their beds.
6 *Let* the high praises of God *be* in their
mouth,
And [a]a two-edged sword in their hand,
7 To execute vengeance on the nations,
And punishments on the peoples;
8 To bind their kings with chains,
And their nobles with fetters of iron;
9 [a]To execute on them the written
judgment—
[b]This honor have all His saints.

Praise the LORD!

PSALM 150

Let All Things Praise the LORD

1 Praise[a] the LORD!

Praise God in His sanctuary;
Praise Him in His mighty firmament!

147:15 [a] [Ps. 107:20] 147:16 [a] Job 37:6 147:18 [a] Job 37:10 147:19 [a] Deut. 33:4 [b] Mal. 4:4 147:20 [a] [Rom. 3:1, 2]
148:4 [a] 1 Kin. 8:27 [b] Gen. 1:7 148:5 [a] Gen. 1:1, 6 148:6 [a] Ps. 89:37 148:7 [a] Is. 43:20 148:9 [a] Is. 44:23; 49:13
148:13 [a] Ps. 8:1 148:14 [a] Ps. 75:10 [b] Ps. 149:9 [c] Eph. 2:17 149:1 [a] Ps. 33:3 149:2 [a] Zech. 9:9 149:3 [a] Ps. 81:2
149:4 [a] Ps. 35:27 [b] Ps. 132:16 149:5 [a] Job 35:10 149:6 [a] Heb. 4:12 149:9 [a] Deut. 7:1, 2 [b] 1 Cor. 6:2 150:1 [a] Ps. 145:5, 6

2 Praise Him for His mighty acts;
Praise Him according to His excellent [a]greatness!

3 Praise Him with the sound of the trumpet;
Praise Him with the lute and harp!
4 Praise Him with the timbrel and dance;
Praise Him with stringed instruments and flutes!
5 Praise Him with loud cymbals;
Praise Him with clashing cymbals!

6 Let everything that has breath praise the LORD.

Praise the LORD!

150:2 [a] Deut. 3:24

THE BOOK OF

PROVERBS

AUTHOR

Solomon's name appears at the beginning of the three sections he wrote: Proverbs 1–9; 10:1—22:16; and 25–29. Only about eight hundred of the more than three thousand proverbs attributed to Solomon are recorded here. It is likely that Solomon collected and edited proverbs other than his own. The collection of Solomonic proverbs in chapters 25–29 was assembled by the scribes of King Hezekiah. Some of the sayings in Proverbs are quite similar to those found in *The Wisdom of Amenemope*, a document of teachings on civil service by an Egyptian who probably lived between 1000 and 600 BC.

TIME

c. 950–700 BC

KEY VERSE

Proverbs 3:5–6

THEME

Proverbs is part of what is commonly called the Wisdom Literature of the Bible. Each society needs a way to pass on to succeeding generations what it understands to be the best way to live. Biblical Wisdom Literature provided that means for the Jewish community. The Book of Proverbs contains nuggets of truth that endure, not only in the Jewish culture, but also in our multifaceted society today. It contains basic wisdom on how to deal with the most common everyday issues we face. The simple truth is that if people followed the advice of Proverbs, which transcends personality and culture, many of their problems would be reduced dramatically.

Much of Proverbs teaches the inextricable bond between truth and peace. We cannot have peace without truth; as the writer said, "Let your heart keep my commands; for length of days and long life and peace they will add to you" (3:1–2). The words "joy" and "rejoice" appear almost three hundred times in the original language of Scripture; for example, Proverbs 12:20: "Deceit is in the heart of those who devise evil, but counselors of peace have joy." Only through God's power will our enemies be at peace with us when we walk with the Lord (16:7). We discover in Proverbs that when we heed the truth, we find peace.

The Beginning of Knowledge

1 The [a]proverbs of Solomon the son of David, king of Israel:

2 To know wisdom and instruction,
To perceive the words of understanding,
3 To receive the instruction of wisdom,
Justice, judgment, and equity;
4 To give prudence to the [a]simple,
To the young man knowledge and discretion—
5 [a]A wise *man* will hear and increase learning,
And a man of understanding will attain wise counsel,
6 To understand a proverb and an enigma,
The words of the wise and their [a]riddles.

7 [a]The fear of the LORD *is* the beginning of knowledge,
But fools despise wisdom and instruction.

Shun Evil Counsel

8 [a]My son, hear the instruction of your father,
And do not forsake the law of your mother;
9 For they *will be* a [a]graceful ornament on your head,
And chains about your neck.

10 My son, if sinners entice you,
[a]Do not consent.
11 If they say, "Come with us,
Let us [a]lie in wait to *shed* blood;
Let us lurk secretly for the innocent without cause;
12 Let us swallow them alive like Sheol,[1]
And whole, [a]like those who go down to the Pit;
13 We shall find all *kinds* of precious possessions,
We shall fill our houses with spoil;
14 Cast in your lot among us,
Let us all have one purse"—
15 My son, [a]do not walk in the way with them,
[b]Keep your foot from their path;
16 [a]For their feet run to evil,
And they make haste to shed blood.
17 Surely, in vain the net is spread
In the sight of any bird;
18 But they lie in wait for their *own* blood,
They lurk secretly for their *own* lives.
19 [a]So *are* the ways of everyone who is greedy for gain;
It takes away the life of its owners.

The Call of Wisdom

20 [a]Wisdom calls aloud outside;
She raises her voice in the open squares.
21 She cries out in the chief concourses,[1]
At the openings of the gates in the city
She speaks her words:
22 "How long, you simple ones, will you love simplicity?
For scorners delight in their scorning,
And fools hate knowledge.
23 Turn at my rebuke;
Surely [a]I will pour out my spirit on you;
I will make my words known to you.
24 [a]Because I have called and you refused,
I have stretched out my hand and no one regarded,
25 Because you [a]disdained all my counsel,
And would have none of my rebuke,
26 [a]I also will laugh at your calamity;
I will mock when your terror comes,
27 When [a]your terror comes like a storm,
And your destruction comes like a whirlwind,
When distress and anguish come upon you.

28 "Then[a] they will call on me, but I will not answer;
They will seek me diligently, but they will not find me.
29 Because they [a]hated knowledge
And did not [b]choose the fear of the LORD,
30 [a]They would have none of my counsel
And despised my every rebuke.
31 Therefore [a]they shall eat the fruit of their own way,
And be filled to the full with their own fancies.
32 For the turning away of the simple will slay them,
And the complacency of fools will destroy them;
33 But whoever listens to me will dwell [a]safely,
And [b]will be secure, without fear of evil."

1:1 [a] 1 Kin. 4:32 1:4 [a] Prov. 9:4 1:5 [a] Prov. 9:9 1:6 [a] Ps. 78:2 1:7 [a] Job 28:28 1:8 [a] Prov. 4:1 1:9 [a] Prov. 3:22 1:10 [a] Gen. 39:7–10 1:11 [a] Jer. 5:26 1:12 [a] Ps. 28:1 [1] Or *the grave* 1:15 [a] Ps. 1:1 [b] Ps. 119:101 1:16 [a] [Is. 59:7] 1:19 [a] [1 Tim. 6:10] 1:20 [a] [John 7:37] 1:21 [1] Septuagint, Syriac, and Targum read *top of the walls;* Vulgate reads *the head of multitudes.* 1:23 [a] Joel 2:28 1:24 [a] Jer. 7:13 1:25 [a] Luke 7:30 1:26 [a] Ps. 2:4 1:27 [a] [Prov. 10:24, 25] 1:28 [a] Is. 1:15 1:29 [a] Job 21:14 [b] Ps. 119:173 1:30 [a] Ps. 81:11 1:31 [a] Job 4:8 1:33 [a] Prov. 3:24–26 [b] Ps. 112:7

The Value of Wisdom

2 My son, if you receive my words,
And [a]treasure my commands within
you,
2 So that you incline your ear to wisdom,
And apply your heart to understanding;
3 Yes, if you cry out for discernment,
And lift up your voice for understanding,
4 [a]If you seek her as silver,
And search for her as *for* hidden
treasures;
5 [a]Then you will understand the fear of
the LORD,
And find the knowledge of God.
6 [a]For the LORD gives wisdom;
From His mouth *come* knowledge and
understanding;
7 He stores up sound wisdom for the
upright;
[a]*He is* a shield to those who walk uprightly;
8 He guards the paths of justice,
And [a]preserves the way of His saints.
9 Then you will understand
righteousness and justice,
Equity *and* every good path.

10 When wisdom enters your heart,
And knowledge is pleasant to your soul,
11 Discretion will preserve you;
[a]Understanding will keep you,
12 To deliver you from the way of evil,
From the man who speaks perverse
things,
13 From those who leave the paths of
uprightness
To [a]walk in the ways of darkness;
14 [a]Who rejoice in doing evil,
And delight in the perversity of the
wicked;
15 [a]Whose ways *are* crooked,
And *who are* devious in their paths;
16 To deliver you from [a]the immoral
woman,
[b]From the seductress *who* flatters with
her words,
17 Who forsakes the companion of her
youth,
And forgets the covenant of her God.
18 For [a]her house leads down to death,
And her paths to the dead;
19 None who go to her return,
Nor do they regain the paths of life—
20 So you may walk in the way of
goodness,
And keep to the paths of righteousness.
21 For the upright will dwell in the [a]land,
And the blameless will remain in it;
22 But the wicked will be cut off from the
earth,
And the unfaithful will be uprooted
from it.

Guidance for the Young

3 My son, do not forget my law,
[a]But let your heart keep my commands;
2 For length of days and long life
And [a]peace they will add to you.

3 Let not mercy and truth forsake you;
[a]Bind them around your neck,
[b]Write them on the tablet of your heart,
4 [a]*And* so find favor and high esteem
In the sight of God and man.

5 [a]Trust in the LORD with all your heart,
[b]And lean not on your own
understanding;
6 [a]In all your ways acknowledge Him,
And He shall direct[1] your paths.

PEACE NOTE

Bad decisions will rob you of God's peace. Pray that the Lord gives you wisdom to make decisions that result in peace.

PROVERBS 3:5-6

7 Do not be wise in your own [a]eyes;
Fear the LORD and depart from evil.
8 It will be health to your flesh,[1]
And [a]strength[2] to your bones.

9 [a]Honor the LORD with your possessions,
And with the firstfruits of all your
increase;
10 [a]So your barns will be filled with plenty,
And your vats will overflow with new
wine.

2:1 [a] [Prov. 4:21] 2:4 [a] [Prov. 3:14] 2:5 [a] [James 1:5, 6] 2:6 [a] 1 Kin. 3:9, 12 2:7 [a] [Ps. 84:11] 2:8 [a] [1 Sam. 2:9] 2:11 [a] Prov. 4:6; 6:22 2:13 [a] [John 3:19, 20] 2:14 [a] [Rom. 1:32] 2:15 [a] Ps. 125:5 2:16 [a] Prov. 5:20; 6:24; 7:5 [b] Prov. 5:3 2:18 [a] Prov. 7:27 2:21 [a] Ps. 37:3 3:1 [a] Deut. 8:1 3:2 [a] Ps. 119:165 3:3 [a] Prov. 6:21 [b] [2 Cor. 3:3] 3:4 [a] Rom. 14:18 3:5 [a] [Ps. 37:3, 5] [b] [Jer. 9:23, 24] 3:6 [a] [1 Chr. 28:9] [1] Or *make smooth* or *straight* 3:7 [a] Rom. 12:16 3:8 [a] Job 21:24 [1] Literally *navel,* figurative of the body [2] Literally *drink* or *refreshment* 3:9 [a] Ex. 22:29 3:10 [a] Deut. 28:8

11 [a]My son, do not despise the chastening
of the LORD,
Nor detest His correction;
12 For whom the LORD loves He corrects,
[a]Just as a father the son *in whom* he
delights.

13 [a]Happy *is* the man *who* finds wisdom,
And the man *who* gains
understanding;
14 [a]For her proceeds *are* better than the
profits of silver,
And her gain than fine gold.
15 She *is* more precious than rubies,
And [a]all the things you may desire
cannot compare with her.
16 [a]Length of days *is* in her right hand,
In her left hand riches and honor.
17 [a]Her ways *are* ways of pleasantness,
And all her paths *are* peace.
18 She *is* [a]a tree of life to those who take
hold of her,
And happy *are all* who retain her.

19 [a]The LORD by wisdom founded the
earth;
By understanding He established the
heavens;
20 By His knowledge the depths were
[a]broken up,
And clouds drop down the dew.

21 My son, let them not depart from your
eyes—
Keep sound wisdom and discretion;
22 So they will be life to your soul
And grace to your neck.
23 [a]Then you will walk safely in your way,
And your foot will not stumble.
24 When you lie down, you will not be afraid;
Yes, you will lie down and your sleep
will be sweet.
25 [a]Do not be afraid of sudden terror,
Nor of trouble from the wicked when it
comes;
26 For the LORD will be your confidence,
And will keep your foot from being
caught.

27 [a]Do not withhold good from those to
whom it is due,
When it is in the power of your hand to
do *so*.
28 [a]Do not say to your neighbor,
"Go, and come back,
And tomorrow I will give *it*,"
When you have it with you.
29 Do not devise evil against your
neighbor,
For he dwells by you for safety's sake.
30 [a]Do not strive with a man without
cause,
If he has done you no harm.

3:11 [a] Job 5:17 **3:12** [a] Deut. 8:5 **3:13** [a] Prov. 8:32, 34, 35 **3:14** [a] Job 28:13 **3:15** [a] Matt. 13:44 **3:16** [a] [1 Tim. 4:8] **3:17** [a] [Matt. 11:29] **3:18** [a] Gen. 2:9 **3:19** [a] Ps. 104:24 **3:20** [a] Gen. 7:11 **3:23** [a] Prov. 10:9 **3:25** [a] Ps. 91:5 **3:27** [a] Rom. 13:7 **3:28** [a] Lev. 19:13 **3:30** [a] [Rom. 12:18]

CHASING AFTER WISDOM

For length of days and long life and peace they will add to you . . . Her ways are ways of pleasantness, and all her paths are peace.

PROVERBS 3:2, 17

The Book of Proverbs is much more than a collection of wise sayings and good advice. Some scholars think the Book of Proverbs originally served as a textbook for young men being educated for service in the court, whether at home or abroad. Proverbs emphasizes the essential role of wisdom, a virtue that became widely recognized and appreciated thanks to Solomon (see 1 Kin. 3). An interesting feature of Proverbs is its presentation of wisdom as personified, as though it is a "she" who resides in heaven and occasionally visits earth. *Young Israelite men* were urged to spend time with Lady Wisdom.

The young man was counseled in Proverbs 3: "My son, do not forget my law, but let your heart keep my commands" (v. 1). Here "law," from *torah*, is probably better understood as "teaching." The benefits of adhering to good teaching are "length of days and long life" as well as "peace" (v. 2). Wisdom's ways, Israel's youth were told, "are ways of pleasantness, and all her paths are peace" (v. 17). The wisdom of God creates peace.

How will you seek wisdom today?

31 [a]Do not envy the oppressor,
And choose none of his ways;
32 For the perverse *person is* an
abomination to the LORD,
[a]But His secret counsel *is* with the
upright.
33 [a]The curse of the LORD *is* on the house
of the wicked,
But [b]He blesses the home of the just.
34 [a]Surely He scorns the scornful,
But gives grace to the humble.
35 The wise shall inherit glory,
But shame shall be the legacy of fools.

Security in Wisdom

4 Hear, [a]*my* children, the instruction of
a father,
And give attention to know
understanding;
2 For I give you good doctrine:
Do not forsake my law.
3 When I was my father's son,
[a]Tender and the only one in the sight of
my mother,
4 [a]He also taught me, and said to me:
"Let your heart retain my words;
[b]Keep my commands, and live.
5 [a]Get wisdom! Get understanding!
Do not forget, nor turn away from the
words of my mouth.
6 Do not forsake her, and she will
preserve you;
[a]Love her, and she will keep you.
7 [a]Wisdom *is* the principal thing;
Therefore get wisdom.
And in all your getting, get
understanding.
8 [a]Exalt her, and she will promote you;
She will bring you honor, when you
embrace her.
9 She will place on your head [a]an
ornament of grace;
A crown of glory she will deliver to you."

10 Hear, my son, and receive my sayings,
[a]And the years of your life will be many.
11 I have [a]taught you in the way of
wisdom;
I have led you in right paths.
12 When you walk, [a]your steps will not be
hindered,
[b]And when you run, you will not stumble.
13 Take firm hold of instruction, do not
let go;
Keep her, for she *is* your life.
14 [a]Do not enter the path of the wicked,
And do not walk in the way of evil.
15 Avoid it, do not travel on it;
Turn away from it and pass on.
16 [a]For they do not sleep unless they have
done evil;
And their sleep is taken away unless
they make *someone* fall.
17 For they eat the bread of wickedness,
And drink the wine of violence.

18 [a]But the path of the just [b]*is* like the
shining sun,[1]
That shines ever brighter unto the
perfect day.
19 [a]The way of the wicked *is* like darkness;
They do not know what makes them
stumble.

20 My son, give attention to my words;
Incline your ear to my sayings.
21 Do not let them depart from your eyes;
Keep them in the midst of your heart;
22 For they *are* life to those who find them,
And health to all their flesh.
23 Keep your heart with all diligence,
For out of it *spring* the issues of [a]life.
24 Put away from you a deceitful mouth,
And put perverse lips far from you.
25 Let your eyes look straight ahead,
And your eyelids look right before you.
26 Ponder the path of your [a]feet,
And let all your ways be established.
27 Do not turn to the right or the left;
Remove your foot from evil.

The Peril of Adultery

5 My son, pay attention to my wisdom;
Lend your ear to my understanding,
2 That you may preserve discretion,
And your lips [a]may keep knowledge.
3 [a]For the lips of an immoral woman drip
honey,
And her mouth *is* [b]smoother than oil;
4 But in the end she is bitter as wormwood,
Sharp as a two-edged sword.
5 Her feet go down to death,
[a]Her steps lay hold of hell.[1]
6 Lest you ponder *her* path of life—
Her ways are unstable;
You do not know *them*.

7 Therefore hear me now, *my* children,
And do not depart from the words of
my mouth.

3:31 [a] Ps. 37:1 **3:32** [a] Ps. 25:14 **3:33** [a] Zech. 5:3, 4 [b] Ps. 1:3 **3:34** [a] James 4:6 **4:1** [a] Ps. 34:11 **4:3** [a] 1 Chr. 29:1 **4:4** [a] 1 Chr. 28:9 [b] Prov. 7:2 **4:5** [a] Prov. 2:2, 3 **4:6** [a] 2 Thess. 2:10 **4:7** [a] Matt. 13:44 **4:8** [a] 1 Sam. 2:30 **4:9** [a] Prov. 3:22 **4:10** [a] Prov. 3:2 **4:11** [a] 1 Sam. 12:23 **4:12** [a] Ps. 18:36 [b] [Ps. 91:11] **4:14** [a] Ps. 1:1 **4:16** [a] Ps. 36:4 **4:18** [a] Matt. 5:14, 45 [b] 2 Sam. 23:4 [1] Literally *light* **4:19** [a] [Is. 59:9, 10] **4:23** [a] [Matt. 12:34; 15:18, 19] **4:26** [a] Heb. 12:13 **5:2** [a] Mal. 2:7 **5:3** [a] Prov. 2:16 [b] Ps. 55:21 **5:5** [a] Prov. 7:27 [1] Or *Sheol*

8 Remove your way far from her,
And do not go near the door of her house,
9 Lest you give your honor to others,
And your years to the cruel *one;*
10 Lest aliens be filled with your wealth,
And your labors *go* to the house of a foreigner;
11 And you mourn at last,
When your flesh and your body are consumed,
12 And say:
"How I have hated instruction,
And my heart despised correction!
13 I have not obeyed the voice of my teachers,
Nor inclined my ear to those who instructed me!
14 I was on the verge of total ruin,
In the midst of the assembly and congregation."

15 Drink water from your own cistern,
And running water from your own well.
16 Should your fountains be dispersed abroad,
Streams of water in the streets?
17 Let them be only your own,
And not for strangers with you.
18 Let your fountain be blessed,
And rejoice with [a]the wife of your youth.
19 [a]*As a* loving deer and a graceful doe,
Let her breasts satisfy you at all times;
And always be enraptured with her love.
20 For why should you, my son, be enraptured by [a]an immoral woman,
And be embraced in the arms of a seductress?

21 [a]For the ways of man *are* before the eyes of the LORD,
And He ponders all his paths.
22 [a]His own iniquities entrap the wicked *man,*
And he is caught in the cords of his sin.
23 [a]He shall die for lack of instruction,
And in the greatness of his folly he shall go astray.

Dangerous Promises

6 My son, [a]if you become surety for your friend,
If you have shaken hands in pledge for a stranger,
2 You are snared by the words of your mouth;
You are taken by the words of your mouth.

PEACE NOTE

When we are humble and vulnerable, God can use our experiences to spread His heavenly peace to others when they hear about the grace of God.

PROVERBS 6:3

3 So do this, my son, and deliver yourself;
For you have come into the hand of your friend:
Go and humble yourself;
Plead with your friend.
4 [a]Give no sleep to your eyes,
Nor slumber to your eyelids.
5 Deliver yourself like a gazelle from the hand *of the hunter,*
And like a bird from the hand of the fowler.[1]

The Folly of Indolence

6 [a]Go to the ant, you sluggard!
Consider her ways and be wise,
7 Which, having no captain,
Overseer or ruler,
8 Provides her supplies in the summer,
And gathers her food in the harvest.
9 [a]How long will you slumber, O sluggard?
When will you rise from your sleep?
10 A little sleep, a little slumber,
A little folding of the hands to sleep—
11 [a]So shall your poverty come on you like a prowler,
And your need like an armed man.

The Wicked Man

12 A worthless person, a wicked man,
Walks with a perverse mouth;
13 [a]He winks with his eyes,
He shuffles his feet,
He points with his fingers;
14 Perversity *is* in his heart,
[a]He devises evil continually,
[b]He sows discord.

5:18 [a] Mal. 2:14 5:19 [a] Song 2:9 5:20 [a] Prov. 2:16 5:21 [a] Hos. 7:2 5:22 [a] Num. 32:23 5:23 [a] Job 4:21 6:1 [a] Prov. 11:15 6:4 [a] Ps. 132:4 6:5 [1] That is, one who catches birds in a trap or snare 6:6 [a] Job 12:7 6:9 [a] Prov. 24:33, 34 6:11 [a] Prov. 10:4 6:13 [a] Job 15:12 6:14 [a] Mic. 2:1 [b] Prov. 6:19

15 Therefore his calamity shall come
[a]suddenly;
Suddenly he shall [b]be broken [c]without
remedy.

16 These six *things* the LORD hates,
Yes, seven *are* an abomination to Him:
17 [a]A proud look,
[b]A lying tongue,
[c]Hands that shed innocent blood,
18 [a]A heart that devises wicked plans,
[b]Feet that are swift in running to evil,
19 [a]A false witness *who* speaks lies,
And one who [b]sows discord among
brethren.

Beware of Adultery

20 [a]My son, keep your father's command,
And do not forsake the law of your
mother.
21 [a]Bind them continually upon your heart;
Tie them around your neck.
22 [a]When you roam, they[1] will lead you;
When you sleep, [b]they will keep you;
And *when* you awake, they will speak
with you.
23 [a]For the commandment *is* a lamp,
And the law a light;
Reproofs of instruction *are* the way of
life,
24 [a]To keep you from the evil woman,
From the flattering tongue of a
seductress.
25 [a]Do not lust after her beauty in your heart,
Nor let her allure you with her eyelids.
26 For [a]by means of a harlot
A man is reduced to a crust of bread;
[b]And an adulteress[1] will [c]prey upon his
precious life.
27 Can a man take fire to his bosom,
And his clothes not be burned?
28 Can one walk on hot coals,
And his feet not be seared?
29 So *is* he who goes in to his neighbor's
wife;
Whoever touches her shall not be
innocent.

30 *People* do not despise a thief
If he steals to satisfy himself when he
is starving.
31 Yet *when* he is found, [a]he must restore
sevenfold;
He may have to give up all the
substance of his house.
32 Whoever commits adultery with a
woman [a]lacks understanding;
He *who* does so destroys his own soul.
33 Wounds and dishonor he will get,
And his reproach will not be wiped away.
34 For [a]jealousy *is* a husband's fury;
Therefore he will not spare in the day
of vengeance.
35 He will accept no recompense,
Nor will he be appeased though you
give many gifts.

7 My son, keep my words,
And [a]treasure my commands within
you.
2 [a]Keep my commands and live,
[b]And my law as the apple of your eye.
3 [a]Bind them on your fingers;
Write them on the tablet of your heart.
4 Say to wisdom, "You *are* my sister,"
And call understanding *your* nearest kin,
5 [a]That they may keep you from the
immoral woman,
From the seductress *who* flatters with
her words.

The Crafty Harlot

6 For at the window of my house
I looked through my lattice,
7 And saw among the simple,
I perceived among the youths,
A young man [a]devoid of
understanding,
8 Passing along the street near her
corner;
And he took the path to her house
9 [a]In the twilight, in the evening,
In the black and dark night.

10 And there a woman met him,
With the attire of a harlot, and a crafty
heart.
11 [a]She *was* loud and rebellious,
[b]Her feet would not stay at home.
12 At times *she was* outside, at times in
the open square,
Lurking at every corner.
13 So she caught him and kissed him;
With an impudent face she said to
him:
14 "*I have* peace offerings with me;
Today I have paid my vows.
15 So I came out to meet you,
Diligently to seek your face,
And I have found you.

6:15 [a] Is. 30:13 [b] Jer. 19:11 [c] 2 Chr. 36:16 **6:17** [a] Ps. 101:5 [b] Ps. 120:2 [c] Is. 1:15 **6:18** [a] Gen. 6:5 [b] Is. 59:7 **6:19** [a] Ps. 27:12 [b] Prov. 6:14 **6:20** [a] Eph. 6:1 **6:21** [a] Prov. 3:3 **6:22** [a] [Prov. 3:23] [b] Prov. 2:11 [1] Literally *it* **6:23** [a] Ps. 19:8 **6:24** [a] Prov. 2:16 **6:25** [a] Matt. 5:28 **6:26** [a] Prov. 29:3 [b] Gen. 39:14 [c] Ezek. 13:18 [1] Literally *a man's wife,* that is, of another **6:31** [a] Ex. 22:1–4 **6:32** [a] Prov. 7:7 **6:34** [a] Song 8:6 **7:1** [a] Prov. 2:1 **7:2** [a] Lev. 18:5 [b] Deut. 32:10 **7:3** [a] Deut. 6:8 **7:5** [a] Prov. 2:16; 5:3 **7:7** [a] [Prov. 6:32; 9:4, 16] **7:9** [a] Job 24:15 **7:11** [a] Prov. 9:13 [b] Titus 2:5

16 I have spread my bed with tapestry,
Colored coverings of [a]Egyptian linen.
17 I have perfumed my bed
With myrrh, aloes, and cinnamon.
18 Come, let us take our fill of love until morning;
Let us delight ourselves with love.
19 For my husband *is* not at home;
He has gone on a long journey;
20 He has taken a bag of money with him,
And will come home on the appointed day."

21 With [a]her enticing speech she caused him to yield,
[b]With her flattering lips she seduced him.
22 Immediately he went after her, as an ox goes to the slaughter,
Or as a fool to the correction of the stocks,[1]
23 Till an arrow struck his liver.
[a]As a bird hastens to the snare,
He did not know it *would cost* his life.

24 Now therefore, listen to me, *my* children;
Pay attention to the words of my mouth:
25 Do not let your heart turn aside to her ways,
Do not stray into her paths;
26 For she has cast down many wounded,
And [a]all who were slain by her were strong *men.*
27 [a]Her house *is* the way to hell,[1]
Descending to the chambers of death.

The Excellence of Wisdom

8 Does not [a]wisdom cry out,
And understanding lift up her voice?
2 She takes her stand on the top of the high hill,
Beside the way, where the paths meet.
3 She cries out by the gates, at the entry of the city,
At the entrance of the doors:
4 "To you, O men, I call,
And my voice *is* to the sons of men.
5 O you simple ones, understand prudence,
And you fools, be of an understanding heart.
6 Listen, for I will speak of [a]excellent things,
And from the opening of my lips *will come* right things;
7 For my mouth will speak truth;
Wickedness *is* an abomination to my lips.
8 All the words of my mouth *are* with righteousness;
Nothing crooked or perverse *is* in them.
9 They *are* all plain to him who understands,
And right to those who find knowledge.
10 Receive my instruction, and not silver,
And knowledge rather than choice gold;
11 [a]For wisdom *is* better than rubies,
And all the things one may desire cannot be compared with her.

12 "I, wisdom, dwell with prudence,
And find out knowledge *and* discretion.
13 [a]The fear of the LORD *is* to hate evil;
[b]Pride and arrogance and the evil way
And [c]the perverse mouth I hate.
14 Counsel *is* mine, and sound wisdom;
I *am* understanding, [a]I have strength.
15 [a]By me kings reign,
And rulers decree justice.
16 By me princes rule, and nobles,
All the judges of the earth.[1]
17 [a]I love those who love me,
And [b]those who seek me diligently will find me.
18 [a]Riches and honor *are* with me,
Enduring riches and righteousness.
19 My fruit *is* better than gold, yes, than fine gold,
And my revenue than choice silver.
20 I traverse the way of righteousness,
In the midst of the paths of justice,
21 That I may cause those who love me to inherit wealth,
That I may fill their treasuries.

22 "The[a] LORD possessed me at the beginning of His way,
Before His works of old.
23 [a]I have been established from everlasting,
From the beginning, before there was ever an earth.

7:16 [a] Is. 19:9 **7:21** [a] Prov. 5:3 [b] Ps. 12:2 **7:22** [1] Septuagint, Syriac, and Targum read *as a dog to bonds;* Vulgate reads *as a lamb . . . to bonds.* **7:23** [a] Eccl. 9:12 **7:26** [a] Neh. 13:26 **7:27** [a] Prov. 2:18; 5:5; 9:18 [1] Or *Sheol* **8:1** [a] Prov. 1:20, 21; 9:3 **8:6** [a] Prov. 22:20 **8:11** [a] Job 28:15 **8:13** [a] Prov. 3:7; 16:6 [b] [Prov. 16:17, 18] [c] Prov. 4:24 **8:14** [a] Eccl. 7:19; 9:16 **8:15** [a] Rom. 13:1 **8:16** [1] Masoretic Text, Syriac, Targum, and Vulgate read *righteousness;* Septuagint, Bomberg, and some manuscripts and editions read *earth.* **8:17** [a] [John 14:21] [b] James 1:5 **8:18** [a] Prov. 3:16 **8:22** [a] Prov. 3:19 **8:23** [a] [Ps. 2:6]

24 When *there were* no depths I was
brought forth,
When *there were* no fountains
abounding with water.
25 [a]Before the mountains were settled,
Before the hills, I was brought forth;
26 While as yet He had not made the earth
or the fields,
Or the primal dust of the world.
27 When He prepared the heavens, I *was*
there,
When He drew a circle on the face of
the deep,
28 When He established the clouds above,
When He strengthened the fountains
of the deep,
29 [a]When He assigned to the sea its limit,
So that the waters would not transgress
His command,
When [b]He marked out the foundations
of the earth,
30 [a]Then I was beside Him *as* a master
craftsman;[1]
[b]And I was daily *His* delight,
Rejoicing always before Him,
31 Rejoicing in His inhabited world,
And [a]my delight *was* with the sons of
men.

32 "Now therefore, listen to me, *my* children,
For [a]blessed *are those who* keep my
ways.
33 Hear instruction and be wise,
And do not disdain *it.*
34 [a]Blessed is the man who listens to me,
Watching daily at my gates,
Waiting at the posts of my doors.
35 For whoever finds me finds life,
And [a]obtains favor from the LORD;
36 But he who sins against me [a]wrongs
his own soul;
All those who hate me love death."

The Way of Wisdom

9 Wisdom has [a]built her house,
She has hewn out her seven pillars;
2 [a]She has slaughtered her meat,
[b]She has mixed her wine,
She has also furnished her table.
3 She has sent out her maidens,
She cries out from the highest places of
the city,
4 "Whoever[a] *is* simple, let him turn in
here!"
As for him who lacks understanding,
she says to him,

PEACE NOTE

Reach out and talk to someone today if you are hurting. Ask a stronger believer in Christ to show you ways you can cultivate the peace of God during suffering and pain.

5 "Come,[a] eat of my bread
And drink of the wine I have mixed.
6 Forsake foolishness and live,
And go in the way of understanding.

7 "He who corrects a scoffer gets shame
for himself,
And he who rebukes a wicked *man only*
harms himself.
8 [a]Do not correct a scoffer, lest he hate you;
[b]Rebuke a wise *man,* and he will love you.
9 Give *instruction* to a wise *man,* and he
will be still wiser;
Teach a just *man,* [a]and he will increase
in learning.

10 "The[a] fear of the LORD *is* the beginning
of wisdom,
And the knowledge of the Holy One *is*
understanding.
11 [a]For by me your days will be multiplied,
And years of life will be added to you.
12 [a]If you are wise, you are wise for
yourself,
And *if* you scoff, you will bear *it* alone."

The Way of Folly

13 [a]A foolish woman is clamorous;
She is simple, and knows nothing.
14 For she sits at the door of her house,
On a seat [a]*by* the highest places of the
city,
15 To call to those who pass by,
Who go straight on their way:
16 "Whoever[a] *is* simple, let him turn in here";
And *as for* him who lacks
understanding, she says to him,

8:25 [a] Job 15:7, 8 **8:29** [a] Gen. 1:9, 10 [b] Job 28:4, 6 **8:30** [a] [John 1:1–3, 18] [b] [Matt. 3:17] [1] A Jewish tradition reads *one brought up.* **8:31** [a] Ps. 16:3 **8:32** [a] Luke 11:28 **8:34** [a] Prov. 3:13, 18 **8:35** [a] [John 17:3] **8:36** [a] Prov. 20:2 **9:1** [a] [Matt. 16:18] **9:2** [a] Matt. 22:4 [b] Prov. 23:30 **9:4** [a] Ps. 19:7 **9:5** [a] Is. 55:1 **9:8** [a] Matt. 7:6 [b] Ps. 141:5 **9:9** [a] [Matt. 13:12] **9:10** [a] Job 28:28 **9:11** [a] Prov. 3:2, 16 **9:12** [a] Job 35:6, 7 **9:13** [a] Prov. 7:11 **9:14** [a] Prov. 9:3 **9:16** [a] Prov. 7:7, 8

17 "Stolen[a] water is sweet,
And bread *eaten* in secret is pleasant."
18 But he does not know that [a]the dead
are there,
That her guests *are* in the depths of
hell.[1]

Wise Sayings of Solomon

10 The proverbs of [a]Solomon:

[b]A wise son makes a glad father,
But a foolish son *is* the grief of his
mother.

2 [a]Treasures of wickedness profit
nothing,
[b]But righteousness delivers from death.
3 [a]The LORD will not allow the righteous
soul to famish,
But He casts away the desire of the
wicked.

4 [a]He who has a slack hand becomes poor,
But [b]the hand of the diligent makes
rich.
5 He who gathers in [a]summer *is* a wise
son;
He who sleeps in harvest *is* [b]a son who
causes shame.

6 Blessings *are* on the head of the
righteous,
But violence covers the mouth of the
wicked.
7 [a]The memory of the righteous *is*
blessed,
But the name of the wicked will rot.

8 The wise in heart will receive commands,
[a]But a prating fool will fall.

9 [a]He who walks with integrity walks
securely,
But he who perverts his ways will
become known.

10 He who winks with the eye causes
trouble,
But a prating fool will fall.

11 The mouth of the righteous *is* a well of
life,
But violence covers the mouth of the
wicked.

12 Hatred stirs up strife,
But [a]love covers all sins.

13 Wisdom is found on the lips of him
who has understanding,
But [a]a rod *is* for the back of him who is
devoid of understanding.

14 Wise *people* store up knowledge,
But [a]the mouth of the foolish *is* near
destruction.

15 The [a]rich man's wealth *is* his strong city;
The destruction of the poor *is* their
poverty.

16 The labor of the righteous *leads* to [a]life,
The wages of the wicked to sin.

17 He who keeps instruction *is in* the way
of life,
But he who refuses correction goes astray.

18 Whoever [a]hides hatred *has* lying lips,
And [b]whoever spreads slander *is* a fool.

19 [a]In the multitude of words sin is not
lacking,
But [b]he who restrains his lips *is* wise.
20 The tongue of the righteous *is* choice
silver;
The heart of the wicked *is worth* little.
21 The lips of the righteous feed many,
But fools die for lack of wisdom.[1]

22 [a]The blessing of the LORD makes *one*
rich,
And He adds no sorrow with it.

23 [a]To do evil *is* like sport to a fool,
But a man of understanding has wisdom.
24 [a]The fear of the wicked will come upon
him,
And [b]the desire of the righteous will be
granted.
25 When the whirlwind passes by, [a]the
wicked *is* no *more,*
But [b]the righteous *has* an everlasting
foundation.

26 As vinegar to the teeth and smoke to
the eyes,
So *is* the lazy *man* to those who send
him.

9:17 [a] Prov. 20:17 **9:18** [a] Prov. 2:18; 7:27 [1] Or *Sheol* **10:1** [a] Prov. 1:1; 25:1 [b] Prov. 15:20; 17:21, 25; 19:13; 29:3, 15 **10:2** [a] [Luke 12:19, 20] [b] Dan. 4:27 **10:3** [a] Ps. 34:9, 10; 37:25 **10:4** [a] Prov. 19:15 [b] Prov. 12:24; 13:4; 21:5 **10:5** [a] Prov. 6:8 [b] Prov. 19:26 **10:7** [a] Eccl. 8:10 **10:8** [a] Prov. 10:10 **10:9** [a] [Ps. 23:4] **10:12** [a] [1 Cor. 13:4–7] **10:13** [a] Prov. 26:3 **10:14** [a] Prov. 18:7 **10:15** [a] Job 31:24 **10:16** [a] Prov. 6:23 **10:18** [a] Prov. 26:24 [b] Ps. 15:3; 101:5 **10:19** [a] Eccl. 5:3 [b] [James 1:19; 3:2] **10:21** [1] Literally *heart* **10:22** [a] Gen. 24:35; 26:12 **10:23** [a] Prov. 2:14; 15:21 **10:24** [a] Job 15:21 [b] Ps. 145:19 **10:25** [a] Ps. 37:9, 10 [b] Ps. 15:5

27 [a]The fear of the LORD prolongs days,
But [b]the years of the wicked will be shortened.
28 The hope of the righteous *will be* gladness,
But the [a]expectation of the wicked will perish.
29 The way of the LORD *is* strength for the upright,
But [a]destruction *will come* to the workers of iniquity.

30 [a]The righteous will never be removed,
But the wicked will not inhabit the earth.
31 [a]The mouth of the righteous brings forth wisdom,
But the perverse tongue will be cut out.
32 The lips of the righteous know what is acceptable,
But the mouth of the wicked *what is* perverse.

11 [a]Dishonest scales *are* an abomination to the LORD,
But a just weight *is* His delight.

2 When pride comes, then comes [a]shame;
But with the humble *is* wisdom.

3 The integrity of the upright will guide [a]them,
But the perversity of the unfaithful will destroy them.
4 [a]Riches do not profit in the day of wrath,
But [b]righteousness delivers from death.
5 The righteousness of the blameless will direct[1] his way aright,
But the wicked will fall by his own [a]wickedness.
6 The righteousness of the upright will deliver them,
But the unfaithful will be caught by *their* lust.

7 When a wicked man dies, *his* expectation will [a]perish,
And the hope of the unjust perishes.
8 [a]The righteous is delivered from trouble,
And it comes to the wicked instead.
9 The hypocrite with *his* mouth destroys *his* neighbor,
But through knowledge the righteous will be delivered.
10 [a]When it goes well with the righteous, the city rejoices;
And when the wicked perish, *there is* jubilation.
11 By the blessing of the upright the city is [a]exalted,
But it is overthrown by the mouth of the wicked.

12 He who is devoid of wisdom despises his neighbor,
But a man of understanding holds his peace.

13 [a]A talebearer reveals secrets,
But he who is of a faithful spirit [b]conceals a matter.

14 [a]Where *there is* no counsel, the people fall;
But in the multitude of counselors *there is* safety.

15 He who is [a]surety for a stranger will suffer,
But one who hates being surety is secure.

16 A gracious woman retains honor,
But ruthless *men* retain riches.
17 [a]The merciful man does good for his own soul,
But *he who is* cruel troubles his own flesh.
18 The wicked *man* does deceptive work,
But [a]he who sows righteousness *will have* a sure reward.
19 As righteousness *leads* to [a]life,
So he who pursues evil *pursues it* to his own [b]death.
20 Those who are of a perverse heart *are* an abomination to the LORD,
But *the* blameless in their ways *are* His delight.
21 [a]*Though they join* forces,[1] the wicked will not go unpunished;
But [b]the posterity of the righteous will be delivered.

22 *As* a ring of gold in a swine's snout,
So is a lovely woman who lacks discretion.

10:27 [a] Prov. 9:11 [b] Job 15:32 **10:28** [a] Job 8:13 **10:29** [a] Ps. 1:6 **10:30** [a] Ps. 37:22 **10:31** [a] Ps. 37:30
11:1 [a] Lev. 19:35, 36 **11:2** [a] Prov. 16:18; 18:12; 29:23 **11:3** [a] Prov. 13:6 **11:4** [a] Ezek. 7:19 [b] Gen. 7:1 **11:5** [a] Prov. 5:22
[1] Or *make smooth* or *straight* **11:7** [a] Prov. 10:28 **11:8** [a] Prov. 21:18 **11:10** [a] Prov. 28:12 **11:11** [a] Prov. 14:34
11:13 [a] Lev. 19:16 [b] Prov. 19:11 **11:14** [a] 1 Kin. 12:1 **11:15** [a] Prov. 6:1, 2 **11:17** [a] [Matt. 5:7; 25:34–36] **11:18** [a] Hos. 10:12
11:19 [a] Prov. 10:16; 12:28 [b] [Rom. 6:23] **11:21** [a] Prov. 16:5 [b] Ps. 112:2 [1] Literally *hand to hand*

23 The desire of the righteous *is* only good,
But the expectation of the wicked [a]*is*
wrath.

24 There is *one* who [a]scatters, yet
increases more;
And there is *one* who withholds more
than is right,
But it *leads* to poverty.
25 [a]The generous soul will be made rich,
[b]And he who waters will also be watered
himself.
26 The people will curse [a]him who
withholds grain,
But [b]blessing *will be* on the head of
him who sells *it.*

27 He who earnestly seeks good finds
favor,
[a]But trouble will come to him who seeks
evil.

28 [a]He who trusts in his riches will fall,
But [b]the righteous will flourish like
foliage.

29 He who troubles his own house [a]will
inherit the wind,
And the fool *will be* [b]servant to the wise
of heart.

30 The fruit of the righteous *is a* tree of
life,
And [a]he who wins souls *is* wise.

31 [a]If the righteous will be recompensed
on the earth,
How much more the ungodly and the
sinner.

12 Whoever loves instruction loves
knowledge,
But he who hates correction *is* stupid.

2 A good *man* obtains favor from the LORD,
But a man of wicked intentions He will
condemn.

3 A man is not established by wickedness,
But the [a]root of the righteous cannot
be moved.

4 [a]An excellent[1] wife *is* the crown of her
husband,
But she who causes shame *is* [b]like
rottenness in his bones.

5 The thoughts of the righteous *are* right,
But the counsels of the wicked *are*
deceitful.
6 [a]The words of the wicked *are,* "Lie in
wait for blood,"
[b]But the mouth of the upright will
deliver them.

7 [a]The wicked are overthrown and *are* no
more,
But the house of the righteous will
stand.

8 A man will be commended according
to his wisdom,
[a]But he who is of a perverse heart will
be despised.

9 [a]Better *is the one* who is slighted but has
a servant,
Than he who honors himself but lacks
bread.

10 [a]A righteous *man* regards the life of his
animal,
But the tender mercies of the wicked
are cruel.

11 [a]He who tills his land will be satisfied
with [b]bread,
But he who follows frivolity [c]*is* devoid
of understanding.[1]

12 The wicked covet the catch of evil
men,
But the root of the righteous yields
fruit.
13 [a]The wicked is ensnared by the
transgression of *his* lips,
[b]But the righteous will come through
trouble.
14 [a]A man will be satisfied with good by
the fruit of *his* mouth,
[b]And the recompense of a man's hands
will be rendered to him.

15 [a]The way of a fool *is* right in his own
eyes,
But he who heeds counsel *is* wise.
16 [a]A fool's wrath is known at once,
But a prudent *man* covers shame.

11:23 [a] Rom. 2:8, 9 **11:24** [a] Ps. 112:9 **11:25** [a] [2 Cor. 9:6, 7] [b] [Matt. 5:7] **11:26** [a] Amos 8:5, 6 [b] Job 29:13 **11:27** [a] Esth. 7:10 **11:28** [a] Job 31:24 [b] Ps. 1:3 **11:29** [a] Eccl. 5:16 [b] Prov. 14:19 **11:30** [a] [Dan. 12:3] **11:31** [a] Jer. 25:29 **12:3** [a] [Prov. 10:25] **12:4** [a] 1 Cor. 11:7 [b] Prov. 14:30 [1] Literally *A wife of valor* **12:6** [a] Prov. 1:11, 18 [b] Prov. 14:3 **12:7** [a] Matt. 7:24–27 **12:8** [a] 1 Sam. 25:17 **12:9** [a] Prov. 13:7 **12:10** [a] Deut. 25:4 **12:11** [a] Gen. 3:19 [b] Prov. 28:19 [c] Prov. 6:32 [1] Literally *heart* **12:13** [a] Prov. 18:7 [b] [2 Pet. 2:9] **12:14** [a] Prov. 13:2; 15:23; 18:20 [b] [Is. 3:10, 11] **12:15** [a] Luke 18:11 **12:16** [a] Prov. 11:13; 29:11

17 [a]He *who* speaks truth declares
righteousness,
But a false witness, deceit.
18 [a]There is one who speaks like the
piercings of a sword,
But the tongue of the wise *promotes*
health.
19 The truthful lip shall be established
forever,
[a]But a lying tongue *is* but for a
moment.
20 Deceit is in the heart of those who
devise evil,
But counselors of peace have joy.
21 [a]No grave trouble will overtake the
righteous,
But the wicked shall be filled with
evil.
22 [a]Lying lips *are* an abomination to the
LORD,
But those who deal truthfully *are* His
delight.

23 [a]A prudent man conceals knowledge,
But the heart of fools proclaims
foolishness.

24 [a]The hand of the diligent will rule,
But the lazy *man* will be put to forced
labor.

25 [a]Anxiety in the heart of man causes
depression,
But [b]a good word makes it glad.
26 The righteous should choose his
friends carefully,
For the way of the wicked leads them
astray.

27 The lazy *man* does not roast what he
took in hunting,
But diligence *is* man's precious
possession.

28 In the way of righteousness *is* life,
And in *its* pathway *there is* no death.

13

A wise son *heeds* his father's
instruction,
[a]But a scoffer does not listen to rebuke.

2 [a]A man shall eat well by the fruit of *his*
mouth,
But the soul of the unfaithful feeds on
violence.
3 [a]He who guards his mouth preserves
his life,
But he who opens wide his lips shall
have destruction.

4 [a]The soul of a lazy *man* desires, and *has*
nothing;
But the soul of the diligent shall be
made rich.

5 A righteous *man* hates lying,
But a wicked *man* is loathsome and
comes to shame.

12:17 [a] Prov. 14:5 12:18 [a] Ps. 57:4 12:19 [a] Prov. 19:9 12:21 [a] 1 Pet. 3:13 12:22 [a] Rev. 22:15 12:23 [a] Prov. 13:16
12:24 [a] Prov. 10:4 12:25 [a] Prov. 15:13 [b] Is. 50:4 13:1 [a] Is. 28:14, 15 13:2 [a] Prov. 12:14 13:3 [a] Prov. 21:23
13:4 [a] Prov. 10:4

THE COUNSEL FOR PEACE

Deceit is in the heart of those who devise evil, but counselors of peace have joy.

PROVERBS 12:20

Chapter 12 begins with a forceful observation: "Whoever loves instruction loves knowledge, but he who hates correction is stupid" (v. 1). This might not be the politest way of making the point, but it is true nonetheless. Given what is at stake, we should not be surprised by such blunt language.

In verse 20, the wise teacher told his students, "Deceit is in the heart of those who devise evil, but counselors of peace have joy." Pursuing and possessing peace results in joy. But how are "counselors of peace" the opposite of "those who devise evil"? "But" indicates the opposition. The context makes clear (vv. 18–19, 21) that devising evil is unhealthy, whereas counseling peace results in goodness and joy. Invariably, peace is both the result and the promoter of blessing.

How will you counsel peace today rather than devising evil? What does that look like for you?

6 [a]Righteousness guards *him whose* way
is blameless,
But wickedness overthrows the sinner.

7 [a]There is one who makes himself rich,
yet *has* nothing;
And one who makes himself poor, yet
has great riches.

8 The ransom of a man's life *is* his
riches,
But the poor does not hear rebuke.

9 The light of the righteous rejoices,
[a]But the lamp of the wicked will be put
out.

10 By pride comes nothing but [a]strife,
But with the well-advised *is* wisdom.

11 [a]Wealth *gained by* dishonesty will be
diminished,
But he who gathers by labor will
increase.

12 Hope deferred makes the heart sick,
But [a]*when* the desire comes, *it is* a tree
of life.

13 He who [a]despises the word will be
destroyed,
But he who fears the commandment
will be rewarded.
14 [a]The law of the wise *is* a fountain of life,
To turn *one* away from [b]the snares of
death.

15 Good understanding gains [a]favor,
But the way of the unfaithful *is* hard.
16 [a]Every prudent *man* acts with
knowledge,
But a fool lays open *his* folly.

17 A wicked messenger falls into trouble,
But [a]a faithful ambassador *brings* health.

18 Poverty and shame *will come* to him
who disdains correction,
But [a]he who regards a rebuke will be
honored.

19 A desire accomplished is sweet to the
soul,
But *it is* an abomination to fools to
depart from evil.

20 He who walks with wise *men* will be wise,
But the companion of fools will be
destroyed.

21 [a]Evil pursues sinners,
But to the righteous, good shall be repaid.

22 A good *man* leaves an inheritance to
his children's children,
But [a]the wealth of the sinner is stored
up for the righteous.

23 [a]Much food *is in* the fallow *ground* of the
poor,
And for lack of justice there is waste.[1]

24 [a]He who spares his rod hates his son,
But he who loves him disciplines him
promptly.

25 [a]The righteous eats to the satisfying of
his soul,
But the stomach of the wicked shall be
in want.

14 The wise woman builds her house,
But the foolish pulls it down with her
hands.

2 He who walks in his uprightness fears
the LORD,
[a]But *he who is* perverse in his ways
despises Him.

3 In the mouth of a fool *is* a rod of pride,
[a]But the lips of the wise will preserve
them.

4 Where no oxen *are,* the trough *is* clean;
But much increase *comes* by the
strength of an ox.

5 A [a]faithful witness does not lie,
But a false witness will utter [b]lies.

6 A scoffer seeks wisdom and does not
find it,
But [a]knowledge *is* easy to him who
understands.
7 Go from the presence of a foolish man,
When you do not perceive *in him* the
lips of [a]knowledge.
8 The wisdom of the prudent *is* to
understand his way,
But the folly of fools *is* deceit.

13:6 [a] Prov. 11:3, 5, 6 **13:7** [a] [Prov. 11:24; 12:9] **13:9** [a] Prov. 24:20 **13:10** [a] Prov. 10:12 **13:11** [a] Prov. 10:2; 20:21 **13:12** [a] Prov. 13:19 **13:13** [a] Num. 15:31 **13:14** [a] Prov. 6:22; 10:11; 14:27 [b] 2 Sam. 22:6 **13:15** [a] Prov. 3:4 **13:16** [a] Prov. 12:23 **13:17** [a] Prov. 25:13 **13:18** [a] Prov. 15:5, 31, 32 **13:21** [a] Ps. 32:10 **13:22** [a] [Eccl. 2:26] **13:23** [a] Prov. 12:11
[1] Literally *what is swept away* **13:24** [a] Prov. 19:18 **13:25** [a] Ps. 34:10 **14:2** [a] [Rom. 2:4] **14:3** [a] Prov. 12:6 **14:5** [a] Rev. 1:5; 3:14 [b] Prov. 6:19; 12:17 **14:6** [a] Prov. 8:9; 17:24 **14:7** [a] Prov. 23:9

9 [a]Fools mock at sin,
But among the upright *there is* favor.

10 The heart knows its own bitterness,
And a stranger does not share its joy.

11 [a]The house of the wicked will be overthrown,
But the tent of the upright will flourish.

12 [a]There is a way *that seems* right to a man,
But [b]its end *is* the way of [c]death.

13 Even in laughter the heart may sorrow,
And [a]the end of mirth *may be* grief.

14 The backslider in heart will be [a]filled with his own ways,
But a good man *will be satisfied* from [b]above.[1]

15 The simple believes every word,
But the prudent considers well his steps.

16 [a]A wise *man* fears and departs from evil,
But a fool rages and is self-confident.

17 A quick-tempered *man* acts foolishly,
And a man of wicked intentions is hated.

18 The simple inherit folly,
But the prudent are crowned with knowledge.

19 The evil will bow before the good,
And the wicked at the gates of the righteous.

20 [a]The poor *man* is hated even by his own neighbor,
But the rich *has* many [b]friends.

21 He who despises his neighbor sins;
[a]But he who has mercy on the poor, happy *is* he.

22 Do they not go astray who devise evil?
But mercy and truth *belong* to those who devise good.

23 In all labor there is profit,
But idle chatter[1] *leads* only to poverty.

24 The crown of the wise is their riches,
But the foolishness of fools *is* folly.

25 A true witness delivers [a]souls,
But a deceitful witness speaks lies.

26 In the fear of the LORD *there is* strong confidence,
And His children will have a place of refuge.

27 [a]The fear of the LORD *is* a fountain of life,
To turn *one* away from the snares of death.

28 In a multitude of people *is* a king's honor,
But in the lack of people *is* the downfall of a prince.

29 [a]*He who is* slow to wrath has great understanding,
But *he who is* impulsive[1] exalts folly.

30 A sound heart *is* life to the body,
But [a]envy *is* [b]rottenness to the bones.

PEACE NOTE

The world so often creates fear, insecurity, and damaged self-esteem. This is the opposite of what God wants for us—"a sound heart" that's full of peace.

PROVERBS 14:30

31 [a]He who oppresses the poor reproaches [b]his Maker,
But he who honors Him has mercy on the needy.

32 The wicked is banished in his wickedness,
But [a]the righteous has a refuge in his death.

33 Wisdom rests in the heart of him who has understanding,
But [a]*what is* in the heart of fools is made known.

34 Righteousness exalts a [a]nation,
But sin *is* a reproach to *any* people.

14:9 [a] Prov. 10:23 **14:11** [a] Job 8:15 **14:12** [a] Prov. 16:25 [b] Rom. 6:21 [c] Prov. 12:15 **14:13** [a] Eccl. 2:1, 2 **14:14** [a] Prov. 1:31; 12:15 [b] Prov. 13:2; 18:20 [1] Literally *from above himself* **14:16** [a] Prov. 22:3 **14:20** [a] Prov. 19:7 [b] Prov. 19:4 **14:21** [a] Ps. 112:9 **14:23** [1] Literally *talk of the lips* **14:25** [a] [Ezek. 3:18–21] **14:27** [a] Prov. 13:14 **14:29** [a] James 1:19 [1] Literally *short of spirit* **14:30** [a] Ps. 112:10 [b] Prov. 12:4 **14:31** [a] Matt. 25:40 [b] [Prov. 22:2] **14:32** [a] Job 13:15 **14:33** [a] Prov. 12:16 **14:34** [a] Prov. 11:11

35 [a]The king's favor *is* toward a wise servant,
But his wrath *is against* him who causes shame.

15 A [a]soft answer turns away wrath,
But [b]a harsh word stirs up anger.
2 The tongue of the wise uses knowledge rightly,
[a]But the mouth of fools pours forth foolishness.

3 [a]The eyes of the LORD *are* in every place,
Keeping watch on the evil and the good.

4 A wholesome tongue *is* a tree of life,
But perverseness in it breaks the spirit.

5 [a]A fool despises his father's instruction,
[b]But he who receives correction is prudent.

6 *In* the house of the righteous *there is* much treasure,
But in the revenue of the wicked is trouble.

7 The lips of the wise disperse knowledge,
But the heart of the fool *does* not *do* so.

8 [a]The sacrifice of the wicked *is* an abomination to the LORD,
But the prayer of the upright *is* His delight.
9 The way of the wicked *is* an abomination to the LORD,
But He loves him who [a]follows righteousness.

10 [a]Harsh discipline *is* for him who forsakes the way,
And [b]he who hates correction will die.

11 [a]Hell[1] and Destruction[2] *are* before the LORD;
So how much more [b]the hearts of the sons of men.

12 [a]A scoffer does not love one who corrects him,
Nor will he go to the wise.

13 [a]A merry heart makes a cheerful countenance,
But [b]by sorrow of the heart the spirit is broken.

14 The heart of him who has understanding seeks knowledge,
But the mouth of fools feeds on foolishness.

15 All the days of the afflicted *are* evil,
[a]But he who is of a merry heart *has* a continual feast.

16 [a]Better *is* a little with the fear of the LORD,
Than great treasure with trouble.
17 [a]Better *is* a dinner of herbs[1] where love is,
Than a fatted calf with hatred.

18 [a]A wrathful man stirs up strife,
But *he who is* slow to anger allays contention.

19 [a]The way of the lazy *man is* like a hedge of thorns,
But the way of the upright *is* a highway.

20 [a]A wise son makes a father glad,
But a foolish man despises his mother.

21 [a]Folly *is* joy *to him who is* destitute of discernment,
[b]But a man of understanding walks uprightly.

22 [a]Without counsel, plans go awry,
But in the multitude of counselors they are established.

23 A man has joy by the answer of his mouth,
And [a]a word *spoken* in due season, how good *it is!*

24 [a]The way of life *winds* upward for the wise,
That he may [b]turn away from hell[1] below.

25 [a]The LORD will destroy the house of the proud,
But [b]He will establish the boundary of the widow.

26 [a]The thoughts of the wicked *are* an abomination to the LORD,
[b]But the words of the pure *are* pleasant.

14:35 [a] Matt. 24:45–47 **15:1** [a] Prov. 25:15 [b] 1 Sam. 25:10 **15:2** [a] Prov. 12:23 **15:3** [a] Job 34:21 **15:5** [a] Prov. 10:1 [b] Prov. 13:18 **15:8** [a] Is. 1:11 **15:9** [a] Prov. 21:21 **15:10** [a] 1 Kin. 22:8 [b] Prov. 5:12 **15:11** [a] Job 26:6 [b] 2 Chr. 6:30 [1] Or *Sheol* [2] Hebrew *Abaddon* **15:12** [a] Amos 5:10 **15:13** [a] Prov. 12:25 [b] Prov. 17:22 **15:15** [a] Prov. 17:22 **15:16** [a] Ps. 37:16 **15:17** [a] Prov. 17:1 [1] Or *vegetables* **15:18** [a] Prov. 26:21 **15:19** [a] Prov. 22:5 **15:20** [a] Prov. 10:1 **15:21** [a] Prov. 10:23 [b] Eph. 5:15 **15:22** [a] Prov. 11:14 **15:23** [a] Prov. 25:11 **15:24** [a] Phil. 3:20 [b] Prov. 14:16 [1] Or *Sheol* **15:25** [a] Prov. 12:7 [b] Ps. 68:5, 6 **15:26** [a] Prov. 6:16, 18 [b] Ps. 37:30

27 [a]He who is greedy for gain troubles his
own house,
But he who hates bribes will live.

28 The heart of the righteous [a]studies how
to answer,
But the mouth of the wicked pours
forth evil.

29 [a]The LORD *is* far from the wicked,
But [b]He hears the prayer of the
righteous.

30 The light of the eyes rejoices the
heart,
And a good report makes the bones
healthy.[1]

31 The ear that hears the rebukes of life
Will abide among the wise.
32 He who disdains instruction despises
his own soul,
But he who heeds rebuke gets
understanding.
33 [a]The fear of the LORD *is* the instruction
of wisdom,
And [b]before honor *is* humility.

16 The [a]preparations of the heart
belong to man,
[b]But the answer of the tongue *is* from
the LORD.

2 All the ways of a man *are* pure in his
own [a]eyes,
But the LORD weighs the spirits.

3 [a]Commit your works to the LORD,
And your thoughts will be
established.

4 The [a]LORD has made all for Himself,
[b]Yes, even the wicked for the day of
doom.

5 [a]Everyone proud in heart *is* an
abomination to the LORD;
Though they join forces,[1] none will go
unpunished.

6 [a]In mercy and truth
Atonement is provided for iniquity;
And [b]by the fear of the LORD *one*
departs from evil.

7 When a man's ways please the
LORD,
He makes even his enemies to be at
peace with him.

8 [a]Better *is* a little with righteousness,
Than vast revenues without justice.

9 [a]A man's heart plans his way,
[b]But the LORD directs his steps.

15:27 [a] Is. 5:8 15:28 [a] 1 Pet. 3:15 15:29 [a] Ps. 10:1; 34:16 [b] Ps. 145:18 15:30 [1] Literally *fat* 15:33 [a] Prov. 1:7 [b] Prov. 18:12 16:1 [a] Jer. 10:23 [b] Matt. 10:19 16:2 [a] Prov. 21:2 16:3 [a] Ps. 37:5 16:4 [a] Is. 43:7 [b] [Rom. 9:22] 16:5 [a] Prov. 6:17; 8:13 [1] Literally *hand to hand* 16:6 [a] Dan. 4:27 [b] Prov. 8:13; 14:16 16:8 [a] Ps. 37:16 16:9 [a] Prov. 19:21 [b] Jer. 10:23

WITH YOUR ENEMIES

When a man's ways please the LORD, He makes even his enemies to be at peace with him.

PROVERBS 16:7

Proverbs points out that peacemaking is beneficial for all concerned—not only for the person to whom peace is extended, but also for the one who extends it. The evil person might see an offering of peace as weakness and so seek to take advantage of it, but in the long run, the person who offers peace is the winner. This is the point that verse 7 makes: "When a man's ways please the LORD, He makes even his enemies to be at peace with him."

One of the sad symptoms of evil is that the wicked, out of their perverse hatred, sometimes oppose the righteous and wish to harm them. The righteous trust God to protect them and make things right (recall what happened to the wicked Haman in the Book of Esther); they do not seek revenge. The peacemaker is called such because he or she makes peace, not war. It is the Lord who will bring judgment as He sees fit. Those who are in positions of influence may have many critics. Commit the critic to the Lord and do not allow him or her to steal your peace. God will fight your battles so much more effectively than you can. Leave those things to the Lord, and move forward in His peace and grace today.

> PEACE NOTE
>
> Like an umpire in a baseball game, God's peace will direct our hearts—for which we can be thankful.
>
> PROVERBS 16:9

10 Divination *is* on the lips of the king;
His mouth must not transgress in judgment.
11 [a]Honest weights and scales *are* the LORD's;
All the weights in the bag *are* His work.
12 *It is* an abomination for kings to commit wickedness,
For [a]a throne is established by righteousness.
13 [a]Righteous lips *are* the delight of kings,
And they love him who speaks *what is* right.
14 As messengers of death *is* the king's wrath,
But a wise man will [a]appease it.
15 In the light of the king's face *is* life,
And his favor *is* like a [a]cloud of the latter rain.

16 [a]How much better to get wisdom than gold!
And to get understanding is to be chosen rather than silver.

17 The highway of the upright *is* to depart from evil;
He who keeps his way preserves his soul.

18 Pride *goes* before destruction,
And a haughty spirit before a fall.
19 Better *to be* of a humble spirit with the lowly,
Than to divide the spoil with the proud.

20 He who heeds the word wisely will find good,
And whoever [a]trusts in the LORD, happy *is* he.

21 The wise in heart will be called prudent,
And sweetness of the lips increases learning.

22 Understanding *is* a wellspring of life to him who has it.
But the correction of fools *is* folly.

23 The heart of the wise teaches his mouth,
And adds learning to his lips.

24 Pleasant words *are like* a honeycomb,
Sweetness to the soul and health to the bones.

25 There is a way *that seems* right to a man,
But its end *is* the way of [a]death.

26 The person who labors, labors for himself,
For his *hungry* mouth drives [a]him *on.*

27 An ungodly man digs up evil,
And *it is* on his lips like a burning [a]fire.
28 A perverse man sows strife,
And [a]a whisperer separates the best of friends.
29 A violent man entices his neighbor,
And leads him in a way *that is* not good.
30 He winks his eye to devise perverse things;
He purses his lips *and* brings about evil.

31 [a]The silver-haired head *is* a crown of glory,
If it is found in the way of righteousness.

32 [a]*He who is* slow to anger *is* better than the mighty,
And he who rules his spirit than he who takes a city.

33 The lot is cast into the lap,
But its every decision *is* from the LORD.

17 Better *is* [a]a dry morsel with quietness,
Than a house full of feasting[1] *with* strife.

2 A wise servant will rule over [a]a son who causes shame,
And will share an inheritance among the brothers.

16:11 [a] Lev. 19:36 16:12 [a] Prov. 25:5 16:13 [a] Prov. 14:35 16:14 [a] Prov. 25:15 16:15 [a] Zech. 10:1 16:16 [a] Prov. 8:10, 11, 19 16:20 [a] Ps. 34:8 16:25 [a] Prov. 14:12 16:26 [a] [Eccl. 6:7] 16:27 [a] [James 3:6] 16:28 [a] Prov. 17:9 16:31 [a] Prov. 20:29 16:32 [a] Prov. 14:29; 19:11 17:1 [a] Prov. 15:17 [1] Or *sacrificial meals* 17:2 [a] Prov. 10:5

3 The refining pot *is* for silver and the furnace for gold,
[a]But the LORD tests the hearts.

4 An evildoer gives heed to false lips;
A liar listens eagerly to a spiteful tongue.

5 [a]He who mocks the poor reproaches his Maker;
[b]He who is glad at calamity will not go unpunished.

6 [a]Children's children *are* the crown of old men,
And the glory of children *is* their father.

7 Excellent speech is not becoming to a fool,
Much less lying lips to a prince.

8 A present *is* a precious stone in the eyes of its possessor;
Wherever he turns, he prospers.

9 [a]He who covers a transgression seeks love,
But [b]he who repeats a matter separates friends.

10 [a]Rebuke is more effective for a wise *man*
Than a hundred blows on a fool.

11 An evil *man* seeks only rebellion;
Therefore a cruel messenger will be sent against him.

12 Let a man meet [a]a bear robbed of her cubs,
Rather than a fool in his folly.

13 Whoever [a]rewards evil for good,
Evil will not depart from his house.

14 The beginning of strife *is like* releasing water;
Therefore [a]stop contention before a quarrel starts.

15 [a]He who justifies the wicked, and he who condemns the just,
Both of them alike *are* an abomination to the LORD.

16 Why *is there* in the hand of a fool the *purchase price of wisdom,*
Since *he has* no heart *for it?*

17 [a]A friend loves at all times,
And a brother is born for adversity.

18 [a]A man devoid of understanding shakes hands in a pledge,
And becomes surety for his friend.

19 He who loves transgression loves strife,
And [a]he who exalts his gate seeks destruction.

20 He who has a deceitful heart finds no good,
And he who has [a]a perverse tongue falls into evil.

21 He who begets a scoffer *does so* to his sorrow,
And the father of a fool has no joy.

22 A [a]merry heart does good, *like* medicine,[1]
But a broken spirit dries the bones.

PEACE NOTE

A person's sense of delight and contentment extends vertically to God and horizontally to God's world. Being happy or merry is a way of having peace.

PROVERBS 17:22

23 A wicked *man* accepts a bribe behind the back[1]
To pervert the ways of justice.

24 [a]Wisdom *is* in the sight of him who has understanding,
But the eyes of a fool *are* on the ends of the earth.

25 A [a]foolish son *is* a grief to his father,
And bitterness to her who bore him.

26 Also, to punish the righteous *is* not good,
Nor to strike princes for *their* uprightness.

17:3 [a] Jer. 17:10 **17:5** [a] Prov. 14:31 [b] Job 31:29 **17:6** [a] [Ps. 127:3; 128:3] **17:9** [a] [Prov. 10:12] [b] Prov. 16:28 **17:10** [a] [Mic. 7:9] **17:12** [a] Hos. 13:8 **17:13** [a] Ps. 109:4, 5 **17:14** [a] [Prov. 20:3] **17:15** [a] Ex. 23:7 **17:17** [a] Ruth 1:16 **17:18** [a] Prov. 6:1 **17:19** [a] Prov. 16:18 **17:20** [a] James 3:8 **17:22** [a] Prov. 12:25; 15:13, 15 [1] Or *makes medicine even better* **17:23** [1] Literally *from the bosom* **17:24** [a] Eccl. 2:14 **17:25** [a] Prov. 10:1; 15:20; 19:13

27 [a]He who has knowledge spares his words,
And a man of understanding is of a calm spirit.
28 [a]Even a fool is counted wise when he holds his peace;
When he shuts his lips, *he is considered* perceptive.

18 A man who isolates himself seeks his own desire;
He rages against all wise judgment.

2 A fool has no delight in understanding,
But in expressing his [a]own heart.

3 When the wicked comes, contempt comes also;
And with dishonor *comes* reproach.

4 [a]The words of a man's mouth *are* deep waters;
[b]The wellspring of wisdom *is* a flowing brook.

5 *It is* not good to show partiality to the wicked,
Or to overthrow the righteous in [a]judgment.

6 A fool's lips enter into contention,
And his mouth calls for blows.
7 [a]A fool's mouth *is* his destruction,
And his lips *are* the snare of his [b]soul.
8 [a]The words of a talebearer *are* like tasty trifles,[1]
And they go down into the inmost body.

9 He who is slothful in his work
Is a brother to him who is a great destroyer.

10 The name of the LORD *is* a strong [a]tower;
The righteous run to it and are safe.
11 The rich man's wealth *is* his strong city,
And like a high wall in his own esteem.

12 [a]Before destruction the heart of a man *is haughty,*
And before honor *is* humility.

13 He who answers a matter before he hears *it,*
It *is* folly and shame to him.

14 The spirit of a man will sustain him in sickness,
But who can bear a broken spirit?

15 The heart of the prudent acquires knowledge,
And the ear of the wise seeks knowledge.

16 [a]A man's gift makes room for him,
And brings him before great men.

17 The first *one* to plead his cause *seems* right,
Until his neighbor comes and examines him.

18 Casting [a]lots causes contentions to cease,
And keeps the mighty apart.

19 A brother offended *is harder to win* than a strong city,
And contentions *are* like the bars of a castle.

20 [a]A man's stomach shall be satisfied from the fruit of his mouth;
From the produce of his lips he shall be filled.

21 [a]Death and life *are* in the power of the tongue,
And those who love it will eat its fruit.

22 [a]*He who* finds a wife finds a good *thing,*
And obtains favor from the LORD.

23 The poor *man* uses entreaties,
But the rich answers [a]roughly.

24 A man *who has* friends must himself be friendly,[1]
[a]But there is a friend *who* sticks closer than a brother.

19 Better [a]*is* the poor who walks in his integrity
Than *one who is* perverse in his lips, and is a fool.

2 Also it is not good *for* a soul *to be* without knowledge,
And he sins who hastens with *his* feet.

17:27 [a] James 1:19 **17:28** [a] Job 13:5 **18:2** [a] Eccl. 10:3 **18:4** [a] Prov. 10:11 [b] [James 3:17] **18:5** [a] Prov. 17:15 **18:7** [a] Prov. 10:14 [b] Eccl. 10:12 **18:8** [a] Prov. 12:18 [1] A Jewish tradition reads *wounds.* **18:10** [a] 2 Sam. 22:2, 3, 33 **18:12** [a] Prov. 15:33; 16:18 **18:16** [a] Gen. 32:20, 21 **18:18** [a] [Prov. 16:33] **18:20** [a] Prov. 12:14; 14:14 **18:21** [a] Matt. 12:37 **18:22** [a] [Prov. 12:4; 19:14] **18:23** [a] James 2:3, 6 **18:24** [a] Prov. 17:17 [1] Following Greek manuscripts, Syriac, Targum, and Vulgate; Masoretic Text reads *may come to ruin.* **19:1** [a] Prov. 28:6

3 The foolishness of a man twists his way,
And his heart frets against the LORD.

4 [a]Wealth makes many friends,
But the poor is separated from his friend.

5 A [a]false witness will not go unpunished,
And *he who* speaks lies will not escape.

6 Many entreat the favor of the nobility,
And every man *is* a friend to one who gives gifts.

7 [a]All the brothers of the poor hate him;
How much more do his friends go [b]far from him!
He may pursue *them with* words, *yet* they abandon *him.*

8 He who gets wisdom loves his own soul;
He who keeps understanding [a]will find good.

PEACE NOTE

You will become like what fills your mind. Fill your mind with good things, and you will notice that your attitude is much more peaceful.

PROVERBS 19:8

9 A false witness will not go unpunished,
And *he who* speaks lies shall perish.

10 Luxury is not fitting for a fool,
Much less [a]for a servant to rule over princes.

11 [a]The discretion of a man makes him slow to anger,
[b]And his glory *is* to overlook a transgression.

12 [a]The king's wrath *is* like the roaring of a lion,
But his favor *is* [b]like dew on the grass.

13 [a]A foolish son *is* the ruin of his father,
[b]And the contentions of a wife *are* a continual dripping.

14 [a]Houses and riches *are* an inheritance from fathers,
But [b]a prudent wife *is* from the LORD.

15 [a]Laziness casts *one* into a deep sleep,
And an idle person will [b]suffer hunger.

16 [a]He who keeps the commandment keeps his soul,
But he who is careless[1] of his ways will die.

17 [a]He who has pity on the poor lends to the LORD,
And He will pay back what he has given.

18 [a]Chasten your son while there is hope,
And do not set your heart on his destruction.[1]

19 *A man of* great wrath will suffer punishment;
For if you rescue *him,* you will have to do it again.

20 Listen to counsel and receive instruction,
That you may be wise [a]in your latter days.

21 There are many plans in a man's heart,
[a]Nevertheless the LORD's counsel—that will stand.

22 What is desired in a man is kindness,
And a poor man is better than a liar.

23 [a]The fear of the LORD *leads* to life,
And *he who has it* will abide in satisfaction;
He will not be visited with evil.

24 [a]A lazy *man* buries his hand in the bowl,[1]
And will not so much as bring it to his mouth again.

19:4 [a] Prov. 14:20 **19:5** [a] Ex. 23:1 **19:7** [a] Prov. 14:20 [b] Ps. 38:11 **19:8** [a] Prov. 16:20 **19:10** [a] Prov. 30:21, 22 **19:11** [a] James 1:19 [b] Eph. 4:32 **19:12** [a] Prov. 16:14 [b] Hos. 14:5 **19:13** [a] Prov. 10:1 [b] Prov. 21:9, 19 **19:14** [a] 2 Cor. 12:14 [b] Prov. 18:22 **19:15** [a] Prov. 6:9 [b] Prov. 10:4 **19:16** [a] Luke 10:28; 11:28 [1] Literally *despises,* figurative of recklessness or carelessness **19:17** [a] [2 Cor. 9:6–8] **19:18** [a] Prov. 13:24 [1] Literally *to put him to death;* a Jewish tradition reads *on his crying.* **19:20** [a] Ps. 37:37 **19:21** [a] Heb. 6:17 **19:23** [a] [1 Tim. 4:8] **19:24** [a] Prov. 15:19 [1] Septuagint and Syriac read *bosom;* Targum and Vulgate read *armpit.*

25 Strike a scoffer, and the simple [a]will
become wary;
[b]Rebuke one who has understanding,
and he will discern knowledge.

26 He who mistreats *his* father *and* chases
away *his* mother
Is [a]a son who causes shame and brings
reproach.

27 Cease listening to instruction, my son,
And you will stray from the words of
knowledge.

28 A disreputable witness scorns justice,
And [a]the mouth of the wicked devours
iniquity.

29 Judgments are prepared for scoffers,
[a]And beatings for the backs of fools.

20 Wine [a]*is* a mocker,
Strong drink *is* a brawler,
And whoever is led astray by it is not
wise.

2 The wrath[1] of a king *is* like the roaring
of a lion;
Whoever provokes him to anger sins
against his own life.

3 [a]*It is* honorable for a man to stop striving,
Since any fool can start a quarrel.

4 [a]The lazy *man* will not plow because of
winter;
[b]He will beg during harvest and *have*
nothing.

5 Counsel in the heart of man *is like* deep
water,
But a man of understanding will draw
it out.

6 Most men will proclaim each his own
goodness,
But who can find a faithful man?

7 [a]The righteous *man* walks in his
integrity;
[b]His children *are* blessed after him.

8 A king who sits on the throne of
judgment
Scatters all evil with his eyes.

9 [a]Who can say, "I have made my heart
clean,
I am pure from my sin"?

10 [a]Diverse weights *and* diverse
measures,
They *are* both alike, an abomination to
the LORD.

11 Even a child is [a]known by his deeds,
Whether what he does *is* pure and
right.

12 [a]The hearing ear and the seeing eye,
The LORD has made them both.

13 [a]Do not love sleep, lest you come to
poverty;
Open your eyes, *and* you will be
satisfied with bread.

14 "*It is* good for nothing,"[1] cries the buyer;
But when he has gone his way, then he
boasts.

15 There is gold and a multitude of rubies,
But [a]the lips of knowledge *are* a
precious jewel.

16 [a]Take the garment of one who is surety
for a stranger,
And hold it as a pledge *when it* is for a
seductress.

17 [a]Bread gained by deceit *is* sweet to a
man,
But afterward his mouth will be filled
with gravel.

18 [a]Plans are established by counsel;
[b]By wise counsel wage war.

19 [a]He who goes about *as* a talebearer
reveals secrets;
Therefore do not associate with one
[b]who flatters with his lips.

20 [a]Whoever curses his father or his
mother,
[b]His lamp will be put out in deep
darkness.

21 [a]An inheritance gained hastily at the
beginning
[b]Will not be blessed at the end.

19:25 [a] Deut. 13:11 [b] Prov. 9:8 **19:26** [a] Prov. 17:2 **19:28** [a] Job 15:16 **19:29** [a] Prov. 26:3 **20:1** [a] Gen. 9:21 **20:2** [1] Literally *fear* or *terror* which is produced by the king's wrath **20:3** [a] Prov. 17:14 **20:4** [a] Prov. 10:4 [b] Prov. 19:15 **20:7** [a] 2 Cor. 1:12 [b] Ps. 37:26 **20:9** [a] [1 Kin. 8:46] **20:10** [a] Deut. 25:13 **20:11** [a] Matt. 7:16 **20:12** [a] Ex. 4:11 **20:13** [a] Rom. 12:11 **20:14** [1] Literally *evil, evil* **20:15** [a] [Prov. 3:13–15] **20:16** [a] Prov. 22:26 **20:17** [a] Prov. 9:17 **20:18** [a] Prov. 24:6 [b] Luke 14:31 **20:19** [a] Prov. 11:13 [b] Rom. 16:18 **20:20** [a] Matt. 15:4 [b] Job 18:5, 6 **20:21** [a] Prov. 28:20 [b] Hab. 2:6

22 [a]Do not say, "I will recompense evil";
[b]Wait for the LORD, and He will save you.

23 Diverse weights *are* an abomination to the LORD,
And dishonest scales *are* not good.

24 A man's steps *are* of the LORD;
How then can a man understand his own way?

25 *It is* a snare for a man to devote rashly *something as* holy,
And afterward to reconsider *his* vows.

26 [a]A wise king sifts out the wicked,
And brings the threshing wheel over them.

27 [a]The spirit of a man *is* the lamp of the LORD,
Searching all the inner depths of his heart.[1]

28 [a]Mercy and truth preserve the king,
And by lovingkindness he upholds his throne.

29 The glory of young men *is* their strength,
And [a]the splendor of old men *is* their gray head.

30 Blows that hurt cleanse away evil,
As *do* stripes the inner depths of the heart.[1]

21 The king's heart *is* in the hand of the LORD,
Like the rivers of water;
He turns it wherever He wishes.

2 [a]Every way of a man *is* right in his own eyes,
[b]But the LORD weighs the hearts.

3 [a]To do righteousness and justice
Is more acceptable to the LORD than sacrifice.

4 [a]A haughty look, a proud heart,
And the plowing[1] of the wicked *are* sin.

5 [a]The plans of the diligent *lead* surely to plenty,

PEACE NOTE

Do you have a personal Peace Plan—an action plan of intentional ways to seek God's tranquility when you lack it?

PROVERBS 21:5

But *those of* everyone *who is* hasty, surely to poverty.

6 [a]Getting treasures by a lying tongue
Is the fleeting fantasy of those who seek death.[1]

7 The violence of the wicked will destroy them,[1]
Because they refuse to do justice.

8 The way of a guilty man *is* perverse;[1]
But *as for* the pure, his work *is* right.

9 Better to dwell in a corner of a housetop,
Than in a house shared with [a]a contentious woman.

10 [a]The soul of the wicked desires evil;
His neighbor finds no favor in his eyes.

11 When the scoffer is punished, the simple is made wise;
But when the [a]wise is instructed, he receives knowledge.

12 The righteous *God* wisely considers the house of the wicked,
Overthrowing the wicked for *their* wickedness.

13 [a]Whoever shuts his ears to the cry of the poor
Will also cry himself and not be heard.

20:22 [a] [Rom. 12:17–19] [b] 2 Sam. 16:12 20:26 [a] Ps. 101:8 20:27 [a] 1 Cor. 2:11 [1] Literally *the rooms of the belly* 20:28 [a] Prov. 21:21 20:29 [a] Prov. 16:31 20:30 [1] Literally *the rooms of the belly* 21:2 [a] Prov. 16:2 [b] Prov. 24:12 21:3 [a] 1 Sam. 15:22 21:4 [a] Prov. 6:17 [1] Or *lamp* 21:5 [a] Prov. 10:4 21:6 [a] 2 Pet. 2:3 [1] Septuagint reads *Pursue vanity on the snares of death;* Vulgate reads *Is vain and foolish, and shall stumble on the snares of death;* Targum reads *They shall be destroyed, and they shall fall who seek death.* 21:7 [1] Literally *drag them away* 21:8 [1] Or *The way of a man is perverse and strange* 21:9 [a] Prov. 19:13 21:10 [a] James 4:5 21:11 [a] Prov. 19:25 21:13 [a] [Matt. 7:2; 18:30–34]

14 A gift in secret pacifies anger,
And a bribe behind the back,[1] strong
wrath.

15 *It is* a joy for the just to do justice,
But destruction *will come* to the
workers of iniquity.

16 A man who wanders from the way of
understanding
Will rest in the assembly of the
[a]dead.

17 He who loves pleasure *will be* a poor
man;
He who loves wine and oil will not be
rich.

18 The wicked *shall be* a ransom for the
righteous,
And the unfaithful for the upright.

19 Better to dwell in the wilderness,
Than with a contentious and angry
woman.

20 [a]*There is* desirable treasure,
And oil in the dwelling of the wise,
But a foolish man squanders it.

21 [a]He who follows righteousness and
mercy
Finds life, righteousness, and honor.

22 A [a]wise *man* scales the city of the
mighty,
And brings down the trusted
stronghold.

23 [a]Whoever guards his mouth and tongue
Keeps his soul from troubles.

24 A proud *and* haughty *man*—"Scoffer" *is*
his name;
He acts with arrogant pride.

25 The [a]desire of the lazy *man* kills him,
For his hands refuse to labor.

26 He covets greedily all day long,
But the righteous [a]gives and does not
spare.

27 [a]The sacrifice of the wicked *is* an
abomination;
How much more *when* he brings it with
wicked intent!

28 A false witness shall perish,
But the man who hears *him* will speak
endlessly.

29 A wicked man hardens his face,
But *as for* the upright, he establishes[1]
his way.

30 [a]*There is* no wisdom or understanding
Or counsel against the LORD.

31 The horse *is* prepared for the day of
battle,
But [a]deliverance *is* of the LORD.

22 A [a]*good* name is to be chosen rather
than great riches,
Loving favor rather than silver and
gold.

2 The [a]rich and the poor have this in
common,
The [b]LORD *is* the maker of them all.

3 A prudent *man* foresees evil and hides
himself,
But the simple pass on and are
[a]punished.

4 By humility *and* the fear of the LORD
Are riches and honor and life.

5 Thorns *and* snares *are* in the way of the
perverse;
He who guards his soul will be far from
them.

6 [a]Train up a child in the way he should go,
And when he is old he will not depart
from it.

7 The [a]rich rules over the poor,
And the borrower *is* servant to the
lender.

8 He who sows iniquity will reap
[a]sorrow,
And the rod of his anger will fail.

9 [a]He who has a generous eye will be
[b]blessed,
For he gives of his bread to the poor.

10 [a]Cast out the scoffer, and contention
will leave;
Yes, strife and reproach will cease.

21:14 [1] Literally *in the bosom* **21:16** [a] Ps. 49:14 **21:20** [a] Ps. 112:3 **21:21** [a] Matt. 5:6 **21:22** [a] Prov. 24:5 **21:23** [a] [James 3:2] **21:25** [a] Prov. 13:4 **21:26** [a] [Prov. 22:9] **21:27** [a] Jer. 6:20 **21:29** [1] Qere and Septuagint read *understands.* **21:30** [a] [Jer. 9:23, 24] **21:31** [a] Ps. 3:8 **22:1** [a] Eccl. 7:1 **22:2** [a] Prov. 29:13 [b] Job 31:15 **22:3** [a] Prov. 27:12 **22:6** [a] Eph. 6:4 **22:7** [a] James 2:6 **22:8** [a] Job 4:8 **22:9** [a] 2 Cor. 9:6 [b] [Prov. 19:17] **22:10** [a] Ps. 101:5

PEACE NOTE

The importance of the mind is anchored in Israel's ancient Scriptures. The intelligent, thinking mind is saturated with God's thoughts.

PROVERBS 22:17

11 [a]He who loves purity of heart
And has grace on his lips,
The king *will be* his friend.

12 The eyes of the LORD preserve knowledge,
But He overthrows the words of the faithless.

13 [a]The lazy *man* says, "*There is* a lion outside!
I shall be slain in the streets!"

14 [a]The mouth of an immoral woman *is* a deep pit;
[b]He who is abhorred by the LORD will fall there.

15 Foolishness *is* bound up in the heart of a child;
[a]The rod of correction will drive it far from him.

16 He who oppresses the poor to increase his *riches,*
And he who gives to the rich, *will* surely *come* to poverty.

Sayings of the Wise

17 Incline your ear and hear the words of the wise,
And apply your heart to my knowledge;
18 For *it is* a pleasant thing if you keep them within you;
Let them all be fixed upon your lips,
19 So that your trust may be in the LORD;
I have instructed you today, even you.
20 Have I not written to you excellent things
Of counsels and knowledge,
21 [a]That I may make you know the certainty of the words of truth,
[b]That you may answer words of truth
To those who send to you?

22 Do not rob the [a]poor because he *is* poor,
Nor oppress the afflicted at the gate;
23 [a]For the LORD will plead their cause,
And plunder the soul of those who plunder them.

24 Make no friendship with an angry man,
And with a [a]furious man do not go,
25 Lest you learn his ways
And set a snare for your soul.

26 [a]Do not be one of those who shakes hands in a pledge,
One of those who is surety for debts;
27 If you have nothing *with which* to pay,
Why should he take away your bed from under you?

28 [a]Do not remove the ancient landmark
Which your fathers have set.

29 Do you see a man *who* excels in his work?
He will stand before kings;
He will not stand before unknown *men.*

23 When you sit down to eat with a ruler,
Consider carefully what *is* before you;
2 And put a knife to your throat
If you *are* a man given to appetite.

PEACE NOTE

The foolish, unthinking mind is caught up with the things and people we idolize, and that is how peace is stolen from our hearts and minds.

PROVERBS 22:17

22:11 [a] Ps. 101:6 22:13 [a] Prov. 26:13 22:14 [a] Prov. 2:16; 5:3; 7:5 [b] Eccl. 7:26 22:15 [a] Prov. 13:24; 23:13, 14
22:21 [a] Luke 1:3, 4 [b] 1 Pet. 3:15 22:22 [a] Ex. 23:6 22:23 [a] 1 Sam. 24:12 22:24 [a] Prov. 29:22 22:26 [a] Prov. 11:15
22:28 [a] Deut. 19:14; 27:17

3 Do not desire his delicacies,
For they *are* deceptive food.

4 [a]Do not overwork to be rich;
[b]Because of your own understanding, cease!
5 Will you set your eyes on that which is not?
For *riches* certainly make themselves wings;
They fly away like an eagle *toward* heaven.

6 Do not eat the bread of [a]a miser,[1]
Nor desire his delicacies;
7 For as he thinks in his heart, so *is* he.
"Eat and drink!" [a]he says to you,
But his heart is not with you.
8 The morsel you have eaten, you will vomit up,
And waste your pleasant words.

9 [a]Do not speak in the hearing of a fool,
For he will despise the wisdom of your words.

10 Do not remove the ancient landmark,
Nor enter the fields of the fatherless;
11 [a]For their Redeemer *is* mighty;
He will plead their cause against you.

12 Apply your heart to instruction,
And your ears to words of knowledge.

13 [a]Do not withhold correction from a child,
For *if* you beat him with a rod, he will not die.
14 You shall beat him with a rod,
And deliver his soul from hell.[1]

15 My son, if your heart is wise,
My heart will rejoice—indeed, I myself;
16 Yes, my inmost being will rejoice
When your lips speak right things.

17 [a]Do not let your heart envy sinners,
But [b]*be zealous* for the fear of the LORD all the day;
18 [a]For surely there is a hereafter,
And your hope will not be cut off.

19 Hear, my son, and be wise;
And guide your heart in the way.
20 [a]Do not mix with winebibbers,
Or with gluttonous eaters of meat;
21 For the drunkard and the glutton will come to poverty,
And drowsiness will clothe *a man* with rags.

22 [a]Listen to your father who begot you,
And do not despise your mother when she is old.
23 [a]Buy the truth, and do not sell *it,*
Also wisdom and instruction and understanding.

24 [a]The father of the righteous will greatly rejoice,
And he who begets a wise *child* will delight in him.
25 Let your father and your mother be glad,
And let her who bore you rejoice.
26 My son, give me your heart,
And let your eyes observe my ways.
27 [a]For a harlot *is* a deep pit,
And a seductress *is* a narrow well.
28 [a]She also lies in wait as *for* a victim,
And increases the unfaithful among men.

29 [a]Who has woe?
Who has sorrow?
Who has contentions?
Who has complaints?
Who has wounds without cause?
Who [b]has redness of eyes?
30 [a]Those who linger long at the wine,
Those who go in search of [b]mixed wine.
31 Do not look on the wine when it is red,
When it sparkles in the cup,
When it swirls around smoothly;
32 At the last it bites like a serpent,
And stings like a viper.
33 Your eyes will see strange things,
And your heart will utter perverse things.
34 Yes, you will be like one who lies down in the midst of the sea,
Or like one who lies at the top of the mast, *saying:*
35 "They[a] have struck me, *but* I was not hurt;
They have beaten me, but I did not feel *it.*
When shall [b]I awake, that I may seek another *drink?*"

24

Do not be [a]envious of evil men,
Nor desire to be with them;
2 For their heart devises violence,
And their lips talk of troublemaking.

23:4 [a] [1 Tim. 6:9, 10] [b] Rom. 12:16 23:6 [a] Deut. 15:9 [1] Literally *one who has an evil eye* 23:7 [a] Prov. 12:2 23:9 [a] Matt. 7:6 23:11 [a] Prov. 22:23 23:13 [a] Prov. 13:24 23:14 [1] Or *Sheol* 23:17 [a] Ps. 37:1 [b] Prov. 28:14 23:18 [a] [Ps. 37:37] 23:20 [a] Is. 5:22 23:22 [a] Prov. 1:8 23:23 [a] [Matt. 13:44] 23:24 [a] Prov. 10:1 23:27 [a] Prov. 22:14 23:28 [a] Prov. 7:12 23:29 [a] Is. 5:11, 22 [b] Gen. 49:12 23:30 [a] [Eph. 5:18] [b] Ps. 75:8 23:35 [a] Jer. 5:3 [b] Eph. 4:19 24:1 [a] Ps. 1:1; 37:1

3 Through wisdom a house is built,
And by understanding it is established;
4 By knowledge the rooms are filled
With all precious and pleasant riches.

5 [a]A wise man *is* strong,
Yes, a man of knowledge increases
strength;
6 [a]For by wise counsel you will wage your
own war,
And in a multitude of counselors *there*
is safety.

7 [a]Wisdom *is* too lofty for a fool;
He does not open his mouth in the gate.

8 He who [a]plots to do evil
Will be called a schemer.
9 The devising of foolishness *is* sin,
And the scoffer *is* an abomination to
men.

10 *If* you [a]faint in the day of adversity,
Your strength *is* small.

11 [a]Deliver *those who* are drawn toward
death,
And hold back *those* stumbling to the
slaughter.
12 If you say, "Surely we did not know this,"
Does not [a]He who weighs the hearts
consider *it?*
He who keeps your soul, does He *not*
know *it?*
And will He *not* render to *each* man
[b]according to his deeds?

13 My son, [a]eat honey because *it is* good,
And the honeycomb *which is* sweet to
your taste;
14 [a]So *shall* the knowledge of wisdom *be* to
your soul;
If you have found *it,* there is a prospect,
And your hope will not be cut off.

15 Do not lie in wait, O wicked *man,*
against the dwelling of the
righteous;
Do not plunder his resting place;
16 [a]For a righteous *man* may fall seven times
And rise again,
[b]But the wicked shall fall by calamity.

17 [a]Do not rejoice when your enemy falls,
And do not let your heart be glad when
he stumbles;
18 Lest the LORD see *it,* and it displease
Him,
And He turn away His wrath from him.

19 [a]Do not fret because of evildoers,
Nor be envious of the wicked;
20 For there will be no prospect for the
evil *man;*
The lamp of the wicked will be
put out.

21 My son, [a]fear the LORD and the king;
Do not associate with those given to
change;
22 For their calamity will rise suddenly,
And who knows the ruin those two can
bring?

Further Sayings of the Wise

23 These *things* also *belong* to the wise:

[a]*It is* not good to show partiality in
judgment.
24 [a]He who says to the wicked, "You *are*
righteous,"
Him the people will curse;
Nations will abhor him.
25 But those who rebuke *the wicked* will
have [a]delight,
And a good blessing will come upon
them.

26 He who gives a right answer kisses the
lips.

27 [a]Prepare your outside work,
Make it fit for yourself in the field;
And afterward build your house.

28 [a]Do not be a witness against your
neighbor without cause,
For would you deceive[1] with your lips?
29 [a]Do not say, "I will do to him just as he
has done to me;
I will render to the man according to
his work."

30 I went by the field of the lazy *man,*
And by the vineyard of the man devoid
of understanding;
31 And there it was, [a]all overgrown with
thorns;
Its surface was covered with nettles;
Its stone wall was broken down.
32 When I saw *it,* I considered *it* well;
I looked on *it and* received instruction:

24:5 [a] Prov. 21:22 **24:6** [a] Luke 14:31 **24:7** [a] Ps. 10:5 **24:8** [a] Rom. 1:30 **24:10** [a] Heb. 12:3 **24:11** [a] Ps. 82:4 **24:12** [a] Prov. 21:2 [b] Ps. 62:12 **24:13** [a] Song 5:1 **24:14** [a] Ps. 19:10; 58:11 **24:16** [a] [Mic. 7:8] [b] Esth. 7:10 **24:17** [a] Obad. 12 **24:19** [a] Ps. 37:1 **24:21** [a] [1 Pet. 2:17] **24:23** [a] Lev. 19:15 **24:24** [a] Is. 5:23 **24:25** [a] Prov. 28:23 **24:27** [a] Prov. 27:23–27 **24:28** [a] Eph. 4:25 [1] Septuagint and Vulgate read *Do not deceive.* **24:29** [a] [Prov. 20:22] **24:31** [a] Gen. 3:18

33 [a]A little sleep, a little slumber,
A little folding of the hands to rest;
34 [a]So shall your poverty come *like* a prowler,
And your need like an armed man.

Further Wise Sayings of Solomon

25 These[a] also *are* proverbs of Solomon which the men of Hezekiah king of Judah copied:

2 [a]*It is* the glory of God to conceal a matter,
But the glory of kings *is* to search out a matter.

3 *As* the heavens for height and the earth for depth,
So the heart of kings *is* unsearchable.

4 [a]Take away the dross from silver,
And it will go to the silversmith *for* jewelry.
5 Take away the wicked from before the king,
And his throne will be established in [a]righteousness.

6 Do not exalt yourself in the presence of the king,
And do not stand in the place of the great;
7 [a]For *it is* better that he say to you,
"Come up here,"
Than that you should be put lower in the presence of the prince,
Whom your eyes have seen.

8 [a]Do not go hastily to court;
For what will you do in the end,
When your neighbor has put you to shame?
9 [a]Debate your case with your neighbor,
And do not disclose the secret to another;
10 Lest he who hears *it* expose your shame,
And your reputation be ruined.

11 A word fitly [a]spoken *is like* apples of gold
In settings of silver.
12 *Like* an earring of gold and an ornament of fine gold
Is a wise rebuker to an obedient ear.

13 [a]Like the cold of snow in time of harvest
Is a faithful messenger to those who send him,
For he refreshes the soul of his masters.

PEACE NOTE

If we are ill, we seek treatment. But when we have struggles in our minds, we hesitate to get help. Help is God's will for us and the path to peace.

PROVERBS 25:13

14 [a]Whoever falsely boasts of giving
Is like [b]clouds and wind without rain.

15 [a]By long forbearance a ruler is persuaded,
And a gentle tongue breaks a bone.

16 Have you found honey?
Eat only as much as you need,
Lest you be filled with it and vomit.

17 Seldom set foot in your neighbor's house,
Lest he become weary of you and hate you.

18 [a]A man who bears false witness against his neighbor
Is like a club, a sword, and a sharp arrow.
19 Confidence in an unfaithful *man* in time of trouble
Is like a bad tooth and a foot out of joint.

20 *Like* one who takes away a garment in cold weather,
And like vinegar on soda,
Is one who [a]sings songs to a heavy heart.

21 [a]If your enemy is hungry, give him bread to eat;
And if he is thirsty, give him water to drink;
22 For *so* you will heap coals of fire on his head,
[a]And the LORD will reward you.

24:33 [a] Prov. 6:9, 10 24:34 [a] Prov. 6:9–11 25:1 [a] 1 Kin. 4:32 25:2 [a] Deut. 29:29 25:4 [a] 2 Tim. 2:21 25:5 [a] Prov. 16:12; 20:8 25:7 [a] Luke 14:7–11 25:8 [a] Matt. 5:25 25:9 [a] [Matt. 18:15] 25:11 [a] Prov. 15:23 25:13 [a] Prov. 13:17 25:14 [a] Prov. 20:6 [b] Jude 12 25:15 [a] Prov. 15:1 25:18 [a] Ps. 57:4 25:20 [a] Dan. 6:18 25:21 [a] Rom. 12:20 25:22 [a] 2 Sam. 16:12

23 The north wind brings forth rain,
And [a]a backbiting tongue an angry countenance.

24 [a]*It is* better to dwell in a corner of a housetop,
Than in a house shared with a contentious woman.

25 *As* cold water to a weary soul,
So *is* [a]good news from a far country.

26 A righteous *man* who falters before the wicked
Is like a murky spring and a polluted well.

27 *It is* not good to eat much honey;
So [a]to seek one's own glory *is not* glory.

28 [a]Whoever *has* no rule over his own spirit
Is like a city broken down, without walls.

26 As snow in summer [a]and rain in harvest,
So honor is not fitting for a fool.

2 Like a flitting sparrow, like a flying swallow,
So [a]a curse without cause shall not alight.

3 [a]A whip for the horse,
A bridle for the donkey,
And a rod for the fool's back.
4 Do not answer a fool according to his folly,
Lest you also be like him.
5 [a]Answer a fool according to his folly,
Lest he be wise in his own eyes.
6 He who sends a message by the hand of a fool
Cuts off *his own* feet *and* drinks violence.
7 *Like* the legs of the lame that hang limp
Is a proverb in the mouth of fools.
8 Like one who binds a stone in a sling
Is he who gives honor to a fool.
9 *Like* a thorn *that* goes into the hand of a drunkard
Is a proverb in the mouth of fools.
10 The great *God* who formed everything
Gives the fool *his* hire and the transgressor *his* wages.[1]
11 [a]As a dog returns to his own vomit,
[b]*So* a fool repeats his folly.
12 [a]Do you see a man wise in his own eyes?
There is more hope for a fool than for him.

13 The lazy *man* says, "*There is* a lion in the road!
A fierce lion *is* in the streets!"
14 *As* a door turns on its hinges,
So *does* the lazy *man* on his bed.

25:23 [a] Ps. 101:5 25:24 [a] Prov. 19:13 25:25 [a] Prov. 15:30 25:27 [a] Prov. 27:2 25:28 [a] Prov. 16:32 26:1 [a] 1 Sam. 12:17 26:2 [a] Deut. 23:5 26:3 [a] Ps. 32:9 26:5 [a] Matt. 16:1–4 26:10 [1] The Hebrew is difficult; ancient and modern translators differ greatly. 26:11 [a] 2 Pet. 2:22 [b] Ex. 8:15 26:12 [a] [Rev. 3:17]

ADVICE FOR PEACEMAKING

For so you will heap coals of fire on his head, and the LORD will reward you.

PROVERBS 25:22

Chapter 25 provides practical advice for peacemaking: "If your enemy is hungry, give him bread to eat; and if he is thirsty, give him water to drink" (v. 21). This advice is contrary to the natural impulse to give an enemy nothing. Why should we help such a person? God's people are guided by a different set of principles. Jesus taught His followers: "I say to you who hear: Love your enemies, do good to those who hate you" (Luke 6:27). This teaching was not original; it is expressed right here in the Book of Proverbs.

The result of this unexpected kindness is described in Proverbs 25:22, a passage not always understood: "For so you will heap coals of fire on his head, and the LORD will reward you." Paul cited this passage in Romans 12:17–22. Instead of seeking revenge against our enemy, we should treat him kindly. In doing this, we "will heap coals of fire on his head," that is, cause his face to burn with shame. The point is not to embarrass our enemy but to make peace with him, as Paul explicitly stated in Romans 12:18: "As much as depends on you, live peaceably with all men."

Is there an enemy you can bless today?

15 The [a]lazy *man* buries his hand in the
bowl;[1]
It wearies him to bring it back to his
mouth.
16 The lazy *man is* wiser in his own eyes
Than seven men who can answer
sensibly.

17 He who passes by *and* meddles in a
quarrel not his own
Is like one who takes a dog by the ears.

18 Like a madman who throws firebrands,
arrows, and death,
19 *Is* the man *who* deceives his neighbor,
And says, [a]"I was only joking!"

20 Where *there is* no wood, the fire goes out;
And where *there is* no talebearer, strife
ceases.
21 [a]*As* charcoal *is* to burning coals, and
wood to fire,
So *is* a contentious man to kindle strife.
22 The words of a talebearer *are* like tasty
trifles,
And they go down into the inmost body.

23 Fervent lips with a wicked heart
Are like earthenware covered with
silver dross.

24 He who hates, disguises *it* with his lips,
And lays up deceit within himself;
25 [a]When he speaks kindly, do not believe
him,
For *there are* seven abominations in his
heart;
26 *Though his* hatred is covered by
deceit,
His wickedness will be revealed before
the assembly.

27 [a]Whoever digs a pit will fall into it,
And he who rolls a stone will have it
roll back on him.

28 A lying tongue hates *those who are*
crushed by it,
And a flattering mouth works [a]ruin.

27 Do[a] not boast about tomorrow,
For you do not know what a day may
bring forth.

2 [a]Let another man praise you, and not
your own mouth;
A stranger, and not your own lips.

3 A stone *is* heavy and sand *is* weighty,
But a fool's wrath *is* heavier than both
of them.

4 Wrath *is* cruel and anger a torrent,
But [a]who *is* able to stand before jealousy?

5 [a]Open rebuke *is* better
Than love carefully concealed.

6 Faithful *are* the wounds of a friend,
But the kisses of an enemy *are* [a]deceitful.

PEACE NOTE

Sometimes I am the one encouraging, admonishing, or challenging others. Sometimes I am the one being encouraged, admonished, or challenged. We should give *and* receive ministry.

PROVERBS 27:6

7 A satisfied soul loathes the
honeycomb,
But to a hungry soul every bitter thing
is sweet.

8 Like a bird that wanders from its nest
Is a man who wanders from his
place.

9 Ointment and perfume delight the
heart,
And the sweetness of a man's friend
gives delight by hearty counsel.

10 Do not forsake your own friend or your
father's friend,
Nor go to your brother's house in the
day of your calamity;
[a]Better *is* a neighbor nearby than a
brother far away.

11 My son, be wise, and make my heart
glad,
[a]That I may answer him who
reproaches me.

26:15 [a] Prov. 19:24 [1] Compare 19:24 **26:19** [a] Eph. 5:4 **26:21** [a] Prov. 15:18 **26:25** [a] Ps. 28:3 **26:27** [a] Ps. 7:15 **26:28** [a] Prov. 29:5 **27:1** [a] James 4:13–16 **27:2** [a] Prov. 25:27 **27:4** [a] 1 John 3:12 **27:5** [a] [Prov. 28:23] **27:6** [a] Matt. 26:49 **27:10** [a] Prov. 17:17; 18:24 **27:11** [a] Prov. 10:1; 23:15–26

PEACE NOTE

The peace of God can come through a helpful friend or mentor who shows me how to get hold of it again.

PROVERBS 27:6

12 A prudent *man* foresees evil *and* hides
himself;
The simple pass on *and* are [a]punished.

13 Take the garment of him who is surety
for a stranger,
And hold it in pledge *when* he is surety
for a seductress.

14 He who blesses his friend with a loud
voice, rising early in the morning,
It will be counted a curse to him.

15 A [a]continual dripping on a very rainy
day
And a contentious woman are alike;
16 Whoever restrains her restrains the wind,
And grasps oil with his right hand.

17 *As* iron sharpens iron,
So a man sharpens the countenance of
his friend.

18 [a]Whoever keeps the fig tree will eat its
fruit;
So he who waits on his master will be
honored.

19 As in water face *reflects* face,
So a man's heart *reveals* the man.

20 [a]Hell[1] and Destruction[2] are never full;
So [b]the eyes of man are never satisfied.

21 [a]The refining pot *is* for silver and the
furnace for gold,
And a man *is valued* by what others say
of him.

22 [a]Though you grind a fool in a mortar
with a pestle along with crushed
grain,
Yet his foolishness will not depart from
him.

23 Be diligent to know the state of your
[a]flocks,
And attend to your herds;
24 For riches *are* not forever,
Nor does a crown *endure* to all
generations.
25 [a]*When* the hay is removed, and the
tender grass shows itself,
And the herbs of the mountains are
gathered in,
26 The lambs *will provide* your
clothing,
And the goats the price of a field;
27 *You shall have* enough goats' milk for
your food,
For the food of your household,
And the nourishment of your
maidservants.

28

The [a]wicked flee when no one
pursues,
But the righteous are bold as a lion.

2 Because of the transgression of a land,
many *are* its princes;
But by a man of understanding *and*
knowledge
Right will be prolonged.

3 [a]A poor man who oppresses the poor
Is like a driving rain which leaves no
food.

4 [a]Those who forsake the law praise the
wicked,
[b]But such as keep the law contend with
them.

5 [a]Evil men do not understand justice,
But [b]those who seek the LORD
understand all.

6 Better *is* the poor who walks in his
integrity
Than one perverse *in his* ways, though
he *be* rich.

7 Whoever keeps the law *is* a discerning
son,
But a companion of gluttons shames
his father.

27:12 [a] Prov. 22:3 27:15 [a] Prov. 19:13 27:18 [a] [1 Cor. 3:8; 9:7–13] 27:20 [a] Hab. 2:5 [b] Eccl. 1:8; 4:8 [1] Or *Sheol* [2] Hebrew *Abaddon* 27:21 [a] Prov. 17:3 27:22 [a] Jer. 5:3 27:23 [a] Prov. 24:27 27:25 [a] Ps. 104:14 28:1 [a] Ps. 53:5 28:3 [a] Matt. 18:28 28:4 [a] Ps. 49:18 [b] 1 Kin. 18:18 28:5 [a] Ps. 92:6 [b] John 17:17

8 One who increases his possessions by
usury and extortion
Gathers it for him who will pity the
poor.

9 One who turns away his ear from
hearing the law,
[a]Even his prayer *is* an abomination.

10 [a]Whoever causes the upright to go
astray in an evil way,
He himself will fall into his own pit;
[b]But the blameless will inherit
good.

11 The rich man *is* wise in his own eyes,
But the poor who has understanding
searches him out.

12 When the righteous rejoice, *there is*
great [a]glory;
But when the wicked arise, men hide
themselves.

13 [a]He who covers his sins will not
prosper,
But whoever confesses and forsakes
them will have mercy.

14 Happy *is* the man who is always
reverent,
But he who hardens his heart will fall
into calamity.

15 [a]*Like* a roaring lion and a charging
bear
[b]*Is* a wicked ruler over poor people.

16 A ruler who lacks understanding *is* a
great [a]oppressor,
But he who hates covetousness will
prolong *his* days.

17 [a]A man burdened with bloodshed will
flee into a pit;
Let no one help him.

18 Whoever walks blamelessly will be
saved,
But he who is perverse *in his* ways will
suddenly fall.

19 [a]He who tills his land will have plenty of
bread,
But he who follows frivolity will have
poverty enough!

20 A faithful man will abound with
blessings,
[a]But he who hastens to be rich will not
go unpunished.

21 [a]To show partiality *is* not good,
[b]Because for a piece of bread a man will
transgress.

22 A man with an evil eye hastens after
riches,
And does not consider that [a]poverty
will come upon him.

23 [a]He who rebukes a man will find more
favor afterward
Than he who flatters with the tongue.

24 Whoever robs his father or his mother,
And says, "*It is* no transgression,"
The same [a]*is* companion to a
destroyer.

25 [a]He who is of a proud heart stirs up
strife,
[b]But he who trusts in the LORD will be
prospered.

26 He who [a]trusts in his own heart is a
fool,
But whoever walks wisely will be
delivered.

27 [a]He who gives to the poor will not lack,
But he who hides his eyes will have
many curses.

28 When the wicked arise, [a]men hide
themselves;
But when they perish, the righteous
increase.

29 He[a] who is often rebuked, *and*
hardens *his* neck,
Will suddenly be destroyed, and that
without remedy.

2 When the righteous are in authority,
the [a]people rejoice;
But when a wicked *man* rules, [b]the
people groan.

3 Whoever loves wisdom makes his
father rejoice,
But a companion of harlots wastes *his*
wealth.

28:9 [a] Prov. 15:8 **28:10** [a] Prov. 26:27 [b] [Matt. 6:33] **28:12** [a] Prov. 11:10; 29:2 **28:13** [a] Ps. 32:3–5 **28:15** [a] 1 Pet. 5:8 [b] Matt. 2:16 **28:16** [a] Eccl. 10:16 **28:17** [a] Gen. 9:6 **28:19** [a] Prov. 12:11; 20:13 **28:20** [a] 1 Tim. 6:9 **28:21** [a] Prov. 18:5 [b] Ezek. 13:19 **28:22** [a] Prov. 21:5 **28:23** [a] Prov. 27:5, 6 **28:24** [a] Prov. 18:9 **28:25** [a] Prov. 13:10 [b] 1 Tim. 6:6 **28:26** [a] Prov. 3:5 **28:27** [a] Deut. 15:7 **28:28** [a] Job 24:4 **29:1** [a] 2 Chr. 36:16 **29:2** [a] Prov. 28:12 [b] Esth. 4:3

4 The king establishes the land by justice,
But he who receives bribes overthrows it.

5 A man who [a]flatters his neighbor
Spreads a net for his feet.

6 By transgression an evil man is snared,
But the righteous sings and rejoices.

7 The righteous [a]considers the cause of the poor,
But the wicked does not understand *such* knowledge.

8 Scoffers [a]set a city aflame,
But wise *men* turn away wrath.

9 *If* a wise man contends with a foolish man,
[a]Whether *the fool* rages or laughs, *there is* no peace.

10 [a]The bloodthirsty hate the blameless,
But the upright seek his well-being.[1]

11 A fool vents all his [a]feelings,[1]
But a wise *man* holds them back.

PEACE NOTE

Feelings are not facts. Preach to your feelings the truth of God. Remind your heart and mind that God is in control so you can be at peace!

PROVERBS 29:11

12 If a ruler pays attention to lies,
All his servants *become* wicked.

13 The poor *man* and the oppressor have this in common:
[a]The LORD gives light to the eyes of both.

14 The king who judges the [a]poor with truth,
His throne will be established forever.

15 The rod and rebuke give [a]wisdom,
But a child left *to himself* brings shame to his mother.

16 When the wicked are multiplied, transgression increases;
But the righteous will see their [a]fall.

17 Correct your son, and he will give you rest;
Yes, he will give delight to your soul.

18 [a]Where *there is* no revelation,[1] the people cast off restraint;
But [b]happy *is* he who keeps the law.

19 A servant will not be corrected by mere words;
For though he understands, he will not respond.

20 Do you see a man hasty in his words?
[a]*There is* more hope for a fool than for him.

21 He who pampers his servant from childhood
Will have him as a son in the end.

22 [a]An angry man stirs up strife,
And a furious man abounds in transgression.

23 [a]A man's pride will bring him low,
But the humble in spirit will retain honor.

24 Whoever is a partner with a thief hates his own life;
[a]He swears to tell the truth,[1] but reveals nothing.

25 [a]The fear of man brings a snare,
But whoever trusts in the LORD shall be safe.

26 [a]Many seek the ruler's favor,
But justice for man *comes* from the LORD.

27 An unjust man *is* an abomination to the righteous,
And *he who is* upright in the way *is* an abomination to the wicked.

29:5 [a] Prov. 26:28 29:7 [a] Job 29:16 29:8 [a] Prov. 11:11 29:9 [a] Matt. 11:17 29:10 [a] 1 John 3:12 [1] Literally *soul*
29:11 [a] Prov. 14:33 [1] Literally *spirit* 29:13 [a] [Matt. 5:45] 29:14 [a] Is. 11:4 29:15 [a] Prov. 22:15 29:16 [a] Ps. 37:34
29:18 [a] 1 Sam. 3:1 [b] John 13:17 [1] Or *prophetic vision* 29:20 [a] Prov. 26:12 29:22 [a] Prov. 26:21 29:23 [a] Is. 66:2
29:24 [a] Lev. 5:1 [1] Literally *hears the adjuration* 29:25 [a] Gen. 12:12; 20:2 29:26 [a] Ps. 20:9

The Wisdom of Agur

30 The words of Agur the son of Jakeh,
his utterance. This man declared to
Ithiel—to Ithiel and Ucal:

2 [a]Surely I *am* more stupid than *any* man,
And do not have the understanding of a man.
3 I neither learned wisdom
Nor have [a]knowledge of the Holy One.

4 [a]Who has ascended into heaven, or descended?
[b]Who has gathered the wind in His fists?
Who has bound the waters in a garment?
Who has established all the ends of the earth?
What *is* His name, and what *is* His Son's name,
If you know?

5 [a]Every word of God *is* pure;
[b]He *is* a shield to those who put their trust in Him.
6 [a]Do not add to His words,
Lest He rebuke you, and you be found a liar.

7 Two *things* I request of You
(Deprive me not before I die):
8 Remove falsehood and lies far from me;
Give me neither poverty nor riches—
[a]Feed me with the food allotted to me;
9 [a]Lest I be full and deny *You,*
And say, "Who *is* the LORD?"
Or lest I be poor and steal,
And profane the name of my God.

10 Do not malign a servant to his master,
Lest he curse you, and you be found guilty.

11 *There is* a generation *that* curses its [a]father,
And does not bless its mother.
12 *There is* a generation [a]*that is* pure in its own eyes,
Yet is not washed from its filthiness.
13 *There is* a generation—oh, how [a]lofty *are their eyes!*
And their eyelids are lifted up.
14 [a]*There is* a generation whose teeth *are like* swords,
And whose fangs *are like* knives,
[b]To devour the poor from off the earth,
And the needy from *among* men.

15 The leech has two daughters—
Give *and* Give!

There are three *things that* are never satisfied,
Four never say, "Enough!":
16 [a]The grave,[1]
The barren womb,
The earth *that* is not satisfied with water—
And the fire never says, "Enough!"

17 [a]The eye *that* mocks *his* father,
And scorns obedience to *his* mother,
The ravens of the valley will pick it out,
And the young eagles will eat it.

18 There are three *things which* are too wonderful for me,
Yes, four *which* I do not understand:
19 The way of an eagle in the air,
The way of a serpent on a rock,
The way of a ship in the midst of the sea,
And the way of a man with a virgin.

20 This *is* the way of an adulterous woman:
She eats and wipes her mouth,
And says, "I have done no wickedness."

21 For three *things* the earth is perturbed,
Yes, for four it cannot bear up:
22 [a]For a servant when he reigns,
A fool when he is filled with food,
23 A hateful *woman* when she is married,
And a maidservant who succeeds her mistress.

24 There are four *things which* are little on the earth,
But they *are* exceedingly wise:
25 [a]The ants *are* a people not strong,
Yet they prepare their food in the summer;
26 [a]The rock badgers[1] are a feeble folk,
Yet they make their homes in the crags;
27 The locusts have no king,
Yet they all advance in ranks;
28 The spider[1] skillfully grasps with its hands,
And it is in kings' palaces.

29 There are three *things which* are majestic in pace,
Yes, four *which* are stately in walk:

30:2 [a] Ps. 73:22 30:3 [a] [Prov. 9:10] 30:4 [a] [John 3:13] [b] Job 38:4 30:5 [a] Ps. 12:6; 19:8; 119:140 [b] Ps. 18:30; 84:11; 115:9–11 30:6 [a] Deut. 4:2; 12:32 30:8 [a] Matt. 6:11 30:9 [a] Deut. 8:12–14 30:11 [a] Ex. 21:17 30:12 [a] Luke 18:11 30:13 [a] Prov. 6:17 30:14 [a] Job 29:17 [b] Amos 8:4 30:16 [a] Prov. 27:20 [1] Or *Sheol* 30:17 [a] Gen. 9:22 30:22 [a] Prov. 19:10 30:25 [a] Prov. 6:6 30:26 [a] Ps. 104:18 [1] Or *hyraxes* 30:28 [1] Or *lizard*

30 A lion, *which is* mighty among beasts
And does not turn away from any;
31 A greyhound,[1]
A male goat also,
And a king *whose* troops *are* with him.[2]

32 If you have been foolish in exalting yourself,
Or if you have devised evil, [a]*put your* hand on *your* mouth.
33 For *as* the churning of milk produces butter,
And wringing the nose produces blood,
So the forcing of wrath produces strife.

The Words of King Lemuel's Mother

31 The words of King Lemuel, the utterance which his mother taught him:

2 What, my son?
And what, son of my womb?
And what, [a]son of my vows?
3 [a]Do not give your strength to women,
Nor your ways [b]to that which destroys kings.

4 [a]*It is* not for kings, O Lemuel,
It is not for kings to drink wine,
Nor for princes intoxicating drink;
5 [a]Lest they drink and forget the law,
And pervert the justice of all the afflicted.
6 [a]Give strong drink to him who is perishing,
And wine to those who are bitter of heart.
7 Let him drink and forget his poverty,
And remember his misery no more.

8 [a]Open your mouth for the speechless,
In the cause of all *who are* appointed to die.[1]
9 Open your mouth, [a]judge righteously,
And [b]plead the cause of the poor and needy.

The Virtuous Wife

10 [a]Who[1] can find a virtuous[2] wife?
For her worth *is* far above rubies.
11 The heart of her husband safely trusts her;
So he will have no lack of gain.
12 She does him good and not evil
All the days of her life.
13 She seeks wool and flax,
And willingly works with her hands.
14 She is like the merchant ships,
She brings her food from afar.
15 [a]She also rises while it is yet night,
And [b]provides food for her household,
And a portion for her maidservants.
16 She considers a field and buys it;
From her profits she plants a vineyard.
17 She girds herself with strength,
And strengthens her arms.
18 She perceives that her merchandise *is* good,
And her lamp does not go out by night.
19 She stretches out her hands to the distaff,
And her hand holds the spindle.
20 [a]She extends her hand to the poor,
Yes, she reaches out her hands to the needy.
21 She is not afraid of snow for her household,
For all her household *is* clothed with scarlet.
22 She makes tapestry for herself;
Her clothing *is* fine linen and purple.
23 [a]Her husband is known in the gates,
When he sits among the elders of the land.
24 She makes linen garments and sells *them,*
And supplies sashes for the merchants.
25 Strength and honor *are* her clothing;
She shall rejoice in time to come.
26 She opens her mouth with wisdom,
And on her tongue *is* the law of kindness.
27 She watches over the ways of her household,
And does not eat the bread of idleness.
28 Her children rise up and call her blessed;
Her husband *also,* and he praises her:
29 "Many daughters have done well,
But you excel them all."
30 Charm *is* deceitful and beauty *is* passing,
But a woman *who* fears the LORD, she shall be praised.
31 Give her of the fruit of her hands,
And let her own works praise her in the gates.

30:31 [1] Exact identity unknown [2] A Jewish tradition reads *a king against whom there is no uprising.* **30:32** [a] Mic. 7:16
31:2 [a] Is. 49:15 **31:3** [a] Prov. 5:9 [b] Deut. 17:17 **31:4** [a] Eccl. 10:17 **31:5** [a] Hos. 4:11 **31:6** [a] Ps. 104:15 **31:8** [a] Job 29:15, 16 [1] Literally *sons of passing away* **31:9** [a] Lev. 19:15 [b] Jer. 22:16 **31:10** [a] Prov. 12:4; 19:14 [1] Verses 10 through 31 are an alphabetic acrostic in Hebrew (compare Psalm 119). [2] Literally *a wife of valor,* in the sense of all forms of excellence
31:15 [a] Rom. 12:11 [b] Luke 12:42 **31:20** [a] Eph. 4:28 **31:23** [a] Prov. 12:4

THE BOOK OF

ECCLESIASTES

AUTHOR

The author calls himself "the Preacher, the son of David, king in Jerusalem" in Ecclesiastes 1:1. Solomonic authorship is the standard Christian position, although some scholars, along with the Talmud, believe the work was later edited during the time of Hezekiah or possibly Ezra. The proverbs in this book are similar to those in the Book of Proverbs (chs. 7; 10). According to 12:9, the Preacher collected and arranged ("set in order") many proverbs, perhaps including the two Solomonic collections in Proverbs.

TIME

c. 935 BC

KEY VERSE

Ecclesiastes 2:24

THEME

Ecclesiastes is a Greek word that is usually translated "the preacher" or "the teacher." The Book of Ecclesiastes was likely written late in Solomon's life when he could see that the glorious era of his kingdom was beginning to decline. He had it all—power, prestige, pleasure—but none of those provide ultimate satisfaction. That fulfillment comes only through a relationship with God and obedience to His Word. It is important to note that the arguments of the book are more thematic than linear. The same topics are addressed in different ways at different points within the work.

"All is vanity" without the peace of God (3:19). Solomon had everything life could offer, but he turned from God and lost the experiential peace of God. In Ecclesiastes we see the ultimate futility of attempting to fill the God-shaped void in our hearts with anything outside of a relationship with God through Jesus Christ. You can have everything and nothing if you do not experience God's peace—this is the lesson of Solomon's life. Nevertheless, life is to be enjoyed to its fullest in the peace of God (3:12–13; 3:22; 5:18–19; 8:15; 9:7–9), so walk with the Lord and find true fulfillment.

The Vanity of Life

1 The words of the Preacher, the son of David, [a]king in Jerusalem.

2 "Vanity[a1] of vanities," says the Preacher;
"Vanity of vanities, [b]all *is* vanity."

3 [a]What profit has a man from all his
labor
In which he toils under the sun?
4 *One* generation passes away, and
another generation comes;
[a]But the earth abides forever.
5 [a]The sun also rises, and the sun goes
down,
And hastens to the place where it
arose.
6 [a]The wind goes toward the south,
And turns around to the north;
The wind whirls about continually,
And comes again on its circuit.
7 [a]All the rivers run into the sea,
Yet the sea *is* not full;
To the place from which the rivers
come,
There they return again.
8 All things *are* full of labor;
Man cannot express *it.*
[a]The eye is not satisfied with seeing,
Nor the ear filled with hearing.

9 [a]That which has been *is* what will be,
That which *is* done is what will be done,
And *there is* nothing new under the sun.
10 Is there anything of which it may be
said,
"See, this *is* new"?
It has already been in ancient times
before us.
11 *There is* [a]no remembrance of former
things,
Nor will there be any remembrance of
things that are to come
By *those* who will come after.

The Grief of Wisdom

12 I, the Preacher, was king over Israel in
Jerusalem. 13 And I set my heart to seek and
[a]search out by wisdom concerning all that is
done under heaven; [b]this burdensome task
God has given to the sons of man, by which
they may be exercised. 14 I have seen all the
works that are done under the sun; and indeed, all *is* vanity and grasping for the wind.

15 [a]*What is* crooked cannot be made
straight,
And what is lacking cannot be
numbered.

16 I communed with my heart, saying,
"Look, I have attained greatness, and have
gained [a]more wisdom than all who were
before me in Jerusalem. My heart has understood great wisdom and knowledge." 17 [a]And
I set my heart to know wisdom and to know
madness and folly. I perceived that this also
is grasping for the wind.

18 For [a]in much wisdom *is* much grief,
And he who increases knowledge
increases sorrow.

The Vanity of Pleasure

2 I said [a]in my heart, "Come now, I will test
you with [b]mirth; therefore enjoy pleasure"; but surely, [c]this also *was* vanity. 2 I
said of laughter—"Madness!"; and of mirth,
"What does it accomplish?" 3 [a]I searched in
my heart *how* to gratify my flesh with wine,
while guiding my heart with wisdom, and
how to lay hold on folly, till I might see what
was [b]good for the sons of men to do under
heaven all the days of their lives.
4 I made my works great, I built myself
[a]houses, and planted myself vineyards. 5 I
made myself gardens and orchards, and I
planted all *kinds* of fruit trees in them. 6 I made
myself water pools from which to water the
growing trees of the grove. 7 I acquired male
and female servants, and had servants born
in my house. Yes, I had greater possessions
of herds and flocks than all who were in Jerusalem before me. 8 [a]I also gathered for myself
silver and gold and the special treasures of
kings and of the provinces. I acquired male
and female singers, the delights of the sons
of men, *and* musical instruments[1] of all kinds.
9 [a]So I became great and excelled [b]more
than all who were before me in Jerusalem.
Also my wisdom remained with me.

10 Whatever my eyes desired I did not
keep from them.
I did not withhold my heart from any
pleasure,
For my heart rejoiced in all my labor;
And [a]this was my reward from all my
labor.

1:1 [a] Prov. 1:1 1:2 [a] Ps. 39:5, 6; 62:9; 144:4 [b] [Rom. 8:20, 21] [1] Or *Absurdity, Frustration, Futility, Nonsense;* and so throughout this book 1:3 [a] Eccl. 2:22; 3:9 1:4 [a] Ps. 104:5; 119:90 1:5 [a] Ps. 19:4–6 1:6 [a] John 3:8 1:7 [a] [Jer. 5:22] 1:8 [a] Prov. 27:20 1:9 [a] Eccl. 3:15 1:11 [a] Eccl. 2:16 1:13 [a] [Eccl. 7:25; 8:16, 17] [b] Eccl. 3:10 1:15 [a] Eccl. 7:13 1:16 [a] 1 Kin. 3:12, 13 1:17 [a] Eccl. 2:3, 12; 7:23, 25 1:18 [a] Eccl. 12:12 2:1 [a] Luke 12:19 [b] [Eccl. 7:4; 8:15] [c] Eccl. 1:2 2:3 [a] Eccl. 1:17 [b] [Eccl. 3:12, 13; 5:18; 6:12] 2:4 [a] 1 Kin. 7:1–12 2:8 [a] 1 Kin. 9:28; 10:10, 14, 21 [1] Exact meaning unknown 2:9 [a] Eccl. 1:16 [b] 2 Chr. 9:22 2:10 [a] Eccl. 3:22; 5:18; 9:9

11 Then I looked on all the works that my
hands had done
And on the labor in which I had toiled;
And indeed all *was* [a]vanity and
grasping for the wind.
There was no profit under the sun.

The End of the Wise and the Fool

12 Then I turned myself to consider
wisdom [a]and madness and folly;
For what *can* the man *do* who succeeds
the king?—
Only what he has already [b]done.
13 Then I saw that wisdom [a]excels folly
As light excels darkness.
14 [a]The wise man's eyes *are* in his head,
But the fool walks in darkness.
Yet I myself perceived
That [b]the same event happens to them
all.

15 So I said in my heart,
"As it happens to the fool,
It also happens to me,
And why was I then more wise?"
Then I said in my heart,
"This also *is* vanity."
16 For *there is* [a]no more remembrance of
the wise than of the fool forever,
Since all that now *is* will be forgotten in
the days to come.
And how does a wise *man* die?
As the fool!

17 Therefore I hated life because the work that
was done under the sun *was* distressing to
me, for all *is* vanity and grasping for the wind.
18 Then I hated all my labor in which I had
toiled under the sun, because [a]I must leave
it to the man who will come after me. 19 And
who knows whether he will be wise or a fool?
Yet he will rule over all my labor in which I
toiled and in which I have shown myself wise
under the sun. This also *is* vanity. 20 Therefore
I turned my heart and despaired of all the labor in which I had toiled under the sun. 21 For
there is a man whose labor *is* with wisdom,
knowledge, and skill; yet he must leave his
heritage to a man who has not labored for it.
This also *is* vanity and a great evil. 22 [a]For what
has man for all his labor, and for the striving
of his heart with which he has toiled under
the sun? 23 For all his days *are* [a]sorrowful, and
his work burdensome; even in the night his
heart takes no rest. This also is vanity.

24 [a]Nothing *is* better for a man *than* that
he should eat and drink, and *that* his soul
should enjoy good in his labor. This also, I
saw, was from the hand of God. 25 For who can
eat, or who can have enjoyment, more than
I?[1] 26 For *God* gives [a]wisdom and knowledge
and joy to a man who *is* good in His sight; but
to the sinner He gives the work of gathering
and collecting, that [b]he may give to *him who*
is good before God. This also *is* vanity and
grasping for the wind.

Everything Has Its Time

3 To everything *there is* a season,
A [a]time for every purpose under
heaven:

2 A time to be born,
And [a]a time to die;
A time to plant,
And a time to pluck *what is* planted;
3 A time to kill,
And a time to heal;
A time to break down,
And a time to build up;
4 A time to [a]weep,
And a time to laugh;
A time to mourn,
And a time to dance;
5 A time to cast away stones,
And a time to gather stones;
[a]A time to embrace,
And a time to refrain from
embracing;
6 A time to gain,
And a time to lose;
A time to keep,
And a time to throw away;
7 A time to tear,
And a time to sew;
[a]A time to keep silence,
And a time to [b]speak;
8 A time to love,
And a time to [a]hate;
A time of war,
And a time of peace.

The God-Given Task

9 [a]What profit has the worker from that in
which he labors? 10 [a]I have seen the God-given
task with which the sons of men are to be
occupied. 11 He has made everything beautiful
in its time. Also He has put eternity in their
hearts, except that [a]no one can find out the
work that God does from beginning to end.

2:11 [a] Eccl. 1:3, 14 **2:12** [a] Eccl. 1:17; 7:25 [b] Eccl. 1:9 **2:13** [a] Eccl. 7:11, 14, 19; 9:18; 10:10 **2:14** [a] Prov. 17:24 [b] Ps. 49:10 **2:16** [a] Eccl. 1:11; 4:16 **2:18** [a] Ps. 49:10 **2:22** [a] Eccl. 1:3; 3:9 **2:23** [a] Job 5:7; 14:1 **2:24** [a] Eccl. 3:12, 13, 22 **2:25** [1] Following Masoretic Text, Targum, and Vulgate; some Hebrew manuscripts, Septuagint, and Syriac read *without Him.* **2:26** [a] Prov. 2:6 [b] Prov. 28:8 **3:1** [a] Eccl. 3:17; 8:6 **3:2** [a] Heb. 9:27 **3:4** [a] Rom. 12:15 **3:5** [a] Joel 2:16 **3:7** [a] Amos 5:13 [b] Prov. 25:11 **3:8** [a] Luke 14:26 **3:9** [a] Eccl. 1:3 **3:10** [a] Eccl. 1:13 **3:11** [a] Rom. 11:33

12 I know that nothing *is* [a]better for them
than to rejoice, and to do good in their lives,
13 and also that [a]every man should eat and
drink and enjoy the good of all his labor—it
is the gift of God.

14 I know that whatever God does,
It shall be forever.
[a]Nothing can be added to it,
And nothing taken from it.
God does *it*, that men should fear
before Him.
15 [a]That which is has already been,
And what is to be has already been;
And God requires an account of what is
past.

Injustice Seems to Prevail

16 Moreover [a]I saw under the sun:

In the place of judgment,
Wickedness *was* there;
And *in* the place of righteousness,
Iniquity *was* there.

17 I said in my heart,

[a]"God shall judge the righteous and the
wicked,
For *there is* a time there for every
purpose and for every work."

18 I said in my heart, "Concerning the condition of the sons of men, God tests them, that
they may see that they themselves are *like*
animals." 19 [a]For what happens to the sons
of men also happens to animals; one thing
befalls them: as one dies, so dies the other.
Surely, they all have one breath; man has no
advantage over animals, for all *is* vanity. 20 All
go to one place: [a]all are from the dust, and
all return to dust. 21 [a]Who knows the spirit of
the sons of men, which goes upward, and the
spirit of the animal, which goes down to the
earth?[1] 22 [a]So I perceived that nothing *is* better
than that a man should rejoice in his own
works, for [b]that *is* his heritage. [c]For who can
bring him to see what will happen after him?

4 Then I returned and considered all the
[a]oppression that is done under the sun:

And look! The tears of the oppressed,
But they have no comforter—
On the side of their oppressors *there is*
power,
But they have no comforter.
2 [a]Therefore I praised the dead who were
already dead,
More than the living who are still alive.
3 [a]Yet, better than both *is he* who has
never existed,
Who has not seen the evil work that is
done under the sun.

The Vanity of Selfish Toil

4 Again, I saw that for all toil and every
skillful work a man is envied by his neighbor.
This also *is* vanity and grasping for the wind.

5 [a]The fool folds his hands
And consumes his own flesh.
6 [a]Better a handful *with* quietness
Than both hands full, *together with* toil
and grasping for the wind.

7 Then I returned, and I saw vanity under
the sun:

8 There is one alone, without
companion:
He has neither son nor brother.
Yet *there is* no end to all his labors,
Nor is his [a]eye satisfied with riches.
But [b]*he never asks,*
"For whom do I toil and deprive myself
of [c]good?"
This also *is* vanity and a grave
misfortune.

The Value of a Friend

9 Two *are* better than one,
Because they have a good reward for
their labor.
10 For if they fall, one will lift up his
companion.
But woe to him *who is* alone when he
falls,
For *he has* no one to help him up.
11 Again, if two lie down together, they
will keep warm;
But how can one be warm *alone?*
12 Though one may be overpowered by
another, two can withstand him.
And a threefold cord is not quickly
broken.

Popularity Passes Away

13 Better a poor and wise youth
Than an old and foolish king who will
be admonished no more.

3:12 [a] Eccl. 2:3, 24 3:13 [a] Eccl. 2:24 3:14 [a] James 1:17 3:15 [a] Eccl. 1:9 3:16 [a] Eccl. 5:8 3:17 [a] [Rom. 2:6–10] 3:19 [a] [Eccl. 2:16] 3:20 [a] Gen. 3:19 3:21 [a] Eccl. 12:7 [1] Septuagint, Syriac, Targum, and Vulgate read *Who knows whether the spirit . . . goes upward, and whether . . . goes downward to the earth?* 3:22 [a] Eccl. 2:24; 5:18 [b] Eccl. 2:10 [c] Eccl. 6:12; 8:7 4:1 [a] Eccl. 3:16; 5:8 4:2 [a] Job 3:17, 18 4:3 [a] Job 3:11–22 4:5 [a] Prov. 6:10; 24:33 4:6 [a] Prov. 15:16, 17; 16:8 4:8 [a] [1 John 2:16] [b] Ps. 39:6 [c] Eccl. 2:18–21

PEACE NOTE

Isolation is the enemy of God's peace. I have to consistently choose to fellowship with the people of God so I can experience His peace in community.

ECCLESIASTES 4:12

14 For he comes out of prison to be king,
Although he was born poor in his
kingdom.
15 I saw all the living who walk under the
sun;
They were with the second youth who
stands in his place.
16 *There was* no end of all the people over
whom he was made king;
Yet those who come afterward will not
rejoice in him.
Surely this also *is* vanity and grasping
for the wind.

Fear God, Keep Your Vows

5 Walk [a]prudently when you go to the house
of God; and draw near to hear rather [b]than
to give the sacrifice of fools, for they do not
know that they do evil.

2 Do not be [a]rash with your mouth,
And let not your heart utter anything
hastily before God.
For God *is* in heaven, and you on earth;
Therefore let your words [b]be few.
3 For a dream comes through much
activity,
And [a]a fool's voice *is known* by *his*
many words.

4 [a]When you make a vow to God, do not
delay to [b]pay it;
For *He has* no pleasure in fools.
Pay what you have vowed—
5 [a]Better not to vow than to vow and not pay.

6 Do not let your [a]mouth cause your flesh to
sin, [b]nor say before the messenger *of God* that
it *was* an error. Why should God be angry at
your excuse[1] and destroy the work of your
hands? 7 For in the multitude of dreams and
many words *there is* also vanity. But [a]fear God.

The Vanity of Gain and Honor

8 If you [a]see the oppression of the poor, and
the violent perversion of justice and righteousness in a province, do not marvel at the
matter; for [b]high official watches over high
official, and higher officials are over them.
9 Moreover the profit of the land is for all;
even the king is served from the field.

10 He who loves silver will not be satisfied
with silver;
Nor he who loves abundance, with
increase.
This also *is* vanity.

11 When goods increase,
They increase who eat them;
So what profit have the owners
Except to see *them* with their eyes?
12 The sleep of a laboring man *is* sweet,
Whether he eats little or much;
But the abundance of the rich will not
permit him to sleep.

13 [a]There is a severe evil *which* I have seen
under the sun:
Riches kept for their owner to his hurt.
14 But those riches perish through
misfortune;
When he begets a son, *there is* nothing
in his hand.
15 [a]As he came from his mother's womb,
naked shall he return,
To go as he came;
And he shall take nothing from his
labor
Which he may carry away in his hand.

16 And this also *is* a severe evil—
Just exactly as he came, so shall he go.
And [a]what profit has he [b]who has
labored for the wind?
17 All his days [a]he also eats in darkness,
And *he has* much sorrow and sickness
and anger.

18 Here is what I have seen: [a]*It is* good and
fitting *for one* to eat and drink, and to enjoy
the good of all his labor in which he toils
under the sun all the days of his life which
God gives him; [b]for it *is* his heritage. 19 As for

5:1 [a] Ex. 3:5 [b] [1 Sam. 15:22] 5:2 [a] Prov. 20:25 [b] Matt. 6:7 5:3 [a] Prov. 10:19 5:4 [a] Num. 30:2 [b] Ps. 66:13, 14
5:5 [a] Acts 5:4 5:6 [a] Prov. 6:2 [b] 1 Cor. 11:10 [1] Literally *voice* 5:7 [a] [Eccl. 12:13] 5:8 [a] Eccl. 3:16 [b] [Ps. 12:5; 58:11; 82:1]
5:13 [a] Eccl. 6:1, 2 5:15 [a] 1 Tim. 6:7 5:16 [a] Eccl. 1:3 [b] Prov. 11:29 5:17 [a] Ps. 127:2 5:18 [a] [1 Tim. 6:17] [b] Eccl. 2:10; 3:22

> **PEACE NOTE**
>
> Christians experience deep loss, pain, and heartache. But the happiness, hope, and peace that the Bible promises go deeper than just emotions.

[a]every man to whom God has given riches
and wealth, and given him power to eat of
it, to receive his heritage and rejoice in his
labor—this *is* the [b]gift of God. 20 For he will not
dwell unduly on the days of his life, because
God keeps *him* busy with the joy of his heart.

6 There[a] is an evil which I have seen under
the sun, and it *is* common among men: 2 A
man to whom God has given riches and wealth
and honor, [a]so that he lacks nothing for himself
of all he desires; [b]yet God does not give him
power to eat of it, but a foreigner consumes it.
This *is* vanity, and it *is* an evil affliction.

3 If a man begets a hundred *children* and
lives many years, so that the days of his
years are many, but his soul is not satisfied
with goodness, or [a]indeed he has no burial,
I say *that* [b]a stillborn child *is* better than
he— 4 for it comes in vanity and departs
in darkness, and its name is covered with
darkness. 5 Though it has not seen the sun
or known *anything,* this has more rest than
that man, 6 even if he lives a thousand years
twice—but has not seen goodness. Do not
all go to one [a]place?

7 [a]All the labor of man *is* for his mouth,
And yet the soul is not satisfied.
8 For what more has the wise *man* than
the fool?
What does the poor man have,
Who knows *how* to walk before the
living?
9 Better *is* the [a]sight of the eyes than the
wandering of desire.
This also *is* vanity and grasping for the
wind.

10 Whatever one is, he has been named
[a]already,
For it is known that he *is* man;
[b]And he cannot contend with Him who
is mightier than he.
11 Since there are many things that
increase vanity,
How *is* man the better?

12 For who knows what *is* good for man
in life, all the days of his vain life which he
passes like [a]a shadow? [b]Who can tell a man
what will happen after him under the sun?

The Value of Practical Wisdom

7 A [a]good name *is* better than precious
ointment,
And the day of death than the day of
one's [b]birth;
2 Better to go to the house of
mourning
Than to go to the house of feasting,
For that *is* the end of all men;
And the living will take *it* to [a]heart.
3 Sorrow *is* better than laughter,
[a]For by a sad countenance the heart is
made better.
4 The heart of the wise *is* in the house of
mourning,
But the heart of fools *is* in the house of
mirth.

5 [a]*It is* better to hear the rebuke of the
wise
Than for a man to hear the song of
fools.
6 [a]For like the crackling of thorns under a
pot,
So *is* the laughter of the fool.
This also is vanity.
7 Surely oppression destroys a wise
man's reason,
[a]And a bribe debases the heart.

8 The end of a thing *is* better than its
beginning;
[a]The patient in spirit *is* better than the
proud in spirit.
9 [a]Do not hasten in your spirit to be
angry,
For anger rests in the bosom of fools.
10 Do not say,
"Why were the former days better than
these?"
For you do not inquire wisely
concerning this.

5:19 [a] [Eccl. 6:2] [b] Eccl. 2:24; 3:13 6:1 [a] Eccl. 5:13 6:2 [a] Job 21:10 [b] Luke 12:20 6:3 [a] Is. 14:19, 20 [b] Job 3:16 6:6 [a] Eccl. 2:14, 15 6:7 [a] Prov. 16:26 6:9 [a] Eccl. 11:9 6:10 [a] Eccl. 1:9; 3:15 [b] Job 9:32 6:12 [a] James 4:14 [b] Eccl. 3:22 7:1 [a] Prov. 22:1 [b] Eccl. 4:2 7:2 [a] [Ps. 90:12] 7:3 [a] [2 Cor. 7:10] 7:5 [a] Ps. 141:5 7:6 [a] Eccl. 2:2 7:7 [a] Ex. 23:8 7:8 [a] Prov. 14:29 7:9 [a] James 1:19

11 Wisdom *is* good with an inheritance,
And profitable [a]to those who see the sun.
12 For wisdom *is* a [a]defense *as* money *is* a defense,
But the excellence of knowledge *is that* wisdom gives [b]life to those who have it.

13 Consider the work of God;
For [a]who can make straight what He has made crooked?
14 [a]In the day of prosperity be joyful,
But in the day of adversity consider:
Surely God has appointed the one as well as the other,
So that man can find out nothing *that will come* after him.

15 I have seen everything in my days of vanity:

[a]There is a just *man* who perishes in his righteousness,
And there is a wicked *man* who prolongs *life* in his wickedness.

16 [a]Do not be overly righteous,
[b]Nor be overly wise:
Why should you destroy yourself?
17 Do not be overly wicked,
Nor be foolish:
[a]Why should you die before your time?
18 *It is* good that you grasp this,
And also not remove your hand from the other;
For he who [a]fears God will escape them all.

19 [a]Wisdom strengthens the wise
More than ten rulers of the city.

20 [a]For *there is* not a just man on earth who does good
And does not sin.

21 Also do not take to heart everything people say,
Lest you hear your servant cursing you.
22 For many times, also, your own heart has known
That even you have cursed others.

23 All this I have proved by wisdom.
[a]I said, "I will be wise";
But it *was* far from me.
24 [a]As for that which is far off and [b]exceedingly deep,
Who can find it out?
25 [a]I applied my heart to know,
To search and seek out wisdom and the reason *of things,*
To know the wickedness of folly,
Even of foolishness *and* madness.
26 [a]And I find more bitter than death
The woman whose heart *is* snares and nets,
Whose hands *are* fetters.
He who pleases God shall escape from her,
But the sinner shall be trapped by her.

27 "Here is what I have found," says [a]the Preacher,
"*Adding* one thing to the other to find out the reason,
28 Which my soul still seeks but I cannot find:
[a]One man among a thousand I have found,
But a woman among all these I have not found.
29 Truly, this only I have found:
[a]That God made man upright,
But [b]they have sought out many schemes."

8 Who *is* like a wise *man?*
And who knows the interpretation of a thing?
[a]A man's wisdom makes his face shine,
And [b]the sternness of his face is changed.

Obey Authorities for God's Sake

2 I *say,* "Keep the king's commandment
[a]for the sake of your oath to God. 3 [a]Do not
be hasty to go from his presence. Do not
take your stand for an evil thing, for he does
whatever pleases him."

4 Where the word of a king *is, there is* power;
And [a]who may say to him, "What are you doing?"
5 He who keeps his command will experience nothing harmful;
And a wise man's heart discerns both time and judgment,
6 Because [a]for every matter there is a time and judgment,
Though the misery of man increases greatly.

7:11 [a] Eccl. 11:7 **7:12** [a] Eccl. 9:18 [b] Prov. 3:18 **7:13** [a] Job 12:14 **7:14** [a] Deut. 28:47 **7:15** [a] Eccl. 8:12–14 **7:16** [a] Prov. 25:16 [b] Rom. 12:3 **7:17** [a] Job 15:32 **7:18** [a] Eccl. 3:14; 5:7; 8:12, 13 **7:19** [a] Prov. 21:22 **7:20** [a] 1 John 1:8 **7:23** [a] Rom. 1:22 **7:24** [a] 1 Tim. 6:16 [b] Rom. 11:33 **7:25** [a] Eccl. 1:17 **7:26** [a] Prov. 5:3, 4 **7:27** [a] Eccl. 1:1, 2 **7:28** [a] Job 33:23 **7:29** [a] Gen. 1:27 [b] Gen. 3:6, 7 **8:1** [a] Acts 6:15 [b] Deut. 28:50 **8:2** [a] 1 Chr. 29:24 **8:3** [a] Eccl. 10:4 **8:4** [a] Job 34:18 **8:6** [a] Eccl. 3:1, 17

7 [a]For he does not know what will
happen;
So who can tell him when it will occur?
8 [a]No one has power over the spirit to
retain the spirit,
And no one has power in the day of
death.
There is [b]no release from that war,
And wickedness will not deliver those
who are given to it.

9 All this I have seen, and applied my heart
to every work that is done under the sun:
There is a time in which one man rules over
another to his own hurt.

Death Comes to All

10 Then I saw the wicked buried, who had
come and gone from the place of holiness,
and they were [a]forgotten[1] in the city where
they had so done. This also *is* vanity. 11 [a]Be-
cause the sentence against an evil work is
not executed speedily, therefore the heart
of the sons of men is fully set in them to do
evil. 12 [a]Though a sinner does evil a hundred
times, and his *days* are prolonged, yet I surely
know that [b]it will be well with those who fear
God, who fear before Him. 13 But it will not
be well with the wicked; nor will he prolong
his days, *which are* as a shadow, because he
does not fear before God.
14 There is a vanity which occurs on earth,
that there are just *men* to whom it [a]happens
according to the work of the wicked; again,
there are wicked *men* to whom it happens
according to the work of the [b]righteous. I
said that this also *is* vanity.
15 [a]So I commended enjoyment, because a
man has nothing better under the sun than to
eat, drink, and be merry; for this will remain
with him in his labor *all* the days of his life
which God gives him under the sun.
16 When I applied my heart to know wisdom
and to see the business that is done on earth,
even though one sees no sleep day or night,
17 then I saw all the work of God, that [a]a man
cannot find out the work that is done under
the sun. For though a man labors to discover
it, yet he will not find *it;* moreover, though
a wise *man* attempts to know *it,* he will not
be able to find *it.*

9 For I considered all this in my heart, so
that I could declare it all: [a]that the righteous and the wise and their works *are* in
the hand of God. People know neither love
nor hatred *by* anything *they see* before them.
2 [a]All things *come* alike to all:

One event *happens* to the righteous
and the wicked;
To the good,[1] the clean, and the unclean;
To him who sacrifices and him who
does not sacrifice.
As is the good, so *is* the sinner;
He who takes an oath as *he* who fears
an oath.

3 This *is* an evil in all that is done under the
sun: that one thing *happens* to all. Truly the
hearts of the sons of men are full of evil;
madness *is* in their hearts while they live, and
after that *they go* to the dead. 4 But for him
who is joined to all the living there is hope,
for a living dog is better than a dead lion.

5 For the living know that they will die;
But [a]the dead know nothing,
And they have no more reward,
For [b]the memory of them is forgotten.
6 Also their love, their hatred, and their
envy have now perished;
Nevermore will they have a share
In anything done under the sun.

7 Go, [a]eat your bread with joy,
And drink your wine with a merry heart;
For God has already accepted your works.
8 Let your garments always be white,
And let your head lack no oil.

9 Live joyfully with the wife whom you
love all the days of your vain life which He
has given you under the sun, all your days of
vanity; [a]for that *is* your portion in life, and in
the labor which you perform under the sun.
10 [a]Whatever your hand finds to do, do
it with your [b]might; for *there is* no work or
device or knowledge or wisdom in the grave
where you are going.
11 I returned [a]and saw under the sun that—

The race *is* not to the swift,
Nor the battle to the strong,
Nor bread to the wise,
Nor riches to men of understanding,
Nor favor to men of skill;
But time and [b]chance happen to them all.
12 For [a]man also does not know his time:
Like fish taken in a cruel net,
Like birds caught in a snare,

8:7 [a] Eccl. 6:12 8:8 [a] Ps. 49:6, 7 [b] Deut. 20:5–8 8:10 [a] Eccl. 2:16; 9:5 [1] Some Hebrew manuscripts, Septuagint, and Vulgate read *praised.* 8:11 [a] Is. 26:10 8:12 [a] Is. 65:20 [b] [Is. 3:10] 8:14 [a] Ps. 73:14 [b] Eccl. 2:14; 7:15; 9:1–3 8:15 [a] Eccl. 2:24 8:17 [a] Rom. 11:33 9:1 [a] Eccl. 8:14 9:2 [a] Mal. 3:15 [1] Septuagint, Syriac, and Vulgate read *good and bad.* 9:5 [a] Is. 63:16 [b] Is. 26:14 9:7 [a] Eccl. 8:15 9:9 [a] Eccl. 2:10 9:10 [a] [Col. 3:17] [b] Rom. 12:11 9:11 [a] Amos 2:14, 15 [b] 1 Sam. 6:9 9:12 [a] Eccl. 8:7

So the sons of men *are* [b]snared in an evil time,
When it falls suddenly upon them.

Wisdom Superior to Folly

13 This wisdom I have also seen under the
sun, and it *seemed* great to me: 14 [a]*There was* a
little city with few men in it; and a great king
came against it, besieged it, and built great
snares[1] around it. 15 Now there was found in
it a poor wise man, and he by his wisdom
delivered the city. Yet no one remembered
that same poor man.
16 Then I said:

"Wisdom *is* better than [a]strength.
Nevertheless [b]the poor man's wisdom *is* despised,
And his words are not heard.
17 Words of the wise, *spoken* quietly, *should be* heard
Rather than the shout of a ruler of fools.
18 Wisdom *is* better than weapons of war;
But [a]one sinner destroys much good."

10

Dead flies putrefy[1] the perfumer's ointment,
And cause it to give off a foul odor;
So does a little folly to one respected for wisdom *and* honor.
2 A wise man's heart *is* at his right hand,
But a fool's heart at his left.
3 Even when a fool walks along the way,
He lacks wisdom,
[a]And he shows everyone *that* he *is* a fool.
4 If the spirit of the ruler rises against you,
[a]Do not leave your post;
For [b]conciliation pacifies great offenses.

5 There is an evil I have seen under the sun,
As an error proceeding from the ruler:
6 [a]Folly is set in great dignity,
While the rich sit in a lowly place.
7 I have seen servants [a]on horses,
While princes walk on the ground like servants.

8 [a]He who digs a pit will fall into it,
And whoever breaks through a wall will be bitten by a serpent.
9 He who quarries stones may be hurt by them,
And he who splits wood may be endangered by it.

> PEACE NOTE
>
> God's perpetual grace never runs dry. It stands as a mighty rushing river, able to move us through any problem. This grace leads us to His perfect peace.

10 If the ax is dull,
And one does not sharpen the edge,
Then he must use more strength;
But wisdom brings success.

11 A serpent may bite [a]when *it is* not charmed;
The babbler is no different.
12 [a]The words of a wise man's mouth *are* gracious,
But [b]the lips of a fool shall swallow him up;
13 The words of his mouth begin with foolishness,
And the end of his talk *is* raving madness.
14 [a]A fool also multiplies words.
No man knows what is to be;
Who can tell him [b]what will be after him?
15 The labor of fools wearies them,
For they do not even know how to go to the city!

16 [a]Woe to you, O land, when your king *is* a child,
And your princes feast in the morning!
17 Blessed *are* you, O land, when your king *is* the son of nobles,
And your [a]princes feast at the proper time—
For strength and not for drunkenness!
18 Because of laziness the building decays,
And [a]through idleness of hands the house leaks.
19 A feast is made for laughter,
And [a]wine makes merry;
But money answers everything.

9:12 [b] Prov. 29:6 **9:14** [a] 2 Sam. 20:16–22 [1] Septuagint, Syriac, and Vulgate read *bulwarks.* **9:16** [a] Eccl. 7:12, 19 [b] Mark 6:2, 3 **9:18** [a] Josh. 7:1–26 **10:1** [1] Targum and Vulgate omit *putrefy.* **10:3** [a] Prov. 13:16; 18:2 **10:4** [a] Eccl. 8:3 [b] 1 Sam. 25:24–33 **10:6** [a] Esth. 3:1 **10:7** [a] Prov. 19:10; 30:22 **10:8** [a] Prov. 26:27 **10:11** [a] Jer. 8:17 **10:12** [a] Prov. 10:32 [b] Prov. 10:14 **10:14** [a] [Prov. 15:2] [b] Eccl. 3:22; 8:7 **10:16** [a] Is. 3:4, 5; 5:11 **10:17** [a] Prov. 31:4 **10:18** [a] Prov. 24:30–34 **10:19** [a] Ps. 104:15

20 [a]Do not curse the king, even in your thought;
Do not curse the rich, even in your bedroom;
For a bird of the air may carry your voice,
And a bird in flight may tell the matter.

The Value of Diligence

11 Cast your bread [a]upon the waters,
[b]For you will find it after many days.
2 [a]Give a serving [b]to seven, and also to eight,
[c]For you do not know what evil will be on the earth.

3 If the clouds are full of rain,
They empty *themselves* upon the earth;
And if a tree falls to the south or the north,
In the place where the tree falls, there it shall lie.
4 He who observes the wind will not sow,
And he who regards the clouds will not reap.

5 As [a]you do not know what *is* the way of the wind,[1]
[b]*Or* how the bones *grow* in the womb of her who is with child,
So you do not know the works of God who makes everything.
6 In the morning sow your seed,
And in the evening do not withhold your hand;
For you do not know which will prosper,
Either this or that,
Or whether both alike *will be* good.

7 Truly the light is sweet,
And *it is* pleasant for the eyes [a]to behold the sun;
8 But if a man lives many years
And [a]rejoices in them all,
Yet let him [b]remember the days of darkness,
For they will be many.
All that is coming *is* vanity.

Seek God in Early Life

9 Rejoice, O young man, in your youth,
And let your heart cheer you in the days of your youth;
[a]Walk in the ways of your heart,
And *in the sight* of your eyes;
But know that for all these
[b]God will bring you into judgment.
10 Therefore remove sorrow from your heart,
And [a]put away evil from your flesh,
[b]For childhood and youth *are* vanity.

12 Remember[a] now your Creator in the days of your youth,
Before the difficult days come,
And the years draw near [b]when you say,
"I have no pleasure in them":
2 While the sun and the light,
The moon and the stars,
Are not darkened,
And the clouds do not return after the rain;
3 In the day when the keepers of the house tremble,
And the strong men bow down;
When the grinders cease because they are few,
And those that look through the windows grow dim;
4 When the doors are shut in the streets,
And the sound of grinding is low;
When one rises up at the sound of a bird,
And all [a]the daughters of music are brought low.
5 Also they are afraid of height,
And of terrors in the way;
When the almond tree blossoms,
The grasshopper is a burden,
And desire fails.
For man goes to [a]his eternal home,
And [b]the mourners go about the streets.

PEACE NOTE

Christians are not naïve about hard times. Solomon clearly prepared his readers "before the difficult days [came]." You will be ready if you're walking in the peace of the Lord.

ECCLESIASTES 12:1

10:20 [a] Acts 23:5 **11:1** [a] Is. 32:20 [b] [Deut. 15:10] **11:2** [a] [1 Tim. 6:18, 19] [b] Mic. 5:5 [c] Eph. 5:16 **11:5** [a] John 3:8 [b] Ps. 139:14 [1] Or *spirit* **11:7** [a] Eccl. 7:11 **11:8** [a] Eccl. 9:7 [b] Eccl. 12:1 **11:9** [a] Num. 15:39 [b] Eccl. 3:17; 12:14 **11:10** [a] 2 Cor. 7:1 [b] Ps. 39:5 **12:1** [a] Lam. 3:27 [b] 2 Sam. 19:35 **12:4** [a] 2 Sam. 19:35 **12:5** [a] Job 17:13 [b] Jer. 9:17

6 *Remember your Creator* before the
silver cord is loosed,[1]
Or the golden bowl is broken,
Or the pitcher shattered at the
fountain,
Or the wheel broken at the well.
7 [a]Then the dust will return to the earth
as it was,
[b]And the spirit will return to God [c]who
gave it.

8 "Vanity[a] of vanities," says the Preacher,
"All *is* vanity."

The Whole Duty of Man

9 And moreover, because the Preacher
was wise, he still taught the people knowledge; yes, he pondered and sought out *and*
[a]set in order many proverbs. 10 The Preacher
sought to find acceptable words; and *what*
was written *was* upright—words of truth.
11 The words of the wise are like goads, and
the words of scholars[1] are like well-driven
nails, given by one Shepherd. 12 And further,
my son, be admonished by these. Of making
many books *there is* no end, and [a]much study
is wearisome to the flesh.
13 Let us hear the conclusion of the whole
matter:

[a]Fear God and keep His commandments,
For this is man's all.
14 For [a]God will bring every work into
judgment,
Including every secret thing,
Whether good or evil.

12:6 [1] Following Qere and Targum; Kethib reads *removed;* Septuagint and Vulgate read *broken.* **12:7** [a] Gen. 3:19 [b] Eccl. 3:21 [c] Job 34:14 **12:8** [a] Ps. 62:9 **12:9** [a] 1 Kin. 4:32 **12:11** [1] Literally *masters of the assemblies* **12:12** [a] Eccl. 1:18 **12:13** [a] [Deut. 6:2; 10:12] **12:14** [a] Matt. 12:36

THE SONG OF SOLOMON

AUTHOR

According to 1 Kings 4:32, Solomon wrote 1,005 songs, but this eulogy of love stood out among them as the "song of songs" (Song 1:1). Tradition strongly favors Solomon as the author of this book. Solomon is specifically mentioned seven times, and he is identified as the groom. There is also evidence in the book of incredible royal luxury and expensive imported goods, things that characterized Solomon's reign.

TIME

c. 965 BC

KEY VERSE

Song of Solomon 7:10

THEME

Song of Solomon, or Song of Songs as it is sometimes known, is a one-of-a-kind love poem that concentrates on elements of the physical attraction between the sexes. It is possible that the Shulamite maiden was Abishag, who attended to David in his last days. Like Jesus' presence at a wedding, Song of Solomon is an indication of God's blessing on the physical union of man and woman. God created us for each other, and we should delight in physical intimacy within the context of marriage that God has sanctioned for us.

According to 1 Kings 4:32, Solomon spoke three thousand proverbs! Indeed, "men of all nations, from all the kings of the earth who had heard of his wisdom, came to hear the wisdom of Solomon" (1 Kin. 4:34). Song of Solomon is a powerful illustration of the beauty of peace in relationship to one's spouse: "Then I became in his eyes as one who found peace" (Song 8:10). The Song was read traditionally at the feast of Passover. For the follower of Christ today, at minimum Song of Solomon illustrates the peace-filled beauty of God-honoring relationships, but even more so, in God-honoring marriage between a man and a woman. A marital relationship with the Lord at the center results in peace, joy, and great memorable experiences that one could sing about!

1 The [a]song of songs, which *is* Solomon's.

The Banquet

The Shulamite[1]

2 Let him kiss me with the kisses of his mouth—
[a]For your[2] love *is* better than wine.
3 Because of the fragrance of your good ointments,
Your name *is* ointment poured forth;
Therefore the virgins love you.
4 [a]Draw me away!

The Daughters of Jerusalem

[b]We will run after you.[1]

The Shulamite

The king [c]has brought me into his chambers.

The Daughters of Jerusalem

We will be glad and rejoice in you.[2]

We will remember your[3] love more than wine.

The Shulamite

Rightly do they love you.[4]

5 I *am* dark, but lovely,
O daughters of Jerusalem,
Like the tents of Kedar,
Like the curtains of Solomon.
6 Do not look upon me, because I *am* dark,
Because the sun has tanned me.
My mother's sons were angry with me;
They made me the keeper of the vineyards,
But my own [a]vineyard I have not kept.

(To Her Beloved)

7 Tell me, O you whom I love,
Where you feed *your flock,*
Where you make *it* rest at noon.
For why should I be as one who veils herself[1]
By the flocks of your companions?

The Beloved

8 If you do not know, [a]O fairest among women,
Follow in the footsteps of the flock,
And feed your little goats
Beside the shepherds' tents.
9 I have compared you, [a]my love,
[b]To my filly among Pharaoh's chariots.
10 [a]Your cheeks are lovely with ornaments,
Your neck with chains *of gold.*

The Daughters of Jerusalem

11 We will make you[1] ornaments of gold
With studs of silver.

The Shulamite

12 While the king *is* at his table,
My spikenard sends forth its fragrance.
13 A bundle of myrrh *is* my beloved to me,
That lies all night between my breasts.
14 My beloved *is* to me a cluster of henna *blooms*
In the vineyards of En Gedi.

The Beloved

15 [a]Behold, you *are* fair, my love!
Behold, you *are* fair!
You *have* dove's eyes.

The Shulamite

16 Behold, you *are* [a]handsome, my beloved!
Yes, pleasant!
Also our bed *is* green.
17 The beams of our houses *are* cedar,
And our rafters of fir.

2 I *am* the rose of Sharon,
And the lily of the valleys.

The Beloved

2 Like a lily among thorns,
So is my love among the daughters.

The Shulamite

3 Like an apple tree among the trees of the woods,
So *is* my beloved among the sons.
I sat down in his shade with great delight,
And [a]his fruit *was* sweet to my taste.

The Shulamite to the Daughters of Jerusalem

4 He brought me to the banqueting house,
And his banner over me *was* love.
5 Sustain me with cakes of raisins,
Refresh me with apples,
For I *am* lovesick.

1:1 [a] 1 Kin. 4:32 **1:2** [a] Song 4:10 [1] A young woman from the town of Shulam or Shunem (compare 6:13). The speaker and audience are identified according to the number, gender, and person of the Hebrew words. Occasionally the identity is not certain. [2] Masculine singular, that is, the Beloved **1:4** [a] Hos. 11:4 [b] Phil. 3:12–14 [c] Ps. 45:14, 15 [1] Masculine singular, that is, the Beloved [2] Feminine singular, that is, the Shulamite [3] Masculine singular, that is, the Beloved [4] Masculine singular, that is, the Beloved **1:6** [a] Song 8:11, 12 **1:7** [1] Septuagint, Syriac, and Vulgate read *wanders.* **1:8** [a] Song 5:9 **1:9** [a] Song 2:2, 10, 13; 4:1, 7 [b] 2 Chr. 1:16 **1:10** [a] Ezek. 16:11 **1:11** [1] Feminine singular, that is, the Shulamite **1:15** [a] Song 4:1; 5:12 **1:16** [a] Song 5:10–16 **2:3** [a] Rev. 22:1, 2

6 [a]His left hand *is* under my head,
And his right hand embraces me.
7 [a]I charge you, O daughters of
Jerusalem,
By the gazelles or by the does of the
field,
Do not stir up nor awaken love
Until it pleases.

The Beloved's Request

The Shulamite

8 The voice of my beloved!
Behold, he comes
Leaping upon the mountains,
Skipping upon the hills.
9 [a]My beloved is like a gazelle or a young
stag.
Behold, he stands behind our wall;
He is looking through the windows,
Gazing through the lattice.

10 My beloved spoke, and said to me:
"Rise up, my love, my fair one,
And come away.
11 For lo, the winter is past,
The rain is over *and* gone.
12 The flowers appear on the earth;
The time of singing has come,
And the voice of the turtledove
Is heard in our land.
13 The fig tree puts forth her green figs,
And the vines *with* the tender grapes
Give a *good* smell.
Rise up, my love, my fair one,
And come away!

14 "O my [a]dove, in the clefts of the rock,
In the secret *places* of the cliff,
Let me see your face,
[b]Let me hear your voice;
For your voice *is* sweet,
And your face *is* lovely."

Her Brothers

15 Catch us [a]the foxes,
The little foxes that spoil the vines,
For our vines *have* tender grapes.

The Shulamite

16 [a]My beloved *is* mine, and I *am* his.
He feeds *his flock* among the lilies.

(To Her Beloved)

17 [a]Until the day breaks
And the shadows flee away,
Turn, my beloved,
And be [b]like a gazelle
Or a young stag
Upon the mountains of Bether.[1]

A Troubled Night

The Shulamite

3 By [a]night on my bed I sought the one
I love;
I sought him, but I did not find him.
2 "I will rise now," *I said,*
"And go about the city;
In the streets and in the squares
I will seek the one I love."
I sought him, but I did not find him.
3 [a]The watchmen who go about the city
found me;
I said,
"Have you seen the one I love?"

4 Scarcely had I passed by them,
When I found the one I love.
I held him and would not let him go,
Until I had brought him to the [a]house
of my mother,
And into the chamber of her who
conceived me.

5 [a]I charge you, O daughters of Jerusalem,
By the gazelles or by the does of the
field,
Do not stir up nor awaken love
Until it pleases.

The Coming of Solomon

The Shulamite

6 [a]Who *is* this coming out of the
wilderness
Like pillars of smoke,
Perfumed with myrrh and
frankincense,
With all the merchant's fragrant
powders?
7 Behold, it *is* Solomon's couch,
With sixty valiant men around it,
Of the valiant of Israel.
8 They all hold swords,
Being expert in war.
Every man *has* his sword on his thigh
Because of fear in the night.

9 Of the wood of Lebanon
Solomon the King
Made himself a palanquin:[1]
10 He made its pillars *of* silver,
Its support *of* gold,
Its seat *of* purple,
Its interior paved *with* love
By the daughters of Jerusalem.

2:6 [a] Song 8:3 **2:7** [a] Song 3:5; 8:4 **2:9** [a] Song 2:17 **2:14** [a] Song 5:2 [b] Song 8:13 **2:15** [a] Ezek. 13:4 **2:16** [a] Song 6:3 **2:17** [a] Song 4:6 [b] Song 8:14 [1] Literally *Separation* **3:1** [a] Is. 26:9 **3:3** [a] Song 5:7 **3:4** [a] Song 8:2 **3:5** [a] Song 2:7; 8:4 **3:6** [a] Song 8:5 **3:9** [1] A portable enclosed chair

11 Go forth, O daughters of Zion,
And see King Solomon with the crown
With which his mother crowned him
On the day of his wedding,
The day of the gladness of his heart.

The Bridegroom Praises the Bride

The Beloved

4 Behold, [a]you *are* fair, my love!
Behold, you *are* fair!
You *have* dove's eyes behind your veil.
Your hair *is* like a [b]flock of goats,
Going down from Mount Gilead.
2 [a]Your teeth *are* like a flock of shorn *sheep*
Which have come up from the washing,
Every one of which bears twins,
And none *is* barren among them.
3 Your lips *are* like a strand of scarlet,
And your mouth is lovely.
[a]Your temples behind your veil
Are like a piece of pomegranate.
4 [a]Your neck *is* like the tower of David,
Built [b]for an armory,
On which hang a thousand bucklers,
All shields of mighty men.
5 [a]Your two breasts *are* like two fawns,
Twins of a gazelle,
Which feed among the lilies.

6 [a]Until the day breaks
And the shadows flee away,
I will go my way to the mountain of myrrh
And to the hill of frankincense.

7 [a]You *are* all fair, my love,
And *there is* no spot in you.
8 Come with me from Lebanon, *my* spouse,
With me from Lebanon.
Look from the top of Amana,
From the top of Senir [a]and Hermon,
From the lions' dens,
From the mountains of the leopards.

9 You have ravished my heart,
My sister, *my* spouse;
You have ravished my heart
With one *look* of your eyes,
With one link of your necklace.
10 How fair is your love,
My sister, *my* spouse!
[a]How much better than wine is your love,
And the scent of your perfumes
Than all spices!
11 Your lips, O *my* spouse,
Drip as the honeycomb;
[a]Honey and milk *are* under your tongue;
And the fragrance of your garments
Is [b]like the fragrance of Lebanon.

12 A garden enclosed
Is my sister, *my* spouse,
A spring shut up,
A fountain sealed.
13 Your plants *are* an orchard of pomegranates
With pleasant fruits,
Fragrant henna with spikenard,
14 Spikenard and saffron,
Calamus and cinnamon,
With all trees of frankincense,
Myrrh and aloes,
With all the chief spices—
15 A fountain of gardens,
A well of [a]living waters,
And streams from Lebanon.

The Shulamite

16 Awake, O north *wind*,
And come, O south!
Blow upon my garden,
That its spices may flow out.
[a]Let my beloved come to his garden
And eat its pleasant [b]fruits.

The Beloved

5 I [a]have come to my garden, my [b]sister, *my* spouse;
I have gathered my myrrh with my spice;
[c]I have eaten my honeycomb with my honey;
I have drunk my wine with my milk.

(To His Friends)

Eat, O [d]friends!
Drink, yes, drink deeply,
O beloved ones!

The Shulamite's Troubled Evening

The Shulamite

2 I sleep, but my heart is awake;
It is the voice of my beloved!
[a]He knocks, *saying*,
"Open for me, my sister, my love,
My dove, my perfect one;
For my head is covered with dew,
My locks with the drops of the night."

4:1 [a] Song 1:15; 5:12 [b] Song 6:5 **4:2** [a] Song 6:6 **4:3** [a] Song 6:7 **4:4** [a] Song 7:4 [b] Neh. 3:19 **4:5** [a] Song 7:3 **4:6** [a] Song 2:17 **4:7** [a] Eph. 5:27 **4:8** [a] Deut. 3:9 **4:10** [a] Song 1:2, 4 **4:11** [a] Prov. 24:13, 14 [b] Hos. 14:6, 7 **4:15** [a] Zech. 14:8 **4:16** [a] Song 5:1 [b] Song 7:13 **5:1** [a] Song 4:16 [b] Song 4:9 [c] Song 4:11 [d] Luke 15:7, 10 **5:2** [a] Rev. 3:20

3 I have taken off my robe;
How can I put it on *again?*
I have washed my feet;
How can I defile them?
4 My beloved put his hand
By the latch *of the door,*
And my heart yearned for him.
5 I arose to open for my beloved,
And my hands dripped *with* myrrh,
My fingers with liquid myrrh,
On the handles of the lock.

6 I opened for my beloved,
But my beloved had turned away *and* was gone.
My heart leaped up when he spoke.
[a]I sought him, but I could not find him;
I called him, but he gave me no answer.
7 [a]The watchmen who went about the city found me.
They struck me, they wounded me;
The keepers of the walls
Took my veil away from me.
8 I charge you, O daughters of Jerusalem,
If you find my beloved,
That you tell him I *am* lovesick!

The Daughters of Jerusalem

9 What *is* your beloved
More than *another* beloved,
[a]O fairest among women?
What *is* your beloved
More than *another* beloved,
That you so charge us?

The Shulamite

10 My beloved *is* white and ruddy,
Chief among ten thousand.
11 His head *is like* the finest gold;
His locks *are* wavy,
And black as a raven.
12 [a]His eyes *are* like doves
By the rivers of waters,
Washed with milk,
And fitly set.
13 His cheeks *are* like a bed of spices,
Banks of scented herbs.
His lips *are* lilies,
Dripping liquid myrrh.

14 His hands *are* rods of gold
Set with beryl.
His body *is* carved ivory
Inlaid *with* sapphires.
15 His legs *are* pillars of marble
Set on bases of fine gold.
His countenance *is* like Lebanon,
Excellent as the cedars.
16 His mouth *is* most sweet,
Yes, he *is* altogether lovely.
This *is* my beloved,
And this *is* my friend,
O daughters of Jerusalem!

The Daughters of Jerusalem

6 Where has your beloved gone,
[a] O fairest among women?
Where has your beloved turned aside,
That we may seek him with you?

The Shulamite

2 My beloved has gone to his [a]garden,
To the beds of spices,
To feed *his flock* in the gardens,
And to gather lilies.
3 [a]I *am* my beloved's,
And my beloved *is* mine.
He feeds *his flock* among the lilies.

Praise of the Shulamite's Beauty

The Beloved

4 O my love, you *are as* beautiful as Tirzah,
Lovely as Jerusalem,
Awesome as *an army* with banners!
5 Turn your eyes away from me,
For they have overcome me.
Your hair *is* [a]like a flock of goats
Going down from Gilead.
6 [a]Your teeth *are* like a flock of sheep
Which have come up from the washing;
Every one bears twins,
And none *is* barren among them.
7 [a]Like a piece of pomegranate
Are your temples behind your veil.

8 There are sixty queens
And eighty concubines,
And [a]virgins without number.
9 My dove, my [a]perfect one,
Is the only one,
The only one of her mother,
The favorite of the one who bore her.
The daughters saw her
And called her blessed,
The queens and the concubines,
And they praised her.

10 Who is she who looks forth as the morning,
Fair as the moon,
Clear as the sun,
[a]Awesome as *an army* with banners?

5:6 [a] Song 3:1 5:7 [a] Song 3:3 5:9 [a] Song 1:8; 6:1 5:12 [a] Song 1:15; 4:1 6:1 [a] Song 1:8; 5:9 6:2 [a] Song 4:16; 5:1
6:3 [a] Song 2:16; 7:10 6:5 [a] Song 4:1 6:6 [a] Song 4:2 6:7 [a] Song 4:3 6:8 [a] Song 1:3 6:9 [a] Song 2:14; 5:2 6:10 [a] Song 6:4

The Shulamite

11 I went down to the garden of nuts
To see the verdure of the valley,
[a]To see whether the vine had budded
And the pomegranates had bloomed.
12 Before I was even aware,
My soul had made me
As the chariots of my noble people.[1]

The Beloved and His Friends

13 Return, return, O Shulamite;
Return, return, that we may look upon you!

The Shulamite

What would you see in the Shulamite—
As it were, the dance of the two camps?[1]

Expressions of Praise

The Beloved

7 How beautiful are your feet in sandals,
[a]O prince's daughter!
The curves of your thighs *are* like jewels,
The work of the hands of a skillful workman.
2 Your navel *is* a rounded goblet;
It lacks no blended beverage.
Your waist *is* a heap of wheat
Set about with lilies.
3 [a]Your two breasts *are* like two fawns,
Twins of a gazelle.
4 [a]Your neck *is* like an ivory tower,
Your eyes *like* the pools in Heshbon
By the gate of Bath Rabbim.
Your nose *is* like the tower of Lebanon
Which looks toward Damascus.
5 Your head *crowns* you like *Mount* Carmel,
And the hair of your head *is* like purple;
A king *is* held captive by *your* tresses.

6 How fair and how pleasant you are,
O love, with your delights!
7 This stature of yours is like a palm tree,
And your breasts *like* its clusters.
8 I said, "I will go up to the palm tree,
I will take hold of its branches."
Let now your breasts be like clusters of the vine,
The fragrance of your breath like apples,
9 And the roof of your mouth like the best wine.

The Shulamite

The wine goes *down* smoothly for my beloved,
Moving gently the lips of sleepers.[1]
10 [a]I *am* my beloved's,
And [b]his desire *is* toward me.

11 Come, my beloved,
Let us go forth to the field;
Let us lodge in the villages.
12 Let us get up early to the vineyards;
Let us [a]see if the vine has budded,
Whether the grape blossoms are open,
And the pomegranates are in bloom.
There I will give you my love.
13 The [a]mandrakes give off a fragrance,
And at our gates [b]*are* pleasant *fruits*,
All manner, new and old,
Which I have laid up for you, my beloved.

8 Oh, that you were like my brother,
Who nursed at my mother's breasts!
If I should find you outside,
I would kiss you;
I would not be despised.
2 I would lead you *and* bring you
Into the [a]house of my mother,
She *who* used to instruct me.
I would cause you to drink of [b]spiced wine,
Of the juice of my pomegranate.

(To the Daughters of Jerusalem)

3 [a]His left hand *is* under my head,
And his right hand embraces me.
4 [a]I charge you, O daughters of Jerusalem,
Do not stir up nor awaken love
Until it pleases.

PEACE NOTE

Wait on God and choose a spouse who loves Jesus. This will bring indescribable peace in your relationship.

SONG OF SOLOMON 8:4

6:11 [a] Song 7:12 **6:12** [1] Hebrew *Ammi Nadib* **6:13** [1] Hebrew *Mahanaim* **7:1** [a] Ps. 45:13 **7:3** [a] Song 4:5 **7:4** [a] Song 4:4 **7:9** [1] Septuagint, Syriac, and Vulgate read *lips and teeth.* **7:10** [a] Song 2:16; 6:3 [b] Ps. 45:11 **7:12** [a] Song 6:11 **7:13** [a] Gen. 30:14 [b] Matt. 13:52 **8:2** [a] Song 3:4 [b] Prov. 9:2 **8:3** [a] Song 2:6 **8:4** [a] Song 2:7; 3:5

LOVELY PEACE

I became in his eyes as one who found peace.

SONG OF SOLOMON 8:10

In the famous biblical love song known as the Song of Solomon, the young woman defended her maturity and value in chapter 8. What I find fascinating is that among her many attributes and assets (including owning property), she asserted, "I became in his eyes as one who found peace." She claims that the man whose judgment she holds in high esteem (Solomon?) saw her as one who savored the wonderful quality of peace (*shalom*). The implication is that this is the young woman's greatest asset. What man would not want her as his wife?

In Proverbs 31:10–31, we find a beautiful description of a hard-to-find wife. Beauty may be passing, the wise man said, "but a woman who fears the LORD, she shall be praised" (v. 30). The good wife has many virtues and many gifts, but the well-known passage in Proverbs says nothing about peace. Song of Solomon does. The young woman of the love song had become in the eyes of him who wooed her as one who possessed peace, and that was "far above rubies" (Prov. 31:10).

What personal qualities do you consider priceless?

Love Renewed in Lebanon

A Relative

5 [a]Who *is* this coming up from the
wilderness,
Leaning upon her beloved?

I awakened you under the apple tree.
There your mother brought you forth;
There she *who* bore you brought *you*
forth.

The Shulamite to Her Beloved

6 [a]Set me as a seal upon your heart,
As a seal upon your arm;
For love *is as* strong as death,
[b]Jealousy *as* cruel as the grave;[1]
Its flames *are* flames of fire,
A most vehement flame.[2]

7 Many waters cannot quench love,
Nor can the floods drown it.
[a]If a man would give for love
All the wealth of his house,
It would be utterly despised.

The Shulamite's Brothers

8 [a]We have a little sister,
And she has no breasts.
What shall we do for our sister
In the day when she is spoken for?
9 If she *is* a wall,
We will build upon her
A battlement of silver;
And if she *is* a door,
We will enclose her
With boards of cedar.

The Shulamite

10 I *am* a wall,
And my breasts like towers;
Then I became in his eyes
As one who found peace.
11 Solomon had a vineyard at Baal Hamon;
[a]He leased the vineyard to keepers;
Everyone was to bring for its fruit
A thousand silver *coins*.

(To Solomon)

12 My own vineyard *is* before me.
You, O Solomon, *may have* a thousand,
And those who tend its fruit two hundred.

The Beloved

13 You who dwell in the gardens,
The companions listen for your voice—
[a]Let me hear it!

The Shulamite

14 [a]Make haste, my beloved,
And [b]be like a gazelle
Or a young stag
On the mountains of spices.

8:5 [a] Song 3:6 8:6 [a] Jer. 22:24 [b] Prov. 6:34, 35 [1] Or *Sheol* [2] Literally *A flame of YAH* (a poetic form of *YHWH, the LORD*)
8:7 [a] Prov. 6:35 8:8 [a] Ezek. 23:33 8:11 [a] Matt. 21:33 8:13 [a] Song 2:14 8:14 [a] Rev. 22:17, 20 [b] Song 2:7, 9, 17

THE BOOK OF ISAIAH

AUTHOR

Although there is much argument regarding the unity of the work, Isaiah is the commonly accepted author of this book. He was from a distinguished Jewish family and his education is evident in his impressive vocabulary and style. The New Testament writers John, Paul, Matthew, and Luke, as well as Jesus Himself, all quoted from the Book of Isaiah and credited him with its authorship. This great poet was uncompromising, sincere, and compassionate. Isaiah maintained close contact with the royal court, but his exhortations against alliances with foreign powers were not always well received.

TIME

c. 740–680 BC

KEY VERSE

Isaiah 9:6–7

THEME

Because of the length of the book and Isaiah's interactions with the politics of the time, we probably get a better picture of Isaiah's ministry than we do of any of the other prophets'. It also contains more well-known, classic prophecy texts than any other book. One commentator calls Isaiah "the Romans of the Old Testament," as in Isaiah we get a broad perspective on how and why God is working in history. Both God's holiness and His grace come clearly into perspective through a careful study of this book.

"I make peace," the Lord said through Isaiah (45:7), and "There is no peace for the wicked" (48:22). The prophet Isaiah spoke the most influential passages in all Scripture on the peace of God. He referred to the peace of God (in Hebrew) more than any other preexilic prophet (nearly fifty times in the original language), but he also prophesied about the coming Messiah using the unique descriptor "Prince of Peace" (9:6). The now famous mantra "Jesus is Lord" finds its origins in 9:7: "Of the increase of His government and peace [*shalom*] there will be no end." Isaiah also made the astounding declaration that the true Messiah would bring an unending peace: thanks to the saving work of Christ, "the work of righteousness will be peace" (32:17), the Lord "will establish peace for us" (26:12), and our minds can be held in "perfect peace" (26:3).

1 The [a]vision of Isaiah the son of Amoz, which he saw concerning Judah and Jerusalem in the [b]days of Uzziah, Jotham, Ahaz, *and* Hezekiah, kings of Judah.

The Wickedness of Judah

2 [a]Hear, O heavens, and give ear, O earth!
For the LORD has spoken:
"I have nourished and brought up children,
And they have rebelled against Me;
3 [a]The ox knows its owner
And the donkey its master's crib;
But Israel [b]does not know,
My people do not consider."

4 Alas, sinful nation,
A people laden with iniquity,
[a]A brood of evildoers,
Children who are corrupters!
They have forsaken the LORD,
They have provoked to anger
The Holy One of Israel,
They have turned away backward.

5 [a]Why should you be stricken again?
You will revolt more and more.
The whole head is sick,
And the whole heart faints.
6 From the sole of the foot even to the head,
There is no soundness in it,
But wounds and bruises and putrefying sores;
They have not been closed or bound up,
Or soothed with ointment.

7 [a]Your country *is* desolate,
Your cities *are* burned with fire;
Strangers devour your land in your presence;
And *it is* desolate, as overthrown by strangers.
8 So the daughter of Zion is left [a]as a booth in a vineyard,
As a hut in a garden of cucumbers,
[b]As a besieged city.
9 [a]Unless the LORD of hosts
Had left to us a very small remnant,
We would have become like [b]Sodom,
We would have been made like Gomorrah.

10 Hear the word of the LORD,
You rulers [a]of Sodom;
Give ear to the law of our God,
You people of Gomorrah:
11 "To what purpose *is* the multitude of your [a]sacrifices to Me?"
Says the LORD.
"I have had enough of burnt offerings of rams
And the fat of fed cattle.
I do not delight in the blood of bulls,
Or of lambs or goats.

12 "When you come [a]to appear before Me,
Who has required this from your hand,
To trample My courts?
13 Bring no more [a]futile sacrifices;
Incense is an abomination to Me.
The New Moons, the Sabbaths, and [b]the calling of assemblies—
I cannot endure iniquity and the sacred meeting.
14 Your [a]New Moons and your [b]appointed feasts
My soul hates;
They are a trouble to Me,
I am weary of bearing *them.*
15 [a]When you spread out your hands,
I will hide My eyes from you;
[b]Even though you make many prayers,
I will not hear.
Your hands are full of blood.

16 "Wash[a] yourselves, make yourselves clean;
Put away the evil of your doings from before My eyes.
[b]Cease to do evil,
17 Learn to do good;
Seek justice,
Rebuke the oppressor;[1]
Defend the fatherless,
Plead for the widow.

18 "Come now, and let us [a]reason together,"
Says the LORD,
"Though your sins are like scarlet,
[b]They shall be as white as snow;
Though they are red like crimson,
They shall be as wool.
19 If you are willing and obedient,
You shall eat the good of the land;
20 But if you refuse and rebel,
You shall be devoured by the sword";
[a]For the mouth of the LORD has spoken.

The Degenerate City

21 [a]How the faithful city has become a harlot!

1:1 [a] Num. 12:6 [b] 2 Chr. 26—32 **1:2** [a] Jer. 2:12 **1:3** [a] Jer. 8:7 [b] Jer. 9:3, 6 **1:4** [a] Matt. 3:7 **1:5** [a] Jer. 5:3 **1:7** [a] Deut. 28:51, 52 **1:8** [a] Job 27:18 [b] Jer. 4:17 **1:9** [a] Lam. 3:22 [b] Gen. 19:24 **1:10** [a] Deut. 32:32 **1:11** [a] [1 Sam. 15:22] **1:12** [a] Ex. 23:17 **1:13** [a] Matt. 15:9 [b] Joel 1:14 **1:14** [a] Num. 28:11 [b] Lam. 2:6 **1:15** [a] Prov. 1:28 [b] Mic. 3:4 **1:16** [a] Jer. 4:14 [b] Rom. 12:9 **1:17** [1] Some ancient versions read *the oppressed.* **1:18** [a] Is. 43:26 [b] Ps. 51:7 **1:20** [a] [Titus 1:2] **1:21** [a] Jer. 2:20

It was full of justice;
Righteousness lodged in it,
But now [b]murderers.
22 [a]Your silver has become dross,
Your wine mixed with water.
23 [a]Your princes *are* rebellious,
And [b]companions of thieves;
[c]Everyone loves bribes,
And follows after rewards.
They [d]do not defend the fatherless,
Nor does the cause of the widow come
before them.

24 Therefore the Lord says,
The LORD of hosts, the Mighty One of
Israel,
"Ah, [a]I will rid Myself of My adversaries,
And take vengeance on My enemies.
25 I will turn My hand against you,
And [a]thoroughly purge away your dross,
And take away all your alloy.
26 I will restore your judges [a]as at the first,
And your counselors as at the
beginning.
Afterward [b]you shall be called the city
of righteousness, the faithful city."

27 Zion shall be redeemed with justice,
And her penitents with righteousness.
28 The [a]destruction of transgressors and
of sinners *shall be* together,
And those who forsake the LORD shall
be consumed.
29 For they[1] shall be ashamed of the
terebinth trees
Which you have desired;
And you shall be embarrassed because
of the gardens
Which you have chosen.
30 For you shall be as a terebinth whose
leaf fades,
And as a garden that has no water.
31 [a]The strong shall be as tinder,
And the work of it as a spark;
Both will burn together,
And no one shall [b]quench *them*.

The Future House of God

2 The word that Isaiah the son of Amoz
saw concerning Judah and Jerusalem.

2 Now [a]it shall come to pass [b]in the latter
days
[c]*That* the mountain of the LORD's house
Shall be established on the top of the
mountains,
And shall be exalted above the hills;
And all nations shall flow to it.
3 Many people shall come and say,
[a]"Come, and let us go up to the mountain
of the LORD,
To the house of the God of Jacob;
He will teach us His ways,
And we shall walk in His paths."
[b]For out of Zion shall go forth the law,
And the word of the LORD from
Jerusalem.
4 He shall judge between the nations,
And rebuke many people;
They shall beat their swords into
plowshares,
And their spears into pruning hooks;
Nation shall not lift up sword against
nation,
Neither shall they learn war anymore.

PEACE NOTE

God promises a robust peace at the end: cessation of war, fresh well-being, and harmonious living for all His restored creation.

ISAIAH 2:4

The Day of the LORD

5 O house of Jacob, come and let us
[a]walk
In the light of the LORD.

6 For You have forsaken Your people, the
house of Jacob,
Because they are filled [a]with eastern
ways;
They *are* [b]soothsayers like the
Philistines,
[c]And they are pleased with the children
of foreigners.
7 [a]Their land is also full of silver and gold,
And there is no end to their treasures;
Their land is also full of horses,
And there is no end to their chariots.

1:21 [b] Mic. 3:1–3 1:22 [a] Jer. 6:28 1:23 [a] Hos. 9:15 [b] Prov. 29:24 [c] Jer. 22:17 [d] Jer. 5:28 1:24 [a] Deut. 28:63 1:25 [a] Mal. 3:3 1:26 [a] Jer. 33:7–11 [b] Zech. 8:3 1:28 [a] [2 Thess. 1:8, 9] 1:29 [1] Following Masoretic Text, Septuagint, and Vulgate; some Hebrew manuscripts and Targum read *you*. 1:31 [a] Ezek. 32:21 [b] Mark 9:43 2:2 [a] Mic. 4:1 [b] Gen. 49:1 [c] Ps. 68:15 2:3 [a] Jer. 50:5 [b] Luke 24:47 2:5 [a] Eph. 5:8 2:6 [a] Num. 23:7 [b] Deut. 18:14 [c] Ps. 106:35 2:7 [a] Deut. 17:16

8 [a]Their land is also full of idols;
They worship the work of their own hands,
That which their own fingers have made.
9 People bow down,
And each man humbles himself;
Therefore do not forgive them.

10 [a]Enter into the rock, and hide in the dust,
From the terror of the LORD
And the glory of His majesty.
11 The lofty looks of man shall be [a]humbled,
The haughtiness of men shall be bowed down,
And the LORD alone shall be exalted [b]in that day.

12 For the day of the LORD of hosts
Shall come upon everything proud and lofty,
Upon everything lifted up—
And it shall be brought low—
13 Upon all [a]the cedars of Lebanon *that are* high and lifted up,
And upon all the oaks of Bashan;
14 [a]Upon all the high mountains,
And upon all the hills *that are* lifted up;
15 Upon every high tower,
And upon every fortified wall;
16 [a]Upon all the ships of Tarshish,
And upon all the beautiful sloops.
17 The loftiness of man shall be bowed down,
And the haughtiness of men shall be brought low;
The LORD alone will be exalted in that day,
18 But the idols He shall utterly abolish.

19 They shall go into the [a]holes of the rocks,
And into the caves of the earth,
[b]From the terror of the LORD
And the glory of His majesty,
When He arises [c]to shake the earth mightily.

20 In that day a man will cast away his idols of silver
And his idols of gold,
Which they made, *each* for himself to worship,
To the moles and bats,
21 To go into the clefts of the rocks,
And into the crags of the rugged rocks,
From the terror of the LORD
And the glory of His majesty,
When He arises to shake the earth mightily.

22 [a]Sever yourselves from such a man,
Whose [b]breath *is* in his nostrils;
For of what account is he?

Judgment on Judah and Jerusalem

3 For behold, the Lord, the LORD of hosts,
[a]Takes away from Jerusalem and from Judah
[b]The stock and the store,
The whole supply of bread and the whole supply of water;
2 [a]The mighty man and the man of war,
The judge and the prophet,
And the diviner and the elder;
3 The captain of fifty and the honorable man,
The counselor and the skillful artisan,
And the expert enchanter.

4 "I will give [a]children *to be* their princes,
And babes shall rule over them.
5 The people will be oppressed,
Every one by another and every one by his neighbor;
The child will be insolent toward the elder,
And the base toward the honorable."

6 When a man takes hold of his brother
In the house of his father, *saying,*
"You have clothing;
You be our ruler,
And *let* these ruins *be* under your power,"[1]
7 In that day he will protest, saying,
"I cannot cure *your* ills,
For in my house *is* neither food nor clothing;
Do not make me a ruler of the people."

8 For [a]Jerusalem stumbled,
And Judah is fallen,
Because their tongue and their doings
Are against the LORD,
To provoke the eyes of His glory.
9 The look on their countenance witnesses against them,
And they declare their sin as [a]Sodom;
They do not hide *it.*
Woe to their soul!
For they have brought evil upon themselves.

10 "Say to the righteous [a]that *it shall be* well *with them,*
[b]For they shall eat the fruit of their doings.

2:8 [a] Jer. 2:28 2:10 [a] Rev. 6:15, 16 2:11 [a] Prov. 16:5 [b] Hos. 2:16 2:13 [a] Zech. 11:1, 2 2:14 [a] Is. 30:25 2:16 [a] 1 Kin. 10:22 2:19 [a] Hos. 10:8 [b] [2 Thess. 1:9] [c] Hag. 2:6, 7 2:22 [a] Jer. 17:5 [b] Job 27:3 3:1 [a] Jer. 37:21 [b] Lev. 26:26 3:2 [a] 2 Kin. 24:14 3:4 [a] Eccl. 10:16 3:6 [1] Literally *hand* 3:8 [a] Mic. 3:12 3:9 [a] Gen. 13:13 3:10 [a] [Eccl. 8:12] [b] Ps. 128:2

11 Woe to the wicked! [a]*It shall be* ill *with him,*
For the reward of his hands shall be given him.
12 *As for* My people, children *are* their oppressors,
And women rule over them.
O My people! [a]Those who lead you cause *you* to err,
And destroy the way of your paths."

Oppression and Luxury Condemned

13 The LORD stands up [a]to plead,
And stands to judge the people.
14 The LORD will enter into judgment
With the elders of His people
And His princes:
"For you have eaten up [a]the vineyard;
The plunder of the poor *is* in your houses.
15 What do you mean by [a]crushing My people
And grinding the faces of the poor?"
Says the Lord GOD of hosts.

16 Moreover the LORD says:

"Because the daughters of Zion are haughty,
And walk with outstretched necks
And wanton eyes,
Walking and mincing *as* they go,
Making a jingling with their feet,
17 Therefore the Lord will strike with [a]a scab
The crown of the head of the daughters of Zion,
And the LORD will [b]uncover their secret parts."

18 In that day the Lord will take away the finery:
The jingling anklets, the scarves, and the [a]crescents;
19 The pendants, the bracelets, and the veils;
20 The headdresses, the leg ornaments, and the headbands;
The perfume boxes, the charms,
21 and the rings;
The nose jewels,
22 the festal apparel, and the mantles;
The outer garments, the purses,
23 and the mirrors;
The fine linen, the turbans, and the robes.

24 And so it shall be:

Instead of a sweet smell there will be a stench;
Instead of a sash, a rope;
Instead of well-set hair, [a]baldness;
Instead of a rich robe, a girding of sackcloth;
And branding instead of beauty.
25 Your men shall fall by the sword,
And your mighty in the war.

26 [a]Her gates shall lament and mourn,
And she *being* desolate [b]shall sit on the ground.

4 And [a]in that day seven women shall take hold of one man, saying,
"We will [b]eat our own food and wear our own apparel;
Only let us be called by your name,
To take away [c]our reproach."

The Renewal of Zion

2 In that day [a]the Branch of the LORD shall be beautiful and glorious;
And the fruit of the earth *shall be* excellent and appealing
For those of Israel who have escaped.

3 And it shall come to pass that *he who is*
left in Zion and remains in Jerusalem [a]will
be called holy—everyone who is [b]recorded
among the living in Jerusalem. 4 When [a]the
Lord has washed away the filth of the daughters of Zion, and purged the blood of Jerusalem from her midst, by the spirit of judgment
and by the spirit of burning, 5 then the LORD
will create above every dwelling place of
Mount Zion, and above her assemblies, [a]a
cloud and smoke by day and [b]the shining of
a flaming fire by night. For over all the glory
there *will be* a covering. 6 And there will be a
tabernacle for shade in the daytime from the
heat, [a]for a place of refuge, and for a shelter
from storm and rain.

God's Disappointing Vineyard

5 Now let me sing to my Well-beloved
A song of my Beloved [a]regarding His vineyard:

My Well-beloved has a vineyard
On a very fruitful hill.
2 He dug it up and cleared out its stones,
And planted it with the choicest vine.

3:11 [a] [Ps. 11:6] **3:12** [a] Is. 9:16 **3:13** [a] Mic. 6:2 **3:14** [a] Matt. 21:33 **3:15** [a] Mic. 3:2, 3 **3:17** [a] Deut. 28:27 [b] Jer. 13:22 **3:18** [a] Judg. 8:21, 26 **3:24** [a] Is. 22:12 **3:26** [a] Jer. 14:2 [b] Lam. 2:10 **4:1** [a] Is. 2:11, 17 [b] 2 Thess. 3:12 [c] Luke 1:25 **4:2** [a] [Jer. 23:5] **4:3** [a] Is. 60:21 [b] Phil. 4:3 **4:4** [a] Mal. 3:2, 3 **4:5** [a] Ex. 13:21, 22 [b] Zech. 2:5 **4:6** [a] Is. 25:4 **5:1** [a] Matt. 21:33

PEACE NOTE

There is an experiential faith link between vulnerability with God and empowerment from God. When we admit our weakness, we make way for His strength.

He built a tower in its midst,
And also made a winepress in it;
[a]So He expected *it* to bring forth *good* grapes,
But it brought forth wild grapes.

3 "And now, O inhabitants of Jerusalem and men of Judah,
[a]Judge, please, between Me and My vineyard.
4 What more could have been done to My vineyard
That I have not done in [a]it?
Why then, when I expected *it* to bring forth *good* grapes,
Did it bring forth wild grapes?
5 And now, please let Me tell you what I will do to My vineyard:
[a]I will take away its hedge, and it shall be burned;
And break down its wall, and it shall be trampled down.
6 I will lay it [a]waste;
It shall not be pruned or dug,
But there shall come up briers and [b]thorns.
I will also command the clouds
That they rain no rain on it."

7 For the vineyard of the LORD of hosts *is* the house of Israel,
And the men of Judah are His pleasant plant.
He looked for justice, but behold, oppression;
For righteousness, but behold, a cry *for help.*

Impending Judgment on Excesses

8 Woe to those who join [a]house to house;
They add field to field,
Till *there is* no place
Where they may dwell alone in the midst of the land!
9 [a]In my hearing the LORD of hosts *said,*
"Truly, many houses shall be desolate,
Great and beautiful ones, without inhabitant.
10 For ten acres of vineyard shall yield one [a]bath,
And a homer of seed shall yield one ephah."

11 [a]Woe to those who rise early in the morning,
That they may follow intoxicating drink;
Who continue until night, *till* wine inflames them!
12 [a]The harp and the strings,
The tambourine and flute,
And wine are in their feasts;
But [b]they do not regard the work of the LORD,
Nor consider the operation of His hands.

13 [a]Therefore my people have gone into captivity,
Because *they have* no [b]knowledge;
Their honorable men *are* famished,
And their multitude dried up with thirst.
14 Therefore Sheol has enlarged itself
And opened its mouth beyond measure;
Their glory and their multitude and their pomp,
And he who is jubilant, shall descend into it.
15 People shall be brought down,
[a]Each man shall be humbled,
And the eyes of the lofty shall be humbled.
16 But the LORD of hosts shall be [a]exalted in judgment,
And God who is holy shall be hallowed in righteousness.
17 Then the lambs shall feed in their pasture,
And in the waste places of [a]the fat ones strangers shall eat.

5:2 [a] Deut. 32:6 5:3 [a] [Rom. 3:4] 5:4 [a] 2 Chr. 36:15, 16 5:5 [a] Ps. 80:12; 89:40, 41 5:6 [a] 2 Chr. 36:19–21 [b] Is. 7:19–25 5:8 [a] Mic. 2:2 5:9 [a] Is. 22:14 5:10 [a] Ezek. 45:11 5:11 [a] Prov. 23:29, 30 5:12 [a] Amos 6:5 [b] Job 34:27 5:13 [a] 2 Kin. 24:14–16 [b] Hos. 4:6 5:15 [a] Is. 2:9, 11 5:16 [a] Is. 2:11 5:17 [a] Is. 10:16

18 Woe to those who draw iniquity with
cords of vanity,
And sin as if with a cart rope;
19 [a]That say, "Let Him make speed *and*
hasten His work,
That we may see *it;*
And let the counsel of the Holy One of
Israel draw near and come,
That we may know *it.*"

20 Woe to those who call evil good, and
good evil;
Who put darkness for light, and light
for darkness;
Who put bitter for sweet, and sweet for
bitter!
21 Woe to *those who are* [a]wise in their own
eyes,
And prudent in their own sight!

22 Woe to men mighty at drinking wine,
Woe to men valiant for mixing
intoxicating drink,
23 Who [a]justify the wicked for a bribe,
And take away justice from the
righteous man!

24 Therefore, [a]as the fire devours the
stubble,
And the flame consumes the chaff,
So [b]their root will be as rottenness,
And their blossom will ascend like
dust;
Because they have rejected the law of
the LORD of hosts,
And despised the word of the Holy One
of Israel.
25 [a]Therefore the anger of the LORD is
aroused against His people;
He has stretched out His hand against
them
And stricken them,
And [b]the hills trembled.
Their carcasses *were* as refuse in the
midst of the streets.

[c]For all this His anger is not turned
away,
But His hand *is* stretched out still.

26 [a]He will lift up a banner to the nations
from afar,
And will [b]whistle to them from [c]the
end of the earth;
Surely [d]they shall come with speed,
swiftly.
27 No one will be weary or stumble among
them,
No one will slumber or sleep;
Nor [a]will the belt on their loins be
loosed,
Nor the strap of their sandals be
broken;
28 [a]Whose arrows *are* sharp,
And all their bows bent;
Their horses' hooves will seem like
flint,
And their wheels like a whirlwind.
29 Their roaring *will be* like a lion,
They will roar like young lions;
Yes, they will roar
And lay hold of the prey;
They will carry *it* away safely,
And no one will deliver.
30 In that day they will roar against them
Like the roaring of the sea.
And if *one* [a]looks to the land,
Behold, darkness *and* sorrow;
And the light is darkened by the
clouds.

Isaiah Called to Be a Prophet

6 In the year that [a]King Uzziah died, I [b]saw
the Lord sitting on a throne, high and
lifted up, and the train of His *robe* filled the
temple. 2 Above it stood seraphim; each one
had six wings: with two he covered his face,
[a]with two he covered his feet, and with two
he flew. 3 And one cried to another and said:

[a]"Holy, holy, holy *is* the LORD of hosts;
[b]The whole earth *is* full of His glory!"

4 And the posts of the door were shaken by
the voice of him who cried out, and the house
was filled with smoke.
5 So I said:

"Woe *is* me, for I am undone!
Because I *am* a man of [a]unclean lips,
And I dwell in the midst of a people of
unclean lips;
For my eyes have seen the King,
The LORD of hosts."

6 Then one of the seraphim flew to me,
having in his hand a live coal *which* he had
taken with the tongs from [a]the altar. 7 And he
[a]touched my mouth *with it,* and said:

"Behold, this has touched your lips;
Your iniquity is taken away,
And your sin purged."

5:19 [a] Jer. 17:15 **5:21** [a] Rom. 1:22; 12:16 **5:23** [a] Prov. 17:15 **5:24** [a] Ex. 15:7 [b] Job 18:16 **5:25** [a] 2 Kin. 22:13, 17 [b] Jer. 4:24 [c] Is. 9:12, 17 **5:26** [a] Is. 11:10, 12 [b] Is. 7:18 [c] Mal. 1:11 [d] Joel 2:7 **5:27** [a] Dan. 5:6 **5:28** [a] Jer. 5:16 **5:30** [a] Is. 8:22 **6:1** [a] 2 Kin. 15:7 [b] John 12:41 **6:2** [a] Ezek. 1:11 **6:3** [a] Rev. 4:8 [b] Num. 14:21 **6:5** [a] Ex. 6:12, 30 **6:6** [a] Rev. 8:3 **6:7** [a] Jer. 1:9

8 Also I heard the voice of the Lord, saying:

"Whom shall I send,
And who will go for [a]Us?"

Then I said, "Here *am* I! Send me."
9 And He said, "Go, and [a]tell this people:

'Keep on hearing, but do not
understand;
Keep on seeing, but do not perceive.'

10 "Make [a]the heart of this people dull,
And their ears heavy,
And shut their eyes;
[b]Lest they see with their eyes,
And hear with their ears,
And understand with their heart,
And return and be healed."

11 Then I said, "Lord, how long?"
And He answered:

[a]"Until the cities are laid waste and
without inhabitant,
The houses are without a man,
The land is utterly desolate,
12 [a]The LORD has removed men far away,
And the forsaken places *are* many in
the midst of the land.
13 But yet a tenth *will be* in it,
And will return and be for consuming,
As a terebinth tree or as an oak,
Whose stump *remains* when it is cut
down.
So [a]the holy seed *shall be* its stump."

Isaiah Sent to King Ahaz

7 Now it came to pass in the days of [a]Ahaz
the son of Jotham, the son of Uzziah, king
of Judah, *that* Rezin king of Syria and Pekah
the son of Remaliah, king of Israel, went up
to Jerusalem to *make* war against [b]it, but
could not prevail against it. 2 And it was told
to the house of David, saying, "Syria's forces
are deployed in Ephraim." So his heart and
the heart of his people were moved as the
trees of the woods are moved with the wind.
3 Then the LORD said to Isaiah, "Go out
now to meet Ahaz, you and Shear-Jashub[1]
your son, at the end of the aqueduct from
the upper pool, on the highway to the Fuller's Field, 4 and say to him: 'Take heed, and
be [a]quiet; do not fear or be fainthearted for
these two stubs of smoking firebrands, for
the fierce anger of Rezin and Syria, and the
son of Remaliah. 5 Because Syria, Ephraim,
and the son of Remaliah have plotted evil
against you, saying, 6 "Let us go up against
Judah and trouble it, and let us make a gap
in its wall for ourselves, and set a king over
them, the son of Tabel"— 7 thus says the Lord
GOD:

[a]"It shall not stand,
Nor shall it come to pass.
8 [a]For the head of Syria *is* Damascus,
And the head of Damascus *is* Rezin.
Within sixty-five years Ephraim will be
broken,
So that it will not *be* a people.
9 The head of Ephraim *is* Samaria,
And the head of Samaria *is* Remaliah's
son.
[a]If you will not believe,
Surely you shall not be established." ' "

The Immanuel Prophecy

10 Moreover the LORD spoke again to Ahaz,
saying, 11 [a]"Ask a sign for yourself from the
LORD your God; ask it either in the depth or
in the height above."
12 But Ahaz said, "I will not ask, nor will I
test the LORD!"
13 Then he said, "Hear now, O house of David! *Is it* a small thing for you to weary men,
but will you weary my God also? 14 Therefore
the Lord Himself will give you a sign: [a]Behold,
the virgin shall conceive and bear [b]a Son,
and shall call His name [c]Immanuel.[1] 15 Curds
and honey He shall eat, that He may know to
refuse the evil and choose the good. 16 [a]For
before the Child shall know to refuse the
evil and choose the good, the land that you
dread will be forsaken by [b]both her kings.
17 [a]The LORD will bring the king of Assyria
upon you and your people and your father's
house—days that have not come since the
day that [b]Ephraim departed from Judah."

18 And it shall come to pass in that day
That the LORD [a]will whistle for the fly
That *is* in the farthest part of the rivers
of Egypt,
And for the bee that *is* in the land of
Assyria.
19 They will come, and all of them will
rest
In the desolate valleys and in [a]the
clefts of the rocks,
And on all thorns and in all
pastures.

6:8 [a] Gen. 1:26 **6:9** [a] Matt. 13:14 **6:10** [a] Ps. 119:70 [b] Jer. 5:21 **6:11** [a] Mic. 3:12 **6:12** [a] 2 Kin. 25:21 **6:13** [a] Ezra 9:2 **7:1** [a] 2 Chr. 28 [b] 2 Kin. 16:5, 9 **7:3** [1] Literally *A Remnant Shall Return* **7:4** [a] Is. 30:15 **7:7** [a] Is. 8:10 **7:8** [a] 2 Sam. 8:6 **7:9** [a] 2 Chr. 20:20 **7:11** [a] Matt. 12:38 **7:14** [a] Matt. 1:23 [b] [Is. 9:6] [c] Is. 8:8, 10 [1] Literally *God-With-Us* **7:16** [a] Is. 8:4 [b] 2 Kin. 15:30 **7:17** [a] 2 Chr. 28:19, 20 [b] 1 Kin. 12:16 **7:18** [a] Is. 5:26 **7:19** [a] Jer. 16:16

20 In the same day the Lord will shave
with a [a]hired [b]razor,
With those from beyond the River,[1]
with the king of Assyria,
The head and the hair of the legs,
And will also remove the beard.

21 It shall be in that day
That a man will keep alive a young cow
and two sheep;
22 So it shall be, from the abundance of
milk they give,
That he will eat curds;
For curds and honey everyone will eat
who is left in the land.

23 It shall happen in that day,
That wherever there could be a
thousand vines
Worth a thousand *shekels* of silver,
[a]It will be for briers and thorns.
24 With arrows and bows *men* will come
there,
Because all the land will become briers
and thorns.

25 And to any hill which could be dug with
the hoe,
You will not go there for fear of briers
and thorns;
But it will become a range for oxen
And a place for sheep to roam.

Assyria Will Invade the Land

8 Moreover the LORD said to me, "Take a
large scroll, and [a]write on it with a man's
pen concerning Maher-Shalal-Hash-Baz.[1]
2 And I will take for Myself faithful witnesses
to record, [a]Uriah the priest and Zechariah
the son of Jeberechiah."
3 Then I went to the prophetess, and she
conceived and bore a son. Then the LORD said
to me, "Call his name Maher-Shalal-Hash-Baz;
4 [a]for before the child shall have knowledge
to cry 'My father' and 'My mother,' [b]the riches
of Damascus and the spoil of Samaria will
be taken away before the king of Assyria."
5 The LORD also spoke to me again, saying:

6 "Inasmuch as these people refused
The waters of [a]Shiloah that flow
softly,
And rejoice [b]in Rezin and in Remaliah's
son;
7 Now therefore, behold, the Lord brings
up over them
The waters of the River,[1] strong and
mighty—
The king of Assyria and all his glory;
He will go up over all his channels
And go over all his banks.
8 He will pass through Judah,
He will overflow and pass over,
[a]He will reach up to the neck;
And the stretching out of his wings
Will fill the breadth of Your land,
O [b]Immanuel.[1]

9 "Be[a] shattered, O you peoples, and be
broken in pieces!
Give ear, all you from far countries.
Gird yourselves, but be broken in pieces;
Gird yourselves, but be broken in pieces.
10 [a]Take counsel together, but it will come
to nothing;
Speak the word, [b]but it will not stand,
[c]For God *is* with us."[1]

Fear God, Heed His Word

11 For the LORD spoke thus to me with a
strong hand, and instructed me that I should
not walk in the way of this people, saying:

12 "Do not say, 'A conspiracy,'
Concerning all that this people call a
conspiracy,
Nor be afraid of their threats, nor be
troubled.
13 The LORD of hosts, Him you shall hallow;
Let Him *be* your fear,
And *let* Him *be* your dread.
14 [a]He will be as a sanctuary,
But [b]a stone of stumbling and a rock of
offense
To both the houses of Israel,
As a trap and a snare to the inhabitants
of Jerusalem.
15 And many among them shall [a]stumble;
They shall fall and be broken,
Be snared and taken."

16 Bind up the testimony,
Seal the law among my disciples.
17 And I will wait on the LORD,
Who [a]hides His face from the house of
Jacob;
And I [b]will hope in Him.
18 [a]Here am I and the children whom the
LORD has given me!
We [b]are for signs and wonders in Israel
From the LORD of hosts,
Who dwells in Mount Zion.

7:20 [a] Is. 10:5, 15 [b] 2 Kin. 16:7 [1] That is, the Euphrates **7:23** [a] Is. 5:6 **8:1** [a] Hab. 2:2 [1] Literally *Speed the Spoil, Hasten the Booty* **8:2** [a] 2 Kin. 16:10 **8:4** [a] 2 Kin. 17:6; Is. 7:16 [b] 2 Kin. 15:29 **8:6** [a] John 9:7 [b] Is. 7:1, 2 **8:7** [1] That is, the Euphrates **8:8** [a] Is. 30:28 [b] Is. 7:14 [1] Literally *God-With-Us* **8:9** [a] Joel 3:9 **8:10** [a] Is. 7:7 [b] Is. 7:14 [c] Rom. 8:31 [1] Hebrew *Immanuel* **8:14** [a] Ezek. 11:16 [b] Luke 2:34; 20:17 **8:15** [a] Matt. 21:44 **8:17** [a] Is. 54:8 [b] Hab. 2:3 **8:18** [a] Heb. 2:13 [b] Ps. 71:7

19 And when they say to you, [a]"Seek those
who are mediums and wizards, [b]who whisper
and mutter," should not a people seek their
God? *Should they* [c]*seek* the dead on behalf of
the living? 20 [a]To the law and to the testimony!
If they do not speak according to this word,
it is because [b]*there is* no light in them.

21 They will pass through it hard-pressed
and hungry; and it shall happen, when they
are hungry, that they will be enraged and
[a]curse their king and their God, and look
upward. 22 Then they will look to the earth,
and see trouble and darkness, gloom of anguish; and *they will be* driven into darkness.

The Government of the Promised Son

9 Nevertheless [a]the gloom *will* not *be*
upon her who *is* distressed,
As when at [b]first He lightly esteemed
The land of Zebulun and the land of
Naphtali,
And [c]afterward more heavily
oppressed *her*,
By the way of the sea, beyond the
Jordan,
In Galilee of the Gentiles.

2 [a]The people who walked in darkness
Have seen a great light;
Those who dwelt in the land of the
shadow of death,
Upon them a light has shined.

3 You have multiplied the nation
And increased its joy;[1]
They rejoice before You
According to the joy of harvest,
As *men* rejoice [a]when they divide the
spoil.

4 For You have broken the yoke of his
burden
And the staff of his shoulder,
The rod of his oppressor,
As in the day of [a]Midian.

5 For every warrior's sandal from the
noisy battle,
And garments rolled in blood,
[a]Will be used for burning *and* fuel of
fire.

6 [a]For unto us a Child is born,
Unto us a [b]Son is given;
And [c]the government will be upon His
shoulder.
And His name will be called
[d]Wonderful, Counselor, [e]Mighty God,
Everlasting Father, [f]Prince of Peace.

8:19 [a] 1 Sam. 28:8 [b] Is. 29:4 [c] Ps. 106:28 **8:20** [a] Luke 16:29 [b] Mic. 3:6 **8:21** [a] Rev. 16:11 **9:1** [a] Is. 8:22 [b] 2 Kin. 15:29 [c] Matt. 4:13–16 **9:2** [a] Matt. 4:16 **9:3** [a] Judg. 5:30 [1] Following Qere and Targum; Kethib and Vulgate read *not increased joy;* Septuagint reads *Most of the people You brought down in Your joy.* **9:4** [a] Judg. 7:22 **9:5** [a] Is. 66:15 **9:6** [a] [Luke 2:11] [b] [John 3:16] [c] [Matt. 28:18] [d] Judg. 13:18 [e] Titus 2:13 [f] Eph. 2:14

THE PRINCE OF PEACE

For unto us a Child is born . . . And His name will be called Wonderful, Counselor, Mighty God, Everlasting Father, Prince of Peace.

ISAIAH 9:6

We have here what may be the single most important prophecy in the Bible. Much of the Book of Isaiah is comprised of oracles of judgment and woe. The book begins by comparing Judah and Jerusalem to an injured man in need of medical attention. In chapter 6 the prophet described his amazing vision of God in the temple. Unfortunately the scene ended on a note of judgment with God telling Isaiah that only a remnant of His people would survive. In chapter 7 the faithless King Ahaz was warned that if he had no faith in the Lord, his throne would not be established. In contrast to the faithlessness of Ahaz is the future King whose "name will be called Wonderful, Counselor, Mighty God, Everlasting Father, Prince of Peace" (9:6). The kingdom that He will establish will never end.

It is very significant that the promised Messiah is called "Prince of *Peace*." He is not the Prince of War or the Prince of Judgment. No, He is the Prince who will bring about a full and lasting peace in the truest sense of this important word. You can begin living in the everlasting peace provided by the Messiah of Peace right now by appropriating this verse in faith: "Lord Jesus, you are the Prince of Peace and I desire today to have Your peace in my life in fresh ways. In Your name I pray, amen."

PEACE NOTE

Shalom originates from God Himself and epitomizes the gospel and the active relationship God initiates, pursues, and perfects with each of us as His followers.

ISAIAH 9:6

7 Of the increase of *His* government and
peace
[a]*There will be* no end,
Upon the throne of David and over His
kingdom,
To order it and establish it with
judgment and justice
From that time forward, even forever.
The [b]zeal of the LORD of hosts will
perform this.

The Punishment of Samaria

8 The Lord sent a word against [a]Jacob,
And it has fallen on Israel.
9 All the people will know—
Ephraim and the inhabitant of Samaria—
Who say in pride and arrogance of heart:
10 "The bricks have fallen down,
But we will rebuild with hewn stones;
The sycamores are cut down,
But we will replace *them* with cedars."
11 Therefore the LORD shall set up
The adversaries of Rezin against him,
And spur his enemies on,
12 The Syrians before and the Philistines
behind;
And they shall devour Israel with an
open mouth.

For all this His anger is not turned away,
But His hand *is* stretched out still.

13 For the people do not turn to Him who
strikes them,
Nor do they seek the LORD of hosts.
14 Therefore the LORD will cut off head
and tail from Israel,
Palm branch and bulrush [a]in one day.
15 The elder and honorable, he *is* the head;
The prophet who teaches lies, he *is* the
tail.
16 For [a]the leaders of this people cause
them to err,
And *those who are* led by them are
destroyed.
17 Therefore the Lord [a]will have no joy in
their young men,
Nor have mercy on their fatherless and
widows;
For everyone *is* a hypocrite and an
evildoer,
And every mouth speaks folly.

[b]For all this His anger is not turned
away,
But His hand *is* stretched out still.

18 For wickedness [a]burns as the fire;
It shall devour the briers and thorns,
And kindle in the thickets of the forest;
They shall mount up *like* rising smoke.
19 Through the wrath of the LORD of hosts
[a]The land is burned up,
And the people shall be as fuel for the
fire;
[b]No man shall spare his brother.
20 And he shall snatch on the right hand
And be hungry;
He shall devour on the left hand
[a]And not be satisfied;
[b]Every man shall eat the flesh of his
own arm.
21 Manasseh *shall devour* Ephraim, and
Ephraim Manasseh;
Together they *shall be* [a]against Judah.

[b]For all this His anger is not turned
away,
But His hand *is* stretched out still.

10 "Woe to those who [a]decree
unrighteous decrees,
Who write misfortune,
Which they have prescribed
2 To rob the needy of justice,
And to take what is right from the poor
of My people,
That widows may be their prey,
And *that* they may rob the fatherless.
3 [a]What will you do in [b]the day of
punishment,
And in the desolation *which* will come
from [c]afar?
To whom will you flee for help?
And where will you leave your glory?

9:7 [a] Dan. 2:44 [b] Is. 37:32 9:8 [a] Gen. 32:28 9:14 [a] Rev. 18:8 9:16 [a] Is. 3:12 9:17 [a] Ps. 147:10 [b] Is. 5:25 9:18 [a] Mal. 4:1 9:19 [a] Is. 8:22 [b] Mic. 7:2, 6 9:20 [a] Lev. 26:26 [b] Jer. 19:9 9:21 [a] 2 Chr. 28:6, 8 [b] Is. 9:12, 17 10:1 [a] Ps. 58:2 10:3 [a] Job 31:14 [b] Hos. 9:7 [c] Is. 5:26

4 Without Me they shall bow down
among the [a]prisoners,
And they shall fall among the slain."

[b]For all this His anger is not turned away,
But His hand *is* stretched out still.

Arrogant Assyria Also Judged

5 "Woe to Assyria, [a]the rod of My anger
And the staff in whose hand is My
indignation.
6 I will send him against [a]an ungodly
nation,
And against the people of My wrath
I will [b]give him charge,
To seize the spoil, to take the prey,
And to tread them down like the mire
of the streets.
7 [a]Yet he does not mean so,
Nor does his heart think so;
But *it is* in his heart to destroy,
And cut off not a few nations.
8 [a]For he says,
'*Are* not my princes altogether kings?
9 *Is* not [a]Calno [b]like Carchemish?
Is not Hamath like Arpad?
Is not Samaria [c]like Damascus?
10 As my hand has found the kingdoms of
the idols,
Whose carved images excelled those of
Jerusalem and Samaria,
11 As I have done to Samaria and her
idols,
Shall I not do also to Jerusalem and
her idols?' "

12 Therefore it shall come to pass, when the
Lord has performed all His work [a]on Mount
Zion and on Jerusalem, *that He will say,* [b]"I
will punish the fruit of the arrogant heart
of the king of Assyria, and the glory of his
haughty looks."
13 [a]For he says:

"By the strength of my hand I have
done *it,*
And by my wisdom, for I am prudent;
Also I have removed the boundaries of
the people,
And have robbed their treasuries;
So I have put down the inhabitants like
a valiant *man.*
14 [a]My hand has found like a nest the
riches of the people,
And as one gathers eggs *that are* left,
I have gathered all the earth;
And there was no one who moved *his*
wing,
Nor opened *his* mouth with even a peep."

15 Shall [a]the ax boast itself against him
who chops with it?
Or shall the saw exalt itself against him
who saws with it?
As if a rod could wield *itself* against
those who lift it up,
Or as if a staff could lift up, *as if it were*
not wood!
16 Therefore the Lord, the Lord[1] of hosts,
Will send leanness among his fat ones;
And under his glory
He will kindle a burning
Like the burning of a fire.
17 So the Light of Israel will be for a fire,
And his Holy One for a flame;
[a]It will burn and devour
His thorns and his briers in one day.
18 And it will consume the glory of his
forest and of [a]his fruitful field,
Both soul and body;
And they will be as when a sick man
wastes away.
19 Then the rest of the trees of his forest
Will be so few in number
That a child may write them.

The Returning Remnant of Israel

20 And it shall come to pass in that day
That the remnant of Israel,
And such as have escaped of the house
of Jacob,
[a]Will never again depend on him who
defeated them,
But will depend on the LORD, the Holy
One of Israel, in truth.
21 The remnant will return, the remnant
of Jacob,
To the [a]Mighty God.
22 [a]For though your people, O Israel, be as
the sand of the sea,
[b]A remnant of them will return;
The destruction decreed shall overflow
with righteousness.
23 [a]For the Lord GOD of hosts
Will make a determined end
In the midst of all the land.

24 Therefore thus says the Lord GOD of
hosts: "O My people, who dwell in Zion, [a]do
not be afraid of the Assyrian. He shall strike
you with a rod and lift up his staff against
you, in the manner of [b]Egypt. 25 For yet a very

10:4 [a] Is. 24:22 [b] Is. 5:25 **10:5** [a] Jer. 51:20 **10:6** [a] Is. 9:17 [b] Jer. 34:22 **10:7** [a] Gen. 50:20 **10:8** [a] 2 Kin. 19:10 **10:9** [a] Amos 6:2 [b] 2 Chr. 35:20 [c] 2 Kin. 16:9 **10:12** [a] 2 Kin. 19:31 [b] Jer. 50:18 **10:13** [a] Is. 37:24–27 **10:14** [a] Job 31:25 **10:15** [a] Jer. 51:20 **10:16** [1] Following Bomberg; Masoretic Text and Dead Sea Scrolls read *YHWH* (*the LORD*). **10:17** [a] Is. 9:18 **10:18** [a] 2 Kin. 19:23 **10:20** [a] 2 Kin. 16:7 **10:21** [a] [Is. 9:6] **10:22** [a] Rom. 9:27, 28 [b] Is. 6:13 **10:23** [a] Dan. 9:27 **10:24** [a] Is. 7:4; 12:2 [b] Ex. 14

little while [a]and the indignation will cease,
as will My anger in their destruction." 26 And
the LORD of hosts will stir up [a]a scourge for
him like the slaughter of [b]Midian at the rock
of Oreb; [c]*as* His rod was on the sea, so will He
lift it up in the manner of Egypt.

27 It shall come to pass in that day
That his burden will be taken away
from your shoulder,
And his yoke from your neck,
And the yoke will be destroyed because
of [a]the anointing oil.

28 He has come to Aiath,
He has passed Migron;
At Michmash he has attended to his
equipment.
29 They have gone along [a]the ridge,
They have taken up lodging at Geba.
Ramah is afraid,
[b]Gibeah of Saul has fled.
30 Lift up your voice,
O daughter [a]of Gallim!
Cause it to be heard as far as [b]Laish—
O poor Anathoth![1]
31 [a]Madmenah has fled,
The inhabitants of Gebim seek refuge.
32 As yet he will remain [a]at Nob that day;
He will [b]shake his fist at the mount of
[c]the daughter of Zion,
The hill of Jerusalem.

33 Behold, the Lord,
The LORD of hosts,
Will lop off the bough with terror;
[a]Those of high stature *will be* hewn
down,
And the haughty will be humbled.
34 He will cut down the thickets of the
forest with iron,
And Lebanon will fall by the Mighty
One.

The Reign of Jesse's Offspring

11 There [a]shall come forth a Rod from
the stem of [b]Jesse,
And [c]a Branch shall grow out of his
roots.
2 [a]The Spirit of the LORD shall rest upon
Him,
The Spirit of wisdom and
understanding,
The Spirit of counsel and might,
The Spirit of knowledge and of the fear
of the LORD.

PEACE NOTE

Jesus' followers will face tribulation. The world will turn against them even as it turned against Jesus Himself.

3 His delight *is* in the fear of the LORD,
And He shall not judge by the sight of
His eyes,
Nor decide by the hearing of His ears;
4 But [a]with righteousness He shall judge
the poor,
And decide with equity for the meek of
the earth;
He shall [b]strike the earth with the rod
of His mouth,
And with the breath of His lips He shall
slay the wicked.
5 Righteousness shall be the belt of His
loins,
And faithfulness the belt of His waist.

6 "The[a] wolf also shall dwell with the
lamb,
The leopard shall lie down with the
young goat,
The calf and the young lion and the
fatling together;
And a little child shall lead them.
7 The cow and the bear shall graze;
Their young ones shall lie down
together;
And the lion shall eat straw like
the ox.
8 The nursing child shall play by the
cobra's hole,
And the weaned child shall put his
hand in the viper's den.
9 [a]They shall not hurt nor destroy in all
My holy mountain,
For [b]the earth shall be full of the
knowledge of the LORD
As the waters cover the sea.

10:25 [a] Dan. 11:36 10:26 [a] 2 Kin. 19:35 [b] Is. 9:4 [c] Ex. 14:26, 27 10:27 [a] Ps. 105:15 10:29 [a] 1 Sam. 13:23 [b] 1 Sam. 11:4 10:30 [a] 1 Sam. 25:44 [b] Judg. 18:7 [1] Following Masoretic Text, Targum, and Vulgate; Septuagint and Syriac read *Listen to her, O Anathoth.* 10:31 [a] Josh. 15:31 10:32 [a] 1 Sam. 21:1 [b] Is. 13:2 [c] Is. 37:22 10:33 [a] Amos 2:9 11:1 [a] [Zech. 6:12] [b] [Acts 13:23] [c] Is. 4:2 11:2 [a] [John 1:32] 11:4 [a] Rev. 19:11 [b] Job 4:9 11:6 [a] Hos. 2:18 11:9 [a] Job 5:23 [b] Hab. 2:14

10 "And[a] in that day [b]there shall be a Root
of Jesse,
Who shall stand as a [c]banner to the
people;
For the [d]Gentiles shall seek Him,
And His resting place shall be glorious."

11 It shall come to pass in that day
That the Lord shall set His hand again
the second time
To recover the remnant of His people
who are left,
[a]From Assyria and Egypt,
From Pathros and Cush,
From Elam and Shinar,
From Hamath and the islands of the sea.

12 He will set up a banner for the nations,
And will assemble the outcasts of Israel,
And gather together [a]the dispersed of
Judah
From the four corners of the earth.
13 Also [a]the envy of Ephraim shall depart,
And the adversaries of Judah shall be
cut off;
Ephraim shall not envy Judah,
And Judah shall not harass Ephraim.
14 But they shall fly down upon the
shoulder of the Philistines toward
the west;
Together they shall plunder the people
of the East;
[a]They shall lay their hand on Edom and
Moab;
And the people of Ammon shall obey
them.
15 The LORD [a]will utterly destroy[1] the
tongue of the Sea of Egypt;
With His mighty wind He will shake
His fist over the River,[2]
And strike it in the seven streams,
And make *men* cross over dry-shod.
16 [a]There will be a highway for the
remnant of His people
Who will be left from Assyria,
[b]As it was for Israel
In the day that he came up from the
land of Egypt.

A Hymn of Praise

12 And [a]in that day you will say:

"O LORD, I will praise You;
Though You were angry with me,
Your anger is turned away, and You
comfort me.
2 Behold, God *is* my salvation,
I will trust and not be afraid;
[a]'For [b]YAH, the LORD, *is* my strength and
song;
He also has become my salvation.' "[1]

3 Therefore with joy you will draw [a]water
From the wells of salvation.

4 And in that day you will say:

[a]"Praise the LORD, call upon His name;
[b]Declare His deeds among the peoples,
Make mention that His [c]name is exalted.
5 [a]Sing to the LORD,
For He has done excellent things;
This *is* known in all the earth.
6 [a]Cry out and shout, O inhabitant of Zion,
For great *is* [b]the Holy One of Israel in
your midst!"

Proclamation Against Babylon

13 The [a]burden against Babylon which
Isaiah the son of Amoz saw.

2 "Lift[a] up a banner [b]on the high
mountain,
Raise your voice to them;
[c]Wave your hand, that they may enter
the gates of the nobles.
3 I have commanded My sanctified ones;
I have also called [a]My mighty ones for
My anger—
Those who [b]rejoice in My exaltation."

4 The [a]noise of a multitude in the
mountains,
Like that of many people!
A tumultuous noise of the kingdoms of
nations gathered together!
The LORD of hosts musters
The army for battle.
5 They come from a far country,
From the end of heaven—
The [a]LORD and His weapons of
indignation,
To destroy the whole [b]land.

6 Wail, [a]for the day of the LORD *is* at
hand!
[b]It will come as destruction from the
Almighty.

11:10 [a] Is. 2:11 [b] Rom. 15:12 [c] Is. 27:12, 13 [d] Rom. 15:10 **11:11** [a] Zech. 10:10 **11:12** [a] John 7:35 **11:13** [a] Jer. 3:18 **11:14** [a] Dan. 11:41 **11:15** [a] Zech. 10:10, 11 [1] Following Masoretic Text and Vulgate; Septuagint, Syriac, and Targum read *dry up*. [2] That is, the Euphrates **11:16** [a] Is. 19:23 [b] Ex. 14:29 **12:1** [a] Is. 2:11 **12:2** [a] Ps. 83:18 [b] Ex. 15:2 [1] Exodus 15:2 **12:3** [a] [John 4:10, 14; 7:37, 38] **12:4** [a] 1 Chr. 16:8 [b] Ps. 145:4–6 [c] Ps. 34:3 **12:5** [a] Ex. 15:1 **12:6** [a] Zeph. 3:14, 15 [b] Ps. 89:18 **13:1** [a] Jer. 50; 51 **13:2** [a] Is. 18:3 [b] Jer. 51:25 [c] Is. 10:32 **13:3** [a] Joel 3:11 [b] Ps. 149:2 **13:4** [a] Is. 17:12 **13:5** [a] Is. 42:13 [b] Is. 24:1; 34:2 **13:6** [a] Zeph. 1:7 [b] Joel 1:15

7 Therefore all hands will be limp,
Every man's heart will melt,
8 And they will be afraid.
[a]Pangs and sorrows will take hold of *them;*
They will be in pain as a woman in
childbirth;
They will be amazed at one another;
Their faces *will be like* flames.

9 Behold, [a]the day of the LORD comes,
Cruel, with both wrath and fierce anger,
To lay the land desolate;
And He will destroy [b]its sinners from it.
10 For the stars of heaven and their
constellations
Will not give their light;
The sun will be [a]darkened in its going
forth,
And the moon will not cause its light to
shine.

11 "I will [a]punish the world for *its* evil,
And the wicked for their iniquity;
[b]I will halt the arrogance of the proud,
And will lay low the haughtiness of the
terrible.
12 I will make a mortal more rare than
fine gold,
A man more than the golden wedge of
Ophir.
13 [a]Therefore I will shake the heavens,
And the earth will move out of her place,
In the wrath of the LORD of hosts
And in [b]the day of His fierce anger.
14 It shall be as the hunted gazelle,
And as a sheep that no man takes up;
[a]Every man will turn to his own people,
And everyone will flee to his own land.
15 Everyone who is found will be thrust
through,
And everyone who is captured will fall
by the sword.
16 Their children also will be [a]dashed to
pieces before their eyes;
Their houses will be plundered
And their wives [b]ravished.

17 "Behold,[a] I will stir up the Medes against
them,
Who will not regard silver;
And *as for* gold, they will not delight in it.
18 Also *their* bows will dash the young
men to pieces,
And they will have no pity on the fruit
of the womb;
Their eye will not spare children.
19 [a]And Babylon, the glory of kingdoms,
The beauty of the Chaldeans' pride,
Will be as when God overthrew [b]Sodom
and Gomorrah.
20 [a]It will never be inhabited,
Nor will it be settled from generation to
generation;
Nor will the Arabian pitch tents there,
Nor will the shepherds make their
sheepfolds there.
21 [a]But wild beasts of the desert will lie
there,
And their houses will be full of owls;
Ostriches will dwell there,
And wild goats will caper there.
22 The hyenas will howl in their citadels,
And jackals in their pleasant palaces.
[a]Her time *is* near to come,
And her days will not be prolonged."

Mercy on Jacob

14 For the LORD [a]will have mercy on Jacob,
and [b]will still choose Israel, and settle
them in their own land. [c]The strangers will
be joined with them, and they will cling to
the house of Jacob. 2 Then people will take
them [a]and bring them to their place, and the
house of Israel will possess them for servants
and maids in the land of the LORD; they will
take them captive whose captives they were,
[b]and rule over their oppressors.

Fall of the King of Babylon

3 It shall come to pass in the day the LORD
gives you rest from your sorrow, and from
your fear and the hard bondage in which
you were made to serve, 4 that you [a]will take

PEACE NOTE

Isaiah predicted Judah's fall to a foreign power due to sin. The prediction included the later promise of inevitable rest. We can have peace even when we endure the Lord's discipline.

ISAIAH 14:3

13:8 [a] Ps. 48:6 13:9 [a] Mal. 4:1 [b] Prov. 2:22 13:10 [a] Joel 2:31 13:11 [a] Is. 26:21 [b] [Is. 2:17] 13:13 [a] Hag. 2:6 [b] Lam. 1:12 13:14 [a] Jer. 50:16; 51:9 13:16 [a] Nah. 3:10 [b] Zech. 14:2 13:17 [a] Dan. 5:28, 31 13:19 [a] Is. 14:4 [b] Gen. 19:24 13:20 [a] Jer. 50:3 13:21 [a] Is. 34:11–15 13:22 [a] Jer. 51:33 14:1 [a] Ps. 102:13 [b] Zech. 1:17; 2:12 [c] Is. 60:4, 5, 10 14:2 [a] Is. 49:22; 60:9; 66:20 [b] Is. 60:14 14:4 [a] Hab. 2:6

up this proverb against the king of Babylon,
and say:

"How the oppressor has ceased,
The [b]golden[1] city ceased!
5 The LORD has broken [a]the staff of the wicked,
The scepter of the rulers;
6 He who struck the people in wrath with a continual stroke,
He who ruled the nations in anger,
Is persecuted *and* no one hinders.
7 The whole earth is at rest *and* quiet;
They break forth into singing.
8 [a]Indeed the cypress trees rejoice over you,
And the cedars of Lebanon,
Saying, 'Since you were cut down,
No woodsman has come up against us.'

9 "Hell[a] from beneath is excited about you,
To meet *you* at your coming;
It stirs up the dead for you,
All the chief ones of the earth;
It has raised up from their thrones
All the kings of the nations.
10 They all shall [a]speak and say to you:
'Have you also become as weak as we?
Have you become like us?
11 Your pomp is brought down to Sheol,
And the sound of your stringed instruments;
The maggot is spread under you,
And worms cover you.'

The Fall of Lucifer

12 "How[a] you are fallen from heaven,
O Lucifer,[1] son of the morning!
How you are cut down to the ground,
You who weakened the nations!
13 For you have said in your heart:
[a]'I will ascend into heaven,
[b]I will exalt my throne above the stars of God;
I will also sit on the [c]mount of the congregation
[d]On the farthest sides of the north;
14 I will ascend above the heights of the clouds,
[a]I will be like the Most High.'
15 Yet you [a]shall be brought down to Sheol,
To the lowest depths of the Pit.

16 "Those who see you will gaze at you,
And consider you, *saying:*
'*Is* this the man who made the earth tremble,
Who shook kingdoms,
17 Who made the world as a wilderness
And destroyed its cities,
Who did not open the house of his prisoners?'

18 "All the kings of the nations,
All of them, sleep in glory,
Everyone in his own house;
19 But you are cast out of your grave
Like an abominable branch,
Like the garment of those who are slain,
Thrust through with a sword,
Who go down to the stones of the pit,
Like a corpse trodden underfoot.
20 You will not be joined with them in burial,
Because you have destroyed your land
And slain your people.
[a]The brood of evildoers shall never be named.
21 Prepare slaughter for his children
[a]Because of the iniquity of their fathers,
Lest they rise up and possess the land,
And fill the face of the world with cities."

Babylon Destroyed

22 "For I will rise up against them," says the LORD of hosts,
"And cut off from Babylon [a]the name and [b]remnant,
[c]And offspring and posterity," says the LORD.
23 "I will also make it a possession for the [a]porcupine,
And marshes of muddy water;
I will sweep it with the broom of destruction," says the LORD of hosts.

Assyria Destroyed

24 The LORD of hosts has sworn, saying,
"Surely, as I have thought, so it shall come to pass,
And as I have purposed, *so* it shall [a]stand:
25 That I will break the [a]Assyrian in My land,
And on My mountains tread him underfoot.
Then [b]his yoke shall be removed from them,
And his burden removed from their shoulders.
26 This *is* the [a]purpose that is purposed against the whole earth,

14:4 [b] Rev. 18:16 [1] Or *insolent* 14:5 [a] Ps. 125:3 14:8 [a] Ezek. 31:16 14:9 [a] Ezek. 32:21 14:10 [a] Ezek. 32:21 14:12 [a] Is. 34:4 [1] Literally *Day Star* 14:13 [a] Ezek. 28:2 [b] Dan. 8:10 [c] Ezek. 28:14 [d] Ps. 48:2 14:14 [a] 2 Thess. 2:4 14:15 [a] Matt. 11:23 14:20 [a] Ps. 21:10; 109:13 14:21 [a] Ex. 20:5 14:22 [a] Prov. 10:7 [b] 1 Kin. 14:10 [c] Job 18:19 14:23 [a] Zeph. 2:14 14:24 [a] Is. 43:13 14:25 [a] Mic. 5:5, 6 [b] Is. 10:27 14:26 [a] Is. 23:9

And this *is* the hand that is stretched
out over all the nations.
27 For the LORD of hosts has [a]purposed,
And who will annul *it?*
His hand *is* stretched out,
And who will turn it back?"

Philistia Destroyed

28 This is the burden which came in the
year that [a]King Ahaz died.

29 "Do not rejoice, all you of Philistia,
[a]Because the rod that struck you is broken;
For out of the serpent's roots will come
forth a viper,
[b]And its offspring *will be* a fiery flying
serpent.
30 The firstborn of the poor will feed,
And the needy will lie down in safety;
I will kill your roots with famine,
And it will slay your remnant.
31 Wail, O gate! Cry, O city!
All you of Philistia *are* dissolved;
For smoke will come from the north,
And no one *will be* alone in his
appointed times."

32 What will they answer the messengers
of the nation?
That [a]the LORD has founded Zion,
And [b]the poor of His people shall take
refuge in it.

Proclamation Against Moab

15 The [a]burden against Moab.

Because in the night [b]Ar of [c]Moab is
laid waste
And destroyed,
Because in the night Kir of Moab is laid
waste
And destroyed,
2 He has gone up to the temple[1] and Dibon,
To the high places to weep.
Moab will wail over Nebo and over
Medeba;
[a]On all their heads *will be* baldness,
And every beard cut off.
3 In their streets they will clothe
themselves with sackcloth;
On the tops of their houses
And in their streets
Everyone will wail, [a]weeping bitterly.
4 Heshbon and Elealeh will cry out,
Their voice shall be heard as far as [a]Jahaz;
Therefore the armed soldiers[1] of Moab
will cry out;
His life will be burdensome to him.

5 "My[a] heart will cry out for Moab;
His fugitives *shall flee* to Zoar,
Like a three-year-old heifer.[1]
For [b]by the Ascent of Luhith
They will go up with weeping;
For in the way of Horonaim
They will raise up a cry of destruction,
6 For the waters [a]of Nimrim will be desolate,
For the green grass has withered away;
The grass fails, there is nothing green.
7 Therefore the abundance they have
gained,
And what they have laid up,
They will carry away to the Brook of the
Willows.
8 For the cry has gone all around the
borders of Moab,
Its wailing to Eglaim
And its wailing to Beer Elim.
9 For the waters of Dimon[1] will be full of
blood;
Because I will bring more upon Dimon,[2]
[a]Lions upon him who escapes from Moab,
And on the remnant of the land."

Moab Destroyed

16 Send [a]the lamb to the ruler of the
land,
[b]From Sela to the wilderness,
To the mount of the daughter of Zion.
2 For it shall be as a [a]wandering bird
thrown out of the nest;
So shall be the daughters of Moab at
the fords of the [b]Arnon.

3 "Take counsel, execute judgment;
Make your shadow like the night in the
middle of the day;
Hide the outcasts,
Do not betray him who escapes.
4 Let My outcasts dwell with you, O Moab;
Be a shelter to them from the face of
the spoiler.
For the extortioner is at an end,
Devastation ceases,
The oppressors are consumed out of
the land.

14:27 [a] Dan. 4:31, 35 **14:28** [a] 2 Kin. 16:20 **14:29** [a] 2 Chr. 26:6 [b] 2 Kin. 18:8 **14:32** [a] Ps. 87:1, 5 [b] Zech. 11:11
15:1 [a] 2 Kin. 3:4 [b] Deut. 2:9 [c] Amos 2:1–3 **15:2** [a] Lev. 21:5 [1] Hebrew *bayith,* literally *house* **15:3** [a] Jer. 48:38
15:4 [a] Jer. 48:34 [1] Following Masoretic Text, Targum, and Vulgate; Septuagint and Syriac read *loins.* **15:5** [a] Jer. 48:31
[b] Jer. 48:5 [1] Or *The Third Eglath,* an unknown city (compare Jeremiah 48:34) **15:6** [a] Num. 32:36 **15:9** [a] 2 Kin. 17:25
[1] Following Masoretic Text and Targum; Dead Sea Scrolls and Vulgate read *Dibon;* Septuagint reads *Rimon.* [2] Following
Masoretic Text and Targum; Dead Sea Scrolls and Vulgate read *Dibon;* Septuagint reads *Rimon.* **16:1** [a] 2 Kin. 3:4
[b] 2 Kin. 14:7 **16:2** [a] Prov. 27:8 [b] Num. 21:13

5 In mercy [a]the throne will be established;
And One will sit on it in truth, in the tabernacle of David,
[b]Judging and seeking justice and hastening [c]righteousness."

6 We have heard of the [a]pride of Moab—
He is very proud—
Of his haughtiness and his pride and his wrath;
[b]*But* his lies *shall* not *be* so.
7 Therefore Moab shall [a]wail for Moab;
Everyone shall wail.
For the foundations [b]of Kir Hareseth you shall mourn;
Surely *they are* stricken.

8 For [a]the fields of Heshbon languish,
And [b]the vine of Sibmah;
The lords of the nations have broken down its choice plants,
Which have reached to Jazer
And wandered through the wilderness.
Her branches are stretched out,
They are gone over the [c]sea.
9 Therefore I will bewail the vine of Sibmah,
With the weeping of Jazer;
I will drench you with my tears,
[a]O Heshbon and Elealeh;
For battle cries have fallen
Over your summer fruits and your harvest.

10 [a]Gladness is taken away,
And joy from the plentiful field;
In the vineyards there will be no singing,
Nor will there be shouting;
No treaders will tread out wine in the presses;
I have made their shouting cease.
11 Therefore [a]my heart shall resound like a harp for Moab,
And my inner being for Kir Heres.

12 And it shall come to pass,
When it is seen that Moab is weary on [a]the high place,
That he will come to his sanctuary to pray;
But he will not prevail.

13 This *is* the word which the LORD has spoken
concerning Moab since that time. 14 But now the
LORD has spoken, saying, "Within three years,
[a]as the years of a hired man, the glory of Moab
will be despised with all that great multitude,
and the remnant *will be* very small *and* feeble."

Proclamation Against Syria and Israel

17 The [a]burden against Damascus.

"Behold, Damascus will cease from *being* a city,
And it will be a ruinous heap.
2 The cities of [a]Aroer *are* forsaken;[1]
They will be for flocks
Which lie down, and [b]no one will make *them* afraid.
3 [a]The fortress also will cease from Ephraim,
The kingdom from Damascus,
And the remnant of Syria;
They will be as the glory of the children of Israel,"
Says the LORD of hosts.

4 "In that day it shall come to pass
That the glory of Jacob will wane,
And [a]the fatness of his flesh grow lean.
5 [a]It shall be as when the harvester gathers the grain,
And reaps the heads with his arm;
It shall be as he who gathers heads of grain
In the Valley of Rephaim.
6 [a]Yet gleaning grapes will be left in it,
Like the shaking of an olive tree,
Two *or* three olives at the top of the uppermost bough,
Four *or* five in its most fruitful branches,"
Says the LORD God of Israel.

7 In that day a man will [a]look to his Maker,
And his eyes will have respect for the Holy One of Israel.
8 He will not look to the altars,
The work of his hands;
He will not respect what his [a]fingers have made,
Nor the wooden images[1] nor the incense altars.

9 In that day his strong cities will be as a forsaken bough[1]
And an uppermost branch,[2]
Which they left because of the children of Israel;
And there will be desolation.

16:5 [a] [Dan. 7:14] [b] Ps. 72:2 [c] Is. 9:7 16:6 [a] Jer. 48:29 [b] Is. 28:15 16:7 [a] Jer. 48:20 [b] 2 Kin. 3:25 16:8 [a] Is. 24:7 [b] Is. 16:9 [c] Jer. 48:32 16:9 [a] Is. 15:4 16:10 [a] Is. 24:8 16:11 [a] Jer. 48:36 16:12 [a] Is. 15:2 16:14 [a] Is. 21:16 17:1 [a] Zech. 9:1 17:2 [a] Num. 32:34 [b] Jer. 7:33 [1] Following Masoretic Text and Vulgate; Septuagint reads *It shall be forsaken forever;* Targum reads *Its cities shall be forsaken and desolate.* 17:3 [a] Is. 7:16; 8:4 17:4 [a] Is. 10:16 17:5 [a] Jer. 51:33 17:6 [a] Is. 24:13 17:7 [a] Mic. 7:7 17:8 [a] Is. 2:8; 31:7 [1] Hebrew *Asherim,* Canaanite deities 17:9 [1] Septuagint reads *Hivites;* Targum reads *laid waste;* Vulgate reads *as the plows.* [2] Septuagint reads *Amorites;* Targum reads *in ruins;* Vulgate reads *corn.*

10 Because you have forgotten [a]the God of
your salvation,
And have not been mindful of the Rock
of your stronghold,
Therefore you will plant pleasant plants
And set out foreign seedlings;
11 In the day you will make your plant to
grow,
And in the morning you will make your
seed to flourish;
But the harvest *will be* a heap of ruins
In the day of grief and desperate sorrow.

12 Woe to the multitude of many people
Who make a noise [a]like the roar of the
seas,
And to the rushing of nations
That make a rushing like the rushing of
mighty waters!
13 The nations will rush like the rushing
of many waters;
But *God* will [a]rebuke them and they will
flee far away,
And [b]be chased like the chaff of the
mountains before the wind,
Like a rolling thing before the whirlwind.
14 Then behold, at eventide, trouble!
And before the morning, he *is* no more.
This *is* the portion of those who
plunder us,
And the lot of those who rob us.

Proclamation Against Ethiopia

18 Woe [a]to the land shadowed with
buzzing wings,
Which *is* beyond the rivers of Ethiopia,
2 Which sends ambassadors by sea,
Even in vessels of reed on the waters,
saying,
"Go, swift messengers, to a nation tall
and smooth *of skin,*
To a people terrible from their
beginning onward,
A nation powerful and treading down,
Whose land the rivers divide."

3 All inhabitants of the world and
dwellers on the earth:
[a]When he lifts up a banner on the
mountains, you see *it;*
And when he blows a trumpet, you
hear *it.*
4 For so the LORD said to me,
"I will take My rest,
And I will look from My dwelling place
Like clear heat in sunshine,
Like a cloud of dew in the heat of harvest."

> PEACE NOTE
>
> Each day we hear of violations of God's plan. Isaiah reminds us that the Lord is not hasty to react. I should rest in the Lord, saying, *I am at peace because I know God is in control and I am not.*
>
> ISAIAH 18:4

5 For before the harvest, when the bud is
perfect
And the sour grape is ripening in the
flower,
He will both cut off the sprigs with
pruning hooks
And take away *and* cut down the
branches.
6 They will be left together for the
mountain birds of prey
And for the beasts of the earth;
The birds of prey will summer on them,
And all the beasts of the earth will
winter on them.

7 In that time [a]a present will be brought
to the LORD of hosts
From[1] a people tall and smooth *of skin,*
And from a people terrible from their
beginning onward,
A nation powerful and treading down,
Whose land the rivers divide—
To the place of the name of the LORD of
hosts,
To Mount Zion.

Proclamation Against Egypt

19 The [a]burden against Egypt.

Behold, the LORD [b]rides on a swift cloud,
And will come into Egypt;
[c]The idols of Egypt will totter at His
presence,
And the heart of Egypt will melt in its
midst.

2 "I will [a]set Egyptians against Egyptians;
Everyone will fight against his brother,

17:10 [a] Ps. 68:19 17:12 [a] Jer. 6:23 17:13 [a] Ps. 9:5 [b] Hos. 13:3 18:1 [a] Zeph. 2:12; 3:10 18:3 [a] Is. 5:26 18:7 [a] Zeph. 3:10 [1] Following Dead Sea Scrolls, Septuagint, and Vulgate; Masoretic Text omits *From;* Targum reads *To.* 19:1 [a] Joel 3:19 [b] Ps. 18:10; 104:3 [c] Jer. 43:12 19:2 [a] Judg. 7:22

And everyone against his neighbor,
City against city, kingdom against kingdom.
3 The spirit of Egypt will fail in its midst;
I will destroy their counsel,
And they will [a]consult the idols and the charmers,
The mediums and the sorcerers.
4 And the Egyptians I will give
[a]Into the hand of a cruel master,
And a fierce king will rule over them,"
Says the Lord, the LORD of hosts.

5 [a]The waters will fail from the sea,
And the river will be wasted and dried up.
6 The rivers will turn foul;
The brooks [a]of defense will be emptied and dried up;
The reeds and rushes will wither.
7 The papyrus reeds by the River,[1] by the mouth of the River,
And everything sown by the River,
Will wither, be driven away, and be no more.
8 The fishermen also will mourn;
All those will lament who cast hooks into the River,
And they will languish who spread nets on the waters.
9 Moreover those who work in [a]fine flax
And those who weave fine fabric will be ashamed;
10 And its foundations will be broken.
All who make wages *will be* troubled of soul.

11 Surely the princes of [a]Zoan *are* fools;
Pharaoh's wise counselors give foolish counsel.
[b]How do you say to Pharaoh, "I *am* the son of the wise,
The son of ancient kings?"
12 [a]Where *are* they?
Where are your wise men?
Let them tell you now,
And let them know what the LORD of hosts has [b]purposed against Egypt.
13 The princes of Zoan have become fools;
[a]The princes of Noph[1] are deceived;
They have also deluded Egypt,
Those who are the mainstay of its tribes.
14 The LORD has mingled [a]a perverse spirit in her midst;
And they have caused Egypt to err in all her work,
As a drunken man staggers in his vomit.
15 Neither will there be *any* work for Egypt,
Which [a]the head or tail,
Palm branch or bulrush, may do.[1]

16 In that day Egypt will [a]be like women,
and will be afraid and fear because of the
waving of the hand of the LORD of hosts,
[b]which He waves over it. 17 And the land of
Judah will be a terror to Egypt; everyone who
makes mention of it will be afraid in himself,
because of the counsel of the LORD of hosts
which He has [a]determined against it.

Egypt, Assyria, and Israel Blessed

18 In that day five cities in the land of
Egypt will [a]speak the language of Canaan
and [b]swear by the LORD of hosts; one will be
called the City of Destruction.[1]
19 In that day [a]there will be an altar to the
LORD in the midst of the land of Egypt, and a
pillar to the [b]LORD at its border. 20 And [a]it will
be for a sign and for a witness to the LORD of
hosts in the land of Egypt; for they will cry
to the LORD because of the oppressors, and
He will send them a [b]Savior and a Mighty
One, and He will deliver them. 21 Then the
LORD will be known to Egypt, and the Egyptians will [a]know the LORD in that day, and
[b]will make sacrifice and offering; yes, they
will make a vow to the LORD and perform
it. 22 And the LORD will strike Egypt, He will
strike and [a]heal *it;* they will return to the
LORD, and He will be entreated by them
and heal them.
23 In that day [a]there will be a highway from
Egypt to Assyria, and the Assyrian will come
into Egypt and the Egyptian into Assyria, and
the Egyptians will [b]serve with the Assyrians.
24 In that day Israel will be one of three with
Egypt and Assyria—a blessing in the midst
of the land, 25 whom the LORD of hosts shall
bless, saying, "Blessed *is* Egypt My people,
and Assyria [a]the work of My hands, and Israel My inheritance."

The Sign Against Egypt and Ethiopia

20 In the year that [a]Tartan[1] came to Ashdod, when Sargon the king of Assyria
sent him, and he fought against Ashdod and
took it, 2 at the same time the LORD spoke

19:3 [a] *Is. 8:19; 47:12* **19:4** [a] *Ezek. 29:19* **19:5** [a] Jer. 51:36 **19:6** [a] 2 Kin. 19:24 **19:7** [1] That is, the Nile **19:9** [a] Prov. 7:16 **19:11** [a] Num. 13:22 [b] 1 Kin. 4:29, 30 **19:12** [a] 1 Cor. 1:20 [b] Ps. 33:11 **19:13** [a] Jer. 2:16 [1] That is, ancient Memphis **19:14** [a] Is. 29:10 **19:15** [a] Is. 9:14–16 [1] Compare Isaiah 9:14–16 **19:16** [a] Nah. 3:13 [b] Is. 11:15 **19:17** [a] Dan. 4:35 **19:18** [a] Zeph. 3:9 [b] Is. 45:23 [1] Some Hebrew manuscripts, Arabic, Dead Sea Scrolls, Targum, and Vulgate read *Sun;* Septuagint reads *Asedek* (literally *Righteousness*). **19:19** [a] Ex. 24:4 [b] Ps. 68:31 **19:20** [a] Josh. 4:20; 22:27 [b] Is. 43:11 **19:21** [a] [Is. 2:3, 4; 11:9] [b] Mal. 1:11 **19:22** [a] Deut. 32:39 **19:23** [a] Is. 11:16; 35:8; 49:11; 62:10 [b] Is. 27:13 **19:25** [a] Is. 29:23 **20:1** [a] 2 Kin. 18:17 [1] Or *the Commander in Chief*

by Isaiah the son of Amoz, saying, "Go, and
remove [a]the sackcloth from your body, and
take your sandals off your feet." And he did
so, [b]walking naked and barefoot.
3 Then the LORD said, "Just as My servant
Isaiah has walked naked and barefoot three
years [a]*for* a sign and a wonder against Egypt
and Ethiopia, 4 so shall the [a]king of Assyria
lead away the Egyptians as prisoners and
the Ethiopians as captives, young and old,
naked and barefoot, [b]with their buttocks
uncovered, to the shame of Egypt. 5 [a]Then
they shall be afraid and ashamed of Ethiopia
their expectation and Egypt their glory. 6 And
the inhabitant of this territory will say in that
day, 'Surely such *is* our expectation, wherever
we flee for [a]help to be delivered from the
king of Assyria; and how shall we escape?' "

The Fall of Babylon Proclaimed

21 The burden against the Wilderness of the Sea.

As [a]whirlwinds in the South pass
through,
So it comes from the desert, from a
terrible land.
2 A distressing vision is declared to me;
[a]The treacherous dealer deals
treacherously,
And the plunderer plunders.
[b]Go up, O Elam!
Besiege, O Media!
All its sighing I have made to cease.

3 Therefore [a]my loins are filled with
pain;
[b]Pangs have taken hold of me, like the
pangs of a woman in labor.
I was distressed when *I* heard *it;*
I was dismayed when *I* saw *it.*
4 My heart wavered, fearfulness
frightened me;
[a]The night for which I longed He turned
into fear for me.
5 [a]Prepare the table,
Set a watchman in the tower,
Eat and drink.
Arise, you princes,
Anoint the shield!

6 For thus has the Lord said to me:
"Go, set a watchman,
Let him declare what he sees."
7 And he saw a chariot *with* a pair of
horsemen,
A chariot of donkeys, *and* a chariot of
camels,
And he listened earnestly with great
care.
8 Then he cried, "A lion,[1] my Lord!
I stand continually on the [a]watchtower
in the daytime;
I have sat at my post every night.
9 And look, here comes a chariot of men
with a pair of horsemen!"
Then he answered and said,
[a]"Babylon is fallen, is fallen!
And [b]all the carved images of her gods
He has broken to the ground."

10 [a]Oh, my threshing and the grain of my
floor!
That which I have heard from the LORD
of hosts,
The God of Israel,
I have declared to you.

Proclamation Against Edom

11 [a]The burden against Dumah.

He calls to me out of [b]Seir,
"Watchman, what of the night?
Watchman, what of the night?"
12 The watchman said,
"The morning comes, and also the
night.
If you will inquire, inquire;
Return! Come back!"

Proclamation Against Arabia

13 [a]The burden against Arabia.

In the forest in Arabia you will lodge,
O you traveling companies [b]of
Dedanites.
14 O inhabitants of the land of Tema,
Bring water to him who is thirsty;
With their bread they met him who
fled.
15 For they fled from the swords, from the
drawn sword,
From the bent bow, and from the
distress of war.

16 For thus the LORD has said to me: "Within a year, [a]according to the year of a hired
man, all the glory of [b]Kedar will fail; 17 and
the remainder of the number of archers,
the mighty men of the people of Kedar, will
be diminished; for the LORD God of Israel
has spoken *it.*"

20:2 [a] Zech. 13:4 [b] 1 Sam. 19:24 **20:3** [a] Is. 8:18 **20:4** [a] Is. 19:4 [b] Jer. 13:22 **20:5** [a] 2 Kin. 18:21 **20:6** [a] Is. 30:5, 7
21:1 [a] Zech. 9:14 **21:2** [a] Is. 33:1 [b] Jer. 49:34 **21:3** [a] Is. 15:5; 16:11 [b] Is. 13:8 **21:4** [a] Deut. 28:67 **21:5** [a] Dan. 5:5
21:8 [a] Hab. 2:1 [1] Dead Sea Scrolls read *Then the observer cried.* **21:9** [a] Jer. 51:8 [b] Is. 46:1 **21:10** [a] Jer. 51:33
21:11 [a] Gen. 25:14 [b] Gen. 32:3 **21:13** [a] Jer. 25:24; 49:28 [b] 1 Chr. 1:9, 32 **21:16** [a] Is. 16:14 [b] Ps. 120:5

PEACE NOTE

Don't get stuck trying to resolve all your doubts. The Bible has so much to say about God's will for us to live in His peace.

Proclamation Against Jerusalem

22 The burden against the Valley of Vision.

What ails you now, that you have all
gone up to the housetops,
2 You who are full of noise,
A tumultuous city, [a]a joyous city?
Your slain *men are* not slain with the
sword,
Nor dead in battle.
3 All your rulers have fled together;
They are captured by the archers.
All who are found in you are bound
together;
They have fled from afar.
4 Therefore I said, "Look away from me,
[a]I will weep bitterly;
Do not labor to comfort me
Because of the plundering of the
daughter of my people."

5 [a]For *it is* a day of trouble and treading
down and perplexity
[b]By the Lord GOD of hosts
In the Valley of Vision—
Breaking down the walls
And of crying to the mountain.
6 [a]Elam bore the quiver
With chariots of men *and*
horsemen,
And [b]Kir uncovered the shield.
7 It shall come to pass *that* your choicest
valleys
Shall be full of chariots,
And the horsemen shall set themselves
in array at the gate.
8 [a]He removed the protection of Judah.
You looked in that day to the armor [b]of
the House of the Forest;
9 [a]You also saw the damage to the city of
David,
That it was great;
And you gathered together the waters
of the lower pool.
10 You numbered the houses of Jerusalem,
And the houses you broke down
To fortify the wall.
11 [a]You also made a reservoir between the
two walls
For the water of the old [b]pool.
But you did not look to its Maker,
Nor did you have respect for Him who
fashioned it long ago.

12 And in that day the Lord GOD of hosts
[a]Called for weeping and for mourning,
[b]For baldness and for girding with
sackcloth.
13 But instead, joy and gladness,
Slaying oxen and killing sheep,
Eating meat and [a]drinking wine:
[b]"Let us eat and drink, for tomorrow we
die!"

14 [a]Then it was revealed in my hearing by
the LORD of hosts,
"Surely for this iniquity there [b]will be no
atonement for you,
Even to your death," says the Lord GOD
of hosts.

The Judgment on Shebna

15 Thus says the Lord GOD of hosts:

"Go, proceed to this steward,
To [a]Shebna, who *is* over the house, *and
say:*
16 'What have you here, and whom have
you here,
That you have hewn a sepulcher here,
As he [a]who hews himself a sepulcher
on high,
Who carves a tomb for himself in a rock?
17 Indeed, the LORD will throw you away
violently,
O mighty man,
[a]And will surely seize you.
18 He will surely turn violently and toss
you like a ball
Into a large country;
There you shall die, and there [a]your
glorious chariots

22:2 [a] Is. 32:13 22:4 [a] Jer. 4:19 22:5 [a] Is. 37:3 [b] Lam. 1:5; 2:2 22:6 [a] Jer. 49:35 [b] Is. 15:1 22:8 [a] 2 Kin. 18:15, 16 [b] 1 Kin. 7:2; 10:17 22:9 [a] 2 Kin. 20:20 22:11 [a] Neh. 3:16 [b] 2 Chr. 32:3, 4 22:12 [a] Joel 1:13; 2:17 [b] Mic. 1:16 22:13 [a] Luke 17:26–29 [b] 1 Cor. 15:32 22:14 [a] Is. 5:9 [b] Ezek. 24:13 22:15 [a] Is. 36:3 22:16 [a] Matt. 27:60 22:17 [a] Esth. 7:8 22:18 [a] Is. 2:7

Shall be the shame of your master's
house.
19 So I will drive you out of your office,
And from your position he will pull you
down.[1]

20 'Then it shall be in that day,
That I will call My servant [a]Eliakim the
son of Hilkiah;
21 I will clothe him with your robe
And strengthen him with your belt;
I will commit your responsibility into
his hand.
He shall be a father to the inhabitants
of Jerusalem
And to the house of Judah.
22 The key of the house of David
I will lay on his [a]shoulder;
So he shall [b]open, and no one shall shut;
And he shall shut, and no one shall open.
23 I will fasten him *as* [a]a peg in a secure
place,
And he will become a glorious throne
to his father's house.

24'They will hang on him all the glory of
his father's house, the offspring and the posterity, all vessels of small quantity, from the
cups to all the pitchers. 25 In that day,' says
the LORD of hosts, 'the peg that is fastened in
the secure place will be removed and be cut
down and fall, and the burden that *was* on
it will be cut off; for the LORD has spoken.' "

Proclamation Against Tyre

23 The [a]burden against Tyre.

Wail, you ships of Tarshish!
For it is laid waste,
So that there is no house, no harbor;
From the land of Cyprus[1] it is revealed
to them.

2 Be still, you inhabitants of the coastland,
You merchants of Sidon,
Whom those who cross the sea have
filled.[1]
3 And on great waters the grain of Shihor,
The harvest of the River,[1] *is* her revenue;
And [a]*she is* a marketplace for the nations.

4 Be ashamed, O Sidon;
For the sea has spoken,
The strength of the sea, saying,
"I do not labor, nor bring forth children;
Neither do I rear young men,
Nor bring up virgins."
5 [a]When the report *reaches* Egypt,
They also will be in agony at the report
of Tyre.

6 Cross over to Tarshish;
Wail, you inhabitants of the coastland!
7 *Is* this your [a]joyous *city,*
Whose antiquity *is* from ancient days,
Whose feet carried her far off to dwell?
8 Who has taken this counsel against
Tyre, [a]the crowning *city,*
Whose merchants *are* princes,
Whose traders *are* the honorable of the
earth?
9 The LORD of hosts has [a]purposed it,
To bring to dishonor the [b]pride of all
glory,
To bring into contempt all the
honorable of the earth.

10 Overflow through your land like the
River,[1]
O daughter of Tarshish;
There is no more strength.
11 He stretched out His hand over the sea,
He shook the kingdoms;
The LORD has given a commandment
[a]against Canaan
To destroy its strongholds.
12 And He said, "You will rejoice no more,
O you oppressed virgin daughter of
Sidon.
Arise, [a]cross over to Cyprus;
There also you will have no rest."

13 Behold, the land of the [a]Chaldeans,
This people *which* was not;
Assyria founded it for [b]wild beasts of
the desert.
They set up its towers,
They raised up its palaces,
And brought it to ruin.

14 [a]Wail, you ships of Tarshish!
For your strength is laid waste.

15 Now it shall come to pass in that day
that Tyre will be forgotten seventy years,
according to the days of one king. At the end
of seventy years it will happen to Tyre as *in*
the song of the harlot:

22:19 [1] Septuagint omits *he will pull you down;* Syriac, Targum, and Vulgate read *I will pull you down.* **22:20** [a] 2 Kin. 18:18 **22:22** [a] Is. 9:6 [b] Job 12:14; Rev. 3:7 **22:23** [a] Ezra 9:8 **23:1** [a] Zech. 9:2, 4 [1] Hebrew *Kittim,* western lands, especially Cyprus **23:2** [1] Following Masoretic Text and Vulgate; Septuagint and Targum read *Passing over the water;* Dead Sea Scrolls read *Your messengers passing over the sea.* **23:3** [a] Ezek. 27:3–23 [1] That is, the Nile **23:5** [a] Is. 19:16 **23:7** [a] Is. 22:2; 32:13 **23:8** [a] Ezek. 28:2, 12 **23:9** [a] Is. 14:26 [b] Dan. 4:37 **23:10** [1] That is, the Nile **23:11** [a] Zech. 9:2–4 **23:12** [a] Rev. 18:22 **23:13** [a] Is. 47:1 [b] Ps. 72:9 **23:14** [a] Ezek. 27:25–30

16 "Take a harp, go about the city,
You forgotten harlot;
Make sweet melody, sing many songs,
That you may be remembered."

17 And it shall be, at the end of seventy years,
that the LORD will deal with Tyre. She will return
to her hire, and [a]commit fornication with all the
kingdoms of the world on the face of the earth.
18 Her gain and her pay [a]will be set apart for the
LORD; it will not be treasured nor laid up, for
her gain will be for those who dwell before the
LORD, to eat sufficiently, and for fine clothing.

Impending Judgment on the Earth

24 Behold, the LORD makes the earth
empty and makes it waste,
Distorts its surface
And scatters abroad its inhabitants.
2 And it shall be:
As with the people, so with the [a]priest;
As with the servant, so with his master;
As with the maid, so with her mistress;
[b]As with the buyer, so with the seller;
As with the lender, so with the borrower;
As with the creditor, so with the debtor.
3 The land shall be entirely emptied and
utterly plundered,
For the LORD has spoken this word.

4 The earth mourns *and* fades away,
The world languishes *and* fades away;
The [a]haughty people of the earth languish.
5 [a]The earth is also defiled under its
inhabitants,
Because they have [b]transgressed the laws,
Changed the ordinance,
Broken the [c]everlasting covenant.
6 Therefore [a]the curse has devoured the
earth,
And those who dwell in it are desolate.
Therefore the inhabitants of the earth
are [b]burned,
And few men *are* left.

7 [a]The new wine fails, the vine languishes,
All the merry-hearted sigh.
8 The mirth [a]of the tambourine ceases,
The noise of the jubilant ends,
The joy of the harp ceases.
9 They shall not drink wine with a song;
Strong drink is bitter to those who
drink it.
10 The city of confusion is broken down;
Every house is shut up, so that none
may go in.
11 *There is* a cry for wine in the streets,
All joy is darkened,
The mirth of the land is gone.
12 In the city desolation is left,
And the gate is stricken with destruction.
13 When it shall be thus in the midst of
the land among the people,
[a]*It shall be* like the shaking of an olive tree,
Like the gleaning of grapes when the
vintage is done.

14 They shall lift up their voice, they shall
sing;
For the majesty of the LORD
They shall cry aloud from the sea.
15 Therefore [a]glorify the LORD in the
dawning light,
[b]The name of the LORD God of Israel in
the coastlands of the sea.
16 From the ends of the earth we have
heard songs:
"Glory to the righteous!"
But I said, "I am ruined, ruined!
Woe to me!
[a]The treacherous dealers have dealt
treacherously,
Indeed, the treacherous dealers have
dealt very treacherously."

17 [a]Fear and the pit and the snare
Are upon you, O inhabitant of the earth.
18 And it shall be
That he who flees from the noise of the
fear
Shall fall into the pit,
And he who comes up from the midst
of the pit
Shall be caught in the snare;
For [a]the windows from on high are open,
And [b]the foundations of the earth are
shaken.

19 [a]The earth is violently broken,
The earth is split open,
The earth is shaken exceedingly.
20 The earth shall [a]reel to and fro like a
drunkard,
And shall totter like a hut;
Its transgression shall be heavy upon it,
And it will fall, and not rise again.

21 It shall come to pass in that day
That the LORD will punish on high the
host of exalted ones,
And on the earth [a]the kings of the
earth.

23:17 [a] Rev. 17:2 23:18 [a] Zech. 14:20, 21 24:2 [a] Hos. 4:9 [b] Ezek. 7:12, 13 24:4 [a] Is. 25:11 24:5 [a] Num. 35:33 [b] Is. 59:12 [c] 1 Chr. 16:14–19 24:6 [a] Mal. 4:6 [b] Is. 9:19 24:7 [a] Joel 1:10, 12 24:8 [a] Ezek. 26:13 24:13 [a] [Is. 17:5, 6; 27:12] 24:15 [a] Is. 25:3 [b] Mal. 1:11 24:16 [a] Jer. 3:20; 5:11 24:17 [a] Jer. 48:43 24:18 [a] Gen. 7:11 [b] Ps. 18:7; 46:2 24:19 [a] Jer. 4:23 24:20 [a] Is. 19:14; 24:1; 28:7 24:21 [a] Ps. 76:12

22 They will be gathered together,
As prisoners are gathered in the pit,
And will be shut up in the prison;
After many days they will be punished.
23 Then the [a]moon will be disgraced
And the sun ashamed;
For the LORD of hosts will [b]reign
On [c]Mount Zion and in Jerusalem
And before His elders, gloriously.

Praise to God

25 O LORD, You *are* my God.
[a]I will exalt You,
I will praise Your name,
[b]For You have done wonderful *things;*
[c]*Your* counsels of old *are* faithfulness
and truth.
2 For You have made [a]a city a ruin,
A fortified city a ruin,
A palace of foreigners to be a city no
more;
It will never be rebuilt.
3 Therefore the strong people will
[a]glorify You;
The city of the terrible nations will fear
You.
4 For You have been a strength to the poor,
A strength to the needy in his distress,
[a]A refuge from the storm,
A shade from the heat;
For the blast of the terrible ones *is* as a
storm *against* the wall.
5 You will reduce the noise of aliens,
As heat in a dry place;
As heat in the shadow of a cloud,
The song of the terrible ones will be
diminished.

6 And in [a]this mountain
[b]The LORD of hosts will make for [c]all
people
A feast of choice pieces,
A feast of wines on the lees,
Of fat things full of marrow,
Of well-refined wines on the lees.
7 And He will destroy on this mountain
The surface of the covering cast over
all people,
And [a]the veil that is spread over all
nations.
8 He will [a]swallow up death forever,
And the Lord GOD will [b]wipe away tears
from all faces;
The rebuke of His people
He will take away from all the earth;
For the LORD has spoken.

9 And it will be said in that day:
"Behold, this *is* our God;
[a]We have waited for Him, and He will
save us.
This *is* the LORD;
We have waited for Him;
[b]We will be glad and rejoice in His
salvation."

10 For on this mountain the hand of the
LORD will rest,
And [a]Moab shall be trampled down
under Him,
As straw is trampled down for the
refuse heap.
11 And He will spread out His hands in
their midst
As a swimmer reaches out to swim,
And He will bring down their [a]pride
Together with the trickery of their hands.
12 The [a]fortress of the high fort of your walls
He will bring down, lay low,
And bring to the ground, down to the dust.

A Song of Salvation

26 In [a]that day this song will be sung in
the land of Judah:

"We have a strong city;
[b]*God* will appoint salvation *for* walls and
bulwarks.
2 [a]Open the gates,
That the righteous nation which keeps
the truth may enter in.
3 You will keep *him* in perfect [a]peace,
Whose mind *is* stayed *on You,*
Because he trusts in You.

PEACE NOTE

One of the most overlooked aspects of balanced Christian living and teaching is the concept of unleashing the *shalom* of God into our lives.

ISAIAH 26:3

24:23 [a] Is. 13:10; 60:19 [b] Rev. 19:4, 6 [c] [Heb. 12:22] 25:1 [a] Ex. 15:2 [b] Ps. 98:1 [c] Num. 23:19 25:2 [a] Jer. 51:37 25:3 [a] Is. 24:15 25:4 [a] Is. 4:6 25:6 [a] [Is. 2:2–4; 56:7] [b] Prov. 9:2 [c] [Dan. 7:14] 25:7 [a] [Eph. 4:18] 25:8 [a] [Hos. 13:14] [b] Rev. 7:17; 21:4 25:9 [a] Gen. 49:18 [b] Ps. 20:5 25:10 [a] Amos 2:1–3 25:11 [a] Is. 24:4; 26:5 25:12 [a] Is. 26:5 26:1 [a] Is. 2:11; 12:1 [b] Is. 60:18 26:2 [a] Ps. 118:19, 20 26:3 [a] Is. 57:19

PERSONALLY PEACEFUL

You will keep him in perfect peace, whose mind is stayed on You.

ISAIAH 26:3

Isaiah often spoke of judgment, but he also spoke of redemption and restoration. In chapter 25 he foretold the day when God would host a great banquet and feed His people (see v. 6). In chapter 26 the prophet declared that on that great day of salvation the redeemed of Israel will say, "Open the gates, that the righteous nation which keeps the truth may enter in" (v. 2). What the New King James Version translates as "truth" is *emunim*, which perhaps is better translated "faith." Those to whom the gates of renewed Jerusalem will open are those who keep faith with God. This correlates better with the next verse: "You will keep him in perfect peace, whose mind is stayed on You, because he trusts in You" (v. 3).

While the restored nation as a whole is addressed in verses 1–2, verse 3 speaks to the individual. The one who places his mind on God and trusts in Him will enjoy abundant peace. I like the focus on the individual. Isaiah's not talking about international peace; he's talking about the peace you and I can have.

How do you feel knowing God desires peace, not just for masses of people but for you as an individual?

4 Trust in the LORD forever,
[a]For in YAH, the LORD, *is* everlasting strength.[1]
5 For He brings down those who dwell on high,
[a]The lofty city;
He lays it low,
He lays it low to the ground,
He brings it down to the dust.
6 The foot shall tread it down—
The feet of the poor
And the steps of the needy."

7 The way of the just *is* uprightness;
[a]O Most Upright,
You weigh the path of the just.
8 Yes, [a]in the way of Your judgments,
O LORD, we have [b]waited for You;
The desire of *our* soul *is* for Your name
And for the remembrance of You.
9 [a]With my soul I have desired You in the night,
Yes, by my spirit within me I will seek You early;
For when Your judgments *are* in the earth,
The inhabitants of the world will learn *righteousness*.

10 [a]Let grace be shown to the wicked,
Yet he will not learn righteousness;
In [b]the land of uprightness he will deal unjustly,
And will not behold the majesty of the LORD.
11 LORD, *when* Your hand is lifted up,
[a]they will not see.
But they will see and be ashamed
For *their* envy of people;
Yes, the fire of Your enemies shall devour them.

12 LORD, You will establish peace for us,
For You have also done all our works in us.
13 O LORD our God, [a]masters besides You
Have had dominion over us;
But by You only we make mention of Your name.
14 *They are* dead, they will not live;
They are deceased, they will not rise.
Therefore You have punished and destroyed them,
And made all their memory to [a]perish.
15 You have increased the nation, O LORD,
You have [a]increased the nation;
You are glorified;
You have expanded all the borders of the land.

16 LORD, [a]in trouble they have visited You,
They poured out a prayer *when* Your chastening *was* upon them.

26:4 [a] Is. 12:2; 45:17 [1] Or *Rock of Ages* 26:5 [a] Is. 25:11, 12 26:7 [a] Ps. 37:23 26:8 [a] Is. 64:5 [b] Is. 25:9; 33:2 26:9 [a] Ps. 63:6
26:10 [a] [Rom. 2:4] [b] Ps. 143:10 26:11 [a] Is. 5:12 26:13 [a] 2 Chr. 12:8 26:14 [a] Eccl. 9:5 26:15 [a] Is. 9:3 26:16 [a] Hos. 5:15

FIRM FOUNDATION

LORD, You will establish peace for us, for You have also done all our works in us.

ISAIAH 26:12

Verses 7–19 describe a vision of the future, when the redeemed of the Lord will experience God's salvation. The vision ends with the hope of resurrection. At the center of the vision is the expression of hope found in verse 12: "LORD, You will establish peace for us, for You have also done all our works in us." The nation of Israel had learned that the power politics of kings like Ahaz and others resulted in disaster. The restored people will recognize that God will deal with Israel's enemies. The vision reveals more of the lessons that exiled Israel learned. In exile, "masters besides [God] . . . had dominion over" them (v. 13). Chastened, Israel would confess only the Lord going forward.

In this passage we once again see the connection between peace and faithfulness. The Israelites' infidelity resulted in their loss of faith. Their renewed commitment to faith in God restored their peace. This important lesson applies not only to the ancient nation of Israel but to us as well. If we do not place our faith in God—confess only the Lord—we can hardly expect to enjoy His peace. Is your faith lacking in any area?

17 As [a]a woman with child
Is in pain and cries out in her pangs,
When she draws near the time of her delivery,
So have we been in Your sight, O LORD.
18 We have been with child, we have been in pain;
We have, as it were, brought forth wind;
We have not accomplished any deliverance in the earth,
Nor have [a]the inhabitants of the world fallen.

19 [a]Your dead shall live;
Together with my dead body[1] they shall arise.
[b]Awake and sing, you who dwell in dust;
For your dew *is like* the dew of herbs,
And the earth shall cast out the dead.

Take Refuge from the Coming Judgment

20 Come, my people, [a]enter your chambers,
And shut your doors behind you;
Hide yourself, as it were, [b]for a little moment,
Until the indignation is past.
21 For behold, the LORD [a]comes out of His place
To punish the inhabitants of the earth for their iniquity;
The earth will also disclose her blood,
And will no more cover her slain.

27 In that day the LORD with His severe sword, great and strong,
Will punish Leviathan the fleeing serpent,
[a]Leviathan that twisted serpent;
And He will slay [b]the reptile that *is* in the sea.

The Restoration of Israel

2 In that day [a]sing to her,
[b]"A vineyard of red wine![1]
3 [a]I, the LORD, keep it,
I water it every moment;
Lest any hurt it,
I keep it night and day.
4 Fury *is* not in Me.
Who would set [a]briers *and* thorns
Against Me in battle?
I would go through them,
I would burn them together.
5 Or let him take hold [a]of My strength,
That he may [b]make peace with Me;
And he shall make peace with Me."

26:17 [a] [John 16:21] **26:18** [a] Ps. 17:14 **26:19** [a] [Ezek. 37:1–14] [b] [Dan. 12:2] [1] Following Masoretic Text and Vulgate; Syriac and Targum read *their dead bodies;* Septuagint reads *those in the tombs.* **26:20** [a] Ex. 12:22, 23 [b] [Ps. 30:5] **26:21** [a] Mic. 1:3 **27:1** [a] Ps. 74:13, 14 [b] Is. 51:9 **27:2** [a] Is. 5:1 [b] Is. 5:7 [1] Following Masoretic Text (Kittel's *Biblia Hebraica*), Bomberg, and Vulgate; Masoretic Text (*Biblia Hebraica Stuttgartensia*), some Hebrew manuscripts, and Septuagint read *delight;* Targum reads *choice vineyard.* **27:3** [a] Is. 31:5 **27:4** [a] 2 Sam. 23:6 **27:5** [a] Is. 25:4 [b] Job 22:21

THE GREAT EXCHANGE

"Let him take hold of My strength, that he may make peace with Me; and he shall make peace with Me."

ISAIAH 27:5

Verses 2–11 describe another vision of future deliverance. It begins with reference to a song about a "vineyard" that the Lord watered (vv. 2–3). This is an unmistakable allusion to the song of judgment pronounced against the Lord's fruitless vineyard that faced ruin (see 5:1–7, where God commanded the clouds to give the vineyard no more rain). Someday in the future, the Lord's vineyard (Israel) will be restored. In the vision, the Lord invited the repentant person, "Let him take hold of My strength, that he may make peace with Me; and he shall make peace with Me" (27:5).

Humanity's ultimate hope is to find peace with God. God's ultimate purpose for humanity is to bring us back to Him in a fellowship of peace. Someday, the prophet foresees, that will happen. But for peace to happen, we must go to God on His terms. We must cast aside the idols that have beguiled us with their false promises of happiness. It is in God alone that we find true peace and joy.

Are there "idols" you've sought while seeking happiness? How can you exchange those for faith in God?

6 Those who come He shall cause [a]to take root in Jacob;
Israel shall blossom and bud,
And fill the face of the world with fruit.

7 [a]Has He struck Israel as He struck those who struck him?
Or has He been slain according to the slaughter of those who were slain by Him?
8 [a]In measure, by sending it away,
You contended with it.
[b]He removes *it* by His rough wind
In the day of the east wind.
9 Therefore by this the iniquity of Jacob will be covered;
And this *is* all the fruit of taking away his sin:
When he makes all the stones of the altar
Like chalkstones that are beaten to dust,
Wooden images[1] and incense altars shall not stand.

10 Yet the fortified city *will be* [a]desolate,
The habitation forsaken and left like a wilderness;
There the calf will feed, and there it will lie down
And consume its branches.
11 When its boughs are withered, they will be broken off;
The women come *and* set them on fire.
For [a]it *is* a people of no understanding;
Therefore He who made them will [b]not have mercy on them,
And [c]He who formed them will show them no favor.

12 And it shall come to pass in that day
That the LORD will thresh,
From the channel of the River[1] to the Brook of Egypt;
And you will be [a]gathered one by one,
O you children of Israel.

13 [a]So it shall be in that day:
[b]The great trumpet will be blown;
They will come, who are about to perish in the land of Assyria,
And they who are outcasts in the land of [c]Egypt,
And shall [d]worship the LORD in the holy mount at Jerusalem.

Woe to Ephraim and Jerusalem

28 Woe to the crown of pride, to the drunkards of Ephraim,
Whose glorious beauty *is* a fading flower
Which *is* at the head of the verdant valleys,

27:6 [a] Is. 37:31 **27:7** [a] Is. 10:12, 17; 30:30–33 **27:8** [a] Job 23:6 [b] [Ps. 78:38] **27:9** [1] Hebrew *Asherim,* Canaanite deities
27:10 [a] Is. 5:6, 17; 32:14 **27:11** [a] Deut. 32:28 [b] Is. 9:17 [c] Deut. 32:18 **27:12** [a] [Is. 11:11; 56:8] [1] That is, the Euphrates
27:13 [a] Is. 2:11 [b] Rev. 11:15 [c] Is. 19:21, 22 [d] Zech. 14:16

To those who are overcome with wine!
2 Behold, the Lord has a mighty and strong one,
[a]Like a tempest of hail and a destroying storm,
Like a flood of mighty waters overflowing,
Who will bring *them* down to the earth with *His* hand.
3 The crown of pride, the drunkards of Ephraim,
Will be trampled underfoot;
4 And the glorious beauty is a fading flower
Which *is* at the head of the verdant valley,
Like the first fruit before the summer,
Which an observer sees;
He eats it up while it is still in his hand.

5 In that day the LORD of hosts will be
For a crown of glory and a diadem of beauty
To the remnant of His people,
6 For a spirit of justice to him who sits in judgment,
And for strength to those who turn back the battle at the gate.

7 But they also [a]have erred through wine,
And through intoxicating drink are out of the way;
[b]The priest and the prophet have erred through intoxicating drink,
They are swallowed up by wine,
They are out of the way through intoxicating drink;
They err in vision, they stumble *in* judgment.
8 For all tables are full of vomit *and* filth;
No place *is clean.*

9 "Whom[a] will he teach knowledge?
And whom will he make to understand the message?
Those *just* weaned from milk?
Those *just* drawn from the breasts?
10 [a]For precept *must be* upon precept, precept upon precept,
Line upon line, line upon line,
Here a little, there a little."
11 For with [a]stammering lips and another tongue
He will speak to this people,
12 To whom He said, "This *is* the [a]rest *with which*
You may cause the weary to rest,"
And, "This *is* the refreshing";
Yet they would not hear.
13 But the word of the LORD was to them,
"Precept upon precept, precept upon precept,
Line upon line, line upon line,
Here a little, there a little,"
That they might go and fall backward, and be broken
And snared and caught.

14 Therefore hear the word of the LORD, you scornful men,
Who rule this people who *are* in Jerusalem,
15 Because you have said, "We have made a covenant with death,
And with Sheol we are in agreement.
When the overflowing scourge passes through,
It will not come to us,
[a]For we have made lies our refuge,
And under falsehood we have hidden ourselves."

A Cornerstone in Zion

16Therefore thus says the Lord GOD:
"Behold, I lay in Zion [a]a stone for a foundation,
A tried stone, a precious cornerstone, a sure foundation;
Whoever believes will not act hastily.
17 Also I will make justice the measuring line,
And righteousness the plummet;
The hail will sweep away the refuge of lies,
And the waters will overflow the hiding place.
18 Your covenant with death will be annulled,
And your agreement with Sheol will not stand;
When the overflowing scourge passes through,
Then you will be trampled down by it.
19 As often as it goes out it will take you;
For morning by morning it will pass over,
And by day and by night;
It will be a terror just to understand the report."
20 For the bed is too short to stretch out *on,*
And the covering so narrow that one cannot wrap himself *in it.*

28:2 [a] Ezek. 13:11 28:7 [a] Hos. 4:11 [b] Is. 56:10, 12 28:9 [a] Jer. 6:10 28:10 [a] [2 Chr. 36:15] 28:11 [a] 1 Cor. 14:21
28:12 [a] Is. 30:15 28:15 [a] Is. 9:15 28:16 [a] Matt. 21:42

21 For the LORD will rise up as *at* Mount
[a]Perazim,
He will be angry as in the Valley of
[b]Gibeon—
That He may do His work, [c]His
awesome work,
And bring to pass His act, His unusual
act.
22 Now therefore, do not be mockers,
Lest your bonds be made strong;
For I have heard from the Lord GOD of
hosts,
[a]A destruction determined even upon
the whole earth.

Listen to the Teaching of God

23 Give ear and hear my voice,
Listen and hear my speech.
24 Does the plowman keep plowing all
day to sow?
Does he keep turning his soil and
breaking the clods?
25 When he has leveled its surface,
Does he not sow the black cummin
And scatter the cummin,
Plant the wheat in rows,
The barley in the appointed place,
And the spelt in its place?
26 For He instructs him in right judgment,
His God teaches him.

27 For the black cummin is not threshed
with a threshing sledge,
Nor is a cartwheel rolled over the cummin;
But the black cummin is beaten out
with a stick,
And the cummin with a rod.
28 Bread *flour* must be ground;
Therefore he does not thresh it forever,
Break *it with* his cartwheel,
Or crush it *with* his horsemen.
29 This also comes from the LORD of hosts,
[a]*Who* is wonderful in counsel *and*
excellent in guidance.

Woe to Jerusalem

29 "Woe [a]to Ariel,[1] to Ariel, the city
[b]*where* David dwelt!
Add year to year;
Let feasts come around.
2 Yet I will distress Ariel;
There shall be heaviness and sorrow,
And it shall be to Me as Ariel.
3 I will encamp against you all around,
I will lay siege against you with a mound,
And I will raise siegeworks against you.
4 You shall be brought down,
You shall speak out of the ground;
Your speech shall be low, out of the dust;
Your voice shall be like a medium's,
[a]out of the ground;
And your speech shall whisper out of
the dust.

5 "Moreover the multitude of your [a]foes
Shall be like fine dust,
And the multitude of the terrible ones
Like [b]chaff that passes away;
Yes, it shall be [c]in an instant, suddenly.
6 [a]You will be punished by the LORD of hosts
With thunder and [b]earthquake and
great noise,
With storm and tempest
And the flame of devouring fire.
7 [a]The multitude of all the nations who
fight against Ariel,
Even all who fight against her and her
fortress,
And distress her,
Shall be [b]as a dream of a night vision.
8 [a]It shall even be as when a hungry man
dreams,
And look—he eats;
But he awakes, and his soul is still empty;
Or as when a thirsty man dreams,
And look—he drinks;
But he awakes, and indeed *he is* faint,
And his soul still craves:
So the multitude of all the nations
shall be,
Who fight against Mount Zion."

The Blindness of Disobedience

9 Pause and wonder!
Blind yourselves and be blind!
[a]They are drunk, [b]but not with wine;
They stagger, but not with intoxicating
drink.
10 For [a]the LORD has poured out on you
The spirit of deep sleep,
And has [b]closed your eyes, namely, the
prophets;
And He has covered your heads,
namely, [c]the seers.

11 The whole vision has become to you like
the words of a book [a]that is sealed, which *men*
deliver to one who is literate, saying, "Read
this, please."
[b]And he says, "I cannot, for it *is* sealed."
12 Then the book is delivered to one who is
illiterate, saying, "Read this, please."

28:21 [a] 2 Sam. 5:20 [b] Josh. 10:10, 12 [c] [Lam. 3:33] **28:22** [a] Is. 10:22 **28:29** [a] Ps. 92:5 **29:1** [a] Ezek. 24:6, 9 [b] 2 Sam. 5:9
[1] That is, Jerusalem **29:4** [a] Is. 8:19 **29:5** [a] Is. 25:5 [b] Job 21:18 [c] Is. 30:13; 47:11 **29:6** [a] Is. 28:2; 30:30 [b] Rev. 16:18, 19
29:7 [a] Mic. 4:11, 12 [b] Job 20:8 **29:8** [a] Ps. 73:20 **29:9** [a] Is. 28:7, 8 [b] Is. 51:21 **29:10** [a] Rom. 11:8 [b] Ps. 69:23 [c] Is. 44:18
29:11 [a] Is. 8:16 [b] Dan. 12:4, 9

And he says, "I am not literate."
13Therefore the Lord said:

[a]"Inasmuch as these people draw near
with their mouths
And honor Me [b]with their lips,
But have removed their hearts far
from Me,
And their fear toward Me is taught by
the commandment of men,
14 [a]Therefore, behold, I will again do a
marvelous work
Among this people,
A marvelous work and a wonder;
[b]For the wisdom of their wise *men* shall
perish,
And the understanding of their
prudent *men* shall be hidden."

15 [a]Woe to those who seek deep to hide
their counsel far from the LORD,
And their works are in the dark;
[b]They say, "Who sees us?" and, "Who
knows us?"
16 Surely you have things turned around!
Shall the potter be esteemed as the clay;
For shall the [a]thing made say of him
who made it,
"He did not make me"?
Or shall the thing formed say of him
who formed it,
"He has no understanding"?

Future Recovery of Wisdom

17 *Is* it not yet a very little while
Till [a]Lebanon shall be turned into a
fruitful field,
And the fruitful field be esteemed as a
forest?
18 [a]In that day the deaf shall hear the
words of the book,
And the eyes of the blind shall see out
of obscurity and out of darkness.
19 [a]The humble also shall increase *their*
joy in the LORD,
And [b]the poor among men shall rejoice
In the Holy One of Israel.
20 For the terrible one is brought to
nothing,
[a]*The scornful one* is consumed,
And all who [b]watch for iniquity are cut
off—
21 Who make a man an offender by a word,
And [a]lay a snare for him who reproves
in the gate,
And turn aside the just [b]by empty words.

22Therefore thus says the LORD, [a]who redeemed Abraham, concerning the house
of Jacob:

"Jacob shall not now be [b]ashamed,
Nor shall his face now grow pale;
23 But when he sees his children,
[a]The work of My hands, in his midst,
They will hallow My name,
And hallow the Holy One of Jacob,
And fear the God of Israel.
24 These also [a]who erred in spirit will
come to understanding,
And those who complained will learn
doctrine."

Futile Confidence in Egypt

30 "Woe to the rebellious children,"
says the LORD,
[a]"Who take counsel, but not of Me,
And who devise plans, but not of My
Spirit,
[b]That they may add sin to sin;
2 [a]Who walk to go down to Egypt,
And [b]have not asked My advice,
To strengthen themselves in the
strength of Pharaoh,
And to trust in the shadow of
Egypt!
3 [a]Therefore the strength of Pharaoh
Shall be your shame,
And trust in the shadow of Egypt
Shall be *your* humiliation.
4 For his princes were at [a]Zoan,
And his ambassadors came to Hanes.
5 [a]They were all ashamed of a people *who*
could not benefit them,
Or be help or benefit,
But a shame and also a reproach."

6[a]The burden against the beasts of the
South.

Through a land of trouble and
anguish,
From which *came* the lioness and lion,
[b]The viper and fiery flying serpent,
They will carry their riches on the
backs of young donkeys,
And their treasures on the humps of
camels,
To a people *who* shall not profit;
7 [a]For the Egyptians shall help in vain
and to no purpose.
Therefore I have called her
Rahab-Hem-Shebeth.[1]

29:13 [a]Ezek. 33:31 [b]Col. 2:22 **29:14** [a]Hab. 1:5 [b]Jer. 49:7 **29:15** [a]Is. 30:1 [b]Ps. 10:11; 94:7 **29:16** [a]Is. 45:9 **29:17** [a]Is. 32:15 **29:18** [a]Is. 35:5 **29:19** [a][Is. 11:4; 61:1] [b][James 2:5] **29:20** [a]Is. 28:14 [b]Mic. 2:1 **29:21** [a]Amos 5:10, 12 [b]Prov. 28:21 **29:22** [a]Josh. 24:3 [b]Is. 45:17 **29:23** [a][Is. 45:11; 49:20–26] **29:24** [a]Is. 28:7 **30:1** [a]Is. 29:15 [b]Deut. 29:19 **30:2** [a]Is. 31:1 [b]Josh. 9:14 **30:3** [a]Is. 20:5 **30:4** [a]Is. 19:11 **30:5** [a]Jer. 2:36 **30:6** [a]Is. 57:9 [b]Deut. 8:15 **30:7** [a]Jer. 37:7 [1]Literally *Rahab Sits Idle*

A Rebellious People

8 Now go, [a]write it before them on a tablet,
And note it on a scroll,
That it may be for time to come,
Forever and ever:
9 That [a]this *is* a rebellious people,
Lying children,
Children *who* will not hear the law of the LORD;
10 [a]Who say to the seers, "Do not see,"
And to the prophets, "Do not prophesy to us right things;
[b]Speak to us smooth things, prophesy deceits.
11 Get out of the way,
Turn aside from the path,
Cause the Holy One of Israel
To cease from before us."

12 Therefore thus says the Holy One of Israel:

"Because you [a]despise this word,
And trust in oppression and perversity,
And rely on them,
13 Therefore this iniquity shall be to you
[a]Like a breach ready to fall,
A bulge in a high wall,
Whose breaking [b]comes suddenly, in an instant.
14 And [a]He shall break it like the breaking of the potter's vessel,
Which is broken in pieces;
He shall not spare.
So there shall not be found among its fragments
A shard to take fire from the hearth,
Or to take water from the cistern."

15 For thus says the Lord GOD, the Holy One of Israel:

[a]"In returning and rest you shall be saved;
In quietness and confidence shall be your strength."
[b]But you would not,
16 And you said, "No, for we will flee on horses"—
Therefore you shall flee!
And, "We will ride on swift *horses*"—
Therefore those who pursue you shall be swift!
17 [a]One thousand *shall flee* at the threat of *one*,
At the threat of five you shall flee,
Till you are left as a pole on top of a mountain
And as a banner on a hill.

God Will Be Gracious

18 Therefore the LORD will wait, that He may be [a]gracious to you;
And therefore He will be exalted, that He may have mercy on you.
For the LORD *is* a God of justice;
[b]Blessed *are* all those who [c]wait for Him.

19 For the people [a]shall dwell in Zion at Jerusalem;
You shall [b]weep no more.
He will be very gracious to you at the sound of your cry;
When He hears it, He will [c]answer you.
20 And *though* the Lord gives you
[a]The bread of adversity and the water of affliction,
Yet [b]your teachers will not be moved into a corner anymore,
But your eyes shall see your teachers.
21 Your ears shall hear a word behind you, saying,
"This *is* the way, walk in it,"
Whenever you [a]turn to the right hand
Or whenever you turn to the left.
22 [a]You will also defile the covering of your images of silver,
And the ornament of your molded images of gold.
You will throw them away as an unclean thing;
[b]You will say to them, "Get away!"

23 [a]Then He will give the rain for your seed
With which you sow the ground,
And bread of the increase of the earth;
It will be fat and plentiful.
In that day your cattle will feed
In large pastures.
24 Likewise the oxen and the young donkeys that work the ground
Will eat cured fodder,
Which has been winnowed with the shovel and fan.
25 There will be [a]on every high mountain
And on every high hill
Rivers *and* streams of waters,
In the day of the [b]great slaughter,
When the towers fall.
26 Moreover [a]the light of the moon will be as the light of the sun,
And the light of the sun will be sevenfold,

30:8 [a] Hab. 2:2 **30:9** [a] Is. 1:2, 4; 65:2 **30:10** [a] Jer. 11:21 [b] 1 Kin. 22:8, 13 **30:12** [a] Is. 5:24 **30:13** [a] Ps. 62:3, 4 [b] Is. 29:5 **30:14** [a] Jer. 19:11 **30:15** [a] Is. 7:4; 28:12 [b] Matt. 23:37 **30:17** [a] Josh. 23:10 **30:18** [a] Is. 33:2 [b] Jer. 17:7 [c] Is. 26:8 **30:19** [a] Is. 65:9 [b] Is. 25:8 [c] Is. 65:24 **30:20** [a] 1 Kin. 22:27 [b] Amos 8:11 **30:21** [a] Josh. 1:7 **30:22** [a] Is. 2:20; 31:7 [b] Hos. 14:8 **30:23** [a] [Matt. 6:33] **30:25** [a] Is. 2:14, 15 [b] Is. 2:10–21; 34:2 **30:26** [a] [Is. 60:19, 20]

As the light of seven days,
In the day that the LORD binds up the bruise of His people
And heals the stroke of their wound.

Judgment on Assyria

27 Behold, the name of the LORD comes from afar,
Burning *with* His anger,
And *His* burden *is* heavy;
His lips are full of indignation,
And His tongue like a devouring fire.
28 [a]His breath is like an overflowing stream,
[b]Which reaches up to the neck,
To sift the nations with the sieve of futility;
And *there shall be* [c]a bridle in the jaws of the people,
Causing *them* to err.

29 You shall have a song
As in the night *when* a holy festival is kept,
And gladness of heart as when one goes with a flute,
To come into [a]the mountain of the LORD,
To the Mighty One of Israel.
30 [a]The LORD will cause His glorious voice to be heard,
And show the descent of His arm,
With the indignation of *His* anger
And the flame of a devouring fire,
With scattering, tempest, [b]and hailstones.
31 For [a]through the voice of the LORD
Assyria will be beaten down,
As He strikes with the [b]rod.
32 And *in* every place where the staff of punishment passes,
Which the LORD lays on him,
It will be with tambourines and harps;
And in battles of [a]brandishing He will fight with it.
33 [a]For Tophet *was* established of old,
Yes, for the king it is prepared.
He has made *it* deep and large;
Its pyre *is* fire with much wood;
The breath of the LORD, like a stream of brimstone,
Kindles it.

The Folly of Not Trusting God

31 Woe to those [a]who go down to Egypt for help,
And [b]rely on horses,
Who trust in chariots because *they are* many,
And in horsemen because they are very strong,
But who do not look to the Holy One of Israel,
[c]Nor seek the LORD!
2 Yet He also *is* wise and will bring disaster,
And [a]will not call back His words,
But will arise against the house of evildoers,
And against the help of those who work iniquity.
3 Now the Egyptians *are* men, and not God;
And their horses are flesh, and not spirit.
When the LORD stretches out His hand,
Both he who helps will fall,
And he who is helped will fall down;
They all will perish [a]together.

God Will Deliver Jerusalem

4For thus the LORD has spoken to me:

[a]"As a lion roars,
And a young lion over his prey
(When a multitude of shepherds is summoned against him,
He will not be afraid of their voice
Nor be disturbed by their noise),
So the LORD of hosts will come down
To fight for Mount Zion and for its hill.
5 [a]Like birds flying about,
So will the LORD of hosts defend Jerusalem.
Defending, He will also deliver *it;*
Passing over, He will preserve *it.*"

6Return *to Him* against whom the children
of Israel have [a]deeply revolted. 7For in that
day every man shall [a]throw away his idols
of silver and his idols of gold—[b]sin, which
your own hands have made for yourselves.

8 "Then Assyria shall [a]fall by a sword not of man,
And a sword not of mankind shall [b]devour him.
But he shall flee from the sword,
And his young men shall become forced labor.
9 [a]He shall cross over to his stronghold for fear,
And his princes shall be afraid of the banner,"
Says the LORD,
Whose fire *is* in Zion
And whose furnace *is* in Jerusalem.

30:28 [a]Is. 11:4 [b]Is. 8:8 [c]Is. 37:29 **30:29** [a][Is. 2:3] **30:30** [a]Is. 29:6 [b]Is. 28:2 **30:31** [a]Is. 14:25; 37:36 [b]Is. 10:5, 24 **30:32** [a]Is. 11:15 **30:33** [a]Jer. 7:31 **31:1** [a]Is. 30:1, 2 [b]Ps. 20:7 [c]Dan. 9:13 **31:2** [a]Num. 23:19 **31:3** [a]Is. 20:6 **31:4** [a]Hos. 11:10 **31:5** [a]Deut. 32:11 **31:6** [a]Hos. 9:9 **31:7** [a]Is. 2:20; 30:22 [b]1 Kin. 12:30 **31:8** [a]2 Kin. 19:35, 36 [b]Is. 37:36 **31:9** [a]Is. 37:37

A Reign of Righteousness

32 Behold, [a]a king will reign in
righteousness,
And princes will rule with justice.
2 A man will be as a hiding place from
the wind,
And [a]a cover from the tempest,
As rivers of water in a dry place,
As the shadow of a great rock in a
weary land.
3 [a]The eyes of those who see will not be
dim,
And the ears of those who hear will listen.
4 Also the heart of the rash will
[a]understand knowledge,
And the tongue of the stammerers will
be ready to speak plainly.

5 The foolish person will no longer be
called generous,
Nor the miser said *to be* bountiful;
6 For the foolish person will speak
foolishness,
And his heart will work [a]iniquity:
To practice ungodliness,
To utter error against the LORD,
To keep the hungry unsatisfied,
And he will cause the drink of the
thirsty to fail.
7 Also the schemes of the schemer *are* evil;
He devises wicked plans
To destroy the poor with [a]lying words,
Even when the needy speaks justice.
8 But a generous man devises generous
things,
And by generosity he shall stand.

Consequences of Complacency

9 Rise up, you women [a]who are at ease,
Hear my voice;
You complacent daughters,
Give ear to my speech.
10 In a year and *some* days
You will be troubled, you complacent
women;
For the vintage will fail,
The gathering will not come.
11 Tremble, you *women* who are at ease;
Be troubled, you complacent ones;
Strip yourselves, make yourselves bare,
And gird *sackcloth* on *your* waists.

12 People shall mourn upon their
breasts
For the pleasant fields, for the fruitful
vine.
13 [a]On the land of my people will come up
thorns *and* briers,
Yes, on all the happy homes *in* [b]the
joyous city;
14 [a]Because the palaces will be forsaken,
The bustling city will be deserted.
The forts and towers will become lairs
forever,
A joy of wild donkeys, a pasture of
flocks—

32:1 [a] Ps. 45:1 **32:2** [a] Is. 4:6 **32:3** [a] Is. 29:18; 35:5 **32:4** [a] Is. 29:24 **32:6** [a] Prov. 24:7–9 **32:7** [a] Jer. 5:26–28
32:9 [a] Amos 6:1 **32:13** [a] Hos. 9:6 [b] Is. 22:2 **32:14** [a] Is. 27:10

MAKE THE CONNECTION

The work of righteousness will be peace, and the effect of righteousness, quietness and assurance forever.

ISAIAH 32:17

Chapter 32 constitutes a moving oracle of Israel's future restoration, when "a king will reign in righteousness, and princes will rule with justice" (v. 1). A word of judgment was spoken in chapter 6, but in 32:3 the judgment has been reversed.

The goal of restoration, as we have seen in other passages of Scripture, is to reconcile humankind with God. This goal is expressed poetically in verse 16: "Then justice will dwell in the wilderness, and righteousness remain in the fruitful field." In other words, justice and righteousness will be everywhere. The key promise is found in verse 17, in which the prophet proclaimed, "The work of righteousness will be peace, and the effect of righteousness, quietness and assurance forever." Once again we must note the close connection between righteousness and peace; the former results in the latter. Too often we expect to enjoy peace but give little thought to righteousness.

Is this true of you? If so, how will you begin to change it?

15 Until [a]the Spirit is poured upon us
from on high,
And [b]the wilderness becomes a fruitful
field,
And the fruitful field is counted as a
forest.

The Peace of God's Reign

16 Then justice will dwell in the
wilderness,
And righteousness remain in the
fruitful field.
17 [a]The work of righteousness will be
peace,
And the effect of righteousness,
quietness and assurance
forever.
18 My people will dwell in a peaceful
habitation,
In secure dwellings, and in quiet
[a]resting places,
19 [a]Though hail comes down [b]on the
forest,
And the city is brought low in
humiliation.

20 Blessed *are* you who sow beside all
waters,
Who send out freely the feet of [a]the ox
and the donkey.

A Prayer in Deep Distress

33 Woe to you [a]who plunder, though
you *have* not *been* plundered;
And you who deal treacherously,
though they have not dealt
treacherously with you!
[b]When you cease plundering,
You will be [c]plundered;
When you make an end of dealing
treacherously,
They will deal treacherously with you.

2 O LORD, be gracious to us;
[a]We have waited for You.
Be their[1] arm every morning,
Our salvation also in the time of
trouble.
3 At the noise of the tumult the people
[a]shall flee;
When You lift Yourself up, the nations
shall be scattered;
4 And Your plunder shall be gathered
Like the gathering of the caterpillar;
As the running to and fro of locusts,
He shall run upon them.

5 [a]The LORD is exalted, for He dwells on
high;
He has filled Zion with justice and
righteousness.

32:15 [a] [Joel 2:28] [b] Is. 29:17 **32:17** [a] James 3:18 **32:18** [a] [Zech. 2:5; 3:10] **32:19** [a] Is. 30:30 [b] Zech. 11:2 **32:20** [a] Is. 30:23, 24 **33:1** [a] Hab. 2:8 [b] Rev. 13:10 [c] Is. 10:12; 14:25; 31:8 **33:2** [a] Is. 25:9; 26:8 [1] Septuagint omits *their;* Syriac, Targum, and Vulgate read *our.* **33:3** [a] Is. 17:13 **33:5** [a] Ps. 97:9

DON'T RESIST REST

My people will dwell in a peaceful habitation, in secure dwellings, and in quiet resting places.

ISAIAH 32:18

In verse 17 the word of the Lord through the prophet declared that "the work of righteousness will be peace." In verse 18 God said through His prophet, "My people will dwell in a peaceful habitation, in secure dwellings, and in quiet resting places." It's a beautiful image. It immediately brings to mind the promise Jesus made to His disciples when He assured them, "In My Father's house are many mansions; if it were not so, I would have told you. I go to prepare a place for you. And if I go and prepare a place for you, I will come again and receive you to Myself; that where I am, there you may be also" (John 14:2–3). What makes this assurance so relevant is that Jesus had warned His disciples of His impending death. They were devastated. An eventual reconciliation in heaven sounded great!

We can live in these dwellings of peace and security, whether on earth or in heaven, thanks to reconciliation with God. And this reconciliation can happen only on God's righteous terms. Peace is not given to those who spurn God and His goodness. Israel learned this truth the hard way.

Is there any way in which you may be resisting God's goodness? How much do you long to live in "a peaceful habitation" (Is. 32:18)? Can you give up resisting for resting?

6 Wisdom and knowledge will be the
stability of your times,
And the strength of salvation;
The fear of the LORD *is* His treasure.

7 Surely their valiant ones shall cry
outside,
[a]The ambassadors of peace shall weep
bitterly.
8 [a]The highways lie waste,
The traveling man ceases.
[b]He has broken the covenant,
He has despised the cities,[1]
He regards no man.
9 [a]The earth mourns *and* languishes,
Lebanon is shamed *and* shriveled;
Sharon is like a wilderness,
And Bashan and Carmel shake off *their*
fruits.

Impending Judgment on Zion

10 "Now[a] I will rise," says the LORD;
"Now I will be exalted,
Now I will lift Myself up.
11 [a]You shall conceive chaff,
You shall bring forth stubble;
Your breath, *as* fire, shall devour you.
12 And the people shall be *like* the
burnings of lime;
[a]*Like* thorns cut up they shall be burned
in the fire.
13 Hear, [a]you *who are* afar off, what I have
done;
And you *who are* near, acknowledge My
might."

14 The sinners in Zion are afraid;
Fearfulness has seized the hypocrites:
"Who among us shall dwell with the
devouring [a]fire?
Who among us shall dwell with
everlasting burnings?"
15 He who [a]walks righteously and speaks
uprightly,
He who despises the gain of oppressions,
Who gestures with his hands, refusing
bribes,
Who stops his ears from hearing of
bloodshed,
And [b]shuts his eyes from seeing evil:
16 He will dwell on high;
His place of defense *will be* the fortress
of rocks;
Bread will be given him,
His water *will be* sure.

The Land of the Majestic King

17 Your eyes will see the King in His
[a]beauty;
They will see the land that is very far off.
18 Your heart will meditate on terror:
[a]"Where *is* the scribe?
Where *is* he who weighs?
Where *is* he who counts the towers?"
19 [a]You will not see a fierce people,
[b]A people of obscure speech, beyond
perception,
Of a stammering tongue *that you*
cannot understand.

20 [a]Look upon Zion, the city of our
appointed feasts;
Your eyes will see [b]Jerusalem, a quiet
home,
A tabernacle *that* will not be taken
down;
[c]Not one of [d]its stakes will ever be
removed,
Nor will any of its cords be broken.
21 But there the majestic LORD *will be* for us
A place of broad rivers *and* streams,
In which no galley with oars will sail,
Nor majestic ships pass by
22 (For the LORD *is* our [a]Judge,
The LORD *is* our [b]Lawgiver,
[c]The LORD *is* our King;
He will save us);
23 Your tackle is loosed,
They could not strengthen their mast,
They could not spread the sail.

Then the prey of great plunder is
divided;
The lame take the prey.
24 And the inhabitant will not say, "I am
sick";
[a]The people who dwell in it *will be*
forgiven *their* iniquity.

Judgment on the Nations

34 Come [a]near, you nations, to hear;
And heed, you people!
[b]Let the earth hear, and all that is in it,
The world and all things that come
forth from it.
2 For the indignation of the LORD *is*
against all nations,
And *His* fury against all their armies;
He has utterly destroyed them,
He has given them over to the
[a]slaughter.

33:7 [a] 2 Kin. 18:18, 37 **33:8** [a] Judg. 5:6 [b] 2 Kin. 18:13–17 [1] Following Masoretic Text and Vulgate; Dead Sea Scrolls read *witnesses;* Septuagint omits *cities;* Targum reads *They have been removed from their cities.* **33:9** [a] Is. 24:4 **33:10** [a] Ps. 12:5 **33:11** [a] [Ps. 7:14] **33:12** [a] Is. 9:18 **33:13** [a] Is. 49:1 **33:14** [a] Heb. 12:29 **33:15** [a] Ps. 15:2; 24:3, 4 [b] Ps. 119:37 **33:17** [a] Ps. 27:4 **33:18** [a] 1 Cor. 1:20 **33:19** [a] 2 Kin. 19:32 [b] Jer. 5:15 **33:20** [a] Ps. 48:12 [b] Ps. 46:5; 125:1 [c] Is. 37:33 [d] Is. 54:2 **33:22** [a] [Acts 10:42] [b] James 4:12 [c] Ps. 89:18 **33:24** [a] Is. 40:2 **34:1** [a] Ps. 49:1 [b] Deut. 32:1 **34:2** [a] Is. 13:5

PEACE NOTE

Christ erased the divisions between Jews and Gentiles by making peace between them—and by *being* "our peace" (Eph. 2:14).

3 Also their slain shall be thrown out;
[a]Their stench shall rise from their corpses,
And the mountains shall be melted
with their blood.
4 [a]All the host of heaven shall be dissolved,
And the heavens shall be rolled up like
a scroll;
[b]All their host shall fall down
As the leaf falls from the vine,
And as [c]*fruit* falling from a fig tree.

5 "For [a]My sword shall be bathed in heaven;
Indeed it [b]shall come down on Edom,
And on the people of My curse, for
judgment.
6 The [a]sword of the LORD is filled with
blood,
It is made overflowing with fatness,
With the blood of lambs and goats,
With the fat of the kidneys of rams.
For [b]the LORD has a sacrifice in Bozrah,
And a great slaughter in the land of
Edom.
7 The wild oxen shall come down with
them,
And the young bulls with the mighty
bulls;
Their land shall be soaked with blood,
And their dust saturated with fatness."

8 *For it is* the day of the LORD's [a]vengeance,
The year of recompense for the cause
of Zion.
9 [a]Its streams shall be turned into pitch,
And its dust into brimstone;
Its land shall become burning pitch.
10 It shall not be quenched night or day;
[a]Its smoke shall ascend forever.
[b]From generation to generation it shall
lie waste;
No one shall pass through it forever
and ever.
11 [a]But the pelican and the porcupine shall
possess it,
Also the owl and the raven shall dwell
in it.
And [b]He shall stretch out over it
The line of confusion and the stones of
emptiness.
12 They shall call its nobles to the kingdom,
But none *shall be* there, and all its
princes shall be nothing.

13 And [a]thorns shall come up in its
palaces,
Nettles and brambles in its fortresses;
[b]It shall be a habitation of jackals,
A courtyard for ostriches.
14 The wild beasts of the desert shall also
meet with the jackals,
And the wild goat shall bleat to its
companion;
Also the night creature shall rest there,
And find for herself a place of rest.
15 There the arrow snake shall make her
nest and lay *eggs*
And hatch, and gather *them* under her
shadow;
There also shall the hawks be gathered,
Every one with her mate.

16 "Search from [a]the book of the LORD,
and read:
Not one of these shall fail;
Not one shall lack her mate.
For My mouth has commanded it, and
His Spirit has gathered them.
17 He has cast the lot for them,
And His hand has divided it among
them with a measuring line.
They shall possess it forever;
From generation to generation they
shall dwell in it."

The Future Glory of Zion

35 The [a]wilderness and the wasteland
shall be glad for them,
And the [b]desert shall rejoice and
blossom as the rose;
2 [a]It shall blossom abundantly and rejoice,
Even with joy and singing.
The glory of Lebanon shall be given to it,
The excellence of Carmel and Sharon.
They shall see the [b]glory of the LORD,
The excellency of our God.

34:3 [a] Joel 2:20 **34:4** [a] Is. 13:13 [b] Is. 14:12 [c] Rev. 6:12–14 **34:5** [a] Jer. 46:10 [b] Mal. 1:4 **34:6** [a] Is. 66:16 [b] Zeph. 1:7 **34:8** [a] Is. 63:4 **34:9** [a] Deut. 29:23 **34:10** [a] Rev. 14:11; 18:18; 19:3 [b] Mal. 1:3, 4 **34:11** [a] Zeph. 2:14 [b] Lam. 2:8 **34:13** [a] Is. 32:13 [b] Is. 13:21 **34:16** [a] [Mal. 3:16] **35:1** [a] Is. 32:15; 55:12 [b] Is. 41:19; 51:3 **35:2** [a] Is. 32:15 [b] Is. 40:5

3 [a]Strengthen the weak hands,
And make firm the feeble knees.
4 Say to those *who are* fearful-hearted,
"Be strong, do not fear!
Behold, your God will come *with* [a]vengeance,
With the recompense of God;
He will come and [b]save you."

5 Then the [a]eyes of the blind shall be opened,
And [b]the ears of the deaf shall be unstopped.
6 Then the [a]lame shall leap like a deer,
And the [b]tongue of the dumb sing.
For [c]waters shall burst forth in the wilderness,
And streams in the desert.
7 The parched ground shall become a pool,
And the thirsty land springs of water;
In [a]the habitation of jackals, where each lay,
There shall be grass with reeds and rushes.

8 A [a]highway shall be there, and a road,
And it shall be called the Highway of Holiness.
[b]The unclean shall not pass over it,
But it *shall be* for others.
Whoever walks the road, although a fool,
Shall not go astray.
9 [a]No lion shall be there,
Nor shall *any* ravenous beast go up on it;
It shall not be found there.
But the redeemed shall walk *there,*
10 And the [a]ransomed of the LORD shall return,
And come to Zion with singing,
With everlasting joy on their heads.
They shall obtain joy and gladness,
And [b]sorrow and sighing shall flee away.

Sennacherib Boasts Against the LORD

36 Now [a]it came to pass in the fourteenth
year of King Hezekiah *that* Sennacherib king of Assyria came up against all the
fortified cities of Judah and took them. 2Then
the king of Assyria sent *the* Rabshakeh[1] with
a great army from Lachish to King Hezekiah
at Jerusalem. And he stood by the aqueduct
from the upper pool, on the highway to the
Fuller's Field. 3And [a]Eliakim the son of Hilkiah, who was over the household, [b]Shebna
the scribe, and Joah the son of Asaph, the
recorder, came out to him.
4[a]Then *the* Rabshakeh said to them, "Say
now to Hezekiah, 'Thus says the great king,
the king of Assyria: "What confidence is this
in which you trust? 5I say you speak of having
plans and power for war; but *they are* mere
words. Now in whom do you trust, that you
rebel against me? 6Look! You are trusting
in the [a]staff of this broken reed, Egypt, on
which if a man leans, it will go into his hand
and pierce it. So *is* Pharaoh king of Egypt to
all who [b]trust in him.
7"But if you say to me, 'We trust in the LORD
our God,' *is it* not He whose high places and
whose altars Hezekiah has taken away, and said
to Judah and Jerusalem, 'You shall worship
before this altar'?"' 8Now therefore, I urge you,
give a pledge to my master the king of Assyria,
and I will give you two thousand horses—if you
are able on your part to put riders on them!
9How then will you repel one captain of the
least of my master's servants, and put your trust
in Egypt for chariots and horsemen? 10Have I
now come up without the LORD against this
land to destroy it? The LORD said to me, 'Go up
against this land, and destroy it.' "
11Then Eliakim, Shebna, and Joah said to
the Rabshakeh, "Please speak to your servants in Aramaic, for we understand *it;* and
do not speak to us in Hebrew[1] in the hearing
of the people who *are* on the wall."
12But *the* Rabshakeh said, "Has my master
sent me to your master and to you to speak
these words, and not to the men who sit on
the wall, who will eat and drink their own
waste with you?"
13Then *the* Rabshakeh stood and called out
with a loud voice in Hebrew, and said, "Hear
the words of the great king, the king of Assyria! 14Thus says the king: 'Do not let Hezekiah
deceive you, for he will not be able to deliver
you; 15nor let Hezekiah make you trust in the
LORD, saying, "The LORD will surely deliver us;
this city will not be given into the hand of the
king of Assyria."' 16Do not listen to Hezekiah;
for thus says the king of Assyria: 'Make *peace*
with me *by a* present and come out to me;
[a]and every one of you eat from his own vine
and every one from his own fig tree, and every
one of you drink the waters of his own cistern;
17until I come and take you away to a land like
your own land, a land of grain and new wine,
a land of bread and vineyards. 18*Beware* lest
Hezekiah persuade you, saying, "The LORD
will deliver us." Has any one of the [a]gods of

35:3 [a] Heb. 12:12 35:4 [a] Is. 34:8 [b] Is. 33:22 35:5 [a] Is. 29:18 [b] [Matt. 11:5] 35:6 [a] Acts 8:7 [b] Is. 32:4 [c] [John 7:38] 35:7 [a] Is. 34:13 35:8 [a] Is. 19:23 [b] Joel 3:17 35:9 [a] Lev. 26:6 35:10 [a] Is. 51:11 [b] [Rev. 7:17; 21:4] 36:1 [a] 2 Chr. 32:1 36:2 [1] A title, probably *Chief of Staff* or *Governor* 36:3 [a] Is. 22:20 [b] Is. 22:15 36:4 [a] 2 Kin. 18:19 36:6 [a] Ezek. 29:6 [b] Ps. 146:3 36:11 [1] Literally *Judean* 36:16 [a] Zech. 3:10 36:18 [a] Is. 37:12

the nations delivered its land from the hand
of the king of Assyria? 19Where *are* the gods
of Hamath and Arpad? Where *are* the gods
of Sepharvaim? Indeed, have they delivered
[a]Samaria from my hand? 20Who among all
the gods of these lands have delivered their
countries from my hand, that the LORD should
deliver Jerusalem from my hand?' "

21But they held their peace and answered
him not a word; for the king's commandment
was, "Do not answer him." 22Then Eliakim
the son of Hilkiah, who *was* over the household, Shebna the scribe, and Joah the son of
Asaph, the recorder, came to Hezekiah with
their clothes torn, and told him the words of
the Rabshakeh.

Isaiah Assures Deliverance

37 And [a]so it was, when King Hezekiah
heard *it,* that he tore his clothes, covered himself with sackcloth, and went into
the house of the LORD. 2Then he sent Eliakim,
who *was* over the household, Shebna the
scribe, and the elders of the priests, covered
with sackcloth, to Isaiah the prophet, the son
of Amoz. 3And they said to him, "Thus says
Hezekiah: 'This day *is* a day of [a]trouble and
rebuke and blasphemy; for the children have
come to birth, but *there is* no strength to bring
them forth. 4It may be that the LORD your
God will hear the words of *the* Rabshakeh,
whom his master the king of Assyria has
sent to [a]reproach the living God, and will
rebuke the words which the LORD your God
has heard. Therefore lift up *your* prayer for
the remnant that is left.' "

5So the servants of King Hezekiah came
to Isaiah. 6And Isaiah said to them, "Thus
you shall say to your master, 'Thus says the
LORD: "Do not be afraid of the words which
you have heard, with which the servants of
the king of Assyria have blasphemed Me.
7Surely I will send a spirit upon him, and
he shall hear a rumor and return to his own
land; and I will cause him to fall by the sword
in his own land." ' "

Sennacherib's Threat and Hezekiah's Prayer

8*Then the* Rabshakeh returned, and found
the king of Assyria warring against Libnah, for
he heard that he had departed from Lachish.
9And the king heard concerning Tirhakah
king of Ethiopia, "He has come out to make
war with you." So when he heard *it,* he sent
messengers to Hezekiah, saying, 10"Thus you
shall speak to Hezekiah king of Judah, saying:
'Do not let your God in whom you trust deceive
you, saying, "Jerusalem shall not be given
into the hand of the king of Assyria." 11Look!
You have heard what the kings of Assyria
have done to all lands by utterly destroying
them; and shall you be delivered? 12Have the
[a]gods of the nations delivered those whom
my fathers have destroyed, Gozan and Haran
and Rezeph, and the people of Eden who *were*
in Telassar? 13Where *is* the king of [a]Hamath,
the king of Arpad, and the king of the city of
Sepharvaim, Hena, and Ivah?' "

14And Hezekiah received the letter from
the hand of the messengers, and read it; and
Hezekiah went up to the house of the LORD,
and spread it before the LORD. 15Then Hezekiah prayed to the LORD, saying: 16"O LORD
of hosts, God of Israel, *the One* who dwells *be-*
tween the cherubim, You *are* God, You [a]alone,
of all the kingdoms of the earth. You have
made heaven and earth. 17[a]Incline Your ear,
O LORD, and hear; open Your eyes, O LORD,
and see; and [b]hear all the words of Sennacherib, which he has sent to reproach the living
God. 18Truly, LORD, the kings of Assyria have
laid waste all the nations and their [a]lands,
19and have cast their gods into the fire; for
they *were* [a]not gods, but the work of men's
hands—wood and stone. Therefore they
destroyed them. 20Now therefore, O LORD
our God, [a]save us from his hand, that all the
kingdoms of the earth may [b]know that You
are the LORD, You alone."

The Word of the LORD Concerning Sennacherib

21Then Isaiah the son of Amoz sent to Hezekiah, saying, "Thus says the LORD God of Israel, 'Because you have prayed to Me against
Sennacherib king of Assyria, 22this *is* the word
which the LORD has spoken concerning him:

"The virgin, the daughter of Zion,
Has despised you, laughed you to scorn;
The daughter of Jerusalem
Has shaken *her* head behind your back!

23 "Whom have you reproached and
blasphemed?
Against whom have you raised *your*
voice,
And lifted up your eyes on high?
Against the Holy One of Israel.
24 By your servants you have reproached
the Lord,
And said, 'By the multitude of my
chariots

36:19 [a] 2 Kin. 17:6 **37:1** [a] 2 Kin. 19:1–37 **37:3** [a] Is. 22:5; 26:16; 33:2 **37:4** [a] Is. 36:15, 18, 20 **37:12** [a] Is. 36:18, 19 **37:13** [a] Is. 49:23 **37:16** [a] Is. 43:10, 11 **37:17** [a] Dan. 9:18 [b] Ps. 74:22 **37:18** [a] 2 Kin. 15:29; 16:9; 17:6, 24 **37:19** [a] Is. 40:19, 20 **37:20** [a] Is. 33:22 [b] Ps. 83:18

I have come up to the height of the mountains,
To the limits of Lebanon;
I will cut down its tall cedars
And its choice cypress trees;
I will enter its farthest height,
To its fruitful forest.
25 I have dug and drunk water,
And with the soles of my feet I have dried up
All the brooks of defense.'

26 "Did you not hear [a]long ago
How I made it,
From ancient times that I formed it?
Now I have brought it to pass,
That you should be
For crushing fortified cities *into* heaps of ruins.
27 Therefore their inhabitants *had* little power;
They were dismayed and confounded;
They were *as* the grass of the field
And the green herb,
As the grass on the housetops
And *grain* blighted before it is grown.

28 "But I know your dwelling place,
Your going out and your coming in,
And your rage against Me.
29 Because your rage against Me and your tumult
Have come up to My ears,
Therefore [a]I will put My hook in your nose
And My bridle in your lips,
And I will [b]turn you back
By the way which you came." '

30"This *shall be* a sign to you:

You shall eat this year such as grows of itself,
And the second year what springs from the same;
Also in the third year sow and reap,
Plant vineyards and eat the fruit of them.
31 And the remnant who have escaped of the house of Judah
Shall again take root downward,
And bear fruit upward.
32 For out of Jerusalem shall go a remnant,
And those who escape from Mount Zion.
The [a]zeal of the LORD of hosts will do this.

33"Therefore thus says the LORD concerning the king of Assyria:

'He shall not come into this city,
Nor shoot an arrow there,
Nor come before it with shield,
Nor build a siege mound against it.
34 By the way that he came,
By the same shall he return;
And he shall not come into this city,'
Says the LORD.
35 'For I will [a]defend this city, to save it
For My own sake and for My servant [b]David's sake.' "

Sennacherib's Defeat and Death

36Then the [a]angel[1] of the LORD went out,
and killed in the camp of the Assyrians one
hundred and eighty-five thousand; and when
people arose early in the morning, there were
the corpses—all dead. 37So Sennacherib king
of Assyria departed and went away, returned
home, and remained at Nineveh. 38Now it came
to pass, as he was worshiping in the house of
Nisroch his god, that his sons Adrammelech
and Sharezer struck him down with the sword;
and they escaped into the land of Ararat. Then
[a]Esarhaddon his son reigned in his place.

Hezekiah's Life Extended

38 In [a]those days Hezekiah was sick and
near death. And Isaiah the prophet,
the son of Amoz, went to him and said to
him, "Thus says the LORD: [b]'Set your house
in order, for you shall die and not live.' "
2Then Hezekiah turned his face toward
the wall, and prayed to the LORD, 3and said,
[a]"Remember now, O LORD, I pray, how I have
walked before You in truth and with a loyal
heart, and have done *what is* good in Your
[b]sight." And Hezekiah wept bitterly.
4And the word of the LORD came to Isaiah,
saying, 5"Go and tell Hezekiah, 'Thus says
the LORD, the God of David your father: "I
have heard your prayer, I have seen your
tears; surely I will add to your days fifteen
years. 6I will deliver you and this city from
the hand of the king of Assyria, and [a]I will
defend this city." ' 7And this *is* [a]the sign to
you from the LORD, that the LORD will do
this thing which He has spoken: 8Behold, I
will bring the shadow on the sundial, which
has gone down with the sun on the sundial
of Ahaz, ten degrees backward." So the sun
returned ten degrees on the dial by which it
had gone down.
9This is the writing of Hezekiah king of

37:26 [a] Is. 25:1; 40:21; 45:21 37:29 [a] Is. 30:28 [b] Ezek. 38:4; 39:2 37:32 [a] 2 Kin. 19:31 37:35 [a] Is. 31:5; 38:6 [b] 1 Kin. 11:13 37:36 [a] 2 Kin. 19:35 [1] Or *Angel* 37:38 [a] Ezra 4:2 38:1 [a] 2 Chr. 32:24 [b] 2 Sam. 17:23 38:3 [a] Neh. 13:14 [b] 2 Kin. 18:5, 6 38:6 [a] Is. 31:5; 37:35 38:7 [a] Is. 7:11

WITH YOUR WHOLE HEART

Remember now, O LORD, I pray, how I have walked before You in truth and with a loyal [peaceful] heart, and have done what is good in Your sight.

ISAIAH 38:3

In chapter 38 King Hezekiah learned that he would soon die (see v. 1). The king was brokenhearted. Not only that, but Jerusalem was also threatened by an expansive, aggressive Assyria. There was no peace there. The king's response was moving: "Then Hezekiah turned his face toward the wall, and prayed to the LORD, and said, 'Remember now, O LORD, I pray, how I have walked before You in truth and with a loyal heart, and have done what is good in Your sight.' And Hezekiah wept bitterly" (vv. 2–3). God heard the king's prayer and sent Isaiah back to the king to tell him He would extend his life for another fifteen years, and Jerusalem would be protected (vv. 4–6).

What is translated as "loyal" is the Hebrew *shalem*, which is from the word *shalom*, meaning "peace" or "wholeness." Hezekiah told God that he had walked in truth and with a whole or complete heart. Hezekiah's faith in God had been real, his commitment full. Can we pray his way? I hope you and I can say to God, "We have walked before You in truth and with complete hearts."

How full is your commitment? Are you willing to up the ante in order to obtain peace?

Judah, when he had been sick and had recovered from his sickness:

10 I said,
"In the prime of my life
I shall go to the gates of Sheol;
I am deprived of the remainder of my years."
11 I said,
"I shall not see YAH,
The LORD[1] [a]in the land of the living;
I shall observe man no more among the inhabitants of the world.[2]
12 [a]My life span is gone,
Taken from me like a shepherd's tent;
I have cut off my life like a weaver.
He cuts me off from the loom;
From day until night You make an end of me.
13 I have considered until morning—
Like a lion,
So He breaks all my bones;
From day until night You make an end of me.
14 Like a crane *or* a swallow, so I chattered;
[a]I mourned like a dove;
My eyes fail *from looking* upward.
O LORD,[1] I am oppressed;
Undertake for me!
15 "What shall I say?
He has both spoken to me,[1]
And He Himself has done *it*.
I shall walk carefully all my years
[a]In the bitterness of my soul.
16 O Lord, by these *things men* live;
And in all these *things is* the life of my spirit;
So You will restore me and make me live.
17 Indeed *it was* for *my own* peace
That I had great bitterness;
But You have lovingly *delivered* my soul from the pit of corruption,
For You have cast all my sins behind Your back.
18 For [a]Sheol cannot thank You,
Death cannot praise You;
Those who go down to the pit cannot hope for Your truth.
19 The living, the living man, he shall praise You,
As I *do* this day;
[a]The father shall make known Your truth to the children.

38:11 [a] Ps. 27:13; 116:9 [1] Hebrew *YAH, YAH* [2] Following some Hebrew manuscripts; Masoretic Text and Vulgate read *rest;* Septuagint omits *among the inhabitants of the world;* Targum reads *land.* **38:12** [a] Job 7:6 **38:14** [a] Is. 59:11 [1] Following Bomberg; Masoretic Text and Dead Sea Scrolls read *Lord.* **38:15** [a] Job 7:11; 10:1 [1] Following Masoretic Text and Vulgate; Dead Sea Scrolls and Targum read *And shall I say to Him;* Septuagint omits first half of this verse. **38:18** [a] Ps. 6:5; 30:9; 88:11; 115:17 **38:19** [a] Deut. 4:9; 6:7

A PEACE-FILLED TURNING

Indeed it was for my own peace that I had great bitterness; but You have lovingly delivered my soul from the pit of corruption, for You have cast all my sins behind Your back.

ISAIAH 38:17

After he recovered from his illness, King Hezekiah wrote a beautiful poem of gratitude to God. He described his initial despair at the thought of his death, and then the joy that God would deliver him: "You will restore me and make me live" (v. 16).

What I find astounding is what the king said about the purpose of his near-fatal illness: "Indeed it was for my own peace that I had great bitterness; but You have lovingly delivered my soul from the pit of corruption, for You have cast all my sins behind Your back" (v. 17). Hezekiah said that, because of his illness, he prayed and repented. And because of his prayer and repentance, not only did God prolong his life, but He forgave the king's sins—or in the king's poetic language, He "cast" them behind His back. I am reminded of what Paul said to the Christians of Rome: "And we know that all things work together for good to those who love God" (Rom. 8:28). It is ironic that Hezekiah's severe illness resulted in spiritual as well as physical healing. I hope I can always say in the face of adversity, "Indeed, it was for my own peace that I repented." Can you say the same?

20 "The LORD *was ready* to save me;
Therefore we will sing my songs with stringed instruments
All the days of our life, in the house of the LORD."

21Now [a]Isaiah had said, "Let them take a
lump of figs, and apply *it* as a poultice on the
boil, and he shall recover."
22And [a]Hezekiah had said, "What *is* the
sign that I shall go up to the house of the
LORD?"

The Babylonian Envoys

39 At [a]that time Merodach-Baladan[1]
the son of Baladan, king of Babylon,
sent letters and a present to Hezekiah, for
he heard that he had been sick and had recovered. 2[a]And Hezekiah was pleased with
them, and showed them the house of his
treasures—the silver and gold, the spices
and precious ointment, and all his armory—
all that was found among his treasures.
There was nothing in his house or in all
his dominion that Hezekiah did not show
them.
3Then Isaiah the prophet went to King
Hezekiah, and said to him, "What did these
men say, and from where did they come to
you?"
So Hezekiah said, "They came to me from
a [a]far country, from Babylon."
4And he said, "What have they seen in
your house?"
So Hezekiah answered, "They have seen
all that *is* in my house; there is nothing
among my treasures that I have not shown
them."
5Then Isaiah said to Hezekiah, "Hear the
word of the LORD of hosts: 6'Behold, the days
are coming [a]when all that *is* in your house,
and what your fathers have accumulated
until this day, shall be carried to Babylon;
nothing shall be left,' says the LORD. 7'And
they shall take away *some* of your [a]sons who
will descend from you, whom you will beget;
and they shall be eunuchs in the palace of
the king of Babylon.'"
8So Hezekiah said to Isaiah, [a]"The word of
the LORD which you have spoken *is* good!"
For he said, "At least there will be peace and
truth in my days."

God's People Are Comforted

40 "Comfort, yes, comfort My people!"
Says your God.
2 "Speak comfort to Jerusalem, and cry out to her,
That her warfare is ended,
That her iniquity is pardoned;
[a]For she has received from the LORD's hand
Double for all her sins."

38:21 [a] 2 Kin. 20:7 38:22 [a] 2 Kin. 20:8 39:1 [a] 2 Kin. 20:12–19 [1] Spelled *Berodach-Baladan* in 2 Kings 20:12
39:2 [a] 2 Chr. 32:25, 31 39:3 [a] Deut. 28:49 39:6 [a] Jer. 20:5 39:7 [a] Dan. 1:1–7 39:8 [a] 1 Sam. 3:18 40:2 [a] Is. 61:7

FOR THE FUTURE GENERATIONS

So Hezekiah said to Isaiah, "The word of the LORD which you have spoken is good!" For he said, "At least there will be peace and truth in my days."

ISAIAH 39:8

Hezekiah had been granted an extension of life and a promise that Assyria would not succeed in capturing the city of Jerusalem, so the king wrote a poem of thanks (see 38:1–20). But Israel's troubles were far from over. Isaiah the prophet warned the king that all that Jerusalem had, including royal sons, would be carried off to Babylon. The prophet was looking ahead more than a century to when the empire of Babylon would rise up, crush Assyria, and become the new world power.

When told this unhappy prophecy, Hezekiah responded, "The word of the LORD which you have spoken is good!" (39:8). He accepted the prophetic word in faith and then expressed gratitude for what God had given him: "At least there will be peace and truth in my days."

Sometimes the road that leads to peace is a bumpy one. One warning from this passage is that all Hezekiah seems to care about is peace in his own day, but at what cost to the generations coming? We should take heed from Hezekiah's example and make sure we are living the peace of God so that His peace remains on our family for generations.

3 [a]The voice of one crying in the wilderness:
[b]"Prepare the way of the LORD;
[c]Make straight in the desert[1]
A highway for our God.
4 Every valley shall be exalted
And every mountain and hill brought low;
[a]The crooked places shall be made straight
And the rough places smooth;
5 The [a]glory of the LORD shall be revealed,
And all flesh shall see *it* together;
For the mouth of the LORD has spoken."

6 The voice said, "Cry out!"
And he[1] said, "What shall I cry?"

[a]"All flesh *is* grass,
And all its loveliness *is* like the flower of the field.
7 The grass withers, the flower fades,
Because the breath of the LORD blows upon it;
Surely the people *are* grass.
8 The grass withers, the flower fades,
But [a]the word of our God stands forever."

9 O Zion,
You who bring good tidings,
Get up into the high mountain;
O Jerusalem,
You who bring good tidings,
Lift up your voice with strength,
Lift *it* up, be not afraid;
Say to the cities of Judah, "Behold your God!"

10 Behold, the Lord GOD shall come with a strong *hand*,
And [a]His arm shall rule for Him;
Behold, [b]His reward *is* with Him,
And His work before Him.
11 He will [a]feed His flock like a shepherd;
He will gather the lambs with His arm,
And carry *them* in His bosom,
And gently lead those who are with young.

12 [a]Who has measured the waters[1] in the hollow of His hand,
Measured heaven with a span
And calculated the dust of the earth in a measure?
Weighed the mountains in scales
And the hills in a balance?
13 [a]Who has directed the Spirit of the LORD,
Or *as* His counselor has taught Him?
14 With whom did He take counsel, and *who* instructed Him,
And [a]taught Him in the path of justice?
Who taught Him knowledge,

40:3 [a] Matt. 3:3 [b] [Mal. 3:1; 4:5, 6] [c] Ps. 68:4 [1] Following Masoretic Text, Targum, and Vulgate; Septuagint omits *in the desert.* **40:4** [a] Is. 45:2 **40:5** [a] Is. 35:2 **40:6** [a] Job 14:2 [1] Following Masoretic Text and Targum; Dead Sea Scrolls, Septuagint, and Vulgate read *I.* **40:8** [a] [John 12:34] **40:10** [a] Is. 59:16, 18 [b] Is. 62:11 **40:11** [a] [John 10:11, 14–16] **40:12** [a] Prov. 30:4 [1] Following Masoretic Text, Septuagint, and Vulgate; Dead Sea Scrolls read *waters of the sea;* Targum reads *waters of the world.* **40:13** [a] [1 Cor. 2:16] **40:14** [a] Job 36:22, 23

And showed Him the way of
understanding?

15 Behold, the nations *are* as a drop in a
bucket,
And are counted as the small dust on
the scales;
Look, He lifts up the isles as a very little
thing.
16 And Lebanon *is* not sufficient to burn,
Nor its beasts sufficient for a burnt
offering.
17 All nations before Him *are* as [a]nothing,
And [b]they are counted by Him less
than nothing and worthless.

18 To whom then will you [a]liken God?
Or what likeness will you compare to
Him?
19 [a]The workman molds an image,
The goldsmith overspreads it with gold,
And the silversmith casts silver chains.
20 Whoever *is* too impoverished for *such* a
contribution
Chooses a tree *that* will not rot;
He seeks for himself a skillful workman
[a]To prepare a carved image *that* will not
totter.

21 [a]Have you not known?
Have you not heard?
Has it not been told you from the
beginning?
Have you not understood from the
foundations of the earth?
22 *It is* He who sits above the circle of the
earth,
And its inhabitants *are* like grasshoppers,
Who [a]stretches out the heavens like a
curtain,
And spreads them out like a [b]tent to
dwell in.
23 He brings the [a]princes to nothing;
He makes the judges of the earth useless.

24 Scarcely shall they be planted,
Scarcely shall they be sown,
Scarcely shall their stock take root in
the earth,
When He will also blow on them,
And they will wither,
And the whirlwind will take them away
like stubble.

25 "To[a] whom then will you liken Me,
Or *to whom* shall I be equal?" says the
Holy One.
26 Lift up your eyes on high,
And see who has created these *things*,
Who brings out their host by number;
[a]He calls them all by name,
By the greatness of His might
And the strength of *His* power;
Not one is missing.

27 [a]Why do you say, O Jacob,
And speak, O Israel:
"My way is hidden from the LORD,
And my just claim is passed over by my
God"?
28 Have you not known?
Have you not heard?
The everlasting God, the LORD,
The Creator of the ends of the earth,
Neither faints nor is weary.
[a]His understanding is unsearchable.
29 He gives power to the weak,
And to *those who have* no might He
increases strength.

PEACE NOTE

Our faith should be an ever-present, positive, moment-by-moment trust in God's power to handle our catastrophes. This is a recipe for peace.

ISAIAH 40:29

30 Even the youths shall faint and be weary,
And the young men shall utterly fall,
31 But those who [a]wait on the LORD
[b]Shall renew *their* strength;
They shall mount up with wings like
eagles,
They shall run and not be weary,
They shall walk and not faint.

Israel Assured of God's Help

41 "Keep [a]silence before Me,
O coastlands,
And let the people renew *their* strength!
Let them come near, then let them speak;
Let us [b]come near together for judgment.

40:17 [a] Dan. 4:35 [b] Ps. 62:9 40:18 [a] Is. 46:5 40:19 [a] Is. 41:7; 44:10 40:20 [a] Is. 41:7; 46:7 40:21 [a] Rom. 1:19 40:22 [a] Jer. 10:12 [b] Ps. 19:4 40:23 [a] Ps. 107:40 40:25 [a] Is. 40:18 40:26 [a] Ps. 147:4 40:27 [a] Is. 54:7, 8 40:28 [a] Rom. 11:33 40:31 [a] Is. 30:15; 49:23 [b] Ps. 103:5 41:1 [a] Zech. 2:13 [b] Is. 1:18

PEACE NOTE

God's Word never says, "God helps those who help themselves." God helps the helpless. Isaiah promises that He gives strength to the weary. Doesn't that inspire peace?

ISAIAH 40:31

2 "Who raised up one [a]from the east?
Who in righteousness called him to His feet?
Who [b]gave the nations before him,
And made *him* rule over kings?
Who gave *them* as the dust *to* his sword,
As driven stubble to his bow?
3 Who pursued them, *and* passed safely
By the way *that* he had not gone with his feet?
4 [a]Who has performed and done *it,*
Calling the generations from the beginning?
'I, the LORD, am [b]the first;
And with the last I *am* [c]He.' "

5 The coastlands saw *it* and feared,
The ends of the earth were afraid;
They drew near and came.
6 [a]Everyone helped his neighbor,
And said to his brother,
"Be of good courage!"
7 [a]So the craftsman encouraged the [b]goldsmith;
He who smooths *with* the hammer
inspired him who strikes the anvil,
Saying, "It *is* ready for the soldering";
Then he fastened it with pegs,
[c]*That* it might not totter.

8 "*But you, Israel, are* My servant,
Jacob whom I have [a]chosen,
The descendants of Abraham My [b]friend.
9 *You* whom I have taken from the ends of the earth,
And called from its farthest regions,
And said to you,
'You *are* My servant,
I have chosen you and have not cast you away:
10 [a]Fear not, [b]for I *am* with you;
Be not dismayed, for I *am* your God.
I will strengthen you,
Yes, I will help you,
I will uphold you with My righteous right hand.'

11 "Behold, all those who were incensed against you
Shall be [a]ashamed and disgraced;
They shall be as nothing,
And those who strive with you shall perish.
12 You shall seek them and not find them—
Those who contended with you.
Those who war against you
Shall be as nothing,
As a nonexistent thing.
13 For I, the LORD your God, will hold your right hand,
Saying to you, 'Fear not, I will help you.'

14 "Fear not, you [a]worm Jacob,
You men of Israel!
I will help you," says the LORD
And your Redeemer, the Holy One of Israel.
15 "Behold, [a]I will make you into a new threshing sledge with sharp teeth;
You shall thresh the mountains and beat *them* small,
And make the hills like chaff.
16 You shall [a]winnow them, the wind shall carry them away,
And the whirlwind shall scatter them;
You shall rejoice in the LORD,
And [b]glory in the Holy One of Israel.

17 "The poor and needy seek water, but *there is* none,
Their tongues fail for thirst.
I, the LORD, will hear them;
I, the God of Israel, will not [a]forsake them.
18 I will open [a]rivers in desolate heights,
And fountains in the midst of the valleys;
I will make the [b]wilderness a pool of water,
And the dry land springs of water.
19 I will plant in the wilderness the cedar and the acacia tree,
The myrtle and the oil tree;

41:2 [a] Is. 46:11 [b] Is. 45:1, 13 **41:4** [a] Is. 41:26 [b] Rev. 1:8, 17; 22:13 [c] Is. 43:10; 44:6 **41:6** [a] Is. 40:19 **41:7** [a] Is. 44:13 [b] Is. 40:19 [c] Is. 40:20 **41:8** [a] Deut. 7:6; 10:15 [b] James 2:23 **41:10** [a] Is. 41:13, 14; 43:5 [b] [Deut. 31:6] **41:11** [a] Zech. 12:3 **41:14** [a] Job 25:6 **41:15** [a] Mic. 4:13 **41:16** [a] Jer. 51:2 [b] Is. 45:25 **41:17** [a] Rom. 11:2 **41:18** [a] Is. 35:6, 7; 43:19; 44:3 [b] Ps. 107:35

I will set in the [a]desert the cypress tree
and the pine
And the box tree together,
20 [a]That they may see and know,
And consider and understand together,
That the hand of the LORD has done this,
And the Holy One of Israel has created it.

The Futility of Idols

21 "Present your case," says the LORD.
"Bring forth your strong *reasons,*" says
the [a]King of Jacob.
22 "Let[a] them bring forth and show us
what will happen;
Let them show the [b]former things,
what they *were,*
That we may consider them,
And know the latter end of them;
Or declare to us things to come.
23 [a]Show the things that are to come
hereafter,
That we may know that you *are* gods;
Yes, [b]do good or do evil,
That we may be dismayed and see *it*
together.
24 Indeed [a]you *are* nothing,
And your work *is* nothing;
He who chooses you *is* an abomination.

25 "I have raised up one from the north,
And he shall come;
From the rising of the sun [a]he shall call
on My name;
[b]And he shall come against princes as
though mortar,
As the potter treads clay.
26 [a]Who has declared from the beginning,
that we may know?
And former times, that we may say, '*He
is* righteous'?
Surely *there is* no one who shows,
Surely *there is* no one who declares,
Surely *there is* no one who hears your
words.
27 [a]The first time [b]*I said* to Zion,
'Look, there they are!'
And I will give to Jerusalem one who
brings good tidings.
28 [a]For I looked, and *there was* no man;
I looked among them, but *there was* no
counselor,
Who, when I asked of them, could
answer a word.
29 [a]Indeed they *are* all worthless;[1]
Their works *are* nothing;
Their molded images *are* wind and
confusion.

The Servant of the LORD

42 "Behold! [a]My Servant whom I
uphold,
My Elect One *in whom* My soul [b]delights!
[c]I have put My Spirit upon Him;
He will bring forth justice to the Gentiles.
2 He will not cry out, nor raise *His voice,*
Nor cause His voice to be heard in the
street.
3 A bruised reed He will not break,
And smoking flax He will not quench;
He will bring forth justice for truth.
4 He will not fail nor be discouraged,
Till He has established justice in the
earth;
[a]And the coastlands shall wait for His
law."

5 Thus says God the LORD,
[a]Who created the heavens and stretched
them out,
Who spread forth the earth and that
which comes from it,
[b]Who gives breath to the people on it,
And spirit to those who walk on it:
6 "I,[a] the LORD, have called You in
righteousness,
And will hold Your hand;
I will keep You [b]and give You as a
covenant to the people,
As [c]a light to the Gentiles,
7 [a]To open blind eyes,
To [b]bring out prisoners from the
prison,
Those who sit in [c]darkness from the
prison house.
8 I *am* the LORD, that *is* My name;
And My [a]glory I will not give to
another,
Nor My praise to carved images.
9 Behold, the former things have come
to pass,
And new things I declare;
Before they spring forth I tell you of
them."

Praise to the LORD

10 [a]Sing to the LORD a new song,
And His praise from the ends of the
earth,
[b]You who go down to the sea, and all
that is in it,

41:19 [a] Is. 35:1 **41:20** [a] Job 12:9 **41:21** [a] Is. 43:15 **41:22** [a] Is. 45:21 [b] Is. 43:9 **41:23** [a] [John 13:19] [b] Jer. 10:5 **41:24** [a] [1 Cor. 8:4] **41:25** [a] Ezra 1:2 [b] Is. 41:2 **41:26** [a] Is. 43:9 **41:27** [a] Is. 41:4 [b] Is. 40:9 **41:28** [a] Is. 63:5 **41:29** [a] Is. 41:24 [1] Following Masoretic Text and Vulgate; Dead Sea Scrolls, Syriac, and Targum read *nothing;* Septuagint omits the first line. **42:1** [a] [Phil. 2:7] [b] Matt. 3:17; 17:5 [c] [Is. 11:2] **42:4** [a] [Gen. 49:10] **42:5** [a] Zech. 12:1 [b] Acts 17:25 **42:6** [a] Is. 43:1 [b] Is. 49:8 [c] Luke 2:32 **42:7** [a] Is. 35:5 [b] Luke 4:18 [c] Is. 9:2 **42:8** [a] Is. 48:11 **42:10** [a] Ps. 33:3; 40:3; 98:1 [b] Ps. 107:23

You coastlands and you inhabitants of
them!
11 Let the wilderness and its cities lift up
their voice,
The villages *that* Kedar inhabits.
Let the inhabitants of Sela sing,
Let them shout from the top of the
mountains.
12 Let them give glory to the LORD,
And declare His praise in the coastlands.
13 The LORD shall go forth like a mighty
man;
He shall stir up *His* zeal like a man of war.
He shall cry out, [a]yes, shout aloud;
He shall prevail against His enemies.

Promise of the LORD's Help

14 "I have held My peace a long time,
I have been still and restrained Myself.
Now I will cry like a woman in labor,
I will pant and gasp at once.
15 I will lay waste the mountains and hills,
And dry up all their vegetation;
I will make the rivers coastlands,
And I will dry up the pools.
16 I will bring the blind by a way they did
not know;
I will lead them in paths they have not
known.
I will make darkness light before them,
And crooked places straight.
These things I will do for them,
And not forsake them.
17 They shall be [a]turned back,
They shall be greatly ashamed,
Who trust in carved images,
Who say to the molded images,
'You *are* our gods.'

18 "Hear, you deaf;
And look, you blind, that you may see.
19 [a]Who *is* blind but My servant,
Or deaf as My messenger *whom* I send?
Who *is* blind as *he who is* perfect,
And blind as the LORD's servant?
20 Seeing many things, [a]but you do not
observe;
Opening the ears, but he does not hear."

Israel's Obstinate Disobedience

21 The LORD is well pleased for His
righteousness' sake;
He will exalt the law and make *it*
honorable.
22 But this *is* a people robbed and plundered;
All of them are snared in holes,
And they are hidden in prison houses;
They are for prey, and no one delivers;
For plunder, and no one says, "Restore!"

23 Who among you will give ear to this?
Who will listen and hear for the time to
come?
24 Who gave Jacob for plunder, and Israel
to the robbers?
Was it not the LORD,
He against whom we have sinned?
[a]For they would not walk in His ways,
Nor were they obedient to His law.
25 Therefore He has poured on him the
fury of His anger
And the strength of battle;
[a]It has set him on fire all around,
[b]Yet he did not know;
And it burned him,
Yet he did not take *it* to [c]heart.

The Redeemer of Israel

43 But now, thus says the LORD, who
created you, O Jacob,
And He who formed you, O Israel:
"Fear not, [a]for I have redeemed you;
[b]I have called *you* by your name;
You *are* Mine.
2 [a]When you pass through the waters, [b]I
will be with you;
And through the rivers, they shall not
overflow you.
When you [c]walk through the fire, you
shall not be burned,
Nor shall the flame scorch you.
3 For I *am* the LORD your God,
The Holy One of Israel, your Savior;
[a]I gave Egypt for your ransom,
Ethiopia and Seba in your place.
4 Since you were precious in My sight,
You have been honored,
And I have [a]loved you;
Therefore I will give men for you,
And people for your life.
5 [a]Fear not, for I *am* with you;
I will bring your descendants from the
east,
And [b]gather you from the west;
6 I will say to the [a]north, 'Give them up!'
And to the south, 'Do not keep them
back!'
Bring My sons from afar,
And My daughters from the ends of the
earth—
7 Everyone who is [a]called by My name,
Whom [b]I have created for My glory;
I have formed him, yes, I have made
him."

42:13 [a] Is. 31:4 **42:17** [a] Ps. 97:7 **42:19** [a] [John 9:39, 41] **42:20** [a] Rom. 2:21 **42:24** [a] Is. 65:2 **42:25** [a] 2 Kin. 25:9 [b] Hos. 7:9 [c] Is. 29:13 **43:1** [a] Is. 43:5; 44:6 [b] Is. 42:6; 45:4 **43:2** [a] [Ps. 66:12; 91:3] [b] [Deut. 31:6] [c] Dan. 3:25 **43:3** [a] [Prov. 11:8; 21:18] **43:4** [a] Is. 63:9 **43:5** [a] Is. 41:10; 44:2 [b] Is. 54:7 **43:6** [a] Is. 49:12 **43:7** [a] James 2:7 [b] [2 Cor. 5:17]

8 [a]Bring out the blind people who have
eyes,
And the [b]deaf who have ears.
9 Let all the nations be gathered together,
And let the people be assembled.
[a]Who among them can declare this,
And show us former things?
Let them bring out their witnesses, that
they may be justified;
Or let them hear and say, "*It is* truth."
10 "You[a] *are* My witnesses," says the LORD,
[b]"And My servant whom I have chosen,
That you may know and [c]believe Me,
And understand that I *am* He.
Before Me there was no God formed,
Nor shall there be after Me.
11 I, *even* I, [a]*am* the LORD,
And besides Me *there is* no savior.
12 I have declared and saved,
I have proclaimed,
And *there was* no [a]foreign *god* among you;
[b]Therefore you *are* My witnesses,"
Says the LORD, "that I *am* God.
13 [a]Indeed before the day *was,* I *am* He;
And *there is* no one who can deliver out
of My hand;
I work, and who will [b]reverse it?"

14 Thus says the LORD, your Redeemer,
The Holy One of Israel:
"For your sake I will send to Babylon,
And bring them all down as fugitives—
The Chaldeans, who rejoice in their ships.
15 I *am* the LORD, your Holy One,
The Creator of Israel, your [a]King."

16 Thus says the LORD, who [a]makes a way
in the sea
And a [b]path through the mighty
waters,
17 Who [a]brings forth the chariot and
horse,
The army and the power
(They shall lie down together, they
shall not rise;
They are extinguished, they are
quenched like a wick):
18 "Do[a] not remember the former things,
Nor consider the things of old.
19 Behold, I will do a [a]new thing,
Now it shall spring forth;
Shall you not know it?
[b]I will even make a road in the
wilderness
And rivers in the desert.
20 The beast of the field will honor Me,
The jackals and the ostriches,
Because [a]I give waters in the
wilderness
And rivers in the desert,
To give drink to My people,
My chosen.
21 [a]This people I have formed for Myself;
They shall declare My [b]praise.

Pleading with Unfaithful Israel

22 "But you have not called upon Me,
O Jacob;
And you [a]have been weary of Me,
O Israel.
23 [a]You have not brought Me the sheep for
your burnt offerings,
Nor have you honored Me with your
sacrifices.
I have not caused you to serve with
grain offerings,
Nor wearied you with incense.
24 You have bought Me no sweet cane
with money,
Nor have you satisfied Me with the fat
of your sacrifices;
But you have burdened Me with your
sins,
You have [a]wearied Me with your
iniquities.

25 "I, *even* I, *am* He who [a]blots out your
transgressions [b]for My own sake;
[c]And I will not remember your sins.
26 Put Me in remembrance;
Let us contend together;
State your *case,* that you may be
acquitted.
27 Your first father sinned,
And your mediators have transgressed
against Me.
28 Therefore I will profane the princes of
the sanctuary;
[a]I will give Jacob to the curse,
And Israel to reproaches.

God's Blessing on Israel

44 "Yet hear now, O Jacob My servant,
And Israel whom I have chosen.
2 Thus says the LORD who made you
And formed you from the womb, *who*
will help you:
'Fear not, O Jacob My servant;
And you, Jeshurun, whom I have
chosen.

43:8 [a] Ezek. 12:2 [b] Is. 29:18 **43:9** [a] Is. 41:21, 22, 26 **43:10** [a] Is. 44:8 [b] Is. 55:4 [c] Is. 41:4; 44:6 **43:11** [a] Hos. 13:4 **43:12** [a] Deut. 32:16 [b] Is. 44:8 **43:13** [a] Ps. 90:2 [b] Job 9:12 **43:15** [a] Is. 41:20, 21 **43:16** [a] Ex. 14:16, 21, 22 [b] Josh. 3:13 **43:17** [a] Ex. 14:4–9, 25 **43:18** [a] Jer. 16:14 **43:19** [a] [2 Cor. 5:17] [b] Ex. 17:6 **43:20** [a] Is. 48:21 **43:21** [a] Ps. 102:18 [b] Jer. 13:11 **43:22** [a] Mal. 1:13; 3:14 **43:23** [a] Amos 5:25 **43:24** [a] Is. 1:14; 7:13 **43:25** [a] Jer. 50:20 [b] Ezek. 36:22 [c] Is. 1:18 **43:28** [a] Dan. 9:11

3 For I will pour water on him who is thirsty,
And floods on the dry ground;
I will pour My Spirit on your descendants,
And My blessing on your offspring;
4 They will spring up among the grass
Like willows by the watercourses.'
5 One will say, 'I *am* the LORD's';
Another will call *himself* by the name of Jacob;
Another will write *with* his hand, 'The LORD's,'
And name *himself* by the name of Israel.

There Is No Other God

6 "Thus says the LORD, the King of Israel,
And his Redeemer, the LORD of hosts:
[a]'I *am* the First and I *am* the Last;
Besides Me *there is* no God.
7 And [a]who can proclaim as I do?
Then let him declare it and set it in order for Me,
Since I appointed the ancient people.
And the things that are coming and shall come,
Let them show these to them.
8 Do not fear, nor be afraid;
[a]Have I not told you from that time, and declared *it?*
[b]You *are* My witnesses.
Is there a God besides Me?
Indeed [c]*there is* no other Rock;
I know not *one.'* "

Idolatry Is Foolishness

9 [a]Those who make an image, all of them *are* useless,
And their precious things shall not profit;
They *are* their own witnesses;
[b]They neither see nor know, that they may be ashamed.
10 Who would form a god or mold an image
[a]*That* profits him nothing?
11 Surely all his companions would be [a]ashamed;
And the workmen, they *are* mere men.
Let them all be gathered together,
Let them stand up;
Yet they shall fear,
They shall be ashamed together.

12 [a]The blacksmith with the tongs works one in the coals,
Fashions it with hammers,
And works it with the strength of his arms.
Even so, he is hungry, and his strength fails;
He drinks no water and is faint.
13 The craftsman stretches out *his* rule,
He marks one out with chalk;
He fashions it with a plane,
He marks it out with the compass,
And makes it like the figure of a man,
According to the beauty of a man, that it may remain in the house.
14 He cuts down cedars for himself,
And takes the cypress and the oak;
He secures *it* for himself among the trees of the forest.
He plants a pine, and the rain nourishes *it.*

15 Then it shall be for a man to burn,
For he will take some of it and warm himself;
Yes, he kindles *it* and bakes bread;
Indeed he makes a god and worships *it;*
He makes it a carved image, and falls down to it.
16 He burns half of it in the fire;
With this half he eats meat;
He roasts a roast, and is satisfied.
He even warms *himself* and says,
"Ah! I am warm,
I have seen the fire."
17 And the rest of it he makes into a god,
His carved image.
He falls down before it and worships *it,*
Prays to it and says,
"Deliver me, for you *are* my god!"

18 [a]They do not know nor understand;
For [b]He has shut their eyes, so that they cannot see,
And their hearts, so that they cannot [c]understand.

PEACE NOTE

The pagan carves up a piece of wood, falls down before it, and worships it. Our minds will lead us away from God and peace and toward other gods if we are not renewed in God's Word.

ISAIAH 44:17

44:6 [a] Is. 41:4 **44:7** [a] Is. 41:4, 22, 26 **44:8** [a] Is. 41:22 [b] Is. 43:10, 12 [c] 1 Sam. 2:2 **44:9** [a] Is. 41:24 [b] Ps. 115:4
44:10 [a] Hab. 2:18 **44:11** [a] Ps. 97:7 **44:12** [a] Jer. 10:3–5 **44:18** [a] Is. 45:20 [b] Is. 6:9, 10; 29:10 [c] Jer. 10:14

19 And no one [a]considers in his heart,
Nor *is there* knowledge nor
understanding to say,
"I have burned half of it in the fire,
Yes, I have also baked bread on its coals;
I have roasted meat and eaten *it;*
And shall I make the rest of it an
abomination?
Shall I fall down before a block of wood?"
20 He feeds on ashes;
[a]A deceived heart has turned him aside;
And he cannot deliver his soul,
Nor say, "*Is there* not a [b]lie in my right
hand?"

Israel Is Not Forgotten

21 "Remember these, O Jacob,
And Israel, for you *are* My servant;
I have formed you, you *are* My servant;
O Israel, you will not be [a]forgotten by Me!
22 [a]I have blotted out, like a thick cloud,
your transgressions,
And like a cloud, your sins.
Return to Me, for [b]I have redeemed you."

23 [a]Sing, O heavens, for the LORD has done *it!*
Shout, you lower parts of the earth;
Break forth into singing, you
mountains,
O forest, and every tree in it!
For the LORD has redeemed Jacob,
And [b]glorified Himself in Israel.

Judah Will Be Restored

24 Thus says the LORD, [a]your Redeemer,
And [b]He who formed you from the
womb:
"I *am* the LORD, who makes all *things,*
[c]Who stretches out the heavens all alone,
Who spreads abroad the earth by Myself;
25 Who [a]frustrates the signs [b]of the
babblers,
And drives diviners mad;
Who turns wise men backward,
[c]And makes their knowledge foolishness;
26 [a]Who confirms the word of His servant,
And performs the counsel of His
messengers;
Who says to Jerusalem, 'You shall be
inhabited,'
To the cities of Judah, 'You shall be built,'
And I will raise up her waste places;
27 [a]Who says to the deep, 'Be dry!
And I will dry up your rivers';
28 Who says of [a]Cyrus, '*He is* My shepherd,
And he shall perform all My pleasure,
Saying to Jerusalem, [b]"You shall be
built,"
And to the temple, "Your foundation
shall be laid." '

Cyrus, God's Instrument

45 "Thus says the LORD to His
anointed,
To [a]Cyrus, whose [b]right hand I have held—
[c]To subdue nations before him
And [d]loose the armor of kings,
To open before him the double doors,
So that the gates will not be shut:
2 'I will go before you
[a]And make the crooked places[1] straight;
[b]I will break in pieces the gates of bronze
And cut the bars of iron.
3 I will give you the treasures of darkness
And hidden riches of secret places,
[a]That you may know that I, the LORD,
Who [b]call *you* by your name,
Am the God of Israel.
4 For [a]Jacob My servant's sake,
And Israel My elect,
I have even called you by your name;
I have named you, though you have
not known Me.
5 I [a]*am* the LORD, and [b]*there is* no other;
There is no God besides Me.
[c]I will gird you, though you have not
known Me,
6 [a]That they may [b]know from the rising of
the sun to its setting
That *there is* none besides Me.
I *am* the LORD, and *there is* no other;
7 I form the light and create darkness,
I make peace and [a]create calamity;
I, the LORD, do all these *things.*'

8 "Rain[a] down, you heavens, from above,
And let the skies pour down
righteousness;
Let the earth open, let them bring forth
salvation,
And let righteousness spring up together.
I, the LORD, have created it.

9 "Woe to him who strives with [a]his Maker!
Let the potsherd *strive* with the
potsherds of the earth!
[b]Shall the clay say to him who forms it,
'What are you making?'

44:19 [a] Is. 46:8 **44:20** [a] 2 Thess. 2:11 [b] Rom. 1:25 **44:21** [a] Is. 49:15 **44:22** [a] Is. 43:25 [b] 1 Cor. 6:20 **44:23** [a] Ps. 69:34 [b] Is. 49:3; 60:21 **44:24** [a] Is. 43:14 [b] Is. 43:1 [c] Job 9:8 **44:25** [a] Is. 47:13 [b] Jer. 50:36 [c] 1 Cor. 1:20, 27 **44:26** [a] Zech. 1:6 **44:27** [a] Jer. 50:38; 51:36 **44:28** [a] Ezra 1:1 [b] Ezra 6:7 **45:1** [a] Is. 44:28 [b] Is. 41:13 [c] Dan. 5:30 [d] Job 12:21 **45:2** [a] Is. 40:4 [b] Ps. 107:16 [1] Dead Sea Scrolls and Septuagint read *mountains;* Targum reads *I will trample down the walls;* Vulgate reads *I will humble the great ones of the earth.* **45:3** [a] Is. 41:23 [b] Ex. 33:12 **45:4** [a] Is. 44:1 **45:5** [a] Deut. 4:35; 32:39 [b] Is. 45:14, 18 [c] Ps. 18:32 **45:6** [a] Mal. 1:11 [b] [Is. 11:9; 52:10] **45:7** [a] Amos 3:6 **45:8** [a] Ps. 85:11 **45:9** [a] Is. 64:8 [b] Jer. 18:6

GOD, OUR CREATOR OF PEACE

"I form the light and create darkness, I make peace and create calamity; I, the LORD, do all these things."

ISAIAH 45:7

The Babylonian exile was over; the people had returned home, and they could rebuild their city and temple. Israel had learned from this experience that God is sovereign; He alone is God. He oversees all, He is Author of all. In His own words, "I form the light and create darkness, I make peace and create calamity; I, the LORD, do all these things."

We wonder at a statement like "I make peace and create calamity." Doesn't God do only good things? How can He be the Author of disaster? The point being made in context—in an oracle addressed to Cyrus, king of the Persians—was that God gives victory and defeat. Cyrus may have thought he was in charge, but in reality the God of Israel rules the earth. True peace comes from Him, not from a human king.

Take a moment and thank the Lord that He creates peace. There is no one in your life who can stop the peace of God from living in your heart right now. Pray this prayer, "Lord, I ask You to make peace in my heart today even while I walk forward in adversity with faith. I know You, O Lord, are the Source of my peace."

Or shall your handiwork *say,* 'He has
no hands'?
10 Woe to him who says to *his* father,
'What are you begetting?'
Or to the woman, 'What have you
brought forth?' "

11 Thus says the LORD,
The Holy One of Israel, and his Maker:
[a]"Ask Me of things to come concerning
[b]My sons;
And concerning [c]the work of My hands,
you command Me.
12 [a]I have made the earth,
And [b]created man on it.
I—My hands—stretched out the
heavens,
And [c]all their host I have commanded.
13 [a]I have raised him up in righteousness,
And I will direct all his ways;
He shall [b]build My city
And let My exiles go free,
[c]Not for price nor reward,"
Says the LORD of hosts.

The LORD, the Only Savior

14 Thus says the LORD:

[a]"The labor of Egypt and merchandise of
Cush
And of the Sabeans, men of stature,
Shall come over to you, and they shall
be yours;
They shall walk behind you,
They shall come over [b]in chains;
And they shall bow down to you.
They will make supplication to you,
saying, [c]'Surely God *is* in you,
And *there is* no other;
[d]*There is* no other God.' "

15 Truly You *are* God, [a]who hide Yourself,
O God of Israel, the Savior!
16 They shall be [a]ashamed
And also disgraced, all of them;
They shall go in confusion together,
Who are makers of idols.
17 [a]*But* Israel shall be saved by the LORD
With an [b]everlasting salvation;
You shall not be ashamed or [c]disgraced
Forever and ever.

18 For thus says the LORD,
[a]Who created the heavens,
Who is God,
Who formed the earth and made it,
Who has established it,
Who did not create it in vain,
Who formed it to be [b]inhabited:
[c]"I *am* the LORD, and *there is* no other.
19 I have not spoken in [a]secret,
In a dark place of the earth;

45:11 [a] Is. 8:19 [b] Jer. 31:9 [c] Is. 29:23; 60:21; 64:8 **45:12** [a] Is. 42:5 [b] Gen. 1:26 [c] Gen. 2:1 **45:13** [a] Is. 41:2 [b] 2 Chr. 36:22 [c] [Rom. 3:24] **45:14** [a] Zech. 8:22, 23 [b] Ps. 149:8 [c] 1 Cor. 14:25 [d] Is. 45:5 **45:15** [a] Ps. 44:24 **45:16** [a] Is. 44:11 **45:17** [a] Is. 26:4 [b] Is. 51:6 [c] Is. 29:22 **45:18** [a] Is. 42:5 [b] Ps. 115:16 [c] Is. 45:5 **45:19** [a] Deut. 30:11

I did not say to the seed of Jacob,
'Seek Me in vain';
[b]I, the LORD, speak righteousness,
I declare things that are right.

20 "Assemble yourselves and come;
Draw near together,
You *who have* escaped from the nations.
[a]They have no knowledge,
Who carry the wood of their carved
image,
And pray to a god *that* cannot save.
21 Tell and bring forth *your case;*
Yes, let them take counsel together.
[a]Who has declared this from ancient time?
Who has told it from that time?
Have not I, the LORD?
[b]And *there is* no other God besides Me,
A just God and a Savior;
There is none besides Me.

22 "Look to Me, and be saved,
[a]All you ends of the earth!
For I *am* God, and *there is* no other.
23 [a]I have sworn by Myself;
The word has gone out of My mouth *in*
righteousness,
And shall not return,
That to Me every [b]knee shall bow,
[c]Every tongue shall take an oath.
24 He shall say,
'Surely in the LORD I have
[a]righteousness and strength.
To Him *men* shall come,
And [b]all shall be ashamed
Who are incensed against Him.
25 [a]In the LORD all the descendants of Israel
Shall be justified, and [b]shall glory.' "

Dead Idols and the Living God

46 Bel [a]bows down, Nebo stoops;
Their idols were on the beasts and
on the cattle.
Your carriages *were* heavily loaded,
[b]A burden to the weary *beast.*
2 They stoop, they bow down together;
They could not deliver the burden,
[a]But have themselves gone into captivity.

3 "Listen to Me, O house of Jacob,
And all the remnant of the house of
Israel,
[a]Who have been upheld *by Me* from birth,
Who have been carried from the womb:
4 Even to *your* old age, [a]I *am* He,
And *even* to gray hairs [b]I will carry *you!*
I have made, and I will bear;
Even I will carry, and will deliver *you.*

5 "To[a] whom will you liken Me, and make
Me equal
And compare Me, that we should be alike?
6 [a]They lavish gold out of the bag,
And weigh silver on the scales;
They hire a [b]goldsmith, and he makes
it a god;
They prostrate themselves, yes, they
worship.
7 [a]They bear it on the shoulder, they carry it
And set it in its place, and it stands;
From its place it shall not move.
Though [b]*one* cries out to it, yet it
cannot answer
Nor save him out of his trouble.

8 "Remember this, and show yourselves men;
[a]Recall to mind, O you transgressors.
9 [a]Remember the former things of old,
For I *am* God, and [b]*there is* no other;
I am God, and *there is* none like Me,
10 [a]Declaring the end from the beginning,
And from ancient times *things* that are
not *yet* done,
Saying, [b]'My counsel shall stand,
And I will do all My pleasure,'
11 Calling a bird of prey [a]from the east,
The man [b]who executes My counsel,
from a far country.
Indeed [c]I have spoken *it;*
I will also bring it to pass.
I have purposed *it;*
I will also do it.

12 "Listen to Me, you [a]stubborn-hearted,
[b]Who *are* far from righteousness:
13 [a]I bring My righteousness near, it shall
not be far off;
My salvation [b]shall not linger.
And I will place [c]salvation in Zion,
For Israel My glory.

The Humiliation of Babylon

47 "Come [a]down and [b]sit in the dust,
O virgin daughter of [c]Babylon;
Sit on the ground without a throne,
O daughter of the Chaldeans!
For you shall no more be called
Tender and delicate.

45:19 [b] Ps. 19:8 **45:20** [a] Is. 44:9; 46:7 **45:21** [a] Is. 41:22; 43:9 [b] Is. 44:8 **45:22** [a] Ps. 22:27; 65:5 **45:23** [a] [Heb. 6:13] [b] Rom. 14:11 [c] Deut. 6:13 **45:24** [a] [1 Cor. 1:30] [b] Is. 41:11 **45:25** [a] Is. 45:17 [b] 1 Cor. 1:31 **46:1** [a] Jer. 50:2 [b] Jer. 10:5 **46:2** [a] Jer. 48:7 **46:3** [a] Ps. 71:6 **46:4** [a] Mal. 3:6 [b] Ps. 48:14 **46:5** [a] Is. 40:18, 25 **46:6** [a] Is. 40:19; 41:6 [b] Is. 44:12 **46:7** [a] Jer. 10:5 [b] Is. 45:20 **46:8** [a] Is. 44:19 **46:9** [a] Deut. 32:7 [b] Is. 45:5, 21 **46:10** [a] Is. 45:21; 48:3 [b] Ps. 33:11 **46:11** [a] Is. 41:2, 25 [b] Is. 44:28 [c] Num. 23:19 **46:12** [a] Ps. 76:5 [b] [Rom. 10:3] **46:13** [a] [Rom. 1:17] [b] Hab. 2:3 [c] Is. 62:11 **47:1** [a] Jer. 48:18 [b] Is. 3:26 [c] Jer. 25:12; 50:1—51:64

2 [a]Take the millstones and grind meal.
Remove your veil,
Take off the skirt,
Uncover the thigh,
Pass through the rivers.
3 [a]Your nakedness shall be uncovered,
Yes, your shame will be seen;
[b]I will take vengeance,
And I will not arbitrate with a man."

4 *As for* [a]our Redeemer, the LORD of
hosts *is* His name,
The Holy One of Israel.

5 "Sit in [a]silence, and go into darkness,
O daughter of the Chaldeans;
[b]For you shall no longer be called
The Lady of Kingdoms.
6 [a]I was angry with My people;
[b]I have profaned My inheritance,
And given them into your hand.
You showed them no mercy;
[c]On the elderly you laid your yoke very
heavily.
7 And you said, 'I shall be [a]a lady forever,'
So that you did not [b]take these *things* to
heart,
[c]Nor remember the latter end of them.

8 "Therefore hear this now, *you who are*
given to pleasures,
Who dwell securely,
Who say in your heart, 'I *am,* and *there*
is no one else besides me;
I shall not sit *as* a widow,
Nor shall I know the loss of children';
9 But these two *things* shall come to you
[a]In a moment, in one day:
The loss of children, and widowhood.
They shall come upon you in their
fullness
Because of the multitude of your
sorceries,
For the great abundance of your
enchantments.

10 "For you have trusted in your wickedness;
You have said, 'No one [a]sees me';
Your wisdom and your knowledge have
warped you;
And you have said in your heart,
'I *am,* and *there is* no one else besides me.'
11 Therefore evil shall come upon you;
You shall not know from where it arises.
And trouble shall fall upon you;
You will not be able to put it off.
And [a]desolation shall come upon you
[b]suddenly,
Which you shall not know.

12 "Stand now with your enchantments
And the multitude of your sorceries,
In which you have labored from your
youth—
Perhaps you will be able to profit,
Perhaps you will prevail.
13 [a]You are wearied in the multitude of
your counsels;
Let now [b]the astrologers, the stargazers,
And the monthly prognosticators
Stand up and save you
From what shall come upon you.
14 Behold, they shall be [a]as stubble,
The fire shall [b]burn them;
They shall not deliver themselves
From the power of the flame;
It shall not *be* a coal to be warmed by,
Nor a fire to sit before!
15 Thus shall they be to you
With whom you have labored,
[a]Your merchants from your youth;
They shall wander each one to his quarter.
No one shall save you.

Israel Refined for God's Glory

48 "Hear this, O house of Jacob,
Who are called by the name of
Israel,
And have come forth from the
wellsprings of Judah;
Who swear by the name of the LORD,
And make mention of the God of
Israel,
But [a]not in truth or in righteousness;
2 For they call themselves [a]after the holy
city,
And [b]lean on the God of Israel;
The LORD of hosts *is* His name:

3 "I have [a]declared the former things
from the beginning;
They went forth from My mouth, and I
caused them to hear it.
Suddenly I did *them,* [b]and they came to
pass.
4 Because I knew that you *were* obstinate,
And [a]your neck *was* an iron sinew,
And your brow bronze,
5 Even from the beginning I have
declared *it* to you;
Before it came to pass I proclaimed *it*
to you,

47:2 [a] Ex. 11:5 **47:3** [a] Is. 3:17; 20:4 [b] [Rom. 12:19] **47:4** [a] Jer. 50:34 **47:5** [a] 1 Sam. 2:9 [b] [Dan. 2:37] **47:6** [a] 2 Sam. 24:14 [b] Is. 43:28 [c] Deut. 28:49, 50 **47:7** [a] Rev. 18:7 [b] Is. 42:25; 46:8 [c] Deut. 32:29 **47:9** [a] 1 Thess. 5:3 **47:10** [a] Is. 29:15 **47:11** [a] 1 Thess. 5:3 [b] Is. 29:5 **47:13** [a] Is. 57:10 [b] Dan. 2:2, 10 **47:14** [a] Nah. 1:10 [b] Jer. 51:58 **47:15** [a] Rev. 18:11 **48:1** [a] Jer. 4:2; 5:2 **48:2** [a] Is. 52:1; 64:10 [b] Mic. 3:11 **48:3** [a] Is. 44:7, 8; 46:10 [b] Josh. 21:45 **48:4** [a] Deut. 31:27

Lest you should say, 'My idol has done them,
And my carved image and my molded image
Have commanded them.'

6 "You have heard;
See all this.
And will you not declare *it?*
I have made you hear new things from this time,
Even hidden things, and you did not know them.
7 They are created now and not from the beginning;
And before this day you have not heard them,
Lest you should say, 'Of course I knew them.'
8 Surely you did not hear,
Surely you did not know;
Surely from long ago your ear was not opened.
For I knew that you would deal very treacherously,
And were called [a]a transgressor from the womb.

9 "For[a] My name's sake [b]I will defer My anger,
And *for* My praise I will restrain it from you,
So that I do not cut you off.
10 Behold, [a]I have refined you, but not as silver;
I have tested you in the [b]furnace of affliction.
11 For My own sake, for My own sake, I will do *it;*
For [a]how should *My name* be profaned?
And [b]I will not give My glory to another.

God's Ancient Plan to Redeem Israel

12 "Listen to Me, O Jacob,
And Israel, My called:
I *am* He, [a]I *am* the [b]First,
I *am* also the Last.
13 Indeed [a]My hand has laid the foundation of the earth,
And My right hand has stretched out the heavens;
When [b]I call to them,
They stand up together.

14 "All of you, assemble yourselves, and hear!
Who among them has declared these *things?*
[a]The LORD loves him;
[b]He shall do His pleasure on Babylon,
And His arm *shall be against* the Chaldeans.
15 I, *even* I, have spoken;
Yes, [a]I have called him,
I have brought him, and his way will prosper.

48:8 [a] Ps. 58:3 48:9 [a] Ezek. 20:9, 14, 22, 44 [b] Ps. 78:38 48:10 [a] Ps. 66:10 [b] Deut. 4:20 48:11 [a] Ezek. 20:9 [b] Is. 42:8 48:12 [a] Deut. 32:39 [b] [Rev. 22:13] 48:13 [a] Ps. 102:25 [b] Is. 40:26 48:14 [a] Is. 45:1 [b] Is. 44:28; 47:1–15 48:15 [a] Is. 45:1, 2

IT'S NOT TOO LATE

"Your peace would have been like a river."

ISAIAH 48:18

Chapter 48 is an oracle that sums up much of what had been disclosed in chapters 40–47. The prophet reviewed Israel's demise as a kingdom, its exile, and its difficult restoration. Speaking through the prophet, the Lord reminded Israel, "I have declared the former things from the beginning . . . Suddenly I did them, and they came to pass" (48:3). This reminder makes it clear that human history is in God's hands. The heart of the oracle is found in verse 18: "Oh, that you had heeded My commandments! Then your peace would have been like a river, and your righteousness like the waves of the sea."

It is not hard to find an application for these sad words. How many of us can say, "Oh, had I only heeded the good advice that was given to me. If only I had listened to the words of Scripture!" Sad words, but not hopeless. The good news is that it is not too late. While we still have breath, we can heed the Word of God and experience His peace flowing like a river.

What counsel have you disregarded only to regret it later? Can you seek God's guidance and peace now?

16 "Come near to Me, hear this:
[a]I have not spoken in secret from the beginning;
From the time that it was, I *was* there.
And now [b]the Lord GOD and His Spirit
Have[1] sent Me."

17 Thus says [a]the LORD, your Redeemer,
The Holy One of Israel:
"I *am* the LORD your God,
Who teaches you to profit,
[b]Who leads you by the way you should go.
18 [a]Oh, that you had heeded My commandments!
[b]Then your peace would have been like a river,
And your righteousness like the waves of the sea.
19 [a]Your descendants also would have been like the sand,
And the offspring of your body like the grains of sand;
His name would not have been cut off
Nor destroyed from before Me."

20 [a]Go forth from Babylon!
Flee from the Chaldeans!
With a voice of singing,
Declare, proclaim this,
Utter it to the end of the earth;
Say, "The LORD has [b]redeemed
His servant Jacob!"
21 And they [a]did not thirst
When He led them through the deserts;
He [b]caused the waters to flow from the rock for them;
He also split the rock, and the waters gushed out.

22 "*There*[a] *is* no peace," says the LORD, "for the wicked."

The Servant, the Light to the Gentiles

49 "Listen, [a]O coastlands, to Me,
And take heed, you peoples from afar!
[b]The LORD has called Me from the womb;
From the matrix of My mother He has made mention of My name.
2 And He has made [a]My mouth like a sharp sword;
[b]In the shadow of His hand He has hidden Me,
And made Me [c]a polished shaft;
In His quiver He has hidden Me."

3 "And He said to me,
[a]'You *are* My servant, O Israel,
[b]In whom I will be glorified.'
4 [a]Then I said, 'I have labored in vain,
I have spent my strength for nothing and in vain;
Yet surely my just reward *is* with the LORD,
And my work with my God.' "

5 "And now the LORD says,
Who formed Me from the womb *to be* His Servant,
To bring Jacob back to Him,

48:16 [a] Is. 45:19 [b] Zech. 2:8, 9, 11 [1] The Hebrew verb is singular. **48:17** [a] Is. 43:14 [b] Ps. 32:8 **48:18** [a] Ps. 81:13 [b] Ps. 119:165 **48:19** [a] Gen. 22:17 **48:20** [a] Zech. 2:6, 7 [b] [Ex. 19:4–6] **48:21** [a] [Is. 41:17, 18] [b] Ex. 17:6 **48:22** [a] [Is. 57:21] **49:1** [a] Is. 41:1 [b] Jer. 1:5 **49:2** [a] Rev. 1:16; 2:12 [b] Is. 51:16 [c] Ps. 45:5 **49:3** [a] [Zech. 3:8] [b] Is. 44:23 **49:4** [a] [Ezek. 3:19]

PURSUE HOLY PEACE

"There is no peace," says the LORD, "for the wicked."

ISAIAH 48:22

In jest we sometimes quote this verse. But alas, in the real world there is nothing funny about this observation. These tragic words (repeated in 57:21) bear witness to a tragic truth: humanity's sin destroys peace. Too often people think they can find peace or wonder why they do not have peace even though their lives are far out of step with God's Word and will.

To find peace we must come to God on His terms to embrace His holiness and His love. We cannot have it both ways, where we want God's peace but we pursue life without Him and in conflict with His holy standards. Peace comes when we surrender to His will and allow His Holy Spirit to work in our lives. Israel had forgotten that truth, and the nation fell into hardship. The people could find neither rest nor peace. This not only applied to the nation as a whole; it also applies to us as individuals. Have you tried to seek peace without pursuing holiness at the same time? What was the result?

So that Israel [a]is gathered to Him[1]
(For I shall be glorious in the eyes of
the LORD,
And My God shall be My strength),
6 Indeed He says,
'It is too small a thing that You should
be My Servant
To raise up the tribes of Jacob,
And to restore the preserved ones of
Israel;
I will also give You as a [a]light to the
Gentiles,
That You should be My salvation to the
ends of the earth.' "

7 Thus says the LORD,
The Redeemer of Israel, their Holy
One,
[a]To Him whom man despises,
To Him whom the nation abhors,
To the Servant of rulers:
[b]"Kings shall see and arise,
Princes also shall worship,
Because of the LORD who is faithful,
The Holy One of Israel;
And He has chosen You."

8 Thus says the LORD:

"In an [a]acceptable time I have heard You,
And in the day of salvation I have
helped You;
I will preserve You [b]and give You
As a covenant to the people,
To restore the earth,
To cause them to inherit the desolate
heritages;
9 That You may say [a]to the prisoners, 'Go
forth,'
To those who *are* in darkness, 'Show
yourselves.'

"They shall feed along the roads,
And their pastures *shall be* on all
desolate heights.
10 They shall neither [a]hunger nor thirst,
[b]Neither heat nor sun shall strike
them;
For He who has mercy on them [c]will
lead them,
Even by the springs of water He will
guide them.
11 [a]I will make each of My mountains a
road,
And My highways shall be elevated.
12 Surely [a]these shall come from afar;
Look! Those from the north and the
west,
And these from the land of Sinim."

13 [a]Sing, O heavens!
Be joyful, O earth!
And break out in singing, O mountains!
For the LORD has comforted His
people,
And will have mercy on His afflicted.

God Will Remember Zion

14 [a]But Zion said, "The LORD has forsaken me,
And my Lord has forgotten me."

15 "Can[a] a woman forget her nursing child,
And not have compassion on the son
of her womb?
Surely they may forget,
[b]Yet I will not forget you.
16 See, [a]I have inscribed you on the palms
of My hands;
Your walls *are* continually before Me.
17 Your sons[1] shall make haste;
Your destroyers and those who laid you
waste
Shall go away from you.
18 [a]Lift up your eyes, look around and see;
All these gather together *and* come to
you.
As I live," says the LORD,
"You shall surely clothe yourselves with
them all [b]as an ornament,
And bind them *on you* as a bride *does.*

19 "For your waste and desolate places,
And the land of your destruction,
[a]Will even now be too small for the
inhabitants;
And those who swallowed you up will
be far away.
20 [a]The children you will have,
[b]After you have lost the others,
Will say again in your ears,
'The place *is* too small for me;
Give me a place where I may dwell.'
21 Then you will say in your heart,
'Who has begotten these for me,
Since I have lost my children and am
desolate,
A captive, and wandering to and fro?
And who has brought these up?
There I was, left alone;
But these, where *were* they?' "

49:5 [a] Matt. 23:37 [1] Qere, Dead Sea Scrolls, and Septuagint read *is gathered to Him;* Kethib reads *is not gathered.* **49:6** [a] [Luke 2:32] **49:7** [a] [Is. 53:3] [b] [Is. 52:15] **49:8** [a] 2 Cor. 6:2 [b] Is. 42:6 **49:9** [a] Is. 61:1 **49:10** [a] Rev. 7:16 [b] Ps. 121:6 [c] Ps. 23:2 **49:11** [a] Is. 40:4 **49:12** [a] Is. 43:5, 6 **49:13** [a] Is. 44:23 **49:14** [a] Is. 40:27 **49:15** [a] Ps. 103:13 [b] Rom. 11:29 **49:16** [a] Song 8:6 **49:17** [1] Dead Sea Scrolls, Septuagint, Targum, and Vulgate read *builders.* **49:18** [a] Is. 60:4 [b] Prov. 17:6 **49:19** [a] Zech. 10:10 **49:20** [a] Is. 60:4 [b] [Rom. 11:11]

22 [a]Thus says the Lord GOD:

"Behold, I will lift My hand in an oath to
the nations,
And set up My standard for the peoples;
They shall bring your sons in *their*
arms,
And your daughters shall be carried on
their shoulders;
23 [a]Kings shall be your foster fathers,
And their queens your nursing
mothers;
They shall bow down to you with *their*
faces to the earth,
And [b]lick up the dust of your feet.
Then you will know that I *am* the LORD,
[c]For they shall not be ashamed who wait
for Me."

24 [a]Shall the prey be taken from the
mighty,
Or the captives of the righteous[1] be
delivered?

25 But thus says the LORD:

"Even the captives of the mighty shall
be taken away,
And the prey of the terrible be
delivered;
For I will contend with him who
contends with you,
And I will save your children.
26 I will [a]feed those who oppress you with
their own flesh,
And they shall be drunk with their own
[b]blood as with sweet wine.
All flesh [c]shall know
That I, the LORD, *am* your Savior,
And your Redeemer, the Mighty One of
Jacob."

The Servant, Israel's Hope

50 Thus says the LORD:

"Where *is* [a]the certificate of your
mother's divorce,
Whom I have put away?
Or which of My [b]creditors *is it* to whom
I have sold you?
For your iniquities [c]you have sold
yourselves,
And for your transgressions your
mother has been put away.
2 Why, when I came, *was there* no man?
Why, when I called, *was there* none to
answer?
Is My hand shortened at all that it
cannot redeem?
Or have I no power to deliver?
Indeed with My [a]rebuke I dry up the sea,
I make the rivers a wilderness;
Their fish stink because *there is* no water,
And die of thirst.
3 [a]I clothe the heavens with blackness,
[b]And I make sackcloth their covering."

4 "The[a] Lord GOD has given Me
The tongue of the learned,
That I should know how to speak
A word in season to *him who is* [b]weary.
He awakens Me morning by morning,
He awakens My ear
To hear as the learned.
5 The Lord GOD [a]has opened My ear;
And I was not [b]rebellious,
Nor did I turn away.
6 [a]I gave My back to those who struck *Me,*
And [b]My cheeks to those who plucked
out the beard;
I did not hide My face from shame and
[c]spitting.

7 "For the Lord GOD will help Me;
Therefore I will not be disgraced;
Therefore [a]I have set My face like a flint,
And I know that I will not be ashamed.
8 [a]*He is* near who justifies Me;
Who will contend with Me?
Let us stand together.
Who *is* My adversary?
Let him come near Me.
9 Surely the Lord GOD will help Me;
Who *is* he *who* will condemn Me?
[a]Indeed they will all grow old like a
garment;
[b]The moth will eat them up.

10 "Who among you fears the LORD?
Who obeys the voice of His Servant?
Who [a]walks in darkness
And has no light?
[b]Let him trust in the name of the LORD
And rely upon his God.
11 Look, all you who kindle a fire,
Who encircle *yourselves* with sparks:
Walk in the light of your fire and in the
sparks you have kindled—
[a]This you shall have from My hand:
You shall lie down [b]in torment.

49:22 [a] Is. 60:4 **49:23** [a] Is. 52:15 [b] Ps. 72:9 [c] [Rom. 5:5] **49:24** [a] Luke 11:21, 22 [1] Following Masoretic Text and Targum; Dead Sea Scrolls, Syriac, and Vulgate read *the mighty;* Septuagint reads *unjustly.* **49:26** [a] Is. 9:20 [b] Rev. 14:20 [c] Ps. 9:16 **50:1** [a] Deut. 24:1 [b] Deut. 32:30; 2 Kin. 4:1 [c] Is. 52:3 **50:2** [a] Nah. 1:4 **50:3** [a] Ex. 10:21 [b] Rev. 6:12 **50:4** [a] Ex. 4:11 [b] Matt. 11:28 **50:5** [a] Ps. 40:6 [b] Matt. 26:39 **50:6** [a] Matt. 27:26 [b] Matt. 26:67; 27:30 [c] Lam. 3:30 **50:7** [a] Ezek. 3:8, 9 **50:8** [a] [Rom. 8:32–34] **50:9** [a] Job 13:28 [b] Is. 51:6, 8 **50:10** [a] Ps. 23:4 [b] 2 Chr. 20:20 **50:11** [a] [John 9:39] [b] Ps. 16:4

The Lord Comforts Zion

51 "Listen to Me, [a]you who follow after righteousness,
You who seek the LORD:
Look to the rock *from which* you were hewn,
And to the hole of the pit *from which* you were dug.
2 [a]Look to Abraham your father,
And to Sarah *who* bore you;
[b]For I called him alone,
And [c]blessed him and increased him."

3 For the LORD will [a]comfort Zion,
He will comfort all her waste places;
He will make her wilderness like Eden,
And her desert [b]like the garden of the LORD;
Joy and gladness will be found in it,
Thanksgiving and the voice of melody.

4 "Listen to Me, My people;
And give ear to Me, O My nation:
[a]For law will proceed from Me,
And I will make My justice rest
[b]As a light of the peoples.
5 [a]My righteousness *is* near,
My salvation has gone forth,
[b]And My arms will judge the peoples;
[c]The coastlands will wait upon Me,
And [d]on My arm they will trust.
6 [a]Lift up your eyes to the heavens,
And look on the earth beneath.
For [b]the heavens will vanish away like smoke,
[c]The earth will grow old like a garment,
And those who dwell in it will die in like manner;
But My salvation will be [d]forever,
And My righteousness will not be abolished.

7 "Listen to Me, you who know righteousness,
You people [a]in whose heart *is* My law:
[b]Do not fear the reproach of men,
Nor be afraid of their insults.
8 For [a]the moth will eat them up like a garment,
And the worm will eat them like wool;
But My righteousness will be forever,
And My salvation from generation to generation."

9 [a]Awake, awake, [b]put on strength,
O arm of the LORD!
Awake [c]as in the ancient days,
In the generations of old.
[d]*Are* You not *the arm* that cut [e]Rahab apart,
And wounded the [f]serpent?
10 *Are* You not *the One* who [a]dried up the sea,
The waters of the great deep;
That made the depths of the sea a road
For the redeemed to cross over?
11 So [a]the ransomed of the LORD shall return,
And come to Zion with singing,
With everlasting joy on their heads.
They shall obtain joy and gladness;
Sorrow and sighing shall flee away.

12 "I, *even* I, *am* He [a]who comforts you.
Who *are* you that you should be afraid
[b]Of a man *who* will die,
And of the son of a man *who* will be made [c]like grass?
13 And [a]you forget the LORD your Maker,
[b]Who stretched out the heavens
And laid the foundations of the earth;
You have feared continually every day
Because of the fury of the oppressor,
When *he has* prepared to destroy.
[c]And where *is* the fury of the oppressor?
14 The captive exile hastens, that he may be loosed,
[a]That he should not die in the pit,
And that his bread should not fail.
15 But I *am* the LORD your God,
Who [a]divided the sea whose waves roared—
The LORD of hosts *is* His name.
16 And [a]I have put My words in your mouth;
[b]I have covered you with the shadow of My hand,
[c]That I may plant the heavens,
Lay the foundations of the earth,
And say to Zion, 'You *are* My people.' "

God's Fury Removed

17 [a]Awake, awake!
Stand up, O Jerusalem,
You who [b]have drunk at the hand of the LORD
The cup of His fury;
You have drunk the dregs of the cup of trembling,
And drained *it* out.

51:1 [a] [Rom. 9:30–32] 51:2 [a] Heb. 11:11 [b] Gen. 12:1 [c] Gen. 24:35 51:3 [a] Is. 40:1; 52:9 [b] Gen. 13:10 51:4 [a] Is. 2:3 [b] Is. 42:6 51:5 [a] Is. 46:13 [b] Ps. 67:4 [c] Is. 60:9 [d] [Rom. 1:16] 51:6 [a] Is. 40:26 [b] Matt. 24:35 [c] Is. 24:19, 20; 50:9 [d] Is. 45:17 51:7 [a] Ps. 37:31 [b] [Matt. 5:11, 12; 10:28] 51:8 [a] Is. 50:9 51:9 [a] Ps. 44:23 [b] Ps. 93:1 [c] Ps. 44:1 [d] Job 26:12 [e] Ps. 87:4 [f] Ps. 74:13 51:10 [a] Ex. 14:21 51:11 [a] Is. 35:10 51:12 [a] 2 Cor. 1:3 [b] Ps. 118:6 [c] Is. 40:6, 7 51:13 [a] Is. 17:10 [b] Ps. 104:2 [c] Job 20:7 51:14 [a] Zech. 9:11 51:15 [a] Job 26:12 51:16 [a] Deut. 18:18 [b] Is. 49:2 [c] Is. 65:17 51:17 [a] Is. 52:1 [b] Job 21:20

18 *There is* no one to guide her
Among all the sons she has brought forth;
Nor *is there any* who takes her by the hand
Among all the sons she has brought up.
19 [a]These two *things* have come to you;
Who will be sorry for you?—
Desolation and destruction, famine and sword—
[b]By whom will I comfort you?
20 [a]Your sons have fainted,
They lie at the head of all the streets,
Like an antelope in a net;
They are full of the fury of the LORD,
The rebuke of your God.

21 Therefore please hear this, you afflicted,
And drunk [a]but not with wine.
22 Thus says your Lord,
The LORD and your God,
Who [a]pleads the cause of His people:
"See, I have taken out of your hand
The cup of trembling,
The dregs of the cup of My fury;
You shall no longer drink it.
23 [a]But I will put it into the hand of those who afflict you,
Who have said to you,[1]
'Lie down, that we may walk over you.'
And you have laid your body like the ground,
And as the street, for those who walk over."

God Redeems Jerusalem

52 Awake, awake!
Put on your strength, O Zion;
Put on your beautiful garments,
O Jerusalem, the holy city!
For the uncircumcised [a]and the unclean
Shall no longer come to you.
2 [a]Shake yourself from the dust, arise;
Sit down, O Jerusalem!
[b]Loose yourself from the bonds of your neck,
O captive daughter of Zion!

3 For thus says the LORD:

[a]"You have sold yourselves for nothing,
And you shall be redeemed [b]without money."

4 For thus says the Lord GOD:

"My people went down at first
Into [a]Egypt to dwell there;
Then the Assyrian oppressed them without cause.
5 Now therefore, what have I here," says the LORD,
"That My people are taken away for nothing?
Those who rule over them
Make them wail,"[1] says the LORD,
"And My name *is* [a]blasphemed continually every day.
6 Therefore My people shall know My name;
Therefore *they shall know* in that day
That I *am* He who speaks:
'Behold, *it is* I.' "

7 [a]How beautiful upon the mountains
Are the feet of him who brings good news,
Who proclaims peace,
Who brings glad tidings of good *things*,
Who proclaims salvation,
Who says to Zion,
[b]"Your God reigns!"
8 Your watchmen shall lift up *their* voices,
With their voices they shall sing together;
For they shall see eye to eye
When the LORD brings back Zion.
9 Break forth into joy, sing together,
You waste places of Jerusalem!
For the LORD has comforted His people,
He has redeemed Jerusalem.

PEACE NOTE

Any time you go out to proclaim the gospel, you are wearing gospel sneakers! The feet of those who bring good news and proclaim peace are beautiful.

ISAIAH 52:7

51:19 [a] Is. 47:9 [b] Amos 7:2 51:20 [a] Lam. 2:11 51:21 [a] Lam. 3:15 51:22 [a] Jer. 50:34 51:23 [a] Zech. 12:2 [1] Literally *your soul* 52:1 [a] [Rev. 21:2–27] 52:2 [a] Is. 3:26 [b] Zech. 2:7 52:3 [a] Ps. 44:12 [b] Is. 45:13 52:4 [a] Gen. 46:6 52:5 [a] Ezek. 36:20, 23 [1] Dead Sea Scrolls read *Mock;* Septuagint reads *Marvel and wail;* Targum reads *Boast themselves;* Vulgate reads *Treat them unjustly.* 52:7 [a] Rom. 10:15 [b] Ps. 93:1

BEAUTIFUL FEET

How beautiful upon the mountains are the feet of him who brings good news, who proclaims peace, who brings glad tidings of good things, who proclaims salvation, who says to Zion, "Your God reigns!"

ISAIAH 52:7

This passage, along with a few others from the Book of Isaiah (40:9; 61:1–2), forms the biblical backdrop of the early church's hope for the kingdom of God. In the Aramaic-speaking synagogue, Isaiah's prophetic announcement, "Your God reigns!" (52:7), was paraphrased, "The kingdom of your God is revealed!" Scholars believe that the Aramaic paraphrase (remember, Jesus' mother tongue was Aramaic) lay behind Jesus' announcement, "The kingdom of God is at hand" (Mark 1:15).

It is God's Messiah who brings ultimate peace to the world. It is this peace that lies at the heart of the Good News (gospel) that Isaiah proclaimed long ago and that Jesus fulfilled in His ministry. It is important to know that *gospel* and *peace* are two sides of the same coin. The good news proclaimed by Isaiah and Jesus is that estranged humanity may be at peace with God. This truth is so simple a young child can understand it. Let's be the people in this passage because "beautiful . . . are the feet of him . . . that publisheth peace" (Is. 52:7 KJV).

10 [a]The LORD has made bare His holy arm
In the eyes of [b]all the nations;
And all the ends of the earth shall see
The salvation of our God.

11 [a]Depart! Depart! Go out from there,
Touch no unclean *thing;*
Go out from the midst of her,
[b]Be clean,
You who bear the vessels of the LORD.
12 For [a]you shall not go out with haste,
Nor go by flight;
[b]For the LORD will go before you,
[c]And the God of Israel *will be* your rear guard.

The Sin-Bearing Servant

13 Behold, [a]My Servant shall deal prudently;
[b]He shall be exalted and extolled and be very high.
14 Just as many were astonished at you,
So His [a]visage was marred more than any man,
And His form more than the sons of men;
15 [a]So shall He sprinkle[1] many nations.
Kings shall shut their mouths at Him;
For [b]what had not been told them they shall see,
And what they had not heard they shall consider.

53 Who [a]has believed our report?
And to whom has the arm of the LORD been revealed?
2 For He shall grow up before Him as a tender plant,
And as a root out of dry ground.
He has no form or comeliness;
And when we see Him,
There is no beauty that we should desire Him.
3 [a]He is despised and rejected by men,
A Man of sorrows and [b]acquainted with grief.
And we hid, as it were, *our* faces from Him;
He was despised, and [c]we did not esteem Him.

4 Surely [a]He has borne our griefs
And carried our sorrows;
Yet we esteemed Him stricken,
Smitten by God, and afflicted.
5 But He *was* [a]wounded for our transgressions,
He was bruised for our iniquities;
The chastisement for our peace *was* upon Him,
And by His [b]stripes we are healed.
6 All we like sheep have gone astray;
We have turned, every one, to his own way;

52:10 [a] Ps. 98:1–3 [b] Luke 3:6 **52:11** [a] Is. 48:20 [b] Lev. 22:2 **52:12** [a] Ex. 12:11, 33 [b] Mic. 2:13 [c] Ex. 14:19, 20 **52:13** [a] Is. 42:1 [b] Phil. 2:9 **52:14** [a] Ps. 22:6, 7 **52:15** [a] Ezek. 36:25 [b] Rom. 15:21 [1] Or *startle* **53:1** [a] John 12:38 **53:3** [a] Ps. 22:6 [b] [Heb. 4:15] [c] [John 1:10, 11] **53:4** [a] [Matt. 8:17] **53:5** [a] [Rom. 4:25] [b] [1 Pet. 2:24, 25]

YOU ARE HEALED

But He was wounded for our transgressions, He was bruised for our iniquities; the chastisement for our peace was upon Him, and by His stripes we are healed.

ISAIAH 53:5

This verse is part of a larger passage in Isaiah (52:13—53:12) that interpreters call the "song of the Suffering Servant". The song is as mysterious as it is beautiful. Some interpreters insist that the Servant is the nation of Israel, but it is hard to see how that can be true when we read "we hid . . . our faces from Him" and "He has borne our griefs and carried our sorrows" (53:3–4). If the Servant is Israel, who is "we"? No, the Servant is someone who suffers *for* Israel as is said in 53:5: "But He was wounded for our transgressions, He was bruised for our iniquities; the chastisement for our peace was upon Him, and by His stripes we are healed."

Because of our transgressions and iniquities, God's Servant was wounded and bruised. The death of Jesus on the cross fulfilled this great prophecy. Jesus was chastised that we might have peace, and He was whipped (given "stripes") that we may be healed. Thanks to Jesus, we have peace with God—but at high cost! Thank Him today.

And the LORD has laid on Him the
iniquity of us all.

7 He was oppressed and He was
afflicted,
Yet [a]He opened not His mouth;
[b]He was led as a lamb to the slaughter,
And as a sheep before its shearers is
silent,
So He opened not His mouth.
8 He was [a]taken from prison and from
judgment,
And who will declare His generation?
For [b]He was cut off from the land of the
living;
For the transgressions of My people He
was stricken.
9 [a]And they[1] made His grave with the
wicked—
But with the rich at His death,
Because He had done no violence,
Nor *was any* [b]deceit in His mouth.

10 Yet it pleased the LORD to bruise Him;
He has put *Him* to grief.
When You make His soul [a]an offering
for sin,
He shall see *His* seed, He shall prolong
His days,
And the pleasure of the LORD shall
prosper in His hand.
11 He shall see the labor of His soul,[1] *and*
be satisfied.
By His knowledge [a]My righteous
[b]Servant shall [c]justify many,
For He shall bear their iniquities.
12 [a]Therefore I will divide Him a portion
with the great,
[b]And He shall divide the spoil with the
strong,
Because He [c]poured out His soul unto
death,
And He was [d]numbered with the
transgressors,
And He bore the sin of many,
And [e]made intercession for the
transgressors.

A Perpetual Covenant of Peace

54 "Sing, O [a]barren,
You *who* have not borne!
Break forth into singing, and cry aloud,
You *who* have not labored with child!
For more *are* the children of the desolate
Than the children of the married
woman," says the LORD.
2 "Enlarge[a] the place of your tent,
And let them stretch out the curtains
of your dwellings;
Do not spare;
Lengthen your cords,
And strengthen your stakes.

53:7 [a] Matt. 26:63; 27:12–14 [b] Acts 8:32, 33 **53:8** [a] Luke 23:1–25 [b] [Dan. 9:26] **53:9** [a] Matt. 27:57–60 [b] 1 Pet. 2:22 [1] Literally *he* or *He* **53:10** [a] [2 Cor. 5:21] **53:11** [a] [1 John 2:1] [b] Is. 42:1 [c] [Rom. 5:15–18] [1] Following Masoretic Text, Targum, and Vulgate; Dead Sea Scrolls and Septuagint read *From the labor of His soul He shall see light.* **53:12** [a] Ps. 2:8 [b] Col. 2:15 [c] Is. 50:6 [d] Matt. 27:38 [e] Luke 23:34 **54:1** [a] Gal. 4:27 **54:2** [a] Is. 49:19, 20

3 For you shall expand to the right and to
the left,
And your descendants will [a]inherit the
nations,
And make the desolate cities inhabited.

4 "Do[a] not fear, for you will not be ashamed;
Neither be disgraced, for you will not
be put to shame;
For you will forget the shame of your
youth,
And will not remember the reproach of
your widowhood anymore.
5 [a]For your Maker *is* your husband,
The LORD of hosts *is* His name;
And your Redeemer *is* the Holy One of
Israel;
He is called [b]the God of the whole earth.
6 For the LORD [a]has called you
Like a woman forsaken and grieved in
spirit,
Like a youthful wife when you were
refused,"
Says your God.
7 "For[a] a mere moment I have forsaken
you,
But with great mercies [b]I will gather you.
8 With a little wrath I hid My face from
you for a moment;
[a]But with everlasting kindness I will
have mercy on you,"
Says the LORD, your Redeemer.
9 "For this *is* like the waters of [a]Noah to Me;
For as I have sworn
That the waters of Noah would no
longer cover the earth,
So have I sworn
That I would not be angry with [b]you,
nor rebuke you.
10 For [a]the mountains shall depart
And the hills be removed,
[b]But My kindness shall not depart from
you,
Nor shall My covenant of peace be
removed,"
Says the LORD, who has mercy on you.

11 "O you afflicted one,
Tossed with tempest, *and* not comforted,
Behold, I will lay your stones with
[a]colorful gems,
And lay your foundations with sapphires.
12 I will make your pinnacles of rubies,
Your gates of crystal,
And all your walls of precious stones.
13 All your children *shall be* [a]taught by the
LORD,
And [b]great *shall be* the peace of your
children.
14 In righteousness you shall be established;
You shall be far from oppression, for
you shall not fear;
And from terror, for it shall not come
near you.

54:3 [a] Is. 14:2; 49:22, 23; 60:9 **54:4** [a] Is. 41:10 **54:5** [a] Jer. 3:14 [b] Zech. 14:9 **54:6** [a] Is. 62:4 **54:7** [a] Is. 26:20; 60:10 [b] [Is. 43:5; 56:8] **54:8** [a] Jer. 31:3 **54:9** [a] Gen. 8:21; 9:11 [b] Ezek. 39:29 **54:10** [a] Is. 51:6 [b] Ps. 89:33, 34 **54:11** [a] Rev. 21:18, 19 **54:13** [a] [John 6:45] [b] Ps. 119:165

THE STRONGEST PEACE

"But My kindness shall not depart from you, nor shall My covenant of peace be removed."

ISAIAH 54:10

Chapter 54 is a song that likens God's relationship with Israel to a tumultuous marriage. God was the faithful Husband; Israel was the fickle, at times faithless bride. During the exile, Israel had been barren but here, the bride is restored. Fruitful Israel was invited to sing (vv. 1–2). Despite its faithlessness, the Lord remained faithful, as seen in verse 10: "My kindness shall not depart from you, nor shall My covenant of peace be removed."

How reassuring! God said this to a stubborn, disobedient people. We may sin, we may stumble, we may feel alienated and alone—yet God's kindness will not be withdrawn; His covenant of peace will not disappear. It is interesting that God called His covenant with His people a "covenant of peace." In keeping with the root meaning of *shalom*, "peace," God was promising never to remove His relationship of wholeness from His people. Simply knowing that this is how God views His relationship with His people should give us a great sense of peace. God's peace in our lives is unstoppable if we live in the truth that God's covenant in Christ is forever. God's peace does not increase or decrease in our position in Christ. This gift is lasting and unbreakable.

AFTER EXILE COMES PEACE

"All your children shall be taught by the LORD, and great shall be the peace of your children."

ISAIAH 54:13

In this, God's song, in which He compares His relationship with Israel to a marriage, God promises restoration and fruitfulness. Not only would Israel, God's bride, be brought back into a peaceful relationship with Him (v. 10), but her children would also be blessed: "All your children shall be taught by the LORD, and great shall be the peace of your children" (v. 13).

As parents we desire that our children will grow up healthy and have wonderful lives and secure futures. God wants the same thing for all of us. When God promised Israel, "Great shall be the peace of your children," we must again remember the root meaning of *shalom*, "peace." The true meaning isn't so much absence of conflict but completeness with nothing essential missing. That is what God wills for us, and that is what we will for our children. Israel lost that peace because of sin and rebellion, but after a period of exile and suffering it was returned. From this we may be assured that if peace is lost, with God's help, we can get it back.

15 Indeed they shall surely assemble, *but*
not because of Me.
Whoever assembles against you shall
[a]fall for your sake.

16 "Behold, I have created the blacksmith
Who blows the coals in the fire,
Who brings forth an instrument for his
work;
And I have created the spoiler to destroy.
17 No weapon formed against you shall
[a]prosper,
And every tongue *which* rises against
you in judgment
You shall condemn.
This *is* the heritage of the servants of
the LORD,
[b]And their righteousness *is* from Me,"
Says the LORD.

An Invitation to Abundant Life

55 "Ho! [a]Everyone who thirsts,
Come to the waters;
And you who have no money,
[b]Come, buy and eat.
Yes, come, buy wine and milk
Without money and without price.
2 Why do you spend money for *what is*
not bread,
And your wages for *what* does not satisfy?
Listen carefully to Me, and eat *what is*
good,
And let your soul delight itself in
abundance.
3 Incline your ear, and [a]come to Me.
Hear, and your soul shall live;
[b]And I will make an everlasting
covenant with you—
The [c]sure mercies of David.
4 Indeed I have given him *as* [a]a witness
to the people,
[b]A leader and commander for the people.
5 [a]Surely you shall call a nation you do
not know,
[b]And nations *who* do not know you shall
run to you,
Because of the LORD your God,
And the Holy One of Israel;
[c]For He has glorified you."

6 [a]Seek the LORD while He may be [b]found,
Call upon Him while He is near.
7 [a]Let the wicked forsake his way,
And the unrighteous man [b]his
thoughts;
Let him return to the LORD,
[c]And He will have mercy on him;
And to our God,
For He will abundantly pardon.

8 "For[a] My thoughts *are* not your
thoughts,
Nor *are* your ways My ways," says the
LORD.
9 "For[a] *as* the heavens are higher than the
earth,
So are My ways higher than your ways,
And My thoughts than your thoughts.

54:15 [a] Is. 41:11–16 **54:17** [a] Is. 17:12–14; 29:8 [b] Is. 45:24, 25; 54:14 **55:1** [a] [John 4:14; 7:37] [b] [Rev. 3:18] **55:3** [a] Matt. 11:28 [b] Jer. 32:40 [c] 2 Sam. 7:8 **55:4** [a] [Rev. 1:5] [b] [Dan. 9:25] **55:5** [a] Eph. 2:11, 12 [b] Is. 60:5 [c] Is. 60:9 **55:6** [a] [Heb. 3:13] [b] Ps. 32:6 **55:7** [a] Is. 1:16 [b] Zech. 8:17 [c] Jer. 3:12 **55:8** [a] 2 Sam. 7:19 **55:9** [a] Ps. 103:11

10 "For [a]as the rain comes down, and the
snow from heaven,
And do not return there,
But water the earth,
And make it bring forth and bud,
That it may give seed to the sower
And bread to the eater,
11 [a]So shall My word be that goes forth
from My mouth;
It shall not return to Me void,
But it shall accomplish what I please,
And it shall [b]prosper *in the thing* for
which I sent it.

12 "For[a] you shall go out with joy,
And be led out with peace;
The mountains and the hills
Shall [b]break forth into singing before you,
And [c]all the trees of the field shall clap
their hands.
13 [a]Instead of [b]the thorn shall come up the
cypress tree,
And instead of the brier shall come up
the myrtle tree;
And it shall be to the LORD [c]for a name,
For an everlasting sign *that* shall not be
cut off."

Salvation for the Gentiles

56 Thus says the LORD:
"Keep justice, and do righteousness,
[a]For My salvation *is* about to come,
And My righteousness to be revealed.
2 Blessed *is* the man *who* does this,
And the son of man *who* lays hold on it;
[a]Who keeps from defiling the Sabbath,
And keeps his hand from doing any evil."

3 Do not let [a]the son of the foreigner
Who has joined himself to the LORD
Speak, saying,
"The LORD has utterly separated me
from His people";
Nor let the [b]eunuch say,
"Here I am, a dry tree."
4 For thus says the LORD:
"To the eunuchs who keep My Sabbaths,
And choose what pleases Me,
And hold fast My covenant,
5 Even to them I will give in [a]My house
And within My walls a place [b]and a name
Better than that of sons and daughters;
I will give them[1] an everlasting name
That shall not be cut off.

6 "Also the sons of the foreigner
Who join themselves to the LORD, to
serve Him,
And to love the name of the LORD, to
be His servants—
Everyone who keeps from defiling the
Sabbath,
And holds fast My covenant—
7 Even them I will [a]bring to My holy
mountain,
And make them joyful in My [b]house of
prayer.

55:10 [a] Deut. 32:2 **55:11** [a] Is. 45:23 [b] Is. 46:9–11 **55:12** [a] Is. 35:10 [b] Ps. 98:8 [c] 1 Chr. 16:33 **55:13** [a] Is. 41:19 [b] Mic. 7:4 [c] Jer. 13:11 **56:1** [a] Matt. 3:2; 4:17 **56:2** [a] Is. 58:13 **56:3** [a] [Eph. 2:12–19] [b] Acts 8:27 **56:5** [a] 1 Tim. 3:15 [b] [1 John 3:1, 2] [1] Literally *him* **56:7** [a] [Is. 2:2, 3; 60:11] [b] Mark 11:17

OPEN THE DOOR

"For you shall go out with joy, and be led out with peace."

ISAIAH 55:12

Chapter 55 looks forward to a time when God's invitation would be extended to the poor and hungry: "Ho! Everyone who thirsts, come to the waters; and you who have no money, come, buy and eat. Yes, come, buy wine and milk without money and without price" (v. 1). The prophet was describing the vision in 25:6, in which God would host a great feast "for all people." The prophet's vision was based on the profound truth that God loves humanity and is committed to our redemption and restoration. For the hungry and destitute, the promise of a delicious feast at no cost would have been very appealing.

The prophet urged God's people to "seek the LORD while He may be found, call upon Him while He is near" (55:6). If they did, then the promise of joy and peace in verse 12 would come to pass. God's peace is at hand, but we must seek Him. How would you rate your desire and willingness to seek the Lord? The truth of the passage cannot be lost on us. The fact is, God is knocking on the door of your heart and wants deeper fellowship with you. Welcome God's fellowship in your life today and seek His peace.

[c]Their burnt offerings and their sacrifices
Will be [d]accepted on My altar;
For [e]My house shall be called a house
of prayer [f]for all nations."
8 The Lord GOD, [a]who gathers the
outcasts of Israel, says,
[b]"Yet I will gather to him
Others besides those who are gathered
to him."

Israel's Irresponsible Leaders

9 [a]All you beasts of the field, come to
devour,
All you beasts in the forest.
10 His watchmen *are* [a]blind,
They are all ignorant;
[b]They *are* all dumb dogs,
They cannot bark;
Sleeping, lying down, loving to slumber.
11 Yes, *they are* [a]greedy dogs
Which [b]never have enough.
And they *are* shepherds
Who cannot understand;
They all look to their own way,
Every one for his own gain,
From his *own* territory.
12 "Come," *one says,* "I will bring wine,
And we will fill ourselves with
intoxicating [a]drink;
[b]Tomorrow will be [c]as today,
And much more abundant."

Israel's Futile Idolatry

57 The righteous perishes,
And no man takes *it* to heart;
[a]Merciful men *are* taken away,
[b]While no one considers
That the righteous is taken away from
evil.
2 He shall enter into peace;
They shall rest in [a]their beds,
Each one walking *in* his uprightness.

3 "But come here,
[a]You sons of the sorceress,
You offspring of the adulterer and the
harlot!
4 Whom do you ridicule?
Against whom do you make a wide mouth
And stick out the tongue?
Are you not children of transgression,
Offspring of falsehood,
5 Inflaming yourselves with gods [a]under
every green tree,
[b]Slaying the children in the valleys,
Under the clefts of the rocks?
6 Among the smooth [a]*stones* of the stream
Is your portion;
They, they, *are* your lot!
Even to them you have poured a drink
offering,
You have offered a grain offering.
Should I receive comfort in [b]these?

56:7 [c][Rom. 12:1] [d]Is. 60:7 [e]Matt. 21:13 [f][Mal. 1:11] **56:8** [a]Is. 11:12; 27:12; 54:7 [b][John 10:16] **56:9** [a]Jer. 12:9 **56:10** [a]Matt. 15:14 [b]Phil. 3:2 **56:11** [a][Mic. 3:5, 11] [b]Ezek. 34:2–10 **56:12** [a]Is. 28:7 [b]Luke 12:19 [c]2 Pet. 3:4 **57:1** [a]Ps. 12:1 [b]1 Kin. 14:13 **57:2** [a]2 Chr. 16:14 **57:3** [a]Matt. 16:4 **57:5** [a]2 Kin. 16:4 [b]Jer. 7:31 **57:6** [a]Jer. 3:9 [b]Jer. 5:9, 29; 9:9

DESTROY YOUR IDOLS

The righteous is taken away from evil. He shall enter into peace; they shall rest in their beds, each one walking in his uprightness.

ISAIAH 57:1-2

Chapter 57 is a grim oracle against idolatry and the wicked, who persecuted the righteous, and who failed to observe that their wicked ways led to destruction. The prophet went on and on in his description of the wicked, who offered up sacrifices and incense to idols and assumed that, because no judgment had yet come upon them, that God must not have noticed their sinful behavior. But judgment would come, and their phony "righteous" deeds and idols would not help them.

What the wicked overlooked, says the prophet, is that "the righteous [person] is taken away from evil. He shall enter into peace; they shall rest in their beds, each one walking in his uprightness." After warning the wicked, the prophet once again promises, "He who puts his trust in Me shall possess the land, and shall inherit My holy mountain" (v. 13). Every follower of Jesus can live in peace right now because the best is yet to come. If you are a Christian, your bad experiences will turn out for good, no matter what. We experience more peace by walking in this truth and trusting God day by day that the best is yet to come.

7 "On[a] a lofty and high mountain
You have set [b]your bed;
Even there you went up
To offer sacrifice.
8 Also behind the doors and their posts
You have set up your remembrance;
For you have uncovered yourself *to those other* than Me,
And have gone up to them;
You have enlarged your bed
And made *a covenant* with them;
[a]You have loved their bed,
Where you saw *their* nudity.[1]
9 [a]You went to the king with ointment,
And increased your perfumes;
You sent your [b]messengers far off,
And *even* descended to Sheol.
10 You are wearied in the length of your way;
[a]*Yet* you did not say, 'There is no hope.'
You have found the life of your hand;
Therefore you were not grieved.

11 "And [a]of whom have you been afraid, or feared,
That you have lied
And not remembered Me,
Nor taken *it* to your heart?
Is it not because [b]I have held My peace from of old
That you do not fear Me?
12 I will declare your righteousness
And your works,
For they will not profit you.
13 When you cry out,
Let your collection *of idols* deliver you.
But the wind will carry them all away,
A breath will take *them.*
But he who puts his trust in Me shall possess the land,
And shall inherit My holy mountain."

Healing for the Backslider

14 And one shall say,
[a]"Heap it up! Heap it up!
Prepare the way,
Take the stumbling block out of the way of My people."

15 For thus says the High and Lofty One
Who inhabits eternity, [a]whose name *is* Holy:
[b]"I dwell in the high and holy *place,*
[c]With him *who* has a contrite and humble spirit,
[d]To revive the spirit of the humble,
And to revive the heart of the contrite ones.
16 [a]For I will not contend forever,
Nor will I always be angry;
For the spirit would fail before Me,
And the souls [b]*which* I have made.

57:7 [a] Ezek. 16:16 [b] Ezek. 23:41 57:8 [a] Ezek. 16:26 [1] Literally *hand,* a euphemism 57:9 [a] Hos. 7:11 [b] Ezek. 23:16, 40 57:10 [a] Jer. 2:25; 18:12 57:11 [a] Is. 51:12, 13 [b] Ps. 50:21 57:14 [a] Is. 40:3; 62:10 57:15 [a] Job 6:10 [b] Zech. 2:13 [c] Ps. 34:18; 51:17 [d] Is. 61:1–3 57:16 [a] [Mic. 7:18] [b] Num. 16:22

THE CALL TO THOSE FAR AWAY

"I create the fruit of the lips: peace, peace to him who is far off and to him who is near," says the LORD, "and I will heal him."

ISAIAH 57:19

The second half of chapter 57 continues contrasting the behavior of the wicked and the righteous and what the results for each will be. For the wicked, "there is no peace" (48:22); they are tossed about in rough seas and dirty water (see 57:20–21). But the righteous will be restored, led, and comforted (v. 18). To the righteous, God says, "'I create the fruit of the lips: peace, peace to him who is far off and to him who is near,' says the LORD, 'and I will heal him'" (v. 19).

In the ancient world, many people were polytheists whose gods possessed power in specific regions. In contrast, the prophet Isaiah knew God was sovereign throughout the entire world. Therefore, He could bring peace to all His people, not just to those in the land of Israel but also to those who remained in exile in faraway lands. In his letter to the Christians of Ephesus, the apostle Paul made the same point by alluding to this passage in Isaiah. Christ is our peace, said the apostle, and His gospel is proclaimed to all, both near and far (Eph. 2:13, 17).

His gospel is proclaimed to *you.* What will you do with it?

17 For the iniquity of [a]his covetousness
I was angry and struck him;
[b]I hid and was angry,
[c]And he went on backsliding in the way
of his heart.
18 I have seen his ways, and [a]will heal him;
I will also lead him,
And restore comforts to him
And to [b]his mourners.

19 "I create [a]the fruit of the lips:
Peace, peace [b]to *him who is* far off and
to *him who is* near,"
Says the LORD,
"And I will heal him."
20 [a]But the wicked *are* like the troubled sea,
When it cannot rest,
Whose waters cast up mire and dirt.

21 "*There*[a] *is* no peace,"
Says my God, "for the wicked."

Fasting that Pleases God

58 "Cry aloud, spare not;
Lift up your voice like a trumpet;
[a]Tell My people their transgression,
And the house of Jacob their sins.
2 Yet they seek Me daily,
And delight to know My ways,
As a nation that did righteousness,
And did not forsake the ordinance of
their God.
They ask of Me the ordinances of justice;
They take delight in approaching God.

PEACE NOTE

When my life is dominated by sin, I will have turmoil. Scripture tells us, "There is no peace . . . for the wicked."

ISAIAH 57:21

3 'Why[a] have we fasted,' *they say,* 'and
You have not seen?
Why have we [b]afflicted our souls, and
You take no notice?'

"In fact, in the day of your fast you find
pleasure,
And exploit all your laborers.
4 [a]Indeed you fast for strife and debate,
And to strike with the fist of
wickedness.
You will not fast as *you do* this day,
To make your voice heard on high.
5 Is [a]it a fast that I have chosen,
[b]A day for a man to afflict his soul?

57:17 [a] Jer. 6:13 [b] Is. 8:17; 45:15; 59:2 [c] Is. 9:13 57:18 [a] Jer. 3:22 [b] Is. 61:2 57:19 [a] Heb. 13:15 [b] Eph. 2:17 57:20 [a] Job 15:20 57:21 [a] Is. 48:22 58:1 [a] Mic. 3:8 58:3 [a] Mal. 3:13–18 [b] Lev. 16:29; 23:27 58:4 [a] 1 Kin. 21:9 58:5 [a] Zech. 7:5 [b] Lev. 16:29

STANDING STRONG FOR TRUE PEACE

"There is no peace," says my God, "for the wicked."

ISAIAH 57:21

The greatest tragedy for a human being is to go through life with no peace. The prophet once again warned the wicked that they would have no peace. The devil lies, saying that living in sin will make us happy and hopeful. Rather, wickedness will eliminate the peace of God from our lives. Therefore, don't ask the Lord for peace, and then willfully open your life up to sinful entertainment and pursuits. The irony in Isaiah is that it was often in the pursuit of political peace that the Israelites chose to do evil—to accommodate pagans, their gods, and their ways. This kind of behavior, says the prophet, will not result in peace. Far from it.

We ourselves can fall into the same trap. Desiring peace with our neighbors or colleagues at work, we compromise. And what results is not peace. Doing what is right sometimes is unpopular and results in conflict. You might not experience peace in the midst of the conflict, but eventually you will. But if you choose the wrong path, peace will elude you.

Is peace elusive to you? Why do you think that is? How can you change that?

Is it to bow down his head like a
bulrush,
And [c]to spread out sackcloth and
ashes?
Would you call this a fast,
And an acceptable day to the LORD?

6 "*Is* this not the fast that I have chosen:
To [a]loose the bonds of wickedness,
[b]To undo the heavy burdens,
[c]To let the oppressed go free,
And that you break every yoke?
7 *Is it* not [a]to share your bread with the
hungry,
And that you bring to your house the
poor who are cast out;
[b]When you see the naked, that you
cover him,
And not hide yourself from [c]your own
flesh?
8 [a]Then your light shall break forth like
the morning,
Your healing shall spring forth
speedily,
And your righteousness shall go before
you;
[b]The glory of the LORD shall be your
rear guard.
9 Then you shall call, and the LORD will
answer;
You shall cry, and He will say, 'Here
I *am*.'

"If you take away the yoke from your
midst,
The pointing of the finger, and
[a]speaking wickedness,
10 *If* you extend your soul to the hungry
And satisfy the afflicted soul,
Then your light shall dawn in the
darkness,
And your darkness shall *be* as the
noonday.
11 The LORD will guide you continually,
And satisfy your soul in drought,
And strengthen your bones;
You shall be like a watered garden,
And like a spring of water, whose
waters do not fail.
12 Those from among you
[a]Shall build the old waste places;
You shall raise up the foundations of
many generations;
And you shall be called the Repairer of
the Breach,
The Restorer of Streets to Dwell In.

13 "If [a]you turn away your foot from the
Sabbath,
From doing your pleasure on My holy
day,
And call the Sabbath a delight,
The holy *day* of the LORD honorable,
And shall honor Him, not doing your
own ways,
Nor finding your own pleasure,
Nor speaking *your own* words,
14 [a]Then you shall delight yourself in the
LORD;
And I will cause you to [b]ride on the
high hills of the earth,
And feed you with the heritage of
Jacob your father.
[c]The mouth of the LORD has spoken."

Separated from God

59 Behold, the LORD's hand is not
[a]shortened,
That it cannot save;
Nor His ear heavy,
That it cannot hear.
2 But your iniquities have separated you
from your God;
And your sins have hidden *His* face
from you,
So that He will [a]not hear.
3 For [a]your hands are defiled with blood,
And your fingers with iniquity;
Your lips have spoken lies,
Your tongue has muttered perversity.

4 No one calls for justice,
Nor does *any* plead for truth.
They trust in [a]empty words and speak lies;
[b]They conceive evil and bring forth
iniquity.
5 They hatch vipers' eggs and weave the
spider's web;
He who eats of their eggs dies,
And *from* that which is crushed a viper
breaks out.

6 [a]Their webs will not become garments,
Nor will they cover themselves with
their works;
Their works *are* works of iniquity,
And the act of violence *is* in their hands.
7 [a]Their feet run to evil,
And they make haste to shed [b]innocent
blood;
[c]Their thoughts *are* thoughts of iniquity;
Wasting and [d]destruction *are* in their
paths.

58:5 [c] Esth. 4:3 **58:6** [a] Luke 4:18, 19 [b] Neh. 5:10–12 [c] Jer. 34:9 **58:7** [a] Ezek. 18:7 [b] Job 31:19–22 [c] Neh. 5:5 **58:8** [a] Job 11:17 [b] Ex. 14:19 **58:9** [a] Ps. 12:2 **58:12** [a] Is. 61:4 **58:13** [a] Is. 56:2, 4, 6 **58:14** [a] Job 22:26 [b] Deut. 32:13; 33:29 [c] Is. 1:20; 40:5 **59:1** [a] Num. 11:23 **59:2** [a] Is. 1:15 **59:3** [a] Ezek. 7:23 **59:4** [a] Jer. 7:4 [b] Job 15:35 **59:6** [a] Job 8:14 **59:7** [a] Rom. 3:15 [b] Prov. 6:17 [c] Is. 55:7 [d] Rom. 3:16, 17

PEACE NOTE

Without Jesus we do not know the way of peace. It is unattainable.

ISAIAH 59:8

8 The way of [a]peace they have not known,
And *there is* no justice in their ways;
[b]They have made themselves crooked paths;
Whoever takes that way shall not know peace.

Sin Confessed

9 Therefore justice is far from us,
Nor does righteousness overtake us;
[a]We look for light, but there is darkness!
For brightness, *but* we walk in blackness!
10 [a]We grope for the wall like the blind,
And we grope as if *we had* no eyes;
We stumble at noonday as at twilight;
We are as dead *men* in desolate places.
11 We all growl like bears,
And [a]moan sadly like doves;
We look for justice, but *there is* none;
For salvation, *but* it is far from us.
12 For our [a]transgressions are multiplied before You,
And our sins testify against us;
For our transgressions *are* with us,
And *as for* our iniquities, we know them:
13 In transgressing and lying against the LORD,
And departing from our God,
Speaking oppression and revolt,
Conceiving and uttering [a]from the heart words of falsehood.
14 Justice is turned back,
And righteousness stands afar off;
For truth is fallen in the street,
And equity cannot enter.
15 So truth fails,
And he *who* departs from evil makes himself a [a]prey.

The Redeemer of Zion

Then the LORD saw *it*, and it displeased Him
That *there was* no justice.

59:8 [a] Is. 57:20, 21 [b] Prov. 2:15 **59:9** [a] Jer. 8:15 **59:10** [a] Job 5:14 **59:11** [a] Ezek. 7:16 **59:12** [a] Is. 24:5; 58:1 **59:13** [a] Matt. 12:34 **59:15** [a] Is. 5:23; 10:2; 29:21; 32:7

CHOOSE THE STRAIGHT PATH

The way of peace they have not known, and there is no justice in their ways; they have made themselves crooked paths; whoever takes that way shall not know peace.

ISAIAH 59:8

Chapter 59 is an oracle in which God, through the prophet, summoned the nation of Israel to repentance. "Your iniquities have separated you from your God," said the prophet, "and your sins have hidden His face from you" (v. 2). This is why the prophet began by saying that "the LORD's hand is not shortened, that it cannot save; nor His ear heavy, that it cannot hear" (v. 1). The wicked had assumed that God hadn't noticed Israel's problems. No, the people's sin was the issue.

Alas, Israel's sins had led the nation so far astray that the prophet could say, "The way of peace they have not known, and there is no justice in their ways" (v. 8). In making his case that all people have sinned and have fallen short of God's righteous standard, Paul cited this very passage in his letter to the Christians of Rome (see Rom. 3:10–18). Let us know "the way of peace" well!

Healthy Christian living is the ability, by the power of the Holy Spirit, to recognize when we are not living in God's peace and to say, "Lord, show me today what is paralyzing me instead of bringing me Your peace."

16 [a]He saw that *there was* no man,
And [b]wondered that *there was* no intercessor;
[c]Therefore His own arm brought salvation for Him;
And His own righteousness, it sustained Him.
17 [a]For He put on righteousness as a breastplate,
And a helmet of salvation on His head;
He put on the garments of vengeance for clothing,
And was clad with zeal as a cloak.
18 [a]According to *their* deeds, accordingly He will repay,
Fury to His adversaries,
Recompense to His enemies;
The coastlands He will fully repay.
19 [a]So shall they fear
The name of the LORD from the west,
And His glory from the rising of the sun;
When the enemy comes in [b]like a flood,
The Spirit of the LORD will lift up a standard against him.

20 "The[a] Redeemer will come to Zion,
And to those who turn from transgression in Jacob,"
Says the LORD.

21"As[a] for Me," says the LORD, "this *is* My
covenant with them: My Spirit who *is* upon
you, and My words which I have put in your
mouth, shall not depart from your mouth,
nor from the mouth of your descendants,
nor from the mouth of your descendants'
descendants," says the LORD, "from this time
and forevermore."

The Gentiles Bless Zion

60 Arise, [a]shine;
For your light has come!
And [b]the glory of the LORD is risen upon you.
2 For behold, the darkness shall cover the earth,
And deep darkness the people;
But the LORD will arise over you,
And His glory will be seen upon you.
3 The [a]Gentiles shall come to your light,
And kings to the brightness of your rising.

4 "Lift[a] up your eyes all around, and see:
They all gather together, [b]they come to you;
Your sons shall come from afar,
And your daughters shall be nursed at *your* side.
5 Then you shall see and become radiant,
And your heart shall swell with joy;
Because [a]the abundance of the sea shall be turned to you,
The wealth of the Gentiles shall come to you.
6 The multitude of camels shall cover your *land,*
The dromedaries of Midian and [a]Ephah;
All those from [b]Sheba shall come;
They shall bring [c]gold and incense,
And they shall proclaim the praises of the LORD.
7 All the flocks of [a]Kedar shall be gathered together to you,
The rams of Nebaioth shall minister to you;
They shall ascend with [b]acceptance on My altar,
And [c]I will glorify the house of My glory.

8 "Who *are* these *who* fly like a cloud,
And like doves to their roosts?
9 [a]Surely the coastlands shall wait for Me;
And the ships of Tarshish *will come* first,
[b]To bring your sons from afar,
[c]Their silver and their gold with them,
To the name of the LORD your God,
And to the Holy One of Israel,
[d]Because He has glorified you.

10 "The[a] sons of foreigners shall build up your walls,
[b]And their kings shall minister to you;
For [c]in My wrath I struck you,
[d]But in My favor I have had mercy on you.
11 Therefore your gates [a]shall be open continually;
They shall not be shut day or night,
That *men* may bring to you the wealth of the Gentiles,
And their kings in procession.
12 [a]For the nation and kingdom which will not serve you shall perish,
And *those* nations shall be utterly ruined.

13 "The[a] glory of Lebanon shall come to you,
The cypress, the pine, and the box tree together,
To beautify the place of My sanctuary;
And I will make [b]the place of My feet glorious.

59:16 [a] Ezek. 22:30 [b] Mark 6:6 [c] Ps. 98:1 **59:17** [a] Eph. 6:14, 17 **59:18** [a] Is. 63:6 **59:19** [a] Mal. 1:11 [b] Rev. 12:15 **59:20** [a] Rom. 11:26 **59:21** [a] [Heb. 8:10; 10:16] **60:1** [a] Eph. 5:14 [b] Mal. 4:2 **60:3** [a] Is. 49:6, 23 **60:4** [a] Is. 49:18 [b] Is. 49:20–22 **60:5** [a] [Rom. 11:25–27] **60:6** [a] Gen. 25:4 [b] Ps. 72:10 [c] Matt. 2:11 **60:7** [a] Gen. 25:13 [b] Is. 56:7 [c] Hag. 2:7, 9 **60:9** [a] Ps. 72:10 [b] [Gal. 4:26] [c] Jer. 3:17 [d] Is. 55:5 **60:10** [a] Zech. 6:15 [b] Rev. 21:24 [c] Is. 57:17 [d] Is. 54:7, 8 **60:11** [a] Rev. 21:25, 26 **60:12** [a] Zech. 14:17 **60:13** [a] Is. 35:2 [b] 1 Chr. 28:2

14 Also the sons of those who afflicted you
Shall come [a]bowing to you,
And all those who despised you shall
[b]fall prostrate at the soles of your feet;
And they shall call you The City of the
LORD,
[c]Zion of the Holy One of Israel.

15 "Whereas you have been forsaken and
hated,
So that no one went through *you,*
I will make you an eternal excellence,
A joy of many generations.
16 You shall drink the milk of the Gentiles,
[a]And milk the breast of kings;
You shall know that [b]I, the LORD, *am*
your Savior
And your Redeemer, the Mighty One of
Jacob.

17 "Instead of bronze I will bring gold,
Instead of iron I will bring silver,
Instead of wood, bronze,
And instead of stones, iron.
I will also make your officers peace,
And your magistrates righteousness.
18 Violence shall no longer be heard in
your land,
Neither wasting nor destruction within
your borders;
But you shall call [a]your walls Salvation,
And your gates Praise.

God the Glory of His People

19 "The [a]sun shall no longer be your light
by day,
Nor for brightness shall the moon give
light to you;
But the LORD will be to you an
everlasting light,
And [b]your God your glory.
20 [a]Your sun shall no longer go down,
Nor shall your moon withdraw itself;
For the LORD will be your everlasting
light,
And the days of your mourning shall
be ended.
21 [a]Also your people *shall* all *be* righteous;
[b]They shall inherit the land forever,
[c]The branch of My planting,
[d]The work of My hands,
That I may be glorified.
22 [a]A little one shall become a thousand,
And a small one a strong nation.
I, the LORD, will hasten it in its time."

The Good News of Salvation

61 "The [a]Spirit of the Lord GOD *is*
upon Me,
Because the LORD [b]has anointed Me
To preach good tidings to the poor;
He has sent Me [c]to heal the brokenhearted,
To proclaim [d]liberty to the captives,
And the opening of the prison to *those*
who are bound;

60:14 [a] Is. 45:14 [b] Rev. 3:9 [c] [Heb. 12:22] **60:16** [a] Is. 49:23 [b] Is. 43:3 **60:18** [a] Is. 26:1 **60:19** [a] Rev. 21:23; 22:5 [b] Zech. 2:5 **60:20** [a] Amos 8:9 **60:21** [a] Rev. 21:27 [b] Ps. 37:11 [c] Is. 61:3 [d] [Eph. 2:10] **60:22** [a] Matt. 13:31, 32 **61:1** [a] Luke 4:18, 19 [b] Luke 7:22 [c] Ps. 147:3 [d] Is. 42:7

THE CORRUPT HAVE NO POWER

"I will also make your officers peace, and your magistrates righteousness."

ISAIAH 60:17

One of the indictments against humanity is the extent of corruption in government and many institutions. Here we witness humankind's fallen nature. Individually and collectively we find it hard to "do righteousness" (Prov. 21:3; Is. 56:1) as we are reminded almost daily in the media.

A big part of Israel's trouble was its government. The king played politics with foreign powers and their gods; the local magistrates accepted bribes and perverted justice, something against which Israel's prophets angrily railed. In 60:1 the prophet pronounced an oracle of restoration: "Arise, shine; for your light has come! And the glory of the LORD is risen upon you." The apostle Paul paraphrased this important passage in his letter to the Christians of Ephesus: "Awake . . . arise . . . and Christ will give you light" (Eph. 5:14). The apostle rightly saw in this passage the hope of redemption for God's people when corruption would be a thing of the past or, as Isaiah put it: "I will also make your officers peace, and your magistrates righteousness" (Is. 60:7).

Hope of future everlasting peace should assure our hearts today.

2 [a]To proclaim the acceptable year of the LORD,
And [b]the day of vengeance of our God;
[c]To comfort all who mourn,
3 To console those who mourn in Zion,
[a]To give them beauty for ashes,
The oil of joy for mourning,
The garment of praise for the spirit of heaviness;
That they may be called trees of righteousness,
[b]The planting of the LORD, [c]that He may be glorified."

4 And they shall [a]rebuild the old ruins,
They shall raise up the former desolations,
And they shall repair the ruined cities,
The desolations of many generations.
5 [a]Strangers shall stand and feed your flocks,
And the sons of the foreigner
Shall be your plowmen and your vinedressers.
6 [a]But you shall be named the priests of the LORD,
They shall call you the servants of our God.
[b]You shall eat the riches of the Gentiles,
And in their glory you shall boast.
7 [a]Instead of your shame *you shall have* double *honor,*
And *instead of* confusion they shall rejoice in their portion.
Therefore in their land they shall possess double;
Everlasting joy shall be theirs.

8 "For [a]I, the LORD, love justice;
[b]I hate robbery for burnt offering;
I will direct their work in truth,
[c]And will make with them an everlasting covenant.
9 Their descendants shall be known among the Gentiles,
And their offspring among the people.
All who see them shall acknowledge them,
[a]That they *are* the posterity *whom* the LORD has blessed."

10 [a]I will greatly rejoice in the LORD,
My soul shall be joyful in my God;
For [b]He has clothed me with the garments of salvation,
He has covered me with the robe of righteousness,
[c]As a bridegroom decks *himself* with ornaments,
And as a bride adorns *herself* with her jewels.
11 For as the earth brings forth its bud,
As the garden causes the things that are sown in it to spring forth,
So the Lord GOD will cause [a]righteousness and [b]praise to spring forth before all the nations.

Assurance of Zion's Salvation

62 For Zion's sake I will not hold My peace,
And for Jerusalem's sake I will not rest,
Until her righteousness goes forth as brightness,
And her salvation as a lamp *that* burns.
2 [a]The Gentiles shall see your righteousness,
And all [b]kings your glory.
[c]You shall be called by a new name,
Which the mouth of the LORD will name.
3 You shall also be [a]a crown of glory
In the hand of the LORD,
And a royal diadem
In the hand of your God.
4 [a]You shall no longer be termed [b]Forsaken,
Nor shall your land any more be termed [c]Desolate;
But you shall be called Hephzibah,[1] and your land Beulah;[2]
For the LORD delights in you,
And your land shall be married.
5 For *as* a young man marries a virgin,
So shall your sons marry you;
And *as* the bridegroom rejoices over the bride,
[a]*So* shall your God rejoice over you.

6 [a]I have set watchmen on your walls, O Jerusalem;
They shall never hold their peace day or night.
You who make mention of the LORD, do not keep silent,
7 And give Him no rest till He establishes
And till He makes Jerusalem [a]a praise in the earth.

61:2 [a] Lev. 25:9 [b] Is. 34:8 [c] Matt. 5:4 **61:3** [a] Ps. 30:11 [b] Is. 60:21 [c] [John 15:8] **61:4** [a] Ezek. 36:33 **61:5** [a] [Eph. 2:12] **61:6** [a] Ex. 19:6 [b] Is. 60:5, 11 **61:7** [a] Zech. 9:12 **61:8** [a] Ps. 11:7 [b] Is. 1:11, 13 [c] Is. 55:3 **61:9** [a] Is. 65:23 **61:10** [a] Hab. 3:18 [b] Ps. 132:9, 16 [c] Is. 49:18 **61:11** [a] Ps. 72:3; 85:11 [b] Is. 60:18; 62:7 **62:2** [a] Is. 60:3 [b] Ps. 102:15, 16; 138:4, 5; 148:11, 13 [c] Is. 62:4, 12; 65:15 **62:3** [a] Zech. 9:16 **62:4** [a] Hos. 1:10 [b] Is. 49:14; 54:6, 7 [c] Is. 54:1 [1] Literally *My Delight Is in Her* [2] Literally *Married* **62:5** [a] Is. 65:19 **62:6** [a] Ezek. 3:17; 33:7 **62:7** [a] Zeph. 3:19, 20

8 The LORD has sworn by His right hand
And by the arm of His strength:
"Surely I will no longer [a]give your grain
As food for your enemies;
And the sons of the foreigner shall not
drink your new wine,
For which you have labored.
9 But those who have gathered it shall
eat it,
And praise the LORD;
Those who have brought it together
shall drink it [a]in My holy courts."

10 Go through,
Go through the gates!
[a]Prepare the way for the people;
Build up,
Build up the highway!
Take out the stones,
[b]Lift up a banner for the peoples!

11 Indeed the LORD has proclaimed
To the end of the world:
[a]"Say to the daughter of Zion,
'Surely your salvation is coming;
Behold, His [b]reward *is* with Him,
And His work before Him.' "
12 And they shall call them The Holy People,
The Redeemed of the LORD;
And you shall be called Sought Out,
A City Not Forsaken.

The LORD in Judgment and Salvation

63 Who *is* this who comes from Edom,
With dyed garments from Bozrah,
This *One who is* glorious in His apparel,
Traveling in the greatness of His
strength?—

PEACE NOTE

Our gospel mission is to bring peace to people who are dominated by sin, conflict, and confusion. They feel far from God.

"I who speak in righteousness, mighty
to save."

2 Why [a]*is* Your apparel red,
And Your garments like one who treads
in the winepress?

3 "I have [a]trodden the winepress alone,
And from the peoples no one *was*
with Me.
For I have trodden them in My anger,
And trampled them in My fury;
Their blood is sprinkled upon My
garments,
And I have stained all My robes.
4 For the [a]day of vengeance *is* in My
heart,
And the year of My redeemed has come.
5 [a]I looked, but [b]*there was* no one to help,
And I wondered
That *there was* no one to uphold;
Therefore My own [c]arm brought
salvation for Me;
And My own fury, it sustained Me.
6 I have trodden down the peoples in My
anger,
Made them drunk in My fury,
And brought down their strength to
the earth."

God's Mercy Remembered

7 I will mention the lovingkindnesses of
the LORD
And the praises of the LORD,
According to all that the LORD has
bestowed on us,
And the great goodness toward the
house of Israel,
Which He has bestowed on them
according to His mercies,
According to the multitude of His
lovingkindnesses.
8 For He said, "Surely they *are* My people,
Children *who* will not lie."
So He became their Savior.
9 [a]In all their affliction He was afflicted,
[b]And the Angel of His Presence saved
them;
[c]In His love and in His pity He
redeemed them;
And [d]He bore them and carried them
All the days of old.
10 But they [a]rebelled and [b]grieved His
Holy Spirit;
[c]So He turned Himself against them as
an enemy,
And He fought against them.

62:8 [a] Deut. 28:31, 33 **62:9** [a] Deut. 12:12; 14:23, 26 **62:10** [a] Is. 40:3; 57:14 [b] Is. 11:12 **62:11** [a] Zech. 9:9 [b] [Rev. 22:12] **63:2** [a] [Rev. 19:13, 15] **63:3** [a] Rev. 14:19, 20; 19:15 **63:4** [a] Is. 34:8; 35:4; 61:2 **63:5** [a] Is. 41:28; 59:16 [b] [John 16:32] [c] Ps. 98:1 **63:9** [a] Judg. 10:16 [b] Ex. 14:19 [c] Deut. 7:7 [d] Ex. 19:4 **63:10** [a] Ex. 15:24 [b] Ps. 78:40 [c] Ex. 23:21

11 Then he [a]remembered the days of old,
Moses *and* his people, *saying:*
"Where *is* He who [b]brought them up out of the sea
With the shepherd of His flock?
[c]Where *is* He who put His Holy Spirit within them,
12 Who led *them* by the right hand of Moses,
[a]With His glorious arm,
[b]Dividing the water before them
To make for Himself an everlasting name,
13 [a]Who led them through the deep,
As a horse in the wilderness,
That they might not stumble?"

14 As a beast goes down into the valley,
And the Spirit of the LORD causes him to rest,
So You lead Your people,
[a]To make Yourself a glorious name.

A Prayer of Penitence

15 [a]Look down from heaven,
And see [b]from Your habitation, holy and glorious.
Where *are* Your zeal and Your strength,
The yearning [c]of Your heart and Your mercies toward me?
Are they restrained?
16 [a]Doubtless You *are* our Father,
Though Abraham [b]was ignorant of us,
And Israel does not acknowledge us.
You, O LORD, *are* our Father;
Our Redeemer from Everlasting *is* Your name.
17 O LORD, why have You [a]made us stray from Your ways,
And hardened our heart from Your fear?
Return for Your servants' sake,
The tribes of Your inheritance.
18 [a]Your holy people have possessed *it* but a little while;
[b]Our adversaries have trodden down Your sanctuary.
19 We have become *like* those of old, over whom You never ruled,
Those who were never called by Your name.

64 Oh, that You would rend the heavens!
That You would come down!
That the mountains might shake at Your [a]presence—
2 As fire burns brushwood,
As fire causes water to boil—
To make Your name known to Your adversaries,
That the nations may tremble at Your presence!
3 When [a]You did awesome things *for which* we did not look,
You came down,
The mountains shook at Your presence.
4 For since the beginning of the world
[a]*Men* have not heard nor perceived by the ear,
Nor has the eye seen any God besides You,
Who acts for the one who waits for Him.
5 You meet him who rejoices and does righteousness,
Who remembers You in Your ways.
You are indeed angry, for we have sinned—
[a]In these ways we continue;
And we need to be saved.

6 But we are all like an unclean *thing,*
And all [a]our righteousnesses *are* like filthy rags;
We all [b]fade as a leaf,
And our iniquities, like the wind,
Have taken us away.
7 And *there is* no one who calls on Your name,
Who stirs himself up to take hold of You;
For You have hidden Your face from us,
And have consumed us because of our iniquities.

8 But now, O LORD,
You *are* our Father;
We *are* the clay, and You our [a]potter;
And all we *are* the work of Your hand.
9 Do not be furious, O LORD,
Nor remember iniquity forever;
Indeed, please look—we all *are* Your people!
10 Your holy cities are a wilderness,
Zion is a wilderness,
Jerusalem a desolation.
11 Our holy and beautiful temple,
Where our fathers praised You,
Is burned up with fire;
And all [a]our pleasant things are laid waste.
12 [a]Will You restrain Yourself because of these *things,* O LORD?
[b]Will You hold Your peace, and afflict us very severely?

63:11 [a] Ps. 106:44, 45 [b] Ex. 14:30 [c] Num. 11:17, 25, 29 **63:12** [a] Ex. 15:6 [b] Ex. 14:21, 22 **63:13** [a] Ps. 106:9 **63:14** [a] 2 Sam. 7:23 **63:15** [a] Deut. 26:15 [b] Ps. 33:14 [c] Jer. 31:20 **63:16** [a] Deut. 32:6 [b] Job 14:21 **63:17** [a] John 12:40 **63:18** [a] Deut. 7:6 [b] Ps. 74:3–7 **64:1** [a] Mic. 1:3, 4 **64:3** [a] Ex. 34:10 **64:4** [a] Ps. 31:19 **64:5** [a] Mal. 3:6 **64:6** [a] [Phil. 3:9] [b] Ps. 90:5, 6 **64:8** [a] Is. 29:16; 45:9 **64:11** [a] Ezek. 24:21 **64:12** [a] Is. 42:14 [b] Ps. 83:1

The Righteousness of God's Judgment

65 "I was [a]sought by *those who* did not
ask *for Me;*
I was found by *those who* did not seek Me.
I said, 'Here I am, here I am,'
To a nation *that* [b]was not called by My
name.
2 [a]I have stretched out My hands all day
long to a [b]rebellious people,
Who [c]walk in a way *that is* not good,
According to their own thoughts;
3 A people [a]who provoke Me to anger
continually to My face;
[b]Who sacrifice in gardens,
And burn incense on altars of brick;
4 [a]Who sit among the graves,
And spend the night in the tombs;
[b]Who eat swine's flesh,
And the broth of abominable things is
in their vessels;
5 [a]Who say, 'Keep to yourself,
Do not come near me,
For I am holier than you!'
These *are* smoke in My nostrils,
A fire that burns all the day.

6 "Behold, [a]*it is* written before Me:
[b]I will not keep silence, [c]but will repay—
Even repay into their bosom—
7 Your iniquities and [a]the iniquities of
your fathers together,"
Says the LORD,
[b]"Who have burned incense on the
mountains
[c]And blasphemed Me on the hills;
Therefore I will measure their former
work into their bosom."

8 Thus says the LORD:

"As the new wine is found in the cluster,
And *one* says, 'Do not destroy it,
For [a]a blessing *is* in it,'
So will I do for My servants' sake,
That I may not destroy them [b]all.
9 I will bring forth descendants from
Jacob,
And from Judah an heir of My mountains;
My [a]elect shall inherit it,
And My servants shall dwell there.
10 [a]Sharon shall be a fold of flocks,
And [b]the Valley of Achor a place for
herds to lie down,
For My people who have [c]sought Me.

11 "But you *are* those who forsake the LORD,
Who forget [a]My holy mountain,
Who prepare [b]a table for Gad,[1]
And who furnish a drink offering for
Meni.[2]
12 Therefore I will number you for the
sword,
And you shall all bow down to the
slaughter;
[a]Because, when I called, you did not
answer;
When I spoke, you did not hear,
But did evil before My eyes,
And chose *that* in which I do not delight."

13 Therefore thus says the Lord GOD:

"Behold, My servants shall eat,
But you shall be hungry;
Behold, My servants shall drink,
But you shall be thirsty;
Behold, My servants shall rejoice,
But you shall be ashamed;
14 Behold, My servants shall sing for joy
of heart,
But you shall cry for sorrow of heart,
And [a]wail for grief of spirit.
15 You shall leave your name [a]as a curse
to [b]My chosen;
For the Lord GOD will slay you,
And [c]call His servants by another
name;
16 [a]So that he who blesses himself in the
earth
Shall bless himself in the God of truth;
And [b]he who swears in the earth
Shall swear by the God of truth;
Because the former troubles are
forgotten,
And because they are hidden from My
eyes.

The Glorious New Creation

17 "For behold, I create [a]new heavens and
a new earth;
And the former shall not be
remembered or come to mind.
18 But be glad and rejoice forever in what
I create;
For behold, I create Jerusalem *as* a
rejoicing,
And her people a joy.
19 [a]I will rejoice in Jerusalem,
And joy in My people;

65:1 [a] Rom. 9:24; 10:20 [b] Is. 63:19 **65:2** [a] Rom. 10:21 [b] Is. 1:2, 23 [c] Is. 42:24 **65:3** [a] Deut. 32:21 [b] Is. 1:29 **65:4** [a] Deut. 18:11 [b] Is. 66:17 **65:5** [a] Matt. 9:11 **65:6** [a] Deut. 32:34 [b] Ps. 50:3 [c] Ps. 79:12 **65:7** [a] Ex. 20:5 [b] Ezek. 18:6 [c] Ezek. 20:27, 28 **65:8** [a] Joel 2:14 [b] Is. 1:9 **65:9** [a] Matt. 24:22 **65:10** [a] Is. 33:9 [b] Josh. 7:24 [c] Is. 55:6 **65:11** [a] Is. 56:7 [b] Ezek. 23:41 [1] Literally *Troop* or *Fortune,* a pagan deity [2] Literally *Number* or *Destiny,* a pagan deity **65:12** [a] Prov. 1:24 **65:14** [a] Matt. 8:12 **65:15** [a] Jer. 29:22 [b] Is. 65:9, 22 [c] [Acts 11:26] **65:16** [a] Jer. 4:2 [b] Zeph. 1:5 **65:17** [a] Rev. 21:1 **65:19** [a] Is. 62:4, 5

The [b]voice of weeping shall no longer
be heard in her,
Nor the voice of crying.

20 "No more shall an infant from there *live*
but a few days,
Nor an old man who has not fulfilled
his days;
For the child shall die one hundred
years old,
[a]But the sinner *being* one hundred years
old shall be accursed.
21 [a]They shall build houses and inhabit *them;*
They shall plant vineyards and eat
their fruit.
22 They shall not build and another
inhabit;
They shall not plant and [a]another eat;
For [b]as the days of a tree, *so shall be* the
days of My people,
And [c]My elect shall long enjoy the work
of their hands.
23 They shall not labor in vain,
[a]Nor bring forth children for trouble;
For [b]they *shall be* the descendants of
the blessed of the LORD,
And their offspring with them.

24 "It shall come to pass
That [a]before they call, I will answer;
And while they are still speaking, I will
[b]hear.
25 The [a]wolf and the lamb shall feed
together,
The lion shall eat straw like the ox,
[b]And dust *shall be* the serpent's food.
They shall not hurt nor destroy in all
My holy mountain,"
Says the LORD.

True Worship and False

66 Thus says the LORD:
[a]"Heaven *is* My throne,
And earth *is* My footstool.
Where *is* the house that you will
build Me?
And where *is* the place of My rest?
2 For all those *things* My hand has made,
And all those *things* exist,"
Says the LORD.
[a]"But on this *one* will I look:
[b]On *him who is* poor and of a contrite
spirit,
And who trembles at My word.

3 "He[a] who kills a bull *is as if* he slays a
man;
He who sacrifices a lamb, *as if* he
[b]breaks a dog's neck;
He who offers a grain offering, *as if he*
offers swine's blood;
He who burns incense, *as if* he blesses
an idol.

65:19 [b] Rev. 7:17; 21:4 **65:20** [a] Eccl. 8:12, 13 **65:21** [a] Amos 9:14 **65:22** [a] Is. 62:8, 9 [b] Ps. 92:12 [c] Is. 65:9, 15 **65:23** [a] Hos. 9:12 [b] Is. 61:9 **65:24** [a] Is. 58:9 [b] Dan. 9:20–23 **65:25** [a] Is. 11:6–9 [b] Gen. 3:14 **66:1** [a] 1 Kin. 8:27 **66:2** [a] [Is. 57:15; 61:1] [b] Ps. 34:18; 51:17 **66:3** [a] [Is. 1:10–17; 58:1–7] [b] Deut. 23:18

HABITATION OF PEACE

"Where is the place of My rest?"

ISAIAH 66:1

The greatness of God is extolled in chapter 66, the book's last chapter: heaven is God's throne, and the earth is His footstool. What house can we build for Him? (v. 1). God is great, so who is the person for whom He has regard? A powerful man? A wealthy man? No, God will look "on him who is poor and of a contrite spirit, and who trembles at My word" (v. 2). God's Word here contradicts the conventional wisdom of antiquity and our own time, too. The ancients believed that the gods were impressed with mighty warriors and great kings. God is not. He honors the humble and those who shake with respect at His word.

God goes on to say in this oracle that He will defend the righteous and punish the wicked, especially those who persecute the righteous (see vv. 3–6). In the middle of the oracle, God *bid His people to rejoice* over Jerusalem as it experiences rebirth. "I will extend peace to her like a river" (v. 12), He promised. What a wonderful picture! Let us pray for that flood of peace, both international and personal. Find the peace and presence of God, move into the center of them, and experience the peace of the Lord.

Just as they have chosen their own
ways,
And their soul delights in their
abominations,
4 So will I choose their delusions,
And bring their fears on them;
[a]Because, when I called, no one
answered,
When I spoke they did not hear;
But they did evil before My eyes,
And chose *that* in which I do not delight."

The LORD Vindicates Zion

5 Hear the word of the LORD,
You who tremble at His word:
"Your brethren who [a]hated you,
Who cast you out for My name's sake,
said,
[b]'Let the LORD be glorified,
That [c]we may see your joy.'
But they shall be ashamed."

6 The sound of noise from the city!
A voice from the temple!
The voice of the LORD,
Who fully repays His enemies!

7 "Before she was in labor, she gave birth;
Before her pain came,
She delivered a male child.
8 Who has heard such a thing?
Who has seen such things?
Shall the earth be made to give birth in
one day?
Or shall a nation be born at once?
For as soon as Zion was in labor,
She gave birth to her children.
9 Shall I bring to the time of birth, and
not cause delivery?" says the LORD.
"Shall I who cause delivery shut up *the
womb?*" says your God.
10 "Rejoice with Jerusalem,
And be glad with her, all you who love
her;
Rejoice for joy with her, all you who
mourn for her;
11 That you may feed and be satisfied
With the consolation of her bosom,
That you may drink deeply and be
delighted
With the abundance of her glory."

12 For thus says the LORD:

"Behold, [a]I will extend peace to her like
a river,
And the glory of the Gentiles like a
flowing stream.
Then you shall [b]feed;
On *her* sides shall you be [c]carried,
And be dandled on *her* knees.
13 As one whom his mother comforts,
So I will [a]comfort you;
And you shall be comforted in
Jerusalem."

The Reign and Indignation of God

14 When you see *this,* your heart shall
rejoice,
And [a]your bones shall flourish like
grass;
The hand of the LORD shall be known
to His servants,
And *His* indignation to His enemies.
15 [a]For behold, the LORD will come with
fire
And with His chariots, like a whirlwind,
To render His anger with fury,
And His rebuke with flames of fire.
16 For by fire and by [a]His sword
The LORD will judge all flesh;
And the slain of the LORD shall be
[b]many.

17 "Those[a] who sanctify themselves and
purify themselves,
To go to the gardens
After an *idol* in the midst,
Eating swine's flesh and the
abomination and the mouse,
Shall be consumed together," says the
LORD.

18 "For I *know* their works and their
[a]thoughts. It shall be that I will [b]gather all
nations and tongues; and they shall come
and see My glory. 19 [a]I will set a sign among
them; and those among them who escape I
will send to the nations: *to* Tarshish and Pul[1]
and Lud, who draw the bow, and Tubal and
Javan, *to* the coastlands afar off who have not
heard My fame nor seen My glory. [b]And they
shall declare My glory among the Gentiles.
20 Then they shall [a]bring all your brethren
[b]for an offering to the LORD out of all nations,
on horses and in chariots and in litters, on
mules and on camels, to My holy mountain
Jerusalem," says the LORD, "as the children
of Israel bring an offering in a clean vessel
into the house of the LORD. 21 And I will also
take some of them for [a]priests *and* Levites,"
says the LORD.

66:4 [a] Is. 65:12 **66:5** [a] Is. 60:15 [b] Is. 5:19 [c] [Titus 2:13] **66:12** [a] Is. 48:18; 60:5 [b] Is. 60:16 [c] Is. 49:22; 60:4 **66:13** [a] Is. 51:3 **66:14** [a] Ezek. 37:1 **66:15** [a] Is. 9:5 **66:16** [a] Is. 27:1 [b] Is. 34:6 **66:17** [a] Is. 65:3–8 **66:18** [a] Is. 59:7 [b] Jer. 3:17 **66:19** [a] Luke 2:34 [b] Mal. 1:11 [1] Following Masoretic Text and Targum; Septuagint reads *Put* (compare Jeremiah 46:9). **66:20** [a] Is. 49:22 [b] [Rom. 15:16] **66:21** [a] Ex. 19:6

22 "For as [a]the new heavens and the new
earth
Which I will make shall remain before
Me," says the LORD,
"So shall your descendants and your
name remain.
23 And [a]it shall come to pass
That from one New Moon to another,
And from one Sabbath to another,
[b]All flesh shall come to worship before
Me," says the LORD.

24 "And they shall go forth and look
Upon the corpses of the men
Who have transgressed against Me.
For their [a]worm does not die,
And their fire is not quenched.
They shall be an abhorrence to all flesh."

66:22 [a] Rev. 21:1 **66:23** [a] Zech. 14:16 [b] Zech. 14:17–21 **66:24** [a] Mark 9:44, 46, 48

THE BOOK OF

JEREMIAH

AUTHOR

Jeremiah was the son of Hilkiah the priest and lived just over two miles north of Jerusalem. The Book of Jeremiah clearly states that he was its author and that he dictated all his prophecies to his secretary Baruch (36:18). A first copy of the work was destroyed by the king, after which Jeremiah and Baruch produced a more complete edition (36:32). The only segment of this book not credited to Jeremiah is chapter 52. This supplement is almost identical to 2 Kings 24:18—25:30 and may have been added by Baruch. Daniel alludes to Jeremiah's prophecy of the seventy-year captivity (Jer. 25:11–14; 29:10; Dan. 9:2), and Jeremiah's authorship is also confirmed by Ecclesiasticus, Josephus, and the Talmud.

TIME

c. 627–580 BC

KEY VERSE

Jeremiah 7:23–24

THEME

In the Book of Jeremiah we get an intimate picture of this prophet's life and thoughts. He was constantly rejected for speaking God's message and often lamented to God. For this fact he is often called "the weeping prophet." His ministry begins in 627 BC during the reign of King Josiah, who brought about reform after finding the Book of the Law (likely all or part of Deuteronomy) in the temple. By that time Judah was a weak kingdom subject to the major political forces of the day, Egypt and Babylon. While Josiah's reform is certainly a step in the right direction, many of the people don't follow through on what the law taught. Jeremiah demonstrates God's perspective on the political upheaval going on throughout Judah in his day.

Are you reluctant to walk through a door God has opened for you (Jer. 1:6)? Ever wanted to quit (1:5)? Questioned why God called you (see 1:5)? Been accused of being too emotional (9:1; 31:16–17)? Is your life characterized by loneliness (16:2)? Have you faced intense persecutions, including physical abuse and imprisonment (36:19–32; 37:11–21)? Jeremiah has been known throughout church history as "the weeping prophet" because of all his difficulties and apparent lack of success. If you can relate to Jeremiah, you and the "weeping prophet" will become fast friends through this incredible book. Notwithstanding the adversity he faced, Jeremiah was one of the most influential prophets in Israel's history because of his faithfulness. No prophet described the peace of God more than Jeremiah in the time of Judah's captivity and destruction (over forty times).

1 The words of Jeremiah the son of Hilkiah,
of the priests who *were* [a]in Anathoth in the
land of Benjamin, 2 to whom the word of the
LORD came in the days of [a]Josiah the son of
Amon, king of Judah, [b]in the thirteenth year of
his reign. 3 It came also in the days of [a]Jehoia-
kim the son of Josiah, king of Judah, [b]until the
end of the eleventh year of Zedekiah the son
of Josiah, king of Judah, [c]until the carrying
away of Jerusalem captive [d]in the fifth month.

The Prophet Is Called

4 Then the word of the LORD came to me,
saying:

5 "Before I [a]formed you in the womb [b]I
knew you;
Before you were born I [c]sanctified you;
I ordained you a prophet to the
nations."

PEACE NOTE

We have to think about and focus on the sources and ramifications of our beliefs. This is how peace happens in God's way.

JEREMIAH 1:4

6 Then said I:

[a]"Ah, Lord GOD!
Behold, I cannot speak, for I *am* a
youth."

7 But the LORD said to me:

"Do not say, 'I *am* a youth,'
For you shall go to all to whom I send
you,
And [a]whatever I command you, you
shall speak.
8 [a]Do not be afraid of their faces,
For [b]*I am with* you to deliver you," says
the LORD.

9 Then the LORD put forth His hand and
[a]touched my mouth, and the LORD said to me:

"Behold, I have [b]put My words in your
mouth.
10 [a]See, I have this day set you over the
nations and over the kingdoms,
To [b]root out and to pull down,
To destroy and to throw down,
To build and to plant."

11 Moreover the word of the LORD came to
me, saying, "Jeremiah, what do you see?"
And I said, "I see a branch of an almond tree."
12 Then the LORD said to me, "You have seen
well, for I am ready to perform My word."
13 And the word of the LORD came to me
the second time, saying, "What do you see?"
And I said, "I see [a]a boiling pot, and it is
facing away from the north."
14 Then the LORD said to me:

"Out of the [a]north calamity shall break
forth
On all the inhabitants of the land.
15 For behold, I am [a]calling
All the families of the kingdoms of the
north," says the LORD;
"They shall come and [b]each one set his
throne
At the entrance of the gates of Jerusalem,
Against all its walls all around,
And against all the cities of Judah.
16 I will utter My judgments
Against them concerning all their
wickedness,
Because [a]they have forsaken Me,
Burned [b]incense to other gods,
And worshiped the works of their own
[c]hands.

17 "Therefore [a]prepare yourself and arise,
And speak to them all that I command
you.
[b]Do not be dismayed before their faces,
Lest I dismay you before them.
18 For behold, I have made you this day
[a]A fortified city and an iron pillar,
And bronze walls against the whole
land—
Against the kings of Judah,
Against its princes,
Against its priests,
And against the people of the land.
19 They will fight against you,
But they shall not prevail against you.

1:1 [a] Josh. 21:18 **1:2** [a] 2 Kin. 21:24 [b] Jer. 25:3 **1:3** [a] 2 Kin. 23:34 [b] Jer. 39:2 [c] Jer. 52:12 [d] 2 Kin. 25:8 **1:5** [a] Is. 49:1, 5 [b] Ex. 33:12 [c] [Luke 1:15] **1:6** [a] Ex. 4:10; 6:12, 30 **1:7** [a] Num. 22:20, 38 **1:8** [a] Ezek. 2:6; 3:9 [b] Ex. 3:12 **1:9** [a] Is. 6:7 [b] Is. 51:16 **1:10** [a] 1 Kin. 19:17 [b] [2 Cor. 10:4, 5] **1:13** [a] Ezek. 11:3; 24:3 **1:14** [a] Jer. 6:1 **1:15** [a] Jer. 6:22; 25:9 [b] Jer. 39:3 **1:16** [a] Deut. 28:20 [b] Jer. 7:9 [c] Is. 37:19 **1:17** [a] Job 38:3 [b] Ezek. 2:6 **1:18** [a] Is. 50:7

For I *am* with you," says the LORD, "to
deliver you."

God's Case Against Israel

2 Moreover the word of the LORD came to
me, saying, [2]"Go and cry in the hearing
of Jerusalem, saying, 'Thus says the LORD:

"I remember you,
The kindness of your [a]youth,
The love of your betrothal,
[b]When you went after Me in the wilderness,
In a land not sown.
3 [a]Israel *was* holiness to the LORD,
[b]The firstfruits of His increase.
[c]All that devour him will offend;
Disaster will [d]come upon them," says
the LORD.'"

[4]Hear the word of the LORD, O house of
Jacob and all the families of the house of
Israel. [5]Thus says the LORD:

[a]"What injustice have your fathers found
in Me,
That they have gone far from Me,
[b]Have followed idols,
And have become idolaters?
6 Neither did they say, 'Where *is* the LORD,
Who [a]brought us up out of the land of
Egypt,
Who led us through [b]the wilderness,
Through a land of deserts and pits,
Through a land of drought and the
shadow of death,
Through a land that no one crossed
And where no one dwelt?'
7 I brought you into [a]a bountiful country,
To eat its fruit and its goodness.
But when you entered, you [b]defiled My
land
And made My heritage an abomination.
8 The priests did not say, 'Where *is* the
LORD?'
And those who handle the [a]law did not
know Me;
The rulers also transgressed against Me;
[b]The prophets prophesied by Baal,
And walked after *things that* do not profit.

9 "Therefore [a]I will yet bring charges
against you," says the LORD,
"And against your children's children I
will bring charges.
10 For pass beyond the coasts of Cyprus[1]
and see,
Send to Kedar[2] and consider diligently,
And see if there has been such *a* [a]*thing.*
11 [a]Has a nation changed *its* gods,
Which *are* [b]not gods?
[c]But My people have changed their Glory
For *what* does not profit.
12 Be astonished, O heavens, at this,
And be horribly afraid;
Be very desolate," says the LORD.
13 "For My people have committed two evils:
They have forsaken Me, the [a]fountain
of living waters,
And hewn themselves cisterns—broken
cisterns that can hold no water.

14 "*Is* Israel [a]a servant?
Is he a homeborn *slave?*
Why is he plundered?
15 [a]The young lions roared at him, *and*
growled;
They made his land waste;
His cities are burned, without inhabitant.
16 Also the people of Noph[1] and [a]Tahpanhes
Have broken the crown of your head.
17 [a]Have you not brought this on yourself,
In that you have forsaken the LORD
your God
When [b]He led you in the way?
18 And now why take [a]the road to Egypt,
To drink the waters of [b]Sihor?
Or why take the road to [c]Assyria,
To drink the waters of the River?[1]
19 Your own wickedness will [a]correct you,
And your backslidings will rebuke you.
Know therefore and see that *it is* an evil
and bitter *thing*
That you have forsaken the LORD your
God,
And the fear of Me *is* not in you,"
Says the Lord GOD of hosts.

20 "For of old I have [a]broken your yoke *and*
burst your bonds;
And [b]you said, 'I will not transgress,'
When [c]on every high hill and under
every green tree
You lay down, [d]playing the harlot.
21 Yet I had [a]planted you a noble vine, a
seed of highest quality.
How then have you turned before Me
Into [b]the degenerate plant of an alien
vine?

2:2 [a] Ezek. 16:8 [b] Deut. 2:7 **2:3** [a] [Ex. 19:5, 6] [b] Rev. 14:4 [c] Jer. 12:14 [d] Is. 41:11 **2:5** [a] Is. 5:4 [b] 2 Kin. 17:15 **2:6** [a] Is. 63:11 [b] Deut. 8:15; 32:10 **2:7** [a] Num. 13:27 [b] Num. 35:33 **2:8** [a] Rom. 2:20 [b] Jer. 23:13 **2:9** [a] Mic. 6:2 **2:10** [a] Jer. 18:13 [1] Hebrew *Kittim,* western lands, especially Cyprus [2] In the northern Arabian desert, representative of the eastern cultures **2:11** [a] Mic. 4:5 [b] Is. 37:19 [c] Rom. 1:23 **2:13** [a] Ps. 36:9 **2:14** [a] [Ex. 4:22] **2:15** [a] Is. 1:7 **2:16** [a] Jer. 43:7–9 [1] That is, Memphis in ancient Egypt **2:17** [a] Jer. 4:18 [b] Deut. 32:10 **2:18** [a] Is. 30:1–3 [b] Josh. 13:3 [c] Hos. 5:13 [1] That is, the Euphrates **2:19** [a] Jer. 4:18 **2:20** [a] Lev. 26:13 [b] Judg. 10:16 [c] Deut. 12:2 [d] Ex. 34:15 **2:21** [a] Ex. 15:17 [b] Is. 5:4

22 For though you wash yourself with lye,
and use much soap,
Yet your iniquity is [a]marked before
Me," says the Lord GOD.

23 "How[a] can you say, 'I am not polluted,
I have not gone after the Baals'?
See your way in the valley;
Know what you have done:
You are a swift dromedary breaking
loose in her ways,
24 A wild donkey used to the wilderness,
That sniffs at the wind in her desire;
In her time of mating, who can turn
her away?
All those who seek her will not weary
themselves;
In her month they will find her.
25 Withhold your foot from being unshod,
and your throat from thirst.
But you said, [a]'There is no hope.
No! For I have loved [b]aliens, and after
them I will go.'

26 "As the thief is ashamed when he is
found out,
So is the house of Israel ashamed;
They and their kings and their princes,
and their priests and their [a]prophets,
27 Saying to a tree, 'You *are* my father,'
And to a [a]stone, 'You gave birth to me.'
For they have turned *their* back to Me,
and not *their* face.
But in the time of their [b]trouble
They will say, 'Arise and save us.'
28 But [a]where *are* your gods that you have
made for yourselves?
Let them arise,
If they [b]can save you in the time of
your trouble;
For [c]*according to* the number of your cities
Are your gods, O Judah.

29 "Why will you plead with Me?
You all have transgressed against Me,"
says the LORD.
30 "In vain I have [a]chastened your children;
They [b]received no correction.
Your sword has [c]devoured your prophets
Like a destroying lion.

31 "O generation, see the word of the LORD!
Have I been a wilderness to Israel,
Or a land of darkness?
Why do My people say, 'We are lords;
[a]We will come no more to You'?
32 Can a virgin forget her ornaments,
Or a bride her attire?
Yet My people [a]have forgotten Me days
without number.

33 "Why do you beautify your way to seek
love?
Therefore you have also taught
The wicked women your ways.
34 Also on your skirts is found
[a]The blood of the lives of the poor
innocents.
I have not found it by secret search,
But plainly on all these things.
35 [a]Yet you say, 'Because I am innocent,
Surely His anger shall turn from me.'
Behold, [b]I will plead My case against you,
[c]Because you say, 'I have not sinned.'
36 [a]Why do you gad about so much to
change your way?
Also [b]you shall be ashamed of Egypt
[c]as you were ashamed of Assyria.
37 Indeed you will go forth from him
With your hands on [a]your head;
For the LORD has rejected your trusted
allies,
And you will [b]not prosper by them.

Israel Is Shameless

3 "They say, 'If a man divorces his wife,
And she goes from him
And becomes another man's,
[a]May he return to her again?'
Would not that [b]land be greatly polluted?
But you have [c]played the harlot with
many lovers;
[d]Yet return to Me," says the LORD.

2 "Lift up your eyes to [a]the desolate
heights and see:
Where have you not lain *with men?*
[b]By the road you have sat for them
Like an Arabian in the wilderness;
[c]And you have polluted the land
With your harlotries and your
wickedness.
3 Therefore the [a]showers have been
withheld,
And there has been no latter rain.
You have had a [b]harlot's forehead;
You refuse to be ashamed.
4 Will you not from this time cry to Me,
'My Father, You *are* [a]the guide of [b]my
youth?

2:22 [a] Job 14:16, 17 **2:23** [a] Prov. 30:12 **2:25** [a] Jer. 18:12 [b] Jer. 3:13 **2:26** [a] Is. 28:7 **2:27** [a] Jer. 3:9 [b] Is. 26:16 **2:28** [a] Judg. 10:14 [b] Is. 45:20 [c] Jer. 11:13 **2:30** [a] Is. 9:13 [b] Jer. 5:3; 7:28 [c] Neh. 9:26 **2:31** [a] Deut. 32:15 **2:32** [a] Ps. 106:21 **2:34** [a] Ps. 106:38 **2:35** [a] Jer. 2:23, 29 [b] Jer. 2:9 [c] [Prov. 28:13] **2:36** [a] Hos. 5:13; 12:1 [b] Is. 30:3 [c] 2 Chr. 28:16 **2:37** [a] 2 Sam. 13:19 [b] Jer. 37:7–10 **3:1** [a] Deut. 24:1–4 [b] Jer. 2:7 [c] Ezek. 16:26 [d] [Zech. 1:3] **3:2** [a] Deut. 12:2 [b] Prov. 23:28 [c] Jer. 2:7 **3:3** [a] Lev. 26:19 [b] Zeph. 3:5 **3:4** [a] Prov. 2:17 [b] Jer. 2:2

5 [a]Will He remain angry forever?
Will He keep it to the end?'
Behold, you have spoken and done evil
things,
As you were able."

A Call to Repentance

6The LORD said also to me in the days of
Josiah the king: "Have you seen what [a]back-
sliding Israel has done? She has [b]gone up
on every high mountain and under every
green tree, and there played the harlot. 7[a]And
I said, after she had done all these *things,*
'Return to Me.' But she did not return. And
her treacherous [b]sister Judah saw it. 8Then
I saw that [a]for all the causes for which backsliding Israel had committed adultery, I had
[b]put her away and given her a certificate of
divorce; [c]yet her treacherous sister Judah
did not fear, but went and played the harlot
also. 9So it came to pass, through her casual
harlotry, that she [a]defiled the land and committed adultery with [b]stones and trees. 10And
yet for all this her treacherous sister Judah
has not turned to Me [a]with her whole heart,
but in pretense," says the LORD.
11Then the LORD said to me, [a]"Backsliding
Israel has shown herself more righteous than
treacherous Judah. 12Go and proclaim these
words toward [a]the north, and say:

'Return, backsliding Israel,' says the
LORD;
'I will not cause My anger to fall on you.
For I *am* [b]merciful,' says the LORD;
'I will not remain angry forever.
13 [a]Only acknowledge your iniquity,
That you have transgressed against the
LORD your God,
And have [b]scattered your charms
To [c]alien deities [d]under every green
tree,
And you have not obeyed My voice,'
says the LORD.

14"Return, O backsliding children," says
the LORD; [a]"for I am married to you. I will
take you, [b]one from a city and two from a
family, and I will bring you to [c]Zion. 15And
I will give you [a]shepherds according to My
heart, who will [b]feed you with knowledge
and understanding.
16"Then it shall come to pass, when you
are multiplied and [a]increased in the land in
those days," says the LORD, "that they will
say no more, 'The ark of the covenant of the
LORD.' [b]It shall not come to mind, nor shall
they remember it, nor shall they visit *it,* nor
shall it be made anymore.
17"At that time Jerusalem shall be called
The Throne of the LORD, and all the nations
shall be gathered to it, [a]to the name of the
LORD, to Jerusalem. No more shall they [b]fol-
low the dictates of their evil hearts.
18"In those days [a]the house of Judah shall
walk with the house of Israel, and they shall
come together out of the land of [b]the north to
[c]the land that I have given as an inheritance
to your fathers.
19"But I said:

'How can I put you among the children
And give you [a]a pleasant land,
A beautiful heritage of the hosts of
nations?'

"And I said:

'You shall call Me, [b]"My Father,"
And not turn away from Me.'
20 Surely, *as* a wife treacherously departs
from her husband,
So [a]have you dealt treacherously
with Me,
O house of Israel," says the LORD.

21 A voice was heard on [a]the desolate
heights,
Weeping *and* supplications of the
children of Israel.
For they have perverted their way;
They have forgotten the LORD their God.

22 "Return, you backsliding children,
And I will [a]heal your backslidings."

"Indeed we do come to You,
For You are the LORD our God.
23 [a]Truly, in vain *is salvation hoped for*
from the hills,
And from the multitude of mountains;
[b]Truly, in the LORD our God
Is the salvation of Israel.
24 [a]For shame has devoured
The labor of our fathers from our
youth—
Their flocks and their herds,
Their sons and their daughters.
25 We lie down in our shame,
And our reproach covers us.

3:5 [a] [Is. 57:16] **3:6** [a] Jer. 7:24 [b] Jer. 2:20 **3:7** [a] 2 Kin. 17:13 [b] Ezek. 16:47, 48 **3:8** [a] Ezek. 23:9 [b] 2 Kin. 17:6 [c] Ezek. 23:11 **3:9** [a] Jer. 2:7 [b] Jer. 2:27 **3:10** [a] Jer. 12:2 **3:11** [a] Ezek. 16:51, 52 **3:12** [a] 2 Kin. 17:6 [b] Ps. 86:15 **3:13** [a] Deut. 30:1, 2 [b] Ezek. 16:15 [c] Jer. 2:25 [d] Deut. 12:2 **3:14** [a] Hos. 2:19, 20 [b] Jer. 31:6 [c] [Rom. 11:5] **3:15** [a] Eph. 4:11 [b] Acts 20:28 **3:16** [a] Is. 49:19 [b] Is. 65:17 **3:17** [a] Is. 60:9 [b] Deut. 29:19; Jer. 7:24 **3:18** [a] Is. 11:13 [b] Jer. 31:8 [c] Amos 9:15 **3:19** [a] Ps. 106:24 [b] Is. 63:16 **3:20** [a] Is. 48:8 **3:21** [a] Is. 15:2 **3:22** [a] Hos. 6:1; 14:4 **3:23** [a] Ps. 121:1, 2 [b] Ps. 3:8 **3:24** [a] Hos. 9:10

[a]For we have sinned against the LORD
our God,
We and our fathers,
From our youth even to this day,
And [b]have not obeyed the voice of the
LORD our God."

4 "If you will return, O Israel," says the
LORD,
[a]"Return to Me;
And if you will put away your
abominations out of My sight,
Then you shall not be moved.
2 [a]And you shall swear, 'The LORD lives,'
[b]In truth, in judgment, and in
righteousness;
[c]The nations shall bless themselves in Him,
And in Him they shall [d]glory."

3For thus says the LORD to the men of
Judah and Jerusalem:

[a]"Break up your fallow ground,
And [b]do not sow among thorns.
4 [a]Circumcise yourselves to the LORD,
And take away the foreskins of your
hearts,
You men of Judah and inhabitants of
Jerusalem,
Lest My fury come forth like fire,
And burn so that no one can quench *it,*
Because of the evil of your doings."

An Imminent Invasion

5Declare in Judah and proclaim in Jerusalem, and say:

[a]"Blow the trumpet in the land;
Cry, 'Gather together,'
And say, [b]'Assemble yourselves,
And let us go into the fortified cities.'
6 Set up the standard toward Zion.
Take refuge! Do not delay!
For I will bring disaster from the
[a]north,
And great destruction."

7 [a]The lion has come up from his thicket,
And [b]the destroyer of nations is on his
way.
He has gone forth from his place
[c]To make your land desolate.
Your cities will be laid waste,
Without inhabitant.
8 For this, [a]clothe yourself with sackcloth,
Lament and wail.
For the fierce anger of the LORD
Has not turned back from us.

9 "And it shall come to pass in that day,"
says the LORD,
"*That* the heart of the king shall perish,
And the heart of the princes;
The priests shall be astonished,
And the prophets shall wonder."

3:25 [a] Ezra 9:6, 7 [b] Jer. 22:21 4:1 [a] Joel 2:12 4:2 [a] Deut. 10:20 [b] Zech. 8:8 [c] [Gen. 22:18] [d] 1 Cor. 1:31 4:3 [a] Hos. 10:12 [b] Matt. 13:7 4:4 [a] Deut. 10:16; 30:6 4:5 [a] Hos. 8:1 [b] Jer. 8:14 4:6 [a] Jer. 1:13–15; 6:1, 22; 50:17 4:7 [a] Dan. 7:4 [b] Jer. 25:9 [c] Is. 1:7; 6:11 4:8 [a] Is. 22:12

DON'T JUST SETTLE

Ah, Lord GOD! Surely You have greatly deceived this people and Jerusalem, saying, "You shall have peace," whereas the sword reaches to the heart.

JEREMIAH 4:10

Some of the Old Testament prophets' hardest-hitting passages appear in Jeremiah. The young prophet did not pull his punches. Jeremiah lived about one century after Isaiah. Whereas Isaiah faced the dangers of an aggressive Assyria, Jeremiah faced the crushing power of Babylon. Assyria brought the northern kingdom of Israel to an end; Babylon would finish the southern kingdom of Judah. But Jeremiah had a lot of work to do before Jerusalem was captured and the famous temple was destroyed.

Verses 5–12 make up an oracle that mimics a call to arms to face the advancing enemy, which brings "disaster from the north, and great destruction" (v. 6). The prophet spoke sarcastically of the false prophets who had promised peace to a sinful nation. Jeremiah alluded to the false sense of peace (see 6:14; 8:11). The great truth here is that false peace is no substitute for the genuine quality.

Have you ever settled for false peace? What happened?

10 Then I said, "Ah, Lord GOD!
[a]Surely You have greatly deceived this people and Jerusalem,
[b]Saying, 'You shall have peace,'
Whereas the sword reaches to the heart."
11 At that time it will be said
To this people and to Jerusalem,
[a]"A dry wind of the desolate heights *blows* in the wilderness
Toward the daughter of My people—
Not to fan or to cleanse—
12 A wind too strong for these will come for Me;
Now [a]I will also speak judgment against them."
13 "Behold, he shall come up like clouds,
And [a]his chariots like a whirlwind.
[b]His horses are swifter than eagles.
Woe to us, for we are plundered!"

14 O Jerusalem, [a]wash your heart from wickedness,
That you may be saved.
How long shall your evil thoughts lodge within you?
15 For a voice declares [a]from Dan
And proclaims affliction from Mount Ephraim:
16 "Make mention to the nations,
Yes, proclaim against Jerusalem,
That watchers come from a [a]far country
And raise their voice against the cities of Judah.
17 [a]Like keepers of a field they are against her all around,
Because she has been rebellious against Me," says the LORD.
18 "Your[a] ways and your doings
Have procured these *things* for you.
This *is* your wickedness,
Because it is bitter,
Because it reaches to your heart."

Sorrow for the Doomed Nation

19 O my [a]soul, my soul!
I am pained in my very heart!
My heart makes a noise in me;
I cannot hold my peace,
Because you have heard, O my soul,
The sound of the trumpet,
The alarm of war.
20 [a]Destruction upon destruction is cried,
For the whole land is plundered.
Suddenly [b]my tents are plundered,
And my curtains in a moment.
21 How long will I see the standard,
And hear the sound of the trumpet?

22 "For My people *are* foolish,
They have not known Me.
They *are* silly children,
And they have no understanding.
[a]They *are* wise to do evil,
But to do good they have no knowledge."

23 [a]I beheld the earth, and indeed *it was* [b]without form, and void;
And the heavens, they *had* no light.
24 [a]I beheld the mountains, and indeed they trembled,
And all the hills moved back and forth.
25 I beheld, and indeed *there was* no man,
And [a]all the birds of the heavens had fled.
26 I beheld, and indeed the fruitful land *was* a [a]wilderness,
And all its cities were broken down
At the presence of the LORD,
By His fierce anger.

27 For thus says the LORD:

"The whole land shall be desolate;
[a]Yet I will not make a full end.
28 For this [a]shall the earth mourn,
And [b]the heavens above be black,
Because I have spoken.
I have [c]purposed and [d]will not relent,
Nor will I turn back from it.
29 The whole city shall flee from the noise of the horsemen and bowmen.
They shall go into thickets and climb up on the rocks.
Every city *shall be* forsaken,
And not a man shall dwell in it.

30 "And *when* you *are* plundered,
What will you do?
Though you clothe yourself with crimson,
Though you adorn *yourself* with ornaments of gold,
[a]Though you enlarge your eyes with paint,
In vain you will make yourself fair;
[b]*Your* lovers will despise you;
They will seek your life.

31 "For I have heard a voice as of a woman in labor,
The anguish as of her who brings forth her first child,

4:10 [a] Ezek. 14:9 [b] Jer. 5:12; 14:13 **4:11** [a] Hos. 13:15 **4:12** [a] Jer. 1:16 **4:13** [a] Is. 5:28 [b] Deut. 28:49 **4:14** [a] James 4:8 **4:15** [a] Jer. 8:16; 50:17 **4:16** [a] Is. 39:3 **4:17** [a] 2 Kin. 25:1, 4 **4:18** [a] Is. 50:1 **4:19** [a] Is. 15:5; 16:11; 21:3; 22:4 **4:20** [a] Ezek. 7:26 [b] Jer. 10:20 **4:22** [a] Rom. 16:19 **4:23** [a] Is. 24:19 [b] Gen. 1:2 **4:24** [a] Ezek. 38:20 **4:25** [a] Zeph. 1:3 **4:26** [a] Jer. 9:10 **4:27** [a] Jer. 5:10, 18; 30:11; 46:28 **4:28** [a] Hos. 4:3 [b] Is. 5:30; 50:3 [c] [Dan. 4:35] [d] [Num. 23:19] **4:30** [a] 2 Kin. 9:30 [b] Jer. 22:20, 22

The voice of the daughter of Zion
bewailing herself;
She [a]spreads her hands, *saying,*
'Woe *is* me now, for my soul is weary
Because of murderers!'

The Justice of God's Judgment

5 "Run to and fro through the streets of
Jerusalem;
See now and know;
And seek in her open places
[a]If you can find a man,
[b]If there is *anyone* who executes
judgment,
Who seeks the truth,
[c]And I will pardon her.
2 [a]Though they say, '*As* [b]the LORD lives,'
Surely they [c]swear falsely."

3 O LORD, *are* not [a]Your eyes on the
truth?
You have [b]stricken them,
But they have not grieved;
You have consumed them,
But [c]they have refused to receive
correction.
They have made their faces harder
than rock;
They have refused to return.

4 Therefore I said, "Surely these *are* poor.
They are foolish;
For [a]they do not know the way of the
LORD,
The judgment of their God.
5 I will go to the great men and speak to
them,
For [a]they have known the way of the
LORD,
The judgment of their God."

But these have altogether [b]broken the
yoke
And burst the bonds.
6 Therefore [a]a lion from the forest shall
slay them,
[b]A wolf of the deserts shall destroy them;
[c]A leopard will watch over their cities.
Everyone who goes out from there
shall be torn in pieces,
Because their transgressions are many;
Their backslidings have increased.

7 "How shall I pardon you for this?
Your children have forsaken Me
And [a]sworn by *those* [b]*that are* not gods.
[c]When I had fed them to the full,
Then they committed adultery
And assembled themselves by troops
in the harlots' houses.
8 [a]They were *like* well-fed lusty stallions;
Every one neighed after his neighbor's
wife.
9 Shall I not punish *them* for these
things?" says the LORD.
"And shall I not [a]avenge Myself on such
a nation as this?

10 "Go up on her walls and destroy,
But do not make a [a]complete end.
Take away her branches,
For they *are* not the LORD's.
11 For [a]the house of Israel and the house
of Judah
Have dealt very treacherously with
Me," says the LORD.

12 [a]They have lied about the LORD,
And said, [b]"*It is* not He.
[c]Neither will evil come upon us,
Nor shall we see sword or famine.
13 And the prophets become wind,
For the word *is* not in them.
Thus shall it be done to them."

14 Therefore thus says the LORD God of hosts:

"Because you speak this word,
[a]Behold, I will make My words in your
mouth fire,
And this people wood,
And it shall devour them.
15 Behold, I will bring a [a]nation against
you [b]from afar,
O house of Israel," says the LORD.
"It *is* a mighty nation,
It *is* an ancient nation,
A nation whose language you do not
know,
Nor can you understand what they say.
16 Their quiver *is* like an open tomb;
They *are* all mighty men.
17 And they shall eat up your [a]harvest and
your bread,
Which your sons and daughters should
eat.
They shall eat up your flocks and your
herds;
They shall eat up your vines and your
fig trees;
They shall destroy your fortified cities,
In which you trust, with the sword.

4:31 [a] Lam. 1:17 5:1 [a] Ezek. 22:30 [b] Gen. 18:23–32 [c] Gen. 18:26 5:2 [a] Titus 1:16 [b] Jer. 4:2 [c] Jer. 7:9 5:3 [a] [2 Chr. 16:9] [b] Is. 1:5; 9:13 [c] Zeph. 3:2 5:4 [a] Jer. 8:7 5:5 [a] Mic. 3:1 [b] Ps. 2:3 5:6 [a] Jer. 4:7 [b] Zeph. 3:3 [c] Hos. 13:7 5:7 [a] Zeph. 1:5 [b] Deut. 32:21 [c] Deut. 32:15 5:8 [a] Ezek. 22:11 5:9 [a] Jer. 9:9 5:10 [a] Jer. 4:27 5:11 [a] Jer. 3:6, 7, 20 5:12 [a] 2 Chr. 36:16 [b] Jer. 23:17 [c] Jer. 14:13 5:14 [a] Jer. 1:9; 23:29 5:15 [a] Deut. 28:49 [b] Jer. 4:16 5:17 [a] Lev. 26:16

18"Nevertheless in those days," says the
LORD, "I [a]will not make a complete end of
you. 19And it will be when you say, [a]'Why
does the LORD our God do all these *things*
to us?' then you shall answer them, 'Just as
you have [b]forsaken Me and served foreign
gods in your land, so [c]you shall serve aliens
in a land *that is* not yours.'

20 "Declare this in the house of Jacob
And proclaim it in Judah, saying,
21 'Hear this now, O [a]foolish people,
Without understanding,
Who have eyes and see not,
And who have ears and hear not:
22 [a]Do you not fear Me?' says the LORD.
'Will you not tremble at My presence,
Who have placed the sand as the
[b]bound of the sea,
By a perpetual decree, that it cannot
pass beyond it?
And though its waves toss to and fro,
Yet they cannot prevail;
Though they roar, yet they cannot pass
over it.
23 But this people has a defiant and
rebellious heart;
They have revolted and departed.
24 They do not say in their heart,
"Let us now fear the LORD our God,
[a]Who gives rain, both the [b]former and
the latter, in its season.
[c]He reserves for us the appointed weeks
of the harvest."
25 [a]Your iniquities have turned these
things away,
And your sins have withheld good
from you.

26 'For among My people are found wicked
men;
They [a]lie in wait as one who sets snares;
They set a trap;
They catch men.
27 As a cage is full of birds,
So their houses *are* full of deceit.
Therefore they have become great and
grown rich.
28 They have grown [a]fat, they are sleek;
Yes, *they surpass* the deeds of the
wicked;
They do not plead [b]the cause,
The cause of the fatherless;
[c]Yet they prosper,
And the right of the needy they do not
defend.
29 [a]Shall I not punish *them* for these
things?' says the LORD.
'Shall I not avenge Myself on such a
nation as this?'

30 "An astonishing and [a]horrible thing
Has been committed in the land:
31 The prophets prophesy [a]falsely,
And the priests rule by their *own*
power;
And My people [b]love *to have it* so.
But what will you do in the end?

Impending Destruction from the North

6 "O you children of Benjamin,
Gather yourselves to flee from the
midst of Jerusalem!
Blow the trumpet in Tekoa,
And set up a signal-fire in [a]Beth
Haccerem;
[b]For disaster appears out of the north,
And great destruction.
2 I have likened the daughter of Zion
To a lovely and delicate woman.
3 The [a]shepherds with their flocks shall
come to her.
They shall pitch *their* tents against her
all around.
Each one shall pasture in his own
place."

4 "Prepare[a] war against her;
Arise, and let us go up [b]at noon.
Woe to us, for the day goes away,
For the shadows of the evening are
lengthening.
5 Arise, and let us go by night,
And let us destroy her palaces."

6For thus has the LORD of hosts said:

"Cut down trees,
And build a mound against
Jerusalem.
This *is* the city to be punished.
She *is* full of oppression in her midst.
7 [a]As a fountain wells up with water,
So she wells up with her wickedness.
[b]Violence and plundering are heard in
her.
Before Me continually *are* grief and
wounds.
8 Be instructed, O Jerusalem,
Lest [a]My soul depart from you;
Lest I make you desolate,
A land not inhabited."

5:18 [a] Jer. 30:11 **5:19** [a] Deut. 29:24–29 [b] Jer. 1:16; 2:13 [c] Deut. 28:48 **5:21** [a] Matt. 13:14 **5:22** [a] [Rev. 15:4] [b] Job 26:10 **5:24** [a] Acts 14:17 [b] Joel 2:23 [c] [Gen. 8:22] **5:25** [a] Jer. 3:3 **5:26** [a] Hab. 1:15 **5:28** [a] Deut. 32:15 [b] Zech. 7:10 [c] Job 12:6 **5:29** [a] Mal. 3:5 **5:30** [a] Hos. 6:10 **5:31** [a] Ezek. 13:6 [b] Mic. 2:11 **6:1** [a] Neh. 3:14 [b] Jer. 4:6 **6:3** [a] 2 Kin. 25:1–4 **6:4** [a] Joel 3:9 [b] Jer. 15:8 **6:7** [a] Is. 57:20 [b] Ps. 55:9 **6:8** [a] Hos. 9:12

9Thus says the LORD of hosts:

"They shall thoroughly glean as a vine
the remnant of Israel;
As a grape-gatherer, put your hand
back into the branches."

10 To whom shall I speak and give warning,
That they may hear?
Indeed their [a]ear *is* uncircumcised,
And they cannot give heed.
Behold, [b]the word of the LORD is a
reproach to them;
They have no delight in it.
11 Therefore I am full of the fury of the
LORD.
[a]I am weary of holding *it* in.
"I will pour it out [b]on the children
outside,
And on the assembly of young men
together;
For even the husband shall be taken
with the wife,
The aged with *him who is* full of days.
12 And [a]their houses shall be turned over
to others,
Fields and wives together;
For I will stretch out My hand
Against the inhabitants of the land,"
says the LORD.

13 "Because from the least of them even to
the greatest of them,
Everyone *is* given to [a]covetousness;
And from the prophet even to the
[b]priest,
Everyone deals falsely.
14 They have also [a]healed the hurt of My
people slightly,
[b]Saying, 'Peace, peace!'
When *there is* no peace.
15 Were they [a]ashamed when they had
committed abomination?
No! They were not at all ashamed;
Nor did they know how to blush.
Therefore they shall fall among those
who fall;
At the time I punish them,
They shall be cast down," says the LORD.

16Thus says the LORD:

"Stand in the ways and see,
And ask for the [a]old paths, where the
good way *is,*
And walk in it;
Then you will find [b]rest for your souls.
But they said, 'We will not walk *in it.*'
17 Also, I set [a]watchmen over you, *saying,*
[b]'Listen to the sound of the trumpet!'
But they said, 'We will not listen.'

6:10 [a] [Acts 7:51] [b] Jer. 8:9; 20:8 **6:11** [a] Jer. 20:9 [b] Jer. 9:21 **6:12** [a] Deut. 28:30 **6:13** [a] Is. 56:11; Jer. 8:10; 22:17 [b] Jer. 5:31; 23:11 **6:14** [a] Jer. 8:11–15 [b] Jer. 4:10; 23:17 **6:15** [a] Jer. 3:3; 8:12 **6:16** [a] Jer. 18:15 [b] Matt. 11:29 **6:17** [a] Hab. 2:1 [b] Deut. 4:1

IDOLS OF ANARCHY

"They have also healed the hurt of My people slightly,
saying, 'Peace, peace!' when there is no peace."

JEREMIAH 6:14

Twice Jeremiah criticized the princes and false prophets of Israel who deceived the people into thinking that all was well. The false prophets offered assurance when they should have been calling for repentance. According to Jeremiah, "They have also healed the hurt of My people slightly, saying, 'Peace, peace!' when there is no peace" (6:14). Jeremiah will repeat this tragic refrain in 8:11. The false prophets had not "healed the hurt" of God's people; they had misled them.

Between these two warnings falls chapter 7, where the prophet warned the people not to assume that they were safe because of the presence of the temple (see 7:4, where the false prophets utter "lying words"). The people viewed the temple almost as a good-luck charm. But Israel's sin would result in the temple's destruction, and for proof of this assertion, the prophet urged the people to visit the ruins of Shiloh, where the house of God once stood (7:12).

How do you know if you are seeking true peace or the false kind? Ask the Holy Spirit to bring about God's true peace in your life and to root out any false peace.

18 Therefore hear, you nations,
And know, O congregation, what *is*
among them.
19 [a]Hear, O earth!
Behold, I will certainly bring [b]calamity
on this people—
[c]The fruit of their thoughts,
Because they have not heeded My
words
Nor My law, but rejected it.
20 [a]For what purpose to Me
Comes frankincense [b]from Sheba,
And [c]sweet cane from a far country?
[d]Your burnt offerings *are* not
acceptable,
Nor your sacrifices sweet to Me."

21Therefore thus says the LORD:

"Behold, I will lay stumbling blocks
before this people,
And the fathers and the sons together
shall fall on them.
The neighbor and his friend shall
perish."

22Thus says the LORD:

"Behold, a people comes from the
[a]north country,
And a great nation will be raised from
the farthest parts of the earth.
23 They will lay hold on bow and spear;
They *are* cruel and have no mercy;
Their voice [a]roars like the sea;
And they ride on horses,
As men of war set in array against you,
O daughter of Zion."

24 We have heard the report of it;
Our hands grow feeble.
[a]Anguish has taken hold of us,
Pain as of a woman in labor.
25 Do not go out into the field,
Nor walk by the way.
Because of the sword of the enemy,
Fear *is* on every side.
26 O daughter of my people,
[a]Dress in sackcloth
[b]*And roll about in ashes!*
[c]Make mourning *as for* an only son,
most bitter lamentation;
For the plunderer will suddenly come
upon us.

27 "I have set you *as* an assayer *and* [a]a
fortress among My people,
That you may know and test their way.
28 [a]They *are* all stubborn rebels, [b]walking
as slanderers.
They are [c]bronze and iron,
They *are* all corrupters;
29 The bellows blow fiercely,
The lead is consumed by the fire;
The smelter refines in vain,
For the wicked are not drawn off.
30 *People* will call them [a]rejected silver,
Because the LORD has rejected them."

Trusting in Lying Words

7 The word that came to Jeremiah from the
LORD, saying, 2[a]"Stand in the gate of the
LORD's house, and proclaim there this word,
and say, 'Hear the word of the LORD, all *you of*
Judah who enter in at these gates to worship
the LORD!' " 3Thus says the LORD of hosts, the
God of Israel: [a]"Amend your ways and your
doings, and I will cause you to dwell in this
place. 4[a]Do not trust in these lying words,
saying, 'The temple of the LORD, the temple
of the LORD, the temple of the LORD *are* these.'
5"For if you thoroughly amend your ways
and your doings, if you thoroughly [a]execute
judgment between a man and his neighbor,
6*if* you do not oppress the stranger, the fatherless, and the widow, and do not shed
innocent blood in this place, [a]or walk after
other gods to your hurt, 7[a]then I will cause
you to dwell in this place, in [b]the land that I
gave to your fathers forever and ever.
8"Behold, you trust in [a]lying words that
cannot profit. 9[a]Will you steal, murder, commit
adultery, swear falsely, burn incense to Baal,
and [b]walk after other gods whom you do not
know, 10[a]and *then* come and stand before Me
in this house [b]which is called by My name, and
say, 'We are delivered to do all these abominations'? 11Has [a]this house, which is called by My
name, become a [b]den of thieves in your eyes?
Behold, I, even I, have seen *it*," says the LORD.
12"But go now to [a]My place which *was* in
Shiloh, [b]where I set My name at the first, and
see [c]what I did to it because of the wickedness
of My people Israel. 13And now, because you
have done all these works," says the LORD,
"and I spoke to you, [a]rising up early and
speaking, but you did not hear, and I [b]called
you, but you did not answer, 14therefore I will
do to the house which is called by My name,

6:19 [a] Is. 1:2 [b] Jer. 19:3, 15 [c] Prov. 1:31 **6:20** [a] Mic. 6:6, 7 [b] Is. 60:6 [c] Is. 43:24 [d] Jer. 7:21–23 **6:22** [a] Jer. 1:15; 10:22; 50:41–43 **6:23** [a] Is. 5:30 **6:24** [a] Jer. 4:31; 13:21; 49:24 **6:26** [a] Jer. 4:8 [b] Mic. 1:10 [c] [Zech. 12:10] **6:27** [a] Jer. 1:18 **6:28** [a] Jer. 5:23 [b] Jer. 9:4 [c] Ezek. 22:18 **6:30** [a] Is. 1:22 **7:2** [a] Jer. 17:19; 26:2 **7:3** [a] Jer. 4:1; 18:11; 26:13 **7:4** [a] Mic. 3:11 **7:5** [a] Jer. 21:12; 22:3 **7:6** [a] Deut. 6:14, 15 **7:7** [a] Deut. 4:40 [b] Jer. 3:18 **7:8** [a] Jer. 5:31; 14:13, 14 **7:9** [a] 1 Kin. 18:21 [b] Ex. 20:3 **7:10** [a] Ezek. 23:39 [b] Jer. 7:11, 14; 32:34; 34:15 **7:11** [a] Is. 56:7 [b] Matt. 21:13 **7:12** [a] Josh. 18:1 [b] Deut. 12:11 [c] 1 Sam. 4:10 **7:13** [a] 2 Chr. 36:15 [b] Prov. 1:24

in which you trust, and to this place which I gave to you and your fathers, as I have done to [a]Shiloh. 15And I will cast you out of My sight, [a]as I have cast out all your brethren—[b]the whole posterity of Ephraim.

16"Therefore [a]do not pray for this people, nor lift up a cry or prayer for them, nor make intercession to Me; [b]for I will not hear you. 17Do you not see what they do in the cities of Judah and in the streets of Jerusalem? 18[a]The children gather wood, the fathers kindle the fire, and the women knead dough, to make cakes for the queen of heaven; and *they* [b]pour out drink offerings to other gods, that they may provoke Me to anger. 19[a]Do they provoke Me to anger?" says the LORD. "*Do they* not *provoke* themselves, to the shame of their own faces?"

20Therefore thus says the Lord GOD: "Behold, My anger and My fury will be poured out on this place—on man and on beast, on the trees of the field and on the fruit of the ground. And it will burn and not be quenched."

21Thus says the LORD of hosts, the God of Israel: [a]"Add your burnt offerings to your sacrifices and eat meat. 22[a]For I did not speak to your fathers, or command them in the day that I brought them out of the land of Egypt, concerning burnt offerings or sacrifices. 23But this is what I commanded them, saying, [a]'Obey My voice, and [b]I will be your God, and you shall be My people. And walk in all the ways that I have commanded you, that it may be well with you.' 24[a]Yet they did not obey or incline their ear, but [b]followed the counsels *and* the dictates of their evil hearts, and [c]went backward and not forward. 25Since the day that your fathers came out of the land of Egypt until this day, I have even [a]sent to you all My servants the prophets, daily rising up early and sending *them*. 26[a]Yet they did not obey Me or incline their ear, but [b]stiffened their neck. [c]They did worse than their fathers.

27"Therefore [a]you shall speak all these words to them, but they will not obey you. You shall also call to them, but they will not answer you.

Judgment on Obscene Religion

28"So you shall say to them, 'This *is* a nation that does not obey the voice of the LORD their God [a]nor receive correction. [b]Truth has perished and has been cut off from their mouth. 29[a]Cut off your hair and cast *it* away, and take up a lamentation on the desolate heights; for the LORD has rejected and forsaken the generation of His wrath.' 30For the children of Judah have done evil in My sight," says the LORD. [a]"They have set their abominations in the house which is called by My name, to pollute it. 31And they have built the [a]high places of Tophet, which *is* in the Valley of the Son of Hinnom, to [b]burn their sons and their daughters in the fire, [c]which I did not command, nor did it come into My heart.

32"Therefore behold, [a]the days are coming," says the LORD, "when it will no more be called Tophet, or the Valley of the Son of Hinnom, but the Valley of Slaughter; [b]for they will bury in Tophet until there is no room. 33The [a]corpses of this people will be food for the birds of the heaven and for the beasts of the earth. And no one will frighten *them away*. 34Then I will cause to [a]cease from the cities of Judah and from the streets of Jerusalem the voice of mirth and the voice of gladness, the voice of the bridegroom and the voice of the bride. For [b]the land shall be desolate.

8 "At that time," says the LORD, "they shall bring out the bones of the kings of Judah, and the bones of its princes, and the bones of the priests, and the bones of the prophets, and the bones of the inhabitants of Jerusalem, out of their graves. 2They shall spread them before the sun and the moon and all the host of heaven, which they have loved and which they have served and after which they have walked, which they have sought and [a]which they have worshiped. They shall not be gathered [b]nor buried; they shall be like refuse on the face of the earth. 3Then [a]death shall be chosen rather than life by all the residue of those who remain of this evil family, who remain in all the places where I have driven them," says the LORD of hosts.

The Peril of False Teaching

4"Moreover you shall say to them, 'Thus says the LORD:

"Will they fall and not rise?
Will one turn away and not return?
5 Why has this people [a]slidden back,
Jerusalem, in a perpetual backsliding?
[b]They hold fast to deceit,
[c]They refuse to return.
6 [a]I listened and heard,
But they do not speak aright.
[b]No man repented of his wickedness,
Saying, 'What have I done?'
Everyone turned to his own course,
As the horse rushes into the battle.

7:14 [a] 1 Sam. 4:10, 11 **7:15** [a] 2 Kin. 17:23 [b] Ps. 78:67 **7:16** [a] Ex. 32:10; Jer. 11:14 [b] Jer. 15:1 **7:18** [a] Jer. 44:17 [b] Jer. 19:13
7:19 [a] Deut. 32:16, 21 **7:21** [a] Jer. 6:20 **7:22** [a] [Hos. 6:6] **7:23** [a] Deut. 6:3 [b] [Ex. 19:5, 6] **7:24** [a] Ps. 81:11 [b] Deut. 29:19 [c] Jer. 32:33
7:25 [a] 2 Chr. 36:15 **7:26** [a] Jer. 11:8 [b] Neh. 9:17 [c] Jer. 16:12 **7:27** [a] Ezek. 2:7 **7:28** [a] Jer. 5:3 [b] Jer. 9:3 **7:29** [a] Mic. 1:16
7:30 [a] Dan. 9:27; 11:31 **7:31** [a] 2 Kin. 23:10 [b] Ps. 106:38 [c] Deut. 17:3 **7:32** [a] Jer. 19:6 [b] 2 Kin. 23:10 **7:33** [a] Jer. 9:22; 19:11
7:34 [a] Is. 24:7, 8 [b] Lev. 26:33 **8:2** [a] 2 Kin. 23:5 [b] Jer. 22:19 **8:3** [a] Rev. 9:6 **8:5** [a] Jer. 7:24 [b] Jer. 9:6 [c] Jer. 5:3 **8:6** [a] Ps. 14:2 [b] Mic. 7:2

7 "Even [a]the stork in the heavens
Knows her appointed times;
And the turtledove, the swift, and the
swallow
Observe the time of their coming.
But [b]My people do not know the
judgment of the LORD.

8 "How can you say, 'We *are* wise,
[a]And the law of the LORD *is* with us'?
Look, the false pen of the scribe
certainly works falsehood.
9 [a]The wise men are ashamed,
They are dismayed and taken.
Behold, they have rejected the word of
the LORD;
So [b]what wisdom do they have?
10 Therefore [a]I will give their wives to others,
And their fields to those who will
inherit *them;*
Because from the least even to the greatest
Everyone is given to [b]covetousness;
From the prophet even to the priest
Everyone deals falsely.
11 For they have [a]healed the hurt of the
daughter of My people slightly,
Saying, [b]'Peace, peace!'
When *there is* no peace.
12 Were they [a]ashamed when they had
committed abomination?
No! They were not at all ashamed,
Nor did they know how to blush.
Therefore they shall fall among those
who fall;
In the time of their punishment
They shall be cast down," says the LORD.

13 "I will surely consume them," says the LORD.
"No grapes *shall be* [a]on the vine,
Nor figs on the [b]fig tree,
And the leaf shall fade;
And *the things* I have given them shall
[c]pass away from them." ' "

14 "Why do we sit still?
[a]Assemble yourselves,
And let us enter the fortified cities,
And let us be silent there.
For the LORD our God has put us to silence
And given us [b]water of gall to drink,
Because we have sinned against the LORD.

15 "*We* [a]looked for peace, but no good *came;*
And for a time of health, and there was
trouble!
16 The snorting of His horses was heard
from [a]Dan.
The whole land trembled at the sound
of the neighing of His [b]strong ones;
For they have come and devoured the
land and all that is in it,
The city and those who dwell in it."

8:7 [a] Song 2:12 [b] Jer. 5:4; 9:3 **8:8** [a] Rom. 2:17 **8:9** [a] Jer. 6:15 [b] Jer. 4:22 **8:10** [a] Deut. 28:30 [b] Is. 56:11; 57:17 **8:11** [a] Jer. 6:14 [b] Ezek. 13:10 **8:12** [a] Jer. 3:3; 6:15 **8:13** [a] Joel 1:17 [b] Matt. 21:19 [c] Deut. 28:39, 40 **8:14** [a] Jer. 4:5 [b] Jer. 9:15 **8:15** [a] Jer. 14:19 **8:16** [a] Jer. 4:15 [b] Jer. 47:3

WITH THE COURAGE OF JEREMIAH

We looked for peace, but no good came; and for a time of health, and there was trouble!

JEREMIAH 8:15

Rebellious Israel, misled by her false prophets and corrupt leaders, "looked for peace" but found nothing good. The nation hoped for "a time of health," but only trouble came. Israel's sin was so great that God called His people "this evil family" (v. 3). Jeremiah built on the tragic image describing the people of Israel as searching in vain for a remedy.

Much of the Book of Jeremiah is negative, and yet the prophet spoke of peace in the original language more than any other prophet. The challenge that the young prophet faced was the preaching of a false peace based on compromise and hidden corruption. Jeremiah simply would not go along with the preferred narrative. His honest proclamation almost got him killed!

I admire this courageous man. He spoke truth to power. He fervently believed that God would someday restore peace to His people. But God's peace must be founded on righteousness and truth. One wonders how much peace Jeremiah actually experienced, but he kept searching and asking. This is a pattern for us today. "Lord, we need Your peace right now. Help us, Lord. Make Your peace apparent in our lives."

17 "For behold, I will send serpents among
you,
Vipers which cannot be [a]charmed,
And they shall bite you," says the LORD.

The Prophet Mourns for the People

18 I would comfort myself in sorrow;
My heart *is* faint in me.
19 Listen! The voice,
The cry of the daughter of my people
From [a]a far country:
"*Is* not the LORD in Zion?
Is not her King in her?"

"Why have they provoked Me to anger
With their carved images—
With foreign idols?"

20 "The harvest is past,
The summer is ended,
And we are not saved!"

21 [a]For the hurt of the daughter of my
people I am hurt.
I am [b]mourning;
Astonishment has taken hold of me.
22 *Is there* no [a]balm in Gilead,
Is there no physician there?
Why then is there no recovery
For the health of the daughter of my
people?

9 Oh, [a]that my head were waters,
And my eyes a fountain of tears,
That I might weep day and night
For the slain of the daughter of my people!
2 Oh, that I had in the wilderness
A lodging place for travelers;
That I might leave my people,
And go from them!
For [a]they *are* all adulterers,
An assembly of treacherous men.

3 "And *like* their bow [a]they have bent their
tongues *for* lies.
They are not valiant for the truth on
the earth.
For they proceed from [b]evil to evil,
And they [c]do not know Me," says the LORD.
4 "Everyone[a] take heed to his neighbor,
And do not trust any brother;
For every brother will utterly supplant,
And every neighbor will [b]walk with
slanderers.
5 Everyone will [a]deceive his neighbor,
And will not speak the truth;
They have taught their tongue to speak
lies;
They weary themselves to commit iniquity.
6 Your dwelling place *is* in the midst of deceit;
Through deceit they refuse to know
Me," says the LORD.

7 Therefore thus says the LORD of hosts:

"Behold, [a]I will refine them and try them;
[b]For how shall I deal with the daughter
of My people?
8 Their tongue *is* an arrow shot out;
It speaks [a]deceit;
One speaks [b]peaceably to his neighbor
with his mouth,
But in his heart he lies in wait.
9 [a]Shall I not punish them for these
things?" says the LORD.
"Shall I not avenge Myself on such a
nation as this?"

10 I will take up a weeping and wailing for
the mountains,
And [a]for the dwelling places of the
wilderness a lamentation,
Because they are burned up,
So that no one can pass through;
Nor can *men* hear the voice of the cattle.
[b]Both the birds of the heavens and the
beasts have fled;
They are gone.

11 "I will make Jerusalem [a]a heap of ruins,
[b]a den of jackals.
I will make the cities of Judah desolate,
without an inhabitant."

12 [a]Who *is* the wise man who may understand this? And *who is he* to whom the mouth
of the LORD has spoken, that he may declare
it? Why does the land perish *and* burn up like
a wilderness, so that no one can pass through?
13 And the LORD said, "Because they have forsaken My law which I set before them, and have
[a]not obeyed My voice, nor walked according
to it, 14 but they have [a]walked according to the
dictates of their own hearts and after the Baals,
[b]which their fathers taught them," 15 therefore
thus says the LORD of hosts, the God of Israel:
"Behold, I will [a]feed them, this people, [b]with
wormwood, and give them water of gall to
drink. 16 I will [a]scatter them also among the
Gentiles, whom neither they nor their fathers
have known. [b]And I will send a sword after
them until I have consumed them."

8:17 [a] Ps. 58:4, 5 8:19 [a] Is. 39:3 8:21 [a] Jer. 9:1 [b] Joel 2:6 8:22 [a] Jer. 46:11 9:1 [a] Is. 22:4 9:2 [a] Jer. 5:7, 8; 23:10
9:3 [a] Ps. 64:3 [b] Jer. 4:22; 13:23 [c] 1 Sam. 2:12 9:4 [a] Mic. 7:5, 6 [b] Jer. 6:28 9:5 [a] Is. 59:4 9:7 [a] Is. 1:25 [b] Hos. 11:8
9:8 [a] Ps. 12:2 [b] Ps. 55:21 9:9 [a] Jer. 5:9, 29 9:10 [a] Hos. 4:3 [b] Jer. 4:25 9:11 [a] Is. 25:2 [b] Is. 13:22; 34:13 9:12 [a] Hos.
14:9 9:13 [a] Jer. 3:25; 7:24 9:14 [a] Jer. 7:24; 11:8 [b] Gal. 1:14 9:15 [a] Ps. 80:5 [b] Lam. 3:15 9:16 [a] Lev. 26:33 [b] Ezek. 5:2

INTEGRITY MATTERS

"Their tongue is an arrow shot out; it speaks deceit; one speaks peaceably to his neighbor with his mouth, but in his heart he lies in wait."

JEREMIAH 9:8

One of the great enemies of peace is hypocrisy. Jeremiah spoke to this problem in chapter 9, in which he said, "Their tongue is an arrow shot out; it speaks deceit; one speaks peaceably to his neighbor with his mouth, but in his heart he lies in wait." The decline of the southern kingdom of Israel (usually called Judah) was due largely to idolatry, but it was also due to a steep decline in morality. People simply ignored much of the ethical code in the Law of Moses. They called on God or on other gods when in danger or in need; otherwise they paid no attention to their covenant's requirements.

Jeremiah was especially critical of those who spoke peaceably (literally "he speaks peace") but didn't mean it. The political peace of the nation's leaders was false and idolatrous; even the peace between individuals was phony. True peace is genuine; it presupposes a whole and complete truth. True peace binds us together as humans and binds us to God. A false peace is no peace at all.

The People Mourn in Judgment

17Thus says the LORD of hosts:

"Consider and call for [a]the mourning
women,
That they may come;
And send for skillful *wailing* women,
That they may come.
18 Let them make haste
And take up a wailing for us,
That [a]our eyes may run with tears,
And our eyelids gush with water.
19 For a voice of wailing is heard from
Zion:
'How we are plundered!
We are greatly ashamed,
Because we have forsaken the land,
Because we have been cast out of [a]our
dwellings.' "

20 Yet hear the word of the LORD,
O women,
And let your ear receive the word of
His mouth;
Teach your daughters wailing,
And everyone her neighbor a
lamentation.
21 For death has come through our windows,
Has entered our palaces,
To kill off [a]the children—*no longer to be*
outside!
And the young men—*no longer* on the
streets!

22Speak, "Thus says the LORD:

'Even the carcasses of men shall fall [a]as
refuse on the open field,
Like cuttings after the harvester,
And no one shall gather *them.*' "

23Thus says the LORD:

[a]"Let not the wise *man* glory in his
wisdom,
Let not the mighty *man* glory in his
[b]might,
Nor let the rich *man* glory in his
riches;
24 But [a]let him who glories glory in
this,
That he understands and
knows Me,
That I *am* the LORD, exercising
lovingkindness, judgment, and
righteousness in the earth.
[b]For in these I delight," says the
LORD.

25"Behold, the days are coming," says the
LORD, "that [a]I will punish all *who are* circumcised with the uncircumcised— 26Egypt,
Judah, Edom, the people of Ammon, Moab,
and all *who are* in the [a]farthest corners, who
dwell in the wilderness. For all *these* nations
are uncircumcised, and all the house of Israel
are [b]uncircumcised in the heart."

9:17 [a] 2 Chr. 35:25 **9:18** [a] Jer. 9:1; 14:17 **9:19** [a] Lev. 18:28 **9:21** [a] Jer. 6:11; 18:21 **9:22** [a] Jer. 8:1, 2 **9:23** [a] [Eccl. 9:11] [b] Ps. 33:16–18 **9:24** [a] 1 Cor. 1:31 [b] Mic. 7:18 **9:25** [a] [Rom. 2:28, 29] **9:26** [a] Jer. 25:23 [b] [Rom. 2:28]

Idols and the True God

10 Hear the word which the LORD speaks
to you, O house of Israel.
2Thus says the LORD:

[a]"Do not learn the way of the Gentiles;
Do not be dismayed at the signs of heaven,
For the Gentiles are dismayed at them.
3 For the customs of the peoples *are* futile;
For [a]*one* cuts a tree from the forest,
The work of the hands of the workman, with the ax.
4 They decorate it with silver and gold;
They [a]fasten it with nails and hammers
So that it will not topple.
5 They *are* upright, like a palm tree,
And [a]they cannot speak;
They must be [b]carried,
Because they cannot go *by themselves.*
Do not be afraid of them,
For [c]they cannot do evil,
Nor can they do any good."

6 Inasmuch as *there is* none [a]like You, O LORD
(You *are* great, and Your name *is* great in might),
7 [a]Who would not fear You, O King of the nations?
For this is Your rightful due.
For [b]among all the wise *men* of the nations,
And in all their kingdoms,
There is none like You.
8 But they are altogether [a]dull-hearted and foolish;
A wooden idol *is* a worthless doctrine.
9 Silver is beaten into plates;
It is brought from Tarshish,
And [a]gold from Uphaz,
The work of the craftsman
And of the hands of the metalsmith;
Blue and purple *are* their clothing;
They *are* all [b]the work of skillful *men.*
10 But the LORD *is* the true God;
He *is* [a]the living God and the [b]everlasting King.
At His wrath the earth will tremble,
And the nations will not be able to *endure His indignation.*

11Thus you shall say to them: [a]"The gods
that have not made the heavens and the earth
[b]shall perish from the earth and from under
these heavens."

12 He [a]has made the earth by His power,
He has [b]established the world by His wisdom,
And [c]has stretched out the heavens at His discretion.
13 [a]When He utters His voice,
There is a multitude of waters in the heavens:
[b]"And He causes the vapors to ascend from the ends of the earth.
He makes lightning for the rain,
He brings the wind out of His treasuries."[1]

14 [a]Everyone is [b]dull-hearted, without knowledge;
[c]Every metalsmith is put to shame by an image;
[d]For his molded image *is* falsehood,
And *there is* no breath in them.
15 They *are* futile, a work of errors;
In the time of their punishment they shall perish.
16 [a]The Portion of Jacob *is* not like them,
For He *is* the Maker of all *things,*
And [b]Israel *is* the tribe of His inheritance;
[c]The LORD of hosts *is* His name.

The Coming Captivity of Judah

17 [a]Gather up your wares from the land,
O inhabitant of the fortress!

18For thus says the LORD:

"Behold, I will [a]throw out at this time
The inhabitants of the land,
And will distress them,
[b]That they may find *it so.*"

19 [a]Woe is me for my hurt!
My wound is severe.
But I say, [b]"Truly this *is* an infirmity,
And [c]I must bear it."
20 [a]My tent is plundered,
And all my cords are broken;
My children have gone from me,
And they *are* [b]no more.
There is no one to pitch my tent anymore,
Or set up my curtains.

10:2 [a] [Lev. 18:3; 20:23] **10:3** [a] Is. 40:19; 45:20 **10:4** [a] Is. 41:7 **10:5** [a] Ps. 115:5 [b] Ps. 115:7 [c] Is. 41:23, 24 **10:6** [a] Ex. 15:11 **10:7** [a] Rev. 15:4 [b] Ps. 89:6 **10:8** [a] Hab. 2:18 **10:9** [a] Dan. 10:5 [b] Ps. 115:4 **10:10** [a] 1 Tim. 6:17 [b] Ps. 10:16 **10:11** [a] Ps. 96:5 [b] Zeph. 2:11 **10:12** [a] Jer. 51:15 [b] Ps. 93:1 [c] Job 9:8 **10:13** [a] Job 38:34 [b] Ps. 135:7 [1] Psalm 135:7 **10:14** [a] Jer. 51:17 [b] Prov. 30:2 [c] Is. 42:17; 44:11 [d] Hab. 2:18 **10:16** [a] Lam. 3:24 [b] Deut. 32:9 [c] Is. 47:4 **10:17** [a] Jer. 6:1 **10:18** [a] 1 Sam. 25:29 [b] Ezek. 6:10 **10:19** [a] Jer. 8:21 [b] Ps. 77:10 [c] Mic. 7:9 **10:20** [a] Jer. 4:20 [b] Jer. 31:15

21 For the shepherds have become
dull-hearted,
And have not sought the LORD;
Therefore they shall not prosper,
And all their flocks shall be [a]scattered.
22 Behold, the noise of the report has come,
And a great commotion out of the
[a]north country,
To make the cities of Judah desolate, a
[b]den of jackals.

23 O LORD, I know the [a]way of man *is* not
in himself;
It is not in man who walks to direct his
own steps.
24 O LORD, [a]correct me, but with justice;
Not in Your anger, lest You bring me to
nothing.
25 [a]Pour out Your fury on the Gentiles,
[b]who do not know You,
And on the families who do not call on
Your name;
For they have eaten up Jacob,
[c]Devoured him and consumed him,
And made his dwelling place desolate.

The Broken Covenant

11 The word that came to Jeremiah from
the LORD, saying, 2"Hear the words of
this covenant, and speak to the men of Judah
and to the inhabitants of Jerusalem; 3and say
to them, 'Thus says the LORD God of Israel:
[a]"Cursed *is* the man who does not obey the
words of this covenant 4which I commanded
your fathers in the day I brought them out
of the land of Egypt, [a]from the iron furnace,
saying, [b]'Obey My voice, and do according to
all that I command you; so shall you be My
people, and I will be your God,' 5that I may
establish the [a]oath which I have sworn to
your fathers, to give them [b]'a land flowing
with milk and honey,'[1] as *it is* this day." ' "
And I answered and said, "So be it, LORD."
6Then the LORD said to me, "Proclaim all
these words in the cities of Judah and in the
streets of Jerusalem, saying: 'Hear the words
of this covenant [a]and do them. 7For I earnestly
exhorted your fathers in the day I brought
them up out of the land of Egypt, until this day,
[a]*rising early and exhorting, saying,* "Obey My
voice." 8[a]Yet they did not obey or incline their
ear, but [b]everyone followed the dictates of his
evil heart; therefore I will bring upon them all
the words of this covenant, which I commanded *them* to do, but *which* they have not done.' "
9And the LORD said to me, [a]"A conspiracy
has been found among the men of Judah
and among the inhabitants of Jerusalem.
10They have turned back to [a]the iniquities
of their forefathers who refused to hear My
words, and they have gone after other gods
to serve them; the house of Israel and the
house of Judah have broken My covenant
which I made with their fathers."
11Therefore thus says the LORD: "Behold,
I will surely bring calamity on them which
they will not be able to escape; and [a]though
they cry out to Me, I will not listen to them.
12Then the cities of Judah and the inhabitants
of Jerusalem will go and [a]cry out to the gods
to whom they offer incense, but they will not
save them at all in the time of their trouble.
13For *according to* the number of your [a]cities
were your gods, O Judah; and *according to* the
number of the streets of Jerusalem you have
set up altars to *that* shameful thing, altars to
burn incense to Baal.
14"So [a]do not pray for this people, or lift
up a cry or prayer for them; for I will not
hear *them* in the time that they cry out to
Me because of their trouble.

15 "What[a] has My beloved to do in My house,
Having [b]done lewd deeds with many?
And [c]the holy flesh has passed from
you.
When you do evil, then you [d]rejoice.
16 The LORD called your name,
[a]Green Olive Tree, Lovely *and* of Good
Fruit.
With the noise of a great tumult
He has kindled fire on it,
And its branches are broken.

17"For the LORD of hosts, [a]who planted you,
has pronounced doom against you for the
evil of the house of Israel and of the house of
Judah, which they have done against themselves to provoke Me to anger in offering
incense to Baal."

Jeremiah's Life Threatened

18Now the LORD gave me knowledge *of it,*
and I know *it;* for You showed me their doings. 19But I *was* like a docile lamb brought
to the slaughter; and I did not know that they
had devised schemes against me, *saying,* "Let
us destroy the tree with its fruit, [a]and let us
cut him off from [b]the land of the living, that
his name may be remembered no more."

10:21 [a] Jer. 23:2 **10:22** [a] Jer. 5:15 [b] Jer. 9:11 **10:23** [a] Prov. 16:1; 20:24 **10:24** [a] Jer. 30:11 **10:25** [a] Ps. 79:6, 7 [b] Job 18:21 [c] Jer. 8:16 **11:3** [a] Deut. 27:26 **11:4** [a] Deut. 4:20 [b] Lev. 26:3 **11:5** [a] Ps. 105:9 [b] Ex. 3:8 [1] Exodus 3:8 **11:6** [a] [Rom. 2:13] **11:7** [a] Jer. 35:15 **11:8** [a] Jer. 7:26 [b] Jer. 13:10 **11:9** [a] Ezek. 22:25 **11:10** [a] Ezek. 20:18 **11:11** [a] Prov. 1:28 **11:12** [a] Deut. 32:37 **11:13** [a] Jer. 2:28 **11:14** [a] Ex. 32:10 **11:15** [a] Ps. 50:16 [b] Ezek. 16:25 [c] [Titus 1:15] [d] Prov. 2:14 **11:16** [a] Ps. 52:8 **11:17** [a] Is. 5:2 **11:19** [a] Ps. 83:4 [b] Ps. 27:13

20 But, O LORD of hosts,
You who judge righteously,
[a]Testing the mind and the heart,
Let me see Your [b]vengeance on them,
For to You I have revealed my cause.

21"Therefore thus says the LORD concerning the men of [a]Anathoth who seek your life,
saying, [b]'Do not prophesy in the name of the
LORD, lest you die by our hand'— 22therefore
thus says the LORD of hosts: 'Behold, I will
punish them. The young men shall die by the
sword, their sons and their daughters shall [a]die
by famine; 23and there shall be no remnant of
them, for I will bring catastrophe on the men of
Anathoth, *even* [a]the year of their punishment.'"

Jeremiah's Question

12 Righteous [a]*are* You, O LORD, when I
plead with You;
Yet let me talk with You about *Your*
judgments.
[b]Why does the way of the wicked prosper?
Why are those happy who deal so
treacherously?
2 You have planted them, yes, they have
taken root;
They grow, yes, they bear fruit.
[a]You *are* near in their mouth
But far from their mind.

3 But You, O LORD, [a]know me;
You have seen me,
And You have [b]tested my heart toward
You.
Pull them out like sheep for the
slaughter,
And prepare them for [c]the day of
slaughter.
4 How long will [a]the land mourn,
And the herbs of every field wither?
[b]The beasts and birds are consumed,
[c]For the wickedness of those who dwell
there,
Because they said, "He will not see our
final end."

The LORD Answers Jeremiah

5 "If you have run with the footmen, and
they have wearied you,
Then how can you contend with horses?
And *if* in the land of peace,
In which you trusted, *they wearied you,*
Then how will you do in [a]the
floodplain[1] of the Jordan?

6 For even [a]your brothers, the house of
your father,
Even they have dealt treacherously
with you;
Yes, they have called a multitude after
you.
[b]Do not believe them,
Even though they speak smooth words
to you.

7 "I have forsaken My house, I have left
My heritage;
I have given the dearly beloved of My
soul into the hand of her enemies.
8 My heritage is to Me like a lion in the
forest;
It cries out against Me;
Therefore I have [a]hated it.
9 My heritage *is* to Me *like* a speckled
vulture;
The vultures all around *are* against her.
Come, assemble all the beasts of the field,
[a]Bring them to devour!

10 "Many [a]rulers[1] have destroyed [b]My
vineyard,
They have [c]trodden My portion
underfoot;
They have made My pleasant portion a
desolate wilderness.
11 They have made it [a]desolate;
Desolate, it mourns to Me;
The whole land is made desolate,
Because [b]no one takes *it* to heart.
12 The plunderers have come
On all the desolate heights in the
wilderness,
For the sword of the LORD shall devour
From *one* end of the land to the *other*
end of the land;
No flesh shall have peace.
13 [a]They have sown wheat but reaped thorns;
They have put themselves to pain *but*
do not profit.
But be ashamed of your harvest
Because of the fierce anger of the LORD."

14Thus says the LORD: "Against all My
evil neighbors who [a]touch the inheritance
which I have caused My people Israel to
inherit—behold, I will [b]pluck them out of
their land and pluck out the house of Judah
from among them. 15[a]Then it shall be, after I
have plucked them out, that I will return and
have compassion on them [b]and bring them

11:20 [a] Ps. 7:9 [b] Jer. 15:15 11:21 [a] Jer. 1:1; 12:5, 6 [b] Mic. 2:6 11:22 [a] Jer. 9:21 11:23 [a] Jer. 23:12 12:1 [a] Ps. 51:4 [b] Mal. 3:15 12:2 [a] Matt. 15:8 12:3 [a] Ps. 17:3 [b] Jer. 11:20 [c] James 5:5 12:4 [a] Hos. 4:3 [b] Jer. 9:10 [c] Ps. 107:34 12:5 [a] Josh. 3:15 [1] Or *thicket* 12:6 [a] Jer. 9:4, 5 [b] Prov. 26:25 12:8 [a] Hos. 9:15 12:9 [a] Lev. 26:22 12:10 [a] Jer. 6:3; 23:1 [b] Is. 5:1–7 [c] Is. 63:18 [1] Literally *shepherds* or *pastors* 12:11 [a] Jer. 10:22; 22:6 [b] Is. 42:25 12:13 [a] Hag. 1:6 12:14 [a] Zech. 2:8 [b] Deut. 30:3 12:15 [a] Ezek. 28:25 [b] Amos 9:14

back, everyone to his heritage and everyone
to his land. 16And it shall be, if they will learn
carefully the ways of My people, [a]to swear by
My name, 'As the LORD lives,' as they taught
My people to swear by Baal, then they shall
be [b]established in the midst of My people.
17But if they do not [a]obey, I will utterly pluck
up and destroy that nation," says the LORD.

Symbol of the Linen Sash

13 Thus the LORD said to me: "Go and get
yourself a linen sash, and put it around
your waist, but do not put it in water." 2So I
got a sash according to the word of the LORD,
and put *it* around my waist.
3And the word of the LORD came to me the
second time, saying, 4"Take the sash that you
acquired, which *is* around your waist, and
arise, go to the Euphrates,[1] and hide it there
in a hole in the rock." 5So I went and hid it by
the Euphrates, as the LORD commanded me.
6Now it came to pass after many days that
the LORD said to me, "Arise, go to the Euphrates, and take from there the sash which
I commanded you to hide there." 7Then I
went to the Euphrates and dug, and I took
the sash from the place where I had hidden
it; and there was the sash, ruined. It was
profitable for nothing.
8Then the word of the LORD came to me,
saying, 9"Thus says the LORD: 'In this manner
[a]I will ruin the pride of Judah and the great
[b]pride of Jerusalem. 10This evil people, who
[a]refuse to hear My words, who [b]follow the
dictates of their hearts, and walk after other
gods to serve them and worship them, shall
be just like this sash which is profitable for
nothing. 11For as the sash clings to the waist
of a man, so I have caused the whole house
of Israel and the whole house of Judah to
cling to Me,' says the LORD, 'that [a]they may
become My people, [b]for renown, for praise,
and for [c]glory; but they would [d]not hear.'

Symbol of the Wine Bottles

12"Therefore you shall speak to them this
word: 'Thus says the LORD God of Israel:
"Every bottle shall be filled with wine." '
"And they will say to you, 'Do we not cer-
tainly know that every bottle will be filled
with wine?'
13"Then you shall say to them, 'Thus says
the LORD: "Behold, I will fill all the inhabitants of this land—even the kings who sit on
David's throne, the priests, the prophets, and
all the inhabitants of Jerusalem—[a]with drunkenness! 14And [a]I will dash them one against
another, even the fathers and the sons together," says the LORD. "I will not pity nor spare nor
have mercy, but will destroy them." ' "

> **PEACE NOTE**
>
> There is no peace in the world, only trouble. We overcome the world through Christ.

Pride Precedes Captivity

15 Hear and give ear:
Do not be proud,
For the LORD has spoken.
16 [a]Give glory to the LORD your God
Before He causes [b]darkness,
And before your feet stumble
On the dark mountains,
And while you are [c]looking for light,
He turns it into [d]the shadow of death
And makes *it* dense darkness.
17 But if you will not hear it,
My soul will [a]weep in secret for *your* pride;
My eyes will weep bitterly
And run down with tears,
Because the LORD's flock has been taken captive.

18 Say to [a]the king and to the queen mother,
"Humble yourselves;
Sit down,
For your rule shall collapse, the crown of your glory."
19 The cities of the South shall be shut up,
And no one shall open *them;*
Judah shall be carried away captive, all of it;
It shall be wholly carried away captive.

20 Lift up your eyes and see
Those who come from the [a]north.
Where *is* the flock *that* was given to you,
Your beautiful sheep?

12:16 [a] [Jer. 4:2] [b] [1 Pet. 2:5] 12:17 [a] Is. 60:12 13:4 [1] Hebrew *Perath* 13:9 [a] Lev. 26:19 [b] Zeph. 3:11 13:10 [a] Jer. 16:12 [b] Jer. 7:24; 16:12 13:11 [a] [Ex. 19:5, 6] [b] Jer. 33:9 [c] Is. 43:21 [d] Jer. 7:13, 24, 26 13:13 [a] Is. 51:17; 63:6 13:14 [a] Jer. 19:9–11 13:16 [a] Josh. 7:19 [b] Amos 8:9 [c] Is. 59:9 [d] Ps. 44:19 13:17 [a] Jer. 9:1; 14:17 13:18 [a] Jer. 22:26 13:20 [a] Jer. 10:22; 46:20

21 What will you say when He punishes you?
For you have taught them
To be chieftains, to be head over you.
Will not [a]pangs seize you,
Like a woman in labor?
22 And if you say in your heart,
[a]"Why have these things come upon me?"
For the greatness of your iniquity
[b]Your skirts have been uncovered,
Your heels made bare.
23 Can the Ethiopian change his skin or the leopard its spots?
Then may you also do good who are accustomed to do evil.

24 "Therefore I will [a]scatter them [b]like stubble
That passes away by the wind of the wilderness.
25 [a]This is your lot,
The portion of your measures from Me," says the LORD,
"Because you have forgotten Me
And trusted in [b]falsehood.
26 Therefore [a]I will uncover your skirts over your face,
That your shame may appear.
27 I have seen your adulteries
And your *lustful* [a]neighings,
The lewdness of your harlotry,
Your abominations [b]on the hills in the fields.
Woe to you, O Jerusalem!
Will you still not be made clean?"

Sword, Famine, and Pestilence

14 The word of the LORD that came to Jeremiah concerning the droughts.

2 "Judah mourns,
And [a]her gates languish;
They [b]mourn for the land,
And [c]the cry of Jerusalem has gone up.
3 Their nobles have sent their lads for water;
They went to the cisterns *and* found no water.
They returned with their vessels empty;
They were [a]ashamed and confounded
[b]And covered their heads.
4 Because the ground is parched,
For there was [a]no rain in the land,
The plowmen were ashamed;
They covered their heads.
5 Yes, the deer also gave birth in the field,
But left because there was no grass.
6 And [a]the wild donkeys stood in the desolate heights;
They sniffed at the wind like jackals;
Their eyes failed because *there was* no grass."

7 O LORD, though our iniquities testify against us,
Do it [a]for Your name's sake;
For our backslidings are many,
We have sinned against You.
8 [a]O the Hope of Israel, his Savior in time of trouble,
Why should You be like a stranger in the land,
And like a traveler *who* turns aside to tarry for a night?
9 Why should You be like a man astonished,
Like a mighty one [a]*who* cannot save?
Yet You, O LORD, [b]*are* in our midst,
And we are called by Your name;
Do not leave us!

10 Thus says the LORD to this people:

[a]"Thus they have loved to wander;
They have not restrained their feet.
Therefore the LORD does not accept them;
[b]He will remember their iniquity now,
And punish their sins."

11 Then the LORD said to me, [a]"Do not pray for
this people, for *their* good. 12 [a]When they fast,
I will not hear their cry; and [b]when they offer
burnt offering and grain offering, I will not
accept them. But [c]I will consume them by the
sword, by the famine, and by the pestilence."
13 [a]Then I said, "Ah, Lord GOD! Behold, the
prophets say to them, 'You shall not see the
sword, nor shall you have famine, but I will
give you assured [b]peace in this place.' "
14 And the LORD said to me, [a]"The prophets
prophesy lies in My name. [b]I have not sent
them, commanded them, nor spoken to them;
they prophesy to you a false vision, divination,
a worthless thing, and the [c]deceit of their heart.
15 Therefore thus says the LORD concerning the
prophets who prophesy in My name, whom I
did not send, [a]and who say, 'Sword and famine
shall not be in this land'—'By sword and famine those prophets shall be consumed! 16 And
the people to whom they prophesy shall be

13:21 [a] Jer. 6:24 13:22 [a] Jer. 16:10 [b] Is. 47:2 13:24 [a] Jer. 9:16 [b] Hos. 13:3 13:25 [a] Job 20:29 [b] Jer. 10:14 13:26 [a] Lam. 1:8 13:27 [a] Jer. 5:7, 8 [b] Is. 65:7; Ezek. 6:13 14:2 [a] Is. 3:26 [b] Jer. 8:21 [c] 1 Sam. 5:12 14:3 [a] Ps. 40:14 [b] 2 Sam. 15:30 14:4 [a] Jer. 3:3 14:6 [a] Jer. 2:24 14:7 [a] Ps. 25:11 14:8 [a] Jer. 17:13 14:9 [a] Is. 59:1 [b] Ex. 29:45 14:10 [a] Jer. 2:23–25 [b] Hos. 8:13 14:11 [a] Ex. 32:10 14:12 [a] Ezek. 8:18 [b] Jer. 6:20 [c] Jer. 9:16 14:13 [a] Jer. 4:10 [b] Jer. 8:11; 23:17 14:14 [a] Jer. 27:10 [b] Jer. 29:8, 9 [c] Jer. 23:16 14:15 [a] Ezek. 14:10

cast out in the streets of Jerusalem because
of the famine and the sword; [a]they will have
no one to bury them—them nor their wives,
their sons nor their daughters—for I will pour
their wickedness on them.'

17"Therefore you shall say this word to
them:

[a]'Let my eyes flow with tears night and day,
And let them not cease;
[b]For the virgin daughter of my people
Has been broken with a mighty stroke,
with a very severe blow.
18 If I go out to [a]the field,
Then behold, those slain with the sword!
And if I enter the city,
Then behold, those sick from famine!
Yes, both prophet and [b]priest go about
in a land they do not know.' "

The People Plead for Mercy

19 [a]Have You utterly rejected Judah?
Has Your soul loathed Zion?
Why have You stricken us so that [b]*there is* no healing for us?
[c]We looked for peace, but *there was* no
good;
And for the time of healing, and there
was trouble.
20 We acknowledge, O LORD, our wickedness
And the iniquity of our [a]fathers,
For [b]we have sinned against You.
21 Do not abhor *us*, for Your name's sake;
Do not disgrace the throne of Your glory.
[a]Remember, do not break Your
covenant with us.
22 [a]Are there any among [b]the idols of the
nations that can cause [c]rain?
Or can the heavens give showers?
[d]*Are* You not He, O LORD our God?
Therefore we will wait for You,
Since You have made all these.

The LORD Will Not Relent

15 Then the LORD said to me, [a]"*Even* if
[b]Moses and [c]Samuel stood before Me,
My mind *would* not *be* favorable toward this
people. Cast *them* out of My sight, and let
them go forth. 2And it shall be, if they say to
you, 'Where should we go?' then you shall
tell them, 'Thus says the LORD:

[a]"Such as *are* for death, to death;
And such as *are* for the sword, to the
sword;
And such as *are* for the famine, to the
famine;
And such as *are* for the [b]captivity, to
the captivity." '

3"And I will [a]appoint over them four forms
of destruction," says the LORD: "the sword to
slay, the dogs to drag, [b]the birds of the heavens and the beasts of the earth to devour and
destroy. 4I will hand them over to [a]trouble,
to all kingdoms of the earth, because of [b]Ma-
nasseh the son of Hezekiah, king of Judah,
for what he did in Jerusalem.

5 "For who will have pity on you,
O Jerusalem?
Or who will bemoan you?
Or who will turn aside to ask how you
are doing?
6 [a]You have forsaken Me," says the LORD,
"You have [b]gone backward.
Therefore I will stretch out My hand
against you and destroy you;
[c]I am weary of relenting!
7 And I will winnow them with a
winnowing fan in the gates of the land;
I will [a]bereave *them* of children;
I will destroy My people,
Since they [b]do not return from their ways.
8 Their widows will be increased to Me
more than the sand of the seas;
I will bring against them,
Against the mother of the young men,
A plunderer at noonday;
I will cause anguish and terror to fall
on them [a]suddenly.

9 "She[a] languishes who has borne seven;
She has breathed her last;
[b]Her sun has gone down
While *it was* yet day;
She has been ashamed and
confounded.
And the remnant of them I will deliver
to the sword
Before their enemies," says the LORD.

Jeremiah's Dejection

10 [a]Woe is me, my mother,
That you have borne me,
A man of strife and a man of
contention to the whole earth!
I have neither lent for interest,
Nor have men lent to me for interest.
Every one of them curses me.

14:16 [a] Ps. 79:2, 3 **14:17** [a] Jer. 9:1; 13:17 [b] Jer. 8:21 **14:18** [a] Ezek. 7:15 [b] Jer. 23:11 **14:19** [a] Lam. 5:22 [b] Jer. 15:18 [c] Jer. 8:15 **14:20** [a] Jer. 3:25 [b] Dan. 9:8 **14:21** [a] Ps. 106:45 **14:22** [a] Zech. 10:1 [b] Deut. 32:21 [c] Jer. 5:24 [d] Ps. 135:7 **15:1** [a] Ezek. 14:14 [b] Ex. 32:11–14 [c] 1 Sam. 7:9 **15:2** [a] Zech. 11:9 [b] Jer. 9:16; 16:13 **15:3** [a] Ezek. 14:21 [b] Jer. 7:33 **15:4** [a] Deut. 28:25 [b] 2 Kin. 24:3, 4 **15:6** [a] Jer. 2:13 [b] Jer. 7:24 [c] Jer. 20:16 **15:7** [a] Jer. 18:21 [b] Is. 9:13 **15:8** [a] Is. 29:5 **15:9** [a] 1 Sam. 2:5 [b] Amos 8:9 **15:10** [a] Job 3:1

11The LORD said:

"Surely it will be well with your remnant;
Surely I will cause [a]the enemy to intercede with you
In the time of adversity and in the time of affliction.
12 Can anyone break iron,
The northern iron and the bronze?
13 Your wealth and your treasures
I will give as [a]plunder without price,
Because of all your sins,
Throughout your territories.
14 And I will make *you* cross over with[1] your enemies
[a]Into a land *which* you do not know;
For a [b]fire is kindled in My anger,
Which shall burn upon you."

15 O LORD, [a]You know;
Remember me and visit me,
And [b]take vengeance for me on my persecutors.
In Your enduring patience, do not take me away.
Know that [c]for Your sake I have suffered rebuke.
16 Your words were found, and I [a]ate them,
And [b]Your word was to me the joy and rejoicing of my heart;
For I am called by Your name,
O LORD God of hosts.
17 [a]I did not sit in the assembly of the mockers,
Nor did I rejoice;
I sat alone because of Your hand,
For You have filled me with indignation.
18 Why is my [a]pain perpetual
And my wound incurable,
Which refuses to be healed?
Will You surely be to me [b]like an unreliable stream,
As waters *that* fail?

The LORD Reassures Jeremiah

19Therefore thus says the LORD:

[a]"If you return,
Then I will bring you back;
You shall [b]stand before Me;
If you [c]take out the precious from the vile,
You shall be as My mouth.
Let them return to you,
But you must not return to them.
20 And I will make you to this people a fortified bronze [a]wall;
And they will fight against you,
But [b]they shall not prevail against you;
For I *am* with you to save you
And deliver you," says the LORD.
21 "I will deliver you from the hand of the wicked,
And I will redeem you from the grip of the terrible."

Jeremiah's Lifestyle and Message

16 The word of the LORD also came to me,
saying, 2"You shall not take a wife, nor
shall you have sons or daughters in this place."
3For thus says the LORD concerning the sons
and daughters who are born in this place, and
concerning their mothers who bore them
and their fathers who begot them in this land:
4"They shall die [a]gruesome deaths; they shall
not be [b]lamented nor shall they be [c]buried, *but*
they shall be [d]like refuse on the face of the earth.
They shall be consumed by the sword and by
famine, and their [e]corpses shall be meat for the
birds of heaven and for the beasts of the earth."
5For thus says the LORD: [a]"Do not enter the
house of mourning, nor go to lament or bemoan them; for I have taken away My peace
from this people," says the LORD, "lovingkindness and mercies. 6Both the great and
the small shall die in this land. They shall
not be buried; [a]neither shall men lament for
them, [b]cut themselves, nor [c]make themselves
bald for them. 7Nor shall *men* break *bread*
in mourning for them, to comfort them for
the dead; nor shall *men* give them the cup of
consolation to [a]drink for their father or their
mother. 8Also you shall not go into the house
of feasting to sit with them, to eat and drink."
9For thus says the LORD of hosts, the God
of Israel: "Behold, [a]I will cause to cease from
this place, before your eyes and in your days,
the voice of mirth and the voice of gladness,
the voice of the bridegroom and the voice
of the bride.
10"And it shall be, when you show this people
all these words, and they say to you, [a]'Why has
the LORD pronounced all this great disaster
against us? Or what *is* our iniquity? Or what
is our sin that we have committed against the
LORD our God?' 11then you shall say to them,
[a]'Because your fathers have forsaken Me,' says
the LORD; 'they have walked after other gods
and have served them and worshiped them, and

15:11 [a] Jer. 40:4, 5 **15:13** [a] Ps. 44:12 **15:14** [a] Jer. 16:13 [b] Deut. 32:22 [1] Following Masoretic Text and Vulgate; Septuagint, Syriac, and Targum read *cause you to serve* (compare 17:4). **15:15** [a] Jer. 12:3 [b] Jer. 20:12 [c] Ps. 69:7–9 **15:16** [a] Ezek. 3:1, 3 [b] [Job 23:12] **15:17** [a] Ps. 26:4, 5 **15:18** [a] Jer. 10:19; 30:15 [b] Job 6:15 **15:19** [a] Zech. 3:7 [b] Jer. 15:1 [c] Ezek. 22:26; 44:23 **15:20** [a] Ezek. 3:9 [b] Jer. 1:8, 19; 20:11; 37:21; 38:13; 39:11, 12 **16:4** [a] Jer. 15:2 [b] Jer. 22:18; 25:33 [c] Jer. 14:16; 19:11 [d] Ps. 83:10 [e] Ps. 79:2 **16:5** [a] Ezek. 24:17, 22, 23 **16:6** [a] Jer. 22:18 [b] Deut. 14:1 [c] Is. 22:12 **16:7** [a] Prov. 31:6 **16:9** [a] Rev. 18:23 **16:10** [a] Deut. 29:24 **16:11** [a] Jer. 22:9

have forsaken Me and not kept My law. 12And you
have done [a]worse than your fathers, for behold,
[b]each one follows the dictates of his own evil
heart, so that no one listens to Me. 13[a]Therefore
I will cast you out of this land [b]into a land that
you do not know, neither you nor your fathers;
and there you shall serve other gods day and
night, where I will not show you favor.'

God Will Restore Israel

14"Therefore behold, the [a]days are coming,"
says the LORD, "that it shall no more be said,
'The LORD lives who brought up the children
of Israel from the land of Egypt,' 15but, 'The
LORD lives who brought up the children of
Israel from the land of the [a]north and from
all the lands where He had driven them.' For
[b]I will bring them back into their land which
I gave to their fathers.

16"Behold, I will send for many [a]fishermen,"
says the LORD, "and they shall fish them; and
afterward I will send for many hunters, and
they shall hunt them from every mountain
and every hill, and out of the holes of the
rocks. 17For My [a]eyes *are* on all their ways;
they are not hidden from My face, nor is their
iniquity hidden from My eyes. 18And first I
will repay [a]double for their iniquity and their
sin, because [b]they have defiled My land; they
have filled My inheritance with the carcasses
of their detestable and abominable idols."

19 O LORD, [a]my strength and my fortress,
[b]My refuge in the day of affliction,
The Gentiles shall come to You
From the ends of the earth and say,
"Surely our fathers have inherited lies,
Worthlessness and [c]unprofitable *things.*"
20 Will a man make gods for himself,
[a]Which *are* not gods?

21 "Therefore behold, I will this once cause
them to know,
I will cause them to know
My hand and My might;
And they shall know that [a]My name *is*
the LORD.

Judah's Sin and Punishment

17 "The sin of Judah *is* [a]written with a
[b]pen of iron;
With the point of a diamond *it is*
[c]engraved
On the tablet of their heart,
And on the horns of your altars,
2 While their children remember
Their altars and their [a]wooden images[1]
By the green trees on the high hills.
3 O My mountain in the field,
I will give as plunder your wealth, all
your treasures,
And your high places of sin within all
your borders.
4 And you, even yourself,
Shall let go of your heritage which I
gave you;
And I will cause you to serve your
enemies
In [a]the land which you do not know;
For [b]you have kindled a fire in My
anger *which* shall burn forever."

5Thus says the LORD:

[a]"Cursed *is* the man who trusts in man
And makes [b]flesh his strength,
Whose heart departs from the LORD.
6 For he shall be [a]like a shrub in the desert,
And [b]shall not see when good comes,
But shall inhabit the parched places in
the wilderness,
[c]*In* a salt land *which is* not inhabited.

7 "Blessed[a] *is* the man who trusts in the
LORD,
And whose hope is the LORD.
8 For he shall be [a]like a tree planted by
the waters,
Which spreads out its roots by the river,
And will not fear[1] when heat comes;
But its leaf will be green,
And will not be anxious in the year of
drought,
Nor will cease from yielding fruit.

9 "The [a]heart *is* deceitful above all *things,*
And desperately wicked;
Who can know it?
10 I, the LORD, [a]search the heart,
I test the mind,
[b]Even to give every man according to
his ways,
According to the fruit of his doings.

11 "*As* a partridge that broods but does not
hatch,
So is he who gets riches, but not by
right;
It [a]will leave him in the midst of his days,
And at his end he will be [b]a fool."

16:12 [a] Jer. 7:26 [b] Jer. 3:17; 18:12 **16:13** [a] Deut. 4:26; 28:36, 63 [b] Jer. 15:14 **16:14** [a] Jer. 23:7, 8 **16:15** [a] Jer. 3:18 [b] Jer. 24:6; 30:3; 32:37 **16:16** [a] Amos 4:2 **16:17** [a] Heb. 4:13 **16:18** [a] Jer. 17:18 [b] [Ezek. 43:7] **16:19** [a] Ps. 18:1, 2 [b] Jer. 17:17 [c] Is. 44:10 **16:20** [a] Gal. 4:8 **16:21** [a] Amos 5:8 **17:1** [a] Jer. 2:22 [b] Job 19:24 [c] 2 Cor. 3:3 **17:2** [a] Judg. 3:7 [1] Hebrew *Asherim,* Canaanite deities **17:4** [a] Jer. 16:13 [b] Jer. 15:14 **17:5** [a] Is. 30:1, 2; 31:1 [b] Is. 31:3 **17:6** [a] Jer. 48:6 [b] Job 20:17 [c] Deut. 29:23 **17:7** [a] [Is. 30:18] **17:8** [a] [Ps. 1:3] [1] Qere and Targum read *see.* **17:9** [a] [Eccl. 9:3] **17:10** [a] Rev. 2:23 [b] Rom. 2:6 **17:11** [a] Ps. 55:23 [b] Luke 12:20

STURDY AND STEADY

"The man who trusts in the LORD . . . will not fear . . . will not be anxious."

JEREMIAH 17:7-8

The prophet Jeremiah wrote about the one whose faith is in God: "He shall be like a tree planted by the waters . . . its leaf will be green . . . [it will not] cease from yielding fruit" (v. 8). Such a person never lacks spiritual nourishment and so always provides spiritual fruit. Jeremiah provides a sobering example of the fruitlessness of trusting in anyone (including ourselves) other than God (vv. 5–6)—he calls him "cursed," like a dead shrub blowing in the wind. The believer's trust is established in the Lord, so he stands steady despite storms and the ravages of time, and his leaves are always a life-giving green.

Clearly this is a person of peace. Though he sees the storms, he finds the fruit of peace inevitably grows when he's locked into the life-giving Source. Are you rooted in your God, sturdy in your trust, and abiding in the Lord (John 15:5)? How can you transform your trust today into something more everlasting?

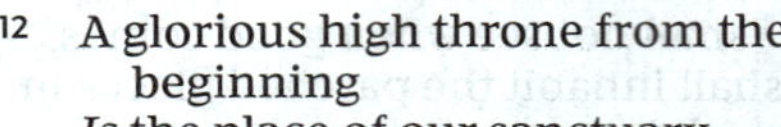

12 A glorious high throne from the
beginning
Is the place of our sanctuary.
13 O LORD, [a]the hope of Israel,
[b]All who forsake You shall be ashamed.

"Those who depart from Me
Shall be [c]written in the earth,
Because they have forsaken the LORD,
The [d]fountain of living waters."

Jeremiah Prays for Deliverance

14 Heal me, O LORD, and I shall be healed;
Save me, and I shall be saved,
For [a]You *are* my praise.
15 Indeed they say to me,
[a]"Where *is* the word of the LORD?
Let it come now!"
16 As for me, [a]I have not hurried away
from *being* a shepherd *who* follows
You,
Nor have I desired the woeful day;
You know what came out of my lips;
It was right there before You.
17 Do not be a terror to me;
[a]You *are* my hope in the day of doom.
18 [a]Let them be ashamed who
persecute me,
But [b]do not let me be put to shame;
Let them be dismayed,
But do not let me be dismayed.
Bring on them the day of doom,
And [c]destroy them with double
destruction!

Hallow the Sabbath Day

19 Thus the LORD said to me: "Go and stand
in the gate of the children of the people, by
which the kings of Judah come in and by
which they go out, and in all the gates of Jerusalem; 20 and say to them, [a]'Hear the word of
the LORD, you kings of Judah, and all Judah,
and all the inhabitants of Jerusalem, who
enter by these gates. 21 Thus says the LORD:
[a]"Take heed to yourselves, and bear no burden
on the Sabbath day, nor bring *it* in by the gates
of Jerusalem; 22 nor carry a burden out of your
houses on the Sabbath day, nor do any work,
but hallow the Sabbath day, as I [a]commanded
your fathers. 23 [a]But they did not obey nor incline their ear, but made their neck stiff, that
they might not hear nor receive instruction.
24 "And it shall be, [a]if you heed Me carefully," says the LORD, "to bring no burden
through the gates of this city on the [b]Sabbath
day, but hallow the Sabbath day, to do no work
in it, 25 [a]then shall enter the gates of this city
kings and princes sitting on the throne of
David, riding in chariots and on horses, they
and their princes, accompanied by the men
of Judah and the inhabitants of Jerusalem;
and this city shall remain forever. 26 And they
shall come from the cities of Judah and from
[a]the places around Jerusalem, from the land
of Benjamin and from [b]the lowland, from the
mountains and from [c]the South, bringing
burnt offerings and sacrifices, grain offerings
and incense, bringing [d]sacrifices of praise to
the house of the LORD.

17:13 [a]Jer. 14:8 [b][Is. 1:28] [c]Luke 10:20 [d]Jer. 2:13 17:14 [a]Deut. 10:21 17:15 [a]Is. 5:19 17:16 [a]Jer. 1:4–12 17:17 [a]Jer. 16:19 17:18 [a]Ps. 35:4; 70:2 [b]Ps. 25:2 [c]Jer. 11:20 17:20 [a]Jer. 19:3, 4 17:21 [a]Neh. 13:19 17:22 [a]Ex. 20:8; 31:13 17:23 [a]Jer. 7:24, 26 17:24 [a]Jer. 11:4; 26:3 [b]Ex. 16:23–30; 20:8–10 17:25 [a]Jer. 22:4 17:26 [a]Jer. 33:13 [b]Zech. 7:7 [c]Judg. 1:9 [d]Ps. 107:22; 116:17

27“But if you will not heed Me to hallow the
Sabbath day, such as not carrying a burden
when entering the gates of Jerusalem on
the Sabbath day, then [a]I will kindle a fire in
its gates, [b]and it shall devour the palaces of
Jerusalem, and it shall not be [c]quenched.” ’ ”

The Potter and the Clay

18 The word which came to Jeremiah from
the LORD, saying: 2“Arise and go down
to the potter’s house, and there I will cause
you to hear My words.” 3Then I went down to
the potter’s house, and there he was, making
something at the wheel. 4And the vessel that
he made of clay was marred in the hand of the
potter; so he made it again into another vessel, as it seemed good to the potter to make.
5Then the word of the LORD came to me,
saying: 6“O house of Israel, [a]can I not do with
you as this potter?” says the LORD. “Look, [b]as
the clay *is* in the potter’s hand, so *are* you in
My hand, O house of Israel! 7The instant I
speak concerning a nation and concerning
a kingdom, to [a]pluck up, to pull down, and to
destroy *it,* 8[a]if that nation against whom I have
spoken turns from its evil, [b]I will relent of the
disaster that I thought to bring upon it. 9And
the instant I speak concerning a nation and
concerning a kingdom, to build and to plant
it, 10if it does evil in My sight so that it does not
obey My voice, then I will relent concerning
the good with which I said I would benefit it.
11“Now therefore, speak to the men of Judah
and to the inhabitants of Jerusalem, saying,
‘Thus says the LORD: “Behold, I am fashioning
a disaster and devising a plan against you.
[a]Return now every one from his evil way, and
make your ways and your doings [b]good.” ’ ”

God’s Warning Rejected

12And they said, [a]“That is hopeless! So we
will walk according to our own plans, and
we will every one obey the [b]dictates of his
evil heart.”
13Therefore thus says the LORD:

[a]“Ask now among the Gentiles,
Who has heard such things?
The virgin of Israel has done [b]a very
horrible thing.
14 Will *a man* leave the snow water of
Lebanon,
Which comes from the rock of the field?
Will the cold flowing waters be
forsaken for strange waters?
15 “Because My people have forgotten [a]Me,
They have burned incense to worthless
idols.
And they have caused themselves to
stumble in their ways,
From the [b]ancient paths,
To walk in pathways and not on a highway,
16 To make their land [a]desolate *and* a
perpetual [b]hissing;
Everyone who passes by it will be
astonished
And shake his head.
17 [a]I will scatter them [b]as with an east
wind before the enemy;
[c]I will show them[1] the back and not the
face
In the day of their calamity.”

Jeremiah Persecuted

18Then they said, [a]“Come and let us devise
plans against Jeremiah; [b]for the law shall not
perish from the priest, nor counsel from the
wise, nor the word from the prophet. Come
and let us attack him with the tongue, and let
us not give heed to any of his words.”

19 Give heed to me, O LORD,
And listen to the voice of those who
contend with me!
20 [a]Shall evil be repaid for good?
For they have [b]dug a pit for my life.
Remember that I [c]stood before You
To speak good for them,
To turn away Your wrath from them.
21 Therefore [a]deliver up their children to
the famine,
And pour out their *blood*
By the force of the sword;
Let their wives *become* widows
And [b]bereaved of their children.
Let their men be put to death,
Their young men *be* slain
By the sword in battle.
22 Let a cry be heard from their houses,
When You bring a troop suddenly upon
them;
For they have dug a pit to take me,
And hidden snares for my feet.
23 Yet, LORD, You know all their counsel
Which is against me, to slay *me.*
[a]Provide no atonement for their iniquity,
Nor blot out their sin from Your sight;
But let them be overthrown before You.
Deal *thus* with them
In the time of Your [b]anger.

17:27 [a] Lam. 4:11 [b] 2 Kin. 25:9 [c] Jer. 7:20 **18:6** [a] Rom. 9:20, 21 [b] Is. 64:8 **18:7** [a] Jer. 1:10 **18:8** [a] [Ezek. 18:21; 33:11] [b] Jer. 26:3 **18:11** [a] 2 Kin. 17:13 [b] Jer. 7:3–7 **18:12** [a] Jer. 2:25 [b] Jer. 3:17; 23:17 **18:13** [a] Jer. 2:10, 11 [b] Jer. 5:30 **18:15** [a] Jer. 2:13, 32 [b] Jer. 6:16 **18:16** [a] Jer. 19:8 [b] 1 Kin. 9:8 **18:17** [a] Jer. 13:24 [b] Ps. 48:7 [c] Jer. 2:27 [1] Following Septuagint, Syriac, Targum, and Vulgate; Masoretic Text reads *look them in.* **18:18** [a] Jer. 11:19 [b] Lev. 10:11 **18:20** [a] Ps. 109:4 [b] Jer. 5:26 [c] Jer. 14:7—15:1 **18:21** [a] Ps. 109:9–20 [b] Jer. 15:7, 8 **18:23** [a] Ps. 35:14; 109:14 [b] Jer. 7:20

The Sign of the Broken Flask

19 Thus says the LORD: "Go and get a potter's earthen flask, and *take* some of the elders of the people and some of the elders of the priests. 2And go out to [a]the Valley of the Son of Hinnom, which *is* by the entry of the Potsherd Gate; and proclaim there the words that I will tell you, 3[a]and say, 'Hear the word of the LORD, O kings of Judah and inhabitants of Jerusalem. Thus says the LORD of hosts, the God of Israel: "Behold, I will bring such a catastrophe on this place, that whoever hears of it, his ears will [b]tingle.

4"Because they [a]have forsaken Me and made this an alien place, because they have burned incense in it to other gods whom neither they, their fathers, nor the kings of Judah have known, and have filled this place with [b]the blood of the innocents 5[a](they have also built the high places of Baal, to burn their sons with fire *for* burnt offerings to Baal, [b]which I did not command or speak, nor did it come into My mind), 6therefore behold, the days are coming," says the LORD, "that this place shall no more be called Tophet or [a]the Valley of the Son of Hinnom, but the Valley of Slaughter. 7And I will make void the counsel of Judah and Jerusalem in this place, [a]and I will cause them to fall by the sword before their enemies and by the hands of those who seek their lives; their [b]corpses I will give as meat for the birds of the heaven and for the beasts of the earth. 8I will make this city [a]desolate and a hissing; everyone who passes by it will be astonished and hiss because of all its plagues. 9And I will cause them to eat the [a]flesh of their sons and the flesh of their daughters, and everyone shall eat the flesh of his friend in the siege and in the desperation with which their enemies and those who seek their lives shall drive them to despair." '

10[a]"Then you shall break the flask in the sight of the men who go with you, 11and say to them, 'Thus says the LORD of hosts: [a]"Even so I will break this people and this city, as *one* breaks a potter's vessel, which cannot be made whole again; and they shall [b]bury *them* in Tophet till *there is* no place to bury. 12Thus I will do to this place," says the LORD, "and to its inhabitants, and make this city like Tophet. 13And the houses of Jerusalem and the houses of the kings of Judah shall be defiled [a]like the place of Tophet, because of all the houses on whose [b]roofs they have burned incense to all the host of heaven, and [c]poured out drink offerings to other gods." ' "

14Then Jeremiah came from Tophet, where the LORD had sent him to prophesy; and he stood in [a]the court of the LORD's house and said to all the people, 15"Thus says the LORD of hosts, the God of Israel: 'Behold, I will bring on this city and on all her towns all the doom that I have pronounced against it, because [a]they have stiffened their necks that they might not hear My words.' "

The Word of God to Pashhur

20 Now [a]Pashhur the son of [b]Immer, the priest who *was* also chief governor in the house of the LORD, heard that Jeremiah prophesied these things. 2Then Pashhur struck Jeremiah the prophet, and put him in the stocks that *were* in the high [a]gate of Benjamin, which *was* by the house of the LORD.

> PEACE NOTE
>
> Sensitive people like Jeremiah need extra spiritual depth to endure life's challenges. But God uses sensitive hearts mightily because they spread the peace of God by example.
>
> JEREMIAH 20:2

3And it happened on the next day that Pashhur brought Jeremiah out of the stocks. Then Jeremiah said to him, "The LORD has not called your name Pashhur, but Magor-Missabib.[1] 4For thus says the LORD: 'Behold, I will make you a terror to yourself and to all your friends; and they shall fall by the sword of their enemies, and your eyes shall see *it*. I will [a]give all Judah into the hand of the king of Babylon, and he shall carry them captive to Babylon and slay them with the sword. 5Moreover I [a]will deliver all the wealth of this city, all its produce, and all its precious things; all the treasures of the kings of Judah I will give into the hand of their enemies, who will plunder them, seize them, and [b]carry them to Babylon. 6And you, Pashhur, and all who dwell in your house, shall go into captivity. You shall go to Babylon,

19:2 [a] Josh. 15:8 **19:3** [a] Jer. 17:20 [b] 1 Sam. 3:11 **19:4** [a] Is. 65:11 [b] 2 Kin. 21:12 **19:5** [a] Jer. 7:31; 32:35 [b] Lev. 18:21 **19:6** [a] Josh. 15:8 **19:7** [a] Lev. 26:17 [b] Ps. 79:2 **19:8** [a] Jer. 18:16; 49:13; 50:13 **19:9** [a] Lev. 26:29 **19:10** [a] Jer. 51:63, 64 **19:11** [a] Is. 30:14 [b] Jer. 7:32 **19:13** [a] 2 Kin. 23:10 [b] Zeph. 1:5 [c] Jer. 7:18 **19:14** [a] 2 Chr. 20:5 **19:15** [a] Neh. 9:17, 29 **20:1** [a] Ezra 2:37, 38 [b] 1 Chr. 24:14 **20:2** [a] Jer. 37:13 **20:3** [1] Literally *Fear on Every Side* **20:4** [a] Jer. 21:4–10 **20:5** [a] 2 Kin. 20:17 [b] Is. 39:6

and there you shall die, and be buried there, you and all your friends, to whom you have [a]prophesied lies.' "

Jeremiah's Unpopular Ministry

7 O LORD, You induced me, and I was
persuaded;
[a]You are stronger than I, and have
prevailed.
[b]I am in derision daily;
Everyone mocks me.
8 For when I spoke, I cried out;
[a]I shouted, "Violence and plunder!"
Because the word of the LORD was
made to me
A reproach and a derision daily.
9 Then I said, "I will not make mention
of Him,
Nor speak anymore in His name."
But *His word* was in my heart like a
[a]burning fire
Shut up in my bones;
I was weary of holding *it* back,
And [b]I could not.
10 [a]For I heard many mocking:
"Fear on every side!"
"Report," *they say,* "and we will report it!"
[b]All my acquaintances watched for my
stumbling, *saying,*
"Perhaps he can be induced;
Then we will prevail against him,
And we will take our revenge on him."

11 But the LORD *is* [a]with me as a mighty,
awesome One.
Therefore my persecutors will stumble,
and will not [b]prevail.
They will be greatly ashamed, for they
will not prosper.
Their [c]everlasting confusion will never
be forgotten.
12 But, O LORD of hosts,
You who [a]test the righteous,
And see the mind and heart,
[b]Let me see Your vengeance on them;
For I have pleaded my cause before You.

13 Sing to the LORD! Praise the LORD!
For [a]He has delivered the life of the
poor
From the hand of evildoers.

14 [a]Cursed *be* the day in which I was born!
Let the day not be blessed in which my
mother bore me!

PEACE NOTE

When "the LORD is with me as a mighty, awesome One," He speaks His peace over my life forevermore.

JEREMIAH 20:11

15 Let the man *be* cursed
Who brought news to my father, saying,
"A male child has been born to you!"
Making him very glad.
16 And let that man be like the cities
Which the LORD [a]overthrew, and did
not relent;
Let him [b]hear the cry in the morning
And the shouting at noon,
17 [a]Because he did not kill me from the
womb,
That my mother might have been my
grave,
And her womb always enlarged *with me.*
18 [a]Why did I come forth from the womb
to [b]see labor and sorrow,
That my days should be consumed
with shame?

Jerusalem's Doom Is Sealed

21 The word which came to Jeremiah from
the LORD when [a]King Zedekiah sent
to him [b]Pashhur the son of Melchiah, and
[c]Zephaniah the son of Maaseiah, the priest,
saying, 2[a]"Please inquire of the LORD for us,
for Nebuchadnezzar[1] king of Babylon makes
war against us. Perhaps the LORD will deal
with us according to all His wonderful works,
that *the king* may go away from us."
3Then Jeremiah said to them, "Thus you
shall say to Zedekiah, 4'Thus says the LORD
God of Israel: "Behold, I will turn back the
weapons of war that *are* in your hands, with
which you fight against the king of Babylon
and the Chaldeans[1] who besiege you outside
the walls; and [a]I will assemble them in the

20:6 [a] Jer. 14:13–15 **20:7** [a] Jer. 1:6, 7 [b] Lam. 3:14 **20:8** [a] Jer. 6:7 **20:9** [a] Ps. 39:3 [b] Job 32:18 **20:10** [a] Ps. 31:13 [b] Ps. 41:9; 55:13, 14 **20:11** [a] Jer. 1:18, 19 [b] Jer. 15:20; 17:18 [c] Jer. 23:40 **20:12** [a] [Jer. 11:20; 17:10] [b] Ps. 54:7; 59:10 **20:13** [a] Ps. 35:9, 10; 109:30, 31 **20:14** [a] Job 3:3 **20:16** [a] Gen. 19:25 [b] Jer. 18:22 **20:17** [a] Job 3:10, 11 **20:18** [a] Job 3:20 [b] Lam. 3:1 **21:1** [a] 2 Kin. 24:17, 18 [b] Jer. 38:1 [c] 2 Kin. 25:18 **21:2** [a] Jer. 37:3, 7 [1] Hebrew *Nebuchadrezzar,* and so elsewhere **21:4** [a] Is. 13:4 [1] Or *Babylonians*

midst of this city. 5I [a]Myself will fight against
you with an [b]outstretched hand and with
a strong arm, even in anger and fury and
great wrath. 6I will strike the inhabitants of
this city, both man and beast; they shall die
of a great pestilence. 7And afterward," says
the LORD, [a]"I will deliver Zedekiah king of
Judah, his servants and the people, and such
as are left in this city from the pestilence and
the sword and the famine, into the hand of
Nebuchadnezzar king of Babylon, into the
hand of their enemies, and into the hand of
those who seek their life; and he shall strike
them with the edge of the sword. [b]He shall
not spare them, or have pity or mercy." '

8"Now you shall say to this people, 'Thus
says the LORD: "Behold, [a]I set before you the
way of life and the way of death. 9He who
[a]remains in this city shall die by the sword, by
famine, and by pestilence; but he who goes out
and defects to the Chaldeans who besiege you,
he shall [b]live, and his life shall be as a prize to
him. 10For I have [a]set My face against this city
for adversity and not for good," says the LORD.
[b]"It shall be given into the hand of the king
of Babylon, and he shall [c]burn it with fire." '

Message to the House of David

11"And concerning the house of the king
of Judah, *say,* 'Hear the word of the LORD,
12O house of David! Thus says the LORD:

[a]"Execute judgment [b]in the morning;
And deliver *him who is* plundered
Out of the hand of the oppressor,
Lest My fury go forth like fire
And burn so that no one can quench *it,*
Because of the evil of your doings.

13 "Behold, [a]I *am* against you, O inhabitant
of the valley,
And rock of the plain," says the LORD,
"Who say, [b]'Who shall come down
against us?
Or who shall enter our dwellings?'
14 But I will punish you according to the
[a]fruit of your doings," says the LORD;
"I will kindle a fire in its forest,
And [b]it shall devour all things
around it." ' "

22 Thus says the LORD: "Go down to the
house of the king of Judah, and there
speak this word, 2and say, [a]'Hear the word of
the LORD, O king of Judah, you who sit on the
throne of David, you and your servants and
your people who enter these gates! 3Thus says
the LORD: [a]"Execute judgment and righteousness, and deliver the plundered out of the
hand of the oppressor. Do no wrong and do
no violence to the stranger, the [b]fatherless,
or the widow, nor shed innocent blood in this
place. 4For if you indeed do this thing, [a]then
shall enter the gates of this house, riding on
horses and in chariots, accompanied by servants and people, kings who sit on the throne
of David. 5But if you will not hear these words,
[a]I swear by Myself," says the LORD, "that this
house shall become a desolation." ' "

6For thus says the LORD to the house of
the king of Judah:

"You *are* [a]Gilead to Me,
The head of Lebanon;
Yet I surely will make you a wilderness,
Cities *which* are not inhabited.
7 I will prepare destroyers against you,
Everyone with his weapons;
They shall cut down [a]your choice
cedars
[b]And cast *them* into the fire.

8And many nations will pass by this city; and
everyone will say to his neighbor, [a]'Why has
the LORD done so to this great city?' 9Then
they will answer, [a]'Because they have forsak-
en the covenant of the LORD their God, and
worshiped other gods and served them.' "

10 Weep not for [a]the dead, nor bemoan
him;
Weep bitterly for him [b]who goes away,
For he shall return no more,
Nor see his native country.

Message to the Sons of Josiah

11For thus says the LORD concerning [a]Shal-
lum[1] the son of Josiah, king of Judah, who
reigned instead of Josiah his father, [b]who
went from this place: "He shall not return
here anymore, 12but he shall die in the place
where they have led him captive, and shall
see this land no more.

13 "Woe[a] to him who builds his house by
unrighteousness
And his chambers by injustice,
[b]*Who* uses his neighbor's service
without wages
And gives him nothing for his work,

21:5 [a] Is. 63:10 [b] Ex. 6:6 21:7 [a] Jer. 37:17; 39:5; 52:9 [b] 2 Chr. 36:17 21:8 [a] Deut. 30:15, 19 21:9 [a] Jer. 38:2 [b] Jer. 39:18 21:10 [a] Amos 9:4 [b] Jer. 38:3 [c] Jer. 34:2, 22; 37:10 21:12 [a] Zech. 7:9 [b] Ps. 101:8 21:13 [a] [Ezek. 13:8] [b] Jer. 49:4 21:14 [a] Is. 3:10, 11 [b] 2 Chr. 36:19 22:2 [a] Jer. 17:20 22:3 [a] Jer. 21:12 [b] Jer. 7:6 22:4 [a] Jer. 17:25 22:5 [a] Heb. 6:13, 17 22:6 [a] Song 4:1 22:7 [a] Is. 37:24 [b] Jer. 21:14 22:8 [a] Deut. 29:24–26 22:9 [a] 2 Chr. 34:25 22:10 [a] 2 Kin. 22:20 [b] Jer. 14:17; 22:11 22:11 [a] 1 Chr. 3:15 [b] 2 Kin. 23:34 [1] Also called *Jehoahaz* 22:13 [a] 2 Kin. 23:35 [b] James 5:4

14 Who says, 'I will build myself a wide
house with spacious chambers,
And cut out windows for it,
Paneling *it* with cedar
And painting *it* with vermilion.'

15 "Shall you reign because you enclose
yourself in cedar?
Did not your father eat and drink,
And do justice and righteousness?
Then [a]*it was* well with him.

16 He judged the cause of the poor and
needy;
Then *it was* well.
Was not this knowing Me?" says the
LORD.

17 "Yet[a] your eyes and your heart *are* for
nothing but your covetousness,
For shedding innocent blood,
And practicing oppression and
violence."

18 Therefore thus says the LORD concerning
Jehoiakim the son of Josiah, king of Judah:

[a]"They shall not lament for him,
Saying, [b]'Alas, my brother!' or 'Alas, my
sister!'
"They shall not lament for him,
Saying, 'Alas, master!' or 'Alas, his
glory!'

19 [a]He shall be buried with the burial of a
donkey,
Dragged and cast out beyond the gates
of Jerusalem.

20 "Go up to Lebanon, and cry out,
And lift up your voice in Bashan;
Cry from Abarim,
For all your lovers are destroyed.

21 I spoke to you in your prosperity,
But you said, 'I will not hear.'
[a]This *has been* your manner from your
youth,
That you did not obey My voice.

22 The wind shall eat up all [a]your rulers,
And your lovers shall go into captivity;
Surely then you will be ashamed and
humiliated
For all your wickedness.

23 O inhabitant of Lebanon,
Making your nest in the cedars,
How gracious will you be when pangs
come upon you,
Like [a]the pain of a woman in labor?

Message to Coniah

24 "*As* I live," says the LORD, [a]"though Coniah[1] the son of Jehoiakim, king of Judah, [b]were
the signet on My right hand, yet I would pluck
you off; 25 [a]and I will give you into the hand of
those who seek your life, and into the hand *of*
those whose face you fear—the hand of Nebuchadnezzar king of Babylon and the hand
of the Chaldeans. 26 [a]So I will cast you out,
and your mother who bore you, into another
country where you were not born; and there
you shall die. 27 But to the land to which they
desire to return, there they shall not return.

28 "Is this man Coniah a despised, broken
idol—
[a]A vessel in which *is* no pleasure?
Why are they cast out, he and his
descendants,
And cast into a land which they do not
know?

29 [a]O earth, earth, earth,
Hear the word of the LORD!

30 Thus says the LORD:
'Write this man down as [a]childless,
A man *who* shall not prosper in his
days;
For [b]none of his descendants shall
prosper,
Sitting on the throne of David,
And ruling anymore in Judah.' "

The Branch of Righteousness

23 "Woe [a]to the shepherds who destroy
and scatter the sheep of My pasture!"
says the LORD. 2 Therefore thus says the LORD
God of Israel against the shepherds who
feed My people: "You have scattered My
flock, driven them away, and not attended
to them. [a]Behold, I will attend to you for the
evil of your doings," says the LORD. 3 "But
[a]I will gather the remnant of My flock out
of all countries where I have driven them,
and bring them back to their folds; and they
shall be fruitful and increase. 4 I will set up
[a]shepherds over them who will feed them;
and they shall fear no more, nor be dismayed,
nor shall they be lacking," says the LORD.

5 "Behold, [a]*the* days are coming," says the
LORD,
"That I will raise to David a Branch of
righteousness;
A King shall reign and prosper,
[b]And execute judgment and
righteousness in the earth.

22:15 [a] Ps. 128:2 **22:17** [a] Ezek. 19:6 **22:18** [a] Jer. 16:4, 6 [b] 1 Kin. 13:30 **22:19** [a] Jer. 36:30 **22:21** [a] Jer. 3:24, 25; 32:30
22:22 [a] Jer. 23:1 **22:23** [a] Jer. 6:24 **22:24** [a] 2 Kin. 24:6, 8 [b] Hag. 2:23 [1] Also called *Jeconiah* and *Jehoiachin* **22:25** [a] Jer. 34:20
22:26 [a] 2 Kin. 24:15 **22:28** [a] Hos. 8:8 **22:29** [a] Deut. 32:1 **22:30** [a] Matt. 1:12 [b] Jer. 36:30 **23:1** [a] Jer. 10:21 **23:2** [a] Ex. 32:34
23:3 [a] Jer. 32:37 **23:4** [a] Jer. 3:15 **23:5** [a] Jer. 33:14; Matt. 1:1, 6; Luke 3:31; [John 1:45; 7:42]; Rev. 22:16 [b] Ps. 72:2

6 [a]In His days Judah will be saved,
And Israel [b]will dwell safely;
Now [c]this *is* His name by which He will
be called:

THE LORD OUR RIGHTEOUSNESS.[1]

7"Therefore, behold, [a]*the* days are coming,"
says the LORD, "that they shall no longer say,
'As the LORD lives who brought up the children of Israel from the land of Egypt,' 8but,
'As the LORD lives who brought up and led
the descendants of the house of Israel from
the north country [a]and from all the countries
where I had driven them.' And they shall
dwell in their own [b]land."

False Prophets and Empty Oracles

9 My heart within me is broken
Because of the prophets;
[a]All my bones shake.
I am like a drunken man,
And like a man whom wine has overcome,
Because of the LORD,
And because of His holy words.
10 For [a]the land is full of adulterers;
For [b]because of a curse the land mourns.
[c]The pleasant places of the wilderness
are dried up.
Their course of life is evil,
And their might *is* not right.

11 "For [a]both prophet and priest are profane;
Yes, [b]in My house I have found their
wickedness," says the LORD.
12 "Therefore[a] their way shall be to them
Like slippery *ways;*
In the darkness they shall be driven on
And fall in them;
For I [b]will bring disaster on them,
The year of their punishment," says the
LORD.
13 "And I have seen folly in the prophets of
Samaria:
[a]They prophesied by Baal
And [b]caused My people Israel to err.
14 Also I have seen a horrible thing in the
prophets of Jerusalem:
[a]They commit adultery and walk in lies;
They also [b]strengthen the hands of
evildoers,
So that no one turns back from his
wickedness.
All of them are like [c]Sodom to Me,
And her inhabitants like Gomorrah.

15"Therefore thus says the LORD of hosts
concerning the prophets:

'Behold, I will feed them with
[a]wormwood,
And make them drink the water of gall;
For from the prophets of Jerusalem
Profaneness has gone out into all the
land.' "

16Thus says the LORD of hosts:

"Do not listen to the words of the
prophets who prophesy to you.
They make you worthless;
[a]They speak a vision of their own heart,
Not from the mouth of the LORD.
17 They continually say to those who
despise Me,
'The LORD has said, [a]"You shall have
peace" ';
And *to* everyone who [b]walks according
to the dictates of his own heart, they
say,
[c]'No evil shall come upon you.' "

18 For [a]who has stood in the counsel of
the LORD,
And has perceived and heard His word?
Who has marked His word and heard *it?*
19 Behold, a [a]whirlwind of the LORD has
gone forth in fury—
A violent whirlwind!
It will fall violently on the head of the
wicked.
20 The [a]anger of the LORD will not turn back
Until He has executed and performed
the thoughts of His heart.
[b]In the latter days you will understand it
perfectly.

21 "I[a] have not sent these prophets, yet
they ran.
I have not spoken to them, yet they
prophesied.
22 But if they had stood in My counsel,
And had caused My people to hear My
words,
Then they would have [a]turned them
from their evil way
And from the evil of their doings.

23 "*Am* I a God near at hand," says the
LORD,
"And not a God afar off?

23:6 [a] Zech. 14:11 [b] Jer. 32:37 [c] [Rom. 3:22; 1 Cor. 1:30] [1] Hebrew *YHWH Tsidkenu* **23:7** [a] Jer. 16:14 **23:8** [a] Is. 43:5, 6 [b] Gen. 12:7 **23:9** [a] Hab. 3:16 **23:10** [a] Jer. 9:2 [b] Hos. 4:2 [c] Jer. 9:10 **23:11** [a] Zeph. 3:4 [b] Jer. 7:30; 32:34 **23:12** [a] [Prov. 4:19] [b] Jer. 11:23 **23:13** [a] Jer. 2:8 [b] Is. 9:16 **23:14** [a] Jer. 29:23 [b] Ezek. 13:22, 23 [c] Is. 1:9, 10 **23:15** [a] Jer. 9:15 **23:16** [a] Jer. 14:14 **23:17** [a] Ezek. 13:10 [b] Deut. 29:19; Jer. 3:17 [c] Mic. 3:11 **23:18** [a] [1 Cor. 2:16] **23:19** [a] Amos 1:14 **23:20** [a] Jer. 30:24 [b] Gen. 49:1 **23:21** [a] Jer. 14:14; 23:32; 27:15 **23:22** [a] Jer. 25:5

24 Can anyone [a]hide himself in secret
places,
So I shall not see him?" says the LORD;
[b]"Do I not fill heaven and earth?" says
the LORD.

25"I have heard what the prophets have
said who prophesy lies in My name, saying, 'I
have dreamed, I have dreamed!' 26How long
will *this* be in the heart of the prophets who
prophesy lies? Indeed *they are* prophets of
the deceit of their own heart, 27who try to
make My people forget My name by their
dreams which everyone tells his neighbor,
[a]as their fathers forgot My name for Baal.

28 "The prophet who has a dream, let him
tell a dream;
And he who has My word, let him speak
My word faithfully.
What *is* the chaff to the wheat?" says
the LORD.
29 "*Is* not My word like a [a]fire?" says the
LORD,
"And like a hammer *that* breaks the rock
in pieces?

30"Therefore behold, [a]I *am* against the
prophets," says the LORD, "who steal My
words every one from his neighbor. 31Behold,
I *am* [a]against the prophets," says the LORD,
"who use their tongues and say, 'He says.'
32Behold, I *am* against those who prophesy
false dreams," says the LORD, "and tell them,
and cause My people to err by their [a]lies and
by [b]their recklessness. Yet I did not send
them or command them; therefore they shall
not [c]profit this people at all," says the LORD.

33"So when these people or the prophet or
the priest ask you, saying, 'What is [a]the oracle
of the LORD?' you shall then say to them,
'What oracle?'[1] I will even forsake you," says
the LORD. 34"And *as for* the prophet and the
priest and the people who say, 'The oracle of
the LORD!' I will even punish that man and his
house. 35Thus every one of you shall say to his
neighbor, and every one to his brother, 'What
has the LORD answered?' and, 'What has the
LORD spoken?' 36And the oracle of the LORD
you shall mention no more. For every man's
word will be his oracle, for you have [a]pervert-
ed the words of the living God, the LORD of
hosts, our God. 37Thus you shall say to the
prophet, 'What has the LORD answered you?'
and, 'What has the LORD spoken?' 38But since
you say, 'The oracle of the LORD!' therefore
thus says the LORD: 'Because you say this
word, "The oracle of the LORD!" and I have
sent to you, saying, "Do not say, 'The oracle
of the LORD!' " 39therefore behold, I, even I,
[a]will utterly forget you and forsake you, and
the city that I gave you and your fathers, and
will cast you out of My presence. 40And I will
bring [a]an everlasting reproach upon you,
and a perpetual [b]shame, which shall not be
forgotten.' "

The Sign of Two Baskets of Figs

24 The [a]LORD showed me, and there were
two baskets of figs set before the temple of the LORD, after Nebuchadnezzar [b]king
of Babylon had carried away captive [c]Jeconi-
ah the son of Jehoiakim, king of Judah, and
the princes of Judah with the craftsmen and
smiths, from Jerusalem, and had brought
them to Babylon. 2One basket *had* very good
figs, like the figs *that are* first ripe; and the
other basket *had* very bad figs which could not
be eaten, they were so [a]bad. 3Then the LORD
said to me, "What do you see, Jeremiah?"

And I said, "Figs, the good figs, very good;
and the bad, very bad, which cannot be eaten,
they are so bad."

4Again the word of the LORD came to me,
saying, 5"Thus says the LORD, the God of Israel: 'Like these good figs, so will I acknowledge
those who are carried away captive from
Judah, whom I have sent out of this place for
their own good, into the land of the Chaldeans. 6For I will set My eyes on them for good,
and [a]I will bring them back to this land; [b]I
will build them and not pull *them* down, and I
will plant them and not pluck *them* up. 7Then

PEACE NOTE

God is always at work in your life. The first deportation of Jews to Babylon came with God's promise: "I will set My eyes on them for good, and I will bring them back."

JEREMIAH 24:6

23:24 [a] [Ps. 139:7] [b] [1 Kin. 8:27] 23:27 [a] Judg. 3:7 23:29 [a] Jer. 5:14 23:30 [a] Deut. 18:20 23:31 [a] Ezek. 13:9 23:32 [a] Lam. 2:14; 3:37 [b] Zeph. 3:4 [c] Jer. 7:8 23:33 [a] Mal. 1:1 [1] Septuagint, Targum, and Vulgate read *'You are the burden.'* 23:36 [a] Deut. 4:2 23:39 [a] Hos. 4:6 23:40 [a] Jer. 20:11 [b] Mic. 3:5–7 24:1 [a] Amos 7:1, 4; 8:1 [b] 2 Kin. 24:12–16 [c] Jer. 22:24–28; 29:2 24:2 [a] Jer. 29:17 24:6 [a] Jer. 12:15; 29:10 [b] Jer. 32:41; 33:7; 42:10

I will give them [a]a heart to know Me, that I *am* the LORD; and they shall be [b]My people, and I will be their God, for they shall return to Me [c]with their whole heart.

8'And as the bad [a]figs which cannot be eaten, they are so bad'—surely thus says the LORD—'so will I give up Zedekiah the king of Judah, his princes, the [b]residue of Jerusalem who remain in this land, and [c]those who dwell in the land of Egypt. 9I will deliver them to [a]trouble into all the kingdoms of the earth, for *their* harm, [b]*to be* a reproach and a byword, a taunt and a curse, in all places where I shall drive them. 10And I will send the sword, the famine, and the pestilence among them, till they are consumed from the land that I gave to them and their fathers.' "

Seventy Years of Desolation

25 The word that came to Jeremiah concerning all the people of Judah, [a]in the fourth year of [b]Jehoiakim the son of Josiah, king of Judah (which *was* the first year of Nebuchadnezzar king of Babylon), 2which Jeremiah the prophet spoke to all the people of Judah and to all the inhabitants of Jerusalem, saying: 3[a]"From the thirteenth year of Josiah the son of Amon, king of Judah, even to this day, this *is* the twenty-third year in which the word of the LORD has come to me; and I have spoken to you, rising early and speaking, [b]but you have not listened. 4And the LORD has sent to you all His servants the prophets, [a]rising early and sending *them,* but you have not listened nor inclined your ear to hear. 5They said, [a]'Repent now everyone of his evil way and his evil doings, and dwell in the land that the LORD has given to you and your fathers forever and ever. 6Do not go after other gods to serve them and worship them, and do not provoke Me to anger with the works of your hands; and I will not harm you.' 7Yet you have not listened to Me," says the LORD, "that you might [a]provoke Me to anger with the works of your hands to your own hurt.

8"Therefore thus says the LORD of hosts: 'Because you have not heard My words, 9behold, I will send and take [a]all the families of the north,' says the LORD, 'and Nebuchadnezzar the king of Babylon, [b]My servant, and will bring them against this land, against its inhabitants, and against these nations all around, and will utterly destroy them, and [c]make them an astonishment, a hissing, and perpetual desolations. 10Moreover I will take from them the [a]voice of mirth and the voice of gladness, the voice of the bridegroom and the voice of the bride, [b]the sound of the millstones and the light of the lamp. 11And this whole land shall be a desolation *and* an astonishment, and these nations shall serve the king of Babylon seventy [a]years.

12'Then it will come to pass, [a]when seventy years are completed, *that* I will punish the king of Babylon and that nation, the land of the Chaldeans, for their iniquity,' says the LORD; [b]'and I will make it a perpetual desolation. 13So I will bring on that land all My words which I have pronounced against it, all that is written in this book, which Jeremiah has prophesied concerning all the nations. 14[a](For many nations [b]and great kings shall [c]be served by them also; [d]and I will repay them according to their deeds and according to the works of their own hands.)' "

Judgment on the Nations

15For thus says the LORD God of Israel to me: "Take this [a]wine cup of fury from My hand, and cause all the nations, to whom I send you, to drink it. 16And [a]they will drink and stagger and go mad because of the sword that I will send among them."

17Then I took the cup from the LORD's hand, and made all the nations drink, to whom the LORD had sent me: 18Jerusalem and the cities of Judah, its kings and its princes, to make them [a]a desolation, an astonishment, a hissing, and [b]a curse, as *it is* this day; 19Pharaoh king of Egypt, his servants, his princes, and all his people; 20all the mixed multitude, all the kings of [a]the land of Uz, all the kings of the land of the [b]Philistines (namely, Ashkelon, Gaza, Ekron, and [c]the remnant of Ashdod); 21[a]Edom, Moab, and the people of Ammon; 22all the kings of [a]Tyre, all the kings of Sidon, and the kings of the coastlands which *are* across the [b]sea; 23[a]Dedan, Tema, Buz, and all *who are* in the farthest corners; 24all the kings of Arabia and all the kings of the [a]mixed multitude who dwell in the desert; 25all the kings of Zimri, all the kings of [a]Elam, and all the kings of the [b]Medes; 26[a]all the kings of the north, far and near, one with another; and all the kingdoms of the world which *are* on the face of the earth. Also the king of Sheshach[1] shall drink after them.

24:7 [a] [Deut. 30:6] [b] Jer. 30:22; 31:33; 32:38 [c] Jer. 29:13 **24:8** [a] Jer. 29:17 [b] Jer. 39:9 [c] Jer. 44:1, 26–30 **24:9** [a] Deut. 28:25, 37 [b] Ps. 44:13, 14 **25:1** [a] Jer. 36:1 [b] 2 Kin. 24:1, 2 **25:3** [a] Jer. 1:2 [b] Jer. 7:13; 11:7, 8, 10 **25:4** [a] Jer. 7:13, 25 **25:5** [a] Jer. 18:11 **25:7** [a] Deut. 32:21 **25:9** [a] Jer. 1:15 [b] Is. 45:1 [c] Jer. 18:16 **25:10** [a] Rev. 18:23 [b] Eccl. 12:4 **25:11** [a] Jer. 29:10 **25:12** [a] Ezra 1:1 [b] Is. 13:20 **25:14** [a] Jer. 50:9; 51:27, 28 [b] Jer. 51:27 [c] Jer. 27:7 [d] Jer. 50:29; 51:6, 24 **25:15** [a] Rev. 14:10 **25:16** [a] Nah. 3:11 **25:18** [a] Jer. 25:9, 11 [b] Jer. 24:9 **25:20** [a] Job 1:1 [b] Jer. 47:1–7 [c] Is. 20:1 **25:21** [a] Jer. 49:7 **25:22** [a] Jer. 47:4 [b] Jer. 49:23 **25:23** [a] Jer. 49:7, 8 **25:24** [a] Ezek. 30:5 **25:25** [a] Jer. 49:34 [b] Jer. 51:11, 28 **25:26** [a] Jer. 50:9 [1] A code word for Babylon (compare 51:41)

27"Therefore you shall say to them, 'Thus
says the LORD of hosts, the God of Israel:
[a]"Drink, [b]be drunk, and vomit! Fall and rise
no more, because of the sword which I will
send among you." ' 28And it shall be, if they
refuse to take the cup from your hand to
drink, then you shall say to them, 'Thus says
the LORD of hosts: "You shall certainly drink!
29For behold, [a]I begin to bring calamity on
the city [b]which is called by My name, and
should you be utterly unpunished? You shall
not be unpunished, for [c]I will call for a sword
on all the inhabitants of the earth," says the
LORD of hosts.'
30"Therefore prophesy against them all
these words, and say to them:

'The LORD will [a]roar from on high,
And utter His voice from [b]His holy
habitation;
He will roar mightily against [c]His fold.
He will give [d]a shout, as those who
tread *the grapes,*
Against all the inhabitants of the earth.
31 A noise will come to the ends of the
earth—
For the LORD has [a]a controversy with
the nations;
[b]He will plead His case with all flesh.
He will give those *who are* wicked to
the sword,' says the LORD."

32Thus says the LORD of hosts:

"Behold, disaster shall go forth
From nation to nation,
And [a]a great whirlwind shall be
raised up
From the farthest parts of the earth.

33[a]And at that day the slain of the LORD shall
be from *one* end of the earth even to the *other*
end of the earth. They shall not be [b]lamented,
[c]or gathered, or buried; they shall become
refuse on the ground.

34 "Wail,[a] shepherds, and cry!
Roll about *in the ashes,*
You leaders of the flock!
For the days of your slaughter and your
dispersions are fulfilled;
You shall fall like a precious vessel.
35 And the shepherds will have no way to
flee,
Nor the leaders of the flock to escape.
36 A voice of the cry of the shepherds,
And a wailing of the leaders to the
flock *will be heard.*
For the LORD has plundered their
pasture,
37 And the peaceful dwellings are cut down
Because of the fierce anger of the LORD.
38 He has left His lair like the lion;
For their land is desolate
Because of the fierceness of the
Oppressor,
And because of His fierce anger."

Jeremiah Saved from Death

26 In the beginning of the reign of Jehoiakim the son of Josiah, king of Judah,
this word came from the LORD, saying, 2"Thus
says the LORD: 'Stand in [a]the court of the
LORD's house, and speak to all the cities of
Judah, which come to worship *in* the LORD's
house, [b]all the words that I command you
to speak to them. [c]Do not diminish a word.
3[a]Perhaps everyone will listen and turn from
his evil way, that I may [b]relent concerning the
calamity which I purpose to bring on them
because of the evil of their doings.' 4And you
shall say to them, 'Thus says the LORD: [a]"If
you will not listen to Me, to walk in My law
which I have set before you, 5to heed the
words of My servants the prophets [a]whom
I sent to you, both rising up early and sending *them* (but you have not heeded), 6then
I will make this house like [a]Shiloh, and will
make this city [b]a curse to all the nations of
the earth." ' "
7So the priests and the prophets and all the
people heard Jeremiah speaking these words
in the house of the LORD. 8Now it happened,
when Jeremiah had made an end of speaking
all that the LORD had commanded *him* to
speak to all the people, that the priests and
the prophets and all the people seized him,
saying, "You will surely die! 9Why have you
prophesied in the name of the LORD, saying,
'This house shall be like Shiloh, and this city
shall be [a]desolate, without an inhabitant'?"
And all the people were gathered against
Jeremiah in the house of the LORD.
10When the princes of Judah heard these
things, they came up from the king's house
to the house of the LORD and sat down in the
entry of the New Gate of the LORD's *house.*
11And the priests and the prophets spoke to
the princes and all the people, saying, "This
man deserves to [a]die! For he has prophesied
against this city, as you have heard with your
ears."

25:27 [a] Hab. 2:16 [b] Is. 63:6 **25:29** [a] Ezek. 9:6 [b] Dan. 9:18 [c] Ezek. 38:21 **25:30** [a] Amos 1:2 [b] Ps. 11:4 [c] 1 Kin. 9:3
[d] Is. 16:9 **25:31** [a] Mic. 6:2 [b] Is. 66:16 **25:32** [a] Jer. 23:19; 30:23 **25:33** [a] Is. 34:2, 3; 66:16 [b] Jer. 16:4, 6 [c] Ps. 79:3
25:34 [a] Jer. 4:8; 6:26 **26:2** [a] Jer. 19:14 [b] Matt. 28:20 [c] Acts 20:27 **26:3** [a] Jer. 36:3–7 [b] Jer. 18:8 **26:4** [a] Lev. 26:14, 15
26:5 [a] Jer. 25:4; 29:19 **26:6** [a] 1 Sam. 4:10, 11 [b] Is. 65:15 **26:9** [a] Jer. 9:11 **26:11** [a] Jer. 38:4

12 Then Jeremiah spoke to all the princes
and all the people, saying: "The LORD sent me
to prophesy against this house and against
this city with all the words that you have
heard. 13 Now therefore, [a]amend your ways
and your doings, and obey the voice of the
LORD your God; then the LORD will relent concerning the doom that He has pronounced
against you. 14 As for me, here [a]I am, in your
hand; do with me as seems good and proper
to you. 15 But know for certain that if you put
me to death, you will surely bring innocent
blood on yourselves, on this city, and on its
inhabitants; for truly the LORD has sent me to
you to speak all these words in your hearing."
16 So the princes and all the people said to
the priests and the prophets, "This man does
not deserve to die. For he has spoken to us
in the name of the LORD our God."
17 [a]Then certain of the elders of the land
rose up and spoke to all the assembly of
the people, saying: 18 [a]"Micah of Moresheth
prophesied in the days of Hezekiah king of
Judah, and spoke to all the people of Judah,
saying, 'Thus says the LORD of hosts:

[b]"Zion shall be plowed *like* a field,
Jerusalem shall become [c]heaps of
ruins,
And the mountain of the temple[1]
Like the bare hills of the forest." '[2]

19 Did Hezekiah king of Judah and all Judah
ever put him to death? [a]Did he not fear the
LORD and [b]seek the LORD's favor? And the
LORD [c]relented concerning the doom which
He had pronounced against them. [d]But we
are doing great evil against ourselves."
20 Now there was also a man who prophesied in the name of the LORD, Urijah the son
of Shemaiah of Kirjath Jearim, who prophesied against this city and against this land
according to all the words of Jeremiah. 21 And
when Jehoiakim the king, with all his mighty
men and all the princes, heard his words, the
king sought to put him to death; but when
Urijah heard *it,* he was afraid and fled, and
went to Egypt. 22 Then Jehoiakim the king
sent men to Egypt: Elnathan the son of Achbor, and *other* men *who went* with him to
Egypt. 23 And they brought Urijah from Egypt
and brought him to Jehoiakim the king, who
killed him with the sword and cast his dead
body into the graves of the common people.
24 Nevertheless [a]the hand of Ahikam the
son of Shaphan was with Jeremiah, so that
they should not give him into the hand of
the people to put him to death.

Symbol of the Bonds and Yokes

27 In the beginning of the reign of Jehoiakim[1] the son of Josiah, [a]king of Judah,
this word came to Jeremiah from the LORD,
saying,[2] 2 "Thus says the LORD to me: 'Make for
yourselves bonds and yokes, [a]and put them on
your neck, 3 and send them to the king of Edom,
the king of Moab, the king of the Ammonites,
the king of Tyre, and the king of Sidon, by the
hand of the messengers who come to Jerusalem to Zedekiah king of Judah. 4 And command
them to say to their masters, "Thus says the
LORD of hosts, the God of Israel—thus you
shall say to your masters: 5 [a]'I have made the
earth, the man and the beast that *are* on the
ground, by My great power and by My outstretched arm, and [b]have given it to whom it
seemed proper to Me. 6 [a]And now I have given
all these lands into the hand of Nebuchadnezzar the king of Babylon, [b]My servant; and
[c]the beasts of the field I have also given him
to serve him. 7 [a]So all nations shall serve him
and his son and his son's son, [b]until the time
of his land comes; [c]and then many nations and
great kings shall make him serve them. 8 And
it shall be, *that* the nation and kingdom which
will not serve Nebuchadnezzar the king of
Babylon, and which will not put its neck under
the yoke of the king of Babylon, that nation I
will punish,' says the LORD, 'with the sword,
the famine, and the pestilence, until I have
consumed them by his hand. 9 Therefore do

PEACE NOTE

Never forget: the way the world defines peace and the way God gives peace are entirely different.

26:13 [a] Jer. 7:3 **26:14** [a] Jer. 38:5 **26:17** [a] Acts 5:34 **26:18** [a] Mic. 1:1 [b] Mic. 3:12 [c] Jer. 9:11 [1] Literally *house* [2] Compare Micah 3:12 **26:19** [a] 2 Chr. 32:26 [b] 2 Kin. 20:1–19 [c] Ex. 32:14 [d] [Acts 5:39] **26:24** [a] 2 Kin. 22:12–14 **27:1** [a] Jer. 27:3, 12, 20; 28:1 [1] Following Masoretic Text, Targum, and Vulgate; some Hebrew manuscripts, Arabic, and Syriac read *Zedekiah* (compare 27:3, 12; 28:1). [2] Septuagint omits verse 1. **27:2** [a] Jer. 28:10, 12 **27:5** [a] Is. 45:12 [b] Dan. 4:17, 25, 32 **27:6** [a] Jer. 28:14 [b] Jer. 25:9; 43:10 [c] Dan. 2:38 **27:7** [a] 2 Chr. 36:20 [b] [Dan. 5:26] [c] Jer. 25:14

not listen to your prophets, your diviners, your dreamers, your soothsayers, or your sorcerers, who speak to you, saying, "You shall not serve the king of Babylon." 10For they prophesy a [a]lie to you, to remove you far from your land; and I will drive you out, and you will perish. 11But the nations that bring their necks under the yoke of the king of Babylon and serve him, I will let them remain in their own land,' says the LORD, 'and they shall till it and dwell in it.' " ' "

12I also spoke to [a]Zedekiah king of Judah according to all these words, saying, "Bring your necks under the yoke of the king of Babylon, and serve him and his people, and live! 13[a]Why will you die, you and your people, by the sword, by the famine, and by the pestilence, as the LORD has spoken against the nation that will not serve the king of Babylon? 14Therefore [a]do not listen to the words of the prophets who speak to you, saying, 'You shall not serve the king of Babylon,' for they prophesy [b]a lie to you; 15for I have [a]not sent them," says the LORD, "yet they prophesy a lie in My name, that I may drive you out, and that you may perish, you and the prophets who prophesy to you."

16Also I spoke to the priests and to all this people, saying, "Thus says the LORD: 'Do not listen to the words of your prophets who prophesy to you, saying, "Behold, [a]the vessels of the LORD's house will now shortly be brought back from Babylon"; for they prophesy a lie to you. 17Do not listen to them; serve the king of Babylon, and live! Why should this city be laid waste? 18But if they *are* prophets, and if the word of the LORD is with them, let them now make intercession to the LORD of hosts, that the vessels which are left in the house of the LORD, *in* the house of the king of Judah, and at Jerusalem, do not go to Babylon.'

19"For thus says the LORD of hosts [a]concerning the pillars, concerning the Sea, concerning the carts, and concerning the remainder of the vessels that remain in this city, 20which Nebuchadnezzar king of Babylon did not take, when he carried away [a]captive Jeconiah the son of Jehoiakim, king of Judah, from Jerusalem to Babylon, and all the nobles of Judah and Jerusalem— 21yes, thus says the LORD of hosts, the God of Israel, *concerning the* [a]vessels that remain in the house of the LORD, and in the house of the king of Judah and of Jerusalem: 22'They shall be [a]carried to Babylon, and there they shall be until the day that I [b]visit them,' says the LORD. 'Then [c]I will bring them up and restore them to this place.' "

Hananiah's Falsehood and Doom

28 And [a]it happened in the same year, at the beginning of the reign of Zedekiah king of Judah, in the [b]fourth year *and* in the fifth month, *that* Hananiah the son of [c]Azur the prophet, who *was* from Gibeon, spoke to me in the house of the LORD in the presence of the priests and of all the people, saying, 2"Thus speaks the LORD of hosts, the God of Israel, saying: 'I have broken [a]the yoke of the king of Babylon. 3[a]Within two full years I will bring back to this place all the vessels of the LORD's house, that Nebuchadnezzar king of Babylon [b]took away from this place and carried to Babylon. 4And I will bring back to this place Jeconiah the son of Jehoiakim, king of Judah, with all the captives of Judah who went to Babylon,' says the LORD, 'for I will break the yoke of the king of Babylon.' "

5Then the prophet Jeremiah spoke to the prophet Hananiah in the presence of the priests and in the presence of all the people who stood in the house of the LORD, 6and the prophet Jeremiah said, [a]"Amen! The LORD do so; the LORD perform your words which you have prophesied, to bring back the vessels of the LORD's house and all who were carried away captive, from Babylon to this place. 7Nevertheless hear now this word that I speak in your hearing and in the hearing of all the people: 8The prophets who have been before me and before you of old prophesied against many countries and great kingdoms—of war and disaster and pestilence. 9As for [a]the prophet who prophesies of [b]peace, when the word of the prophet comes to pass, the prophet will be known *as* one whom the LORD has truly sent."

10Then Hananiah the prophet took the [a]yoke off the prophet Jeremiah's neck and broke it. 11And Hananiah spoke in the presence of all the people, saying, "Thus says the LORD: 'Even so I will break the yoke of Nebuchadnezzar king of Babylon [a]from the neck of all nations within the space of two full years.' " And the prophet Jeremiah went his way.

12Now the word of the LORD came to Jeremiah, after Hananiah the prophet had broken the yoke from the neck of the prophet Jeremiah, saying, 13"Go and tell Hananiah, saying, 'Thus says the LORD: "You have broken the yokes of wood, but you have made in their place yokes of iron." 14For thus says the LORD of hosts, the God of Israel: [a]"I have put a yoke of iron on the neck of all these nations, that they may serve Nebuchadnezzar king of Babylon; and they shall serve him. [b]I have given him the beasts of the field also." ' "

27:10 [a] Jer. 23:16, 32; 28:15 **27:12** [a] Jer. 28:1; 38:17 **27:13** [a] [Ezek. 18:31] **27:14** [a] Jer. 23:16 [b] Jer. 14:14; 23:21; 29:8, 9 **27:15** [a] Jer. 23:21; 29:9 **27:16** [a] Dan. 1:2 **27:19** [a] 2 Kin. 25:13–17 **27:20** [a] Jer. 24:1 **27:21** [a] Jer. 20:5 **27:22** [a] 2 Kin. 25:13 [b] 2 Chr. 36:21; Jer. 29:10; 32:5 [c] Ezra 1:7; 7:19 **28:1** [a] Jer. 27:1 [b] Jer. 51:59 [c] Ezek. 11:1 **28:2** [a] Jer. 27:12 **28:3** [a] Jer. 27:16 [b] Dan. 1:2 **28:6** [a] 1 Kin. 1:36 **28:9** [a] Deut. 18:22 [b] Jer. 23:17 **28:10** [a] Jer. 27:2 **28:11** [a] Jer. 27:7 **28:14** [a] Deut. 28:48 [b] Jer. 27:6

15Then the prophet Jeremiah said to Hananiah the prophet, "Hear now, Hananiah, the
LORD has not sent you, but [a]you make this
people trust in a [b]lie. 16Therefore thus says the
LORD: 'Behold, I will cast you from the face
of the earth. This year you shall [a]die, because
you have taught [b]rebellion against the LORD.' "
17So Hananiah the prophet died the same
year in the seventh month.

Jeremiah's Letter to the Captives

29 Now these *are* the words of the letter
that Jeremiah the prophet sent from
Jerusalem to the remainder of the elders who
were [a]carried away captive—to the priests,
the prophets, and all the people whom Nebuchadnezzar had carried away captive from
Jerusalem to Babylon. 2(This happened after
[a]Jeconiah the king, the [b]queen mother, the
eunuchs, the princes of Judah and Jerusalem,
the craftsmen, and the smiths had departed
from Jerusalem.) 3*The letter was sent* by the
hand of Elasah the son of [a]Shaphan, and
Gemariah the son of Hilkiah, whom Zedekiah
king of Judah sent to Babylon, to Nebuchadnezzar king of Babylon, saying,

4 Thus says the LORD of hosts, the God
of Israel, to all who were carried away
captive, whom I have caused to be
carried away from Jerusalem to Babylon:

5 Build houses and dwell *in them;* plant
gardens and eat their fruit. 6Take wives
and beget sons and daughters; and
take wives for your sons and give your
daughters to husbands, so that they may
bear sons and daughters—that you may
be increased there, and not diminished.
7And seek the peace of the city where
I have caused you to be carried away
captive, [a]and pray to the LORD for it; for
in its peace you will have peace. 8For
thus says the LORD of hosts, the God of
Israel: Do not let your prophets and your
diviners who are in your midst [a]deceive
you, nor listen to your dreams which you
cause to be dreamed. 9For they prophesy
[a]falsely to you in My name; I have not
sent them, says the LORD.

10 For thus says the LORD: After [a]seventy
years are completed at Babylon, I will
visit you and perform My good word
toward you, and cause you to [b]return
to this place. 11For I know the thoughts
that I think toward you, says the LORD,
thoughts of peace and not of evil, to give
you a future and a hope. 12Then you will
[a]call upon Me and go and pray to Me,
and I will [b]listen to you. 13And [a]you will
seek Me and find *Me,* when you search
for Me [b]with all your heart. 14[a]I will be
found by you, says the LORD, and I will
bring you back from your captivity; [b]I
will gather you from all the nations and
from all the places where I have driven
you, says the LORD, and I will bring you
to the place from which I cause you to be
carried away captive.

15 Because you have said, "The LORD
has raised up prophets for us in
Babylon"— 16[a]therefore thus says the
LORD concerning the king who sits on
the throne of David, concerning all
the people who dwell in this city, and
concerning your brethren who have not
gone out with you into captivity— 17thus
says the LORD of hosts: Behold, I will
send on them the sword, the famine,
and the pestilence, and will make them
like [a]rotten figs that cannot be eaten,
they are so bad. 18And I will pursue them
with the sword, with famine, and with
pestilence; and I [a]will deliver them to
trouble among all the kingdoms of the
earth—to be [b]a curse, an astonishment,
a hissing, and a reproach among all
the nations where I have driven them,
19because they have not heeded My
words, says the LORD, which [a]I sent
to them by My servants the prophets,
rising up early and sending *them;*
neither would you heed, says the LORD.
20Therefore hear the word of the LORD,
all you of the captivity, whom I have sent
from Jerusalem to Babylon.

21 Thus says the LORD of hosts, the God
of Israel, concerning Ahab the son
of Kolaiah, and Zedekiah the son of
Maaseiah, who prophesy a [a]lie to you
in My name: Behold, I will deliver them
into the hand of Nebuchadnezzar king
of Babylon, and he shall slay them
before your eyes. 22[a]And because of
them a curse shall be taken up by all the
captivity of Judah who *are* in Babylon,
saying, "The LORD make you like
Zedekiah and Ahab, [b]whom the king of
Babylon roasted in the fire"; 23because

28:15 [a] Ezek. 13:22 [b] Jer. 27:10; 29:9 **28:16** [a] Jer. 20:6 [b] Deut. 13:5 **29:1** [a] Jer. 27:20 **29:2** [a] 2 Kin. 24:12–16 [b] Jer. 13:18 **29:3** [a] 2 Chr. 34:8 **29:7** [a] 1 Tim. 2:2 **29:8** [a] Eph. 5:6 **29:9** [a] Jer. 28:15; 37:19 **29:10** [a] Dan. 9:2 [b] [Jer. 24:6, 7] **29:12** [a] Ps. 50:15 [b] Ps. 145:19 **29:13** [a] Deut. 30:1–3 [b] Jer. 24:7 **29:14** [a] [Is. 55:6, 7] [b] Jer. 23:8; 32:37 **29:16** [a] Jer. 38:2, 3, 17–23 **29:17** [a] Jer. 24:3, 8–10 **29:18** [a] Deut. 28:25 [b] Jer. 26:6; 42:18 **29:19** [a] Jer. 25:4; 26:5; 35:15 **29:21** [a] Lam. 2:14 **29:22** [a] Is. 65:15 [b] Dan. 3:6, 21

[a]they have done disgraceful things in
Israel, have committed adultery with
their neighbors' wives, and have spoken
lying words in My name, which I have
not commanded them. Indeed I [b]know,
and *am* a witness, says the LORD.

24 You shall also speak to Shemaiah the
Nehelamite, saying, 25Thus speaks
the LORD of hosts, the God of Israel,
saying: You have sent letters in your
name to all the people who *are* at
Jerusalem, [a]to Zephaniah the son of
Maaseiah the priest, and to all the
priests, saying, 26"The LORD has made
you priest instead of Jehoiada the
priest, so that there should be [a]officers
in the house of the LORD over every
man *who* is [b]demented and considers
himself a prophet, that you should
[c]put him in prison and in the stocks.
27Now therefore, why have you not
rebuked Jeremiah of Anathoth who
makes himself a prophet to you? 28For
he has sent to us *in* Babylon, saying,
'This *captivity is* long; build houses and
dwell *in them,* and plant gardens and
eat their fruit.'"

29Now Zephaniah the priest read this letter
in the hearing of Jeremiah the prophet. 30Then
the word of the LORD came to Jeremiah, saying: 31Send to all those in captivity, saying, Thus
says the LORD concerning Shemaiah the Nehelamite: Because Shemaiah has prophesied
to you, [a]and I have not sent him, and he has
caused you to trust in a [b]lie— 32therefore thus
says the LORD: Behold, I will punish Shemaiah the Nehelamite and his family: he shall
not have anyone to dwell among this people,
nor shall he see the good that I will do for My
people, says the LORD, [a]because he has taught
rebellion against the LORD.

Restoration of Israel and Judah

30 The word that came to Jeremiah from
the LORD, saying, 2"Thus speaks the
LORD God of Israel, saying: 'Write in a book
for yourself all the words that I have spoken
to you. 3For behold, the days are coming,'
says the LORD, 'that [a]I will bring back from
captivity My people Israel and Judah,' says
the LORD. [b]'And I will cause them to return
to the land that I gave to their fathers, and
they shall possess it.'"

4Now these *are* the words that the LORD
spoke concerning Israel and Judah.

> **PEACE NOTE**
>
> I need to develop my care team: Who is helping me manage the stress of daily living? Who can help me seek the Lord's peace and depend on Him?

5"For thus says the LORD:

'We have heard a voice of trembling,
Of fear, and not of peace.
6 Ask now, and see,
Whether a man is ever in labor with
child?
So why do I see every man *with* his
hands on his loins
[a]Like a woman in labor,
And all faces turned pale?
7 [a]Alas! For that day *is* great,
[b]So that none *is* like it;
And it *is* the time of Jacob's trouble,
But he shall be saved out of it.

8 'For it shall come to pass in that day,'
Says the LORD of hosts,
'*That* I will break his yoke from your
neck,
And will burst your bonds;
Foreigners shall no more enslave them.
9 But they shall serve the LORD their God,
And [a]David their king,
Whom I will [b]raise up for them.

10 'Therefore [a]do not fear, O My servant
Jacob,' says the LORD,
'Nor be dismayed, O Israel;
For behold, I will save you from afar,
And your seed [b]from the land of their
captivity.
Jacob shall return, have rest and be quiet,
And no one shall make *him* afraid.
11 For I *am* with [a]you,' says the LORD, 'to
save you;
[b]Though I make a full end of all nations
where I have scattered you,

29:23 [a] Jer. 23:14 [b] [Prov. 5:21] **29:25** [a] Jer. 21:1 **29:26** [a] Jer. 20:1 [b] John 10:20 [c] Jer. 20:1, 2 **29:31** [a] Jer. 28:15 [b] Ezek. 13:8–16, 22, 23 **29:32** [a] Jer. 28:16 **30:3** [a] Ezek. 39:25 [b] Jer. 16:15 **30:6** [a] Jer. 4:31; 6:24 **30:7** [a] Amos 5:18 [b] Dan. 9:12; 12:1 **30:9** [a] Hos. 3:5 [b] [Luke 1:69] **30:10** [a] Is. 41:13; 43:5; 44:2 [b] Jer. 3:18 **30:11** [a] [Is. 43:2–5] [b] Amos 9:8

[c]Yet I will not make a complete end of
you.
But I will correct you [d]in justice,
And will not let you go altogether
unpunished.'

12"For thus says the LORD:

[a]'Your affliction *is* incurable,
Your wound *is* severe.
13 *There is* no one to plead your cause,
That you may be bound up;
[a]You have no healing medicines.
14 [a]All your lovers have forgotten you;
They do not seek you;
For I have wounded you with the
wound [b]of an enemy,
With the chastisement [c]of a cruel one,
For the multitude of your iniquities,
[d]*Because* your sins have increased.
15 Why [a]do you cry about your affliction?
Your sorrow *is* incurable.
Because of the multitude of your
iniquities,
Because your sins have increased,
I have done these things to you.

16 'Therefore all those who devour you
[a]shall be devoured;
And all your adversaries, every one of
them, shall go into [b]captivity;
Those who plunder you shall become
[c]plunder,
And all who prey upon you I will make
a [d]prey.
17 [a]For I will restore health to you
And heal you of your wounds,' says the
LORD,
'Because they called you an outcast
saying:
"This *is* Zion;
No one seeks her." '

18"Thus says the LORD:

'Behold, I will bring back the captivity
of Jacob's tents,
And [a]have mercy on his dwelling
places;
The city shall be built upon its own
mound,
And the palace shall remain according
to its own plan.
19 Then [a]out of them shall proceed
thanksgiving
And the voice of those who make merry;
[b]I will multiply them, and they shall not
diminish;
I will also glorify them, and they shall
not be small.
20 Their children also shall be [a]as before,
And their congregation shall be
established before Me;
And I will punish all who oppress them.
21 Their nobles shall be from among
them,
[a]And their governor shall come from
their midst;
Then I will [b]cause him to draw near,
And he shall approach Me;
For who *is* this who pledged his heart
to approach Me?' says the LORD.
22 'You shall be [a]My people,
And I will be your God.' "

23 Behold, the [a]whirlwind of the LORD
Goes forth with fury,
A continuing whirlwind;
It will fall violently on the head of the
wicked.
24 The fierce anger of the LORD will not
return until He has done it,
And until He has performed the
intents of His heart.

[a]In the latter days you will consider it.

The Remnant of Israel Saved

31 "At [a]the same time," says the LORD, [b]"I
will be the God of all the families of Israel, and they shall be My people."
2Thus says the LORD:

"The people who survived the sword
Found grace in the wilderness—
Israel, when [a]I went to give him rest."

3 The LORD has appeared of old to me,
saying:
"Yes, [a]I have loved you with [b]an
everlasting love;
Therefore with lovingkindness I have
[c]drawn you.
4 Again [a]I will build you, and you shall be
rebuilt,
O virgin of Israel!
You shall again be adorned with your
[b]tambourines,
And shall go forth in the dances of
those who rejoice.

30:11 [c] Jer. 4:27; 46:27, 28 [d] Ps. 6:1 **30:12** [a] Jer. 15:18 **30:13** [a] Jer. 8:22 **30:14** [a] Lam. 1:2 [b] Job 13:24; 16:9; 19:11 [c] Job 30:21 [d] Jer. 5:6 **30:15** [a] Jer. 15:18 **30:16** [a] Jer. 10:25 [b] Is. 14:2 [c] Ezek. 39:10 [d] Jer. 2:3 **30:17** [a] Jer. 33:6 **30:18** [a] Ps. 102:13 **30:19** [a] Is. 51:11 [b] Zech. 10:8 **30:20** [a] Is. 1:26 **30:21** [a] Gen. 49:10 [b] Num. 16:5 **30:22** [a] Ezek. 36:28 **30:23** [a] Jer. 23:19, 20; 25:32 **30:24** [a] Gen. 49:1 **31:1** [a] Jer. 30:24 [b] Jer. 30:22 **31:2** [a] Num. 10:33 **31:3** [a] Mal. 1:2 [b] Rom. 11:28 [c] Hos. 11:4 **31:4** [a] Jer. 33:7 [b] Judg. 11:34

5 [a]You shall yet plant vines on the
mountains of Samaria;
The planters shall plant and eat *them*
as ordinary food.
6 For there shall be a day
When the watchmen will cry on Mount
Ephraim,
[a]'Arise, and let us go up *to* Zion,
To the LORD our God.' "

7For thus says the LORD:

[a]"Sing with gladness for Jacob,
And shout among the chief of the nations;
Proclaim, give praise, and say,
'O LORD, save Your people,
The remnant of Israel!'
8 Behold, I will bring them [a]from the
north country,
And [b]gather them from the ends of the
earth,
Among them the blind and the lame,
The woman with child
And the one who labors with child,
together;
A great throng shall return there.
9 [a]They shall come with weeping,
And with supplications I will lead
them.
I will cause them to walk [b]by the rivers
of waters,
In a straight way in which they shall
not stumble;
For I am a Father to Israel,
And Ephraim *is* My [c]firstborn.

10 "Hear the word of the LORD, O nations,
And declare *it* in the isles afar off, and
say,
'He who scattered Israel [a]will gather
him,
And keep him as a shepherd *does* his
flock.'
11 For [a]the LORD has redeemed Jacob,
And ransomed him [b]from the hand of
one stronger than he.
12 Therefore they shall come and sing in
[a]the height of Zion,
Streaming to [b]the goodness of the
LORD—
For wheat and new wine and oil,
For the young of the flock and the
herd;
Their souls shall be like a [c]well-watered
garden,
[d]And they shall sorrow no more at all.

13 "Then shall the virgin rejoice in the
dance,
And the young men and the old,
together;
For I will turn their mourning to joy,
Will comfort them,
And make them rejoice rather than
sorrow.
14 I will satiate the soul of the priests with
abundance,
And My people shall be satisfied with
My goodness, says the LORD."

Mercy on Ephraim

15Thus says the LORD:

[a]"A voice was heard in [b]Ramah,
Lamentation *and* bitter [c]weeping,
Rachel weeping for her children,
Refusing to be comforted for her
children,
Because [d]they *are* no more."

16Thus says the LORD:

"Refrain your voice from [a]weeping,
And your eyes from tears;
For your work shall be rewarded, says
the LORD,
And they shall come back from the
land of the enemy.
17 There is [a]hope in your future, says the
LORD,
That *your* children shall come back to
their own border.

18 "I have surely heard Ephraim
bemoaning himself:
'You have [a]chastised me, and I was
chastised,
Like an untrained bull;
[b]Restore me, and I will return,
For You *are* the LORD my God.
19 Surely, [a]after my turning, I repented;
And after I was instructed, I struck
myself on the thigh;
I was [b]ashamed, yes, even humiliated,
Because I bore the reproach of my
youth.'
20 *Is* Ephraim My dear son?
Is he a pleasant child?
For though I spoke against him,
I earnestly remember him still;
[a]Therefore My heart yearns for him;
[b]I will surely have mercy on him, says
the LORD.

31:5 [a]Amos 9:14 **31:6** [a][Mic. 4:2] **31:7** [a]Is. 12:5, 6 **31:8** [a]Jer. 3:12, 18; 23:8 [b]Ezek. 20:34, 41; 34:13 **31:9** [a][Jer. 50:4] [b]Is. 35:8; 43:19; 49:10, 11 [c]Ex. 4:22 **31:10** [a]Is. 40:11 **31:11** [a]Is. 44:23; 48:20 [b]Is. 49:24 **31:12** [a]Ezek. 17:23 [b]Hos. 3:5 [c]Is. 58:11 [d]Is. 35:10; 65:19 **31:15** [a]Matt. 2:17, 18 [b]Josh. 18:25 [c]Gen. 37:35 [d]Jer. 10:20 **31:16** [a][Is. 25:8; 30:19] **31:17** [a]Jer. 29:11 **31:18** [a]Ps. 94:12 [b]Lam. 5:21 **31:19** [a]Deut. 30:2 [b]Ezek. 36:31 **31:20** [a]Is. 63:15 [b][Hos. 14:4]

21 "Set up signposts,
Make landmarks;
[a]Set your heart toward the highway,
The way in *which* you went.
Turn back, O virgin of Israel,
Turn back to these your cities.
22 How long will you [a]gad about,
O you [b]backsliding daughter?
For the LORD has created a new thing
in the earth—
A woman shall encompass a man."

Future Prosperity of Judah

23 Thus says the LORD of hosts, the God of
Israel: "They shall again use this speech in
the land of Judah and in its cities, when I
bring back their captivity: [a]'The LORD bless
you, O home of justice, *and* [b]mountain of
holiness!' 24 And there shall dwell in Judah
itself, and [a]in all its cities together, farmers
and those going out with flocks. 25 For I have
satiated the weary soul, and I have replen-
ished every sorrowful soul."

26 After this I awoke and looked around,
and my sleep was [a]sweet to me.

27 "Behold, the days are coming, says the
LORD, that [a]I will sow the house of Israel and
the house of Judah with the seed of man and
the seed of beast. 28 And it shall come to pass,
that as I have [a]watched over them [b]to pluck
up, to break down, to throw down, to destroy,
and to afflict, so I will watch over them [c]to
build and to plant, says the LORD. 29 [a]In those
days they shall say no more:

'The fathers have eaten sour grapes,
And the children's teeth are set on edge.'

30 [a]But every one shall die for his own iniquity; every man who eats the sour grapes, his
teeth shall be set on edge.

A New Covenant

31 "Behold, the [a]days are coming, says the
LORD, when I will make a new covenant with
the house of Israel and with the house of
Judah— 32 not according to the covenant that
I made with their fathers in the day *that* [a]I
took them by the hand to lead them out of
the land of Egypt, My covenant which they
broke, though I was a husband to them,[1] says
the LORD. 33 [a]But this *is* the covenant that
I will make with the house of Israel after
those days, says the LORD: [b]I will put My law
in their minds, and write it on their hearts;
[c]and I will be their God, and they shall be My
people. 34 No more shall every man teach his
neighbor, and every man his brother, saying,
'Know the LORD,' for [a]they all shall know Me,
from the least of them to the greatest of them,
says the LORD. For [b]I will forgive their iniquity, and their sin I will remember no more."

35 Thus says the LORD,
[a]Who gives the sun for a light by day,
The ordinances of the moon and the
stars for a light by night,
Who disturbs [b]the sea,
And its waves roar
[c](The LORD of hosts *is* His name):
36 "If [a]those ordinances depart
From before Me, says the LORD,
Then the seed of Israel shall also cease
From being a nation before Me forever."

37 Thus says the LORD:

[a]"If heaven above can be measured,
And the foundations of the earth
searched out beneath,
I will also [b]cast off all the seed of Israel
For all that they have done, says the
LORD.

38 "Behold, the days are coming, says the
LORD, that the city shall be built for the LORD
[a]from the Tower of Hananel to the Corner
Gate. 39 [a]The surveyor's line shall again extend
straight forward over the hill Gareb; then it
shall turn toward Goath. 40 And the whole
valley of the dead bodies and of the ashes,
and all the fields as far as the Brook Kidron,
[a]to the corner of the Horse Gate toward the
east, [b]*shall be* holy to the LORD. It shall not be
plucked up or thrown down anymore forever."

Jeremiah Buys a Field

32 The word that came to Jeremiah from
the LORD [a]in the tenth year of Zedekiah king of Judah, which was the eighteenth
year of Nebuchadnezzar. 2 For then the king of
Babylon's army besieged Jerusalem, and Jeremiah the prophet was shut up [a]in the court
of the prison, which *was in* the king of Judah's
house. 3 For Zedekiah king of Judah had shut

31:21 [a] Jer. 50:5 ***31:22*** [a] Jer. 2:18, 23, 36 [b] Jer. 3:6, 8, 11, 12, 14, 22 ***31:23*** [a] Is. 1:26 [b] [Zech. 8:3] ***31:24*** [a] Jer. 33:12 ***31:26*** [a] Prov. 3:24 ***31:27*** [a] Ezek. 36:9–11 ***31:28*** [a] Jer. 44:27 [b] Jer. 1:10; 18:7 [c] Jer. 24:6 ***31:29*** [a] Ezek. 18:2, 3 ***31:30*** [a] [Gal. 6:5, 7] ***31:31*** [a] Heb. 8:8–12; 10:16, 17 ***31:32*** [a] Deut. 1:31 [1] Following Masoretic Text, Targum, and Vulgate; Septuagint and Syriac read *and I turned away from them.* ***31:33*** [a] Jer. 32:40 [b] Ps. 40:8 [c] Jer. 24:7; 30:22; 32:38 ***31:34*** [a] [John 6:45] [b] [Rom. 11:27] ***31:35*** [a] Gen. 1:14–18 [b] Is. 51:15 [c] Jer. 10:16 ***31:36*** [a] Ps. 148:6 ***31:37*** [a] Jer. 33:22 [b] [Rom. 11:2–5, 26, 27] ***31:38*** [a] Zech. 14:10 ***31:39*** [a] Zech. 2:1, 2 ***31:40*** [a] Neh. 3:28 [b] [Joel 3:17] ***32:1*** [a] Jer. 39:1, 2 ***32:2*** [a] Jer. 33:1; 37:21; 39:14

him up, saying, "Why do you [a]prophesy and say, 'Thus says the LORD: [b]"Behold, I will give this city into the hand of the king of Babylon, and he shall take it; 4and Zedekiah king of Judah [a]shall not escape from the hand of the Chaldeans, but shall surely be delivered into the hand of the king of Babylon, and shall speak with him face to face,[1] and see him [b]eye to eye; 5then he shall [a]lead Zedekiah to Babylon, and there he shall be [b]until I visit him," says the LORD; [c]"though you fight with the Chaldeans, you shall not succeed" '?"

6And Jeremiah said, "The word of the LORD came to me, saying, 7'Behold, Hanamel the son of Shallum your uncle will come to you, saying, "Buy my field which *is* in Anathoth, for the [a]right of redemption *is* yours to buy *it.*" ' 8Then Hanamel my uncle's son came to me in the court of the prison according to the word of the LORD, and said to me, 'Please buy my field that *is* in Anathoth, which *is* in the country of Benjamin; for the right of inheritance *is* yours, and the redemption yours; buy *it* for yourself.' Then I knew that this was the word of the LORD. 9So I bought the field from Hanamel, the son of my uncle who *was* in Anathoth, and [a]weighed *out to* him the money—seventeen shekels of silver. 10And I signed the deed and sealed *it,* took witnesses, and weighed the money on the scales. 11So I took the purchase deed, *both* that which was sealed *according* to the law and custom, and that which was open; 12and I gave the purchase deed to [a]Baruch the son of Neriah, son of Mahseiah, in the presence of Hanamel my uncle's *son,* and in the presence of the [b]witnesses who signed the purchase deed, before all the Jews who sat in the court of the prison.

13"Then I charged [a]Baruch before them, saying, 14'Thus says the LORD of hosts, the God of Israel: "Take these deeds, both this purchase deed which is sealed and this deed which is open, and put them in an earthen vessel, that they may last many days." 15For thus says the LORD of hosts, the God of Israel: "Houses and fields and vineyards shall be [a]possessed again in this land." '

Jeremiah Prays for Understanding

16"Now when I had delivered the purchase deed to Baruch the son of Neriah, I prayed to the LORD, saying: 17'Ah, Lord GOD! Behold, [a]You have made the heavens and the earth by Your great power and outstretched arm. [b]There is nothing too hard for You. 18*You* show [a]lovingkindness to thousands, and repay the iniquity of the fathers into the bosom of their children after them—the Great, [b]the Mighty God, whose name *is* [c]the LORD of hosts. 19*You are* [a]great in counsel and mighty in work, for Your [b]eyes *are* open to all the ways of the sons of men, [c]to give everyone according to his ways and according to the fruit of his doings. 20You have set signs and wonders in the land of Egypt, to this day, and in Israel and among *other* men; and You have made Yourself [a]a name, as it is this day. 21You [a]have brought Your people Israel out of the land of Egypt with signs and wonders, with a strong hand and an outstretched arm, and with great terror; 22You have given them this land, of which You swore to their fathers to give them—[a]"a land flowing with milk and honey."[1] 23And they came in and took possession of it, but [a]they have not obeyed Your voice or walked in Your law. They have done nothing of all that You commanded them to do; therefore You have caused all this calamity to come upon them.

24'Look, the siege mounds! They have come to the city to take it; and the city has been given into the hand of the Chaldeans who fight against it, because of [a]the sword and famine and pestilence. What You have spoken has happened; there You see *it!* 25And You have said to me, O Lord GOD, "Buy the field for money, and take witnesses"!—yet the city has been given into the hand of the Chaldeans.' "

God's Assurance of the People's Return

26Then the word of the LORD came to Jeremiah, saying, 27"Behold, I *am* the LORD, the [a]God of all flesh. Is there anything too hard for Me? 28Therefore thus says the LORD: 'Behold, I will give this city into the hand of the Chaldeans, into the hand of Nebuchadnezzar king of Babylon, and he shall take it. 29And the Chaldeans who fight against this city shall come and [a]set fire to this city and burn it, with the houses [b]on whose roofs they have offered incense to Baal and poured out drink offerings to other gods, to provoke Me to anger; 30because the children of Israel and the children of Judah [a]have done only evil before Me from their youth. For the children of Israel have provoked Me only to anger with the work of their hands,' says the LORD. 31'For this city has been to Me *a provocation of* My anger and My fury from the day that they built it, even to this day; [a]so I will remove it

32:3 [a] Jer. 26:8, 9 [b] Jer. 21:3–7; 34:2 **32:4** [a] Jer. 34:3; 38:18, 23; 39:5; 52:9 [b] Jer. 39:5 [1] Literally *mouth to mouth* **32:5** [a] Ezek. 12:12, 13 [b] Jer. 27:22 [c] Jer. 21:4; 33:5 **32:7** [a] Ruth 4:4 **32:9** [a] Zech. 11:12 **32:12** [a] Jer. 36:4 [b] Is. 8:2 **32:13** [a] Jer. 36:4 **32:15** [a] [Jer. 31:5, 12, 14] **32:17** [a] 2 Kin. 19:15 [b] Luke 18:27 **32:18** [a] Deut. 5:9, 10 [b] [Is. 9:6] [c] Jer. 10:16 **32:19** [a] Is. 28:29 [b] Prov. 5:21 [c] Jer. 17:10 **32:20** [a] Is. 63:12 **32:21** [a] Ex. 6:6 **32:22** [a] Ex. 3:8, 17 [1] Exodus 3:8 **32:23** [a] [Neh. 9:26] **32:24** [a] Jer. 14:12 **32:27** [a] [Num. 16:22] **32:29** [a] 2 Chr. 36:19 [b] Jer. 19:13 **32:30** [a] Jer. 2:7; 3:25; 7:22–26 **32:31** [a] 2 Kin. 23:27; 24:3

from before My face 32because of all the evil
of the children of Israel and the children of
Judah, which they have done to provoke Me
to anger—[a]they, their kings, their princes,
their priests, [b]their prophets, the men of
Judah, and the inhabitants of Jerusalem.
33And they have turned to Me the [a]back, and
not the face; though I taught them, [b]rising
up early and teaching *them,* yet they have
not listened to receive instruction. 34But they
[a]set their abominations in the house which
is called by My name, to defile it. 35And they
built the high places of Baal which *are* in the
Valley of the Son of Hinnom, to [a]cause their
sons and their daughters to pass through *the
fire* to [b]Molech, [c]which I did not command
them, nor did it come into My mind that
they should do this abomination, to cause
Judah to sin.'
36"Now therefore, thus says the LORD, the
God of Israel, concerning this city of which
you say, 'It shall be delivered into the hand
of the king of Babylon by the sword, by the
famine, and by the pestilence: 37Behold, I
will [a]gather them out of all countries where
I have driven them in My anger, in My fury,
and in great wrath; I will bring them back
to this place, and I will cause them [b]to dwell
safely. 38They shall be [a]My people, and I
will be their God; 39then I will [a]give them
one heart and one way, that they may fear
Me forever, for the good of them and their
children after them. 40And [a]I will make an
everlasting covenant with them, that I will
not turn away from doing them good; but
[b]I will put My fear in their hearts so that
they will not depart from Me. 41Yes, [a]I will
rejoice over them to do them good, and [b]I
will assuredly plant them in this land, with
all My heart and with all My soul.'
42"For thus says the LORD: [a]'Just as I have
brought all this great calamity on this people,
so I will bring on them all the good that I have
promised them. 43And fields will be bought
in this land [a]of which you say, "*It is* desolate,
without man or beast; it has been given into
the hand of the Chaldeans." 44Men will buy
fields for money, sign deeds and seal *them,*
and take witnesses, in [a]the land of Benjamin,
in the places around Jerusalem, in the cities
of Judah, in the cities of the mountains, in
the cities of the lowland, and in the cities of
the South; for [b]I will cause their captives to
return,' says the LORD."

Excellence of the Restored Nation

33 Moreover the word of the LORD came
to Jeremiah a second time, while he
was still [a]shut up in the court of the prison,
saying, 2"Thus says the LORD [a]who made it,
the LORD who formed it to establish it [b](the
LORD *is* His name): 3[a]'Call to Me, and I will
answer you, and show you great and mighty
things, which you do not know.'
4"For thus says the LORD, the God of Israel, concerning the houses of this city and
the houses of the kings of Judah, which have
been pulled down *to fortify*[1] against [a]the siege
mounds and the sword: 5'They come to fight
with the Chaldeans, but *only* to [a]fill their places[1] with the dead bodies of men whom I will
slay in My anger and My fury, all for whose
wickedness I have hidden My face from this
city. 6Behold, [a]I will bring it health and healing; I will heal them and reveal to them the
abundance of peace and truth. 7And [a]I will
cause the captives of Judah and the captives
of Israel to return, and will rebuild those places [b]as at the first. 8I will [a]cleanse them from
all their iniquity by which they have sinned
against Me, and I will pardon all their iniquities by which they have sinned and by which
they have transgressed against Me. 9[a]Then it
shall be to Me a name of joy, a praise, and an
honor before all nations of the earth, who
shall hear all the good that I do to them; they
shall [b]fear and tremble for all the goodness
and all the prosperity that I provide for it.'
10"Thus says the LORD: 'Again there shall
be heard in this place—[a]of which you say,

PEACE NOTE

Peace and happiness come when our lives are anchored to God's unchanging truth.

JEREMIAH 33:6

32:32 [a] Dan. 9:8 [b] Jer. 23:14 **32:33** [a] Jer. 2:27; 7:24 [b] Jer. 7:13 **32:34** [a] Jer. 7:10–12, 30; 23:11 **32:35** [a] Jer. 7:31; 19:5 [b] Lev. 18:21 [c] Jer. 7:31 **32:37** [a] Deut. 30:3 [b] Jer. 33:16 **32:38** [a] [Jer. 24:7; 30:22; 31:33] **32:39** [a] [Ezek. 11:19] **32:40** [a] Is. 55:3 [b] [Jer. 31:33] **32:41** [a] Deut. 30:9 [b] Amos 9:15 **32:42** [a] Jer. 31:28 **32:43** [a] Jer. 33:10 **32:44** [a] Jer. 17:26 [b] Jer. 33:7, 11 **33:1** [a] Jer. 32:2, 3 **33:2** [a] Is. 37:26 [b] Ex. 15:3 **33:3** [a] Jer. 29:12 **33:4** [a] Is. 22:10 [1] Compare Isaiah 22:10 **33:5** [a] 2 Kin. 23:14 [1] Compare 2 Kings 23:14 **33:6** [a] Jer. 30:17 **33:7** [a] Jer. 30:3; 32:44 [b] Is. 1:26 **33:8** [a] Zech. 13:1 **33:9** [a] Is. 62:7 [b] Is. 60:5 **33:10** [a] Jer. 32:43

"It *is* desolate, without man and without
beast"—in the cities of Judah, in the streets
of Jerusalem that are desolate, without man
and without inhabitant and without beast,
11 the [a]voice of joy and the voice of gladness,
the voice of the bridegroom and the voice
of the bride, the voice of those who will say:

[b]"Praise the LORD of hosts,
For the LORD *is* good,
For His mercy *endures* forever"—

and of those *who will* bring [c]the sacrifice of
praise into the house of the LORD. For I will
cause the captives of the land to return as at
the first,' says the LORD.

12 "Thus says the LORD of hosts: [a]'In this
place which is desolate, without man and
without beast, and in all its cities, there shall
again be a dwelling place of shepherds causing
their flocks to lie down. 13 [a]In the cities of the
mountains, in the cities of the lowland, in the
cities of the South, in the land of Benjamin, in
the places around Jerusalem, and in the cities
of Judah, the flocks shall again [b]pass under the
hands of him who counts *them*,' says the LORD.
14 [a]'Behold, the days are coming,' says the
LORD, 'that [b]I will perform that good thing
which I have promised to the house of Israel
and to the house of Judah:

15 'In those days and at that time
I will cause to grow up to David
A [a]Branch of righteousness;
He shall execute judgment and
righteousness in the earth.
16 In those days Judah will be saved,
And Jerusalem will dwell safely.
And this *is the name* by which she will
be called:

THE LORD OUR RIGHTEOUSNESS.'[1]

17 "For thus says the LORD: 'David shall
never [a]lack a man to sit on the throne of the
house of Israel; 18 nor shall the [a]priests, the
Levites, lack a man to [b]offer burnt offerings
before Me, to kindle grain offerings, and to
sacrifice continually.' "

The Permanence of God's Covenant

19 And the word of the LORD came to Jeremiah, saying, 20 "Thus says the LORD: 'If you
can break My covenant with the day and My
covenant with the night, so that there will
not be day and night in their season, 21 then
[a]My covenant may also be broken with David
My servant, so that he shall not have a son
to reign on his throne, and with the Levites,
the priests, My ministers. 22 As [a]the host of
heaven cannot be numbered, nor the sand
of the sea measured, so will I [b]multiply the
descendants of David My servant and the
[c]Levites who minister to Me.' "

23 Moreover the word of the LORD came to
Jeremiah, saying, 24 "Have you not considered
what these people have spoken, saying, 'The
two families which the LORD has chosen,
He has also cast them off'? Thus they have
[a]despised My people, as if they should no
more be a nation before them.

25 "Thus says the LORD: 'If [a]My covenant *is*
not with day and night, *and if* I have not [b]ap-
pointed the ordinances of heaven and earth,
26 [a]then I will [b]cast away the descendants of
Jacob and David My servant, *so* that I will not
take *any* of his descendants *to be* rulers over
the descendants of Abraham, Isaac, and Jacob. For I will cause their captives to return,
and will have mercy on them.' "

Zedekiah Warned by God

34 The word which came to Jeremiah from
the LORD, [a]when Nebuchadnezzar king
of Babylon and all his army, [b]all the kingdoms
of the earth under his dominion, and all the
people, fought against Jerusalem and all its
cities, saying, 2 "Thus says the LORD, the God
of Israel: 'Go and [a]speak to Zedekiah king
of Judah and tell him, "Thus says the LORD:
'Behold, [b]I will give this city into the hand of
the king of Babylon, and he shall burn it with
fire. 3 And [a]you shall not escape from his hand,
but shall surely be taken and delivered into
his hand; your eyes shall see the eyes of the
king of Babylon, he shall speak with you [b]face
to face,[1] and you shall go to Babylon.' " ' 4 Yet
hear the word of the LORD, O Zedekiah king of
Judah! Thus says the LORD concerning you:
'You shall not die by the sword. 5 You shall
die in peace; as in [a]the ceremonies of your
fathers, the former kings who were before
you, [b]so they shall burn *incense* for you and
[c]lament for you, *saying*, "Alas, lord!" For I
have pronounced the word, says the LORD.' "

6 Then Jeremiah the prophet spoke all
these words to Zedekiah king of Judah in
Jerusalem, 7 when the king of Babylon's army

33:11 [a] Rev. 18:23 [b] Is. 12:4 [c] Lev. 7:12 **33:12** [a] Is. 65:10 **33:13** [a] Jer. 17:26; 32:44 [b] Lev. 27:32 **33:14** [a] Jer. 23:5; 31:27, 31 [b] Jer. 29:10; 32:42 **33:15** [a] Jer. 23:5 **33:16** [1] Compare 23:5, 6 **33:17** [a] 2 Sam. 7:16 **33:18** [a] Ezek. 44:15 [b] [1 Pet. 2:5, 9] **33:21** [a] 2 Sam. 23:5; Ps. 89:34 **33:22** [a] Gen. 15:5; 22:17 [b] Jer. 30:19 [c] Is. 66:21 **33:24** [a] Esth. 3:6–8 **33:25** [a] Gen. 8:22 [b] Ps. 74:16; 104:19 **33:26** [a] Jer. 31:37 [b] Rom. 11:1, 2 **34:1** [a] 2 Kin. 25:1 [b] Jer. 1:15; 25:9 **34:2** [a] 2 Chr. 36:11, 12 [b] Jer. 21:10; 32:3, 28 **34:3** [a] 2 Kin. 25:4, 5 [b] Jer. 32:4; 39:5, 6 [1] Literally *mouth to mouth* **34:5** [a] 2 Chr. 16:14; 21:19 [b] Dan. 2:46 [c] Jer. 22:18

fought against Jerusalem and all the cities of
Judah that were left, against Lachish and Azekah; for *only* [a]these fortified cities remained
of the cities of Judah.

Treacherous Treatment of Slaves

8*This is* the word that came to Jeremiah
from the LORD, after King Zedekiah had made
a covenant with all the people who *were* at Jerusalem to proclaim [a]liberty to them: 9[a]that
every man should set free his male and female
slave—a Hebrew man or woman—[b]that no
one should keep a Jewish brother in bondage.
10Now when all the princes and all the people,
who had entered into the covenant, heard
that everyone should set free his male and
female slaves, that no one should keep them
in bondage anymore, they obeyed and let *them*
go. 11But afterward they changed their minds
and made the male and female slaves return,
whom they had set free, and brought them
into subjection as male and female slaves.

12Therefore the word of the LORD came
to Jeremiah from the LORD, saying, 13"Thus
says the LORD, the God of Israel: 'I made a
[a]covenant with your fathers in the day that
I brought them out of the land of Egypt, out
of the house of bondage, saying, 14"At the end
of [a]seven years let every man set free his Hebrew brother, who has been sold to him; and
when he has served you six years, you shall
let him go free from you." But your fathers
did not obey Me nor incline their ear. 15Then
you recently turned and did what was right
in My sight—every man proclaiming liberty
to his neighbor; and you [a]made a covenant
before Me [b]in the house which is called by
My name. 16Then you turned around and
[a]profaned My name, and every one of you
brought back his male and female slaves,
whom you had set at liberty, at their pleasure,
and brought them back into subjection, to
be your male and female slaves.'

17"Therefore thus says the LORD: 'You have
not obeyed Me in proclaiming liberty, every
one to his brother and every one to his neighbor. [a]Behold, I proclaim liberty to you,' says
the LORD—[b]'to the sword, to pestilence, and
to famine! And I will deliver you to [c]trouble
among all the kingdoms of the earth. 18And I
will give the men who have transgressed My
covenant, who have not performed the words
of the covenant which they made before Me,
when [a]they cut the calf in two and passed between the parts of it— 19the princes of Judah,
the princes of Jerusalem, the eunuchs, the
priests, and all the people of the land who
passed between the parts of the calf— 20I will
[a]give them into the hand of their enemies and
into the hand of those who seek their life. Their
[b]dead bodies shall be for meat for the birds of
the heaven and the beasts of the earth. 21And I
will give Zedekiah king of Judah and his princes into the hand of their enemies, into the hand
of those who seek their life, and into the hand
of the king of Babylon's army [a]which has gone
back from you. 22[a]Behold, I will command,' says
the LORD, 'and cause them to return to this city.
They will fight against it [b]and take it and burn
it with fire; and [c]I will make the cities of Judah
a desolation without inhabitant.' "

The Obedient Rechabites

35 The word which came to Jeremiah
from the LORD in the days of Jehoiakim the son of Josiah, king of Judah, saying,
2"Go to the house of the [a]Rechabites, speak
to them, and bring them into the house of
the LORD, into one of [b]the chambers, and
give them wine to drink."

3Then I took Jaazaniah the son of Jeremiah,
the son of Habazziniah, his brothers and all his
sons, and the whole house of the Rechabites,
4and I brought them into the house of the
LORD, into the chamber of the sons of Hanan
the son of Igdaliah, a man of God, which *was* by
the chamber of the princes, above the chamber
of Maaseiah the son of Shallum, [a]the keeper
of the door. 5Then I set before the sons of the
house of the Rechabites bowls full of wine,
and cups; and I said to them, "Drink wine."

6But they said, "We will drink no wine, for
[a]Jonadab the son of Rechab, our father, commanded us, saying, 'You shall drink [b]no wine,
you nor your sons, forever. 7You shall not
build a house, sow seed, plant a vineyard, nor
have *any of these;* but all your days you shall
dwell in tents, [a]that you may live many days in
the land where you are sojourners.' 8Thus we
have [a]obeyed the voice of Jonadab the son of
Rechab, our father, in all that he charged us, to
drink no wine all our days, we, our wives, our
sons, or our daughters, 9nor to build ourselves
houses to dwell in; nor do we have vineyard,
field, or seed. 10But we have dwelt in tents, and
have obeyed and done according to all that
Jonadab our father commanded us. 11But it
came to pass, when Nebuchadnezzar king of
Babylon came up into the land, that we said,
'Come, let us [a]go to Jerusalem for fear of the

34:7 [a] 2 Kin. 18:13; 19:8 **34:8** [a] Ex. 21:2 **34:9** [a] Neh. 5:11 [b] Lev. 25:39–46 **34:13** [a] Ex. 24:3, 7, 8 **34:14** [a] Deut. 15:12 **34:15** [a] Neh. 10:29 [b] Jer. 7:10 **34:16** [a] Ex. 20:7 **34:17** [a] [Matt. 7:2] [b] Jer. 32:24, 36 [c] Deut. 28:25, 64 **34:18** [a] Gen. 15:10, 17 **34:20** [a] Jer. 22:25 [b] Jer. 7:33; 16:4; 19:7 **34:21** [a] Jer. 37:5–11; 39:4–7 **34:22** [a] Jer. 37:8, 10 [b] Jer. 38:3; 39:1, 2, 8; 52:7, 13 [c] Jer. 9:11; 44:2, 6 **35:2** [a] 1 Chr. 2:55 [b] 1 Kin. 6:5, 8 **35:4** [a] 1 Chr. 9:18, 19 **35:6** [a] 2 Kin. 10:15, 23 [b] Luke 1:15 **35:7** [a] Ex. 20:12 **35:8** [a] [Col. 3:20] **35:11** [a] Jer. 4:5–7; 8:14

army of the Chaldeans and for fear of the army
of the Syrians.' So we dwell at Jerusalem."
12Then came the word of the LORD to Jeremiah, saying, 13"Thus says the LORD of hosts,
the God of Israel: 'Go and tell the men of
Judah and the inhabitants of Jerusalem,
"Will you not [a]receive instruction to obey My
words?" says the LORD. 14"The words of Jonadab the son of Rechab, which he commanded
his sons, not to drink wine, are performed;
for to this day they drink none, and obey their
father's commandment. [a]But although I have
spoken to you, [b]rising early and speaking,
you did not obey Me. 15I have also sent to
you all My [a]servants the prophets, rising
up early and sending *them,* saying, [b]'Turn
now everyone from his evil way, amend your
doings, and do not go after other gods to
serve them; then you will [c]dwell in the land
which I have given you and your fathers.' But
you have not inclined your ear, nor obeyed
Me. 16Surely the sons of Jonadab the son of
Rechab have performed the commandment
of their [a]father, which he commanded them,
but this people has not obeyed Me." '
17"Therefore thus says the LORD God of
hosts, the God of Israel: 'Behold, I will bring
on Judah and on all the inhabitants of Jerusalem all the doom that I have pronounced
against them; [a]because I have spoken to them
but they have not heard, and I have called to
them but they have not answered.' "
18And Jeremiah said to the house of the
Rechabites, "Thus says the LORD of hosts, the
God of Israel: 'Because you have obeyed the
commandment of Jonadab your father, and
kept all his precepts and done according to
all that he commanded you, 19therefore thus
says the LORD of hosts, the God of Israel:
"Jonadab the son of Rechab shall not lack a
man to [a]stand before Me forever." ' "

The Scroll Read in the Temple

36 Now it came to pass in the [a]fourth year
of Jehoiakim the son of Josiah, king
of Judah, *that* this word came to Jeremiah
from the LORD, saying: 2"Take a [a]scroll of
a book and [b]write on it all the words that I
have spoken to you against Israel, against
Judah, and against [c]all the nations, from the
day I spoke to you, from the days of [d]Josiah
even to this day. 3It [a]may be that the house
of Judah will hear all the adversities which
I purpose to bring upon them, that everyone may [b]turn from his evil way, that I may
forgive their iniquity and their sin."

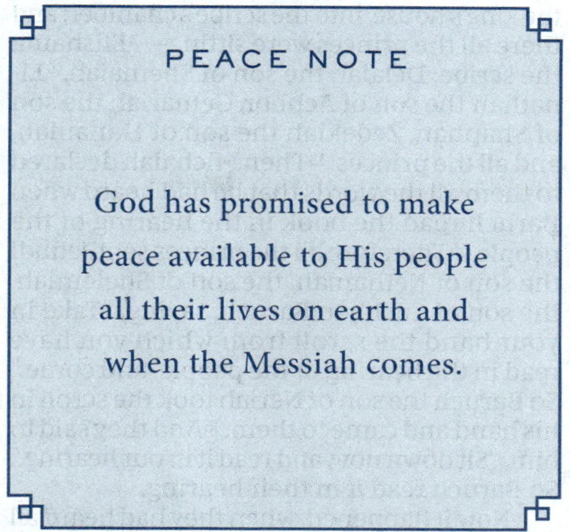

4Then Jeremiah [a]called Baruch the son of
Neriah; and [b]Baruch wrote on a scroll of a book,
at the instruction of Jeremiah,[1] all the words of
the LORD which He had spoken to him. 5And
Jeremiah commanded Baruch, saying, "I *am*
confined, I cannot go into the house of the
LORD. 6You go, therefore, and read from the
scroll which you have written at my instruction,[1] the words of the LORD, in the hearing of
the people in the LORD's house on [a]the day of
fasting. And you shall also read them in the
hearing of all Judah who come from their cities.
7It may be that they will present their supplication before the LORD, and everyone will turn
from his evil way. For great *is* the anger and the
fury that the LORD has pronounced against
this people." 8And Baruch the son of Neriah
did according to all that Jeremiah the prophet
commanded him, reading from the book the
words of the LORD in the LORD's house.
9Now it came to pass in the fifth year of
Jehoiakim the son of Josiah, king of Judah,
in the ninth month, *that* they proclaimed
a fast before the LORD to all the people in
Jerusalem, and to all the people who came
from the cities of Judah to Jerusalem. 10Then
Baruch read from the book the words of
Jeremiah in the house of the LORD, in the
chamber of Gemariah the son of Shaphan
the scribe, in the upper court at the [a]entry
of the New Gate of the LORD's house, in the
hearing of all the people.

The Scroll Read in the Palace

11When Michaiah the son of Gemariah, the
son of Shaphan, heard all the words of the
LORD from the book, 12he then went down to

35:13 [a] Jer. 6:10; 17:23; 32:33 **35:14** [a] 2 Chr. 36:15 [b] Jer. 7:13; 25:3 **35:15** [a] Jer. 26:4, 5; 29:19 [b] Jer. 18:11; 25:5, 6 [c] Jer. 7:7; 25:5, 6 **35:16** [a] [Heb. 12:9] **35:17** [a] Prov. 1:24 **35:19** [a] Jer. 15:19 **36:1** [a] Jer. 25:1, 3; 45:1 **36:2** [a] Zech. 5:1 [b] Jer. 30:2 [c] Jer. 25:15 [d] Jer. 25:3 **36:3** [a] Jer. 26:3 [b] Jon. 3:8 **36:4** [a] Jer. 32:12 [b] Jer. 45:1 [1] Literally *from Jeremiah's mouth* **36:6** [a] Acts 27:9 [1] Literally *from my mouth* **36:10** [a] Jer. 26:10

the king's house, into the scribe's chamber; and there all the princes were sitting—[a]Elishama the scribe, Delaiah the son of Shemaiah, [b]Elnathan the son of Achbor, Gemariah the son of Shaphan, Zedekiah the son of Hananiah, and all the princes. 13Then Michaiah declared to them all the words that he had heard when Baruch read the book in the hearing of the people. 14Therefore all the princes sent Jehudi the son of Nethaniah, the son of Shelemiah, the son of Cushi, to Baruch, saying, "Take in your hand the scroll from which you have read in the hearing of the people, and come." So Baruch the son of Neriah took the scroll in his hand and came to them. 15And they said to him, "Sit down now, and read it in our hearing." So Baruch read *it* in their hearing.

16Now it happened, when they had heard all the words, that they looked in fear from one to another, and said to Baruch, "We will surely tell the king of all these words." 17And they asked Baruch, saying, "Tell us now, how did you write all these words—at his instruction?"[1]

18So Baruch answered them, "He proclaimed with his mouth all these words to me, and I wrote *them* with ink in the book."

19Then the princes said to Baruch, "Go and hide, you and Jeremiah; and let no one know where you are."

The King Destroys Jeremiah's Scroll

20And they went to the king, into the court; but they stored the scroll in the chamber of Elishama the scribe, and told all the words in the hearing of the king. 21So the king sent Jehudi to bring the scroll, and he took it from Elishama the scribe's chamber. And Jehudi read it in the hearing of the king and in the hearing of all the princes who stood beside the king. 22Now the king was sitting in [a]the winter house in the ninth month, with *a fire* burning on the hearth before him. 23And it happened, when Jehudi had read three or four columns, *that the king* cut it with the scribe's knife and cast *it* into the fire that *was* on the hearth, until all the scroll was consumed in the fire that *was* on the hearth. 24Yet they were [a]not afraid, nor did they [b]tear their garments, the king nor any of his servants who heard all these words. 25Nevertheless Elnathan, Delaiah, and Gemariah implored the king not to burn the scroll; but he would not listen to them. 26And the king commanded Jerahmeel the king's[1] son, Seraiah the son of Azriel, and Shelemiah the son of Abdeel, to seize Baruch the scribe and Jeremiah the prophet, but the LORD hid them.

Jeremiah Rewrites the Scroll

27Now after the king had burned the scroll with the words which Baruch had written at the instruction of Jeremiah,[1] the word of the LORD came to Jeremiah, saying: 28"Take yet another scroll, and write on it all the former words that were in the first scroll which Jehoiakim the king of Judah has burned. 29And you shall say to Jehoiakim king of Judah, 'Thus says the LORD: "You have burned this scroll, saying, [a]'Why have you written in it that the king of Babylon will certainly come and destroy this land, and cause man and beast to [b]cease from here?' " 30Therefore thus says the LORD concerning Jehoiakim king of Judah: [a]"He shall have no one to sit on the throne of David, and his dead body shall be [b]cast out to the heat of the day and the frost of the night. 31I will punish him, his family, and his servants for their iniquity; and I will bring on them, on the inhabitants of Jerusalem, and on the men of Judah all the doom that I have pronounced against them; but they did not heed." ' "

32Then Jeremiah took another scroll and gave it to Baruch the scribe, the son of Neriah, who wrote on it at the instruction of Jeremiah[1] all the words of the book which Jehoiakim king of Judah had burned in the fire. And besides, there were added to them many similar words.

Zedekiah's Vain Hope

37 Now King [a]Zedekiah the son of Josiah reigned instead of Coniah the son of Jehoiakim, whom Nebuchadnezzar king of Babylon made king in the land of Judah. 2[a]But neither he nor his servants nor the people of the land gave heed to the words of the LORD which He spoke by the prophet Jeremiah.

3And Zedekiah the king sent Jehucal the son of Shelemiah, and [a]Zephaniah the son of Maaseiah, the priest, to the prophet Jeremiah, saying, [b]"Pray now to the LORD our God for us." 4Now Jeremiah was coming and going among the people, for they had not *yet* put him in prison. 5Then [a]Pharaoh's army came up from Egypt; and when the Chaldeans who were besieging Jerusalem heard news of them, they departed from Jerusalem.

6Then the word of the LORD came to the prophet Jeremiah, saying, 7"Thus says the LORD, the God of Israel, 'Thus you shall say to the king of Judah, [a]who sent you to Me to inquire of Me: "Behold, Pharaoh's army which has come up to help you will return to Egypt, to their own land. 8[a]And the Chaldeans shall

36:12 [a] Jer. 41:1 [b] Jer. 26:22 **36:17** [1] Literally *with his mouth* **36:22** [a] Amos 3:15 **36:24** [a] [Ps. 36:1] [b] Is. 36:22; 37:1 **36:26** [1] Hebrew *Hammelech* **36:27** [1] Literally *from Jeremiah's mouth* **36:29** [a] Jer. 32:3 [b] Jer. 25:9–11; 26:9 **36:30** [a] Jer. 22:30 [b] Jer. 22:19 **36:32** [1] Literally *from Jeremiah's mouth* **37:1** [a] 2 Kin. 24:17 **37:2** [a] 2 Chr. 36:12–16 **37:3** [a] Jer. 21:1, 2; 29:25; 52:24 [b] Jer. 42:2 **37:5** [a] Ezek. 17:15 **37:7** [a] Jer. 21:2 **37:8** [a] Jer. 34:22

come back and fight against this city, and take it and burn it with fire." ' [9]Thus says the LORD: 'Do not deceive yourselves, saying, "The Chaldeans will surely depart from us," for they will not depart. [10][a]For though you had defeated the whole army of the Chaldeans who fight against you, and there remained *only* wounded men among them, they would rise up, every man in his tent, and burn the city with fire.' "

Jeremiah Imprisoned

[11]And it happened, when the army of the Chaldeans left *the siege* of Jerusalem for fear of Pharaoh's army, [12]that Jeremiah went out of Jerusalem to go into the land of Benjamin to claim his property there among the people. [13]And when he was in the Gate of Benjamin, a captain of the guard *was* there whose name *was* Irijah the son of Shelemiah, the son of Hananiah; and he seized Jeremiah the prophet, saying, "You are defecting to the Chaldeans!"

[14]Then Jeremiah said, "False! I am not defecting to the Chaldeans." But he did not listen to him.

So Irijah seized Jeremiah and brought him to the princes. [15]Therefore the princes were angry with Jeremiah, and they struck him [a]and put him in prison in the [b]house of Jonathan the scribe. For they had made that the prison.

[16]When Jeremiah entered [a]the dungeon and the cells, and Jeremiah had remained there many days, [17]then Zedekiah the king sent and took him *out.* The king asked him secretly in his house, and said, "Is there *any* word from the LORD?"

And Jeremiah said, "There is." Then he said, "You shall be [a]delivered into the hand of the king of Babylon!"

[18]Moreover Jeremiah said to King Zedekiah, "What offense have I committed against you, against your servants, or against this people, that you have put me in prison? [19]Where now *are* your prophets who prophesied to you, saying, 'The king of Babylon will not come against you or against this land'? [20]Therefore please hear now, O my lord the king. Please, let my petition be accepted before you, and do not make me return to the house of Jonathan the scribe, lest I die there."

[21]Then Zedekiah the king commanded that they should commit Jeremiah [a]to the court of the prison, and that they should give him daily a piece of bread from the bakers' street, [b]until all the bread in the city was gone. Thus Jeremiah remained in the court of the prison.

Jeremiah in the Dungeon

38 Now Shephatiah the son of Mattan, Gedaliah the son of Pashhur, [a]Jucal[1] the son of Shelemiah, and [b]Pashhur the son of Malchiah [c]heard the words that Jeremiah had spoken to all the people, saying, [2]"Thus says the LORD: [a]'He who remains in this city shall die by the sword, by famine, and by pestilence; but he who goes over to the Chaldeans shall live; his life shall be as a prize to him, and he shall live.'[1] [3]Thus says the LORD: [a]'This city shall surely be [b]given into the hand of the king of Babylon's army, which shall take it.' "

[4]Therefore the princes said to the king, "Please, [a]let this man be put to death, for thus he weakens the hands of the men of war who remain in this city, and the hands of all the people, by speaking such words to them. For this man does not seek the welfare of this people, but their harm."

[5]Then Zedekiah the king said, "Look, he *is* in your hand. For the king can *do* nothing against you." [6][a]So they took Jeremiah and cast him into the dungeon of Malchiah the king's[1] son, which *was* in the court of the prison, and they let Jeremiah down with ropes. And in the dungeon *there was* no water, but mire. So Jeremiah sank in the mire.

[7][a]Now Ebed-Melech the Ethiopian, one of the eunuchs, who was in the king's house, heard that they had put Jeremiah in the dungeon. When the king was sitting at the Gate of Benjamin, [8]Ebed-Melech went out of the king's house and spoke to the king, saying: [9]"My lord the king, these men have done evil in all that they have done to Jeremiah the prophet, whom they have cast into the dungeon, and he is likely to die from hunger in the place where he is. For *there is* [a]no more bread in the city." [10]Then the king commanded Ebed-Melech the Ethiopian, saying, "Take from here thirty men with you, and lift Jeremiah the prophet out of the dungeon before he dies." [11]So Ebed-Melech took the men with him and went into the house of the king under the treasury, and took from there old clothes and old rags, and let them down by ropes into the dungeon to Jeremiah. [12]Then Ebed-Melech the Ethiopian said to Jeremiah, "Please put these old clothes and rags under your armpits, under the ropes." And Jeremiah did so. [13]So they pulled Jeremiah up with ropes and lifted him out of the dungeon. And Jeremiah remained [a]in the court of the prison.

37:10 [a] Jer. 21:4, 5 **37:15** [a] Jer. 20:2 [b] Jer. 38:26 **37:16** [a] Jer. 38:6 **37:17** [a] Jer. 21:7 **37:21** [a] Jer. 32:2; 38:13, 28 [b] Jer. 38:9; 52:6 **38:1** [a] Jer. 37:3 [b] Jer. 21:1 [c] Jer. 21:8 [1] Same as *Jehucal* (compare 37:3) **38:2** [a] Jer. 21:9 [1] Compare 21:9 **38:3** [a] Jer. 21:10; 32:3 [b] Jer. 34:2 **38:4** [a] Jer. 26:11 **38:6** [a] Jer. 37:21 [1] Hebrew *Hammelech* **38:7** [a] Jer. 39:16 **38:9** [a] Jer. 37:21 **38:13** [a] Jer. 37:21

Zedekiah's Fears and Jeremiah's Advice

14Then Zedekiah the king sent and had Jeremiah the prophet brought to him at the third entrance of the house of the LORD. And the king said to Jeremiah, "I will [a]ask you something. Hide nothing from me."

15Jeremiah said to Zedekiah, "If I declare *it* to you, will you not surely put me to death? And if I give you advice, you will not listen to me."

16So Zedekiah the king swore secretly to Jeremiah, saying, "*As* the LORD lives, [a]who made our very souls, I will not put you to death, nor will I give you into the hand of these men who seek your life."

17Then Jeremiah said to Zedekiah, "Thus says the LORD, the God of hosts, the God of Israel: 'If you surely [a]surrender [b]to the king of Babylon's princes, then your soul shall live; this city shall not be burned with fire, and you and your house shall live. 18But if you do not surrender to the king of Babylon's princes, then this city shall be given into the hand of the Chaldeans; they shall burn it with fire, and [a]you shall not escape from their hand.' "

19And Zedekiah the king said to Jeremiah, "I am afraid of the Jews who have [a]defected to the Chaldeans, lest they deliver me into their hand, and they [b]abuse me."

20But Jeremiah said, "They shall not deliver *you*. Please, obey the voice of the LORD which I speak to you. So it shall be [a]well with you, and your soul shall live. 21But if you refuse to surrender, this *is* the word that the LORD has shown me: 22'Now behold, all the [a]women who are left in the king of Judah's house *shall be* surrendered to the king of Babylon's princes, and those *women* shall say:

"Your close friends have set upon you
And prevailed against you;
Your feet have sunk in the mire,
And they have turned away again."

23'So they shall surrender all your wives and [a]children to the Chaldeans. [b]You shall not escape from their hand, but shall be taken by the hand of the king of Babylon. And you shall cause this city to be burned with fire.' "

24Then Zedekiah said to Jeremiah, "Let no one know of these words, and you shall not die. 25But if the princes hear that I have talked with you, and they come to you and say to you, 'Declare to us now what you have said to the king, and also what the king said to you; do not hide *it* from us, and we will not put you to death,' 26then you shall say to them, [a]'I presented my request before the king, that he would not make me return [b]to Jonathan's house to die there.' "

27Then all the princes came to Jeremiah and asked him. And he told them according to all these words that the king had commanded. So they stopped speaking with him, for the conversation had not been heard. 28Now [a]Jeremiah remained in the court of the prison until the day that Jerusalem was taken. And he was *there* when Jerusalem was taken.

The Fall of Jerusalem

39 In the [a]ninth year of Zedekiah king of Judah, in the tenth month, Nebuchadnezzar king of Babylon and all his army came against Jerusalem, and besieged it. 2In the [a]eleventh year of Zedekiah, in the fourth month, on the ninth *day* of the month, the city was penetrated.

3[a]Then all the princes of the king of Babylon came in and sat in the Middle Gate: Nergal-Sharezer, Samgar-Nebo, Sarsechim, Rabsaris,[1] Nergal-Sarezer, Rabmag,[2] with the rest of the princes of the king of Babylon.

4[a]So it was, when Zedekiah the king of Judah and all the men of war saw them, that they fled and went out of the city by night, by way of the king's garden, by the gate between the two walls. And he went out by way of the plain.[1] 5But the Chaldean army pursued them and [a]overtook Zedekiah in the plains of Jericho. And when they had captured him, they brought him up to Nebuchadnezzar king of Babylon, to [b]Riblah in the land of Hamath, where he

PEACE NOTE

Gratitude is a form of prayer. We are thankful to God. The Lord blesses us with peace when we praise Him.

38:14 [a] Jer. 21:1, 2; 37:17 38:16 [a] Is. 57:16 38:17 [a] 2 Kin. 24:12 [b] Jer. 39:3 38:18 [a] Jer. 32:4; 34:3 38:19 [a] Jer. 39:9 [b] 1 Sam. 31:4 38:20 [a] Jer. 40:9 38:22 [a] Jer. 8:10 38:23 [a] Jer. 39:6; 41:10 [b] Jer. 39:5 38:26 [a] Jer. 37:20 [b] Jer. 37:15 38:28 [a] Jer. 37:21; 39:14 39:1 [a] 2 Kin. 25:1–12 39:2 [a] Jer. 1:3 39:3 [a] Jer. 1:15; 38:17 [1] A title, probably *Chief Officer;* also verse 13 [2] A title, probably *Troop Commander;* also verse 13 39:4 [a] Jer. 52:7 [1] Or *the Arabah,* that is, the Jordan Valley 39:5 [a] Jer. 21:7; 32:4; 38:18, 23 [b] 2 Kin. 23:33

pronounced judgment on him. 6Then the king
of Babylon killed the sons of Zedekiah before
his [a]eyes in Riblah; the king of Babylon also
killed all the [b]nobles of Judah. 7Moreover [a]he
put out Zedekiah's eyes, and bound him with
bronze fetters to carry him off to Babylon.
8[a]And the Chaldeans burned the king's house
and the houses of the people with [b]fire, and
broke down the [c]walls of Jerusalem. 9[a]Then
Nebuzaradan the captain of the guard carried
away captive to Babylon the remnant of the
people who remained in the city and those
who [b]defected to him, with the rest of the
people who remained. 10But Nebuzaradan the
captain of the guard left in the land of Judah
the [a]poor people, who had nothing, and gave
them vineyards and fields at the same time.

Jeremiah Goes Free

11Now Nebuchadnezzar king of Babylon
gave charge concerning Jeremiah to Nebuzaradan the captain of the guard, saying,
12"Take him and look after him, and do him no
[a]harm; but do to him just as he says to you."
13So Nebuzaradan the captain of the guard
sent Nebushasban, Rabsaris, Nergal-Sharezer,
Rabmag, and all the king of Babylon's chief
officers; 14then they sent *someone* [a]to take
Jeremiah from the court of the prison, and
committed him [b]to Gedaliah the son of [c]Ahi-
kam, the son of Shaphan, that he should take
him home. So he dwelt among the people.
15Meanwhile the word of the LORD had
come to Jeremiah while he was shut up in the
court of the prison, saying, 16"Go and speak
to [a]Ebed-Melech the Ethiopian, saying, 'Thus
says the LORD of hosts, the God of Israel:
"Behold, [b]I will bring My words upon this city
for adversity and not for good, and they shall
be *performed* in that day before you. 17But I
will deliver you in that day," says the LORD,
"and you shall not be given into the hand of
the men of whom you *are* afraid. 18For I will
surely deliver you, and you shall not fall by
the sword; but [a]your life shall be as a prize
to you, [b]because you have put your trust in
Me," says the LORD.' "

Jeremiah with Gedaliah the Governor

40 The word that came to Jeremiah from
the LORD [a]after Nebuzaradan the captain of the guard had let him go from Ramah,
when he had taken him bound in chains
among all who were carried away captive
from Jerusalem and Judah, who were carried
away captive to Babylon.
2And the captain of the guard took Jeremiah and [a]said to him: "The LORD your God has
pronounced this doom on this place. 3Now the
LORD has brought *it,* and has done just as He
said. [a]Because you *people* have sinned against
the LORD, and not obeyed His voice, therefore
this thing has come upon you. 4And now look,
I free you this day from the chains that *were*
on your hand. [a]If it seems good to you to come
with me to Babylon, come, and I will look after
you. But if it seems wrong for you to come with
me to Babylon, remain here. See, [b]all the land
is before you; wherever it seems good and
convenient for you to go, go there."
5Now while Jeremiah had not yet gone back,
Nebuzaradan said, "Go back to [a]Gedaliah the
son of Ahikam, the son of Shaphan, [b]whom
the king of Babylon has made governor over
the cities of Judah, and dwell with him among
the people. Or go wherever it seems convenient for you to go." So the captain of the
guard gave him rations and a gift and let him
go. 6[a]Then Jeremiah went to Gedaliah the son
of Ahikam, to [b]Mizpah, and dwelt with him
among the people who were left in the land.
7[a]And when all the captains of the armies
who *were* in the fields, they and their men,
heard that the king of Babylon had made Gedaliah the son of Ahikam governor in the land,
and had committed to him men, women, children, and [b]the poorest of the land who had not
been carried away captive to Babylon, 8then
they came to Gedaliah at Mizpah—[a]Ishmael
the son of Nethaniah, [b]Johanan and Jonathan
the sons of Kareah, Seraiah the son of Tanhumeth, the sons of Ephai the Netophathite,
and [c]Jezaniah[1] the son of a [d]Maachathite, they
and their men. 9And Gedaliah the son of Ahikam, the son of Shaphan, took an oath before
them and their men, saying, "Do not be afraid
to serve the Chaldeans. Dwell in the land and
serve the king of Babylon, and it shall be [a]well
with you. 10As for me, I will indeed dwell at
Mizpah and serve the Chaldeans who come
to us. But you, gather wine and summer fruit
and oil, put *them* in your vessels, and dwell in
your cities that you have taken." 11Likewise,
when all the Jews who *were* in Moab, among
the Ammonites, in Edom, and who *were* in all
the countries, heard that the king of Babylon
had left a remnant of Judah, and that he had
set over them Gedaliah the son of Ahikam, the

39:6 [a] Deut. 28:34 [b] Jer. 34:19–21 **39:7** [a] Ezek. 12:13 **39:8** [a] 2 Kin. 25:9 [b] Jer. 21:10 [c] Neh. 1:3 **39:9** [a] 2 Kin. 25:8, 11, 12, 20 [b] Jer. 38:19 **39:10** [a] Jer. 40:7 **39:12** [a] Jer. 1:18, 19; 15:20, 21 **39:14** [a] Jer. 38:28 [b] Jer. 40:5 [c] Jer. 26:24 **39:16** [a] Jer. 38:7, 12 [b] [Dan. 9:12] **39:18** [a] Jer. 21:9; 45:5 [b] Ps. 37:40 **40:1** [a] Jer. 39:9, 11 **40:2** [a] Jer. 50:7 **40:3** [a] Dan. 9:11 **40:4** [a] Jer. 39:12 [b] Gen. 20:15 **40:5** [a] Jer. 39:14 [b] Jer. 41:10 **40:6** [a] Jer. 39:14 [b] Judg. 20:1 **40:7** [a] 2 Kin. 25:23, 24 [b] Jer. 39:10 **40:8** [a] Jer. 41:1–10 [b] Jer. 41:11; 43:2 [c] Jer. 42:1 [d] Deut. 3:14 [1] Spelled *Jaazaniah* in 2 Kings 25:23 **40:9** [a] Jer. 27:11; 38:17–20

son of Shaphan, 12then all the Jews [a]returned
out of all places where they had been driven,
and came to the land of Judah, to Gedaliah
at Mizpah, and gathered wine and summer
fruit in abundance.
13Moreover Johanan the son of Kareah and
all the captains of the forces that *were* in the
fields came to Gedaliah at Mizpah, 14and said
to him, "Do you certainly know that [a]Baalis the
king of the Ammonites has sent Ishmael the
son of Nethaniah to murder you?" But Gedaliah the son of Ahikam did not believe them.
15Then Johanan the son of Kareah spoke
secretly to Gedaliah in Mizpah, saying, "Let
me go, please, and I will kill Ishmael the son
of Nethaniah, and no one will know *it.* Why
should he murder you, so that all the Jews
who are gathered to you would be scattered,
and the [a]remnant in Judah perish?"
16But Gedaliah the son of Ahikam said to
Johanan the son of Kareah, "You shall not do
this thing, for you speak falsely concerning
Ishmael."

Insurrection Against Gedaliah

41 Now it came to pass in the seventh
month [a]*that* Ishmael the son of Nethaniah, the son of Elishama, of the royal family
and of the officers of the king, came with
ten men to Gedaliah the son of Ahikam, at
[b]Mizpah. And there they ate bread together in
Mizpah. 2Then Ishmael the son of Nethaniah,
and the ten men who were with him, arose
and [a]struck Gedaliah the son of [b]Ahikam, the
son of Shaphan, with the sword, and killed
him whom the king of Babylon had made
[c]governor over the land. 3Ishmael also struck
down all the Jews who were with him, *that is,*
with Gedaliah at Mizpah, and the Chaldeans
who were found there, the men of war.
4And it happened, on the second day after he had killed Gedaliah, when as yet no
one knew *it,* 5that certain men came from
Shechem, from Shiloh, and from Samaria,
eighty men [a]with their beards shaved and
their clothes torn, having cut themselves,
with offerings and incense in their hand, to
bring *them* to [b]the house of the LORD. 6Now
Ishmael the son of Nethaniah went out from
Mizpah to meet them, weeping as he went
along; and it happened as he met them that
he said to them, "Come to Gedaliah the son
of Ahikam!" 7So it was, when they came into
the midst of the city, that Ishmael the son of
Nethaniah [a]killed them *and cast them* into the
midst of a pit, he and the men who were with
him. 8But ten men were found among them
who said to Ishmael, "Do not kill us, for we
have treasures of wheat, barley, oil, and honey
in the field." So he desisted and did not kill
them among their brethren. 9Now the pit into
which Ishmael had cast all the dead bodies
of the men whom he had slain, because of
Gedaliah, *was* [a]the same one Asa the king
had made for fear of Baasha king of Israel.
Ishmael the son of Nethaniah filled it with *the*
slain. 10Then Ishmael carried away captive all
the [a]rest of the people who *were* in Mizpah,
[b]the king's daughters and all the people who
remained in Mizpah, [c]whom Nebuzaradan
the captain of the guard had committed to
Gedaliah the son of Ahikam. And Ishmael the
son of Nethaniah carried them away captive
and departed to go over to [d]the Ammonites.
11But when [a]Johanan the son of Kareah
and all the captains of the forces that *were*
with him heard of all the evil that Ishmael
the son of Nethaniah had done, 12they took
all the men and went to fight with Ishmael
the son of Nethaniah; and they found him by
[a]the great pool that *is* in Gibeon. 13So it was,
when all the people who *were* with Ishmael
saw Johanan the son of Kareah, and all the
captains of the forces who *were* with him, that
they were glad. 14Then all the people whom
Ishmael had carried away captive from Mizpah turned around and came back, and went
to Johanan the son of Kareah. 15But Ishmael
the son of Nethaniah escaped from Johanan
with eight men and went to the Ammonites.
16Then Johanan the son of Kareah, and all
the captains of the forces that were with him,
took from Mizpah all the [a]rest of the people
whom he had recovered from Ishmael the
son of Nethaniah after he had murdered Gedaliah the son of Ahikam—the mighty men of
war and the women and the children and the
eunuchs, whom he had brought back from
Gibeon. 17And they departed and dwelt in the
habitation of [a]Chimham, which is near Bethlehem, as they went on their way to [b]Egypt,
18because of the Chaldeans; for they were
afraid of them, because Ishmael the son of
Nethaniah had murdered Gedaliah the son
of Ahikam, [a]whom the king of Babylon had
made governor in the land.

The Flight to Egypt Forbidden

42 Now all the captains of the forces,
[a]Johanan the son of Kareah, Jezaniah
the son of Hoshaiah, and all the people, from
the least to the greatest, came near 2and said

40:12 [a] Jer. 43:5 **40:14** [a] Jer. 41:10 **40:15** [a] Jer. 42:2 **41:1** [a] 2 Kin. 25:25 [b] Jer. 40:6, 10 **41:2** [a] 2 Kin. 25:25 [b] Jer. 26:24 [c] Jer. 40:5 **41:5** [a] Deut. 14:1 [b] 1 Sam. 1:7 **41:7** [a] Ps. 55:23 **41:9** [a] 1 Kin. 15:22 **41:10** [a] Jer. 40:11, 12 [b] Jer. 43:6 [c] Jer. 40:7 [d] Jer. 40:14 **41:11** [a] Jer. 40:7, 8, 13–16 **41:12** [a] 2 Sam. 2:13 **41:16** [a] Jer. 40:11, 12; 43:4–7 **41:17** [a] 2 Sam. 19:37, 38 [b] Jer. 43:7 **41:18** [a] Jer. 40:5 **42:1** [a] Jer. 40:8, 13; 41:11

to Jeremiah the prophet, [a]"Please, let our
petition be acceptable to you, and [b]pray for
us to the LORD your God, for all this remnant
(since we are left *but* [c]a few of many, as you
can see), 3that the LORD your God may show
us [a]the way in which we should walk and the
thing we should do."
4Then Jeremiah the prophet said to them,
"I have heard. Indeed, I will pray to the LORD
your God according to your words, and it shall
be, *that* [a]whatever the LORD answers you, I
will declare *it* to you. I will [b]keep nothing
back from you."
5So they said to Jeremiah, [a]"Let the LORD
be a true and faithful witness between us, if
we do not do according to everything which
the LORD your God sends us by you. 6Whether
it is pleasing or displeasing, we will [a]obey the
voice of the LORD our God to whom we send
you, [b]that it may be well with us when we obey
the voice of the LORD our God."
7And it happened after ten days that the
word of the LORD came to Jeremiah. 8Then
he called Johanan the son of Kareah, all the
captains of the forces which *were* with him,
and all the people from the least even to the
greatest, 9and said to them, "Thus says the
LORD, the God of Israel, to whom you sent me
to present your petition before Him: 10'If you
will still remain in this land, then [a]I will build
you and not pull *you* down, and I will plant you
and not pluck *you* up. For I [b]relent concerning
the disaster that I have brought upon you. 11Do
not be afraid of the king of Babylon, of whom
you are afraid; do not be afraid of him,' says
the LORD, [a]'for I *am* with you, to save you and
deliver you from his hand. 12And [a]I will show

PEACE NOTE

When Jeremiah interceded on behalf of the Lord's people, God did not answer for ten days. The peace of God gives us the patience to wait on God. Let Him answer in His time.

JEREMIAH 42:7

you mercy, that he may have mercy on you
and cause you to return to your own land.'
13"But if [a]you say, 'We will not dwell in this
land,' disobeying the voice of the LORD your
God, 14saying, 'No, but we will go to the land of
[a]Egypt where we shall see no war, nor hear the
sound of the trumpet, nor be hungry for bread,
and there we will dwell'— 15Then hear now the
word of the LORD, O remnant of Judah! Thus
says the LORD of hosts, the God of Israel: 'If
you [a]wholly set [b]your faces to enter Egypt,
and go to dwell there, 16then it shall be *that*
the [a]sword which you feared shall overtake
you there in the land of Egypt; the famine of
which you were afraid shall follow close after
you there *in* Egypt; and there you shall die.
17So shall it be with all the men who set their
faces to go to Egypt to dwell there. They shall
die by the sword, by famine, and by pestilence.
And [a]none of them shall remain or escape
from the disaster that I will bring upon them.'
18"For thus says the LORD of hosts, the God
of Israel: 'As My anger and My fury have been
[a]poured out on the inhabitants of Jerusalem,
so will My fury be poured out on you when
you enter Egypt. And [b]you shall be an oath,
an astonishment, a curse, and a reproach;
and you shall see this place no more.'
19"The LORD has said concerning you,
O remnant of Judah, [a]'Do not go to Egypt!'
Know certainly that I have admonished you
this day. 20For you were hypocrites in your
hearts when you sent me to the LORD your
God, saying, 'Pray for us to the LORD our
God, and according to all that the LORD your
God says, so declare to us and we will do *it*.'
21And I have this day declared *it* to you, but
you have [a]not obeyed the voice of the LORD
your God, or anything which He has sent you
by me. 22Now therefore, know certainly that
you [a]shall die by the sword, by famine, and
by pestilence in the place where you desire
to go to dwell."

Jeremiah Taken to Egypt

43 Now it happened, when Jeremiah had
stopped speaking to all the people all
the [a]words of the LORD their God, for which the
LORD their God had sent him to them, all these
words, 2[a]that Azariah the son of Hoshaiah,
Johanan the son of Kareah, and all the proud
men spoke, saying to Jeremiah, "You speak
falsely! The LORD our God has not sent you to
say, 'Do not go to Egypt to dwell there.' 3But
[a]Baruch the son of Neriah has set you against
us, to deliver us into the hand of the Chaldeans,

42:2 [a] Jer. 15:11 [b] Is. 37:4 [c] Lev. 26:22 **42:3** [a] Ezra 8:21 **42:4** [a] 1 Kin. 22:14 [b] 1 Sam. 3:17, 18 **42:5** [a] Gen. 31:50 **42:6** [a] Ex. 24:7 [b] Jer. 7:23 **42:10** [a] Jer. 24:6; 31:28; 33:7 [b] [Jer. 18:8] **42:11** [a] Rom. 8:31 **42:12** [a] Ps. 106:46 **42:13** [a] Jer. 44:16 **42:14** [a] Jer. 41:17; 43:7 **42:15** [a] Deut. 17:16 [b] Luke 9:51 **42:16** [a] Ezek. 11:8 **42:17** [a] Jer. 44:14, 28 **42:18** [a] Jer. 7:20 [b] Is. 65:15 **42:19** [a] Deut. 17:16 **42:21** [a] Is. 30:1–7 **42:22** [a] Ezek. 6:11 **43:1** [a] Jer. 42:9–18 **43:2** [a] Jer. 42:1 **43:3** [a] Jer. 36:4; 45:1

that they may put us to death or carry us away captive to Babylon." 4So Johanan the son of Kareah, all the captains of the forces, and all the people would [a]not obey the voice of the LORD, to remain in the land of Judah. 5But Johanan the son of Kareah and all the captains of the forces took [a]all the remnant of Judah who had returned to dwell in the land of Judah, from all nations where they had been driven— 6men, women, children, [a]the king's daughters, [b]and every person whom Nebuzaradan the captain of the guard had left with Gedaliah the son of Ahikam, the son of Shaphan, and Jeremiah the prophet and Baruch the son of Neriah. 7[a]So they went to the land of Egypt, for they did not obey the voice of the LORD. And they went as far as [b]Tahpanhes.

8Then the [a]word of the LORD came to Jeremiah in Tahpanhes, saying, 9"Take large stones in your hand, and hide them in the sight of the men of Judah, in the clay in the brick courtyard which *is* at the entrance to Pharaoh's house in Tahpanhes; 10and say to them, 'Thus says the LORD of hosts, the God of Israel: "Behold, I will send and bring Nebuchadnezzar the king of Babylon, [a]My servant, and will set his throne above these stones that I have hidden. And he will spread his royal pavilion over them. 11[a]When he comes, he shall strike the land of Egypt *and deliver* to death [b]*those appointed* for death, and to captivity *those appointed* for captivity, and to the sword *those appointed* for the sword. 12I[1] will kindle a fire in the houses of [a]the gods of Egypt, and he shall burn them and carry them away captive. And he shall array himself with the land of Egypt, as a shepherd puts on his garment, and he shall go out from there in peace. 13He shall also break the *sacred* pillars of Beth Shemesh[1] that *are* in the land of Egypt; and the houses of the gods of the Egyptians he shall burn with fire." ' "

Israelites Will Be Punished in Egypt

44 The word that came to Jeremiah concerning all the Jews who dwell in the land of Egypt, who dwell at [a]Migdol, at [b]Tahpanhes, at [c]Noph,[1] and in the country of [d]Pathros, saying, 2"Thus says the LORD of hosts, the God of Israel: 'You have seen all the calamity that I have brought on Jerusalem and on all the cities of Judah; and behold, this day they *are* [a]a desolation, and no one dwells in them, 3because of their wickedness which they have committed to provoke Me to anger, in that they went [a]to burn incense *and* to [b]serve other gods whom they did not know, they nor you nor your fathers. 4However [a]I have sent to you all My servants the prophets, rising early and sending *them,* saying, "Oh, do not do this abominable thing that I hate!" 5But they did not listen or incline their ear to turn from their wickedness, to burn no incense to other gods. 6So My fury and My anger were poured out and kindled in the cities of Judah and in the streets of Jerusalem; and they are wasted *and* desolate, as it is this day.'

7"Now therefore, thus says the LORD, the God of hosts, the God of Israel: 'Why do you commit *this* great evil [a]against yourselves, to cut off from you man and woman, child and infant, out of Judah, leaving none to remain, 8in that you [a]provoke Me to wrath with the works of your hands, burning incense to other gods in the land of Egypt where you have gone to dwell, that you may cut yourselves off and be [b]a curse and a reproach among all the nations of the earth? 9Have you forgotten the wickedness of your fathers, the wickedness of the kings of Judah, the wickedness of their wives, your own wickedness, and the wickedness of your wives, which they committed in the land of Judah and in the streets of Jerusalem? 10They have not been [a]humbled, to this day, nor have they [b]feared; they have not walked in My law or in My statutes that I set before you and your fathers.'

11"Therefore thus says the LORD of hosts, the God of Israel: 'Behold, [a]I will set My face against you for catastrophe and for cutting off all Judah. 12And I will take the remnant of Judah who have set their faces to go into the land of Egypt to dwell there, and [a]they shall all be consumed *and* fall in the land of Egypt. They shall be consumed by the sword *and* by famine. They shall die, from the least to the greatest, by the sword and by famine; and [b]they shall be an oath, an astonishment, a curse and a reproach! 13[a]For I will punish those who dwell in the land of Egypt, as I have punished Jerusalem, by the sword, by famine, and by pestilence, 14so that none of the remnant of Judah who have gone into the land of Egypt to dwell there shall escape or survive, lest they return to the land of Judah, to which they [a]desire to return and dwell. For [b]none shall return except those who escape.' "

43:4 [a] 2 Kin. 25:26 **43:5** [a] Jer. 40:11, 12 **43:6** [a] Jer. 41:10 [b] Jer. 39:10; 40:7 **43:7** [a] Jer. 42:19 [b] Jer. 2:16; 44:1 **43:8** [a] Jer. 44:1–30 **43:10** [a] Jer. 25:9; 27:6 **43:11** [a] Jer. 25:15–19; 44:13; 46:1, 2, 13–26 [b] Jer. 15:2 **43:12** [a] Jer. 46:25 [1] Following Masoretic Text and Targum; Septuagint, Syriac, and Vulgate read *He.* **43:13** [1] Literally *House of the Sun,* ancient On; later called Heliopolis **44:1** [a] Jer. 46:14 [b] Jer. 43:7 [c] Is. 19:13 [d] Ezek. 29:14; 30:14 [1] That is, ancient Memphis **44:2** [a] Jer. 4:7; 9:11; 34:22 **44:3** [a] Jer. 19:4 [b] Deut. 13:6; 32:17 **44:4** [a] Jer. 7:25; 25:4; 26:5; 29:19 **44:7** [a] Num. 16:38 **44:8** [a] Jer. 25:6, 7; 44:3 [b] Jer. 42:18 **44:10** [a] Jer. 6:15; 8:12 [b] [Prov. 28:14] **44:11** [a] Amos 9:4 **44:12** [a] Jer. 42:15–17, 22 [b] Is. 65:15 **44:13** [a] Jer. 43:11 **44:14** [a] Jer. 22:26, 27 [b] Jer. 44:28

15Then all the men who knew that their
wives had burned incense to other gods, with
all the women who stood by, a great multitude, and all the people who dwelt in the land
of Egypt, in Pathros, answered Jeremiah, saying: 16"*As for* the word that you have spoken
to us in the name of the LORD, [a]we will not
listen to you! 17But we will certainly do [a]what-
ever has gone out of our own mouth, to burn
incense to the [b]queen of heaven and pour out
drink offerings to her, as we have done, we
and our fathers, our kings and our princes,
in the cities of Judah and in the streets of
Jerusalem. For *then* we had plenty of food,
were well-off, and saw no trouble. 18But since
we stopped burning incense to the queen
of heaven and pouring out drink offerings
to her, we have lacked everything and have
been consumed by the sword and by famine."
19*The women also said,* [a]"And when we
burned incense to the queen of heaven and
poured out drink offerings to her, did we
make cakes for her, to worship her, and pour
out drink offerings to her without our husbands' *permission?*"
20Then Jeremiah spoke to all the people—
the men, the women, and all the people who
had given him *that* answer—saying: 21"The
incense that you burned in the cities of Judah
and in the streets of Jerusalem, you and your
fathers, your kings and your princes, and
the people of the land, did not the LORD
remember them, and did it *not* come into
His mind? 22So the LORD could no longer
bear *it,* because of the evil of your doings
and because of the abominations which you
committed. Therefore your land is a desolation, an astonishment, a curse, and without
an inhabitant, [a]as *it is* this day. 23Because
you have burned incense and because you
have sinned against the LORD, and have not
obeyed the voice of the LORD or walked in
His law, in His statutes or in His testimonies,
[a]therefore this calamity has happened to
you, as *at* this day."
24Moreover Jeremiah said to all the people
and to all the women, "Hear the word of the
LORD, all Judah who *are* in the land of Egypt!
25Thus says the LORD of hosts, the God of Israel, *saying:* 'You and your wives have spoken
with your mouths and fulfilled with your
hands, saying, "We will surely keep our vows
that we have made, to burn incense to the
queen of heaven and pour out drink offerings
to her." You will surely keep your vows and
perform your vows!' 26Therefore hear the
word of the LORD, all Judah who dwell in the
land of Egypt: 'Behold, [a]I have sworn by My
[b]great name,' says the LORD, 'that [c]My name
shall no more be named in the mouth of any
man of Judah in all the land of Egypt, saying,
"The Lord GOD lives." 27Behold, I will watch
over them for adversity and not for good. And
all the men of Judah who *are* in the land of
Egypt [a]shall be consumed by the sword and
by famine, until there is an end to them. 28Yet
[a]a small number who escape the sword shall
return from the land of Egypt to the land of
Judah; and all the remnant of Judah, who
have gone to the land of Egypt to dwell there,
shall know whose words will stand, Mine or
theirs. 29And this *shall be* a sign to you,' says
the LORD, 'that I will punish you in this place,
that you may know that My words will surely
[a]stand against you for adversity.'
30"Thus says the LORD: 'Behold, [a]I will give
Pharaoh Hophra king of Egypt into the hand
of his enemies and into the hand of those
who seek his life, as I gave [b]Zedekiah king of
Judah into the hand of Nebuchadnezzar king
of Babylon, his enemy who sought his life.' "

Assurance to Baruch

45 The [a]word that Jeremiah the prophet
spoke to [b]Baruch the son of Neriah,
when he had written these words in a book
at the instruction of Jeremiah,[1] in the [c]fourth
year of Jehoiakim the son of Josiah, king of
Judah, saying, 2"Thus says the LORD, the God
of Israel, to you, O Baruch: 3'You said, "Woe
is me now! For the LORD has added grief to
my sorrow. I [a]fainted in my sighing, and I
find no rest." '

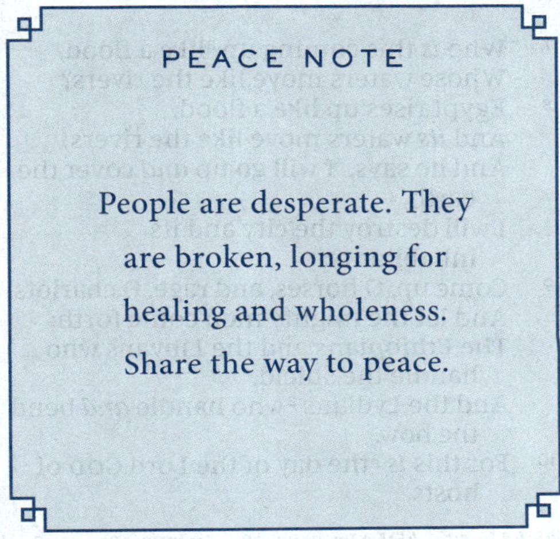

44:16 [a] Jer. 6:16 **44:17** [a] Num. 30:12 [b] Jer. 7:18 **44:19** [a] Jer. 7:18 **44:22** [a] Jer. 25:11, 18, 38 **44:23** [a] Dan. 9:11, 12
44:26 [a] Heb. 6:13 [b] Jer. 10:6 [c] Ezek. 20:39 **44:27** [a] Ezek. 7:6 **44:28** [a] Is. 10:19; 27:12, 13 **44:29** [a] [Ps. 33:11]
44:30 [a] Ezek. 29:3; 30:21 [b] Jer. 39:5 **45:1** [a] Jer. 36:1, 4, 32 [b] Jer. 32:12, 16; 43:3 [c] Jer. 25:1; 36:1; 46:2 [1] Literally *from Jeremiah's mouth* **45:3** [a] Ps. 6:6; 69:3

4"Thus you shall say to him, 'Thus says the
LORD: "Behold, [a]what I have built I will break
down, and what I have planted I will pluck
up, that is, this whole land. 5And do you seek
great things for yourself? Do not seek *them;*
for behold, [a]I will bring adversity on all flesh,"
says the LORD. "But I will give your [b]life to you
as a prize in all places, wherever you go." ' "

Judgment on Egypt

46 The word of the LORD which came to
Jeremiah the prophet against [a]the
nations. 2Against [a]Egypt.
[b]Concerning the army of Pharaoh Necho,
king of Egypt, which was by the River Euphrates in Carchemish, and which Nebuchadnezzar king of Babylon [c]defeated in the
[d]fourth year of Jehoiakim the son of Josiah,
king of Judah:

3 "Order the buckler and shield,
And draw near to battle!
4 Harness the horses,
And mount up, you horsemen!
Stand forth with *your* helmets,
Polish the spears,
[a]Put on the armor!
5 Why have I seen them dismayed *and*
turned back?
Their mighty ones are beaten down;
They have speedily fled,
And did not look back,
For [a]fear *was* all around," says the LORD.
6 "Do not let the swift flee away,
Nor the mighty man escape;
They will [a]stumble and fall
Toward the north, by the River
Euphrates.

7 "Who *is* this coming up [a]like a flood,
Whose waters move like the rivers?
8 Egypt rises up like a flood,
And *its* waters move like the rivers;
And he says, 'I will go up *and* cover the
earth,
I will destroy the city and its
inhabitants.'
9 Come up, O horses, and rage, O chariots!
And let the mighty men come forth:
The Ethiopians and the Libyans who
handle the shield,
And the Lydians [a]who handle *and* bend
the bow.
10 For this *is* [a]the day of the Lord GOD of
hosts,
A day of vengeance,
That He may avenge Himself on His
adversaries.
[b]The sword shall devour;
It shall be satiated and made drunk
with their blood;
For the Lord GOD of hosts [c]has a sacrifice
In the north country by the River
Euphrates.

11 "Go[a] up to Gilead and take balm,
[b]O virgin, the daughter of Egypt;
In vain you will use many medicines;
[c]You shall not be cured.
12 The nations have heard of your [a]shame,
And your cry has filled the land;
For the mighty man has stumbled
against the mighty;
They both have fallen together."

Babylonia Will Strike Egypt

13The word that the LORD spoke to Jeremiah the prophet, how Nebuchadnezzar
king of Babylon would come *and* [a]strike the
land of Egypt.

14 "Declare in Egypt, and proclaim in [a]Migdol;
Proclaim in Noph[1] and in [b]Tahpanhes;
Say, 'Stand fast and prepare yourselves,
For the sword devours all around you.'
15 Why are your valiant *men* swept away?
They did not stand
Because the LORD drove them away.
16 He made many fall;
Yes, [a]one fell upon another.
And they said, 'Arise!
[b]Let us go back to our own people
And to the land of our nativity
From the oppressing sword.'
17 They cried there,
'Pharaoh, king of Egypt, *is but* a noise.
He has passed by the appointed time!'

18 "*As* I live," says the King,
[a]Whose name *is* the LORD of hosts,
"Surely as Tabor *is* among the mountains
And as Carmel by the sea, *so* he shall come.
19 O [a]you daughter dwelling in Egypt,
Prepare yourself [b]to go into captivity!
For Noph[1] shall be waste and desolate,
without inhabitant.

20 "Egypt *is* a very pretty [a]heifer,
But destruction comes, it comes [b]from
the north.

45:4 [a] Is. 5:5 **45:5** [a] Jer. 25:17–26 [b] Jer. 21:9; 38:2; 39:18 **46:1** [a] Jer. 25:15 **46:2** [a] Jer. 25:17–19 [b] 2 Kin. 23:33–35 [c] 2 Chr. 35:20 [d] Jer. 45:1 **46:4** [a] Jer. 51:11, 12 **46:5** [a] Jer. 49:29 **46:6** [a] Dan. 11:19 **46:7** [a] Jer. 47:2 **46:9** [a] Is. 66:19 **46:10** [a] Joel 1:15 [b] Deut. 32:42 [c] Is. 34:6 **46:11** [a] Jer. 8:22 [b] Is. 47:1 [c] Ezek. 30:21 **46:12** [a] Jer. 2:36 **46:13** [a] Is. 19:1 **46:14** [a] Jer. 44:1 [b] Ezek. 30:18 [1] That is, ancient Memphis **46:16** [a] Lev. 26:36, 37 [b] Jer. 51:9 **46:18** [a] Jer. 48:15 **46:19** [a] Jer. 48:18 [b] Is. 20:4 [1] That is, ancient Memphis **46:20** [a] Hos. 10:11 [b] Jer. 1:14

21 Also her mercenaries are in her midst
like fat bulls,
For they also are turned back,
They have fled away together.
They did not stand,
For [a]the day of their calamity had come
upon them,
The time of their punishment.
22 [a]Her noise shall go like a serpent,
For they shall march with an army
And come against her with axes,
Like those who chop wood.

23 "They shall [a]cut down her forest," says
the LORD,
"Though it cannot be searched,
Because they *are* innumerable,
And more numerous than
[b]grasshoppers.
24 The daughter of Egypt shall be
ashamed;
She shall be delivered into the hand
Of [a]the people of the north."

25The LORD of hosts, the God of Israel, says:
"Behold, I will bring punishment on Amon[1]
of [a]No,[2] and Pharaoh and Egypt, [b]with their
gods and their kings—Pharaoh and those
who [c]trust in him. 26[a]And I will deliver them
into the hand of those who seek their lives,
into the hand of Nebuchadnezzar king of
Babylon and the hand of his servants. [b]Af-
terward it shall be inhabited as in the days
of old," says the LORD.

God Will Preserve Israel

27 "But[a] do not fear, O My servant Jacob,
And do not be dismayed, O Israel!
For behold, I will [b]save you from afar,
And your offspring from the land of
their captivity;
Jacob shall return, have rest and be at
ease;
No one shall make *him* afraid.
28 Do not fear, O Jacob My servant," says
the LORD,
"For I *am* with you;
For I will make a complete end of all
the nations
To which I have driven you,
But I will not make [a]a complete end of
you.
I will rightly [b]correct you,
For I will not leave you wholly
unpunished."

Judgment on Philistia

47 The word of the LORD that came
to Jeremiah the prophet [a]against
the Philistines, [b]before Pharaoh attacked
Gaza.
2Thus says the LORD:

"Behold, [a]waters rise [b]out of the north,
And shall be an overflowing flood;
They shall overflow the land and all
that is in it,
The city and those who dwell within;
Then the men shall cry,
And all the inhabitants of the land
shall wail.
3 At the [a]noise of the stamping hooves of
his strong horses,
At the rushing of his chariots,
At the rumbling of his wheels,
The fathers will not look back for *their*
children,
Lacking courage,
4 Because of the day that comes to
plunder all the [a]Philistines,
To cut off from [b]Tyre and Sidon every
helper who remains;
For the LORD shall plunder the
Philistines,
[c]The remnant of the country of
[d]Caphtor.
5 [a]Baldness has come upon Gaza,
[b]Ashkelon is cut off
With the remnant of their valley.
How long will you cut yourself?

6 "O you [a]sword of the LORD,
How long until you are quiet?
Put yourself up into your scabbard,
Rest and be still!
7 How can it be quiet,
Seeing the LORD has [a]given it a charge
Against Ashkelon and against the
seashore?
There He has [b]appointed it."

Judgment on Moab

48 Against [a]Moab.
Thus says the LORD of hosts, the God
of Israel:

"Woe to [b]Nebo!
For it is plundered,
[c]Kirjathaim is shamed *and* taken;
The high stronghold[1] is shamed and
dismayed—

46:21 [a] [Ps. 37:13] **46:22** [a] [Is. 29:4] **46:23** [a] Is. 10:34 [b] Judg. 6:5; 7:12 **46:24** [a] Jer. 1:15 **46:25** [a] Ezek. 30:14–16 [b] Jer. 43:12, 13 [c] Is. 30:1–5; 31:1–3 [1] A sun god [2] That is, ancient Thebes **46:26** [a] Ezek. 32:11 [b] Ezek. 29:8–14 **46:27** [a] Is. 41:13, 14; 43:5; 44:2 [b] Is. 11:11 **46:28** [a] Amos 9:8, 9 [b] Jer. 30:11 **47:1** [a] Zeph. 2:4, 5 [b] Amos 1:6 **47:2** [a] Is. 8:7, 8 [b] Jer. 1:14 **47:3** [a] Jer. 8:16 **47:4** [a] Is. 14:29–31 [b] Jer. 25:22 [c] Ezek. 25:16 [d] Gen. 10:14 **47:5** [a] Mic. 1:16 [b] Jer. 25:20 **47:6** [a] Ezek. 21:3–5 **47:7** [a] Ezek. 14:17 [b] Mic. 6:9 **48:1** [a] Is. 15:1—16:14; 25:10 [b] Is. 15:2 [c] Num. 32:37 [1] Hebrew *Misgab*

PEACE NOTE

There are differences between spiritual struggles, human weaknesses, and mental illness. We can bring comfort, peace, and encouragement to people's lives.

2 [a]No more praise of Moab.
In [b]Heshbon they have devised evil
against her:
'Come, and let us cut her off as a nation.'
You also shall be cut down, O [c]Madmen![1]
The sword shall pursue you;
3 A voice of crying *shall be* from
[a]Horonaim:
'Plundering and great
destruction!'

4 "Moab is destroyed;
Her little ones have caused a cry to be
heard;[1]
5 [a]For in the Ascent of Luhith they ascend
with continual weeping;
For in the descent of Horonaim
the enemies have heard a cry of
destruction.

6 "Flee, save your lives!
And be like the [a]juniper[1] in the
wilderness.
7 For because you have trusted in your
works and your [a]treasures,
You also shall be taken.
And [b]Chemosh shall go forth into
captivity,
His [c]priests and his princes together.
8 And [a]the plunderer shall come against
every city;
No one shall escape.
The valley also shall perish,
And the plain shall be destroyed,
As the LORD has spoken.

9 "Give[a] wings to Moab,
That she may flee and get away;
For her cities shall be desolate,
Without any to dwell in them.
10 [a]Cursed *is* he who does the work of the
LORD deceitfully,
And cursed *is* he who keeps back his
sword from blood.

11 "Moab has been at ease from his[1] youth;
He [a]has settled on his dregs,
And has not been emptied from vessel
to vessel,
Nor has he gone into captivity.
Therefore his taste remained in him,
And his scent has not changed.

12 "Therefore behold, the days are
coming," says the LORD,
"That I shall send him wine-workers
Who will tip him over
And empty his vessels
And break the bottles.
13 Moab shall be ashamed of [a]Chemosh,
As the house of Israel [b]was ashamed of
[c]Bethel, their confidence.

14 "How can you say, [a]'We *are* mighty
And strong men for the war'?
15 Moab is plundered and gone up *from*
her cities;
Her chosen young men have [a]gone
down to the slaughter," says [b]the King,
Whose name *is* the LORD of hosts.

16 "The calamity of Moab *is* near at hand,
And his affliction comes quickly.
17 Bemoan him, all you who are around
him;
And all you who know his name,
Say, [a]'How the strong staff is broken,
The beautiful rod!'

18 "O [a]daughter inhabiting [b]Dibon,
Come down from *your* glory,
And sit in thirst;
For the plunderer of Moab has come
against you,
He has destroyed your strongholds.
19 O inhabitant of [a]Aroer,
[b]Stand by the way and watch;
Ask him who flees
And her who escapes;
Say, 'What has happened?'

48:2 [a] Is. 16:14 [b] Jer. 49:3 [c] Is. 10:31 [1] A city of Moab **48:3** [a] Is. 15:5 **48:4** [1] Following Masoretic Text, Targum, and Vulgate; Septuagint reads *Proclaim it in Zoar.* **48:5** [a] Is. 15:5 **48:6** [a] Jer. 17:6 [1] Or *Aroer,* a city of Moab **48:7** [a] Jer. 9:23 [b] Jer. 48:13 [c] Jer. 49:3 **48:8** [a] Jer. 6:26 **48:9** [a] Ps. 55:6 **48:10** [a] 1 Sam. 15:3, 9 **48:11** [a] Zeph. 1:12 [1] The Hebrew uses masculine and feminine pronouns interchangeably in this chapter. **48:13** [a] 1 Kin. 11:7 [b] Hos. 10:6 [c] 1 Kin. 12:29; 13:32–34 **48:14** [a] Is. 16:6 **48:15** [a] Jer. 50:27 [b] Jer. 46:18; 51:57 **48:17** [a] Is. 9:4; 14:4, 5 **48:18** [a] Is. 47:1 [b] Is. 15:2 **48:19** [a] Deut. 2:36 [b] 1 Sam. 4:13, 14, 16

20 Moab is shamed, for he is broken down.
[a]Wail and cry!
Tell it in [b]Arnon, that Moab is plundered.

21 "And judgment has come on the plain country:
On Holon and Jahzah and Mephaath,
22 On Dibon and Nebo and Beth Diblathaim,
23 On Kirjathaim and Beth Gamul and Beth Meon,
24 On [a]Kerioth and Bozrah,
On all the cities of the land of Moab,
Far or near.
25 [a]The horn of Moab is cut off,
And his [b]arm is broken," says the LORD.

26 "Make[a] him drunk,
Because he exalted *himself* against the LORD.
Moab shall wallow in his vomit,
And he shall also be in derision.
27 For [a]was not Israel a derision to you?
[b]Was he found among thieves?
For whenever you speak of him,
You shake *your head in* [c]*scorn.*
28 You who dwell in Moab,
Leave the cities and [a]dwell in the rock,
And be like [b]the dove *which* makes her nest
In the sides of the cave's mouth.

29 "We have heard the [a]pride of Moab
(He *is* exceedingly proud),
Of his loftiness and arrogance and [b]pride,
And of the haughtiness of his heart."

30 "I know his wrath," says the LORD,
"But it *is* not right;
[a]His lies have made nothing right.
31 Therefore [a]I will wail for Moab,
And I will cry out for all Moab;
I[1] will mourn for the men of Kir Heres.
32 [a]O vine of Sibmah! I will weep for you with the weeping of [b]Jazer.
Your plants have gone over the sea,
They reach to the sea of Jazer.
The plunderer has fallen on your summer fruit and your vintage.
33 [a]Joy and gladness are taken
From the plentiful field
And from the land of Moab;
I have caused wine to fail from the winepresses;
No one will tread with joyous shouting—
Not joyous shouting!

34 "From[a] the cry of Heshbon to [b]Elealeh and to Jahaz
They have uttered their voice,
[c]From Zoar to Horonaim,
Like a three-year-old heifer;[1]
For the waters of Nimrim also shall be desolate.

35 "Moreover," says the LORD,
"I will cause to cease in Moab
[a]The one who offers *sacrifices* in the high places
And burns incense to his gods.
36 Therefore [a]My heart shall wail like flutes for Moab,
And like flutes My heart shall wail
For the men of Kir Heres.
Therefore [b]the riches they have acquired have perished.

37 "For [a]every head *shall be* bald, and every beard clipped;
On all the hands *shall be* cuts, and [b]on the loins sackcloth—
38 A general lamentation
On all the [a]housetops of Moab,
And in its streets;
For I have [b]broken Moab like a vessel in which *is* no pleasure," says the LORD.
39 "They shall wail:
'How she is broken down!
How Moab has turned her back with shame!'
So Moab shall be a derision
And a dismay to all those about her."

40 For thus says the LORD:

"Behold, [a]one shall fly like an eagle,
And [b]spread his wings over Moab.
41 Kerioth is taken,
And the strongholds are surprised;
[a]The mighty men's hearts in Moab on that day shall be
Like the heart of a woman in birth pangs.
42 And Moab shall be destroyed [a]as a people,
Because he exalted *himself* against the LORD.

48:20 [a] Is. 16:7 [b] Num. 21:13 **48:24** [a] Amos 2:2 **48:25** [a] Ps. 75:10 [b] Ezek. 30:21 **48:26** [a] Jer. 25:15 **48:27** [a] Zeph. 2:8 [b] Jer. 2:26 [c] Lam. 2:15 **48:28** [a] Ps. 55:6, 7 [b] Song 2:14 **48:29** [a] Is. 16:6 [b] Jer. 49:16 **48:30** [a] Jer. 50:36 **48:31** [a] Is. 15:5; 16:7, 11 [1] Following Dead Sea Scrolls, Septuagint, and Vulgate; Masoretic Text reads *He.* **48:32** [a] Is. 16:8, 9 [b] Num. 21:32 **48:33** [a] Joel 1:12 **48:34** [a] Is. 15:4–6 [b] Num. 32:3, 37 [c] Is. 15:5, 6 [1] Or *The Third Eglath,* an unknown city (compare Isaiah 15:5) **48:35** [a] Is. 15:2; 16:12 **48:36** [a] Is. 15:5; 16:11 [b] Is. 15:7 **48:37** [a] Is. 15:2, 3 [b] Gen. 37:34 **48:38** [a] Is. 15:3 [b] Jer. 22:28 **48:40** [a] Deut. 28:49 [b] Is. 8:8 **48:41** [a] Is. 13:8; 21:3 **48:42** [a] Ps. 83:4

43 [a]Fear and the pit and the snare *shall be*
upon you,
O inhabitant of Moab," says the LORD.
44 "He who flees from the fear shall fall
into the pit,
And he who gets out of the pit shall be
caught in the [a]snare.
For upon Moab, upon it [b]I will bring
The year of their punishment," says the
LORD.

45 "Those who fled stood under the
shadow of Heshbon
Because of exhaustion.
But [a]a fire shall come out of Heshbon,
A flame from the midst of [b]Sihon,
And [c]shall devour the brow of Moab,
The crown of the head of the sons of
tumult.
46 [a]Woe to you, O Moab!
The people of Chemosh perish;
For your sons have been taken captive,
And your daughters captive.

47 "Yet I will bring back the captives of Moab
[a]In the latter days," says the LORD.

Thus far *is* the judgment of Moab.

Judgment on Ammon

49 Against the [a]Ammonites.
Thus says the LORD:

"Has Israel no sons?
Has he no heir?
Why *then* does Milcom[1] inherit [b]Gad,
And his people dwell in its cities?
2 [a]Therefore behold, the days are
coming," says the LORD,
"That I will cause to be heard an alarm
of war
In [b]Rabbah of the Ammonites;
It shall be a desolate mound,
And her villages shall be burned with
fire.
Then Israel shall take possession of his
inheritance," says the LORD.

3 "Wail, O [a]Heshbon, for Ai is plundered!
Cry, you daughters of Rabbah,
[b]Gird yourselves with sackcloth!
Lament and run to and fro by the walls;
For Milcom shall go into captivity
With his [c]priests and his princes together.
4 Why [a]do you boast in the valleys,
Your flowing valley, O [b]backsliding
daughter?
Who trusted in her [c]treasures, [d]*saying,*
'Who will come against me?'
5 Behold, I will bring fear upon you,"
Says the Lord GOD of hosts,
"From all those who are around you;
You shall be driven out, everyone
headlong,
And no one will gather those who
wander off.
6 But [a]afterward I will bring back
The captives of the people of Ammon,"
says the LORD.

Judgment on Edom

7 [a]Against Edom.
Thus says the LORD of hosts:

[b]"*Is* wisdom no more in Teman?
[c]Has counsel perished from the prudent?
Has their wisdom [d]vanished?
8 Flee, turn back, dwell in the depths,
O inhabitants of [a]Dedan!
For I will bring the calamity of Esau
upon him,
The time *that* I will punish him.
9 [a]If grape-gatherers came to you,
Would they not leave *some* gleaning
grapes?
If thieves by night,
Would they not destroy until they have
enough?
10 [a]But I have made Esau bare;
I have uncovered his secret places,[1]
And he shall not be able to hide
himself.
His descendants are plundered,
His brethren and his neighbors,
And [b]he *is* no more.
11 Leave your fatherless children,
I will preserve *them* alive;
And let your widows trust in Me."

12 For thus says the LORD: "Behold, [a]those
whose judgment *was* not to drink of the cup
have assuredly drunk. And *are* you the one
who will altogether go unpunished? You
shall not go unpunished, but you shall surely
drink *of it.* 13 For [a]I have sworn by Myself,"
says the LORD, "that [b]Bozrah shall become a
desolation, a reproach, a waste, and a curse.
And all its cities shall be perpetual wastes."

48:43 [a] Is. 24:17, 18 **48:44** [a] Is. 24:18 [b] Jer. 11:23 **48:45** [a] Num. 21:28, 29 [b] Ps. 135:11 [c] Num. 24:17 **48:46** [a] Num. 21:29 **48:47** [a] Jer. 49:6, 39 **49:1** [a] Ezek. 21:28–32; 25:1–7 [b] Amos 1:13–15 [1] Hebrew *Malcam,* literally *their king,* a god of the Ammonites; also called *Molech* (compare verse 3) **49:2** [a] Amos 1:13–15 [b] Ezek. 25:5 **49:3** [a] Jer. 48:2 [b] Is. 32:11 [c] Jer. 48:7 **49:4** [a] Jer. 9:23 [b] Jer. 3:14 [c] Jer. 48:7 [d] Jer. 21:13 **49:6** [a] Jer. 48:47 **49:7** [a] Ezek. 25:12–14; 35:1–15 [b] Gen. 36:11 [c] Is. 19:11 [d] Jer. 8:9 **49:8** [a] Jer. 25:23 **49:9** [a] Obad. 5, 6 **49:10** [a] Mal. 1:3 [b] Is. 17:14 [1] Compare Obadiah 5, 6 **49:12** [a] Jer. 25:29 **49:13** [a] Amos 6:8 [b] Is. 34:6; 63:1

14 [a]I have heard a message from the LORD,
And an ambassador has been sent to the nations:
"Gather together, come against her,
And rise up to battle!

15 "For indeed, I will make you small among nations,
Despised among men.
16 Your fierceness has deceived you,
The [a]pride of your heart,
O you who dwell in the clefts of the rock,
Who hold the height of the hill!
[b]Though you make your [c]nest as high as the eagle,
[d]I will bring you down from there," says the LORD.[1]

17 "Edom also shall be an astonishment;
[a]Everyone who goes by it will be astonished
And will hiss at all its plagues.
18 [a]As in the overthrow of Sodom and Gomorrah
And their neighbors," says the LORD,
"No one shall remain there,
Nor shall a son of man dwell in it.

19 "Behold,[a] he shall come up like a lion from [b]the floodplain[1] of the Jordan
Against the dwelling place of the strong;
But I will suddenly make him run away from her.
And who *is* a chosen *man that* I may appoint over her?
For [c]who *is* like Me?
Who will arraign Me?
And [d]who *is* that shepherd
Who will withstand Me?"

20 [a]Therefore hear the counsel of the LORD that He has taken against Edom,
And His purposes that He has proposed against the inhabitants of Teman:
Surely the least of the flock shall draw them out;
Surely He shall make their dwelling places desolate with them.
21 [a]The earth shakes at the noise of their *fall;*
At the cry its noise is heard at the Red Sea.
22 Behold, [a]He shall come up and fly like the eagle,
And spread His wings over Bozrah;
The heart of the mighty men of Edom in that day shall be
Like the heart of a woman in birth pangs.

Judgment on Damascus

23 [a]Against Damascus.

[b]"Hamath and Arpad are shamed,
For they have heard bad news.
They are fainthearted;
[c]*There is* trouble on the sea;
It cannot be quiet.
24 Damascus has grown feeble;
She turns to flee,
And fear has seized *her.*
[a]Anguish and sorrows have taken her like a woman in labor.
25 Why is [a]the city of praise not deserted, the city of My joy?
26 [a]Therefore her young men shall fall in her streets,
And all the men of war shall be cut off in that day," says the LORD of hosts.
27 "I[a] will kindle a fire in the wall of Damascus,
And it shall consume the palaces of Ben-Hadad."[1]

Judgment on Kedar and Hazor

28 [a]Against Kedar and against the kingdoms of Hazor, which Nebuchadnezzar king of Babylon shall strike.
Thus says the LORD:

"Arise, go up to Kedar,
And devastate [b]the men of the East!
29 Their [a]tents and their flocks they shall take away.
They shall take for themselves their curtains,
All their vessels and their camels;
And they shall cry out to them,
[b]'Fear *is* on every side!'

30 "Flee, get far away! Dwell in the depths,
O inhabitants of Hazor!" says the LORD.
"For Nebuchadnezzar king of Babylon has taken counsel against you,
And has conceived a plan against you.

31 "Arise, go up to [a]the wealthy nation that dwells securely," says the LORD,
"Which has neither gates nor bars,
[b]Dwelling alone.

49:14 [a] Obad. 1–4 **49:16** [a] Jer. 48:29 [b] Obad. 3, 4 [c] Job 39:27 [d] Amos 9:2 [1] Compare Obadiah 3, 4 **49:17** [a] Jer. 18:16; 49:13; 50:13 **49:18** [a] Deut. 29:23 **49:19** [a] Jer. 50:44 [b] Jer. 12:5 [c] Ex. 15:11 [d] Job 41:10 [1] Or *thicket* **49:20** [a] Jer. 50:45 **49:21** [a] Jer. 50:46 **49:22** [a] Jer. 48:40, 41 **49:23** [a] Amos 1:3, 5 [b] Jer. 39:5 [c] [Is. 57:20] **49:24** [a] Is. 13:8 **49:25** [a] Jer. 33:9 **49:26** [a] Jer. 50:30 **49:27** [a] Amos 1:4 [1] Compare Amos 1:4 **49:28** [a] Ezek. 27:21 [b] Judg. 6:3 **49:29** [a] Ps. 120:5 [b] Jer. 46:5 **49:31** [a] Ezek. 38:11 [b] Num. 23:9

32 Their camels shall be for booty,
And the multitude of their cattle for plunder.
I will [a]scatter to all winds those in the farthest corners,
And I will bring their calamity from all its sides," says the LORD.
33 "Hazor [a]shall be a dwelling for jackals, a desolation forever;
No one shall reside there,
Nor son of man dwell in it."

Judgment on Elam

34The word of the LORD that came to Jeremiah the prophet against [a]Elam, in the
[b]beginning of the reign of Zedekiah king of
Judah, saying, 35"Thus says the LORD of hosts:

'Behold, I will break [a]the bow of Elam,
The foremost of their might.
36 Against Elam I will bring the four winds
From the four quarters of heaven,
And scatter them toward all those winds;
There shall be no nations where the outcasts of Elam will not go.
37 For I will cause Elam to be dismayed before their enemies
And before those who seek their life.
[a]I will bring disaster upon them,
My fierce anger,' says the LORD;
'And I will send the sword after them
Until I have consumed them.
38 I will [a]set My throne in Elam,
And will destroy from there the king and the princes,' says the LORD.

39 'But it shall come to pass [a]in the latter days:
I will bring back the captives of Elam,' says the LORD."

Judgment on Babylon and Babylonia

50 The word that the LORD spoke [a]against Babylon *and* against the land of the Chaldeans by Jeremiah the prophet.

2 "Declare among the nations,
Proclaim, and set up a standard;
Proclaim—do not conceal *it*—
Say, 'Babylon is [a]taken, [b]Bel is shamed.
Merodach[1] is broken in pieces;
[c]Her idols are humiliated,
Her images are broken in pieces.'
3 [a]For out of the north [b]a nation comes up against her,
Which shall make her land desolate,
And no one shall dwell therein.
They shall move, they shall depart,
Both man and beast.

4 "In those days and in that time," says the LORD,
"The children of Israel shall come,
[a]They and the children of Judah together;
[b]With continual weeping they shall come,
[c]And seek the LORD their God.
5 They shall ask the way to Zion,
With their faces toward it, *saying,*
'Come and let us join ourselves to the LORD
In [a]a perpetual covenant
That will not be forgotten.'

6 "My people have been [a]lost sheep.
Their shepherds have led them [b]astray;
They have turned them away *on* [c]the mountains.
They have gone from mountain to hill;
They have forgotten their resting place.
7 All who found them have [a]devoured them;
And [b]their adversaries said, [c]'We have not offended,
Because they have sinned against the LORD, [d]the habitation of justice,
The LORD, [e]the hope of their fathers.'

8 "Move[a] from the midst of Babylon,
Go out of the land of the Chaldeans;
And be like the rams before the flocks.
9 [a]For behold, I will raise and cause to come up against Babylon
An assembly of great nations from the north country,
And they shall array themselves against her;
From there she shall be captured.
Their arrows *shall be* like *those* of an expert warrior;[1]
[b]None shall return in vain.
10 And Chaldea shall become plunder;
[a]All who plunder her shall be satisfied," says the LORD.

11 "Because[a] you were glad, because you rejoiced,
You destroyers of My heritage,
Because you have grown fat [b]like a heifer threshing grain,
And you bellow like bulls,

49:32 [a] Ezek. 5:10 49:33 [a] Mal. 1:3 49:34 [a] Jer. 25:25 [b] 2 Kin. 24:17, 18 49:35 [a] Is. 22:6 49:37 [a] Jer. 9:16 49:38 [a] Jer. 43:10 49:39 [a] Jer. 48:47 50:1 [a] Is. 13:1; 47:1 50:2 [a] Is. 21:9 [b] Is. 46:1 [c] Jer. 43:12, 13 [1] A Babylonian god; sometimes spelled *Marduk* 50:3 [a] Jer. 51:48 [b] Is. 13:17, 18, 20 50:4 [a] Hos. 1:11 [b] Ezra 3:12, 13 [c] Hos. 3:5 50:5 [a] Jer. 31:31 50:6 [a] Is. 53:6 [b] Jer. 23:1 [c] [Jer. 2:20; 3:6, 23] 50:7 [a] Ps. 79:7 [b] Zech. 11:5 [c] Jer. 2:3 [d] [Ps. 90:1; 91:1] [e] Ps. 22:4 50:8 [a] Is. 48:20 50:9 [a] Jer. 15:14; 51:27 [b] 2 Sam. 1:22 [1] Following some Hebrew manuscripts, Septuagint, and Syriac; Masoretic Text, Targum, and Vulgate read *a warrior who makes childless.* 50:10 [a] [Rev. 17:16] 50:11 [a] Is. 47:6 [b] Hos. 10:11

12 Your mother shall be deeply ashamed;
She who bore you shall be ashamed.
Behold, the least of the nations *shall be*
a [a]wilderness,
A dry land and a desert.
13 Because of the wrath of the LORD
She shall not be inhabited,
[a]But she shall be wholly desolate.
[b]Everyone who goes by Babylon shall be
horrified
And hiss at all her plagues.

14 "Put[a] yourselves in array against
Babylon all around,
All you who bend the bow;
Shoot at her, spare no arrows,
For she has sinned against the LORD.
15 Shout against her all around;
She has [a]given her hand,
Her foundations have fallen,
[b]Her walls are thrown down;
For [c]it *is* the vengeance of the LORD.
Take vengeance on her.
As she has done, so do to her.
16 Cut off the sower from Babylon,
And him who handles the sickle at
harvest time.
For fear of the oppressing sword
[a]Everyone shall turn to his own people,
And everyone shall flee to his own land.

PEACE NOTE

We can have righteous peace as God judges sin. Babylon was decimated just like many other nations that punished Israel, God's chosen people in God's chosen land.

JEREMIAH 50:14

17 "Israel *is* like [a]scattered sheep;
[b]The lions have driven *him* away.
First [c]the king of Assyria devoured
him;
Now at last this [d]Nebuchadnezzar king
of Babylon has broken his bones."

18 Therefore thus says the LORD of hosts,
the God of Israel:

"Behold, I will punish the king of
Babylon and his land,
As I have punished the king of [a]Assyria.
19 [a]But I will bring back Israel to his home,
And he shall feed on Carmel and
Bashan;
His soul shall be satisfied on Mount
Ephraim and Gilead.
20 In those days and in that time," says
the LORD,
[a]"The iniquity of Israel shall be sought,
but *there shall be* none;
And the sins of Judah, but they shall
not be found;
For I will pardon those [b]whom I preserve.

21 "Go up against the land of Merathaim,
against it,
And against the inhabitants of [a]Pekod.
Waste and utterly destroy them," says
the LORD,
"And do [b]according to all that I have
commanded you.
22 [a]A sound of battle *is* in the land,
And of great destruction.
23 How [a]the hammer of the whole earth
has been cut apart and broken!
How Babylon has become a desolation
among the nations!
24 I have laid a snare for you;
You have indeed been [a]trapped,
O Babylon,
And you were not aware;
You have been found and also caught,
Because you have [b]contended against
the LORD.
25 The LORD has opened His armory,
And has brought out [a]the weapons of
His indignation;
For this *is* the work of the Lord GOD of
hosts
In the land of the Chaldeans.
26 Come against her from the farthest
border;
Open her storehouses;
Cast her up as heaps of ruins,
And destroy her utterly;
Let nothing of her be left.
27 Slay all her [a]bulls,
Let them go down to the slaughter.
Woe to them!
For their day has come, the time of
[b]their punishment.

50:12 [a] Jer. 51:43 **50:13** [a] Jer. 25:12 [b] Jer. 49:17 **50:14** [a] Jer. 51:2 **50:15** [a] Lam. 5:6 [b] Jer. 51:58 [c] Jer. 51:6, 11 **50:16** [a] Is. 13:14 **50:17** [a] 2 Kin. 24:10, 14 [b] Jer. 2:15 [c] 2 Kin. 15:29; 17:6; 18:9–13 [d] 2 Kin. 24:10–14; 25:1–7 **50:18** [a] Ezek. 31:3, 11, 12 **50:19** [a] Is. 65:10 **50:20** [a] [Jer. 31:34] [b] Is. 1:9 **50:21** [a] Ezek. 23:23 [b] 2 Sam. 16:11 **50:22** [a] Jer. 51:54 **50:23** [a] Jer. 51:20–24 **50:24** [a] Dan. 5:30 [b] [Is. 45:9] **50:25** [a] Is. 13:5 **50:27** [a] Is. 34:7 [b] Jer. 48:44

28 The voice of those who flee and escape
from the land of Babylon
[a]Declares in Zion the vengeance of the
LORD our God,
The vengeance of His temple.

29 "Call together the archers against Babylon.
All you who bend the bow, encamp
against it all around;
Let none of them escape.[1]
[a]Repay her according to her work;
According to all she has done, do to her;
[b]For she has been proud against the LORD,
Against the Holy One of Israel.
30 [a]Therefore her young men shall fall in
the streets,
And all her men of war shall be cut off
in that day," says the LORD.
31 "Behold, I *am* against you,
O most haughty one!" says the Lord
GOD of hosts;
"For your day has come,
The time *that* I will punish you.[1]
32 The most [a]proud shall stumble and fall,
And no one will raise him up;
[b]I will kindle a fire in his cities,
And it will devour all around him."

33 Thus says the LORD of hosts:

"The children of Israel *were* oppressed,
Along with the children of Judah;
All who took them captive have held
them fast;
They have refused to let them go.
34 [a]Their Redeemer *is* strong;
[b]The LORD of hosts *is* His name.
He will thoroughly plead their [c]case,
That He may give rest to the land,
And disquiet the inhabitants of
Babylon.

35 "A sword *is* against the Chaldeans," says
the LORD,
"Against the inhabitants of Babylon,
And [a]against her princes and [b]her wise
men.
36 A sword *is* [a]against the soothsayers,
and they will be fools.
A sword *is* against her mighty men, and
they will be dismayed.
37 A sword *is* against their horses,
Against their chariots,
And against all [a]the mixed peoples who
are in her midst;
And [b]they will become like women.
A sword *is* against her treasures, and
they will be robbed.
38 [a]A drought[1] *is* against her waters, and
they will be dried up.
For it *is* the land of carved images,
And they are insane with *their* idols.

39 "Therefore[a] the wild desert beasts shall
dwell *there* with the jackals,
And the ostriches shall dwell in it.
[b]It shall be inhabited no more forever,
Nor shall it be dwelt in from generation
to generation.
40 [a]As God overthrew Sodom and Gomorrah
And their neighbors," says the LORD,
"*So* no one shall reside there,
Nor son of man [b]dwell in it.

41 "Behold,[a] a people shall come from the
north,
And a great nation and many kings
Shall be raised up from the ends of the
earth.
42 [a]They shall hold the bow and the lance;
[b]They *are* cruel and shall not show mercy.
[c]Their voice shall roar like the sea;
They shall ride on horses,
Set in array, like a man for the battle,
Against you, O daughter of Babylon.

43 "The king of Babylon has [a]heard the
report about them,
And his hands grow feeble;
Anguish has taken hold of him,
Pangs as of a woman in [b]childbirth.

44 "Behold,[a] he shall come up like a lion
from the floodplain[1] of the Jordan
Against the dwelling place of the strong;
But I will make them suddenly run
away from her.
And who *is* a chosen *man that* I may
appoint over her?
For who *is* like Me?
Who will arraign Me?
And [b]who *is* that shepherd
Who will withstand Me?"

45 Therefore hear [a]the counsel of the LORD
that He has taken against Babylon,

50:28 [a] *Jer. 51:10* ***50:29*** [a] *Jer. 51:56* [b] *[Is. 47:10]* [1] Qere, some Hebrew manuscripts, Septuagint, and Targum add *to her*. **50:30** [a] Jer. 49:26; 51:4 **50:31** [1] Following Masoretic Text and Targum; Septuagint and Vulgate read *The time of your punishment.* **50:32** [a] Mal. 4:1 [b] Jer. 21:14 **50:34** [a] Rev. 18:8 [b] Is. 47:4 [c] Jer. 51:36; Mic. 7:9 **50:35** [a] Dan. 5:30 [b] Is. 47:13 **50:36** [a] Is. 44:25 **50:37** [a] Jer. 25:20 [b] Jer. 51:30 **50:38** [a] Rev. 16:12 [1] Following Masoretic Text, Targum, and Vulgate; Syriac reads *sword;* Septuagint omits *A drought is.* **50:39** [a] Rev. 18:2 [b] Is. 13:20 **50:40** [a] Is. 13:19 [b] Is. 13:20 **50:41** [a] Jer. 6:22; 25:14; 51:27 **50:42** [a] Jer. 6:23 [b] Is. 13:18 [c] Is. 5:30 **50:43** [a] Jer. 51:31 [b] Jer. 6:24 **50:44** [a] Jer. 49:19–21 [b] Job 41:10 [1] Or *thicket* **50:45** [a] Jer. 51:10, 11

And His [b]purposes that He has
proposed against the land of the
Chaldeans:
[c]Surely the least of the flock shall draw
them out;
Surely He will make their dwelling
place desolate with them.
46 [a]At the noise of the taking of Babylon
The earth trembles,
And the cry is heard among the nations.

The Utter Destruction of Babylon

51 Thus says the LORD:
"Behold, I will raise up against [a]Babylon,
Against those who dwell in Leb Kamai,[1]
[b]A destroying wind.
2 And I will send [a]winnowers to Babylon,
Who shall winnow her and empty her
land.
[b]For in the day of doom
They shall be against her all around.
3 Against *her* [a]let the archer bend his bow,
And lift himself up against *her* in his
armor.
Do not spare her young men;
[b]Utterly destroy all her army.
4 Thus the slain shall fall in the land of
the Chaldeans,
[a]And *those* thrust through in her streets.
5 For Israel is [a]not forsaken, nor Judah,
By his God, the LORD of hosts,
Though their land was filled with sin
against the Holy One of Israel."

6 [a]Flee from the midst of Babylon,
And every one save his life!
Do not be cut off in her iniquity,
For [b]this *is* the time of the LORD's
vengeance;
[c]He shall recompense her.
7 [a]Babylon *was* a golden cup in the
LORD's hand,
That made all the earth drunk.
[b]The nations drank her wine;
Therefore the nations [c]are deranged.
8 Babylon has suddenly [a]fallen and been
destroyed.
[b]Wail for her!
[c]Take balm for her pain;
Perhaps she may be healed.

9 We would have healed Babylon,
But she is not healed.
Forsake her, and [a]let us go everyone to
his own country;
[b]For her judgment reaches to heaven
and is lifted up to the skies.
10 The LORD has [a]revealed our
righteousness.
Come and let us [b]declare in Zion the
work of the LORD our God.

11 [a]Make the arrows bright!
Gather the shields!
[b]The LORD has raised up the spirit of
the kings of the Medes.
[c]For His plan *is* against Babylon to
destroy it,
Because it *is* [d]the vengeance of the LORD,
The vengeance for His temple.
12 [a]Set up the standard on the walls of
Babylon;
Make the guard strong,
Set up the watchmen,
Prepare the ambushes.
For the LORD has both devised and done
What He spoke against the inhabitants
of Babylon.
13 [a]O you who dwell by many waters,
Abundant in treasures,
Your end has come,
The measure of your covetousness.
14 [a]The LORD of hosts has sworn by Himself:
"Surely I will fill you with men, [b]as with
locusts,
And they shall lift [c]up a shout against
you."

15 [a]He has made the earth by His power;
He has established the world by His
wisdom,
And [b]stretched out the heaven by His
understanding.
16 When He utters *His* voice—
There is a multitude of waters in the
heavens:
[a]"He causes the vapors to ascend from
the ends of the earth;
He makes lightnings for the rain;
He brings the wind out of His treasuries."[1]

17 [a]Everyone is dull-hearted, without
knowledge;
Every metalsmith is put to shame by
the carved image;
[b]For his molded image *is* falsehood,
And *there is* no breath in them.

50:45 [b] Jer. 51:29 [c] Jer. 49:19, 20 **50:46** [a] Rev. 18:9 **51:1** [a] Is. 47:1 [b] Jer. 4:11 [1] A code word for Chaldea (Babylonia); may be translated *The Midst of Those Who Rise Up Against Me* **51:2** [a] Jer. 15:7 [b] Jer. 50:14 **51:3** [a] Jer. 50:14, 29 [b] Jer. 50:21 **51:4** [a] Jer. 49:26; 50:30, 37 **51:5** [a] [Jer. 33:24–26; 46:28] **51:6** [a] Rev. 18:4 [b] Jer. 50:15 [c] Jer. 25:14 **51:7** [a] Rev. 17:4 [b] Rev. 14:8 [c] Jer. 25:16 **51:8** [a] Is. 21:9 [b] Rev. 18:9, 11, 19 [c] Jer. 46:11 **51:9** [a] Is. 13:14 [b] Rev. 18:5 **51:10** [a] Ps. 37:6 [b] Jer. 50:28 **51:11** [a] Jer. 46:4, 9 [b] Is. 13:17 [c] Jer. 50:45 [d] Jer. 50:28 **51:12** [a] Nah. 2:1; 3:14 **51:13** [a] Rev. 17:1, 15 **51:14** [a] Jer. 49:13 [b] Nah. 3:15 [c] Jer. 50:15 **51:15** [a] Gen. 1:1, 6 [b] Job 9:8 **51:16** [a] Ps. 135:7 [1] Psalm 135:7 **51:17** [a] Jer. 10:14 [b] Jer. 50:2

18 They *are* futile, a work of errors;
In the time of their punishment they shall perish.
19 The Portion of Jacob *is* not like them,
For He *is* the Maker of all things;
And *Israel is* the tribe of His inheritance.
The LORD of hosts *is* His name.

20 "You[a] *are* My battle-ax *and* weapons of war:
For with you I will break the nation in pieces;
With you I will destroy kingdoms;
21 With you I will break in pieces the horse and its rider;
With you I will break in pieces the chariot and its rider;
22 With you also I will break in pieces man and woman;
With you I will break in pieces [a]old and young;
With you I will break in pieces the young man and the maiden;
23 With you also I will break in pieces the shepherd and his flock;
With you I will break in pieces the farmer and his yoke of oxen;
And with you I will break in pieces governors and rulers.

24 "And[a] I will repay Babylon
And all the inhabitants of Chaldea
For all the evil they have done
In Zion in your sight," says the LORD.

25 "Behold, I *am* against you, [a]O destroying mountain,
Who destroys all the earth," says the LORD.
"And I will stretch out My hand against you,
Roll you down from the rocks,
[b]And make you a burnt mountain.
26 They shall not take from you a stone for a corner
Nor a stone for a foundation,
[a]But you shall be desolate forever," says the LORD.

27 [a]Set up a banner in the land,
Blow the trumpet among the nations!
[b]Prepare the nations against her,
Call [c]the kingdoms together against her:
Ararat, Minni, and Ashkenaz.
Appoint a general against her;
Cause the horses to come up like the bristling locusts.
28 Prepare against her the nations,
With the kings of the Medes,
Its governors and all its rulers,
All the land of his dominion.
29 And the land will tremble and sorrow;
For every [a]purpose of the LORD shall be performed against Babylon,
[b]To make the land of Babylon a desolation without inhabitant.
30 The mighty men of Babylon have ceased fighting,
They have remained in their strongholds;
Their might has failed,
[a]They became *like* women;
They have burned her dwelling places,
[b]The bars of her *gate* are broken.
31 [a]One runner will run to meet another,
And one messenger to meet another,
To show the king of Babylon that his city is taken on *all* sides;
32 [a]The passages are blocked,
The reeds they have burned with fire,
And the men of war are terrified.

33 For thus says the LORD of hosts, the God of Israel:

"The daughter of Babylon *is* [a]like a threshing floor
When [b]*it is* time to thresh her;
Yet a little while
[c]And the time of her harvest will come."

34 "Nebuchadnezzar the king of Babylon
Has [a]devoured me, he has crushed me;
He has made me an [b]empty vessel,
He has swallowed me up like a monster;
He has filled his stomach with my delicacies,
He has spit me out.
35 Let the violence *done* to me and my flesh *be* upon Babylon,"
The inhabitant of Zion will say;
"And my blood be upon the inhabitants of Chaldea!"
Jerusalem will say.

36 Therefore thus says the LORD:

"Behold, [a]I will plead your case and take vengeance for you.
[b]I will dry up her sea and make her springs dry.

51:20 [a] Is. 10:5, 15 **51:22** [a] 2 Chr. 36:17 **51:24** [a] Jer. 50:15, 29 **51:25** [a] Zech. 4:7 [b] Rev. 8:8 **51:26** [a] Jer. 50:26, 40 **51:27** [a] Is. 13:2 [b] Jer. 25:14 [c] Jer. 50:41, 42 **51:29** [a] Jer. 50:45 [b] Jer. 50:13; 51:26, 43 **51:30** [a] Is. 19:16 [b] Lam. 2:9 **51:31** [a] Jer. 50:24 **51:32** [a] Jer. 50:38 **51:33** [a] Is. 21:10 [b] Hab. 3:12 [c] Rev. 14:15 **51:34** [a] Jer. 50:17 [b] Is. 24:1–3 **51:36** [a] Jer. 50:34 [b] Jer. 50:38

37 [a]Babylon shall become a heap,
A dwelling place for jackals,
[b]An astonishment and a hissing,
Without an inhabitant.
38 They shall roar together like lions,
They shall growl like lions' whelps.
39 In their excitement I will prepare their
feasts;
[a]I will make them drunk,
That they may rejoice,
And sleep a perpetual sleep
And not awake," says the LORD.
40 "I will bring them down
Like lambs to the slaughter,
Like rams with male goats.

41 "Oh, how [a]Sheshach[1] is taken!
Oh, how [b]the praise of the whole earth
is seized!
How Babylon has become desolate
among the nations!
42 [a]The sea has come up over Babylon;
She is covered with the multitude of its
waves.
43 [a]Her cities are a desolation,
A dry land and a wilderness,
A land where [b]no one dwells,
Through which no son of man passes.
44 I will punish [a]Bel in Babylon,
And I will bring out of his mouth what
he has swallowed;
And the nations shall not stream to
him anymore.
Yes, [b]the wall of Babylon shall fall.

45 "My[a] people, go out of the midst of her!
And let everyone deliver himself from
the fierce anger of the LORD.
46 And lest your heart faint,
And you fear [a]for the rumor that *will be*
heard in the land
(A rumor will come *one* year,
And after that, in *another* year
A rumor *will come,*
And violence in the land,
Ruler against ruler),
47 Therefore behold, the days are coming
That I will bring judgment on the
carved images of Babylon;
Her whole land *shall* be ashamed,
And all her slain shall fall in her midst.
48 Then [a]the heavens and the earth and
all that *is* in them
Shall sing joyously over Babylon;
[b]For the plunderers shall come to her
from the north," says the LORD.
49 As Babylon *has caused* the slain of
Israel to fall,
So at Babylon the slain of all the earth
shall fall.
50 [a]You who have escaped the sword,
Get away! Do not stand still!
[b]Remember the LORD afar off,
And let Jerusalem come to your
mind.

51 [a]We are ashamed because we have
heard reproach.
Shame has covered our faces,
For strangers [b]have come into the
sanctuaries of the LORD's house.

52 "Therefore behold, the days are
coming," says the LORD,
"That I will bring judgment on her
carved images,
And throughout all her land the
wounded shall groan.
53 [a]Though Babylon were to mount up to
heaven,
And though she were to fortify the
height of her strength,
Yet from Me plunderers would come to
her," says the LORD.

54 [a]The sound of a cry *comes* from
Babylon,
And great destruction from the land of
the Chaldeans,
55 Because the LORD is plundering
Babylon
And silencing her loud voice,
Though her waves roar like great
waters,
And the noise of their voice is
uttered,
56 Because the plunderer comes against
her, against Babylon,
And her mighty men are taken.
Every one of their bows is broken;
[a]For the LORD *is* the God of
recompense,
He will surely repay.

57 "And I will make drunk
Her princes and [a]wise men,
Her governors, her deputies, and her
mighty men.
And they shall sleep a perpetual
sleep
And not awake," says [b]the King,
Whose name *is* the LORD of hosts.

51:37 [a] Is. 13:22 [b] Jer. 25:9, 11 **51:39** [a] Jer. 51:57 **51:41** [a] Jer. 25:26 [b] Is. 13:19 [1] A code word for Babylon (compare Jeremiah 25:26) **51:42** [a] Is. 8:7, 8 **51:43** [a] Jer. 50:39, 40 [b] Is. 13:20 **51:44** [a] Jer. 50:2 [b] Jer. 50:15 **51:45** [a] [Rev. 18:4] **51:46** [a] 2 Kin. 19:7 **51:48** [a] Is. 44:23; 48:20; 49:13 [b] Jer. 50:3, 41 **51:50** [a] Jer. 44:28 [b] [Deut. 4:29–31] **51:51** [a] Ps. 44:15; 79:4 [b] Lam. 1:10 **51:53** [a] Amos 9:2 **51:54** [a] Jer. 50:22 **51:56** [a] Jer. 50:29 **51:57** [a] Jer. 50:35 [b] Jer. 46:18; 48:15

58Thus says the LORD of hosts:

"The broad walls of Babylon shall be
utterly [a]broken,
And her high gates shall be burned
with fire;
[b]The people will labor in vain,
And the nations, because of the fire;
And they shall be weary."

Jeremiah's Command to Seraiah

59The word which Jeremiah the prophet
commanded Seraiah the son of [a]Neriah, the
son of Mahseiah, when he went with Zedekiah the king of Judah to Babylon in the fourth
year of his reign. And Seraiah *was* the quarter-
master. 60So Jeremiah [a]wrote in a book all
the evil that would come upon Babylon, all
these words that are written against Babylon.
61And Jeremiah said to Seraiah, "When you
arrive in Babylon and see it, and read all these
words, 62then you shall say, 'O LORD, You have
spoken against this place to cut it off, so that
[a]none shall remain in it, neither man nor
beast, but it shall be desolate forever.' 63Now
it shall be, when you have finished reading
this book, [a]*that* you shall tie a stone to it and
throw it out into the Euphrates. 64Then you
shall say, 'Thus Babylon shall sink and not rise
from the catastrophe that I will bring upon
her. And they shall be weary.' "

Thus far *are* the words of Jeremiah.

The Fall of Jerusalem Reviewed

52 Zedekiah *was* [a]twenty-one years old
when he became king, and he reigned
eleven years in Jerusalem. His mother's name
was Hamutal the daughter of Jeremiah of
[b]Libnah. 2He also did evil in the sight of the
LORD, according to all that Jehoiakim had
done. 3For because of the anger of the LORD
this happened in Jerusalem and Judah, till He
finally cast them out from His presence. Then
Zedekiah [a]rebelled against the king of Babylon.

4Now it came to pass in the [a]ninth year of
his reign, in the tenth month, on the tenth
day of the month, *that* Nebuchadnezzar king
of Babylon and all his army came against
Jerusalem and encamped against it; and
they built a siege wall against it all around.
5So the city was besieged until the eleventh
year of King Zedekiah. 6By the fourth month,
on the ninth day of the month, the famine
had become so severe in the city that there
was no food for the people of the land. 7Then
the city *wall* was broken through, and all the
men of war fled and went out of the city at
night by way of the gate between the two
walls, which *was* by the king's garden, even
though the Chaldeans *were* near the city all
around. And they went by way of the plain.[1]

8But the army of the Chaldeans pursued
the king, and they overtook Zedekiah in
the plains of Jericho. All his army was scattered from him. 9[a]So they took the king and
brought him up to the king of Babylon at
Riblah in the land of Hamath, and he pronounced judgment on him. 10[a]Then the king
of Babylon killed the sons of Zedekiah before
his eyes. And he killed all the princes of Judah
in Riblah. 11He also [a]put out the eyes of Zedekiah; and the king of Babylon bound him
in bronze fetters, took him to Babylon, and
put him in prison till the day of his death.

The Temple and City Plundered and Burned

12[a]Now in the fifth month, on the tenth *day*
of the month ([b]which *was* the nineteenth
year of King Nebuchadnezzar king of Babylon), [c]Nebuzaradan, the captain of the guard,
who served the king of Babylon, came to
Jerusalem. 13He burned the house of the
LORD and the king's house; all the houses of
Jerusalem, that is, all the houses of the great,
he burned with fire. 14And all the army of the
Chaldeans who *were* with the captain of the
guard broke down all the walls of Jerusalem
all around. 15[a]Then Nebuzaradan the captain
of the guard carried away captive *some* of
the poor people, the rest of the people who
remained in the city, the defectors who had
deserted to the king of Babylon, and the rest
of the craftsmen. 16But Nebuzaradan the
captain of the guard left *some* of the poor of
the land as vinedressers and farmers.

17[a]The [b]bronze pillars that *were* in the
house of the LORD, and the carts and the
bronze Sea that *were* in the house of the
LORD, the Chaldeans broke in pieces, and
carried all their bronze to Babylon. 18They
also took away [a]the pots, the shovels, the
trimmers, the bowls, the spoons, and all
the bronze utensils with which the *priests*
ministered. 19The basins, the firepans, the
bowls, the pots, the lampstands, the spoons,
and the cups, whatever *was* solid gold and
whatever *was* solid silver, the captain of the
guard took away. 20The two pillars, one Sea,
the twelve bronze bulls which *were* under *it,*
and the carts, which King Solomon had made
for the house of the LORD—[a]the bronze of

51:58 [a] Jer. 50:15 [b] Hab. 2:13 **51:59** [a] Jer. 32:12 **51:60** [a] Jer. 36:2 **51:62** [a] Jer. 50:3, 39 **51:63** [a] Rev. 18:21
52:1 [a] 2 Kin. 24:18 [b] Josh. 10:29 **52:3** [a] 2 Chr. 36:13 **52:4** [a] Jer. 39:1 **52:7** [1] Or *the Arabah,* that is, the Jordan Valley **52:9** [a] Jer. 32:4; 39:5 **52:10** [a] Ezek. 12:13 **52:11** [a] Ezek. 12:13 **52:12** [a] 2 Kin. 25:8–21 [b] Jer. 52:29 [c] Jer. 39:9
52:15 [a] Jer. 39:9 **52:17** [a] Jer. 27:19 [b] 1 Kin. 7:15, 23, 27, 50 **52:18** [a] Ex. 27:3 **52:20** [a] 1 Kin. 7:47

all these articles was beyond measure. 21Now
concerning the [a]pillars: the height of one
pillar *was* eighteen cubits, a measuring line
of twelve cubits could measure its circumference, and its thickness *was* four fingers;
it was hollow. 22A capital of bronze *was* on it;
and the height of one capital *was* five cubits,
with a network and pomegranates all around
the capital, all of bronze. The second pillar,
with pomegranates was the same. 23There
were ninety-six pomegranates on the sides;
[a]all the pomegranates, all around on the
network, *were* one hundred.

The People Taken Captive to Babylonia

24[a]The captain of the guard took Seraiah the
chief priest, [b]Zephaniah the second priest, and
the three doorkeepers. 25He also took out of
the city an officer who had charge of the men
of war, seven men of the king's close associates who were found in the city, the principal
scribe of the army who mustered the people
of the land, and sixty men of the people of
the land who were found in the midst of the
city. 26And Nebuzaradan the captain of the
guard took these and brought them to the
king of Babylon at Riblah. 27Then the king of
Babylon struck them and put them to death
at Riblah in the land of Hamath. Thus Judah
was carried away captive from its own land.

28[a]These *are* the people whom Nebuchadnezzar carried away captive: [b]in the seventh
year, [c]three thousand and twenty-three Jews;
29[a]in the eighteenth year of Nebuchadnezzar he carried away captive from Jerusalem
eight hundred and thirty-two persons; 30in
the twenty-third year of Nebuchadnezzar,
Nebuzaradan the captain of the guard carried
away captive of the Jews seven hundred and
forty-five persons. All the persons *were* four
thousand six hundred.

Jehoiachin Released from Prison

31[a]Now it came to pass in the thirty-
seventh year of the captivity of Jehoiachin
king of Judah, in the twelfth month, on the
twenty-fifth *day* of the month, *that* Evil-
Merodach[1] king of Babylon, in the *first* year
of his reign, [b]lifted up the head of Jehoiachin king of Judah and brought him out of
prison. 32And he spoke kindly to him and
gave him a more prominent seat than those
of the kings who *were* with him in Babylon.
33So Jehoiachin changed from his prison
garments, [a]and he ate bread regularly before
the *king* all the days of his life. 34And as for
his provisions, there was a regular ration
given him by the king of Babylon, a portion
for each day until the day of his death, all
the days of his life.

52:21 [a] 2 Kin. 25:17 **52:23** [a] 1 Kin. 7:20 **52:24** [a] 2 Kin. 25:18 [b] Jer. 21:1; 29:25 **52:28** [a] 2 Kin. 24:2 [b] 2 Kin. 24:12 [c] 2 Kin. 24:14 **52:29** [a] Jer. 39:9 **52:31** [a] 2 Kin. 25:27–30 [b] Gen. 40:13, 20 [1] Or *Awil-Marduk* **52:33** [a] 2 Sam. 9:7, 13

THE BOOK OF LAMENTATIONS

AUTHOR

The universal consensus of early Jewish and Christian tradition attributes this book to Jeremiah. Even though the author is unnamed in the book, the superscription to Lamentations in the Septuagint states: "And it came to pass, after Israel had been carried away captive and Jerusalem had become desolate, that Jeremiah sat weeping, and lamented with this lamentation over Jerusalem." The Talmud, as well as many other ancient sources, also supports this position.

TIME

c. 586 BC

KEY VERSE

Lamentations 3:22–23

THEME

A lament is a vehicle for working through sorrow. While grief is expressed in words, its resolution is in God and the hope He gives for the future. In a way, the lamentation process is one of coming to grips with all that God wants us to see about our present circumstances. For the people of Judah to lose a country meant not only the loss of their homeland but also the loss of God's presence and power to sustain the people in that land. It is hard for people who have never experienced such loss to understand the depth of grief expressed in this book.

In the five prayers of "lament," Jeremiah exemplifies how to pray in times of desperation when God seems absent or distant. He says, "You have moved my soul far from peace; I have forgotten prosperity" (3:17). We can be creative in how we cry out to God, like Jeremiah, who composed acrostic poems about opening his heart to the Lord. The prophet's unique way to cope with his difficulties involved the artistic skills God blessed him with. Perhaps from Jeremiah we can learn to use the gifts and talents God has given to us as helpful coping mechanisms when anxiety tries to steal our peace.

Jerusalem in Affliction

1 How lonely sits the city
That was full of people!
[a] *How* like a widow is she,
Who *was* great among the nations!
The [b]princess among the provinces
Has become a slave!

2 She [a]weeps bitterly in the [b]night,
Her tears *are* on her cheeks;
Among all her lovers
She has none to comfort *her.*
All her friends have dealt treacherously
with her;
They have become her enemies.

3 [a]Judah has gone into captivity,
Under affliction and hard servitude;
[b]She dwells among the nations,
She finds no [c]rest;
All her persecutors overtake her in dire
straits.

4 The roads to Zion mourn
Because no one comes to the set feasts.
All her gates are [a]desolate;
Her priests sigh,
Her virgins are afflicted,
And she *is* in bitterness.

5 Her adversaries [a]have become the
master,
Her enemies prosper;
For the LORD has afflicted her
[b]Because of the multitude of her
transgressions.
Her [c]children have gone into captivity
before the enemy.

6 And from the daughter of Zion
All her splendor has departed.
Her princes have become like deer
That find no pasture,
That flee without strength
Before the pursuer.

7 In the days of her affliction and roaming,
Jerusalem [a]remembers all her pleasant
things
That she had in the days of old.
When her people fell into the hand of
the enemy,
With no one to help her,
The adversaries saw her
And mocked at her downfall.[1]

8 [a]Jerusalem has sinned gravely,
Therefore she has become vile.[1]
All who honored her despise her
Because [b]they have seen her nakedness;
Yes, she sighs and turns away.

9 Her uncleanness *is* in her skirts;
She [a]did not consider her destiny;
Therefore her collapse was awesome;
She had no comforter.
"O LORD, behold my affliction,
For *the* enemy is exalted!"

10 The adversary has spread his hand
Over all her pleasant things;
For she has seen [a]the nations enter her
sanctuary,
Those whom You commanded
[b]Not to enter Your assembly.

11 All her people sigh,
[a]They seek bread;
They have given their valuables for
food to restore life.
"See, O LORD, and consider,
For I am scorned."

12 "*Is it* nothing to you, all you who pass by?
Behold and see
[a]If there is any sorrow like my sorrow,
Which has been brought on me,
Which the LORD has inflicted
In the day of His fierce anger.

13 "From above He has sent fire into my bones,
And it overpowered them;
He has [a]spread a net for my feet
And turned me back;
He has made me desolate
And faint all the day.

14 "The[a] yoke of my transgressions was
bound;[1]
They were woven together by His hands,
And thrust upon my neck.
He made my strength fail;
The Lord delivered me into the hands of
those whom I am not able to withstand.

15 "The Lord has trampled underfoot all
my mighty *men* in my midst;
He has called an assembly against me
To crush my young men;
[a]The Lord trampled *as* in a winepress
The virgin daughter of Judah.

1:1 [a] Is. 47:7–9 [b] Ezra 4:20 **1:2** [a] Jer. 13:17 [b] Job 7:3 **1:3** [a] Jer. 52:27 [b] Lam. 2:9 [c] Deut. 28:65 **1:4** [a] Is. 27:10 **1:5** [a] Deut. 28:43 [b] Dan. 9:7, 16 [c] Jer. 52:28 **1:7** [a] Ps. 137:1 [1] Vulgate reads *her Sabbaths.* **1:8** [a] [1 Kin. 8:46] [b] Ezek. 16:37 [1] Septuagint and Vulgate read *moved* or *removed.* **1:9** [a] Is. 47:7 **1:10** [a] Jer. 51:51 [b] Deut. 23:3 **1:11** [a] Jer. 38:9; 52:6 **1:12** [a] Dan. 9:12 **1:13** [a] Ezek. 12:13; 17:20 **1:14** [a] Deut. 28:48 [1] Following Masoretic Text and Targum; Septuagint, Syriac, and Vulgate read *watched over.* **1:15** [a] [Rev. 14:19]

16 "For these *things* I weep;
My eye, [a]my eye overflows with water;
Because the comforter, who should restore my life,
Is far from me.
My children are desolate
Because the enemy prevailed."

17 [a]Zion spreads out her hands,
But no one comforts her;
The LORD has commanded concerning Jacob
That those [b]around him *become* his adversaries;
Jerusalem has become an unclean thing among them.

18 "The LORD is [a]righteous,
For I [b]rebelled against His commandment.
Hear now, all peoples,
And behold my sorrow;
My virgins and my young men
Have gone into captivity.

19 "I called for my lovers,
But they deceived me;
My priests and my elders
Breathed their last in the city,
While they sought food
To restore their life.

20 "See, O LORD, that I *am* in distress;
My [a]soul is troubled;
My heart is overturned within me,
For I have been very rebellious.
[b]Outside the sword bereaves,
At home *it is* like death.

21 "They have heard that I sigh,
But no one comforts me.
All my enemies have heard of my trouble;
They are [a]glad that You have done *it*.
Bring on [b]the day You have announced,
That they may become like me.

22 "Let[a] all their wickedness come before You,
And do to them as You have done to me
For all my transgressions;
For my sighs are many,
And my heart *is* faint."

God's Anger with Jerusalem

2 How the Lord has covered the daughter of Zion
With a [a]cloud in His anger!
[b]He cast down from heaven to the earth
[c]The beauty of Israel,
And did not remember [d]His footstool
In the day of His anger.

2 The Lord has swallowed up and has [a]not pitied
All the dwelling places of Jacob.
He has thrown down in His wrath
The strongholds of the daughter of Judah;
He has brought *them* down to the ground;
[b]He has profaned the kingdom and its princes.

3 He has cut off in fierce anger
Every horn of Israel;
[a]He has drawn back His right hand
From before the enemy.
[b]He has blazed against Jacob like a flaming fire
Devouring all around.

4 [a]Standing like an enemy, He has bent His bow;
With His right hand, like an adversary,
He has slain [b]all *who were* pleasing to His eye;
On the tent of the daughter of Zion,
He has poured out His fury like fire.

5 [a]The Lord was like an enemy.
He has swallowed up Israel,
He has swallowed up all her palaces;
[b]He has destroyed her strongholds,
And has increased mourning and lamentation
In the daughter of Judah.

6 He has done violence [a]to His tabernacle,
[b]*As if it were* a garden;
He has destroyed His place of assembly;
The LORD has caused
The appointed feasts and Sabbaths to be forgotten in Zion.
In His burning indignation He has [c]spurned the king and the priest.

7 The Lord has spurned His altar,
He has [a]abandoned His sanctuary;
He has given up the walls of her palaces
Into the hand of the enemy.

1:16 [a] Eccl. 4:1 **1:17** [a] Jer. 4:31 [b] 2 Kin. 24:2–4 **1:18** [a] Dan. 9:7, 14 [b] 1 Sam. 12:14, 15 **1:20** [a] Is. 16:11 [b] Ezek. 7:15 **1:21** [a] Ps. 35:15 [b] [Jer. 46] **1:22** [a] Ps. 109:15; 137:7, 8 **2:1** [a] [Lam. 3:44] [b] Matt. 11:23 [c] 2 Sam. 1:19 [d] Ps. 99:5 **2:2** [a] Lam. 3:43 [b] Ps. 89:39, 40 **2:3** [a] Ps. 74:11 [b] Ps. 89:46 **2:4** [a] Is. 63:10 [b] Ezek. 24:25 **2:5** [a] Jer. 30:14 [b] Jer. 52:13 **2:6** [a] Ps. 80:12; 89:40 [b] Is. 1:8 [c] Is. 43:28 **2:7** [a] Ezek. 24:21

[b]They have made a noise in the house of
the LORD
As on the day of a set feast.

8 The LORD has purposed to destroy
The [a]wall of the daughter of Zion.
[b]He has stretched out a line;
He has not withdrawn His hand from
destroying;
Therefore He has caused the rampart
and wall to lament;
They languished together.

9 Her gates have sunk into the ground;
He has destroyed and [a]broken her bars.
[b]Her king and her princes *are* among
the nations;
[c]The Law *is* no *more,*
And her [d]prophets find no vision from
the LORD.

10 The elders of the daughter of Zion
[a]Sit on the ground *and* keep silence;
They [b]throw dust on their heads
And [c]gird themselves with sackcloth.
The virgins of Jerusalem
Bow their heads to the ground.

11 [a]My eyes fail with tears,
My heart is troubled;
[b]My bile is poured on the ground
Because of the destruction of the
daughter of my people,
Because [c]the children and the infants
Faint in the streets of the city.

12 They say to their mothers,
"Where *is* grain and wine?"
As they swoon like the wounded
In the streets of the city,
As their life is poured out
In their mothers' bosom.

13 How shall I [a]console you?
To what shall I liken you,
O daughter of Jerusalem?
What shall I compare with you, that I
may comfort you,
O virgin daughter of Zion?
For your ruin *is* spread wide as the sea;
Who can heal you?

14 Your [a]prophets have seen for you
False and deceptive visions;
They have not [b]uncovered your iniquity,
To bring back your captives,
But have envisioned for you false
[c]prophecies and delusions.

15 All who pass by [a]clap *their* hands at you;
They hiss [b]and shake their heads
At the daughter of Jerusalem:
"*Is* this the city that is called
[c]'The perfection of beauty,
The joy of the whole earth'?"

16 [a]All your enemies have opened their
mouth against you;
They hiss and gnash *their* teeth.
They say, [b]"We have swallowed *her* up!
Surely this *is* the [c]day we have waited for;
We have found *it,* [d]we have seen *it!*"

17 The LORD has done what He
[a]purposed;
He has fulfilled His word
Which He commanded in days of old.
He has thrown down and has not pitied,
And He has caused an enemy to
[b]rejoice over you;
He has exalted the horn of your
adversaries.

18 Their heart cried out to the Lord,
"O wall of the daughter of Zion,
[a]Let tears run down like a river day and
night;
Give yourself no relief;
Give your eyes no rest.

19 "Arise, [a]cry out in the night,
At the beginning of the watches;
[b]Pour out your heart like water before
the face of the Lord.
Lift your hands toward Him
For the life of your young children,
Who faint from hunger [c]at the head of
every street."

20 "See, O LORD, and consider!
To whom have You done this?
[a]Should the women eat their offspring,
The children they have cuddled?[1]
Should the priest and prophet be slain
In the sanctuary of the Lord?

21 "Young[a] and old lie
On the ground in the streets;
My virgins and my young men
Have fallen by the [b]sword;

2:7 [b] Ps. 74:3–8 **2:8** [a] Jer. 52:14 [b] [Is. 34:11] **2:9** [a] Jer. 51:30 [b] Deut. 28:36 [c] 2 Chr. 15:3 [d] Ps. 74:9 **2:10** [a] Is. 3:26 [b] Job 2:12 [c] Is. 15:3 **2:11** [a] Lam. 3:48 [b] Job 16:13 [c] Lam. 4:4 **2:13** [a] Lam. 1:12 **2:14** [a] Jer. 2:8; 23:25–29; 29:8, 9; 37:19 [b] Is. 58:1 [c] Jer. 23:33–36 **2:15** [a] Ezek. 25:6 [b] Ps. 44:14 [c] [Ps. 48:2; 50:2] **2:16** [a] Job 16:9, 10 [b] Ps. 56:2; 124:3 [c] Lam. 1:21 [d] Ps. 35:21 **2:17** [a] Lev. 26:16 [b] Ps. 38:16 **2:18** [a] Jer. 14:17 **2:19** [a] Ps. 119:147 [b] Ps. 42:4; 62:8 [c] Is. 51:20 **2:20** [a] Lev. 26:29 [1] Vulgate reads *a span long.* **2:21** [a] 2 Chr. 36:17 [b] Jer. 18:21

You have slain *them* in the day of Your
anger,
You have slaughtered *and* not pitied.

22 "You have invited as to a feast day
[a]The terrors that surround me.
In the day of the LORD's anger
There was no refugee or survivor.
[b]Those whom I have borne and
brought up
My enemies have [c]destroyed."

The Prophet's Anguish and Hope

3 I *am* the man *who* has seen affliction
by the rod of His wrath.
2 He has led me and made *me* walk
In darkness and not *in* light.
3 Surely He has turned His hand against me
Time and time again throughout the day.

4 He has aged [a]my flesh and my skin,
And [b]broken my bones.
5 He has besieged me
And surrounded *me* with bitterness
and woe.
6 [a]He has set me in dark places
Like the dead of long ago.

7 [a]He has hedged me in so that I cannot
get out;
He has made my chain heavy.
8 Even [a]when I cry and shout,
He shuts out my prayer.
9 He has blocked my ways with hewn stone;
He has made my paths crooked.

10 [a]He *has been* to me a bear lying in wait,
Like a lion in ambush.
11 He has turned aside my ways and [a]torn
me in pieces;
He has made me desolate.
12 He has bent His bow
And [a]set me up as a target for the arrow.

13 He has caused [a]the arrows of His quiver
To pierce my loins.[1]
14 I have become the [a]ridicule of all my
people—
[b]Their taunting song all the day.
15 [a]He has filled me with bitterness,
He has made me drink wormwood.

16 He has also broken my teeth [a]with
gravel,
And covered me with ashes.
17 You have moved my soul far from peace;
I have forgotten prosperity.
18 [a]And I said, "My strength and my hope
Have perished from the LORD."

19 Remember my affliction and roaming,
[a]The wormwood and the gall.
20 My soul still remembers
And sinks within me.

2:22 [a] Ps. 31:13 [b] Hos. 9:12 [c] Jer. 16:2–4; 44:7 **3:4** [a] Job 16:8 [b] Ps. 51:8 **3:6** [a] [Ps. 88:5, 6; 143:3] **3:7** [a] Hos. 2:6 **3:8** [a] Job 30:20 **3:10** [a] Is. 38:13 **3:11** [a] Hos. 6:1 **3:12** [a] Job 7:20; 16:12 **3:13** [a] Job 6:4 [1] Literally *kidneys* **3:14** [a] Jer. 20:7 [b] Job 30:9 **3:15** [a] Jer. 9:15 **3:16** [a] [Prov. 20:17] **3:18** [a] Ps. 31:22 **3:19** [a] Jer. 9:15

THE FATE OF THE SEEN

You have moved my soul far from peace; I have forgotten prosperity.

LAMENTATIONS 3:17

In the aftermath of the destruction of Jerusalem and the city's magnificent temple (2 Kin. 25:9–10), the prophet Jeremiah penned a lamentation: "How lonely sits the city that was full of people! How like a widow is she . . . She weeps bitterly in the night" (Lam. 1:1–2). The roads that led to Jerusalem were empty; no one went there to celebrate the feasts. "All her splendor has departed" (1:6).

Perhaps the saddest verse is where the prophet complained to God, "You have moved my soul far from peace; I have forgotten prosperity" (3:17). Another way of translating this verse is "My life was deprived of peace; I forgot goodness." The capture of Jerusalem and the destruction of the temple were so catastrophic that the prophet lamented that peace, or well-being, were no longer part of his life.

God already knows everything about us. His awareness of us should comfort us because He stays with us through every situation and trial and provides us with His true peace. Lean into the peace of God today.

21 This I recall to my mind,
Therefore I have [a]hope.
22 [a]*Through* the LORD's mercies we are not consumed,
Because His compassions [b]fail not.
23 *They are* new [a]every morning;
Great *is* Your faithfulness.
24 "The LORD *is* my [a]portion," says my soul,
"Therefore I [b]hope in Him!"

25 The LORD *is* good to those who [a]wait for Him,
To the soul *who* seeks Him.
26 *It is* good that *one* should [a]hope [b]and wait quietly
For the salvation of the LORD.
27 [a]*It is* good for a man to bear
The yoke in his youth.

28 [a]Let him sit alone and keep silent,
Because *God* has laid *it* on him;
29 [a]Let him put his mouth in the dust—
There may yet be hope.
30 [a]Let him give *his* cheek to the one who strikes him,
And be full of reproach.
31 [a]For the Lord will not cast off forever.
32 Though He causes grief,
Yet He will show compassion
According to the multitude of His mercies.
33 For [a]He does not afflict willingly,
Nor grieve the children of men.

34 To crush under one's feet
All the prisoners of the earth,
35 To turn aside the justice *due* a man
Before the face of the Most High,
36 Or subvert a man in his cause—
[a]The Lord does not approve.

37 Who *is* he [a]*who* speaks and it comes to pass,
When the Lord has not commanded *it?*
38 *Is it* not from the mouth of the Most High
That [a]woe and well-being proceed?
39 [a]Why should a living man complain,
[b]A man for the punishment of his sins?

40 Let us search out and examine our ways,
And turn back to the LORD;

PEACE NOTE

Review your personal values. How much emphasis are you placing on living in the peace of God in your life, calendar, and planning?

LAMENTATIONS 3:40

41 [a]Let us lift our hearts and hands
To God in heaven.
42 [a]We have transgressed and rebelled;
You have not pardoned.

43 You have covered *Yourself* with anger
And pursued us;
You have slain *and* not pitied.
44 You have covered Yourself with a cloud,
That prayer should not pass through.
45 You have made us an [a]offscouring and refuse
In the midst of the peoples.

46 [a]All our enemies
Have opened their mouths against us.
47 [a]Fear and a snare have come upon us,
[b]Desolation and destruction.
48 [a]My eyes overflow with rivers of water
For the destruction of the daughter of my people.

49 [a]My eyes flow and do not cease,
Without interruption,
50 Till the LORD from heaven
[a]Looks down and sees.
51 My eyes bring suffering to my soul
Because of all the daughters of my city.

52 My enemies [a]without cause
Hunted me down like a bird.
53 They silenced[1] my life [a]in the pit
And [b]threw stones at me.
54 [a]The waters flowed over my head;
[b]I said, "I am cut off!"

3:21 [a] Ps. 130:7 **3:22** [a] [Mal. 3:6] [b] Ps. 78:38 **3:23** [a] Is. 33:2 **3:24** [a] Ps. 16:5; 73:26; 119:57 [b] Mic. 7:7 **3:25** [a] Is. 30:18 **3:26** [a] [Rom. 4:16–18] [b] Ps. 37:7 **3:27** [a] Ps. 94:12 **3:28** [a] Jer. 15:17 **3:29** [a] Job 42:6 **3:30** [a] Is. 50:6 **3:31** [a] Ps. 77:7; 94:14 **3:33** [a] [Ezek. 33:11] **3:36** [a] [Hab. 1:13] **3:37** [a] [Ps. 33:9–11] **3:38** [a] Job 2:10 **3:39** [a] Prov. 19:3 [b] Mic. 7:9 **3:41** [a] Ps. 86:4 **3:42** [a] Dan. 9:5 **3:45** [a] 1 Cor. 4:13 **3:46** [a] Lam. 2:16 **3:47** [a] Is. 24:17, 18 [b] Is. 51:19 **3:48** [a] Jer. 4:19; 14:17 **3:49** [a] Jer. 14:17 **3:50** [a] Is. 63:15 **3:52** [a] Ps. 35:7, 19 **3:53** [a] Jer. 37:16 [b] Dan. 6:17 [1] Septuagint reads *put to death.* **3:54** [a] Ps. 69:2 [b] Is. 38:10

55 [a]I called on Your name, O LORD,
From the lowest [b]pit.
56 [a]You have heard my voice:
"Do not hide Your ear
From my sighing, from my cry for help."
57 You [a]drew near on the day I called on You,
And said, [b]"Do not fear!"

58 O Lord, You have [a]pleaded the case for my soul;
[b]You have redeemed my life.
59 O LORD, You have seen *how* I am wronged;
[a]Judge my case.
60 You have seen all their vengeance,
All their [a]schemes against me.

61 You have heard their reproach, O LORD,
All their schemes against me,
62 The lips of my enemies
And their whispering against me all the day.
63 Look at their [a]sitting down and their rising up;
I *am* their taunting song.

64 [a]Repay them, O LORD,
According to the work of their hands.
65 Give them a veiled[1] heart;
Your curse *be* upon them!
66 In Your anger,
Pursue and destroy them
[a]From under the heavens of the [b]LORD.

The Degradation of Zion

4 How the gold has become dim!
How changed the fine gold!
The stones of the sanctuary are scattered
At the head of every street.

2 The precious sons of Zion,
Valuable as fine gold,
How they are regarded [a]as clay pots,
The work of the hands of the potter!

3 Even the jackals present their breasts
To nurse their young;
But the daughter of my people *is* cruel,
[a]Like ostriches in the wilderness.

4 The tongue of the infant clings
To the roof of its mouth for thirst;
[a]The young children ask for bread,
But no one breaks it for them.

5 Those who ate delicacies
Are desolate in the streets;
Those who were brought up in scarlet
[a]Embrace ash heaps.

6 The punishment of the iniquity of the daughter of my people
Is greater than the punishment of the [a]sin of Sodom,
Which was [b]overthrown in a moment,
With no hand to help her!

7 Her Nazirites[1] were brighter than snow
And whiter than milk;
They were more ruddy in body than rubies,
Like sapphire in their appearance.

8 *Now* their appearance is blacker than soot;
They go unrecognized in the streets;
[a]Their skin clings to their bones,
It has become as dry as wood.

9 *Those* slain by the sword are better off
Than *those* who die of hunger;
For these [a]pine away,
Stricken *for lack* of the fruits of the [b]field.

10 The hands of the [a]compassionate women
Have cooked their [b]own children;
They became [c]food for them
In the destruction of the daughter of my people.

11 The LORD has fulfilled His fury,
[a]He has poured out His fierce anger.
[b]He kindled a fire in Zion,
And it has devoured its foundations.

12 The kings of the earth,
And all inhabitants of the world,
Would not have believed
That the adversary and the enemy
Could [a]enter the gates of Jerusalem—

13 [a]Because of the sins of her prophets
And the iniquities of her priests,
[b]Who shed in her midst
The blood of the just.

14 They wandered blind in the streets;
[a]They have defiled themselves with blood,
[b]So that no one would touch their garments.

3:55 [a] Ps. 130:1 [b] Jer. 38:6–13 **3:56** [a] Ps. 3:4 **3:57** [a] James 4:8 [b] Is. 41:10, 14 **3:58** [a] Jer. 51:36 [b] Ps. 71:23 **3:59** [a] Ps. 9:4 **3:60** [a] Jer. 11:19 **3:63** [a] Ps. 139:2 **3:64** [a] Ps. 28:4 **3:65** [1] A Jewish tradition reads *sorrow of.* **3:66** [a] Deut. 25:19 [b] Ps. 8:3 **4:2** [a] Is. 30:14 **4:3** [a] Job 39:14–17 **4:4** [a] Ps. 22:15 **4:5** [a] Job 24:8 **4:6** [a] Ezek. 16:48 [b] Gen. 19:25 **4:7** [1] Or *nobles* **4:8** [a] Ps. 102:5 **4:9** [a] Lev. 26:39 [b] Jer. 16:4 **4:10** [a] Lam. 2:20 [b] Is. 49:15 [c] Deut. 28:57 **4:11** [a] Jer. 7:20 [b] Deut. 32:22 **4:12** [a] Jer. 21:13 **4:13** [a] Jer. 5:31 [b] Matt. 23:31 **4:14** [a] Jer. 2:34 [b] Num. 19:16

15 They cried out to them,
"Go away, [a]unclean!
Go away, go away,
Do not touch us!"
When they fled and wandered,
Those among the nations said,
"They shall no longer dwell *here.*"

16 The face[1] of the LORD scattered them;
He no longer regards them.
[a]*The people* do not respect the priests
Nor show favor to the elders.

17 Still [a]our eyes failed us,
Watching vainly for our help;
In our watching we watched
For a nation *that* could not save *us.*

18 [a]They tracked our steps
So that we could not walk in our streets.
[b]Our end was near;
Our days were over,
For our end had come.

19 Our pursuers were [a]swifter
Than the eagles of the heavens.
They pursued us on the mountains
And lay in wait for us in the wilderness.

20 The [a]breath of our nostrils, the anointed of the LORD,
[b]Was caught in their pits,
Of whom we said, "Under his shadow
We shall live among the nations."

21 Rejoice and be glad, O daughter of [a]Edom,
You who dwell in the land of Uz!
[b]The cup shall also pass over to you
And you shall become drunk and make yourself naked.

22 [a]*The punishment of* your iniquity is accomplished,
O daughter of Zion;
He will no longer send you into captivity.
[b]He will punish your iniquity,
O daughter of Edom;
He will uncover your sins!

Prayer for Restoration

5 Remember, [a]O LORD, what has come upon us;
Look, and behold [b]our reproach!
2 [a]Our inheritance has been turned over to aliens,
And our houses to foreigners.
3 We have become orphans and waifs,
Our mothers *are* like [a]widows.

4 We pay for the water we drink,
And our wood comes at a price.
5 [a]*They* pursue at our heels;[1]
We labor *and* have no rest.
6 [a]We have given our hand [b]*to* the Egyptians
And the [c]Assyrians, to be satisfied with bread.

7 [a]Our fathers sinned *and are* no more,
But we bear their iniquities.
8 Servants rule over us;
There is none to deliver *us* from their hand.
9 We get our bread *at the risk* of our lives,
Because of the sword in the wilderness.

10 Our skin is hot as an oven,
Because of the fever of famine.
11 They [a]ravished the women in Zion,
The maidens in the cities of Judah.
12 Princes were hung up by their hands,
And elders were not respected.
13 Young men [a]ground at the millstones;
Boys staggered under *loads of* wood.
14 The elders have ceased *gathering at* the gate,
And the young men from their [a]music.

15 The joy of our heart has ceased;
Our dance has turned into [a]mourning.
16 [a]The crown has fallen *from* our head.
Woe to us, for we have sinned!
17 Because of this our heart is faint;
[a]Because of these *things* our eyes grow dim;
18 Because of Mount Zion which is [a]desolate,
With foxes walking about on it.

19 You, O LORD, [a]remain forever;
[b]Your throne from generation to generation.
20 [a]Why do You forget us forever,
And forsake us for so long a time?
21 [a]Turn us back to You, O LORD, and we will be restored;
Renew our days as of old,
22 Unless You have utterly rejected us,
And are very angry with us!

4:15 [a] Lev. 13:45, 46 **4:16** [a] Lam. 5:12 [1] Targum reads *anger.* **4:17** [a] 2 Kin. 24:7 **4:18** [a] 2 Kin. 25:4 [b] Ezek. 7:2, 3, 6 **4:19** [a] Deut. 28:49 **4:20** [a] Gen. 2:7 [b] Jer. 52:9 **4:21** [a] Ps. 83:3–6 [b] Jer. 25:15 **4:22** [a] [Is. 40:2] [b] Ps. 137:7 **5:1** [a] Ps. 89:50 [b] Lam. 2:15 **5:2** [a] Ps. 79:1 **5:3** [a] Jer. 15:8; 18:21 **5:5** [a] Jer. 28:14 [1] Literally *necks* **5:6** [a] Gen. 24:2 [b] Hos. 9:3; 12:1 [c] Hos. 5:13 **5:7** [a] Jer. 31:29 **5:11** [a] Zech. 14:2 **5:13** [a] Judg. 16:21 **5:14** [a] Jer. 7:34 **5:15** [a] Amos 8:10 **5:16** [a] Ps. 89:39 **5:17** [a] Ps. 6:7 **5:18** [a] Is. 27:10 **5:19** [a] Ps. 9:7 [b] Ps. 45:6 **5:20** [a] Ps. 13:1; 44:24 **5:21** [a] Jer. 31:18

THE BOOK OF

EZEKIEL

AUTHOR

There is strong evidence in favor of Ezekiel's authorship of this book. The first-person singular point of view is used throughout the book, indicating that it is the work of one person. This person is actually identified in Ezekiel 1:3 and 24:24 as Ezekiel. The unity and integrity of Ezekiel's prophetic record are supported and the style, language, and thematic development are consistent throughout the book. Like Jeremiah, Ezekiel was a priest who was called to be a prophet of the Lord. Ezekiel was privileged to receive a number of visions of the power and plan of God, and he was careful and artistic in his written presentation.

TIME

c. 592–570 BC

KEY VERSE

Ezekiel 36:33–35

THEME

Ezekiel was an exilic prophet, meaning he prophesied to the exiles in Babylon. He was one of the ten thousand taken there by Nebuchadnezzar in 597 BC (2 Kin. 24:14). The book contains a series of prophetic messages that represent a lifetime of ministry to the exiles in Babylon. Ezekiel sees himself as a watchman or lookout compelled to warn people of coming danger and the need for personal responsibility to an awesome, all-seeing, all-knowing God. The last half of the book is more concerned with encouraging the people to hope for God's promise of restoration back to the land of Israel. The restoration of the temple is a key element of Ezekiel 40–48.

God did not call Ezekiel into ministry until his thirtieth birthday (1:1–3). Ezekiel suffered while he ministered to the people of God in Babylonian exile (sixth century BC), especially over the death of his wife (ch. 24), and he even had to struggle with his own speech impediment (3:26–27; 24:27; 33:22). The prophet also contended with false prophets: they "have seduced [God's] people, saying, 'Peace!' when there is no peace" (13:10) and they "see visions of peace for [Jerusalem] when there is no peace" (13:16). Yet like his contemporary Jeremiah, Ezekiel found the peace of God practical and immediate, so he proclaimed repeatedly that God would establish a "covenant of peace" with His people (34:25; 37:26).

Ezekiel's Vision of God

1 Now it came to pass in the thirtieth year, in the fourth *month,* on the fifth *day* of the month, as I *was* among the captives by [a]the River Chebar, *that* [b]the heavens were opened and I saw [c]visions[1] of God. 2On the fifth *day* of the month, which *was* in the fifth year of King Jehoiachin's captivity, 3the word of the LORD came expressly to Ezekiel the priest, the son of Buzi, in the land of the Chaldeans[1] by the River Chebar; and [a]the hand of the LORD was upon him there.

4Then I looked, and behold, [a]a whirlwind was coming [b]out of the north, a great cloud with raging fire engulfing itself; and brightness *was* all around it and radiating out of its midst like the color of amber, out of the midst of the fire. 5[a]Also from within it *came* the likeness of four living creatures. And [b]this *was* their appearance: they had [c]the likeness of a man. 6Each one had four faces, and each one had four wings. 7Their legs *were* straight, and the soles of their feet *were* like the soles of calves' feet. They sparkled [a]like the color of burnished bronze. 8[a]The hands of a man *were* under their wings on their four sides; and each of the four had faces and wings. 9Their wings touched one another. *The creatures* did not turn when they went, but each one went straight [a]forward.

10As for [a]the likeness of their faces, *each* [b]had the face of a man; each of the four had [c]the face of a lion on the right side, [d]each of the four had the face of an ox on the left side, [e]and each of the four had the face of an eagle. 11Thus *were* their faces. Their wings stretched upward; two *wings* of each one touched one another, and [a]two covered their bodies. 12And [a]each one went straight forward; they went wherever the spirit wanted to go, and they did not turn when they went.

13As for the likeness of the living creatures, their appearance *was* like burning coals of fire, [a]like the appearance of torches going back and forth among the living creatures. The fire was bright, and out of the fire went lightning. 14And the living creatures ran back and forth, [a]in appearance like a flash of lightning.

15Now as I looked at the living creatures, behold, [a]a wheel *was* on the earth beside each living creature with its four faces. 16[a]The appearance of the wheels and their workings *was* [b]like the color of beryl, and all four had the same likeness. The appearance of their workings *was,* as it were, a wheel in the middle of a wheel. 17When they moved, they went toward any one of four directions; they did not turn aside when they went. 18As for their rims, they were so high they were awesome; and their rims *were* [a]full of eyes, all around the four of them. 19[a]When the living creatures went, the wheels went beside them; and when the living creatures were lifted up from the earth, the wheels were lifted up. 20Wherever the spirit wanted to go, they went, *because* there the spirit went; and the wheels were lifted together with them, [a]for the spirit of the living creatures[1] *was* in the wheels. 21When those went, *these* went; when those stood, *these* stood; and when those were lifted up from the earth, the wheels were lifted up together with them, for the spirit of the living creatures[1] *was* in the wheels.

22[a]The likeness of the firmament above the heads of the living creatures[1] *was* like the color of an awesome [b]crystal, stretched out [c]over their heads. 23And under the firmament their wings *spread out* straight, one toward another. Each one had two which covered one side, and each one had two which covered the other side of the body. 24[a]When they went, I heard the noise of their wings, [b]like the noise of many waters, like [c]the voice of the Almighty, a tumult like the noise of an army; and when they stood still, they let down their wings. 25A voice came from above the firmament that *was* over their heads; whenever they stood, they let down their wings.

26[a]And above the firmament over their heads *was* the likeness of a throne, [b]in appearance like a sapphire stone; on the likeness of the throne *was* a likeness with the appearance of a man high above [c]it. 27Also from the appearance of His waist and upward [a]I saw, as it were, the color of amber with the appearance of fire all around within it; and from the appearance of His waist and downward I saw, as it were, the appearance of fire with brightness all around. 28[a]Like the appearance of a rainbow in a cloud on a rainy day, so *was* the appearance of the brightness all around it. [b]This *was* the appearance of the likeness of the glory of the LORD.

1:1 [a] Ezek. 3:15, 23; 10:15 [b] Rev. 4:1; 19:11 [c] Ezek. 8:3 [1] Following Masoretic Text, Septuagint, and Vulgate; Syriac and Targum read *a vision.* **1:3** [a] Ezek. 3:14, 22 [1] Or *Babylonians,* and so elsewhere in this book **1:4** [a] Jer. 23:19; 25:32 [b] Jer. 1:14 **1:5** [a] Rev. 4:6–8 [b] Ezek. 10:8 [c] Ezek. 10:14 **1:7** [a] Dan. 10:6 **1:8** [a] Ezek. 10:8, 21 **1:9** [a] Ezek. 1:12; 10:20–22 **1:10** [a] Rev. 4:7 [b] Num. 2:10 [c] Num. 2:3 [d] Num. 2:18 [e] Num. 2:25 **1:11** [a] Is. 6:2 **1:12** [a] Ezek. 10:11, 22 **1:13** [a] Rev. 4:5 **1:14** [a] [Matt. 24:27] **1:15** [a] Ezek. 10:9 **1:16** [a] Ezek. 10:9, 10 [b] Dan. 10:6 **1:18** [a] Ezek. 10:12 **1:19** [a] Ezek. 10:16, 17 **1:20** [a] Ezek. 10:17 [1] Literally *living creature;* Septuagint and Vulgate read *spirit of life;* Targum reads *creatures.* **1:21** [1] Literally *living creature;* Septuagint and Vulgate read *spirit of life;* Targum reads *creatures.* **1:22** [a] Ezek. 10:1 [b] Rev. 4:6 [c] Ezek. 10:1 [1] Following Septuagint, Targum, and Vulgate; Masoretic Text reads *living creature.* **1:24** [a] Ezek. 3:13; 10:5 [b] Rev. 1:15 [c] Job 37:4, 5 **1:26** [a] Ezek. 10:1 [b] Ex. 24:10, 16 [c] Ezek. 8:2 **1:27** [a] Ezek. 8:2 **1:28** [a] Rev. 4:3; 10:1 [b] Ezek. 3:23; 8:4

Ezekiel Sent to Rebellious Israel

So when I saw *it,* [c]I fell on my face, and I heard a voice of One speaking.

2 And He said to me, "Son of man, [a]stand on your feet, and I will speak to you." 2Then [a]the Spirit entered me when He spoke to me, and set me on my feet; and I heard Him who spoke to me. 3And He said to me: "Son of man, I am sending you to the children of Israel, to a rebellious nation that has [a]rebelled against Me; [b]they and their fathers have transgressed against Me to this very day. 4[a]For *they are* impudent and stubborn children. I am sending you to them, and you shall say to them, 'Thus says the Lord GOD.' 5[a]As for them, whether they hear or whether they refuse—for they *are* a [b]rebellious house—yet they [c]will know that a prophet has been among them.

6"And you, son of man, [a]do not be afraid of them nor be afraid of their words, though [b]briers and thorns *are* with you and you dwell among scorpions; [c]do not be afraid of their words or dismayed by their looks, [d]though they *are* a rebellious house. 7[a]You shall speak My words to them, whether they hear or whether they refuse, for they *are* rebellious. 8But you, son of man, hear what I say to you. Do not be rebellious like that rebellious house; open your mouth and [a]eat what I give you."

9Now when I looked, there was [a]a hand stretched out to me; and behold, [b]a scroll of a book *was* in it. 10Then He spread it before me; and *there was* writing on the inside and on the outside, and written on it *were* lamentations and mourning and woe.

3 Moreover He said to me, "Son of man, eat what you find; [a]eat this scroll, and go, speak to the house of Israel." 2So I opened my mouth, and He caused me to eat that scroll.

3And He said to me, "Son of man, feed your belly, and fill your stomach with this scroll that I give you." So I [a]ate, and it was in my mouth [b]like honey in sweetness.

4Then He said to me: "Son of man, go to the house of Israel and speak with My words to them. 5For you *are* not sent to a people of unfamiliar speech and of hard language, *but* to the house of Israel, 6not to many people of unfamiliar speech and of hard language, whose words you cannot understand. Surely, [a]had I sent you to them, they would have listened to you. 7But the house of Israel will not listen to you, [a]because they will not listen to Me; [b]for all the house of Israel *are* impudent and hard-*hearted.* 8*Behold, I have* made your face strong against their faces, and your forehead strong against their foreheads. 9[a]Like adamant stone, harder than flint, I have made your forehead; [b]do not be afraid of them, nor be dismayed at their looks, though they *are* a rebellious house."

10Moreover He said to me: "Son of man, receive into your heart all My words that I speak to you, and hear with your ears. 11And go, get to the captives, to the children of your people, and speak to them and tell them, [a]'Thus says the Lord GOD,' whether they hear, or whether they refuse."

12Then [a]the Spirit lifted me up, and I heard behind me a great thunderous voice: "Blessed *is* the [b]glory of the LORD from His place!" 13*I* also *heard* the [a]noise of the wings of the living creatures that touched one another, and the noise of the wheels beside them, and a great thunderous noise. 14So the Spirit lifted me up and took me away, and I went in bitterness, in the heat of my spirit; but [a]the hand of the LORD was strong upon me. 15Then I came to the captives at Tel Abib, who dwelt by the River Chebar; and [a]I sat where they sat, and remained there astonished among them seven days.

> **PEACE NOTE**
>
> God's peace is not dependent on circumstances. It is a deep and abiding assurance that He will make "all things work together for good to those who love God" (Rom. 8:28).

Ezekiel Is a Watchman

16Now it [a]came to pass at the end of seven days that the word of the LORD came to me, saying, 17[a]"Son of man, I have made you [b]a watchman for the house of Israel; therefore hear a word from My mouth, and give them [c]warning from Me: 18When I say to the wicked, 'You shall surely die,' and you give him no warning, nor speak to warn the wicked from his wicked way, to save his life, that

1:28 [c] Dan. 8:17 **2:1** [a] Dan. 10:11 **2:2** [a] Ezek. 3:24 **2:3** [a] Ezek. 5:6; 20:8, 13, 18 [b] Jer. 3:25 **2:4** [a] Ezek. 3:7 **2:5** [a] Ezek. 3:11, 26, 27 [b] Ezek. 3:26 [c] Ezek. 33:33 **2:6** [a] Jer. 1:8, 17 [b] Mic. 7:4 [c] [1 Pet. 3:14] [d] Ezek. 3:9, 26, 27 **2:7** [a] Jer. 1:7, 17 **2:8** [a] Rev. 10:9 **2:9** [a] [Ezek. 8:3] [b] Ezek. 3:1 **3:1** [a] Ezek. 2:8, 9 **3:3** [a] Rev. 10:9 [b] Ps. 19:10; 119:103 **3:6** [a] Matt. 11:21 **3:7** [a] John 15:20, 21 [b] Ezek. 2:4 **3:9** [a] Mic. 3:8 [b] Jer. 1:8, 17 **3:11** [a] Ezek. 2:5, 7 **3:12** [a] Acts 8:39 [b] Ezek. 1:28; 8:4 **3:13** [a] Ezek. 1:24; 10:5 **3:14** [a] 2 Kin. 3:15 **3:15** [a] Job 2:13 **3:16** [a] Jer. 42:7 **3:17** [a] Ezek. 33:7–9 [b] Jer. 6:17 [c] [Lev. 19:17]

same wicked *man* [a]shall die in his iniquity; but his blood I will require at your hand. 19Yet, if you warn the wicked, and he does not turn from his wickedness, nor from his wicked way, he shall die in his iniquity; [a]but you have delivered your soul.

20"Again, when a [a]righteous *man* turns from his righteousness and commits iniquity, and I lay a stumbling block before him, he shall die; because you did not give him warning, he shall die in his sin, and his righteousness which he has done shall not be remembered; but his blood I will require at your hand. 21Nevertheless if you warn the righteous *man* that the righteous should not sin, and he does not sin, he shall surely live because he took warning; also you will have delivered your soul."

22[a]Then the hand of the LORD was upon me there, and He said to me, "Arise, go out [b]into the plain, and there I shall talk with you."

23So I arose and went out into the plain, and behold, [a]the glory of the LORD stood there, like the glory which I [b]saw by the River Chebar; [c]and I fell on my face. 24Then [a]the Spirit entered me and set me on my feet, and spoke with me and said to me: "Go, shut yourself inside your house. 25And you, O son of man, surely [a]they will put ropes on you and bind you with them, so that you cannot go out among them. 26[a]I will make your tongue cling to the roof of your mouth, so that you shall be mute and [b]not be one to rebuke them, [c]for they *are* a rebellious house. 27[a]But when I speak with you, I will open your mouth, and you shall say to them, [b]'Thus says the Lord GOD.' He who hears, let him hear; and he who refuses, let him refuse; for they *are* a rebellious house.

The Siege of Jerusalem Portrayed

4 "You also, son of man, take a clay tablet and lay it before you, and portray on it a city, Jerusalem. 2[a]Lay siege against it, build a [b]siege wall against it, and heap up a mound against it; set camps against it also, and place battering rams against it all around. 3Moreover take for yourself an iron plate, and set it *as* an iron wall between you and the city. Set your face against it, and it shall be [a]besieged, and you shall lay siege against it. [b]This *will be a sign to the house* of Israel.

4"Lie also on your left side, and lay the iniquity of the house of Israel upon it. *According* to the number of the days that you lie on it, you shall bear their iniquity. 5For I have laid on you the years of their iniquity, according to the number of the days, three hundred and ninety days; [a]so you shall bear the iniquity of the house of Israel. 6And when you have completed them, lie again on your right side; then you shall bear the iniquity of the house of Judah forty days. I have laid on you a day for each year.

7"Therefore you shall set your face toward the siege of Jerusalem; your arm *shall be* uncovered, and you shall prophesy against it. 8[a]And surely I will restrain you so that you cannot turn from one side to another till you have ended the days of your siege.

9"Also take for yourself wheat, barley, beans, lentils, millet, and spelt; put them into one vessel, and make bread of them for yourself. *During* the number of days that you lie on your side, three hundred and ninety days, you shall eat it. 10And your food which you eat *shall be* by weight, twenty shekels a day; from time to time you shall eat it. 11You shall also drink water by measure, one-sixth of a hin; from time to time you shall drink. 12And you shall eat it *as* barley cakes; and bake it using fuel of human waste in their sight."

13Then the LORD said, "So [a]shall the children of Israel eat their defiled bread among the Gentiles, where I will drive them."

14So I said, [a]"Ah, Lord GOD! Indeed I have never defiled myself from my youth till now; I have never eaten [b]what died of itself or was torn by beasts, nor has [c]abominable flesh ever come into my mouth."

15Then He said to me, "See, I am giving you cow dung instead of human waste, and you shall prepare your bread over it."

16Moreover He said to me, "Son of man, surely I will cut off the [a]supply of bread in Jerusalem; they shall [b]eat bread by weight and with anxiety, and shall [c]drink water by measure and with dread, 17that they may lack bread and water, and be dismayed with one another, and [a]waste away because of their iniquity.

A Sword Against Jerusalem

5 "And you, son of man, take a sharp sword, take it as a barber's razor, [a]and pass *it* over your head and your beard; then take scales to weigh and divide the *hair*. 2[a]You shall burn with fire one-third in the midst of [b]the city, when [c]the days of the siege are finished; then you shall take one-third and strike around *it* with the sword, and one-third you shall scatter in the wind: I will draw out a sword after [d]them.

3:18 [a] [John 8:21, 24] **3:19** [a] Acts 18:6; 20:26 **3:20** [a] Ezek. 18:24; 33:18 **3:22** [a] Ezek. 1:3 [b] Ezek. 8:4 **3:23** [a] Ezek. 1:28 [b] Ezek. 1:1 [c] Ezek. 1:28 **3:24** [a] Ezek. 2:2 **3:25** [a] Ezek. 4:8 **3:26** [a] Luke 1:20, 22 [b] Hos. 4:17 [c] Ezek. 2:5–7 **3:27** [a] Ezek. 24:27; 33:22 [b] Ezek. 3:11 **4:2** [a] Jer. 6:6 [b] 2 Kin. 25:1 **4:3** [a] Jer. 39:1, 2 [b] Ezek. 12:6, 11; 24:24, 27 **4:5** [a] Num. 14:34 **4:8** [a] Ezek. 3:25 **4:13** [a] Hos. 9:3 **4:14** [a] Acts 10:14 [b] Lev. 17:15; 22:8 [c] Deut. 14:3 **4:16** [a] Is. 3:1 [b] Ezek. 4:10, 11; 12:19 [c] Ezek. 4:11 **4:17** [a] Lev. 26:39 **5:1** [a] Is. 7:20 **5:2** [a] Ezek. 5:12 [b] Ezek. 4:1 [c] Ezek. 4:8, 9 [d] Lev. 26:25

3[a]You shall also take a small number of them
and bind them in the edge of your *garment.*
4Then take some of them again and [a]throw
them into the midst of the fire, and burn them
in the fire. From there a fire will go out into
all the house of Israel.

5"Thus says the Lord GOD: 'This *is* Jerusalem; I have set her in the midst of the nations
and the countries all around her. 6She has
rebelled against My judgments by doing wickedness more than the nations, and against
My statutes more than the countries that
are all around her; for they have refused My
judgments, and they have not walked in My
statutes.' 7Therefore thus says the Lord GOD:
'Because you have multiplied *disobedience*
more than the nations that *are* all around you,
have not walked in My statutes [a]nor kept My
judgments, nor even done[1] according to the
judgments of the nations that *are* all around
you'— 8therefore thus says the Lord GOD: 'Indeed I, even I, *am* against you and will execute
judgments in your midst in the sight of the
nations. 9[a]And I will do among you what I have
never done, and the like of which I will never
do again, because of all your abominations.
10Therefore fathers [a]shall eat *their* sons in your
midst, and sons shall eat their fathers; and I
will execute judgments among you, and all of
you who remain I will [b]scatter to all the winds.

11"Therefore, *as* I live,' says the Lord GOD,
'surely, because you have [a]defiled My sanctuary with all your [b]detestable things and
with all your abominations, therefore I will
also diminish *you;* [c]My eye will not spare, nor
will I have any pity. 12[a]One-third of you shall
die of the pestilence, and be consumed with
famine in your midst; and one-third shall
fall by the sword all around you; and [b]I will
scatter another third to all the winds, and I
will draw out a sword after [c]them.

13"Thus shall My anger [a]be spent, and I will
[b]cause My fury to rest upon them, [c]and I will
be avenged; [d]and they shall know that I, the
LORD, have spoken *it* in My zeal, when I have
spent My fury upon them. 14Moreover [a]I will
make you a waste and a reproach among the
nations that *are* all around you, in the sight
of all who pass by.

15'So it[1] shall be a [a]reproach, a taunt, a [b]les-
son, and an astonishment to the nations
that *are* all around you, when I execute
judgments among you in anger and in fury
and in [c]furious rebukes. I, the LORD, have
spoken. 16When I [a]send against them the
terrible arrows of famine which shall be for
destruction, which I will send to destroy you,
I will increase the famine upon you and cut
off your [b]supply of bread. 17So I will send
against you famine and [a]wild beasts, and they
will bereave you. [b]Pestilence and blood shall
pass through you, and I will bring the sword
against you. I, the LORD, have spoken.' "

Judgment on Idolatrous Israel

6 Now the word of the LORD came to me,
saying: 2"Son of man, [a]set your face toward the [b]mountains of Israel, and prophesy
against them, 3and say, 'O mountains of Israel,
hear the word of the Lord GOD! Thus says the
Lord GOD to the mountains, to the hills, to the
ravines, and to the valleys: "Indeed I, *even*
I, will bring a sword against you, and [a]I will
destroy your high places. 4Then your altars
shall be desolate, your incense altars shall be
broken, and [a]I will cast down your slain *men*
before your idols. 5And I will lay the corpses
of the children of Israel before their idols,
and I will scatter your bones all around your
altars. 6In all your dwelling places the cities
shall be laid waste, and the high places shall
be desolate, so that your altars may be laid
waste and made desolate, your idols may be
broken and made to cease, your incense altars
may be cut down, and your works may be
abolished. 7The slain shall fall in your midst,
and [a]you shall know that I *am* the LORD.

8[a]"Yet I will leave a remnant, so that you
may have *some* who escape the sword among
the nations, when you are [b]scattered through
the countries. 9Then those of you who escape will [a]remember Me among the nations
where they are carried captive, because [b]I
was crushed by their adulterous heart which
has departed from Me, and [c]by their eyes
which play the harlot after their idols; [d]they
will loathe themselves for the evils which
they committed in all their abominations.
10And they shall know that I *am* the LORD; I
have not said in vain that I would bring this
calamity upon them."

11"Thus says the Lord GOD: [a]"Pound your
fists and stamp your feet, and say, 'Alas, for all
the evil abominations of the house of Israel!
[b]For they shall fall by the sword, by famine,
and by pestilence. 12He who is far off shall

5:3 [a] *Jer. 40:6; 52:16* *5:4* [a] Jer. 41:1, 2; 44:14 **5:7** [a] Jer. 2:10, 11 [1] Following Masoretic Text, Septuagint, Targum, and Vulgate; many Hebrew manuscripts and Syriac read *but have done* (compare 11:12). **5:9** [a] [Amos 3:2] **5:10** [a] Jer. 19:9 [b] Zech. 2:6; 7:14 **5:11** [a] [Jer. 7:9–11] [b] Ezek. 11:21 [c] Ezek. 7:4, 9; 8:18; 9:10 **5:12** [a] Ezek. 6:12 [b] Jer. 9:16 [c] Jer. 43:10, 11; 44:27 **5:13** [a] Lam. 4:11 [b] Ezek. 21:17 [c] Is. 1:24 [d] Ezek. 36:6; 38:19 **5:14** [a] Lev. 26:31 **5:15** [a] Jer. 24:9 [b] [Is. 26:9] [c] Ezek. 5:8; 25:17 [1] Septuagint, Syriac, Targum, and Vulgate read *you.* **5:16** [a] Deut. 32:23 [b] Lev. 26:26 **5:17** [a] Lev. 26:22 [b] Ezek. 38:22 **6:2** [a] Ezek. 20:46; 21:2; 25:2 [b] Ezek. 36:1 **6:3** [a] Lev. 26:30 **6:4** [a] Lev. 26:30 **6:7** [a] Ezek. 7:4, 9 **6:8** [a] Jer. 44:28 [b] Ezek. 5:12 **6:9** [a] [Deut. 4:29] [b] Ps. 78:40 [c] Ezek. 20:7, 24 [d] Ezek. 20:43; 36:31 **6:11** [a] Ezek. 21:14 [b] Ezek. 5:12

die by the pestilence, he who is near shall
fall by the sword, and he who remains and is
besieged shall die by the famine. [a]Thus will I
spend My fury upon them. 13Then you shall
know that I *am* the LORD, when their slain are
among their idols all around their altars, [a]on
every high hill, [b]on all the mountaintops, [c]un-
der every green tree, and under every thick
oak, wherever they offered sweet incense to
all their idols. 14So I will [a]stretch out My hand
against them and make the land desolate, yes,
more desolate than the wilderness toward
[b]Diblah, in all their dwelling places. Then they
shall know that I *am* the LORD.' " ' "

Judgment on Israel Is Near

7 Moreover the word of the LORD came to
me, saying, 2"And you, son of man, thus
says the Lord GOD to the land of Israel:

[a]'An end! The end has come upon the
four corners of the land.
3 Now the end *has come* upon you,
And I will send My anger against you;
I will judge you [a]according to your ways,
And I will repay you for all your
abominations.
4 [a]My eye will not spare you,
Nor will I have pity;
But I will repay your ways,
And your abominations will be in your
midst;
[b]Then you shall know that I *am* the LORD!'

5"Thus says the Lord GOD:

'A disaster, a singular [a]disaster;
Behold, it has come!
6 An end has come,
The end has come;
It has dawned for you;
Behold, it has come!
7 [a]Doom has come to you, you who dwell
in the land;
[b]The time has come,
A day of trouble *is* near,
And not of rejoicing in the mountains.
8 Now upon you I will soon [a]pour out My
fury,
And spend My anger upon you;
I will judge you according to your ways,
And I will repay you for all your
abominations.

9 'My eye will not spare,
Nor will I have pity;
I will repay you according to your ways,
And your abominations will be in your
midst.
Then you shall know that I *am* the
LORD who strikes.

10 'Behold, the day!
Behold, it has come!
[a]Doom has gone out;
The rod has blossomed,
Pride has budded.
11 [a]Violence has risen up into a rod of
wickedness;
None of them *shall remain,*
None of their multitude,
None of them;
[b]Nor *shall there be* wailing for them.
12 The time has come,
The day draws near.

'Let not the buyer [a]rejoice,
Nor the seller [b]mourn,
For wrath *is* on their whole multitude.
13 For the seller shall not return to what
has been sold,
Though he may still be alive;
For the vision concerns the whole
multitude,
And it shall not turn back;
No one will strengthen himself
Who lives in iniquity.

14 'They have blown the trumpet and
made everyone ready,
But no one goes to battle;
For My wrath *is* on all their multitude.
15 [a]The sword *is* outside,
And the pestilence and famine within.
Whoever *is* in the field
Will die by the sword;
And whoever *is* in the city,
Famine and pestilence will devour him.

16 'Those who [a]survive will escape and be
on the mountains
Like doves of the valleys,
All of them mourning,
Each for his iniquity.
17 Every [a]hand will be feeble,
And every knee will be *as* weak *as*
water.
18 They will also [a]be girded with
sackcloth;
Horror will cover them;
Shame *will be* on every face,
Baldness on all their heads.

6:12 [a] Ezek. 5:13 **6:13** [a] Jer. 2:20; 3:6 [b] Hos. 4:13 [c] Is. 57:5 **6:14** [a] Is. 5:25 [b] Num. 33:46 **7:2** [a] Amos 8:2, 10
7:3 [a] [Rom. 2:6] **7:4** [a] Ezek. 5:11 [b] Ezek. 12:20 **7:5** [a] 2 Kin. 21:12, 13 **7:7** [a] Ezek. 7:10 [b] Zeph. 1:14, 15 **7:8** [a] Ezek. 20:8, 21
7:10 [a] Ezek. 7:7 **7:11** [a] Jer. 6:7 [b] Jer. 16:5, 6 **7:12** [a] Prov. 20:14 [b] Is. 24:2 **7:15** [a] Jer. 14:18 **7:16** [a] Ezek. 6:8; 14:22
7:17 [a] Is. 13:7 **7:18** [a] Amos 8:10

19 'They will throw their silver into the
streets,
And their gold will be like refuse;
Their [a]silver and their gold will not be
able to deliver them
In the day of the wrath of the LORD;
They will not satisfy their souls,
Nor fill their stomachs,
Because it became their stumbling
block of iniquity.

20 'As for the beauty of his ornaments,
He set it in majesty;
[a]But they made from it
The images of their abominations—
Their detestable things;
Therefore I have made it
Like refuse to them.
21 I will give it as [a]plunder
Into the hands of strangers,
And to the wicked of the earth as spoil;
And they shall defile it.
22 I will turn My face from them,
And they will defile My secret place;
For robbers shall enter it and defile it.

23 'Make a chain,
For [a]the land is filled with crimes of
blood,
And the city is full of violence.
24 Therefore I will bring the [a]worst of the
Gentiles,
And they will possess their houses;
I will cause the pomp of the strong to
cease,
And their holy places shall be [b]defiled.
25 Destruction comes;
They will seek peace, but *there shall be*
none.
26 [a]Disaster will come upon disaster,
And rumor will be upon rumor.
[b]Then they will seek a vision from a
prophet;
But the law will perish from the priest,
And counsel from the elders.

27 'The king will mourn,
The prince will be clothed with desolation,
And the hands of the common people
will tremble.
I will do to them according to their way,
And according to what they deserve I
will judge them;
Then they shall know that I *am* the
LORD!' "

Abominations in the Temple

8 And it came to pass in the sixth year, in
the sixth *month*, on the fifth *day* of the
month, as I sat in my house with [a]the elders
of Judah sitting before me, that [b]the hand
of the Lord GOD fell upon me there. 2 [a]Then
I looked, and there was a likeness, like the
appearance of fire—from the appearance
of His waist and downward, fire; and from
His waist and upward, like the appearance

7:19 [a] Zeph. 1:18 7:20 [a] Jer. 7:30 7:21 [a] 2 Kin. 24:13 7:23 [a] 2 Kin. 21:16 7:24 [a] Ezek. 21:31; 28:7 [b] Ezek. 24:21
7:26 [a] Jer. 4:20 [b] Ps. 74:9 8:1 [a] Ezek. 14:1; 20:1; 33:31 [b] Ezek. 1:3; 3:22 8:2 [a] Ezek. 1:26, 27

TAKE ACTION

"Destruction comes; they will seek peace, but there shall be none."

EZEKIEL 7:25

Ezekiel had many negative things to say about apostate Judah and her wicked leaders. Chapter 7 announced the end of that kingdom. The Lord said to Ezekiel, "An end! The end has come upon the four corners of the land" (v. 2). All that remained, including the city of Jerusalem itself, would fall to the approaching Babylonian army. The situation was so bad that the prophet could offer no hope: "Destruction comes," he warned, "they will seek peace, but there shall be none" (v. 25).

That's about as bad as it can get. Disaster will follow disaster, the prophet foretold. Desperate people would seek advice from prophet, priest, and elder to no avail.

If nothing else, this sad passage shows how important peace is. Why would anyone let it slip away? Draw near to God now. Don't wait. Seek His peace. But how? Read the Scriptures daily. Memorize a promise of God because there is a promise of Scripture for every problem you face. Fellowship with believers. Worship the Lord in church. These are the immediate ways you can live in the peace of God every day.

of brightness, [b]like the color of amber. 3He
[a]stretched out the form of a hand, and took
me by a lock of my hair; and [b]the Spirit lifted me up between earth and heaven, and
[c]brought me in visions of God to Jerusalem,
to the door of the north gate of the inner
court, [d]where the seat of the image of jealousy *was,* which [e]provokes to jealousy. 4And
behold, the [a]glory of the God of Israel *was*
there, like the vision that I [b]saw in the plain.
5Then He said to me, "Son of man, lift
your eyes now toward the north." So I lifted
my eyes toward the north, and there, north
of the altar gate, was this image of jealousy
in the entrance.
6Furthermore He said to me, "Son of
man, do you see what they are doing, the
great [a]abominations that the house of Israel
commits here, to make Me go far away from
My sanctuary? Now turn again, you will see
greater abominations." 7So He brought me
to the door of the court; and when I looked,
there was a hole in the wall. 8Then He said
to me, "Son of man, dig into the wall"; and
when I dug into the wall, there was a door.
9And He said to me, "Go in, and see the wicked abominations which they are doing there."
10So I went in and saw, and there—every [a]sort
of [b]creeping thing, abominable beasts, and all
the idols of the house of Israel, portrayed all
around on the walls. 11And there stood before
them [a]seventy men of the elders of the house
of Israel, and in their midst stood Jaazaniah
the son of Shaphan. Each man had a censer
in his hand, and a thick cloud of incense went
up. 12Then He said to me, "Son of man, have
you seen what the elders of the house of Israel
do in the dark, every man in the room of his
idols? For they say, [a]'The LORD does not see
us, the LORD has forsaken the land.' "
13And He said to me, "Turn again, *and* you
will see greater abominations that they are
doing." 14So He brought me to the door of the
north gate of the LORD's house; and to my
dismay, women were sitting there weeping
for Tammuz.
15Then He said to me, "Have you seen *this,*
O son of man? Turn again, you will see greater
abominations than these." 16So He brought
me into the inner court of the LORD's house;
and there, at the door of the temple of the
LORD, [a]between the porch and the altar, [b]*were*
about twenty-five men [c]with their backs toward the temple of the LORD and their faces
toward the east, and they were worshiping
[d]the sun toward the east.
17And He said to me, "Have you seen *this,*
O son of man? Is it a trivial thing to the house
of Judah to commit the abominations which
they commit here? For they have [a]filled the
land with violence; then they have returned
to provoke Me to anger. Indeed they put the
branch to their nose. 18[a]Therefore I also will
act in fury. My [b]eye will not spare nor will I
have pity; and though they [c]cry in My ears
with a loud voice, I will not hear them."

The Wicked Are Slain

9 Then He called out in my hearing with a
loud voice, saying, "Let those who have
charge over the city draw near, each *with* a
deadly weapon in his hand." 2And suddenly
six men came from the direction of the upper
gate, which faces north, each with his battle-
ax in his hand. [a]One man among them *was*
clothed with linen and had a writer's inkhorn
at his side. They went in and stood beside
the bronze altar.
3Now [a]the glory of the God of Israel had gone
up from the cherub, where it had been, to the
threshold of the temple.[1] And He called to the
man clothed with linen, who *had* the writer's
inkhorn at his side; 4and the LORD said to him,
"Go through the midst of the city, through the
midst of Jerusalem, and put [a]a mark on the
foreheads of the men [b]who sigh and cry over
all the abominations that are done within it."
5To the others He said in my hearing, "Go
after him through the city and [a]kill; [b]do not
let your eye spare, nor have any pity. 6[a]Utterly
slay old *and* young men, maidens and little
children and women; but [b]do not come near
anyone on whom *is* the mark; and [c]begin
at My sanctuary." [d]So they began with the
elders who *were* before the temple. 7Then
He said to them, "Defile the temple, and fill
the courts with the slain. Go out!" And they
went out and killed in the city.
8So it was, that while they were killing
them, I was left *alone;* and I [a]fell on my face
and cried out, and said, [b]"Ah, Lord GOD! Will
You destroy all the remnant of Israel in pouring out Your fury on Jerusalem?"
9Then He said to me, "The iniquity of the
house of Israel and Judah *is* exceedingly
great, and [a]the land is full of bloodshed, and
the city full of perversity; for they say, [b]'The
LORD has forsaken the land, and [c]the LORD

8:2 [b] Ezek. 1:4, 27 **8:3** [a] Dan. 5:5 [b] Ezek. 3:14 [c] Ezek. 11:1, 24; 40:2 [d] Ezek. 5:11 [e] Deut. 32:16, 21 **8:4** [a] Ezek. 3:12; 9:3 [b] Ezek. 1:28; 3:22, 23 **8:6** [a] 2 Kin. 23:4, 5 **8:10** [a] Ex. 20:4 [b] Rom. 1:23 **8:11** [a] Num. 11:16, 25 **8:12** [a] Ezek. 9:9 **8:16** [a] Joel 2:17 [b] Ezek. 11:1 [c] Jer. 2:27; 32:33 [d] Deut. 4:19 **8:17** [a] Ezek. 9:9 **8:18** [a] Ezek. 5:13; 16:42; 24:13 [b] Ezek. 5:11; 7:4, 9; 9:5, 10 [c] Mic. 3:4 **9:2** [a] Lev. 16:4 **9:3** [a] Ezek. 3:23; 8:4; 10:4, 18; 11:22, 23 [1] Literally *house* **9:4** [a] Rev. 7:2, 3; 9:4; 14:1 [b] Jer. 13:17 **9:5** [a] Ezek. 7:9 [b] Ezek. 5:11 **9:6** [a] 2 Chr. 36:17 [b] Rev. 9:4 [c] Jer. 25:29 [d] Ezek. 8:11, 12, 16 **9:8** [a] Josh. 7:6 [b] Ezek. 11:13 **9:9** [a] 2 Kin. 21:16 [b] Ezek. 8:12 [c] Is. 29:15

does not see!' 10And as for Me also, My [a]eye will neither spare, nor will I have pity, *but* [b]I will recompense their deeds on their own head."

11Just then, the man clothed with linen, who *had* the inkhorn at his side, reported back and said, "I have done as You commanded me."

The Glory Departs from the Temple

10 And I looked, and there in the [a]firmament that was above the head of the cherubim, there appeared something like a sapphire stone, having the appearance of the likeness of a throne. 2[a]Then He spoke to the man clothed with linen, and said, "Go in among the wheels, under the cherub, fill your hands with [b]coals of fire from among the cherubim, and [c]scatter *them* over the city." And he went in as I watched.

3Now the cherubim were standing on the south side of the temple[1] when the man went in, and the [a]cloud filled the inner court. 4[a]Then the glory of the LORD went up from the cherub, *and paused* over the threshold of the temple; and [b]the house was filled with the cloud, and the court was full of the brightness of the LORD's [c]glory. 5And the [a]sound of the wings of the cherubim was heard *even* in the outer court, like [b]the voice of Almighty God when He speaks.

6Then it happened, when He commanded the man clothed in linen, saying, "Take fire from among the wheels, from among the cherubim," that he went in and stood beside the wheels. 7And the cherub stretched out his hand from among the cherubim to the fire that *was* among the cherubim, and took *some of it* and put *it* into the hands of the *man* clothed with linen, who took *it* and went out. 8[a]The cherubim appeared to have the form of a man's hand under their wings.

9[a]And when I looked, there were four wheels by the cherubim, one wheel by one cherub and another wheel by each other cherub; the wheels appeared *to have* the color of a [b]beryl stone. 10*As for* their appearance, all four looked alike—as it were, a wheel in the middle of a wheel. 11[a]When they went, they went toward *any of* their four directions; they did not turn aside when they went, but followed in the direction the head was facing. They did not turn aside when they went. 12And their whole body, with their back, their hands, their wings, and the wheels that the four had, *were* [a]full of eyes all around. 13As for the wheels, they were called in my hearing, "Wheel."

14[a]Each one had four faces: the first face *was* the face of a cherub, the second face the face of a man, the third the face of a lion, and the fourth the face of an eagle. 15And the cherubim were lifted up. This *was* [a]the living creature I saw by the River Chebar. 16[a]When the cherubim went, the wheels went beside them; and when the cherubim lifted their wings to mount up from the earth, the same wheels also did not turn from beside them. 17[a]When *the cherubim*[1] stood still, *the wheels* stood still, and when *one*[2] was lifted up, *the other*[3] lifted itself up, for the spirit of the living creature *was* in them.

18Then [a]the glory of the LORD [b]departed from the threshold of the temple and stood over the cherubim. 19And [a]the cherubim lifted their wings and mounted up from the earth in my sight. When they went out, the wheels *were* beside them; and they stood at the door of the [b]east gate of the LORD's house, and the glory of the God of Israel *was* above them.

20[a]This *is* the living creature I saw under the God of Israel [b]by the River Chebar, and I knew they *were* cherubim. 21[a]Each one had four faces and each one four wings, and the likeness of the hands of a man *was* under their wings. 22And [a]the likeness of their faces *was* the same *as* the faces which I had seen by the River Chebar, their appearance and their persons. [b]They each went straight forward.

PEACE NOTE

A path to God's *shalom* is living in a state of gratitude. Make a list of all the good things in your life and read through them often. Count your blessings.

9:10 [a] Ezek. 5:11; 7:4; 8:18 [b] Ezek. 11:21 **10:1** [a] Ezek. 1:22, 26 **10:2** [a] Dan. 10:5 [b] Ezek. 1:13 [c] Rev. 8:5 **10:3** [a] 1 Kin. 8:10, 11 [1] Literally *house,* also in verses 4 and 18 **10:4** [a] Ezek. 1:28 [b] Ezek. 43:5 [c] Ezek. 11:22, 23 **10:5** [a] Ezek. 1:24 [b] [Ps. 29:3] **10:8** [a] Ezek. 1:8; 10:21 **10:9** [a] Ezek. 1:15 [b] Ezek. 1:16 **10:11** [a] Ezek. 1:17 **10:12** [a] Rev. 4:6, 8 **10:14** [a] Ezek. 1:6, 10, 11 **10:15** [a] Ezek. 1:3, 5 **10:16** [a] Ezek. 1:19 **10:17** [a] Ezek. 1:12, 20, 21 [1] Literally *they* [2] Literally *they* [3] Literally *they* **10:18** [a] Ezek. 10:4 [b] Hos. 9:12 **10:19** [a] Ezek. 11:22 [b] Ezek. 11:1 **10:20** [a] Ezek. 1:22 [b] Ezek. 1:1 **10:21** [a] Ezek. 1:6, 8; 10:14; 41:18, 19 **10:22** [a] Ezek. 1:10 [b] Ezek. 1:9, 12

Judgment on Wicked Counselors

11 Then [a]the Spirit lifted me up and brought me to [b]the East Gate of the LORD's house, which faces eastward; and there [c]at the door of the gate were twenty-five men, among whom I saw Jaazaniah the son of Azzur, and Pelatiah the son of Benaiah, princes of the people. 2And He said to me: "Son of man, these *are* the men who devise iniquity and give wicked counsel in this city, 3who say, '*The time is* not [a]near to build houses; [b]this *city is* the caldron, and we *are* the meat.' 4Therefore prophesy against them, prophesy, O son of man!"

5Then [a]the Spirit of the LORD fell upon me, and said to me, "Speak! 'Thus says the LORD: "Thus you have said, O house of Israel; for [b]I know the things that come into your mind. 6[a]You have multiplied your slain in this city, and you have filled its streets with the slain." 7Therefore thus says the Lord GOD: [a]"Your slain whom you have laid in its midst, they *are* the meat, and this *city is* the caldron; [b]but I shall bring you out of the midst of it. 8You have [a]feared the sword; and I will bring a sword upon you," says the Lord GOD. 9"And I will bring you out of its midst, and deliver you into the hands of strangers, and [a]execute judgments on you. 10[a]You shall fall by the sword. I will judge you at [b]the border of Israel. [c]Then you shall know that I *am* the LORD. 11[a]This *city* shall not be your caldron, nor shall you be the meat in its midst. I will judge you at the border of Israel. 12And you shall know that I *am* the LORD; for you have not walked in My statutes nor executed My judgments, but [a]have done according to the customs of the Gentiles which *are* all around you." ' "

13Now it happened, while I was prophesying, that [a]Pelatiah the son of Benaiah died. Then [b]I fell on my face and cried with a loud voice, and said, "Ah, Lord GOD! Will You make a complete end of the remnant of Israel?"

God Will Restore Israel

14Again the word of the LORD came to me, saying, 15"Son of man, your brethren, your relatives, your countrymen, and all the house of Israel in its entirety, *are* those about whom the inhabitants of Jerusalem have said, 'Get far away from the LORD; this land has been given to us as a possession.' 16Therefore say, 'Thus says the Lord GOD: "Although I have cast them far off among the Gentiles, and although I have scattered them among the countries, [a]yet I shall be a little sanctuary for them in the countries where they have gone." ' 17Therefore say, 'Thus says the Lord GOD: [a]"I will gather you from the peoples, assemble you from the countries where you have been scattered, and I will give you the land of Israel." ' 18And they will go there, and they will take away all its [a]detestable things and all its abominations from there. 19Then [a]I will give them one heart, and I will put [b]a new spirit within them,[1] and take [c]the stony heart out of their flesh, and give them a heart of flesh, 20[a]that they may walk in My statutes and keep My judgments and do them; [b]and they shall be My people, and I will be their God. 21But *as for those* whose hearts follow the desire for their detestable things and their abominations, [a]I will recompense their deeds on their own heads," says the Lord GOD.

22So the cherubim [a]lifted up their wings, with the wheels beside them, and the glory of the God of Israel *was* high above them. 23And [a]the glory of the LORD went up from the midst of the city and stood [b]on the mountain, [c]which *is* on the east side of the city.

24Then [a]the Spirit took me up and brought me in a vision by the Spirit of God into Chaldea,[1] to those in captivity. And the vision that I had seen went up from me. 25So I spoke to those in captivity of all the things the LORD had shown me.

Judah's Captivity Portrayed

12 Now the word of the LORD came to me, saying: 2"Son of man, you dwell in the midst of [a]a rebellious house, which [b]has eyes to see but does not see, and ears to hear but does not hear; [c]for they *are* a rebellious house.

3"Therefore, son of man, prepare your belongings for captivity, and go into captivity by day in their sight. You shall go from your place into captivity to another place in their sight. It may be that they will consider, though they *are* a rebellious house. 4By day you shall bring out your belongings in their sight, as though going into captivity; and at evening you shall go in their sight, like those who go into captivity. 5Dig through the wall in their sight, and carry *your belongings* out through it. 6In their sight you shall bear *them* on *your* shoulders *and* carry *them* out at twilight; you shall cover your face, so that you cannot see the ground, [a]for I have made you a sign to the house of Israel."

11:1 [a] Ezek. 3:12, 14 [b] Ezek. 10:19 [c] Ezek. 8:16 **11:3** [a] 2 Pet. 3:4 [b] Jer. 1:13 **11:5** [a] Ezek. 2:2; 3:24 [b] [Jer. 16:17; 17:10] **11:6** [a] Ezek. 7:23; 22:2–6, 9, 12, 27 **11:7** [a] Mic. 3:2, 3 [b] Ezek. 11:9 **11:8** [a] Jer. 42:16 **11:9** [a] Ezek. 5:8 **11:10** [a] Jer. 39:6; 52:10 [b] 2 Kin. 14:25 [c] Ps. 9:16 **11:11** [a] Ezek. 11:3, 7 **11:12** [a] Deut. 12:30, 31 **11:13** [a] Acts 5:5 [b] Ezek. 9:8 **11:16** [a] Is. 8:14 **11:17** [a] Jer. 3:12, 18; 24:5 **11:18** [a] Ezek. 37:23 **11:19** [a] Jer. 32:39 [b] Ezek. 18:31 [c] Zech. 7:12 [1] Literally *you* **11:20** [a] Ps. 105:45 [b] Jer. 24:7 **11:21** [a] Ezek. 9:10 **11:22** [a] Ezek. 1:19 **11:23** [a] Ezek. 8:4; 9:3 [b] Zech. 14:4 [c] Ezek. 43:2 **11:24** [a] Ezek. 8:3 [1] Or *Babylon*, and so elsewhere in this book **12:2** [a] Ezek. 2:3, 6–8 [b] Jer. 5:21 [c] Ezek. 2:5 **12:6** [a] Ezek. 4:3; 24:24

7So I did as I was commanded. I brought out my belongings by day, as though going into captivity, and at evening I dug through the wall with my hand. I brought *them* out at twilight, *and* I bore *them* on *my* shoulder in their sight.

8And in the morning the word of the LORD came to me, saying, 9"Son of man, has not the house of Israel, [a]the rebellious house, said to you, [b]'What are you doing?' 10Say to them, 'Thus says the Lord GOD: "This [a]burden *concerns* the prince in Jerusalem and all the house of Israel who are among them." ' 11Say, [a]'I *am* a sign to you. As I have done, so shall it be done to them; [b]they shall be carried away into captivity.' 12And [a]the prince who *is* among them shall bear *his belongings* on *his* shoulder at twilight and go out. They shall dig through the wall to carry *them* out through it. He shall cover his face, so that he cannot see the ground with *his* eyes. 13I will also spread My [a]net over him, and he shall be caught in My snare. [b]I will bring him to Babylon, *to* the land of the Chaldeans; yet he shall not see it, though he shall die there. 14[a]I will scatter to every wind all who *are* around him to help him, and all his troops; and [b]I will draw out the sword after them.

15[a]"Then they shall know that I *am* the LORD, when I scatter them among the nations and disperse them throughout the countries. 16[a]But I will spare a few of their men from the sword, from famine, and from pestilence, that they may declare all their abominations among the Gentiles wherever they go. Then they shall know that I *am* the LORD."

Judgment Not Postponed

17Moreover the word of the LORD came to me, saying, 18"Son of man, [a]eat your bread with quaking, and drink your water with trembling and anxiety. 19And say to the people of the land, 'Thus says the Lord GOD to the inhabitants of Jerusalem *and* to the land of Israel: "They shall eat their bread with anxiety, and drink their water with dread, so that her land may [a]be emptied of all who are in it, [b]because of the violence of all those who dwell in it. 20Then the cities that are inhabited shall be laid waste, and the land shall become desolate; and you shall know that I *am* the LORD." ' "

21And the word of the LORD came to me, saying, 22"Son of man, what *is* this proverb *that* you *people* have about the land of Israel, which says, [a]'The days are prolonged, and every vision fails'? 23Tell them therefore, 'Thus says the Lord GOD: "I will lay this proverb to rest, and they shall no more use it as a proverb in Israel." ' But say to them, ' [a]"The days are at hand, and the fulfillment of every vision. 24For [a]no more shall there be any [b]false vision or flattering divination within the house of Israel. 25For I *am* the LORD. I speak, and [a]the word which I speak will come to pass; it will no more be postponed; for in your days, O rebellious house, I will say the word and [b]perform it," says the Lord GOD.' "

26Again the word of the LORD came to me, saying, 27[a]"Son of man, look, the house of Israel is saying, 'The vision that he sees *is* [b]for many days *from now,* and he prophesies of times far off.' 28[a]Therefore say to them, 'Thus says the Lord GOD: "None of My words will be postponed any more, but the word which I speak [b]will be done," says the Lord GOD.' "

Woe to Foolish Prophets

13 And the word of the LORD came to me, saying, 2"Son of man, prophesy [a]against the prophets of Israel who prophesy, and say to [b]those who prophesy out of their own [c]heart, 'Hear the word of the LORD!' "

3Thus says the Lord GOD: "Woe to the foolish prophets, who follow their own spirit and have seen nothing! 4O Israel, your prophets are [a]like foxes in the deserts. 5You [a]have not gone up into the gaps to build a wall for the house of Israel to stand in battle on the day of the LORD. 6[a]They have envisioned futility and false divination, saying, 'Thus says the LORD!' But the LORD has [b]not sent them; yet they hope that the word may be confirmed. 7Have you not seen a futile vision, and have you not spoken false divination? You say, 'The LORD says,' but I have not spoken."

8Therefore thus says the Lord GOD: "Because you have spoken nonsense and envisioned lies, therefore I *am* indeed against you," says the Lord GOD. 9"My hand will be [a]against the prophets who envision futility and who [b]divine lies; they shall not be in the assembly of My people, [c]nor be written in the record of the house of Israel, [d]nor shall they enter into the land of Israel. [e]Then you shall know that I *am* the Lord GOD.

10"Because, indeed, because they have seduced My people, saying, [a]'Peace!' when *there is* no peace—and one builds a wall, and they

12:9 [a] Ezek. 2:5 [b] Ezek. 17:12; 24:19 **12:10** [a] Mal. 1:1 **12:11** [a] Ezek. 12:6 [b] 2 Kin. 25:4, 5, 7 **12:12** [a] Jer. 39:4; 52:7 **12:13** [a] Jer. 52:9 [b] Jer. 52:11 **12:14** [a] Ezek. 5:10 [b] Ezek. 5:2, 12 **12:15** [a] Ezek. 6:7, 14; 12:16, 20 **12:16** [a] Ezek. 6:8–10 **12:18** [a] Ezek. 4:16 **12:19** [a] Zech. 7:14 [b] Ps. 107:34 **12:22** [a] Ezek. 11:3; 12:27 **12:23** [a] Zeph. 1:14 **12:24** [a] Ezek. 13:6 [b] Lam. 2:14 **12:25** [a] [Luke 21:33] [b] [Is. 14:24] **12:27** [a] Ezek. 12:22 [b] Dan. 10:14 **12:28** [a] Ezek. 12:23, 25 [b] Jer. 4:7 **13:2** [a] Ezek. 22:25–28 [b] Ezek. 13:17 [c] Jer. 14:14; 23:16, 26 **13:4** [a] Song 2:15 **13:5** [a] Ps. 106:23 **13:6** [a] Ezek. 22:28 [b] Jer. 27:8–15 **13:9** [a] Jer. 23:30 [b] Jer. 20:3–6 [c] Ezra 2:59, 62 [d] Jer. 20:3–6 [e] Ezek. 11:10, 12 **13:10** [a] Jer. 6:14; 8:11

[b]plaster it with untempered *mortar*— 11say to those who plaster *it* with untempered *mortar,* that it will fall. [a]There will be flooding rain, and you, O great hailstones, shall fall; and a stormy wind shall tear *it* down. 12Surely, when the wall has fallen, will it not be said to you, 'Where *is* the mortar with which you plastered *it?*' "

13Therefore thus says the Lord GOD: "I will cause a stormy wind to break forth in My fury; and there shall be a flooding rain in My anger, and great hailstones in fury to consume *it.* 14So I will break down the wall you have plastered with untempered *mortar,* and bring it down to the ground, so that its foundation will be uncovered; it will fall, and you shall be consumed in the midst of it. [a]Then you shall know that I *am* the LORD.

15"Thus will I accomplish My wrath on the wall and on those who have plastered it with untempered *mortar;* and I will say to you, 'The wall *is* no *more,* nor those who plastered it, 16*that is,* the prophets of Israel who prophesy concerning Jerusalem, and who [a]see visions of peace for her when *there is* no peace,' " says the Lord GOD.

17"Likewise, son of man, [a]set your face against the daughters of your people, [b]who prophesy out of their own heart; prophesy against them, 18and say, 'Thus says the Lord GOD: "Woe to the *women* who sew *magic* charms on their sleeves[1] and make veils for the heads of people of every height to hunt souls! Will you [a]hunt the souls of My people, and keep yourselves alive? 19And will you profane Me among My people [a]for handfuls of barley and for pieces of bread, killing people who should not die, and keeping people alive who should not live, by your lying to My people who listen to lies?"

20"Therefore thus says the Lord GOD: "Behold, I *am* against your *magic* charms by which you hunt souls there like birds. I will tear them from your arms, and let the souls go, the souls you hunt like birds. 21I will also tear off your veils and deliver My people out of your hand, and they shall no longer be as prey in your hand. [a]Then you shall know that I *am* the LORD.

22"Because with [a]lies you have made the heart of the righteous sad, whom I have not made sad; and you have [b]strengthened the hands of the wicked, so that he does not turn from his wicked way to save his life. 23Therefore [a]you shall no longer envision futility nor practice divination; for I will deliver My people out of your hand, and you shall know that I *am* the LORD." ' "

Idolatry Will Be Punished

14 Now [a]some of the elders of Israel came to me and sat before me. 2And the word of the LORD came to me, saying, 3"Son of man, these men have set up their idols in their hearts, and put before them [a]that which causes them to stumble into iniquity. [b]Should I let Myself be inquired of at all by them?

13:10 [b] Ezek. 22:28 13:11 [a] Ezek. 38:22 13:14 [a] Ezek. 13:9, 21, 23; 14:8 13:16 [a] Jer. 6:14; 8:11; 28:9 13:17 [a] Ezek. 20:46; 21:2 [b] Ezek. 13:2 13:18 [a] [2 Pet. 2:14] [1] Literally *over all the joints of My hands;* Vulgate reads *under every elbow;* Septuagint and Targum read *on all elbows of the hands.* 13:19 [a] Mic. 3:5 13:21 [a] Ezek. 13:9 13:22 [a] Jer. 28:15 [b] Jer. 23:14 13:23 [a] Mic. 3:5, 6 14:1 [a] Ezek. 8:1; 20:1; 33:31 14:3 [a] Ezek. 7:19 [b] Ezek. 20:3, 31

BE A FAITHFUL BRIDE

"They have seduced My people, saying, 'Peace!' when there is no peace . . . The prophets of Israel . . . see visions of peace for her when there is no peace."

EZEKIEL 13:10, 16

All of us need to make sure we are in churches that really teach God's Word if we are going to live in God's peace. We should take spiritual inventory of what is said from the pulpit. Do teaching and worship reflect the Word of God? If so, we are in the right place. If not, it's time to find a new church community.

Like Jeremiah, the prophet Ezekiel railed against the priests and false prophets who assured a sinful people of peace when there was none. The people built a flimsy wall around Jerusalem, daubed it with whitewash ("plaster," v. 10) to make it look impressive, and hoped it would hold back the invaders from the north. But it would not; it would fall.

One of the reasons so many Christians lack peace is that they commit spiritual adultery every week by sitting under false teachers' preaching. If that is you, it's time to move on. Be addicted to the truths of Scripture to find the peace of God.

PEACE NOTE

Our faith should constantly bring us ultimate peace because we are "persuaded that [Jesus] is able to keep what [we] have committed to Him until that Day" (2 Tim. 1:12).

4"Therefore speak to them, and say to them, 'Thus says the Lord GOD: "Everyone of the house of Israel who sets up his idols in his heart, and puts before him what causes him to stumble into iniquity, and then comes to the prophet, I the LORD will answer him who comes, according to the multitude of his idols, 5that I may seize the house of Israel by their heart, because they are all estranged from Me by their idols." '

6"Therefore say to the house of Israel, 'Thus says the Lord GOD: "Repent, turn away from your idols, and [a]turn your faces away from all your abominations. 7For anyone of the house of Israel, or of the strangers who dwell in Israel, who separates himself from Me and sets up his idols in his heart and puts before him what causes him to stumble into iniquity, then comes to a prophet to inquire of him concerning Me, I the LORD will answer him by Myself. 8[a]I will set My face against that man and make him a [b]sign and a proverb, and I will cut him off from the midst of My people. [c]Then you shall know that I *am* the LORD.

9"And if the prophet is induced to speak anything, I the LORD [a]have induced that prophet, and I will stretch out My hand against him and destroy him from among My people Israel. 10And they shall bear their iniquity; the punishment of the prophet shall be the same as the punishment of the one who inquired, 11that the house of Israel may [a]no longer stray from Me, nor be profaned anymore with all their transgressions, [b]but that they may be My people and I may be their God," says the Lord GOD.' "

Judgment on Persistent Unfaithfulness

12The word of the LORD came again to me, saying: 13"Son of man, when a land sins against Me by persistent unfaithfulness, I will stretch out My hand against it; I will cut off its [a]supply of bread, send famine on it, and cut off man and beast from it. 14[a]Even *if* these three men, Noah, Daniel, and Job, were in it, they would deliver *only* themselves [b]by their righteousness," says the Lord GOD.

15"If I cause [a]wild beasts to pass through the land, and they empty it, and make it so desolate that no man may pass through because of the beasts, 16*even* [a]*though* these three men *were* in it, *as* I live," says the Lord GOD, "they would deliver neither sons nor daughters; only they would be delivered, and the land would be [b]desolate.

17"Or *if* [a]I bring a sword on that land, and say, 'Sword, go through the land,' and I [b]cut off man and beast from it, 18even [a]*though* these three men *were* in it, *as* I live," says the Lord GOD, "they would deliver neither sons nor daughters, but only they themselves would be delivered.

19"Or *if* I send [a]a pestilence into that land and [b]pour out My fury on it in blood, and cut off from it man and beast, 20even [a]*though* Noah, Daniel, and Job *were* in it, *as* I live," says the Lord GOD, "they would deliver neither son nor daughter; they would deliver *only* themselves by their righteousness."

21For thus says the Lord GOD: "How much more it shall be when [a]I send My four severe judgments on Jerusalem—the sword and famine and wild beasts and pestilence—to cut off man and beast from it? 22[a]Yet behold, there shall be left in it a remnant who will be [b]brought out, *both* sons and daughters; surely they will come out to you, and [c]you will see their ways and their doings. Then you will be comforted concerning the disaster that I have brought upon Jerusalem, all that I have brought upon it. 23And they will comfort you, when you see their ways and their doings; and you shall know that I have done nothing [a]without cause that I have done in it," says the Lord GOD.

The Outcast Vine

15 Then the word of the LORD came to me, saying: 2"Son of man, how is the wood of the vine *better* than any other wood, the vine branch which is among the trees of the forest? 3Is wood taken from it to make any object? Or can *men* make a peg from it to hang

14:6 [a] Is. 2:20; 30:22; 55:6, 7 **14:8** [a] Jer. 44:11 [b] Num. 26:10 [c] Ezek. 6:7; 13:14 **14:9** [a] 2 Thess. 2:11 **14:11** [a] 2 Pet. 2:15 [b] Ezek. 11:20; 37:27 **14:13** [a] Is. 3:1 **14:14** [a] Jer. 15:1 [b] [Prov. 11:4] **14:15** [a] Lev. 26:22 **14:16** [a] Ezek. 14:14, 18, 20 [b] Ezek. 15:8; 33:28, 29 **14:17** [a] Lev. 26:25 [b] Zeph. 1:3 **14:18** [a] Ezek. 14:14 **14:19** [a] 2 Sam. 24:15 [b] Ezek. 7:8 **14:20** [a] Ezek. 14:14 **14:21** [a] Ezek. 5:17; 33:27 **14:22** [a] Ezek. 12:16; 36:20 [b] Ezek. 6:8 [c] Ezek. 20:43 **14:23** [a] Jer. 22:8, 9

any vessel on? 4Instead, [a]it is thrown into the
fire for fuel; the fire devours both ends of it,
and its middle is burned. Is it useful for *any*
work? 5Indeed, when it was whole, no object
could be made from it. How much less will
it be useful for *any* work when the fire has
devoured it, and it is burned?

6"Therefore thus says the Lord GOD: 'Like
the wood of the vine among the trees of the
forest, which I have given to the fire for fuel,
so I will give up the inhabitants of Jerusalem;
7and [a]I will set My face against them. [b]They
will go out from *one* fire, but *another* fire shall
devour them. [c]Then you shall know that I *am*
the LORD, when I set My face against them.
8Thus I will make the land desolate, because
they have persisted in unfaithfulness,' says
the Lord GOD."

God's Love for Jerusalem

16 Again the word of the LORD came to
me, saying, 2"Son of man, [a]cause Jerusalem to know her abominations, 3and say,
'Thus says the Lord GOD to Jerusalem: "Your
birth [a]and your nativity *are* from the land of
Canaan; [b]your father *was* an Amorite and
your mother a Hittite. 4*As for* your nativity,
[a]on the day you were born your navel cord
was not cut, nor were you washed in water to
cleanse *you;* you were not rubbed with salt nor
wrapped in swaddling cloths. 5No eye pitied
you, to do any of these things for you, to have
compassion on you; but you were thrown out
into the open field, when you yourself were
loathed on the day you were born.

6"And when I passed by you and saw you
struggling in your own blood, I said to you
in your blood, 'Live!' Yes, I said to you in your
blood, 'Live!' 7[a]I made you thrive like a plant in
the field; and you grew, matured, and became
very beautiful. *Your* breasts were formed,
your hair grew, but you *were* naked and bare.

8"When I passed by you again and looked
upon you, indeed your time *was* the time of
love; [a]so I spread My wing over you and covered your nakedness. Yes, I [b]swore an oath to
you and entered into a [c]covenant with you,
and [d]you became Mine," says the Lord GOD.

9"Then I washed you in water; yes, I thoroughly washed off your blood, and I anointed
you with oil. 10I clothed you in embroidered
cloth and gave you sandals of badger skin; I
clothed you with fine linen and covered you
with silk. 11I adorned you with ornaments,
[a]put bracelets on your wrists, [b]and a chain on
your neck. 12And I put a jewel in your nose,
earrings in your ears, and a beautiful crown
on your head. 13Thus you were adorned with
gold and silver, and your clothing *was of* fine
linen, silk, and embroidered cloth. [a]You ate
pastry of fine flour, honey, and oil. You were
exceedingly [b]beautiful, and succeeded to
royalty. 14[a]Your fame went out among the
nations because of your beauty, for it *was*
perfect through My splendor which I had
bestowed on you," says the Lord GOD.

Jerusalem's Harlotry

15[a]"But you trusted in your own beauty,
[b]played the harlot because of your fame, and
poured out your harlotry on everyone passing
by who *would have* it. 16[a]You took some of your
garments and adorned multicolored high
places for yourself, and played the harlot on
them. *Such* things should not happen, nor be.
17You have also taken your beautiful jewelry
from My gold and My silver, which I had given
you, and made for yourself male images and
played the harlot with them. 18You took your
embroidered garments and covered them,
and you set My oil and My incense before
them. 19Also [a]My food which I gave you—the
pastry of fine flour, oil, and honey *which* I fed
you—you set it before them as sweet incense;
and *so* it was," says the Lord GOD.

20[a]"Moreover you took your sons and your
daughters, whom you bore to Me, and these
you sacrificed to them to be devoured. *Were*
your *acts* of harlotry a small matter, 21that
you have slain My children and offered them
up to them by causing them to pass through
the [a]*fire?* 22And in all your abominations and
acts of harlotry you did not remember the
days of your [a]youth, [b]when you were naked
and bare, struggling in your blood.

23"Then it was so, after all your wickedness—
'Woe, woe to you!' says the Lord GOD— 24*that*
[a]you also built for yourself a shrine, and
[b]made a high place for yourself in every
street. 25You built your high places [a]at the
head of every road, and made your beauty to
be abhorred. You offered yourself to everyone
who passed by, and multiplied your acts of
harlotry. 26You also committed harlotry with
[a]the Egyptians, your very fleshly neighbors,
and increased your acts of harlotry to [b]pro-
voke Me to anger.

27"Behold, therefore, I stretched out My
hand against you, diminished your allotment,
and gave you up to the will of those who hate

15:4 [a] [John 15:6] **15:7** [a] Ezek. 14:8 [b] Is. 24:18 [c] Ezek. 7:4 **16:2** [a] Ezek. 20:4; 22:2 **16:3** [a] Ezek. 21:30 [b] Ezek. 16:45
16:4 [a] Hos. 2:3 **16:7** [a] Ex. 1:7 **16:8** [a] Ruth 3:9 [b] Gen. 22:16–18 [c] Ex. 24:6–8 [d] [Ex. 19:5] **16:11** [a] Gen. 24:22, 47
[b] Prov. 1:9 **16:13** [a] Deut. 32:13, 14 [b] Ps. 48:2 **16:14** [a] Lam. 2:15 **16:15** [a] Mic. 3:11 [b] Is. 1:21; 57:8 **16:16** [a] Ezek. 7:20
16:19 [a] Hos. 2:8 **16:20** [a] Jer. 7:31 **16:21** [a] Jer. 19:5 **16:22** [a] Jer. 2:2 [b] Ezek. 16:4–6 **16:24** [a] Jer. 11:13 [b] Jer. 2:20; 3:2
16:25 [a] Prov. 9:14 **16:26** [a] Ezek. 16:26; 20:7, 8 [b] Deut. 31:20

you, [a]the daughters of the Philistines, who were ashamed of your lewd behavior. 28You also played the harlot with the [a]Assyrians, because you were insatiable; indeed you played the harlot with them and still were not satisfied. 29Moreover you multiplied your acts of harlotry as far as the land of the trader, [a]Chaldea; and even then you were not satisfied.

30"How degenerate is your heart!" says the Lord GOD, "seeing you do all these *things,* the deeds of a brazen harlot.

Jerusalem's Adultery

31[a]"You erected your shrine at the head of every road, and built your high place in every street. Yet you were not like a harlot, because you scorned [b]payment. 32*You are* an adulterous wife, *who* takes strangers instead of her husband. 33Men make payment to all harlots, but [a]you made your payments to all your lovers, and hired them to come to you from all around for your harlotry. 34You are the opposite of *other* women in your harlotry, because no one solicited you to be a harlot. In that you gave payment but no payment was given you, therefore you are the opposite."

Jerusalem's Lovers Will Abuse Her

35'Now then, O harlot, hear the word of the LORD! 36Thus says the Lord GOD: "Because your filthiness was poured out and your nakedness uncovered in your harlotry with your lovers, and with all your abominable idols, and because of [a]the blood of your children which you gave to them, 37surely, therefore, [a]I will gather all your lovers with whom you took pleasure, all those you loved, *and* all those you hated; I will gather them from all around against you and will uncover your nakedness to them, that they may see all your nakedness. 38And I will judge you as [a]women who break wedlock or [b]shed blood are judged; I will bring blood upon you in fury and jealousy. 39I will also give you into their hand, and they shall throw down your shrines and break down [a]your high places. [b]They shall also strip you of your clothes, take your beautiful jewelry, and leave you naked and bare.

40[a]"They shall also bring up an assembly against you, [b]and they shall stone you with stones and thrust you through with their swords. 41They shall [a]burn your houses with fire, and [b]execute judgments on you in the sight of many women; and I will make you [c]cease playing the harlot, and you shall no longer hire lovers. 42So [a]I will lay to rest My fury toward you, and My jealousy shall depart from you. I will be quiet, and be angry no more. 43Because [a]you did not remember the days of your youth, but agitated Me[1] with all these *things,* surely [b]I will also recompense your deeds on *your own* head," says the Lord GOD. "And you shall not commit lewdness in addition to all your abominations.

More Wicked than Samaria and Sodom

44"Indeed everyone who quotes proverbs will use *this* proverb against you: 'Like mother, like daughter!' 45You *are* your mother's daughter, loathing husband and children; and you *are* the [a]sister of your sisters, who loathed their husbands and children; [b]your mother *was* a Hittite and your father an Amorite.

46"Your elder sister *is* Samaria, who dwells with her daughters to the north of you; and [a]your younger sister, who dwells to the south of you, *is* Sodom and her daughters. 47You did not walk in their ways nor act according to their abominations; but, as *if that were* too little, [a]you became more corrupt than they in all your ways.

48"*As* I live," says the Lord GOD, "neither [a]your sister Sodom nor her daughters have done as you and your daughters have done. 49Look, this was the iniquity of your sister Sodom: She and her daughter had pride, [a]fullness of food, and abundance of idleness; neither did she strengthen the hand of the poor and needy. 50And they were haughty and [a]committed abomination before Me; therefore [b]I took them away as I saw *fit.*[1]

51"Samaria did not commit [a]half of your sins; but you have multiplied your abominations more than they, and [b]have justified your sisters by all the abominations which you have done. 52You who judged your sisters, bear your own shame also, because the sins which you committed were more abominable than theirs; they are more righteous than you. Yes, be disgraced also, and bear your own shame, because you justified your sisters.

53[a]"When I bring back their captives, the captives of Sodom and her daughters, and the captives of Samaria and her daughters, then *I will also bring back* [b]the captives of your captivity among them, 54that you may bear

16:27 [a] Ezek. 16:57 **16:28** [a] Jer. 2:18, 36 **16:29** [a] Ezek. 23:14–17 **16:31** [a] Ezek. 16:24, 39 [b] Is. 52:3 **16:33** [a] Hos. 8:9, 10 **16:36** [a] Jer. 2:34 **16:37** [a] Lam. 1:8 **16:38** [a] Lev. 20:10 [b] Gen. 9:6 **16:39** [a] Ezek. 16:24, 31 [b] Hos. 2:3 **16:40** [a] Ezek. 23:45–47 [b] John 8:5, 7 **16:41** [a] Deut. 13:16 [b] Ezek. 5:8; 23:10, 48 [c] Ezek. 23:27 **16:42** [a] Ezek. 5:13; 21:17 **16:43** [a] Ps. 78:42 [b] Ezek. 9:10; 11:21; 22:31 [1] Following Septuagint, Syriac, Targum, and Vulgate; Masoretic Text reads *were agitated with Me.* **16:45** [a] Ezek. 23:2–4 [b] Ezek. 16:3 **16:46** [a] Is. 1:10 **16:47** [a] Ezek. 5:6, 7 **16:48** [a] Matt. 10:15; 11:24 **16:49** [a] Gen. 13:10 **16:50** [a] Gen. 13:13; 18:20; 19:5 [b] Gen. 19:24 [1] Vulgate reads *you saw;* Septuagint reads *he saw;* Targum reads *as was revealed to Me.* **16:51** [a] Ezek. 23:11 [b] Jer. 3:8–11 **16:53** [a] Is. 1:9 [b] Jer. 20:16

your own shame and be disgraced by all that
you did when [a]you comforted them. 55When
your sisters, Sodom and her daughters, return
to their former state, and Samaria and her
daughters return to their former state, then
you and your daughters will return to your
former state. 56For your sister Sodom was not
a byword in your mouth in the days of your
pride, 57before your wickedness was uncovered. It was like the time of the [a]reproach of
the daughters of Syria[1] and all *those* around
her, and of [b]the daughters of the Philistines,
who despise you everywhere. 58[a]You have paid
for your lewdness and your abominations,"
says the LORD. 59For thus says the Lord GOD:
"I will deal with you as you have done, who
[a]despised [b]the oath by breaking the covenant.

An Everlasting Covenant

60"Nevertheless I will [a]remember My covenant with you in the days of your youth, and
I will establish [b]an everlasting covenant with
you. 61Then [a]you will remember your ways
and be ashamed, when you receive your older
and your younger sisters; for I will give them
to you for [b]daughters, [c]but not because of My
covenant with you. 62[a]And I will establish My
covenant with you. Then you shall know that I
am the LORD, 63that you may [a]remember and
be ashamed, [b]and never open your mouth
anymore because of your shame, when I
provide you an atonement for all you have
done," says the Lord GOD.' "

The Eagles and the Vine

17 And the word of the LORD came to me,
saying, 2"Son of man, pose a riddle, and
speak a [a]parable to the house of Israel, 3and
say, 'Thus says the Lord GOD:

[a]"A great eagle with large wings and long
pinions,
Full of feathers of various colors,
Came to Lebanon
And [b]took from the cedar the highest
branch.
4 He cropped off its topmost young twig
And carried it to a land of trade;
He set it in a city of merchants.
5 Then he took some of the seed of the land
And planted it in [a]a fertile field;
He placed *it* by abundant waters
And set it [b]like a willow tree.
6 And it grew and became a spreading
vine [a]of low stature;
Its branches turned toward him,
But its roots were under it.
So it became a vine,
Brought forth branches,
And put forth shoots.

7 "But there was another[1] great eagle with
large wings and many feathers;
And behold, [a]this vine bent its roots
toward him,
And stretched its branches toward him,
From the garden terrace where it had
been planted,
That he might water it.
8 It was planted in good soil by many
waters,
To bring forth branches, bear fruit,
And become a majestic vine." '

9"Say, 'Thus says the Lord GOD:

"Will it thrive?
[a]Will he not pull up its roots,
Cut off its fruit,
And leave it to wither?
All of its spring leaves will wither,
And no great power or many people
Will be needed to pluck it up by its
roots.
10 Behold, *it is* planted,
Will it thrive?
[a]Will it not utterly wither when the east
wind touches it?
It will wither in the garden terrace
where it grew." ' "

11Moreover the word of the LORD came
to me, saying, 12"Say now to [a]the rebellious
house: 'Do you not know what these *things*
mean?' Tell *them,* 'Indeed [b]the king of Babylon went to Jerusalem and took its king and
princes, and led them with him to Babylon.
13[a]And he took the king's offspring, made a
covenant with him, [b]and put him under oath.
He also took away the mighty of the land,
14that the kingdom might be [a]brought low
and not lift itself up, *but* that by keeping his
covenant it might stand. 15But [a]he rebelled
against him by sending his ambassadors
to Egypt, [b]that they might give him horses
and many people. [c]Will he prosper? Will he

16:54 [a] Ezek. 14:22 **16:57** [a] 2 Kin. 16:5 [b] Ezek. 16:27 [1] Following Masoretic Text, Septuagint, Targum, and Vulgate; many Hebrew manuscripts and Syriac read *Edom.* **16:58** [a] Ezek. 23:49 **16:59** [a] Ezek. 17:13 [b] Deut. 29:12 **16:60** [a] Ps. 106:45 [b] Is. 55:3 **16:61** [a] Ezek. 20:43; 36:31 [b] [Gal. 4:26] [c] Jer. 31:31 **16:62** [a] Hos. 2:19, 20 **16:63** [a] Ezek. 36:31, 32 [b] [Rom. 3:19] **17:2** [a] Ezek. 20:49; 24:3 **17:3** [a] Ezek. 17:12 [b] 2 Kin. 24:12 **17:5** [a] Deut. 8:7–9 [b] Is. 44:4 **17:6** [a] Ezek. 17:14 **17:7** [a] Ezek. 17:15 [1] Following Septuagint, Syriac, and Vulgate; Masoretic Text and Targum read *one.* **17:9** [a] 2 Kin. 25:7 **17:10** [a] Hos. 13:15 **17:12** [a] Ezek. 2:3–5; 12:9 [b] 2 Kin. 24:11–16 **17:13** [a] 2 Kin. 24:17 [b] 2 Chr. 36:13 **17:14** [a] Ezek. 29:14 **17:15** [a] 2 Kin. 24:20 [b] Deut. 17:16 [c] Ezek. 17:9

who does such *things* escape? Can he break
a covenant and still be delivered?

16 '*As* I live,' says the Lord GOD, 'surely [a]in
the place *where* the king *dwells* who made
him king, whose oath he despised and whose
covenant he broke—with him in the midst
of Babylon he shall die. 17 [a]Nor will Pharaoh
with *his* mighty army and great company
do anything in the war, [b]when they heap
up a siege mound and build a wall to cut off
many persons. 18 Since he despised the oath
by breaking the covenant, and in fact [a]gave
his hand and still did all these *things,* he shall
not escape.' "

19 Therefore thus says the Lord GOD: "*As* I
live, surely My oath which he despised, and
My covenant which he broke, I will recompense on his own head. 20 I will [a]spread My
net over him, and he shall be taken in My
snare. I will bring him to Babylon and [b]try
him there for the treason which he committed against Me. 21 [a]All his fugitives[1] with all his
troops shall fall by the sword, and those who
remain shall be [b]scattered to every wind; and
you shall know that I, the LORD, have spoken."

Israel Exalted at Last

22 Thus says the Lord GOD: "I will take also
one of the highest [a]branches of the high cedar
and set *it* out. I will crop off from the topmost
of its young twigs [b]a tender one, and will [c]plant
it on a high and prominent mountain. 23 [a]On
the mountain height of Israel I will plant it; and
it will bring forth boughs, and bear fruit, and
be a majestic cedar. [b]Under it will dwell birds of
every sort; in the shadow of its branches they
will dwell. 24 And all the trees of the field shall
know that I, the LORD, [a]have brought down the
high tree and exalted the low tree, dried up
the green tree and made the dry tree flourish;
[b]I, the LORD, have spoken and have done *it.*"

A False Proverb Refuted

18 The word of the LORD came to me
again, saying, 2 "What do you mean
when you use this proverb concerning the
land of Israel, saying:

'The [a]fathers have eaten sour grapes,
And the children's teeth are set on
edge'?

3 "*As* I live," says the Lord GOD, "you shall
no longer use this proverb in Israel.

4 "Behold, all souls are [a]Mine;
The soul of the father
As well as the soul of the son is Mine;
[b]The soul who sins shall die.
5 But if a man is just
And does what is lawful and right;
6 [a]If he has not eaten on the mountains,
Nor lifted up his eyes to the idols of the
house of Israel,
Nor [b]defiled his neighbor's wife,
Nor approached [c]a woman during her
impurity;
7 If he has not [a]oppressed anyone,
But has restored to the debtor his [b]pledge;
Has robbed no one by violence,
But has [c]given his bread to the hungry
And covered the naked with [d]clothing;
8 If he has not exacted [a]usury
Nor taken any increase,
But has withdrawn his hand from
iniquity
And [b]executed true judgment between
man and man;
9 *If* he has walked in My statutes
And kept My judgments faithfully—
He *is* just;
He shall surely [a]live!"
Says the Lord GOD.

PEACE NOTE

Just like Ezekiel, who perhaps wondered if God's peace would truly come, we must walk forward with faith in the Lord even when the road is rocky.

EZEKIEL 18:9

10 "If he begets a son *who is* a robber
Or [a]a shedder of blood,
Who does any of these *things*
11 And does none of those *duties,*
But has eaten on the mountains
Or defiled his neighbor's wife;

17:16 [a] Ezek. 12:13 **17:17** [a] Jer. 37:7 [b] Jer. 52:4 **17:18** [a] 1 Chr. 29:24 **17:20** [a] Ezek. 12:13 [b] Ezek. 20:36 **17:21** [a] Ezek. 12:14 [b] Ezek. 12:15; 22:15 [1] Following Masoretic Text and Vulgate; many Hebrew manuscripts and Syriac read *choice men;* Targum reads *mighty men;* Septuagint omits *All his fugitives.* **17:22** [a] [Zech. 3:8] [b] Is. 53:2 [c] [Ps. 2:6] **17:23** [a] [Is. 2:2, 3] [b] Dan. 4:12 **17:24** [a] Amos 9:11 [b] Ezek. 22:14 **18:2** [a] Lam. 5:7 **18:4** [a] Num. 16:22; 27:16 [b] [Rom. 6:23] **18:6** [a] Ezek. 22:9 [b] Lev. 18:20; 20:10 [c] Lev. 18:19; 20:18 **18:7** [a] Ex. 22:21 [b] Deut. 24:12 [c] Deut. 15:7, 11 [d] Is. 58:7 **18:8** [a] Ex. 22:25 [b] Zech. 8:16 **18:9** [a] Amos 5:4 **18:10** [a] Num. 35:31

12 If he has oppressed the poor and needy,
Robbed by violence,
Not restored the pledge,
Lifted his eyes to the idols,
Or [a]committed abomination;
13 If he has exacted usury
Or taken increase—
Shall he then live?
He shall not live!
If he has done any of these
abominations,
He shall surely die;
[a]His blood shall be upon him.

14 "*If,* however, he begets a son
Who sees all the sins which his father
has done,
And considers but does not do
likewise;
15 [a]*Who* has not eaten on the
mountains,
Nor lifted his eyes to the idols of the
house of Israel,
Nor defiled his neighbor's wife;
16 Has not oppressed anyone,
Nor withheld a pledge,
Nor robbed by violence,
But has given his bread to the hungry
And covered the naked with clothing;
17 *Who* has withdrawn his hand from the
poor[1]
And not received usury or increase,
But has executed My judgments
And walked in My statutes—
He shall not die for the iniquity of his
father;
He shall surely live!

18 "*As for* his father,
Because he cruelly oppressed,
Robbed his brother by violence,
And did what *is* not good among his
people,
Behold, [a]he shall die for his iniquity.

Turn and Live

19"Yet you say, 'Why [a]should the son not
bear the guilt of the father?' Because the son
has done what is lawful and right, and has
kept all My statutes and observed them, he
shall surely live. 20[a]The soul who sins shall
die. [b]The son shall not bear the guilt of the
father, nor the father bear the guilt of the
son. [c]The righteousness of the righteous
shall be upon himself, [d]and the wickedness
of the wicked shall be upon himself.
21"But [a]if a wicked man turns from all his
sins which he has committed, keeps all My
statutes, and does what is lawful and right, he
shall surely live; he shall not die. 22[a]None of
the transgressions which he has committed
shall be remembered against him; because of
the righteousness which he has done, he shall
[b]live. 23[a]Do I have any pleasure at all that the
wicked should die?" says the Lord GOD, "*and*
not that he should turn from his ways and live?
24"But [a]when a righteous man turns away
from his righteousness and commits iniquity,
and does according to all the abominations
that the wicked *man* does, shall he live? [b]All
the righteousness which he has done shall not
be remembered; because of the unfaithfulness of which he is guilty and the sin which he
has committed, because of them he shall die.
25"Yet you say, [a]'The way of the Lord is not
fair.' Hear now, O house of Israel, is it not My
way which is fair, and your ways which are
not fair? 26[a]When a righteous *man* turns away
from his righteousness, commits iniquity, and
dies in it, it is because of the iniquity which he
has done that he dies. 27Again, [a]when a wicked
man turns away from the wickedness which
he committed, and does what is lawful and
right, he preserves himself alive. 28Because
he [a]considers and turns away from all the
transgressions which he committed, he shall
surely live; he shall not die. 29[a]Yet the house
of Israel says, 'The way of the Lord is not fair.'
O house of Israel, is it not My ways which are
fair, and your ways which are not fair?
30[a]"Therefore I will judge you, O house
of Israel, every one according to his ways,"
says the Lord GOD. [b]"Repent, and turn from
all your transgressions, so that iniquity will
not be your ruin. 31[a]Cast away from you all
the transgressions which you have committed, and get yourselves a [b]new heart and a
new spirit. For why should you die, O house
of Israel? 32For [a]I have no pleasure in the
death of one who dies," says the Lord GOD.
"Therefore turn and [b]live!"

Israel Degraded

19 "Moreover [a]take up a lamentation for
the princes of Israel, 2and say:

'What *is* your mother? A lioness:
She lay down among the lions;

18:12 [a] Ezek. 8:6, 17 18:13 [a] Lev. 20:9, 11–13, 16, 27 18:15 [a] Ezek. 18:6 18:17 [1] Following Masoretic Text, Targum, and Vulgate; Septuagint reads *iniquity* (compare verse 8). 18:18 [a] Ezek. 3:18 18:19 [a] Ex. 20:5 18:20 [a] Ezek. 18:4 [b] Deut. 24:16 [c] Is. 3:10, 11 [d] Rom. 2:6–9 18:21 [a] Ezek. 18:27; 33:12, 19 18:22 [a] Ezek. 18:24; 33:16 [b] [Ps. 18:20–24] 18:23 [a] [Ezek. 18:32; 33:11] 18:24 [a] Ezek. 3:20; 18:26; 33:18 [b] [2 Pet. 2:20] 18:25 [a] Ezek. 18:29; 33:17, 20 18:26 [a] Ezek. 18:24 18:27 [a] Ezek. 18:21 18:28 [a] Ezek. 18:14 18:29 [a] Ezek. 18:25 18:30 [a] Ezek. 7:3; 33:20 [b] Matt. 3:2 18:31 [a] Eph. 4:22, 23 [b] Jer. 32:39 18:32 [a] Lam. 3:33 [b] [Prov. 4:2, 5, 6] 19:1 [a] Ezek. 26:17; 27:2

Among the young lions she nourished
her cubs.
3 She brought up one of her cubs,
And [a]he became a young lion;
He learned to catch prey,
And he devoured men.
4 The nations also heard of him;
He was trapped in their pit,
And they brought him with chains to
the land of [a]Egypt.

5 'When she saw that she waited, *that* her
hope was lost,
She took [a]another of her cubs *and*
made him a young lion.
6 [a]He roved among the lions,
And [b]became a young lion;
He learned to catch prey;
He devoured men.
7 He knew their desolate places,[1]
And laid waste their cities;
The land with its fullness was desolated
By the noise of his roaring.
8 [a]Then the nations set against him from
the provinces on every side,
And spread their net over him;
[b]He was trapped in their pit.
9 [a]They put him in a cage with chains,
And brought him to the king of
Babylon;
They brought him in nets,
That his voice should no longer be
heard on [b]the mountains of Israel.

10 'Your mother *was* [a]like a vine in your
bloodline,[1]
Planted by the waters,
[b]Fruitful and full of branches
Because of many waters.
11 She had strong branches for scepters
of rulers.
[a]She towered in stature above the thick
branches,
And was seen in her height amid the
dense foliage.
12 But she was [a]plucked up in fury,
She was cast down to the ground,
And the [b]east wind dried her fruit.
Her strong branches were broken and
withered;
The fire consumed them.
13 And now she *is* planted in the wilderness,
In a dry and thirsty land.
14 [a]Fire has come out from a rod of her
branches
And devoured her fruit,
So that she has no strong branch—a
scepter for ruling.' "

[b]This *is* a lamentation, and has become a
lamentation.

The Rebellions of Israel

20 It came to pass in the seventh year, in
the fifth *month,* on the tenth *day* of the
month, *that* [a]certain of the elders of Israel
came to inquire of the LORD, and sat before
me. 2Then the word of the LORD came to me,
saying, 3"Son of man, speak to the elders of
Israel, and say to them, 'Thus says the Lord
GOD: "Have you come to inquire of Me? *As* I
live," says the Lord GOD, [a]"I will not be inquired
of by you." ' 4Will you judge them, son of man,
will you judge *them?* Then [a]make known to
them the abominations of their fathers.
5"Say to them, 'Thus says the Lord GOD:
"On the day when [a]I chose Israel and raised
My hand in an oath to the descendants of the
house of Jacob, and made Myself [b]known to
them in the land of Egypt, I raised My hand
in an oath to them, saying, [c]'I *am* the LORD
your God.' 6On that day I raised My hand in
an oath to them, [a]to bring them out of the
land of Egypt into a land that I had searched
out for them, [b]'flowing with milk and honey,'[1]
[c]the glory of all lands. 7Then I said to them,
'Each of you, [a]throw away [b]the abominations
which are before his eyes, and do not defile
yourselves with [c]the idols of Egypt. I *am* the
LORD your God.' 8But they rebelled against Me
and would not obey Me. They did not all cast
away the abominations which were before
their eyes, nor did they forsake the idols of
Egypt. Then I said, 'I will [a]pour out My fury on
them and fulfill My anger against them in the
midst of the land of Egypt.' 9[a]But I acted for
My name's sake, that it should not be profaned
before the Gentiles among whom they *were,*
in whose sight I had made Myself [b]known to
them, to bring them out of the land of Egypt.
10"Therefore I [a]made them go out of the
land of Egypt and brought them into the wilderness. 11[a]And I gave them My statutes and
showed them My judgments, [b]'which, *if* a man

19:3 [a] 2 Kin. 23:31, 32 **19:4** [a] 2 Kin. 23:33, 34 **19:5** [a] 2 Kin. 23:34 **19:6** [a] 2 Kin. 24:8, 9 [b] Ezek. 19:3 **19:7** [1] Septuagint reads *He stood in insolence;* Targum reads *He destroyed its palaces;* Vulgate reads *He learned to make widows.* **19:8** [a] 2 Kin. 24:2, 11 [b] Ezek. 19:4 **19:9** [a] 2 Chr. 36:6 [b] Ezek. 6:2 **19:10** [a] Ezek. 17:6 [b] Deut. 8:7–9 [1] Literally *blood,* following Masoretic Text, Syriac, and Vulgate; Septuagint reads *like a flower on a pomegranate tree;* Targum reads *in your likeness.* **19:11** [a] Dan. 4:11 **19:12** [a] Jer. 31:27, 28 [b] Hos. 13:5 **19:14** [a] Judg. 9:15 [b] Lam. 2:5 **20:1** [a] Ezek. 8:1, 11, 12; 14:1 **20:3** [a] Ezek. 7:26; 14:3 **20:4** [a] Ezek. 16:2; 22:2 **20:5** [a] Ex. 6:6–8 [b] Deut. 4:34 [c] Ex. 20:2 **20:6** [a] Jer. 32:22 [b] Ex. 3:8 [c] Jer. 11:5; 32:22 [1] Exodus 3:8 **20:7** [a] Ezek. 18:31 [b] 2 Chr. 15:8 [c] Lev. 18:3 **20:8** [a] Ezek. 7:8 **20:9** [a] Num. 14:13 [b] Josh. 2:10; 9:9, 10 **20:10** [a] Ex. 13:18 **20:11** [a] Neh. 9:13 [b] Lev. 18:5

does, he shall live by them.'[1] 12Moreover I also
gave them My [a]Sabbaths, to be a sign between
them and Me, that they might know that I *am*
the LORD who sanctifies them. 13Yet the house
of Israel [a]rebelled against Me in the wilderness; they did not walk in My statutes; they
[b]despised My judgments, [c]'which, *if* a man
does, he shall live by them';[1] and they greatly
[d]defiled My Sabbaths. Then I said I would pour
out My fury on them in the [e]wilderness, to
consume them. 14[a]But I acted for My name's
sake, that it should not be profaned before the
Gentiles, in whose sight I had brought them
out. 15So [a]I also raised My hand in an oath
to them in the wilderness, that I would not
bring them into the land which I had given
them, [b]'flowing with milk and honey,'[1] [c]the
glory of all lands, 16[a]because they despised My
judgments and did not walk in My statutes,
but profaned My Sabbaths; for [b]their heart
went after their idols. 17[a]Nevertheless My eye
spared them from destruction. I did not make
an end of them in the wilderness.

18"But I said to their children in the wilderness, 'Do not walk in the statutes of your
fathers, nor observe their judgments, nor
defile yourselves with their idols. 19I *am* the
LORD your God: [a]Walk in My statutes, keep
My judgments, and do them; 20[a]hallow My
Sabbaths, and they will be a sign between
Me and you, that you may know that I *am*
the LORD your God.'

21"Notwithstanding, [a]the children rebelled
against Me; they did not walk in My statutes,
and were not careful to observe My judgments, [b]'which, *if* a man does, he shall live by
them';[1] but they profaned My Sabbaths. Then
I said I would pour out My fury on them and
fulfill My anger against them in the wilderness. 22Nevertheless I withdrew My hand and
acted for My name's sake, that it should not
be profaned in the sight of the Gentiles, in
whose sight I had brought them out. 23Also
I raised My hand in an oath to those in the
wilderness, that [a]I would scatter them among
the Gentiles and disperse them throughout
the countries, 24[a]because they had not executed My judgments, but had despised My
statutes, profaned My Sabbaths, and [b]their
eyes were fixed on their fathers' idols.

25"Therefore [a]I also gave them up to statutes *that were* not good, and judgments by
which they could not live; 26and I pronounced
them unclean because of their ritual gifts, in
that they caused all their firstborn to pass
[a]through *the fire,* that I might make them
desolate and that they [b]might know that I
am the LORD." '

27"Therefore, son of man, speak to the
house of Israel, and say to them, 'Thus says
the Lord GOD: "In this too your fathers have
[a]blasphemed Me, by being unfaithful to Me.
28When I brought them into the land *concern-*
ing which I had raised My hand in an oath to
give them, and [a]they saw all the high hills and
all the thick trees, there they offered their sacrifices and provoked Me with their offerings.
There they also sent up their [b]sweet aroma
and poured out their drink offerings. 29Then I
said to them, 'What *is* this high place to which
you go?' So its name is called Bamah[1] to this
day." ' 30Therefore say to the house of Israel,
'Thus says the Lord GOD: "Are you defiling
yourselves in the manner of your [a]fathers,
and committing harlotry according to their
[b]abominations? 31For when you offer [a]your
gifts and make your sons pass through the fire,
you defile yourselves with all your idols, even
to this day. So shall I be inquired of by you,
O house of Israel? *As* I live," says the Lord GOD,
"I will [b]not be inquired of by you. 32[a]What you
have in your mind shall never be, when you say,
'We will be like the Gentiles, like the families
in other countries, serving wood and stone.'

God Will Restore Israel

33"*As* I live," says the Lord GOD, "surely with
a mighty hand, [a]with an outstretched arm,
and with fury poured out, I will rule over you.
34I will bring you out from the peoples and
gather you out of the countries where you
are scattered, with a mighty hand, with an
outstretched arm, and with fury poured out.
35And I will bring you into the wilderness of
the peoples, and there [a]I will plead My case
with you face to face. 36[a]Just as I pleaded
My case with your fathers in the wilderness
of the land of Egypt, so I will plead My case
with you," says the Lord GOD.

37"I will make you [a]pass under the rod, and
I will bring you into the bond of the [b]cov-
enant; 38[a]I will purge the rebels from among
you, and those who transgress against Me; I
will bring them out of the country where they
dwell, but [b]they shall not enter the land of
Israel. Then you will know that I *am* the LORD.

20:11 [1] Leviticus 18:5 **20:12** [a] Deut. 5:12 **20:13** [a] Num. 14:22 [b] Prov. 1:25 [c] Lev. 18:5 [d] Ex. 16:27 [e] Num. 14:29 [1] Leviticus 18:5 **20:14** [a] Ezek. 20:9, 20 **20:15** [a] Num. 14:28 [b] Ex. 3:8 [c] Ezek. 20:6 [1] Exodus 3:8 **20:16** [a] Ezek. 20:13, 24 [b] Amos 5:25 **20:17** [a] [Ps. 78:38] **20:19** [a] Deut. 5:32 **20:20** [a] Jer. 17:22 **20:21** [a] Num. 25:1 [b] Lev. 18:5 [1] Leviticus 18:5 **20:23** [a] Lev. 26:33 **20:24** [a] Ezek. 20:13, 16 [b] Ezek. 6:9 **20:25** [a] Rom. 1:24 **20:26** [a] Jer. 32:35 [b] Ezek. 6:7; 20:12, 20 **20:27** [a] Rom. 2:24 **20:28** [a] Ezek. 6:13 [b] Ezek. 16:19 **20:29** [1] Literally *High Place* **20:30** [a] Judg. 2:19 [b] Jer. 7:26; 16:12 **20:31** [a] Ezek. 16:20; 20:26 [b] Ezek. 20:3 **20:32** [a] Ezek. 11:5 **20:33** [a] Jer. 21:5 **20:35** [a] Jer. 2:9, 35; Ezek. 17:20 **20:36** [a] Num. 14:21–23, 28 **20:37** [a] Lev. 27:32 [b] Ps. 89:30–34 **20:38** [a] Ezek. 34:17 [b] Jer. 44:14

39"As for you, O house of Israel," thus says
the Lord GOD: [a]"Go, serve every one of you his
idols—and hereafter—if you will not obey Me;
[b]but profane My holy name no more with your
gifts and your idols. 40For [a]on My holy mountain, on the mountain height of Israel," says
the Lord GOD, "there [b]all the house of Israel,
all of them in the land, shall serve Me; there [c]I
will accept them, and there I will require your
offerings and the firstfruits of your sacrifices,
together with all your holy things. 41I will accept you as a [a]sweet aroma when I bring you
out from the peoples and gather you out of the
countries where you have been scattered; and
I will be hallowed in you before the Gentiles.
42[a]Then you shall know that I *am* the LORD,
[b]when I bring you into the land of Israel, into
the country *for* which I raised My hand in
an oath to give to your fathers. 43And [a]there
you shall remember your ways and all your
doings with which you were defiled; and [b]you
shall loathe yourselves in your own sight because of all the evils that you have committed.
44[a]Then you shall know that I *am* the LORD,
when I have dealt with you [b]for My name's
sake, not according to your wicked ways nor
according to your corrupt doings, O house of
Israel," says the Lord GOD.' "

Fire in the Forest

45Furthermore the word of the LORD came
to me, saying, 46[a]"Son of man, set your face
toward the south; preach against the south
and prophesy against the forest land, the
South,[1] 47and say to the forest of the South,
'Hear the word of the LORD! Thus says the
Lord GOD: "Behold, [a]I will kindle a fire in
you, and it shall devour [b]every green tree
and every dry tree in you; the blazing flame
shall not be quenched, and all faces [c]from
the south to the north shall be scorched by
it. 48All flesh shall see that I, the LORD, have
kindled it; it shall not be quenched." ' "
49Then I said, "Ah, Lord GOD! They say of
me, 'Does he not speak [a]parables?' "

Babylon, the Sword of God

21 And the word of the LORD came to me,
saying, 2[a]"Son of man, set your face toward Jerusalem, [b]preach against the holy places, and prophesy against the land of Israel; 3and
say to the land of Israel, 'Thus says the LORD:
"Behold, I *am* [a]against you, and I will draw My
sword out of its sheath and cut off both [b]righ-
teous and wicked from you. 4Because I will
cut off both righteous and wicked from you,
therefore My sword shall go out of its sheath
against all flesh [a]from south *to* north, 5that all
flesh may know that I, the LORD, have drawn
My sword out of its sheath; it [a]shall not return
anymore." ' 6[a]Sigh therefore, son of man, with a
breaking heart, and sigh with bitterness before
their eyes. 7And it shall be when they say to you,
'Why are you sighing?' that you shall answer,
'Because of the news; when it comes, every
heart will melt, [a]all hands will be feeble, every
spirit will faint, and all knees will be weak *as*
water. Behold, it is coming and shall be brought
to pass,' says the Lord GOD."
8Again the word of the LORD came to me,
saying, 9"Son of man, prophesy and say, 'Thus
says the LORD!' Say:

[a]'A sword, a sword is sharpened
And also polished!
10 Sharpened to make a dreadful
slaughter,
Polished to flash like lightning!
Should we then make mirth?
It despises the scepter of My son,
As it does all wood.
11 And He has given it to be polished,
That it may be handled;
This sword is sharpened, and it is
polished
To be given into the hand of [a]the slayer.'

12 "Cry and wail, son of man;
For it will be against My people,
Against all the princes of Israel.
Terrors including the sword will be
against My people;
Therefore [a]strike *your* thigh.

13 "Because *it is* [a]a testing,
And what if *the sword* despises even
the scepter?
[b]*The scepter* shall be no *more*,"

says the Lord GOD.

14 "You therefore, son of man, prophesy,
And [a]strike *your* hands together.
The third time let the sword do double
damage.
It *is* the sword *that* slays,
The sword that slays the great *men*,
That enters their [b]private chambers.
15 I have set the point of the sword
against all their gates,

20:39 [a] Amos 4:4 [b] Is. 1:13–15 **20:40** [a] Is. 2:2, 3 [b] Ezek. 37:22 [c] Zech. 8:20–22 **20:41** [a] Phil. 4:18 **20:42** [a] Ezek. 36:23; 38:23 [b] Ezek. 11:17; 34:13; 36:24 **20:43** [a] Ezek. 16:61 [b] Lev. 26:39 **20:44** [a] Ezek. 24:24 [b] Ezek. 36:22 **20:46** [a] Ezek. 21:2 [1] Hebrew *Negev* **20:47** [a] Jer. 21:14 [b] Luke 23:31 [c] Ezek. 21:4 **20:49** [a] Ezek. 12:9; 17:2 **21:2** [a] Ezek. 20:46 [b] Amos 7:16 **21:3** [a] Ezek. 5:8 [b] Job 9:22 **21:4** [a] Ezek. 20:47 **21:5** [a] [Is. 45:23; 55:11] **21:6** [a] Is. 22:4 **21:7** [a] Ezek. 7:17 **21:9** [a] Deut. 32:41 **21:11** [a] Ezek. 21:19 **21:12** [a] Jer. 31:19 **21:13** [a] Job 9:23 [b] Ezek. 21:27 **21:14** [a] Num. 24:10 [b] 1 Kin. 20:30

That the heart may melt and many may
stumble.
Ah! [a]*It is* made bright;
It is grasped for slaughter:

16 "Swords[a] at the ready!
Thrust right!
Set your blade!
Thrust left—
Wherever your edge is ordered!

17 "I also will [a]beat My fists together,
And [b]I will cause My fury to rest;
I, the LORD, have spoken."

18The word of the LORD came to me again,
saying: 19"And son of man, appoint for yourself
two ways for the sword of the king of Babylon to
go; both of them shall go from the same land.
Make a sign; put *it* at the head of the road to
the city. 20Appoint a road for the sword to go to
[a]Rabbah of the Ammonites, and to Judah, into
fortified Jerusalem. 21For the king of Babylon
stands at the parting of the road, at the fork of
the two roads, to use divination: he shakes the
arrows, he consults the images, he looks at the
liver. 22In his right hand is the divination for
Jerusalem: to set up battering rams, to call for
a slaughter, to [a]lift the voice with shouting, [b]to
set battering rams against the gates, to heap up
a *siege* mound, and to build a wall. 23And it will
be to them like a false divination in the eyes of
those who [a]have sworn oaths with them; but
he will bring their iniquity to remembrance,
that they may be taken.

24"Therefore thus says the Lord GOD: 'Because you have made your iniquity to be
remembered, in that your transgressions
are uncovered, so that in all your doings
your sins appear—because you have come
to remembrance, you shall be taken in hand.

25'Now to you, O [a]profane, wicked prince of
Israel, [b]whose day has come, whose iniquity
shall end, 26thus says the Lord GOD:

"Remove the turban, and take off the
crown;
Nothing *shall remain* the same.
[a]Exalt the humble, and humble the
exalted.
27 Overthrown, overthrown,
I will make it overthrown!
[a]It shall be no *longer,*
Until He comes whose right it is,
And I will give it *to* [b]*Him.*" '

A Sword Against the Ammonites

28"And you, son of man, prophesy and say,
'Thus says the Lord GOD [a]concerning the
Ammonites and concerning their reproach,'
and say:

'A sword, a sword *is* drawn,
Polished for slaughter,
For consuming, for flashing—
29 While they [a]see false visions for you,
While they divine a lie to you,
To bring you on the necks of the
wicked, the slain
[b]Whose day has come,
Whose iniquity *shall* end.

30 'Return[a] *it* to its sheath.
[b]I will judge you
In the place where you were created,
[c]In the land of your nativity.
31 I will [a]pour out My indignation on you;
I will [b]blow against you with the fire of
My wrath,
And deliver you into the hands of
brutal men *who are* skillful to
[c]destroy.
32 You shall be fuel for the fire;
Your blood shall be in the midst of the
land.
[a]You shall not be remembered,
For I the LORD have spoken.' "

Sins of Jerusalem

22 Moreover the word of the LORD came
to me, saying, 2"Now, son of man, [a]will
you judge, will you judge [b]the bloody city?
Yes, show her all her abominations! 3Then
say, 'Thus says the Lord GOD: "The city sheds
[a]blood in her own midst, that her time may
come; and she makes idols within herself to
defile herself. 4You have become guilty by
the blood which you have [a]shed, and have
defiled yourself with the idols which you
have made. You have caused your days to
draw near, and have come to *the end of* your
years; [b]therefore I have made you a reproach
to the nations, and a mockery to all countries.
5*Those* near and *those* far from you will mock
you as infamous *and* full of tumult.

6"Look, [a]the princes of Israel: each one
has used his power to shed blood in you.
7In you they have [a]made light of father and
mother; in your midst they have [b]oppressed
the stranger; in you they have mistreated
the fatherless and the widow. 8You have

21:15 [a] Ezek. 21:10, 28 **21:16** [a] Ezek. 14:17 **21:17** [a] Ezek. 22:13 [b] Ezek. 5:13; 16:42; 24:13 **21:20** [a] Jer. 49:2 **21:22** [a] Jer. 51:14 [b] Ezek. 4:2 **21:23** [a] Ezek. 17:16, 18 **21:25** [a] Jer. 52:2 [b] Ezek. 21:29 **21:26** [a] Luke 1:52 **21:27** [a] [Luke 1:32, 33] [b] [Jer. 23:5, 6] **21:28** [a] Ezek. 25:1–7 **21:29** [a] Ezek. 12:24; 13:6–9; 22:28 [b] Job 18:20 **21:30** [a] Jer. 47:6, 7 [b] Gen. 15:14 [c] Ezek. 16:3 **21:31** [a] Ezek. 7:8 [b] Ezek. 22:20, 21 [c] Hab. 1:6–10 **21:32** [a] Ezek. 25:10 **22:2** [a] Ezek. 20:4 [b] Nah. 3:1 **22:3** [a] Ezek. 24:6, 7 **22:4** [a] 2 Kin. 21:16 [b] Deut. 28:37 **22:6** [a] Is. 1:23 **22:7** [a] Lev. 20:9 [b] Ex. 22:22

despised My holy things and [a]profaned My
Sabbaths. 9In you are [a]men who slander
to cause bloodshed; [b]in you are those who
eat on the mountains; in your midst they
commit lewdness. 10In you men [a]uncover
their fathers' nakedness; in you they violate
women who are [b]set apart during their impurity. 11One commits abomination [a]with his
neighbor's wife; [b]another lewdly defiles his
daughter-in-law; and another in you violates
his sister, his father's [c]daughter. 12In you
[a]they take bribes to shed blood; [b]you take
usury and increase; you have made profit
from your neighbors by extortion, and [c]have
forgotten Me," says the Lord GOD.

13"Behold, therefore, I [a]beat My fists at the
dishonest profit which you have made, and at
the bloodshed which has been in your midst.
14[a]Can your heart endure, or can your hands
remain strong, in the days when I shall deal with
you? [b]I, the LORD, have spoken, and will do *it.*
15[a]I will scatter you among the nations, disperse
you throughout the countries, and [b]remove
your filthiness completely from you. 16You shall
defile yourself in the sight of the nations; then
[a]you shall know that I *am* the LORD." ' "

Israel in the Furnace

17The word of the LORD came to me, saying, 18"Son of man, [a]the house of Israel has
become dross to Me; they *are* all bronze, tin,
iron, and lead, in the midst of a [b]furnace; they
have become dross from silver. 19Therefore
thus says the Lord GOD: 'Because you have
all become dross, therefore behold, I will
gather you into the midst of Jerusalem. 20*As
men* gather silver, bronze, iron, lead, and tin
into the midst of a furnace, to blow fire on it,
to [a]melt *it;* so I will gather *you* in My anger
and in My fury, and I will leave *you there* and
melt you. 21Yes, I will gather you and blow on
you with the fire of My wrath, and you shall
be melted in its midst. 22As silver is melted in
the midst of a furnace, so shall you be melted
in its midst; then you shall know that I, the
LORD, have [a]poured out My fury on you.' "

Israel's Wicked Leaders

23And the word of the LORD came to me,
saying, 24"Son of man, say to her: 'You *are* a
land that is [a]not cleansed[1] or rained on in the
day of indignation.' 25[a]The conspiracy of her
prophets[1] in her midst is like a roaring lion
tearing the prey; they [b]have devoured people; [c]they have taken treasure and precious
things; they have made many widows in her
midst. 26[a]Her priests have violated My law and
[b]profaned My holy things; they have not [c]dis-
tinguished between the holy and unholy, nor
have they made known *the difference* between
the unclean and the clean; and they have hidden their eyes from My Sabbaths, so that I am
profaned among them. 27Her [a]princes in her
midst *are* like wolves tearing the prey, to shed
blood, to destroy people, and to get dishonest
gain. 28[a]Her prophets plastered them with
untempered *mortar,* [b]seeing false visions, and
divining [c]lies for them, saying, 'Thus says the
Lord GOD,' when the LORD had not spoken.
29The people of the land have used oppressions, committed robbery, and mistreated the
poor and needy; and they wrongfully [a]oppress
the stranger. 30[a]So I sought for a man among
them who would [b]make a wall, and [c]stand in
the gap before Me on behalf of the land, that
I should not destroy it; but I found no one.
31Therefore I have [a]poured out My indignation
on them; I have consumed them with the fire
of My wrath; and I have recompensed [b]their
deeds on their own heads," says the Lord GOD.

Two Harlot Sisters

23 The word of the LORD came again to
me, saying:

2 "Son of man, there were [a]two women,
The daughters of one mother.

PEACE NOTE

God is still looking for any man or woman who will stand in the gap before Him. Intercession is a major highway to bring peace to societies.

EZEKIEL 22:30

22:8 [a] Lev. 19:30 **22:9** [a] Lev. 19:16 [b] Ezek. 18:6, 11 **22:10** [a] Lev. 18:7, 8 [b] Lev. 18:19; 20:18 **22:11** [a] Ezek. 18:11 [b] Lev. 18:15 [c] Lev. 18:9 **22:12** [a] Ex. 23:8 [b] Ex. 22:25 [c] Ezek. 23:35 **22:13** [a] Ezek. 21:17 **22:14** [a] Ezek. 21:7 [b] Ezek. 17:24 **22:15** [a] Deut. 4:27 [b] Ezek. 23:27, 48 **22:16** [a] Ps. 9:16 **22:18** [a] Is. 1:22 [b] Prov. 17:3 **22:20** [a] Is. 1:25 **22:22** [a] Ezek. 20:8, 33 **22:24** [a] Ezek. 24:13 [1] Following Masoretic Text, Syriac, and Vulgate; Septuagint reads *showered upon.* **22:25** [a] Hos. 6:9 [b] Matt. 23:14 [c] Mic. 3:11 [1] Following Masoretic Text and Vulgate; Septuagint reads *princes;* Targum reads *scribes.* **22:26** [a] Mal. 2:8 [b] 1 Sam. 2:29 [c] Lev. 10:10 **22:27** [a] Is. 1:23 **22:28** [a] Ezek. 13:10 [b] Ezek. 13:6, 7 [c] Jer. 23:25–32 **22:29** [a] Ex. 23:9 **22:30** [a] Jer. 5:1 [b] Ezek. 13:5 [c] Ps. 106:23 **22:31** [a] Ezek. 22:22 [b] Ezek. 9:10 **23:2** [a] Ezek. 16:44–46

3 [a]They committed harlotry in Egypt,
They committed harlotry in [b]their youth;
Their breasts were there embraced,
Their virgin bosom was there pressed.
4 Their names: Oholah[1] the elder and Oholibah[2] [a]her sister;
[b]They were Mine,
And they bore sons and daughters.
As for their names,
Samaria *is* Oholah, and Jerusalem *is* Oholibah.

The Older Sister, Samaria

5 "Oholah played the harlot even though she was Mine;
And she lusted for her lovers, the neighboring [a]Assyrians,
6 *Who were* clothed in purple,
Captains and rulers,
All of them desirable young men,
Horsemen riding on horses.
7 Thus she committed her harlotry with them,
All of them choice men of Assyria;
And with all for whom she lusted,
With all their idols, she defiled herself.
8 She has never given up her harlotry *brought* [a]from Egypt,
For in her youth they had lain with her,
Pressed her virgin bosom,
And poured out their immorality upon her.

9 "Therefore I have delivered her
Into the hand of her lovers,
Into the hand of the [a]Assyrians,
For whom she lusted.
10 They uncovered her nakedness,
Took away her sons and daughters,
And slew her with the sword;
She became a byword among women,
For they had executed judgment on her.

The Younger Sister, Jerusalem

11 "Now [a]although her sister Oholibah saw
this, [b]she became more corrupt in her lust
than she, and in her harlotry more corrupt
than her sister's harlotry.

12 "She lusted for the neighboring [a]Assyrians,
[b]Captains and rulers,
Clothed most gorgeously,
Horsemen riding on horses,
All of them desirable young men.
13 Then I saw that she was defiled;
Both *took* the same way.
14 But she increased her harlotry;
She looked at men portrayed on the wall,
Images of [a]Chaldeans portrayed in vermilion,
15 Girded with belts around their waists,
Flowing turbans on their heads,
All of them looking like captains,
In the manner of the Babylonians of Chaldea,
The land of their nativity.
16 [a]As soon as her eyes saw them,
She lusted for them
And sent [b]messengers to them in Chaldea.

17 "Then the Babylonians came to her, into the bed of love,
And they defiled her with their immorality;
So she was defiled by them, [a]and alienated herself from them.
18 She revealed her harlotry and uncovered her nakedness.
Then [a]I [b]alienated Myself from her,
As I had alienated Myself from her sister.

19 "Yet she multiplied her harlotry
In calling to remembrance the days of her youth,
[a]When she had played the harlot in the land of Egypt.
20 For she lusted for her paramours,
Whose flesh *is like* the flesh of donkeys,
And whose issue *is like* the issue of horses.
21 Thus you called to remembrance the lewdness of your youth,
When the [a]Egyptians pressed your bosom
Because of your youthful breasts.

Judgment on Jerusalem

22 "Therefore, Oholibah, thus says the Lord
GOD:

[a]'Behold, I will stir up your lovers against you,
From whom you have alienated yourself,
And I will bring them against you from every side:

23:3 [a] Lev. 17:7 [b] Ezek. 16:22 **23:4** [a] Jer. 3:6, 7 [b] Ezek. 16:8, 20 [1] Literally *Her Own Tabernacle* [2] Literally *My Tabernacle Is in Her* **23:5** [a] Hos. 5:13; 8:9, 10 **23:8** [a] Ezek. 23:3, 19 **23:9** [a] 2 Kin. 17:3 **23:11** [a] Jer. 3:8 [b] Jer. 3:8–11 **23:12** [a] 2 Kin. 16:7, 8 [b] Ezek. 23:6, 23 **23:14** [a] Ezek. 8:10; 16:29 **23:16** [a] 2 Kin. 24:1 [b] Is. 57:9 **23:17** [a] Ezek. 23:22, 28 **23:18** [a] Jer. 6:8 [b] Jer. 12:8 **23:19** [a] Ezek. 23:2 **23:21** [a] Ezek. 16:26 **23:22** [a] Ezek. 16:37–41; 23:28

23 The Babylonians,
All the Chaldeans,
[a]Pekod, Shoa, Koa,
[b]All the Assyrians with them,
All of them desirable young men,
Governors and rulers,
Captains and men of renown,
All of them riding on horses.
24 And they shall come against you
With chariots, wagons, and war-horses,
With a horde of people.
They shall array against you
Buckler, shield, and helmet all around.

'I will delegate judgment to them,
And they shall judge you according to
their judgments.
25 I will set My [a]jealousy against you,
And they shall deal furiously with you;
They shall remove your nose and your
ears,
And your remnant shall fall by the sword;
They shall take your sons and your
daughters,
And your remnant shall be devoured
by fire.
26 [a]They shall also strip you of your clothes
And take away your beautiful jewelry.

27 'Thus [a]I will make you cease your
lewdness and your [b]harlotry
Brought from the land of Egypt,
So that you will not lift your eyes to
them,
Nor remember Egypt anymore.'

28"For thus says the Lord GOD: 'Surely I will
deliver you into the hand of [a]those you hate,
into the hand *of those* [b]from whom you alienated yourself. 29[a]They will deal hatefully with
you, take away all you have worked for, and
[b]leave you naked and bare. The nakedness of
your harlotry shall be uncovered, both your
lewdness and your harlotry. 30I will do these
things to you because you have [a]gone as a
harlot after the Gentiles, because you have
become defiled by their idols. 31You have
walked in the way of your sister; therefore I
will put her [a]cup in your hand.'
32"Thus says the Lord GOD:

'You shall drink of your sister's cup,
The deep and wide one;
[a]You shall be laughed to scorn
And held in derision;
It contains much.
33 You will be filled with drunkenness and
sorrow,
The cup of horror and desolation,
The cup of your sister Samaria.
34 You shall [a]drink and drain it,
You shall break its shards,
And tear at your own breasts;
For I have spoken,'
Says the Lord GOD.

35"Therefore thus says the Lord GOD:

'Because you [a]have forgotten Me and
[b]cast Me behind your back,
Therefore you shall bear the *penalty*
Of your lewdness and your
harlotry.'"

Both Sisters Judged

36The LORD also said to me: "Son of man,
will you [a]judge Oholah and Oholibah? Then
[b]declare to them their abominations. 37For they
have committed adultery, and [a]blood *is* on their
hands. They have committed adultery with
their idols, and even *sacrificed* their sons [b]whom
they bore to Me, passing them through *the fire,*
to devour *them.* 38Moreover they have done this
to Me: They have [a]defiled My sanctuary on the
same day and [b]profaned My Sabbaths. 39For
after they had slain their children for their idols,
on the same day they came into My sanctuary
to profane it; and indeed [a]thus they have done
in the midst of My house.
40"Furthermore you sent for men to come
from afar, [a]to whom a messenger *was* sent; and
there they came. And you [b]washed yourself
for them, [c]painted your eyes, and adorned
yourself with ornaments. 41You sat on a stately
[a]couch, with a table prepared before it, [b]on
which you had set My incense and My oil. 42The
sound of a carefree multitude *was* with her,
and Sabeans *were* brought from the wilderness with men of the common sort, who put
bracelets on their wrists and beautiful crowns
on their heads. 43Then I said concerning *her*
who had grown old in adulteries, 'Will they
commit harlotry with her now, and she *with*
them?' 44Yet they went in to her, as men go in to
a woman who plays the harlot; thus they went
in to Oholah and Oholibah, the lewd women.
45But righteous men will [a]judge them after the
manner of adulteresses, and after the manner
of women who shed blood, because they *are*
adulteresses, and [b]blood *is* on their hands.

23:23 [a] Jer. 50:21 [b] Ezek. 23:12 **23:25** [a] Ex. 34:14 **23:26** [a] Is. 3:18–23 **23:27** [a] Ezek. 16:41; 22:15 [b] Ezek. 23:3, 19
23:28 [a] Ezek. 16:37–41 [b] Ezek. 23:17 **23:29** [a] Deut. 28:48 [b] Ezek. 16:39 **23:30** [a] Ezek. 6:9 **23:31** [a] Jer. 7:14, 15; 25:15
23:32 [a] Ezek. 22:4, 5 **23:34** [a] Is. 51:17 **23:35** [a] Jer. 3:21 [b] 1 Kin. 14:9 **23:36** [a] Ezek. 20:4; 22:2 [b] Is. 58:1 **23:37** [a] Ezek.
16:38 [b] Ezek. 16:20, 21, 36, 45; 20:26, 31 **23:38** [a] 2 Kin. 21:4, 7 [b] Ezek. 22:8 **23:39** [a] 2 Kin. 21:2–8 **23:40** [a] Is. 57:9
[b] Ruth 3:3 [c] Jer. 4:30 **23:41** [a] Is. 57:7 [b] Prov. 7:17 **23:45** [a] Ezek. 16:38 [b] Ezek. 23:37

[46]"For thus says the Lord GOD: [a]'Bring up
an assembly against them, give them up to
trouble and plunder. [47][a]The assembly shall
stone them with stones and execute them
with their swords; [b]they shall slay their sons
and their daughters, and burn their houses
with fire. [48]Thus [a]I will cause lewdness to
cease from the land, [b]that all women may be
taught not to practice your lewdness. [49]They
shall repay you for your lewdness, and you
shall [a]pay for your idolatrous sins. [b]Then you
shall know that I *am* the Lord GOD.' "

Symbol of the Cooking Pot

24 Again, in the ninth year, in the tenth
month, on the tenth *day* of the month,
the word of the LORD came to me, saying,
[2]"Son of man, write down the name of the
day, this very day—the king of Babylon started his siege against Jerusalem [a]this very day.
[3][a]And utter a parable to the rebellious house,
and say to them, 'Thus says the Lord GOD:

[b]"Put on a pot, set *it* on,
And also pour water into it.
4 Gather pieces *of meat* in it,
Every good piece,
The thigh and the shoulder.
Fill *it* with choice cuts;
5 Take the choice of the flock.
Also pile *fuel* bones under it,
Make it boil well,
And let the cuts simmer in it."

[6]'Therefore thus says the Lord GOD:

"Woe to [a]the bloody city,
To the pot whose scum *is* in it,
And whose scum is not gone from it!
Bring it out piece by piece,
On which no [b]lot has fallen.
7 For her blood is in her midst;
She set it on top of a rock;
[a]She did not pour it on the ground,
To cover it with dust.
8 That it may raise up fury and take
vengeance,
[a]I have set her blood on top of a rock,
That it may not be covered."

[9]'Therefore thus says the Lord GOD:

[a]"Woe to the bloody city!
I too will make the pyre great.
10 Heap on the wood,
Kindle the fire;
Cook the meat well,
Mix in the spices,
And let the cuts be burned up.

11 "Then set the pot empty on the coals,
That it may become hot and its bronze
may burn,
That [a]its filthiness may be melted in it,
That its scum may be consumed.
12 She has grown weary with lies,
And her great scum has not gone from
her.
Let her scum *be* in the fire!
13 In your [a]filthiness *is* lewdness.
Because I have cleansed you, and you
were not cleansed,
You will [b]not be cleansed of your
filthiness anymore,
[c]Till I have caused My fury to rest upon
you.
14 [a]I, the LORD, have spoken *it;*
[b]It shall come to pass, and I will do *it;*
I will not hold back,
[c]Nor will I spare,
Nor will I relent;
According to your ways
And according to your deeds
They[1] will judge you,"
Says the Lord GOD.' "

The Prophet's Wife Dies

[15]Also the word of the LORD came to me,
saying, [16]"Son of man, behold, I take away
from you the desire of your eyes with one
stroke; yet you shall [a]neither mourn nor
weep, nor shall your tears run down. [17]Sigh
in silence, [a]make no mourning for the dead;
[b]bind your turban on your head, and [c]put
your sandals on your feet; [d]do not cover
your lips, and do not eat man's bread *of
sorrow.*"

[18]So I spoke to the people in the morning,
and at evening my wife died; and the next
morning I did as I was commanded.

[19]And the people said to me, [a]"Will you not
tell us what these *things signify* to us, that
you behave so?"

[20]Then I answered them, "The word of
the LORD came to me, saying, [21]'Speak to the
house of Israel, "Thus says the Lord GOD:
'Behold, [a]I will profane My sanctuary, your
arrogant boast, the desire of your eyes, the
delight of your soul; [b]and your sons and
daughters whom you left behind shall fall

23:46 [a] Ezek. 16:40 **23:47** [a] Ezek. 16:40 [b] Ezek. 24:21 **23:48** [a] Ezek. 22:15 [b] Deut. 13:11 **23:49** [a] Ezek. 23:35 [b] Ezek. 20:38, 42, 44; 25:5 **24:2** [a] 2 Kin. 25:1 **24:3** [a] Ezek. 17:12 [b] Jer. 1:13 **24:6** [a] Ezek. 22:2, 3, 27 [b] Nah. 3:10 **24:7** [a] Lev. 17:13 **24:8** [a] [Matt. 7:2] **24:9** [a] Hab. 2:12 **24:11** [a] Ezek. 22:15 **24:13** [a] Ezek. 23:36–48 [b] Jer. 6:28–30 [c] Ezek. 5:13; 8:18; 16:42 **24:14** [a] [1 Sam. 15:29] [b] Is. 55:11 [c] Ezek. 5:11 [1] Septuagint, Syriac, Targum, and Vulgate read *I.* **24:16** [a] Jer. 16:5 **24:17** [a] Jer. 16:5 [b] Lev. 10:6; 21:10 [c] 2 Sam. 15:30 [d] Mic. 3:7 **24:19** [a] Ezek. 12:9; 37:18 **24:21** [a] Jer. 7:14 [b] Ezek. 23:25, 47

PEACE NOTE

It's hard to imagine that what I am facing today may be a platform I use, by God's grace, to live in His peace and minister that same peace to others!

by the sword. 22And you shall do as I have done; [a]you shall not cover *your* lips nor eat man's bread *of sorrow.* 23Your turbans shall be on your heads and your sandals on your feet; [a]you shall neither mourn nor weep, but [b]you shall pine away in your iniquities and mourn with one another. 24Thus [a]Ezekiel is a sign to you; according to all that he has done you shall do; [b]and when this comes, [c]you shall know that I *am* the Lord GOD.' "

25'And you, son of man—*will it* not *be* in the day when I take from them [a]their stronghold, their joy and their glory, the desire of their eyes, and that on which they set their minds, their sons and their daughters: 26*that* on that day [a]one who escapes will come to you to let *you* hear *it* with *your* ears? 27[a]On that day your mouth will be opened to him who has escaped; you shall speak and no longer be mute. Thus you will be a sign to them, and they shall know that I *am* the LORD.' "

Proclamation Against Ammon

25 The word of the LORD came to me, saying, 2"Son of man, [a]set your face [b]against the Ammonites, and prophesy against them. 3Say to the Ammonites, 'Hear the word of the Lord GOD! Thus says the Lord GOD: [a]"Because you said, 'Aha!' against My sanctuary when it was profaned, and against the land of Israel when it was desolate, and against the house of Judah when they went into captivity, 4indeed, therefore, I will deliver you as a possession to the men of the East, and they shall set their encampments among you and make their dwellings among you; they shall eat your fruit, and they shall drink your milk. 5And I will make [a]Rabbah [b]a stable for camels and Ammon a resting place for flocks. [c]Then you shall know that I *am* the LORD."

6'For thus says the Lord GOD: "Because you [a]clapped *your* hands, stamped your feet, and [b]rejoiced in heart with all your disdain for the land of Israel, 7indeed, therefore, I will [a]stretch out My hand against you, and give you as plunder to the nations; I will cut you off from the peoples, and I will cause you to perish from the countries; I will destroy you, and you shall know that I *am* the LORD."

Proclamation Against Moab

8"Thus says the Lord GOD: "Because [a]Moab and [b]Seir say, 'Look! The house of Judah *is* like all the nations,' 9therefore, behold, I will clear the territory of Moab of cities, of the cities on its frontier, the glory of the country, Beth Jeshimoth, Baal Meon, and [a]Kirjathaim. 10[a]To the men of the East I will give it as a possession, together with the Ammonites, that the Ammonites [b]may not be remembered among the nations. 11And I will execute judgments upon Moab, and they shall know that I *am* the LORD."

Proclamation Against Edom

12"Thus says the Lord GOD: [a]"Because of what Edom did against the house of Judah by taking vengeance, and has greatly offended by avenging itself on them," 13therefore thus says the Lord GOD: "I will also stretch out My hand against Edom, cut off man and beast from it, and make it desolate from Teman; Dedan shall fall by the sword. 14[a]I will lay My vengeance on Edom by the hand of My people Israel, that they may do in Edom according to My anger and according to My fury; and they shall know My vengeance," says the Lord GOD.

Proclamation Against Philistia

15"Thus says the Lord GOD: [a]"Because [b]the Philistines dealt vengefully and took vengeance with a spiteful heart, to destroy because of the old hatred," 16therefore thus says the Lord GOD: [a]"I will stretch out My hand against the Philistines, and I will cut off the [b]Cherethites [c]and destroy the remnant of the seacoast. 17I will [a]execute great vengeance on them with furious rebukes; [b]and they shall know that I *am* the LORD, when I lay My vengeance upon them." ' "

24:22 [a] Jer. 16:6, 7 **24:23** [a] Job 27:15 [b] Lev. 26:39 **24:24** [a] Is. 20:3 [b] Jer. 17:15 [c] Ezek. 6:7; 25:5 **24:25** [a] Ezek. 24:21 **24:26** [a] Ezek. 33:21 **24:27** [a] Ezek. 3:26; 33:22 **25:2** [a] Ezek. 35:2 [b] Jer. 49:1 **25:3** [a] Ezek. 26:2 **25:5** [a] Ezek. 21:20 [b] Is. 17:2 [c] Ezek. 24:24 **25:6** [a] Job 27:23 [b] Ezek. 36:5 **25:7** [a] Ezek. 35:3 **25:8** [a] Amos 2:1, 2 [b] Ezek. 35:2, 5 **25:9** [a] Jer. 48:23 **25:10** [a] Ezek. 25:4 [b] Ezek. 21:32 **25:12** [a] Obad. 10–14 **25:14** [a] Is. 11:14 **25:15** [a] Jer. 25:20 [b] 2 Chr. 28:18 **25:16** [a] Zeph. 2:4 [b] 1 Sam. 30:14 [c] Jer. 47:4 **25:17** [a] Ezek. 5:15 [b] Ps. 9:16

Proclamation Against Tyre

26 And it came to pass in the eleventh
year, on the first *day* of the month,
that the word of the LORD came to me, saying,
2“Son of man, [a]because Tyre has said against
Jerusalem, [b]‘Aha! She is broken who *was* the
gateway of the peoples; now she is turned
over to me; I shall be filled; she is laid waste.’
3“Therefore thus says the Lord GOD: ‘Behold, I *am* against you, O Tyre, and will cause
many nations to come up against you, as the
sea causes its waves to come up. 4And they
shall destroy the walls of Tyre and break
down her towers; I will also scrape her dust
from her, and [a]make her like the top of a rock.
5It shall be *a place for* spreading nets [a]in the
midst of the sea, for I have spoken,’ says
the Lord GOD; ‘it shall become plunder for
the nations. 6Also her daughter *villages* which
are in the fields shall be slain by the sword.
[a]Then they shall know that I am the LORD.’
7“For thus says the Lord GOD: ‘Behold, I will
bring against Tyre from the north [a]Nebuchad-
nezzar[1] king of Babylon, [b]king of kings, with
horses, with chariots, and with horsemen, and
an army with many people. 8He will slay with
the sword your daughter *villages* in the fields;
he will [a]heap up a siege mound against you,
build a wall against you, and raise a defense
against you. 9He will direct his battering rams
against your walls, and with his axes he will
break down your towers. 10Because of the
abundance of his horses, their dust will cover
you; your walls will shake at the noise of the
horsemen, the wagons, and the chariots, when
he enters your gates, as men enter a city that
has been breached. 11With the hooves of his
[a]horses he will trample all your streets; he will
slay your people by the sword, and your strong
pillars will fall to the ground. 12They will plunder your riches and pillage your merchandise;
they will break down your walls and destroy
your pleasant houses; they will lay your stones,
your timber, and your soil in the [a]midst of the
water. 13[a]I will put an end to the sound of [b]your
songs, and the sound of your harps shall be
heard no more. 14[a]I will make you like the top
of a rock; you shall be *a place for* spreading
nets, and you shall never be rebuilt, for I the
LORD have spoken,’ says the Lord GOD.
15“Thus says the Lord GOD to Tyre: ‘Will the
coastlands not [a]shake at the sound of your
fall, when the wounded cry, when slaughter
is made in the midst of you? 16Then all the
[a]princes of the sea will [b]come down from
their thrones, lay aside their robes, and take
off their embroidered garments; they will
clothe themselves with trembling; [c]they will
sit on the ground, [d]tremble *every* moment,
and [e]be astonished at you. 17And they will take
up a [a]lamentation for you, and say to you:

“How you have perished,
O one inhabited by seafaring men,
O renowned city,
Who was [b]strong at sea,
She and her inhabitants,
Who caused their terror *to be* on all her
inhabitants!
18 Now [a]the coastlands tremble on the
day of your fall;
Yes, the coastlands by the sea are
troubled at your departure.” ’

19“For thus says the Lord GOD: ‘When I make
you a desolate city, like cities that are not inhabited, when I bring the deep upon you, and
great waters cover you, 20then I will bring you
down [a]with those who descend into the Pit, to
the people of old, and I will make you dwell in
the lowest part of the earth, in places desolate
from antiquity, with those who go down to
the Pit, so that you may never be inhabited;
and I shall establish glory [b]in the land of the
living. 21[a]I will make you a terror, and you *shall*
be no *more;* [b]though you are sought for, you
will never be found again,’ says the Lord GOD.”

Lamentation for Tyre

27 The word of the LORD came again to
me, saying, 2“Now, son of man, [a]take
up a lamentation for Tyre, 3and say to Tyre,
[a]‘You who are situated at the entrance of
the sea, [b]merchant of the peoples on many
coastlands, thus says the Lord GOD:

“O Tyre, you have said,
[c]‘I *am* perfect in beauty.’
4 Your borders *are* in the midst of the
seas.
Your builders have perfected your
beauty.
5 They made all *your* planks of fir trees
from [a]Senir;
They took a cedar from Lebanon to
make you a mast.
6 *Of* [a]oaks from Bashan they made your
oars;

26:2 [a] Jer. 25:22 [b] Ezek. 25:3 **26:4** [a] Ezek. 26:14 **26:5** [a] Ezek. 27:32 **26:6** [a] Ezek. 25:5 **26:7** [a] Jer. 27:3–6 [b] Dan. 2:37, 47 [1] Hebrew *Nebuchadrezzar,* and so elsewhere in this book **26:8** [a] Ezek. 21:22 **26:11** [a] Hab. 1:8 **26:12** [a] Ezek. 27:27, 32 **26:13** [a] Is. 14:11; 24:8 [b] Rev. 18:22 **26:14** [a] Ezek. 26:4, 5 **26:15** [a] Jer. 49:21 **26:16** [a] Is. 23:8 [b] Jon. 3:6 [c] Job 2:13 [d] Ezek. 32:10 [e] Ezek. 27:35 **26:17** [a] Ezek. 27:2–36 [b] Is. 23:4 **26:18** [a] Ezek. 26:15 **26:20** [a] Ezek. 32:18 [b] Ezek. 32:23 **26:21** [a] Ezek. 27:36; 28:19 [b] Ps. 37:10, 36 **27:2** [a] Ezek. 26:17 **27:3** [a] Ezek. 26:17; 28:2 [b] Is. 23:3 [c] Ezek. 28:12 **27:5** [a] Deut. 3:9 **27:6** [a] Is. 2:12, 13

The company of Ashurites have inlaid
your planks
With ivory from [b]the coasts of Cyprus.[1]
7 Fine embroidered linen from Egypt
was what you spread for your sail;
Blue and purple from the coasts of
Elishah was what covered you.

8 "Inhabitants of Sidon and Arvad were
your oarsmen;
Your wise men, O Tyre, were in you;
They became your pilots.
9 Elders of [a]Gebal and its wise men
Were in you to caulk your seams;
All the ships of the sea
And their oarsmen were in you
To market your merchandise.

10 "Those from Persia, Lydia,[1] and Libya[2]
Were in your army as men of war;
They hung shield and helmet in you;
They gave splendor to you.
11 Men of Arvad with your army *were* on
your walls *all* around,
And the men of Gammad were in your
towers;
They hung their shields on your walls
all around;
They made [a]your beauty perfect.

12 [a]"Tarshish *was* your merchant because
of your many luxury goods. They gave you
silver, iron, tin, and lead for your goods.
13 [a]Javan, Tubal, and Meshech *were* your traders. They bartered [b]human lives and vessels
of bronze for your merchandise. 14 Those
from the house of [a]Togarmah traded for your
wares with horses, steeds, and mules. 15 The
men of [a]Dedan *were* your traders; many
isles *were* the market of your hand. They
brought you ivory tusks and ebony as payment. 16 Syria *was* your merchant because
of the abundance of goods you made. They
gave you for your wares emeralds, purple,
embroidery, fine linen, corals, and rubies.
17 Judah and the land of Israel *were* your
traders. They traded for your merchandise
wheat of [a]Minnith, millet, honey, oil, and
[b]balm. 18 Damascus *was* your merchant because of the abundance of goods you made,
because of your many luxury items, with
the wine of Helbon and with white wool.
19 Dan and Javan paid for your wares, tra-
versing back and forth. Wrought iron, cassia,
and cane were among your merchandise.
20 [a]Dedan *was* your merchant in saddlecloths
for riding. 21 Arabia and all the princes of
[a]Kedar *were* your regular merchants. They
traded with you in lambs, rams, and goats.
22 The merchants of [a]Sheba and Raamah
were your merchants. They traded for your
wares the choicest spices, all kinds of precious stones, and gold. 23 [a]Haran, Canneh,
Eden, the merchants of [b]Sheba, Assyria, *and*
Chilmad *were* your merchants. 24 These *were*
your merchants in choice items—in purple
clothes, in embroidered garments, in chests
of multicolored apparel, in sturdy woven
cords, which were in your marketplace.

25 "The [a]ships of Tarshish were carriers of
your merchandise.
You were filled and very glorious [b]in
the midst of the seas.
26 Your oarsmen brought you into many
waters,
But [a]the east wind broke you in the
midst of the seas.

27 "Your [a]riches, wares, and merchandise,
Your mariners and pilots,
Your caulkers and merchandisers,
All your men of war who *are* in you,
And the entire company which *is* in
your midst,
Will fall into the midst of the seas on
the day of your ruin.
28 The [a]common-land will shake at the
sound of the cry of your pilots.

29 "All [a]who handle the oar,
The mariners,
All the pilots of the sea
Will come down from their ships *and*
stand on the shore.
30 They will make their voice heard
because of you;
They will cry bitterly and [a]cast dust on
their heads;
They [b]will roll about in ashes;
31 They will [a]shave themselves
completely bald because of you,
Gird themselves with sackcloth,
And weep for you
With bitterness of heart *and* bitter wailing.
32 In their wailing for you
They will [a]take up a lamentation,
And lament for you:
[b]'What *city is* like Tyre,
Destroyed in the midst of the sea?

27:6 [b] Jer. 2:10 [1] Hebrew *Kittim,* western lands, especially Cyprus 27:9 [a] 1 Kin. 5:18 27:10 [1] Hebrew *Lud* [2] Hebrew *Put* 27:11 [a] Ezek. 27:3 27:12 [a] Gen. 10:4 27:13 [a] Gen. 10:2 [b] Rev. 18:13 27:14 [a] Gen. 10:3 27:15 [a] Gen. 10:7 27:17 [a] Judg. 11:33 [b] Jer. 8:22 27:20 [a] Gen. 25:3 27:21 [a] Is. 60:7 27:22 [a] Gen. 10:7 27:23 [a] 2 Kin. 19:12 [b] Gen. 25:3 27:25 [a] Is. 2:16 [b] Ezek. 27:4 27:26 [a] Ps. 48:7 27:27 [a] [Prov. 11:4] 27:28 [a] Ezek. 26:15 27:29 [a] Rev. 18:17 27:30 [a] Rev. 18:19 [b] Jer. 6:26 27:31 [a] Ezek. 29:18 27:32 [a] Ezek. 26:17 [b] Rev. 18:18

33 'When[a] your wares went out by sea,
You satisfied many people;
You enriched the kings of the earth
With your many luxury goods and your merchandise.
34 But [a]you are broken by the seas in the depths of the waters;
[b]Your merchandise and the entire company will fall in your midst.
35 [a]All the inhabitants of the isles will be astonished at you;
Their kings will be greatly afraid,
And *their* countenance will be troubled.
36 The merchants among the peoples
[a]will hiss at you;
[b]You will become a horror, and *be* no
[c]more forever.' " ' "

Proclamation Against the King of Tyre

28 The word of the LORD came to me again, saying, 2"Son of man, say to the prince of Tyre, 'Thus says the Lord GOD:

"Because your heart *is* [a]lifted up,
And [b]you say, 'I *am* a god,
I sit *in* the seat of gods,
[c]In the midst of the seas,'
[d]Yet you *are* a man, and not a god,
Though you set your heart as the heart of a god
3 (Behold, [a]you *are* wiser than Daniel!
There is no secret that can be hidden from you!
4 With your wisdom and your understanding
You have gained [a]riches for yourself,
And gathered gold and silver into your treasuries;
5 [a]By your great wisdom in trade you have increased your riches,
And your heart is lifted up because of your riches),"

6'Therefore thus says the Lord GOD:

"Because you have set your heart as the heart of a god,
7 Behold, therefore, I will bring
[a]strangers against you,
[b]The most terrible of the nations;
And they shall draw their swords against the beauty of your wisdom,
And defile your splendor.
8 They shall throw you down into the
[a]Pit,
And you shall die the death of the slain
In the midst of the seas.

9 "Will you still [a]say before him who slays you,
'I *am* a god'?
But you *shall be* a man, and not a god,
In the hand of him who slays you.
10 You shall die the death of [a]the uncircumcised
By the hand of aliens;
For I have spoken," says the Lord GOD.' "

Lamentation for the King of Tyre

11Moreover the word of the LORD came to
me, saying, 12"Son of man, [a]take up a lamentation for the king of Tyre, and say to him, 'Thus says the Lord GOD:

[b]"You *were* the seal of perfection,
Full of wisdom and perfect in beauty.
13 You were in [a]Eden, the garden of God;
Every precious stone *was* your covering:
The sardius, topaz, and diamond,
Beryl, onyx, and jasper,
Sapphire, turquoise, and emerald with gold.
The workmanship of [b]your timbrels and pipes
Was prepared for you on the day you were created.

14 "You *were* the anointed [a]cherub who covers;
I established you;
You were on [b]the holy mountain of God;
You walked back and forth in the midst of fiery stones.
15 You *were* perfect in your ways from the day you were created,
Till [a]iniquity was found in you.

16 "By the abundance of your trading
You became filled with violence within,
And you sinned;
Therefore I cast you as a profane thing
Out of the mountain of God;
And I destroyed you, [a]O covering cherub,
From the midst of the fiery stones.

27:33 [a] Rev. 18:19 **27:34** [a] Ezek. 26:19 [b] Ezek. 27:27 **27:35** [a] Ezek. 26:15, 16 **27:36** [a] Jer. 18:16 [b] Ezek. 26:2 [c] Ps. 37:10, 36 **28:2** [a] Jer. 49:16 [b] Ezek. 28:9 [c] Ezek. 27:3, 4 [d] Is. 31:3 **28:3** [a] Dan. 1:20; 2:20–23, 28; 5:11, 12 **28:4** [a] Zech. 9:1–3 **28:5** [a] Ps. 62:10 **28:7** [a] Ezek. 26:7 [b] Ezek. 7:24; 21:31; 30:11 **28:8** [a] Is. 14:15 **28:9** [a] Ezek. 28:2 **28:10** [a] Ezek. 31:18; 32:19, 21, 25, 27 **28:12** [a] Ezek. 27:2 [b] Ezek. 27:3; 28:3 **28:13** [a] Ezek. 31:8, 9; 36:35 [b] Ezek. 26:13 **28:14** [a] Ex. 25:20 [b] Ezek. 20:40 **28:15** [a] [Is. 14:12] **28:16** [a] Ezek. 28:14

PEACE NOTE

Satan, our adversary, wants to steal God's peace from our hearts. How does he do this? Chiefly by sending lies to our minds. Anchor your mind and emotions in God's Word.

EZEKIEL 28:15

17 "Your [a]heart was lifted up because of
your beauty;
You corrupted your wisdom for the
sake of your splendor;
I cast you to the ground,
I laid you before kings,
That they might gaze at you.

18 "You defiled your sanctuaries
By the multitude of your iniquities,
By the iniquity of your trading;
Therefore I brought fire from your midst;
It devoured you,
And I turned you to ashes upon the
earth
In the sight of all who saw you.
19 All who knew you among the peoples
are astonished at you;
[a]You have become a horror,
And *shall be* no [b]more forever." ' "

Proclamation Against Sidon

20 Then the word of the LORD came to me,
saying, 21 "Son of man, [a]set your face [b]toward
Sidon, and prophesy against her, 22 and say,
'Thus says the Lord GOD:

[a]"Behold, I *am* against you, O Sidon;
I will be glorified in your midst;
And [b]they shall know that I *am* the LORD,
When I execute judgments in her and
am [c]hallowed in her.
23 [a]For I will send pestilence upon her,
And blood in her streets;
The wounded shall be judged in her
midst
By the sword against her on every side;
Then they shall know that I *am* the
LORD.

24 "And there shall no longer be a pricking
brier or [a]a painful thorn for the house of Israel from among all *who are* around them,
who [b]despise them. Then they shall know
that I *am* the Lord GOD."

Israel's Future Blessing

25 'Thus says the Lord GOD: "When I have
[a]gathered the house of Israel from the peoples among whom they are scattered, and am
[b]hallowed in them in the sight of the Gentiles,
then they will dwell in their own land which
I gave to My servant Jacob. 26 And they will
[a]dwell safely there, [b]build houses, and [c]plant
vineyards; yes, they will dwell securely, when
I execute judgments on all those around
them who despise them. Then they shall
know that I *am* the LORD their God." ' "

Proclamation Against Egypt

29 In the tenth year, in the tenth *month,*
on the twelfth *day* of the month, the
word of the LORD came to me, saying, 2 "Son
of man, [a]set your face against Pharaoh king
of Egypt, and prophesy against him, and
[b]against all Egypt. 3 Speak, and say, 'Thus
says the Lord GOD:

[a]"Behold, I *am* against you,
O Pharaoh king of Egypt,
O great [b]monster who lies in the midst
of his rivers,
[c]Who has said, 'My River[1] *is* my own;
I have made *it* for myself.'
4 But [a]I will put hooks in your jaws,
And cause the fish of your rivers to
stick to your scales;
I will bring you up out of the midst of
your rivers,
And all the fish in your rivers will stick
to your scales.
5 I will leave you in the wilderness,
You and all the fish of your rivers;
You shall fall on the open [a]field;
[b]You shall not be picked up or gathered.[1]
[c]I have given you as food
To the beasts of the field
And to the birds of the heavens.

6 "Then all the inhabitants of Egypt
Shall know that I *am* the LORD,

28:17 [a] Ezek. 28:2, 5 **28:19** [a] Ezek. 26:21 [b] Ezek. 27:36 **28:21** [a] Ezek. 6:2; 25:2; 29:2 [b] Is. 23:2, 4, 12 **28:22** [a] Ex. 14:4, 17 [b] Ps. 9:16 [c] Ezek. 28:25 **28:23** [a] Ezek. 38:22 **28:24** [a] Josh. 23:13 [b] Ezek. 16:57; 25:6, 7 **28:25** [a] Is. 11:12, 13 [b] Ezek. 28:22 **28:26** [a] Jer. 23:6 [b] Amos 9:13, 14 [c] Jer. 31:5 **29:2** [a] Ezek. 28:21 [b] Is. 19:1 **29:3** [a] Jer. 44:30 [b] Ps. 74:13, 14 [c] Ezek. 28:2 [1] That is, the Nile **29:4** [a] Ezek. 38:4 **29:5** [a] Ezek. 32:4–6 [b] Jer. 8:2; 16:4; 25:33 [c] Jer. 7:33; 34:20 [1] Following Masoretic Text, Septuagint, and Vulgate; some Hebrew manuscripts and Targum read *buried.*

Because they have been a [a]staff of reed
to the house of Israel.
7 [a]When they took hold of you with the
hand,
You broke and tore all their shoulders;[1]
When they leaned on you,
You broke and made all their backs
quiver."

8 'Therefore thus says the Lord GOD: "Surely
I will bring [a]a sword upon you and cut off
from you man and beast. 9 And the land of
Egypt shall become [a]desolate and waste;
then they will know that I *am* the LORD, because he said, 'The River *is* mine, and I have
made *it*.' 10 Indeed, therefore, I *am* against
you and against your rivers, [a]and I will make
the land of Egypt utterly waste and desolate,
[b]from Migdol[1] *to* Syene, as far as the border
of Ethiopia. 11 [a]Neither foot of man shall pass
through it nor foot of beast pass through
it, and it shall be uninhabited forty years.
12 [a]I will make the land of Egypt desolate in
the midst of the countries *that are* desolate;
and among the cities *that are* laid waste, her
cities shall be desolate forty years; and I will
[b]scatter the Egyptians among the nations and
disperse them throughout the countries."
13 'Yet, thus says the Lord GOD: "At the [a]end
of forty years I will gather the Egyptians from
the peoples among whom they were scattered.
14 I will bring back the captives of Egypt and
cause them to return to the land of Pathros, to
the land of their origin, and there they shall be
a [a]lowly kingdom. 15 It shall be the lowliest of
kingdoms; it shall never again exalt itself above
the nations, for I will diminish them so that
they will not rule over the nations anymore.
16 No longer shall it be [a]the confidence of the
house of Israel, but will remind them of *their*
iniquity when they turned to follow them. Then
they shall know that I *am* the Lord GOD." ' "

Babylonia Will Plunder Egypt

17 And it came to pass in the twenty-seventh
year, in the first *month*, on the first *day* of
the month, *that* the word of the LORD came
to me, saying, 18 "Son of man, [a]Nebuchad-
nezzar king of Babylon caused his army to
labor strenuously against Tyre; every head
was made [b]bald, and every shoulder rubbed
raw; yet neither he nor his army received
wages from Tyre, for the labor which they
expended on it. 19 Therefore thus says the
Lord GOD: 'Surely I will give the land of Egypt
to [a]Nebuchadnezzar king of Babylon; he shall
take away her wealth, carry off her spoil, and
remove her pillage; and that will be the wages
for his army. 20 I have given him the land of
Egypt *for* his labor, because they [a]worked for
Me,' says the Lord GOD.
21 'In that day [a]I will cause the horn of the
house of Israel to spring forth, and I will
[b]open your mouth to speak in their midst.
Then they shall know that I *am* the LORD.' "

Egypt and Her Allies Will Fall

30 The word of the LORD came to me
again, saying, 2 "Son of man, prophesy
and say, 'Thus says the Lord GOD:

[a]"Wail, 'Woe to the day!'
3 For [a]the day *is* near,
Even the day of the LORD *is* near;
It will be a day of clouds, the time of
the Gentiles.
4 The sword shall come upon Egypt,
And great anguish shall be in Ethiopia,
When the slain fall in Egypt,
And they [a]take away her wealth,
And [b]her foundations are broken down.

5 "Ethiopia, Libya,[1] Lydia,[2] [a]all the mingled
people, Chub, and the men of the lands who
are allied, shall fall with them by the sword."
6 'Thus says the LORD:

"Those who uphold Egypt shall fall,
And the pride of her power shall come
down.
[a]From Migdol *to* Syene
Those within her shall fall by the sword,"
Says the Lord GOD.

7 "They[a] shall be desolate in the midst of
the desolate countries,
And her cities shall be in the midst of
the cities *that are* laid waste.
8 Then they will know that I *am* the LORD,
When I have set a fire in Egypt
And all her helpers are destroyed.
9 On that day [a]messengers shall go forth
from Me in ships
To make the careless Ethiopians afraid,
And great anguish shall come upon
them,
As on the day of Egypt;
For indeed it is coming!"

29:6 [a] Is. 36:6 **29:7** [a] Ezek. 17:17 [1] Following Masoretic Text and Vulgate; Septuagint and Syriac read *hand*.
29:8 [a] Ezek. 14:17; 32:11–13 **29:9** [a] Ezek. 30:7, 8 **29:10** [a] Ezek. 30:12 [b] Ezek. 30:6 [1] Or *tower* **29:11** [a] Ezek. 32:13
29:12 [a] Ezek. 30:7, 26 [b] Ezek. 30:23, 26 **29:13** [a] Jer. 46:26 **29:14** [a] Ezek. 17:6, 14 **29:16** [a] Is. 30:2, 3; 36:4, 6
29:18 [a] Jer. 25:9; 27:6 [b] Ezek. 27:31 **29:19** [a] Jer. 43:10–13 **29:20** [a] Jer. 25:9 **29:21** [a] Ps. 92:10; 132:17 [b] Ezek. 24:27
30:2 [a] Is. 13:6; 15:2 **30:3** [a] Joel 2:1 **30:4** [a] Ezek. 29:19 [b] Jer. 50:15 **30:5** [a] Jer. 25:20, 24 [1] Hebrew *Put* [2] Hebrew *Lud*
30:6 [a] Ezek. 29:10 **30:7** [a] Ezek. 29:12 **30:9** [a] Is. 18:1, 2

10 'Thus says the Lord GOD:

[a]"I will also make a multitude of Egypt to
cease
By the hand of Nebuchadnezzar king of
Babylon.
11 He and his people with him, [a]the most
terrible of the nations,
Shall be brought to destroy the land;
They shall draw their swords against
Egypt,
And fill the land with the slain.
12 [a]I will make the rivers dry,
And [b]sell the land into the hand of the
wicked;
I will make the land waste, and all that
is in it,
By the hand of aliens.
I, the LORD, have spoken."

13 'Thus says the Lord GOD:

"I will also [a]destroy the idols,
And cause the images to cease from
Noph;[1]
[b]There shall no longer be princes from
the land of Egypt;
[c]I will put fear in the land of Egypt.
14 I will make [a]Pathros desolate,
Set fire to [b]Zoan,
[c]And execute judgments in No.[1]
15 I will pour My fury on Sin,[1] the strength
of Egypt;
[a]I will cut off the multitude of No,
16 And [a]set a fire in Egypt;
Sin shall have great pain,
No shall be split open,
And Noph *shall be in* distress daily.
17 The young men of Aven[1] and Pi Beseth
shall fall by the sword,
And these *cities* shall go into captivity.
18 [a]At Tehaphnehes[1] the day shall also be
darkened,[2]
When I break the yokes of Egypt there.
And her arrogant strength shall cease
in her;
As for her, a cloud shall cover her,
And her daughters shall go into
captivity.
19 Thus I will [a]execute judgments on
Egypt,
Then they shall know that I *am* the
LORD." ' "

Proclamation Against Pharaoh

20 And it came to pass in the eleventh year,
in the first *month,* on the seventh *day* of the
month, *that* the word of the LORD came to
me, saying, 21 "Son of man, I have [a]broken the
arm of Pharaoh king of Egypt; and see, [b]it has
not been bandaged for healing, nor a splint
put on to bind it, to make it strong enough
to hold a sword. 22 Therefore thus says the
Lord GOD: 'Surely I *am* [a]against Pharaoh king
of Egypt, and will [b]break his arms, both the
strong one and the one that was broken; and
I will make the sword fall out of his hand. 23 [a]I
will scatter the Egyptians among the nations,
and disperse them throughout the countries.
24 I will strengthen the arms of the king of
Babylon and put My sword in his hand; but I
will break Pharaoh's arms, and he will groan
before him with the groanings of a mortally
wounded *man.* 25 Thus I will strengthen the
arms of the king of Babylon, but the arms
of Pharaoh shall fall down; [a]they shall know
that I *am* the LORD, when I put My sword
into the hand of the king of Babylon and he
stretches it out against the land of Egypt. 26 [a]I
will scatter the Egyptians among the nations
and disperse them throughout the countries.
Then they shall know that I *am* the LORD.' "

Egypt Cut Down Like a Great Tree

31 Now it came to pass in the [a]eleventh
year, in the third *month,* on the first *day*
of the month, *that* the word of the LORD came
to me, saying, 2 "Son of man, say to Pharaoh
king of Egypt and to his multitude:

[a]'Whom are you like in your greatness?
3 [a]Indeed Assyria *was* a cedar in Lebanon,
With fine branches that shaded the
forest,
And of high stature;
And its top was among the thick
boughs.
4 [a]The waters made it grow;
Underground waters gave it height,
With their rivers running around the
place where it was planted,
And sent out rivulets to all the trees of
the field.

5 'Therefore [a]its height was exalted above
all the trees of the field;
Its boughs were multiplied,

30:10 [a] *Ezek. 29:19* **30:11** [a] Ezek. 28:7; 31:12 **30:12** [a] Is. 19:5, 6 [b] Is. 19:4 **30:13** [a] Is. 19:1 [b] Zech. 10:11 [c] Is. 19:16 [1] That is, ancient Memphis **30:14** [a] Ezek. 29:14 [b] Ps. 78:12, 43 [c] Nah. 3:8–10 [1] That is, ancient Thebes **30:15** [a] Jer. 46:25 [1] That is, ancient Pelusium **30:16** [a] Ezek. 30:8 **30:17** [1] That is, ancient On (Heliopolis) **30:18** [a] Jer. 2:16 [1] Spelled *Tahpanhes* in Jeremiah 43:7 and elsewhere [2] Following many Hebrew manuscripts, Bomberg, Septuagint, Syriac, Targum, and Vulgate; Masoretic Text reads *refrained.* **30:19** [a] [Ps. 9:16] **30:21** [a] Jer. 48:25 [b] Jer. 46:11 **30:22** [a] Jer. 46:25 [b] Ps. 37:17 **30:23** [a] Ezek. 29:12; 30:17, 18, 26 **30:25** [a] Ps. 9:16 **30:26** [a] Ezek. 29:12 **31:1** [a] Ezek. 30:20; 32:1 **31:2** [a] Ezek. 31:18 **31:3** [a] Dan. 4:10, 20–23 **31:4** [a] Jer. 51:36 **31:5** [a] Dan. 4:11

And its branches became long because
of the abundance of water,
As it sent them out.
6 All the [a]birds of the heavens made
their nests in its boughs;
Under its branches all the beasts of the
field brought forth their young;
And in its shadow all great nations
made their home.

7 'Thus it was beautiful in greatness and
in the length of its branches,
Because its roots reached to abundant
waters.
8 The cedars in the [a]garden of God could
not hide it;
The fir trees were not like its boughs,
And the chestnut[1] trees were not like
its branches;
No tree in the garden of God was like it
in beauty.
9 I made it beautiful with a multitude of
branches,
So that all the trees of Eden envied it,
That *were* in the garden of God.'

10"Therefore thus says the Lord GOD: 'Because you have increased in height, and it
set its top among the thick boughs, and [a]its
heart was lifted up in its height, 11therefore
I will deliver it into the hand of the [a]mighty
one of the nations, and he shall surely deal
with it; I have driven it out for its wickedness.
12And aliens, [a]the most terrible of the nations,
have cut it down and left it; its branches have
fallen [b]on the mountains and in all the valleys; its boughs lie [c]broken by all the rivers
of the land; and all the peoples of the earth
have gone from under its shadow and left it.

13 'On [a]its ruin will remain all the birds of
the heavens,
And all the beasts of the field will come
to its branches—

14So that no trees by the waters may ever
again exalt themselves for their height, nor
set their tops among the thick boughs, that
no tree which drinks water may ever be high
enough to reach up to them.

'For [a]they have all been delivered to death,
[b]To the depths of the earth,
Among the children of men who go
down to the Pit.'

15"Thus says the Lord GOD: 'In the day when it
[a]went down to hell, I caused mourning. I covered
the deep because of it. I restrained its rivers,
and the great waters were held back. I caused
Lebanon to mourn for it, and all the trees of the
field wilted because of it. 16I made the nations
[a]shake at the sound of its fall, when I [b]cast it
down to hell together with those who descend
into the Pit; and [c]all the trees of Eden, the choice
and best of Lebanon, all that drink water, [d]were
comforted in the depths of the earth. 17They also
went down to hell with it, with those slain by the
sword; and *those who were* its *strong* arm [a]dwelt
in its shadows among the nations.
18[a]'To which of the trees in Eden will you
then be likened in glory and greatness? Yet
you shall be brought down with the trees of
Eden to the depths of the earth; [b]you shall
lie in the midst of the uncircumcised, with
those slain by the sword. This *is* Pharaoh and
all his multitude,' says the Lord GOD."

Lamentation for Pharaoh and Egypt

32 And it came to pass in the twelfth
year, in the [a]twelfth *month,* on the first
day of the month, *that* the word of the LORD
came to me, saying, 2"Son of man, [a]take up
a lamentation for Pharaoh king of Egypt,
and say to him:

[b]'You are like a young lion among the
nations,
And [c]you *are* like a monster in the seas,
[d]Bursting forth in your rivers,
Troubling the waters with your feet,
And [e]fouling their rivers.

3'Thus says the Lord GOD:

"I will therefore [a]spread My net over you
with a company of many people,
And they will draw you up in My net.
4 Then [a]I will leave you on the land;
I will cast you out on the open fields,
[b]And cause to settle on you all the birds
of the heavens.
And with you I will fill the beasts of the
whole earth.
5 I will lay your flesh [a]on the mountains,
And fill the valleys with your carcass.

6 "I will also water the land with the flow
of your blood,
Even to the mountains;
And the riverbeds will be full of you.

31:6 [a] Dan. 4:12, 21 **31:8** [a] Gen. 2:8, 9; 13:10 [1] Hebrew *armon* **31:10** [a] Dan. 5:20 **31:11** [a] Ezek. 30:10 **31:12** [a] Ezek. 28:7; 30:11; 32:12 [b] Ezek. 32:5; 35:8 [c] Ezek. 30:24, 25 **31:13** [a] Is. 18:6 **31:14** [a] Ps. 82:7 [b] Ezek. 32:18 **31:15** [a] Ezek. 32:22, 23 **31:16** [a] Ezek. 26:15 [b] Is. 14:15 [c] Is. 14:8 [d] Ezek. 32:31 **31:17** [a] Lam. 4:20 **31:18** [a] Ezek. 32:19 [b] Ezek. 28:10; 32:19, 21 **32:1** [a] Ezek. 31:1; 33:21 **32:2** [a] Ezek. 27:2 [b] Ezek. 19:2–6 [c] Ezek. 29:3 [d] Jer. 46:7, 8 [e] Ezek. 34:18 **32:3** [a] Ezek. 12:13; 17:20 **32:4** [a] Ezek. 29:5 [b] Is. 18:6; Ezek. 31:13 **32:5** [a] Ezek. 31:12

7 When *I* put out your light,
[a]I will cover the heavens, and make its stars dark;
I will cover the sun with a cloud,
And the moon shall not give her light.
8 All the bright lights of the heavens I will make dark over you,
And bring darkness upon your land,'
Says the Lord GOD.

9'I will also trouble the hearts of many peoples, when I bring your destruction among
the nations, into the countries which you
have not known. 10Yes, I will make many peoples astonished at you, and their kings shall
be horribly afraid of you when I brandish My
sword before them; and [a]they shall tremble
every moment, every man for his own life,
in the day of your fall.

PEACE NOTE

God's power is clearly revealed in His control, discipline, and blessing of every nation.

The power of God causes us to seek the peace of God in our lives every day.

EZEKIEL 32:9

11[a]"For thus says the Lord GOD: 'The sword
of the king of Babylon shall come upon you.
12By the swords of the mighty warriors, all of
them [a]the most terrible of the nations, I will
cause your multitude to fall.

[b]'They shall plunder the pomp of Egypt,
And all its multitude shall be destroyed.
13 Also I will destroy all its animals
From beside its great waters;
[a]The foot of man shall muddy them no more,
Nor shall the hooves of animals muddy them.
14 Then I will make their waters clear,
And make their rivers run like oil,'
Says the Lord GOD.

15 'When I make the land of Egypt desolate,
And the country is destitute of all that once filled it,
When I strike all who dwell in it,
[a]Then they shall know that I *am* the LORD.

16 'This *is* the [a]lamentation
With which they shall lament her;
The daughters of the nations shall lament her;
They shall lament for her, for Egypt,
And for all her multitude,'
Says the Lord GOD."

Egypt and Others Consigned to the Pit

17It came to pass also in the twelfth year,
on the fifteenth *day* of the month, [a]*that* the
word of the LORD came to me, saying:

18 "Son of man, wail over the multitude of Egypt,
And [a]cast them down to the depths of the earth,
Her and the daughters of the famous nations,
With those who go down to the Pit:
19 'Whom [a]do you surpass in beauty?
[b]Go down, be placed with the uncircumcised.'

20 "They shall fall in the midst of *those* slain by the sword;
She is delivered to the sword,
[a]Drawing her and all her multitudes.
21 [a]The strong among the mighty
Shall speak to him out of the midst of hell
With those who help him:
'They have [b]gone down,
They lie with the uncircumcised, slain by the sword.'

22 "Assyria[a] *is* there, and all her company,
With their graves all around her,
All of them slain, fallen by the sword.
23 [a]Her graves are set in the recesses of the Pit,
And her company is all around her grave,
All of them slain, fallen by the sword,
Who [b]caused terror in the land of the living.

24 "There *is* [a]Elam and all her multitude,
All around her grave,

32:7 [a] Rev. 6:12, 13; 8:12 32:10 [a] Ezek. 26:16 32:11 [a] Jer. 46:26 32:12 [a] Ezek. 28:7; 30:11; 31:12 [b] Ezek. 29:19
32:13 [a] Ezek. 29:11 32:15 [a] Ps. 9:16 32:16 [a] Ezek. 26:17 32:17 [a] Ezek. 32:1; 33:21 32:18 [a] Ezek. 26:20; 31:14
32:19 [a] Ezek. 31:2, 18 [b] Ezek. 28:10 32:20 [a] Ps. 28:3 32:21 [a] Is. 1:31; 14:9, 10 [b] Ezek. 32:19, 25 32:22 [a] Ezek. 31:3, 16
32:23 [a] Is. 14:15 [b] Ezek. 32:24–27, 32 32:24 [a] Jer. 25:25; 49:34–39

All of them slain, fallen by the sword,
Who have [b]gone down uncircumcised
to the lower parts of the earth,
[c]Who caused their terror in the land of
the living;
Now they bear their shame with those
who go down to the Pit.
25 They have set her [a]bed in the midst of
the slain,
With all her multitude,
With her graves all around it,
All of them uncircumcised, slain by the
sword;
Though their terror was caused
In the land of the living,
Yet they bear their shame
With those who go down to the Pit;
It was put in the midst of the slain.

26 "There *are* [a]Meshech and Tubal and all
their multitudes,
With all their graves around it,
All of them [b]uncircumcised, slain by
the sword,
Though they caused their terror in the
land of the living.
27 [a]They do not lie with the mighty
Who are fallen of the uncircumcised,
Who have gone down to hell with their
weapons of war;
They have laid their swords under their
heads,
But their iniquities will be on their
bones,
Because of the terror of the mighty in
the land of the living.
28 Yes, you shall be broken in the midst of
the uncircumcised,
And lie with *those* slain by the sword.

29 "There *is* [a]Edom,
Her kings and all her princes,
Who despite their might
Are laid beside *those* slain by the
sword;
They shall lie with the uncircumcised,
And with those who go down to the Pit.
30 [a]There *are* the princes of the north,
All of them, and all the [b]Sidonians,
Who have gone down with the slain
In shame at the terror which they
caused by their might;
They lie uncircumcised with *those* slain
by the sword,
And bear their shame with those who
go down to the Pit.

31 "Pharaoh will see them
And be [a]comforted over all his
multitude,
Pharaoh and all his army,
Slain by the sword,"
Says the Lord GOD.

32 "For I have caused My terror in the land
of the living;
And he shall be placed in the midst of
the uncircumcised
With *those* slain by the sword,
Pharaoh and all his multitude,"
Says the Lord GOD.

The Watchman and His Message

33 Again the word of the LORD came to me,
saying, 2"Son of man, speak to [a]the children of your people, and say to them: [b]'When
I bring the sword upon a land, and the people
of the land take a man from their territory and
make him their [c]watchman, 3when he sees the
sword coming upon the land, if he blows the
trumpet and warns the people, 4then whoever
hears the sound of the trumpet and does [a]not
take warning, if the sword comes and takes
him away, [b]his blood shall be on his *own* head.
5He heard the sound of the trumpet, but did
not take warning; his blood shall be upon
himself. But he who takes warning will save
his life. 6But if the watchman sees the sword
coming and does not blow the trumpet, and
the people are not warned, and the sword
comes and takes *any* person from among
them, [a]he is taken away in his iniquity; but his
blood I will require at the watchman's hand.'

7[a]"So you, son of man: I have made you a
watchman for the house of Israel; therefore
you shall hear a word from My mouth and
warn them for Me. 8When I say to the wicked,
'O wicked *man*, you shall surely die!' and you
do not speak to warn the wicked from his way,
that wicked *man* shall die in his iniquity; but his
blood I will require at your hand. 9Nevertheless
if you warn the wicked to turn from his way, and
he does not turn from his way, he shall die in
his iniquity; but you have delivered your soul.

10"Therefore you, O son of man, say to the
house of Israel: 'Thus you say, "If our transgressions and our sins *lie* upon us, and we
[a]pine away in them, [b]how can we then live?" '
11Say to them: '*As* I live,' says the Lord GOD, [a]'I
have no pleasure in the death of the wicked,
but that the wicked [b]turn from his way and
live. Turn, turn from your evil ways! For [c]why
should you die, O house of Israel?'

32:24 [b] Ezek. 32:21 [c] Ezek. 32:23 **32:25** [a] Ps. 139:8 **32:26** [a] Gen. 10:2 [b] Ezek. 32:19 **32:27** [a] Is. 14:18, 19 **32:29** [a] Ezek. 25:12–14 **32:30** [a] Jer. 1:15; 25:26 [b] Ezek. 28:21–23 **32:31** [a] Ezek. 14:22; 31:16 **33:2** [a] Ezek. 3:11 [b] Ezek. 14:17 [c] 2 Sam. 18:24, 25 **33:4** [a] Zech. 1:4 [b] [Acts 18:6] **33:6** [a] Ezek. 33:8 **33:7** [a] Is. 62:6 **33:10** [a] Ezek. 24:23 [b] Is. 49:14 **33:11** [a] [2 Sam. 14:14] [b] [Acts 3:19] [c] Ezek. 18:30, 31

The Fairness of God's Judgment

12 "Therefore you, O son of man, say to the children of your people: 'The [a]righteousness of the righteous man shall not deliver him in the day of his transgression; as for the wickedness of the wicked, [b]he shall not fall because of it in the day that he turns from his wickedness; nor shall the righteous be able to live because of *his righteousness* in the day that he sins.' 13 When I say to the righteous *that* he shall surely live, [a]but he trusts in his own righteousness and commits iniquity, none of his righteous works shall be remembered; but because of the iniquity that he has committed, he shall die. 14 Again, [a]when I say to the wicked, 'You shall surely die,' if he turns from his sin and does what is lawful and right, 15 *if* the wicked [a]restores the pledge, [b]gives back what he has stolen, and walks in [c]the statutes of life without committing iniquity, he shall surely live; he shall not die. 16 [a]None of his sins which he has committed shall be remembered against him; he has done what is lawful and right; he shall surely live.

17 [a]"Yet the children of your people say, 'The way of the Lord is not fair.' But it is their way which is not fair! 18 [a]When the righteous turns from his righteousness and commits iniquity, he shall die because of it. 19 But when the wicked turns from his wickedness and does what is lawful and right, he shall live because of it. 20 Yet you say, [a]'The way of the Lord is not fair.' O house of Israel, I will judge every one of you according to his own ways."

The Fall of Jerusalem

21 And it came to pass in the twelfth year [a]of our captivity, in the tenth *month,* on the fifth *day* of the month, [b]*that* one who had escaped from Jerusalem came to me and said, [c]"The city has been captured!"

22 Now [a]the hand of the LORD had been upon me the evening before the man came who had escaped. And He had [b]opened my mouth; so when he came to me in the morning, my mouth was opened, and I was no longer mute.

The Cause of Judah's Ruin

23 Then the word of the LORD came to me, saying: 24 "Son of man, [a]they who inhabit those [b]ruins in the land of Israel are saying, [c]'Abraham was only one, and he inherited the land. [d]But we *are* many; the land has been given to us as a [e]possession.'

25 "Therefore say to them, 'Thus says the Lord GOD: [a]"You eat *meat* with blood, you [b]lift up your eyes toward your idols, and [c]shed blood. Should you then possess the [d]land? 26 You rely on your sword, you commit abominations, and you [a]defile one another's wives. Should you then possess the land?" '

27 "Say thus to them, 'Thus says the Lord GOD: *"As* I live, surely [a]those who *are* in the ruins shall fall by the sword, and the one who *is* in the open field [b]I will give to the beasts to be devoured, and those who *are* in the strongholds and [c]caves shall die of the pestilence. 28 [a]For I will make the land most desolate, her [b]arrogant strength shall cease, and [c]the mountains of Israel shall be so desolate that no one will pass through. 29 Then they shall know that I *am* the LORD, when I have made the land most desolate because of all their abominations which they have committed." '

Hearing and Not Doing

30 "As for you, son of man, the children of your people are talking about you beside the walls and in the doors of the houses; and they [a]speak to one another, everyone saying to his brother, 'Please come and hear what the word is that comes from the LORD.' 31 So [a]they come to you as people do, they [b]sit before you *as* My people, and they [c]hear your words, but they do not do them; [d]for with their mouth they show much love, *but* [e]their hearts pursue their *own* gain. 32 Indeed you *are* to them as a very lovely song of one who has a pleasant voice and can play well on an instrument; for they hear your words, but they do [a]not do them. 33 [a]And when this comes to pass—surely it will come—then [b]they will know that a prophet has been among them."

Irresponsible Shepherds

34 And the word of the LORD came to me, saying, 2 "Son of man, prophesy against the shepherds of Israel, prophesy and say to them, 'Thus says the Lord GOD to the shepherds: [a]"Woe to the shepherds of Israel who feed themselves! Should not the shepherds feed the flocks? 3 [a]You eat the fat and clothe yourselves with the wool; you [b]slaughter the fatlings, *but* you do not feed the flock. 4 [a]The weak you have not strengthened, nor have you healed those who were sick, nor bound up the broken, nor brought

33:12 [a] *Ezek. 3:20; 18:24, 26* [b] *[2 Chr. 7:14]* **33:13** [a] Ezek. 3:20; 18:24 **33:14** [a] Ezek. 3:18, 19; 18:27 **33:15** [a] Ezek. 18:7 [b] Lev. 6:2, 4, 5 [c] Ezek. 20:11, 13, 21 **33:16** [a] [Is. 1:18; 43:25] **33:17** [a] Ezek. 18:25, 29 **33:18** [a] Ezek. 18:26 **33:20** [a] Ezek. 18:25, 29 **33:21** [a] Ezek. 1:2 [b] Ezek. 24:26 [c] 2 Kin. 25:4 **33:22** [a] Ezek. 1:3; 8:1; 37:1 [b] Ezek. 24:27 **33:24** [a] Ezek. 34:2 [b] Ezek. 36:4 [c] Is. 51:2 [d] [Matt. 3:9] [e] Ezek. 11:15 **33:25** [a] Lev. 3:17; 7:26; 17:10–14; 19:26 [b] Ezek. 18:6 [c] Ezek. 22:6, 9 [d] Deut. 29:28 **33:26** [a] Ezek. 18:6; 22:11 **33:27** [a] Ezek. 33:24 [b] Ezek. 39:4 [c] 1 Sam. 13:6 **33:28** [a] Jer. 44:2, 6, 22 [b] Ezek. 7:24; 24:21 [c] Ezek. 6:2, 3, 6 **33:30** [a] Is. 29:13 **33:31** [a] Ezek. 14:1 [b] Ezek. 8:1 [c] Is. 58:2 [d] Ps. 78:36, 37 [e] [Matt. 13:22] **33:32** [a] [Matt. 7:21–28] **33:33** [a] 1 Sam. 3:20 [b] Ezek. 2:5 **34:2** [a] Zech. 11:17 **34:3** [a] Zech. 11:16 [b] Ezek. 33:25, 26 **34:4** [a] Zech. 11:16

back what was driven away, nor [b]sought what
was lost; but with [c]force and cruelty you
have ruled them. 5 [a]So they were [b]scattered
because *there was* no shepherd; [c]and they
became food for all the beasts of the field
when they were scattered. 6 My sheep [a]wan-
dered through all the mountains, and on
every high hill; yes, My flock was scattered
over the whole face of the earth, and no one
was seeking or searching *for them.*"

7 "Therefore, you shepherds, hear the word
of the LORD: 8 "*As* I live," says the Lord GOD,
"surely because My flock became a prey, and
My flock [a]became food for every beast of the
field, because *there was* no shepherd, nor did
My shepherds search for My flock, [b]but the
shepherds fed themselves and did not feed
My flock"— 9 therefore, O shepherds, hear the
word of the LORD! 10 Thus says the Lord GOD:
"Behold, I *am* [a]against the shepherds, and [b]I
will require My flock at their hand; I will cause
them to cease feeding the sheep, and the
shepherds shall [c]feed themselves no more;
for I will [d]deliver My flock from their mouths,
that they may no longer be food for them."

God, the True Shepherd

11 'For thus says the Lord GOD: "Indeed I Myself will search for My sheep and seek them out.
12 As a [a]shepherd seeks out his flock on the day
he is among his scattered sheep, so will I seek
out My sheep and deliver them from all the
places where they were scattered on [b]a cloudy
and dark day. 13 And [a]I will bring them out from
the peoples and gather them from the countries, and will bring them to their own land; I
will feed them on the mountains of Israel, in
the valleys and in all the inhabited places of
the country. 14 [a]I will feed them in good pasture,
and their fold shall be on the high mountains
of Israel. [b]There they shall lie down in a good
fold and feed in rich pasture on the mountains
of Israel. 15 I will feed My flock, and I will make
them lie down," says the Lord GOD. 16 [a]"I will
seek what was lost and bring back what was
driven away, bind up the broken and strengthen
what was sick; but I will destroy [b]the fat and the
strong, and feed them [c]in judgment."

17 'And *as for* you, O My flock, thus says the
Lord GOD: [a]"Behold, I shall judge between
sheep and sheep, between rams and goats.
18 *Is it* too little for you to have eaten up the
good pasture, that you must tread down with
your feet the residue of your pasture—and to
have drunk of the clear waters, that you must
foul the residue with your feet? 19 And *as for*
My flock, they eat what you have trampled
with your feet, and they drink what you have
fouled with your feet."

20 'Therefore thus says the Lord GOD to
them: [a]"Behold, I Myself will judge between
the fat and the lean sheep. 21 Because you
have pushed with side and shoulder, butted
all the weak ones with your horns, and scattered them abroad, 22 therefore I will save
My flock, and they shall no longer be a prey;
and I will judge between sheep and sheep.
23 I will establish one [a]shepherd over them,

34:4 [b] Luke 15:4 [c] [1 Pet. 5:3] **34:5** [a] Ezek. 33:21 [b] Matt. 9:36 [c] Is. 56:9 **34:6** [a] 1 Pet. 2:25 **34:8** [a] Ezek. 34:5, 6 [b] Ezek. 34:2, 10 **34:10** [a] Jer. 21:13; 52:24–27 [b] Heb. 13:17 [c] Ezek. 34:2, 8 [d] Ezek. 13:23 **34:12** [a] Jer. 31:10 [b] Ezek. 30:3 **34:13** [a] Jer. 23:3 **34:14** [a] [John 10:9] [b] Jer. 33:12 **34:16** [a] Mic. 4:6 [b] Is. 10:16 [c] Jer. 10:24 **34:17** [a] [Matt. 25:32] **34:20** [a] Ezek. 34:17 **34:23** [a] [Is. 40:11]

YOUR SHEPHERD KING

"I will establish one shepherd over them, and he shall feed them—My servant David."

EZEKIEL 34:23

Not all the visions and oracles in Ezekiel contain bad news. God also gave the prophet extraordinary visions of redemption and renewal. Here in chapter 34 the promise of a new Shepherd is one of the most hopeful passages in the Book of Ezekiel.

Hope creates peace. Ezekiel's vision announces a new "David": "I will establish one shepherd over them, and he shall feed them—My servant David." For a defeated people suffering the loss of their great city and their famous temple and now facing exile to a foreign land, God's promise of a new David, a righteous king, must have been very uplifting. Of course, this "David" is not the old king raised from the dead but his supernatural descendant, Jesus the Son of God. Our hope for a lasting and fully satisfying peace rests on this new King.

What gives you hope today? How does that give you peace?

and he shall feed them—[b]My servant David.
He shall feed them and be their shepherd.
[24]And [a]I, the LORD, will be their God, and My
servant David [b]a prince among them; I, the
LORD, have spoken.
[25][a]"I will make a covenant of peace with
them, and [b]cause wild beasts to cease from
the land; and they [c]will dwell safely in the wilderness and sleep in the woods. [26]I will make
them and the places all around [a]My hill [b]a
blessing; and I will [c]cause showers to come
down in their season; there shall be [d]showers
of blessing. [27]Then [a]the trees of the field shall
yield their fruit, and the earth shall yield her
increase. They shall be safe in their land; and
they shall know that I *am* the LORD, when I have
[b]broken the bands of their yoke and delivered
them from the hand of those who [c]enslaved
them. [28]And they shall no longer be a prey for
the nations, nor shall beasts of the land devour
them; but [a]they shall dwell safely, and no one
shall make *them* afraid. [29]I will raise up for
them a [a]garden of renown, and they shall [b]no
longer be consumed with hunger in the land,
[c]nor bear the shame of the Gentiles anymore.
[30]Thus they shall know that [a]I, the LORD their
God, *am* with them, and they, the house of Israel, *are* [b]My people," says the Lord GOD.'
[31]"You are My [a]flock, the flock of My pasture; you *are* men, *and* I *am* your God," says
the Lord GOD.

Judgment on Mount Seir

35 Moreover the word of the LORD came to
me, saying, [2]"Son of man, set your face
against [a]Mount Seir and [b]prophesy against
it, [3]and say to it, 'Thus says the Lord GOD:

"Behold, O Mount Seir, I *am* against you;
[a]I will stretch out My hand against you,
And make you most desolate;
4 I shall lay your cities waste,
And you shall be desolate.
Then you shall know that I *am* the LORD.

[5][a]"Because you have had an ancient hatred,
and have shed *the blood of* the children of Israel by the power of the sword at the time of
their calamity, [b]when their iniquity *came to an*
end, [6]therefore, *as* I live," says the Lord GOD,
"I will prepare you for [a]blood, and blood shall
pursue you; [b]since you have not hated blood,
therefore blood shall pursue you. [7]Thus I will
make Mount Seir most desolate, and cut off
from it the [a]one who leaves and the one who
returns. [8]And I will fill its mountains with the
slain; on your hills and in your valleys and in
all your ravines those who are slain by the
sword shall fall. [9][a]I will make you perpetually
desolate, and your cities shall be uninhabited;
[b]then you shall know that I *am* the LORD.
[10]"Because you have said, 'These two nations and these two countries shall be mine,

34:23 [b] Jer. 30:9 **34:24** [a] Ex. 29:45 [b] Ezek. 37:24, 25 **34:25** [a] Ezek. 37:26 [b] Is. 11:6–9 [c] Jer. 23:6 **34:26** [a] Is. 56:7 [b] Zech. 8:13 [c] Lev. 26:4 [d] Ps. 68:9 **34:27** [a] Is. 4:2 [b] Jer. 2:20 [c] Jer. 25:14 **34:28** [a] Jer. 30:10 **34:29** [a] [Is. 11:1] [b] Ezek. 36:29 [c] Ezek. 36:3, 6, 15 **34:30** [a] Ezek. 34:24 [b] Ezek. 14:11; 36:28 **34:31** [a] Ps. 100:3 **35:2** [a] Ezek. 25:12–14 [b] Amos 1:11 **35:3** [a] Ezek. 6:14 **35:5** [a] Ezek. 25:12 [b] Ps. 137:7 **35:6** [a] Is. 63:1–6 [b] Ps. 109:17 **35:7** [a] Judg. 5:6 **35:9** [a] Jer. 49:13 [b] Ezek. 36:11

THE PEACE COVENANT

"I will make a covenant of peace with them . . . and they will dwell safely."

EZEKIEL 34:25

Besides the promise of a new David, which Christian interpreters understand to be fulfilled in Jesus Christ, chapter 34 also promises covenant renewal: "I will make a covenant of peace with them . . . and they will dwell safely." After what the people of Israel had been through, they must have received a promise like this with great joy and renewed hope.

To have a "covenant of peace" with God is the ultimate goal and purpose of His redemptive plan for humanity. Our sin and defiance broke the peace we enjoyed with God and with creation. Though wronged, God initiated a plan to draw us back to Himself so that we might be redeemed and have peace restored. God's openness to apostate Israel and His wooing of His estranged people—and ultimately of us—reveal His love and willingness to forgive. Just knowing this wonderful reality is reason for having hope and finding peace.

Have you ever felt as though your covenant of peace with God was broken or in jeopardy? How did you handle it? Is that peace restored today, or do you need forgiveness to start again?

and we will [a]possess them,' although [b]the
LORD was there, 11therefore, *as* I live," says the
Lord GOD, "I will do [a]according to your anger
and according to the envy which you showed
in your hatred against them; and I will make
Myself known among them when I judge you.
12[a]Then you shall know that I *am* the LORD. I
have [b]heard all your [c]blasphemies which you
have spoken against the mountains of Israel, saying, 'They are desolate; they are given
to us to consume.' 13Thus [a]with your mouth
you have boasted against Me and multiplied
your [b]words against Me; I have heard *them*."
14"Thus says the Lord GOD: [a]"The whole
earth will rejoice when I make you desolate.
15[a]As you rejoiced because the inheritance of
the house of Israel was desolate, [b]so I will do
to you; you shall be desolate, O Mount Seir,
as well as all of Edom—all of it! Then they
shall know that I *am* the LORD." '

Blessing on Israel

36 "And you, son of man, prophesy to
the [a]mountains of Israel, and say,
'O mountains of Israel, hear the word of the
LORD! 2Thus says the Lord GOD: "Because [a]the
enemy has said of you, 'Aha! [b]The ancient
heights [c]have become our possession,' " '
3therefore prophesy, and say, 'Thus says the
Lord GOD: "Because they made *you* desolate and swallowed you up on every side,
so that you became the possession of the
rest of the nations, [a]and you are taken up
by the lips of [b]talkers and slandered by the
people"— 4therefore, O mountains of Israel, hear the word of the Lord GOD! Thus says
the Lord GOD to the mountains, the hills, the
rivers, the valleys, the desolate wastes, and
the cities that have been forsaken, which
[a]became plunder and [b]mockery to the rest
of the nations all around— 5therefore thus
says the Lord GOD: [a]"Surely I have spoken
in My burning jealousy against the rest of
the nations and against all Edom, [b]who gave
My land to themselves as a possession, with
wholehearted joy *and* spiteful minds, in order
to plunder its open country." '
6"Therefore prophesy concerning the land
of Israel, and say to the mountains, the hills,
the rivers, and the valleys, 'Thus says the Lord
GOD: "Behold, I have spoken in My jealousy
and My fury, because you have [a]borne the
shame of the nations." 7Therefore thus says
the Lord GOD: "I have [a]raised My hand in an
oath that surely the nations that *are* around
you shall [b]bear their own shame. 8But you,
O mountains of Israel, you shall shoot forth
your branches and yield your fruit to My people Israel, for they are about to come. 9For
indeed I *am* for you, and I will turn to you, and
you shall be tilled and sown. 10I will multiply
men upon you, all the house of Israel, all of
it; and the cities shall be inhabited and [a]the
ruins rebuilt. 11[a]I will multiply upon you man
and beast; and they shall increase and bear
young; I will make you inhabited as in former
times, and do [b]better *for you* than at your beginnings. [c]Then you shall know that I *am* the
LORD. 12Yes, I will cause men to walk on you,
My people Israel; [a]they shall take possession
of you, and you shall be their inheritance; no
more shall you [b]bereave them *of children*."
13"Thus says the Lord GOD: "Because they
say to you, [a]'You devour men and bereave
your nation *of children*,' 14therefore you shall
devour men no more, nor bereave your nation anymore," says the Lord GOD. 15[a]"Nor will
I let you hear the taunts of the nations anymore, nor bear the reproach of the peoples
anymore, nor shall you cause your nation
to stumble anymore," says the Lord GOD.' "

The Renewal of Israel

16Moreover the word of the LORD came to
me, saying: 17"Son of man, when the house of
Israel dwelt in their own land, [a]they defiled it
by their own ways and deeds; to Me their way
was like [b]the uncleanness of a woman in her
customary impurity. 18Therefore I poured out
My fury on them [a]for the blood they had shed
on the land, and for their idols *with which* they
had defiled it. 19So I [a]scattered them among
the nations, and they were dispersed throughout the countries; I judged them [b]according
to their ways and their deeds. 20When they
came to the nations, wherever they went, they
[a]profaned My holy name—when they said of
them, 'These *are* the people of the LORD, *and*
yet they have gone out of His land.' 21But I had
concern [a]for My holy name, which the house
of Israel had profaned among the nations
wherever they went.
22"Therefore say to the house of Israel,
'Thus says the Lord GOD: "I do not do *this*
for your sake, O house of Israel, [a]but for My
holy name's sake, which you have profaned

35:10 [a] Ps. 83:4–12 [b] [Ps. 48:1–3; 132:13, 14] **35:11** [a] [James 2:13] **35:12** [a] Ps. 9:16 [b] Zeph. 2:8 [c] Is. 52:5 **35:13** [a] [1 Sam. 2:3] [b] Ezek. 36:3 **35:14** [a] Is. 65:13, 14 **35:15** [a] Obad. 12, 15 [b] Lam. 4:21 **36:1** [a] Ezek. 6:2, 3 **36:2** [a] Ezek. 25:3; 26:2 [b] Deut. 32:13 [c] Ezek. 35:10 **36:3** [a] Deut. 28:37 [b] Ezek. 35:13 **36:4** [a] Ezek. 34:8, 28 [b] Ps. 79:4 **36:5** [a] Deut. 4:24 [b] Ezek. 35:10, 12 **36:6** [a] Ps. 74:10; 123:3, 4 **36:7** [a] Ezek. 20:5 [b] Jer. 25:9, 15, 29 **36:10** [a] Amos 9:14 **36:11** [a] Jer. 31:27; 33:12 [b] Is. 51:3 [c] Ezek. 35:9; 37:6, 13 **36:12** [a] Obad. 17 [b] Jer. 15:7 **36:13** [a] Num. 13:32 **36:15** [a] Ezek. 34:29 **36:17** [a] Jer. 2:7 [b] Lev. 15:19 **36:18** [a] Ezek. 16:36, 38; 23:37 **36:19** [a] Deut. 28:64 [b] [Rom. 2:6] **36:20** [a] Rom. 2:24 **36:21** [a] Ezek. 20:9, 14 **36:22** [a] Ps. 106:8

among the nations wherever you went. 23 And I will sanctify My great name, which has been profaned among the nations, which you have profaned in their midst; and the nations shall know that I *am* the LORD," says the Lord GOD, "when I am [a]hallowed in you before their eyes. 24 For [a]I will take you from among the nations, gather you out of all countries, and bring you into your own land. 25 [a]Then I will sprinkle clean water on you, and you shall be clean; I will cleanse you [b]from all your filthiness and from all your idols. 26 I will give you a [a]new heart and put a new spirit within you; I will take the heart of stone out of your flesh and give you a heart of flesh. 27 I will put My [a]Spirit within you and cause you to walk in My statutes, and you will keep My judgments and do *them.* 28 [a]Then you shall dwell in the land that I gave to your fathers; [b]you shall be My people, and I will be your God. 29 I will [a]deliver you from all your uncleannesses. [b]I will call for the grain and multiply it, and [c]bring no famine upon you. 30 [a]And I will multiply the fruit of your trees and the increase of your fields, so that you need never again bear the reproach of famine among the nations. 31 Then [a]you will remember your evil ways and your deeds that *were* not good; and you [b]will loathe yourselves in your own sight, for your iniquities and your abominations. 32 [a]Not for your sake do I do *this,*" says the Lord GOD, "let it be known to you. Be ashamed and confounded for your own ways, O house of Israel!"

33 "Thus says the Lord GOD: "On the day that I cleanse you from all your iniquities, I will also enable *you* to dwell in the cities, [a]and the ruins shall be rebuilt. 34 The desolate land shall be tilled instead of lying desolate in the sight of all who pass by. 35 So they will say, 'This land that was desolate has become like the garden of [a]Eden; and the wasted, desolate, and ruined cities *are now* fortified *and* inhabited.' 36 Then the nations which are left all around you shall know that I, the LORD, have rebuilt the ruined places *and* planted what was desolate. [a]I, the LORD, have spoken *it,* and I will do *it.*"

37 "Thus says the Lord GOD: [a]"I will also let the house of Israel inquire of Me to do this for them: I will [b]increase their men like a flock. 38 Like a flock *offered as* holy *sacrifices,* like the flock at Jerusalem on its feast days, so shall the ruined cities be filled with flocks of men. Then they shall know that I *am* the LORD." ' "

The Dry Bones Live

37 The [a]hand of the LORD came upon me and brought me out [b]in the Spirit of the LORD, and set me down in the midst of the valley; and it *was* full of bones. 2 Then He caused me to pass by them all around, and behold, *there were* very many in the open valley; and indeed *they were* very dry. 3 And He said to me, "Son of man, can these bones live?"

So I answered, "O Lord GOD, [a]You know."

4 Again He said to me, "Prophesy to these bones, and say to them, 'O dry bones, hear the word of the LORD! 5 Thus says the Lord GOD to these bones: "Surely I will [a]cause breath to enter into you, and you shall live. 6 I will put sinews on you and bring flesh upon you, cover you with skin and put breath in you; and you shall live. [a]Then you shall know that I *am* the LORD." ' "

7 So I prophesied as I was commanded; and as I prophesied, there was a noise, and suddenly a rattling; and the bones came together, bone to bone. 8 Indeed, as I looked, the sinews and the flesh came upon them, and the skin covered them over; but *there was* no breath in them.

9 Also He said to me, "Prophesy to the breath, prophesy, son of man, and say to the breath, 'Thus says the Lord GOD: [a]"Come from the four winds, O breath, and breathe on these slain, that they may live." ' " 10 So I prophesied as He commanded me, [a]and breath came into them, and they lived, and stood upon their feet, an exceedingly great army.

11 Then He said to me, "Son of man, these bones are the [a]whole house of Israel. They indeed say, [b]'Our bones are dry, our hope is lost, and we ourselves are cut off!' 12 Therefore prophesy and say to them, 'Thus says the Lord GOD: "Behold, [a]O My people, I will open your graves and cause you to come up from your graves, and [b]bring you into the land of Israel. 13 Then you shall know that I *am* the LORD, when I have opened your graves, O My people, and brought you up from your graves. 14 I [a]will put My Spirit in you, and you shall live, and I will place you in your own land. Then you shall know that I, the LORD, have spoken *it* and performed *it,*" says the LORD.' "

One Kingdom, One King

15 Again the word of the LORD came to me, saying, 16 "As for you, son of man, [a]take a stick for yourself and write on it: 'For Judah and for [b]the children of Israel, his companions.'

36:23 [a] Ezek. 20:41; 28:22 **36:24** [a] Ezek. 34:13; 37:21 **36:25** [a] Heb. 9:13, 19; 10:22 [b] Jer. 33:8 **36:26** [a] Ezek. 11:19 **36:27** [a] Ezek. 11:19; 37:14 **36:28** [a] Ezek. 28:25; 37:25 [b] Jer. 30:22 **36:29** [a] [Rom. 11:26] [b] Ps. 105:16 [c] Ezek. 34:27, 29 **36:30** [a] Ezek. 34:27 **36:31** [a] Ezek. 16:61, 63 [b] Ezek. 6:9; 20:43 **36:32** [a] Deut. 9:5 **36:33** [a] Ezek. 36:10 **36:35** [a] Joel 2:3 **36:36** [a] Ezek. 17:24; 22:14; 37:14 **36:37** [a] Ezek. 14:3; 20:3, 31 [b] Ezek. 36:10 **37:1** [a] Ezek. 1:3 [b] Ezek. 3:14; 8:3; 11:24 **37:3** [a] [1 Sam. 2:6] **37:5** [a] Ps. 104:29, 30 **37:6** [a] Joel 2:27; 3:17 **37:9** [a] [Ps. 104:30] **37:10** [a] Rev. 11:11 **37:11** [a] Ezek. 36:10 [b] Ps. 141:7 **37:12** [a] Is. 26:19; 66:14 [b] Ezek. 36:24 **37:14** [a] Ezek. 36:27 **37:16** [a] Num. 17:2, 3 [b] 2 Chr. 11:12, 13, 16; 15:9; 30:11, 18

Then take another stick and write on it, 'For
Joseph, the stick of Ephraim, and *for* all the
house of Israel, his companions.' 17Then [a]join
them one to another for yourself into one
stick, and they will become one in your hand.
18"And when the children of your people
speak to you, saying, [a]'Will you not show us what
you *mean* by these?'— 19[a]say to them, 'Thus says
the Lord GOD: "Surely I will take [b]the stick of
Joseph, which *is* in the hand of Ephraim, and
the tribes of Israel, his companions; and I will
join them with it, with the stick of Judah, and
make them one stick, and they will be one in
My hand." ' 20And the sticks on which you write
will be in your hand [a]before their eyes.
21"Then say to them, 'Thus says the Lord
GOD: "Surely [a]I will take the children of Israel
from among the nations, wherever they have
gone, and will gather them from every side
and bring them into their own land; 22and
[a]I will make them one nation in the land, on
the mountains of Israel; and [b]one king shall
be king over them all; they shall no longer
be two nations, nor shall they ever be divided into two kingdoms again. 23[a]They shall
not defile themselves anymore with their
idols, nor with their detestable things, nor
with any of their transgressions; but [b]I will
deliver them from all their dwelling places
in which they have sinned, and will cleanse
them. Then they shall be My people, and I
will be their God.
24[a]"David My servant *shall be* king over them,
and [b]they shall all have one shepherd; [c]they
shall also walk in My judgments and observe
My statutes, and do them. 25[a]Then they shall
dwell in the land that I have given to Jacob My
servant, where your fathers dwelt; and they
shall dwell there, they, their children, and their
children's children, [b]forever; and [c]My servant
David *shall be* their prince forever. 26Moreover I
will make [a]a covenant of peace with them, and
it shall be an everlasting covenant with them;
I will establish them and [b]multiply them, and
I will set My [c]sanctuary in their midst forevermore. 27[a]My tabernacle also shall be with them;
indeed I will be [b]their God, and they shall be
My people. 28[a]The nations also will know that I,
the LORD, [b]sanctify Israel, when My sanctuary
is in their midst forevermore." ' "

Gog and Allies Attack Israel

38 Now the word of the LORD came to me,
saying, 2[a]"Son of man, [b]set your face
against [c]Gog, of the land of [d]Magog, the prince
of Rosh,[1] [e]Meshech, and Tubal, and prophesy
against him, 3and say, 'Thus says the Lord
GOD: "Behold, I *am* against you, O Gog, the
prince of Rosh, Meshech, and Tubal. 4[a]I will
turn you around, put hooks into your jaws,

37:17 [a] Hos. 1:11 **37:18** [a] Ezek. 12:9; 24:19 **37:19** [a] Zech. 10:6 [b] Ezek. 37:16, 17 **37:20** [a] Ezek. 12:3 **37:21** [a] Ezek. 36:24 **37:22** [a] Jer. 3:18 [b] Ezek. 34:23 **37:23** [a] Ezek. 36:25 [b] Ezek. 36:28, 29 **37:24** [a] Is. 40:11; [Luke 1:32]; 1 Pet. 2:25 [b] [John 10:16] [c] Ezek. 36:27 **37:25** [a] Ezek. 36:28; Rev. 21:3; 22:3 [b] Is. 60:21 [c] John 12:34 **37:26** [a] Is. 55:3 [b] Ezek. 36:10 [c] [2 Cor. 6:16] **37:27** [a] [John 1:14] [b] Ezek. 11:20 **37:28** [a] Ezek. 36:23 [b] Ezek. 20:12 **38:2** [a] Ezek. 39:1 [b] Ezek. 35:2, 3 [c] Rev. 20:8 [d] Gen. 10:2 [e] Ezek. 32:26 [1] Targum, Vulgate, and Aquila read *chief prince of* (also verse 3). **38:4** [a] 2 Kin. 19:28

MEET YOUR SHEPHERD

"David My servant shall be king over them, and they shall all have one shepherd."

EZEKIEL 37:24

In 34:23 the prophet promised that someday God would raise up a new David. Here in 37:24, Ezekiel called him "king" and "shepherd." The promise that someday Israel would "all have one shepherd" must have resonated very positively. The shepherd imagery goes back to Israel's very beginning. In the wilderness Moses prayed for a successor so that the nation "may not be like sheep which have no shepherd" (Num. 27:17). When David arose as Israel's new king, God told him, "You shall shepherd My people Israel, and be ruler over Israel" (2 Sam. 5:2; see Ps. 78:71). Of course, ultimately it is God Himself who has been Israel's Shepherd (see Pss. 23:1; 28:9; 80:1).

Jesus' appearance fulfilled the promise of a coming Shepherd. It was to Ezekiel's prophecy that Jesus alluded when He told His disciples, "I am the good shepherd" (John 10:11, 14). Ezekiel complained of Israel's wicked shepherds, who failed to feed and protect the sheep (Ezek. 34:2, 7–10). Jesus the Good Shepherd would protect and even give His life for His flock (John 10:11). Knowing that we have such a Shepherd should give us a great sense of peace.

and [b]lead you out, with all your army, horses, and horsemen, [c]all splendidly clothed, a great company *with* bucklers and shields, all of them handling swords. 5 Persia, Ethiopia,[1] and Libya[2] are with them, all of them *with* shield and helmet; 6 [a]Gomer and all its troops; the house of [b]Togarmah *from* the far north and all its troops—many people *are* with you.

7 [a]"Prepare yourself and be ready, you and all your companies that are gathered about you; and be a guard for them. 8 [a]After many days [b]you will be visited. In the latter years you will come into the land of those brought back from the sword [c]*and* gathered from many people on [d]the mountains of Israel, which had long been desolate; they were brought out of the nations, and now all of them [e]dwell safely. 9 You will ascend, coming [a]like a storm, covering the [b]land like a cloud, you and all your troops and many peoples with you."

10 'Thus says the Lord GOD: "On that day it shall come to pass *that* thoughts will arise in your mind, and you will make an evil plan: 11 You will say, 'I will go up against a land of [a]unwalled villages; I will [b]go to a peaceful people, [c]who dwell safely, all of them dwelling without walls, and having neither bars nor gates'— 12 to take plunder and to take booty, to stretch out your hand against the waste places *that are again* inhabited, [a]and against a people gathered from the nations, who have acquired livestock and goods, who dwell in the midst of the land. 13 [a]Sheba, [b]Dedan, the merchants [c]of Tarshish, and all [d]their young lions will say to you, 'Have you come to take plunder? Have you gathered your army to take booty, to carry away silver and gold, to take away livestock and goods, to take great plunder?' " '

14 "Therefore, son of man, prophesy and say to Gog, 'Thus says the Lord GOD: [a]"On that day when My people Israel [b]dwell safely, will you not know *it?* 15 [a]Then you will come from your place out of the far north, you and many peoples with you, all of them riding on horses, a great company and a mighty army. 16 You will come up against My people Israel like a cloud, to cover the land. It will be in the latter days that I will bring you against My land, so that the nations may [a]know Me, when I am [b]hallowed in you, O Gog, before their eyes." 17 Thus says the Lord GOD: "Are *you* he of whom I have spoken in former days by My servants the prophets of Israel, who prophesied for years in those days that I would bring you against them?

Judgment on Gog

18 "And it will come to pass at the same time, when Gog comes against the land of Israel," says the Lord GOD, "*that* My fury will show in My face. 19 For [a]in My jealousy [b]*and* in the fire of My wrath I have spoken: [c]'Surely in that day there shall be a great earthquake in the land of Israel, 20 so that [a]the fish of the sea, the birds of the heavens, the beasts of the field, all creeping things that creep on the earth, and all men who *are* on the face of the earth shall shake at My presence. [b]The mountains shall be thrown down, the steep places shall fall, and every wall shall fall to the ground.' 21 I will [a]call for [b]a sword against Gog throughout all My mountains," says the Lord GOD. [c]"Every man's sword will be against his brother. 22 And I will [a]bring him to judgment with [b]pestilence and bloodshed; [c]I will rain down on him, on his troops, and on the many peoples who *are* with him, flooding rain, [d]great hailstones, fire, and brimstone. 23 Thus I will magnify Myself and [a]sanctify Myself, [b]and I will be known in the eyes of many nations. Then they shall know that I *am* the LORD." '

Gog's Armies Destroyed

39 "And [a]you, son of man, prophesy against Gog, and say, 'Thus says the Lord GOD: "Behold, I *am* against you, O Gog, the prince of Rosh,[1] Meshech, and Tubal; 2 and I will [a]turn you around and lead you on, [b]bringing you up from the far north, and bring you against the mountains of Israel. 3 Then I will knock the bow out of your left hand, and cause the arrows to fall out of your right hand. 4 [a]You shall fall upon the mountains of Israel, you and all your troops and the peoples who *are* with you; [b]I will give you to birds of prey of every sort and *to* the beasts of the field to be devoured. 5 You shall fall on the open field; for I have spoken," says the Lord GOD. 6 [a]"And I will send fire on Magog and on those who live in security in [b]the coastlands. Then they shall know that I *am* the LORD. 7 [a]So I will make My holy name known in the midst of My people Israel, and I will not *let them* [b]profane My holy name anymore. [c]Then the

38:4 [b] Is. 43:17 [c] Ezek. 23:12 **38:5** [1] Hebrew *Cush* [2] Hebrew *Put* **38:6** [a] Gen. 10:2 [b] Ezek. 27:14 **38:7** [a] Is. 8:9, 10 **38:8** [a] Is. 24:22 [b] Is. 29:6 [c] Ezek. 34:13 [d] Ezek. 36:1, 4 [e] Ezek. 34:25; 39:26 **38:9** [a] Is. 28:2 [b] Jer. 4:13 **38:11** [a] Zech. 2:4 [b] Jer. 49:31 [c] Ezek. 38:8 **38:12** [a] Ezek. 38:8 **38:13** [a] Ezek. 27:22 [b] Ezek. 27:15, 20 [c] Ezek. 27:12 [d] Ezek. 19:3, 5 **38:14** [a] Is. 4:1 [b] Ezek. 38:8, 11 **38:15** [a] Ezek. 39:2 **38:16** [a] Ezek. 35:11 [b] Ezek. 28:22 **38:19** [a] Ezek. 36:5, 6 [b] Ps. 89:46 [c] Rev. 16:18 **38:20** [a] Hos. 4:3 [b] Jer. 4:24 **38:21** [a] Ps. 105:16 [b] Ezek. 14:17 [c] 1 Sam. 14:20 **38:22** [a] Is. 66:16 [b] Ezek. 5:17 [c] Ps. 11:6 [d] Rev. 16:21 **38:23** [a] Ezek. 36:23 [b] Ezek. 37:28; 38:16 **39:1** [a] Ezek. 38:2, 3 [1] Targum, Vulgate and Aquila read *chief prince of.* **39:2** [a] Ezek. 38:8 [b] Ezek. 38:15 **39:4** [a] Ezek. 38:4, 21 [b] Ezek. 33:27 **39:6** [a] Amos 1:4, 7, 10 [b] Ps. 72:10 **39:7** [a] Ezek. 39:25 [b] Lev. 18:21 [c] Ezek. 38:16

nations shall know that *I am* the LORD, the
Holy One in Israel. 8 [a]Surely it is coming, and
it shall be done," says the Lord GOD. "This *is*
the day [b]of which I have spoken.
9 "Then those who dwell in the cities of Israel will go out and set on fire and burn the
weapons, both the shields and bucklers, the
bows and arrows, the javelins and spears; and
they will make fires with them for seven years.
10 They will not take wood from the field nor cut
down *any* from the forests, because they will
make fires with the weapons; [a]and they will
plunder those who plundered them, and pillage
those who pillaged them," says the Lord GOD.

The Burial of Gog

11 "It will come to pass in that day *that* I will
give Gog a burial place there in Israel, the
valley of those who pass by east of the sea;
and it will obstruct travelers, because there
they will bury Gog and all his multitude.
Therefore they will call *it* the Valley of Hamon
Gog.[1] 12 For seven months the house of Israel
will be burying them, [a]in order to cleanse the
land. 13 Indeed all the people of the land will
be burying, and they will gain [a]renown for
it on the day that [b]I am glorified," says the
Lord GOD. 14 "They will set apart men regularly
employed, with the help of a search party,[1] to
pass through the land and bury those bodies
remaining on the ground, in order [a]to cleanse
it. At the end of seven months they will make
a search. 15 The search party will pass through
the land; and *when anyone* sees a man's bone,
he shall set up a marker by it, till the buriers
have buried it in the Valley of Hamon Gog.
16 *The* name of *the* city *will* also *be* Hamonah.
Thus they shall [a]cleanse the land." '

A Triumphant Festival

17 "And as for you, son of man, thus says
the Lord GOD, [a]'Speak to every sort of bird
and to every beast of the field:

[b]"Assemble yourselves and come;
Gather together from all sides to My
[c]sacrificial meal
Which I am sacrificing for you,
A great sacrificial meal [d]on the
mountains of Israel,
That you may eat flesh and drink blood.
18 [a]You shall eat the flesh of the mighty,
Drink the blood of the princes of the
earth,
Of rams and lambs,
Of goats and bulls,
All of them [b]fatlings of Bashan.
19 You shall eat fat till you are full,
And drink blood till you are drunk,
At My sacrificial meal
Which I am sacrificing for you.
20 [a]You shall be filled at My table
With horses and riders,
[b]With mighty men
And with all the men of war," says the
Lord GOD.

Israel Restored to the Land

21 [a]"I will set My glory among the nations;
all the nations shall see My judgment which
I have executed, and [b]My hand which I have
laid on them. 22 [a]So the house of Israel shall
know that I *am* the LORD their God from that
day forward. 23 [a]The Gentiles shall know that
the house of Israel went into captivity for
their iniquity; because they were unfaithful
to Me, therefore [b]I hid My face from them. I
[c]gave them into the hand of their enemies,
and they all fell by the sword. 24 [a]According
to their uncleanness and according to their
transgressions I have dealt with them, and
hidden My face from them." '
25 "Therefore thus says the Lord GOD: [a]'Now
I will bring back the captives of Jacob, and
have mercy on the [b]whole house of Israel;
and I will be jealous for My holy name—
26 [a]after they have borne their shame, and
all their unfaithfulness in which they were
unfaithful to Me, when they [b]dwelt safely in
their *own* land and no one made *them* afraid.
27 [a]When I have brought them back from the
peoples and gathered them out of their enemies' lands, and I [b]am hallowed in them in
the sight of many nations, 28 [a]then they shall
know that I *am* the LORD their God, who sent
them into captivity among the nations, but
also brought them back to their land, and
left none of them captive any longer. 29 [a]And
I will not hide My face from them anymore;
for I shall have [b]poured out My Spirit on the
house of Israel,' says the Lord GOD."

A New City, a New Temple

40 In the twenty-fifth year of our captivity,
at the beginning of the year, on the
tenth *day* of the month, in the fourteenth year
after [a]the city was captured, on the very same
day [b]the hand of the LORD was upon me; and

39:8 [a] Rev. 16:17; 21:6 [b] Ezek. 38:17 **39:10** [a] Is. 14:2; 33:1 **39:11** [1] Literally *The Multitude of Gog* **39:12** [a] Deut. 21:23 **39:13** [a] Zeph. 3:19, 20 [b] Ezek. 28:22 **39:14** [a] Ezek. 39:12 [1] Literally *those who pass through* **39:16** [a] Ezek. 39:12 **39:17** [a] Rev. 19:17, 18 [b] Is. 18:6 [c] Zeph. 1:7 [d] Ezek. 39:4 **39:18** [a] Rev. 19:18 [b] Deut. 32:14 **39:20** [a] Ps. 76:5, 6 [b] Rev. 19:18 **39:21** [a] Ezek. 36:23; 38:23 [b] Ex. 7:4 **39:22** [a] Ex. 39:7, 28 **39:23** [a] Ezek. 36:18–20, 23 [b] Is. 1:15; 59:2 [c] Lev. 26:25 **39:24** [a] Ezek. 36:19 **39:25** [a] Ezek. 34:13; 36:24 [b] Hos. 1:11 **39:26** [a] Dan. 9:16 [b] Lev. 26:5, 6 **39:27** [a] Ezek. 28:25, 26 [b] Ezek. 36:23, 24; 38:16 **39:28** [a] Ezek. 34:30 **39:29** [a] Is. 54:8, 9 [b] [Joel 2:28] **40:1** [a] Ezek. 33:21 [b] Ezek. 1:3; 3:14, 22; 37:1

PEACE NOTE

When we submit our lives to Jesus Christ, peace will result, but we must contend for it moment by moment in our faith.

He took me there. 2 [a]In the visions of God He took me into the land of Israel and [b]set me on a very high mountain; on it toward the south *was* something like the structure of a city. 3 He took me there, and behold, *there was* a man whose appearance *was* [a]like the appearance of bronze. [b]He had a line of flax [c]and a measuring rod in his hand, and he stood in the gateway.

4 And the man said to me, [a]"Son of man, look with your eyes and hear with your ears, and fix your mind on everything I show you; for you *were* brought here so that I might show *them* to you. [b]Declare to the house of Israel everything you see." 5 Now there was [a]a wall all around the outside of the temple.[1] In the man's hand was a measuring rod six cubits *long, each being a* cubit and a handbreadth; and he measured the width of the wall structure, one rod; and the height, one rod.

The Eastern Gateway of the Temple

6 Then he went to the gateway which faced [a]east; and he went up its stairs and measured the threshold of the gateway, *which was* one rod wide, and the other threshold *was* one rod wide. 7 Each gate chamber *was* one rod long and one rod wide; between the gate chambers *was a space of* five cubits; and the threshold of the gateway by the vestibule of the inside gate *was* one rod. 8 He also measured the vestibule of the inside gate, one rod. 9 Then he measured the vestibule of the gateway, eight cubits; and the gateposts, two cubits. The vestibule of the gate *was* on the inside. 10 In the eastern gateway *were* three gate chambers on one *side and three on the other;* the three *were* all the same size; also the gateposts were of the same size on this side and that side.

11 He measured the width of the entrance to the gateway, ten cubits; *and* the length of the gate, thirteen cubits. 12 *There was* a space in front of the gate chambers, one cubit *on this side* and one cubit on that side; the gate chambers *were* six cubits on this side and six cubits on that side. 13 Then he measured the gateway from the roof of *one* gate chamber to the roof of the other; the width *was* twenty-five cubits, as door faces door. 14 He measured the gateposts, sixty cubits high, and the court all around the gateway *extended* to the gatepost. 15 *From* the front of the entrance gate to the front of the vestibule of the inner gate *was* fifty cubits. 16 *There were* [a]beveled window *frames* in the gate chambers and in their intervening archways on the inside of the gateway all around, and likewise in the vestibules. *There were* windows all around on the inside. And on each gatepost *were* [b]palm trees.

The Outer Court

17 Then he brought me into [a]the outer court; and *there were* [b]chambers and a pavement made all around the court; [c]thirty chambers faced the pavement. 18 The pavement was by the side of the gateways, corresponding to the length of the gateways; *this was* the lower pavement. 19 Then he measured the width from the front of the lower gateway to the front of the inner court exterior, one hundred cubits toward the east and the north.

The Northern Gateway

20 On the outer court was also a gateway facing north, and he measured its length and its width. 21 Its gate chambers, three on this side and three on that side, its gateposts and its archways, had the same measurements as the first gate; its length *was* fifty cubits and its width twenty-five cubits. 22 Its windows and those of its archways, and also its palm trees, *had* the same measurements as the gateway facing east; it was ascended by seven steps, and its archway *was* in front of it. 23 A gate of the inner court was opposite the northern gateway, just as the eastern *gateway;* and he measured from gateway to gateway, one hundred cubits.

The Southern Gateway

24 After that he brought me toward the south, and there a gateway was facing south; and he measured its gateposts and archways according to these same measurements. 25 *There were* windows in it and in its archways all around like those windows; its length *was* fifty cubits and its width twenty-five cubits. 26 Seven steps

40:2 [a] Ezek. 1:1; 3:14; 8:3; 37:1 [b] Rev. 21:10 **40:3** [a] Dan. 10:6 [b] Ezek. 47:3 [c] Rev. 11:1; 21:15 **40:4** [a] Ezek. 44:5 [b] Ezek. 43:10 **40:5** [a] Ezek. 42:20 [1] Literally *house,* and so elsewhere in this book **40:6** [a] Ezek. 43:1 **40:16** [a] 1 Kin. 6:4 [b] 1 Kin. 6:29, 32, 35 **40:17** [a] Rev. 11:2 [b] 1 Kin. 6:5 [c] Ezek. 45:5

led up to it, and its archway *was* in front of them; and it had palm trees on its gateposts, one on this side and one on that side. 27*There was* also a gateway on the inner court, facing south; and he measured from gateway to gateway toward the south, one hundred cubits.

Gateways of the Inner Court

28Then he brought me to the inner court through the southern gateway; he measured the southern gateway according to these same measurements. 29Also its gate chambers, its gateposts, and its archways *were* according to these same measurements; *there were* windows in it and in its archways all around; *it was* fifty cubits long and twenty-five cubits wide. 30*There were* archways all around, [a]twenty-five cubits long and five cubits wide. 31Its archways faced the outer court, palm trees *were* on its gateposts, and going up to it *were* eight steps.

32And he brought me into the inner court facing east; he measured the gateway according to these same measurements. 33Also its gate chambers, its gateposts, and its archways *were* according to these same measurements; and *there were* windows in it and in its archways all around; *it was* fifty cubits long and twenty-five cubits wide. 34Its archways faced the outer court, and palm trees *were* on its gateposts on this side and on that side; and going up to it *were* eight steps.

35Then he brought me to the north gateway and measured *it* according to these same measurements— 36also its gate chambers, its gateposts, and its archways. It had windows all around; its length *was* fifty cubits and its width twenty-five cubits. 37Its gateposts faced the outer court, palm trees *were* on its gateposts on this side and on that side, and going up to it *were* eight steps.

Where Sacrifices Were Prepared

38*There was* a chamber and its entrance by the gateposts of the gateway, where they [a]washed the burnt offering. 39In the vestibule of the gateway *were* two tables on this side and two tables on that side, on which to slay the burnt offering, [a]the sin offering, and [b]the trespass offering. 40At the outer side of the *vestibule,* as one goes up to the entrance of the northern gateway, *were* two tables; and on the other side of the vestibule of the gateway *were* two tables. 41Four tables *were* on this side and four tables on that side, by the side of the gateway, eight tables on which they slaughtered *the sacrifices.* 42*There were* also four tables of hewn stone for the burnt offering, one cubit and a half long, one cubit and a half wide, and one cubit high; on these they laid the instruments with which they slaughtered the burnt offering and the sacrifice. 43Inside *were* hooks, a handbreadth wide, fastened all around; and the flesh of the sacrifices *was* on the tables.

Chambers for Singers and Priests

44Outside the inner gate *were* the chambers for [a]the singers in the inner court, one facing south at the side of the northern gateway, and the other facing north at the side of the southern[1] gateway. 45Then he said to me, "This chamber which faces south *is* for [a]the priests who have charge of the temple. 46The chamber which faces north *is* for the priests [a]who have charge of the altar; these *are* the sons of [b]Zadok, from the sons of Levi, who come near the LORD to minister to Him."

Dimensions of the Inner Court and Vestibule

47And he measured the court, one hundred cubits long and one hundred cubits wide, foursquare. The altar *was* in front of the temple. 48Then he brought me to the [a]vestibule of the temple and measured the doorposts of the vestibule, five cubits on this side and five cubits on that side; and the width of the gateway was three cubits on this side and three cubits on that side. 49[a]The length of the vestibule *was* twenty cubits, and the width eleven cubits; and by the steps which led up to it *there were* [b]pillars by the doorposts, one on this side and another on that side.

Dimensions of the Sanctuary

41 Then he [a]brought me into the sanctuary[1] and measured the doorposts, six cubits wide on one side and six cubits wide on the other side—the width of the tabernacle. 2The width of the entryway *was* ten cubits, and the side walls of the entrance *were* five cubits on this side and five cubits on the other side; and he measured its length, forty cubits, and its width, twenty cubits.

3Also he went inside and measured the doorposts, two cubits; and the entrance, six cubits *high;* and the width of the entrance, seven cubits. 4[a]He measured the length, twenty cubits; and the width, twenty cubits, beyond the sanctuary; and he said to me, "This *is* the Most Holy *Place.*"

40:30 [a] Ezek. 40:21, 25, 33, 36 **40:38** [a] 2 Chr. 4:6 **40:39** [a] Lev. 4:2, 3 [b] Lev. 5:6; 6:6; 7:1 **40:44** [a] 1 Chr. 6:31, 32; 16:41–43; 25:1–7 [1] Following Septuagint; Masoretic Text and Vulgate read *eastern.* **40:45** [a] Lev. 8:35 **40:46** [a] Num. 18:5 [b] 1 Kin. 2:35 **40:48** [a] 1 Kin. 6:3 **40:49** [a] 1 Kin. 6:3 [b] 1 Kin. 7:15–22 **41:1** [a] Ezek. 40:2, 3, 17 [1] Hebrew *heykal,* here the main room of the temple, sometimes called the *holy place* (compare Exodus 26:33) **41:4** [a] 1 Kin. 6:20

The Side Chambers on the Wall
5 Next, he measured the wall of the temple,
six cubits. The width of each side chamber all
around the temple *was* four cubits on every
side. 6 [a]The side chambers *were* in three stories, one above the other, thirty chambers in
each story; they rested on ledges which *were*
for the side chambers all around, that they
might be supported, but [b]not fastened to the
wall of the temple. 7 As one went up from story
to story, the side chambers [a]became wider
all around, because their supporting ledges
in the wall of the temple ascended like steps;
therefore the width of the structure increased
as one went up *from* the lowest *story* to the
highest by way of the middle one. 8 I also saw
an elevation all around the temple; it was
the foundation of the side chambers, [a]a full
rod, *that is,* six cubits *high.* 9 The thickness of
the outer wall of the side chambers *was* five
cubits, and so also the remaining terrace by
the place of the side chambers of the temple. 10 And between *it and* the *wall* chambers
was a width of twenty cubits all around the
temple on every side. 11 The doors of the side
chambers opened on the terrace, one door
toward the north and another toward the
south; and the width of the terrace *was* five
cubits all around.

The Building at the Western End
12 The building that faced the separating
courtyard at its western end *was* seventy
cubits wide; the wall of the building *was*
five cubits thick all around, and its length
ninety cubits.

Dimensions and Design of the Temple Area
13 So he measured the temple, one [a]hun-
dred cubits long; and the separating courtyard with the building and its walls *was* one
hundred cubits long; 14 also the width of the
eastern face of the temple, including the separating courtyard, *was* one hundred cubits.
15 He measured the length of the building behind it, facing the separating courtyard, with
its [a]galleries on the one side and on the other
side, one hundred cubits, as well as the inner
temple and the porches of the court, 16 their
doorposts and [a]the beveled window frames.
And the galleries all around their three stories opposite the threshold were paneled with
[b]wood from the ground to the windows—the
windows were covered— 17 from the space
above the door, even to the inner room,[1] as
well as outside, and on every wall all around,
inside and outside, by measure.
18 And *it was* made [a]with cherubim and
[b]palm trees, a palm tree between cherub and
cherub. *Each* cherub had two faces, 19 [a]so that
the face of a man *was* toward a palm tree on
one side, and the face of a young lion toward a
palm tree on the other side; thus *it was* made
throughout the temple all around. 20 From
the floor to the space above the door, and
on the wall of the sanctuary, cherubim and
palm trees *were* carved.
21 The [a]doorposts of the temple *were*
square, *as was* the front of the sanctuary;
their appearance was similar. 22 [a]The altar
was of wood, three cubits high, and its length
two cubits. Its corners, its length, and its sides
were of wood; and he said to me, "This *is* [b]the
table that *is* [c]before the LORD."
23 [a]The temple and the sanctuary had two
doors. 24 The doors had two [a]panels *apiece,*
two folding panels: two *panels* for one door
and two panels for the other *door.* 25 Cherubim and palm trees *were* carved on the
doors of the temple just as they *were* carved
on the walls. A wooden canopy *was* on the
front of the vestibule outside. 26 *There were*
[a]beveled window *frames* and palm trees on
one side and on the other, on the sides of the
vestibule—also on the side chambers of the
temple and on the canopies.

The Chambers for the Priests
42 Then he [a]brought me out into the
outer court, by the way toward the
[b]north; and he brought me into [c]the chamber
which *was* opposite the separating courtyard, and which *was* opposite the building
toward the north. 2 Facing the length, *which*
was one hundred cubits (the width was fifty
cubits), was the north door. 3 Opposite the
inner court of twenty *cubits,* and opposite the
[a]pavement of the outer court, *was* [b]gallery
against gallery in three *stories.* 4 In front of
the chambers, toward the inside, *was* a walk
ten cubits wide, at a distance of one cubit;
and their doors faced north. 5 Now the upper
chambers *were* shorter, because the galleries
took away *space* from them more than from
the lower and middle stories of the building.
6 For they *were* in three *stories* and did not
have pillars like the pillars of the courts;
therefore *the upper level* was shortened more
than the lower and middle levels from the

41:6 [a] 1 Kin. 6:5–10 [b] 1 Kin. 6:6, 10 **41:7** [a] 1 Kin. 6:8 **41:8** [a] Ezek. 40:5 **41:13** [a] Ezek. 40:47 **41:15** [a] Ezek. 42:3, 5 **41:16** [a] Ezek. 40:16, 25 [b] 1 Kin. 6:15 **41:17** [1] Literally *house,* here *the Most Holy Place* **41:18** [a] 1 Kin. 6:29 [b] Ezek. 40:16 **41:19** [a] Ezek. 1:10; 10:14 **41:21** [a] 1 Kin. 6:33 **41:22** [a] Ex. 30:1–3 [b] Ex. 25:23, 30 [c] Ex. 30:8 **41:23** [a] 1 Kin. 6:31–35 **41:24** [a] 1 Kin. 6:34 **41:26** [a] Ezek. 40:16 **42:1** [a] Ezek. 41:1 [b] Ezek. 40:20 [c] Ezek. 41:12, 15 **42:3** [a] Ezek. 40:17 [b] Ezek. 41:15, 16; 42:5

ground up. 7And a wall which *was* outside
ran parallel to the chambers, at the front of
the chambers, toward the outer court; its
length *was* fifty cubits. 8The length of the
chambers toward the outer court *was* fifty
cubits, whereas that facing the temple *was*
one [a]hundred cubits. 9At the lower chambers
was the entrance on the east side, as one goes
into them from the outer court.

10Also *there were* chambers in the thickness of the wall of the court toward the east,
opposite the separating courtyard and opposite the building. 11[a]*There was* a walk in
front of them also, and their appearance
was like the chambers which *were* toward
the north; they *were* as long and as wide as
the others, and all their exits and entrances
were according to plan. 12And corresponding
to the doors of the chambers that *were* facing
south, as one enters them, *there was* a door
in front of the walk, the way directly in front
of the wall toward the east.

13Then he said to me, "The north chambers
and the south chambers, which *are* opposite
the separating courtyard, *are* the holy chambers where the priests who approach the
LORD [a]shall eat the most holy offerings. There
they shall lay the most holy offerings—[b]the
grain offering, the sin offering, and the trespass offering—for the place *is* holy. 14[a]When
the priests enter them, they shall not go out
of the holy *chamber* into the outer court;
but there they shall leave their garments in
which they minister, for they *are* holy. They
shall put on other garments; then they may
approach *that* which *is* for the people."

Outer Dimensions of the Temple

15Now when he had finished measuring
the inner temple, he brought me out through
the gateway that faces toward the [a]east, and
measured it all around. 16He measured the
east side with the measuring rod,[1] five hundred rods by the measuring rod all around.
17He measured the north side, five hundred
rods by the measuring rod all around. 18He
measured the south side, five hundred rods
by the measuring rod. 19He came around to
the west side *and* measured five hundred
rods by the measuring rod. 20He measured
it on the four sides; [a]it had a wall all around,
[b]five hundred *cubits* long and five hundred
wide, to separate the holy areas from the
common.

The Temple, the LORD's Dwelling Place

43 Afterward he brought me to the gate,
the gate [a]that faces toward the east.
2[a]And behold, the glory of the God of Israel
came from the way of the east. [b]His voice
was like the sound of many waters; [c]and
the earth shone with His glory. 3*It was* [a]like
the appearance of the vision which I saw—
like the vision which I saw when I[1] came [b]to
destroy the city. The visions *were* like the
vision which I saw [c]by the River Chebar;
and I fell on my face. 4[a]And the glory of the
LORD came into the temple by way of the
gate which faces toward the east. 5[a]The Spirit
lifted me up and brought me into the inner
court; and behold, [b]the glory of the LORD
filled the temple.

6Then I heard *Him* speaking to me from
the temple, while [a]a man stood beside me.
7And He said to me, "Son of man, *this is* [a]the
place of My throne and [b]the place of the
soles of My feet, [c]where I will dwell in the
midst of the children of Israel forever. [d]No
more shall the house of Israel defile My holy
name, they nor their kings, by their harlotry
or with [e]the carcasses of their kings on their
high places. 8[a]When they set their threshold
by My threshold, and their doorpost by My
doorpost, with a wall between them and Me,
they defiled My holy name by the abominations which they committed; therefore I have
consumed them in My anger. 9Now let them
put their harlotry and the carcasses of their
kings far away from Me, and I will dwell in
their midst forever.

10"Son of man, [a]describe the temple to the
house of Israel, that they may be ashamed
of their iniquities; and let them measure the
pattern. 11And if they are ashamed of all that
they have done, make known to them the
design of the temple and its arrangement,
its exits and its entrances, its entire design
and all its [a]ordinances, all its forms and all
its laws. Write *it* down in their sight, so that
they may keep its whole design and all its
ordinances, and [b]perform them. 12This *is* the
law of the temple: The whole area surrounding [a]the mountaintop *is* most holy. Behold,
this *is* the law of the temple.

Dimensions of the Altar

13"These are the measurements of the [a]al-
tar in cubits [b](the cubit *is* one cubit and a
handbreadth): the base one cubit high and

42:8 [a] Ezek. 41:13, 14 **42:11** [a] Ezek. 42:4 **42:13** [a] Lev. 6:16, 26; 24:9 [b] Lev. 2:3, 10; 6:14, 17, 25 **42:14** [a] Ezek. 44:19 **42:15** [a] Ezek. 40:6; 43:1 **42:16** [1] Compare 40:5 **42:20** [a] Ezek. 40:5 [b] Ezek. 45:2 **43:1** [a] Ezek. 10:19; 46:1 **43:2** [a] Ezek. 11:23 [b] Rev. 1:15; 14:2 [c] Rev. 18:1 **43:3** [a] Ezek. 1:4–28 [b] Jer. 1:10 [c] Ezek. 1:28; 3:23 [1] Some Hebrew manuscripts and Vulgate read *He.* **43:4** [a] Ezek. 10:19; 11:23 **43:5** [a] Ezek. 3:12, 14; 8:3 [b] 1 Kin. 8:10, 11 **43:6** [a] Ezek. 1:26; 40:3 **43:7** [a] Ps. 99:1 [b] 1 Chr. 28:2 [c] Joel 3:17 [d] Ezek. 39:7 [e] Lev. 26:30 **43:8** [a] Ezek. 8:3; 23:39; 44:7 **43:10** [a] Ezek. 40:4 **43:11** [a] Ezek. 44:5 [b] Ezek. 11:20 **43:12** [a] Ezek. 40:2 **43:13** [a] Ex. 27:1–8 [b] Ezek. 41:8

one cubit wide, with a rim all around its edge
of one span. This *is* the height of the altar:
14from the base on the ground to the lower
ledge, two cubits; the width of the ledge, one
cubit; from the smaller ledge to the larger
ledge, four cubits; and the width of the ledge,
one cubit. 15The altar hearth *is* four cubits
high, with four [a]horns extending upward
from the hearth. 16The altar hearth *is* twelve
cubits long, twelve wide, [a]square at its four
corners; 17the ledge, fourteen *cubits* long and
fourteen wide on its four sides, with a rim of
half a cubit around it; its base, one cubit all
around; and [a]its steps face toward the east."

Consecrating the Altar

18And He said to me, "Son of man, thus
says the Lord GOD: 'These *are* the ordinances
for the altar on the day when it is made, for
sacrificing [a]burnt offerings on it, and for
[b]sprinkling blood on it. 19You shall give [a]a
young bull for a sin offering to [b]the priests,
the Levites, who are of the seed of [c]Zadok,
who approach Me to minister to Me,' says the
Lord GOD. 20'You shall take some of its blood
and put *it* on the four horns of the altar, on
the four corners of the ledge, and on the rim
around it; thus you shall cleanse it and make
atonement for it. 21Then you shall also take
the bull of the sin offering, and [a]burn it in
the appointed place of the temple, [b]outside
the sanctuary. 22On the second day you shall
offer a kid of the goats without blemish for a
sin offering; and they shall cleanse the altar,
as they cleansed *it* with the bull. 23When you
have finished cleansing *it,* you shall offer a
young bull without blemish, and a ram from
the flock without blemish. 24When you offer
them before the LORD, [a]the priests shall throw
salt on them, and they will offer them up *as*
a burnt offering to the LORD. 25Every day for
[a]seven days you shall prepare a goat *for* a sin
offering; they shall also prepare a young bull
and a ram from the flock, both without blemish. 26Seven days they shall make atonement
for the altar and purify it, and so consecrate
it. 27[a]When these days are over it shall be,
on the eighth day and thereafter, that the
priests shall offer your burnt offerings and
your peace offerings on the altar; and I will
[b]accept you,' says the Lord GOD."

The East Gate and the Prince

44 Then He brought me back to the outer
gate of the sanctuary [a]which faces
toward the east, but it *was* shut. 2And the
LORD said to me, "This gate shall be shut; it
shall not be opened, and no man shall enter
by it, [a]because the LORD God of Israel has
entered by it; therefore it shall be shut. 3*As
for* the [a]prince, *because* he *is* the prince, he
may sit in it to [b]eat bread before the LORD;
he shall enter by way of the vestibule of the
gateway, and go out the same way."

43:15 [a] Ex. 27:2 **43:16** [a] Ex. 27:1 **43:17** [a] Ex. 20:26 **43:18** [a] Ex. 40:29 [b] Lev. 1:5, 11 **43:19** [a] Lev. 8:14 [b] Ezek. 44:15, 16 [c] Ezek. 40:46 **43:21** [a] Ex. 29:14 [b] Heb. 13:11 **43:24** [a] Lev. 2:13 **43:25** [a] Ex. 29:35 **43:27** [a] Lev. 9:1–4 [b] Ezek. 20:40, 41 **44:1** [a] Ezek. 43:1 **44:2** [a] Ezek. 43:2–4 **44:3** [a] Gen. 31:54 [b] Ezek. 46:2, 8

GRACE ABOUNDING

"When these days are over it shall be . . . that the priests shall offer your burnt offerings and your peace offerings on the altar; and I will accept you."

EZEKIEL 43:27

Through His prophet Ezekiel, God promised the defeated and frightened Israelites that once again they would present peace offerings and God would accept them. As it so happened, the exile did end and the people of Israel were permitted to return to their homeland, rebuild Jerusalem and the temple, and present peace offerings to God.

But Ezekiel's vision also says something to us today. It reveals God's goodness and graciousness: He is willing to give people another chance. This should give us hope that, no matter the circumstances, no matter our failings, we can find our way back to God and enjoy His peace. This is the great value of many of the Old Testament stories and the oracles of the prophets. Again and again we hear the message of God's grace and forgiveness, that God is a God of the second, third, and fourth chance. Where sin abounds, God's super-grace abounds more! This is why we can have that reassuring peace that says, *All is right between you and God.*

Those Admitted to the Temple

4 Also He brought me by way of the north gate to the front of the temple; so I looked, and [a]behold, the glory of the LORD filled the house of the LORD; [b]and I fell on my face. 5 And the LORD said to me, [a]"Son of man, mark well, see with your eyes and hear with your ears, all that I say to you concerning all the [b]ordinances of the house of the LORD and all its laws. Mark well who may enter the house and all who go out from the sanctuary.

6 "Now say to the [a]rebellious, to the house of Israel, 'Thus says the Lord GOD: "O house of Israel, [b]let Us have no more of all your abominations. 7 [a]When you brought in [b]foreigners, [c]uncircumcised in heart and uncircumcised in flesh, to be in My sanctuary to defile it—My house—and when you offered [d]My food, [e]the fat and the blood, then they broke My covenant because of all your abominations. 8 And you have not [a]kept charge of My holy things, but you have set *others* to keep charge of My sanctuary for you." 9 Thus says the Lord GOD: [a]"No foreigner, uncircumcised in heart or uncircumcised in flesh, shall enter My sanctuary, including any foreigner who *is* among the children of Israel.

Laws Governing Priests

10 [a]"And the Levites who went far from Me, when Israel went astray, who strayed away from Me after their idols, they shall bear their iniquity. 11 Yet they shall be ministers in My sanctuary, [a]*as* gatekeepers of the house and ministers of the house; [b]they shall slay the burnt offering and the sacrifice for the people, and [c]they shall stand before them to minister to them. 12 Because they ministered to them before their idols and [a]caused the house of Israel to fall into iniquity, therefore I have [b]raised My hand in an oath against them," says the Lord GOD, "that they shall bear their iniquity. 13 [a]And they shall not come near Me to minister to Me as priest, nor come near any of My holy things, nor into the Most Holy *Place;* but they shall [b]bear their shame and their abominations which they have committed. 14 Nevertheless I will make them [a]keep charge of the temple, for all its work, and for all that has to be done in it.

15 [a]"But the priests, the Levites, [b]the sons of Zadok, who kept charge of My sanctuary [c]when the children of Israel went astray from Me, they shall come near Me to minister to Me; and they [d]shall stand before Me to offer to Me the [e]fat and the blood," says the Lord GOD. 16 "They shall [a]enter My sanctuary, and they shall come near [b]My table to minister to Me, and they shall keep My charge. 17 And it shall be, whenever they enter the gates of the inner court, that [a]they shall put on linen garments; no wool shall come upon them while they minister within the gates of the inner court or within the house. 18 [a]They shall have linen turbans on their heads and linen trousers on their bodies; they shall not clothe themselves with *anything that causes* sweat. 19 When they go out to the outer court, to the outer court to the people, [a]they shall take off their garments in which they have ministered, leave them in the holy chambers, and put on other garments; and in their holy garments they shall [b]not sanctify the people.

20 [a]"They shall neither shave their heads nor let their hair grow [b]long, but they shall keep their hair well trimmed. 21 [a]No priest shall drink wine when he enters the inner court. 22 They shall not take as wife a [a]widow or a divorced woman, but take virgins of the descendants of the house of Israel, or widows of priests.

23 "And [a]they shall teach My people *the difference* between the holy and the unholy, and cause them to [b]discern between the unclean and the clean. 24 [a]In controversy they shall stand as judges, *and* judge it according to My judgments. They shall keep My laws and My statutes in all My appointed meetings, [b]and they shall hallow My Sabbaths.

25 "They shall not defile *themselves* by coming near a dead person. Only for father or mother, for son or daughter, for brother or unmarried sister may they defile themselves. 26 [a]After he is cleansed, they shall count seven days for him. 27 And on the day that he goes to the sanctuary to minister in the sanctuary, [a]he must offer his sin offering [b]in the inner court," says the Lord GOD.

28 "It shall be, in regard to their inheritance, *that* I [a]*am* their inheritance. You shall give them no [b]possession in Israel, for I *am* their possession. 29 [a]They shall eat the grain offering, the sin offering, and the trespass offering; [b]every dedicated thing in Israel shall be theirs. 30 The [a]best of all firstfruits of any kind, and every sacrifice of any kind from

44:4 [a] Ezek. 3:23; 43:5 [b] Ezek. 1:28; 43:3 **44:5** [a] Ezek. 40:4 [b] Ezek. 43:10, 11 **44:6** [a] Ezek. 2:5 [b] 1 Pet. 4:3 **44:7** [a] Acts 21:28 [b] Lev. 22:25 [c] Lev. 26:41 [d] Lev. 21:17 [e] Lev. 3:16 **44:8** [a] Lev. 22:2 **44:9** [a] Ezek. 44:7 **44:10** [a] 2 Kin. 23:8 **44:11** [a] 1 Chr. 26:1–19 [b] 2 Chr. 29:34; 30:17 [c] Num. 16:9 **44:12** [a] Is. 9:16 [b] Ps. 106:26 **44:13** [a] 2 Kin. 23:9 [b] Ezek. 32:30 **44:14** [a] Num. 18:4 **44:15** [a] Ezek. 40:46 [b] [1 Sam. 2:35] [c] Ezek. 44:10 [d] Deut. 10:8 [e] Ezek. 44:7 **44:16** [a] Num. 18:5, 7, 8 [b] Ezek. 41:22 **44:17** [a] Ex. 28:39–43; 39:27–29 **44:18** [a] Ex. 28:40; 39:28 **44:19** [a] Ezek. 42:14 [b] Lev. 6:27 **44:20** [a] Lev. 21:5 [b] Num. 6:5 **44:21** [a] Lev. 10:9 **44:22** [a] Lev. 21:7, 13, 14 **44:23** [a] Mal. 2:6–8 [b] Lev. 20:25 **44:24** [a] Deut. 17:8, 9 [b] Ezek. 22:26 **44:26** [a] Num. 6:10; 19:11, 13–19 **44:27** [a] Lev. 5:3, 6 [b] Ezek. 44:17 **44:28** [a] Num. 18:20 [b] Ezek. 45:4 **44:29** [a] Lev. 7:6 [b] Lev. 27:21, 28 **44:30** [a] Num. 3:13; 18:12

all your sacrifices, shall be the priest's; also you [b]shall give to the priest the first of your ground meal, [c]to cause a blessing to rest on your house. 31The priests shall not eat anything, bird or beast, that [a]died naturally or was torn *by wild beasts.*

The Holy District

45 "Moreover, when you [a]divide the land by lot into inheritance, you shall [b]set apart a district for the LORD, a holy section of the land; its length *shall be* twenty-five thousand *cubits,* and the width ten thousand. It *shall be* holy throughout its territory all around. 2Of this there shall be a square plot for the sanctuary, [a]five hundred by five hundred *rods,* with fifty cubits around it for an open space. 3So this is the district you shall measure: twenty-five thousand *cubits* long and ten thousand wide; [a]in it shall be the sanctuary, the Most Holy *Place.* 4It shall be [a]a holy *section* of the land, belonging to the priests, the ministers of the sanctuary, who come near to minister to the LORD; it shall be a place for their houses and a holy place for the sanctuary. 5[a]*An area* twenty-five thousand *cubits* long and ten thousand wide shall belong to the Levites, the ministers of the temple; they shall have [b]twenty chambers as a possession.[1]

Properties of the City and the Prince

6[a]"You shall appoint as the property of the city *an area* five thousand *cubits* wide and twenty-five thousand long, adjacent to the district of the holy *section;* it shall belong to the whole house of Israel.

7[a]"The prince shall have *a section* on one side and the other of the holy district and the city's property; and bordering on the holy district and the city's property, extending westward on the west side and eastward on the east side, the length *shall be* side by side with one of the *tribal* portions, from the west border to the east border. 8The land shall be his possession in Israel; and [a]My princes shall no more oppress My people, but they shall give *the rest of* the land to the house of Israel, according to their tribes."

Laws Governing the Prince

9'Thus says the Lord GOD: [a]"Enough, O princes of Israel! [b]Remove violence and plundering, execute justice and righteousness, and stop dispossessing My people," says the Lord GOD. 10"You shall have [a]honest scales, an honest ephah, and an honest bath. 11The ephah and the bath shall be of the same measure, so that the bath contains one-tenth of a homer, and the ephah one-tenth of a homer; their measure shall be according to the homer. 12The [a]shekel *shall be* twenty gerahs; twenty shekels, twenty-five shekels, *and* fifteen shekels shall be your mina.

13"This *is* the offering which you shall offer: you shall give one-sixth of an ephah from a homer of wheat, and one-sixth of an ephah from a homer of barley. 14The ordinance concerning oil, the bath of oil, *is* one-tenth of a bath from a kor. *A kor is* a homer or ten baths, for ten baths *are* a homer. 15And one lamb shall be given from a flock of two hundred, from the rich pastures of Israel. These shall be for grain offerings, burnt offerings, and peace offerings, [a]to make atonement for them," says the Lord GOD. 16"All the people of the land shall give this offering for the prince in Israel. 17Then it shall be the [a]prince's part *to give* burnt offerings, grain offerings, and drink offerings, at the feasts, the New Moons, the Sabbaths, and at all the appointed seasons of the house of Israel. He shall prepare the sin offering, the grain offering, the burnt offering, and the peace offerings to make atonement for the house of Israel."

Keeping the Feasts

18'Thus says the Lord GOD: "In the first *month,* on the first *day* of the month, you shall take a young bull without blemish and [a]cleanse the sanctuary. 19[a]The priest shall take some of the blood of the sin offering and put *it* on the doorposts of the temple, on the four corners of the ledge of the altar, and on the gateposts of the gate of the inner court. 20And so you shall do on the seventh *day* of the month [a]for everyone who has sinned unintentionally or in ignorance. Thus you shall make atonement for the temple.

21[a]"In the first *month,* on the fourteenth day of the month, you shall observe the Passover, a feast of seven days; unleavened bread shall be eaten. 22And on that day the prince shall prepare for himself and for all the people of the land [a]a bull *for* a sin offering. 23On the [a]seven days of the feast he shall prepare a burnt offering to the LORD, seven bulls and seven rams without blemish, daily for seven days, [b]and a kid of the goats daily *for* a sin offering. 24[a]And he shall prepare a grain offering of one

44:30 [b] Neh. 10:37 [c] [Mal. 3:10] **44:31** [a] Lev. 22:8 **45:1** [a] Ezek. 47:22 [b] Ezek. 48:8, 9 **45:2** [a] Ezek. 42:20 **45:3** [a] Ezek. 48:10 **45:4** [a] Ezek. 48:10, 11 **45:5** [a] Ezek. 48:13 [b] Ezek. 40:17 [1] Following Masoretic Text, Targum, and Vulgate; Septuagint reads *a possession, cities of dwelling.* **45:6** [a] Ezek. 48:15 **45:7** [a] Ezek. 48:21 **45:8** [a] Ezek. 22:27 **45:9** [a] Ezek. 44:6 [b] Jer. 22:3 **45:10** [a] Lev. 19:36 **45:12** [a] Ex. 30:13 **45:15** [a] Lev. 1:4; 6:30 **45:17** [a] Ezek. 46:4–12 **45:18** [a] Lev. 16:16, 33 **45:19** [a] Ezek. 43:20 **45:20** [a] Lev. 4:27 **45:21** [a] Ex. 12:18 **45:22** [a] Lev. 4:14 **45:23** [a] Lev. 23:8 [b] Num. 28:15, 22, 30; 29:5, 11, 16, 19 **45:24** [a] Ezek. 46:5, 7

SUPERHIGHWAY OF PEACE

"He shall prepare . . . the peace offerings to make atonement for the house of Israel."

EZEKIEL 45:17

Israel's sin against God was so egregious that the prophets Isaiah and Jeremiah proclaimed, "There will be no atonement for you" (Is. 22:14), and "Provide no atonement for their iniquity" (Jer. 18:23). Understood in context, these prophets announced to apostate Israel that judgment could not be averted. The nation would fall to her enemies. Of course, that judgment was spoken against the nation as a whole and at a specific time in the nation's history. Ezekiel was thinking of a future repentant remnant when he spoke of "peace offerings to make atonement" (Ezek. 45:17). Isaiah's dreadful announcement that atonement no longer existed would someday be annulled. Someday Israel could once again make peace offerings and enjoy a right relationship with God.

The good news today is that, in the death of Jesus Christ, the ultimate peace offering was made. In Him we can find atonement and lasting peace. You may feel as though God has forgotten you. Don't forget, God built a superhighway to save you and bring you tidings of peace (see Is. 40:1–8). Nothing will stand in the way of Jesus forgiving you and bringing His peace to your life if you trust in Him, repent of all sins, and follow Him.

ephah for each bull and one ephah for each
ram, together with a hin of oil for each ephah.
25"In the seventh *month*, on the fifteenth
day of the month, at the [a]feast, he shall do
likewise for seven days, according to the
sin offering, the burnt offering, the grain
offering, and the oil."

The Manner of Worship

46 'Thus says the Lord GOD: "The gateway
of the inner court that faces toward the
east shall be shut the six [a]working days; but
on the Sabbath it shall be opened, and on the
day of the New Moon it shall be opened. 2[a]The
prince shall enter by way of the vestibule of
the gateway from the outside, and stand by
the gatepost. The priests shall prepare his
burnt offering and his peace offerings. He
shall worship at the threshold of the gate.
Then he shall go out, but the gate shall not
be shut until evening. 3Likewise the people
of the land shall worship at the entrance to
this gateway before the LORD on the Sabbaths
and the New Moons. 4The burnt offering that
[a]*the prince offers to the* LORD on the [b]Sab-
bath day *shall be* six lambs without blemish,
and a ram without blemish; 5[a]and the grain
offering *shall be one* ephah for a ram, and the
grain offering for the lambs, as much as he
wants to give, as well as a hin of oil with every
ephah. 6On the day of the New Moon *it shall
be* a young bull without blemish, six lambs,
and a ram; they shall be without blemish. 7He
shall prepare a grain offering of an ephah
for a bull, an ephah for a ram, as much as he
wants to give for the lambs, and a hin of oil
with every ephah. 8[a]When the prince enters,
he shall go in by way of the vestibule of the
gateway, and go out the same way.
9"But when the people of the land [a]come
before the LORD on the appointed feast days,
whoever enters by way of the north [b]gate to
worship shall go out by way of the south gate;
and whoever enters by way of the south gate
shall go out by way of the north gate. He shall
not return by way of the gate through which
he came, but shall go out through the opposite
gate. 10The prince shall then be in their midst.
When they go in, he shall go in; and when they
go out, he shall go out. 11At the festivals and the
appointed feast days [a]the grain offering shall
be an ephah for a bull, an ephah for a ram, as
much as he wants to give for the lambs, and
a hin of oil with every ephah.
12"Now when the prince makes a voluntary
burnt offering or voluntary peace offering to
the LORD, the gate that faces toward the east
[a]shall then be opened for him; and he shall prepare his burnt offering and his peace offerings
as he did on the Sabbath day. Then he shall go
out, and after he goes out the gate shall be shut.
13[a]"You shall daily make a burnt offering to
the LORD *of* a lamb of the first year without
blemish; you shall prepare it every morning.

45:25 [a] Num. 29:12 **46:1** [a] Ex. 20:9 **46:2** [a] Ezek. 44:3 **46:4** [a] Ezek. 45:17 [b] Num. 28:9, 10 **46:5** [a] Ezek. 45:24; 46:7, 11 **46:8** [a] Ezek. 44:3; 46:2 **46:9** [a] Ex. 23:14–17; 34:23 [b] Ezek. 48:31, 33 **46:11** [a] Ezek. 46:5, 7 **46:12** [a] Ezek. 44:3; 46:1, 2, 8 **46:13** [a] Num. 28:3–5

14 And you shall prepare a grain offering with it every morning, a sixth of an ephah, and a third of a hin of oil to moisten the fine flour. This grain offering is a perpetual ordinance, to be made regularly to the LORD. 15 Thus they shall prepare the lamb, the grain offering, and the oil, *as* a [a]regular burnt offering every morning."

The Prince and Inheritance Laws

16 'Thus says the Lord GOD: "If the prince gives a gift *of some* of his inheritance to any of his sons, it shall belong to his sons; it is their possession by inheritance. 17 But if he gives a gift of some of his inheritance to one of his servants, it shall be his until [a]the year of liberty, after which it shall return to the prince. But his inheritance shall belong to his sons; it shall become theirs. 18 Moreover [a]the prince shall not take any of the people's inheritance by evicting them from their property; he shall provide an inheritance for his sons from his own property, so that none of My people may be scattered from his property." ' "

How the Offerings Were Prepared

19 Now he brought me through the entrance, which *was* at the side of the gate, into the holy [a]chambers of the priests which face toward the north; and there a place *was* situated at their extreme western end. 20 And he said to me, "This *is* the place where the priests shall [a]boil the trespass offering and the sin offering, *and* where they shall [b]bake the grain offering, so that they do not bring *them* out into the outer court [c]to sanctify the people."

21 Then he brought me out into the outer court and caused me to pass by the four corners of the court; and in fact, in every corner of the court *there was another* court. 22 In the four corners of the court *were* enclosed courts, forty *cubits* long and thirty wide; all four corners *were* the same size. 23 *There was* a row *of building stones* all around in them, all around the four of them; and cooking hearths were made under the rows of stones all around. 24 And he said to me, "These *are* the kitchens where the ministers of the temple shall [a]boil the sacrifices of the people."

The Healing Waters and Trees

47 Then he brought me back to the door of the temple; and there was [a]water, flowing from under the threshold of the temple toward the east, for the front of the temple *faced* east; the water was flowing from under the right side of the temple, south of the altar. 2 He brought me out by way of the north gate,

PEACE NOTE

Jesus can break anything that keeps us in bondage! Stop and pray for a person who needs to turn from Satan's power to God so he or she can find Jesus' everlasting peace.

and led me around on the outside to the outer gateway that faces [a]east; and there was water, running out on the right side.

3 And when [a]the man went out to the east with the line in his hand, he measured one thousand cubits, and he brought me through the waters; the water *came up to my* ankles. 4 Again he measured one thousand and brought me through the waters; the water *came up to my* knees. Again he measured one thousand and brought me through; the water *came up to my* waist. 5 Again he measured one thousand, *and it was* a river that I could not cross; for the water was too deep, water in which one must swim, a river that could not be crossed. 6 He said to me, "Son of man, have you seen *this?*" Then he brought me and returned me to the bank of the river.

7 When I returned, there, along the bank of the river, *were* very many [a]trees on one side and the other. 8 Then he said to me: "This water flows toward the eastern region, goes down into the valley, and enters the sea. *When it* reaches the sea, *its* waters are healed. 9 And it shall be *that* every living thing that moves, wherever the rivers go, will live. There will be a very great multitude of fish, because these waters go there; for they will be healed, and everything will live wherever the river goes. 10 It shall be *that* fishermen will stand by it from En Gedi to En Eglaim; they will be *places* for spreading their nets. Their fish will be of the same kinds as the fish [a]of the Great Sea, exceedingly many. 11 But its swamps and marshes will not be healed; they will be given over to salt. 12 [a]Along the bank of the river, on this side and that, will grow all *kinds of* trees used for food; [b]their leaves will not

46:15 [a] Ex. 29:42 **46:17** [a] Lev. 25:10 **46:18** [a] Ezek. 45:8 **46:19** [a] Ezek. 42:13 **46:20** [a] 2 Chr. 35:13 [b] Lev. 2:4, 5, 7 [c] Ezek. 44:19 **46:24** [a] Ezek. 46:20 **47:1** [a] Joel 3:18 **47:2** [a] Ezek. 44:1, 2 **47:3** [a] Ezek. 40:3 **47:7** [a] [Rev. 22:2] **47:10** [a] Num. 34:3 **47:12** [a] Ezek. 47:7 [b] [Jer. 17:8]

wither, and their fruit will not fail. They will bear fruit every month, because their water flows from the sanctuary. Their fruit will be for food, and their leaves for [c]medicine."

Borders of the Land

13Thus says the Lord GOD: "These *are* the [a]borders by which you shall divide the land as an inheritance among the twelve tribes of Israel. [b]Joseph *shall have two* portions. 14You shall inherit it equally with one another; for I [a]raised My hand in an oath to give it to your fathers, and this land shall [b]fall to you as your inheritance.

15"This *shall be* the border of the land on the north: from the Great Sea, *by* [a]the road to Hethlon, as one goes to [b]Zedad, 16[a]Hamath, [b]Berothah, Sibraim (which *is* between the border of Damascus and the border of Hamath), to Hazar Hatticon (which *is* on the border of Hauran). 17Thus the boundary shall be from the Sea to [a]Hazar Enan, the border of Damascus; and as for the north, northward, it is the border of Hamath. *This is* the north side.

18"On the east side you shall mark out the border from between Hauran and Damascus, and between Gilead and the land of Israel, along the Jordan, and along the eastern side of the sea. *This is* the east side.

19"The south side, toward the South,[1] *shall be* from Tamar to [a]the waters of Meribah by Kadesh, along the brook to the Great Sea. *This is* the south side, toward the South.

20"The west side *shall be* the Great Sea, from the *southern* boundary until one comes to a point opposite Hamath. This *is* the west side.

21"Thus you shall [a]divide this land among yourselves according to the tribes of Israel. 22It shall be that you will divide it by [a]lot as an inheritance for yourselves, [b]and for the strangers who dwell among you and who bear children among you. [c]They shall be to you as native-born among the children of Israel; they shall have an inheritance with you among the tribes of Israel. 23And it shall be *that* in whatever tribe the stranger dwells, there you shall give *him* his inheritance," says the Lord GOD.

Division of the Land

48 "Now these *are* the names of the tribes: [a]From the northern border along the road to Hethlon at the entrance of Hamath, to Hazar Enan, the border of Damascus northward, in the direction of Hamath, *there shall be* one *section for* [b]Dan from its east to its west side; 2by the border of Dan, from the east side to the west, one *section for* [a]Asher; 3by the border of Asher, from the east side to the west, one *section for* [a]Naphtali; 4by the border of Naphtali, from the east side to the west, one *section for* [a]Manasseh; 5by the border of Manasseh, from the east side to the west, one *section for* [a]Ephraim; 6by the border of Ephraim, from the east side to the west, one *section for* [a]Reuben; 7by the border of Reuben, from the east side to the west, one *section for* [a]Judah; 8by the border of Judah, from the east side to the west, shall be [a]the district which you shall set apart, twenty-five thousand *cubits* in width, and *in* length the same as one of the *other* portions, from the east side to the west, with the [b]sanctuary in the center.

9"The district that you shall set apart for the LORD *shall be* twenty-five thousand *cubits* in length and ten thousand in width. 10To these—to the priests—the holy district shall belong: on the north twenty-five thousand *cubits in length,* on the west ten thousand in width, on the east ten thousand in width, and on the south twenty-five thousand in length. The sanctuary of the LORD shall be in the center. 11[a]*It shall be* for the priests of the sons of Zadok, who are sanctified, who have kept My charge, who did not go astray when the children of Israel went astray, [b]as the Levites went astray. 12And *this* district of land that is set apart shall be to them a thing most [a]holy by the border of the Levites.

13"Opposite the border of the priests, the [a]Levites *shall have an area* twenty-five thousand *cubits* in length and ten thousand in width; its entire length *shall be* twenty-five thousand and its width ten thousand. 14[a]And they shall not sell or exchange any of it; they may not alienate this best *part* of the land, for *it is* holy to the LORD.

15[a]"The five thousand *cubits* in width that remain, along the edge of the twenty-five thousand, shall be [b]for general use by the city, for dwellings and common-land; and the city shall be in the center. 16These *shall be* its measurements: the north side four thousand five hundred *cubits,* the south side four thousand five hundred, the east side four thousand five hundred, and the west side four thousand five hundred.

47:12 [c] [Rev. 22:2] **47:13** [a] Num. 34:1–29 [b] Gen. 48:5 **47:14** [a] Ezek. 20:5, 6, 28, 42 [b] Ezek. 48:29 **47:15** [a] Ezek. 48:1 [b] Num. 34:7, 8 **47:16** [a] Num. 34:8 [b] 2 Sam. 8:8 **47:17** [a] Num. 34:9 **47:19** [a] Ps. 81:7 [1] Hebrew *Negev* **47:21** [a] Ezek. 45:1 **47:22** [a] Num. 26:55, 56 [b] [Eph. 3:6] [c] [Col. 3:11] **48:1** [a] Ezek. 47:15 [b] Josh. 19:40–48 **48:2** [a] Josh. 19:24–31 **48:3** [a] Josh. 19:32–39 **48:4** [a] Josh. 13:29–31; 17:1–11, 17, 18 **48:5** [a] Josh. 16:5–10; 17:8–10, 14–18 **48:6** [a] Josh. 13:15–23 **48:7** [a] Josh. 15:1–63; 19:9 **48:8** [a] Ezek. 45:1–6 [b] [Is. 12:6; 33:20–22] **48:11** [a] Ezek. 40:46; 44:15 [b] Ezek. 44:10, 12 **48:12** [a] Ezek. 45:4 **48:13** [a] Ezek. 45:5 **48:14** [a] Lev. 27:10, 28, 33 **48:15** [a] Ezek. 45:6 [b] Ezek. 42:20

17The common-land of the city shall be: to the north two hundred and fifty *cubits,* to the south two hundred and fifty, to the east two hundred and fifty, and to the west two hundred and fifty. 18The rest of the length, alongside the district of the holy *section, shall be* ten thousand *cubits* to the east and ten thousand to the west. It shall be adjacent to the district of the holy *section,* and its produce shall be food for the workers of the city. 19[a]The workers of the city, from all the tribes of Israel, shall cultivate it. 20The entire district *shall be* twenty-five thousand *cubits* by twenty-five thousand *cubits,* foursquare. You shall set apart the holy district with the property of the city.

21[a]"The rest *shall belong* to the prince, on one side and on the other of the holy district and of the city's property, next to the twenty-five thousand *cubits* of the *holy* district as far as the eastern border, and westward next to the twenty-five thousand as far as the western border, adjacent to the *tribal* portions; *it shall belong* to the prince. It shall be the holy district, [b]and the sanctuary of the temple *shall be* in the center. 22Moreover, apart from the possession of the Levites and the possession of the city *which are* in the midst of what *belongs* to the prince, *the area* between the border of Judah and the border of [a]Benjamin shall belong to the prince.

23"As for the rest of the tribes, from the east side to the west, Benjamin *shall have* one *section;* 24by the border of Benjamin, from the east side to the west, [a]Simeon *shall have* one *section;* 25by the border of Simeon, from the east side to the west, [a]Issachar *shall have* one *section;* 26by the border of Issachar, from the east side to the west, [a]Zebulun *shall have* one *section;* 27by the border of Zebulun, from the east side to the west, [a]Gad *shall have* one *section;* 28by the border of Gad, on the south side, toward the South,[1] the border shall be from Tamar *to* [a]the waters of Meribah *by* Kadesh, along the brook to the [b]Great Sea. 29[a]This *is* the land which you shall divide by lot as an inheritance among the tribes of Israel, and these *are* their portions," says the Lord GOD.

The Gates of the City and Its Name

30"These *are* the exits of the city. On the north side, measuring four thousand five hundred *cubits* 31[a](the gates of the city *shall be* named after the tribes of Israel), the three gates northward: one gate for Reuben, one gate for Judah, and one gate for Levi; 32on the east side, four thousand five hundred *cubits,* three gates: one gate for Joseph, one gate for Benjamin, and one gate for Dan; 33on the south side, measuring four thousand five hundred *cubits,* three gates: one gate for Simeon, one gate for Issachar, and one gate for Zebulun; 34on the west side, four thousand five hundred *cubits* with their three gates: one gate for Gad, one gate for Asher, and one gate for Naphtali. 35All the way around *shall be* eighteen thousand *cubits;* [a]and the name of the city from *that* day *shall be:* [b]THE LORD *IS* THERE."[1]

48:19 [a] Ezek. 45:6 **48:21** [a] Ezek. 34:24; 45:7; 48:22 [b] Ezek. 48:8, 10 **48:22** [a] Josh. 18:21–28 **48:24** [a] Josh. 19:1–9 **48:25** [a] Josh. 19:17–23 **48:26** [a] Josh. 19:10–16 **48:27** [a] Josh. 13:24–28 **48:28** [a] Ezek. 47:19 [b] Ezek. 47:10, 15, 19, 20 [1] Hebrew *Negev* **48:29** [a] Ezek. 47:14, 21, 22 **48:31** [a] [Rev. 21:10–14] **48:35** [a] Jer. 23:6; 33:16 [b] Joel 3:21 [1] Hebrew *YHWH Shammah*

THE BOOK OF DANIEL

AUTHOR

Daniel's life and ministry bridge the entire seventy-year period of Babylonian captivity. This book claims Daniel as author, and it is written in the first person from Daniel 7:2 onward. The Jewish Talmud supports this claim, and Christ attributed a quote from 9:27 to "Daniel the prophet" (Matt. 24:15). Daniel's wisdom and divinely given interpretive abilities brought him into a position of prominence, especially in the courts of Nebuchadnezzar and Darius.

TIME

c. 605–536 BC

KEY VERSE

Daniel 2:20–22

THEME

Daniel is one of very few heroes in the Bible whose record is flawless. He is an example of how to live and work as a believer in a hostile environment; he was a man of action while at the same time fully aware of his dependence on God. The important prophecies in Daniel have inspired many interpretations over the years. Many have attempted to identify the various elements of the prophecies and apply them to contemporary figures.

The peace of God arrived in a most unique way in the Book of Daniel: through angelic visitation! Gabriel appeared to Daniel in response to his prayers to God and said, "O man greatly beloved, fear not! Peace be to you; be strong, yes, be strong!" (10:19). The result was divine and immediate replenishing for Daniel as he reported, "The one having the likeness of a man touched me and strengthened me . . . When he spoke to me I was strengthened" (10:18–19). What we will learn from Daniel's faithfulness to God is that the Lord sends angels to minister to us, too, and they speak words of peace in response to our prayers, trust in the Lord, and faithful obedience. We are vividly reminded of how the peace of God can immediately renew us.

Daniel and His Friends Obey God

1 In the third year of the reign of [a]Jehoiakim king of Judah, Nebuchadnezzar king of Babylon came to Jerusalem and besieged it. 2 And the Lord gave Jehoiakim king of Judah into his hand, with [a]some of the articles of the house of God, which he carried [b]into the land of Shinar to the house of his god; [c]and he brought the articles into the treasure house of his god.

3 Then the king instructed Ashpenaz, the master of his eunuchs, to bring [a]some of the children of Israel and some of the king's descendants and some of the nobles, 4 young men [a]in whom *there was* no blemish, but good-looking, gifted in all wisdom, possessing knowledge and quick to understand, who *had* ability to serve in the king's palace, and [b]whom they might teach the language and literature of the Chaldeans. 5 And the king appointed for them a daily provision of the king's delicacies and of the wine which he drank, and three years of training for them, so that at the end of *that time* they might [a]serve before the king. 6 Now from among those of the sons of Judah were Daniel, Hananiah, Mishael, and Azariah. 7 [a]To them the chief of the eunuchs gave names: [b]he gave Daniel *the name* Belteshazzar; to Hananiah, Shadrach; to Mishael, Meshach; and to Azariah, Abed-Nego.

8 But Daniel purposed in his heart that he would not defile himself [a]with the portion of the king's delicacies, nor with the wine which he drank; therefore he requested of the chief of the eunuchs that he might not defile himself. 9 Now [a]God had brought Daniel into the favor and goodwill of the chief of the eunuchs. 10 And the chief of the eunuchs said to Daniel, "I fear my lord the king, who has appointed your food and drink. For why should he see your faces looking worse than the young men who *are* your age? Then you would endanger my head before the king."

11 So Daniel said to the steward[1] whom the chief of the eunuchs had set over Daniel, Hananiah, Mishael, and Azariah, 12 "Please test your servants for ten days, and let them give us vegetables to eat and water to drink. 13 Then let our appearance be examined before you, and the appearance of the young men who eat the portion of the king's delicacies; and as you see fit, *so* deal with your servants." 14 So he consented with them in this matter, and tested them ten days.

15 And at the end of ten days their features appeared better and fatter in flesh than all the young men who ate the portion of the king's delicacies. 16 Thus the steward took away their portion of delicacies and the wine that they were to drink, and gave them vegetables.

1:1 [a] 2 Kin. 24:1, 2 **1:2** [a] Jer. 27:19, 20 [b] Zech. 5:11 [c] 2 Chr. 36:7 **1:3** [a] Is. 39:7 **1:4** [a] Lev. 24:19, 20 [b] Acts 7:22 **1:5** [a] Dan. 1:19 **1:7** [a] 2 Kin. 24:17 [b] Dan. 2:26; 4:8; 5:12 **1:8** [a] Hos. 9:3 **1:9** [a] Gen. 39:21 **1:11** [1] Hebrew *Melzar,* also in verse 16

DECIDING FOR PEACE WITH GOD

Daniel purposed in his heart that he would not defile himself with the portion of the king's delicacies.

DANIEL 1:8

The young Daniel found himself exiled to Babylon along with thousands of Jews after the army of Nebuchadnezzar conquered Jerusalem and destroyed the temple. Daniel and several other elite Jewish young men were to receive training in Babylonian ways, but some of these ways, including the food they ate, were contrary to God's law. Daniel was in a tough spot. He could go along with his new employers' expectations—and probably thrive and enjoy advancement—or he could stand by his convictions and possibly suffer negative consequences. Daniel chose the latter. As it turned out, God blessed Daniel and his companions: "God had brought Daniel into the favor and goodwill of the chief of the eunuchs" (v. 9).

Lasting peace comes from doing the right thing despite enormous pressure to do otherwise. This is what a character of peace requires. You have the ability to turn away from the Lord at any time, but instead you choose the narrow way of following Jesus. That is the way of peace. Choose it every day.

Have you turned down "the portion of the king's delicacies" (v. 8)? What was the result?

17As for these four young men, [a]God gave
them [b]knowledge and skill in all literature
and wisdom; and Daniel had [c]understanding
in all visions and dreams.

18Now at the end of the days, when the
king had said that they should be brought
in, the chief of the eunuchs brought them
in before Nebuchadnezzar. 19Then the king
interviewed[1] them, and among them all none
was found like Daniel, Hananiah, Mishael,
and Azariah; therefore [a]they served before
the king. 20[a]And in all matters of wisdom
and understanding about which the king
examined them, he found them ten times
better than all the magicians *and* astrologers
who *were* in all his realm. 21[a]Thus Daniel
continued until the first year of King Cyrus.

Nebuchadnezzar's Dream

2 Now in the second year of Nebuchadnezzar's reign, Nebuchadnezzar had dreams;
[a]and his spirit was *so* troubled that [b]his sleep
left him. 2[a]Then the king gave the command
to call the magicians, the astrologers, the
sorcerers, and the Chaldeans to tell the king
his dreams. So they came and stood before
the king. 3And the king said to them, "I have
had a dream, and my spirit is anxious to
know the dream."

4Then the Chaldeans spoke to the king
in Aramaic,[1] [a]"O king, live forever! Tell your
servants the dream, and we will give the
interpretation."

5The king answered and said to the Chaldeans, "My decision is firm: if you do not make
known the dream to me, and its interpretation, you shall be [a]cut in pieces, and your
houses shall be made an ash heap. 6[a]Howev-
er, if you tell the dream and its interpretation,
you shall receive from me gifts, rewards, and
great honor. Therefore tell me the dream and
its interpretation."

7They answered again and said, "Let the
king tell his servants the dream, and we will
give its interpretation."

8The king answered and said, "I know for
certain that you would gain time, because
you see that my decision is firm: 9if you do
not make known the dream to me, *there is*
only one decree for you! For you have agreed
to speak lying and corrupt words before me
till the time has changed. Therefore tell me
the dream, and I shall know that you can give
me its interpretation."

10The Chaldeans answered the king, and
said, "There is not a man on earth who can
tell the king's matter; therefore no king, lord,
or ruler has *ever* asked such things of any
magician, astrologer, or Chaldean. 11*It is* a difficult thing that the king requests, and there
is no other who can tell it to the king [a]except
the gods, whose dwelling is not with flesh."

12For this reason the king was angry and
very furious, and gave the command to destroy all the wise *men* of Babylon. 13So the
decree went out, and they began killing the
wise *men;* and they sought [a]Daniel and his
companions, to kill *them.*

God Reveals Nebuchadnezzar's Dream

14Then with counsel and wisdom Daniel
answered Arioch, the captain of the king's
guard, who had gone out to kill the wise *men*
of Babylon; 15he answered and said to Arioch
the king's captain, "Why is the decree from
the king so urgent?" Then Arioch made the
decision known to Daniel.

16So Daniel went in and asked the king to
give him time, that he might tell the king
the interpretation. 17Then Daniel went to his
house, and made the decision known to Hananiah, Mishael, and Azariah, his companions,
18[a]that they might seek mercies from the God
of heaven concerning this secret, so that Daniel and his companions might not perish with
the rest of the wise *men* of Babylon. 19Then
the secret was revealed to Daniel [a]in a night
vision. So Daniel blessed the God of heaven.

20Daniel answered and said:

[a]"Blessed be the name of God forever
and ever,
[b]For wisdom and might are His.
21 And He changes [a]the times and the
seasons;
[b]He removes kings and raises up kings;
[c]He gives wisdom to the wise
And knowledge to those who have
understanding.
22 [a]He reveals deep and secret things;
[b]He knows what *is* in the darkness,
And [c]light dwells with Him.

23 "I thank You and praise You,
O God of my fathers;
You have given me wisdom and might,
And have now made known to me what
we [a]asked of You,
For You have made known to us the
king's demand."

1:17 [a] [James 1:5–7] [b] Acts 7:22 [c] 2 Chr. 26:5 **1:19** [a] Gen. 41:46 [1] Literally *talked with them* **1:20** [a] 1 Kin. 10:1
1:21 [a] Dan. 6:28; 10:1 **2:1** [a] Gen. 40:5–8; 41:1, 8 [b] Esth. 6:1 **2:2** [a] Ex. 7:11 **2:4** [a] Dan. 3:9; 5:10; 6:6, 21 [1] The original language of Daniel 2:4b through 7:28 is Aramaic. **2:5** [a] Ezra 6:11 **2:6** [a] Dan. 5:16 **2:11** [a] Dan. 5:11 **2:13** [a] Dan. 1:19, 20
2:18 [a] [Matt. 18:19] **2:19** [a] Job 33:15 **2:20** [a] Ps. 113:2 [b] [Jer. 32:19] **2:21** [a] Esth. 1:13 [b] [Ps. 75:6, 7] [c] [James 1:5]
2:22 [a] Ps. 25:14 [b] [Heb. 4:13] [c] Dan. 5:11, 14 **2:23** [a] Dan. 2:18, 29, 30

Daniel Explains the Dream

24 Therefore Daniel went to Arioch, whom the king had appointed to destroy the wise *men* of Babylon. He went and said thus to him: "Do not destroy the wise *men* of Babylon; take me before the king, and I will tell the king the interpretation."

25 Then Arioch quickly brought Daniel before the king, and said thus to him, "I have found a man of the captives[1] of Judah, who will make known to the king the interpretation."

26 The king answered and said to Daniel, whose name *was* Belteshazzar, "Are you able to make known to me the dream which I have seen, and its interpretation?"

27 Daniel answered in the presence of the king, and said, "The secret which the king has demanded, the wise *men,* the astrologers, the magicians, and the soothsayers cannot declare to the king. 28 [a]But there is a God in heaven who reveals secrets, and He has made known to King Nebuchadnezzar [b]what will be in the latter days. Your dream, and the visions of your head upon your bed, were these: 29 As for you, O king, thoughts came *to* your *mind while* on your bed, *about* what would come to pass after this; [a]and He who reveals secrets has made known to you what will be. 30 [a]But as for me, this secret has not been revealed to me because I have more wisdom than anyone living, but for *our* sakes who make known the interpretation to the king, [b]and that you may know the thoughts of your heart.

31 "You, O king, were watching; and behold, a great image! This great image, whose splendor *was* excellent, stood before you; and its form *was* awesome. 32 [a]This image's head *was* of fine gold, its chest and arms of silver, its belly and thighs[1] of bronze, 33 its legs of iron, its feet partly of iron and partly of clay.[1] 34 You watched while a stone was cut out [a]without hands, which struck the image on its feet of iron and clay, and broke them in pieces. 35 [a]Then the iron, the clay, the bronze, the silver, and the gold were crushed together, and became [b]like chaff from the summer threshing floors; the wind carried them away so that [c]no trace of them was found. And the stone that struck the image [d]became a great mountain [e]and filled the whole earth.

36 "This *is* the dream. Now we will tell the interpretation of it before the king. 37 [a]You, O king, *are* a king of kings. [b]For the God of heaven has given you a kingdom, power, strength, and glory; 38 [a]and wherever the children of men dwell, or the beasts of the field and the birds of the heaven, He has given *them* into your hand, and has made you ruler over them all—[b]you *are* this head of gold. 39 But after you shall arise [a]another kingdom [b]inferior to yours; then another, a third kingdom of bronze, which shall rule over all the earth.

2:25 [1] Literally *of the sons of the captivity* **2:28** [a] Gen. 40:8 [b] Gen. 49:1 **2:29** [a] [Dan. 2:22, 28] **2:30** [a] Acts 3:12 [b] Dan. 2:47 **2:32** [a] Dan. 2:38, 45 [1] Or *sides* **2:33** [1] Or *baked clay,* and so in verses 34, 35, and 42 **2:34** [a] [Zech. 4:6] **2:35** [a] [Rev. 16:14] [b] Hos. 13:3 [c] Ps. 37:10, 36 [d] [Is. 2:2, 3] [e] Ps. 80:9 **2:37** [a] Jer. 27:6, 7 [b] Ezra 1:2 **2:38** [a] Dan. 4:21, 22 [b] Dan. 2:32 **2:39** [a] Dan. 5:28, 31 [b] Dan. 2:32

PEACEFUL FOREVER

The God of heaven will set up a kingdom which shall never be destroyed.

DANIEL 2:44

For Daniel, a Jewish exile in Babylon, hope for a restored Jerusalem and nation of Israel could not have seemed more remote. Daniel had resolved not to eat the king's food when it violated Jewish food laws. Daniel was vindicated. Soon after, he found himself advanced in the Babylonian king's government. His talents were soon put to the test.

Nebuchadnezzar had a terrifying dream that none of his wise men could decipher. Daniel (after praying to God, who revealed it to him) explained it to the king and was rewarded. For Daniel, his Jewish friends, and for us today, the truly important part of the king's dream was the "stone . . . cut out without hands, which struck the image" and smashed it to pieces (vv. 34–35). The meaning, Daniel told the king, is that "the God of heaven will set up a kingdom which shall never be destroyed" (v. 44).

The kingdom of God will eventually supplant the kingdoms of this world. Imagine a world filled with God's peace! This is your destiny and future reward for a life of faith in Christ today.

40And [a]the fourth kingdom shall be as strong as iron, inasmuch as iron breaks in pieces and shatters everything; and like iron that crushes, *that kingdom* will break in pieces and crush all the others. 41Whereas you saw the feet and toes, partly of potter's clay and partly of iron, the kingdom shall be divided; yet the strength of the iron shall be in it, just as you saw the iron mixed with ceramic clay. 42And *as* the toes of the feet *were* partly of iron and partly of clay, [a]*so* the kingdom shall be partly strong and partly fragile. 43As you saw iron mixed with ceramic clay, they will mingle with the seed of men; but they will not adhere to one another, just as iron does not mix with clay. 44And in the days of these kings [a]the God of heaven will set up a kingdom [b]which shall never be destroyed; and the kingdom shall not be left to other people; [c]it shall break in pieces and consume all these kingdoms, and it shall stand forever. 45[a]Inasmuch as you saw that the stone was cut out of the mountain without hands, and that it broke in pieces the iron, the bronze, the clay, the silver, and the gold—the great God has made known to the king what will come to pass after this. The dream is certain, and its interpretation is sure."

Daniel and His Friends Promoted

46[a]Then King Nebuchadnezzar fell on his face, prostrate before Daniel, and commanded that they should present an offering [b]and incense to him. 47The king answered Daniel, and said, "Truly [a]your God *is* the God of [b]gods, the Lord of kings, and a revealer of secrets, since you could reveal this secret." 48[a]Then the king promoted Daniel [b]and gave him many great gifts; and he made him ruler over the whole province of Babylon, and [c]chief administrator over all the wise *men* of Babylon. 49Also Daniel petitioned the king, [a]and he set Shadrach, Meshach, and Abed-Nego over the affairs of the province of Babylon; but Daniel [b]*sat* in the gate[1] of the king.

The Image of Gold

3 Nebuchadnezzar the king made an image of gold, whose height *was* sixty cubits *and* its width six cubits. He set it up in the plain of Dura, in the province of Babylon. 2And King Nebuchadnezzar sent *word* to gather together the satraps, the administrators, the governors, the counselors, the treasurers, the judges, the magistrates, and all the officials of the provinces, to come to the dedication of the image which King Nebuchadnezzar had set up. 3So the satraps, the administrators, the governors, the counselors, the treasurers, the judges, the magistrates, and all the officials of the provinces gathered together for the dedication of the image that King Nebuchadnezzar had set up; and they stood before the image that Nebuchadnezzar had set up. 4Then a herald cried aloud: "To you it is commanded, [a]O peoples, nations, and languages, 5*that* at the time you hear the sound of the horn, flute, harp, lyre, *and* psaltery, in symphony with all kinds of music, you shall fall down and worship the gold image that King Nebuchadnezzar has set up; 6and whoever does not fall down and worship shall [a]be cast immediately into the midst of a burning fiery furnace."

7So at that time, when all the people heard the sound of the horn, flute, harp, *and* lyre, in symphony with all kinds of music, all the people, nations, and languages fell down *and* worshiped the gold image which King Nebuchadnezzar had set up.

Daniel's Friends Disobey the King

8Therefore at that time certain Chaldeans [a]came forward and accused the Jews. 9They spoke and said to King Nebuchadnezzar, [a]"O king, live forever! 10You, O king, have made a decree that everyone who hears the sound of the horn, flute, harp, lyre, *and* psaltery, in symphony with all kinds of music, shall fall down and worship the gold image; 11and whoever does not fall down and worship shall be cast into the midst of a burning fiery furnace. 12[a]There are certain Jews whom you have set over the affairs of the province of Babylon: Shadrach, Meshach, and Abed-Nego; these men, O king, have [b]not paid due regard to you. They do not serve your gods or worship the gold image which you have set up."

13Then Nebuchadnezzar, in [a]rage and fury, gave the command to bring Shadrach, Meshach, and Abed-Nego. So they brought these men before the king. 14Nebuchadnezzar spoke, saying to them, "*Is it* true, Shadrach, Meshach, and Abed-Nego, *that* you do not serve my gods or worship the gold image which I have set up? 15Now if you are ready at the time you hear the sound of the horn, flute, harp, lyre, *and* psaltery, in symphony with all kinds of music, and you fall down and worship the image which I have made, [a]*good!* But if you do not worship, you shall be cast immediately into the midst of a burning fiery furnace. [b]And who *is* the god who will deliver you from my hands?"

2:40 [a] Dan. 7:7, 23 **2:42** [a] Dan. 7:24 **2:44** [a] Dan. 2:28, 37 [b] [Luke 1:32, 33] [c] Is. 60:12 **2:45** [a] Dan. 2:35 **2:46** [a] Acts 10:25; 14:13 [b] Ezra 6:10 **2:47** [a] Dan. 3:28, 29; 4:34–37 [b] [Deut. 10:17] **2:48** [a] [Prov. 14:35; 21:1] [b] Dan. 2:6 [c] Dan. 4:9; 5:11 **2:49** [a] Dan. 1:7; 3:12 [b] Esth. 2:19, 21; 3:2 [1] That is, the king's court **3:4** [a] Dan. 4:1; 6:25 **3:6** [a] Jer. 29:22 **3:8** [a] Dan. 6:12, 13 **3:9** [a] Dan. 2:4; 5:10; 6:6, 21 **3:12** [a] Dan. 2:49 [b] Dan. 1:8; 6:12, 13 **3:13** [a] Dan. 2:12; 3:19 **3:15** [a] Luke 13:9 [b] Ex. 5:2

16Shadrach, Meshach, and Abed-Nego answered and said to the king, "O Nebuchadnezzar, [a]we have no need to answer you in this matter. 17If that *is the case,* our [a]God whom we serve is able to [b]deliver us from the burning fiery furnace, and He will deliver *us* from your hand, O king. 18But if not, let it be known to you, O king, that we do not serve your gods, nor will we [a]worship the gold image which you have set up."

PEACE NOTE

Do you have an "even if He doesn't save us" kind of faith? Like Shadrach, Meshach, and Abed-Nego, we must choose to serve only the one true God of the Bible. Only He gives peace.

DANIEL 3:16-18

Saved in Fiery Trial

19Then Nebuchadnezzar was full of fury, and the expression on his face changed toward Shadrach, Meshach, and Abed-Nego. He spoke and commanded that they heat the furnace seven times more than it was usually heated. 20And he commanded certain mighty men of valor who *were* in his army to bind Shadrach, Meshach, and Abed-Nego, *and* cast *them* into the burning fiery furnace. 21Then these men were bound in their coats, their trousers, their turbans, and their *other* garments, and were cast into the midst of the burning fiery furnace. 22Therefore, because the king's command was urgent, and the furnace exceedingly hot, the flame of the fire killed those men who took up Shadrach, Meshach, and Abed-Nego. 23And these three men, Shadrach, Meshach, and Abed-Nego, fell down bound into the midst of the burning fiery furnace.

24Then King Nebuchadnezzar was astonished; and he rose in haste *and* spoke, saying to his counselors, "Did we not cast three men bound into the midst of the fire?"

They answered and said to the king, "True, O king."

25"Look!" he answered, "I see four men loose, [a]walking in the midst of the fire; and they are not hurt, and the form of the fourth is like [b]the Son of God."[1]

Nebuchadnezzar Praises God

26Then Nebuchadnezzar went near the mouth of the burning fiery furnace *and* spoke, saying, "Shadrach, Meshach, and Abed-Nego, servants of the [a]Most High God, come out, and come *here.*" Then Shadrach, Meshach, and Abed-Nego came from the midst of the fire. 27And the satraps, administrators, governors, and the king's counselors gathered together, and they saw these men [a]on whose bodies the fire had no power; the hair of their head was not singed nor were their garments affected, and the smell of fire was not on them.

28Nebuchadnezzar spoke, saying, "Blessed be the God of Shadrach, Meshach, and Abed-Nego, who sent His [a]Angel[1] and delivered His servants who trusted in Him, and they have frustrated the king's word, and yielded their bodies, that they should not serve nor worship any god except their own God! 29[a]Therefore I make a decree that any people, nation, or language which speaks anything amiss against the [b]God of Shadrach, Meshach, and Abed-Nego shall be [c]cut in pieces, and their houses shall be made an ash heap; [d]because there is no other God who can deliver like this."

30Then the king promoted Shadrach, Meshach, and Abed-Nego in the province of Babylon.

Nebuchadnezzar's Second Dream

4 Nebuchadnezzar the king,

[a] To all peoples, nations, and languages
that dwell in all the earth:

Peace be multiplied to you.

2 I thought it good to declare the signs
and wonders [a]that the Most High God
has worked for me.

3 [a]How great *are* His signs,
And how mighty His wonders!
His kingdom *is* [b]an everlasting
kingdom,
And His dominion *is* from generation
to generation.

4 I, Nebuchadnezzar, was at rest in my
house, and flourishing in my palace.
5I saw a dream which made me afraid,

3:16 [a] [Matt. 10:19] 3:17 [a] [Is. 26:3, 4] [b] 1 Sam. 17:37 3:18 [a] Job 13:15 3:25 [a] Is. 43:2 [b] [Ps. 34:7] [1] Or *a son of the gods* 3:26 [a] [Dan. 4:2, 3, 17, 34, 35] 3:27 [a] Heb. 11:34 3:28 [a] [Ps. 34:7, 8] [1] Or *angel* 3:29 [a] Dan. 6:26 [b] Dan. 2:46, 47; 4:34–37 [c] Dan. 2:5 [d] Dan. 6:27 4:1 [a] Dan. 3:4; 6:25 4:2 [a] Dan. 3:26 4:3 [a] 2 Sam. 7:16 [b] [Dan. 2:44; 4:34; 6:26]

[a]and the thoughts on my bed and
the visions of my head [b]troubled me.
6Therefore I issued a decree to bring
in all the wise *men* of Babylon before
me, that they might make known to me
the interpretation of the dream. 7[a]Then
the magicians, the astrologers, the
Chaldeans, and the soothsayers came in,
and I told them the dream; but they did
not make known to me its interpretation.
8But at last Daniel came before me [a](his
name *is* Belteshazzar, according to the
name of my god; [b]in him *is* the Spirit
of the Holy God), and I told the dream
before him, *saying:* 9"Belteshazzar, [a]chief
of the magicians, because I know that
the Spirit of the Holy God *is* in you, and
no secret troubles you, explain to me the
visions of my dream that I have seen,
and its interpretation.

10 "These *were* the visions of my head
while on my bed:

I was looking, and behold,
[a]A tree in the midst of the earth,
And its height was great.
11 The tree grew and became strong;
Its height reached to the heavens,
And it could be seen to the ends of all
the earth.
12 Its leaves *were* lovely,
Its fruit abundant,
And in it *was* food for all.
[a]The beasts of the field found shade
under it,
The birds of the heavens dwelt in its
branches,
And all flesh was fed from it.

13 "I saw in the visions of my head *while*
on my bed, and there was [a]a watcher, [b]a
holy one, coming down from heaven.
14He cried aloud and said thus:

[a]'Chop down the tree and cut off its
branches,
Strip off its leaves and scatter its fruit.
[b]Let the beasts get out from under it,
And the birds from its branches.
15 Nevertheless leave the stump and roots
in the earth,
Bound with a band of iron and bronze,
In the tender grass of the field.
Let it be wet with the dew of heaven,
And *let* him graze with the beasts
On the grass of the earth.
16 Let his heart be changed from *that of* a
man,
Let him be given the heart of a beast,
And let seven [a]times[1] pass over him.

17 'This decision *is* by the decree of the
watchers,
And the sentence by the word of the
holy ones,
In order [a]that the living may know
[b]That the Most High rules in the
kingdom of men,
[c]Gives it to whomever He will,
And sets over it the [d]lowest of men.'

18 "This dream I, King Nebuchadnezzar,
have seen. Now you, Belteshazzar,
declare its interpretation, [a]since all
the wise *men* of my kingdom are
not able to make known to me the
interpretation; but you *are* able, [b]for
the Spirit of the Holy God *is* in you."

Daniel Explains the Second Dream

19 Then Daniel, [a]whose name *was*
Belteshazzar, was astonished for a
time, and his thoughts [b]troubled
him. *So* the king spoke, and said,
"Belteshazzar, do not let the dream or
its interpretation trouble you."
Belteshazzar answered and said, "My
lord, *may* [c]the dream concern those
who hate you, and its interpretation
concern your enemies!

20 [a]"The tree that you saw, which grew and
became strong, whose height reached
to the heavens and which *could be*
seen by all the earth, 21whose leaves
were lovely and its fruit abundant, in
which *was* food for all, under which the
beasts of the field dwelt, and in whose
branches the birds of the heaven had
their home— 22[a]it *is* you, O king, who
have grown and become strong; for
your greatness has grown and reaches
to the heavens, [b]and your dominion to
the end of the earth.
23 [a]"And inasmuch as the king saw a
watcher, a holy one, coming down from
heaven and saying, 'Chop down the tree
and destroy it, but leave its stump and
roots in the earth, *bound* with a band

4:5 [a] Dan. 2:28, 29 [b] Dan. 2:1 **4:7** [a] Dan. 2:2 **4:8** [a] Dan. 1:7 [b] Dan. 2:11; 4:18; 5:11, 14 **4:9** [a] Dan. 2:48; 5:11 **4:10** [a] Ezek. 31:3 **4:12** [a] Lam. 4:20 **4:13** [a] [Dan. 4:17, 23] [b] Deut. 33:2 **4:14** [a] Ezek. 31:10–14 [b] Ezek. 31:12, 13 **4:16** [a] Dan. 11:13; 12:7 [1] Possibly *seven years,* and so in verses 23, 25, and 32 **4:17** [a] Ps. 9:16; 83:18 [b] Dan. 2:21; 4:25, 32; 5:21 [c] Jer. 27:5–7 [d] 1 Sam. 2:8 **4:18** [a] Gen. 41:8, 15 [b] Dan. 4:8, 9; 5:11, 14 **4:19** [a] Dan. 4:8 [b] Dan. 7:15, 28; 8:27 [c] 2 Sam. 18:32 **4:20** [a] Dan. 4:10–12 **4:22** [a] Dan. 2:37, 38 [b] Jer. 27:6–8 **4:23** [a] Dan. 4:13–15

of iron and bronze in the tender grass
of the field; let it be wet with the dew
of heaven, [b]and let him graze with the
beasts of the field, till seven times pass
over him'; [24]this is the interpretation,
O king, and this is the decree of the
Most High, which has come upon my
lord the king: [25]They shall [a]drive you
from men, your dwelling shall be with
the beasts of the field, and they shall
make you [b]eat grass like oxen. They
shall wet you with the dew of heaven,
and seven times shall pass over you,
[c]till you know that the Most High rules
in the kingdom of men, and [d]gives it to
whomever He chooses.
26 "And inasmuch as they gave the
command to leave the stump *and* roots
of the tree, your kingdom shall be
assured to you, after you come to know
that [a]Heaven rules. [27]Therefore, O king,
let my advice be acceptable to you;
[a]break off your sins by *being* righteous,
and your iniquities by showing mercy
to *the* poor. [b]Perhaps there may be [c]a
lengthening of your prosperity."

Nebuchadnezzar's Humiliation

28 All *this* came upon King
Nebuchadnezzar. [29]At the end of the
twelve months he was walking about
the royal palace of Babylon. [30]The
king [a]spoke, saying, "Is not this great
Babylon, that I have built for a royal
dwelling by my mighty power and for
the honor of my majesty?"
31 [a]While the word *was still* in the king's
mouth, [b]a voice fell from heaven: "King
Nebuchadnezzar, to you it is spoken: the
kingdom has departed from you! [32]And
[a]they shall drive you from men, and
your dwelling *shall be* with the beasts of
the field. They shall make you eat grass
like oxen; and seven times shall pass
over you, until you know that the Most
High rules in the kingdom of men, and
gives it to whomever He chooses."
33 That very hour the word was fulfilled
concerning Nebuchadnezzar; he was
driven from men and ate grass like
oxen; his body was wet with the dew of
heaven till his hair had grown like eagles'
feathers and his nails like birds' *claws.*

Nebuchadnezzar Praises God

34 And [a]at the end of the time[1] I,
Nebuchadnezzar, lifted my eyes
to heaven, and my understanding
returned to me; and I blessed the Most
High and praised and honored Him
[b]who lives forever:

For His dominion *is* [c]an everlasting
dominion,
And His kingdom *is* from generation to
generation.

4:23 [b] Dan. 5:21 **4:25** [a] Dan. 4:32; 5:21 [b] Ps. 106:20 [c] Dan. 4:2, 17, 32 [d] Jer. 27:5 **4:26** [a] Matt. 21:25 **4:27** [a] [1 Pet. 4:8] [b] [Ps. 41:1–3] [c] 1 Kin. 21:29 **4:30** [a] Prov. 16:18 **4:31** [a] Luke 12:20 [b] Dan. 4:24 **4:32** [a] [Dan. 4:25] **4:34** [a] Dan. 4:26 [b] [Rev. 4:10] [c] [Luke 1:33] [1] Literally *days*

IN HIS HANDS

His dominion is an everlasting dominion.

DANIEL 4:34

In chapter 4, Daniel the Jewish captive and wise man interpreted another dream for Nebuchadnezzar, king of Babylon. In this dream the king and his realm were likened to a great tree that filled the earth but was then brought low (vv. 19–23). Daniel told the king he was that tree and for a season, he would lose his mind and wander around like an animal (vv. 24–25).

One year later, the dream was fulfilled. Puffed up with his imagined greatness, Nebuchadnezzar was struck with madness. Later, once he'd repented, his sanity and kingdom were restored and he praised God. The king acknowledged God's rule: "His dominion is an everlasting dominion, and His kingdom is from generation to generation" (v. 34).

We find God's peace by resting in His complete control of our lives. From Nebuchadnezzar's dream and experience we learn that humans do not control their destiny—the Ruler of heaven and earth does. Our future is in His hands.

35 [a]All the inhabitants of the earth *are*
reputed as nothing;
[b]He does according to His will in the
army of heaven
And *among* the inhabitants of the
earth.
[c]No one can restrain His hand
Or say to Him, [d]"What have You done?"
36 At the same time my reason returned
to me, [a]and for the glory of my
kingdom, my honor and splendor
returned to me. My counselors and
nobles resorted to me, I was [b]restored
to my kingdom, and excellent
majesty was [c]added to me. 37 Now I,
Nebuchadnezzar, [a]praise and extol and
honor the King of heaven, [b]all of whose
works *are* truth, and His ways justice.
[c]And those who walk in pride He is able
to put down.

Belshazzar's Feast

5 Belshazzar the king [a]made a great feast for a
thousand of his lords, and drank wine in the
presence of the thousand. 2 While he tasted the
wine, Belshazzar gave the command to bring
the gold and silver vessels [a]which his father
Nebuchadnezzar had taken from the temple
which *had been* in Jerusalem, that the king and
his lords, his wives, and his concubines might
drink from them. 3 Then they brought the gold
[a]vessels that had been taken from the temple
of the house of God which *had been* in Jerusalem; and the king and his lords, his wives, and
his concubines drank from them. 4 They drank
wine, [a]and praised the gods of gold and silver,
bronze and iron, wood and stone.
5 [a]In the same hour the fingers of a man's
hand appeared and wrote opposite the lampstand on the plaster of the wall of the king's
palace; and the king saw the part of the hand
that wrote. 6 Then the king's countenance
changed, and his thoughts troubled him,
so that the joints of his hips were loosened
and his [a]knees knocked against each other.
7 [a]The king cried aloud to bring in [b]the astrologers, the Chaldeans, and the soothsayers.
The king spoke, saying to the wise *men* of
Babylon, "Whoever reads this writing, and
tells me its interpretation, shall be clothed
with purple and *have* a chain of gold around
his neck; [c]and he shall be the third ruler in
the kingdom." 8 Now all the king's wise *men*
came, [a]but they could not read the writing,
or make known to the king its interpretation.
9 Then King Belshazzar was greatly [a]troubled,
his countenance was changed, and his lords
were astonished.
10 The queen, because of the words of the
king and his lords, came to the banquet hall.
The queen spoke, saying, "O king, live forever!
Do not let your thoughts trouble you, nor let
your countenance change. 11 [a]There is a man
in your kingdom in whom *is* the Spirit of the
Holy God. And in the days of your father, light
and understanding and wisdom, like the wisdom of the gods, were found in him; and King
Nebuchadnezzar your father—your father
the king—made him chief of the magicians,
astrologers, Chaldeans, *and* soothsayers.
12 Inasmuch as an excellent spirit, knowledge,
understanding, interpreting dreams, solving
riddles, and explaining enigmas[1] were found
in this Daniel, [a]whom the king named Belteshazzar, now let Daniel be called, and he
will give the interpretation."

The Writing on the Wall Explained

13 Then Daniel was brought in before the
king. The king spoke, and said to Daniel, "*Are*
you that Daniel who is one of the captives[1]
from Judah, whom my father the king brought
from Judah? 14 I have heard of you, that [a]the
Spirit of God *is* in you, and *that* light and understanding and excellent wisdom are found in
you. 15 Now [a]the wise *men*, the astrologers, have
been brought in before me, that they should
read this writing and make known to me its
interpretation, but they could not give the
interpretation of the thing. 16 And I have heard
of you, that you can give interpretations and
explain enigmas. [a]Now if you can read the writing and make known to me its interpretation,
you shall be clothed with purple and *have* a
chain of gold around your neck, and shall be
the third ruler in the kingdom."
17 Then Daniel answered, and said before
the king, "Let your gifts be for yourself, and
give your rewards to another; yet I will read
the writing to the king, and make known to
him the interpretation. 18 O king, [a]the Most
High God gave Nebuchadnezzar your father a
kingdom and majesty, glory and honor. 19 And
because of the majesty that He gave him, [a]all
peoples, nations, and languages trembled and
feared before him. Whomever he wished, he
[b]executed; whomever he wished, he kept alive;

4:35 [a] Is. 40:15, 17 [b] Ps. 115:3; 135:6 [c] Job 34:29 [d] Rom. 9:20 **4:36** [a] Dan. 4:26 [b] 2 Chr. 20:20 [c] [Prov. 22:4] **4:37** [a] Dan. 2:46, 47; 3:28, 29 [b] [Ps. 33:4] [c] Ex. 18:11 **5:1** [a] Esth. 1:3 **5:2** [a] Dan. 1:2 **5:3** [a] 2 Chr. 36:10 **5:4** [a] Rev. 9:20 **5:5** [a] Dan. 4:31 **5:6** [a] Ezek. 7:17; 21:7 **5:7** [a] Dan. 4:6, 7; 5:11, 15 [b] Is. 47:13 [c] Dan. 6:2, 3 **5:8** [a] Dan. 2:27; 4:7; 5:15 **5:9** [a] Dan. 2:1; 5:6 **5:11** [a] Dan. 2:48; 4:8, 9, 18 **5:12** [a] Dan. 1:7; 4:8 [1] Literally *untying knots,* and so in verse 16 **5:13** [1] Literally *of the sons of the captivity* **5:14** [a] Dan. 4:8, 9, 18; 5:11, 12 **5:15** [a] Dan. 5:7, 8 **5:16** [a] Dan. 5:7, 29 **5:18** [a] Dan. 2:37, 38; 4:17, 22, 25 **5:19** [a] Jer. 27:7 [b] Dan. 2:12, 13; 3:6

whomever he wished, he set up; and whomever he wished, he put down. 20 [a]But when his heart was lifted up, and his spirit was hardened in pride, he was deposed from his kingly throne, and they took his glory from him. 21 Then he was [a]driven from the sons of men, his heart was made like the beasts, and his dwelling *was* with the wild donkeys. They fed him with grass like oxen, and his body was wet with the dew of heaven, [b]till he knew that the Most High God rules in the kingdom of men, and appoints over it whomever He chooses.

22 "But you his son, Belshazzar, [a]have not humbled your heart, although you knew all this. 23 [a]And you have lifted yourself up against the Lord of heaven. They have brought the [b]vessels of His house before you, and you and your lords, your wives and your concubines, have drunk wine from them. And you have praised the gods of silver and gold, bronze and iron, wood and stone, [c]which do not see or hear or know; and the God who *holds* your breath in His hand [d]and owns all your ways, you have not glorified. 24 Then the fingers[1] of the hand were sent from Him, and this writing was written.

25 "And this is the inscription that was written:

MENE,[1] MENE, TEKEL,[2] UPHARSIN.[3]

26 This *is* the interpretation of *each* word. MENE: God has numbered your kingdom, and finished it; 27 TEKEL: [a]You have been weighed in the balances, and found wanting; 28 PERES: Your kingdom has been divided, and given to the [a]Medes and [b]Persians."[1] 29 Then Belshazzar gave the command, and they clothed Daniel with purple and *put* a chain of gold around his neck, and made a proclamation concerning him [a]that he should be the third ruler in the kingdom.

Belshazzar's Fall

30 [a]That very night Belshazzar, king of the Chaldeans, was slain. 31 [a]And Darius the Mede received the kingdom, *being* about sixty-two years old.

The Plot Against Daniel

6 It pleased Darius to set over the kingdom one hundred and twenty satraps, to be over the whole kingdom; 2 and over these, three governors, of whom Daniel *was* one, that the satraps might give account to them, so that the king would suffer no loss. 3 Then this Daniel distinguished himself above the governors and satraps, [a]because an excellent spirit *was* in him; and the king gave thought to setting him over the whole realm. 4 [a]So the governors and satraps sought to find *some* charge against Daniel concerning the kingdom; but they could find no charge or fault, because he *was* faithful; nor was there any error or fault found in him. 5 Then these men said, "We shall not find any charge against this Daniel unless we find *it* against him concerning the law of his God."

6 So these governors and satraps thronged before the king, and said thus to him: [a]"King Darius, live forever! 7 All the governors of the kingdom, the administrators and satraps, the counselors and advisors, have [a]consulted together to establish a royal statute and to make a firm decree, that whoever petitions any god or man for thirty days, except you, O king, shall be cast into the den of lions. 8 Now, O king, establish the decree and sign the writing, so that it cannot be changed, according to the [a]law of the Medes and Persians, which does not alter." 9 Therefore King Darius signed the written decree.

Daniel in the Lions' Den

10 Now when Daniel knew that the writing was signed, he went home. And in his upper room, with his windows open [a]toward Jerusalem, he knelt down on his knees [b]three times that day, and prayed and gave thanks before his God, as was his custom since early days.

11 Then these men assembled and found Daniel praying and making supplication before his God. 12 [a]And they went before the king, and spoke concerning the king's decree: "Have you not signed a decree that every man who petitions any god or man within thirty days, except you, O king, shall be cast into the den of lions?"

The king answered and said, "The thing *is* true, [b]according to the law of the Medes and Persians, which does not alter."

13 So they answered and said before the king, "That Daniel, [a]who is one of the captives[1] from Judah, [b]does not show due regard for you, O king, or for the decree that you have signed, but makes his petition three times a day."

5:20 [a] Dan. 4:30, 37 **5:21** [a] Dan. 4:32, 33 [b] Ezek. 17:24 **5:22** [a] 2 Chr. 33:23; 36:12 **5:23** [a] Dan. 5:3, 4 [b] Ex. 40:9 [c] Ps. 115:5, 6 [d] [Jer. 10:23] **5:24** [1] Literally *palm* **5:25** [1] Literally *a mina* (50 shekels) from the verb "to number" [2] Literally *a shekel* from the verb "to weigh" [3] Literally *and half-shekels* from the verb "to divide" **5:27** [a] Ps. 62:9 **5:28** [a] Dan. 5:31; 9:1 [b] Dan. 6:28 [1] Aramaic *Paras,* consonant with *Peres* **5:29** [a] Dan. 5:7, 16 **5:30** [a] Jer. 51:31, 39, 57 **5:31** [a] Dan. 2:39; 9:1 **6:3** [a] Dan. 5:12 **6:4** [a] Eccl. 4:4 **6:6** [a] Neh. 2:3 **6:7** [a] Ps. 59:3; 62:4; 64:2–6 **6:8** [a] Esth. 1:19; 8:8 **6:10** [a] Jon. 2:4 [b] Ps. 55:17 **6:12** [a] Dan. 3:8–12 [b] Dan. 6:8, 15 **6:13** [a] Dan. 1:6; 5:13 [b] Dan. 3:12 [1] Literally *of the sons of the captivity*

14And the king, when he heard *these* words,
[a]was greatly displeased with himself, and
set *his* heart on Daniel to deliver him; and
he labored till the going down of the sun to
deliver him. 15Then these men approached
the king, and said to the king, "Know, O king,
that *it is* [a]the law of the Medes and Persians
that no decree or statute which the king establishes may be changed."

16So the king gave the command, and they
brought Daniel and cast *him* into the den of
lions. *But* the king spoke, saying to Daniel,
"Your God, whom you serve continually,
He will deliver you." 17[a]Then a stone was
brought and laid on the mouth of the den,
[b]and the king sealed it with his own signet
ring and with the signets of his lords, that
the purpose concerning Daniel might not
be changed.

Daniel Saved from the Lions

18Now the king went to his palace and spent
the night fasting; and no musicians[1] were
brought before him. [a]Also his sleep went
from him. 19Then the [a]king arose very early
in the morning and went in haste to the den
of lions. 20And when he came to the den, he
cried out with a lamenting voice to Daniel.
The king spoke, saying to Daniel, "Daniel,
servant of the living God, [a]has your God,
whom you serve continually, been able to
deliver you from the lions?"

21Then Daniel said to the king, [a]"O king,
live forever! 22[a]My God sent His angel and
[b]shut the lions' mouths, so that they have
not hurt me, because I was found innocent
before Him; and also, O king, I have done no
wrong before you."

23Now the king was exceedingly glad for
him, and commanded that they should take
Daniel up out of the den. So Daniel was taken
up out of the den, and no injury whatever
was found on him, [a]because he believed in
his God.

Darius Honors God

24And the king gave the command, [a]and
they brought those men who had accused
Daniel, and they cast *them* into the den of
lions—them, [b]their children, and their wives;
and the lions overpowered them, and broke
all their bones in pieces before they ever
came to the bottom of the den.

25[a]Then King Darius wrote:

To all peoples, nations, and languages
that dwell in all the earth:

Peace be multiplied to you.

26 [a]I make a decree that in every dominion
of my kingdom *men must* [b]tremble and
fear before the God of Daniel.

[c]For He *is* the living God,
And steadfast forever;
His kingdom *is the one* which shall not
be [d]destroyed,
And His dominion *shall endure* to the
end.
27 He delivers and rescues,
[a]And He works signs and wonders
In heaven and on earth,
Who has delivered Daniel from the
power of the lions.

28So this Daniel prospered in the reign
of Darius [a]and in the reign of [b]Cyrus the
Persian.

Vision of the Four Beasts

7 In the first year of Belshazzar king of Babylon, [a]Daniel had a dream and [b]visions
of his head *while* on his bed. Then he wrote
down the dream, telling the main facts.[1]

2Daniel spoke, saying, "I saw in my vision
by night, and behold, the four winds of heav-
en were stirring up the Great Sea. 3And four
great beasts [a]came up from the sea, each
different from the other. 4The first *was* [a]like
a lion, and had eagle's wings. I watched till its
wings were plucked off; and it was lifted up
from the earth and made to stand on two feet
like a man, and a [b]man's heart was given to it.

5[a]"And suddenly another beast, a second,
like a bear. It was raised up on one side, and *had*
three ribs in its mouth between its teeth. And
they said thus to it: 'Arise, devour much flesh!'

6"After this I looked, and there was another, like a leopard, which had on its back
four wings of a bird. The beast also had [a]four
heads, and dominion was given to it.

7"After this I saw in the night visions, and
behold, [a]a fourth beast, dreadful and terrible,
exceedingly strong. It had huge iron teeth;
it was devouring, breaking in pieces, and
trampling the residue with its feet. It *was*
different from all the beasts that *were* before
it, [b]and it had ten horns. 8I was considering

6:14 [a] Mark 6:26 **6:15** [a] Dan. 6:8, 12 **6:17** [a] Lam. 3:53 [b] Matt. 27:66 **6:18** [a] Dan. 2:1 [1] Exact meaning unknown **6:19** [a] Dan. 3:24 **6:20** [a] Dan. 3:17 **6:21** [a] Dan. 2:4; 6:6 **6:22** [a] Dan. 3:28 [b] Heb. 11:33 **6:23** [a] Heb. 11:33 **6:24** [a] Deut. 19:18, 19 [b] Deut. 24:16 **6:25** [a] Dan. 4:1 **6:26** [a] Dan. 3:29 [b] Ps. 99:1 [c] Dan. 4:34; 6:20 [d] Dan. 2:44; 4:3; 7:14, 27 **6:27** [a] Dan. 4:2, 3 **6:28** [a] Dan. 1:21 [b] Ezra 1:1, 2 **7:1** [a] [Amos 3:7] [b] [Dan. 2:28] [1] Literally *the head* (or *chief*) *of the words* **7:3** [a] Rev. 13:1; 17:8 **7:4** [a] Deut. 28:49 [b] Dan. 4:16, 34 **7:5** [a] Dan. 2:39 **7:6** [a] Dan. 8:8, 22 **7:7** [a] Dan. 2:40 [b] Rev. 12:3; 13:1

the horns, and [a]there was another horn, a
little one, coming up among them, before
whom three of the first horns were plucked
out by the roots. And there, in this horn, *were*
eyes like the eyes [b]of a man, [c]and a mouth
speaking pompous words.

Vision of the Ancient of Days

9 "I[a] watched till thrones were put in place,
And [b]the Ancient of Days was seated;
[c]His garment *was* white as snow,
And the hair of His head *was* like pure wool.
His throne *was* a fiery flame,
[d]Its wheels a burning fire;
10 [a]A fiery stream issued
And came forth from before Him.
[b]A thousand thousands ministered to Him;
Ten thousand times ten thousand stood before Him.
[c]The court[1] was seated,
And the books were opened.

11"I watched then because of the sound
of the pompous words which the horn was
speaking; [a]I watched till the beast was slain,
and its body destroyed and given to the burning flame. 12As for the rest of the beasts, they
had their dominion taken away, yet their
lives were prolonged for a season and a time.

13 "I was watching in the night visions,
And behold, [a]*One* like the Son of Man,
Coming with the clouds of heaven!
He came to the Ancient of Days,
And they brought Him near before Him.
14 [a]Then to Him was given dominion and glory and a kingdom,
That all [b]peoples, nations, and languages should serve Him.
His dominion *is* [c]an everlasting dominion,
Which shall not pass away,
And His kingdom *the one*
Which shall not be destroyed.

Daniel's Visions Interpreted

15"I, Daniel, was grieved in my spirit within
my body, and the visions of my head troubled
me. 16I came near to one of those who stood
by, and asked him the truth of all this. So he
told me and made known to me the interpretation of these things: 17"Those great beasts,
which are four, *are* four kings[1] *which* arise
out of the earth. 18But [a]the saints of the Most
High shall receive the kingdom, and possess
the kingdom forever, even forever and ever.'
19"Then I wished to know the truth about
the fourth beast, which was different from
all the others, exceedingly dreadful, *with* its
teeth of iron and its nails of bronze, *which*
devoured, broke in pieces, and trampled the

7:8 [a] Dan. 8:9 [b] Rev. 9:7 [c] Rev. 13:5, 6 **7:9** [a] [Rev. 20:4] [b] Ps. 90:2 [c] Rev. 1:14 [d] Ezek. 1:15 **7:10** [a] Is. 30:33; 66:15 [b] Rev. 5:11 [c] [Rev. 20:11–15] [1] Or *judgment* **7:11** [a] [Rev. 19:20; 20:10] **7:13** [a] [Matt. 24:30; 26:64; Mark 13:26; 14:62; Luke 21:27; Rev. 1:7, 12; 14:14] **7:14** [a] [Matt. 28:18; John 3:35, 36; 1 Cor. 15:27; Eph. 1:22; Phil. 2:9–11; Rev. 1:6; 11:15] [b] Dan. 3:4 [c] Mic. 4:7; [Luke 1:33]; John 12:34; Heb. 12:28 **7:17** [1] Representing their kingdoms (compare verse 23) **7:18** [a] Is. 60:12–14

PEACE FROM THE ANCIENT OF DAYS

Behold, One like the Son of Man, [was] coming with the clouds of heaven!

DANIEL 7:13

One of the most startling passages in the Old Testament is Daniel's night vision in which the sage saw the throne of God and the appearance of "One like the Son of Man, coming with the clouds of heaven." What Daniel saw was a humanlike figure—in contrast to the terrible beasts he had seen earlier—who approached the very throne of God, whom Daniel described as the "Ancient of Days." This figure received kingdom and authority and would eventually establish God's rule on earth.

In the New Testament Gospels, we learn that Daniel's vision was fulfilled in Jesus of Nazareth, who referred to Himself as "the Son of Man." Jesus exercised the authority He received in heaven, which included proclaiming the kingdom of God and forgiving sin. Our peace is guaranteed by this Son of Man!

Still, peace is a discipline we must develop every day. Maintain faith-centric peer support; maintain an active relationship with an accountability partner. Always check your thoughts against Scripture. These are immediate steps to developing God's peace.

residue with its feet; 20and the ten horns that
were on its head, and the other *horn* which
came up, before which three fell, namely,
that horn which had eyes and a mouth which
spoke pompous words, whose appearance
was greater than his fellows.
21"I was watching; [a]and the same horn was
making war against the saints, and prevailing
against them, 22until the Ancient of Days
came, [a]and a judgment was made *in favor*
of the saints of the Most High, and the time
came for the saints to possess the kingdom.
23"Thus he said:

'The fourth beast shall be
[a]A fourth kingdom on earth,
Which shall be different from all *other*
kingdoms,
And shall devour the whole earth,
Trample it and break it in pieces.
24 [a]The ten horns *are* ten kings
Who shall arise from this kingdom.
And another shall rise after them;
He shall be different from the first *ones,*
And shall subdue three kings.
25 [a]He shall speak *pompous* words against
the Most High,
Shall [b]persecute[1] the saints of the Most
High,
And shall [c]intend to change times and
law.
Then [d]*the saints* shall be given into his
hand
[e]For a time and times and half a time.
26 'But[a] the court shall be seated,
And they shall [b]take away his dominion,
To consume and destroy *it* forever.
27 Then the [a]kingdom and dominion,
And the greatness of the kingdoms
under the whole heaven,
Shall be given to the people, the saints
of the Most High.
[b]His kingdom *is* an everlasting kingdom,
[c]And all dominions shall serve and obey
Him.'

28"This *is* the end of the account.[1] As for me,
Daniel, [a]my thoughts greatly troubled me,
and my countenance changed; but I [b]kept the
matter in my heart."

Vision of a Ram and a Goat

8 In the third year of the reign of King Belshazzar a vision appeared *to* me—to me,
Daniel—after the one that appeared to me
[a]the first time. 2I saw in the vision, and it so
happened while I was looking, that I *was* in
[a]Shushan, the citadel, which *is* in the province
of Elam; and I saw in the vision that I was by
the River Ulai. 3Then I lifted my eyes and saw,
and there, standing beside the river, was a ram

7:21 [a] Rev. 11:7; 13:7; 17:14 **7:22** [a] [Rev. 1:6] **7:23** [a] Dan. 2:40 **7:24** [a] Rev. 13:1; 17:12 **7:25** [a] Rev. 13:1–6 [b] Rev. 17:6 [c] Dan. 2:21 [d] Rev. 13:7; 18:24 [e] Rev. 12:14 [1] Literally *wear out* **7:26** [a] [Dan. 2:35; 7:10, 22] [b] Rev. 19:20 **7:27** [a] Dan. 7:14, 18, 22 [b] [Luke 1:33, 34] [c] Is. 60:12 **7:28** [a] Dan. 8:27 [b] Luke 2:19, 51 [1] Literally *the word* **8:1** [a] Dan. 7:1 **8:2** [a] Esth. 1:2; 2:8

THE WAY OF PEACE

Then the kingdom and dominion . . . shall be given to the people, the saints of the Most High.

DANIEL 7:27

In his lifetime Daniel saw the kingdom of Judah collapse. He saw the city of Jerusalem captured and the temple of Solomon destroyed. He, along with thousands of other Jews, was taken to Babylon as an exile. No one, not even Daniel, has perfect faith. But each time we look to the Lord in faith, we have peace. It's that simple—and profound. Daniel apparently never lost his faith in God. He knew that God was with him and would someday restore the nation's fortunes.

Under the leadership of "One like the Son of Man" (Jesus, Dan. 7:13; see Matt. 26:64), the kingdom would be secured for God's people. In his vision Daniel was told, "Then the kingdom and dominion . . . shall be given to the people, the saints of the Most High" (Dan. 7:27). What great news! Daniel was entrusted by God, in spite of how terrifying these visions were, to know that the kingdoms of Babylon, Persia, Macedonia, and Rome would not have the last word. God would prevail!

Daniel was called by God, but he still needed the Lord moment by moment. He trusted in the Lord, and so should we. That's the way of peace.

which had two horns, and the two horns *were*
high; but one *was* [a]higher than the other, and
the higher *one* came up last. 4 I saw the ram
pushing westward, northward, and southward,
so that no animal could withstand him; nor *was*
there any that could deliver from his hand, [a]but
he did according to his will and became great.

5 And as I was considering, suddenly a male
goat came from the west, across the surface of
the whole earth, without touching the ground;
and the goat *had* a notable [a]horn between his
eyes. 6 Then he came to the ram that had two
horns, which I had seen standing beside the
river, and ran at him with furious power. 7 And
I saw him confronting the ram; he was moved
with rage against him, attacked the ram, and
broke his two horns. There was no power in the
ram to withstand him, but he cast him down to
the ground and trampled him; and there was no
one that could deliver the ram from his hand.

8 Therefore the male goat grew very great;
but when he became strong, the large horn
was broken, and in place of it [a]four notable
ones came up toward the four winds of heav-
en. 9 [a]And out of one of them came a little
horn which grew exceedingly great toward
the south, [b]toward the east, and toward the
[c]Glorious *Land.* 10 [a]And it grew up to [b]the
host of heaven; and [c]it cast down *some* of the
host and *some* of the stars to the ground, and
trampled them. 11 [a]He even exalted *himself* as
high as [b]the Prince of the host; [c]and by him
[d]the daily *sacrifices* were taken away, and the
place of His sanctuary was cast down. 12 Because of transgression, [a]an army was given
over *to the horn* to oppose the daily *sacrifices;*
and he cast [b]truth down to the ground. He
[c]did *all this* and prospered.

13 Then I heard [a]a holy one speaking; and
another holy one said to that certain *one* who
was speaking, "How long *will* the vision *be,*
concerning the daily *sacrifices* and the transgression of desolation, the giving of both
the sanctuary and the host to be trampled
underfoot?"

14 And he said to me, "For two thousand
three hundred days;[1] then the sanctuary
shall be cleansed."

Gabriel Interprets the Vision

15 Then it happened, when I, Daniel, had
seen the vision and [a]was seeking the meaning, that suddenly there stood before me
[b]one having the appearance of a man. 16 And
I heard a man's voice [a]between *the banks*
of the Ulai, who called, and said, [b]"Gabriel,
make this *man* understand the vision." 17 So
he came near where I stood, and when he
came I was afraid and [a]fell on my face; but
he said to me, "Understand, son of man,
that the vision *refers* to the time of the end."

18 [a]Now, as he was speaking with me, I was
in a deep sleep with my face to the ground;
[b]but he touched me, and stood me upright.
19 And he said, "Look, I am making known to
you what shall happen in the latter time of
the indignation; [a]for at the appointed time
the end *shall be.* 20 The ram which you saw,
having the two horns—*they are* the kings of
Media and Persia. 21 And the male goat *is* the
kingdom[1] of Greece. The large horn that *is*
between its eyes [a]*is* the first king. 22 [a]As for
the broken *horn* and the four that stood up
in its place, four kingdoms shall arise out of
that nation, but not with its power.

23 "And in the latter time of their kingdom,
When the transgressors have reached
their fullness,
A king shall arise,
[a]Having fierce features,
Who understands sinister schemes.
24 His power shall be mighty, [a]but not by
his own power;
He shall destroy fearfully,
[b]And shall prosper and thrive;
[c]He shall destroy the mighty, and *also*
the holy people.

25 "Through[a] his cunning
He shall cause deceit to prosper under
his rule;[1]
[b]And he shall exalt *himself* in his heart.
He shall destroy many in *their*
prosperity.
[c]He shall even rise against the Prince of
princes;
But he shall be [d]broken without *human*
means.[2]

26 "And the vision of the evenings and
mornings
Which was told is true;
[a]Therefore seal up the vision,
For *it refers* to many days *in the*
future."

8:3 [a] Dan. 7:5 **8:4** [a] Dan. 5:19 **8:5** [a] Dan. 8:8, 21; 11:3 **8:8** [a] Dan. 7:6; 8:22; 11:4 **8:9** [a] Dan. 11:21 [b] Dan. 11:25 [c] Ps. 48:2 **8:10** [a] Dan. 11:28 [b] Is. 14:13 [c] Rev. 12:4 **8:11** [a] Dan. 8:25; 11:36, 37 [b] Josh. 5:14 [c] Dan. 11:31; 12:11 [d] Ex. 29:38 **8:12** [a] Dan. 11:31 [b] Is. 59:14 [c] Dan. 8:4; 11:36 **8:13** [a] Dan. 4:13, 23 **8:14** [1] Literally *evening-mornings* **8:15** [a] 1 Pet. 1:10 [b] Ezek. 1:26 **8:16** [a] Dan. 12:6, 7 [b] Luke 1:19, 26 **8:17** [a] Rev. 1:17 **8:18** [a] Luke 9:32 [b] Ezek. 2:2 **8:19** [a] Hab. 2:3 **8:21** [a] Dan. 11:3 [1] Literally *king,* representing his kingdom (compare 7:17, 23) **8:22** [a] Dan. 11:4 **8:23** [a] Deut. 28:50 **8:24** [a] Rev. 17:13 [b] Dan. 11:36 [c] Dan. 7:25 **8:25** [a] Dan. 11:21 [b] Dan. 8:11–13; 11:36; 12:7 [c] Rev. 19:19, 20 [d] Job 34:20 [1] Literally *hand* [2] Literally *hand* **8:26** [a] Ezek. 12:27

27 [a]And I, Daniel, fainted and was sick for
days; afterward I arose and went about the
king's business. I was astonished by the vision, but no one understood it.

Daniel's Prayer for the People

9 In the first year [a]of Darius the son of
Ahasuerus, of the lineage of the Medes,
who was made king over the realm of the
Chaldeans— 2 in the first year of his reign I,
Daniel, understood by the books the num-
ber of the years *specified* by the word of the
LORD through [a]Jeremiah the prophet, that
He would accomplish seventy years in the
desolations of Jerusalem.

3 [a]Then I set my face toward the Lord God
to make request by prayer and supplications,
with fasting, sackcloth, and ashes. 4 And I
prayed to the LORD my God, and made confession, and said, "O [a]Lord, great and awesome
God, who keeps His covenant and mercy with
those who love Him, and with those who keep
His commandments, 5 [a]we have sinned and
committed iniquity, we have done wickedly
and rebelled, even by departing from Your
precepts and Your judgments. 6 [a]Neither have
we heeded Your servants the prophets, who
spoke in Your name to our kings and our
princes, to our fathers and all the people of
the land. 7 O Lord, [a]righteousness *belongs* to
You, but to us shame of face, as *it is* this day—
to the men of Judah, to the inhabitants of
Jerusalem and all Israel, those near and those
far off in all the countries to which You have
driven them, because of the unfaithfulness
which they have committed against You.

8 "O Lord, to us *belongs* shame of face, to our
kings, our princes, and our fathers, because
we have sinned against You. 9 [a]To the Lord our
God *belong* mercy and forgiveness, though
we have rebelled against Him. 10 We have not
obeyed the voice of the LORD our God, to walk
in His laws, which He set before us by His
servants the prophets. 11 Yes, [a]all Israel has
transgressed Your law, and has departed so
as not to obey Your voice; therefore the curse
and the oath written in the [b]Law of Moses the
servant of God have been poured out on us,
because we have sinned against Him. 12 And
He has [a]confirmed His words, which He spoke
against us and against our judges who judged
us, by bringing upon us a great disaster; [b]for
under the whole heaven such has never been
done as what has been done to Jerusalem.

13 [a]"As *it is* written in the Law of Moses, all
this disaster has come upon us; [b]yet we have
not made our prayer before the LORD our
God, that we might turn from our iniquities
and understand Your truth. 14 Therefore the
LORD has [a]kept the disaster in mind, and
brought it upon us; for [b]the LORD our God
is righteous in all the works which He does,
though we have not obeyed His voice. 15 And
now, O Lord our God, [a]who brought Your
people out of the land of Egypt with a mighty
hand, and made Yourself [b]a name, as *it is* this
day—we have sinned, we have done wickedly!

16 "O Lord, [a]according to all Your righteousness, I pray, let Your anger and Your fury be
turned away from Your city Jerusalem, [b]Your
holy mountain; because for our sins, [c]and
for the iniquities of our fathers, [d]Jerusalem
and Your people [e]*are* a reproach to all *those*
around us. 17 Now therefore, our God, hear the
prayer of Your servant, and his supplications,
[a]and [b]for the Lord's sake cause Your face to
shine on Your sanctuary, [c]which is desolate.
18 [a]O my God, incline Your ear and hear; open
Your eyes [b]and see our desolations, and the
city [c]which is called by Your name; for we
do not present our supplications before You
because of our righteous deeds, but because
of Your great mercies. 19 O Lord, hear! O Lord,
forgive! O Lord, listen and act! Do not delay
for Your own sake, my God, for Your city and
Your people are called by Your name."

The Seventy-Weeks Prophecy

20 Now while I *was* speaking, praying, and
confessing my sin and the sin of my people
Israel, and presenting my supplication before
the LORD my God for the holy mountain of my
God, 21 yes, while I *was* speaking in prayer, the
man [a]Gabriel, whom I had seen in the vision
at the beginning, being caused to fly swiftly,
reached me about the time of the evening
offering. 22 And he informed *me,* and talked
with me, and said, "O Daniel, I have now come
forth to give you skill to understand. 23 At the
beginning of your supplications the command went out, and I have come to tell *you,* for
you *are* greatly [a]beloved; therefore [b]consider
the matter, and understand the vision:

24 "Seventy weeks[1] are determined
For your people and for your holy city,
To finish the transgression,
To make an end of[2] sins,

8:27 [a] Dan. 7:28; 8:17 **9:1** [a] Dan. 1:21 **9:2** [a] 2 Chr. 36:21 **9:3** [a] Neh. 1:4 **9:4** [a] Ex. 20:6 **9:5** [a] 1 Kin. 8:47, 48
9:6 [a] 2 Chr. 36:15 **9:7** [a] Neh. 9:33 **9:9** [a] [Ps. 130:4, 7] **9:11** [a] Is. 1:3–6 [b] Lev. 26:14 **9:12** [a] Zech. 1:6 [b] Lam. 1:12; 2:13
9:13 [a] Deut. 28:15–68 [b] Is. 9:13 **9:14** [a] Jer. 31:28; 44:27 [b] Neh. 9:33 **9:15** [a] Neh. 1:10 [b] Neh. 9:10 **9:16** [a] 1 Sam. 12:7
[b] Zech. 8:3 [c] Ex. 20:5 [d] Lam. 2:16 [e] Ps. 79:4 **9:17** [a] Num. 6:24–26 [b] Lam. 5:18 [c] [John 16:24] **9:18** [a] Is. 37:17 [b] Ex. 3:7
[c] Jer. 25:29 **9:21** [a] Dan. 8:16 **9:23** [a] Dan. 10:11, 19 [b] Matt. 24:15 **9:24** [1] Literally *sevens,* and so throughout the chapter
[2] Following Qere, Septuagint, Syriac, and Vulgate; Kethib and Theodotion read *To seal up.*

[a]To make reconciliation for iniquity,
[b]To bring in everlasting righteousness,
To seal up vision and prophecy,
[c]And to anoint the Most Holy.

25 "Know therefore and understand,
That from the going forth of the command
To restore and build Jerusalem
Until [a]Messiah [b]the Prince,
There shall be seven weeks and sixty-two weeks;
The street[1] shall be built again, and the wall,[2]
Even in troublesome times.

26 "And after the sixty-two weeks
[a]Messiah shall be cut off, [b]but not for Himself;
And [c]the people of the prince who is to come
[d]Shall destroy the city and the sanctuary.
The end of it *shall be* with a flood,
And till the end of the war desolations are determined.
27 Then he shall confirm [a]a covenant with [b]many for one week;
But in the middle of the week
He shall bring an end to sacrifice and offering.
And on the wing of abominations shall be one who makes desolate,
[c]Even until the consummation, which is determined,
Is poured out on the desolate."

Vision of the Glorious Man

10 In the third year of Cyrus king of Persia a message was revealed to Daniel,
whose [a]name was called Belteshazzar. The
message *was* true, but the appointed time
was long;[1] and he understood the message,
and had understanding of the vision. 2In
those days I, Daniel, was mourning three full
weeks. 3I ate no pleasant food, no meat or
wine came into my mouth, nor did I anoint
myself at all, till three whole weeks were
fulfilled.
4Now on the twenty-fourth day of the first
month, as I was by the side of the great river, that *is*, the Tigris,[1] 5I lifted my eyes and
looked, and behold, a certain man clothed
in [a]linen, whose waist *was* [b]girded with gold
of *Uphaz!* 6His body *was* like beryl, his face
like the appearance of lightning, his eyes
like torches of fire, his arms and feet like
burnished bronze in color, [a]and the sound
of his words like the voice of a multitude.
7And I, Daniel, alone saw the vision, for
the men who were with me did not see the
vision; but a great terror fell upon them, so
that they fled to hide themselves. 8Therefore
I was left alone when I saw this great vision,
and no strength remained in me; for my vigor
was turned to frailty in me, and I retained no
strength. 9Yet I heard the sound of his words;
and while I heard the sound of his words I
was in a deep sleep on my face, with my face
to the ground.

PEACE NOTE

Feelings come and go, but the peace (*shalom*) promised in the Bible stems from a relationship with the One who created us.

Prophecies Concerning Persia and Greece

10[a]Suddenly, a hand touched me, which
made me tremble on my knees and *on* the
palms of my hands. 11And he said to me,
"O Daniel, [a]man greatly beloved, understand
the words that I speak to you, and stand upright, for I have now been sent to you." While
he was speaking this word to me, I stood
trembling.
12Then he said to me, [a]"Do not fear, Daniel,
for from the first day that you set your heart
to understand, and to humble yourself before
your God, [b]your words were heard; and I
have come because of your words. 13[a]But the
prince of the kingdom of Persia withstood
me twenty-one days; and behold, [b]Michael,
one of the chief princes, came to help me,
for I had been left alone there with the kings
of Persia. 14Now I have come to make you

9:24 [a] [Is. 53:10] [b] Rev. 14:6 [c] Ps. 45:7 **9:25** [a] John 1:41; 4:25 [b] Is. 55:4 [1] Or *open square* [2] Or *moat* **9:26** [a] [Is. 53:8]; Matt. 27:50; Mark 9:12; 15:37; [Luke 23:46; 24:26]; John 19:30; Acts 8:32 [b] [1 Pet. 2:21] [c] Matt. 22:7 [d] Matt. 24:2; Mark 13:2; Luke 19:43, 44 **9:27** [a] Is. 42:6 [b] [Matt. 26:28] [c] Dan. 11:36 **10:1** [a] Dan. 1:7 [1] Or *and of great conflict* **10:4** [1] Hebrew *Hiddekel* **10:5** [a] Ezek. 9:2; 10:2 [b] Rev. 1:13; 15:6 **10:6** [a] [Rev. 1:15] **10:10** [a] Dan. 9:21 **10:11** [a] Dan. 9:23 **10:12** [a] Rev. 1:17 [b] Acts 10:4 **10:13** [a] Dan. 10:20 [b] Dan. 10:21; 12:1

understand what will happen to your people [a]in the latter days, [b]for the vision *refers* to *many* days yet *to come*."

15 When he had spoken such words to me, [a]I turned my face toward the ground and became speechless. 16 And suddenly, [a]*one* having the likeness of the sons[1] of men [b]touched my lips; then I opened my mouth and spoke, saying to him who stood before me, "My lord, because of the vision [c]my sorrows have overwhelmed me, and I have retained no strength. 17 For how can this servant of my lord talk with you, my lord? As for me, no strength remains in me now, nor is any breath left in me."

18 Then again, *the one* having the likeness of a man touched me and strengthened me. 19 [a]And he said, "O man greatly beloved, [b]fear not! Peace *be* to you; be strong, yes, be strong!"

So when he spoke to me I was strengthened, and said, "Let my lord speak, for you have strengthened me."

20 Then he said, "Do you know why I have come to you? And now I must return to fight [a]with the prince of Persia; and when I have gone forth, indeed the prince of Greece will come. 21 But I will tell you what is noted in the Scripture of Truth. (No one upholds me against these, [a]except Michael your prince.

11 "Also [a]in the first year of [b]Darius the Mede, I, *even* I, stood up to confirm and strengthen him.) 2 And now I will tell you the truth: Behold, three more kings will arise in Persia, and the fourth shall be far richer than *them* all; by his strength, through his riches, he shall stir up all against the realm of Greece. 3 Then [a]a mighty king shall arise, who shall rule with great dominion, and [b]do according to his will. 4 And when he has arisen, [a]his kingdom shall be broken up and divided toward the four winds of heaven, but not among his posterity [b]nor according to his dominion with which he ruled; for his kingdom shall be uprooted, even for others besides these.

Warring Kings of North and South

5 "Also the king of the South shall become strong, as well as *one* of his princes; and he shall gain power over him and have dominion. His dominion *shall be* a great dominion. 6 And at the end of *some* years they shall join forces, for the daughter of the king of the South shall go to the king of the North to make an agreement; but she shall not retain the power of her authority,[1] and neither he nor his authority[2] shall stand; but she shall be given up, with those who brought her, and with him who begot her, and with him who strengthened her in *those* times. 7 But from a branch of her roots *one* shall arise in his place, who shall come with an army, enter the fortress of the king of the North, and deal with them and prevail. 8 And he shall also carry their gods captive to Egypt, with their princes[1] *and* their precious articles of silver and gold; and he shall continue *more* years than the king of the North.

9 "Also *the king of the North* shall come to the kingdom of the king of the South, but shall return to his own land. 10 However his sons shall stir up strife, and assemble a multitude of great forces; and *one* shall certainly come [a]and overwhelm and pass through; then he shall return [b]to his fortress and stir up strife.

11 "And the king of the South shall be [a]moved with rage, and go out and fight with him, with the king of the North, who shall muster a great multitude; but the [b]multitude shall be given into the hand of his *enemy*. 12 When he has taken away the multitude, his heart will be lifted up; and he will cast down tens of thousands, but he will not prevail. 13 For the king of the North will return and muster a multitude greater than the former, and shall certainly come at the end of some years with a great army and much equipment.

14 "Now in those times many shall rise up against the king of the South. Also, violent men[1] of your people shall exalt themselves in fulfillment of the vision, but they shall [a]fall. 15 So the king of the North shall come and [a]build a siege mound, and take a fortified city; and the forces[1] of the South shall not withstand *him*. Even his choice troops *shall have* no strength to resist. 16 But he who comes against him [a]shall do according to his own will, and [b]no one shall stand against him. He shall stand in the Glorious Land with destruction in his power.[1]

17 "He shall also [a]set his face to enter with the strength of his whole kingdom, and upright ones[1] with him; thus shall he do. And he shall give him the daughter of women to destroy it; but she shall not stand *with him*, [b]or be for him. 18 After this he shall turn his

10:14 [a] Dan. 2:28 [b] Dan. 8:26; 10:1 **10:15** [a] Dan. 8:18; 10:9 **10:16** [a] Dan. 8:15 [b] Jer. 1:9 [c] Dan. 10:8, 9 [1] Theodotion and Vulgate read *the son;* Septuagint reads *a hand.* **10:19** [a] Dan. 10:11 [b] Judg. 6:23 **10:20** [a] Dan. 10:13 **10:21** [a] [Rev. 12:7] **11:1** [a] Dan. 9:1 [b] Dan. 5:31 **11:3** [a] Dan. 7:6; 8:5 [b] Dan. 8:4; 11:16, 36 **11:4** [a] Zech. 2:6 [b] Dan. 8:22 **11:6** [1] Literally *arm* [2] Literally *arm* **11:8** [1] Or *molded images* **11:10** [a] Is. 8:8 [b] Dan. 11:7 **11:11** [a] Prov. 16:14 [b] [Ps. 33:10, 16] **11:14** [a] Job 9:13 [1] Or *robbers,* literally *sons of breakage* **11:15** [a] Ezek. 4:2; 17:17 [1] Literally *arms* **11:16** [a] Dan. 8:4, 7 [b] Josh. 1:5 [1] Literally *hand* **11:17** [a] 2 Chr. 20:3 [b] Dan. 9:26 [1] Or *bring equitable terms*

face to the coastlands, and shall take many.
But a ruler shall bring the reproach against
them to an end; and with the reproach removed, he shall turn back on him. 19Then
he shall turn his face toward the fortress of
his own land; but he shall [a]stumble and fall,
[b]and not be found.

20"There shall arise in his place one who
imposes taxes *on* the glorious kingdom; but
within a few days he shall be destroyed, but
not in anger or in battle. 21And in his place
[a]shall arise a vile person, to whom they will
not give the honor of royalty; but he shall
come in peaceably, and seize the kingdom
by intrigue. 22With the force[1] of a [a]flood they
shall be swept away from before him and be
broken, [b]and also the prince of the covenant.
23And after the league *is made* with him [a]he
shall act deceitfully, for he shall come up and
become strong with a small *number of* people. 24He shall enter peaceably, even into the
richest places of the province; and he shall
do *what* his fathers have not done, nor his
forefathers: he shall disperse among them
the plunder, spoil, and riches; and he shall
devise his plans against the strongholds, but
only for a time.

25"He shall stir up his power and his courage
against the king of the South with a great army.
And the king of the South shall be stirred up
to battle with a very great and mighty army;
but he shall not stand, for they shall devise
plans against him. 26Yes, those who eat of the
portion of his delicacies shall destroy him; his
army shall be swept away, and many shall fall
down slain. 27Both these kings' hearts *shall be*
bent on evil, and they shall speak lies at the
same table; but it shall not prosper, for the end
will still *be* at the [a]appointed time. 28While returning to his land with great riches, his heart
shall be *moved* against the holy covenant; so
he shall do *damage* and return to his own
land.

The Northern King's Blasphemies

29"At the appointed time he shall return
and go toward the south; but it shall not be
like the former or the latter. 30[a]For ships from
Cyprus[1] shall come against him; therefore he
shall be grieved, and return in rage against
the holy covenant, and do *damage.*

"So he shall return and show regard for
those who forsake the holy covenant. 31And
forces[1] shall be mustered by him, [a]and they
shall defile the sanctuary fortress; then they
shall take away the daily *sacrifices,* and place
there the abomination of desolation. 32Those
who do wickedly against the covenant he
shall corrupt with flattery; but the people
who know their God shall be strong, and carry
out *great exploits.* 33And those of the people
who understand shall instruct many; yet *for
many* days they shall fall by sword and flame,
by captivity and plundering. 34Now when
they fall, they shall be aided with a little help;
but many shall join with them by intrigue.
35And *some* of those of understanding shall
fall, [a]to refine them, purify *them,* and make
them white, *until* the time of the end; because
it is still for the appointed time.

36"Then the king shall do according to his
own will: he shall [a]exalt and magnify himself
above every god, shall speak blasphemies
against the God of gods, and shall prosper till
the wrath has been accomplished; for what
has been determined shall be done. 37He
shall regard neither the God[1] of his fathers
nor the desire of women, [a]nor regard any
god; for he shall exalt himself above *them*
all. 38But in their place he shall honor a god
of fortresses; and a god which his fathers did
not know he shall honor with gold and silver,
with precious stones and pleasant things.
39Thus he shall act against the strongest
fortresses with a foreign god, which he shall
acknowledge, *and* advance *its* glory; and
he shall cause them to rule over many, and
divide the land for gain.

The Northern King's Conquests

40"At the [a]time of the end the king of the
South shall attack him; and the king of the
North shall come against him [b]like a whirlwind, with chariots, [c]horsemen, and with
many ships; and he shall enter the countries,
overwhelm *them,* and pass through. 41He
shall also enter the Glorious Land, and many
countries shall be overthrown; but these shall
escape from his hand: [a]Edom, Moab, and the
prominent people of Ammon. 42He shall
stretch out his hand against the countries,
and the land of [a]Egypt shall not escape. 43He
shall have power over the treasures of gold
and silver, and over all the precious things of
Egypt; also the Libyans and Ethiopians *shall
follow* [a]at his heels. 44But news from the east
and the north shall trouble him; therefore
he shall go out with great fury to destroy
and annihilate many. 45And he shall plant
the tents of his palace between the seas and
[a]the glorious holy mountain; [b]yet he shall
come to his end, and no one will help him.

11:19 [a] Jer. 46:6 [b] Ps. 37:36 **11:21** [a] Dan. 7:8 **11:22** [a] Dan. 9:26 [b] Dan. 8:10, 11 [1] Literally *arms* **11:23** [a] Dan. 8:25 **11:27** [a] Hab. 2:3 **11:30** [a] Jer. 2:10 [1] Hebrew *Kittim,* western lands, especially Cyprus **11:31** [a] Dan. 8:11–13; 12:11 [1] Literally *arms* **11:35** [a] Dan. 12:10 **11:36** [a] Dan. 7:8, 25 **11:37** [a] Is. 14:13 [1] Or *gods* **11:40** [a] Dan. 11:27, 35; 12:4, 9 [b] Is. 21:1 [c] Rev. 9:16 **11:41** [a] Is. 11:14 **11:42** [a] Joel 3:19 **11:43** [a] Ex. 11:8 **11:45** [a] Ps. 48:2 [b] Rev. 19:20

Prophecy of the End Time

12 "At that time Michael shall stand up,
The great prince who stands *watch*
over the sons of your people;
[a]And there shall be a time of trouble,
Such as never was since there was a
nation,
Even to that time.
And at that time your people [b]shall be
delivered,
Every one who is found [c]written in the
book.
2 And many of those who sleep in the
dust of the earth shall awake,
[a]Some to everlasting life,
Some to shame [b]*and* everlasting
contempt.
3 Those who are wise shall [a]shine
Like the brightness of the firmament,
[b]And those who turn many to
righteousness
[c]Like the stars forever and ever.

4"But you, Daniel, [a]shut up the words, and
seal the book until the time of the end; many
shall [b]run to and fro, and knowledge shall
increase."
5Then I, Daniel, looked; and there stood
two others, one on this riverbank and the
other on that [a]riverbank. 6And *one* said to
the man clothed in [a]linen, who *was* above
the waters of the river, [b]"How long shall the
fulfillment of these wonders *be?*"
7Then I heard the man clothed in linen,
who *was* above the waters of the river, when
he [a]held up his right hand and his left hand to
heaven, and swore by Him [b]who lives forever,
[c]that *it shall be* for a time, times, and half *a
time;* [d]and when the power of [e]the holy people has been completely shattered, all these
things shall be finished.
8Although I heard, I did not understand.
Then I said, "My lord, what *shall be* the end
of these *things?*"
9And he said, "Go *your way*, Daniel, for
the words *are* closed up and sealed till the
time of the end. 10[a]Many shall be purified,
made white, and refined, [b]but the wicked
shall do wickedly; and none of the wicked shall understand, but [c]the wise shall
understand.
11"And from the time *that* the daily *sacrifice*
is taken away, and the abomination of desolation is set up, *there shall be* one thousand
two hundred and ninety days. 12Blessed *is* he
who waits, and comes to the one thousand
three hundred and thirty-five days.
13"But you, go *your way* till the end; [a]for you
shall rest, [b]and will arise to your inheritance
at the end of the days."

12:1 [a] Jer. 30:7 [b] Rom. 11:26 [c] Ex. 32:32 **12:2** [a] [John 5:28, 29] [b] [Is. 66:24] **12:3** [a] Matt. 13:43 [b] [James 5:19, 20] [c] 1 Cor. 15:41 **12:4** [a] Rev. 22:10 [b] Amos 8:12 **12:5** [a] Dan. 10:4 **12:6** [a] Ezek. 9:2 [b] Dan. 8:13; 12:8 **12:7** [a] Deut. 32:40 [b] Dan. 4:34 [c] Dan. 7:25 [d] Luke 21:24 [e] Dan. 8:24 **12:10** [a] Zech. 13:9 [b] Is. 32:6, 7 [c] John 7:17; 8:47 **12:13** [a] Rev. 14:13 [b] Ps. 1:5

THE BOOK OF

HOSEA

AUTHOR

Few critics argue with the claim in Hosea 1:1 that Hosea is the author of this book. The author's place of birth is not given but his familiarity and obvious concern with the northern kingdom point to his living in Israel, rather than in Judah. Hosea had a real compassion for his people. His personal suffering because of his wife, Gomer, gave him some understanding of God's grief over the people's sin, and this grief becomes the source of the unique tenderness and hope that characterize Hosea's book.

TIME

c. 755–710 BC

KEY VERSE

Hosea 4:1

THEME

Hosea was a contemporary of Isaiah, prophesying near the end of Israel's existence. It is clear from reading the text that Assyria was about to take over. In the second verse of Hosea, God tells Hosea to marry a prostitute to provide a living illustration of God's faithfulness and Israel's unfaithfulness. By this, Hosea demonstrates that God loves us as He did Israel: knowingly and in spite of all our propensities to reject His love for us.

The prophet Hosea originated the worshipful and familiar phrase: "For we will offer the sacrifices of our lips" (14:2). The verb "offer" (*shalam*), which is from the same root word as "peace," inspires us to worship God in words of confession and praise and petition. It is striking that we learn from Hosea's prophecies the importance of finding peace after asking the Lord to "receive us graciously" (14:2). We also see a mirror of our culture in Hosea's indictment of sinful Israel: "There is no truth or mercy or knowledge of God in the land" (4:1). In Hosea we find the recipe for national peace: truth + God's faithful love + knowledge of God in the land.

1 The word of the LORD that came to Hosea the son of Beeri, in the days of [a]Uzziah, [b]Jotham, [c]Ahaz, *and* [d]Hezekiah, kings of Judah, and in the days of [e]Jeroboam the son of Joash, king of Israel.

The Family of Hosea

2 When the LORD began to speak by Hosea, the LORD said to Hosea:

[a]"Go, take yourself a wife of harlotry
And children of harlotry,
For [b]the land has committed great harlotry
By departing from the LORD."

3 So he went and took Gomer the daughter of Diblaim, and she conceived and bore him a son. 4 Then the LORD said to him:

"Call his name Jezreel,
For in a little *while*
[a]I will avenge the bloodshed of Jezreel on the house of Jehu,
[b]And bring an end to the kingdom of the house of Israel.
5 [a]It shall come to pass in that day
That I will break the bow of Israel in the Valley of Jezreel."

6 And she conceived again and bore a daughter. Then *God* said to him:

"Call her name Lo-Ruhamah,[1]
[a]For I will no longer have mercy on the house of Israel,
But I will utterly take them away.[2]
7 [a]Yet I will have mercy on the house of Judah,
Will save them by the LORD their God,
And [b]will not save them by bow,
Nor by sword or battle,
By horses or horsemen."

8 Now when she had weaned Lo-Ruhamah, she conceived and bore a son. 9 Then *God* said:

"Call his name Lo-Ammi,[1]
For you *are* not My people,
And I will not be your *God*.

The Restoration of Israel

10 "Yet [a]the number of the children of Israel
Shall be as the sand of the sea,
Which cannot be measured or numbered.
[b]And it shall come to pass
In the place where it was said to them,
'You *are* not My [c]people,'[1]
There it shall be said to them,
'*You are* [d]sons of the living God.'
11 [a]Then the children of Judah and the children of Israel
Shall be gathered together,
And appoint for themselves one head;
And they shall come up out of the land,
For great *will be* the day of Jezreel!

2 Say to your brethren, 'My people,'[1]
And to your sisters, 'Mercy[2] *is shown*.'

God's Unfaithful People

2 "Bring charges against your mother, bring charges;
For [a]she *is* not My wife, nor *am* I her Husband!
Let her put away her [b]harlotries from her sight,
And her adulteries from between her breasts;
3 Lest [a]I strip her naked
And expose her, as in the day she was [b]born,
And make her like a wilderness,
And set her like a dry land,
And slay her with [c]thirst.

4 "I will not have mercy on her children,
For they *are* the [a]children of harlotry.
5 For their mother has played the harlot;
She who conceived them has behaved shamefully.
For she said, 'I will go after my lovers,
[a]Who give *me* my bread and my water,
My wool and my linen,
My oil and my drink.'

6 "Therefore, behold,
[a]I will hedge up your way with thorns,
And wall her in,
So that she cannot find her paths.
7 She will chase her lovers,
But not overtake them;
Yes, she will seek them, but not find *them*.
Then she will say,
[a]'I will go and return to my [b]first husband,
For then *it was* better for me than now.'

1:1 [a] Amos 1:1 [b] 2 Chr. 27 [c] 2 Chr. 28 [d] 2 Chr. 29:1—32:33 [e] 2 Kin. 13:13; 14:23–29 **1:2** [a] Hos. 3:1 [b] Jer. 2:13 **1:4** [a] 2 Kin. 10:11 [b] 2 Kin. 15:8–10; 17:6, 23; 18:11 **1:5** [a] 2 Kin. 15:29 **1:6** [a] 2 Kin. 17:6 [1] Literally *No-Mercy* [2] Or *That I may forgive them at all* **1:7** [a] 2 Kin. 19:29–35 [b] [Zech. 4:6] **1:9** [1] Literally *Not-My-People* **1:10** [a] Gen. 22:17; 32:12 [b] 1 Pet. 2:10 [c] Rom. 9:26 [d] [John 1:12] [1] Hebrew *lo-ammi* (compare verse 9) **1:11** [a] Is. 11:11–13 **2:1** [1] Hebrew *Ammi* (compare 1:9, 10) [2] Hebrew *Ruhamah* (compare 1:6) **2:2** [a] Is. 50:1 [b] Ezek. 16:25 **2:3** [a] Jer. 13:22, 26 [b] Ezek. 16:4–7, 22 [c] Amos 8:11–13 **2:4** [a] John 8:41 **2:5** [a] Hos. 2:8, 12 **2:6** [a] Lam. 3:7, 9 **2:7** [a] Luke 15:17, 18 [b] Ezek. 16:8; 23:4

8 For she did not [a]know
That I gave her grain, new wine, and oil,
And multiplied her silver and gold—
Which they prepared for Baal.

9 "Therefore I will return and take away
My grain in its time
And My new wine in its season,
And will take back My wool and My linen,
Given to cover her nakedness.
10 Now [a]I will uncover her lewdness in the sight of her lovers,
And no one shall deliver her from My hand.
11 [a]I will also cause all her mirth to cease,
Her feast days,
Her New Moons,
Her Sabbaths—
All her appointed feasts.

12 "And I will destroy her vines and her fig trees,
Of which she has said,
'These *are* my wages that my lovers have given me.'
So I will make them a forest,
And the beasts of the field shall eat them.
13 I will punish her
For the days of the Baals to which she burned incense.
She decked herself with her earrings and jewelry,
And went after her lovers;
But Me she forgot," says the LORD.

God's Mercy on His People

14 "Therefore, behold, I will allure her,
Will bring her into the wilderness,
And speak comfort to her.
15 I will give her her vineyards from there,
And [a]the Valley of Achor as a door of hope;
She shall sing there,
As in [b]the days of her youth,
[c]As in the day when she came up from the land of Egypt.

16 "And it shall be, in that day,"
Says the LORD,
"*That* you will call Me 'My Husband,'[1]
And no longer call Me 'My Master,'[2]
17 For [a]I will take from her mouth the names of the Baals,
And they shall be remembered by their name no more.
18 In that day I will make a [a]covenant for them
With the beasts of the field,
With the birds of the air,
And *with* the creeping things of the ground.
Bow and sword of battle [b]I will shatter from the earth,
To make them [c]lie down safely.

19 "I will betroth you to Me forever;
Yes, I will betroth you to Me
In righteousness and justice,
In lovingkindness and mercy;
20 I will betroth you to Me in faithfulness,
And [a]you shall know the LORD.

21 "It shall come to pass in that day
That [a]I will answer," says the LORD;
"I will answer the heavens,
And they shall answer the earth.
22 The earth shall answer
With grain,
With new wine,
And with oil;
They shall answer Jezreel.[1]
23 Then [a]I will sow her for Myself in the earth,
[b]And I will have mercy on *her who had* not obtained mercy;[1]
Then [c]I will say to *those who were* not My people,[2]
'You *are* My people!'
And they shall say, '*You are* my God!' "

Israel Will Return to God

3 Then the LORD said to me, "Go again,
love a woman *who is* loved by a [a]lover[1]
and is committing adultery, just like the love
of the LORD for the children of Israel, who
look to other gods and love *the* raisin cakes
of the pagans."
2 So I bought her for myself for fifteen *shek-*
els of silver, and one and one-half homers
of barley. 3 And I said to her, "You shall [a]stay
with me many days; you shall not play the
harlot, nor shall you have a man—so, too,
will I *be* toward you."
4 For the children of Israel shall abide
many days [a]without king or prince, without
sacrifice or *sacred* pillar, without [b]ephod or
[c]teraphim. 5 Afterward the children of Israel
shall return and [a]seek the LORD their God
and [b]David their king. They shall fear the
LORD and His goodness in the [c]latter days.

2:8 [a] Is. 1:3 2:10 [a] Ezek. 16:37 2:11 [a] Amos 5:21; 8:10 2:15 [a] Josh. 7:26 [b] Ezek. 16:8–14 [c] Ex. 15:1 2:16 [1] Hebrew *Ishi* [2] Hebrew *Baali* 2:17 [a] Ex. 23:13 2:18 [a] Job 5:23 [b] Is. 2:4 [c] Lev. 26:5 2:20 [a] [Jer. 31:33, 34] 2:21 [a] Zech. 8:12 2:22 [1] Literally *God Will Sow* 2:23 [a] Jer. 31:27 [b] Hos. 1:6 [c] Hos. 1:10 [1] Hebrew *lo-ruhamah* [2] Hebrew *lo-ammi* 3:1 [a] Jer. 3:20 [1] Literally *friend* or *husband* 3:3 [a] Deut. 21:13 3:4 [a] Hos. 10:3 [b] Ex. 28:4–12 [c] Judg. 17:5; 18:14, 17 3:5 [a] Jer. 50:4 [b] Jer. 30:9 [c] [Is. 2:2, 3]

PEACE FOR GOD'S FAMILY

"I will have mercy on her who had not obtained mercy; then I will say . . . 'You are My people!'"

HOSEA 2:23

You've probably surmised that the life of an Old Testament prophet was not easy. Hosea's was especially challenging. He married an adulteress—and that was by God's design (see 1:2–3)! Hosea's faithless wife exemplified Israel and her infidelity in her relationship to God. Like a cheating wife chasing after lovers, Israel ran after other gods. Israel's sin was so bad it led to separation.

But God was merciful nonetheless. The prophet foretold the day when "Not-My-People" ("Lo-Ammi," 1:9) would be called "sons of the living God" (1:10). God's willingness to bring back into the heavenly fold people who had so grievously sinned should give us assurance and hope. It is proof that God's will is our restoration. The devil's lie is that you have lost God's forgiveness or love. A lie destroys your peace if you believe it. Repent and return to the Lord, and you will find His peace again and again.

God's Charge Against Israel

4 Hear the word of the LORD,
You children of Israel,
For the LORD *brings* a [a]charge against
the inhabitants of the land:

"There is no truth or mercy
Or [b]knowledge of God in the land.
2 *By* swearing and lying,
Killing and stealing and committing
adultery,
They break all restraint,
With bloodshed upon bloodshed.
3 Therefore [a]the land will mourn;
And [b]everyone who dwells there will
waste away
With the beasts of the field
And the birds of the air;
Even the fish of the sea will be taken
away.

4 "Now let no man contend, or rebuke
another;
For your people *are* like those [a]who
contend with the priest.
5 Therefore you shall stumble [a]in the
day;
The prophet also shall stumble with
you in the night;
And I will destroy your mother.
6 [a]My people are destroyed for lack of
knowledge.
Because you have rejected knowledge,
I also will reject you from being priest
for Me;
[b]Because you have forgotten the law of
your God,
I also will forget your children.

7 "The more they increased,
The more they sinned against Me;
[a]I will change[1] their glory[2] into shame.
8 They eat up the sin of My people;
They set their heart on their iniquity.
9 And it shall be: [a]like people, like priest.
So I will punish them for their ways,
And reward them for their deeds.
10 For [a]they shall eat, but not have enough;
They shall commit harlotry, but not
increase;
Because they have ceased obeying the
LORD.

The Idolatry of Israel

11 "Harlotry, wine, and new wine [a]enslave
the heart.
12 My people ask counsel from their
[a]wooden *idols,*
And their staff informs them.
For [b]the spirit of harlotry has caused
them to stray,
And they have played the harlot
against their God.
13 [a]They offer sacrifices on the
mountaintops,
And burn incense on the hills,

4:1 [a] Is. 1:18 [b] Jer. 4:22 **4:3** [a] Amos 5:16; 8:8 [b] Zeph. 1:3 **4:4** [a] Deut. 17:12 **4:5** [a] Jer. 15:8 **4:6** [a] Is. 5:13 [b] Ezek. 22:26 **4:7** [a] 1 Sam. 2:30 [1] Following Masoretic Text, Septuagint, and Vulgate; scribal tradition, Syriac, and Targum read *They will change.* [2] Following Masoretic Text, Septuagint, Syriac, Targum, and Vulgate; scribal tradition reads *My glory.* **4:9** [a] Is. 24:2 **4:10** [a] Lev. 26:26 **4:11** [a] Is. 5:12; 28:7 **4:12** [a] Jer. 2:27 [b] Is. 44:19, 20 **4:13** [a] Is. 1:29; 57:5, 7

Under oaks, poplars, and terebinths,
Because their shade *is* good.
[b]Therefore your daughters commit harlotry,
And your brides commit adultery.

14 "I will not punish your daughters when they commit harlotry,
Nor your brides when they commit adultery;
For *the men* themselves go apart with harlots,
And offer sacrifices with a [a]ritual harlot.[1]
Therefore people *who* do not understand will be trampled.

15 "Though you, Israel, play the harlot,
Let not Judah offend.
[a]Do not come up to Gilgal,
Nor go up to [b]Beth Aven,
[c]Nor swear an oath, *saying,* 'As the LORD lives'—

16 "For Israel [a]is stubborn
Like a stubborn calf;
Now the LORD will let them forage
Like a lamb in open country.

17 "Ephraim *is* joined to idols,
[a]Let him alone.
18 Their drink is rebellion,
They commit harlotry continually.
[a]Her rulers dearly[1] love dishonor.
19 [a]The wind has wrapped her up in its wings,
And [b]they shall be ashamed because of their sacrifices.

Impending Judgment on Israel and Judah

5 "Hear this, O priests!
Take heed, O house of Israel!
Give ear, O house of the king!
For yours *is* the judgment,
Because [a]you have been a snare to Mizpah
And a net spread on Tabor.
2 The revolters are [a]deeply involved in slaughter,
Though I rebuke them all.
3 [a]I know Ephraim,
And Israel is not hidden from Me;
For now, O Ephraim, [b]you commit harlotry;
Israel is defiled.

4 "They do not direct their deeds
Toward turning to their God,
For [a]the spirit of harlotry is in their midst,
And they do not know the LORD.
5 The [a]pride of Israel testifies to his face;
Therefore Israel and Ephraim stumble in their iniquity;
Judah also stumbles with them.

6 "With their flocks and herds
[a]They shall go to seek the LORD,
But they will not find *Him;*
He has withdrawn Himself from them.
7 They have [a]dealt treacherously with the LORD,
For they have begotten pagan children.
Now a New Moon shall devour them and their heritage.

8 "Blow[a] the ram's horn in Gibeah,
The trumpet in Ramah!
[b]Cry aloud *at* [c]Beth Aven,
'*Look* behind you, O Benjamin!'
9 Ephraim shall be desolate in the day of rebuke;
Among the tribes of Israel I make known what is sure.

10 "The princes of Judah are like those who [a]remove a landmark;
I will pour out My wrath on them like water.
11 Ephraim is [a]oppressed *and* broken in judgment,
Because he willingly walked by [b]*human* precept.
12 Therefore I *will be* to Ephraim like a moth,
And to the house of Judah [a]like rottenness.

13 "When Ephraim saw his sickness,
And Judah *saw* his [a]wound,
Then Ephraim went [b]to Assyria
And sent to King Jareb;
Yet he cannot cure you,
Nor heal you of your wound.
14 For [a]I *will be* like a lion to Ephraim,
And like a young lion to the house of Judah.
[b]I, *even* I, will tear *them* and go away;
I will take *them* away, and no one shall rescue.

4:13 [b] Amos 7:17 **4:14** [a] Deut. 23:18 [1] Compare Deuteronomy 23:18 **4:15** [a] Hos. 9:15; 12:11 [b] 1 Kin. 12:29 [c] Amos 8:14 **4:16** [a] Jer. 3:6; 7:24; 8:5 **4:17** [a] Matt. 15:14 **4:18** [a] Mic. 3:11 [1] Hebrew is difficult; a Jewish tradition reads *Her rulers shamefully love, 'Give!'* **4:19** [a] Jer. 51:1 [b] Is. 1:29 **5:1** [a] Hos. 6:9 **5:2** [a] Is. 29:15 **5:3** [a] Amos 3:2; 5:12 [b] Hos. 4:17 **5:4** [a] Hos. 4:12 **5:5** [a] Hos. 7:10 **5:6** [a] Prov. 1:28 **5:7** [a] Jer. 3:20 **5:8** [a] Joel 2:1 [b] Is. 10:30 [c] Josh. 7:2 **5:10** [a] Deut. 19:14; 27:17 **5:11** [a] Deut. 28:33 [b] Mic. 6:16 **5:12** [a] Prov. 12:4 **5:13** [a] Jer. 30:12–15 [b] 2 Kin. 15:19 **5:14** [a] Lam. 3:10 [b] Ps. 50:22

15 I will return again to My place
Till they acknowledge their offense.
Then they will seek My face;
In their affliction they will earnestly seek Me."

A Call to Repentance

6 Come,[a] and let us return to the LORD;
For [b]He has torn, but [c]He will heal us;
He has stricken, but He will bind us up.
2 [a]After two days He will revive us;
On the third day He will raise us up,
That we may live in His sight.
3 [a]Let us know,
Let us pursue the knowledge of the LORD.
His going forth is established [b]as the morning;
[c]He will come to us [d]like the rain,
Like the latter *and* former rain to the earth.

Impenitence of Israel and Judah

4 "O Ephraim, what shall I do to you?
O Judah, what shall I do to you?
For your faithfulness is like a morning cloud,
And like the early dew it goes away.
5 Therefore I have hewn *them* by the prophets,
I have slain them by [a]the words of My mouth;
And your judgments *are like* light *that* goes forth.
6 For I desire [a]mercy and [b]not sacrifice,
And the [c]knowledge of God more than burnt offerings.

7 "But like men[1] they transgressed the covenant;
There they dealt treacherously with Me.
8 [a]Gilead *is* a city of evildoers
And defiled with blood.
9 As bands of robbers lie in wait for a man,
So the company of [a]priests [b]murder on the way to Shechem;
Surely they commit [c]lewdness.
10 I have seen a horrible thing in the house of Israel:
There *is* the harlotry of Ephraim;
Israel is defiled.
11 Also, O Judah, a harvest is appointed for you,
When I return the captives of My people.

7 "When I would have healed Israel,
Then the iniquity of Ephraim was uncovered,
And the wickedness of Samaria.
For [a]they have committed fraud;
A thief comes in;
A band of robbers takes spoil outside.

6:1 [a] Is. 1:18 [b] Deut. 32:39 [c] Jer. 30:17 **6:2** [a] Luke 24:26; Acts 10:40; [1 Cor. 15:4] **6:3** [a] Is. 54:13 [b] 2 Sam. 23:4 [c] Ps. 72:6 [d] Job 29:23 **6:5** [a] [Jer. 23:29] **6:6** [a] Matt. 9:13; 12:7 [b] [Mic. 6:6–8] [c] [John 17:3] **6:7** [1] Or *like Adam* **6:8** [a] Hos. 12:11 **6:9** [a] Hos. 5:1 [b] Jer. 7:9, 10 [c] Ezek. 22:9; 23:27 **7:1** [a] Hos. 5:1

IMMERSED IN PEACE

"I desire mercy and not sacrifice."

HOSEA 6:6

When King Saul disobeyed Samuel and then tried to make up for it by offering a sacrifice, he was told: "Has the LORD as great delight in burnt offerings and sacrifices, as in obeying the voice of the LORD? Behold, to obey is better than sacrifice" (1 Sam. 15:22). Samuel's rebuke contains a huge, important truth that we find echoed here in Hosea 6:6 more than a century later. The prophet said, "I desire mercy and not sacrifice, and the knowledge of God more than burnt offerings." In essence, God was saying that the attitude was far more important than ritual.

Samuel's and Hosea's words were of great relevance in their respective times and places, but these words are just as important for us today. Peace with God cannot be reduced to a ritual, formula, or routine. Peace with God grows out of a living and loving relationship that includes obeying God (as Samuel says) and showing mercy to others (as Hosea says). This reflects true "knowledge of God" and the way to be immersed in His peace.

Are there areas in which you need to obey and/or show mercy today?

2 They do not consider in their hearts
That [a]I remember all their wickedness;
Now their own deeds have surrounded
them;
They are before My face.
3 They make a [a]king glad with their
wickedness,
And princes [b]with their lies.

4 "They[a] *are* all adulterers.
Like an oven heated by a baker—
He ceases stirring *the fire* after
kneading the dough,
Until it is leavened.
5 In the day of our king
Princes have made *him* sick, inflamed
with [a]wine;
He stretched out his hand with scoffers.
6 They prepare their heart like an oven,
While they lie in wait;
Their baker[1] sleeps all night;
In the morning it burns like a flaming
fire.
7 They are all hot, like an oven,
And have devoured their judges;
All their kings have fallen.
[a]None among them calls upon Me.

8 "Ephraim [a]has mixed himself among
the peoples;
Ephraim is a cake unturned.
9 [a]Aliens have devoured his strength,
But he does not know *it;*
Yes, gray hairs are here and there on
him,
Yet he does not know *it.*
10 And the [a]pride of Israel testifies to his
face,
But [b]they do not return to the LORD
their God,
Nor seek Him for all this.

Futile Reliance on the Nations

11 "Ephraim[a] also is like a silly dove,
without sense—
[b]They call to Egypt,
They go to [c]Assyria.
12 Wherever they go, I will [a]spread My net
on them;
I will bring them down like birds of the
air;
I will chastise them
[b]According to what their congregation
has heard.

13 "Woe to them, for they have fled from Me!
Destruction to them,
Because they have transgressed
against Me!
Though [a]I redeemed them,
Yet they have spoken lies against Me.
14 [a]They did not cry out to Me with their
heart
When they wailed upon their beds.

"They assemble together for[1] grain and
new [b]wine,
They rebel against Me;[2]
15 Though I disciplined *and* strengthened
their arms,
Yet they devise evil against Me;
16 They return, *but* not to the Most High;[1]
[a]They are like a treacherous bow.
Their princes shall fall by the sword
For the [b]cursings of their tongue.
This *shall be* their derision [c]in the land
of Egypt.

The Apostasy of Israel

8 "*Set* the trumpet[1] to your mouth!
He shall come [a]like an eagle against
the house of the LORD,
Because they have transgressed My
covenant
And rebelled against My law.
2 [a]Israel will cry to Me,
'My God, [b]we know You!'
3 Israel has rejected the good;
The enemy will pursue him.

4 "They[a] set up kings, but not by Me;
They made princes, but I did not
acknowledge *them.*
From their silver and gold
They made idols for themselves—
That they might be cut off.
5 Your calf is rejected, O Samaria!
My anger is aroused against them—
[a]How long until they attain to
innocence?
6 For from Israel *is* even this:
A [a]workman made it, and it *is* not God;
But the calf of Samaria shall be broken
to pieces.

7:2 [a] Jer. 14:10; 17:1 **7:3** [a] Hos. 1:1 [b] [Rom. 1:32] **7:4** [a] Jer. 9:2; 23:10 **7:5** [a] Is. 28:1, 7 **7:6** [1] Following Masoretic Text and Vulgate; Syriac and Targum read *Their anger;* Septuagint reads *Ephraim.* **7:7** [a] Is. 64:7 **7:8** [a] Ps. 106:35 **7:9** [a] Hos. 8:7 **7:10** [a] Hos. 5:5 [b] Is. 9:13 **7:11** [a] Hos. 11:11 [b] Is. 30:3 [c] Hos. 5:13; 8:9 **7:12** [a] Ezek. 12:13 [b] Lev. 26:14 **7:13** [a] Mic. 6:4 **7:14** [a] Job 35:9, 10 [b] Amos 2:8 [1] Following Masoretic Text and Targum; Vulgate reads *thought upon;* Septuagint reads *slashed themselves for* (compare 1 Kings 18:28). [2] Following Masoretic Text, Syriac, and Targum; Septuagint omits *They rebel against Me;* Vulgate reads *They departed from Me.* **7:16** [a] Ps. 78:57 [b] Ps. 73:9 [c] Hos. 8:13; 9:3 [1] Or *upward* **8:1** [a] Deut. 28:49 [1] Hebrew *shophar,* ram's horn **8:2** [a] Ps. 78:34 [b] Titus 1:16 **8:4** [a] 2 Kin. 15:23, 25 **8:5** [a] Jer. 13:27 **8:6** [a] Is. 40:19

7 "They[a] sow the wind,
And reap the whirlwind.
The stalk has no bud;
It shall never produce meal.
If it should produce,
[b]Aliens would swallow it up.
8 [a]Israel is swallowed up;
Now they are among the Gentiles
[b]Like a vessel in which *is* no pleasure.
9 For they have gone up to Assyria,
Like [a]a wild donkey alone by itself;
Ephraim [b]has hired lovers.
10 Yes, though they have hired among the nations,
Now [a]I will gather them;
And they shall sorrow a little,[1]
Because of the burden[2] of [b]the king of princes.

11 "Because Ephraim has made many altars for sin,
They have become for him altars for sinning.
12 I have written for him [a]the great things of My law,
But they were considered a strange thing.
13 *For* the sacrifices of My offerings [a]they sacrifice flesh and eat *it,*
[b]*But* the LORD does not accept them.
[c]Now He will remember their iniquity and punish their sins.
They shall return to Egypt.

14 "For[a] Israel has forgotten [b]his Maker,
And has built temples;[1]
Judah also has multiplied [c]fortified cities;
But [d]I will send fire upon his cities,
And it shall devour his palaces."

Judgment of Israel's Sin

9 Do[a] not rejoice, O Israel, with joy like *other* peoples,
For you have played the harlot against your God.
You have made love *for* [b]hire on every threshing floor.
2 The threshing floor and the winepress
Shall not feed them,
And the new wine shall fail in her.

3 They shall not dwell in [a]the LORD's land,
[b]But Ephraim shall return to Egypt,
And [c]shall eat unclean *things* in Assyria.

PEACE NOTE

We can change the way we think! This is the promise of God's Word.

4 They shall not offer wine *offerings* to the LORD,
Nor [a]shall their [b]sacrifices be pleasing to Him.
It shall be like bread of mourners to them;
All who eat it shall be defiled.
For their bread *shall be* for their *own* life;
It shall not come into the house of the LORD.

5 What will you do in the appointed day,
And in the day of the feast of the LORD?
6 For indeed they are gone because of destruction.
Egypt shall gather them up;
Memphis shall bury them.
[a]Nettles shall possess their valuables of silver;
Thorns *shall be* in their tents.

7 The [a]days of punishment have come;
The days of recompense have come.
Israel knows!
The prophet *is* a [b]fool,
[c]The spiritual man *is* insane,
Because of the greatness of your iniquity and great enmity.
8 The [a]watchman of Ephraim *is* with my God;
But the prophet *is* a fowler's[1] snare in all his ways—
Enmity in the house of his God.
9 [a]They are deeply corrupted,
As in the days of [b]Gibeah.
He will remember their iniquity;
He will punish their sins.

8:7 [a] Prov. 22:8 [b] Hos. 7:9 **8:8** [a] 2 Kin. 17:6 [b] Jer. 22:28; 25:34 **8:9** [a] Jer. 2:24 [b] Ezek. 16:33, 34 **8:10** [a] Ezek. 16:37; 22:20 [b] Is. 10:8 [1] Or *begin to diminish* [2] Or *oracle* **8:12** [a] [Deut. 4:6–8] **8:13** [a] Zech. 7:6 [b] Jer. 14:10 [c] Amos 8:7 **8:14** [a] Deut. 32:18 [b] Is. 29:23 [c] Num. 32:17 [d] Jer. 17:27 [1] Or *palaces* **9:1** [a] Is. 22:12, 13 [b] Jer. 44:17 **9:3** [a] [Lev. 25:23] [b] Hos. 7:16; 8:13 [c] Ezek. 4:13 **9:4** [a] Jer. 6:20 [b] Hos. 8:13 **9:6** [a] Is. 5:6; 7:23 **9:7** [a] Is. 10:3 [b] Lam. 2:14 [c] Mic. 2:11 **9:8** [a] Ezek. 3:17; 33:7 [1] That is, one who catches birds in a trap or snare **9:9** [a] Hos. 10:9 [b] Judg. 19:22

10 "I found Israel
Like grapes in the [a]wilderness;
I saw your fathers
As the [b]firstfruits on the fig tree in its first season.
But they went to [c]Baal Peor,
And separated themselves *to that* shame;
[d]They became an abomination like the thing they loved.
11 *As for* Ephraim, their glory shall fly away like a bird—
No birth, no pregnancy, and no conception!
12 Though they bring up their children,
Yet I will bereave them to the last man.
Yes, [a]woe to them when I depart from them!
13 Just [a]as I saw Ephraim like Tyre, planted in a pleasant place,
So Ephraim will bring out his children to the murderer."

14 Give them, O LORD—
What will You give?
Give them [a]a miscarrying womb
And dry breasts!

15 "All their wickedness *is* in [a]Gilgal,
For there I hated them.
Because of the evil of their deeds
I will drive them from My house;
I will love them no more.
[b]All their princes *are* rebellious.
16 Ephraim is [a]stricken,
Their root is dried up;
They shall bear no fruit.
Yes, were they to bear children,
I would kill the darlings of their womb."

17 My God will [a]cast them away,
Because they did not obey Him;
And they shall be [b]wanderers among the nations.

Israel's Sin and Captivity

10 Israel [a]empties *his* vine;
He brings forth fruit for himself.
According to the multitude of his fruit
[b]He has increased the altars;
According to the bounty of his land
They have embellished *his sacred* pillars.
2 Their heart is [a]divided;
Now they are held guilty.
He will break down their altars;
He will ruin their *sacred* pillars.

3 For now they say,
"We have no king,
Because we did not fear the LORD.
And as for a king, what would he do for us?"
4 They have spoken words,
Swearing falsely in making a covenant.
Thus judgment springs up [a]like hemlock in the furrows of the field.

5 The inhabitants of Samaria fear
Because of the [a]calf[1] of Beth Aven.
For its people mourn for it,
And its priests shriek for it—
Because its [b]glory has departed from it.
6 *The idol* also shall be carried to Assyria
As a present for King [a]Jareb.
Ephraim shall receive shame,
And Israel shall be ashamed of his own counsel.

7 *As for* Samaria, her king is cut off
Like a twig on the water.
8 Also the [a]high places of Aven, [b]the sin of Israel,
Shall be destroyed.
The thorn and thistle shall grow on their altars;
[c]They shall say to the mountains, "Cover us!"
And to the hills, "Fall on us!"

9 "O Israel, you have sinned from the days of [a]Gibeah;
There they stood.
The [b]battle in Gibeah against the children of iniquity[1]
Did not overtake them.
10 When *it is* My desire, I will chasten them.
[a]Peoples shall be gathered against them
When I bind them for their two transgressions.[1]
11 Ephraim *is* [a]a trained heifer
That loves to thresh *grain;*
But I harnessed her fair neck,
I will make Ephraim pull *a plow.*
Judah shall plow;
Jacob shall break his clods."

9:10 [a] Jer. 2:2 [b] Is. 28:4 [c] Num. 25:3 [d] Ps. 81:12 **9:12** [a] Deut. 31:17 **9:13** [a] Ezek. 26—28 **9:14** [a] Luke 23:29 **9:15** [a] Hos. 4:15; 12:11 [b] Is. 1:23 **9:16** [a] Hos. 5:11 **9:17** [a] [Zech. 10:6] [b] Lev. 26:33 **10:1** [a] Nah. 2:2 [b] Jer. 2:28 **10:2** [a] 1 Kin. 18:21 **10:4** [a] Amos 5:7 **10:5** [a] Hos. 8:5, 6; 13:2 [b] Hos. 9:11 [1] Literally *calves* **10:6** [a] Hos. 5:13 **10:8** [a] Hos. 4:15 [b] 1 Kin. 13:34 [c] Luke 23:30 **10:9** [a] Hos. 9:9 [b] Judg. 20 [1] So read many Hebrew manuscripts, Septuagint, and Vulgate; Masoretic Text reads *unruliness.* **10:10** [a] Jer. 16:16 [1] Or *in their two habitations* **10:11** [a] [Mic. 4:13]

12 Sow for yourselves righteousness;
Reap in mercy;
[a]Break up your fallow ground,
For *it is* time to seek the LORD,
Till He [b]comes and rains righteousness
on you.

13 [a]You have plowed wickedness;
You have reaped iniquity.
You have eaten the fruit of lies,
Because you trusted in your own way,
In the multitude of your mighty men.
14 Therefore tumult shall arise among
your people,
And all your fortresses shall be
plundered
As Shalman plundered Beth Arbel in
the day of battle—
A mother dashed in pieces upon *her*
children.
15 Thus it shall be done to you, O Bethel,
Because of your great wickedness.
At dawn the king of Israel
Shall be cut off utterly.

God's Continuing Love for Israel

11 "When Israel *was* a child, I loved him,
And out of Egypt [a]I called My [b]son.
2 *As* they called them,[1]
So they [a]went from them;[2]
They sacrificed to the Baals,
And burned incense to carved images.

3 "I[a] taught Ephraim to walk,
Taking them by their arms;[1]
But they did not know that [b]I healed
them.
4 I drew them with gentle cords,[1]
With bands of love,
And [a]I was to them as those who take
the yoke from their neck.[2]
[b]I stooped *and* fed them.

5 "He shall not return to the land of Egypt;
But the Assyrian shall be his king,
Because they refused to repent.
6 And the sword shall slash in his cities,
Devour his districts,
And consume *them,*
Because of their own counsels.
7 My people are bent on [a]backsliding
from Me.
Though they call to the Most High,[1]
None at all exalt *Him.*

8 "How[a] can I give you up, Ephraim?
How can I hand you over, Israel?
How can I make you like [b]Admah?
How can I set you like Zeboiim?
My heart churns within Me;
My sympathy is stirred.
9 I will not execute the fierceness of My
anger;
I will not again destroy Ephraim.
[a]For I *am* God, and not man,
The Holy One in your midst;
And I will not come with terror.[1]

10 "They shall walk after the LORD.
[a]He will roar like a lion.
When He roars,
Then *His* sons shall come trembling
from the west;
11 They shall come trembling like a bird
from Egypt,
[a]Like a dove from the land of Assyria.
[b]And I will let them dwell in their
houses,"
Says the LORD.

God's Charge Against Ephraim

12 "Ephraim has encircled Me with lies,
And the house of Israel with deceit;
But Judah still walks with God,
Even with the Holy One[1] *who is*
faithful.

12 "Ephraim [a]feeds on the wind,
And pursues the east wind;
He daily increases lies and desolation.
[b]Also they make a covenant with the
Assyrians,
And [c]oil is carried to Egypt.

2 "The[a] LORD also *brings* a charge against
Judah,
And will punish Jacob according to his
ways;
According to his deeds He will
recompense him.
3 He took his brother [a]by the heel in the
womb,
And in his strength he [b]struggled with
God.[1]

10:12 [a] Jer. 4:3 [b] Hos. 6:3 **10:13** [a] [Prov. 22:8] **11:1** [a] Matt. 2:15 [b] Ex. 4:22, 23 **11:2** [a] 2 Kin. 17:13–15 [1] Following Masoretic Text and Vulgate; Septuagint reads *Just as I called them;* Targum interprets as *I sent prophets to a thousand of them.* [2] Following Masoretic Text, Targum, and Vulgate; Septuagint reads *from My face.* **11:3** [a] Deut. 1:31; 32:10, 11 [b] Ex. 15:26 [1] Some Hebrew manuscripts, Septuagint, Syriac, and Vulgate read *My arms.* **11:4** [a] Lev. 26:13 [b] Ps. 78:25 [1] Literally *cords of a man* [2] Literally *jaws* **11:7** [a] Jer. 3:6, 7; 8:5 [1] Or *upward* **11:8** [a] Jer. 9:7 [b] Gen. 14:8; 19:24, 25 **11:9** [a] Num. 23:19 [1] Or *I will not enter a city* **11:10** [a] [Joel 3:16] **11:11** [a] Is. 11:11; 60:8 [b] Ezek. 28:25, 26; 34:27, 28 **11:12** [1] Or *holy ones* **12:1** [a] Job 15:2, 3 [b] 2 Kin. 17:4 [c] Is. 30:6 **12:2** [a] Mic. 6:2 **12:3** [a] Gen. 25:26 [b] Gen. 32:24–28 [1] Compare Genesis 32:28

4 Yes, he struggled with the Angel and
prevailed;
He wept, and sought favor from Him.
He found Him *in* [a]Bethel,
And there He spoke to us—
5 That is, the LORD God of hosts.
The LORD *is* His [a]memorable name.
6 [a]So you, by *the help of* your God,
return;
Observe mercy and justice,
And wait on your God continually.

7 "A cunning Canaanite!
[a]Deceitful scales *are* in his hand;
He loves to oppress.
8 And Ephraim said,
[a]'Surely I have become rich,
I have found wealth for myself;
In all my labors
They shall find in me no iniquity that *is*
sin.'

9 "But I *am* the LORD your God,
Ever since the land of Egypt;
[a]I will again make you dwell in tents,
As in the days of the appointed
feast.
10 [a]I have also spoken by the prophets,
And have multiplied visions;
I have given symbols through the
witness of the prophets."

11 Though [a]Gilead *has* idols—
Surely they are vanity—
Though they sacrifice bulls in [b]Gilgal,
Indeed their altars *shall be* heaps in the
furrows of the field.

12 Jacob [a]fled to the country of Syria;
[b]Israel served for a spouse,
And for a wife he tended *sheep.*
13 [a]By a prophet the LORD brought Israel
out of Egypt,
And by a prophet he was preserved.
14 Ephraim [a]provoked *Him* to anger most
bitterly;
Therefore his Lord will leave the guilt
of his bloodshed upon him,
[b]And return his reproach upon him.

Relentless Judgment on Israel

13 When Ephraim spoke, trembling,
He exalted *himself* in Israel;
But when he offended through Baal
worship, he died.

> **PEACE NOTE**
>
> The prerequisite to God's peace is believing by faith, not relying on feelings!

2 Now they sin more and more,
And have made for themselves molded
images,
Idols of their silver, according to their
skill;
All of it *is* the work of craftsmen.
They say of them,
"Let the men who sacrifice[1] kiss the calves!"
3 Therefore they shall be like the
morning cloud
And like the early dew that passes
away,
[a]Like chaff blown off from a threshing
floor
And like smoke from a chimney.

4 "Yet [a]I *am* the LORD your God
Ever since the land of Egypt,
And you shall know no God but Me;
For [b]*there is* no savior besides Me.
5 [a]I knew you in the wilderness,
[b]In the land of great drought.
6 [a]When they had pasture, they were
filled;
They were filled and their heart was
exalted;
Therefore they forgot Me.

7 "So [a]I will be to them like a lion;
Like [b]a leopard by the road I will lurk;
8 I will meet them [a]like a bear deprived
of her cubs;
I will tear open their rib cage,
And there I will devour them like a
lion.
The wild beast shall tear them.

12:4 [a] [Gen. 28:12–19; 35:9–15] **12:5** [a] Ex. 3:15 **12:6** [a] Mic. 6:8 **12:7** [a] Amos 8:5 **12:8** [a] Rev. 3:17 **12:9** [a] Lev. 23:42 **12:10** [a] 2 Kin. 17:13 **12:11** [a] Hos. 6:8 [b] Hos. 9:15 **12:12** [a] Gen. 28:5 [b] Gen. 29:20, 28 **12:13** [a] Ex. 12:50, 51; 13:3 **12:14** [a] Ezek. 18:10–13 [b] Dan. 11:18 **13:2** [1] Or *those who offer human sacrifice* **13:3** [a] Dan. 2:35 **13:4** [a] Is. 43:11 [b] Is. 43:11; 45:21, 22 **13:5** [a] Deut. 2:7; 32:10 [b] Deut. 8:15 **13:6** [a] Deut. 8:12, 14; 32:13–15 **13:7** [a] Lam. 3:10 [b] Jer. 5:6 **13:8** [a] 2 Sam. 17:8

9 "O Israel, you are destroyed,[1]
But your help[2] *is* from Me.
10 I will be your King;[1]
[a]Where *is any other,*
That he may save you in all your cities?
And your judges to whom [b]you said,
'Give me a king and princes'?
11 [a]I gave you a king in My anger,
And took *him* away in My wrath.

12 "The[a] iniquity of Ephraim *is* bound up;
His sin *is* stored up.
13 [a]The sorrows of a woman in childbirth
shall come upon him.
He *is* an unwise son,
For he should not stay long where
children are born.

14 "I will ransom them from the power of
the grave;[1]
I will redeem them from death.
[a]O Death, I will be your plagues![2]
O Grave,[3] I will be your destruction![4]
[b]Pity is hidden from My eyes."

15 Though he is fruitful among *his* brethren,
[a]An east wind shall come;
The wind of the LORD shall come up
from the wilderness.
Then his spring shall become dry,
And his fountain shall be dried up.
He shall plunder the treasury of every
desirable prize.
16 Samaria is held guilty,[1]
For she has [a]rebelled against her God.
They shall fall by the sword,
Their infants shall be dashed in pieces,
And their women with child [b]ripped
open.

Israel Restored at Last

14 O Israel, [a]return to the LORD your
God,
For you have stumbled because of your
iniquity;
2 Take words with you,
And return to the LORD.
Say to Him,
"Take away all iniquity;
Receive *us* graciously,
For we will offer the [a]sacrifices[1] of our
lips.
3 Assyria shall [a]not save us,
[b]We will not ride on horses,
Nor will we say anymore to the work of
our hands, '*You are* our gods.'
[c]For in You the fatherless finds mercy."

4 "I will heal their [a]backsliding,
I will [b]love them freely,
For My anger has turned away from
him.
5 I will be like the [a]dew to Israel;
He shall grow like the lily,
And lengthen his roots like Lebanon.
6 His branches shall spread;
[a]His beauty shall be like an olive
tree,
And [b]his fragrance like Lebanon.
7 [a]Those who dwell under his shadow
shall return;
They shall be revived *like* grain,
And grow like a vine.
Their scent[1] *shall be* like the wine of
Lebanon.

8 "Ephraim *shall say,* 'What have I to do
anymore with idols?'
I have heard and observed him.
I *am* like a green cypress tree;
[a]Your fruit is found in Me."

9 Who *is* wise?
Let him understand these things.
Who is prudent?
Let him know them.
For [a]the ways of the LORD *are* right;
The righteous walk in them,
But transgressors stumble in
them.

13:9 [1] Literally *it* or *he destroyed you* [2] Literally *in your help* **13:10** [a] Deut. 32:38 [b] 1 Sam. 8:5, 6 [1] Septuagint, Syriac, Targum, and Vulgate read *Where is your king?* **13:11** [a] 1 Sam. 8:7; 10:17–24 **13:12** [a] Deut. 32:34, 35 **13:13** [a] Is. 13:8 **13:14** [a] [1 Cor. 15:54, 55] [b] Jer. 15:6 [1] Or *Sheol* [2] Septuagint reads *where is your punishment?* [3] Or *Sheol* [4] Septuagint reads *where is your sting?* **13:15** [a] Jer. 4:11, 12 **13:16** [a] 2 Kin. 18:12 [b] 2 Kin. 15:16 [1] Septuagint reads *shall be disfigured* **14:1** [a] [Joel 2:13] **14:2** [a] [Heb. 13:15] [1] Literally *bull calves;* Septuagint reads *fruit.* **14:3** [a] Hos. 7:11; 10:13; 12:1 [b] [Ps. 33:17] [c] Ps. 10:14; 68:5 **14:4** [a] Jer. 14:7 [b] [Eph. 1:6] **14:5** [a] Prov. 19:12 **14:6** [a] Ps. 52:8; 128:3 [b] Gen. 27:27 **14:7** [a] Dan. 4:12 [1] Literally *remembrance* **14:8** [a] [John 15:4] **14:9** [a] [Prov. 10:29]

THE BOOK OF

JOEL

AUTHOR

Although there are several other Joels in the Bible, the prophet Joel is known only from this book. It has been suggested that he lived not far from Jerusalem and some think that Joel was possibly a priest as well as a prophet due to references to the priesthood throughout the book (1:13–14; 2:17).

TIME

c. 835 BC

KEY VERSE

Joel 2:11

THEME

For the true agrarian society, crops are life itself. It is hard to imagine how devastating the natural disasters described in Joel are, and he uses these painful events as a megaphone to get the attention of the people. There is urgency in this call because the day of the Lord is coming. This day will be a day of judgment or a day of blessing, depending on where one stands with God.

Joel was an influential writer promising the Holy Spirit (2:28) as well as peace with God (2:32) for anyone who calls upon the name of the Lord, and he was quoted by both Luke (Acts 2:17) and Paul (Rom. 10:13). One of the most vivid pictures of restoration ("completeness," "wholeness"—all definitions of *shalom*, "peace") from the Lord is heard in the promise, "So I will restore to you the years that the swarming locust has eaten" (Joel 2:25). The occasion of Joel's writing was a plague of locusts in the land along with a severe drought, so a promise of the Lord bringing restoration for the seeming "lost years" would have been medicinal to the hearts of the people who had suffered. Joel prophetically describes that, after national repentance, God promised, "I will pour out My Spirit on all flesh" so that young and old alike will proclaim the greatness and power of God's salvation (2:28–32). This book shows us that the Lord's peace is always available for those who turn to God because of His unfailing love and faithful character.

1 The word of the LORD that came to [a]Joel the son of Pethuel.

The Land Laid Waste

2 Hear this, you elders,
And give ear, all you inhabitants of the land!
[a]Has *anything like* this happened in your days,
Or even in the days of your fathers?
3 [a]Tell your children about it,
Let your children *tell* their children,
And their children another generation.

4 [a]What the chewing locust[1] left, the [b]swarming locust has eaten;
What the swarming locust left, the crawling locust has eaten;
And what the crawling locust left, the consuming locust has eaten.

5 Awake, you [a]drunkards, and weep;
And wail, all you drinkers of wine,
Because of the new wine,
[b]For it has been cut off from your mouth.
6 For [a]a nation has come up against My land,
Strong, and without number;
[b]His teeth *are* the teeth of a lion,
And he has the fangs of a fierce lion.
7 He has [a]laid waste My vine,
And ruined My fig tree;
He has stripped it bare and thrown *it* away;
Its branches are made white.

8 [a]Lament like a virgin girded with sackcloth
For [b]the husband of her youth.
9 [a]The grain offering and the drink offering
Have been cut off from the house of the LORD;
The priests [b]mourn, who minister to the LORD.
10 The field is wasted,
[a]The land mourns;
For the grain is ruined,
[b]The new wine is dried up,
The oil fails.

11 [a]Be ashamed, you farmers,
Wail, you vinedressers,
For the wheat and the barley;
Because the harvest of the field has perished.
12 [a]The vine has dried up,
And the fig tree has withered;
The pomegranate tree,
The palm tree also,
And the apple tree—
All the trees of the field are withered;
Surely [b]joy has withered away from the sons of men.

Mourning for the Land

13 [a]Gird yourselves and lament, you priests;
Wail, you who minister before the altar;
Come, lie all night in sackcloth,
You who minister to my God;
For the grain offering and the drink offering
Are withheld from the house of your God.
14 [a]Consecrate a fast,
Call [b]a sacred assembly;
Gather the elders
And [c]all the inhabitants of the land
Into the house of the LORD your God,
And cry out to the LORD.

15 [a]Alas for the day!
For [b]the day of the LORD *is* at hand;
It shall come as destruction from the Almighty.
16 Is not the food [a]cut off before our eyes,
[b]Joy and gladness from the house of our God?
17 The seed shrivels under the clods,
Storehouses are in shambles;
Barns are broken down,
For the grain has withered.
18 How [a]the animals groan!
The herds of cattle are restless,
Because they have no pasture;
Even the flocks of sheep suffer punishment.[1]

19 O LORD, [a]to You I cry out;
For [b]fire has devoured the open pastures,
And a flame has burned all the trees of the field.
20 The beasts of the field also [a]cry out to You,
For [b]the water brooks are dried up,
And fire has devoured the open pastures.

1:1 [a] Acts 2:16 **1:2** [a] Joel 2:2 **1:3** [a] Ps. 78:4 **1:4** [a] Deut. 28:38 [b] Is. 33:4 [1] Exact identity of these locusts is unknown. **1:5** [a] Is. 5:11; 28:1 [b] Is. 32:10 **1:6** [a] Joel 2:2, 11, 25 [b] Rev. 9:8 **1:7** [a] Is. 5:6 **1:8** [a] Is. 22:12 [b] Jer. 3:4 **1:9** [a] Joel 1:13; 2:14 [b] Joel 2:17 **1:10** [a] Jer. 12:11 [b] Is. 24:7 **1:11** [a] Jer. 14:3, 4 **1:12** [a] Joel 1:10 [b] Jer. 48:33 **1:13** [a] Jer. 4:8 **1:14** [a] Joel 2:15, 16 [b] Lev. 23:36 [c] 2 Chr. 20:13 **1:15** [a] [Jer. 30:7] [b] Is. 13:6 **1:16** [a] Is. 3:1 [b] Deut. 12:7 **1:18** [a] Hos. 4:3 [1] Septuagint and Vulgate read *are made desolate.* **1:19** [a] [Ps. 50:15] [b] Jer. 9:10 **1:20** [a] Ps. 104:21; 147:9 [b] 1 Kin. 17:7; 18:5

The Day of the LORD

2 Blow [a]the trumpet in Zion,
And [b]sound an alarm in My holy
mountain!
Let all the inhabitants of the land
tremble;
For [c]the day of the LORD is coming,
For it is at hand:
2 [a]A day of darkness and gloominess,
A day of clouds and thick darkness,
Like the morning *clouds* spread over
the mountains.
[b]A people *come,* great and strong,
[c]The like of whom has never been;
Nor will there ever be any *such* after
them,
Even for many successive generations.

3 A fire devours before them,
And behind them a flame burns;
The land *is* like [a]the Garden of Eden
before them,
[b]And behind them a desolate
wilderness;
Surely nothing shall escape them.
4 [a]Their appearance is like the
appearance of horses;
And like swift steeds, so they run.
5 [a]With a noise like chariots
Over mountaintops they leap,
Like the noise of a flaming fire that
devours the stubble,
Like a strong people set in battle array.

6 Before them the people writhe in pain;
[a]All faces are drained of color.[1]
7 They run like mighty men,
They climb the wall like men of war;
Every one marches in formation,
And they do not break [a]ranks.
8 They do not push one another;
Every one marches in his own column.[1]
Though they lunge between the weapons,
They are not cut down.[2]
9 They run to and fro in the city,
They run on the wall;
They climb into the houses,
They [a]enter at the windows [b]like a thief.

10 [a]The earth quakes before them,
The heavens tremble;
[b]The sun and moon grow dark,
And the stars diminish their
brightness.

11 [a]The LORD gives voice before His army,
For His camp is very great;
[b]For strong *is the One* who executes His
word.
For the [c]day of the LORD *is* great and
very terrible;
[d]Who can endure it?

A Call to Repentance

12 "Now, therefore," says the LORD,
[a]"Turn to Me with all your heart,
With fasting, with weeping, and with
mourning."
13 So [a]rend your heart, and not [b]your
garments;
Return to the LORD your God,
For He *is* [c]gracious and merciful,
Slow to anger, and of great kindness;
And He relents from doing harm.
14 [a]Who knows *if* He will turn and relent,
And leave [b]a blessing behind Him—
[c]A grain offering and a drink offering
For the LORD your God?

15 [a]Blow the trumpet in Zion,
[b]Consecrate a fast,
Call a sacred assembly;
16 Gather the people,
[a]Sanctify the congregation,
Assemble the elders,
Gather the children and nursing babes;
[b]Let the bridegroom go out from his
chamber,
And the bride from her dressing room.
17 Let the priests, who minister to the
LORD,
Weep [a]between the porch and the altar;
Let them say, [b]"Spare Your people,
O LORD,
And do not give Your heritage to
reproach,
That the nations should rule over them.
[c]Why should they say among the
peoples,
'Where *is* their God?' "

The Land Refreshed

18 Then the LORD will [a]be zealous for His
land,
And pity His people.
19 The LORD will answer and say to His
people,
"Behold, I will send you [a]grain and new
wine and oil,

2:1 [a] Jer. 4:5 [b] Num. 10:5 [c] [Obad. 15] **2:2** [a] Amos 5:18 [b] Joel 1:6; 2:11, 25 [c] Dan. 9:12; 12:1 **2:3** [a] Is. 51:3 [b] Zech. 7:14 **2:4** [a] Rev. 9:7 **2:5** [a] Rev. 9:9 **2:6** [a] Nah. 2:10 [1] Septuagint, Targum, and Vulgate read *gather blackness.* **2:7** [a] Prov. 30:27 **2:8** [1] Literally *his own highway* [2] That is, they are not halted by losses **2:9** [a] Jer. 9:21 [b] John 10:1 **2:10** [a] Ps. 18:7 [b] Is. 13:10; 34:4 **2:11** [a] Jer. 25:30 [b] Rev. 18:8 [c] Amos 5:18 [d] [Mal. 3:2] **2:12** [a] Jer. 4:1 **2:13** [a] [Ps. 34:18; 51:17] [b] Gen. 37:34 [c] [Ex. 34:6] **2:14** [a] Jer. 26:3 [b] Hag. 2:19 [c] Joel 1:9, 13 **2:15** [a] Num. 10:3 [b] Joel 1:14 **2:16** [a] Ex. 19:10 [b] Ps. 19:5 **2:17** [a] Matt. 23:35 [b] Ex. 32:11, 12 [c] Ps. 42:10 **2:18** [a] [Is. 60:10; 63:9, 15] **2:19** [a] [Mal. 3:10]

PROOF OF PEACE

Return to the LORD your God, for He is gracious and merciful.

JOEL 2:13

Interpreters believe that one event leading to Joel's prophecy was a plague of locusts (see 1:4, 10–11). In antiquity, drought and locusts were an agrarian people's great enemies. Whole crops could be wiped out in a day. Joel saw in this calamity a lesson for Israel: *If you think this is bad, just wait till you see the "day of the* LORD*"* (see 1:15; 2:1, 11, 31; 3:14). Accordingly, the prophet called the people to repent.

Readers of the New Testament are familiar with Joel because Peter cited the prophet's promise that God would pour out his Spirit "on all flesh" (2:28), a promise fulfilled on the day of Pentecost (see Acts 2:17–21). What is often overlooked is the prophet's appeal: "Return to the LORD your God, for He is gracious and merciful" (Joel 2:13). The prophets were often thought of as messengers of doom, but they were also messengers of grace, mercy, and hope. The proof of God's grace and mercy is seen in the generous outpouring of His Spirit—and in His granting of peace.

And you will be satisfied by them;
I will no longer make you a reproach
among the nations.

20 "But [a]I will remove far from you [b]the
northern *army,*
And will drive him away into a barren
and desolate land,
With his face toward the eastern sea
And his back [c]toward the western sea;
His stench will come up,
And his foul odor will rise,
Because he has done monstrous things."

21 Fear not, O land;
Be glad and rejoice,
For the LORD has done marvelous things!
22 Do not be afraid, you beasts of the field;
For [a]the open pastures are springing up,
And the tree bears its fruit;
The fig tree and the vine yield their
strength.
23 Be glad then, you children of Zion,
And [a]rejoice in the LORD your God;
For He has given you the former rain
faithfully,[1]
And He [b]will cause the rain to come
down for you—
The former rain,
And the latter rain in the first *month.*
24 The threshing floors shall be full of wheat,
And the vats shall overflow with new
wine and oil.

25 "So I will restore to you the years [a]that
the swarming locust has eaten,
The crawling locust,
The consuming locust,
And the chewing locust,[1]
My great army which I sent among
you.
26 You shall [a]eat in plenty and be
satisfied,
And praise the name of the LORD your
God,
Who has dealt wondrously with you;
And My people shall never be put to
[b]shame.
27 Then you shall know that I *am* [a]in the
midst of Israel:
[b]I *am* the LORD your God
And there is no other.
My people shall never be put to
shame.

God's Spirit Poured Out

28 "And[a] it shall come to pass afterward
That [b]I will pour out My Spirit on all
flesh;
[c]Your sons and your [d]daughters shall
prophesy,
Your old men shall dream dreams,
Your young men shall see visions.
29 And also on *My* [a]menservants and on
My maidservants
I will pour out My Spirit in those
days.

2:20 [a] Ex. 10:19 [b] Jer. 1:14, 15 [c] Deut. 11:24 **2:22** [a] Joel 1:19 **2:23** [a] Is. 41:16 [b] Lev. 26:4 [1] Or *the teacher of righteousness* **2:25** [a] Joel 1:4–7; 2:2–11 [1] Compare 1:4 **2:26** [a] Lev. 26:5 [b] Is. 45:17 **2:27** [a] Lev. 26:11, 12 [b] [Is. 45:5, 6] **2:28** [a] Ezek. 39:29 [b] Zech. 12:10 [c] Is. 54:13 [d] Acts 21:9 **2:29** [a] [Gal. 3:28]

PEACE POURED OUT

"I will pour out My Spirit on all flesh."

JOEL 2:28

In his first letter to the Christians of Corinth, the apostle Paul offered instruction about the gifts of the Spirit (1 Cor. 12:1–11). In his letter to the churches of Galatia the apostle listed what he called the "fruit of the Spirit" (Gal. 5:22–23). There would be no gifts or fruit of the Spirit if God had not poured out His Spirit "on all flesh" (Joel 2:28). Have you ever thought of that?

It is also important to understand that Joel's remarkable prophecy was not limited to a one-day event, the day of Pentecost, when Peter boldly proclaimed the gospel and the church was born. The outpouring of the Holy Spirit has been a continuous reality as He goes on filling believers and empowering the church to do its work. Without God's Holy Spirit there would be no peace. God in His grace and mercy poured out His Spirit as part of His redemptive, saving plan. Let us thank Him for His Spirit and for the peace that He gives.

30 "And [a]I will show wonders in the heavens and in the earth:
Blood and fire and pillars of smoke.
31 [a]The sun shall be turned into darkness,
And the moon into blood,
[b]Before the coming of the great and awesome day of the LORD.
32 And it shall come to pass
That [a]whoever calls on the name of the LORD
Shall be saved.
For [b]in Mount Zion and in Jerusalem there shall be deliverance,
As the LORD has said,
Among [c]the remnant whom the LORD calls.

God Judges the Nations

3 "For behold, [a]in those days and at that time,
When I bring back the captives of Judah and Jerusalem,
2 [a]I will also gather all nations,
And bring them down to the Valley of Jehoshaphat;
And I [b]will enter into judgment with them there
On account of My people, My heritage Israel,
Whom they have scattered among the nations;
They have also divided up My land.
3 They have [a]cast lots for My people,
Have given a boy *as payment* for a harlot,
And sold a girl for wine, that they may drink.

4 "Indeed, what have you to do with Me,
[a]O Tyre and Sidon, and all the coasts of Philistia?
Will you retaliate against Me?
But if you retaliate against Me,
Swiftly and speedily I will return your retaliation upon your own head;
5 Because you have taken My silver and My gold,
And have carried into your temples My prized possessions.
6 Also the people of Judah and the people of Jerusalem
You have sold to the Greeks,
That you may remove them far from their borders.

7 "Behold, [a]I will raise them
Out of the place to which you have sold them,
And will return your retaliation upon your own head.
8 I will sell your sons and your daughters
Into the hand of the people of Judah,
And they will sell them to the [a]Sabeans,[1]
To a people [b]far off;
For the LORD has spoken."

2:30 [a] Matt. 24:29 2:31 [a] Is. 13:9, 10; 34:4 [b] [Mal. 4:1, 5, 6] 2:32 [a] Rom. 10:13 [b] Is. 46:13 [c] [Mic. 4:7] 3:1 [a] Jer. 30:3 3:2 [a] Zech. 14:2 [b] Is. 66:16 3:3 [a] Nah. 3:10 3:4 [a] Amos 1:6–8 3:7 [a] Jer. 23:8 3:8 [a] Ezek. 23:42 [b] Jer. 6:20 [1] Literally *Shebaites* (compare Isaiah 60:6 and Ezekiel 27:22)

9 [a]Proclaim this among the nations:
"Prepare for war!
Wake up the mighty men,
Let all the men of war draw near,
Let them come up.
10 [a]Beat your plowshares into swords
And your pruning hooks into
spears;
[b]Let the weak say, 'I *am* strong.'"
11 Assemble and come, all you nations,
And gather together all around.
Cause [a]Your mighty ones to go down
there, O LORD.

12 "Let the nations be wakened, and come
up to the Valley of Jehoshaphat;
For there I will sit to [a]judge all the
surrounding nations.
13 [a]Put in the sickle, for [b]the harvest is
ripe.
Come, go down;
For the [c]winepress is full,
The vats overflow—
For their wickedness *is* great."

14 Multitudes, multitudes in the valley of
decision!
For [a]the day of the LORD *is* near in the
valley of decision.
15 The sun and moon will grow dark,
And the stars will diminish their
brightness.
16 The LORD also will roar from Zion,
And utter His voice from Jerusalem;
The heavens and earth will shake;
[a]But the LORD will be a shelter for His
people,
And the strength of the children of
Israel.

17 "So you shall know that I *am* the LORD
your God,
Dwelling in Zion My [a]holy mountain.
Then Jerusalem shall be holy,
And no aliens shall ever pass through
her again."

God Blesses His People

18 And it will come to pass in that day
That the mountains shall drip with new
wine,
The hills shall flow with milk,
And all the brooks of Judah shall be
flooded with water;
A [a]fountain shall flow from the house
of the LORD
And water the Valley of Acacias.

19 "Egypt shall be a desolation,
And Edom a desolate wilderness,
Because of violence *against* the people
of Judah,
For they have shed innocent blood in
their land.
20 But Judah shall abide forever,
And Jerusalem from generation to
generation.
21 For I will [a]acquit them of the guilt of
bloodshed, whom I had not acquitted;
For the LORD dwells in Zion."

3:9 [a] Ezek. 38:7 **3:10** [a] [Is. 2:4] [b] Zech. 12:8 **3:11** [a] Is. 13:3 **3:12** [a] Is. 2:4 **3:13** [a] Rev. 14:15 [b] Jer. 51:33 [c] [Is. 63:3]
3:14 [a] Joel 2:1 **3:16** [a] [Is. 51:5, 6] **3:17** [a] Zech. 8:3 **3:18** [a] Ezek. 47:1 **3:21** [a] Is. 4:4

THE BOOK OF AMOS

AUTHOR

The only Old Testament appearance of the name Amos is in this book. Amos's objective appraisal of Israel's spiritual condition was not well received, not least because he was just a farmer from Judah. The author said of his background, "I was no prophet, nor was I a son of a prophet, but I was a sheepbreeder and a tender of sycamore fruit" (Amos 7:14). He delivered his message in Bethel because it was the residence of the king of Israel and a center of idolatry.

TIME

c. 760–753 BC

KEY VERSE

Amos 3:1–2

THEME

Amos was a contemporary of Isaiah and Hosea. The unusual aspect of his ministry is that he was a farmer and herdsman from Judah prophesying to the northern kingdom of Israel. The issues he addresses are the usual prophetic concerns, but with a heavy emphasis on social justice. When injustice is rampant, expect God's judgment. No one is immune. In fact, the more God has given, the more God expects in response.

The people of God in the northern tribes were prosperous and materially blessed, but they suffered from brokenness and spiritual bankruptcy. It was no real sacrifice for Israel to offer material possessions to the Lord. "Though you offer Me burnt offerings and your grain offerings, I will not accept them, nor will I regard your fattened peace [*shalom*] offerings" (5:22). Under Jeroboam II's kingship, the historic boundaries of Israel returned to the original borders of Solomon's empire, yet, instead of turning to God and walking in His ways, God's people resisted the Lord and grew hard in heart. Amos is a stark reminder to never put our trust for peace in our possessions and to always look to the Lord in obedience and faithfulness in both times of blessing and times of need.

1 The words of Amos, who was among the
[a]sheepbreeders[1] of [b]Tekoa, which he saw
concerning Israel in the days of [c]Uzziah king
of Judah, and in the days of [d]Jeroboam the
son of Joash, king of Israel, two years before
the [e]earthquake.
2 And he said:

"The LORD [a]roars from Zion,
And utters His voice from
Jerusalem;
The pastures of the shepherds
mourn,
And the top of [b]Carmel withers."

Judgment on the Nations

3 Thus says the LORD:

"For three transgressions of [a]Damascus,
and for four,
I will not turn away its *punishment,*
Because they have [b]threshed Gilead
with implements of iron.
4 [a]But I will send a fire into the house of
Hazael,
Which shall devour the palaces of
[b]Ben-Hadad.
5 I will also break the *gate* [a]bar of
Damascus,
And cut off the inhabitant from the
Valley of Aven,
And the one who holds the scepter
from Beth Eden.
The people of Syria shall go captive to
Kir,"
Says the LORD.

6 Thus says the LORD:

"For three transgressions of [a]Gaza, and
for four,
I will not turn away its *punishment,*
Because they took captive the whole
captivity
To deliver *them* up to Edom.
7 [a]But I will send a fire upon the wall of
Gaza,
Which shall devour its palaces.
8 I will cut off the inhabitant [a]from
Ashdod,
And the one who holds the scepter
from Ashkelon;
I will [b]turn My hand against Ekron,
And [c]the remnant of the Philistines
shall perish,"
Says the Lord GOD.

9 Thus says the LORD:

"For three transgressions of [a]Tyre, and
for four,
I will not turn away its *punishment,*
Because they delivered up the whole
captivity to Edom,
And did not remember the covenant of
brotherhood.
10 But I will send a fire upon the wall of Tyre,
Which shall devour its palaces."

11 Thus says the LORD:

"For three transgressions of [a]Edom, and
for four,
I will not turn away its *punishment,*
Because he pursued his [b]brother with
the sword,
And cast off all pity;
His anger tore perpetually,
And he kept his wrath forever.
12 But [a]I will send a fire upon Teman,
Which shall devour the palaces of
Bozrah."

13 Thus says the LORD:

"For three transgressions of [a]the people
of Ammon, and for four,
I will not turn away its *punishment,*
Because they ripped open the women
with child in Gilead,
That they might enlarge their territory.
14 But I will kindle a fire in the wall of
[a]Rabbah,
And it shall devour its palaces,
[b]Amid shouting in the day of battle,
And a tempest in the day of the
whirlwind.
15 [a]Their king shall go into captivity,
He and his princes together,"
Says the LORD.

2 Thus says the LORD:

[a]"For three transgressions of Moab, and
for four,
I will not turn away its *punishment,*
Because he [b]burned the bones of the
king of Edom to lime.
2 But I will send a fire upon Moab,
And it shall devour the palaces of
[a]Kerioth;
Moab shall die with tumult,
With shouting *and* trumpet sound.

1:1 [a] 2 Kin. 3:4; Amos 7:14 [b] 2 Sam. 14:2 [c] 2 Chr. 26:1–23 [d] Amos 7:10 [e] Zech. 14:5 [1] Compare 2 Kings 3:4 **1:2** [a] Joel 3:16 [b] 1 Sam. 25:2 **1:3** [a] Is. 8:4; 17:1–3 [b] 2 Kin. 10:32, 33 **1:4** [a] Jer. 49:27; 51:30 [b] 2 Kin. 6:24 **1:5** [a] Jer. 51:30 **1:6** [a] Jer. 47:1, 5 **1:7** [a] Jer. 47:1 **1:8** [a] Zeph. 2:4 [b] Ps. 81:14 [c] Ezek. 25:16 **1:9** [a] Is. 23:1–18 **1:11** [a] Is. 21:11 [b] Obad. 10–12 **1:12** [a] Obad. 9, 10 **1:13** [a] Ezek. 25:2 **1:14** [a] Deut. 3:11 [b] Amos 2:2 **1:15** [a] Jer. 49:3 **2:1** [a] Zeph. 2:8–11 [b] 2 Kin. 3:26, 27 **2:2** [a] Jer. 48:24, 41

PEACE NOTE

Paul's vulnerability and humility increased his ministry. Let's follow his example.

3 And I will cut off [a]the judge from its
midst,
And slay all its princes with him,"
Says the LORD.

Judgment on Judah

[4]Thus says the LORD:

"For three transgressions of [a]Judah, and
for four,
I will not turn away its *punishment*,
[b]Because they have despised the law of
the LORD,
And have not kept His commandments.
[c]Their lies lead them astray,
Lies [d]which their fathers followed.
5 [a]But I will send a fire upon Judah,
And it shall devour the palaces of
Jerusalem."

Judgment on Israel

[6]Thus says the LORD:

"For three transgressions of [a]Israel, and
for four,
I will not turn away its *punishment*,
Because [b]they sell the righteous for
silver,
And the [c]poor for a pair of sandals.
7 They pant after[1] the dust of the earth
which is on the head of the poor,
And [a]pervert the way of the humble.
[b]A man and his father go in to the *same*
girl,
[c]To defile My holy name.
8 They lie down [a]by every altar on
clothes [b]taken in pledge,
And drink the wine of the condemned
in the house of their god.
9 "Yet *it was* I *who* destroyed the [a]Amorite
before them,
Whose height *was* like the [b]height of
the cedars,
And he *was as* strong as the oaks;
Yet I [c]destroyed his fruit above
And his roots beneath.
10 Also *it was* [a]I *who* brought you up from
the land of Egypt,
And [b]led you forty years through the
wilderness,
To possess the land of the Amorite.
11 I raised up some of your sons as
[a]prophets,
And some of your young men as
[b]Nazirites.
Is it not so, O you children of Israel?"
Says the LORD.
12 "But you gave the Nazirites wine to
drink,
And commanded the prophets [a]saying,
'Do not prophesy!'

13 "Behold,[a] I am weighed down by you,
As a cart full of sheaves is weighed
down.
14 [a]Therefore flight shall perish from the
swift,
The strong shall not strengthen his
power,
[b]Nor shall the mighty deliver himself;
15 He shall not stand who handles the
bow,
The swift of foot shall not escape,
Nor shall he who rides a horse deliver
himself.
16 The most courageous men of might
Shall flee naked in that day,"
Says the LORD.

Authority of the Prophet's Message

3 Hear this word that the LORD has spoken
against you, O children of Israel, against
the whole family which I brought up from
the land of Egypt, saying:

2 "You[a] only have I known of all the
families of the earth;
[b]Therefore I will punish you for all your
iniquities."
3 Can two walk together, unless they are
agreed?

2:3 [a] Num. 24:17 2:4 [a] Hos. 12:2 [b] Lev. 26:14 [c] Jer. 16:19 [d] Ezek. 20:13, 16, 18 2:5 [a] Hos. 8:14 2:6 [a] 2 Kin. 17:7–18; 18:12 [b] Is. 29:21 [c] Amos 4:1; 5:11; 8:6 2:7 [a] Amos 5:12 [b] Ezek. 22:11 [c] Lev. 20:3 [1] Or *trample on* 2:8 [a] 1 Cor. 8:10 [b] Ex. 22:26 2:9 [a] Num. 21:25 [b] Ezek. 31:3 [c] [Mal. 4:1] 2:10 [a] Ex. 12:51 [b] Deut. 2:7 2:11 [a] Num. 12:6 [b] Num. 6:2, 3 2:12 [a] Is. 30:10 2:13 [a] Is. 1:14 2:14 [a] Jer. 46:6 [b] Ps. 33:16 3:2 [a] [Deut. 7:6] [b] [Rom. 2:9]

4 Will a lion roar in the forest, when he
has no prey?
Will a young lion cry out of his den, if
he has caught nothing?
5 Will a bird fall into a snare on the
earth, where there is no trap for it?
Will a snare spring up from the earth, if
it has caught nothing at all?
6 If a trumpet is blown in a city, will not
the people be afraid?
[a]If there is calamity in a city, will not the
LORD have done *it?*

7 Surely the Lord GOD does nothing,
Unless [a]He reveals His secret to His
servants the prophets.
8 A lion has roared!
Who will not fear?
The Lord GOD has spoken!
[a]Who can but prophesy?

Punishment of Israel's Sins

9 "Proclaim in the palaces at Ashdod,[1]
And in the palaces in the land of Egypt,
and say:
'Assemble on the mountains of
Samaria;
See great tumults in her midst,
And the oppressed within her.
10 For they [a]do not know to do right,'
Says the LORD,
'Who store up violence and robbery in
their palaces.'"

11 Therefore thus says the Lord GOD:

"An adversary *shall be* all around the
land;
He shall sap your strength from you,
And your palaces shall be plundered."

12 Thus says the LORD:

"As a shepherd takes from the mouth of
a lion
Two legs or a piece of an ear,
So shall the children of Israel be taken
out
Who dwell in Samaria—
In the corner of a bed and on the edge[1]
of a couch!
13 Hear and testify against the house of
Jacob,"
Says the Lord GOD, the God of hosts,
14 "That in the day I punish Israel for their
transgressions,
I will also visit *destruction* on the altars
of [a]Bethel;
And the horns of the altar shall be cut
off
And fall to the ground.
15 I will destroy [a]the winter house along
with [b]the summer house;
The [c]houses of ivory shall perish,
And the great houses shall have an
end,"
Says the LORD.

4 Hear this word, you [a]cows of Bashan,
who *are* on the mountain of Samaria,
Who oppress the [b]poor,
Who crush the needy,
Who say to your husbands,[1] "Bring
wine, let us [c]drink!"
2 [a]The Lord GOD has sworn by His
holiness:
"Behold, the days shall come upon you
When He will take you away [b]with
fishhooks,
And your posterity with fishhooks.
3 [a]You will go out *through* broken *walls,*
Each one straight ahead of her,
And you will be cast into Harmon,"
Says the LORD.

4 "Come[a] to Bethel and transgress,
At [b]Gilgal multiply transgression;
[c]Bring your sacrifices every morning,
[d]Your tithes every three days.[1]
5 [a]Offer a sacrifice of thanksgiving with
leaven,
Proclaim *and* announce [b]the freewill
offerings;
For this you love,
You children of Israel!"
Says the Lord GOD.

Israel Did Not Accept Correction

6 "Also I gave you cleanness of teeth in all
your cities,
And lack of bread in all your places;
[a]Yet you have not returned to Me,"
Says the LORD.

7 "I also withheld rain from you,
When *there were* still three months to
the harvest.
I made it rain on one city,
I withheld rain from another city.
One part was rained upon,
And where it did not rain the part
withered.

3:6 [a] Is. 45:7 **3:7** [a] [John 15:15] **3:8** [a] Acts 4:20 **3:9** [1] Following Masoretic Text; Septuagint reads *Assyria.* **3:10** [a] Jer. 4:22 **3:12** [1] The Hebrew is uncertain. **3:14** [a] Amos 4:4 **3:15** [a] Jer. 36:22 [b] Judg. 3:20 [c] 1 Kin. 22:39 **4:1** [a] Ps. 22:12 [b] Amos 2:6 [c] Prov. 23:20 [1] Literally *their lords* or *their masters* **4:2** [a] Ps. 89:35 [b] Jer. 16:16 **4:3** [a] Ezek. 12:5 **4:4** [a] Ezek. 20:39 [b] Hos. 4:15 [c] Num. 28:3 [d] Deut. 14:28 [1] Or *years* (compare Deuteronomy 14:28) **4:5** [a] Lev. 7:13 [b] Lev. 22:18 **4:6** [a] Jer. 5:3

8 So two *or* three cities wandered to
another city to drink water,
But they were not satisfied;
Yet you have not returned to Me,"
Says the LORD.

9 "I[a] blasted you with blight and
mildew.
When your gardens increased,
Your vineyards,
Your fig trees,
And your olive trees,
[b]The locust devoured *them;*
Yet you have not returned to Me,"
Says the LORD.

10 "I sent among you a plague [a]after the
manner of Egypt;
Your young men I killed with a
sword,
Along with your captive horses;
I made the stench of your camps come
up into your nostrils;
Yet you have not returned to Me,"
Says the LORD.

11 "I overthrew *some* of you,
As God overthrew [a]Sodom and
Gomorrah,
And you were like a firebrand plucked
from the burning;
Yet you have not returned to Me,"
Says the LORD.

12 "Therefore thus will I do to you,
O Israel;
Because I will do this to you,
[a]Prepare to meet your God, O Israel!"

13 For behold,
He who forms mountains,
And creates the wind,
[a]Who declares to man what his[1]
thought *is,*
And makes the morning darkness,
[b]Who treads the high places of the
earth—
[c]The LORD God of hosts *is* His name.

A Lament for Israel

5 Hear this word which I [a]take up against
you, a lamentation, O house of Israel:

2 The virgin of Israel has fallen;
She will rise no more.
She lies forsaken on her land;
There is no one to raise her up.

3For thus says the Lord GOD:

"The city that goes out by a thousand
Shall have a hundred left,
And that which goes out by a hundred
Shall have ten left to the house of
Israel."

A Call to Repentance

4For thus says the LORD to the house of
Israel:

[a]"Seek Me [b]and live;
5 But do not seek [a]Bethel,
Nor enter Gilgal,
Nor pass over to [b]Beersheba;
For Gilgal shall surely go into captivity,
And [c]Bethel shall come to nothing.
6 [a]Seek the LORD and live,
Lest He break out like fire *in* the house
of Joseph,
And devour *it,*
With no one to quench *it* in Bethel—
7 You who [a]turn justice to
wormwood,
And lay righteousness to rest in the
earth!"

8 He made the [a]Pleiades and Orion;
He turns the shadow of death into
morning
[b]And makes the day dark as night;
He [c]calls for the waters of the sea
And pours them out on the face of the
earth;
[d]The LORD *is* His name.
9 He rains ruin upon the strong,
So that fury comes upon the fortress.

PEACE NOTE

The majestic, creative power of God calls us to seek His peace. Yes, God created billions of stars and galaxies. But He also created you and knows your every need.

AMOS 5:8

4:9 [a] Hag. 2:17 [b] Joel 1:4, 7 4:10 [a] Ps. 78:50 4:11 [a] Is. 13:19 4:12 [a] Jer. 5:22 4:13 [a] Ps. 139:2 [b] Mic. 1:3 [c] Is. 47:4 [1] Or *His* 5:1 [a] Jer. 7:29; 9:10, 17 5:4 [a] [Jer. 29:13] [b] [Is. 55:3] 5:5 [a] Amos 4:4 [b] Amos 8:14 [c] Hos. 4:15 5:6 [a] [Is. 55:3, 6, 7] 5:7 [a] Amos 6:12 5:8 [a] Job 9:9; 38:31 [b] Ps. 104:20 [c] Job 38:34 [d] [Amos 4:13]

10 [a]They hate the one who rebukes in the gate,
And they [b]abhor the one who speaks uprightly.
11 [a]Therefore, because you tread down the poor
And take grain taxes from him,
Though [b]you have built houses of hewn stone,
Yet you shall not dwell in them;
You have planted pleasant vineyards,
But you shall not drink wine from them.
12 For I [a]know your manifold transgressions
And your mighty sins:
[b]Afflicting the just *and* taking bribes;
[c]Diverting the poor *from justice* at the gate.
13 Therefore [a]the prudent keep silent at that time,
For it *is* an evil time.

14 Seek good and not evil,
That you may live;
So the LORD God of hosts will be with you,
[a]As you have spoken.
15 [a]Hate evil, love good;
Establish justice in the gate.
[b]It may be that the LORD God of hosts
Will be gracious to the remnant of Joseph.

The Day of the LORD

16Therefore the LORD God of hosts, the Lord, says this:

"*There shall be* wailing in all streets,
And they shall say in all the highways,
'Alas! Alas!'
They shall call the farmer to mourning,
[a]And skillful lamenters to wailing.
17 In all vineyards *there shall be* wailing,
For [a]I will pass through you,"
Says the LORD.

18 [a]Woe to you who desire the day of the LORD!
For what good *is* [b]the day of the LORD to you?
It *will be* darkness, and not light.
19 It *will be* [a]as though a man fled from a lion,
And a bear met him!
Or *as though* he went into the house,
Leaned his hand on the wall,
And a serpent bit him!
20 *Is* not the day of the LORD darkness, and not light?
Is it not very dark, with no brightness in it?

21 "I[a] hate, I despise your feast days,
And [b]I do not savor your sacred assemblies.
22 [a]Though you offer Me burnt offerings and your grain offerings,
I will not accept *them,*
Nor will I regard your fattened peace offerings.
23 Take away from Me the noise of your songs,
For I will not hear the melody of your stringed instruments.
24 [a]But let justice run down like water,
And righteousness like a mighty stream.

25 "Did[a] you offer Me sacrifices and offerings
In the wilderness forty years, O house of Israel?
26 You also carried Sikkuth[1] [a]your king[2]
And Chiun,[3] your idols,
The star of your gods,
Which you made for yourselves.
27 Therefore I will send you into captivity [a]beyond Damascus,"
Says the LORD, [b]whose name *is* the God of hosts.

Warnings to Zion and Samaria

6 Woe [a]to you *who are* at [b]ease in Zion,
And [c]trust in Mount Samaria,
Notable persons in the [d]chief nation,
To whom the house of Israel comes!
2 [a]Go over to [b]Calneh and see;
And from there go to [c]Hamath the great;
Then go down to Gath of the Philistines.
[d]*Are you* better than these kingdoms?
Or is their territory greater than your territory?

3 *Woe to* you who [a]put far off the day of [b]doom,
[c]Who cause [d]the seat of violence to come near;

5:10 [a] Is. 29:21; 66:5 [b] 1 Kin. 22:8 **5:11** [a] Amos 2:6 [b] Mic. 6:15 **5:12** [a] Hos. 5:3 [b] Amos 2:6 [c] Is. 29:21 **5:13** [a] Amos 6:10 **5:14** [a] Mic. 3:11 **5:15** [a] Rom. 12:9 [b] Joel 2:14 **5:16** [a] Jer. 9:17 **5:17** [a] Ex. 12:12 **5:18** [a] Is. 5:19 [b] Joel 2:2 **5:19** [a] Jer. 48:44 **5:21** [a] Is. 1:11–16 [b] Lev. 26:31 **5:22** [a] Mic. 6:6, 7 **5:24** [a] Mic. 6:8 **5:25** [a] Deut. 32:17 **5:26** [a] 1 Kin. 11:33 [1] A pagan deity [2] Septuagint and Vulgate read *tabernacle of Moloch.* [3] A pagan deity **5:27** [a] 2 Kin. 17:6 [b] Amos 4:13 **6:1** [a] Luke 6:24 [b] Zeph. 1:12 [c] Is. 31:1 [d] Ex. 19:5 **6:2** [a] Jer. 2:10 [b] Is. 10:9 [c] 2 Kin. 18:34 [d] Nah. 3:8 **6:3** [a] Is. 56:12 [b] Amos 5:18 [c] Amos 5:12 [d] Ps. 94:20

4 Who lie on beds of ivory,
Stretch out on your couches,
Eat lambs from the flock
And calves from the midst of the stall;
5 [a]Who sing idly to the sound of stringed instruments,
And invent for yourselves [b]musical instruments [c]like David;
6 Who [a]drink wine from bowls,
And anoint yourselves with the best ointments,
[b]But are not grieved for the affliction of Joseph.
7 Therefore they shall now go [a]captive as the first of the captives,
And those who recline at banquets shall be removed.

8 [a]The Lord GOD has sworn by Himself,
The LORD God of hosts says:
"I abhor [b]the pride of Jacob,
And hate his palaces;
Therefore I will deliver up *the* city
And all that is in it."

9Then it shall come to pass, that if ten
men remain in one house, they shall die.
10And when a relative *of the dead,* with one
who will burn *the bodies,* picks up the bodies[1]
to take them out of the house, he will say to
one inside the house, "*Are there* any more
with you?"

Then someone will say, "None."

And he will say, [a]"Hold your tongue! [b]For we dare not mention the name of the LORD."

11 For behold, [a]the LORD gives a command:
[b]He will break the great house into bits,
And the little house into pieces.

12 Do horses run on rocks?
Does *one* plow *there* with oxen?
Yet [a]you have turned justice into gall,
And the fruit of righteousness into wormwood,
13 You who rejoice over Lo Debar,[1]
Who say, "Have we not taken Karnaim[2] for ourselves
By our own strength?"

14 "But, behold, [a]I will raise up a nation against you,
O house of Israel,"
Says the LORD God of hosts;
"And they will afflict you from the [b]entrance of Hamath
To the Valley of the Arabah."

Vision of the Locusts

7 Thus the Lord GOD showed me: Behold,
He formed locust swarms at the beginning of the late crop; indeed *it was* the late
crop after the king's mowings. 2And so it was,
when they had finished eating the grass of
the land, that I said:

"O Lord GOD, forgive, I pray!
[a]Oh, that Jacob may stand,
For he *is* small!"
3 *So* [a]the LORD relented concerning this.
"It shall not be," said the LORD.

Vision of the Fire

4Thus the Lord GOD showed me: Behold,
the Lord GOD called for conflict by fire, and
it consumed the great deep and devoured
the territory. 5Then I said:

"O Lord GOD, cease, I pray!
[a]Oh, that Jacob may stand,
For he *is* small!"
6 *So* the LORD relented concerning this.
"This also shall not be," said the Lord GOD.

Vision of the Plumb Line

7Thus He showed me: Behold, the Lord
stood on a wall *made* with a plumb line, with
a plumb line in His hand. 8And the LORD said
to me, "Amos, what do you see?"

And I said, "A plumb line."

Then the Lord said:

"Behold, [a]I am setting a plumb line
In the midst of My people Israel;
[b]I will not pass by them anymore.
9 [a]The high places of Isaac shall be desolate,
And the sanctuaries of Israel shall be laid waste.
[b]I will rise with the sword against the house of Jeroboam."

Amaziah's Complaint

10Then Amaziah the [a]priest of [b]Bethel sent
to [c]Jeroboam king of Israel, saying, "Amos
has conspired against you in the midst of
the house of Israel. The land is not able to
bear all his words. 11For thus Amos has said:

'Jeroboam shall die by the sword,

6:5 [a] Is. 5:12; Amos 5:23 [b] 1 Chr. 15:16; 16:42 [c] 1 Chr. 23:5 **6:6** [a] Amos 2:8; 4:1 [b] Gen. 37:25 **6:7** [a] Amos 5:27 **6:8** [a] Jer. 51:14 [b] Amos 8:7 **6:10** [a] Amos 5:13 [b] Amos 8:3 [1] Literally *bones* **6:11** [a] Is. 55:11 [b] Amos 3:15 **6:12** [a] Hos. 10:4 **6:13** [1] Literally *Nothing* [2] Literally *Horns,* symbol of strength **6:14** [a] Jer. 5:15 [b] 1 Kin. 8:65 **7:2** [a] Is. 51:19 **7:3** [a] Jon. 3:10 **7:5** [a] Amos 7:2, 3 **7:8** [a] 2 Kin. 21:13 [b] Mic. 7:18 **7:9** [a] Gen. 46:1 [b] 2 Kin. 15:8–10 **7:10** [a] 1 Kin. 12:31, 32; 13:33 [b] Amos 4:4 [c] 2 Kin. 14:23

And Israel shall surely be led away
[a]captive
From their own land.' "

12Then Amaziah said to Amos:

"Go, you seer!
Flee to the land of Judah.
There eat bread,
And there prophesy.
13 But [a]never again prophesy at Bethel,
[b]For it *is* the king's sanctuary,
And it *is* the royal residence."

14Then Amos answered, and said to Amaziah:

"I *was* no prophet,
Nor *was* I [a]a son of a prophet,
But I *was* a [b]sheepbreeder[1]
And a tender of sycamore fruit.
15 Then the LORD took me as I followed
the flock,
And the LORD said to me,
'Go, [a]prophesy to My people Israel.'
16 Now therefore, hear the word of the
LORD:
You say, 'Do not prophesy against Israel,
And [a]do not spout against the house of
Isaac.'

17"Therefore[a] thus says the LORD:

[b]'Your wife shall be a harlot in the city;
Your sons and daughters shall fall by
the sword;
Your land shall be divided by *survey* line;
You shall die in a [c]defiled land;
And Israel shall surely be led away
captive
From his own land.' "

Vision of the Summer Fruit

8 Thus the Lord GOD showed me: Behold,
a basket of summer fruit. 2And He said,
"Amos, what do you see?"
So I said, "A basket of summer fruit."
Then the LORD said to me:

[a]"The end has come upon My people
Israel;
[b]I will not pass by them anymore.
3 And [a]the songs of the temple
Shall be wailing in that day,"
Says the Lord GOD—
"Many dead bodies everywhere,
[b]They shall be thrown out in silence."

4 Hear this, you who swallow up[1] the needy,
And make the poor of the land fail,

5Saying:

"When will the New Moon be past,
That we may sell grain?
And [a]the Sabbath,
That we may trade wheat?
[b]Making the ephah small and the shekel
large,
Falsifying the scales by [c]deceit,
6 That we may buy the poor for [a]silver,
And the needy for a pair of sandals—
Even sell the bad wheat?"

7 The LORD has sworn by [a]the pride of
Jacob:
"Surely [b]I will never forget any of their
works.
8 [a]Shall the land not tremble for this,
And everyone mourn who dwells in it?
All of it shall swell like the River,[1]
Heave and subside
[b]Like the River of Egypt.

9 "And it shall come to pass in that day,"
says the Lord GOD,
[a]"That I will make the sun go down at noon,
And I will darken the earth in broad
daylight;
10 I will turn your feasts into [a]mourning,
[b]And all your songs into lamentation;
[c]I will bring sackcloth on every waist,
And baldness on every head;
I will make it like mourning for an only
son,
And its end like a bitter day.

11 "Behold, the days are coming," says the
Lord GOD,
"That I will send a famine on the land,
Not a famine of bread,
Nor a thirst for water,
But [a]of hearing the words of the LORD.
12 They shall wander from sea to sea,
And from north to east;
They shall run to and fro, seeking the
word of the LORD,
But shall [a]not find *it*.

7:11 [a] Amos 5:27; 6:7 **7:13** [a] Amos 2:12 [b] 1 Kin. 12:29, 32 **7:14** [a] 1 Kin. 20:35 [b] Zech. 13:5 [1] Compare 2 Kings 3:4 **7:15** [a] Amos 3:8 **7:16** [a] Ezek. 21:2 **7:17** [a] Jer. 28:12; 29:21, 32 [b] Zech. 14:2 [c] Hos. 9:3 **8:2** [a] Ezek. 7:2 [b] Amos 7:8 **8:3** [a] Amos 5:23 [b] Amos 6:9, 10 **8:4** [1] Or *trample on* (compare 2:7) **8:5** [a] Neh. 13:15 [b] Mic. 6:10, 11 [c] Lev. 19:35, 36 **8:6** [a] Amos 2:6 **8:7** [a] Amos 6:8 [b] Hos. 7:2; 8:13 **8:8** [a] Hos. 4:3 [b] Amos 9:5 [1] That is, the Nile; some Hebrew manuscripts, Septuagint, Syriac, Targum, and Vulgate read *River;* Masoretic Text reads *the light.* **8:9** [a] Job 5:14 **8:10** [a] Ezek. 7:18 [b] Ezek. 27:31 [c] [Zech. 12:10] **8:11** [a] Ezek. 7:26 **8:12** [a] Hos. 5:6

13 "In that day the fair virgins
And strong young men
Shall faint from thirst.
14 Those who [a]swear by [b]the sin[1] of Samaria,
Who say,
'As your god lives, O Dan!'
And, 'As the way of [c]Beersheba lives!'
They shall fall and never rise again."

The Destruction of Israel

9 I saw the Lord standing by the altar, and He said:

"Strike the doorposts, that the thresholds may shake,
And [a]break them on the heads of them all.
I will slay the last of them with the sword.
[b]He who flees from them shall not get away,
And he who escapes from them shall not be delivered.

2 "Though[a] they dig into hell,[1]
From there My hand shall take them;
[b]Though they climb up to heaven,
From there I will bring them down;
3 And though they [a]hide themselves on top of Carmel,
From there I will search and take them;
Though they hide from My sight at the bottom of the sea,
From there I will command the serpent, and it shall bite them;
4 Though they go into captivity before their enemies,
From there [a]I will command the sword,
And it shall slay them.
[b]I will set My eyes on them for harm and not for good."

5 The Lord GOD of hosts,
He who touches the earth and it [a]melts,
[b]And all who dwell there mourn;
All of it shall swell like the River,[1]
And subside like the River of Egypt.
6 He who builds His [a]layers in the sky,
And has founded His strata in the earth;
Who [b]calls for the waters of the sea,
And pours them out on the face of the earth—
[c]The LORD *is* His name.

7 "*Are* you not like the people of Ethiopia to Me,
O children of Israel?" says the LORD.
"Did I not bring up Israel from the land of Egypt,
The [a]Philistines from [b]Caphtor,
And the Syrians from [c]Kir?

8:14 [a] Hos. 4:15 [b] Deut. 9:21 [c] Amos 5:5 [1] Or *Ashima,* a Syrian goddess **9:1** [a] Hab. 3:13 [b] Amos 2:14 **9:2** [a] Ps. 139:8 [b] Jer. 51:53 [1] Or *Sheol* **9:3** [a] Jer. 23:24 **9:4** [a] Lev. 26:33 [b] Jer. 21:10; 39:16; 44:11 **9:5** [a] Mic. 1:4 [b] Amos 8:8 [1] That is, the Nile **9:6** [a] Ps. 104:3, 13 [b] Amos 5:8 [c] Amos 4:13; 5:27 **9:7** [a] Jer. 47:4 [b] Deut. 2:23 [c] Amos 1:5

OUT OF THE RUINS

"I will raise up the tabernacle of David."

AMOS 9:11

God raised up Amos to preach against corruption and sin. In chapters 7–9 the prophet proclaimed his visions of Israel's coming doom, but in chapter 9, Amos also prophesied the future restoration of Israel when the nation would become what God had intended all along. The prophet said, "I will raise up the tabernacle of David, which has fallen down, and repair its damages; I will raise up its ruins, and rebuild it as in the days of old" (v. 11).

Human failure does not prevent God from accomplishing His redemptive plan. The fallen tabernacle of David will be fully restored in the coming of Jesus Christ, the Prince of Peace. Maybe you think God has abandoned you because you feel far from God; Israel might have felt this way during the time of Amos. The great truth of today is that you live on the right side of the cross. Jesus has done everything necessary to deliver you through His death and resurrection. You can know that God will bring peace to your life when there seems to be no way.

Pain moves people in different directions: it will either break your back or bend your knee. Allow your pain to bring you to the foot of the cross again so you can find His peace.

8 "Behold, [a]the eyes of the Lord GOD *are*
on the sinful kingdom,
And I [b]will destroy it from the face of
the earth;
Yet I will not utterly destroy the house
of Jacob,"
Says the LORD.

9 "For surely I will command,
And will sift the house of Israel among
all nations,
As *grain* is sifted in a sieve;
[a]Yet not the smallest grain shall fall to
the ground.
10 All the sinners of My people shall die
by the sword,
[a]Who say, 'The calamity shall not
overtake nor confront us.'

Israel Will Be Restored

11 "On[a] that day I will raise up
The tabernacle[1] of David, which has
fallen down,
And repair its damages;
I will raise up its ruins,
And rebuild it as in the days of old;
12 [a]That they may possess the remnant of
[b]Edom,[1]
And all the Gentiles who are called by
My name,"
Says the LORD who does this
thing.

13 "Behold, [a]the days are coming," says the
LORD,
"When the plowman shall overtake the
reaper,
And the treader of grapes him who
sows seed;
[b]The mountains shall drip with sweet
wine,
And all the hills shall flow *with it.*
14 [a]I will bring back the captives of My
people Israel;
[b]They shall build the waste cities and
inhabit *them;*
They shall plant vineyards and drink
wine from them;
They shall also make gardens and eat
fruit from them.
15 I will plant them in their land,
[a]And no longer shall they be
pulled up
From the land I have given
them,"
Says the LORD your God.

9:8 [a] Amos 9:4 [b] Jer. 5:10; 30:11 **9:9** [a] [Is. 65:8–16] **9:10** [a] Amos 6:3 **9:11** [a] Acts 15:16–18 [1] Literally *booth,* figure of a deposed dynasty **9:12** [a] Obad. 19 [b] Num. 24:18 [1] Septuagint reads *mankind.* **9:13** [a] Lev. 26:5 [b] Joel 3:18 **9:14** [a] Jer. 30:3, 18 [b] Is. 61:4 **9:15** [a] Ezek. 34:28; 37:25

THE BOOK OF

OBADIAH

AUTHOR

Obadiah was an obscure prophet who probably lived in the southern kingdom of Judah. It is assumed, however, that he was not a priest, since his father is not mentioned and nothing is given of his background. There are thirteen Obadiahs in the Old Testament. Four of the better prospects for this Obadiah are (1) the officer in Ahab's palace who hid God's prophets in a cave (1 Kin. 18:3); (2) one of the officials Jehoshaphat sent out to teach the law in the cities of Judah (2 Chr. 17:7); (3) one of the overseers who took part in repairing the temple under Josiah (2 Chr. 34:12); or (4) a priest in the time of Nehemiah (Neh. 10:5).

TIME

c. 840 BC

KEY VERSE

Obadiah v. 10

THEME

Obadiah is a prophecy against Edom, the nation that descended from Esau. Edom included the area south and east of the Dead Sea. Throughout most of Old Testament history, if Edom is mentioned, it is in the context of some kind of skirmish. This friction started when the king of Edom refused to let the Israelites cross his territory as they journeyed toward the Promised Land in Numbers 20:14–21. When Israel and Judah were taken into exile, Edom stood by and watched. The purpose of Obadiah seems clear: he is encouraging the Israelites in the context of captivity. God will rescue His people.

In the classic film *Indiana Jones and the Last Crusade* (1989), the climactic scene takes place inside the rock-city of Petra (in modern-day Jordan), where one of Israel's archenemies—the Edomites—originally settled. The scene offers a great visual to go with this prophecy: Obadiah, in the shortest book of the Old Testament, proclaimed, "You who dwell in the clefts of the rock, whose habitation is high; you . . . say in your heart, 'Who will bring me down to the ground?'" And God responded, "I will bring you down" (vv. 3–4). We also see that alliances made without God at the center bring calamity; the prophet further announced, "The men at peace with you shall deceive you" (v. 7). In these we see the utter vacuousness of placing our trust for peace in any stronghold other than God Himself.

The Coming Judgment on Edom

The vision of Obadiah.
Thus says the Lord GOD [a]concerning Edom
[b](We have heard a report from the LORD,
And a messenger has been sent among the nations, *saying,*
"Arise, and let us rise up against her for battle"):

2 "Behold, I will make you small among the nations;
You shall be greatly despised.
3 The [a]pride of your heart has deceived you,
You who dwell in the clefts of the rock,
Whose habitation is high;
[b]*You* who say in your heart, 'Who will bring me down to the ground?'
4 [a]Though you ascend *as* high as the eagle,
And though you [b]set your nest among the stars,
From there I will bring you down," says the LORD.

5 "If [a]thieves had come to you,
If robbers by night—
Oh, how you will be cut off!—
Would they not have stolen till they had enough?
If grape-gatherers had come to you,
[b]Would they not have left *some* gleanings?

6 "Oh, how Esau shall be searched out!
How his hidden treasures shall be sought after!
7 All the men in your confederacy
Shall force you to the border;
[a]The men at peace with you
Shall deceive you *and* prevail against you.
Those who eat your bread shall lay a trap[1] for you.
[b]No one is aware of it.

8 "Will[a] I not in that day," says the LORD,
"Even destroy the wise *men* from Edom,
And understanding from the mountains of Esau?
9 Then your [a]mighty men, O [b]Teman, shall be dismayed,
To the end that everyone from the mountains of Esau
May be cut off by slaughter.

Edom Mistreated His Brother

10 "For [a]violence against your brother Jacob,
Shame shall cover you,
And [b]you shall be cut off forever.
11 In the day that you [a]stood on the other side—
In the day that strangers carried captive his forces,
When foreigners entered his gates
And [b]cast lots for Jerusalem—
Even you *were* as one of them.

12 "But you should not have [a]gazed on the day of your brother
In the day of his captivity;[1]
Nor should you have [b]rejoiced over the children of Judah
In the day of their destruction;
Nor should you have spoken proudly
In the day of distress.
13 You should not have entered the gate of My people
In the day of their calamity.
Indeed, you should not have gazed on their affliction
In the day of their calamity,
Nor laid *hands* on their substance
In the day of their calamity.
14 You should not have stood at the crossroads
To cut off those among them who escaped;
Nor should you have delivered up those among them who remained
In the day of distress.

15 "For[a] the day of the LORD upon all the nations *is* near;
[b]As you have done, it shall be done to you;
Your reprisal shall return upon your own head.
16 [a]For as you drank on My holy mountain,
So shall all the nations drink continually;
Yes, they shall drink, and swallow,
And they shall be as though they had never been.

Israel's Final Triumph

17 "But on Mount Zion there [a]shall be deliverance,
And there shall be holiness;
The house of Jacob shall possess their possessions.

1 [a] Is. 21:11 [b] Jer. 49:14–16 **3** [a] Jer. 49:16 [b] Rev. 18:7 **4** [a] Job 20:6 [b] Hab. 2:9 **5** [a] Jer. 49:9 [b] Deut. 24:21 **7** [a] Jer. 38:22 [b] Is. 19:11 [1] Or *wound,* or *plot* **8** [a] [Job 5:12–14] **9** [a] Ps. 76:5 [b] Jer. 49:7 **10** [a] Gen. 27:41 [b] Ezek. 35:9 **11** [a] Ps. 83:5–8 [b] Nah. 3:10 **12** [a] Mic. 4:11; 7:10 [b] [Prov. 17:5] [1] Literally *On the day he became a foreigner* **15** [a] Ezek. 30:3 [b] Hab. 2:8 **16** [a] Joel 3:17 **17** [a] Amos 9:8

18 The house of Jacob shall be a fire,
And the house of Joseph [a]a flame;
But the house of Esau *shall be* stubble;
They shall kindle them and devour them,
And no survivor shall *remain* of the house of Esau,"
For the LORD has spoken.

19 The South[1] [a]shall possess the mountains of Esau,
[b]And the Lowland shall possess Philistia.
They shall possess the fields of Ephraim
And the fields of Samaria.
Benjamin *shall possess* Gilead.
20 And the captives of this host of the children of Israel
Shall possess the land of the Canaanites
As [a]far as Zarephath.
The captives of Jerusalem who are in Sepharad
[b]Shall possess the cities of the South.[1]
21 Then [a]saviors[1] shall come to Mount Zion
To judge the mountains of Esau,
And the [b]kingdom shall be the LORD's.

18 [a] Zech. 12:6 **19** [a] Is. 11:14 [b] Zeph. 2:7 [1] Hebrew *Negev* **20** [a] 1 Kin. 17:9 [b] Jer. 32:44 [1] Hebrew *Negev* **21** [a] [James 5:20] [b] [Rev. 11:15] [1] Or *deliverers*

THE BOOK OF JONAH

AUTHOR

Jonah was "the son of Amittai" (Jon. 1:1) and nothing more would be known about him were it not for a reference in 2 Kings 14:25 calling him a prophet in the reign of Jeroboam II of Israel. Jonah was a Galilean, contrary to the Pharisees' claim that "no prophet has arisen out of Galilee" (John 7:52). One Jewish tradition says that Jonah was the son of the widow of Zarephath whom Elijah raised from the dead (1 Kin. 17:8–24).

TIME

c. 760 BC

KEY VERSE

Jonah 2:8–9

THEME

The Book of Jonah directs us toward God's greatness and mercy. He will go to any lengths to assure that His message is heard. He makes it possible for people to repent and be redeemed no matter how decadent and far away from God they are. Jonah himself is a prime example of the power of storytelling as he gives us an amazingly visual and memorable image of God's far-reaching grace and His involvement in individual lives to accomplish His purposes.

Second Kings 14:25 explicitly states that Jonah was a God-called prophet from Gath Hepher (near Nazareth). The reluctant prophet Jonah used the word for peace (*shalom*) in a prayer (Jon. 2:9) he offered inside the belly of a "great fish" (1:17). Throughout his story Jonah seesawed from obedience to disobedience, commitment to compromise, but he ultimately followed God's will for his life. Jonah proves it is far easier to obey God than to trust Him; however, we must trust God to experience His peace. In Jonah we learn of God's providential control (1:17), the plant (4:6), a worm (4:7), and the east wind (4:8). The Lord used it all to get Jonah's attention, but also to show Jonah His love and care for the whole world, even Israel's enemies (the Assyrians). God even used Jonah to bring about a revival in the Assyrians.

The Bible reader wonders if Jonah himself ever experienced the peace of God; if he had, why did he so often rebel? Jonah reminds us that God's peace will show up in the most unexpected places. Fascinatingly, Jesus referred to the "sign of the prophet Jonah" (Matt. 12:39) as the only response that the Pharisees would receive when they antagonistically sought some signal from the Lord.

Jonah's Disobedience

1 Now the word of the LORD came to [a]Jonah
the son of Amittai, saying, 2“Arise, go to
[a]Nineveh, that [b]great city, and cry out against it;
for [c]their wickedness has come up before Me.”
3But Jonah arose to flee to Tarshish from the
presence of the LORD. He went down to [a]Joppa,
and found a ship going to Tarshish; so he paid
the fare, and went down into it, to go with them
to [b]Tarshish [c]from the presence of the LORD.

The Storm at Sea

4But [a]the LORD sent out a great wind on the
sea, and there was a mighty tempest on the
sea, so that the ship was about to be broken up.
5Then the mariners were afraid; and every
man cried out to his god, and threw the cargo
that *was* in the ship into the sea, to lighten
the load.[1] But Jonah had gone down [a]into the
lowest parts of the ship, had lain down, and
was fast asleep.

6So the captain came to him, and said to
him, “What do you mean, sleeper? Arise, [a]call
on your God; [b]perhaps your God will consider
us, so that we may not perish.”

7And they said to one another, “Come, let us
[a]cast lots, that we may know for whose cause
this trouble *has come* upon us.” So they cast
lots, and the lot fell on Jonah. 8Then they said
to him, [a]“Please tell us! For whose cause *is* this
trouble upon us? What is your occupation?
And where do you come from? What is your
country? And of what people are you?”

9So he said to them, “I *am* a Hebrew; and I
fear the LORD, the God of heaven, [a]who made
the sea and the dry *land*.”

Jonah Thrown into the Sea

10Then the men were exceedingly afraid,
and said to him, “Why have you done this?”
For the men knew that he fled from the presence of the LORD, because he had told them.
11Then they said to him, “What shall we do to
you that the sea may be calm for us?”—for the
sea was growing more tempestuous.

12And he said to them, [a]“Pick me up and
throw me into the sea; then the sea will become calm for you. For I know that this great
tempest *is* because of me.”

13Nevertheless the men rowed hard to return to land, [a]but they could not, for the sea
continued to grow more tempestuous against
them. 14Therefore they cried out to the LORD
and said, “We pray, O LORD, please do not let
us perish for this man's life, and [a]do not charge
us with innocent blood; for You, O LORD, [b]have
done as it pleased You.” 15So they picked up
Jonah and threw him into the sea, [a]and the
sea ceased from its raging. 16Then the men
[a]feared the LORD exceedingly, and offered a
sacrifice to the LORD and took vows.

Jonah's Prayer and Deliverance

17Now the LORD had prepared a great fish
to swallow Jonah. And [a]Jonah was in the
belly of the fish three days and three nights.

2 Then Jonah prayed to the LORD his God
from the fish's belly. 2And he said:

“I [a]cried out to the LORD because of my
affliction,
[b]And He answered me.

“Out of the belly of Sheol I cried,
And You heard my voice.
3 [a]For You cast me into the deep,
Into the heart of the seas,
And the floods surrounded me;
[b]All Your billows and Your waves passed
over me.
4 [a]Then I said, ‘I have been cast out of
Your sight;
Yet I will look again [b]toward Your holy
temple.’
5 The [a]waters surrounded me, *even* to
my soul;
The deep closed around me;
Weeds were wrapped around my head.
6 I went down to the moorings of the
mountains;
The earth with its bars *closed* behind
me forever;
Yet You have brought up my [a]life from
the pit,
O LORD, my God.

7 “When my soul fainted within me,
I remembered the LORD;
[a]And my prayer went *up* to You,
Into Your holy temple.

8 “Those who regard [a]worthless idols
Forsake their own Mercy.
9 But I will [a]sacrifice to You
With the voice of thanksgiving;
I will pay what I have [b]vowed.
[c]Salvation *is* of the [d]LORD.”

10So the LORD spoke to the fish, and it vomited Jonah onto dry *land*.

1:1 [a] 2 Kin. 14:25 1:2 [a] Is. 37:37 [b] Gen. 10:11, 12 [c] Gen. 18:20 1:3 [a] Josh. 19:46 [b] Is. 23:1 [c] Gen. 4:16 1:4 [a] Ps. 107:25 1:5 [a] 1 Sam. 24:3 [1] Literally *from upon them* 1:6 [a] Ps. 107:28 [b] Joel 2:14 1:7 [a] Josh. 7:14 1:8 [a] Josh. 7:19 1:9 [a] [Neh. 9:6] 1:12 [a] John 11:50 1:13 [a] [Prov. 21:30] 1:14 [a] Deut. 21:8 [b] Ps. 115:3 1:15 [a] [Ps. 89:9; 107:29] 1:16 [a] Acts 5:11 1:17 [a] [Matt. 12:40] 2:2 [a] Ps. 120:1 [b] Ps. 65:2 2:3 [a] Ps. 88:6 [b] Ps. 42:7 2:4 [a] Ps. 31:22 [b] 1 Kin. 8:38 2:5 [a] Lam. 3:54 2:6 [a] [Ps. 16:10] 2:7 [a] Ps. 18:6 2:8 [a] Jer. 10:8 2:9 [a] Hos. 14:2 [b] [Eccl. 5:4, 5] [c] Ps. 3:8 [d] [Jer. 3:23]

CRY OUT FOR PEACE

I cried out to the LORD because of my affliction, and He answered me.

JONAH 2:2

The account of the prophet Jonah is one of the first Bible stories children hear. The fleeing prophet was swallowed by a fish and still ended up preaching in Nineveh, which he'd been avoiding. Worse yet the people repented, which he'd also been avoiding! People debate the literalness of the story, but what is not debated is the important truth that this little book teaches: God loves all humanity and does not want anyone to perish—not even the wicked.

Something I really like about Jonah is his prayer in chapter 2. Jonah had flagrantly disobeyed God's command to go to Nineveh. For a prophet, he showed an outrageous level of disobedience. That he didn't want the people of Nineveh to repent, lest God forgive them, was even more outrageous. Finding himself in the belly of the fish, which Jonah compared to being in hell, the prophet said, "I cried out to the LORD because of my affliction, and He answered me . . . You heard my voice" (v. 1). That God will hear the prayer of someone so obstinate, so disobedient, should give us all a sense of peace.

What does this mean to you? Would you describe yourself as obstinate, disobedient, or unworthy to be heard?

Jonah Preaches at Nineveh

3 Now the word of the LORD came to Jonah
the second time, saying, 2"Arise, go to
Nineveh, that great city, and preach to it the
message that I tell you." 3So Jonah arose and
went to Nineveh, according to the word of
the LORD. Now Nineveh was an exceedingly
great city, a three-day journey[1] *in extent.* 4And
Jonah began to enter the city on the first day's
walk. Then [a]he cried out and said, "Yet forty
days, and Nineveh shall be overthrown!"

The People of Nineveh Believe

5So the [a]people of Nineveh believed God,
proclaimed a fast, and put on sackcloth, from
the greatest to the least of them. 6Then word
came to the king of Nineveh; and he arose
from his throne and laid aside his robe, covered *himself* with sackcloth [a]and sat in ashes.
7[a]And he caused *it* to be proclaimed and
published throughout Nineveh by the decree
of the king and his nobles, saying,

> Let neither man nor beast, herd nor
> flock, taste anything; do not let them
> eat, or drink water. 8But let man and
> beast be covered with sackcloth, and
> cry mightily to God; yes, [a]let every one
> turn from his evil way and from [b]the
> violence that is in his hands. 9[a]Who
> can tell *if* God will turn and relent, and
> turn away from His fierce anger, so
> that we may not perish?

10[a]Then God saw their works, that they
turned from their evil way; and God relented
from the disaster that He had said He would
bring upon them, and He did not do it.

Jonah's Anger and God's Kindness

4 But it displeased Jonah exceedingly, and
he became angry. 2So he prayed to the
LORD, and said, "Ah, LORD, was not this what I
said when I was still in my country? Therefore
I [a]fled previously to Tarshish; for I know that
You *are* a [b]gracious and merciful God, slow to
anger and abundant in lovingkindness, One
who relents from doing harm. 3[a]Therefore
now, O LORD, please take my life from me,
for [b]*it is* better for me to die than to live!"
4Then the LORD said, "*Is it* right for you
to be angry?"
5So Jonah went out of the city and sat on
the east side of the city. There he made himself a shelter and sat under it in the shade,
till he might see what would become of the
city. 6And the LORD God prepared a plant[1] and
made it come up over Jonah, that it might
be shade for his head to deliver him from
his misery. So Jonah was very grateful for
the plant. 7But as morning dawned the next
day God prepared a worm, and it *so* damaged

3:3 [1] Exact meaning unknown **3:4** [a] [Deut. 18:22] **3:5** [a] [Matt. 12:41] **3:6** [a] Job 2:8 **3:7** [a] 2 Chr. 20:3 **3:8** [a] Is. 58:6 [b] Is. 59:6 **3:9** [a] Joel 2:14 **3:10** [a] Jer. 18:8 **4:2** [a] Jon. 1:3 [b] Joel 2:13 **4:3** [a] 1 Kin. 19:4 [b] Jon. 4:8 **4:6** [1] Hebrew *kikayon,* exact identity unknown

GOD'S DESIRE FOR YOUR PEACE

Then God saw their works, that they turned from their evil way; and God relented from the disaster that He had said He would bring upon them.

JONAH 3:10

What Jonah feared happened: the Ninevites repented—and God forgave them! "Then God saw their works, that they turned from their evil way; and God relented from the disaster that He had said He would bring upon them." Jonah was angry. He suspected that Nineveh's survival would someday mean disaster for Israel (and eventually it did). Jonah was so unhappy he asked God to take his life (4:3, 8–9). The prophet was indulging in the ultimate pity party! God shamed Jonah by pointing out that the prophet cared more about the plant that gave him shade than he did about the people of Nineveh. "And should I not pity Nineveh," the Lord asked, "that great city, in which are more than one hundred and twenty thousand persons?" (4:11).

The Book of Jonah ends abruptly, but its message is clear enough: God loves all humanity and desires our salvation, no matter how estranged from Him we might be. I invite you to reflect on God's love and mercy and on His desire for your salvation. What can give us peace more than knowing God loves us and desires our salvation?

the plant that it withered. 8And it happened,
when the sun arose, that God prepared a
vehement east wind; and the sun beat on
Jonah's head, so that he grew faint. Then he
wished death for himself, and said, [a]"*It is*
better for me to die than to live."
9Then God said to Jonah, "*Is it* right for
you to be angry about the plant?"
And he said, "*It is* right for me to be angry,
even to death!"

10But the LORD said, "You have had pity
on the plant for which you have not labored,
nor made it grow, which came up in a night
and perished in a night. 11And should I not
pity Nineveh, [a]that great city, in which are
more than one hundred and twenty thousand persons [b]who cannot discern between
their right hand and their left—and much
livestock?"

4:8 [a] Jon. 4:3 **4:11** [a] Jon. 1:2; 3:2, 3 [b] Deut. 1:39

THE BOOK OF

MICAH

AUTHOR

Micah was from Moresheth Gath (Mic. 1:1, 14) which was located about twenty-five miles southwest of Jerusalem, near Gath. Although Micah was not as politically aware as Isaiah or Daniel, he showed a profound concern for the suffering of the people and had a clear sense of his prophetic calling. A contemporary of Isaiah and Hosea, Micah may have been a farmer-turned-prophet like Amos.

TIME

c. 735–710 BC

KEY VERSE

Micah 6:8

THEME

Micah was from a town in southwestern Judah. His message was directed at both capital cities, Samaria and Jerusalem. He was probably around when the Assyrians destroyed Samaria in 722 BC and may even have lived through Assyria's siege of Jerusalem. Micah's message comes out of unique visions from God. In effect, he saw things that others couldn't, such as the prophecy of Bethlehem as the birthplace of Christ (5:2).

False teaching is an enemy to finding God's peace in our lives. Absolute truth from God is always the prerequisite to experiencing the peace of God. Micah spewed prophetic fire over the false prophets "who make my people stray; who chant 'Peace' while they . . . prepare war" (3:5). Again, in a phase of national apostasy and unbelief, Micah offered hope in a coming Redeemer Messiah, the "One [who] shall be peace" (5:5). We look forward to the day when King Jesus returns in His glorious Second Coming and is our Shepherd once and for all (5:4). He will protect us from all enemies (5:5–6).

1 The word of the LORD that came to [a]Micah of Moresheth in the days of [b]Jotham, Ahaz, *and* Hezekiah, kings of Judah, which he saw concerning Samaria and Jerusalem.

The Coming Judgment on Israel

2 Hear, all you peoples!
Listen, O earth, and all that is in it!
Let the Lord GOD be a witness against you,
The Lord from [a]His holy temple.

3 For behold, the LORD is coming out of His place;
He will come down
And tread on the high places of the earth.
4 [a]The mountains will melt under Him,
And the valleys will split
Like wax before the fire,
Like waters poured down a steep place.
5 All this is for the transgression of Jacob
And for the sins of the house of Israel.
What *is* the transgression of Jacob?
Is it not Samaria?
And what *are* the [a]high places of Judah?
Are they not Jerusalem?

6 "Therefore I will make Samaria [a]a heap of ruins in the field,
Places for planting a vineyard;
I will pour down her stones into the valley,
And I will [b]uncover her foundations.
7 All her carved images shall be beaten to pieces,
And all her [a]pay as a harlot shall be burned with the fire;
All her idols I will lay desolate,
For she gathered *it* from the pay of a harlot,
And they shall return to the [b]pay of a harlot."

Mourning for Israel and Judah

8 Therefore I will wail and howl,
I will go stripped and naked;
[a]I will make a wailing like the jackals
And a mourning like the ostriches,
9 For her wounds *are* incurable.
For [a]it has come to Judah;
It has come to the gate of My people—
To Jerusalem.

10 [a]Tell *it* not in Gath,
Weep not at all;
In Beth Aphrah[1]
Roll yourself in the dust.
11 Pass by in naked shame, you inhabitant of Shaphir;
The inhabitant of Zaanan[1] does not go out.
Beth Ezel mourns;
Its place to stand is taken away from you.

12 For the inhabitant of Maroth pined[1] for good,
But [a]disaster came down from the LORD
To the gate of Jerusalem.
13 O inhabitant of [a]Lachish,
Harness the chariot to the swift steeds
(She *was* the beginning of sin to the daughter of Zion),
For the transgressions of Israel were [b]found in you.

14 Therefore you shall [a]give presents to Moresheth Gath;[1]
The houses of [b]Achzib[2] *shall be* a lie to the kings of Israel.
15 I will yet bring an heir to you,
O inhabitant of [a]Mareshah;[1]
The glory of Israel shall come to [b]Adullam.
16 Make yourself [a]bald and cut off your hair,
Because of your [b]precious children;
Enlarge your baldness like an eagle,
For they shall go from you into [c]captivity.

Woe to Evildoers

2 Woe to those who devise iniquity,
And work out evil on their beds!
At [a]morning light they practice it,
Because it is in the power of their hand.
2 They [a]covet fields and take *them* by violence,
Also houses, and seize *them*.
So they oppress a man and his house,
A man and his inheritance.

3 Therefore thus says the LORD:

"Behold, against this [a]family I am devising [b]disaster,
From which you cannot remove your necks;
Nor shall you walk haughtily,
For this *is* an evil time.

1:1 [a] Jer. 26:18 [b] Is. 1:1 **1:2** [a] [Ps. 11:4] **1:4** [a] Amos 9:5 **1:5** [a] Deut. 32:13; 33:29 **1:6** [a] 2 Kin. 19:25 [b] Ezek. 13:14 **1:7** [a] Hos. 2:5 [b] Deut. 23:18 **1:8** [a] Ps. 102:6 **1:9** [a] 2 Kin. 18:13 **1:10** [a] 2 Sam. 1:20 [1] Literally *House of Dust* **1:11** [1] Literally *Going Out* **1:12** [a] Is. 59:9–11 [1] Literally *was sick* **1:13** [a] Is. 36:2 [b] Ezek. 23:11 **1:14** [a] 2 Sam. 8:2 [b] Josh. 15:44 [1] Literally *Possession of Gath* [2] Literally *Lie* **1:15** [a] Josh. 15:44 [b] 2 Chr. 11:7 [1] Literally *Inheritance* **1:16** [a] Job 1:20 [b] Lam. 4:5 [c] Amos 7:11, 17 **2:1** [a] Hos. 7:6, 7 **2:2** [a] Is. 5:8 **2:3** [a] Jer. 8:3 [b] Amos 5:13

4 In that day *one* shall take up a proverb
against you,
And [a]lament with a bitter lamentation,
saying:
'We are utterly destroyed!
He has changed the heritage of my
people;
How He has removed *it* from me!
To a turncoat He has divided our
fields.' "

5 Therefore you will have no one to
determine boundaries[1] by lot
In the assembly of the LORD.

Lying Prophets

6 "Do not prattle," *you say to those* who
prophesy.
So they shall not prophesy to you;[1]
They shall not return insult for insult.[2]
7 *You who are* named the house of Jacob:
"Is the Spirit of the LORD restricted?
Are these His doings?
Do not My words do good
To him who walks uprightly?

8 "Lately My people have risen up as an
enemy—
You pull off the robe with the garment
From those who trust *you,* as they pass
by,
Like men returned from war.
9 The women of My people you cast out
From their pleasant houses;
From their children
You have taken away My glory forever.

10 "Arise and depart,
For this *is* not *your* [a]rest;
Because it is [b]defiled, it shall destroy,
Yes, with utter destruction.
11 If a man should walk in a false spirit
And speak a lie, *saying,*
'I will prophesy to you of wine and
drink,'
Even he would be the [a]prattler of this
people.

Israel Restored

12 "I[a] will surely assemble all of you, O Jacob,
I will surely gather the remnant of
Israel;
I will put them together [b]like sheep of
the fold,[1]
Like a flock in the midst of their pasture;
[c]They shall make a loud noise because
of *so many* people.
13 The one who breaks open will come up
before them;
They will break out,
Pass through the gate,
And go out by it;
[a]Their king will pass before them,
[b]With the LORD at their head."

2:4 [a] 2 Sam. 1:17 2:5 [1] Literally *one casting a surveyor's line* 2:6 [1] Literally *to these* [2] Vulgate reads *He shall not take shame.* 2:10 [a] Deut. 12:9 [b] Lev. 18:25 2:11 [a] Is. 30:10 2:12 [a] [Mic. 4:6, 7] [b] Jer. 31:10 [c] Ezek. 33:22; 36:37 [1] Hebrew *Bozrah* 2:13 [a] [Hos. 3:5] [b] Is. 52:12

LIVE BY PEACE

"I will surely assemble all of you, O Jacob, I will surely gather the remnant of Israel."

MICAH 2:12

The prophet Micah was a younger contemporary of the great prophet Isaiah. In chapter 2 he railed against Israel's corrupt elite and leaders. One of their faults was seizing a poor man's property (see v. 2). Micah mockingly said, "If a man should walk in a false spirit and speak a lie . . . he would be the prattler of this people" (v. 11). Liars and false prophets were just what that generation wanted!

But Micah also voiced hope. Judgment would not have the last word: "I will surely assemble all of you, O Jacob, I will surely gather the remnant of Israel; I will put them together like sheep of the fold" (v. 12). God's grace is greater than our sin. If we let Him, He will gather us as a shepherd gathers his flock. This should give us peace.

God wants you to develop the discipline of His peace the way you develop a muscle. You need to flex that muscle of peace from time to time to keep it strong. Life gives us plenty of opportunities to decide to live in the peace of God no matter what: each time we trust Him like a Shepherd to gather and keep us, we develop our peace muscle.

Wicked Rulers and Prophets

3 And I said:

"Hear now, O heads of Jacob,
And you [a]rulers of the house of Israel:
[b]*Is it* not for you to know justice?
2 You who hate good and love evil;
Who strip the skin from My people,[1]
And the flesh from their bones;
3 Who also [a]eat the flesh of My people,
Flay their skin from them,
Break their bones,
And chop *them* in pieces
Like *meat* for the pot,
[b]Like flesh in the caldron."

4 Then [a]they will cry to the LORD,
But He will not hear them;
He will even hide His face from them
at that time,
Because they have been evil in their
deeds.

5 Thus says the LORD [a]concerning the
prophets
Who make my people stray;
Who chant "Peace"
While they [b]chew with their teeth,
But who prepare war against him
[c]Who puts nothing into their mouths:
6 "Therefore[a] you shall have night
without vision,
And you shall have darkness without
divination;
The sun shall go down on the prophets,
And the day shall be dark for [b]them.
7 So the seers shall be ashamed,
And the diviners abashed;
Indeed they shall all cover their lips;
[a]For *there is* no answer from God."

8 But truly I am full of power by the
Spirit of the LORD,
And of justice and might,
[a]To declare to Jacob his transgression
And to Israel his sin.
9 Now hear this,
You heads of the house of Jacob
And rulers of the house of Israel,
Who abhor justice
And pervert all equity,
10 [a]Who build up Zion with [b]bloodshed
And Jerusalem with iniquity:
11 [a]Her heads judge for a bribe,
[b]Her priests teach for pay,
And her prophets divine for money.
[c]Yet they lean on the LORD, and say,
"Is not the LORD among us?
No harm can come upon us."
12 Therefore because of you
Zion shall be [a]plowed *like* a field,
[b]Jerusalem shall become heaps of ruins,
And [c]the mountain of the temple[1]
Like the bare hills of the forest.

3:1 [a] Ezek. 22:27 [b] Jer. 5:4, 5 **3:2** [1] Literally *them* **3:3** [a] Ps. 14:4; 27:2 [b] Ezek. 11:3, 6, 7 **3:4** [a] Jer. 11:11 **3:5** [a] Ezek. 13:10, 19 [b] Matt. 7:15 [c] Ezek. 13:18 **3:6** [a] Is. 8:20–22; 29:10–12 [b] Is. 29:10 **3:7** [a] Amos 8:11 **3:8** [a] Is. 58:1 **3:10** [a] Jer. 22:13, 17 [b] Hab. 2:12 **3:11** [a] Is. 1:23 [b] Jer. 6:13 [c] Is. 48:2 **3:12** [a] Jer. 26:18 [b] Ps. 79:1 [c] Mic. 4:1, 2 [1] Literally *house*

GOD CHAMPIONS YOUR PEACE

The prophets who make my people stray; who chant "Peace" . . . judge for a bribe . . . [and] teach for pay.

MICAH 3:5, 11

In the third chapter, Micah took a swipe at the false prophets and the corrupt judges of the southern kingdom. God was angry at "the prophets who make My people stray; who chant 'Peace' . . . [and at leaders who] judge for a bribe . . . [and at priests who] teach for pay." The sin of kings can bring judgment, but the sins of corrupt managers and bureaucrats can destroy a kingdom, too (and the same is true in a church). Hezekiah was a good king, but he failed to rein in the corruption and idolatry in his kingdom.

Like other prophets (notably Jeremiah a century later), Micah was especially critical of the false prophets who proclaimed a false peace because there was no wholeness in the kingdom—only corruption and oppression. When the powerful step on the poor and vulnerable, God takes notice.

We should take heart. God is a Champion of justice and a Defender of the weak. Embrace His righteous ways, and you will find Him and His peace in your corner.

The LORD's Reign in Zion

4 Now [a]it shall come to pass in the latter days
That the mountain of the LORD's house
Shall be established on the top of the mountains,
And shall be exalted above the hills;
And peoples shall flow to it.
2 Many nations shall come and say,
"Come, and let us go up to the mountain of the LORD,
To the house of the God of Jacob;
He will teach us His ways,
And we shall walk in His paths."
For out of Zion the law shall go forth,
And the word of the LORD from Jerusalem.
3 He shall judge between many peoples,
And rebuke strong nations afar off;
They shall beat their swords into [a]plowshares,
And their spears into pruning hooks;
Nation shall not lift up sword against nation,
[b]Neither shall they learn war anymore.[1]

4 [a]But everyone shall sit under his vine and under his fig tree,
And no one shall make *them* afraid;
For the mouth of the LORD of hosts has spoken.
5 For all people walk each in the name of his god,
But [a]we will walk in the name of the LORD our God
Forever and ever.

Zion's Future Triumph

6 "In that day," says the LORD,
[a]"I will assemble the lame,
[b]I will gather the outcast
And those whom I have afflicted;
7 I will make the lame [a]a remnant,
And the outcast a strong nation;
So the LORD [b]will reign over them in Mount Zion
From now on, even forever.
8 And you, O tower of the flock,
The stronghold of the daughter of Zion,
To you shall it come,
Even the former dominion shall come,
The kingdom of the daughter of Jerusalem."

9 Now why do you cry aloud?
[a]*Is there* no king in your midst?
Has your counselor perished?
For [b]pangs have seized you like a woman in labor.
10 Be in pain, and labor to bring forth,
O daughter of Zion,
Like a woman in birth pangs.
For now you shall go forth from the city,
You shall dwell in the field,
And to [a]Babylon you shall go.
There you shall be delivered;
There the [b]LORD will [c]redeem you
From the hand of your enemies.

11 [a]Now also many nations have gathered against you,
Who say, "Let her be defiled,
And let our eye [b]look upon Zion."
12 But they do not know [a]the thoughts of the LORD,
Nor do they understand His counsel;
For He will gather them [b]like sheaves to the threshing floor.

13 "Arise[a] and [b]thresh, O daughter of Zion;
For I will make your horn iron,
And I will make your hooves bronze;
You shall [c]beat in pieces many peoples;
[d]I will consecrate their gain to the LORD,
And their substance to [e]the Lord of the whole earth."

5 Now gather yourself in troops,
O daughter of troops;
He has laid siege against us;
They will [a]strike the judge of Israel with a rod on the cheek.

The Coming Messiah

2 "But you, [a]Bethlehem [b]Ephrathah,
Though you are little [c]among the [d]thousands of Judah,
Yet out of you shall come forth to Me
The One to be [e]Ruler in Israel,
[f]Whose goings forth *are* from of old,
From everlasting."

3 Therefore He shall give them up,
Until the time *that* [a]she who is in labor has given birth;
Then [b]the remnant of His brethren
Shall return to the children of Israel.

4:1 [a] Is. 2:2–4 **4:3** [a] Is. 2:4 [b] Ps. 72:7 [1] Compare Isaiah 2:2–4 **4:4** [a] Zech. 3:10 **4:5** [a] Zech. 10:12 **4:6** [a] Ezek. 34:16 [b] Ps. 147:2 **4:7** [a] Mic. 2:12 [b] [Is. 9:6; 24:23] **4:9** [a] Jer. 8:19 [b] Is. 13:8 **4:10** [a] Amos 5:27 [b] [Is. 45:13] [c] Ps. 18:17 **4:11** [a] Lam. 2:16 [b] Obad. 12 **4:12** [a] [Is. 55:8, 9] [b] Is. 21:10 **4:13** [a] Jer. 51:33 [b] Is. 41:15 [c] Dan. 2:44 [d] Is. 18:7 [e] Zech. 4:14 **5:1** [a] Lam. 3:30; Matt. 27:30; Mark 15:19 **5:2** [a] John 7:42 [b] Gen. 35:19; 48:7 [c] 1 Sam. 23:23 [d] Ex. 18:25 [e] [Is. 9:6] [f] Ps. 90:2; [John 1:1] **5:3** [a] Mic. 4:10 [b] Mic. 4:7; 7:18

4 And He shall stand and [a]feed *His flock*
In the strength of the LORD,
In the majesty of the name of the LORD
His God;
And they shall abide,
For now He [b]shall be great
To the ends of the earth;
5 And this *One* [a]shall be peace.

Judgment on Israel's Enemies

When the Assyrian comes into our
land,
And when he treads in our palaces,
Then we will raise against him
Seven shepherds and eight princely
men.
6 They shall waste with the sword the
land of Assyria,
And the land of [a]Nimrod at its
entrances;
Thus He shall [b]deliver *us* from the
Assyrian,
When he comes into our land
And when he treads within our
borders.

7 Then [a]the remnant of Jacob
Shall be in the midst of many peoples,
[b]Like dew from the LORD,
Like showers on the grass,
That tarry for no man
Nor wait for the sons of men.
8 And the remnant of Jacob
Shall be among the Gentiles,
In the midst of many peoples,
Like a [a]lion among the beasts of the
forest,
Like a young lion among flocks of
sheep,
Who, if he passes through,
Both treads down and tears in pieces,
And none can deliver.
9 Your hand shall be lifted against your
adversaries,
And all your enemies shall be cut off.

10 "And it shall be in that day," says the
LORD,
"That I will [a]cut off your [b]horses from
your midst
And destroy your [c]chariots.
11 I will cut off the cities of your land
And throw down all your strongholds.
12 I will cut off sorceries from your hand,
And you shall have no [a]soothsayers.
13 [a]Your carved images I will also cut off,
And your *sacred* pillars from your
midst;
You shall [b]no more worship the work
of your hands;
14 I will pluck your wooden images[1] from
your midst;
Thus I will destroy your cities.
15 And I will [a]execute vengeance in anger
and fury
On the nations that have not heard."[1]

God Pleads with Israel

6 Hear now what the LORD says:

"Arise, plead your case before the
mountains,
And let the hills hear your voice.
2 [a]Hear, O you mountains, [b]the LORD's
complaint,
And you strong foundations of the
earth;
For [c]the LORD has a complaint against
His people,
And He will contend with Israel.

3 "O My people, what [a]have I done to you?
And how have I [b]wearied you?
Testify against Me.
4 [a]For I brought you up from the land of
Egypt,
I redeemed you from the house of
bondage;
And I sent before you Moses, Aaron,
and Miriam.
5 O My people, remember now
What [a]Balak king of Moab counseled,
And what Balaam the son of Beor
answered him,
From Acacia Grove[1] to Gilgal,
That you may know [b]the righteousness
of the LORD."

6 With what shall I come before the LORD,
And bow myself before the High God?
Shall I come before Him with burnt
offerings,
With calves a year old?
7 [a]Will the LORD be pleased with
thousands of rams,
Ten thousand [b]rivers of oil?
[c]Shall I give my firstborn *for* my
transgression,
The fruit of my body *for* the sin of my
soul?

5:4 [a] [Is. 40:11; 49:9] [b] Ps. 72:8 **5:5** [a] [Is. 9:6] **5:6** [a] Gen. 10:8–11 [b] Is. 14:25 **5:7** [a] Mic. 5:3 [b] Deut. 32:2 **5:8** [a] Num. 24:9 **5:10** [a] Zech. 9:10 [b] Deut. 17:16 [c] Is. 2:7; 22:18 **5:12** [a] Is. 2:6 **5:13** [a] Zech. 13:2 [b] Is. 2:8 **5:14** [1] Hebrew *Asherim,* Canaanite deities **5:15** [a] [2 Thess. 1:8] [1] Or *obeyed* **6:2** [a] Ps. 50:1, 4 [b] Hos. 12:2 [c] [Is. 1:18] **6:3** [a] Jer. 2:5, 31 [b] Is. 43:22, 23 **6:4** [a] [Deut. 4:20] **6:5** [a] Num. 22:5, 6 [b] Judg. 5:11 [1] Hebrew *Shittim* (compare Numbers 25:1; Joshua 2:1; 3:1) **6:7** [a] Is. 1:11 [b] Job 29:6 [c] 2 Kin. 16:3

8 He has [a]shown you, O man, what *is* good;
And what does the LORD require of you
But [b]to do justly,
To love mercy,
And to walk humbly with your God?

Punishment of Israel's Injustice

9 The LORD's voice cries to the city—
Wisdom shall see Your name:

"Hear the rod!
Who has appointed it?
10 Are there yet the treasures of wickedness
In the house of the wicked,
And the short measure *that is* an abomination?
11 Shall I count pure *those* with [a]the wicked scales,
And with the bag of deceitful weights?
12 For her rich men are full of [a]violence,
Her inhabitants have spoken lies,
And [b]their tongue is deceitful in their mouth.

13 "Therefore I will also [a]make *you* sick by striking you,
By making *you* desolate because of your sins.
14 [a]You shall eat, but not be satisfied;
Hunger[1] *shall be* in your midst.
You may carry *some* away,[2] but shall not save *them;*
And what you do rescue I will give over to the sword.

15 "You shall [a]sow, but not reap;
You shall tread the olives, but not anoint yourselves with oil;
And *make* sweet wine, but not drink wine.
16 For the statutes of [a]Omri are [b]kept;
All the works of Ahab's house *are done;*
And you walk in their counsels,
That I may make you a desolation,
And your inhabitants a hissing.
Therefore you shall bear the [c]reproach of My people."[1]

Sorrow for Israel's Sins

7 Woe is me!
For I am like those who gather summer fruits,
Like those who [a]glean vintage grapes;
There is no cluster to eat
Of the first-ripe fruit *which* [b]my soul desires.
2 The [a]faithful *man* has perished from the earth,
And *there is* no one upright among men.
They all lie in wait for blood;
[b]Every man hunts his brother with a net.

6:8 [a] [Deut. 10:12] [b] Gen. 18:19 **6:11** [a] Hos. 12:7 **6:12** [a] Mic. 2:1, 2 [b] Jer. 9:2–6, 8 **6:13** [a] Lev. 26:16 **6:14** [a] Lev. 26:26 [1] Or *Emptiness* or *Humiliation* [2] Targum and Vulgate read *You shall take hold.* **6:15** [a] Amos 5:11 **6:16** [a] 1 Kin. 16:25, 26 [b] Hos. 5:11 [c] Is. 25:8 [1] Following Masoretic Text, Targum, and Vulgate; Septuagint reads *of nations.* **7:1** [a] Is. 17:6 [b] Is. 28:4 **7:2** [a] Is. 57:1 [b] Hab. 1:15

ACT, LOVE, WALK

He has shown you, O man, what is good.

MICAH 6:8

Please read verses 6–8 prayerfully. Let the words sink in. This is one of the most moving passages in the Bible. Here's the context: the wealthy oppressors of Micah's day brought their sacrifices to the temple believing that their grand offerings compensated for their avarice and injustice. The prophet asked sarcastically, "Will the LORD be pleased with thousands of rams, ten thousand rivers of oil? Shall I give my firstborn?" (v. 7).

Micah's point is hard to miss. Is it possible to buy off God? Can we inundate Him with so many sacrifices that no matter what we do, He will forgive us? No, Micah said. "He has shown you, O man, what is good; and what does the LORD require of you but to do justly, to love mercy, and to walk humbly with your God?" (v. 8).

Act justly, love mercy, and walk with Him humbly. Do this and you will live a life of grace and peace. But don't forget the word "walk." "We walk by faith, not by sight" (2 Cor. 5:7). We keep walking in the direction of our faith to find the peace of God, even if peace seems elusive at times.

3 That they may successfully do evil with
both hands—
The prince asks *for gifts,*
The judge *seeks* a [a]bribe,
And the great *man* utters his evil desire;
So they scheme together.
4 The best of them *is* [a]like a brier;
The most upright *is sharper* than a
thorn hedge;
The day of your watchman and your
punishment comes;
Now shall be their perplexity.

5 [a]Do not trust in a friend;
Do not put your confidence in a
companion;
Guard the doors of your mouth
From her who lies in your [b]bosom.
6 For [a]son dishonors father,
Daughter rises against her mother,
Daughter-in-law against her
mother-in-law;
A man's enemies *are* the men of his
own household.
7 Therefore I will look to the LORD;
I will [a]wait for the God of my salvation;
My God will hear me.

Israel's Confession and Comfort

8 [a]Do not rejoice over me, my enemy;
[b]When I fall, I will arise;
When I sit in darkness,
The LORD *will be* a light to me.
9 [a]I will bear the indignation of the LORD,
Because I have sinned against Him,
Until He pleads my [b]case
And executes justice for me.
He will bring me forth to the light;
I will see His righteousness.
10 Then *she who is* my enemy will see,
And [a]shame will cover her who said to me,
[b]"Where is the LORD your God?"
My eyes will see her;
Now she will be trampled down
Like mud in the streets.

11 *In* the day when your [a]walls are to be
built,
In that day the decree shall go far and
wide.[1]
12 *In* that day [a]they[1] shall come to you
From Assyria and the fortified cities,[2]
From the fortress[3] to the River,[4]
From sea to sea,
And mountain *to* mountain.
13 Yet the land shall be desolate
Because of those who dwell in it,
And [a]for the fruit of their deeds.

God Will Forgive Israel

14 Shepherd Your people with Your staff,
The flock of Your heritage,

7:3 [a] Mic. 3:11; Luke 1:72, 73 **7:4** [a] Ezek. 2:6 **7:5** [a] Jer. 9:4 [b] Deut. 28:56 **7:6** [a] Matt. 10:36 **7:7** [a] Is. 25:9 **7:8** [a] Prov. 24:17 [b] [Prov. 24:16] **7:9** [a] Lam. 3:39, 40 [b] Jer. 50:34 **7:10** [a] Ps. 35:26 [b] Ps. 42:3 **7:11** [a] [Amos 9:11] [1] Or *the boundary shall be extended* **7:12** [a] [Is. 11:16; 19:23–25] [1] Literally *he,* collective of the captives [2] Hebrew *arey mazor,* possibly *cities of Egypt* [3] Hebrew *mazor,* possibly *Egypt* [4] That is, the Euphrates **7:13** [a] Jer. 21:14

WHERE ARE YOU LOOKING?

I will look to the LORD; I will wait for the God of my salvation.

MICAH 7:7

In verses 1–6 Micah the prophet describes the final decline of the southern kingdom as it drifted toward its inevitable destruction. The decline was not military; it was moral. "The faithful man has perished from the earth, and there is no one upright . . . They all lie in wait for blood" (v. 2). Princes and judges asked for bribes. Friends could not be trusted. Even the family unit had disintegrated.

I suspect most people without God would view circumstances like these as hopeless. The picture that Micah paints in chapter 7 is so gloomy, Jesus Himself used verse 6 as a sign of the last generation before the day of judgment (see Matt. 10:21, 35–36). So did the rabbis and others.

But Micah 7:1–6 was not the last word. The prophet had hope: "I will look to the LORD; I will wait for the God of my salvation; my God will hear me" (v. 7). Micah gave us a model for faith and prayer. We, too, must look to the Lord, knowing that God will hear our prayers. Prayer in difficult times is what keeps our peace close.

WE ARE GOD'S HERITAGE

Who is a God like You, pardoning iniquity?

MICAH 7:18

The last part of chapter 7 is an addendum that reflects the postexilic period. The people of the southern kingdom had returned to their land. They had begun to rebuild Jerusalem, her walls, and her temple. Verses 8–20 are a response to Israel's enemies who mocked her defeat and exile. Israel had been reduced to a small, struggling remnant. The might of David and the glory of Solomon were long gone. All that remained was a small population of refugees and settlers whose future was uncertain.

But the prophet saw much more. He saw in the return to the land the fulfillment of God's promise in 2:12 ("I will surely gather the remnant of Israel"). God had done that! Not only did God fulfill His promise, but He even pardoned sinful Israel. The stunned prophet asked, "Who is a God like You, pardoning iniquity and passing over the transgression of the remnant of His heritage?" (v. 18).

I love how the prophet referred to God's people as "His heritage." The implication of this language is profound. God sees us as His children. We are His heritage! Isn't it great that God is never ashamed to call us His children? This truth should bring us peace right now.

Who dwell solitarily *in* a [a]woodland,
In the midst of Carmel;
Let them feed *in* Bashan and Gilead,
As in days of old.

15 "As[a] in the days when you came out of
the land of Egypt,
I will show them[1] [b]wonders."

16 The nations [a]shall see and be ashamed
of all their might;
[b]They shall put *their* hand over *their*
mouth;
Their ears shall be deaf.
17 They shall lick the [a]dust like a serpent;
[b]They shall crawl from their holes like
snakes of the earth.
[c]They shall be afraid of the LORD our
God,
And shall fear because of You.
18 [a]Who *is* a God like You,
[b]Pardoning iniquity
And passing over the transgression of
[c]the remnant of His heritage?

[d]He does not retain His anger
forever,
Because He delights *in* [e]mercy.
19 He will again have compassion on us,
And will subdue our iniquities.

You will cast all our[1] sins
Into the depths of the sea.
20 [a]You will give truth to Jacob
And mercy to Abraham,
[b]Which You have sworn to our
fathers
From days of old.

7:14 [a] Is. 37:24 **7:15** [a] Ps. 68:22; 78:12 [b] Ex. 34:10 [1] Literally *him,* collective for the captives **7:16** [a] Is. 26:11 [b] Job 21:5 **7:17** [a] [Is. 49:23] [b] Ps. 18:45 [c] Jer. 33:9 **7:18** [a] Ex. 15:11 [b] Ex. 34:6, 7, 9 [c] Mic. 4:7 [d] Ps. 103:8, 9, 13 [e] [Ezek. 33:11] **7:19** [1] Literally *their* **7:20** [a] Luke 1:72, 73 [b] Ps. 105:9

THE BOOK OF

NAHUM

AUTHOR

The only mention of Nahum in the Old Testament is found in Nahum 1:1, where he is called an Elkoshite. Scholars have been unable to determine the exact location of Elkosh and numerous theories exist, but due to his interest in the triumph of Judah (1:15; 2:2), some believe Nahum to be a prophet of the southern kingdom.

TIME

c. 600 BC

KEY VERSE

Nahum 1:7–8

THEME

Nahum is unique in that it is a prophecy addressed completely to a nation other than Israel: Assyria and its capital, Nineveh. While Nineveh may be powerful, its day of destruction is coming. Nineveh is not invincible. The message is that God's standards apply to all nations, not just Israel and Judah. They need to be prepared to live by those standards or face judgment.

One hundred years after Jonah, God called the prophet Nahum to preach against the apostate Assyrians who had destroyed the northern kingdom of Israel. This great prophetic book reminds us that everlasting peace is coming: "Behold, on the mountains the feet of him who brings good tidings, who proclaims peace!" (1:15). Nahum invites us to see the Lord just over the horizon, racing toward us, proclaiming everlasting peace through His presence. We also find inspiration to be like the heralds in 1:15 and proclaim peace to a world in desperate need of forgiveness and hope through faith in Jesus Christ.

1 The burden[1] [a]against Nineveh. The book of the vision of Nahum the Elkoshite.

God's Wrath on His Enemies

2 God *is* [a]jealous, and the LORD avenges;
The LORD avenges and *is* furious.
The LORD will take vengeance on His adversaries,
And He reserves *wrath* for His enemies;
3 The LORD *is* [a]slow to anger and [b]great in power,
And will not at all acquit *the wicked.*

[c]The LORD has His way
In the whirlwind and in the storm,
And the clouds *are* the dust of His feet.
4 [a]He rebukes the sea and makes it dry,
And dries up all the rivers.
[b]Bashan and Carmel wither,
And the flower of Lebanon wilts.
5 The mountains quake before Him,
The hills melt,
And the earth heaves[1] at His presence,
Yes, the world and all who dwell in it.

6 Who can stand before His indignation?
And [a]who can endure the fierceness of His anger?
His fury is poured out like fire,
And the rocks are thrown down by Him.

7 [a]The LORD *is* good,
A stronghold in the day of trouble;
And [b]He knows those who trust in Him.
8 But with an overflowing flood
He will make an utter end of its place,
And darkness will pursue His enemies.

9 [a]What do you conspire against the LORD?
[b]He will make an utter end *of it.*
Affliction will not rise up a second time.
10 For while tangled [a]*like* thorns,
[b]And while drunken *like* drunkards,
[c]They shall be devoured like stubble fully dried.
11 From you comes forth *one*
Who plots evil against the LORD,
A wicked counselor.

12 Thus says the LORD:

"Though *they are* safe, and likewise many,
Yet in this manner they will be [a]cut down
When he passes through.
Though I have afflicted you,
I will afflict you no more;
13 For now I will break off his yoke from you,
And burst your bonds apart."

14 The LORD has given a command concerning you:
"Your name shall be perpetuated no longer.

1:1 [a] Zeph. 2:13 [1] Or *oracle* **1:2** [a] Ex. 20:5 **1:3** [a] Ex. 34:6, 7 [b] [Job 9:4] [c] Ps. 18:17 **1:4** [a] Matt. 8:26 [b] Is. 33:9 **1:5** [1] Targum reads *burns.* **1:6** [a] [Mal. 3:2] **1:7** [a] [Jer. 33:11] [b] 2 Tim. 2:19 **1:9** [a] Ps. 2:1 [b] 1 Sam. 3:12 **1:10** [a] 2 Sam. 23:6 [b] Nah. 3:11 [c] Mal. 4:1 **1:12** [a] [Is. 10:16–19, 33, 34]

TRUST GOD'S JUST WAYS

The LORD is slow to anger and great in power, and will not at all acquit the wicked.

NAHUM 1:3

Nahum witnessed what the prophet Jonah longed to see: the destruction of the Assyrian Empire. Several times in the prophets' writings we hear words of grace and mercy, but we should never forget that sin does have consequences. Israel lost her city, her temple, and her land for almost two generations—and then, through the sovereignty of God, got all of it back.

Assyria also received grace. Though the city of Nineveh repented at Jonah's preaching, the capital city of Asshur never did. In the words of Nahum the prophet, "The LORD is slow to anger and great in power, and will not at all acquit the wicked" (v. 3). Jonah witnessed God's slowness to anger; Nahum saw His refusal to excuse the evil.

Divine justice strengthens our sense of well-being and our peace. This is where we must develop the peace-of-God perspective and acknowledge that the Lord works in mysterious ways. How can you reframe a troubling situation today using the peace-of-God perspective? Maybe He's doing something unexpectedly, explosively positive behind the scenes!

Out of the house of your gods
I will cut off the carved image and the molded image.
I will dig your [a]grave,
For you are [b]vile."

15 Behold, on the mountains
The [a]feet of him who brings good tidings,
Who proclaims peace!
O Judah, keep your appointed feasts,
Perform your vows.
For the wicked one shall no more pass through you;
He is [b]utterly cut off.

The Destruction of Nineveh

2 He who scatters[1] has come up before your face.
Man the fort!
Watch the road!
Strengthen *your* flanks!
Fortify *your* power mightily.

2 For the LORD will restore the excellence of Jacob
Like the excellence of Israel,
For the emptiers have emptied them out
And ruined their vine branches.

3 The shields of his mighty men *are* made red,
The valiant men *are* in scarlet.
The chariots *come* with flaming torches
In the day of his preparation,
And the spears are brandished.[1]
4 The chariots rage in the streets,
They jostle one another in the broad roads;
They seem like torches,
They run like lightning.

5 He remembers his nobles;
They stumble in their walk;
They make haste to her walls,
And the defense is prepared.
6 The gates of the rivers are opened,
And the palace is dissolved.
7 It is decreed:[1]
She shall be led away captive,
She shall be brought up;
And her maidservants shall lead *her* as with the voice of doves,
Beating their breasts.

8 Though Nineveh of old *was* like a pool of water,
Now they flee away.
"Halt! Halt!" *they cry;*
But no one turns back.

1:14 [a] Ezek. 32:22, 23 [b] Nah. 3:6 1:15 [a] Rom. 10:15 [b] Is. 29:7, 8 2:1 [1] Vulgate reads *He who destroys.* 2:3 [1] Literally *the cypresses are shaken;* Septuagint and Syriac read *the horses rush about;* Vulgate reads *the drivers are stupefied.* 2:7 [1] Hebrew *Huzzab*

PEACE-OF-GOD WORLDVIEW

Behold, on the mountains the feet of him who brings good tidings, who proclaims peace!

NAHUM 1:15

When news of Assyria's destruction reached Israel, the people rejoiced. Israel's prophets had foretold coming judgment on the oppressive and violent empire. Nahum himself had reminded the peoples that although God was slow in judgment, He would accomplish it. So word of the empire's demise was heard: "Behold, on the mountains the feet of him who brings good tidings, who proclaims peace!" (1:15). The peace that the prophet announced was much more than an end to warfare; it was the peace that God had promised—the peace that fulfills and makes one whole and complete.

This is of course the truest part of the glad tidings (or "good news"). It isn't simply that Assyria had been defeated and was no more. Other tyrannical kingdoms would take Assyria's place. The good news is that God was and is supreme. Kingdoms that oppose Him and oppress His people will come to an end. The peace that God brings will never end—and that is truly good news.

Ask the Lord to help you with a renewed peace-of-God worldview to see your problems as opportunities for the Lord to work in your life. That will change your attitude and your heart.

9 Take spoil of silver!
Take spoil of [a]gold!
There is no end of treasure,
Or wealth of every desirable prize.
10 She is empty, desolate, and waste!
The heart melts, and the knees shake;
Much pain *is* in every side,
And all their faces are drained of color.[1]

11 Where *is* the dwelling of the [a]lions,
And the feeding place of the young lions,
Where the lion walked, the lioness *and* lion's cub,
And no one made *them* afraid?
12 The lion tore in pieces enough for his cubs,
Killed for his lionesses,
[a]Filled his caves with prey,
And his dens with flesh.

13"Behold, [a]I *am* against you," says the
LORD of hosts, "I will burn your[1] chariots
in smoke, and the sword shall devour your
young lions; I will cut off your prey from the
earth, and the voice of your [b]messengers
shall be heard no more."

The Woe of Nineveh

3 Woe to the [a]bloody city!
It *is* all full of lies *and* robbery.
Its victim never departs.
2 The noise of a whip
And the noise of rattling wheels,
Of galloping horses,
Of clattering chariots!
3 Horsemen charge with bright sword and glittering spear.
There is a multitude of slain,
A great number of bodies,
Countless corpses—
They stumble over the corpses—
4 Because of the multitude of harlotries of the seductive harlot,
[a]The mistress of sorceries,
Who sells nations through her harlotries,
And families through her sorceries.

5 "Behold, I *am* [a]against you," says the LORD of hosts;
[b]"I will lift your skirts over your face,
I will show the nations your nakedness,
And the kingdoms your shame.
6 I will cast abominable filth upon you,
Make you [a]vile,
And make you [b]a spectacle.
7 It shall come to pass *that* all who look upon you
[a]Will flee from you, and say,
[b]'Nineveh is laid waste!
[c]Who will bemoan her?'
Where shall I seek comforters for you?"

8 [a]Are you better than [b]No Amon[1]
That was situated by the River,[2]
That had the waters around her,
Whose rampart *was* the sea,
Whose wall *was* the sea?
9 Ethiopia and Egypt *were* her strength,
And *it was* boundless;
[a]Put and Lubim were your[1] helpers.
10 Yet she *was* carried away,
She went into captivity;
[a]Her young children also were dashed to pieces
[b]At the head of every street;
They [c]cast lots for her honorable men,
And all her great men were bound in chains.
11 You also will be [a]drunk;
You will be hidden;
You also will seek refuge from the enemy.

12 All your strongholds *are* [a]fig trees with ripened figs:
If they are shaken,
They fall into the mouth of the eater.
13 Surely, [a]your people in your midst *are* women!
The gates of your land are wide open for your enemies;
Fire shall devour the [b]bars of your *gates*.

14 Draw your water for the siege!
[a]Fortify your strongholds!
Go into the clay and tread the mortar!
Make strong the brick kiln!
15 There the fire will devour you,
The sword will cut you off;
It will eat you up like a [a]locust.

Make yourself many—like the locust!
Make yourself many—like the *swarming* locusts!
16 You have multiplied your [a]merchants more than the stars of heaven.
The locust plunders and flies away.

2:9 [a] Zeph. 1:18 **2:10** [1] Compare Joel 2:6 **2:11** [a] Job 4:10, 11 **2:12** [a] Jer. 51:34 **2:13** [a] Nah. 3:5 [b] 2 Kin. 18:17–25; 19:9–13, 23 [1] Literally *her* **3:1** [a] Hab. 2:12 **3:4** [a] Is. 47:9–12 **3:5** [a] Nah. 2:13 [b] Is. 47:2, 3 **3:6** [a] Nah. 1:14 [b] Heb. 10:33 **3:7** [a] Rev. 18:10 [b] Jon. 3:3; 4:11 [c] Jer. 15:5 **3:8** [a] Amos 6:2 [b] Jer. 46:25 [1] That is, ancient Thebes; Targum and Vulgate read *populous Alexandria.* [2] Literally *rivers,* that is, the Nile and the surrounding canals **3:9** [a] Ezek. 27:10 [1] Septuagint reads *her.* **3:10** [a] Hos. 13:16 [b] Lam. 2:19 [c] Joel 3:3 **3:11** [a] Nah. 1:10 **3:12** [a] Rev. 6:12, 13 **3:13** [a] Is. 19:16 [b] Jer. 51:30 **3:14** [a] Nah. 2:1 **3:15** [a] Joel 1:4 **3:16** [a] Rev. 18:3, 11–19

17 [a]Your commanders *are* like *swarming* locusts,
And your generals like great grasshoppers,
Which camp in the hedges on a cold day;
When the sun rises they flee away,
And the place where they *are* is not known.

18 [a]Your shepherds slumber, O [b]king of Assyria;
Your nobles rest *in the dust.*
Your people are [c]scattered on the mountains,
And no one gathers them.
19 Your injury *has* no healing,
[a]Your wound is severe.
[b]All who hear news of you
Will clap *their* hands over you,
For upon whom has not your wickedness passed continually?

3:17 [a] Rev. 9:7 3:18 [a] Ps. 76:5, 6 [b] Jer. 50:18 [c] 1 Kin. 22:17 3:19 [a] Mic. 1:9 [b] Lam. 2:15

THE BOOK OF

HABAKKUK

AUTHOR

In both the introduction to this book (Hab. 1:1) and the closing psalm (3:1), the author identifies himself as Habakkuk the prophet. It is believed that he might have been a priest, as he mentions in the closing psalm, "To the Chief Musician. With my stringed instruments" (3:19). Also, in the apocryphal book of Bel and the Dragon, Daniel is rescued a second time by the prophet Habakkuk.

TIME

c. 607 BC

KEY VERSE

Habakkuk 2:4

THEME

This whole Book of Habakkuk is really devoted to the question of why, if the Lord is all-powerful, He allows evil to exist. The events that seem to be precipitating this question are the victories of Babylon. God was using Babylon, a nation without God, to punish Israel, God's own people. The answers God gives in Habakkuk solidly point us in one direction, but ultimately the answers are in faith in Him alone.

The fifty-six verses of Habakkuk are truly a prayer journal because, in them, the prophet addresses only God. Habakkuk essentially opened his first prayer by asking God a very human question: *Are You dead? Why aren't You listening?* (1:2). The Lord's answer caused Habakkuk to issue a holy hush: "The Lord is in His holy temple. Let all the earth keep silence before Him" (2:20). The prophet requested an explanation from the Lord, yet when God began attempting to explain, Habakkuk nearly collapsed (3:16). Very interestingly, this is one of only five books in the Old Testament in which the word "peace" does not occur. Yet the book is a call to live by God's promises, not explanations, in order to find peace. God told Habakkuk, "The just shall live by his faith" (2:4), a verse that all of Romans, Galatians, and Hebrews fully support and teach us to appreciate, understand, and apply. Faith leads to the peace of God.

1 The burden[1] which the prophet Habakkuk saw.

The Prophet's Question

2 O LORD, how long shall I cry,
[a]And You will not hear?
Even cry out to You, [b]"Violence!"
And You will [c]not save.
3 Why do You show me iniquity,
And cause *me* to see trouble?
For plundering and violence *are* before me;
There is strife, and contention arises.
4 Therefore the law is powerless,
And justice never goes forth.
For the [a]wicked surround the righteous;
Therefore perverse judgment proceeds.

The LORD's Reply

5 "Look[a] among the nations and watch—
Be utterly astounded!
For *I will* work a work in your days
Which you would not believe, though it were told *you.*
6 For indeed I am [a]raising up the Chaldeans,
A bitter and hasty [b]nation
Which marches through the breadth of the earth,
To possess dwelling places *that are* not theirs.
7 They are terrible and dreadful;
Their judgment and their dignity proceed from themselves.
8 Their horses also are [a]swifter than leopards,
And more fierce than evening wolves.
Their chargers charge ahead;
Their cavalry comes from afar;
They fly as the [b]eagle *that* hastens to eat.

9 "They all come for violence;
Their faces are set *like* the east wind.
They gather captives like sand.
10 They scoff at kings,
And princes are scorned by them.
They deride every stronghold,
For they heap up earthen *mounds* and seize it.
11 Then *his* mind[1] changes, and he transgresses;
He commits offense,
[a]*Ascribing* this power to his god."

The Prophet's Second Question

12 Are You not [a]from everlasting,
O LORD my God, my Holy One?
We shall not die.
O LORD, [b]You have appointed them for judgment;
O Rock, You have marked them for [c]correction.
13 *You are* of purer eyes than to behold evil,
And cannot look on wickedness.
Why do You look on those who deal treacherously,
And hold Your tongue when the wicked devours
A *person* more righteous than he?
14 *Why* do You make men like fish of the sea,
Like creeping things *that have* no ruler over them?

15 They take up all of them with a hook,
They catch them in their net,
And gather them in their dragnet.
Therefore they rejoice and are glad.
16 Therefore [a]they sacrifice to their net,
And burn incense to their dragnet;
Because by them their share *is* sumptuous
And their food plentiful.
17 Shall they therefore empty their net,
And continue to slay nations without pity?

2 I will [a]stand my watch
And set myself on the rampart,
And watch to see what He will say to me,
And what I will answer when I am corrected.

PEACE NOTE

Habakkuk wrote down his own personal Peace Plan. So we should prayerfully write down steps to refocus on living in the peace of God through our daily habits, decisions, and lifestyles.

HABAKKUK 2:2

1:1 [1] Or *oracle* 1:2 [a] Lam. 3:8 [b] Mic. 2:1, 2; 3:1–3 [c] [Job 21:5–16] 1:4 [a] Jer. 12:1 1:5 [a] Is. 29:14 1:6 [a] 2 Kin. 24:2 [b] Ezek. 7:24; 21:31 1:8 [a] Jer. 4:13 [b] Hos. 8:1 1:11 [a] Dan. 5:4 [1] Literally *spirit* or *wind* 1:12 [a] Ps. 90:2; 93:2 [b] Is. 10:5–7 [c] Jer. 25:9 1:16 [a] Deut. 8:17 2:1 [a] Is. 21:8, 11

The Just Live by Faith

2 Then the LORD answered me and said:

[a]"Write the vision
And make *it* plain on tablets,
That he may run who reads it.
3 For [a]the vision *is* yet for an appointed time;
But at the end it will speak, and it will [b]not lie.
Though it tarries, [c]wait for it;
Because it will [d]surely come,
It will not tarry.

4 "Behold the proud,
His soul is not upright in him;
But the [a]just shall live by his faith.

Woe to the Wicked

5 "Indeed, because he transgresses by wine,
He is a proud man,
And he does not stay at home.
Because he [a]enlarges his desire as hell,[1]
And he *is* like death, and cannot be satisfied,
He gathers to himself all nations
And heaps up for himself all peoples.

6 "Will not all these [a]take up a proverb against him,
And a taunting riddle against him, and say,
'Woe to him who increases
What is not his—how long?
And to him who loads himself with many pledges'?[1]
7 Will not your creditors[1] rise up suddenly?
Will they not awaken who oppress you?
And you will become their booty.
8 [a]Because you have plundered many nations,

PEACE NOTE

"The just shall live by his faith."

Peace comes by believing in the facts of Scripture.

HABAKKUK 2:4

2:2 [a] Is. 8:1 2:3 [a] Dan. 8:17, 19; 10:14 [b] Ezek. 12:24, 25 [c] [Heb. 10:37, 38] [d] [2 Pet. 3:9] 2:4 [a] [John 3:36]; Rom. 1:17
2:5 [a] Is. 5:11–15 [1] Or *Sheol* 2:6 [a] Mic. 2:4 [1] Syriac and Vulgate read *thick clay.* 2:7 [1] Literally *those who bite you*
2:8 [a] Is. 33:1

HOW WILL YOU NOW LIVE?

"The just shall live by his faith."

HABAKKUK 2:4

Have you ever wanted God to explain all your problems? Habakkuk did. God first warned the prophet, *You cannot handle the explanation* (see 1:5). Then God started to offer an explanation, and Habakkuk nearly collapsed (3:16). That led Habakkuk to declare the word of the Lord that we don't put faith in explanations; rather, we put faith in God's promises. This is what it means that "the just shall live by his faith" (2:4).

The meaning of verse 4 has been much discussed. Literally the Hebrew reads, "The righteous person shall live by its faithfulness," that is, he would live by the faithfulness of the vision that God revealed to His prophet. Of course, to live by it requires faith in God who gave it. We have here a remarkable reciprocity between God and the believer. We must have faith that God is Himself faithful.

Habakkuk had to make a decision, and so do we: *I will face this bad news in the peace of God.* Not only are we saved by faith, but we are to live by faith in His "exceedingly great and precious promises" (2 Pet. 1:4)! Therein we find peace.

All the remnant of the people shall
plunder you,
Because of men's blood
And the violence of the land *and* the
city,
And of all who dwell in it.

9 "Woe to him who covets evil gain for his
house,
That he may [a]set his nest on high,
That he may be delivered from the
power of disaster!
10 You give shameful counsel to your
house,
Cutting off many peoples,
And sin *against* your soul.
11 For the stone will cry out from the wall,
And the beam from the timbers will
answer it.

12 "Woe to him who builds a town with
bloodshed,
Who establishes a city by iniquity!
13 Behold, *is it* not of the LORD of hosts
That the peoples labor to feed the fire,[1]
And nations weary themselves in vain?
14 For the earth will be filled
With the knowledge of the glory of the
LORD,
As the waters cover the sea.

15 "Woe to him who gives drink to his
neighbor,
Pressing[1] *him to* your [a]bottle,
Even to make *him* drunk,
That you may look on his nakedness!
16 You are filled with shame instead of
glory.
You also—drink!
And be exposed as uncircumcised![1]
The cup of the LORD's right hand *will
be* turned against you,
And utter shame will be on your glory.
17 For the violence *done to* Lebanon will
cover you,
And the plunder of beasts *which* made
them afraid,
Because of men's blood
And the violence of the land *and* the
city,
And of all who dwell in it.

18 "What profit is the image, that its maker
should carve it,
The molded image, a teacher of lies,
That the maker of its mold should trust
in it,
To make mute idols?
19 Woe to him who says to wood,
'Awake!'
To silent stone, 'Arise! It shall teach!'
Behold, it is overlaid with gold and
silver,
Yet in it there is no breath at all.

20 "But[a] the LORD is in His holy temple.
Let all the earth keep silence before
Him."

2:9 [a] Obad. 4 2:13 [1] Literally *for what satisfies fire,* that is, for what is of no lasting value 2:15 [a] Hos. 7:5 [1] Literally *Attaching* or *Joining* 2:16 [1] Dead Sea Scrolls and Septuagint read *And reel!;* Syriac and Vulgate read *And fall fast asleep!* 2:20 [a] Zeph. 1:7

THE EARTH FILLED WITH PEACE

"For the earth will be filled with the knowledge of the glory of the LORD."

HABAKKUK 2:14

In chapter 1 Habakkuk complained to God about the violence and injustice that filled the earth. But in chapter 2, God gave the prophet a vision that (if trusted) would enable the righteous person to live (see 2:4). Those who thought they prospered through violence and theft would in the end have nothing. How did the prophet know this? Because God had promised that He would change the world: "For the earth will be filled with the knowledge of the glory of the LORD, as the waters cover the sea" (2:14). God's glory will encompass the earth!

Neither new economic policies nor new technologies will transform the earth. What will is better understanding of the God who created the earth. Habakkuk inspires us to look at the *Who* when we do not understand the *why* behind what's happening. This is what the peace of God will do for us today—help us focus on our faithful God and not on a cosmic understanding of world events. He is where we find peace.

The Prophet's Prayer

3 A prayer of Habakkuk the prophet, on Shigionoth.[1]

2 O LORD, I have heard Your speech *and* was afraid;
O LORD, revive Your work in the midst of the years!
In the midst of the years make *it* known;
In wrath remember mercy.

3 God came from Teman,
The Holy One from Mount Paran. *Selah*

His glory covered the heavens,
And the earth was full of His praise.
4 *His* brightness was like the light;
He had rays *flashing* from His hand,
And there His power *was* hidden.
5 Before Him went pestilence,
And fever followed at His feet.

6 He stood and measured the earth;
He looked and startled the nations.
[a]And the everlasting mountains were scattered,
The perpetual hills bowed.
His ways *are* everlasting.
7 I saw the tents of Cushan in affliction;
The curtains of the land of Midian trembled.

8 O LORD, were *You* displeased with the rivers,
Was Your anger against the rivers,
Was Your wrath against the sea,
That You rode on Your horses,
Your chariots of salvation?
9 Your bow was made quite ready;
Oaths were sworn over *Your* arrows.[1] *Selah*

You divided the earth with rivers.
10 The mountains saw You *and* trembled;
The overflowing of the water passed by.
The deep uttered its voice,
And [a]lifted its hands on high.
11 The [a]sun and moon stood still in their habitation;
At the light of Your arrows they went,
At the shining of Your glittering spear.

12 You marched through the land in indignation;
You trampled the nations in anger.
13 You went forth for the salvation of Your people,
For salvation with Your Anointed.
You struck the head from the house of the wicked,
By laying bare from foundation to neck. *Selah*

14 You thrust through with his own arrows
The head of his villages.
They came out like a whirlwind to scatter me;
Their rejoicing was like feasting on the poor in secret.
15 [a]You walked through the sea with Your horses,
Through the heap of great waters.

16 When I heard, [a]my body trembled;
My lips quivered at *the* voice;
Rottenness entered my bones;
And I trembled in myself,
That I might rest in the day of trouble.
When he comes up to the people,
He will invade them with his troops.

A Hymn of Faith

17 Though the fig tree may not blossom,
Nor fruit be on the vines;

PEACE NOTE

We cannot follow Jesus without our faith being tested. God will either deliver us from the problem we are facing, or He will sustain us through it. Ask for His peace.

HABAKKUK 3:17

3:1 [1] Exact meaning unknown **3:6** [a] Nah. 1:5 **3:9** [1] Literally *rods* or *tribes* (compare verse 14) **3:10** [a] Ex. 14:22
3:11 [a] Josh. 10:12–14 **3:15** [a] Ps. 77:19 **3:16** [a] Ps. 119:120

Though the labor of the olive may
fail,
And the fields yield no food;
Though the flock may be cut off from
the fold,
And there be no herd in the stalls—
18 Yet I will [a]rejoice in the LORD,
I will joy in the God of my salvation.

19 The LORD God[1] is my strength;
He will make my feet like [a]deer's *feet*,
And He will make me [b]walk on my high
hills.

To the Chief Musician. With my stringed instruments.

PEACE NOTE

It is God's will for every follower of Jesus to have His peace (*shalom*). It is not God's will for us to live in conflict, confusion, or anxiety.

HABAKKUK 3:18

3:18 [a] Is. 41:16; 61:10 3:19 [a] 2 Sam. 22:34 [b] Deut. 32:13; 33:29 [1] Hebrew *YHWH Adonai*

THE BOOK OF

ZEPHANIAH

AUTHOR

In the beginning of this book, Zephaniah traces his lineage back four generations to the godly King Hezekiah. This would make him the only prophet of royal descent. His use of the phrase "this place" in reference to Jerusalem (Zeph. 1:4) indicates that he was probably an inhabitant of Judah's royal city.

TIME

c. 630 BC

KEY VERSE

Zephaniah 1:14–15

THEME

Contemporary with Jeremiah, Zephaniah wrote during the reign of Josiah, one of the good kings of Judah. The book follows a fairly familiar pattern for the prophets. Judgment is pronounced on Judah as well as several surrounding nations. After the judgment of the first two chapters, the third declares a restoration process that sounds strongly encouraging.

"The Lord will be awesome to them" (2:11) has to be one of the greatest passages in all Scripture. Zephaniah's powerful preaching preceded the peace and revival experienced under the good King Josiah in 621 BC. Himself a great-great-grandson of King Hezekiah, Zephaniah was of noble birth and lived up to his family heritage in condemning Judah's vast idolatry. This is one of five books in the Old Testament where the word "peace" is absent from the text, and this is a direct result of the context of the book. Ungodly Kings Manasseh and Amon had plunged Judah into apostasy for nearly half a century. No peace was in the land, and there would be no peace in the hearts of the people of God until they repented and turned to the Lord in truth. Zephaniah's influence led to Josiah's leading the people of God in revival (2 Chr. 34:3). One of the applications from this book is a reminder of the need for absolute truth in every culture and society, and truth, grace, and peace are found only in Scripture. We see from Zephaniah what happens when a society forgets God.

1 The word of the LORD which came to Zephaniah the son of Cushi, the son of Gedaliah, the son of Amariah, the son of Hezekiah, in the days of [a]Josiah the son of Amon, king of Judah.

The Great Day of the LORD

2 "I will utterly consume everything
From the face of the land,"
Says the LORD;
3 "I[a] will consume man and beast;
I will consume the birds of the heavens,
The fish of the sea,
And the stumbling blocks[1] along with the wicked.
I will cut off man from the face of the land,"
Says the LORD.

4 "I will stretch out My hand against Judah,
And against all the inhabitants of Jerusalem.
I will cut off every trace of Baal from this place,
The names of the [a]idolatrous priests[1] with the *pagan* priests—
5 Those [a]who worship the host of heaven on the housetops;
Those who worship and swear *oaths* by the LORD,
But who *also* swear [b]by Milcom;[1]
6 [a]Those who have turned back from *following* the LORD,
And [b]have not sought the LORD, nor inquired of Him."

7 [a]Be silent in the presence of the Lord GOD;
[b]For the day of the LORD *is* at hand,
For [c]the LORD has prepared a sacrifice;
He has invited[1] His guests.

8 "And it shall be,
In the day of the LORD's sacrifice,
That I will punish [a]the princes and the king's children,
And all such as are clothed with foreign apparel.
9 In the same day I will punish
All those who [a]leap over the threshold,[1]
Who fill their masters' houses with violence and deceit.

10 "And there shall be on that day," says the LORD,
"The sound of a mournful cry from [a]the Fish Gate,
A wailing from the Second Quarter,
And a loud crashing from the hills.
11 [a]Wail, you inhabitants of Maktesh![1]
For all the merchant people are cut down;
All those who handle money are cut off.

12 "And it shall come to pass at that time
That I will search Jerusalem with lamps,
And punish the men
Who are [a]settled in complacency,[1]
[b]Who say in their heart,
'The LORD will not do good,
Nor will He do evil.'
13 Therefore their goods shall become booty,
And their houses a desolation;
They shall build houses, but not inhabit *them;*
They shall plant vineyards, but [a]not drink their wine."

14 [a]The great day of the LORD *is* near;
It is near and hastens quickly.
The noise of the day of the LORD is bitter;
There the mighty men shall cry out.
15 [a]That day *is* a day of wrath,
A day of trouble and distress,
A day of devastation and desolation,
A day of darkness and gloominess,
A day of clouds and thick darkness,
16 A day of [a]trumpet and alarm
Against the fortified cities
And against the high towers.

17 "I will bring distress upon men,
And they shall [a]walk like blind men,
Because they have sinned against the LORD;
Their blood shall be poured out like dust,
And their flesh like refuse."

18 [a]Neither their silver nor their gold
Shall be able to deliver them
In the day of the LORD's wrath;
But the whole land shall be devoured
By the fire of His jealousy,
For He will make speedy riddance
Of all those who dwell in the land.

1:1 [a] 2 Kin. 22:1, 2 **1:3** [a] Hos. 4:3 [1] Figurative of idols **1:4** [a] Hos. 10:5 [1] Hebrew *chemarim* **1:5** [a] 2 Kin. 23:12 [b] Josh. 23:7 [1] Or *Malcam,* an Ammonite god, also called *Molech* (compare Leviticus 18:21) **1:6** [a] Is. 1:4 [b] Hos. 7:7 **1:7** [a] Zech. 2:13 [b] Is. 13:6 [c] Jer. 46:10 [1] Literally *set apart, consecrated* **1:8** [a] Jer. 39:6 **1:9** [a] 1 Sam. 5:5 [1] Compare 1 Samuel 5:5 **1:10** [a] 2 Chr. 33:14 **1:11** [a] James 5:1 [1] Literally *Mortar,* a market district of Jerusalem **1:12** [a] Jer. 48:11 [b] Ps. 94:7 [1] Literally *on their lees,* that is, settled like the dregs of wine **1:13** [a] Deut. 28:39 **1:14** [a] Joel 2:1, 11 **1:15** [a] Is. 22:5 **1:16** [a] Jer. 4:19 **1:17** [a] Deut. 28:29 **1:18** [a] Ezek. 7:19

A Call to Repentance

2 Gather[a] yourselves together, yes,
gather together,
O undesirable[1] nation,
2 Before the decree is issued,
Or the day passes like chaff,
Before the LORD's fierce anger comes
upon you,
Before the day of the LORD's anger
comes upon you!
3 [a]Seek the LORD, [b]all you meek of the
earth,
Who have upheld His justice.
Seek righteousness, seek humility.
[c]It may be that you will be hidden
In the day of the LORD's anger.

Judgment on Nations

4 For [a]Gaza shall be forsaken,
And Ashkelon desolate;
They shall drive out Ashdod [b]at
noonday,
And Ekron shall be uprooted.
5 Woe to the inhabitants of [a]the seacoast,
The nation of the Cherethites!
The word of the LORD *is* against you,
O [b]Canaan, land of the Philistines:
"I will destroy you;
So there shall be no inhabitant."

6 The seacoast shall be pastures,
With shelters[1] for shepherds [a]and folds
for flocks.
7 The coast shall be for [a]the remnant of
the house of Judah;
They shall feed *their* flocks there;
In the houses of Ashkelon they shall lie
down at evening.
For the LORD their God will [b]intervene
for them,
And [c]return their captives.

8 "I[a] have heard the reproach of Moab,
And [b]the insults of the people of
Ammon,
With which they have reproached My
people,
And [c]made arrogant threats against
their borders.
9 Therefore, as I live,"
Says the LORD of hosts, the God of
Israel,
"Surely [a]Moab shall be like Sodom,
And [b]the people of Ammon like
Gomorrah—
[c]Overrun with weeds and saltpits,
And a perpetual desolation.
The residue of My people shall plunder
them,
And the remnant of My people shall
possess them."

10 This they shall have [a]for their pride,
Because they have reproached and
made arrogant threats
Against the people of the LORD of
hosts.
11 The LORD *will be* awesome to them,
For He will reduce to nothing all the
gods of the earth;
[a]*People* shall worship Him,
Each one from his place,
Indeed all [b]the shores of the nations.

12 "You[a] Ethiopians also,
You shall be slain by [b]My sword."

13 And He will stretch out His hand
against the north,
[a]Destroy Assyria,
And make Nineveh a desolation,
As dry as the wilderness.
14 The herds shall lie down in her
midst,
[a]Every beast of the nation.
Both the [b]pelican and the bittern
Shall lodge on the capitals *of* her
pillars;
Their voice shall sing in the
windows;
Desolation *shall be* at the threshold;
For He will lay bare the [c]cedar work.
15 This is the rejoicing city
[a]That dwelt securely,
[b]That said in her heart,
"I *am it,* and *there is* none
besides me."
How has she become a desolation,
A place for beasts to lie down!
Everyone who passes by her
[c]Shall hiss and [d]shake his fist.

The Wickedness of Jerusalem

3 Woe to her who is rebellious and
polluted,
To the oppressing city!
2 She has not obeyed *His* voice,
She has not received correction;
She has not trusted in the LORD,
She has not drawn near to her God.

2:1 [a] Joel 1:14; 2:16 [1] Or *shameless* **2:3** [a] Amos 5:6 [b] Ps. 76:9 [c] Amos 5:14, 15 **2:4** [a] Zech. 9:5 [b] Jer. 6:4 **2:5** [a] Ezek. 25:15–17 [b] Josh. 13:3 **2:6** [a] Is. 17:2 [1] Literally *excavations,* either underground huts or cisterns **2:7** [a] [Mic. 5:7, 8] [b] Luke 1:68 [c] Jer. 29:14 **2:8** [a] Jer. 48:27 [b] Ezek. 25:3 [c] Jer. 49:1 **2:9** [a] Is. 15:1–9 [b] Amos 1:13 [c] Deut. 29:23 **2:10** [a] Is. 16:6 **2:11** [a] Mal. 1:11 [b] Gen. 10:5 **2:12** [a] Is. 18:1–7 [b] Ps. 17:13 **2:13** [a] Is. 10:5–27; 14:24–27 **2:14** [a] Is. 13:21 [b] Is. 14:23; 34:11 [c] Jer. 22:14 **2:15** [a] Is. 47:8 [b] Rev. 18:7 [c] Lam. 2:15 [d] Nah. 3:19

3 [a]Her princes in her midst *are* roaring
lions;
Her judges *are* [b]evening wolves
That leave not a bone till morning.
4 Her [a]prophets are insolent,
treacherous people;
Her priests have polluted the
sanctuary,
They have done [b]violence to the
law.
5 The LORD *is* righteous in her midst,
He will do no unrighteousness.
Every morning He brings His justice to
light;
He never fails,
But [a]the unjust knows no shame.

6 "I have cut off nations,
Their fortresses are devastated;
I have made their streets desolate,
With none passing by.
Their cities are destroyed;
There is no one, no inhabitant.
7 [a]I said, 'Surely you will fear Me,
You will receive instruction'—
So that her dwelling would not be cut
off,
Despite everything for which I
punished her.
But they rose early and [b]corrupted all
their deeds.

A Faithful Remnant

8 "Therefore [a]wait for Me," says the LORD,
"Until the day I rise up for plunder;[1]
My determination *is* to [b]gather the
nations
To My assembly of kingdoms,
To pour on them My indignation,
All My fierce anger;
All the earth [c]shall be devoured
With the fire of My jealousy.

9 "For then I will restore to the peoples [a]a
pure language,
That they all may call on the name of
the LORD,
To serve Him with one accord.
10 [a]From beyond the rivers of Ethiopia
My worshipers,
The daughter of My dispersed ones,
Shall bring My offering.
11 In that day you shall not be shamed for
any of your deeds
In which you transgress against Me;
For then I will take away from your midst
Those who [a]rejoice in your pride,
And you shall no longer be haughty
In My holy mountain.
12 I will leave in your midst
[a]A meek and humble people,
And they shall trust in the name of the
LORD.

3:3 [a] Ezek. 22:27 [b] Hab. 1:8 3:4 [a] Hos. 9:7 [b] Ezek. 22:26 3:5 [a] Jer. 3:3 3:7 [a] Jer. 8:6 [b] Gen. 6:12 3:8 [a] Hab. 2:3 [b] Joel 3:2 [c] Zeph. 1:18 [1] Septuagint and Syriac read *for witness;* Targum reads *for the day of My revelation for judgment;* Vulgate reads *for the day of My resurrection that is to come.* 3:9 [a] Is. 19:18; 57:19 3:10 [a] Ps. 68:31 3:11 [a] Is. 2:12; 5:15 3:12 [a] Is. 14:32

WORTH THE WAIT

"Therefore wait for Me," says the LORD.

ZEPHANIAH 3:8

Were you impatient when you were a child? "Just a minute," your parent said. But the child can't wait one minute. We become more patient with age and maturity, but we can still be uneasy, especially if patience means waiting years. Zephaniah warned the elite of their sinfulness: the prophets were faithless, the priests were profane, and the unjust showed no shame (see vv. 1–5).

I imagine that Zephaniah felt as if he was about to jump out of his skin. But God was looking for the right moment. "'Therefore wait for Me,' says the LORD, 'until the day I rise up for plunder'" (v. 8). God would gather up the nations and give them what for. But God's purpose is redemption, not destruction.

We should rejoice in God's redemptive purposes. We are privileged to have a part in them. Each time you experience anxiety, take a moment to discern any lies you may be believing and instead focus on a promise of God. This is how we wait on the Lord and find His peace in every situation and difficulty.

THE BOOK OF

HAGGAI

AUTHOR

The authorship of this book is virtually uncontested as Haggai's name is mentioned nine times. Haggai is known only from this book and two other references to him in Ezra 5:1 and 6:14. Haggai returned from Babylon with the remnant and may well have been one of the few people who could remember the former temple before its destruction. Haggai was therefore very instrumental in the rebuilding of the temple.

TIME

c. 520 BC

KEY VERSE

Haggai 1:7–8

THEME

Haggai is the first of the postexilic prophets, and he addressed the immediate problem of rebuilding the temple. The people had returned about twenty years earlier, but apathy and opposition kept the work from being completed. Haggai's concern is that neglect of the temple is a symptom of a bigger problem: God has dropped out of the Israelites' sight as a priority. The people are more concerned with building their materialistic lifestyles than they are with their relationship with God.

The preservation of David's messianic line and the restoration of the temple were at great risk in the postexilic time in which God raised up the prophet Haggai. If Satan could wipe out Judah's bloodline to the Savior, he could make God a liar and block the redemption coming with the Messiah. The Lord called Haggai to inspire God's people to stop being selfish; he raged that while they prospered, the Lord's temple remained in ruins (Hag. 1:4–6). Haggai and Zechariah returned to the land of Israel by Cyrus's decree in 538 BC with fifty thousand Jewish countryman, yet the people flinched and didn't finish building the temple. Haggai's words of peace looked forward to the temple's completion but even more to the peace Jesus would win for us on Calvary's cross: "'The glory of this latter temple shall be greater than the former . . . And in this place I will give peace,' says the Lord of hosts" (2:9).

SHOUT FOR JOY

Sing, O daughter of Zion! Shout, O Israel! Be glad and rejoice
with all your heart, O daughter of Jerusalem!

ZEPHANIAH 3:14

God's redemptive, restorative work is something to sing about. God will set the earth back in order. The wicked will be punished, the righteous will be vindicated, prophecies and promises will be fulfilled. Therefore, "sing, O daughter of Zion! Shout, O Israel! . . . The LORD your God in your midst . . . Will give you fame and praise among all the peoples of the earth" (3:14, 17, 20).

Zephaniah's call to rejoice and sing applies as much to us today as it did to the Israelites of old. Although the prophet's message spoke to a long-past period in Israel, the truth behind it remains relevant. Israel's experience of falling and then being restored gives us insight into God's faithfulness and His enduring love and mercy for His people.

I find it amazing how, so often in Scripture, we are told to rejoice and sing and even be loud about it. Whispering or talking in a quiet voice doesn't cut it. When God acts, we need to shout! The peace that God brings to His people is simply overwhelming. Have you ever shouted for gladness for your salvation? Start doing so today! Peace can sometimes be noisy!

13 [a]The remnant of Israel [b]shall do no
unrighteousness
[c]And speak no lies,
Nor shall a deceitful tongue be found
in their mouth;
For [d]they shall feed *their* flocks and lie
down,
And no one shall make *them* afraid."

Joy in God's Faithfulness

14 [a]Sing, O daughter of Zion!
Shout, O Israel!
Be glad and rejoice with all *your* heart,
O daughter of Jerusalem!
15 The LORD has taken away your
judgments,
He has cast out your enemy.
[a]The King of Israel, the LORD, [b]*is* in your
midst;
You shall see[1] disaster no more.

16 In that day [a]it shall be said to
Jerusalem:
"Do not fear;
Zion, [b]let not your hands be weak.
17 The LORD your God [a]in your midst,
The Mighty One, will save;
[b]He will rejoice over you with gladness,
He will quiet *you* with His love,
He will rejoice over you with singing."

18 "I will gather those who [a]sorrow over
the appointed assembly,
Who are among you,
To whom its reproach *is* a burden.
19 Behold, at that time
I will deal with all who afflict you;
I will save the [a]lame,
And gather those who were driven out;
I will appoint them for praise and
fame
In every land where they were put to
shame.
20 At that time [a]I will bring you back,
Even at the time I gather you;
For I will give you fame and praise
Among all the peoples of the earth,
When I return your captives before
your eyes,"
Says the LORD.

3:13 [a] [Mic. 4:7] [b] Is. 60:21 [c] Rev. 14:5 [d] Ezek. 34:13–15, 28 **3:14** [a] Is. 12:6 **3:15** [a] [John 1:49] [b] Ezek. 48:35 [1] Some Hebrew manuscripts, Septuagint, and Bomberg read *see;* Masoretic Text and Vulgate read *fear.* **3:16** [a] Is. 35:3, 4 [b] Heb. 12:12 **3:17** [a] Zeph. 3:5, 15 [b] Is. 62:5; 65:19 **3:18** [a] Lam. 2:6 **3:19** [a] [Mic. 4:6, 7] **3:20** [a] Is. 11:12

The Command to Build God's House

1 In [a]the second year of King Darius, in the
sixth month, on the first day of the month,
the word of the LORD came by [b]Haggai the
prophet to [c]Zerubbabel the son of Shealtiel,
governor of Judah, and to [d]Joshua the son of
[e]Jehozadak, the high priest, saying, 2 "Thus
speaks the LORD of hosts, saying: 'This people
says, "The time has not come, the time that
the LORD's house should be built." ' "
3 Then the word of the LORD [a]came by Haggai the prophet, saying, 4 "*Is it* [a]time for you
yourselves to dwell in your paneled houses,
and this temple[1] *to lie* in ruins?" 5 Now therefore, thus says the LORD of hosts: [a]"Consider
your ways!

6 "You have [a]sown much, and bring in little;
You eat, but do not have enough;
You drink, but you are not filled with
drink;
You clothe yourselves, but no one is
warm;
And [b]he who earns wages,
Earns wages *to put* into a bag with holes."

7 Thus says the LORD of hosts: "Consider
your ways! 8 Go up to the [a]mountains and
bring wood and build the temple, that I may
take pleasure in it and be glorified," says the
LORD. 9 [a]"*You* looked for much, but indeed
it came to little; and when you brought it
home, [b]I blew it away. Why?" says the LORD
of hosts. "Because of My house that *is in* ruins, while every one of you runs to his own
house. 10 Therefore [a]the heavens above you
withhold the dew, and the earth withholds
its fruit. 11 For I [a]called for a drought on the
land and the mountains, on the grain and
the new wine and the oil, on whatever the
ground brings forth, on men and livestock,
and on [b]all the labor of *your* hands."

The People's Obedience

12 [a]Then Zerubbabel the son of Shealtiel,
and Joshua the son of Jehozadak, the high
priest, with all the remnant of the people,
obeyed the voice of the LORD their God, and
the words of Haggai the prophet, as the LORD
their God had sent him; and the people feared
the presence of the LORD. 13 Then Haggai, the
LORD's messenger, spoke the LORD's message
to the people, saying, [a]"I *am* with you, says the
LORD." 14 So [a]the LORD stirred up the spirit of
Zerubbabel the son of Shealtiel, [b]governor of
Judah, and the spirit of Joshua the son of Jehozadak, the high priest, and the spirit of all
the remnant of the people; [c]and they came
and worked on the house of the LORD of hosts,
their God, 15 on the twenty-fourth day of the
sixth month, in the second year of King Darius.

The Coming Glory of God's House

2 In the seventh *month,* on the twenty-first
of the month, the word of the LORD came
by Haggai the prophet, saying: 2 "Speak now
to Zerubbabel the son of Shealtiel, governor
of Judah, and to Joshua the son of Jehozadak, the high priest, and to the remnant of
the people, saying: 3 [a]'Who is left among you
who saw this temple[1] in its former glory? And
how do you see it now? In comparison with
it, [b]*is this* not in your eyes as nothing? 4 Yet
now [a]be strong, Zerubbabel,' says the LORD;
'and be strong, Joshua, son of Jehozadak, the
high priest; and be strong, all you people of
the land,' says the LORD, 'and work; for I *am*
with you,' says the LORD of hosts. 5 [a]'*According
to* the word that I covenanted with you when
you came out of Egypt, so [b]My Spirit remains
among you; do not fear!'
6 "For thus says the LORD of hosts: [a]'Once
more (it *is* a little while) [b]I will shake heaven
and earth, the sea and dry land; 7 and I will
shake all nations, and they shall come to
[a]the Desire of All Nations,[1] and I will fill this
temple with [b]glory,' says the LORD of hosts.
8 'The silver *is* Mine, and the gold *is* Mine,' says
the LORD of hosts. 9 [a]'The glory of this latter
temple shall be greater than the former,' says
the LORD of hosts. 'And in this place I will give
[b]peace,' says the LORD of hosts."

The People Are Defiled

10 On the twenty-fourth *day* of the ninth
month, in the second year of Darius, the word
of the LORD came by Haggai the prophet, saying, 11 "Thus says the LORD of hosts: 'Now, [a]ask
the priests *concerning the* law, saying, 12 "If one
carries holy meat in the fold of his garment,
and with the edge he touches bread or stew,
wine or oil, or any food, will it become holy?" ' "
Then the priests answered and said, "No."
13 And Haggai said, "If *one who is* [a]unclean
because of a dead body touches any of these,
will it be unclean?"
So the priests answered and said, "It shall
be unclean."

1:1 [a] Ezra 4:24 [b] Ezra 5:1; 6:14 [c] Ezra 2:2 [d] Ezra 5:2, 3 [e] 1 Chr. 6:15 **1:3** [a] Ezra 5:1 **1:4** [a] 2 Sam. 7:2 [1] Literally *house,* and so in verse 8 **1:5** [a] Lam. 3:40 **1:6** [a] Deut. 28:38–40 [b] Zech. 8:10 **1:8** [a] Ezra 3:7 **1:9** [a] Hag. 2:16 [b] Hag. 2:17 **1:10** [a] Deut. 28:23 **1:11** [a] 1 Kin. 17:1 [b] Hag. 2:17 **1:12** [a] Ezra 5:2 **1:13** [a] [Matt. 28:20] **1:14** [a] Ezra 1:1 [b] Hag. 2:21 [c] Ezra 5:2, 8 **2:3** [a] Ezra 3:12, 13 [b] Zech. 4:10 [1] Literally *house,* and so in verses 7 and 9 **2:4** [a] Zech. 8:9 **2:5** [a] Ex. 29:45, 46 [b] [Neh. 9:20] **2:6** [a] Heb. 12:26 [b] [Joel 3:16] **2:7** [a] Gen. 49:10 [b] Is. 60:7 [1] Or *the desire of all nations* **2:9** [a] [John 1:14] [b] Ps. 85:8, 9 **2:11** [a] Mal. 2:7 **2:13** [a] Num. 19:11, 22

THE GIVER OF PEACE

"The glory of this latter temple shall be greater than the former . . .
And in this place I will give peace," says the LORD of hosts.

HAGGAI 2:9

The temple that King Solomon built and dedicated was something to behold. The description of it in 1 Kings is astounding—in terms of its design and size as well as the materials that went into it. Solomon's Temple was so well known that emissaries from distant lands went to see it and meet the man who built it. But the Babylonians destroyed this great temple in 586 BC. The glory of Jerusalem existed no more.

When the Persian king allowed the Jewish people to return to their homeland in 538 BC, they eventually rebuilt the temple (completed in 515 BC) thanks in part to the prophet Haggai. The second temple was nothing like the first one. Yet the prophet boldly declared, "'The glory of this latter temple shall be greater than the former,' says the LORD of hosts. 'And in this place I will give peace'" (Hag. 2:9).

Haggai knew something no one else did. The second temple was nowhere near as grand as the first, yet the Lord promised that a later one—not the second one the Israelites constructed—would be more amazing than Solomon's. In that temple God will give us peace. This promise was fulfilled in Jesus, God's Son, the Prince of Peace!

14 Then Haggai answered and said, [a]"'So is
this people, and so is this nation before Me,'
says the LORD, 'and so is every work of their
hands; and what they offer there is unclean.

Promised Blessing

15 'And now, carefully [a]consider from this
day forward: from before stone was laid upon
stone in the temple of the LORD— 16 since
those *days,* [a]when *one* came to a heap of twenty ephahs, there were *but* ten; when *one* came
to the wine vat to draw out fifty baths from
the press, there were *but* twenty. 17 [a]I struck
you with blight and mildew and hail [b]in all
the labors of your hands; [c]yet you did not *turn*
to Me,' says the LORD. 18 'Consider now from
this day forward, from the twenty-fourth day
of the ninth month, from [a]the day that the
foundation of the LORD's temple was laid—
consider it: 19 [a]Is the seed still in the barn? As
yet the vine, the fig tree, the pomegranate,
and the olive tree have not yielded *fruit. But*
from this day I will [b]bless *you.*'"

Zerubbabel Chosen as a Signet

20 And again the word of the LORD came
to Haggai on the twenty-fourth day of the
month, saying, 21 "Speak to Zerubbabel, [a]gov-
ernor of Judah, saying:

[b]'I will shake heaven and earth.
22 [a]I will overthrow the throne of
kingdoms;
I will destroy the strength of the
Gentile kingdoms.
[b]I will overthrow the chariots
And those who ride in them;
The horses and their riders shall come
down,
Every one by the sword of his
brother.

23 'In that day,' says the LORD of hosts, 'I
will take you, Zerubbabel My servant, the son
of Shealtiel,' says the LORD, [a]'and will make
you like a signet *ring;* for [b]I have chosen you,'
says the LORD of hosts."

2:14 [a] [Titus 1:15] **2:15** [a] Hag. 1:5, 7; 2:18 **2:16** [a] Zech. 8:10 **2:17** [a] Deut. 28:22 [b] Hag. 1:11 [c] Amos 4:6–11
2:18 [a] Zech. 8:9 **2:19** [a] Zech. 8:12 [b] [Mal. 3:10] **2:21** [a] Zech. 4:6–10 [b] Hag. 2:6, 7 **2:22** [a] [Dan. 2:44] [b] Mic. 5:10
2:23 [a] Song 8:6 [b] Is. 42:1; 43:10

THE BOOK OF

ZECHARIAH

AUTHOR

The universal testimony of the Jewish and Christian tradition affirms Zechariah as the author of this entire book. Like Jeremiah and Ezekiel, he was of priestly lineage and was a young man when he was called to prophesy. According to Jewish tradition, Zechariah was a member of the Great Synagogue that collected and preserved the canon of revealed Scripture. He was born in Babylon and brought to the Holy Land by his grandfather when the Jewish exiles returned under Zerubbabel and Joshua the high priest.

TIME

520–470 BC

KEY VERSE

Zechariah 9:9

THEME

Zechariah's writings were designed to encourage the Israelites and inspire energy, identity, and vision during the rebuilding of the temple. Like the prophecies of Isaiah, Daniel, and Ezekiel, Zechariah's messages are characterized by visions of God and the future. In this context, many would describe the book as apocalyptic with similarities to Revelation. Probably more than any of the other books, Zechariah makes concrete predictions about Christ that are fulfilled in the New Testament. He also makes some startling predictions about Israel in the end times that have already seen fulfillment.

"Therefore love truth and peace" is a wonderful summary of Zechariah (8:19). None of the minor prophets used the term "peace" (*shalom*) more frequently than Zechariah, which is fitting because he led the Levites, who led God's people in worshiping the Lord. The book includes seven prophecies of Christ, including a key promise of God's peace through Jesus' atonement and resurrection: "And I will pour on the house of David and on the inhabitants of Jerusalem the Spirit of grace and supplication; then they will look on Me whom they pierced" (12:10). There are also numerous references to the ultimate peace we will experience with Jesus' Second Coming: "He shall speak peace to the nations" (9:10).

A Call to Repentance

1 In the eighth month [a]of the second year of Darius, the word of the LORD came [b]to Zechariah the son of Berechiah, the son of [c]Iddo the prophet, saying, 2“The LORD has been very angry with your fathers. 3Therefore say to them, ‘Thus says the LORD of hosts: “Return [a]to Me,” says the LORD of hosts, “and I will return to you,” says the LORD of hosts. 4“Do not be like your fathers, [a]to whom the former prophets preached, saying, ‘Thus says the LORD of hosts: [b]“Turn now from your evil ways and your evil deeds.” ’ But they did not hear nor heed Me,” says the LORD.

5 “Your fathers, where *are* they?
And the prophets, do they live forever?
6 Yet surely [a]My words and My statutes,
Which I commanded My servants the prophets,
Did they not overtake your fathers?

“So they returned and said:

[b]‘Just as the LORD of hosts determined to do to us,
According to our ways and according to our deeds,
So He has dealt with us.’ ” ’ ”

Vision of the Horses

7On the twenty-fourth day of the eleventh month, which is the month Shebat, in the second year of Darius, the word of the LORD came to Zechariah the son of Berechiah, the son of Iddo the prophet: 8I saw by night, and behold, [a]a man riding on a red horse, and it stood among the myrtle trees in the hollow; and behind him *were* [b]horses: red, sorrel, and white. 9Then I said, [a]“My lord, what *are* these?” So the angel who talked with me said to me, “I will show you what they *are*.”

10And the man who stood among the myrtle trees answered and said, [a]“These *are the ones* whom the LORD has sent to walk to and fro throughout the earth.”

11[a]So they answered the Angel of the LORD, who stood among the myrtle trees, and said, “We have walked to and fro throughout the earth, and behold, all the earth is resting quietly.”

The LORD Will Comfort Zion

12Then the Angel of the LORD answered and said, “O LORD of hosts, [a]how long will You not have mercy on Jerusalem and on the cities of Judah, against which You were angry [b]these seventy years?”

13And the LORD answered the angel who talked to me, *with* [a]good *and* comforting words. 14So the angel who spoke with me said to me, “Proclaim, saying, ‘Thus says the LORD of hosts:

“I am [a]zealous for Jerusalem
And for Zion with great zeal.
15 I am exceedingly angry with the nations at ease;
For [a]I was a little angry,
And they helped—*but* with evil *intent*.”

16‘Therefore thus says the LORD:

[a]“I am returning to Jerusalem with mercy;
My [b]house [c]shall be built in it,” says the LORD of hosts,
“And [d]a *surveyor’s* line shall be stretched out over Jerusalem.” ’

17“Again proclaim, saying, ‘Thus says the LORD of hosts:

“My cities shall again spread out through prosperity;
[a]The LORD will again comfort Zion,
And [b]will again choose Jerusalem.” ’ ”

Vision of the Horns

18Then I raised my eyes and looked, and there *were* four [a]horns. 19And I said to the angel who talked with me, “What *are* these?”

So he answered me, [a]“These *are* the horns that have scattered Judah, Israel, and Jerusalem.”

20Then the LORD showed me four craftsmen. 21And I said, “What are these coming to do?”

So he said, “These *are* the [a]horns that scattered Judah, so that no one could lift up his head; but the craftsmen[1] are coming to terrify them, to cast out the horns of the nations that [b]lifted up *their* horn against the land of Judah to scatter it.”

Vision of the Measuring Line

2 Then I raised my eyes and looked, and behold, [a]a man with a measuring line in his hand. 2So I said, “Where are you going?”

And he said to me, [a]“To measure Jerusalem, to see what *is* its width and what *is* its length.”

1:1 [a] Zech. 7:1 [b] Matt. 23:35 [c] Neh. 12:4, 16 1:3 [a] [Mal. 3:7–10] 1:4 [a] 2 Chr. 36:15, 16 [b] Is. 31:6 1:6 [a] [Is. 55:11] [b] Lam. 1:18; 2:17 1:8 [a] [Rev. 6:4] [b] [Zech. 6:2–7] 1:9 [a] Zech. 4:4, 5, 13; 6:4 1:10 [a] [Heb. 1:14] 1:11 [a] [Ps. 103:20, 21] 1:12 [a] Ps. 74:10 [b] Jer. 25:11, 12; 29:10 1:13 [a] Jer. 29:10 1:14 [a] Zech. 8:2 1:15 [a] Is. 47:6 1:16 [a] [Zech. 2:10; 8:3] [b] Ezra 6:14, 15 [c] Is. 44:28 [d] Zech. 2:1–3 1:17 [a] [Is. 40:1, 2; 51:3] [b] Zech. 2:12 1:18 [a] [Lam. 2:17] 1:19 [a] Ezra 4:1, 4, 7 1:21 [a] [Ps. 75:10] [b] Ps. 75:4, 5 [1] Literally *these* 2:1 [a] Jer. 31:39 2:2 [a] Rev. 11:1

3And there *was* the angel who talked with
me, going out; and another angel was coming
out to meet him, 4who said to him, "Run, speak
to this young man, saying: [a]'Jerusalem shall be
inhabited *as* towns without walls, because of
the multitude of men and livestock in it. 5For I,'
says the LORD, 'will be [a]a wall of fire all around
her, [b]and I will be the glory in her midst.'"

Future Joy of Zion and Many Nations

6"Up, up! Flee [a]from the land of the north,"
says the LORD; "for I have [b]spread you abroad
like the four winds of heaven," says the LORD.
7"Up, Zion! [a]Escape, you who dwell with the
daughter of Babylon."

8For thus says the LORD of hosts: "He sent
Me after glory, to the nations which plunder
you; for he who [a]touches you touches the
apple of His eye. 9For surely I will [a]shake My
hand against them, and they shall become
spoil for their servants. Then [b]you will know
that the LORD of hosts has sent Me.

10[a]"Sing and rejoice, O daughter of Zion!
For behold, I am coming and I [b]will dwell in
your midst," says the LORD. 11[a]"Many nations
shall be joined to the LORD [b]in that day, and
they shall become [c]My people. And I will
dwell in your midst. Then [d]you will know that
the LORD of hosts has sent Me to you. 12And
the LORD will [a]take possession of Judah as
His inheritance in the Holy Land, and will
again choose Jerusalem. 13[a]Be silent, all flesh,
before the LORD, for He is aroused [b]from His
holy habitation!"

Vision of the High Priest

3 Then he showed me [a]Joshua the high
priest standing before the Angel of the
LORD, and [b]Satan standing at his right hand
to oppose him. 2And the LORD said to Satan,
[a]"The LORD rebuke you, Satan! The LORD who
[b]has chosen Jerusalem rebuke you! [c]*Is* this
not a brand plucked from the fire?"

3Now Joshua was clothed with [a]filthy garments, and was standing before the Angel.

4Then He answered and spoke to those
who stood before Him, saying, "Take away
the filthy garments from him." And to him He
said, "See, I have removed your iniquity from
you, [a]and I will clothe you with rich robes."

5And I said, "Let them put a clean [a]turban
on his head."

So they put a clean turban on his head, and
they put the clothes on him. And the Angel
of the LORD stood by.

The Coming Branch

6Then the Angel of the LORD admonished
Joshua, saying, 7"Thus says the LORD of hosts:

'If you will walk in My ways,
And if you will [a]keep My command,
Then you shall also [b]judge My house,
And likewise have charge of My courts;

2:4 [a] Jer. 31:27 **2:5** [a] [Is. 26:1] [b] [Is. 60:19] **2:6** [a] Is. 48:20 [b] Deut. 28:64 **2:7** [a] Is. 48:20 **2:8** [a] Deut. 32:10 **2:9** [a] Is. 19:16 [b] Zech. 4:9 **2:10** [a] Is. 12:6 [b] [Lev. 26:12] **2:11** [a] [Is. 2:2, 3] [b] Zech. 3:10 [c] Ex. 12:49 [d] Ezek. 33:33 **2:12** [a] [Deut. 32:9] **2:13** [a] Hab. 2:20 [b] Ps. 68:5 **3:1** [a] Hag. 1:1 [b] Ps. 109:6 **3:2** [a] [Jude 9] [b] [Rom. 8:33] [c] Amos 4:11 **3:3** [a] Is. 64:6 **3:4** [a] Is. 61:10 **3:5** [a] Ex. 29:6 **3:7** [a] Lev. 8:35 [b] Deut. 17:9, 12

FIND PEACE IN SERVING

"I am bringing forth My Servant the BRANCH."

ZECHARIAH 3:8

The prophet Zechariah announced that God would provide to Israel someone very special: "I am bringing forth My Servant the BRANCH." The word "branch" comes from the Hebrew word *semah* that first appears in Isaiah 4:2: "In that day the Branch of the LORD shall be beautiful and glorious." Jeremiah made clear that this Person would be a descendant of King David: "I will raise to David a Branch of righteousness" (Jer. 23:5; see 33:15).

In this postexilic setting the prophet Zechariah, Haggai's contemporary, announced hope to the Jewish people as they struggled to rebuild their nation. The task was daunting, the future uncertain. But do not be dismayed, the prophet said, God will bring His Servant the Branch! Our hope and peace are founded on this game-changing promise. The Branch is not just another descendant of David; He is the Savior, the Son of God!

Since our Savior is called the "Servant" (Zech. 3:8), we should endeavor to follow His example by serving others. This is a helpful step to walking in the peace of God!

I will give you places to walk
Among these who [c]stand here.

8 'Hear, O Joshua, the high priest,
You and your companions who sit
before you,
For they are [a]a wondrous sign;
For behold, I am bringing forth [b]My
Servant the [c]BRANCH.
9 For behold, the stone
That I have laid before Joshua:
[a]Upon the stone *are* [b]seven eyes.
Behold, I will engrave its inscription,'
Says the LORD of hosts,
'And [c]I will remove the iniquity of that
land in one day.
10 [a]In that day,' says the LORD of hosts,
'Everyone will invite his neighbor
[b]Under his vine and under his fig tree.' "

Vision of the Lampstand and Olive Trees

4 Now [a]the angel who talked with me came
back and wakened me, [b]as a man who is
wakened out of his sleep. 2And he said to me,
"What do you see?"
So I said, "I am looking, and there *is* [a]a
lampstand of solid gold with a bowl on top of
it, [b]and on the *stand* seven lamps with seven
pipes to the seven lamps. 3[a]Two olive trees
are by it, one at the right of the bowl and the
other at its left." 4So I answered and spoke to
the angel who talked with me, saying, "What
are these, my lord?"
5Then the angel who talked with me answered and said to me, "Do you not know
what these are?"
And I said, "No, my lord."
6So he answered and said to me:

"This *is* the word of the LORD to
[a]Zerubbabel:
[b]'Not by might nor by power, but by My
Spirit,'
Says the LORD of hosts.
7 'Who *are* you, [a]O great mountain?
Before Zerubbabel *you shall become* a
plain!
And he shall bring forth [b]the capstone
[c]With shouts of "Grace, grace to it!" ' "

8Moreover the word of the LORD came to
me, saying:

9 "The hands of Zerubbabel
[a]Have laid the foundation of this temple;[1]
His hands [b]shall also finish *it*.

3:7 [c] Zech. 3:4 3:8 [a] Ps. 71:7 [b] Is. 42:1 [c] Is. 11:1; 53:2; Jer. 23:5 3:9 [a] [Zech. 4:10] [b] Ps. 118:22 [c] Jer. 31:34; 50:20 3:10 [a] Zech. 2:11 [b] Is. 36:16 4:1 [a] Zech. 1:9; 2:3 [b] Dan. 8:18 4:2 [a] Rev. 1:12 [b] [Rev. 4:5] 4:3 [a] Rev. 11:3, 4 4:6 [a] Hag. 1:1 [b] Hos. 1:7 4:7 [a] Jer. 51:25 [b] Ps. 118:22 [c] Ezra 3:10, 11, 13 4:9 [a] Ezra 3:8–10; 5:16 [b] Ezra 6:14, 15 [1] Literally *house*

IMPOSSIBLE TO FAIL

"Not by might nor by power, but by My Spirit," says the LORD of hosts. "Who are you, O great mountain? Before Zerubbabel you shall become a plain!"

ZECHARIAH 4:6-7

God's fickle people, the Israelites, found themselves in a sore spot: exile in Persia, among pagans, far from their glorious temple and center of worship. When finally the king allowed them to return home, under Zerubbabel's leadership, so they could rebuild what had been destroyed in Jerusalem, it seemed like a dream come true. It was . . . except there were few participants, limited resources, and opposing forces. The work started but dragged, and the Israelites were tempted to quit. Never One to abandon His people, God sent a prophet, Zechariah, to stir their hearts. His message: the rebuilding would be accomplished and "not by might nor by power, but by My Spirit."

What a relief this message must have been to the weary, discouraged people! Their power wasn't going to complete the work, God's was! Human willpower was as weak as could be, but God's strength was endless. Failure was, in fact, impossible. All of Zerubbabel's problems and challenges were likened to "a great mountain," yet God promised him a *plain in place of the mountain.*

This same power is yours for the asking. Don't think your mountain is too high for the Lord to bulldoze! Rely on the supernatural Spirit of God for all you need—which includes your peace.

Then [c]you will know
That the [d]LORD of hosts has sent Me to you.
10 For who has despised the day of [a]small things?
For these seven rejoice to see
The plumb line in the hand of Zerubbabel.
[b]They are the eyes of the LORD,
Which scan to and fro throughout the whole earth."

11 Then I answered and said to him, "What *are* these [a]two olive trees—at the right of the lampstand and at its left?" 12 And I further answered and said to him, "What *are these* two olive branches that *drip* into the receptacles[1] of the two gold pipes from which the golden *oil* drains?"

13 Then he answered me and said, "Do you not know what these *are?*"

And I said, "No, my lord."

14 So he said, [a]"These *are* the two anointed ones, [b]who stand beside the Lord of the whole earth."

Vision of the Flying Scroll

5 Then I turned and raised my eyes, and saw there a flying [a]scroll.

2 And he said to me, "What do you see?"

So I answered, "I see a flying scroll. Its length *is* twenty cubits and its width ten cubits."

3 Then he said to me, "This *is* the [a]curse that goes out over the face of the whole earth: 'Every thief shall be expelled,' according *to* this side of *the scroll;* and, 'Every perjurer shall be expelled,' according *to* that side of it."

4 "I will send out *the curse,*" says the LORD of hosts;
"It shall enter the house of the [a]thief
And the house of [b]the one who swears falsely by My name.
It shall remain in the midst of his house
And consume [c]it, with its timber and stones."

Vision of the Woman in a Basket

5 Then the angel who talked with me came out and said to me, "Lift your eyes now, and see what this *is* that goes forth."

6 So I asked, "What *is* it?" And he said, "It *is* a basket[1] that is going forth."

He also said, "This *is* their resemblance throughout the earth: 7 Here *is* a lead disc lifted up, and this *is* a woman sitting inside the basket"; 8 then he said, "This *is* Wickedness!" And he thrust her down into the basket, and threw the lead cover[1] over its mouth. 9 Then I raised my eyes and looked, and there *were* two women, coming with the wind in their wings; for they had wings like the wings of a [a]stork, and they lifted up the basket between earth and heaven.

4:9 [c] Zech. 2:9, 11; 6:15 [d] [Is. 43:16] **4:10** [a] Hag. 2:3 [b] 2 Chr. 16:9 **4:11** [a] Zech. 4:3 **4:12** [1] Literally *into the hands of* **4:14** [a] Rev. 11:4 [b] Zech. 3:1–7 **5:1** [a] Ezek. 2:9 **5:3** [a] Mal. 4:6 **5:4** [a] Ex. 20:15 [b] Lev. 19:12 [c] Lev. 14:34, 35 **5:6** [1] Hebrew *ephah,* a measuring container, and so elsewhere **5:8** [1] Literally *stone* **5:9** [a] Lev. 11:13, 19

LEADERS FOR PEACE

"These are the two anointed ones, who stand beside the Lord of the whole earth."

ZECHARIAH 4:14

God again spoke about the future when He explained to Zechariah the meaning of the two olive trees that the prophet saw in a vision: "These are the two anointed ones," two men who had been anointed for service. Interpreters debate the meaning of this expression, for it is not the usual way Scripture speaks of the anointed Messiah. In his vision Zechariah saw two figures—one an anointed king and one an anointed high priest.

The image symbolized Israel's restoration when the nation at its zenith prospered under the rule of King Solomon and Zadok, the high priest. Zechariah's vision was then fulfilled in Jesus who, having ascended to heaven, stands at God's right and intercedes for His people. Jesus serves both as King and as High Priest (as is clearly taught in the Book of Hebrews).

The immediate interpretation is that the verse refers to Zerubbabel and Jeshua, who led captives from Babylon back to their homeland (Ezra 2:2)—servants God raised up to lead God's people. Pray for the Lord to raise up other "anointed ones" (Zech. 4:14) to be leaders.

10 So I said to the [a]angel who talked with
me, "Where are they carrying the basket?"
11 And he said to me, "To [a]build a house for
it in [b]the land of Shinar;[1] when it is ready, *the
basket* will be set there on its base."

Vision of the Four Chariots

6 Then I turned and raised my eyes and
looked, and behold, four chariots *were*
coming from between two mountains, and
the mountains *were* mountains of bronze.
2 With the first chariot *were* [a]red horses, with
the second chariot [b]black horses, 3 with the
third chariot white horses, and with the
fourth chariot dappled horses—strong
steeds. 4 Then I answered [a]and said to the
angel who talked with me, "What *are* these,
my lord?"
5 And the angel answered and said to me,
[a]"These *are* four spirits of heaven, who go
out from *their* [b]station before the Lord of
all the earth. 6 The one with the black horses
is going to [a]the north country, the white
are going after them, and the dappled are
going toward the south country." 7 Then the
strong *steeds* went out, eager to go, that
they might [a]walk to and fro throughout
the earth. And He said, "Go, walk to and
fro throughout the earth." So they walked
to and fro throughout the earth. 8 And He
called to me, and spoke to me, saying, "See,
those who go toward the north country
have given rest to My [a]Spirit in the north
country."

The Command to Crown Joshua

9 Then the word of the LORD came to me,
saying: 10 "Receive *the gift* from the captives—
from Heldai, Tobijah, and Jedaiah, who have
come from Babylon—and go the same day
and enter the house of Josiah the son of
Zephaniah. 11 Take the silver and gold, make
[a]an elaborate crown, and set *it* on the head
of [b]Joshua the son of Jehozadak, the high
priest. 12 Then speak to him, saying, 'Thus
says the LORD of hosts, saying:

"Behold, [a]the Man whose name *is* the
[b]BRANCH!
From His place He shall branch out,
[c]And He shall build the temple of the
LORD;
13 Yes, He shall build the temple of the
LORD.
He [a]shall bear the glory,
And shall sit and rule on His throne;
So [b]He shall be a priest on His throne,
And the counsel of peace shall be
between them both." '

14 "Now the elaborate crown shall be [a]for
a memorial in the temple of the LORD for
Helem,[1] Tobijah, Jedaiah, and Hen the son
of Zephaniah. 15 Even [a]those from afar shall
come and build the temple of the LORD. Then
you shall know that the LORD of hosts has
sent Me to you. And *this* shall come to pass
if you diligently obey the voice of the LORD
your God."

5:10 [a] Zech. 5:5 **5:11** [a] Jer. 29:5, 28 [b] Gen. 10:10 [1] That is, Babylon **6:2** [a] Zech. 1:8 [b] Rev. 6:5 **6:4** [a] Zech. 5:10 **6:5** [a] [Heb. 1:7, 14] [b] Dan. 7:10 **6:6** [a] Jer. 1:14 **6:7** [a] Zech. 1:10 **6:8** [a] Eccl. 10:4 **6:11** [a] Ex. 29:6 [b] Hag. 1:1 **6:12** [a] John 1:45 [b] Zech. 3:8 [c] [Matt. 16:18; Eph. 2:20; Heb. 3:3] **6:13** [a] Is. 22:24 [b] Ps. 110:4; [Heb. 3:1] **6:14** [a] Ex. 12:14 [1] Following Masoretic Text, Targum, and Vulgate; Syriac reads *for Heldai* (compare verse 10); Septuagint reads *for the patient ones.* **6:15** [a] Is. 57:19

THE BRANCH OF PEACE

"Behold, the Man whose name is the BRANCH! . . . He shall build the temple."

ZECHARIAH 6:12

Zechariah prophesied the coming of someone called the "BRANCH." We've seen that Jewish and Christian interpreters believe Zechariah was talking about the Messiah. Christians, of course, believe that Jesus was the Messiah. Jesus Himself said—possibly alluding to this very passage—that He would raise up a temple not built by human hands (see John 2:19, 21). It wasn't that Jesus pointed to the temple but that the temple pointed to Jesus. And the peace of God finds us through Jesus, the Branch.

Our hope and our peace are based on God's faithfulness and the assurance that He will fulfill all that He has promised. Through the agency of His Son, the earth will be renewed and our lives transformed. The Branch is the peace of God manifested in a Person. Knowing that our destiny is in the hands of God gives me a great sense of peace.

Obedience Better than Fasting

7 Now in the fourth year of King Darius it came to pass *that* the word of the LORD came to Zechariah, on the fourth *day* of the ninth month, Chislev, 2when *the people*[1] sent Sherezer,[2] with Regem-Melech and his men, *to* the house of God,[3] to pray before the LORD, 3*and* to [a]ask the priests who *were* in the house of the LORD of hosts, and the prophets, saying, "Should I weep in [b]the fifth month and fast as I have done for so many years?"

4Then the word of the LORD of hosts came to me, saying, 5"Say to all the people of the land, and to the priests: 'When you [a]fasted and mourned in the fifth [b]and seventh *months* [c]during those seventy years, did you really fast [d]for Me—for Me? 6[a]When you eat and when you drink, do you not eat and drink *for yourselves*? 7*Should you* not *have obeyed* the words which the LORD proclaimed through the [a]former prophets when Jerusalem and the cities around it were inhabited and prosperous, and [b]the South[1] and the Lowland were inhabited?' "

Disobedience Resulted in Captivity

8Then the word of the LORD came to Zechariah, saying, 9"Thus says the LORD of hosts:

[a]'Execute true justice,
Show mercy and compassion
Everyone to his brother.
10 [a]Do not oppress the widow or the fatherless,
The alien or the poor.
[b]Let none of you plan evil in his heart
Against his brother.'

11"But they refused to heed, [a]shrugged their shoulders, and [b]stopped their ears so that they could not hear. 12Yes, they made their [a]hearts like flint, [b]refusing to hear the law and the words which the LORD of hosts had sent by His Spirit through the former prophets. [c]Thus great wrath came from the LORD of hosts. 13Therefore it happened, *that* just as He proclaimed and they would not hear, so [a]they called out and I would not listen," says the LORD of hosts. 14"But [a]I scattered them with a whirlwind among all the nations which they had not known. Thus the land became desolate after them, so that no one passed through or returned; for they made the pleasant land desolate."

Jerusalem, Holy City of the Future

8 Again the word of the LORD of hosts came, saying, 2"Thus says the LORD of hosts:

[a]'I am zealous for Zion with great zeal;
With great fervor I am zealous for her.'

7:2 [1] Literally *they* (compare verse 5) [2] Or *Sar-Ezer* [3] Hebrew *Bethel* **7:3** [a] Mal. 2:7 [b] Zech. 8:19 **7:5** [a] [Is. 58:1–9] [b] Jer. 41:1 [c] Zech. 1:12 [d] [Rom. 14:6] **7:6** [a] 1 Chr. 29:22 **7:7** [a] Zech. 1:4 [b] Jer. 17:26 [1] Hebrew *Negev* **7:9** [a] Jer. 7:28 **7:10** [a] Ex. 22:22 [b] Mic. 2:1 **7:11** [a] Neh. 9:29 [b] Jer. 17:23 **7:12** [a] Ezek. 11:19 [b] Neh. 9:29, 30 [c] Dan. 9:11, 12 **7:13** [a] Prov. 1:24–28 **7:14** [a] Deut. 4:27; 28:64 **8:2** [a] Zech. 1:14

BE AN INSTRUMENT OF PEACE

Thus says the LORD of hosts: "Execute true justice, show mercy and compassion."

ZECHARIAH 7:9

Everyone wants peace, but there are prerequisites. Zechariah spells them out! If you are not committed to personal righteousness—or if you are unconcerned about injustice around you—you can't have peace. To enjoy peace we have to *promote* peace among family and neighbors.

This is the point that the prophet Zechariah shared when he said, "Thus says the LORD of hosts: 'Execute true justice, show mercy and compassion.'" If you've read the Old Testament *prophets, you will immediately* think of Micah 6:8 and several other passages. The prophets made clear again and again that religious practice and rituals don't make for peace; truth and righteousness do. If we do everything in our power to execute genuine justice, we shall have peace in our hearts.

Giving peace to others will create peace in yourself. Whom can you help today in the spirit of showing real mercy and compassion? It doesn't have to be a monetary gift. Whom can you find to encourage? Ask the Lord to help you find someone today at his or her greatest point of need and show the love of Jesus Christ. Peace rises from acts like that.

3"Thus says the LORD:

[a]'I will return to Zion,
And [b]dwell in the midst of Jerusalem.
Jerusalem [c]shall be called the City of Truth,
[d]The Mountain of the LORD of hosts,
[e]The Holy Mountain.'

4"Thus says the LORD of hosts:

[a]'Old men and old women shall again sit
In the streets of Jerusalem,
Each one with his staff in his hand
Because of great age.
5 The streets of the city
Shall be [a]full of boys and girls
Playing in its streets.'

6"Thus says the LORD of hosts:

'If it is marvelous in the eyes of the remnant of this people in these days,
[a]Will it also be marvelous in My eyes?'
Says the LORD of hosts.

7"Thus says the LORD of hosts:

'Behold, [a]I will save My people from the land of the east
And from the land of the west;
8 I will [a]bring them *back,*
And they shall dwell in the midst of Jerusalem.
[b]They shall be My people
And I will be their God,
[c]In truth and righteousness.'

9"Thus says the LORD of hosts:

[a]'Let your hands be strong,
You who have been hearing in these days
These words by the mouth of [b]the prophets,
Who *spoke* in [c]the day the foundation was laid
For the house of the LORD of hosts,
That the temple might be built.
10 For before these days
There were no [a]wages for man nor any hire for beast;
There was no peace from the enemy for whoever went out or came in;
For I set all men, everyone, against his neighbor.

11[a]But now I *will* not *treat* the remnant of this
people as in the former days,' says the LORD
of hosts.

12 'For[a] the seed *shall be* prosperous,
The vine shall give its fruit,

8:3 [a] Zech. 1:16 [b] Zech. 2:10, 11 [c] Is. 1:21 [d] [Is. 2:2, 3] [e] Jer. 31:23 8:4 [a] Is. 65:20 8:5 [a] Jer. 30:19, 20 8:6 [a] [Luke 1:37] 8:7 [a] Is. 11:11 8:8 [a] Zeph. 3:20 [b] [Jer. 30:22; 31:1, 33] [c] Jer. 4:2 8:9 [a] Hag. 2:4 [b] Ezra 5:1, 2; 6:14 [c] Hag. 2:18 8:10 [a] Hag. 1:6, 9 8:11 [a] Hag. 2:15–19 8:12 [a] Joel 2:22

A COSTLY PEACE

"For the seed shall be prosperous, the vine shall give its fruit, the ground shall give her increase."

ZECHARIAH 8:12

The prophet Zechariah foresaw a time of restoration for Israel. But Israel's renewal foreshadows God's redemptive work throughout the world. This is a very important point: the future of the church is closely tied to the future of Israel. The prophecies and promises of restoration that relate to the latter also have great importance for the former. When John in the Book of Revelation said, "I saw a new heaven and a new earth" (Rev. 21:1), he was alluding to the Old Testament prophecies like this one in Zechariah: "For the seed shall be prosperous, the vine shall give its fruit, the ground shall give her increase" (Zech. 8:12).

It is important to note that what the NKJV translates as "prosperous" in the Hebrew is that wonderful word *shalom,* "peace." The new earth that God has planned will be not only peaceful but also complete. Nothing good, nothing wholesome will be missing. All will be as it should be, as God intended it at creation.

Our personal peace is closely linked to God's redemptive work of restoration of the very earth itself. Peace cost God something—the death of His precious Son. So please don't take the peace of God for granted.

[b]The ground shall give her increase,
And [c]the heavens shall give their dew—
I will cause the remnant of this people
To possess all these.
13 And it shall come to pass
That just as you were [a]a curse among the nations,
O house of Judah and house of Israel,
So I will save you, and [b]you shall be a blessing.
Do not fear,
Let your hands be strong.'

14"For thus says the LORD of hosts:

[a]'Just as I determined to punish you
When your fathers provoked Me to wrath,'
Says the LORD of hosts,
[b]'And I would not relent,
15 So again in these days
I am determined to do good
To Jerusalem and to the house of Judah.
Do not fear.
16 These *are* the things you shall [a]do:
[b]Speak each man the truth to his neighbor;
Give judgment in your gates for truth, justice, and peace;
17 [a]Let none of you think evil in your[1] heart against your neighbor;
And do not love a false oath.
For all these *are things* that I hate,'
Says the LORD."

18Then the word of the LORD of hosts came
to me, saying, 19"Thus says the LORD of hosts:

[a]'The fast of the fourth *month,*
[b]The fast of the fifth,
[c]The fast of the seventh,
[d]And the fast of the tenth,
Shall be [e]joy and gladness and cheerful feasts
For the house of Judah.
[f]Therefore love truth and peace.'

20"Thus says the LORD of hosts:

'Peoples shall yet come,
Inhabitants of many cities;
21 The inhabitants of one *city* shall go to another, saying,
[a]"Let us continue to go and pray before the LORD,
And seek the LORD of hosts.
I myself will go also."
22 Yes, [a]many peoples and strong nations
Shall come to seek the LORD of hosts in Jerusalem,
And to pray before the LORD.'

23"Thus says the LORD of hosts: 'In those
days ten men [a]from every language of the
nations shall [b]grasp the sleeve of a Jewish
man, saying, "Let us go with you, for we have
heard [c]*that* God *is* with you." ' "

Israel Defended Against Enemies

9 The burden[1] of the word of the LORD
Against the land of Hadrach,
And [a]Damascus its resting place

8:12 [b] Ps. 67:6 [c] Hag. 1:10 **8:13** [a] Jer. 42:18 [b] Gen. 12:2 **8:14** [a] Jer. 31:28 [b] [2 Chr. 36:16] **8:16** [a] Zech. 7:9, 10 [b] [Eph. 4:25] **8:17** [a] Prov. 3:29 [1] Literally *his* **8:19** [a] Jer. 52:6 [b] Jer. 52:12 [c] 2 Kin. 25:25 [d] Jer. 52:4 [e] Esth. 8:17 [f] Zech. 8:16 **8:21** [a] [Is. 2:2, 3] **8:22** [a] Is. 60:3; 66:23 **8:23** [a] Is. 3:6 [b] [Is. 45:14] [c] 1 Cor. 14:25 **9:1** [a] Is. 17:1 [1] Or *oracle*

PEACE FROM INTEGRITY

"These are the things you shall do: Speak each man the truth to his neighbor;. give judgment in your gates for truth, justice, and peace."

ZECHARIAH 8:16

Zechariah prophesied a new day for Israel. The day of judgment was past, restoration lay ahead. As the Israelites renewed their faith, they were instructed: "Speak each man the truth to his neighbor; give judgment in your gates for truth, justice, and peace." These are exactly the things we must do! If we speak truth to friends and neighbors (no lying, cheating, dirty deals) and if we promote "truth, justice, and peace" in society (in our courts or wherever we have influence), we fulfill God's law and will.

Promoting justice and peace is also a good way to enjoy personal peace. Do you want an overflowing peace? Treat people the way God treats people.

SPEAK WORDS OF PROMISE AND PEACE

Thus says the LORD of hosts . . . "Love truth and peace."

ZECHARIAH 8:19

When it comes to promoting restorative peace, the prophet Zechariah was on a roll! He declared, "Thus says the LORD of hosts . . . 'Love truth and peace.'" Earnest pursuit of truth and peace leads to positive, healthy relationships that, in turn, enhance your own sense of peace. A generous soul is a happy soul. Building peace in others does not diminish your own. On the contrary, it enhances your peace!

The gods of Israel's ancient neighbors promoted war and oppression. The gods of the violent empires like Assyria and Babylon inspired their armies to conquer the peoples of the ancient Near East. Brute strength was praised. The God of Israel is Himself a Mighty Warrior when He has to be, but His core essence is grace and the restorative peace, which He offers all people. Ultimately, our peace does not originate with us but with our Creator.

If you are low on peace, consider enhancing others' sense of peace. Speak words of promise and hope. Try this formula for peace today! The math always works.

(For [b]the eyes of men
And all the tribes of Israel
Are on the LORD);
2 Also *against* [a]Hamath, *which* borders on it,
And *against* [b]Tyre and [c]Sidon, though they are very [d]wise.

3 For Tyre built herself a tower,
Heaped up silver like the dust,
And gold like the mire of the streets.
4 Behold, [a]the Lord will cast her out;
He will destroy [b]her power in the sea,
And she will be devoured by fire.

5 Ashkelon shall see *it* and fear;
Gaza also shall be very sorrowful;
And [a]Ekron, for He dried up her expectation.
The king shall perish from Gaza,
And Ashkelon shall not be inhabited.

6 "A mixed race shall settle [a]in Ashdod,
And I will cut off the pride of the [b]Philistines.
7 I will take away the blood from his mouth,
And the abominations from between his teeth.
But he who remains, even he *shall be* for our God,
And shall be like a leader in Judah,
And Ekron like a Jebusite.

8 [a]I will camp around My house
Because of the army,
Because of him who passes by and him who returns.
No more shall an oppressor pass through them,
For now I have seen with My eyes.

The Coming King

9 "Rejoice [a]greatly, O daughter of Zion!
Shout, O daughter of Jerusalem!
Behold, [b]your King is coming to you;
He *is* just and having salvation,
Lowly and riding on a donkey,
A colt, the foal of a donkey.
10 I [a]will cut off the chariot from Ephraim
And the horse from Jerusalem;
The [b]battle bow shall be cut off.
He shall speak peace to the nations;
His dominion *shall be* [c]'from sea to sea,
And from the River to the ends of the earth.'[1]

God Will Save His People

11 "As for you also,
Because of the blood of your covenant,
I will set your [a]prisoners free from the waterless pit.
12 Return to the stronghold,
[a]You prisoners of hope.
Even today I declare
That I will restore [b]double to you.

9:1 [b] Amos 1:3–5 9:2 [a] Jer. 49:23 [b] Is. 23 [c] 1 Kin. 17:9 [d] Ezek. 28:3 9:4 [a] Is. 23:1 [b] Ezek. 26:17 9:5 [a] Zeph. 2:4, 5 9:6 [a] Amos 1:8 [b] Ezek. 25:15–17 9:8 [a] [Ps. 34:7] 9:9 [a] Zech. 2:10 [b] [Jer. 23:5, 6]; Matt. 21:5; Mark 11:7, 9; Luke 19:35–38; John 12:15 9:10 [a] Hos. 1:7 [b] Hos. 2:18 [c] Ps. 72:8 [1] Psalm 72:8 9:11 [a] Is. 42:7 9:12 [a] Is. 49:9 [b] Is. 61:7

BE THE WITNESS TO PEACE

"He shall speak peace to the nations; His dominion shall be 'from sea to sea, and from the River to the ends of the earth.'"

ZECHARIAH 9:10

The prophet Jonah did not want peace for the mighty Assyrian city of Nineveh (see the devotions on Jon. 2:2; 3:10). But God wanted that city's inhabitants to have the chance to repent. We hear the same generous sentiment expressed here in Zechariah 9:10: "He shall speak peace to the nations." These are the very nations that trampled over Israel. Yes, there are times of judgment, when God acts decisively against the wicked. But God also appeals to the nations, that is, to the Gentiles, the people who are not part of Israel. All people are invited to embrace God and His healing, life-transforming peace.

The evangelism of the early church, which reached out to Jew and Gentile alike, is rooted in these prophetic oracles that envisioned God speaking peace to the whole inhabited earth. We call this the Great Commission: "Go therefore and make disciples of all the nations," the risen Jesus told His disciples (Matt. 28:19). In proclaiming the gospel we proclaim peace.

To whom can you proclaim peace today?

13 For I have bent Judah, My *bow,*
Fitted the bow with Ephraim,
And raised up your sons, O Zion,
Against your sons, O Greece,
And made you like the sword of a mighty man."

14 Then the LORD will be seen over them,
And [a]His arrow will go forth like lightning.
The Lord GOD will blow the trumpet,
And go [b]with whirlwinds from the south.
15 The LORD of hosts will [a]defend them;
They shall devour and subdue with slingstones.
They shall drink *and* roar as if with wine;
They shall be filled *with blood* like basins,
Like the corners of the altar.
16 The LORD their God will [a]save them in that day,
As the flock of His people.
For [b]they *shall be like* the jewels of a crown,
[c]Lifted like a banner over His land—
17 For [a]how great is its[1] goodness
And how great its[2] [b]beauty!
[c]Grain shall make the young men thrive,
And new wine the young women.

Restoration of Judah and Israel

10 Ask [a]the LORD for [b]rain
In [c]the time of the latter rain.[1]
The LORD will make flashing clouds;
He will give them showers of rain,
Grass in the field for everyone.

2 For the [a]idols[1] speak delusion;
The diviners envision [b]lies,
And tell false dreams;
They [c]comfort in vain.
Therefore *the people* wend their way like [d]sheep;
They are in trouble [e]because *there is* no shepherd.

3 "My anger is kindled against the [a]shepherds,
[b]And I will punish the goatherds.
For the LORD of hosts [c]will visit His flock,
The house of Judah,
And [d]will make them as His royal horse in the battle.
4 From him comes [a]the cornerstone,
From him [b]the tent peg,
From him the battle bow,
From him every ruler[1] together.
5 They shall be like mighty men,
Who [a]tread down *their enemies*
In the mire of the streets in the battle.

9:14 [a] Ps. 18:14 [b] Is. 21:1 **9:15** [a] Zech. 12:8 **9:16** [a] Jer. 31:10, 11 [b] Is. 62:3 [c] Is. 11:12 **9:17** [a] [Ps. 31:19] [b] [Ps. 45:1–16] [c] Joel 3:18 [1] Or *His* [2] Or *His* **10:1** [a] [Jer. 14:22] [b] [Deut. 11:13, 14] [c] [Joel 2:23] [1] That is, spring rain **10:2** [a] Jer. 10:8 [b] Jer. 27:9 [c] Job 13:4 [d] Jer. 50:6, 17 [e] Ezek. 34:5–8 [1] Hebrew *teraphim* **10:3** [a] Jer. 25:34–36 [b] Ezek. 34:17 [c] Luke 1:68 [d] Song 1:9 **10:4** [a] Is. 28:16 [b] Is. 22:23 [1] Or *despot* **10:5** [a] Ps. 18:42

They shall fight because the LORD is with them,
And the riders on horses shall be put to shame.

6 "I will strengthen the house of Judah,
And I will save the house of Joseph.
[a]I will bring them back,
Because I [b]have mercy on them.
They shall be as though I had not cast them aside;
For I *am* the LORD their God,
And I [c]will hear them.
7 *Those of* Ephraim shall be like a mighty man,
And their [a]heart shall rejoice as if with wine.
Yes, their children shall see *it* and be glad;
Their heart shall rejoice in the LORD.
8 I will [a]whistle for them and gather them,
For I will redeem them;
[b]And they shall increase as they once increased.

9 "I[a] will sow them among the peoples,
And they shall [b]remember Me in far countries;
They shall live, together with their children,
And they shall return.
10 [a]I will also bring them back from the land of Egypt,
And gather them from Assyria.
I will bring them into the land of Gilead and Lebanon,
[b]Until no *more room* is found for them.
11 [a]He shall pass through the sea with affliction,
And strike the waves of the sea:
All the depths of the River[1] shall dry up.
Then [b]the pride of Assyria shall be brought down,
And [c]the scepter of Egypt shall depart.

12 "So I will strengthen them in the LORD,
And [a]they shall walk up and down in His name,"
Says the LORD.

Desolation of Israel

11 Open [a]your doors, O Lebanon,
That fire may devour your cedars.
2 Wail, O cypress, for the [a]cedar has fallen,
Because the mighty *trees* are ruined.
Wail, O oaks of Bashan,
[b]For the thick forest has come down.
3 *There is* the sound of wailing [a]shepherds!
For their glory is in ruins.
There is the sound of roaring lions!
For the pride[1] of the Jordan is in ruins.

PEACE NOTE

Disciples who enjoy God's *shalom* are cheerful despite hardship and persecution. They look forward to a "great . . . reward in heaven" (Matt. 5:12).

Prophecy of the Shepherds

4Thus says the LORD my God, "Feed the
flock for slaughter, 5whose owners slaughter
them and [a]feel no guilt; those who sell them
[b]say, 'Blessed be the LORD, for I am rich'; and
their shepherds do [c]not pity them. 6For I will
no longer pity the inhabitants of the land,"
says the LORD. "But indeed I will give everyone into his neighbor's hand and into the
hand of his king. They shall attack the land,
and I will not deliver *them* from their hand."
7So I fed the flock for slaughter, in particular [a]the poor of the flock.[1] I took for myself
two staffs: the one I called Beauty,[2] and the
other I called Bonds;[3] and I fed the flock. 8I
dismissed the three shepherds [a]in one month.
My soul loathed them, and their soul also abhorred me. 9Then I said, "I will not feed you.
[a]Let what is dying die, and what is perishing
perish. Let those that are left eat each other's
flesh." 10And I took my staff, Beauty, and cut
it in two, that I might break the covenant
which I had made with all the peoples. 11So it
was broken on that day. Thus [a]the poor[1] of the
flock, who were watching me, knew that it *was*
the word of the LORD. 12Then I said to them,
"If it is agreeable to you, give *me* my wages;

10:6 [a] Jer. 3:18 [b] Hos. 1:7 [c] Zech. 13:9 10:7 [a] Ps. 104:15 10:8 [a] Is. 5:26 [b] Ezek. 36:37 10:9 [a] Hos. 2:23 [b] Deut. 30:1 10:10 [a] Is. 11:11 [b] Is. 49:19, 20 10:11 [a] Is. 11:15 [b] Zeph. 2:13 [c] Ezek. 30:13 [1] That is, the Nile 10:12 [a] Mic. 4:5 11:1 [a] Zech. 10:10 11:2 [a] Ezek. 31:3 [b] Is. 32:19 11:3 [a] Jer. 25:34–36 [1] Or *floodplain, thicket* 11:5 [a] [Jer. 2:3]; 50:7 [b] Hos. 12:8 [c] Ezek. 34:2, 3 11:7 [a] Zeph. 3:12 [1] Following Masoretic Text, Targum, and Vulgate; Septuagint reads *for the Canaanites.* [2] Or *Grace,* and so in verse 10 [3] Or *Unity,* and so in verse 14 11:8 [a] Hos. 5:7 11:9 [a] Jer. 15:2 11:11 [a] Zeph. 3:12 [1] Following Masoretic Text, Targum, and Vulgate; Septuagint reads *the Canaanites.*

and if not, refrain." So they [a]weighed out for my wages thirty *pieces* of silver.

13 And the LORD said to me, "Throw it to the [a]potter"—that princely price they set on me. So I took the thirty *pieces* of silver and threw them into the house of the LORD for the potter. 14 Then I cut in two my other staff, Bonds, that I might break the brotherhood between Judah and Israel.

15 And the LORD said to me, [a]"Next, take for yourself the implements of a foolish shepherd. 16 For indeed I will raise up a shepherd in the land *who* will not care for those who are cut off, nor seek the young, nor heal those that are broken, nor feed those that still stand. But he will eat the flesh of the fat and tear their hooves in [a]pieces.

17 "Woe[a] to the worthless shepherd,
Who leaves the flock!
A sword *shall be* against his arm
And against his right eye;
His arm shall completely wither,
And his right eye shall be totally
blinded."

The Coming Deliverance of Judah

12 The burden[1] of the word of the LORD against Israel. Thus says the LORD, [a]who stretches out the heavens, lays the foundation of the earth, and [b]forms the spirit of man within him: 2 "Behold, I will make Jerusalem [a]a cup of drunkenness to all the surrounding peoples, when they lay siege against Judah and Jerusalem. 3 [a]And it shall happen in that day that I will make Jerusalem [b]a very heavy stone for all peoples; all who would heave it away will surely be cut in pieces, though all nations of the earth are gathered against it. 4 In that day," says the LORD, [a]"I will strike every horse with confusion, and its rider with madness; I will open My eyes on the house of Judah, and will strike every horse of the peoples with blindness. 5 And the governors of Judah shall say in their heart, 'The inhabitants of Jerusalem *are* my strength in the LORD of hosts, their God.' 6 In that day I will make the governors of Judah [a]like a firepan in the woodpile, and like a fiery torch in the sheaves; they shall devour all the surrounding peoples on the right hand and on the left, but Jerusalem shall be inhabited again in her own place—Jerusalem.

7 "The LORD will save the tents of Judah first, so that the glory of the house of David and the glory of the inhabitants of Jerusalem shall not become greater than that of Judah. 8 In that day the LORD will defend the inhabitants of Jerusalem; the one who is feeble among them in that day shall be like David, and the house of David *shall be* like God, like the Angel of the LORD before them. 9 It shall be in that day *that* I will seek to [a]destroy all the nations that come against Jerusalem.

Mourning for the Pierced One

10 [a]"And I will pour on the house of David and on the inhabitants of Jerusalem the Spirit of grace and supplication; then they will [b]look on Me whom they pierced. Yes, they will mourn for Him [c]as one mourns for *his* only *son,* and grieve for Him as one grieves for a firstborn. 11 In that day there shall be a great [a]mourning in Jerusalem, [b]like the mourning at Hadad Rimmon in the plain of Megiddo.[1] 12 [a]And the land shall mourn, every family by itself: the family of the house of David by itself, and their wives by themselves; the family of the house of [b]Nathan by itself, and their wives by themselves; 13 the family of the house of Levi by itself, and their wives by themselves; the family of Shimei by itself, and their wives by themselves; 14 all the families that remain, every family by itself, and their wives by themselves.

Idolatry Cut Off

13 "In that [a]day [b]a fountain shall be opened for the house of David and for the inhabitants of Jerusalem, for sin and for [c]uncleanness.

2 "It shall be in that day," says the LORD of hosts, "*that* I will [a]cut off the names of the idols from the land, and they shall no longer be remembered. I will also cause [b]the prophets and the unclean spirit to depart from the land. 3 It shall come to pass *that* if anyone still prophesies, then his father and mother who begot him will say to him, 'You shall [a]not live, because you have spoken lies in the name of the LORD.' And his father and mother who begot him [b]shall thrust him through when he prophesies.

4 "And it shall be in that day *that* [a]every prophet will be ashamed of his vision when he prophesies; they will not wear [b]a robe of coarse hair to deceive. 5 [a]But he will say, 'I *am* no prophet, I *am* a farmer; for a man taught me to keep cattle from my youth.' 6 And *one* will say to him, 'What are these

11:12 [a] Ex. 21:32; Matt. 26:15; 27:9, 10 **11:13** [a] Matt. 27:3–10 **11:15** [a] Is. 56:11 **11:16** [a] Ezek. 34:1–10 **11:17** [a] Jer. 23:1
12:1 [a] Is. 42:5; 44:24 [b] [Is. 57:16] [1] Or *oracle* **12:2** [a] Is. 51:17 **12:3** [a] Zech. 12:4, 6, 8; 13:1 [b] Matt. 21:44 **12:4** [a] Ezek. 38:4
12:6 [a] Obad. 18 **12:9** [a] Hag. 2:22 **12:10** [a] [Joel 2:28, 29] [b] John 19:34, 37; 20:27; [Rev. 1:7] [c] Jer. 6:26 **12:11** [a] [Rev. 1:7]
[b] 2 Kin. 23:29 [1] Hebrew *Megiddon* **12:12** [a] [Matt. 24:30] [b] Luke 3:31 **13:1** [a] [Rev. 21:6, 7] [b] [Heb. 9:14] [c] Ezek. 36:25
13:2 [a] Ex. 23:13 [b] Jer. 23:14, 15 **13:3** [a] Deut. 18:20 [b] Deut. 13:6–11 **13:4** [a] [Mic. 3:6, 7] [b] 2 Kin. 1:8 **13:5** [a] Amos 7:14

PEACE NOTE

Today, ask the Lord to heal you of whatever is troubling you that may be hijacking His peace in your life.

wounds between your arms?'[1] Then he will answer, '*Those* with which I was wounded in the house of my friends.'

The Shepherd Savior

7 "Awake, O sword, against [a]My Shepherd,
Against the Man [b]who is My
Companion,"
Says the LORD of hosts.
[c]"Strike the Shepherd,
And the sheep will be scattered;
Then I will turn My hand against [d]the
little ones.
8 And it shall come to pass in all the
land,"
Says the LORD,
"*That* [a]two-thirds in it shall be cut off
and die,
[b]But *one*-third shall be left in it:
9 I will bring the *one*-third [a]through the
fire,
Will [b]refine them as silver is refined,
And test them as gold is tested.
[c]They will call on My name,
And I will answer them.
[d]I will say, 'This *is* My people';
And each one will say, 'The LORD *is* my
God.' "

The Day of the LORD

14 Behold, [a]the day of the LORD is
coming,
And your spoil will be divided in your
midst.
2 For [a]I will gather all the nations to
battle against Jerusalem;
The city shall be taken,
The houses rifled,
And the women ravished.
Half of the city shall go into
captivity,
But the remnant of the people shall not
be cut off from the city.

3 Then the LORD will go forth
And fight against those nations,
As He fights in the day of battle.
4 And in that day His feet will stand [a]on
the Mount of Olives,
Which faces Jerusalem on the east.
And the Mount of Olives shall be split
in two,
From east to west,
[b]*Making* a very large valley;
Half of the mountain shall move
toward the north
And half of it toward the south.

5 Then you shall flee *through* My
mountain valley,
For the mountain valley shall reach to
Azal.
Yes, you shall flee
As you fled from the [a]earthquake
In the days of Uzziah king of Judah.

[b]Thus the LORD my God will come,
And [c]all the saints with You.[1]

6 It shall come to pass in that day
That there will be no light;
The lights will diminish.
7 It shall be one day
[a]Which is known to the LORD—
Neither day nor night.
But at [b]evening time it shall happen
That it will be light.

8 And in that day it shall be
That living [a]waters shall flow from
Jerusalem,
Half of them toward the eastern sea
And half of them toward the western
sea;
In both summer and winter it shall
occur.
9 And the LORD shall be [a]King over all
the earth.
In that day it shall be—
[b]"The LORD *is* one,"[1]
And His name one.

13:6 [1] Or *hands* 13:7 [a] Is. 40:11 [b] [John 10:30] [c] Matt. 26:31, 56, 67; Mark 14:27; 1 Pet. 5:4; Rev. 7:16, 17 [d] Luke 12:32
13:8 [a] Ezek. 5:2, 4, 12 [b] [Rom. 11:5] 13:9 [a] Is. 48:10 [b] 1 Pet. 1:6, 7 [c] Ps. 50:15 [d] Hos. 2:23 14:1 [a] [Is. 13:6, 9]
14:2 [a] Zech. 12:2, 3 14:4 [a] Ezek. 11:23 [b] Joel 3:12 14:5 [a] Amos 1:1 [b] Matt. 24:30, 31; 25:31 [c] Joel 3:11 [1] Or *you;*
Septuagint, Targum, and Vulgate read *Him.* 14:7 [a] Matt. 24:36 [b] Is. 30:26 14:8 [a] Ezek. 47:1–12 14:9 [a] [Rev. 11:15]
[b] Deut. 6:4 [1] Compare Deuteronomy 6:4

10 All the land shall be turned into a plain
from Geba to Rimmon south of Jerusalem.
Jerusalem[1] shall be raised up and [a]inhabited
in her place from Benjamin's Gate to the
place of the First Gate and the Corner Gate,
[b]and *from* the Tower of Hananel to the king's
winepresses.

11 *The people* shall dwell in it;
And [a]no longer shall there be utter
 destruction,
[b]But Jerusalem shall be safely
 inhabited.

12 And this shall be the plague with which
the LORD will strike all the people who fought
against Jerusalem:

Their flesh shall dissolve while they
 stand on their feet,
Their eyes shall dissolve in their
 sockets,
And their tongues shall dissolve in
 their mouths.

13 It shall come to pass in that day
That [a]a great panic from the LORD will
 be among them.
Everyone will seize the hand of his
 neighbor,
And raise [b]his hand against his
 neighbor's hand;
14 Judah also will fight at Jerusalem.
[a]And the wealth of all the surrounding
 nations
Shall be gathered together:
Gold, silver, and apparel in great
 abundance.

15 [a]Such also shall be the plague
On the horse *and* the mule,
On the camel and the donkey,
And on all the cattle that will be in
 those camps.
So *shall* this plague *be.*

The Nations Worship the King

16 And it shall come to pass *that* everyone
who is left of all the nations which came
against Jerusalem shall [a]go up from year to
year to [b]worship the King, the LORD of hosts,
and to keep [c]the Feast of Tabernacles. 17 [a]And
it shall be *that* whichever of the families of
the earth do not come up to Jerusalem to
worship the King, the LORD of hosts, on them
there will be no rain. 18 If the family of [a]Egypt
will not come up and enter in, [b]they *shall have*
no *rain;* they shall receive the plague with
which the LORD strikes the nations who do
not come up to keep the Feast of Tabernacles.
19 This shall be the punishment of Egypt and
the punishment of all the nations that do not
come up to keep the Feast of Tabernacles.
20 In that day [a]"HOLINESS TO THE LORD"
shall be *engraved* on the bells of the horses.
The [b]pots in the LORD's house shall be like
the bowls before the altar. 21 Yes, every pot in
Jerusalem and Judah shall be holiness to the
LORD of hosts.[1] Everyone who sacrifices shall
come and take them and cook in them. In
that day there shall no longer be a [a]Canaanite
[b]in the house of the LORD of hosts.

14:10 [a] Zech. 12:6 [b] Jer. 31:38 [1] Literally *She* **14:11** [a] Jer. 31:40 [b] Jer. 23:6 **14:13** [a] 1 Sam. 14:15, 20 [b] Judg. 7:22 **14:14** [a] Ezek. 39:10, 17 **14:15** [a] Zech. 14:12 **14:16** [a] [Is. 2:2, 3; 60:6–9; 66:18–21] [b] Is. 27:13 [c] Lev. 23:34–44 **14:17** [a] Is. 60:12 **14:18** [a] Is. 19:21 [b] Deut. 11:10 **14:20** [a] Is. 23:18 [b] Ezek. 46:20 **14:21** [a] Is. 35:8 [b] [Eph. 2:19–22] [1] Or *on every pot . . . shall be (engraved) "HOLINESS TO THE LORD OF HOSTS"*

THE BOOK OF

MALACHI

AUTHOR

The only Old Testament mention of Malachi is in Malachi 1:1. Nothing else is known of this prophet, not even his father's name. But tradition holds that he, like Zechariah, was a member of the Great Synagogue. He is generally accepted as the author of this book. It is likely that Malachi proclaimed his message when Nehemiah was absent from Judah between 432 and 425 BC, almost a century after Haggai and Zechariah began to prophesy. Thus, because of its place in history and the Old Testament, Malachi is a transitional book. Its primary themes are consistent with the rest of the Old Testament, but it also serves as a precursor to the New Testament.

TIME

c. 432–425 BC

KEY VERSE

Malachi 2:17

THEME

In Malachi, the days of political upheaval are past, and the country is living in an uneventful waiting period. The people are waiting for the Messiah to bring the glorious restoration of their nation to the renewed prominence of the Davidic and Solomonic periods. But there is a sense that the people are losing touch with God. The old problem with idol worship is gone, but other problems have taken its place. Malachi's role is to call the people back to a genuine, enduring faith in God. His dominant admonition is for a personal relationship with the living God, who seeks people to walk with Him (2:6).

Deceit and complacency were causing God's people to be inconsistent in their worship and unwilling to give their gifts of tithes and offerings (3:8), yet they simply couldn't figure out why God's peace was not with them. God "cursed" their routine, hollow "blessings" (2:2) because their hearts were far from Him. Malachi challenges us to see that the peace of God is not found in ritual and empty religious formalities. He offers all of us the description of one who would find true *shalom*: "My covenant was with him, one of life and peace . . . The law of truth was in his mouth, and injustice was not found on his lips. He walked with Me in peace and equity, and turned many away from iniquity" (2:5–6).

1 The burden[1] of the word of the LORD to Israel by Malachi.

Israel Beloved of God

2 "I[a] have loved you," says the LORD.
"Yet you say, 'In what way have You loved us?'
Was not Esau Jacob's brother?"
Says the LORD.
"Yet [b]Jacob I have loved;
3 But Esau I have hated,
And [a]laid waste his mountains and his heritage
For the jackals of the wilderness."

4 Even though Edom has said,
"We have been impoverished,
But we will return and build the desolate places,"
Thus says the LORD of hosts:

"They may build, but I will [a]throw down;
They shall be called the Territory of Wickedness,
And the people against whom the LORD will have indignation forever.
5 Your eyes shall see,
And you shall say,
[a]'The LORD is magnified beyond the border of Israel.'

Polluted Offerings

6 "A son [a]honors *his* father,
And a servant *his* master.
[b]If then I am the Father,
Where *is* My honor?
And if I *am* a Master,
Where *is* My reverence?
Says the LORD of hosts
To you priests who despise My name.
[c]Yet you say, 'In what way have we despised Your name?'

7 "You offer [a]defiled food on My altar,
But say,
'In what way have we defiled You?'
By saying,
[b]'The table of the LORD is contemptible.'
8 And [a]when you offer the blind as a sacrifice,
Is it not evil?
And when you offer the lame and sick,
Is it not evil?
Offer it then to your governor!
Would he be pleased with you?
Would he [b]accept you favorably?"
Says the LORD of hosts.

9 "But now entreat God's favor,
That He may be gracious to us.
[a]*While* this is being *done* by your hands,
Will He accept you favorably?"
Says the LORD of hosts.
10 "Who *is there* even among you who would shut the doors,
[a]So that you would not kindle fire *on* My altar in vain?
I have no pleasure in you,"
Says the LORD of hosts,

1:1 [1] Or *oracle* 1:2 [a] Deut. 4:37; 7:8; 23:5 [b] Rom. 9:13 1:3 [a] Jer. 49:18 1:4 [a] Jer. 49:16–18 1:5 [a] Ps. 35:27 1:6 [a] [Ex. 20:12] [b] Luke 6:46 [c] Mal. 2:14 1:7 [a] Deut. 15:21 [b] Ezek. 41:22 1:8 [a] Lev. 22:22 [b] [Job 42:8] 1:9 [a] Hos. 13:9 1:10 [a] 1 Cor. 9:13

FREE FROM ANXIETY

"My covenant was with him, one of life and peace."

MALACHI 2:5

Malachi is perhaps the most mysterious of the Old Testament prophets. We are not sure who he was. In Hebrew, Malachi means "My Messenger," and this prophet had an important message. Malachi railed against corruption among the priests. He reminded them of God's covenant with Aaron, Israel's first high priest (using the name Levi, the father of the priests and Levites): "My covenant was with him, one of life and peace." The thought is beautiful! The whole purpose of God's saving work is to promote life and peace. In sharp contrast, sin and rebellion promote death and sorrow.

This is why God made a covenant with Israel. It wasn't to lay a heavy burden of laws and rituals on Israel; it was to set His people free, to make it possible for them to have a right relationship with God. *Freedom* is another descriptor from living in the peace of God. I've struggled with anxiety, but God has given me freedom. Freedom is a gift within the peace of God that can be yours today.

[b]"Nor will I accept an offering from your
hands.
11 For [a]from the rising of the sun, even to
its going down,
My name *shall be* great [b]among the
Gentiles;
[c]In every place [d]incense *shall be* offered
to My name,
And a pure offering;
[e]For My name shall be great among the
nations,"
Says the LORD of hosts.

12 "But you profane it,
In that you say,
[a]'The table of the LORD[1] is defiled;
And its fruit, its food, *is* contemptible.'
13 You also say,
'Oh, what a [a]weariness!'
And you sneer at it,"
Says the LORD of hosts.
"And you bring the stolen, the lame, and
the sick;
Thus you bring an offering!
[b]Should I accept this from your hand?"
Says the LORD.
14 "But cursed *be* [a]the deceiver
Who has in his flock a male,
And takes a vow,
But sacrifices to the Lord [b]what is
blemished—
For [c]I *am* a great King,"
Says the LORD of hosts,
"And My name *is to be* feared among the
nations.

Corrupt Priests

2 "And now, O [a]priests, this
commandment is for you.
2 [a]If you will not hear,
And if you will not take *it* to heart,
To give glory to My name,"
Says the LORD of hosts,
"I will send a curse upon you,
And I will curse your blessings.
Yes, I have cursed them [b]already,
Because you do not take *it* to heart.

3 "Behold, I will rebuke your descendants
And spread [a]refuse on your faces,
The refuse of your solemn feasts;
And *one* will [b]take you away with it.
4 Then you shall know that I have sent
this commandment to you,
That My covenant with Levi may continue,"
Says the LORD of hosts.
5 "My[a] covenant was with him, *one* of life
and peace,
And I gave them to him [b]*that he might*
fear *Me;*
So he feared Me
And was reverent before My name.
6 [a]The law of truth[1] was in his mouth,
And injustice was not found on his lips.
He walked with Me in peace and equity,
And [b]turned many away from iniquity.

1:10 [b] Is. 1:11 **1:11** [a] Is. 59:19 [b] Is. 60:3, 5 [c] 1 Tim. 2:8 [d] Rev. 8:3 [e] Is. 66:18, 19 **1:12** [a] Mal. 1:7 [1] Following Bomberg; Masoretic Text reads *Lord.* **1:13** [a] Is. 43:22 [b] Lev. 22:20 **1:14** [a] Mal. 1:8 [b] Lev. 22:18–20 [c] Ps. 47:2 **2:1** [a] Mal. 1:6 **2:2** [a] [Deut. 28:15] [b] Mal. 3:9 **2:3** [a] Ex. 29:14 [b] 1 Kin. 14:10 **2:5** [a] Num. 25:12 [b] Deut. 33:9 **2:6** [a] Deut. 33:10 [b] Jer. 23:22 [1] Or *true instruction*

WALK WITH THE GOD OF PEACE

"The law of truth was in his mouth, and injustice was not found on his lips. He walked with Me in peace and equity."

MALACHI 2:6

Malachi had more to say about Aaron, Moses' brother and Israel's first high priest (using the name Levi, the father of the priests and Levites). "The law of truth was in his mouth, and injustice was not found on his lips," the prophet said. "He walked with Me in peace and equity." Malachi reminded the priests of this great legacy because they were not living up to it: "For the lips of a priest should keep knowledge . . . he is the messenger of the LORD of hosts" (v. 7).

These are awesome words. Everyone who labors in Christian ministry should heed this exhortation. Like the priests of old, today's ministers of the gospel should proclaim the truth and keep (or guard) the knowledge of God. If we do, then, like Aaron of old, we will walk with God in peace and justice. Peace can flourish in our lives, and we can unleash it in a hurting world.

7 "For[a] the lips of a priest should keep
knowledge,
And *people* should seek the law from
his mouth;
[b]For he is the messenger of the LORD of
hosts.
8 But you have departed from the way;
You [a]have caused many to stumble at
the law.
[b]You have corrupted the covenant of
Levi,"
Says the LORD of hosts.
9 "Therefore [a]I also have made you
contemptible and base
Before all the people,
Because you have not kept My ways
But have shown [b]partiality in the law."

Treachery of Infidelity

10 [a]Have we not all one Father?
[b]Has not one God created us?
Why do we deal treacherously with one
another
By profaning the covenant of the
fathers?
11 Judah has dealt treacherously,
And an abomination has been
committed in Israel and in Jerusalem,
For Judah has [a]profaned
The LORD's holy *institution* which He
loves:
He has married the daughter of a
foreign god.
12 May the LORD cut off from the tents of
Jacob
The man who does this, being awake
and aware,[1]
Yet [a]who brings an offering to the
LORD of hosts!

13 And this is the second thing you do:
You cover the altar of the LORD with
tears,
With weeping and crying;
So He does not regard the offering
anymore,
Nor receive *it* with goodwill from your
hands.
14 Yet you say, "For what reason?"
Because the LORD has been witness
Between you and [a]the wife of your
youth,
With whom you have dealt treacherously;
[b]Yet she is your companion
And your wife by covenant.
15 But [a]did He not make *them* one,
Having a remnant of the Spirit?
And why one?
He seeks [b]godly offspring.
Therefore take heed to your spirit,
And let none deal treacherously with
the wife of his youth.

16 "For [a]the LORD God of Israel says
That He hates divorce,
For it covers one's garment with
violence,"
Says the LORD of hosts.
"Therefore take heed to your spirit,
That you do not deal treacherously."

2:7 [a] Deut. 17:8–11 [b] [Gal. 4:14] **2:8** [a] Jer. 18:15 [b] Neh. 13:29 **2:9** [a] 1 Sam. 2:30 [b] Deut. 1:17 **2:10** [a] 1 Cor. 8:6 [b] Job 31:15 **2:11** [a] Ezra 9:1, 2 **2:12** [a] Neh. 13:29 [1] Talmud and Vulgate read *teacher and student.* **2:14** [a] Mal. 3:5 [b] Prov. 2:17 **2:15** [a] Matt. 19:4, 5 [b] [1 Cor. 7:14] **2:16** [a] [Matt. 5:31; 19:6–8]

THE WAY OF PEACE PREPARED

"Behold, I send My messenger, and he will prepare the way before Me."

MALACHI 3:1

The prophet Malachi knew that the day of reckoning would someday come. God's desire, which the prophet of course shared, was that the people would make things right *before* that day arrived. Perhaps in reference to himself, Malachi relayed God's prophecy: "Behold, I send My messenger, and he will prepare the way before Me." It is important to be ready, for the prophet asked, "Who can endure the day of His coming? And who can stand when He appears?" (v. 2). The day will come for all of us, and when it does, you want to be ready.

We must ask ourselves these questions. Of course, Malachi primarily had in mind the priests of his day as he made clear later in the oracle: "He will purify the sons of Levi" (v. 3). But just because the prophet addressed the priests did not mean his warning had no relevance for the rest of us. The messenger God sent was John the Baptist, whose ministry was to prepare Israel for the Lord, the Messiah Jesus. Embrace the Prince of Peace.

17 [a]You have wearied the LORD with your
words;
Yet you say,
"In what way have we wearied *Him?*"
In that you say,
[b]"Everyone who does evil
Is good in the sight of the LORD,
And He delights in them,"
Or, "Where *is* the God of justice?"

The Coming Messenger

3 "Behold, [a]I send My messenger,
And he will [b]prepare the way before Me.
And the Lord, whom you seek,
Will suddenly come to His temple,
[c]Even the Messenger of the covenant,
In whom you delight.
Behold, [d]He is coming,"
Says the LORD of hosts.

2 "But who can endure [a]the day of His
coming?
And [b]who can stand when He appears?
For [c]He *is* like a refiner's fire
And like launderers' soap.
3 [a]He will sit as a refiner and a purifier of
silver;
He will purify the sons of Levi,
And purge them as gold and silver,
That they may [b]offer to the LORD
An offering in righteousness.

4 "Then [a]the offering of Judah and
Jerusalem
Will be pleasant to the LORD,
As in the days of old,
As in former years.
5 And I will come near you for
judgment;
I will be a swift witness
Against sorcerers,
Against adulterers,
[a]Against perjurers,
Against those who [b]exploit wage
earners and [c]widows and orphans,
And against those who turn away an
alien—
Because they do not fear Me,"
Says the LORD of hosts.

6 "For I *am* the LORD, [a]I do not change;
[b]Therefore you are not consumed,
O sons of Jacob.

PEACE NOTE

I don't live by feelings; I live by faith in the facts of God's unchanging Word and character. This brings peace.

MALACHI 3:6

2:17 [a] Is. 43:22, 24 [b] Is. 5:20 **3:1** [a] Matt. 11:10; Mark 1:2; Luke 1:76; 7:27; John 1:23; 2:14, 15 [b] [Is. 40:3] [c] Is. 63:9 [d] Hab. 2:7 **3:2** [a] [Mal. 4:1] [b] Rev. 6:17 [c] [Matt. 3:10–12] **3:3** [a] Is. 1:25 [b] [1 Pet. 2:5] **3:4** [a] Mal. 1:11 **3:5** [a] Zech. 5:4 [b] James 5:4 [c] Ex. 22:22 **3:6** [a] [Rom. 11:29] [b] [Lam. 3:22]

THE STEADFAST WAY OF GOD

"For I am the LORD, I do not change . . . Return to Me, and I will return to you."

MALACHI 3:6-7

In his oracles Malachi hammered away at the priesthood to return to the knowledge of God and His ways of peace and justice. The prophet warned the priests that a day of reckoning would come. The good news, however, is that God wanted to redeem His servants. He wanted them back on board, speaking truth and administrating justice. Through the prophet God said, "Return to Me, and I will return to you."

I find God's declaration very reassuring. God is not fickle. He remains steadfast and true. This passage is reflected in the thief on the cross, who had the boldness to simply say, "Lord, remember me when You come into Your kingdom" (Luke 23:42). Today, if you lack the peace of God, pray the thief's prayer and ask Jesus to "remember you." He promises He will in the Word of God through Malachi.

PEACE NOTE

When God promises *shalom*, He means it.

MALACHI 3:6

7 Yet from the days of [a]your fathers
You have gone away from My ordinances
And have not kept *them*.
[b]Return to Me, and I will return to you,"
Says the LORD of hosts.
[c]"But you said,
'In what way shall we return?'

Do Not Rob God

8 "Will a man rob God?
Yet you have robbed Me!
But you say,
'In what way have we robbed You?'
[a]In tithes and offerings.
9 You are cursed with a curse,
For you have robbed Me,
Even this whole nation.
10 [a]Bring all the tithes into the [b]storehouse,
That there may be food in My house,
And try Me now in this,"
Says the LORD of hosts,
"If I will not open for you the [c]windows
of heaven
And [d]pour out for you *such* blessing
That *there will* not *be room* enough *to receive it.*

11 "And I will rebuke [a]the devourer for
your sakes,
So that he will not destroy the fruit of
your ground,
Nor shall the vine fail to bear fruit for
you in the field,"
Says the LORD of hosts;
12 "And all nations will call you blessed,
For you will be [a]a delightful land,"
Says the LORD of hosts.

The People Complain Harshly

13 "Your[a] words have been harsh against Me,"
Says the LORD,
"Yet you say,
'What have we spoken against You?'
14 [a]You have said,
'It is useless to serve God;
What profit *is it* that we have kept His
ordinance,
And that we have walked as mourners
Before the LORD of hosts?

3:7 [a] Acts 7:51 [b] Zech. 1:3 [c] Mal. 1:6 **3:8** [a] Neh. 13:10–12 **3:10** [a] Prov. 3:9, 10 [b] 1 Chr. 26:20 [c] Gen. 7:11 [d] 2 Chr. 31:10
3:11 [a] Amos 4:9 **3:12** [a] Dan. 8:9 **3:13** [a] Mal. 2:17 **3:14** [a] Job 21:14

TURN YOUR HEART TO PEACE

"Behold, I will send you Elijah the prophet . . . He will turn the hearts of the fathers to the children."

MALACHI 4:5-6

God commissioned Malachi to prepare Israel's backslid priests for the coming day of judgment. They would be wise to listen. But it was Elijah himself who came and began God's redemptive ministry to a lost world. Malachi said, "He will turn the hearts of the fathers to the children." In Hebrew the word for "turn" or "return" is *shuv*. It also means "repent." Elijah would initiate a season of repentance.

John the Baptist came in fulfillment of this prophecy, calling for repentance and baptizing all who came to him (see Matt. 3:1–12). In doing these things he prepared the way for the Lord. Then Jesus appeared, announcing the Good News of the kingdom of God (see Matt. 4:17). Repentance—returning to God—makes peace possible. To acquire God's peace requires preparation, and that preparation is repentance.

Have you pursued God's peace without first repenting?

15 So now [a]we call the proud blessed,
For those who do wickedness are raised up;
They even [b]tempt God and go free.' "

A Book of Remembrance

16 Then those [a]who feared the LORD [b]spoke to one another,
And the LORD listened and heard *them;*
So [c]a book of remembrance was written before Him
For those who fear the LORD
And who meditate on His name.

17 "They[a] shall be Mine," says the LORD of hosts,
"On the day that I make them My [b]jewels.[1]
And [c]I will spare them
As a man spares his own son who serves him."
18 [a]Then you shall again discern
Between the righteous and the wicked,
Between one who serves God
And one who does not serve Him.

The Great Day of God

4 "For behold, [a]the day is coming,
Burning like an oven,
And all [b]the proud, yes, all who do wickedly will be [c]stubble.
And the day which is coming shall burn them up,"
Says the LORD of hosts,
"That will [d]leave them neither root nor branch.
2 But to you who [a]fear My name
The [b]Sun of Righteousness shall arise
With healing in His wings;
And you shall go out
And grow fat like stall-fed calves.
3 [a]You shall trample the wicked,
For they shall be ashes under the soles of your feet
On the day that I do *this,*"
Says the LORD of hosts.

4 "Remember the [a]Law of Moses, My servant,
Which I commanded him in Horeb for all Israel,
With [b]*the* statutes and judgments.
5 Behold, I will send you [a]Elijah the prophet
[b]Before the coming of the great and dreadful day of the LORD.
6 And [a]he will turn
The hearts of the fathers to the children,
And the hearts of the children to their fathers,
Lest I come and [b]strike the earth with [c]a curse."

3:15 [a] Ps. 73:12 [b] Ps. 95:9 3:16 [a] Ps. 66:16 [b] Heb. 3:13 [c] Ps. 56:8 3:17 [a] Ex. 19:5 [b] Is. 62:3 [c] Ps. 103:13 [1] Literally *special treasure* 3:18 [a] [Ps. 58:11] 4:1 [a] [2 Pet. 3:7] [b] Mal. 3:18 [c] Obad. 18 [d] Amos 2:9 4:2 [a] Mal. 3:16 [b] Luke 1:78 4:3 [a] Mic. 7:10 4:4 [a] Ex. 20:3 [b] Deut. 4:10 4:5 [a] [Matt. 11:14; 17:10–13; Mark 9:11–13; Luke 1:17]; John 1:21 [b] Joel 2:31 4:6 [a] Luke 1:17 [b] Zech. 14:12 [c] Zech. 5:3

THE NEW TESTAMENT

WORDS OF CHRIST IN RED

THE GOSPEL ACCORDING TO

MATTHEW

AUTHOR

The early church uniformly attributed this Gospel to Matthew, and no tradition to the contrary ever emerged. This book was known early and accepted quickly. Matthew occupied the unpopular post of tax collector for the Roman government in Capernaum, and as a result, he was no doubt disliked by his Jewish countrymen. He was chosen as one of the twelve apostles, and the last appearance of his name in the Bible is in Acts 1:13. Matthew's life from that point on is veiled in tradition.

TIME

c. 4 BC–AD 33

KEY VERSE

Matthew 16:16–19

THEME

Matthew is typically described as the story of Jesus written by a Jew for Jewish people. In this context it contains the most references to Jewish culture and the Old Testament of the Gospels. The author's main purpose seems to be proving to his Jewish readers that Jesus is their Messiah. Matthew is also the fullest systematic account of Christ's teachings. These five "blocks" of teaching are one of the key differences from the other Gospels: chapters 5–7, the Sermon on the Mount; chapter 10, the Mission Charge; chapter 13, the Parables of the Kingdom; chapter 18, the Church; chapters 23–25, Judgment and the End of the Age.

In Jesus' ministry and teaching, we often find the word *peace* used in its Old Testament sense of completion and wholeness. Jesus taught that peace *with* God will result in the peace *of* God, and "everyone who is of the truth hears My voice" (John 18:37). In Matthew's Gospel we learn that when Jesus commissioned His apostles to go throughout Israel preaching the Good News of the kingdom of God, He instructed them in how to respond to rejection: "If the household is worthy," Jesus said, "let your peace come upon it. But if it is not worthy, let your peace return to you" (Matt. 10:13). What does Jesus mean by "peace" in this context? Obviously He did not mean the absence of conflict or the end of war. The idea that Jesus' peace can remain on a house (that is, on the people who live in the house—which then meant an extended family) implies something almost tangible about the *shalom* that Jesus offers to every home and family. The peace of God experienced is summed up by Matthew in 6:33, "But seek first the kingdom of God and His righteousness, and all these things shall be added to you."

The Genealogy of Jesus Christ

1 The book of the [a]genealogy of Jesus Christ,
[b]the Son of David, [c]the Son of Abraham:
2 [a]Abraham begot Isaac, [b]Isaac begot Jacob,
and Jacob begot [c]Judah and his brothers.
3 [a]Judah begot Perez and Zerah by Tamar,
[b]Perez begot Hezron, and Hezron begot Ram.
4 Ram begot Amminadab, Amminadab begot Nahshon, and Nahshon begot Salmon.
5 Salmon begot [a]Boaz by Rahab, Boaz begot
Obed by Ruth, Obed begot Jesse, 6 and [a]Jesse
begot David the king.
[b]David the king begot Solomon by her *who
had been the wife*[1] of Uriah. 7 [a]Solomon begot
Rehoboam, Rehoboam begot [b]Abijah, and
Abijah begot Asa.[1] 8 Asa begot [a]Jehoshaphat,
Jehoshaphat begot Joram, and Joram begot
[b]Uzziah. 9 Uzziah begot Jotham, Jotham begot
[a]Ahaz, and Ahaz begot Hezekiah. 10 [a]Hezekiah
begot Manasseh, Manasseh begot Amon,[1] and
Amon begot [b]Josiah. 11 [a]Josiah begot Jeconiah
and his brothers about the time they were
[b]carried away to Babylon.
12 And after they were brought to Babylon,
[a]Jeconiah begot Shealtiel, and Shealtiel begot [b]Zerubbabel. 13 Zerubbabel begot Abiud,
Abiud begot Eliakim, and Eliakim begot Azor.
14 Azor begot Zadok, Zadok begot Achim, and
Achim begot Eliud. 15 Eliud begot Eleazar,
Eleazar begot Matthan, and Matthan begot
Jacob. 16 And Jacob begot Joseph the husband
of [a]Mary, of whom was born Jesus who is
called Christ.
17 So all the generations from Abraham to
David *are* fourteen generations, from David
until the captivity in Babylon *are* fourteen
generations, and from the captivity in Babylon until the Christ *are* fourteen generations.

Christ Born of Mary

18 Now the [a]birth of Jesus Christ was as follows: After His mother Mary was betrothed to
Joseph, before they came together, she was
found with child [b]of the Holy Spirit. 19 Then
Joseph her husband, being a just *man,* and
not wanting [a]to make her a public example,
was minded to put her away secretly. 20 But
while he thought about these things, behold,
an angel of the Lord appeared to him in a
dream, saying, "Joseph, son of David, do not
be afraid to take to you Mary your wife, [a]for
that which is conceived in her is of the Holy
Spirit. 21 [a]And she will bring forth a Son, and
you shall call His name JESUS, [b]for He will
save His people from their sins."
22 So all this was done that it might be fulfilled which was spoken by the Lord through
the prophet, saying: 23 [a]"Behold, the virgin

1:1 [a] Luke 3:23 [b] John 7:42 [c] Gen. 12:3; 22:18 **1:2** [a] Gen. 21:2, 12 [b] Gen. 25:26; 28:14 [c] Gen. 29:35 **1:3** [a] Gen. 38:27; 49:10 [b] Ruth 4:18–22 **1:5** [a] Ruth 2:1; 4:1–13 **1:6** [a] 1 Sam. 16:1 [b] 2 Sam. 7:12; 12:24 [1] Words in italic type have been added for clarity. They are not found in the original Greek. **1:7** [a] 1 Chr. 3:10 [b] 2 Chr. 11:20 [1] NU-Text reads *Asaph.* **1:8** [a] 1 Chr. 3:10 [b] 2 Kin. 15:13 **1:9** [a] 2 Kin. 15:38 **1:10** [a] 2 Kin. 20:21 [b] 1 Kin. 13:2 [1] NU-Text reads *Amos.* **1:11** [a] 1 Chr. 3:15, 16 [b] 2 Kin. 24:14–16 **1:12** [a] 1 Chr. 3:17 [b] Ezra 3:2 **1:16** [a] Matt. 13:55 **1:18** [a] Luke 1:27 [b] Luke 1:35 **1:19** [a] Deut. 24:1 **1:20** [a] Luke 1:35 **1:21** [a] Luke 1:31; 2:21 [b] John 1:29 **1:23** [a] Is. 7:14

THE SAVIOR HAS ARRIVED!

And she will bring forth a Son, and you shall call His name JESUS, for He will save His people from their sins.

MATTHEW 1:21

People love hearing birth announcements. Something about them makes us smile and reminds us that life goes on, that there is a future. When a family hears the words, "I'm expecting," they rejoice. But Mary's being found with child *before* her wedding was no occasion for joy. Joseph's consternation was understandable. He decided to break off the engagement quietly so as not to shame Mary. But God directed him otherwise, explaining that Mary, his betrothed, would "bring forth a Son, and you shall call His name JESUS, for He will save His people from their sins."

What a birth announcement! Joseph and Mary were promised a Son. They were to name *Him Jesus (Hebrew, Yeshua)*, which means "The Lord Saves." The angel did not tell Joseph that Jesus would save Israel from the Romans. No, God knows what people truly need. Sin is the enemy, and it needs to be vanquished if we are to find peace with God. Ask Jesus to forgive you today for any sin that may be preempting His peace in your life.

shall be with child, and bear a Son, and they
shall call His name Immanuel,"[1] which is
translated, "God with us."
24Then Joseph, being aroused from sleep,
did as the angel of the Lord commanded him
and took to him his wife, 25and did not know
her till she had brought forth [a]her firstborn
Son.[1] And he called His name JESUS.

Wise Men from the East

2 Now after [a]Jesus was born in Bethlehem
of Judea in the days of Herod the king,
behold, wise men [b]from the East came to
Jerusalem, 2saying, [a]"Where is He who has
been born King of the Jews? For we have
seen [b]His star in the East and have come to
worship Him."
3When Herod the king heard *this,* he was
troubled, and all Jerusalem with him. 4And
when he had gathered all [a]the chief priests
and [b]scribes of the people together, [c]he inquired of them where the Christ was to be
born.
5So they said to him, "In Bethlehem of
Judea, for thus it is written by the prophet:

6 'But[a] you, Bethlehem, *in* the land of
Judah,
Are not the least among the rulers of
Judah;
For out of you shall come a Ruler
[b]Who will shepherd My people
Israel.' "[1]

7Then Herod, when he had secretly called
the wise men, determined from them what
time the [a]star appeared. 8And he sent them
to Bethlehem and said, "Go and search carefully for the young Child, and when you have
found *Him,* bring back word to me, that I may
come and worship Him also."
9When they heard the king, they departed;
and behold, the star which they had seen
in the East went before them, till it came
and stood over where the young Child was.
10When they saw the star, they rejoiced with
exceedingly great joy. 11And when they had
come into the house, they saw the young
Child with Mary His mother, and fell down
and worshiped Him. And when they had
opened their treasures, [a]they presented gifts
to Him: gold, frankincense, and myrrh.
12Then, being divinely warned [a]in a dream
that they should not return to Herod, they
departed for their own country another way.

The Flight into Egypt

13Now when they had departed, behold,
an angel of the Lord appeared to Joseph in
a dream, saying, "Arise, take the young Child
and His mother, flee to Egypt, and stay there
until I bring you word; for Herod will seek
the young Child to destroy Him."
14When he arose, he took the young Child
and His mother by night and departed for
Egypt, 15and was there until the death of
Herod, that it might be fulfilled which was

1:23 [1] Isaiah 7:14 **1:25** [a] Luke 2:7, 21 [1] NU-Text reads *a Son.* **2:1** [a] Mic. 5:2; Luke 2:4 [b] Gen. 25:6 **2:2** [a] Luke 2:11 [b] [Num. 24:17] **2:4** [a] 2 Chr. 36:14 [b] 2 Chr. 34:13 [c] Mal. 2:7 **2:6** [a] Mic. 5:2 [b] [Rev. 2:27] [1] Micah 5:2 **2:7** [a] Num. 24:17 **2:11** [a] Is. 60:6 **2:12** [a] Matt. 1:20

THE ULTIMATE PEACE GIFT

I indeed baptize you with water unto repentance, but He who is coming after me is mightier than I . . . He will baptize you with the Holy Spirit and fire.

MATTHEW 3:11

John the Baptist came on the scene to fulfill Malachi's prophecy (Mal. 3:1; 4:5–6). He had good news to proclaim: "The kingdom of heaven is at hand!" (Matt. 3:1). But this good news required repentance, so John invited all to come and be baptized as a sign of their spiritual renewal. John said, "I indeed baptize you with water unto repentance, but He who is coming after me is mightier than I . . . He will baptize you with the Holy Spirit and fire" (Matt. 3:11). John's water baptism prepares the repentant person for the Giver of the Holy Spirit and the Spirit's cleansing fire (John 20:22; Acts 2:3–4).

Jesus, who "is mightier than" (Matt. 3:11) John, will save us from the consequences of sin, which is separation from God. Through His saving work, Jesus brings us back to God and makes genuine peace a reality. Take a moment to thank God for salvation and, if you have not, accept this gift of His forgiveness and eternal life.

spoken by the Lord through the prophet,
saying, [a]"Out of Egypt I called My Son."[1]

Massacre of the Innocents

16 Then Herod, when he saw that he was
deceived by the wise men, was exceedingly
angry; and he sent forth and put to death all
the male children who were in Bethlehem
and in all its districts, from two years old
and under, according to the time which he
had determined from the wise men. 17 Then
was fulfilled what was spoken by Jeremiah
the prophet, saying:

18 "A [a]voice was heard in Ramah,
Lamentation, weeping, and great
mourning,
Rachel weeping *for* her children,
Refusing to be comforted,
Because they are no more."[1]

The Home in Nazareth

19 Now when Herod was dead, behold, an
angel of the Lord appeared in a dream to
Joseph in Egypt, 20 [a]saying, "Arise, take the
young Child and His mother, and go to the
land of Israel, for those who [b]sought the
young Child's life are dead." 21 Then he arose,
took the young Child and His mother, and
came into the land of Israel.
22 But when he heard that Archelaus was
reigning over Judea instead of his father
Herod, he was afraid to go there. And being
warned by God in a [a]dream, he turned aside
[b]into the region of Galilee. 23 And he came
and dwelt in a city called [a]Nazareth, that it
might be fulfilled [b]which was spoken by the
prophets, "He shall be called a Nazarene."

John the Baptist Prepares the Way

3 In those days [a]John the Baptist came
preaching [b]in the wilderness of Judea,
2 and saying, "Repent, for [a]the kingdom of
heaven is at hand!" 3 For this is he who was
spoken of by the prophet Isaiah, saying:

[a]"The voice of one crying in the
wilderness:
[b]'Prepare the way of the LORD;
Make His paths straight.'"[1]

4 Now [a]John himself was clothed in camel's
hair, with a leather belt around his waist;
and his food was [b]locusts and [c]wild honey. 5 [a]Then Jerusalem, all Judea, and all the
region around the Jordan went out to him
6 [a]and were baptized by him in the Jordan,
confessing their sins.
7 But when he saw many of the Pharisees
and Sadducees coming to his baptism, he
said to them, [a]"Brood of vipers! Who warned
you to flee from [b]the wrath to come? 8 Therefore bear fruits worthy of repentance, 9 and
do not think to say to yourselves, [a]'We have

2:15 [a] Hos. 11:1 [1] Hosea 11:1 2:18 [a] Jer. 31:15 [1] Jeremiah 31:15 2:20 [a] Luke 2:39 [b] Matt. 2:16 2:22 [a] Matt. 2:12, 13, 19 [b] Luke 2:39 2:23 [a] John 1:45, 46 [b] Judg. 13:5 3:1 [a] Mark 1:3–8 [b] Josh. 14:10 3:2 [a] Dan. 2:44 3:3 [a] Is. 40:3 [b] Luke 1:76 [1] Isaiah 40:3 3:4 [a] Mark 1:6 [b] Lev. 11:22 [c] 1 Sam. 14:25, 26 3:5 [a] Mark 1:5 3:6 [a] Acts 19:4, 18 3:7 [a] Matt. 12:34 [b] [1 Thess. 1:10] 3:9 [a] John 8:33

EMPOWERED FOR PEACE

"This is My beloved Son, in whom I am well pleased."

MATTHEW 3:17

With these words it wasn't John the Baptist who recognized Jesus, it was God Himself. When Jesus emerged from the waters of baptism, the voice from heaven declared, "This is My beloved Son, in whom I am well pleased." The ancient rabbis believed that when something legitimately important was said or done, God would speak to confirm it. This is what happened at the baptism of Jesus. And what He spoke confirmed the prophetic Psalm 2, written and sung back in the days of David: "I will declare the decree: The LORD has said to Me, 'You are My Son, today I have begotten You'" (Ps. 2:7).

Matthew's early readers would have instantly seen the importance of the words spoken at the baptism. Jesus had been identified as the Lord's unique Son. Who else can save us from our sins? David saved his people from the Philistines, but his great descendant, the Son of God, saves us from sin and separation from God! Review the difficult temptations confronting you today, and then ask the Lord to empower you with His peace to face them down with holiness.

Abraham as *our* father.' For I say to you that
God is able to raise up children to Abraham
from these stones. 10 And even now the ax is
laid to the root of the trees. [a]Therefore every
tree which does not bear good fruit is cut
down and thrown into the fire. 11 [a]I indeed
baptize you with water unto repentance,
but He who is coming after me is mightier
than I, whose sandals I am not worthy to
carry. [b]He will baptize you with the Holy
Spirit and fire.[1] 12 [a]His winnowing fan *is* in
His hand, and He will thoroughly clean out
His threshing floor, and gather His wheat
into the barn; but He will [b]burn up the chaff
with unquenchable fire."

John Baptizes Jesus

13 [a]Then Jesus came [b]from Galilee to John at
the Jordan to be baptized by him. 14 And John
tried to prevent Him, saying, "I need to be
baptized by You, and are You coming to me?"
15 But Jesus answered and said to him,
"Permit *it to be so* now, for thus it is fitting
for us to fulfill all righteousness." Then he
allowed Him.
16 [a]When He had been baptized, Jesus came
up immediately from the water; and behold,
the heavens were opened to Him, and He[1]
saw [b]the Spirit of God descending like a dove
and alighting upon Him. 17 [a]And suddenly a
voice *came* from heaven, saying, [b]"This is
My beloved Son, in whom I am well pleased."

Satan Tempts Jesus

4 Then [a]Jesus was led up by [b]the Spirit into
the wilderness to be tempted by the devil.
2 And when He had fasted forty days and forty
nights, afterward He was hungry. 3 Now when
the tempter came to Him, he said, "If You are
the Son of God, command that these stones
become bread."
4 But He answered and said, "It is written,
[a]'Man shall not live by bread alone, but by every
word that proceeds from the mouth of God.' "[1]
5 Then the devil took Him up [a]into the holy
city, set Him on the pinnacle of the temple,
6 and said to Him, "If You are the Son of God,
throw Yourself down. For it is written:

> [a]'He shall give His angels charge over
> you,'

and,

> [b]'In *their* hands they shall bear you up,
> Lest you dash your foot against a
> stone.' "[1]

7 Jesus said to him, "It is written again,
[a]'You shall not tempt the LORD your God.' "[1]

3:10 [a] Matt. 7:19 **3:11** [a] Luke 3:16 [b] [Acts 2:3, 4] [1] M-Text omits *and fire.* **3:12** [a] Mal. 3:3 [b] Matt. 13:30 **3:13** [a] Mark 1:9–11 [b] Matt. 2:22 **3:16** [a] Mark 1:10 [b] [Is. 11:2]; John 1:32 [1] Or *he* **3:17** [a] John 12:28 [b] Ps. 2:7 **4:1** [a] Mark 1:12 [b] Ezek. 3:14 **4:4** [a] Deut. 8:3 [1] Deuteronomy 8:3 **4:5** [a] Neh. 11:1, 18 **4:6** [a] Ps. 91:11 [b] Ps. 91:12 [1] Psalm 91:11, 12 **4:7** [a] Deut. 6:16 [1] Deuteronomy 6:16

TRUE TO THE MISSION

Then Jesus said to him, "Away with you, Satan! For it is written, 'You shall worship the LORD your God, and Him only you shall serve.'"

MATTHEW 4:10

After His baptism, Jesus went into the desert, where Satan tried to tempt Him. The devil threw at Jesus three pretty serious temptations. First, because Jesus had been fasting and was hungry, Satan suggested that Jesus prove His divine sonship by turning stones into bread. It was a wickedly clever idea. How could turning stones into bread be a bad thing? Next, Satan suggested that Jesus prove His faith in God by casting Himself off the pinnacle of the temple. Finally, Satan offered Jesus the kingdoms of the world if He would just fall down and worship him. That, of course, was the big one!

Had Jesus yielded to the third temptation, to achieve what most Israelites of His time hoped for, His ministry would have been ruined and His divine sonship called into question. To all three temptations Jesus replied with Scripture and said No! Have you wondered what might have been, had Jesus given in? There would have been no forgiveness of sins, no salvation, no reconciliation with God, and no peace. Jesus remained true to His mission of redemption in order to purchase your peace. Now is a wonderful moment to pause and worship Him and thank Him for His steadfast love toward you.

8 Again, the devil took Him up on an exceedingly high mountain, and [a]showed Him
all the kingdoms of the world and their glory.
9 And he said to Him, "All these things I will
give You if You will fall down and worship me."
10 Then Jesus said to him, "Away with you,[1]
Satan! For it is written, [a]'You shall worship
the LORD your God, and Him only you shall
serve.' "[2]
11 Then the devil [a]left Him, and behold,
[b]angels came and ministered to Him.

Jesus Begins His Galilean Ministry

12 [a]Now when Jesus heard that John had
been put in prison, He departed to Galilee.
13 And leaving Nazareth, He came and dwelt
in Capernaum, which is by the sea, in the
regions of Zebulun and Naphtali, 14 that it
might be fulfilled which was spoken by Isaiah the prophet, saying:

15 "The[a] land of Zebulun and the land of
Naphtali,
By the way of the sea, beyond the
Jordan,
Galilee of the Gentiles:
16 [a]The people who sat in darkness have
seen a great light,
And upon those who sat in the region
and shadow of death
Light has dawned."[1]

17 [a]From that time Jesus began to preach
and to say, [b]"Repent, for the kingdom of
heaven is at hand."

Four Fishermen Called as Disciples

18 [a]And Jesus, walking by the Sea of Galilee, saw two brothers, Simon [b]called Peter,
and Andrew his brother, casting a net into
the sea; for they were fishermen. 19 Then He
said to them, "Follow Me, and [a]I will make
you fishers of men." 20 [a]They immediately
left *their* nets and followed Him.
21 [a]Going on from there, He saw two other
brothers, James *the son* of Zebedee, and John
his brother, in the boat with Zebedee their
father, mending their nets. He called them,
22 and immediately they left the boat and
their father, and followed Him.

Jesus Heals a Great Multitude

23 And Jesus went about all Galilee, [a]teach-
ing in their synagogues, preaching [b]the
gospel of the kingdom, [c]and healing all
kinds of sickness and all kinds of disease
among the people. 24 Then His fame went
throughout all Syria; and they [a]brought to
Him all sick people who were afflicted with
various diseases and torments, and those
who were demon-possessed, epileptics, and
paralytics; and He healed them. 25 [a]Great
multitudes followed Him—from Galilee,

4:8 [a] [1 John 2:15–17] **4:10** [a] Deut. 6:13; 10:20 [1] M-Text reads *Get behind Me.* [2] Deuteronomy 6:13 **4:11** [a] [James 4:7] [b] [Heb. 1:14] **4:12** [a] John 4:43 **4:15** [a] Is. 9:1, 2 **4:16** [a] Luke 2:32 [1] Isaiah 9:1, 2 **4:17** [a] Mark 1:14, 15 [b] Matt. 3:2; 10:7 **4:18** [a] Mark 1:16–20 [b] John 1:40–42 **4:19** [a] Luke 5:10 **4:20** [a] Mark 10:28 **4:21** [a] Mark 1:19 **4:23** [a] Matt. 9:35 [b] [Matt. 24:14] [c] Mark 1:34 **4:24** [a] Luke 4:40 **4:25** [a] Mark 3:7, 8

FROM DEFLATED TO TRIUMPHANT

"Blessed are the poor in spirit."

MATTHEW 5:3

Jesus began His famous Sermon on the Mount with a series of beatitudes or statements of blessing. In the Old Testament we find a few passages where two beatitudes appear together, and among the Dead Sea Scrolls we find one passage that has a cluster of five or so beatitudes. The list Jesus articulated is the longest known in ancient Jewish literature. Depending on how you count them, there are as few as eight or as many as ten.

What makes Jesus' beatitudes so extraordinary is that they pronounce blessings on people who seem particularly lacking. At least in the eyes of the public, these people don't seem blessed. The first one says, "Blessed are the poor in spirit, for theirs is the kingdom of heaven." What does "poor in spirit" mean? I suspect it means people who are deflated emotionally. They have little optimism. I doubt they *feel* blessed. But they are, said Jesus. Why? Because they have nothing in their lives that will prevent them from entering the kingdom of heaven—or from engaging God's wonderful peace! Take the circumstances that are trying to deflate you and allow the light and peace of Christ to change your view of them. Let your heart find comfort.

and *from* Decapolis, Jerusalem, Judea, and beyond the Jordan.

The Beatitudes

5 And seeing the multitudes, [a]He went up on a mountain, and when He was seated His disciples came to Him. 2Then He opened His mouth and [a]taught them, saying:

3 "Blessed[a] *are* the poor in spirit,
For theirs is the kingdom of heaven.
4 [a]Blessed *are* those who mourn,
For they shall be comforted.
5 [a]Blessed *are* the meek,
For [b]they shall inherit the earth.
6 Blessed *are* those who [a]hunger and thirst for righteousness,
[b]For they shall be filled.
7 Blessed *are* the merciful,
[a]For they shall obtain mercy.
8 [a]Blessed *are* the pure in heart,
For [b]they shall see God.
9 Blessed *are* the peacemakers,
For they shall be called sons of God.
10 [a]Blessed *are* those who are persecuted for righteousness' sake,
For theirs is the kingdom of heaven.

PEACE NOTE

Jesus' Sermon on the Mount is a theological blueprint instructing us in peace and happiness (*shalom*) that is sorely lacking in so many Christian lives today.

MATTHEW 5:2

11[a]Blessed are you when they revile and persecute you, and say all kinds of [b]evil against
you falsely for My sake. 12[a]Rejoice and be
exceedingly glad, for great *is* your reward in
heaven, for [b]so they persecuted the prophets
who were before you.

Believers Are Salt and Light

13"You are the salt of the earth; [a]but if the
salt loses its flavor, how shall it be seasoned?
It is then good for nothing but to be thrown
out and trampled underfoot by men.
14[a]"You are the light of the world. A city
that is set on a hill cannot be hidden. 15Nor do
they [a]light a lamp and put it under a basket,
but on a lampstand, and it gives light to all
who are in the house. 16Let your light so shine
before men, [a]that they may see your good
works and [b]glorify your Father in heaven.

Christ Fulfills the Law

17[a]"Do not think that I came to destroy the
Law or the Prophets. I did not come to destroy

5:1 [a] Mark 3:13 **5:2** [a] [Matt. 7:29] **5:3** [a] Luke 6:20–23 **5:4** [a] Rev. 21:4 **5:5** [a] Ps. 37:11 [b] [Rom. 4:13] **5:6** [a] Luke 1:53 [b] [Is. 55:1; 65:13] **5:7** [a] Ps. 41:1 **5:8** [a] Ps. 15:2; 24:4 [b] 1 Cor. 13:12 **5:10** [a] 1 Pet. 3:14 **5:11** [a] Luke 6:22 [b] 1 Pet. 4:14 **5:12** [a] 1 Pet. 4:13, 14 [b] Acts 7:52 **5:13** [a] Luke 14:34 **5:14** [a] [John 8:12] **5:15** [a] Luke 8:16 **5:16** [a] 1 Pet. 2:12 [b] [John 15:8] **5:17** [a] Rom. 10:4

THE COMFORT FROM CHRIST

"Blessed are those who mourn, for they shall be comforted."

MATTHEW 5:4

Who feels blessed when they mourn? Do you feel fortunate at a funeral? I have read hundreds of epitaphs from antiquity, and few express joy. Many of the pagan epitaphs express unmitigated grief. "I am no more," some of these sad epitaphs declare. "Don't grieve. No one lives forever!" others say. "Here lies so-and-so. Nothing remains but a little ash." It is pitiful. There is no hope.

Must it be that way? Not at all, said Jesus. "Blessed are those who mourn, for they shall be comforted." Those who mourn will be comforted because *there is hope*. The good news is that redemption and salvation are possible. We can be reconciled to God, and death will not have the last word! Our hope in Christ provides the antidote to mourning because He comforts us at the worst moments of our lives. Be honest today with God and tell Him what is bringing grief to your heart so you can receive His comforting peace in return.

PEACE NOTE

The happy were enjoined to "rejoice and be exceedingly glad" because they stood in the company of the prophets. The obedient prophets enjoyed happy relationships with God.

MATTHEW 5:12

but to fulfill. 18 For assuredly, I say to you, [a]till
heaven and earth pass away, one jot or one
tittle will by no means pass from the law till
all is fulfilled. 19 [a]Whoever therefore breaks
one of the least of these commandments,
and teaches men so, shall be called least in
the kingdom of heaven; but whoever does
and teaches *them,* he shall be called great in
the kingdom of heaven. 20 For I say to you,
that unless your righteousness exceeds [a]*the
righteousness* of the scribes and Pharisees, you
will by no means enter the kingdom of heaven.

Murder Begins in the Heart

21 "You have heard that it was said to those
of old, [a]'You shall not murder,'[1] and whoever
murders will be in danger of the judgment.'
22 But I say to you that [a]whoever is angry
with his brother without a cause[1] shall be in
danger of the judgment. And whoever says
to his brother, [b]'Raca!' shall be in danger of
the council. But whoever says, 'You fool!'
shall be in danger of hell fire. 23 Therefore
[a]if you bring your gift to the altar, and there
remember that your brother has something
against you, 24 [a]leave your gift there before
the altar, and go your way. First be reconciled to your brother, and then come and
offer your gift. 25 [a]Agree with your adversary
quickly, [b]while you are on the way with him,
lest your adversary deliver you to the judge,
the judge hand you over to the officer, and
you be thrown into prison. 26 Assuredly, I say
to you, you will by no means get out of there
till you have paid the last penny.

Adultery in the Heart

27 "You have heard that it was said to those
of old,[1] [a]'You shall not commit adultery.'[2]
28 But I say to you that whoever [a]looks at a
woman to lust for her has already committed
adultery with her in his heart. 29 [a]If your right
eye causes you to sin, [b]pluck it out and cast
it from you; for it is more profitable for you

5:18 [a] Luke 16:17 **5:19** [a] [James 2:10] **5:20** [a] [Rom. 10:3] **5:21** [a] Ex. 20:13; Deut. 5:17 [1] Exodus 20:13; Deuteronomy 5:17 **5:22** [a] [1 John 3:15] [b] [James 2:20; 3:6] [1] NU-Text omits *without a cause.* **5:23** [a] Matt. 8:4 **5:24** [a] [Job 42:8] **5:25** [a] Luke 12:58, 59 [b] [Is. 55:6] **5:27** [a] Ex. 20:14; Deut. 5:18 [1] NU-Text and M-Text omit *to those of old.* [2] Exodus 20:14; Deuteronomy 5:18 **5:28** [a] Prov. 6:25 **5:29** [a] Mark 9:43 [b] [Col. 3:5]

THE BLESSING OF MEEKNESS

"Blessed are the meek, for they shall inherit the earth."

MATTHEW 5:5

According to the wisdom of the ancients (and probably moderns too), the meek quake before the strong and aggressive. The meek are bullied. They are pushed around. And in a world where "might makes right" is the norm, the meek usually don't inherit anything. It was somewhat different in Israel—or at least it was supposed to be. The law of Moses protected the vulnerable and powerless. But the influential and powerful didn't follow Moses' law in Jesus' day.

Contrary to the wisdom of the age, Jesus pronounced, "Blessed are the meek, for they shall inherit the earth." His third beatitude echoed Psalm 37:9–11, where the psalmist predicted that "evildoers shall be cut off" (v. 9), the wicked shall disappear, and "the meek *shall inherit the earth*" (v. 11). Jesus agreed. The meek are blessed. Why? Because the era of the Holy Spirit had come; redemption and renewal were under way. All of us—the meek included—have reason to hope because we can rely on the strength of God and the peace offered by His rulership.

that one of your members perish, than for
your whole body to be cast into hell. 30And
if your right hand causes you to sin, cut it off
and cast *it* from you; for it is more profitable
for you that one of your members perish,
than for your whole body to be cast into hell.

Marriage Is Sacred and Binding

31"Furthermore it has been said, [a]'Whoever
divorces his wife, let him give her a certificate
of divorce.' 32But I say to you that [a]whoever
divorces his wife for any reason except sexual
immorality[1] causes her to commit adultery;
and whoever marries a woman who is divorced commits adultery.

Jesus Forbids Oaths

33"Again you have heard that [a]it was said
to those of old, [b]'You shall not swear falsely,
but [c]shall perform your oaths to the Lord.'
34But I say to you, [a]do not swear at all: neither
by heaven, for it is [b]God's throne; 35nor by
the earth, for it is His footstool; nor by Jerusalem, for it is the city of [a]the great King.
36Nor shall you swear by your head, because
you cannot make one hair white or black.
37[a]But let your 'Yes' be 'Yes,' and your 'No,'
'No.' For whatever is more than these is from
the evil one.

Go the Second Mile

38"You have heard that it was said, [a]'An eye
for an eye and a tooth for a tooth.'[1] 39[a]But I tell
you not to resist an evil person. [b]But whoever
slaps you on your right cheek, turn the other
to him also. 40If anyone wants to sue you
and take away your tunic, let him have *your*
cloak also. 41And whoever [a]compels you to
go one mile, go with him two. 42Give to him
who asks you, and [a]from him who wants to
borrow from you do not turn away.

Love Your Enemies

43"You have heard that it was said, [a]'You
shall love your neighbor[1] [b]and hate your
enemy.' 44But I say to you, [a]love your enemies, bless those who curse you, [b]do good to
those who hate you, and pray [c]for those who
spitefully use you and persecute you,[1] 45that
you may be sons of your Father in heaven;
for [a]He makes His sun rise on the evil and on
the good, and sends rain on the just and on
the unjust. 46[a]For if you love those who love
you, what reward have you? Do not even the
tax collectors do the same? 47And if you greet
your brethren[1] only, what do you do more
than others? Do not even the tax collectors[2]
do so? 48[a]Therefore you shall be perfect, just
[b]as your Father in heaven is perfect.

5:31 [a] Deut. 24:1 **5:32** [a] [Luke 16:18] [1] Or *fornication* **5:33** [a] Matt. 23:16 [b] Lev. 19:12 [c] Deut. 23:23 **5:34** [a] James 5:12 [b] Is. 66:1 **5:35** [a] Ps. 48:2 **5:37** [a] [Col. 4:6] **5:38** [a] Ex. 21:24; Lev. 24:20; Deut. 19:21 [1] Exodus 21:24; Leviticus 24:20; Deuteronomy 19:21 **5:39** [a] Luke 6:29 [b] Is. 50:6 **5:41** [a] Matt. 27:32 **5:42** [a] Luke 6:30–34 **5:43** [a] Lev. 19:18 [b] Deut. 23:3–6 [1] Compare Leviticus 19:18 **5:44** [a] Luke 6:27 [b] [Rom. 12:20] [c] Acts 7:60 [1] NU-Text omits three clauses from this verse, leaving, *"But I say to you, love your enemies and pray for those who persecute you."* **5:45** [a] Job 25:3 **5:46** [a] Luke 6:32 **5:47** [1] M-Text reads *friends.* [2] NU-Text reads *Gentiles.* **5:48** [a] [Col. 1:28; 4:12] [b] Eph. 5:1

HUNGRY FOR GOD'S GOODNESS

"Blessed are those who hunger and thirst for righteousness, for they shall be filled."

MATTHEW 5:6

The world of Jesus was a world of hunger. Most got enough to eat; many didn't. Hunger and malnutrition were common problems. Roman emperors curried the favor of the masses by offering free food and drink. The prophet Isaiah foresaw the arrival of God's kingdom as a great banquet in which all are offered food and drink at no cost (Is. 25:6; 55:1–2). On two occasions Jesus fed a multitude to reveal His divine ability to provide.

"Blessed are those who hunger and thirst for righteousness," Jesus said (Matt. 5:6). Why is that? Because "they shall be filled." Yes, the literal hungry and thirsty will receive food and drink in the kingdom of heaven, but it will be those who hunger and thirst for God's righteousness who will be truly and fully blessed.

Are you hungry for God and His holiness? That's where you will find true food (John 6:27). Today, when you think about what you lack, turn that sensation to an opportunity to praise God for His provision, both physical and spiritual. Don't forget to praise Him for His peace.

Do Good to Please God

6 "Take heed that you do not do your charitable deeds before men, to be seen by
them. Otherwise you have no reward from
your Father in heaven. 2Therefore, [a]when
you do a charitable deed, do not sound a
trumpet before you as the hypocrites do in
the synagogues and in the streets, that they
may have glory from men. Assuredly, I say to
you, they have their reward. 3But when you
do a charitable deed, do not let your left hand
know what your right hand is doing, 4that
your charitable deed may be in secret; and
your Father who sees in secret [a]will Himself
reward you openly.[1]

The Model Prayer

5"And when you pray, you shall not be like
the hypocrites. For they love to pray standing
in the synagogues and on the corners of the
streets, that they may be seen by men. Assuredly, I say to you, they have their reward.
6But you, when you pray, [a]go into your room,
and when you have shut your door, pray to
your Father who *is* in the secret *place;* and
your Father who sees in secret will reward
you openly.[1] 7And when you pray, [a]do not
use vain repetitions as the heathen *do.* [b]For
they think that they will be heard for their
many words.
8"Therefore do not be like them. For your
Father [a]knows the things you have need
of before you ask Him. 9In this [a]manner,
therefore, pray:

[b]Our Father in heaven,
Hallowed be Your [c]name.
10 Your kingdom come.
[a]Your will be done
On earth [b]as *it is* in heaven.
11 Give us this day our [a]daily bread.

PEACE NOTE

Happiness is a lifestyle. The happy know that Jesus does not want phony religion but requires sincere righteousness—which brings peace.

MATTHEW 6:1

6:2 [a] Rom. 12:8 6:4 [a] Luke 14:12–14 [1] NU-Text omits *openly.* 6:6 [a] 2 Kin. 4:33 [1] NU-Text omits *openly.* 6:7 [a] Eccl. 5:2 [b] 1 Kin. 18:26 6:8 [a] [Rom. 8:26, 27] 6:9 [a] Luke 11:2–4 [b] [Matt. 5:9, 16] [c] Mal. 1:11 6:10 [a] Matt. 26:42 [b] Ps. 103:20 6:11 [a] Prov. 30:8

MERCIFUL SOULS

"Blessed are the merciful, for they shall obtain mercy."

MATTHEW 5:7

When Jesus said, "Blessed are the merciful, for they shall obtain mercy," He echoed His own teaching in Luke 6:36: "Be merciful, just as your Father also is merciful." God's people are to be like God Himself, extending mercy to others. The Jewish people well remembered God's grace extended to them when He said to Moses, "The LORD, the LORD God, merciful and gracious, longsuffering, and abounding in goodness and truth, keeping mercy for thousands" (Ex. 34:6–7).

Jesus' promise is well founded. The kingdom of heaven has drawn near. The law of God will replace the oppressive and unjust laws of human societies that favor the wealthy and powerful. It will be the merciful who obtain mercy, not the violent and the wicked. Although the beatitude sounds a note of hope, it also implies a stern warning. Many of the Jewish authorities were not merciful, among them the ruling priests who lived in mansions in Jerusalem and opposed those who—like Jesus—called for reform and warned of coming judgment. Jesus' followers must resist the impulse to respond in anger. The way to peace is in extending mercy.

Where can you introduce mercy today?

12 And [a]forgive us our debts,
As we forgive our debtors.
13 [a]And do not lead us into temptation,
But [b]deliver us from the evil one.
For Yours is the kingdom and the
power and the glory forever. Amen.[1]

14[a]“For if you forgive men their trespasses, your heavenly Father will also forgive
you. 15But [a]if you do not forgive men their
trespasses, neither will your Father forgive
your trespasses.

Fasting to Be Seen Only by God

16“Moreover, [a]when you fast, do not be like
the hypocrites, with a sad countenance. For
they disfigure their faces that they may appear to men to be fasting. Assuredly, I say to
you, they have their reward. 17But you, when
you fast, [a]anoint your head and wash your
face, 18so that you do not appear to men to
be fasting, but to your Father who *is* in the
secret *place;* and your Father who sees in
secret will reward you openly.[1]

Lay Up Treasures in Heaven

19[a]“Do not lay up for yourselves treasures
on earth, where moth and rust destroy and
where thieves break in and steal; 20[a]but lay
up for yourselves treasures in heaven, where
neither moth nor rust destroys and where
thieves do not break in and steal. 21For where
your treasure is, there your heart will be also.

The Lamp of the Body

22[a]“The lamp of the body is the eye. If
therefore your eye is good, your whole body
will be full of light. 23But if your eye is bad,
your whole body will be full of darkness. If
therefore the light that is in you is darkness,
how great *is* that darkness!

You Cannot Serve God and Riches

24[a]“No one can serve two masters; for either he will hate the one and love the other, or
else he will be loyal to the one and despise the
other. [b]You cannot serve God and mammon.

Do Not Worry

25“Therefore I say to you, [a]do not worry
about your life, what you will eat or what
you will drink; nor about your body, what
you will put on. Is not life more than food
and the body more than clothing? 26[a]Look at
the birds of the air, for they neither sow nor
reap nor gather into barns; yet your heavenly
Father feeds them. Are you not of more value
than they? 27Which of you by worrying can
add one cubit to his stature?

28“So why do you worry about clothing?
Consider the lilies of the field, how they grow:
they neither toil nor spin; 29and yet I say to
you that even Solomon in all his glory was
not arrayed like one of these. 30Now if God so
clothes the grass of the field, which today is,
and tomorrow is thrown into the oven, *will He*
not much more *clothe* you, O you of little faith?

6:12 [a] [Matt. 18:21, 22] **6:13** [a] [2 Pet. 2:9] [b] John 17:15 [1] NU-Text omits *For Yours* through *Amen.* **6:14** [a] Mark 11:25 **6:15** [a] Matt. 18:35 **6:16** [a] Is. 58:3–7 **6:17** [a] Ruth 3:3 **6:18** [1] NU-Text and M-Text omit *openly.* **6:19** [a] Prov. 23:4 **6:20** [a] Matt. 19:21 **6:22** [a] Luke 11:34, 35 **6:24** [a] Luke 16:9, 11, 13 [b] [Gal. 1:10] **6:25** [a] Luke 12:22 **6:26** [a] Luke 12:24

TO SEE GOD AND HIS KINGDOM

“Blessed are the pure in heart, for they shall see God.”

MATTHEW 5:8

Moral purity seems to be scarcer than ever. It grieves me to see the steep moral decline in our society. The crude, blasphemous speech, the animalistic sexual ethics, our leaders’ cynicism, and the insane ideas expressed by people who ought to know better. I wonder where it will end.

I think this is why the sixth beatitude is my favorite. Jesus told His disciples, “Blessed are the pure in heart, for they shall see God.” Jesus once again alluded to the Book of Psalms. The psalmist asked, “Who may ascend into the hill of the LORD? Or who may stand in His holy place?” He answered his own question, “He who has clean hands and a pure heart” (Ps. 24:3–4).

Moses was told, “You cannot see My face; for no man shall see Me, and live” (Ex. 33:20). Yet, Jesus says, the pure in heart will enter the kingdom of heaven and will see God. I can’t wait! Ask the Lord to purify your heart today and grant you the peace that should live there.

31“Therefore do not worry, saying, ‘What
shall we eat?’ or ‘What shall we drink?’ or
‘What shall we wear?’ 32For after all these
things the Gentiles seek. For your heavenly
Father knows that you need all these things.
33But [a]seek first the kingdom of God and
His righteousness, and all these things shall
be added to you. 34Therefore do not worry
about tomorrow, for tomorrow will worry
about its own things. Sufficient for the day
is its own trouble.

Do Not Judge

7 “Judge [a]not, that you be not judged. 2For
with what judgment you judge, you will
be judged; [a]and with the measure you use, it
will be measured back to you. 3[a]And why do
you look at the speck in your brother’s eye,
but do not consider the plank in your own
eye? 4Or how can you say to your brother, ‘Let
me remove the speck from your eye’; and
look, a plank *is* in your own eye? 5Hypocrite!
First remove the plank from your own eye,
and then you will see clearly to remove the
speck from your brother’s eye.
6[a]“Do not give what is holy to the dogs;
nor cast your pearls before swine, lest they
trample them under their feet, and turn and
tear you in pieces.

Keep Asking, Seeking, Knocking

7[a]“Ask, and it will be given to you; seek, and
you will find; knock, and it will be opened to
you. 8For [a]everyone who asks receives, and
he who seeks finds, and to him who knocks it
will be opened. 9[a]Or what man is there among
you who, if his son asks for bread, will give
him a stone? 10Or if he asks for a fish, will he
give him a serpent? 11If you then, [a]being evil,
know how to give good gifts to your children,
how much more will your Father who is in
heaven give good things to those who ask
Him! 12Therefore, [a]whatever you want men
to do to you, do also to them, for [b]this is the
Law and the Prophets.

The Narrow Way

13[a]“Enter by the narrow gate; for wide *is*
the gate and broad *is* the way that leads to
destruction, and there are many who go in by
it. 14Because[1] narrow *is* the gate and difficult
is the way which leads to life, and there are
few who find it.

You Will Know Them by Their Fruits

15[a]“Beware of false prophets, [b]who come
to you in sheep’s clothing, but inwardly they
are ravenous wolves. 16[a]You will know them
by their fruits. [b]Do men gather grapes from
thornbushes or figs from thistles? 17Even so,
[a]every good tree bears good fruit, but a bad
tree bears bad fruit. 18A good tree cannot bear
bad fruit, nor *can* a bad tree bear good fruit.
19[a]Every tree that does not bear good fruit is
cut down and thrown into the fire. 20There-
fore by their fruits you will know them.

I Never Knew You

21“Not everyone who says to Me, [a]‘Lord,
Lord,’ shall enter the kingdom of heaven,

6:33 [a] [1 Tim. 4:8] **7:1** [a] Rom. 14:3 **7:2** [a] Luke 6:38 **7:3** [a] Luke 6:41 **7:6** [a] Prov. 9:7, 8 **7:7** [a] [Mark 11:24] **7:8** [a] Prov. 8:17 **7:9** [a] Luke 11:11 **7:11** [a] Gen. 6:5; 8:21 **7:12** [a] Luke 6:31 [b] Gal. 5:14 **7:13** [a] Luke 13:24 **7:14** [1] NU-Text and M-Text read *How . . . !* **7:15** [a] Jer. 23:16 [b] Mic. 3:5 **7:16** [a] Matt. 7:20; 12:33 [b] Luke 6:43 **7:17** [a] Matt. 12:33 **7:19** [a] [John 15:2, 6] **7:21** [a] Luke 6:46

SPREAD PEACE

“Blessed are the peacemakers, for they shall be called sons of God.”

MATTHEW 5:9

In Leviticus God instructed Moses to say to the people of Israel, “‘You shall be holy, for I the Lord your God am holy’” (Lev. 19:2). Interpreters call this part of Leviticus the Holiness Code. The command to be holy because God is holy makes sense. After all, we were made in God’s image, so shouldn’t we be like God in ethics and morals?

One of God’s characteristics is peace. He makes peace. So should we. Peacemaking is very strong evidence that you are one of His children and one of Jesus’ disciples (Is. 9:6; Zech. 9:10). If you’re a peacemaker, then you are part of the team and you will be blessed. A spiritually mature follower of Jesus will always seek peace.

How are you seeking or spreading peace today?

but he who [b]does the will of My Father in
heaven. 22 Many will say to Me in that day,
'Lord, Lord, have we [a]not prophesied in Your
name, cast out demons in Your name, and
done many wonders in Your name?' 23 And
[a]then I will declare to them, 'I never knew
you; [b]depart from Me, you who practice
lawlessness!'

Build on the Rock

24 "Therefore [a]whoever hears these sayings
of Mine, and does them, I will liken him to a
wise man who built his house on the rock:
25 and the rain descended, the floods came, and
the winds blew and beat on that house; and
it did not fall, for it was founded on the rock.
26 "But everyone who hears these sayings
of Mine, and does not do them, will be like a
foolish man who built his house on the sand:
27 and the rain descended, the floods came,
and the winds blew and beat on that house;
and it fell. And great was its fall."
28 And so it was, when Jesus had ended
these sayings, that [a]the people were astonished
at His teaching, 29 [a]for He taught
them as one having authority, and not as
the scribes.

Jesus Cleanses a Leper

8 When He had come down from the mountain,
great multitudes followed Him.
2 [a]And behold, a leper came and [b]worshiped
Him, saying, "Lord, if You are willing, You
can make me clean."
3 Then Jesus put out *His* hand and touched
him, saying, "I am willing; be cleansed." Immediately
his leprosy [a]was cleansed.
4 And Jesus said to him, [a]"See that you
tell no one; but go your way, show yourself
to the priest, and offer the gift that [b]Moses
[c]commanded, as a testimony to them."

Jesus Heals a Centurion's Servant

5 [a]Now when Jesus had entered Capernaum,
a [b]centurion came to Him, pleading
with Him, 6 saying, "Lord, my servant is
lying at home paralyzed, dreadfully tormented."
7 And Jesus said to him, "I will come and
heal him."
8 The centurion answered and said, "Lord,
[a]I am not worthy that You should come under
my roof. But only [b]speak a word, and my
servant will be healed. 9 For I also am a man
under authority, having soldiers under me.
And I say to this *one,* 'Go,' and he goes; and
to another, 'Come,' and he comes; and to my
servant, 'Do this,' and he does *it.*"
10 When Jesus heard *it,* He marveled, and
said to those who followed, "Assuredly, I say
to you, I have not found such great faith,
not even in Israel! 11 And I say to you that
[a]many will come from east and west, and sit

7:21 [b] Rom. 2:13 **7:22** [a] Num. 24:4 **7:23** [a] [2 Tim. 2:19] [b] Ps. 5:5; 6:8 **7:24** [a] Luke 6:47–49 **7:28** [a] Matt. 13:54 **7:29** [a] [John 7:46] **8:2** [a] Mark 1:40–45 [b] John 9:38 **8:3** [a] Luke 4:27 **8:4** [a] Mark 5:43 [b] Luke 5:14 [c] Deut. 24:8 **8:5** [a] Luke 7:1–3 [b] Matt. 27:54 **8:8** [a] Luke 15:19, 21 [b] Ps. 107:20 **8:11** [a] Is. 2:2, 3; Mal. 1:11

THE HIDDEN BLESSING

"Blessed are those who are persecuted for righteousness' sake, for theirs is the kingdom of heaven."

MATTHEW 5:10

Have you ever been falsely accused? It causes a special kind of hurt. But to be accused, even persecuted, for doing what is right is about the toughest thing you can experience. Jesus referred to this very thing in His eighth beatitude: "Blessed are those who are persecuted for righteousness' sake, for theirs is the kingdom of heaven."

I wonder if some of His listeners rolled their eyes. Many faithful Jews had suffered persecution in the generations leading up to the time of Jesus. They were not only falsely accused but imprisoned, tortured, and executed. How can that be described as "blessed"?

The point is that being persecuted for righteousness is evidence that you are one of God's children. To be one of God's children—no matter what life throws at you—is to be blessed. *That* is something to be happy about! Stop and consider the everlasting blessing of being called a child of God, and let it bring you peace.

down with Abraham, Isaac, and Jacob in the
kingdom of heaven. 12But [a]the sons of the
kingdom [b]will be cast out into outer darkness. There will be weeping and gnashing
of teeth." 13Then Jesus said to the centurion,
"Go your way; and as you have believed, *so*
let it be done for you." And his servant was
healed that same hour.

Peter's Mother-in-Law Healed

14[a]Now when Jesus had come into Peter's
house, He saw [b]his wife's mother lying sick
with a fever. 15So He touched her hand, and
the fever left her. And she arose and served
them.[1]

Many Healed in the Evening

16[a]When evening had come, they brought
to Him many who were demon-possessed.
And He cast out the spirits with a word, and
healed all who were sick, 17that it might be
fulfilled which was spoken by Isaiah the
prophet, saying:

> [a]"He Himself took our infirmities
> And bore *our* sicknesses."[1]

The Cost of Discipleship

18And when Jesus saw great multitudes
about Him, He gave a command to depart to
the other side. 19[a]Then a certain scribe came
and said to Him, "Teacher, I will follow You
wherever You go."

20And Jesus said to him, "Foxes have holes
and birds of the air *have* nests, but the Son of
Man has nowhere to lay *His* head."

21[a]Then another of His disciples said to
Him, "Lord, [b]let me first go and bury my
father."

22But Jesus said to him, "Follow Me, and
let the dead bury their own dead."

Wind and Wave Obey Jesus

23Now when He got into a boat, His disciples followed Him. 24[a]And suddenly a great
tempest arose on the sea, so that the boat
was covered with the waves. But He was
asleep. 25Then His disciples came to *Him*
and awoke Him, saying, "Lord, save us! We
are perishing!"

26But He said to them, "Why are you fearful, O you of little faith?" Then [a]He arose and
rebuked the winds and the sea, and there was
a great calm. 27So the men marveled, saying,
"Who can this be, that even the winds and
the sea obey Him?"

Two Demon-Possessed Men Healed

28[a]When He had come to the other side,
to the country of the Gergesenes,[1] there met
Him two demon-possessed *men,* coming
out of the tombs, exceedingly fierce, so that

8:12 [a] [Matt. 21:43] [b] Luke 13:28 8:14 [a] Mark 1:29–31 [b] 1 Cor. 9:5 8:15 [1] NU-Text and M-Text read *Him.* 8:16 [a] Luke 4:40, 41 8:17 [a] Is. 53:4 [1] Isaiah 53:4 8:19 [a] Luke 9:57, 58 8:21 [a] Luke 9:59, 60 [b] 1 Kin. 19:20 8:24 [a] Mark 4:37 8:26 [a] Ps. 65:7; 89:9; 107:29 8:28 [a] Mark 5:1–4 [1] NU-Text reads *Gadarenes.*

FOR THE SAKE OF CHRIST

"Blessed are you when they revile and persecute you, and say all kinds of evil against you falsely for My sake."

MATTHEW 5:11

Jesus' ninth beatitude is related to the one that precedes it. It, too, is startling: "Blessed are you when they revile and persecute you, and say all kinds of evil against you falsely for My sake." Not too many people feel blessed when they are reviled and spoken of hatefully. To suffer this kind of abuse is painful. The apostle Peter heard this beatitude and passed it on to those who had not heard it before: "But even if you should suffer for righteousness' sake," the apostle said, "you are blessed" (1 Pet. 3:14).

What makes this beatitude special is that Jesus referred to evil raining down on His followers because of their loyalty to Him ("for My sake"; Matt. 5:11). In verse 10 the blessing followed persecution for doing good; in verse 11 the blessing followed serving Jesus. Don't miss the *parallelism: doing what* is right and being loyal to Jesus are closely related. Our world is fallen, and as a result, people don't always want what is righteous or accept Jesus. If you are persecuted for your faith today, know that God will give you His strength, wisdom, and peace. You are blessed.

no one could pass that way. 29And suddenly
they cried out, saying, "What have we to do
with You, Jesus, You Son of God? Have You
come here to torment us before the time?"
30Now a good way off from them there
was a herd of many swine feeding. 31So the
demons begged Him, saying, "If You cast
us out, permit us to go away[1] into the herd
of swine."
32And He said to them, "Go." So when they
had come out, they went into the herd of
swine. And suddenly the whole herd of swine
ran violently down the steep place into the
sea, and perished in the water.
33Then those who kept *them* fled; and they
went away into the city and told everything,
including what *had happened* to the demon-
possessed *men.* 34And behold, the whole
city came out to meet Jesus. And when they
saw Him, [a]they begged *Him* to depart from
their region.

Jesus Forgives and Heals a Paralytic

9 So He got into a boat, crossed over, [a]and
came to His own city. 2[a]Then behold, they
brought to Him a paralytic lying on a bed.
[b]When Jesus saw their faith, He said to the
paralytic, "Son, be of good cheer; your sins
are forgiven you."
3And at once some of the scribes said within themselves, "This Man blasphemes!"
4But Jesus, [a]knowing their thoughts, said,
"Why do you think evil in your hearts? 5For
which is easier, to say, '*Your* sins are forgiven
you,' or to say, 'Arise and walk'? 6But that you
may know that the Son of Man has power on
earth to forgive sins"—then He said to the
paralytic, "Arise, take up your bed, and go
to your house." 7And he arose and departed
to his house.
8Now when the multitudes saw *it,* they
[a]marveled[1] and glorified God, who had given
such power to men.

Matthew the Tax Collector

9[a]As Jesus passed on from there, He saw a
man named Matthew sitting at the tax office.
And He said to him, "Follow Me." So he arose
and followed Him.
10[a]Now it happened, as Jesus sat at the
table in the house, *that* behold, many tax
collectors and sinners came and sat down
with Him and His disciples. 11And when the
Pharisees saw *it,* they said to His disciples,
"Why does your Teacher eat with [a]tax collectors and [b]sinners?"
12When Jesus heard *that,* He said to them,
"Those who are well have no need of a physician, but those who are sick. 13But go and
learn what *this* means: [a]'I desire mercy and
not sacrifice.'[1] For I did not come to call the
righteous, [b]but sinners, to repentance."[2]

8:31 [1] NU-Text reads *send us.* **8:34** [a] Luke 5:8; Acts 16:39 **9:1** [a] Matt. 4:13; 11:23 **9:2** [a] Luke 5:18–26 [b] Matt. 8:10 **9:4** [a] Matt. 12:25 **9:8** [a] John 7:15 [1] NU-Text reads *were afraid.* **9:9** [a] Luke 5:27 **9:10** [a] Mark 2:15 **9:11** [a] Matt. 11:19 [b] [Gal. 2:15] **9:13** [a] Hos. 6:6 [b] 1 Tim. 1:15 [1] Hosea 6:6 [2] NU-Text omits *to repentance.*

OUR GREAT REWARD

"Rejoice and be exceedingly glad, for great is your reward in heaven,
for so they persecuted the prophets who were before you."

MATTHEW 5:12

Jesus' tenth exhortation is not a beatitude (the word "blessed" or "happy" does not appear); it is a summary of all the beatitudes, especially those in verses 10–11. Instead of being down in the dumps over persecution and slander, we should, Jesus said, "rejoice and be exceedingly glad" (v. 12). Why? To be persecuted is to find oneself in the company of the prophets, whom the wicked often persecuted. In Jesus' time the prophets of old were admired; they were thought of as being especially close to God. Well, said Jesus, they were persecuted for telling the truth and living in accordance with God's righteousness. So don't be surprised if, in being a person of truth and living righteously, you, too, are persecuted.

What Jesus didn't say, but it runs throughout all His beatitudes, is that living with integrity, living righteously, is medicine for the soul. Integrity is the food on which peace feeds. If you seek peace, then live with integrity and do what is right. You will be blessed, and you will have peace.

Jesus Is Questioned About Fasting

14Then the disciples of John came to Him,
saying, [a]"Why do we and the Pharisees fast
often,[1] but Your disciples do not fast?"
15And Jesus said to them, "Can [a]the friends
of the bridegroom mourn as long as the
bridegroom is with them? But the days will
come when the bridegroom will be taken
away from them, and [b]then they will fast. 16No
one puts a piece of unshrunk cloth on an old
garment; for the patch pulls away from the
garment, and the tear is made worse. 17Nor
do they put new wine into old wineskins, or
else the wineskins break, the wine is spilled,
and the wineskins are ruined. But they put
new wine into new wineskins, and both are
preserved."

A Girl Restored to Life and a Woman Healed

18[a]While He spoke these things to them,
behold, a ruler came and worshiped Him,
saying, "My daughter has just died, but come
and lay Your hand on her and she will live."
19So Jesus arose and followed him, and so
did His [a]disciples.
20[a]And suddenly, a woman who had a flow
of blood for twelve years came from behind
and [b]touched the hem of His garment. 21For
she said to herself, "If only I may touch His
garment, I shall be made well." 22But Jesus
turned around, and when He saw her He said,
"Be of good cheer, daughter; [a]your faith has
made you well." And the woman was made
well from that hour.
23[a]When Jesus came into the ruler's house,
and saw [b]the flute players and the noisy crowd
wailing, 24He said to them, [a]"Make room, for
the girl is not dead, but sleeping." And they
ridiculed Him. 25But when the crowd was
put outside, He went in and [a]took her by the
hand, and the girl arose. 26And the [a]report
of this went out into all that land.

Two Blind Men Healed

27When Jesus departed from there, [a]two
blind men followed Him, crying out and
saying, [b]"Son of David, have mercy on us!"
28And when He had come into the house,
the blind men came to Him. And Jesus said
to them, "Do you believe that I am able to
do this?"
They said to Him, "Yes, Lord."
29Then He touched their eyes, saying, "According to your faith let it be to you." 30And
their eyes were opened. And Jesus sternly warned them, saying, [a]"See *that* no one
knows *it*." 31[a]But when they had departed, they
spread the news about Him in all that country.

A Mute Man Speaks

32[a]As they went out, behold, they brought
to Him a man, mute and demon-possessed.
33And when the demon was cast out, the
mute spoke. And the multitudes marveled,
saying, "It was never seen like this in Israel!"

9:14 [a] Luke 5:33–35; 18:12 [1] NU-Text brackets *often* as disputed. **9:15** [a] John 3:29 [b] Acts 13:2, 3; 14:23 **9:18** [a] Luke 8:41–56 **9:19** [a] Matt. 10:2–4 **9:20** [a] Luke 8:43 [b] Matt. 14:36; 23:5 **9:22** [a] Luke 7:50; 8:48; 17:19; 18:42 **9:23** [a] Mark 5:38 [b] 2 Chr. 35:25 **9:24** [a] Acts 20:10 **9:25** [a] Mark 1:31 **9:26** [a] Matt. 4:24 **9:27** [a] Matt. 20:29–34 [b] Luke 18:38, 39 **9:30** [a] Matt. 8:4 **9:31** [a] Mark 7:36 **9:32** [a] Matt. 12:22, 24

LIGHT UP THE WORLD WITH PEACE

"You are the light of the world . . . Let your light so shine before men, that they may see your good works and glorify your Father in heaven."

MATTHEW 5:14, 16

We have here one of the greatest compliments Jesus paid His followers: "You are the light of the world . . . Let your light so shine before men, that they may see your good works and glorify your Father in heaven." What a beautiful picture! These words underscore the importance of our testimony. When people see believers, they, in a sense, see Jesus. What do they see in you? If they see light and good works, they will glorify God. They will praise God by thinking and saying good things about Him. "God must be good—look at the way George and Jane live. I wish I could live that way!"

With Jesus' words comes huge responsibility. When people look at believers, do they see lives that are blessed, that mirror God's grace and goodness? Do they see lives characterized by God's peace? In a sense, our lives are the windows of heaven. When people look at you, what do they see?

34But the Pharisees said, [a]"He casts out
demons by the ruler of the demons."

The Compassion of Jesus

35Then Jesus went about all the cities
and villages, [a]teaching in their synagogues,
preaching the gospel of the kingdom, and
healing every sickness and every disease
among the people.[1] 36[a]But when He saw
the multitudes, He was moved with compassion for them, because they were weary[1] and scattered, [b]like sheep having no
shepherd. 37Then He said to His disciples,
[a]"The harvest truly *is* plentiful, but the laborers *are* few. 38[a]Therefore pray the Lord
of the harvest to send out laborers into His
harvest."

The Twelve Apostles

10 And [a]when He had called His twelve
disciples to *Him,* He gave them power
over unclean spirits, to cast them out, and to
heal all kinds of sickness and all kinds of disease. 2Now the names of the twelve apostles
are these: first, Simon, [a]who is called Peter,
and Andrew his brother; James the *son* of
Zebedee, and John his brother; 3Philip and
Bartholomew; Thomas and Matthew the tax
collector; James the *son* of Alphaeus, and
Lebbaeus, whose surname was[1] Thaddaeus;
4[a]Simon the Cananite,[1] and Judas [b]Iscariot,
who also betrayed Him.

Sending Out the Twelve

5These twelve Jesus sent out and commanded them, saying: [a]"Do not go into the
way of the Gentiles, and do not enter a city of
[b]the Samaritans. 6[a]But go rather to the [b]lost
sheep of the house of Israel. 7[a]And as you go,
preach, saying, [b]'The kingdom of heaven is
at hand.' 8Heal the sick, cleanse the lepers,
raise the dead,[1] cast out demons. [a]Freely you
have received, freely give. 9[a]Provide neither
gold nor silver nor [b]copper in your money
belts, 10nor bag for *your* journey, nor two

PEACE NOTE

Our ministry to harassed people begins with an empathetic heart. If we are not moved by compassion for the suffering, we will not fully embrace all the peace God has for us.

MATTHEW 9:36

9:34 [a] Luke 11:15 **9:35** [a] Matt. 4:23 [1] NU-Text omits *among the people.* **9:36** [a] Mark 6:34 [b] Num. 27:17 [1] NU-Text and M-Text read *harassed.* **9:37** [a] Luke 10:2 **9:38** [a] 2 Thess. 3:1 **10:1** [a] Luke 6:13 **10:2** [a] John 1:42 **10:3** [1] NU-Text omits *Lebbaeus, whose surname was.* **10:4** [a] Acts 1:13 [b] John 13:2, 26 [1] NU-Text reads *Cananaean.* **10:5** [a] Matt. 4:15 [b] John 4:9 **10:6** [a] Matt. 15:24 [b] Jer. 50:6 **10:7** [a] Luke 9:2 [b] Matt. 3:2 **10:8** [a] [Acts 8:18] [1] NU-Text reads *raise the dead, cleanse the lepers;* M-Text omits *raise the dead.* **10:9** [a] 1 Sam. 9:7 [b] Mark 6:8

OUR CONFIDENCE IN PRAYER

"And when you pray, do not use vain repetitions as the heathen do . . . For your Father knows the things you have need of before you ask Him."

MATTHEW 6:7-8

Jesus taught His disciples, *When you pray, don't repeat yourself.* Most interpreters think Jesus probably had in mind the prayers of Baal's prophets as they screamed for their god to answer them (as though their god couldn't take notice unless they made a lot of noise, as in 1 Kin. 18:20–29). These "vain repetitions" (Matt. 6:7) are not what Paul was talking about when he urged the Thessalonian Christians to "pray without ceasing" (1 Thess. 5:17).

Shouting at God, begging Him to listen, informing Him of your wants and needs is not necessary, "for your Father knows the things you have need of before you ask Him" (Matt. 6:8). Students have asked, "If God knows before I ask, why pray?" I reply, "Would you pray to God if He had no idea of your needs until you informed Him?" And that's the point: pray with confidence, knowing that God hears you and will answer according to His will. Live in the peace and good care of God.

tunics, nor sandals, nor staffs; [a]for a worker
is worthy of his food.
11[a]"Now whatever city or town you enter,
inquire who in it is worthy, and stay there
till you go out. 12And when you go into a
household, greet it. 13[a]If the household is
worthy, let your peace come upon it. [b]But
if it is not worthy, let your peace return to
you. 14[a]And whoever will not receive you nor
hear your words, when you depart from that
house or city, [b]shake off the dust from your
feet. 15Assuredly, I say to you, [a]it will be more
tolerable for the land of Sodom and Gomorrah in the day of judgment than for that city!

Persecutions Are Coming

16[a]"Behold, I send you out as sheep in the
midst of wolves. [b]Therefore be wise as serpents and [c]harmless as doves. 17But beware of
men, for [a]they will deliver you up to councils
and [b]scourge you in their synagogues. 18[a]You
will be brought before governors and kings
for My sake, as a testimony to them and to
the Gentiles. 19[a]But when they deliver you up,
do not worry about how or what you should
speak. For [b]it will be given to you in that hour
what you should speak; 20[a]for it is not you
who speak, but the Spirit of your Father who
speaks in you.
21[a]"Now brother will deliver up brother to
death, and a father *his* child; and children
will rise up against parents and cause them
to be put to death. 22And [a]you will be hated
by all for My name's sake. [b]But he who endures to the end will be saved. 23[a]When they
persecute you in this city, flee to another.
For assuredly, I say to you, you will not have
[b]gone through the cities of Israel [c]before the
Son of Man comes.
24[a]"A disciple is not above *his* teacher, nor a
servant above his master. 25It is enough for a

PEACE NOTE

The idea that Jesus' peace can remain on a house implies something almost tangible about the *shalom* He offers.

MATTHEW 10:13

10:10 [a] 1 Tim. 5:18 **10:11** [a] Luke 10:8 **10:13** [a] Luke 10:5 [b] Ps. 35:13 **10:14** [a] Mark 6:11 [b] Acts 13:51 **10:15** [a] Matt. 11:22, 24 **10:16** [a] Luke 10:3 [b] Eph. 5:15 [c] [Phil. 2:14–16] **10:17** [a] Mark 13:9 [b] Acts 5:40; 22:19; 26:11 **10:18** [a] 2 Tim. 4:16 **10:19** [a] Luke 12:11, 12; 21:14, 15 [b] Ex. 4:12 **10:20** [a] 2 Sam. 23:2 **10:21** [a] Mic. 7:6 **10:22** [a] Luke 21:17 [b] Mark 13:13 **10:23** [a] Acts 8:1 [b] [Mark 13:10] [c] Matt. 16:28 **10:24** [a] John 15:20

SET YOUR PRIORITIES

"But seek first the kingdom of God and His righteousness, and all these things shall be added to you."

MATTHEW 6:33

Have you ever heard "He who dies with the most toys wins"? Everyone knows it's a joke, but many people live as though this nonsensical epigram is true. Of course, Jesus said nothing about toys; He spoke about necessities and taught His disciples that life was much more than clothing and food, that the pursuit of possessions and wealth was ultimately futile. He said, "Seek first the kingdom of God and His righteousness, and all these things shall be added to you."

This is one of my favorite verses in the Bible. When I recite it I can't help but think of Solomon's dream in which God offered the young monarch whatever he wanted—wealth, fame, power, whatever. Solomon requested wisdom so that he might rule God's people well. God was pleased, telling the son of David, "I have given you a wise and understanding *heart . . . And I have* also given you what you have not asked: both riches and honor" (1 Kin. 3:12–13). Peace comes to your life when you prioritize your walk with God. Take a moment and determine what it will take—on this day—to prioritize God's glory, power, and kingdom above every other thing. See if acting on that brings peace.

disciple that he be like his teacher, and a servant like his master. If [a]they have called the master of the house Beelzebub,[1] how much more *will they call* those of his household! 26 Therefore do not fear them. [a]For there is nothing covered that will not be revealed, and hidden that will not be known.

Jesus Teaches the Fear of God

27 "Whatever I tell you in the dark, [a]speak in the light; and what you hear in the ear, preach on the housetops. 28 [a]And do not fear those who kill the body but cannot kill the soul. But rather [b]fear Him who is able to destroy both soul and body in hell. 29 Are not two [a]sparrows sold for a copper coin? And not one of them falls to the ground apart from your Father's will. 30 [a]But the very hairs of your head are all numbered. 31 Do not fear therefore; you are of more value than many sparrows.

Confess Christ Before Men

32 [a]"Therefore whoever confesses Me before men, [b]him I will also confess before My Father who is in heaven. 33 [a]But whoever denies Me before men, him I will also deny before My Father who is in heaven.

Christ Brings Division

34 [a]"Do not think that I came to bring peace on earth. I did not come to bring peace but a sword. 35 For I have come to [a]'set a man against his father, a daughter against her mother, and a daughter-in-law against her mother-in-law'; 36 and [a]'a man's enemies *will be* those of his *own* household.'[1] 37 [a]He who loves father or mother more than Me is not worthy of Me. And he who loves son or daughter more than Me is not worthy of Me. 38 [a]And he who does not take his cross and follow after Me is not worthy of Me. 39 [a]He who finds his life will lose it, and he who loses his life for My sake will find it.

A Cup of Cold Water

40 [a]"He who receives you receives Me, and he who receives Me receives Him who sent Me. 41 [a]He who receives a prophet in the name of a prophet shall receive a prophet's reward. And he who receives a righteous man in the name of a righteous man shall receive a righteous man's reward. 42 [a]And whoever gives one of these little ones only a cup of cold *water* in the name of a disciple, assuredly, I say to you, he shall by no means lose his reward."

John the Baptist Sends Messengers to Jesus

11 Now it came to pass, when Jesus finished commanding His twelve disciples, that He departed from there to [a]teach and to preach in their cities.

10:25 [a] John 8:48, 52 [1] NU-Text and M-Text read *Beelzebul.* **10:26** [a] Mark 4:22 **10:27** [a] Acts 5:20 **10:28** [a] Luke 12:4 [b] Luke 12:5 **10:29** [a] Luke 12:6, 7 **10:30** [a] Luke 21:18 **10:32** [a] Luke 12:8 [b] [Rev. 3:5] **10:33** [a] 2 Tim. 2:12 **10:34** [a] [Luke 12:49] **10:35** [a] Mic. 7:6 **10:36** [a] John 13:18 [1] Micah 7:6 **10:37** [a] Luke 14:26 **10:38** [a] [Mark 8:34] **10:39** [a] John 12:25 **10:40** [a] Luke 9:48 **10:41** [a] 1 Kin. 17:10 **10:42** [a] Mark 9:41 **11:1** [a] Luke 23:5

ASK FOR PEACE

"Ask, and it will be given to you; seek, and you will find; knock, and it will be opened to you. For everyone who asks receives, and he who seeks finds, and to him who knocks it will be opened."

MATTHEW 7:7–8

Jesus famously promised His disciples that if they asked, they would receive, if they sought, they would find, and if they knocked, the door of answered prayer would be opened to them. Jesus was not promoting a false prosperity theology—if you do this or that, God will make you rich. Rather Jesus taught His disciples that they often experienced want because they neglected to pray and ask God. They simply didn't ask for God's provision. Or they asked wrongly. James, Jesus' brother, said: "You ask and do not receive, because you ask amiss, that you may spend it on your pleasures" (James 4:3). His comment is an unmistakable allusion to Jesus' teaching here in Matthew 7.

Jesus promised riches in godly things. But we must seek them, we must ask for them, and we must do so in faith. For what do we ask? Things sometimes, but mostly for God's leading and for His grace. We ask for opportunities to serve, for ways to help people, and for ways to advance His kingdom. You should also ask for peace! Perhaps you don't have it because you've not actively asked for it. Today, see if the Lord will let His peace fall on you.

2[a]And when John had heard [b]in prison
about the works of Christ, he sent two of[1]
his disciples 3and said to Him, "Are You [a]the
Coming One, or do we look for another?"
4Jesus answered and said to them, "Go and
tell John the things which you hear and see:
5[a]*The* blind see and *the* lame walk; *the* lepers are cleansed and *the* deaf hear; *the* dead
are raised up and [b]*the* poor have the gospel
preached to them. 6And blessed is he who is
not [a]offended because of Me."
7[a]As they departed, Jesus began to say to
the multitudes concerning John: "What did
you go out into the wilderness to see? [b]A reed
shaken by the wind? 8But what did you go
out to see? A man clothed in soft garments?
Indeed, those who wear soft *clothing* are in
kings' houses. 9But what did you go out to
see? A prophet? Yes, I say to you, [a]and more
than a prophet. 10For this is *he* of whom it
is written:

> [a]'Behold, I send My messenger before
> Your face,
> Who will prepare Your way
> before You.'[1]

11"Assuredly, I say to you, among those
born of women there has not risen one greater than John the Baptist; but he who is least
in the kingdom of heaven is greater than he.
12[a]And from the days of John the Baptist until
now the kingdom of heaven suffers violence,
and the violent take it by force. 13[a]For all the
prophets and the law prophesied until John.
14And if you are willing to receive *it,* he is
[a]Elijah who is to come. 15[a]He who has ears
to hear, let him hear!
16[a]"But to what shall I liken this generation? It is like children sitting in the marketplaces and calling to their companions,
17and saying:

> 'We played the flute for you,
> And you did not dance;
> We mourned to you,
> And you did not lament.'

PEACE NOTE

Let's take our doubts directly to Jesus. Notice how John involved his buddies: when we feel full of anxiety, we should reach out to a friend for biblical reminders of how to recover God's peace.

MATTHEW 11:3

11:2 [a] Luke 7:18–35 [b] Matt. 4:12; 14:3 [1] NU-Text reads *by* for *two of.* **11:3** [a] John 6:14 **11:5** [a] Is. 29:18; 35:4–6 [b] Ps. 22:26; Is. 61:1 **11:6** [a] [Rom. 9:32] **11:7** [a] Luke 7:24 [b] [Eph. 4:14] **11:9** [a] Luke 1:76; 20:6 **11:10** [a] Mal. 3:1 [1] Malachi 3:1 **11:12** [a] Luke 16:16 **11:13** [a] Mal. 4:4–6 **11:14** [a] Luke 1:17 **11:15** [a] Luke 8:8 **11:16** [a] Luke 7:31

CHRIST, OUR FIRM FOUNDATION

"Therefore whoever hears these sayings of Mine, and does them, I will liken him to a wise man who built his house on the rock."

MATTHEW 7:24

If you own a house, you probably have insurance. If you live somewhere near water or where heavy rains fall, you probably have flood insurance. But insurance is a modern concept; there wasn't any in ancient times. This is why Jesus told the parable of the wise man and the fool at the end of His well-known Sermon on the Mount. The wise man, Jesus said, "built his house on the rock: and the rain descended, the floods came, and the winds blew and beat on that house; and it did not fall, for it was founded on the rock" (vv. 24–25). The man who ignores Jesus is like a fool who builds his house on sand; when the rains and flood come, his house falls (vv. 26–27).

We all want our lives, not just our houses, to be founded on solid rock. I cannot live in God's peace today unless I find all my security in Christ. Every moment you spend seeking the peace of God is an investment in securing your life on the Rock that is Christ.

[18]For John came neither eating nor drinking,
and they say, 'He has a demon.' [19]The Son of
Man came eating and drinking, and they say,
'Look, a glutton and a winebibber, [a]a friend
of tax collectors and sinners!' [b]But wisdom
is justified by her children."[1]

Woe to the Impenitent Cities

[20a]Then He began to rebuke the cities in
which most of His mighty works had been
done, because they did not repent: [21]"Woe to
you, Chorazin! Woe to you, Bethsaida! For if
the mighty works which were done in you had
been done in Tyre and Sidon, they would have
repented long ago [a]in sackcloth and ashes.
[22]But I say to you, [a]it will be more tolerable
for Tyre and Sidon in the day of judgment
than for you. [23]And you, Capernaum, [a]who
are exalted to heaven, will be[1] brought down
to Hades; for if the mighty works which were
done in you had been done in Sodom, it would
have remained until this day. [24]But I say to you
[a]that it shall be more tolerable for the land of
Sodom in the day of judgment than for you."

Jesus Gives True Rest

[25a]At that time Jesus answered and said, "I
thank You, Father, Lord of heaven and earth,
that [b]You have hidden these things from *the*
wise and prudent [c]and have revealed them
to babes. [26]Even so, Father, for so it seemed
good in Your sight. [27a]All things have been
delivered to Me by My Father, and no one
knows the Son except the Father. [b]Nor does
anyone know the Father except the Son, and
the one to whom the Son wills to reveal *Him.*
[28]Come to [a]Me, all *you* who labor and are
heavy laden, and I will give you rest. [29]Take
My yoke upon you [a]and learn from Me, for I

PEACE NOTE

We can find rest for our souls only when we take on the yoke of Jesus. I have to *learn* to let Jesus take control of my life.

MATTHEW 11:29

11:19 [a] Matt. 9:10 [b] Luke 7:35 [1] NU-Text reads *works.* **11:20** [a] Luke 10:13–15, 18 **11:21** [a] Jon. 3:6–8 **11:22** [a] Matt. 10:15; 11:24 **11:23** [a] Is. 14:13 [1] NU-Text reads *will you be exalted to heaven? No, you will be.* **11:24** [a] Matt. 10:15 **11:25** [a] Luke 10:21, 22 [b] Ps. 8:2 [c] Matt. 16:17 **11:27** [a] Matt. 28:18 [b] John 1:18; 6:46; 10:15 **11:28** [a] [John 6:35–37] **11:29** [a] [Phil. 2:5]

YOUR TESTIMONY OF PEACE

Now when the multitudes saw it, they marveled and glorified God, who had given such power to men.

MATTHEW 9:8

Jesus was well known as a Healer. Given the grim health realities of the ancient world, I am not surprised crowds followed Him. Some of the healings were especially amazing. When Jesus healed a paralyzed man by merely speaking a word, the people "marveled and glorified God, who had given such power to men." Jesus did not beg God to hear Him, did not use medicines and gimmicks. He simply spoke a word or touched someone and healing took place—and it happened fairly quickly, not over a period of days or weeks. The people who followed Jesus had never seen or heard anything like it.

When we think of Jesus, we usually think of His resurrection and the forgiveness of our sin. Those are, of course, hugely significant. But let's not forget that Jesus ministered to people, He blessed people, He restored people—and He is still doing those things. The ministry of Jesus continues through His church. We should be greatly comforted that One like no other cares about us and seeks our good. How do you need Jesus to minister to you? Make a specific request to Jesus today that goes right to the heart of the matter where you need peace.

am gentle and [b]lowly in heart, [c]and you will
find rest for your souls. 30 [a]For My yoke *is*
easy and My burden is light."

Jesus Is Lord of the Sabbath

12 At that time [a]Jesus went through the
grainfields on the Sabbath. And His
disciples were hungry, and began to [b]pluck
heads of grain and to eat. 2 And when the
Pharisees saw *it*, they said to Him, "Look,
Your disciples are doing what is not lawful
to do on the Sabbath!"
3 But He said to them, "Have you not read
[a]what David did when he was hungry, he and
those who were with him: 4 how he entered
the house of God and ate [a]the showbread
which was not lawful for him to eat, nor for
those who were with him, [b]but only for the
priests? 5 Or have you not read in the [a]law
that on the Sabbath the priests in the temple
profane the Sabbath, and are blameless?
6 Yet I say to you that in this place there is
[a]*One* greater than the temple. 7 But if you
had known what *this* means, [a]'I desire mercy
and not sacrifice,'[1] you would not have condemned the guiltless. 8 For the Son of Man
is Lord even[1] of the Sabbath."

Healing on the Sabbath

9 [a]Now when He had departed from there,
He went into their synagogue. 10 And behold,
there was a man who had a withered hand. And
they asked Him, saying, [a]"Is it lawful to heal on
the Sabbath?"—that they might accuse Him.
11 Then He said to them, "What man is there
among you who has one sheep, and if it falls
into a pit on the Sabbath, will not lay hold of
it and lift *it* out? 12 Of how much more value
then is a man than a sheep? Therefore it is
lawful to do good on the Sabbath." 13 Then
He said to the man, "Stretch out your hand."
And he stretched *it* out, and it was restored
as whole as the other. 14 Then [a]the Pharisees
went out and plotted against Him, how they
might destroy Him.

Behold, My Servant

15 But when Jesus knew *it*, [a]He withdrew
from there. [b]And great multitudes[1] followed Him, and He healed them all. 16 Yet
He [a]warned them not to make Him known,
17 that it might be fulfilled which was spoken
by Isaiah the prophet, saying:

18 "Behold![a] My Servant whom I have
chosen,
My Beloved [b]in whom My soul is well
pleased!
I will put My Spirit upon Him,
And He will declare justice to the
Gentiles.
19 He will not quarrel nor cry out,
Nor will anyone hear His voice in the
streets.

11:29 [b] Zech. 9:9 [c] Jer. 6:16 11:30 [a] [1 John 5:3] 12:1 [a] Luke 6:1–5 [b] Deut. 23:25 12:3 [a] 1 Sam. 21:6 12:4 [a] Lev. 24:5 [b] Ex. 29:32 12:5 [a] Num. 28:9 12:6 [a] [Is. 66:1, 2] 12:7 [a] [Hos. 6:6] [1] Hosea 6:6 12:8 [1] NU-Text and M-Text omit *even.* 12:9 [a] Mark 3:1–6 12:10 [a] John 9:16 12:14 [a] Mark 3:6 12:15 [a] Mark 3:7 [b] Matt. 19:2 [1] NU-Text brackets *multitudes* as disputed. 12:16 [a] Matt. 8:4; 9:30; 17:9 12:18 [a] Is. 42:1–4; 49:3 [b] Matt. 3:17; 17:5

TAKE THE PEACE OF GOD WITH YOU

"If the household is worthy, let your peace come upon it. But if it is not worthy, let your peace return to you."

MATTHEW 10:13

Do you know someone whose very presence brings peace, a peace that you can almost feel? The presence of Jesus and His chosen apostles had that effect on people. Jesus sent them out to proclaim the kingdom of God. The apostles not only proclaimed the kingdom of God, but they also brought with them the peace of God. But God's peace is never forced on anyone. If a person (or household) accepts the healing, redemptive peace that God offers, His peace lingers. But if it is rejected, it will not remain.

It may seem strange to us, but the human condition is such that people often push away the peace that God offers. Why? It's like a sick person refusing the medicine that will cure them. But if it is received, healing results. If the peace of God is received, everything changes.

God's peace means salvation; it brings completeness. Have you asked for this peace? If not, why not?

20 A bruised reed He will not break,
And smoking flax He will not quench,
Till He sends forth justice to victory;
21 And in His name Gentiles will trust."[1]

A House Divided Cannot Stand

22 [a]Then one was brought to Him who was
demon-possessed, blind and mute; and He
healed him, so that the blind and[1] mute man
both spoke and saw. 23 And all the multitudes
were amazed and said, "Could this be the
[a]Son of David?"
24 [a]Now when the Pharisees heard *it* they
said, "This *fellow* does not cast out demons except by Beelzebub,[1] the ruler of the demons."
25 But Jesus [a]knew their thoughts, and said
to them: "Every kingdom divided against
itself is brought to desolation, and every city
or house divided against itself will not stand.
26 If Satan casts out Satan, he is divided against
himself. How then will his kingdom stand?
27 And if I cast out demons by Beelzebub, by
whom do your sons cast *them* out? Therefore
they shall be your judges. 28 But if I cast out demons by the Spirit of God, [a]surely the kingdom
of God has come upon you. 29 [a]Or how can one
enter a strong man's house and plunder his
goods, unless he first binds the strong man?
And then he will plunder his house. 30 He who
is not with Me is against Me, and he who does
not gather with Me scatters abroad.

The Unpardonable Sin

31 "Therefore I say to you, [a]every sin and
blasphemy will be forgiven men, [b]but the
blasphemy *against* the Spirit will not be forgiven men. 32 Anyone who [a]speaks a word
against the Son of Man, [b]it will be forgiven
him; but whoever speaks against the Holy
Spirit, it will not be forgiven him, either in
this age or in the *age* to come.

A Tree Known by Its Fruit

33 "Either make the tree good and [a]its fruit
good, or else make the tree bad and its fruit
bad; for a tree is known by *its* fruit. 34 [a]Brood
of vipers! How can you, being evil, speak
good things? [b]For out of the abundance of
the heart the mouth speaks. 35 A good man
out of the good treasure of his heart[1] brings
forth good things, and an evil man out of the
evil treasure brings forth evil things. 36 But I
say to you that for every idle word men may
speak, they will give account of it in the day
of judgment. 37 For by your words you will
be justified, and by your words you will be
condemned."

The Scribes and Pharisees Ask for a Sign

38 [a]Then some of the scribes and Pharisees
answered, saying, "Teacher, we want to see
a sign from You."
39 But He answered and said to them, "An

12:21 [1] Isaiah 42:1–4 **12:22** [a] Luke 11:14, 15 [1] NU-Text omits *blind and.* **12:23** [a] Matt. 9:27; 21:9 **12:24** [a] Matt. 9:34 [1] NU-Text and M-Text read *Beelzebul.* **12:25** [a] Matt. 9:4 **12:28** [a] [Dan. 2:44; 7:14] **12:29** [a] Is. 49:24 **12:31** [a] Mark 3:28–30 [b] Acts 7:51 **12:32** [a] John 7:12, 52 [b] 1 Tim. 1:13 **12:33** [a] Matt. 7:16–18 **12:34** [a] Matt. 3:7; 23:33 [b] Luke 6:45 **12:35** [1] NU-Text and M-Text omit *of his heart.* **12:38** [a] Mark 8:11

OUTCASTS GET RESTORED

"Go and tell John the things which you hear and see: The blind see and the lame walk; the lepers are cleansed . . . Blessed is he who is not offended because of Me."

MATTHEW 11:4-6

This is one of the most remarkable exchanges recorded in the Gospels. John the Baptist had been imprisoned for publicly criticizing Herod Antipas, the ruler of Galilee. Jesus was active in ministry, preaching, teaching, and healing. The discouraged John sent messengers to Jesus, asking, "Are You the Coming One, or do we look for another?" (v. 3). Jesus said, "Go and tell John the things which you hear and see: The blind see and the lame walk; the lepers are cleansed . . . Blessed is he who is not offended because of Me" (vv. 4–6).

Jesus' reply to John alluded to Isaiah's prophecies (Is. 35:5–6; 61:1–2). The implied answer to John's question is clearly Yes—yes, Jesus was indeed the Coming One! But Jesus added the beatitude, "Blessed is he who is not offended because of Me" (Matt. 11:6). Why? Many in Israel expected the Messiah to destroy the wicked. But Jesus instead ministered to all, including Gentiles. His messianic task was one of redemption and restoration, not vengeance and punishment. He was indeed the Prince of Peace. Thank God that Jesus' mission was restoring enemies of God—because at one time, we were all His enemies.

evil and [a]adulterous generation seeks after a sign, and no sign will be given to it except the sign of the prophet Jonah. 40 [a]For as Jonah was three days and three nights in the belly of the great fish, so will the Son of Man be three days and three nights in the heart of the earth. 41 [a]The men of Nineveh will rise up in the judgment with this generation and [b]condemn it, [c]because they repented at the preaching of Jonah; and indeed a greater than Jonah *is* here. 42 [a]The queen of the South will rise up in the judgment with this generation and condemn it, for she came from the ends of the earth to hear the wisdom of Solomon; and indeed a greater than Solomon *is* here.

An Unclean Spirit Returns

43 [a]"When an unclean spirit goes out of a man, [b]he goes through dry places, seeking rest, and finds none. 44 Then he says, 'I will return to my house from which I came.' And when he comes, he finds *it* empty, swept, and put in order. 45 Then he goes and takes with him seven other spirits more wicked than himself, and they enter and dwell there; [a]and the last *state* of that man is worse than the first. So shall it also be with this wicked generation."

Jesus' Mother and Brothers Send for Him

46 While He was still talking to the multitudes, [a]behold, His mother and [b]brothers stood outside, seeking to speak with Him. 47 Then one said to Him, "Look, [a]Your mother and Your brothers are standing outside, seeking to speak with You."

48 But He answered and said to the one who told Him, "Who is My mother and who are My brothers?" 49 And He stretched out His hand toward His disciples and said, "Here are My mother and My [a]brothers! 50 For [a]whoever does the will of My Father in heaven is My brother and sister and mother."

The Parable of the Sower

13 On the same day Jesus went out of the house [a]and sat by the sea. 2 [a]And great multitudes were gathered together to Him, so that [b]He got into a boat and sat; and the whole multitude stood on the shore.

3 Then He spoke many things to them in parables, saying: [a]"Behold, a sower went out to sow. 4 And as he sowed, some *seed* fell by the wayside; and the birds came and devoured them. 5 Some fell on stony places, where they did not have much earth; and they immediately sprang up because they had no depth of earth. 6 But when the sun was up they were scorched, and because they had no root they withered away. 7 And some fell among thorns, and the thorns sprang up and choked them. 8 But others fell on good ground and yielded a crop: some [a]a hundredfold, some sixty, some thirty. 9 [a]He who has ears to hear, let him hear!"

The Purpose of Parables

10 And the disciples came and said to Him, "Why do You speak to them in parables?"

12:39 [a] Matt. 16:4 **12:40** [a] Jon. 1:17 **12:41** [a] Luke 11:32 [b] Jer. 3:11 [c] Jon. 3:5 **12:42** [a] 1 Kin. 10:1–13 **12:43** [a] Luke 11:24–26 [b] [1 Pet. 5:8] **12:45** [a] [2 Pet. 2:20–22] **12:46** [a] Luke 8:19–21 [b] John 2:12; 7:3, 5 **12:47** [a] Matt. 13:55, 56 **12:49** [a] John 20:17 **12:50** [a] John 15:14 **13:1** [a] Mark 4:1–12 **13:2** [a] Luke 8:4 [b] Luke 5:3 **13:3** [a] Luke 8:5 **13:8** [a] Gen. 26:12 **13:9** [a] Matt. 11:15

TO LIGHTEN YOUR BURDEN

"Come to Me, all you who labor and are heavy laden, and I will give you rest."

MATTHEW 11:28

In Israel's rich Books of Proverbs and Ecclesiastes, wisdom is sometimes personified, that is, wisdom acts like a person, not just an abstract concept. For example, in Proverbs 8 wisdom "cries out by the gates" (v. 3), urges fools to hear her (v. 5), and declares that she was in the presence of God at creation itself (v. 22). In this literature, wisdom invites the wise to follow her, to take her yoke upon themselves, and to learn.

It is to this manner of speaking that Jesus alluded when He said, "Come to Me, all you who labor and are heavy laden, and I will give you rest. Take My yoke upon you and *learn from Me, for I* am gentle and lowly in heart, and you will find rest for your souls" (Matt. 11:28–29). Jesus spoke as the personification of God's wisdom. He summoned those who will listen to, learn from, and follow Him. His teaching is not for the proud but for the humble. Following Him leads to peace.

11He answered and said to them, "Because [a]it
has been given to you to know the mysteries of
the kingdom of heaven, but to them it has not
been given. 12[a]For whoever has, to him more
will be given, and he will have abundance; but
whoever does not have, even what he has will
be taken away from him. 13Therefore I speak
to them in parables, because seeing they do
not see, and hearing they do not hear, nor do
they understand. 14And in them the prophecy
of Isaiah is fulfilled, which says:

[a]'Hearing you will hear and shall not
understand,
And seeing you will see and not
[b]perceive;
15 For the hearts of this people have
grown dull.
Their ears [a]are hard of hearing,
And their eyes they have [b]closed,
Lest they should see with *their* eyes and
hear with *their* ears,
Lest they should understand with *their*
hearts and turn,
So that I should[1] [c]heal them.'[2]

16But [a]blessed *are* your eyes for they see, and
your ears for they hear; 17for assuredly, I say to
you [a]that many prophets and righteous *men*
desired to see what you see, and did not see *it*,
and to hear what you hear, and did not hear *it*.

The Parable of the Sower Explained

18[a]"Therefore hear the parable of the sower: 19When anyone hears the word [a]of the
kingdom, and does not understand *it*, then
the wicked *one* comes and snatches away
what was sown in his heart. This is he who
received seed by the wayside. 20But he who
received the seed on stony places, this is he
who hears the word and immediately [a]re-
ceives it with joy; 21yet he has no root in himself, but endures only for a while. For when
[a]tribulation or persecution arises because of
the word, immediately [b]he stumbles. 22Now
[a]he who received seed [b]among the thorns is
he who hears the word, and the cares of this
world and the deceitfulness of riches choke
the word, and he becomes unfruitful. 23But
he who received seed on the good ground is
he who hears the word and understands *it*,
who indeed bears [a]fruit and produces: some
a hundredfold, some sixty, some thirty."

The Parable of the Wheat and the Tares

24Another parable He put forth to them,
saying: "The kingdom of heaven is like a man
who sowed good seed in his field; 25but while
men slept, his enemy came and sowed tares
among the wheat and went his way. 26But
when the grain had sprouted and produced
a crop, then the tares also appeared. 27So the
servants of the owner came and said to him,
'Sir, did you not sow good seed in your field?
How then does it have tares?' 28He said to
them, 'An enemy has done this.' The servants
said to him, 'Do you want us then to go and
gather them up?' 29But he said, 'No, lest while
you gather up the tares you also uproot the
wheat with them. 30Let both grow together

13:11 [a] Mark 4:10, 11 **13:12** [a] Matt. 25:29 **13:14** [a] Is. 6:9, 10; Ezek. 12:2 [b] [John 3:36] **13:15** [a] Heb. 5:11 [b] Luke 19:42 [c] Acts 28:26, 27 [1] NU-Text and M-Text read *would.* [2] Isaiah 6:9, 10 **13:16** [a] Luke 10:23, 24 **13:17** [a] Heb. 11:13 **13:18** [a] Mark 4:13–20 **13:19** [a] Matt. 4:23 **13:20** [a] Is. 58:2 **13:21** [a] [Acts 14:22] [b] Matt. 11:6 **13:22** [a] 1 Tim. 6:9 [b] Jer. 4:3 **13:23** [a] Col. 1:6

FOR THE SALVATION OF ALL

In His name Gentiles will trust.

MATTHEW 12:21

The evangelist Matthew quoted Isaiah 42:1–4, one of the longest excerpts of Old Testament Scripture in the Gospels. It is a wonderful prophecy, a beautiful passage in which the Messiah, the Lord's Servant, is called "chosen," "Beloved," One who would not "quarrel nor cry out" but instead would bring "forth justice" (Matt. 12:18–20). The quotation concludes with the remarkable words, "And in His name Gentiles will trust" (v. 21).

The popular expectation was that the Messiah would come and crush the Romans and Gentiles. Instead, the true Messiah would be *trusted* by the Gentiles, who historically were Israel's enemies. This is the ultimate Dale Carnegie "how to win friends and influence people" outcome. The mission of Jesus is not to conquer humans but to save them, not to punish but to forgive, not to rattle them but to give them peace. He is our Savior and Redeemer, our Friend and Good Shepherd.

until the harvest, and at the time of harvest I
will say to the reapers, "First gather together
the tares and bind them in bundles to burn
them, but [a]gather the wheat into my barn." ' "

The Parable of the Mustard Seed

31Another parable He put forth to them,
saying: [a]"The kingdom of heaven is like a
mustard seed, which a man took and sowed
in his field, 32which indeed is the least of all
the seeds; but when it is grown it is greater than the herbs and becomes a [a]tree, so
that the birds of the air come and nest in
its branches."

The Parable of the Leaven

33[a]Another parable He spoke to them: "The
kingdom of heaven is like leaven, which a
woman took and hid in three measures[1] of
meal till [b]it was all leavened."

Prophecy and the Parables

34[a]All these things Jesus spoke to the multitude in parables; and without a parable He did
not speak to them, 35that it might be fulfilled
which was spoken by the prophet, saying:

[a]"I will open My mouth in parables;
[b]I will utter things kept secret from the
foundation of the world."[1]

The Parable of the Tares Explained

36Then Jesus sent the multitude away and
went into the house. And His disciples came
to Him, saying, "Explain to us the parable of
the tares of the field."

37He answered and said to them: "He who
sows the good seed is the Son of Man. 38[a]The
field is the world, the good seeds are the sons
of the kingdom, but the tares are [b]the sons
of the wicked *one.* 39The enemy who sowed
them is the devil, [a]the harvest is the end
of the age, and the reapers are the angels.
40Therefore as the tares are gathered and
burned in the fire, so it will be at the end
of this age. 41The Son of Man will send out
His angels, [a]and they will gather out of His
kingdom all things that offend, and those
who practice lawlessness, 42[a]and will cast
them into the furnace of fire. [b]There will be
wailing and gnashing of teeth. 43[a]Then the
righteous will shine forth as the sun in the
kingdom of their Father. [b]He who has ears
to hear, let him hear!

The Parable of the Hidden Treasure

44"Again, the kingdom of heaven is like
treasure hidden in a field, which a man found
and hid; and for joy over it he goes and [a]sells
all that he has and [b]buys that field.

13:30 [a] Matt. 3:12 **13:31** [a] Luke 13:18, 19 **13:32** [a] Ezek. 17:22–24; 31:3–9 **13:33** [a] Luke 13:20, 21 [b] [1 Cor. 5:6] [1] Greek *sata,* approximately two pecks in all **13:34** [a] Ps. 78:2; Mark 4:33, 34 **13:35** [a] Ps. 78:2 [b] Eph. 3:9 [1] Psalm 78:2 **13:38** [a] Rom. 10:18 [b] John 8:44 **13:39** [a] Rev. 14:15 **13:41** [a] Matt. 18:7 **13:42** [a] Rev. 19:20; 20:10 [b] Matt. 8:12; 13:50 **13:43** [a] [Dan. 12:3] [b] Matt. 13:9 **13:44** [a] Phil. 3:7, 8 [b] [Is. 55:1]

THE TRUE AND BETTER KING

"The queen of the South . . . came from the ends of the earth to hear the wisdom of Solomon; and indeed a greater than Solomon is here."

MATTHEW 12:42

In verses 38–42 Jesus compared His life with the lives of two celebrated Old Testament figures—the prophet Jonah and King Solomon. His comparisons are extraordinary. Jonah enjoyed the reputation of one of Israel's most successful prophets. The entire city of Nineveh repented in response to this preacher. Yet, Jesus declared, one "greater than Jonah is here" (v. 41). Solomon enjoyed a reputation as Israel's greatest king, whose wisdom was unequaled. Yet One "greater than Solomon is here," Jesus said (v. 42). What God was doing through Jesus—His preaching and His mighty deeds—was even more astounding than what God had done through Jonah and Solomon.

In making these comparisons, Jesus was not boasting but upbraiding His contemporaries, *especially the religious* leaders. They simply could not recognize who was in their midst. God was at work, and they were missing it. All of us have longed for redemption and peace. Well, here it is! Let's embrace the peace of God today by trusting in the superiority of Jesus Christ over all things!

The Parable of the Pearl of Great Price

45"Again, the kingdom of heaven is like a
merchant seeking beautiful pearls, 46who,
when he had found [a]one pearl of great price,
went and sold all that he had and bought it.

The Parable of the Dragnet

47"Again, the kingdom of heaven is like a
dragnet that was cast into the sea and [a]gath-
ered some of every kind, 48which, when it was
full, they drew to shore; and they sat down
and gathered the good into vessels, but threw
the bad away. 49So it will be at the end of the
age. The angels will come forth, [a]separate
the wicked from among the just, 50and cast
them into the furnace of fire. There will be
wailing and gnashing of teeth."

51Jesus said to them,[1] "Have you understood all these things?"

They said to Him, "Yes, Lord."[2]

52Then He said to them, "Therefore every
scribe instructed concerning[1] the kingdom of
heaven is like a householder who brings out
of his treasure [a]*things* new and old."

Jesus Rejected at Nazareth

53Now it came to pass, when Jesus had
finished these parables, that He departed
from there. 54[a]When He had come to His
own country, He taught them in their synagogue, so that they were astonished and
said, "Where did this *Man* get this wisdom
and *these* mighty works? 55[a]Is this not the
carpenter's son? Is not His mother called
Mary? And [b]His brothers [c]James, Joses,[1]
Simon, and Judas? 56And His sisters, are
they not all with us? Where then did this
Man get all these things?" 57So they [a]were
offended at Him.

But Jesus said to them, [b]"A prophet is not
without honor except in his own country and
in his own house." 58Now [a]He did not do many
mighty works there because of their unbelief.

John the Baptist Beheaded

14 At that time [a]Herod the tetrarch heard
the report about Jesus 2and said to his
servants, "This is John the Baptist; he is risen
from the dead, and therefore these powers
are at work in him." 3[a]For Herod had laid
hold of John and bound him, and put *him* in
prison for the sake of Herodias, his brother
Philip's wife. 4Because John had said to him,
[a]"It is not lawful for you to have her." 5And
although he wanted to put him to death, he
feared the multitude, [a]because they counted
him as a prophet.

6But when Herod's birthday was celebrated, the daughter of Herodias danced before
them and pleased Herod. 7Therefore he
promised with an oath to give her whatever
she might ask.

8So she, having been prompted by her
mother, said, "Give me John the Baptist's
head here on a platter."

9And the king was sorry; nevertheless, because of the oaths and because of those who
sat with him, he commanded *it* to be given
to *her*. 10So he sent and had John beheaded
in prison. 11And his head was brought on a
platter and given to the girl, and she brought
it to her mother. 12Then his disciples came
and took away the body and buried it, and
went and told Jesus.

Feeding the Five Thousand

13[a]When Jesus heard *it*, He departed from
there by boat to a deserted place by Himself. But when the multitudes heard it, they
followed Him on foot from the cities. 14And
when Jesus went out He saw a great multitude; and He [a]was moved with compassion
for them, and healed their sick. 15[a]When it
was evening, His disciples came to Him,
saying, "This is a deserted place, and the
hour is already late. Send the multitudes
away, that they may go into the villages and
buy themselves food."

16But Jesus said to them, "They do not need
to go away. You give them something to eat."

17And they said to Him, "We have here only
five loaves and two fish."

18He said, "Bring them here to Me." 19Then
He commanded the multitudes to sit down
on the grass. And He took the five loaves
and the two fish, and looking up to heaven,
[a]He blessed and broke and gave the loaves
to the disciples; and the disciples gave to the
multitudes. 20So they all ate and were filled,
and they took up twelve baskets full of the
fragments that remained. 21Now those who
had eaten were about five thousand men,
besides women and children.

Jesus Walks on the Sea

22Immediately Jesus made His disciples
get into the boat and go before Him to the
other side, while He sent the multitudes
away. 23[a]And when He had sent the multitudes away, He went up on the mountain by

13:46 [a] Prov. 2:4; 3:14, 15; 8:10, 19 **13:47** [a] Matt. 22:9, 10 **13:49** [a] Matt. 25:32 **13:51** [1] NU-Text omits *Jesus said to them.* [2] NU-Text omits *Lord.* **13:52** [a] Song 7:13 [1] Or *for* **13:54** [a] Luke 4:16 **13:55** [a] John 6:42 [b] Matt. 12:46 [c] Mark 15:40 [1] NU-Text reads *Joseph.* **13:57** [a] Matt. 11:6 [b] Luke 4:24 **13:58** [a] Mark 6:5, 6 **14:1** [a] Mark 6:14–29 **14:3** [a] Luke 3:19, 20 **14:4** [a] Lev. 18:16; 20:21 **14:5** [a] Luke 20:6 **14:13** [a] John 6:1, 2 **14:14** [a] Mark 6:34 **14:15** [a] Luke 9:12 **14:19** [a] Matt. 15:36; 26:26 **14:23** [a] Mark 6:46

Himself to pray. [b]Now when evening came, He was alone there. 24But the boat was now in the middle of the sea,[1] tossed by the waves, for the wind was contrary.

25Now in the fourth watch of the night Jesus went to them, walking on the sea. 26And when the disciples saw Him [a]walking on the sea, they were troubled, saying, "It is a ghost!" And they cried out for fear.

27But immediately Jesus spoke to them, saying, "Be of good [a]cheer! It is I; do not be afraid."

28And Peter answered Him and said, "Lord, if it is You, command me to come to You on the water."

29So He said, "Come." And when Peter had come down out of the boat, he walked on the water to go to Jesus. 30But when he saw that the wind *was* boisterous,[1] he was afraid; and beginning to sink he cried out, saying, "Lord, save me!"

31And immediately Jesus stretched out *His* hand and caught him, and said to him, "O you of [a]little faith, why did you doubt?" 32And when they got into the boat, the wind ceased.

33Then those who were in the boat came and[1] worshiped Him, saying, "Truly [a]You are the Son of God."

Many Touch Him and Are Made Well

34[a]When they had crossed over, they came to the land of[1] Gennesaret. 35And when the men of that place recognized Him, they sent out into all that surrounding region, brought to Him all who were sick, 36and begged Him that they might only [a]touch the hem of His garment. And [b]as many as touched *it* were made perfectly well.

Defilement Comes from Within

15 Then [a]the scribes and Pharisees who were from Jerusalem came to Jesus, saying, 2[a]"Why do Your disciples transgress the tradition of the elders? For they do not wash their hands when they eat bread."

3He answered and said to them, "Why do you also transgress the commandment of God because of your tradition? 4For God commanded, saying, [a]'Honor your father and your mother';[1] and, [b]'He who curses father or mother, let him be put to death.'[2] 5But you say, 'Whoever says to his father or mother, [a]"Whatever profit you might have received from me *is* a gift *to God*"— 6then he need not honor his father or mother.'[1] Thus you have made the commandment[2] of God of no effect by your tradition. 7[a]Hypocrites! Well did Isaiah prophesy about you, saying:

8 'These[a] people draw near to Me with
 their mouth,
And[1] honor Me with *their* lips,
But their heart is far from Me.
9 And in vain they worship Me,
[a]Teaching *as* doctrines the
 commandments of men.'"[1]

10[a]When He had called the multitude to *Himself,* He said to them, "Hear and understand: 11[a]Not what goes into the mouth defiles a man; but what comes out of the mouth, this defiles a man."

12Then His disciples came and said to Him, "Do You know that the Pharisees were offended when they heard this saying?"

13But He answered and said, [a]"Every plant which My heavenly Father has not planted will be uprooted. 14Let them alone. [a]They are blind leaders of the blind. And if the blind leads the blind, both will fall into a ditch."

15[a]Then Peter answered and said to Him, "Explain this parable to us."

16So Jesus said, [a]"Are you also still without understanding? 17Do you not yet understand that [a]whatever enters the mouth goes into the stomach and is eliminated? 18But [a]those things which proceed out of the mouth come from the heart, and they defile a man. 19[a]For out of the heart proceed evil thoughts, murders, adulteries, fornications, thefts, false witness, blasphemies. 20These are *the things* which defile a man, but to eat with unwashed hands does not defile a man."

A Gentile Shows Her Faith

21[a]Then Jesus went out from there and departed to the region of Tyre and Sidon. 22And behold, a woman of Canaan came from that region and cried out to Him, saying, "Have mercy on me, O Lord, [a]Son of David! My daughter is severely demon-possessed."

23But He answered her not a word.

And His disciples came and urged Him, saying, "Send her away, for she cries out after us."

14:23 [b] John 6:16 **14:24** [1] NU-Text reads *many furlongs away from the land.* **14:26** [a] Job 9:8 **14:27** [a] Acts 23:11; *27:22, 25, 36* **14:30** [1] *NU-Text brackets that* and *boisterous* as disputed. **14:31** [a] Matt. 6:30; 8:26 **14:33** [a] Ps. 2:7 [1] NU-Text omits *came and.* **14:34** [a] Mark 6:53 [1] NU-Text reads *came to land at.* **14:36** [a] [Mark 5:24–34] [b] [Luke 6:19] **15:1** [a] Mark 7:1 **15:2** [a] Mark 7:5 **15:4** [a] [Deut. 5:16] [b] Ex. 21:17 [1] Exodus 20:12; Deuteronomy 5:16 [2] Exodus 21:17 **15:5** [a] Mark 7:11, 12 **15:6** [1] NU-Text omits *or mother.* [2] NU-Text reads *word.* **15:7** [a] Mark 7:6 **15:8** [a] Ps. 78:36; Is. 29:13 [1] NU-Text omits *draw near to Me with their mouth, And.* **15:9** [a] [Col. 2:18–22] [1] Isaiah 29:13 **15:10** [a] Mark 7:14 **15:11** [a] [Acts 10:15] **15:13** [a] [John 15:2] **15:14** [a] Luke 6:39 **15:15** [a] Mark 7:17 **15:16** [a] Matt. 16:9 **15:17** [a] [1 Cor. 6:13] **15:18** [a] [James 3:6] **15:19** [a] Prov. 6:14 **15:21** [a] Mark 7:24–30 **15:22** [a] Matt. 1:1; 22:41, 42

24But He answered and said, [a]"I was not
sent except to the lost sheep of the house
of Israel."
25Then she came and worshiped Him,
saying, "Lord, help me!"
26But He answered and said, "It is not good
to take the children's bread and throw *it* to
the little [a]dogs."
27And she said, "Yes, Lord, yet even the
little dogs eat the crumbs which fall from
their masters' table."
28Then Jesus answered and said to her,
"O woman, [a]great *is* your faith! Let it be to
you as you desire." And her daughter was
healed from that very hour.

Jesus Heals Great Multitudes

29[a]Jesus departed from there, [b]skirted the
Sea of Galilee, and went up on the mountain
and sat down there. 30[a]Then great multitudes came to Him, having with them *the*
lame, blind, mute, maimed, and many others;
and they laid them down at Jesus' [b]feet, and
He healed them. 31So the multitude marveled when they saw *the* mute speaking, *the*
maimed made whole, *the* lame walking, and
the blind seeing; and they [a]glorified the God
of Israel.

Feeding the Four Thousand

32[a]Now Jesus called His disciples to *Himself* and said, "I have compassion on the
multitude, because they have now continued
with Me three days and have nothing to eat.
And I do not want to send them away hungry,
lest they faint on the way."
33[a]Then His disciples said to Him, "Where
could we get enough bread in the wilderness
to fill such a great multitude?"
34Jesus said to them, "How many loaves
do you have?"
And they said, "Seven, and a few little fish."
35So He commanded the multitude to sit
down on the ground. 36And [a]He took the
seven loaves and the fish and [b]gave thanks,
broke *them* and gave *them* to His disciples;
and the disciples *gave* to the multitude. 37So
they all ate and were filled, and they took
up seven large baskets full of the fragments
that were left. 38Now those who ate were four
thousand men, besides women and children.
39[a]And He sent away the multitude, got into
the boat, and came to the region of Magdala.[1]

The Pharisees and Sadducees Seek a Sign

16 Then the [a]Pharisees and Sadducees
came, and testing Him asked that He
would show them a sign from heaven. 2He
answered and said to them, "When it is evening you say, '*It will be* fair weather, for the
sky is red'; 3and in the morning, '*It will be*
foul weather today, for the sky is red and
threatening.' Hypocrites![1] You know how to

15:24 [a] Matt. 10:5, 6 **15:26** [a] Matt. 7:6 **15:28** [a] Luke 7:9 **15:29** [a] Mark 7:31–37 [b] Matt. 4:18 **15:30** [a] Is. 35:5, 6 [b] Luke 7:38; 8:41; 10:39 **15:31** [a] Luke 5:25, 26; 19:37, 38 **15:32** [a] Mark 8:1–10 **15:33** [a] 2 Kin. 4:43 **15:36** [a] Matt. 14:19; 26:27 [b] Luke 22:19 **15:39** [a] Mark 8:10 [1] NU-Text reads *Magadan.* **16:1** [a] Mark 8:11 **16:3** [1] NU-Text omits *Hypocrites.*

YOU CAN HAVE GREAT FAITH

"O woman, great is your faith! Let it be to you as you desire."

MATTHEW 15:28

At the outset of His public ministry Jesus made it clear that the Good News and the blessings that came with it were to be made available first to the "lost sheep of the house of Israel" (10:6). Only later would the gospel of messianic blessings be shared with Gentiles (28:18–20). Paul echoed the same idea in his letter to the Roman Christians: the gospel was "for the Jew first and also for the Greek" (Rom. 1:16).

So when the Greek-speaking Gentile woman beseeched Jesus on behalf of her tormented daughter, Jesus replied, "I was not sent except to the lost sheep of the house of Israel" (Matt. 15:24). But the woman's response so impressed Jesus, He praised the troubled mother and granted her request, saying, "O woman, great is your faith! Let it be to you as you desire" (v. 28). Her daughter was healed. What amazes me is the woman's faith—and how it moved Jesus.

Express your faith! Tell God you trust Him, and don't take no for an answer. Like Jacob, wrestle with God for His peace and don't let go until He blesses you.

discern the face of the sky, but you cannot
discern the signs of the times. 4[a]A wicked and
adulterous generation seeks after a sign, and
no sign shall be given to it except the sign of
the prophet[1] Jonah." And He left them and
departed.

The Leaven of the Pharisees and Sadducees

5Now [a]when His disciples had come to the
other side, they had forgotten to take bread.
6Then Jesus said to them, [a]"Take heed and
beware of the leaven of the Pharisees and
the Sadducees."
7And they reasoned among themselves,
saying, "*It is* because we have taken no bread."
8But Jesus, being aware of *it*, said to them,
"O you of little faith, why do you reason
among yourselves because you have brought
no bread?[1] 9[a]Do you not yet understand, or
remember the five loaves of the five thousand and how many baskets you took up?
10[a]Nor the seven loaves of the four thousand
and how many large baskets you took up?
11How is it you do not understand that I did
not speak to you concerning bread?—*but* to
beware of the leaven of the Pharisees and
Sadducees." 12Then they understood that He
did not tell *them* to beware of the leaven of
bread, but of the doctrine of the Pharisees
and Sadducees.

Peter Confesses Jesus as the Christ

13When Jesus came into the region of
Caesarea Philippi, He asked His disciples,
saying, [a]"Who do men say that I, the Son of
Man, am?"
14So they said, [a]"Some *say* John the Baptist,
some Elijah, and others Jeremiah or [b]one of
the prophets."
15He said to them, "But who do [a]you say
that I am?"
16Simon Peter answered and said, [a]"You
are the Christ, the Son of the living God."
17Jesus answered and said to him, "Blessed
are you, Simon Bar-Jonah, [a]for flesh and
blood has not revealed *this* to you, but [b]My
Father who is in heaven. 18And I also say to
you that [a]you are Peter, and [b]on this rock I
will build My church, and [c]the gates of Hades
shall not prevail against it. 19[a]And I will give
you the keys of the kingdom of heaven, and
whatever you bind on earth will be bound
in heaven, and whatever you loose on earth
will be loosed[1] in heaven."
20[a]Then He commanded His disciples that
they should tell no one that He was Jesus
the Christ.

16:4 [a] Matt. 12:39 [1] NU-Text omits *the prophet.* **16:5** [a] Mark 8:14 **16:6** [a] Luke 12:1 **16:8** [1] NU-Text reads *you have no bread.* **16:9** [a] Matt. 14:15–21 **16:10** [a] Matt. 15:32–38 **16:13** [a] Luke 9:18 **16:14** [a] Matt. 14:2 [b] Matt. 21:11 **16:15** [a] John 6:67 **16:16** [a] Acts 8:37; 9:20 **16:17** [a] [Eph. 2:8] [b] Gal. 1:16 **16:18** [a] John 1:42 [b] [Eph. 2:20] [c] Is. 38:10 **16:19** [a] Matt. 18:18 [1] Or *will have been bound . . . will have been loosed* **16:20** [a] Luke 9:21

MAKE THIS YOUR CONFESSION

You are the Christ.

MATTHEW 16:16

This is one of the most memorable passages in the Gospel of Matthew. In keeping with the Jewish custom of modesty and reluctance to make presumptuous assertions about oneself, Jesus asked His disciples, "Who do men say that I, the Son of Man, am?" (v. 13). The disciples had heard a number of opinions (14:1–2), so they offered, "Some say John the Baptist, some Elijah, and others Jeremiah or one of the prophets" (13:14). Yes, that's what people were saying: John the Baptist raised from the dead, perhaps Elijah who was thought to be the herald of the last day, maybe Jeremiah who had foretold the destruction of Solomon's temple, or perhaps some other prophet.

"But who do you say that I am?" Jesus asked (v. 15). Simon Peter answered, "You are the Christ, the Son of the living God" (v. 16). Peter didn't always get it right, but on this occasion *he hit the ball out of the park.* Jesus replied, "Blessed are you, Simon Bar-Jonah, for flesh and blood has not revealed this to you, but My Father who is in heaven" (v. 17). This single title, "the Christ," is another term for peace, for it comes from the word meaning "Messiah" or "Savior." The Christ has blessed us with His peace. Are you experiencing it today?

Jesus Predicts His Death and Resurrection

21 From that time Jesus began [a]to show to His disciples that He must go to Jerusalem, and suffer many things from the elders and chief priests and scribes, and be killed, and be raised the third day.

22 Then Peter took Him aside and began to rebuke Him, saying, "Far be it from You, Lord; this shall not happen to You!"

23 But He turned and said to Peter, "Get behind Me, [a]Satan! [b]You are an offense to Me, for you are not mindful of the things of God, but the things of men."

Take Up the Cross and Follow Him

24 [a]Then Jesus said to His disciples, "If anyone desires to come after Me, let him deny himself, and take up his cross, and [b]follow Me. 25 For [a]whoever desires to save his life will lose it, but whoever loses his life for My sake will find it. 26 For what [a]profit is it to a man if he gains the whole world, and loses his own soul? Or [b]what will a man give in exchange for his soul? 27 For [a]the Son of Man will come in the glory of His Father [b]with His angels, [c]and then He will reward each according to his works. 28 Assuredly, I say to you, [a]there are some standing here who shall not taste death till they see the Son of Man coming in His kingdom."

Jesus Transfigured on the Mount

17 Now [a]after six days Jesus took Peter, James, and John his brother, led them up on a high mountain by themselves; 2 and He was transfigured before them. His face shone like the sun, and His clothes became as white as the light. 3 And behold, Moses and Elijah appeared to them, talking with Him. 4 Then Peter answered and said to Jesus, "Lord, it is good for us to be here; if You wish, let us[1] make here three tabernacles: one for You, one for Moses, and one for Elijah."

5 [a]While he was still speaking, behold, a bright cloud overshadowed them; and suddenly a voice came out of the cloud, saying, [b]"This is My beloved Son, [c]in whom I am well pleased. [d]Hear Him!" 6 [a]And when the disciples heard *it,* they fell on their faces and were greatly afraid. 7 But Jesus came and [a]touched them and said, "Arise, and do not be afraid." 8 When they had lifted up their eyes, they saw no one but Jesus only.

9 Now as they came down from the mountain, Jesus commanded them, saying, "Tell the vision to no one until the Son of Man is risen from the dead."

10 And His disciples asked Him, saying, [a]"Why then do the scribes say that Elijah must come first?"

11 Jesus answered and said to them, "Indeed, Elijah is coming first[1] and will [a]restore all things. 12 [a]But I say to you that Elijah has come already, and they [b]did not know him but did to him whatever they wished. Likewise [c]the Son of Man is also about to suffer at their hands." 13 [a]Then the disciples understood that He spoke to them of John the Baptist.

A Boy Is Healed

14 [a]And when they had come to the multitude, a man came to Him, kneeling down to Him and saying, 15 "Lord, have mercy on my son, for he is an epileptic[1] and suffers severely; for he often falls into the fire and often into the water. 16 So I brought him to Your disciples, but they could not cure him."

17 Then Jesus answered and said, "O faithless and [a]perverse generation, how long shall I be with you? How long shall I bear with you? Bring him here to Me." 18 And Jesus [a]rebuked the demon, and it came out of him; and the child was cured from that very hour.

19 Then the disciples came to Jesus privately and said, "Why could we not cast it out?"

20 So Jesus said to them, "Because of your unbelief;[1] for assuredly, I say to you, [a]if you have faith as a mustard seed, you will say to this mountain, 'Move from here to there,' and it will move; and nothing will be impossible for you. 21 However, this kind does not go out except by prayer and fasting."[1]

Jesus Again Predicts His Death and Resurrection

22 [a]Now while they were staying[1] in Galilee, Jesus said to them, "The Son of Man is about to be betrayed into the hands of men, 23 and they will kill Him, and the third day He will be raised up." And they were exceedingly [a]sorrowful.

Peter and His Master Pay Their Taxes

24 [a]When they had come to Capernaum,[1] those who received the *temple* tax came to

16:21 [a] Luke 9:22; 18:31; 24:46 **16:23** [a] Matt. 4:10 [b] [Rom. 8:7] **16:24** [a] [2 Tim. 3:12] [b] [1 Pet. 2:21] **16:25** [a] John 12:25 **16:26** [a] Luke 12:20, 21 [b] Ps. 49:7, 8 **16:27** [a] Mark 8:38 [b] [Dan. 7:10] [c] Rom. 2:6 **16:28** [a] Luke 9:27 **17:1** [a] Mark 9:2–8 **17:4** [1] NU-Text reads *I will.* **17:5** [a] 2 Pet. 1:17 [b] Mark 1:11 [c] Matt. 3:17; 12:18 [d] [Deut. 18:15, 19] **17:6** [a] 2 Pet. 1:18 **17:7** [a] Dan. 8:18 **17:10** [a] Mal. 4:5 **17:11** [a] [Mal. 4:6] [1] NU-Text omits *first.* **17:12** [a] Mark 9:12, 13 [b] Matt. 14:3, 10 [c] Matt. 16:21 **17:13** [a] Matt. 11:14 **17:14** [a] Mark 9:14–28 **17:15** [1] Literally *moonstruck* **17:17** [a] Phil. 2:15 **17:18** [a] Luke 4:41 **17:20** [a] Luke 17:6 [1] NU-Text reads *little faith.* **17:21** [1] NU-Text omits this verse. **17:22** [a] Mark 8:31 [1] NU-Text reads *gathering together.* **17:23** [a] John 16:6; 19:30 **17:24** [a] Mark 9:33 [1] NU-Text reads *Capharnaum* (here and elsewhere).

Peter and said, "Does your Teacher not pay
the *temple* tax?"
25 He said, "Yes."
And when he had come into the house,
Jesus anticipated him, saying, "What do you
think, Simon? From whom do the kings of
the earth take customs or taxes, from their
sons or from [a]strangers?"
26 Peter said to Him, "From strangers."
Jesus said to him, "Then the sons are free.
27 Nevertheless, lest we offend them, go to
the sea, cast in a hook, and take the fish that
comes up first. And when you have opened
its mouth, you will find a piece of money;[1]
take that and give it to them for Me and you."

Who Is the Greatest?

18 At [a]that time the disciples came to
Jesus, saying, "Who then is greatest
in the kingdom of heaven?"
2 Then Jesus called a little [a]child to Him,
set him in the midst of them, 3 and said, "Assuredly, I say to you, [a]unless you are converted and become as little children, you will
by no means enter the kingdom of heaven.
4 [a]Therefore whoever humbles himself as this
little child is the greatest in the kingdom of
heaven. 5 [a]Whoever receives one little child
like this in My name receives Me.

Jesus Warns of Offenses

6 [a]"But whoever causes one of these little
ones who believe in Me to sin, it would be better for him if a millstone were hung around
his neck, and he were drowned in the depth
of the sea. 7 Woe to the world because of offenses! For [a]offenses must come, but [b]woe
to that man by whom the offense comes!
8 [a]"If your hand or foot causes you to sin,
cut it off and cast *it* from you. It is better
for you to enter into life lame or maimed,
rather than having two hands or two feet, to
be cast into the everlasting fire. 9 And if your
eye causes you to sin, pluck it out and cast *it*
from you. It is better for you to enter into life
with one eye, rather than having two eyes,
to be cast into hell fire.

The Parable of the Lost Sheep

10 "Take heed that you do not despise one
of these little ones, for I say to you that in
heaven [a]their angels always [b]see the face of
My Father who is in heaven. 11 [a]For the Son of
Man has come to save that which was lost.[1]
12 [a]"What do you think? If a man has a hundred sheep, and one of them goes astray, does
he not leave the ninety-nine and go to the
mountains to seek the one that is straying?
13 And if he should find it, assuredly, I say to
you, he rejoices more over that *sheep* than
over the ninety-nine that did not go astray.
14 Even so it is not the [a]will of your Father
who is in heaven that one of these little ones
should perish.

Dealing with a Sinning Brother

15 "Moreover [a]if your brother sins against
you, go and tell him his fault between you

17:25 [a] [Is. 60:10–17] **17:27** [1] Greek *stater,* the exact amount to pay the temple tax (didrachma) for two **18:1** [a] Luke 9:46–48; 22:24–27 **18:2** [a] Matt. 19:14 **18:3** [a] Luke 18:16 **18:4** [a] [Matt. 20:27; 23:11] **18:5** [a] [Matt. 10:42] **18:6** [a] Mark 9:42 **18:7** [a] [1 Cor. 11:19] [b] Matt. 26:24; 27:4, 5 **18:8** [a] Matt. 5:29, 30 **18:10** [a] [Heb. 1:14] [b] Luke 1:19 **18:11** [a] Luke 9:56 [1] NU-Text omits this verse. **18:12** [a] Luke 15:4–7 **18:14** [a] [1 Tim. 2:4] **18:15** [a] Lev. 19:17

GOD DESIRES PEACE

"It is not the will of your Father who is in heaven that one of these little ones should perish."

MATTHEW 18:14

Jesus' words have never been more relevant or more urgent than in today's world of sex trafficking, child porn, and abuse. He taught His disciples, "It is not the will of your Father who is in heaven that one of these little ones should perish." Interpreters debate who the "little ones" are. Are they new believers? Are they children? Most interpreters think children were in view. On other occasions Jesus showed affection for children and welcomed them (Matt. 18:2–5; 19:13–16; Mark 9:36–37).

In ancient times children's lives were at risk due to abortion, exposure, enslavement, and illness. *These facts reflect* the grim realities of poverty and hardship. But in Jesus' eyes every life was precious; every child was wanted and loved. One essential aspect of living in the peace of God is to proclaim the truth that every human being is valuable and loved. Every person can find self-esteem and peace in Him.

and him alone. If he hears you, [b]you have
gained your brother. 16But if he will not hear,
take with you one or two more, that [a]'by the
mouth of two or three witnesses every word
may be established.'[1] 17And if he refuses to
hear them, tell *it* to the church. But if he
refuses even to hear the church, let him be
to you like a [a]heathen and a tax collector.

18"Assuredly, I say to you, [a]whatever you
bind on earth will be bound in heaven, and
whatever you loose on earth will be loosed
in heaven.

19[a]"Again I say[1] to you that if two of you
agree on earth concerning anything that
they ask, [b]it will be done for them by My Father in heaven. 20For where two or three are
gathered [a]together in My name, I am there
in the midst of them."

The Parable of the Unforgiving Servant

21Then Peter came to Him and said, "Lord,
how often shall my brother sin against me,
and I forgive him? [a]Up to seven times?"

22Jesus said to him, "I do not say to you, [a]up
to seven times, but up to seventy times seven.
23Therefore the kingdom of heaven is like a
certain king who wanted to settle accounts
with his servants. 24And when he had begun to
settle accounts, one was brought to him who
owed him ten thousand talents. 25But as he
was not able to pay, his master commanded
[a]that he be sold, with his wife and children and
all that he had, and that payment be made.
26The servant therefore fell down before him,
saying, 'Master, have patience with me, and
I will pay you all.' 27Then the master of that
servant was moved with compassion, released
him, and forgave him the debt.

28"But that servant went out and found
one of his fellow servants who owed him a
hundred denarii; and he laid hands on him
and took *him* by the throat, saying, 'Pay me
what you owe!' 29So his fellow servant fell
down at his feet[1] and begged him, saying,
'Have patience with me, and I will pay you
all.'[2] 30And he would not, but went and threw
him into prison till he should pay the debt.
31So when his fellow servants saw what had
been done, they were very grieved, and came
and told their master all that had been done.
32Then his master, after he had called him,
said to him, 'You wicked servant! I forgave
you [a]all that debt because you begged me.
33Should you not also have had compassion
on your fellow servant, just as I had pity on
you?' 34And his master was angry, and delivered him to the torturers until he should
pay all that was due to him.

35[a]"So My heavenly Father also will do to
you if each of you, from his heart, does not
forgive his brother his trespasses."[1]

Marriage and Divorce

19 Now it came to pass, [a]when Jesus had
finished these sayings, *that* He departed from Galilee and came to the region
of Judea beyond the Jordan. 2[a]And great
multitudes followed Him, and He healed
them there.

3The Pharisees also came to Him, testing
Him, and saying to Him, "Is it lawful for a
man to divorce his wife for *just* any reason?"
4And He answered and said to them, "Have
you not read that He who made[1] *them* at the
beginning [a]'made them male and female,'[2]
5and said, [a]'For this reason a man shall leave
his father and mother and be joined to his
wife, and [b]the two shall become one flesh'?[1]
6So then, they are no longer two but one flesh.
Therefore what God has joined together, let
not man separate."

7They said to Him, [a]"Why then did Moses
command to give a certificate of divorce, and
to put her away?"

8He said to them, "Moses, because of the
[a]hardness of your hearts, permitted you to
divorce your [b]wives, but from the beginning
it was not so. 9[a]And I say to you, whoever
divorces his wife, except for sexual immorality,[1] and marries another, commits adultery;
and whoever marries her who is divorced
commits adultery."

10His disciples said to Him, [a]"If such is
the case of the man with *his* wife, it is better
not to marry."

Jesus Teaches on Celibacy

11But He said to them, [a]"All cannot accept
this saying, but only *those* to whom it has
been given: 12For there are eunuchs who were
born thus from *their* mother's womb, and
[a]there are eunuchs who were made eunuchs
by men, and there are eunuchs who have
made themselves eunuchs for the kingdom
of heaven's sake. He who is able to accept *it*,
let him accept *it*."

18:15 [b] [James 5:20] **18:16** [a] Deut. 17:6; 19:15 [1] Deuteronomy 19:15 **18:17** [a] [2 Thess. 3:6, 14] **18:18** [a] [John 20:22, 23]
18:19 [a] [1 Cor. 1:10] [b] [1 John 3:22; 5:14] [1] NU-Text and M-Text read *Again, assuredly, I say.* **18:20** [a] Acts 20:7
18:21 [a] Luke 17:4 **18:22** [a] Col. 3:13 **18:25** [a] 2 Kin. 4:1 **18:29** [1] NU-Text omits *at his feet.* [2] NU-Text and M-Text omit *all.*
18:32 [a] Luke 7:41–43 **18:35** [a] James 2:13 [1] NU-Text omits *his trespasses.* **19:1** [a] Mark 10:1–12 **19:2** [a] Matt. 12:15
19:4 [a] Gen. 1:27; 5:2 [1] NU-Text reads *created.* [2] Genesis 1:27; 5:2 **19:5** [a] Gen. 2:24 [b] [1 Cor. 6:16; 7:2] [1] Genesis 2:24
19:7 [a] Deut. 24:1–4 **19:8** [a] Heb. 3:15 [b] Mal. 2:16 **19:9** [a] [Matt. 5:32] [1] Or *fornication* **19:10** [a] [Prov. 21:19]
19:11 [a] [1 Cor. 7:2, 7, 9, 17] **19:12** [a] [1 Cor. 7:32]

Jesus Blesses Little Children

13 [a]Then little children were brought to Him
that He might put *His* hands on them and
pray, but the disciples rebuked them. 14 But
Jesus said, "Let the little children come to
Me, and do not forbid them; for [a]of such is
the kingdom of heaven." 15 And He laid *His*
hands on them and departed from there.

Jesus Counsels the Rich Young Ruler

16 [a]Now behold, one came and said to Him,
[b]"Good[1] Teacher, what good thing shall I do
that I may have eternal life?"
17 So He said to him, "Why do you call Me
good?[1] No one *is* [a]good but One, *that is,* God.[2]
But if you want to enter into life, [b]keep the
commandments."
18 He said to Him, "Which ones?"
Jesus said, [a]" 'You shall not murder,' 'You
shall not commit adultery,' 'You shall not
steal,' 'You shall not bear false witness,'
19 [a]'Honor your father and *your* mother,'[1] and,
[b]'You shall love your neighbor as yourself.' "[2]
20 The young man said to Him, "All these
things I have [a]kept from my youth.[1] What
do I still lack?"
21 Jesus said to him, "If you want to be perfect, [a]go, sell what you have and give to the
poor, and you will have treasure in heaven;
and come, follow Me."
22 But when the young man heard that
saying, he went away sorrowful, for he had
great possessions.

With God All Things Are Possible

23 Then Jesus said to His disciples, "Assuredly, I say to you that [a]it is hard for a rich
man to enter the kingdom of heaven. 24 And
again I say to you, it is easier for a camel to
go through the eye of a needle than for a rich
man to enter the kingdom of God."
25 When His disciples heard *it,* they were
greatly astonished, saying, "Who then can
be saved?"
26 But Jesus looked at *them* and said to
them, "With men this is impossible, but [a]with
God all things are possible."
27 Then Peter answered and said to Him,
"See, [a]we have left all and followed You.
Therefore what shall we have?"
28 So Jesus said to them, "Assuredly I say
to you, that in the regeneration, when the
Son of Man sits on the throne of His glory,
[a]you who have followed Me will also sit on
twelve thrones, judging the twelve tribes of
Israel. 29 [a]And everyone who has left houses
or brothers or sisters or father or mother
or wife[1] or children or lands, for My name's
sake, shall receive a hundredfold, and inherit

19:13 [a] Luke 18:15 **19:14** [a] Matt. 18:3, 4 **19:16** [a] Mark 10:17–30 [b] Luke 10:25 [1] NU-Text omits *Good.* **19:17** [a] Nah. 1:7 [b] Lev. 18:5 [1] NU-Text reads *Why do you ask Me about what is good?* [2] NU-Text reads *There is One who is good.* **19:18** [a] Ex. 20:13–16 **19:19** [a] Ex. 20:12–16; Deut. 5:16–20 [b] Lev. 19:18 [1] Exodus 20:12–16; Deuteronomy 5:16–20 [2] Leviticus 19:18 **19:20** [a] [Phil. 3:6, 7] [1] NU-Text omits *from my youth.* **19:21** [a] Acts 2:45; 4:34, 35 **19:23** [a] [1 Tim. 6:9] **19:26** [a] Jer. 32:17 **19:27** [a] Deut. 33:9 **19:28** [a] Luke 22:28–30 **19:29** [a] Mark 10:29, 30 [1] NU-Text omits *or wife.*

WITH CHILDLIKE FAITH

"Let the little children come to Me."

MATTHEW 19:14

Society in the ancient world was hierarchical. Children were at the bottom. People clamored for the attention of the rich and powerful and ignored the poor and marginal.

The disciples of Jesus often acted as "handlers" for their well-known and much-sought-after Rabbi. Although Jesus was instructing them, they had much to learn. We see this in how they reacted to anxious parents who brought their children to Jesus so that He might lay His hands on them and pray for them. Given the high mortality rate for infants and young children, I can't blame them. But the disciples rebuked those parents, probably claiming that Jesus was too busy to spend time with children.

The disciples were wrong. Jesus said, "Let the little children come to Me . . . for of such is *the kingdom of heaven" (v. 14).* The gates of heaven are open to all who knock, no matter how great or small. Perhaps the most overlooked aspect of this passage is the beauty and the intelligence of a childlike faith. Take time to cast all your burdens on the Lord today in childlike faith, and rest in the peace of Jesus.

eternal life. 30[a]But many *who are* first will be
last, and the last first.

The Parable of the Workers in the Vineyard

20 "For the kingdom of heaven is like a
landowner who went out early in the
morning to hire laborers for his vineyard.
2Now when he had agreed with the laborers
for a denarius a day, he sent them into his
vineyard. 3And he went out about the third
hour and saw others standing idle in the
marketplace, 4and said to them, 'You also go
into the vineyard, and whatever is right I will
give you.' So they went. 5Again he went out
about the sixth and the ninth hour, and did
likewise. 6And about the eleventh hour he
went out and found others standing idle,[1] and
said to them, 'Why have you been standing
here idle all day?' 7They said to him, 'Because
no one hired us.' He said to them, 'You also
go into the vineyard, and whatever is right
you will receive.'[1]
8"So when evening had come, the owner
of the vineyard said to his steward, 'Call the
laborers and give them *their* wages, beginning
with the last to the first.' 9And when those
came who *were hired* about the eleventh hour,
they each received a denarius. 10But when the
first came, they supposed that they would
receive more; and they likewise received each
a denarius. 11And when they had received
it, they complained against the landowner,
12saying, 'These last *men* have worked *only*
one hour, and you made them equal to us
who have borne the burden and the heat of
the day.' 13But he answered one of them and
said, 'Friend, I am doing you no wrong. Did
you not agree with me for a denarius? 14Take
what is yours and go your way. I wish to give
to this last man *the same* as to you. 15[a]Is it
not lawful for me to do what I wish with my
own things? Or [b]is your eye evil because I am
good?' 16[a]So the last will be first, and the first
last. [b]For many are called, but few chosen."[1]

Jesus a Third Time Predicts His Death and Resurrection

17[a]Now Jesus, going up to Jerusalem,
took the twelve disciples aside on the road
and said to them, 18[a]"Behold, we are going
up to Jerusalem, and the Son of Man will
be betrayed to the chief priests and to the
scribes; and they will condemn Him to death,
19[a]and deliver Him to the Gentiles to [b]mock
and to [c]scourge and to [d]crucify. And the third
day He will [e]rise again."

Greatness Is Serving

20[a]Then the mother of [b]Zebedee's sons
came to Him with her sons, kneeling down
and asking something from Him.
21And He said to her, "What do you wish?"
She said to Him, "Grant that these two sons
of mine [a]may sit, one on Your right hand
and the other on the left, in Your kingdom."
22But Jesus answered and said, "You do not
know what you ask. Are you able to drink [a]the
cup that I am about to drink, and be baptized
with [b]the baptism that I am baptized with?"[1]
They said to Him, "We are able."
23So He said to them, [a]"You will indeed
drink My cup, and be baptized with the baptism that I am baptized with;[1] but to sit on
My right hand and on My left is not Mine to
give, but *it is for those* for whom it is prepared
by My Father."
24[a]And when the ten heard *it,* they were
greatly displeased with the two brothers.
25But Jesus called them to *Himself* and said,
"You know that the rulers of the Gentiles
lord it over them, and those who are great
exercise authority over them. 26Yet [a]it shall
not be so among you; but [b]whoever desires
to become great among you, let him be your
servant. 27[a]And whoever desires to be first
among you, let him be your slave— 28[a]just as
the [b]Son of Man did not come to be served,
[c]but to serve, and [d]to give His life a ransom
[e]for many."

Two Blind Men Receive Their Sight

29[a]Now as they went out of Jericho, a great
multitude followed Him. 30And behold, [a]two
blind men sitting by the road, when they
heard that Jesus was passing by, cried out,
saying, "Have mercy on us, O Lord, [b]Son of
David!"
31Then the multitude [a]warned them that
they should be quiet; but they cried out all
the more, saying, "Have mercy on us, O Lord,
Son of David!"
32So Jesus stood still and called them, and
said, "What do you want Me to do for you?"

19:30 [a] Luke 13:30 **20:6** [1] NU-Text omits *idle.* **20:7** [1] NU-Text omits the last clause of this verse. **20:15** [a] [Rom. 9:20, 21] [b] Deut. 15:9 **20:16** [a] Matt. 19:30 [b] Matt. 22:14 [1] NU-Text omits the last sentence of this verse. **20:17** [a] Mark 10:32–34 **20:18** [a] Matt. 16:21; 26:47–57 **20:19** [a] Matt. 27:2 [b] Matt. 26:67, 68; 27:29, 41 [c] Matt. 27:26 [d] Acts 3:13–15 [e] Matt. 28:5, 6 **20:20** [a] Mark 10:35–45 [b] Matt. 4:21; 10:2 **20:21** [a] [Matt. 19:28] **20:22** [a] Luke 22:42 [b] Luke 12:50 [1] NU-Text omits *and be baptized with the baptism that I am baptized with.* **20:23** [a] [Acts 12:2] [1] NU-Text omits *and be baptized with the baptism that I am baptized with.* **20:24** [a] Mark 10:41 **20:26** [a] [1 Pet. 5:3] [b] Matt. 23:11 **20:27** [a] [Matt. 18:4] **20:28** [a] John 13:4 [b] [Phil. 2:6, 7] [c] Luke 22:27 [d] [Is. 53:10, 11] [e] [Rom. 5:15, 19] **20:29** [a] Mark 10:46–52 **20:30** [a] Matt. 9:27 [b] [Ezek. 37:21–25] **20:31** [a] Matt. 19:13

33They said to Him, "Lord, that our eyes
may be opened." 34So Jesus had [a]compassion
and touched their eyes. And immediately
their eyes received sight, and they followed
Him.

The Triumphal Entry

21 Now [a]when they drew near Jerusalem,
and came to Bethphage,[1] at [b]the Mount
of Olives, then Jesus sent two disciples, 2say-
ing to them, "Go into the village opposite you,
and immediately you will find a donkey tied,
and a colt with her. Loose *them* and bring
them to Me. 3And if anyone says anything
to you, you shall say, 'The Lord has need of
them,' and immediately he will send them."
4All[1] this was done that it might be fulfilled
which was spoken by the prophet, saying:

5 "Tell[a] the daughter of Zion,
'Behold, your King is coming to you,
Lowly, and sitting on a donkey,
A colt, the foal of a donkey.'"[1]

6[a]So the disciples went and did as Jesus
commanded them. 7They brought the donkey
and the colt, [a]laid their clothes on them, and
set *Him*[1] on them. 8And a very great multitude
spread their clothes on the road; [a]others cut
down branches from the trees and spread
them on the road. 9Then the multitudes who
went before and those who followed cried
out, saying:

"Hosanna to the Son of David!
[a]'Blessed *is* He who comes in the name
of the LORD!'[1]
Hosanna in the highest!"

10[a]And when He had come into Jerusalem,
all the city was moved, saying, "Who is this?"
11So the multitudes said, "This is Jesus, [a]the
prophet from Nazareth of Galilee."

Jesus Cleanses the Temple

12[a]Then Jesus went into the temple of God[1]
and drove out all those who bought and sold
in the temple, and overturned the tables of the
[b]money changers and the seats of those who
sold doves. 13And He said to them, "It is written,
[a]'My house shall be called a house of prayer,'[1]
but you have made it a [b]'den of thieves.'"[2]
14Then *the* blind and *the* lame came to
Him in the temple, and He healed them.
15But when the chief priests and scribes saw
the wonderful things that He did, and the
children crying out in the temple and saying,
"Hosanna to the [a]Son of David!" they were
indignant 16and said to Him, "Do You hear
what these are saying?"

20:34 [a] Matt. 9:36; 14:14; 15:32; 18:27 **21:1** [a] Luke 19:29–38 [b] [Zech. 14:4] [1] M-Text reads *Bethsphage.* **21:4** [1] NU-Text omits *All.* **21:5** [a] Zech. 9:9 [1] Zechariah 9:9 **21:6** [a] Mark 11:4 **21:7** [a] 2 Kin. 9:13 [1] NU-Text reads *and He sat.* **21:8** [a] Lev. 23:40 **21:9** [a] Ps. 118:26; Matt. 23:39 [1] Psalm 118:26 **21:10** [a] John 2:13, 15 **21:11** [a] John 6:14; 7:40; 9:17 **21:12** [a] Mark 11:15–18 [b] Deut. 14:25 [1] NU-Text omits *of God.* **21:13** [a] Is. 56:7 [b] Jer. 7:11 [1] Isaiah 56:7 [2] Jeremiah 7:11 **21:15** [a] John 7:42

SAVE US, WE PRAY!

Hosanna to the Son of David! "Blessed is He who comes in the name of the LORD!"

MATTHEW 21:9

Jesus' final week on earth, known as Passion Week, began with His entrance into the city of Jerusalem on what came to be called Palm Sunday in either AD 30 or 33. Jesus' ministry in Galilee in the north, along with the southward journey that took Him through Jericho, resulted in throngs of people accompanying Him. As Jesus entered the gates of Jerusalem, the people with Him sang, "Hosanna to the Son of David! 'Blessed is He who comes in the name of the LORD!'" The people quoted parts of Psalm 118:25–26. "Hosanna," which means "save now," is from verse 25, the beatitude from verse 26. David is not explicitly mentioned in Psalm 118, but ancient Jewish interpreters believed the psalm was about his going up to the Temple Mount to be crowned king.

The application of Psalm 118 to Jesus is quite fitting. Citing the one word "hosanna" is *spot-on, for that is what Jesus'* whole ministry had been about. He was named Jesus, which means "The Lord Saves" or "Savior" (Matt. 1:21), and with His arrival in Jerusalem it was time to "save now"! Jesus' saving work hasn't stopped. He still saves people from their sins. To find God's peace today, pray "Hosanna!" and know that it means "Save us, we pray!"

And Jesus said to them, "Yes. Have you never read,

[a]'Out of the mouth of babes and nursing infants
You have perfected praise'?"[1]

17 Then He left them and [a]went out of the city to Bethany, and He lodged there.

The Fig Tree Withered

18 [a]Now in the morning, as He returned to the city, He was hungry. 19 [a]And seeing a fig tree by the road, He came to it and found nothing on it but leaves, and said to it, "Let no fruit grow on you ever again." Immediately the fig tree withered away.

The Lesson of the Withered Fig Tree

20 [a]And when the disciples saw *it,* they marveled, saying, "How did the fig tree wither away so soon?"

21 So Jesus answered and said to them, "Assuredly, I say to you, [a]if you have faith and [b]do not doubt, you will not only do what was done to the fig tree, [c]but also if you say to this mountain, 'Be removed and be cast into the sea,' it will be done. 22 And [a]whatever things you ask in prayer, believing, you will receive."

Jesus' Authority Questioned

23 [a]Now when He came into the temple, the chief priests and the elders of the people confronted Him as He was teaching, and [b]said, "By what authority are You doing these things? And who gave You this authority?"

24 But Jesus answered and said to them, "I also will ask you one thing, which if you tell Me, I likewise will tell you by what authority I do these things: 25 The [a]baptism of [b]John—where was it from? From heaven or from men?"

And they reasoned among themselves, saying, "If we say, 'From heaven,' He will say to us, 'Why then did you not believe him?' 26 But if we say, 'From men,' we [a]fear the multitude, [b]for all count John as a prophet." 27 So they answered Jesus and said, "We do not know."

And He said to them, "Neither will I tell you by what authority I do these things.

The Parable of the Two Sons

28 "But what do you think? A man had two sons, and he came to the first and said, 'Son, go, work today in my [a]vineyard.' 29 He answered and said, 'I will not,' but afterward he regretted it and went. 30 Then he came to the second and said likewise. And he answered and said, 'I *go,* sir,' but he did not go. 31 Which of the two did the will of *his* father?"

They said to Him, "The first."

Jesus said to them, [a]"Assuredly, I say to you that tax collectors and harlots enter the kingdom of God before you. 32 For [a]John came to you in the way of righteousness, and you did not believe him; [b]but tax collectors and harlots believed him; and when you saw *it,* you did not afterward relent and believe him.

The Parable of the Wicked Vinedressers

33 "Hear another parable: There was a certain landowner [a]who planted a vineyard and set a hedge around it, dug a winepress in it and built a tower. And he leased it to vinedressers and [b]went into a far country. 34 Now when vintage-time drew near, he sent his servants to the vinedressers, that they might receive its fruit. 35 [a]And the vinedressers took his servants, beat one, killed one, and stoned another. 36 Again he sent other servants, more than the first, and they did likewise to them. 37 Then last of all he sent his [a]son to them, saying, 'They will respect my son.' 38 But when the vinedressers saw the son, they said among themselves, [a]'This is the heir. [b]Come, let us kill him and seize his inheritance.' 39 [a]So they took him and cast *him* out of the vineyard and killed *him.*

40 "Therefore, when the owner of the vineyard comes, what will he do to those vinedressers?"

41 [a]They said to Him, [b]"He will destroy those wicked men miserably, [c]and lease *his* vineyard to other vinedressers who will render to him the fruits in their seasons."

42 Jesus said to them, "Have you never read in the Scriptures:

[a]'The stone which the builders rejected
Has become the chief cornerstone.
This was the LORD's doing,
And it is marvelous in our eyes'?[1]

43 "Therefore I say to you, [a]the kingdom of God will be taken from you and given to a nation bearing the fruits of it. 44 And [a]whoever falls on this stone will be broken; but on whomever it falls, [b]it will grind him to powder."

21:16 [a] Ps. 8:2 [1] Psalm 8:2 **21:17** [a] John 11:1, 18; 12:1 **21:18** [a] Mark 11:12–14, 20–24 **21:19** [a] Mark 11:13 **21:20** [a] Mark 11:20 **21:21** [a] Matt. 17:20 [b] James 1:6 [c] 1 Cor. 13:2 **21:22** [a] Matt. 7:7–11 **21:23** [a] Luke 20:1–8 [b] Ex. 2:14 **21:25** [a] [John 1:29–34] [b] John 1:15–28 **21:26** [a] Matt. 14:5; 21:46 [b] Mark 6:20 **21:28** [a] Matt. 20:1; 21:33 **21:31** [a] Luke 7:29, 37–50 **21:32** [a] Luke 3:1–12; 7:29 [b] Luke 3:12, 13 **21:33** [a] Luke 20:9–19 [b] Matt. 25:14 **21:35** [a] [1 Thess. 2:15] **21:37** [a] [John 3:16] **21:38** [a] [Heb. 1:2] [b] John 11:53 **21:39** [a] [Acts 2:23] **21:41** [a] Luke 20:16 [b] [Luke 21:24] [c] [Acts 13:46] **21:42** [a] Ps. 118:22, 23 [1] Psalm 118:22, 23 **21:43** [a] [Matt. 8:12] **21:44** [a] Is. 8:14, 15 [b] [Dan. 2:44]

45 Now when the chief priests and Pharisees heard His parables, they perceived that
He was speaking of them. 46 But when they
sought to lay hands on Him, they [a]feared
the multitudes, because [b]they took Him for
a prophet.

The Parable of the Wedding Feast

22 And Jesus answered [a]and spoke to
them again by parables and said:
2 "The kingdom of heaven is like a certain
king who arranged a marriage for his son,
3 and sent out his servants to call those who
were invited to the wedding; and they were
not willing to come. 4 Again, he sent out other
servants, saying, 'Tell those who are invited,
"See, I have prepared my dinner; [a]my oxen
and fatted cattle *are* killed, and all things
are ready. Come to the wedding." ' 5 But they
made light of it and went their ways, one to
his own farm, another to his business. 6 And
the rest seized his servants, treated *them*
spitefully, and killed *them*. 7 But when the
king heard *about it,* he was furious. And he
sent out [a]his armies, destroyed those murderers, and burned up their city. 8 Then he
said to his servants, 'The wedding is ready,
but those who were invited were not [a]wor-
thy. 9 Therefore go into the highways, and as
many as you find, invite to the wedding.' 10 So
those servants went out into the highways
and [a]gathered together all whom they found,
both bad and good. And the wedding *hall* was
filled with guests.

11 "But when the king came in to see the
guests, he saw a man there [a]who did not have
on a wedding garment. 12 So he said to him,
'Friend, how did you come in here without a
wedding garment?' And he was [a]speechless.
13 Then the king said to the servants, 'Bind
him hand and foot, take him away, and[1] cast
him [a]into outer darkness; there will be weeping and gnashing of teeth.'

14 [a]"For many are called, but few *are* chosen."

The Pharisees: Is It Lawful to Pay Taxes to Caesar?

15 [a]Then the Pharisees went and plotted
how they might entangle Him in *His* talk.
16 And they sent to Him their disciples with
the [a]Herodians, saying, "Teacher, we know
that You are true, and teach the way of God
in truth; nor do You care about anyone, for
You do not regard the person of men. 17 Tell
us, therefore, what do You think? Is it lawful
to pay taxes to Caesar, or not?"

18 But Jesus perceived their wickedness,
and said, "Why do you test Me, *you* hypocrites? 19 Show Me the tax money."

So they brought Him a denarius.

20 And He said to them, "Whose image and
inscription *is* this?"

21 They said to Him, "Caesar's."

And He said to them, [a]"Render therefore
to Caesar the things that are [b]Caesar's, and
to God the things that are [c]God's." 22 When
they had heard *these words,* they marveled,
and left Him and went their way.

The Sadducees: What About the Resurrection?

23 [a]The same day the Sadducees, [b]who say
there is no resurrection, came to Him and
asked Him, 24 saying: "Teacher, [a]Moses said
that if a man dies, having no children, his
brother shall marry his wife and raise up
offspring for his brother. 25 Now there were
with us seven brothers. The first died after
he had married, and having no offspring, left
his wife to his brother. 26 Likewise the second
also, and the third, even to the seventh. 27 Last
of all the woman died also. 28 Therefore, in
the resurrection, whose wife of the seven will
she be? For they all had her."

29 Jesus answered and said to them, "You
are mistaken, [a]not knowing the Scriptures
nor the power of God. 30 For in the resurrection they neither marry nor are given
in marriage, but [a]are like angels of God[1] in
heaven. 31 But concerning the resurrection of
the dead, have you not read what was spoken
to you by God, saying, 32 [a]'I am the God of
Abraham, the God of Isaac, and the God of
Jacob'?[1] God is not the God of the dead, but of
the living." 33 And when the multitudes heard
this, [a]they were astonished at His teaching.

The Scribes: Which Is the First Commandment of All?

34 [a]But when the Pharisees heard that He
had silenced the Sadducees, they gathered
together. 35 Then one of them, [a]a lawyer, asked
Him a question, testing Him, and saying,
36 "Teacher, which *is* the great commandment
in the law?"

37 Jesus said to him, [a]" 'You shall love the
LORD your God with all your heart, with all
your soul, and with all your mind.'[1] 38 This is

21:46 [a] Matt. 21:26 [b] Matt. 21:11 **22:1** [a] [Rev. 19:7–9] **22:4** [a] Prov. 9:2 **22:7** [a] [Dan. 9:26] **22:8** [a] Matt. 10:11 **22:10** [a] Matt. 13:38, 47, 48 **22:11** [a] [Col. 3:10, 12] **22:12** [a] [Rom. 3:19] **22:13** [a] Matt. 8:12; 25:30 [1] NU-Text omits *take him away, and.* **22:14** [a] Matt. 20:16 **22:15** [a] Mark 12:13–17 **22:16** [a] Mark 3:6; 8:15; 12:13 **22:21** [a] Matt. 17:25 [b] [Rom. 13:1–7] [c] [1 Cor. 3:23; 6:19, 20; 12:27] **22:23** [a] Luke 20:27–40 [b] Acts 23:8 **22:24** [a] Deut. 25:5 **22:29** [a] John 20:9 **22:30** [a] [1 John 3:2] [1] NU-Text omits *of God.* **22:32** [a] Ex. 3:6, 15 [1] Exodus 3:6, 15 **22:33** [a] Matt. 7:28 **22:34** [a] Mark 12:28–31 **22:35** [a] Luke 7:30; 10:25; 11:45, 46, 52; 14:3 **22:37** [a] Deut. 6:5; 10:12; 30:6 [1] Deuteronomy 6:5

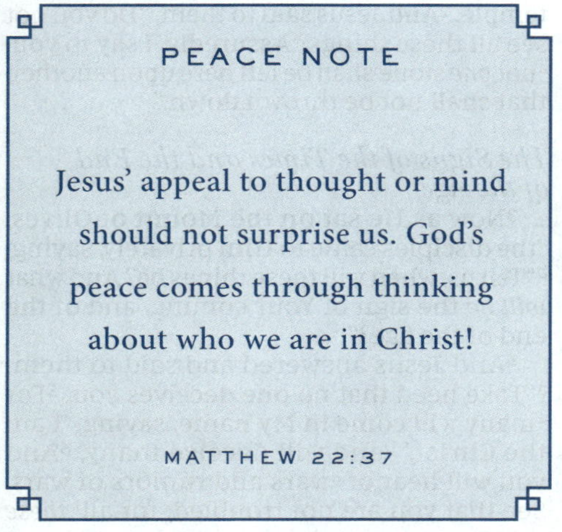

the first and great commandment. 39 And *the*
second *is* like it: [a]'You shall love your neighbor as yourself.'[1] 40 [a]On these two commandments hang all the Law and the Prophets."

Jesus: How Can David Call His Descendant "Lord"?

41 [a]While the Pharisees were gathered together, Jesus asked them, 42 saying, "What
do you think about the Christ? Whose Son
is He?"

They said to Him, "*The* [a]*Son* of David."
43 He said to them, "How then does David
in the Spirit call Him 'Lord,' saying:

44 'The[a] LORD said to my Lord,
"Sit at My right hand,
Till I make Your enemies Your
footstool" '?[1]

45 If David then calls Him 'Lord,' how is He his
Son?" 46 [a]And no one was able to answer Him
a word, [b]nor from that day on did anyone
dare question Him anymore.

Woe to the Scribes and Pharisees

23 Then Jesus spoke to the multitudes
and to His disciples, 2 saying: [a]"The
scribes and the Pharisees sit in Moses' seat.
3 Therefore whatever they tell you to observe,[1]
that observe and do, but do not do according
to their works; for [a]they say, and do not do.
4 [a]For they bind heavy burdens, hard to bear,
and lay *them* on men's shoulders; but they
themselves will not move them with one of
their fingers. 5 But all their works they do
to [a]be seen by men. They make their phy-
lacteries broad and enlarge the borders of
their garments. 6 [a]They love the best places
at feasts, the best seats in the synagogues,
7 greetings in the marketplaces, and to be
called by men, 'Rabbi, Rabbi.' 8 [a]But you, do
not be called 'Rabbi'; for One is your Teacher,
the Christ,[1] and you are all brethren. 9 Do not
call anyone on earth your father; [a]for One is
your Father, He who is in heaven. 10 And do
not be called teachers; for One is your Teacher, the Christ. 11 But [a]he who is greatest among
you shall be your servant. 12 [a]And whoever
exalts himself will be humbled, and he who
humbles himself will be exalted.

13 "But [a]woe to you, scribes and Pharisees,
hypocrites! For you shut up the kingdom of
heaven against men; for you neither go in
yourselves, nor do you allow those who are
entering to go in. 14 Woe to you, scribes and
Pharisees, hypocrites! [a]For you devour widows' houses, and for a pretense make long
prayers. Therefore you will receive greater
condemnation.[1]

15 "Woe to you, scribes and Pharisees, hypocrites! For you travel land and sea to win one
proselyte, and when he is won, you make him
twice as much a son of hell as yourselves.

16 "Woe to you, [a]blind guides, who say,
[b]'Whoever swears by the temple, it is nothing; but whoever swears by the gold of the
temple, he is obliged *to perform it.*' 17 Fools
and blind! For which is greater, the gold [a]or
the temple that sanctifies[1] the gold? 18 And,
'Whoever swears by the altar, it is nothing;
but whoever swears by the gift that is on it,
he is obliged *to perform it.*' 19 Fools and blind!
For which is greater, the gift [a]or the altar that
sanctifies the gift? 20 Therefore he who swears
by the altar, swears by it and by all things on
it. 21 He who swears by the temple, swears by it
and by [a]Him who dwells[1] in it. 22 And he who
swears by heaven, swears by [a]the throne of
God and by Him who sits on it.

23 "Woe to you, scribes and Pharisees,
hypocrites! [a]For you pay tithe of mint and
anise and cummin, and [b]have neglected
the weightier *matters* of the law: justice and
mercy and faith. These you ought to have
done, without leaving the others undone.
24 Blind guides, who strain out a gnat and
swallow a camel!

25 "Woe to you, scribes and Pharisees,

22:39 [a] Lev. 19:18 [1] Leviticus 19:18 **22:40** [a] [Matt. 7:12] **22:41** [a] Luke 20:41–44 **22:42** [a] Matt. 1:1; 21:9 **22:44** [a] Ps. 110:1 [1] Psalm 110:1 **22:46** [a] Luke 14:6 [b] Mark 12:34 **23:2** [a] Neh. 8:4, 8 **23:3** [a] [Rom. 2:19] [1] NU-Text omits *to observe.* **23:4** [a] Luke 11:46 **23:5** [a] [Matt. 6:1–6, 16–18] **23:6** [a] Luke 11:43; 20:46 **23:8** [a] [James 3:1] [1] NU-Text omits *the Christ.* **23:9** [a] [Mal. 1:6] **23:11** [a] Matt. 20:26, 27 **23:12** [a] Luke 14:11; 18:14 **23:13** [a] Luke 11:52 **23:14** [a] Mark 12:40 [1] NU-Text omits this verse. **23:16** [a] Matt. 15:14; 23:24 [b] [Matt. 5:33, 34] **23:17** [a] Ex. 30:29 [1] NU-Text reads *sanctified.* **23:19** [a] Ex. 29:37 **23:21** [a] 1 Kin. 8:13 [1] M-Text reads *dwelt.* **23:22** [a] Matt. 5:34 **23:23** [a] Luke 11:42; 18:12 [b] [Hos. 6:6]

hypocrites! [a]For you cleanse the outside of the cup and dish, but inside they are full of extortion and self-indulgence.[1] 26 Blind Pharisee, first cleanse the inside of the cup and dish, that the outside of them may be clean also.

27 "Woe to you, scribes and Pharisees, hypocrites! [a]For you are like whitewashed tombs which indeed appear beautiful outwardly, but inside are full of dead *men's* bones and all uncleanness. 28 Even so you also outwardly appear righteous to men, but inside you are full of hypocrisy and lawlessness.

29 [a]"Woe to you, scribes and Pharisees, hypocrites! Because you build the tombs of the prophets and adorn the monuments of the righteous, 30 and say, 'If we had lived in the days of our fathers, we would not have been partakers with them in the blood of the prophets.'

31 "Therefore you are witnesses against yourselves that [a]you are sons of those who murdered the prophets. 32 [a]Fill up, then, the measure of your fathers' *guilt*. 33 Serpents, [a]brood of vipers! How can you escape the condemnation of hell? 34 [a]Therefore, indeed, I send you prophets, wise men, and scribes: [b]*some* of them you will kill and crucify, and [c]*some* of them you will scourge in your synagogues and persecute from city to city, 35 [a]that on you may come all the righteous blood shed on the earth, [b]from the blood of righteous Abel to [c]the blood of Zechariah, son of Berechiah, whom you murdered between the temple and the altar. 36 Assuredly, I say to you, all these things will come upon this generation.

Jesus Laments over Jerusalem

37 [a]"O Jerusalem, Jerusalem, the one who kills the prophets [b]and stones those who are sent to her! How often [c]I wanted to gather your children together, as a hen gathers her chicks [d]under *her* wings, but you were not willing! 38 See! Your house is left to you desolate; 39 for I say to you, you shall see Me no more till you say, [a]'Blessed *is* He who comes in the name of the LORD!' "[1]

Jesus Predicts the Destruction of the Temple

24 Then [a]Jesus went out and departed from the temple, and His disciples came up to show Him the buildings of the temple. 2 And Jesus said to them, "Do you not see all these things? Assuredly, I say to you, [a]not *one* stone shall be left here upon another, that shall not be thrown down."

The Signs of the Times and the End of the Age

3 Now as He sat on the Mount of Olives, [a]the disciples came to Him privately, saying, [b]"Tell us, when will these things be? And what *will be* the sign of Your coming, and of the end of the age?"

4 And Jesus answered and said to them: [a]"Take heed that no one deceives you. 5 For [a]many will come in My name, saying, 'I am the Christ,' [b]and will deceive many. 6 And you will hear of [a]wars and rumors of wars. See that you are not troubled; for all[1] *these things* must come to pass, but the end is not yet. 7 For [a]nation will rise against nation, and kingdom against kingdom. And there will be [b]famines, pestilences,[1] and earthquakes in various places. 8 All these *are* the beginning of sorrows.

9 [a]"Then they will deliver you up to tribulation and kill you, and you will be hated by all nations for My name's sake. 10 And then many will be offended, will betray one another, and will hate one another. 11 Then [a]many false prophets will rise up and [b]deceive many. 12 And because lawlessness will abound, the love of many will grow [a]cold. 13 [a]But he who endures to the end shall be saved. 14 And this [a]gospel of the kingdom [b]will be preached in all the world as a witness to all the nations, and then the end will come.

The Great Tribulation

15 [a]"Therefore when you see the [b]'abomination of desolation,'[1] spoken of by Daniel the prophet, standing in the holy place" [c](whoever reads, let him understand), 16 "then let those who are in Judea flee to the mountains. 17 Let him who is on the housetop not go down to take anything out of his house. 18 And let him who is in the field not go back to get his clothes. 19 But [a]woe to those who are pregnant and to those who are nursing babies in those days! 20 And pray that your flight may not be in winter or on the Sabbath. 21 For [a]then there will be great tribulation, such as has not been since the

23:25 [a] Luke 11:39 [1] M-Text reads *unrighteousness.* **23:27** [a] Acts 23:3 **23:29** [a] Luke 11:47, 48 **23:31** [a] [Acts 7:51, 52] **23:32** [a] *[1 Thess. 2:16]* **23:33** [a] *Matt. 3:7; 12:34* **23:34** [a] Luke 11:49 [b] Acts 7:54–60; 22:19 [c] 2 Cor. 11:24, 25 **23:35** [a] Rev. 18:24 [b] Gen. 4:8 [c] 2 Chr. 24:20, 21 **23:37** [a] Luke 13:34, 35 [b] 2 Chr. 24:20, 21; 36:15, 16 [c] Deut. 32:11, 12 [d] Ps. 17:8; 91:4 **23:39** [a] Ps. 118:26 [1] Psalm 118:26 **24:1** [a] Mark 13:1 **24:2** [a] Luke 19:44 **24:3** [a] Mark 13:3 [b] [1 Thess. 5:1–3] **24:4** [a] [Col. 2:8, 18] **24:5** [a] John 5:43 [b] Matt. 24:11 **24:6** [a] [Rev. 6:2–4] [1] NU-Text omits *all.* **24:7** [a] Hag. 2:22 [b] Rev. 6:5, 6 [1] NU-Text omits *pestilences.* **24:9** [a] Matt. 10:17 **24:11** [a] 2 Pet. 2:1 [b] [1 Tim. 4:1] **24:12** [a] [2 Thess. 2:3] **24:13** [a] Matt. 10:22 **24:14** [a] Matt. 4:23 [b] Rom. 10:18 **24:15** [a] Mark 13:14 [b] Dan. 9:27; 11:31; 12:11 [c] Dan. 9:23 [1] Daniel 11:31; 12:11 **24:19** [a] Luke 23:29 **24:21** [a] Dan. 9:26

beginning of the world until this time, no,
nor ever shall be. 22And unless those days
were shortened, no flesh would be saved;
[a]but for the elect's sake those days will be
shortened.
23[a]"Then if anyone says to you, 'Look, here
is the Christ!' or 'There!' do not believe *it.*
24For [a]false christs and false prophets will
rise and show great signs and wonders to
deceive, [b]if possible, even the elect. 25See, I
have told you beforehand.
26"Therefore if they say to you, 'Look, He
is in the desert!' do not go out; *or* 'Look, *He is*
in the inner rooms!' do not believe *it.* 27[a]For
as the lightning comes from the east and
flashes to the west, so also will the coming
of the Son of Man be. 28[a]For wherever the
carcass is, there the eagles will be gathered
together.

The Coming of the Son of Man

29[a]"Immediately after the tribulation of
those days [b]the sun will be darkened, and the
moon will not give its light; the stars will fall
from heaven, and the powers of the heavens
will be shaken. 30[a]Then the sign of the Son of
Man will appear in heaven, [b]and then all the
tribes of the earth will mourn, and they will
see the Son of Man coming on the clouds of
heaven with power and great glory. 31[a]And
He will send His angels with a great sound
of a trumpet, and they will gather together
His elect from the four winds, from one end
of heaven to the other.

The Parable of the Fig Tree

32"Now learn [a]this parable from the fig
tree: When its branch has already become
tender and puts forth leaves, you know that
summer *is* near. 33So you also, when you
see all these things, know [a]that it[1] is near—
at the doors! 34Assuredly, I say to you, [a]this
generation will by no means pass away till
all these things take place. 35[a]Heaven and
earth will pass away, but My words will by
no means pass away.

No One Knows the Day or Hour

36[a]"But of that day and hour no one
knows, not even the angels of heaven,[1]
[b]but My Father only. 37But as the days of
Noah *were,* so also will the coming of the
Son of Man be. 38[a]For as in the days before
the flood, they were eating and drinking,

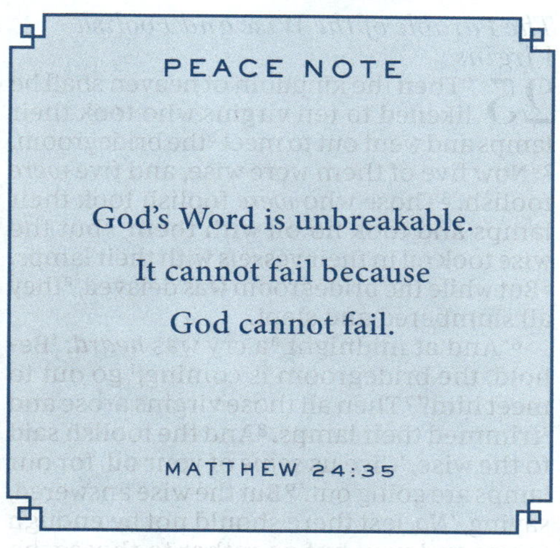

marrying and giving in marriage, until the
day that Noah entered the ark, 39and did not
know until the flood came and took them
all away, so also will the coming of the Son
of Man be. 40[a]Then two *men* will be in the
field: one will be taken and the other left.
41Two *women will be* grinding at the mill:
one will be taken and the other left. 42[a]Watch
therefore, for you do not know what hour[1]
your Lord is coming. 43[a]But know this, that
if the master of the house had known what
hour the thief would come, he would have
watched and not allowed his house to be
broken into. 44[a]Therefore you also be ready,
for the Son of Man is coming at an hour you
do not expect.

The Faithful Servant and the Evil Servant

45[a]"Who then is a faithful and wise servant, whom his master made ruler over his
household, to give them food in due season? 46[a]Blessed *is* that servant whom his
master, when he comes, will find so doing.
47Assuredly, I say to you that [a]he will make
him ruler over all his goods. 48But if that
evil servant says in his heart, 'My master [a]is
delaying his coming,'[1] 49and begins to beat
his fellow servants, and to eat and drink with
the drunkards, 50the master of that servant
will come on a day when he is not looking
for *him* and at an hour that he is [a]not aware
of, 51and will cut him in two and appoint *him*
his portion with the hypocrites. [a]There shall
be weeping and gnashing of teeth.

24:22 [a] Is. 65:8, 9 **24:23** [a] Luke 17:23 **24:24** [a] [2 Thess. 2:9] [b] [2 Tim. 2:19] **24:27** [a] Luke 17:24 **24:28** [a] Luke 17:37 **24:29** [a] [Dan. 7:11] [b] Ezek. 32:7 **24:30** [a] [Dan. 7:13, 14] [b] Zech. 12:12 **24:31** [a] [1 Cor. 15:52] **24:32** [a] Luke 21:29 **24:33** [a] [James 5:9] [1] Or *He* **24:34** [a] [Matt. 10:23; 16:28; 23:36] **24:35** [a] Luke 21:33 **24:36** [a] Acts 1:7 [b] Zech. 14:7 [1] NU-Text adds *nor the Son.* **24:38** [a] [Gen. 6:3–5] **24:40** [a] Luke 17:34 **24:42** [a] Matt. 25:13 [1] NU-Text reads *day.* **24:43** [a] Luke 12:39 **24:44** [a] [1 Thess. 5:6] **24:45** [a] Luke 12:42–46 **24:46** [a] Rev. 16:15 **24:47** [a] Matt. 25:21, 23 **24:48** [a] [2 Pet. 3:4–9] [1] NU-Text omits *his coming.* **24:50** [a] Mark 13:32 **24:51** [a] Matt. 8:12; 25:30

The Parable of the Wise and Foolish Virgins

25 "Then the kingdom of heaven shall be
likened to ten virgins who took their
lamps and went out to meet [a]the bridegroom.
2 [a]Now five of them were wise, and five *were*
foolish. 3 Those who *were* foolish took their
lamps and took no oil with them, 4 but the
wise took oil in their vessels with their lamps.
5 But while the bridegroom was delayed, [a]they
all slumbered and slept.
6 "And at midnight [a]a cry was *heard:* 'Behold, the bridegroom is coming;[1] go out to
meet him!' 7 Then all those virgins arose and
[a]trimmed their lamps. 8 And the foolish said
to the wise, 'Give us *some* of your oil, for our
lamps are going out.' 9 But the wise answered,
saying, '*No,* lest there should not be enough
for us and you; but go rather to those who
sell, and buy for yourselves.' 10 And while
they went to buy, the bridegroom came, and
those who were ready went in with him to the
wedding; and [a]the door was shut.
11 "Afterward the other virgins came also,
saying, [a]'Lord, Lord, open to us!' 12 But he
answered and said, 'Assuredly, I say to you,
[a]I do not know you.'
13 [a]"Watch therefore, for you [b]know neither
the day nor the hour[1] in which the Son of
Man is coming.

The Parable of the Talents

14 [a]"For *the kingdom of heaven is* [b]like a man
traveling to a far country, *who* called his own
servants and delivered his goods to them.
15 And to one he gave five talents, to another
two, and to another one, [a]to each according
to his own ability; and immediately he went
on a journey. 16 Then he who had received the
five talents went and traded with them, and
made another five talents. 17 And likewise he
who *had received* two gained two more also.
18 But he who had received one went and
dug in the ground, and hid his lord's money.
19 After a long time the lord of those servants
came and settled accounts with them.
20 "So he who had received five talents
came and brought five other talents, saying,
'Lord, you delivered to me five talents; look, I
have gained five more talents besides them.'
21 His lord said to him, 'Well *done,* good and
faithful servant; you were [a]faithful over a
few things, [b]I will make you ruler over many
things. Enter into [c]the joy of your lord.' 22 He
also who had received two talents came and
said, 'Lord, you delivered to me two talents;
look, I have gained two more talents besides
them.' 23 His lord said to him, [a]'Well *done,*
good and faithful servant; you have been
faithful over a few things, I will make you
ruler over many things. Enter into [b]the joy
of your lord.'
24 "Then he who had received the one talent
came and said, 'Lord, I knew you to be a hard
man, reaping where you have not sown, and
gathering where you have not scattered seed.
25 And I was afraid, and went and hid your
talent in the ground. Look, *there* you have
what is yours.'
26 "But his lord answered and said to him,
'You [a]wicked and lazy servant, you knew that
I reap where I have not sown, and gather
where I have not scattered seed. 27 So you
ought to have deposited my money with
the bankers, and at my coming I would have
received back my own with interest. 28 So take
the talent from him, and give *it* to him who
has ten talents.
29 [a]'For to everyone who has, more will be
given, and he will have abundance; but from
him who does not have, even what he has will
be taken away. 30 And cast the unprofitable
servant [a]into the outer darkness. [b]There will
be weeping and [c]gnashing of teeth.'

The Son of Man Will Judge the Nations

31 [a]"When the Son of Man comes in His
glory, and all the holy[1] angels with Him, then
He will sit on the throne of His glory. 32 [a]All
the nations will be gathered before Him, and
[b]He will separate them one from another,
as a shepherd divides *his* sheep from the
goats. 33 And He will set the [a]sheep on His
right hand, but the goats on the left. 34 Then
the King will say to those on His right hand,
'Come, you blessed of My Father, [a]inherit the
kingdom [b]prepared for you from the foundation of the world: 35 [a]for I was hungry and
you gave Me food; I was thirsty and you gave
Me drink; [b]I was a stranger and you took Me
in; 36 I *was* [a]naked and you clothed Me; I was
sick and you visited Me; [b]I was in prison and
you came to Me.'
37 "Then the righteous will answer Him,
saying, 'Lord, when did we see You hungry
and feed *You,* or thirsty and give *You* drink?

25:1 [a] [Eph. 5:29, 30] **25:2** [a] Matt. 13:47; 22:10 **25:5** [a] 1 Thess. 5:6 **25:6** [a] [1 Thess. 4:16] [1] NU-Text omits *is coming.* **25:7** [a] Luke 12:35 **25:10** [a] Luke 13:25 **25:11** [a] [Matt. 7:21–23] **25:12** [a] [Hab. 1:13] **25:13** [a] Mark 13:35 [b] Matt. 24:36, 42 [1] NU-Text omits the rest of this verse. **25:14** [a] Luke 19:12–27 [b] Matt. 21:33 **25:15** [a] [Rom. 12:6] **25:21** [a] [1 Cor. 4:2] [b] [Luke 12:44; 22:29, 30] [c] [Heb. 12:2] **25:23** [a] Matt. 24:45, 47; 25:21 [b] [Ps. 16:11] **25:26** [a] Matt. 18:32 **25:29** [a] Matt. 13:12 **25:30** [a] Matt. 8:12; 22:13 [b] Matt. 7:23; 8:12; 24:51 [c] Ps. 112:10 **25:31** [a] [1 Thess. 4:16] [1] NU-Text omits *holy.* **25:32** [a] [2 Cor. 5:10] [b] Ezek. 20:38 **25:33** [a] [John 10:11, 27, 28] **25:34** [a] [Rom. 8:17] [b] Mark 10:40 **25:35** [a] Is. 58:7 [b] [Heb. 13:2] **25:36** [a] [James 2:15, 16] [b] 2 Tim. 1:16

38When did we see You a stranger and take *You* in, or naked and clothe *You?* 39Or when did we see You sick, or in prison, and come to You?' 40And the King will answer and say to them, 'Assuredly, I say to you, [a]inasmuch as you did *it* to one of the least of these My brethren, you did *it* to Me.'

41"Then He will also say to those on the left hand, [a]'Depart from Me, you cursed, [b]into the everlasting fire prepared for [c]the devil and his angels: 42for I was hungry and you gave Me no food; I was thirsty and you gave Me no drink; 43I was a stranger and you did not take Me in, naked and you did not clothe Me, sick and in prison and you did not visit Me.'

44"Then they also will answer Him,[1] saying, 'Lord, when did we see You hungry or thirsty or a stranger or naked or sick or in prison, and did not minister to You?' 45Then He will answer them, saying, 'Assuredly, I say to you, [a]inasmuch as you did not do *it* to one of the least of these, you did not do *it* to Me.' 46And [a]these will go away into everlasting punishment, but the righteous into eternal life."

The Plot to Kill Jesus

26 Now it came to pass, when Jesus had finished all these sayings, *that* He said to His disciples, 2[a]"You know that after two days is the Passover, and the Son of Man will be delivered up to be crucified."

3[a]Then the chief priests, the scribes,[1] and the elders of the people assembled at the palace of the high priest, who was called Caiaphas, 4and [a]plotted to take Jesus by trickery and kill *Him.* 5But they said, "Not during the feast, lest there be an uproar among the [a]people."

The Anointing at Bethany

6And when Jesus was in [a]Bethany at the house of Simon the leper, 7a woman came to Him having an alabaster flask of very costly fragrant oil, and she poured *it* on His head as He sat *at the table.* 8[a]But when His disciples saw *it,* they were indignant, saying, "Why this waste? 9For this fragrant oil might have been sold for much and given to *the* poor."

10But when Jesus was aware of *it,* He said to them, "Why do you trouble the woman? For she has done a good work for Me. 11[a]For you have the poor with you always, but [b]Me you do not have always. 12For in pouring this fragrant oil on My body, she did *it* for My [a]burial. 13Assuredly, I say to you, wherever this gospel is preached in the whole world, what this woman has done will also be told as a memorial to her."

Judas Agrees to Betray Jesus

14[a]Then one of the twelve, called [b]Judas Iscariot, went to the chief priests 15and said, [a]"What are you willing to give me if I deliver Him to you?" And they counted out to him thirty pieces of silver. 16So from that time he sought opportunity to betray Him.

25:40 [a] Mark 9:41 **25:41** [a] Matt. 7:23 [b] Matt. 13:40, 42 [c] [2 Pet. 2:4] **25:44** [1] NU-Text and M-Text omit *Him.* **25:45** [a] Prov. 14:31 **25:46** [a] [Dan. 12:2] **26:2** [a] Luke 22:1, 2 **26:3** [a] John 11:47 [1] NU-Text omits *the scribes.* **26:4** [a] Acts 4:25–28 **26:5** [a] Matt. 21:26 **26:6** [a] Mark 14:3–9 **26:8** [a] John 12:4 **26:11** [a] [Deut. 15:11] [b] [John 13:33; 14:19; 16:5, 28; 17:11] **26:12** [a] John 19:38–42 **26:14** [a] Mark 14:10, 11; Luke 22:3–6 [b] Matt. 10:4 **26:15** [a] Zech. 11:12

TO THE LEAST OF THESE

"Inasmuch as you did it to one of the least of these My brethren, you did it to Me."

MATTHEW 25:40

The apostle Paul is well known for describing the church as the "body of Christ" (Rom. 7:4; 1 Cor. 12:27). The idea may have occurred to him when he met the risen Christ on the road to Damascus and Jesus asked, "Why are you persecuting Me?" (Acts 9:4). In persecuting the church, Paul was persecuting Jesus. But Jesus' teaching in Matthew 25:34–40 may have contributed to it as well. In this teaching He said people will ask Him, "When did we see You sick, or in prison, and come to You?" (v. 39) and King Jesus will answer, "Inasmuch as you did it to one of the least of these My brethren, you did it to Me" (v. 40).

To give nourishment or assistance to one of Jesus' disciples, even one of the least "important," is the same as giving nourishment or assistance to Jesus Himself. It is a beautiful picture. It is said that kindness is often its own reward, but imagine kindness extended to Christ via one of His followers—that's hard to beat. How much time do you take to serve others? Perhaps this is what is missing in your life right now and why you have no peace.

Jesus Celebrates Passover with His Disciples

17[a]Now on the first *day of the Feast* of the Unleavened Bread the disciples came to Jesus, saying to Him, "Where do You want us to prepare for You to eat the Passover?"

18And He said, "Go into the city to a certain man, and say to him, 'The Teacher says, [a]"My time is at hand; I will keep the Passover at your house with My disciples." ' "

19So the disciples did as Jesus had directed them; and they prepared the Passover.

20[a]When evening had come, He sat down with the twelve. 21Now as they were eating, He said, "Assuredly, I say to you, one of you will [a]betray Me."

22And they were exceedingly sorrowful, and each of them began to say to Him, "Lord, is it I?"

23He answered and said, [a]"He who dipped *his* hand with Me in the dish will betray Me. 24The Son of Man indeed goes just [a]as it is written of Him, but [b]woe to that man by whom the Son of Man is betrayed! [c]It would have been good for that man if he had not been born."

25Then Judas, who was betraying Him, answered and said, "Rabbi, is it I?"

He said to him, "You have said it."

Jesus Institutes the Lord's Supper

26[a]And as they were eating, [b]Jesus took bread, blessed[1] and broke *it,* and gave *it* to the disciples and said, "Take, eat; [c]this is My body."

27Then He took the cup, and gave thanks, and gave *it* to them, saying, [a]"Drink from it, all of you. 28For [a]this is My blood [b]of the new[1] covenant, which is shed [c]for many for the remission of sins. 29But [a]I say to you, I will not drink of this fruit of the vine from now on [b]until that day when I drink it new with you in My Father's kingdom."

30[a]And when they had sung a hymn, they went out to the Mount of Olives.

Jesus Predicts Peter's Denial

31Then Jesus said to them, [a]"All of you will [b]be made to stumble because of Me this night, for it is written:

[c]'I will strike the Shepherd,
And the sheep of the flock will be
scattered.'[1]

32But after I have been raised, [a]I will go before you to Galilee."

33Peter answered and said to Him, "Even if all are made to stumble because of You, I will never be made to stumble."

34Jesus said to him, [a]"Assuredly, I say to you that this night, before the rooster crows, you will deny Me three times."

35Peter said to Him, "Even if I have to die with You, I will not deny You!"

And so said all the disciples.

The Prayer in the Garden

36[a]Then Jesus came with them to a place called Gethsemane, and said to the disciples, "Sit here while I go and pray over there." 37And He took with Him Peter and [a]the two sons of Zebedee, and He began to be sorrowful and deeply distressed. 38Then He said to them, [a]"My soul is exceedingly sorrowful, even to death. Stay here and watch with Me."

39He went a little farther and fell on His face, and [a]prayed, saying, [b]"O My Father, if it is possible, [c]let this cup pass from Me; nevertheless, [d]not as I will, but as You *will.*"

40Then He came to the disciples and found them sleeping, and said to Peter, "What! Could you not watch with Me one hour? 41[a]Watch and pray, lest you enter into temptation. [b]The spirit indeed *is* willing, but the flesh *is* weak."

42Again, a second time, He went away and prayed, saying, "O My Father, if this cup cannot pass away from Me unless[1] I drink it, Your will be done." 43And He came and found them asleep again, for their eyes were heavy.

44So He left them, went away again, and prayed the third time, saying the same words. 45Then He came to His disciples and said to them, "Are *you* still sleeping and resting? Behold, the hour is at hand, and the Son of Man is being [a]betrayed into the hands of sinners. 46Rise, let us be going. See, My betrayer is at hand."

Betrayal and Arrest in Gethsemane

47And [a]while He was still speaking, behold, Judas, one of the twelve, with a great multitude with swords and clubs, came from the chief priests and elders of the people.

48Now His betrayer had given them a sign, saying, "Whomever I kiss, He is the One; seize Him." 49Immediately he went up to Jesus and said, "Greetings, Rabbi!" [a]and kissed Him.

26:17 [a] Ex. 12:6, 18–20 **26:18** [a] Luke 9:51 **26:20** [a] Mark 14:17–21 **26:21** [a] John 6:70, 71; 13:21 **26:23** [a] Ps. 41:9 **26:24** [a] 1 Cor. 15:3 [b] Luke 17:1 [c] John 17:12 **26:26** [a] Mark 14:22–25 [b] 1 Cor. 11:23–25 [c] [1 Pet. 2:24] [1] M-Text reads *gave thanks for.* **26:27** [a] Mark 14:23 **26:28** [a] [Ex. 24:8] [b] Jer. 31:31 [c] Matt. 20:28 [1] NU-Text omits *new.* **26:29** [a] Mark 14:25 [b] Acts 10:41 **26:30** [a] Mark 14:26–31 **26:31** [a] John 16:32 [b] [Matt. 11:6] [c] Zech. 13:7 [1] Zechariah 13:7 **26:32** [a] Matt. 28:7, 10, 16 **26:34** [a] John 13:38 **26:36** [a] Mark 14:32–35 **26:37** [a] Matt. 4:21; 17:1 **26:38** [a] John 12:27 **26:39** [a] [Heb. 5:7–9] [b] John 12:27 [c] Matt. 20:22 [d] John 5:30; 6:38 **26:41** [a] Luke 22:40, 46 [b] [Gal. 5:17] **26:42** [1] NU-Text reads *if this may not pass away unless.* **26:45** [a] Matt. 17:22, 23; 20:18, 19 **26:47** [a] Acts 1:16 **26:49** [a] 2 Sam. 20:9

50 But Jesus said to him, [a]"Friend, why have you come?"

Then they came and laid hands on Jesus and took Him. 51 And suddenly, [a]one of those *who were* with Jesus stretched out *his* hand and drew his sword, struck the servant of the high priest, and cut off his ear.

52 But Jesus said to him, "Put your sword in its place, [a]for all who take the sword will perish[1] by the sword. 53 Or do you think that I cannot now pray to My Father, and He will provide Me with [a]more than twelve legions of angels? 54 How then could the Scriptures be fulfilled, [a]that it must happen thus?"

55 In that hour Jesus said to the multitudes, "Have you come out, as against a robber, with swords and clubs to take Me? I sat daily with you, teaching in the temple, and you did not seize Me. 56 But all this was done that the [a]Scriptures of the prophets might be fulfilled."

Then [b]all the disciples forsook Him and fled.

Jesus Faces the Sanhedrin

57 [a]And those who had laid hold of Jesus led *Him* away to Caiaphas the high priest, where the scribes and the elders were assembled. 58 But [a]Peter followed Him at a distance to the high priest's courtyard. And he went in and sat with the servants to see the end.

59 Now the chief priests, the elders,[1] and all the council sought [a]false testimony against Jesus to put Him to death, 60 but found none. Even though [a]many false witnesses came forward, they found none.[1] But at last [b]two false witnesses[2] came forward 61 and said, "This *fellow* said, [a]'I am able to destroy the temple of God and to build it in three days.' "

62 [a]And the high priest arose and said to Him, "Do You answer nothing? What *is it* these men testify against You?" 63 But [a]Jesus kept silent. And the high priest answered and said to Him, [b]"I put You under oath by the living God: Tell us if You are the Christ, the Son of God!"

64 Jesus said to him, "*It is as* you said. Nevertheless, I say to you, [a]hereafter you will see the Son of Man [b]sitting at the right hand of the Power, and coming on the clouds of heaven."

65 [a]Then the high priest tore his clothes, saying, "He has spoken blasphemy! What further need do we have of witnesses? Look, now you have heard His [b]blasphemy! 66 What do you think?"

They answered and said, [a]"He is deserving of death."

67 [a]Then they spat in His face and beat Him; and [b]others struck *Him* with the palms of their hands, 68 saying, [a]"Prophesy to us, Christ! Who is the one who struck You?"

Peter Denies Jesus, and Weeps Bitterly

69 [a]Now Peter sat outside in the courtyard. And a servant girl came to him, saying, "You also were with Jesus of Galilee."

70 But he denied it before *them* all, saying, "I do not know what you are saying."

71 And when he had gone out to the gateway, another *girl* saw him and said to those *who were* there, "This *fellow* also was with Jesus of Nazareth."

72 But again he denied with an oath, "I do not know the Man!"

73 And a little later those who stood by came up and said to Peter, "Surely you also are *one* of them, for your [a]speech betrays you."

74 Then [a]he began to curse and swear, *saying,* "I do not know the Man!"

Immediately a rooster crowed. 75 And Peter remembered the word of Jesus who had said to him, [a]"Before the rooster crows, you will deny Me three times." So he went out and wept bitterly.

Jesus Handed Over to Pontius Pilate

27 When morning came, [a]all the chief priests and elders of the people plotted against Jesus to put Him to death. 2 And when they had bound Him, they led Him away and [a]delivered Him to Pontius[1] Pilate the governor.

Judas Hangs Himself

3 [a]Then Judas, His betrayer, seeing that He had been condemned, was remorseful and brought back the thirty [b]pieces of silver to the chief priests and elders, 4 saying, "I have sinned by betraying innocent blood."

And they said, "What *is that* to us? You see *to it!*"

5 Then he threw down the pieces of silver in the temple and [a]departed, and went and hanged himself.

26:50 [a] Ps. 41:9; 55:13 **26:51** [a] John 18:10 **26:52** [a] Rev. 13:10 [1] M-Text reads *die.* **26:53** [a] Dan. 7:10 **26:54** [a] Is. 50:6; 53:2–11 **26:56** [a] Lam. 4:20 [b] John 18:15 **26:57** [a] John 18:12, 19–24 **26:58** [a] John 18:15, 16 **26:59** [a] Ps. 35:11 [1] NU-Text omits *the elders.* **26:60** [a] Mark 14:55 [b] Deut. 19:15 [1] NU-Text puts a comma after *but found none,* does not capitalize *Even,* and omits *they found none.* [2] NU-Text omits *false witnesses.* **26:61** [a] John 2:19 **26:62** [a] Mark 14:60 **26:63** [a] Is. 53:7 [b] Lev. 5:1 **26:64** [a] Dan. 7:13 [b] [Acts 7:55] **26:65** [a] 2 Kin. 18:37 [b] John 10:30–36 **26:66** [a] Lev. 24:16 **26:67** [a] Is. 50:6; 53:3 [b] Luke 22:63–65 **26:68** [a] Mark 14:65 **26:69** [a] John 18:16–18, 25–27 **26:73** [a] Luke 22:59 **26:74** [a] Mark 14:71 **26:75** [a] Matt. 26:34 **27:1** [a] John 18:28 **27:2** [a] Acts 3:13 [1] NU-Text omits *Pontius.* **27:3** [a] Matt. 26:14 [b] Matt. 26:15 **27:5** [a] Acts 1:18

6 But the chief priests took the silver pieces and said, "It is not lawful to put them into the treasury, because they are the price of blood." 7 And they consulted together and bought with them the potter's field, to bury strangers in. 8 Therefore that field has been called [a]the Field of Blood to this day.

9 Then was fulfilled what was spoken by Jeremiah the prophet, saying, [a]"And they took the thirty pieces of silver, the value of Him who was priced, whom they of the children of Israel priced, 10 and [a]gave them for the potter's field, as the LORD directed me."[1]

Jesus Faces Pilate

11 Now Jesus stood before the governor. [a]And the governor asked Him, saying, "Are You the King of the Jews?"

Jesus said to him, [b]"*It is as* you say." 12 And while He was being accused by the chief priests and elders, [a]He answered nothing.

13 Then Pilate said to Him, [a]"Do You not hear how many things they testify against You?" 14 But He answered him not one word, so that the governor marveled greatly.

Taking the Place of Barabbas

15 [a]Now at the feast the governor was accustomed to releasing to the multitude one prisoner whom they wished. 16 And at that time they had a notorious prisoner called Barabbas.[1] 17 Therefore, when they had gathered together, Pilate said to them, "Whom do you want me to release to you? Barabbas, or Jesus who is called Christ?" 18 For he knew that they had handed Him over because of [a]envy.

19 While he was sitting on the judgment seat, his wife sent to him, saying, "Have nothing to do with that just Man, for I have suffered many things today in a dream because of Him."

20 [a]But the chief priests and elders persuaded the multitudes that they should ask for Barabbas and destroy Jesus. 21 The governor answered and said to them, "Which of the two do you want me to release to you?"

They said, [a]"Barabbas!"

22 Pilate said to them, "What then shall I do with Jesus who is called Christ?"

They all said to him, "Let Him be crucified!"

23 Then the governor said, [a]"Why, what evil has He done?"

But they cried out all the more, saying, "Let Him be crucified!"

24 When Pilate saw that he could not prevail at all, but rather *that* a tumult was rising, he [a]took water and washed *his* hands before the multitude, saying, "I am innocent of the blood of this just Person.[1] You see *to it*."

25 And all the people answered and said, [a]"His blood *be* on us and on our children."

26 Then he released Barabbas to them; and when [a]he had scourged Jesus, he delivered *Him* to be crucified.

The Soldiers Mock Jesus

27 [a]Then the soldiers of the governor took Jesus into the Praetorium and gathered the whole garrison around Him. 28 And they [a]stripped Him and [b]put a scarlet robe on Him. 29 [a]When they had twisted a crown of thorns, they put *it* on His head, and a reed in His right hand. And they bowed the knee before Him and mocked Him, saying, "Hail, King of the Jews!" 30 Then [a]they spat on Him, and took the reed and struck Him on the head. 31 And when they had mocked Him, they took the robe off Him, put His *own* clothes on Him, [a]and led Him away to be crucified.

The King on a Cross

32 [a]Now as they came out, [b]they found a man of Cyrene, Simon by name. Him they compelled to bear His cross. 33 [a]And when they had come to a place called Golgotha, that is to say, Place of a Skull, 34 [a]they gave Him sour[1] wine mingled with gall to drink. But when He had tasted *it*, He would not drink.

35 [a]Then they crucified Him, and divided His garments, casting lots,[1] that it might be fulfilled which was spoken by the prophet:

[b]"They divided My garments among them,
And for My clothing they cast lots."[2]

36 [a]Sitting down, they kept watch over Him there. 37 And they [a]put up over His head the accusation written against Him:

THIS IS JESUS THE KING OF THE JEWS.

38 [a]Then two robbers were crucified with Him, one on the right and another on the left.

39 And [a]those who passed by blasphemed

27:8 [a] Acts 1:19 **27:9** [a] Zech. 11:12 **27:10** [a] Jer. 32:6–9; Zech. 11:12, 13 [1] Jeremiah 32:6–9 **27:11** [a] Mark 15:2–5 [b] John 18:37 **27:12** [a] John 19:9 **27:13** [a] Matt. 26:62 **27:15** [a] Luke 23:17–25 **27:16** [1] NU-Text reads *Jesus Barabbas.* **27:18** [a] Matt. 21:38 **27:20** [a] Acts 3:14 **27:21** [a] Acts 3:14 **27:23** [a] Acts 3:13 **27:24** [a] Deut. 21:6–8 [1] NU-Text omits *just.* **27:25** [a] Josh. 2:19 **27:26** [a] [Is. 50:6; 53:5] **27:27** [a] Mark 15:16–20 **27:28** [a] John 19:2 [b] Luke 23:11 **27:29** [a] Is. 53:3 **27:30** [a] Matt. 26:67 **27:31** [a] Is. 53:7 **27:32** [a] Heb. 13:12 [b] Mark 15:21 **27:33** [a] John 19:17 **27:34** [a] Ps. 69:21 [1] NU-Text omits *sour.* **27:35** [a] Luke 23:34 [b] Ps. 22:18 [1] NU-Text and M-Text omit the rest of this verse. [2] Psalm 22:18 **27:36** [a] Matt. 27:54 **27:37** [a] John 19:19 **27:38** [a] Is. 53:9, 12 **27:39** [a] Mark 15:29

Him, wagging their heads 40and saying, [a]"You
who destroy the temple and build *it* in three
days, save Yourself! [b]If You are the Son of
God, come down from the cross."
41Likewise the chief priests also, mocking
with the scribes and elders,[1] said, 42"He [a]saved
others; Himself He cannot save. If He is the
King of Israel,[1] let Him now come down from
the cross, and we will believe Him.[2] 43[a]He
trusted in God; let Him deliver Him now if
He will have Him; for He said, 'I am the Son
of God.' "
44[a]Even the robbers who were crucified
with Him reviled Him with the same thing.

Jesus Dies on the Cross

45[a]Now from the sixth hour until the ninth
hour there was darkness over all the land.
46And about the ninth hour [a]Jesus cried out
with a loud voice, saying, "Eli, Eli, lama sabachthani?" that is, [b]"My God, My God, why
have You forsaken Me?"[1]
47Some of those who stood there, when
they heard *that,* said, "This Man is calling for
Elijah!" 48Immediately one of them ran and
took a sponge, [a]filled *it* with sour wine and
put *it* on a reed, and offered it to Him to drink.
49The rest said, "Let Him alone; let us see
if Elijah will come to save Him."
50And Jesus [a]cried out again with a loud
voice, and [b]yielded up His spirit.
51Then, behold, [a]the veil of the temple
was torn in two from top to bottom; and
the earth quaked, and the rocks were split,
52and the graves were opened; and many
bodies of the saints who had fallen asleep
were raised; 53and coming out of the graves
after His resurrection, they went into the
holy city and appeared to many.
54[a]So when the centurion and those with
him, who were guarding Jesus, saw the earthquake and the things that had happened,
they feared greatly, saying, [b]"Truly this was
the Son of God!"
55And many women [a]who followed Jesus
from Galilee, ministering to Him, were there
looking on from afar, 56[a]among whom were
Mary Magdalene, Mary the mother of James
and Joses,[1] and the mother of Zebedee's sons.

Jesus Buried in Joseph's Tomb

57Now [a]when evening had come, there
came a rich man from Arimathea, named
Joseph, who himself had also become a disciple of Jesus. 58This man went to Pilate and
asked for the body of Jesus. Then Pilate commanded the body to be given to him. 59When
Joseph had taken the body, he wrapped it in
a clean linen cloth, 60and [a]laid it in his new
tomb which he had hewn out of the rock;
and he rolled a large stone against the door
of the tomb, and departed. 61And Mary Magdalene was there, and the other Mary, sitting
opposite the tomb.

Pilate Sets a Guard

62On the next day, which followed the Day
of Preparation, the chief priests and Pharisees gathered together to Pilate, 63saying,
"Sir, we remember, while He was still alive,
how that deceiver said, [a]'After three days
I will rise.' 64Therefore command that the
tomb be made secure until the third day, lest
His disciples come by night[1] and steal Him
away, and say to the people, 'He has risen
from the dead.' So the last deception will be
worse than the first."
65Pilate said to them, "You have a guard; go
your way, make *it* as secure as you know how."
66So they went and made the tomb secure,
[a]sealing the stone and setting the guard.

He Is Risen

28 Now [a]after the Sabbath, as the first
day of the week began to dawn, Mary
Magdalene [b]and the other Mary came to see
the tomb. 2And behold, there was a great
earthquake; for [a]an angel of the Lord descended from heaven, and came and rolled
back the stone from the door,[1] and sat on it.
3[a]His countenance was like lightning, and his
clothing as white as snow. 4And the guards
shook for fear of him, and became like [a]dead
men.
5But the angel answered and said to the
women, "Do not be afraid, for I know that
you seek Jesus who was crucified. 6He is not
here; for He is risen, [a]as He said. Come, see
the place where the Lord lay. 7And go quickly
and tell His disciples that He is risen from
the dead, and indeed [a]He is going before you
into Galilee; there you will see Him. Behold,
I have told you."
8So they went out quickly from the tomb
with fear and great joy, and ran to bring His
disciples word.

27:40 [a] John 2:19 [b] Matt. 26:63 **27:41** [1] M-Text reads *with the scribes, the Pharisees, and the elders.* **27:42** [a] [John 3:14, 15] [1] NU-Text reads *He is the King of Israel!* [2] NU-Text and M-Text read *we will believe in Him.* **27:43** [a] Ps. 22:8 **27:44** [a] Luke 23:39–43 **27:45** [a] Mark 15:33–41 **27:46** [a] [Heb. 5:7] [b] Ps. 22:1 [1] Psalm 22:1 **27:48** [a] Ps. 69:21 **27:50** [a] Luke 23:46 [b] [John 10:18] **27:51** [a] Ex. 26:31 **27:54** [a] Mark 15:39 [b] Matt. 14:33 **27:55** [a] Luke 8:2, 3 **27:56** [a] Mark 15:40, 47; 16:9 [1] NU-Text reads *Joseph.* **27:57** [a] John 19:38–42 **27:60** [a] Is. 53:9 **27:63** [a] Mark 8:31; 10:34 **27:64** [1] NU-Text omits *by night.* **27:66** [a] Dan. 6:17 **28:1** [a] Luke 24:1–10 [b] Matt. 27:56, 61 **28:2** [a] Mark 16:5 [1] NU-Text omits *from the door.* **28:3** [a] Dan. 7:9; 10:6 **28:4** [a] Rev. 1:17 **28:6** [a] Matt. 12:40; 16:21; 17:23; 20:19 **28:7** [a] Mark 16:7

The Women Worship the Risen Lord

9And as they went to tell His disciples,[1]
behold, [a]Jesus met them, saying, "Rejoice!"
So they came and held Him by the feet and
worshiped Him. 10Then Jesus said to them,
"Do not be afraid. Go *and* tell [a]My brethren
to go to Galilee, and there they will see Me."

The Soldiers Are Bribed

11Now while they were going, behold, some
of the guard came into the city and reported
to the chief priests all the things that had
happened. 12When they had assembled with
the elders and consulted together, they gave a
large sum of money to the soldiers, 13saying,
"Tell them, 'His disciples came at night and
stole Him *away* while we slept.' 14And if this
comes to the governor's ears, we will appease
him and make you secure." 15So they took the
money and did as they were instructed; and
this saying is commonly reported among the
Jews until this day.

The Great Commission

16Then the eleven disciples went away into
Galilee, to the mountain [a]which Jesus had
appointed for them. 17When they saw Him,
they worshiped Him; but some [a]doubted.
18And Jesus came and spoke to them, saying, [a]"All authority has been given to Me in
heaven and on earth. 19[a]Go therefore[1] and
[b]make disciples of all the nations, baptizing
them in the name of the Father and of the
Son and of the Holy Spirit, 20[a]teaching them
to observe all things that I have commanded
you; and lo, I am [b]with you always, *even* to
the end of the age." Amen.[1]

28:9 [a] John 20:14 [1] NU-Text omits the first clause of this verse. **28:10** [a] John 20:17 **28:16** [a] Matt. 26:32; 28:7, 10
28:17 [a] John 20:24–29 **28:18** [a] [Dan. 7:13, 14] **28:19** [a] Mark 16:15 [b] Luke 24:47 [1] M-Text omits *therefore.*
28:20 [a] [Acts 2:42] [b] [Acts 4:31; 18:10; 23:11] [1] NU-Text omits *Amen.*

THE GOSPEL ACCORDING TO

MARK

AUTHOR

According to Acts 12:12, Mark's mother Mary had a large house that was used as a meeting place for believers in Jerusalem. Barnabas was Mark's cousin (Col. 4:10), but Peter may have been the person that led him to Christ (Peter called him "Mark my son" in 1 Pet. 5:13). It was this close association with Peter that lent apostolic authority to Mark's Gospel, since Peter was evidently Mark's primary source of information. It has been suggested that Mark was referring to himself in his account of a "certain young man" in Gethsemane (Mark 14:51). Since all the disciples had abandoned Jesus (14:50), this little incident may have been a firsthand account.

TIME

c. AD 29–33

KEY VERSE

Mark 8:34–37

THEME

Mark is the shortest and simplest of the Gospels. He doesn't seem to be telling the story in a way that appeals to a particular audience the way Matthew did. He also does not use the well-developed thematic structure that characterizes John. One of the most common terms in the book is translated "immediately" or "at once." He uses this frequently as he moves from one anecdote to another. Mark's quickly paced Gospel is often confrontational as he tells the story of the gospel as clearly as possible. He wants the reader to respond and almost seems to be saying, *Here is the truth! Believe it, and let's get on with following Jesus.*

Faith locked into the peace of Jesus saves us. In Mark we learn how rich Jesus' peace is. We see this in the apostle's story of the woman who suffered from a hemorrhage. This woman reached out to Jesus in faith, touched Him, and was healed. But it wasn't simply a healing power that went out from Jesus. He said to her: "Daughter, your faith has made you well. Go in peace, and be healed of your affliction" (5:34). While the NKJV translates it as "your faith has made you well," the Greek literally reads, "Your faith has saved you." When Jesus said, "Go in peace," He was not saying, "Have a good day." The peace of which Jesus spoke is life changing. The healed woman will possess for the rest of her life the restorative, fulfilling *shalom* that Jesus offers. In Mark we see how His peace fulfills, restores, heals, and makes complete.

John the Baptist Prepares the Way

1 The [a]beginning of the gospel of Jesus
Christ, [b]the Son of God. 2As it is written
in the Prophets:[1]

> [a]"Behold, I send My messenger before
> Your face,
> Who will prepare Your way before
> You."[2]
>
> 3 "The[a] voice of one crying in the
> wilderness:
> 'Prepare the way of the LORD;
> Make His paths straight.' "[1]

4[a]John came baptizing in the wilderness
and preaching a baptism of repentance for
the remission of sins. 5[a]Then all the land of
Judea, and those from Jerusalem, went out
to him and were all baptized by him in the
Jordan River, confessing their sins.
6Now John was [a]clothed with camel's hair
and with a leather belt around his waist,
and he ate locusts and wild honey. 7And he
preached, saying, [a]"There comes One after
me who is mightier than I, whose sandal strap
I am not worthy to stoop down and loose. 8[a]I
indeed baptized you with water, but He will
baptize you [b]with the Holy Spirit."

John Baptizes Jesus

9[a]It came to pass in those days *that* Jesus
came from Nazareth of Galilee, and was baptized by John in the Jordan. 10[a]And immediately, coming up from[1] the water, He saw the
heavens parting and the Spirit [b]descending
upon Him like a dove. 11Then a voice came
from heaven, [a]"You are My beloved Son, in
whom I am well pleased."

Satan Tempts Jesus

12[a]Immediately the Spirit drove Him into
the wilderness. 13And He was there in the
wilderness forty days, tempted by Satan,
and was with the wild beasts; [a]and the angels
ministered to Him.

Jesus Begins His Galilean Ministry

14[a]Now after John was put in prison, Jesus
came to Galilee, [b]preaching the gospel of the
kingdom[1] of God, 15and saying, [a]"The time is
fulfilled, and [b]the kingdom of God is at hand.
Repent, and believe in the gospel."

Four Fishermen Called as Disciples

16[a]And as He walked by the Sea of Galilee, He saw Simon and Andrew his brother
casting a net into the sea; for they were
fishermen. 17Then Jesus said to them, "Follow

1:1 [a] Luke 3:22 [b] Matt. 14:33 **1:2** [a] Mal. 3:1 [1] NU-Text reads *Isaiah the prophet.* [2] Malachi 3:1 **1:3** [a] Is. 40:3 [1] Isaiah 40:3 **1:4** [a] Matt. 3:1 **1:5** [a] Matt. 3:5 **1:6** [a] Matt. 3:4 **1:7** [a] John 1:27 **1:8** [a] Acts 1:5; 11:16 [b] Is. 44:3 **1:9** [a] Matt. 3:13–17 **1:10** [a] Matt. 3:16 [b] Acts 10:38 [1] NU-Text reads *out of.* **1:11** [a] Matt. 3:17; 12:18 **1:12** [a] Matt. 4:1–11 **1:13** [a] Matt. 4:10, 11 **1:14** [a] Matt. 4:12 [b] Matt. 4:23 [1] NU-Text omits *of the kingdom.* **1:15** [a] [Gal. 4:4] [b] Matt. 3:2; 4:17 **1:16** [a] Luke 5:2–11

A NEW ERA OF PEACE

The beginning of the gospel of Jesus Christ, the Son of God.

MARK 1:1

Mark's Gospel begins with an ears-burning, eye-popping announcement: "The beginning of the gospel of Jesus Christ, the Son of God." Expanded and paraphrased, the verse says, *The beginning of the Good News for the world is brought by Jesus, the Anointed One, not Caesar. And by the way, Jesus, not Caesar, is also the true Son of God.* Mark directly challenged the Roman imperial cult of Caesar, the alleged son of a god (probably Zeus) whose reign prompted the arrival of the Golden Age.

To apply such exalted and well-recognized language to Jesus rather than to Caesar was very bold, almost reckless. But Mark knew Jesus was the Messiah because of His amazing ministry of healing and teaching and because of the resurrection. The good news is that the Good News of Jesus is true and that a whole new era really had begun. Romans sought peace; Mark told them they would find it in Jesus.

Just like the Romans in biblical days, everyone on your street is looking for peace and most in the wrong places. Take a moment today and pray for your neighborhood to find the peace of God in Jesus. When you have the opportunity, show them the way.

Me, and I will make you become [a]fishers of
men." [18][a]They immediately left their nets
and followed Him.
[19]When He had gone a little farther from
there, He saw James the *son* of Zebedee, and
John his brother, who also *were* in the boat
mending their nets. [20]And immediately He
called them, and they left their father Zebedee in the boat with the hired servants, and
went after Him.

Jesus Casts Out an Unclean Spirit

[21][a]Then they went into Capernaum, and
immediately on the Sabbath He entered the
[b]synagogue and taught. [22][a]And they were
astonished at His teaching, for He taught
them as one having authority, and not as
the scribes.
[23]Now there was a man in their synagogue
with an [a]unclean spirit. And he cried out,
[24]saying, "Let *us* alone! [a]What have we to do
with You, Jesus of Nazareth? Did You come
to destroy us? I [b]know who You are—the
[c]Holy One of God!"
[25]But Jesus [a]rebuked him, saying, "Be
quiet, and come out of him!" [26]And when
the unclean spirit [a]had convulsed him and
cried out with a loud voice, he came out of
him. [27]Then they were all amazed, so that
they questioned among themselves, saying,
"What is this? What new doctrine *is* this?
For with authority[1] He commands even the
unclean spirits, and they obey Him." [28]And
immediately His [a]fame spread throughout
all the region around Galilee.

Peter's Mother-in-Law Healed

[29][a]Now as soon as they had come out of
the synagogue, they entered the house of
Simon and Andrew, with James and John.
[30]But Simon's wife's mother lay sick with a
fever, and they told Him about her at once.
[31]So He came and took her by the hand and
lifted her up, and immediately the fever left
her. And she served them.

Many Healed After Sabbath Sunset

[32][a]At evening, when the sun had set, they
brought to Him all who were sick and those
who were demon-possessed. [33]And the whole
city was gathered together at the door. [34]Then
He healed many who were sick with various
diseases, and [a]cast out many demons; and He
[b]did not allow the demons to speak, because
they knew Him.

Preaching in Galilee

[35]Now [a]in the morning, having risen a
long while before daylight, He went out and
departed to a solitary place; and there He

1:17 [a] Matt. 13:47, 48 **1:18** [a] [Luke 14:26] **1:21** [a] Luke 4:31–37 [b] Matt. 4:23 **1:22** [a] Matt. 7:28, 29; 13:54 **1:23** [a] [Matt. 12:43] **1:24** [a] Matt. 8:28, 29 [b] James 2:19 [c] Ps. 16:10 **1:25** [a] [Luke 4:39] **1:26** [a] Mark 9:20 **1:27** [1] NU-Text reads *What is this? A new doctrine with authority.* **1:28** [a] Matt. 4:24; 9:31 **1:29** [a] Luke 4:38, 39 **1:32** [a] Matt. 8:16, 17 **1:34** [a] Luke 13:32 [b] Acts 16:17, 18 **1:35** [a] Luke 4:42, 43

BAPTIZED WITH THE HOLY SPIRIT

I indeed baptized you with water, but He will baptize you with the Holy Spirit.

MARK 1:8

The Jewish historian and apologist Josephus (c. AD 37–100) told his readers that almost everyone in Israel admired John the Baptist. When Herod Antipas put John to death and then suffered a serious military defeat, some people assumed it was divine vengeance! Maybe it was!

Given John's excellent reputation, what he said about Jesus in contrast to himself is all the more remarkable. John told the crowds who went to him, "I indeed baptized you with water, but He will baptize you with the Holy Spirit." Jesus—not John—was the main event. John prepared; Jesus fulfilled. I suspect John recognized Jesus when he saw the Spirit come upon him and heard the divine voice speak from heaven (John 1:29–34).

Jesus' ministry began and ended in the power of the Holy Spirit, which raised Him up. This is why we can look to Him to bring us peace and blessing. John loved Isaiah 40; in fact, he quoted from it in this chapter (Mark 1:2–3). To find the peace of God the way John the Baptist did, read Isaiah 40 today, which begins with a wonderful word: "Comfort!" (v. 1).

[b]prayed. 36And Simon and those *who were*
with Him searched for Him. 37When they
found Him, they said to Him, [a]"Everyone [b]is
looking for You."
38But He said to them, [a]"Let us go into the
next towns, that I may preach there also,
because [b]for this purpose I have come forth."
39[a]And He was preaching in their synagogues throughout all Galilee, and [b]casting
out demons.

Jesus Cleanses a Leper

40[a]Now a leper came to Him, imploring
Him, kneeling down to Him and saying to
Him, "If You are willing, You can make me
clean."
41Then Jesus, moved with [a]compassion,
stretched out *His* hand and touched him,
and said to him, "I am willing; be cleansed."
42As soon as He had spoken, [a]immediately
the leprosy left him, and he was cleansed.
43And He strictly warned him and sent him
away at once, 44and said to him, "See that
you say nothing to anyone; but go your way,
show yourself to the priest, and offer for
your cleansing those things [a]which Moses
commanded, as a testimony to them."
45[a]However, he went out and began to
proclaim *it* freely, and to spread the matter,
so that Jesus could no longer openly enter
the city, but was outside in deserted places;
[b]and they came to Him from every direction.

Jesus Forgives and Heals a Paralytic

2 And again [a]He entered Capernaum after
some days, and it was heard that He was
in the house. 2Immediately[1] many gathered
together, so that there was no longer room
to receive *them,* not even near the door.
And He preached the word to them. 3Then
they came to Him, bringing a [a]paralytic
who was carried by four *men.* 4And when
they could not come near Him because of
the crowd, they uncovered the roof where
He was. So when they had broken through,
they let down the bed on which the paralytic
was lying.
5When Jesus saw their faith, He said to the
paralytic, "Son, your sins are forgiven you."
6And some of the scribes were sitting there
and reasoning in their hearts, 7"Why does
this *Man* speak blasphemies like this? [a]Who
can forgive sins but God alone?"
8But immediately, when Jesus perceived
in His spirit that they reasoned thus within
themselves, He said to them, "Why do you
reason about these things in your hearts?
9[a]Which is easier, to say to the paralytic,

1:35 [b] Luke 5:16; 6:12; 9:28, 29 **1:37** [a] John 3:26; 12:19 [b] [Heb. 11:6] **1:38** [a] Luke 4:43 [b] [Is. 61:1, 2] **1:39** [a] Matt. 4:23; 9:35 [b] Mark 5:8, 13; 7:29, 30 **1:40** [a] Luke 5:12–14 **1:41** [a] Luke 7:13 **1:42** [a] Matt. 15:28 **1:44** [a] Lev. 14:1–32 **1:45** [a] Luke 5:15 [b] Mark 2:2, 13; 3:7 **2:1** [a] Matt. 9:1 **2:2** [1] NU-Text omits *Immediately.* **2:3** [a] Matt. 4:24; 8:6 **2:7** [a] Is. 43:25 **2:9** [a] Matt. 9:5

GOD'S TRUTH DELIVERING OUR PEACE

We never saw anything like this!

MARK 2:12

Jesus was not the only healer in Israel. Indeed, Mark tells us about a professional exorcist who attempted to cast out evil spirits in Jesus' name (9:38–40). This is important evidence that Jesus' power had become well known long before the resurrection.

The people of first-century Israel had seen would-be healers and would-be exorcists. No doubt pious leaders of the synagogues prayed for the ill and some recovered. But people had never seen works of power like Jesus'. In 2:1–12 we have the story of the paralyzed man. Jesus healed him and ordered him to pick up the bed on which he had been carried and take it home with him. The man did, and the people who witnessed it exclaimed, "We never saw anything like this!" (v. 12). No, I am sure they had not!

Most healers prescribed medicines and made use of paraphernalia. Jesus simply spoke: "I say to you, arise" (v. 11), and the man was healed instantly. There was no period of recovery. No medicines or therapies were prescribed. That is power, and that is what we have in Jesus. What is one way you can live in the transforming power of Jesus today? Truth. Truth conquers the lies that destroy our peace. Walk in God's truth to experience His peace in your life today.

'Your sins are forgiven you,' or to say, 'Arise,
take up your bed and walk'? 10But that you
may know that the Son of Man has power
on earth to forgive sins"—He said to the
paralytic, 11"I say to you, arise, take up your
bed, and go to your house." 12Immediately he
arose, took up the bed, and went out in the
presence of them all, so that all were amazed
and [a]glorified God, saying, "We never saw
anything like this!"

Matthew the Tax Collector

13[a]Then He went out again by the sea; and
all the multitude came to Him, and He taught
them. 14[a]As He passed by, He saw Levi the *son*
of Alphaeus sitting at the tax office. And He
said to him, [b]"Follow Me." So he arose and
[c]followed Him.
15[a]Now it happened, as He was dining in
Levi's house, that many tax collectors and
sinners also sat together with Jesus and His
disciples; for there were many, and they
followed Him. 16And when the scribes and[1]
Pharisees saw Him eating with the tax collectors and sinners, they said to His disciples,
"How *is it* that He eats and drinks with tax
collectors and sinners?"
17When Jesus heard *it,* He said to them,
[a]"Those who are well have no need of a
physician, but those who are sick. I did not
come to call *the* righteous, but sinners, to
repentance."[1]

Jesus Is Questioned About Fasting

18[a]The disciples of John and of the Pharisees were fasting. Then they came and said to
Him, "Why do the disciples of John and of the
Pharisees fast, but Your disciples do not fast?"
19And Jesus said to them, "Can the friends
of the bridegroom fast while the bridegroom
is with them? As long as they have the bridegroom with them they cannot fast. 20But the
days will come when the bridegroom will be
[a]taken away from them, and then they will
fast in those days. 21No one sews a piece of
unshrunk cloth on an old garment; or else
the new piece pulls away from the old, and
the tear is made worse. 22And no one puts
new wine into old wineskins; or else the new
wine bursts the wineskins, the wine is spilled,
and the wineskins are ruined. But new wine
must be put into new wineskins."

Jesus Is Lord of the Sabbath

23[a]Now it happened that He went through
the grainfields on the Sabbath; and as they
went His disciples began [b]to pluck the heads
of grain. 24And the Pharisees said to Him,
"Look, why do they do what is [a]not lawful
on the Sabbath?"
25But He said to them, "Have you never
read [a]what David did when he was in need and
hungry, he and those with him: 26how he went
into the house of God *in the days* of Abiathar
the high priest, and ate the showbread, [a]which

2:12 [a] [Phil. 2:11] **2:13** [a] Matt. 9:9 **2:14** [a] Luke 5:27–32 [b] John 1:43; 12:26; 21:22 [c] Luke 18:28 **2:15** [a] Matt. 9:10 **2:16** [1] NU-Text reads *of the.* **2:17** [a] Matt. 9:12, 13; 18:11 [1] NU-Text omits *to repentance.* **2:18** [a] Luke 5:33–38 **2:20** [a] Acts 1:9; 13:2, 3; 14:23 **2:23** [a] Luke 6:1–5 [b] Deut. 23:25 **2:24** [a] Ex. 20:10; 31:15 **2:25** [a] 1 Sam. 21:1–6 **2:26** [a] Lev. 24:5–9

JESUS CAME FOR YOU

"I did not come to call the righteous, but sinners, to repentance."

MARK 2:17

Celebrities seem to surround themselves with important, influential people. Jesus was different. He frequently associated with the "losers" of His day, people called "sinners," a group that included tax collectors, prostitutes, and others thought to be indifferent toward the law of Moses. It is not surprising that religious leaders and scholars who took the law of Moses very seriously found Jesus' choice of company questionable: "How is it that He eats and drinks with tax collectors and sinners?" (v. 16). How indeed?

I love Jesus' answer: "I did not come to call the righteous, but sinners, to repentance" (v. 17). Jesus did not sweep sin under the rug. No, He ate and drank with "sinners," not only to show that God loved them but to lead them to repentance, restoration, and salvation. That was Jesus' ministry. He wished to save us all by bringing us back into a peaceful and loving relationship with our heavenly Father.

Jesus had a heart of compassion; no wonder He lived in the peace of God. Express compassion today, and you will be walking in the peace of God.

is not lawful to eat except for the priests, and also gave some to those who were with him?"

27 And He said to them, "The Sabbath was made for man, and not man for the [a]Sabbath. 28 Therefore [a]the Son of Man is also Lord of the Sabbath."

Healing on the Sabbath

3 And [a]He entered the synagogue again, and a man was there who had a withered hand. 2 So they [a]watched Him closely, whether He would [b]heal him on the Sabbath, so that they might accuse Him. 3 And He said to the man who had the withered hand, "Step forward." 4 Then He said to them, "Is it lawful on the Sabbath to do good or to do evil, to save life or to kill?" But they kept silent. 5 And when He had looked around at them with anger, being grieved by the [a]hardness of their hearts, He said to the man, "Stretch out your hand." And he stretched *it* out, and his hand was restored as whole as the other.[1] 6 [a]Then the Pharisees went out and immediately plotted with [b]the Herodians against Him, how they might destroy Him.

A Great Multitude Follows Jesus

7 But Jesus withdrew with His disciples to the sea. And a great multitude from Galilee followed Him, [a]and from Judea 8 and Jerusalem and Idumea and beyond the Jordan; and those from Tyre and Sidon, a great multitude, when they heard how [a]many things He was doing, came to Him. 9 So He told His disciples that a small boat should be kept ready for Him because of the multitude, lest they should crush Him. 10 For He healed [a]many, so that as many as had afflictions pressed about Him to [b]touch Him. 11 [a]And the unclean spirits, whenever they saw Him, fell down before Him and cried out, saying, [b]"You are the Son of God." 12 But [a]He sternly warned them that they should not make Him known.

The Twelve Apostles

13 [a]And He went up on the mountain and called to *Him* those He Himself wanted. And they came to Him. 14 Then He appointed twelve,[1] that they might be with Him and that He might send them out to preach, 15 and to have power to heal sicknesses and[1] to cast out demons: 16 Simon,[1] [a]to whom He gave the name Peter; 17 James the *son* of Zebedee and John the brother of James, to whom He gave the name Boanerges, that is, "Sons of Thunder"; 18 Andrew, Philip, Bartholomew, Matthew, Thomas, James the *son* of Alphaeus, Thaddaeus, Simon the Cananite; 19 and Judas Iscariot, who also betrayed Him. And they went into a house.

A House Divided Cannot Stand

20 Then the multitude came together again, [a]so that they could not so much as eat bread. 21 But when His [a]own people heard *about this,* they went out to lay hold of Him, [b]for they said, "He is out of His mind."

22 And the scribes who came down from Jerusalem said, [a]"He has Beelzebub," and, "By the [b]ruler of the demons He casts out demons."

23 [a]So He called them to *Himself* and said to them in parables: "How can Satan cast out Satan? 24 If a kingdom is divided against itself, that kingdom cannot stand. 25 And if a house is divided against itself, that house cannot stand. 26 And if Satan has risen up against himself, and is divided, he cannot stand, but has an end. 27 [a]No one can enter a strong man's house and plunder his goods, unless he first binds the strong man. And then he will plunder his house.

The Unpardonable Sin

28 [a]"Assuredly, I say to you, all sins will be forgiven the sons of men, and whatever blasphemies they may utter; 29 but he who blasphemes against the Holy Spirit never has forgiveness, but is subject to eternal condemnation"— 30 because they [a]said, "He has an unclean spirit."

Jesus' Mother and Brothers Send for Him

31 [a]Then His brothers and His mother came, and standing outside they sent to Him, calling Him. 32 And a multitude was sitting around Him; and they said to Him, "Look, Your mother and Your brothers[1] are outside seeking You."

33 But He answered them, saying, "Who is My mother, or My brothers?" 34 And He looked around in a circle at those who sat about Him, and said, "Here are My mother and My brothers! 35 For whoever does the [a]will of God is My brother and My sister and mother."

2:27 [a] Deut. 5:14 **2:28** [a] Matt. 12:8 **3:1** [a] Luke 6:6–11 **3:2** [a] Luke 14:1; 20:20 [b] Luke 13:14 **3:5** [a] Zech. 7:12 [1] NU-Text omits *as whole as the other.* **3:6** [a] Mark 12:13 [b] Matt. 22:16 **3:7** [a] Luke 6:17 **3:8** [a] Mark 5:19 **3:10** [a] Luke 7:21 [b] Matt. 9:21; 14:36 **3:11** [a] Luke 4:41 [b] Matt. 8:29; 14:33 **3:12** [a] Mark 1:25, 34 **3:13** [a] Luke 9:1 **3:14** [1] NU-Text adds *whom He also named apostles.* **3:15** [1] NU-Text omits *to heal sicknesses and.* **3:16** [a] John 1:42 [1] NU-Text reads *and He appointed the twelve: Simon ....* **3:20** [a] Mark 6:31 **3:21** [a] Mark 6:3 [b] John 7:5; 10:20 **3:22** [a] Matt. 9:34; 10:25 [b] [John 12:31; 14:30; 16:11] **3:23** [a] Matt. 12:25–29 **3:27** [a] [Is. 49:24, 25] **3:28** [a] Luke 12:10 **3:30** [a] Matt. 9:34 **3:31** [a] Matt. 12:46–50 **3:32** [1] NU-Text and M-Text add *and Your sisters.* **3:35** [a] Eph. 6:6

BECOMING PART OF THE FAMILY

"Whoever does the will of God is My brother and My sister and mother."

MARK 3:35

Nepotism and favoritism were not issues for Jesus. Yes, I am sure He loved his biological family. At least two of His brothers—James and Jude (called Judas in Matt. 13:55; Mark 6:3)—became leaders in the church. But the mere fact of biological relationship did not cause Him to set aside faith and obedience.

Jesus made this important point clear after people told Him, "Your mother and Your brothers are outside seeking You" (3:32). Jesus then defined who truly made up His "family": "He looked around in a circle at those who sat about Him, and said, 'Here are My mother and My brothers! For whoever does the will of God is My brother and My sister and mother'" (vv. 34–35). No disrespect was intended, but to be part of Jesus' family in a way that eternally matters, you have to do the will of God.

The good news is that anyone can be part of Jesus' family! You may think you've messed up for the five hundredth time. We all mess up. "Whoever" means you, and it means me. Return to the Father today in repentance, ask Him to forgive you, and thank Him for His peace, knowing that God always keeps His Word.

The Parable of the Sower

4 And [a]again He began to teach by the sea.
And a great multitude was gathered to
Him, so that He got into a boat and sat *in*
it on the sea; and the whole multitude was
on the land facing the sea. 2Then He taught
them many things by parables, [a]and said to
them in His teaching:
3"Listen! Behold, a sower went out to sow.
4And it happened, as he sowed, *that* some
seed fell by the wayside; and the birds of the
air[1] came and devoured it. 5Some fell on stony
ground, where it did not have much earth;
and immediately it sprang up because it had
no depth of earth. 6But when the sun was up
it was scorched, and because it had no root
it withered away. 7And some *seed* fell among
thorns; and the thorns grew up and choked
it, and it yielded no crop. 8But other *seed*
fell on good ground and yielded a crop that
sprang up, increased and produced: some
thirtyfold, some sixty, and some a hundred."
9And He said to them,[1] "He who has ears
to hear, let him hear!"

The Purpose of Parables

10[a]But when He was alone, those around
Him with the twelve asked Him about the
parable. 11And He said to them, "To you it
has been given to [a]know the mystery of the
kingdom of God; but to [b]those who are outside, all things come in parables, 12so that

[a]'Seeing they may see and not perceive,
And hearing they may hear and not
understand;
Lest they should turn,
And *their* sins be forgiven them.' "[1]

The Parable of the Sower Explained

13And He said to them, "Do you not understand this parable? How then will you understand all the parables? 14[a]The sower sows
the word. 15And these are the ones by the
wayside where the word is sown. When they
hear, Satan comes immediately and takes
away the word that was sown in their hearts.
16These likewise are the ones sown on stony
ground who, when they hear the word, immediately receive it with gladness; 17and they
have no root in themselves, and so endure
only for a time. Afterward, when tribulation
or persecution arises for the word's sake,
immediately they stumble. 18Now these are
the ones sown among thorns; *they are* the
ones who hear the word, 19and the [a]cares of
this world, [b]the deceitfulness of riches, and
the desires for other things entering in choke
the word, and it becomes unfruitful. 20But
these are the ones sown on good ground,

4:1 [a] Luke 8:4–10 **4:2** [a] Mark 12:38 **4:4** [1] NU-Text and M-Text omit *of the air.* **4:9** [1] NU-Text and M-Text omit *to them.* **4:10** [a] Luke 8:9 **4:11** [a] [1 Cor. 2:10–16] [b] [Col. 4:5] **4:12** [a] Is. 6:9, 10; 43:8 [1] Isaiah 6:9, 10 **4:14** [a] Matt. 13:18–23 **4:19** [a] Luke 21:34 [b] 1 Tim. 6:9, 10, 17

those who hear the word, accept *it,* and bear
[a]fruit: some thirtyfold, some sixty, and some
a hundred."

Light Under a Basket

21 [a]Also He said to them, "Is a lamp brought
to be put under a basket or under a bed? Is it
not to be set on a lampstand? 22 [a]For there is
nothing hidden which will not be revealed,
nor has anything been kept secret but that it
should come to light. 23 [a]If anyone has ears
to hear, let him hear."
24 Then He said to them, "Take heed what
you hear. [a]With the same measure you use,
it will be measured to you; and to you who
hear, more will be given. 25 [a]For whoever has,
to him more will be given; but whoever does
not have, even what he has will be taken away
from him."

The Parable of the Growing Seed

26 And He said, [a]"The kingdom of God is as
if a man should scatter seed on the ground,
27 and should sleep by night and rise by day,
and the seed should sprout and [a]grow, he
himself does not know how. 28 For the earth
[a]yields crops by itself: first the blade, then
the head, after that the full grain in the head.
29 But when the grain ripens, immediately
[a]he puts in the sickle, because the harvest
has come."

The Parable of the Mustard Seed

30 Then He said, [a]"To what shall we liken
the kingdom of God? Or with what parable
shall we picture it? 31 *It is* like a mustard seed
which, when it is sown on the ground, is
smaller than all the seeds on earth; 32 but
when it is sown, it grows up and becomes
greater than all herbs, and shoots out large
branches, so that the birds of the air may
nest under its shade."

Jesus' Use of Parables

33 [a]And with many such parables He spoke
the word to them as they were able to hear
it. 34 But without a parable He did not speak
to them. And when they were alone, [a]He
explained all things to His disciples.

Wind and Wave Obey Jesus

35 [a]On the same day, when evening had
come, He said to them, "Let us cross over to
the other side." 36 Now when they had left the
multitude, they took Him along in the boat
as He was. And other little boats were also
with Him. 37 And a great windstorm arose,
and the waves beat into the boat, so that it
was already filling. 38 But He was in the stern,
asleep on a pillow. And they awoke Him and
said to Him, [a]"Teacher, [b]do You not care that
we are perishing?"
39 Then He arose and [a]rebuked the wind,

4:20 [a] [Rom. 7:4] **4:21** [a] Matt. 5:15 **4:22** [a] Matt. 10:26, 27 **4:23** [a] Matt. 11:15; 13:9, 43 **4:24** [a] Matt. 7:2 **4:25** [a] Luke 8:18; 19:26 **4:26** [a] [Matt. 13:24–30, 36–43] **4:27** [a] [2 Pet. 3:18] **4:28** [a] [John 12:24] **4:29** [a] Rev. 14:15 **4:30** [a] Matt. 13:31, 32 **4:33** [a] Matt. 13:34, 35 **4:34** [a] Luke 24:27, 45 **4:35** [a] Luke 8:22, 25 **4:38** [a] [Matt. 23:8–10] [b] Ps. 44:23 **4:39** [a] Luke 4:39

FINDING STILLNESS IN THE STORM

"Peace, be still!"

MARK 4:39

We love our dog, Buster. He is always so excited to see us. I tell Buster I love him. We snuggle with him. We rub his tummy. Even so, oftentimes Buster doesn't calm down. He is just too excited. So we have to say, "Buster! Calm down. Relax. We are here."

When Jesus said, "Peace, be still," He told those waves to calm down the way we tell Buster to relax. And the waves listened to Jesus the way Buster listens to us! Crossing the Sea of Galilee in a violent storm gave the disciples a view of Jesus' power at work in a way that exceeded their expectation and experience. In response to their fearful cry for help, Jesus spoke and the storm was stilled. Stunned, the disciples asked, "Who can this be, that even the wind and the sea obey Him!" (v. 41).

The disciples knew then that Jesus was much more than a gifted Teacher. They knew the Old Testament Scriptures spoke of God's power over creation. He who stills storms can also still our hearts. Waves may not be stealing your peace today, but something else might be nipping at your heels (like Buster). Whatever it is, ask Jesus to say to that worry, "Peace, be still."

and said to the sea, [b]"Peace, be still!" And the
wind ceased and there was a great calm. 40But
He said to them, "Why are you so fearful?
[a]How *is it* that you have no faith?"[1] 41And they
feared exceedingly, and said to one another,
"Who can this be, that even the wind and the
sea obey Him!"

A Demon-Possessed Man Healed

5 Then [a]they came to the other side of the
sea, to the country of the Gadarenes.[1] 2And
when He had come out of the boat, immediately there met Him out of the tombs a man
with an [a]unclean spirit, 3who had *his* dwelling
among the tombs; and no one could bind him,[1]
not even with chains, 4because he had often
been bound with shackles and chains. And
the chains had been pulled apart by him, and
the shackles broken in pieces; neither could
anyone tame him. 5And always, night and day,
he was in the mountains and in the tombs,
crying out and cutting himself with stones.
6When he saw Jesus from afar, he ran and
worshiped Him. 7And he cried out with a loud
voice and said, "What have I to do with You,
Jesus, Son of the Most High God? I [a]implore
You by God that You do not torment me."
8For He said to him, [a]"Come out of the
man, unclean spirit!" 9Then He asked him,
"What *is* your name?"
And he answered, saying, "My name *is*
Legion; for we are many." 10Also he begged
Him earnestly that He would not send them
out of the country.
11Now a large herd of [a]swine was feeding
there near the mountains. 12So all the demons begged Him, saying, "Send us to the
swine, that we may enter them." 13And at
once Jesus[1] gave them permission. Then
the unclean spirits went out and entered the
swine (there were about two thousand); and
the herd ran violently down the steep place
into the sea, and drowned in the sea.
14So those who fed the swine fled, and they
told *it* in the city and in the country. And
they went out to see what it was that had
happened. 15Then they came to Jesus, and
saw the one *who had been* [a]demon-possessed
and had the legion, [b]sitting and [c]clothed and
in his right mind. And they were afraid. 16And
those who saw it told them how it happened
to him *who had been* demon-possessed, and
about the swine. 17Then [a]they began to plead
with Him to depart from their region.
18And when He got into the boat, [a]he who
had been demon-possessed begged Him that
he might be with Him. 19However, Jesus did
not permit him, but said to him, "Go home to
your friends, and tell them what great things
the Lord has done for you, and how He has

4:39 [b] Ps. 65:7; 89:9; 93:4; 104:6, 7 **4:40** [a] Matt. 14:31, 32 [1] NU-Text reads *Have you still no faith?* **5:1** [a] Matt. 8:28–34 [1] NU-Text reads *Gerasenes.* **5:2** [a] Mark 1:23; 7:25 **5:3** [1] NU-Text adds *anymore.* **5:7** [a] Acts 19:13 **5:8** [a] Mark 1:25; 9:25 **5:11** [a] Deut. 14:8 **5:13** [1] NU-Text reads *And He gave.* **5:15** [a] Matt. 4:24; 8:16 [b] Luke 10:39 [c] [Is. 61:10] **5:17** [a] Acts 16:39 **5:18** [a] Luke 8:38, 39

DESPERATION AS THE DOORWAY

And He said to her, "Daughter, your faith has made you well.
Go in peace, and be healed of your affliction."

MARK 5:34

Have you asked for one thing, then received something else? Or perhaps you received something above and beyond what you requested! We find this in the story of the woman with the hemorrhage.

The ill woman had spent everything she had on doctors and found no relief. In fact, her condition only grew worse. Desperate, she snuck up behind Jesus in the crowd and touched His garment. Suddenly she sensed that she had been healed. Jesus asked, "Who touched My clothes?" (v. 30). The woman knelt before Jesus and told all. He replied, "Daughter, your faith has made you well" (v. 34). Calling her "daughter" affirmed that she was indeed family—the family of God—and Jesus' affirming her faith was what she hoped would happen.

But then Jesus added, "Go in peace." This was the icing on the cake! The woman received healing, but she also received God's peace. Another physician might have been able to cure her, but only Jesus Christ could give her the peace of God. The woman reached out in faith and received more than she anticipated. You can too. Go ahead—touch His garment (ask)!

had compassion on you." 20And he departed
and began to [a]proclaim in Decapolis all that
Jesus had done for him; and all [b]marveled.

A Girl Restored to Life and a Woman Healed

21[a]Now when Jesus had crossed over again
by boat to the other side, a great multitude
gathered to Him; and He was by the sea.
22[a]And behold, one of the rulers of the synagogue came, Jairus by name. And when he
saw Him, he fell at His feet 23and begged Him
earnestly, saying, "My little daughter lies at
the point of death. Come and [a]lay Your hands
on her, that she may be healed, and she will
live." 24So *Jesus* went with him, and a great
multitude followed Him and thronged Him.
25Now a certain woman [a]had a flow of
blood for twelve years, 26and had suffered
many things from many physicians. She had
spent all that she had and was no better, but
rather grew worse. 27When she heard about
Jesus, she came behind *Him* in the crowd
and [a]touched His garment. 28For she said,
"If only I may touch His clothes, I shall be
made well."
29Immediately the fountain of her blood
was dried up, and she felt in *her* body that
she was healed of the affliction. 30And Jesus,
immediately knowing in Himself that [a]power
had gone out of Him, turned around in the
crowd and said, "Who touched My clothes?"
31But His disciples said to Him, "You see
the multitude thronging You, and You say,
'Who touched Me?' "
32And He looked around to see her who
had done this thing. 33But the woman, [a]fear-
ing and trembling, knowing what had happened to her, came and fell down before
Him and told Him the whole truth. 34And
He said to her, "Daughter, [a]your faith has
made you well. [b]Go in peace, and be healed
of your affliction."
35[a]While He was still speaking, *some* came
from the ruler of the synagogue's *house* who
said, "Your daughter is dead. Why trouble the
Teacher any further?"
36As soon as Jesus heard the word that
was spoken, He said to the ruler of the synagogue, "Do not be afraid; only [a]believe."
37And He permitted no one to follow Him
except Peter, James, and John the brother of
James. 38Then He came to the house of the
ruler of the synagogue, and saw a tumult and
those who [a]wept and wailed loudly. 39When

> **PEACE NOTE**
>
> Suffering people reached out to Jesus in faith and were healed. Some received more than health: some received Jesus' peace.
>
> MARK 5:34

He came in, He said to them, "Why make this
commotion and weep? The child is not dead,
but [a]sleeping."
40And they ridiculed Him. [a]But when He
had put them all outside, He took the father
and the mother of the child, and those *who
were* with Him, and entered where the child
was lying. 41Then He took the child by the
hand, and said to her, "Talitha, cumi," which
is translated, "Little girl, I say to you, arise."
42Immediately the girl arose and walked, for
she was twelve years *of age.* And they were
[a]overcome with great amazement. 43But [a]He
commanded them strictly that no one should
know it, and said that *something* should be
given her to eat.

Jesus Rejected at Nazareth

6 Then [a]He went out from there and came
to His own country, and His disciples
followed Him. 2And when the Sabbath had
come, He began to teach in the synagogue.
And many hearing *Him* were [a]astonished,
saying, [b]"Where *did* this Man *get* these
things? And what wisdom *is* this which is
given to Him, that such mighty works are
performed by His hands! 3Is this not the
carpenter, the Son of Mary, and [a]brother of
James, Joses, Judas, and Simon? And are
not His sisters here with us?" So they [b]were
offended at Him.
4But Jesus said to them, [a]"A prophet is not
without honor except in his own country,
among his own relatives, and in his own
house." 5[a]Now He could do no mighty work
there, except that He laid His hands on a

5:20 [a] Ps. 66:16 [b] Matt. 9:8, 33 5:21 [a] Luke 8:40 5:22 [a] Matt. 9:18–26 5:23 [a] Acts 9:17; 28:8 5:25 [a] Lev. 15:19, 25 5:27 [a] Matt. 14:35, 36 5:30 [a] Luke 6:19; 8:46 5:33 [a] [Ps. 89:7] 5:34 [a] Matt. 9:22 [b] Luke 7:50; 8:48 5:35 [a] Luke 8:49 5:36 [a] [John 11:40] 5:38 [a] Acts 9:39 5:39 [a] John 11:4, 11 5:40 [a] Acts 9:40 5:42 [a] Mark 1:27; 7:37 5:43 [a] [Matt. 8:4; 12:16–19; 17:9] 6:1 [a] Matt. 13:54 6:2 [a] Matt. 7:28 [b] John 6:42 6:3 [a] Matt. 12:46 [b] [Matt. 11:6] 6:4 [a] John 4:44 6:5 [a] Gen. 19:22; 32:25

few sick people and healed *them.* 6And [a]He
marveled because of their unbelief. [b]Then He
went about the villages in a circuit, teaching.

Sending Out the Twelve

7[a]And He called the twelve to *Himself,* and
began to send them out [b]two *by* two, and
gave them power over unclean spirits. 8He
commanded them to take nothing for the
journey except a staff—no bag, no bread, no
copper in *their* money belts— 9but [a]to wear
sandals, and not to put on two tunics.

10[a]Also He said to them, "In whatever place
you enter a house, stay there till you depart
from that place. 11[a]And whoever[1] will not
receive you nor hear you, when you depart
from there, [b]shake off the dust under your
feet as a testimony against them.[2] Assuredly, I say to you, it will be more tolerable for
Sodom and Gomorrah in the day of judgment
than for that city!"

12So they went out and preached that *peo-*
ple should repent. 13And they cast out many
demons, [a]and anointed with oil many who
were sick, and healed *them.*

John the Baptist Beheaded

14[a]Now King Herod heard *of Him,* for His
name had become well known. And he said,
"John the Baptist is risen from the dead, and
therefore [b]these powers are at work in him."

15[a]Others said, "It is Elijah."

And others said, "It is the Prophet, [b]or[1] like
one of the prophets."

16[a]But when Herod heard, he said, "This is
John, whom I beheaded; he has been raised
from the dead!" 17For Herod himself had sent
and laid hold of John, and bound him in prison for the sake of Herodias, his brother Philip's wife; for he had married her. 18Because
John had said to Herod, [a]"It is not lawful for
you to have your brother's wife."

19Therefore Herodias held it against him
and wanted to kill him, but she could not;
20for Herod [a]feared John, knowing that he
was a just and holy man, and he protected
him. And when he heard him, he did many
things, and heard him gladly.

21[a]Then an opportune day came when
Herod [b]on his birthday gave a feast for his
nobles, the high officers, and the chief *men*
of Galilee. 22And when Herodias' daughter
herself came in and danced, and pleased
Herod and those who sat with him, the king
said to the girl, "Ask me whatever you want,
and I will give *it* to you." 23He also swore to
her, [a]"Whatever you ask me, I will give you,
up to half my kingdom."

24So she went out and said to her mother,
"What shall I ask?"

And she said, "The head of John the Baptist!"

25Immediately she came in with haste to
the king and asked, saying, "I want you to
give me at once the head of John the Baptist
on a platter."

26[a]And the king was exceedingly sorry; *yet,*
because of the oaths and because of those who
sat with him, he did not want to refuse her.
27Immediately the king sent an executioner
and commanded his head to be brought.
And he went and beheaded him in prison,
28brought his head on a platter, and gave it
to the girl; and the girl gave it to her mother.
29When his disciples heard *of it,* they came
and [a]took away his corpse and laid it in a tomb.

Feeding the Five Thousand

30[a]Then the apostles gathered to Jesus
and told Him all things, both what they had
done and what they had taught. 31[a]And He
said to them, "Come aside by yourselves to
a deserted place and rest a while." For [b]there
were many coming and going, and they did
not even have time to eat. 32[a]So they departed
to a deserted place in the boat by themselves.

33But the multitudes[1] saw them departing,
and many [a]knew Him and ran there on foot
from all the cities. They arrived before them
and came together to Him. 34[a]And Jesus,
when He came out, saw a great multitude
and was moved with compassion for them,
because they were like [b]sheep not having a
shepherd. So [c]He began to teach them many
things. 35[a]When the day was now far spent,
His disciples came to Him and said, "This
is a deserted place, and already the hour *is*
late. 36Send them away, that they may go
into the surrounding country and villages
and buy themselves bread;[1] for they have
nothing to eat."

37But He answered and said to them, "You
give them something to eat."

And they said to Him, [a]"Shall we go and
buy two hundred denarii worth of bread and
give them *something* to eat?"

6:6 [a] Is. 59:16 [b] Matt. 9:35 **6:7** [a] Mark 3:13, 14 [b] [Eccl. 4:9, 10] **6:9** [a] [Eph. 6:15] **6:10** [a] Matt. 10:11 **6:11** [a] Matt. 10:14 [b] Acts 13:51; 18:6 [1] NU-Text reads *whatever place.* [2] NU-Text omits the rest of this verse. **6:13** [a] [James 5:14] **6:14** [a] Luke 9:7–9 [b] Luke 19:37 **6:15** [a] Mark 8:28 [b] Matt. 21:11 [1] NU-Text and M-Text omit *or.* **6:16** [a] Luke 3:19 **6:18** [a] Lev. 18:16; 20:21 **6:20** [a] Matt. 14:5; 21:26 **6:21** [a] Matt. 14:6 [b] Gen. 40:20 **6:23** [a] Esth. 5:3, 6; 7:2 **6:26** [a] Matt. 14:9 **6:29** [a] 1 Kin. 13:29, 30 **6:30** [a] Luke 9:10 **6:31** [a] Matt. 14:13 [b] Mark 3:20 **6:32** [a] Matt. 14:13–21 **6:33** [a] [Col. 1:6] [1] NU-Text and M-Text read *they.* **6:34** [a] Matt. 9:36; 14:14 [b] Num. 27:17 [c] Luke 9:11 **6:35** [a] Matt. 14:15 **6:36** [1] NU-Text reads *something to eat* and omits the rest of this verse. **6:37** [a] 2 Kin. 4:43

38 But He said to them, "How many loaves
do you have? Go and see."
And when they found out they said, [a]"Five,
and two fish."
39 Then He [a]commanded them to make
them all sit down in groups on the green
grass. 40 So they sat down in ranks, in hundreds and in fifties. 41 And when He had taken
the five loaves and the two fish, He [a]looked up
to heaven, [b]blessed and broke the loaves, and
gave *them* to His disciples to set before them;
and the two fish He divided among *them* all.
42 So they all ate and were filled. 43 And they
took up twelve baskets full of fragments and
of the fish. 44 Now those who had eaten the
loaves were about[1] five thousand men.

Jesus Walks on the Sea

45 [a]Immediately He made His disciples get
into the boat and go before Him to the other
side, to Bethsaida, while He sent the multitude away. 46 And when He had sent them
away, He [a]departed to the mountain to pray.
47 Now when evening came, the boat was in
the middle of the sea; and He *was* alone on
the land. 48 Then He saw them straining at
rowing, for the wind was against them. Now
about the fourth watch of the night He came
to them, walking on the sea, and [a]would have
passed them by. 49 And when they saw Him
walking on the sea, they supposed it was a
[a]ghost, and cried out; 50 for they all saw Him
and were troubled. But immediately He talked
with them and said to them, [a]"Be of good
cheer! It is I; do not be [b]afraid." 51 Then He
went up into the boat to them, and the wind
[a]ceased. And they were greatly [b]amazed in
themselves beyond measure, and marveled.
52 For [a]they had not understood about the
loaves, because their [b]heart was hardened.

Many Touch Him and Are Made Well

53 [a]When they had crossed over, they came
to the land of Gennesaret and anchored
there. 54 And when they came out of the
boat, immediately the people recognized
Him, 55 ran through that whole surrounding region, and began to carry about on
beds those who were sick to wherever they
heard He was. 56 Wherever He entered, into
villages, cities, or the country, they laid the
sick in the marketplaces, and begged Him
that [a]they might just touch the [b]hem of His
garment. And as many as touched Him were
made well.

Defilement Comes from Within

7 Then [a]the Pharisees and some of the
scribes came together to Him, having
come from Jerusalem. 2 Now when[1] they saw
some of His disciples eat bread with defiled,
that is, with [a]unwashed hands, they found
fault. 3 For the Pharisees and all the Jews do
not eat unless they wash *their* hands in a special way, holding the [a]tradition of the elders.
4 *When they come* from the marketplace, they
do not eat unless they wash. And there are
many other things which they have received
and hold, *like* the washing of cups, pitchers,
copper vessels, and couches.
5 [a]Then the Pharisees and scribes asked
Him, "Why do Your disciples not walk according to the tradition of the elders, but eat
bread with unwashed hands?"
6 He answered and said to them, "Well did
Isaiah prophesy of you [a]hypocrites, as it is
written:

[b]'This people honors Me with *their* lips,
But their heart is far from Me.
7 And in vain they worship Me,
Teaching *as* doctrines the
commandments of men.'[1]

8 For laying aside the commandment of God,
you hold the tradition of men[1]—the washing
of pitchers and cups, and many other such
things you do."
9 He said to them, "*All too* well [a]you reject
the commandment of God, that you may
keep your tradition. 10 For Moses said, [a]'Hon-
or your father and your mother';[1] and, [b]'He
who curses father or mother, let him be put
to death.'[2] 11 But you say, 'If a man says to
his father or mother, [a]"Whatever profit you
might have received from me *is* Corban"—'
(that is, a gift *to God*), 12 then you no longer let
him do anything for his father or his mother,
13 making the word of God of no effect through
your tradition which you have handed down.
And many such things you do."
14 [a]When He had called all the multitude
to *Himself*, He said to them, "Hear Me, everyone, and [b]understand: 15 There is nothing that
enters a man from outside which can defile
him; but the things which come out of him,

6:38 [a] *John 6:9* **6:39** [a] Matt. 15:35 **6:41** [a] John 11:41, 42 [b] Matt. 15:36; 26:26 **6:44** [1] NU-Text and M-Text omit *about*. **6:45** [a] John 6:15–21 **6:46** [a] Luke 5:16 **6:48** [a] Luke 24:28 **6:49** [a] Matt. 14:26 **6:50** [a] Matt. 9:2 [b] Is. 41:10 **6:51** [a] Ps. 107:29 [b] Mark 1:27; 2:12; 5:42; 7:37 **6:52** [a] Mark 8:17, 18 [b] Mark 3:5; 16:14 **6:53** [a] Matt. 14:34–36 **6:56** [a] Matt. 9:20 [b] Num. 15:38, 39 **7:1** [a] Matt. 15:1–20 **7:2** [a] Matt. 15:20 [1] NU-Text omits *when* and *they found fault*. **7:3** [a] Gal. 1:14 **7:5** [a] Matt. 15:2 **7:6** [a] Matt. 23:13–29 [b] Is. 29:13 **7:7** [1] Isaiah 29:13 **7:8** [1] NU-Text omits the rest of this verse. **7:9** [a] Prov. 1:25 **7:10** [a] Ex. 20:12; Deut. 5:16 [b] Ex. 21:17 [1] Exodus 20:12; Deuteronomy 5:16 [2] Exodus 21:17 **7:11** [a] Matt. 15:5; 23:18 **7:14** [a] Matt. 15:10 [b] Matt. 16:9, 11, 12

those are the things that [a]defile a man. 16[a]If
anyone has ears to hear, let him hear!"[1]
17[a]When He had entered a house away from
the crowd, His disciples asked Him concerning
the parable. 18So He said to them, [a]"Are you
thus without understanding also? Do you not
perceive that whatever enters a man from
outside cannot defile him, 19because it does
not enter his heart but his stomach, and is
eliminated, *thus* purifying all foods?"[1] 20And He
said, [a]"What comes out of a man, that defiles
a man. 21[a]For from within, out of the heart of
men, [b]proceed evil thoughts, [c]adulteries, [d]for-
nications, murders, 22thefts, [a]covetousness,
wickedness, [b]deceit, [c]lewdness, an evil eye,
[d]blasphemy, [e]pride, foolishness. 23All these evil
things come from within and defile a man."

A Gentile Shows Her Faith

24[a]From there He arose and went to the
region of Tyre and Sidon.[1] And He entered a
house and wanted no one to know *it,* but He
could not be [b]hidden. 25For a woman whose
young daughter had an unclean spirit heard
about Him, and she came and [a]fell at His feet.
26The woman was a Greek, a Syro-Phoenician
by birth, and she kept asking Him to cast the
demon out of her daughter. 27But Jesus said
to her, "Let the children be filled first, for it
is not good to take the children's bread and
throw *it* to the little dogs."

28And she answered and said to Him, "Yes,
Lord, yet even the little dogs under the table
eat from the children's crumbs."

29Then He said to her, "For this saying go
your way; the demon has gone out of your
daughter."

30And when she had come to her house,
she found the demon gone out, and her
daughter lying on the bed.

Jesus Heals a Deaf-Mute

31[a]Again, departing from the region of Tyre
and Sidon, He came through the midst of
the region of Decapolis to the Sea of Galilee.
32Then [a]they brought to Him one who was
deaf and had an impediment in his speech,
and they begged Him to put His hand on him.
33And He took him aside from the multitude,
and put His fingers in his ears, and [a]He spat
and touched his tongue. 34Then, [a]looking
up to heaven, [b]He sighed, and said to him,
"Ephphatha," that is, "Be opened."
35[a]Immediately his ears were opened, and
the impediment of his tongue was loosed,
and he spoke plainly. 36Then [a]He commanded them that they should tell no one; but
the more He commanded them, the more
widely they proclaimed *it.* 37And they were
[a]astonished beyond measure, saying, "He
has done all things well. He [b]makes both the
deaf to hear and the mute to speak."

Feeding the Four Thousand

8 In those days, [a]the multitude being very
great and having nothing to eat, Jesus
called His disciples *to Him* and said to them,
2"I have [a]compassion on the multitude, because they have now continued with Me three
days and have nothing to eat. 3And if I send
them away hungry to their own houses, they
will faint on the way; for some of them have
come from afar."

4Then His disciples answered Him, "How
can one satisfy these people with bread here
in the wilderness?"

5[a]He asked them, "How many loaves do
you have?"

And they said, "Seven."

6So He commanded the multitude to sit
down on the ground. And He took the seven
loaves and gave thanks, broke *them* and gave
them to His disciples to set before *them;* and
they set *them* before the multitude. 7They
also had a few small fish; and [a]having blessed
them, He said to set them also before *them.*
8So they ate and were filled, and they took
up seven large baskets of leftover fragments.
9Now those who had eaten were about four
thousand. And He sent them away, 10[a]imme-
diately got into the boat with His disciples,
and came to the region of Dalmanutha.

The Pharisees Seek a Sign

11[a]Then the Pharisees came out and began to dispute with Him, seeking from Him
a sign from heaven, testing Him. 12But He
[a]sighed deeply in His spirit, and said, "Why
does this generation seek a sign? Assuredly,
I say to you, [b]no sign shall be given to this
generation."

Beware of the Leaven of the Pharisees and Herod

13And He left them, and getting into the
boat again, departed to the other side. 14[a]Now

7:15 [a] Is. 59:3 **7:16** [a] Matt. 11:15 [1] NU-Text omits this verse. **7:17** [a] Matt. 15:15 **7:18** [a] [Heb. 5:11–14] **7:19** [1] NU-Text ends quotation with *eliminated,* setting off the final clause as Mark's comment that Jesus has declared all foods clean. **7:20** [a] Ps. 39:1 **7:21** [a] Gen. 6:5; 8:21 [b] [Gal. 5:19–21] [c] 2 Pet. 2:14 [d] 1 Thess. 4:3 **7:22** [a] Luke 12:15 [b] Rom. 1:28, 29 [c] 1 Pet. 4:3 [d] Rev. 2:9 [e] 1 John 2:16 **7:24** [a] Matt. 15:21 [b] Mark 2:1, 2 [1] NU-Text omits *and Sidon.* **7:25** [a] John 11:32 **7:31** [a] Matt. 15:29 **7:32** [a] Luke 11:14 **7:33** [a] Mark 8:23 **7:34** [a] Mark 6:41 [b] John 11:33, 38 **7:35** [a] Is. 35:5, 6 **7:36** [a] Mark 5:43 **7:37** [a] Mark 6:51; 10:26 [b] Matt. 12:22 **8:1** [a] Matt. 15:32–39 **8:2** [a] Mark 1:41; 6:34 **8:5** [a] Mark 6:38 **8:7** [a] Matt. 14:19 **8:10** [a] Matt. 15:39 **8:11** [a] Matt. 12:38; 16:1 **8:12** [a] Mark 7:34 [b] Matt. 12:39 **8:14** [a] Matt. 16:5

the disciples[1] had forgotten to take bread, and
they did not have more than one loaf with
them in the boat. 15[a]Then He charged them,
saying, "Take heed, beware of the leaven of
the Pharisees and the leaven of Herod."
16And they reasoned among themselves,
saying, "*It is* because we have no bread."
17But Jesus, being aware of *it,* said to them,
"Why do you reason because you have no
bread? [a]Do you not yet perceive nor understand? Is your heart still[1] hardened? 18Having
eyes, do you not see? And having ears, do
you not hear? And do you not remember?
19[a]When I broke the five loaves for the five
thousand, how many baskets full of fragments did you take up?"
They said to Him, "Twelve."
20"Also, [a]when I broke the seven for the
four thousand, how many large baskets full
of fragments did you take up?"
And they said, "Seven."
21So He said to them, "How *is it* [a]you do
not understand?"

A Blind Man Healed at Bethsaida

22Then He came to Bethsaida; and they
brought a [a]blind man to Him, and begged
Him to [b]touch him. 23So He took the blind
man by the hand and led him out of the town.
And when [a]He had spit on his eyes and put
His hands on him, He asked him if he saw
anything.
24And he looked up and said, "I see men
like trees, walking."
25Then He put *His* hands on his eyes again
and made him look up. And he was restored
and saw everyone clearly. 26Then He sent
him away to his house, saying, "Neither go
into the town, [a]nor tell anyone in the town."[1]

Peter Confesses Jesus as the Christ

27[a]Now Jesus and His disciples went out
to the towns of Caesarea Philippi; and on the
road He asked His disciples, saying to them,
"Who do men say that I am?"
28So they answered, [a]"John the Baptist;
but some *say,* [b]Elijah; and others, one of
the prophets."
29He said to them, "But who do you say
that I am?"
Peter answered and said to Him, [a]"You
are the Christ."
30[a]Then He strictly warned them that they
should tell no one about Him.

Jesus Predicts His Death and Resurrection

31And [a]He began to teach them that the
Son of Man must suffer many things, and be
[b]rejected by the elders and chief priests and
scribes, and be [c]killed, and after three days
rise again. 32He spoke this word openly. Then
Peter took Him aside and began to rebuke
Him. 33But when He had turned around and
looked at His disciples, He [a]rebuked Peter,
saying, "Get behind Me, Satan! For you are
not mindful of the things of God, but the
things of men."

Take Up the Cross and Follow Him

34When He had called the people to *Himself,* with His disciples also, He said to them,
[a]"Whoever desires to come after Me, let him
deny himself, and take up his cross, and
follow Me. 35For [a]whoever desires to save his
life will lose it, but whoever loses his life for
My sake and the gospel's will save it. 36For
what will it profit a man if he gains the whole
world, and loses his own soul? 37Or what will
a man give in exchange for his soul? 38[a]For
whoever [b]is ashamed of Me and My words
in this adulterous and sinful generation, of
him the Son of Man also will be ashamed
when He comes in the glory of His Father
with the holy angels."

9 And He said to them, [a]"Assuredly, I say
to you that there are some standing here
who will not taste death till they see [b]the
kingdom of God present with power."

Jesus Transfigured on the Mount

2[a]Now after six days Jesus took Peter,
James, and John, and led them up on a high
mountain apart by themselves; and He was
transfigured before them. 3His clothes became shining, exceedingly [a]white, like snow,
such as no launderer on earth can whiten
them. 4And Elijah appeared to them with
Moses, and they were talking with Jesus.
5Then Peter answered and said to Jesus,
"Rabbi, it is good for us to be here; and let
us make three tabernacles: one for You, one
for Moses, and one for Elijah"— 6because
he did not know what to say, for they were
greatly afraid.
7And a [a]cloud came and overshadowed
them; and a voice came out of the cloud,
saying, "This is [b]My beloved Son. [c]Hear Him!"
8Suddenly, when they had looked around,

8:14 [1] NU-Text and M-Text read *they.* **8:15** [a] Luke 12:1 **8:17** [a] Mark 6:52; 16:14 [1] NU-Text omits *still.* **8:19** [a] Matt. 14:20 **8:20** [a] Matt. 15:37 **8:21** [a] [Mark 6:52] **8:22** [a] John 9:1 [b] Luke 18:15 **8:23** [a] Mark 7:33 **8:26** [a] Mark 5:43; 7:36 [1] NU-Text reads *"Do not even go into the town."* **8:27** [a] Luke 9:18–20 **8:28** [a] Matt. 14:2 [b] Luke 9:7, 8 **8:29** [a] John 1:41; 4:42; 6:69; 11:27 **8:30** [a] Matt. 8:4; 16:20 **8:31** [a] Matt. 16:21; 20:19 [b] Mark 10:33 [c] Mark 9:31; 10:34 **8:33** [a] [Rev. 3:19] **8:34** [a] Luke 14:27 **8:35** [a] John 12:25 **8:38** [a] Matt. 10:33 [b] 2 Tim. 1:8, 9; 2:12 **9:1** [a] Luke 9:27 [b] [Matt. 24:30] **9:2** [a] Matt. 17:1–8 **9:3** [a] Dan. 7:9 **9:7** [a] Ex. 40:34 [b] Mark 1:11 [c] Acts 3:22

SPIRITUAL PROFIT

"For what will it profit a man if he gains the whole world, and loses his own soul? Or what will a man give in exchange for his soul?"

MARK 8:36-37

Right after Simon Peter confessed Jesus as the Messiah, Jesus told His disciples that He would suffer and die. And although He also said that He would be raised up, Peter strenuously objected (v. 32). Jesus rebuked Peter, then said to His disciples, "Whoever desires to come after Me, let him deny himself, and take up his cross, and follow Me" (v. 34). From Peter's point of view, this only raised more concerns.

Jesus responded to His disciples by putting the whole matter into the context of eternity: "For what will it profit a man if he gains the whole world, and loses his own soul? Or what will a man give in exchange for his soul?" (vv. 36–37). The reasoning makes sense. After all, the material things we strive for will not follow us into eternity. But we've all been guilty of prioritizing things that do not make for peace in our lives.

Today, the grace of God is available for you so you can reprioritize your day with a focus on eternity and gaining God's transforming peace. What is one thing you can do to add more peace in your life today? Make the adjustment.

they saw no one anymore, but only Jesus
with themselves.
9[a]Now as they came down from the mountain, He commanded them that they should
tell no one the things they had seen, till the
Son of Man had risen from the dead. 10So they
kept this word to themselves, questioning
[a]what the rising from the dead meant.
11And they asked Him, saying, "Why do
the scribes say [a]that Elijah must come first?"
12Then He answered and told them, "Indeed, Elijah is coming first and restores all
things. And [a]how is it written concerning
the Son of Man, that He must suffer many
things and [b]be treated with contempt? 13But
I say to you that [a]Elijah has also come, and
they did to him whatever they wished, as it
is written of him."

A Boy Is Healed

14[a]And when He came to the disciples,
He saw a great multitude around them, and
scribes disputing with them. 15Immediate-
ly, when they saw Him, all the people were
greatly amazed, and running to *Him,* greeted
Him. 16And He asked the scribes, "What are
you discussing with them?"
17Then [a]one of the crowd answered and
said, "Teacher, I brought You my son, who
has a mute spirit. 18And wherever it seizes
him, it throws him down; he foams at the
mouth, gnashes his teeth, and becomes rigid.
So I spoke to Your disciples, that they should
cast it out, but they could not."
19He answered him and said, "O [a]faithless
generation, how long shall I be with you?
How long shall I bear with you? Bring him to
Me." 20Then they brought him to Him. And
[a]when he saw Him, immediately the spirit
convulsed him, and he fell on the ground
and wallowed, foaming at the mouth.
21So He asked his father, "How long has
this been happening to him?"
And he said, "From childhood. 22And often
he has thrown him both into the fire and
into the water to destroy him. But if You
can do anything, have compassion on us
and help us."
23Jesus said to him, [a]"If you can believe,[1]
all things *are* possible to him who believes."
24Immediately the father of the child cried
out and said with tears, "Lord, I believe; [a]help
my unbelief!"
25When Jesus saw that the people came
running together, He [a]rebuked the unclean
spirit, saying to it, "Deaf and dumb spirit, I
command you, come out of him and enter
him no more!" 26Then *the spirit* cried out,
convulsed him greatly, and came out of him.
And he became as one dead, so that many
said, "He is dead." 27But Jesus took him by
the hand and lifted him up, and he arose.

9:9 [a] Matt. 17:9–13 **9:10** [a] John 2:19–22 **9:11** [a] Mal. 4:5 **9:12** [a] Is. 53:3 [b] Phil. 2:7 **9:13** [a] Luke 1:17 **9:14** [a] Matt. 17:14–19 **9:17** [a] Luke 9:38 **9:19** [a] John 4:48 **9:20** [a] Mark 1:26 **9:23** [a] John 11:40 [1] NU-Text reads "*'If You can!' All things . . . .*" **9:24** [a] Luke 17:5 **9:25** [a] Mark 1:25

28 [a]And when He had come into the house, His disciples asked Him privately, "Why could we not cast it out?"

29 So He said to them, "This kind can come out by nothing but [a]prayer and fasting."[1]

Jesus Again Predicts His Death and Resurrection

30 Then they departed from there and passed through Galilee, and He did not want anyone to know *it.* 31 [a]For He taught His disciples and said to them, "The Son of Man is being betrayed into the hands of men, and they will [b]kill Him. And after He is killed, He will [c]rise the third day." 32 But they [a]did not understand this saying, and were afraid to ask Him.

Who Is the Greatest?

33 [a]Then He came to Capernaum. And when He was in the house He asked them, "What was it you disputed among yourselves on the road?" 34 But they kept silent, for on the road they had [a]disputed among themselves who *would be the* [b]greatest. 35 And He sat down, called the twelve, and said to them, [a]"If anyone desires to be first, he shall be last of all and servant of all." 36 Then [a]He took a little child and set him in the midst of them. And when He had taken him in His arms, He said to them, 37 "Whoever receives one of these little children in My name receives Me; and [a]whoever receives Me, receives not Me but Him who sent Me."

Jesus Forbids Sectarianism

38 [a]Now John answered Him, saying, "Teacher, we saw someone who does not follow us casting out demons in Your name, and we forbade him because he does not follow us."

39 But Jesus said, "Do not forbid him, [a]for no one who works a miracle in My name can soon afterward speak evil of Me. 40 For [a]he who is not against us is on our[1] side. 41 [a]For whoever gives you a cup of water to drink in My name, because you belong to Christ, assuredly, I say to you, he will by no means lose his reward.

Jesus Warns of Offenses

42 [a]"But whoever causes one of these little ones who believe in Me to stumble, it would be better for him if a millstone were hung around his neck, and he were thrown into the sea. 43 [a]If your hand causes you to sin, cut it off. It is better for you to enter into life maimed, rather than having two hands, to go to hell, into the fire that shall never be quenched— 44 where

> [a]'Their worm does not die,
> And the fire is not quenched.'[1]

45 And if your foot causes you to sin, cut it off. It is better for you to enter life lame, rather than having two feet, to be cast into hell, into the fire that shall never be quenched— 46 where

> [a]'Their worm does not die,
> And the fire is not quenched.'[1]

47 And if your eye causes you to sin, pluck it out. It is better for you to enter the kingdom of God with one eye, rather than having two eyes, to be cast into hell fire— 48 where

> [a]'Their worm does not die,
> And the [b]fire is not quenched.'[1]

Tasteless Salt Is Worthless

49 "For everyone will be [a]seasoned with fire,[1] [b]and every sacrifice will be seasoned with salt. 50 [a]Salt *is* good, but if the salt loses its flavor, how will you season it? [b]Have salt in yourselves, and [c]have peace with one another."

Marriage and Divorce

10 Then [a]He arose from there and came to the region of Judea by the other side of the Jordan. And multitudes gathered to Him again, and as He was accustomed, He taught them again.

2 [a]The Pharisees came and asked Him, "Is it lawful for a man to divorce *his* wife?" testing Him.

3 And He answered and said to them, "What did Moses command you?"

4 They said, [a]"Moses permitted *a man* to write a certificate of divorce, and to dismiss *her.*"

5 And Jesus answered and said to them, "Because of the hardness of your heart he wrote you this precept. 6 But from the

9:28 [a] Matt. 17:19 **9:29** [a] [James 5:16] [1] NU-Text omits *and fasting.* **9:31** [a] Luke 9:44 [b] Matt. 16:21; 27:50 [c] 1 Cor. 15:4 **9:32** [a] Luke 2:50; 18:34 **9:33** [a] Matt. 18:1–5 **9:34** [a] [Prov. 13:10] [b] Luke 22:24; 23:46; 24:46 **9:35** [a] Luke 22:26, 27 **9:36** [a] Mark 10:13–16 **9:37** [a] Matt. 10:40 **9:38** [a] Num. 11:27–29 **9:39** [a] 1 Cor. 12:3 **9:40** [a] [Matt. 12:30] [1] M-Text reads *against you is on your side.* **9:41** [a] Matt. 10:42 **9:42** [a] Luke 17:1, 2 **9:43** [a] Matt. 5:29, 30; 18:8, 9 **9:44** [a] Is. 66:24 [1] NU-Text omits this verse. **9:46** [a] Is. 66:24 [1] NU-Text omits the last clause of verse 45 and all of verse 46. **9:48** [a] Is. 66:24 [b] Jer. 7:20 [1] Isaiah 66:24 **9:49** [a] [Matt. 3:11] [b] Lev. 2:13 [1] NU-Text omits the rest of this verse. **9:50** [a] Matt. 5:13 [b] Col. 4:6 [c] Rom. 12:18; 14:19 **10:1** [a] Matt. 19:1–9 **10:2** [a] Matt. 19:3 **10:4** [a] Deut. 24:1–4

SALTY PEACE

"Have salt in yourselves, and have peace with one another."

MARK 9:50

In the context of His strange instruction to have "salt in[themselves]," Jesus warned His listeners of sins that cause division and harm. "If your hand causes you to sin, cut it off" (v. 43). Interpreters recognize that Jesus was speaking metaphorically (people should not literally maim themselves), but He was speaking seriously. A fractured, divided church will fail in its mission. Believers must think of themselves as sacrifices offered to God (see Paul's similar comment in Rom. 12:1–2). Recall that Jesus commanded His followers to be the "salt of the earth" (Matt. 5:13). So here in Mark, Jesus urged His followers to be well salted—meaning to promote unity and to "have peace with one another" (Mark 9:50).

"Salty" believers will be able to form a community of peace-filled fellowship. How are you already well salted? Where do you need more seasoning? As Christians we should mark those who cause divisions in the church and avoid them. Sometimes our peace is stolen because we are in proximity with people who are not committed to God's peace. It can be difficult at first, but focus on friends who seek peace if you want it yourself.

beginning of the creation, God [a]'made them
male and female.'[1] 7[a]'For this reason a man
shall leave his father and mother and be
joined to his wife, 8and the two shall become
one flesh';[1] so then they are no longer two,
but one flesh. 9Therefore what God has joined
together, let not man separate."
10In the house His disciples also asked Him
again about the same *matter.* 11So He said
to them, [a]"Whoever divorces his wife and
marries another commits adultery against
her. 12And if a woman divorces her husband
and marries another, she commits adultery."

Jesus Blesses Little Children

13[a]Then they brought little children to Him,
that He might touch them; but the disciples
rebuked those who brought *them.* 14But when
Jesus saw *it,* He was greatly displeased and
said to them, "Let the little children come to
Me, and do not forbid them; for [a]of such is
the kingdom of God. 15Assuredly, I say to you,
[a]whoever does not receive the kingdom of
God as a little child will [b]by no means enter
it." 16And He took them up in His arms, laid
His hands on them, and blessed them.

Jesus Counsels the Rich Young Ruler

17[a]Now as He was going out on the road,
one came running, knelt before Him, and
asked Him, "Good Teacher, what shall I [b]do
that I may inherit eternal life?"
18So Jesus said to him, "Why do you call Me
good? No one *is* good but One, *that is,* [a]God.
19You know the commandments: [a]'Do not
commit adultery,' 'Do not murder,' 'Do not
steal,' 'Do not bear false witness,' 'Do not defraud,' 'Honor your father and your mother.' "[1]
20And he answered and said to Him,
"Teacher, all these things I have [a]kept from
my youth."
21Then Jesus, looking at him, loved him,
and said to him, "One thing you lack: Go your
way, [a]sell whatever you have and give to the
poor, and you will have [b]treasure in heaven;
and come, [c]take up the cross, and follow Me."
22But he was sad at this word, and went
away sorrowful, for he had great possessions.

With God All Things Are Possible

23[a]Then Jesus looked around and said to
His disciples, "How hard it is for those who
have riches to enter the kingdom of God!"
24And the disciples were astonished at His
words. But Jesus answered again and said
to them, "Children, how hard it is for those
[a]who trust in riches[1] to enter the kingdom of
God! 25It is easier for a camel to go through
the eye of a needle than for a [a]rich man to
enter the kingdom of God."

10:6 [a] Gen. 1:27; 5:2 [1] Genesis 1:27; 5:2 **10:7** [a] Gen. 2:24 **10:8** [1] Genesis 2:24 **10:11** [a] [Matt. 5:32; 19:9] **10:13** [a] Luke 18:15–17 **10:14** [a] [1 Pet. 2:2] **10:15** [a] Matt. 18:3, 4; 19:14 [b] Luke 13:28 **10:17** [a] Matt. 19:16–30 [b] John 6:28 **10:18** [a] 1 Sam. 2:2 **10:19** [a] Ex. 20:12–16; Deut. 5:16–20 [1] Exodus 20:12–16; Deuteronomy 5:16–20 **10:20** [a] Phil. 3:6 **10:21** [a] [Luke 12:33; 16:9] [b] Matt. 6:19, 20; 19:21 [c] [Mark 8:34] **10:23** [a] Matt. 19:23 **10:24** [a] [1 Tim. 6:17] [1] NU-Text omits *for those who trust in riches.* **10:25** [a] [Matt. 13:22; 19:24]

26 And they were greatly astonished, saying among themselves, "Who then can be saved?"

27 But Jesus looked at them and said, "With men *it is* impossible, but not [a]with God; for with God all things are possible."

28 [a]Then Peter began to say to Him, "See, we have left all and followed You."

29 So Jesus answered and said, "Assuredly, I say to you, there is no one who has left house or brothers or sisters or father or mother or wife[1] or children or lands, for My sake and the gospel's, 30 [a]who shall not receive a hundredfold now in this time—houses and brothers and sisters and mothers and children and lands, with [b]persecutions—and in the age to come, eternal life. 31 [a]But many *who are* first will be last, and the last first."

Jesus a Third Time Predicts His Death and Resurrection

32 [a]Now they were on the road, going up to Jerusalem, and Jesus was going before them; and they were amazed. And as they followed they were afraid. [b]Then He took the twelve aside again and began to tell them the things that would happen to Him: 33 "Behold, we are going up to Jerusalem, and the Son of Man will be betrayed to the chief priests and to the scribes; and they will condemn Him to death and deliver Him to the Gentiles; 34 and they will mock Him, and scourge Him, and spit on Him, and kill Him. And the third day He will rise again."

Greatness Is Serving

35 [a]Then James and John, the sons of Zebedee, came to Him, saying, "Teacher, we want You to do for us whatever we ask."

36 And He said to them, "What do you want Me to do for you?"

37 They said to Him, "Grant us that we may sit, one on Your right hand and the other on Your left, in Your glory."

38 But Jesus said to them, "You do not know what you ask. Are you able to drink the [a]cup that I drink, and be baptized with the [b]baptism that I am baptized with?"

39 They said to Him, "We are able."

So Jesus said to them, [a]"You will indeed drink the cup that I drink, and with the baptism I am baptized with you will be baptized; 40 but to sit on My right hand and on My left is not Mine to give, but *it is for those* [a]for whom it is prepared."

41 [a]And when the ten heard *it*, they began to be greatly displeased with James and John. 42 But Jesus called them to *Himself* and said to them, [a]"You know that those who are considered rulers over the Gentiles lord it over them, and their great ones exercise authority over them. 43 [a]Yet it shall not be so

10:27 [a] Jer. 32:17 **10:28** [a] Luke 18:28 **10:29** [1] NU-Text omits *or wife.* **10:30** [a] Luke 18:29, 30 [b] [1 Pet. 4:12, 13] **10:31** [a] Luke 13:30 **10:32** [a] Matt. 20:17–19 [b] Mark 8:31; 9:31 **10:35** [a] [James 4:3] **10:38** [a] John 18:11 [b] Luke 12:50 **10:39** [a] Acts 12:2 **10:40** [a] [Heb. 11:16] **10:41** [a] Matt. 20:24 **10:42** [a] Luke 22:25 **10:43** [a] Mark 9:35

PURCHASING YOUR PEACE

"For even the Son of Man did not come to be served, but to serve, and to give His life a ransom for many."

MARK 10:45

The rich and powerful seek wealth and power to be served, not to serve. But Jesus turned the world's assumptions on their head when He taught His disciples, "For even the Son of Man did not come to be served, but to serve, and to give His life a ransom for many." Jesus' philosophy would have struck most of His contemporaries—especially Greeks and Romans—as naïve, even silly. Who wants to serve? Yet Jesus, God's Son, said He had come "to serve, and to give His life" for humanity. No Greek king or Roman Caesar ever said anything like that.

Jesus' focus was on eternity, not the present age. He invited His disciples (and us) to join Him. Have you ever wondered why you felt so good when you helped someone? When you encouraged someone? You are made in the image of God, and when you serve others, you have peace.

What God-things might you undertake today in an effort to encourage someone and to sustain yourself with God's peace?

among you; but whoever desires to become
great among you shall be your servant. [44]And
whoever of you desires to be first shall be
slave of all. [45]For even [a]the Son of Man did
not come to be served, but to serve, and [b]to
give His life a ransom for many."

Jesus Heals Blind Bartimaeus

[46a]Now they came to Jericho. As He went
out of Jericho with His disciples and a great
multitude, blind Bartimaeus, the son of Ti-
maeus, sat by the road begging. [47]And when
he heard that it was Jesus of Nazareth, he began to cry out and say, "Jesus, [a]Son of David,
[b]have mercy on me!"

[48]Then many warned him to be quiet; but
he cried out all the more, "Son of David, have
mercy on me!"

[49]So Jesus stood still and commanded
him to be called.

Then they called the blind man, saying to
him, "Be of good cheer. Rise, He is calling
you."

[50]And throwing aside his garment, he rose
and came to Jesus.

[51]So Jesus answered and said to him, "What
do you want Me to do for you?"

The blind man said to Him, "Rabboni, that
I may receive my sight."

[52]Then Jesus said to him, "Go your way;
[a]your faith has made you well." And immediately he received his sight and followed
Jesus on the road.

The Triumphal Entry

11 Now [a]when they drew near Jerusalem, to
Bethphage[1] and Bethany, at the Mount
of Olives, He sent two of His disciples; [2]and
He said to them, "Go into the village opposite
you; and as soon as you have entered it you
will find a colt tied, on which no one has sat.
Loose it and bring *it*. [3]And if anyone says to
you, 'Why are you doing this?' say, 'The Lord
has need of it,' and immediately he will send
it here."

[4]So they went their way, and found the[1]
colt tied by the door outside on the street,
and they loosed it. [5]But some of those who
stood there said to them, "What are you doing, loosing the colt?"

[6]And they spoke to them just as Jesus had
commanded. So they let them go. [7]Then they
brought the colt to Jesus and threw their
clothes on it, and He sat on it. [8a]And many
spread their clothes on the road, and others
cut down leafy branches from the trees and
spread *them* on the road. [9]Then those who
went before and those who followed cried
out, saying:

"Hosanna!
[a]'Blessed *is* He who comes in the name
of the LORD!'[1]
10 Blessed *is* the kingdom of our father
David
That comes in the name of the Lord![1]
[a]Hosanna in the highest!"

10:45 [a] [Phil. 2:7, 8] [b] [Titus 2:14] **10:46** [a] Luke 18:35–43 **10:47** [a] Rev. 22:16 [b] Matt. 15:22 **10:52** [a] Matt. 9:22 **11:1** [a] Matt. 21:1–9 [1] M-Text reads *Bethsphage.* **11:4** [1] NU-Text and M-Text read *a.* **11:8** [a] Matt. 21:8 **11:9** [a] Ps. 118:25, 26 [1] Psalm 118:26 **11:10** [a] Ps. 148:1 [1] NU-Text omits *in the name of the Lord.*

THE ANXIOUS CRY FOR PEACE

Jesus, Son of David, have mercy on me!

MARK 10:47

Jesus told His disciples that He was on His way to Jerusalem, where He would be rejected, He would suffer, and He would die (see 8:31). He also taught His disciples that He came to serve, not to be served (10:45). Well, on His way to Jerusalem, Jesus served people such as blind Bartimaeus, who, because of his disability, was reduced to begging. When he heard that Jesus was passing by, he cried out, "Jesus, Son of David, have mercy on me!" (v. 47; see v. 48). The crowds told him to be quiet (apparently they had missed a lot of Jesus' earlier teaching!), but Jesus summoned him and healed him.

I love how Bartimaeus addressed Jesus: "Son of David"! In saying those words, the blind man expressed his faith that Jesus was the fulfillment of messianic prophecy. The irony here is that a blind man could see so clearly while many with perfect eyesight couldn't see at all. Bartimaeus's faith (and insight) was rewarded. His blindness was gone. Today, the Lord offers you the chance to be healed from anxiety so you can enjoy God's peace. Don't miss it.

11[a]And Jesus went into Jerusalem and into
the temple. So when He had looked around
at all things, as the hour was already late, He
went out to Bethany with the twelve.

The Fig Tree Withered

12[a]Now the next day, when they had come
out from Bethany, He was hungry. 13[a]And
seeing from afar a fig tree having leaves, He
went to see if perhaps He would find something on it. When He came to it, He found
nothing but leaves, for it was not the season
for figs. 14In response Jesus said to it, "Let no
one eat fruit from you ever again."
And His disciples heard *it*.

Jesus Cleanses the Temple

15[a]So they came to Jerusalem. Then Jesus
went into the temple and began to drive out
those who bought and sold in the temple,
and overturned the tables of the money
changers and the seats of those who sold
[b]doves. 16And He would not allow anyone
to carry wares through the temple. 17Then
He taught, saying to them, "Is it not written,
[a]'My house shall be called a house of prayer
for all nations'?[1] But you have made it a [b]'den
of thieves.' "[2]
18And [a]the scribes and chief priests heard
it and sought how they might destroy Him;
for they feared Him, because [b]all the people
were astonished at His teaching. 19When
evening had come, He went out of the city.

The Lesson of the Withered Fig Tree

20[a]Now in the morning, as they passed
by, they saw the fig tree dried up from the
roots. 21And Peter, remembering, said to Him,
"Rabbi, look! The fig tree which You cursed
has withered away."
22So Jesus answered and said to them,
"Have faith in God. 23For [a]assuredly, I say
to you, whoever says to this mountain, 'Be
removed and be cast into the sea,' and does
not doubt in his heart, but believes that
those things he says will be done, he will
have whatever he says. 24Therefore I say
to you, [a]whatever things you ask when you
pray, believe that you receive *them*, and you
will have *them*.

Forgiveness and Prayer

25"And whenever you stand praying, [a]if you
have anything against anyone, forgive him,
that your Father in heaven may also forgive
you your trespasses. 26But [a]if you do not
forgive, neither will your Father in heaven
forgive your trespasses."[1]

Jesus' Authority Questioned

27Then they came again to Jerusalem. [a]And
as He was walking in the temple, the chief
priests, the scribes, and the elders came to
Him. 28And they said to Him, "By what [a]au-
thority are You doing these things? And who
gave You this authority to do these things?"
29But Jesus answered and said to them, "I
also will ask you one question; then answer
Me, and I will tell you by what authority I do
these things: 30The [a]baptism of John—was
it from heaven or from men? Answer Me."
31And they reasoned among themselves,
saying, "If we say, 'From heaven,' He will say,
'Why then did you not believe him?' 32But if
we say, 'From men' "—they feared the people,
for [a]all counted John to have been a prophet
indeed. 33So they answered and said to Jesus,
"We do not know."
And Jesus answered and said to them,
"Neither will I tell you by what authority I
do these things."

The Parable of the Wicked Vinedressers

12 Then [a]He began to speak to them in
parables: "A man planted a vineyard
and set a hedge around *it*, dug *a place for* the
wine vat and built a tower. And he leased it
to vinedressers and went into a far country.
2Now at vintage-time he sent a servant to
the vinedressers, that he might receive some
of the fruit of the vineyard from the vinedressers. 3And they took *him* and beat him
and sent *him* away empty-handed. 4Again he

PEACE NOTE

Sometimes we let emotions cloud biblical truth, which opens a door to anxiety and closes the door to peace.

MARK 11:24

11:11 [a] Matt. 21:12 11:12 [a] Matt. 21:18–22 11:13 [a] Matt. 21:19 11:15 [a] John 2:13–16 [b] Lev. 14:22 11:17 [a] Is. 56:7 [b] Jer. 7:11 [1] Isaiah 56:7 [2] Jeremiah 7:11 11:18 [a] Matt. 21:45, 46 [b] Matt. 7:28 11:20 [a] Matt. 21:19–22 11:23 [a] Matt. 17:20; 21:21 11:24 [a] Matt. 7:7 11:25 [a] [Col. 3:13] 11:26 [a] Matt. 6:15; 18:35 [1] NU-Text omits this verse. 11:27 [a] Luke 20:1–8 11:28 [a] John 5:27 11:30 [a] Luke 7:29, 30 11:32 [a] Matt. 3:5; 14:5 12:1 [a] Luke 20:9–19

sent them another servant, and at him they
threw stones,[1] wounded *him* in the head, and
sent *him* away shamefully treated. 5And again
he sent another, and him they killed; and
many others, [a]beating some and killing some.
6Therefore still having one son, his beloved,
he also sent him to them last, saying, 'They
will respect my son.' 7But those vinedressers
said among themselves, 'This is the heir.
Come, let us kill him, and the inheritance
will be ours.' 8So they took him and [a]killed
him and cast *him* out of the vineyard.
9"Therefore what will the owner of the
vineyard do? He will come and destroy the
vinedressers, and give the vineyard to others. 10Have you not even read this Scripture:

[a]'The stone which the builders rejected
Has become the chief cornerstone.
11 This was the LORD's doing,
And it is marvelous in our eyes'?"[1]

12[a]And they sought to lay hands on Him, but
feared the multitude, for they knew He had
spoken the parable against them. So they left
Him and went away.

The Pharisees: Is It Lawful to Pay Taxes to Caesar?

13[a]Then they sent to Him some of the Pharisees and the Herodians, to catch Him in *His*
words. 14When they had come, they said to
Him, "Teacher, we know that You are true,
and care about no one; for You do not regard
the person of men, but teach the [a]way of God
in truth. Is it lawful to pay taxes to Caesar,
or not? 15Shall we pay, or shall we not pay?"
But He, knowing their [a]hypocrisy, said to
them, "Why do you test Me? Bring Me a denarius that I may see *it*." 16So they brought *it*.
And He said to them, "Whose image and
inscription *is* this?" They said to Him, "Caesar's."
17And Jesus answered and said to them,
"Render to Caesar the things that are Caesar's,
and to [a]God the things that are God's."
And they marveled at Him.

The Sadducees: What About the Resurrection?

18[a]Then *some* Sadducees, [b]who say there
is no resurrection, came to Him; and they
asked Him, saying: 19"Teacher, [a]Moses wrote
to us that if a man's brother dies, and leaves
his wife behind, and leaves no children, his
brother should take his wife and raise up
offspring for his brother. 20Now there were
seven brothers. The first took a wife; and
dying, he left no offspring. 21And the second
took her, and he died; nor did he leave any
offspring. And the third likewise. 22So the
seven had her and left no offspring. Last of
all the woman died also. 23Therefore, in the
resurrection, when they rise, whose wife will
she be? For all seven had her as wife."
24Jesus answered and said to them, "Are
you not therefore mistaken, because you do
not know the Scriptures nor the power of
God? 25For when they rise from the dead, they
neither marry nor are given in marriage, but
[a]are like angels in heaven. 26But concerning
the dead, that they [a]rise, have you not read
in the book of Moses, in the *burning* bush
passage, how God spoke to him, saying, [b]'I
am the God of Abraham, the God of Isaac,
and the God of Jacob'?[1] 27He is not the God
of the dead, but the God of the living. You
are therefore greatly mistaken."

The Scribes: Which Is the First Commandment of All?

28[a]Then one of the scribes came, and having heard them reasoning together, perceiv-
ing[1] that He had answered them well, asked
Him, "Which is the first commandment of
all?"
29Jesus answered him, "The first of all
the commandments *is:* [a]'Hear, O Israel, the
LORD our God, the LORD is one. 30And you
shall [a]love the LORD your God with all your
heart, with all your soul, with all your mind,
and with all your strength.'[1] This *is* the first
commandment.[2] 31And the second, like *it,*
is this: [a]'You shall love your neighbor as
yourself.'[1] There is no other commandment
greater than [b]these."
32So the scribe said to Him, "Well *said,*
Teacher. You have spoken the truth, for there
is one God, [a]and there is no other but He.
33And to love Him with all the heart, with all
the understanding, with all the soul,[1] and with
all the strength, and to love one's neighbor
as oneself, [a]is more than all the whole burnt
offerings and sacrifices."
34Now when Jesus saw that he answered
wisely, He said to him, "You are not far from
the kingdom of God."
[a]But after that no one dared question Him.

12:4 [1] NU-Text omits *and at him they threw stones.* **12:5** [a] 2 Chr. 36:16 **12:8** [a] [Acts 2:23] **12:10** [a] Ps. 118:22, 23 **12:11** [1] Psalm 118:22, 23 **12:12** [a] John 7:25, 30, 44 **12:13** [a] Luke 20:20–26 **12:14** [a] Acts 18:26 **12:15** [a] Luke 12:1 **12:17** [a] [Eccl. 5:4, 5] **12:18** [a] Luke 20:27–38 [b] Acts 23:8 **12:19** [a] Deut. 25:5 **12:25** [a] [1 Cor. 15:42, 49, 52] **12:26** [a] [Rev. 20:12, 13] [b] Ex. 3:6, 15 [1] Exodus 3:6, 15 **12:28** [a] Matt. 22:34–40 [1] NU-Text reads *seeing.* **12:29** [a] Deut. 6:4, 5 **12:30** [a] [Deut. 10:12; 30:6] [1] Deuteronomy 6:4, 5 [2] NU-Text omits this sentence. **12:31** [a] Lev. 19:18 [b] [Rom. 13:9] [1] Leviticus 19:18 **12:32** [a] Deut. 4:39 **12:33** [a] [Hos. 6:6] [1] NU-Text omits *with all the soul.* **12:34** [a] Matt. 22:46

Jesus: How Can David Call His Descendant "Lord"?

35[a]Then Jesus answered and said, while
He taught in the temple, "How *is it* that the
scribes say that the Christ is the Son of David?
36For David himself said [a]by the Holy Spirit:

> [b]'The LORD said to my Lord,
> "Sit at My right hand,
> Till I make Your enemies Your
> footstool." '[1]

37Therefore David himself calls Him 'Lord';
how is He *then* his [a]Son?"
And the common people heard Him gladly.

Beware of the Scribes

38Then [a]He said to them in His teaching,
[b]"Beware of the scribes, who desire to go
around in long robes, [c]*love* greetings in the
marketplaces, 39the [a]best seats in the synagogues, and the best places at feasts, 40[a]who
devour widows' houses, and for a pretense
make long prayers. These will receive greater
condemnation."

The Widow's Two Mites

41[a]Now Jesus sat opposite the treasury and
saw how the people put money [b]into the treasury. And many *who were* rich put in much.
42Then one poor widow came and threw in
two mites,[1] which make a quadrans. 43So He
called His disciples to *Himself* and said to
them, "Assuredly, I say to you that [a]this poor
widow has put in more than all those who have
given to the treasury; 44for they all put in out
of their abundance, but she out of her poverty
put in all that she had, [a]her whole livelihood."

Jesus Predicts the Destruction of the Temple

13 Then [a]as He went out of the temple, one
of His disciples said to Him, "Teacher,
see what manner of stones and what buildings *are here!*"
2And Jesus answered and said to him, "Do
you see these great buildings? [a]Not *one* stone
shall be left upon another, that shall not be
thrown down."

The Signs of the Times and the End of the Age

3Now as He sat on the Mount of Olives opposite the temple, [a]Peter, [b]James, [c]John, and
[d]Andrew asked Him privately, 4[a]"Tell us, when
will these things be? And what *will be* the sign
when all these things will be fulfilled?"
5And Jesus, answering them, began to say:
[a]"Take heed that no one deceives you. 6For
many will come in My name, saying, 'I am *He,*'

12:35 [a] Luke 20:41–44 12:36 [a] 2 Sam. 23:2 [b] Ps. 110:1 [1] Psalm 110:1 12:37 [a] [Acts 2:29–31] 12:38 [a] Mark 4:2 [b] Matt. 23:1–7 [c] Matt. 23:7 12:39 [a] Luke 14:7 12:40 [a] Matt. 23:14 12:41 [a] Luke 21:1–4 [b] 2 Kin. 12:9 12:42 [1] Greek *lepta,* very small copper coins worth a fraction of a penny 12:43 [a] [2 Cor. 8:12] 12:44 [a] Deut. 24:6 13:1 [a] Luke 21:5–36 13:2 [a] Luke 19:44 13:3 [a] Matt. 16:18 [b] Mark 1:19 [c] Mark 1:19 [d] John 1:40 13:4 [a] Matt. 24:3 13:5 [a] Eph. 5:6

FOCUS ON THE KING

"The LORD said to my Lord, 'Sit at My right hand, till I make Your enemies Your footstool.'"

MARK 12:36

While blind Bartimaeus addressed Jesus as "Son of David" (10:47), Israel's great King David addressed Jesus as "my Lord" (12:36). What? Where did David address Jesus? In Psalm 110:1, which Jesus quoted in Mark 12:36. Most interpreters believe that this psalm was prophetic and referred to the awaited Messiah. But they overlooked the significance of what David said—and Jesus pointed this out to the scholars and priests who questioned Him.

Jesus asked why the scribes called the Messiah the "Son of David" (v. 35). In that culture, to be "son of" somebody implied a rank lower than the father's. Jesus corrected this idea by pointing out that David, speaking "by the Holy Spirit" (v. 36), said "The LORD," that is, God the Father, "said to my Lord," that is, God spoke to David's Lord, implying that the Son was greater than David. This is huge.

The Messiah is God's Son and your Lord. He is somebody you can trust. God will deal with your detractors. You can lose the peace of God by trying to keep up with everyone who has hurt you. Let it go. Leave those people to the Lord. Make Jesus and His peace your focus today.

and will deceive many. 7 But when you hear of wars and rumors of wars, do not be troubled; for *such things* must happen, but the end *is* not yet. 8 For nation will rise against nation, and [a]kingdom against kingdom. And there will be earthquakes in various places, and there will be famines and troubles.[1] [b]These *are* the beginnings of sorrows.

9 "But [a]watch out for yourselves, for they will deliver you up to councils, and you will be beaten in the synagogues. You will be brought[1] before rulers and kings for My sake, for a testimony to them. 10 And [a]the gospel must first be preached to all the nations. 11 [a]But when they arrest *you* and deliver you up, do not worry beforehand, or premeditate[1] what you will speak. But whatever is given you in that hour, speak that; for it is not you who speak, [b]but the Holy Spirit. 12 Now [a]brother will betray brother to death, and a father *his* child; and children will rise up against parents and cause them to be put to death. 13 [a]And you will be hated by all for My name's sake. But [b]he who endures to the end shall be saved.

The Great Tribulation

14 [a]"So when you see the [b]'abomination of desolation,'[1] spoken of by Daniel the prophet,[2] standing where it ought not" (let the reader understand), "then [c]let those who are in Judea flee to the mountains. 15 Let him who is on the housetop not go down into the house, nor enter to take anything out of his house. 16 And let him who is in the field not go back to get his clothes. 17 [a]But woe to those who are pregnant and to those who are nursing babies in those days! 18 And pray that your flight may not be in winter. 19 [a]For *in* those days there will be tribulation, such as has not been since the beginning of the creation which God created until this time, nor ever shall be. 20 And unless the Lord had shortened those days, no flesh would be saved; but for the elect's sake, whom He chose, He shortened the days.

21 [a]"Then if anyone says to you, 'Look, here *is* the Christ!' or, 'Look, *He is* there!' do not believe it. 22 For false christs and false prophets will rise and show signs and [a]wonders to deceive, if possible, even the elect. 23 But [a]take heed; see, I have told you all things beforehand.

The Coming of the Son of Man

24 [a]"But in those days, after that tribulation, the sun will be darkened, and the moon will not give its light; 25 the stars of heaven will fall, and the powers in the heavens will be [a]shaken. 26 [a]Then they will see the Son of Man coming in the clouds with great power and glory. 27 And then He will send His angels, and gather together His elect from the four winds, from the farthest part of earth to the farthest part of heaven.

The Parable of the Fig Tree

28 [a]"Now learn this parable from the fig tree: When its branch has already become tender, and puts forth leaves, you know that summer is near. 29 So you also, when you see these things happening, know that it[1] is near—at the doors! 30 Assuredly, I say to you, this generation will by no means pass away till all these things take place. 31 Heaven and earth will pass away, but [a]My words will by no means pass away.

No One Knows the Day or Hour

32 "But of that day and hour [a]no one knows, not even the angels in heaven, nor the Son, but only the [b]Father. 33 [a]Take heed, watch and pray; for you do not know when the time is. 34 [a]*It is* like a man going to a far country, who left his house and gave [b]authority to his servants, and to each his work, and commanded the doorkeeper to watch. 35 [a]Watch therefore, for you do not know when the master of the house is coming—in the evening, at midnight, at the crowing of the rooster, or in the morning— 36 lest, coming suddenly, he find you sleeping. 37 And what I say to you, I say to all: Watch!"

The Plot to Kill Jesus

14 After [a]two days it was the Passover and [b]*the Feast* of Unleavened Bread. And the chief priests and the scribes sought how they might take Him by trickery and put *Him* to death. 2 But they said, "Not during the feast, lest there be an uproar of the people."

The Anointing at Bethany

3 [a]And being in Bethany at the house of Simon the leper, as He sat at the table, a woman came having an alabaster flask of very costly oil of spikenard. Then she broke

13:8 [a] Hag. 2:22 [b] Matt. 24:8 [1] NU-Text omits *and troubles.* **13:9** [a] Matt. 10:17, 18; 24:9 [1] NU-Text and M-Text read *will stand.* **13:10** [a] Matt. 24:14 **13:11** [a] Luke 12:11; 21:12–17 [b] Acts 2:4; 4:8, 31 [1] NU-Text omits *or premeditate.* **13:12** [a] Mic. 7:6 **13:13** [a] Luke 21:17 [b] Matt. 10:22; 24:13 **13:14** [a] Matt. 24:15 [b] Dan. 9:27; 11:31; 12:11 [c] Luke 21:21 [1] Daniel 11:31; 12:11 [2] NU-Text omits *spoken of by Daniel the prophet.* **13:17** [a] Luke 21:23 **13:19** [a] Dan. 9:26; 12:1 **13:21** [a] Luke 17:23; 21:8 **13:22** [a] Rev. 13:13, 14 **13:23** [a] [2 Pet. 3:17] **13:24** [a] Zeph. 1:15 **13:25** [a] Is. 13:10; 34:4 **13:26** [a] [Dan. 7:13, 14] **13:28** [a] Luke 21:29 **13:29** [1] Or *He* **13:31** [a] Is. 40:8 **13:32** [a] Matt. 25:13 [b] Acts 1:7 **13:33** [a] 1 Thess. 5:6 **13:34** [a] Matt. 24:45; 25:14 [b] [Matt. 16:19] **13:35** [a] Matt. 24:42, 44 **14:1** [a] Luke 22:1, 2 [b] Ex. 12:1–27 **14:3** [a] Luke 7:37

the flask and poured *it* on His head. 4But
there were some who were indignant among
themselves, and said, "Why was this fragrant
oil wasted? 5For it might have been sold for
more than three hundred [a]denarii and given
to the poor." And they [b]criticized her sharply.
6But Jesus said, "Let her alone. Why do you
trouble her? She has done a good work for Me.
7[a]For you have the poor with you always, and
whenever you wish you may do them good;
[b]but Me you do not have always. 8She has
done what she could. She has come beforehand to anoint My body for burial. 9Assuredly,
I say to you, wherever this gospel is [a]preached
in the whole world, what this woman has
done will also be told as a memorial to her."

Judas Agrees to Betray Jesus

10[a]Then Judas Iscariot, one of the twelve,
went to the chief priests to betray Him to them.
11And when they heard *it,* they were glad, and
promised to give him money. So he sought
how he might conveniently betray Him.

Jesus Celebrates the Passover with His Disciples

12[a]Now on the first day of Unleavened
Bread, when they killed the Passover *lamb,*
His disciples said to Him, "Where do You
want us to go and prepare, that You may eat
the Passover?"
13And He sent out two of His disciples and
said to them, "Go into the city, and a man will
meet you carrying a pitcher of water; follow
him. 14Wherever he goes in, say to the master
of the house, 'The Teacher says, "Where is the
guest room in which I may eat the Passover
with My disciples?"' 15Then he will show you
a large upper room, furnished *and* prepared;
there make ready for us."
16So His disciples went out, and came into
the city, and found it just as He had said to
them; and they prepared the Passover.
17[a]In the evening He came with the twelve.
18Now as they sat and ate, Jesus said, "Assuredly, I say to you, [a]one of you who eats
with Me will betray Me."
19And they began to be sorrowful, and to
say to Him one by one, "*Is* it I?" And another
said, "*Is* it I?"[1]
20He answered and said to them, "*It is*
one of the twelve, who dips with Me in the
dish. 21[a]The Son of Man indeed goes just as
it is written of Him, but woe to that man by
whom the Son of Man is betrayed! It would
have been good for that man if he had never
been born."

Jesus Institutes the Lord's Supper

22[a]And as they were eating, Jesus took
bread, blessed and broke *it,* and gave *it* to
them and said, "Take, eat;[1] this is My [b]body."

14:5 [a] Matt. 18:28 [b] John 6:61 **14:7** [a] Deut. 15:11 [b] [John 7:33; 8:21; 14:2, 12; 16:10, 17, 28] **14:9** [a] Luke 24:47 **14:10** [a] Matt. 10:2–4 **14:12** [a] Matt. 26:17–19 **14:17** [a] Matt. 26:20–24 **14:18** [a] John 6:70, 71; 13:18 **14:19** [1] NU-Text omits this sentence. **14:21** [a] Luke 22:22 **14:22** [a] 1 Cor. 11:23–25 [b] [1 Pet. 2:24] [1] NU-Text omits *eat.*

ACTIVATE YOUR FAITH

"Wherever this gospel is preached in the whole world, what this woman has done will also be told as a memorial to her."

MARK 14:9

In Jesus' last evening and meal with His disciples, a woman poured expensive oil (sometimes called ointment) on His head. The disciples were annoyed. Jesus rebuked His disciples, telling them, "She has done a good work for Me" (v. 6).

I am deeply moved by the unnamed woman's act of devotion. Her act should be understood as an anointing. She recognized Jesus as Israel's Messiah. But the disciples, worried about the trials that lay ahead, could think of it only as a waste. What a shame. They failed to see that this woman had stepped into history, seizing a moment that would never be repeated. Jesus saw it, saying, "Wherever this gospel is preached in the whole world, what this woman has done will also be told as a memorial to her" (v. 9). His prophecy has been fulfilled countless times since.

Our faith is not a passive one. We must also seize unexpected opportunities to serve and honor Jesus. If you desire God's peace, why don't you look for surprise moments when you might offer Jesus your service or worship?

23Then He took the cup, and when He had given thanks He gave *it* to them, and they all drank from it. 24And He said to them, "This is My blood of the new[1] covenant, which is shed for many. 25Assuredly, I say to you, I will no longer drink of the fruit of the vine until that day when I drink it new in the kingdom of God."

26[a]And when they had sung a hymn, they went out to the Mount of Olives.

Jesus Predicts Peter's Denial

27[a]Then Jesus said to them, "All of you will be made to stumble because of Me this night,[1] for it is written:

> [b]'I will strike the Shepherd,
> And the sheep will be scattered.'[2]

28"But [a]after I have been raised, I will go before you to Galilee."

29[a]Peter said to Him, "Even if all are made to stumble, yet I *will* not *be*."

30Jesus said to him, "Assuredly, I say to you that today, *even* this night, before the rooster crows twice, you will deny Me three times."

31But he spoke more vehemently, "If I have to die with You, I will not deny You!"

And they all said likewise.

The Prayer in the Garden

32[a]Then they came to a place which was named Gethsemane; and He said to His disciples, "Sit here while I pray." 33And He [a]took Peter, James, and John with Him, and He began to be troubled and deeply distressed. 34Then He said to them, [a]"My soul is exceedingly sorrowful, *even* to death. Stay here and watch."

35He went a little farther, and fell on the ground, and prayed that if it were possible, the hour might pass from Him. 36And He said, [a]"Abba, Father, [b]all things *are* possible for You. Take this cup away from Me; [c]nevertheless, not what I will, but what You *will*."

37Then He came and found them sleeping, and said to Peter, "Simon, are you sleeping? Could you not watch one hour? 38[a]Watch and pray, lest you enter into temptation. [b]The spirit indeed *is* willing, but the flesh *is* weak."

39Again He went away and prayed, and spoke the same words. 40And when He returned, He found them asleep again, for their eyes were heavy; and they did not know what to answer Him.

41Then He came the third time and said to them, "Are you still sleeping and resting? It is enough! [a]The hour has come; behold, the Son of Man is being betrayed into the hands of sinners. 42[a]Rise, let us be going. See, My betrayer is at hand."

Betrayal and Arrest in Gethsemane

43[a]And immediately, while He was still speaking, Judas, one of the twelve, with a great multitude with swords and clubs, came from the chief priests and the scribes and the elders. 44Now His betrayer had given them a signal, saying, "Whomever I [a]kiss, He is the One; seize Him and lead *Him* away safely."

45As soon as he had come, immediately he went up to Him and said to Him, "Rabbi, Rabbi!" and kissed Him.

46Then they laid their hands on Him and took Him. 47And one of those who stood by drew his sword and struck the servant of the high priest, and cut off his ear.

48[a]Then Jesus answered and said to them, "Have you come out, as against a robber, with swords and clubs to take Me? 49I was daily with you in the temple [a]teaching, and you did not seize Me. But [b]the Scriptures must be fulfilled."

50[a]Then they all forsook Him and fled.

A Young Man Flees Naked

51Now a certain young man followed Him, having a linen cloth thrown around *his* naked *body*. And the young men laid hold of him, 52and he left the linen cloth and fled from them naked.

Jesus Faces the Sanhedrin

53[a]And they led Jesus away to the high priest; and with him were [b]assembled all the [c]chief priests, the elders, and the scribes. 54But [a]Peter followed Him at a distance, right into the courtyard of the high priest. And he sat with the servants and warmed himself at the fire.

55[a]Now the chief priests and all the council sought testimony against Jesus to put Him to death, but found none. 56For many bore [a]false witness against Him, but their testimonies did not agree.

57Then some rose up and bore false witness against Him, saying, 58"We heard Him say, [a]'I will destroy this temple made with hands, and within three days I will build

14:24 [1] NU-Text omits *new*. **14:26** [a] Matt. 26:30 **14:27** [a] Matt. 26:31–35 [b] Zech. 13:7 [1] NU-Text omits *because of Me this night*. [2] Zechariah 13:7 **14:28** [a] Mark 16:7 **14:29** [a] John 13:37, 38 **14:32** [a] Luke 22:40–46 **14:33** [a] Mark 5:37; 9:2; 13:3 **14:34** [a] John 12:27 **14:36** [a] Gal. 4:6 [b] [Heb. 5:7] [c] John 5:30; 6:38 **14:38** [a] Luke 21:36 [b] [Rom. 7:18, 21–24] **14:41** [a] John 13:1; 17:1 **14:42** [a] John 13:21; 18:1, 2 **14:43** [a] Luke 22:47–53 **14:44** [a] [Prov. 27:6] **14:48** [a] Matt. 26:55 **14:49** [a] Matt. 21:23 [b] Is. 53:7 **14:50** [a] Ps. 88:8 **14:53** [a] Matt. 26:57–68 [b] Mark 15:1 [c] John 7:32; 18:3; 19:6 **14:54** [a] John 18:15 **14:55** [a] Matt. 26:59 **14:56** [a] Ex. 20:16 **14:58** [a] John 2:19

another made without hands.' " 59But not
even then did their testimony agree.
60[a]And the high priest stood up in the
midst and asked Jesus, saying, "Do You answer nothing? What *is it* these men testify
against You?" 61But [a]He kept silent and answered nothing.
[b]Again the high priest asked Him, saying
to Him, "Are You the Christ, the Son of the
Blessed?"
62Jesus said, "I am. [a]And you will see
the Son of Man sitting at the right hand of
the Power, and coming with the clouds of
heaven."
63Then the high priest tore his clothes
and said, "What further need do we have of
witnesses? 64You have heard the [a]blasphemy!
What do you think?"
And they all condemned Him to be deserving of [b]death.
65Then some began to [a]spit on Him, and
to blindfold Him, and to beat Him, and to say
to Him, "Prophesy!" And the officers struck
Him with the palms of their hands.[1]

Peter Denies Jesus, and Weeps

66[a]Now as Peter was below in the courtyard, one of the servant girls of the high
priest came. 67And when she saw Peter warm-
ing himself, she looked at him and said, "You
also were with [a]Jesus of Nazareth."
68But he denied it, saying, "I neither know
nor understand what you are saying." And he
went out on the porch, and a rooster crowed.
69[a]And the servant girl saw him again, and
began to say to those who stood by, "This is
one of them." 70But he denied it again.
[a]And a little later those who stood by said
to Peter again, "Surely you are *one* of them;
[b]for you are a Galilean, and your speech
shows *it*."[1]
71Then he began to curse and swear, "I
do not know this Man of whom you speak!"
72[a]A second time *the* rooster crowed. Then
Peter called to mind the word that Jesus had
said to him, "Before the rooster crows twice,
you will deny Me three times." And when he
thought about it, he wept.

Jesus Faces Pilate

15 Immediately, [a]in the morning, the chief
priests held a consultation with the
elders and scribes and the whole council;
and they bound Jesus, led *Him* away, and
[b]delivered *Him* to Pilate. 2[a]Then Pilate asked
Him, "Are You the King of the Jews?"
He answered and said to him, "*It is as* you
say."
3And the chief priests accused Him of
many things, but He [a]answered nothing.
4[a]Then Pilate asked Him again, saying, "Do
You answer nothing? See how many things
they testify against You!"[1] 5[a]But Jesus still
answered nothing, so that Pilate marveled.

Taking the Place of Barabbas

6Now [a]at the feast he was accustomed to
releasing one prisoner to them, whomever
they requested. 7And there was one named
Barabbas, *who was* chained with his fellow
rebels; they had committed murder in the
rebellion. 8Then the multitude, crying aloud,[1]
began to ask *him to do* just as he had always
done for them. 9But Pilate answered them,
saying, "Do you want me to release to you
the King of the Jews?" 10For he knew that the
chief priests had handed Him over because
of envy.
11But [a]the chief priests stirred up the crowd,
so that he should rather release Barabbas
to them. 12Pilate answered and said to them
again, "What then do you want me to do *with
Him* whom you call the [a]King of the Jews?"
13So they cried out again, "Crucify Him!"
14Then Pilate said to them, "Why, [a]what
evil has He done?"
But they cried out all the more, "Crucify
Him!"
15[a]So Pilate, wanting to gratify the crowd,
released Barabbas to them; and he delivered Jesus, after he had scourged *Him*, to
be [b]crucified.

The Soldiers Mock Jesus

16[a]Then the soldiers led Him away into
the hall called Praetorium, and they called
together the whole garrison. 17And they
clothed Him with purple; and they twisted
a crown of thorns, put it on His *head*, 18and
began to salute Him, "Hail, King of the Jews!"
19Then they [a]struck Him on the head with a
reed and spat on Him; and bowing the knee,
they worshiped Him. 20And when they had
[a]mocked Him, they took the purple off Him,
put His own clothes on Him, and led Him
out to crucify Him.

14:60 [a] Matt. 26:62 **14:61** [a] Is. 53:7 [b] Luke 22:67–71 **14:62** [a] Luke 22:69 **14:64** [a] John 10:33, 36 [b] John 19:7 **14:65** [a] Is. 50:6; 52:14 [1] NU-Text reads *received Him with slaps.* **14:66** [a] John 18:16–18, 25–27 **14:67** [a] John 1:45 **14:69** [a] Matt. 26:71 **14:70** [a] Luke 22:59 [b] Acts 2:7 [1] NU-Text omits *and your speech shows it.* **14:72** [a] Matt. 26:75 **15:1** [a] Ps. 2:2 [b] Acts 3:13 **15:2** [a] Matt. 27:11–14 **15:3** [a] John 19:9 **15:4** [a] Matt. 27:13 [1] NU-Text reads *of which they accuse You.* **15:5** [a] Is. 53:7 **15:6** [a] Matt. 27:15–26 **15:8** [1] NU-Text reads *going up.* **15:11** [a] Acts 3:14 **15:12** [a] Mic. 5:2 **15:14** [a] 1 Pet. 2:21–23 **15:15** [a] Matt. 27:26 [b] [Is. 53:8] **15:16** [a] Matt. 27:27–31 **15:19** [a] [Is. 50:6; 52:14; 53:5] **15:20** [a] Luke 22:63; 23:11

The King on a Cross

21[a]Then they compelled a certain man,
Simon a Cyrenian, the father of Alexander
and Rufus, as he was coming out of the country and passing by, to bear His cross. 22[a]And
they brought Him to the place Golgotha,
which is translated, Place of a Skull. 23[a]Then
they gave Him wine mingled with myrrh to
drink, but He did not take *it.* 24And when they
crucified Him, [a]they divided His garments,
casting lots for them *to determine* what every
man should take.
25Now [a]it was the third hour, and they crucified Him. 26And [a]the inscription of His
accusation was written above:

THE KING OF THE JEWS.

27[a]With Him they also crucified two robbers,
one on His right and the other on His left.
28So the Scripture was fulfilled[1] which says,
[a]"And He was numbered with the transgressors."[2]
29And [a]those who passed by blasphemed
Him, [b]wagging their heads and saying, "Aha!
[c]*You* who destroy the temple and build *it* in
three days, 30save Yourself, and come down
from the cross!"
31Likewise the chief priests also, [a]mocking
among themselves with the scribes, said, "He
saved [b]others; Himself He cannot save. 32Let
the Christ, the King of Israel, descend now
from the cross, that we may see and believe."[1]
Even [a]those who were crucified with Him
reviled Him.

Jesus Dies on the Cross

33Now [a]when the sixth hour had come,
there was darkness over the whole land until the ninth hour. 34And at the ninth hour
Jesus cried out with a loud voice, saying,
"Eloi, Eloi, lama sabachthani?" which is
translated, [a]"My God, My God, why have
You forsaken Me?"[1]
35Some of those who stood by, when they
heard *that,* said, "Look, He is calling for
Elijah!" 36Then [a]someone ran and filled a
sponge full of sour wine, put *it* on a reed,
and [b]offered *it* to Him to drink, saying, "Let
Him alone; let us see if Elijah will come to
take Him down."
37[a]And Jesus cried out with a loud voice,
and breathed His last.
38Then [a]the veil of the temple was torn
in two from top to bottom. 39So [a]when the
centurion, who stood opposite Him, saw that
He cried out like this and breathed His last,[1]
he said, "Truly this Man was the Son of God!"
40[a]There were also women looking
on [b]from afar, among whom were Mary

15:21 [a] Matt. 27:32 **15:22** [a] John 19:17–24 **15:23** [a] Matt. 27:34 **15:24** [a] Ps. 22:18 **15:25** [a] John 19:14 **15:26** [a] Matt. 27:37 **15:27** [a] Luke 22:37 **15:28** [a] Is. 53:12 [1] Isaiah 53:12 [2] NU-Text omits this verse. **15:29** [a] Ps. 22:6, 7; 69:7 [b] Ps. 109:25 [c] John 2:19–21 **15:31** [a] Luke 18:32 [b] John 11:43, 44 **15:32** [a] Matt. 27:44 [1] M-Text reads *believe Him.* **15:33** [a] Luke 23:44–49 **15:34** [a] Ps. 22:1 [1] Psalm 22:1 **15:36** [a] John 19:29 [b] Ps. 69:21 **15:37** [a] Matt. 27:50 **15:38** [a] Ex. 26:31–33 **15:39** [a] Luke 23:47 [1] NU-Text reads *that He thus breathed His last.* **15:40** [a] Matt. 27:55 [b] Ps. 38:11

THE CONFESSION WE MUST MAKE

Truly this Man was the Son of God!

MARK 15:39

Several times, Jesus foretold His suffering and death. Not surprisingly, the disciples had difficulty understanding these predictions (9:10, 32). Peter even tried to talk Jesus out of it (8:32–33). Jesus also foretold His resurrection, but that hardly reassured the disciples. What about the here and now?

Jesus' grim prophecy came to fulfillment, of course, on a Roman cross. As Jesus suffered, ruling priests mocked, "He saved others; Himself He cannot save" (15:31). But at the moment of His death, the veil of the temple tore, and the centurion overseeing the execution cried out, "Truly this Man was the Son of God!" (v. 39). Even in death, Jesus' glory shone.

The resurrection Sunday morning removed all doubt: Jesus truly was the Son of God. For me, this is a big peace-builder—that even when Jesus died, an unbeliever could see who He was. Recognizing who Jesus is may be the most powerful tool for walking in the peace of God. J. B. Phillips wrote a book famously titled, *Your God Is Too Small*! Perhaps your Jesus is too small. See Jesus in His proper place and find His rest.

Magdalene, Mary the mother of James the
Less and of Joses, and Salome, [41]who also
[a]followed Him and ministered to Him when
He was in Galilee, and many other women
who came up with Him to Jerusalem.

Jesus Buried in Joseph's Tomb

[42][a]Now when evening had come, because
it was the Preparation Day, that is, the day
before the Sabbath, [43]Joseph of Arimathea, a
prominent council member, who [a]was himself waiting for the kingdom of God, coming
and taking courage, went in to Pilate and
asked for the body of Jesus. [44]Pilate marveled
that He was already dead; and summoning
the centurion, he asked him if He had been
dead for some time. [45]So when he found out
from the centurion, he granted the body to
Joseph. [46][a]Then he bought fine linen, took
Him down, and wrapped Him in the linen.
And he laid Him in a tomb which had been
hewn out of the rock, and rolled a stone
against the door of the tomb. [47]And Mary
Magdalene and Mary *the mother* of Joses
observed where He was laid.

He Is Risen

16 Now [a]when the Sabbath was past, Mary
Magdalene, Mary *the mother* of James,
and Salome [b]bought spices, that they might
come and anoint Him. [2][a]Very early in the
morning, on the first *day* of the week, they
came to the tomb when the sun had risen.
[3]And they said among themselves, "Who
will roll away the stone from the door of
the tomb for us?" [4]But when they looked
up, they saw that the stone had been rolled
away—for it was very large. [5][a]And entering
the tomb, they saw a young man clothed in
a long white robe sitting on the right side;
and they were alarmed.

[6][a]But he said to them, "Do not be alarmed.
You seek Jesus of Nazareth, who was crucified. He is risen! He is not here. See the
place where they laid Him. [7]But go, tell His
disciples—and Peter—that He is going before
you into Galilee; there you will see Him, [a]as
He said to you."

[8]So they went out quickly[1] and fled from
the tomb, for they trembled and were
amazed. [a]And they said nothing to anyone,
for they were afraid.

Mary Magdalene Sees the Risen Lord

[9]Now when *He* rose early on the first *day*
of the week, He appeared first to Mary Magdalene, [a]out of whom He had cast seven demons. [10][a]She went and told those who had
been with Him, as they mourned and wept.
[11][a]And when they heard that He was alive and
had been seen by her, they did not believe.

Jesus Appears to Two Disciples

[12]After that, He appeared in another form
[a]to two of them as they walked and went into
the country. [13]And they went and told *it* to
the rest, *but* they did not believe them either.

The Great Commission

[14][a]Later He appeared to the eleven as they
sat at the table; and He rebuked their unbelief
and hardness of heart, because they did not
believe those who had seen Him after He
had risen. [15][a]And He said to them, "Go into
all the world [b]and preach the gospel to every
creature. [16][a]He who believes and is baptized
will be saved; [b]but he who does not believe
will be condemned. [17]And these [a]signs will
follow those who believe: [b]In My name they
will cast out demons; [c]they will speak with
new tongues; [18][a]they[1] will take up serpents;
and if they drink anything deadly, it will by
no means hurt them; [b]they will lay hands on
the sick, and they will recover."

Christ Ascends to God's Right Hand

[19]So then, [a]after the Lord had spoken to
them, He was [b]received up into heaven, and
[c]sat down at the right hand of God. [20]And they
went out and preached everywhere, the Lord
working with *them* [a]and confirming the word
through the accompanying signs. Amen.[1]

15:41 [a] Luke 8:2, 3 **15:42** [a] John 19:38–42 **15:43** [a] Luke 2:25, 38; 23:51 **15:46** [a] Matt. 27:59, 60 **16:1** [a] John 20:1–8 [b] Luke 23:56 **16:2** [a] Luke 24:1 **16:5** [a] John 20:11, 12 **16:6** [a] Matt. 28:6 **16:7** [a] Matt. 26:32; 28:16, 17 **16:8** [a] Matt. 28:8 [1] NU-Text and M-Text omit *quickly.* **16:9** [a] Luke 8:2 **16:10** [a] Luke 24:10 **16:11** [a] Luke 24:11, 41 **16:12** [a] Luke 24:13–35 **16:14** [a] 1 Cor. 15:5 **16:15** [a] Matt. 28:19 [b] [Col. 1:23] **16:16** [a] [John 3:18, 36] [b] [John 12:48] **16:17** [a] Acts 5:12 [b] Luke 10:17 [c] [Acts 2:4] **16:18** [a] Acts 28:3–6 [b] James 5:14 [1] NU-Text reads *and in their hands they will.* **16:19** [a] Acts 1:2, 3 [b] Luke 9:51; 24:51 [c] [Ps. 110:1] **16:20** [a] [Heb. 2:4] [1] Verses 9–20 are bracketed in NU-Text as not original. They are lacking in Codex Sinaiticus and Codex Vaticanus, although nearly all other manuscripts of Mark contain them.

THE GOSPEL ACCORDING TO

LUKE

AUTHOR

It is evident from the prologues to Luke and Acts (Luke 1:1–4; Acts 1:1–5) that both books were addressed to a man called Theophilus as a two-volume work. Acts begins with a summary of Luke and continues the story from where the Gospel of Luke concludes. Luke may have been a Hellenistic Jew, but it is more likely that he was a Gentile (this would make him the only Gentile contributor to the New Testament). It has been suggested that Luke may have been a Greek physician to a Roman family who at some point was set free and given Roman citizenship. Luke was not an eyewitness of the events in his Gospel, but he relied on the testimony of apostolic eyewitnesses and reliable written sources.

TIME

c. 4 BC–AD 33

KEY VERSE

Luke 19:10

THEME

The beginning of Luke mentions that there was a great deal of oral tradition concerning Jesus circulating during the first century. The rapid growth of the church (by over three thousand on the day of Pentecost alone) meant that there would have been potential for significant variety in stories about Jesus. Luke's stated agenda is reliability. Where Matthew goes to great lengths to tie Jesus' story to the history of the Jews, Luke is more interested in where the story fits in the history of the human race. Throughout the book, Christ reaches out to people from a variety of social strata, nationalities, and cultures. Luke sees Jesus as the Savior of the whole world.

Luke's Gospel uses the word "peace" in two-thirds of the twenty-four chapters, but the power of God's restorative peace appears on every page (for example, the Incarnation, the angels' announcement, and the parables of the good Samaritan and the prodigal son). The exchange between Jesus and the "woman . . . who was a sinner" in Luke 7 is one of the most moving scenes in all Scripture. Jesus blessed her with spiritual healing. The woman's sins were forgiven, she was saved, and she could then "go in peace" (7:50). The peace that Jesus gave her is the same that He gave the woman who had suffered from the hemorrhage (Mark 5), and it is the same that He offers to everyone who receives the Good News of the kingdom of God. In Luke we are reminded again and again that to receive the peace of Jesus is to be made whole, to lack nothing.

Dedication to Theophilus

1 Inasmuch as many have taken in hand to
set in order a narrative of those [a]things
which have been fulfilled[1] among us, 2just as
those who [a]from the beginning were [b]eye-
witnesses and ministers of the word [c]de-
livered them to us, 3it seemed good to me
also, having had perfect understanding of all
things from the very first, to write to you an
orderly account, [a]most excellent Theophilus,
4[a]that you may know the certainty of those
things in which you were instructed.

John's Birth Announced to Zacharias

5There was [a]in the days of Herod, the king
of Judea, a certain priest named Zacharias,
[b]of the division of [c]Abijah. His [d]wife *was* of
the daughters of Aaron, and her name *was*
Elizabeth. 6And they were both righteous before God, walking in all the commandments
and ordinances of the Lord blameless. 7But
they had no child, because Elizabeth was
barren, and they were both well advanced
in years.

8So it was, that while he was serving as
priest before God in the order of his division,
9according to the custom of the priesthood,
his lot fell [a]to burn incense when he went
into the temple of the Lord. 10[a]And the whole
multitude of the people was praying outside
at the hour of incense. 11Then an angel of
the Lord appeared to him, standing on the
right side of [a]the altar of incense. 12And when
Zacharias saw *him,* [a]he was troubled, and fear
fell upon him.

13But the angel said to him, "Do not be
afraid, Zacharias, for your prayer is heard;
and your wife Elizabeth will bear you a son,
and [a]you shall call his name John. 14And you
will have joy and gladness, and [a]many will
rejoice at his birth. 15For he will be [a]great in
the sight of the Lord, and [b]shall drink neither
wine nor strong drink. He will also be filled
with the Holy Spirit, [c]even from his mother's
womb. 16And he will turn many of the children of Israel to the Lord their God. 17[a]He will
also go before Him in the spirit and power
of Elijah, 'to turn the hearts of the fathers
to the children,'[1] and the disobedient to the
wisdom of the just, to make ready a people
prepared for the Lord."

18And Zacharias said to the angel, [a]"How
shall I know this? For I am an old man, and
my wife is well advanced in years."

19And the angel answered and said to him,
"I am [a]Gabriel, who stands in the presence of
God, and was sent to speak to you and bring
you these glad [b]tidings. 20But behold, [a]you
will be mute and not able to speak until the
day these things take place, because you did
not believe my words which will be fulfilled
in their own time."

21And the people waited for Zacharias,
and marveled that he lingered so long in the
temple. 22But when he came out, he could
not speak to them; and they perceived that
he had seen a vision in the temple, for he
beckoned to them and remained speechless.

23So it was, as soon as [a]the days of his service were completed, that he departed to his
own house. 24Now after those days his wife
Elizabeth conceived; and she hid herself five
months, saying, 25"Thus the Lord has dealt
with me, in the days when He looked on *me,*
to [a]take away my reproach among people."

Christ's Birth Announced to Mary

26Now in the sixth month the angel Gabriel
was sent by God to a city of Galilee named
Nazareth, 27to a virgin [a]betrothed to a man
whose name was Joseph, of the house of
David. The virgin's name *was* Mary. 28And
having come in, the angel said to her, [a]"Rejoice, highly favored *one,* [b]the Lord *is* with
you; blessed *are* you among women!"[1]

29But when she saw *him,*[1] [a]she was troubled at his saying, and considered what
manner of greeting this was. 30Then the
angel said to her, "Do not be afraid, Mary,
for you have found [a]favor with God. 31[a]And
behold, you will conceive in your womb and
bring forth a Son, and [b]shall call His name
JESUS. 32He will be great, [a]and will be called
the Son of the Highest; and [b]the Lord God
will give Him the [c]throne of His [d]father
David. 33[a]And He will reign over the house
of Jacob forever, and of His kingdom there
will be no end."

34Then Mary said to the angel, "How can
this be, since I do not know a man?"

35And the angel answered and said to her,
[a]"*The* Holy Spirit will come upon you, and
the power of the Highest will overshadow
you; therefore, also, that Holy One who is
to be born will be called [b]the Son of God.

1:1 [a] *John 20:31* [1] Or *are most surely believed* **1:2** [a] Acts 1:21, 22 [b] Acts 1:2 [c] Heb. 2:3 **1:3** [a] Acts 1:1 **1:4** [a] [John 20:31] **1:5** [a] Matt. 2:1 [b] 1 Chr. 24:1, 10 [c] Neh. 12:4 [d] Lev. 21:13, 14 **1:9** [a] Ex. 30:7, 8 **1:10** [a] Lev. 16:17 **1:11** [a] Ex. 30:1 **1:12** [a] Luke 2:9 **1:13** [a] Luke 1:57, 60, 63 **1:14** [a] Luke 1:58 **1:15** [a] [Luke 7:24–28] [b] Num. 6:3 [c] Jer. 1:5 **1:17** [a] Mal. 4:5, 6; Matt. 3:2; 11:14 [1] Malachi 4:5, 6 **1:18** [a] Gen. 17:17 **1:19** [a] Dan. 8:16 [b] Luke 2:10 **1:20** [a] Ezek. 3:26; 24:27 **1:23** [a] 2 Kin. 11:5 **1:25** [a] Gen. 30:23 **1:27** [a] Matt. 1:18 **1:28** [a] Dan. 9:23 [b] Judg. 6:12 [1] NU-Text omits *blessed are you among women.* **1:29** [a] Luke 1:12 [1] NU-Text omits *when she saw him.* **1:30** [a] Luke 2:52 **1:31** [a] Is. 7:14 [b] Luke 2:21 **1:32** [a] Mark 5:7 [b] 2 Sam. 7:12, 13, 16 [c] 2 Sam. 7:14–17 [d] Matt. 1:1 **1:33** [a] [Dan. 2:44] **1:35** [a] Matt. 1:20 [b] [Heb. 1:2, 8]

36 Now indeed, Elizabeth your relative has
also conceived a son in her old age; and
this is now the sixth month for her who was
called barren. 37 For [a]with God nothing will
be impossible."
38 Then Mary said, "Behold the maidservant of the Lord! Let it be to me according to your word." And the angel departed
from her.

Mary Visits Elizabeth

39 Now Mary arose in those days and went
into the hill country with haste, [a]to a city of
Judah, 40 and entered the house of Zacharias
and greeted Elizabeth. 41 And it happened,
when Elizabeth heard the greeting of Mary,
that the babe leaped in her womb; and Elizabeth was [a]filled with the Holy Spirit. 42 Then
she spoke out with a loud voice and said,
[a]"Blessed *are* you among women, and blessed
is the fruit of your womb! 43 But why *is* this
granted to me, that the mother of my Lord
should come to me? 44 For indeed, as soon
as the voice of your greeting sounded in my
ears, the babe leaped in my womb for joy.
45 [a]Blessed *is* she who believed, for there will
be a fulfillment of those things which were
told her from the Lord."

The Song of Mary

46 And Mary said:

[a]"My soul magnifies the Lord,
47 And my spirit has [a]rejoiced in [b]God my
Savior.
48 For [a]He has regarded the lowly state of
His maidservant;
For behold, henceforth [b]all generations
will call me blessed.
49 For He who is mighty [a]has done great
things for me,
And [b]holy *is* His name.
50 And [a]His mercy *is* on those who fear
Him
From generation to generation.
51 [a]He has shown strength with His arm;
[b]He has scattered *the* proud in the
imagination of their hearts.
52 [a]He has put down the mighty from *their*
thrones,
And exalted *the* lowly.
53 He has [a]filled *the* hungry with good
things,
And *the* rich He has sent away
empty.
54 He has helped His [a]servant Israel,
[b]In remembrance of *His* mercy,
55 [a]As He spoke to our [b]fathers,
To Abraham and to his [c]seed
forever."

56 And Mary remained with her about three
months, and returned to her house.

Birth of John the Baptist

57 Now Elizabeth's full time came for her
to be delivered, and she brought forth a son.
58 When her neighbors and relatives heard
how the Lord had shown great mercy to her,
they [a]rejoiced with her.

Circumcision of John the Baptist

59 So it was, [a]on the eighth day, that they
came to circumcise the child; and they would
have called him by the name of his father,
Zacharias. 60 His mother answered and said,
[a]"No; he shall be called John."
61 But they said to her, "There is no one
among your relatives who is called by this
name." 62 So they made signs to his father—
what he would have him called.
63 And he asked for a writing tablet, and
wrote, saying, "His name is John." So they
all marveled. 64 Immediately his mouth was
opened and his tongue *loosed,* and he spoke,
praising God. 65 Then fear came on all who
dwelt around them; and all these sayings
were discussed throughout all the hill country of Judea. 66 And all those who heard *them*
[a]kept *them* in their hearts, saying, "What kind
of child will this be?" And [b]the hand of the
Lord was with him.

Zacharias' Prophecy

67 Now his father Zacharias [a]was filled with
the Holy Spirit, and prophesied, saying:

68 "Blessed[a] *is* the Lord God of Israel,
For [b]He has visited and redeemed His
people,
69 [a]And has raised up a horn of salvation
for us
In the house of His servant David,
70 [a]As He spoke by the mouth of His holy
prophets,
Who *have been* [b]since the world began,
71 That we should be saved from our
enemies
And from the hand of all who
hate us,

1:37 [a] Jer. 32:17 **1:39** [a] Josh. 21:9 **1:41** [a] Acts 6:3 **1:42** [a] Judg. 5:24 **1:45** [a] John 20:29 **1:46** [a] 1 Sam. 2:1–10
1:47 [a] Hab. 3:18 [b] 1 Tim. 1:1; 2:3 **1:48** [a] Ps. 138:6 [b] Luke 11:27 **1:49** [a] Ps. 71:19; 126:2, 3 [b] Ps. 111:9 **1:50** [a] Ps. 103:17
1:51 [a] Ps. 98:1; 118:15 [b] [1 Pet. 5:5] **1:52** [a] 1 Sam. 2:7, 8 **1:53** [a] [Matt. 5:6] **1:54** [a] Is. 41:8 [b] [Jer. 31:3] **1:55** [a] Gen. 17:19
[b] [Rom. 11:28] [c] Gen. 17:7 **1:58** [a] [Rom. 12:15] **1:59** [a] Gen. 17:12 **1:60** [a] Luke 1:13, 63 **1:66** [a] Luke 2:19 [b] Acts 11:21
1:67 [a] Joel 2:28 **1:68** [a] 1 Kin. 1:48 [b] Ex. 3:16 **1:69** [a] Ps. 132:17 **1:70** [a] Rom. 1:2 [b] Acts 3:21

72 [a]To perform the mercy *promised* to
our fathers
And to remember His holy covenant,
73 [a]The oath which He swore to our
father Abraham:
74 To grant us that we,
Being delivered from the hand of our
enemies,
Might [a]serve Him without fear,
75 [a]In holiness and righteousness before
Him all the days of our life.

76 "And you, child, will be called the
[a]prophet of the Highest;
For [b]you will go before the face of the
Lord to prepare His ways,
77 To give [a]knowledge of salvation to
His people
By the remission of their sins,
78 Through the tender mercy of
our God,
With which the Dayspring from on
high has visited[1] us;
79 [a]To give light to those who sit in
darkness and the shadow of
death,
To [b]guide our feet into the way of
peace."

80 So [a]the child grew and became strong
in spirit, and [b]was in the deserts till the day
of his manifestation to Israel.

Christ Born of Mary

2 And it came to pass in those days *that* a
decree went out from Caesar Augustus
that all the world should be registered. 2 [a]This
census first took place while Quirinius was
governing Syria. 3 So all went to be registered,
everyone to his own city.
4 Joseph also went up from Galilee, out of
the city of Nazareth, into Judea, to [a]the city of
David, which is called Bethlehem, [b]because
he was of the house and lineage of David, 5 to
be registered with Mary, [a]his betrothed wife,[1]
who was with child. 6 So it was, that while they
were there, the days were completed for her
to be delivered. 7 And [a]she brought forth her
firstborn Son, and wrapped Him in swaddling
cloths, and laid Him in a manger, because
there was no room for them in the inn.

Glory in the Highest

8 Now there were in the same country
shepherds living out in the fields, keeping
watch over their flock by night. 9 And behold,[1]
an angel of the Lord stood before them, and

1:72 [a] Lev. 26:42 1:73 [a] Gen. 12:3; 22:16–18 1:74 [a] [Heb. 9:14] 1:75 [a] [Eph. 4:24] 1:76 [a] Matt. 3:3; 11:9 [b] Is. 40:3
1:77 [a] [Mark 1:4] 1:78 [1] NU-Text reads *shall visit.* 1:79 [a] Is. 9:2 [b] [John 10:4; 14:27; 16:33] 1:80 [a] Luke 2:40 [b] Matt. 3:1
2:2 [a] Acts 5:37 2:4 [a] 1 Sam. 16:1 [b] Matt. 1:16 2:5 [a] [Matt. 1:18] [1] NU-Text omits *wife.* 2:7 [a] Matt. 1:25
2:9 [1] NU-Text omits *behold.*

PRAY FOR LIGHT

You will go before the face of the Lord . . . to give light to those who sit in darkness and the shadow of death, to guide our feet into the way of peace.

LUKE 1:76, 79

Have you ever been lost in the dark and then, much to your relief, found the light? In the Bible, estrangement from God is sometimes likened to sitting in darkness. Indeed, there were times when the whole nation of Israel was lost in the shadows, wondering when the light would return.

Before the birth of Jesus, Israel was under the thumb of the Roman Empire and the empire's client king, Herod the Great. Many in Israel longed for the appearance of the Lord's Anointed, the Messiah! The years went by. Then suddenly the aged priest Zacharias received a prophecy announcing news he and his wife had been waiting to hear for years. But he couldn't believe it! That's the way we all are sometimes. We pray and ask God for something, but when it comes, we can't take it in. Due to Zacharias's unbelief, an angel declared that he wouldn't be able to speak until his son was born. At the birth, he then thanked God for giving light and leading His people into "the way of peace" (v. 79).

With the help of God, we, too, emerge from darkness into the light and find ourselves on the way of peace. What is the way of peace like for you?

the glory of the Lord shone around them,
[a]and they were greatly afraid. 10 Then the
angel said to them, [a]"Do not be afraid, for
behold, I bring you good tidings of great
joy [b]which will be to all people. 11 [a]For there
is born to you this day in the city of David
[b]a Savior, [c]who is Christ the Lord. 12 And
this *will be* the sign to you: You will find a
Babe wrapped in swaddling cloths, lying in
a manger."
13 [a]And suddenly there was with the angel
a multitude of the heavenly host praising
God and saying:

14 "Glory[a] to God in the highest,
And on earth [b]peace, [c]goodwill toward
men!"[1]

15 So it was, when the angels had gone away
from them into heaven, that the shepherds
said to one another, "Let us now go to Bethlehem and see this thing that has come to
pass, which the Lord has made known to us."
16 And they came with haste and found Mary
and Joseph, and the Babe lying in a manger.
17 Now when they had seen *Him,* they made
widely[1] known the saying which was told
them concerning this Child. 18 And all those
who heard *it* marveled at those things which
were told them by the shepherds. 19 [a]But Mary
kept all these things and pondered *them* in
her heart. 20 Then the shepherds returned,
glorifying and [a]praising God for all the things
that they had heard and seen, as it was told
them.

Circumcision of Jesus

21 [a]And when eight days were completed for
the circumcision of the Child,[1] His name was
called [b]JESUS, the name given by the angel
[c]before He was conceived in the womb.

Jesus Presented in the Temple

22 Now when [a]the days of her purification
according to the law of Moses were completed, they brought Him to Jerusalem to present
Him to the Lord 23 [a](as it is written in the law of
the Lord, [b]"Every male who opens the womb
shall be called holy to the LORD"),[1] 24 and to
offer a sacrifice according to what is said in
the law of the Lord, [a]"A pair of turtledoves
or two young pigeons."[1]

Simeon Sees God's Salvation

25 And behold, there was a man in Jerusalem whose name *was* Simeon, and this
man *was* just and devout, [a]waiting for the
Consolation of Israel, and the Holy Spirit
was upon him. 26 And it had been revealed to
him by the Holy Spirit that he would not [a]see
death before he had seen the Lord's Christ.
27 So he came [a]by the Spirit into the temple.

2:9 [a] Luke 1:12 **2:10** [a] Luke 1:13, 30 [b] Gen. 12:3 **2:11** [a] Is. 9:6 [b] Matt. 1:21 [c] Acts 2:36 **2:13** [a] Dan. 7:10 **2:14** [a] Luke 19:38 [b] Is. 57:19 [c] [Eph. 2:4, 7] [1] NU-Text reads *toward men of goodwill.* **2:17** [1] NU-Text omits *widely.* **2:19** [a] Gen. 37:11 **2:20** [a] Luke 19:37 **2:21** [a] Lev. 12:3 [b] [Matt. 1:21] [c] Luke 1:31 [1] NU-Text reads *for His circumcision.* **2:22** [a] Lev. 12:2–8 **2:23** [a] Deut. 18:4 [b] Ex. 13:2, 12, 15 [1] Exodus 13:2, 12, 15 **2:24** [a] Lev. 12:2, 8 [1] Leviticus 12:8 **2:25** [a] Mark 15:43 **2:26** [a] [Heb. 11:5] **2:27** [a] Matt. 4:1

WHEN ANGELS DECLARE PEACE

Glory to God in the highest, and on earth peace, goodwill toward men!

LUKE 2:14

When Christmas rolls around, do you have a sense of peace? Does the angelic announcement come to mind? Their message underscores the importance of peace for humankind. The angels could have pronounced many other things for needy humanity, but it was *peace* that came first (see 19:38). In Jesus' coming, the world received a Savior. At long last peace was a possibility.

In the Roman world the angelic announcement would have been viewed as a challenge to Caesar's authority. When Jesus was born, Augustus had been ruler of the known world for a few decades. He was regarded as a god, and his rule brought peace to the empire.

Who has secured peace for you? You will find peace in the true Son of God, Jesus. Sometimes when we're harried and worried—maybe especially at Christmas—we should stop and ask, *Does the Lord require this of me right now?* If not, slow down and find *shalom* rest.

And when the parents brought in the Child
Jesus, to do for Him according to the custom
of the law, 28he took Him up in his arms and
blessed God and said:

29 "Lord, [a]now You are letting Your servant
depart in peace,
According to Your word;
30 For my eyes [a]have seen Your salvation
31 Which You have prepared before the
face of all peoples,
32 [a]A light to *bring* revelation to the
Gentiles,
And the glory of Your people Israel."

33And Joseph and His mother[1] marveled
at those things which were spoken of Him.
34Then Simeon blessed them, and said to
Mary His mother, "Behold, this *Child* is destined for the [a]fall and rising of many in Israel,
and for [b]a sign which will be spoken against
35(yes, [a]a sword will pierce through your own
soul also), that the thoughts of many hearts
may be revealed."

Anna Bears Witness to the Redeemer

36Now there was one, Anna, a prophetess, the daughter of Phanuel, of the tribe
of [a]Asher. She was of a great age, and had
lived with a husband seven years from her
virginity; 37and this woman *was* a widow of
about eighty-four years,[1] who did not depart
from the temple, but served *God* with fastings
and prayers [a]night and day. 38And coming
in that instant she gave thanks to the Lord,[1]
and spoke of Him to all those who [a]looked
for redemption in Jerusalem.

The Family Returns to Nazareth

39So when they had performed all things
according to the law of the Lord, they returned to Galilee, to their *own* city, Nazareth.
40[a]And the Child grew and became strong in
spirit,[1] filled with wisdom; and the grace of
God was upon Him.

The Boy Jesus Amazes the Scholars

41His parents went to [a]Jerusalem [b]every
year at the Feast of the Passover. 42And when
He was twelve years old, they went up to Jerusalem according to the [a]custom of the feast.
43When they had finished the [a]days, as they
returned, the Boy Jesus lingered behind in Jerusalem. And Joseph and His mother[1] did not
know *it;* 44but supposing Him to have been
in the company, they went a day's journey,
and sought Him among *their* relatives and
acquaintances. 45So when they did not find
Him, they returned to Jerusalem, seeking
Him. 46Now so it was *that* after three days they
found Him in the temple, sitting in the midst
of the teachers, both listening to them and

2:29 [a] Gen. 46:30 2:30 [a] [Is. 52:10] 2:32 [a] Acts 10:45; 13:47; 28:28 2:33 [1] NU-Text reads *And His father and mother.* 2:34 [a] [1 Pet. 2:7, 8] [b] Acts 4:2; 17:32; 28:22 2:35 [a] Ps. 42:10 2:36 [a] Josh. 19:24 2:37 [a] 1 Tim. 5:5 [1] NU-Text reads *a widow until she was eighty-four.* 2:38 [a] Mark 15:43 [1] NU-Text reads *to God.* 2:40 [a] Luke 1:80; 2:52 [1] NU-Text omits *in spirit.* 2:41 [a] John 4:20 [b] Deut. 16:1, 16 2:42 [a] Ex. 23:14, 15 2:43 [a] Ex. 12:15 [1] NU-Text reads *And His parents.*

THE WORD BRINGS PEACE

Lord, now You are letting Your servant depart in peace, according to Your word.

LUKE 2:29

If you were on your deathbed, what would be your last words? Would you speak of peace? Would you have peace? You should think about it.

Shortly after Jesus' birth, His parents took him to Jerusalem to fulfill the law's requirement. When an old man named Simeon saw Jesus, he said he was ready to die because he saw in the Infant the fulfillment of his hopes. The righteous and devout Simeon had regularly visited the temple and prayed for the redemption of Israel, so here, his mission was accomplished. Simeon knew he could depart his physical life in confident assurance that all was right, that God's redemptive purposes were at work. "For my eyes have seen Your salvation," he declared (v. 30). Indeed they had! This special Infant was the Light of the World and the Glory of Israel.

With the peace Jesus brought, everything can change for you, too. Simeon loved the Word of God, and it was the foundation of his hope in Christ. Memorize a Scripture promise today that helps increase your peace.

asking them questions. 47And [a]all who heard
Him were astonished at His understanding
and answers. 48So when they saw Him, they
were amazed; and His mother said to Him,
"Son, why have You done this to us? Look,
Your father and I have sought You anxiously."
49And He said to them, "Why did you seek
Me? Did you not know that I must be [a]about
[b]My Father's business?" 50But [a]they did not
understand the statement which He spoke
to them.

Jesus Advances in Wisdom and Favor

51Then He went down with them and came
to Nazareth, and was subject to them, but His
mother [a]kept all these things in her heart.
52And Jesus [a]increased in wisdom and stature, [b]and in favor with God and men.

John the Baptist Prepares the Way

3 Now in the fifteenth year of the reign of
Tiberius Caesar, [a]Pontius Pilate being
governor of Judea, Herod being tetrarch of
Galilee, his brother Philip tetrarch of Iturea
and the region of Trachonitis, and Lysanias
tetrarch of Abilene, 2while [a]Annas and Caiaphas were high priests,[1] the word of God
came to [b]John the son of Zacharias in the
wilderness. 3[a]And he went into all the region
around the Jordan, preaching a baptism of
repentance [b]for the remission of sins, 4as it
is written in the book of the words of Isaiah
the prophet, saying:

[a]"The voice of one crying in the
wilderness:
'Prepare the way of the LORD;
Make His paths straight.
5 Every valley shall be filled
And every mountain and hill brought
low;
The crooked places shall be made
straight
And the rough ways smooth;
6 And [a]all flesh shall see the salvation of
God.' "[1]

John Preaches to the People

7Then he said to the multitudes that came
out to be baptized by him, [a]"Brood of vipers!
Who warned you to flee from the wrath to
come? 8Therefore bear fruits [a]worthy of repentance, and do not begin to say to yourselves, 'We have Abraham as *our* father.' For
I say to you that God is able to raise up children to Abraham from these stones. 9And
even now the ax is laid to the root of the
trees. Therefore [a]every tree which does not
bear good fruit is cut down and thrown into
the fire."
10So the people asked him, saying, [a]"What
shall we do then?"
11He answered and said to them, [a]"He who
has two tunics, let him give to him who has
none; and he who has food, [b]let him do likewise."
12Then [a]tax collectors also came to be baptized, and said to him, "Teacher, what shall
we do?"
13And he said to them, [a]"Collect no more
than what is appointed for you."
14Likewise the soldiers asked him, saying,
"And what shall we do?"
So he said to them, "Do not intimidate
anyone [a]or accuse falsely, and be content
with your wages."
15Now as the people were in expectation,
and all reasoned in their hearts about John,
whether he was the Christ *or* not, 16John
answered, saying to all, [a]"I indeed baptize
you with water; but One mightier than I is
coming, whose sandal strap I am not worthy
to loose. He will [b]baptize you with the Holy
Spirit and fire. 17His winnowing fan *is* in His
hand, and He will thoroughly clean out His
threshing floor, and [a]gather the wheat into
His barn; but the chaff He will burn with
unquenchable fire."
18And with many other exhortations he
preached to the people. 19[a]But Herod the
tetrarch, being rebuked by him concerning
Herodias, his brother Philip's wife,[1] and for
all the evils which Herod had done, 20also
added this, above all, that he shut John up
in prison.

John Baptizes Jesus

21When all the people were baptized, [a]it
came to pass that Jesus also was baptized;
and while He prayed, the heaven was opened.
22And the Holy Spirit descended in bodily
form like a dove upon Him, and a voice came
from heaven which said, "You are My beloved
Son; in You I am [a]well pleased."

The Genealogy of Jesus Christ

23Now Jesus Himself began *His ministry*
at [a]about thirty years of age, being (as was

2:47 [a] Matt. 7:28; 13:54; 22:33 **2:49** [a] John 9:4 [b] [Luke 4:22, 32] **2:50** [a] John 7:15, 46 **2:51** [a] Dan. 7:28 **2:52** [a] [Col. 2:2, 3] [b] 1 Sam. 2:26 **3:1** [a] Matt. 27:2 **3:2** [a] Acts 4:6 [b] Luke 1:13 [1] NU-Text and M-Text read *in the high priesthood of Annas and Caiaphas.* **3:3** [a] Mark 1:4 [b] Luke 1:77 **3:4** [a] Is. 40:3–5 **3:6** [a] Is. 52:10 [1] Isaiah 40:3–5 **3:7** [a] Matt. 3:7; 12:34; 23:33 **3:8** [a] [2 Cor. 7:9–11] **3:9** [a] Matt. 7:19 **3:10** [a] [Acts 2:37, 38; 16:30, 31] **3:11** [a] 2 Cor. 8:14 [b] Is. 58:7 **3:12** [a] Luke 7:29 **3:13** [a] Luke 19:8 **3:14** [a] Ex. 20:16; 23:1 **3:16** [a] Matt. 3:11, 12 [b] John 7:39; 20:22 **3:17** [a] Matt. 13:24–30 **3:19** [a] Mark 6:17 [1] NU-Text reads *his brother's wife.* **3:21** [a] Matt. 3:13–17 **3:22** [a] 2 Pet. 1:17 **3:23** [a] [Num. 4:3, 35, 39, 43, 47] supposed) [b]*the* son of Joseph, *the son* of Heli, 24*the son* of Matthat,[1] *the son* of Levi, *the son* of Melchi, *the son* of Janna, *the son* of Joseph, 25*the son* of Mattathiah, *the son* of Amos, *the son* of Nahum, *the son* of Esli, *the son* of Naggai, 26*the son* of Maath, *the son* of Mattathiah, *the son* of Semei, *the son* of Joseph, *the son* of Judah, 27*the son* of Joannas, *the son* of Rhesa, *the son* of [a]Zerubbabel, *the son* of Shealtiel, *the son* of Neri, 28*the son* of Melchi, *the son* of Addi, *the son* of Cosam, *the son* of Elmodam, *the son* of Er, 29*the son* of Jose, *the son* of Eliezer, *the son* of Jorim, *the son* of Matthat, *the son* of Levi, 30*the son* of Simeon, *the son* of Judah, *the son* of Joseph, *the son* of Jonan, *the son* of Eliakim, 31*the son* of Melea, *the son* of Menan, *the son* of Mattathah, *the son* of [a]Nathan, [b]*the son* of David, 32[a]*the son* of Jesse, *the son* of Obed, *the son* of Boaz, *the son* of Salmon, *the son* of Nahshon, 33*the son* of Amminadab, *the son* of Ram, *the son* of Hezron, *the son* of Perez, *the son* of Judah, 34*the son* of Jacob, *the son* of Isaac, *the son* of Abraham, [a]*the son* of Terah, *the son* of Nahor, 35*the son* of Serug, *the son* of Reu, *the son* of Peleg, *the son* of Eber, *the son* of Shelah, 36[a]*the son* of Cainan, *the son* of [b]Arphaxad, [c]*the son* of Shem, *the son* of Noah, *the son* of Lamech, 37*the son* of Methuselah, *the son* of Enoch, *the son* of Jared, *the son* of Mahalalel, *the son* of Cainan, 38*the son* of Enosh, *the son* of Seth, *the son* of Adam, [a]*the son* of God.

Satan Tempts Jesus

4 Then [a]Jesus, being filled with the Holy Spirit, returned from the Jordan and [b]was led by the Spirit into[1] the wilderness, 2being tempted for forty days by the devil. And [a]in those days He ate nothing, and afterward, when they had ended, He was hungry.

3And the devil said to Him, "If You are [a]the Son of God, command this stone to become bread."

4But Jesus answered him, saying,[1] "It is written, [a]'Man shall not live by bread alone, but by every word of God.' "[2]

5Then the devil, taking Him up on a high mountain, showed Him[1] all the kingdoms of the world in a moment of time. 6And the devil said to Him, "All this authority I will give You, and their glory; for [a]*this* has been delivered to me, and I give it to whomever I wish. 7Therefore, if You will worship before me, all will be Yours."

8And Jesus answered and said to him, "Get behind Me, Satan![1] For[2] it is written, [a]'You shall worship the LORD your God, and Him only you shall serve.' "[3]

9[a]Then he brought Him to Jerusalem, set Him on the pinnacle of the temple, and said to Him, "If You are the Son of God, throw Yourself down from here. 10For it is written:

[a]'He shall give His angels charge over
you,
To keep you,'

11and,

[a]'In *their* hands they shall bear you up,
Lest you dash your foot against a
stone.' "[1]

12And Jesus answered and said to him, "It has been said, [a]'You shall not tempt the LORD your God.' "[1]

13Now when the devil had ended every temptation, he departed from Him [a]until an opportune time.

Jesus Begins His Galilean Ministry

14[a]Then Jesus returned [b]in the power of the Spirit to [c]Galilee, and [d]news of Him went out through all the surrounding region. 15And He [a]taught in their synagogues, [b]being glorified by all.

Jesus Rejected at Nazareth

16So He came to [a]Nazareth, where He had been brought up. And as His custom was, [b]He went into the synagogue on the Sabbath day, and stood up to read. 17And He was handed the book of the prophet Isaiah. And when He had opened the book, He found the place where it was written:

18 "The[a] Spirit of the LORD *is* upon Me,
Because He has anointed Me
To preach the gospel to *the* poor;
He has sent Me to heal the
brokenhearted,[1]
To proclaim liberty to *the* captives

3:23 [b] John 6:42 3:24 [1] This and several other names in the genealogy are spelled somewhat differently in the NU-Text. Since the New King James Version uses the Old Testament spelling for persons mentioned in the New Testament, these variations, which come from the Greek, have not been footnoted. 3:27 [a] Ezra 2:2; 3:8 3:31 [a] Zech. 12:12 [b] 2 Sam. 5:14; 7:12 3:32 [a] Ruth 4:18–22 3:34 [a] Gen. 11:24, 26–30; 12:3 3:36 [a] Gen. 11:12 [b] Gen. 10:22, 24; 11:10–13 [c] Gen. 5:6–32; 9:27; 11:10 3:38 [a] Gen. 5:1, 2 4:1 [a] Matt. 4:1–11 [b] Luke 2:27 [1] NU-Text reads *in.* 4:2 [a] Ex. 34:28 4:3 [a] John 20:31 4:4 [a] Deut. 8:3 [1] Deuteronomy 8:3 [2] NU-Text omits *but by every word of God.* 4:5 [1] NU-Text reads *And taking Him up, he showed Him.* 4:6 [a] [Rev. 13:2, 7] 4:8 [a] Deut. 6:13; 10:20 [1] NU-Text omits *Get behind Me, Satan.* [2] NU-Text and M-Text omit *For.* [3] Deuteronomy 6:13 4:9 [a] Matt. 4:5–7 4:10 [a] Ps. 91:11 4:11 [a] Ps. 91:12 [1] Psalm 91:11, 12 4:12 [a] Deut. 6:16 [1] Deuteronomy 6:16 4:13 [a] [Heb. 4:15] 4:14 [a] Matt. 4:12 [b] John 4:43 [c] Acts 10:37 [d] Matt. 4:24 4:15 [a] Matt. 4:23 [b] Is. 52:13 4:16 [a] Mark 6:1 [b] Acts 13:14–16; 17:2 4:18 [a] Is. 49:8, 9; 61:1, 2 [1] NU-Text omits *to heal the brokenhearted.*

And recovery of sight to *the* blind,
To [b]set at liberty those who are
oppressed;
19 To proclaim the acceptable year of the
LORD."[1]

20Then He closed the book, and gave *it* back
to the attendant and sat down. And the eyes
of all who were in the synagogue were fixed
on Him. 21And He began to say to them,
"Today this Scripture is [a]fulfilled in your
hearing." 22So all bore witness to Him, and
[a]marveled at the gracious words which proceeded out of His mouth. And they said, [b]"Is
this not Joseph's son?"
23He said to them, "You will surely say
this proverb to Me, 'Physician, heal yourself!
Whatever we have heard done in [a]Caperna-
um,[1] do also here in [b]Your country.'" 24Then
He said, "Assuredly, I say to you, no [a]prophet
is accepted in his own country. 25But I tell
you truly, [a]many widows were in Israel in the
days of Elijah, when the heaven was shut up
three years and six months, and there was a
great famine throughout all the land; 26but
to none of them was Elijah sent except to
Zarephath,[1] *in the region* of Sidon, to a woman
who was a widow. 27[a]And many lepers were
in Israel in the time of Elisha the prophet,
and none of them was cleansed except Naaman the Syrian."
28So all those in the synagogue, when they
heard these things, were [a]filled with wrath,
29[a]and rose up and thrust Him out of the
city; and they led Him to the brow of the
hill on which their city was built, that they
might throw Him down over the cliff. 30Then
[a]passing through the midst of them, He went
His way.

Jesus Casts Out an Unclean Spirit

31Then [a]He went down to Capernaum, a
city of Galilee, and was teaching them on the
Sabbaths. 32And they were [a]astonished at His
teaching, [b]for His word was with authority.
33[a]Now in the synagogue there was a man
who had a spirit of an unclean demon. And
he cried out with a loud voice, 34saying, "Let
us alone! What have we to do with You, Jesus
of Nazareth? *Did* You *come* to destroy us? [a]I
know who You are—[b]the Holy One of God!"
35But Jesus rebuked him, saying, "Be quiet,
and come out of him!" And when the demon
had thrown him in *their* midst, it came out of
him and did not hurt him. 36Then they were
all amazed and spoke among themselves,
saying, "What a word this *is!* For with authority and power He commands the unclean
spirits, and they come out." 37And the report
about Him went out into every place in the
surrounding region.

Peter's Mother-in-Law Healed

38[a]Now He arose from the synagogue and
entered Simon's house. But Simon's wife's
mother was sick with a high fever, and they
[b]made request of Him concerning her. 39So
He stood over her and [a]rebuked the fever,
and it left her. And immediately she arose
and served them.

Many Healed After Sabbath Sunset

40[a]When the sun was setting, all those
who had any that were sick with various
diseases brought them to Him; and He laid
His hands on every one of them and healed
them. 41[a]And demons also came out of many,
crying out and saying, [b]"You are the Christ,[1]
the Son of God!"
And He, [c]rebuking *them,* did not allow
them to speak, for they knew that He was
the Christ.

Jesus Preaches in Galilee

42[a]Now when it was day, He departed and
went into a deserted place. And the crowd
sought Him and came to Him, and tried to
keep Him from leaving them; 43but He said to
them, "I must [a]preach the kingdom of God to
the other cities also, because for this purpose
I have been sent." 44[a]And He was preaching
in the synagogues of Galilee.[1]

Four Fishermen Called as Disciples

5 So [a]it was, as the multitude pressed about
Him to [b]hear the word of God, that He
stood by the Lake of Gennesaret, 2and saw two
boats standing by the lake; but the fishermen
had gone from them and were washing *their*
nets. 3Then He got into one of the boats,
which was Simon's, and asked him to put
out a little from the land. And He [a]sat down
and taught the multitudes from the boat.
4When He had stopped speaking, He said
to Simon, [a]"Launch out into the deep and let
down your nets for a catch."

4:18 [b] [Dan. 9:24] **4:19** [1] Isaiah 61:1, 2 **4:21** [a] Acts 13:29 **4:22** [a] [Ps. 45:2] [b] John 6:42 **4:23** [a] Matt. 4:13; 11:23 [b] Matt. 13:54 [1] Here and elsewhere the NU-Text spelling is *Capharnaum.* **4:24** [a] John 4:44 **4:25** [a] 1 Kin. 17:9 **4:26** [1] Greek *Sarepta* **4:27** [a] 2 Kin. 5:1–14 **4:28** [a] Luke 6:11 **4:29** [a] John 8:37; 10:31 **4:30** [a] John 8:59; 10:39 **4:31** [a] Matt. 4:13 **4:32** [a] Matt. 7:28, 29 [b] [John 6:63; 7:46; 8:26, 28, 38, 47; 12:49, 50] **4:33** [a] Mark 1:23 **4:34** [a] Luke 4:41 [b] Ps. 16:10 **4:38** [a] Mark 1:29–31 [b] Mark 5:23 **4:39** [a] Luke 8:24 **4:40** [a] Matt. 8:16, 17 **4:41** [a] Mark 1:34; 3:11 [b] Mark 8:29 [c] Mark 1:25, 34; 3:11 [1] NU-Text omits *the Christ.* **4:42** [a] Mark 1:35–38 **4:43** [a] [John 9:4] **4:44** [a] Matt. 4:23; 9:35 [1] NU-Text reads *Judea.* **5:1** [a] Mark 1:16–20 [b] Acts 13:44 **5:3** [a] John 8:2 **5:4** [a] John 21:6

5But Simon answered and said to Him,
"Master, we have toiled all night and caught
[a]nothing; nevertheless [b]at Your word I will
let down the net." 6And when they had done
this, they caught a great number of fish, and
their net was breaking. 7So they signaled to
their partners in the other boat to come and
help them. And they came and filled both
the boats, so that they began to sink. 8When
Simon Peter saw *it,* he fell down at Jesus'
knees, saying, [a]"Depart from me, for I am a
sinful man, O Lord!"

9For he and all who were with him were
[a]astonished at the catch of fish which they
had taken; 10and so also *were* James and John,
the sons of Zebedee, who were partners with
Simon. And Jesus said to Simon, "Do not be
afraid. [a]From now on you will catch men."
11So when they had brought their boats to
land, [a]they forsook all and followed Him.

Jesus Cleanses a Leper

12[a]And it happened when He was in a certain city, that behold, a man who was full of
[b]leprosy saw Jesus; and he fell on *his* face
and implored Him, saying, "Lord, if You are
willing, You can make me clean."

13Then He put out *His* hand and touched
him, saying, "I am willing; be cleansed."[a]Im-
mediately the leprosy left him. 14[a]And He
charged him to tell no one, "But go and show
yourself to the priest, and make an offering
for your cleansing, as a testimony to them,
[b]just as Moses commanded."

15However, [a]the report went around concerning Him all the more; and [b]great multitudes came together to hear, and to be
healed by Him of their infirmities. 16[a]So He
Himself *often* withdrew into the wilderness
and [b]prayed.

Jesus Forgives and Heals a Paralytic

17Now it happened on a certain day, as He
was teaching, that there were Pharisees and
teachers of the law sitting by, who had come
out of every town of Galilee, Judea, and Jerusalem. And the power of the Lord was *present*
to heal them.[1] 18[a]Then behold, men brought
on a bed a man who was paralyzed, whom
they sought to bring in and lay before Him.
19And when they could not find how they
might bring him in, because of the crowd,
they went up on the housetop and let him
down with *his* bed through the tiling into the
midst [a]before Jesus.

20When He saw their faith, He said to him,
"Man, your sins are forgiven you."

21[a]And the scribes and the Pharisees began
to reason, saying, "Who is this who speaks
blasphemies? [b]Who can forgive sins but God
alone?"

22But when Jesus [a]perceived their
thoughts, He answered and said to them,
"Why are you reasoning in your hearts?
23 Which is easier, to say, 'Your sins are forgiven you,' or to say, 'Rise up and walk'?24 But
that you may know that the Son of Man has
power on earth to forgive sins"—He said to
the man who was paralyzed, [a]"I say to you,
arise, take up your bed, and go to your house."

25Immediately he rose up before them,
took up what he had been lying on, and departed to his own house, [a]glorifying God.
26And they were all amazed, and they [a]glo-
rified God and were filled with fear, saying,
"We have seen strange things today!"

Matthew the Tax Collector

27[a]After these things He went out and saw
a tax collector named Levi, sitting at the tax
office. And He said to him, [b]"Follow Me."
28So he left all, rose up, and [a]followed Him.

29[a]Then Levi gave Him a great feast in his
own house. And [b]there were a great number
of tax collectors and others who sat down
with them. 30And their scribes and the Pharisees[1] complained against His disciples, saying, [a]"Why do You eat and drink with tax
collectors and sinners?"

31Jesus answered and said to them, "Those
who are well have no need of a physician, but
those who are sick. 32 [a]I have not come to call
the righteous, but sinners, to repentance."

Jesus Is Questioned About Fasting

33Then they said to Him, [a]"Why do[1] the
disciples of John fast often and make prayers,
and likewise those of the Pharisees, but Yours
eat and drink?"

34And He said to them, "Can you make
the friends of the bridegroom fast while the
[a]bridegroom is with them? 35 But the days will
come when the bridegroom will be taken away
from them; then they will fast in those days."

36[a]Then He spoke a parable to them: "No
one puts a piece from a new garment on an

5:5 [a] John 21:3 [b] Ps. 33:9 **5:8** [a] 1 Kin. 17:18 **5:9** [a] Mark 5:42; 10:24, 26 **5:10** [a] Matt. 4:19 **5:11** [a] Matt. 4:20; 19:27 **5:12** [a] Mark 1:40–44 [b] Lev. 13:14 **5:13** [a] John 5:9 **5:14** [a] Matt. 8:4 [b] Lev. 13:1–3; 14:2–32 **5:15** [a] Mark 1:45 [b] John 6:2 **5:16** [a] Luke 9:10 [b] Matt. 14:23 **5:17** [1] NU-Text reads *present with Him to heal.* **5:18** [a] Mark 2:3–12 **5:19** [a] Matt. 15:30 **5:21** [a] Mark 2:6, 7 [b] Is. 43:25 **5:22** [a] John 2:25 **5:24** [a] Luke 7:14 **5:25** [a] Acts 3:8 **5:26** [a] Luke 1:65; 7:16 **5:27** [a] Matt. 9:9–17 [b] John 12:26; 21:19, 22 **5:28** [a] Mark 10:28 **5:29** [a] Matt. 9:9, 10 [b] Luke 15:1 **5:30** [a] Luke 15:2 [1] NU-Text reads *But the Pharisees and their scribes.* **5:32** [a] 1 Tim. 1:15 **5:33** [a] Matt. 9:14 [1] NU-Text omits *Why do,* making the verse a statement. **5:34** [a] John 3:29 **5:36** [a] Mark 2:21, 22

old one;[1] otherwise the new makes a tear, and
also the piece that was *taken* out of the new
does not match the old. 37And no one puts
new wine into old wineskins; or else the new
wine will burst the wineskins and be spilled,
and the wineskins will be ruined. 38But new
wine must be put into new wineskins, and
both are preserved.[1] 39And no one, having
drunk old *wine,* immediately[1] desires new;
for he says, 'The old is better.' "[2]

Jesus Is Lord of the Sabbath

6 Now [a]it happened on the second Sabbath
after the first[1] that He went through the
grainfields. And His disciples plucked the
heads of grain and ate *them,* rubbing *them*
in *their* hands. 2And some of the Pharisees
said to them, "Why are you doing [a]what is
not lawful to do on the Sabbath?"

3But Jesus answering them said, "Have you
not even read this, [a]what David did when he
was hungry, he and those who were with him:
4how he went into the house of God, took and
ate the showbread, and also gave some to
those with him, [a]which is not lawful for any
but the priests to eat?" 5And He said to them,
"The Son of Man is also Lord of the Sabbath."

Healing on the Sabbath

6[a]Now it happened on another Sabbath,
also, that He entered the synagogue and
taught. And a man was there whose right
hand was withered. 7So the scribes and Pharisees watched Him closely, whether He would
[a]heal on the Sabbath, that they might find
an [b]accusation against Him. 8But He [a]knew
their thoughts, and said to the man who had
the withered hand, "Arise and stand here."
And he arose and stood. 9Then Jesus said to
them, "I will ask you one thing: [a]Is it lawful
on the Sabbath to do good or to do evil, to
save life or to destroy?"[1] 10And when He had
looked around at them all, He said to the
man,[1] "Stretch out your hand." And he did
so, and his hand was restored as whole as
the other.[2] 11But they were filled with rage,
and discussed with one another what they
might do to Jesus.

The Twelve Apostles

12Now it came to pass in those days that
He went out to the mountain to pray, and
continued all night in [a]prayer to God. 13And
when it was day, He called His disciples to
Himself; [a]and from them He chose [b]twelve
whom He also named apostles: 14Simon,
[a]whom He also named Peter, and Andrew
his brother; James and John; Philip and Bartholomew; 15Matthew and Thomas; James
the *son* of Alphaeus, and Simon called the
Zealot; 16Judas [a]*the son* of James, and [b]Judas
Iscariot who also became a traitor.

Jesus Heals a Great Multitude

17And He came down with them and stood
on a level place with a crowd of His disciples
[a]and a great multitude of people from all
Judea and Jerusalem, and from the seacoast
of Tyre and Sidon, who came to hear Him
and be healed of their diseases, 18as well as
those who were tormented with unclean
spirits. And they were healed. 19And the whole
multitude [a]sought to [b]touch Him, for [c]power
went out from Him and healed *them* all.

The Beatitudes

20Then He lifted up His eyes toward His
disciples, and said:

[a]"Blessed *are you* poor,
For yours is the kingdom of God.
21 [a]Blessed *are you* who hunger now,
For you shall be [b]filled.
[c]Blessed *are you* who weep now,
For you shall [d]laugh.
22 [a]Blessed are you when men hate you,
And when they [b]exclude you,
And revile *you,* and cast out your
name as evil,
For the Son of Man's sake.
23 [a]Rejoice in that day and leap for joy!
For indeed your reward *is* great in
heaven,
For [b]in like manner their fathers did
to the prophets.

Jesus Pronounces Woes

24 "But[a] woe to you [b]who are rich,
For [c]you have received your
consolation.
25 [a]Woe to you who are full,
For you shall hunger.
[b]Woe to you who laugh now,
For you shall mourn and [c]weep.

5:36 [1] NU-Text reads *No one tears a piece from a new garment and puts it on an old one.* **5:38** [1] NU-Text omits *and both are preserved.* **5:39** [1] NU-Text omits *immediately.* [2] NU-Text reads *good.* **6:1** [a] Matt. 12:1–8 [1] NU-Text reads *on a Sabbath.* **6:2** [a] Ex. 20:10 **6:3** [a] 1 Sam. 21:6 **6:4** [a] Lev. 24:9 **6:6** [a] Mark 3:1–6 **6:7** [a] Luke 13:14; 14:1–6 [b] Luke 20:20 **6:8** [a] Matt. 9:4 **6:9** [a] John 7:23 [1] M-Text reads *to kill.* **6:10** [1] NU-Text and M-Text read *to him.* [2] NU-Text omits *as whole as the other.* **6:12** [a] Mark 1:35 **6:13** [a] John 6:70 [b] Matt. 10:1 **6:14** [a] John 1:42 **6:16** [a] Jude 1 [b] Luke 22:3–6 **6:17** [a] Mark 3:7, 8 **6:19** [a] Matt. 9:21; 14:36 [b] Mark 5:27, 28 [c] Luke 8:46 **6:20** [a] Matt. 5:3–12; [11:5] **6:21** [a] Is. 55:1; 65:13 [b] [Rev. 7:16] [c] [Is. 61:3] [d] Ps. 126:5 **6:22** [a] 1 Pet. 2:19; 3:14; 4:14 [b] [John 16:2] **6:23** [a] James 1:2 [b] Acts 7:51 **6:24** [a] James 5:1–6 [b] Luke 12:21 [c] Luke 16:25 **6:25** [a] [Is. 65:13] [b] [Prov. 14:13] [c] James 4:9

26 [a]Woe to you[1] when all[2] men speak well
of you,
For so did their fathers to the false
prophets.

Love Your Enemies

27 [a]"But I say to you who hear: Love your
enemies, do good to those who hate you,
28 [a]bless those who curse you, and [b]pray for
those who spitefully use you. 29 [a]To him who
strikes you on the *one* cheek, offer the other
also. [b]And from him who takes away your
cloak, do not withhold *your* tunic either.
30 [a]Give to everyone who asks of you. And
from him who takes away your goods do not
ask *them* back. 31 [a]And just as you want men
to do to you, you also do to them likewise.
32 [a]"But if you love those who love you, what
credit is that to you? For even sinners love
those who love them. 33 And if you do good to
those who do good to you, what credit is that
to you? For even sinners do the same. 34 [a]And
if you lend *to those* from whom you hope to
receive back, what credit is that to you? For
even sinners lend to sinners to receive as
much back. 35 But [a]love your enemies, [b]do
good, and [c]lend, hoping for nothing in return;
and your reward will be great, and [d]you will
be sons of the Most High. For He is kind to
the unthankful and evil. 36 [a]Therefore be
merciful, just as your Father also is merciful.

Do Not Judge

37 [a]"Judge not, and you shall not be
judged. Condemn not, and you shall not be
condemned. [b]Forgive, and you will be forgiv-
en. 38 [a]Give, and it will be given to you: good
measure, pressed down, shaken together, and
running over will be put into your [b]bosom.
For [c]with the same measure that you use, it
will be measured back to you."
39 And He spoke a parable to them: [a]"Can
the blind lead the blind? Will they not both
fall into the ditch? 40 [a]A disciple is not above
his teacher, but everyone who is perfectly
trained will be like his teacher. 41 [a]And why do
you look at the speck in your brother's eye,
but do not perceive the plank in your own
eye? 42 Or how can you say to your brother,
'Brother, let me remove the speck that *is* in
your eye,' when you yourself do not see the
plank that *is* in your own eye? Hypocrite!
First remove the plank from your own eye,
and then you will see clearly to remove the
speck that is in your brother's eye.

A Tree Is Known by Its Fruit

43 [a]"For a good tree does not bear bad fruit,
nor does a bad tree bear good fruit. 44 For
[a]every tree is known by its own fruit. For
men do not gather figs from thorns, nor do
they gather grapes from a bramble bush.
45 [a]A good man out of the good treasure of
his heart brings forth good; and an evil man
out of the evil treasure of his heart[1] brings
forth evil. For out [b]of the abundance of the
heart his mouth speaks.

Build on the Rock

46 [a]"But why do you call Me 'Lord, Lord,'
and not do the things which I say? 47 [a]Who-
ever comes to Me, and hears My sayings and
does them, I will show you whom he is like:
48 He is like a man building a house, who dug
deep and laid the foundation on the rock.
And when the flood arose, the stream beat
vehemently against that house, and could
not shake it, for it was founded on the rock.[1]
49 But he who heard and did nothing is like a
man who built a house on the earth without
a foundation, against which the stream beat
vehemently; and immediately it fell.[1] And the
ruin of that house was great."

Jesus Heals a Centurion's Servant

7 Now when He concluded all His sayings in
the hearing of the people, He [a]entered Capernaum. 2 And a certain centurion's servant,
who was dear to him, was sick and ready to

PEACE NOTE

Followers of Jesus love their enemies and persecutors. A forgiving Christian is a peaceful Christian.

LUKE 6:28

6:26 [a] [John 15:19] [1] NU-Text and M-Text omit *to you.* [2] M-Text omits *all.* **6:27** [a] Rom. 12:20 **6:28** [a] Rom. 12:14 [b] Acts 7:60 **6:29** [a] Matt. 5:39–42 [b] [1 Cor. 6:7] **6:30** [a] Deut. 15:7, 8 **6:31** [a] Matt. 7:12 **6:32** [a] Matt. 5:46 **6:34** [a] Matt. 5:42 **6:35** [a] [Rom. 13:10] [b] Heb. 13:16 [c] Ps. 37:26 [d] Matt. 5:46 **6:36** [a] Matt. 5:48 **6:37** [a] Matt. 7:1–5 [b] Matt. 18:21–35 **6:38** [a] [Prov. 19:17; 28:27] [b] Ps. 79:12 [c] James 2:13 **6:39** [a] Matt. 15:14; 23:16 **6:40** [a] [John 13:16; 15:20] **6:41** [a] Matt. 7:3 **6:43** [a] Matt. 7:16–18, 20 **6:44** [a] Matt. 12:33 **6:45** [a] Matt. 12:35 [b] Matt. 12:34 [1] NU-Text omits *treasure of his heart.* **6:46** [a] Mal. 1:6 **6:47** [a] James 1:22–25 **6:48** [1] NU-Text reads *for it was well built.* **6:49** [1] NU-Text reads *collapsed.* **7:1** [a] Matt. 8:5–13

die. 3So when he heard about Jesus, he sent elders of the Jews to Him, pleading with Him to come and heal his servant. 4And when they came to Jesus, they begged Him earnestly, saying that the one for whom He should do this was deserving, 5"for he loves our nation, and has built us a synagogue."

6Then Jesus went with them. And when He was already not far from the house, the centurion sent friends to Him, saying to Him, "Lord, do not trouble Yourself, for I am not worthy that You should enter under my roof. 7Therefore I did not even think myself worthy to come to You. But [a]say the word, and my servant will be healed. 8For I also am a man placed under [a]authority, having soldiers under me. And I say to one, 'Go,' and he goes; and to another, 'Come,' and he comes; and to my servant, 'Do this,' and he does *it.*"

9When Jesus heard these things, He marveled at him, and turned around and said to the crowd that followed Him, "I say to you, I have not found such great faith, not even in Israel!" 10And those who were sent, returning to the house, found the servant well who had been sick.[1]

Jesus Raises the Son of the Widow of Nain

11Now it happened, the day after, *that* He went into a city called Nain; and many of His disciples went with Him, and a large crowd. 12And when He came near the gate of the city, behold, a dead man was being carried out, the only son of his mother; and she was a widow. And a large crowd from the city was with her. 13When the Lord saw her, He had [a]compassion on her and said to her, [b]"Do not weep." 14Then He came and touched the open coffin, and those who carried *him* stood still. And He said, "Young man, I say to you, [a]arise." 15So he who was dead [a]sat up and began to speak. And He [b]presented him to his mother.

16[a]Then fear came upon all, and they [b]glorified God, saying, [c]"A great prophet has risen up among us"; and, [d]"God has visited His people." 17And this report about Him went throughout all Judea and all the surrounding region.

John the Baptist Sends Messengers to Jesus

18[a]Then the disciples of John reported to him concerning all these things. 19And John, calling two of his disciples to *him,* sent *them* to Jesus,[1] saying, "Are You [a]the Coming One, or do we look for another?"

20When the men had come to Him, they said, "John the Baptist has sent us to You, saying, 'Are You the Coming One, or do we look for another?' " 21And that very hour He cured many of infirmities, afflictions, and evil spirits; and to many blind He gave sight.

22[a]Jesus answered and said to them, "Go and tell John the things you have seen and

7:7 [a] Ps. 33:9; 107:20 **7:8** [a] [Mark 13:34] **7:10** [1] NU-Text omits *who had been sick.* **7:13** [a] John 11:35 [b] Luke 8:52 **7:14** [a] Acts 9:40 **7:15** [a] John 11:44 [b] 2 Kin. 4:36 **7:16** [a] Luke 1:65 [b] Luke 5:26 [c] Luke 24:19 [d] Luke 1:68 **7:18** [a] Matt. 11:2–19 **7:19** [a] [Zech. 9:9] [1] NU-Text reads *the Lord.* **7:22** [a] Matt. 11:4

THE VISITATION OF PEACE

When the Lord saw her, He had compassion on her.

LUKE 7:13

In the ancient Near East, the worst possible social and economic situation was that of a childless widow. Without a spouse or son, the woman had no source of income or security. This grim reality is well illustrated in the Book of Ruth, in which Naomi lost her husband and her two sons. We encounter the same sad scenario in Luke 7:11–17, in which Jesus encountered a widow who had lost her only son. She and everyone in the village were taking the boy out to bury him. Thus, when Jesus encountered her, her grief was at its rawest.

But with Jesus, hope is never lost. He said, "Do not weep" (v. 13). Jesus then spoke to the deceased, "Young man, I say to you, arise" (v. 14), and the son revived and sat up. Needless to say, the crowd was blown away, exclaiming that "God has visited His people" (v. 16). "Visited" is a good word. In the Bible it means God checks things out and assists as needed. Thanks to Christ, we can call on God and know that He will visit us and give us all we need—including everlasting life and peace!

heard: [b]that *the* blind [c]see, *the* lame [d]walk, *the* lepers are [e]cleansed, *the* deaf [f]hear, *the* dead are raised, [g]*the* poor have the gospel preached to them. 23 And blessed is *he* who is not offended because of Me."

24 [a]When the messengers of John had departed, He began to speak to the multitudes concerning John: "What did you go out into the wilderness to see? A reed shaken by the wind? 25 But what did you go out to see? A man clothed in soft garments? Indeed those who are gorgeously appareled and live in luxury are in kings' courts. 26 But what did you go out to see? A prophet? Yes, I say to you, and more than a prophet. 27 This is *he* of whom it is written:

> [a]'Behold, I send My messenger before Your face,
> Who will prepare Your way before You.'[1]

28 For I say to you, among those born of women there is not a [a]greater prophet than John the Baptist;[1] but he who is least in the kingdom of God is greater than he."

29 And when all the people heard *Him,* even the tax collectors justified God, [a]having been baptized with the baptism of John. 30 But the Pharisees and lawyers rejected [a]the will of God for themselves, not having been baptized by him.

31 And the Lord said,[1] [a]"To what then shall I liken the men of this generation, and what are they like? 32 They are like children sitting in the marketplace and calling to one another, saying:

> 'We played the flute for you,
> And you did not dance;
> We mourned to you,
> And you did not weep.'

33 For [a]John the Baptist came [b]neither eating bread nor drinking wine, and you say, 'He has a demon.' 34 The Son of Man has come [a]eating and drinking, and you say, 'Look, a glutton and a winebibber, a friend of tax collectors and sinners!' 35 [a]But wisdom is justified by all her children."

A Sinful Woman Forgiven

36 [a]Then one of the Pharisees asked Him to eat with him. And He went to the Pharisee's house, and sat down to eat. 37 And behold, a woman in the city who was a sinner, when she knew that *Jesus* sat at the table in the Pharisee's house, brought an alabaster flask of fragrant oil, 38 and stood at His feet behind *Him* weeping; and she began to wash His feet with her tears, and wiped *them* with the hair of her head; and she kissed His feet and anointed *them* with the fragrant oil. 39 Now

7:22 [b] Is. 35:5 [c] John 9:7 [d] Matt. 15:31 [e] Luke 17:12–14 [f] Mark 7:37 [g] [Is. 61:1–3] **7:24** [a] Matt. 11:7 **7:27** [a] Mal. 3:1 [1] Malachi 3:1 **7:28** [a] [Luke 1:15] [1] NU-Text reads *there is none greater than John.* **7:29** [a] Luke 3:12 **7:30** [a] Acts 20:27 **7:31** [a] Matt. 11:16 [1] NU-Text and M-Text omit *And the Lord said.* **7:33** [a] Matt. 3:1 [b] Luke 1:15 **7:34** [a] Luke 15:2 **7:35** [a] Matt. 11:19 **7:36** [a] John 11:2

EXTRAVAGANT FORGIVENESS

"For she loved much."

LUKE 7:47

Jesus' encounter with the "woman . . . who was a sinner" (v. 37) is one of the most beautiful stories in the Gospels. Jesus was invited to the home of Simon, a Pharisee, to have dinner. We may assume that Jesus had preached in the local synagogue and that this meal was a reception that was open to the people of the village. Neighbors gathered about, eager to hear what Jesus might say. One of these was a woman known as "a sinner."

The woman washed Jesus' feet with her tears and perfume. She dried His feet with her hair. Simon the host suspected Jesus didn't know who and what this woman really was. He was wrong. "Do you see this woman?" Jesus asked Simon (v. 44). "Her sins, which are many, are forgiven, for she loved much" (v. 47). Proof that the woman experienced God's grace was seen, Jesus said, in her display of extravagant love. Therefore, Jesus could say to her, "Your faith has saved you. Go in peace" (v. 50).

Imagine that Jesus is addressing you today, saying, "Your faith has saved you. Go in peace." Will you do that?

when the Pharisee who had invited Him
saw *this,* he spoke to himself, saying, [a]“This
Man, if He were a prophet, would know who
and what manner of woman *this is* who is
touching Him, for she is a sinner.”
40And Jesus answered and said to him,
“Simon, I have something to say to you.”
So he said, “Teacher, say it.”
41“There was a certain creditor who had two
debtors. One owed five hundred [a]denarii, and
the other fifty. 42And when they had nothing
with which to repay, he freely forgave them
both. Tell Me, therefore, which of them will
love him more?”
43Simon answered and said, “I suppose
the *one* whom he forgave more.”
And He said to him, “You have rightly
judged.” 44Then He turned to the woman
and said to Simon, “Do you see this woman?
I entered your house; you gave Me no [a]water
for My feet, but she has washed My feet with
her tears and wiped *them* with the hair of her
head. 45You gave Me no [a]kiss, but this woman
has not ceased to kiss My feet since the time I
came in. 46[a]You did not anoint My head with
oil, but this woman has anointed My feet with
fragrant oil. 47[a]Therefore I say to you, her
sins, *which are* many, are forgiven, for she
loved much. But to whom little is forgiven,
the same loves little.”
48Then He said to her, [a]“Your sins are forgiven.”
49And those who sat at the table with Him
began to say to themselves, [a]“Who is this who
even forgives sins?”
50Then He said to the woman, [a]“Your faith
has saved you. Go in peace.”

PEACE NOTE

In this story we see spiritual healing. The woman’s sins were forgiven, she was “saved,” and she could then “go in peace.”

LUKE 7:50

Many Women Minister to Jesus

8 Now it came to pass, afterward, that He went
through every city and village, preaching
and bringing the glad tidings of the kingdom
of God. And the twelve *were* with Him, 2and
[a]certain women who had been healed of evil
spirits and infirmities—Mary called Magdalene, [b]out of whom had come seven demons,
3and Joanna the wife of Chuza, Herod’s steward, and Susanna, and many others who provided for Him[1] from their substance.

The Parable of the Sower

4[a]And when a great multitude had gathered, and they had come to Him from every
city, He spoke by a parable: 5“A sower went
out to sow his seed. And as he sowed, some
fell by the wayside; and it was trampled down,
and the birds of the air devoured it. 6Some
fell on rock; and as soon as it sprang up, it
withered away because it lacked moisture.
7And some fell among thorns, and the thorns
sprang up with it and choked it. 8But others
fell on good ground, sprang up, and yielded
a crop a hundredfold.” When He had said
these things He cried, [a]“He who has ears to
hear, let him hear!”

The Purpose of Parables

9[a]Then His disciples asked Him, saying,
“What does this parable mean?”
10And He said, “To you it has been given to
know the mysteries of the kingdom of God,
but to the rest *it is given* in parables, that

[a]‘Seeing they may not see,
And hearing they may not
understand.’[1]

The Parable of the Sower Explained

11[a]“Now the parable is this: The seed is the
[b]word of God. 12Those by the wayside are the
ones who hear; then the devil comes and
takes away the word out of their hearts, lest
they should believe and be saved. 13But the
ones on the rock *are those* who, when they
hear, receive the word with joy; and these
have no root, who believe for a while and in
time of temptation fall away. 14Now the ones
that fell among thorns are those who, when
they have heard, go out and are choked with
cares, [a]riches, and pleasures of life, and bring
no fruit to maturity. 15But the ones *that* fell
on the good ground are those who, having
heard the word with a noble and good heart,
keep *it* and bear fruit with [a]patience.

7:39 [a] Luke 15:2 **7:41** [a] Matt. 18:28 **7:44** [a] Gen. 18:4; 19:2; 43:24 **7:45** [a] Rom. 16:16 **7:46** [a] Ps. 23:5 **7:47** [a] [1 Tim. 1:14]
7:48 [a] Matt. 9:2 **7:49** [a] Luke 5:21 **7:50** [a] Matt. 9:22 **8:2** [a] Matt. 27:55 [b] Mark 16:9 **8:3** [1] NU-Text and M-Text read *them.*
8:4 [a] Mark 4:1–9 **8:8** [a] Luke 14:35 **8:9** [a] Matt. 13:10–23 **8:10** [a] Is. 6:9 [1] Isaiah 6:9 **8:11** [a] [1 Pet. 1:23] [b] Luke 5:1; 11:28
8:14 [a] 1 Tim. 6:9, 10 **8:15** [a] [Heb. 10:36–39]

The Parable of the Revealed Light

16[a]"No one, when he has lit a lamp, covers
it with a vessel or puts *it* under a bed, but sets
it on a lampstand, that those who enter may
see the [b]light. 17[a]For nothing is secret that
will not be [b]revealed, nor *anything* hidden
that will not be known and come to light.
18Therefore take heed how you hear. [a]For
whoever has, to him *more* will be given; and
whoever does not have, even what he seems
to [b]have will be taken from him."

Jesus' Mother and Brothers Come to Him

19[a]Then His mother and brothers came to
Him, and could not approach Him because
of the crowd. 20And it was told Him *by some,*
who said, "Your mother and Your brothers
are standing outside, desiring to see You."
21But He answered and said to them, "My
mother and My brothers are these who hear
the word of God and do it."

Wind and Wave Obey Jesus

22[a]Now it happened, on a certain day, that
He got into a boat with His disciples. And He
said to them, "Let us cross over to the other
side of the lake." And they launched out. 23But
as they sailed He fell asleep. And a windstorm
came down on the lake, and they were filling
with water, and were in jeopardy. 24And they
came to Him and awoke Him, saying, "Master,
Master, we are perishing!"

Then He arose and rebuked the wind and
the raging of the water. And they ceased,
and there was a calm. 25But He said to them,
[a]"Where is your faith?"

And they were afraid, and marveled, saying
to one another, [b]"Who can this be? For He
commands even the winds and water, and
they obey Him!"

A Demon-Possessed Man Healed

26[a]Then they sailed to the country of the
Gadarenes,[1] which is opposite Galilee. 27And
when He stepped out on the land, there met
Him a certain man from the city who had demons for a long time. And he wore no clothes,[1]
nor did he live in a house but in the tombs.
28When he saw Jesus, he [a]cried out, fell down
before Him, and with a loud voice said, [b]"What
have I to do with [c]You, Jesus, Son of the Most
High God? I beg You, do not torment me!" 29For
He had commanded the unclean spirit to come
out of the man. For it had often seized him, and
he was kept under guard, bound with chains
and shackles; and he broke the bonds and
was driven by the demon into the wilderness.
30Jesus asked him, saying, "What is your
name?"

And he said, "Legion," because many demons had entered him. 31And they begged
Him that He would not command them to
go out [a]into the abyss.
32Now a herd of many [a]swine was feeding
there on the mountain. So they begged Him
that He would permit them to enter them.
And He permitted them. 33Then the demons
went out of the man and entered the swine,
and the herd ran violently down the steep
place into the lake and drowned.
34When those who fed *them* saw what had
happened, they fled and told *it* in the city and
in the country. 35Then they went out to see
what had happened, and came to Jesus, and
found the man from whom the demons had
departed, [a]sitting at the [b]feet of Jesus, clothed
and in his [c]right mind. And they were afraid.
36They also who had seen *it* told them by what
means he who had been demon-possessed
was healed. 37[a]Then the whole multitude of
the surrounding region of the Gadarenes[1]
[b]asked Him to [c]depart from them, for they
were seized with great [d]fear. And He got into
the boat and returned.
38Now [a]the man from whom the demons
had departed begged Him that he might be
with Him. But Jesus sent him away, saying,
39"Return to your own house, and tell what
great things God has done for you." And he went
his way and proclaimed throughout the whole
city what great things Jesus had done for him.

A Girl Restored to Life and a Woman Healed

40So it was, when Jesus returned, that the
multitude welcomed Him, for they were all
waiting for Him. 41[a]And behold, there came
a man named Jairus, and he was a ruler of
the synagogue. And he fell down at Jesus'
feet and begged Him to come to his house,
42for he had an only daughter about twelve
years of age, and she [a]was dying.

But as He went, the multitudes thronged
Him. 43[a]Now a woman, having a [b]flow of
blood for twelve years, who had spent all
her livelihood on physicians and could not
be healed by any, 44came from behind and

8:16 [a] Luke 11:33 [b] Matt. 5:14 **8:17** [a] Luke 12:2 [b] [2 Cor. 5:10] **8:18** [a] Matt. 25:29 [b] Matt. 13:12 **8:19** [a] Mark 3:31–35 **8:22** [a] Matt. 8:23–27 **8:25** [a] Luke 9:41 [b] Luke 4:36; 5:26 **8:26** [a] Mark 5:1–17 [1] NU-Text reads *Gerasenes.* **8:27** [1] NU-Text reads *who had demons and for a long time wore no clothes.* **8:28** [a] Mark 1:26; 9:26 [b] Mark 1:23, 24 [c] Luke 4:41 **8:31** [a] [Rev. 20:1, 3] **8:32** [a] Lev. 11:7 **8:35** [a] [Matt. 11:28] [b] Luke 10:39; 17:16 [c] [2 Tim. 1:7] **8:37** [a] Matt. 8:34 [b] Luke 4:34 [c] Acts 16:39 [d] Luke 5:26 [1] NU-Text reads *Gerasenes.* **8:38** [a] Mark 5:18–20 **8:41** [a] Mark 5:22–43 **8:42** [a] Luke 7:2 **8:43** [a] Matt. 9:20 [b] Luke 15:19–22

[a]touched the border of His garment. And
immediately her flow of blood stopped.
45 And Jesus said, "Who touched Me?"
When all denied it, Peter and those with
him[1] said, "Master, the multitudes throng and
press You, and You say, 'Who touched Me?' "[2]
46 But Jesus said, "Somebody touched Me,
for I perceived [a]power going out from Me."
47 Now when the woman saw that she was
not hidden, she came trembling; and falling
down before Him, she declared to Him in
the presence of all the people the reason she
had touched Him and how she was healed
immediately.
48 And He said to her, "Daughter, be of good
cheer;[1] [a]your faith has made you well. [b]Go
in peace."

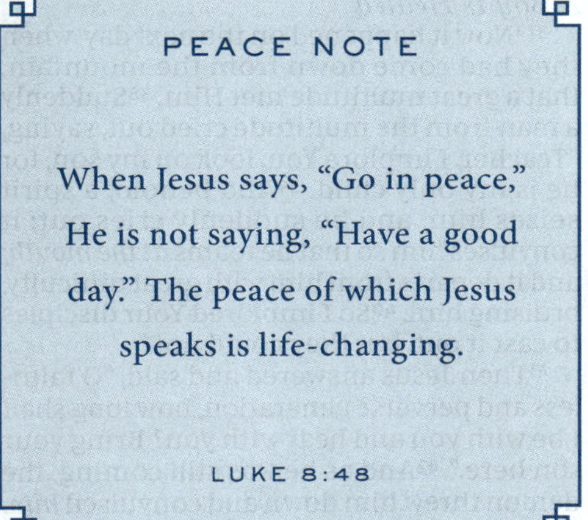

49 [a]While He was still speaking, someone
came from the ruler of the synagogue's *house,*
saying to him, "Your daughter is dead. Do
not trouble the Teacher."[1]
50 But when Jesus heard *it,* He answered
him, saying, "Do not be afraid; [a]only believe,
and she will be made well." 51 When He came
into the house, He permitted no one to go in[1]
except Peter, James, and John,[2] and the father
and mother of the girl. 52 Now all wept and
mourned for her; but He said, [a]"Do not weep;
she is not dead, [b]but sleeping." 53 And they
ridiculed Him, knowing that she was dead.
54 But He put them all outside,[1] took her
by the hand and called, saying, "Little girl,
[a]arise." 55 Then her spirit returned, and she
arose immediately. And He commanded that
she be given *something* to eat. 56 And her parents were astonished, but [a]He charged them
to tell no one what had happened.

Sending Out the Twelve

9 Then [a]He called His twelve disciples together and [b]gave them power and authority over all demons, and to cure diseases.
2 [a]He sent them to preach the kingdom of God
and to heal the sick. 3 [a]And He said to them,
"Take nothing for the journey, neither staffs
nor bag nor bread nor money; and do not
have two tunics apiece.
4 [a]"Whatever house you enter, stay there,
and from there depart. 5 [a]And whoever will
not receive you, when you go out of that city,
[b]shake off the very dust from your feet as a
testimony against them."
6 [a]So they departed and went through the
towns, preaching the gospel and healing
everywhere.

Herod Seeks to See Jesus

7 [a]Now Herod the tetrarch heard of all that
was done by Him; and he was perplexed,
because it was said by some that John had
risen from the dead, 8 and by some that Elijah
had appeared, and by others that one of the
old prophets had risen again. 9 Herod said,
"John I have beheaded, but who is this of
whom I hear such things?" [a]So he sought
to see Him.

Feeding the Five Thousand

10 [a]And the apostles, when they had returned, told Him all that they had done.
[b]Then He took them and went aside privately
into a deserted place belonging to the city
called Bethsaida. 11 But when the multitudes
knew *it,* they followed Him; and He received
them and spoke to them about the kingdom
of God, and healed those who had need of
healing. 12 [a]When the day began to wear away,
the twelve came and said to Him, "Send the
multitude away, that they may go into the
surrounding towns and country, and lodge
and get provisions; for we are in a deserted
place here."
13 But He said to them, "You give them
something to eat."
And they said, "We have no more than five
loaves and two fish, unless we go and buy
food for all these people." 14 For there were
about five thousand men.

8:44 [a] Mark 6:56 **8:45** [1] NU-Text omits *and those with him.* [2] NU-Text omits *and You say, 'Who touched Me?'*
8:46 [a] Mark 5:30 **8:48** [a] Luke 7:50 [b] John 8:11 [1] NU-Text omits *be of good cheer.* **8:49** [a] Mark 5:35 [1] NU-Text adds *anymore.* **8:50** [a] [Mark 11:22–24] **8:51** [1] NU-Text adds *with Him.* [2] NU-Text and M-Text read *Peter, John, and James.*
8:52 [a] Luke 7:13 [b] [John 11:11, 13] **8:54** [a] John 11:43 [1] NU-Text omits *put them all outside.* **8:56** [a] Matt. 8:4; 9:30
9:1 [a] Matt. 10:1, 2 [b] [John 14:12] **9:2** [a] Matt. 10:7, 8 **9:3** [a] Luke 10:4–12; 22:35 **9:4** [a] Mark 6:10 **9:5** [a] Matt. 10:14 [b] Acts 13:51 **9:6** [a] Mark 6:12 **9:7** [a] Matt. 14:1, 2 **9:9** [a] Luke 23:8 **9:10** [a] Mark 6:30 [b] Matt. 14:13 **9:12** [a] John 6:1, 5

Then He said to His disciples, "Make them sit down in groups of fifty." 15And they did so, and made them all sit down.

16Then He took the five loaves and the two fish, and looking up to heaven, He [a]blessed and broke them, and gave *them* to the disciples to set before the multitude. 17So they all ate and were filled, and twelve baskets of the leftover fragments were taken up by them.

Peter Confesses Jesus as the Christ

18[a]And it happened, as He was alone praying, *that* His disciples joined Him, and He asked them, saying, "Who do the crowds say that I am?"

19So they answered and said, [a]"John the Baptist, but some *say* Elijah; and others *say* that one of the old prophets has risen again."

20He said to them, "But who do you say that I am?"

[a]Peter answered and said, "The Christ of God."

Jesus Predicts His Death and Resurrection

21[a]And He strictly warned and commanded them to tell this to no one, 22saying, [a]"The Son of Man must suffer many things, and be rejected by the elders and chief priests and scribes, and be killed, and be raised the third day."

Take Up the Cross and Follow Him

23[a]Then He said to *them* all, "If anyone desires to come after Me, let him deny himself, and take up his cross daily,[1] and follow Me. 24[a]For whoever desires to save his life will lose it, but whoever loses his life for My sake will save it. 25[a]For what profit is it to a man if he gains the whole world, and is himself destroyed or lost? 26[a]For whoever is ashamed of Me and My words, of him the Son of Man will be [b]ashamed when He comes in His *own* glory, and *in His* Father's, and of the holy angels. 27[a]But I tell you truly, there are some standing here who shall not taste death till they see the kingdom of God."

Jesus Transfigured on the Mount

28[a]Now it came to pass, about eight days after these sayings, that He took Peter, John, and James and went up on the mountain to pray. 29As He prayed, the appearance of His face was altered, and His robe *became* white *and* glistening. 30And behold, two men talked with Him, who were [a]Moses and [b]Elijah, 31who appeared *in glory and spoke of His* decease which He was about to accomplish at Jerusalem. 32But Peter and those with him [a]were heavy with sleep; and when they were fully awake, they saw His glory and the two men who stood with Him. 33Then it happened, as they were parting from Him, *that* Peter said to Jesus, "Master, it is good for us to be here; and let us make three tabernacles: one for You, one for Moses, and one for Elijah"—not knowing what he said.

34While he was saying this, a cloud came and overshadowed them; and they were fearful as they entered the [a]cloud. 35And a voice came out of the cloud, saying, [a]"This is My beloved Son.[1] [b]Hear Him!" 36When the voice had ceased, Jesus was found alone. [a]But they kept quiet, and told no one in those days any of the things they had seen.

A Boy Is Healed

37[a]Now it happened on the next day, when they had come down from the mountain, that a great multitude met Him. 38Suddenly a man from the multitude cried out, saying, "Teacher, I implore You, look on my son, for he is my only child. 39And behold, a spirit seizes him, and he suddenly cries out; it convulses him so that he foams *at the mouth;* and it departs from him with great difficulty, bruising him. 40So I implored Your disciples to cast it out, but they could not."

41Then Jesus answered and said, "O faithless and perverse generation, how long shall I be with you and bear with you? Bring your son here." 42And as he was still coming, the demon threw him down and convulsed *him.* Then Jesus rebuked the unclean spirit, healed the child, and gave him back to his father.

Jesus Again Predicts His Death

43And they were all amazed at the majesty of God.

But while everyone marveled at all the things which Jesus did, He said to His disciples, 44[a]"Let these words sink down into your ears, for the Son of Man is about to be betrayed into the hands of men." 45[a]But they did not understand this saying, and it was hidden from them so that they did not perceive it; and they were afraid to ask Him about this saying.

Who Is the Greatest?

46[a]Then a dispute arose among them as to which of them would be greatest. 47And Jesus, [a]perceiving the thought of their heart, took a [b]little child and set him by Him, 48and

9:16 [a] Luke 22:19; 24:30 **9:18** [a] Matt. 16:13–16 **9:19** [a] Matt. 14:2 **9:20** [a] John 6:68, 69 **9:21** [a] Matt. 8:4; 16:20 **9:22** [a] Matt. 16:21; 17:22 **9:23** [a] Matt. 10:38; 16:24 [1] M-Text omits *daily.* **9:24** [a] [John 12:25] **9:25** [a] Mark 8:36 **9:26** [a] [Rom. 1:16] [b] Matt. 10:33 **9:27** [a] Matt. 16:28 **9:28** [a] Mark 9:2–8 **9:30** [a] Heb. 11:23–29 [b] 2 Kin. 2:1–11 **9:32** [a] Dan. 8:18; 10:9 **9:34** [a] Ex. 13:21 **9:35** [a] [Matt. 3:17; 12:18] [b] Acts 3:22 [1] NU-Text reads *This is My Son, the Chosen One.* **9:36** [a] Matt. 17:9 **9:37** [a] Mark 9:14–27 **9:44** [a] Matt. 17:22 **9:45** [a] Mark 9:32 **9:46** [a] Matt. 18:1–5 **9:47** [a] Matt. 9:4 [b] Luke 18:17

said to them, [a]"Whoever receives this little
child in My name receives Me; and [b]whoever
receives Me [c]receives Him who sent Me. [d]For
he who is least among you all will be great."

Jesus Forbids Sectarianism

49 [a]Now John answered and said, "Master,
we saw someone casting out demons in Your
name, and we forbade him because he does
not follow with us."

50 But Jesus said to him, "Do not forbid *him,*
for [a]he who is not against us[1] is on our[2] side."

A Samaritan Village Rejects the Savior

51 Now it came to pass, when the time had
come for [a]Him to be received up, that He
steadfastly set His face to go to Jerusalem,
52 and sent messengers before His face. And
as they went, they entered a village of the
Samaritans, to prepare for Him. 53 But [a]they
did not receive Him, because His face was
set for the journey to Jerusalem. 54 And when
His disciples [a]James and John saw *this,* they
said, "Lord, do You want us to command fire
to come down from heaven and consume
them, just as [b]Elijah did?"[1]

55 But He turned and rebuked them,[1] and
said, "You do not know what manner of
[a]spirit you are of. 56 For [a]the Son of Man did
not come to destroy men's lives but to save
them."[1] And they went to another village.

The Cost of Discipleship

57 [a]Now it happened as they journeyed on
the road, *that* someone said to Him, "Lord,
I will follow You wherever You go."

58 And Jesus said to him, "Foxes have holes
and birds of the air *have* nests, but the Son of
Man [a]has nowhere to lay *His* head."

59 [a]Then He said to another, "Follow Me."

But he said, "Lord, let me first go and bury
my father."

60 Jesus said to him, "Let the dead bury
their own dead, but you go and preach the
kingdom of God."

61 And another also said, "Lord, [a]I will follow You, but let me first go *and* bid them
farewell who are at my house."

62 But Jesus said to him, "No one, having
put his hand to the plow, and looking back,
is [a]fit for the kingdom of God."

The Seventy Sent Out

10 After these things the Lord appointed
seventy others also,[1] and [a]sent them two
by two before His face into every city and place
where He Himself was about to go. 2 Then He
said to them, [a]"The harvest truly *is* great, but
the laborers *are* few; therefore [b]pray the Lord
of the harvest to send out laborers into His
harvest. 3 Go your way; [a]behold, I send you
out as lambs among wolves. 4 [a]Carry neither
money bag, knapsack, nor sandals; and [b]greet
no one along the road. 5 [a]But whatever house
you enter, first say, 'Peace to this house.' 6 And
if a son of peace is there, your peace will rest
on it; if not, it will return to you. 7 [a]And remain
in the same house, [b]eating and drinking such
things as they give, for [c]the laborer is worthy
of his wages. Do not go from house to house.
8 Whatever city you enter, and they receive
you, eat such things as are set before you.
9 [a]And heal the sick there, and say to them,
[b]'The kingdom of God has come near to you.'
10 But whatever city you enter, and they do
not receive you, go out into its streets and
say, 11 [a]'The very dust of your city which clings
to us[1] we wipe off against you. Nevertheless
know this, that the kingdom of God has come
near you.' 12 But[1] I say to you that [a]it will be
more tolerable in that Day for Sodom than
for that city.

Woe to the Impenitent Cities

13 [a]"Woe to you, Chorazin! Woe to you, Bethsaida! [b]For if the mighty works which were
done in you had been done in Tyre and Sidon,
they would have repented long ago, sitting
in sackcloth and ashes. 14 But it will be more
tolerable for Tyre and Sidon at the judgment
than for you. 15 [a]And you, Capernaum, who
are [b]exalted to heaven, [c]will be brought down
to Hades.[1] 16 [a]He who hears you hears Me,
[b]he who rejects you rejects Me, and [c]he who
rejects Me rejects Him who sent Me."

The Seventy Return with Joy

17 Then [a]the seventy[1] returned with joy,
saying, "Lord, even the demons are subject
to us in Your name."

18 And He said to them, [a]"I saw Satan fall
like lightning from heaven. 19 Behold, [a]I give
you the authority to trample on serpents and

9:48 [a] Matt. 18:5 [b] John 12:44 [c] John 13:20 [d] Eph. 3:8 **9:49** [a] Mark 9:38–40 **9:50** [a] Luke 11:23 [1] NU-Text reads *you.* [2] NU-Text reads *your.* **9:51** [a] Mark 16:19 **9:53** [a] John 4:4, 9 **9:54** [a] Mark 3:17 [b] 2 Kin. 1:10, 12 [1] NU-Text omits *just as Elijah did.* **9:55** [a] [2 Tim. 1:7] [1] NU-Text omits the rest of this verse. **9:56** [a] John 3:17; 12:47 [1] NU-Text omits the first sentence of this verse. **9:57** [a] Matt. 8:19–22 **9:58** [a] Luke 2:7; 8:23 **9:59** [a] Matt. 8:21, 22 **9:61** [a] 1 Kin. 19:20 **9:62** [a] 2 Tim. 4:10 **10:1** [a] Mark 6:7 [1] NU-Text reads *seventy-two others.* **10:2** [a] John 4:35 [b] 2 Thess. 3:1 **10:3** [a] Matt. 10:16 **10:4** [a] Luke 9:3–5 [b] 2 Kin. 4:29 **10:5** [a] Matt. 10:12 **10:7** [a] Matt. 10:11 [b] 1 Cor. 10:27 [c] 1 Tim. 5:18 **10:9** [a] Mark 3:15 [b] Matt. 3:2; 10:7 **10:11** [a] Acts 13:51 [1] NU-Text reads *our feet.* **10:12** [a] Matt. 10:15; 11:24 [1] NU-Text and M-Text omit *But.* **10:13** [a] Matt. 11:21–23 [b] Ezek. 3:6 **10:15** [a] Matt. 11:23 [b] Is. 14:13–15 [c] Ezek. 26:20 [1] NU-Text reads *will you be exalted to heaven? You will be thrust down to Hades!* **10:16** [a] John 13:20 [b] 1 Thess. 4:8 [c] John 5:23 **10:17** [a] Luke 10:1 [1] NU-Text reads *seventy-two.* **10:18** [a] John 12:31 **10:19** [a] Mark 16:18

EMPOWERED FOR OUR BATTLES

"I give you the authority to trample on serpents and scorpions."

LUKE 10:19

When the disciples completed their mission to go out and preach, they returned with joy. Why, even the evil spirits had been subject to them in the name of Jesus! Jesus said, "I saw Satan fall like lightning from heaven. Behold, I give you the authority . . . over all the power of the enemy" (vv. 18–19). What does this mean?

Jesus assured His disciples that they had "the authority to trample on serpents and scorpions" (v. 19). In Jewish antiquity, evil spirits were sometimes referred to as serpents (or snakes—Satan himself being the great serpent) and scorpions. Thus Jesus told His disciples that as His followers, they had power over evil spirits. In the Book of Acts we see the disciples, especially Peter and Paul, exercise this authority.

It's a powerful encouragement to us that Jesus has not left us unprepared for the spiritual battles we face. Through studying the Word and being filled with the Spirit, we can go with peace and confidence into the spiritual fray. As an exercise, memorize a verse about peace that you can lean on when the spiritual battle rages around you. Use it as a reminder that God's authority is already at work.

scorpions, and over all the power of the enemy, and nothing shall by any means hurt you.
20Nevertheless do not rejoice in this, that the spirits are subject to you, but rather[1] rejoice because [a]your names are written in heaven."

Jesus Rejoices in the Spirit

21[a]In that hour Jesus rejoiced in the Spirit and said, "I thank You, Father, Lord of heaven and earth, that You have hidden these things from *the* wise and prudent and revealed them to babes. Even so, Father, for so it seemed
good in Your sight. 22[a]All[1] things have been delivered to Me by My Father, and [b]no one knows who the Son is except the Father, and who the Father is except the Son, and *the one* to whom the Son wills to reveal *Him.*"
23Then He turned to *His* disciples and said privately, [a]"Blessed *are* the eyes which see
the things you see; 24for I tell you [a]that many prophets and kings have desired to see what you see, and have not seen *it,* and to hear what you hear, and have not heard *it.*"

The Parable of the Good Samaritan

25And behold, a certain lawyer stood up and tested Him, saying, [a]"Teacher, what shall I do to inherit eternal life?"
26He said to him, "What is written in the law? What is your reading *of it?*"
27So he answered and said, [a]"'You shall love the LORD your God with all your heart, with all your soul, with all your strength, and with all your mind,'[1] and [b]'your neighbor as yourself.'"[2]
28And He said to him, "You have answered rightly; do this and [a]you will live."
29But he, wanting to [a]justify himself, said to Jesus, "And who is my neighbor?"
30Then Jesus answered and said: "A certain *man* went down from Jerusalem to Jericho, and fell among thieves, who stripped him of his clothing, wounded *him,* and departed, leaving *him* half dead.
31Now by chance a certain priest came down that road. And when he saw him, [a]he passed by on the other
side. 32Likewise a Levite, when he arrived at the place, came and looked, and passed by
on the other side. 33But a certain [a]Samaritan, as he journeyed, came where he was. And when he saw him, he had [b]compassion.
34So he went to *him* and bandaged his wounds, pouring on oil and wine; and he set him on his own animal, brought him to an inn, and
took care of him. 35On the next day, when he departed,[1] he took out two [a]denarii, gave *them* to the innkeeper, and said to him, 'Take care of him; and whatever more you spend, when
I come again, I will repay you.' 36So which of these three do you think was neighbor to him who fell among the thieves?"

10:20 [a] Is. 4:3 [1] NU-Text and M-Text omit *rather.* **10:21** [a] Matt. 11:25–27 **10:22** [a] John 3:35; 5:27; 17:2 [b] [John 1:18; 6:44, 46] [1] M-Text reads *And turning to the disciples He said, "All . . . .* **10:23** [a] Matt. 13:16, 17 **10:24** [a] 1 Pet. 1:10, 11 **10:25** [a] Matt. 19:16–19; 22:35 **10:27** [a] Deut. 6:5 [b] Lev. 19:18 [1] Deuteronomy 6:5 [2] Leviticus 19:18 **10:28** [a] Ezek. 20:11, 13, 21 **10:29** [a] Luke 16:15 **10:31** [a] Ps. 38:11 **10:33** [a] John 4:9 [b] Luke 15:20 **10:35** [a] Matt. 20:2 [1] NU-Text omits *when he departed.*

UNEXPECTED COMPASSION

"But a certain Samaritan . . . had compassion."

LUKE 10:33

Getting past ethnic prejudices is hard in today's divided, angry society. In the first century it was just as difficult. In the Holy Land the sharpest ethnic division was between Jews and Samaritans. The latter believed they were legitimate descendants of Abraham, the survivors of the northern kingdom of Israel. First-century Jews didn't buy it. They regarded the Samaritans as half breeds at best, law-breakers at worst. You need to know this to appreciate fully Jesus' parable of the good Samaritan (vv. 30–37).

A Jewish scholar asked Jesus which neighbor he was to love as Scripture commanded (see Lev. 19:18). Jesus answered by telling the parable and—you guessed it—the man who proved to be the neighbor to the beaten man turned out to be a Samaritan. The Samaritan fulfilled the Law of Moses (and followed the example of another good Samaritan; see 2 Chr. 28:8–15).

If we follow the example of the Samaritan, ethnic rancor disappears. Living in peace with those who are different is the call of God. Choose a person who is different from you in your neighborhood or at work and be a source of peace for him or her today for the sake of the gospel.

37And he said, "He who showed mercy
on him."
Then Jesus said to him, [a]"Go and do likewise."

Mary and Martha Worship and Serve

38Now it happened as they went that He
entered a certain village; and a certain woman
named [a]Martha welcomed Him into her
house. 39And she had a sister called Mary, [a]who
also [b]sat at Jesus'[1] feet and heard His word.
40But Martha was distracted with much serving, and she approached Him and said, "Lord,
do You not care that my sister has left me to
serve alone? Therefore tell her to help me."
41And Jesus[1] answered and said to her,
"Martha, Martha, you are worried and troubled about many things. 42But [a]one thing
is needed, and Mary has chosen that good
part, which will not be taken away from her."

The Model Prayer

11 Now it came to pass, as He was praying
in a certain place, when He ceased, *that*
one of His disciples said to Him, "Lord, teach
us to pray, as John also taught his disciples."
2So He said to them, "When you pray, say:

[a]Our Father in heaven,[1]
Hallowed be Your name.
Your kingdom come.[2]
Your will be done
On earth as *it is* in heaven.
3 Give us day by day our daily bread.
4 And [a]forgive us our sins,
For we also forgive everyone who is
indebted to us.
And do not lead us into temptation,
But deliver us from the evil one."[1]

A Friend Comes at Midnight

5And He said to them, "Which of you shall
have a friend, and go to him at midnight and
say to him, 'Friend, lend me three loaves;
6for a friend of mine has come to me on his
journey, and I have nothing to set before
him'; 7and he will answer from within and
say, 'Do not trouble me; the door is now shut,
and my children are with me in bed; I cannot
rise and give to you'? 8I say to you, [a]though
he will not rise and give to him because he is
his friend, yet because of his persistence he
will rise and give him as many as he needs.

Keep Asking, Seeking, Knocking

9[a]"So I say to you, ask, and it will be given
to you; [b]seek, and you will find; knock, and
it will be opened to you. 10For everyone who
asks receives, and he who seeks finds, and to
him who knocks it will be opened. 11[a]If a son

10:37 [a] Prov. 14:21 **10:38** [a] John 11:1; 12:2, 3 **10:39** [a] [1 Cor. 7:32–40] [b] Acts 22:3 [1] NU-Text reads *the Lord's.* **10:41** [1] NU-Text reads *the Lord.* **10:42** [a] [Ps. 27:4] **11:2** [a] Matt. 6:9–13 [1] NU-Text omits *Our* and *in heaven.* [2] NU-Text omits the rest of this verse. **11:4** [a] [Eph. 4:32] [1] NU-Text omits *But deliver us from the evil one.* **11:8** [a] [Luke 18:1–5] **11:9** [a] [John 15:7] [b] Is. 55:6 **11:11** [a] Matt. 7:9

LET GO OF WORRY

"You are worried and troubled about many things."

LUKE 10:41

Only the evangelist Luke provided us with the endearing story of the two sisters Mary and Martha who hosted Jesus in their home. While Martha busied herself in the kitchen, Mary sat at Jesus' feet to hear His teaching. Exasperated, Martha complained that Mary wasn't helping her. Jesus replied, "Martha, Martha, you are worried and troubled about many things. But one thing is needed, and Mary has chosen that good part, which will not be taken away from her" (vv. 41–42).

My sympathies definitely lie with Martha; her complaint was legitimate. But the point Jesus made is of great importance and has obvious application. Do we not often become so caught up with the daily concerns of life that we miss the opportunities and big moments to hear from Jesus? Mary recognized that sitting at the Savior's feet was a rare opportunity. How can we expect to find peace when we neglect the things that are truly "needed"?

We, too, can sit at the feet of Jesus when we read the Gospels and hear His words. Or are we too busy? Take extra time today to seek God's peace by meditating on His Word.

asks for bread[1] from any father among you,
will he give him a stone? Or if *he asks* for a
fish, will he give him a serpent instead of a
fish? 12 Or if he asks for an egg, will he offer
him a scorpion? 13 If you then, being evil,
know how to give [a]good gifts to your children,
how much more will *your* heavenly Father
give the Holy Spirit to those who ask Him!"

A House Divided Cannot Stand

14 [a]And He was casting out a demon, and
it was mute. So it was, when the demon had
gone out, that the mute spoke; and the multitudes marveled. 15 But some of them said,
[a]"He casts out demons by Beelzebub,[1] the
ruler of the demons."

16 Others, testing *Him,* [a]sought from Him a
sign from heaven. 17 [a]But [b]He, knowing their
thoughts, said to them: "Every kingdom divided against itself is brought to desolation,
and a house *divided* against a house falls. 18 If
Satan also is divided against himself, how
will his kingdom stand? Because you say I
cast out demons by Beelzebub. 19 And if I cast
out demons by Beelzebub, by whom do your
sons cast *them* out? Therefore they will be
your judges. 20 But if I cast out demons [a]with
the finger of God, surely the kingdom of God
has come upon you. 21 [a]When a strong man,
fully armed, guards his own palace, his goods
are in peace. 22 But [a]when a stronger than
he comes upon him and overcomes him,
he takes from him all his armor in which he
trusted, and divides his spoils. 23 [a]He who is
not with Me is against Me, and he who does
not gather with Me scatters.

An Unclean Spirit Returns

24 [a]"When an unclean spirit goes out of a
man, he goes through dry places, seeking
rest; and finding none, he says, 'I will return
to my house from which I came.' 25 And when
he comes, he finds *it* swept and put in order.
26 Then he goes and takes with *him* seven
other spirits more wicked than himself, and
they enter and dwell there; and [a]the last *state*
of that man is worse than the first."

Keeping the Word

27 And it happened, as He spoke these
things, that a certain woman from the crowd
raised her voice and said to Him, [a]"Blessed
is the womb that bore You, and *the* breasts
which nursed You!"

28 But He said, [a]"More than that, blessed *are*
those who hear the word of God and keep it!"

Seeking a Sign

29 [a]And while the crowds were thickly gathered together, He began to say, "This is an evil
generation. It seeks a [b]sign, and no sign will
be given to it except the sign of Jonah the

11:11 [1] NU-Text omits the words from *bread* through *for* in the next sentence. **11:13** [a] James 1:17 **11:14** [a] Matt. 9:32–34; 12:22, 24 **11:15** [a] Matt. 9:34; 12:24 [1] NU-Text and M-Text read *Beelzebul.* **11:16** [a] Matt. 12:38; 16:1 **11:17** [a] Matt. 12:25–29 [b] John 2:25 **11:20** [a] Ex. 8:19 **11:21** [a] Mark 3:27 **11:22** [a] [Is. 53:12] **11:23** [a] Matt. 12:30 **11:24** [a] Matt. 12:43–45 **11:26** [a] [2 Pet. 2:20] **11:27** [a] Luke 1:28, 48 **11:28** [a] [Luke 8:21] **11:29** [a] Matt. 12:38–42 [b] 1 Cor. 1:22

PEACE NOTE

The woman was not wrong in honoring Jesus' mother, but His larger point is that happiness rests on people who hear the Word of God and take it to heart.

LUKE 11:28

prophet.[1] 30 For as [a]Jonah became a sign to
the Ninevites, so also the Son of Man will be
to this generation. 31 [a]The queen of the South
will rise up in the judgment with the men of
this generation and condemn them, for she
came from the ends of the earth to hear the
wisdom of Solomon; and indeed a [b]greater
than Solomon *is* here. 32 The men of Nineveh
will rise up in the judgment with this generation and condemn it, for [a]they repented at
the preaching of Jonah; and indeed a greater
than Jonah *is* here.

The Lamp of the Body

33 [a]"No one, when he has lit a lamp, puts *it*
in a secret place or under a [b]basket, but on
a lampstand, that those who come in may
see the light. 34 [a]The lamp of the body is the
eye. Therefore, when your eye is good, your
whole body also is full of light. But when *your*
eye is bad, your body also *is* full of darkness.
35 Therefore take heed that the light which is
in you is not darkness. 36 If then your whole
body *is* full of light, having no part dark, *the*
whole *body* will be full of light, as when the
bright shining of a lamp gives you light."

Woe to the Pharisees and Lawyers

37 And as He spoke, a certain Pharisee asked
Him to dine with him. So He went in and sat
down to eat. 38 [a]When the Pharisee saw *it*,
he marveled that He had not first washed
before dinner.

39 [a]Then the Lord said to him, "Now you
Pharisees make the outside of the cup and
dish clean, but [b]your inward part is full of
greed and wickedness. 40 Foolish ones! Did
not [a]He who made the outside make the
inside also? 41 [a]But rather give alms of such
things as you have; then indeed all things
are clean to you.

42 [a]"But woe to you Pharisees! For you tithe
mint and rue and all manner of herbs, and
[b]pass by justice and the [c]love of God. These
you ought to have done, without leaving the
others undone. 43 [a]Woe to you Pharisees! For
you love the best seats in the synagogues
and greetings in the marketplaces. 44 [a]Woe
to you, scribes and Pharisees, hypocrites![1]
[b]For you are like graves which are not seen,
and the men who walk over *them* are not
aware *of them*."

45 Then one of the lawyers answered and
said to Him, "Teacher, by saying these things
You reproach us also."

46 And He said, "Woe to you also, lawyers!
[a]For you load men with burdens hard to
bear, and you yourselves do not touch the
burdens with one of your fingers. 47 [a]Woe to
you! For you build the tombs of the prophets,
and your fathers killed them. 48 In fact, you
bear witness that you approve the deeds of
your fathers; for they indeed killed them,
and you build their tombs. 49 Therefore the
wisdom of God also said, [a]'I will send them
prophets and apostles, and *some* of them
they will kill and persecute,' 50 that the blood
of all the prophets which was shed from the
foundation of the world may be required of
this generation, 51 [a]from the blood of Abel
to [b]the blood of Zechariah who perished
between the altar and the temple. Yes, I say
to you, it shall be required of this generation.

52 [a]"Woe to you lawyers! For you have taken
away the key of knowledge. You did not enter
in yourselves, and those who were entering
in you hindered."

53 And as He said these things to them,[1]
the scribes and the Pharisees began to assail
Him vehemently, and to cross-examine Him
about many things, 54 lying in wait for Him,
and [a]seeking to catch Him in something He
might say, that they might accuse Him.[1]

Beware of Hypocrisy

12 In [a]the meantime, when an innumerable multitude of people had gathered
together, so that they trampled one another,
He began to say to His disciples first *of all*,

11:29 [1] NU-Text omits *the prophet.* **11:30** [a] Jon. 1:17; 2:10; 3:3–10 **11:31** [a] 1 Kin. 10:1–9 [b] [Rom. 9:5] **11:32** [a] Jon. 3:5 **11:33** [a] Mark 4:21 [b] Matt. 5:15 **11:34** [a] Matt. 6:22, 23 **11:38** [a] Mark 7:2, 3 **11:39** [a] Matt. 23:25 [b] Titus 1:15 **11:40** [a] Gen. 1:26, 27 **11:41** [a] [Luke 12:33; 16:9] **11:42** [a] Matt. 23:23 [b] [Mic. 6:7, 8] [c] John 5:42 **11:43** [a] Mark 12:38, 39 **11:44** [a] Matt. 23:27 [b] Ps. 5:9 [1] NU-Text omits *scribes and Pharisees, hypocrites.* **11:46** [a] Matt. 23:4 **11:47** [a] Matt. 23:29 **11:49** [a] Matt. 23:34 **11:51** [a] Gen. 4:8 [b] 2 Chr. 24:20, 21 **11:52** [a] Matt. 23:13 **11:53** [1] NU-Text reads *And when He left there.* **11:54** [a] Mark 12:13 [1] NU-Text omits *and seeking* and *that they might accuse Him.* **12:1** [a] Mark 8:15

[b]"Beware of the leaven of the Pharisees, which
is hypocrisy. 2 [a]For there is nothing covered
that will not be revealed, nor hidden that will
not be known. 3 Therefore whatever you have
spoken in the dark will be heard in the light,
and what you have spoken in the ear in inner
rooms will be proclaimed on the housetops.

Jesus Teaches the Fear of God

4 [a]"And I say to you, [b]My friends, do not be
afraid of those who kill the body, and after
that have no more that they can do. 5 But I
will show you whom you should fear: Fear
Him who, after He has killed, has power to
cast into hell; yes, I say to you, [a]fear Him!
6 "Are not five sparrows sold for two copper
coins?[1] And [a]not one of them is forgotten
before God. 7 But the very hairs of your head
are all numbered. Do not fear therefore; you
are of more value than many sparrows.

Confess Christ Before Men

8 [a]"Also I say to you, whoever confesses Me
[b]before men, him the Son of Man also will
confess before the angels of God. 9 But he
who [a]denies Me before men will be denied
before the angels of God.
10 "And [a]anyone who speaks a word against
the Son of Man, it will be forgiven him; but
to him who blasphemes against the Holy
Spirit, it will not be forgiven.
11 [a]"Now when they bring you to the synagogues and magistrates and authorities,
do not worry about how or what you should
answer, or what you should say. 12 For the Holy
Spirit will [a]teach you in that very hour what
you ought to say."

The Parable of the Rich Fool

13 Then one from the crowd said to Him,
"Teacher, tell my brother to divide the inheritance with me."
14 But He said to him, [a]"Man, who made
Me a judge or an arbitrator over you?" 15 And
He said to them, [a]"Take heed and beware of
covetousness,[1] for one's life does not consist
in the abundance of the things he possesses."
16 Then He spoke a parable to them, saying:
"The ground of a certain rich man yielded
plentifully. 17 And he thought within himself,
saying, 'What shall I do, since I have no room
to store my crops?' 18 So he said, 'I will do this:
I will pull down my barns and build greater,
and there I will store all my crops and my
goods. 19 And I will say to my soul, [a]"Soul, you
have many goods laid up for many years;
take your ease; [b]eat, drink, *and* be merry." '
20 But God said to him, 'Fool! This night [a]your
soul will be required of you; [b]then whose will
those things be which you have provided?'
21 "So *is* he who lays up treasure for himself,
[a]and is not rich toward God."

12:1 [b] Matt. 16:12 **12:2** [a] Matt. 10:26; [1 Cor. 4:5] **12:4** [a] Is. 51:7, 8, 12, 13 [b] [John 15:13–15] **12:5** [a] Ps. 119:120 **12:6** [a] Matt. 6:26 [1] Greek *assarion,* a coin of very small value **12:8** [a] Matt. 10:32 [b] Ps. 119:46 **12:9** [a] Matt. 10:33 **12:10** [a] [Matt. 12:31, 32] **12:11** [a] Mark 13:11 **12:12** [a] [John 14:26] **12:14** [a] [John 18:36] **12:15** [a] [1 Tim. 6:6–10] [1] NU-Text reads *all covetousness.* **12:19** [a] Eccl. 11:9 [b] [Eccl. 2:24; 3:13; 5:18; 8:15] **12:20** [a] Ps. 52:7 [b] Ps. 39:6 **12:21** [a] [James 2:5; 5:1–5]

FROM FEAR TO PEACE

"I say to you, My friends, do not be afraid of those who kill the body."

LUKE 12:4

People in the time of Jesus also had much to be anxious about. They worried about the essentials of life—food, clothing, shelter. And they often suffered injustice and oppression. Indeed, physical brutality and death were real threats. In response to those frightening realities, Jesus encouraged His disciples, "I say to you, My friends, do not be afraid of those who kill the body, and after that have no more that they can do" (v. 4). Jesus reminded them that it was far more important to fear (respect) Him who had power over life and death.

This is something to remember when we face pressures at work or school. Peer pressure is very real, but so are the negative consequences. We can stand up to bad influences and evil counselors when we remember the One who is Master of this life and the next. Take a moment with pen and paper to make two lists: one of the circumstances that drain peace from your life and one of the ways that Jesus answers those circumstances. Carry it with you, and praise Christ for being the Prince of Peace in your daily circumstances.

PROSPERITY IN PEACE

"[Be] rich toward God."

LUKE 12:21

In a world of poverty and want, I can understand why the rich man in Jesus' parable was so relieved and pleased that his crops were plentiful. What farmer would feel otherwise? To have full barns after harvest is the farmer's dream. But the man's prosperity blinded him to the reality of eternity. Yes, he had such a large harvest that he may have had to build bigger barns and so could enjoy enough food and wealth for many years, but what if eternity arrived that night?

To be sure, there is nothing wrong with working, building, saving, and providing for oneself and for one's family. The Bible commends it (see 1 Tim. 5:8; 2 Thess. 3:6–13). But in doing these things, don't lose sight of eternity. When we leave this life, the goods that we have stockpiled will not come with us. Rather, as Jesus taught His disciples, be "rich toward God" (Luke 12:21). Wealth tucked away in heaven's vaults will, in the long run, give us more peace than the wealth we accumulate in the vaults of earth. Today, seek out a way to share the peace of God with one person within your circle of friends.

Do Not Worry

22Then He said to His disciples, "Therefore
I say to you, [a]do not worry about your life,
what you will eat; nor about the body, what
you will put on. 23Life is more than food, and
the body *is more* than clothing. 24Consider
the ravens, for they neither sow nor reap,
which have neither storehouse nor barn; and
[a]God feeds them. Of how much more value
are you than the birds? 25And which of you
by worrying can add one cubit to his stature?
26If you then are not able to do *the* least, why
are you anxious for the rest? 27Consider the
lilies, how they grow: they neither toil nor
spin; and yet I say to you, even [a]Solomon
in all his glory was not arrayed like one of
these. 28If then God so clothes the grass,
which today is in the field and tomorrow is
thrown into the oven, how much more *will
He clothe* you, O *you* of [a]little faith?
29"And do not seek what you should eat or
what you should drink, nor have an anxious
mind. 30For all these things the nations of
the world seek after, and your Father [a]knows
that you need these things. 31[a]But seek the
kingdom of God, and all these things[1] shall
be added to you.
32"Do not fear, little flock, for [a]it is your
Father's good pleasure to give you the kingdom. 33[a]Sell what you have and give [b]alms;
[c]provide yourselves money bags which do
not grow old, a treasure in the heavens that
does not fail, where no thief approaches nor
moth destroys. 34For where your treasure is,
there your heart will be also.

The Faithful Servant and the Evil Servant

35[a]"Let your waist be girded and [b]*your*
lamps burning; 36and you yourselves be
like men who wait for their master, when
he will return from the wedding, that when
he comes and knocks they may open to him
immediately. 37[a]Blessed *are* those servants
whom the master, when he comes, will find
watching. Assuredly, I say to you that he will
gird himself and have them sit down *to eat,*
and will come and serve them. 38And if he
should come in the second watch, or come
in the third watch, and find *them* so, blessed
are those servants. 39[a]But know this, that if
the master of the house had known what
hour the thief would come, he would have
watched and[1] not allowed his house to be
broken into. 40[a]Therefore you also be ready,
for the Son of Man is coming at an hour you
do not expect."
41Then Peter said to Him, "Lord, do You
speak this parable *only* to us, or to all *people?*"
42And the Lord said, [a]"Who then is that
faithful and wise steward, whom *his* master
will make ruler over his household, to give

12:22 [a] Matt. 6:25–33 **12:24** [a] Job 38:41 **12:27** [a] 1 Kin. 10:4–7 **12:28** [a] Matt. 6:30; 8:26; 14:31; 16:8 **12:30** [a] Matt. 6:31, 32 **12:31** [a] Matt. 6:33 [1] NU-Text reads *His kingdom, and these things.* **12:32** [a] [Matt. 11:25, 26] **12:33** [a] Matt. 19:21 [b] Luke 11:41 [c] Matt. 6:20 **12:35** [a] [1 Pet. 1:13] [b] [Matt. 25:1–13] **12:37** [a] Matt. 24:46 **12:39** [a] Rev. 3:3; 16:15 [1] NU-Text reads *he would not have allowed.* **12:40** [a] Mark 13:33 **12:42** [a] Matt. 24:45, 46; 25:21

them their portion of food in due season? 43 Blessed *is* that servant whom his master will find so doing when he comes. 44 [a]Truly, I say to you that he will make him ruler over all that he has. 45 [a]But if that servant says in his heart, 'My master is delaying his coming,' and begins to beat the male and female servants, and to eat and drink and be drunk, 46 the master of that servant will come on a [a]day when he is not looking for *him,* and at an hour when he is not aware, and will cut him in two and appoint *him* his portion with the unbelievers. 47 And [a]that servant who [b]knew his master's will, and did not prepare *himself* or do according to his will, shall be beaten with many *stripes.* 48 [a]But he who did not know, yet committed things deserving of stripes, shall be beaten with few. For everyone to whom much is given, from him much will be required; and to whom much has been committed, of him they will ask the more.

Christ Brings Division

49 [a]"I came to send fire on the earth, and how I wish it were already kindled! 50 But [a]I have a baptism to be baptized with, and how distressed I am till it is [b]accomplished! 51 [a]Do *you* suppose that I came to give peace on earth? I tell you, not at all, [b]but rather division. 52 [a]For from now on five in one house will be divided: three against two, and two against three. 53 [a]Father will be divided against son and son against father, mother against daughter and daughter against mother, mother-in-law against her daughter-in-law and daughter-in-law against her mother-in-law."

Discern the Time

54 Then He also said to the multitudes, [a]"Whenever you see a cloud rising out of the west, immediately you say, 'A shower is coming'; and so it is. 55 And when you see the [a]south wind blow, you say, 'There will be hot weather'; and there is. 56 Hypocrites! You can discern the face of the sky and of the earth, but how *is it* you do not discern [a]this time?

Make Peace with Your Adversary

57 "Yes, and why, even of yourselves, do you not judge what is right? 58 [a]When you go with your adversary to the magistrate, make every effort [b]along the way to settle with him, lest he drag you to the judge, the judge deliver you to the officer, and the officer throw you into prison. 59 I tell you, you shall not depart from there till you have paid the very last mite."

Repent or Perish

13 There were present at that season some who told Him about the Galileans whose blood Pilate had mingled with their sacrifices. 2 And Jesus answered and said to them, "Do you suppose that these Galileans were worse sinners than all *other* Galileans, because they suffered such things? 3 I tell you, no; but unless you repent you will all likewise perish. 4 Or those eighteen on whom the tower in Siloam fell and killed them, do you think that they were worse sinners than all *other* men who dwelt in Jerusalem? 5 I tell you, no; but unless you repent you will all likewise perish."

The Parable of the Barren Fig Tree

6 He also spoke this parable: [a]"A certain *man* had a fig tree planted in his vineyard, and he came seeking fruit on it and found none. 7 Then he said to the keeper of his vineyard, 'Look, for three years I have come seeking fruit on this fig tree and find none. Cut it down; why does it use up the ground?' 8 But he answered and said to him, 'Sir, let it alone this year also, until I dig around it and fertilize *it.* 9 And if it bears fruit, *well.* But if not, after that[1] you can [a]cut it down.' "

A Spirit of Infirmity

10 Now He was teaching in one of the synagogues on the Sabbath. 11 And behold, there was a woman who had a spirit of infirmity eighteen years, and was bent over and could in no way raise *herself* up. 12 But when Jesus saw her, He called *her* to *Him* and said to her, "Woman, you are loosed from your [a]infirmity." 13 [a]And He laid *His* hands on her, and immediately she was made straight, and glorified God.

14 But the ruler of the synagogue answered with indignation, because Jesus had [a]healed on the Sabbath; and he said to the crowd, [b]"There are six days on which men ought to work; therefore come and be healed on them, and [c]not on the Sabbath day."

15 The Lord then answered him and said, "Hypocrite![1] [a]Does not each one of you on the Sabbath loose his ox or donkey from the stall, and lead *it* away to water it? 16 So ought not

12:44 [a] Matt. 24:47; 25:21 **12:45** [a] 2 Pet. 3:3, 4 **12:46** [a] 1 Thess. 5:3 **12:47** [a] Deut. 25:2 [b] [James 4:17] **12:48** [a] [Lev. 5:17] **12:49** [a] Luke 12:51 **12:50** [a] Mark 10:38 [b] John 12:27; 19:30 **12:51** [a] Matt. 10:34–36 [b] John 7:43; 9:16; 10:19 **12:52** [a] Mark 13:12 **12:53** [a] Matt. 10:21, 36 **12:54** [a] Matt. 16:2, 3 **12:55** [a] Job 37:17 **12:56** [a] Luke 19:41–44 **12:58** [a] Prov. 25:8 [b] [Is. 55:6] **13:6** [a] Matt. 21:19 **13:9** [a] [John 15:2] [1] NU-Text reads *And if it bears fruit after that, well. But if not, you can cut it down.* **13:12** [a] Luke 7:21; 8:2 **13:13** [a] Acts 9:17 **13:14** [a] [Luke 6:6–11; 14:1–6] [b] Ex. 20:9; 23:12 [c] Mark 3:2 **13:15** [a] Luke 14:5 [1] NU-Text and M-Text read *Hypocrites.*

this woman, [a]being a daughter of Abraham,
whom Satan has bound—think of it—for
eighteen years, be loosed from this bond
on the Sabbath?" 17And when He said these
things, all His adversaries were put to shame;
and all the multitude rejoiced for all the glorious things that were [a]done by Him.

The Parable of the Mustard Seed

18[a]Then He said, "What is the kingdom of
God like? And to what shall I compare it? 19It
is like a mustard seed, which a man took and
put in his garden; and it grew and became
a large[1] tree, and the birds of the air nested
in its branches."

The Parable of the Leaven

20And again He said, "To what shall I liken
the kingdom of God? 21It is like leaven, which
a woman took and hid in three [a]measures[1]
of meal till it was all leavened."

The Narrow Way

22[a]And He went through the cities and
villages, teaching, and journeying toward
Jerusalem. 23Then one said to Him, "Lord,
are there [a]few who are saved?"

And He said to them, 24[a]"Strive to enter
through the narrow gate, for [b]many, I say to
you, will seek to enter and will not be able.
25[a]When once the Master of the house has
risen up and [b]shut the door, and you begin to
stand outside and knock at the door, saying,
[c]'Lord, Lord, open for us,' and He will answer
and say to you, [d]'I do not know you, where you
are from,' 26then you will begin to say, 'We ate
and drank in Your presence, and You taught
in our streets.' 27[a]But He will say, 'I tell you I
do not know you, where you are from. [b]Depart
from Me, all you workers of iniquity.' 28[a]There
will be weeping and gnashing of teeth, [b]when
you see Abraham and Isaac and Jacob and
all the prophets in the kingdom of God, and
yourselves thrust out. 29They will come from
the east and the west, from the north and the
south, and sit down in the kingdom of God.
30[a]And indeed there are last who will be first,
and there are first who will be last."

31On that very day[1] some Pharisees came,
saying to Him, "Get out and depart from here,
for Herod wants to kill You."

32And He said to them, "Go, tell that fox,
'Behold, I cast out demons and perform cures
today and tomorrow, and the third *day* [a]I
shall be perfected.' 33Nevertheless I must
journey today, tomorrow, and the *day* following; for it cannot be that a prophet should
perish outside of Jerusalem.

Jesus Laments over Jerusalem

34[a]"O Jerusalem, Jerusalem, the one who
kills the prophets and stones those who are

13:16 [a] Luke 19:9 **13:17** [a] Mark 5:19, 20 **13:18** [a] Mark 4:30–32 **13:19** [1] NU-Text omits *large.* **13:21** [a] Matt. 13:33 [1] Greek *sata,* approximately two pecks in all **13:22** [a] Mark 6:6 **13:23** [a] [Matt. 7:14; 20:16] **13:24** [a] [Matt. 7:13] [b] [John 7:34; 8:21; 13:33] **13:25** [a] Is. 55:6 [b] Matt. 25:10 [c] Luke 6:46 [d] Matt. 7:23; 25:12 **13:27** [a] [Matt. 7:23; 25:41] [b] Ps. 6:8 **13:28** [a] Matt. 8:12; 13:42; 24:51 [b] Matt. 8:11 **13:30** [a] [Matt. 19:30; 20:16] **13:31** [1] NU-Text reads *In that very hour.* **13:32** [a] [Heb. 2:10; 5:9; 7:28] **13:34** [a] Matt. 23:37–39

WHEN CHRIST BRINGS YOU HOME

"Ought not this woman . . . be loosed from this bond on the Sabbath?"

LUKE 13:16

The story of Jesus' healing the woman with a crooked spine (possibly a case of scoliosis) is found only in Luke 13 and may reflect the evangelist's special interest in medicine. The woman was described as "bent over" and unable to "raise herself up" (v. 11). Jesus said to her, "Woman, you are loosed from your infirmity" (v. 12). He laid hands on her and healed her.

Because it was the Sabbath, someone objected, arguing that she should have been healed on another day. I love how Jesus replied, "Ought not this woman, being a daughter of Abraham, whom Satan has bound—think of it—for eighteen years, be loosed from this bond on the Sabbath?" (v. 16). In calling this woman a "daughter of Abraham," Jesus made it clear that she was family! Think what those words meant to her! Her life would suddenly, finally be one of *shalom.*

How do you feel knowing that Jesus calls you "family"? Does it bring you peace? Rest in the truth of God today that you are part of His family, and the hallmark of that family is peace.

sent to her! How often I wanted to gather your
children together, as a hen *gathers* her brood
under *her* wings, but you were not willing!
35See! [a]Your house is left to you desolate; and
assuredly,[1] I say to you, you shall not see Me
until *the time* comes when you say, [b]'Blessed
is He who comes in the name of the LORD!' "[2]

A Man with Dropsy Healed on the Sabbath

14 Now it happened, as He went into the
house of one of the rulers of the Pharisees to eat bread on the Sabbath, that they
watched Him closely. 2And behold, there was
a certain man before Him who had dropsy.
3And Jesus, answering, spoke to the lawyers
and Pharisees, saying, [a]"Is it lawful to heal
on the Sabbath?"[1]

4But they kept silent. And He took *him*
and healed him, and let him go. 5Then He
answered them, saying, [a]"Which of you, having a donkey[1] or an ox that has fallen into a
pit, will not immediately pull him out on the
Sabbath day?" 6And they could not answer
Him regarding these things.

Take the Lowly Place

7So He told a parable to those who were
invited, when He noted how they chose the
best places, saying to them: 8"When you are
invited by anyone to a wedding feast, do not
sit down in the best place, lest one more
honorable than you be invited by him; 9and
he who invited you and him come and say to
you, 'Give place to this man,' and then you
begin with shame to take the lowest place.
10[a]But when you are invited, go and sit down
in the lowest place, so that when he who invited you comes he may say to you, 'Friend,
go up higher.' Then you will have glory in
the presence of those who sit at the table
with you. 11[a]For whoever exalts himself will
be humbled, and he who humbles himself
will be exalted."

12Then He also said to him who invited
Him, "When you give a dinner or a supper,
do not ask your friends, your brothers, your
relatives, nor rich neighbors, lest they also
invite you back, and you be repaid. 13But
when you give a feast, invite [a]*the* poor, *the*
maimed, *the* lame, *the* blind. 14And you will
be [a]blessed, because they cannot repay you;
for you shall be repaid at the resurrection
of the just."

The Parable of the Great Supper

15Now when one of those who sat at the
table with Him heard these things, he said
to Him, [a]"Blessed *is* he who shall eat bread[1]
in the kingdom of God!"
16[a]Then He said to him, "A certain man
gave a great supper and invited many, 17and
[a]sent his servant at supper time to say to
those who were invited, 'Come, for all things
are now ready.' 18But they all with one *accord*
began to make excuses. The first said to him,

13:35 [a] Lev. 26:31, 32 [b] Ps. 118:26; Matt. 21:9 [1] NU-Text and M-Text omit *assuredly.* [2] Psalm 118:26 **14:3** [a] Matt. 12:10 [1] NU-Text adds *or not.* **14:5** [a] [Ex. 23:5] [1] NU-Text and M-Text read *son.* **14:10** [a] Prov. 25:6, 7 **14:11** [a] Matt. 23:12 **14:13** [a] Neh. 8:10, 12 **14:14** [a] [Matt. 25:34–40] **14:15** [a] Rev. 19:9 [1] M-Text reads *dinner.* **14:16** [a] Matt. 22:2–14 **14:17** [a] Prov. 9:2, 5

JUST BE KIND

"You shall be repaid at the resurrection of the just."

LUKE 14:14

On one occasion, Jesus observed what is all too common: people choosing places of honor and climbing the social ladder. *Show some humility*, Jesus taught. "When you give a feast, invite the poor, the maimed, the lame, the blind. And you will be blessed" (vv. 13–14). The hope of *quid pro quo* ("something for something") lies at the heart of social climbing: *What can I get out of this? I'll show courtesy and generosity to the wealthy and influential because this will benefit me down the road.*

But Jesus recommended a different philosophy: *invite those who can't repay you.* Instead of getting anything back in this life, "you shall be repaid at the resurrection of the just" (v. 14). If there is repayment, let it come from God. After all, "it is more blessed to give than to receive" (Acts 20:35). Showing kindness because it is the God-thing to do is a real peace-builder. Is there someone today in need of your presence and the love of God in and through you?

'I have bought a piece of ground, and I must
go and see it. I ask you to have me excused.'
19And another said, 'I have bought five yoke
of oxen, and I am going to test them. I ask
you to have me excused.' 20Still another said,
'I have married a wife, and therefore I cannot
come.' 21So that servant came and reported
these things to his master. Then the master
of the house, being angry, said to his servant,
'Go out quickly into the streets and lanes of
the city, and bring in here *the* poor and *the*
maimed and *the* lame and *the* blind.' 22And
the servant said, 'Master, it is done as you
commanded, and still there is room.' 23Then
the master said to the servant, 'Go out into the
highways and hedges, and compel *them* to
come in, that my house may be filled. 24For I
say to you [a]that none of those men who were
invited shall taste my supper.' "

Leaving All to Follow Christ

25Now great multitudes went with Him.
And He turned and said to them, 26[a]"If anyone comes to Me [b]and does not hate his father and mother, wife and children, brothers
and sisters, [c]yes, and his own life also, he
cannot be My disciple. 27And [a]whoever does
not bear his cross and come after Me cannot
be My disciple. 28For [a]which of you, intending
to build a tower, does not sit down first and
count the cost, whether he has *enough* to
finish *it*— 29lest, after he has laid the foundation, and is not able to finish, all who see
it begin to mock him, 30saying, 'This man
began to build and was not able to finish'?
31Or what king, going to make war against
another king, does not sit down first and consider whether he is able with ten thousand
to meet him who comes against him with
twenty thousand? 32Or else, while the other
is still a great way off, he sends a delegation
and asks conditions of peace. 33So likewise,
whoever of you [a]does not forsake all that he
has cannot be My disciple.

Tasteless Salt Is Worthless

34[a]"Salt *is* good; but if the salt has lost its
flavor, how shall it be seasoned? 35It is neither fit for the land nor for the dunghill, *but*
men throw it out. He who has ears to hear,
let him hear!"

The Parable of the Lost Sheep

15 Then [a]all the tax collectors and the
sinners drew near to Him to hear Him.
2And the Pharisees and scribes complained,
saying, "This Man receives sinners [a]and eats
with them." 3So He spoke this parable to
them, saying:
4[a]"What man of you, having a hundred
sheep, if he loses one of them, does not leave
the ninety-nine in the wilderness, and go after the one which is lost until he finds it? 5And
when he has found *it,* he lays *it* on his shoulders, rejoicing. 6And when he comes home,
he calls together *his* friends and neighbors,

14:24 [a] [Acts 13:46] **14:26** [a] Deut. 13:6; 33:9 [b] Rom. 9:13 [c] Rev. 12:11 **14:27** [a] Luke 9:23 **14:28** [a] Prov. 24:27 **14:33** [a] Matt. 19:27 **14:34** [a] [Mark 9:50] **15:1** [a] [Matt. 9:10–13] **15:2** [a] Gal. 2:12 **15:4** [a] Matt. 18:12–14

JOIN THE PARTY

"Go out into the highways and hedges, and compel them to come in."

LUKE 14:23

Did Jesus create some awkward moments after His comments about showing humility (vv. 7–11) and inviting the poor to dinner instead of the wealthy? I suspect He did. One of the men at the banquet cried out, "Blessed is he who shall eat bread in the kingdom of God!" (v. 15). I like what he said. But if his intent was to move Jesus away from the theme of the poor and what constitutes doing God's will, he failed. After all, eating bread in the kingdom of God is very much a messianic theme (see Is. 25:6).

Jesus told His fellow banqueters a parable about the great banquet of the future when God will summon people to His table. The wealthy ignored the divine invitation—they were too preoccupied with their possessions. But the poor and hungry gladly accepted. The point is that wealth is no certain sign of blessing, and poverty is no certain sign of judgment. God invites us—rich and poor, healthy and sick—to enter His kingdom and find true fulfillment.

Perhaps you are missing the peace of God because you are missing time with God's people. Get out of your rut and get some fellowship!

saying to them, [a]'Rejoice with me, for I have
found my sheep [b]which was lost!' 7 I say to
you that likewise there will be more joy in
heaven over one sinner who repents [a]than
over ninety-nine just persons who [b]need no
repentance.

The Parable of the Lost Coin

8 "Or what woman, having ten silver coins,[1]
if she loses one coin, does not light a lamp,
sweep the house, and search carefully until
she finds *it?* 9 And when she has found *it,*
she calls *her* friends and neighbors together,
saying, 'Rejoice with me, for I have found the
piece which I lost!' 10 Likewise, I say to you,
there is joy in the presence of the angels of
God over one sinner who repents."

The Parable of the Lost Son

11 Then He said: "A certain man had two
sons. 12 And the younger of them said to *his*
father, 'Father, give me the portion of goods
that falls *to me.*' So he divided to them [a]*his*
livelihood. 13 And not many days after, the
younger son gathered all together, journeyed to a far country, and there wasted
his possessions with prodigal living. 14 But
when he had spent all, there arose a severe
famine in that land, and he began to be in
want. 15 Then he went and joined himself to
a citizen of that country, and he sent him
into his fields to feed swine. 16 And he would
gladly have filled his stomach with the pods
that the swine ate, and no one gave him
anything.
17 "But when he came to himself, he said,
'How many of my father's hired servants have
bread enough and to spare, and I perish with
hunger! 18 I will arise and go to my father, and
will say to him, "Father, [a]I have sinned against
heaven and before you, 19 and I am no longer
worthy to be called your son. Make me like
one of your hired servants." '
20 "And he arose and came to his father. But
[a]when he was still a great way off, his father
saw him and had compassion, and ran and
fell on his neck and kissed him. 21 And the son
said to him, 'Father, I have sinned against
heaven [a]and in your sight, and am no longer
worthy to be called your son.'
22 "But the father said to his servants,
'Bring[1] out the best robe and put *it* on him,
and put a ring on his hand and sandals on *his*
feet. 23 And bring the fatted calf here and kill
it, and let us eat and be merry; 24 [a]for this my
son was dead and is alive again; he was lost
and is found.' And they began to be merry.
25 "Now his older son was in the field. And
as he came and drew near to the house, he
heard music and dancing. 26 So he called one
of the servants and asked what these things
meant. 27 And he said to him, 'Your brother
has come, and because he has received him
safe and sound, your father has killed the
fatted calf.'
28 "But he was angry and would not go in.

15:6 [a] [Rom. 12:15] [b] [1 Pet. 2:10, 25] **15:7** [a] [Luke 5:32] [b] [Mark 2:17] **15:8** [1] Greek *drachma,* a valuable coin often worn in a ten-piece garland by married women **15:12** [a] Mark 12:44 **15:18** [a] 2 Sam. 12:13; 24:10, 17 **15:20** [a] [Eph. 2:13, 17] **15:21** [a] Ps. 51:4 **15:22** [1] NU-Text reads *Quickly bring.* **15:24** [a] Luke 9:60; 15:32

CELEBRATE OTHERS' RESTORATION

"Son, you are always with me, and all that I have is yours."

LUKE 15:31

The parable of the prodigal son could be Jesus' best known. The older son, the one who obeyed his father and never let him down, is often overlooked. Somehow in the tears of joy over the prodigal's return we lose sight of the young man who was faithful and—understandably—resentful of the extraordinary grace extended to his brother.

I like the older son and I understand his annoyance that his father, family, and servants celebrated the wasteful, sinning son. How many of us have lost our joy because of an embarrassing relative? I encourage you to hear the words of the father: "Son, you are always with me, and all that I have is yours." Here, our heavenly Father is telling us that His generous grace extended to the wayward takes nothing from those who serve Him faithfully. He sees and honors all our service.

Be at peace over the wayward even as you pray for their restoration—and thank God for the peace that is always available to you.

Therefore his father came out and pleaded
with him. 29 So he answered and said to *his*
father, 'Lo, these many years I have been serving you; I never transgressed your commandment at any time; and yet you never gave me
a young goat, that I might make merry with
my friends. 30 But as soon as this son of yours
came, who has devoured your livelihood with
harlots, you killed the fatted calf for him.'
31 "And he said to him, 'Son, you are always
with me, and all that I have is yours. 32 It was
right that we should make merry and be glad,
[a]for your brother was dead and is alive again,
and was lost and is found.' "

The Parable of the Unjust Steward

16 He also said to His disciples: "There was
a certain rich man who had a steward,
and an accusation was brought to him that
this man was wasting his goods. 2 So he called
him and said to him, 'What is this I hear about
you? Give an [a]account of your stewardship,
for you can no longer be steward.'
3 "Then the steward said within himself,
'What shall I do? For my master is taking the
stewardship away from me. I cannot dig; I am
ashamed to beg. 4 I have resolved what to do,
that when I am put out of the stewardship,
they may receive me into their houses.'
5 "So he called every one of his master's
debtors to *him,* and said to the first, 'How
much do you owe my master?' 6 And he said,
'A hundred measures[1] of oil.' So he said to
him, 'Take your bill, and sit down quickly
and write fifty.' 7 Then he said to another,
'And how much do you owe?' So he said, 'A
hundred measures[1] of wheat.' And he said
to him, 'Take your bill, and write eighty.' 8 So
the master commended the unjust steward
because he had dealt shrewdly. For the sons
of this world are more shrewd in their generation than [a]the sons of light.
9 "And I say to you, [a]make friends for yourselves by unrighteous mammon, that when
you fail,[1] they may receive you into an everlasting home. 10 [a]He who *is* faithful in *what is*
least is faithful also in much; and he who is
unjust in *what is* least is unjust also in much.
11 Therefore if you have not been faithful in
the unrighteous mammon, who will commit
to your trust the true *riches?* 12 And if you have
not been faithful in what is another man's,
who will give you what is your [a]own?
13 [a]"No servant can serve two masters; for
either he will hate the one and love the other,
or else he will be loyal to the one and despise the other. You cannot serve God and
mammon."

The Law, the Prophets, and the Kingdom

14 Now the Pharisees, [a]who were lovers of
money, also heard all these things, and they

15:32 [a] Luke 15:24 **16:2** [a] [Rom. 14:12] **16:6** [1] Greek *batos,* eight or nine gallons each (Old Testament *bath*) **16:7** [1] Greek *koros,* ten or twelve bushels each (Old Testament *kor*) **16:8** [a] [Eph. 5:8] **16:9** [a] Dan. 4:27 [1] NU-Text reads *it fails.* **16:10** [a] Matt. 25:21 **16:12** [a] [1 Pet. 1:3, 4] **16:13** [a] Matt. 6:24 **16:14** [a] Matt. 23:14

THE FINAL REWARD

"The beggar died, and was carried by the angels to Abraham's bosom."

LUKE 16:22

In Israel in the time of Jesus it was widely assumed that health and prosperity were indicators of righteous standing before God. Indeed, many people today—above all, televangelists—believe poverty and ill health indicate a lack of God's blessing. Jesus pushed back against such thinking. We see His most jarring challenge to unfair assumptions in His parable of the rich man and Lazarus.

In the parable the rich man lives like a king (some interpreters wonder if Jesus had in mind Herod Antipas, ruler of Galilee). He feasts daily and wears costly, comfortable clothes. Outside his gate lies the poor man Lazarus, covered in sores, who eats garbage scraps. Yet when the men die, Lazarus is taken to heaven and the rich man is cast into hell. Jesus showed that our external circumstances are no sure indicator of our standing before God.

You may struggle with health or finances, but that does not indicate your spiritual health. Your standing with God is guaranteed by God's Word. If you have accepted Jesus as your personal Savior and Lord, you are His, and His peace is yours. Seek it today.

derided Him. 15And He said to them, "You are those who [a]justify yourselves [b]before men, but [c]God knows your hearts. For [d]what is highly esteemed among men is an abomination in the sight of God.

16[a]"The law and the prophets *were* until John. Since that time the kingdom of God has been preached, and everyone is pressing into it. 17[a]And it is easier for heaven and earth to pass away than for one tittle of the law to fail.

18[a]"Whoever divorces his wife and marries another commits adultery; and whoever marries her who is divorced from *her* husband commits adultery.

The Rich Man and Lazarus

19"There was a certain rich man who was clothed in purple and fine linen and fared sumptuously every day. 20But there was a certain beggar named Lazarus, full of sores, who was laid at his gate, 21desiring to be fed with the crumbs which fell[1] from the rich man's table. Moreover the dogs came and licked his sores. 22So it was that the beggar died, and was carried by the angels to [a]Abraham's bosom. The rich man also died and was buried. 23And being in torments in Hades, he lifted up his eyes and saw Abraham afar off, and Lazarus in his bosom.

24"Then he cried and said, 'Father Abraham, have mercy on me, and send Lazarus that he may dip the tip of his finger in water and [a]cool my tongue; for I [b]am tormented in this flame.' 25But Abraham said, 'Son, [a]remember that in your lifetime you received your good things, and likewise Lazarus evil things; but now he is comforted and you are tormented. 26And besides all this, between us and you there is a great gulf fixed, so that those who want to pass from here to you cannot, nor can those from there pass to us.'

27"Then he said, 'I beg you therefore, father, that you would send him to my father's house, 28for I have five brothers, that he may testify to them, lest they also come to this place of torment.' 29Abraham said to him, [a]'They have Moses and the prophets; let them hear them.' 30And he said, 'No, father Abraham; but if one goes to them from the dead, they will repent.' 31But he said to him, [a]'If they do not hear Moses and the prophets, [b]neither will they be persuaded though one rise from the dead.' "

Jesus Warns of Offenses

17 Then He said to the disciples, [a]"It is impossible that no offenses should come, but [b]woe *to him* through whom they do come! 2It would be better for him if a millstone were hung around his neck, and he were thrown into the sea, than that he should offend one of these little ones. 3Take heed to yourselves. [a]If your brother sins against you,[1] [b]rebuke him; and if he repents, forgive him. 4And if he sins against you seven times in a day, and seven times in a day returns to you,[1] saying, 'I repent,' you shall forgive him."

Faith and Duty

5And the apostles said to the Lord, "Increase our faith."

6[a]So the Lord said, "If you have faith as a mustard seed, you can say to this mulberry tree, 'Be pulled up by the roots and be planted in the sea,' and it would obey you. 7And which of you, having a servant plowing or tending sheep, will say to him when he has come in from the field, 'Come at once and sit down to eat'? 8But will he not rather say to him, 'Prepare something for my supper, and gird yourself [a]and serve me till I have eaten and drunk, and afterward you will eat and drink'? 9Does he thank that servant because he did the things that were commanded him? I think not.[1] 10So likewise you, when you have done all those things which you are commanded, say, 'We are [a]unprofitable servants. We have done what was our duty to do.' "

Ten Lepers Cleansed

11Now it happened [a]as He went to Jerusalem that He passed through the midst of Samaria and Galilee. 12Then as He entered a certain village, there met Him ten men who were lepers, [a]who stood afar off. 13And they lifted up *their* voices and said, "Jesus, Master, have mercy on us!"

14So when He saw *them,* He said to them, [a]"Go, show yourselves to the priests." And so it was that as they went, they were cleansed.

15And one of them, when he saw that he was healed, returned, and with a loud voice [a]glorified God, 16and fell down on *his* face at His feet, giving Him thanks. And he was a [a]Samaritan.

17So Jesus answered and said, "Were there not ten cleansed? But where *are* the nine?

16:15 [a] Luke 10:29 [b] [Matt. 6:2, 5, 16] [c] Ps. 7:9 [d] 1 Sam. 16:7 **16:16** [a] Matt. 3:1–12; 4:17; 11:12, 13 **16:17** [a] Is. 40:8; 51:6 **16:18** [a] 1 Cor. 7:10, 11 **16:21** [1] NU-Text reads *with what fell.* **16:22** [a] Matt. 8:11 **16:24** [a] Zech. 14:12 [b] [Mark 9:42–48] **16:25** [a] Luke 6:24 **16:29** [a] Acts 15:21; 17:11 **16:31** [a] [John 5:46] [b] John 12:10, 11 **17:1** [a] [1 Cor. 11:19] [b] [2 Thess. 1:6] **17:3** [a] [Matt. 18:15, 21] [b] [Prov. 17:10] [1] NU-Text omits *against you.* **17:4** [1] M-Text omits *to you.* **17:6** [a] [Mark 9:23; 11:23] **17:8** [a] [Luke 12:37] **17:9** [1] NU-Text ends verse with *commanded;* M-Text omits *him.* **17:10** [a] Rom. 3:12; 11:35 **17:11** [a] Luke 9:51, 52 **17:12** [a] Lev. 13:46 **17:14** [a] Matt. 8:4 **17:15** [a] Luke 5:25; 18:43 **17:16** [a] 2 Kin. 17:24

A GRATEFUL PEOPLE

"Were there not ten cleansed?"

LUKE 17:17

The evangelist Luke gathered stories about Jesus and His teaching that challenged assumptions about who is righteous before God. The story of the lepers' healing (found only in Luke's Gospel) is a good example. Keeping their distance, as lepers were required to do, they cried out to Jesus for mercy. Jesus did not touch them; He did not even approach them. He simply said, "Go, show yourselves to the priest" (v. 14), something people who'd had serious skin problems did when they thought they were well. As they went on their way, to their astonishment, they discovered that they had been healed! But only one of the ten—the Samaritan—returned to thank Jesus.

Grace and gratitude go hand in hand. In fact, the words *grace*, *gratitude*, and *thanks* are from the same root. Responding with thanks to acts of grace promotes spiritual growth that in turn nurtures peace. Thankless people are not happy people. If we want to be people of peace, may we always be thankful for the blessings that come our way.

18 Were there not any found who returned
to give glory to God except this foreigner?"
19 [a]And He said to him, "Arise, go your way.
Your faith has made you well."

The Coming of the Kingdom

20 Now when He was asked by the Pharisees
when the kingdom of God would come, He
answered them and said, "The kingdom of
God does not come with observation; 21 [a]nor
will they say, 'See here!' or 'See there!'[1] For
indeed, [b]the kingdom of God is within you."
22 Then He said to the disciples, [a]"The days
will come when you will desire to see one
of the days of the Son of Man, and you will
not see *it.* 23 [a]And they will say to you, 'Look
here!' or 'Look there!'[1] Do not go after *them*
or follow *them.* 24 [a]For as the lightning that
flashes out of one *part* under heaven shines
to the other *part* under heaven, so also the
Son of Man will be in His day. 25 [a]But first He
must suffer many things and be [b]rejected
by this generation. 26 [a]And as it [b]was in the
[c]days of [d]Noah, so it will be also in the days of
the Son of Man: 27 They ate, they drank, they
married wives, they were given in marriage,
until the [a]day that Noah entered the ark,
and the flood came and [b]destroyed them
all. 28 [a]Likewise as it was also in the days of
Lot: They ate, they drank, they bought, they
sold, they planted, they built; 29 but on [a]the
day that Lot went out of Sodom it rained fire
and brimstone from heaven and destroyed
them all. 30 Even so will it be in the day when
the Son of Man [a]is revealed.
31 "In that day, he [a]who is on the housetop,
and his goods *are* in the house, let him not
come down to take them away. And likewise
the one who is in the field, let him not turn
back. 32 [a]Remember Lot's wife. 33 [a]Whoever
seeks to save his life will lose it, and whoever
loses his life will preserve it. 34 [a]I tell you, in
that night there will be two *men* in one bed:

PEACE NOTE

Jesus' ministry was certainly spiritual, but He first gained fame as a miracle-worker who healed physical suffering as well.

LUKE 17:19

17:19 [a] Matt. 9:22 **17:21** [a] Luke 17:23 [b] [Rom. 14:17] [1] NU-Text reverses *here* and *there.* **17:22** [a] Matt. 9:15
17:23 [a] Matt. 24:23 [1] NU-Text reverses *here* and *there.* **17:24** [a] Matt. 24:27 **17:25** [a] Mark 8:31; 9:31; 10:33 [b] Luke 9:22
17:26 [a] Matt. 24:37–39 [b] [Gen. 6:5–7] [c] [Gen. 6:8–13] [d] 1 Pet. 3:20 **17:27** [a] Gen. 7:1–16 [b] Gen. 7:19–23 **17:28** [a] Gen. 19
17:29 [a] Gen. 19:16, 24, 29 **17:30** [a] [2 Thess. 1:7] **17:31** [a] Mark 13:15 **17:32** [a] Gen. 19:26 **17:33** [a] Matt. 10:39; 16:25
17:34 [a] [1 Thess. 4:17]

the one will be taken and the other will be
left. 35[a]Two *women* will be grinding together:
the one will be taken and the other left. 36Two
men will be in the field: the one will be taken
and the other left."[1]
37And they answered and said to Him,
[a]"Where, Lord?"
So He said to them, "Wherever the body is,
there the eagles will be gathered together."

The Parable of the Persistent Widow

18 Then He spoke a parable to them, that
men [a]always ought to pray and not lose
heart, 2saying: "There was in a certain city a
judge who did not fear God nor regard man.
3Now there was a widow in that city; and
she came to him, saying, 'Get justice for me
from my adversary.' 4And he would not for a
while; but afterward he said within himself,
'Though I do not fear God nor regard man,
5[a]yet because this widow troubles me I will
avenge her, lest by her continual coming she
weary me.' "
6Then the Lord said, "Hear what the unjust
judge said. 7And [a]shall God not avenge His
own elect who cry out day and night to Him,
though He bears long with them? 8I tell you
[a]that He will avenge them speedily. Nevertheless, when the Son of Man comes, will He
really find faith on the earth?"

The Parable of the Pharisee and the Tax Collector

9Also He spoke this parable to some [a]who
trusted in themselves that they were righteous, and despised others: 10"Two men went
up to the temple to pray, one a Pharisee
and the other a tax collector. 11The Pharisee
[a]stood and prayed thus with himself, [b]'God,
I thank You that I am not like other men—
extortioners, unjust, adulterers, or even
as this tax collector. 12I fast twice a week;
I give tithes of all that I possess.' 13And the
tax collector, standing afar off, would not
so much as raise *his* eyes to heaven, but
beat his breast, saying, 'God, be merciful
to me a sinner!' 14I tell you, this man went
down to his house justified *rather* than the
other; [a]for everyone who exalts himself will
be humbled, and he who humbles himself
will be exalted."

Jesus Blesses Little Children

15[a]Then they also brought infants to Him
that He might touch them; but when the
disciples saw *it,* they rebuked them. 16But
Jesus called them to *Him* and said, "Let the
little children come to Me, and do not forbid
them; for [a]of such is the kingdom of God.
17[a]Assuredly, I say to you, whoever does not
receive the kingdom of God as a little child
will by no means enter it."

17:35 [a] Matt. 24:40, 41 **17:36** [1] NU-Text and M-Text omit verse 36. **17:37** [a] Matt. 24:28 **18:1** [a] Luke 11:5–10 **18:5** [a] Luke 11:8 **18:7** [a] Rev. 6:10 **18:8** [a] Heb. 10:37 **18:9** [a] Luke 10:29; 16:15 **18:11** [a] Ps. 135:2 [b] Is. 1:15; 58:2 **18:14** [a] Luke 14:11 **18:15** [a] Mark 10:13–16 **18:16** [a] 1 Pet. 2:2 **18:17** [a] Mark 10:15

THE RIGHTEOUS JUDGE CARES FOR YOU

Men always ought to pray and not lose heart.

LUKE 18:1

The parable of the widow and the unjust judge is one of my favorites. I can just imagine an angry old lady shaking her umbrella at an indifferent judge who finally gives in and gives the woman what she demands. I can't help but chuckle. I wouldn't be surprised if the people who heard Jesus tell it also laughed.

The point Jesus made is a good one: if a callous, indifferent human judge finally gives justice to a persistent widow—a nobody in the ancient world—then we should be confident that God, the ultimate righteous Judge, will certainly give justice to His people, whom He loves. It's a great parable with a great message.

This parable builds faith and, in turn, peace. Being reminded that God is caring, in contrast to many humans who are not, encourages us to go to God, knowing that He will hear us and respond in our best interest. We need this reminder because, in times of discouragement, we are more likely to give ear to Satan's lie that God is indifferent about us. Here's a peace-giving thought: *God does care about us, and deeply.* How would your fully embracing this truth change your life and give you peace?

Jesus Counsels the Rich Young Ruler

18 [a]Now a certain ruler asked Him, saying, "Good Teacher, what shall I do to inherit eternal life?"

19 So Jesus said to him, "Why do you call Me good? No one *is* good but [a]One, *that is,* God. 20 You know the commandments: [a]'Do not commit adultery,' 'Do not murder,' 'Do not steal,' 'Do not bear false witness,' [b]'Honor your father and your mother.' "[1]

21 And he said, "All [a]these things I have kept from my youth."

22 So when Jesus heard these things, He said to him, "You still lack one thing. [a]Sell all that you have and distribute to the poor, and you will have treasure in heaven; and come, follow Me."

23 But when he heard this, he became very sorrowful, for he was very rich.

With God All Things Are Possible

24 And when Jesus saw that he became very sorrowful, He said, [a]"How hard it is for those who have riches to enter the kingdom of God! 25 For it is easier for a camel to go through the eye of a needle than for a rich man to enter the kingdom of God."

26 And those who heard it said, "Who then can be saved?"

27 But He said, [a]"The things which are impossible with men are possible with God."

28 [a]Then Peter said, "See, we have left all[1] and followed You."

29 So He said to them, "Assuredly, I say to you, [a]there is no one who has left house or parents or brothers or wife or children, for the sake of the kingdom of God, 30 [a]who shall not receive many times more in this present time, and in the age to come eternal life."

Jesus a Third Time Predicts His Death and Resurrection

31 [a]Then He took the twelve aside and said to them, "Behold, we are going up to Jerusalem, and all things [b]that are written by the prophets concerning the Son of Man will be accomplished. 32 For [a]He will be delivered to the Gentiles and will be mocked and insulted and spit upon. 33 They will scourge *Him* and kill Him. And the third day He will rise again."

34 [a]But they understood none of these things; this saying was hidden from them, and they did not know the things which were spoken.

A Blind Man Receives His Sight

35 [a]Then it happened, as He was coming near Jericho, that a certain blind man sat by the road begging. 36 And hearing a multitude passing by, he asked what it meant. 37 So they told him that Jesus of Nazareth was passing by. 38 And he cried out, saying, "Jesus, [a]Son of David, have mercy on me!"

39 Then those who went before warned him that he should be quiet; but he cried out all the more, "Son of David, have mercy on me!"

18:18 [a] Matt. 19:16–29 **18:19** [a] Ps. 86:5; 119:68 **18:20** [a] Ex. 20:12–16; Deut. 5:16–20 [b] Eph. 6:2; Col. 3:20 [1] Exodus 20:12–16; Deuteronomy 5:16–20 **18:21** [a] Phil. 3:6 **18:22** [a] Matt. 6:19, 20; 19:21 **18:24** [a] Mark 10:23 **18:27** [a] Jer. 32:17 **18:28** [a] Matt. 19:27 [1] NU-Text reads *our own.* **18:29** [a] Deut. 33:9 **18:30** [a] Job 42:10 **18:31** [a] Matt. 16:21; 17:22; 20:17 [b] Ps. 22 **18:32** [a] Acts 3:13 **18:34** [a] Luke 2:50; 9:45 **18:35** [a] Matt. 20:29–34 **18:38** [a] Matt. 9:27

OUR COMMON PLEA

God, be merciful to me a sinner!

LUKE 18:13

One of the most moving yet overlooked parables is that of the Pharisee and the tax collector. This parable contains both warning and assurance: warning against arrogant presumption ("God, I thank You that I am not like other men," v. 11) and assurance for the penitent ("God, be merciful to me a sinner!"; v. 13). The door to forgiveness stands wide open. Some may want to make entry difficult by adding various rituals and requirements, but according to Jesus, all that is required is repentance. The Pharisee bragged of his righteousness and faithfulness; the tax collector begged for God's mercy. The former lost sight of his sin and shortcomings while the latter was fully aware of his guilt and appealed to God's grace.

The teaching of this parable builds in me a sense of peace because it reminds me in such a simple way that God is gracious. "If we confess our sins, He is faithful and just to forgive us our sins and to cleanse us from all unrighteousness" (1 John 1:9). That is what the tax collector did, and he no doubt experienced peace as a result. We can do the same.

40So Jesus stood still and commanded him
to be brought to Him. And when he had come
near, He asked him, 41saying, "What do you
want Me to do for you?"
He said, "Lord, that I may receive my sight."
42Then Jesus said to him, "Receive your
sight; [a]your faith has made you well." 43And
immediately he received his sight, and followed Him, [a]glorifying God. And all the people, when they saw *it,* gave praise to God.

Jesus Comes to Zacchaeus' House

19 Then *Jesus* entered and passed through
[a]Jericho. 2Now behold, *there was* a man
named Zacchaeus who was a chief tax collector, and he was rich. 3And he sought to [a]see
who Jesus was, but could not because of the
crowd, for he was of short stature. 4So he ran
ahead and climbed up into a sycamore tree to
see Him, for He was going to pass that *way.*
5And when Jesus came to the place, He looked
up and saw him,[1] and said to him, "Zacchaeus, make haste and come down, for today I
must stay at your house." 6So he made haste
and came down, and received Him joyfully.
7But when they saw *it,* they all complained,
saying, [a]"He has gone to be a guest with a
man who is a sinner."
8Then Zacchaeus stood and said to the
Lord, "Look, Lord, I give half of my goods
to the [a]poor; and if I have taken anything
from anyone by [b]false accusation, [c]I restore
fourfold."
9And Jesus said to him, "Today salvation
has come to this house, because [a]he also is
[b]a son of Abraham; 10[a]for the Son of Man has
come to seek and to save that which was lost."

The Parable of the Minas

11Now as they heard these things, He spoke
another parable, because He was near Jerusalem and because [a]they thought the kingdom
of God would appear immediately. 12[a]There-
fore He said: "A certain nobleman went into
a far country to receive for himself a kingdom and to return. 13So he called ten of his
servants, delivered to them ten minas,[1] and
said to them, 'Do business till I come.' 14[a]But
his citizens hated him, and sent a delegation
after him, saying, 'We will not have this *man*
to reign over us.'
15"And so it was that when he returned,
having received the kingdom, he then commanded these servants, to whom he had
given the money, to be called to him, that
he might know how much every man had
gained by trading. 16Then came the first,
saying, 'Master, your mina has earned ten
minas.' 17And he said to him, [a]'Well *done,* good
servant; because you were [b]faithful in a very
little, have authority over ten cities.' 18And
the second came, saying, 'Master, your mina

18:42 [a] Luke 17:19 **18:43** [a] Luke 5:26 **19:1** [a] Josh. 6:26 **19:3** [a] John 12:21 **19:5** [1] NU-Text omits *and saw him.* **19:7** [a] Luke 5:30; 15:2 **19:8** [a] [Ps. 41:1] [b] Luke 3:14 [c] Ex. 22:1 **19:9** [a] [Gal. 3:7] [b] [Luke 13:16] **19:10** [a] Matt. 18:11 **19:11** [a] Acts 1:6 **19:12** [a] Matt. 25:14–30 **19:13** [1] The *mina* (Greek *mna,* Hebrew *minah*) was worth about three months' salary. **19:14** [a] [John 1:11] **19:17** [a] Matt. 25:21, 23 [b] Luke 16:10

WHEN JESUS VISITS A SINNER

"Today salvation has come to this house."

LUKE 19:9

Every child in Sunday school hears the story of Zacchaeus, the chief tax collector. Perhaps it is because he was short and found it necessary to climb a tree so he could glimpse Jesus, the famous Teacher. Jesus told Zacchaeus to come down, saying, "Today I must stay at your house" (v. 5). Zacchaeus was thrilled, but the crowd wasn't: "He has gone to be a guest with a man who is a sinner" (v. 7). The crowd assumed that because Zacchaeus was a loathed tax collector, he was probably dishonest.

The criticism leveled against Zacchaeus was prejudicial and assumed crimes the man may not have committed. He responded: "Lord, I give half of my goods to the poor; and if I have taken anything from anyone by false accusation, I restore fourfold" (v. 8). Zacchaeus was doing his best to follow Moses, and Jesus commended him for it.

We learn from this story how easy it is to judge someone and make assumptions. In doing this, we may rob worthy people of their peace. We also learn that anyone's repentance is welcome in God's sight—peace is available to all who are penitent.

has earned five minas.' 19Likewise he said to
him, 'You also be over five cities.'
20"Then another came, saying, 'Master,
here is your mina, which I have kept put
away in a handkerchief. 21[a]For I feared you,
because you are an austere man. You collect
what you did not deposit, and reap what you
did not sow.' 22And he said to him, [a]'Out of
your own mouth I will judge you, *you* wicked
servant. [b]You knew that I was an austere man,
collecting what I did not deposit and reaping
what I did not sow. 23Why then did you not
put my money in the bank, that at my coming
I might have collected it with interest?'
24"And he said to those who stood by, 'Take
the mina from him, and give *it* to him who
has ten minas.' 25(But they said to him, 'Master, he has ten minas.') 26'For I say to you,
[a]that to everyone who has will be given; and
from him who does not have, even what he
has will be taken away from him. 27But bring
here those enemies of mine, who did not
want me to reign over them, and slay *them*
before me.' "

The Triumphal Entry

28When He had said this, [a]He went on
ahead, going up to Jerusalem. 29[a]And it came
to pass, when He drew near to Bethphage[1] and
[b]Bethany, at the mountain called [c]Olivet, *that*
He sent two of His disciples, 30saying, "Go
into the village opposite *you,* where as you
enter you will find a colt tied, on which no one
has ever sat. Loose it and bring *it here.* 31And
if anyone asks you, 'Why are you loosing *it?*'
thus you shall say to him, 'Because the Lord
has need of it.' "
32So those who were sent went their way and
found *it* just [a]as He had said to them. 33But
as they were loosing the colt, the owners of it
said to them, "Why are you loosing the colt?"
34And they said, "The Lord has need of
him." 35Then they brought him to Jesus.
[a]And they threw their own clothes on the
colt, and they set Jesus on him. 36And as He
went, *many* spread their clothes on the road.
37Then, as He was now drawing near the
descent of the Mount of Olives, the whole
multitude of the disciples began to [a]rejoice
and praise God with a loud voice for all the
mighty works they had seen, 38saying:

[a]" 'Blessed *is* the King who comes in the
name of the LORD!'[1]
[b]Peace in heaven and glory in the
highest!"

39And some of the Pharisees called to Him
from the crowd, "Teacher, rebuke Your disciples."

19:21 [a] Matt. 25:24 19:22 [a] Job 15:6 [b] Matt. 25:26 19:26 [a] Luke 8:18 19:28 [a] Mark 10:32 19:29 [a] Matt. 21:1 [b] John 12:1 [c] Acts 1:12 [1] M-Text reads *Bethsphage.* 19:32 [a] Luke 22:13 19:35 [a] 2 Kin. 9:13 19:37 [a] Luke 13:17; 18:43 19:38 [a] Ps. 118:26 [b] [Eph. 2:14] [1] Psalm 118:26

SHOUTING FOR JOY

"Blessed is the King who comes in the name of the LORD!"
Peace in heaven and glory in the highest!

LUKE 19:38

With all the division, hatred, and strife on earth, have you wondered what heaven is like? When Jesus entered Jerusalem amidst shouts of joy and the acclamation, "Blessed is the King who comes in the name of LORD!" the people called for "peace in heaven." Does that mean there is no peace in heaven? And at the beginning of Luke's Gospel, the angels appeared to the startled shepherds and sang, "Glory to God in the highest, and on earth peace, goodwill toward men!" (2:14). Announcing peace "on earth" makes sense because peace is very much needed on earth. But "in heaven"?

Elsewhere in Luke Jesus said he saw Satan fall from heaven (10:18). The people praising Jesus knew, from Old Testament books like Daniel, that there is war in heaven. The battle between light and darkness is not limited to earth. Scripture assures us that God will prevail, that peace will become a reality in heaven and on earth, and that peace will come about through the work of His Son, Jesus Christ.

The peace that Christ offers is powerful. Can you join the joyful shouts of those who have received Jesus and His peace?

PEACE NOTE

In a heart-wrenching scene, Luke records Jesus' weeping over Jerusalem. Like Him we recognize the landscape of anxiety, despair, and depression. Pray for God's peace throughout the world.

LUKE 19:41

40But He answered and said to them, "I
tell you that if these should keep silent, [a]the
stones would immediately cry out."

Jesus Weeps over Jerusalem

41Now as He drew near, He saw the city and
[a]wept over it, 42saying, "If you had known,
even you, especially in this [a]your day, the
things *that* [b]*make* for your [c]peace! But now
they are hidden from your eyes. 43For days
will come upon you when your enemies will
[a]build an embankment around you, surround you and close you in on every side,
44[a]and level you, and your children within
you, to the ground; and [b]they will not leave
in you one stone upon another, [c]because you
did not know the time of your visitation."

Jesus Cleanses the Temple

45[a]Then He went into the temple and began
to drive out those who bought and sold in it,[1]
46saying to them, "It is written, [a]'My house
is[1] a house of prayer,'[2] but you have made it
a [b]'den of thieves.' "[3]

47And He [a]was teaching daily in the temple.
But [b]the chief priests, the scribes, and the

PEACE NOTE

What are these "things that make for . . . peace"? Repentance and faith. If Jerusalem had responded to the message of the kingdom, then the peace of God would have come upon the city.

LUKE 19:42

19:40 [a] Hab. 2:11 **19:41** [a] John 11:35 **19:42** [a] Heb. 3:13 [b] [Acts 10:36] [c] [Rom. 5:1] **19:43** [a] Jer. 6:3, 6 **19:44** [a] 1 Kin. 9:7, 8 [b] Matt. 24:2 [c] [1 Pet. 2:12] **19:45** [a] Mark 11:11, 15–17 [1] NU-Text reads *those who were selling.* **19:46** [a] Is. 56:7 [b] Jer. 7:11 [1] NU-Text reads *shall be.* [2] Isaiah 56:7 [3] Jeremiah 7:11 **19:47** [a] Luke 21:37; 22:53 [b] John 7:19; 8:37

IF YOU ONLY KNEW

"If you had known, even you, especially in this your day, the things that make for your peace! But now they are hidden from your eyes."

LUKE 19:42

Have you faced a crisis in your life and wondered what you could do to get or regain peace? You're not alone. In our fallen world marked by division and strife, the things that make for peace are hard to find. They are hidden from our eyes. Prime ministers and presidents can't seem to create peace. Lasting worldwide peace will not be found until the arrival of the Prince of Peace.

What makes Jesus' words here in verses 41–44 so sad is that He uttered them over the city of Jerusalem. Standing on the Mount of Olives and looking down on the Temple Mount, the heart and soul of the ancient city, Jesus wept. It was widely believed that the name *Jerusalem meant something like* "sacred peace." And yet there would be no peace for Jerusalem. Rejecting the peace that Jesus offered, the city would soon find itself surrounded by armies who would "not leave in [it] one stone upon another" (v. 44). Peace is found in Jesus. I invite you to embrace the peace that Jesus offered Jerusalem. Make it your own.

leaders of the people sought to destroy Him, 48and were unable to do anything; for all the people were very attentive to [a]hear Him.

Jesus' Authority Questioned

20 Now [a]it happened on one of those days, as He taught the people in the temple and preached the gospel, *that* the chief priests and the scribes, together with the elders, confronted *Him* 2and spoke to Him, saying, "Tell us, [a]by what authority are You doing these things? Or who is he who gave You this authority?"

3But He answered and said to them, "I also will ask you one thing, and answer Me: 4The [a]baptism of John—was it from heaven or from men?"

5And they reasoned among themselves, saying, "If we say, 'From heaven,' He will say, 'Why then[1] did you not believe him?' 6But if we say, 'From men,' all the people will stone us, [a]for they are persuaded that John was a prophet." 7So they answered that they did not know where *it was* from.

8And Jesus said to them, "Neither will I tell you by what authority I do these things."

The Parable of the Wicked Vinedressers

9Then He began to tell the people this parable: [a]"A certain man planted a vineyard, leased it to vinedressers, and went into a far country for a long time. 10Now at vintage-time he [a]sent a servant to the vinedressers, that they might give him some of the fruit of the vineyard. But the vinedressers beat him and sent *him* away empty-handed. 11Again he sent another servant; and they beat him also, treated *him* shamefully, and sent *him* away empty-handed. 12And again he sent a third; and they wounded him also and cast *him* out.

13"Then the owner of the vineyard said, 'What shall I do? I will send my beloved son. Probably they will respect *him* when they see him.' 14But when the vinedressers saw him, they reasoned among themselves, saying, 'This is the [a]heir. Come, [b]let us kill him, that the inheritance may be [c]ours.' 15So they cast him out of the vineyard and [a]killed *him*. Therefore what will the owner of the vineyard do to them? 16He will come and destroy those vinedressers and give the vineyard to [a]others."

And when they heard *it* they said, "Certainly not!"

17Then He looked at them and said, "What then is this that is written:

[a]'The stone which the builders rejected
Has become the chief cornerstone'?[1]

18Whoever falls on that stone will be [a]broken; but [b]on whomever it falls, it will grind him to powder."

19And the chief priests and the scribes that very hour sought to lay hands on Him, but they feared the people[1]—for they knew He had spoken this parable against them.

The Pharisees: Is It Lawful to Pay Taxes to Caesar?

20[a]So they watched *Him*, and sent spies who pretended to be righteous, that they might seize on His words, in order to deliver Him to the power and the authority of the governor.

21Then they asked Him, saying, [a]"Teacher, we know that You say and teach rightly, and You do not show personal favoritism, but teach the way of God in truth: 22Is it lawful for us to pay taxes to Caesar or not?"

23But He perceived their craftiness, and said to them, "Why do you test Me?[1] 24Show Me a denarius. Whose image and inscription does it have?"

They answered and said, "Caesar's."

25And He said to them, [a]"Render therefore to Caesar the things that are Caesar's, and to God the things that are God's."

26But they could not catch Him in His words in the presence of the people. And they marveled at His answer and kept silent.

The Sadducees: What About the Resurrection?

27[a]Then some of the Sadducees, [b]who deny that there is a resurrection, came to *Him* and asked Him, 28saying: "Teacher, Moses wrote to us *that* if a man's brother dies, having a wife, and he dies without children, his brother should take his wife and raise up offspring for his brother. 29Now there were seven brothers. And the first took a wife, and died without children. 30And the second[1] took her as wife, and he died childless. 31Then the third took her, and in like manner the seven also; and they left no children,[1] and died. 32Last of all the woman died also. 33Therefore, in the resurrection, whose wife does she become? For all seven had her as wife."

19:48 [a] Luke 21:38 **20:1** [a] Matt. 21:23–27 **20:2** [a] Acts 4:7; 7:27 **20:4** [a] John 1:26, 31 **20:5** [1] NU-Text and M-Text omit *then.* **20:6** [a] Luke 7:24–30 **20:9** [a] Mark 12:1–12 **20:10** [a] [1 Thess. 2:15] **20:14** [a] [Heb. 1:1–3] [b] Matt. 27:21–23 [c] John 11:47, 48 **20:15** [a] Luke 23:33 **20:16** [a] Rom. 11:1, 11 **20:17** [a] Ps. 118:22 [1] Psalm 118:22 **20:18** [a] Is. 8:14, 15 [b] [Dan. 2:34, 35, 44, 45] **20:19** [1] M-Text reads *but they were afraid.* **20:20** [a] Matt. 22:15 **20:21** [a] Mark 12:14 **20:23** [1] NU-Text omits *Why do you test Me?* **20:25** [a] [1 Pet. 2:13–17] **20:27** [a] Mark 12:18–27 [b] Acts 23:6, 8 **20:30** [1] NU-Text ends verse 30 here. **20:31** [1] NU-Text and M-Text read *the seven also left no children.*

34Jesus answered and said to them, "The
sons of this age marry and are given in marriage. 35But those who are [a]counted worthy
to attain that age, and the resurrection from
the dead, neither marry nor are given in
marriage; 36nor can they die anymore, for
[a]they are equal to the angels and are sons of
God, [b]being sons of the resurrection. 37But
even Moses showed in the *burning* bush *passage* that the dead are raised, when he called
the Lord [a]'the God of Abraham, the God of
Isaac, and the God of Jacob.'[1] 38For He is not
the God of the dead but of the living, for [a]all
live to Him."

39Then some of the scribes answered and
said, "Teacher, You have spoken well." 40But
after that they dared not question Him anymore.

Jesus: How Can David Call His Descendant "Lord"?

41And He said to them, [a]"How can they say
that the Christ is the Son of David? 42Now
David himself said in the Book of Psalms:

> [a]'The LORD said to my Lord,
> "Sit at My right hand,
> 43 Till I make Your enemies Your
> footstool." '[1]

44Therefore David calls Him 'Lord'; [a]how is
He then his Son?"

Beware of the Scribes

45[a]Then, in the hearing of all the people,
He said to His disciples, 46[a]"Beware of the
scribes, who desire to go around in long
robes, [b]love greetings in the marketplaces,
the best seats in the synagogues, and the best
places at feasts, 47[a]who devour widows' houses, and for a [b]pretense make long prayers.
These will receive greater condemnation."

The Widow's Two Mites

21 And He looked up [a]and saw the rich
putting their gifts into the treasury,
2and He saw also a certain [a]poor widow putting in two [b]mites. 3So He said, "Truly I say
to you [a]that this poor widow has put in more
than all; 4for all these out of their abundance
have put in offerings for God,[1] but she out
of her poverty put in [a]all the livelihood that
she had."

Jesus Predicts the Destruction of the Temple

5[a]Then, as some spoke of the temple, how
it was adorned with beautiful stones and
donations, He said, 6"These things which you
see—the days will come in which [a]not *one*
stone shall be left upon another that shall
not be thrown down."

The Signs of the Times and the End of the Age

7So they asked Him, saying, "Teacher, but
when will these things be? And what sign
will there be when these things are about to
take place?"

8And He said: [a]"Take heed that you not be
deceived. For many will come in My name,
saying, 'I am *He,*' and, 'The time has drawn
near.' Therefore[1] do not go after them. 9But
when you hear of [a]wars and commotions,
do not be terrified; for these things must
come to pass first, but the end *will not come*
immediately."

10[a]Then He said to them, "Nation will rise
against nation, and kingdom against kingdom. 11And there will be great [a]earthquakes in
various places, and famines and pestilences;
and there will be fearful sights and great
signs from heaven. 12[a]But before all these
things, they will lay their hands on you and
persecute *you,* delivering *you* up to the synagogues and [b]prisons. [c]You will be brought
before kings and rulers [d]for My name's sake.
13But [a]it will turn out for you as an occasion
for testimony. 14[a]Therefore settle *it* in your
hearts not to meditate beforehand on what
you will answer; 15for I will give you a mouth
and wisdom [a]which all your adversaries will
not be able to contradict or resist. 16[a]You will
be betrayed even by parents and brothers,
relatives and friends; and they will put [b]*some*
of you to death. 17And [a]you will be hated by
all for My name's sake. 18[a]But not a hair of
your head shall be lost. 19By your patience
possess your souls.

The Destruction of Jerusalem

20[a]"But when you see Jerusalem surrounded by armies, then know that its desolation is
near. 21Then let those who are in Judea flee
to the mountains, let those who are in the
midst of her depart, and let not those who
are in the country enter her. 22For these are

20:35 [a] *Phil. 3:11* *20:36* [a] *[1 John 3:2]* [b] Rom. 8:23 **20:37** [a] Ex. 3:1–6, 15 [1] Exodus 3:6, 15 **20:38** [a] [Rom. 6:10, 11; 14:8, 9] **20:41** [a] Matt. 22:41–46 **20:42** [a] Ps. 110:1 **20:43** [1] Psalm 110:1 **20:44** [a] Rom. 1:3; 9:4, 5 **20:45** [a] Matt. 23:1–7 **20:46** [a] Matt. 23:5 [b] Luke 11:43; 14:7 **20:47** [a] Matt. 23:14 [b] [Matt. 6:5, 6] **21:1** [a] Mark 12:41–44 **21:2** [a] [2 Cor. 6:10] [b] Mark 12:42 **21:3** [a] [2 Cor. 8:12] **21:4** [a] [2 Cor. 8:12] [1] NU-Text omits *for God.* **21:5** [a] Mark 13:1 **21:6** [a] Luke 19:41–44 **21:8** [a] Eph. 5:6 [1] NU-Text omits *Therefore.* **21:9** [a] Rev. 6:4 **21:10** [a] Matt. 24:7 **21:11** [a] Rev. 6:12 **21:12** [a] [Rev. 2:10] [b] Acts 4:3; 5:18; 12:4; 16:24 [c] Acts 25:23 [d] 1 Pet. 2:13 **21:13** [a] [Phil. 1:12–14, 28] **21:14** [a] Luke 12:11 **21:15** [a] Acts 6:10 **21:16** [a] Mic. 7:6 [b] Acts 7:59; 12:2 **21:17** [a] Matt. 10:22 **21:18** [a] Matt. 10:30 **21:20** [a] Mark 13:14

the days of vengeance, that [a]all things which
are written may be fulfilled. 23[a]But woe to
those who are pregnant and to those who are
nursing babies in those days! For there will
be great distress in the land and wrath upon
this people. 24And they will fall by the edge
of the sword, and be led away captive into
all nations. And Jerusalem will be trampled
by Gentiles [a]until the times of the Gentiles
are fulfilled.

The Coming of the Son of Man

25[a]"And there will be signs in the sun, in
the moon, and in the stars; and on the earth
distress of nations, with perplexity, the sea
and the waves roaring; 26men's hearts failing
them from fear and the expectation of those
things which are coming on the earth, [a]for
the powers of the heavens will be shaken.
27Then they will see the Son of Man [a]coming
in a cloud with power and great glory. 28Now
when these things begin to happen, look
up and lift up your heads, because [a]your
redemption draws near."

The Parable of the Fig Tree

29[a]Then He spoke to them a parable: "Look
at the fig tree, and all the trees. 30When they
are already budding, you see and know for
yourselves that summer is now near. 31So you
also, when you see these things happening,
know that the kingdom of God is near. 32As-
suredly, I say to you, this generation will by
no means pass away till all things take place.
33[a]Heaven and earth will pass away, but My
[b]words will by no means pass away.

The Importance of Watching

34"But [a]take heed to yourselves, lest your
hearts be weighed down with carousing,
drunkenness, and [b]cares of this life, and that
Day come on you unexpectedly. 35For [a]it will
come as a snare on all those who dwell on the
face of the whole earth. 36[a]Watch therefore,
and [b]pray always that you may be counted
[c]worthy[1] to escape all these things that will
come to pass, and [d]to stand before the Son
of Man."

37[a]And in the daytime He was teaching in
the temple, but [b]at night He went out and
stayed on the mountain called Olivet. 38Then
early in the morning all the people came to
Him in the temple to hear Him.

The Plot to Kill Jesus

22 Now [a]the Feast of Unleavened Bread
drew near, which is called Passover.
2And [a]the chief priests and the scribes sought
how they might kill Him, for they feared the
people.

3[a]Then Satan entered Judas, surnamed
Iscariot, who was numbered among the
[b]twelve. 4So he went his way and conferred
with the chief priests and captains, how he
might betray Him to them. 5And they were
glad, and [a]agreed to give him money. 6So he
promised and sought opportunity to [a]betray
Him to them in the absence of the multitude.

Jesus and His Disciples Prepare the Passover

7[a]Then came the Day of Unleavened Bread,
when the Passover must be killed. 8And He
sent Peter and John, saying, "Go and prepare
the Passover for us, that we may eat."

9So they said to Him, "Where do You want
us to prepare?"

10And He said to them, "Behold, when you
have entered the city, a man will meet you
carrying a pitcher of water; follow him into
the house which he enters. 11Then you shall
say to the master of the house, 'The Teacher
says to you, "Where is the guest room where
I may eat the Passover with My disciples?" '
12Then he will show you a large, furnished
upper room; there make ready."

13So they went and [a]found it just as He had
said to them, and they prepared the Passover.

Jesus Institutes the Lord's Supper

14[a]When the hour had come, He sat down,
and the twelve[1] apostles with Him. 15Then
He said to them, "With *fervent* desire I have
desired to eat this Passover with you before I
suffer; 16for I say to you, I will no longer eat of
it [a]until it is fulfilled in the kingdom of God."

17Then He took the cup, and gave thanks,
and said, "Take this and divide *it* among
yourselves; 18for [a]I say to you,[1] I will not drink
of the fruit of the vine until the kingdom of
God comes."

19[a]And He took bread, gave thanks and
broke *it*, and gave *it* to them, saying, "This
is My [b]body which is given for you; [c]do this
in remembrance of Me."

20Likewise He also *took* the cup after supper, saying, [a]"This cup *is* the new covenant

21:22 [a] [Dan. 9:24–27] **21:23** [a] Matt. 24:19 **21:24** [a] [Dan. 9:27; 12:7] **21:25** [a] [2 Pet. 3:10–12] **21:26** [a] Matt. 24:29 **21:27** [a] Rev. 1:7; 14:14 **21:28** [a] [Rom. 8:19, 23] **21:29** [a] Mark 13:28 **21:33** [a] Matt. 24:35 [b] Is. 40:8 **21:34** [a] 1 Thess. 5:6 [b] Luke 8:14 **21:35** [a] Rev. 3:3; 16:15 **21:36** [a] Matt. 24:42; 25:13 [b] Luke 18:1 [c] Luke 20:35 [d] [Eph. 6:13] [1] NU-Text reads *may have strength.* **21:37** [a] John 8:1, 2 [b] Luke 22:39 **22:1** [a] Matt. 26:2–5 **22:2** [a] John 11:47 **22:3** [a] Mark 14:10, 11 [b] Matt. 10:2–4 **22:5** [a] Zech. 11:12 **22:6** [a] Ps. 41:9 **22:7** [a] Matt. 26:17–19 **22:13** [a] Luke 19:32 **22:14** [a] Mark 14:17 [1] NU-Text omits *twelve.* **22:16** [a] [Rev. 19:9] **22:18** [a] Mark 14:25 [1] NU-Text adds *from now on.* **22:19** [a] Matt. 26:26 [b] [1 Pet. 2:24] [c] 1 Cor. 11:23–26 **22:20** [a] 1 Cor. 10:16

in My blood, which is shed for you. 21[a]But behold, the hand of My betrayer *is* with Me on the table. 22[a]And truly the Son of Man goes [b]as it has been determined, but woe to that man by whom He is betrayed!"

23[a]Then they began to question among themselves, which of them it was who would do this thing.

The Disciples Argue About Greatness

24[a]Now there was also a dispute among them, as to which of them should be considered the greatest. 25[a]And He said to them, "The kings of the Gentiles exercise lordship over them, and those who exercise authority over them are called 'benefactors.' 26[a]But not so *among* you; on the contrary, [b]he who is greatest among you, let him be as the younger, and he who governs as he who serves. 27[a]For who *is* greater, he who sits at the table, or he who serves? *Is* it not he who sits at the table? Yet [b]I am among you as the One who serves.

28"But you are those who have continued with Me in [a]My trials. 29And [a]I bestow upon you a kingdom, just as My Father bestowed *one* upon Me, 30that [a]you may eat and drink at My table in My kingdom, [b]and sit on thrones judging the twelve tribes of Israel."

Jesus Predicts Peter's Denial

31And the Lord said,[1] "Simon, Simon! Indeed, [a]Satan has asked for you, that he may [b]sift *you* as wheat. 32But [a]I have prayed for you, that your faith should not fail; and when you have returned to *Me,* [b]strengthen your brethren."

33But he said to Him, "Lord, I am ready to go with You, both to prison and to death."

34[a]Then He said, "I tell you, Peter, the rooster shall not crow this day before you will deny three times that you know Me."

Supplies for the Road

35[a]And He said to them, "When I sent you without money bag, knapsack, and sandals, did you lack anything?"

So they said, "Nothing."

36Then He said to them, "But now, he who has a money bag, let him take *it,* and likewise a knapsack; and he who has no sword, let him sell his garment and buy one. 37For I say to you that this which is written must still be accomplished in Me: [a]'And He was numbered with the transgressors.'[1] For the things concerning Me have an end."

38So they said, "Lord, look, here *are* two swords."

And He said to them, "It is enough."

The Prayer in the Garden

39[a]Coming out, [b]He went to the Mount of Olives, as He was accustomed, and His disciples also followed Him. 40[a]When He came to the place, He said to them, "Pray that you may not enter into temptation."

41[a]And He was withdrawn from them about a stone's throw, and He knelt down and prayed, 42saying, "Father, if it is Your will, take this cup away from Me; nevertheless [a]not My will, but Yours, be done." 43Then [a]an angel appeared to Him from heaven, strengthening Him. 44[a]And being in agony, He prayed more earnestly. Then His sweat became like great drops of blood falling down to the ground.[1]

45When He rose up from prayer, and had come to His disciples, He found them sleeping from sorrow. 46Then He said to them, "Why [a]do you sleep? Rise and [b]pray, lest you enter into temptation."

Betrayal and Arrest in Gethsemane

47And while He was still speaking, [a]behold, a multitude; and he who was called [b]Judas, one of the twelve, went before them and drew near to Jesus to kiss Him. 48But Jesus said to him, "Judas, are you betraying the Son of Man with a [a]kiss?"

49When those around Him saw what was going to happen, they said to Him, "Lord, shall we strike with the sword?" 50And [a]one of them struck the servant of the high priest and cut off his right ear.

51But Jesus answered and said, "Permit even this." And He touched his ear and healed him.

52[a]Then Jesus said to the chief priests, captains of the temple, and the elders who had come to Him, "Have you come out, as against a [b]robber, with swords and clubs? 53When I was with you daily in the [a]temple, you did not try to seize Me. But this is your [b]hour, and the power of darkness."

22:21 [a] John 13:21, 26, 27 **22:22** [a] Matt. 26:24 [b] Acts 2:23 **22:23** [a] John 13:22, 25 **22:24** [a] Mark 9:34 **22:25** [a] Mark 10:42–45 **22:26** [a] [1 Pet. 5:3] [b] Luke 9:48 **22:27** [a] [Luke 12:37] [b] Phil. 2:7 **22:28** [a] [Heb. 2:18; 4:15] **22:29** [a] Matt. 24:47 **22:30** [a] [Matt. 8:11] [b] [Rev. 3:21] **22:31** [a] 1 Pet. 5:8 [b] Amos 9:9 [1] NU-Text omits *And the Lord said.* **22:32** [a] [John 17:9, 11, 15] [b] John 21:15–17 **22:34** [a] John 13:37, 38 **22:35** [a] Matt. 10:9 **22:37** [a] Is. 53:12 [1] Isaiah 53:12 **22:39** [a] John 18:1 [b] Luke 21:37 **22:40** [a] Mark 14:32–42 **22:41** [a] Matt. 26:39 **22:42** [a] John 4:34; 5:30; 6:38; 8:29 **22:43** [a] Matt. 4:11 **22:44** [a] [Heb. 5:7] [1] NU-Text brackets verses 43 and 44 as not in the original text. **22:46** [a] Luke 9:32 [b] Luke 22:40 **22:47** [a] John 18:3–11 [b] Acts 1:16, 17 **22:48** [a] [Prov. 27:6] **22:50** [a] Matt. 26:51 **22:52** [a] Matt. 26:55 [b] Luke 23:32 **22:53** [a] Luke 19:47, 48 [b] [John 12:27]

Peter Denies Jesus, and Weeps Bitterly

54 [a]Having arrested Him, they led *Him* and brought Him into the high priest's house. [b]But Peter followed at a distance. 55 [a]Now when they had kindled a fire in the midst of the courtyard and sat down together, Peter sat among them. 56 And a certain servant girl, seeing him as he sat by the fire, looked intently at him and said, "This man was also with Him."

57 But he denied Him,[1] saying, "Woman, I do not know Him."

58 [a]And after a little while another saw him and said, "You also are of them."

But Peter said, "Man, I am not!"

59 [a]Then after about an hour had passed, another confidently affirmed, saying, "Surely this *fellow* also was with Him, for he is a [b]Galilean."

60 But Peter said, "Man, I do not know what you are saying!"

Immediately, while he was still speaking, the rooster[1] crowed. 61 And the Lord turned and looked at Peter. Then [a]Peter remembered the word of the Lord, how He had said to him, [b]"Before the rooster crows,[1] you will deny Me three times." 62 So Peter went out and wept bitterly.

Jesus Mocked and Beaten

63 [a]Now the men who held Jesus mocked Him and [b]beat Him. 64 And having blindfolded Him, they [a]struck Him on the face and asked Him,[1] saying, "Prophesy! Who is the one who struck You?" 65 And many other things they blasphemously spoke against Him.

Jesus Faces the Sanhedrin

66 [a]As soon as it was day, [b]the elders of the people, both chief priests and scribes, came together and led Him into their council, saying, 67 [a]"If You are the Christ, tell us."

But He said to them, "If I tell you, you will [b]by no means believe. 68 And if I also ask *you,* you will by no means answer Me or let *Me* go.[1] 69 [a]Hereafter the Son of Man will sit on the right hand of the power of God."

70 Then they all said, "Are You then the Son of God?"

So He said to them, [a]"You *rightly* say that I am."

71 [a]And they said, "What further testimony do we need? For we have heard it ourselves from His own mouth."

Jesus Handed Over to Pontius Pilate

23 Then [a]the whole multitude of them arose and led Him to [b]Pilate. 2 And they began to [a]accuse Him, saying, "We found this *fellow* [b]perverting the[1] nation, and [c]forbidding to pay taxes to Caesar, saying [d]that He Himself is Christ, a King."

3 [a]Then Pilate asked Him, saying, "Are You the King of the Jews?"

He answered him and said, "*It is as* you say."

4 So Pilate said to the chief priests and the crowd, [a]"I find no fault in this Man."

5 But they were the more fierce, saying, "He stirs up the people, teaching throughout all Judea, beginning from [a]Galilee to this place."

Jesus Faces Herod

6 When Pilate heard of Galilee,[1] he asked if the Man were a Galilean. 7 And as soon as he knew that He belonged to [a]Herod's jurisdiction, he sent Him to Herod, who was also in Jerusalem at that time. 8 Now when Herod saw Jesus, [a]he was exceedingly glad; for he had desired for a long *time* to see Him, because [b]he had heard many things about Him, and he hoped to see some miracle done by Him. 9 Then he questioned Him with many words, but He answered him [a]nothing. 10 And the chief priests and scribes stood and vehemently accused Him. 11 [a]Then Herod, with his men of war, treated Him with contempt and mocked *Him,* arrayed Him in a gorgeous robe, and sent Him back to Pilate. 12 That very day [a]Pilate and Herod became friends with each other, for previously they had been at enmity with each other.

Taking the Place of Barabbas

13 [a]Then Pilate, when he had called together the chief priests, the rulers, and the people, 14 said to them, [a]"You have brought this Man to me, as one who misleads the people. And indeed, [b]having examined *Him* in your presence, I have found no fault in this Man concerning those things of which you accuse Him; 15 no, neither did Herod, for I sent you back to him;[1] and indeed nothing deserving

22:54 [a] Matt. 26:57 [b] John 18:15 **22:55** [a] Mark 14:66–72 **22:57** [1] NU-Text reads *denied it.* **22:58** [a] John 18:25 **22:59** [a] Mark 14:70 [b] Acts 1:11; 2:7 **22:60** [1] NU-Text and M-Text read *a rooster.* **22:61** [a] Matt. 26:75 [b] John 13:38 [1] NU-Text adds *today.* **22:63** [a] Ps. 69:1, 4, 7–9 [b] Is. 50:6 **22:64** [a] Zech. 13:7 [1] NU-Text reads *And having blindfolded Him, they asked Him.* **22:66** [a] Matt. 27:1 [b] Acts 4:26 **22:67** [a] Matt. 26:63–66 [b] Luke 20:5–7 **22:68** [1] NU-Text omits *also* and *Me or let Me go.* **22:69** [a] Heb. 1:3; 8:1 **22:70** [a] Matt. 26:64; 27:11 **22:71** [a] Mark 14:63 **23:1** [a] John 18:28 [b] Luke 3:1; 13:1 **23:2** [a] Acts 24:2 [b] Acts 17:7 [c] Matt. 17:27 [d] John 19:12 [1] NU-Text reads *our.* **23:3** [a] 1 Tim. 6:13 **23:4** [a] [1 Pet. 2:22] **23:5** [a] John 7:41 **23:6** [1] NU-Text omits *of Galilee.* **23:7** [a] Luke 3:1; 9:7; 13:31 **23:8** [a] Luke 9:9 [b] Matt. 14:1 **23:9** [a] John 19:9 **23:11** [a] Is. 53:3 **23:12** [a] Acts 4:26, 27 **23:13** [a] Mark 15:14 **23:14** [a] Luke 23:1, 2 [b] Luke 23:4 **23:15** [1] NU-Text reads *for he sent Him back to us.*

of death has been done by Him. 16 [a]I will therefore chastise Him and release *Him*" 17 [a](for it
was necessary for him to release one to them
at the feast).[1]

18 And [a]they all cried out at once, saying,
"Away with this *Man,* and release to us Barabbas"— 19 who had been thrown into prison
for a certain rebellion made in the city, and
for murder.

20 Pilate, therefore, wishing to release
Jesus, again called out to them. 21 But they
shouted, saying, "Crucify *Him,* crucify Him!"

22 Then he said to them the third time,
"Why, what evil has He done? I have found
no reason for death in Him. I will therefore
chastise Him and let *Him* go."

23 But they were insistent, demanding with
loud voices that He be crucified. And the
voices of these men and of the chief priests
prevailed.[1] 24 So [a]Pilate gave sentence that it
should be as they requested. 25 [a]And he released to them[1] the one they requested, who
for rebellion and murder had been thrown
into prison; but he delivered Jesus to their will.

The King on a Cross

26 [a]Now as they led Him away, they laid
hold of a certain man, Simon a Cyrenian,
who was coming from the country, and on
him they laid the cross that he might bear
it after Jesus.

27 And a great multitude of the people followed Him, and women who also mourned
and lamented Him. 28 But Jesus, turning to
them, said, "Daughters of Jerusalem, do not
weep for Me, but weep for yourselves and
for your children. 29 [a]For indeed the days
are coming in which they will say, 'Blessed
are the barren, wombs that never bore, and
breasts which never nursed!' 30 Then they will
begin [a]'to say to the mountains, "Fall on us!"
and to the hills, "Cover us!" '[1] 31 [a]For if they do
these things in the green wood, what will be
done in the dry?"

32 [a]There were also two others, criminals,
led with Him to be put to death. 33 And [a]when
they had come to the place called Calvary,
there they crucified Him, and the criminals,
one on the right hand and the other on the
left. 34 Then Jesus said, "Father, [a]forgive them,
for [b]they do not know what they do."[1]

And [c]they divided His garments and cast
lots. 35 And [a]the people stood looking on. But
even the [b]rulers with them sneered, saying,
"He saved others; let Him save Himself if He
is the Christ, the chosen of God."

36 The soldiers also mocked Him, coming
and offering Him [a]sour wine, 37 and saying, "If
You are the King of the Jews, save Yourself."

38 [a]And an inscription also was written over
Him in letters of Greek, Latin, and Hebrew:[1]

THIS IS THE KING OF THE JEWS.

39 [a]Then one of the criminals who were
hanged blasphemed Him, saying, "If You are
the Christ,[1] save Yourself and us."

40 But the other, answering, rebuked him,
saying, "Do you not even fear God, seeing you
are under the same condemnation? 41 And
we indeed justly, for we receive the due reward of our deeds; but this Man has done
[a]nothing wrong." 42 Then he said to Jesus,
"Lord,[1] remember me when You come into
Your kingdom."

43 And Jesus said to him, "Assuredly, I say to
you, today you will be with Me in [a]Paradise."

Jesus Dies on the Cross

44 [a]Now it was[1] about the sixth hour, and
there was darkness over all the earth until
the ninth hour. 45 Then the sun was darkened,[1]
and [a]the veil of the temple was torn in two.
46 And when Jesus had cried out with a loud
voice, He said, "Father, [a]'into Your hands I
commit My spirit.' "[1] [b]Having said this, He
breathed His last.

47 [a]So when the centurion saw what had
happened, he glorified God, saying, "Certainly this was a righteous Man!"

48 And the whole crowd who came together
to that sight, seeing what had been done,
beat their breasts and returned. 49 [a]But all
His acquaintances, and the women who followed Him from Galilee, stood at a distance,
watching these things.

Jesus Buried in Joseph's Tomb

50 [a]Now behold, *there was* a man named
Joseph, a council member, a good and just
man. 51 He had not consented to their decision and deed. *He was* from Arimathea, a city

23:16 [a] John 19:1 **23:17** [a] John 18:39 [1] NU-Text omits verse 17. **23:18** [a] Acts 3:13–15 **23:23** [1] NU-Text omits *and of the chief priests.* **23:24** [a] Mark 15:15 **23:25** [a] Is. 53:8 [1] NU-Text and M-Text omit *to them.* **23:26** [a] Matt. 27:32 **23:29** [a] Matt. 24:19 **23:30** [a] Hos. 10:8; Rev. 6:16, 17; 9:6 [1] Hosea 10:8 **23:31** [a] [Jer. 25:29] **23:32** [a] Is. 53:9, 12 **23:33** [a] John 19:17–24 **23:34** [a] 1 Cor. 4:12 [b] Acts 3:17 [c] Matt. 27:35 [1] NU-Text brackets the first sentence as a later addition. **23:35** [a] Ps. 22:17 [b] Matt. 27:39 **23:36** [a] Ps. 69:21 **23:38** [a] John 19:19 [1] NU-Text omits *written* and *in letters of Greek, Latin, and Hebrew.* **23:39** [a] Mark 15:32 [1] NU-Text reads *Are You not the Christ?* **23:41** [a] [Heb. 7:26] **23:42** [1] NU-Text reads *And he said, "Jesus, remember me.* **23:43** [a] [Rev. 2:7] **23:44** [a] Matt. 27:45–56 [1] NU-Text adds *already.* **23:45** [a] Matt. 27:51 [1] NU-Text reads *obscured.* **23:46** [a] Ps. 31:5 [b] John 19:30 [1] Psalm 31:5 **23:47** [a] Mark 15:39 **23:49** [a] Ps. 38:11 **23:50** [a] Matt. 27:57–61

of the Jews, [a]who himself was also waiting[1] for the kingdom of God. 52This man went to Pilate and asked for the body of Jesus. 53[a]Then he took it down, wrapped it in linen, and laid it in a tomb *that was* hewn out of the rock, where no one had ever lain before. 54That day was [a]the Preparation, and the Sabbath drew near.

55And the women [a]who had come with Him from Galilee followed after, and [b]they observed the tomb and how His body was laid. 56Then they returned and [a]prepared spices and fragrant oils. And they rested on the Sabbath [b]according to the commandment.

He Is Risen

24 Now [a]on the first *day* of the week, very early in the morning, they, and certain *other women* with them,[1] came to the tomb [b]bringing the spices which they had prepared. 2[a]But they found the stone rolled away from the tomb. 3[a]Then they went in and did not find the body of the Lord Jesus. 4And it happened, as they were greatly[1] perplexed about this, that [a]behold, two men stood by them in shining garments. 5Then, as they were afraid and bowed *their* faces to the earth, they said to them, "Why do you seek the living among the dead? 6He is not here, but is risen! [a]Remember how He spoke to you when He was still in Galilee, 7saying, 'The Son of Man must be [a]delivered into the hands of sinful men, and be crucified, and the third day rise again.' "

8And [a]they remembered His words. 9[a]Then they returned from the tomb and told all these things to the eleven and to all the rest. 10It was Mary Magdalene, [a]Joanna, Mary *the mother* of James, and the other *women* with them, who told these things to the apostles. 11[a]And their words seemed to them like idle tales, and they did not believe them. 12[a]But Peter arose and ran to the tomb; and stooping down, he saw the linen cloths lying[1] by themselves; and he departed, marveling to himself at what had happened.

The Road to Emmaus

13[a]Now behold, two of them were traveling that same day to a village called Emmaus, which was seven miles[1] from Jerusalem. 14And they talked together of all these things which had happened. 15So it was, while they conversed and reasoned, that [a]Jesus Himself drew near and went with them. 16But [a]their eyes were restrained, so that they did not know Him.

17And He said to them, "What kind of conversation *is* this that you have with one another as you walk and are sad?"[1]

18Then the one [a]whose name was Cleopas answered and said to Him, "Are You the only stranger in Jerusalem, and have You not known the things which happened there in these days?"

19And He said to them, "What things?"

So they said to Him, "The things concerning Jesus of Nazareth, [a]who was a Prophet [b]mighty in deed and word before God and all the people, 20[a]and how the chief priests and our rulers delivered Him to be condemned to death, and crucified Him. 21But we were hoping [a]that it was He who was going to redeem Israel. Indeed, besides all this, today is the third day since these things happened. 22Yes, and [a]certain women of our company, who arrived at the tomb early, astonished us. 23When they did not find His body, they came saying that they had also seen a vision of angels who said He was alive. 24And [a]certain of those *who were* with us went to the tomb and found *it* just as the women had said; but Him they did not see."

25Then He said to them, "O foolish ones, and slow of heart to believe in all that the prophets have spoken! 26[a]Ought not the Christ to have suffered these things and to enter into His [b]glory?" 27And beginning at [a]Moses and [b]all the Prophets, He expounded to them in all the Scriptures the things concerning Himself.

The Disciples' Eyes Opened

28Then they drew near to the village where they were going, and [a]He indicated that He would have gone farther. 29But [a]they constrained Him, saying, [b]"Abide with us, for it is toward evening, and the day is far spent." And He went in to stay with them.

30Now it came to pass, as [a]He sat at the table with them, that He took bread, blessed

23:51 [a] Luke 2:25, 38 [1] NU-Text reads *who was waiting.* **23:53** [a] Mark 15:46 **23:54** [a] Matt. 27:62 **23:55** [a] Luke 8:2 [b] Mark 15:47 **23:56** [a] Mark 16:1 [b] Ex. 20:10 **24:1** [a] John 20:1–8 [b] Luke 23:56 [1] NU-Text omits *and certain other women with them.* **24:2** [a] Mark 16:4 **24:3** [a] Mark 16:5 **24:4** [a] John 20:12 [1] NU-Text omits *greatly.* **24:6** [a] Luke 9:22 **24:7** [a] Luke 9:44; 11:29, 30; 18:31–33 **24:8** [a] John 2:19–22 **24:9** [a] Mark 16:10 **24:10** [a] Luke 8:3 **24:11** [a] Luke 24:25 **24:12** [a] John 20:3–6 [1] NU-Text omits *lying.* **24:13** [a] Mark 16:12 [1] Literally *sixty stadia* **24:15** [a] [Matt. 18:20] **24:16** [a] John 20:14; 21:4 **24:17** [1] NU-Text reads *as you walk? And they stood still, looking sad.* **24:18** [a] John 19:25 **24:19** [a] Matt. 21:11 [b] Acts 7:22 **24:20** [a] Acts 13:27, 28 **24:21** [a] Luke 1:68; 2:38 **24:22** [a] Mark 16:10 **24:24** [a] Luke 24:12 **24:26** [a] Acts 17:2, 3 [b] [1 Pet. 1:10–12] **24:27** [a] [Deut. 18:15] [b] [Is. 7:14; 9:6] **24:28** [a] Mark 6:48 **24:29** [a] Gen. 19:2, 3 [b] [John 14:23] **24:30** [a] Matt. 14:19

and broke *it,* and gave it to them. 31Then their
eyes were opened and they knew Him; and
He vanished from their sight.
32And they said to one another, "Did not
our heart burn within us while He talked
with us on the road, and while He opened
the Scriptures to us?" 33So they rose up that
very hour and returned to Jerusalem, and
found the eleven and those *who were* with
them gathered together, 34saying, "The Lord
is risen indeed, and [a]has appeared to Simon!"
35And they told about the things *that had happened* on the road, and how He was known
to them in the breaking of bread.

Jesus Appears to His Disciples

36[a]Now as they said these things, Jesus
Himself stood in the midst of them, and said
to them, "Peace to you." 37But they were terrified and frightened, and supposed they had
seen [a]a spirit. 38And He said to them, "Why
are you troubled? And why do doubts arise
in your hearts? 39Behold My hands and My
feet, that it is I Myself. [a]Handle Me and see,
for a [b]spirit does not have flesh and bones
as you see I have."
40When He had said this, He showed them
His hands and His feet.[1] 41But while they still
did not believe [a]for joy, and marveled, He
said to them, [b]"Have you any food here?"
42So they gave Him a piece of a broiled fish
and some honeycomb.[1] 43[a]And He took *it* and
ate in their presence.

The Scriptures Opened

44Then He said to them, [a]"These *are* the
words which I spoke to you while I was still
with you, that all things must be fulfilled
which were written in the Law of Moses and
the Prophets and *the* Psalms concerning Me."
45And [a]He opened their understanding, that
they might comprehend the Scriptures.
46Then He said to them, [a]"Thus it is written,

> **PEACE NOTE**
>
> Only in the physical, bodily resurrection of Jesus does the full expression of *shalom* come true.
>
> LUKE 24:36

24:34 [a] 1 Cor. 15:5 24:36 [a] Mark 16:14 24:37 [a] Mark 6:49 24:39 [a] John 20:20, 27 [b] [1 Cor. 15:50] 24:40 [1] Some printed New Testaments omit this verse. It is found in nearly all Greek manuscripts. 24:41 [a] Gen. 45:26 [b] John 21:5 24:42 [1] NU-Text omits *and some honeycomb.* 24:43 [a] Acts 10:39–41 24:44 [a] Matt. 16:21; 17:22; 20:18 24:45 [a] Acts 16:14 24:46 [a] Acts 17:3

JESUS' DECLARATION OF PEACE

Now as they said these things, Jesus Himself stood in the midst of them, and said to them, "Peace to you."

LUKE 24:36

Peace sometimes comes as a big surprise and a huge relief. Have you experienced those moments when all seems lost, and then suddenly and unexpectedly something happens that brings you peace? The way peace and joy sneak up on us sometimes is a powerful argument, not only for the existence of God, but also for God's love for humanity. We are made in His image, and as a result, we have an awareness of God that can bring us peace when circumstances dictate otherwise. The atheist cannot explain this peace. After Jesus had been betrayed, tried as a criminal, and put to death on a cross, the glorious movement He had launched appeared to be over. And then unexpectedly He appeared to His disciples and said, "Peace to you."

Can you imagine what the apostles thought? The word *peace* took on a whole new meaning. It can for you, too, if you let it. Make yourself more aware of who you are in Christ (Eph. 2), and you will find a deeper level of peace.

and thus it was necessary for the Christ to
suffer and to rise[1] from the dead the third
day, 47and that repentance and [a]remission
of sins should be preached in His name [b]to
all nations, beginning at Jerusalem. 48And
[a]you are witnesses of these things. 49[a]Behold,
I send the Promise of My Father upon you;
but tarry in the city of Jerusalem[1] until you
are endued with power from on high."

The Ascension

50And He led them out [a]as far as Bethany,
and He lifted up His hands and blessed them.
51[a]Now it came to pass, while He blessed
them, that He was parted from them and carried up into heaven. 52[a]And they worshiped
Him, and returned to Jerusalem with great
joy, 53and were continually [a]in the temple
praising and[1] blessing God. Amen.[2]

24:46 [1] NU-Text reads *written, that the Christ should suffer and rise.* **24:47** [a] Acts 5:31; 10:43; 13:38; 26:18 [b] [Jer. 31:34] **24:48** [a] [Acts 1:8] **24:49** [a] Joel 2:28 [1] NU-Text omits *of Jerusalem.* **24:50** [a] Acts 1:12 **24:51** [a] Mark 16:19 **24:52** [a] Matt. 28:9 **24:53** [a] Acts 2:46 [1] NU-Text omits *praising and.* [2] NU-Text omits *Amen.*

THE GOSPEL ACCORDING TO

JOHN

AUTHOR

Jesus nicknamed John and his brother James the "Sons of Thunder" (Mark 3:17). John was evidently among the Galileans who followed John the Baptist until they were called to follow Jesus at the outset of His public ministry. These Galileans were later called to become full-time disciples of the Lord (Luke 5:1–11), and John was among the twelve men who were selected to be apostles (Luke 6:12–16). The author of this Gospel is identified only as the disciple "whom Jesus loved" (John 13:23; 19:26; 21:7), but attention to detail concerning geography and Jewish culture in the Gospel lend credibility to the author's claim to be an eyewitness. The strong testimony of the early church connects this eyewitness to the apostle John.

TIME

c. AD 29–33

KEY VERSE

John 20:30–31

THEME

John is a great book for new or young Christians because it helps the reader understand Jesus' significance. What becomes increasingly clear as you read the Gospel of John is that Jesus is not simply a nice moral teacher. Only a lunatic would make the claims He makes for Himself unless He is who He says He is. John leaves no room for indecision. Like the many people Jesus encounters in the book, as you read you must either reject Him or accept Him and say, in the end, like Thomas, "My Lord and my God!" (20:28). This Gospel is an incredibly powerful presentation of Jesus.

John's Gospel reveals the explicit contrast between the peace Jesus gives and the faux peace the world delivers. Only God, through His unique Son, Jesus, can provide genuine peace and security. Jesus offers His disciples *His* peace and calls us not to worry: "My peace I give to you" (14:27). This is not the phony, unsatisfying peace of the world around us; it is the saving, fulfilling peace that comes from a Savior who suffered and died for His people. The richest words of experiencing the peace of Jesus are found in chapters 13–17 and can be prayerfully applied to the life of every believer: "Let not your heart be troubled" (14:1).

The Eternal Word

1 In the beginning [a]was the Word, and the
[b]Word was [c]with God, and the Word was
[d]God. 2 [a]He was in the beginning with God. 3 [a]All
things were made through Him, and without
Him nothing was made that was made. 4 [a]In
Him was life, and [b]the life was the light of men.
5 And [a]the light shines in the darkness, and the
darkness did not comprehend[1] it.

John's Witness: The True Light

6 There was a [a]man sent from God, whose
name *was* John. 7 This man came for a [a]wit-
ness, to bear witness of the Light, that all
through him might [b]believe. 8 He was not
that Light, but *was sent* to bear witness of that
[a]Light. 9 [a]That was the true Light which gives
light to every man coming into the world.[1]
10 He was in the world, and the world was
made through Him, and [a]the world did not
know Him. 11 [a]He came to His own,[1] and His
own[2] did not receive Him. 12 But [a]as many as
received Him, to them He gave the right to
become children of God, to those who believe
in His name: 13 [a]who were born, not of blood,
nor of the will of the flesh, nor of the will of
man, but of God.

The Word Becomes Flesh

14 [a]And the Word [b]became [c]flesh and dwelt
among us, and [d]we beheld His glory, the glory
as of the only begotten of the Father, [e]full of
grace and truth.
15 [a]John bore witness of Him and cried out,
saying, "This was He of whom I said, [b]'He who
comes after me is preferred before me, [c]for
He was before me.' "
16 And[1] of His [a]fullness we have all received,
and grace for grace. 17 For [a]the law was given
through Moses, *but* [b]grace and [c]truth came
through Jesus Christ. 18 [a]No one has seen
God at any time. [b]The only begotten Son,[1]
who is in the bosom of the Father, He has
declared *Him*.

A Voice in the Wilderness

19 Now this is [a]the testimony of John, when
the Jews sent priests and Levites from Jerusalem to ask him, "Who are you?"
20 [a]He confessed, and did not deny, but
confessed, "I am not the Christ."
21 And they asked him, "What then? Are
you Elijah?"
He said, "I am not."
"Are you [a]the Prophet?"

1:1 [a] 1 John 1:1 [b] Rev. 19:13 [c] [John 17:5] [d] [1 John 5:20] **1:2** [a] Gen. 1:1 **1:3** [a] [Col. 1:16, 17] **1:4** [a] [1 John 5:11] [b] John 8:12; 9:5; 12:46 **1:5** [a] [John 3:19] [1] Or *overcome* **1:6** [a] Matt. 3:1–17 **1:7** [a] John 3:25–36; 5:33–35 [b] [John 3:16] **1:8** [a] Is. 9:2; 49:6 **1:9** [a] Is. 49:6 [1] Or *That was the true Light which, coming into the world, gives light to every man.* **1:10** [a] Heb. 1:2 **1:11** [a] Is. 53:3; [Luke 19:14] [1] That is, His own things or domain [2] That is, His own people **1:12** [a] Gal. 3:26 **1:13** [a] [1 Pet. 1:23] **1:14** [a] Rev. 19:13 [b] Gal. 4:4 [c] Heb. 2:11 [d] Is. 40:5 [e] [John 8:32; 14:6; 18:37] **1:15** [a] John 3:32 [b] [Matt. 3:11] [c] [Col. 1:17] **1:16** [a] [Col. 1:19; 2:9] [1] NU-Text reads *For.* **1:17** [a] [Ex. 20:1] [b] [Rom. 5:21; 6:14] [c] [John 8:32; 14:6; 18:37] **1:18** [a] Ex. 33:20 [b] 1 John 4:9 [1] NU-Text reads *only begotten God.* **1:19** [a] John 5:33 **1:20** [a] Luke 3:15 **1:21** [a] Deut. 18:15, 18

THE GOD OF PEACE COMES TO EARTH

The Word became flesh and dwelt among us.

JOHN 1:14

Apart from creation itself, the greatest event in human history was the Incarnation: the appearance of God in human form. The evangelist John spoke of this: "And the Word became flesh and dwelt among us, and we beheld His glory, the glory as of the only begotten of the Father, full of grace and truth" (v. 14). Those last words, "full of grace and truth," allude to the very words of God when He passed before Moses: "The LORD, LORD . . . abounding in grace and truth" (Ex. 34:6, rendered literally).

We have hope and peace because a God of grace and forgiveness took it upon Himself to redeem and restore a lost humanity. This task could not be delegated to angels or mere mortals but required the action of the triune God. This tells us that, in God's eyes, humanity is sacred. We are not mindless creatures but human beings made in His image. To know that God "so loved the world" (John 3:16) that He "became flesh and dwelt among us" (1:14) should give us peace.

How are you affected by John 1:14? Is it an affirmation of peace for you or an invitation to try this peace? How will you respond?

And he answered, "No."
22Then they said to him, "Who are you, that
we may give an answer to those who sent us?
What do you say about yourself?"
23He said: [a]"I *am*

[b]'The voice of one crying in the
wilderness:
"Make straight the way of the LORD," '[1]

as the prophet Isaiah said."
24Now those who were sent were from the
Pharisees. 25And they asked him, saying,
"Why then do you baptize if you are not the
Christ, nor Elijah, nor the Prophet?"
26John answered them, saying, [a]"I baptize
with water, [b]but there stands One among
you whom you do not know. 27[a]It is He who,
coming after me, is preferred before me,
whose sandal strap I am not worthy to loose."
28These things were done [a]in Bethabara[1]
beyond the Jordan, where John was baptizing.

The Lamb of God

29The next day John saw Jesus coming
toward him, and said, "Behold! [a]The Lamb
of God [b]who takes away the sin of the world!
30This is He of whom I said, 'After me comes
a Man who is preferred before me, for He was
before me.' 31I did not know Him; but that
He should be revealed to Israel, [a]therefore
I came baptizing with water."
32[a]And John bore witness, saying, "I saw
the Spirit descending from heaven like a
dove, and He remained upon Him. 33I did not
know Him, but He who sent me to baptize
with water said to me, 'Upon whom you see
the Spirit descending, and remaining on
Him, [a]this is He who baptizes with the Holy
Spirit.' 34And I have seen and testified that
this is the [a]Son of God."

The First Disciples

35Again, the next day, John stood with two
of his disciples. 36And looking at Jesus as He
walked, he said, [a]"Behold the Lamb of God!"
37The two disciples heard him speak, and
they [a]followed Jesus. 38Then Jesus turned,
and seeing them following, said to them,
"What do you seek?"
They said to Him, "Rabbi" (which is to
say, when translated, Teacher), "where are
You staying?"
39He said to them, "Come and see." They
came and saw where He was staying, and remained with Him that day (now it was about
the tenth hour).
40One of the two who heard John *speak,*
and followed Him, was [a]Andrew, Simon Peter's brother. 41He first found his own brother
Simon, and said to him, "We have found the
Messiah" (which is translated, the Christ).
42And he brought him to Jesus.
Now when Jesus looked at him, He said,
"You are Simon the son of Jonah.[1] [a]You shall be
called Cephas" (which is translated, A Stone).

Philip and Nathanael

43The following day Jesus wanted to go to
Galilee, and He found [a]Philip and said to him,
"Follow Me." 44Now [a]Philip was from Bethsaida, the city of Andrew and Peter. 45Philip
found [a]Nathanael and said to him, "We have
found Him of whom [b]Moses in the law, and
also the [c]prophets, wrote—Jesus [d]of Nazareth, the [e]son of Joseph."
46And Nathanael said to him, [a]"Can anything good come out of Nazareth?"
Philip said to him, "Come and see."
47Jesus saw Nathanael coming toward
Him, and said of him, "Behold, [a]an Israelite
indeed, in whom is no deceit!"
48Nathanael said to Him, "How do You
know me?"
Jesus answered and said to him, "Before
Philip called you, when you were under the
fig tree, I saw you."
49Nathanael answered and said to Him,
"Rabbi, [a]You are the Son of God! You are [b]the
King of Israel!"

PEACE NOTE

Jesus Christ, the Lamb of God, shed His blood to cleanse us from all sin and make peace with God on our behalf.

JOHN 1:29

1:23 [a] Matt. 3:3 [b] Is. 40:3 [1] Isaiah 40:3 **1:26** [a] Matt. 3:11 [b] Mal. 3:1 **1:27** [a] Acts 19:4 **1:28** [a] Judg. 7:24 [1] NU-Text and M-Text read *Bethany.* **1:29** [a] Rev. 5:6–14 [b] [1 Pet. 2:24] **1:31** [a] Matt. 3:6 **1:32** [a] Mark 1:10 **1:33** [a] Is. 42:1; 61:1; Matt. 3:11 **1:34** [a] John 11:27 **1:36** [a] John 1:29 **1:37** [a] Matt. 4:20, 22 **1:40** [a] Matt. 4:18 **1:42** [a] Matt. 16:18 [1] NU-Text reads *John.* **1:43** [a] John 6:5; 12:21, 22; 14:8, 9 **1:44** [a] John 12:21 **1:45** [a] John 21:2 [b] Luke 24:27 [c] [Zech. 6:12] [d] [Matt. 2:23] [e] Luke 3:23 **1:46** [a] John 7:41, 42, 52 **1:47** [a] Ps. 32:2; 73:1 **1:49** [a] Matt. 14:33 [b] Matt. 21:5

50Jesus answered and said to him, "Because I said to you, 'I saw you under the fig
tree,' do you believe? You will see greater
things than these." 51And He said to him,
"Most assuredly, I say to you, [a]hereafter[1] you
shall see heaven open, and the angels of
God ascending and descending upon the
Son of Man."

Water Turned to Wine

2 On the third day there was a [a]wedding in
[b]Cana of Galilee, and the [c]mother of Jesus
was there. 2Now both Jesus and His disciples
were invited to the wedding. 3And when they
ran out of wine, the mother of Jesus said to
Him, "They have no wine."
4Jesus said to her, [a]"Woman, [b]what does
your concern have to do with Me? [c]My hour
has not yet come."
5His mother said to the servants, "Whatever He says to you, do *it.*"
6Now there were set there six waterpots of
stone, [a]according to the manner of purification of the Jews, containing twenty or thirty
gallons apiece. 7Jesus said to them, "Fill the
waterpots with water." And they filled them
up to the brim. 8And He said to them, "Draw
some out now, and take *it* to the master of the
feast." And they took *it.* 9When the master
of the feast had tasted [a]the water that was
made wine, and did not know where it came
from (but the servants who had drawn the
water knew), the master of the feast called
the bridegroom. 10And he said to him, "Every
man at the beginning sets out the good wine,
and when the *guests* have well drunk, then
the inferior. You have kept the good wine
until now!"
11This [a]beginning of signs Jesus did in Cana
of Galilee, [b]and manifested His glory; and
His disciples believed in Him.
12After this He went down to [a]Capernaum,
He, His mother, [b]His brothers, and His disciples; and they did not stay there many days.

Jesus Cleanses the Temple

13[a]Now the Passover of the Jews was at hand,
and Jesus went up to Jerusalem. 14[a]And He
found in the temple those who sold oxen and
sheep and doves, and the money changers
doing business. 15When He had made a whip
of cords, He drove them all out of the temple,
with the sheep and the oxen, and poured out
the changers' money and overturned the
tables. 16And He said to those who sold doves,
"Take these things away! Do not make [a]My Father's house a house of merchandise!" 17Then
His disciples remembered that it was written,
[a]"Zeal for Your house has eaten[1] Me up."[2]
18So the Jews answered and said to Him,
[a]"What sign do You show to us, since You do
these things?"
19Jesus answered and said to them, [a]"Destroy this temple, and in three days I will
raise it up."
20Then the Jews said, "It has taken forty-six
years to build this temple, and will You raise
it up in three days?"
21But He was speaking [a]of the temple of His
body. 22Therefore, when He had risen from
the dead, [a]His disciples remembered that He
had said this to them;[1] and they believed the
Scripture and the word which Jesus had said.

The Discerner of Hearts

23Now when He was in Jerusalem at the
Passover, during the feast, many believed in
His name when they saw the [a]signs which He
did. 24But Jesus did not commit Himself to
them, because He [a]knew all *men,* 25and had
no need that anyone should testify of man,
for [a]He knew what was in man.

The New Birth

3 There was a man of the Pharisees named
Nicodemus, a ruler of the Jews. 2[a]This
man came to Jesus by night and said to Him,
"Rabbi, we know that You are a teacher come
from God; for [b]no one can do these signs that
You do unless [c]God is with him."
3Jesus answered and said to him, "Most
assuredly, I say to you, [a]unless one is born
again, he cannot see the kingdom of God."
4Nicodemus said to Him, "How can a man
be born when he is old? Can he enter a second
time into his mother's womb and be born?"
5Jesus answered, "Most assuredly, I say
to you, [a]unless one is born of water and the
Spirit, he cannot enter the kingdom of God.
6That which is born of the flesh is [a]flesh, and
that which is born of the Spirit is spirit. 7Do
not marvel that I said to you, 'You must be
born again.' 8[a]The wind blows where it wishes, and you hear the sound of it, but cannot
tell where it comes from and where it goes.
So is everyone who is born of the Spirit."
9Nicodemus answered and said to Him,
[a]"How can these things be?"

1:51 [a] Gen. 28:12 [1] NU-Text omits *hereafter.* 2:1 [a] [Heb. 13:4] [b] John 4:46 [c] John 19:25 2:4 [a] John 19:26 [b] 2 Sam. 16:10 [c] John 7:6, 8, 30; 8:20 2:6 [a] [Mark 7:3] 2:9 [a] John 4:46 2:11 [a] John 4:54 [b] [John 1:14] 2:12 [a] Matt. 4:13 [b] Matt. 12:46; 13:55 2:13 [a] Deut. 16:1–6 2:14 [a] Mark 11:15, 17 2:16 [a] Luke 2:49 2:17 [a] Ps. 69:9 [1] NU-Text and M-Text read *will eat.* [2] Psalm 69:9 2:18 [a] Matt. 12:38 2:19 [a] Matt. 26:61; 27:40 2:21 [a] [1 Cor. 3:16; 6:19] 2:22 [a] Luke 24:8 [1] NU-Text and M-Text omit *to them.* 2:23 [a] [Acts 2:22] 2:24 [a] Rev. 2:23 2:25 [a] Matt. 9:4 3:2 [a] John 7:50; 19:39 [b] John 9:16, 33 [c] [Acts 10:38] 3:3 [a] [1 Pet. 1:23] 3:5 [a] [Acts 2:38] 3:6 [a] 1 Cor. 15:50 3:8 [a] Eccl. 11:5 3:9 [a] John 6:52, 60

10Jesus answered and said to him, "Are
you the teacher of Israel, and do not know
these things? 11[a]Most assuredly, I say to you,
We speak what We know and testify what
We have seen, and [b]you do not receive Our
witness. 12If I have told you earthly things
and you do not believe, how will you believe
if I tell you heavenly things? 13[a]No one has
ascended to heaven but He who came down
from heaven, *that is,* the Son of Man who
is in heaven.[1] 14[a]And as Moses lifted up the
serpent in the wilderness, even so [b]must
the Son of Man be lifted up, 15that whoever
[a]believes in Him should not perish but[1] [b]have
eternal life. 16[a]For God so loved the world
that He gave His only begotten [b]Son, that
whoever believes in Him should not perish
but have everlasting life. 17[a]For God did not
send His Son into the world to condemn
the world, but that the world through Him
might be saved.
18[a]"He who believes in Him is not condemned; but he who does not believe is condemned already, because he has not believed
in the name of the only begotten Son of God.
19And this is the condemnation, [a]that the
light has come into the world, and men loved
darkness rather than light, because their
deeds were evil. 20For [a]everyone practicing
evil hates the light and does not come to the
light, lest his deeds should be exposed. 21But
he who does the truth comes to the light, that
his deeds may be clearly seen, that they have
been [a]done in God."

John the Baptist Exalts Christ

22After these things Jesus and His disciples
came into the land of Judea, and there He remained with them [a]and baptized. 23Now John
also was baptizing in Aenon near [a]Salim,
because there was much water there. [b]And
they came and were baptized. 24For [a]John
had not yet been thrown into prison.
25Then there arose a dispute between *some*
of John's disciples and the Jews about purification. 26And they came to John and said
to him, "Rabbi, He who was with you beyond
the Jordan, [a]to whom you have testified—
behold, He is baptizing, and all [b]are coming
to Him!"
27John answered and said, [a]"A man can
receive nothing unless it has been given to
him from heaven. 28You yourselves bear me
witness, that I said, [a]'I am not the Christ,'
but, [b]'I have been sent before Him.' 29[a]He
who has the bride is the bridegroom; but
[b]the friend of the bridegroom, who stands
and hears him, rejoices greatly because of
the bridegroom's voice. Therefore this joy
of mine is fulfilled. 30[a]He must increase,
but I *must* decrease. 31[a]He who comes from
above [b]is above all; [c]he who is of the earth
is earthly and speaks of the earth. [d]He who
comes from heaven is above all. 32And [a]what
He has seen and heard, that He testifies; and
no one receives His testimony. 33He who has
received His testimony [a]has certified that
God is true. 34[a]For He whom God has sent
speaks the words of God, for God does not
give the Spirit [b]by measure. 35[a]The Father
loves the Son, and has given all things into
His hand. 36[a]He who believes in the Son has
everlasting life; and he who does not believe
the Son shall not see life, but the [b]wrath of
God abides on him."

PEACE NOTE

A distorted view of God will crumble God's peace in your life. Make sure that everything you believe to be true about God can be traced back specifically to Scripture.

JOHN 3:17

A Samaritan Woman Meets Her Messiah

4 Therefore, when the Lord knew that the
Pharisees had heard that Jesus made and
[a]baptized more disciples than John 2(though
Jesus Himself did not baptize, but His disciples), 3He left Judea and departed again
to Galilee. 4But He needed to go through
Samaria.
5So He came to a city of Samaria which is
called Sychar, near the plot of ground that

3:11 [a] [Matt. 11:27] [b] John 3:32; 8:14 **3:13** [a] Eph. 4:9 [1] NU-Text omits *who is in heaven.* **3:14** [a] Num. 21:9 [b] John 8:28; 12:34; 19:18 **3:15** [a] John 6:47 [b] John 3:36 [1] NU-Text omits *not perish but.* **3:16** [a] Rom. 5:8 [b] [Is. 9:6] **3:17** [a] Luke 9:56 **3:18** [a] John 5:24; 6:40, 47; 20:31 **3:19** [a] [John 1:4, 9–11] **3:20** [a] Eph. 5:11, 13 **3:21** [a] 1 Cor. 15:10 **3:22** [a] John 4:1, 2 **3:23** [a] 1 Sam. 9:4 [b] Matt. 3:5, 6 **3:24** [a] Matt. 4:12; 14:3 **3:26** [a] John 1:7, 15, 27, 34 [b] Mark 2:2; 3:10; 5:24 **3:27** [a] 1 Cor. 3:5, 6; 4:7 **3:28** [a] John 1:19–27 [b] Mal. 3:1 **3:29** [a] [2 Cor. 11:2] [b] Song 5:1 **3:30** [a] [Is. 9:7] **3:31** [a] John 3:13; 8:23 [b] Matt. 28:18 [c] 1 Cor. 15:47 [d] John 6:33 **3:32** [a] John 3:11; 15:15 **3:33** [a] 1 John 5:10 **3:34** [a] Deut. 18:18; John 7:16 [b] John 1:16 **3:35** [a] [Heb. 2:8] **3:36** [a] John 3:16, 17; 6:47 [b] Rom. 1:18 **4:1** [a] John 3:22, 26

[a]Jacob [b]gave to his son Joseph. 6Now Jacob's well was there. Jesus therefore, being wearied from *His* journey, sat thus by the well. It was about the sixth hour.

7A woman of Samaria came to draw water. Jesus said to her, "Give Me a drink." 8For His disciples had gone away into the city to buy food.

9Then the woman of Samaria said to Him, "How is it that You, being a Jew, ask a drink from me, a Samaritan woman?" For [a]Jews have no dealings with [b]Samaritans.

10Jesus answered and said to her, "If you knew the [a]gift of God, and who it is who says to you, 'Give Me a drink,' you would have asked Him, and He would have given you [b]living water."

11The woman said to Him, "Sir, You have nothing to draw with, and the well is deep. Where then do You get that living water? 12Are You greater than our father Jacob, who gave us the well, and drank from it himself, as well as his sons and his livestock?"

13Jesus answered and said to her, "Whoever drinks of this water will thirst again, 14but [a]whoever drinks of the water that I shall give him will never thirst. But the water that I shall give him [b]will become in him a fountain of water springing up into everlasting life."

15[a]The woman said to Him, "Sir, give me this water, that I may not thirst, nor come here to draw."

16Jesus said to her, "Go, call your husband, and come here."

17The woman answered and said, "I have no husband."

Jesus said to her, "You have well said, 'I have no husband,' 18for you have had five husbands, and the one whom you now have is not your husband; in that you spoke truly."

19The woman said to Him, "Sir, [a]I perceive that You are a prophet. 20Our fathers worshiped on [a]this mountain, and you *Jews* say that in [b]Jerusalem is the place where one ought to worship."

21Jesus said to her, "Woman, believe Me, the hour is coming [a]when you will neither on this mountain, nor in Jerusalem, worship the Father. 22You worship [a]what you do not know; we know what we worship, for [b]salvation is of the Jews. 23But the hour is coming, and now is, when the true worshipers will [a]worship the Father in [b]spirit [c]and truth; for the Father is seeking such to worship Him. 24[a]God *is* Spirit, and those who worship Him must worship in spirit and truth."

25The woman said to Him, "I know that Messiah [a]is coming" (who is called Christ). "When He comes, [b]He will tell us all things."

26Jesus said to her, [a]"I who speak to you am *He*."

The Whitened Harvest

27And at this *point* His disciples came, and they marveled that He talked with a woman; yet no one said, "What do You seek?" or, "Why are You talking with her?"

28The woman then left her waterpot, went her way into the city, and said to the men, 29"Come, see a Man [a]who told me all things that I ever did. Could this be the Christ?" 30Then they went out of the city and came to Him.

31In the meantime His disciples urged Him, saying, "Rabbi, eat."

32But He said to them, "I have food to eat of which you do not know."

33Therefore the disciples said to one another, "Has anyone brought Him *anything* to eat?"

34Jesus said to them, [a]"My food is to do the will of Him who sent Me, and to [b]finish His work. 35Do you not say, 'There are still four months and *then* comes [a]the harvest'? Behold, I say to you, lift up your eyes and look at the fields, [b]for they are already white for harvest! 36[a]And he who reaps receives wages, and gathers fruit for eternal life, that [b]both he who sows and he who reaps may rejoice together. 37For in this the saying is true: [a]'One sows and another reaps.' 38I sent you to reap that for which you have not labored; [a]others have labored, and you have entered into their labors."

The Savior of the World

39And many of the Samaritans of that city believed in Him [a]because of the word of the woman who testified, "He told me all that I *ever* did." 40So when the Samaritans had come to Him, they urged Him to stay with them; and He stayed there two days. 41And many more believed because of His own [a]word.

42Then they said to the woman, "Now we believe, not because of what you said, for [a]we ourselves have heard *Him* and we know that this is indeed the Christ,[1] the Savior of the world."

4:5 [a] Gen. 33:19 [b] Gen. 48:22 **4:9** [a] Acts 10:28 [b] 2 Kin. 17:24 **4:10** [a] [Rom. 5:15] [b] Is. 12:3; 44:3 **4:14** [a] [John 6:35, 58] [b] John 7:37, 38 **4:15** [a] John 6:34, 35; 17:2, 3 **4:19** [a] Luke 7:16, 39; 24:19 **4:20** [a] Judg. 9:7 [b] Deut. 12:5, 11 **4:21** [a] 1 Tim. 2:8 **4:22** [a] [2 Kin. 17:28–41] [b] [Rom. 3:1; 9:4, 5] **4:23** [a] [Heb. 13:10–14] [b] Phil. 3:3 [c] [John 1:17] **4:24** [a] 2 Cor. 3:17 **4:25** [a] Deut. 18:15 [b] John 4:29, 39 **4:26** [a] Matt. 26:63, 64 **4:29** [a] John 4:25 **4:34** [a] Ps. 40:7, 8 [b] [John 6:38; 17:4; 19:30] **4:35** [a] Gen. 8:22 [b] Matt. 9:37 **4:36** [a] Dan. 12:3 [b] 1 Thess. 2:19 **4:37** [a] 1 Cor. 3:5–9 **4:38** [a] [1 Pet. 1:12] **4:39** [a] John 4:29 **4:41** [a] Luke 4:32 **4:42** [a] 1 John 4:14 [1] NU-Text omits *the Christ*.

Welcome at Galilee

43Now after the two days He departed from there and went to Galilee. 44For [a]Jesus Himself testified that a prophet has no honor in his own country. 45So when He came to Galilee, the Galileans received Him, [a]having seen all the things He did in Jerusalem at the feast; [b]for they also had gone to the feast.

A Nobleman's Son Healed

46So Jesus came again to Cana of Galilee [a]where He had made the water wine. And there was a certain nobleman whose son was sick at Capernaum. 47When he heard that Jesus had come out of Judea into Galilee, he went to Him and implored Him to come down and heal his son, for he was at the point of death. 48Then Jesus said to him, [a]"Unless you *people* see signs and wonders, you will by no means believe."

49The nobleman said to Him, "Sir, come down before my child dies!"

50Jesus said to him, "Go your way; your son lives." So the man believed the word that Jesus spoke to him, and he went his way. 51And as he was now going down, his servants met him and told *him,* saying, "Your son lives!"

52Then he inquired of them the hour when he got better. And they said to him, "Yesterday at the seventh hour the fever left him." 53So the father knew that *it was* at the same hour in which Jesus said to him, "Your son lives." And he himself believed, and his whole household.

54This again *is* the second sign Jesus did when He had come out of Judea into Galilee.

A Man Healed at the Pool of Bethesda

5 After [a]this there was a feast of the Jews, and Jesus [b]went up to Jerusalem. 2Now there is in Jerusalem [a]by the Sheep *Gate* a pool, which is called in Hebrew, Bethesda,[1] having five porches. 3In these lay a great multitude of sick people, blind, lame, paralyzed, waiting for the moving of the water. 4For an angel went down at a certain time into the pool and stirred up the water; then whoever stepped in first, after the stirring of the water, was made well of whatever disease he had.[1] 5Now a certain man was there who had an infirmity thirty-eight years. 6When Jesus saw him lying there, and knew that he already had been *in that condition* a long time, He said to him, "Do you want to be made well?"

7The sick man answered Him, "Sir, I have no man to put me into the pool when the water is stirred up; but while I am coming, another steps down before me."

8Jesus said to him, [a]"Rise, take up your bed and walk." 9And immediately the man was made well, took up his bed, and walked.

And [a]that day was the Sabbath. 10The Jews therefore said to him who was cured, "It is the Sabbath; [a]it is not lawful for you to carry your bed."

11He answered them, "He who made me well said to me, 'Take up your bed and walk.' "

12Then they asked him, "Who is the Man who said to you, 'Take up your bed and walk'?" 13But the one who was [a]healed did not know who it was, for Jesus had withdrawn, a multitude being in *that* place. 14Afterward Jesus found him in the temple, and said to him, "See, you have been made well. [a]Sin no more, lest a worse thing come upon you."

15The man departed and told the Jews that it was Jesus who had made him well.

Honor the Father and the Son

16For this reason the Jews [a]persecuted Jesus, and sought to kill Him,[1] because He had done these things on the Sabbath. 17But Jesus answered them, [a]"My Father has been working until now, and I have been working."

18Therefore the Jews [a]sought all the more to kill Him, because He not only broke the Sabbath, but also said that God was His Father, [b]making Himself equal with God. 19Then Jesus answered and said to them, "Most assuredly, I say to you, [a]the Son can do nothing of Himself, but what He sees the Father do; for whatever He does, the Son also does in like manner. 20For [a]the Father loves the Son, and [b]shows Him all things that He Himself does; and He will show Him greater works than these, that you may marvel. 21For as the Father raises the dead and gives life to *them,* [a]even so the Son gives life to whom He will. 22For the Father judges no one, but [a]has committed all judgment to the Son, 23that all should honor the Son just as they honor the Father. [a]He who does not honor the Son does not honor the Father who sent Him.

Life and Judgment Are Through the Son

24"Most assuredly, I say to you, [a]he who hears My word and believes in Him who sent Me has everlasting life, and shall not

4:44 [a] Matt. 13:57 **4:45** [a] John 2:13, 23; 3:2 [b] Deut. 16:16 **4:46** [a] John 2:1, 11 **4:48** [a] 1 Cor. 1:22 **5:1** [a] Deut. 16:16 [b] John 2:13 **5:2** [a] Neh. 3:1, 32; 12:39 [1] NU-Text reads *Bethzatha.* **5:4** [1] NU-Text omits *waiting for the moving of the water* at the end of verse 3, and all of verse 4. **5:8** [a] Luke 5:24 **5:9** [a] John 9:14 **5:10** [a] Jer. 17:21, 22 **5:13** [a] Luke 13:14; 22:51 **5:14** [a] John 8:11 **5:16** [a] John 8:37; 10:39 [1] NU-Text omits *and sought to kill Him.* **5:17** [a] [John 9:4; 17:4] **5:18** [a] John 7:1, 19 [b] John 10:30 **5:19** [a] John 5:30; 6:38; 8:28; 12:49; 14:10 **5:20** [a] Matt. 3:17 [b] [Matt. 11:27] **5:21** [a] [John 11:25] **5:22** [a] [Acts 17:31] **5:23** [a] 1 John 2:23 **5:24** [a] John 3:16, 18; 6:47

PEACE NOTE

We put our faith in Jesus Christ, who is worthy of our trust, honor, and faith. He is the only One who can grant true peace.

JOHN 5:24

come into judgment, [b]but has passed from death into life. 25Most assuredly, I say to you, the hour is coming, and now is, when [a]the dead will hear the voice of the Son of God; and those who hear will live. 26For [a]as the Father has life in Himself, so He has granted the Son to have [b]life in Himself, 27and [a]has given Him authority to execute judgment also, [b]because He is the Son of Man. 28Do not marvel at this; for the hour is coming in which all who are in the graves will [a]hear His voice 29[a]and come forth—[b]those who have done good, to the resurrection of life, and those who have done evil, to the resurrection of condemnation. 30[a]I can of Myself do nothing. As I hear, I judge; and My judgment is righteous, because [b]I do not seek My own will but the will of the Father who sent Me.

The Fourfold Witness

31[a]"If I bear witness of Myself, My witness is not true. 32[a]There is another who bears witness of Me, and I know that the witness which He witnesses of Me is true. 33You have sent to John, [a]and he has borne witness to the truth. 34Yet I do not receive testimony from man, but I say these things that you may be saved. 35He was the burning and [a]shining lamp, and [b]you were willing for a time to rejoice in his light. 36But [a]I have a greater witness than John's; for [b]the works which the Father has given Me to finish—the very [c]works that I do—bear witness of Me, that the Father has sent Me. 37And the Father Himself, who sent Me, [a]has testified of Me. You have neither heard His voice at any time, [b]nor seen His form. 38But you do not have His word abiding in you, because whom He sent, Him you do not believe. 39[a]You search the Scriptures, for in them you think you have eternal life; and [b]these are they which testify of Me. 40[a]But you are not willing to come to Me that you may have life.

41[a]"I do not receive honor from men. 42But I know you, that you do not have the love of God in you. 43I have come in My Father's name, and you do not receive Me; if another comes in his own name, him you will receive. 44[a]How can you believe, who receive honor from one another, and do not seek [b]the honor that *comes* from the only God? 45Do not think that I shall accuse you to the Father; [a]there is *one* who accuses you—Moses, in whom you trust. 46For if you believed Moses, you would believe Me; [a]for he wrote about Me. 47But if you [a]do not believe his writings, how will you believe My words?"

Feeding the Five Thousand

6 After [a]these things Jesus went over the Sea of Galilee, which is *the Sea* of [b]Tiberias. 2Then a great multitude followed Him, because they saw His signs which He performed on those who were [a]diseased. 3And Jesus went up on the mountain, and there He sat with His disciples.

4[a]Now the Passover, a feast of the Jews, was near. 5[a]Then Jesus lifted up *His* eyes, and seeing a great multitude coming toward Him, He said to [b]Philip, "Where shall we buy bread, that these may eat?" 6But this He said to test him, for He Himself knew what He would do.

7Philip answered Him, [a]"Two hundred denarii worth of bread is not sufficient for them, that every one of them may have a little."

8One of His disciples, [a]Andrew, Simon Peter's brother, said to Him, 9"There is a lad here who has five barley loaves and two small fish, [a]but what are they among so many?"

10Then Jesus said, "Make the people sit down." Now there was much grass in the place. So the men sat down, in number about five thousand. 11And Jesus took the loaves, and when He had given thanks He distributed *them* to the disciples, and the disciples[1] to those sitting down; and likewise of the fish, as much as they wanted. 12So when they were

5:24 [b] [1 John 3:14] **5:25** [a] [Col. 2:13] **5:26** [a] Ps. 36:9 [b] 1 Cor. 15:45 **5:27** [a] [Acts 10:42; 17:31] [b] Dan. 7:13 **5:28** [a] [1 Thess. 4:15–17] **5:29** [a] Is. 26:19 [b] Dan. 12:2 **5:30** [a] John 5:19 [b] Matt. 26:39 **5:31** [a] John 8:14 **5:32** [a] [Matt. 3:17] **5:33** [a] [John 1:15, 19, 27, 32] **5:35** [a] 2 Pet. 1:19 [b] Mark 6:20 **5:36** [a] 1 John 5:9 [b] John 3:2; 10:25; 17:4 [c] John 9:16; 10:38 **5:37** [a] Matt. 3:17 [b] 1 John 4:12 **5:39** [a] Is. 8:20; 34:16 [b] Luke 24:27 **5:40** [a] [John 1:11; 3:19] **5:41** [a] 1 Thess. 2:6 **5:44** [a] John 12:43 [b] [Rom. 2:29] **5:45** [a] Rom. 2:12 **5:46** [a] Deut. 18:15, 18 **5:47** [a] Luke 16:29, 31 **6:1** [a] Mark 6:32 [b] John 6:23; 21:1 **6:2** [a] Matt. 4:23; 8:16; 9:35; 14:36; 15:30; 19:2 **6:4** [a] Deut. 16:1 **6:5** [a] Matt. 14:14 [b] John 1:43 **6:7** [a] Num. 11:21, 22 **6:8** [a] John 1:40 **6:9** [a] 2 Kin. 4:43 **6:11** [1] NU-Text omits *to the disciples, and the disciples.*

filled, He said to His disciples, "Gather up the fragments that remain, so that nothing is lost." 13Therefore they gathered *them* up, and filled twelve baskets with the fragments of the five barley loaves which were left over by those who had eaten. 14Then those men, when they had seen the sign that Jesus did, said, "This is truly [a]the Prophet who is to come into the world."

Jesus Walks on the Sea

15Therefore when Jesus perceived that they were about to come and take Him by force to make Him [a]king, He departed again to the mountain by Himself alone.

16[a]Now when evening came, His disciples went down to the sea, 17got into the boat, and went over the sea toward Capernaum. And it was already dark, and Jesus had not come to them. 18Then the sea arose because a great wind was blowing. 19So when they had rowed about three or four miles,[1] they saw Jesus walking on the sea and drawing near the boat; and they were [a]afraid. 20But He said to them, [a]"It is I; do not be afraid." 21Then they willingly received Him into the boat, and immediately the boat was at the land where they were going.

The Bread from Heaven

22On the following day, when the people who were standing on the other side of the sea saw that there was no other boat there, except that one which His disciples had entered,[1] and that Jesus had not entered the boat with His disciples, but His disciples had gone away alone— 23however, other boats came from Tiberias, near the place where they ate bread after the Lord had given thanks— 24when the people therefore saw that Jesus was not there, nor His disciples, they also got into boats and came to Capernaum, [a]seeking Jesus. 25And when they found Him on the other side of the sea, they said to Him, "Rabbi, when did You come here?"

26Jesus answered them and said, "Most assuredly, I say to you, you seek Me, not because you saw the signs, but because you ate of the loaves and were filled. 27[a]Do not labor for the food which perishes, but [b]for the food which endures to everlasting life, which the Son of Man will give you, [c]because God the Father has set His seal on Him."

28Then they said to Him, "What shall we do, that we may work the works of God?"

29Jesus answered and said to them, [a]"This is the work of God, that you believe in Him whom He sent."

30Therefore they said to Him, [a]"What sign will You perform then, that we may see it and believe You? What work will You do? 31[a]Our fathers ate the manna in the desert; as it is written, [b]'He gave them bread from heaven to eat.' "[1]

32Then Jesus said to them, "Most assuredly, I say to you, Moses did not give you the bread from heaven, but [a]My Father gives you the true bread from heaven. 33For the bread of God is He who comes down from heaven and gives life to the world."

34[a]Then they said to Him, "Lord, give us this bread always."

35And Jesus said to them, [a]"I am the bread of life. [b]He who comes to Me shall never hunger, and he who believes in Me shall never [c]thirst. 36[a]But I said to you that you have seen Me and yet [b]do not believe. 37[a]All that the Father gives Me will come to Me, and [b]the one who comes to Me I will by no means cast out. 38For I have come down from heaven, [a]not to do My own will, [b]but the will of Him who sent Me. 39This is the will of the Father who sent Me, [a]that of all He has given Me I should lose nothing, but should raise it up at the last day. 40And this is the will of Him who sent Me, [a]that everyone who sees the Son and believes in Him may have everlasting life; and I will raise him up at the last day."

Rejected by His Own

41The Jews then complained about Him, because He said, "I am the bread which came down from heaven." 42And they said, [a]"Is not this Jesus, the son of Joseph, whose father and mother we know? How is it then that He says, 'I have come down from heaven'?"

43Jesus therefore answered and said to them, "Do not murmur among yourselves. 44[a]No one can come to Me unless the Father who sent Me [b]draws him; and I will raise him up at the last day. 45It is written in the prophets, [a]'And they shall all be taught by God.'[1] [b]Therefore everyone who has heard and learned[2] from the Father comes to Me. 46[a]Not that anyone has seen the Father, [b]except He who is from God; He has seen

6:14 [a] Gen. 49:10 **6:15** [a] [*John 18:36*] **6:16** [a] Matt. 14:23 **6:19** [a] Matt. 17:6 [1] Literally *twenty-five or thirty stadia* **6:20** [a] Is. 43:1, 2 **6:22** [1] NU-Text omits *that* and *which His disciples had entered.* **6:24** [a] Luke 4:42 **6:27** [a] Matt. 6:19 [b] John 4:14 [c] Acts 2:22 **6:29** [a] [1 John 3:23] **6:30** [a] Matt. 12:38; 16:1 **6:31** [a] Ex. 16:15 [b] Ex. 16:4, 15; Neh. 9:15; Ps. 78:24 [1] Exodus 16:4; Nehemiah 9:15; Psalm 78:24 **6:32** [a] John 3:13, 16 **6:34** [a] John 4:15 **6:35** [a] John 6:48, 58 [b] John 4:14; 7:37 [c] Is. 55:1, 2 **6:36** [a] John 6:26, 64; 15:24 [b] John 10:26 **6:37** [a] John 6:45 [b] 2 Tim. 2:19 **6:38** [a] Matt. 26:39 [b] John 4:34 **6:39** [a] John 10:28; 17:12; 18:9 **6:40** [a] John 3:15, 16; 4:14; 6:27, 47, 54 **6:42** [a] Matt. 13:55 **6:44** [a] Song 1:4 [b] [Phil. 1:29; 2:12, 13] **6:45** [a] Is. 54:13 [b] John 6:37 [1] Isaiah 54:13 [2] M-Text reads *hears and has learned.* **6:46** [a] John 1:18 [b] Matt. 11:27

the Father. 47Most assuredly, I say to you,
[a]he who believes in Me[1] has everlasting life.
48[a]I am the bread of life. 49[a]Your fathers ate
the manna in the wilderness, and are dead.
50[a]This is the bread which comes down from
heaven, that one may eat of it and not die. 51I
am the living bread [a]which came down from
heaven. If anyone eats of this bread, he will
live forever; and [b]the bread that I shall give
is My flesh, which I shall give for the life of
the world."

52The Jews therefore [a]quarreled among
themselves, saying, "How can this Man give
us *His* flesh to eat?"

53Then Jesus said to them, "Most assuredly,
I say to you, unless [a]you eat the flesh of the
Son of Man and drink His blood, you have
no life in you. 54[a]Whoever eats My flesh and
drinks My blood has eternal life, and I will
raise him up at the last day. 55For My flesh is
food indeed,[1] and My blood is drink indeed.
56He who eats My flesh and drinks My blood
[a]abides in Me, and I in him. 57As the living
Father sent Me, and I live because of the Father, so he who feeds on Me will live because
of Me. 58[a]This is the bread which came down
from heaven—not [b]as your fathers ate the
manna, and are dead. He who eats this bread
will live forever."

59These things He said in the synagogue
as He taught in Capernaum.

Many Disciples Turn Away

60[a]Therefore many of His disciples, when
they heard *this,* said, "This is a hard saying;
who can understand it?"

61When Jesus knew in Himself that His
disciples complained about this, He said to
them, "Does this offend you? 62[a]*What* then if
you should see the Son of Man ascend where
He was before? 63[a]It is the Spirit who gives
life; the [b]flesh profits nothing. The [c]words
that I speak to you are spirit, and *they* are
life. 64But [a]there are some of you who do
not believe." For [b]Jesus knew from the beginning who they were who did not believe,
and who would betray Him. 65And He said,
"Therefore [a]I have said to you that no one
can come to Me unless it has been granted
to him by My Father."

66[a]From that *time* many of His disciples
went back and walked with Him no more.
67Then Jesus said to the twelve, "Do you also
want to go away?"

68But Simon Peter answered Him, "Lord,
to whom shall we go? You have [a]the words of
eternal life. 69[a]Also we have come to believe
and know that You are the Christ, the Son of
the living God."[1]

70Jesus answered them, [a]"Did I not choose
you, the twelve, [b]and one of you is a devil?" 71He spoke of [a]Judas Iscariot, *the son* of
Simon, for it was he who would [b]betray Him,
being one of the twelve.

Jesus' Brothers Disbelieve

7 After these things Jesus walked in Galilee;
for He did not want to walk in Judea, [a]be-
cause the Jews[1] sought to kill Him. 2[a]Now the
Jews' Feast of Tabernacles was at hand. 3[a]His
brothers therefore said to Him, "Depart from
here and go into Judea, that Your disciples
also may see the works that You are doing.
4For no one does anything in secret while he
himself seeks to be known openly. If You do
these things, show Yourself to the world." 5For
[a]even His [b]brothers did not believe in Him.

6Then Jesus said to them, [a]"My time has
not yet come, but your time is always ready.
7[a]The world cannot hate you, but it hates Me
[b]because I testify of it that its works are evil.
8You go up to this feast. I am not yet[1] going
up to this feast, [a]for My time has not yet fully
come." 9When He had said these things to
them, He remained in Galilee.

The Heavenly Scholar

10But when His brothers had gone up, then
He also went up to the feast, not openly, but
as it were in secret. 11Then [a]the Jews sought
Him at the feast, and said, "Where is He?"
12And [a]there was much complaining among
the people concerning Him. [b]Some said, "He
is good"; others said, "No, on the contrary,
He deceives the people." 13However, no one
spoke openly of Him [a]for fear of the Jews.

14Now about the middle of the feast Jesus
went up into the temple and [a]taught. 15[a]And
the Jews marveled, saying, "How does this
Man know letters, having never studied?"

16Jesus[1] answered them and said, [a]"My
doctrine is not Mine, but His who sent Me.

6:47 [a] [John 3:16, 18] [1] NU-Text omits *in Me.* **6:48** [a] John 6:33, 35 **6:49** [a] John 6:31, 58 **6:50** [a] John 6:51, 58 **6:51** [a] John 3:13 [b] Heb. 10:5 **6:52** [a] John 7:43; 9:16; 10:19 **6:53** [a] Matt. 26:26 **6:54** [a] John 4:14; 6:27, 40 **6:55** [1] NU-Text reads *true food* and *true drink.* **6:56** [a] [1 John 3:24; 4:15, 16] **6:58** [a] John 6:49–51 [b] Ex. 16:14–35 **6:60** [a] John 6:66 **6:62** [a] Acts 1:9; 2:32, 33 **6:63** [a] 2 Cor. 3:6 [b] John 3:6 [c] [John 6:68; 14:24] **6:64** [a] John 6:36 [b] John 2:24, 25; 13:11 **6:65** [a] John 6:37, 44, 45 **6:66** [a] Luke 9:62 **6:68** [a] Acts 5:20 **6:69** [a] Luke 9:20 [1] NU-Text reads *You are the Holy One of God.* **6:70** [a] Luke 6:13 [b] [John 13:27] **6:71** [a] John 12:4; 13:2, 26 [b] Matt. 26:14–16 **7:1** [a] John 5:18; 7:19, 25; 8:37, 40 [1] That is, the ruling authorities **7:2** [a] Lev. 23:34 **7:3** [a] Matt. 12:46 **7:5** [a] Ps. 69:8; Mic. 7:6 [b] Mark 3:21 **7:6** [a] John 2:4; 8:20 **7:7** [a] [John 15:19] [b] John 3:19 **7:8** [a] John 8:20 [1] NU-Text omits *yet.* **7:11** [a] John 11:56 **7:12** [a] John 9:16; 10:19 [b] Luke 7:16 **7:13** [a] [John 9:22; 12:42; 19:38] **7:14** [a] Ps. 22:22; Mark 6:34 **7:15** [a] Matt. 13:54 **7:16** [a] John 3:11 [1] NU-Text and M-Text read *So Jesus.*

17 [a]If anyone wills to do His will, he shall know concerning the doctrine, whether it is from God or *whether* I speak on My own *authority.* 18 [a]He who speaks from himself seeks his own glory; but He who [b]seeks the glory of the One who sent Him is true, and [c]no unrighteousness is in Him. 19 [a]Did not Moses give you the law, yet none of you keeps the law? [b]Why do you seek to kill Me?"

20 The people answered and said, [a]"You have a demon. Who is seeking to kill You?"

21 Jesus answered and said to them, "I did one work, and you all marvel. 22 [a]Moses therefore gave you circumcision (not that it is from Moses, [b]but from the fathers), and you circumcise a man on the Sabbath. 23 If a man receives circumcision on the Sabbath, so that the law of Moses should not be broken, are you angry with Me because [a]I made a man completely well on the Sabbath? 24 [a]Do not judge according to appearance, but judge with righteous judgment."

Could This Be the Christ?

25 Now some of them from Jerusalem said, "Is this not He whom they seek to [a]kill? 26 But look! He speaks boldly, and they say nothing to Him. [a]Do the rulers know indeed that this is truly[1] the Christ? 27 [a]However, we know where this Man is from; but when the Christ comes, no one knows where He is from."

28 Then Jesus cried out, as He taught in the temple, saying, [a]"You both know Me, and you know where I am from; and [b]I have not come of Myself, but He who sent Me [c]is true, [d]whom you do not know. 29 But[1] [a]I know Him, for I am from Him, and He sent Me."

30 Therefore [a]they sought to take Him; but [b]no one laid a hand on Him, because His hour had not yet come. 31 And [a]many of the people believed in Him, and said, "When the Christ comes, will He do more signs than these which this *Man* has done?"

Jesus and the Religious Leaders

32 The Pharisees heard the crowd murmuring these things concerning Him, and the Pharisees and the chief priests sent officers to take Him. 33 Then Jesus said to them,[1] [a]"I shall be with you a little while longer, and *then* I [b]go to Him who sent Me. 34 You [a]will seek Me and not find *Me,* and where I am you [b]cannot come."

35 Then the Jews said among themselves, "Where does He intend to go that we shall not find Him? Does He intend to go to [a]the Dispersion among the Greeks and teach the Greeks? 36 What is this thing that He said, 'You will seek Me and not find Me, and where I am you cannot come'?"

The Promise of the Holy Spirit

37 [a]On the last day, that great *day* of the feast, Jesus stood and cried out, saying, [b]"If anyone thirsts, let him come to Me and drink. 38 [a]He who believes in Me, as the Scripture has said, [b]out of his heart will flow rivers of living water." 39 [a]But this He spoke concerning the Spirit, whom those believing[1] in Him would receive; for the Holy[2] Spirit was not yet *given,* because Jesus was not yet [b]glorified.

Who Is He?

40 Therefore many[1] from the crowd, when they heard this saying, said, "Truly this is [a]the Prophet." 41 Others said, "This is [a]the Christ."

But some said, "Will the Christ come out of Galilee? 42 [a]Has not the Scripture said that the Christ comes from the seed of David and from the town of Bethlehem, [b]where David was?" 43 So [a]there was a division among the people because of Him. 44 Now [a]some of them wanted to take Him, but no one laid hands on Him.

Rejected by the Authorities

45 Then the officers came to the chief priests and Pharisees, who said to them, "Why have you not brought Him?"

46 The officers answered, [a]"No man ever spoke like this Man!"

47 Then the Pharisees answered them, "Are you also deceived? 48 Have any of the rulers or the Pharisees believed in Him? 49 But this crowd that does not know the law is accursed."

50 Nicodemus [a](he who came to Jesus by night,[1] being one of them) said to them, 51 [a]"Does our law judge a man before it hears him and knows what he is doing?"

52 They answered and said to him, "Are you also from Galilee? Search and look, for [a]no prophet has arisen[1] out of Galilee."

7:17 [a] John 3:21; 8:43 **7:18** [a] John 5:41 [b] John 8:50 [c] [2 Cor. 5:21] **7:19** [a] Deut. 33:4 [b] Matt. 12:14 **7:20** [a] John 8:48, 52 **7:22** [a] Lev. 12:3 [b] Gen. 17:9–14 **7:23** [a] John 5:8, 9, 16 **7:24** [a] Prov. 24:23 **7:25** [a] Matt. 21:38; 26:4 **7:26** [a] John 7:48 [1] NU-Text *omits truly.* **7:27** [a] Luke 4:22 **7:28** [a] John 8:14 [b] John 5:43 [c] Rom. 3:4 [d] John 1:18; 8:55 **7:29** [a] Matt. 11:27 [1] NU-Text and M-Text omit *But.* **7:30** [a] Mark 11:18 [b] John 7:32, 44; 8:20; 10:39 **7:31** [a] Matt. 12:23 **7:33** [a] John 13:33 [b] [1 Pet. 3:22] [1] NU-Text and M-Text omit *to them.* **7:34** [a] Hos. 5:6 [b] [Matt. 5:20] **7:35** [a] James 1:1 **7:37** [a] Lev. 23:36 [b] [Is. 55:1] **7:38** [a] Deut. 18:15 [b] Is. 12:3; 43:20; 44:3; 55:1 **7:39** [a] Is. 44:3 [b] John 12:16; 13:31; 17:5 [1] NU-Text reads *who believed.* [2] NU-Text omits *Holy.* **7:40** [a] Deut. 18:15, 18 [1] NU-Text reads *some.* **7:41** [a] John 4:42; 6:69 **7:42** [a] Mic. 5:2 [b] 1 Sam. 16:1, 4 **7:43** [a] John 7:12 **7:44** [a] John 7:30 **7:46** [a] Luke 4:22 **7:50** [a] John 3:1, 2; 19:39 [1] NU-Text reads *before.* **7:51** [a] Deut. 1:16, 17; 19:15 **7:52** [a] [Is. 9:1, 2] [1] NU-Text reads *is to rise.*

An Adulteress Faces the Light of the World

53And everyone went to his *own* house.[1]
8 But Jesus went to the Mount of Olives.
2Now early[1] in the morning He came again
into the temple, and all the people came to
Him; and He sat down and [a]taught them.
3Then the scribes and Pharisees brought to
Him a woman caught in adultery. And when
they had set her in the midst, 4they said to
Him, "Teacher, this woman was caught[1] in
[a]adultery, in the very act. 5[a]Now Moses, in
the law, commanded[1] us that such should
be stoned.[2] But what do You say?"[3] 6This
they said, testing Him, that they [a]might have
something of which to accuse Him. But Jesus
stooped down and wrote on the ground with
His finger, as though He did not hear.[1]
7So when they continued asking Him, He
raised Himself up[1] and said to them, [a]"He
who is without sin among you, let him throw
a stone at her first." 8And again He stooped
down and wrote on the ground. 9Then those
who heard *it,* [a]being convicted by *their* conscience,[1] went out one by one, beginning
with the oldest *even* to the last. And Jesus
was left alone, and the woman standing in
the midst. 10When Jesus had raised Himself
up and saw no one but the woman, He said
to her,[1] "Woman, where are those accusers of
yours?[2] Has no one condemned you?"
11She said, "No one, Lord."
And Jesus said to her, [a]"Neither do I condemn you; go and[1] [b]sin no more."
12Then Jesus spoke to them again, saying,
[a]"I am the light of the world. He who [b]follows
Me shall not walk in darkness, but have the
light of life."

Jesus Defends His Self-Witness

13The Pharisees therefore said to Him,
[a]"You bear witness of Yourself; Your witness
is not true."
14Jesus answered and said to them, "Even
if I bear witness of Myself, My witness is true,
for I know where I came from and where I
am going; but [a]you do not know where I
come from and where I am going. 15[a]You
judge according to the flesh; [b]I judge no
one. 16And yet if I do judge, My judgment
is true; for [a]I am not alone, but I *am* with
the Father who sent Me. 17[a]It is also written
in your law that the testimony of two men
is true. 18I am One who bears witness of

7:53 [1] The words *And everyone* through *sin no more* (8:11) are bracketed by NU-Text as not original. They are present in over 900 manuscripts. **8:2** [a] John 8:20; 18:20 [1] M-Text reads *very early.* **8:4** [a] Ex. 20:14 [1] M-Text reads *we found this woman.* **8:5** [a] Lev. 20:10 [1] M-Text reads *in our law Moses commanded.* [2] NU-Text and M-Text read *to stone such.* [3] M-Text adds *about her.* **8:6** [a] Matt. 22:15 [1] NU-Text and M-Text omit *as though He did not hear.* **8:7** [a] Deut. 17:7 [1] M-Text reads *He looked up.* **8:9** [a] Rom. 2:22 [1] NU-Text and M-Text omit *being convicted by their conscience.* **8:10** [1] NU-Text omits *and saw no one but the woman;* M-Text reads *He saw her and said.* [2] NU-Text and M-Text omit *of yours.* **8:11** [a] [John 3:17] [b] [John 5:14] [1] NU-Text and M-Text add *from now on.* **8:12** [a] John 1:4; 9:5; 12:35 [b] 1 Thess. 5:5 **8:13** [a] John 5:31 **8:14** [a] John 7:28; 9:29 **8:15** [a] John 7:24 [b] [John 3:17; 12:47; 18:36] **8:16** [a] John 16:32 **8:17** [a] Deut. 17:6; 19:15

DARKNESS NEVER HAD A CHANCE

"I am the light of the world."

JOHN 8:12

The modern world is filled with turmoil. Terrorists commit acts of violence. Strange opinions, some of which are obviously false, attract followers. We hear statements like "This is my truth" or "That is your truth." Many people are unsettled by these assertions. Is there really no truth?

In the world of Jesus and His followers, philosophers and politicians voiced arguable ideas. The popular pagan beliefs about the gods were contradictory and nonsensical. Pontius Pilate, the Roman governor who sent Jesus to the cross, cynically asked, "What is truth?" (18:38). Pushing back against the ignorance, Jesus boldly declared, "I am the light of the world. He who follows Me shall not walk in darkness, but have the light of life" (8:12; see 9:5).

Real peace is based on truth, not fad or personal preference. In Christ, the Light of the World, we have authentic peace. Commit to memorizing one of Jesus' sayings in John's Gospel that will reinforce His truth and peace in your life.

Myself, and [a]the Father who sent Me bears witness of Me."

19Then they said to Him, "Where is Your Father?"

Jesus answered, [a]"You know neither Me nor My Father. [b]If you had known Me, you would have known My Father also." 20These words Jesus spoke in [a]the treasury, as He taught in the temple; and [b]no one laid hands on Him, for [c]His hour had not yet come.

Jesus Predicts His Departure

21Then Jesus said to them again, "I am going away, and [a]you will seek Me, and [b]will die in your sin. Where I go you cannot come."

22So the Jews said, "Will He kill Himself, because He says, 'Where I go you cannot come'?"

23And He said to them, [a]"You are from beneath; I am from above. [b]You are of this world; I am not of this world. 24[a]Therefore I said to you that you will die in your sins; [b]for if you do not believe that I am *He,* you will die in your sins."

25Then they said to Him, "Who are You?"

And Jesus said to them, "Just what I [a]have been saying to you from the beginning. 26I have many things to say and to judge concerning you, but [a]He who sent Me is true; and [b]I speak to the world those things which I heard from Him."

27They did not understand that He spoke to them of the Father.

28Then Jesus said to them, "When you [a]lift up the Son of Man, [b]then you will know that I am *He,* and [c]*that* I do nothing of Myself; but [d]as My Father taught Me, I speak these things. 29And [a]He who sent Me is with Me. [b]The Father has not left Me alone, [c]for I always do those things that please Him." 30As He spoke these words, [a]many believed in Him.

The Truth Shall Make You Free

31Then Jesus said to those Jews who believed Him, "If you [a]abide in My word, you are My disciples indeed. 32And you shall know the [a]truth, and [b]the truth shall make you free."

33They answered Him, [a]"We are Abraham's descendants, and have never been in bondage to anyone. How *can* You say, 'You will be made free'?"

34Jesus answered them, "Most assuredly, I say to you, [a]whoever commits sin is a slave of sin. 35And [a]a slave does not abide in the house forever, *but* a son abides forever. 36[a]Therefore if the Son makes you free, you shall be free indeed.

Abraham's Seed and Satan's

37"I know that you are Abraham's descendants, but [a]you seek to kill Me, because My word has no place in you. 38[a]I speak what I have seen with My Father, and you do what you have seen with[1] your father."

39They answered and said to Him, [a]"Abraham is our father."

Jesus said to them, [b]"If you were Abraham's children, you would do the works of Abraham. 40[a]But now you seek to kill Me, a Man who has told you the truth [b]which I heard from God. Abraham did not do this. 41You do the deeds of your father."

Then they said to Him, "We were not born of fornication; [a]we have one Father—God."

42Jesus said to them, [a]"If God were your Father, you would love Me, for [b]I proceeded forth and came from God; [c]nor have I come of Myself, but He sent Me. 43[a]Why do you not understand My speech? Because you are not able to listen to My word. 44[a]You are of *your* father the devil, and the [b]desires of your father you want to [c]do. He was a murderer from the beginning, and [d]does not stand in the truth, because there is no truth in him.

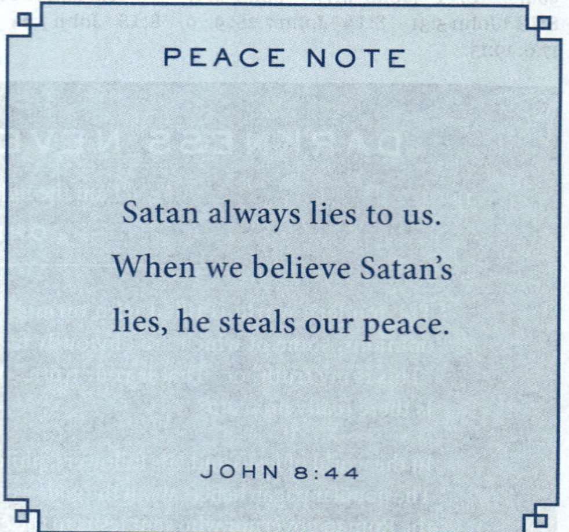

8:18 [a]John 5:37 **8:19** [a]John 16:3 [b]John 14:7 **8:20** [a]Mark 12:41, 43 [b]John 2:4; 7:30 [c]John 7:8 **8:21** [a]John 7:34; *13:33* [b]*John 8:24* **8:23** [a]*John 3:31* [b]1 John 4:5 **8:24** [a]John 8:21 [b][Mark 16:16] **8:25** [a]John 4:26 **8:26** [a]John 7:28 [b]John 3:32; 15:15 **8:28** [a]John 3:14; 12:32; 19:18 [b][Rom. 1:4] [c]John 5:19, 30 [d]John 3:11 **8:29** [a]John 14:10 [b]John 8:16; 16:32 [c]John 4:34; 5:30; 6:38 **8:30** [a]John 7:31; 10:42; 11:45 **8:31** [a][John 14:15, 23] **8:32** [a][John 1:14, 17; 14:6] [b][Rom. 6:14, 18, 22] **8:33** [a][Matt. 3:9] **8:34** [a]2 Pet. 2:19 **8:35** [a]Gal. 4:30 **8:36** [a]Gal. 5:1 **8:37** [a]John 7:19 **8:38** [a][John 3:32; 5:19, 30; 14:10, 24] [1]NU-Text reads *heard from.* **8:39** [a]Matt. 3:9 [b][Rom. 2:28] **8:40** [a]John 8:37 [b]John 8:26 **8:41** [a]Is. 63:16 **8:42** [a]1 John 5:1 [b]John 16:27; 17:8, 25 [c]Gal. 4:4 **8:43** [a][John 7:17] **8:44** [a]Matt. 13:38 [b]1 John 2:16, 17 [c][1 John 3:8–10, 15] [d][Jude 6]

When he speaks a lie, he speaks from his own
resources, for he is a liar and the father of it.
45But because I tell the truth, you do not
believe Me. 46Which of you convicts Me of
sin? And if I tell the truth, why do you not
believe Me? 47[a]He who is of God hears God's
words; therefore you do not hear, because
you are not of God."

Before Abraham Was, I AM

48Then the Jews answered and said to Him,
"Do we not say rightly that You are a Samaritan and [a]have a demon?"
49Jesus answered, "I do not have a demon;
but I honor My Father, and [a]you dishonor Me.
50And [a]I do not seek My *own* glory; there is
One who seeks and judges. 51Most assuredly, I say to you, [a]if anyone keeps My word he
shall never see death."
52Then the Jews said to Him, "Now we
know that You [a]have a demon! [b]Abraham
is dead, and the prophets; and You say, 'If
anyone keeps My word he shall never taste
death.' 53Are You greater than our father
Abraham, who is dead? And the prophets are
dead. [a]Who do You make Yourself out to be?"
54Jesus answered, [a]"If I honor Myself, My
honor is nothing. [b]It is My Father who honors Me, of whom you say that He is your[1]
God. 55Yet [a]you have not known Him, but I
know Him. And if I say, 'I do not know Him,'
I shall be a liar like you; but I do know Him
and [b]keep His word. 56Your father Abraham
[a]rejoiced to see My day, [b]and he saw *it* and
was glad."
57Then the Jews said to Him, "You are not
yet fifty years old, and have You seen Abraham?"
58Jesus said to them, "Most assuredly, I say
to you, [a]before Abraham was, [b]I AM."
59Then [a]they took up stones to throw at
Him; but Jesus hid Himself and went out
of the temple,[1] [b]going through the midst of
them, and so passed by.

A Man Born Blind Receives Sight

9 Now as *Jesus* passed by, He saw a man who
was blind from birth. 2And His disciples
asked Him, saying, "Rabbi, [a]who sinned, this
man or his parents, that he was born blind?"
3Jesus answered, "Neither this man nor his
parents sinned, [a]but that the works of God
should be revealed in him. 4[a]I[1] must work the
works of Him who sent Me while it is [b]day;
the night is coming when no one can work.
5As long as I am in the world, [a]I am the light
of the world."
6When He had said these things, [a]He spat
on the ground and made clay with the saliva;
and He anointed the eyes of the blind man
with the clay. 7And He said to him, "Go, wash
[a]in the pool of Siloam" (which is translated,
Sent). So [b]he went and washed, and came
back seeing.
8Therefore the neighbors and those who
previously had seen that he was blind[1] said,
"Is not this he who sat and begged?"
9Some said, "This is he." Others *said,* "He
is like him."[1]
He said, "I am *he.*"
10Therefore they said to him, "How were
your eyes opened?"
11He answered and said, [a]"A Man called
Jesus made clay and anointed my eyes and
said to me, 'Go to the pool of[1] Siloam and
wash.' So I went and washed, and I received
sight."
12Then they said to him, "Where is He?"
He said, "I do not know."

The Pharisees Excommunicate the Healed Man

13They brought him who formerly was
blind to the Pharisees. 14Now it was a Sabbath when Jesus made the clay and opened
his eyes. 15Then the Pharisees also asked
him again how he had received his sight. He
said to them, "He put clay on my eyes, and I
washed, and I see."
16Therefore some of the Pharisees said,
"This Man is not from God, because He does
not keep the Sabbath."
Others said, [a]"How can a man who is a
sinner do such signs?" And [b]there was a division among them.
17They said to the blind man again, "What
do you say about Him because He opened
your eyes?"
He said, [a]"He is a prophet."
18But the Jews did not believe concerning
him, that he had been blind and received his
sight, until they called the parents of him
who had received his sight. 19And they asked
them, saying, "Is this your son, who you say
was born blind? How then does he now see?"
20His parents answered them and said,

8:47 [a] 1 John 4:6 **8:48** [a] John 7:20; 10:20 **8:49** [a] John 5:41 **8:50** [a] John 5:41; 7:18 **8:51** [a] John 5:24; 11:26
8:52 [a] John 7:20; 10:20 [b] Zech. 1:5 **8:53** [a] John 10:33; 19:7 **8:54** [a] John 5:31, 32 [b] Acts 3:13 [1] NU-Text and M-Text read *our.*
8:55 [a] John 7:28, 29 [b] [John 15:10] **8:56** [a] Luke 10:24 [b] Heb. 11:13 **8:58** [a] Mic. 5:2 [b] Rev. 1:8 **8:59** [a] John 10:31; 11:8
[b] Luke 4:30 [1] NU-Text omits the rest of this verse. **9:2** [a] John 9:34 **9:3** [a] John 11:4 **9:4** [a] [John 4:34; 5:19, 36; 17:4]
[b] John 11:9, 10; 12:35 [1] NU-Text reads *We.* **9:5** [a] [John 1:5, 9; 3:19; 8:12; 12:35, 46] **9:6** [a] Mark 7:33; 8:23 **9:7** [a] Neh. 3:15
[b] 2 Kin. 5:14 **9:8** [1] NU-Text reads *a beggar.* **9:9** [1] NU-Text reads *"No, but he is like him."* **9:11** [a] John 9:6, 7
[1] NU-Text omits *the pool of.* **9:16** [a] John 3:2; 9:33 [b] John 7:12, 43; 10:19 **9:17** [a] [John 4:19; 6:14]

"We know that this is our son, and that he was born blind; [21]but by what means he now sees we do not know, or who opened his eyes we do not know. He is of age; ask him. He will speak for himself." [22]His parents said these *things* because [a]they feared the Jews, for the Jews had agreed already that if anyone confessed *that* He *was* Christ, he [b]would be put out of the synagogue. [23]Therefore his parents said, "He is of age; ask him."

[24]So they again called the man who was blind, and said to him, [a]"Give God the glory! [b]We know that this Man is a sinner."

[25]He answered and said, "Whether He is a sinner *or not* I do not know. One thing I know: that though I was blind, now I see."

[26]Then they said to him again, "What did He do to you? How did He open your eyes?"

[27]He answered them, "I told you already, and you did not listen. Why do you want to hear *it* again? Do you also want to become His disciples?"

[28]Then they reviled him and said, "You are His disciple, but we are Moses' disciples. [29]We know that God [a]spoke to [b]Moses; *as for* this *fellow,* [c]we do not know where He is from."

[30]The man answered and said to them, [a]"Why, this is a marvelous thing, that you do not know where He is from; yet He has opened my eyes! [31]Now we know that [a]God does not hear sinners; but if anyone is a worshiper of God and does His will, He hears him. [32]Since the world began it has been unheard of that anyone opened the eyes of one who was born blind. [33][a]If this Man were not from God, He could do nothing."

[34]They answered and said to him, [a]"You were completely born in sins, and are you teaching us?" And they cast him out.

True Vision and True Blindness

[35]Jesus heard that they had cast him out; and when He had [a]found him, He said to him, "Do you [b]believe in [c]the Son of God?"[1]

[36]He answered and said, "Who is He, Lord, that I may believe in Him?"

[37]And Jesus said to him, "You have both seen Him and [a]it is He who is talking with you."

[38]Then he said, "Lord, I believe!" And he [a]worshiped Him.

[39]And Jesus said, [a]"For judgment I have come into this world, [b]that those who do not see may see, and that those who see may be made blind."

[40]Then *some* of the Pharisees who were with Him heard these words, [a]and said to Him, "Are we blind also?"

[41]Jesus said to them, [a]"If you were blind, you would have no sin; but now you say, 'We see.' Therefore your sin remains.

Jesus the True Shepherd

10 "Most assuredly, I say to you, he who does not enter the sheepfold by the door, but climbs up some other way, the same is a thief and a robber. [2]But he who enters by the door is the shepherd of the sheep. [3]To him the doorkeeper opens, and the sheep hear his voice; and he calls his own sheep by [a]name and leads them out. [4]And when he brings out his own sheep, he goes before them; and the sheep follow him, for they know his voice. [5]Yet they will by no means follow a [a]stranger, but will flee from him, for they do not know the voice of strangers." [6]Jesus used this illustration, but they did not understand the things which He spoke to them.

Jesus the Good Shepherd

[7]Then Jesus said to them again, "Most assuredly, I say to you, I am the door of the sheep. [8]All who *ever* came before Me[1] are thieves and robbers, but the sheep did not hear them. [9][a]I am the door. If anyone enters by Me, he will be saved, and will go in and out and find pasture. [10]The thief does not come except to steal, and to kill, and to destroy. I have come that they may have life, and that they may have *it* more abundantly.

[11][a]"I am the good shepherd. The good shepherd gives His life for the sheep. [12]But a hireling, *he who is* not the shepherd, one who does not own the sheep, sees the wolf coming and [a]leaves the sheep and flees; and the wolf catches the sheep and scatters them. [13]The hireling flees because he is a hireling and does not care about the sheep. [14]I am the good shepherd; and [a]I know My *sheep,* and [b]am known by My own. [15][a]As the Father knows Me, even so I know the Father; [b]and I lay down My life for the sheep. [16]And [a]other sheep I have which are not of this fold; them also I must bring, and they will hear My voice; [b]and there will be one flock *and* one shepherd.

[17]"Therefore My Father [a]loves Me, [b]because I lay down My life that I may take it again. [18]No one takes it from Me, but I lay it down

9:22 [a] Acts 5:13 [b] John 16:2 **9:24** [a] Josh. 7:19 [b] John 9:16 **9:29** [a] Num. 12:6–8 [b] [John 5:45–47] [c] John 7:27, 28; 8:14 **9:30** [a] John 3:10 **9:31** [a] Zech. 7:13 **9:33** [a] John 3:2; 9:16 **9:34** [a] John 9:2 **9:35** [a] John 5:14 [b] John 1:7; 16:31 [c] Matt. 14:33; 16:16 [1] NU-Text reads *Son of Man.* **9:37** [a] John 4:26 **9:38** [a] Matt. 8:2 **9:39** [a] [John 3:17; 5:22, 27; 12:47] [b] Matt. 13:13; 15:14 **9:40** [a] [Rom. 2:19] **9:41** [a] John 15:22, 24 **10:3** [a] John 20:16 **10:5** [a] [2 Cor. 11:13–15] **10:8** [1] M-Text omits *before Me.* **10:9** [a] [Eph. 2:18] **10:11** [a] Is. 40:11 **10:12** [a] Zech. 11:16, 17 **10:14** [a] 2 Tim. 2:19 [b] 2 Tim. 1:12 **10:15** [a] Matt. 11:27 [b] [John 15:13; 19:30] **10:16** [a] Is. 42:6; 56:8 [b] Eph. 2:13–18 **10:17** [a] John 5:20 [b] [Heb. 2:9]

THE PEACE-DELIVERING SHEPHERD

"I am the good shepherd. The good shepherd gives His life."

JOHN 10:11

Moses long before had begged God to set up a leader for the Israelites so they would not become "like sheep which have no shepherd" (Num. 27:17). Alas, in later times, the leaders of Israel were corrupt and violent (Ezek. 34:2, 7–10). Even in the years leading up to Jesus' ministry, Jewish writings bitterly complained of Israel's avaricious leaders. But the prophet Ezekiel prophesied to the discouraged people of Israel that one day God Himself would be Israel's Shepherd: "As a shepherd seeks out his flock on the day he is among his scattered sheep, so will I seek out My sheep and deliver them" (Ezek. 34:12).

Jesus' bold declaration would have been understood in light of these prophetic oracles when He said, "I am the good shepherd. The good shepherd gives His life for the sheep" (John 10:11). In contrast to those who robbed and exploited God's people, Jesus protected His people and even laid down His life for them. The well-being of His people is Jesus' chief concern. Herein lie the grounds for hope and peace: "If God is for us, who can be against us?" (Rom. 8:31).

What does this mean for you? Can any problem or peace-thief be bigger than God's presence and love?

of Myself. I [a]have power to lay it down, and I
have power to take it again. [b]This command
I have received from My Father."
19Therefore [a]there was a division again
among the Jews because of these sayings.
20And many of them said, [a]"He has a demon
and is mad. Why do you listen to Him?"
21Others said, "These are not the words of
one who has a demon. [a]Can a demon [b]open
the eyes of the blind?"

The Shepherd Knows His Sheep

22Now it was the Feast of Dedication in
Jerusalem, and it was winter. 23And Jesus
walked in the temple, [a]in Solomon's porch.
24Then the Jews surrounded Him and said
to Him, "How long do You keep us in doubt?
If You are the Christ, tell us plainly."
25Jesus answered them, "I told you, and
you do not believe. [a]The works that I do in
My Father's name, they [b]bear witness of Me.
26But [a]you do not believe, because you are
not of My sheep, as I said to you.[1] 27[a]My sheep
hear My voice, and I know them, and they
follow Me. 28And I give them eternal life, and
they shall never perish; neither shall anyone
snatch them out of My hand. 29[a]My Father,
[b]who has given *them* to Me, is greater than all;
and no one is able to snatch *them* out of My
Father's hand. 30[a]I and *My* Father are one."

Renewed Efforts to Stone Jesus

31Then [a]the Jews took up stones again to
stone Him. 32Jesus answered them, "Many
good works I have shown you from My Father.
For which of those works do you stone Me?"
33The Jews answered Him, saying, "For

PEACE NOTE

Jesus protects us from the great enemy who tries to seize us. Reflect on the promise of Jesus' eternal hold on us. What a reason for peace!

JOHN 10:28

10:18 [a] [John 2:19; 5:26] [b] [John 6:38; 14:31; 17:4; Acts 2:24, 32] **10:19** [a] John 7:43; 9:16 **10:20** [a] John 7:20 **10:21** [a] [Ex. 4:11] [b] John 9:6, 7, 32, 33 **10:23** [a] Acts 3:11; 5:12 **10:25** [a] John 5:36; 10:38 [b] Matt. 11:4 **10:26** [a] [John 8:47] [1] NU-Text omits *as I said to you.* **10:27** [a] John 10:4, 14 **10:29** [a] John 14:28 [b] [John 17:2, 6, 12, 24] **10:30** [a] John 17:11, 21–24 **10:31** [a] John 8:59

a good work we do not stone You, but for
[a]blasphemy, and because You, being a Man,
[b]make Yourself God."
34 Jesus answered them, "Is it not written
in your law, [a]'I said, "You are gods" '?[1] 35 If
He called them gods, [a]to whom the word
of God came (and the Scripture [b]cannot be
broken), 36 do you say of Him [a]whom the
Father sanctified and [b]sent into the world,
'You are blaspheming,' [c]because I said, 'I am
[d]the Son of God'? 37 [a]If I do not do the works
of My Father, do not believe Me; 38 but if I do,
though you do not believe Me, [a]believe the
works, that you may know and believe[1] [b]that
the Father *is* in Me, and I in Him." 39 [a]There-
fore they sought again to seize Him, but He
escaped out of their hand.

The Believers Beyond Jordan

40 And He went away again beyond the Jordan to the place [a]where John was baptizing
at first, and there He stayed. 41 Then many
came to Him and said, "John performed no
sign, [a]but all the things that John spoke about
this Man were true." 42 And many believed in
Him there.

The Death of Lazarus

11 Now a certain *man* was sick, Lazarus
of Bethany, the town of [a]Mary and her
sister Martha. 2 [a]It was *that* Mary who anointed the Lord with fragrant oil and wiped His
feet with her hair, whose brother Lazarus
was sick. 3 Therefore the sisters sent to Him,
saying, "Lord, behold, he whom You love
is sick."
4 When Jesus heard *that,* He said, "This
sickness is not unto death, but for the glory
of God, that the Son of God may be glorified
through it."
5 Now Jesus loved Martha and her sister
and Lazarus. 6 So, when He heard that he was
sick, [a]He stayed two more days in the place
where He was. 7 Then after this He said to *the*
disciples, "Let us go to Judea again."
8 *The* disciples said to Him, "Rabbi, lately
the Jews sought to [a]stone You, and are You
going there again?"
9 Jesus answered, "Are there not twelve
hours in the day? [a]If anyone walks in the day,
he does not stumble, because he sees the
[b]light of this world. 10 But [a]if one walks in the
night, he stumbles, because the light is not
in him." 11 These things He said, and after that
He said to them, "Our friend Lazarus [a]sleeps,
but I go that I may wake him up."
12 Then His disciples said, "Lord, if he sleeps
he will get well." 13 However, Jesus spoke of his
death, but they thought that He was speaking
about taking rest in sleep.
14 Then Jesus said to them plainly, "Lazarus is dead. 15 And I am glad for your sakes
that I was not there, that you may believe.
Nevertheless let us go to him."
16 Then [a]Thomas, who is called the Twin,
said to his fellow disciples, "Let us also go,
that we may die with Him."

I Am the Resurrection and the Life

17 So when Jesus came, He found that he
had already been in the tomb four days.
18 Now Bethany was near Jerusalem, about
two miles[1] away. 19 And many of the Jews had
joined the women around Martha and Mary,
to comfort them concerning their brother.
20 Then Martha, as soon as she heard that
Jesus was coming, went and met Him, but
Mary was sitting in the house. 21 Now Martha
said to Jesus, "Lord, if You had been here, my
brother would not have died. 22 But even now
I know that [a]whatever You ask of God, God
will give You."
23 Jesus said to her, "Your brother will rise
again."
24 Martha said to Him, [a]"I know that he will
rise again in the resurrection at the last day."
25 Jesus said to her, "I am [a]the resurrection
and the life. [b]He who believes in Me, though
he may [c]die, he shall live. 26 And whoever
lives and believes in Me shall never die. Do
you believe this?"
27 She said to Him, "Yes, Lord, [a]I believe
that You are the Christ, the Son of God, who
is to come into the world."

Jesus and Death, the Last Enemy

28 And when she had said these things, she
went her way and secretly called Mary her
sister, saying, "The Teacher has come and is
calling for you." 29 As soon as she heard *that,*
she arose quickly and came to Him. 30 Now
Jesus had not yet come into the town, but
was[1] in the place where Martha met Him.
31 [a]Then the Jews who were with her in the
house, and comforting her, when they saw
that Mary rose up quickly and went out,

10:33 [a] Matt. 9:3 [b] John 5:18 **10:34** [a] Ps. 82:6 [1] Psalm 82:6 **10:35** [a] Matt. 5:17, 18 [b] 1 Pet. 1:25 **10:36** [a] John 6:27 [b] John 3:17 [c] John 5:17, 18 [d] Luke 1:35 **10:37** [a] John 10:25; 15:24 **10:38** [a] John 5:36 [b] John 14:10, 11 [1] NU-Text reads *understand.* **10:39** [a] John 7:30, 44 **10:40** [a] John 1:28 **10:41** [a] [John 1:29, 36; 3:28–36; 5:33] **11:1** [a] Luke 10:38, 39 **11:2** [a] Matt. 26:7 **11:6** [a] John 10:40 **11:8** [a] John 8:59; 10:31 **11:9** [a] John 9:4; 12:35 [b] Is. 9:2 **11:10** [a] John 12:35 **11:11** [a] Matt. 9:24 **11:16** [a] John 14:5; 20:26–28 **11:18** [1] Literally *fifteen stadia* **11:22** [a] [John 9:31; 11:41] **11:24** [a] [John 5:29] **11:25** [a] John 5:21; 6:39, 40, 44 [b] 1 John 5:10 [c] 1 Cor. 15:22 **11:27** [a] Matt. 16:16 **11:30** [1] NU-Text adds *still.* **11:31** [a] John 11:19, 33

DO YOU BELIEVE?

"I am the resurrection and the life."

JOHN 11:25

One of the saddest stories in the Gospels is the death of Lazarus, brother of Mary and Martha, all friends of Jesus who lived near Jerusalem. Lazarus had been ill for some time. Jesus arrived four days after his death.

Martha reproached Jesus for taking so long: "Lord, if You had been here, my brother would not have died" (v. 21). The sisters' grief was so pitiful that even "Jesus wept" (v. 35). Jesus promised the sisters that their brother would live again, and they assured Him they believed that he would "rise again in the resurrection at the last day" (v. 24). But Jesus asserted, "I am the resurrection and the life . . . Whoever lives and believes in Me shall never die. Do you believe this?" (v. 25). And then He raised Lazarus from the dead.

Jesus' question is a good one. Do you believe in Him? We have hope and peace because Jesus is the resurrection and the life. Identify any barrier you have to a fuller faith in Jesus and surrender it to Him.

followed her, saying, "She is going to the
tomb to weep there."[1]
32 Then, when Mary came where Jesus was,
and saw Him, she [a]fell down at His feet, saying to Him, [b]"Lord, if You had been here, my
brother would not have died."
33 Therefore, when Jesus saw her weeping,
and the Jews who came with her weeping,
He groaned in the spirit and was troubled.
34 And He said, "Where have you laid him?"
They said to Him, "Lord, come and see."
35 [a]Jesus wept. 36 Then the Jews said, "See
how He loved him!"
37 And some of them said, "Could not this
Man, [a]who opened the eyes of the blind, also
have kept this man from dying?"

Lazarus Raised from the Dead

38 Then Jesus, again groaning in Himself,
came to the tomb. It was a cave, and a [a]stone
lay against it. 39 Jesus said, "Take away the
stone."
Martha, the sister of him who was dead,
said to Him, "Lord, by this time there is a
stench, for he has been *dead* four days."
40 Jesus said to her, "Did I not say to you
that if you would believe you would [a]see the
glory of God?" 41 Then they took away the
stone *from the place* where the dead man was
lying.[1] And Jesus lifted up *His* eyes and said,
"Father, I thank You that You have heard Me.
42 And I know that You always hear Me, but
[a]because of the people who are standing by
I said *this,* that they may believe that You
sent Me." 43 Now when He had said these
things, He cried with a loud voice, "Lazarus,
come forth!" 44 And he who had died came
out bound hand and foot with [a]graveclothes,
and [b]his face was wrapped with a cloth. Jesus
said to them, "Loose him, and let him go."

The Plot to Kill Jesus

45 Then many of the Jews who had come
to Mary, [a]and had seen the things Jesus did,
believed in Him. 46 But some of them went
away to the Pharisees and [a]told them the
things Jesus did. 47 [a]Then the chief priests
and the Pharisees gathered a council and
said, [b]"What shall we do? For this Man works
many signs. 48 If we let Him alone like this,
everyone will believe in Him, and the Romans will come and take away both our place
and nation."
49 And one of them, [a]Caiaphas, being high
priest that year, said to them, "You know
nothing at all, 50 [a]nor do you consider that it
is expedient for us[1] that one man should die
for the people, and not that the whole nation
should perish." 51 Now this he did not say on
his own *authority;* but being high priest that
year he prophesied that Jesus would die for
the nation, 52 and [a]not for that nation only,

11:31 [1] NU-Text reads *supposing that she was going to the tomb to weep there.* **11:32** [a] Rev. 1:17 [b] John 11:21 **11:35** [a] Luke 19:41 **11:37** [a] John 9:6, 7 **11:38** [a] Matt. 27:60, 66 **11:40** [a] [John 11:4, 23] **11:41** [1] NU-Text omits *from the place where the dead man was lying.* **11:42** [a] John 12:30; 17:21 **11:44** [a] John 19:40 [b] John 20:7 **11:45** [a] John 2:23; 10:42; 12:11, 18 **11:46** [a] John 5:15 **11:47** [a] Ps. 2:2 [b] Acts 4:16 **11:49** [a] Luke 3:2 **11:50** [a] John 18:14 [1] NU-Text reads *you.* **11:52** [a] Is. 49:6

but [b]also that He would gather together in one the children of God who were scattered abroad.

53 Then, from that day on, they plotted to [a]put Him to death. 54 [a]Therefore Jesus no longer walked openly among the Jews, but went from there into the country near the wilderness, to a city called [b]Ephraim, and there remained with His disciples.

55 [a]And the Passover of the Jews was near, and many went from the country up to Jerusalem before the Passover, to [b]purify themselves. 56 [a]Then they sought Jesus, and spoke among themselves as they stood in the temple, "What do you think—that He will not come to the feast?" 57 Now both the chief priests and the Pharisees had given a command, that if anyone knew where He was, he should report *it,* that they might [a]seize Him.

The Anointing at Bethany

12 Then, six days before the Passover, Jesus came to Bethany, [a]where Lazarus was who had been dead,[1] whom He had raised from the dead. 2 [a]There they made Him a supper; and Martha served, but Lazarus was one of those who sat at the table with Him. 3 Then [a]Mary took a pound of very costly oil of [b]spikenard, anointed the feet of Jesus, and wiped His feet with her hair. And the house was filled with the fragrance of the oil.

4 But one of His disciples, [a]Judas Iscariot, Simon's *son,* who would betray Him, said, 5 "Why was this fragrant oil not sold for three hundred denarii[1] and given to the poor?" 6 This he said, not that he cared for the poor, but because he was a thief, and [a]had the money box; and he used to take what was put in it.

7 But Jesus said, "Let her alone; she has kept[1] this for the day of My burial. 8 For [a]the poor you have with you always, but Me you do not have always."

The Plot to Kill Lazarus

9 Now a great many of the Jews knew that He was there; and they came, not for Jesus' sake only, but that they might also see Lazarus, [a]whom He had raised from the dead. 10 [a]But the chief priests plotted to put Lazarus to death also, 11 [a]because on account of him many of the Jews went away and believed in Jesus.

The Triumphal Entry

12 [a]The next day a great multitude that had come to the feast, when they heard that Jesus was coming to Jerusalem, 13 took branches of palm trees and went out to meet Him, and cried out:

"Hosanna!
[a]'Blessed *is* He who comes in the name
of the LORD!'[1]
The King of Israel!"

14 [a]Then Jesus, when He had found a young donkey, sat on it; as it is written:

15 "Fear[a] not, daughter of Zion;
Behold, your King is coming,
Sitting on a donkey's colt."[1]

16 [a]His disciples did not understand these things at first; [b]but when Jesus was glorified, [c]then they remembered that these things were written about Him and *that* they had done these things to Him.

17 Therefore the people, who were with Him when He called Lazarus out of his tomb and raised him from the dead, bore witness. 18 [a]For this reason the people also met Him, because they heard that He had done this sign. 19 The Pharisees therefore said among themselves, [a]"You see that you are accomplishing nothing. Look, the world has gone after Him!"

The Fruitful Grain of Wheat

20 Now there [a]were certain Greeks among those [b]who came up to worship at the feast. 21 Then they came to Philip, [a]who was from Bethsaida of Galilee, and asked him, saying, "Sir, we wish to see Jesus."

22 Philip came and told Andrew, and in turn Andrew and Philip told Jesus.

23 But Jesus answered them, saying, [a]"The hour has come that the Son of Man should be glorified. 24 Most assuredly, I say to you, [a]unless a grain of wheat falls into the ground and dies, it remains alone; but if it dies, it produces much grain. 25 [a]He who loves his life will lose it, and he who hates his life in this world will keep it for eternal life. 26 If anyone serves Me, let him [a]follow Me; and [b]where I am, there My servant will be also. If anyone serves Me, him *My* Father will honor.

11:52 [b] [Eph. 2:14–17] **11:53** [a] Matt. 26:4 **11:54** [a] John 4:1, 3; 7:1 [b] 2 Chr. 13:19 **11:55** [a] John 2:13; 5:1; 6:4 [b] Num. 9:10, 13; 31:19, 20 **11:56** [a] John 7:11 **11:57** [a] Matt. 26:14–16 **12:1** [a] John 11:1, 43 [1] NU-Text omits *who had been dead.* **12:2** [a] Mark 14:3; Luke 10:38–41 **12:3** [a] John 11:2 [b] Song 1:12 **12:4** [a] John 13:26 **12:5** [1] About one year's wages for a worker **12:6** [a] John 13:29 **12:7** [1] NU-Text reads *that she may keep.* **12:8** [a] Mark 14:7 **12:9** [a] John 11:43, 44 **12:10** [a] Luke 16:31 **12:11** [a] John 11:45; 12:18 **12:12** [a] Matt. 21:4–9 **12:13** [a] Ps. 118:25, 26 [1] Psalm 118:26 **12:14** [a] Matt. 21:7 **12:15** [a] Is. 40:9; Zech. 9:9 [1] Zechariah 9:9 **12:16** [a] Luke 18:34 [b] John 7:39; 12:23 [c] [John 14:26] **12:18** [a] John 12:11 **12:19** [a] John 11:47, 48 **12:20** [a] Acts 17:4 [b] 1 Kin. 8:41, 42 **12:21** [a] John 1:43, 44; 14:8–11 **12:23** [a] John 13:32 **12:24** [a] 1 Cor. 15:36 **12:25** [a] Mark 8:35 **12:26** [a] [Matt. 16:24] [b] John 14:3; 17:24

Jesus Predicts His Death on the Cross

27[a]"Now My soul is troubled, and what shall
I say? 'Father, save Me from this hour'? [b]But
for this purpose I came to this hour. 28Father,
glorify Your name."

[a]Then a voice came from heaven, *saying,*
"I have both glorified *it* and will glorify *it*
again."

29Therefore the people who stood by and
heard *it* said that it had thundered. Others
said, "An angel has spoken to Him."

30Jesus answered and said, [a]"This voice did
not come because of Me, but for your sake.
31Now is the judgment of this world; now [a]the
ruler of this world will be cast out. 32And I, [a]if
I am lifted up from the earth, will draw [b]all
peoples to Myself." 33[a]This He said, signifying
by what death He would die.

34The people answered Him, [a]"We have
heard from the law that the Christ remains
forever; and how *can* You say, 'The Son of
Man must be lifted up'? Who is this Son of
Man?"

35Then Jesus said to them, "A little while
longer [a]the light is with you. [b]Walk while you
have the light, lest darkness overtake you;
[c]he who walks in darkness does not know
where he is going. 36While you have the light,
believe in the light, that you may become
[a]sons of light." These things Jesus spoke,
and departed, and [b]was hidden from them.

Who Has Believed Our Report?

37But although He had done so many
[a]signs before them, they did not believe in
Him, 38that the word of Isaiah the prophet
might be fulfilled, which he spoke:

> [a]"Lord, who has believed our report?
> And to whom has the arm of the LORD
> been revealed?"[1]

39Therefore they could not believe, because Isaiah said again:

> 40 "He[a] has blinded their eyes and
> hardened their hearts,
> [b]Lest they should see with *their* eyes,
> Lest they should understand with *their*
> hearts and turn,
> So that I should heal them."[1]

41[a]These things Isaiah said when[1] he saw His
glory and spoke of Him.

Walk in the Light

42Nevertheless even among the rulers
many believed in Him, but [a]because of the
Pharisees they did not confess *Him,* lest they
should be put out of the synagogue; 43[a]for
they loved the praise of men more than the
praise of God.

44Then Jesus cried out and said, [a]"He who
believes in Me, [b]believes not in Me [c]but in
Him who sent Me. 45And [a]he who sees Me sees
Him who sent Me. 46[a]I have come *as* a light
into the world, that whoever believes in Me
should not abide in darkness. 47And if anyone
hears My words and does not believe,[1] [a]I do
not judge him; for [b]I did not come to judge
the world but to save the world. 48[a]He who
rejects Me, and does not receive My words,
has that which judges him—[b]the word that
I have spoken will judge him in the last day.
49For [a]I have not spoken on My own *authority;*
but the Father who sent Me gave Me a command, [b]what I should say and what I should
speak. 50And I know that His command is
everlasting life. Therefore, whatever I speak,
just as the Father has told Me, so I [a]speak."

Jesus Washes the Disciples' Feet

13 Now [a]before the Feast of the Passover,
when Jesus knew that [b]His hour had
come that He should depart from this world
to the Father, having loved His own who were
in the world, He [c]loved them to the end.

2And supper being ended,[1] [a]the devil having already put it into the heart of Judas
Iscariot, Simon's *son,* to betray Him, 3Jesus,
knowing [a]that the Father had given all things
into His hands, and that He [b]had come from
God and [c]was going to God, 4[a]rose from supper and laid aside His garments, took a towel
and girded Himself. 5After that, He poured
water into a basin and began to wash the
disciples' feet, and to wipe *them* with the
towel with which He was girded. 6Then He
came to Simon Peter. And *Peter* said to Him,
[a]"Lord, are You washing my feet?"

7Jesus answered and said to him, "What I
am doing you [a]do not understand now, [b]but
you will know after this."

12:27 [a] [Matt. 26:38, 39] [b] Luke 22:53 **12:28** [a] Matt. 3:17; 17:5 **12:30** [a] John 11:42 **12:31** [a] [2 Cor. 4:4] **12:32** [a] John 3:14; 8:28 [b] [Rom. 5:18] **12:33** [a] John 18:32; 21:19 **12:34** [a] Mic. 4:7 **12:35** [a] [John 1:9; 7:33; 8:12] [b] Eph. 5:8 [c] [1 John 2:9–11] **12:36** [a] Luke 16:8 [b] John 8:59 **12:37** [a] John 11:47 **12:38** [a] Is. 53:1 [1] Isaiah 53:1 **12:40** [a] Is. 6:9, 10 [b] Matt. 13:14 [1] Isaiah 6:10 **12:41** [a] Is. 6:1 [1] NU-Text reads *because.* **12:42** [a] John 7:13; 9:22 **12:43** [a] John 5:41, 44 **12:44** [a] Mark 9:37 [b] [John 3:16, 18, 36; 11:25, 26] [c] [John 5:24] **12:45** [a] [John 14:9] **12:46** [a] John 1:4, 5; 8:12; 12:35, 36 **12:47** [a] John 5:45 [b] John 3:17 [1] NU-Text reads *keep them.* **12:48** [a] [Luke 10:16] [b] Deut. 18:18, 19 **12:49** [a] John 8:38 [b] Deut. 18:18 **12:50** [a] John 5:19; 8:28 **13:1** [a] Matt. 26:2 [b] John 12:23; 17:1 [c] John 15:9 **13:2** [a] Luke 22:3 [1] NU-Text reads *And during supper.* **13:3** [a] Acts 2:36 [b] John 8:42; 16:28 [c] John 17:11; 20:17 **13:4** [a] [Luke 22:27] **13:6** [a] Matt. 3:14 **13:7** [a] John 12:16; 16:12 [b] John 13:19

8 Peter said to Him, "You shall never wash
my feet!"
Jesus answered him, [a]"If I do not wash
you, you have no part with Me."
9 Simon Peter said to Him, "Lord, not my
feet only, but also *my* hands and *my* head!"
10 Jesus said to him, "He who is bathed
needs only to wash *his* feet, but is completely
clean; and [a]you are clean, but not all of you."
11 For [a]He knew who would betray Him; therefore He said, "You are not all clean."
12 So when He had washed their feet, taken
His garments, and sat down again, He said
to them, "Do you know what I have done
to you? 13 [a]You call Me Teacher and Lord,
and you say well, for *so* I am. 14 [a]If I then,
your Lord and Teacher, have washed your
feet, [b]you also ought to wash one another's
feet. 15 For [a]I have given you an example,
that you should do as I have done to you.
16 [a]Most assuredly, I say to you, a servant is
not greater than his master; nor is he who
is sent greater than he who sent him. 17 [a]If
you know these things, blessed are you if
you do them.

Jesus Identifies His Betrayer

18 "I do not speak concerning all of you.
I know whom I have chosen; but that the
[a]Scripture may be fulfilled, [b]'He who eats
bread with Me[1] has lifted up his heel against
Me.'[2] 19 [a]Now I tell you before it comes, that
when it does come to pass, you may believe
that I am *He.* 20 [a]Most assuredly, I say to you,
he who receives whomever I send receives
Me; and he who receives Me receives Him
who sent Me."
21 [a]When Jesus had said these things, [b]He
was troubled in spirit, and testified and said,
"Most assuredly, I say to you, [c]one of you will
betray Me." 22 Then the disciples looked at one
another, perplexed about whom He spoke.
23 Now [a]there was leaning on Jesus' bosom
one of His disciples, whom Jesus loved.
24 Simon Peter therefore motioned to him
to ask who it was of whom He spoke.
25 Then, leaning back[1] on Jesus' breast, he
said to Him, "Lord, who is it?"
26 Jesus answered, "It is he to whom I shall
give a piece of bread when I have dipped *it.*"
And having dipped the bread, He gave *it* to
[a]Judas Iscariot, *the son* of Simon. 27 [a]Now
after the piece of bread, Satan entered him.
Then Jesus said to him, "What you do, do
quickly." 28 But no one at the table knew for
what reason He said this to him. 29 For some
thought, because [a]Judas had the money box,
that Jesus had said to him, "Buy *those things*
we need for the feast," or that he should give
something to the poor.
30 Having received the piece of bread, he
then went out immediately. And it was night.

The New Commandment

31 So, when he had gone out, Jesus said,
[a]"Now the Son of Man is glorified, and [b]God is
glorified in Him. 32 If God is glorified in Him,
God will also glorify Him in Himself, and
[a]glorify Him immediately. 33 Little children,
I shall be with you a [a]little while longer. You
will seek Me; [b]and as I said to the Jews, 'Where
I am going, you cannot come,' so now I say to
you. 34 [a]A new commandment I give to you,
that you love one another; as I have loved
you, that you also love one another. 35 [a]By
this all will know that you are My disciples,
if you have love for one another."

Jesus Predicts Peter's Denial

36 Simon Peter said to Him, "Lord, where
are You going?"
Jesus answered him, "Where I [a]am going
you cannot follow Me now, but [b]you shall
follow Me afterward."
37 Peter said to Him, "Lord, why can I not
follow You now? I will [a]lay down my life for
Your sake."
38 Jesus answered him, "Will you lay down
your life for My sake? Most assuredly, I say to
you, the rooster shall not [a]crow till you have
denied Me three times.

The Way, the Truth, and the Life

14 "Let [a]not your heart be troubled; you
believe in God, believe also in Me. 2 In
My Father's house are many mansions;[1] if
it were not *so,* I would have told you. [a]I go
to prepare a place for you.[2] 3 And if I go and
prepare a place for you, [a]I will come again
and receive you to Myself; that [b]where I am,
there you may be also. 4 And where I go you
know, and the way you know."

13:8 [a] [1 Cor. 6:11] **13:10** [a] [John 15:3] **13:11** [a] John 6:64; 18:4 **13:13** [a] Matt. 23:8, 10 **13:14** [a] Luke 22:27 [b] [Rom. 12:10] **13:15** [a] [1 Pet. 2:21–24] **13:16** [a] Matt. 10:24 **13:17** [a] [James 1:25] **13:18** [a] John 15:25; 17:12 [b] Ps. 41:9 [1] NU-Text reads *My bread.* [2] *Psalm 41:9* **13:19** [a] John 14:29; 16:4 **13:20** [a] Matt. 10:40 **13:21** [a] Luke 22:21 [b] John 12:27 [c] 1 John 2:19 **13:23** [a] John 19:26; 20:2; 21:7, 20 **13:25** [1] NU-Text and M-Text add *thus.* **13:26** [a] John 6:70, 71; 12:4 **13:27** [a] Luke 22:3 **13:29** [a] John 12:6 **13:31** [a] John 12:23 [b] [1 Pet. 4:11] **13:32** [a] John 12:23 **13:33** [a] John 12:35; 14:19; 16:16–19 [b] [John 7:34; 8:21] **13:34** [a] 1 Thess. 4:9 **13:35** [a] 1 John 2:5 **13:36** [a] John 13:33; 14:2; 16:5 [b] 2 Pet. 1:14 **13:37** [a] Mark 14:29–31 **13:38** [a] John 18:25–27 **14:1** [a] [John 14:27; 16:22, 24] **14:2** [a] John 13:33, 36 [1] Literally *dwellings* [2] NU-Text adds a word which would cause the text to read either *if it were not so, would I have told you that I go to prepare a place for you?* or *if it were not so I would have told you; for I go to prepare a place for you.* **14:3** [a] [Acts 1:11] [b] [John 12:26]

PEACE NOTE

You won't find peace in the church, in Christian service, or in any expected place. Peace comes from Jesus, "the way, the truth, and the life."

JOHN 14:6

5[a]Thomas said to Him, "Lord, we do not
know where You are going, and how can we
know the way?"
6Jesus said to him, "I am [a]the way, [b]the
truth, and [c]the life. [d]No one comes to the
Father [e]except through Me.

The Father Revealed

7[a]"If you had known Me, you would have
known My Father also; and from now on you
know Him and have seen Him."
8Philip said to Him, "Lord, show us the
Father, and it is sufficient for us."
9Jesus said to him, "Have I been with you
so long, and yet you have not known Me, Philip? [a]He who has seen Me has seen the Father;
so how can you say, 'Show us the Father'? 10Do
you not believe that [a]I am in the Father, and
the Father in Me? The words that I speak to
you [b]I do not speak on My own *authority;* but
the Father who dwells in Me does the works.
11Believe Me that I *am* in the Father and the
Father in Me, [a]or else believe Me for the sake
of the works themselves.

The Answered Prayer

12[a]"Most assuredly, I say to you, he who
believes in Me, the works that I do he will do
also; and greater *works* than these he will do,
because I go to My Father. 13[a]And whatever
you ask in My name, that I will do, that the
Father may be [b]glorified in the Son. 14If you
ask[1] anything in My name, I will do *it.*

Jesus Promises Another Helper

15[a]"If you love Me, keep[1] My commandments. 16And I will pray the Father, and [a]He
will give you another Helper, that He may
abide with you forever—17[a]the Spirit of truth,
[b]whom the world cannot receive, because it
neither sees Him nor knows Him; but you

14:5 [a] Matt. 10:3 **14:6** [a] [Heb. 9:8; 10:19, 20] [b] [John 1:14, 17; 8:32; 18:37] [c] [John 11:25] [d] 1 Tim. 2:5 [e] [John 10:7–9] **14:7** [a] John 8:19 **14:9** [a] Col. 1:15 **14:10** [a] John 10:38; 14:11, 20 [b] John 5:19; 14:24 **14:11** [a] John 5:36; 10:38 **14:12** [a] Luke 10:17 **14:13** [a] Matt. 7:7 [b] John 13:31 **14:14** [1] NU-Text adds *Me.* **14:15** [a] 1 John 5:3 [1] NU-Text reads *you will keep.* **14:16** [a] Rom. 8:15 **14:17** [a] [1 John 4:6; 5:7] [b] [1 Cor. 2:14]

THE PERSONAL PEACE OF JESUS

"Peace I leave with you, My peace I give to you; not as the world gives do I give to you. Let not your heart be troubled, neither let it be afraid."

JOHN 14:27

If a loved one told you that he or she was about to die, would you have peace? Would it make any difference if he or she offered you *his* or *her* peace? What would that mean? I'm not sure it would give me much assurance if I didn't already possess the peace that surpasses understanding, that is, the peace Jesus Christ offers.

In what is called the Farewell Discourse in the Gospel of John, Jesus gave His disciples—soon to be apostles—His final teaching. Among other things, He assured them that they would receive the Holy Spirit, who would guide and teach them. But what about when Jesus was gone and His disciples were left behind? What could replace Jesus?

The only thing that comes close is the peace of His presence experienced through His Spirit. "My peace," Jesus says, "I give to you." It is a peace that the world can't provide. Rome could defeat an enemy and end a war. That creates peace of a sort, but it is not the redemptive, healing peace that Jesus offers you and me. Will you receive it? Tell Him now.

know Him, for He dwells with you [c]and will be in you. 18 [a]I will not leave you orphans; [b]I will come to you.

Indwelling of the Father and the Son

19 "A little while longer and the world will see Me no more, but [a]you will see Me. [b]Because I live, you will live also. 20 At that day you will know that [a]I *am* in My Father, and you in Me, and I in you. 21 [a]He who has My commandments and keeps them, it is he who loves Me. And he who loves Me will be loved by My Father, and I will love him and manifest Myself to him."

22 [a]Judas (not Iscariot) said to Him, "Lord, how is it that You will manifest Yourself to us, and not to the world?"

23 Jesus answered and said to him, "If anyone loves Me, he will keep My word; and My Father will love him, [a]and We will come to him and make Our home with him. 24 He who does not love Me does not keep My words; and [a]the word which you hear is not Mine but the Father's who sent Me.

The Gift of His Peace

25 "These things I have spoken to you while being present with you. 26 But [a]the Helper, the Holy Spirit, whom the Father will [b]send in My name, [c]He will teach you all things, and bring to your [d]remembrance all things that I said to you. 27 [a]Peace I leave with you, My peace I give to you; not as the world gives do I give to you. Let not your heart be troubled, neither let it be afraid. 28 You have heard Me [a]say to you, 'I am going away and coming *back* to you.' If you loved Me, you would rejoice because I said,[1] [b]'I am going to the Father,' for [c]My Father is greater than I.

29 "And [a]now I have told you before it comes, that when it does come to pass, you may believe. 30 I will no longer talk much with you, [a]for the ruler of this world is coming, and he has [b]nothing in Me. 31 But that the world may know that I love the Father, and [a]as the Father gave Me commandment, so I do. Arise, let us go from here.

> PEACE NOTE
>
> One of the greatest promises of Jesus for believers walking in peace is the fact that we are not only "in Christ" (see Eph. 1–3), but Jesus also lives in us: "I in you."
>
> JOHN 14:20

The True Vine

15 "I am the true vine, and My Father is the vinedresser. 2 [a]Every branch in Me that does not bear fruit He takes away;[1] and every *branch* that bears fruit He prunes, that it may bear [b]more fruit. 3 [a]You are already clean because of the word which I have spoken to you. 4 [a]Abide in Me, and I in you. As the branch cannot bear fruit of itself, unless it abides in the vine, neither can you, unless you abide in Me.

5 "I am the vine, you *are* the branches. He who abides in Me, and I in him, bears much [a]fruit; for without Me you can do [b]nothing. 6 If anyone does not abide in Me, [a]he is cast out as a branch and is withered; and they gather them and throw *them* into the fire, and they are burned. 7 If you abide in Me, and My words [a]abide in you, [b]you will[1] ask what you desire, and it shall be done for you. 8 [a]By this My Father is glorified, that you bear much fruit; [b]so you will be My disciples.

Love and Joy Perfected

9 "As the Father [a]loved Me, I also have loved you; abide in My love. 10 [a]If you keep My commandments, you will abide in My love, just as I have kept My Father's commandments and abide in His love.

11 "These things I have spoken to you, that My joy may remain in you, and [a]*that* your joy may be full. 12 [a]This is My [b]commandment, that you love one another as I have loved you. 13 [a]Greater love has no one than this, than to lay down one's life for his friends. 14 [a]You are My friends if you do whatever I command you. 15 No longer do I call you servants, for

14:17 [c] [1 John 2:27] **14:18** [a] [Matt. 28:20] [b] [John 14:3, 28] **14:19** [a] John 16:16, 22 [b] [1 Cor. 15:20] **14:20** [a] John *10:38; 14:11* ***14:21*** [a] *1 John 2:5* **14:22** [a] Luke 6:16 **14:23** [a] Rev. 3:20; 21:3 **14:24** [a] John 5:19 **14:26** [a] Luke 24:49 [b] John 15:26 [c] 1 Cor. 2:13 [d] John 2:22; 12:16 **14:27** [a] [Phil. 4:7] **14:28** [a] John 14:3, 18 [b] John 16:16 [c] [Phil. 2:6] [1] NU-Text omits *I said.* **14:29** [a] John 13:19 **14:30** [a] [John 12:31] [b] [Heb. 4:15] **14:31** [a] Is. 50:5; John 10:18 **15:2** [a] Matt. 15:13 [b] [Matt. 13:12] [1] Or *lifts up* **15:3** [a] [John 13:10; 17:17] **15:4** [a] [Col. 1:23] **15:5** [a] Hos. 14:8 [b] 2 Cor. 3:5 **15:6** [a] Matt. 3:10 **15:7** [a] 1 John 2:14 [b] John 14:13; 16:23 [1] NU-Text omits *you will.* **15:8** [a] [Matt. 5:16] [b] John 8:31 **15:9** [a] John 5:20; 17:26 **15:10** [a] John 14:15 **15:11** [a] 1 John 1:4 **15:12** [a] 1 John 3:11 [b] Rom. 12:9 **15:13** [a] 1 John 3:16 **15:14** [a] [Matt. 12:50; 28:20]

ABIDING WITH CHRIST

"I am the vine, you are the branches."

JOHN 15:5

The disciples' greatest fear was perhaps abandonment. Jesus had told them that He would soon depart (14:3; 16:7). Although He promised to send them the Comforter (the Holy Spirit) to take His place, they were not consoled. The big point Jesus made is that even if He departed, His disciples could nevertheless abide in Him. Jesus may be physically absent, but His Spirit dwells in His followers. This makes all the difference in the world!

Jesus likened this important truth to a grapevine: "I am the vine, you are the branches. He who abides in Me, and I in him, bears much fruit" (15:5). In a region well known for its viticulture, Jesus could hardly have chosen a better metaphor. The mature, choice vine will produce excellent fruit through its branches getting life from the vine.

We can enjoy the same close fellowship with Jesus that His disciples enjoyed after His resurrection and ascension. His abiding Spirit generates peace within us. To magnify your sense of peace, use this moment to enjoy Christ's presence in a time of personal worship through song and/or prayer.

a servant does not know what his master is doing; but I have called you friends, [a]for all things that I heard from My Father I have made known to you. 16 [a]You did not choose Me, but I chose you and [b]appointed you that you should go and bear fruit, and *that* your fruit should remain, that whatever you ask the Father [c]in My name He may give you. 17 These things I command you, that you love one another.

The World's Hatred

18 [a]"If the world hates you, you know that it hated Me before *it hated* you. 19 [a]If you were of the world, the world would love its own. Yet [b]because you are not of the world, but I chose you out of the world, therefore the world hates you. 20 Remember the word that I said to you, [a]'A servant is not greater than his master.' If they persecuted Me, they will also persecute you. [b]If they kept My word, they will keep yours also. 21 But [a]all these things they will do to you for My name's sake, because they do not know Him who sent Me. 22 [a]If I had not come and spoken to them, they would have no sin, [b]but now they have no excuse for their sin. 23 [a]He who hates Me hates My Father also. 24 If I had not done among them [a]the works which no one else did, they would have no sin; but now they have [b]seen and also hated both Me and My Father. 25 But *this happened* that the word might be fulfilled which is written in their law, [a]'They hated Me without a cause.'[1]

The Coming Rejection

26 [a]"But when the Helper comes, whom I shall send to you from the Father, the Spirit of truth who proceeds from the Father, [b]He will testify of Me. 27 And [a]you also will bear witness, because [b]you have been with Me from the beginning.

16 "These things I have spoken to you, that you [a]should not be made to stumble. 2 [a]They will put you out of the synagogues; yes, the time is coming [b]that whoever kills you will think that he offers God service. 3 And [a]these things they will do to you[1] because they have not known the Father nor Me. 4 But these things I have told you, that when the[1] time comes, you may remember that I told you of them.

"And these things I did not say to you at the beginning, because I was with you.

The Work of the Holy Spirit

5 "But now I [a]go away to Him who sent Me, and none of you asks Me, 'Where are You going?' 6 But because I have said these things to you, [a]sorrow has filled your heart.

15:15 [a] Gen. 18:17 **15:16** [a] John 6:70; 13:18; 15:19 [b] [Col. 1:6] [c] John 14:13; 16:23, 24 **15:18** [a] 1 John 3:13 **15:19** [a] 1 John 4:5 [b] John 17:14 **15:20** [a] John 13:16 [b] Ezek. 3:7 **15:21** [a] Matt. 10:22; 24:9 **15:22** [a] John 9:41; 15:24 [b] [James 4:17] **15:23** [a] 1 John 2:23 **15:24** [a] John 3:2 [b] John 14:9 **15:25** [a] Ps. 35:19; 69:4; 109:3–5 [1] Psalm 69:4 **15:26** [a] Luke 24:49 [b] 1 John 5:6 **15:27** [a] Luke 24:48 [b] Luke 1:2 **16:1** [a] Matt. 11:6 **16:2** [a] John 9:22 [b] Acts 8:1 **16:3** [a] John 8:19; 15:21 [1] NU-Text and M-Text omit *to you.* **16:4** [1] NU-Text reads *their.* **16:5** [a] John 7:33; 13:33; 14:28; 17:11 **16:6** [a] [John 16:20, 22]

7 Nevertheless I tell you the truth. It is to
your advantage that I go away; for if I do
not go away, the Helper will not come to
you; but [a]if I depart, I will send Him to you.
8 And when He has [a]come, He will convict
the world of sin, and of righteousness, and
of judgment: 9 [a]of sin, because they do not
believe in Me; 10 [a]of righteousness, [b]because
I go to My Father and you see Me no more;
11 [a]of judgment, because [b]the ruler of this
world is judged.

12 "I still have many things to say to you,
[a]but you cannot bear *them* now. 13 However,
when He, [a]the Spirit of truth, has come, [b]He
will guide you into all truth; for He will not
speak on His own *authority*, but whatever
He hears He will speak; and He will tell you
things to come. 14 [a]He will glorify Me, for He
will take of what is Mine and declare *it* to you.
15 [a]All things that the Father has are Mine.
Therefore I said that He will take of Mine
and declare *it* to you.[1]

Sorrow Will Turn to Joy

16 "A [a]little while, and you will not see Me;
and again a little while, and you will see Me,
[b]because I go to the Father."

17 Then *some* of His disciples said among
themselves, "What is this that He says to us,
'A little while, and you will not see Me; and
again a little while, and you will see Me'; and,
'because I go to the Father'?" 18 They said
therefore, "What is this that He says, 'A little
while'? We do not know what He is saying."

> **PEACE NOTE**
>
> The antidote to deceit is "the Spirit of truth" who "will guide you into all truth." Truth + freedom = God's peace in my life.
>
> JOHN 16:13

19 Now Jesus knew that they desired to ask
Him, and He said to them, "Are you inquiring
among yourselves about what I said, 'A little
while, and you will not see Me; and again a
little while, and you will see Me'? 20 Most assuredly, I say to you that you will weep and
[a]lament, but the world will rejoice; and you
will be sorrowful, but your sorrow will be
turned into [b]joy. 21 [a]A woman, when she is
in labor, has sorrow because her hour has
come; but as soon as she has given birth
to the child, she no longer remembers the
anguish, for joy that a human being has been
born into the world. 22 Therefore you now
have sorrow; but I will see you again and
[a]your heart will rejoice, and your joy no one
will take from you.

23 "And in that day you will ask Me nothing.
[a]Most assuredly, I say to you, whatever you
ask the Father in My name He will give you.
24 Until now you have asked nothing in My
name. Ask, and you will receive, [a]that your
joy may be [b]full.

Jesus Christ Has Overcome the World

25 "These things I have spoken to you in
figurative language; but the time is coming
when I will no longer speak to you in figurative language, but I will tell you [a]plainly
about the Father. 26 In that day you will ask
in My name, and I do not say to you that I
shall pray the Father for you; 27 [a]for the Father
Himself loves you, because you have loved
Me, and [b]have believed that I came forth
from God. 28 [a]I came forth from the Father
and have come into the world. Again, I leave
the world and go to the Father."

29 His disciples said to Him, "See, now You
are speaking plainly, and using no figure of
speech! 30 Now we are sure that [a]You know all
things, and have no need that anyone should
question You. By this [b]we believe that You
came forth from God."

31 Jesus answered them, "Do you now believe? 32 [a]Indeed the hour is coming, yes, has
now come, that you will be scattered, [b]each to
his own, and will leave Me alone. And [c]yet I
am not alone, because the Father is with Me.
33 These things I have spoken to you, that [a]in
Me you may have peace. [b]In the world you
will[1] have tribulation; but be of good cheer,
[c]I have overcome the world."

16:7 [a] *Acts 2:33* ***16:8*** [a] *Acts 1:8; 2:1–4, 37* **16:9** [a] Acts 2:22 **16:10** [a] Acts 2:32 [b] John 5:32 **16:11** [a] Acts 26:18 [b] [Luke 10:18] **16:12** [a] Mark 4:33 **16:13** [a] [John 14:17] [b] John 14:26 **16:14** [a] John 15:26 **16:15** [a] Matt. 11:27
[1] NU-Text and M-Text read *He takes of Mine and will declare it to you.* **16:16** [a] John 7:33; 12:35; 13:33; 14:19; 19:40–42; 20:19 [b] John 13:3 **16:20** [a] Mark 16:10 [b] Luke 24:32, 41 **16:21** [a] Is. 13:8; 26:17; 42:14 **16:22** [a] 1 Pet. 1:8 **16:23** [a] Matt. 7:7 **16:24** [a] John 17:13 [b] John 15:11 **16:25** [a] John 7:13 **16:27** [a] [John 14:21, 23] [b] John 3:13 **16:28** [a] John 13:1, 3; 16:5, 10, 17 **16:30** [a] John 21:17 [b] John 17:8 **16:32** [a] Matt. 26:31, 56 [b] John 20:10 [c] John 8:29 **16:33** [a] [Eph. 2:14] [b] 2 Tim. 3:12 [c] Rom. 8:37 [1] NU-Text and M-Text omit *will.*

PEACE NO MATTER WHAT

"These things I have spoken to you, that in Me you may have peace. In the world you will have tribulation; but be of good cheer, I have overcome the world."

JOHN 16:33

Worried? Who can blame you? Most days the headlines aren't very encouraging. When you think of what is happening in the world, the first word that comes to mind probably isn't *peace.*

As challenging as things are for us today, they were far more frightening in the days of Jesus and His disciples. Not only was Israel under the Roman thumb, but Jesus' followers faced persecution even from their own people. In Jesus' appearance, they rightly perceived the arrival of the "Prince of Peace" (Is. 9:6), but in the aftermath of Easter and Jesus' ascension, the young church experienced very little peace, at least in terms of how the world reckons it.

Jesus knew this was coming. This is why, in His farewell teaching (John 14–16), He prepared and reassured His disciples about what lay ahead. Jesus knew the world would offer them no peace; on the contrary, they would experience tribulation. It was Jesus who would provide the peace that "surpasses all understanding" (Phil. 4:7). His followers then and now—including you—can know that in their Master they will have real, fathomless peace because He had "overcome the world" (John 16:33).

Jesus Prays for Himself

17 Jesus spoke these words, lifted up His
eyes to heaven, and said: "Father, [a]the
hour has come. Glorify Your Son, that Your
Son also may glorify You, 2 [a]as You have given
Him authority over all flesh, that He should[1]
give eternal life to as many [b]as You have given
Him. 3 And [a]this is eternal life, that they may
know You, [b]the only true God, and Jesus Christ
[c]whom You have sent. 4 [a]I have glorified You
on the earth. [b]I have finished the work [c]which
You have given Me to do. 5 And now, O Father,
glorify Me together with Yourself, with the glory [a]which I had with You before the world was.

Jesus Prays for His Disciples

6 [a]"I have manifested Your name to the
men [b]whom You have given Me out of the
world. [c]They were Yours, You gave them to
Me, and they have kept Your word. 7 Now they
have known that all things which You have
given Me are from You. 8 For I have given
to them the words [a]which You have given
Me; and they have received *them,* [b]and have
known surely that I came forth from You;
and they have believed that [c]You sent Me.
9 "I pray for them. [a]I do not pray for the world
but for those whom You have given Me, for
they are Yours. 10 And all Mine are Yours, and
[a]Yours are Mine, and I am glorified in them.
11 [a]Now I am no longer in the world, but these
are in the world, and I come to You. Holy Father, [b]keep through Your name those whom
You have given Me,[1] that they may be one [c]as
We *are.* 12 While I was with them in the world,[1]
[a]I kept them in Your name. Those whom You
gave Me I have kept;[2] and [b]none of them is
lost [c]except the son of perdition, [d]that the
Scripture might be fulfilled. 13 But now I come
to You, and these things I speak in the world,
that they may have My joy fulfilled in themselves. 14 I have given them Your word; [a]and the
world has hated them because they are not of
the world, [b]just as I am not of the world. 15 I do
not pray that You should take them out of the
world, but [a]that You should keep them from
the evil one. 16 They are not of the world, just as
I am not of the world. 17 [a]Sanctify them by Your
truth. [b]Your word is truth. 18 [a]As You sent Me
into the world, I also have sent them into the
world. 19 And [a]for their sakes I sanctify Myself,
that they also may be sanctified by the truth.

17:1 [a] John 12:23 **17:2** [a] John 3:35 [b] John 6:37, 39; 17:6, 9, 24 [1] M-Text reads *shall.* **17:3** [a] Jer. 9:23, 24 [b] 1 Cor. 8:4 [c] John 3:34 **17:4** [a] John 13:31 [b] John 4:34; 19:30 [c] John 14:31 **17:5** [a] Phil. 2:6 **17:6** [a] Ps. 22:22 [b] John 6:37 [c] Ezek. 18:4 **17:8** [a] John 8:28 [b] John 8:42; 16:27, 30 [c] Deut. 18:15, 18 **17:9** [a] [1 John 5:19] **17:10** [a] John 16:15 **17:11** [a] John 13:1 [b] [1 Pet. 1:5] [c] John 10:30 [1] NU-Text and M-Text read *keep them through Your name which You have given Me.* **17:12** [a] Heb. 2:13 [b] 1 John 2:19 [c] John 6:70 [d] Ps. 41:9; 109:8 [1] NU-Text omits *in the world.* [2] NU-Text reads *in Your name which You gave Me. And I guarded them;* (or *it;*). **17:14** [a] John 15:19 [b] John 8:23 **17:15** [a] 1 John 5:18 **17:17** [a] [Eph. 5:26] [b] Ps. 119:9, 142, 151 **17:18** [a] John 4:38; 20:21 **17:19** [a] [Heb. 10:10]

Jesus Prays for All Believers

20 “I do not pray for these alone, but also for
those who will[1] believe in Me through their
word; 21 [a]that they all may be one, as [b]You,
Father, *are* in Me, and I in You; that they also
may be one in Us, that the world may believe
that You sent Me. 22 And the [a]glory which You
gave Me I have given them, [b]that they may be
one just as We are one: 23 I in them, and You in
Me; [a]that they may be made perfect in one, and
that the world may know that You have sent
Me, and have loved them as You have loved Me.
24 [a]“Father, I desire that they also whom You
gave Me may be with Me where I am, that they
may behold My glory which You have given
Me; [b]for You loved Me before the foundation
of the world. 25 O righteous Father! [a]The world
has not known You, but [b]I have known You;
and [c]these have known that You sent Me.
26 [a]And I have declared to them Your name,
and will declare *it,* that the love [b]with which
You loved Me may be in them, and I in them.”

Betrayal and Arrest in Gethsemane

18 When Jesus had spoken these words,
[a]He went out with His disciples over [b]the
Brook Kidron, where there was a garden, which
He and His disciples entered. 2 And Judas, who
betrayed Him, also knew the place; [a]for Jesus
often met there with His disciples. 3 [a]Then
Judas, having received a detachment *of troops,*
and officers from the chief priests and Pharisees, came there with lanterns, torches, and
weapons. 4 Jesus therefore, [a]knowing all things
that would come upon Him, went forward
and said to them, “Whom are you seeking?”
5 They answered Him, [a]“Jesus of Nazareth.”
Jesus said to them, “I am *He.*” And Judas,
who [b]betrayed Him, also stood with them.
6 Now when He said to them, “I am *He,*” they
drew back and fell to the ground.
7 Then He asked them again, “Whom are
you seeking?”
And they said, “Jesus of Nazareth.”
8 Jesus answered, “I have told you that I
am *He.* Therefore, if you seek Me, let these go
their way,” 9 that the saying might be fulfilled
which He spoke, [a]“Of those whom You gave
Me I have lost none.”
10 [a]Then Simon Peter, having a sword, drew
it and struck the high priest’s servant, and
cut off his right ear. The servant’s name was
Malchus.
11 So Jesus said to Peter, “Put your sword
into the sheath. Shall I not drink [a]the cup
which My Father has given Me?”

Before the High Priest

12 Then the detachment *of troops* and the
captain and the officers of the Jews arrested
Jesus and bound Him. 13 And [a]they led Him
away to [b]Annas first, for he was the father-
in-law of [c]Caiaphas who was high priest that
year. 14 [a]Now it was Caiaphas who advised
the Jews that it was expedient that one man
should die for the people.

17:20 [1] NU-Text and M-Text omit *will.* **17:21** [a] [Gal. 3:28] [b] John 10:38; 17:11, 23 **17:22** [a] 1 John 1:3 [b] [2 Cor. 3:18] **17:23** [a] [Col. 3:14] **17:24** [a] [1 Thess. 4:17] [b] John 17:5 **17:25** [a] John 15:21 [b] John 7:29; 8:55; 10:15 [c] John 3:17; 17:3, 8, 18, 21, 23 **17:26** [a] John 17:6 [b] John 15:9 **18:1** [a] Mark 14:26, 32 [b] 2 Sam. 15:23 **18:2** [a] Luke 21:37; 22:39 **18:3** [a] Luke 22:47–53 **18:4** [a] John 6:64; 13:1, 3; 19:28 **18:5** [a] Matt. 21:11 [b] Ps. 41:9 **18:9** [a] [John 6:39; 17:12] **18:10** [a] Matt. 26:51 **18:11** [a] Matt. 20:22; 26:39 **18:13** [a] Matt. 26:57 [b] Luke 3:2 [c] Matt. 26:3 **18:14** [a] John 11:50

TO BE LOVED BY GOD

“I have declared to them Your name, and will declare it, that the love with which You loved Me may be in them.”

JOHN 17:26

One of the most serene, spiritually moving passages in all the Bible is found in John 17 in what is called the High Priestly Prayer. What grips my heart is the last verse in this prayer. Jesus said to His Father in heaven, “I have declared to them Your name, and will declare it, that the love with which You loved Me may be in them.” That is powerful!

In the final petition of His prayer Jesus asked that His heavenly Father love the disciples with the same love with which He loved His only Son, Jesus Christ. Can you imagine? To be *loved by God as much* as God loved His Son! I can scarcely comprehend this. This is something to remember any time you feel unloved, unwanted, or “unpeaceful.” Remember that if you are in Christ, then God in heaven loves you as much as He loved Jesus. Peace is part of the gift. Ask for it.

Peter Denies Jesus

15 [a]And Simon Peter followed Jesus, and
so *did* [b]another[1] disciple. Now that disciple
was known to the high priest, and went with
Jesus into the courtyard of the high priest.
16 [a]But Peter stood at the door outside. Then
the other disciple, who was known to the
high priest, went out and spoke to her who
kept the door, and brought Peter in. 17 Then
the servant girl who kept the door said to
Peter, "You are not also *one* of this Man's
disciples, are you?"

He said, "I am [a]not."

18 Now the servants and officers who had
made a fire of coals stood there, for it was
cold, and they warmed themselves. And Peter
stood with them and warmed himself.

Jesus Questioned by the High Priest

19 The high priest then asked Jesus about
His disciples and His doctrine.

20 Jesus answered him, [a]"I spoke openly to
the world. I always taught [b]in synagogues and
[c]in the temple, where the Jews always meet,[1]
and in secret I have said nothing. 21 Why do
you ask Me? Ask [a]those who have heard Me
what I said to them. Indeed they know what
I said."

22 And when He had said these things, one
of the officers who stood by [a]struck Jesus
with the palm of his hand, saying, "Do You
answer the high priest like that?"

23 Jesus answered him, "If I have spoken
evil, bear witness of the evil; but if well, why
do you strike Me?"

24 [a]Then Annas sent Him bound to [b]Caia-
phas the high priest.

Peter Denies Twice More

25 Now Simon Peter stood and warmed
himself. [a]Therefore they said to him, "You
are not also *one* of His disciples, are you?"

He denied *it* and said, "I am not!"

26 One of the servants of the high priest, a
relative *of him* whose ear Peter cut off, said,
"Did I not see you in the garden with Him?"
27 Peter then denied again; and [a]immediately
a rooster crowed.

In Pilate's Court

28 [a]Then they led Jesus from Caiaphas to
the Praetorium, and it was early morning.
[b]But they themselves did not go into the
Praetorium, lest they should be defiled, but
that they might eat the Passover. 29 [a]Pilate
then went out to them and said, "What accusation do you bring against this Man?"

30 They answered and said to him, "If He
were not an evildoer, we would not have
delivered Him up to you."

31 Then Pilate said to them, "You take Him
and judge Him according to your law."

Therefore the Jews said to him, "It is not
lawful for us to put anyone to death," 32 [a]that
the saying of Jesus might be fulfilled which He
spoke, [b]signifying by what death He would die.

33 [a]Then Pilate entered the Praetorium
again, called Jesus, and said to Him, "Are
You the King of the Jews?"

34 Jesus answered him, "Are you speaking
for yourself about this, or did others tell you
this concerning Me?"

35 Pilate answered, "Am I a Jew? Your own
nation and the chief priests have delivered
You to me. What have You done?"

36 [a]Jesus answered, [b]"My kingdom is not of
this world. If My kingdom were of this world,
My servants would fight, so that I should
not be delivered to the Jews; but now My
kingdom is not from here."

37 Pilate therefore said to Him, "Are You
a king then?"

Jesus answered, "You say *rightly* that I
am a king. For this cause I was born, and for
this cause I have come into the world, [a]that I
should bear [b]witness to the truth. Everyone
who [c]is of the truth [d]hears My voice."

38 Pilate said to Him, "What is truth?" And
when he had said this, he went out again to
the Jews, and said to them, [a]"I find no fault
in Him at all.

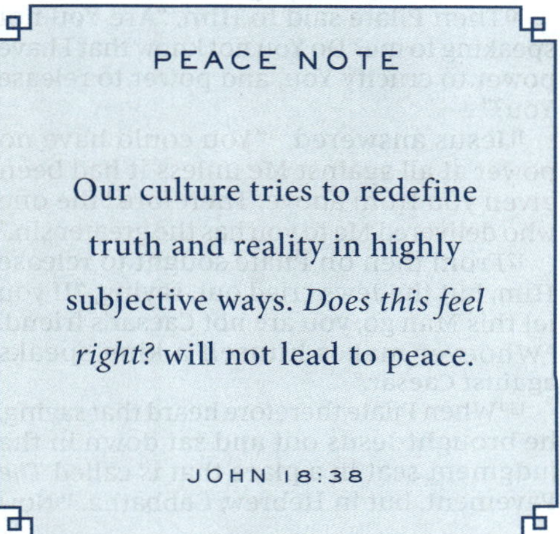

18:15 [a] Mark 14:54 [b] John 20:2–5 [1] M-Text reads *the other.* **18:16** [a] Matt. 26:69 **18:17** [a] Matt. 26:34 **18:20** [a] Luke 4:15 [b] John 6:59 [c] Mark 14:49 [1] NU-Text reads *where all the Jews meet.* **18:21** [a] Mark 12:37 **18:22** [a] Jer. 20:2 **18:24** [a] Matt. 26:57 [b] John 11:49 **18:25** [a] Luke 22:58–62 **18:27** [a] John 13:38 **18:28** [a] Mark 15:1 [b] Acts 10:28; 11:3 **18:29** [a] Matt. 27:11–14 **18:32** [a] Matt. 20:17–19; 26:2 [b] John 3:14; 8:28; 12:32, 33 **18:33** [a] Matt. 27:11 **18:36** [a] 1 Tim. 6:13 [b] [Dan. 2:44; 7:14] **18:37** [a] [Matt. 5:17; 20:28] [b] Is. 55:4 [c] [John 14:6] [d] John 8:47; 10:27 **18:38** [a] John 19:4, 6

Taking the Place of Barabbas

39 [a]“But you have a custom that I should
release someone to you at the Passover. Do
you therefore want me to release to you the
King of the Jews?”
40 [a]Then they all cried again, saying, “Not
this Man, but Barabbas!” [b]Now Barabbas
was a robber.

The Soldiers Mock Jesus

19 So then [a]Pilate took Jesus and scourged
Him. 2 And the soldiers twisted a crown
of thorns and put *it* on His head, and they
put on Him a purple robe. 3 Then they said,[1]
“Hail, King of the Jews!” And they [a]struck
Him with their hands.
4 Pilate then went out again, and said to
them, “Behold, I am bringing Him out to
you, [a]that you may know that I find no fault
in Him.”

Pilate’s Decision

5 Then Jesus came out, wearing the crown
of thorns and the purple robe. And *Pilate* said
to them, “Behold the Man!”
6 [a]Therefore, when the chief priests and
officers saw Him, they cried out, saying, “Crucify *Him,* crucify *Him!*”
Pilate said to them, “You take Him and
crucify *Him,* for I find no fault in Him.”
7 The Jews answered him, [a]“We have a law,
and according to our[1] law He ought to die,
because [b]He made Himself the Son of God.”
8 Therefore, when Pilate heard that saying,
he was the more afraid, 9 and went again into
the Praetorium, and said to Jesus, “Where are
You from?” [a]But Jesus gave him no answer.
10 Then Pilate said to Him, “Are You not
speaking to me? Do You not know that I have
power to crucify You, and power to release
You?”
11 Jesus answered, [a]“You could have no
power at all against Me unless it had been
given you from above. Therefore [b]the one
who delivered Me to you has the greater sin.”
12 From then on Pilate sought to release
Him, but the Jews cried out, saying, “If you
let this Man go, you are not Caesar’s friend.
[a]Whoever makes himself a king speaks
against Caesar.”
13 [a]When Pilate therefore heard that saying,
he brought Jesus out and sat down in the
judgment seat in a place that is called *The*
Pavement, but in Hebrew, Gabbatha. 14 Now
[a]it was the Preparation Day of the Passover,
and about the sixth hour. And he said to the
Jews, “Behold your King!”
15 But they cried out, “Away with *Him,* away
with *Him!* Crucify Him!”
Pilate said to them, “Shall I crucify your
King?”
The chief priests answered, [a]“We have no
king but Caesar!”
16 [a]Then he delivered Him to them to be
crucified. Then they took Jesus and led *Him*
away.[1]

The King on a Cross

17 [a]And He, bearing His cross, [b]went out
to a place called *the Place* of a Skull, which
is called in Hebrew, Golgotha, 18 where they
crucified Him, and [a]two others with Him,
one on either side, and Jesus in the center.
19 [a]Now Pilate wrote a title and put *it* on the
cross. And the writing was:

JESUS OF NAZARETH, THE KING
OF THE JEWS.

20 Then many of the Jews read this title, for
the place where Jesus was crucified was near
the city; and it was written in Hebrew, Greek,
and Latin.
21 Therefore the chief priests of the Jews
said to Pilate, “Do not write, ‘The King of
the Jews,’ but, ‘He said, “I am the King of
the Jews.” ’ ”
22 Pilate answered, “What I have written,
I have written.”
23 [a]Then the soldiers, when they had crucified Jesus, took His garments and made
four parts, to each soldier a part, and also
the tunic. Now the tunic was without seam,
woven from the top in one piece. 24 They said
therefore among themselves, “Let us not tear
it, but cast lots for it, whose it shall be,” that
the Scripture might be fulfilled which says:

[a]“They divided My garments among
them,
And for My clothing they cast lots.”[1]

Therefore the soldiers did these things.

Behold Your Mother

25 [a]Now there stood by the cross of Jesus
His mother, and His mother’s sister, Mary the
wife of [b]Clopas, and Mary Magdalene. 26 When

18:39 [a] Luke 23:17–25 **18:40** [a] Acts 3:14 [b] Luke 23:19 **19:1** [a] Matt. 20:19; 27:26 **19:3** [a] Is. 50:6 [1] NU-Text reads *And they came up to Him and said.* **19:4** [a] John 18:33, 38 **19:6** [a] Acts 3:13 **19:7** [a] Lev. 24:16 [b] Matt. 26:63–66 [1] NU-Text reads *the law.* **19:9** [a] Is. 53:7 **19:11** [a] [Luke 22:53] [b] Rom. 13:1 **19:12** [a] Luke 23:2 **19:13** [a] 1 Sam. 15:24 **19:14** [a] Matt. 27:62 **19:15** [a] [Gen. 49:10] **19:16** [a] Luke 23:24 [1] NU-Text omits *and led Him away.* **19:17** [a] Mark 15:21, 22 [b] Num. 15:36 **19:18** [a] Is. 53:12 **19:19** [a] Matt. 27:37 **19:23** [a] Luke 23:34 **19:24** [a] Ps. 22:18 [1] Psalm 22:18 **19:25** [a] Mark 15:40 [b] Luke 24:18

Jesus therefore saw His mother, and [a]the disciple whom He loved standing by, He said to His mother, [b]"Woman, behold your son!" 27 Then He said to the disciple, "Behold your mother!" And from that hour that disciple took her [a]to his own *home.*

It Is Finished

28 After this, Jesus, knowing[1] that all things were now accomplished, [a]that the Scripture might be fulfilled, said, "I thirst!" 29 Now a vessel full of sour wine was sitting there; and [a]they filled a sponge with sour wine, put *it* on hyssop, and put *it* to His mouth. 30 So when Jesus had received the sour wine, He said, [a]"It is finished!" And bowing His head, He gave up His spirit.

Jesus' Side Is Pierced

31 [a]Therefore, because it was the Preparation *Day,* [b]that the bodies should not remain on the cross on the Sabbath (for that Sabbath was a [c]high day), the Jews asked Pilate that their legs might be broken, and *that* they might be taken away. 32 Then the soldiers came and broke the legs of the first and of the other who was crucified with Him. 33 But when they came to Jesus and saw that He was already dead, they did not break His legs. 34 But one of the soldiers pierced His side with a spear, and immediately [a]blood and water came out. 35 And he who has seen has testified, and his testimony is [a]true; and he knows that he is telling the truth, so that you may [b]believe. 36 For these things were done that the Scripture should be fulfilled, [a]"Not *one* of His bones shall be broken."[1] 37 And again another Scripture says, [a]"They shall look on Him whom they pierced."[1]

Jesus Buried in Joseph's Tomb

38 [a]After this, Joseph of Arimathea, being a disciple of Jesus, but secretly, [b]for fear of the Jews, asked Pilate that he might take away the body of Jesus; and Pilate gave *him* permission. So he came and took the body of Jesus. 39 And [a]Nicodemus, who at first came to Jesus by night, also came, bringing a mixture of [b]myrrh and aloes, about a hundred pounds. 40 Then they took the body of Jesus, and [a]bound it in strips of linen with the spices, as the custom of the Jews is to bury. 41 Now in the place where He was crucified there was a garden, and in the garden a new tomb in which no one had yet been laid. 42 So [a]there they laid Jesus, [b]because of the Jews' Preparation *Day,* for the tomb was nearby.

The Empty Tomb

20 Now the [a]first *day* of the week Mary Magdalene went to the tomb early, while it was still dark, and saw *that* the [b]stone had been taken away from the tomb. 2 Then she ran and came to Simon Peter, and to the [a]other disciple, [b]whom Jesus loved, and said to them, "They have taken away the Lord out of the tomb, and we do not know where they have laid Him."

3 [a]Peter therefore went out, and the other disciple, and were going to the tomb. 4 So they both ran together, and the other disciple outran Peter and came to the tomb first. 5 And he, stooping down and looking in, saw [a]the linen cloths lying *there;* yet he did not go in. 6 Then Simon Peter came, following him, and went into the tomb; and he saw the linen cloths lying *there,* 7 and [a]the handkerchief that had been around His head, not lying with the linen cloths, but folded together in a place by itself. 8 Then the [a]other disciple, who came to the tomb first, went in also; and he saw and believed. 9 For as yet they did not know the [a]Scripture, that He must rise again from the dead. 10 Then the disciples went away again to their own homes.

Mary Magdalene Sees the Risen Lord

11 [a]But Mary stood outside by the tomb weeping, and as she wept she stooped down *and looked* into the tomb. 12 And she saw two angels in white sitting, one at the head and the other at the feet, where the body of Jesus had lain. 13 Then they said to her, "Woman, why are you weeping?"

She said to them, "Because they have taken away my Lord, and I do not know where they have laid Him."

14 [a]Now when she had said this, she turned around and saw Jesus standing *there,* and [b]did not know that it was Jesus. 15 Jesus said to her, "Woman, why are you weeping? Whom are you seeking?"

She, supposing Him to be the gardener, said to Him, "Sir, if You have carried Him

19:26 [a] John 13:23; 20:2; 21:7, 20, 24 [b] John 2:4 **19:27** [a] John 1:11; 16:32 **19:28** [a] Ps. 22:15 [1] M-Text reads *seeing.* **19:29** [a] Ps. 69:21; Matt. 27:48, 50 **19:30** [a] John 17:4 **19:31** [a] Mark 15:42 [b] Deut. 21:23 [c] Ex. 12:16; [Ex. 12:46; Num. 9:12]; Ps. 34:20 **19:34** [a] [1 John 5:6, 8] **19:35** [a] John 21:24 [b] [John 20:31] **19:36** [a] [Ex. 12:46; Num. 9:12]; Ps. 34:20 [1] Exodus 12:46; Numbers 9:12; Psalm 34:20 **19:37** [a] Ps. 22:16, 17; Zech. 12:10; 13:6 [1] Zechariah 12:10 **19:38** [a] Luke 23:50–56 [b] [John 7:13; 9:22; 12:42] **19:39** [a] John 3:1, 2; 7:50 [b] Matt. 2:11 **19:40** [a] John 20:5, 7 **19:42** [a] Is. 53:9 [b] John 19:14, 31 **20:1** [a] Matt. 28:1–8 [b] Matt. 27:60, 66; 28:2 **20:2** [a] John 21:23, 24 [b] John 13:23; 19:26; 21:7, 20, 24 **20:3** [a] Luke 24:12 **20:5** [a] John 19:40 **20:7** [a] John 11:44 **20:8** [a] John 21:23, 24 **20:9** [a] Ps. 16:10 **20:11** [a] Mark 16:5 **20:14** [a] Matt. 28:9 [b] John 21:4

away, tell me where You have laid Him, and
I will take Him away."
16 Jesus said to her, [a]"Mary!"
She turned and said to Him,[1] "Rabboni!"
(which is to say, Teacher).
17 Jesus said to her, "Do not cling to Me, for
I have not yet [a]ascended to My Father; but
go to [b]My brethren and say to them, [c]'I am
ascending to My Father and your Father, and
to [d]My God and your God.' "
18 [a]Mary Magdalene came and told the disciples that she had seen the Lord,[1] and *that*
He had spoken these things to her.

The Apostles Commissioned

19 [a]Then, the same day at evening, being the
first *day* of the week, when the doors were
shut where the disciples were assembled,[1] for
[b]fear of the Jews, Jesus came and stood in the
midst, and said to them, [c]"Peace *be* with you."
20 When He had said this, He [a]showed them
His hands and His side. [b]Then the disciples
were glad when they saw the Lord.
21 So Jesus said to them again, "Peace
to you! [a]As the Father has sent Me, I also
send you." 22 And when He had said this, He
breathed on *them*, and said to them, "Receive
the Holy Spirit. 23 [a]If you forgive the sins of
any, they are forgiven them; if you retain the
sins of any, they are retained."

Seeing and Believing

24 Now Thomas, [a]called the Twin, one of
the twelve, was not with them when Jesus
came. 25 The other disciples therefore said
to him, "We have seen the Lord."
So he said to them, "Unless I see in His
hands the print of the nails, and put my finger
into the print of the nails, and put my hand
into His side, I will not believe."
26 And after eight days His disciples were
again inside, and Thomas with them. Jesus
came, the doors being shut, and stood in
the midst, and said, "Peace to you!" 27 Then
He said to Thomas, "Reach your finger here,
and look at My hands; and [a]reach your hand
here, and put *it* into My side. Do not be [b]un-
believing, but believing."
28 And Thomas answered and said to Him,
"My Lord and my God!"
29 Jesus said to him, "Thomas,[1] because you
have seen Me, you have believed. [a]Blessed *are*
those who have not seen and *yet* have believed."

That You May Believe

30 And [a]truly Jesus did many other signs in
the presence of His disciples, which are not
written in this book; 31 [a]but these are written
that [b]you may believe that Jesus [c]is the Christ,
the Son of God, [d]and that believing you may
have life in His name.

20:16 [a] John 10:3 [1] NU-Text adds *in Hebrew*. **20:17** [a] Heb. 4:14 [b] Heb. 2:11 [c] John 16:28; 17:11 [d] Eph. 1:17 **20:18** [a] Luke 24:10, 23 [1] NU-Text reads *disciples, "I have seen the Lord,"* . . . . **20:19** [a] Luke 24:36 [b] John 9:22; 19:38 [c] John 14:27; 16:33 [1] NU-Text omits *assembled*. **20:20** [a] Acts 1:3 [b] John 16:20, 22 **20:21** [a] John 17:18, 19 **20:23** [a] Matt. 16:19; 18:18 **20:24** [a] John 11:16 **20:27** [a] 1 John 1:1 [b] Mark 16:14 **20:29** [a] 1 Pet. 1:8 [1] NU-Text and M-Text omit *Thomas*. **20:30** [a] John 21:25 **20:31** [a] Luke 1:4 [b] 1 John 5:13 [c] Luke 2:11 [d] John 3:15, 16; 5:24

SENT IN PEACE WITH PURPOSE

So Jesus said to them again, "Peace to you! As the Father has sent Me, I also send you."

JOHN 20:21

Have you ever had your hopes dashed? One day all is well with the world, and the next day everything falls apart. True to what Jesus had told His disciples, His ministry came to a sudden and violent end. Jesus was arrested, tried, and condemned to a cruel cross. But three days after His death, Jesus appeared to His disciples. Hiding because of fear of arrest, the disciples were startled to see Him standing among them and speaking a word of assurance: "Peace to you."

When you've been knocked to the ground, a friendly word of encouragement is enormously helpful. Jesus' ministry had not ended with the cross—it was reignited with His resurrection!

Jesus said, "As the Father has sent Me, I also send you." Out of peace comes mission and purpose. This is quite a turnaround. One moment the disciples were at a complete loss without plan or direction. A moment later peace was restored, and the original mission that had given meaning to their lives was relaunched. Peace isn't simply tranquility; it is motivating.

REASSURANCE FROM CHRIST

And after eight days His disciples were again inside, and Thomas with them. Jesus came, the doors being shut, and stood in the midst, and said, "Peace to you!"

JOHN 20:26

Do you know someone who is a Doubting Thomas—perhaps *you?* Doubt isn't necessarily bad. Thinking and asking tough questions are good things to do. I can hardly fault Thomas. After all, people have always told ghost stories. People are gullible. A few people said they'd seen Jesus. So what? Maybe this was nothing more than wishful thinking.

Whatever was going on, Thomas found himself with the other disciples as they were keeping out of sight. Then Jesus suddenly appeared before them and uttered those reassuring words, "Peace to you!" This time Thomas himself saw Jesus. He didn't have to take anyone else's word; he was an eyewitness. Jesus invited Thomas to inspect the marks of crucifixion, but Thomas declared, "My Lord and my God!" (v. 28). He had seen and believed. Said Jesus, "Blessed are those who have not seen and yet have believed" (v. 29).

Those who believe receive the peace that the risen Jesus offers. Does that include you?

Breakfast by the Sea

21 After these things Jesus showed Himself again to the disciples at the [a]Sea
of Tiberias, and in this way He showed *Himself:* 2Simon Peter, [a]Thomas called the Twin,
[b]Nathanael of [c]Cana in Galilee, [d]the *sons* of
Zebedee, and two others of His disciples were
together. 3Simon Peter said to them, "I am
going fishing."

They said to him, "We are going with you
also." They went out and immediately[1] got
into the boat, and that night they caught nothing. 4But when the morning had now come,
Jesus stood on the shore; yet the disciples
[a]did not know that it was Jesus. 5Then [a]Jesus
said to them, "Children, have you any food?"

They answered Him, "No."

6And He said to them, [a]"Cast the net on the
right side of the boat, and you will find *some.*"
So they cast, and now they were not able to
draw it in because of the multitude of fish.

7Therefore [a]that disciple whom Jesus
loved said to Peter, "It is the Lord!" Now when
Simon Peter heard that it was the Lord, he
put on *his* outer garment (for he had removed
it), and plunged into the sea. 8But the other
disciples came in the little boat (for they were
not far from land, but about two hundred
cubits), dragging the net with fish. 9Then,
as soon as they had come to land, they saw
a fire of coals there, and fish laid on it, and
bread. 10Jesus said to them, "Bring some of
the fish which you have just caught."

11Simon Peter went up and dragged the
net to land, full of large fish, one hundred
and fifty-three; and although there were so
many, the net was not broken. 12Jesus said to
them, [a]"Come *and* eat breakfast." Yet none
of the disciples dared ask Him, "Who are
You?"—knowing that it was the Lord. 13Jesus
then came and took the bread and gave it to
them, and likewise the fish.

14This *is* now [a]the third time Jesus showed
Himself to His disciples after He was raised
from the dead.

Jesus Restores Peter

15So when they had eaten breakfast, Jesus
said to Simon Peter, "Simon, *son* of Jonah,[1]
do you love Me more than these?"

He said to Him, "Yes, Lord; You know that
I love You."

He said to him, [a]"Feed My lambs."

16He said to him again a second time,
"Simon, *son* of Jonah,[1] do you love Me?"

He said to Him, "Yes, Lord; You know that
I love You."

[a]He said to him, "Tend My [b]sheep."

17He said to him the third time, "Simon,
son of Jonah,[1] do you love Me?" Peter was
grieved because He said to him the third
time, "Do you love Me?"

21:1 [a] John 6:1 **21:2** [a] John 20:24 [b] John 1:45–51 [c] John 2:1 [d] Matt. 4:21 **21:3** [1] NU-Text omits *immediately.*
21:4 [a] John 20:14 **21:5** [a] Luke 24:41 **21:6** [a] Luke 5:4, 6, 7 **21:7** [a] John 13:23; 20:2 **21:12** [a] Acts 10:41 **21:14** [a] John 20:19, 26 **21:15** [a] Acts 20:28 [1] NU-Text reads *John.* **21:16** [a] Heb. 13:20 [b] Ps. 79:13 [1] NU-Text reads *John.*
21:17 [1] NU-Text reads *John.*

And he said to Him, "Lord, [a]You know all
things; You know that I love You."
Jesus said to him, "Feed My sheep. 18[a]Most
assuredly, I say to you, when you were younger, you girded yourself and walked where
you wished; but when you are old, you will
stretch out your hands, and another will gird
you and carry *you* where you do not wish."
19This He spoke, signifying [a]by what death he
would glorify God. And when He had spoken
this, He said to him, [b]"Follow Me."

The Beloved Disciple and His Book

20Then Peter, turning around, saw the
disciple [a]whom Jesus loved following, [b]who
also had leaned on His breast at the supper,
and said, "Lord, who is the one who betrays
You?" 21Peter, seeing him, said to Jesus, "But
Lord, what *about* this man?"
22Jesus said to him, "If I will that he remain
[a]till I come, what *is that* to you? You follow Me."
23Then this saying went out among the
brethren that this disciple would not die. Yet
Jesus did not say to him that he would not
die, but, "If I will that he remain till I come,
what *is that* to you?"
24This is the disciple who [a]testifies of these
things, and wrote these things; and we know
that his testimony is true.
25[a]And there are also many other things
that Jesus did, which if they were written one
by one, [b]I suppose that even the world itself
could not contain the books that would be
written. Amen.

21:17 [a] John 2:24, 25; 16:30 **21:18** [a] Acts 12:3, 4 **21:19** [a] 2 Pet. 1:13, 14 [b] [Matt. 4:19; 16:24] **21:20** [a] John 13:23; 20:2 [b] John 13:25 **21:22** [a] [Rev. 2:25; 3:11; 22:7, 20] **21:24** [a] John 19:35 **21:25** [a] John 20:30 [b] Amos 7:10

THE ACTS OF THE APOSTLES

AUTHOR

There are many "we" sections in Acts that imply the author was present for these events (Acts 16:10–17; 20:5—21:18; 27:1—28:16). These sections of Acts are the historical record of an eyewitness. For the remainder of this book, Luke no doubt followed the same careful investigative procedures that he used in writing his Gospel (Luke 1:1–4). As a close traveling companion of Paul, Luke had access to the principal eyewitness for Acts 13–18. It is also likely that he had opportunities to interview such key witnesses in Jerusalem as Peter and John for the information in chapters 13–28. Modern archaeological discoveries have strikingly confirmed the trustworthiness and precision of Luke as a historian.

TIME

c. AD 33–62

KEY VERSE

Acts 2:42–47

THEME

Acts is the record of how the events surrounding Jesus' life and death and resurrection resulted in this worldwide movement called *the church*. The book is certainly not a comprehensive history. Acts is more like a photo album of snapshots. It is the record of an eyewitness who wrote about what he saw—what seemed to be the critical events in the church's beginnings and its movement out of Jerusalem to the rest of the world. One could say that the Book of Acts is an elaboration on 1:8: "But you shall receive power when the Holy Spirit has come upon you; and you shall be witnesses to Me in Jerusalem, and in all Judea and Samaria, and to the end of the earth."

In Acts we learn not only the power of the Holy Spirit but the ways in which the peace of the Holy Spirit sustained the new church movement. We see in Acts how His Spirit fed and inspired the early believers: "Then the churches throughout all Judea, Galilee, and Samaria had peace and were edified. And walking in the fear of the Lord and in the comfort of the Holy Spirit, they were multiplied" (9:31). We also witness the opening of the gospel to non-Jews via Peter's dynamic vision, which he explained this way: "God shows no partiality. But in every nation whoever fears Him and works righteousness is *accepted by Him*" (10:34–35). In Acts Jesus brings peace because He is Lord, and the result is comfort in and motivation from Him.

Prologue

1 The former account I made, O [a]Theoph-
ilus, of all that Jesus began both to do
and teach, 2 [a]until the day in which He was
taken up, after He through the Holy Spirit
[b]had given commandments to the apostles
whom He had chosen, 3 [a]to whom He also
presented Himself alive after His suffering
by many infallible proofs, being seen by them
during forty days and speaking of the things
pertaining to the kingdom of God.

The Holy Spirit Promised

4 [a]And being assembled together with
them, He commanded them not to depart
from Jerusalem, but to wait for the Promise
of the Father, "which," *He said,* "you have
[b]heard from Me; 5 [a]for John truly baptized
with water, [b]but you shall be baptized with
the Holy Spirit not many days from now."
6 Therefore, when they had come together,
they asked Him, saying, "Lord, will You at this
time restore the kingdom to Israel?" 7 And
He said to them, [a]"It is not for you to [b]know
times or seasons which the Father has put
in His own authority. 8 [a]But you shall receive
power [b]when the Holy Spirit has come upon
you; and [c]you shall be witnesses to Me[1] in
Jerusalem, and in all Judea and [d]Samaria,
and to the [e]end of the earth."

Jesus Ascends to Heaven

9 [a]Now when He had spoken these things,
while they watched, [b]He was taken up, and a
cloud received Him out of their sight. 10 And
while they looked steadfastly toward heaven
as He went up, behold, two men stood by
them [a]in white apparel, 11 who also said, "Men
of Galilee, why do you stand gazing up into
heaven? This *same* Jesus, who was taken up
from you into heaven, [a]will so come in like
manner as you saw Him go into heaven."

The Upper Room Prayer Meeting

12 [a]Then they returned to Jerusalem from
the mount called Olivet, which is near Jerusalem, a Sabbath day's journey. 13 And when they
had entered, they went up [a]into the upper
room where they were staying: [b]Peter, James,
John, and Andrew; Philip and Thomas; Bartholomew and Matthew; James *the son* of
Alphaeus and [c]Simon the Zealot; and [d]Judas
the son of James. 14 [a]These all continued with
one accord in prayer and supplication,[1] with
[b]the women and Mary the mother of Jesus,
and with [c]His brothers.

Matthias Chosen

15 And in those days Peter stood up in the
midst of the disciples[1] (altogether the number
[a]of names was about a hundred and twenty),
and said, 16 "Men *and* brethren, this Scripture
had to be fulfilled, [a]which the Holy Spirit
spoke before by the mouth of David concerning Judas, [b]who became a guide to those
who arrested Jesus; 17 for [a]he was numbered
with us and obtained a part in [b]this ministry."
18 [a](Now this man purchased a field with
[b]the wages of iniquity; and falling headlong,
he burst open in the middle and all his entrails gushed out. 19 And it became known to
all those dwelling in Jerusalem; so that field
is called in their own language, Akel Dama,
that is, Field of Blood.)
20 "For it is written in the Book of Psalms:

[a]'Let his dwelling place be desolate,
And let no one live in it';[1]

and,

[b]'Let[2] another take his office.'[3]

21 "Therefore, of these men who have accompanied us all the time that the Lord Jesus
went in and out among us, 22 beginning from
the baptism of John to that day when [a]He was
taken up from us, one of these must [b]become
a witness with us of His resurrection."
23 And they proposed two: Joseph called
[a]Barsabas, who was surnamed Justus, and
Matthias. 24 And they prayed and said, "You,
O Lord, [a]who know the hearts of all, show
which of these two You have chosen 25 [a]to
take part in this ministry and apostleship
from which Judas by transgression fell, that
he might go to his own place." 26 And they cast
their lots, and the lot fell on Matthias. And
he was numbered with the eleven apostles.

Coming of the Holy Spirit

2 When [a]the Day of Pentecost had fully
come, [b]they were all with one accord[1] in
one place. 2 And suddenly there came a sound

1:1 [a] Luke 1:3 **1:2** [a] Mark 16:19 [b] Matt. 28:19 **1:3** [a] Mark 16:12, 14 **1:4** [a] Luke 24:49 [b] [John 14:16, 17, 26; 15:26] *1:5* [a] Matt. 3:11 [b] *[Joel 2:28]* **1:7** [a] 1 Thess. 5:1 [b] Matt. 24:36 **1:8** [a] [Acts 2:1, 4] [b] Luke 24:49 [c] Luke 24:48 [d] Acts 8:1, 5, 14 [e] Col. 1:23 [1] NU-Text reads *My witnesses.* **1:9** [a] Luke 24:50, 51 [b] Acts 1:2 **1:10** [a] John 20:12 **1:11** [a] Dan. 7:13 **1:12** [a] Luke 24:52 **1:13** [a] Acts 9:37, 39; 20:8 [b] Matt. 10:2–4 [c] Luke 6:15 [d] Jude 1 **1:14** [a] Acts 2:1, 46 [b] Luke 23:49, 55 [c] Matt. 13:55 [1] NU-Text omits *and supplication.* **1:15** [a] Rev. 3:4 [1] NU-Text reads *brethren.* **1:16** [a] Ps. 41:9 [b] Luke 22:47 **1:17** [a] Matt. 10:4 [b] Acts 1:25 **1:18** [a] Matt. 27:3–10 [b] Mark 14:21 **1:20** [a] Ps. 69:25 [b] Ps. 109:8 [1] Psalm 69:25 [2] Psalm 109:8 [3] Greek *episkopen,* position of overseer **1:22** [a] Acts 1:9 [b] Acts 1:8; 2:32 **1:23** [a] Acts 15:22 **1:24** [a] 1 Sam. 16:7 **1:25** [a] Acts 1:17 **2:1** [a] Lev. 23:15 [b] Acts 1:14 [1] NU-Text reads *together.*

from heaven, as of a rushing mighty wind,
and [a]it filled the whole house where they were
sitting. 3Then there appeared to them divided
tongues, as of fire, and *one* sat upon each
of them. 4And [a]they were all filled with the
Holy Spirit and began [b]to speak with other
tongues, as the Spirit gave them utterance.

The Crowd's Response

5And there were dwelling in Jerusalem
Jews, [a]devout men, from every nation under
heaven. 6And when this sound occurred, the
[a]multitude came together, and were confused, because everyone heard them speak
in his own language. 7Then they were all
amazed and marveled, saying to one another,
"Look, are not all these who speak [a]Galileans?
8And how *is it that* we hear, each in our own
language in which we were born? 9Parthians
and Medes and Elamites, those dwelling in
Mesopotamia, Judea and [a]Cappadocia, Pontus and Asia, 10Phrygia and Pamphylia, Egypt
and the parts of Libya adjoining Cyrene,
visitors from Rome, both Jews and proselytes, 11Cretans and Arabs—we hear them
speaking in our own tongues the wonderful
works of God." 12So they were all amazed and
perplexed, saying to one another, "Whatever
could this mean?"
13Others mocking said, "They are full of
new wine."

Peter's Sermon

14But Peter, standing up with the eleven,
raised his voice and said to them, "Men of
Judea and all who dwell in Jerusalem, let this
be known to you, and heed my words. 15For
these are not drunk, as you suppose, [a]since
it is *only* the third hour of the day. 16But this
is what was spoken by the prophet Joel:

17 'And[a] it shall come to pass in the last
days, says God,
[b]That I will pour out of My Spirit on all
flesh;
Your sons and [c]your daughters shall
prophesy,
Your young men shall see visions,
Your old men shall dream dreams.
18 And on My menservants and on My
maidservants
I will pour out My Spirit in those days;
[a]And they shall prophesy.
19 [a]I will show wonders in heaven above
And signs in the earth beneath:
Blood and fire and vapor of smoke.
20 [a]The sun shall be turned into darkness,
And the moon into blood,
Before the coming of the great and
awesome day of the LORD.
21 And it shall come to pass
That [a]whoever calls on the name of the
LORD
Shall be saved.'[1]

22"Men of Israel, hear these words: Jesus
of Nazareth, a Man attested by God to you [a]by
miracles, wonders, and signs which God did
through Him in your midst, as you yourselves
also know— 23Him, [a]being delivered by the
determined purpose and foreknowledge of
God, [b]you have taken[1] by lawless hands, have
crucified, and put to death; 24[a]whom God
raised up, having loosed the pains of death,
because it was not possible that He should be
held by it. 25For David says concerning Him:

[a]'I foresaw the LORD always before my
face,
For He is at my right hand, that I may
not be shaken.
26 Therefore my heart rejoiced, and my
tongue was glad;
Moreover my flesh also will rest in
hope.
27 For You will not leave my soul in
Hades,
Nor will You allow Your Holy One to see
[a]corruption.
28 You have made known to me the ways
of life;
You will make me full of joy in Your
presence.'[1]

29"Men *and* brethren, let *me* speak freely
to you [a]of the patriarch David, that he is both
dead and buried, and his tomb is with us to
this day. 30Therefore, being a prophet, [a]and
knowing that God had sworn with an oath to
him that of the fruit of his body, according
to the flesh, He would raise up the Christ to
sit on his throne,[1] 31he, foreseeing this, spoke
concerning the resurrection of the Christ,
[a]that His soul was not left in Hades, nor did
His flesh see corruption. 32[a]This Jesus God
has raised up, [b]of which we are all witnesses.
33Therefore [a]being exalted to [b]the right hand
of God, and [c]having received from the Father

2:2 [a] Acts 4:31 **2:4** [a] Acts 1:5 [b] Mark 16:17 **2:5** [a] Acts 8:2 **2:6** [a] Acts 4:32 **2:7** [a] Acts 1:11 **2:9** [a] 1 Pet. 1:1 **2:15** [a] 1 Thess. 5:7 **2:17** [a] Joel 2:28–32 [b] Acts 10:45 [c] Acts 21:9 **2:18** [a] 1 Cor. 12:10 **2:19** [a] Joel 2:30 **2:20** [a] Matt. 24:29 **2:21** [a] Rom. 10:13 [1] Joel 2:28–32 **2:22** [a] John 3:2; 5:6 **2:23** [a] Luke 22:22 [b] Acts 5:30 [1] NU-Text omits *have taken.* **2:24** [a] [Rom. 8:11] **2:25** [a] Ps. 16:8–11 **2:27** [a] Acts 13:30–37 **2:28** [1] Psalm 16:8–11 **2:29** [a] Acts 13:36 **2:30** [a] Ps. 132:11 [1] NU-Text omits *according to the flesh, He would raise up the Christ* and completes the verse with *He would seat one on his throne.* **2:31** [a] Ps. 16:10 **2:32** [a] Acts 2:24 [b] Acts 1:8; 3:15 **2:33** [a] [Acts 5:31] [b] [Heb. 10:12] [c] [John 14:26]

the promise of the Holy Spirit, He [d]poured
out this which you now see and hear.
34"For David did not ascend into the heavens, but he says himself:

[a]'The LORD said to my Lord,
"Sit at My right hand,
35 Till I make Your enemies Your
footstool." '[1]

36"Therefore let all the house of Israel
know assuredly that God has made this Jesus,
whom you crucified, both Lord and Christ."
37Now when they heard *this,* [a]they were
cut to the heart, and said to Peter and the
rest of the apostles, "Men *and* brethren, what
shall we do?"
38Then Peter said to them, [a]"Repent, and
let every one of you be baptized in the name
of Jesus Christ for the remission of sins; and
you shall receive the gift of the Holy Spirit.
39For the promise is to you and [a]to your children, and [b]to all who are afar off, as many as
the Lord our God will call."

A Vital Church Grows

40And with many other words he testified
and exhorted them, saying, "Be saved from
this perverse generation." 41Then those who
gladly[1] received his word were baptized; and
that day about three thousand souls were
added *to them.* 42[a]And they continued steadfastly in the apostles' doctrine and fellowship,
in the breaking of bread, and in prayers.
43Then fear came upon every soul, and [a]many
wonders and signs were done through the
apostles. 44Now all who believed were together, and [a]had all things in common, 45and sold
their possessions and goods, and [a]divided
them among all, as anyone had need.
46[a]So continuing daily with one accord [b]in
the temple, and [c]breaking bread from house
to house, they ate their food with gladness
and simplicity of heart, 47praising God and
having favor with all the people. And [a]the
Lord added to the church[1] daily those who
were being saved.

A Lame Man Healed

3 Now Peter and John went up together
[a]to the temple at the hour of prayer, [b]the
ninth *hour.* 2And [a]a certain man lame from
his mother's womb was carried, whom they
laid daily at the gate of the temple which is
called Beautiful, [b]to ask alms from those who
entered the temple; 3who, seeing Peter and
John about to go into the temple, asked for
alms. 4And fixing his eyes on him, with John,
Peter said, "Look at us." 5So he gave them his
attention, expecting to receive something
from them. 6Then Peter said, "Silver and gold
I do not have, but what I do have I give you:

2:33 [d] Acts 2:1–11, 17; 10:45 **2:34** [a] Ps. 68:18; 110:1 **2:35** [1] Psalm 110:1 **2:37** [a] Luke 3:10, 12, 14 **2:38** [a] Luke 24:47
2:39 [a] Joel 2:28, 32 [b] Eph. 2:13 **2:41** [1] NU-Text omits *gladly.* **2:42** [a] Acts 1:14 **2:43** [a] Acts 2:22 **2:44** [a] Acts 4:32, 34, 37; 5:2 **2:45** [a] Is. 58:7 **2:46** [a] Acts 1:14 [b] Luke 24:53 [c] Acts 2:42; 20:7 **2:47** [a] Acts 5:14 [1] NU-Text omits *to the church.*
3:1 [a] Acts 2:46 [b] Ps. 55:17 **3:2** [a] Acts 14:8 [b] John 9:8

GIVING AWAY GOD'S PEACE

Peter said, "Silver and gold I do not have, but what I do have I give you."

ACTS 3:6

Christian faith is not about prosperity; it is about redemption and peace. The one creates the other. The church officially began on the day of Pentecost with the outpouring of the Holy Spirit. The apostle Peter preached a sermon and three thousand people responded in faith. A day or two later Peter and John went up to the temple to pray and encountered a man who couldn't walk begging for money. Peter said, "Silver and gold I do not have, but what I do have I give you: In the name of Jesus Christ of Nazareth, rise up and walk" (Acts 3:6). Immediately, the man's legs were strengthened and he was able to stand, walk, and even run—much to everyone's amazement.

What I like about this story is what Peter said: "What I do have I give you." That's what God asks of us. He doesn't ask for what you and I do not have. We can all serve Him in big ways and small. You may not have a lot of money, but what you have—the peace of Christ—you can share with the one who has no peace.

With whom can you share it today?

[a]In the name of Jesus Christ of Nazareth, rise up and walk." 7And he took him by the right hand and lifted *him* up, and immediately his feet and ankle bones received strength. 8So he, [a]leaping up, stood and walked and entered the temple with them—walking, leaping, and praising God. 9[a]And all the people saw him walking and praising God. 10Then they knew that it was he who [a]sat begging alms at the Beautiful Gate of the temple; and they were filled with wonder and amazement at what had happened to him.

Preaching in Solomon's Portico

11Now as the lame man who was healed held on to Peter and John, all the people ran together to them in the porch [a]which is called Solomon's, greatly amazed. 12So when Peter saw *it,* he responded to the people: "Men of Israel, why do you marvel at this? Or why look so intently at us, as though by our own power or godliness we had made this man walk? 13[a]The God of Abraham, Isaac, and Jacob, the God of our fathers, [b]glorified His Servant Jesus, whom you [c]delivered up and [d]denied in the presence of Pilate, when he was determined to let *Him* go. 14But you denied [a]the Holy One [b]and the Just, and [c]asked for a murderer to be granted to you, 15and killed the Prince of life, [a]whom God raised from the dead, [b]of which we are witnesses. 16[a]And His name, through faith in His name, has made this man strong, whom you see and know. Yes, the faith which *comes* through Him has given him this perfect soundness in the presence of you all.

17"Yet now, brethren, I know that [a]you did *it* in ignorance, as *did* also your rulers. 18But [a]those things which God foretold [b]by the mouth of all His prophets, that the Christ would suffer, He has thus fulfilled. 19[a]Repent therefore and be converted, that your sins may be blotted out, so that times of refreshing may come from the presence of the Lord, 20and that He may send Jesus Christ, who was preached to you before,[1] 21[a]whom heaven must receive until the times of [b]restoration of all things, [c]which God has spoken by the mouth of all His holy prophets since the world began. 22For Moses truly said to the fathers, [a]'The LORD your God will raise up for you a Prophet like me from your brethren. Him you shall hear in all things, whatever He says to you. 23And it shall be *that* every soul who will not hear that Prophet shall be utterly destroyed from among the people.'[1] 24Yes, and [a]all the prophets, from Samuel and those who follow, as many as have spoken, have also foretold[1] these days. 25[a]You are sons of the prophets, and of the covenant which God made with our fathers, saying to Abraham, [b]'And in your seed all the families of the earth shall be blessed.'[1] 26To you [a]first, God, having raised up His Servant Jesus, sent Him to bless you, [b]in turning away every one *of you* from your iniquities."

Peter and John Arrested

4 Now as they spoke to the people, the priests, the captain of the temple, and the [a]Sadducees came upon them, 2being greatly disturbed that they taught the people and preached in Jesus the resurrection from the dead. 3And they laid hands on them, and put *them* in custody until the next day, for it was already evening. 4However, many of those who heard the word believed; and the number of the men came to be about five thousand.

Addressing the Sanhedrin

5And it came to pass, on the next day, that their rulers, elders, and scribes, 6as well as [a]Annas the high priest, Caiaphas, John, and Alexander, and as many as were of the family of the high priest, were gathered together at Jerusalem. 7And when they had set them in the midst, they asked, [a]"By what power or by what name have you done this?"

8[a]Then Peter, filled with the Holy Spirit, said to them, "Rulers of the people and elders of Israel: 9If we this day are judged for a good deed *done* to a helpless man, by what means he has been made well, 10let it be known to you all, and to all the people of Israel, [a]that by the name of Jesus Christ of Nazareth, whom you crucified, [b]whom God raised from the dead, by Him this man stands here before you whole. 11This is the [a]'stone which was rejected by you builders, which has become the chief cornerstone.'[1] 12[a]Nor is there salvation in any other, for there is no other name under heaven given among men by which we must be saved."

3:6 [a] Acts 4:10 **3:8** [a] Is. 35:6 **3:9** [a] Acts 4:16, 21 **3:10** [a] John 9:8 **3:11** [a] John 10:23 **3:13** [a] John 5:30 [b] John 7:39; 12:23; 13:31 [c] Matt. 27:2 [d] Matt. 27:20 **3:14** [a] Mark 1:24 [b] Acts 7:52 [c] John 18:40 **3:15** [a] Acts 2:24 [b] Acts 2:32 **3:16** [a] Matt. 9:22 **3:17** [a] Luke 23:34 **3:18** [a] Acts 26:22 [b] 1 Pet. 1:10 **3:19** [a] [Acts 2:38; 26:20] **3:20** [1] NU-Text and M-Text read *Christ Jesus, who was ordained for you before.* **3:21** [a] Acts 1:11 [b] Matt. 17:11 [c] Luke 1:70 **3:22** [a] Deut. 18:15, 18, 19 **3:23** [1] Deuteronomy 18:15, 18, 19 **3:24** [a] Luke 24:25 [1] NU-Text and M-Text read *proclaimed.* **3:25** [a] [Rom. 9:4, 8] [b] Gen. 12:3; 18:18; 22:18; 26:4; 28:14 [1] Genesis 22:18; 26:4; 28:14 **3:26** [a] [Rom. 1:16; 2:9] [b] Matt. 1:21 **4:1** [a] Matt. 22:23 **4:6** [a] Luke 3:2 **4:7** [a] Matt. 21:23 **4:8** [a] Luke 12:11, 12 **4:10** [a] Acts 2:22; 3:6, 16 [b] Acts 2:24 **4:11** [a] Ps. 118:22 [1] Psalm 118:22 **4:12** [a] [1 Tim. 2:5, 6]

The Name of Jesus Forbidden

13Now when they saw the boldness of Peter
and John, [a]and perceived that they were un-
educated and untrained men, they marveled.
And they realized that they had been with
Jesus. 14And seeing the man who had been
healed [a]standing with them, they could say
nothing against it. 15But when they had commanded them to go aside out of the council,
they conferred among themselves, 16saying,
[a]"What shall we do to these men? For, indeed,
that a notable miracle has been done through
them *is* [b]evident to all who dwell in Jerusalem, and we cannot deny *it.* 17But so that it
spreads no further among the people, let us
severely threaten them, that from now on
they speak to no man in this name."

18[a]So they called them and commanded
them not to speak at all nor teach in the name
of Jesus. 19But Peter and John answered and
said to them, [a]"Whether it is right in the sight
of God to listen to you more than to God, you
judge. 20[a]For we cannot but speak the things
which [b]we have seen and heard." 21So when
they had further threatened them, they let
them go, finding no way of punishing them,
[a]because of the people, since they all [b]glo-
rified God for [c]what had been done. 22For
the man was over forty years old on whom
this miracle of healing had been performed.

Prayer for Boldness

23And being let go, [a]they went to their own
companions and reported all that the chief
priests and elders had said to them. 24So
when they heard that, they raised their voice
to God with one accord and said: "Lord, [a]You
are God, who made heaven and earth and
the sea, and all that is in them, 25who by the
mouth of Your servant David[1] have said:

[a]'Why did the nations rage,
And the people plot vain things?
26 The kings of the earth took their stand,
And the rulers were gathered together
Against the LORD and against His
Christ.'[1]

27"For [a]truly against [b]Your holy Servant
Jesus, [c]whom You anointed, both Herod
and Pontius Pilate, with the Gentiles and the
people of Israel, were gathered together 28[a]to
do whatever Your hand and Your purpose
determined before to be done. 29Now, Lord,
look on their threats, and grant to Your servants [a]that with all boldness they may speak
Your word, 30by stretching out Your hand
to heal, [a]and that signs and wonders may
be done [b]through the name of [c]Your holy
Servant Jesus."

31And when they had prayed, [a]the place
where they were assembled together was
shaken; and they were all filled with the Holy
Spirit, [b]and they spoke the word of God with
boldness.

Sharing in All Things

32Now the multitude of those who believed
[a]were of one heart and one soul; [b]neither did
anyone say that any of the things he possessed was his own, but they had all things in
common. 33And with [a]great power the apostles gave [b]witness to the resurrection of the
Lord Jesus. And [c]great grace was upon them
all. 34Nor was there anyone among them
who lacked; [a]for all who were possessors
of lands or houses sold them, and brought
the proceeds of the things that were sold,
35[a]and laid *them* at the apostles' feet; [b]and
they distributed to each as anyone had need.

36And Joses,[1] who was also named Barnabas by the apostles (which is translated Son
of Encouragement), a Levite of the country of
Cyprus, 37[a]having land, sold *it,* and brought
the money and laid *it* at the apostles' feet.

Lying to the Holy Spirit

5 But a certain man named Ananias, with
Sapphira his wife, sold a possession. 2And
he kept back *part* of the proceeds, his wife
also being aware *of it,* and brought a certain
part and laid *it* at the apostles' feet. 3[a]But
Peter said, "Ananias, why has [b]Satan filled
your heart to lie to the Holy Spirit and keep
back *part* of the price of the land for yourself?
4While it remained, was it not your own?
And after it was sold, was it not in your own
control? Why have you conceived this thing
in your heart? You have not lied to men but
to God."

5Then Ananias, hearing these words, [a]fell
down and breathed his last. So great fear
came upon all those who heard these things.
6And the young men arose and [a]wrapped him
up, carried *him* out, and buried *him.*

7Now it was about three hours later when

4:13 [a] [1 Cor. 1:27] **4:14** [a] Acts 3:11 **4:16** [a] John 11:47 [b] Acts 3:7–10 **4:18** [a] Acts 5:28, 40 **4:19** [a] Acts 5:29 **4:20** [a] Acts 1:8; 2:32 [b] [1 John 1:1, 3] **4:21** [a] Acts 5:26 [b] Matt. 15:31 [c] Acts 3:7, 8 **4:23** [a] Acts 2:44–46; 12:12 **4:24** [a] Ex. 20:11 **4:25** [a] Ps. 2:1, 2 [1] NU-Text reads *who through the Holy Spirit, by the mouth of our father, Your servant David.* **4:26** [1] Psalm 2:1, 2 **4:27** [a] Luke 22:2; 23:1, 8 [b] [Luke 1:35] [c] John 10:36 **4:28** [a] Acts 2:23; 3:18 **4:29** [a] Acts 4:13, 31; 9:27; 13:46; 14:3; 19:8; 26:26 **4:30** [a] Acts 2:43; 5:12 [b] Acts 3:6, 16 [c] Acts 4:27 **4:31** [a] Acts 2:2, 4; 16:26 [b] Acts 4:29 **4:32** [a] Rom. 15:5, 6 [b] Acts 2:44 **4:33** [a] [Acts 1:8] [b] Acts 1:22 [c] Rom. 6:15 **4:34** [a] Acts 2:45 **4:35** [a] Acts 4:37; 5:2 [b] Acts 2:45; 6:1 **4:36** [1] NU-Text reads *Joseph.* **4:37** [a] Acts 4:34, 35; 5:1, 2 **5:3** [a] Deut. 23:21 [b] Luke 22:3 **5:5** [a] Acts 5:10, 11 **5:6** [a] John 19:40

his wife came in, not knowing what had happened. 8And Peter answered her, "Tell me whether you sold the land for so much?"

She said, "Yes, for so much."

9Then Peter said to her, "How is it that you have agreed together [a]to test the Spirit of the Lord? Look, the feet of those who have buried your husband *are* at the door, and they will carry you out." 10[a]Then immediately she fell down at his feet and breathed her last. And the young men came in and found her dead, and carrying *her* out, buried *her* by her husband. 11[a]So great fear came upon all the church and upon all who heard these things.

Continuing Power in the Church

12And [a]through the hands of the apostles many signs and wonders were done among the people. [b]And they were all with one accord in Solomon's Porch. 13Yet [a]none of the rest dared join them, [b]but the people esteemed them highly. 14And believers were increasingly added to the Lord, multitudes of both men and women, 15so that they brought the sick out into the streets and laid *them* on beds and couches, [a]that at least the shadow of Peter passing by might fall on some of them. 16Also a multitude gathered from the surrounding cities to Jerusalem, bringing [a]sick people and those who were tormented by unclean spirits, and they were all healed.

Imprisoned Apostles Freed

17[a]Then the high priest rose up, and all those who *were* with him (which is the sect of the Sadducees), and they were filled with indignation, 18[a]and laid their hands on the apostles and put them in the common prison. 19But at night [a]an angel of the Lord opened the prison doors and brought them out, and said, 20"Go, stand in the temple and speak to the people [a]all the words of this life."

21And when they heard *that,* they entered the temple early in the morning and taught. [a]But the high priest and those with him came and called the council together, with all the elders of the children of Israel, and sent to the prison to have them brought.

Apostles on Trial Again

22But when the officers came and did not find them in the prison, they returned and reported, 23saying, "Indeed we found the prison shut securely, and the guards standing outside[1] before the doors; but when we opened them, we found no one inside!" 24Now when the high priest,[1] [a]the captain of the temple, and the chief priests heard these things, they wondered what the outcome would be. 25So one came and told them, saying,[1] "Look, the men whom you put in prison are standing in the temple and teaching the people!"

5:9 [a] Acts 5:3, 4 **5:10** [a] Acts 5:5 **5:11** [a] Acts 2:43; 5:5; 19:17 **5:12** [a] Acts 2:43; 4:30; 6:8; 14:3; 15:12 [b] Acts 3:11; 4:32 **5:13** [a] John 9:22 [b] Acts 2:47; 4:21 **5:15** [a] Acts 19:12 **5:16** [a] Mark 16:17, 18 **5:17** [a] Acts 4:1, 2, 6 **5:18** [a] Luke 21:12 **5:19** [a] Acts 12:7; 16:26 **5:20** [a] [John 6:63, 68; 17:3] **5:21** [a] Acts 4:5, 6 **5:23** [1] NU-Text and M-Text omit *outside.* **5:24** [a] Acts 4:1; 5:26 [1] NU-Text omits *the high priest.* **5:25** [1] NU-Text and M-Text omit *saying.*

BE BOLD IN YOUR OBEDIENCE

We ought to obey God rather than men.

ACTS 5:29

In our increasingly post-Judeo-Christian world it is becoming harder to follow Christ in the public sphere. In schools and the workplace we are expected to say and not say certain things. We are asked to embrace ideologies that are dubious, even immoral. To say, "I follow Christ, so I will do this and will not do that," could result in expulsion or dismissal. We who have historically enjoyed freedom have never experienced anything like it.

In Acts we read of the world of first-century Christianity. Jesus' apostles faced extreme opposition. Their religious leaders (the ruling priests and members of the Jewish council) ordered them to stop proclaiming Jesus. These leaders were not just unbelievers; they had persuaded the Roman governor to put Jesus to death. How could they then say proclaiming Jesus as Messiah was okay?

Speaking for the apostles, Peter replied, "We ought to obey God rather than men." I applaud his boldness. Would that more people today possessed such courage. The lesson here is that sometimes you have to make a difficult choice: peace with God or peace with the world.

26Then the captain went with the officers
and brought them without violence, [a]for
they feared the people, lest they should be
stoned. 27And when they had brought them,
they set *them* before the council. And the
high priest asked them, 28saying, [a]"Did we
not strictly command you not to teach in this
name? And look, you have filled Jerusalem
with your doctrine, [b]and intend to bring this
Man's [c]blood on us!"
29But Peter and the *other* apostles answered and said: [a]"We ought to obey God
rather than men. 30[a]The God of our fathers
raised up Jesus whom you murdered by
[b]hanging on a tree. 31[a]Him God has exalted
to His right hand *to be* [b]Prince and [c]Savior,
[d]to give repentance to Israel and forgiveness
of sins. 32And [a]we are His witnesses to these
things, and *so* also *is* the Holy Spirit [b]whom
God has given to those who obey Him."

Gamaliel's Advice

33When they heard *this,* they were [a]furious
and plotted to kill them. 34Then one in the
council stood up, a Pharisee named [a]Gama-
liel, a teacher of the law held in respect by
all the people, and commanded them to put
the apostles outside for a little while. 35And
he said to them: "Men of Israel, take heed to
yourselves what you intend to do regarding
these men. 36For some time ago Theudas rose
up, claiming to be somebody. A number of
men, about four hundred, joined him. He was
slain, and all who obeyed him were scattered
and came to nothing. 37After this man, Judas
of Galilee rose up in the days of the census,
and drew away many people after him. He
also perished, and all who obeyed him were
dispersed. 38And now I say to you, keep away
from these men and let them alone; for if
this plan or this work is of men, it will come
to nothing; 39[a]but if it is of God, you cannot
overthrow it—lest you even be found [b]to
fight against God."
40And they agreed with him, and when
they had [a]called for the apostles [b]and beaten
them, they commanded that they should not
speak in the name of Jesus, and let them go.
41So they departed from the presence of the
council, [a]rejoicing that they were counted
worthy to suffer shame for His[1] name. 42And
daily [a]in the temple, and in every house, [b]they
did not cease teaching and preaching Jesus
as the Christ.

Seven Chosen to Serve

6 Now in those days, [a]when *the number*
of the disciples was multiplying, there
arose a complaint against the Hebrews by
the [b]Hellenists,[1] because their widows were
neglected [c]in the daily distribution. 2Then
the twelve summoned the multitude of the
disciples and said, [a]"It is not desirable that
we should leave the word of God and serve
tables. 3Therefore, brethren, [a]seek out from
among you seven men of *good* reputation,
full of the Holy Spirit and wisdom, whom we
may appoint over this [b]business; 4but we [a]will
give ourselves continually to prayer and to
the ministry of the word."
5And the saying pleased the whole multitude. And they chose Stephen, [a]a man full of
faith and the Holy Spirit, and [b]Philip, Proch-
orus, Nicanor, Timon, Parmenas, and [c]Nic-
olas, a proselyte from Antioch, 6whom they
set before the apostles; and [a]when they had
prayed, [b]they laid hands on them.
7Then [a]the word of God spread, and the
number of the disciples multiplied greatly in
Jerusalem, and a great many [b]of the priests
were obedient to the faith.

Stephen Accused of Blasphemy

8And Stephen, full of faith[1] and power, did
great [a]wonders and signs among the people.
9Then there arose some from what is called
the Synagogue of the Freedmen (Cyrenians,
Alexandrians, and those from Cilicia and Asia),
disputing with Stephen. 10And [a]they were not
able to resist the wisdom and the Spirit by
which he spoke. 11[a]Then they secretly induced
men to say, "We have heard him speak blasphemous words against Moses and God." 12And
they stirred up the people, the elders, and the
scribes; and they came upon *him,* seized him,
and brought *him* to the council. 13They also
set up false witnesses who said, "This man
does not cease to speak blasphemous[1] words
against this holy place and the law; 14[a]for we
have heard him say that this Jesus of Nazareth
will destroy this place and change the customs
which Moses delivered to us." 15And all who
sat in the council, looking steadfastly at him,
saw his face as the face of an angel.

5:26 [a] Matt. 21:26 **5:28** [a] Acts 4:17, 18 [b] Acts 2:23, 36 [c] Matt. 23:35 **5:29** [a] Acts 4:19 **5:30** [a] Acts 3:13, 15 [b] [1 Pet. 2:24] **5:31** [a] [Acts 2:33, 36] [b] Acts 3:15 [c] Matt. 1:21 [d] Luke 24:47 **5:32** [a] John 15:26, 27 [b] Acts 2:4; 10:44 **5:33** [a] Acts 2:37; 7:54 **5:34** [a] Acts 22:3 **5:39** [a] 1 Cor. 1:25 [b] Acts 7:51; 9:5 **5:40** [a] Acts 4:18 [b] Matt. 10:17 **5:41** [a] [1 Pet. 4:13–16] [1] NU-Text reads *the name;* M-Text reads *the name of Jesus.* **5:42** [a] Acts 2:46 [b] Acts 4:20, 29 **6:1** [a] Acts 2:41; 4:4 [b] Acts 9:29; 11:20 [c] Acts 4:35; 11:29 [1] That is, Greek-speaking Jews **6:2** [a] Ex. 18:17 **6:3** [a] 1 Tim. 3:7 [b] 1 Tim. 3:8–13 **6:4** [a] Acts 2:42 **6:5** [a] Acts 6:3; 11:24 [b] Acts 8:5, 26; 21:8 [c] Rev. 2:6, 15 **6:6** [a] Acts 1:24 [b] [2 Tim. 1:6] **6:7** [a] Acts 12:24 [b] John 12:42 **6:8** [a] Acts 2:43; 5:12; 8:15; 14:3 [1] NU-Text reads *grace.* **6:10** [a] Luke 21:15 **6:11** [a] 1 Kin. 21:10, 13 **6:13** [1] NU-Text omits *blasphemous.* **6:14** [a] Acts 10:38; 25:8

Stephen's Address: The Call of Abraham

7 Then the high priest said, "Are these
things so?"
2And he said, [a]"Brethren and fathers, listen:
The [b]God of glory appeared to our father Abraham when he was in Mesopotamia, before he
dwelt in [c]Haran, 3and said to him, [a]'Get out
of your country and from your relatives, and
come to a land that I will show you.'[1] 4Then
[a]he came out of the land of the Chaldeans
and dwelt in Haran. And from there, when
his father was [b]dead, He moved him to this
land in which you now dwell. 5And *God* gave
him no inheritance in it, not even *enough* to
set his foot on. But even when *Abraham* had
no child, [a]He promised to give it to him for a
possession, and to his descendants after him.
6But God spoke in this way: [a]that his descendants would dwell in a foreign land, and that
they would bring them into [b]bondage and
oppress *them* four hundred years. 7[a]'And the
nation to whom they will be in bondage I will
[b]judge,'[1] said God, [c]'and after that they shall
come out and serve Me in this place.'[2] 8[a]Then
He gave him the covenant of circumcision;
[b]and so *Abraham* begot Isaac and circumcised
him on the eighth day; [c]and Isaac *begot* Jacob, and [d]Jacob *begot* the twelve patriarchs.

The Patriarchs in Egypt

9[a]"And the patriarchs, becoming envious,
[b]sold Joseph into Egypt. [c]But God was with
him 10and delivered him out of all his troubles, [a]and gave him favor and wisdom in the
presence of Pharaoh, king of Egypt; and he
made him governor over Egypt and all his
house. 11[a]Now a famine and great trouble
came over all the land of Egypt and Canaan,
and our fathers found no sustenance. 12[a]But
when Jacob heard that there was grain in
Egypt, he sent out our fathers first. 13And
the [a]second *time* Joseph was made known
to his brothers, and Joseph's family became
known to the Pharaoh. 14[a]Then Joseph sent
and called his father Jacob and [b]all his relatives to *him*, seventy-five[1] people. 15[a]So Jacob
went down to Egypt; [b]and he died, he and
our fathers. 16And [a]they were carried back to
Shechem and laid in [b]the tomb that Abraham
bought for a sum of money from the sons of
Hamor, *the father* of Shechem.

God Delivers Israel by Moses

17"But when [a]the time of the promise drew
near which God had sworn to Abraham, [b]the
people grew and multiplied in Egypt 18till
another king [a]arose who did not know Joseph. 19This man dealt treacherously with
our people, and oppressed our forefathers,
[a]making them expose their babies, so that
they might not live. 20[a]At this time Moses was
born, and [b]was well pleasing to God; and he
was brought up in his father's house for three
months. 21But [a]when he was set out, [b]Phar-
aoh's daughter took him away and brought
him up as her own son. 22And Moses was
learned in all the wisdom of the Egyptians,
and was [a]mighty in words and deeds.
23[a]"Now when he was forty years old, it
came into his heart to visit his brethren, the
children of Israel. 24And seeing one of *them*
suffer wrong, he defended and avenged him
who was oppressed, and struck down the
Egyptian. 25For he supposed that his brethren would have understood that God would
deliver them by his hand, but they did not
understand. 26And the next day he appeared
to *two of* them as they were fighting, and
tried to reconcile them, saying, 'Men, you are
brethren; why do you wrong one another?'
27But he who did his neighbor wrong pushed
him away, saying, [a]'Who made you a ruler and
a judge over us? 28Do you want to kill me as
you did the Egyptian yesterday?'[1] 29[a]Then, at
this saying, Moses fled and became a dweller
in the land of Midian, where he [b]had two sons.
30[a]"And when forty years had passed, an
Angel of the Lord[1] appeared to him in a flame
of fire in a bush, in the wilderness of Mount
Sinai. 31When Moses saw *it*, he marveled at
the sight; and as he drew near to observe,
the voice of the Lord came to him, 32*saying*,
[a]'I *am* the God of your fathers—the God of
Abraham, the God of Isaac, and the God of
Jacob.'[1] And Moses trembled and dared not
look. 33[a]'Then the LORD said to him, "Take
your sandals off your feet, for the place where
you stand is holy ground. 34I have surely
[a]seen the oppression of My people who are
in Egypt; I have heard their groaning and
have come down to deliver them. And now
come, I will [b]send you to Egypt." '[1]
35"This Moses whom they rejected, saying,

7:2 [a] Acts 22:1 [b] Ps. 29:3 [c] Gen. 11:31, 32 **7:3** [a] Gen. 12:1 [1] Genesis 12:1 **7:4** [a] Gen. 11:31; 15:7 [b] Gen. 11:32 **7:5** [a] Gen. 12:7; 13:15; 15:3, 18; 17:8; 26:3 **7:6** [a] Gen. 15:13, 14, 16; 47:11, 12 [b] Ex. 1:8–14; 12:40, 41 **7:7** [a] Gen. 15:14 [b] Ex. 14:13–31 [c] Ex. 3:12 [1] Genesis 15:14 [2] Exodus 3:12 **7:8** [a] Gen. 17:9–14 [b] Gen. 21:1–5 [c] Gen. 25:21–26 [d] Gen. 29:31—30:24; 35:18, 22–26 **7:9** [a] Gen. 37:4, 11, 28 [b] Gen. 37:28 [c] Gen. 39:2, 21, 23 **7:10** [a] Gen. 41:38–44 **7:11** [a] Gen. 41:54; 42:5 **7:12** [a] Gen. 42:1, 2 **7:13** [a] Gen. 45:4, 16 **7:14** [a] Gen. 45:9, 27 [b] Deut. 10:22 [1] Or *seventy* (compare Exodus 1:5) **7:15** [a] Gen. 46:1–7 [b] Gen. 49:33 **7:16** [a] Josh. 24:32 [b] Gen. 23:16 **7:17** [a] Gen. 15:13 [b] Ex. 1:7–9 **7:18** [a] Ex. 1:8 **7:19** [a] Ex. 1:22 **7:20** [a] Ex. 2:1, 2 [b] Heb. 11:23 **7:21** [a] Ex. 2:3, 4 [b] Ex. 2:5–10 **7:22** [a] Luke 24:19 **7:23** [a] Ex. 2:11, 12 **7:27** [a] Ex. 2:14 **7:28** [1] Exodus 2:14 **7:29** [a] Heb. 11:27 [b] Ex. 2:15, 21, 22; 4:20; 18:3 **7:30** [a] Ex. 3:1–10 [1] NU-Text omits *of the Lord.* **7:32** [a] Ex. 3:6, 15 [1] Exodus 3:6, 15 **7:33** [a] Ex. 3:5, 7, 8, 10 **7:34** [a] Ex. 2:24, 25 [b] Ps. 105:26 [1] Exodus 3:5, 7, 8, 10

[a]'Who made you a ruler and a judge?'[1] is the
one God sent *to be* a ruler and a deliverer
[b]by the hand of the Angel who appeared to
him in the bush. 36 [a]He brought them out,
after he had [b]shown wonders and signs in
the land of Egypt, [c]and in the Red Sea, [d]and
in the wilderness forty years.

Israel Rebels Against God

37 "This is that Moses who said to the children of Israel,[1] [a]'The LORD your God will raise
up for you a Prophet like me from your brethren. [b]Him you shall hear.'[2]
38 [a]"This is he who was in the congregation
in the wilderness with [b]the Angel who spoke to
him on Mount Sinai, and *with* our fathers, [c]the
one who received the living [d]oracles to give to
us, 39 whom our fathers [a]would not obey, but
rejected. And in their hearts they turned back
to Egypt, 40 [a]saying to Aaron, 'Make us gods to
go before us; *as for* this Moses who brought
us out of the land of Egypt, we do not know
what has become of him.'[1] 41 [a]And they made
a calf in those days, offered sacrifices to the
idol, and [b]rejoiced in the works of their own
hands. 42 Then [a]God turned and gave them up
to worship [b]the host of heaven, as it is written
in the book of the Prophets:

[c]'Did you offer Me slaughtered animals
and sacrifices *during* forty years in
the wilderness,
O house of Israel?
43 You also took up the tabernacle of
Moloch,
And the star of your god Remphan,
Images which you made to worship;
And [a]I will carry you away beyond
Babylon.'[1]

God's True Tabernacle

44 "Our fathers had the tabernacle of witness in the wilderness, as He appointed,
instructing Moses [a]to make it according to
the pattern that he had seen, 45 [a]which our fathers, having received it in turn, also brought
with Joshua into the land possessed by the
Gentiles, [b]whom God drove out before the
face of our fathers until the [c]days of David,
46 [a]who found favor before God and [b]asked
to find a dwelling for the God of Jacob. 47 [a]But
Solomon built Him a house.
48 "However, [a]the Most High does not dwell
in temples made with hands, as the prophet
says:

49 'Heaven[a] *is* My throne,
And earth *is* My footstool.
What house will you build for Me? says
the LORD,
Or what *is* the place of My rest?
50 Has My hand not [a]made all these
things?'[1]

Israel Resists the Holy Spirit

51 "*You* [a]stiff-necked and [b]uncircumcised
in heart and ears! You always resist the Holy
Spirit; as your fathers *did,* so *do* you. 52 [a]Which
of the prophets did your fathers not persecute? And they killed those who foretold the
coming of [b]the Just One, of whom you now
have become the betrayers and murderers,
53 [a]who have received the law by the direction
of angels and have not kept *it.*"

Stephen the Martyr

54 [a]When they heard these things they were
cut to the heart, and they gnashed at him with
their teeth. 55 But he, [a]being full of the Holy
Spirit, gazed into heaven and saw the [b]glory
of God, and Jesus standing at the right hand
of God, 56 and said, "Look! [a]I see the heavens
opened and the [b]Son of Man standing at the
right hand of God!"
57 Then they cried out with a loud voice,
stopped their ears, and ran at him with one
accord; 58 and they cast *him* out of the city
and stoned *him.* And [a]the witnesses laid
down their clothes at the feet of a young
man named Saul. 59 And they stoned Stephen
as he was calling on *God* and saying, "Lord
Jesus, [a]receive my spirit." 60 Then he knelt
down and cried out with a loud voice, [a]"Lord,
do not charge them with this sin." And when
he had said this, he fell asleep.

Saul Persecutes the Church

8 Now Saul was consenting to his death.
At that time a great persecution arose
against the church which was at Jerusalem;
and [a]they were all scattered throughout the
regions of Judea and Samaria, except the apostles. 2 And devout men carried Stephen *to his
burial,* and [a]made great lamentation over him.

7:35 [a] Ex. 2:14 [b] Ex. 14:21 [1] Exodus 2:14 **7:36** [a] Ex. 12:41; 33:1 [b] Ps. 105:27 [c] Ex. 14:21 [d] Ex. 16:1, 35 **7:37** [a] Deut. 18:15, 18, 19 [b] *Matt. 17:5* [1] *Deuteronomy 18:15* [2] *NU-Text and M-Text omit Him you shall hear.* **7:38** [a] Ex. 19:3 [b] Gal. 3:19 [c] Deut. 5:27 [d] Heb. 5:12 **7:39** [a] Ps. 95:8–11 **7:40** [a] Ex. 32:1, 23 [1] Exodus 32:1, 23 **7:41** [a] Deut. 9:16 [b] Ex. 32:6, 18, 19 **7:42** [a] [2 Thess. 2:11] [b] 2 Kin. 21:3 [c] Amos 5:25–27 **7:43** [a] Jer. 25:9–12 [1] Amos 5:25–27 **7:44** [a] [Heb. 8:5] **7:45** [a] Josh. 3:14; 18:1; 23:9 [b] Ps. 44:2 [c] 2 Sam. 6:2–15 **7:46** [a] 2 Sam. 7:1–13 [b] 1 Chr. 22:7 **7:47** [a] 1 Kin. 6:1–38; 8:20, 21 **7:48** [a] 1 Kin. 8:27 **7:49** [a] Is. 66:1, 2 **7:50** [a] Ps. 102:25 [1] Isaiah 66:1, 2 **7:51** [a] Ex. 32:9 [b] Lev. 26:41 **7:52** [a] 2 Chr. 36:16 [b] Acts 3:14; 22:14 **7:53** [a] Ex. 20:1 **7:54** [a] Acts 5:33 **7:55** [a] Acts 6:5 [b] [Ex. 24:17] **7:56** [a] Matt. 3:16 [b] Dan. 7:13 **7:58** [a] Acts 22:20 **7:59** [a] Ps. 31:5 **7:60** [a] Matt. 5:44 **8:1** [a] Acts 8:4; 11:19 **8:2** [a] Gen. 23:2

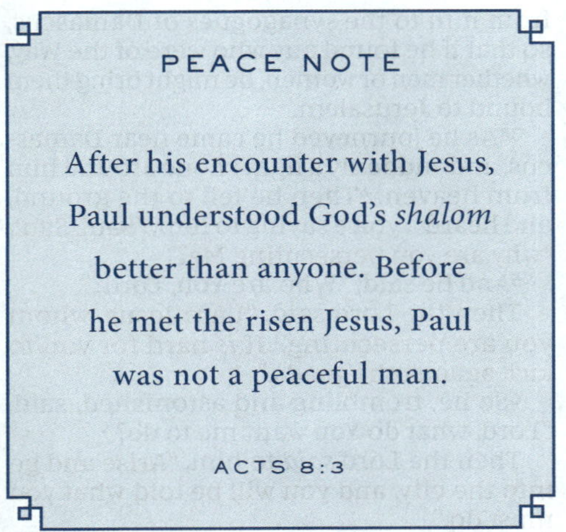

3As for Saul, [a]he made havoc of the church, entering every house, and dragging off men and women, committing *them* to prison.

Christ Is Preached in Samaria

4Therefore [a]those who were scattered went everywhere preaching the word. 5Then [a]Philip went down to the[1] city of Samaria and preached Christ to them. 6And the multitudes with one accord heeded the things spoken by Philip, hearing and seeing the miracles which he did. 7For [a]unclean spirits, crying with a loud voice, came out of many who were possessed; and many who were paralyzed and lame were healed. 8And there was great joy in that city.

The Sorcerer's Profession of Faith

9But there was a certain man called Simon, who previously [a]practiced sorcery in the city and [b]astonished the people of Samaria, claiming that he was someone great, 10to whom they all gave heed, from the least to the greatest, saying, "This man is the great power of God." 11And they heeded him because he had astonished them with his sorceries for a long time. 12But when they believed Philip as he preached the things [a]concerning the kingdom of God and the name of Jesus Christ, both men and women were baptized. 13Then Simon himself also believed; and when he was baptized he continued with Philip, and was amazed, seeing the miracles and signs which were done.

The Sorcerer's Sin

14Now when the [a]apostles who were at Jerusalem heard that Samaria had received the word of God, they sent Peter and John to them, 15who, when they had come down, prayed for them [a]that they might receive the Holy Spirit. 16For [a]as yet He had fallen upon none of them. [b]They had only been baptized in [c]the name of the Lord Jesus. 17Then [a]they laid hands on them, and they received the Holy Spirit.

18And when Simon saw that through the laying on of the apostles' hands the Holy Spirit was given, he offered them money, 19saying, "Give me this power also, that anyone on whom I lay hands may receive the Holy Spirit."

20But Peter said to him, "Your money perish with you, because [a]you thought that [b]the gift of God could be purchased with money! 21You have neither part nor portion in this matter, for your [a]heart is not right in the sight of God. 22Repent therefore of this your wickedness, and pray God [a]if perhaps the thought of your heart may be forgiven you. 23For I see that you are [a]poisoned by bitterness and bound by iniquity."

24Then Simon answered and said, [a]"Pray to the Lord for me, that none of the things which you have spoken may come upon me."

25So when they had testified and preached the word of the Lord, they returned to Jerusalem, preaching the gospel in many villages of the Samaritans.

Christ Is Preached to an Ethiopian

26Now an angel of the Lord spoke to [a]Philip, saying, "Arise and go toward the south along the road which goes down from Jerusalem to Gaza." This is desert. 27So he arose and went.

PEACE NOTE

The Holy Spirit empowers, equips, energizes, and inspires believers to share the gospel of peace with others.

ACTS 8:12

8:3 [a] Phil. 3:6 **8:4** [a] Matt. 10:23 **8:5** [a] Acts 6:5; 8:26, 30 [1] Or *a* **8:7** [a] Mark 16:17 **8:9** [a] Acts 8:11; 13:6 [b] Acts 5:36 **8:12** [a] Acts 1:3; 8:4 **8:14** [a] Acts 5:12, 29, 40 **8:15** [a] Acts 2:38; 19:2 **8:16** [a] Acts 19:2 [b] Matt. 28:19 [c] Acts 10:48; 19:5 **8:17** [a] Acts 6:6; 19:6 **8:20** [a] [Matt. 10:8] [b] [Acts 2:38; 10:45; 11:17] **8:21** [a] Jer. 17:9 **8:22** [a] 2 Tim. 2:25 **8:23** [a] Heb. 12:15 **8:24** [a] James 5:16 **8:26** [a] Acts 6:5

And behold, [a]a man of Ethiopia, a eunuch of
great authority under Candace the queen
of the Ethiopians, who had charge of all her
treasury, and [b]had come to Jerusalem to
worship, 28was returning. And sitting in his
chariot, he was reading Isaiah the prophet.
29Then the Spirit said to Philip, "Go near and
overtake this chariot."
30So Philip ran to him, and heard him
reading the prophet Isaiah, and said, "Do you
understand what you are reading?"
31And he said, "How can I, unless someone
guides me?" And he asked Philip to come up
and sit with him. 32The place in the Scripture
which he read was this:

[a]"He was led as a sheep to the slaughter;
And as a lamb before its shearer *is*
silent,
[b]So He opened not His mouth.
33 In His humiliation His [a]justice was
taken away,
And who will declare His generation?
For His life is [b]taken from the earth."[1]

34So the eunuch answered Philip and said,
"I ask you, of whom does the prophet say this,
of himself or of some other man?" 35Then
Philip opened his mouth, [a]and beginning
at this Scripture, preached Jesus to him.
36Now as they went down the road, they came
to some water. And the eunuch said, "See,
here is water. [a]What hinders me from being
baptized?"
37Then Philip said, [a]"If you believe with all
your heart, you may."
And he answered and said, [b]"I believe that
Jesus Christ is the Son of God."[1]
38So he commanded the chariot to stand
still. And both Philip and the eunuch went
down into the water, and he baptized him.
39Now when they came up out of the water,
[a]the Spirit of the Lord caught Philip away,
so that the eunuch saw him no more; and
he went on his way rejoicing. 40But Philip
was found at Azotus. And passing through,
he preached in all the cities till he came to
[a]Caesarea.

The Damascus Road: Saul Converted

9 Then [a]Saul, still breathing threats and
murder against the disciples of the Lord,
went to the high priest 2and asked [a]letters
from him to the synagogues of Damascus,
so that if he found any who were of the Way,
whether men or women, he might bring them
bound to Jerusalem.
3[a]As he journeyed he came near Damascus, and suddenly a light shone around him
from heaven. 4Then he fell to the ground,
and heard a voice saying to him, "Saul, Saul,
[a]why are you persecuting Me?"
5And he said, "Who are You, Lord?"
Then the Lord said, "I am Jesus, whom
you are persecuting.[1] It *is* hard for you to
kick against the goads."
6So he, trembling and astonished, said,
"Lord, what do You want me to do?"
Then the Lord *said* to him, "Arise and go
into the city, and you will be told what you
must do."
7And [a]the men who journeyed with him
stood speechless, hearing a voice but seeing
no one. 8Then Saul arose from the ground,
and when his eyes were opened he saw
no one. But they led him by the hand and
brought *him* into Damascus. 9And he was
three days without sight, and neither ate
nor drank.

Ananias Baptizes Saul

10Now there was a certain disciple at Damascus [a]named Ananias; and to him the
Lord said in a vision, "Ananias."
And he said, "Here I am, Lord."
11So the Lord *said* to him, "Arise and go to
the street called Straight, and inquire at the
house of Judas for *one* called Saul [a]of Tarsus,
for behold, he is praying. 12And in a vision
he has seen a man named Ananias coming
in and putting *his* hand on him, so that he
might receive his sight."
13Then Ananias answered, "Lord, I have
heard from many about this man, [a]how much
harm he has done to Your saints in Jerusalem. 14And here he has authority from the
chief priests to bind all [a]who call on Your
name."
15But the Lord said to him, "Go, for [a]he is
a chosen vessel of Mine to bear My name
before [b]Gentiles, [c]kings, and the [d]children
of Israel. 16For [a]I will show him how many
things he must suffer for My [b]name's sake."
17[a]And Ananias went his way and entered
the house; and [b]laying his hands on him
he said, "Brother Saul, the Lord Jesus,[1] who

8:27 [a] *Ps. 68:31; 87:4* [b] *John 12:20* **8:32** [a] Is. 53:7, 8 [b] John 19:9 **8:33** [a] Luke 23:1–25 [b] Luke 23:33–46 [1] Isaiah 53:7, 8 **8:35** [a] Luke 24:27 **8:36** [a] Acts 10:47; 16:33 **8:37** [a] [Mark 16:16] [b] Matt. 16:16 [1] NU-Text and M-Text omit this verse. It is found in Western texts, including the Latin tradition. **8:39** [a] Ezek. 3:12, 14 **8:40** [a] Acts 21:8 **9:1** [a] Acts 7:57; 8:1, 3; 26:10, 11 **9:2** [a] Acts 22:5 **9:3** [a] 1 Cor. 15:8 **9:4** [a] [Matt. 25:40] **9:5** [1] NU-Text and M-Text omit the last sentence of verse 5 and begin verse 6 with *But arise and go.* **9:7** [a] [Acts 22:9; 26:13] **9:10** [a] Acts 22:12 **9:11** [a] Acts 21:39; 22:3 **9:13** [a] Acts 9:1 **9:14** [a] Acts 7:59; 9:2, 21 **9:15** [a] Eph. 3:7, 8 [b] Rom. 1:5; 11:13 [c] Acts 25:22, 23; 26:1 [d] Rom. 1:16; 9:1–5 **9:16** [a] Acts 20:23 [b] 2 Cor. 4:11 **9:17** [a] Acts 22:12, 13 [b] Acts 8:17 [1] M-Text omits *Jesus.*

appeared to you on the road as you came, has
sent me that you may receive your sight and
[c]be filled with the Holy Spirit." 18 Immediately
there fell from his eyes *something* like scales,
and he received his sight at once; and he
arose and was baptized.
19 So when he had received food, he was
strengthened. [a]Then Saul spent some days
with the disciples at Damascus.

Saul Preaches Christ

20 Immediately he preached the Christ[1] in
the synagogues, that He is the Son of God.
21 Then all who heard were amazed, and
said, [a]"Is this not he who destroyed those
who called on this name in Jerusalem, and
has come here for that purpose, so that he
might bring them bound to the chief priests?"
22 But Saul increased all the more in strength,
[a]and confounded the Jews who dwelt in Damascus, proving that this *Jesus* is the Christ.

Saul Escapes Death

23 Now after many days were past, [a]the Jews
plotted to kill him. 24 [a]But their plot became
known to Saul. And they watched the gates
day and night, to kill him. 25 Then the disciples took him by night and [a]let *him* down
through the wall in a large basket.

Saul at Jerusalem

26 And [a]when Saul had come to Jerusalem,
he tried to join the disciples; but they were
all afraid of him, and did not believe that
he was a disciple. 27 [a]But Barnabas took him
and brought *him* to the apostles. And he
declared to them how he had seen the Lord
on the road, and that He had spoken to him,
[b]and how he had preached boldly at Damascus in the name of Jesus. 28 So [a]he was with
them at Jerusalem, coming in and going out.
29 And he spoke boldly in the name of the Lord
Jesus and disputed against the [a]Hellenists,
[b]but they attempted to kill him. 30 When the
brethren found out, they brought him down
to Caesarea and sent him out to Tarsus.

The Church Prospers

31 [a]Then the churches[1] throughout all
Judea, Galilee, and Samaria had peace and
were [b]edified. And walking in the [c]fear of the
Lord and in the [d]comfort of the Holy Spirit,
they were [e]multiplied.

Aeneas Healed

32 Now it came to pass, as Peter went
[a]through all *parts of the country,* that he
also came down to the saints who dwelt
in Lydda. 33 There he found a certain man

9:17 [c] Acts 2:4; 4:31; 8:17; 13:52 **9:19** [a] Acts 26:20 **9:20** [1] NU-Text reads *Jesus.* **9:21** [a] Gal. 1:13, 23 **9:22** [a] Acts 18:28 **9:23** [a] 2 Cor. 11:26 **9:24** [a] 2 Cor. 11:32 **9:25** [a] Josh. 2:15 **9:26** [a] Acts 22:17–20; 26:20 **9:27** [a] Acts 4:36; 13:2 [b] Acts 9:20, 22 **9:28** [a] Gal. 1:18 **9:29** [a] Acts 6:1; 11:20 [b] 2 Cor. 11:26 **9:31** [a] Acts 5:11; 8:1; 16:5 [b] [Eph. 4:16, 29] [c] Ps. 34:9 [d] John 14:16 [e] Acts 16:5 [1] NU-Text reads *church . . . was edified.* **9:32** [a] Acts 8:14

COMFORTED BY THE HOLY SPIRIT

Walking in the fear of the Lord and in the comfort of the
Holy Spirit, [the churches] were multiplied.

ACTS 9:31

I love those moments of peace when I can sit back in my office and quietly read or write. There are seasons in life when all is well, and everyone seems to be at peace. These are periods of blessing and growth. The church experiences these seasons too.

In the early years of the church the believers faced persecution, to be sure, but they also experienced periods when the leaders could evangelize, preach, and teach. That was when the church grew rapidly, and its membership expanded. The author of the Book of Acts, who gave us the history of the church's first thirty years, wrote of a such a time in chapter 9. The angry Saul of Tarsus, who had tried to crush the church, was confronted by the risen Jesus and had himself become one of the apostles. With Saul the persecutor out of the way, the church enjoyed a time of tranquility and membership began to expand. The church's leaders had time to study and grow in the faith, and they could all enjoy "the comfort of the Holy Spirit."

The Holy Spirit is often the least understood member of the Trinity. The Holy Spirit is a Person, not an "it" or a force. Ask the Holy Spirit to fill you today.

named Aeneas, who had been bedridden
eight years and was paralyzed. 34And Peter
said to him, "Aeneas, [a]Jesus the Christ heals
you. Arise and make your bed." Then he arose
immediately. 35So all who dwelt at Lydda and
[a]Sharon saw him and [b]turned to the Lord.

Dorcas Restored to Life

36At Joppa there was a certain disciple
named Tabitha, which is translated Dorcas.
This woman was full [a]of good works and charitable deeds which she did. 37But it happened
in those days that she became sick and died.
When they had washed her, they laid *her*
in [a]an upper room. 38And since Lydda was
near Joppa, and the disciples had heard that
Peter was there, they sent two men to him,
imploring *him* not to delay in coming to them.
39Then Peter arose and went with them. When
he had come, they brought *him* to the upper
room. And all the widows stood by him weeping, showing the tunics and garments which
Dorcas had made while she was with them.
40But Peter [a]put them all out, and [b]knelt down
and prayed. And turning to the body he [c]said,
"Tabitha, arise." And she opened her eyes,
and when she saw Peter she sat up. 41Then
he gave her *his* hand and lifted her up; and
when he had called the saints and widows, he
presented her alive. 42And it became known
throughout all Joppa, [a]and many believed
on the Lord. 43So it was that he stayed many
days in Joppa with [a]Simon, a tanner.

Cornelius Sends a Delegation

10 There was a certain man in [a]Caesarea
called Cornelius, a centurion of what
was called the Italian Regiment, 2[a]a devout
man and one who [b]feared God with all his
household, who gave alms generously to the
people, and prayed to God always. 3About
the ninth hour of the day [a]he saw clearly in a
vision an angel of God coming in and saying
to him, "Cornelius!"

4And when he observed him, he was afraid,
and said, "What is it, lord?"

So he said to him, "Your prayers and your
alms have come up for a memorial before
God. 5Now [a]send men to Joppa, and send
for Simon whose surname is Peter. 6He is
lodging with [a]Simon, a tanner, whose house
is by the sea.[1] [b]He will tell you what you must
do." 7And when the angel who spoke to him
had departed, Cornelius called two of his
household servants and a devout soldier
from among those who waited on him continually. 8So when he had explained all *these*
things to them, he sent them to Joppa.

9:34 [a] [Acts 3:6, 16; 4:10] **9:35** [a] 1 Chr. 5:16; 27:29 [b] Acts 11:21; 15:19 **9:36** [a] 1 Tim. 2:10 **9:37** [a] Acts 1:13; 9:39 **9:40** [a] Matt. 9:25 [b] Acts 7:60 [c] Mark 5:41, 42 **9:42** [a] John 11:45 **9:43** [a] Acts 10:6 **10:1** [a] Acts 8:40; 23:23 **10:2** [a] Acts 8:2; 9:22; 22:12 [b] [Acts 10:22, 35; 13:16, 26] **10:3** [a] Acts 10:30; 11:13 **10:5** [a] Acts 11:13, 14 **10:6** [a] Acts 9:43 [b] Acts 11:14

[1] NU-Text and M-Text omit the last sentence of this verse.

PREACH THE PEACE OF CHRIST

The word which God sent to the children of Israel, preaching peace through Jesus Christ—He is Lord of all—that word you know.

ACTS 10:36

In popular culture the Christian evangelist is often portrayed as preaching hellfire and damnation. But that's not really what the Christian proclamation is about. Death, disaster, and the fear of damnation are all around us. People try to avoid thinking about these grim realities. They seek distractions, exchange comforting bromides, or perhaps take shelter in agnosticism and skepticism. These are not remedies, of course, they are mere avoidance strategies.

The Christian message is often called the Good News because it is a message of peace. When Peter shared the gospel with Cornelius, the Roman centurion stationed at Caesarea Maritima, he described it as "preaching peace through Jesus Christ." He did not say "preaching damnation." Like many pagans, Cornelius knew he was lost; he wanted to find salvation. And he could! Jesus made peace possible between God and all humankind. In Jesus the peace that Isaiah proclaimed long ago (Is. 52:7) is fulfilled.

Understand today that your peace with God is a gift, not something you have to earn or fear losing. If you need a refill, ask for it!

Peter's Vision

9 The next day, as they went on their journey and drew near the city, [a]Peter went up on the housetop to pray, about the sixth hour. 10 Then he became very hungry and wanted to eat; but while they made ready, he fell into a trance 11 and [a]saw heaven opened and an object like a great sheet bound at the four corners, descending to him and let down to the earth. 12 In it were all kinds of four-footed animals of the earth, wild beasts, creeping things, and birds of the air. 13 And a voice came to him, "Rise, Peter; kill and eat."

14 But Peter said, "Not so, Lord! [a]For I have never eaten anything common or unclean."

15 And a voice *spoke* to him again the second time, [a]"What God has cleansed you must not call common." 16 This was done three times. And the object was taken up into heaven again.

Summoned to Caesarea

17 Now while Peter wondered within himself what this vision which he had seen meant, behold, the men who had been sent from Cornelius had made inquiry for Simon's house, and stood before the gate. 18 And they called and asked whether Simon, whose surname was Peter, was lodging there.

19 While Peter thought about the vision, [a]the Spirit said to him, "Behold, three men are seeking you. 20 [a]Arise therefore, go down and go with them, doubting nothing; for I have sent them."

21 Then Peter went down to the men who had been sent to him from Cornelius,[1] and said, "Yes, I am he whom you seek. For what reason have you come?"

22 And they said, "Cornelius *the* centurion, a just man, one who fears God and [a]has a good reputation among all the nation of the Jews, was divinely instructed by a holy angel to summon you to his house, and to hear words from you." 23 Then he invited them in and lodged *them.*

On the next day Peter went away with them, [a]and some brethren from Joppa accompanied him.

Peter Meets Cornelius

24 And the following day they entered Caesarea. Now Cornelius was waiting for them, and had called together his relatives and close friends. 25 As Peter was coming in, Cornelius met him and fell down at his feet and worshiped *him.* 26 But Peter lifted him up, saying, [a]"Stand up; I myself am also a man." 27 And as he talked with him, he went in and found many who had come together. 28 Then he said to them, "You know how [a]unlawful it is for a Jewish man to keep company with or go to one of another nation. But [b]God has shown me that I should not call any man common or unclean. 29 Therefore I came without objection as soon as I was sent for. I ask, then, for what reason have you sent for me?"

30 So Cornelius said, "Four days ago I was fasting until this hour; and at the ninth hour[1] I prayed in my house, and behold, [a]a man stood before me [b]in bright clothing, 31 and said, 'Cornelius, [a]your prayer has been heard, and [b]your alms are remembered in the sight of God. 32 Send therefore to Joppa and call Simon here, whose surname is Peter. He is lodging in the house of Simon, a tanner, by the sea.[1] When he comes, he will speak to you.' 33 So I sent to you immediately, and you have done well to come. Now therefore, we are all present before God, to hear all the things commanded you by God."

Preaching to Cornelius' Household

34 Then Peter opened *his* mouth and said: [a]"In truth I perceive that God shows no partiality. 35 But [a]in every nation whoever fears Him and works righteousness is [b]accepted by Him. 36 The word which *God* sent to the children of Israel, [a]preaching peace through Jesus Christ—[b]He is Lord of all— 37 that word

PEACE NOTE

Isaiah's gospel of peace is heard in Peter's reference to "the word which God sent to the children of Israel, preaching peace through Jesus Christ—He is Lord of all."

ACTS 10:36

10:9 [a] Acts 10:9–32; 11:5–14 **10:11** [a] Acts 7:56 **10:14** [a] Deut. 14:3, 7 **10:15** [a] [Rom. 14:14] **10:19** [a] Acts 11:12 **10:20** [a] Acts 15:7–9 **10:21** [1] NU-Text and M-Text omit *who had been sent to him from Cornelius.* **10:22** [a] Acts 22:12 **10:23** [a] Acts 10:45; 11:12 **10:26** [a] Acts 14:14, 15 **10:28** [a] John 4:9; 18:28 [b] [Acts 10:14, 35; 15:8, 9] **10:30** [a] Acts 1:10 [b] Matt. 28:3 [1] NU-Text reads *Four days ago to this hour, at the ninth hour.* **10:31** [a] Dan. 10:12 [b] Heb. 6:10 **10:32** [1] NU-Text omits the last sentence of this verse. **10:34** [a] Deut. 10:17 **10:35** [a] [Eph. 2:13] [b] Ps. 15:1, 2 **10:36** [a] Is. 57:19 [b] Rom. 10:12

you know, which was proclaimed throughout
all Judea, and [a]began from Galilee after the
baptism which John preached: 38how [a]God
anointed Jesus of Nazareth with the Holy
Spirit and with power, who [b]went about doing
good and healing all who were oppressed by
the devil, [c]for God was with Him. 39And we are
[a]witnesses of all things which He did both in
the land of the Jews and in Jerusalem, whom
they[1] [b]killed by hanging on a tree. 40Him [a]God
raised up on the third day, and showed Him
openly, 41[a]not to all the people, but to witnesses chosen before by God, *even* to us [b]who ate
and drank with Him after He arose from the
dead. 42And [a]He commanded us to preach to
the people, and to testify [b]that it is He who was
ordained by God *to be* Judge [c]of the living and
the dead. 43[a]To Him all the prophets witness
that, through His name, [b]whoever believes in
Him will receive [c]remission of sins."

The Holy Spirit Falls on the Gentiles

44While Peter was still speaking these
words, [a]the Holy Spirit fell upon all those
who heard the word. 45[a]And those of the
circumcision who believed were astonished,
as many as came with Peter, [b]because the gift
of the Holy Spirit had been poured out on the
Gentiles also. 46For they heard them speak
with tongues and magnify God.
Then Peter answered, 47"Can anyone forbid water, that these should not be baptized
who have received the Holy Spirit [a]just as
we *have?*" 48[a]And he commanded them to
be baptized [b]in the name of the Lord. Then
they asked him to stay a few days.

Peter Defends God's Grace

11 Now the apostles and brethren who were
in Judea heard that the Gentiles had
also received the word of God. 2And when
Peter came up to Jerusalem, [a]those of the
circumcision contended with him, 3saying,
[a]"You went in to uncircumcised men [b]and
ate with them!"
4But Peter explained *it* to them [a]in order
from the beginning, saying: 5[a]"I was in the
city of Joppa praying; and in a trance I saw
a vision, an object descending like a great
sheet, let down from heaven by four corners; and it came to me. 6When I observed
it intently and considered, I saw four-footed
animals of the earth, wild beasts, creeping
things, and birds of the air. 7And I heard a
voice saying to me, 'Rise, Peter; kill and eat.'
8But I said, 'Not so, Lord! For nothing common or unclean has at any time entered my
mouth.' 9But the voice answered me again
from heaven, 'What God has cleansed you
must not call common.' 10Now this was done

10:37 [a] Luke 4:14 **10:38** [a] Luke 4:18 [b] Matt. 4:23 [c] John 3:2; 8:29 **10:39** [a] Acts 1:8 [b] Acts 2:23 [1] NU-Text and M-Text add *also.* **10:40** [a] Acts 2:24 **10:41** [a] [John 14:17, 19, 22; 15:27] [b] Luke 24:30, 41–43 **10:42** [a] Matt. 28:19 [b] John 5:22, 27 [c] 1 Pet. 4:5 **10:43** [a] Zech. 13:1 [b] Gal. 3:22 [c] Acts 13:38, 39 **10:44** [a] Acts 4:31 **10:45** [a] Acts 10:23 [b] Acts 11:18 **10:47** [a] Acts 2:4; 10:44; 11:17; 15:8 **10:48** [a] 1 Cor. 1:14–17 [b] Acts 2:38; 8:16; 19:5 **11:2** [a] Acts 10:45 **11:3** [a] Acts 10:28 [b] Gal. 2:12 **11:4** [a] Luke 1:3 **11:5** [a] Acts 10:9

FAITH = PEACE

[Barnabas] was a good man, full of the Holy Spirit and of faith . . . Then [he] departed for Tarsus to seek Saul.

ACTS 11:24-25

Barnabas, a celebrated member of the early church, exemplified a special part of God's nature: he bore a great hope despite circumstances and past history. For example, we see in this passage from Acts that Barnabas "departed for Tarsus to seek Saul." Why is this noteworthy? Saul, you may remember, had recently been *murdering Christians.* His zeal for the law and hatred for believers made him dangerous and fearsome. Most in the early church avoided him because they were partial to living!

But the news had arrived that Saul (later to be called Paul) had had a change of heart. He now sought to add believers to the fold, not to annihilate them. Barnabas believed that such a change was possible through God's power, and he brought Saul back to Antioch for training and spiritual nurturing. Apparently, not another soul had that kind of faith in God's work.

The person with faith was the person with peace. Is there someone for whom you need to have more faith today?

three times, and all were drawn up again into heaven. 11At that very moment, three men stood before the house where I was, having been sent to me from Caesarea. 12Then [a]the Spirit told me to go with them, doubting nothing. Moreover [b]these six brethren accompanied me, and we entered the man's house. 13[a]And he told us how he had seen an angel standing in his house, who said to him, 'Send men to Joppa, and call for Simon whose surname is Peter, 14who will tell you words by which you and all your household will be saved.' 15And as I began to speak, the Holy Spirit fell upon them, [a]as upon us at the beginning. 16Then I remembered the word of the Lord, how He said, [a]'John indeed baptized with water, but [b]you shall be baptized with the Holy Spirit.' 17[a]If therefore God gave them the same gift as *He gave* us when we believed on the Lord Jesus Christ, [b]who was I that I could withstand God?"

18When they heard these things they became silent; and they glorified God, saying, [a]"Then God has also granted to the Gentiles repentance to life."

Barnabas and Saul at Antioch

19[a]Now those who were scattered after the persecution that arose over Stephen traveled as far as Phoenicia, Cyprus, and Antioch, preaching the word to no one but the Jews only. 20But some of them were men from Cyprus and Cyrene, who, when they had come to Antioch, spoke to [a]the Hellenists, preaching the Lord Jesus. 21And [a]the hand of the Lord was with them, and a great number believed and [b]turned to the Lord.

22Then news of these things came to the ears of the church in Jerusalem, and they sent out [a]Barnabas to go as far as Antioch. 23When he came and had seen the grace of God, he was glad, and [a]encouraged them all that with purpose of heart they should continue with the Lord. 24For he was a good man, [a]full of the Holy Spirit and of faith. [b]And a great many people were added to the Lord.

25Then Barnabas departed for [a]Tarsus to seek Saul. 26And when he had found him, he brought him to Antioch. So it was that for a whole year they assembled with the church and taught a great many people. And the disciples were first called Christians in Antioch.

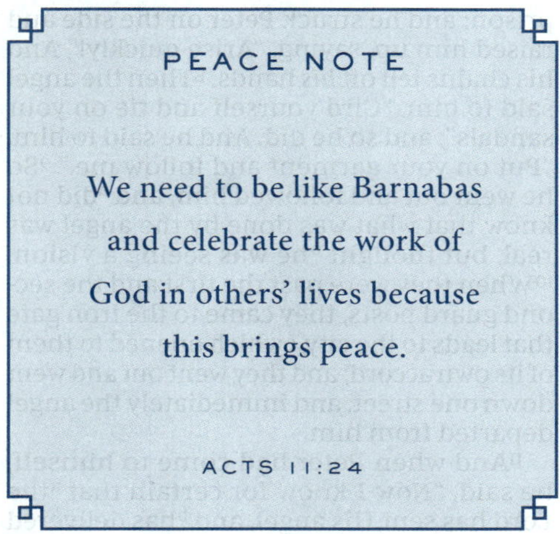

Relief to Judea

27And in these days [a]prophets came from Jerusalem to Antioch. 28Then one of them, named [a]Agabus, stood up and showed by the Spirit that there was going to be a great famine throughout all the world, which also happened in the days of [b]Claudius Caesar. 29Then the disciples, each according to his ability, determined to send [a]relief to the brethren dwelling in Judea. 30[a]This they also did, and sent it to the elders by the hands of Barnabas and Saul.

Herod's Violence to the Church

12 Now about that time Herod the king stretched out *his* hand to harass some from the church. 2Then he killed James [a]the brother of John with the sword. 3And because he saw that it pleased the Jews, he proceeded further to seize Peter also. Now it was *during* [a]the Days of Unleavened Bread. 4So [a]when he had arrested him, he put *him* in prison, and delivered *him* to four squads of soldiers to keep him, intending to bring him before the people after Passover.

Peter Freed from Prison

5Peter was therefore kept in prison, but constant[1] prayer was offered to God for him by the church. 6And when Herod was about to bring him out, that night Peter was sleeping, bound with two chains between two soldiers; and the guards before the door were keeping the prison. 7Now behold, [a]an angel of the Lord stood by *him,* and a light shone in the

11:12 [a] [John 16:13] [b] Acts 10:23 **11:13** [a] Acts 10:30 **11:15** [a] Acts 2:1–4; 15:7–9 **11:16** [a] John 1:26, 33 [b] Is. 44:3
11:17 [a] [Acts 15:8, 9] [b] Acts 10:47 **11:18** [a] Rom. 10:12, 13; 15:9, 16 **11:19** [a] Acts 8:1, 4 **11:20** [a] Acts 6:1; 9:29
11:21 [a] Luke 1:66 [b] Acts 9:35; 14:1 **11:22** [a] Acts 4:36; 9:27 **11:23** [a] Acts 13:43; 14:22 **11:24** [a] Acts 6:5 [b] Acts 5:14; 11:21
11:25 [a] Acts 9:11, 30 **11:27** [a] 1 Cor. 12:28 **11:28** [a] Acts 21:10 [b] Acts 18:2 **11:29** [a] 1 Cor. 16:1 **11:30** [a] Acts 12:25
12:2 [a] Matt. 4:21; 20:23 **12:3** [a] Ex. 12:15; 23:15 **12:4** [a] John 21:18 **12:5** [1] NU-Text reads *constantly* (or *earnestly*).
12:7 [a] Acts 5:19

prison; and he struck Peter on the side and
raised him up, saying, "Arise quickly!" And
his chains fell off *his* hands. 8Then the angel
said to him, "Gird yourself and tie on your
sandals"; and so he did. And he said to him,
"Put on your garment and follow me." 9So
he went out and followed him, and [a]did not
know that what was done by the angel was
real, but thought [b]he was seeing a vision.
10When they were past the first and the second guard posts, they came to the iron gate
that leads to the city, [a]which opened to them
of its own accord; and they went out and went
down one street, and immediately the angel
departed from him.

11And when Peter had come to himself,
he said, "Now I know for certain that [a]the
Lord has sent His angel, and [b]has delivered
me from the hand of Herod and *from* all the
expectation of the Jewish people."

12So, when he had considered *this,* [a]he
came to the house of Mary, the mother of
[b]John whose surname was Mark, where many
were gathered together [c]praying. 13And as
Peter knocked at the door of the gate, a girl
named Rhoda came to answer. 14When she
recognized Peter's voice, because of *her* gladness she did not open the gate, but ran in
and announced that Peter stood before the
gate. 15But they said to her, "You are beside
yourself!" Yet she kept insisting that it was
so. So they said, [a]"It is his angel."

16Now Peter continued knocking; and when
they opened *the door* and saw him, they were
astonished. 17But [a]motioning to them with
his hand to keep silent, he declared to them
how the Lord had brought him out of the
prison. And he said, "Go, tell these things to
James and to the brethren." And he departed
and went to another place.

18Then, as soon as it was day, there was
no small stir among the soldiers about what
had become of Peter. 19But when Herod had
searched for him and not found him, he
examined the guards and commanded that
they should be put to death.

And he went down from Judea to Caesarea,
and stayed *there.*

Herod's Violent Death

20Now Herod had been very angry with
the people of [a]Tyre and Sidon; but they came
to him with one accord, and having made
Blastus the king's personal aide their friend,
they asked for peace, because [b]their country
was supplied with food by the king's *country.*

21So on a set day Herod, arrayed in royal
apparel, sat on his throne and gave an oration
to them. 22And the people kept shouting,
"The voice of a god and not of a man!" 23Then
immediately an angel of the Lord [a]struck
him, because [b]he did not give glory to God.
And he was eaten by worms and died.

24But [a]the word of God grew and multiplied.

Barnabas and Saul Appointed

25And [a]Barnabas and Saul returned from[1]
Jerusalem when they had [b]fulfilled *their*
ministry, and they also [c]took with them [d]John
whose surname was Mark.

13 Now [a]in the church that was at Antioch there were certain prophets and
teachers: [b]Barnabas, Simeon who was called
Niger, [c]Lucius of Cyrene, Manaen who had
been brought up with Herod the tetrarch,
and Saul. 2As they ministered to the Lord and
fasted, the Holy Spirit said, [a]"Now separate
to Me Barnabas and Saul for the work [b]to
which I have called them." 3Then, [a]having
fasted and prayed, and laid hands on them,
they sent *them* away.

Preaching in Cyprus

4So, being sent out by the Holy Spirit, they
went down to Seleucia, and from there they
sailed to [a]Cyprus. 5And when they arrived in
Salamis, [a]they preached the word of God in
the synagogues of the Jews. They also had
[b]John as *their* assistant.

6Now when they had gone through the
island[1] to Paphos, they found [a]a certain sorcerer, a false prophet, a Jew whose name
was Bar-Jesus, 7who was with the proconsul,
Sergius Paulus, an intelligent man. This man
called for Barnabas and Saul and sought
to hear the word of God. 8But [a]Elymas the
sorcerer (for so his name is translated) withstood them, seeking to turn the proconsul
away from the faith. 9Then Saul, who also
is called Paul, [a]filled with the Holy Spirit,
looked intently at him 10and said, "O full
of all deceit and all fraud, [a]*you* son of the
devil, *you* enemy of all righteousness, will
you not cease perverting the straight ways
of the Lord? 11And now, indeed, [a]the hand of
the Lord *is* upon you, and you shall be blind,
not seeing the sun for a time."

12:9 [a] Ps. 126:1 [b] Acts 10:3, 17; 11:5 **12:10** [a] Acts 5:19; 16:26 **12:11** [a] [Ps. 34:7] [b] Job 5:19 **12:12** [a] Acts 4:23 [b] Acts 13:5, 13; 15:37 [c] Acts 12:5 **12:15** [a] [Matt. 18:10] **12:17** [a] Acts 13:16; 19:33; 21:40 **12:20** [a] Matt. 11:21 [b] Ezek. 27:17 **12:23** [a] 2 Sam. 24:16, 17 [b] Ps. 115:1 **12:24** [a] Acts 6:7; 19:20 **12:25** [a] Acts 11:30 [b] Acts 11:30 [c] Acts 13:5, 13 [d] Acts 12:12; 15:37 [1] NU-Text and M-Text read *to.* **13:1** [a] Acts 14:26 [b] Acts 11:22 [c] Rom. 16:21 **13:2** [a] Gal. 1:15; 2:9 [b] Heb. 5:4 **13:3** [a] Acts 6:6 **13:4** [a] Acts 4:36 **13:5** [a] [Acts 13:46] [b] Acts 12:25; 15:37 **13:6** [a] Acts 8:9 [1] NU-Text reads *the whole island.* **13:8** [a] Ex. 7:11 **13:9** [a] Acts 2:4; 4:8 **13:10** [a] Matt. 13:38 **13:11** [a] 1 Sam. 5:6

And immediately a dark mist fell on him,
and he went around seeking someone to
lead him by the hand. 12Then the proconsul
believed, when he saw what had been done,
being astonished at the teaching of the Lord.

At Antioch in Pisidia

13Now when Paul and his party set sail from
Paphos, they came to Perga in Pamphylia;
and [a]John, departing from them, returned
to Jerusalem. 14But when they departed from
Perga, they came to Antioch in Pisidia, and
[a]went into the synagogue on the Sabbath
day and sat down. 15And [a]after the reading of
the Law and the Prophets, the rulers of the
synagogue sent to them, saying, "Men *and*
brethren, if you have [b]any word of exhortation for the people, say on."

16Then Paul stood up, and motioning with
his hand said, "Men of Israel, and [a]you who
fear God, listen: 17The God of this people
Israel[1] [a]chose our fathers, and exalted the
people [b]when they dwelt as strangers in the
land of Egypt, and with an uplifted arm He
[c]brought them out of it. 18Now [a]for a time of
about forty years He put up with their ways in
the wilderness. 19And when He had destroyed
[a]seven nations in the land of Canaan, [b]He
distributed their land to them by allotment.

20"After that [a]He gave *them* judges for
about four hundred and fifty years, [b]until
Samuel the prophet. 21[a]And afterward they
asked for a king; so God gave them [b]Saul the
son of Kish, a man of the tribe of Benjamin,
for forty years. 22And [a]when He had removed
him, [b]He raised up for them David as king,
to whom also He gave testimony and said, [c]'I
have found David[1] the *son* of Jesse, [d]a man
after My *own* heart, who will do all My will.'[2]
23[a]From this man's seed, according [b]to *the*
promise, God raised up for Israel [c]a Savior—
Jesus—[1] 24[a]after John had first preached, before His coming, the baptism of repentance
to all the people of Israel. 25And as John was
finishing his course, he said, [a]'Who do you
think I am? I am not *He.* But behold, [b]there
comes One after me, the sandals of whose
feet I am not worthy to loose.'

26"Men *and* brethren, sons of the family of
Abraham, and [a]those among you who fear
God, [b]to you the word of this salvation has
been sent. 27For those who dwell in Jerusalem,
and their rulers, [a]because they did not know
Him, nor even the voices of the Prophets
which are read every Sabbath, have fulfilled
them in condemning *Him.* 28[a]And though they
found no cause for death *in Him,* they asked
Pilate that He should be put to death. 29[a]Now
when they had fulfilled all that was written
concerning Him, [b]they took *Him* down from
the tree and laid *Him* in a tomb. 30[a]But God
raised Him from the dead. 31[a]He was seen
for many days by those who came up with
Him from Galilee to Jerusalem, who are His
witnesses to the people. 32And we declare to
you glad tidings—[a]that promise which was
made to the fathers. 33God has fulfilled this
for us their children, in that He has raised up
Jesus. As it is also written in the second Psalm:

> [a]'You are My Son,
> Today I have begotten You.'[1]

34And that He raised Him from the dead,
no more to return to corruption, He has
spoken thus:

> [a]'I will give you the sure mercies of
> David.'[1]

35Therefore He also says in another *Psalm:*

> [a]'You will not allow Your Holy One to see
> corruption.'[1]

36"For David, after he had served his own
generation by the will of God, [a]fell asleep,
was buried with his fathers, and saw corruption; 37but He whom God raised up saw
no corruption. 38Therefore let it be known
to you, brethren, that [a]through this Man is
preached to you the forgiveness of sins; 39and
[a]by Him everyone who believes is justified
from all things from which you could not
be justified by the law of Moses. 40Beware
therefore, lest what has been spoken in the
prophets come upon you:

> 41 'Behold,[a] you despisers,
> Marvel and perish!
> For I work a work in your days,
> A work which you will by no means
> believe,
> Though one were to declare it to you.' "[1]

13:13 [a] Acts 15:38 **13:14** [a] Acts 16:13 **13:15** [a] Luke 4:16 [b] Heb. 13:22 **13:16** [a] Acts 10:35 **13:17** [a] Deut. 7:6–8 [b] Acts 7:17 [c] Ex. 14:8 [1] M-Text omits *Israel.* **13:18** [a] Num. 14:34 **13:19** [a] Deut. 7:1 [b] Josh. 14:1, 2; 19:51 **13:20** [a] Judg. 2:16 [b] 1 Sam. 3:20 **13:21** [a] 1 Sam. 8:5 [b] 1 Sam. 10:20–24 **13:22** [a] 1 Sam. 15:23, 26, 28 [b] 1 Sam. 16:1, 12, 13 [c] Ps. 89:20 [d] 1 Sam. 13:14 [1] Psalm 89:20 [2] 1 Samuel 13:14 **13:23** [a] Is. 11:1 [b] Ps. 132:11 [c] [Matt. 1:21] [1] M-Text reads *for Israel salvation.* **13:24** [a] [Luke 3:3] **13:25** [a] Mark 1:7 [b] John 1:20, 27 **13:26** [a] Ps. 66:16 [b] Matt. 10:6 **13:27** [a] Luke 23:34 **13:28** [a] Matt. 27:22, 23 **13:29** [a] Luke 18:31 [b] Matt. 27:57–61 **13:30** [a] Matt. 12:39, 40; 28:6 **13:31** [a] Acts 1:3, 11 **13:32** [a] [Gen. 3:15] **13:33** [a] Ps. 2:7 [1] Psalm 2:7 **13:34** [a] Is. 55:3 [1] Isaiah 55:3 **13:35** [a] Ps. 16:10 [1] Psalm 16:10 **13:36** [a] Acts 2:29 **13:38** [a] Jer. 31:34 **13:39** [a] [Is. 53:11] **13:41** [a] Hab. 1:5 [1] Habakkuk 1:5

Blessing and Conflict at Antioch

42So when the Jews went out of the synagogue,[1] the Gentiles begged that these words
might be preached to them the next Sabbath.
43Now when the congregation had broken
up, many of the Jews and devout proselytes
followed Paul and Barnabas, who, speaking
to them, [a]persuaded them to continue in
[b]the grace of God.
44On the next Sabbath almost the whole
city came together to hear the word of God.
45But when the Jews saw the multitudes,
they were filled with envy; and contradicting
and blaspheming, they [a]opposed the things
spoken by Paul. 46Then Paul and Barnabas
grew bold and said, [a]"It was necessary that
the word of God should be spoken to you first;
but [b]since you reject it, and judge yourselves
unworthy of everlasting life, behold, [c]we
turn to the Gentiles. 47For so the Lord has
commanded us:

> [a]'I have set you as a light to the Gentiles,
> That you should be for salvation to the
> ends of the earth.' "[1]

48Now when the Gentiles heard this, they
were glad and glorified the word of the Lord.
[a]And as many as had been appointed to eternal life believed.
49And the word of the Lord was being
spread throughout all the region. 50But the
Jews stirred up the devout and prominent
women and the chief men of the city, [a]raised
up persecution against Paul and Barnabas,
and expelled them from their region. 51[a]But
they shook off the dust from their feet against
them, and came to Iconium. 52And the disciples [a]were filled with joy and [b]with the
Holy Spirit.

At Iconium

14 Now it happened in Iconium that they
went together to the synagogue of the
Jews, and so spoke that a great multitude
both of the Jews and of the [a]Greeks believed.
2But the unbelieving Jews stirred up the
Gentiles and poisoned their minds against
the brethren. 3Therefore they stayed there a
long time, speaking boldly in the Lord, [a]who
was bearing witness to the word of His grace,
granting signs and [b]wonders to be done by
their hands.
4But the multitude of the city was [a]divid-
ed: part sided with the Jews, and part with
the [b]apostles. 5And when a violent attempt
was made by both the Gentiles and Jews,
with their rulers, [a]to abuse and stone them,
6they became aware of it and [a]fled to Lystra
and Derbe, cities of Lycaonia, and to the

13:42 [1] Or *And when they went out of the synagogue of the Jews;* NU-Text reads *And when they went out, they begged.*
13:43 [a] Acts 11:23 [b] Titus 2:11 **13:45** [a] 1 Pet. 4:4 **13:46** [a] Rom. 1:16 [b] Ex. 32:10 [c] Acts 18:6 **13:47** [a] Is. 42:6; 49:6
[1] Isaiah 49:6 **13:48** [a] [Acts 2:47] **13:50** [a] 2 Tim. 3:11 **13:51** [a] Matt. 10:14 **13:52** [a] John 16:22 [b] Acts 2:4; 4:8, 31; 13:9
14:1 [a] Acts 18:4 **14:3** [a] Heb. 2:4 [b] Acts 5:12 **14:4** [a] Luke 12:51 [b] Acts 13:2, 3 **14:5** [a] 2 Tim. 3:11 **14:6** [a] Matt. 10:23

THE GOSPEL OF PEACE

"I have set you as a light to the Gentiles . . ." Now when the Gentiles heard this, they were glad and glorified the word of the Lord.

ACTS 13:47-48

Long ago the prophet Isaiah spoke of a day when peace would be extended to those who were "far off" as well as those who were "near" (Is. 57:19), an important passage to which Paul alluded in one of his letters (Eph. 2:17). The people who were far from God were the Gentiles. The people who were near were the Jewish people, the people of God's special covenant at Sinai.

On a missionary journey, Paul found himself preaching Jesus in a synagogue in Antioch. At the end of his preaching, Paul quoted another passage from Isaiah: "'I have set you as a light to the Gentiles . . .' Now when the Gentiles heard this, they were glad and glorified the word of the Lord" (Acts 13:47–48). In Christ, the "light of the world" (John 8:12), the Gentiles who once were far off had been brought near. The Good News was for them, too.

God's peace is available for everyone! This great truth rocked the church and the world. The church, unified and mobilized, is the greatest force for God on earth and you, as a follower of Christ, are included! Let's get moving and share the gospel.

surrounding region. 7And they were preaching the gospel there.

Idolatry at Lystra

8[a]And in Lystra a certain man without
strength in his feet was sitting, a cripple from
his mother's womb, who had never walked.
9*This* man heard Paul speaking. Paul, observing him intently and seeing that he had faith
to be healed, 10said with a loud voice, [a]"Stand
up straight on your feet!" And he leaped and
walked. 11Now when the people saw what Paul
had done, they raised their voices, saying
in the Lycaonian *language,* [a]"The gods have
come down to us in the likeness of men!"
12And Barnabas they called Zeus, and Paul,
Hermes, because he was the chief speaker.
13Then the priest of Zeus, whose temple was
in front of their city, brought oxen and gar-
lands to the gates, [a]intending to sacrifice
with the multitudes.

14But when the apostles Barnabas and Paul
heard this, [a]they tore their clothes and ran in
among the multitude, crying out 15and saying, "Men, [a]why are you doing these things?
[b]We also are men with the same nature as
you, and preach to you that you should turn
from [c]these useless things [d]to the living God,
[e]who made the heaven, the earth, the sea,
and all things that are in them, 16[a]who in
bygone generations allowed all nations to
walk in their own ways. 17[a]Nevertheless He
did not leave Himself without witness, in that
He did good, [b]gave us rain from heaven and
fruitful seasons, filling our hearts with [c]food
and gladness." 18And with these sayings they
could scarcely restrain the multitudes from
sacrificing to them.

Stoning, Escape to Derbe

19[a]Then Jews from Antioch and Iconium
came there; and having persuaded the multitudes, [b]they stoned Paul *and* dragged *him*
out of the city, supposing him to be [c]dead.
20However, when the disciples gathered
around him, he rose up and went into the
city. And the next day he departed with Barnabas to Derbe.

Strengthening the Converts

21And when they had preached the gospel
to that city [a]and made many disciples, they
returned to Lystra, Iconium, and Antioch,
22strengthening the souls of the disciples,
[a]exhorting *them* to continue in the faith, and
saying, [b]"We must through many tribulations enter the kingdom of God." 23So when
they had [a]appointed elders in every church,
and prayed with fasting, they commended
them to the Lord in whom they had believed.
24And after they had passed through Pisidia,
they came to Pamphylia. 25Now when they
had preached the word in Perga, they went
down to Attalia. 26From there they sailed to
Antioch, where they had been commended
to the grace of God for the work which they
had completed.

27Now when they had come and gathered
the church together, [a]they reported all that
God had done with them, and that He had
[b]opened the door of faith to the Gentiles.
28So they stayed there a long time with the
disciples.

Conflict over Circumcision

15 And [a]certain *men* came down from
Judea and taught the brethren, [b]"Unless you are circumcised according to the
custom of Moses, you cannot be saved."
2Therefore, when Paul and Barnabas had
no small dissension and dispute with them,
they determined that [a]Paul and Barnabas
and certain others of them should go up to
Jerusalem, to the apostles and elders, about
this question.

3So, [a]being sent on their way by the church,
they passed through Phoenicia and Samaria,
[b]describing the conversion of the Gentiles;
and they caused great joy to all the brethren.
4And when they had come to Jerusalem, they
were received by the church and the apostles
and the elders; and they reported all things
that God had done with them. 5But some of
the sect of the Pharisees who believed rose
up, saying, "It is necessary to circumcise
them, and to command *them* to keep the
law of Moses."

The Jerusalem Council

6Now the apostles and elders came together to consider this matter. 7And when there
had been much dispute, Peter rose up *and*
said to them: [a]"Men *and* brethren, you know
that a good while ago God chose among us,
that by my mouth the Gentiles should hear
the word of the gospel and believe. 8So God,
[a]who knows the heart, acknowledged them
by [b]giving them the Holy Spirit, just as *He did*
to us, 9[a]and made no distinction between us
and them, [b]purifying their hearts by faith.

14:8 [a] Acts 3:2 **14:10** [a] [Is. 35:6] **14:11** [a] Acts 8:10; 28:6 **14:13** [a] Dan. 2:46 **14:14** [a] Matt. 26:65 **14:15** [a] Acts 10:26 [b] James 5:17 [c] 1 Cor. 8:4 [d] 1 Thess. 1:9 [e] Rev. 14:7 **14:16** [a] Ps. 81:12 **14:17** [a] Rom. 1:19, 20 [b] Deut. 11:14 [c] Ps. 145:16 **14:19** [a] Acts 13:45, 50; 14:2–5 [b] 2 Cor. 11:25 [c] [2 Cor. 12:1–4] **14:21** [a] Matt. 28:19 **14:22** [a] Acts 11:23 [b] [2 Tim. 2:12; 3:12] **14:23** [a] Titus 1:5 **14:27** [a] Acts 15:4, 12 [b] 2 Cor. 2:12 **15:1** [a] Gal. 2:12 [b] Phil. 3:2 **15:2** [a] Gal. 2:1 **15:3** [a] Rom. 15:24 [b] Acts 14:27; 15:4, 12 **15:7** [a] Acts 10:20 **15:8** [a] Acts 1:24 [b] Acts 2:4; 10:44, 47 **15:9** [a] Rom. 10:12 [b] Acts 10:15, 28

10Now therefore, why do you test God [a]by
putting a yoke on the neck of the disciples
which neither our fathers nor we were able
to bear? 11But [a]we believe that through the
grace of the Lord Jesus Christ[1] we shall be
saved in the same manner as they."
12Then all the multitude kept silent and
listened to Barnabas and Paul declaring
how many miracles and wonders God had
[a]worked through them among the Gentiles.
13And after they had become silent, [a]James
answered, saying, "Men *and* brethren, listen
to me: 14[a]Simon has declared how God at
the first visited the Gentiles to take out of
them a people for His name. 15And with this
the words of the prophets agree, just as it
is written:

16 'After[a] this I will return
And will rebuild the tabernacle of
David, which has fallen down;
I will rebuild its ruins,
And I will set it up;
17 So that the rest of mankind may seek
the LORD,
Even all the Gentiles who are called by
My name,
Says the LORD who does all these
things.'[1]

18"Known to God from eternity are all His
works.[1] 19Therefore [a]I judge that we should
not trouble those from among the Gentiles
who [b]are turning to God, 20but that we [a]write
to them to abstain [b]from things polluted by
idols, [c]*from* sexual immorality,[1] [d]*from* things
strangled, and *from* blood. 21For Moses has
had throughout many generations those who
preach him in every city, [a]being read in the
synagogues every Sabbath."

The Jerusalem Decree

22Then it pleased the apostles and elders,
with the whole church, to send chosen men
of their own company to Antioch with Paul
and Barnabas, *namely,* Judas who was also
named [a]Barsabas,[1] and Silas, leading men
among the brethren.
23They wrote this *letter* by them:

The apostles, the elders, and the
brethren,
To the brethren who are of the Gentiles
in Antioch, Syria, and Cilicia:

Greetings.

24 Since we have heard that [a]some who
went out from us have troubled you
with words, [b]unsettling your souls,
saying, "*You must* be circumcised and
keep the law"[1]—to whom we gave no
such commandment— 25it seemed
good to us, being assembled with one
accord, to send chosen men to you
with our beloved Barnabas and Paul,
26[a]men who have risked their lives for
the name of our Lord Jesus Christ. 27We
have therefore sent Judas and Silas,
who will also report the same things
by word of mouth. 28For it seemed
good to the Holy Spirit, and to us, to lay
upon you no greater burden than these
necessary things: 29[a]that you abstain
from things offered to idols, [b]from
blood, from things strangled, and
from [c]sexual immorality.[1] If you keep
yourselves from these, you will do well.

Farewell.

Continuing Ministry in Syria

30So when they were sent off, they came
to Antioch; and when they had gathered the
multitude together, they delivered the letter.
31When they had read it, they rejoiced over
its encouragement. 32Now Judas and Silas,
themselves being [a]prophets also, [b]exhorted
and strengthened the brethren with many
words. 33And after they had stayed *there* for
a time, they were [a]sent back with greetings
from the brethren to the apostles.[1]
34However, it seemed good to Silas to remain there.[1] 35[a]Paul and Barnabas also remained in Antioch, teaching and preaching
the word of the Lord, with many others also.

Division over John Mark

36Then after some days Paul said to Barnabas, "Let us now go back and visit our brethren in every city where we have preached
the word of the Lord, *and see* how they are
doing." 37Now Barnabas was determined to
take with them [a]John called Mark. 38But Paul

15:10 [a] Matt. 23:4 **15:11** [a] Rom. 3:4; 5:15 [1] NU-Text and M-Text omit *Christ.* **15:12** [a] Acts 14:27; 15:3, 4 **15:13** [a] Acts 12:17 **15:14** [a] Acts 15:7 **15:16** [a] Amos 9:11, 12 **15:17** [1] Amos 9:11, 12 **15:18** [1] NU-Text (combining with verse 17) reads *Says the Lord, who makes these things known from eternity (of old).* **15:19** [a] Acts 15:28; 21:25 [b] 1 Thess. 1:9 **15:20** [a] Acts 21:25 [b] [1 Cor. 8:1; 10:20, 28] [c] [1 Cor. 6:9] [d] Lev. 3:17 [1] Or *fornication* **15:21** [a] Acts 13:15, 27 **15:22** [a] Acts 1:23 [1] NU-Text and M-Text read *Barsabbas.* **15:24** [a] Titus 1:10, 11 [b] Gal. 1:7; 5:10 [1] NU-Text omits *saying, "You must be circumcised and keep the law."* **15:26** [a] Acts 13:50; 14:19 **15:29** [a] Acts 15:20; 21:25 [b] Lev. 17:14 [c] Col. 3:5 [1] Or *fornication* **15:32** [a] Eph. 4:11 [b] Acts 14:22; 18:23 **15:33** [a] Heb. 11:31 [1] NU-Text reads *to those who had sent them.* **15:34** [1] NU-Text and M-Text omit this verse. **15:35** [a] Acts 13:1 **15:37** [a] Acts 12:12, 25

insisted that they should not take with them
[a]the one who had departed from them in
Pamphylia, and had not gone with them to
the work. 39 Then the contention became so
sharp that they parted from one another. And
so Barnabas took Mark and sailed to [a]Cyprus;
40 but Paul chose Silas and departed, [a]being
commended by the brethren to the grace of
God. 41 And he went through Syria and Cilicia,
[a]strengthening the churches.

Timothy Joins Paul and Silas

16 Then he came to [a]Derbe and Lystra.
And behold, a certain disciple was
there, [b]named Timothy, [c]*the* son of a certain Jewish woman who believed, but his
father *was* Greek. 2 He was well spoken of by
the brethren who were at Lystra and Iconium. 3 Paul wanted to have him go on with
him. And he [a]took *him* and circumcised
him because of the Jews who were in that
region, for they all knew that his father was
Greek. 4 And as they went through the cities,
they delivered to them the [a]decrees to keep,
[b]which were determined by the apostles and
elders at Jerusalem. 5 [a]So the churches were
strengthened in the faith, and increased in
number daily.

The Macedonian Call

6 Now when they had gone through Phrygia
and the region of [a]Galatia, they were forbidden by the Holy Spirit to preach the word in
Asia. 7 After they had come to Mysia, they tried
to go into Bithynia, but the Spirit[1] did not permit them. 8 So passing by Mysia, they [a]came
down to Troas. 9 And a vision appeared to
Paul in the night. A [a]man of Macedonia stood
and pleaded with him, saying, "Come over to
Macedonia and help us." 10 Now after he had
seen the vision, immediately we sought to
go [a]to Macedonia, concluding that the Lord
had called us to preach the gospel to them.

Lydia Baptized at Philippi

11 Therefore, sailing from Troas, we ran a
straight course to Samothrace, and the next
day came to Neapolis, 12 and from there to
[a]Philippi, which is the foremost city of that
part of Macedonia, a colony. And we were
staying in that city for some days. 13 And on
the Sabbath day we went out of the city to
the riverside, where prayer was custom-
arily made; and we sat down and spoke to
the women who met *there.* 14 Now a certain
woman named Lydia heard *us.* She was a
seller of purple from the city of [a]Thyatira,
who worshiped God. [b]The Lord opened her
heart to heed the things spoken by Paul.
15 And when she and her household were
baptized, she begged *us,* saying, "If you have
judged me to be faithful to the Lord, come to
my house and stay." So [a]she persuaded us.

Paul and Silas Imprisoned

16 Now it happened, as we went to prayer,
that a certain slave girl [a]possessed with a
spirit of divination met us, who brought
her masters [b]much profit by fortune-telling.
17 This girl followed Paul and us, and cried out,
saying, "These men are the servants of the
Most High God, who proclaim to us the way of
salvation." 18 And this she did for many days.

But Paul, [a]greatly annoyed, turned and
said to the spirit, "I command you in the
name of Jesus Christ to come out of her."
[b]And he came out that very hour. 19 But [a]when
her masters saw that their hope of profit
was gone, they seized Paul and Silas and
[b]dragged *them* into the marketplace to the
authorities.

20 And they brought them to the magistrates, and said, "These men, being Jews,
[a]exceedingly trouble our city; 21 and they
teach customs which are not lawful for us,
being Romans, to receive or observe." 22 Then
the multitude rose up together against them;
and the magistrates tore off their clothes
[a]and commanded *them* to be beaten with
rods. 23 And when they had laid many stripes
on them, they threw *them* into prison, commanding the jailer to keep them securely.
24 Having received such a charge, he put them
into the inner prison and fastened their feet
in the stocks.

The Philippian Jailer Saved

25 But at midnight Paul and Silas were
praying and singing hymns to God, and the
prisoners were listening to them. 26 [a]Sud-
denly there was a great earthquake, so that
the foundations of the prison were shaken;
and immediately [b]all the doors were opened
and everyone's chains were loosed. 27 And the
keeper of the prison, awaking from sleep and
seeing the prison doors open, supposing the
prisoners had fled, drew his sword and was
about to kill himself. 28 But Paul called with
a loud voice, saying, "Do yourself no harm,
for we are all here."

15:38 [a] Acts 13:13 **15:39** [a] Acts 4:36; 13:4 **15:40** [a] Acts 11:23; 14:26 **15:41** [a] Acts 16:5 **16:1** [a] Acts 14:6 [b] Rom. 16:21 [c] 2 Tim. 1:5; 3:15 **16:3** [a] [Gal. 2:3; 5:2] **16:4** [a] Acts 15:19–21 [b] Acts 15:28, 29 **16:5** [a] Acts 2:47; 15:41 **16:6** [a] Gal. 1:1, 2 **16:7** [1] NU-Text adds *of Jesus.* **16:8** [a] 2 Cor. 2:12 **16:9** [a] Acts 10:30 **16:10** [a] 2 Cor. 2:13 **16:12** [a] Phil. 1:1 **16:14** [a] Rev. 1:11; 2:18, 24 [b] Luke 24:45 **16:15** [a] Judg. 19:21 **16:16** [a] 1 Sam. 28:3, 7 [b] Acts 19:24 **16:18** [a] Mark 1:25, 34 [b] Mark 16:17 **16:19** [a] Acts 16:16; 19:25, 26 [b] Matt. 10:18 **16:20** [a] Acts 17:8 **16:22** [a] 1 Thess. 2:2 **16:26** [a] Acts 4:31 [b] Acts 5:19; 12:7, 10

PEACE NOTE

Jesus says people are happy—and at peace!—for doing the right and just thing even if they are persecuted (or prosecuted, even imprisoned) for doing it.

ACTS 16:25

29Then he called for a light, ran in, and fell
down trembling before Paul and Silas. 30And
he brought them out and said, [a]"Sirs, what
must I do to be saved?"
31So they said, [a]"Believe on the Lord Jesus
Christ, and you will be saved, you and your
household." 32Then they spoke the word of
the Lord to him and to all who were in his
house. 33And he took them the same hour
of the night and washed *their* stripes. And
immediately he and all his *family* were baptized. 34Now when he had brought them into
his house, [a]he set food before them; and he
rejoiced, having believed in God with all his
household.

Paul Refuses to Depart Secretly

35And when it was day, the magistrates
sent the officers, saying, "Let those men go."
36So the keeper of the prison reported
these words to Paul, saying, "The magistrates
have sent to let you go. Now therefore depart,
and go in peace."
37But Paul said to them, "They have beaten
us openly, uncondemned [a]Romans, *and* have
thrown *us* into prison. And now do they put
us out secretly? No indeed! Let them come
themselves and get us out."
38And the officers told these words to the
magistrates, and they were afraid when they
heard that they were Romans. 39Then they
came and pleaded with them and brought
them out, and [a]asked *them* to depart from
the city. 40So they went out of the prison
[a]and entered *the house of* Lydia; and when
they had seen the brethren, they encouraged
them and departed.

Preaching Christ at Thessalonica

17 Now when they had passed through
Amphipolis and Apollonia, they came
to [a]Thessalonica, where there was a synagogue of the Jews. 2Then Paul, as his custom
was, [a]went in to them, and for three Sabbaths
[b]reasoned with them from the Scriptures,
3explaining and demonstrating [a]that the
Christ had to suffer and rise again from the
dead, and *saying,* "This Jesus whom I preach
to you is the Christ." 4[a]And some of them
were persuaded; and a great multitude of the

16:30 [a] Acts 2:37; 9:6; 22:10 16:31 [a] [John 3:16, 36; 6:47] 16:34 [a] Luke 5:29; 19:6 16:37 [a] Acts 22:25–29 16:39 [a] Matt. 8:34 16:40 [a] Acts 16:14 17:1 [a] 1 Thess. 1:1 17:2 [a] Luke 4:16 [b] 1 Thess. 2:1–16 17:3 [a] Acts 18:5, 28 17:4 [a] Acts 28:24

THE GREATEST QUESTION OF ALL TIME

Sirs, what must I do to be saved?

ACTS 16:30

Falsely accused, assaulted, and thrown into prison, Paul and his companions continued to experience the peace of God. In fact, Paul was so at peace that he and "Silas were praying and singing hymns to God, and the prisoners were listening to them" (v. 25). Then an earthquake shook the prison and knocked open the gates. When the jailer saw what had happened, he assumed that the prisoners had escaped and was ready to commit suicide. But Paul assured him that all were present. The jailer was so moved by the experience and Paul's evident care that he cried out, "Sirs, what must I do to be saved?" (v. 30).

Paul told the jailer to believe in Jesus, and he did. Paul baptized him, and the jailer washed and dressed Paul's and Silas's wounds and fed them. We have in this brief story the power of the gospel on full display. We see how it brings about peace and reconciliation. The jailer was now Paul's friend and, more importantly, he was blessed with the peace that Paul had. The gospel of peace does that.

devout Greeks, and not a few of the leading
women, joined Paul and [b]Silas.

Assault on Jason's House

5But the Jews who were not persuaded,
becoming [a]envious,[1] took some of the evil
men from the marketplace, and gathering a
mob, set all the city in an uproar and attacked
the house of [b]Jason, and sought to bring
them out to the people. 6But when they did
not find them, they dragged Jason and some
brethren to the rulers of the city, crying out,
[a]"These who have turned the world upside
down have come here too. 7Jason has har-
bored them, and these are all acting contrary
to the decrees of Caesar, [a]saying there is
another king—Jesus." 8And they troubled
the crowd and the rulers of the city when
they heard these things. 9So when they had
taken security from Jason and the rest, they
let them go.

Ministering at Berea

10Then [a]the brethren immediately sent
Paul and Silas away by night to Berea. When
they arrived, they went into the synagogue
of the Jews. 11These were more fair-minded
than those in Thessalonica, in that they
received the word with all readiness, and
[a]searched the Scriptures daily *to find out*
whether these things were so. 12Therefore
many of them believed, and also not a few
of the Greeks, prominent women as well as
men. 13But when the Jews from Thessalonica
learned that the word of God was preached
by Paul at Berea, they came there also and
stirred up the crowds. 14[a]Then immediately
the brethren sent Paul away, to go to the sea;
but both Silas and Timothy remained there.
15So those who conducted Paul brought him
to Athens; and [a]receiving a command for
Silas and Timothy to come to him with all
speed, they departed.

The Philosophers at Athens

16Now while Paul waited for them at Athens, [a]his spirit was provoked within him
when he saw that the city was given over to
idols. 17Therefore he reasoned in the synagogue with the Jews and with the *Gentile*
worshipers, and in the marketplace daily
with those who happened to be there. 18Then[1]
certain Epicurean and Stoic philosophers
encountered him. And some said, "What
does this babbler want to say?"

Others said, "He seems to be a proclaimer
of foreign gods," because he preached to
them [a]Jesus and the resurrection.

19And they took him and brought him to
the Areopagus, saying, "May we know what
this new doctrine *is* of which you speak? 20For
you are bringing some strange things to our
ears. Therefore we want to know what these
things mean." 21For all the Athenians and the

17:4 [b] Acts 15:22, 27, 32, 40 **17:5** [a] Acts 13:45 [b] Rom. 16:21 [1] NU-Text omits *who were not persuaded;* M-Text omits *becoming envious.* **17:6** [a] [Acts 16:20] **17:7** [a] 1 Pet. 2:13 **17:10** [a] Acts 9:25; 17:14 **17:11** [a] John 5:39 **17:14** [a] Matt. 10:23 **17:15** [a] Acts 18:5 **17:16** [a] 2 Pet. 2:8 **17:18** [a] 1 Cor. 15:12 [1] NU-Text and M-Text add *also.*

LIGHT FOR THOSE WHO DOUBT

The One whom you worship without knowing, Him I proclaim to you.

ACTS 17:23

I love the story of Paul's walking through the forum of Athens just below the Acropolis, on which was perched the iconic Parthenon. Anyone walking through the Athens agora even today will see the statues and inscribed bases. Paul recognized the pagan polytheism of the city. When he saw an inscription "TO THE UNKNOWN GOD" (v. 23), he took the opportunity to proclaim the Good News. Paul announced, "The One whom you worship without knowing, Him I proclaim to you." Paul then described the one God, the Creator of heaven and earth, who does not dwell in a temple, nor does He need anything. When Paul mentioned Jesus' resurrection, many "mocked" (v. 32), but a few were interested in hearing more.

I have to give Paul high marks for creativity. He went up against a tough crowd, but at least he got some of them thinking, and a few of those became believers. We face much the same today in our post-Christian world where anything goes. We encounter skepticism and mockery, but the gospel of God's redemption and peace is compelling and when it's shared, invariably some will see the light.

foreigners who were there spent their time in nothing else but either to tell or to hear some new thing.

Addressing the Areopagus

22 Then Paul stood in the midst of the Areopagus and said, "Men of Athens, I perceive that in all things you are very religious; 23 for as I was passing through and considering the objects of your worship, I even found an altar with this inscription:

TO THE UNKNOWN GOD.

Therefore, the One whom you worship without knowing, Him I proclaim to you: 24 [a]God, who made the world and everything in it, since He is [b]Lord of heaven and earth, [c]does not dwell in temples made with hands. 25 Nor is He worshiped with men's hands, as though He needed anything, since He [a]gives to all life, breath, and all things. 26 And He has made from one blood[1] every nation of men to dwell on all the face of the earth, and has determined their preappointed times and [a]the boundaries of their dwellings, 27 [a]so that they should seek the Lord, in the hope that they might grope for Him and find Him, [b]though He is not far from each one of us; 28 for [a]in Him we live and move and have our being, [b]as also some of your own poets have said, 'For we are also His offspring.' 29 Therefore, since we are the offspring of God, [a]we ought not to think that the Divine Nature is like gold or silver or stone, something shaped by art and man's devising. 30 Truly, [a]these times of ignorance God overlooked, but [b]now commands all men everywhere to repent, 31 because He has appointed a day on which [a]He will judge the world in righteousness by the Man whom He has ordained. He has given assurance of this to all by [b]raising Him from the dead."

32 And when they heard of the resurrection of the dead, some mocked, while others said, "We will hear you again on this *matter.*" 33 So Paul departed from among them. 34 However, some men joined him and believed, among them Dionysius the Areopagite, a woman named Damaris, and others with them.

Ministering at Corinth

18 After these things Paul departed from Athens and went to Corinth. 2 And he found a certain Jew named [a]Aquila, born in Pontus, who had recently come from Italy with his wife Priscilla (because Claudius had commanded all the Jews to depart from Rome); and he came to them. 3 So, because he was of the same trade, he stayed with them [a]and worked; for by occupation they were tentmakers. 4 [a]And he reasoned in the synagogue every Sabbath, and persuaded both Jews and Greeks.

5 [a]When Silas and Timothy had come from Macedonia, Paul was [b]compelled by the Spirit, and testified to the Jews *that* Jesus *is* the Christ. 6 But [a]when they opposed him and blasphemed, [b]he shook *his* garments and said to them, [c]"Your blood *be* upon your *own* heads; [d]I *am* clean. [e]From now on I will go to the Gentiles." 7 And he departed from there and entered the house of a certain *man* named Justus,[1] *one* who worshiped God, whose house was next door to the synagogue. 8 [a]Then Crispus, the ruler of the synagogue, believed on the Lord with all his household. And many of the Corinthians, hearing, believed and were baptized.

9 Now [a]the Lord spoke to Paul in the night by a vision, "Do not be afraid, but speak, and do not keep silent; 10 [a]for I am with you, and no one will attack you to hurt you; for I have many people in this city." 11 And he continued *there* a year and six months, teaching the word of God among them.

12 When Gallio was proconsul of Achaia, the Jews with one accord rose up against Paul and brought him to the judgment seat, 13 saying, "This *fellow* persuades men to worship God contrary to the law."

14 And when Paul was about to open *his* mouth, Gallio said to the Jews, "If it were a matter of wrongdoing or wicked crimes, O Jews, there would be reason why I should bear with you. 15 But if it is a [a]question of words and names and your own law, look *to it* yourselves; for I do not want to be a judge of such *matters.*" 16 And he drove them from the judgment seat. 17 Then all the Greeks[1] took [a]Sosthenes, the ruler of the synagogue, and beat *him* before the judgment seat. But Gallio took no notice of these things.

Paul Returns to Antioch

18 So Paul still remained a good while. Then he took leave of the brethren and sailed for Syria, and Priscilla and Aquila *were* with him. [a]He had *his* hair cut off at [b]Cenchrea, for he

17:24 [a] Acts 14:15 [b] Matt. 11:25 [c] Acts 7:48–50 **17:25** [a] Is. 42:5 **17:26** [a] Deut. 32:8 [1] NU-Text omits *blood.* **17:27** [a] [Rom. 1:20] [b] Jer. 23:23, 24 **17:28** [a] [Heb. 1:3] [b] Titus 1:12 **17:29** [a] Is. 40:18, 19 **17:30** [a] [Rom. 3:25] [b] [Titus 2:11, 12] **17:31** [a] Acts 10:42 [b] Acts 2:24 **18:2** [a] 1 Cor. 16:19 **18:3** [a] Acts 20:34 **18:4** [a] Acts 17:2 **18:5** [a] Acts 17:14, 15 [b] Acts 18:28 **18:6** [a] Acts 13:45 [b] Neh. 5:13 [c] 2 Sam. 1:16 [d] [Ezek. 3:18, 19] [e] Acts 13:46–48; 28:28 **18:7** [1] NU-Text reads *Titius Justus.* **18:8** [a] 1 Cor. 1:14 **18:9** [a] Acts 23:11 **18:10** [a] Jer. 1:18, 19 **18:15** [a] Acts 23:29; 25:19 **18:17** [a] 1 Cor. 1:1 [1] NU-Text reads *they all.* **18:18** [a] Acts 21:24 [b] Rom. 16:1

had taken a vow. 19And he came to Ephesus, and left them there; but he himself entered the synagogue and reasoned with the Jews. 20When they asked *him* to stay a longer time with them, he did not consent, 21but took leave of them, saying, [a]"I must by all means keep this coming feast in Jerusalem;[1] but I will return again to you, [b]God willing." And he sailed from Ephesus.

22And when he had landed at [a]Caesarea, and gone up and greeted the church, he went down to Antioch. 23After he had spent some time *there,* he departed and went over the region of [a]Galatia and Phrygia in order, [b]strengthening all the disciples.

Ministry of Apollos

24[a]Now a certain Jew named Apollos, born at Alexandria, an eloquent man *and* mighty in the Scriptures, came to Ephesus. 25This man had been instructed in the way of the Lord; and being [a]fervent in spirit, he spoke and taught accurately the things of the Lord, [b]though he knew only the baptism of John. 26So he began to speak boldly in the synagogue. When Aquila and Priscilla heard him, they took him aside and explained to him the way of God more accurately. 27And when he desired to cross to Achaia, the brethren wrote, exhorting the disciples to receive him; and when he arrived, [a]he greatly helped those who had believed through grace; 28for he vigorously refuted the Jews publicly, [a]showing from the Scriptures that Jesus is the Christ.

Paul at Ephesus

19 And it happened, while [a]Apollos was at Corinth, that Paul, having passed through [b]the upper regions, came to Ephesus. And finding some disciples 2he said to them, "Did you receive the Holy Spirit when you believed?"

So they said to him, [a]"We have not so much as heard whether there is a Holy Spirit."

3And he said to them, "Into what then were you baptized?"

So they said, [a]"Into John's baptism."

4Then Paul said, [a]"John indeed baptized with a baptism of repentance, saying to the people that they should believe on Him who would come after him, that is, on Christ Jesus."

5When they heard *this,* they were baptized [a]in the name of the Lord Jesus. 6And when Paul had [a]laid hands on them, the Holy Spirit came upon them, and [b]they spoke with tongues and prophesied. 7Now the men were about twelve in all.

8[a]And he went into the synagogue and spoke boldly for three months, reasoning and persuading [b]concerning the things of the kingdom of God. 9But [a]when some were hardened and did not believe, but spoke evil [b]of the Way before the multitude, he departed from them and withdrew the disciples, reasoning daily in the school of Tyrannus. 10And [a]this continued for two years, so that all who dwelt in Asia heard the word of the Lord Jesus, both Jews and Greeks.

Miracles Glorify Christ

11Now [a]God worked unusual miracles by the hands of Paul, 12[a]so that even handkerchiefs or aprons were brought from his body to the sick, and the diseases left them and the evil spirits went out of them. 13[a]Then some of the itinerant Jewish exorcists [b]took it upon themselves to call the name of the Lord Jesus over those who had evil spirits, saying, "We[1] exorcise you by the Jesus whom Paul [c]preaches." 14Also there were seven sons of Sceva, a Jewish chief priest, who did so.

15And the evil spirit answered and said, "Jesus I know, and Paul I know; but who are you?"

16Then the man in whom the evil spirit was leaped on them, overpowered[1] them, and prevailed against them,[2] so that they fled out of that house naked and wounded. 17This became known both to all Jews and Greeks dwelling in Ephesus; and [a]fear fell on them all, and the name of the Lord Jesus was magnified. 18And many who had believed came [a]confessing and telling their deeds. 19Also, many of those who had practiced magic brought their books together and burned *them* in the sight of all. And they counted up the value of them, and *it* totaled fifty thousand *pieces* of silver. 20[a]So the word of the Lord grew mightily and prevailed.

The Riot at Ephesus

21[a]When these things were accomplished, Paul [b]purposed in the Spirit, when he had passed through [c]Macedonia and Achaia, to go to Jerusalem, saying, "After I have been there, [d]I must also see Rome." 22So he sent

18:21 [a] Acts 19:21; 20:16 [b] 1 Cor. 4:19 [1] NU-Text omits *I must* through *Jerusalem.* **18:22** [a] Acts 8:40 **18:23** [a] Gal. 1:2 [b] Acts 14:22; 15:32, 41 **18:24** [a] Titus 3:13 **18:25** [a] Rom. 12:11 [b] Acts 19:3 **18:27** [a] 1 Cor. 3:6 **18:28** [a] Acts 9:22; 17:3; 18:5 **19:1** [a] 1 Cor. 1:12; 3:5, 6 [b] Acts 18:23 **19:2** [a] 1 Sam. 3:7 **19:3** [a] Acts 18:25 **19:4** [a] Matt. 3:11 **19:5** [a] Acts 8:12, 16; 10:48 **19:6** [a] Acts 6:6; 8:17 [b] Acts 2:4; 10:46 **19:8** [a] Acts 17:2; 18:4 [b] Acts 1:3; 28:23 **19:9** [a] 2 Tim. 1:15 [b] Acts 9:2; 19:23; 22:4; 24:14 **19:10** [a] Acts 19:8; 20:31 **19:11** [a] Mark 16:20 **19:12** [a] Acts 5:15 **19:13** [a] Matt. 12:27 [b] Mark 9:38 [c] 1 Cor. 1:23; 2:2 [1] NU-Text reads *I.* **19:16** [1] M-Text reads *and they overpowered.* [2] NU-Text reads *both of them.* **19:17** [a] Luke 1:65; 7:16 **19:18** [a] Matt. 3:6 **19:20** [a] Acts 6:7; 12:24 **19:21** [a] Rom. 15:25 [b] Acts 20:22 [c] Acts 20:1 [d] Rom. 1:13; 15:22–29

into Macedonia two of those who ministered to him, [a]Timothy and [b]Erastus, but he himself stayed in Asia for a time.

23And [a]about that time there arose a great commotion about [b]the Way. 24For a certain man named Demetrius, a silversmith, who made silver shrines of Diana,[1] brought [a]no small profit to the craftsmen. 25He called them together with the workers of similar occupation, and said: "Men, you know that we have our prosperity by this trade. 26Moreover you see and hear that not only at Ephesus, but throughout almost all Asia, this Paul has persuaded and turned away many people, saying that [a]they are not gods which are made with hands. 27So not only is this trade of ours in danger of falling into disrepute, but also the temple of the great goddess Diana may be despised and her magnificence destroyed,[1] whom all Asia and the world worship."

28Now when they heard *this,* they were full of wrath and cried out, saying, "Great *is* Diana of the Ephesians!" 29So the whole city was filled with confusion, and rushed into the theater with one accord, having seized [a]Gaius and [b]Aristarchus, Macedonians, Paul's travel companions. 30And when Paul wanted to go in to the people, the disciples would not allow him. 31Then some of the officials of Asia, who were his friends, sent to him pleading that he would not venture into the theater. 32Some therefore cried one thing and some another, for the assembly was confused, and most of them did not know why they had come together. 33And they drew Alexander out of the multitude, the Jews putting him forward. And [a]Alexander [b]motioned with his hand, and wanted to make his defense to the people. 34But when they found out that he was a Jew, all with one voice cried out for about two hours, "Great *is* Diana of the Ephesians!"

35And when the city clerk had quieted the crowd, he said: "Men of Ephesus, what man is there who does not know that the city of the Ephesians is temple guardian of the great goddess Diana, and of the *image* which fell down from Zeus? 36Therefore, since these things cannot be denied, you ought to be quiet and do nothing rashly. 37For you have brought these men here who are neither robbers of temples nor blasphemers of your[1] goddess. 38Therefore, if Demetrius and his fellow craftsmen have a case against anyone, the courts are open and there are proconsuls. Let them bring charges against one another. 39But if you have any other inquiry to make, it shall be determined in the lawful assembly. 40For we are in danger of being called in question for today's uproar, there being no reason which we may give to account for this disorderly gathering." 41And when he had said these things, he dismissed the assembly.

Journeys in Greece

20 After the uproar had ceased, Paul called the disciples to *himself,* embraced *them,* and [a]departed to go to Macedonia. 2Now when he had gone over that region and encouraged them with many words, he came to [a]Greece 3and stayed three months. And [a]when the Jews plotted against him as he was about to sail to Syria, he decided to return through Macedonia. 4And Sopater of Berea accompanied him to Asia—also [a]Aristarchus and Secundus of the Thessalonians, and [b]Gaius of Derbe, and [c]Timothy, and [d]Tychicus and [e]Trophimus of Asia. 5These men, going ahead, waited for us at [a]Troas. 6But we sailed away from Philippi after [a]the Days of Unleavened Bread, and in five days joined them [b]at Troas, where we stayed seven days.

Ministering at Troas

7Now on [a]the first *day* of the week, when the disciples came together [b]to break bread, Paul, ready to depart the next day, spoke to them and continued his message until midnight. 8There were many lamps [a]in the upper room where they[1] were gathered together. 9And in a window sat a certain young man named Eutychus, who was sinking into a deep sleep. He was overcome by sleep; and as Paul continued speaking, he fell down from the third story and was taken up dead. 10But Paul went down, [a]fell on him, and embracing *him* said, [b]"Do not trouble yourselves, for his life is in him." 11Now when he had come up, had broken bread and eaten, and talked a long while, even till daybreak, he departed. 12And they brought the young man in alive, and they were not a little comforted.

From Troas to Miletus

13Then we went ahead to the ship and sailed to Assos, there intending to take Paul on board; for so he had given orders, intending himself to go on foot. 14And when he met us at Assos, we took him on board and came

19:22 [a] 1 Tim. 1:2 [b] Rom. 16:23 **19:23** [a] 2 Cor. 1:8 [b] Acts 9:2 **19:24** [a] Acts 16:16, 19 [1] Greek *Artemis* **19:26** [a] Is. 44:10–20 **19:27** [1] NU-Text reads *she be deposed from her magnificence.* **19:29** [a] Rom. 16:23 [b] Col. 4:10 **19:33** [a] 2 Tim. 4:14 [b] Acts 12:17 **19:37** [1] NU-Text reads *our.* **20:1** [a] 1 Tim. 1:3 **20:2** [a] Acts 17:15; 18:1 **20:3** [a] 2 Cor. 11:26 **20:4** [a] Col. 4:10 [b] Acts 19:29 [c] Acts 16:1 [d] Eph. 6:21 [e] 2 Tim. 4:20 **20:5** [a] 2 Tim. 4:13 **20:6** [a] Ex. 12:14, 15 [b] 2 Tim. 4:13 **20:7** [a] 1 Cor. 16:2 [b] Acts 2:42, 46; 20:11 **20:8** [a] Acts 1:13 [1] NU-Text and M-Text read *we.* **20:10** [a] 1 Kin. 17:21 [b] Matt. 9:23, 24

to Mitylene. 15We sailed from there, and the
next *day* came opposite Chios. The following
day we arrived at Samos and stayed at Tro-
gyllium. The next *day* we came to Miletus.
16For Paul had decided to sail past Ephesus,
so that he would not have to spend time in
Asia; for [a]he was hurrying [b]to be at Jerusalem, if possible, on [c]the Day of Pentecost.

The Ephesian Elders Exhorted

17From Miletus he sent to Ephesus and
called for the elders of the church. 18And
when they had come to him, he said to them:
"You know, [a]from the first day that I came to
Asia, in what manner I always lived among
you, 19serving the Lord with all humility,
with many tears and trials which happened
to me [a]by the plotting of the Jews; 20how
[a]I kept back nothing that was helpful, but
proclaimed it to you, and taught you publicly
and from house to house, 21[a]testifying to
Jews, and also to Greeks, [b]repentance toward
God and faith toward our Lord Jesus Christ.
22And see, now [a]I go bound in the spirit to
Jerusalem, not knowing the things that will
happen to me there, 23except that [a]the Holy
Spirit testifies in every city, saying that chains
and tribulations await me. 24But [a]none of
these things move me; nor do I count my life
dear to myself,[1] [b]so that I may finish my race
with joy, [c]and the ministry [d]which I received
from the Lord Jesus, to testify to the gospel
of the grace of God.
25"And indeed, now I know that you all,

PEACE NOTE

When he was warned of great danger, the great apostle stated, "None of these things move me." A spiritually mature Paul lived daily in the peace of God.

ACTS 20:24

among whom I have gone preaching the
kingdom of God, will see my face no more.
26Therefore I testify to you this day that I
am [a]innocent of the blood of all *men.* 27For
I have not shunned to declare to you [a]the
whole counsel of God. 28[a]Therefore take heed
to yourselves and to all the flock, among
which the Holy Spirit [b]has made you overseers, to shepherd the church of God[1] [c]which
He purchased [d]with His own blood. 29For I
know this, that after my departure [a]savage
wolves will come in among you, not sparing
the flock. 30Also [a]from among yourselves
men will rise up, speaking perverse things,
to draw away the disciples after themselves.
31Therefore watch, and remember that [a]for
three years I did not cease to warn everyone
night and day with tears.
32"So now, brethren, I commend you to
God and [a]to the word of His grace, which is
able [b]to build you up and give you [c]an inheritance among all those who are sanctified.
33I have coveted no one's silver or gold or apparel. 34Yes,[1] you yourselves know [a]that these
hands have provided for my necessities, and
for those who were with me. 35I have shown
you in every way, [a]by laboring like this, that
you must support the weak. And remember
the words of the Lord Jesus, that He said,
'It is more blessed to give than to receive.' "
36And when he had said these things, he
knelt down and prayed with them all. 37Then
they all [a]wept freely, and [b]fell on Paul's neck
and kissed him, 38sorrowing most of all for
the words which he spoke, that they would
see his face no more. And they accompanied
him to the ship.

Warnings on the Journey to Jerusalem

21 Now it came to pass, that when we had
departed from them and set sail, running a straight course we came to Cos, the
following *day* to Rhodes, and from there
to Patara. 2And finding a ship sailing over
to Phoenicia, we went aboard and set sail.
3When we had sighted Cyprus, we passed it
on the left, sailed to Syria, and landed at Tyre;
for there the ship was to unload her cargo.
4And finding disciples,[1] we stayed there seven
days. [a]They told Paul through the Spirit not
to go up to Jerusalem. 5When we had come
to the end of those days, we departed and
went on our way; and they all accompanied

20:16 [a] Acts 18:21; 19:21; 21:4 [b] Acts 24:17 [c] Acts 2:1 **20:18** [a] Acts 18:19; 19:1, 10; 20:4, 16 **20:19** [a] Acts 20:3 **20:20** [a] Acts 20:27 **20:21** [a] Acts 18:5; 19:10 [b] Mark 1:15 **20:22** [a] Acts 19:21 **20:23** [a] Acts 21:4, 11 **20:24** [a] Acts 21:13 [b] 2 Tim. 4:7 [c] Acts 1:17 [d] Gal. 1:1 [1] NU-Text reads *But I do not count my life of any value or dear to myself.* **20:26** [a] Acts 18:6 **20:27** [a] Luke 7:30 **20:28** [a] 1 Pet. 5:2 [b] 1 Cor. 12:28 [c] Eph. 1:7, 14 [d] Heb. 9:14 [1] M-Text reads *of the Lord and God.* **20:29** [a] Matt. 7:15 **20:30** [a] 1 Tim. 1:20 **20:31** [a] Acts 19:8, 10; 24:17 **20:32** [a] Heb. 13:9 [b] Acts 9:31 [c] [Heb. 9:15] **20:34** [a] Acts 18:3 [1] NU-Text and M-Text omit *Yes.* **20:35** [a] Rom. 15:1 **20:37** [a] Acts 21:13 [b] Gen. 45:14 **21:4** [a] [Acts 20:23; 21:12] [1] NU-Text reads *the disciples.*

us, with wives and children, till *we were* out
of the city. And [a]we knelt down on the shore
and prayed. 6When we had taken our leave of
one another, we boarded the ship, and they
returned [a]home.

7And when we had finished *our* voyage
from Tyre, we came to Ptolemais, greeted the
brethren, and stayed with them one day. 8On
the next *day* we who were Paul's companions[1]
departed and came to [a]Caesarea, and entered
the house of Philip [b]the evangelist, [c]who was
one of the seven, and stayed with him. 9Now
this man had four virgin daughters [a]who
prophesied. 10And as we stayed many days, a
certain prophet named [a]Agabus came down
from Judea. 11When he had come to us, he
took Paul's belt, bound his *own* hands and
feet, and said, "Thus says the Holy Spirit, [a]'So
shall the Jews at Jerusalem bind the man
who owns this belt, and deliver *him* into the
hands of the Gentiles.' "

12Now when we heard these things, both
we and those from that place pleaded with
him not to go up to Jerusalem. 13Then Paul
answered, [a]"What do you mean by weeping
and breaking my heart? For I am ready not
only to be bound, but also to die at Jerusalem
for the name of the Lord Jesus."

14So when he would not be persuaded, we
ceased, saying, [a]"The will of the Lord be done."

Paul Urged to Make Peace

15And after those days we packed and went
up to Jerusalem. 16Also some of the disciples
from Caesarea went with us and brought
with them a certain Mnason of Cyprus, an
early disciple, with whom we were to lodge.

17[a]And when we had come to Jerusalem,
the brethren received us gladly. 18On the
following *day* Paul went in with us to [a]James,
and all the elders were present. 19When he
had greeted them, [a]he told in detail those
things which God had done among the Gentiles [b]through his ministry. 20And when they
heard *it,* they glorified the Lord. And they
said to him, "You see, brother, how many
myriads of Jews there are who have believed,
and they are all [a]zealous for the law; 21but
they have been informed about you that
you teach all the Jews who are among the
Gentiles to forsake Moses, saying that they
ought not to circumcise *their* children nor to
walk according to the customs. 22What then?
The assembly must certainly meet, for they
will[1] hear that you have come. 23Therefore do
what we tell you: We have four men who have
taken a vow. 24Take them and be purified
with them, and pay their expenses so that
they may [a]shave *their* heads, and that all may
know that those things of which they were
informed concerning you are nothing, but
that you yourself also walk orderly and keep
the law. 25But concerning the Gentiles who
believe, [a]we have written *and* decided that
they should observe no such thing, except[1]
that they should keep themselves from *things*
offered to idols, from blood, from things
strangled, and from sexual immorality."

Arrested in the Temple

26Then Paul took the men, and the next
day, having been purified with them, [a]entered
the temple [b]to announce the expiration of
the days of purification, at which time an offering should be made for each one of them.

27Now when the seven days were almost
ended, [a]the Jews from Asia, seeing him in the
temple, stirred up the whole crowd and [b]laid
hands on him, 28crying out, "Men of Israel,
help! This is the man [a]who teaches all *men*
everywhere against the people, the law, and
this place; and furthermore he also brought
Greeks into the temple and has defiled this
holy place." 29(For they had previously[1] seen
[a]Trophimus the Ephesian with him in the
city, whom they supposed that Paul had
brought into the temple.)

30And [a]all the city was disturbed; and the
people ran together, seized Paul, and dragged
him out of the temple; and immediately the
doors were shut. 31Now as they were [a]seeking
to kill him, news came to the commander
of the garrison that all Jerusalem was in
an uproar. 32[a]He immediately took soldiers
and centurions, and ran down to them. And
when they saw the commander and the soldiers, they stopped beating Paul. 33Then
the [a]commander came near and took him,
and [b]commanded *him* to be bound with two
chains; and he asked who he was and what he
had done. 34And some among the multitude
cried one thing and some another.

So when he could not ascertain the truth
because of the tumult, he commanded him
to be taken into the barracks. 35When he
reached the stairs, he had to be carried by the

21:5 [a] Acts 9:40; 20:36 **21:6** [a] John 1:11 **21:8** [a] Acts 8:40; 21:16 [b] Eph. 4:11 [c] Acts 6:5 [1] NU-Text omits *who were Paul's companions.* **21:9** [a] Joel 2:28 **21:10** [a] Acts 11:28 **21:11** [a] Acts 20:23; 21:33; 22:25 **21:13** [a] Acts 20:24, 37 **21:14** [a] Luke 11:2; 22:42 **21:17** [a] Acts 15:4 **21:18** [a] Gal. 1:19; 2:9 **21:19** [a] Rom. 15:18, 19 [b] Acts 1:17; 20:24 **21:20** [a] Acts 15:1; 22:3 **21:22** [1] NU-Text reads *What then is to be done? They will certainly.* **21:24** [a] Acts 18:18 **21:25** [a] Acts 15:19, 20, 29 [1] NU-Text omits *that they should observe no such thing, except.* **21:26** [a] Acts 21:24; 24:18 [b] Num. 6:13 **21:27** [a] Acts 20:19; 24:18 [b] Acts 26:21 **21:28** [a] Acts 6:13; 24:6 **21:29** [a] Acts 20:4 [1] M-Text omits *previously.* **21:30** [a] Acts 16:19; 26:21 **21:31** [a] 2 Cor. 11:23 **21:32** [a] Acts 23:27; 24:7 **21:33** [a] Acts 24:7 [b] Acts 20:23; 21:11

soldiers because of the violence of the mob.
36For the multitude of the people followed
after, crying out, [a]"Away with him!"

Addressing the Jerusalem Mob

37Then as Paul was about to be led into the
barracks, he said to the commander, "May I
speak to you?"

He replied, "Can you speak Greek? 38[a]Are
you not the Egyptian who some time ago
stirred up a rebellion and led the four thousand assassins out into the wilderness?"

39But Paul said, [a]"I am a Jew from Tarsus,
in Cilicia, a citizen of no mean city; and I implore you, permit me to speak to the people."

40So when he had given him permission,
Paul stood on the stairs and [a]motioned with
his hand to the people. And when there was
a great silence, he spoke to *them* in the [b]He-
brew language, saying,

22 "Brethren[a] and fathers, hear my defense before you now." 2And when they
heard that he spoke to them in the [a]Hebrew
language, they kept all the more silent.

Then he said: 3[a]"I am indeed a Jew, born in
Tarsus of Cilicia, but brought up in this city
[b]at the feet of [c]Gamaliel, taught [d]according
to the strictness of our fathers' law, and [e]was
zealous toward God [f]as you all are today. 4[a]I
persecuted this Way to the death, binding
and delivering into prisons both men and
women, 5as also the high priest bears me
witness, and [a]all the council of the elders,
[b]from whom I also received letters to the
brethren, and went to Damascus [c]to bring
in chains even those who were there to Jerusalem to be punished.

6"Now [a]it happened, as I journeyed and
came near Damascus at about noon, suddenly a great light from heaven shone around
me. 7And I fell to the ground and heard a
voice saying to me, 'Saul, Saul, why are you
persecuting Me?' 8So I answered, 'Who are
You, Lord?' And He said to me, 'I am Jesus of
Nazareth, whom you are persecuting.'

9"And [a]those who were with me indeed
saw the light and were afraid,[1] but they did
not hear the voice of Him who spoke to me.
10So I said, 'What shall I do, Lord?' And the
Lord said to me, 'Arise and go into Damascus,
and there you will be told all things which are
appointed for you to do.' 11And since I could
not see for the glory of that light, being led
by the hand of those who were with me, I
came into Damascus.

12"Then [a]a certain Ananias, a devout man
according to the law, [b]having a good testimony
with all the [c]Jews who dwelt *there,* 13came to
me; and he stood and said to me, 'Brother Saul,
receive your sight.' And at that same hour I
looked up at him. 14Then he said, [a]'The God of
our fathers [b]has chosen you that you should
[c]know His will, and [d]see the Just One, [e]and
hear the voice of His mouth. 15[a]For you will be
His witness to all men of [b]what you have seen
and heard. 16And now why are you waiting?
Arise and be baptized, [a]and wash away your
sins, [b]calling on the name of the Lord.'

17"Now [a]it happened, when I returned to
Jerusalem and was praying in the temple,
that I was in a trance 18and [a]saw Him saying
to me, [b]'Make haste and get out of Jerusalem
quickly, for they will not receive your testimony concerning Me.' 19So I said, 'Lord, [a]they
know that in every synagogue I imprisoned
and [b]beat those who believe on You. 20[a]And
when the blood of Your martyr Stephen was
shed, I also was standing by [b]consenting to
his death,[1] and guarding the clothes of those
who were killing him.' 21Then He said to me,
'Depart, [a]for I will send you far from here to
the Gentiles.' "

Paul's Roman Citizenship

22And they listened to him until this word,
and *then* they raised their voices and said,
[a]"Away with such a *fellow* from the earth, for
[b]he is not fit to live!" 23Then, as they cried out
and tore off *their* clothes and threw dust into
the air, 24the commander ordered him to be
brought into the barracks, and said that he
should be examined under scourging, so that
he might know why they shouted so against
him. 25And as they bound him with thongs,
Paul said to the centurion who stood by, [a]"Is
it lawful for you to scourge a man who is a
Roman, and uncondemned?"

26When the centurion heard *that,* he went
and told the commander, saying, "Take care
what you do, for this man is a Roman."

27Then the commander came and said to
him, "Tell me, are you a Roman?"

He said, "Yes."

28The commander answered, "With a large
sum I obtained this citizenship."

And Paul said, "But I was born *a citizen.*"

21:36 [a] John 19:15 **21:38** [a] Acts 5:36 **21:39** [a] Acts 9:11; 22:3 **21:40** [a] Acts 12:17 [b] Acts 22:2 **22:1** [a] Acts 7:2 **22:2** [a] Acts 21:40 **22:3** [a] 2 Cor. 11:22 [b] Deut. 33:3 [c] Acts 5:34 [d] Acts 23:6; 26:5 [e] Gal. 1:14 [f] [Rom. 10:2] **22:4** [a] 1 Tim. 1:13 **22:5** [a] Acts 23:14; 24:1; 25:15 [b] Luke 22:66 [c] Acts 9:2 **22:6** [a] Acts 9:3; 26:12, 13 **22:9** [a] Acts 9:7 [1] NU-Text omits *and were afraid.* **22:12** [a] Acts 9:17 [b] Acts 10:22 [c] 1 Tim. 3:7 **22:14** [a] Acts 3:13; 5:30 [b] Acts 9:15; 26:16 [c] Acts 3:14; 7:52 [d] 1 Cor. 9:1; 15:8 [e] Gal. 1:12 **22:15** [a] Acts 23:11 [b] Acts 4:20; 26:16 **22:16** [a] Heb. 10:22 [b] Rom. 10:13 **22:17** [a] Acts 9:26; 26:20 **22:18** [a] Acts 22:14 [b] Matt. 10:14 **22:19** [a] Acts 8:3; 22:4 [b] Matt. 10:17 **22:20** [a] Acts 7:54—8:1 [b] Luke 11:48 [1] NU-Text omits *to his death.* **22:21** [a] Acts 9:15 **22:22** [a] Acts 21:36 [b] Acts 25:24 **22:25** [a] Acts 16:37

29Then immediately those who were about
to examine him withdrew from him; and the
commander was also afraid after he found
out that he was a Roman, and because he
had bound him.

The Sanhedrin Divided

30The next day, because he wanted to know
for certain why he was accused by the Jews,
he released him from *his* bonds, and commanded the chief priests and all their council
to appear, and brought Paul down and set
him before them.

23 Then Paul, looking earnestly at the
council, said, "Men *and* brethren, [a]I
have lived in all good conscience before God
until this day." 2And the high priest Ananias commanded those who stood by him [a]to
strike him on the mouth. 3Then Paul said to
him, "God will strike you, *you* whitewashed
wall! For you sit to judge me according to the
law, and [a]do you command me to be struck
contrary to the law?"
4And those who stood by said, "Do you
revile God's high priest?"
5Then Paul said, [a]"I did not know, brethren,
that he was the high priest; for it is written,
[b]'You shall not speak evil of a ruler of your
people.' "[1]
6But when Paul perceived that one part
were Sadducees and the other Pharisees,
he cried out in the council, "Men *and* brethren, [a]I am a Pharisee, the son of a Pharisee;
[b]concerning the hope and resurrection of
the dead I am being judged!"
7And when he had said this, a dissension
arose between the Pharisees and the Sadducees; and the assembly was divided. 8[a]For
Sadducees say that there is no resurrection—
and no angel or spirit; but the Pharisees
confess both. 9Then there arose a loud outcry.
And the scribes of the Pharisees' party arose
and protested, saying, [a]"We find no evil in this
man; but [b]if a spirit or an angel has spoken
to him, [c]let us not fight against God."[1]
10Now when there arose a great dissension,
the commander, fearing lest Paul might be
pulled to pieces by them, commanded the
soldiers to go down and take him by force
from among them, and bring *him* into the
barracks.

The Plot Against Paul

11But [a]the following night the Lord stood
by him and said, "Be of good cheer, Paul; for

PEACE NOTE

One of Paul's character qualities that made him so effective was that he lived in "good conscience" before God. The peace of God ruling our lives produces a clear conscience.

ACTS 23:1

as you have testified for Me in [b]Jerusalem,
so you must also bear witness at [c]Rome."
12And when it was day, [a]some of the Jews
banded together and bound themselves under an oath, saying that they would neither
eat nor drink till they had [b]killed Paul. 13Now
there were more than forty who had formed
this conspiracy. 14They came to the chief
priests and [a]elders, and said, "We have bound
ourselves under a great oath that we will eat
nothing until we have killed Paul. 15Now you,
therefore, together with the council, suggest
to the commander that he be brought down
to you tomorrow,[1] as though you were going
to make further inquiries concerning him;
but we are ready to kill him before he comes
near."
16So when Paul's sister's son heard of their
ambush, he went and entered the barracks
and told Paul. 17Then Paul called one of the
centurions to *him* and said, "Take this young
man to the commander, for he has something
to tell him." 18So he took him and brought
him to the commander and said, "Paul the
prisoner called me to *him* and asked *me* to
bring this young man to you. He has something to say to you."
19Then the commander took him by the
hand, went aside, and asked privately, "What
is it that you have to tell me?"
20And he said, [a]"The Jews have agreed to
ask that you bring Paul down to the council tomorrow, as though they were going to
inquire more fully about him. 21But do not
yield to them, for more than forty of them
lie in wait for him, men who have bound

23:1 [a] 2 Tim. 1:3 **23:2** [a] John 18:22 **23:3** [a] Deut. 25:1, 2 **23:5** [a] Lev. 5:17, 18 [b] Ex. 22:28 [1] Exodus 22:28 **23:6** [a] Phil. 3:5 [b] Acts 24:15, 21; 26:6; 28:20 **23:8** [a] Matt. 22:23 **23:9** [a] Acts 25:25; 26:31 [b] Acts 22:6, 7, 17, 18 [c] Acts 5:39 [1] NU-Text omits last clause and reads *what if a spirit or an angel has spoken to him?* **23:11** [a] Acts 18:9; 27:23, 24 [b] Acts 21:18, 19; 22:1–21 [c] Acts 28:16, 17, 23 **23:12** [a] Acts 23:21, 30; 25:3 [b] Acts 9:23, 24; 25:3; 26:21; 27:42 **23:14** [a] Acts 4:5, 23; 6:12; 22:5; 24:1; 25:15 **23:15** [1] NU-Text omits *tomorrow.* **23:20** [a] Acts 23:12

themselves by an oath that they will neither
eat nor drink till they have killed him; and
now they are ready, waiting for the promise
from you."
22So the commander let the young man
depart, and commanded *him,* "Tell no one
that you have revealed these things to me."

Sent to Felix

23And he called for two centurions, saying, "Prepare two hundred soldiers, seventy
horsemen, and two hundred spearmen to go
to [a]Caesarea at the third hour of the night;
24and provide mounts to set Paul on, and
bring *him* safely to Felix the governor." 25He
wrote a letter in the following manner:

26 Claudius Lysias,

To the most excellent governor Felix:

Greetings.

27 [a]This man was seized by the Jews
and was about to be killed by them.
Coming with the troops I rescued
him, having learned that he was a
Roman. 28[a]And when I wanted to
know the reason they accused him,
I brought him before their council.
29I found out that he was accused
[a]concerning questions of their law,
[b]but had nothing charged against
him deserving of death or chains.
30And [a]when it was told me that the
Jews lay in wait for the man,[1] I sent
him immediately to you, and [b]also
commanded his accusers to state
before you the charges against him.

Farewell.

31Then the soldiers, as they were commanded, took Paul and brought *him* by night
to Antipatris. 32The next day they left the
horsemen to go on with him, and returned to
the barracks. 33When they came to [a]Caesarea
and had delivered the [b]letter to the governor, they also presented Paul to him. 34And
when the governor had read *it,* he asked what
province he was from. And when he understood that *he was* from [a]Cilicia, 35he said, [a]"I
will hear you when your accusers also have
come." And he commanded him to be kept
in [b]Herod's Praetorium.

Accused of Sedition

24 Now after [a]five days [b]Ananias the high
priest came down with the elders and
a certain orator *named* Tertullus. These gave
evidence to the governor against Paul.
2And when he was called upon, Tertullus
began his accusation, saying: "Seeing that
through you we enjoy great peace, and prosperity is being brought to this nation by your
foresight, 3we accept *it* always and in all places, most noble Felix, with all thankfulness.
4Nevertheless, not to be tedious to you any
further, I beg you to hear, by your courtesy,
a few words from us. 5[a]For we have found
this man a plague, a creator of dissension
among all the Jews throughout the world,
and a ringleader of the sect of the Nazarenes.
6[a]He even tried to profane the temple, and
we seized him,[1] and wanted [b]to judge him
according to our law. 7[a]But the commander Lysias came by and with great violence
took *him* out of our hands, 8[a]commanding
his accusers to come to you. By examining
him yourself you may ascertain all these
things of which we accuse him." 9And the
Jews also assented,[1] maintaining that these
things were so.

The Defense Before Felix

10Then Paul, after the governor had nod-
ded to him to speak, answered: "Inasmuch
as I know that you have been for many years
a judge of this nation, I do the more cheer-
fully answer for myself, 11because you may
ascertain that it is no more than twelve days
since I went up to Jerusalem [a]to worship.
12[a]And they neither found me in the temple
disputing with anyone nor inciting the crowd,
either in the synagogues or in the city. 13Nor
can they prove the things of which they now
accuse me. 14But this I confess to you, that
according to [a]the Way which they call a sect,
so I worship the [b]God of my fathers, believing
all things which are written in [c]the Law and
in the Prophets. 15[a]I have hope in God, which
they themselves also accept, [b]that there will
be a resurrection of *the* dead,[1] both of *the*
just and *the* unjust. 16[a]This *being* so, I myself
always strive to have a conscience without
offense toward God and men.

23:23 [a] Acts 8:40; 23:33 **23:27** [a] Acts 21:30, 33; 24:7 **23:28** [a] Acts 22:30 **23:29** [a] Acts 18:15; 25:19 [b] Acts 25:25; 26:31 **23:30** [a] Acts 23:20 [b] Acts 24:8; 25:6 [1] NU-Text reads *there would be a plot against the man.* **23:33** [a] Acts 8:40 [b] Acts 23:26–30 **23:34** [a] Acts 6:9; 21:39 **23:35** [a] Acts 24:1, 10; 25:16 [b] Matt. 27:27 **24:1** [a] Acts 21:27 [b] Acts 23:2, 30, 35; 25:2 **24:5** [a] 1 Pet. 2:12, 15 **24:6** [a] Acts 21:28 [b] John 18:31 [1] NU-Text ends the sentence here and omits the rest of verse 6, all of verse 7, and the first clause of verse 8. **24:7** [a] Acts 21:33; 23:10 **24:8** [a] Acts 23:30 **24:9** [1] NU-Text and M-Text read *joined the attack.* **24:11** [a] Acts 21:15, 18, 26, 27; 24:17 **24:12** [a] Acts 25:8; 28:17 **24:14** [a] Acts 9:2; 24:22 [b] 2 Tim. 1:3 [c] Acts 26:22; 28:23 **24:15** [a] Acts 23:6; 26:6, 7; 28:20 [b] [Dan. 12:2] [1] NU-Text omits *of the dead.* **24:16** [a] Acts 23:1

17"Now after many years [a]I came to bring
alms and offerings to my nation, 18[a]in the
midst of which some Jews from Asia found
me [b]purified in the temple, neither with a
mob nor with tumult. 19[a]They ought to have
been here before you to object if they had
anything against me. 20Or else let those who
are *here* themselves say if they found any
wrongdoing[1] in me while I stood before the
council, 21unless *it is* for this one statement
which I cried out, standing among them,
[a]'Concerning the resurrection of the dead I
am being judged by you this day.' "

Felix Procrastinates

22But when Felix heard these things, having more accurate knowledge of *the* [a]Way, he
adjourned the proceedings and said, "When
[b]Lysias the commander comes down, I will
make a decision on your case." 23So he commanded the centurion to keep Paul and to let
him have liberty, and [a]told him not to forbid
any of his friends to provide for or visit him.
24And after some days, when Felix came
with his wife Drusilla, who was Jewish, he
sent for Paul and heard him concerning the
[a]faith in Christ. 25Now as he reasoned about
righteousness, self-control, and the judgment to come, Felix was afraid and answered,
"Go away for now; when I have a convenient
time I will call for you." 26Meanwhile he also
hoped that [a]money would be given him by
Paul, that he might release him.[1] Therefore
he sent for him more often and conversed
with him.
27But after two years Porcius Festus succeeded Felix; and Felix, [a]wanting to do the
Jews a favor, left Paul bound.

Paul Appeals to Caesar

25 Now when Festus had come to the
province, after three days he went up
from [a]Caesarea to Jerusalem. 2[a]Then the
high priest[1] and the chief men of the Jews
informed him against Paul; and they petitioned him, 3asking a favor against him, that
he would summon him to Jerusalem—[a]while
they lay in ambush along the road to kill him.
4But Festus answered that Paul should be
kept at Caesarea, and that he himself was
going *there* shortly. 5"Therefore," he said,
"let those who have authority among you go
down with *me* and accuse this man, to see [a]if
there is any fault in him."
6And when he had remained among them
more than ten days, he went down to Caesarea. And the next day, sitting on the judgment
seat, he commanded Paul to be brought.
7When he had come, the Jews who had come
down from Jerusalem stood about [a]and laid
many serious complaints against Paul, which
they could not prove, 8while he answered for
himself, [a]"Neither against the law of the Jews,
nor against the temple, nor against Caesar
have I offended in anything at all."
9But Festus, [a]wanting to do the Jews a
favor, answered Paul and said, [b]"Are you
willing to go up to Jerusalem and there be
judged before me concerning these things?"
10So Paul said, "I stand at Caesar's judgment seat, where I ought to be judged. To
the Jews I have done no wrong, as you very
well know. 11[a]For if I am an offender, or have
committed anything deserving of death, I do
not object to dying; but if there is nothing
in these things of which these men accuse
me, no one can deliver me to them. [b]I appeal
to Caesar."
12Then Festus, when he had conferred with
the council, answered, "You have appealed
to Caesar? To Caesar you shall go!"

Paul Before Agrippa

13And after some days King Agrippa and
Bernice came to Caesarea to greet Festus.
14When they had been there many days, Festus laid Paul's case before the king, saying:
[a]"There is a certain man left a prisoner by
Felix, 15[a]about whom the chief priests and
the elders of the Jews informed *me,* when
I was in Jerusalem, asking for a judgment
against him. 16[a]To them I answered, 'It is
not the custom of the Romans to deliver
any man to destruction[1] before the accused
meets the accusers face to face, and has opportunity to answer for himself concerning
the charge against him.' 17Therefore when
they had come together, [a]without any delay, the next day I sat on the judgment seat
and commanded the man to be brought in.
18When the accusers stood up, they brought
no accusation against him of such things
as I supposed, 19[a]but had some questions
against him about their own religion and

24:17 [a] Rom. 15:25–28 **24:18** [a] Acts 21:27; 26:21 [b] Acts 21:26 **24:19** [a] [Acts 23:30; 25:16] **24:20** [1] NU-Text and M-Text read *say what wrongdoing they found.* **24:21** [a] [Acts 23:6; 24:15; 28:20] **24:22** [a] Acts 9:2; 18:26; 19:9, 23; 22:4 [b] Acts 23:26; 24:7 **24:23** [a] Acts 23:16; 27:3; 28:16 **24:24** [a] [Rom. 10:9] **24:26** [a] Ex. 23:8 [1] NU-Text omits *that he might release him.* **24:27** [a] Acts 12:3; 23:35; 25:9, 14 **25:1** [a] Acts 8:40; 25:4, 6, 13 **25:2** [a] Acts 24:1; 25:15 [1] NU-Text reads *chief priests.* **25:3** [a] Acts 23:12, 15 **25:5** [a] Acts 18:14; 25:18 **25:7** [a] Acts 24:5, 13 **25:8** [a] Acts 6:13; 24:12; 28:17 **25:9** [a] Acts 12:2; 24:27 [b] Acts 25:20 **25:11** [a] Acts 18:14; 23:29; 25:25; 26:31 [b] Acts 26:32; 28:19 **25:14** [a] Acts 24:27 **25:15** [a] Acts 24:1; 25:2, 3 **25:16** [a] Acts 25:4, 5 [1] NU-Text omits *to destruction,* although it is implied. **25:17** [a] Acts 25:6, 10 **25:19** [a] Acts 18:14, 15; 23:29

about a certain Jesus, who had died, whom
Paul affirmed to be alive. 20And because I was
uncertain of such questions, I asked whether
he was willing to go to Jerusalem and there
be judged concerning these matters. 21But
when Paul [a]appealed to be reserved for the
decision of Augustus, I commanded him to
be kept till I could send him to Caesar."
22Then [a]Agrippa said to Festus, "I also
would like to hear the man myself."
"Tomorrow," he said, "you shall hear him."
23So the next day, when Agrippa and Bernice had come with great pomp, and had entered the auditorium with the commanders
and the prominent men of the city, at Festus' command [a]Paul was brought in. 24And
Festus said: "King Agrippa and all the men
who are here present with us, you see this
man about whom [a]the whole assembly of
the Jews petitioned me, both at Jerusalem
and here, crying out that he was [b]not fit to
live any longer. 25But when I found that [a]he
had committed nothing deserving of death,
[b]and that he himself had appealed to Augustus, I decided to send him. 26I have nothing
certain to write to my lord concerning him.
Therefore I have brought him out before you,
and especially before you, King Agrippa, so
that after the examination has taken place I
may have something to write. 27For it seems
to me unreasonable to send a prisoner and
not to specify the charges against him."

Paul's Early Life

26 Then Agrippa said to Paul, "You are
permitted to speak for yourself."
So Paul stretched out his hand and answered for himself: 2"I think myself [a]happy,
King Agrippa, because today I shall answer
[b]for myself before you concerning all the
things of which I am [c]accused by the Jews,
3especially because you are expert in all customs and questions which have to do with the
Jews. Therefore I beg you to hear me patiently.
4"My manner of life from my youth, which
was spent from the beginning among my own
nation at Jerusalem, all the Jews know. 5They
knew me from the first, if they were willing
to testify, that according to [a]the strictest sect
of our religion I lived a Pharisee. 6[a]And now
I stand and am judged for the hope of [b]the
promise made by God to our fathers. 7To this
promise [a]our twelve tribes, earnestly serving
God [b]night and day, [c]hope to attain. For this
hope's sake, King Agrippa, I am accused by
the Jews. 8Why should it be thought incredible by you that God raises the dead?
9[a]"Indeed, I myself thought I must do
many things contrary to the name of [b]Jesus
of Nazareth. 10[a]This I also did in Jerusalem,
and many of the saints I shut up in prison,
having received authority [b]from the chief
priests; and when they were put to death,
I cast my vote against *them.* 11[a]And I punished them often in every synagogue and
compelled *them* to blaspheme; and being
exceedingly enraged against them, I persecuted *them* even to foreign cities.

Paul Recounts His Conversion

12[a]"While thus occupied, as I journeyed to
Damascus with authority and commission
from the chief priests, 13at midday, O king,
along the road I saw a light from heaven,
brighter than the sun, shining around me and
those who journeyed with me. 14And when we
all had fallen to the ground, I heard a voice
speaking to me and saying in the Hebrew
language, 'Saul, Saul, why are you persecuting Me? *It is* hard for you to kick against the
goads.' 15So I said, 'Who are You, Lord?' And
He said, 'I am Jesus, whom you are persecuting. 16But rise and stand on your feet; for
I have appeared to you for this purpose, [a]to
make you a minister and a witness both of the
things which you have seen and of the things
which I will yet reveal to you. 17I will deliver
you from the *Jewish* people, as well as *from*
the Gentiles, [a]to whom I now[1] send you, 18[a]to
open their eyes, *in order* [b]to turn *them* from
darkness to light, and *from* the power of Satan
to God, [c]that they may receive forgiveness of
sins and [d]an inheritance among those who
are [e]sanctified by faith in Me.'

Paul's Post-Conversion Life

19"Therefore, King Agrippa, I was not
disobedient to the heavenly vision, 20but
[a]declared first to those in Damascus and in
Jerusalem, and throughout all the region
of Judea, and *then* to the Gentiles, that they
should repent, turn to God, and do [b]works
befitting repentance. 21For these reasons the
Jews seized me in the temple and tried to kill
me. 22Therefore, having obtained help from
God, to this day I stand, witnessing both to
small and great, saying no other things than
those [a]which the prophets and [b]Moses said

25:21 [a] Acts 25:11, 12 **25:22** [a] Acts 9:15 **25:23** [a] Acts 9:15 **25:24** [a] Acts 25:2, 3, 7 [b] Acts 21:36; 22:22 **25:25** [a] Acts 23:9, 29; 26:31 [b] Acts 25:11, 12 **26:2** [a] [1 Pet. 3:14; 4:14] [b] [1 Pet. 3:15, 16] [c] Acts 21:28; 24:5, 6 **26:5** [a] Phil. 3:5 **26:6** [a] Acts 23:6 [b] Acts 13:32 **26:7** [a] James 1:1 [b] 1 Thess. 3:10 [c] Phil. 3:11 **26:9** [a] 1 Tim. 1:12, 13 [b] Acts 2:22; 10:38 **26:10** [a] Acts 8:1–3; 9:13 [b] Acts 9:14 **26:11** [a] Acts 22:19 **26:12** [a] Acts 9:3–8; 22:6–11; 26:12–18 **26:16** [a] Acts 22:15 **26:17** [a] Acts 22:21 [1] NU-Text and M-Text omit *now.* **26:18** [a] Is. 35:5; 42:7, 16 [b] 1 Pet. 2:9 [c] Luke 1:77 [d] Col. 1:12 [e] Acts 20:32 **26:20** [a] Acts 9:19, 20, 22; 11:26 [b] Matt. 3:8 **26:22** [a] Rom. 3:21 [b] John 5:46

would come— 23[a]that the Christ would suffer, [b]that He would be the first to rise from the dead, and [c]would proclaim light to the *Jewish* people and to the Gentiles."

Agrippa Parries Paul's Challenge

24Now as he thus made his defense, Festus said with a loud voice, "Paul, [a]you are beside yourself! Much learning is driving you mad!"

25But he said, "I am not mad, most noble Festus, but speak the words of truth and reason. 26For the king, before whom I also speak freely, [a]knows these things; for I am convinced that none of these things escapes his attention, since this thing was not done in a corner. 27King Agrippa, do you believe the prophets? I know that you do believe."

28Then Agrippa said to Paul, "You almost persuade me to become a Christian."

29And Paul said, [a]"I would to God that not only you, but also all who hear me today, might become both almost and altogether such as I am, except for these chains."

30When he had said these things, the king stood up, as well as the governor and Bernice and those who sat with them; 31and when they had gone aside, they talked among themselves, saying, [a]"This man is doing nothing deserving of death or chains."

32Then Agrippa said to Festus, "This man might have been set [a]free [b]if he had not appealed to Caesar."

The Voyage to Rome Begins

27 And when [a]it was decided that we should sail to Italy, they delivered Paul and some other prisoners to *one* named Julius, a centurion of the Augustan Regiment. 2So, entering a ship of Adramyttium, we put to sea, meaning to sail along the coasts of Asia. [a]Aristarchus, a Macedonian of Thessalonica, was with us. 3And the next *day* we landed at Sidon. And Julius [a]treated Paul kindly and gave *him* liberty to go to his friends and receive care. 4When we had put to sea from there, we sailed under *the shelter of* Cyprus, because the winds were contrary. 5And when we had sailed over the sea which is off Cilicia and Pamphylia, we came to Myra, *a city* of Lycia. 6There the centurion found [a]an Alexandrian ship sailing to Italy, and he put us on board.

7When we had sailed slowly many days, and arrived with difficulty off Cnidus, the wind not permitting us to proceed, we sailed under *the shelter of* [a]Crete off Salmone. 8Passing it with difficulty, we came to a place called Fair Havens, near the city *of* Lasea.

Paul's Warning Ignored

9Now when much time had been spent, and sailing was now dangerous [a]because the Fast was already over, Paul advised them, 10saying, "Men, I perceive that this voyage will end with disaster and much loss, not only of the cargo and ship, but also our lives." 11Nevertheless the centurion was more persuaded by the helmsman and the owner of the ship than by the things spoken by Paul. 12And because the harbor was not suitable to winter in, the majority advised to set sail from there also, if by any means they could reach Phoenix, a harbor of Crete opening toward the southwest and northwest, *and* winter *there.*

In the Tempest

13When the south wind blew softly, supposing that they had obtained *their* desire, putting out to sea, they sailed close by Crete. 14But not long after, a tempestuous head wind arose, called Euroclydon.[1] 15So when the ship was caught, and could not head into the wind, we let *her* drive. 16And running under *the shelter of* an island called Clauda,[1] we secured the skiff with difficulty. 17When they had taken it on board, they used cables to undergird the ship; and fearing lest they should run aground on the Syrtis[1] *Sands,* they struck sail and so were driven. 18And because we were exceedingly tempest-tossed, the next *day* they lightened the ship. 19On the third *day* [a]we threw the ship's tackle overboard with our own hands. 20Now when neither sun nor stars appeared for many days, and no small tempest beat on *us,* all hope that we would be saved was finally given up.

21But after long abstinence from food, then Paul stood in the midst of them and said, "Men, you should have listened to me, and not have sailed from Crete and incurred this disaster and loss. 22And now I urge you to take heart, for there will be no loss of life among you, but only of the ship. 23[a]For there stood by me this night an angel of the God to whom I belong and [b]whom I serve, 24saying, 'Do not be afraid, Paul; you must be brought before Caesar; and indeed God has granted you all those who sail with you.' 25Therefore take heart, men, [a]for I believe God that it will be just as it was told me. 26However, [a]we must run aground on a certain island."

26:23 [a] Luke 24:26 [b] 1 Cor. 15:20, 23 [c] Luke 2:32 **26:24** [a] [1 Cor. 1:23; 2:13, 14; 4:10] **26:26** [a] Acts 26:3 **26:29** [a] 1 Cor. 7:7 **26:31** [a] Acts 23:9, 29; 25:25 **26:32** [a] Acts 28:18 [b] Acts 25:11 **27:1** [a] Acts 25:12, 25 **27:2** [a] Acts 19:29 **27:3** [a] Acts 24:23; 28:16 **27:6** [a] Acts 28:11 **27:7** [a] Titus 1:5, 12 **27:9** [a] Lev. 16:29–31; 23:27–29 **27:14** [1] NU-Text reads *Euraquilon.* **27:16** [1] NU-Text reads *Cauda.* **27:17** [1] M-Text reads *Syrtes.* **27:19** [a] Jon. 1:5 **27:23** [a] Acts 18:9; 23:11 [b] Dan. 6:16 **27:25** [a] Rom. 4:20, 21 **27:26** [a] Acts 28:1

27Now when the fourteenth night had
come, as we were driven up and down in
the Adriatic *Sea,* about midnight the sailors
sensed that they were drawing near some
land. 28And they took soundings and found
it to be twenty fathoms; and when they had
gone a little farther, they took soundings
again and found *it* to be fifteen fathoms.
29Then, fearing lest we should run aground
on the rocks, they dropped four anchors
from the stern, and prayed for day to come.
30And as the sailors were seeking to escape
from the ship, when they had let down the
skiff into the sea, under pretense of putting
out anchors from the prow, 31Paul said to the
centurion and the soldiers, "Unless these
men stay in the ship, you cannot be saved."
32Then the soldiers cut away the ropes of the
skiff and let it fall off.

33And as day was about to dawn, Paul implored *them* all to take food, saying, "Today
is the fourteenth day you have waited and
continued without food, and eaten nothing.
34Therefore I urge you to take nourishment,
for this is for your survival, [a]since not a hair
will fall from the head of any of you." 35And
when he had said these things, he took bread
and [a]gave thanks to God in the presence of
them all; and when he had broken *it* he began to eat. 36Then they were all encouraged,
and also took food themselves. 37And in all
we were two hundred and seventy-six [a]per-
sons on the ship. 38So when they had eaten
enough, they lightened the ship and threw
out the wheat into the sea.

Shipwrecked on Malta

39When it was day, they did not recognize
the land; but they observed a bay with a beach,
onto which they planned to run the ship if
possible. 40And they let go the anchors and
left *them* in the sea, meanwhile loosing the
rudder ropes; and they hoisted the mainsail
to the wind and made for shore. 41But striking
a place where two seas met, [a]they ran the
ship aground; and the prow stuck fast and
remained immovable, but the stern was being broken up by the violence of the waves.

42And the soldiers' plan was to kill the
prisoners, lest any of them should swim away
and escape. 43But the centurion, wanting to
save Paul, kept them from *their* purpose,
and commanded that those who could swim
should jump *overboard* first and get to land,
44and the rest, some on boards and some on
parts of the ship. And so it was [a]that they all
escaped safely to land.

Paul's Ministry on Malta

28 Now when they had escaped, they then
found out that [a]the island was called
Malta. 2And the [a]natives showed us unusual
kindness; for they kindled a fire and made
us all welcome, because of the rain that was
falling and because of the cold. 3But when
Paul had gathered a bundle of sticks and laid
them on the fire, a viper came out because of
the heat, and fastened on his hand. 4So when
the natives saw the creature hanging from
his hand, they said to one another, "No doubt
this man is a murderer, whom, though he has
escaped the sea, yet justice does not allow
to live." 5But he shook off the creature into
the fire and [a]suffered no harm. 6However,
they were expecting that he would swell up
or suddenly fall down dead. But after they
had looked for a long time and saw no harm
come to him, they changed their minds and
[a]said that he was a god.

7In that region there was an estate of the
leading citizen of the island, whose name was
Publius, who received us and entertained
us courteously for three days. 8And it happened that the father of Publius lay sick of a
fever and dysentery. Paul went in to him and
[a]prayed, and [b]he laid his hands on him and
healed him. 9So when this was done, the rest
of those on the island who had diseases also
came and were healed. 10They also honored
us in many [a]ways; and when we departed,
they provided such things as were [b]necessary.

Arrival at Rome

11After three months we sailed in [a]an Alexandrian ship whose figurehead was the
Twin Brothers, which had wintered at the
island. 12And landing at Syracuse, we stayed
three days. 13From there we circled round
and reached Rhegium. And after one day the
south wind blew; and the next day we came
to Puteoli, 14where we found [a]brethren, and
were invited to stay with them seven days.
And so we went toward Rome. 15And from
there, when the brethren heard about us,
they came to meet us as far as Appii Forum
and Three Inns. When Paul saw them, he
thanked God and took courage.

16Now when we came to Rome, the centurion delivered the prisoners to the captain of
the guard; but [a]Paul was permitted to dwell
by himself with the soldier who guarded him.

Paul's Ministry at Rome

17And it came to pass after three days that
Paul called the leaders of the Jews together.

27:34 [a] [Matt. 10:30] **27:35** [a] [1 Tim. 4:3, 4] **27:37** [a] Acts 2:41; 7:14 **27:41** [a] 2 Cor. 11:25 **27:44** [a] Acts 27:22, 31
28:1 [a] Acts 27:26 **28:2** [a] Col. 3:11 **28:5** [a] Mark 16:18 **28:6** [a] Acts 12:22; 14:11 **28:8** [a] [James 5:14, 15] [b] Mark 5:23; 6:5;
7:32; 16:18 **28:10** [a] Matt. 15:6 [b] [Phil. 4:19] **28:11** [a] Acts 27:6 **28:14** [a] Rom. 1:8 **28:16** [a] Acts 23:11; 24:25; 27:3

So when they had come together, he said to
them: "Men *and* brethren, [a]though I have
done nothing against our people or the customs of our fathers, yet [b]I was delivered as
a prisoner from Jerusalem into the hands
of the Romans, 18who, [a]when they had examined me, wanted to let *me* go, because
there was no cause for putting me to death.
19But when the Jews[1] spoke against *it,* [a]I was
compelled to appeal to Caesar, not that I had
anything of which to accuse my nation. 20For
this reason therefore I have called for you, to
see *you* and speak with *you,* because [a]for the
hope of Israel I am bound with [b]this chain."
21Then they said to him, "We neither received letters from Judea concerning you,
nor have any of the brethren who came reported or spoken any evil of you. 22But we
desire to hear from you what you think; for
concerning this sect, we know that [a]it is spoken against everywhere."
23So when they had appointed him a day,
many came to him at *his* lodging, [a]to whom he
explained and solemnly testified of the kingdom of God, persuading them concerning
Jesus [b]from both the Law of Moses and the
Prophets, from morning till evening. 24And
[a]some were persuaded by the things which
were spoken, and some disbelieved. 25So
when they did not agree among themselves,
they departed after Paul had said one word:
"The Holy Spirit spoke rightly through Isaiah
the prophet to our[1] fathers, 26saying,

[a]'Go to this people and say:
"Hearing you will hear, and shall not
understand;
And seeing you will see, and not
perceive;
27 For the hearts of this people have
grown dull.
Their ears are hard of hearing,
And their eyes they have closed,
Lest they should see with *their* eyes and
hear with *their* ears,
Lest they should understand with *their*
hearts and turn,
So that I should heal them."'[1]

28"Therefore let it be known to you that
the salvation of God has been sent [a]to the
Gentiles, and they will hear it!" 29And when
he had said these words, the Jews departed
and had a great dispute among themselves.[1]
30Then Paul dwelt two whole years in his
own rented house, and received all who came
to him, 31[a]preaching the kingdom of God
and teaching the things which concern the
Lord Jesus Christ with all confidence, no one
forbidding him.

28:17 [a] Acts 23:29; 24:12, 13; 26:31 [b] Acts 21:33 **28:18** [a] Acts 22:24; 24:10; 25:8; 26:32 **28:19** [a] Acts 25:11, 21, 25 [1] That is, the ruling authorities **28:20** [a] Acts 26:6, 7 [b] Eph. 3:1; 4:1; 6:20 **28:22** [a] [1 Pet. 2:12; 3:16; 4:14, 16] **28:23** [a] Luke 24:27 [b] Acts 26:6, 22 **28:24** [a] Acts 14:4; 19:9 **28:25** [1] NU-Text reads *your.* **28:26** [a] Is. 6:9, 10 **28:27** [1] Isaiah 6:9, 10 **28:28** [a] Rom. 11:11 **28:29** [1] NU-Text omits this verse. **28:31** [a] Eph. 6:19

EQUIPPED WITH PEACE FOR TRYING TIMES

[Paul preached] the kingdom of God and [taught] the things which concern the Lord Jesus Christ with all confidence, no one forbidding him.

ACTS 28:31

The Book of Acts ends on an optimistic note. Though Paul had been taken into custody, charged with sedition, and at his own request sent to Rome to make his case before the emperor, nothing dampened his spirits. At every turn of events, Paul seized the opportunity to proclaim Jesus.

The evangelist Luke concluded his account noting that Paul lived in Rome "two whole years . . . preaching the kingdom" (vv. 30–31). I am greatly impressed by Paul's faith, his dependence on God's leading, and his ability to roll with the punches. Beginning with his dramatic conversion on the road to Damascus (Acts 9:2–7) and continuing through his arrival at Rome under house arrest, the apostle Paul maintained a steady course. He suffered beatings, assaults, imprisonment, hunger, cold, and was even shipwrecked three times!

The most important thing you can do today is get busy exactly where you are. Know that God can use you today, and let it increase your peace.

THE EPISTLE OF PAUL THE APOSTLE TO THE

ROMANS

AUTHOR

All critical schools agree on the Pauline authorship of this foundational book. The vocabulary, style, logic, and theological development are consistent with Paul's other epistles. He wrote Romans in AD 57, near the end of his third missionary journey, evidently during his three-month stay in Greece (Acts 20:3–6), more specifically, in Corinth. The church in Rome was well known (Rom. 1:8), and it had been established for several years by the time of this letter. The believers were probably numerous and evidently, they met in several places (16:1–16). The historian Tacitus even referred to the Christians who were persecuted there under Nero in AD 64 as an "immense multitude" as the gospel filled the gap left by the practically defunct polytheism of the Romans.

TIME

c. AD 57

KEY VERSE

Romans 1:16–17

THEME

Most scholars think that Paul probably wrote this letter from Corinth shortly before going to Jerusalem with the relief funds for the believers there. At this point in his life and ministry, his theology has been fully developed through years of study and interaction with people as he preached the gospel. Romans systematically explains what Christ did, why He did it, and what resulted. It speaks to what we are as humans and how God has interacted with us through Christ. It lays out God's plan for the world, clarifying what has happened and is still happening in biblical history. In this way, Paul forces us to deal with all the false versions of reality inspired by our fallen human nature as opposed to God's gracious, sustaining plan.

Paul mentions peace several times in his letter to the Christians of Rome. Believers are "justified by faith" in the Messiah, Jesus, Paul said, therefore "we have peace with God" (5:1). What a glorious truth! That peace had eluded Paul in the years before his conversion, but meeting the risen Jesus changed everything. In the Messiah he found joy. He found life. He found peace, and he found his purpose. From then on Paul traveled around the ancient world sharing the Messiah with any who would listen. And he knowingly wrote to the Roman Christians that, "to be carnally minded is death, but to be spiritually minded is life and peace" (8:6).

Greeting

1 Paul, a bondservant of Jesus Christ, [a]called
to be an apostle, [b]separated to the gospel
of God 2 [a]which He promised before [b]through
His prophets in the Holy Scriptures, 3 concerning His Son Jesus Christ our Lord, who
was [a]born of the seed of David according
to the flesh, 4 *and* [a]declared *to be* the Son
of God with power according [b]to the Spirit
of holiness, by the resurrection from the
dead. 5 Through Him [a]we have received grace
and apostleship for [b]obedience to the faith
among all nations [c]for His name, 6 among
whom you also are the called of Jesus Christ;

7 To all who are in Rome, beloved of God,
[a]called *to be* saints:

[b]Grace to you and peace from God our
Father and the Lord Jesus Christ.

Desire to Visit Rome

8 First, [a]I thank my God through Jesus
Christ for you all, that [b]your faith is spoken
of throughout the whole world. 9 For [a]God is
my witness, [b]whom I serve with my spirit in
the gospel of His Son, that [c]without ceasing I
make mention of you always in my prayers,
10 making request if, by some means, now
at last I may find a way in the will of God to
come to you. 11 For I long to see you, that [a]I
may impart to you some spiritual gift, so
that you may be established— 12 that is, that
I may be encouraged together with you by
[a]the mutual faith both of you and me.

13 Now I do not want you to be unaware,
brethren, that I often planned to come to you
(but [a]was hindered until now), that I might have
some [b]fruit among you also, just as among the
other Gentiles. 14 I am a debtor both to Greeks
and to barbarians, both to wise and to unwise.
15 So, as much as is in me, *I am* ready to preach
the gospel to you who are in Rome also.

The Just Live by Faith

16 For [a]I am not ashamed of the gospel of
Christ,[1] for [b]it is the power of God to salvation
for everyone who believes, [c]for the Jew first
and also for the Greek. 17 For [a]in it the righteousness of God is revealed from faith to faith;
as it is written, [b]"The just shall live by faith."[1]

God's Wrath on Unrighteousness

18 [a]For the wrath of God is revealed from
heaven against all ungodliness and [b]unrigh-
teousness of men, who suppress the truth in
unrighteousness, 19 because [a]what may be
known of God is manifest in them, for [b]God
has shown *it* to them. 20 For since the creation of the world [a]His invisible *attributes* are

1:1 [a] 1 Tim. 1:11 [b] Acts 9:15; 13:2 **1:2** [a] Acts 26:6 [b] Gal. 3:8 **1:3** [a] Gal. 4:4 **1:4** [a] Acts 9:20; 13:33 [b] [Heb. 9:14] **1:5** [a] Eph. 3:8 [b] Acts 6:7 [c] Acts 9:15 **1:7** [a] 1 Cor. 1:2, 24 [b] 1 Cor. 1:3 **1:8** [a] 1 Cor. 1:4 [b] Rom. 16:19 **1:9** [a] Rom. 9:1 [b] Acts 27:23 [c] 1 Thess. 3:10 **1:11** [a] Rom. 15:29 **1:12** [a] Titus 1:4 **1:13** [a] [1 Thess. 2:18] [b] Phil. 4:17 **1:16** [a] Ps. 40:9, 10 [b] 1 Cor. 1:18, 24 [c] Acts 3:26 [1] NU-Text omits *of Christ*. **1:17** [a] Rom. 3:21; 9:30 [b] Hab. 2:4 [1] Habakkuk 2:4 **1:18** [a] [Acts 17:30] [b] 2 Thess. 2:10 **1:19** [a] [Acts 14:17; 17:24] [b] [John 1:9] **1:20** [a] Ps. 19:1–6

THE SOURCE OF LASTING PEACE

To all who are in Rome, beloved of God, called to be saints: Grace to you and peace from God our Father and the Lord Jesus Christ.

ROMANS 1:7

You may remember the hippies and "peaceniks" of the 1960s and 1970s. "Peace, bro!" was the greeting, often with two fingers raised in the shape of a *V*. It seems so corny now. For some of those folks, peace came through mind-numbing and mind-altering drugs. That was the fashion then and for some, it still is. No true peace is found in drugs bought and sold in these days of "progressive" thinking. The peace of Christ is the real article.

In most of his letters, the apostle Paul greeted those he wrote to with the words "Grace to you and peace" from God the Father and/or the Lord Jesus Christ. Paul found peace—for the first time, true and lasting peace—in Jesus Christ when he encountered Him on the road to Damascus. After that, his greeting, whether in person or in his letters, was "Peace," and Paul knew what he was talking about. Drugs had nothing to do with it.

Have you ever sought peace in drugs, fads, other people, or ideas? How did that work out? Where do you find peace today?

CONFIDENCE IN A KING

I am not ashamed of the gospel of Christ, for it is the power of God to salvation for everyone.

ROMANS 1:16

In Paul's day—and in ours—shame was something to avoid. No one likes to be singled out, put on the spot, identified as having done or said something embarrassing, and subjected to public scrutiny. Haven't all of us had moments of that in our lives, moments that left us determined never to be humiliated that way again? Things like defeat, punishment, and mockery were and are awful things to experience. Did you notice—Paul experienced all of those things?

Yet Paul announced that he was "not ashamed." He even wrote to his protégé, Timothy, again that he was "not ashamed, for I know whom I have believed" (2 Tim. 1:12). What was Paul's secret? Confidence in the King! He knew in his deepest heart that his ministry was not a vain effort but a sublime testimony to God's love and power. His was a life of victory, not shame!

Do you need to put away shame and build your confidence in the Lord? Joy—and peace—will result.

clearly seen, being understood by the things
that are made, *even* His eternal power and
Godhead, so that they are without excuse,
21 because, although they knew God, they did
not glorify *Him* as God, nor were thankful, but
[a]became futile in their thoughts, and their
foolish hearts were darkened. 22 [a]Professing
to be wise, they became fools, 23 and changed
the glory of the [a]incorruptible [b]God into an
image made like corruptible man—and birds
and four-footed animals and creeping things.
24 [a]Therefore God also gave them up to
uncleanness, in the lusts of their hearts, [b]to
dishonor their bodies [c]among themselves,
25 who exchanged [a]the truth of God [b]for the lie,
and worshiped and served the creature rather
than the Creator, who is blessed forever. Amen.
26 For this reason God gave them up to [a]vile
passions. For even their women exchanged
the natural use for what is against nature.
27 Likewise also the men, leaving the natural
use of the woman, burned in their lust for one
another, men with men committing what is
shameful, and receiving in themselves the
penalty of their error which was due.
28 And even as they did not like to retain God
in *their* knowledge, God gave them over to a de-
based mind, to do those things [a]which are not
fitting; 29 being filled with all unrighteousness,
sexual immorality,[1] wickedness, covetousness,
maliciousness; full of envy, murder, strife,
deceit, evil-mindedness; *they are* whisperers,
30 backbiters, haters of God, violent, proud,
boasters, inventors of evil things, disobedient
to parents, 31 undiscerning, untrustworthy,
unloving, unforgiving,[1] unmerciful; 32 who,
[a]knowing the righteous judgment of God, that
those who practice such things [b]are deserving
of death, not only do the same but also [c]ap-
prove of those who practice them.

God's Righteous Judgment

2 Therefore you are [a]inexcusable, O man,
whoever you are who judge, [b]for in whatever you judge another you condemn yourself;
for you who judge practice the same things.
2 But we know that the judgment of God is
according to truth against those who practice
such things. 3 And do you think this, O man,
you who judge those practicing such things,
and doing the same, that you will escape the
judgment of God? 4 Or do you despise [a]the riches of His goodness, [b]forbearance, and [c]long-
suffering, [d]not knowing that the goodness of
God leads you to repentance? 5 But in accordance with your hardness and your impenitent
heart [a]you are treasuring up for yourself wrath
in the day of wrath and revelation of the righteous judgment of God, 6 who [a]"will render to
each one according to his deeds":[1] 7 eternal life
to those who by patient continuance in doing
good seek for glory, honor, and immortality;

1:21 [a] Jer. 2:5 **1:22** [a] Jer. 10:14 **1:23** [a] 1 Tim. 1:17; 6:15, 16 [b] Deut. 4:16–18 **1:24** [a] Eph. 4:18, 19 [b] 1 Cor. 6:18 [c] Lev. 18:22 **1:25** [a] 1 Thess. 1:9 [b] Is. 44:20 **1:26** [a] Lev. 18:22 **1:28** [a] Eph. 5:4 **1:29** [1] NU-Text omits *sexual immorality.* **1:31** [1] NU-Text omits *unforgiving.* **1:32** [a] [Rom. 2:2] [b] [Rom. 6:21] [c] Hos. 7:3 **2:1** [a] [Rom. 1:20] [b] [Matt. 7:1–5] **2:4** [a] [Eph. 1:7, 18; 2:7] [b] [Rom. 3:25] [c] Ex. 34:6 [d] Is. 30:18 **2:5** [a] [Deut. 32:34] **2:6** [a] Ps. 62:12; Prov. 24:12 [1] Psalm 62:12; Proverbs 24:12

8 but to those who are self-seeking and [a]do not obey the truth, but obey unrighteousness—indignation and wrath, 9 tribulation and anguish, on every soul of man who does evil, of the Jew [a]first and also of the Greek; 10 [a]but glory, honor, and peace to everyone who works what is good, to the Jew first and also to the Greek. 11 For [a]there is no partiality with God.

12 For as many as have sinned without law will also perish without law, and as many as have sinned in the law will be judged by the law 13 (for [a]not the hearers of the law *are* just in the sight of God, but the doers of the law will be justified; 14 for when Gentiles, who do not have the law, by nature do the things in the law, these, although not having the law, are a law to themselves, 15 who show the [a]work of the law written in their hearts, their [b]conscience also bearing witness, and between themselves *their* thoughts accusing or else excusing *them*) 16 [a]in the day when God will judge the secrets of men [b]by Jesus Christ, [c]according to my gospel.

The Jews Guilty as the Gentiles

17 Indeed[1] [a]you are called a Jew, and [b]rest on the law, [c]and make your boast in God, 18 and [a]know *His* will, and [b]approve the things that are excellent, being instructed out of the law, 19 and [a]are confident that you yourself are a guide to the blind, a light to those who are in darkness, 20 an instructor of the foolish, a teacher of babes, [a]having the form of knowledge and truth in the law. 21 [a]You, therefore, who teach another, do you not teach yourself? You who preach that a man should not steal, do you steal? 22 You who say, "Do not commit adultery," do you commit adultery? You who abhor idols, [a]do you rob temples? 23 You who [a]make your boast in the law, do you dishonor God through breaking the law? 24 For [a]"the name of God is [b]blasphemed among the Gentiles because of you,"[1] as it is written.

Circumcision of No Avail

25 [a]For circumcision is indeed profitable if you keep the law; but if you are a breaker of the law, your circumcision has become uncircumcision. 26 Therefore, [a]if an uncircumcised man keeps the righteous requirements of the law, will not his uncircumcision be counted as circumcision? 27 And will not the physically uncircumcised, if he fulfills the law, [a]judge you who, *even* with *your* written *code* and circumcision, *are* a transgressor of the law? 28 For [a]he is not a Jew who *is one* outwardly, nor *is* circumcision that which *is* outward in the flesh; 29 but *he is* a Jew [a]who *is one* inwardly; and [b]circumcision *is that* of the heart, [c]in the Spirit, not in the letter; [d]whose praise *is* not from men but from God.

2:8 [a] [2 Thess. 1:8] **2:9** [a] 1 Pet. 4:17 **2:10** [a] [1 Pet. 1:7] **2:11** [a] Deut. 10:17 **2:13** [a] [James 1:22, 25] **2:15** [a] 1 Cor. 5:1 [b] Acts 24:25 **2:16** [a] [Matt. 25:31] [b] Acts 10:42; 17:31 [c] 1 Tim. 1:11 **2:17** [a] John 8:33 [b] Mic. 3:11 [c] Is. 48:1, 2 [1] NU-Text reads *But if.* **2:18** [a] Deut. 4:8 [b] Phil. 1:10 **2:19** [a] Matt. 15:14 **2:20** [a] [2 Tim. 3:5] **2:21** [a] Matt. 23:3 **2:22** [a] Mal. 3:8 **2:23** [a] Rom. 2:17; 9:4 **2:24** [a] Ezek. 16:27 [b] Is. 52:5; Ezek. 36:22 [1] Isaiah 52:5; Ezekiel 36:22 **2:25** [a] [Gal. 5:3] **2:26** [a] [Acts 10:34] **2:27** [a] Matt. 12:41 **2:28** [a] [Gal. 6:15] **2:29** [a] [1 Pet. 3:4] [b] Phil. 3:3 [c] Deut. 30:6 [d] [1 Cor. 4:5]

BECOMING WHOLE

Glory, honor, and peace to everyone who works what is good, to the Jew first and also to the Greek.

ROMANS 2:10

"No good deed goes unpunished," says the cynic. How many times have you heard that? In our fallen world there is, alas, some truth to it, but in God's world it is utterly false.

The apostle affirmed in his letter to the Christians of Rome that "everyone who works what is good" will receive "peace." This is the second time the word *peace* appears in Paul's letter. It will appear ten more times. The word occurs often because it is an integral part of the Good News. Paul warned that the wicked, including those who disobeyed the truth, could expect God's wrath, while the righteous who obeyed the truth could expect eternal life along with "glory, honor, and peace." Good deeds will in fact be rewarded, not punished.

Does it strike you as odd that peace would be coupled with words like *glory* and *honor*? The first time I read this verse, that question crossed my mind. Then it occurred to me: peace in this context means wholeness and completion, not passive tranquility. God will reward the righteous with a life that lacks nothing. How does this fact affect your mood today?

God's Judgment Defended

3 What advantage then has the Jew, or what
is the profit of circumcision? 2 Much in
every way! Chiefly because [a]to them were
committed the oracles of God. 3 For what if
[a]some did not believe? [b]Will their unbelief
make the faithfulness of God without effect?
4 [a]Certainly not! Indeed, let [b]God be true but
[c]every man a liar. As it is written:

[d]"That You may be justified in Your
words,
And may overcome when You are
judged."[1]

5 But if our unrighteousness demonstrates
the righteousness of God, what shall we say?
Is God unjust who inflicts wrath? [a](I speak as
a man.) 6 Certainly not! For then [a]how will
God judge the world?

7 For if the truth of God has increased
through my lie to His glory, why am I also
still judged as a sinner? 8 And *why* not *say*,
[a]"Let us do evil that good may come"?—as we
are slanderously reported and as some affirm
that we say. Their condemnation is just.

All Have Sinned

9 What then? Are we better *than they?* Not
at all. For we have previously charged both
Jews and Greeks that [a]they are all under sin.
10 As it is written:

[a]"There is none righteous, no, not one;
11 There is none who understands;
There is none who seeks after God.
12 They have all turned aside;
They have together become
unprofitable;
There is none who does good, no, not
one."[1]
13 "Their[a] throat *is* an open tomb;
With their tongues they have practiced
deceit";[1]
[b]"The poison of asps *is* under their lips";[2]
14 "Whose[a] mouth *is* full of cursing and
bitterness."[1]
15 "Their[a] feet *are* swift to shed blood;
16 Destruction and misery *are* in their
ways;
17 And the way of peace they have not
known."[1]
18 "There[a] is no fear of God before their
eyes."[1]

19 Now we know that whatever [a]the law
says, it says to those who are under the law,
that [b]every mouth may be stopped, and all
the world may become guilty before God.
20 Therefore [a]by the deeds of the law no flesh
will be justified in His sight, for by the law *is*
the knowledge of sin.

3:2 [a] Deut. 4:5–8 **3:3** [a] Heb. 4:2 [b] [2 Tim. 2:13] **3:4** [a] Job 40:8 [b] [John 3:33] [c] Ps. 62:9 [d] Ps. 51:4 [1] Psalm 51:4 **3:5** [a] Gal. 3:15 **3:6** [a] [Gen. 18:25] **3:8** [a] Rom. 5:20 **3:9** [a] Gal. 3:22 **3:10** [a] Ps. 14:1–3; 53:1–3; Eccl. 7:20 **3:12** [1] Psalms 14:1–3; 53:1–3; Ecclesiastes 7:20 **3:13** [a] Ps. 5:9 [b] Ps. 140:3 [1] Psalm 5:9 [2] Psalm 140:3 **3:14** [a] Ps. 10:7 [1] Psalm 10:7 **3:15** [a] Prov. 1:16; Is. 59:7, 8 **3:17** [1] Isaiah 59:7, 8 **3:18** [a] Ps. 36:1 [1] Psalm 36:1 **3:19** [a] John 10:34 [b] Job 5:16 **3:20** [a] [Gal. 2:16]

THE ONLY WAY TO PEACE

And the way of peace they have not known.

ROMANS 3:17

In verses 10–18 Paul quoted hard-hitting passages from Isaiah and the Psalms that declared all humankind sinful and in need of salvation. He hammered away at this because not all people see themselves as sinful, including fellow Jews, who believed they were righteous and didn't need the forgiveness that God's Messiah brought. So Paul cited one Scripture after another to show that, in reality, every human is indeed sinful.

Here in verses 16–17 Paul cited Isaiah 59:7–8, in which poetic language says that "wasting and destruction" are in the paths of the wicked and that the "way of peace" is something the people have not known. Paul's point is that peace inevitably eludes the wicked. Through conniving and deceit, they may acquire wealth. Polite society may even hold them in high esteem, but they will never find peace.

Peace comes through repentance and the forgiveness that Jesus Christ offers. Have you received this peace? Have you shared it recently?

God's Righteousness Through Faith

21 But now [a]the righteousness of God apart
from the law is revealed, [b]being witnessed
by the Law [c]and the Prophets, 22 even the
righteousness of God, through faith in Jesus
Christ, to all and on all[1] who believe. For [a]there
is no difference; 23 for [a]all have sinned and
fall short of the glory of God, 24 being justified
freely [a]by His grace [b]through the redemption
that is in Christ Jesus, 25 whom God set forth
[a]*as* a propitiation [b]by His blood, through faith,
to demonstrate His righteousness, because in
His forbearance God had passed over [c]the sins
that were previously committed, 26 to demonstrate at the present time His righteousness, that He might be just and the justifier
of the one who has faith in Jesus.

Boasting Excluded

27 [a]Where *is* boasting then? It is excluded.
By what law? Of works? No, but by the law of
faith. 28 Therefore we conclude [a]that a man is
justified by faith apart from the deeds of the
law. 29 Or *is He* the God of the Jews only? *Is He*
not also the God of the Gentiles? Yes, of the
Gentiles also, 30 since [a]*there is* one God who
will justify the circumcised by faith and the
uncircumcised through faith. 31 Do we then
make void the law through faith? Certainly
not! On the contrary, we establish the law.

Abraham Justified by Faith

4 What then shall we say that [a]Abraham our
[b]father has found according to the flesh?[1]
2 For if Abraham was [a]justified by works, he has
something to boast about, but not before God.
3 For what does the Scripture say? [a]"Abraham
believed God, and it was accounted to him for
righteousness."[1] 4 Now [a]to him who works, the
wages are not counted as grace but as debt.

David Celebrates the Same Truth

5 But to him who [a]does not work but believes
on Him who justifies [b]the ungodly, his faith is
accounted for righteousness, 6 just as David also
[a]describes the blessedness of the man to whom
God imputes righteousness apart from works:

7 "Blessed[a] *are those* whose lawless deeds
are forgiven,
And whose sins are covered;
8 Blessed *is the* man to whom the LORD
shall not impute sin."[1]

Abraham Justified Before Circumcision

9 *Does* this blessedness then *come* upon the
circumcised *only,* or upon the uncircumcised
also? For we say that faith was accounted to
Abraham for righteousness. 10 How then was it
accounted? While he was circumcised, or uncircumcised? Not while circumcised, but while

3:21 [a] Acts 15:11 [b] John 5:46 [c] 1 Pet. 1:10 **3:22** [a] [Col. 3:11] [1] NU-Text omits *and on all.* **3:23** [a] Gal. 3:22 **3:24** [a] [Eph. 2:8] [b] [Heb. 9:12, 15] **3:25** [a] Lev. 16:15 [b] Col. 1:20 [c] Acts 14:16; 17:30 **3:27** [a] [1 Cor. 1:29] **3:28** [a] Gal. 2:16 **3:30** [a] [Gal. 3:8, 20] **4:1** [a] Is. 51:2 [b] James 2:21 [1] Or *Abraham our (fore)father according to the flesh has found?* **4:2** [a] Rom. 3:20, 27 **4:3** [a] Gen. 15:6 [1] Genesis 15:6 **4:4** [a] Rom. 11:6 **4:5** [a] [Eph. 2:8, 9] [b] Josh. 24:2 **4:6** [a] Ps. 32:1, 2 **4:7** [a] Ps. 32:1, 2 **4:8** [1] Psalm 32:1, 2

FORGIVEN AND FREE

Blessed is the man to whom the LORD shall not impute sin.

ROMANS 4:8

Would people describe you as a happy soul? Is your heart light or weighted with cares? Does happiness seem elusive—even impossible? Do you ever hear the words, "You stress me out"?

Those who possess God's peace are rarely unhappy. Consider the apostle Paul. Prior to meeting Christ for himself, he was an angry man who sent Christians to their deaths. Once he'd embraced the risen Christ, Paul knew that he was forgiven for all his crimes so he said, "Blessed is the man to whom the LORD shall not impute sin" (v. 8). Having experienced the peace, the *shalom* of God, Paul discovered what true happiness was—a state of genuine, meaningful delight. Paul in fact exhorted the church to follow his example, saying, "Rejoice in the Lord always. Again I will say, rejoice!" (Phil. 4:4).

If you haven't found the true happiness that Christ offers, I invite you to place your faith in Him. Pray this prayer: "Lord Jesus, I trust in You as my Savior and Lord and ask You to forgive me for my sins. I know that I am forgiven because You paid for them on the cross and rose from the grave. Thank You for the peace I now have with God through You, Lord Jesus. Amen."

uncircumcised. 11 And [a]he received the sign of
circumcision, a seal of the righteousness of the
faith which *he had while still* uncircumcised,
that [b]he might be the father of all those who
believe, though they are uncircumcised, that
righteousness might be imputed to them also,
12 and the father of circumcision to those who
not only *are* of the circumcision, but who also
walk in the steps of the faith which our father
[a]Abraham *had while still* uncircumcised.

The Promise Granted Through Faith

13 For the promise that he would be the
[a]heir of the world *was* not to Abraham or to
his seed through the law, but through the
righteousness of faith. 14 For [a]if those who
are of the law *are* heirs, faith is made void
and the promise made of no effect, 15 because
[a]the law brings about wrath; for where there
is no law *there is* no transgression.
16 Therefore *it is* of faith that *it might be* [a]ac-
cording to grace, [b]so that the promise might
be sure to all the seed, not only to those who
are of the law, but also to those who are of the
faith of Abraham, [c]who is the father of us all
17 (as it is written, [a]"I have made you a father of
many nations"[1]) in the presence of Him whom
he believed—God, [b]who gives life to the dead
and calls those [c]things which do not exist as
though they did; 18 who, contrary to hope, in
hope believed, so that he became the father of
many nations, according to what was spoken,
[a]"So shall your descendants be."[1] 19 And not
being weak in faith, [a]he did not consider his
own body, already dead (since he was about a
hundred years old), [b]and the deadness of Sarah's womb. 20 He did not waver at the promise
of God through unbelief, but was strengthened
in faith, giving glory to God, 21 and being fully
convinced that what He had promised [a]He was
also able to perform. 22 And therefore [a]"it was
accounted to him for righteousness."[1]
23 Now [a]it was not written for his sake alone
that it was imputed to him, 24 but also for us.
It shall be imputed to us who believe [a]in Him
who raised up Jesus our Lord from the dead,
25 [a]who was delivered up because of our offenses, and [b]was raised because of our justification.

Faith Triumphs in Trouble

5 Therefore, [a]having been justified by faith,
we have[1] [b]peace with God through our
Lord Jesus Christ, 2 [a]through whom also we
have access by faith into this grace [b]in which

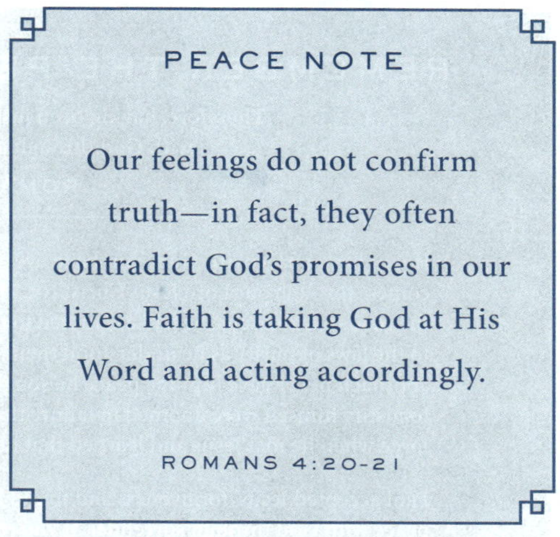

we stand, and [c]rejoice in hope of the glory of
God. 3 And not only *that,* but [a]we also glory
in tribulations, [b]knowing that tribulation
produces perseverance; 4 [a]and perseverance,
character; and character, hope. 5 [a]Now hope
does not disappoint, [b]because the love of
God has been poured out in our hearts by
the Holy Spirit who was given to us.

Christ in Our Place

6 For when we were still without strength,
in due time [a]Christ died for the ungodly. 7 For
scarcely for a righteous man will one die; yet
perhaps for a good man someone would even
dare to die. 8 But [a]God demonstrates His own
love toward us, in that while we were still

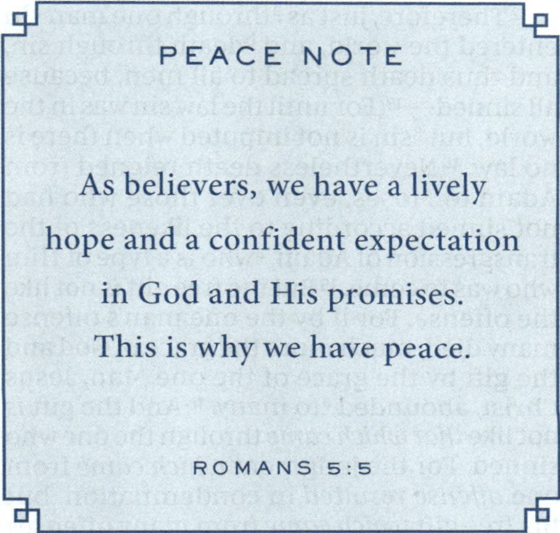

4:11 [a] Gen. 17:10 [b] Luke 19:9 **4:12** [a] Rom. 4:18–22 **4:13** [a] Gen. 17:4–6; 22:17 **4:14** [a] Gal. 3:18 **4:15** [a] Rom. 3:20 **4:16** [a] [Rom. 3:24] [b] [Gal. 3:22] [c] Is. 51:2 **4:17** [a] Gen. 17:5 [b] [Rom. 8:11] [c] Rom. 9:26 [1] Genesis 17:5 **4:18** [a] Gen. 15:5 [1] Genesis 15:5 **4:19** [a] Gen. 17:17 [b] Heb. 11:11 **4:21** [a] [Heb. 11:19] **4:22** [a] Gen. 15:6 [1] Genesis 15:6 **4:23** [a] Rom. 15:4 **4:24** [a] Acts 2:24 **4:25** [a] Is. 53:4, 5 [b] [1 Cor. 15:17] **5:1** [a] Is. 32:17 [b] [Eph. 2:14] [1] Another ancient reading is, *let us have peace.* **5:2** [a] [Eph. 2:18; 3:12] [b] 1 Cor. 15:1 [c] Heb. 3:6 **5:3** [a] Matt. 5:11, 12 [b] James 1:3 **5:4** [a] [James 1:12] **5:5** [a] Phil. 1:20 [b] 2 Cor. 1:22 **5:6** [a] [Rom. 4:25; 5:8; 8:32] **5:8** [a] [John 3:16; 15:13]

REMEMBER THE PEACE GIVEN TO YOU

Therefore, having been justified by faith, we have peace with God through our Lord Jesus Christ.

ROMANS 5:1

If you have peace with God, you have everything. Paul rightly said that peace with God comes "through our Lord Jesus Christ" (v. 1). Before his encounter with the risen Christ on the road to Damascus, he had attempted to find this peace through scrupulous attendance to the laws of purity as he understood them. I have no doubt that Paul was sincere. But his approach never gave him the peace he sought. It wasn't until he realized that his attempts to justify himself were doomed to failure that his eyes were opened. This happened in full force when he met Jesus and learned that he had been going about it all wrong.

Paul accepted Jesus' forgiveness and found lasting peace. You can too. Take a step toward peace with God through surrender. If you're a Christian already, assess what areas of your life are not fully under God's control. If you are not yet a Christian, today is the day to find eternal peace with God through Christ's sacrifice on the cross. (For more information, please see the article "How to Find God and His Peace.")

sinners, Christ died for us. 9 Much more then,
having now been justified [a]by His blood, we
shall be saved [b]from wrath through Him.
10 For [a]if when we were enemies [b]we were
reconciled to God through the death of His
Son, much more, having been reconciled,
we shall be saved [c]by His life. 11 And not only
that, but we also [a]rejoice in God through our
Lord Jesus Christ, through whom we have
now received the reconciliation.

Death in Adam, Life in Christ

12 Therefore, just as [a]through one man sin
entered the world, and [b]death through sin,
and thus death spread to all men, because
all sinned— 13 (For until the law sin was in the
world, but [a]sin is not imputed when there is
no law. 14 Nevertheless death reigned from
Adam to Moses, even over those who had
not sinned according to the likeness of the
transgression of Adam, [a]who is a type of Him
who was to come. 15 But the free gift *is* not like
the offense. For if by the one man's offense
many died, much more the grace of God and
the gift by the grace of the one Man, Jesus
Christ, abounded [a]to many. 16 And the gift *is*
not like *that which came* through the one who
sinned. For the judgment *which came* from
one *offense resulted* in condemnation, but
the free gift *which came* from many offenses
resulted in justification. 17 For if by the one
man's offense death reigned through the one,
much more those who receive abundance of
grace and of the gift of righteousness will
reign in life through the One, Jesus Christ.)
18 Therefore, as through one man's offense
judgment came to all men, resulting in condemnation, even so through [a]one Man's
righteous act *the free gift came* [b]to all men,
resulting in justification of life. 19 For as by
one man's disobedience many were made
sinners, so also by [a]one Man's obedience
many will be made righteous.
20 Moreover [a]the law entered that the offense might abound. But where sin abounded, grace [b]abounded much more, 21 so that
as sin reigned in death, even so grace might
reign through righteousness to eternal life
through Jesus Christ our Lord.

Dead to Sin, Alive to God

6 What shall we say then? [a]Shall we continue in sin that grace may abound? 2 Certainly not! How shall we who [a]died to sin live
any longer in it? 3 Or do you not know that [a]as
many of us as were baptized into Christ Jesus
[b]were baptized into His death? 4 Therefore we
were [a]buried with Him through baptism into
death, that [b]just as Christ was raised from the
dead by [c]the glory of the Father, [d]even so we
also should walk in newness of life.
5 [a]For if we have been united together in
the likeness of His death, certainly we also
shall be *in the likeness* of *His* resurrection,

5:9 [a] Eph. 2:13 [b] 1 Thess. 1:10 **5:10** [a] [Rom. 8:32] [b] 2 Cor. 5:18 [c] John 14:19 **5:11** [a] [Gal. 4:9] **5:12** [a] [1 Cor. 15:21] [b] Gen. 2:17 **5:13** [a] 1 John 3:4 **5:14** [a] [1 Cor. 15:21, 22] **5:15** [a] [Is. 53:11] **5:18** [a] [1 Cor. 15:21, 45] [b] [John 12:32] **5:19** [a] [Phil. 2:8] **5:20** [a] John 15:22 [b] 1 Tim. 1:14 **6:1** [a] Rom. 3:8; 6:15 **6:2** [a] [Gal. 2:19] **6:3** [a] [Gal. 3:27] [b] [1 Cor. 15:29] **6:4** [a] Col. 2:12 [b] 1 Cor. 6:14 [c] John 2:11 [d] [Gal. 6:15] **6:5** [a] Phil. 3:10

6 knowing this, that [a]our old man was crucified with *Him,* that [b]the body of sin might be done away with, that we should no longer be slaves of sin. 7 For [a]he who has died has been freed from sin. 8 Now [a]if we died with Christ, we believe that we shall also live with Him, 9 knowing that [a]Christ, having been raised from the dead, dies no more. Death no longer has dominion over Him. 10 For *the death* that He died, [a]He died to sin once for all; but *the life* that He lives, [b]He lives to God. 11 Likewise you also, reckon yourselves to be [a]dead indeed to sin, but [b]alive to God in Christ Jesus our Lord.

12 [a]Therefore do not let sin reign in your mortal body, that you should obey it in its lusts. 13 And do not present your [a]members *as* instruments of unrighteousness to sin, but [b]present yourselves to God as being alive from the dead, and your members *as* instruments of righteousness to God. 14 For [a]sin shall not have dominion over you, for you are not under law but under grace.

From Slaves of Sin to Slaves of God

15 What then? Shall we sin [a]because we are not under law but under grace? Certainly not! 16 Do you not know that [a]to whom you present yourselves slaves to obey, you are that one's slaves whom you obey, whether of sin *leading* to death, or of obedience *leading* to righteousness? 17 But God be thanked that *though* you were slaves of sin, yet you obeyed from the heart [a]that form of doctrine to which you were delivered. 18 And [a]having been set free from sin, you became slaves of righteousness. 19 I speak in human *terms* because of the weakness of your flesh. For just as you presented your members *as* slaves of uncleanness, and of lawlessness *leading* to *more* lawlessness, so now present your members *as* slaves *of* righteousness for holiness.

20 For when you were [a]slaves of sin, you were free in regard to righteousness. 21 [a]What fruit did you have then in the things of which you are now ashamed? For [b]the end of those things *is* death. 22 But now [a]having been set free from sin, and having become slaves of God, you have your fruit to holiness, and the end, everlasting life. 23 For [a]the wages of sin *is* death, but [b]the gift of God *is* eternal life in Christ Jesus our Lord.

Freed from the Law

7 Or do you not know, brethren (for I speak to those who know the law), that the law has dominion over a man as long as he lives? 2 For [a]the woman who has a husband is bound by the law to *her* husband as long as he lives. But if the husband dies, she is released from the law of *her* husband. 3 So then [a]if, while *her* husband lives, she marries another man, she will be called an adulteress; but if her husband dies, she is free from that law, so that she is no adulteress, though she has married another man. 4 Therefore, my brethren, you also have become [a]dead to the law through the body of Christ, that you may be married to another—to Him who was raised from the dead, that we should [b]bear fruit to God. 5 For when we were in the flesh, the sinful passions which were aroused by the law [a]were at work in our members [b]to bear fruit to death. 6 But now we have been delivered from the law, having died to what we were held by, so that we should serve [a]in the newness of the Spirit and not *in* the oldness of the letter.

Sin's Advantage in the Law

7 What shall we say then? *Is* the law sin? Certainly not! On the contrary, [a]I would not have known sin except through the law. For I would not have known covetousness unless the law had said, [b]"You shall not covet."[1] 8 But [a]sin, taking opportunity by the commandment, produced in me all *manner of evil* desire. For [b]apart from the law sin *was* dead. 9 I was alive once without the law, but when the commandment came, sin revived and I died. 10 And the commandment, [a]which *was* to *bring* life, I found to *bring* death. 11 For sin, taking occasion by the commandment, deceived me, and by it killed *me.* 12 Therefore [a]the law *is* holy, and the commandment holy and just and good.

Law Cannot Save from Sin

13 Has then what is good become death to me? Certainly not! But sin, that it might appear sin, was producing death in me through what is good, so that sin through the commandment might become exceedingly sinful. 14 For we know that the law is spiritual, but I am carnal, [a]sold under sin. 15 For what I am doing, I do not understand. [a]For what I will to do, that I do not practice; but what I hate, that I do. 16 If, then, I do what I will not to do, I agree with the law

6:6 [a] Gal. 2:20; 5:24; 6:14 [b] Col. 2:11 **6:7** [a] 1 Pet. 4:1 **6:8** [a] 2 Tim. 2:11 **6:9** [a] Rev. 1:18 **6:10** [a] Heb. 9:27 [b] Luke 20:38 **6:11** [a] [Rom. 6:2; 7:4, 6] [b] [Gal. 2:19] **6:12** [a] Ps. 19:13 **6:13** [a] Col. 3:5 [b] 1 Pet. 2:24; 4:2 **6:14** [a] [Gal. 5:18] **6:15** [a] 1 Cor. 9:21 **6:16** [a] 2 Pet. 2:19 **6:17** [a] 2 Tim. 1:13 **6:18** [a] John 8:32 **6:20** [a] John 8:34 **6:21** [a] Rom. 7:5 [b] Rom. 1:32 **6:22** [a] Rom. 6:18; 8:2 **6:23** [a] Gen. 2:17 [b] 1 Pet. 1:4 **7:2** [a] 1 Cor. 7:39 **7:3** [a] [Matt. 5:32] **7:4** [a] Gal. 2:19; 5:18 [b] Gal. 5:22 **7:5** [a] Rom. 6:13 [b] James 1:15 **7:6** [a] Rom. 2:29 **7:7** [a] Rom. 3:20 [b] Ex. 20:17; Deut. 5:21; Acts 20:33 [1] Exodus 20:17; Deuteronomy 5:21 **7:8** [a] Rom. 4:15 [b] 1 Cor. 15:56 **7:10** [a] Lev. 18:5 **7:12** [a] Ps. 19:8 **7:14** [a] 2 Kin. 17:17 **7:15** [a] [Gal. 5:17]

that *it is* good. 17 But now, *it is* no longer I who
do it, but sin that dwells in me. 18 For I know
that [a]in me (that is, in my flesh) nothing good
dwells; for to will is present with me, but *how*
to perform what is good I do not find. 19 For
the good that I will *to do,* I do not do; but the
evil I will not *to do,* that I practice. 20 Now if I
do what I will not *to do,* it is no longer I who
do it, but sin that dwells in me.

21 I find then a law, that evil is present with
me, the one who wills to do good. 22 For I
[a]delight in the law of God according to [b]the
inward man. 23 But [a]I see another law in
[b]my members, warring against the law of
my mind, and bringing me into captivity
to the law of sin which is in my members.
24 O wretched man that I am! Who will deliver me [a]from this body of death? 25 [a]I thank
God—through Jesus Christ our Lord!

So then, with the mind I myself serve the
law of God, but with the flesh the law of sin.

Free from Indwelling Sin

8 *There is* therefore now no condemnation
to those who are in Christ Jesus,[1] [a]who do
not walk according to the flesh, but according
to the Spirit. 2 For [a]the law of [b]the Spirit of
life in Christ Jesus has made me free from
[c]the law of sin and death. 3 For [a]what the law
could not do in that it was weak through the
flesh, [b]God *did* by sending His own Son in
the likeness of sinful flesh, on account of
sin: He condemned sin in the flesh, 4 that
the righteous requirement of the law might
be fulfilled in us who [a]do not walk according to the flesh but according to the Spirit.
5 For [a]those who live according to the flesh
set their minds on the things of the flesh,
but those *who live* according to the Spirit,
[b]the things of the Spirit. 6 For [a]to be carnally
minded *is* death, but to be spiritually minded
is life and peace. 7 Because [a]the carnal mind
is enmity against God; for it is not subject to
the law of God, [b]nor indeed can be. 8 So then,
those who are in the flesh cannot please God.

9 But you are not in the flesh but in the
Spirit, if indeed the Spirit of God dwells in
you. Now if anyone does not have the Spirit
of Christ, he is not His. 10 And if Christ *is* in
you, the body *is* dead because of sin, but the
Spirit *is* life because of righteousness. 11 But
if the Spirit of [a]Him who raised Jesus from
the dead dwells in you, [b]He who raised Christ
from the dead will also give life to your mortal
bodies through His Spirit who dwells in you.

Sonship Through the Spirit

12 [a]Therefore, brethren, we are debtors—not
to the flesh, to live according to the flesh. 13 For
[a]if you live according to the flesh you will die;
but if by the Spirit you [b]put to death the deeds
of the body, you will live. 14 For [a]as many as are
led by the Spirit of God, these are sons of God.
15 For [a]you did not receive the spirit of bondage
again [b]to fear, but you received the [c]Spirit of
adoption by whom we cry out, [d]"Abba, Father."

7:18 [a] [Gen. 6:5; 8:21] **7:22** [a] Ps. 1:2 [b] [2 Cor. 4:16] **7:23** [a] [Gal. 5:17] [b] Rom. 6:13, 19 **7:24** [a] [1 Cor. 15:51, 52] **7:25** [a] 1 Cor. 15:57 **8:1** [a] Gal. 5:16 [1] NU-Text omits the rest of this verse. **8:2** [a] Rom. 6:18, 22 [b] [1 Cor. 15:45] [c] Rom. 7:24, 25 **8:3** [a] Acts 13:39 [b] [2 Cor. 5:21] **8:4** [a] Gal. 5:16, 25 **8:5** [a] John 3:6 [b] [Gal. 5:22–25] **8:6** [a] Gal. 6:8 **8:7** [a] James 4:4 [b] 1 Cor. 2:14 **8:11** [a] Acts 2:24 [b] 1 Cor. 6:14 **8:12** [a] [Rom. 6:7, 14] **8:13** [a] Gal. 6:8 [b] Eph. 4:22 **8:14** [a] [Gal. 5:18] **8:15** [a] Heb. 2:15 [b] 2 Tim. 1:7 [c] [Is. 56:5] [d] Mark 14:36

FIXING YOUR MIND ON PEACE

For to be carnally minded is death, but to be spiritually minded is life and peace.

ROMANS 8:6

"You are what you eat," we hear from time to time. Obviously a healthy diet is important. You also are what you think. How you think affects your work, your mood, your relationships. "You are what you eat" holds true when it comes to spirituality, which is what Paul was talking about in chapter 8. "To be carnally minded," Paul said, "is death" (v. 6). The Greek text actually says, "The mind of the flesh is death." In the Bible and in Paul's theological lexicon, flesh is the antithesis of spirit. The former is sinful and subject to death; the latter leads to life. That's the apostle's point: if your mind is set on fleshly things, the end result is death, but if your mind is set on spiritual things you will have life. But Paul doesn't leave it at that: he says, "to be spiritually minded is life and peace."

What the Spirit provides is not just life—which is great—but the Spirit also provides *peace*, which means life fully redeemed and restored. Is your mind leading toward death or life?

16 [a]The Spirit Himself bears witness with our spirit that we are children of God, 17 and if children, then [a]heirs—heirs of God and joint heirs with Christ, [b]if indeed we suffer with *Him,* that we may also be glorified together.

From Suffering to Glory

18 For I consider that [a]the sufferings of this present time are not worthy *to be compared* with the glory which shall be revealed in us. 19 For [a]the earnest expectation of the creation eagerly waits for the revealing of the sons of God. 20 For [a]the creation was subjected to futility, not willingly, but because of Him who subjected *it* in hope; 21 because the creation itself also will be delivered from the bondage of corruption into the glorious [a]liberty of the children of God. 22 For we know that the whole creation [a]groans and labors with birth pangs together until now. 23 Not only *that,* but we also who have [a]the firstfruits of the Spirit, [b]even we ourselves groan [c]within ourselves, eagerly waiting for the adoption, the [d]redemption of our body. 24 For we were saved in this hope, but [a]hope that is seen is not hope; for why does one still hope for what he sees? 25 But if we hope for what we do not see, we eagerly wait for *it* with perseverance.

26 Likewise the Spirit also helps in our weaknesses. For [a]we do not know what we should pray for as we ought, but [b]the Spirit Himself makes intercession for us[1] with groanings which cannot be uttered. 27 Now [a]He who searches the hearts knows what the mind of the Spirit *is,* because He makes intercession for the saints [b]according to *the will of* God.

28 And we know that all things work together for good to those who love God, to those [a]who are the called according to *His* purpose. 29 For whom [a]He foreknew, [b]He also predestined [c]*to be* conformed to the image of His Son, [d]that He might be the firstborn among many brethren. 30 Moreover whom He predestined, these He also [a]called; whom He called, these He also [b]justified; and whom He justified, these He also [c]glorified.

God's Everlasting Love

31 What then shall we say to these things? [a]If God *is* for us, who *can be* against us? 32 [a]He who did not spare His own Son, but [b]delivered Him up for us all, how shall He not with Him also freely give us all things? 33 Who shall bring a charge against God's elect? [a]*It is* God who justifies. 34 [a]Who *is* he who condemns? *It is* Christ who died, and furthermore is also risen, [b]who is even at the right hand of God, [c]who also makes intercession for us. 35 Who shall separate us from the love of Christ? *Shall* tribulation, or distress, or persecution, or famine, or nakedness, or peril, or sword? 36 As it is written:

[a]"For Your sake we are killed all day long;
We are accounted as sheep for the
slaughter."[1]

37 [a]Yet in all these things we are more than conquerors through Him who loved us. 38 For I am persuaded that neither death nor life, nor angels nor [a]principalities nor powers, nor things present nor things to come, 39 nor height nor depth, nor any other created thing, shall be able to separate us from the love of God which is in Christ Jesus our Lord.

PEACE NOTE

"We are more than conquerors through Him who loved us." We can wrap ourselves in this truth, walk in God's peace, and face whatever today holds.

ROMANS 8:37

Israel's Rejection of Christ

9 I [a]tell the truth in Christ, I am not lying, my conscience also bearing me witness in the Holy Spirit, 2 [a]that I have great sorrow and continual grief in my heart. 3 For [a]I could wish that I myself were accursed from Christ for my brethren, my countrymen[1] according to the flesh, 4 who are Israelites, [a]to whom *pertain* the adoption, [b]the glory, [c]the covenants, [d]the giving of the law, [e]the service *of God,* and [f]the promises; 5 [a]of whom *are* the fathers and from [b]whom, according to

8:16 [a] Eph. 1:13 **8:17** [a] Acts 26:18 [b] Phil. 1:29 **8:18** [a] 2 Cor. 4:17 **8:19** [a] [2 Pet. 3:13] **8:20** [a] Gen. 3:17–19 **8:21** [a] [2 Cor. 3:17] **8:22** [a] Jer. 12:4, 11 **8:23** [a] 2 Cor. 5:5 [b] 2 Cor. 5:2, 4 [c] [Luke 20:36] [d] Eph. 1:14; 4:30 **8:24** [a] Heb. 11:1 **8:26** [a] Matt. 20:22 [b] Eph. 6:18 [1] NU-Text omits *for us.* **8:27** [a] 1 Chr. 28:9 [b] 1 John 5:14 **8:28** [a] 2 Tim. 1:9 **8:29** [a] 2 Tim. 2:19 [b] Eph. 1:5, 11 [c] [2 Cor. 3:18] [d] Heb. 1:6 **8:30** [a] [1 Pet. 2:9; 3:9] [b] [Gal. 2:16] [c] John 17:22 **8:31** [a] Num. 14:9 **8:32** [a] Rom. 5:6, 10 [b] [Rom. 4:25] **8:33** [a] Is. 50:8, 9 **8:34** [a] John 3:18 [b] Mark 16:19 [c] Heb. 7:25; 9:24 **8:36** [a] Ps. 44:22 [1] Psalm 44:22 **8:37** [a] 1 Cor. 15:57 **8:38** [a] [Eph. 1:21] **9:1** [a] 2 Cor. 1:23 **9:2** [a] Rom. 10:1 **9:3** [a] Ex. 32:32 [1] Or *relatives* **9:4** [a] Ex. 4:22 [b] 1 Sam. 4:21 [c] Acts 3:25 [d] Ps. 147:19 [e] Heb. 9:1, 6 [f] [Acts 2:39; 13:32] **9:5** [a] Deut. 10:15 [b] [Luke 1:34, 35; 3:23]

the flesh, Christ *came,* [c]who is over all, *the*
eternally blessed God. Amen.

Israel's Rejection and God's Purpose

6 [a]But it is not that the word of God has
taken no effect. For [b]they *are* not all Israel
who *are* of Israel, 7 [a]nor *are they* all children
because they are the seed of Abraham; but,
[b]"In Isaac your seed shall be called."[1] 8 That is,
those who *are* the children of the flesh, these
are not the children of God; but [a]the children
of the promise are counted as the seed. 9 For
this *is* the word of promise: [a]"At this time I
will come and Sarah shall have a son."[1]
10 And not only *this,* but when [a]Rebecca
also had conceived by one man, *even* by our
father Isaac 11 (for *the children* not yet being
born, nor having done any good or evil, that
the purpose of God according to election
might stand, not of works but of [a]Him who
calls), 12 it was said to her, [a]"The older shall
serve the younger."[1] 13 As it is written, [a]"Jacob
I have loved, but Esau I have hated."[1]

Israel's Rejection and God's Justice

14 What shall we say then? [a]*Is there* unrighteousness with God? Certainly not!
15 For He says to Moses, [a]"I will have mercy
on whomever I will have mercy, and I will
have compassion on whomever I will have
compassion."[1] 16 So then *it is* not of him who
wills, nor of him who runs, but of God who
shows mercy. 17 For [a]the Scripture says to
the Pharaoh, [b]"For this very purpose I have
raised you up, that I may show My power in
you, and that My name may be declared in
all the earth."[1] 18 Therefore He has mercy
on whom He wills, and whom He wills He
[a]hardens.
19 You will say to me then, "Why does He
still find fault? For [a]who has resisted His
will?" 20 But indeed, O man, who are you to
reply against God? [a]Will the thing formed say
to him who formed *it,* "Why have you made
me like this?" 21 Does not the [a]potter have
power over the clay, from the same lump
to make [b]one vessel for honor and another
for dishonor?
22 *What* if God, wanting to show *His* wrath
and to make His power known, endured with
much longsuffering [a]the vessels of wrath
[b]prepared for destruction, 23 and that He
might make known [a]the riches of His glory
on the vessels of mercy, which He had [b]pre-
pared beforehand for glory, 24 even us whom
He [a]called, [b]not of the Jews only, but also of
the Gentiles?
25 As He says also in Hosea:

[a]"I will call them My people, who were
not My people,
And her beloved, who was not
beloved."[1]
26 "And[a] it shall come to pass in the place
where it was said to them,
'*You are* not My people,'
There they shall be called sons of the
living God."[1]

27 Isaiah also cries out concerning Israel:[1]

[a]"Though the number of the children of
Israel be as the sand of the sea,
[b]The remnant will be saved.
28 For He will finish the work and cut *it*
short in righteousness,
[a]Because the LORD will make a short
work upon the earth."[1]

29 And as Isaiah said before:

[a]"Unless the LORD of Sabaoth[1] had left us
a seed,
[b]We would have become like Sodom,
And we would have been made like
Gomorrah."[2]

Present Condition of Israel

30 What shall we say then? [a]That Gentiles,
who did not pursue righteousness, have attained to righteousness, [b]even the righteousness of faith; 31 but Israel, [a]pursuing the law
of righteousness, [b]has not attained to the
law of righteousness.[1] 32 Why? Because *they*
did not *seek it* by faith, but as it were, by the
works of the law.[1] For [a]they stumbled at that
stumbling stone. 33 As it is written:

[a]"Behold, I lay in Zion a stumbling stone
and rock of offense,
And [b]whoever believes on Him will not
be put to shame."[1]

9:5 [c] Jer. 23:6 **9:6** [a] Num. 23:19 [b] [Gal. 6:16] **9:7** [a] [Gal. 4:23] [b] Gen. 21:12 [1] Genesis 21:12 **9:8** [a] Gal. 4:28 **9:9** [a] Gen. 18:10, 14 [1] Genesis 18:10, 14 **9:10** [a] Gen. 25:21 **9:11** [a] [Rom. 4:17; 8:28] **9:12** [a] Gen. 25:23 [1] Genesis 25:23 **9:13** [a] Mal. 1:2, 3 [1] Malachi 1:2, 3 **9:14** [a] Deut. 32:4 **9:15** [a] Ex. 33:19 [1] Exodus 33:19 **9:17** [a] Gal. 3:8 [b] Ex. 9:16 [1] Exodus 9:16 **9:18** [a] Ex. 4:21 **9:19** [a] 2 Chr. 20:6 **9:20** [a] Is. 29:16 **9:21** [a] Prov. 16:4 [b] 2 Tim. 2:20 **9:22** [a] [1 Thess. 5:9] [b] [1 Pet. 2:8] **9:23** [a] [Col. 1:27] [b] [Rom. 8:28–30] **9:24** [a] [Rom. 8:28] [b] Rom. 3:29 **9:25** [a] Hos. 2:23 [1] Hosea 2:23 **9:26** [a] Hos. 1:10 [1] Hosea 1:10 **9:27** [a] Is. 10:22, 23 [b] Rom. 11:5 [1] Isaiah 10:22, 23 **9:28** [a] Is. 10:23; 28:22 [1] NU-Text reads *For the LORD will finish the work and cut it short upon the earth.* **9:29** [a] Is. 1:9 [b] Is. 13:19 [1] Literally, in Hebrew, *Hosts* [2] Isaiah 1:9 **9:30** [a] Rom. 4:11 [b] Rom. 1:17; 3:21; 10:6 **9:31** [a] [Rom. 10:2–4] [b] [Gal. 5:4] [1] NU-Text omits *of righteousness.* **9:32** [a] [1 Cor. 1:23] [1] NU-Text reads *by works.* **9:33** [a] Is. 8:14; 28:16 [b] Rom. 5:5; 10:11 [1] Isaiah 8:14; 28:16

Israel Needs the Gospel

10 Brethren, my heart's desire and prayer
to God for Israel[1] is that they may be
saved. 2 For I bear them witness [a]that they
have a zeal for God, but not according to
knowledge. 3 For they being ignorant of [a]God's
righteousness, and seeking to establish their
own [b]righteousness, have not submitted to
the righteousness of God. 4 For [a]Christ *is* the
end of the law for righteousness to everyone
who believes.
5 For Moses writes about the righteousness which is of the law, [a]"The man who does
those things shall live by them."[1] 6 But the
righteousness of faith speaks in this way,
[a]"Do not say in your heart, 'Who will ascend
into heaven?' "[1] (that is, to bring Christ down
from above) 7 or, [a]" 'Who will descend into the
abyss?' "[1] (that is, to bring Christ up from the
dead). 8 But what does it say? [a]"The word is
near you, in your mouth and in your heart"[1]
(that is, the word of faith which we preach):
9 that [a]if you confess with your mouth the
Lord Jesus and believe in your heart that
God has raised Him from the dead, you will
be saved. 10 For with the heart one believes
unto righteousness, and with the mouth
confession is made unto salvation. 11 For the
Scripture says, [a]"Whoever believes on Him
will not be put to shame."[1] 12 For [a]there is no
distinction between Jew and Greek, for [b]the
same Lord over all [c]is rich to all who call upon
Him. 13 For [a]"whoever calls [b]on the name of
the LORD shall be saved."[1]

Israel Rejects the Gospel

14 How then shall they call on Him in whom
they have not believed? And how shall they
believe in Him of whom they have not heard?
And how shall they hear [a]without a preacher?
15 And how shall they preach unless they are
sent? As it is written:

> [a]"How beautiful are the feet of those who
> preach the gospel of peace,[1]
> Who bring glad tidings of good things!"[2]

16 But they have not all obeyed the gospel.
For Isaiah says, [a]"LORD, who has believed our
report?"[1] 17 So then faith *comes* by hearing,
and hearing by the word of God.
18 But I say, have they not heard? Yes indeed:

> [a]"Their sound has gone out to all the
> earth,
> And their words to the ends of the
> world."[1]

10:1 [1] NU-Text reads *them.* **10:2** [a] Acts 21:20 **10:3** [a] [Rom. 1:17] [b] [Phil. 3:9] **10:4** [a] [Gal. 3:24; 4:5] **10:5** [a] Lev. 18:5 [1] Leviticus 18:5 **10:6** [a] Deut. 30:12–14 [1] Deuteronomy 30:12 **10:7** [a] Deut. 30:13 [1] Deuteronomy 30:13 **10:8** [a] Deut. 30:14 [1] Deuteronomy 30:14 **10:9** [a] Luke 12:8 **10:11** [a] Is. 28:16 [1] Isaiah 28:16 **10:12** [a] Rom. 3:22, 29 [b] Acts 10:36 [c] Eph. 1:7 **10:13** [a] Joel 2:32 [b] Acts 9:14 [1] Joel 2:32 **10:14** [a] Titus 1:3 **10:15** [a] Is. 52:7; Nah. 1:15 [1] NU-Text omits *preach the gospel of peace, Who.* [2] Isaiah 52:7; Nahum 1:15 **10:16** [a] Is. 53:1 [1] Isaiah 53:1 **10:18** [a] Ps. 19:4 [1] Psalm 19:4

SURRENDER YOUR ANXIETY

And how shall they preach unless they are sent? As it is written: "How beautiful are the feet of those who preach the gospel of peace, who bring glad tidings of good things!"

ROMANS 10:15

"Clothes make the man," we used to hear. Now I wonder if it's the shoes. Shoes for men and women, boys and girls have never been more varied and exotic (and expensive!).

Isaiah long ago spoke of beautiful feet. What shoes those feet were wearing I am not sure, but the feet were beautiful because of what their owner was proclaiming—the glad tidings, or Good News, of a happy announcement of peace. In this passage in Romans Paul quotes Isaiah 52:7, which says that the oppressive kings of Assyria and Babylonia have no power; "God reigns!" Nothing has changed about humanity; we are always trying to rule or looking for a ruler who will fulfill our personal wants and wishes. Again, we are looking for a way to control life and bring us peace.

Paul shows us that if we embrace the kingdom of God, we discover a kingdom of peace. One way to embrace God's kingdom is by surrendering the need to control everything. Today, choose one anxiety that is birthed from your control habits and let it go by remembering that Christ truly rules all.

19 But I say, did Israel not know? First Moses
says:

[a]"I will provoke you to jealousy by *those*
who are not a nation,
I will move you to anger by a [b]foolish
nation."[1]

20 But Isaiah is very bold and says:

[a]"I was found by those who did not
seek Me;
I was made manifest to those who did
not ask for Me."[1]

21 But to Israel he says:

[a]"All day long I have stretched out My
hands
To a disobedient and contrary
people."[1]

Israel's Rejection Not Total

11 I say then, [a]has God cast away His people? [b]Certainly not! For [c]I also am an
Israelite, of the seed of Abraham, *of* the tribe
of Benjamin. 2 God has not cast away His
people whom [a]He foreknew. Or do you not
know what the Scripture says of Elijah, how
he pleads with God against Israel, saying,
3 [a]"LORD, they have killed Your prophets and
torn down Your altars, and I alone am left,
and they seek my life"?[1] 4 But what does the
divine response say to him? [a]"I have reserved
for Myself seven thousand men who have
not bowed the knee to Baal."[1] 5 [a]Even so then,
at this present time there is a remnant according to the election of grace. 6 And [a]if by
grace, then *it is* no longer of works; otherwise
grace is no longer grace.[1] But if *it is* of works,
it is no longer grace; otherwise work is no
longer work.
7 What then? [a]Israel has not obtained
what it seeks; but the elect have obtained
it, and the rest were [b]blinded. 8 Just as it is
written:

[a]"God has given them a spirit of
stupor,
[b]Eyes that they should not see
And ears that they should not
hear,
To this very day."[1]

9 And David says:

[a]"Let their table become a snare and a trap,
A stumbling block and a recompense
to them.
10 Let their eyes be darkened, so that they
do not see,
And bow down their back always."[1]

Israel's Rejection Not Final

11 I say then, have they stumbled that they
should fall? Certainly not! But [a]through their
fall, to provoke them to [b]jealousy, salvation
has come to the Gentiles. 12 Now if their fall *is*
riches for the world, and their failure riches for
the Gentiles, how much more their fullness!
13 For I speak to you Gentiles; inasmuch as
[a]I am an apostle to the Gentiles, I magnify
my ministry, 14 if by any means I may provoke
to jealousy *those who are* my flesh and [a]save
some of them. 15 For if their being cast away
is the reconciling of the world, what *will* their
acceptance *be* [a]but life from the dead?
16 For if [a]the firstfruit *is* holy, the lump *is*
also *holy;* and if the root *is* holy, so *are* the
branches. 17 And if [a]some of the branches
were broken off, [b]and you, being a wild olive
tree, were grafted in among them, and with
them became a partaker of the root and fatness of the olive tree, 18 [a]do not boast against
the branches. But if you do boast, *remember*
that you do not support the root, but the root
supports you.
19 You will say then, "Branches were broken
off that I might be grafted in." 20 Well *said.*
Because of [a]unbelief they were broken off, and
you stand by faith. Do not be haughty, but fear.
21 For if God did not spare the natural branches, He may not spare you either. 22 Therefore
consider the goodness and severity of God:
on those who fell, severity; but toward you,
goodness,[1] [a]if you continue in *His* goodness.
Otherwise [b]you also will be cut off. 23 And they
also, [a]if they do not continue in unbelief, will
be grafted in, for God is able to graft them in
again. 24 For if you were cut out of the olive
tree which is wild by nature, and were grafted
contrary to nature into a cultivated olive tree,
how much more will these, who *are* natural
branches, be grafted into their own olive tree?
25 For I do not desire, brethren, that you
should be ignorant of this mystery, lest you
should be [a]wise in your own opinion, that

10:19 [a] Deut. 32:21 [b] *Titus 3:3* [1] *Deuteronomy 32:21* **10:20** [a] Is. 65:1 [1] Isaiah 65:1 **10:21** [a] Is. 65:2 [1] Isaiah 65:2 **11:1** [a] Jer. 46:28 [b] 1 Sam. 12:22 [c] 2 Cor. 11:22 **11:2** [a] [Rom. 8:29] **11:3** [a] 1 Kin. 19:10, 14 [1] 1 Kings 19:10, 14 **11:4** [a] 1 Kin. 19:18 [1] 1 Kings 19:18 **11:5** [a] Rom. 9:27 **11:6** [a] Rom. 4:4 [1] NU-Text omits the rest of this verse. **11:7** [a] Rom. 9:31 [b] 2 Cor. 3:14 **11:8** [a] Is. 29:10, 13 [b] Deut. 29:3, 4 [1] Deuteronomy 29:4; Isaiah 29:10 **11:9** [a] Ps. 69:22, 23 **11:10** [1] Psalm 69:22, 23 **11:11** [a] Is. 42:6, 7 [b] Rom. 10:19 **11:13** [a] Acts 9:15; 22:21 **11:14** [a] 1 Cor. 9:22 **11:15** [a] [Is. 26:16–19] **11:16** [a] Lev. 23:10 **11:17** [a] Jer. 11:16 [b] [Eph. 2:12] **11:18** [a] [1 Cor. 10:12] **11:20** [a] Heb. 3:19 **11:22** [a] 1 Cor. 15:2 [b] [John 15:2] [1] NU-Text adds *of God.* **11:23** [a] [2 Cor. 3:16] **11:25** [a] Rom. 12:16

[b]blindness in part has happened to Israel
[c]until the fullness of the Gentiles has come in.
26 And so all Israel will be saved,[1] as it is written:

[a]"The Deliverer will come out of Zion,
And He will turn away ungodliness
from Jacob;
27 For [a]this *is* My covenant with them,
When I take away their sins."[1]

28 Concerning the gospel *they are* enemies
for your sake, but concerning the election *they*
are [a]beloved for the sake of the fathers. 29 For
the gifts and the calling of God *are* [a]irrevoca-
ble. 30 For as you [a]were once disobedient to
God, yet have now obtained mercy through
their disobedience, 31 even so these also have
now been disobedient, that through the mercy
shown you they also may obtain mercy. 32 For
God has committed them [a]all to disobedience,
that He might have mercy on all.
33 Oh, the depth of the riches both of the
wisdom and knowledge of God! How unsearchable *are* His judgments and His ways
past finding out!

34 "For who has known the [a]mind of the
LORD?
Or [b]who has become His counselor?"[1]
35 "Or[a] who has first given to Him
And it shall be repaid to him?"[1]

36 For [a]of Him and through Him and to
Him *are* all things, [b]to whom *be* glory forever. Amen.

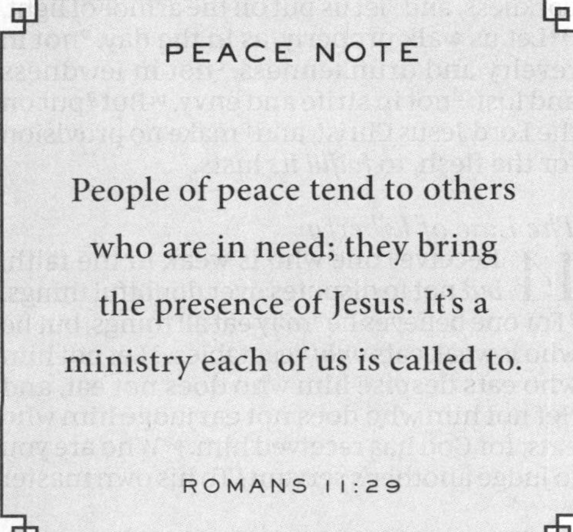

Living Sacrifices to God

12 I [a]beseech you therefore, brethren, by
the mercies of God, that you present
your bodies [b]a living sacrifice, holy, acceptable to God, *which is* your reasonable service.
2 And [a]do not be conformed to this world,
but [b]be transformed by the renewing of your
mind, that you may [c]prove what *is* that good
and acceptable and perfect will of God.

PEACE NOTE

Christians lead chaotic lives when their minds have not been renewed. Present yourself as a living sacrifice today, and ask God to renew His peace in your life.

ROMANS 12:1-2

Serve God with Spiritual Gifts

3 For I say, [a]through the grace given to me,
to everyone who is among you, [b]not to think
of himself more highly than he ought to think,
but to think soberly, as God has dealt [c]to each
one a measure of faith. 4 For [a]as we have many
members in one body, but all the members
do not have the same function, 5 so [a]we, *being*
many, are one body in Christ, and individually members of one another. 6 Having then
gifts differing according to the grace that is
[a]given to us, *let us use them:* if prophecy, *let*
us [b]*prophesy* in proportion to our faith; 7 or
ministry, *let us use it* in *our* ministering; [a]he
who teaches, in teaching; 8 [a]he who exhorts,
in exhortation; [b]he who gives, with liberality;
[c]he who leads, with diligence; he who shows
mercy, [d]with cheerfulness.

Behave Like a Christian

9 [a]*Let* love *be* without hypocrisy. [b]Abhor
what is evil. Cling to what is good. 10 [a]*Be* kindly
affectionate to one another with brotherly
love, [b]in honor giving preference to one
another; 11 not lagging in diligence, fervent

11:25 [b] 2 Cor. 3:14 [c] Luke 21:24 **11:26** [a] Is. 59:20, 21 [1] Or *delivered* **11:27** [a] Is. 27:9 [1] Isaiah 59:20, 21 **11:28** [a] Deut. 7:8; 10:15 **11:29** [a] Num. 23:19 **11:30** [a] [Eph. 2:2] **11:32** [a] [Gal. 3:22] **11:34** [a] Is. 40:13; Jer. 23:18 [b] Job 36:22 [1] Isaiah 40:13; Jeremiah 23:18 **11:35** [a] Job 41:11 [1] Job 41:11 **11:36** [a] Heb. 2:10 [b] Heb. 13:21 **12:1** [a] 2 Cor. 10:1–4 [b] Heb. 10:18, 20 **12:2** [a] 1 John 2:15 [b] Eph. 4:23 [c] [1 Thess. 4:3] **12:3** [a] Gal. 2:9 [b] Prov. 25:27 [c] [Eph. 4:7] **12:4** [a] 1 Cor. 12:12–14 **12:5** [a] [1 Cor. 10:17] **12:6** [a] [John 3:27] [b] Acts 11:27 **12:7** [a] Eph. 4:11 **12:8** [a] Acts 15:32 [b] [Matt. 6:1–3] [c] [Acts 20:28] [d] 2 Cor. 9:7 **12:9** [a] 1 Tim. 1:5 [b] Ps. 34:14 **12:10** [a] Heb. 13:1 [b] Phil. 2:3

in spirit, serving the Lord; 12 [a]rejoicing in hope, [b]patient in tribulation, [c]continuing steadfastly in prayer; 13 [a]distributing to the needs of the saints, [b]given to hospitality.

14 [a]Bless those who persecute you; bless and do not curse. 15 [a]Rejoice with those who rejoice, and weep with those who weep. 16 [a]Be of the same mind toward one another. [b]Do not set your mind on high things, but associate with the humble. Do not be wise in your own opinion.

17 [a]Repay no one evil for evil. [b]Have regard for good things in the sight of all men. 18 If it is possible, as much as depends on you, [a]live peaceably with all men. 19 Beloved, [a]do not avenge yourselves, but *rather* give place to wrath; for it is written, [b]"Vengeance *is* Mine, I will repay,"[1] says the Lord. 20 Therefore

[a]"If your enemy is hungry, feed him;
If he is thirsty, give him a drink;
For in so doing you will heap coals of
fire on his head."[1]

21 Do not be overcome by evil, but [a]overcome evil with good.

PEACE NOTE

Christians should seek to live at peace with other human beings, but ultimately, peace comes as a result of Jesus' work and thus is a gift given by God.

ROMANS 12:18

Submit to Government

13 Let every soul be [a]subject to the governing authorities. For there is no authority except from God, and the authorities that exist are appointed by God. 2 Therefore whoever resists [a]the authority resists the ordinance of God, and those who resist will bring judgment on themselves. 3 For rulers are not a terror to good works, but to evil. Do you want to be unafraid of the authority? [a]Do what is good, and you will have praise from the same. 4 For he is God's minister to you for good. But if you do evil, be afraid; for he does not bear the sword in vain; for he is God's minister, an avenger to *execute* wrath on him who practices evil. 5 Therefore [a]*you* must be subject, not only because of wrath [b]but also for conscience' sake. 6 For because of this you also pay taxes, for they are God's ministers attending continually to this very thing. 7 [a]Render therefore to all their due: taxes to whom taxes *are due,* customs to whom customs, fear to whom fear, honor to whom honor.

Love Your Neighbor

8 Owe no one anything except to love one another, for [a]he who loves another has fulfilled the law. 9 For the commandments, [a]"You shall not commit adultery," "You shall not murder," "You shall not steal," "You shall not bear false witness,"[1] "You shall not covet,"[2] and if *there is* any other commandment, are *all* summed up in this saying, namely, [b]"You shall love your neighbor as yourself."[3] 10 Love does no harm to a neighbor; therefore [a]love *is* the fulfillment of the law.

Put on Christ

11 And *do* this, knowing the time, that now *it is* high time [a]to awake out of sleep; for now our salvation *is* nearer than when we *first* believed. 12 The night is far spent, the day is at hand. [a]Therefore let us cast off the works of darkness, and [b]let us put on the armor of light. 13 [a]Let us walk properly, as in the day, [b]not in revelry and drunkenness, [c]not in lewdness and lust, [d]not in strife and envy. 14 But [a]put on the Lord Jesus Christ, and [b]make no provision for the flesh, to *fulfill its* lusts.

The Law of Liberty

14 Receive[a] one who is weak in the faith, *but* not to disputes over doubtful things. 2 For one believes he [a]may eat all things, but he who is weak eats *only* vegetables. 3 Let not him who eats despise him who does not eat, and [a]let not him who does not eat judge him who eats; for God has received him. 4 [a]Who are you to judge another's servant? To his own master

12:12 [a] Luke 10:20 [b] Luke 21:19 [c] Luke 18:1 **12:13** [a] 1 Cor. 16:1 [b] 1 Tim. 3:2 **12:14** [a] [Matt. 5:44] **12:15** [a] [1 Cor. 12:26] **12:16** [a] [Phil. 2:2; 4:2] [b] *Jer. 45:5* **12:17** [a] [Matt. 5:39] [b] 2 Cor. 8:21 **12:18** [a] Heb. 12:14 **12:19** [a] Lev. 19:18 [b] Deut. 32:35 [1] Deuteronomy 32:35 **12:20** [a] Prov. 25:21, 22 [1] Proverbs 25:21, 22 **12:21** [a] [Rom. 12:1, 2] **13:1** [a] 1 Pet. 2:13 **13:2** [a] [Titus 3:1] **13:3** [a] 1 Pet. 2:14 **13:5** [a] Eccl. 8:2 [b] [1 Pet. 2:13, 19] **13:7** [a] Matt. 22:21 **13:8** [a] [Gal. 5:13, 14] **13:9** [a] Ex. 20:13–17; Deut. 5:17–21 [b] Lev. 19:18 [1] NU-Text omits *"You shall not bear false witness."* [2] Exodus 20:13–15, 17; Deuteronomy 5:17–19, 21 [3] Leviticus 19:18 **13:10** [a] [Matt. 7:12; 22:39, 40] **13:11** [a] [1 Cor. 15:34] **13:12** [a] Eph. 5:11 [b] [Eph. 6:11, 13] **13:13** [a] Phil. 4:8 [b] Prov. 23:20 [c] [1 Cor. 6:9] [d] James 3:14 **13:14** [a] Gal. 3:27 [b] [Gal. 5:16] **14:1** [a] [1 Cor. 8:9; 9:22] **14:2** [a] [Titus 1:15] **14:3** [a] [Col. 2:16] **14:4** [a] James 4:11, 12

he stands or falls. Indeed, he will be made
to stand, for God is able to make him stand.
5 [a]One person esteems *one* day above another; another esteems every day *alike.* Let
each be fully convinced in his own mind.
6 He who [a]observes the day, observes *it* to
the Lord;[1] and he who does not observe the
day, to the Lord he does not observe *it.* He
who eats, eats to the Lord, for [b]he gives God
thanks; and he who does not eat, to the Lord
he does not eat, and gives God thanks. 7 For
[a]none of us lives to himself, and no one dies
to himself. 8 For if we [a]live, we live to the Lord;
and if we die, we die to the Lord. Therefore,
whether we live or die, we are the Lord's. 9 For
[a]to this end Christ died and rose[1] and lived
again, that He might be [b]Lord of both the dead
and the living. 10 But why do you judge your
brother? Or why do you show contempt for
your brother? For [a]we shall all stand before
the judgment seat of Christ.[1] 11 For it is written:

> [a]"*As* I live, says the LORD,
> Every knee shall bow to Me,
> And every tongue shall confess to God."[1]

12 So then [a]each of us shall give account of
himself to God. 13 Therefore let us not judge
one another anymore, but rather resolve this,
[a]not to put a stumbling block or a cause to
fall in *our* brother's way.

The Law of Love

14 I know and am convinced by the Lord Jesus
[a]that *there is* nothing unclean of itself; but to
him who considers anything to be unclean, to
him *it is* unclean. 15 Yet if your brother is grieved
because of *your* food, you are no longer walking
in love. [a]Do not destroy with your food the one
for whom Christ died. 16 [a]Therefore do not let
your good be spoken of as evil; 17 [a]for the kingdom of God is not eating and drinking, but righteousness and [b]peace and joy in the Holy Spirit.
18 For he who serves Christ in these things[1] [a]*is*
acceptable to God and approved by men.
19 [a]Therefore let us pursue the things *which
make* for peace and the things by which [b]one
may edify another. 20 [a]Do not destroy the work
of God for the sake of food. [b]All things indeed *are*
pure, [c]but *it is* evil for the man who eats with offense. 21 *It is* good neither to eat [a]meat nor drink
wine nor *do anything* by which your brother
stumbles or is offended or is made weak.[1] 22 Do
you have faith? Have[1] *it* to yourself before God.
[a]Happy *is* he who does not condemn himself
in what he approves. 23 But he who doubts is
condemned if he eats, because *he does* not *eat*
from faith; for [a]whatever *is* not from faith is sin.[1]

14:5 [a] Gal. 4:10 **14:6** [a] Gal. 4:10 [b] [1 Tim. 4:3] [1] NU-Text omits the rest of this sentence. **14:7** [a] [Gal. 2:20] **14:8** [a] 2 Cor. 5:14, 15 **14:9** [a] 2 Cor. 5:15 [b] Acts 10:36 [1] NU-Text omits *and rose.* **14:10** [a] 2 Cor. 5:10 [1] NU-Text reads *of God.* **14:11** [a] Is. 45:23 [1] Isaiah 45:23 **14:12** [a] 1 Pet. 4:5 **14:13** [a] 1 Cor. 8:9 **14:14** [a] 1 Cor. 10:25 **14:15** [a] 1 Cor. 8:11 **14:16** [a] [Rom. 12:17] **14:17** [a] 1 Cor. 8:8 [b] [Rom. 8:6] **14:18** [a] 2 Cor. 8:21 [1] NU-Text reads *this.* **14:19** [a] Rom. 12:18 [b] 1 Cor. 14:12 **14:20** [a] Rom. 14:15 [b] Acts 10:15 [c] 1 Cor. 8:9–12 **14:21** [a] 1 Cor. 8:13 [1] NU-Text omits *or is offended or is made weak.* **14:22** [a] [1 John 3:21] [1] NU-Text reads *The faith which you have—have.* **14:23** [a] Titus 1:15 [1] M-Text puts Romans 16:25–27 here.

THE REIGN OF OUR PEACE-GIVING GOD

For the kingdom of God is not eating and drinking, but
righteousness and peace and joy in the Holy Spirit.

ROMANS 14:17

Finding the right diet has become a way of life for many people in our overfed Western society. Believe it or not, what people should or shouldn't eat was a problem in the early church. Paul exhorted the Roman Christians not to judge one another in the matter of food and drink. That may sound strange to us, but in a time when the church was a mix of Jews and Gentiles with very different rules regarding food, conflict was inevitable. But that isn't how it should be in the church, especially if we understand the gospel properly.

One of the signs of the presence of God's rule or kingdom is peace. And one of the signs of true fellowship among believers from all ethnicities and social classes is eating together. Paul reminded the Christians of Rome that the kingdom of God really isn't about tangibles like food and drink but about righteousness and peace, including joy in the Holy Spirit.

Does your life reflect God's kingdom peace? Is food an issue in your circle? How can you promote peace rather than conflict in that situation?

BEING CHURCHES OF PEACE

Therefore let us pursue the things which make for peace and
the things by which one may edify another.

ROMANS 14:19

Are you a peacemaker or an agitator? Jesus told His followers, "Blessed are the peacemakers, for they shall be called sons of God" (Matt. 5:9).

Paul echoed this sentiment. Whatever believers do, they are to "pursue the things which make for peace and the things by which one may edify another" (Rom. 14:19). This is the same advice the apostle gave the Corinthians with regard to spiritual gifts. Gifts are to be exercised for the edification of the church, not the glorification of the gifted person. If believers are guided by the principle of peacemaking and edifying, the church will be strengthened and blessed by peace. Paul exhorted believers to "examine" and "test" themselves to make sure that what they did proceeded from faith (2 Cor. 13:5).

Let's commit ourselves to making our churches congregations of peace, where members encourage and edify one another. One immediate step toward peacemaking is to pray for someone with whom you may have a conflict. See if that small act doesn't reap big rewards.

Bearing Others' Burdens

15 We [a]then who are strong ought to bear
with the scruples of the weak, and not to
please ourselves. 2 [a]Let each of us please *his*
neighbor for *his* good, leading to edification.
3 [a]For even Christ did not please Himself; but
as it is written, [b]"The reproaches of those who
reproached You fell on Me."[1] 4 For [a]whatever
things were written before were written for
our learning, that we through the patience
and comfort of the Scriptures might have
hope. 5 [a]Now may the God of patience and
comfort grant you to be like-minded toward
one another, according to Christ Jesus, 6 that
you may [a]with one mind *and* one mouth
glorify the God and Father of our Lord Jesus
Christ.

Glorify God Together

7 Therefore [a]receive one another, just [b]as
Christ also received us,[1] to the glory of God.
8 Now I say that [a]Jesus Christ has become a
servant to the circumcision for the truth of
God, [b]to confirm the promises *made* to the
fathers, 9 and [a]that the Gentiles might glorify
God for *His* mercy, as it is written:

> [b]"For this reason I will confess to You
> among the Gentiles,
> And sing to Your name."[1]

10 And again he says:

> [a]"Rejoice, O Gentiles, with His people!"[1]

11 And again:

> [a]"Praise the LORD, all you Gentiles!
> Laud Him, all you peoples!"[1]

12 And again, Isaiah says:

> [a]"There shall be a root of Jesse;
> And He who shall rise to reign over the
> Gentiles,
> In Him the Gentiles shall hope."[1]

13 Now may the God of hope fill you with
all [a]joy and peace in believing, that you may
abound in hope by the power of the Holy Spirit.

From Jerusalem to Illyricum

14 Now [a]I myself am confident concerning
you, my brethren, that you also are full of
goodness, [b]filled with all knowledge, able
also to admonish one another.[1] 15 Nevertheless, brethren, I have written more boldly
to you on *some* points, as reminding you,
[a]because of the grace given to me by God,
16 that [a]I might be a minister of Jesus Christ
to the Gentiles, ministering the gospel of

15:1 [a] [Gal. 6:1, 2] **15:2** [a] 1 Cor. 9:22; 10:24, 33 **15:3** [a] Matt. 26:39 [b] Ps. 69:9 [1] Psalm 69:9 **15:4** [a] 1 Cor. 10:11 **15:5** [a] 1 Cor. 1:10 **15:6** [a] Acts 4:24 **15:7** [a] Rom. 14:1, 3 [b] Rom. 5:2 [1] NU-Text and M-Text read *you.* **15:8** [a] Matt. 15:24 [b] 2 Cor. 1:20 **15:9** [a] John 10:16 [b] 2 Sam. 22:50; Ps. 18:49 [1] 2 Samuel 22:50; Psalm 18:49 **15:10** [a] Deut. 32:43 [1] Deuteronomy 32:43 **15:11** [a] Ps. 117:1 [1] Psalm 117:1 **15:12** [a] Is. 11:1, 10 [1] Isaiah 11:10 **15:13** [a] Rom. 12:12; 14:17 **15:14** [a] 2 Pet. 1:12 [b] 1 Cor. 1:5; 8:1, 7, 10 [1] M-Text reads *others.* **15:15** [a] Rom. 1:5; 12:3 **15:16** [a] Rom. 11:13

PEACE NOTE

Our God of hope will fill us with joy and peace when we trust in Him.

ROMANS 15:13

God, that the [b]offering of the Gentiles might be acceptable, sanctified by the Holy Spirit. 17 Therefore I have reason to glory in Christ Jesus [a]in the things *which pertain* to God. 18 For I will not dare to speak of any of those things [a]which Christ has not accomplished through me, in word and deed, [b]to make the Gentiles obedient— 19 [a]in mighty signs and wonders, by the power of the Spirit of God, so that from Jerusalem and round about to Illyricum I have fully preached the gospel of Christ. 20 And so I have made it my aim to preach the gospel, not where Christ was named, [a]lest I should build on another man's foundation, 21 but as it is written:

[a]"To whom He was not announced, they
shall see;
And those who have not heard shall
understand."[1]

Plan to Visit Rome

22 For this reason [a]I also have been much hindered from coming to you. 23 But now no longer having a place in these parts, and [a]having a great desire these many years to come to you, 24 whenever I journey to Spain, I shall come to you.[1] For I hope to see you on my journey, [a]and to be helped on my way there by you, if first I may [b]enjoy your *company* for a while. 25 But now [a]I am going to Jerusalem to minister to the saints. 26 For [a]it pleased those from Macedonia and Achaia to make a certain contribution for the poor among the saints who are in Jerusalem. 27 It pleased them indeed, and they are their debtors. For [a]if the Gentiles have been partakers of their spiritual things, [b]their duty is also to minister to them in material things. 28 Therefore, when I have performed this and have sealed to them [a]this fruit, I shall go by way of you to Spain. 29 [a]But I know that when I come to you, I shall come in the fullness of the blessing of the gospel[1] of Christ.

30 Now I beg you, brethren, through the Lord Jesus Christ, and [a]through the love of the Spirit, [b]that you strive together with me in prayers to God for me, 31 [a]that I may be delivered from those in Judea who do not

15:16 [b] [Is. 66:20] **15:17** [a] Heb. 2:17; 5:1 **15:18** [a] Acts 15:12; 21:19 [b] Rom. 1:5 **15:19** [a] Acts 19:11 **15:20** [a] [2 Cor. 10:13, 15, 16] **15:21** [a] Is. 52:15 [1] Isaiah 52:15 **15:22** [a] Rom. 1:13 **15:23** [a] Acts 19:21; 23:11 **15:24** [a] Acts 15:3 [b] Rom. 1:12 [1] NU-Text omits *I shall come to you* (and joins *Spain* with the next sentence). **15:25** [a] Acts 19:21 **15:26** [a] 1 Cor. 16:1 **15:27** [a] Rom. 11:17 [b] 1 Cor. 9:11 **15:28** [a] Phil. 4:17 **15:29** [a] [Rom. 1:11] [1] NU-Text omits *of the gospel.* **15:30** [a] Phil. 2:1 [b] 2 Cor. 1:11 **15:31** [a] 2 Tim. 3:11; 4:17

THE GOD WHO GIVES

Now may the God of hope fill you with all joy and peace in believing, that you may abound in hope by the power of the Holy Spirit.

ROMANS 15:13

Have you experienced a time in which you felt no hope about the desperate situations in life, yours and others'? Is that time now? Paul spoke of the Father as "the God of hope." That's another wonderful characteristic of the gospel: it brings hope to the hopeless. In the Roman world much contributed to a sense of despair: poverty, slavery, abuse, oppression, hunger, illness. But the God of hope, Paul said, fills His people "with all joy and peace." Here again we find that important word! Paul's prayer on behalf of the Christians of Rome was that God would fill them "with all joy and peace in believing." That is, that their faith would give them joy and peace that, in turn, would increase their hope.

That is how it works! One positive leads to another, and in the middle of it all is the peace that God gives. Whatever you lack, seek God for it today. He is a giving God.

CRUSHING THE WORKS OF THE DEVIL

And the God of peace will crush Satan under your feet shortly.
The grace of our Lord Jesus Christ be with you. Amen.

ROMANS 16:20

At the end of his letter to the Christians in Rome, Paul once again referred to God as "the God of peace." What I like about this reference is that he assured his readers that God would "crush Satan" under their feet. I love it! Do you notice the paradox? God is a God of *peace*, but that doesn't mean He won't crack some heads. Paul alluded to Genesis 3:15, where God spoke to the serpent that deceived Eve. Ancient interpreters believed that the serpent was Satan, and that the woman's Seed would be the Messiah. "He shall bruise your head," God told the serpent. "And you shall bruise His heel."

Interpreters see the crucifixion of Jesus as the bruising of the Messiah's heel and the coming judgment of Satan and his minions as the bruising of the serpent's head. To bring peace sometimes requires the destruction of the one who opposes peace. When the Holy Spirit convicts you of something in your life that is stealing your peace, do not rationalize it or negotiate. Eliminate it.

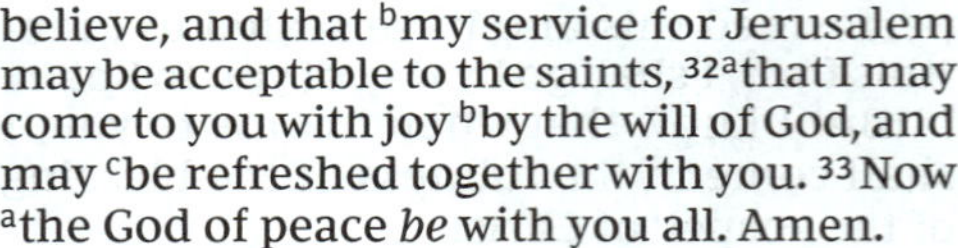

believe, and that [b]my service for Jerusalem
may be acceptable to the saints, 32 [a]that I may
come to you with joy [b]by the will of God, and
may [c]be refreshed together with you. 33 Now
[a]the God of peace *be* with you all. Amen.

Sister Phoebe Commended

16 I commend to you Phoebe our sister,
who is a servant of the church in [a]Cen-
chrea, 2 [a]that you may receive her in the Lord
[b]in a manner worthy of the saints, and assist
her in whatever business she has need of you;
for indeed she has been a helper of many
and of myself also.

Greeting Roman Saints

3 Greet [a]Priscilla and Aquila, my fellow workers in Christ Jesus, 4 who risked their own necks
for my life, to whom not only I give thanks, but
also all the churches of the Gentiles. 5 Likewise
greet [a]the church that is in their house.
Greet my beloved Epaenetus, who is [b]the
firstfruits of Achaia[1] to Christ. 6 Greet Mary,
who labored much for us. 7 Greet Andro-
nicus and Junia, my countrymen and my
fellow prisoners, who are of note among the
[a]apostles, who also [b]were in Christ before me.
8 Greet Amplias, my beloved in the Lord.
9 Greet Urbanus, our fellow worker in Christ,
and Stachys, my beloved. 10 Greet Apelles,
approved in Christ. Greet those who are of the
household of Aristobulus. 11 Greet Herodion,
my countryman.[1] Greet those who are of the
household of Narcissus who are in the Lord.
12 Greet Tryphena and Tryphosa, who have
labored in the Lord. Greet the beloved Per-
sis, who labored much in the Lord. 13 Greet
Rufus, [a]chosen in the Lord, and his mother
and mine. 14 Greet Asyncritus, Phlegon, Her-
mas, Patrobas, Hermes, and the brethren who
are with them. 15 Greet Philologus and Julia,
Nereus and his sister, and Olympas, and all
the saints who are with them.
16 [a]Greet one another with a holy kiss. The[1]
churches of Christ greet you.

Avoid Divisive Persons

17 Now I urge you, brethren, note those
[a]who cause divisions and offenses, contrary to the doctrine which you learned, and
[b]avoid them. 18 For those who are such do not
serve our Lord Jesus[1] Christ, but [a]their own
belly, and [b]by smooth words and flattering
speech deceive the hearts of the simple.
19 For [a]your obedience has become known
to all. Therefore I am glad on your behalf;
but I want you to be [b]wise in what is good,
and simple concerning evil. 20 And [a]the God
of peace [b]will crush Satan under your feet
shortly.
[c]The grace of our Lord Jesus Christ *be* with
you. Amen.

15:31 [b] 2 Cor. 8:4 **15:32** [a] Rom. 1:10 [b] Acts 18:21 [c] 1 Cor. 16:18 **15:33** [a] 1 Cor. 14:33 **16:1** [a] Acts 18:18 **16:2** [a] Phil. 2:29 [b] Phil. 1:27 **16:3** [a] Acts 18:2, 18, 26 **16:5** [a] 1 Cor. 16:19 [b] 1 Cor. 16:15 [1] NU-Text reads *Asia.* **16:7** [a] Acts 1:13, 26 [b] Gal. 1:22 **16:11** [1] Or *relative* **16:13** [a] 2 John 1 **16:16** [a] 1 Cor. 16:20 [1] NU-Text reads *All the churches.* **16:17** [a] [Acts 15:1] [b] [1 Cor. 5:9] **16:18** [a] Phil. 3:19 [b] Col. 2:4 [1] NU-Text and M-Text omit *Jesus.* **16:19** [a] Rom. 1:8 [b] Matt. 10:16 **16:20** [a] Rom. 15:33 [b] Gen. 3:15 [c] 1 Cor. 16:23

Greetings from Paul's Friends

21[a]Timothy, my fellow worker, and [b]Lucius, [c]Jason, and [d]Sosipater, my countrymen,
greet you.
22 I, Tertius, who wrote *this* epistle, greet
you in the Lord.
23[a]Gaius, my host and *the host* of the whole
church, greets you. [b]Erastus, the treasurer of
the city, greets you, and Quartus, a brother.
24[a]The grace of our Lord Jesus Christ *be* with
you all. Amen.[1]

Benediction

25 Now [a]to Him who is able to establish you
[b]according to my gospel and the preaching
of Jesus Christ, [c]according to the revelation
of the mystery [d]kept secret since the world
began 26 but [a]now made manifest, and by
the prophetic Scriptures made known to all
nations, according to the commandment of
the everlasting God, for [b]obedience to the
faith— 27 to [a]God, alone wise, *be* glory through
Jesus Christ forever. Amen.[1]

16:21 [a] Acts 16:1 [b] Acts 13:1 [c] Acts 17:5 [d] Acts 20:4 **16:23** [a] 1 Cor. 1:14 [b] Acts 19:22 **16:24** [a] 1 Thess. 5:28 [1] NU-Text omits this verse. **16:25** [a] [Eph. 3:20] [b] Rom. 2:16 [c] Eph. 1:9 [d] Col. 1:26; 2:2; 4:3 **16:26** [a] Eph. 1:9 [b] Rom. 1:5 **16:27** [a] Jude 25 [1] M-Text puts Romans 16:25–27 after Romans 14:23.

THE FIRST EPISTLE OF PAUL THE APOSTLE TO THE

CORINTHIANS

AUTHOR

Pauline authorship of 1 Corinthians is almost universally accepted. Instances of this widely held belief can be found as early as AD 95, when Clement of Rome wrote to the Corinthian church and cited this epistle in regard to the continuing problem of factions among them. Paul taught the truth of Christ in Corinth for eighteen months in AD 51–52, leaving Apollos to preach and teach in his absence. When Paul was in Ephesus during his third missionary journey, he became disturbed by reports of discord in the church of Corinth. First Corinthians is a record of Paul's initial response to these problems.

TIME

c. AD 56

KEY VERSE

1 Corinthians 1:10

THEME

The basic theme of this epistle is the application of Christian principles to carnality in the individual as well as in the church. Paul is responding to a letter he received from the Corinthians concerning five behavioral problems causing dissension: (1) divisions in the church, (2) a case of incest, (3) court cases between members, (4) the abuse of Christian "freedom," and (5) the chaos occurring in connection with celebration of the Lord's Supper. Paul's ethical responses to the various behaviors of the Corinthian church are based on a theological understanding of what it means to be a part of the people of God in a complex, multicultural, pagan environment.

Paul's first letter to the Christians at Corinth is a striking treatise on what God wants for every believer: "God has called us to peace" (7:15). In the face of the Corinthian church's competing factions, disunity, and quarreling, Paul admonished that congregation and all believers with the reminder that "God is not the author of confusion but of peace, as in all the churches of the saints" (14:33). He also recommended that the church send out missionaries and those called of God "in peace" (16:11). While 1 Corinthians is known primarily for its Love Chapter (ch. 13), peace proves another worthy theme.

Greeting

1 Paul, [a]called *to be* an apostle of Jesus Christ
[b]through the will of God, and [c]Sosthenes
our brother,

2 To the church of God which is at Corinth,
to those who [a]are sanctified in Christ Jesus,
[b]called *to be* saints, with all who in every place
call on the name of Jesus Christ [c]our Lord,
[d]both theirs and ours:

3 [a]Grace to you and peace from God our
Father and the Lord Jesus Christ.

Spiritual Gifts at Corinth

4 [a]I thank my God always concerning you
for the grace of God which was given to you
by Christ Jesus, 5 that you were enriched in
everything by Him [a]in all utterance and all
knowledge, 6 even as [a]the testimony of Christ
was confirmed in you, 7 so that you come short
in no gift, eagerly [a]waiting for the revelation of
our Lord Jesus Christ, 8 [a]who will also confirm
you to the end, [b]*that you may be* blameless
in the day of our Lord Jesus Christ. 9 [a]God *is*
faithful, by whom you were called into [b]the
fellowship of His Son, Jesus Christ our Lord.

Sectarianism Is Sin

10 Now I plead with you, brethren, by the
name of our Lord Jesus Christ, [a]that you
all speak the same thing, and *that* there be
no divisions among you, but *that* you be
perfectly joined together in the same mind
and in the same judgment. 11 For it has been
declared to me concerning you, my brethren,
by those of Chloe's *household,* that there are
contentions among you. 12 Now I say this,
that [a]each of you says, "I am of Paul," or "I
am of [b]Apollos," or "I am of [c]Cephas," or "I
am of Christ." 13 [a]Is Christ divided? Was Paul
crucified for you? Or were you baptized in
the name of Paul?

14 I thank God that I baptized [a]none of you
except [b]Crispus and [c]Gaius, 15 lest anyone
should say that I had baptized in my own
name. 16 Yes, I also baptized the household of
[a]Stephanas. Besides, I do not know whether I
baptized any other. 17 For Christ did not send
me to baptize, but to preach the gospel, [a]not
with wisdom of words, lest the cross of Christ
should be made of no effect.

Christ the Power and Wisdom of God

18 For the message of the cross is [a]foolish-
ness to [b]those who are perishing, but to us
[c]who are being saved it is the [d]power of God.
19 For it is written:

> [a]"I will destroy the wisdom of the wise,
> And bring to nothing the
> understanding of the prudent."[1]

20 [a]Where *is* the wise? Where *is* the scribe?
Where *is* the disputer of this age? [b]Has not
God made foolish the wisdom of this world?
21 For since, in the [a]wisdom of God, the world
through wisdom did not know God, it pleased
God through the foolishness of the message
preached to save those who believe. 22 For
[a]Jews request a sign, and Greeks seek after
wisdom; 23 but we preach Christ crucified, [a]to
the Jews a stumbling block and to the Greeks[1]
[b]foolishness, 24 but to those who are called,
both Jews and Greeks, Christ [a]the power of
God and [b]the wisdom of God. 25 Because the
foolishness of God is wiser than men, and
the weakness of God is stronger than men.

Glory Only in the Lord

26 For you see your calling, brethren, [a]that
not many wise according to the flesh, not
many mighty, not many noble, *are called.*
27 But [a]God has chosen the foolish things of
the world to put to shame the wise, and God
has chosen the weak things of the world to put
to shame the things which are mighty; 28 and
the base things of the world and the things
which are despised God has chosen, and the
things which are not, to bring to nothing the
things that are, 29 that no flesh should glory in
His presence. 30 But of Him you are in Christ
Jesus, who became for us wisdom from God—
and [a]righteousness and sanctification and
redemption— 31 that, as it is written, [a]"He who
glories, let him glory in the LORD."[1]

Christ Crucified

2 And I, brethren, when I came to you, did
not come with excellence of speech or of
wisdom declaring to you the testimony[1] of
God. 2 For I determined not to know anything
among you [a]except Jesus Christ and Him
crucified. 3 [a]I was with you [b]in weakness,
in fear, and in much trembling. 4 And my

1:1 [a] Rom. 1:1 [b] 2 Cor. 1:1 [c] Acts 18:17 **1:2** [a] [Acts 15:9] [b] Rom. 1:7 [c] [1 Cor. 8:6] [d] [Rom. 3:22] **1:3** [a] Rom. 1:7 **1:4** [a] Rom. 1:8 **1:5** [a] [1 Cor. 12:8] **1:6** [a] 2 Tim. 1:8 **1:7** [a] Phil. 3:20 **1:8** [a] 1 Thess. 3:13; 5:23 [b] Col. 1:22; 2:7 **1:9** [a] Is. 49:7 [b] [John 15:4] **1:10** [a] 2 Cor. 13:11 **1:12** [a] 1 Cor. 3:4 [b] Acts 18:24 [c] John 1:42 **1:13** [a] 2 Cor. 11:4 **1:14** [a] John 4:2 [b] Acts 18:8 [c] Rom. 16:23 **1:16** [a] 1 Cor. 16:15, 17 **1:17** [a] [1 Cor. 2:1, 4, 13] **1:18** [a] 1 Cor. 2:14 [b] 2 Cor. 2:15 [c] [1 Cor. 15:2] [d] Rom. 1:16 **1:19** [a] Is. 29:14 [1] Isaiah 29:14 **1:20** [a] Is. 19:12; 33:18 [b] Job 12:17 **1:21** [a] Dan. 2:20 **1:22** [a] Matt. 12:38 **1:23** [a] Luke 2:34 [b] [1 Cor. 2:14] [1] NU-Text reads *Gentiles.* **1:24** [a] [Rom. 1:4] [b] Col. 2:3 **1:26** [a] John 7:48 **1:27** [a] Matt. 11:25 **1:30** [a] [2 Cor. 5:21] **1:31** [a] Jer. 9:23, 24 [1] Jeremiah 9:24 **2:1** [1] NU-Text reads *mystery.* **2:2** [a] Gal. 6:14 **2:3** [a] Acts 18:1 [b] [2 Cor. 4:7]

PEACE NOTE

The beautiful by-product of God's peace is sanctification. When I live in the peace of God, I will walk in the holiness of God.

1 CORINTHIANS 1:30

speech and my preaching [a]*were* not with
persuasive words of human[1] wisdom, [b]but
in demonstration of the Spirit and of power,
5 that your faith should not be in the wisdom
of men but in the [a]power of God.

Spiritual Wisdom

6 However, we speak wisdom among those
who are mature, yet not the wisdom of this
age, nor of the rulers of this age, who are
coming to nothing. 7 But we speak the wisdom of God in a mystery, the hidden *wisdom*
which God ordained before the ages for our
glory, 8 which none of the rulers of this age
knew; for [a]had they known, they would not
have [b]crucified the Lord of glory.
9 But as it is written:

[a]"Eye has not seen, nor ear heard,
Nor have entered into the heart of man
The things which God has prepared for
those who love Him."[1]

10 But [a]God has revealed *them* to us through
His Spirit. For the Spirit searches all things,
yes, the deep things of God. 11 For what man
knows the things of a man except the [a]spirit
of the man which is in him? [b]Even so no one
knows the things of God except the Spirit of
God. 12 Now we have received, not the spirit
of the world, but [a]the Spirit who is from God,
that we might know the things that have been
freely given to us by God.
13 These things we also speak, not in words
which man's wisdom teaches but which the
Holy[1] Spirit teaches, comparing spiritual
things with spiritual. 14 [a]But the natural man
does not receive the things of the Spirit of
God, for they are foolishness to him; nor can
he know *them,* because they are spiritually
discerned. 15 But he who is spiritual judges
all things, yet he himself is *rightly* judged by
no one. 16 For [a]"who has known the mind of
the LORD that he may instruct Him?"[1] [b]But
we have the mind of Christ.

Sectarianism Is Carnal

3 And I, brethren, could not speak to you as
to spiritual *people* but as to carnal, as to
[a]babes in Christ. 2 I fed you with [a]milk and not
with solid food; [b]for until now you were not
able *to receive it,* and even now you are still
not able; 3 for you are still carnal. For where
there are envy, strife, and divisions among
you, are you not carnal and behaving like *mere*
men? 4 For when one says, "I am of Paul," and
another, "I *am* of Apollos," are you not carnal?

Watering, Working, Warning

5 Who then is Paul, and who *is* Apollos,
but [a]ministers through whom you believed,
as the Lord gave to each one? 6 [a]I planted,
[b]Apollos watered, [c]but God gave the increase.
7 So then [a]neither he who plants is anything,
nor he who waters, but God who gives the
increase. 8 Now he who plants and he who
waters are one, [a]and each one will receive
his own reward according to his own labor.
9 For [a]we are God's fellow workers; you are
God's field, *you are* [b]God's building. 10 [a]Accord-
ing to the grace of God which was given to
me, as a wise master builder I have laid [b]the

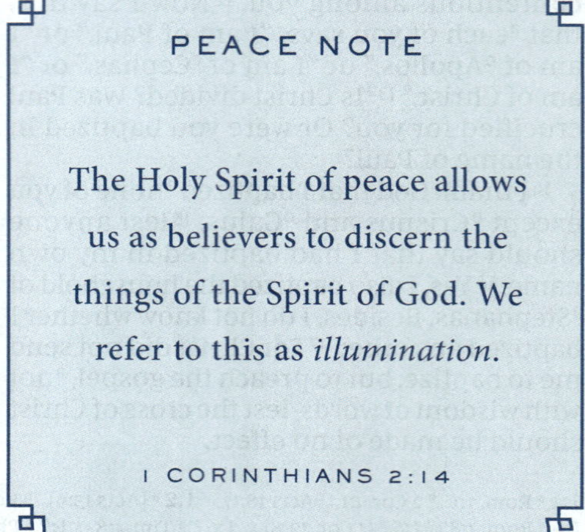

2:4 [a] 2 Pet. 1:16 [b] Rom. 15:19 [1] NU-Text omits *human.* **2:5** [a] 1 Thess. 1:5 **2:8** [a] Luke 23:34 [b] Matt. 27:33–50 **2:9** [a] [Is. 64:4; 65:17] [1] Isaiah 64:4 **2:10** [a] Matt. 11:25; 13:11; 16:17 **2:11** [a] [James 2:26] [b] Rom. 11:33 **2:12** [a] [Rom. 8:15] **2:13** [1] NU-Text omits *Holy.* **2:14** [a] Matt. 16:23 **2:16** [a] Is. 40:13 [b] [John 15:15] [1] Isaiah 40:13 **3:1** [a] Heb. 5:13 **3:2** [a] 1 Pet. 2:2 [b] John 16:12 **3:5** [a] 2 Cor. 3:3, 6; 4:1; 5:18; 6:4 **3:6** [a] Acts 18:4 [b] Acts 18:24–27 [c] [2 Cor. 3:5] **3:7** [a] [Gal. 6:3] **3:8** [a] Ps. 62:12 **3:9** [a] 2 Cor. 6:1 [b] [Eph. 2:20–22] **3:10** [a] Rom. 1:5 [b] 1 Cor. 4:15

PEACE NOTE

The peace of the Lord in our lives gives us the guarantee of the Second Coming of the Lord Jesus Christ.

1 CORINTHIANS 4:5

foundation, and another builds on it. But let
each one take heed how he builds on it. 11For
no other foundation can anyone lay than [a]that
which is laid, [b]which is Jesus Christ. 12Now if
anyone builds on this foundation *with* gold,
silver, precious stones, wood, hay, straw, 13each
one's work will become clear; for the Day [a]will
declare it, because [b]it will be revealed by fire;
and the fire will test each one's work, of what
sort it is. 14If anyone's work which he has built
on *it* endures, he will receive a reward. 15If
anyone's work is burned, he will suffer loss; but
he himself will be saved, yet so as through fire.
16[a]Do you not know that you are the temple
of God and *that* the Spirit of God dwells in
you? 17If anyone defiles the temple of God,
God will destroy him. For the temple of God
is holy, which *temple* you are.

Avoid Worldly Wisdom

18[a]Let no one deceive himself. If anyone
among you seems to be wise in this age, let
him become a fool that he may become wise.
19For the wisdom of this world is foolishness with God. For it is written, [a]"He catches the wise in their *own* craftiness";[1] 20and
again, [a]"The LORD knows the thoughts of the
wise, that they are futile."[1] 21Therefore let no
one boast in men. For [a]all things are yours:
22whether Paul or Apollos or Cephas, or the
world or life or death, or things present or
things to come—all are yours. 23And [a]you
are Christ's, and Christ *is* God's.

Stewards of the Mysteries of God

4 Let a man so consider us, as [a]servants of
Christ [b]and stewards of the mysteries of
God. 2Moreover it is required in stewards that
one be found faithful. 3But with me it is a very
small thing that I should be judged by you or
by a human court.[1] In fact, I do not even judge
myself. 4For I know of nothing against myself,
yet I am not justified by this; but He who judges me is the Lord. 5[a]Therefore judge nothing
before the time, until the Lord comes, who will
both bring to [b]light the hidden things of darkness and [c]reveal the counsels of the hearts.
[d]Then each one's praise will come from God.

Fools for Christ's Sake

6Now these things, brethren, I have figu-
ratively transferred to myself and Apollos
for your sakes, that you may learn in us not
to think beyond what is written, that none of
you may be puffed up on behalf of one against
the other. 7For who makes you differ *from*
another? And [a]what do you have that you did
not receive? Now if you did indeed receive *it,*
why do you boast as if you had not received *it?*
8You are already full! [a]You are already rich!
You have reigned as kings without us—and
indeed I could wish you did reign, that we
also might reign with you! 9For I think that
God has displayed us, the apostles, last, as
men condemned to death; for we have been
made a [a]spectacle to the world, both to angels
and to men. 10We *are* [a]fools for Christ's sake,
but you *are* wise in Christ! [b]We *are* weak, but
you *are* strong! You *are* distinguished, but
we *are* dishonored! 11To the present hour we
both hunger and thirst, and we are poorly
clothed, and beaten, and homeless. 12[a]And
we labor, working with our own hands. [b]Be-
ing reviled, we bless; being persecuted, we
endure; 13being defamed, we entreat. [a]We
have been made as the filth of the world, the
offscouring of all things until now.

Paul's Paternal Care

14I do not write these things to shame you,
but [a]as my beloved children I warn *you.* 15For
though you might have ten thousand in-
structors in Christ, yet *you do* not *have* many
fathers; for [a]in Christ Jesus I have begotten
you through the gospel. 16Therefore I urge
you, [a]imitate me. 17For this reason I have sent
[a]Timothy to you, [b]who is my beloved and
faithful son in the Lord, who will [c]remind you
of my ways in Christ, as I [d]teach everywhere
[e]in every church.
18[a]Now some are puffed up, as though I

3:11 [a] Is. 28:16 [b] Eph. 2:20 **3:13** [a] 1 Pet. 1:7 [b] Luke 2:35 **3:16** [a] 2 Cor. 6:16 **3:18** [a] Prov. 3:7 **3:19** [a] Job 5:13 [1] Job 5:13 **3:20** [a] Ps. 94:11 [1] Psalm 94:11 **3:21** [a] [2 Cor. 4:5] **3:23** [a] 2 Cor. 10:7 **4:1** [a] Col. 1:25 [b] Titus 1:7 **4:3** [1] Literally *day* **4:5** [a] Matt. 7:1 [b] Matt. 10:26 [c] 1 Cor. 3:13 [d] Rom. 2:29 **4:7** [a] John 3:27 **4:8** [a] Rev. 3:17 **4:9** [a] Heb. 10:33 **4:10** [a] Acts 17:18; 26:24 [b] 2 Cor. 13:9 **4:12** [a] Acts 18:3; 20:34 [b] Matt. 5:44 **4:13** [a] Lam. 3:45 **4:14** [a] 1 Thess. 2:11 **4:15** [a] Gal. 4:19 **4:16** [a] [1 Cor. 11:1] **4:17** [a] Acts 19:22 [b] 1 Tim. 1:2, 18 [c] 1 Cor. 11:2 [d] 1 Cor. 7:17 [e] 1 Cor. 14:33 **4:18** [a] 1 Cor. 5:2

were not coming to you. 19 [a]But I will come
to you shortly, [b]if the Lord wills, and I will
know, not the word of those who are puffed
up, but the power. 20 For [a]the kingdom of God
is not in word but in [b]power. 21 What do you
want? [a]Shall I come to you with a rod, or in
love and a spirit of gentleness?

Immorality Defiles the Church

5 It is actually reported *that there is* sexual
immorality among you, and such sexual
immorality as is not even named[1] among the
Gentiles—that a man has his father's [a]wife!
2 [a]And you are puffed up, and have not rather
[b]mourned, that he who has done this deed
might be taken away from among you. 3 [a]For I
indeed, as absent in body but present in spirit,
have already judged (as though I were present)
him who has so done this deed. 4 In the [a]name
of our Lord Jesus Christ, when you are gathered
together, along with my spirit, [b]with the power
of our Lord Jesus Christ, 5 [a]deliver such a one to
[b]Satan for the destruction of the flesh, that his
spirit may be saved in the day of the Lord Jesus.[1]
6 [a]Your glorying *is* not good. Do you not
know that [b]a little leaven leavens the whole
lump? 7 Therefore purge out the old leaven,
that you may be a new lump, since you truly
are unleavened. For indeed [a]Christ, our [b]Pass-
over, was sacrificed for us.[1] 8 Therefore [a]let us
keep the feast, [b]not with old leaven, nor [c]with
the leaven of malice and wickedness, but with
the unleavened *bread* of sincerity and truth.

Immorality Must Be Judged

9 I wrote to you in my epistle [a]not to keep
company with sexually immoral people. 10 Yet
I certainly *did* not *mean* with the sexually
immoral people of this world, or with the
covetous, or extortioners, or idolaters, since
then you would need to go [a]out of the world.
11 But now I have written to you not to keep
company [a]with anyone named a brother,
who is sexually immoral, or covetous, or
an idolater, or a reviler, or a drunkard, or
an extortioner—[b]not even to eat with such
a person.
12 For what *have* I *to do* with judging those
also who are outside? Do you not judge those
who are inside? 13 But those who are outside
God judges. Therefore [a]"put away from yourselves the evil person."[1]

Do Not Sue the Brethren

6 Dare any of you, having a matter against
another, go to law before the unrighteous,
and not before the [a]saints? 2 Do you not know
that [a]the saints will judge the world? And
if the world will be judged by you, are you
unworthy to judge the smallest matters? 3 Do
you not know that we shall [a]judge angels?
How much more, things that pertain to this
life? 4 If then you have judgments concerning
things pertaining to this life, do you appoint
those who are least esteemed by the church
to judge? 5 I say this to your shame. Is it so,
that there is not a wise man among you, not
even one, who will be able to judge between
his brethren? 6 But brother goes to law against
brother, and that before unbelievers!
7 Now therefore, it is already an utter failure
for you that you go to law against one another.
[a]Why do you not rather accept wrong? Why do
you not rather *let yourselves* be cheated? 8 No,
you yourselves do wrong and cheat, and *you
do* these things *to your* brethren! 9 Do you not
know that the unrighteous will not inherit the
kingdom of God? Do not be deceived. [a]Neither
fornicators, nor idolaters, nor adulterers, nor
homosexuals,[1] nor sodomites, 10 nor thieves,
nor covetous, nor drunkards, nor revilers, nor
extortioners will inherit the kingdom of God.
11 And such were [a]some of you. [b]But you were
washed, but you were sanctified, but you were
justified in the name of the Lord Jesus and
by the Spirit of our God.

Glorify God in Body and Spirit

12 [a]All things are lawful for me, but all things
are not helpful. All things are lawful for me,
but I will not be brought under the power of
any. 13 [a]Foods for the stomach and the stomach for foods, but God will destroy both it
and them. Now the body *is* not for [b]sexual
immorality but [c]for the Lord, [d]and the Lord
for the body. 14 And [a]God both raised up the
Lord and will also raise us up [b]by His power.
15 Do you not know that [a]your bodies are
members of Christ? Shall I then take the
members of Christ and make *them* members
of a harlot? Certainly not! 16 Or do you not
know that he who is joined to a harlot is one
body *with her?* For [a]"the two," He says, "shall
become one flesh."[1] 17 [a]But he who is joined
to the Lord is one spirit *with Him.*

4:19 [a] Acts 19:21; 20:2 [b] Acts 18:21 **4:20** [a] 1 Thess. 1:5 [b] 1 Cor. 2:4 **4:21** [a] 2 Cor. 10:2 **5:1** [a] Lev. 18:6–8 [1] NU-Text omits *named.* **5:2** [a] 1 Cor. 4:18 [b] 2 Cor. 7:7–10 **5:3** [a] Col. 2:5 **5:4** [a] [Matt. 18:20] [b] [John 20:23] **5:5** [a] 1 Tim. 1:20 [b] [Acts 26:18] [1] NU-Text omits *Jesus.* **5:6** [a] 1 Cor. 3:21 [b] Gal. 5:9 **5:7** [a] Is. 53:7 [b] John 19:14 [1] NU-Text omits *for us.* **5:8** [a] Ex. 12:15 [b] Deut. 16:3 [c] Matt. 16:6 **5:9** [a] 2 Cor. 6:14 **5:10** [a] John 17:15 **5:11** [a] Matt. 18:17 [b] Gal. 2:12 **5:13** [a] Deut. 13:5; 17:7, 12; 19:19; 21:21; 22:21, 24; 24:7 [1] Deuteronomy 17:7; 19:19; 22:21, 24; 24:7 **6:1** [a] Dan. 7:22 **6:2** [a] Ps. 49:14 **6:3** [a] 2 Pet. 2:4 **6:7** [a] [Prov. 20:22] **6:9** [a] Gal. 5:21 [1] That is, catamites **6:11** [a] [1 Cor. 12:2] [b] Heb. 10:22 **6:12** [a] 1 Cor. 10:23 **6:13** [a] Matt. 15:17 [b] Gal. 5:19 [c] 1 Thess. 4:3 [d] [Eph. 5:23] **6:14** [a] 2 Cor. 4:14 [b] Eph. 1:19 **6:15** [a] Rom. 12:5 **6:16** [a] Gen. 2:24 [1] Genesis 2:24 **6:17** [a] [John 17:21–23]

18 [a]Flee sexual immorality. Every sin that a man does is outside the body, but he who commits sexual immorality sins [b]against his own body. 19 Or [a]do you not know that your body is the temple of the Holy Spirit *who is* in you, whom you have from God, [b]and you are not your own? 20 For [a]you were bought at a price; therefore glorify God in your body[1] and in your spirit, which are God's.

Principles of Marriage

7 Now concerning the things of which you wrote to me:
[a]*It is* good for a man not to touch a woman. 2 Nevertheless, because of sexual immorality, let each man have his own wife, and let each woman have her own husband. 3 [a]Let the husband render to his wife the affection due her, and likewise also the wife to her husband. 4 The wife does not have authority over her own body, but the husband *does.* And likewise the husband does not have authority over his own body, but the wife *does.* 5 [a]Do not deprive one another except with consent for a time, that you may give yourselves to fasting and prayer; and come together again so that [b]Satan does not tempt you because of your lack of self-control. 6 But I say this as a concession, [a]not as a commandment. 7 For [a]I wish that all men were even as I myself. But each one has his own gift from God, one in this manner and another in that.

8 But I say to the unmarried and to the widows: [a]It is good for them if they remain even as I am; 9 but [a]if they cannot exercise self-control, let them marry. For it is better to marry than to burn *with passion.*

Keep Your Marriage Vows

10 Now to the married I command, *yet* not I but the [a]Lord: [b]A wife is not to depart from *her* husband. 11 But even if she does depart, let her remain unmarried or be reconciled to *her* husband. And a husband is not to divorce *his* wife.

12 But to the rest I, not the Lord, say: If any brother has a wife who does not believe, and she is willing to live with him, let him not divorce her. 13 And a woman who has a husband who does not believe, if he is willing to live with her, let her not divorce him. 14 For the unbelieving husband is sanctified by the wife, and the unbelieving wife is sanctified by the husband; otherwise [a]your children would be unclean, but now they are holy. 15 But if the unbeliever departs, let him depart; a brother or a sister is not under bondage in such *cases.* But God has called us [a]to peace. 16 For how do you know, O wife, whether you will [a]save *your* husband? Or how do you know, O husband, whether you will save *your* wife?

6:18 [a] Heb. 13:4 [b] Rom. 1:24 **6:19** [a] 2 Cor. 6:16 [b] Rom. 14:7 **6:20** [a] 2 Pet. 2:1 [1] NU-Text ends the verse at *body.*
7:1 [a] 1 Cor. 7:8, 26 **7:3** [a] Ex. 21:10 **7:5** [a] Joel 2:16 [b] 1 Thess. 3:5 **7:6** [a] 2 Cor. 8:8 **7:7** [a] Acts 26:29 **7:8** [a] 1 Cor. 7:1, 26
7:9 [a] 1 Tim. 5:14 **7:10** [a] Mark 10:6–10 [b] [Matt. 5:32] **7:14** [a] Mal. 2:15 **7:15** [a] Rom. 12:18 **7:16** [a] 1 Pet. 3:1

THE FRUIT OF GRACIOUSNESS

But if the unbeliever departs, let him depart; a brother or a sister is not under bondage in such cases. But God has called us to peace.

I CORINTHIANS 7:15

The death of a marriage is a tragedy. In antiquity divorce was every bit as messy as it is today—bitterness, strife, litigation. In those days, marriages often involved contracts and dowries. In the event that a partner was unfaithful or tried to leave the marriage, the consequences could be ugly.

Life then was intertwined with phony gods. People feared the gods and wished above all not to offend them. This meant offering sacrifices to them, giving money to their priests, and other acts and rituals designed to appease the easily offended deities. When a pagan became a Christian, belief in and appeasement of the gods ended—which terrified one's partner who was still a pagan. This is what Paul is talking about in chapter 7. Christian conversion could destabilize a pagan marriage.

Paul counseled believing spouses to remain faithful and loving, but if unbelieving partners wished to leave, to let them. God has called us to peace, not conflict. The gracious response of the believing spouse toward the unbelieving spouse can lead to conversion and a redeemed marriage. Obey the Lord and watch for good fruit to come of it.

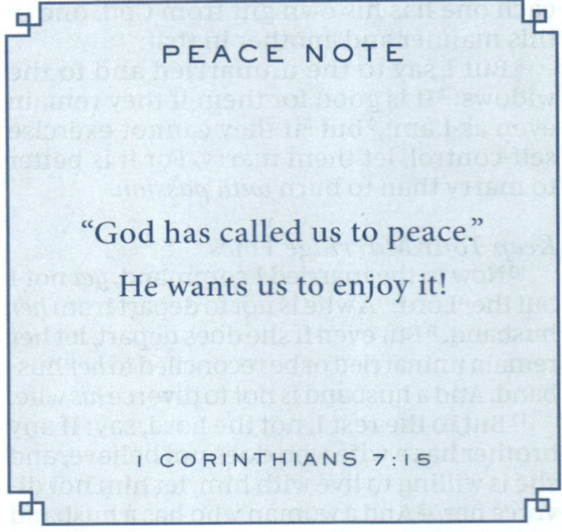

Live as You Are Called

17 But as God has distributed to each one,
as the Lord has called each one, so let him
walk. And [a]so I ordain in all the churches.
18 Was anyone called while circumcised? Let
him not become uncircumcised. Was anyone
called while uncircumcised? [a]Let him not
be circumcised. 19 [a]Circumcision is nothing
and uncircumcision is nothing, but [b]keeping
the commandments of God *is what matters.*
20 Let each one remain in the same calling in
which he was called. 21 Were you called *while*
a slave? Do not be concerned about it; but
if you can be made free, rather use *it.* 22 For
he who is called in the Lord *while* a slave is
[a]the Lord's freedman. Likewise he who is
called *while* free is [b]Christ's slave. 23 [a]You were
bought at a price; do not become slaves of
men. 24 Brethren, let each one remain with
[a]God in that *state* in which he was called.

To the Unmarried and Widows

25 Now concerning virgins: [a]I have no commandment from the Lord; yet I give judgment
as one [b]whom the Lord in His mercy has made
[c]trustworthy. 26 I suppose therefore that this
is good because of the present distress—[a]that
it is good for a man to remain as he is: 27 Are
you bound to a wife? Do not seek to be loosed.
Are you loosed from a wife? Do not seek a
wife. 28 But even if you do marry, you have not
sinned; and if a virgin marries, she has not
sinned. Nevertheless such will have trouble
in the flesh, but I would spare you.
29 But [a]this I say, brethren, the time *is* short,
so that from now on even those who have wives
should be as though they had none, 30 those
who weep as though they did not weep, those
who rejoice as though they did not rejoice,
those who buy as though they did not possess,
31 and those who use this world as not [a]misusing
it. For [b]the form of this world is passing away.
32 But I want you to be without care. [a]He
who is unmarried cares for the things of the
Lord—how he may please the Lord. 33 But
he who is married cares about the things
of the world—how he may please *his* wife.
34 There is[1] a difference between a wife and a
virgin. The unmarried woman [a]cares about
the things of the Lord, that she may be holy
both in body and in spirit. But she who is
married cares about the things of the world—
how she may please *her* husband. 35 And this
I say for your own profit, not that I may put a
leash on you, but for what is proper, and that
you may serve the Lord without distraction.
36 But if any man thinks he is behaving
improperly toward his virgin, if she is past
the flower of youth, and thus it must be, let
him do what he wishes. He does not sin; let
them marry. 37 Nevertheless he who stands
steadfast in his heart, having no necessity,
but has power over his own will, and has so
determined in his heart that he will keep his
virgin,[1] does well. 38 [a]So then he who gives *her*[1]
in marriage does well, but he who does not
give *her* in marriage does better.
39 [a]A wife is bound by law as long as her husband lives; but if her husband dies, she is at liberty to be married to whom she wishes, [b]only
in the Lord. 40 But she is happier if she remains
as she is, [a]according to my judgment—and [b]I
think I also have the Spirit of God.

Be Sensitive to Conscience

8 Now [a]concerning things offered to idols:
We know that we all have [b]knowledge.
[c]Knowledge puffs up, but love edifies. 2 And
[a]if anyone thinks that he knows anything, he
knows nothing yet as he ought to know. 3 But if
anyone loves God, this one is known by Him.
4 Therefore concerning the eating of things
offered to idols, we know that [a]an idol *is* nothing in the world, [b]and that *there is* no other
God but one. 5 For even if there are [a]so-called
gods, whether in heaven or on earth (as there
are many gods and many lords), 6 yet [a]for us
there is one God, the Father, [b]of whom *are* all
things, and we for Him; and [c]one Lord Jesus

7:17 [a] 1 Cor. 4:17 **7:18** [a] Acts 15:1 **7:19** [a] [Gal. 3:28; 5:6; 6:15] [b] [John 15:14] **7:22** [a] [John 8:36] [b] 1 Pet. 2:16 **7:23** [a] 1 Pet. 1:18, 19 **7:24** [a] [Col. 3:22–24] **7:25** [a] 2 Cor. 8:8 [b] 1 Tim. 1:13, 16 [c] 1 Tim. 1:12 **7:26** [a] 1 Cor. 7:1, 8 **7:29** [a] 1 Pet. 4:7 **7:31** [a] 1 Cor. 9:18 [b] [1 John 2:17] **7:32** [a] 1 Tim. 5:5 **7:34** [a] Luke 10:40 [1] M-Text adds *also.* **7:37** [1] Or *virgin daughter* **7:38** [a] Heb. 13:4 [1] NU-Text reads *his own virgin.* **7:39** [a] Rom. 7:2 [b] 2 Cor. 6:14 **7:40** [a] 1 Cor. 7:6, 25 [b] 1 Thess. 4:8 **8:1** [a] Acts 15:20 [b] Rom. 14:14 [c] Rom. 14:3 **8:2** [a] [1 Cor. 13:8–12] **8:4** [a] Is. 41:24 [b] Deut. 4:35, 39; 6:4 **8:5** [a] [John 10:34] **8:6** [a] Mal. 2:10 [b] Acts 17:28 [c] John 13:13

Christ, [d]through whom *are* all things, and
[e]through whom we *live.*
7 However, *there is* not in everyone that
knowledge; for some, [a]with consciousness
of the idol, until now eat *it* as a thing offered
to an idol; and their conscience, being weak,
is [b]defiled. 8 But [a]food does not commend us
to God; for neither if we eat are we the better,
nor if we do not eat are we the worse.
9 But [a]beware lest somehow this liberty of
yours become [b]a stumbling block to those
who are weak. 10 For if anyone sees you who
have knowledge eating in an idol's temple,
will not [a]the conscience of him who is weak
be emboldened to eat those things offered to
idols? 11 And [a]because of your knowledge shall
the weak brother perish, for whom Christ
died? 12 But [a]when you thus sin against the
brethren, and wound their weak conscience,
you sin against Christ. 13 Therefore, [a]if food
makes my brother stumble, I will never again
eat meat, lest I make my brother stumble.

A Pattern of Self-Denial

9 Am [a]I not an apostle? Am I not free?
[b]Have I not seen Jesus Christ our Lord?
[c]Are you not my work in the Lord? 2 If I am
not an apostle to others, yet doubtless I am to
you. For you are [a]the seal of my apostleship
in the Lord.
3 My defense to those who examine me is
this: 4 [a]Do we have no right to eat and drink?
5 Do we have no right to take along a believing wife, as *do* also the other apostles, [a]the
brothers of the Lord, and [b]Cephas? 6 Or *is*
it only Barnabas and I [a]*who* have no right
to refrain from working? 7 Who ever [a]goes
to war at his own expense? Who [b]plants a
vineyard and does not eat of its fruit? Or
who [c]tends a flock and does not drink of the
milk of the flock?
8 Do I say these things as a *mere* man? Or
does not the law say the same also? 9 For it is
written in the law of Moses, [a]"You shall not
muzzle an ox while it treads out the grain."[1] Is
it oxen God is concerned about? 10 Or does He
say *it* altogether for our sakes? For our sakes,
no doubt, *this* is written, that [a]he who plows
should plow in hope, and he who threshes
in hope should be partaker of his hope. 11 [a]If
we have sown spiritual things for you, *is it* a
great thing if we reap your material things?
12 If others are partakers of *this* right over
you, *are* we not even more?
[a]Nevertheless we have not used this right,
but endure all things [b]lest we hinder the
gospel of Christ. 13 [a]Do you not know that
those who minister the holy things eat *of the*
things of the [b]temple, and those who serve at
the altar partake of *the offerings of* the altar?
14 Even so [a]the Lord has commanded [b]that
those who preach the gospel should live
from the gospel.
15 But [a]I have used none of these things,
nor have I written these things that it should
be done so to me; for [b]it *would be* better for
me to die than that anyone should make my
boasting void. 16 For if I preach the gospel, I
have nothing to boast of, for [a]necessity is laid
upon me; yes, woe is me if I do not preach
the gospel! 17 For if I do this willingly, [a]I have
a reward; but if against my will, [b]I have been
entrusted with a stewardship. 18 What is my
reward then? That [a]when I preach the gospel,
I may present the gospel of Christ[1] without
charge, that I [b]may not abuse my authority
in the gospel.

Serving All Men

19 For though I am [a]free from all *men,* [b]I
have made myself a servant to all, [c]that I
might win the more; 20 and [a]to the Jews I
became as a Jew, that I might win Jews; to
those *who are* under the law, as under the
law,[1] that I might win those *who are* under
the law; 21 [a]to [b]those *who are* without law, as
without law [c](not being without law toward
God,[1] but under law toward Christ[2]), that I
might win those *who are* without law; 22 [a]to
the weak I became as[1] weak, that I might win
the weak. [b]I have become all things to all *men,*
[c]that I might by all means save some. 23 Now
this I do for the gospel's sake, that I may be
partaker of it with *you.*

Striving for a Crown

24 Do you not know that those who run
in a race all run, but one receives the prize?
[a]Run in such a way that you may obtain *it.*
25 And everyone who competes *for the prize*
is temperate in all things. Now they *do it* to
obtain a perishable crown, but we *for* [a]an

8:6 [d] John 1:3 [e] Rom. 5:11 **8:7** [a] [1 Cor. 10:28] [b] Rom. 14:14, 22 **8:8** [a] [Rom. 14:17] **8:9** [a] Gal. 5:13 [b] Rom. 14:13, 21 **8:10** [a] 1 Cor. 10:28 **8:11** [a] Rom. 14:15, 20 **8:12** [a] Matt. 25:40 **8:13** [a] Rom. 14:21 **9:1** [a] Acts 9:15 [b] 1 Cor. 15:8 [c] 1 Cor. 3:6; 4:15 **9:2** [a] 2 Cor. 12:12 **9:4** [a] [1 Thess. 2:6, 9] **9:5** [a] Matt. 13:55 [b] Matt. 8:14 **9:6** [a] Acts 4:36 **9:7** [a] 2 Cor. 10:4 [b] Deut. 20:6 [c] John 21:15 **9:9** [a] Deut. 25:4 [1] Deuteronomy 25:4 **9:10** [a] 2 Tim. 2:6 **9:11** [a] Rom. 15:27 **9:12** [a] [Acts 18:3; 20:33] [b] 2 Cor. 11:12 **9:13** [a] Lev. 6:16, 26; 7:6, 31 [b] Num. 18:8–31 **9:14** [a] Matt. 10:10 [b] Rom. 10:15 **9:15** [a] Acts 18:3; 20:33 [b] 2 Cor. 11:10 **9:16** [a] [Rom. 1:14] **9:17** [a] 1 Cor. 3:8, 14; 9:18 [b] Gal. 2:7 **9:18** [a] 1 Cor. 10:33 [b] 1 Cor. 7:31; 9:12 [1] NU-Text omits *of Christ.* **9:19** [a] 1 Cor. 9:1 [b] Gal. 5:13 [c] Matt. 18:15 **9:20** [a] Acts 16:3; 21:23–26 [1] NU-Text adds *though not being myself under the law.* **9:21** [a] [Gal. 2:3; 3:2] [b] [Rom. 2:12, 14] [c] [1 Cor. 7:22] [1] NU-Text reads *God's law.* [2] NU-Text reads *Christ's law.* **9:22** [a] Rom. 14:1; 15:1 [b] 1 Cor. 10:33 [c] Rom. 11:14 [1] NU-Text omits *as.* **9:24** [a] Gal. 2:2 **9:25** [a] James 1:12

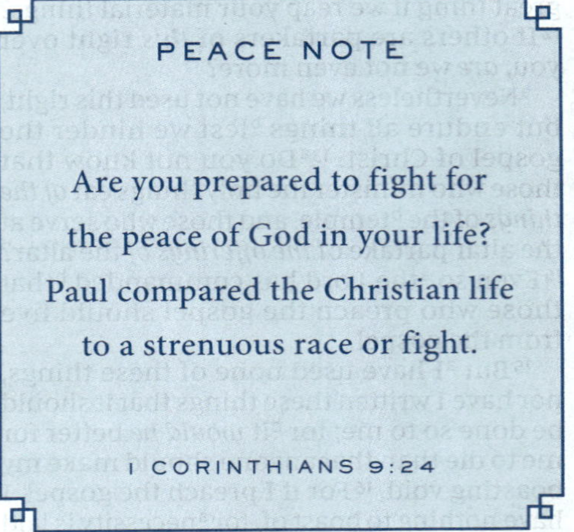

imperishable *crown.* 26 Therefore I run thus:
[a]not with uncertainty. Thus I fight: not as
one who beats the air. 27 [a]But I discipline my
body and [b]bring *it* into subjection, lest, when
I have preached to others, I myself should
become [c]disqualified.

Old Testament Examples

10 Moreover, brethren, I do not want you
to be unaware that all our fathers were
under [a]the cloud, all passed through [b]the sea,
2 all were baptized into Moses in the cloud
and in the sea, 3 all ate the same [a]spiritual
food, 4 and all drank the same [a]spiritual drink.
For they drank of that spiritual Rock that
followed them, and that Rock was Christ.
5 But with most of them God was not well
pleased, for *their bodies* [a]were scattered in
the wilderness.
6 Now these things became our examples,
to the intent that we should not lust after
evil things as [a]they also lusted. 7 [a]And do
not become idolaters as *were* some of them.
As it is written, [b]"The people sat down to
eat and drink, and rose up to play."[1] 8 [a]Nor
let us commit sexual immorality, as [b]some
of them did, and [c]in one day twenty-three
thousand fell; 9 nor let us tempt Christ, as
[a]some of them also tempted, and [b]were
destroyed by serpents; 10 nor complain,
as [a]some of them also complained, and
[b]were destroyed by [c]the destroyer. 11 Now
all[1] these things happened to them as examples, and [a]they were written for our
admonition, [b]upon whom the ends of the
ages have come.
12 Therefore [a]let him who thinks he stands
take heed lest he fall. 13 No temptation has
overtaken you except such as is common
to man; but [a]God *is* faithful, [b]who will not
allow you to be tempted beyond what you
are able, but with the temptation will also
make the way of escape, that you may be
able to bear *it.*

Flee from Idolatry

14 Therefore, my beloved, [a]flee from idolatry. 15 I speak as to [a]wise men; judge for
yourselves what I say. 16 [a]The cup of blessing
which we bless, is it not the communion of
the blood of Christ? [b]The bread which we
break, is it not the communion of the body
of Christ? 17 For [a]we, *though* many, are one
bread *and* one body; for we all partake of
that one bread.
18 Observe [a]Israel [b]after the flesh: [c]Are not
those who eat of the sacrifices partakers of
the altar? 19 What am I saying then? [a]That
an idol is anything, or what is offered to
idols is anything? 20 Rather, that the things
which the Gentiles [a]sacrifice [b]they sacrifice
to demons and not to God, and I do not want
you to have fellowship with demons. 21 [a]You
cannot drink the cup of the Lord and [b]the
cup of demons; you cannot partake of the
[c]Lord's table and of the table of demons.
22 Or do we [a]provoke the Lord to jealousy?
[b]Are we stronger than He?

PEACE NOTE

An impure thought or a temptation may lead to a sinful deed or word. The temptation isn't the sin; it's the yielding to it. That choice kills peace.

1 CORINTHIANS 10:13

9:26 [a] 2 Tim. 2:5 9:27 [a] [Rom. 8:13] [b] [Rom. 6:18] [c] Jer. 6:30 10:1 [a] Ex. 13:21, 22 [b] Ex. 14:21, 22, 29 10:3 [a] Ex. 16:4, 15, 35 10:4 [a] Ex. 17:5–7 10:5 [a] Num. 14:29, 37; 26:65 10:6 [a] Num. 11:4, 34 10:7 [a] 1 Cor. 5:11; 10:14 [b] Ex. 32:6 [1] Exodus 32:6 10:8 [a] Rev. 2:14 [b] Num. 25:1–9 [c] Ps. 106:29 10:9 [a] Ex. 17:2, 7 [b] Num. 21:6–9 10:10 [a] Ex. 16:2 [b] Num. 14:37 [c] Ex. 12:23 10:11 [a] Rom. 15:4 [b] Phil. 4:5 [1] NU-Text omits *all.* 10:12 [a] Rom. 11:20 10:13 [a] 1 Cor. 1:9 [b] Ps. 125:3 10:14 [a] 2 Cor. 6:17 10:15 [a] 1 Cor. 8:1 10:16 [a] Matt. 26:26–28 [b] Acts 2:42 10:17 [a] 1 Cor. 12:12, 27 10:18 [a] Rom. 4:12 [b] Rom. 4:1 [c] Lev. 3:3; 7:6, 14 10:19 [a] 1 Cor. 8:4 10:20 [a] Lev. 17:7 [b] Deut. 32:17 10:21 [a] 2 Cor. 6:15, 16 [b] Deut. 32:38 [c] [1 Cor. 11:23–29] 10:22 [a] Deut. 32:21 [b] Ezek. 22:14

All to the Glory of God

23 All things are lawful for me,[1] but not all
things are [a]helpful; all things are lawful for
me,[2] but not all things edify. 24 Let no one seek
his own, but each one [a]the other's *well-being.*
25 [a]Eat whatever is sold in the meat market,
asking no questions for conscience' sake; 26 for
[a]"the earth *is* the LORD's, and all its fullness."[1]
27 If any of those who do not believe invites
you *to dinner,* and you desire to go, [a]eat whatever is set before you, asking no question
for conscience' sake. 28 But if anyone says to
you, "This was offered to idols," do not eat
it [a]for the sake of the one who told you, and
for conscience' sake;[1] for [b]"the earth *is* the
LORD's, and all its fullness."[2] 29 "Conscience,"
I say, not your own, but that of the other. For
[a]why is my liberty judged by another *man's*
conscience? 30 But if I partake with thanks,
why am I evil spoken of for *the food* [a]over
which I give thanks?
31 [a]Therefore, whether you eat or drink, or
whatever you do, do all to the glory of God.
32 [a]Give no offense, either to the Jews or to
the Greeks or to the church of God, 33 just [a]as
I also please all *men* in all *things,* not seeking
my own profit, but the *profit* of many, that
they may be saved.

11 Imitate[a] me, just as I also *imitate* Christ.

Head Coverings

2 Now I praise you, brethren, that you remember me in all things and keep the traditions just as I delivered *them* to you. 3 But I
want you to know that [a]the head of every man
is Christ, [b]the head of woman *is* man, and [c]the
head of Christ *is* God. 4 Every man praying
or [a]prophesying, having *his* head covered,
dishonors his head. 5 But every woman who
prays or prophesies with *her* head uncovered
dishonors her head, for that is one and the
same as if her head were [a]shaved. 6 For if a
woman is not covered, let her also be shorn.
But if it is [a]shameful for a woman to be shorn
or shaved, let her be covered. 7 For a man indeed ought not to cover *his* head, since [a]he is
the image and glory of God; but woman is the
glory of man. 8 For man is not from woman,
but woman [a]from man. 9 Nor was man created
for the woman, but woman [a]for the man. 10 For
this reason the woman ought to have *a symbol
of* authority on *her* head, because of the angels.
11 Nevertheless, [a]neither *is* man independent
of woman, nor woman independent of man,
in the Lord. 12 For as woman *came* from man,
even so man also *comes* through woman; but
all things are from God.
13 Judge among yourselves. Is it proper
for a woman to pray to God with her head
uncovered? 14 Does not even nature itself
teach you that if a man has long hair, it is a
dishonor to him? 15 But if a woman has long
hair, it is a glory to her; for *her* hair is given
to her[1] for a covering. 16 But [a]if anyone seems
to be contentious, we have no such custom,
[b]nor *do* the churches of God.

Conduct at the Lord's Supper

17 Now in giving these instructions I do not
praise *you,* since you come together not for
the better but for the worse. 18 For first of all,
when you come together as a church, [a]I hear
that there are divisions among you, and in part
I believe it. 19 For [a]there must also be factions
among you, [b]that those who are approved may
be recognized among you. 20 Therefore when
you come together in one place, it is not to eat
the Lord's Supper. 21 For in eating, each one
takes his own supper ahead of *others;* and one is
hungry and [a]another is drunk. 22 What! Do you
not have houses to eat and drink in? Or do you
despise [a]the church of God and [b]shame those
who have nothing? What shall I say to you?
Shall I praise you in this? I do not praise *you.*

Institution of the Lord's Supper

23 For [a]I received from the Lord that which I
also delivered to you: [b]that the Lord Jesus on
the *same* night in which He was betrayed took
bread; 24 and when He had given thanks, He
broke *it* and said, "Take, eat;[1] this is My body
which is broken[2] for you; do this in remembrance of Me." 25 In the same manner *He* also
took the cup after supper, saying, "This cup
is the new covenant in My blood. This do, as
often as you drink *it,* in remembrance of Me."
26 For as often as you eat this bread and
drink this cup, you proclaim the Lord's death
[a]till He comes.

Examine Yourself

27 Therefore whoever eats [a]this bread or
drinks *this* cup of the Lord in an unworthy
manner will be guilty of the body and blood[1]

10:23 [a] 1 Cor. 6:12 [1] NU-Text omits *for me.* [2] NU-Text omits *for me.* **10:24** [a] Phil. 2:4 **10:25** [a] [1 Tim. 4:4] **10:26** [a] Ps. 24:1 [1] Psalm 24:1 **10:27** [a] Luke 10:7, 8 **10:28** [a] [1 Cor. 8:7, 10, 12] [b] Ps. 24:1 [1] NU-Text omits the rest of this verse. [2] Psalm 24:1 **10:29** [a] Rom. 14:16 **10:30** [a] Rom. 14:6 **10:31** [a] Col. 3:17 **10:32** [a] Rom. 14:13 **10:33** [a] Rom. 15:2 **11:1** [a] Eph. 5:1 **11:3** [a] Eph. 1:22; 4:15; 5:23 [b] Gen. 3:16 [c] John 14:28 **11:4** [a] 1 Cor. 12:10 **11:5** [a] Deut. 21:12 **11:6** [a] Num. 5:18 **11:7** [a] Gen. 1:26, 27; 5:1; 9:6 **11:8** [a] Gen. 2:21–23 **11:9** [a] Gen. 2:18 **11:11** [a] [Gal. 3:28] **11:15** [1] M-Text omits *to her.* **11:16** [a] 1 Tim. 6:4 [b] 1 Cor. 7:17 **11:18** [a] 1 Cor. 1:10–12; 3:3 **11:19** [a] 1 Tim. 4:1 [b] [Deut. 13:3] **11:21** [a] Jude 12 **11:22** [a] 1 Cor. 10:32 [b] James 2:6 **11:23** [a] 1 Cor. 15:3 [b] Matt. 26:26–28 **11:24** [1] NU-Text omits *Take, eat.* [2] NU-Text omits *broken.* **11:26** [a] John 14:3 **11:27** [a] [John 6:51] [1] NU-Text and M-Text read *the blood.*

of the Lord. 28 But [a]let a man examine himself, and so let him eat of the bread and drink of the cup. 29 For he who eats and drinks in an unworthy manner[1] eats and drinks judgment to himself, not discerning the Lord's[2] body. 30 For this reason many *are* weak and sick among you, and many sleep. 31 For [a]if we would judge ourselves, we would not be judged. 32 But when we are judged, [a]we are chastened by the Lord, that we may not be condemned with the world.

33 Therefore, my brethren, when you [a]come together to eat, wait for one another. 34 But if anyone is hungry, let him eat at home, lest you come together for judgment. And the rest I will set in order when I come.

Spiritual Gifts: Unity in Diversity

12 Now [a]concerning spiritual *gifts,* brethren, I do not want you to be ignorant: 2 You know [a]that[1] you were Gentiles, carried away to these [b]dumb idols, however you were led. 3 Therefore I make known to you that no one speaking by the Spirit of God calls Jesus accursed, and [a]no one can say that Jesus is Lord except by the Holy Spirit.

4 [a]There are diversities of gifts, but [b]the same Spirit. 5 [a]There are differences of ministries, but the same Lord. 6 And there are diversities of activities, but it is the same God [a]who works all in all. 7 But the manifestation of the Spirit is given to each one for the profit *of all:* 8 for to one is given [a]the word of wisdom through the Spirit, to another [b]the word of knowledge through the same Spirit, 9 [a]to another faith by the same Spirit, to another [b]gifts of healings by the same[1] Spirit, 10 [a]to another the working of miracles, to another [b]prophecy, to another [c]discerning of spirits, to another [d]*different* kinds of tongues, to another the interpretation of tongues. 11 But one and the same Spirit works all these things, [a]distributing to each one individually [b]as He wills.

Unity and Diversity in One Body

12 For [a]as the body is one and has many members, but all the members of that one body, being many, are one body, [b]so also *is* Christ. 13 For [a]by one Spirit we were all baptized into one body—[b]whether Jews or Greeks, whether slaves or free—and [c]have all been made to drink into[1] one Spirit. 14 For in fact the body is not one member but many.

15 If the foot should say, "Because I am not a hand, I am not of the body," is it therefore not of the body? 16 And if the ear should say, "Because I am not an eye, I am not of the body," is it therefore not of the body? 17 If the whole body *were* an eye, where *would be* the hearing? If the whole *were* hearing, where *would be* the smelling? 18 But now [a]God has set the members, each one of them, in the body [b]just as He pleased. 19 And if they were all one member, where *would* the body *be?*

20 But now indeed *there are* many members, yet one body. 21 And the eye cannot say to the hand, "I have no need of you"; nor again the head to the feet, "I have no need of you." 22 No, much rather, those members of the body which seem to be weaker are necessary. 23 And those *members* of the body which we think to be less honorable, on these we bestow greater honor; and our unpresentable *parts* have greater modesty, 24 but our presentable *parts* have no need. But God composed the body, having given greater honor to that *part* which lacks it, 25 that there should be no schism in the body, but *that* the members should have the same care for one another. 26 And if one member suffers, all the members suffer with *it;* or if one member is honored, all the members rejoice with *it.*

27 Now [a]you are the body of Christ, and [b]members individually. 28 And [a]God has appointed these in the church: first [b]apostles, second [c]prophets, third teachers, after that [d]miracles, then [e]gifts of healings, [f]helps, [g]administrations, varieties of tongues. 29 *Are* all apostles? *Are* all prophets? *Are* all teachers? *Are* all workers of miracles? 30 Do all have gifts of healings? Do all speak with tongues? Do all interpret? 31 But [a]earnestly desire the best[1] gifts. And yet I show you a more excellent way.

The Greatest Gift

13 Though I speak with the tongues of men and of angels, but have not love, I have become sounding brass or a clanging cymbal. 2 And though I have *the gift of* [a]prophecy, and understand all mysteries and all knowledge, and though I have all faith, [b]so that I could remove mountains, but have not love, I am nothing. 3 And [a]though I bestow all my goods to feed *the poor,* and though I give my body to be burned,[1] but have not love, it profits me nothing.

11:28 [a] 2 Cor. 13:5 **11:29** [1] NU-Text omits *in an unworthy manner.* [2] NU-Text omits *Lord's.* **11:31** [a] [1 John 1:9] ***11:32*** [a] *Ps. 94:12* ***11:33*** [a] 1 Cor. 14:26 **12:1** [a] 1 Cor. 12:4; 14:1, 37 **12:2** [a] Eph. 2:11 [b] Ps. 115:5 [1] NU-Text and M-Text add *when.* **12:3** [a] Matt. 16:17 **12:4** [a] Rom. 12:3–8 [b] Eph. 4:4 **12:5** [a] Rom. 12:6 **12:6** [a] 1 Cor. 15:28 **12:8** [a] 1 Cor. 2:6, 7 [b] Rom. 15:14 **12:9** [a] 2 Cor. 4:13 [b] Mark 3:15; 16:18 [1] NU-Text reads *one.* **12:10** [a] Mark 16:17 [b] Rom. 12:6 [c] 1 John 4:1 [d] Acts 2:4–11 **12:11** [a] Rom. 12:6 [b] [John 3:8] **12:12** [a] Rom. 12:4, 5 [b] [Gal. 3:16] **12:13** [a] [Rom. 6:5] [b] Col. 3:11 [c] [John 7:37–39] [1] NU-Text omits *into.* **12:18** [a] 1 Cor. 12:28 [b] Rom. 12:3 **12:27** [a] Rom. 12:5 [b] Eph. 5:30 **12:28** [a] Eph. 4:11 [b] [Eph. 2:20; 3:5] [c] Acts 13:1 [d] 1 Cor. 12:10, 29 [e] 1 Cor. 12:9, 30 [f] Num. 11:17 [g] Rom. 12:8 **12:31** [a] 1 Cor. 14:1, 39 [1] NU-Text reads *greater.* **13:2** [a] 1 Cor. 12:8–10, 28; 14:1 [b] Matt. 17:20; 21:21 **13:3** [a] Matt. 6:1, 2 [1] NU-Text reads *so I may boast.*

4 [a]Love suffers long *and* is [b]kind; love [c]does not envy; love does not parade itself, is not puffed up; 5 does not behave rudely, [a]does not seek its own, is not provoked, thinks no evil; 6 [a]does not rejoice in iniquity, but [b]rejoices in the truth; 7 [a]bears all things, believes all things, hopes all things, endures all things.

8 Love never fails. But whether *there are* prophecies, they will fail; whether *there are* tongues, they will cease; whether *there is* knowledge, it will vanish away. 9 [a]For we know in part and we prophesy in part. 10 But when that which is perfect has come, then that which is in part will be done away.

11 When I was a child, I spoke as a child, I understood as a child, I thought as a child; but when I became a man, I put away childish things. 12 For [a]now we see in a mirror, dimly, but then [b]face to face. Now I know in part, but then I shall know just as I also am known.

13 And now abide faith, hope, love, these three; but the greatest of these *is* love.

Prophecy and Tongues

14 Pursue love, and [a]desire spiritual *gifts,* [b]but especially that you may prophesy. 2 For he who [a]speaks in a tongue does not speak to men but to God, for no one understands *him;* however, in the spirit he speaks mysteries. 3 But he who prophesies speaks [a]edification and [b]exhortation and comfort to men. 4 He who speaks in a tongue edifies himself, but he who prophesies edifies the church. 5 I wish you all spoke with tongues, but even more that you prophesied; for[1] he who prophesies *is* greater than he who speaks with tongues, unless indeed he interprets, that the church may receive edification.

Tongues Must Be Interpreted

6 But now, brethren, if I come to you speaking with tongues, what shall I profit you unless I speak to you either by [a]revelation, by knowledge, by prophesying, or by teaching? 7 Even things without life, whether flute or harp, when they make a sound, unless they make a distinction in the sounds, how will it be known what is piped or played? 8 For if the trumpet makes an uncertain sound, who will prepare for battle? 9 So likewise you, unless you utter by the tongue words easy to understand, how will it be known what is spoken? For you will be speaking into the air. 10 There are, it may be, so many kinds of languages in the world, and none of them *is* without significance. 11 Therefore, if I do not know the meaning of the language, I shall be a foreigner to him who speaks, and he who speaks *will be* a foreigner to me. 12 Even so you, since you are zealous for spiritual *gifts, let it be* for the edification of the church *that* you seek to excel.

13 Therefore let him who speaks in a tongue pray that he may [a]interpret. 14 For if I pray in a tongue, my spirit prays, but my understanding is unfruitful. 15 What is *the conclusion* then? I will pray with the spirit, and I will also pray with the understanding. [a]I will sing with the spirit, and I will also sing [b]with the understanding. 16 Otherwise, if you bless with the spirit, how will he who occupies the place of the uninformed say "Amen" [a]at your giving of thanks, since he does not understand what you say? 17 For you indeed give thanks well, but the other is not edified.

18 I thank my God I speak with tongues more than you all; 19 yet in the church I would rather speak five words with my understanding, that I may teach others also, than ten thousand words in a tongue.

Tongues a Sign to Unbelievers

20 Brethren, [a]do not be children in understanding; however, in malice [b]be babes, but in understanding be mature.

21 [a]In the law it is written:

[b]"With *men of* other tongues and other
lips
I will speak to this people;
And yet, for all that, they will not
hear Me,"[1]

says the Lord.

22 Therefore tongues are for a [a]sign, not to those who believe but to unbelievers; but prophesying is not for unbelievers but for those who believe. 23 Therefore if the whole church comes together in one place, and all speak with tongues, and there come in *those who are* uninformed or unbelievers, [a]will they not say that you are out of your mind? 24 But if all prophesy, and an unbeliever or an uninformed person comes in, he is convinced by all, he is convicted by all. 25 And thus[1] the secrets of his heart are revealed; and so, falling down on *his* face, he will worship God and report [a]that God is truly among you.

13:4 [a] Prov. 10:12; 17:9 [b] Eph. 4:32 [c] Gal. 5:26 **13:5** [a] 1 Cor. 10:24 **13:6** [a] Rom. 1:32 [b] 2 John 4 **13:7** [a] Gal. 6:2 **13:9** [a] 1 Cor. 8:2; 13:12 **13:12** [a] Phil. 3:12 [b] [1 John 3:2] **14:1** [a] 1 Cor. 12:31; 14:39 [b] Num. 11:25, 29 **14:2** [a] Acts 2:4; 10:46 **14:3** [a] Rom. 14:19; 15:2 [b] 1 Tim. 4:13 **14:5** [1] NU-Text reads *and.* **14:6** [a] 1 Cor. 14:26 **14:13** [a] 1 Cor. 12:10 **14:15** [a] Col. 3:16 [b] Ps. 47:7 **14:16** [a] 1 Cor. 11:24 **14:20** [a] Ps. 131:2 [b] [1 Pet. 2:2] **14:21** [a] John 10:34 [b] Is. 28:11, 12 [1] Isaiah 28:11, 12 **14:22** [a] Mark 16:17 **14:23** [a] Acts 2:13 **14:25** [a] Is. 45:14 [1] NU-Text omits *And thus.*

Order in Church Meetings

26 How is it then, brethren? Whenever you
come together, each of you has a psalm, [a]has
a teaching, has a tongue, has a revelation, has
an interpretation. [b]Let all things be done for
edification. 27 If anyone speaks in a tongue,
let there be two or at the most three, *each* in
turn, and let one interpret. 28 But if there is no
interpreter, let him keep silent in church, and
let him speak to himself and to God. 29 Let two
or three prophets speak, and [a]let the others
judge. 30 But if *anything* is revealed to another
who sits by, [a]let the first keep silent. 31 For you
can all prophesy one by one, that all may learn
and all may be encouraged. 32 And [a]the spirits
of the prophets are subject to the prophets.
33 For God is not *the author* of confusion but
of peace, [a]as in all the churches of the saints.
34 [a]Let your[1] women keep silent in the
churches, for they are not permitted to speak;
but *they are* to be submissive, as the [b]law also
says. 35 And if they want to learn something,
let them ask their own husbands at home; for
it is shameful for women to speak in church.
36 Or did the word of God come *originally*
from you? Or *was it* you only that it reached?
37 [a]If anyone thinks himself to be a prophet or
spiritual, let him acknowledge that the things
which I write to you are the commandments
of the Lord. 38 But if anyone is ignorant, let
him be ignorant.[1]
39 Therefore, brethren, [a]desire earnestly
to prophesy, and do not forbid to speak with
tongues. 40 [a]Let all things be done decently
and in order.

The Risen Christ, Faith's Reality

15 Moreover, brethren, I declare to you the
gospel [a]which I preached to you, which
also you received and [b]in which you stand,
2 [a]by which also you are saved, if you hold fast
that word which I preached to you—unless
[b]you believed in vain.
3 For [a]I delivered to you first of all that [b]which
I also received: that Christ died for our sins
[c]according to the Scriptures, 4 and that He was
buried, and that He rose again the third day
[a]according to the Scriptures, 5 [a]and that He was
seen by Cephas, then [b]by the twelve. 6 After that
He was seen by over five hundred brethren at
once, of whom the greater part remain to the
present, but some have fallen asleep. 7 After
that He was seen by James, then [a]by all the
apostles. 8 [a]Then last of all He was seen by me
also, as by one born out of due time.
9 For I am [a]the least of the apostles, who am
not worthy to be called an apostle, because [b]I
persecuted the church of God. 10 But [a]by the
grace of God I am what I am, and His grace
toward me was not in vain; but I labored
more abundantly than they all, [b]yet not I,
but the grace of God *which was* with me.

14:26 [a] 1 Cor. 12:8–10; 14:6 [b] [2 Cor. 12:19] **14:29** [a] 1 Cor. 12:10 **14:30** [a] [1 Thess. 5:19, 20] **14:32** [a] 1 John 4:1 **14:33** [a] 1 Cor. 11:16 **14:34** [a] 1 Tim. 2:11 [b] Gen. 3:16 [1] NU-Text omits *your.* **14:37** [a] 2 Cor. 10:7 **14:38** [1] NU-Text reads *if anyone does not recognize this, he is not recognized.* **14:39** [a] 1 Cor. 12:31 **14:40** [a] 1 Cor. 14:33 **15:1** [a] [Gal. 1:11] [b] [Rom. 5:2; 11:20] **15:2** [a] Rom. 1:16 [b] Gal. 3:4 **15:3** [a] 1 Cor. 11:2, 23 [b] [Gal. 1:12] [c] Ps. 22:15 **15:4** [a] Ps. 16:9–11; 68:18; 110:1 **15:5** [a] Luke 24:34 [b] Matt. 28:17 **15:7** [a] Acts 1:3, 4 **15:8** [a] [Acts 9:3–8; 22:6–11; 26:12–18] **15:9** [a] Eph. 3:8 [b] Acts 8:3 **15:10** [a] Eph. 3:7, 8 [b] Phil. 2:13

GUIDED BY THE AUTHOR OF PEACE

God is not the author of confusion but of peace, as in all the churches of the saints.

I CORINTHIANS 14:33

Know anybody who shouts the loudest in a group? Which ones insist they're always right? I do, and I admit that I find it very difficult not to outshout them!

Paul encountered a similar problem in the large, gifted church in Corinth. He had trained and taught the new Christians for a year and a half, and then other Christian leaders visited. The result was a large but very divided congregation. Even their spiritual gifts were a cause of division: Whose gift was the most important? Who should do most of the talking?

Paul responded by writing some letters. He urged the Christians of Corinth to love one another and to use their gifts to edify the body of Christ, not splinter it. And when it came to speaking, all was to be done in order, each taking a turn, each listening with respect. After all, God is not "the author of confusion but of peace," and peace is the essence of the gospel.

Are you a shouter or a listener? How can you bring more peace to your own congregation?

PEACE NOTE

Concern yourself with the direction you are moving. Be okay with saying, *While I am not holy yet, I am pursuing it by God's grace!* Then you'll have peace.

1 CORINTHIANS 15:10

11 Therefore, whether *it was* I or they, so we preach and so you believed.

The Risen Christ, Our Hope

12 Now if Christ is preached that He has been raised from the dead, how do some among you say that there is no resurrection of the dead? 13 But if there is no resurrection of the dead, [a]then Christ is not risen. 14 And if Christ is not risen, then our preaching *is* empty and your faith *is* also empty. 15 Yes, and we are found false witnesses of God, because [a]we have testified of God that He raised up Christ, whom He did not raise up—if in fact the dead do not rise. 16 For if *the* dead do not rise, then Christ is not risen. 17 And if Christ is not risen, your faith *is* futile; [a]you are still in your sins! 18 Then also those who have fallen [a]asleep in Christ have perished. 19 [a]If in this life only we have hope in Christ, we are of all men the most pitiable.

The Last Enemy Destroyed

20 But now [a]Christ is risen from the dead, *and* has become [b]the firstfruits of those who have fallen asleep. 21 For [a]since by man *came* death, [b]by Man also *came* the resurrection of the dead. 22 For as in Adam all die, even so in Christ all shall [a]be made alive. 23 But [a]each one in his own order: Christ the firstfruits, afterward those *who are* Christ's at His coming. 24 Then *comes* the end, when He delivers [a]the kingdom to God the Father, when He puts an end to all rule and all authority and power. 25 For He must reign [a]till He has put all enemies under His feet. 26 [a]The last enemy *that* will be destroyed *is* death. 27 For [a]"He has put all things under His feet."[1] But when He says "all things are put under *Him*," *it is* evident that He who put all things under Him is excepted. 28 [a]Now when all things are made subject to Him, then [b]the Son Himself will also be subject to Him who put all things under Him, that God may be all in all.

Effects of Denying the Resurrection

29 Otherwise, what will they do who are baptized for the dead, if the dead do not rise at all? Why then are they baptized for the dead? 30 And [a]why do we stand in jeopardy every hour? 31 I affirm, by [a]the boasting in you which I have in Christ Jesus our Lord, [b]I die daily. 32 If, in the manner of men, [a]I have fought with beasts at Ephesus, what advantage *is it* to me? If *the* dead do not rise, [b]"Let us eat and drink, for tomorrow we die!"[1]

33 Do not be deceived: [a]"Evil company corrupts good habits." 34 [a]Awake to righteousness, and do not sin; [b]for some do not have the knowledge of God. [c]I speak *this* to your shame.

A Glorious Body

35 But someone will say, [a]"How are the dead raised up? And with what body do they come?" 36 Foolish one, [a]what you sow is not made alive unless it dies. 37 And what you sow, you do not sow that body that shall be, but mere grain—perhaps wheat or some other *grain*. 38 But God gives it a body as He pleases, and to each seed its own body.

39 All flesh *is* not the same flesh, but *there is* one *kind of* flesh[1] of men, another flesh of animals, another of fish, *and* another of birds.

40 *There are* also celestial bodies and terrestrial bodies; but the glory of the celestial *is* one, and the *glory* of the terrestrial *is* another. 41 *There is* one glory of the sun, another glory of the moon, and another glory of the stars; for *one* star differs from *another* star in glory.

42 [a]So also *is* the resurrection of the dead. *The body* is sown in corruption, it is raised in incorruption. 43 [a]It is sown in dishonor, it is raised in glory. It is sown in weakness, it is raised in power. 44 It is sown a natural body, it is raised a spiritual body. There is a natural body, and there is a spiritual body. 45 And so it is written, [a]"The first man Adam became a living being."[1] [b]The last Adam *became* [c]a life-giving spirit.

15:13 [a] [1 Thess. 4:14] **15:15** [a] Acts 2:24 **15:17** [a] [Rom. 4:25] **15:18** [a] Job 14:12 **15:19** [a] 2 Tim. 3:12 **15:20** [a] 1 Pet. 1:3 [b] Acts 26:23 **15:21** [a] Rom. 5:12; 6:23 [b] John 11:25 **15:22** [a] [John 5:28, 29] **15:23** [a] [1 Thess. 4:15–17] **15:24** [a] [Dan. 2:44; 7:14, 27] **15:25** [a] Ps. 110:1 **15:26** [a] [2 Tim. 1:10] **15:27** [a] Ps. 8:6 [1] Psalm 8:6 **15:28** [a] [Phil. 3:21] [b] 1 Cor. 3:23; 11:3; 12:6 **15:30** [a] 2 Cor. 11:26 **15:31** [a] 1 Thess. 2:19 [b] Rom. 8:36 **15:32** [a] 2 Cor. 1:8 [b] Is. 22:13; 56:12 [1] Isaiah 22:13 **15:33** [a] [1 Cor. 5:6] **15:34** [a] Rom. 13:11 [b] [1 Thess. 4:5] [c] 1 Cor. 6:5 **15:35** [a] Ezek. 37:3 **15:36** [a] John 12:24 **15:39** [1] NU-Text and M-Text omit *of flesh.* **15:42** [a] [Dan. 12:3] **15:43** [a] [Phil. 3:21] **15:45** [a] Gen. 2:7 [b] [Rom. 5:14] [c] John 5:21; 6:57 [1] Genesis 2:7

46 However, the spiritual is not first, but the
natural, and afterward the spiritual. 47 [a]The
first man *was* of the earth, [b]*made* of dust; the
second Man *is* the Lord[1] [c]from heaven. 48 As
was the *man* of dust, so also *are* those *who are*
made of dust; [a]and as *is* the heavenly *Man,* so
also *are* those *who are* heavenly. 49 And [a]as we
have borne the image of the *man* of dust, [b]we
shall also bear[1] the image of the heavenly *Man.*

Our Final Victory

50 Now this I say, brethren, that [a]flesh and
blood cannot inherit the kingdom of God;
nor does corruption inherit incorruption.
51 Behold, I tell you a mystery: [a]We shall not
all sleep, [b]but we shall all be changed— 52 in
a moment, in the twinkling of an eye, at the
last trumpet. [a]For the trumpet will sound,
and the dead will be raised incorruptible, and
we shall be changed. 53 For this corruptible
must put on incorruption, and [a]this mortal
must put on immortality. 54 So when this
corruptible has put on incorruption, and
this mortal has put on immortality, then
shall be brought to pass the saying that is
written: [a]"Death is swallowed up in victory."[1]

55 "O[a] Death, where *is* your sting?[1]
O Hades, where *is* your victory?"[2]

56 The sting of death *is* sin, and [a]the strength of
sin *is* the law. 57 [a]But thanks *be* to God, who gives
us [b]the victory through our Lord Jesus Christ.
58 [a]Therefore, my beloved brethren, be
steadfast, immovable, always abounding
in the work of the Lord, knowing [b]that your
labor is not in vain in the Lord.

Collection for the Saints

16 Now concerning [a]the collection for the
saints, as I have given orders to the
churches of Galatia, so you must do also: 2 [a]On
the first *day* of the week let each one of you
lay something aside, storing up as he may
prosper, that there be no collections when
I come. 3 And when I come, [a]whomever you
approve by *your* letters I will send to bear
your gift to Jerusalem. 4 [a]But if it is fitting
that I go also, they will go with me.

Personal Plans

5 Now I will come to you [a]when I pass
through Macedonia (for I am passing
through Macedonia). 6 And it may be that I
will remain, or even spend the winter with
you, that you may [a]send me on my journey,
wherever I go. 7 For I do not wish to see you
now on the way; but I hope to stay a while
with you, [a]if the Lord permits.

15:47 [a] John 3:31 [b] Gen. 2:7; 3:19 [c] John 3:13 [1] NU-Text omits *the Lord.* **15:48** [a] Phil. 3:20 **15:49** [a] Gen. 5:3 [b] Rom. 8:29 [1] M-Text reads *let us also bear.* **15:50** [a] [John 3:3, 5] **15:51** [a] [1 Thess. 4:15] [b] [Phil. 3:21] **15:52** [a] Matt. 24:31 **15:53** [a] 2 Cor. 5:4 **15:54** [a] Is. 25:8 [1] Isaiah 25:8 **15:55** [a] Hos. 13:14 [1] Hosea 13:14 [2] NU-Text reads *O Death, where is your victory? O Death, where is your sting?* **15:56** [a] [Rom. 3:20; 4:15; 7:8] **15:57** [a] [Rom. 7:25] [b] [1 John 5:4] **15:58** [a] 2 Pet. 3:14 [b] [1 Cor. 3:8] **16:1** [a] Gal. 2:10 **16:2** [a] Acts 20:7 **16:3** [a] 2 Cor. 3:1; 8:18 **16:4** [a] 2 Cor. 8:4, 19 **16:5** [a] 2 Cor. 1:15, 16 **16:6** [a] Acts 15:3 **16:7** [a] James 4:15

A GENEROUS PEACE

Therefore let no one despise him. But send him on his journey in peace,
that he may come to me; for I am waiting for him with the brethren.

1 CORINTHIANS 16:11

Once when I attended a conference and found a seat, someone brusquely told me the seat was for someone else. Then he saw my name badge and realized I was the speaker! He was embarrassed and insisted I sit. My "big shot" status apparently made all the difference.

Paul encountered this kind of thing in his long and productive ministry. He himself was not always treated with respect; nor were his fellow workers. Timothy, whom Paul loved dearly, was on his way to Corinth (v. 10). He was younger than Paul and he wasn't an apostle. In a church of people who imagined themselves to be quite gifted—super saints if there ever were any!—Paul knew that Timothy might not receive respect. "Therefore," the apostle said, "let no one despise him" (v. 11). When Timothy's work in Corinth was finished, the congregation was to "send him on his journey in peace." Paul implied that the church was to assist Timothy financially so that he could travel to meet Paul.

We learn here that "peace" can also mean *generosity*. Are you generous—with your time, your energy, your finances?

8 But I will tarry in Ephesus until [a]Pen-
tecost. 9 For [a]a great and effective door has
opened to me, and [b]*there are* many adversaries.
10 And [a]if Timothy comes, see that he may
be with you without fear; for [b]he does the
work of the Lord, as I also *do*. 11 [a]Therefore
let no one despise him. But send him on his
journey [b]in peace, that he may come to me;
for I am waiting for him with the brethren.
12 Now concerning *our* brother [a]Apollos, I
strongly urged him to come to you with the
brethren, but he was quite unwilling to come
at this time; however, he will come when he
has a convenient time.

Final Exhortations

13 [a]Watch, [b]stand fast in the faith, be brave,
[c]be strong. 14 [a]Let all *that* you *do* be done
with love.
15 I urge you, brethren—you know [a]the
household of Stephanas, that it is [b]the firstfruits of Achaia, and *that* they have devoted
themselves to [c]the ministry of the saints—
16 [a]that you also submit to such, and to everyone who works and [b]labors with *us*.
17 I am glad about the coming of Stephanas, Fortunatus, and Achaicus, [a]for what was
lacking on your part they supplied. 18 [a]For
they refreshed my spirit and yours. Therefore
[b]acknowledge such men.

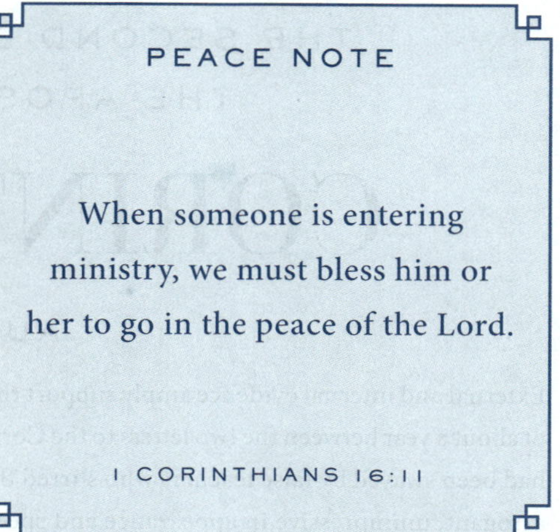
PEACE NOTE

When someone is entering ministry, we must bless him or her to go in the peace of the Lord.

1 CORINTHIANS 16:11

Greetings and a Solemn Farewell

19 The churches of Asia greet you. Aquila
and Priscilla greet you heartily in the Lord,
[a]with the church that is in their house. 20 All
the brethren greet you.
[a]Greet one another with a holy kiss.
21 [a]The salutation with my own hand—Paul's.
22 If anyone [a]does not love the Lord Jesus
Christ, [b]let him be accursed.[1] [c]O Lord, come![2]
23 [a]The grace of our Lord Jesus Christ *be*
with you. 24 My love *be* with you all in Christ
Jesus. Amen.

16:8 [a] Lev. 23:15–22 **16:9** [a] Acts 14:27 [b] Acts 19:9 **16:10** [a] Acts 19:22 [b] Phil. 2:20 **16:11** [a] 1 Tim. 4:12 [b] Acts 15:33 **16:12** [a] 1 Cor. 1:12; 3:5 **16:13** [a] Matt. 24:42 [b] Phil. 1:27; 4:1 [c] [Eph. 3:16; 6:10] **16:14** [a] [1 Pet. 4:8] **16:15** [a] 1 Cor. 1:16 [b] Rom. 16:5 [c] 2 Cor. 8:4 **16:16** [a] Heb. 13:17 [b] [Heb. 6:10] **16:17** [a] 2 Cor. 11:9 **16:18** [a] Col. 4:8 [b] Phil. 2:29 **16:19** [a] Rom. 16:5 **16:20** [a] Rom. 16:16 **16:21** [a] Col. 4:18 **16:22** [a] Eph. 6:24 [b] Gal. 1:8, 9 [c] Jude 14, 15 [1] Greek *anathema* [2] Aramaic *Maranatha* **16:23** [a] Rom. 16:20

THE SECOND EPISTLE OF PAUL THE APOSTLE TO THE

CORINTHIANS

AUTHOR

External and internal evidence amply support the Pauline authorship of this letter. There is an interval of about a year between the two letters to the Corinthians. Since Paul's first letter, the Corinthian church had been swayed by false teachers who stirred the people up against Paul. They claimed he was fickle, arrogant, unimpressive in appearance and speech, and unqualified to be an apostle of Jesus Christ. During this time Paul had paid them what must have been an unpleasant visit and then wrote them another letter, which we do not have (2 Cor. 2:1–4). Paul wrote 2 Corinthians in AD 56 in Macedonia and sent the letter to the church with Titus and another brother (8:16).

TIME

c. AD 56

KEY VERSE

2 Corinthians 4:5–6

THEME

As Paul writes this letter, he is looking forward to yet another visit, and it appears that the Corinthians have listened to him and things are improving. But there are still some problems. The key issue seems to be Paul's leadership. He spends a good deal of the letter establishing his authority and the need to exercise it, which makes the letter intensely personal. In it we can see the depth of his relationship with the Corinthians, and we get an understanding of the hardships Paul went through for these people on his missionary journeys. Most importantly we see a faith that is so focused that Paul is ready to endure anything to see it spread.

Nothing we endure compares to what we have in Christ: this is the thrust of 2 Corinthians, and it should reverberate in our lives as we seek God. Paul has often been referred to as "the Job of the New Testament" because he faced so many challenges and adversities. In fact, when Paul wrote to the Corinthian church he had founded in AD 50, he was hurting so deeply that only God could comfort him. Yet he acknowledged, "As the sufferings of Christ abound in us, so our consolation also abounds through Christ" (1:5). We learn of Paul's pain as we open 2 Corinthians and then we read of the ever-present help of God's peace no matter what he faced. "We do not lose heart," he stated, for we "live in peace; and the God of love and peace" is with us always (4:1; 13:11).

Greeting

1 Paul, [a]an apostle of Jesus Christ by the will
of God, and [b]Timothy *our* brother,

To the church of God which is at Corinth,
[c]with all the saints who are in all Achaia:

2 [a]Grace to you and peace from God our
Father and the Lord Jesus Christ.

Comfort in Suffering

3 [a]Blessed *be* the God and Father of our
Lord Jesus Christ, the Father of mercies and
God of all comfort, 4 who [a]comforts us in
all our tribulation, that we may be able to
comfort those who are in any trouble, with
the comfort with which we ourselves are
comforted by God. 5 For as [a]the sufferings
of Christ abound in us, so our consolation
also abounds through Christ. 6 Now if we
are afflicted, [a]*it is* for your consolation and
salvation, which is effective for enduring the
same sufferings which we also suffer. Or if we
are comforted, *it is* for your consolation and
salvation. 7 And our hope for you *is* steadfast,
because we know that [a]as you are partakers
of the sufferings, so also *you will partake* of
the consolation.

PEACE NOTE

To live in the peace of God, we must constantly remind ourselves of all God has done, is doing, and will do for us.

2 CORINTHIANS 1:7

Delivered from Suffering

8 For we do not want you to be ignorant,
brethren, of [a]our trouble which came to us
in Asia: that we were burdened beyond measure, above strength, so that we despaired
even of life. 9 Yes, we had the sentence of
death in ourselves, that we should [a]not trust
in ourselves but in God who raises the dead,
10 [a]who delivered us from so great a death,
and does[1] deliver us; in whom we trust that
He will still deliver *us,* 11 you also [a]helping
together in prayer for us, that thanks may be
given by many persons on our[1] behalf [b]for
the gift *granted* to us through many.

Paul's Sincerity

12 For our boasting is this: the testimony of
our conscience that we conducted ourselves
in the world in simplicity and [a]godly sincerity, [b]not with fleshly wisdom but by the grace
of God, and more abundantly toward you.
13 For we are not writing any other things to
you than what you read or understand. Now
I trust you will understand, even to the end
14 (as also you have understood us in part),
[a]that we are your boast as [b]you also *are* ours,
in the day of the Lord Jesus.

Sparing the Church

15 And in this confidence [a]I intended to
come to you before, that you might have [b]a
second benefit— 16 to pass by way of you to
Macedonia, [a]to come again from Macedonia to you, and be helped by you on my way
to Judea. 17 Therefore, when I was planning
this, did I do it lightly? Or the things I plan,
do I plan [a]according to the flesh, that with
me there should be Yes, Yes, and No, No?
18 But *as* God *is* [a]faithful, our word to you
was not Yes and No. 19 For [a]the Son of God,
Jesus Christ, who was preached among you
by us—by me, [b]Silvanus, and [c]Timothy—was
not Yes and No, [d]but in Him was Yes. 20 [a]For

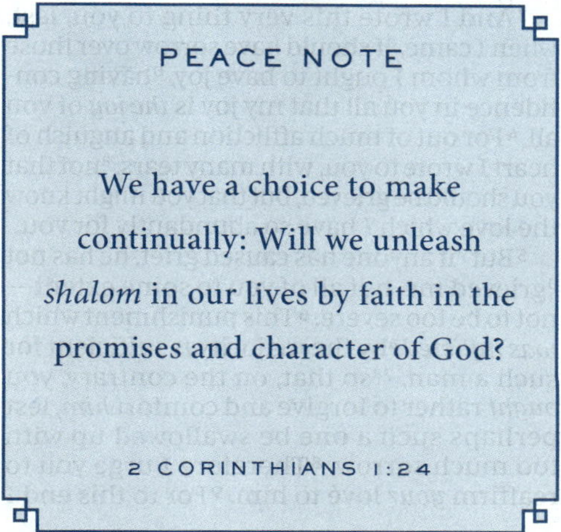

1:1 [a] 2 Tim. 1:1 [b] 1 Cor. 16:10 [c] Col. 1:2 1:2 [a] Rom. 1:7 1:3 [a] 1 Pet. 1:3 1:4 [a] Is. 51:12; 66:13 1:5 [a] 2 Cor. 4:10
1:6 [a] 2 Cor. 4:15; 12:15 1:7 [a] [Rom. 8:17] 1:8 [a] Acts 19:23 1:9 [a] Jer. 17:5, 7 1:10 [a] [2 Pet. 2:9] [1] NU-Text reads
shall. 1:11 [a] Rom. 15:30 [b] 2 Cor. 4:15; 9:11 [1] M-Text reads *your behalf.* 1:12 [a] 2 Cor. 2:17 [b] [1 Cor. 2:4] 1:14 [a] 2 Cor.
5:12 [b] Phil. 2:16 1:15 [a] 1 Cor. 4:19 [b] Rom. 1:11; 15:29 1:16 [a] 1 Cor. 16:3–6 1:17 [a] 2 Cor. 10:2; 11:18 1:18 [a] 1 John 5:20
1:19 [a] Mark 1:1 [b] 1 Pet. 5:12 [c] 2 Cor. 1:1 [d] [Heb. 13:8] 1:20 [a] [Rom. 15:8, 9]

PEACE NOTE

Did you ever suspect Paul was a worrier? Even the great apostle may have experienced panic attacks, and he learned to overcome. This can be your story too.

2 CORINTHIANS 2:13

all the promises of God in Him *are* Yes, and
in Him Amen, to the glory of God through
us. 21 Now He who establishes us with you in
Christ and [a]has anointed us *is* God, 22 who
[a]also has sealed us and [b]given us the Spirit
in our hearts as a guarantee.
23 Moreover [a]I call God as witness against
my soul, [b]that to spare you I came no more
to Corinth. 24 Not [a]that we have dominion
over your faith, but are fellow workers for
your joy; for [b]by faith you stand.
2 But I determined this within myself, [a]that
I would not come again to you in sorrow.
2 For if I make you [a]sorrowful, then who is he
who makes me glad but the one who is made
sorrowful by me?

Forgive the Offender

3 And I wrote this very thing to you, lest,
when I came, [a]I should have sorrow over those
from whom I ought to have joy, [b]having confidence in you all that my joy is *the joy* of you
all. 4 For out of much affliction and anguish of
heart I wrote to you, with many tears, [a]not that
you should be grieved, but that you might know
the love which I have so abundantly for you.
5 But [a]if anyone has caused grief, he has not
[b]grieved me, but all of you to some extent—
not to be too severe. 6 This punishment which
was inflicted [a]by the majority *is* sufficient for
such a man, 7 [a]so that, on the contrary, you
ought rather to forgive and comfort *him*, lest
perhaps such a one be swallowed up with
too much sorrow. 8 Therefore I urge you to
reaffirm *your* love to him. 9 For to this end I
also wrote, that I might put you to the test,
whether you are [a]obedient in all things. 10 Now
whom you forgive anything, I also *forgive*. For
if indeed I have forgiven anything, I have forgiven that one[1] for your sakes in the presence
of Christ, 11 lest Satan should take advantage
of us; for we are not ignorant of his devices.

Triumph in Christ

12 Furthermore, [a]when I came to Troas
to *preach* Christ's gospel, and [b]a door was
opened to me by the Lord, 13 [a]I had no rest
in my spirit, because I did not find Titus
my brother; but taking my leave of them, I
departed for Macedonia.
14 Now thanks *be* to God who always leads
us in triumph in Christ, and through us dif-
fuses the fragrance of His knowledge in every
place. 15 For we are to God the fragrance of
Christ [a]among those who are being saved and
[b]among those who are perishing. 16 [a]To the one
we are the aroma of death *leading* to death,
and to the other the aroma of life *leading* to
life. And [b]who *is* sufficient for these things?
17 For we are not, as so many,[1] [a]peddling the
word of God; but as [b]of sincerity, but as from
God, we speak in the sight of God in Christ.

Christ's Epistle

3 Do [a]we begin again to commend ourselves? Or do we need, as some *others*,
[b]epistles of commendation to you or *letters*
of commendation from you? 2 [a]You are our
epistle written in our hearts, known and
read by all men; 3 clearly you are an epistle

PEACE NOTE

Our vulnerability drives us to greater dependency on Jesus Christ. He makes us adequate for His service. Doesn't that give you peace?

2 CORINTHIANS 3:5

1:21 [a] [1 John 2:20, 27] **1:22** [a] [Eph. 4:30] [b] [Eph. 1:14] **1:23** [a] Gal. 1:20 [b] 1 Cor. 4:21 **1:24** [a] [1 Pet. 5:3] [b] Rom. 11:20 **2:1** [a] 2 Cor. 1:23 **2:2** [a] 2 Cor. 7:8 **2:3** [a] 2 Cor. 12:21 [b] Gal. 5:10 **2:4** [a] [2 Cor. 2:9; 7:8, 12] **2:5** [a] [1 Cor. 5:1] [b] Gal. 4:12 **2:6** [a] 1 Cor. 5:4, 5 **2:7** [a] Gal. 6:1 **2:9** [a] 2 Cor. 7:15; 10:6 **2:10** [1] NU-Text reads *For indeed, what I have forgiven, if I have forgiven anything, I did it.* **2:12** [a] Acts 16:8 [b] 1 Cor. 16:9 **2:13** [a] 2 Cor. 7:6, 13; 8:6 **2:15** [a] [1 Cor. 1:18] [b] [2 Cor. 4:3] **2:16** [a] Luke 2:34 [b] [1 Cor. 15:10] **2:17** [a] 2 Pet. 2:3 [b] 2 Cor. 1:12 [1] M-Text reads *the rest.* **3:1** [a] 2 Cor. 5:12; 10:12, 18; 12:11 [b] Acts 18:27 **3:2** [a] 1 Cor. 9:2

of Christ, [a]ministered by us, written not with ink but by the Spirit of the living God, not [b]on tablets of stone but [c]on tablets of flesh, *that is,* of the heart.

The Spirit, Not the Letter

4 And we have such trust through Christ toward God. 5 [a]Not that we are sufficient of ourselves to think of anything as *being* from ourselves, but [b]our sufficiency *is* from God, 6 who also made us sufficient as [a]ministers of [b]the new covenant, not [c]of the letter but of the Spirit;[1] for [d]the letter kills, [e]but the Spirit gives life.

Glory of the New Covenant

7 But if [a]the ministry of death, [b]written *and* engraved on stones, was glorious, [c]so that the children of Israel could not look steadily at the face of Moses because of the glory of his countenance, which *glory* was passing away, 8 how will [a]the ministry of the Spirit not be more glorious? 9 For if the ministry of condemnation *had* glory, the ministry [a]of righteousness exceeds much more in glory. 10 For even what was made glorious had no glory in this respect, because of the glory that excels. 11 For if what is passing away *was* glorious, what remains *is* much more glorious.

12 Therefore, since we have such hope, [a]we use great boldness of speech— 13 unlike Moses, [a]*who* put a veil over his face so that the children of Israel could not look steadily at [b]the end of what was passing away. 14 But [a]their minds were blinded. For until this day the same veil remains unlifted in the reading of the Old Testament, because the *veil* is taken away in Christ. 15 But even to this day, when Moses is read, a veil lies on their heart. 16 Nevertheless [a]when one turns to the Lord, [b]the veil is taken away. 17 Now [a]the Lord is the Spirit; and where the Spirit of the Lord *is,* there *is* [b]liberty. 18 But we all, with unveiled face, beholding [a]as in a mirror [b]the glory of the Lord, [c]are being transformed into the same image from glory to glory, just as by the Spirit of the Lord.

The Light of Christ's Gospel

4 Therefore, since we have this ministry, [a]as we have received mercy, we [b]do not lose heart. 2 But we have renounced the hidden things of shame, not walking in craftiness nor

PEACE NOTE

The Holy Spirit provides joy and peace. He is constantly transforming us to be more and more like Christ.

2 CORINTHIANS 3:18

handling the word of God deceitfully, but by manifestation of the truth [a]commending ourselves to every man's conscience in the sight of God. 3 But even if our gospel is veiled, [a]it is veiled to those who are perishing, 4 whose minds [a]the god of this age [b]has blinded, who do not believe, lest [c]the light of the gospel of the glory of Christ, [d]who is the image of God, should shine on them. 5 [a]For we do not preach ourselves, but Christ Jesus the Lord, and [b]ourselves your bondservants for Jesus' sake. 6 For it is the God [a]who commanded light to shine out of darkness, who has [b]shone in our hearts to *give* the light of the knowledge of the glory of God in the face of Jesus Christ.

Cast Down but Unconquered

7 But we have this treasure in earthen vessels, [a]that the excellence of the power may be of God and not of us. 8 *We are* [a]hard-pressed on every side, yet not crushed; *we are* perplexed, but not in despair; 9 persecuted, but not [a]forsaken; [b]struck down, but not destroyed— 10 [a]always carrying about in the body the dying of the Lord Jesus, [b]that the life of Jesus also may be manifested in our body. 11 For we who live [a]are always delivered to death for Jesus' sake, that the life of Jesus also may be manifested in our mortal flesh. 12 So then death is working in us, but life in you.

13 And since we have [a]the same spirit of faith, according to what is written, [b]"I believed and therefore I spoke,"[1] we also believe and therefore speak, 14 knowing that [a]He who

3:3 [a] 1 Cor. 3:5 [b] Ex. 24:12; 31:18; 32:15 [c] Ps. 40:8 **3:5** [a] [John 15:5] [b] 1 Cor. 15:10 **3:6** [a] 1 Cor. 3:5 [b] Jer. 31:31 [c] Rom. 2:27 [d] Gal. 3:10 [e] John 6:63 [1] Or *spirit* **3:7** [a] Rom. 7:10 [b] Ex. 34:1 [c] Ex. 34:29 **3:8** [a] [Gal. 3:5] **3:9** [a] [Rom. 1:17; 3:21] **3:12** [a] Eph. 6:19 **3:13** [a] Ex. 34:33–35 [b] [Gal. 3:23] **3:14** [a] Acts 28:26 **3:16** [a] Rom. 11:23 [b] Is. 25:7 **3:17** [a] [1 Cor. 15:45] [b] Gal. 5:1, 13 **3:18** [a] 1 Cor. 13:12 [b] [2 Cor. 4:4, 6] [c] [Rom. 8:29, 30] **4:1** [a] 1 Cor. 7:25 [b] 2 Cor. 4:16 **4:2** [a] 2 Cor. 5:11 **4:3** [a] [1 Cor. 1:18] **4:4** [a] John 12:31 [b] John 12:40 [c] [2 Cor. 3:8, 9] [d] [John 1:18] **4:5** [a] 1 Cor. 1:13 [b] 1 Cor. 9:19 **4:6** [a] Gen. 1:3 [b] 2 Pet. 1:19 **4:7** [a] 1 Cor. 2:5 **4:8** [a] 2 Cor. 1:8; 7:5 **4:9** [a] [Heb. 13:5] [b] Ps. 37:24 **4:10** [a] Phil. 3:10 [b] Rom. 8:17 **4:11** [a] Rom. 8:36 **4:13** [a] 2 Pet. 1:1 [b] Ps. 116:10 [1] Psalm 116:10 **4:14** [a] [Rom. 8:11]

PEACE NOTE

If you have put your faith in Jesus Christ, then God has adopted you. You are completely forgiven in Christ. Now move forward in God's peace armed and reassured.

2 CORINTHIANS 5:17

raised up the Lord Jesus will also raise us up
with Jesus, and will present *us* with you. 15 For
[a]all things *are* for your sakes, that [b]grace,
having spread through the many, may cause
thanksgiving to abound to the glory of God.

Seeing the Invisible

16 Therefore we [a]do not lose heart. Even
though our outward man is perishing, yet
the inward *man* is [b]being renewed day by
day. 17 For [a]our light affliction, which is but for
a moment, is working for us a far more exceeding *and* eternal weight of glory, 18 [a]while
we do not look at the things which are seen,
but at the things which are not seen. For the
things which are seen *are* temporary, but the
things which are not seen *are* eternal.

Assurance of the Resurrection

5 For we know that if [a]our earthly house,
this tent, is destroyed, we have a building
from God, a house [b]not made with hands,
eternal in the heavens. 2 For in this [a]we groan,
earnestly desiring to be clothed with our
habitation which is from heaven, 3 if indeed,
[a]having been clothed, we shall not be found
naked. 4 For we who are in *this* tent groan,
being burdened, not because we want to be
unclothed, [a]but further clothed, that mortality may be swallowed up by life. 5 Now He who
has prepared us for this very thing *is* God, who
also [a]has given us the Spirit as a guarantee.
6 So *we are* always confident, knowing
that while we are at home in the body we are
absent from the Lord. 7 For [a]we walk by faith,
not by sight. 8 We are confident, yes, [a]well
pleased rather to be absent from the body
and to be present with the Lord.

The Judgment Seat of Christ

9 Therefore we make it our aim, whether
present or absent, to be well pleasing to Him.
10 [a]For we must all appear before the judgment
seat of Christ, [b]that each one may receive the
things *done* in the body, according to what he
has done, whether good or bad. 11 Knowing,
therefore, [a]the terror of the Lord, we persuade
men; but we are well known to God, and I also
trust are well known in your consciences.

Be Reconciled to God

12 For [a]we do not commend ourselves again
to you, but give you opportunity [b]to boast on
our behalf, that you may have *an answer* for
those who boast in appearance and not in
heart. 13 For [a]if we are beside ourselves, *it is* for
God; or if we are of sound mind, *it is* for you.
14 For the love of Christ compels us, because
we judge thus: that [a]if One died for all, then
all died; 15 and He died for all, [a]that those who
live should live no longer for themselves, but
for Him who died for them and rose again.
16 [a]Therefore, from now on, we regard no
one according to the flesh. Even though we
have known Christ according to the flesh, [b]yet
now we know *Him thus* no longer. 17 Therefore,
if anyone [a]*is* in Christ, *he is* [b]a new creation;
[c]old things have passed away; behold, all
things have become [d]new. 18 Now all things
are of God, [a]who has reconciled us to Himself through Jesus Christ, and has given us
the ministry of reconciliation, 19 that is, that

PEACE NOTE

We experience the peace of God through faith in Jesus Christ and His finished work on the cross. The gospel is Good News.

2 CORINTHIANS 5:21

4:15 [a] Col. 1:24 [b] 2 Cor. 1:11 4:16 [a] 2 Cor. 4:1 [b] [Is. 40:29, 31] 4:17 [a] Rom. 8:18 4:18 [a] [Heb. 11:1, 13] 5:1 [a] Job 4:19 [b] Mark 14:58 5:2 [a] Rom. 8:23 5:3 [a] Rev. 3:18 5:4 [a] 1 Cor. 15:53 5:5 [a] Rom. 8:23 5:7 [a] Heb. 11:1 5:8 [a] Phil. 1:23 5:10 [a] Rom. 2:16; 14:10, 12 [b] Eph. 6:8 5:11 [a] [Heb. 10:31; 12:29] 5:12 [a] 2 Cor. 3:1 [b] 2 Cor. 1:14 5:13 [a] 2 Cor. 11:1, 16; 12:11 5:14 [a] [Rom. 5:15; 6:6] 5:15 [a] [Rom. 6:11] 5:16 [a] 2 Cor. 10:3 [b] [Matt. 12:50] 5:17 [a] [John 6:63] [b] [Rom. 8:9] [c] Is. 43:18; 65:17 [d] [Rom. 6:3–10] 5:18 [a] Rom. 5:10

[a]God was in Christ reconciling the world to
Himself, not imputing their trespasses to
them, and has committed to us the word of
reconciliation.
20 Now then, we are [a]ambassadors for
Christ, as though God were pleading through
us: we implore *you* on Christ's behalf, be
reconciled to God. 21 For [a]He made Him who
knew no sin *to be* sin for us, that we might
become [b]the righteousness of God in Him.

Marks of the Ministry

6 We then, *as* [a]workers together *with Him*
also [b]plead with *you* not to receive the
grace of God in vain. 2 For He says:

> [a]"In an acceptable time I have heard you,
> And in the day of salvation I have
> helped you."[1]

Behold, now *is* the accepted time; behold,
now *is* the day of salvation.
3 [a]We give no offense in anything, that our
ministry may not be blamed. 4 But in all *things*
we commend ourselves [a]as ministers of God:
in much patience, in tribulations, in needs, in
distresses, 5 [a]in stripes, in imprisonments, in
tumults, in labors, in sleeplessness, in fastings;
6 by purity, by knowledge, by longsuffering, by
kindness, by the Holy Spirit, by sincere love,
7 [a]by the word of truth, by [b]the power of God, by
[c]the armor of righteousness on the right hand
and on the left, 8 by honor and dishonor, by
evil report and good report; as deceivers, and
yet true; 9 as unknown, and [a]*yet* well known;
[b]as dying, and behold we live; [c]as chastened,
and *yet* not killed; 10 as sorrowful, yet always
rejoicing; as poor, yet making many [a]rich; as
having nothing, and *yet* possessing all things.

Be Holy

11 O Corinthians! We have spoken openly to
you, [a]our heart is wide open. 12 You are not restricted by us, but [a]you are restricted by your
own affections. 13 Now in return for the same
[a](I speak as to children), you also be open.
14 [a]Do not be unequally yoked together
with unbelievers. For [b]what fellowship has
righteousness with lawlessness? And what
communion has light with darkness? 15 And
what accord has Christ with Belial? Or what
part has a believer with an unbeliever? 16 And
what agreement has the temple of God with
idols? For [a]you[1] are the temple of the living
God. As God has said:

> [b]"I will dwell in them
> And walk among *them*.
> I will be their God,
> And they shall be My people."[2]

17 Therefore

> [a]"Come out from among them
> And be separate, says the Lord.
> Do not touch what is unclean,
> And I will receive you."[1]
> 18 "I [a]will be a Father to you,
> And you shall be My [b]sons and
> daughters,
> Says the LORD Almighty."[1]

7 Therefore,[a] having these promises, beloved, let us cleanse ourselves from all
filthiness of the flesh and spirit, perfecting
holiness in the fear of God.

The Corinthians' Repentance

2 Open *your hearts* to us. We have wronged
no one, we have corrupted no one, [a]we have
cheated no one. 3 I do not say *this* to condemn; for [a]I have said before that you are in
our hearts, to die together and to live together. 4 [a]Great *is* my boldness of speech toward
you, [b]great *is* my boasting on your behalf.
[c]I am filled with comfort. I am exceedingly
joyful in all our tribulation.

> **PEACE NOTE**
>
> The idolator reflects a mind not guided by the truth of God. This is a mind suffering from spiritual disease—a mind that is infected by deceit repels the experience of God's peace.
>
> 2 CORINTHIANS 6:16

5:19 [a] [Rom. 3:24] **5:20** [a] Eph. 6:20 **5:21** [a] Is. 53:6, 9 [b] [Rom. 1:17; 3:21] **6:1** [a] 1 Cor. 3:9 [b] 2 Cor. 5:20 **6:2** [a] Is. 49:8 [1] Isaiah 49:8 **6:3** [a] Rom. 14:13 **6:4** [a] 1 Cor. 4:1 **6:5** [a] 2 Cor. 11:23 **6:7** [a] 2 Cor. 7:14 [b] 1 Cor. 2:4 [c] 2 Cor. 10:4 **6:9** [a] 2 Cor. 4:2; 5:11 [b] 1 Cor. 4:9, 11 [c] Ps. 118:18 **6:10** [a] [2 Cor. 8:9] **6:11** [a] 2 Cor. 7:3 **6:12** [a] 2 Cor. 12:15 **6:13** [a] 1 Cor. 4:14 **6:14** [a] 1 Cor. 5:9 [b] Eph. 5:6, 7, 11 **6:16** [a] [1 Cor. 3:16, 17; 6:19] [b] Ezek. 37:26, 27 [1] NU-Text reads *we*. [2] Leviticus 26:12; Jeremiah 32:38; Ezekiel 37:27 **6:17** [a] Is. 52:11 [1] Isaiah 52:11; Ezekiel 20:34, 41 **6:18** [a] 2 Sam. 7:14 [b] [Rom. 8:14] [1] 2 Samuel 7:14 **7:1** [a] [1 John 3:3] **7:2** [a] Acts 20:33 **7:3** [a] 2 Cor. 6:11, 12 **7:4** [a] 2 Cor. 3:12 [b] 1 Cor. 1:4 [c] Phil. 2:17

PEACE NOTE

The Bible is a missile. Its promises are aimed at the lies of the world, the flesh, and the devil. Use those missiles to obliterate the weapons stealing your peace.

2 CORINTHIANS 7:1

5 For indeed, [a]when we came to Macedonia,
our bodies had no rest, but [b]we were troubled
on every side. [c]Outside *were* conflicts, inside
were fears. 6 Nevertheless [a]God, who comforts
the downcast, comforted us by [b]the coming
of Titus, 7 and not only by his coming, but
also by the consolation with which he was
comforted in you, when he told us of your
earnest desire, your mourning, your zeal for
me, so that I rejoiced even more.
8 For even if I made you [a]sorry with my
letter, I do not regret it; [b]though I did regret it.
For I perceive that the same epistle made you
sorry, though only for a while. 9 Now I rejoice,
not that you were made sorry, but that your
sorrow led to repentance. For you were made
sorry in a godly manner, that you might suffer
loss from us in nothing. 10 For [a]godly sorrow
produces repentance *leading* to salvation, not
to be regretted; [b]but the sorrow of the world
produces death. 11 For observe this very thing,
that you sorrowed in a godly manner: What
diligence it produced in you, *what* [a]clearing *of
yourselves, what* indignation, *what* fear, *what*
vehement desire, *what* zeal, *what* vindication!
In all *things* you proved yourselves to be [b]clear
in this matter. 12 Therefore, although I wrote
to you, *I did* not *do it* for the sake of him who
had done the wrong, nor for the sake of him
who suffered wrong, [a]but that our care for
you in the sight of God might appear to you.

The Joy of Titus

13 Therefore we have been comforted in
your comfort. And we rejoiced exceedingly
more for the joy of Titus, because his spirit
[a]has been refreshed by you all. 14 For if in
anything I have boasted to him about you, I
am not ashamed. But as we spoke all things to
you in truth, even so our boasting to Titus was
found true. 15 And his affections are greater
for you as he remembers [a]the obedience of
you all, how with fear and trembling you
received him. 16 Therefore I rejoice that [a]I
have confidence in you in everything.

Excel in Giving

8 Moreover, brethren, we make known to
you the grace of God bestowed on the
churches of Macedonia: 2 that in a great trial
of affliction the abundance of their joy and
[a]their deep poverty abounded in the riches
of their liberality. 3 For I bear witness that according to *their* ability, yes, and beyond *their*
ability, *they were* freely willing, 4 imploring
us with much urgency that we would receive[1]
the gift and [a]the fellowship of the ministering
to the saints. 5 And not *only* as we had hoped,
but they first [a]gave themselves to the Lord,
and *then* to us by the [b]will of God. 6 So [a]we
urged Titus, that as he had begun, so he would
also complete this grace in you as well. 7 But
as [a]you abound in everything—in faith, in
speech, in knowledge, in all diligence, and
in your love for us—*see* [b]that you abound
in this grace also.

Christ Our Pattern

8 [a]I speak not by commandment, but I
am testing the sincerity of your love by the
diligence of others. 9 For you know the grace
of our Lord Jesus Christ, [a]that though He
was rich, yet for your sakes He became poor,
that you through His poverty might become
[b]rich.
10 And in this [a]I give advice: [b]It is to your
advantage not only to be doing what you
began and [c]were desiring to do a year ago;
11 but now you also must complete the doing
of it; that as *there was* a readiness to desire
it, so *there* also *may be* a completion out of
what *you* have. 12 For [a]if there is first a willing mind, *it is* accepted according to what
one has, *and* not according to what he does
not have.
13 For *I do* not *mean* that others should be
eased and you burdened; 14 but by an equality,
that now at this time your abundance *may
supply* their lack, that their abundance also

7:5 [a] 2 Cor. 2:13 [b] 2 Cor. 4:8 [c] Deut. 32:25 **7:6** [a] 2 Cor. 1:3, 4 [b] 2 Cor. 2:13; 7:13 **7:8** [a] 2 Cor. 2:2 [b] 2 Cor. 2:4 **7:10** [a] Matt. 26:75 [b] Prov. 17:22 **7:11** [a] Eph. 5:11 [b] 2 Cor. 2:5–11 **7:12** [a] 2 Cor. 2:4 **7:13** [a] Rom. 15:32 **7:15** [a] 2 Cor. 2:9 **7:16** [a] 2 Thess. 3:4 **8:2** [a] Mark 12:44 **8:4** [a] Rom. 15:25, 26 [1] NU-Text and M-Text omit *that we would receive,* thus changing text to *urgency for the favor and fellowship . . . .* **8:5** [a] [Rom. 12:1, 2] [b] [Eph. 6:6] **8:6** [a] 2 Cor. 8:17; 12:18 **8:7** [a] [1 Cor. 1:5; 12:13] [b] 2 Cor. 9:8 **8:8** [a] 1 Cor. 7:6 **8:9** [a] Phil. 2:6, 7 [b] Rom. 9:23 **8:10** [a] 1 Cor. 7:25, 40 [b] [Heb. 13:16] [c] 2 Cor. 9:2 **8:12** [a] Mark 12:43, 44

may *supply* your lack—that there may be
equality. 15 As it is written, [a]"He who *gath-*
ered much had nothing left over, and he who
gathered little had no lack."[1]

Collection for the Judean Saints

16 But thanks *be* to God who puts[1] the same
earnest care for you into the heart of Titus.
17 For he not only accepted the exhortation,
but being more diligent, he went to you of
his own accord. 18 And we have sent with
him [a]the brother whose praise *is* in the gospel throughout all the churches, 19 and not
only *that,* but who was also [a]chosen by the
churches to travel with us with this gift, which
is administered by us [b]to the glory of the
Lord Himself and *to show* your ready mind,
20 avoiding this: that anyone should blame
us in this lavish gift which is administered
by us— 21 [a]providing honorable things, not
only in the sight of the Lord, but also in the
sight of men.

22 And we have sent with them our brother
whom we have often proved diligent in many
things, but now much more diligent, because
of the great confidence which *we have* in you.
23 If *anyone inquires* about [a]Titus, *he is* my
partner and fellow worker concerning you.
Or if our brethren *are inquired about, they*
are [b]messengers of the churches, the glory
of Christ. 24 Therefore show to them, and[1]
before the churches, the proof of your love
and of our [a]boasting on your behalf.

Administering the Gift

9 Now concerning [a]the ministering to the
saints, it is superfluous for me to write
to you; 2 for I know your willingness, about
which I boast of you to the Macedonians, that
Achaia was ready a [a]year ago; and your zeal
has stirred up the majority. 3 [a]Yet I have sent
the brethren, lest our boasting of you should
be in vain in this respect, that, as I said, you
may be ready; 4 lest if *some* Macedonians
come with me and find you unprepared, we
(not to mention you!) should be ashamed
of this confident boasting.[1] 5 Therefore I
thought it necessary to exhort the brethren
to go to you ahead of time, and prepare your
generous gift beforehand, which *you had*
previously promised, that it may be ready as
a matter of generosity and not as a grudging
obligation.

The Cheerful Giver

6 [a]But this *I say:* He who sows sparingly
will also reap sparingly, and he who sows
bountifully will also reap bountifully. 7 *So let*
each one *give* as he purposes in his heart, [a]not
grudgingly or of necessity; for [b]God loves a
cheerful giver. 8 [a]And God *is* able to make all
grace abound toward you, that you, always
having all sufficiency in all *things,* may have
an abundance for every good work. 9 As it
is written:

[a]"He has dispersed abroad,
He has given to the poor;
His righteousness endures forever."[1]

10 Now may[1] He who [a]supplies seed to the
sower, and bread for food, supply and multiply the seed you have *sown* and increase
the fruits of your [b]righteousness, 11 while *you*
are enriched in everything for all liberality,
[a]which causes thanksgiving through us to
God. 12 For the administration of this service
not only [a]supplies the needs of the saints,
but also is abounding through many thanks-
givings to God, 13 while, through the proof
of this ministry, they [a]glorify God for the
obedience of your confession to the gospel
of Christ, and for *your* liberal [b]sharing with
them and all *men,* 14 and by their prayer for
you, who long for you because of the exceeding [a]grace of God in you. 15 Thanks *be* to God
[a]for His indescribable gift!

The Spiritual War

10 Now [a]I, Paul, myself am pleading with
you by the meekness and gentleness of
Christ—[b]who in presence *am* lowly among
you, but being absent am bold toward you.
2 But I beg *you* [a]that when I am present I may
not be bold with that confidence by which I
intend to be bold against some, who think
of us as if we walked according to the flesh.
3 For though we walk in the flesh, we do not
war according to the flesh. 4 [a]For the weapons
[b]of our warfare *are* not carnal but [c]mighty in
God [d]for pulling down strongholds, 5 [a]casting
down arguments and every high thing that
exalts itself against the knowledge of God,
bringing every thought into captivity to the
obedience of Christ, 6 [a]and being ready to
punish all disobedience when [b]your obedience is fulfilled.

8:15 [a] Ex. 16:18 [1] Exodus 16:18 **8:16** [1] NU-Text reads *has put.* **8:18** [a] 2 Cor. 12:18 **8:19** [a] 1 Cor. 16:3, 4 [b] 2 Cor. 4:15 **8:21** [a] Rom. 12:17 **8:23** [a] 2 Cor. 7:13, 14 [b] Phil. 2:25 **8:24** [a] 2 Cor. 7:4, 14; 9:2 [1] NU-Text and M-Text omit *and.* **9:1** [a] Gal. 2:10 **9:2** [a] 2 Cor. 8:10 **9:3** [a] 2 Cor. 8:6, 17 **9:4** [1] NU-Text reads *this confidence.* **9:6** [a] Prov. 11:24; 22:9 **9:7** [a] Deut. 15:7 [b] Rom. 12:8 **9:8** [a] [Prov. 11:24] **9:9** [a] Ps. 112:9 [1] Psalm 112:9 **9:10** [a] Is. 55:10 [b] Hos. 10:12 [1] NU-Text reads *Now He who supplies . . . will supply . . . .* **9:11** [a] 2 Cor. 1:11 **9:12** [a] 2 Cor. 8:14 **9:13** [a] [Matt. 5:16] [b] [Heb. 13:16] **9:14** [a] 2 Cor. 8:1 **9:15** [a] [James 1:17] **10:1** [a] Rom. 12:1 [b] 1 Thess. 2:7 **10:2** [a] 1 Cor. 4:21 **10:4** [a] Eph. 6:13 [b] 1 Tim. 1:18 [c] Acts 7:22 [d] Jer. 1:10 **10:5** [a] 1 Cor. 1:19 **10:6** [a] 2 Cor. 13:2, 10 [b] 2 Cor. 7:15

PEACE NOTE

The battle for our *shalom* is won or lost in the mind, and we have weapons at our disposal that are mighty through God.

2 CORINTHIANS 10:4

Reality of Paul's Authority

7 [a]Do you look at things according to the
outward appearance? [b]If anyone is convinced
in himself that he is Christ's, let him again
consider this in himself, that just as he *is*
Christ's, even so [c]we *are* Christ's.[1] 8 For even
if I should boast somewhat more [a]about
our authority, which the Lord gave us[1] for
edification and not for your destruction, [b]I
shall not be ashamed— 9 lest I seem to terrify
you by letters. 10 "For *his* letters," they say,
"*are* weighty and powerful, but [a]*his* bodily
presence *is* weak, and *his* [b]speech contemptible." 11 Let such a person consider this, that
what we are in word by letters when we are
absent, such *we will* also *be* in deed when
we are present.

Limits of Paul's Authority

12 [a]For we dare not class ourselves or compare ourselves with those who commend
themselves. But they, measuring themselves
by themselves, and comparing themselves
among themselves, are not wise. 13 [a]We, however, will not boast beyond measure, but
within the limits of the sphere which God
appointed us—a sphere which especially
includes you. 14 For we are not overextending
ourselves (as though *our authority* did not
extend to you), [a]for it was to you that we came
with the gospel of Christ; 15 not boasting of
things beyond measure, *that is*, [a]in other
men's labors, but having hope, *that* as your
faith is increased, we shall be greatly enlarged
by you in our sphere, 16 to preach the gospel
in the *regions* beyond you, *and* not to boast
in another man's sphere of accomplishment.
17 But [a]"he who glories, let him glory in the
LORD."[1] 18 For [a]not he who commends himself
is approved, but [b]whom the Lord commends.

Concern for Their Faithfulness

11 Oh, that you would bear with me in a
little [a]folly—and indeed you do bear
with me. 2 For I am [a]jealous for you with godly
jealousy. For [b]I have betrothed you to one
husband, [c]that I may present *you* [d]*as* a chaste
virgin to Christ. 3 But I fear, lest somehow, as
[a]the serpent deceived Eve by his craftiness, so
your minds [b]may be corrupted from the simplicity[1] that is in Christ. 4 For if he who comes
preaches another Jesus whom we have not
preached, or *if* you receive a different spirit
which you have not received, or a [a]different
gospel which you have not accepted—you
may well put up with it!

Paul and False Apostles

5 For I consider that [a]I am not at all inferior
to the most eminent apostles. 6 Even though
[a]*I am* untrained in speech, yet *I am* not [b]in
knowledge. But [c]we have been thoroughly
manifested[1] among you in all things.
7 Did I commit sin in humbling myself that
you might be exalted, because I preached the
gospel of God to you [a]free of charge? 8 I robbed
other churches, taking wages *from them* to
minister to you. 9 And when I was present
with you, and in need, [a]I was a burden to no
one, for what I lacked [b]the brethren who came

PEACE NOTE

It is possible to bring "every thought into captivity." We ignore intrusive thoughts and focus on God's peace by saying, "Lord, what do You have for me today?"

2 CORINTHIANS 10:5

10:7 [a] [John 7:24] [b] 1 Cor. 1:12; 14:37 [c] 1 Cor. 3:23 [1] NU-Text reads *even as we are.* **10:8** [a] 2 Cor. 13:10 [b] 2 Cor. 7:14 [1] NU-Text omits *us.* **10:10** [a] Gal. 4:13 [b] 2 Cor. 11:6 **10:12** [a] 2 Cor. 5:12 **10:13** [a] 2 Cor. 10:15 **10:14** [a] 1 Cor. 3:5, 6 **10:15** [a] Rom. 15:20 **10:17** [a] Jer. 9:24 [1] Jeremiah 9:24 **10:18** [a] Prov. 27:2 [b] Rom. 2:29 **11:1** [a] 2 Cor. 11:4, 16, 19 **11:2** [a] Gal. 4:17 [b] Hos. 2:19 [c] Col. 1:28 [d] Lev. 21:13 **11:3** [a] Gen. 3:4, 13 [b] Eph. 6:24 [1] NU-Text adds *and purity.* **11:4** [a] Gal. 1:6–8 **11:5** [a] 2 Cor. 12:11 **11:6** [a] [1 Cor. 1:17] [b] [Eph. 3:4] [c] [2 Cor. 12:12] [1] NU-Text omits *been.* **11:7** [a] 1 Cor. 9:18 **11:9** [a] Acts 20:33 [b] Phil. 4:10

from Macedonia supplied. And in everything
I kept myself from being burdensome to you,
and so I will keep *myself.* 10 [a]As the truth of
Christ is in me, [b]no one shall stop me from
this boasting in the regions of Achaia. 11 Why?
[a]Because I do not love you? God knows!
12 But what I do, I will also continue to do,
[a]that I may cut off the opportunity from
those who desire an opportunity to be regarded just as we are in the things of which
they boast. 13 For such [a]*are* false apostles,
[b]deceitful workers, transforming themselves
into apostles of Christ. 14 And no wonder! For
Satan himself transforms himself into [a]an
angel of light. 15 Therefore *it is* no great thing
if his ministers also transform themselves
into ministers of righteousness, [a]whose end
will be according to their works.

Reluctant Boasting

16 I say again, let no one think me a fool. If
otherwise, at least receive me as a fool, that I
also may boast a little. 17 What I speak, [a]I speak
not according to the Lord, but as it were, foolishly, in this confidence of boasting. 18 Seeing
that many boast according to the flesh, I also
will boast. 19 For you put up with fools gladly,
[a]since you *yourselves* are wise! 20 For you put
up with it [a]if one brings you into bondage, if
one devours *you,* if one takes *from you,* if one
exalts himself, if one strikes you on the face.
21 To *our* shame [a]I say that we were too weak
for that! But [b]in whatever anyone is bold—I
speak foolishly—I am bold also.

Suffering for Christ

22 Are they [a]Hebrews? So *am* I. Are they Israelites? So *am* I. Are they the seed of Abraham? So
am I. 23 Are they ministers of Christ?—I speak as
a fool—I *am* more: [a]in labors more abundant,
[b]in stripes above measure, in prisons more
frequently, [c]in deaths often. 24 From the Jews
five times I received [a]forty [b]*stripes* minus one.
25 Three times I was [a]beaten with rods; [b]once I
was stoned; three times I [c]was shipwrecked; a
night and a day I have been in the deep; 26 *in*
journeys often, *in* perils of waters, *in* perils of
robbers, [a]*in* perils of *my own* countrymen,
[b]*in* perils of the Gentiles, *in* perils in the city,
in perils in the wilderness, *in* perils in the sea,
in perils among false brethren; 27 in weariness
and toil, [a]in sleeplessness often, [b]in hunger
and thirst, in [c]fastings often, in cold and nakedness— 28 besides the other things, what
comes upon me daily: [a]my deep concern for
all the churches. 29 [a]Who is weak, and I am not
weak? Who is made to stumble, and I do not
burn *with indignation?*
30 If I must boast, [a]I will boast in the things
which concern my infirmity. 31 [a]The God and
Father of our Lord Jesus Christ, [b]who is blessed
forever, knows that I am not lying. 32 [a]In Damascus the governor, under Aretas the king,
was guarding the city of the Damascenes with
a garrison, desiring to arrest me; 33 but I was
let down in a basket through a window in the
wall, and escaped from his hands.

The Vision of Paradise

12 It is doubtless[1] not profitable for me to
boast. I will come to [a]visions and [b]rev-
elations of the Lord: 2 I know a man [a]in Christ
who fourteen years ago—whether in the body
I do not know, or whether out of the body I
do not know, God knows—such a one [b]was
caught up to the third heaven. 3 And I know
such a man—whether in the body or out of
the body I do not know, God knows— 4 how
he was caught up into [a]Paradise and heard
inexpressible words, which it is not lawful for
a man to utter. 5 Of such a one I will boast; yet
of myself I will not [a]boast, except in my infirmities. 6 For though I might desire to boast,
I will not be a fool; for I will speak the truth.
But I refrain, lest anyone should think of me
above what he sees me *to be* or hears from me.

The Thorn in the Flesh

7 And lest I should be exalted above measure
by the abundance of the revelations, a [a]thorn
in the flesh was given to me, [b]a messenger
of Satan to buffet me, lest I be exalted above
measure. 8 [a]Concerning this thing I pleaded
with the Lord three times that it might depart
from me. 9 And He said to me, "My grace is
sufficient for you, for My strength is made
perfect in weakness." Therefore most gladly
[a]I will rather boast in my infirmities, [b]that the
power of Christ may rest upon me. 10 Therefore
[a]I take pleasure in infirmities, in reproaches, in
needs, in persecutions, in distresses, for Christ's
sake. [b]For when I am weak, then I am strong.

11:10 [a] Rom. 1:9; 9:1 [b] 1 Cor. 9:15 **11:11** [a] 2 Cor. 6:11; 12:15 **11:12** [a] 1 Cor. 9:12 **11:13** [a] Phil. 1:15 [b] Phil. 3:2 **11:14** [a] Gal. 1:8 **11:15** [a] [Phil. 3:19] **11:17** [a] 1 Cor. 7:6 **11:19** [a] 1 Cor. 4:10 **11:20** [a] [Gal. 2:4; 4:3, 9; 5:1] **11:21** [a] 2 Cor. 10:10 [b] Phil. 3:4 **11:22** [a] Phil. 3:4–6 **11:23** [a] 1 Cor. 15:10 [b] Acts 9:16 [c] 1 Cor. 15:30 **11:24** [a] Deut. 25:3 [b] 2 Cor. 6:5 **11:25** [a] Acts 16:22, 23; 21:32 [b] Acts 14:5, 19 [c] Acts 27:1–44 **11:26** [a] Acts 9:23, 24; 13:45, 50; 17:5, 13 [b] Acts 14:5, 19; 19:23; 27:42 **11:27** [a] Acts 20:31 [b] 1 Cor. 4:11 [c] Acts 9:9; 13:2, 3; 14:23 **11:28** [a] Acts 20:18 **11:29** [a] [1 Cor. 8:9, 13; 9:22] **11:30** [a] [2 Cor. 12:5, 9, 10] **11:31** [a] 1 Thess. 2:5 [b] Rom. 9:5 **11:32** [a] Acts 9:19–25 **12:1** [a] Acts 16:9; 18:9; 22:17, 18; 23:11; 26:13–15; 27:23 [b] [Gal. 1:12; 2:2] [1] NU-Text reads *necessary, though not profitable, to boast.* **12:2** [a] Rom. 16:7 [b] Acts 22:17 **12:4** [a] Luke 23:43 **12:5** [a] 2 Cor. 11:30 **12:7** [a] Ezek. 28:24 [b] Job 2:7 **12:8** [a] Matt. 26:44 **12:9** [a] 2 Cor. 11:30 [b] [1 Pet. 4:14] **12:10** [a] [Rom. 5:3; 8:35] [b] 2 Cor. 13:4

OUR LIMITS, HIS SUPPLY

I pleaded with the Lord three times that it might depart from me.

2 CORINTHIANS 12:8

The great apostle Paul suffered from an unnamed nemesis in his physical body. He referred to it as "a messenger of Satan" (v. 7) that served to keep him humble—and probably reliant on the Lord to keep it from hindering his ministry. Some might speculate that this "messenger" was evidence that God had forsaken Paul; after all, God often removes pain and heals when we ask Him. But Paul was sure of God's presence with him, and we can be too.

God's hand was with Paul. Jesus promised us trouble and opposition (Matt. 5:11–12; John 16:33), and Paul himself declared boldly, "I bear on my body the marks of Jesus" (Gal. 6:17). He even found satisfaction in his suffering because it gave him a chance to show off God's goodness: "I take pleasure in infirmities . . . For when I am weak, I am strong" (2 Cor. 12:10). In fact, he stated, "our sufficiency is from God" (1 Cor. 3:5).

That kind of man will know God's peace. He's discovered that it's available in the midst of anything and everything he faces. Let pain drive you toward, not away from, God.

Signs of an Apostle

[11]I have become [a]a fool in boasting;[1] you
have compelled me. For I ought to have been
commended by you; for [b]in nothing was I
behind the most eminent apostles, though
[c]I am nothing. [12][a]Truly the signs of an apostle were accomplished among you with all
perseverance, in signs and [b]wonders and
mighty [c]deeds. [13]For what is it in which you
were inferior to other churches, except that I
myself was not burdensome to you? Forgive
me this wrong!

PEACE NOTE

I define Christian vulnerability as *God's strength through my weakness*. Today, claim God's strength in your weakness and have more of His peace.

2 CORINTHIANS 12:10

Love for the Church

[14][a]Now *for* the third time I am ready to
come to you. And I will not be burdensome
to you; for [b]I do not seek yours, but you. [c]For
the children ought not to lay up for the parents, but the parents for the children. [15]And I
will very gladly spend and be spent [a]for your
souls; though [b]the more abundantly I love
you, the less I am loved.

[16]But be that *as it may,* [a]I did not burden
you. Nevertheless, being crafty, I caught you
by cunning! [17]Did I take advantage of you by
any of those whom I sent to you? [18]I urged
Titus, and sent our [a]brother with *him.* Did
Titus take advantage of you? Did we not walk
in the same spirit? Did *we* not *walk* in the
same steps?

[19][a]Again, do you think[1] that we excuse
ourselves to you? [b]We speak before God in
Christ. [c]But *we do* all things, beloved, for your
edification. [20]For I fear lest, when I come, I
shall not find you such as I wish, and *that*
[a]I shall be found by you such as you do not
wish; lest *there be* contentions, jealousies,
outbursts of wrath, selfish ambitions, backbitings, whisperings, conceits, tumults; [21]lest,
when I come again, my God [a]will humble me
among you, and I shall mourn for many [b]who
have sinned before and have not repented of
the uncleanness, [c]fornication, and lewdness
which they have practiced.

12:11 [a] 2 Cor. 5:13; 11:1, 16; 12:6 [b] 2 Cor. 11:5 [c] 1 Cor. 3:7; 13:2; 15:9 [1] NU-Text omits *in boasting.* **12:12** [a] Rom. 15:18 [b] Acts 15:12 [c] Acts 14:8–10; 16:16–18; 19:11, 12; 20:6–12; 28:1–10 **12:14** [a] 2 Cor. 1:15; 13:1, 2 [b] [1 Cor. 10:24–33] [c] 1 Cor. 4:14 **12:15** [a] [2 Tim. 2:10] [b] 2 Cor. 6:12, 13 **12:16** [a] 2 Cor. 11:9 **12:18** [a] 2 Cor. 8:18 **12:19** [a] 2 Cor. 5:12 [b] [Rom. 9:1, 2] [c] 1 Cor. 10:33 [1] NU-Text reads *You have been thinking for a long time . . . .* **12:20** [a] 1 Cor. 4:21 **12:21** [a] 2 Cor. 2:1, 4 [b] 2 Cor. 13:2 [c] 1 Cor. 5:1

Coming with Authority

13 This *will be* [a]the third *time* I am coming
to you. [b]"By the mouth of two or three
witnesses every word shall be established."[1] 2 [a]I
have told you before, and foretell as if I were
present the second time, and now being absent I write[1] to those [b]who have sinned before,
and to all the rest, that if I come again [c]I will
not spare— 3 since you seek a proof of Christ
[a]speaking in me, who is not weak toward you,
but mighty [b]in you. 4 [a]For though He was crucified in weakness, yet [b]He lives by the power of
God. For [c]we also are weak in Him, but we shall
live with Him by the power of God toward you.
5 Examine yourselves *as to* whether you
are in the faith. Test yourselves. Do you not
know yourselves, [a]that Jesus Christ is in you?—
unless indeed you are [b]disqualified. 6 But I trust
that you will know that we are not disqualified.

Paul Prefers Gentleness

7 Now I[1] pray to God that you do no evil,
not that we should appear approved, but
that you should do what is honorable,
though [a]we may seem disqualified. 8 For
we can do nothing against the truth, but
for the truth. 9 For we are glad [a]when we
are weak and you are strong. And this also
we pray, [b]that you may be made complete.
10 [a]Therefore I write these things being absent, lest being present I should use sharpness, according to the [b]authority which the
Lord has given me for edification and not
for destruction.

Greetings and Benediction

11 Finally, brethren, farewell. Become complete. [a]Be of good comfort, be of one mind,
live in peace; and the God of love [b]and peace
will be with you.
12 [a]Greet one another with a holy kiss.
13 All the saints greet you.
14 [a]The grace of the Lord Jesus Christ, and
the love of God, and [b]the communion of the
Holy Spirit *be* with you all. Amen.

13:1 [a] 2 Cor. 12:14 [b] Deut. 17:6; 19:15 [1] Deuteronomy 19:15 **13:2** [a] 2 Cor. 10:2 [b] 2 Cor. 12:21 [c] 2 Cor. 1:23; 10:11 [1] NU-Text omits *I write.* **13:3** [a] Matt. 10:20 [b] [1 Cor. 9:2] **13:4** [a] [1 Pet. 3:18] [b] [Rom. 1:4; 6:4] [c] [2 Cor. 10:3, 4] **13:5** [a] [Gal. 4:19] [b] 1 Cor. 9:27 **13:7** [a] 2 Cor. 6:9 [1] NU-Text reads *we.* **13:9** [a] 1 Cor. 4:10 [b] [1 Thess. 3:10] **13:10** [a] 1 Cor. 4:21 [b] 2 Cor. 10:8 **13:11** [a] Rom. 12:16, 18 [b] Rom. 15:33 **13:12** [a] Rom. 16:16 **13:14** [a] Rom. 16:24 [b] Phil. 2:1

THE EPISTLE OF PAUL THE APOSTLE TO THE

GALATIANS

AUTHOR

The Pauline authorship and the unity of this epistle are virtually unchallenged. The first verse clearly identifies the author as "Paul, an apostle" (Gal. 1:1), as does 5:2: "I, Paul, say to you." In fact, Paul actually wrote, or at least finished, Galatians by his own hand (6:11) instead of dictating it to a secretary, as was his usual practice. There is some controversy as to whether Paul was writing to the northern Galatians or the southern Galatians. If the former theory is correct, this epistle was written sometime during Paul's third missionary journey in AD 53–56. If the latter theory is correct, this epistle was written before the Jerusalem council (Acts 15) in AD 49, right after the first missionary journey. Regardless of the timing of its writing, Galatians affords us a clear glimpse into the ministry and theology of Paul as a Jewish Christian.

TIME

c. AD 49–53

KEY VERSE

Galatians 2:20–21

THEME

The big question for the church in its first generation was whether a person had to become a Jew before he or she could become a Christian. Many Jews thought this was the case. Three things happened to move the church away from this perspective: Peter's vision as recorded in Acts 10; the decision of the Jerusalem council in Acts 15 that Gentiles didn't need to adopt all the Jewish customs; and Paul's received revelation that he was to deliver to the Gentiles. Even with all this evidence, there were still some Jews who followed Paul around and attempted to teach Jewish regulations to his newly planted churches. Paul was furious at these events and used this letter to set the record straight. Christ brought freedom and died for people of all cultures, an idea that was a new paradigm for many of the Jews who were stuck in a "God loves us most" mode. Paul goes to great lengths to review with the Galatians what he has taught them and where this teaching came from.

We live the Christian life as we "walk in the Spirit," Paul told the Galatians (5:16), but how do we know we are doing that? Peace! Peace is a fruit (evidence) of the Spirit and Spirit-filled living—in fact, Paul put it in the first three qualities he listed: "The fruit of the Spirit is love, joy, peace" (5:22). Galatians tells all disciples that when we walk according to the Spirit, we live by the rule of peace: "And as many as walk according to this rule, peace and mercy be upon them" (6:16). Perhaps the greatest contribution to understanding the results of God's peace is the promise of 3:28—complete unity in Jesus Christ—and we should mirror this unity in our lives, families, communities, churches, and societies.

Greeting

1 Paul, an apostle (not from men nor
through man, but [a]through Jesus Christ
and God the Father [b]who raised Him from the
dead), 2 and all the brethren who are with me,

To the churches of Galatia:

3 Grace to you and peace from God the
Father and our Lord Jesus Christ, 4 [a]who gave
Himself for our sins, that He might deliver
us [b]from this present evil age, according to
the will of our God and Father, 5 to whom *be*
glory forever and ever. Amen.

> **PEACE NOTE**
>
> The use of "peace" in the greeting of a letter assured the readers of the presence of God's peace, which comes to us through the redemptive activity of Jesus.
>
> GALATIANS 1:3

Only One Gospel

6 I marvel that you are turning away so
soon [a]from Him who called you in the grace
of Christ, to a different gospel, 7 [a]which is not
another; but there are some [b]who trouble you
and want to [c]pervert the gospel of Christ. 8 But
even if [a]we, or an angel from heaven, preach
any other gospel to you than what we have
preached to you, let him be accursed. 9 As we
have said before, so now I say again, if anyone
preaches any other gospel to you [a]than what
you have received, let him be accursed.
10 For [a]do I now [b]persuade men, or God? Or
[c]do I seek to please men? For if I still pleased
men, I would not be a bondservant of Christ.

Call to Apostleship

11 [a]But I make known to you, brethren, that
the gospel which was preached by me is not
according to man. 12 For [a]I neither received
it from man, nor was I taught *it,* but *it came*
[b]through the revelation of Jesus Christ.
13 For you have heard of my former conduct
in Judaism, how [a]I persecuted the church of
God beyond measure and [b]*tried to* destroy it.
14 And I advanced in Judaism beyond many
of my contemporaries in my own nation,
[a]being more exceedingly zealous [b]for the
traditions of my fathers.
15 But when it pleased God, [a]who separated
me from my mother's womb and called *me*
through His grace, 16 [a]to reveal His Son in me,
that [b]I might preach Him among the Gentiles,
I did not immediately confer with [c]flesh and
blood, 17 nor did I go up to Jerusalem to those
who were apostles before me; but I went to
Arabia, and returned again to Damascus.

Contacts at Jerusalem

18 Then after three years [a]I went up to Jerusalem to see Peter,[1] and remained with him
fifteen days. 19 But [a]I saw none of the other
apostles except [b]James, the Lord's brother.
20 (Now *concerning* the things which I write to
you, indeed, before God, I do not lie.)
21 [a]Afterward I went into the regions of
Syria and Cilicia. 22 And I was unknown by
face to the churches of Judea which [a]*were*
in Christ. 23 But they were [a]hearing only, "He
who formerly [b]persecuted us now preaches
the faith which he once *tried to* destroy."
24 And they [a]glorified God in me.

Defending the Gospel

2 Then after fourteen years [a]I went up
again to Jerusalem with Barnabas, and
also took Titus with *me.* 2 And I went up by
revelation, and communicated to them that
gospel which I preach among the Gentiles,
but [a]privately to those who were of reputation, lest by any means [b]I might run, or had
run, in vain. 3 Yet not even Titus who *was*
with me, being a Greek, was compelled to be
circumcised. 4 And *this occurred* because of
[a]false brethren secretly brought in (who came
in by stealth to spy out our [b]liberty which we
have in Christ Jesus, [c]that they might bring
us into bondage), 5 to whom we did not yield
submission even for an hour, that [a]the truth
of the gospel might continue with you.
6 But from those [a]who seemed to be
something—whatever they were, it makes no
difference to me; [b]God shows personal favoritism to no man—for those who seemed *to be*

1:1 [a] Acts 9:6 [b] Acts 2:24 **1:4** [a] [Matt. 20:28] [b] Heb. 2:5 **1:6** [a] Gal. 1:15; 5:8 **1:7** [a] 2 Cor. 11:4 [b] Gal. 5:10, 12 [c] 2 Cor. 2:17 **1:8** [a] 1 Cor. 16:22 **1:9** [a] Deut. 4:2 **1:10** [a] 1 Thess. 2:4 [b] 1 Sam. 24:7 [c] 1 Thess. 2:4 **1:11** [a] 1 Cor. 15:1 **1:12** [a] 1 Cor. 15:1 [b] [Eph. 3:3–5] **1:13** [a] Acts 9:1 [b] Acts 8:3; 22:4, 5 **1:14** [a] Acts 26:9 [b] Jer. 9:14 **1:15** [a] Is. 49:1, 5 **1:16** [a] [2 Cor. 4:5–7] [b] Acts 9:15 [c] Matt. 16:17 **1:18** [a] Acts 9:26 [1] NU-Text reads *Cephas.* **1:19** [a] 1 Cor. 9:5 [b] Matt. 13:55 **1:21** [a] Acts 9:30 **1:22** [a] Rom. 16:7 **1:23** [a] Acts 9:20, 21 [b] Acts 8:3 **1:24** [a] Acts 11:18 **2:1** [a] Acts 15:2 **2:2** [a] Acts 15:1–4 [b] Phil. 2:16 **2:4** [a] Acts 15:1, 24 [b] Gal. 3:25; 5:1, 13 [c] Gal. 4:3, 9 **2:5** [a] [Gal. 1:6; 2:14; 3:1] **2:6** [a] Gal. 2:9; 6:3 [b] Acts 10:34

something [c]added nothing to me. 7 But on the contrary, [a]when they saw that the gospel for the uncircumcised [b]had been committed to me, as *the gospel* for the circumcised *was* to Peter 8 (for He who worked effectively in Peter for the apostleship to the [a]circumcised [b]also [c]worked effectively in me toward the Gentiles), 9 and when James, Cephas, and John, who seemed to be [a]pillars, perceived [b]the grace that had been given to me, they gave me and Barnabas the right hand of fellowship, [c]that we *should go* to the Gentiles and they to the circumcised. 10 *They desired* only that we should remember the poor, [a]the very thing which I also was eager to do.

No Return to the Law

11 [a]Now when Peter[1] had come to Antioch, I withstood him to his face, because he was to be blamed; 12 for before certain men came from James, [a]he would eat with the Gentiles; but when they came, he withdrew and separated himself, fearing those who were of the circumcision. 13 And the rest of the Jews also played the hypocrite with him, so that even Barnabas was carried away with their hypocrisy.

14 But when I saw that they were not straightforward about [a]the truth of the gospel, I said to Peter [b]before *them* all, [c]"If you, being a Jew, live in the manner of Gentiles and not as the Jews, why do you[1] compel Gentiles to live as Jews?[2] 15 [a]We *who are* Jews by nature, and not [b]sinners of the Gentiles, 16 [a]knowing that a man is not justified by the works of the law but [b]by faith in Jesus Christ, even we have believed in Christ Jesus, that we might be justified by faith in Christ and not [c]by the works of the law; for by the works of the law no flesh shall be justified.

17 "But if, while we seek to be justified by Christ, we ourselves also are found [a]sinners, *is* Christ therefore a minister of sin? Certainly not! 18 For if I build again those things which I destroyed, I make myself a transgressor. 19 For I [a]through the law [b]died to the law that I might [c]live to God. 20 I have been [a]crucified with Christ; it is no longer I who live, but Christ lives in me; and the *life* which I now live in the flesh [b]I live by faith in the Son of God, [c]who loved me and gave Himself for me. 21 I do not set aside the grace of God; for [a]if righteousness *comes* through the law, then Christ died in vain."

Justification by Faith

3 O foolish Galatians! Who has bewitched you that you should not obey the truth,[1] before whose eyes Jesus Christ was clearly portrayed among you[2] as crucified? 2 This only I want to learn from you: Did you receive the Spirit by the works of the law, [a]or by the hearing of faith? 3 Are you so foolish? [a]Having begun in the Spirit, are you now being made perfect by [b]the flesh? 4 [a]Have you suffered so many things in vain—if indeed *it was* in vain?

5 Therefore He who supplies the Spirit to you and works miracles among you, *does He do it* by the works of the law, or by the hearing of faith?— 6 just as Abraham [a]"believed God, and it was accounted to him for righteousness."[1] 7 Therefore know that *only* [a]those who are of faith are sons of Abraham. 8 And [a]the Scripture, foreseeing that God would justify the Gentiles by faith, preached the gospel to Abraham beforehand, *saying,* [b]"In you all the nations shall be blessed."[1] 9 So then those who *are* of faith are blessed with believing Abraham.

The Law Brings a Curse

10 For as many as are of the works of the law are under the curse; for it is written, [a]"Cursed *is* everyone who does not continue in all things which are written in the book of the law, to do them."[1] 11 But that no one is justified by the law in the sight of God *is* evident, for [a]"the just shall live by faith."[1] 12 Yet [a]the law is not of faith, but [b]"the man who does them shall live by them."[1]

13 [a]Christ has redeemed us from the curse of the law, having become a curse for us (for it is written, [b]"Cursed *is* everyone who hangs on a tree"[1]), 14 [a]that the blessing of Abraham might come upon the [b]Gentiles in Christ Jesus, that we might receive [c]the promise of the Spirit through faith.

The Changeless Promise

15 Brethren, I speak in the manner of men: [a]Though *it is* only a man's covenant, yet *if it is* confirmed, no one annuls or adds to it. 16 Now to Abraham and his Seed were the promises made. He does not say, "And to seeds," as of many, but as of [a]one, [b]"And to your Seed,"[1] who is [c]Christ. 17 And this I say, *that* the law, [a]which was four hundred and thirty years later, cannot

2:6 [c] 2 Cor. 11:5; 12:11 **2:7** [a] Acts 9:15; 13:46; 22:21 [b] 1 Thess. 2:4 **2:8** [a] 1 Pet. 1:1 [b] Acts 9:15 [c] [Gal. 3:5] **2:9** [a] Matt. 16:18 [b] Rom. 1:5 [c] Acts 13:3 **2:10** [a] Acts 11:30 **2:11** [a] Acts 15:35 [1] NU-Text reads *Cephas.* **2:12** [a] [Acts 10:28; 11:2, 3] **2:14** [a] Gal. 1:6; 2:5 [b] 1 Tim. 5:20 [c] [Acts 10:28] [1] NU-Text reads *how can you.* [2] Some interpreters stop the quotation here. **2:15** [a] [Acts 15:10] [b] Matt. 9:11 **2:16** [a] Acts 13:38, 39 [b] Rom. 1:17 [c] Ps. 143:2 **2:17** [a] [1 John 3:8] **2:19** [a] Rom. 8:2 [b] [Rom. 6:2, 14; 7:4] [c] [Rom. 6:11] **2:20** [a] [Rom. 6:6] [b] 2 Cor. 5:15 [c] Eph. 5:2 **2:21** [a] Heb. 7:11 **3:1** [1] NU-Text omits *that you should not obey the truth.* [2] NU-Text omits *among you.* **3:2** [a] Rom. 10:16, 17 **3:3** [a] [Gal. 4:9] [b] Heb. 7:16 **3:4** [a] Heb. 10:35 **3:6** [a] Gen. 15:6 [1] Genesis 15:6 **3:7** [a] John 8:39 **3:8** [a] Rom. 9:17 [b] Gen. 12:3; 18:18; 22:18; 26:4; 28:14 [1] Genesis 12:3; 18:18; 22:18; 26:4; 28:14 **3:10** [a] Deut. 27:26 [1] Deuteronomy 27:26 **3:11** [a] Hab. 2:4 [1] Habakkuk 2:4 **3:12** [a] Rom. 4:4, 5 [b] Lev. 18:5 [1] Leviticus 18:5 **3:13** [a] [Rom. 8:3] [b] Deut. 21:23 [1] Deuteronomy 21:23 **3:14** [a] Gen. 12:3; 22:18; [Rom. 4:1–5, 9, 16] [b] Is. 49:6; Rom. 3:29, 30 [c] Is. 32:15 **3:15** [a] Heb. 9:17 **3:16** [a] Gen. 22:18 [b] Gen. 12:3, 7; 13:15; 24:7 [c] [1 Cor. 12:12] [1] Genesis 12:7; 13:15; 24:7 **3:17** [a] Ex. 12:40

annul the covenant that was confirmed before
by God in Christ,[1] [b]that it should make the
promise of no effect. 18 For if [a]the inheritance
is of the law, [b]*it is* no longer of promise; but
God gave *it* to Abraham by promise.

Purpose of the Law

19 What purpose then *does* the law *serve?* [a]It
was added because of transgressions, till the
[b]Seed should come to whom the promise was
made; *and it was* [c]appointed through angels
by the hand [d]of a mediator. 20 Now a mediator
does not *mediate* for one *only,* [a]but God is one.

21 *Is* the law then against the promises of
God? Certainly not! For if there had been a
law given which could have given life, truly
righteousness would have been by the law.
22 But the Scripture has confined [a]all under
sin, [b]that the promise by faith in Jesus Christ
might be given to those who believe. 23 But
before faith came, we were kept under guard
by the law, kept for the faith which would
afterward be revealed. 24 Therefore [a]the law
was our tutor *to bring us* to Christ, [b]that we
might be justified by faith. 25 But after faith
has come, we are no longer under a tutor.

Sons and Heirs

26 For you [a]are all sons of God through
faith in Christ Jesus. 27 For [a]as many of you as
were baptized into Christ [b]have put on Christ.
28 [a]There is neither Jew nor Greek, [b]there is
neither slave nor free, there is neither male
nor female; for you are all [c]one in Christ
Jesus. 29 And [a]if you *are* Christ's, then you
are Abraham's [b]seed, and [c]heirs according
to the promise.

4 Now I say *that* the heir, as long as he
is a child, does not differ at all from a
slave, though he is master of all, 2 but is under guardians and stewards until the time
appointed by the father. 3 Even so we, when
we were children, [a]were in bondage under
the elements of the world. 4 But [a]when the
fullness of the time had come, God sent forth
His Son, [b]born[1] [c]of a woman, [d]born under
the law, 5 [a]to redeem those who were under
the law, [b]that we might receive the adoption
as sons.

6 And because you are sons, God has sent
forth [a]the Spirit of His Son into your hearts,
crying out, "Abba, Father!" 7 Therefore you
are no longer a slave but a son, [a]and if a son,
then an heir of[1] God through Christ.

Fears for the Church

8 But then, indeed, [a]when you did not know
God, [b]you served those which by nature are
not gods. 9 But now [a]after you have known
God, or rather are known by God, [b]how *is it*
that you turn again to [c]the weak and beggarly
elements, to which you desire again to be in
bondage? 10 [a]You observe days and months
and seasons and years. 11 I am afraid for you,
[a]lest I have labored for you in vain.

12 Brethren, I urge you to become like me,
for I *became* like you. [a]You have not injured
me at all. 13 You know that [a]because of physical infirmity I preached the gospel to you
at the first. 14 And my trial which was in my
flesh you did not despise or reject, but you
received me [a]as an angel of God, [b]*even* as
Christ Jesus. 15 What[1] then was the blessing
you *enjoyed?* For I bear you witness that, if
possible, you would have plucked out your
own eyes and given them to me. 16 Have I
therefore become your enemy because I tell
you the truth?

17 They [a]zealously court you, *but* for no
good; yes, they want to exclude you, that you
may be zealous for them. 18 But it is good to
be zealous in a good thing always, and not
only when I am present with you. 19 [a]My little
children, for whom I labor in birth again until
Christ is formed in you, 20 I would like to be
present with you now and to change my tone;
for I have doubts about you.

Two Covenants

21 Tell me, you who desire to be under the
law, do you not hear the law? 22 For it is written that Abraham had two sons: [a]the one by
a bondwoman, [b]the other by a freewoman.
23 But he *who was* of the bondwoman [a]was
born according to the flesh, [b]and he of the
freewoman through promise, 24 which things
are symbolic. For these are the[1] two covenants: the one from Mount [a]Sinai which
gives birth to bondage, which is Hagar— 25 for
this Hagar is Mount Sinai in Arabia, and
corresponds to Jerusalem which now is, and
is in bondage with her children— 26 but the

3:17 [b] [Rom. 4:13] [1] NU-Text omits *in Christ.* **3:18** [a] [Rom. 8:17] [b] Rom. 4:14 **3:19** [a] John 15:22 [b] Gal. 4:4 [c] Acts 7:53 [d] Ex. 20:19 **3:20** [a] [Rom. 3:29] **3:22** [a] Rom. 11:32 [b] Rom. 4:11 **3:24** [a] Rom. 10:4 [b] Acts 13:39 **3:26** [a] John 1:12 **3:27** [a] [Rom. 6:3] [b] Rom. 10:12; 13:14 **3:28** [a] Col. 3:11 [b] [1 Cor. 12:13] [c] [Eph. 2:15, 16] **3:29** [a] Gen. 21:10 [b] Rom. 4:11; Gal. 3:7 [c] Gen. 12:3; 18:18; Rom. 8:17 **4:3** [a] Col. 2:8, 20 **4:4** [a] [Gen. 49:10] [b] [John 1:14] [c] Gen. 3:15; [Is. 7:14; Matt. 1:25] [d] [Matt. 5:17]; Luke 2:21, 27 [1] Or *made* **4:5** [a] [Matt. 20:28] [b] [John 1:12] **4:6** [a] [Rom. 5:5; 8:9, 15, 16] **4:7** [a] [Rom. 8:16, 17] [1] NU-Text reads *through God* and omits *through Christ.* **4:8** [a] Eph. 2:12 [b] Rom. 1:25 **4:9** [a] [1 Cor. 8:3] [b] Col. 2:20 [c] Heb. 7:18 **4:10** [a] Rom. 14:5 **4:11** [a] 1 Thess. 3:5 **4:12** [a] 2 Cor. 2:5 **4:13** [a] 1 Cor. 2:3 **4:14** [a] Mal. 2:7 [b] [Luke 10:16] **4:15** [1] NU-Text reads *Where.* **4:17** [a] Rom. 10:2 **4:19** [a] 1 Cor. 4:15 **4:22** [a] Gen. 16:15 [b] Gen. 21:2 **4:23** [a] Rom. 9:7, 8 [b] Heb. 11:11 **4:24** [a] Deut. 33:2 [1] NU-Text and M-Text omit *the.*

[a]Jerusalem above is free, which is the mother
of us all. 27 For it is written:

[a]"Rejoice, O barren,
You who do not bear!
Break forth and shout,
You who are not in labor!
For the desolate has many more
children
Than she who has a husband."[1]

28 Now [a]we, brethren, as Isaac *was,* are
[b]children of promise. 29 But, as [a]he who was
born according to the flesh then persecuted
him *who was born* according to the Spirit, [b]even so *it is* now. 30 Nevertheless what
does [a]the Scripture say? [b]"Cast out the bondwoman and her son, for [c]the son of the bondwoman shall not be heir with the son of the
freewoman."[1] 31 So then, brethren, we are not
children of the bondwoman but of the free.

Christian Liberty

5 [a]Stand fast therefore in the liberty by
which Christ has made us free,[1] and do
not be entangled again with a [b]yoke of bondage. 2 Indeed I, Paul, say to you that [a]if you
become circumcised, Christ will profit you
nothing. 3 And I testify again to every man
who becomes circumcised [a]that he is a debtor
to keep the whole law. 4 [a]You have become
estranged from Christ, you who *attempt to*
be justified by law; [b]you have fallen from
grace. 5 For we through the Spirit eagerly
[a]wait for the hope of righteousness by faith.
6 For [a]in Christ Jesus neither circumcision
nor uncircumcision avails anything, but
[b]faith working through love.

Love Fulfills the Law

7 You [a]ran well. Who hindered you from
obeying the truth? 8 This persuasion does
not *come* from Him who calls you. 9 [a]A little leaven leavens the whole lump. 10 I have
confidence in you, in the Lord, that you will
have no other mind; but he who troubles
you shall bear his judgment, whoever he is.
11 And I, brethren, if I still preach circumcision, [a]why do I still suffer persecution?
Then [b]the offense of the cross has ceased.
12 [a]I could wish that those [b]who trouble you
would even cut themselves off!
13 For you, brethren, have been called to
liberty; only [a]do not *use* liberty as an [b]oppor-
tunity for the flesh, but [c]through love serve
one another. 14 For [a]all the law is fulfilled
in one word, *even* in this: [b]"You shall love
your neighbor as yourself."[1] 15 But if you bite
and devour one another, beware lest you be
consumed by one another!

Walking in the Spirit

16 I say then: [a]Walk in the Spirit, and you
shall not fulfill the lust of the flesh. 17 For

4:26 [a] [Is. 2:2] **4:27** [a] Is. 54:1 [1] Isaiah 54:1 **4:28** [a] Gal. 3:29 [b] Acts 3:25 **4:29** [a] Gen. 21:9 [b] Gal. 5:11 **4:30** [a] [Gal. 3:8, 22] [b] Gen. 21:10, 12 [c] [John 8:35] [1] Genesis 21:10 **5:1** [a] Phil. 4:1 [b] Acts 15:10 [1] NU-Text reads *For freedom Christ has made us free; stand fast therefore.* **5:2** [a] Acts 15:1 **5:3** [a] [Rom. 2:25] **5:4** [a] [Rom. 9:31] [b] Heb. 12:15 **5:5** [a] Rom. 8:24 **5:6** [a] [Gal. 6:15] [b] 1 Thess. 1:3 **5:7** [a] 1 Cor. 9:24 **5:9** [a] 1 Cor. 5:6 **5:11** [a] 1 Cor. 15:30 [b] [1 Cor. 1:23] **5:12** [a] Josh. 7:25 [b] Acts 15:1, 2 **5:13** [a] 1 Cor. 8:9 [b] 1 Pet. 2:16 [c] 1 Cor. 9:19 **5:14** [a] Matt. 7:12; 22:40 [b] Lev. 19:18 [1] Leviticus 19:18 **5:16** [a] Rom. 6:12

A FRUITFUL LIFE

But the fruit of the Spirit is love, joy, peace, longsuffering, kindness, goodness, faithfulness, gentleness, self-control. Against such there is no law.

GALATIANS 5:22-23

Long ago Jesus told His followers that "a tree is known by its fruit" (Matt. 12:33). The fruit produced by God's Spirit is "love, joy, peace, longsuffering, kindness, goodness, faithfulness" (Gal. 5:22), and much more. The first three attributes in Paul's list—love, joy, and peace—are closely related. In fact, joy and peace are almost interchangeable. All three of these attributes reflect a state of being. They are not actions; they provide the essence and energy that leads to actions such as "kindness, goodness, faithfulness," and the like. The reason the world is in short supply of these acts of kindness and goodness is because love, joy, and peace are in short supply.

By embracing the love, joy, and peace that God offers, you can find the energy to make a positive difference in our world. Are you willing?

[a]the flesh lusts against the Spirit, and the
Spirit against the flesh; and these are contrary to one another, [b]so that you do not
do the things that you wish. 18 But [a]if you
are led by the Spirit, you are not under
the law.

19 Now [a]the works of the flesh are evident,
which are: adultery,[1] fornication, uncleanness, lewdness, 20 idolatry, sorcery, hatred,
contentions, jealousies, outbursts of wrath,
selfish ambitions, dissensions, heresies,
21 envy, murders,[1] drunkenness, revelries,
and the like; of which I tell you beforehand,
just as I also told *you* in time past, that [a]those
who practice such things will not inherit the
kingdom of God.

22 But [a]the fruit of the Spirit is [b]love, joy,
peace, longsuffering, kindness, [c]goodness,
[d]faithfulness, 23 gentleness, self-control.
[a]Against such there is no law. 24 And
those *who are* Christ's [a]have crucified the
flesh with its passions and desires. 25 [a]If
we live in the Spirit, let us also walk in
the Spirit. 26 [a]Let us not become conceit-
ed, provoking one another, envying one
another.

Bear and Share Burdens

6 Brethren, if a man is overtaken in any
trespass, you who *are* spiritual restore
such a one in a spirit of [a]gentleness, considering yourself lest you also be tempted.
2 [a]Bear one another's burdens, and so fulfill
[b]the law of Christ. 3 For [a]if anyone thinks
himself to be something, when [b]he is nothing, he deceives himself. 4 But [a]let each one
examine his own work, and then he will
have rejoicing in himself alone, and [b]not in
another. 5 For [a]each one shall bear his own
load.

Be Generous and Do Good

6 [a]Let him who is taught the word share in
all good things with him who teaches.

7 Do not be deceived, God is not mocked;
for [a]whatever a man sows, that he will also
reap. 8 For he who sows to his flesh will of
the flesh reap corruption, but he who sows
to the Spirit will of the Spirit reap [a]ever-
lasting life. 9 And [a]let us not grow weary
while doing good, for in due season we shall
reap [b]if we do not lose heart. 10 [a]Therefore,
as we have opportunity, [b]let us do good
to all, [c]especially to those who are of the
household of faith.

Glory Only in the Cross

11 See with what large letters I have written to you with my own hand! 12 As many as
desire to make a good showing in the flesh,
these *would* compel you to be circumcised,
[a]only that they may not suffer persecution
for the cross of Christ. 13 For not even those
who are circumcised keep the law, but they

5:17 [a] Rom. 7:18, 22, 23; 8:5 [b] Rom. 7:15 **5:18** [a] [Rom. 6:14; 7:4; 8:14] **5:19** [a] Eph. 5:3, 11 [1] NU-Text omits *adultery.*
5:21 [a] 1 Cor. 6:9, 10 [1] NU-Text omits *murders.* **5:22** [a] [John 15:2] [b] [Col. 3:12–15] [c] Rom. 15:14 [d] 1 Cor. 13:7
5:23 [a] 1 Tim. 1:9 **5:24** [a] Rom. 6:6 **5:25** [a] [Rom. 8:4, 5] **5:26** [a] Phil. 2:3 **6:1** [a] Eph. 4:2 **6:2** [a] Rom. 15:1 [b] [James 2:8]
6:3 [a] Rom. 12:3 [b] [2 Cor. 3:5] **6:4** [a] 1 Cor. 11:28 [b] Luke 18:11 **6:5** [a] [Rom. 2:6] **6:6** [a] 1 Cor. 9:11, 14 **6:7** [a] [Rom. 2:6]
6:8 [a] [Rom. 6:8] **6:9** [a] 1 Cor. 15:58 [b] [James 5:7, 8] **6:10** [a] Prov. 3:27 [b] Titus 3:8 [c] Rom. 12:13 **6:12** [a] Gal. 5:11

YOU: AMBASSADOR OF PEACE

And as many as walk according to this rule, peace and mercy be upon them, and upon the Israel of God.

GALATIANS 6:16

In his letter to the churches of Galatia, Paul underscored the need for the unity of believers—Jewish and non-Jewish. What upset Paul was Peter's cowardly decision not to eat with non-Jewish believers because their food and food preparation probably didn't meet the Jews' strict food laws and traditions. Instead of promoting peace, as Peter intended, he created division and robbed some churches of their well-being. "There is neither Jew nor Greek . . . in Christ," Paul proclaimed (3:28). Surely Peter knew that, didn't he?

If believers recognize that it is okay for Jews to be Jews and Gentiles to be Gentiles, then the church will be united in mission and, as Paul says, "peace and mercy" (6:16) will be upon it.

The same applies to all of us. If we can accept our brothers and sisters, we also will be blessed with the peace of God. Make a mental list of those you'll encounter today whom you, as an ambassador of God's peace, need to accept.

desire to have you circumcised that they may
boast in your flesh. 14 But God forbid that I
should boast except in the [a]cross of our Lord
Jesus Christ, by whom[1] the world has been
crucified to me, and [b]I to the world. 15 For
[a]in Christ Jesus neither circumcision nor
uncircumcision avails anything, but a new
creation.

Blessing and a Plea

16 And as many as walk according to this
rule, peace and mercy *be* upon them, and
upon the Israel of God.
17 From now on let no one trouble me, for I
bear in my body the marks of the Lord Jesus.
18 Brethren, the grace of our Lord Jesus
Christ *be* with your spirit. Amen.

6:14 [a] [1 Cor. 1:18] [b] Col. 2:20 [1] Or *by which* (the cross) 6:15 [a] 1 Cor. 7:19

PEACE NOTE

The experiences that scarred Paul became, by God's healing and redeeming grace, his greatest marks of victory. We can view our now-healed emotional scars as memorials to God's faithfulness.

GALATIANS 6:17

THE EPISTLE OF PAUL THE APOSTLE TO THE

EPHESIANS

AUTHOR

All internal and external evidence strongly supports the Pauline authorship of Ephesians. In recent years, however, critics have turned to internal grounds to challenge this unanimous ancient tradition. It has been argued that the vocabulary and style are different from other Pauline epistles, but this overlooks Paul's flexibility under different circumstances (see, for example, Romans and 2 Corinthians). The theology of Ephesians in some ways reflects a later development, but this must be attributed to Paul's own growth and meditation on the church as the body of Christ. Ephesians was written during his first Roman imprisonment in AD 60–61, perhaps around the same time as Philippians, Colossians, and Philemon.

TIME

c. AD 60–61

KEY VERSE

Ephesians 4:1–3

THEME

Ephesians is like a grand landscape whose subject is the whole world. Paul paints a richly textured picture of God's plan to bless the world through Christ. God is bringing light to darkness, healing to brokenness, and reconciliation to the separated. Central to this teaching is the role of the church in the world and the gifts God has given it. God will bring about these things through the church. Once we understand and believe all that God has done and is doing, it is our responsibility to obey and live in light of His actions. Paul gives us much more than theory in Ephesians. He makes critical connections between big-picture theology and the practical implications for living the day-to-day Christian life.

Paul opened and closed this beloved letter with the bookends of peace: "peace from God our father and the Lord Jesus Christ" and "peace to the brethren [the church]" (Eph. 1:2; 6:23). In fact, peace bells ring throughout the letter! Ephesians firmly plants us in the truth that Jesus is our *shalom* now and forevermore: "For He Himself is our peace" because Jesus Himself made peace for us (2:14–15). Further, Jesus "preached peace" to all "who were afar off and to those who were near" (2:17). Faithful Christians will pursue peace by "endeavoring to keep the unity of the Spirit in the bond of peace" (4:3). And finally, believers should always stand ready because our feet are "shod" with the "preparation of the gospel of peace" (6:15).

Greeting

1 Paul, an apostle of Jesus Christ by the
will of God,

To the saints who are in Ephesus, and faithful in Christ Jesus:

2 Grace to you and peace from God our
Father and the Lord Jesus Christ.

Redemption in Christ

3 [a]Blessed *be* the God and Father of our Lord
Jesus Christ, who has blessed us with every spiritual blessing in the heavenly *places* in Christ,
4 just as [a]He chose us in Him [b]before the foundation of the world, that we should [c]be holy and
without blame before Him in love, 5 [a]having predestined us to [b]adoption as sons by Jesus Christ
to Himself, [c]according to the good pleasure of
His will, 6 to the praise of the glory of His grace,
[a]by which He made us accepted in [b]the Beloved.
7 [a]In Him we have redemption through
His blood, the forgiveness of sins, according to [b]the riches of His grace 8 which He
made to abound toward us in all wisdom and
prudence, 9 [a]having made known to us the
mystery of His will, according to His good
pleasure [b]which He purposed in Himself,
10 that in the dispensation of [a]the fullness of
the times [b]He might gather together in one
[c]all things in Christ, both[1] which are in heaven
and which are on earth—in Him. 11 [a]In Him
also we have obtained an inheritance, being
predestined according to [b]the purpose of Him
who works all things according to the counsel
of His will, 12 [a]that we [b]who first trusted in
Christ should be to the praise of His glory.
13 In Him you also *trusted,* after you heard
[a]the word of truth, the gospel of your salvation; in whom also, having believed, [b]you
were sealed with the Holy Spirit of promise,
14 [a]who[1] is the guarantee of our inheritance
[b]until the redemption of [c]the purchased
possession, [d]to the praise of His glory.

Prayer for Spiritual Wisdom

15 Therefore I also, [a]after I heard of your
faith in the Lord Jesus and your love for all
the saints, 16 [a]do not cease to give thanks for

PEACE NOTE

Biblical happiness is not laughter or amusement. It is a delight that wells up within one's heart as a result of coming into contact with God and experiencing His restorative, life-changing *shalom.*

EPHESIANS 1:18

1:3 [a] 2 Cor. 1:3 **1:4** [a] Rom. 8:28 [b] 1 Pet. 1:2 [c] Luke 1:75 **1:5** [a] [Rom. 8:29] [b] John 1:12 [c] [1 Cor. 1:21] **1:6** [a] [Rom. 3:24] [b] Matt. 3:17 **1:7** [a] [Heb. 9:12] [b] [Rom. 3:24, 25] **1:9** [a] [Rom. 16:25] [b] [2 Tim. 1:9] **1:10** [a] Gal. 4:4 [b] 1 Cor. 3:22 [c] [Col. 1:16, 20] [1] NU-Text and M-Text omit *both.* **1:11** [a] Rom. 8:17 [b] Is. 46:10 **1:12** [a] 2 Thess. 2:13 [b] James 1:18 **1:13** [a] John 1:17 [b] [2 Cor. 1:22] **1:14** [a] 2 Cor. 5:5 [b] Rom. 8:23 [c] [Acts 20:28] [d] 1 Pet. 2:9 [1] NU-Text reads *which.* **1:15** [a] Col. 1:4 **1:16** [a] Rom. 1:9

HE BROUGHT US NEAR

Now in Christ Jesus you who once were far off have been brought near by the blood of Christ.

EPHESIANS 2:13

At some point in our lives, each of us has felt the sting of being the outsider in a group: the new kid at school, the new family at church, the one who looks or talks a little differently, the trainee at work, the weakest link on the sports team, the one who sings out of tune in the choir. That's so uncomfortable, isn't it? To feel unaccepted and even unacceptable is a certain kind of anguish we all want to avoid.

This is the beauty of our Creator. He builds bridges. He draws people close. He responds to our efforts to reach Him. He even takes the initiative to bring us into His family (John 3:16; Eph. 2:13). Have you experienced joining God's "in crowd"? If not, see the article "Find God and His Peace: The Plan of Salvation." If you've forgotten how good He is, reach out and find Him (James 4:8). That's where all the love and peace are. Perhaps you can be bring the peace of God to someone today: Could you include someone today who may feel excluded?

you, making mention of you in my prayers:
17 that [a]the God of our Lord Jesus Christ, the
Father of glory, [b]may give to you the spirit
of wisdom and revelation in the knowledge
of Him, 18 [a]the eyes of your understanding[1]
being enlightened; that you may know what
is [b]the hope of His calling, what are the riches
of the glory of His inheritance in the saints,
19 and what *is* the exceeding greatness of His
power toward us who believe, [a]according to
the working of His mighty power 20 which He
worked in Christ when [a]He raised Him from
the dead and [b]seated *Him* at His right hand
in the heavenly *places,* 21 [a]far above all [b]prin-
cipality and power and might and dominion,
and every name that is named, not only in this
age but also in that which is to come.
22 And [a]He put all *things* under His feet,
and gave Him [b]*to be* head over all *things* to
the church, 23 [a]which is His body, [b]the fullness
of Him [c]who fills all in all.

By Grace Through Faith

2 And [a]you *He made alive,* [b]who were dead
in trespasses and sins, 2 [a]in which you
once walked according to the course of this
world, according to [b]the prince of the power
of the air, the spirit who now works in [c]the
sons of disobedience, 3 [a]among whom also
we all once conducted ourselves in [b]the lusts
of our flesh, fulfilling the desires of the flesh
and of the mind, and [c]were by nature children
of wrath, just as the others.
4 But God, [a]who is rich in mercy, because of
His [b]great love with which He loved us, 5 [a]even
when we were dead in trespasses, [b]made us
alive together with Christ (by grace you have
been saved), 6 and raised *us* up together, and
made *us* sit together [a]in the heavenly *places*
in Christ Jesus, 7 that in the ages to come He
might show the exceeding riches of His grace
in [a]*His* kindness toward us in Christ Jesus.
8 [a]For by grace you have been saved [b]through
faith, and that not of yourselves; [c]*it is* the gift
of God, 9 not of [a]works, lest anyone should
[b]boast. 10 For we are [a]His workmanship, created in Christ Jesus for good works, which
God prepared beforehand that we should
walk in them.

Brought Near by His Blood

11 Therefore remember that you, once Gentiles in the flesh—who are called Uncircumcision by what is called [a]the Circumcision made
in the flesh by hands— 12 that at that time you
were without Christ, being aliens from the

1:17 [a] John 20:17 [b] Col. 1:9 **1:18** [a] Acts 26:18 [b] Eph. 2:12 [1] NU-Text and M-Text read *hearts.* **1:19** [a] Col. 2:12 **1:20** [a] Acts 2:24 [b] Ps. 110:1 **1:21** [a] Phil. 2:9, 10 [b] [Rom. 8:38, 39] **1:22** [a] Ps. 8:6; 110:1; Matt. 28:18; 1 Cor. 15:27 [b] Heb. 2:7, 8 **1:23** [a] Rom. 12:5 [b] Col. 2:9 [c] [1 Cor. 12:6] **2:1** [a] Col. 2:13 [b] Eph. 4:18 **2:2** [a] Col. 1:21 [b] Eph. 6:12 [c] Col. 3:6 **2:3** [a] 1 Pet. 4:3 [b] Gal. 5:16 [c] [Ps. 51:5] **2:4** [a] Rom. 10:12 [b] John 3:16 **2:5** [a] Rom. 5:6, 8 [b] [Rom. 6:4, 5] **2:6** [a] Eph. 1:20 **2:7** [a] Titus 3:4 **2:8** [a] [2 Tim. 1:9] [b] Rom. 4:16 [c] [John 1:12, 13] **2:9** [a] Rom. 4:4, 5; 11:6 [b] Rom. 3:27 **2:10** [a] Is. 19:25 **2:11** [a] [Col. 2:11]

RECONCILE WITH ONE ANOTHER

For He Himself is our peace, who has made both one, and has broken down the middle wall of separation.

EPHESIANS 2:14

Fifty years ago missionary Don Richardson published his remarkable book *Peace Child* (Baker Publishing Group, 2005). In it he told the story of how, in western New Guinea, he and his wife were able to help the Sawi, an ancient people who practiced betrayal, deceit, murder, and cannibalism, understand the gospel. The Richardsons' ministry was far from easy. In the Sawi way of thinking, Judas the betrayer was a hero! Treachery was admired! How could the gospel be explained to a people like that?

Eventually Don learned that the Sawi made peace by offering a son to an enemy. The son was called a "peace child." That was it! Paul said Jesus "is our peace." Yes, He is God's Peace Child. Don explained to the Sawi that this is what God did to reconcile sinful humanity—He offered His Son. This opened the eyes of the Sawi, who embraced the gospel and found peace. Over half of them become followers of Jesus, reconciled to the God of Peace.

If God can reconcile the Sawi, he can reconcile anyone, including you and me. Is there any relationship in your life in which reconciliation could bring peace?

commonwealth of Israel and strangers from the covenants of promise, having no hope and without God in the world. 13 But now in Christ Jesus you who once were far off have been brought near by the blood of Christ.

Christ Our Peace

14 For He Himself is our peace, who has made both one, and has broken down the middle wall of separation, 15 having abolished in His flesh the enmity, *that is,* the law of commandments *contained* in ordinances, so as to create in Himself one [a]new man *from* the two, *thus* making peace, 16 and that He might [a]reconcile them both to God in one body through the cross, thereby [b]putting to death the enmity. 17 And He came and preached peace to you who were afar off and to those who were near. 18 For [a]through Him we both have access [b]by one Spirit to the Father.

Christ Our Cornerstone

19 Now, therefore, you are no longer strangers and foreigners, but fellow citizens with the saints and members of the household of God, 20 having been [a]built [b]on the foundation of the [c]apostles and prophets, Jesus Christ Himself being [d]the chief corner*stone,* 21 in whom the whole building, being fitted together, grows into [a]a holy temple in the Lord, 22 [a]in whom you also are being built together for a [b]dwelling place of God in the Spirit.

The Mystery Revealed

3 For this reason I, Paul, the prisoner of Christ Jesus for you Gentiles— 2 if indeed you have heard of the dispensation of the grace of God [a]which was given to me for you, 3 [a]how that by revelation [b]He made known to me the mystery (as I have briefly written already, 4 by which, when you read, you may understand my knowledge in the mystery of Christ), 5 which in other ages was not made known to the sons of men, as it has now been revealed by the Spirit to His holy apostles and prophets: 6 that the Gentiles [a]should be fellow heirs, of the same body, and partakers of His promise in Christ through the gospel, 7 [a]of which I became a minister [b]according to the gift of the grace of God given to me by [c]the effective working of His power.

Purpose of the Mystery

8 To me, [a]who am less than the least of all the saints, this grace was given, that I should preach among the Gentiles [b]the unsearchable riches of Christ, 9 and to make all see what *is* the fellowship[1] of the mystery, which from the beginning of the ages has been hidden in God who [a]created all things through Jesus Christ;[2] 10 [a]to the intent that now [b]the manifold wisdom of God might be made known by the church [c]to the principalities and powers in the

2:15 [a] Gal. 6:15 **2:16** [a] [Col. 1:20–22] [b] [Rom. 6:6] **2:18** [a] John 10:9 [b] 1 Cor. 12:13 **2:20** [a] 1 Pet. 2:4 [b] Matt. 16:18; 1 Cor. 3:10, 11 [c] 1 Cor. 12:28 [d] Ps. 118:22; Luke 20:17 **2:21** [a] 1 Cor. 3:16, 17 **2:22** [a] 1 Pet. 2:5 [b] John 17:23 **3:2** [a] Acts 9:15 **3:3** [a] Acts 22:17, 21; 26:16 [b] [Rom. 11:25; 16:25] **3:6** [a] Gal. 3:28, 29 **3:7** [a] Rom. 15:16 [b] Rom. 1:5 [c] Rom. 15:18 **3:8** [a] [1 Cor. 15:9] [b] [Col. 1:27; 2:2, 3] **3:9** [a] Heb. 1:2 [1] NU-Text and M-Text read *stewardship* (dispensation). [2] NU-Text omits *through Jesus Christ.* **3:10** [a] 1 Pet. 1:12 [b] [1 Tim. 3:16] [c] Col. 1:16; 2:10, 15

GRACISM OVER RACISM

[For Jesus] abolished in His flesh the enmity, that is, the law of commandments contained in ordinances, so as to create in Himself one new man from the two, thus making peace.

EPHESIANS 2:15

Are you discouraged by the divisions you see in the world? It makes me wonder when people will get their act together. It is all so unnecessary. We can thank God that Jesus did what was needed to make peace happen.

Paul said that Jesus "abolished in His flesh the enmity," that is, the commandments that separated people. The apostle was, of course, speaking of the separation of Jew from Gentile, but the principle applies to all (see Gal. 3:28, where the apostle says, "you are all one in Christ").

The means to ending racism and division is the peace that God makes available in Christ. In Him we become one. In Him there is only one people, a people redeemed and made new. I want to be part of this peace plan. How about you?

PEACE FOR THOSE NEAR OR FAR

And He came and preached peace to you who were afar off and to those who were near.

EPHESIANS 2:17

Has God ever seemed far away? Perhaps even out of reach? Israel's great kingdom that King David established was crushed by the Babylonians in 586 BC. The city of Jerusalem was captured, the temple that Solomon built was destroyed, and the people were carried away into exile. Many Israelites believed their nation was finished, never to exist again. But God raised up prophets who spoke of a coming day when the scattered people would be regathered. Israel's Messiah would collect His people from the east and west. Here in verse 17, Paul alludes to this prophetic hope, along with Isaiah's prophecy of the messenger who announces peace. This prophecy was fulfilled in Christ's resurrection and His apostles' preaching. God's peace was and is proclaimed to those far away and to those nearby.

In reality God is always near, no matter how you feel. You, too, can feel His presence at any time, along with the comfort that His peace brings. Just ask for it. The Scriptures say that "faith comes by hearing" (Rom. 10:17). I need to spend time in the Word of God to have my faith increased in the peace of God. Are you truly abiding in the Word of God?

heavenly *places,* 11[a]according to the eternal
purpose which He accomplished in Christ
Jesus our Lord, 12 in whom we have boldness
and access [a]with confidence through faith
in Him. 13[a]Therefore I ask that you do not
lose heart at my tribulations for you, [b]which
is your glory.

Appreciation of the Mystery

14 For this reason I bow my knees to the
[a]Father of our Lord Jesus Christ,[1] 15 from
whom the whole family in heaven and
earth is named, 16 that He would grant you,
[a]according to the riches of His glory, [b]to be
strengthened with might through His Spirit
in [c]the inner man, 17[a]that Christ may dwell in
your hearts through faith; that you, [b]being
rooted and grounded in love, 18[a]may be able
to comprehend with all the saints [b]what *is*
the width and length and depth and height—
19 to know the love of Christ which passes
knowledge; that you may be filled [a]with all
the fullness of God.

20 Now [a]to Him who is able to do exceed-
ingly abundantly [b]*above all that* we ask or
think, [c]according to the power that works
in us, 21[a]to Him *be* glory in the church by
Christ Jesus to all generations, forever and
ever. Amen.

Walk in Unity

4 I, therefore, the prisoner of the Lord,
beseech you to [a]walk worthy of the calling with which you were called, 2 with all
lowliness and gentleness, with longsuffering,
bearing with one another in love, 3 endeavoring to keep the unity of the Spirit [a]in the
bond of peace. 4[a]*There is* one body and one
Spirit, just as you were called in one hope
of your calling; 5[a]one Lord, [b]one faith, [c]one
baptism; 6[a]one God and Father of all, who *is*
above all, and [b]through all, and in you[1] all.

Spiritual Gifts

7 But [a]to each one of us grace was given
according to the measure of Christ's gift.
8 Therefore He says:

[a]"When He ascended on high,
He led captivity captive,
And gave gifts to men."[1]

9[a](Now this, "He ascended"—what does it
mean but that He also first[1] descended into the
lower parts of the earth? 10 He who descended
is also the One [a]who ascended far above all
the heavens, [b]that He might fill all things.)
11 And He Himself gave some *to be* apostles,
some prophets, some evangelists, and some

3:11 [a] [Eph. 1:4, 11] **3:12** [a] Heb. 4:16; 10:19, 35 **3:13** [a] Phil. 1:14 [b] 2 Cor. 1:6 **3:14** [a] Eph. 1:3 [1] NU-Text omits *of our Lord Jesus Christ.* **3:16** [a] [Phil. 4:19] [b] Col. 1:11 [c] Rom. 7:22 **3:17** [a] John 14:23 [b] Col. 1:23 **3:18** [a] Eph. 1:18 [b] Rom. 8:39 **3:19** [a] Eph. 1:23 **3:20** [a] Rom. 16:25 [b] 1 Cor. 2:9 [c] Col. 1:29 **3:21** [a] Rom. 11:36 **4:1** [a] 1 Thess. 2:12 **4:3** [a] Col. 3:14 **4:4** [a] Rom. 12:5 **4:5** [a] 1 Cor. 1:13 [b] Jude 3 [c] [Heb. 6:6] **4:6** [a] Mal. 2:10 [b] Rom. 11:36 [1] NU-Text omits *you;* M-Text reads *us.* **4:7** [a] [1 Cor. 12:7, 11] **4:8** [a] Ps. 68:18; Mark 16:19; Acts 1:9; [1 Cor. 12:4–11] [1] Psalm 68:18 **4:9** [a] John 3:13; 20:17 [1] NU-Text omits *first.* **4:10** [a] Ps. 68:18; Acts 1:9 [b] [Acts 2:33; Eph. 1:23]

UNIFIED BY THE SPIRIT OF PEACE

[Bear] with one another in love, endeavoring to keep the unity of the Spirit in the bond of peace.

EPHESIANS 4:2-3

A key ingredient to finding and maintaining peace in your life, family, and church is humility and treating others with respect. We draw insight from passages like this (vv. 1–7), where Paul called for believers to keep "unity . . . in the bond of peace," which requires humility and patience to help us put up with "one another in love" (v. 3). If we are at peace with God, then we can be at peace with ourselves and others. This peace process is ultimately founded on the reconciliation that God provides through His Son, Jesus Christ, who died for us and eliminated the list of charges against us. With the slate wiped clean, we can enter into a peaceful relationship with God and with one another.

Do your relationships reflect peace or chaos? How could God help change that? We are divisive by nature. It is always easier to go negative. So I have to remind myself daily to seek unity and to protect the peace of God in my life and in my relationships.

pastors and teachers, 12 for the equipping of the
saints for the work of ministry, [a]for the edifying
of [b]the body of Christ, 13 till we all come to the
unity of the faith [a]and of the knowledge of the
Son of God, to [b]a perfect man, to the measure
of the stature of the fullness of Christ; 14 that we
should no longer be [a]children, tossed to and fro
and carried about with every wind of doctrine,
by the trickery of men, in the cunning craftiness
of [b]deceitful plotting, 15 but, speaking the truth
in love, may grow up in all things into Him who
is the [a]head—Christ— 16 [a]from whom the whole
body, joined and knit together by what every
joint supplies, according to the effective working
by which every part does its share, causes growth
of the body for the edifying of itself in love.

The New Man

17 This I say, therefore, and testify in the
Lord, that you should [a]no longer walk as
the rest of[1] the Gentiles walk, in the futility
of their mind, 18 having their understanding darkened, being alienated from the life
of God, because of the ignorance that is in
them, because of the [a]blindness of their
heart; 19 [a]who, being past feeling, [b]have given
themselves over to lewdness, to work all
uncleanness with greediness.
20 But you have not so learned Christ, 21 if
indeed you have heard Him and have been
taught by Him, as the truth is in Jesus: 22 that
you [a]put off, concerning your former conduct,
the old man which grows corrupt according
to the deceitful lusts, 23 and [a]be renewed in
the spirit of your mind, 24 and that you [a]put
on the new man which was created according
to God, in true righteousness and holiness.

Do Not Grieve the Spirit

25 Therefore, putting away lying, [a]"*Let* each
one *of you* speak truth with his neighbor,"[1]
for [b]we are members of one another. 26 [a]"Be
angry, and do not sin":[1] do not let the sun go
down on your wrath, 27 [a]nor give place to the
devil. 28 Let him who stole steal no longer, but
rather [a]let him labor, working with *his* hands
what is good, that he may have something [b]to
give him who has need. 29 [a]Let no corrupt word
proceed out of your mouth, but [b]what is good
for necessary edification, [c]that it may impart
grace to the hearers. 30 And [a]do not grieve the
Holy Spirit of God, by whom you were sealed
for the day of redemption. 31 [a]Let all bitterness,
wrath, anger, clamor, and [b]evil speaking be put
away from you, [c]with all malice. 32 And [a]be kind
to one another, tenderhearted, [b]forgiving one
another, even as God in Christ forgave you.

Walk in Love

5 Therefore[a] be imitators of God as dear
[b]children. 2 And [a]walk in love, [b]as Christ
also has loved us and given Himself for us, an
offering and a sacrifice to God [c]for a sweet-
smelling aroma.

4:12 [a] 1 Cor. 14:26 [b] Col. 1:24 **4:13** [a] Col. 2:2 [b] 1 Cor. 14:20 **4:14** [a] 1 Cor. 14:20 [b] Rom. 16:18 **4:15** [a] Eph. 1:22 **4:16** [a] Col. 2:19 **4:17** [a] Eph. 2:2; 4:22 [1] NU-Text omits *the rest of.* **4:18** [a] Rom. 1:21 **4:19** [a] 1 Tim. 4:2 [b] 1 Pet. 4:3 **4:22** [a] Col. 3:8 **4:23** [a] [Rom. 12:2] **4:24** [a] [Rom. 6:4; 7:6; 12:2] **4:25** [a] Zech. 8:16 [b] Rom. 12:5 [1] Zechariah 8:16 **4:26** [a] Ps. 4:4; 37:8 [1] Psalm 4:4 **4:27** [a] [Rom. 12:19] **4:28** [a] Acts 20:35 [b] Luke 3:11 **4:29** [a] Col. 3:8 [b] 1 Thess. 5:11 [c] Col. 3:16 **4:30** [a] Is. 7:13 **4:31** [a] Col. 3:8, 19 [b] James 4:11 [c] Titus 3:3 **4:32** [a] 2 Cor. 6:10 [b] [Mark 11:25] **5:1** [a] Luke 6:36 [b] 1 Pet. 1:14–16 **5:2** [a] 1 Thess. 4:9 [b] Gal. 1:4 [c] 2 Cor. 2:14, 15

3 But fornication and all [a]uncleanness or
[b]covetousness, let it not even be named among
you, as is fitting for saints; 4 [a]neither filthiness,
nor [b]foolish talking, nor coarse jesting, [c]which
are not fitting, but rather [d]giving of thanks.
5 For this you know,[1] that no fornicator, unclean
person, nor covetous man, who is an idolater,
has any [a]inheritance in the kingdom of Christ
and God. 6 Let no one deceive you with empty
words, for because of these things the wrath
of God comes upon the sons of disobedience.
7 Therefore do not be [a]partakers with them.

Walk in Light

8 For you were once darkness, but now *you
are* [a]light in the Lord. Walk as children of light
9 (for [a]the fruit of the Spirit[1] *is* in all goodness,
righteousness, and truth), 10 [a]finding out what
is acceptable to the Lord. 11 And have [a]no fellowship with the unfruitful works of darkness, but
rather expose *them.* 12 [a]For it is shameful even to
speak of those things which are done by them
in secret. 13 But [a]all things that are exposed are
made manifest by the light, for whatever makes
manifest is light. 14 Therefore He says:

[a]"Awake, you who sleep,
Arise from the dead,
And Christ will give you light."

Walk in Wisdom

15 [a]See then that you walk circumspectly,
not as fools but as wise, 16 [a]redeeming the
time, [b]because the days are evil.

> **PEACE NOTE**
>
> "Walk as children of light."
> When you shine, others
> will be drawn to you.
>
> EPHESIANS 5:8

17 [a]Therefore do not be unwise, but [b]under-
stand [c]what the will of the Lord *is.* 18 And [a]do
not be drunk with wine, in which is dissipation; but be filled with the Spirit, 19 speaking
to one another [a]in psalms and hymns and
spiritual songs, singing and making [b]melody
in your heart to the Lord, 20 [a]giving thanks
always for all things to God the Father [b]in the
name of our Lord Jesus Christ, 21 [a]submitting
to one another in the fear of God.[1]

Marriage—Christ and the Church

22 Wives, [a]submit to your own husbands,
as to the Lord. 23 For [a]the husband is head of
the wife, as also [b]Christ is head of the church;

5:3 [a] Col. 3:5–7 [b] [Luke 12:15] **5:4** [a] Matt. 12:34, 35 [b] Titus 3:9 [c] Rom. 1:28 [d] Phil. 4:6 **5:5** [a] 1 Cor. 6:9, 10 [1] NU-Text reads *For know this.* **5:7** [a] 1 Tim. 5:22 **5:8** [a] 1 Thess. 5:5 **5:9** [a] Gal. 5:22 [1] NU-Text reads *light.* **5:10** [a] [Rom. 12:1, 2] **5:11** [a] 2 Cor. 6:14 **5:12** [a] Rom. 1:24 **5:13** [a] [John 3:20, 21] **5:14** [a] [Is. 26:19; 60:1] **5:15** [a] Col. 4:5 **5:16** [a] Col. 4:5 [b] Eccl. 11:2 **5:17** [a] Col. 4:5 [b] [Rom. 12:2] [c] 1 Thess. 4:3 **5:18** [a] Prov. 20:1; 23:31 **5:19** [a] Acts 16:25 [b] James 5:13 **5:20** [a] Ps. 34:1 [b] [1 Pet. 2:5] **5:21** [a] [Phil. 2:3] [1] NU-Text reads *Christ.* **5:22** [a] Col. 3:18—4:1 **5:23** [a] [1 Cor. 11:3] [b] Col. 1:18

BE A MISSIONARY OF PEACE

Stand . . . having shod your feet with the preparation of the gospel of peace.

EPHESIANS 6:14-15

The phrase "having girded your waist with truth" (v. 14) is the key element that holds all the armor of God together in our lives. Note that in the armor there is no protection for *our backs,* which means Christians are never to retreat. We can keep standing against everything we face because we walk in the gospel and protection of God's peace. Don't run away. The Lord is calling us to make our stand in the peace of God and attach all we are to the truth of God's Word.

We must gird our waists with truth, put on the breastplate of righteousness, take up the shield of faith, put on the helmet of salvation, and take up the sword of the Spirit (vv. 14–17). The mention of "feet" (v. 15) refers to the work of the missionary, who goes from place to place proclaiming the gospel. How do you give yourself to the gospel of peace?

and He is the Savior of the body. 24 Therefore, just as the church is subject to Christ, so *let* the wives *be* to their own husbands [a]in everything.

25 [a]Husbands, love your wives, just as Christ also loved the church and [b]gave Himself for her, 26 that He might sanctify and cleanse her [a]with the washing of water [b]by the word, 27 [a]that He might present her to Himself a glorious church, [b]not having spot or wrinkle or any such thing, but that she should be holy and without blemish. 28 So husbands ought to love their own wives as their own bodies; he who loves his wife loves himself. 29 For no one ever hated his own flesh, but nourishes and cherishes it, just as the Lord *does* the church. 30 For [a]we are members of His body,[1] of His flesh and of His bones. 31 [a]"For this reason a man shall leave his father and mother and be joined to his wife, and the [b]two shall become one flesh."[1] 32 This is a great mystery, but I speak concerning Christ and the church. 33 Nevertheless [a]let each one of you in particular so love his own wife as himself, and let the wife *see* that she [b]respects *her* husband.

Children and Parents

6 Children, [a]obey your parents in the Lord, for this is right. 2 [a]"Honor your father and mother," which is the first commandment with promise: 3 "that it may be well with you and you may live long on the earth."[1]

4 And [a]you, fathers, do not provoke your children to wrath, but [b]bring them up in the training and admonition of the Lord.

Bondservants and Masters

5 [a]Bondservants, be obedient to those who are your masters according to the flesh, [b]with fear and trembling, [c]in sincerity of heart, as to Christ; 6 [a]not with eyeservice, as men-pleasers, but as bondservants of Christ, doing the will of God from the heart, 7 with goodwill doing service, as to the Lord, and not to men, 8 [a]knowing that whatever good anyone does, he will receive the same from the Lord, whether *he is* a slave or free.

9 And you, masters, do the same things to them, giving up threatening, knowing that your own [a]Master also[1] is in heaven, and [b]there is no partiality with Him.

The Whole Armor of God

10 Finally, my brethren, be strong in the Lord and in the power of His might. 11 [a]Put on the whole armor of God, that you may be able to stand against the wiles of the devil. 12 For we do not wrestle against flesh and blood, but against [a]principalities, against powers, against [b]the rulers of the darkness of this age,[1] against spiritual *hosts* of wickedness in the heavenly *places*. 13 [a]Therefore take up the whole armor of God, that you may be able to withstand [b]in the evil day, and having done all, to stand.

5:24 [a] Titus 2:4, 5 **5:25** [a] Col. 3:19 [b] Acts 20:28 **5:26** [a] John 3:5 [b] [John 15:3; 17:17] **5:27** [a] Col. 1:22 [b] Song 4:7 **5:30** [a] Gen. 2:23 [1] NU-Text omits the rest of this verse. **5:31** [a] Gen. 2:24 [b] [1 Cor. 6:16] [1] Genesis 2:24 **5:33** [a] Col. 3:19 [b] 1 Pet. 3:1, 6 **6:1** [a] Col. 3:20 **6:2** [a] Deut. 5:16 **6:3** [1] Deuteronomy 5:16 **6:4** [a] Col. 3:21 [b] Gen. 18:19 **6:5** [a] [1 Tim. 6:1] [b] 2 Cor. 7:15 [c] 1 Chr. 29:17 **6:6** [a] Col. 3:22 **6:8** [a] Rom. 2:6 **6:9** [a] Col. 4:1 [b] Rom. 2:11 [1] NU-Text reads *He who is both their Master and yours.* **6:11** [a] [2 Cor. 6:7] **6:12** [a] Rom. 8:38 [b] Luke 22:53 [1] NU-Text reads *rulers of this darkness.* **6:13** [a] [2 Cor. 10:4] [b] Eph. 5:16

RADIATING PEACE

Peace to the brethren, and love with faith, from God the Father and the Lord Jesus Christ.

EPHESIANS 6:23

Do you know people who seem full of grace and peace? I do, and I love being with them.

Sometimes the word "grace" (v. 24) has a tangible quality about it. The Old Testament talks about seeing or finding grace in someone. It is as though you can even touch it. Similarly the word "peace" (v. 23) has an almost tangible dimension. People can sense peace. It puts them at ease. It pushes away anxiety and fear and replaces these negatives with hope and assurance. In whose presence do you feel calm instead of worry? What persons help blow away nervousness and replace it with relaxation?

For Paul that was how Christian life should be: it is the experience of peace from start to finish, from morning to night. Is this your experience? Is it an experience you help others have? Can you become a person who exudes peace?

14 Stand therefore, [a]having girded your
waist with truth, [b]having put on the breastplate of righteousness, 15 [a]and having shod
your feet with the preparation of the gospel of
peace; 16 above all, taking [a]the shield of faith
with which you will be able to quench all the
fiery darts of the wicked one. 17 And [a]take the
helmet of salvation, and [b]the sword of the
Spirit, which is the word of God; 18 [a]praying
always with all prayer and supplication in
the Spirit, [b]being watchful to this end with
all perseverance and [c]supplication for all the
saints— 19 and for me, that utterance may
be given to me, [a]that I may open my mouth
boldly to make known the mystery of the
gospel, 20 for which [a]I am an ambassador
in chains; that in it I may speak boldly, as I
ought to speak.

PEACE NOTE

God's protective power was such that Paul spoke of the shield, the sword, the breastplate, the helmet, and other military equipment—all to give us peace.

EPHESIANS 6:13-17

A Gracious Greeting

21 But that you also may know my affairs
and how I am doing, [a]Tychicus, a beloved
brother and [b]faithful minister in the Lord,
will make all things known to you; 22 [a]whom
I have sent to you for this very purpose, that
you may know our affairs, and *that* he may
[b]comfort your hearts.
23 Peace to the brethren, and love with
faith, from God the Father and the Lord Jesus
Christ. 24 Grace *be* with all those who love our
Lord Jesus Christ in sincerity. Amen.

6:14 [a] Is. 11:5 [b] Is. 59:17 **6:15** [a] Is. 52:7 **6:16** [a] 1 John 5:4 **6:17** [a] 1 Thess. 5:8 [b] [Heb. 4:12] **6:18** [a] Luke 18:1 [b] [Matt. 26:41] [c] Phil. 1:4 **6:19** [a] Col. 4:3 **6:20** [a] 2 Cor. 5:20 **6:21** [a] Acts 20:4 [b] 1 Cor. 4:1, 2 **6:22** [a] Col. 4:8 [b] 2 Cor. 1:6

THE EPISTLE OF PAUL THE APOSTLE TO THE

PHILIPPIANS

AUTHOR

The external and internal evidence for the Pauline authorship of Philippians is very strong, and there is scarcely any doubt that anyone but Paul wrote it. Paul's "Macedonian call" in Troas during his second missionary journey led to his ministry in Philippi with the conversion of Lydia and others (Acts 16). Internal evidence suggests that the epistle was written from Rome (Phil. 1:3; 4:22), although some commentators argue for Caesarea or Ephesus. It seems that during the writing of this letter Paul's life was at stake, and he was evidently awaiting the verdict of the imperial court (2:20–26).

TIME

c. AD 62

KEY VERSE

Philippians 4:4–7

THEME

Even though Paul probably wrote this letter while imprisoned in Rome, the letter is often called the "epistle of joy." It gives us valuable insight by helping us understand how we should identify with Christ in a variety of circumstances. We learn what the content of our prayers for each other should be. Philippians also provides great inspiration for setting spiritual direction and determining spiritual priorities. Christians desiring to mature in the Lord will study it often.

Peace is a steady theme in this beloved book. Here we find the greatest antianxiety chapter in all the Bible—chapter 4. Further, we learn of Paul's peace plan (4:6–9), what he removed from his mind in order to maintain the peace of God (4:6), and the truths he continually filled his mind with to walk in the peace of the Lord (4:8). In Philippians we come to understand that living in the peace of God is a discipline, and it happens through an action verb: *think*! But think about what, exactly? In 4:9, Paul gave every believer a promise of peace, but note that it is preceded by learning: "The things which you learned and received and heard and saw in me, these do, and the God of peace will be with you." A key application of Philippians is that, by ridding your mind of anxiety and foul thoughts, you make room for God's peace.

Greeting

1 Paul and Timothy, bondservants of Jesus Christ,

To all the saints in Christ Jesus who are in Philippi, with the bishops[1] and [a]deacons:

2 Grace to you and peace from God our Father and the Lord Jesus Christ.

Thankfulness and Prayer

3 [a]I thank my God upon every remembrance of you, 4 always in [a]every prayer of mine making request for you all with joy, 5 [a]for your fellowship in the gospel from the first day until now, 6 being confident of this very thing, that He who has begun [a]a good work in you will complete *it* until the day of Jesus Christ; 7 just as it is right for me to think this of you all, because I have you in my heart, inasmuch as both in my chains and in the defense and confirmation of the gospel, you all are partakers with me of grace. 8 For God is my witness, how greatly I long for you all with the affection of Jesus Christ.

9 And this I pray, that your love may abound still more and more in knowledge and all discernment, 10 that you may approve the things that are excellent, that you may be sincere and without offense till the day of Christ, 11 being filled with the fruits of righteousness [a]which *are* by Jesus Christ, [b]to the glory and praise of God.

Christ Is Preached

12 But I want you to know, brethren, that the things *which happened* to me have actually turned out for the furtherance of the gospel, 13 so that it has become evident [a]to the whole palace guard, and to all the rest, that my chains are in Christ; 14 and most of the brethren in the Lord, having become confident by my chains, are much more bold to speak the word without fear.

15 Some indeed preach Christ even from envy and strife, and some also from goodwill: 16 The former[1] preach Christ from selfish ambition, not sincerely, supposing to add affliction to my chains; 17 but the latter out of love, knowing that I am appointed for the defense of the gospel. 18 What then? Only *that* in every way, whether in pretense or in truth, Christ is preached; and in this I rejoice, yes, and will rejoice.

> **PEACE NOTE**
>
> The *shalom* of God is the assurance that He who started a "good work" in us will be faithful to "complete it until the day of Jesus Christ."
>
> PHILIPPIANS 1:6

To Live Is Christ

19 For I know that [a]this will turn out for my deliverance through your prayer and the supply of the Spirit of Jesus Christ, 20 according to my earnest expectation and hope that in nothing I shall be ashamed, but [a]with all boldness, as always, so now also Christ will be magnified in my body, whether by life [b]or by death. 21 For to me, to live *is* Christ, and to die *is* gain. 22 But if *I* live on in the flesh, this *will mean* fruit from *my* labor; yet what I shall choose I cannot tell. 23 For[1] I am hard-pressed between the two, having a [a]desire to depart and be with Christ, *which is* [b]far better. 24 Nevertheless to remain in the flesh *is* more needful for you. 25 And being confident of this, I know that I shall remain and continue with you all for your progress and joy of faith, 26 that [a]your rejoicing for me may be more abundant in Jesus Christ by my coming to you again.

Striving and Suffering for Christ

27 Only [a]let your conduct be worthy of the gospel of Christ, so that whether I come and see you or am absent, I may hear of your affairs, that you stand fast in one spirit, [b]with one mind [c]striving together for the faith of the gospel, 28 and not in any way terrified by your adversaries, which is to them a proof of perdition, but to you of salvation,[1] and that from God. 29 For to you [a]it has been granted on behalf of Christ, [b]not only to believe in Him, but also to [c]suffer for His sake, 30 [a]having the same conflict [b]which you saw in me and now hear *is* in me.

1:1 [a] [1 Tim. 3:8–13] [1] Literally *overseers* **1:3** [a] 1 Cor. 1:4 **1:4** [a] Eph. 1:16 **1:5** [a] [Rom. 12:13] **1:6** [a] [John 6:29] **1:11** [a] Col. 1:6 [b] John 15:8 **1:13** [a] Phil. 4:22 **1:16** [1] NU-Text reverses the contents of verses 16 and 17. **1:19** [a] Job 13:16, LXX **1:20** [a] Eph. 6:19, 20 [b] [Rom. 14:8] **1:23** [a] [2 Cor. 5:2, 8] [b] [Ps. 16:11] [1] NU-Text and M-Text read *But.* **1:26** [a] 2 Cor. 1:14 **1:27** [a] Eph. 4:1 [b] Eph. 4:3 [c] Jude 3 **1:28** [1] NU-Text reads *of your salvation.* **1:29** [a] [Matt. 5:11, 12] [b] Eph. 2:8 [c] [2 Tim. 3:12] **1:30** [a] Col. 1:29; 2:1 [b] Acts 16:19–40

Unity Through Humility

2 Therefore if *there is* any consolation in
Christ, if any comfort of love, if any fellowship of the Spirit, if any [a]affection and mercy,
2 [a]fulfill my joy [b]by being like-minded, having
the same love, *being* of [c]one accord, of one
mind. 3 [a]*Let* nothing *be done* through selfish
ambition or conceit, but [b]in lowliness of mind
let each esteem others better than himself.
4 [a]Let each of you look out not only for his own
interests, but also for the interests of [b]others.

The Humbled and Exalted Christ

5 [a]Let this mind be in you which was also
in Christ Jesus, 6 who, [a]being in the form of
God, did not consider it robbery to be equal
with God, 7 [a]but made Himself of no reputation, taking the form [b]of a bondservant,
and [c]coming in the likeness of men. 8 And
being found in appearance as a man, He
humbled Himself and [a]became [b]obedient
to *the point of* death, even the death of the
cross. 9 [a]Therefore God also [b]has highly exalted Him and [c]given Him the name which
is above every name, 10 [a]that at the name of
Jesus every knee should bow, of those in
heaven, and of those on earth, and of those
under the earth, 11 and [a]*that* every tongue
should confess that Jesus Christ *is* Lord, to
the glory of God the Father.

Light Bearers

12 Therefore, my beloved, [a]as you have always obeyed, not as in my presence only, but
now much more in my absence, [b]work out
your own salvation with [c]fear and trembling;
13 for [a]it is God who works in you both to will
and to do [b]for *His* good pleasure.
14 Do all things [a]without complaining and
[b]disputing, 15 that you may become blameless
and harmless, children of God without fault
in the midst of a crooked and perverse generation, among whom you shine as [a]lights in
the world, 16 holding fast the word of life, so
that [a]I may rejoice in the day of Christ that
[b]I have not run in vain or labored in [c]vain.
17 Yes, and if [a]I am being poured out *as a*
drink offering on the sacrifice [b]and service of
your faith, [c]I am glad and rejoice with you
all. 18 For the same reason you also be glad
and rejoice with me.

Timothy Commended

19 But I trust in the Lord Jesus to send
[a]Timothy to you shortly, that I also may be
encouraged when I know your state. 20 For I
have no one [a]like-minded, who will sincerely
care for your state. 21 For all seek their own,
not the things which are of Christ Jesus. 22 But
you know his proven character, [a]that as a
son with *his* father he served with me in the
gospel. 23 Therefore I hope to send him at
once, as soon as I see how it goes with me.
24 But I trust in the Lord that I myself shall
also come shortly.

Epaphroditus Praised

25 Yet I considered it necessary to send to
you [a]Epaphroditus, my brother, fellow worker, and [b]fellow soldier, [c]but your messenger
and [d]the one who ministered to my need;
26 [a]since he was longing for you all, and was
distressed because you had heard that he
was sick. 27 For indeed he was sick almost
unto death; but God had mercy on him, and
not only on him but on me also, lest I should
have sorrow upon sorrow. 28 Therefore I sent
him the more eagerly, that when you see
him again you may rejoice, and I may be
less sorrowful. 29 Receive him therefore in
the Lord with all gladness, and hold such
men in esteem; 30 because for the work of
Christ he came close to death, not regarding
his life, [a]to supply what was lacking in your
service toward me.

All for Christ

3 Finally, my brethren, [a]rejoice in the Lord.
For me to write the same things to you *is*
not tedious, but for you *it is* safe.
2 [a]Beware of dogs, beware of [b]evil workers, [c]beware of the mutilation! 3 For we are
[a]the circumcision, [b]who worship God in the
Spirit,[1] rejoice in Christ Jesus, and have no
confidence in the flesh, 4 though [a]I also might
have confidence in the flesh. If anyone else
thinks he may have confidence in the flesh, I
[b]more so: 5 circumcised the eighth day, of the
stock of Israel, [a]*of* the tribe of Benjamin, [b]a
Hebrew of the Hebrews; concerning the law,
[c]a Pharisee; 6 concerning zeal, [a]persecuting
the church; concerning the righteousness
which is in the law, blameless.

2:1 [a] Col. 3:12 **2:2** [a] John 3:29 [b] Rom. 12:16 [c] Phil. 4:2 **2:3** [a] Gal. 5:26 [b] Rom. 12:10 **2:4** [a] 1 Cor. 13:5 [b] Rom. 15:1, 2 **2:5** [a] [Matt. 11:29] **2:6** [a] 2 Cor. 4:4 **2:7** [a] Ps. 22:6 [b] Is. 42:1 [c] [John 1:14] **2:8** [a] Matt. 26:39 [b] Heb. 5:8 **2:9** [a] Heb. 2:9 [b] *Ps. 68:18; 110:1; Is. 52:13; Acts 2:33* [c] Eph. 1:21 **2:10** [a] Is. 45:23 **2:11** [a] John 13:13; [Rom. 10:9; 14:9] **2:12** [a] Phil. 1:5, 6; 4:15 [b] John 6:27, 29 [c] Eph. 6:5 **2:13** [a] Heb. 13:20, 21 [b] Eph. 1:5 **2:14** [a] 1 Pet. 4:9 [b] Rom. 14:1 **2:15** [a] Matt. 5:15, 16 **2:16** [a] 2 Cor. 1:14 [b] Gal. 2:2 [c] 1 Thess. 3:5 **2:17** [a] 2 Tim. 4:6 [b] Rom. 15:16 [c] 2 Cor. 7:4 **2:19** [a] Rom. 16:21 **2:20** [a] 2 Tim. 3:10 **2:22** [a] 1 Cor. 4:17 **2:25** [a] Phil. 4:18 [b] Philem. 2 [c] 2 Cor. 8:23 [d] 2 Cor. 11:9 **2:26** [a] Phil. 1:8 **2:30** [a] 1 Cor. 16:17 **3:1** [a] 1 Thess. 5:16 **3:2** [a] Gal. 5:15 [b] Ps. 119:115 [c] Rom. 2:28 **3:3** [a] Deut. 30:6 [b] Rom. 7:6 [1] NU-Text and M-Text read *who worship in the Spirit of God.* **3:4** [a] 2 Cor. 5:16; 11:18 [b] 2 Cor. 11:22, 23 **3:5** [a] Rom. 11:1 [b] 2 Cor. 11:22 [c] Acts 23:6 **3:6** [a] Acts 8:3; 22:4, 5; 26:9–11

PEACE NOTE

There is no perfect faith, only faith in a perfect Savior, Jesus Christ! Don't stop believing! Jesus calls on you to have greater faith in the power of His peace in your life day by day.

PHILIPPIANS 3:10

7 But [a]what things were gain to me, these
I have counted loss for Christ. 8 Yet indeed I
also count all things loss [a]for the excellence
of the knowledge of Christ Jesus my Lord, for
whom I have suffered the loss of all things,
and count them as rubbish, that I may gain
Christ 9 and be found in Him, not having [a]my
own righteousness, which *is* from the law,
but [b]that which *is* through faith in Christ, the
righteousness which is from God by faith;
10 that I may know Him and the [a]power of
His resurrection, and [b]the fellowship of His
sufferings, being conformed to His death,
11 if, by any means, I may [a]attain to the resurrection from the dead.

Pressing Toward the Goal

12 Not that I have already [a]attained, or am
already [b]perfected; but I press on, that I may
lay hold of that for which Christ Jesus has
also laid hold of me. 13 Brethren, I do not
count myself to have apprehended; but one
thing *I do,* [a]forgetting those things which
are behind and [b]reaching forward to those
things which are ahead, 14 [a]I press toward the
goal for the prize of [b]the upward call of God
in Christ Jesus.
15 Therefore let us, as many as are [a]mature,
[b]have this mind; and if in anything you think
otherwise, [c]God will reveal even this to you.
16 Nevertheless, to *the degree* that we have
already attained, [a]let us walk [b]by the same
rule,[1] let us be of the same mind.

Our Citizenship in Heaven

17 Brethren, [a]join in following my example,
and note those who so walk, as [b]you have
us for a pattern. 18 For many walk, of whom
I have told you often, and now tell you even
weeping, *that they are* [a]the enemies of the
cross of Christ: 19 [a]whose end *is* destruction,
[b]whose god *is their* belly, and [c]*whose* glory
is in their shame—[d]who set their mind on
earthly things. 20 For [a]our citizenship is in
heaven, [b]from which we also [c]eagerly wait

3:7 [a] Matt. 13:44 **3:8** [a] Jer. 9:23 **3:9** [a] Rom. 10:3 [b] Rom. 1:17 **3:10** [a] Eph. 1:19, 20 [b] [Rom. 6:3–5] **3:11** [a] Acts 26:6–8 **3:12** [a] [1 Tim. 6:12, 19] [b] Heb. 12:23 **3:13** [a] Luke 9:62 [b] Heb. 6:1 **3:14** [a] 2 Tim. 4:7 [b] Heb. 3:1 **3:15** [a] 1 Cor. 2:6 [b] Gal. 5:10 [c] Hos. 6:3 **3:16** [a] Gal. 6:16 [b] Rom. 12:16; 15:5 [1] NU-Text omits *rule* and the rest of the verse. **3:17** [a] [1 Cor. 4:16; 11:1] [b] Titus 2:7, 8 **3:18** [a] Gal. 1:7 **3:19** [a] 2 Cor. 11:15 [b] 1 Tim. 6:5 [c] Hos. 4:7 [d] Rom. 8:5 **3:20** [a] Eph. 2:6, 19 [b] Acts 1:11 [c] 1 Cor. 1:7

PEACE BEYOND IMAGINATION

The peace of God, which surpasses all understanding, will guard your hearts and minds through Christ Jesus . . . If there is anything praiseworthy—meditate on these things.

PHILIPPIANS 4:7-8

I think Paul may have been a moody person. He suffered a lot (if you need some examples, read 2 Cor. 1). He had so many troubles, he has often been called "the Job of the New Testament." I am encouraged that if Paul could find peace, so can I.

Paul used a vivid military metaphor to describe how the peace of God will allow us to relax and rest. The "peace of God . . . will guard" us (Phil. 4:7)—imagine soldiers surrounding a city to protect it from invasion. In his letter to the Philippians, Paul urged his readers to access this peace by setting their minds on lovely, pure things (v. 8). Minds that dwell on the things of God tend to have clear consciences and receptivity to God's peace.

When we submit our lives to Jesus Christ and His lordship, peace will be the result, but it is something we must contend for—especially those of us who are moody—moment by moment in our faith walk with God. Think on good things, and accept the peace that follows.

PEACE NOTE

Philippians 4 is the greatest anti-anxiety chapter in all the Bible. Read it and memorize it! Peace is closer than you think.

PHILIPPIANS 4:6

for the Savior, the Lord Jesus Christ, [21][a]who
will transform our lowly body that it may be
[b]conformed to His glorious body, [c]according
to the working by which He is able even to
[d]subdue all things to Himself.
4 Therefore, my beloved and [a]longed-for
brethren, [b]my joy and crown, so [c]stand
fast in the Lord, beloved.

Be United, Joyful, and in Prayer

[2]I implore Euodia and I implore Syntyche
[a]to be of the same mind in the Lord. [3]And[1]
I urge you also, true companion, help these
women who [a]labored with me in the gospel,
with Clement also, and the rest of my fellow
workers, whose names *are* in [b]the Book of
Life.
[4][a]Rejoice in the Lord always. Again I will
say, rejoice!
[5]Let your gentleness be known to all men.
[a]The Lord *is* at hand.
[6][a]Be anxious for nothing, but in everything
by prayer and supplication, with [b]thanks-
giving, let your requests be made known to
God; [7]and [a]the peace of God, which surpasses
all understanding, will guard your hearts and
minds through Christ Jesus.

PEACE NOTE

Paul used a vivid military metaphor to describe how the peace of God will allow us to relax and rest: imagine soldiers surrounding a city to protect it from invasion.

PHILIPPIANS 4:7

3:21 [a] [1 Cor. 15:43–53] [b] 1 John 3:2 [c] Eph. 1:19 [d] [1 Cor. 15:28] **4:1** [a] Phil. 1:8 [b] 2 Cor. 1:14 [c] Phil. 1:27 **4:2** [a] Phil. 2:2; 3:16 **4:3** [a] Rom. 16:3 [b] Luke 10:20 [1] NU-Text and M-Text read *Yes.* **4:4** [a] Rom. 12:12 **4:5** [a] [James 5:7–9] **4:6** [a] Matt. 6:25 [b] [1 Thess. 5:17, 18] **4:7** [a] [John 14:27]

THE PEACEFUL PRESENCE OF GOD

The things which you learned and received and heard and saw in me, these do, and the God of peace will be with you.

PHILIPPIANS 4:9

You have probably realized that true, lasting peace is not generated within us but is sourced in God. What brings peace is not a series of rituals or ideas, as such, but it is the work of the Holy Spirit. A big problem in today's world is the never-ending, fruitless quest for peace and joy—money, entertainment, cuisine, adventures, and experiences—yet nothing satisfies.

When the apostle Paul found himself in prison, his peace and joy did not come from himself and they certainly did not come from money or entertainment: they came from God. Paul urged believers to follow his example by thinking on what is good and honorable. If they thought on and then did such things as Paul taught them, "the God of peace" would be with them.

When one does what is right and good, one is blessed with God's peace. Don't believe it? Try it and see.

Meditate on These Things
8 Finally, brethren, whatever things are
[a]true, whatever things *are* [b]noble, whatever
things *are* [c]just, [d]whatever things *are* pure,
whatever things *are* [e]lovely, whatever things
are of good report, if *there is* any virtue and if
there is anything praiseworthy—meditate on
these things. 9 The things which you learned
and received and heard and saw in me,
these do, and [a]the God of peace will be with
you.

Philippian Generosity
10 But I rejoiced in the Lord greatly that
now at last [a]your care for me has flourished
again; though you surely did care, but you
lacked opportunity. 11 Not that I speak in regard to need, for I have learned in whatever
state I am, [a]to be content: 12 [a]I know how to
be abased, and I know how to abound. Everywhere and in all things I have learned both to
be full and to be hungry, both to abound and
to suffer need. 13 I can do all things [a]through
Christ[1] who strengthens me.
14 Nevertheless you have done well that
[a]you shared in my distress. 15 Now you Philippians know also that in the beginning of
the gospel, when I departed from Macedonia, [a]no church shared with me concerning
giving and receiving but you only. 16 For even
in Thessalonica you sent *aid* once and again
for my necessities. 17 Not that I seek the gift,
but I seek [a]the fruit that abounds to your
account. 18 Indeed I have all and abound. I
am full, having received from [a]Epaphroditus
the things *sent* from you, [b]a sweet-smelling
aroma, [c]an acceptable sacrifice, well pleasing to God. 19 And my God [a]shall supply all
your need according to His riches in glory by
Christ Jesus. 20 [a]Now to our God and Father
be glory forever and ever. Amen.

Greeting and Blessing
21 Greet every saint in Christ Jesus. The
brethren [a]who are with me greet you. 22 All
the saints greet you, but especially those who
are of Caesar's household.
23 The grace of our Lord Jesus Christ be
with you all.[1] Amen.

PEACE NOTE

Peace happens through an action verb: *meditate*. Meditate on what? "If there is anything praiseworthy—meditate on these things."

PHILIPPIANS 4:8

4:8 [a] Eph. 4:25 [b] 2 Cor. 8:21 [c] Deut. 16:20 [d] 1 Thess. 5:22 [e] 1 Cor. 13:4–7 **4:9** [a] Rom. 15:33 **4:10** [a] 2 Cor. 11:9
4:11 [a] 1 Tim. 6:6, 8 **4:12** [a] 1 Cor. 4:11 **4:13** [a] John 15:5 [1] NU-Text reads *Him who.* **4:14** [a] Phil. 1:7 **4:15** [a] 2 Cor. 11:8, 9
4:17 [a] Titus 3:14 **4:18** [a] Phil. 2:25 [b] Heb. 13:16 [c] 2 Cor. 9:12 **4:19** [a] Ps. 23:1 **4:20** [a] Rom. 16:27 **4:21** [a] Gal. 1:2
4:23 [1] NU-Text reads *your spirit.*

THE EPISTLE OF PAUL THE APOSTLE TO THE

COLOSSIANS

AUTHOR

The external testimony to the Pauline authorship of Colossians is ancient and consistent, and the internal evidence is also very good. It not only claims to be written by Paul (Col. 1:1, 23; 4:18), but the personal details and close parallels with Ephesians and Philemon make the case even stronger. It is evident from 1:4–8 and 2:1 that Paul had never visited the church at Colosse, which was founded by Epaphras. On his third missionary journey, Paul devoted almost three years to an Asian ministry centered in Ephesus (Acts 19:10; 20:31), and Epaphras probably came to Christ during this time. He then carried the gospel to cities like Colosse in the Lycus Valley. Epaphras visited Paul in prison (Col. 4:12) and his report concerning the church in Colosse prompted this epistle.

TIME

c. AD 60–61

KEY VERSE

Colossians 2:9–10

THEME

The problem of the Colossian church was similar to what we experience in many churches today. This is often called *syncretism*, which is the tendency to regard other philosophies and religions as equally valid with Christianity. The people in Colosse wanted to believe Christian truth, but they also wanted to keep their old beliefs by blending them with the gospel. Paul's purpose in this letter is to settle once and for all the issue of Christ's supremacy. He writes to restore Jesus the Messiah to the center of these believers' lives. Here we can see Paul's unwavering confidence in the incomparability of Christ as it has completely shaped his views on all aspects of life. He writes to introduce the Colossians to this same vision.

In Colossians Paul gave a most forceful command regarding God's *shalom*: "And let the peace of God rule in your hearts, to which also you were called in one body; and be thankful" (3:15). In recent times we've realized what should be common sense: grateful people, those who focus on blessings, are happier, more peaceful individuals. Even though this may seem to be a new phenomenon, the Scriptures elucidated the power combination of peace and gratitude. Colossians calls us to count our blessings one by one, and then we will experience the peace of God, which will "rule" our hearts!

Greeting

1 Paul, [a]an apostle of Jesus Christ by the will
of God, and Timothy our brother,

2 To the saints [a]and faithful brethren in
Christ *who are* in Colosse:

[b]Grace to you and peace from God our
Father and the Lord Jesus Christ.[1]

Their Faith in Christ

3 [a]We give thanks to the God and Father of
our Lord Jesus Christ, praying always for you,
4 [a]since we heard of your faith in Christ Jesus
and of [b]your love for all the saints; 5 because
of the hope [a]which is laid up for you in heav-
en, of which you heard before in the word
of the truth of the gospel, 6 which has come
to you, [a]as *it has* also in all the world, and
[b]is bringing forth fruit,[1] as *it is* also among
you since the day you heard and knew [c]the
grace of God in truth; 7 as you also learned
from [a]Epaphras, our dear fellow servant,
who is [b]a faithful minister of Christ on your
behalf, 8 who also declared to us your [a]love
in the Spirit.

Preeminence of Christ

9 [a]For this reason we also, since the day
we heard it, do not cease to pray for you,
and to ask [b]that you may be filled with [c]the
knowledge of His will [d]in all wisdom and
spiritual understanding; 10 [a]that you may
walk worthy of the Lord, [b]fully pleasing
Him, [c]being fruitful in every good work
and increasing in the [d]knowledge of God;
11 [a]strengthened with all might, according
to His glorious power, [b]for all patience and
longsuffering [c]with joy; 12 [a]giving thanks
to the Father who has qualified us to be
partakers of [b]the inheritance of the saints
in the light. 13 He has delivered us from [a]the
power of darkness [b]and conveyed *us* into the
kingdom of the Son of His love, 14 [a]in whom
we have redemption through His blood,[1] the
forgiveness of sins.

15 He is [a]the image of the invisible God,
[b]the firstborn over all creation. 16 For [a]by Him
all things were created that are in heaven
and that are on earth, visible and invisible,
whether thrones or [b]dominions or principalities or powers. All things were created
[c]through Him and for Him. 17 [a]And He is
before all things, and in Him [b]all things
consist. 18 And [a]He is the head of the body, the
church, who is the beginning, [b]the firstborn
from the dead, that in all things He may have
the preeminence.

1:1 [a] Eph. 1:1 **1:2** [a] 1 Cor. 4:17 [b] Gal. 1:3 [1] NU-Text omits *and the Lord Jesus Christ.* **1:3** [a] Phil. 1:3 **1:4** [a] Eph. 1:15 [b] [Heb. 6:10] **1:5** [a] [1 Pet. 1:4] **1:6** [a] Matt. 24:14 [b] John 15:16 [c] Eph. 3:2 [1] NU-Text and M-Text add *and growing.* **1:7** [a] Philem. 23 [b] 2 Cor. 11:23 **1:8** [a] Rom. 15:30 **1:9** [a] Eph. 1:15–17 [b] 1 Cor. 1:5 [c] [Rom. 12:2] [d] Eph. 1:8 **1:10** [a] Eph. 4:1 [b] 1 Thess. 4:1 [c] Heb. 13:21 [d] 2 Pet. 3:18 **1:11** [a] [Eph. 3:16; 6:10] [b] Eph. 4:2 [c] [Acts 5:41] **1:12** [a] [Eph. 5:20] [b] Eph. 1:11 **1:13** [a] Eph. 6:12 [b] 2 Pet. 1:11 **1:14** [a] Eph. 1:7 [1] NU-Text and M-Text omit *through His blood.* **1:15** [a] 2 Cor. 4:4 [b] Rev. 3:14 **1:16** [a] Heb. 1:2, 3 [b] [Eph. 1:20, 21] [c] Heb. 2:10 **1:17** [a] [John 17:5] [b] Heb. 1:3 **1:18** [a] Eph. 1:22 [b] Rev. 1:5

BEING A GENUINE CHRISTIAN

To the saints and faithful brethren in Christ who are in Colosse: Grace to you and peace.

COLOSSIANS 1:2

How many "holy ones" do you know? I ask this because the Greek word *hagioi* translated as "saints" in this verse literally means "holy ones." In the Latin, the word is *sancti,* which in English comes out as "saints."

What makes a "saint" a *saint*? Well, in the Old Testament, the holy one was a person set apart from average folk. The holy person was not profane. He or she lived according to *God's values, not man's. "You shall be holy, for I the Lord your God am holy,"* said the Lord in Leviticus 19:2. This He said to the whole nation of Israel! All followers of God are saints, not just a canonized few—did you know that? Similarly, in the early church all believers were viewed as holy ones or saints.

Paul also called the Christians of Colosse "faithful brethren" (Col. 1:2). The Greek word for "faithful" is *pistos,* which means "genuine." It was to the holy and faithful, the saints, that Paul asked God to extend His grace and peace. That means you. How can you live more completely as a holy one?

Reconciled in Christ

19 For it pleased *the Father that* [a]in Him all the fullness should dwell, 20 and [a]by Him to reconcile [b]all things to Himself, by Him, whether things on earth or things in heaven, [c]having made peace through the blood of His cross.

21 And you, [a]who once were alienated and enemies in your mind [b]by wicked works, yet now He has [c]reconciled 22 [a]in the body of His flesh through death, [b]to present you holy, and blameless, and above reproach in His sight— 23 if indeed you continue [a]in the faith, grounded and steadfast, and are [b]not moved away from the hope of the gospel which you heard, [c]which was preached to every creature under heaven, [d]of which I, Paul, became a minister.

Sacrificial Service for Christ

24 [a]I now rejoice in my sufferings [b]for you, and fill up in my flesh [c]what is lacking in the afflictions of Christ, for [d]the sake of His body, which is the church, 25 of which I became a minister according to [a]the stewardship from God which was given to me for you, to fulfill the word of God, 26 [a]the mystery which has been hidden from ages and from generations, [b]but now has been revealed to His saints. 27 [a]To them God willed to make known what are [b]the riches of the glory of this mystery among the Gentiles: which[1] is [c]Christ in you, [d]the hope of glory. 28 Him we preach, [a]warning every man and teaching every man in all wisdom, [b]that we may present every man perfect in Christ Jesus. 29 To this *end* I also labor, striving according to His working which works in me [a]mightily.

Not Philosophy but Christ

2 For I want you to know what a great [a]conflict I have for you and those in Laodicea, and *for* as many as have not seen my face in the flesh, 2 that their hearts may be encouraged, being knit together in love, and *attaining* to all riches of the full assurance of understanding, to the knowledge of the mystery of God, both of the Father and[1] of Christ, 3 [a]in whom are hidden all the treasures of wisdom and knowledge.

4 Now this I say [a]lest anyone should deceive you with persuasive words. 5 For [a]though I am absent in the flesh, yet I am with you in spirit, rejoicing to see [b]your *good* order and the [c]steadfastness of your faith in Christ.

> **PEACE NOTE**
>
> The healing, forgiving, loving relationship Jesus won for us at the cross penetrates every aspect of our lives—spiritual, mental, physical, and emotional—and brings completeness (and peace).
>
> COLOSSIANS 2:2

6 [a]As you therefore have received Christ Jesus the Lord, so walk in Him, 7 [a]rooted and built up in Him and established in the faith, as you have been taught, abounding in it[1] with thanksgiving.

8 Beware lest anyone cheat you through philosophy and empty deceit, according to [a]the tradition of men, according to the [b]basic principles of the world, and not according to Christ. 9 For [a]in Him dwells all the fullness of the Godhead bodily; 10 and you are complete in Him, who is the [a]head of all principality and power.

Not Legalism but Christ

11 In Him you were also [a]circumcised with the circumcision made without hands, by [b]putting off the body of the sins[1] of the flesh, by the circumcision of Christ, 12 [a]buried with Him in baptism, in which you also were raised with *Him* through [b]faith in the working of God, [c]who raised Him from the dead. 13 And you, being dead in your trespasses and the uncircumcision of your flesh, He has made alive together with Him, having forgiven you all trespasses, 14 [a]having wiped out the handwriting of requirements that was against us, which was contrary to us. And He has taken it out of the way, having nailed it to the cross. 15 [a]Having disarmed [b]principalities and powers, He made a public spectacle of them, triumphing over them in it.

16 So let no one [a]judge you in food or in drink, or regarding a festival or a new moon or sabbaths, 17 [a]which are a shadow of things

1:19 [a] John 1:16 **1:20** [a] Eph. 2:14 [b] 2 Cor. 5:18 [c] Eph. 1:10 **1:21** [a] [Eph. 2:1] [b] Titus 1:15 [c] 2 Cor. 5:18, 19 **1:22** [a] 2 Cor. 5:18 [b] [Eph. 5:27] **1:23** [a] Eph. 3:17 [b] [John 15:6] [c] Col. 1:6 [d] Col. 1:25 **1:24** [a] 2 Cor. 7:4 [b] Eph. 3:1, 13 [c] [2 Cor. 1:5; 12:15] [d] Eph. 1:23 **1:25** [a] Gal. 2:7 **1:26** [a] [1 Cor. 2:7] [b] [2 Tim. 1:10] **1:27** [a] 2 Cor. 2:14 [b] Rom. 9:23 [c] [Rom. 8:10, 11] [d] 1 Tim. 1:1 [1] M-Text reads *who.* **1:28** [a] Acts 20:20 [b] Eph. 5:27 **1:29** [a] Eph. 3:7 **2:1** [a] Phil. 1:30 **2:2** [1] NU-Text omits *both of the Father and.* **2:3** [a] 1 Cor. 1:24, 30 **2:4** [a] Rom. 16:18 **2:5** [a] 1 Thess. 2:17 [b] 1 Cor. 14:40 [c] 1 Pet. 5:9 **2:6** [a] 1 Thess. 4:1 **2:7** [a] Eph. 2:21 [1] NU-Text omits *in it.* **2:8** [a] Gal. 1:14 [b] Gal. 4:3, 9, 10 **2:9** [a] [John 1:14] **2:10** [a] [Eph. 1:20, 21] **2:11** [a] Deut. 10:16 [b] Rom. 6:6; 7:24 [1] NU-Text omits *of the sins.* **2:12** [a] Rom. 6:4 [b] Eph. 1:19, 20 [c] Acts 2:24 **2:14** [a] [Eph. 2:15, 16] **2:15** [a] [Is. 53:12] [b] Eph. 6:12 **2:16** [a] Rom. 14:3 **2:17** [a] Heb. 8:5; 10:1

to come, but the substance is of Christ. 18 Let
no one cheat you of your reward, taking delight in *false* humility and worship of angels,
intruding into those things which he has not[1]
seen, vainly puffed up by his fleshly mind,
19 and not holding fast to [a]the Head, from
whom all the body, nourished and knit together by joints and ligaments, [b]grows with
the increase *that is* from God.

20 Therefore,[1] if you [a]died with Christ from
the basic principles of the world, [b]why, as
though living in the world, do you subject
yourselves to regulations— 21 [a]"Do not touch,
do not taste, do not handle," 22 which all concern things which perish with the using—[a]ac-
cording to the commandments and doctrines
of men? 23 [a]These things indeed have an appearance of wisdom in self-imposed religion,
false humility, and neglect of the body, *but are*
of no value against the indulgence of the flesh.

Not Carnality but Christ

3 If then you were [a]raised with Christ, seek
those things which are above, [b]where
Christ is, sitting at the right hand of God. 2 Set
your mind on things above, not on things
on the [a]earth. 3 [a]For you died, [b]and your life
is hidden with Christ in God. 4 [a]When Christ
who is [b]our life appears, then you also will
appear with Him in [c]glory.

5 [a]Therefore put to death [b]your members
which are on the earth: [c]fornication, uncleanness, passion, evil desire, and covetousness,
[d]which is idolatry. 6 [a]Because of these things
the wrath of God is coming upon [b]the sons
of disobedience, 7 [a]in which you yourselves
once walked when you lived in them.

8 [a]But now you yourselves are to put off all
these: anger, wrath, malice, blasphemy, filthy
language out of your mouth. 9 Do not lie to one
another, since you have put off the old man
with his deeds, 10 and have put on the new *man*
who [a]is renewed in knowledge [b]according to
the image of Him who [c]created him, 11 where
there is neither [a]Greek nor Jew, circumcised
nor uncircumcised, barbarian, Scythian, slave
nor free, [b]but Christ *is* all and in all.

Character of the New Man

12 Therefore, [a]as *the* elect of God, holy and
beloved, [b]put on tender mercies, kindness,
humility, meekness, longsuffering; 13 [a]bearing
with one another, and forgiving one another,
if anyone has a complaint against another;
even as Christ forgave you, so you also *must*
do. 14 [a]But above all these things [b]put on love,
which is the [c]bond of perfection. 15 And let
[a]the peace of God rule in your hearts, [b]to
which also you were called [c]in one body;
and [d]be thankful. 16 Let the word of Christ
dwell in you richly in all wisdom, teaching
and admonishing one another [a]in psalms
and hymns and spiritual songs, singing
with grace in your hearts to the Lord. 17 And
[a]whatever you do in word or deed, *do* all in
the name of the Lord Jesus, giving thanks to
God the Father through Him.

The Christian Home

18 [a]Wives, submit to your own husbands,
[b]as is fitting in the Lord.

19 [a]Husbands, love your wives and do not
be [b]bitter toward them.

20 [a]Children, obey your parents [b]in all
things, for this is well pleasing to the Lord.

21 [a]Fathers, do not provoke your children,
lest they become discouraged.

22 [a]Bondservants, obey in all things your
masters according to the flesh, not with eyeservice, as men-pleasers, but in sincerity
of heart, fearing God. 23 [a]And whatever you
do, do it heartily, as to the Lord and not to
men, 24 [a]knowing that from the Lord you will
receive the reward of the inheritance; [b]for[1]
you serve the Lord Christ. 25 But he who does

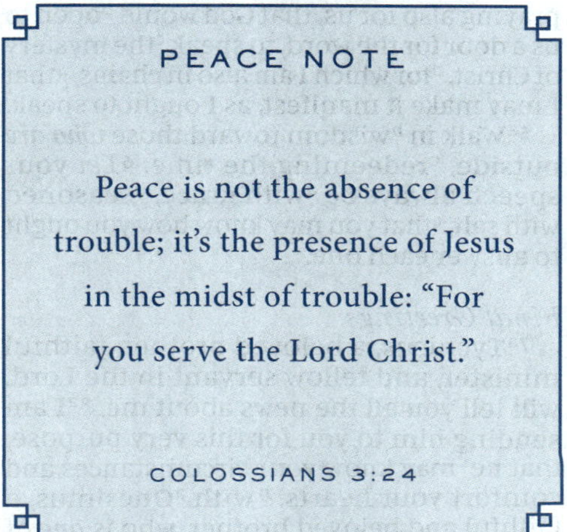

2:18 [1] NU-Text omits *not.* **2:19** [a] Eph. 4:15 [b] Eph. 1:23; 4:16 **2:20** [a] Rom. 6:2–5 [b] Gal. 4:3, 9 [1] NU-Text and M-Text omit *Therefore.* **2:21** [a] 1 Tim. 4:3 **2:22** [a] Titus 1:14 **2:23** [a] 1 Tim. 4:8 **3:1** [a] Col. 2:12 [b] Ps. 68:18; 110:1; Eph. 1:20 **3:2** [a] [Matt. 6:19–21] **3:3** [a] [Rom. 6:2] [b] [2 Cor. 5:7] **3:4** [a] [1 John 3:2] [b] John 14:6 [c] 1 Cor. 15:43 **3:5** [a] [Rom. 8:13] [b] [Rom. 6:13] [c] Eph. 5:3 [d] Eph. 4:19; 5:3, 5 **3:6** [a] Rom. 1:18 [b] [Eph. 2:2] **3:7** [a] 1 Cor. 6:11 **3:8** [a] Eph. 4:22 **3:10** [a] Rom. 12:2 [b] [Rom. 8:29] [c] [Eph. 2:10] **3:11** [a] Gal. 3:27, 28 [b] Eph. 1:23 **3:12** [a] [1 Pet. 1:2] [b] 1 John 3:17 **3:13** [a] [Mark 11:25] **3:14** [a] 1 Pet. 4:8 [b] [1 Cor. 13] [c] Eph. 4:3 **3:15** [a] [John 14:27] [b] 1 Cor. 7:15 [c] Eph. 4:4 [d] [1 Thess. 5:18] **3:16** [a] Eph. 5:19 **3:17** [a] 1 Cor. 10:31 **3:18** [a] 1 Pet. 3:1 [b] [Eph. 5:22—6:9] **3:19** [a] [Eph. 5:25] [b] Eph. 4:31 **3:20** [a] Eph. 6:1 [b] Eph. 5:24 **3:21** [a] Eph. 6:4 **3:22** [a] Eph. 6:5 **3:23** [a] [Eccl. 9:10] **3:24** [a] Eph. 6:8 [b] 1 Cor. 7:22 [1] NU-Text omits *for.*

WHAT RULES YOUR HEART

Let the peace of God rule in your hearts, to which also you were called in one body; and be thankful.

COLOSSIANS 3:15

What rules your heart? Who gives you "orders" when you get up in the morning and plan your day? You may not want to admit it, but you are not always in control of your decisions and impulses. Paul talks about our struggle with sinful impulses in chapter 7.

In baseball, there is always an umpire in the center of the action. He allows the players to pitch, catch, and bat, but they all heed his rulings. If God rules your heart, then His peace will play umpire in helping you find and follow the will of God. Why is that? It is because the will of God is a peacemaking one: He wants to redeem us and bring us into a tranquil relationship with Him and with one another.

So, I ask you again, who rules your heart? Does your life reflect tangled relationships with others or peaceful interactions? Think over the Scriptures you've read lately or heard taught in church services. Apply those parts of God's Word to your walk this week in order to find more peace. "And be thankful" (3:15).

wrong will be repaid for what he has done, and [a]there is no partiality.

4 Masters,[a] give your bondservants what is just and fair, knowing that you also have a Master in heaven.

Christian Graces

2 [a]Continue earnestly in prayer, being vigilant in it [b]with thanksgiving; 3 [a]meanwhile praying also for us, that God would [b]open to us a door for the word, to speak [c]the mystery of Christ, [d]for which I am also in chains, 4 that I may make it manifest, as I ought to speak.

5 [a]Walk in [b]wisdom toward those *who are* outside, [c]redeeming the time. 6 *Let* your speech always *be* [a]with grace, [b]seasoned with salt, [c]that you may know how you ought to answer each one.

Final Greetings

7 [a]Tychicus, a beloved brother, faithful minister, and fellow servant in the Lord, will tell you all the news about me. 8 [a]I am sending him to you for this very purpose, that he[1] may know your circumstances and comfort your hearts, 9 with [a]Onesimus, a faithful and beloved brother, who is *one* of you. They will make known to you all things which *are happening* here.

10 [a]Aristarchus my fellow prisoner greets you, with [b]Mark the cousin of Barnabas (about whom you received instructions: if he comes to you, welcome him), 11 and Jesus who is called Justus. These *are my* only fellow workers for the kingdom of God who are of the circumcision; they have proved to be a comfort to me. 12 [a]Epaphras, who is *one* of you, a bondservant of Christ, greets you, always [b]laboring fervently for you in prayers, that you may stand [c]perfect and complete[1] in all the will of God. 13 For I bear him witness that he has a great zeal[1] for you, and those who are in Laodicea, and those in Hierapolis. 14 [a]Luke the beloved physician and [b]Demas greet you. 15 Greet the brethren who are in Laodicea, and Nymphas and [a]the church that *is* in his[1] house.

Closing Exhortations and Blessing

16 Now when [a]this epistle is read among you, see that it is read also in the church of the Laodiceans, and that you likewise read the *epistle* from Laodicea. 17 And say to [a]Archippus, "Take heed to [b]the ministry which you have received in the Lord, that you may fulfill it."

18 [a]This salutation by my own hand—Paul. [b]Remember my chains. Grace *be* with you. Amen.

3:25 [a] Rom. 2:11 **4:1** [a] Eph. 6:9 **4:2** [a] Luke 18:1 [b] Col. 2:7 **4:3** [a] Eph. 6:19 [b] 1 Cor. 16:9 [c] Eph. 3:3, 4; 6:19 [d] Eph. 6:20 **4:5** [a] Eph. 5:15 [b] [Matt. 10:16] [c] Eph. 5:16 **4:6** [a] Eccl. 10:12 [b] Mark 9:50 [c] 1 Pet. 3:15 **4:7** [a] 2 Tim. 4:12 **4:8** [a] Eph. 6:22 [1] NU-Text reads *you may know our circumstances and he may.* **4:9** [a] Philem. 10 **4:10** [a] Acts 19:29; 20:4; 27:2 [b] 2 Tim. 4:11 **4:12** [a] Philem. 23 [b] Rom. 15:30 [c] Matt. 5:48 [1] NU-Text reads *fully assured.* **4:13** [1] NU-Text reads *concern.* **4:14** [a] 2 Tim. 4:11 [b] 2 Tim. 4:10 **4:15** [a] Rom. 16:5 [1] NU-Text reads *Nympha . . . her house.* **4:16** [a] 1 Thess. 5:27 **4:17** [a] Philem. 2 [b] 2 Tim. 4:5 **4:18** [a] 1 Cor. 16:21 [b] Heb. 13:3

THE FIRST EPISTLE OF PAUL THE APOSTLE TO THE

THESSALONIANS

AUTHOR

First Thessalonians went unchallenged as a Pauline epistle until the nineteenth century, when radical critics claimed that its lack of doctrinal content made its authenticity suspect. But this is a weak objection on two counts: (1) the proportion of doctrinal teaching in Paul's epistles varies widely, and (2) 1 Thessalonians 4:13—5:11 is a foundational passage for New Testament eschatology (study of future events). Paul had quickly grounded the Thessalonians in Christian doctrine, and the only problematic issue when this epistle was written concerned the matter of Christ's return. Paul planted the Thessalonian church on his second missionary journey and wrote this epistle as a response to a good report from Timothy in AD 51 regarding the church.

TIME

c. AD 51

KEY VERSE

1 Thessalonians 3:12–13

THEME

Since Paul's time in Thessalonica was cut short, Paul used these letters to clarify some of his teaching. After a review of the basics, the primary issues covered in 1 Thessalonians are about what happens when people die and the timing of the Second Coming of Christ. Because so many people at that time had seen Jesus, the promise of His return was met with anxious expectation. We tend to be blasé about it because we have watched so many predictions concerning the end times come and go, but this book will sharpen and renew our expectations.

Paul echoed the prophets of the Old Testament, such as Joel, Ezekiel, and Jeremiah, in warning the Thessalonians about the Antichrist and false peace tempting our world. A peace that may seem spiritual but is void of truth is dangerous, as Paul warned, "For when [false teachers] say, 'Peace and safety!' then sudden destruction comes upon them" (5:3). A Christ-centered peace will always bring us closer to the Lord Jesus. Note how comprehensive the peace of God is: "May the God of peace Himself sanctify you completely; and may your whole spirit, soul, and body be preserved blameless at the coming of our Lord Jesus Christ" (5:23). First Thessalonians steers us away from the false (teachers, teachings, tranquility) and toward the true (teachers, teaching, peace).

Greeting

1 Paul, [a]Silvanus, and Timothy,

To the church of the [b]Thessalonians in
God the Father and the Lord Jesus Christ:

Grace to you and peace from God our Father and the Lord Jesus Christ.[1]

Their Good Example

2 [a]We give thanks to God always for you
all, making mention of you in our prayers,
3 remembering without ceasing [a]your work
of faith, [b]labor of love, and patience of hope
in our Lord Jesus Christ in the sight of our
God and Father, 4 knowing, beloved brethren,
[a]your election by God. 5 For [a]our gospel did
not come to you in word only, but also in
power, [b]and in the Holy Spirit [c]and in much
assurance, as you know what kind of men we
were among you for your sake.
6 And [a]you became followers of us and of
the Lord, having received the word in much
affliction, [b]with joy of the Holy Spirit, 7 so that
you became examples to all in Macedonia
and Achaia who believe. 8 For from you the
word of the Lord [a]has sounded forth, not
only in Macedonia and Achaia, but also [b]in
every place. Your faith toward God has gone
out, so that we do not need to say anything.
9 For they themselves declare concerning us
[a]what manner of entry we had to you, [b]and
how you turned to God from idols to serve
the living and true God, 10 and [a]to wait for His
Son from heaven, whom He raised from the
dead, *even* Jesus who delivers us [b]from the
wrath to come.

Paul's Conduct

2 For you yourselves know, brethren, that
our coming to you was not in vain. 2 But
even[1] after we had suffered before and were
spitefully treated at [a]Philippi, as you know,

PEACE NOTE

Your faith is purest when you inconvenience yourself to help someone who is barely hanging on. You are an agent of God's peace, and the Lord will bless you when you meet others' needs.

1:1 [a] 1 Pet. 5:12 [b] Acts 17:1–9 [1] NU-Text omits *from God our Father and the Lord Jesus Christ.* **1:2** [a] Rom. 1:8 **1:3** [a] John 6:29 [b] Rom. 16:6 **1:4** [a] Col. 3:12 **1:5** [a] Mark 16:20 [b] 2 Cor. 6:6 [c] Heb. 2:3 **1:6** [a] 1 Cor. 4:16; 11:1 [b] Acts 5:41; 13:52 **1:8** [a] Rom. 10:18 [b] Rom. 1:8; 16:19 **1:9** [a] 1 Thess. 2:1 [b] 1 Cor. 12:2 **1:10** [a] [Rom. 2:7] [b] Rom. 5:9 **2:2** [a] Acts 14:5; 16:19–24 [1] NU-Text and M-Text omit *even.*

CALL ON THE LORD

Paul, Silvanus, and Timothy, to the church of the Thessalonians in God the Father and the Lord Jesus Christ.

1 THESSALONIANS 1:1

Paul's favorite term for Jesus, indeed, the key name for Jesus in the New Testament, is "the Lord." In one of his letters, Paul assured new believers that *the Lord is faithful; He will strengthen you and guard you from evil* (see 2 Thess. 3:3). Paul had visited Thessalonica during his tumultuous second missionary journey and was there scarcely one month before being driven away. Paul did not experience the outward ministry success in Thessalonica that he had in other locations, but he must have learned something powerful by then about the peace of God, given how much he mentions that topic.

You may be in Thessalonica spiritually right now. You may not be experiencing the success you are accustomed to. Perhaps God is strengthening your inward life instead. Call on Jesus as Lord of your life in this moment. Ask Jesus to help you to be faithful: "Jesus, I don't understand why I am experiencing the unrest I am, but I do trust You. You are the Lord of my life, and I surrender to You. Give me the strength to keep moving forward like Paul in Thessalonica. In Your name, amen."

we were [b]bold in our God to speak to you
the gospel of God in much conflict. 3 [a]For
our exhortation *did* not *come* from error or
uncleanness, nor *was it* in deceit.
4 But as [a]we have been approved by God
[b]to be entrusted with the gospel, even so we
speak, [c]not as pleasing men, but God [d]who
tests our hearts. 5 For [a]neither at any time
did we use flattering words, as you know, nor
a cloak for covetousness—[b]God *is* witness.
6 [a]Nor did we seek glory from men, either
from you or from others, when [b]we might
have [c]made demands [d]as apostles of Christ.
7 But [a]we were gentle among you, just as a
nursing *mother* cherishes her own children.
8 So, affectionately longing for you, we were
well pleased [a]to impart to you not only the
gospel of God, but also [b]our own lives, because you had become dear to us. 9 For you
remember, brethren, our [a]labor and toil; for
laboring night and day, [b]that we might not
be a burden to any of you, we preached to
you the gospel of God.
10 [a]You *are* witnesses, and God *also,* [b]how
devoutly and justly and blamelessly we behaved ourselves among you who believe; 11 as
you know how we exhorted, and comforted,
and charged[1] every one of you, as a father
does his own children, 12 [a]that you would walk
worthy of God [b]who calls you into His own
kingdom and glory.

Their Conversion

13 For this reason we also thank God
[a]without ceasing, because when you [b]re-
ceived the word of God which you heard
from us, you welcomed *it* [c]not *as* the word
of men, but as it is in truth, the word of
God, which also effectively [d]works in you
who believe. 14 For you, brethren, became
imitators [a]of the churches of God which
are in Judea in Christ Jesus. For [b]you also
suffered the same things from your own
countrymen, just as they *did* from the Ju-
deans, 15 [a]who killed both the Lord Jesus
and [b]their own prophets, and have persecuted us; and they do not please God [c]and
are contrary to all men, 16 [a]forbidding us
to speak to the Gentiles that they may be
saved, so as always [b]to fill up *the measure
of* their sins; [c]but wrath has come upon
them to the uttermost.

Longing to See Them

17 But we, brethren, having been taken away
from you for a short time [a]in presence, not in
heart, endeavored more eagerly to see your
face with great desire. 18 Therefore we wanted
to come to you—even I, Paul, time and again—
but [a]Satan hindered us. 19 For [a]what *is* our hope,
or joy, or [b]crown of rejoicing? *Is it* not even you
in the [c]presence of our Lord Jesus Christ [d]at
His coming? 20 For you are our glory and joy.

Concern for Their Faith

3 Therefore, when we could no longer
endure it, we thought it good to be left
in Athens alone, 2 and sent [a]Timothy, our
brother and minister of God, and our fellow
laborer in the gospel of Christ, to establish
you and encourage you concerning your
faith, 3 [a]that no one should be shaken by these
afflictions; for you yourselves know that [b]we
are appointed to this. 4 [a]For, in fact, we told
you before when we were with you that we
would suffer tribulation, just as it happened,
and you know. 5 For this reason, when I could
no longer endure it, I sent to know your faith,
[a]lest by some means the tempter had tempted
you, and [b]our labor might be in vain.

Encouraged by Timothy

6 [a]But now that Timothy has come to us
from you, and brought us good news of your
faith and love, and that you always have good
remembrance of us, greatly desiring to see
us, [b]as we also *to see* you— 7 therefore, brethren, in all our affliction and distress [a]we were
comforted concerning you by your faith. 8 For
now we live, if you [a]stand fast in the Lord.
9 For what thanks can we render to God for
you, for all the joy with which we rejoice for
your sake before our God, 10 night and day
praying exceedingly that we may see your
face [a]and perfect what is lacking in your faith?

Prayer for the Church

11 Now may our God and Father Himself,
and our Lord Jesus Christ, [a]direct our way to
you. 12 And may the Lord make you increase
and [a]abound in love to one another and to
all, just as we *do* to you, 13 so that He may
establish [a]your hearts blameless in holiness
before our God and Father at the coming
of our Lord Jesus Christ with all His saints.

2:2 [b] Acts 17:1–9 **2:3** [a] 2 Cor. 7:2 **2:4** [a] 1 Cor. 7:25 [b] Titus 1:3 [c] Gal. 1:10 [d] Prov. 17:3 **2:5** [a] 2 Cor. 2:17 [b] Rom. 1:9 **2:6** [a] 1 Tim. 5:17 [b] 1 Cor. 9:4 [c] 2 Cor. 11:9 [d] 1 Cor. 9:1 **2:7** [a] 1 Cor. 2:3 **2:8** [a] Rom. 1:11 [b] 2 Cor. 12:15 **2:9** [a] Acts 18:3; 20:34, 35 [b] 2 Cor. 12:13 **2:10** [a] 1 Thess. 1:5 [b] 2 Cor. 7:2 **2:11** [1] NU-Text and M-Text read *implored.* **2:12** [a] Eph. 4:1 [b] 1 Cor. 1:9 **2:13** [a] 1 Thess. 1:2, 3 [b] Mark 4:20 [c] [Gal. 4:14] [d] [1 Pet. 1:23] **2:14** [a] Gal. 1:22 [b] Acts 17:5 **2:15** [a] Acts 2:23 [b] Matt. 5:12; 23:34, 35 [c] Esth. 3:8 **2:16** [a] Luke 11:52 [b] Gen. 15:16 [c] Matt. 24:6 **2:17** [a] 1 Cor. 5:3 **2:18** [a] Rom. 1:13; 15:22 **2:19** [a] 2 Cor. 1:14 [b] Prov. 16:31 [c] Jude 24 [d] 1 Cor. 15:23 **3:2** [a] Rom. 16:21 **3:3** [a] Eph. 3:13 [b] Acts 9:16; 14:22 **3:4** [a] Acts 20:24 **3:5** [a] 1 Cor. 7:5 [b] Gal. 2:2 **3:6** [a] Acts 18:5 [b] Phil. 1:8 **3:7** [a] 2 Cor. 1:4 **3:8** [a] Phil. 4:1 **3:10** [a] 2 Cor. 13:9 **3:11** [a] Mark 1:3 **3:12** [a] Phil. 1:9 **3:13** [a] 2 Thess. 2:17

Plea for Purity

4 Finally then, brethren, we urge and exhort in the Lord Jesus [a]that you should
abound more and more, [b]just as you received
from us how you ought to walk and to please
God; 2 for you know what commandments we
gave you through the Lord Jesus.
3 For this is [a]the will of God, [b]your sanctification: [c]that you should abstain from sexual
immorality; 4 [a]that each of you should know
how to possess his own vessel in sanctification and honor, 5 [a]not in passion of lust,
[b]like the Gentiles [c]who do not know God;
6 that no one should take advantage of and
defraud his brother in this matter, because
the Lord [a]*is* the avenger of all such, as we also
forewarned you and testified. 7 For God did
not call us to uncleanness, [a]but in holiness.
8 [a]Therefore he who rejects *this* does not
reject man, but God, [b]who has also given[1]
us His Holy Spirit.

A Brotherly and Orderly Life

9 But concerning brotherly love you have
no need that I should write to you, for [a]you
yourselves are taught by God [b]to love one
another; 10 and indeed you do so toward all
the brethren who are in all Macedonia. But
we urge you, brethren, [a]that you increase
more and more; 11 that you also aspire to lead
a quiet life, [a]to mind your own business, and
[b]to work with your own hands, as we commanded you, 12 [a]that you may walk properly
toward those who are outside, and *that* you
may lack nothing.

The Comfort of Christ's Coming

13 But I do not want you to be ignorant,
brethren, concerning those who have fallen
asleep, lest you sorrow [a]as others [b]who have
no hope. 14 For [a]if we believe that Jesus died
and rose again, even so God will bring with
Him [b]those who sleep in Jesus.[1]
15 For this we say to you [a]by the word of
the Lord, that [b]we who are alive *and* remain
until the coming of the Lord will by no means
precede those who are asleep. 16 For [a]the Lord
Himself will descend from heaven with a
shout, with the voice of an archangel, and
with [b]the trumpet of God. [c]And the dead
in Christ will rise first. 17 [a]Then we who are
alive *and* remain shall be caught up together
with them [b]in the clouds to meet the Lord
in the air. And thus [c]we shall always be with
the Lord. 18 [a]Therefore comfort one another
with these words.

4:1 [a] 1 Cor. 15:58 [b] Phil. 1:27 **4:3** [a] [Rom. 12:2] [b] Eph. 5:27 [c] [1 Cor. 6:15–20] **4:4** [a] Rom. 6:19 **4:5** [a] Col. 3:5 [b] Eph. 4:17, 18 [c] 1 Cor. 15:34 **4:6** [a] 2 Thess. 1:8 **4:7** [a] Lev. 11:44 **4:8** [a] Luke 10:16 [b] 1 Cor. 2:10 [1] NU-Text reads *who also gives.* **4:9** [a] [Jer. 31:33, 34] [b] Matt. 22:39 **4:10** [a] 1 Thess. 3:12 **4:11** [a] 2 Thess. 3:11 [b] Acts 20:35 **4:12** [a] Rom. 13:13 **4:13** [a] Lev. 19:28 [b] [Eph. 2:12] **4:14** [a] 1 Cor. 15:13 [b] 1 Cor. 15:20, 23 [1] Or *those who through Jesus sleep* **4:15** [a] 1 Kin. 13:17; 20:35 [b] 1 Cor. 15:51, 52 **4:16** [a] [Matt. 24:30, 31] [b] [1 Cor. 15:52] [c] [1 Cor. 15:23] **4:17** [a] [1 Cor. 15:51–53] [b] Acts 1:9 [c] John 14:3; 17:24 **4:18** [a] 1 Thess. 5:11

DISCERN TRUE PEACE

For when they say, "Peace and safety!" then sudden destruction comes upon them, as labor pains upon a pregnant woman. And they shall not escape.

1 THESSALONIANS 5:3

With the rise of AI (artificial intelligence), where and how we source truth has never been more important to our lives. Truth is often obscure. We are so easily deceived. Paul warned the believers of Thessalonica to be careful where they found "peace and safety." Every age has experienced "sudden destruction."

Today's world leaders promise peace, but they cannot guarantee it. Discernment is a crucial aspect of living in the peace of God. Ask the Lord to give you a discerning heart for all the information you receive each day. Ask the Lord to help you make decisions that increase your peace with God and others. *Discernment* means *choosing wisely*. The great news is that as we meditate on God's Word, we increase our discernment. Another way is through *seeking the godly* counsel of a pastor or mature believer. And finally, ask the Spirit to give you discernment and increase the peace of God in your life.

No need for AI when you have the Word and Spirit of God to guide you in every decision!

The Day of the Lord

5 But concerning [a]the times and the seasons, brethren, you have no need that I
should write to you. 2 For you yourselves know
perfectly that [a]the day of the Lord so comes as
a thief in the night. 3 For when they say, "Peace
and safety!" then [a]sudden destruction comes
upon them, [b]as labor pains upon a pregnant
woman. And they shall not escape. 4 [a]But you,
brethren, are not in darkness, so that this Day
should overtake you as a thief. 5 You are all
[a]sons of light and sons of the day. We are not
of the night nor of darkness. 6 [a]Therefore let
us not sleep, as others *do,* but [b]let us watch
and be sober. 7 For [a]those who sleep, sleep at
night, and those who get drunk [b]are drunk at
night. 8 But let us who are of the day be sober,
[a]putting on the breastplate of faith and love,
and *as* a helmet the hope of salvation. 9 For
[a]God did not appoint us to wrath, [b]but to obtain salvation through our Lord Jesus Christ,
10 [a]who died for us, that whether we wake or
sleep, we should live together with Him.

11 Therefore comfort each other and edify
one another, just as you also are doing.

Various Exhortations

12 And we urge you, brethren, [a]to recognize
those who labor among you, and are over
you in the Lord and admonish you, 13 and
to esteem them very highly in love for their
work's sake. [a]Be at peace among yourselves.

> **PEACE NOTE**
>
> Start a gratitude journal today by simply writing down something every day you are thankful for. You will have more peace when you focus on your blessings.
>
> I THESSALONIANS 5:18

14 Now we exhort you, brethren, [a]warn
those who are unruly, [b]comfort the fainthearted, [c]uphold the weak, [d]be patient with
all. 15 [a]See that no one renders evil for evil
to anyone, but always [b]pursue what is good
both for yourselves and for all.

16 [a]Rejoice always, 17 [a]pray without ceasing,
18 in everything give thanks; for this is the will
of God in Christ Jesus for you.

19 [a]Do not quench the Spirit. 20 [a]Do not
despise prophecies. 21 [a]Test all things; [b]hold
fast what is good. 22 Abstain from every form
of evil.

5:1 [a] Matt. 24:3 **5:2** [a] [2 Pet. 3:10] **5:3** [a] Is. 13:6–9 [b] Hos. 13:13 **5:4** [a] 1 John 2:8 **5:5** [a] Eph. 5:8 **5:6** [a] Matt. 25:5 [b] [1 Pet. 5:8] **5:7** [a] [Luke 21:34] [b] Acts 2:15 **5:8** [a] Eph. 6:14 **5:9** [a] Rom. 9:22 [b] [2 Thess. 2:13] **5:10** [a] 2 Cor. 5:15 **5:12** [a] 1 Cor. 16:18 **5:13** [a] Mark 9:50 **5:14** [a] 2 Thess. 3:6, 7, 11 [b] Heb. 12:12 [c] Rom. 14:1; 15:1 [d] Gal. 5:22 **5:15** [a] Lev. 19:18 [b] Gal. 6:10 **5:16** [a] [2 Cor. 6:10] **5:17** [a] Eph. 6:18 **5:19** [a] Eph. 4:30 **5:20** [a] 1 Cor. 14:1, 31 **5:21** [a] 1 John 4:1 [b] Phil. 4:8

PEACE FOR YOUR WHOLE LIFE

Now may the God of peace Himself sanctify you completely; and may your whole spirit, soul, and body be preserved blameless at the coming of our Lord Jesus Christ.

I THESSALONIANS 5:23

The peace of God in our lives is the presence of God Himself. Wow! That is an incredible truth. The peace of God also sanctifies us, which means God makes us holier through His peace. There is a connection between peace and holiness. When I grow in Christ, I become more sacred or separated from the life I once lived without God. As I move away from the *old life, I embrace a new life in Christ full of God's peace.*

As the "God of peace" sanctifies or makes holy His people, Paul prayed that believers' "whole spirit, soul, and body [would] be preserved blameless" at the coming of the Lord Jesus Christ (5:23). This is the hope that creates peace; it's the hope that Christ provides. The peace of God is for the whole person. Every aspect of your life: your spirit, your soul, and your body can be affected by the peace of God. Today, rededicate your whole self to the peace of God in the presence of God.

Blessing and Admonition

23 Now may [a]the God of peace Himself
[b]sanctify you completely; and may your
whole spirit, soul, and body [c]be preserved
blameless at the coming of our Lord Jesus
Christ. 24 He who calls you *is* [a]faithful, who
also will [b]do *it.*

25 Brethren, pray for us.

26 Greet all the brethren with a holy kiss.

27 I charge you by the Lord that this epistle
be read to all the holy[1] brethren.

28 The grace of our Lord Jesus Christ *be*
with you. Amen.

5:23 [a] Phil. 4:9 [b] 1 Thess. 3:13 [c] 1 Cor. 1:8, 9 5:24 [a] [1 Cor. 10:13] [b] Phil. 1:6 5:27 [1] NU-Text omits *holy.*

THE SECOND EPISTLE OF PAUL THE APOSTLE TO THE

THESSALONIANS

AUTHOR

The external attestation to the authenticity of 2 Thessalonians as a Pauline epistle is even stronger than that for 1 Thessalonians. Internally the vocabulary, style, and doctrinal content support the claims in 2 Thessalonians 1:1 and 3:17 that it was written by Paul. This letter was probably written a few months after 1 Thessalonians, while Paul was still in Corinth with Silas and Timothy (Acts 18:5; 2 Thess. 1:1).

TIME

c. AD 51

KEY VERSE

2 Thessalonians 2:2–3

THEME

This letter to the Thessalonians appears to have been written fairly soon after the first one. Paul provides further clarification on some of the same issues he addressed in the first letter; there appeared to still be some confusion about the events of the end times. He also wisely encourages the believers in the basics he has taught them in his role as a caring pastor.

At a particularly difficult moment in Paul's life he was alone, even abandoned in a human sense, but even so, he affirmed, "The Lord stood with me" (2 Tim. 4:17). Paul still had the peace of God because Jesus Himself stood with Paul. No matter what we are going through, no matter how difficult the challenge, 2 Thessalonians reminds us that we do not face anything by ourselves. How can we be certain? Because when Paul prayed one of the most beautiful prayers in the Bible in 2 Thessalonians, he said, "May the Lord of peace Himself give you peace always in every way. The Lord be with you all" (3:16).

Greeting

1 Paul, Silvanus, and Timothy,

To the church of the Thessalonians in God
our Father and the Lord Jesus Christ:

2 [a]Grace to you and peace from God our
Father and the Lord Jesus Christ.

God's Final Judgment and Glory

3 We are bound to thank God always for
you, brethren, as it is fitting, because your
faith grows exceedingly, and the love of every
one of you all abounds toward each other, 4 so
that [a]we ourselves boast of you among the
churches of God [b]for your patience and faith
[c]in all your persecutions and tribulations that
you endure, 5 *which is* [a]manifest evidence
of the righteous judgment of God, that you
may be counted worthy of the kingdom of
God, [b]for which you also suffer; 6 [a]since *it is* a
righteous thing with God to repay with tribulation those who trouble you, 7 and to *give*
you who are troubled [a]rest with us when [b]the
Lord Jesus is revealed from heaven with His
mighty angels, 8 in flaming fire taking vengeance on those who do not know God, and
on those who do not obey the gospel of our
Lord Jesus Christ. 9 [a]These shall be punished
with everlasting destruction from the presence of the Lord and [b]from the glory of His
power, 10 when He comes, in that Day, [a]to be
[b]glorified in His saints and to be admired
among all those who believe,[1] because our
testimony among you was believed.
11 Therefore we also pray always for you
that our God would [a]count you worthy of
this calling, and fulfill all the good pleasure
of *His* goodness and [b]the work of faith with
power, 12 [a]that the name of our Lord Jesus
Christ may be glorified in you, and you in
Him, according to the grace of our God and
the Lord Jesus Christ.

The Great Apostasy

2 Now, brethren, [a]concerning the coming
of our Lord Jesus Christ [b]and our gathering together to Him, we ask you, 2 [a]not to be
soon shaken in mind or troubled, either by
spirit or by word or by letter, as if from us, as
though the day of Christ[1] had come. 3 Let no
one deceive you by any means; for *that Day*
will not come [a]unless the falling away comes
first, and [b]the man of sin[1] is revealed, [c]the
son of perdition, 4 who opposes and [a]exalts
himself [b]above all that is called God or that is
worshiped, so that he sits as God[1] in the temple of God, showing himself that he is God.

1:2 [a] 1 Cor. 1:3 **1:4** [a] 2 Cor. 7:4 [b] 1 Thess. 1:3 [c] 1 Thess. 2:14 **1:5** [a] Phil. 1:28 [b] 1 Thess. 2:14 **1:6** [a] Rev. 6:10 **1:7** [a] Rev. 14:13 [b] Jude 14 **1:9** [a] Phil. 3:19 [b] Deut. 33:2 **1:10** [a] Matt. 25:31 [b] John 17:10 [1] NU-Text and M-Text read *have believed.* **1:11** [a] Col. 1:12 [b] 1 Thess. 1:3 **1:12** [a] [Col. 3:17] **2:1** [a] [1 Thess. 4:15–17] [b] Matt. 24:31 **2:2** [a] Matt. 24:4 [1] NU-Text reads *the Lord.* **2:3** [a] 1 Tim. 4:1 [b] Dan. 7:25; 8:25; 11:36 [c] John 17:12 [1] NU-Text reads *lawlessness.* **2:4** [a] Is. 14:13, 14 [b] 1 Cor. 8:5 [1] NU-Text omits *as God.*

THE POWER OF YOUR TESTIMONY

We ourselves boast of you among the churches of God for your patience and faith in all your persecutions and tribulations that you endure.

2 THESSALONIANS 1:4

Popular preachers sometimes try to assign a date to Jesus' return to earth. But Jesus Himself issued a warning to His disciples that no one knows the day or the hour when He will return (except, He said, "My Father only," Matt. 24:36).

Paul addressed this question in both his letters to the believers in Thessalonica. In 1 Thessalonians 4:13–18, Paul assured the Christians that believers who die before the coming of Jesus will not miss out on His glorious return. In 2 Thessalonians he warned believers not to be deceived by rumors that the day of the Lord had arrived. It has not and it will not until certain unmistakable signs take place, including the appearance of the "son of perdition," who will oppose God and His people (2 Thess. 2:3). Paul routinely prayed for peace for those who received his letters.

In these days of prevalent violence and frequent fear, Paul's prayer for peace is especially welcome, as is his praise for the overcoming Thessalonians. How do you ask God for strength—and peace?

5 Do you not remember that when I was still with you I told you these things? 6 And now you know what is restraining, that he may be revealed in his own time. 7 For [a]the mystery of lawlessness is already at work; only He[1] who now restrains *will do so* until He[2] is taken out of the way. 8 And then the lawless one will be revealed, [a]whom the Lord will consume [b]with the breath of His mouth and destroy [c]with the brightness of His coming. 9 The coming of the *lawless one* is [a]according to the working of Satan, with all power, [b]signs, and lying wonders, 10 and with all unrighteous deception among [a]those who perish, because they did not receive [b]the love of the truth, that they might be saved. 11 And [a]for this reason God will send them strong delusion, [b]that they should believe the lie, 12 that they all may be condemned who did not believe the truth but [a]had pleasure in unrighteousness.

Stand Fast

13 But we are bound to give thanks to God always for you, brethren beloved by the Lord, because God [a]from the beginning [b]chose you for salvation [c]through sanctification by the Spirit and belief in the truth, 14 to which He called you by our gospel, for [a]the obtaining of the glory of our Lord Jesus Christ. 15 Therefore, brethren, [a]stand fast and hold [b]the traditions which you were taught, whether by word or our epistle.

16 Now may our Lord Jesus Christ Himself, and our God and Father, [a]who has loved us and given *us* everlasting consolation and [b]good hope by grace, 17 comfort your hearts [a]and establish you in every good word and work.

Pray for Us

3 Finally, brethren, [a]pray for us, that the word of the Lord may run *swiftly* and be glorified, just as *it is* with you, 2 and [a]that we may be delivered from unreasonable and wicked men; [b]for not all have faith.

3 But [a]the Lord is faithful, who will establish you and [b]guard *you* from the evil one. 4 And [a]we have confidence in the Lord concerning you, both that you do and will do the things we command you.

5 Now may [a]the Lord direct your hearts into the love of God and into the patience of Christ.

Warning Against Idleness

6 But we command you, brethren, in the name of our Lord Jesus Christ, [a]that you withdraw [b]from every brother who walks [c]disorderly and not according to the tradition which he[1]

2:7 [a] 1 John 2:18 [1] Or *he* [2] Or *he* **2:8** [a] Dan. 7:10 [b] Is. 11:4 [c] Heb. 10:27 **2:9** [a] John 8:41 [b] Deut. 13:1 **2:10** [a] 2 Cor. 2:15 [b] 1 Cor. 16:22 **2:11** [a] Rom. 1:28 [b] 1 Tim. 4:1 **2:12** [a] Rom. 1:32 **2:13** [a] Eph. 1:4 [b] 1 Thess. 1:4 [c] [1 Pet. 1:2] **2:14** [a] 1 Pet. 5:10 **2:15** [a] 1 Cor. 16:13 [b] 1 Cor. 11:2 **2:16** [a] [Rev. 1:5] [b] 1 Pet. 1:3 **2:17** [a] 1 Cor. 1:8 **3:1** [a] Eph. 6:19 **3:2** [a] Rom. 15:31 [b] Acts 28:24 **3:3** [a] 1 Cor. 1:9 [b] John 17:15 **3:4** [a] 2 Cor. 7:16 **3:5** [a] 1 Chr. 29:18 **3:6** [a] Rom. 16:17 [b] 1 Cor. 5:1 [c] 1 Thess. 4:11

[1] NU-Text and M-Text read *they*.

PRAYING AMID HOSTILITIES

Now may the Lord of peace Himself give you peace always in every way. The Lord be with you all.

2 THESSALONIANS 3:16

For Christians in the hostile Roman Empire, day-to-day living, as well as the uncertain future, gave them enough to worry about, but rumors that "the day of Christ had come" (2 Thess. 2:2) would have been very destabilizing. Paul's prayer for the Thessalonians' peace and well-being would have been much appreciated. But his language was also countercultural, for it flew in the face of the Roman cult of the divine emperor (called "lord") who supposedly guaranteed peace.

It's speculation, but I wonder if the Thessalonian church struggled with anxious believers. Why? Paul repeats himself in his second letter: "Now may the Lord of peace Himself" (3:16), which sounds familiar—in his first letter he wrote, "May the God of peace Himself" (1 Thess. 5:23). Paul stressed that the peace of God is not abstract but embodied in the Lord Jesus. We can spell peace: J-e-s-u-s. True peace and security, Paul said, were given by the "Lord of peace" (2 Thess. 3:16).

Are you a partaker of peace even when the news is bad? Ask God to help you with this.

received from us. [7]For you yourselves know
how you ought to follow us, for we were not
disorderly among you; [8]nor did we eat anyone's bread free of charge, but worked with
[a]labor and toil night and day, that we might
not be a burden to any of you, [9]not because we
do not have [a]authority, but to make ourselves
an example of how you should follow us.

[10]For even when we were with you, we
commanded you this: If anyone will not
work, neither shall he eat. [11]For we hear that
there are some who walk among you in a
disorderly manner, not working at all, but
are [a]busybodies. [12]Now those who are such
we command and exhort through our Lord
Jesus Christ [a]that they work in quietness and
eat their own bread.

[13]But *as for* you, brethren, [a]do not grow
weary *in* doing good. [14]And if anyone does
not obey our word in this epistle, note that
person and [a]do not keep company with him,
that he may be ashamed. [15a]Yet do not count
him as an enemy, [b]but admonish *him* as a
brother.

Benediction

[16]Now may [a]the Lord of peace Himself give
you peace always in every way. The Lord *be*
with you all.

[17a]The salutation of Paul with my own
hand, which is a sign in every epistle; so I
write.

[18a]The grace of our Lord Jesus Christ *be*
with you all. Amen.

3:8 [a] 1 Thess. 2:9 3:9 [a] 1 Cor. 9:4, 6–14 3:11 [a] 1 Pet. 4:15 3:12 [a] Eph. 4:28 3:13 [a] Gal. 6:9 3:14 [a] Matt. 18:17
3:15 [a] Lev. 19:17 [b] Titus 3:10 3:16 [a] Rom. 15:33 3:17 [a] 1 Cor. 16:21 3:18 [a] Rom. 16:20, 24

THE FIRST EPISTLE OF PAUL
THE APOSTLE TO

TIMOTHY

AUTHOR

The external evidence solidly supports the position that Paul wrote the letters to Timothy and Titus. Only Romans and 1 Corinthians have better attestation among the Pauline Epistles. Pauline authorship of the Pastoral Epistles requires Paul's release from his Roman imprisonment (Acts 28), the continuation of his missionary endeavors, and his imprisonment for a second time in Rome. Unfortunately, the order of events can only be reconstructed from hints because there is no concurrent history paralleling Acts to chronicle the last years of the apostle. It is most probable that Paul wrote 1 Timothy from Macedonia in AD 62 or 63 while Timothy was serving as his representative in Ephesus.

TIME

c. AD 62–63

KEY VERSE

1 Timothy 3:15–16

THEME

The letters to Timothy and Titus are generally called the Pastoral Epistles. They are pastoral in tone and subject matter. While covering much of the apostolic instruction on the life and doctrine of the church, they also provide some guidelines on how Christians in the church should relate to society. One of the overriding concerns of these books is that truth be valued and guarded. Too often today, truth is subjective and culturally conditioned to the point where people don't even have problems believing mutually contradictory ideas. Paul speaks of the value of truth in his own apostolic role, and he stands against false teachers who would distort the truth for their own ends.

Paul mentored Timothy, "a true son in the faith" (1:2), in the peace of God. We all need mentors to guide us in our walk with Christ and into a fruitful life. Because there are quite a few gimmicks, superstitions, rabbits' feet, and other false tokens of security in the world, both ancient and contemporary, Paul warned Timothy to give no "heed to fables and endless genealogies" and to "reject profane and old wives' fables, and exercise [himself] toward godliness" (1:4; 4:7). First Timothy also describes the attributes of a life lived in the way of peace in chapter 3, and Paul encourages believers to follow them so that even those who are outside the Christian faith will respect their godly character (v. 7). Whether you have a human *mentor or spiritual* one (the Lord of Peace Himself), follow Paul's advice to skip meaningless worldly ways and become someone who exemplifies the way to live God's peace.

Greeting

1 Paul, an apostle of Jesus Christ, by the commandment of God our Savior and the Lord Jesus Christ, our hope,

2 To Timothy, a [a]true son in the faith:

[b]Grace, mercy, *and* peace from God our Father and Jesus Christ our Lord.

No Other Doctrine

3 As I urged you [a]when I went into Macedonia—remain in Ephesus that you may charge some [b]that they teach no other doctrine, 4 [a]nor give heed to fables and endless genealogies, which cause disputes rather than godly edification which is in faith. 5 Now [a]the purpose of the commandment is love [b]from a pure heart, *from* a good conscience, and *from* sincere faith, 6 from which some, having strayed, have turned aside to [a]idle talk, 7 desiring to be teachers of the law, understanding neither what they say nor the things which they affirm.

8 But we know that the law *is* [a]good if one uses it lawfully, 9 knowing this: that the law is not made for a righteous person, but for *the* lawless and insubordinate, for *the* ungodly and for sinners, for *the* unholy and profane, for murderers of fathers and murderers of mothers, for manslayers, 10 for fornicators, for sodomites, for kidnappers, for liars, for perjurers, and if there is any other thing that is contrary to sound doctrine, 11 according to the glorious gospel of the [a]blessed God which was [b]committed to my trust.

Glory to God for His Grace

12 And I thank Christ Jesus our Lord who has [a]enabled me, [b]because He counted me faithful, [c]putting *me* into the ministry, 13 although [a]I was formerly a blasphemer, a persecutor, and an insolent man; but I obtained mercy because [b]I did *it* ignorantly in unbelief. 14 [a]And the grace of our Lord was exceedingly abundant, [b]with faith and love which are in Christ Jesus. 15 [a]This *is* a faithful saying and worthy of all acceptance, that [b]Christ Jesus came into the world to save sinners, of whom I am chief. 16 However, for this reason I obtained mercy, that in me first Jesus Christ might show all longsuffering, as a pattern to those who are going to believe on Him for everlasting life. 17 Now to [a]the King eternal, [b]immortal, [c]invisible, to God [d]who alone is wise,[1] [e]*be* honor and glory forever and ever. Amen.

Fight the Good Fight

18 This charge I commit to you, son Timothy, according to the prophecies previously made concerning you, that by them you

1:2 [a] Titus 1:4 [b] Gal. 1:3 **1:3** [a] Acts 20:1, 3 [b] Gal. 1:6, 7 **1:4** [a] Titus 1:14 **1:5** [a] Rom. 13:8–10 [b] Eph. 6:24 **1:6** [a] 1 Tim. 6:4, 20 **1:8** [a] Rom. 7:12, 16 **1:11** [a] 1 Tim. 6:15 [b] 1 Cor. 9:17 **1:12** [a] 1 Cor. 15:10 [b] 1 Cor. 7:25 [c] Col. 1:25 **1:13** [a] Acts 8:3 [b] John 4:21 **1:14** [a] Rom. 5:20 [b] 2 Tim. 1:13; 2:22 **1:15** [a] 2 Tim. 2:11 [b] Matt. 1:21; 9:13 **1:17** [a] Ps. 10:16 [b] Rom. 1:23 [c] Heb. 11:27 [d] Rom. 16:27 [e] 1 Chr. 29:11 [1] NU-Text reads *to the only God.*

TAKE PEACE TO YOUR FRIENDS

To Timothy, a true son in the faith: Grace, mercy, and peace from God our Father and Jesus Christ our Lord.

I TIMOTHY 1:2

How "true" are your friends? Who forms your community of peace (*shalom*)? True companions (see Phil. 4:3) walk with you through life's joys and sorrows. One of the ways to be a great friend is to keep confidences. A peace-filled Christian can be trusted with information. A peace-filled Christian speaks with wisdom, not brashly or impulsively.

A life of peace is invariably peopled by friends who are "true." What does that mean? Here in 1 Timothy 1:2, Paul referred to the young man as his "true son" (see Titus 1:4). In Philippians 4:3, Paul referred to a fellow worker as a "true companion." Real friends and colleagues can and should be part of your world of genuine peace. I admire Paul's focus on truth in relationships and friendships. So many aspects of relating to others are built on lies or social media highlight reels. True friendship is walking in the door when everyone else is leaving. Be a true friend and God will guide you to be an ambassador of His peace, like Timothy.

Are *you* an authentic friend to those around you? How so? How can you improve?

may wage the good warfare, 19 having faith
and a good conscience, which some having
rejected, concerning the faith have suffered
shipwreck, 20 of whom are [a]Hymenaeus and
[b]Alexander, whom I delivered to Satan that
they may learn not to [c]blaspheme.

Pray for All Men

2 Therefore I exhort first of all that supplications, prayers, intercessions, *and* giving
of thanks be made for all men, 2 [a]for kings and
[b]all who are in authority, that we may lead a
quiet and peaceable life in all godliness and
reverence. 3 For this *is* [a]good and acceptable in
the sight [b]of God our Savior, 4 [a]who desires all
men to be saved [b]and to come to the knowledge of the truth. 5 [a]For *there is* one God and
[b]one Mediator between God and men, *the* Man
Christ Jesus, 6 [a]who gave Himself a ransom for
all, to be testified in due time, 7 [a]for which I was
appointed a preacher and an apostle—I am
speaking the truth in Christ[1] *and* not lying—[b]a
teacher of the Gentiles in faith and truth.

Men and Women in the Church

8 I desire therefore that the men pray
[a]everywhere, [b]lifting up holy hands, without wrath and doubting; 9 in like manner
also, that the [a]women adorn themselves in
modest apparel, with propriety and moder-
ation, not with braided hair or gold or pearls
or costly clothing, 10 [a]but, which is proper
for women professing godliness, with good
works. 11 Let a woman learn in silence with all
submission. 12 And [a]I do not permit a woman
to teach or to have authority over a man, but
to be in silence. 13 For Adam was formed first,
then Eve. 14 And Adam was not deceived, but
the woman being deceived, fell into transgression. 15 Nevertheless she will be saved in
childbearing if they continue in faith, love,
and holiness, with self-control.

Qualifications of Overseers

3 This *is* a faithful saying: If a man desires
the position of a bishop,[1] he desires a good
work. 2 A bishop then must be blameless,
the husband of one wife, temperate, sober-
minded, of good behavior, hospitable, able
to teach; 3 not given to wine, not violent, not
greedy for money,[1] but gentle, not quarrel-
some, not covetous; 4 one who rules his own
house well, having *his* children in submission
with all reverence 5 (for if a man does not
know how to rule his own house, how will
he take care of the church of God?); 6 not a
novice, lest being puffed up with pride he
fall into the *same* condemnation as the devil.
7 Moreover he must have a good testimony
among those who are outside, lest he fall into
reproach and the [a]snare of the devil.

Qualifications of Deacons

8 Likewise deacons *must be* reverent, not
double-tongued, [a]not given to much wine,
not greedy for money, 9 holding the mystery
of the faith with a pure conscience. 10 But
let these also first be tested; then let them
serve as deacons, being *found* blameless.
11 Likewise, *their* wives *must be* reverent, not
slanderers, temperate, faithful in all things.
12 Let deacons be the husbands of one wife,
ruling *their* children and their own houses
well. 13 For those who have served well as deacons [a]obtain for themselves a good standing
and great boldness in the faith which is in
Christ Jesus.

The Great Mystery

14 These things I write to you, though I
hope to come to you shortly; 15 but if I am
delayed, *I write* so that you may know how
you ought to conduct yourself in the house
of God, which is the church of the living God,
the pillar and ground of the truth. 16 And
without controversy great is the mystery of
godliness:

> [a]God[1] was manifested in the flesh,
> [b]Justified in the Spirit,
> [c]Seen by angels,
> [d]Preached among the Gentiles,
> [e]Believed on in the world,
> [f]Received up in glory.

The Great Apostasy

4 Now the Spirit expressly says that in latter
times some will depart from the faith, giving heed [a]to deceiving spirits and doctrines of
demons, 2 [a]speaking lies in hypocrisy, having
their own conscience [b]seared with a hot iron,
3 forbidding to marry, *and commanding* to
abstain from foods which God created to be
received with thanksgiving by those who believe and know the truth. 4 For every creature
of God *is* good, and nothing is to be refused
if it is received with thanksgiving; 5 for it is
sanctified by the word of God and prayer.

1:20 [a] 2 Tim. 2:17, 18 [b] 2 Tim. 4:14 [c] Acts 13:45 **2:2** [a] Ezra 6:10 [b] [Rom. 13:1] **2:3** [a] Rom. 12:2 [b] 2 Tim. 1:9 **2:4** [a] Ezek. 18:23, 32 [b] [John 17:3] **2:5** [a] Gal. 3:20 [b] [Heb. 9:15] **2:6** [a] Mark 10:45 **2:7** [a] Eph. 3:7, 8 [b] [Gal. 1:15, 16] [1] NU-Text omits *in Christ.* **2:8** [a] Luke 23:34 [b] Ps. 134:2 **2:9** [a] 1 Pet. 3:3 **2:10** [a] 1 Pet. 3:4 **2:12** [a] 1 Cor. 14:34 **3:1** [1] Literally *overseer* **3:3** [1] NU-Text omits *not greedy for money.* **3:7** [a] 2 Tim. 2:26 **3:8** [a] Ezek. 44:21 **3:13** [a] Matt. 25:21 **3:16** [a] [John 1:14] [b] [Matt. 3:16] [c] Matt. 28:2 [d] Rom. 10:18 [e] Col. 1:6, 23 [f] Luke 24:51 [1] NU-Text reads *Who.* **4:1** [a] Rev. 16:14 **4:2** [a] Matt. 7:15 [b] Eph. 4:19

A Good Servant of Jesus Christ

6 If you instruct the brethren in these
things, you will be a good minister of Jesus
Christ, [a]nourished in the words of faith and
of the good doctrine which you have carefully followed. 7 But [a]reject profane and old
wives' fables, and [b]exercise yourself toward
godliness. 8 For [a]bodily exercise profits a little, but godliness is profitable for all things,
[b]having promise of the life that now is and
of that which is to come. 9 This *is* a faithful
saying and worthy of all acceptance. 10 For to
this *end* we both labor and suffer reproach,[1]
because we trust in the living God, [a]who is
the Savior of all men, especially of those who
believe. 11 These things command and teach.

Take Heed to Your Ministry

12 Let no one despise your youth, but be an
[a]example to the believers in word, in conduct,
in love, in spirit,[1] in faith, in purity. 13 Till I
come, give attention to reading, to exhortation, to doctrine. 14 [a]Do not neglect the
gift that is in you, which was given to you by
prophecy [b]with the laying on of the hands of
the eldership. 15 Meditate on these things; give
yourself entirely to them, that your progress
may be evident to all. 16 Take heed to yourself
and to the doctrine. Continue in them, for in
doing this you will save both yourself and
those who hear you.

> PEACE NOTE
>
> Paul's exhortation here may have been an allusion to Joshua 1:9: "Be strong and manly; do not be cowardly or frightened, for the LORD your God is with you in all places where you go" (*Greek Old Testament*).
>
> 1 TIMOTHY 4:12

Treatment of Church Members

5 Do not rebuke an older man, but exhort
him as a father, younger men as brothers,
2 older women as mothers, younger women
as sisters, with all purity.

Honor True Widows

3 Honor widows who are really widows.
4 But if any widow has children or grandchildren, let them first learn to show piety at
home and [a]to repay their parents; for this is
good and[1] acceptable before God. 5 Now she
who is really a widow, and left alone, trusts
in God and continues in supplications and
prayers [a]night and day. 6 But she who lives
in pleasure is dead while she lives. 7 And
these things command, that they may be
blameless. 8 But if anyone does not provide
for his own, [a]and especially for those of his
household, [b]he has denied the faith [c]and is
worse than an unbeliever.

9 Do not let a widow under sixty years old be
taken into the number, *and not unless* she has
been the wife of one man, 10 well reported for
good works: if she has brought up children, if
she has lodged strangers, if she has washed the
saints' feet, if she has relieved the afflicted, if
she has diligently followed every good work.

11 But refuse *the* younger widows; for when
they have begun to grow wanton against
Christ, they desire to marry, 12 having condemnation because they have cast off their
first faith. 13 And besides they learn *to be*
idle, wandering about from house to house,
and not only idle but also gossips and busybodies, saying things which they ought not.
14 Therefore I desire that *the* younger *widows*
marry, bear children, manage the house, give
no opportunity to the adversary to speak reproachfully. 15 For some have already turned
aside after Satan. 16 If any believing man or[1]
woman has widows, let them relieve them,
and do not let the church be burdened, that
it may relieve those who are really widows.

Honor the Elders

17 Let the elders who rule well be counted
worthy of double honor, especially those
who labor in the word and doctrine. 18 For
the Scripture says, [a]"You shall not muzzle
an ox while it treads out the grain,"[1] and,
[b]"The laborer *is* worthy of his wages."[2] 19 Do
not receive an accusation against an elder
except [a]from two or three witnesses. 20 Those
who are sinning rebuke in the presence of
all, that the rest also may fear.

21 I charge *you* before God and the Lord
Jesus Christ and the elect angels that you
observe these things without [a]prejudice,
doing nothing with partiality. 22 Do not lay
hands on anyone hastily, nor [a]share in other
people's sins; keep yourself pure.

4:6 [a] 2 Tim. 3:14 **4:7** [a] 2 Tim. 2:16 [b] Heb. 5:14 **4:8** [a] 1 Cor. 8:8 [b] Ps. 37:9 **4:10** [a] Ps. 36:6 [1] NU-Text reads *we labor and strive.* **4:12** [a] 1 Pet. 5:3 [1] NU-Text omits *in spirit.* **4:14** [a] 2 Tim. 1:6 [b] Acts 6:6 **5:4** [a] Gen. 45:10 [1] NU-Text and M-Text omit *good and.* **5:5** [a] Acts 26:7 **5:8** [a] Is. 58:7 [b] 2 Tim. 3:5 [c] Matt. 18:17 **5:16** [1] NU-Text omits *man or.* **5:18** [a] Deut. 25:4 [b] Luke 10:7 [1] Deuteronomy 25:4 [2] Luke 10:7 **5:19** [a] Deut. 17:6; 19:15 **5:21** [a] Deut. 1:17 **5:22** [a] Eph. 5:6, 7

[23]No longer drink only water, but use a little wine for your stomach's sake and your frequent infirmities.

[24]Some men's sins are [a]clearly evident, preceding *them* to judgment, but those of some *men* follow later. [25]Likewise, the good works *of some* are clearly evident, and those that are otherwise cannot be hidden.

Honor Masters

6 Let as many [a]bondservants as are under the yoke count their own masters worthy of all honor, so that the name of God and *His* doctrine may not be blasphemed. [2]And those who have believing masters, let them not despise *them* because they are brethren, but rather serve *them* because those who are benefited are believers and beloved. Teach and exhort these things.

Error and Greed

[3]If anyone teaches otherwise and does not consent to [a]wholesome words, *even* the words of our Lord Jesus Christ, [b]and to the doctrine which accords with godliness, [4]he is proud, knowing nothing, but is obsessed with disputes and arguments over words, from which come envy, strife, reviling, evil suspicions, [5]useless wranglings[1] of men of corrupt minds and destitute of the truth, who suppose that godliness is a *means of* gain. From [a]such withdraw yourself.[2]

[6]Now godliness with [a]contentment is great gain. [7]For we brought nothing into *this* world, *and it is* [a]certain[1] we can carry nothing out. [8]And having food and clothing, with these we shall be [a]content. [9]But those who desire to be rich fall into temptation and a snare, and *into* many foolish and harmful lusts which drown men in destruction and perdition. [10]For the love of money is a root of all *kinds of* evil, for which some have strayed from the faith in their greediness, and pierced themselves through with many sorrows.

The Good Confession

[11]But you, O man of God, flee these things and pursue righteousness, godliness, faith, love, patience, gentleness. [12]Fight the good fight of faith, lay hold on eternal life, to which you were also called and have confessed the good confession in the presence of many witnesses. [13]I urge you in the sight of God who gives life to all things, and *before* Christ Jesus [a]who witnessed the good confession before Pontius Pilate, [14]that you keep *this* commandment without spot, blameless until our Lord Jesus Christ's appearing, [15]which He will manifest in His own time, *He who is* the blessed and only Potentate, the King of kings and Lord of lords, [16]who alone has immortality, dwelling in [a]unapproachable light, [b]whom no man has seen or can see, to whom *be* honor and everlasting power. Amen.

Instructions to the Rich

[17]Command those who are rich in this present age not to be haughty, nor to trust in uncertain [a]riches but in the living God, who gives us richly all things [b]to enjoy. [18]*Let them* do good, that they be rich in good works, ready to give, willing to share, [19][a]storing up for themselves a good foundation for the time to come, that they may lay hold on eternal life.

Guard the Faith

[20]O Timothy! [a]Guard what was committed to your trust, [b]avoiding the profane *and* idle babblings and contradictions of what is falsely called knowledge— [21]by professing it some have strayed concerning the faith.

Grace *be* with you. Amen.

5:24 [a] Gal. 5:19–21 **6:1** [a] Eph. 6:5 **6:3** [a] 2 Tim. 1:13 [b] Titus 1:1 **6:5** [a] 2 Tim. 3:5 [1] NU-Text and M-Text read *constant friction.* [2] NU-Text omits this sentence. **6:6** [a] Heb. 13:5 **6:7** [a] Job 1:21 [1] NU-Text omits *and it is certain.* **6:8** [a] Prov. 30:8, 9 **6:13** [a] John 18:36, 37 **6:16** [a] Dan. 2:22 [b] John 6:46 **6:17** [a] Jer. 9:23; 48:7 [b] Eccl. 5:18, 19 **6:19** [a] [Matt. 6:20, 21; 19:21] **6:20** [a] [2 Tim. 1:12, 14] [b] Titus 1:14

THE SECOND EPISTLE OF PAUL

THE APOSTLE TO

TIMOTHY

AUTHOR

Fearing for their own lives, the Asian believers failed to support Paul after his second Roman imprisonment and his first defense before the imperial court (2 Tim. 1:15; 4:16). Here, he was in a cold Roman cell (4:13) without hope of acquittal, in spite of the success of his initial defense. Under these conditions, Paul wrote this epistle in the fall of AD 67, hoping that Timothy would be able to visit him before the approaching winter (4:21).

TIME

c. AD 66–67

KEY VERSE

2 Timothy 3:14–17

THEME

This is likely the last of Paul's writings that we have. In ancient Rome there existed a maximum-security dungeon called the Carcer. It is possible that Paul was placed in that prison during Nero's reign. He writes this letter from a cell where he is being kept like a common criminal. He knows that his work on earth is nearing its conclusion, and these are his last words of counsel to his trusted companion in ministry. One can sense Paul's weariness but also his strongly held conviction about what is necessary for the continued growth of the church. One can also clearly see the hope that sustains him as he looks forward to going home to Christ.

When Paul wrote 2 Timothy, he issued strong words to bolster his young protégé's confidence for ministry. Paul knew this letter was his final opportunity, so he sought to encourage, comfort, charge, and challenge Timothy to fulfill his divinely given task. Make no mistake, he warned the young man, "God has not given us a spirit of fear, but . . . of love and of a sound mind" (1:7); therefore, we can boldly "pursue righteousness, faith, love, [and] peace" (2:22). Paul's reference to timidity is a deliberate allusion to the opening words of the Book of Joshua, where God charged the successor of Moses: "Be strong and manly; do not be cowardly or frightened, for the LORD your God is with you in all places where you go" (Josh. 1:9, Septuagint). In essence, Paul exhorted Timothy not to be a coward. He must remember that God has given him "a spirit of . . . power [*dynameos*]" (2 Tim. 1:7). Possessing this power, Timothy could fulfill his mission and do the work of the ministry (2 Tim. 4:5), and that same power is available to every follower of Jesus.

Greeting

1 Paul, an apostle of Jesus Christ[1] by the will
of God, according to the [a]promise of life
which is in Christ Jesus,

2 To Timothy, a [a]beloved son:

Grace, mercy, *and* peace from God the
Father and Christ Jesus our Lord.

Timothy's Faith and Heritage

3 I thank God, whom I serve with a pure
conscience, as *my* [a]forefathers *did,* as without
ceasing I remember you in my prayers night
and day, 4 greatly desiring to see you, being
mindful of your tears, that I may be filled
with joy, 5 when I call to remembrance [a]the
genuine faith that is in you, which dwelt first
in your grandmother Lois and [b]your mother
Eunice, and I am persuaded is in you also.
6 Therefore I remind you [a]to stir up the gift
of God which is in you through the laying
on of my hands. 7 For [a]God has not given us
a spirit of fear, [b]but of power and of love and
of a sound mind.

PEACE NOTE

Mentorship leads to God's peace in our lives! Seek to have older, wiser mentors like Paul who trained Timothy. These teachers can speak truth (and peace) into your life at critical moments.

2 TIMOTHY 1:5

PEACE NOTE

Paul exhorted Timothy to remember that God had given him a spirit "of power and of love and of a sound mind." We need the same reminder today. Fear is never from God.

2 TIMOTHY 1:7

Not Ashamed of the Gospel

8 [a]Therefore do not be ashamed of [b]the
testimony of our Lord, nor of me [c]His prisoner, but share with me in the sufferings for
the gospel according to the power of God,
9 who has saved us and called *us* with a holy
calling, [a]not according to our works, but
[b]according to His own purpose and grace
which was given to us in Christ Jesus [c]before
time began, 10 but [a]has now been revealed
by the appearing of our Savior Jesus Christ,
who has abolished death and brought life
and immortality to light through the gospel,
11 [a]to which I was appointed a preacher, an
apostle, and a teacher of the Gentiles.[1] 12 For
this reason I also suffer these things; nevertheless I am not ashamed, [a]for I know whom
I have believed and am persuaded that He is
able to keep what I have committed to Him
until that Day.

Be Loyal to the Faith

13 [a]Hold fast [b]the pattern of [c]sound words
which you have heard from me, in faith and
love which are in Christ Jesus. 14 That good
thing which was committed to you, keep by
the Holy Spirit who dwells in us.

15 This you know, that all those in Asia have
turned away from me, among whom are
Phygellus and Hermogenes. 16 The Lord grant
mercy to the [a]household of Onesiphorus, for
he often refreshed me, and was not ashamed
of my chain; 17 but when he arrived in Rome,
he sought me out very zealously and found
me. 18 The Lord [a]grant to him that he may
find mercy from the Lord [b]in that Day—
and you know very well how many ways he
[c]ministered *to me*[1] at Ephesus.

Be Strong in Grace

2 You therefore, [a]my son, [b]be strong in the
grace that is in Christ Jesus. 2 And the
things that you have heard from me among
many witnesses, commit these to faithful
men who will be able to teach others also.
3 You therefore must [a]endure[1] hardship [b]as

1:1 [a] Titus 1:2 [1] NU-Text and M-Text read *Christ Jesus.* 1:2 [a] 1 Tim. 1:2 1:3 [a] Acts 24:14 1:5 [a] 1 Tim. 1:5; 4:6 [b] Acts 16:1 1:6 [a] 1 Tim. 4:14 1:7 [a] Rom. 8:15 [b] [Acts 1:8] 1:8 [a] [Rom. 1:16] [b] 1 Tim. 2:6 [c] Eph. 3:1 1:9 [a] [Rom. 3:20] [b] Rom. 8:28 [c] Rom. 16:25 1:10 [a] Eph. 1:9 1:11 [a] Acts 9:15 [1] NU-Text omits *of the Gentiles.* 1:12 [a] 1 Pet. 4:19 1:13 [a] Titus 1:9 [b] Rom. 2:20; 6:17 [c] 1 Tim. 6:3 1:16 [a] 2 Tim. 4:19 1:18 [a] Mark 9:41 [b] 2 Thess. 1:10 [c] Heb. 6:10 [1] *To me* is from the Vulgate and a few Greek manuscripts. 2:1 [a] 1 Tim. 1:2 [b] Eph. 6:10 2:3 [a] 2 Tim. 4:5 [b] 1 Tim. 1:18 [1] NU-Text reads *You must share.*

a good soldier of Jesus Christ. 4[a]No one engaged in warfare entangles himself with the
affairs of *this* life, that he may please him who
enlisted him as a soldier. 5 And also [a]if anyone competes in athletics, he is not crowned
unless he competes according to the rules.
6 The hardworking farmer must be first to
partake of the crops. 7 Consider what I say,
and may[1] the Lord [a]give you understanding
in all things.

8 Remember that Jesus Christ, [a]of the seed
of David, [b]was raised from the dead [c]ac-
cording to my gospel, 9[a]for which I suffer
trouble as an evildoer, [b]*even* to the point of
chains; [c]but the word of God is not chained.
10 Therefore [a]I endure all things for the sake
of the elect, [b]that they also may obtain the
salvation which is in Christ Jesus with eternal
glory.

11 *This is* a faithful saying:

For [a]if we died with *Him,*
We shall also live with *Him.*
12 [a]If we endure,
We shall also reign with *Him.*
[b]If we deny *Him,*
He also will deny us.
13 If we are faithless,
He remains faithful;
He [a]cannot deny Himself.

Approved and Disapproved Workers

14 Remind *them* of these things, [a]charging
them before the Lord not to strive about
words to no profit, to the ruin of the hearers.
15[a]Be diligent to present yourself approved
to God, a worker who does not need to be
ashamed, rightly dividing the word of truth.
16 But shun profane *and* idle babblings, for
they will increase to more ungodliness. 17 And
their message will spread like cancer. [a]Hy-
menaeus and Philetus are of this sort, 18 who
have strayed concerning the truth, [a]saying
that the resurrection is already past; and they
overthrow the faith of some. 19 Nevertheless
[a]the solid foundation of God stands, having
this seal: "The Lord [b]knows those who are
His," and, "Let everyone who names the name
of Christ[1] depart from iniquity."

20 But in a great house there are not only
[a]vessels of gold and silver, but also of wood
and clay, some for honor and some for dishonor. 21 Therefore if anyone cleanses himself
from the latter, he will be a vessel for honor,
sanctified and useful for the Master, [a]prepared
for every good work. 22[a]Flee also youthful
lusts; but pursue righteousness, faith, love,
peace with those who call on the Lord out of
a pure heart. 23 But avoid foolish and ignorant
disputes, knowing that they generate strife.
24 And [a]a servant of the Lord must not quarrel

2:4 [a] [2 Pet. 2:20] **2:5** [a] [1 Cor. 9:25] **2:7** [a] Prov. 2:6 [1] NU-Text reads *the Lord will give you.* **2:8** [a] Rom. 1:3, 4 [b] 1 Cor. 15:4 [c] Rom. 2:16 **2:9** [a] Acts 9:16 [b] Eph. 3:1 [c] Acts 28:31 **2:10** [a] Eph. 3:13 [b] 2 Cor. 1:6 **2:11** [a] Rom. 6:5, 8 **2:12** [a] [Rom. 5:17; 8:17] [b] Matt. 10:33 **2:13** [a] Num. 23:19 **2:14** [a] Titus 3:9 **2:15** [a] 2 Pet. 1:10 **2:17** [a] 1 Tim. 1:20 **2:18** [a] 1 Cor. 15:12 **2:19** [a] [1 Cor. 3:11] [b] [Nah. 1:7] [1] NU-Text and M-Text read *the Lord.* **2:20** [a] Rom. 9:21 **2:21** [a] 2 Tim. 3:17 **2:22** [a] 1 Tim. 6:11 **2:24** [a] Titus 3:2

GIVE PEACE A CHANCE

Flee . . . youthful lusts; but pursue righteousness, faith, love, peace with those who call on the Lord out of a pure heart.

2 TIMOTHY 2:22

At nineteen I decided to say farewell to youthful folly and angry impulses and pursue instead a life of faith and righteousness. I admit that I didn't give peace much thought at first, but it wasn't long before I discovered that peace was part of the package. I found, too, that living the life God wants us to live puts love in our hearts (for family, friends, and eventually for the woman I married!).

One of Paul's best-known statements is this: "And now abide faith, hope, love, these three; but the greatest of these is love" (1 Cor. 13:13). There can be no holy love without peace. So we need to be those who are pursuing God's peace as He is pursuing us with His peace.

After all, it's His peace that creates in our hearts that love of which the apostle Paul spoke. Is your soul at peace? Can you tell by the love it is generating? Find a way to serve a family member today through your spiritual gift or through some spiritual action. Spread God's peace to those you love dearly.

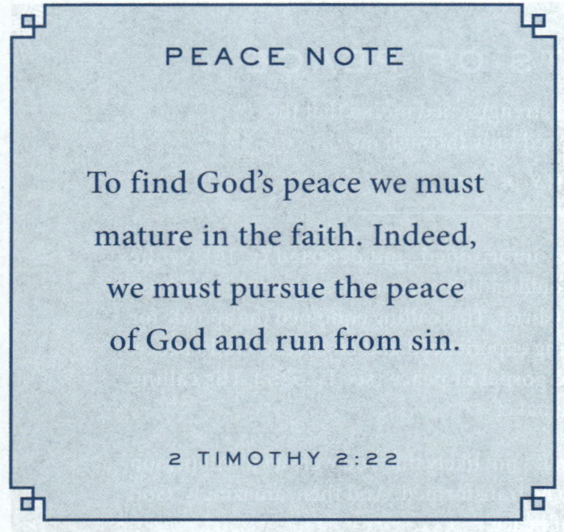

but be gentle to all, [b]able to teach, [c]patient,
25 [a]in humility correcting those who are in
opposition, [b]if God perhaps will grant them
repentance, [c]so that they may know the truth,
26 and *that* they may come to their senses *and*
[a]*escape* the snare of the devil, having been
taken captive by him to *do* his will.

Perilous Times and Perilous Men

3 But know this, that [a]in the last days perilous times will come: 2 For men will be lovers of themselves, lovers of money, boasters,
proud, blasphemers, disobedient to parents,
unthankful, unholy, 3 unloving, unforgiving,
slanderers, without self-control, brutal, de-
spisers of good, 4 [a]traitors, headstrong, haughty, lovers of pleasure rather than lovers of God,
5 [a]having a form of godliness but [b]denying
its power. And [c]from such people turn away!
6 For [a]of this sort are those who creep into
households and make captives of gullible
women loaded down with sins, led away by
various lusts, 7 always learning and never able
[a]to come to the knowledge of the truth. 8 [a]Now
as Jannes and Jambres resisted Moses, so do
these also resist the truth: [b]men of corrupt
minds, [c]disapproved concerning the faith;
9 but they will progress no further, for their
folly will be manifest to all, [a]as theirs also was.

The Man of God and the Word of God

10 [a]But you have carefully followed my
doctrine, manner of life, purpose, faith,
longsuffering, love, perseverance, 11 persecutions, afflictions, which happened to me [a]at
Antioch, [b]at Iconium, [c]at Lystra—what persecutions I endured. And [d]out of *them* all the Lord
delivered me. 12 Yes, and [a]all who desire to live
godly in Christ Jesus will suffer persecution.
13 [a]But evil men and impostors will grow worse
and worse, deceiving and being deceived. 14 But
you must [a]continue in the things which you
have learned and been assured of, knowing
from whom you have learned *them,* 15 and that
from childhood you have known [a]the Holy
Scriptures, which are able to make you wise for
salvation through faith which is in Christ Jesus.
16 [a]All Scripture *is* given by inspiration of
God, [b]and *is* profitable for doctrine, for reproof,
for correction, for instruction in righteousness, 17 [a]that the man of God may be complete,
[b]thoroughly equipped for every good work.

Preach the Word

4 I [a]charge *you* therefore before God and
the Lord Jesus Christ, [b]who will judge the
living and the dead at[1] His appearing and
His kingdom: 2 Preach the word! Be ready in
season *and* out of season. [a]Convince, [b]rebuke,
[c]exhort, with all longsuffering and teaching.
3 [a]For the time will come when they will not
endure [b]sound doctrine, [c]but according to
their own desires, *because* they have itching
ears, they will heap up for themselves teachers;
4 and they will turn *their* ears away from the
truth, and [a]be turned aside to fables. 5 But you
be watchful in all things, [a]endure afflictions, do
the work of [b]an evangelist, fulfill your ministry.

Paul's Valedictory

6 For [a]I am already being poured out as a
drink offering, and the time of [b]my departure
is at hand. 7 [a]I have fought the good fight, I
have finished the race, I have kept the faith.
8 Finally, there is laid up for me [a]the crown
of righteousness, which the Lord, the righteous [b]Judge, will give to me [c]on that Day,
and not to me only but also to all who have
loved His appearing.

The Abandoned Apostle

9 Be diligent to come to me quickly; 10 for
[a]Demas has forsaken me, [b]having loved this
present world, and has departed for Thessalonica—Crescens for Galatia, Titus for

2:24 [b] Titus 1:9 [c] 1 Tim. 3:3 **2:25** [a] Gal. 6:1 [b] Acts 8:22 [c] 1 Tim. 2:4 **2:26** [a] 1 Tim. 3:7 **3:1** [a] 1 Tim. 4:1 **3:4** [a] 2 Pet. 2:10 **3:5** [a] Titus 1:16 [b] 1 Tim. 5:8 [c] 2 Thess. 3:6 **3:6** [a] Matt. 23:14 **3:7** [a] 1 Tim. 2:4 **3:8** [a] Ex. 7:11, 12, 22; 8:7; 9:11 [b] 1 Tim. 6:5 [c] Rom. 1:28 **3:9** [a] Ex. 7:11, 12; 8:18; 9:11 **3:10** [a] 1 Tim. 4:6 **3:11** [a] Acts 13:44–52 [b] Acts 14:1–6, 19 [c] Acts 14:8–20 [d] Ps. 34:19 **3:12** [a] [Ps. 34:19] **3:13** [a] 2 Thess. 2:11 **3:14** [a] 2 Tim. 1:13 **3:15** [a] John 5:39 **3:16** [a] [2 Pet. 1:20] [b] Rom. 4:23; 15:4 **3:17** [a] 1 Tim. 6:11 [b] 2 Tim. 2:21 **4:1** [a] 1 Tim. 5:21 [b] Acts 10:42 [1] NU-Text omits *therefore* and reads *and by* for *at.* **4:2** [a] Titus 2:15 [b] 1 Tim. 5:20 [c] 1 Tim. 4:13 **4:3** [a] 2 Tim. 3:1 [b] 1 Tim. 1:10 [c] 2 Tim. 3:6 **4:4** [a] 1 Tim. 1:4 **4:5** [a] 2 Tim. 1:8 [b] Acts 21:8 **4:6** [a] Phil. 2:17 [b] [Phil. 1:23] **4:7** [a] 1 Cor. 9:24–27 **4:8** [a] James 1:12 [b] John 5:22 [c] 2 Tim. 1:12 **4:10** [a] Col. 4:14 [b] 1 John 2:15

WE ARE AGENTS OF PEACE

But the Lord stood with me and strengthened me, so that the message might be preached fully through me.

2 TIMOTHY 4:17

Paul found himself knocked about, opposed, imprisoned, and deserted (v. 16), yet he experienced God's comforting presence. Paul could endure opposition and setbacks because of his transforming experience of life in Jesus Christ. This calling equipped the apostle for the challenging ministry that lay ahead. Having experienced and embraced God's peace, the apostle Paul became an evangelist of the gospel of peace (see Is. 52:7). His calling transformed him from violent zealot to peacemaker.

God's calling can transform Paul, you, and me. It's not likely that you were a violent person who persecuted Christians, but we all need to be transformed. And then, amazingly, God wants to deploy each of us into His mission of peace.

Just tell your story of finding peace in God. This week, pick your friend, pray that the Lord will strengthen you, invite him or her for coffee or lunch. Ask God to open up a time for you to share about the peace you have because of Jesus. Just talk about peace!

PEACE NOTE

If you have felt alone in your pursuit of peace, I pray that you will feel seen and know that God cares about your pain and wants you to experience His *shalom*.

2 TIMOTHY 4:17

Dalmatia. 11 Only Luke is with me. Get [a]Mark
and bring him with you, for he is useful to
me for ministry. 12 And [a]Tychicus I have sent
to Ephesus. 13 Bring the cloak that I left with
Carpus at Troas when you come—and the
books, especially the parchments.
14 [a]Alexander the coppersmith did me much
harm. May the Lord repay him according to
his works. 15 You also must beware of him, for
he has greatly resisted our words.
16 At my first defense no one stood with me,
but all forsook me. [a]May it not be charged
against them.

The Lord Is Faithful

17 [a]But the Lord stood with me and
strengthened me, [b]so that the message might
be preached fully through me, and *that* all the
Gentiles might hear. Also I was delivered [c]out
of the mouth of the lion. 18 [a]And the Lord will
deliver me from every evil work and preserve
me for His heavenly kingdom. [b]To Him *be*
glory forever and ever. Amen!

Come Before Winter

19 Greet [a]Prisca and Aquila, and the household of [b]Onesiphorus. 20 [a]Erastus stayed in Corinth, but [b]Trophimus I have left in Miletus sick.
21 Do your utmost to come before winter.
Eubulus greets you, as well as Pudens,
Linus, Claudia, and all the brethren.

Farewell

22 The Lord Jesus Christ[1] be with your spirit.
Grace be with you. Amen.

4:11 [a] Acts 12:12, 25; 15:37–39 **4:12** [a] Acts 20:4 **4:14** [a] 1 Tim. 1:20 **4:16** [a] Acts 7:60 **4:17** [a] Acts 23:11 [b] Acts 9:15 [c] 1 Sam. 17:37 **4:18** [a] Ps. 121:7 [b] Rom. 11:36 **4:19** [a] Acts 18:2 [b] 2 Tim. 1:16 **4:20** [a] Rom. 16:23 [b] Acts 20:4; 21:29
4:22 [1] NU-Text omits *Jesus Christ.*

THE EPISTLE OF PAUL THE APOSTLE TO

TITUS

AUTHOR

Titus was one of Paul's Gentile converts. He probably worked with Paul during his time at Ephesus on his third missionary journey. Later he also worked in Corinth and this letter indicates that Paul is commissioning him to work on the island of Crete. Paul wrote this letter about AD 63, perhaps from Corinth, taking advantage of the journey of Zenas and Apollos (Titus 3:13), whose destination would take them by way of Crete.

TIME

c. AD 63

KEY VERSE

Titus 3:8

THEME

Paul's instructions to Titus are similar to those he gave to Timothy. He delivers instructions about the leadership and organization of the church and guidance in dealing with the opposition of those who contradict his teaching. His tone is that of a seasoned leader passing on the essential directions to a valued disciple.

Paul was close to Titus and referred to him as "a true son in our common faith" (1:4). We've all found ourselves in a place where there is a legitimate cause for concern. Paul learned of false teaching (asceticism and useless speculation) and so urged his friend Titus to teach "sound doctrine" (2:1) and to strengthen church leadership (hence the interest in church officers in these letters; see ch. 1). The immediate application of Titus is the importance of developing leaders grounded in truth (2:1–8), and then experiencing the peace of God because the Holy Spirit has been "abundantly" poured out to us in our Messiah, "Jesus Christ our Savior" (3:6).

Greeting

1 Paul, a bondservant of God and an apostle
of Jesus Christ, according to the faith of
God's elect and [a]the acknowledgment of the
truth [b]which accords with godliness, 2 in hope
of eternal life which God, who [a]cannot lie,
promised before time began, 3 but has in due
time manifested His word through preaching, which was committed to me according
to the commandment of God our Savior;

4 To [a]Titus, a true son in *our* common faith:

Grace, mercy, *and* peace from God the
Father and the Lord Jesus Christ[1] our Savior.

Qualified Elders

5 For this reason I left you in Crete, that
you should [a]set in order the things that are
lacking, and appoint elders in every city as I
commanded you— 6 if a man is blameless, the
husband of one wife, [a]having faithful children
not accused of dissipation or insubordination.
7 For a bishop[1] must be blameless, as a steward
of God, not self-willed, not quick-tempered,
[a]not given to wine, not violent, not greedy for
money, 8 but hospitable, a lover of what is good,
sober-minded, just, holy, self-controlled, 9 holding fast the faithful word as he has been taught,
that he may be able, by sound doctrine, both
to exhort and convict those who contradict.

The Elders' Task

10 For there are many insubordinate, both
idle [a]talkers and deceivers, especially those
of the circumcision, 11 whose mouths must
be stopped, who subvert whole households,
teaching things which they ought not, [a]for
the sake of dishonest gain. 12 [a]One of them, a
prophet of their own, said, "Cretans *are* always
liars, evil beasts, lazy gluttons." 13 This testimony is true. [a]Therefore rebuke them sharply, that
they may be sound in the faith, 14 not giving
heed to Jewish fables and [a]commandments of
men who turn from the truth. 15 [a]To the pure all
things are pure, but to those who are defiled
and unbelieving nothing is pure; but even
their mind and conscience are defiled. 16 They
profess to [a]know God, but [b]in works they deny
Him, being abominable, disobedient, [c]and
disqualified for every good work.

Qualities of a Sound Church

2 But as for you, speak the things which
are proper for sound doctrine: 2 that the
older men be sober, reverent, temperate,
sound in faith, in love, in patience; 3 the older
women likewise, that they be reverent in
behavior, not slanderers, not given to much
wine, teachers of good things— 4 that they
admonish the young women to love their
husbands, to love their children, 5 *to be* dis-
creet, chaste, [a]homemakers, good, [b]obedient
to their own husbands, [c]that the word of God
may not be blasphemed.

6 Likewise, exhort the young men to be
sober-minded, 7 in all things showing yourself
to be [a]a pattern of good works; in doctrine
showing integrity, reverence, [b]incorruptibili-
ty,[1] 8 sound speech that cannot be condemned,
that one who is an opponent may be ashamed,
having nothing evil to say of you.[1]

1:1 [a] 2 Tim. 2:25 [b] [1 Tim. 3:16] **1:2** [a] Num. 23:19 **1:4** [a] 2 Cor. 2:13; 8:23 [1] NU-Text reads *and Christ Jesus.* **1:5** [a] 1 Cor. 11:34 **1:6** [a] 1 Tim. 3:2–4 **1:7** [a] Lev. 10:9 [1] Literally *overseer* **1:10** [a] James 1:26 **1:11** [a] 1 Tim. 6:5 **1:12** [a] Acts 17:28 **1:13** [a] 2 Cor. 13:10 **1:14** [a] Is. 29:13 **1:15** [a] 1 Cor. 6:12 **1:16** [a] Matt. 7:20–23; 25:12 [b] [2 Tim. 3:5, 7] [c] Rom. 1:28 **2:5** [a] 1 Tim. 5:14 [b] 1 Cor. 14:34 [c] Rom. 2:24 **2:7** [a] 1 Tim. 4:12 [b] Eph. 6:24 [1] NU-Text omits *incorruptibility.* **2:8** [1] NU-Text and M-Text read *us.*

INVEST IN THE COMMUNITY OF FAITH

To Titus, a true son in our common faith.

TITUS 1:4

We all need a Paul-Titus friendship in our lives. What do I mean? Sometimes our family of faith can be even closer to us than our biological family. Christians shares a brotherhood and bond that can feel stronger than relational ties. Paul called Titus "a true son in our common faith." We can only speculate, but perhaps Paul was not as close to his own family after coming to faith in Christ. God blessed him with new connections within the body of Christ.

Watching church online can be an encouragement, but it is no replacement for being in fellowship with believers. We serve together, we suffer together, we believe together; we live the Christian life in community. Whom do you need to befriend today in your church? Make that your next step so you can establish faith friendships and experience peace together.

PEACE NOTE

We need those who are younger or less mature than we are (as Timothy was for Paul) whom we are mentoring in God's peace.

TITUS 2:6-7

[9] *Exhort* [a]bondservants to be obedient to their own masters, to be well pleasing in all *things,* not answering back, [10] not pilfering, but showing all good fidelity, that they may adorn the doctrine of God our Savior in all things.

Trained by Saving Grace

[11] For [a]the grace of God that brings salvation has appeared to all men, [12] teaching
us that, denying ungodliness and worldly lusts, we should live soberly, righteously,
and godly in the present age, [13a]looking for
the blessed [b]hope and glorious appearing of
our great God and Savior Jesus Christ, [14a]who
gave Himself for us, that He might redeem us from every lawless deed [b]and purify for Himself [c]*His* own special people, zealous for good works.
[15] Speak these things, [a]exhort, and rebuke
with all authority. Let no one despise you.

Graces of the Heirs of Grace

3 Remind them [a]to be subject to rulers
and authorities, to obey, [b]to be ready for
every good work, [2] to speak evil of no one,
to be peaceable, gentle, showing all humility to all men. [3] For [a]we ourselves were also
once foolish, disobedient, deceived, serving various lusts and pleasures, living in malice and envy, hateful and hating one another.
[4] But when [a]the kindness and the love of
[b]God our Savior toward man appeared, [5a]not
by works of righteousness which we have done, but according to His mercy He saved us, through [b]the washing of regeneration and renewing of the Holy Spirit, [6a]whom
He poured out on us abundantly through Jesus Christ our Savior, [7] that having been
justified by His grace [a]we should become heirs according to the hope of eternal life.
[8a]This is a faithful saying, and these things
I want you to affirm constantly, that those who have believed in God should be careful to maintain good works. These things are good and profitable to men.

2:9 [a] 1 Tim. 6:1 **2:11** [a] [Rom. 5:15] **2:13** [a] 1 Cor. 1:7 [b] [Col. 3:4] **2:14** [a] Gal. 1:4 [b] [Heb. 1:3; 9:14] [c] Ex. 15:16 **2:15** [a] 2 Tim. 4:2 **3:1** [a] 1 Pet. 2:13 [b] Col. 1:10 **3:3** [a] 1 Cor. 6:11 **3:4** [a] Titus 2:11 [b] 1 Tim. 2:3 **3:5** [a] [Rom. 3:20] [b] John 3:3 **3:6** [a] Ezek. 36:26 **3:7** [a] [Rom. 8:17, 23, 24] **3:8** [a] 1 Tim. 1:15

HE SAVED US

When the kindness and the love of God our Savior toward man appeared . . . according to His mercy He saved us.

TITUS 3:4-5

After Rome's civil wars were ended, Roman statesmen spoke of "Roman peace." Of course, Rome was very much engaged in conquest and expansion of its authority and power. For those conquered by Rome, life was hardly peaceful. Those whose beliefs were viewed as threats to the Roman peace found themselves in prison. That's where Paul was when he wrote to Titus, a pastor of a Christian church.

The kingdom of God is very different from the world we live in. Peace is found not in gathering land or spoils via war or bringing societies into submission. Peace is found, oddly enough, in the accomplishments of another—Jesus Christ. Titus wrote of "our great God and Savior Jesus Christ, who gave Himself for us, that He might redeem us" (Titus 2:13–14). Jesus' sacrificial death on the cross and subsequent resurrection made our means of salvation. How wonderful that such a kindly, loving God is our Source of peace. Every other source shall come up empty.

Avoid Dissension

9 But [a]avoid foolish disputes, genealogies,
contentions, and strivings about the law; for
they are unprofitable and useless. 10 [a]Reject
a divisive man after the first and second
admonition, 11 knowing that such a person is
warped and sinning, being self-condemned.

Final Messages

12 When I send Artemas to you, or [a]Tychi-
cus, be diligent to come to me at Nicopolis,
for I have decided to spend the winter there.
13 Send Zenas the lawyer and [a]Apollos on
their journey with haste, that they may lack
nothing. 14 And let our *people* also learn to
maintain good works, to *meet* urgent needs,
that they may not be unfruitful.

Farewell

15 All who *are* with me greet you. Greet
those who love us in the faith.

Grace *be* with you all. Amen.

3:9 [a] 2 Tim. 2:23 3:10 [a] Matt. 18:17 3:12 [a] Acts 20:4 3:13 [a] Acts 18:24

THE EPISTLE OF PAUL THE APOSTLE TO

PHILEMON

AUTHOR

Though some critics deny its authenticity, the general consensus of scholarship recognizes Philemon as Paul's work. There could have been no doctrinal motive for its forgery, and it is supported externally by consistent tradition and internally by no fewer than three references to Paul (Philem. vv. 1, 9, 19).

TIME

c. AD 60–61

KEY VERSE

Philemon vv. 16–17

THEME

Paul wrote this letter to a slave owner in the church at Colosse. Apparently Onesimus, the slave of Philemon, had stolen from him and had run away, an act punishable by death under Roman law. Onesimus had since met Paul and become a Christian. Paul's letter is a personal appeal to help them reconcile and renew their relationship.

In Philemon we learn how the peace of God brings freedom. According to Dr. J. Rufus Fears, not until the dawn of the Bible did ideas of universal freedom—freedom as a right for all people—begin to take hold. Closely related to Colossians, Philemon was probably written about the same time. In fact, it may have served as the cover letter for the longer letter. The main reason Paul wrote to Philemon, a man whom the apostle had converted, was to exhort him to let his runaway slave, Onesimus, return to him as a brother in the Lord. Although Paul did not directly attack the evils of slavery, his directions imply that, in Christ, such an institution has no place. This is the peace of God in action.

Greeting

Paul, a [a]prisoner of Christ Jesus, and Timothy *our* brother,

To Philemon our beloved *friend* and fellow
laborer, 2 to the beloved[1] Apphia, [a]Archip-
pus our fellow soldier, and to the church in
your house:

3 Grace to you and peace from God our
Father and the Lord Jesus Christ.

Philemon's Love and Faith

4 [a]I thank my God, making mention of
you always in my prayers, 5 [a]hearing of your
love and faith which you have toward the
Lord Jesus and toward all the saints, 6 that
the sharing of your faith may become effective [a]by the acknowledgment of [b]every good
thing which is in you[1] in Christ Jesus. 7 For
we have[1] great joy[2] and consolation in your
love, because the hearts of the saints have
been refreshed by you, brother.

The Plea for Onesimus

8 Therefore, though I might be very bold in
Christ to command you what is fitting, 9 *yet* for
love's sake I rather appeal *to you*—being such a
one as Paul, the aged, and now also a prisoner
of Jesus Christ— 10 I appeal to you for my son
[a]Onesimus, whom I have begotten *while* in
my chains, 11 who once was unprofitable to
you, but now is profitable to you and to me.
12 I am sending him back.[1] You therefore
receive him, that is, my own heart, 13 whom
I wished to keep with me, that on your behalf he might minister to me in my chains
for the gospel. 14 But without your consent I
wanted to do nothing, [a]that your good deed
might not be by compulsion, as it were, but
voluntary.
15 For perhaps he departed for a while for
this *purpose,* that you might receive him
forever, 16 no longer as a slave but more than
a slave—a beloved brother, especially to me
but how much more to you, both in the [a]flesh
and in the Lord.

Philemon's Obedience Encouraged

17 If then you count me as a partner, receive him as *you would* me. 18 But if he has
wronged you or owes anything, put that on
my account. 19 I, Paul, am writing with my
own [a]hand. I will repay—not to mention
to you that you owe me even your own self
besides. 20 Yes, brother, let me have joy from
you in the Lord; refresh my heart in the Lord.
21 [a]Having confidence in your obedience, I
write to you, knowing that you will do even
more than I say. 22 But, meanwhile, also prepare a guest room for me, for [a]I trust that
[b]through your prayers I shall be granted
to you.

Farewell

23 [a]Epaphras, my fellow prisoner in Christ
Jesus, greets you, 24 *as do* [a]Mark, [b]Aristarchus,
[c]Demas, [d]Luke, my fellow laborers.
25 [a]The grace of our Lord Jesus Christ *be*
with your spirit. Amen.

1 [a] Eph. 3:1 **2** [a] Col. 4:17 [1] NU-Text reads *to our sister Apphia.* **4** [a] 2 Thess. 1:3 **5** [a] Col. 1:4 **6** [a] Phil. 1:9 [b] [1 Thess. 5:18] [1] NU-Text and M-Text read *us.* **7** [1] NU-Text reads *had.* [2] M-Text reads *thanksgiving.* **10** [a] Col. 4:9 **12** [1] NU-Text reads *back to you in person, that is, my own heart.* **14** [a] 2 Cor. 9:7 **16** [a] Col. 3:22 **19** [a] 1 Cor. 16:21 **21** [a] 2 Cor. 7:16 **22** [a] Phil. 1:25; 2:24 [b] 2 Cor. 1:11 **23** [a] Col. 1:7; 4:12 **24** [a] Acts 12:12, 25; 15:37–39 [b] Acts 19:29; 27:2 [c] Col. 4:14 [d] 2 Tim. 4:11 **25** [a] 2 Tim. 4:22

THE EPISTLE TO THE

HEBREWS

AUTHOR

The origin of Hebrews is unknown. Uncertainty plagues not only its authorship but also its date and its readership. Hebrews 13:18–24 tells us that this book was not anonymous to the original readers; they evidently knew the author. For some reason, however, early church tradition is divided over the identity of the author. Part of the church attributed it to Paul, others preferred Barnabas, Luke, or Clement, and some chose anonymity. Some aspects of the language style and theology of Hebrews are very similar to Paul's epistles, but significant stylistic differences have led many biblical scholars to reject Pauline authorship of this book.

TIME

c. AD 64–68

KEY VERSE

Hebrews 4:14–16

THEME

Hebrews was written for a group of Jewish Christians who were thinking about returning to their original faith. The author goes to great lengths to convince them to stay with their new beliefs. Point by point he shows how Judaism was a foreshadowing of Christ. The new way is the superior way, as Christ and the faith that He established supersedes what has gone before. Understanding Jewish belief and practice and the roles of Moses and Aaron in biblical history are prerequisites to understanding Hebrews.

In this letter, the author warned and exhorted his readers who were slothful and despondent. Lacking enthusiasm for the faith, a desire to grow, and vital spiritual discernment, they often skipped assemblies and had even fallen prey to strange teaching. Now they were in danger of drifting away from the faith and thus incurring God's judgment. Peace to the rescue! The author urged his readers to continue in their faith: "Pursue peace . . . without which no one will see the Lord" (12:14). This is illustrated in the Hall of Faith in chapter 11, including faith in the God who brings peace, because, "without faith it is impossible to please Him" (11:6). In chapter 12 Jesus Himself is cited as the chief example of endurance and peace; the author of Hebrews said to look "unto Jesus, the author and finisher of our faith, who for the joy that was set before Him endured the cross" (v. 2). While Hebrews describes a people unfocused and failing, it also points the way to Jesus, Prince of Peace, and center of their faith. He would get them back in shape.

God's Supreme Revelation

1 God, who at various times and [a]in various
ways spoke in time past to the fathers by
the prophets, 2 has in these last days spoken
to us by *His* Son, whom He has appointed heir
of all things, through whom also He made
the worlds; 3 [a]who being the brightness of *His*
glory and the express [b]image of His person,
and [c]upholding all things by the word of His
power, [d]when He had by Himself[1] purged our[2]
sins, [e]sat down at the right hand of the Majesty on high, 4 having become so much better
than the angels, as [a]He has by inheritance
obtained a more excellent name than they.

The Son Exalted Above Angels

5 For to which of the angels did He ever say:

[a]"You are My Son,
Today I have begotten You"?[1]

And again:

[b]"I will be to Him a Father,
And He shall be to Me a Son"?[2]

6 But when He again brings [a]the firstborn
into the world, He says:

[b]"Let all the angels of God worship Him."[1]

7 And of the angels He says:

[a]"Who makes His angels spirits
And His ministers a flame of fire."[1]

8 But to the Son *He says:*

[a]"Your throne, O God, *is* forever and ever;
A scepter of righteousness *is* the
scepter of Your kingdom.
9 You have loved righteousness and
hated lawlessness;
Therefore God, Your God, [a]has
anointed You
With the oil of gladness more than
Your companions."[1]

10 And:

[a]"You, LORD, in the beginning laid the
foundation of the earth,
And the heavens are the work of Your
hands.
11 [a]They will perish, but You
remain;
And [b]they will all grow old like a
garment;
12 Like a cloak You will fold
them up,
And they will be changed.
But You are the [a]same,
And Your years will not fail."[1]

13 But to which of the angels has He ever
said:

[a]"Sit at My right hand,
Till I make Your enemies Your
footstool"?[1]

14 [a]Are they not all ministering spirits sent
forth to minister for those who will [b]inherit
salvation?

Do Not Neglect Salvation

2 Therefore we must give the more earnest heed to the things we have heard,
lest we drift away. 2 For if the word [a]spoken
through angels proved steadfast, and [b]every
transgression and disobedience received
a just reward, 3 [a]how shall we escape if we
neglect so great a salvation, [b]which at the
first began to be spoken by the Lord, and
was [c]confirmed to us by those who heard
Him, 4 [a]God also bearing witness [b]both with
signs and wonders, with various miracles,
and [c]gifts of the Holy Spirit, [d]according to
His own will?

PEACE NOTE

We must give careful attention to anything or anyone that robs us of the peace of God. Spiritual mindfulness on a daily basis prevents us from forgetting God's truth.

HEBREWS 2:1

1:1 [a] Num. 12:6, 8 1:3 [a] John 1:14 [b] 2 Cor. 4:4 [c] Col. 1:17 [d] [Heb. 7:27] [e] Ps. 110:1 [1] NU-Text omits *by Himself.* [2] NU-Text omits *our.* 1:4 [a] [Phil. 2:9, 10] 1:5 [a] Ps. 2:7 [b] 2 Sam. 7:14 [1] Psalm 2:7 [2] 2 Samuel 7:14 1:6 [a] [Rom. 8:29] [b] Deut. 32:43, LXX, DSS; Ps. 97:7 [1] Deuteronomy 32:43 (Septuagint, Dead Sea Scrolls); Psalm 97:7 1:7 [a] Ps. 104:4 [1] Psalm 104:4 1:8 [a] Ps. 45:6, 7 1:9 [a] Is. 61:1, 3 [1] Psalm 45:6, 7 1:10 [a] Ps. 102:25–27 1:11 [a] [Is. 34:4] [b] Is. 50:9; 51:6 1:12 [a] Heb. 13:8 [1] Psalm 102:25–27 1:13 [a] Ps. 110:1 [1] Psalm 110:1 1:14 [a] Ps. 103:20 [b] Rom. 8:17 2:2 [a] Acts 7:53 [b] Num. 15:30 2:3 [a] Heb. 10:28 [b] Matt. 4:17 [c] Luke 1:2 2:4 [a] Mark 16:20 [b] Acts 2:22, 43 [c] 1 Cor. 12:4, 7, 11 [d] Eph. 1:5, 9

The Son Made Lower than Angels

5 For He has not put [a]the world to come,
of which we speak, in subjection to angels.
6 But one testified in a certain place, saying:

[a]"What is man that You are mindful of
him,
Or the son of man that You take care of
him?
7 You have made him a little lower than
the angels;
You have crowned him with glory and
honor,[1]
And set him over the works of Your
hands.
8 [a]You have put all things in subjection
under his feet."[1]

For in that He put all in subjection under
him, He left nothing *that is* not put under
him. But now [b]we do not yet see all things
put under him. 9 But we see Jesus, [a]who was
made a little lower than the angels, for the
suffering of death [b]crowned with glory and
honor, that He, by the grace of God, might
taste death [c]for everyone.

Bringing Many Sons to Glory

10 For it was fitting for Him, [a]for whom
are all things and by whom *are* all things,
in bringing many sons to glory, to make the
captain of their salvation [b]perfect through
sufferings. 11 For [a]both He who sanctifies and
those who are being sanctified [b]*are* all of one,
for which reason [c]He is not ashamed to call
them brethren, 12 saying:

[a]"I will declare Your name to My brethren;
In the midst of the assembly I will sing
praise to You."[1]

13 And again:

[a]"I will put My trust in Him."[1]

And again:

[b]"Here am I and the children whom God
has given Me."[2]

14 Inasmuch then as the children have par-
taken of flesh and blood, He [a]Himself likewise
shared in the same, [b]that through death He
might destroy him who had the power of
[c]death, that is, the devil, 15 and release those
who [a]through fear of death were all their
lifetime subject to bondage. 16 For indeed He
does not give aid to angels, but He does give
aid to the seed of Abraham. 17 Therefore, in all
things He had [a]to be made like *His* brethren,
that He might be [b]a merciful and faithful High
Priest in things *pertaining* to God, to make
propitiation for the sins of the people. 18 [a]For
in that He Himself has suffered, being tempted, He is able to aid those who are tempted.

The Son Was Faithful

3 Therefore, holy brethren, partakers of the
heavenly calling, consider the Apostle and
High Priest of our confession, Christ Jesus,
2 who was faithful to Him who appointed Him,
as [a]Moses also *was faithful* in all His house.
3 For this One has been counted worthy of
more glory than Moses, inasmuch as [a]He
who built the house has more honor than the
house. 4 For every house is built by someone,
but [a]He who built all things *is* God. 5 [a]And
Moses indeed *was* faithful in all His house as
[b]a servant, [c]for a testimony of those things
which would be spoken *afterward,* 6 but Christ
as [a]a Son over His own house, [b]whose house
we are [c]if we hold fast the confidence and the
rejoicing of the hope firm to the end.[1]

Be Faithful

7 Therefore, as [a]the Holy Spirit says:

[b]"Today, if you will hear His voice,
8 Do not harden your hearts as in the
rebellion,
In the day of trial in the wilderness,
9 Where your fathers tested Me, tried Me,
And saw My works forty years.
10 Therefore I was angry with that
generation,
And said, 'They always go astray in
their heart,
And they have not known My ways.'
11 So I swore in My wrath,
'They shall not enter My rest.'"[1]

12 Beware, brethren, lest there be in any
of you an evil heart of unbelief in departing
from the living God; 13 but exhort one another
daily, while it is called "Today," lest any of you
be hardened through the deceitfulness of sin.

2:5 [a] [2 Pet. 3:13] **2:6** [a] Ps. 8:4–6 **2:7** [1] NU-Text and M-Text omit the rest of verse 7. **2:8** [a] Matt. 28:18 [b] 1 Cor. 15:25, 27 [1] Psalm 8:4–6 **2:9** [a] Phil. 2:7–9 [b] Acts 2:33; 3:13 [c] [John 3:16] **2:10** [a] Col. 1:16 [b] Heb. 5:8, 9; 7:28 **2:11** [a] Heb. 10:10 [b] Acts 17:26 [c] Matt. 28:10 **2:12** [a] Ps. 22:22 [1] Psalm 22:22 **2:13** [a] 2 Sam. 22:3; Is. 8:17 [b] Is. 8:18 [1] 2 Samuel 22:3; Isaiah 8:17 [2] Isaiah 8:18 **2:14** [a] John 1:14 [b] Col. 2:15 [c] 2 Tim. 1:10 **2:15** [a] [Luke 1:74] **2:17** [a] Phil. 2:7 [b] [Heb. 4:15; 5:1–10] **2:18** [a] [Heb. 4:15, 16] **3:2** [a] Num. 12:7 **3:3** [a] Zech. 6:12, 13 **3:4** [a] [Eph. 2:10] **3:5** [a] Heb. 3:2 [b] Ex. 14:31 [c] Deut. 18:15, 18, 19 **3:6** [a] Heb. 1:2 [b] [1 Cor. 3:16] [c] [Matt. 10:22] [1] NU-Text omits *firm to the end.* **3:7** [a] Acts 1:16 [b] Ps. 95:7–11 **3:11** [1] Psalm 95:7–11

14 For we have become partakers of Christ if
we hold the beginning of our confidence
steadfast to the end, 15 while it is said:

[a]"Today, if you will hear His voice,
Do not harden your hearts as in the
rebellion."[1]

Failure of the Wilderness Wanderers

16 [a]For who, having heard, rebelled? Indeed,
was it not all who came out of Egypt, *led* by
Moses? 17 Now with whom was He angry forty
years? *Was it* not with those who sinned,
[a]whose corpses fell in the wilderness? 18 And
[a]to whom did He swear that they would not
enter His rest, but to those who did not obey?
19 So we see that they could not enter in because of [a]unbelief.

The Promise of Rest

4 Therefore, since a promise remains of
entering His rest, [a]let us fear lest any
of you seem to have come short of it. 2 For
indeed the gospel was preached to us as well
as to them; but the word which they heard
did not profit them,[1] not being mixed with
faith in those who heard *it.* 3 For we who have
believed do enter that rest, as He has said:

[a]"So I swore in My wrath,
'They shall not enter My rest,' "[1]

although the works were finished from the
foundation of the world. 4 For He has spoken
in a certain place of the seventh *day* in this
way: [a]"And God rested on the seventh day
from all His works";[1] 5 and again in this *place:*
[a]"They shall not enter My rest."[1]
6 Since therefore it remains that some
must enter it, and those to whom it was first
preached did not enter because of disobedience, 7 again He designates a certain day,
saying in David, "Today," after such a long
time, as it has been said:

[a]"Today, if you will hear His voice,
Do not harden your hearts."[1]

8 For if Joshua had [a]given them rest, then
He would not afterward have spoken of another day. 9 There remains therefore a rest for
the people of God. 10 For he who has entered
His rest has himself also ceased from his
works as God *did* from His.

The Word Discovers Our Condition

11 [a]Let us therefore be diligent to enter that
rest, lest anyone fall according to the same
example of disobedience. 12 For the word of
God *is* [a]living and powerful, and [b]sharper than
any [c]two-edged sword, piercing even to the
division of soul and spirit, and of joints and
marrow, and is [d]a discerner of the thoughts
and intents of the heart. 13 [a]And there is no
creature hidden from His sight, but all things
are [b]naked and open to the eyes of Him to
whom we *must give* account.

Our Compassionate High Priest

14 Seeing then that we have a great [a]High
Priest who has passed through the heavens,
Jesus the Son of God, [b]let us hold fast *our* confession. 15 For [a]we do not have a High Priest
who cannot sympathize with our weaknesses,
but [b]was in all *points* tempted as *we are,* [c]*yet*
without sin. 16 [a]Let us therefore come boldly
to the throne of grace, that we may obtain
mercy and find grace to help in time of need.

PEACE NOTE

Jesus hurts when we hurt, especially when we are deceived like the religious folks whose religion keeps them from the true experience of peace with God.

HEBREWS 4:15

Qualifications for High Priesthood

5 For every high priest taken from among
men [a]is appointed for men in things *per-*
taining to God, that he may offer both gifts and
sacrifices for sins. 2 He can have compassion
on those who are ignorant and going astray,
since he himself is also subject to [a]weakness.
3 Because of this he is required as for the people, so also for [a]himself, to offer *sacrifices* for
sins. 4 And no man takes this honor to himself,
but he who is called by God, just as [a]Aaron *was.*

3:15 [a] Ps. 95:7, 8 [1] Psalm 95:7, 8 **3:16** [a] Num. 14:2, 11, 30 **3:17** [a] Num. 14:22, 23 **3:18** [a] Num. 14:30 **3:19** [a] 1 Cor. 10:11, 12
4:1 [a] Heb. 12:15 **4:2** [1] NU-Text and M-Text read *profit them, since they were not united by faith with those who heeded it.*
4:3 [a] Ps. 95:11 [1] Psalm 95:11 **4:4** [a] Gen. 2:2 [1] Genesis 2:2 **4:5** [a] Ps. 95:11 [1] Psalm 95:11 **4:7** [a] Ps. 95:7, 8 [1] Psalm 95:7, 8
4:8 [a] Josh. 22:4 **4:11** [a] 2 Pet. 1:10 **4:12** [a] Ps. 147:15 [b] Is. 49:2 [c] Eph. 6:17 [d] 1 Cor. 14:24, 25 **4:13** [a] Ps. 33:13–15; 90:8
[b] Job 26:6 **4:14** [a] Heb. 2:17; 7:26 [b] Heb. 10:23 **4:15** [a] Is. 53:3–5 [b] Luke 22:28 [c] 2 Cor. 5:21 **4:16** [a] [Eph. 2:18]
5:1 [a] Heb. 2:17; 8:3 **5:2** [a] Heb. 7:28 **5:3** [a] Lev. 9:7; 16:6 **5:4** [a] Ex. 28:1

A Priest Forever

5 [a]So also Christ did not glorify Himself to become High Priest, but *it was* He who said to Him:

[b]"You are My Son,
Today I have begotten You."[1]

6 As *He* also says in another *place:*

[a]"You *are* a priest forever
According to the order of
Melchizedek";[1]

7 who, in the days of His flesh, when He had [a]offered up prayers and supplications, [b]with vehement cries and tears to Him [c]who was able to save Him from death, and was heard [d]because of His godly fear, 8 though He was a Son, *yet* He learned [a]obedience by the things which He suffered. 9 And [a]having been perfected, He became the author of eternal salvation to all who obey Him, 10 called by God as High Priest [a]"according to the order of Melchizedek," 11 of whom [a]we have much to say, and hard to explain, since you have become [b]dull of hearing.

Spiritual Immaturity

12 For though by this time you ought to be teachers, you need *someone* to teach you again the first principles of the oracles of God; and you have come to need [a]milk and not solid food. 13 For everyone who partakes *only* of milk *is* unskilled in the word of righteousness, for he is [a]a babe. 14 But solid food belongs to those who are of full age, *that is,* those who by reason of use have their senses exercised [a]to discern both good and evil.

The Peril of Not Progressing

6 Therefore, [a]leaving the discussion of the elementary *principles* of Christ, let us go on to perfection, not laying again the foundation of repentance from [b]dead works and of faith toward God, 2 [a]of the doctrine of baptisms, [b]of laying on of hands, [c]of resurrection of the dead, [d]and of eternal judgment. 3 And this we will[1] do if God permits.

4 For *it is* impossible for those who were once enlightened, and have tasted [a]the heavenly gift, and [b]have become partakers of the Holy Spirit, 5 and have tasted the good word of God and the powers of the age to come, 6 if they fall away,[1] to renew them again to repentance, [a]since they crucify again for themselves the Son of God, and put *Him* to an open shame.

7 For the earth which drinks in the rain that often comes upon it, and bears herbs useful for those by whom it is cultivated, [a]receives blessing from God; 8 [a]but if it bears thorns and briers, *it is* rejected and near to being cursed, whose end *is* to be burned.

A Better Estimate

9 But, beloved, we are confident of better things concerning you, yes, things that accompany salvation, though we speak in this manner. 10 For [a]God *is* not unjust to forget [b]your work and labor of[1] love which you have shown toward His name, *in that* you have [c]ministered to the saints, and do minister. 11 And we desire that each one of you show the same diligence [a]to the full assurance of hope until the end, 12 that you do not become sluggish, but imitate those who through faith and patience [a]inherit the promises.

God's Infallible Purpose in Christ

13 For when God made a promise to Abraham, because He could swear by no one greater, [a]He swore by Himself, 14 saying, [a]"Surely blessing I will bless you, and multiplying I will multiply you."[1] 15 And so, after he had patiently endured, he obtained the [a]promise. 16 For men indeed swear by the greater, and [a]an oath for confirmation *is* for them an end of all dispute. 17 Thus God, determining to show more abundantly to [a]the heirs of promise [b]the immutability of His counsel, confirmed *it* by an oath, 18 that by two immutable things, in which it *is* impossible for God to [a]lie, we might[1] have strong consolation, who have fled for refuge to lay hold of the hope [b]set before *us.*

19 This *hope* we have as an anchor of the soul, both sure and steadfast, [a]and which enters the *Presence* behind the veil, 20 [a]where the forerunner has entered for us, *even* Jesus, [b]having become High Priest forever according to the order of Melchizedek.

5:5 [a] John 8:54 [b] Ps. 2:7 [1] Psalm 2:7 **5:6** [a] Ps. 110:4 [1] Psalm 110:4 **5:7** [a] Matt. 26:39, 42, 44 [b] Ps. 22:1 [c] Matt. 26:53 [d] Matt. 26:39 **5:8** [a] Phil. 2:8 **5:9** [a] Heb. 2:10 **5:10** [a] Ps. 110:4 **5:11** [a] [John 16:12] [b] [Matt. 13:15] **5:12** [a] 1 Cor. 3:1–3 **5:13** [a] Eph. 4:14 **5:14** [a] Is. 7:15 **6:1** [a] Heb. 5:12 [b] [Heb. 9:14] **6:2** [a] Acts 19:3–5 [b] [Acts 8:17] [c] Acts 17:31 [d] Acts 24:25 **6:3** [1] M-Text reads *let us do.* **6:4** [a] [John 4:10] [b] [Gal. 3:2, 5] **6:6** [a] Heb. 10:29 [1] Or *and have fallen away* **6:7** [a] Ps. 65:10 **6:8** [a] Is. 5:6 **6:10** [a] Rom. 3:4 [b] 1 Thess. 1:3 [c] Rom. 15:25 [1] NU-Text omits *labor of.* **6:11** [a] Col. 2:2 **6:12** [a] Heb. 10:36 **6:13** [a] Gen. 22:16, 17 **6:14** [a] Gen. 22:16, 17 [1] Genesis 22:17 **6:15** [a] Gen. 12:4; 21:5 **6:16** [a] Ex. 22:11 **6:17** [a] Heb. 11:9 [b] Rom. 11:29 **6:18** [a] Num. 23:19 [b] [Col. 1:5] [1] M-Text omits *might.* **6:19** [a] Lev. 16:2, 15 **6:20** [a] [Heb. 4:14] [b] Heb. 3:1; 5:10, 11

PEACE NOTE

Hope in God, as much as faith in God, is the hallmark of the believer's new life in Christ. Hope brings peace.

HEBREWS 6:19

The King of Righteousness

7 For this [a]Melchizedek, king of Salem,
priest of the Most High God, who met
Abraham returning from the slaughter of
the kings and blessed him, 2 to whom also
Abraham gave a tenth part of all, first being
translated "king of righteousness," and then
also king of Salem, meaning "king of peace,"
3 without father, without mother, without
genealogy, having neither beginning of days
nor end of life, but made like the Son of God,
remains a priest continually.
4 Now consider how great this man *was,*
to whom even the patriarch Abraham gave
a tenth of the spoils. 5 And indeed [a]those
who are of the sons of Levi, who receive the
priesthood, have a commandment to receive
tithes from the people according to the law,
that is, from their brethren, though they have
come from the loins of Abraham; 6 but he
whose genealogy is not derived from them
received tithes from Abraham [a]and blessed
[b]him who had the promises. 7 Now beyond
all contradiction the lesser is blessed by the
better. 8 Here mortal men receive tithes, but
there he *receives them,* [a]of whom it is witnessed that he lives. 9 Even Levi, who receives
tithes, paid tithes through Abraham, so to
speak, 10 for he was still in the loins of his
father when Melchizedek met him.

Need for a New Priesthood

11 [a]Therefore, if perfection were through the
Levitical priesthood (for under it the people
received the law), what further need *was there*
that another priest should rise according to
the order of Melchizedek, and not be called
according to the order of Aaron? 12 For the
priesthood being changed, of necessity there is
also a change of the law. 13 For He of whom these
things are spoken belongs to another tribe,
from which no man has officiated at the altar.
14 For *it is* evident that [a]our Lord arose from
[b]Judah, of which tribe Moses spoke nothing
concerning priesthood.[1] 15 And it is yet far
more evident if, in the likeness of Melchizedek, there arises another priest 16 who has
come, not according to the law of a fleshly
commandment, but according to the power
of an endless life. 17 For He testifies:[1]

[a]"You *are* a priest forever
According to the order of Melchizedek."[2]

18 For on the one hand there is an annul-
ling of the former commandment because
of [a]its weakness and unprofitableness, 19 for
[a]the law made nothing perfect; on the other
hand, *there is the* bringing in of [b]a better
hope, through which [c]we draw near to God.

Greatness of the New Priest

20 And inasmuch as *He was* not *made priest*
without an oath 21 (for they have become
priests without an oath, but He with an oath
by Him who said to Him:

[a]"The LORD has sworn
And will not relent,
'You *are* a priest forever[1]
According to the order of
Melchizedek' "),[2]

22 by so much more Jesus has become a surety of a [a]better covenant.
23 Also there were many priests, because
they were prevented by death from continuing. 24 But He, because He continues forever,
has an unchangeable priesthood. 25 Therefore
He is also [a]able to save to the uttermost those
who come to God through Him, since He
always lives [b]to make intercession for them.
26 For such a High Priest was fitting for us,
[a]*who is* holy, harmless, undefiled, separate
from sinners, [b]and has become higher than
the heavens; 27 who does not need daily, as
those high priests, to offer up sacrifices, first
for His [a]own sins and then for the people's,
for this He did once for all when He offered
up Himself. 28 For the law appoints as high
priests men who have weakness, but the word
of the oath, which came after the law, *appoints*
the Son who has been perfected forever.

7:1 [a] Gen. 14:18–20 **7:5** [a] Num. 18:21–26 **7:6** [a] Gen. 14:19, 20 [b] [Rom. 4:13] **7:8** [a] Heb. 5:6; 6:20 **7:11** [a] Heb. 7:18; 8:7 **7:14** [a] Is. 1:1 [b] Matt. 1:2 [1] NU-Text reads *priests.* **7:17** [a] Ps. 110:4 [1] NU-Text reads *it is testified.* [2] Psalm 110:4 **7:18** [a] [Rom. 8:3] **7:19** [a] [Acts 13:39] [b] Heb. 6:18, 19 [c] Rom. 5:2 **7:21** [a] Ps. 110:4 [1] NU-Text ends the quotation here. [2] Psalm 110:4 **7:22** [a] Heb. 8:6 **7:25** [a] Jude 24 [b] Rom. 8:34 **7:26** [a] Heb. 4:15 [b] Eph. 1:20 **7:27** [a] Lev. 9:7; 16:6

The New Priestly Service

8 Now *this is* the main point of the things
we are saying: We have such a High
Priest, [a]who is seated at the right hand of
the throne of the Majesty in the heavens,
2 a Minister of [a]the sanctuary and of [b]the
true tabernacle which the Lord erected, and
not man.

3 For [a]every high priest is appointed to offer
both gifts and sacrifices. Therefore [b]*it is* necessary that this One also have something to
offer. 4 For if He were on earth, He would not
be a priest, since there are priests who offer
the gifts according to the law; 5 who serve [a]the
copy and [b]shadow of the heavenly things, as
Moses was divinely instructed when he was
about to make the tabernacle. For He said,
[c]"See *that* you make all things according to
the pattern shown you on the mountain."[1]
6 But now [a]He has obtained a more excellent
ministry, inasmuch as He is also Mediator of
a [b]better covenant, which was established on
better promises.

A New Covenant

7 For if that [a]first *covenant* had been faultless, then no place would have been sought
for a second. 8 Because finding fault with
them, He says: [a]"Behold, the days are coming, says the LORD, when I will make a new
covenant with the house of Israel and with
the house of Judah— 9 not according to the
covenant that I made with their fathers in
the day when I took them by the hand to
lead them out of the land of Egypt; because
they did not continue in My covenant, and
I disregarded them, says the LORD. 10 For
this *is* the covenant that I will make with
the house of Israel after those days, says
the [a]LORD: I will put My laws in their mind
and write them on their hearts; and [b]I will
be their God, and they shall be My people.
11 [a]None of them shall teach his neighbor,
and none his brother, saying, 'Know the
[b]LORD,' for all shall know Me, from the least
of them to the greatest of them. 12 For I will
be merciful to their unrighteousness, [a]and
their sins and their lawless deeds[1] I will
remember no more."[2]

13 [a]In that He says, "A new *covenant*," He
has made the first obsolete. Now what is
becoming obsolete and growing old is ready
to vanish away.

The Earthly Sanctuary

9 Then indeed, even the first *covenant* had
ordinances of divine service and [a]the
earthly sanctuary. 2 For a tabernacle was
prepared: the first *part,* in which *was* the
lampstand, the table, and the showbread,
which is called the sanctuary; 3 [a]and behind
the second veil, the part of the tabernacle
which is called the Holiest of All, 4 which
had the [a]golden censer and [b]the ark of the
covenant overlaid on all sides with gold,
in which *were* [c]the golden pot that had the
manna, [d]Aaron's rod that budded, and [e]the
tablets of the covenant; 5 and [a]above it were
the cherubim of glory overshadowing the
mercy seat. Of these things we cannot now
speak in detail.

Limitations of the Earthly Service

6 Now when these things had been thus
prepared, [a]the priests always went into the
first part of the tabernacle, performing the
services. 7 But into the second part the high
priest *went* alone [a]once a year, not without
blood, which he offered for [b]himself and *for*
the people's sins *committed* in ignorance;
8 the Holy Spirit indicating this, that [a]the
way into the Holiest of All was not yet made
manifest while the first tabernacle was still
standing. 9 It *was* symbolic for the present
time in which both gifts and sacrifices are
offered [a]which cannot make him who performed the service perfect in regard to the
conscience— 10 *concerned* only with [a]foods
and drinks, [b]various washings, [c]and fleshly
ordinances imposed until the time of ref-
ormation.

The Heavenly Sanctuary

11 But Christ came *as* High Priest of [a]the
good things to come,[1] with the greater and
more perfect tabernacle not made with
hands, that is, not of this creation. 12 Not [a]with
the blood of goats and calves, but [b]with His
own blood He entered the Most Holy Place
[c]once for all, [d]having obtained eternal redemption. 13 For if [a]the blood of bulls and
goats and [b]the ashes of a heifer, sprinkling
the unclean, sanctifies for the purifying of
the flesh, 14 how much more shall the blood of
Christ, who through the eternal Spirit offered
Himself without spot to God, [a]cleanse your
conscience from [b]dead works [c]to serve the

8:1 [a] Col. 3:1 **8:2** [a] Heb. 9:8, 12 [b] Heb. 9:11, 24 **8:3** [a] Heb. 5:1; 8:4 [b] [Eph. 5:2] **8:5** [a] Heb. 9:23, 24 [b] Col. 2:17 [c] Ex. 25:40 [1] Exodus 25:40 **8:6** [a] [2 Cor. 3:6–8] [b] Heb. 7:22 **8:7** [a] Ex. 3:8; 19:5 **8:8** [a] Jer. 31:31–34 **8:10** [a] Jer. 31:33 [b] Zech. 8:8 **8:11** [a] Is. 54:13 [b] Jer. 31:34 **8:12** [a] Rom. 11:27 [1] NU-Text omits *and their lawless deeds.* [2] Jeremiah 31:31–34 **8:13** [a] [2 Cor. 5:17] **9:1** [a] Ex. 25:8 **9:3** [a] Ex. 26:31–35; 40:3 **9:4** [a] Lev. 16:12 [b] Ex. 25:10 [c] Ex. 16:33 [d] Num. 17:1–10 [e] Ex. 25:16; 34:29 **9:5** [a] Lev. 16:2 **9:6** [a] Num. 18:2–6; 28:3 **9:7** [a] Ex. 30:10 [b] Heb. 5:3 **9:8** [a] [John 14:6] **9:9** [a] Heb. 7:19 **9:10** [a] Col. 2:16 [b] Num. 19:7 [c] Eph. 2:15 **9:11** [a] Heb. 10:1 [1] NU-Text reads *that have come.* **9:12** [a] Heb. 10:4 [b] Eph. 1:7 [c] Zech. 3:9 [d] [Dan. 9:24] **9:13** [a] Lev. 16:14, 15 [b] Num. 19:2 **9:14** [a] 1 John 1:7 [b] Heb. 6:1 [c] Luke 1:74

living God? 15 And for this reason [a]He is the
Mediator of the new covenant, by means of
death, for the redemption of the transgressions under the first covenant, that [b]those
who are called may receive the promise of
the eternal inheritance.

The Mediator's Death Necessary

16 For where there *is* a testament, there
must also of necessity be the death of the testator. 17 For [a]a testament *is* in force after men
are dead, since it has no power at all while
the testator lives. 18 [a]Therefore not even the
first *covenant* was dedicated without blood.
19 For when Moses had spoken every precept
to all the people according to the law, [a]he took
the blood of calves and goats, [b]with water,
scarlet wool, and hyssop, and sprinkled both
the book itself and all the people, 20 saying,
[a]"This *is* the [b]blood of the covenant which
God has commanded you."[1] 21 Then likewise
[a]he sprinkled with blood both the tabernacle
and all the vessels of the ministry. 22 And
according to the law almost all things are
purified with blood, and [a]without shedding
of blood there is no remission.

Greatness of Christ's Sacrifice

23 Therefore *it was* necessary that [a]the
copies of the things in the heavens should be
purified with these, but the heavenly things
themselves with better sacrifices than these.
24 For [a]Christ has not entered the holy places
made with hands, *which are* copies of [b]the
true, but into heaven itself, now [c]to appear
in the presence of God for us; 25 not that He
should offer Himself often, as [a]the high priest
enters the Most Holy Place every year with
blood of another— 26 He then would have
had to suffer often since the foundation of
the world; but now, once at the end of the
ages, He has appeared to put away sin by the
sacrifice of Himself. 27 [a]And as it is appointed
for men to die once, [b]but after this the judgment, 28 so [a]Christ was [b]offered once to bear
the sins [c]of many. To those who [d]eagerly wait
for Him He will appear a second time, apart
from sin, for salvation.

Animal Sacrifices Insufficient

10 For the law, having a [a]shadow of the
good things to come, *and* not the very
image of the things, [b]can never with these
same sacrifices, which they offer continually
year by year, make those who approach perfect. 2 For then would they not have ceased to
be offered? For the worshipers, once purified,
would have had no more consciousness of
sins. 3 But in those *sacrifices there is* a reminder of sins every year. 4 For [a]*it is* not possible
that the blood of bulls and goats could take
away sins.

Christ's Death Fulfills God's Will

5 Therefore, when He came into the world,
He said:

[a]"Sacrifice and offering You did not
desire,
But a body You have prepared for Me.
6 In burnt offerings and *sacrifices* for
sin
You had no pleasure.
7 Then I said, 'Behold, I have come—
In the volume of the book it is written
of Me—
To do Your will, O God.' "[1]

8 Previously saying, "Sacrifice and offering,
burnt offerings, and *offerings* for sin You did
not desire, nor had pleasure *in them*" (which
are offered according to the law), 9 then He
said, "Behold, I have come to do Your will,
O God."[1] He takes away the first that He may
establish the second. 10 [a]By that will we have
been sanctified [b]through the offering of the
body of Jesus Christ once *for all.*

Christ's Death Perfects the Sanctified

11 And every priest stands [a]ministering
daily and offering repeatedly the same sacrifices, which can never take away sins. 12 [a]But
this Man, after He had offered one sacrifice
for sins forever, sat down [b]at the right hand
of God, 13 from that time waiting [a]till His enemies are made His footstool. 14 For by one
offering He has perfected forever those who
are being sanctified.

15 But the Holy Spirit also witnesses to us;
for after He had said before,

16 [a]"This *is* the covenant that I will make
with them after those days, says the LORD:
I will put My laws into their hearts, and in
their minds I will write them,"[1] 17 *then He
adds,* [a]"Their sins and their lawless deeds I
will remember no more."[1] 18 Now where there
is remission of these, *there is* no longer an
offering for sin.

9:15 [a] Rom. 3:25 [b] Heb. 3:1 **9:17** [a] Gal. 3:15 **9:18** [a] Ex. 24:6 **9:19** [a] Ex. 24:5, 6 [b] Lev. 14:4, 7 **9:20** [a] [Matt. 26:28] [b] Ex. 24:3–8 [1] Exodus 24:8 **9:21** [a] Ex. 29:12, 36 **9:22** [a] Lev. 17:11 **9:23** [a] Heb. 8:5 **9:24** [a] Heb. 6:20 [b] Heb. 8:2 [c] Rom. 8:34 **9:25** [a] Heb. 9:7 **9:27** [a] Gen. 3:19 [b] [2 Cor. 5:10] **9:28** [a] Rom. 6:10 [b] 1 Pet. 2:24 [c] Matt. 26:28 [d] Titus 2:13 **10:1** [a] Heb. 8:5 [b] Heb. 7:19; 9:9 **10:4** [a] Mic. 6:6, 7 **10:5** [a] Ps. 40:6–8 **10:7** [1] Psalm 40:6–8 **10:9** [1] NU-Text and M-Text omit *O God.* **10:10** [a] John 17:19 [b] [Heb. 9:12] **10:11** [a] Num. 28:3 **10:12** [a] Col. 3:1 [b] Ps. 110:1 **10:13** [a] Ps. 110:1 **10:16** [a] Jer. 31:33, 34 [1] Jeremiah 31:33 **10:17** [a] Jer. 31:34 [1] Jeremiah 31:34

Hold Fast Your Confession

19 Therefore, brethren, having [a]boldness
to enter [b]the Holiest by the blood of Jesus,
20 by a new and [a]living way which He consecrated for us, through the veil, that is, His
flesh, 21 and *having* a High Priest over the
house of God, 22 let us [a]draw near with a true
heart [b]in full assurance of faith, having our
hearts sprinkled from an evil conscience and
our bodies washed with pure water. 23 Let us
hold fast the confession of *our* hope without
wavering, for [a]He who promised *is* faithful.
24 And let us consider one another in order to
stir up love and good works, 25 [a]not forsaking
the assembling of ourselves together, as *is* the
manner of some, but exhorting *one another,*
and [b]so much the more as you see [c]the Day
approaching.

The Just Live by Faith

26 For [a]if we sin willfully [b]after we have
received the knowledge of the truth, there
[c]no longer remains a sacrifice for sins, 27 but
a certain fearful expectation of judgment,
and [a]fiery indignation which will devour the
adversaries. 28 Anyone who has rejected Moses' law dies without mercy on *the testimony*
of two or three [a]witnesses. 29 [a]Of how much
worse punishment, do you suppose, will he
be thought worthy who has trampled the Son
of God underfoot, [b]counted the blood of the
covenant by which he was sanctified a common thing, [c]and insulted the Spirit of grace?
30 For we know Him who said, [a]"Vengeance
is Mine, I will repay,"[1] says the Lord.[2] And
again, [b]"The LORD will judge His people."[3]
31 [a]It is a fearful thing to fall into the hands
of the living God.

32 But [a]recall the former days in which,
after you were illuminated, you endured
a great struggle with sufferings: 33 partly
while you were made [a]a spectacle both by
reproaches and tribulations, and partly
while [b]you became companions of those
who were so treated; 34 for you had compassion on me[1] [a]in my chains, and [b]joyfully
accepted the plundering of your goods,
knowing that [c]you have a better and an
enduring possession for yourselves in
heaven.[2] 35 Therefore do not cast away your
confidence, [a]which has great reward. 36 [a]For
you have need of endurance, so that after
you have done the will of God, [b]you may
receive the promise:

37 "For [a]yet a little while,
And [b]He[1] who is coming will come and
will not tarry.
38 Now [a]the[1] just shall live by faith;
But if *anyone* draws back,
My soul has no pleasure in
him."[2]

39 But we are not of those [a]who draw back to
perdition, but of those who [b]believe to the
saving of the soul.

PEACE NOTE

We were designed to thrive in
community. There is no greater
peace than that experienced
among the people of God, both
now and for all eternity.

HEBREWS 10:25

10:19 [a] [Eph. 2:18] [b] Heb. 9:8, 12 **10:20** [a] John 14:6 **10:22** [a] Heb. 7:19; 10:1 [b] Eph. 3:12 **10:23** [a] 1 Cor. 1:9; 10:13 **10:25** [a] Acts 2:42 [b] Rom. 13:11 [c] Phil. 4:5 **10:26** [a] Num. 15:30 [b] 2 Pet. 2:20 [c] Heb. 6:6 **10:27** [a] Zeph. 1:18 **10:28** [a] Deut. 17:2–6; 19:15 **10:29** [a] [Heb. 2:3] [b] 1 Cor. 11:29 [c] [Matt. 12:31] **10:30** [a] Deut. 32:35 [b] Deut. 32:36 [1] Deuteronomy 32:35 [2] NU-Text omits *says the Lord.* [3] Deuteronomy 32:36 **10:31** [a] [Luke 12:5] **10:32** [a] Gal. 3:4 **10:33** [a] 1 Cor. 4:9 [b] Phil. 1:7 **10:34** [a] 2 Tim. 1:16 [b] Matt. 5:12 [c] Matt. 6:20 [1] NU-Text reads *the prisoners* instead of *me in my chains.* [2] NU-Text omits *in heaven.* **10:35** [a] Matt. 5:12 **10:36** [a] Luke 21:19 [b] [Col. 3:24] **10:37** [a] Luke 18:8 [b] Hab. 2:3, 4 [1] Or *that which* **10:38** [a] Rom. 1:17 [1] NU-Text reads *My just one.* [2] Habakkuk 2:3, 4 **10:39** [a] 2 Pet. 2:20 [b] Acts 16:31

> **PEACE NOTE**
>
> Let's be clear: faith is faith because it's based on belief in what we don't yet see. I have God's peace by trusting and waiting on the Lord.
>
> HEBREWS 11:1

By Faith We Understand

11 Now faith is the substance of things hoped for, the evidence [a]of things not seen. 2 For by it the elders obtained a *good* testimony.

3 By faith we understand that [a]the worlds were framed by the word of God, so that the things which are seen were not made of things which are visible.

Faith at the Dawn of History

4 By faith [a]Abel offered to God a more excellent sacrifice than Cain, through which he obtained witness that he was righteous, God testifying of his gifts; and through it he being dead still [b]speaks.

5 By faith Enoch was taken away so that he did not see death, [a]"and was not found, because God had taken him";[1] for before he was taken he had this testimony, that he pleased God. 6 But without faith *it is* impossible to please *Him,* for he who comes to God must believe that He is, and *that* He is a rewarder of those who diligently seek Him.

7 By faith [a]Noah, being divinely warned of things not yet seen, moved with godly fear, [b]prepared an ark for the saving of his household, by which he condemned the world and became heir of [c]the righteousness which is according to faith.

Faithful Abraham

8 By faith [a]Abraham obeyed when he was called to go out to the place which he would receive as an inheritance. And he went out, not knowing where he was going. 9 By faith he dwelt in the land of promise as *in* a foreign country, [a]dwelling in tents with Isaac and Jacob, [b]the heirs with him of the same promise; 10 for he waited for [a]the city which has foundations, [b]whose builder and maker *is* God.

11 By faith [a]Sarah herself also received strength to conceive seed, and [b]she bore a child[1] when she was past the age, because she judged Him [c]faithful who had promised. 12 Therefore from one man, and him as good as [a]dead, were born *as many* as the [b]stars of the sky in multitude—innumerable as the sand which is by the seashore.

The Heavenly Hope

13 These all died in faith, [a]not having received the [b]promises, but [c]having seen them afar off were assured of them,[1] embraced *them* and [d]confessed that they were strangers and pilgrims on the earth. 14 For those who say such things [a]declare plainly that they seek a homeland. 15 And truly if they had called to mind [a]that *country* from which they had come out, they would have had opportunity to return. 16 But now they desire a better, that is, a heavenly *country.* Therefore God is not ashamed [a]to be called their God, for He has [b]prepared a city for them.

The Faith of the Patriarchs

17 By faith Abraham, [a]when he was tested, offered up Isaac, and he who had received the promises offered up his only begotten *son,* 18 of whom it was said, [a]"In Isaac your seed shall be called,"[1] 19 concluding that God [a]*was* able to raise *him* up, even from the dead, from which he also received him in a figurative sense.

20 By faith [a]Isaac blessed Jacob and Esau concerning things to come.

21 By faith Jacob, when he was dying, [a]blessed each of the sons of Joseph, and worshiped, *leaning* on the top of his staff.

22 By faith [a]Joseph, when he was dying, made mention of the departure of the children of Israel, and gave instructions concerning his bones.

The Faith of Moses

23 By faith [a]Moses, when he was born, was hidden three months by his parents, because they saw *he was* a beautiful child; and they were not afraid of the king's [b]command.

11:1 [a] Rom. 8:24 **11:3** [a] Ps. 33:6 **11:4** [a] Gen. 4:3–5 [b] Heb. 12:24 **11:5** [a] Gen. 5:21–24 [1] Genesis 5:24 **11:7** [a] Gen. 6:13–22 [b] 1 Pet. 3:20 [c] Rom. 3:22 **11:8** [a] Gen. 12:1–4 **11:9** [a] Gen. 12:8; 13:3, 18; 18:1, 9 [b] Heb. 6:17 **11:10** [a] [Heb. 12:22; 13:14] [b] [Rev. 21:10] **11:11** [a] Gen. 17:19; 18:11–14; 21:1, 2 [b] Luke 1:36 [c] Heb. 10:23 [1] NU-Text omits *she bore a child.* **11:12** [a] Rom. 4:19 [b] Gen. 15:5; 22:17; 32:12 **11:13** [a] Heb. 11:39 [b] Gen. 12:7 [c] John 8:56 [d] Ps. 39:12 [1] NU-Text and M-Text omit *were assured of them.* **11:14** [a] Heb. 13:14 **11:15** [a] Gen. 11:31 **11:16** [a] Ex. 3:6, 15; 4:5 [b] [Rev. 21:2] **11:17** [a] James 2:21 **11:18** [a] Gen. 21:12 [1] Genesis 21:12 **11:19** [a] Rom. 4:17 **11:20** [a] Gen. 27:26–40 **11:21** [a] Gen. 48:1, 5, 16, 20 **11:22** [a] Gen. 50:24, 25 **11:23** [a] Ex. 2:1–3 [b] Ex. 1:16, 22

[24]By faith [a]Moses, when he became of age,
refused to be called the son of Pharaoh's
daughter, [25]choosing rather to suffer affliction with the people of God than to enjoy the
passing pleasures of sin, [26]esteeming [a]the
reproach of Christ greater riches than the treasures in[1] Egypt; for he looked to the [b]reward.
[27]By faith [a]he forsook Egypt, not fearing
the wrath of the king; for he endured as seeing Him who is invisible. [28]By faith [a]he kept
the Passover and the sprinkling of blood,
lest he who destroyed the firstborn should
touch them.
[29]By faith [a]they passed through the Red
Sea as by dry *land, whereas* the Egyptians,
attempting to do so, were drowned.

By Faith They Overcame

[30]By faith [a]the walls of Jericho fell down
after they were encircled for seven days. [31]By
faith [a]the harlot Rahab did not perish with
those who did not believe, when [b]she had
received the spies with peace.
[32]And what more shall I say? For the time
would fail me to tell of [a]Gideon and [b]Barak and
[c]Samson and [d]Jephthah, also *of* [e]David and
[f]Samuel and the prophets: [33]who through faith
subdued kingdoms, worked righteousness,
obtained promises, [a]stopped the mouths of
lions, [34][a]quenched the violence of fire, escaped
the edge of the sword, out of weakness were
made strong, became valiant in battle, turned
to flight the armies of the aliens. [35][a]Women
received their dead raised to life again.
Others were [b]tortured, not accepting deliverance, that they might obtain a better
resurrection. [36]Still others had trial of mock-
ings and scourgings, yes, and [a]of chains and
imprisonment. [37][a]They were stoned, they
were sawn in two, were tempted,[1] were slain
with the sword. [b]They wandered about [c]in
sheepskins and goatskins, being destitute,
afflicted, tormented— [38]of whom the world
was not worthy. They wandered in deserts and
mountains, [a]*in* dens and caves of the earth.
[39]And all these, [a]having obtained a good
testimony through faith, did not receive the
promise, [40]God having provided something
better for us, that they should not be [a]made
perfect apart from us.

The Race of Faith

12 Therefore we also, since we are surrounded by so great a cloud of witnesses, [a]let us lay aside every weight, and
the sin which so easily ensnares *us,* and [b]let

11:24 [a] Ex. 2:11–15 **11:26** [a] Heb. 13:13 [b] Rom. 8:18 [1] NU-Text and M-Text read *of.* **11:27** [a] Ex. 10:28 **11:28** [a] Ex. 12:21 **11:29** [a] Ex. 14:22–29 **11:30** [a] Josh. 6:20 **11:31** [a] Josh. 2:9; 6:23 [b] Josh. 2:1 **11:32** [a] Judg. 6:11; 7:1–25 [b] Judg. 4:6–24 [c] Judg. 13:24—16:31 [d] Judg. 11:1–29; 12:1–7 [e] 1 Sam. 16; 17 [f] 1 Sam. 7:9–14 **11:33** [a] Dan. 6:22 **11:34** [a] Dan. 3:23–28 **11:35** [a] 1 Kin. 17:22 [b] Acts 22:25 **11:36** [a] Gen. 39:20 **11:37** [a] 1 Kin. 21:13 [b] 2 Kin. 1:8 [c] Zech. 13:4 [1] NU-Text omits *were tempted.* **11:38** [a] 1 Kin. 18:4, 13; 19:9 **11:39** [a] Heb. 11:2, 13 **11:40** [a] Heb. 5:9 **12:1** [a] Col. 3:8 [b] 1 Cor. 9:24

FROM TRUST TO TRIUMPH

By faith the harlot Rahab did not perish with those who did not believe, when she had received the spies with peace.

HEBREWS 11:31

A Canaanite prostitute named Rahab made a tough decision. She recognized that God was with the approaching Israelites. But she didn't just believe it; she acted on it. At considerable risk to herself, she hid the Israelite spies, and when the walls of Jericho collapsed and the Israelite army entered the city, she was saved.

We can only guess what her life had been like before the arrival of the people of Israel. We may assume that she had had enough of pagan society and the misery that went with it. She sensed something very different about the God of Israel and decided to embrace Him. I believe she then found lasting peace.

You can make the same choice. We will never have total knowledge of a situation, but to live in the peace of God, we have to trust that the Lord has revealed enough for us to trust Him no matter what. All faith is a risk assessment. Rahab had to make a quick decision, and quick decisions are never easy. Let's focus on what we know and not on what we don't. God has revealed enough about Himself for us to trust Him and, like Rahab, act "by faith" (v. 31) and be blessed.

TWO WORDS

And all these . . . obtained a good testimony through faith.

HEBREWS 11:39

All the heroes of Scripture faced enormous obstacles and deadly threats. You can see this in the verses describing their exploits in Hebrews 11. These men and women "subdued kingdoms, worked righteousness, obtained promises, stopped the mouths of lions" (v. 33)—and the list goes on! "They were stoned, they were sawn in two, were tempted, were slain with the sword" (v. 37). How many of us could develop "a good testimony" through all of that?

You don't have to be heroic to face the worst of the world. Hebrews' author tells us how to do it in two words: "through faith." Romans 10:17 promises, "Faith comes by hearing and hearing by the word of God." The most effective way to increase our faith is to ring out the sponge of God's Word on our hearts and minds each day and then speak it with our lips! What hardships weigh on you today? Practicing faith will drive you away from despair and toward a good testimony. Those heroes did it; you can too. And peace is part of the deal.

PEACE NOTE

Take the next logical step. Keep moving in the direction of your faith. Endurance brings more and more peace because we have more experience with God's reliability.

HEBREWS 12:1

us run [c]with endurance the race that is set
before us, 2 looking unto Jesus, the author
and finisher of *our* faith, [a]who for the joy
that was set before Him [b]endured the cross,
despising the shame, and [c]has sat down at
the right hand of the throne of God.

The Discipline of God

3 [a]For consider Him who endured such hostility from sinners against Himself, [b]lest you
become weary and discouraged in your souls.
4 [a]You have not yet resisted to bloodshed, striving against sin. 5 And you have forgotten the
exhortation which speaks to you as to sons:

[a]"My son, do not despise the chastening
of the LORD,
Nor be discouraged when you are
rebuked by Him;
6 For [a]whom the LORD loves He chastens,
And scourges every son whom He
receives."[1]

7 [a]If[1] you endure chastening, God deals
with you as with sons; for what [b]son is there
whom a father does not chasten? 8 But if you
are without chastening, [a]of which all have become partakers, then you are illegitimate and
not sons. 9 Furthermore, we have had human
fathers who corrected *us,* and we paid *them*
respect. Shall we not much more readily be in
subjection to [a]the Father of spirits and live?
10 For they indeed for a few days chastened *us*
as seemed *best* to them, but He for *our* profit,
[a]that *we* may be partakers of His holiness.
11 Now no chastening seems to be joyful for the
present, but painful; nevertheless, afterward
it yields [a]the peaceable fruit of righteousness
to those who have been trained by it.

Renew Your Spiritual Vitality

12 Therefore [a]strengthen the hands which
hang down, and the feeble knees, 13 and make
straight paths for your feet, so that what is lame
may not be dislocated, but rather be healed.
14 [a]Pursue peace with all *people,* and holiness,
[b]without which no one will see the Lord: 15 looking carefully lest anyone [a]fall short of the grace

12:1 [c] Rom. 12:12 **12:2** [a] Luke 24:26 [b] Phil. 2:8 [c] Ps. 110:1 **12:3** [a] Matt. 10:24 [b] Gal. 6:9 **12:4** [a] [1 Cor. 10:13] **12:5** [a] Prov. 3:11, 12 **12:6** [a] Rev. 3:19 [1] Proverbs 3:11, 12 **12:7** [a] Deut. 8:5 [b] Prov. 13:24; 19:18; 23:13 [1] NU-Text and M-Text read *It is for discipline that you endure; God . . . .* **12:8** [a] 1 Pet. 5:9 **12:9** [a] [Job 12:10] **12:10** [a] Lev. 11:44 **12:11** [a] James 3:17, 18 **12:12** [a] Is. 35:3 **12:14** [a] Ps. 34:14 [b] Matt. 5:8 **12:15** [a] Heb. 4:1

of God; lest any [b]root of bitterness springing up cause trouble, and by this many become defiled; 16 lest there *be* any [a]fornicator or profane person like Esau, [b]who for one morsel of food sold his birthright. 17 For you know that afterward, when he wanted to inherit the blessing, he was [a]rejected, for he found no place for repentance, though he sought it diligently with tears.

The Glorious Company

18 For you have not come to [a]the mountain that[1] may be touched and that burned with fire, and to blackness and darkness[2] and tempest, 19 and the sound of a trumpet and the voice of words, so that those who heard *it* [a]begged that the word should not be spoken to them anymore. 20 (For they could not endure what was commanded: [a]"And if so much as a beast touches the mountain, it shall be stoned[1] or shot with an arrow."[2] 21 And so terrifying was the sight *that* Moses said, [a]"I am exceedingly afraid and trembling."[1])

22 But you have come to Mount Zion and to the city of the living God, the heavenly Jerusalem, to an innumerable company of angels, 23 to the general assembly and church of [a]the firstborn [b]*who are* registered in heaven, to God [c]the Judge of all, to the spirits of just men [d]made perfect, 24 to Jesus [a]the Mediator of the new covenant, and to [b]the blood of sprinkling that speaks better things [c]than *that of* Abel.

Hear the Heavenly Voice

25 See that you do not refuse Him who speaks. For [a]if they did not escape who refused Him who spoke on earth, much more *shall we not escape* if we turn away from Him who *speaks* from heaven, 26 whose voice then shook the earth; but now He has promised, saying, [a]"Yet once more I shake[1] not only the earth, but also heaven."[2] 27 Now this, "Yet once more," indicates the [a]removal of those things that are being shaken, as of things that are made, that the things which cannot be shaken may remain.

28 Therefore, since we are receiving a kingdom which cannot be shaken, let us have grace, by which we may[1] [a]serve God acceptably with reverence and godly fear. 29 For [a]our God *is* a consuming fire.

Concluding Moral Directions

13 Let [a]brotherly love continue. 2 [a]Do not forget to entertain strangers, for by so *doing* [b]some have unwittingly entertained angels. 3 [a]Remember the prisoners as if chained with them—those who are mistreated—since you yourselves are in the body also.

12:15 [b] Deut. 29:18 **12:16** [a] [1 Cor. 6:13–18] [b] Gen. 25:33 **12:17** [a] Gen. 27:30–40 **12:18** [a] Deut. 4:11; 5:22 [1] NU-Text reads *to that which.* [2] NU-Text reads *gloom.* **12:19** [a] Ex. 20:18–26 **12:20** [a] Ex. 19:12, 13 [1] NU-Text and M-Text omit the rest of this verse. [2] Exodus 19:12, 13 **12:21** [a] Deut. 9:19 [1] Deuteronomy 9:19 **12:23** [a] [James 1:18] [b] Luke 10:20 [c] Ps. 50:6; 94:2 [d] [Phil. 3:12] **12:24** [a] Heb. 8:6; 9:15 [b] Ex. 24:8 [c] Gen. 4:10 **12:25** [a] Heb. 2:2, 3 **12:26** [a] Hag. 2:6 [1] NU-Text reads *will shake.* [2] Haggai 2:6 **12:27** [a] [Is. 34:4; 54:10; 65:17] **12:28** [a] Heb. 13:15, 21 [1] M-Text omits *may.* **12:29** [a] Ex. 24:17 **13:1** [a] Rom. 12:10 **13:2** [a] Matt. 25:35 [b] Gen. 18:1–22; 19:1 **13:3** [a] Matt. 25:36

ANGELIC ENCOUNTERS

Do not forget to entertain strangers, for by so doing some have unwittingly entertained angels.

HEBREWS 13:2

Have you ever experienced God's protection in your life? Would a situation have turned out differently without God's intervention? I firmly believe I experienced an angel's help after an automobile accident. This verse says, "Some have unwittingly entertained angels." My father and I were in a head-on collision. We finally came to a screeching stop against a median, and an eerie silence filled the vehicle. I began to panic. My father looked dead. His head was awkwardly leaning against the headrest, his mouth was open, and he wasn't moving.

I screamed. It felt like a bad dream. The powder from the airbags made me think our car was about to explode. Suddenly, the car door was yanked open by an African American man who pulled me and my father out of the wreck. We had both survived. After emergency services arrived, no one saw the man who helped us. This reminds me that sometimes we experience the peace and help of God through angels.

Consider whether you may have experienced an angelic encounter. One reason we can experience God's *shalom* and happiness in our lives is that we have God's divine protection.

PEACE NOTE

A peace-filled thought: Jesus will never, never, never, never, never, never leave or forsake you. God is faithful. God is good. God is loving. God is reliable.

HEBREWS 13:5

4 [a]Marriage *is* honorable among all, and the bed undefiled; [b]but fornicators and adulterers God will judge.

5 *Let your* conduct *be* without covetousness; *be* content with such things as you have. For He Himself has said, [a]"I will never leave you nor forsake you."[1] 6 So we may boldly say:

[a]"The LORD *is* my helper;
I will not fear.
What can man do to me?"[1]

Concluding Religious Directions

7 Remember those who rule over you, who have spoken the word of God to you, whose faith follow, considering the outcome of *their* conduct. 8 Jesus Christ *is* [a]the same yesterday, today, and forever. 9 Do not be carried about[1] with various and strange doctrines. For *it is* good that the heart be established by grace, not with foods which have not profited those who have been occupied with them.

10 We have an altar from which those who serve the tabernacle have no right to eat. 11 For the bodies of those animals, whose blood is brought into the sanctuary by the high priest for sin, are burned outside the camp. 12 Therefore Jesus also, that He might sanctify the people with His own blood, suffered outside the gate. 13 Therefore let us go forth to Him, outside the camp, bearing [a]His reproach. 14 For here we have no continuing city, but we seek the one to come. 15 [a]Therefore by Him let us continually offer [b]the sacrifice of praise to God, that is, [c]the fruit of *our* lips, giving thanks to His name. 16 [a]But do not forget to do good and to share, for [b]with such sacrifices God is well pleased.

17 [a]Obey those who rule over you, and be submissive, for [b]they watch out for your souls, as those who must give account. Let them do so with joy and not with grief, for that would be unprofitable for you.

Prayer Requested

18 [a]Pray for us; for we are confident that we have [b]a good conscience, in all things desiring to live honorably. 19 But I especially urge *you* to do this, that I may be restored to you the sooner.

Benediction, Final Exhortation, Farewell

20 Now may [a]the God of peace [b]who brought up our Lord Jesus from the dead, [c]that great Shepherd of the sheep, [d]through the blood of the everlasting covenant, 21 make you complete in every good work to do His will, [a]working in you[1] what is well pleasing in His sight, through Jesus Christ, to whom *be* glory forever and ever. Amen.

22 And I appeal to you, brethren, bear with the word of exhortation, for I have written to you in few words. 23 Know that *our* brother Timothy has been set free, with whom I shall see you if he comes shortly.

24 Greet all those who rule over you, and all the saints. Those from Italy greet you.

25 Grace *be* with you all. Amen.

PEACE NOTE

The God of peace brought Jesus back from the dead. The peace of God will raise me up when I feel as if I cannot go on.

HEBREWS 13:20

13:4 [a] Prov. 5:18, 19 [b] 1 Cor. 6:9 **13:5** [a] Deut. 31:6, 8; Josh. 1:5 [1] Deuteronomy 31:6, 8; Joshua 1:5 **13:6** [a] Ps. 27:1; 118:6 [1] Psalm 118:6 **13:8** [a] Heb. 1:12 **13:9** [1] NU-Text and M-Text read *away.* **13:13** [a] 1 Pet. 4:14 **13:15** [a] Eph. 5:20 [b] Lev. 7:12 [c] Hos. 14:2 **13:16** [a] Rom. 12:13 [b] Phil. 4:18 **13:17** [a] Phil. 2:29 [b] Ezek. 3:17 **13:18** [a] Eph. 6:19 [b] Acts 23:1 **13:20** [a] Rom. 5:1, 2, 10; 15:33 [b] Rom. 4:24 [c] 1 Pet. 2:25; 5:4 [d] Zech. 9:11 **13:21** [a] Phil. 2:13 [1] NU-Text and M-Text read *us.*

THE EPISTLE OF

JAMES

AUTHOR

Four men are named James in the New Testament, one of which is the Lord's brother (Matt. 13:55; Mark 6:3; Gal. 1:19). Tradition points to this prominent figure as the author of the epistle, and this best fits the evidence of Scripture. The brevity and limited doctrinal emphasis of James kept it from wide circulation, and by the time it became known in the church as a whole, there was uncertainty about the identity of the "James" in James 1:1. Growing recognition that it was written by the Lord's brother led to its acceptance as a canonical book.

TIME

c. AD 46–49

KEY VERSE

James 1:19–22

THEME

The Book of James is for the practical person. While most of Paul's epistles have a theological and practical focus, there isn't much theoretical or systematic theology in this book. The subject matter covered in James includes the issues we face daily if not hourly: How do we respond to trials and temptation? What are we doing with our money? Do we keep our tongues under control? Are we acting on our faith? What are we doing with our prayer lives? The main point of all these questions James raises is that saving faith needs to result in changed behavior.

James, the earthly brother of Jesus, provided one of the oldest New Testament writings. Functionally, this helpful letter could be a commentary to Jesus' Sermon on the Mount (Matt. 5–7). How do we live in peace? James let us know: "The fruit of righteousness is sown in peace by those who make peace" (James 3:18). It does no good to say to a neighbor, "Depart in peace, be warmed and filled," and then to withhold the things they need to do so (2:16). The lesson: if you wish peace for someone, give him the tools he needs to obtain it. The peace of God is always practical, reachable, applicable, and achievable. Those who find the peace of God must not only continue in it but, like a farmer, they must sow the peace of God to everyone, everywhere in order to see a harvest.

Greeting to the Twelve Tribes

1 James, [a]a bondservant of God and of the Lord Jesus Christ,

To the twelve tribes which are scattered abroad:

Greetings.

Profiting from Trials

2 My brethren, [a]count it all joy [b]when you fall into various trials, 3 [a]knowing that the testing of your faith produces patience. 4 But let patience have *its* perfect work, that you may be perfect and complete, lacking nothing. 5 [a]If any of you lacks wisdom, [b]let him ask of God, who gives to all liberally and without reproach, and [c]it will be given to him. 6 [a]But let him ask in faith, with no doubting, for he who doubts is like a wave of the sea driven and tossed by the wind. 7 For let not that man suppose that he will receive anything from the Lord; 8 *he is* [a]a double-minded man, unstable in all his ways.

PEACE NOTE

Ask God to give you wisdom on how to bring more peace to your life. Ask God to reorder your plans and values to be more focused on peace. God says, "Ask Me."

JAMES 1:5

The Perspective of Rich and Poor

9 Let the lowly brother glory in his exaltation, 10 but the rich in his humiliation, because [a]as a flower of the field he will pass away. 11 For no sooner has the sun risen with a burning heat than it withers the grass; its flower falls, and its beautiful appearance perishes. So the rich man also will fade away in his pursuits.

Loving God Under Trials

12 [a]Blessed *is* the man who endures temptation; for when he has been approved, he will receive [b]the crown of life [c]which the Lord has promised to those who love Him. 13 Let no one say when he is tempted, "I am tempted by God"; for God cannot be tempted by evil, nor does He Himself tempt anyone. 14 But each one is tempted when he is drawn away by his own desires and enticed. 15 Then, [a]when desire has conceived, it gives birth to sin; and sin, when it is full-grown, [b]brings forth death.

16 Do not be deceived, my beloved brethren. 17 [a]Every good gift and every perfect gift is from above, and comes down from the Father of lights, [b]with whom there is no variation or shadow of turning. 18 [a]Of His own will He brought us forth by the [b]word of truth, [c]that we might be a kind of firstfruits of His creatures.

Qualities Needed in Trials

19 So then,[1] my beloved brethren, let every man be swift to hear, [a]slow to speak, [b]slow to wrath; 20 for the wrath of man does not produce the righteousness of God.

Doers—Not Hearers Only

21 Therefore [a]lay aside all filthiness and overflow of wickedness, and receive with meekness the implanted word, [b]which is able to save your souls.

22 But [a]be doers of the word, and not hearers only, deceiving yourselves. 23 For [a]if anyone is a hearer of the word and not a doer, he is like a man observing his natural face in a mirror; 24 for he observes himself, goes away, and immediately forgets what kind of man he was. 25 But [a]he who looks into the perfect law of liberty and continues *in it,* and is not a forgetful hearer but a doer of the work, [b]this one will be blessed in what he does.

26 If anyone among you[1] thinks he is religious, and [a]does not bridle his tongue but deceives his own heart, this one's religion *is* useless. 27 [a]Pure and undefiled religion before God and the Father is this: [b]to visit orphans and widows in their trouble, [c]*and* to keep oneself unspotted from the world.

Beware of Personal Favoritism

2 My brethren, do not hold the faith of our Lord Jesus Christ, [a]*the Lord* of glory, with [b]partiality. 2 For if there should come into your assembly a man with gold rings, in fine

1:1 [a] Acts 12:17 **1:2** [a] Acts 5:41 [b] 1 Pet. 1:6 **1:3** [a] Rom. 5:3–5 **1:5** [a] 1 Kin. 3:9 [b] Matt. 7:7 [c] Jer. 29:12 **1:6** [a] [Mark 11:23, 24] **1:8** [a] James 4:8 **1:10** [a] Job 14:2 **1:12** [a] James 5:11 [b] [1 Cor. 9:25] [c] Matt. 10:22 **1:15** [a] Job 15:35 [b] [Rom. 5:12; 6:23] **1:17** [a] John 3:27 [b] Num. 23:19 **1:18** [a] John 1:13 [b] [1 Pet. 1:3, 23] [c] [Eph. 1:12, 13] **1:19** [a] Prov. 10:19; 17:27 [b] Prov. 14:17; 16:32 [1] NU-Text reads *Know this* or *This you know.* **1:21** [a] Col. 3:8 [b] Acts 13:26 **1:22** [a] Matt. 7:21–28 **1:23** [a] Luke 6:47 **1:25** [a] James 2:12 [b] John 13:17 **1:26** [a] Ps. 34:13 [1] NU-Text omits *among you.* **1:27** [a] Matt. 25:34–36 [b] Is. 1:17 [c] [Rom. 12:2] **2:1** [a] 1 Cor. 2:8 [b] Lev. 19:15

BLESSED INCONVENIENCE

Pure and undefiled religion before God and the Father is this: to visit orphans and widows in their trouble, and to keep oneself unspotted from the world.

JAMES 1:27

Peace is not static or inert. It may bring serenity and calm, but it is not the same as passivity or inaction. Peace is much more than a platitude. Peace is constructive.

James, Jesus' brother, was deeply concerned with the treatment of the poor. Genuine faith, he said, results in works of love. The same is true of peace.

Real peace transforms every aspect of life. Genuine peace provides the needs of life to the one who is suffering; it isn't talk, it is love in action. Perhaps you, like me, can remember specific moments in your life when believers showed up at just the right moment. They spoke a word of encouragement. They believed in you. They forgave. They loved when you did not deserve it. And they did so in Jesus' name.

Your faith is never more real or your peace more constructive than when you inconvenience yourself to help someone who is barely hanging on. When has someone reached beyond platitudes to really meet your needs? How can you do that for someone else today?

apparel, and there should also come in a poor
man in filthy clothes, 3 and you pay attention
to the one wearing the fine clothes and say to
him, "You sit here in a good place," and say
to the poor man, "You stand there," or, "Sit
here at my footstool," 4 have you not shown
partiality among yourselves, and become
judges with evil thoughts?
5 Listen, my beloved brethren: [a]Has God
not chosen the poor of this world *to be* [b]rich
in faith and heirs of the kingdom [c]which
He promised to those who love Him? 6 But
[a]you have dishonored the poor man. Do not
the rich oppress you [b]and drag you into the
courts? 7 Do they not blaspheme that noble
name by which you are [a]called?
8 If you really fulfill *the* royal law according
to the Scripture, [a]"You shall love your neighbor
as yourself,"[1] you do well; 9 but if you show partiality, you commit sin, and are convicted by the
law as [a]transgressors. 10 For whoever shall keep
the whole law, and yet [a]stumble in one *point*,
[b]he is guilty of all. 11 For He who said, [a]"Do not
commit adultery,"[1] also said, [b]"Do not murder."[2]
Now if you do not commit adultery, but you do
murder, you have become a transgressor of the
law. 12 So speak and so do as those who will be
judged by [a]the law of liberty. 13 For [a]judgment
is without mercy to the one who has shown
[b]no [c]mercy. [d]Mercy triumphs over judgment.

Faith Without Works Is Dead

14 [a]What *does it* profit, my brethren, if
someone says he has faith but does not have
works? Can faith save him? 15 [a]If a brother or
sister is naked and destitute of daily food,
16 and [a]one of you says to them, "Depart in
peace, be warmed and filled," but you do
not give them the things which are needed
for the body, what *does it* profit? 17 Thus also
faith by itself, if it does not have works, is
dead.

PEACE NOTE

Spreading the peace of God requires us to take people by the hand and show them the path to it.

JAMES 2:16

2:5 [a] 1 Cor. 1:27 [b] Luke 12:21 [c] Ex. 20:6 **2:6** [a] 1 Cor. 11:22 [b] Acts 13:50 **2:7** [a] 1 Pet. 4:16 **2:8** [a] Lev. 19:18 [1] Leviticus 19:18 **2:9** [a] Deut. 1:17 **2:10** [a] Gal. 3:10 [b] Deut. 27:26 **2:11** [a] Ex. 20:14; Deut. 5:18 [b] Ex. 20:13; Deut. 5:17 [1] Exodus 20:14; Deuteronomy 5:18 [2] Exodus 20:13; Deuteronomy 5:17 **2:12** [a] James 1:25 **2:13** [a] Job 22:6 [b] Prov. 21:13 [c] Mic. 7:18 [d] Rom. 12:8 **2:14** [a] Matt. 7:21–23, 26; 21:28–32 **2:15** [a] Luke 3:11 **2:16** [a] [1 John 3:17, 18]

18 But someone will say, "You have faith, and I have works." [a]Show me your faith without your[1] works, [b]and I will show you my faith by my[2] works. 19 You believe that there is one God. You do well. Even the demons believe—and tremble! 20 But do you want to know, O foolish man, that faith without works is dead?[1] 21 Was not Abraham our father justified by works [a]when he offered Isaac his son on the altar? 22 Do you see [a]that faith was working together with his works, and by [b]works faith was made perfect? 23 And the Scripture was fulfilled which says, [a]"Abraham believed God, and it was accounted to him for righteousness."[1] And he was called [b]the friend of God. 24 You see then that a man is justified by works, and not by faith only.

25 Likewise, [a]was not Rahab the harlot also justified by works when she received the messengers and sent *them* out another way?

26 For as the body without the spirit is dead, so faith without works is dead also.

The Untamable Tongue

3 My brethren, [a]let not many of you become teachers, [b]knowing that we shall receive a stricter judgment. 2 For [a]we all stumble in many things. [b]If anyone does not stumble in word, [c]he *is* a perfect man, able also to bridle the whole body. 3 Indeed,[1] [a]we put bits in horses' mouths that they may obey us, and we turn their whole body. 4 Look also at ships: although they are so large and are driven by fierce winds, they are turned by a very small rudder wherever the pilot desires. 5 Even so [a]the tongue is a little member and [b]boasts great things.

See how great a forest a little fire kindles! 6 And [a]the tongue *is* a fire, a world of iniquity. The tongue is so set among our members that it [b]defiles the whole body, and sets on fire the course of nature; and it is set on fire by hell. 7 For every kind of beast and bird, of reptile and creature of the sea, is tamed and has been tamed by mankind. 8 But no man can tame the tongue. *It is* an unruly evil, [a]full of deadly poison. 9 With it we bless our God and Father, and with it we curse men, who have been made [a]in the similitude of God. 10 Out of the same mouth proceed blessing and cursing. My brethren, these things ought not to be so. 11 Does a spring send forth fresh *water* and bitter from the same opening? 12 Can a [a]fig tree, my brethren, bear olives, or a grapevine bear figs? Thus no spring yields both salt water and fresh.[1]

Heavenly Versus Demonic Wisdom

13 [a]Who *is* wise and understanding among you? Let him show by good conduct *that* his works *are done* in the meekness of wisdom. 14 But if you have [a]bitter envy and self-seeking in your hearts, [b]do not boast and lie against the truth. 15 [a]This wisdom does not descend from above, but *is* earthly, sensual, demonic. 16 For [a]where envy and self-seeking *exist,* confusion

2:18 [a] Heb. 6:10 [b] James 3:13 [1] NU-Text omits *your.* [2] NU-Text omits *my.* **2:20** [1] NU-Text reads *useless.* **2:21** [a] Gen. 22:9, 10, 12, 16–18 **2:22** [a] Heb. 11:17 [b] John 8:39 **2:23** [a] Gen. 15:6 [b] 2 Chr. 20:7 [1] Genesis 15:6 **2:25** [a] Heb. 11:31 **3:1** [a] [Matt. 23:8] [b] Luke 6:37 **3:2** [a] 1 Kin. 8:46 [b] Ps. 34:13 [c] [Matt. 12:34–37] **3:3** [a] Ps. 32:9 [1] NU-Text reads *Now if.* **3:5** [a] Prov. 12:18; 15:2 [b] Ps. 12:3; 73:8 **3:6** [a] Prov. 16:27 [b] [Matt. 12:36; 15:11, 18] **3:8** [a] Ps. 140:3 **3:9** [a] Gen. 1:26; 5:1; 9:6 **3:12** [a] Matt. 7:16–20 [1] NU-Text reads *Neither can a salty spring produce fresh water.* **3:13** [a] Gal. 6:4 **3:14** [a] Rom. 13:13 [b] Rom. 2:17 **3:15** [a] Phil. 3:19 **3:16** [a] 1 Cor. 3:3

SOWING AND REAPING

Now the fruit of righteousness is sown in peace by those who make peace.

JAMES 3:18

Growing up I often heard the maxim, "You reap what you sow." It is a truism based on seasonal observation. Fig trees produce figs; grapevines produce grapes. That is just the way it is.

James, Jesus' brother, taught that the "fruit of righteousness is sown in peace." That is, justice produces fruit but only if it is sown in peace. The Christian isn't interested simply in his or her own personal peace, but in the peace that produces the fruit of righteousness and justice in society in general.

I have found that making peace in the setting in which I live reinforces the peace that dwells within me. It's a win-win! How can you contribute to peace in society?

and every evil thing *are* there. 17 But [a]the wisdom that is from above is first pure, then peaceable, gentle, willing to yield, full of mercy and
good fruits, [b]without partiality [c]and without
hypocrisy. 18 [a]Now the fruit of righteousness
is sown in peace by those who make peace.

Pride Promotes Strife

4 Where do wars and fights *come* from
among you? Do *they* not *come* from your
desires for pleasure [a]that war in your members? 2 You lust and do not have. You murder
and covet and cannot obtain. You fight and
war. Yet[1] you do not have because you do not
ask. 3 [a]You ask and do not receive, [b]because
you ask amiss, that you may spend *it* on your
pleasures. 4 Adulterers and[1] adulteresses!
Do you not know that [a]friendship with the
world is enmity with God? [b]Whoever therefore wants to be a friend of the world makes
himself an enemy of God. 5 Or do you think
that the Scripture says in vain, [a]"The Spirit
who dwells in us yearns jealously"?

6 But He gives more grace. Therefore He
says:

[a]"God resists the proud,
But gives grace to the humble."[1]

Humility Cures Worldliness

7 Therefore submit to God. [a]Resist the devil
and he will flee from you. 8 [a]Draw near to God
and He will draw near to you. [b]Cleanse *your*
hands, *you* sinners; and [c]purify *your* hearts,
you double-minded. 9 [a]Lament and mourn

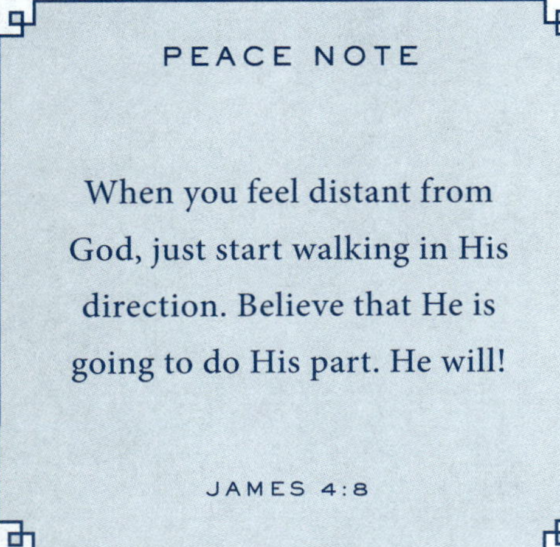

PEACE NOTE

Vulnerability will always lead me to glory in Christ—who will lead me to peace.

JAMES 4:10

and weep! Let your laughter be turned to
mourning and *your* joy to gloom. 10 [a]Humble
yourselves in the sight of the Lord, and He
will lift you up.

Do Not Judge a Brother

11 [a]Do not speak evil of one another, brethren. He who speaks evil of a brother [b]and
judges his brother, speaks evil of the law and
judges the law. But if you judge the law, you
are not a doer of the law but a judge. 12 There
is one Lawgiver,[1] [a]who is able to save and to
destroy. [b]Who[2] are you to judge another?[3]

Do Not Boast About Tomorrow

13 Come now, you who say, "Today or tomorrow we will[1] go to such and such a city,
spend a year there, buy and sell, and make
a profit"; 14 whereas you do not know what
will happen tomorrow. For what *is* your life?
[a]It is even a vapor that appears for a little
time and then vanishes away. 15 Instead you
ought to say, [a]"If the Lord wills, we shall live
and do this or that." 16 But now you boast in
your arrogance. [a]All such boasting is evil.
17 Therefore, [a]to him who knows to do good
and does not do *it*, to him it is sin.

Rich Oppressors Will Be Judged

5 Come now, *you* [a]rich, weep and howl for
your miseries that are coming upon *you*!
2 Your [a]riches are corrupted, and [b]your garments are moth-eaten. 3 Your gold and silver
are corroded, and their corrosion will be a
witness against you and will eat your flesh

3:17 [a] 1 Cor. 2:6, 7 [b] James 2:1 [c] Rom. 12:9 **3:18** [a] Prov. 11:18 **4:1** [a] Rom. 7:23 **4:2** [1] NU-Text and M-Text omit *Yet.* **4:3** [a] Job 27:8, 9 [b] [Ps. 66:18] **4:4** [a] 1 John 2:15 [b] Gal. 1:4 [1] NU-Text omits *Adulterers and.* **4:5** [a] Gen. 6:5 **4:6** [a] Prov. 3:34 [1] Proverbs 3:34 **4:7** [a] [Eph. 4:27; 6:11] **4:8** [a] 2 Chr. 15:2 [b] Is. 1:16 [c] 1 Pet. 1:22 **4:9** [a] Matt. 5:4 **4:10** [a] Job 22:29 **4:11** [a] 1 Pet. 2:1–3 [b] [Matt. 7:1–5] **4:12** [a] [Matt. 10:28] [b] Rom. 14:4 [1] NU-Text adds *and Judge.* [2] NU-Text and M-Text read *But who.* [3] NU-Text reads *a neighbor.* **4:13** [1] M-Text reads *let us.* **4:14** [a] Job 7:7 **4:15** [a] Acts 18:21 **4:16** [a] 1 Cor. 5:6 **4:17** [a] [Luke 12:47] **5:1** [a] [Luke 6:24] **5:2** [a] Matt. 6:19 [b] Job 13:28

like fire. [a]You have heaped up treasure in the last days. 4 Indeed [a]the wages of the laborers who mowed your fields, which you kept back by fraud, cry out; and [b]the cries of the reapers have reached the ears of the Lord of Sabaoth.[1] 5 You have lived on the earth in pleasure and luxury; you have fattened your hearts as[1] in a day of slaughter. 6 You have condemned, you have murdered the just; he does not resist you.

Be Patient and Persevering

7 Therefore be patient, brethren, until the coming of the Lord. See *how* the farmer waits for the precious fruit of the earth, waiting patiently for it until it receives the early and latter rain. 8 You also be patient. Establish your hearts, for the coming of the Lord is at hand.

9 Do not grumble against one another, brethren, lest you be condemned.[1] Behold, the Judge is standing at the door! 10 [a]My brethren, take the prophets, who spoke in the name of the Lord, as an example of suffering and [b]patience. 11 Indeed [a]we count them blessed who [b]endure. You have heard of [c]the perseverance of Job and seen [d]the end *intended by* the Lord—that [e]the Lord is very compassionate and merciful.

12 But above all, my brethren, [a]do not swear, either by heaven or by earth or with any other oath. But let your "Yes" be "Yes," and *your* "No," "No," lest you fall into judgment.[1]

Meeting Specific Needs

13 Is anyone among you suffering? Let him [a]pray. Is anyone cheerful? [b]Let him sing psalms. 14 Is anyone among you sick? Let him call for the elders of the church, and let them pray over him, [a]anointing him with oil in the name of the Lord. 15 And the prayer of faith will save the sick, and the Lord will raise him up. [a]And if he has committed sins, he will be forgiven. 16 Confess *your* trespasses[1] to one another, and pray for one another, that you may be healed. [a]The effective, fervent prayer of a righteous man avails much. 17 Elijah was a man [a]with a nature like ours, and [b]he prayed earnestly that it would not rain; and it did not rain on the land for three years and six months. 18 And he prayed [a]again, and the heaven gave rain, and the earth produced its fruit.

Bring Back the Erring One

19 Brethren, if anyone among you wanders from the truth, and someone [a]turns him back, 20 let him know that he who turns a sinner from the error of his way [a]will save a soul[1] from death and [b]cover a multitude of sins.

5:3 [a] Rom. 2:5 **5:4** [a] Lev. 19:13 [b] Deut. 24:15 [1] Literally, in Hebrew, *Hosts* **5:5** [1] NU-Text omits *as.* **5:9** [1] NU-Text and M-Text read *judged.* **5:10** [a] Matt. 5:12 [b] Heb. 10:36 **5:11** [a] [Ps. 94:12] [b] [James 1:12] [c] Job 1:21, 22; 2:10 [d] Job 42:10 [e] Num. 14:18 **5:12** [a] Matt. 5:34–37 [1] M-Text reads *hypocrisy.* **5:13** [a] Ps. 50:14, 15 [b] Eph. 5:19 **5:14** [a] Mark 6:13; 16:18 **5:15** [a] Is. 33:24 **5:16** [a] Num. 11:2 [1] NU-Text reads *Therefore confess your sins.* **5:17** [a] Acts 14:15 [b] 1 Kin. 17:1; 18:1 **5:18** [a] 1 Kin. 18:1, 42 **5:19** [a] Gal. 6:1 **5:20** [a] Rom. 11:14 [b] [1 Pet. 4:8] [1] NU-Text reads *his soul.*

THE FIRST EPISTLE OF

PETER

AUTHOR

The early church universally acknowledged the authenticity and authority of 1 Peter. It is likely that Peter used Silvanus (also called Silas) as his scribe (1 Pet. 5:12). This epistle was addressed to Christians throughout Asia Minor, indicating the spread of the gospel in regions not evangelized when Acts was written. It was written from Babylon (5:13), but scholars are divided as to whether this refers literally to Babylon in Mesopotamia or symbolically to Rome. It is probably the latter, as tradition consistently indicates that Peter spent the last few years of his life in Rome.

TIME

c. AD 63–64

KEY VERSE

1 Peter 4:12–13

THEME

First Peter was probably written to the Roman provinces of Turkey at the beginning of Nero's persecutions of Christians. Its primary message is one of comfort, hope, and encouragement. Peter asks the readers to hold fast to the faith in the midst of the coming persecution. In these letters we get a picture of a mature Peter who has incorporated Christ's crucifixion and death and resurrection into his thinking about suffering. He fully understands and even looks forward to the glory that is to come after this life's suffering.

The peace of God makes hope possible. In Peter's first letter, we learn that believers receive "a living hope through the resurrection of Jesus" (1:3); therefore, we must be well acquainted with peace. Peter invokes Paul's instruction from Romans 12:18 to "live peaceably" by encouraging believers to "seek peace and pursue it" (1 Pet. 3:11). Even in suffering we are blessed. Isaiah 8:12 was on Peter's heart as he clarified the protection of God's peace: we need "not be afraid of . . . threats, nor be troubled" (1 Pet. 3:14) because we continually "sanctify the Lord God in [our] hearts" and are always prepared to respond to "everyone who asks [us] a reason for the hope that is in [us]" (3:15). First Peter reminds us of the relationship between these two blessings, hope and peace.

Greeting to the Elect Pilgrims

1 Peter, an apostle of Jesus Christ,

To the pilgrims [a]of the Dispersion in Pontus, Galatia, Cappadocia, Asia, and Bithynia, 2 [a]elect [b]according to the foreknowledge of God the Father, [c]in sanctification of the Spirit, for [d]obedience and [e]sprinkling of the blood of Jesus Christ:

[f]Grace to you and peace be multiplied.

A Heavenly Inheritance

3 [a]Blessed *be* the God and Father of our Lord Jesus Christ, who [b]according to His abundant mercy [c]has begotten us again to a living hope [d]through the resurrection of Jesus Christ from the dead, 4 to an inheritance incorruptible and undefiled and that does not fade away, [a]reserved in heaven for you, 5 [a]who are kept by the power of God through faith for salvation ready to be revealed in the last time.

6 [a]In this you greatly rejoice, though now [b]for a little while, if need be, [c]you have been grieved by various trials, 7 that [a]the genuineness of your faith, *being* much more precious than gold that perishes, though [b]it is tested by fire, [c]may be found to praise, honor, and glory at the revelation of Jesus Christ, 8 [a]whom having not seen[1] you love. [b]Though now you do not see *Him,* yet believing, you rejoice with joy inexpressible and full of glory, 9 receiving the end of your faith—the salvation of *your* souls.

10 Of this salvation the prophets have inquired and searched carefully, who prophesied of the grace *that would come* to you, 11 searching what, or what manner of time, [a]the Spirit of Christ who was in them was indicating when He testified beforehand the sufferings of Christ and the glories that would follow. 12 To them it was revealed that, not to themselves, but to us[1] they were ministering the things which now have been reported to you through those who have preached the gospel to you by the Holy Spirit sent from heaven—things which [a]angels desire to look into.

Living Before God Our Father

13 Therefore gird up the loins of your mind, be sober, and rest *your* hope fully upon the grace that is to be brought to you at the revelation of Jesus Christ; 14 as obedient children, not [a]conforming yourselves to the former lusts, *as* in your ignorance; 15 [a]but as He who called you *is* holy, you also be holy in all *your* conduct, 16 because it is written, [a]"Be holy, for I am holy."[1]

17 And if you call on the Father, who [a]without partiality judges according to each one's work, conduct yourselves throughout the time of your stay *here* in fear; 18 knowing that you were not redeemed with corruptible things, *like* silver or gold, from your aimless conduct *received* by tradition from your fathers, 19 but [a]with the

1:1 [a] James 1:1 **1:2** [a] Eph. 1:4 [b] [Rom. 8:29] [c] 2 Thess. 2:13 [d] Rom. 1:5 [e] Heb. 10:22; 12:24 [f] Rom. 1:7 **1:3** [a] Eph. 1:3 [b] Gal. 6:16 [c] [John 3:3, 5] [d] 1 Cor. 15:20 **1:4** [a] Col. 1:5 **1:5** [a] John 10:28 **1:6** [a] Matt. 5:12 [b] 2 Cor. 4:17 [c] James 1:2 **1:7** [a] James 1:3 [b] Job 23:10 [c] [Rom. 2:7] **1:8** [a] 1 John 4:20 [b] John 20:29 [1] M-Text reads *known.* **1:11** [a] 2 Pet. 1:21 **1:12** [a] Eph. 3:10 [1] NU-Text and M-Text read *you.* **1:14** [a] [Rom. 12:2] **1:15** [a] [2 Cor. 7:1] **1:16** [a] Lev. 11:44, 45; 19:2; 20:7 [1] Leviticus 11:44, 45; 19:2; 20:7 **1:17** [a] Acts 10:34 **1:19** [a] Acts 20:28

MULTIPLYING PEACE

Grace to you and peace be multiplied.

I PETER 1:2

Peter, the leading apostle of Jesus, began his first letter with a richly theological introduction: God's people are chosen, they are intimately known by God, they are in the process of being made holy by God's Spirit, and their sins are washed away by the blood of Jesus.

It was to people such as these that the apostle Peter extended grace and expressed his prayer that "peace be multiplied." What gives me assurance is that all of this is God's work; it's not mine. The reception of so many blessings, including a multiplying peace, requires humility. Arrogance or the attitude of *I can do it myself* pushes away the blessings God wants to give us.

It is the arrogant person who finds his or her own path and inevitably gets lost. If we humble ourselves before Jesus and keep our minds fixed on all that is ours in Christ, we will receive the *multiplied* peace He offers. How can you humble yourself before God today?

THE LIVING HOPE OF JESUS

[God's] abundant mercy has begotten us again to a living hope.

I PETER 1:3

Remarkable as it may seem, the word "hope" is used as a descriptor for the believer in Christ dozens of times in the New Testament. What's fascinating is that hope in God, like faith in God, is a hallmark of our lives in Christ: "Through Him [you] believe in God, who raised Him from the dead and gave Him glory, so that your faith and hope are in God" (v. 21).

As we trust in God, we must wrap ourselves in the truth that our hope stands: Jesus Christ shattered the gates of death for us and now reigns as our living Lord. He is alive. We are, right now, alive with Him. In other words, our living hope is based on the historical, unchangeable fact of Jesus' physical, bodily resurrection from the dead.

Are you a believer who brings hope to those around you? As a believer, do you base your hope on feelings or on the objective fact of God's unchanging Word? This hope is something to share. It endures. It will carry us through our most challenging moments. Let's share this living hope with others every chance we get.

precious blood of Christ, [b]as of a lamb without
blemish and without spot. 20 [a]He indeed was
foreordained before the foundation of the
world, but was manifest [b]in these last times
for you 21 who through Him believe in God,
[a]who raised Him from the dead and [b]gave Him
glory, so that your faith and hope are in God.

The Enduring Word

22 Since you [a]have purified your souls in
obeying the truth through the Spirit[1] in sincere [b]love of the brethren, love one another
fervently with a pure heart, 23 [a]having been
born again, not of corruptible seed but incorruptible, [b]through the word of God which
lives and abides forever,[1] 24 because

[a]"All flesh *is* as grass,
And all the glory of man[1] as the flower
of the grass.
The grass withers,
And its flower falls away,
25 [a]But the word of the LORD endures
forever."[1]

[b]Now this is the word which by the gospel
was preached to you.

2 Therefore, [a]laying aside all malice, all deceit, hypocrisy, envy, and all evil speaking,
2 [a]as newborn babes, desire the pure [b]milk
of the word, that you may grow thereby,[1]
3 if indeed you have [a]tasted that the Lord *is*
gracious.

The Chosen Stone and His Chosen People

4 Coming to Him *as to* a living stone, [a]re-
jected indeed by men, but chosen by God *and*
precious, 5 you also, as living stones, are being
built up a spiritual house, a holy priesthood,
to offer up spiritual sacrifices acceptable to
God through Jesus Christ. 6 Therefore it is
also contained in the Scripture,

[a]"Behold, I lay in Zion
A chief cornerstone, elect, precious,
And he who believes on Him will by no
means be put to shame."[1]

7 Therefore, to you who believe, *He is* precious; but to those who are disobedient,[1]

[a]"The stone which the builders rejected
Has become the chief cornerstone,"[2]

8 and

[a]"A stone of stumbling
And a rock of offense."[1]

[b]They stumble, being disobedient to the
word, [c]to which they also were appointed.

1:19 [b] Ex. 12:5 **1:20** [a] Rom. 3:25 [b] Gal. 4:4 **1:21** [a] Acts 2:24 [b] Acts 2:33 **1:22** [a] Acts 15:9 [b] Heb. 13:1 [1] NU-Text omits *through the Spirit.* **1:23** [a] John 1:13 [b] James 1:18 [1] NU-Text omits *forever.* **1:24** [a] Is. 40:6–8 [1] NU-Text reads *all its glory.* **1:25** [a] Is. 40:8 [b] [John 1:1] [1] Isaiah 40:6–8 **2:1** [a] Heb. 12:1 **2:2** [a] [Matt. 18:3; 19:14] [b] 1 Cor. 3:2 [1] NU-Text adds *up to salvation.* **2:3** [a] Heb. 6:5 **2:4** [a] Ps. 118:22 **2:6** [a] Is. 28:16 [1] Isaiah 28:16 **2:7** [a] Ps. 118:22 [1] NU-Text reads *to those who disbelieve.* [2] Psalm 118:22 **2:8** [a] Is. 8:14 [b] 1 Cor. 1:23 [c] Rom. 9:22 [1] Isaiah 8:14

9 But you *are* a chosen generation, a royal
priesthood, a holy nation, His own special
people, that you may proclaim the praises of
Him who called you out of [a]darkness into His
marvelous light; 10 [a]who once *were* not a people
but *are* now the people of God, who had not
obtained mercy but now have obtained mercy.

Living Before the World

11 Beloved, I beg *you* as sojourners and
pilgrims, abstain from fleshly lusts [a]which
war against the soul, 12 [a]having your conduct
honorable among the Gentiles, that when
they speak against you as evildoers, [b]they
may, by *your* good works which they observe,
glorify God in the day of visitation.

Submission to Government

13 [a]Therefore submit yourselves to every
ordinance of man for the Lord's sake, whether
to the king as supreme, 14 or to governors, as
to those who are sent by him for the punishment of evildoers and *for the* praise of those
who do good. 15 For this is the will of God,
that by doing good you may put to silence
the ignorance of foolish men— 16 [a]as free, yet
not [b]using liberty as a cloak for vice, but as
bondservants of God. 17 Honor all *people.* Love
the brotherhood. Fear [a]God. Honor the king.

Submission to Masters

18 [a]Servants, *be* submissive to *your* masters
with all fear, not only to the good and gentle, but also to the harsh. 19 For this *is* [a]com-
mendable, if because of conscience toward
God one endures grief, suffering wrongfully.
20 For [a]what credit *is it* if, when you are beat-
en for your faults, you take it patiently? But
when you do good and suffer, if you take it
patiently, this *is* commendable before God.
21 For [a]to this you were called, because Christ
also suffered for us,[1] [b]leaving us[2] an example,
that you should follow His steps:

22 "Who[a] committed no sin,
Nor was deceit found in His mouth";[1]

23 [a]who, when He was reviled, did not revile in return; when He suffered, He did not
threaten, but [b]committed *Himself* to Him who
judges righteously; 24 [a]who Himself bore our
sins in His own body on the tree, [b]that we,
having died to sins, might live for righteousness—[c]by whose stripes you were healed.

> PEACE NOTE
>
> Jesus' most countercultural trait: He could not be provoked. He lived in God's peace on the daily, and so should we.
>
> 1 PETER 2:23

25 For [a]you were like sheep going astray, but
have now returned [b]to the Shepherd and
Overseer[1] of your souls.

Submission to Husbands

3 Wives, likewise, *be* [a]submissive to your
own husbands, that even if some do not
obey the word, [b]they, without a word, may [c]be
won by the conduct of their wives, 2 [a]when
they observe your chaste conduct *accompanied* by fear. 3 [a]Do not let your adornment be
merely outward—arranging the hair, wearing
gold, or putting on *fine* apparel— 4 rather *let
it be* [a]the hidden person of the heart, with the
incorruptible *beauty* of a gentle and quiet
spirit, which is very precious in the sight of
God. 5 For in this manner, in former times, the
holy women who trusted in God also adorned
themselves, being submissive to their own
husbands, 6 as Sarah obeyed Abraham, [a]call-
ing him lord, whose daughters you are if you
do good and are not afraid with any terror.

A Word to Husbands

7 [a]Husbands, likewise, dwell with *them* with
understanding, giving honor to the wife, [b]as
to the weaker vessel, and as *being* heirs together of the grace of life, [c]that your prayers
may not be hindered.

Called to Blessing

8 Finally, all *of you be* of one mind, having compassion for one another; love as
brothers, *be* tenderhearted, *be* courteous;[1]
9 [a]not returning evil for evil or reviling for

2:9 [a] [Acts 26:18] **2:10** [a] Hos. 1:9, 10; 2:23 **2:11** [a] James 4:1 **2:12** [a] Phil. 2:15 [b] Matt. 5:16; 9:8 **2:13** [a] Matt. 22:21 **2:16** [a] Rom. 6:14, 20, 22 [b] Gal. 5:13 **2:17** [a] Prov. 24:21 **2:18** [a] Eph. 6:5–8 **2:19** [a] Matt. 5:10 **2:20** [a] Luke 6:32–34 **2:21** [a] Matt. 16:24 [b] [1 John 2:6] [1] NU-Text reads *you.* [2] NU-Text and M-Text read *you.* **2:22** [a] Is. 53:9 [1] Isaiah 53:9 **2:23** [a] Is. 53:7 [b] Luke 23:46 **2:24** [a] [Heb. 9:28] [b] Rom. 7:6 [c] Is. 53:5 **2:25** [a] Is. 53:5, 6 [b] [Ezek. 34:23] [1] Greek *Episkopos* **3:1** [a] Eph. 5:22 [b] 1 Cor. 7:16 [c] Matt. 18:15 **3:2** [a] 1 Pet. 2:12; 3:6 **3:3** [a] 1 Tim. 2:9 **3:4** [a] Rom. 2:29 **3:6** [a] Gen. 18:12 **3:7** [a] [Eph. 5:25] [b] 1 Cor. 12:23 [c] Job 42:8 **3:8** [1] NU-Text reads *humble.* **3:9** [a] [Prov. 17:13]

reviling, but on the contrary [b]blessing, knowing that you were called to this, [c]that you may inherit a blessing. 10 For

[a]"He who would love life
And see good days,
[b]Let him refrain his tongue from evil,
And his lips from speaking deceit.
11 Let him [a]turn away from evil and do good;
[b]Let him seek peace and pursue it.
12 For the eyes of the LORD *are* on the righteous,
[a]And His ears *are open* to their prayers;
But the face of the LORD *is* against those who do evil."[1]

Suffering for Right and Wrong

13 [a]And who *is* he who will harm you if you become followers of what is good? 14 [a]But even if you should suffer for righteousness' sake, *you are* blessed. [b]"And do not be afraid of their threats, nor be troubled."[1] 15 But sanctify the Lord God[1] in your hearts, and always [a]*be* ready to *give* a defense to everyone who asks you a reason for the [b]hope that is in you, with meekness and fear; 16 [a]having a good conscience, that when they defame you as evildoers, those who revile your good conduct in Christ may be ashamed. 17 For *it is* better, if it is the will of God, to suffer for doing good than for doing evil.

Christ's Suffering and Ours

18 For Christ also suffered once for sins, the just for the unjust, that He might bring us[1] to God, being put to death in the flesh but made alive by the Spirit, 19 by whom also He went and preached to the spirits in prison, 20 who formerly were disobedient, when once the Divine longsuffering waited[1] in the days of Noah, while *the* ark was being prepared, in which a few, that is, eight souls, were saved through water. 21 [a]There is also an antitype which now saves us—baptism [b](not the removal of the filth of the flesh, [c]but the answer of a good conscience toward God), through the resurrection of Jesus Christ, 22 who has gone into heaven and [a]is at the right hand of God, [b]angels and authorities and powers having been made subject to Him.

4 Therefore, since Christ suffered for us[1] in the flesh, arm yourselves also with the same mind, for he who has suffered in the flesh has ceased from sin, 2 that he no longer should live the rest of *his* time in the flesh for the lusts of men, [a]but for the will of God. 3 For we *have spent* enough of our past lifetime[1] in doing the will of the Gentiles—when we walked in lewdness, lusts, drunkenness, revelries, drinking parties, and abominable idolatries. 4 In regard to these, they think it strange that you do not run with *them* in the same flood of dissipation, speaking evil of *you*. 5 They will give an account to Him who is ready [a]to judge the living and the dead. 6 For this reason [a]the gospel was preached also to those who are dead, that they might be judged according to men in the flesh, but [b]live according to God in the spirit.

3:9 [b] Matt. 5:44 [c] Matt. 25:34 **3:10** [a] Ps. 34:12–16 [b] James 1:26 **3:11** [a] Ps. 37:27 [b] Rom. 12:18 **3:12** [a] John 9:31 [1] Psalm 34:12–16 **3:13** [a] Prov. 16:7 **3:14** [a] James 1:12 [b] Is. 8:12 [1] Isaiah 8:12 **3:15** [a] Ps. 119:46 [b] [Titus 3:7] [1] NU-Text reads *Christ as Lord.* **3:16** [a] Heb. 13:18 **3:18** [1] NU-Text and M-Text read *you.* **3:20** [1] NU-Text and M-Text read *when the longsuffering of God waited patiently.* **3:21** [a] Eph. 5:26 [b] [Titus 3:5] [c] [Rom. 10:10] **3:22** [a] Ps. 110:1 [b] Rom. 8:38 **4:1** [1] NU-Text omits *for us.* **4:2** [a] John 1:13 **4:3** [1] NU-Text reads *time.* **4:5** [a] Acts 10:42 **4:6** [a] 1 Pet. 1:12; 3:19 [b] [Rom. 8:9, 13]

READY TO GIVE AN ANSWER

Be ready to give a defense to everyone who asks you a reason for the hope that is in you.

I PETER 3:15

Not all people expect to find love and peace in this life. In 1 Peter, we are reminded that *Jesus' bodily resurrection* secures our present and future with a "living hope" (1:3), a "better hope" (Heb. 7:19), and a "sure and steadfast" hope (Heb. 6:19). Indeed, this living hope is such that we must be prepared to explain it when we are challenged by a hopeless world.

This hope gives us purpose. Our whole lives can be poured out in a God-serving way. That's what the resurrection does for us: we are and continue to become the people who bring hope. Hope is found only in Christ, in people used by God's Spirit to share the Word of God. Do you realize what a gift you bear? Do you understand how hungry the people around you are for life-giving peace and hope? Can you share these in some small way today?

Serving for God's Glory

7 But [a]the end of all things is at hand; therefore be serious and watchful in your prayers. 8 And above all things have fervent love for one another, for [a]"love will cover a multitude of sins."[1] 9 [a]*Be* hospitable to one another [b]without grumbling. 10 [a]As each one has received a gift, minister it to one another, [b]as good stewards of [c]the manifold grace of God. 11 [a]If anyone speaks, *let him speak* as the oracles of God. If anyone ministers, *let him do it* as with the ability which God supplies, that [b]in all things God may be glorified through Jesus Christ, to whom belong the glory and the dominion forever and ever. Amen.

Suffering for God's Glory

12 Beloved, do not think it strange concerning the fiery trial which is to try you, as though some strange thing happened to you; 13 but rejoice [a]to the extent that you partake of Christ's sufferings, that [b]when His glory is revealed, you may also be glad with exceeding joy. 14 If you are reproached for the name of Christ, [a]blessed *are you,* for the Spirit of glory and of God rests upon you.[1] On their part He is blasphemed, [b]but on your part He is glorified. 15 But let none of you suffer as a murderer, a thief, an evildoer, or as a busybody in other people's matters. 16 Yet if *anyone suffers* as a Christian, let him not be ashamed, but let him glorify God in this matter.[1]

17 For the time *has come* [a]for judgment to begin at the house of God; and if *it begins* with us first, [b]what will *be* the end of those who do not obey the gospel of God? 18 Now

[a]"If the righteous one is scarcely saved,
Where will the ungodly and the sinner appear?"[1]

19 Therefore let those who suffer according to the will of God [a]commit their souls *to Him* in doing good, as to a faithful Creator.

Shepherd the Flock

5 The elders who are among you I exhort, I who am a fellow elder and a [a]witness of the sufferings of Christ, and also a partaker of the [b]glory that will be revealed: 2 [a]Shepherd the flock of God which is among you, serving as overseers, [b]not by compulsion but willingly,[1] [c]not for dishonest gain but eagerly; 3 nor as [a]being lords over [b]those entrusted to you, but [c]being examples to the flock; 4 and when [a]the Chief Shepherd appears, you will receive [b]the crown of glory that does not fade away.

Submit to God, Resist the Devil

5 Likewise you younger people, submit yourselves to *your* elders. Yes, [a]all of *you* be submissive to one another, and be clothed with humility, for

[b]"God resists the proud,
But [c]gives grace to the humble."[1]

4:7 [a] Rom. 13:11 **4:8** [a] [Prov. 10:12] [1] Proverbs 10:12 **4:9** [a] Heb. 13:2 [b] 2 Cor. 9:7 **4:10** [a] Rom. 12:6–8 [b] 1 Cor. 4:1, 2 [c] [1 Cor. 12:4] **4:11** [a] Eph. 4:29 [b] [1 Cor. 10:31] **4:13** [a] James 1:2 [b] 2 Tim. 2:12 **4:14** [a] Matt. 5:11 [b] Matt. 5:16 [1] NU-Text omits the rest of this verse. **4:16** [1] NU-Text reads *name.* **4:17** [a] Is. 10:12 [b] Luke 10:12 **4:18** [a] Prov. 11:31 [1] Proverbs 11:31 **4:19** [a] 2 Tim. 1:12 **5:1** [a] Matt. 26:37 [b] Rom. 8:17, 18 **5:2** [a] Acts 20:28 [b] 1 Cor. 9:17 [c] 1 Tim. 3:3 [1] NU-Text adds *according to God.* **5:3** [a] Ezek. 34:4 [b] Ps. 33:12 [c] Phil. 3:17 **5:4** [a] Heb. 13:20 [b] 2 Tim. 4:8 **5:5** [a] Eph. 5:21 [b] Prov. 3:34 [c] Is. 57:15 [1] Proverbs 3:34

KISS OF PEACE

Greet one another with a kiss of love. Peace to you all who are in Christ Jesus.

1 PETER 5:14

I kiss my wife and children, but I never kiss anyone else. In antiquity, kissing was the way people greeted each other; it was a sign of respect and friendship. When Peter speaks of a "kiss of love," he means more than a mere formality. Rather he speaks of a Christian greeting that included, as we might expect, a prayer for peace—for the fullness and completeness that God provides.

A "kiss of peace" needn't be literal to be effective. Whom can you greet today with a blessing for their peace? What words would best communicate your desire for their emotional and spiritual tranquility? Who has given you such a greeting? What difference did it make? Remember that you may be the one person someone sees today who is eager to pass the peace. Don't hesitate to bless others from a pure heart.

[6]Therefore humble yourselves under the
mighty hand of God, that He may exalt you
in due time, [7]casting all your care upon Him,
for He cares for you.
[8]Be sober, be vigilant; because[1] your adversary the devil walks about like a roaring
lion, seeking whom he may devour. [9]Re-
sist him, steadfast in the faith, knowing
that the same sufferings are experienced
by your brotherhood in the world. [10]But
may[1] the God of all grace, [a]who called us[2]
to His eternal glory by Christ Jesus, after
you have suffered a while, perfect, establish, strengthen, and settle *you*. [11][a]To Him
be the glory and the dominion forever and
ever. Amen.

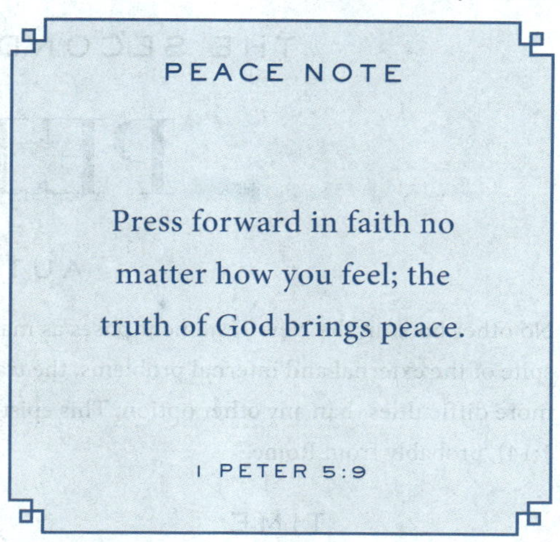

Farewell and Peace

[12]By [a]Silvanus, our faithful brother as I
consider him, I have written to you briefly,
exhorting and testifying [b]that this is the true
grace of God in which you stand.
[13]She who is in Babylon, elect together
with *you*, greets you; and *so does* [a]Mark my
son. [14]Greet one another with a kiss of love.
Peace to you all who are in Christ Jesus.
Amen.

5:8 [1] NU-Text and M-Text omit *because*. 5:10 [a] 1 Cor. 1:9 [1] NU-Text reads *But the God of all grace . . . will perfect, establish, strengthen, and settle you.* [2] NU-Text and M-Text read *you*. 5:11 [a] Rev. 1:6 5:12 [a] 2 Cor. 1:19 [b] Acts 20:24
5:13 [a] Acts 12:12, 25; 15:37, 39

THE SECOND EPISTLE OF

PETER

AUTHOR

No other book in the New Testament poses as many problems of authenticity as does 2 Peter. But in spite of the external and internal problems, the traditional position of Petrine authorship overcomes more difficulties than any other option. This epistle was written just before the apostle's death (2 Pet. 1:14), probably from Rome.

TIME

c. AD 64–66

KEY VERSE

2 Peter 1:20–21

THEME

While 1 Peter deals with suffering and persecution caused by people outside the church, 2 Peter deals more with the need for true spiritual knowledge and maturity in the face of false teachers who would distort the faith from inside the church. He gives his readers insight into the false teachers' thinking and encourages opposition to them. He also urges watchfulness for Christ's return through all the events at the end of the age.

Godless people will always mock the peace of God. In fact, they will attempt to question God's promises, as Peter warned us, "Scoffers will come in the last days . . . saying, 'Where is the promise of His coming?'" (3:3–4). Peter explains that people "willfully forget" the ways in which God miraculously works in our world (3:5). The apostle reminds us that, even when we feel emotionally out of sorts, Scripture says that, because of Christ, God's always got us (3:14). After all, "His divine power has given to us all things that pertain to life and godliness," especially His "great and precious promises" that are at work in us (1:3–4). These promises include providing the peace we need (John 14:27; Phil. 4:7) because we are "established in the present truth" (2 Pet. 1:12).

Greeting the Faithful

1 Simon Peter, a bondservant and [a]apostle of Jesus Christ,

To those who have obtained [b]like precious faith with us by the righteousness of our God and Savior Jesus Christ:

2 [a]Grace and peace be multiplied to you in the knowledge of God and of Jesus our Lord, 3 as His [a]divine power has given to us all things that *pertain* to life and godliness, through the knowledge of Him [b]who called us by glory and virtue, 4 [a]by which have been given to us exceedingly great and precious promises, that through these you may be [b]partakers of the divine nature, having escaped the corruption *that is* in the world through lust.

Fruitful Growth in the Faith

5 But also for this very reason, [a]giving all diligence, add to your faith virtue, to virtue [b]knowledge, 6 to knowledge self-control, to self-control perseverance, to perseverance godliness, 7 to godliness brotherly kindness, and [a]to brotherly kindness love. 8 For if these things are yours and abound, *you* will be neither barren [a]nor unfruitful in the knowledge of our Lord Jesus Christ. 9 For he who lacks these things is [a]shortsighted, even to blindness, and has forgotten that he was cleansed from his old sins.

PEACE NOTE

With God there are no hopeless situations, and that is why we can be assured of His peace.

2 PETER 1:4

10 Therefore, brethren, be even more diligent [a]to make your call and election sure, for if you do these things you will never stumble; 11 for so an entrance will be supplied to you abundantly into the everlasting kingdom of our Lord and Savior Jesus Christ.

Peter's Approaching Death

12 For this reason [a]I will not be negligent to remind you always of these things, [b]though you know and are established in the present truth. 13 Yes, I think it is right, [a]as long as I am in this tent, [b]to stir you up by reminding

1:1 [a] Gal. 2:8 [b] Eph. 4:5 **1:2** [a] Dan. 4:1 **1:3** [a] 1 Pet. 1:5 [b] 1 Thess. 2:12 **1:4** [a] 2 Cor. 1:20; 7:1 [b] [2 Cor. 3:18] **1:5** [a] 2 Pet. 3:18 [b] 2 Pet. 1:2 **1:7** [a] Gal. 6:10 **1:8** [a] [John 15:2] **1:9** [a] 1 John 2:9–11 **1:10** [a] 1 John 3:19 **1:12** [a] Phil. 3:1 [b] 1 Pet. 5:12 **1:13** [a] [2 Cor. 5:1, 4] [b] 2 Pet. 3:1

IMMEASURABLE PEACE

Grace and peace be multiplied to you in the knowledge of God and of Jesus our Lord.

2 PETER 1:2

One of the things I like about publishing a book is that it multiplies how many I can encourage. When I speak in a church or at a conference, a few hundred hear me. But a book is read by thousands, and it sometimes remains in print for many years, so it can be read by many more people. That's multiplication.

Peace does the same thing. It is never used up. It's sourced in God, whose resources are *never exhausted. It changes* our broken world into the world that God intended all along. Of course Peter qualified this multiplying peace by saying it is found "in the knowledge of God and of Jesus our Lord, which confirms we cannot have grace or peace independent of Jesus Christ. In this short letter, Peter mentions knowledge of our Lord Jesus Christ three additional times (1:3, 8; 2:20). The more we know of Christ, the more peace we have available to us.

Genuine peace produces grace, peace, and holiness. Dig into the Bible, and your knowledge will grow and your peace will be multiplied.

you, 14 [a]knowing that shortly I *must* put off my tent, just as [b]our Lord Jesus Christ showed me. 15 Moreover I will be careful to ensure that you always have a reminder of these things after my decease.

The Trustworthy Prophetic Word

16 For we did not follow [a]cunningly devised fables when we made known to you the [b]power and [c]coming of our Lord Jesus Christ, but were [d]eyewitnesses of His majesty. 17 For He received from God the Father honor and glory when such a voice came to Him from the Excellent Glory: [a]"This is My beloved Son, in whom I am well pleased." 18 And we heard this voice which came from heaven when we were with Him on [a]the holy mountain.

19 And so we have the prophetic word confirmed,[1] which you do well to heed as a [a]light that shines in a dark place, [b]until [c]the day dawns and the morning star rises in your [d]hearts; 20 knowing this first, that [a]no prophecy of Scripture is of any private interpretation,[1] 21 for [a]prophecy never came by the will of man, [b]but holy men of God[1] spoke *as they were* moved by the Holy Spirit.

Destructive Doctrines

2 But there were also false prophets among the people, even as there will be [a]false teachers among you, who will secretly bring in destructive heresies, even denying the Lord who bought them, *and* bring on themselves swift destruction. 2 And many will follow their destructive ways, because of whom the way of truth will be blasphemed. 3 By covetousness they will exploit you with deceptive words; for a long time their judgment has not been idle, and their destruction does[1] not slumber.

Doom of False Teachers

4 For if God did not spare the angels who sinned, but cast *them* down to hell and delivered *them* into chains of darkness, to be reserved for judgment; 5 and did not spare the ancient world, but saved Noah, *one of* eight *people,* a preacher of righteousness, bringing in the flood on the world of the ungodly; 6 and turning the cities of [a]Sodom and Gomorrah into ashes, condemned *them* to destruction, making *them* an example to those who afterward would live ungodly; 7 and [a]delivered righteous Lot, *who was* oppressed by the filthy conduct of the wicked 8 (for that righteous man, dwelling among them, [a]tormented *his* righteous soul from day to day by seeing and hearing *their* lawless deeds)— 9 *then* [a]the Lord knows how to deliver the godly out of temptations and to reserve the unjust under punishment for the day of judgment, 10 and especially [a]those who walk according to the flesh in the lust of uncleanness and despise authority. [b]*They are* presumptuous, self-willed. They are not afraid to speak evil of dignitaries, 11 whereas [a]angels, who are greater in power and might, do not bring a reviling accusation against them before the Lord.

PEACE NOTE

If you allow a tempting thought to take up permanent residence in your mind, you are no longer living in the peace of God. Ask for His help.

2 PETER 2:9

Depravity of False Teachers

12 But these, [a]like natural brute beasts made to be caught and destroyed, speak evil of the things they do not understand, and will utterly perish in their own corruption, 13 [a]*and* will receive the wages of unrighteousness, *as* those who count it pleasure [b]to carouse in the daytime. [c]*They are* spots and blemishes, carousing in their own deceptions while [d]they feast with you, 14 having eyes full of adultery and that cannot cease from sin, enticing unstable souls. [a]They have a heart trained in covetous practices, *and are* accursed children. 15 They have forsaken the right way and gone astray, following the way of [a]Balaam the *son* of Beor, who loved the wages of unrighteousness; 16 but he was rebuked for his iniquity: a dumb donkey

1:14 [a] [2 Tim. 4:6] [b] John 13:36; 21:18, 19 **1:16** [a] 1 Cor. 1:17 [b] [Eph. 1:19–22] [c] [1 Pet. 5:4] [d] Matt. 17:1–5 **1:17** [a] Matt. 17:5 **1:18** [a] Matt. 17:1 **1:19** [a] [John 1:4, 5, 9] [b] Prov. 4:18 [c] Rev. 2:28; 22:16 [d] [2 Cor. 4:5–7] [1] Or *We also have the more sure prophetic word.* **1:20** [a] [Rom. 12:6] [1] Or *origin* **1:21** [a] [2 Tim. 3:16] [b] 2 Sam. 23:2 [1] NU-Text reads *but men spoke from God.* **2:1** [a] 1 Tim. 4:1, 2 **2:3** [1] M-Text reads *will not.* **2:6** [a] Gen. 19:1–26 **2:7** [a] Gen. 19:16, 29 **2:8** [a] Ps. 119:139 **2:9** [a] Ps. 34:15–19 **2:10** [a] Jude 4, 7, 8 [b] Jude 8 **2:11** [a] Jude 9 **2:12** [a] Jude 10 **2:13** [a] Phil. 3:19 [b] Rom. 13:13 [c] Jude 12 [d] 1 Cor. 11:20, 21 **2:14** [a] Jude 11 **2:15** [a] Num. 22:5, 7

speaking with a man's voice restrained the
madness of the prophet.
17 [a]These are wells without water, clouds[1]
carried by a tempest, for whom is reserved
the blackness of darkness forever.[2]

Deceptions of False Teachers

18 For when they speak great swelling *words*
of emptiness, they allure through the lusts
of the flesh, through lewdness, the ones who
have actually escaped[1] from those who live
in error. 19 While they promise them liberty,
they themselves are slaves of corruption;
[a]for by whom a person is overcome, by him
also he is brought into bondage. 20 For if,
after they [a]have escaped the pollutions of
the world through the knowledge of the Lord
and Savior Jesus Christ, they are [b]again entangled in them and overcome, the latter
end is worse for them than the beginning.
21 For [a]it would have been better for them
not to have known the way of righteousness,
than having known *it,* to turn from the holy
commandment delivered to them. 22 But it
has happened to them according to the true
proverb: [a]"A dog returns to his own vomit,"[1]
and, "a sow, having washed, to her wallowing
in the mire."

God's Promise Is Not Slack

3 Beloved, I now write to you this second
epistle (in *both of* which [a]I stir up your
pure minds by way of reminder), 2 that you
may be mindful of the words [a]which were
spoken before by the holy prophets, [b]and
of the commandment of us,[1] the apostles of
the Lord and Savior, 3 knowing this first: that
scoffers will come in the last days, [a]walking
according to their own lusts, 4 and saying,
"Where is the promise of His coming? For
since the fathers fell asleep, all things continue as *they were* from the beginning of
[a]creation." 5 For this they willfully forget:
that [a]by the word of God the heavens were
of old, and the earth [b]standing out of water
and in the water, 6 [a]by which the world *that*
then existed perished, being flooded with
water. 7 But [a]the heavens and the earth *which*
are now preserved by the same word, are
reserved for [b]fire until the day of judgment
and perdition of ungodly men.
8 But, beloved, do not forget this one thing,
that with the Lord one day *is* as a thousand
years, and [a]a thousand years as one day. 9 [a]The
Lord is not slack concerning *His* promise, as
some count slackness, but [b]is longsuffering
toward us,[1] [c]not willing that any should perish but [d]that all should come to repentance.

2:17 [a] Jude 12, 13 [1] NU-Text reads *and mists.* [2] NU-Text omits *forever.* **2:18** [1] NU-Text reads *are barely escaping.* **2:19** [a] John 8:34 **2:20** [a] Matt. 12:45 [b] [Heb. 6:4–6] **2:21** [a] Luke 12:47 **2:22** [a] Prov. 26:11 [1] Proverbs 26:11 **3:1** [a] 2 Pet. 1:13 **3:2** [a] 2 Pet. 1:21 [b] Jude 17 [1] NU-Text and M-Text read *commandment of the apostles of your Lord and Savior* or *commandment of your apostles of the Lord and Savior.* **3:3** [a] 2 Pet. 2:10 **3:4** [a] Gen. 6:1–7 **3:5** [a] Gen. 1:6, 9 [b] Ps. 24:2; 136:6 **3:6** [a] Gen. 7:11, 12, 21–23 **3:7** [a] 2 Pet. 3:10, 12 [b] [2 Thess. 1:8] **3:8** [a] Ps. 90:4 **3:9** [a] Hab. 2:3 [b] Is. 30:18 [c] Ezek. 33:11 [d] [Rom. 2:4] [1] NU-Text reads *you.*

PEACE THAT STANDS

Beloved, do not forget this one thing, that with the Lord one day is as a thousand years, and a thousand years as one day. The Lord is not slack concerning His promise.

2 PETER 3:8-9

Remarkable as it may seem, nearly one hundred times in the New Testament the word "hope" is used as a descriptor for the believer in Christ. What's fascinating is that hope in God, as much as faith in God, is the hallmark of our lives in Christ, "Through Him [you] believe in God, who raised Him from the dead and gave Him glory, so that your faith and hope are in God" (1 Pet. 1:21). As we trust in God, we must wrap ourselves in the truth that our hope *stands*: Jesus Christ shattered the gates of death for us and now reigns as our living Lord. He is alive. We are, right now, alive with Him. In other words, our living hope is based on the historical, unchangeable fact of Jesus's physical, bodily resurrection from the dead (see 1 Peter 1:3).

Aren't you relieved that your hope is eternal and based on an ageless God and the facts of the Gospel? Doesn't that inspire you to "joy and peace in believing"? (Rom. 15:13). Let your trust in our resurrecting God lead you into His unfathomable peace.

SEEK TO FIND

Beloved, looking forward to these things, be diligent to be found by Him in peace, without spot and blameless.

2 PETER 3:14

Peter the apostle knew well the dangers faced by his readers. Early Christians not only multiplied in the face of opposition that resulted in social, political, and economic disadvantages, they also risked imprisonment, torture, and martyrdom. Yet the church grew by leaps and bounds. Why? Though some struggled with crippling fear and some exhibited bravado, some had genuine courage and some showed admirable perseverance by reflecting, of all things, peace. Imagine that! Could you be quiet in soul and countenance if someone were barking insults at you or threatening physical harm?

It may seem unfair for Peter to exhort his readers to "be found by Him in peace" when, humanly speaking, they might be shaking in their sandals. But his order to "be diligent" shows his humanity—he knew peace sometimes had to be sought and fought for, and believers are never alone in a spiritual battle. Peter knew the Spirit would empower his readers to find this precious commodity. In our worst moments, what is lovelier than peace? Whether you face literal threats or figurative ones today, how can you work with the Holy Spirit to seek and fight for your peace?

The Day of the Lord

10 But [a]the day of the Lord will come as a thief
in the night, in which [b]the heavens will pass
away with a great noise, and the elements will
melt with fervent heat; both the earth and the
works that are in it will be burned up.[1] 11 Therefore, since all these things will be dissolved,
what manner *of persons* ought you to be [a]in
holy conduct and godliness, 12 [a]looking for and
hastening the coming of the day of God, because of which the heavens will [b]be dissolved,
being on fire, and the elements will [c]melt with
fervent heat? 13 Nevertheless we, according to
His promise, look for [a]new heavens and a [b]new
earth in which righteousness dwells.

Be Steadfast

14 Therefore, beloved, looking forward to
these things, be diligent [a]to be found by Him
in peace, without spot and blameless; 15 and
consider *that* [a]the longsuffering of our Lord *is*
salvation—as also our beloved brother Paul,
according to the wisdom given to him, has
written to you, 16 as also in all his [a]epistles,
speaking in them of these things, in which
are some things hard to understand, which
untaught and unstable *people* twist to their
own destruction, as *they do* also the [b]rest of
the Scriptures.

17 You therefore, beloved, [a]since you know
this beforehand, [b]beware lest you also fall
from your own steadfastness, being led away
with the error of the wicked; 18 [a]but grow in
the grace and knowledge of our Lord and
Savior Jesus Christ.

[b]To Him *be* the glory both now and forever. Amen.

3:10 [a] Rev. 3:3; 16:15 [b] Ps. 102:25, 26 [1] NU-Text reads *laid bare* (literally *found*). **3:11** [a] 1 Pet. 1:15 **3:12** [a] 1 Cor. 1:7, 8 [b] Ps. 50:3 [c] Mic. 1:4 **3:13** [a] Is. 65:17; 66:22 [b] Rev. 21:1 **3:14** [a] 1 Cor. 1:8; 15:58 **3:15** [a] Rom. 2:4 **3:16** [a] 1 Cor. 15:24 [b] 2 Tim. 3:16 **3:17** [a] Mark 13:23 [b] Eph. 4:14 **3:18** [a] Eph. 4:15 [b] 2 Tim. 4:18

THE FIRST EPISTLE OF JOHN

AUTHOR

First John was universally accepted without dispute as authoritative by the early church. The internal evidence supports this tradition because the "we" (apostles), "you" (readers), and "they" (false teachers) phraseology places the writer in the sphere of apostolic eyewitness (1 John 1:1–3; 4:1, 14). John's name was well known to the readers, and it was unnecessary for him to mention it. The style and vocabulary of 1 John are so similar to those of the fourth Gospel that most scholars acknowledge these books to be by the same hand. First John was probably written in Ephesus after the Gospel of John, but the date cannot be fixed with certainty.

TIME

c. AD 89–95

KEY VERSE

1 John 1:3–4

THEME

Shortly after the church began, people like the Gnostics continually tried to recast the gospel in their own terms. Gnosticism made a distinction between the material or carnal, which was evil to them, and the spiritual, which was pure. John writes as one who was acquainted with Jesus personally, physically, and spiritually. He wants the readers to take the Christ he knew at face value and believe the truth of his experience of Jesus and not the Gnostics' philosophical speculation. In these letters we see the same themes as in John's Gospel—light and darkness, truth and falsehood, life and death, love and hate. John weaves these themes together with straightforward skill and fatherly care.

An attribute of living in the *shalom* of God is the absence of panic: "There is no fear in love; but perfect love casts out fear" (4:18). God loves us perfectly, and therefore, we can live fearless lives. A person committed to the peace of God loves everyone and cannot hold on to a grudge (4:9–11). First John explores love and its connection to peace.

What Was Heard, Seen, and Touched

1 That [a]which was from the beginning,
which we have heard, which we have [b]seen
with our eyes, [c]which we have looked upon,
and [d]our hands have handled, concerning
the [e]Word of life— 2 [a]the life [b]was manifested,
and we have seen, [c]and bear witness, and declare to you that eternal life which was [d]with
the Father and was manifested to us— 3 that
which we have seen and heard we declare
to you, that you also may have fellowship
with us; and truly our fellowship *is* [a]with the
Father and with His Son Jesus Christ. 4 And
these things we write to you [a]that your[1] joy
may be full.

Fellowship with Him and One Another

5 [a]This is the message which we have heard
from Him and declare to you, that [b]God is
light and in Him is no darkness at all. 6 [a]If we
say that we have fellowship with Him, and
walk in darkness, we lie and do not practice
the truth. 7 But if we [a]walk in the light as He
is in the light, we have fellowship with one
another, and [b]the blood of Jesus Christ His
Son cleanses us from all sin.
8 If we say that we have no sin, we deceive
ourselves, and the truth is not in us. 9 If we
[a]confess our sins, He is [b]faithful and just to
forgive us *our* sins and to [c]cleanse us from
all unrighteousness. 10 If we say that we have
not sinned, we [a]make Him a liar, and His
word is not in us.

2 My little children, these things I write
to you, so that you may not sin. And if
anyone sins, [a]we have an Advocate with the
Father, Jesus Christ the righteous. 2 And [a]He
Himself is the propitiation for our sins, and
not for ours only but [b]also for the whole world.

The Test of Knowing Him

3 Now by this we know that we know Him,
if we keep His commandments. 4 He who
says, "I know Him," and does not keep His
commandments, is a [a]liar, and the truth is
not in him. 5 But [a]whoever keeps His word,
truly the love of God is perfected [b]in him. By
this we know that we are in Him. 6 [a]He who
says he abides in Him [b]ought himself also
to walk just as He walked.
7 Brethren,[1] I write no new commandment
to you, but an old commandment which you
have had [a]from the beginning. The old commandment is the word which you heard from
the beginning.[2] 8 Again, [a]a new commandment I write to you, which thing is true in Him
and in you, [b]because the darkness is passing
away, and [c]the true light is already shining.
9 [a]He who says he is in the light, and hates
his brother, is in darkness until now. 10 [a]He
who loves his brother abides in the light,
and [b]there is no cause for stumbling in him.
11 But he who [a]hates his brother is in darkness
and [b]walks in darkness, and does not know
where he is going, because the darkness has
blinded his eyes.

1:1 [a] [John 1:1] [b] John 1:14 [c] 2 Pet. 1:16 [d] Luke 24:39 [e] [John 1:1, 4, 14] **1:2** [a] John 1:4 [b] Rom. 16:26 [c] John 21:24 [d] [John 1:1, 18; 16:28] **1:3** [a] 1 Cor. 1:9 **1:4** [a] John 15:11; 16:24 [1] NU-Text and M-Text read *our.* **1:5** [a] 1 John 3:11 [b] [1 Tim. 6:16] **1:6** [a] [1 John 2:9–11] **1:7** [a] Is. 2:5 [b] [1 Cor. 6:11] **1:9** [a] Prov. 28:13 [b] [Rom. 3:24–26] [c] Ps. 51:2 **1:10** [a] 1 John 5:10 **2:1** [a] Heb. 7:25; 9:24 **2:2** [a] [Rom. 3:25] [b] John 1:29 **2:4** [a] Rom. 3:4 **2:5** [a] John 14:21, 23 [b] [1 John 4:12] **2:6** [a] John 15:4 [b] 1 Pet. 2:21 **2:7** [a] 1 John 3:11, 23; 4:21 [1] NU-Text reads *Beloved.* [2] NU-Text omits *from the beginning.* **2:8** [a] John 13:34; 15:12 [b] Rom. 13:12 [c] [John 1:9; 8:12; 12:35] **2:9** [a] [1 Cor. 13:2] **2:10** [a] [1 John 3:14] [b] 2 Pet. 1:10 **2:11** [a] [1 John 2:9; 3:15; 4:20] [b] John 12:35

DARKNESS DISPELLED

God is light and in Him is no darkness at all.

I JOHN 1:5

When you were a child, were you afraid of the dark? Did that fear follow you into adulthood? Christians can do more than buy another flashlight; they can turn to the Light of the world for help. The overpowering truth of God in our lives is "the light [that] shines in the darkness," and the darkness cannot overcome it (John 1:5). When I open my life to the light of God's Word, darkness cannot take me down.

John the apostle wrote that "God is light" without a shred of darkness to make us afraid. As John the *disciple,* he recorded Jesus' words: "He who follows Me shall not walk in darkness, but have the light of life" (John 8:12). And David the psalmist exclaimed that in God's presence, "night shines as the day" (Ps. 139:12). Whether you fear physical darkness or a more figurative one, turn to the Light. He's waiting to brighten your life and grant you peace.

Their Spiritual State

12 I write to you, little children,
Because [a]your sins are forgiven you
for His name's sake.
13 I write to you, fathers,
Because you have known Him *who is*
[a]from the beginning.
I write to you, young men,
Because you have overcome the
wicked one.
I write to you, little children,
Because you have [b]known the Father.
14 I have written to you, fathers,
Because you have known Him *who is*
from the beginning.
I have written to you, young men,
Because [a]you are strong, and the word
of God abides in you,
And you have overcome the wicked one.

Do Not Love the World

15 [a]Do not love the world or the things in
the world. [b]If anyone loves the world, the love
of the Father is not in him. 16 For all that *is* in
the world—the lust of the flesh, [a]the lust of
the eyes, and the pride of life—is not of the
Father but is of the world. 17 And [a]the world
is passing away, and the lust of it; but he who
does the will of God abides forever.

Deceptions of the Last Hour

18 [a]Little children, [b]it is the last hour; and as
you have heard that [c]the[1] Antichrist is coming,
[d]even now many antichrists have come, by
which we know [e]that it is the last hour. 19 [a]They
went out from us, but they were not of us;
for [b]if they had been of us, they would have
continued with us; but *they went out* [c]that
they might be made manifest, that none of
them were of us.
20 But [a]you have an anointing [b]from the
Holy One, and [c]you know all things.[1] 21 I have
not written to you because you do not know
the truth, but because you know it, and that
no lie is of the truth.
22 [a]Who is a liar but he who denies that
[b]Jesus is the Christ? He is antichrist who denies

PEACE NOTE

Following Christ assures us of God's peace, protection, and presence, yet we are constantly targeted by the flesh, the world, and the devil.

1 JOHN 2:16

2:12 [a] [1 Cor. 6:11] **2:13** [a] John 1:1 [b] [Rom. 8:15–17] **2:14** [a] Eph. 6:10 **2:15** [a] [Rom. 12:2] [b] James 4:4 **2:16** [a] [Eccl. 5:10, 11] **2:17** [a] 1 Cor. 7:31 **2:18** [a] John 21:5 [b] 1 Pet. 4:7 [c] 2 Thess. 2:3 [d] 2 John 7 [e] 1 Tim. 4:1 [1] NU-Text omits *the.* **2:19** [a] Deut. 13:13 [b] Matt. 24:24 [c] 1 Cor. 11:19 **2:20** [a] 2 Cor. 1:21 [b] Acts 3:14 [c] [John 16:13] [1] NU-Text reads *you all know.* **2:22** [a] 2 John 7 [b] 1 John 4:3

DON'T QUIT

My little children, these things I write to you, so that you may not sin.

1 JOHN 2:1

I felt inspired at the burial site of John in Ephesus. John had worked in the mines and marble quarry while exiled by Emperor Domitian to Patmos, and yet he stayed faithful, and God rewarded his faithfulness. In one of the last New Testament writings, John exhorted his readers to stay the course—and he exemplified this in his own life. The Christians faced threatening opposition as well as false teaching that could drive them away from faith and good doctrine. John longed to see his friends experience success in their Christian lives, and it comes from faithfulness to God.

Have you ever been on the verge of faltering, on giving up on your faith and hope due to discouragement, someone's criticism, or your own disappointment in unanswered prayers? Don't give up. You may be an inch away from a long-awaited success, a reached goal, or a life-altering insight. Ask for strength, don't sin, and keep the faith. Be encouraged that other believers have stayed faithful to God, and so can you. It's the only path to peace.

the Father and the Son. 23[a]Whoever denies the Son does not have the [b]Father either; [c]he who acknowledges the Son has the Father also.

Let Truth Abide in You

24 Therefore let that abide in you [a]which you heard from the beginning. If what you heard from the beginning abides in you, [b]you also will abide in the Son and in the Father. 25[a]And this is the promise that He has promised us—eternal life.

26 These things I have written to you concerning those who *try to* deceive you. 27 But the [a]anointing which you have received from Him abides in you, and [b]you do not need that anyone teach you; but as the same anointing [c]teaches you concerning all things, and is true, and is not a lie, and just as it has taught you, you will[1] abide in Him.

The Children of God

28 And now, little children, abide in Him, that when[1] He appears, we may have [a]confidence and not be ashamed before Him at His coming. 29[a]If you know that He is righteous, you know that [b]everyone who practices righteousness is born of Him.

3 Behold [a]what manner of love the Father has bestowed on us, that [b]we should be called children of God![1] Therefore the world does not know us,[2] [c]because it did not know Him. 2 Beloved, [a]now we are children of God; and [b]it has not yet been revealed what we shall be, but we know that when He is revealed, [c]we shall be like Him, for [d]we shall see Him as He is. 3[a]And everyone who has this hope in Him purifies himself, just as He is pure.

Sin and the Child of God

4 Whoever commits sin also commits lawlessness, and [a]sin is lawlessness. 5 And you know [a]that He was manifested [b]to take away our sins, and [c]in Him there is no sin. 6 Whoever abides in Him does not sin. Whoever sins has neither seen Him nor known Him.

7 Little children, let no one deceive you. He who practices righteousness is righteous, just as He is righteous. 8[a]He who sins is of the devil, for the devil has sinned from the beginning. For this purpose the Son of God was manifested, [b]that He might destroy the works of the devil. 9 Whoever has been [a]born of God does not sin, for [b]His seed remains in him; and he cannot sin, because he has been born of God.

The Imperative of Love

10 In this the children of God and the children of the devil are manifest: Whoever does not practice righteousness is not of God, nor *is* he who does not love his brother. 11 For this is the message that you heard from the beginning, [a]that we should love one another, 12 not as [a]Cain *who* was of the wicked one and murdered his brother. And why did he murder him? Because his works were evil and his brother's righteous.

13 Do not marvel, my brethren, if [a]the world hates you. 14 We know that we have passed from death to life, because we love the brethren. He who does not love *his* brother[1] abides in death. 15[a]Whoever hates his brother is a murderer, and you know that [b]no murderer has eternal life abiding in him.

The Outworking of Love

16[a]By this we know love, [b]because He laid down His life for us. And we also ought to lay down *our* lives for the brethren. 17 But [a]whoever has this world's goods, and sees his brother in need, and shuts up his heart from him, how does the love of God abide in him?

18 My little children, [a]let us not love in word or in tongue, but in deed and in truth. 19 And by this we know[1] [a]that we are of the truth, and shall assure our hearts before Him. 20[a]For if our heart condemns us, God is greater than

PEACE NOTE

Jesus regularly emphasized our need to be heralds of peace and the Good News. Let's bring peace, not confusion or conflict, to everyone we encounter.

1 JOHN 3:17

2:23 [a] John 15:23 [b] John 5:23 [c] 1 John 4:15; 5:1 **2:24** [a] 2 John 5, 6 [b] John 14:23 **2:25** [a] John 3:14–16; 6:40; 17:2, 3 **2:27** [a] [John 14:16; 16:13] [b] [Jer. 31:33] [c] [John 14:16] [1] NU-Text reads *you abide.* **2:28** [a] 1 John 3:21; 4:17; 5:14 [1] NU-Text reads *if.* **2:29** [a] Acts 22:14 [b] 1 John 3:7, 10 **3:1** [a] [1 John 4:10] [b] [John 1:12] [c] John 15:18, 21; 16:3 [1] NU-Text adds *And we are.* [2] M-Text reads *you.* **3:2** [a] [Rom. 8:15, 16] [b] [Rom. 8:18, 19, 23] [c] Rom. 8:29 [d] [Ps. 16:11] **3:3** [a] 1 John 4:17 **3:4** [a] Rom. 4:15 **3:5** [a] 1 John 1:2; 3:8 [b] John 1:29 [c] [2 Cor. 5:21] **3:8** [a] Matt. 13:38 [b] Luke 10:18 **3:9** [a] John 1:3; 3:3 [b] 1 Pet. 1:23 **3:11** [a] [John 13:34; 15:12] **3:12** [a] Gen. 4:4, 8 **3:13** [a] [John 15:18; 17:14] **3:14** [1] NU-Text omits *his brother.* **3:15** [a] Matt. 5:21 [b] [Gal. 5:20, 21] **3:16** [a] [John 3:16] [b] John 10:11; 15:13 **3:17** [a] Deut. 15:7 **3:18** [a] Ezek. 33:31 **3:19** [a] John 18:37 [1] NU-Text reads *we shall know.* **3:20** [a] [1 Cor. 4:4, 5]

PROOF POSITIVE

We know that we have passed from death to life, because we love the brethren.

1 JOHN 3:14

Have you struggled to believe you're saved? Worried that your prayer of repentance was worded incorrectly or that your heart wasn't completely confident in the God you prayed to? So many people lack peace about their salvation thanks to grace-less individuals who tried to insert doubt, stir fear, and create panic. You are not at the mercy of such people—you live in the mercy of God! That is where salvation—and peace—come from!

John the apostle offers a very simple test for salvation: Do you love? This is love that provides for people's needs, longs for their happiness and wholeness, and reaches out in tangible ways to see them succeed. If you have not a smidgen of care for those around you, check the authenticity of your salvation. If, though, you act toward others in love—a kind word, a financial gift, an offering of time, energy, or prayers—then you reflect the God of salvation. Seek His peace and assurance, trust in His promise (1 John 2:25), and love the people of God!

our heart, and knows all things. 21 Beloved,
if our heart does not condemn us, [a]we have
confidence toward God. 22 And [a]whatever we
ask we receive from Him, because we keep
His commandments [b]and do those things
that are pleasing in His sight. 23 And this is
His commandment: that we should believe
on the name of His Son Jesus Christ [a]and love
one another, as He gave us[1] commandment.

The Spirit of Truth and the Spirit of Error

24 Now [a]he who keeps His commandments
[b]abides in Him, and He in him. And [c]by this
we know that He abides in us, by the Spirit
whom He has given us.

4 Beloved, do not believe every spirit, but
[a]test the spirits, whether they are of God;
because [b]many false prophets have gone out
into the world. 2 By this you know the Spirit
of God: [a]Every spirit that confesses that Jesus
Christ has come in the flesh is of God, 3 and every
spirit that does not confess that[1] Jesus Christ has
come in the flesh is not of God. And this is the
spirit of the Antichrist, which you have heard
was coming, and is now already in the world.

4 You are of God, little children, and have
overcome them, because He who is in you is
greater than [a]he who is in the world. 5 [a]They
are of the world. Therefore they speak *as* of
the world, and [b]the world hears them. 6 We
are of God. He who knows God hears us; he
who is not of God does not hear us. [a]By this we
know the spirit of truth and the spirit of error.

Knowing God Through Love

7 [a]Beloved, let us love one another, for love
is of God; and everyone who [b]loves is born
of God and knows God. 8 He who does not
love does not know God, for God is love. 9 [a]In
this the love of God was manifested toward
us, that God has sent His only begotten [b]Son
into the world, that we might live through
Him. 10 In this is love, [a]not that we loved God,
but that He loved us and sent His Son [b]*to
be* the propitiation for our sins. 11 Beloved,
[a]if God so loved us, we also ought to love
one another.

PEACE NOTE

Never forget that God, whose Spirit dwells within believers, is greater than the evil one, who dwells within the world.

1 JOHN 4:4

3:21 [a] [1 John 2:28; 5:14] **3:22** [a] Ps. 34:15 [b] John 8:29 **3:23** [a] Matt. 22:39 [1] M-Text omits *us.* **3:24** [a] John 14:23 [b] John 14:21; 17:21 [c] Rom. 8:9, 14, 16 **4:1** [a] 1 Cor. 14:29 [b] Matt. 24:5 **4:2** [a] 1 Cor. 12:3 **4:3** [1] NU-Text omits *that* and *Christ has come in the flesh.* **4:4** [a] John 14:30; 16:11 **4:5** [a] John 3:31 [b] John 15:19; 17:14 **4:6** [a] [1 Cor. 2:12–16] **4:7** [a] 1 John 3:10, 11, 23 [b] 1 Thess. 4:9 **4:9** [a] Rom. 5:8 [b] John 3:16 **4:10** [a] Titus 3:5 [b] 1 John 2:2 **4:11** [a] Matt. 18:33

Seeing God Through Love

12 [a]No one has seen God at any time. If we love one another, God abides in us, and His love has been perfected in us. 13 [a]By this we know that we abide in Him, and He in us, because He has given us of His Spirit. 14 And [a]we have seen and testify that [b]the Father has sent the Son *as* Savior of the world. 15 [a]Whoever confesses that Jesus is the Son of God, God abides in him, and he in God. 16 And we have known and believed the love that God has for us. God is love, and [a]he who abides in love abides in God, and God [b]in him.

The Consummation of Love

17 Love has been perfected among us in this: that [a]we may have boldness in the day of judgment; because as He is, so are we in this world. 18 There is no fear in love; but perfect love casts out fear, because fear involves torment. But he who fears has not been made perfect in love. 19 [a]We love Him[1] because He first loved us.

Obedience by Faith

20 [a]If someone says, "I love God," and hates his brother, he is a liar; for he who does not love his brother whom he has seen, how can[1] he love God [b]whom he has not seen? 21 And [a]this commandment we have from Him: that he who loves God *must* love his brother also.

5 Whoever believes that [a]Jesus is the Christ is [b]born of God, and everyone who loves Him who begot also loves him who is begotten of Him. 2 By this we know that we love the children of God, when we love God and [a]keep His commandments. 3 [a]For this is the love of God, that we keep His commandments. And [b]His commandments are not burdensome. 4 For [a]whatever is born of God overcomes the world. And this is the victory that [b]has overcome the world—our[1] faith. 5 Who is he who overcomes the world, but [a]he who believes that Jesus is the Son of God?

The Certainty of God's Witness

6 This is He who came [a]by water and blood—Jesus Christ; not only by water, but by water and blood. [b]And it is the Spirit who bears witness, because the Spirit is truth. 7 For there are three that bear witness in heaven: the Father, [a]the Word, and the Holy Spirit; [b]and these three are one. 8 And there are three that bear witness on earth:[1] [a]the Spirit, the water, and the blood; and these three agree as one.

9 If we receive [a]the witness of men, the witness of God is greater; [b]for this is the witness of God which[1] He has testified of His Son. 10 He who believes in the Son of God [a]has the witness in himself; he who does not believe God [b]has made Him a liar, because he has not believed the testimony that God has given of His Son. 11 And this is the testimony: that God has given us eternal life, and this life is in His Son. 12 [a]He who has the Son has life; he who does not have the Son of God does not have life. 13 These things I have written to you who believe in the name of the Son of God, that you may know that you have eternal life,[1] and that you may *continue to* believe in the name of the Son of God.

Confidence and Compassion in Prayer

14 Now this is the confidence that we have in Him, that [a]if we ask anything according to His will, He hears us. 15 And if we know that He hears us, whatever we ask, we know that we have the petitions that we have asked of Him.

16 If anyone sees his brother sinning a sin *which does* not *lead* to death, he will ask, and [a]He will give him life for those who commit sin not *leading* to death. [b]There is sin *leading* to death. [c]I do not say that he should pray about that. 17 [a]All unrighteousness is sin, and there is sin not *leading* to death.

Knowing the True—Rejecting the False

18 We know that [a]whoever is born of God does not sin; but he who has been born of God [b]keeps himself,[1] and the wicked one does not touch him.

19 We know that we are of God, and [a]the whole world lies *under the sway of* the wicked one.

20 And we know that the [a]Son of God has come and [b]has given us an understanding, [c]that we may know Him who is true; and we are in Him who is true, in His Son Jesus Christ. [d]This is the true God [e]and eternal life.

21 Little children, keep yourselves from idols. Amen.

4:12 [a] John 1:18 **4:13** [a] John 14:20 **4:14** [a] John 1:14 [b] John 3:17; 4:42 **4:15** [a] [Rom. 10:9] **4:16** [a] [1 John 3:24] [b] [John 14:23] **4:17** [a] 1 John 2:28 **4:19** [a] 1 John 4:10 [1] NU-Text omits *Him.* **4:20** [a] [1 John 2:4] [b] 1 John 4:12 [1] NU-Text reads *he cannot.* **4:21** [a] [Matt. 5:43, 44; 22:39] **5:1** [a] 1 John 2:22; 4:2, 15 [b] John 1:13 **5:2** [a] John 15:10 **5:3** [a] John 14:15 [b] Matt. 11:30; 23:4 **5:4** [a] John 16:33 [b] 1 John 2:13; 4:4 [1] M-Text reads *your.* **5:5** [a] 1 Cor. 15:57 **5:6** [a] John 1:31–34 [b] [John 14:17] **5:7** [a] [John 1:1] [b] John 10:30 **5:8** [a] John 15:26 [1] NU-Text and M-Text omit the words from *in heaven* (verse 7) through *on earth* (verse 8). Only four or five very late manuscripts contain these words in Greek. **5:9** [a] John 5:34, 37; 8:17, 18 [b] [Matt. 3:16, 17] [1] NU-Text reads *God, that.* **5:10** [a] [Rom. 8:16] [b] John 3:18, 33 **5:12** [a] [John 3:15, 36; 6:47; 17:2, 3] **5:13** [1] NU-Text omits the rest of this verse. **5:14** [a] [1 John 2:28; 3:21, 22] **5:16** [a] Job 42:8 [b] [Matt. 12:31] [c] Jer. 7:16; 14:11 **5:17** [a] 1 John 3:4 **5:18** [a] [1 Pet. 1:23] [b] James 1:27 [1] NU-Text reads *him.* **5:19** [a] Gal. 1:4 **5:20** [a] 1 John 4:2 [b] Luke 24:45 [c] John 17:3 [d] Is. 9:6 [e] 1 John 5:11, 12

THE SECOND EPISTLE OF

JOHN

AUTHOR

Second John was not widely circulated at first because of its brevity and subject matter. Its strong resemblance to the tone and style of 1 John and the fourth Gospel support the early tradition that John was the author of this epistle sometime after AD 90.

TIME

c. AD 90–95

KEY VERSE

2 John vv. 9–10

THEME

The addressee of 2 John is a woman in a local church who apparently had a strong friendship with John. The apostle writes to warn her about showing hospitality to false teachers. He cautions her against unwittingly aiding these teachers who were sowing seeds of heresy and hurting the church.

Scripture commands us to live in peace and tells us that if our minds are fixed on Christ, we will have "perfect peace" (Is. 26:3). So why is there so little peace in the world, even among Christians? Have we forgotten these truths, these commands hiding in plain sight in Scripture? John reminds us that peace—with God and with each other—is an essential characteristic of the Christian life (1 John 4:11; Gal. 5:22). Peacemaking should be our passion and our calling (Matt. 5:9).

We live in an anxious time. But John's epistles remind us that being Christians means that love pushes fear out of the picture (1 John 4:18). God's peace is always available; therefore, we should unleash it in a hurting world: "Grace, mercy, and peace will be with you from God the Father and from the Lord Jesus Christ, the Son of the Father, in truth and love" (2 John v. 3). We can't give it unless we have it, and we won't have it if we don't ask for it (James 4:2). Perfect peace is often just a prayer away.

Greeting the Elect Lady

The Elder,

To the elect lady and her children, whom
I love in truth, and not only I, but also all
those who have known [a]the truth, 2 because
of the truth which abides in us and will be
with us forever:

3 [a]Grace, mercy, *and* peace will be with you[1]
from God the Father and from the Lord Jesus
Christ, the Son of the Father, in truth and
love.

Walk in Christ's Commandments

4 I [a]rejoiced greatly that I have found *some*
of your children walking in truth, as we received commandment from the Father. 5 And
now I plead with you, lady, not as though I
wrote a new commandment to you, but that
which we have had from the beginning: [a]that
we love one another. 6 [a]This is love, that we
walk according to His commandments. This
is the commandment, that [b]as you have heard
from the beginning, you should walk in it.

Beware of Antichrist Deceivers

7 For [a]many deceivers have gone out into
the world [b]who do not confess Jesus Christ
as coming in the flesh. [c]This is a deceiver and
an antichrist. 8 [a]Look to yourselves, [b]that we[1]
do not lose those things we worked for, but
that we[2] may receive a full reward.
9 [a]Whoever transgresses[1] and does not
abide in the doctrine of Christ does not have
God. He who abides in the doctrine of Christ
has both the Father and the Son. 10 If anyone
comes to you and [a]does not bring this doctrine, do not receive him into your house nor
greet him; 11 for he who greets him shares in
his evil deeds.

John's Farewell Greeting

12 [a]Having many things to write to you, I
did not wish *to do so* with paper and ink; but
I hope to come to you and speak face to face,
[b]that our joy may be full.
13 [a]The children of your elect sister greet
you. Amen.

PEACE NOTE

If need be, refer struggling friends to helpers—counselors, clergy, mentors—who can care for them and lead them toward the peace of God.

1 [a] Col. 1:5 3 [a] 1 Tim. 1:2 [1] NU-Text and M-Text read *us.* 4 [a] 3 John 3, 4 5 [a] [John 13:34, 35; 15:12, 17] 6 [a] 1 John 2:5; 5:3 [b] 1 John 2:24 7 [a] 1 John 2:19; 4:1 [b] 1 John 4:2 [c] 1 John 2:22 8 [a] Mark 13:9 [b] Gal. 3:4 [1] NU-Text reads *you.* [2] NU-Text reads *you.* 9 [a] John 7:16; 8:31 [1] NU-Text reads *goes ahead.* 10 [a] Rom. 16:17 12 [a] 3 John 13, 14 [b] John 17:13 13 [a] 1 Pet. 5:13

THE THIRD EPISTLE OF

JOHN

AUTHOR

Much like 2 John, this letter had a very limited circulation in the early church but was accepted as authoritative on account of its apostolic authorship. Its style and vocabulary strongly resemble that of John's Gospel and other epistles.

TIME

c. AD 90–95

KEY VERSE

3 John v. 11

THEME

Third John has two main purposes. The first is to commend Gaius for being hospitable to itinerant missionaries. The second is to advise Gaius about Diotrephes, a man in the church who refuses to help the same kind of missionaries and who even gossips about them.

Jesus is the Prince of Peace. In Christ, peace is the hallmark of all our relationships: "I hope to see you shortly, and we shall speak face to face. Peace to you. Our friends greet you. Greet the friends by name" (3 John v. 14). "I pray that you may prosper in all things . . . just as your soul prospers" (v. 2). How will you know if your soul is prospering? A good sign is peace. "For I rejoiced greatly [that] you walk in the truth" (v. 3). How do you know if you are walking in truth? You have peace—not confusion. John told Gaius that "if you send [the people you meet] forward on their journey in a manner worthy of God, you will do well" (v. 6). What is a manner worthy of God? Peace. "Imitate . . . what is good. He who does good is of God" (v. 11). What is something good that I can do? Sow peace. Reflect the Prince of Peace and show the world what He looks like.

Greeting to Gaius

The Elder,

To the beloved Gaius, [a]whom I love in
truth:

2 Beloved, I pray that you may prosper in
all things and be in health, just as your soul
prospers. 3 For I [a]rejoiced greatly when brethren came and testified of the truth *that is* in
you, just as you walk in the truth. 4 I have no
greater [a]joy than to hear that [b]my children
walk in truth.[1]

Gaius Commended for Generosity

5 Beloved, you do faithfully whatever you
do for the brethren and[1] for strangers, 6 who
have borne witness of your love before the
church. *If* you send them forward on their
journey in a manner worthy of God, you
will do well, 7 because they went forth for
His name's sake, [a]taking nothing from the
Gentiles. 8 We therefore ought to [a]receive[1]
such, that we may become fellow workers
for the truth.

Diotrephes and Demetrius

9 I wrote to the church, but Diotrephes, who
loves to have the preeminence among them,
does not receive us. 10 Therefore, if I come,
I will call to mind his deeds which he does,
[a]prating against us with malicious words.
And not content with that, he himself does
not receive the brethren, and forbids those
who wish to, putting *them* out of the church.

11 Beloved, [a]do not imitate what is evil, but
what is good. [b]He who does good is of God,
but[1] he who does evil has not seen [c]God.
12 Demetrius [a]has a *good* testimony from
all, and from the truth itself. And we also
bear witness, [b]and you know that our testimony is true.

Farewell Greeting

13 [a]I had many things to write, but I do not
wish to write to you with pen and ink; 14 but I
hope to see you shortly, and we shall speak
face to face.
Peace to you. Our friends greet you. Greet
the friends by name.

1 [a] 2 John 1 **3** [a] 2 John 4 **4** [a] 1 Thess. 2:19, 20 [b] [1 Cor. 4:15] [1] NU-Text reads *the truth.* **5** [1] NU-Text adds *especially.* **7** [a] 1 Cor. 9:12, 15 **8** [a] Matt. 10:40 [1] NU-Text reads *support.* **10** [a] Prov. 10:8, 10 **11** [a] Ps. 34:14; 37:27 [b] [1 John 2:29; 3:10] [c] [1 John 3:10] [1] NU-Text and M-Text omit *but.* **12** [a] 1 Tim. 3:7 [b] John 19:35; 21:24 **13** [a] 2 John 12

PEACE NOTE

Jesus taught wellness before anyone, but He used a different word—*shalom*—the best form of health there is.

3 JOHN v. 2

LOOKING AHEAD

I hope to see you shortly, and we shall speak face to face. Peace to you. Our friends greet you. Greet the friends by name.

3 JOHN v. 14

I've had moments in my life, especially in ministry, where things go sideways. These moments are not conducive to a sense of peace! Not much can be done about the past, so I find that I must focus on what lies ahead. That's what John is saying in his brief letter—despite the setbacks, he hoped to see his companions in the faith. In the meantime, he wished them peace.

Paul expressed a similar idea in Philippians 3:13 when he said he was "forgetting those things which are behind and reaching forward to those things which are ahead." How can you begin letting go of the past and reaching toward what's ahead? When you do that, how is your peace increased?

THE EPISTLE OF

JUDE

AUTHOR

In spite of its limited subject matter and size, Jude was accepted as authentic and quoted by early church fathers. It is unlikely that the author is the apostle Jude (Luke 6:16), but rather Jude, the brother of Jesus and James (called Judas in Matt. 13:55 and Mark 6:3). Because of the silence of the New Testament and tradition concerning Jude's later years, we cannot know where or when this epistle was written.

TIME

c. AD 66–80

KEY VERSE

Jude v. 3

THEME

Jude's letter is hard-hitting, short, and right to the point. False teachers are on the loose in the church, and Jude wants his readers to understand the destructive implications of their teaching. He urges Christians to resist these teachers and to defend the faith and the body of truth received from the apostles that they have come to know and believe. He finishes by reminding them of the hope they have in knowing that Christ is coming again.

Jude, Jesus' earthly brother, sums up a theology of peace within one chapter through some very descriptive phrases. It's important not to overlook the word "contend" (Jude v. 3) because, if we are going to live lives full of the Holy Spirit and experience all God's promised peace, we have to take action! Peace is a reality in the life of every believer walking in fellowship with God. This is why Jude could say, "Mercy, peace, and love be multiplied to you" (v. 2). Remember that the believer's sins are forgiven, and believers keep themselves "in the love of God" (v. 21). The fruit of keeping ourselves in the atmosphere of God's love is constantly being reminded of our God's perfect love for us, and the truth of this results in our experiencing His peace.

Greeting to the Called

Jude, a bondservant of Jesus Christ, and
[a]brother of James,

To those who are [b]called, sanctified[1] by God
the Father, and [c]preserved in Jesus Christ:

2 Mercy, [a]peace, and love be multiplied
to you.

Contend for the Faith

3 Beloved, while I was very diligent to write
to you [a]concerning our common salvation, I
found it necessary to write to you exhorting
[b]you to contend earnestly for the faith which
was once for all delivered to the saints. 4 For
certain men have crept in unnoticed, who
long ago were marked out for this condemnation, ungodly men, who turn the grace of
our God into lewdness and deny the only
Lord God[1] and our Lord Jesus Christ.

Old and New Apostates

5 But I want to remind you, though you
once knew this, that [a]the Lord, having saved
the people out of the land of Egypt, afterward
destroyed those who did not believe. 6 And
the angels who did not keep their proper
domain, but left their own abode, He has
reserved in everlasting chains under darkness for the judgment of the great day; 7 as
[a]Sodom and Gomorrah, and the cities around
them in a similar manner to these, having
given themselves over to sexual immorality
and gone after strange flesh, are set forth
as an example, suffering the vengeance of
eternal fire.

8 [a]Likewise also these dreamers defile the
flesh, reject authority, and [b]speak evil of dignitaries. 9 Yet Michael the archangel, in contend-
ing with the devil, when he disputed about the
body of Moses, dared not bring against him a
reviling accusation, but said, [a]"The Lord rebuke you!" 10 [a]But these speak evil of whatever
they do not know; and whatever they know
naturally, like brute beasts, in these things
they corrupt themselves. 11 Woe to them! For
they have gone in the way [a]of Cain, [b]have run
greedily in the error of Balaam for profit, and
perished [c]in the rebellion of Korah.

Apostates Depraved and Doomed

12 These are spots in your love feasts, while
they feast with you without fear, serving *only*
themselves. *They are* clouds without water,
carried about[1] by the winds; late autumn trees
without fruit, twice dead, pulled up by the
roots; 13 [a]raging waves of the sea, [b]foaming up
their own shame; wandering stars [c]for whom
is reserved the blackness of darkness forever.
14 Now Enoch, the seventh from Adam,
prophesied about these men also, saying,
"Behold, the Lord comes with ten thousands
of His saints, 15 to execute judgment on all,
to convict all who are ungodly among them
of all their ungodly deeds which they have
committed in an ungodly way, and of all the
[a]harsh things which ungodly sinners have
spoken against Him."

Apostates Predicted

16 These are grumblers, complainers, walking
according to their own lusts; and they [a]mouth
great swelling *words*, [b]flattering people to gain

1 [a] Acts 1:13 [b] Rom. 1:7 [c] John 17:11, 12 [1] NU-Text reads *beloved.* 2 [a] 1 Pet. 1:2 3 [a] Titus 1:4 [b] Phil. 1:27 4 [1] NU-Text omits *God.* 5 [a] 1 Cor. 10:5–10 7 [a] Gen. 19:24 8 [a] 2 Pet. 2:10 [b] Ex. 22:28 9 [a] Zech. 3:2 10 [a] 2 Pet. 2:12 11 [a] Gen. 4:3–8 [b] 2 Pet. 2:15 [c] Num. 16:1–3, 31–35 12 [1] NU-Text and M-Text read *along.* 13 [a] Is. 57:20 [b] [Phil. 3:19] [c] 2 Pet. 2:17 15 [a] 1 Sam. 2:3 16 [a] 2 Pet. 2:18 [b] Prov. 28:21

MORE AND MORE

Mercy, peace, and love be multiplied to you.

JUDE v. 2

I love how early Christian leaders spoke of the multiplication of God's blessings, like mercy, peace, and love. At the very least it implies that these blessings are never in short supply. Yet sometimes in my life when I feel as though the wonderful things are dwindling, not multiplying, it's good to be reminded by the words of Scripture that feelings can be deceiving.

The song of hope keeps singing. The ultimate source of human hope is God, whose mercy, peace, and love are unlimited. Jude, Jesus' brother, could express this hope for his readers because they were followers of Jesus. For them, mercy, peace, and love would be multiplied. They are multiplied for us, too. How does knowing this affect your peace?

advantage. 17 [a]But you, beloved, remember the
words which were spoken before by the apostles of our Lord Jesus Christ: 18 how they told
you that [a]there would be mockers in the last
time who would walk according to their own
ungodly lusts. 19 These are sensual persons, who
cause divisions, not having the Spirit.

Maintain Your Life with God

20 But you, beloved, [a]building yourselves
up on your most holy faith, [b]praying in the
Holy Spirit, 21 keep yourselves in the love of
God, [a]looking for the mercy of our Lord Jesus
Christ unto eternal life.
22 And on some have compassion, making
a distinction;[1] 23 but [a]others save with fear,
[b]pulling *them* out of the fire,[1] hating even
[c]the garment defiled by the flesh.

Glory to God

24 [a]Now to Him who is able to keep you[1]
from stumbling,
And [b]to present *you* faultless
Before the presence of His glory with
exceeding joy,
25 To God our Savior,[1]
Who alone is wise,[2]
Be glory and majesty,
Dominion and power,[3]
Both now and forever.
Amen.

PEACE NOTE

We can be enveloped by the peace of God—a peace so transforming and overwhelming it simply surpasses our ability to understand it.

JUDE V. 21

17 [a] 2 Pet. 3:2 **18** [a] [1 Tim. 4:1] **20** [a] Col. 2:7 [b] [Rom. 8:26] **21** [a] Titus 2:13 **22** [1] NU-Text reads *who are doubting* (or *making distinctions*). **23** [a] Rom. 11:14 [b] Amos 4:11 [c] [Zech. 3:4, 5] [1] NU-Text adds *and on some have mercy with fear* and omits *with fear* in first clause. **24** [a] [Eph. 3:20] [b] Col. 1:22 [1] M-Text reads *them.* **25** [1] NU-Text reads *To the only God our Savior.* [2] NU-Text omits *Who . . . is wise* and adds *Through Jesus Christ our Lord.* [3] NU-Text adds *Before all time.*

THE REVELATION OF JESUS CHRIST

AUTHOR

The style, symmetry, and plan of Revelation show that it was written by one author, named four times as "John" (Rev. 1:1, 4, 9; 22:8). Because of its contents and its address to seven churches, Revelation quickly circulated and became widely known and accepted in the early church. From the beginning, it was considered an authentic work of the apostle John, the same John who wrote the Gospel and Epistles named for him. Revelation was written at a time when Roman hostility to Christianity was erupting into overt persecution. It is likely that John wrote this book in AD 95 or 96 when the severe persecution of Christians began under the emperor Domitian.

TIME

c. AD 95–96

KEY VERSE

Revelation 19:11–15

THEME

John wrote this book late in his life while in exile on the island of Patmos off the coast of Asia. It is safe to say that no book of the Bible has generated more theories of interpretation over the last two millennia. In this context, probably one of the best approaches to interpreting and understanding Revelation is to concentrate on the major themes, such as worship. When the reader does that, he or she finds great assurance. Many scholars think the book is meant to provide comfort in the midst of persecution and difficult times and communicate hope through symbolic imagery.

The greeting John extended to the seven churches in 1:4–5 begins, "Grace to you and peace," which is the greatest possible blessing in Revelation. Grace and peace from whom? "From Him who is and who was and who is to come," the greatest possible Source of overflowing peace—Jesus. And who is He? He is "the firstborn from the dead, and the ruler over the kings of the earth," which eludes to the greatest possible purpose—eternal peace in Jesus in the re-created heaven and earth. The Jesus described in Revelation brings peace forevermore—no more sin, no more crying, no more death, no more disappointment—because of His faithfulness to us now and forever. John vividly described the resurrected and reigning Jesus as He who is "called Faithful and True" and the One who "has on His robe and on His thigh a name written: KING OF KINGS AND LORD OF LORDS" (19:11, 16). This is He who has peace to give and who promises, "Surely I am coming quickly" (22:20).

Introduction and Benediction

1 The Revelation of Jesus Christ, [a]which
God gave Him to show His servants—
things which must shortly take place. And
[b]He sent and signified *it* by His angel to His
servant John, 2 [a]who bore witness to the word
of God, and to the testimony of Jesus Christ,
to all things [b]that he saw. 3 [a]Blessed *is* he who
reads and those who hear the words of this
prophecy, and keep those things which are
written in it; for [b]the time *is* near.

Greeting the Seven Churches

4 John, to the seven churches which are
in Asia:

Grace to you and peace from Him [a]who is
and [b]who was and who is to come, [c]and from
the seven Spirits who are before His throne,
5 and from Jesus Christ, [a]the faithful [b]witness,
the [c]firstborn from the dead, and [d]the ruler
over the kings of the earth.

To Him [e]who loved us [f]and washed[1] us
from our sins in His own blood, 6 and has
[a]made us kings[1] and priests to His God and
Father, [b]to Him *be* glory and dominion forever and ever. Amen.

7 Behold, He is coming with [a]clouds, and
every eye will see Him, even [b]they who
pierced Him. And all the tribes of the earth
will mourn because of Him. Even so, Amen.

8 [a]"I am the Alpha and the Omega, *the* Beginning and *the* End,"[1] says the Lord,[2] [b]"who
is and who was and who is to come, the [c]Al-
mighty."

Vision of the Son of Man

9 I, John, both[1] your brother and [a]com-
panion in the tribulation and [b]kingdom and
patience of Jesus Christ, was on the island
that is called Patmos for the word of God and
for the testimony of Jesus Christ. 10 [a]I was
in the Spirit on [b]the Lord's Day, and I heard
behind me [c]a loud voice, as of a trumpet,
11 saying, "I am the Alpha and the Omega, the
First and the Last," and,[1] "What you see, write
in a book and send *it* to the seven churches
which are in Asia:[2] to Ephesus, to Smyrna,
to Pergamos, to Thyatira, to Sardis, to Philadelphia, and to Laodicea."

12 Then I turned to see the voice that spoke
with me. And having turned [a]I saw seven
golden lampstands, 13 [a]and in the midst of the
seven lampstands [b]*One* like the Son of Man,
[c]clothed with a garment down to the feet and
[d]girded about the chest with a golden band.
14 His head and [a]hair *were* white like wool, as
white as snow, and [b]His eyes like a flame of fire;

1:1 [a] John 3:32 [b] Rev. 22:6 **1:2** [a] 1 Cor. 1:6 [b] 1 John 1:1 **1:3** [a] Luke 11:28 [b] James 5:8 **1:4** [a] Ex. 3:14 [b] John 1:1 [c] [Is. 11:2] **1:5** [a] John 8:14 [b] Is. 55:4 [c] [Col. 1:18] [d] Rev. 17:14 [e] John 13:34 [f] Heb. 9:14 [1] NU-Text reads *loves us and freed;* M-Text reads *loves us and washed.* **1:6** [a] 1 Pet. 2:5, 9 [b] 1 Tim. 6:16 [1] NU-Text and M-Text read *a kingdom.* **1:7** [a] Matt. 24:30 [b] Zech. 12:10–14 **1:8** [a] Is. 41:4 [b] Rev. 4:8; 11:17 [c] Is. 9:6 [1] NU-Text and M-Text omit *the Beginning and the End.* [2] NU-Text and M-Text add *God.* **1:9** [a] Phil. 1:7 [b] [2 Tim. 2:12] [1] NU-Text and M-Text omit *both.* **1:10** [a] Acts 10:10 [b] Acts 20:7 [c] Rev. 4:1 **1:11** [1] NU-Text and M-Text omit *I am* through third *and.* [2] NU-Text and M-Text omit *which are in Asia.* **1:12** [a] Ex. 25:37 **1:13** [a] Rev. 2:1 [b] Ezek. 1:26 [c] Dan. 10:5 [d] Rev. 15:6 **1:14** [a] Dan. 7:9 [b] Dan. 10:6

LOOK FIRST TO JESUS

Grace to you and peace from Him who is and who was and who is to come.

REVELATION 1:4

I live in Texas, so I know a thing or two about violent weather. I have experienced firsthand hurricanes, tornadoes, and flooding. I mention this because of what John says in his Revelation of the risen Christ. What John discloses in chapters 6–19 is truly frightening. Yet he extended to his struggling readers, who faced threats on their lives, grace and peace. *What?* Given the tribulation that would eventually come upon these churches—earthly and spiritual mayhem—how could he speak of soothing ideas like grace and peace?

The answer is in the rest of the verse. Where can any believer, in any circumstance, find peace and grace? "In Him who is and who was and who is to come." In short, from the Lord Jesus. John was assured of Jesus' wise control of his life even as he received this revelation on the rugged, volcanic-rock island of Patmos. In stressing Jesus' eternal existence and wise control, John reminds us that this One who lives forever is living today in us. This is the same Jesus who promised peace (John 14:27) and presence (Matt. 28:20). If you lack peace, look first to Jesus.

15 [a]His feet *were* like fine brass, as if refined in a
furnace, and [b]His voice as the sound of many
waters; 16 [a]He had in His right hand seven stars,
[b]out of His mouth went a sharp two-edged
sword, [c]and His countenance *was* like the sun
shining in its strength. 17 And [a]when I saw Him,
I fell at His feet as dead. But [b]He laid His right
hand on me, saying to me,[1] "Do not be afraid;
[c]I am the First and the Last. 18 [a]I *am* He who
lives, and was dead, and behold, [b]I am alive
forevermore. Amen. And [c]I have the keys of
Hades and of Death. 19 Write[1] the things which
you have [a]seen, [b]and the things which are, [c]and
the things which will take place after this. 20 The
mystery of the seven stars which you saw in My
right hand, and the seven golden lampstands:
The seven stars are [a]the angels of the seven
churches, and [b]the seven lampstands which
you saw[1] are the seven churches.

The Loveless Church

2 "To the angel of the church of Ephesus
write,
'These things says [a]He who holds the seven
stars in His right hand, [b]who walks in the
midst of the seven golden lampstands: 2 [a]"I
know your works, your labor, your patience,
and that you cannot bear those who are evil.
And [b]you have tested those [c]who say they are
apostles and are not, and have found them
liars; 3 and you have persevered and have patience, and have labored for My name's sake
and have [a]not become weary. 4 Nevertheless I
have *this* against you, that you have left your
first love. 5 Remember therefore from where
you have fallen; repent and do the first works,
[a]or else I will come to you quickly and remove
your lampstand from its place—unless you
repent. 6 But this you have, that you hate the
deeds of the Nicolaitans, which I also hate.
7 [a]"He who has an ear, let him hear what the
Spirit says to the churches. To him who overcomes I will give [b]to eat from [c]the tree of life,
which is in the midst of the Paradise of God." '

The Persecuted Church

8 "And to the angel of the church in Smyrna write,
'These things says [a]the First and the Last,
who was dead, and came to life: 9 "I know your
works, tribulation, and poverty (but you are
[a]rich); and *I know* the blasphemy of [b]those
who say they are Jews and are not, [c]but *are* a
synagogue of Satan. 10 [a]Do not fear any of those
things which you are about to suffer. Indeed,
the devil is about to throw *some* of you into
prison, that you may be tested, and you will
have tribulation ten days. [b]Be faithful until
death, and I will give you [c]the crown of life.
11 [a]"He who has an ear, let him hear what the
Spirit says to the churches. He who overcomes
shall not be hurt by [b]the second death." '

The Compromising Church

12 "And to the angel of the church in Pergamos write,
'These things says [a]He who has the sharp
two-edged sword: 13 "I know your works, and
where you dwell, where Satan's throne *is.*
And you hold fast to My name, and did not
deny My faith even in the days in which Antipas *was* My faithful martyr, who was killed
among you, where Satan dwells. 14 But I have
a few things against you, because you have
there those who hold the doctrine of [a]Ba-
laam, who taught Balak to put a stumbling
block before the children of Israel, [b]to eat
things sacrificed to idols, [c]and to commit sexual immorality. 15 Thus you also have those
who hold the doctrine of the Nicolaitans,
which thing I hate.[1] 16 Repent, or else I will
come to you quickly and [a]will fight against
them with the sword of My mouth.
17 "He who has an ear, let him hear what the
Spirit says to the churches. To him who overcomes I will give some of the hidden [a]manna
to eat. And I will give him a white stone, and
on the stone [b]a new name written which no
one knows except him who receives *it.*" '

The Corrupt Church

18 "And to the angel of the church in Thyatira write,
'These things says the Son of God, [a]who
has eyes like a flame of fire, and His feet
like fine brass: 19 [a]"I know your works, love,
service, faith,[1] and your patience; and *as* for
your works, the last *are* more than the first.
20 Nevertheless I have a few things against
you, because you allow[1] that woman[2] [a]Jeze-
bel, who calls herself a prophetess, to teach
and seduce[3] My servants [b]to commit sexual

1:15 [a] Ezek. 1:7 [b] Ezek. 1:24; 43:2 **1:16** [a] Rev. 1:20; 2:1; 3:1 [b] Is. 49:2 [c] Matt. 17:2 **1:17** [a] Ezek. 1:28 [b] Dan. 8:18; 10:10, 12 [c] Is. 41:4; 44:6; 48:12 [1] NU-Text and M-Text omit *to me.* **1:18** [a] Rom. 6:9 [b] Rev. 4:9 [c] Ps. 68:20 **1:19** [a] Rev. 1:9–18 [b] Rev. 2:1 [c] Rev. 4:1 [1] NU-Text and M-Text read *Therefore, write.* **1:20** [a] Rev. 2:1 [b] Zech. 4:2 [1] NU-Text and M-Text omit *which you saw.* **2:1** [a] Rev. 1:16 [b] Rev. 1:13 **2:2** [a] Ps. 1:6 [b] 1 John 4:1 [c] 2 Cor. 11:13 **2:3** [a] Gal. 6:9 **2:5** [a] Matt. 21:41 **2:7** [a] Matt. 11:15 [b] [Rev. 22:2, 14] [c] [Gen. 2:9; 3:22] **2:8** [a] Rev. 1:8, 17, 18 **2:9** [a] Luke 12:21 [b] Rom. 2:17 [c] Rev. 3:9 **2:10** [a] Matt. 10:22 [b] Matt. 24:13 [c] James 1:12 **2:11** [a] Rev. 13:9 [b] [Rev. 20:6, 14; 21:8] **2:12** [a] Rev. 1:16; 2:16 **2:14** [a] Num. 31:16 [b] Acts 15:29 [c] 1 Cor. 6:13 **2:15** [1] NU-Text and M-Text read *likewise* for *which thing I hate.* **2:16** [a] 2 Thess. 2:8 **2:17** [a] Ex. 16:33, 34 [b] Rev. 3:12 **2:18** [a] Rev. 1:14, 15 **2:19** [a] Rev. 2:2 [1] NU-Text and M-Text read *faith, service.* **2:20** [a] 1 Kin. 16:31; 21:25 [b] Ex. 34:15 [1] NU-Text and M-Text read *I have against you that you tolerate.* [2] M-Text reads *your wife Jezebel.* [3] NU-Text and M-Text read *and teaches and seduces.*

immorality and eat things sacrificed to idols.
21 And I gave her time [a]to repent of her sexual
immorality, and she did not repent.[1] 22 Indeed
I will cast her into a sickbed, and those who
commit adultery with her into great tribulation, unless they repent of their[1] deeds.
23 I will kill her children with death, and all
the churches shall know that I am He who
[a]searches the minds and hearts. And I will give
to each one of you according to your works.
24 "Now to you I say, and[1] to the rest in Thyatira, as many as do not have this doctrine,
who have not known the [a]depths of Satan, as
they say, [b]I will[2] put on you no other burden.
25 But hold fast [a]what you have till I come.
26 And he who overcomes, and keeps [a]My
works until the end, [b]to him I will give power
over the nations—

27 'He[a] shall rule them with a rod
of iron;
They shall be dashed to pieces like the
potter's vessels'[1]—

as I also have received from My Father; 28 and
I will give him [a]the morning star.
29 "He who has an ear, let him hear what
the Spirit says to the churches." '

The Dead Church

3 "And to the angel of the church in Sardis write,
'These things says He who [a]has the seven
Spirits of God and the seven stars: "I know
your works, that you have a name that you
are alive, but you are dead. 2 Be watchful,
and strengthen the things which remain,
that are ready to die, for I have not found
your works perfect before God.[1] 3 [a]Remember
therefore how you have received and heard;
hold fast and [b]repent. [c]Therefore if you will
not watch, I will come upon you [d]as a thief,
and you will not know what hour I will come
upon you. 4 You[1] have [a]a few names even in
Sardis who have not [b]defiled their garments;
and they shall walk with Me [c]in white, for
they are worthy. 5 He who overcomes [a]shall
be clothed in white garments, and I will not
[b]blot out his name from the [c]Book of Life;
but [d]I will confess his name before My Father
and before His angels.

> **PEACE NOTE**
>
> Some future glorious day, all will be peaceful in the eternal kingdom of our Lord Jesus Christ! Imagine perfect harmony and peace among the redeemed from hundreds of nations.

6 [a]"He who has an ear, let him hear what
the Spirit says to the churches." '

The Faithful Church

7 "And to the angel of the church in Philadelphia write,
'These things says [a]He who is holy, [b]He who
is true, [c]"He who has the key of David, [d]He
who opens and no one shuts, and [e]shuts and
no one opens":[1] 8 [a]"I know your works. See, I
have set before you [b]an open door, and no one
can shut it;[1] for you have a little strength, have
kept My word, and have not denied My name.
9 Indeed I will make [a]*those* of the synagogue
of Satan, who say they are Jews and are not,
but lie—indeed [b]I will make them come and
worship before your feet, and to know that I
have loved you. 10 Because you have kept My
command to persevere, [a]I also will keep you
from the hour of trial which shall come upon
[b]the whole world, to test those who dwell [c]on
the earth. 11 Behold,[1] [a]I am coming quickly!
[b]Hold fast what you have, that no one may
take [c]your crown. 12 He who overcomes, I will
make him [a]a pillar in the temple of My God,
and he shall [b]go out no more. [c]I will write
on him the name of My God and the name
of the city of My God, the [d]New Jerusalem,
which [e]comes down out of heaven from My
God. [f]And *I will write on him* My new name.
13 [a]"He who has an ear, let him hear what
the Spirit says to the churches." '

2:21 [a] Rev. 9:20; 16:9, 11 [1] NU-Text and M-Text read *time to repent, and she does not want to repent of her sexual immorality.* **2:22** [1] NU-Text and M-Text read *her.* **2:23** [a] Jer. 11:20; 17:10 **2:24** [a] 2 Tim. 3:1–9 [b] Acts 15:28 [1] NU-Text and M-Text omit *and.* [2] NU-Text and M-Text omit *will.* **2:25** [a] Rev. 3:11 **2:26** [a] [John 6:29] [b] [Matt. 19:28] **2:27** [a] Ps. 2:8, 9 [1] Psalm 2:9 **2:28** [a] 2 Pet. 1:19 **3:1** [a] Rev. 1:4, 16 **3:2** [1] NU-Text and M-Text read *My God.* **3:3** [a] 1 Tim. 6:20 [b] Rev. 3:19 [c] Matt. 24:42, 43 [d] [Rev. 16:15] **3:4** [a] Acts 1:15 [b] [Jude 23] [c] Rev. 4:4; 6:11 [1] NU-Text and M-Text read *Nevertheless you have a few names in Sardis.* **3:5** [a] [Rev. 19:8] [b] Ex. 32:32 [c] Phil. 4:3 [d] Luke 12:8 **3:6** [a] Rev. 2:7 **3:7** [a] Acts 3:14 [b] 1 John 5:20 [c] Is. 9:7; 22:22 [d] [Matt. 16:19] [e] Job 12:14 [1] Isaiah 22:22 **3:8** [a] Rev. 3:1 [b] 1 Cor. 16:9 [1] NU-Text and M-Text read *which no one can shut.* **3:9** [a] Rev. 2:9 [b] Is. 45:14; 49:23; 60:14 **3:10** [a] 2 Pet. 2:9 [b] Luke 2:1 [c] Is. 24:17 **3:11** [a] Phil. 4:5 [b] Rev. 2:25 [c] [Rev. 2:10] [1] NU-Text and M-Text omit *Behold.* **3:12** [a] 1 Kin. 7:21 [b] Ps. 23:6 [c] [Rev. 14:1; 22:4] [d] [Heb. 12:22] [e] Rev. 21:2 [f] [Rev. 2:17; 22:4] **3:13** [a] Rev. 2:7

The Lukewarm Church

14"And to the angel of the church of the
Laodiceans[1] write,
[a]'These things says the Amen, [b]the Faithful and True Witness, [c]the Beginning of the
creation of God: 15[a]"I know your works, that
you are neither cold nor hot. I could wish you
were cold or hot. 16So then, because you are
lukewarm, and neither cold nor hot,[1] I will
vomit you out of My mouth. 17Because you
say, [a]'I am rich, have become wealthy, and
have need of nothing'—and do not know
that you are wretched, miserable, poor, blind,
and naked— 18I counsel you [a]to buy from
Me gold refined in the fire, that you may be
rich; and [b]white garments, that you may be
clothed, *that* the shame of your nakedness
may not be revealed; and anoint your eyes
with eye salve, that you may see. 19[a]As many
as I love, I rebuke and [b]chasten. Therefore be
zealous and repent. 20Behold, [a]I stand at the
door and knock. [b]If anyone hears My voice
and opens the door, [c]I will come in to him
and dine with him, and he with Me. 21To him
who overcomes [a]I will grant to sit with Me on
My throne, as I also overcame and sat down
with My Father on His throne.
22[a]"He who has an ear, let him hear what
the Spirit says to the churches." ' "

The Throne Room of Heaven

4 After these things I looked, and behold, a
door *standing* [a]open in heaven. And the
first voice which I heard *was* like a [b]trumpet
speaking with me, saying, "Come up here,
and I will show you things which must take
place after this."
2Immediately [a]I was in the Spirit; and behold, [b]a throne set in heaven, and *One* sat on
the throne. 3And He who sat there was[1] [a]like a
jasper and a sardius stone in appearance; [b]and
there was a rainbow around the throne, in appearance like an emerald. 4[a]Around the throne
were twenty-four thrones, and on the thrones
I saw twenty-four elders sitting, [b]clothed in
white robes; and they had crowns[1] of gold on
their heads. 5And from the throne proceeded
[a]lightnings, thunderings, and voices.[1] [b]Seven
lamps of fire *were* burning before the throne,
which are [c]the[2] seven Spirits of God.
6Before the throne *there was*[1] [a]a sea of
glass, like crystal. [b]And in the midst of the
throne, and around the throne, *were* four living creatures full of eyes in front and in back.
7[a]The first living creature *was* like a lion, the
second living creature like a calf, the third
living creature had a face like a man, and the
fourth living creature *was* like a flying eagle.
8*The* four living creatures, each having [a]six
wings, were full of eyes around and within.
And they do not rest day or night, saying:

[b]"Holy, holy, holy,[1]
[c]Lord God Almighty,
[d]Who was and is and is to come!"

9Whenever the living creatures give glory
and honor and thanks to Him who sits on the
throne, [a]who lives forever and ever, 10[a]the
twenty-four elders fall down before Him
who sits on the throne and worship Him who
lives forever and ever, and cast their crowns
before the throne, saying:

11 "You[a] are worthy, O Lord,[1]
To receive glory and honor and power;
[b]For You created all things,
And by [c]Your will they exist[2] and were
created."

The Lamb Takes the Scroll

5 And I saw in the right *hand* of Him who sat
on the throne [a]a scroll written inside and
on the back, [b]sealed with seven seals. 2Then
I saw a strong angel proclaiming with a loud
voice, [a]"Who is worthy to open the scroll and
to loose its seals?" 3And no one in heaven or
on the earth or under the earth was able to
open the scroll, or to look at it.
4So I wept much, because no one was found
worthy to open and read[1] the scroll, or to look
at it. 5But one of the elders said to me, "Do
not weep. Behold, [a]the Lion of the tribe of
[b]Judah, [c]the Root of David, has [d]prevailed to
open the scroll [e]and to loose[1] its seven seals."
6And I looked, and behold,[1] in the midst of
the throne and of the four living creatures,
and in the midst of the elders, stood [a]a Lamb
as though it had been slain, having seven
horns and [b]seven eyes, which are [c]the seven

3:14 [a] 2 Cor. 1:20 [b] Rev. 1:5; 3:7; 19:11 [c] [Col. 1:15] [1] NU-Text and M-Text read *in Laodicea.* **3:15** [a] Rev. 3:1 **3:16** [1] NU-Text and M-Text read *hot nor cold.* **3:17** [a] Hos. 12:8 **3:18** [a] Is. 55:1 [b] 2 Cor. 5:3 **3:19** [a] Job 5:17 [b] Heb. 12:6 **3:20** [a] Song 5:2 [b] Luke 12:36, 37 [c] [John 14:23] **3:21** [a] Matt. 19:28 **3:22** [a] Rev. 2:7 **4:1** [a] Ezek. 1:1 [b] Rev. 1:10 **4:2** [a] Rev. 1:10 [b] Is. 6:1 **4:3** [a] Rev. 21:11 [b] Ezek. 1:28 [1] M-Text omits *And He who sat there was* (which makes the description in verse 3 modify the throne rather than God). **4:4** [a] Rev. 11:16 [b] Rev. 3:4, 5 [1] NU-Text and M-Text read *robes, with crowns.* **4:5** [a] Rev. 8:5; 11:19; 16:18 [b] Ex. 37:23 [c] [Rev. 1:4] [1] NU-Text and M-Text read *voices, and thunderings.* [2] M-Text omits *the.* **4:6** [a] Rev. 15:2 [b] Ezek. 1:5 [1] NU-Text and M-Text add *something like.* **4:7** [a] Ezek. 1:10; 10:14 **4:8** [a] Is. 6:2 [b] Is. 6:3 [c] Rev. 1:8 [d] Rev. 1:4 [1] M-Text has *holy* nine times. **4:9** [a] Rev. 1:18 **4:10** [a] Rev. 5:8, 14; 7:11; 11:16; 19:4 **4:11** [a] Rev. 1:6; 5:12 [b] Gen. 1:1 [c] Col. 1:16 [1] NU-Text and M-Text read *our Lord and God.* [2] NU-Text and M-Text read *existed.* **5:1** [a] Ezek. 2:9, 10 [b] Is. 29:11 **5:2** [a] Rev. 4:11; 5:9 **5:4** [1] NU-Text and M-Text omit *and read.* **5:5** [a] Gen. 49:9 [b] Heb. 7:14 [c] Is. 11:1, 10 [d] Rev. 3:21 [e] Rev. 6:1 [1] NU-Text and M-Text omit *to loose.* **5:6** [a] [John 1:29] [b] Zech. 3:9; 4:10 [c] Rev. 1:4; 3:1; 4:5 [1] NU-Text and M-Text read *I saw in the midst . . . a Lamb standing.*

Spirits of God sent out into all the earth.
7 Then He came and took the scroll out of the
right hand [a]of Him who sat on the throne.

Worthy Is the Lamb

8 Now when He had taken the scroll, [a]the
four living creatures and the twenty-four
elders fell down before the Lamb, each having a harp, and golden bowls full of incense,
which are the [b]prayers of the saints. 9 And
[a]they sang a new song, saying:

[b]"You are worthy to take the scroll,
And to open its seals;
For You were slain,
And [c]have redeemed us to God [d]by
Your blood
Out of every tribe and tongue and
people and nation,
10 And have made us[1] [a]kings[2] and [b]priests
to our God;
And we[3] shall reign on the earth."

11 Then I looked, and I heard the voice of
many angels around the throne, the living
creatures, and the elders; and the number of
them was ten thousand times ten thousand,
and thousands of thousands, 12 saying with
a loud voice:

"Worthy is the Lamb who was slain
To receive power and riches and
wisdom,
And strength and honor and glory and
blessing!"

13 And [a]every creature which is in heaven
and on the earth and under the earth and
such as are in the sea, and all that are in
them, I heard saying:

[b]"Blessing and honor and glory and
power
Be to Him [c]who sits on the throne,
And to the Lamb, forever and
ever!"[1]

14 Then the four living creatures said,
"Amen!" And the twenty-four[1] elders fell
down and worshiped Him who lives forever
and ever.[2]

First Seal: The Conqueror

6 Now [a]I saw when the Lamb opened one of
the seals;[1] and I heard [b]one of the four living creatures saying with a voice like thunder,
"Come and see." 2 And I looked, and behold,
[a]a white horse. [b]He who sat on it had a bow;
[c]and a crown was given to him, and he went
out [d]conquering and to conquer.

Second Seal: Conflict on Earth

3 When He opened the second seal, [a]I heard
the second living creature saying, "Come and
see."[1] 4 [a]Another horse, fiery red, went out.
And it was granted to the one who sat on it
to [b]take peace from the earth, and that *people*
should kill one another; and there was given
to him a great sword.

Third Seal: Scarcity on Earth

5 When He opened the third seal, [a]I heard
the third living creature say, "Come and see."
So I looked, and behold, [b]a black horse, and he
who sat on it had a pair of [c]scales in his hand.
6 And I heard a voice in the midst of the four
living creatures saying, "A quart[1] of wheat for a
denarius,[2] and three quarts of barley for a denarius; and [a]do not harm the oil and the wine."

Fourth Seal: Widespread Death on Earth

7 When He opened the fourth seal, [a]I heard
the voice of the fourth living creature saying,
"Come and see." 8 [a]So I looked, and behold, a
pale horse. And the name of him who sat on
it was Death, and Hades followed with him.
And power was given to them over a fourth
of the earth, [b]to kill with sword, with hunger,
with death, [c]and by the beasts of the earth.

Fifth Seal: The Cry of the Martyrs

9 When He opened the fifth seal, I saw under [a]the altar [b]the souls of those who had
been slain [c]for the word of God and for [d]the
testimony which they held. 10 And they cried
with a loud voice, saying, [a]"How long, O Lord,
[b]holy and true, [c]until You judge and avenge
our blood on those who dwell on the earth?"
11 Then a [a]white robe was given to each of them;
and it was said to them [b]that they should rest
a little while longer, until both *the number of*
their fellow servants and their brethren, who
would be killed as they *were,* was completed.

5:7 [a] Rev. 4:2 **5:8** [a] Rev. 4:8–10; 19:4 [b] Rev. 8:3 **5:9** [a] Rev. 14:3 [b] Rev. 4:11 [c] John 1:29 [d] [Heb. 9:12] **5:10** [a] Ex. 19:6 [b] Is. 61:6 [1] NU-Text and M-Text read *them.* [2] NU-Text reads *a kingdom.* [3] NU-Text and M-Text read *they.* **5:13** [a] Phil. 2:10 [b] 1 Chr. 29:11 [c] Rev. 4:2, 3; 6:16; 20:11 [1] M-Text adds *Amen.* **5:14** [1] NU-Text and M-Text omit *twenty-four.* [2] NU-Text and M-Text omit *Him who lives forever and ever.* **6:1** [a] [Rev. 5:5–7, 12; 13:8] [b] Rev. 4:7 [1] NU-Text and M-Text read *seven seals.* **6:2** [a] Zech. 1:8; 6:3 [b] Ps. 45:4, 5, LXX [c] Zech. 6:11 [d] Matt. 24:5 **6:3** [a] Rev. 4:7 [1] NU-Text and M-Text omit *and see.* **6:4** [a] Zech. 1:8; 6:2 [b] Matt. 24:6, 7 **6:5** [a] Rev. 4:7 [b] Zech. 6:2, 6 [c] Matt. 24:7 **6:6** [a] Rev. 7:3; 9:4 [1] Greek *choinix;* that is, approximately one quart [2] This was approximately one day's wage for a worker. **6:7** [a] Rev. 4:7 **6:8** [a] Zech. 6:3 [b] Ezek. 5:12, 17; 14:21; 29:5 [c] Lev. 26:22 **6:9** [a] Rev. 8:3 [b] [Rev. 20:4] [c] Rev. 1:2, 9 [d] 2 Tim. 1:8 **6:10** [a] Zech. 1:12 [b] Rev. 3:7 [c] Rev. 11:18 **6:11** [a] Rev. 3:4, 5; 7:9 [b] Heb. 11:40

BE READY FOR THE END

Another horse, fiery red, went out. And it was granted to the one who sat on it to take peace from the earth, and that people should kill one another.

REVELATION 6:4

Politicians and world leaders often speak of peace. They assure us that, thanks to their policies and leadership, there will be peace. Yet peace is quite rare. It seems that there is war or a threat of war somewhere in our broken world all the time. National governments and people groups routinely deplore violence but are largely ineffective in preventing or ending it.

John's revelation from the risen Christ warned of dangerous times ahead. It's clear from Revelation that those who don't know Christ will not know peace. Indeed, according to this verse, the man who sits on the "fiery red" horse will "take peace from the earth" with the result that "people should kill one another."

But the peace that this villain takes away is not the peace that God gives to His people. That peace no villain, not even the Antichrist himself, can take away. This is true even though the church will face awful tribulation (and it often has throughout history). Faith in Christ is the key to surviving the coming tribulation, and the peace of Christ is what makes it endurable.

Sixth Seal: Cosmic Disturbances

12 I looked when He opened the sixth seal,
[a]and behold,[1] there was a great earthquake;
and [b]the sun became black as sackcloth
of hair, and the moon[2] became like blood.
13 [a]And the stars of heaven fell to the earth, as
a fig tree drops its late figs when it is shaken
by a mighty wind. 14 [a]Then the sky receded as
a scroll when it is rolled up, and [b]every mountain and island was moved out of its place.
15 And the [a]kings of the earth, the great men,
the rich men, the commanders,[1] the mighty
men, every slave and every free man, [b]hid
themselves in the caves and in the rocks of
the mountains, 16 [a]and said to the mountains
and rocks, "Fall on us and hide us from the
face of Him who [b]sits on the throne and
from the wrath of the Lamb! 17 For the great
day of His wrath has come, [a]and who is able
to stand?"

The Sealed of Israel

7 After these things I saw four angels standing at the four corners of the earth, [a]hold-
ing the four winds of the earth, [b]that the wind
should not blow on the earth, on the sea,
or on any tree. 2 Then I saw another angel
ascending from the east, having the seal of
the living God. And he cried with a loud voice
to the four angels to whom it was granted to
harm the earth and the sea, 3 saying, [a]"Do
not harm the earth, the sea, or the trees till
we have sealed the servants of our God [b]on
their foreheads." 4 [a]And I heard the number
of those who were sealed. [b]One hundred *and*
forty-four thousand [c]of all the tribes of the
children of Israel *were* sealed:

5 of the tribe of Judah twelve thousand
were sealed;[1]
of the tribe of Reuben twelve thousand
were sealed;
of the tribe of Gad twelve thousand
were sealed;
6 of the tribe of Asher twelve thousand
were sealed;
of the tribe of Naphtali twelve
thousand *were* sealed;
of the tribe of Manasseh twelve
thousand *were* sealed;
7 of the tribe of Simeon twelve thousand
were sealed;
of the tribe of Levi twelve thousand
were sealed;
of the tribe of Issachar twelve
thousand *were* sealed;
8 of the tribe of Zebulun twelve thousand
were sealed;

6:12 [a] Matt. 24:7 [b] Joel 2:10, 31; 3:15 [1] NU-Text and M-Text omit *behold.* [2] NU-Text and M-Text read *the whole moon.* 6:13 [a] Rev. 8:10; 9:1 6:14 [a] Is. 34:4 [b] Rev. 16:20 6:15 [a] Ps. 2:2–4 [b] Is. 2:10, 19, 21; 24:21 [1] NU-Text and M-Text read *the commanders, the rich men.* 6:16 [a] Luke 23:29, 30 [b] Rev. 20:11 6:17 [a] Zeph. 1:14 7:1 [a] Dan. 7:2 [b] Rev. 7:3; 8:7; 9:4 7:3 [a] Rev. 6:6 [b] Rev. 22:4 7:4 [a] Rev. 9:16 [b] Rev. 14:1, 3 [c] Gen. 49:1–27 7:5 [1] In NU-Text and M-Text *were sealed* is stated only in verses 5a and 8c; the words are understood in the remainder of the passage.

of the tribe of Joseph twelve thousand
were sealed;
of the tribe of Benjamin twelve
thousand *were* sealed.

A Multitude from the Great Tribulation

9 After these things I looked, and behold, [a]a
great multitude which no one could number,
[b]of all nations, tribes, peoples, and tongues,
standing before the throne and before the
Lamb, [c]clothed with white robes, with palm
branches in their hands, 10 and crying out
with a loud voice, saying, [a]"Salvation *belongs*
to our God [b]who sits on the throne, and to
the Lamb!" 11 [a]All the angels stood around
the throne and the elders and the four living
creatures, and fell on their faces before the
throne and [b]worshiped God, 12 [a]saying:

"Amen! Blessing and glory and wisdom,
Thanksgiving and honor and power
and might,
Be to our God forever and ever.
Amen."

13 Then one of the elders answered, saying to me, "Who are these arrayed in [a]white
robes, and where did they come from?"
14 And I said to him, "Sir,[1] you know."
So he said to me, [a]"These are the ones
who come out of the great tribulation, and
[b]washed their robes and made them white in
the blood of the Lamb. 15 Therefore they are
before the throne of God, and serve Him day
and night in His temple. And He who sits on
the throne will [a]dwell among them. 16 [a]They
shall neither hunger anymore nor thirst
anymore; [b]the sun shall not strike them, nor
any heat; 17 for the Lamb who is in the midst
of the throne [a]will shepherd them and lead
them to living fountains of waters.[1] [b]And God
will wipe away every tear from their eyes."

Seventh Seal: Prelude to the Seven Trumpets

8 When[a] He opened the seventh seal, there
was silence in heaven for about half an
hour. 2 [a]And I saw the seven angels who stand
before God, [b]and to them were given seven
trumpets. 3 Then another angel, having a
golden censer, came and stood at the altar.
He was given much incense, that he should
offer *it* with [a]the prayers of all the saints

> PEACE NOTE
>
> Jesus came not to destroy Israel's enemies but to save and redeem all, Israel and the Gentile nations alike. His mission and our Great Commission are to spread the gospel of peace to the nations!
>
> REVELATION 7:9

upon [b]the golden altar which was before the
throne. 4 And [a]the smoke of the incense, with
the prayers of the saints, ascended before
God from the angel's hand. 5 Then the angel
took the censer, filled it with fire from the
altar, and threw *it* to the earth. And [a]there
were noises, thunderings, [b]lightnings, [c]and
an earthquake.
6 So the seven angels who had the seven
trumpets prepared themselves to sound.

First Trumpet: Vegetation Struck

7 The first angel sounded: [a]And hail and
fire followed, mingled with blood, and they
were thrown [b]to the earth.[1] And a third [c]of
the trees were burned up, and all green grass
was burned up.

Second Trumpet: The Seas Struck

8 Then the second angel sounded: [a]And
something like a great mountain burning with
fire was thrown into the sea, [b]and a third of
the sea [c]became blood. 9 [a]And a third of the
living creatures in the sea died, and a third
of the ships were destroyed.

Third Trumpet: The Waters Struck

10 Then the third angel sounded: [a]And a
great star fell from heaven, burning like a
torch, [b]and it fell on a third of the rivers and
on the springs of water. 11 [a]The name of the
star is Wormwood. [b]A third of the waters
became wormwood, and many men died
from the water, because it was made bitter.

7:9 [a] Rom. 11:25 [b] Rev. 5:9 [c] Rev. 3:5, 18; 4:4; 6:11 **7:10** [a] Ps. 3:8 [b] Rev. 5:13 **7:11** [a] Rev. 4:6 [b] Rev. 4:11; 5:9, 12, 14; 11:16 **7:12** [a] Rev. 5:13, 14 **7:13** [a] Rev. 7:9 **7:14** [a] Rev. 6:9 [b] [Heb. 9:14] [1] NU-Text and M-Text read *My lord.* **7:15** [a] Is. 4:5, 6 **7:16** [a] Is. 49:10 [b] Ps. 121:6 **7:17** [a] Ps. 23:1 [b] Rev. 21:4 [1] NU-Text and M-Text read *to fountains of the waters of life.* **8:1** [a] Rev. 6:1 **8:2** [a] [Matt. 18:10] [b] 2 Chr. 29:25–28 **8:3** [a] Rev. 5:8 [b] Ex. 30:1 **8:4** [a] Ps. 141:2 **8:5** [a] Rev. 11:19; 16:18 [b] Rev. 4:5 [c] 2 Sam. 22:8 **8:7** [a] Ezek. 38:22 [b] Rev. 16:2 [c] Rev. 9:4, 15–18 [1] NU-Text and M-Text add *and a third of the earth was burned up.* **8:8** [a] Jer. 51:25 [b] Ex. 7:17 [c] Ezek. 14:19 **8:9** [a] Rev. 16:3 **8:10** [a] Is. 14:12 [b] Rev. 14:7; 16:4 **8:11** [a] Ruth 1:20 [b] Ex. 15:23

Fourth Trumpet: The Heavens Struck

12[a]Then the fourth angel sounded: And
a third of the sun was struck, a third of the
moon, and a third of the stars, so that a third
of them were darkened. A third of the day did
not shine, and likewise the night.

13 And I looked, [a]and I heard an angel[1] flying through the midst of heaven, saying with
a loud voice, [b]"Woe, woe, woe to the inhabitants of the earth, because of the remaining
blasts of the trumpet of the three angels who
are about to sound!"

Fifth Trumpet: The Locusts from the Bottomless Pit

9 Then the fifth angel sounded: [a]And I saw
a star fallen from heaven to the earth. To
him was given the key to [b]the bottomless
pit. 2 And he opened the bottomless pit, and
smoke arose out of the pit like the smoke of
a great furnace. So the [a]sun and the air were
darkened because of the smoke of the pit.
3 Then out of the smoke locusts came upon
the earth. And to them was given power, [a]as
the scorpions of the earth have power. 4 They
were commanded [a]not to harm [b]the grass of
the earth, or any green thing, or any tree, but
only those men who do not have [c]the seal of
God on their foreheads. 5 And they were not
given *authority* to kill them, [a]but to torment
them *for* five months. Their torment *was* like
the torment of a scorpion when it strikes a
man. 6 In those days [a]men will seek death
and will not find it; they will desire to die,
and death will flee from them.

7[a]The shape of the locusts was like horses
prepared for battle. [b]On their heads were
crowns of something like gold, [c]and their faces *were* like the faces of men. 8 They had hair
like women's hair, and [a]their teeth were like
lions' *teeth.* 9 And they had breastplates like
breastplates of iron, and the sound of their
wings *was* [a]like the sound of chariots with
many horses running into battle. 10 They had
tails like scorpions, and there were stings in
their tails. Their power *was* to hurt men five
months. 11 And they had as king over them
[a]the angel of the bottomless pit, whose name
in Hebrew *is* Abaddon, but in Greek he has
the name Apollyon.

12[a]One woe is past. Behold, still two more
woes are coming after these things.

Sixth Trumpet: The Angels from the Euphrates

13 Then the sixth angel sounded: And I heard
a voice from the four horns of the [a]golden altar
which is before God, 14 saying to the sixth angel
who had the trumpet, "Release the four angels
who are bound [a]at the great river Euphrates."
15 So the four angels, who had been prepared
for the hour and day and month and year, were
released to kill a [a]third of mankind. 16 Now [a]the
number of the army [b]of the horsemen *was*
two hundred million; [c]I heard the number of
them. 17 And thus I saw the horses in the vision:
those who sat on them had breastplates of
fiery red, hyacinth blue, and sulfur yellow;
[a]and the heads of the horses *were* like the
heads of lions; and out of their mouths came
fire, smoke, and brimstone. 18 By these three
plagues a third of mankind was killed—by the
fire and the smoke and the brimstone which
came out of their mouths. 19 For their power[1]
is in their mouth and in their tails; [a]for their
tails *are* like serpents, having heads; and with
them they do harm.

20 But the rest of mankind, who were not
killed by these plagues, [a]did not repent of the
works of their hands, that they should not
worship [b]demons, [c]and idols of gold, silver,
brass, stone, and wood, which can neither see
nor hear nor walk. 21 And they did not repent
of their murders [a]or their sorceries[1] or their
sexual immorality or their thefts.

The Mighty Angel with the Little Book

10 I saw still another mighty angel coming
down from heaven, clothed with a cloud.
[a]And a rainbow *was* on [b]his head, his face *was*
like the sun, and [c]his feet like pillars of fire. 2 He
had a little book open in his hand. [a]And he set
his right foot on the sea and *his* left *foot* on the
land, 3 and cried with a loud voice, as *when* a
lion roars. When he cried out, [a]seven thunders
uttered their voices. 4 Now when the seven
thunders uttered their voices,[1] I was about to
write; but I heard a voice from heaven saying
to me,[2] [a]"Seal up the things which the seven
thunders uttered, and do not write them."

5 The angel whom I saw standing on the
sea and on the land [a]raised up his hand[1] to
heaven 6 and swore by Him who lives forever
and ever, [a]who created heaven and the things
that are in it, the earth and the things that are

8:12 [a] Is. 13:10 **8:13** [a] Rev. 14:6; 19:17 [b] Rev. 9:12; 11:14; 12:12 [1] NU-Text and M-Text read *eagle.* **9:1** [a] Rev. 8:10 [b] Luke 8:31 **9:2** [a] Joel 2:2, 10 **9:3** [a] Judg. 7:12 **9:4** [a] Rev. 6:6 [b] Rev. 8:7 [c] Rev. 7:2, 3 **9:5** [a] [Rev. 9:10; 11:7] **9:6** [a] Jer. 8:3 **9:7** [a] Joel 2:4 [b] Nah. 3:17 [c] Dan. 7:8 **9:8** [a] Joel 1:6 **9:9** [a] Joel 2:5–7 **9:11** [a] Eph. 2:2 **9:12** [a] Rev. 8:13; 11:14 **9:13** [a] Rev. 8:3 **9:14** [a] Rev. 16:12 **9:15** [a] Rev. 8:7–9; 9:18 **9:16** [a] Dan. 7:10 [b] Ezek. 38:4 [c] Rev. 7:4 **9:17** [a] Is. 5:28, 29 **9:19** [a] Is. 9:15 [1] NU-Text and M-Text read *the power of the horses.* **9:20** [a] Deut. 31:29 [b] 1 Cor. 10:20 [c] Dan. 5:23 **9:21** [a] Rev. 21:8; 22:15 [1] NU-Text and M-Text read *drugs.* **10:1** [a] Rev. 4:3 [b] Rev. 1:16 [c] Rev. 1:15 **10:2** [a] Matt. 28:18 **10:3** [a] Ps. 29:3–9 **10:4** [a] Dan. 8:26; 12:4, 9 [1] NU-Text and M-Text read *sounded.* [2] NU-Text and M-Text omit *to me.* **10:5** [a] Dan. 12:7 [1] NU-Text and M-Text read *right hand.* **10:6** [a] Rev. 4:11

in it, and the sea and the things that are in it, [b]that there should be delay no longer, 7 but [a]in the days of the sounding of the seventh angel, when he is about to sound, the mystery of God would be finished, as He declared to His servants the prophets.

John Eats the Little Book

8 Then the voice which I heard from heaven spoke to me again and said, "Go, take the little book which is open in the hand of the angel who stands on the sea and on the earth."

9 So I went to the angel and said to him, "Give me the little book."

And he said to me, [a]"Take and eat it; and it will make your stomach bitter, but it will be as sweet as honey in your mouth."

10 Then I took the little book out of the angel's hand and ate it, [a]and it was as sweet as honey in my mouth. But when I had eaten it, [b]my stomach became bitter. 11 And he[1] said to me, "You must prophesy again about many peoples, nations, tongues, and kings."

The Two Witnesses

11 Then I was given [a]a reed like a measuring rod. And the angel stood,[1] saying, [b]"Rise and measure the temple of God, the altar, and those who worship there. 2 But leave out [a]the court which is outside the temple, and do not measure it, [b]for it has been given to the Gentiles. And they will [c]tread the holy city underfoot *for* [d]forty-two months. 3 And I will give *power* to my two [a]witnesses, [b]and they will prophesy [c]one thousand two hundred and sixty days, clothed in sackcloth."

4 These are the [a]two olive trees and the two lampstands standing before the God[1] of the earth. 5 And if anyone wants to harm them, [a]fire proceeds from their mouth and devours their enemies. [b]And if anyone wants to harm them, he must be killed in this manner. 6 These [a]have power to shut heaven, so that no rain falls in the days of their prophecy; and they have power over waters to turn them to blood, and to strike the earth with all plagues, as often as they desire.

The Witnesses Killed

7 When they [a]finish their testimony, [b]the *beast that ascends* [c]*out of the bottomless pit* [d]will make war against them, overcome them, and kill them. 8 And their dead bodies *will lie* in the street of [a]the great city which spiritually is called Sodom and Egypt, [b]where also our[1] Lord was crucified. 9 [a]Then *those* from the peoples, tribes, tongues, and nations will see their dead bodies three-and-a-half days, [b]and not allow[1] their dead bodies to be put into graves. 10 [a]And those who dwell on the earth will rejoice over them, make merry, [b]and send gifts to one another, [c]because these two prophets tormented those who dwell on the earth.

The Witnesses Resurrected

11 [a]Now after the three-and-a-half days [b]the breath of life from God entered them, and they stood on their feet, and great fear fell on those who saw them. 12 And they[1] heard a loud voice from heaven saying to them, "Come up here." [a]And they ascended to heaven [b]in a cloud, [c]and their enemies saw them. 13 In the same hour [a]there was a great earthquake, [b]and a tenth of the city fell. In the earthquake seven thousand people were killed, and the rest were afraid [c]and gave glory to the God of heaven.

14 [a]The second woe is past. Behold, the third woe is coming quickly.

Seventh Trumpet: The Kingdom Proclaimed

15 Then [a]the seventh angel sounded: [b]And there were loud voices in heaven, saying, [c]"The kingdoms[1] of this world have become *the kingdoms* of our Lord and of His Christ, [d]and He shall reign forever and ever!" 16 And [a]the twenty-four elders who sat before God on their thrones fell on their faces and [b]worshiped God, 17 saying:

"We give You thanks, O Lord God Almighty,
The One [a]who is and who was and who is to come,[1]
Because You have taken Your great power [b]and reigned.
18 The nations were [a]angry, and Your wrath has come,
And the time of the [b]dead, that they should be judged,
And that You should reward Your servants the prophets and the saints,

10:6 [b] Rev. 16:17 **10:7** [a] Rev. 11:15 **10:9** [a] Jer. 15:16 **10:10** [a] Ezek. 3:3 [b] Ezek. 2:10 **10:11** [1] NU-Text and M-Text read *they.* **11:1** [a] Ezek. 40:3—42:20 [b] Num. 23:18 [1] NU-Text and M-Text omit *And the angel stood.* **11:2** [a] Ezek. 40:17, 20 [b] Ps. 79:1 [c] Dan. 8:10 [d] Rev. 12:6; 13:5 **11:3** [a] Rev. 20:4 [b] Rev. 19:10 [c] Rev. 12:6 **11:4** [a] Zech. 4:2, 3, 11, 14 [1] NU-Text and M-Text read *Lord.* **11:5** [a] 2 Kin. 1:10–12 [b] Num. 16:29 **11:6** [a] 1 Kin. 17:1 **11:7** [a] Luke 13:32 [b] Rev. 13:1, 11; 17:8 [c] Rev. 9:1, 2 [d] Dan. 7:21 **11:8** [a] Rev. 14:8 [b] Heb. 13:12 [1] NU-Text and M-Text read *their.* **11:9** [a] Rev. 17:15 [b] Ps. 79:2, 3 [1] NU-Text and M-Text read *nations see . . . and will not allow.* **11:10** [a] Rev. 12:12 [b] Esth. 9:19, 22 [c] Rev. 16:10 **11:11** [a] Rev. 11:9 [b] Ezek. 37:5, 9, 10 **11:12** [a] Is. 14:13 [b] Acts 1:9 [c] 2 Kin. 2:11, 12 [1] M-Text reads *I.* **11:13** [a] Rev. 6:12; 8:5; 11:19; 16:18 [b] Rev. 16:19 [c] Rev. 14:7; 16:9; 19:7 **11:14** [a] Rev. 8:13; 9:12 **11:15** [a] Rev. 8:2; 10:7 [b] Is. 27:13 [c] Rev. 12:10 [1] NU-Text and M-Text read *kingdom . . . has become.* [d] Ex. 15:18 **11:16** [a] Rev. 4:4 [b] Rev. 4:11; 5:9, 12, 14; 7:11 **11:17** [a] Rev. 16:5 [b] Rev. 19:6 [1] NU-Text and M-Text omit *and who is to come.* **11:18** [a] Ps. 2:1 [b] Dan. 7:10

And those who fear Your name, small
and great,
And should destroy those who destroy
the earth."

19 Then [a]the temple of God was opened in heaven, and the ark of His covenant[1] was seen in His temple. And [b]there were lightnings, noises, thunderings, an earthquake, [c]and great hail.

The Woman, the Child, and the Dragon

12 Now a great sign appeared in heaven: a woman clothed with the sun, with the moon under her feet, and on her head a garland of twelve stars. 2 Then being with child, she cried out [a]in labor and in pain to give birth.

3 And another sign appeared in heaven: behold, [a]a great, fiery red dragon having seven heads and ten horns, and seven diadems on his heads. 4 [a]His tail drew a third [b]of the stars of heaven [c]and threw them to the earth. And the dragon stood [d]before the woman who was ready to give birth, [e]to devour her Child as soon as it was born. 5 She bore a male Child [a]who was to rule all nations with a rod of iron. And her Child was [b]caught up to God and His throne. 6 Then [a]the woman fled into the wilderness, where she has a place prepared by God, that they should feed her there [b]one thousand two hundred and sixty days.

Satan Thrown Out of Heaven

7 And war broke out in heaven: [a]Michael and his angels fought [b]with the dragon; and the dragon and his angels fought, 8 but they did not prevail, nor was a place found for them[1] in heaven any longer. 9 So [a]the great dragon was cast out, [b]that serpent of old, called the Devil and Satan, [c]who deceives the whole world; [d]he was cast to the earth, and his angels were cast out with him.

10 Then I heard a loud voice saying in heaven, [a]"Now salvation, and strength, and the kingdom of our God, and the power of His Christ have come, for the accuser of our brethren, [b]who accused them before our God day and night, has been cast down. 11 And [a]they overcame him by the blood of the Lamb and by the word of their testimony, [b]and they did not love their lives to the death. 12 Therefore [a]rejoice, O heavens, and you who dwell in them! [b]Woe to the inhabitants of the earth and the sea! For the devil has come down to you, having great wrath, [c]because he knows that he has a short time."

The Woman Persecuted

13 Now when the dragon saw that he had been cast to the earth, he persecuted [a]the woman who gave birth to the male *Child.* 14 [a]But the woman was given two wings of a great eagle, [b]that she might fly [c]into the wilderness to her place, where she is nourished [d]for a time and times and half a time, from the presence of the serpent. 15 So the serpent [a]spewed water out of his mouth like a flood after the woman, that he might cause her to be carried away by the flood. 16 But the earth helped the woman, and the earth opened its mouth and swallowed up the flood which the dragon had spewed out of his mouth. 17 And the dragon was enraged with the woman, and he went to make war with the rest of her offspring, who keep the commandments of God and have the testimony of Jesus Christ.[1]

The Beast from the Sea

13 Then I[1] stood on the sand of the sea. And I saw [a]a beast rising up out of the sea, [b]having seven heads and ten horns,[2] and on his horns ten crowns, and on his heads a [c]blasphemous name. 2 Now the beast which I saw was like a leopard, his feet were like *the feet of* a bear, and his mouth like the mouth of a lion. The [a]dragon gave him his power,

PEACE NOTE

If you pursue the peace of God in an all-or-nothing fashion (*I'm doing it perfectly* or *I'm failing*), you will never feel successful.

11:19 [a] Rev. 4:1; 15:5, 8 [b] Rev. 8:5 [c] Rev. 16:21 [1] M-Text reads *the covenant of the Lord.* **12:2** [a] Is. 26:17; 66:6–9 **12:3** [a] Rev. 13:1; 17:3, 7, 9 **12:4** [a] Rev. 9:10, 19 [b] Rev. 8:7, 12 [c] Dan. 8:10 [d] Rev. 12:2 [e] Matt. 2:16 **12:5** [a] Ps. 2:9 [b] Acts 1:9–11 **12:6** [a] Rev. 12:4, 14 [b] Rev. 11:3; 13:5 **12:7** [a] Dan. 10:13, 21; 12:1 [b] Rev. 20:2 **12:8** [1] M-Text reads *him.* **12:9** [a] John 12:31 [b] Gen. 3:1, 4 [c] Rev. 20:3 [d] Rev. 9:1 **12:10** [a] Rev. 11:15 [b] Zech. 3:1 **12:11** [a] Rom. 16:20 [b] Luke 14:26 **12:12** [a] Ps. 96:11 [b] Rev. 8:13 [c] Rev. 10:6 **12:13** [a] Rev. 12:5 **12:14** [a] Ex. 19:4 [b] Rev. 12:6 [c] Rev. 17:3 [d] Dan. 7:25; 12:7 **12:15** [a] Is. 59:19 **12:17** [1] NU-Text and M-Text omit *Christ.* **13:1** [a] Dan. 7:2, 7 [b] Rev. 12:3 [c] Rev. 17:3 [1] NU-Text reads *he.* [2] NU-Text and M-Text read *ten horns and seven heads.* **13:2** [a] Rev. 12:3, 9; 13:4, 12

his throne, and great authority. 3 And I saw
one of his heads [a]as if it had been mortally
wounded, and his deadly wound was healed.
And [b]all the world marveled and followed
the beast. 4 So they worshiped the dragon
who gave authority to the beast; and they
worshiped the beast, saying, [a]"Who *is* like the
beast? Who is able to make war with him?"
5 And he was given [a]a mouth speaking great
things and blasphemies, and he was given
authority to continue[1] for [b]forty-two months.
6 Then he opened his mouth in blasphemy
against God, to blaspheme His name, [a]His
tabernacle, and those who dwell in heaven.
7 It was granted to him [a]to make war with the
saints and to overcome them. And [b]author-
ity was given him over every tribe,[1] tongue,
and nation. 8 All who dwell on the earth will
worship him, [a]whose names have not been
written in the Book of Life of the Lamb slain
[b]from the foundation of the world.
9 [a]If anyone has an ear, let him hear. 10 [a]He
who leads into captivity shall go into captivity; [b]he who kills with the sword must be
killed with the sword. [c]Here is the patience
and the faith of the saints.

The Beast from the Earth

11 Then I saw another beast [a]coming up out
of the earth, and he had two horns like a lamb
and spoke like a dragon. 12 And he exercises all
the authority of the first beast in his presence,
and causes the earth and those who dwell in
it to worship the first beast, [a]whose deadly wound was healed. 13 [a]He performs great
signs, [b]so that he even makes fire come down
from heaven on the earth in the sight of men.
14 [a]And he deceives those[1] who dwell on the
earth [b]by those signs which he was granted to
do in the sight of the beast, telling those who
dwell on the earth to make an image to the
beast who was wounded by the sword [c]and
lived. 15 He was granted *power* to give breath
to the image of the beast, that the image of
the beast should both speak [a]and cause as
many as would not worship the image of the
beast to be killed. 16 He causes all, both small
and great, rich and poor, free and slave, [a]to
receive a mark on their right hand or on their
foreheads, 17 and that no one may buy or sell
except one who has the mark or[1] [a]the name
of the beast, [b]or the number of his name.
18 [a]Here is wisdom. Let him who has
[b]understanding calculate [c]the number of
the beast, [d]for it is the number of a man: His
number *is* 666.

The Lamb and the 144,000

14 Then I looked, and behold, a[1] [a]Lamb
standing on Mount Zion, and with
Him [b]one hundred *and* forty-four thousand,
having[2] His Father's name [c]written on their
foreheads. 2 And I heard a voice from heaven,
[a]like the voice of many waters, and like the
voice of loud thunder. And I heard the sound
of [b]harpists playing their harps. 3 They sang
as it were a new song before the throne, before the four living creatures, and the elders;
and no one could learn that song [a]except
the hundred *and* forty-four thousand who
were redeemed from the earth. 4 These are
the ones who were not defiled with women,
[a]for they are virgins. These are the ones [b]who
follow the Lamb wherever He goes. These
[c]were redeemed[1] from *among* men, [d]*being*
firstfruits to God and to the Lamb. 5 And [a]in
their mouth was found no deceit,[1] for [b]they
are without fault before the throne of God.[2]

The Proclamations of Three Angels

6 Then I saw another angel [a]flying in the
midst of heaven, [b]having the everlasting gospel
to preach to those who dwell on the earth—[c]to
every nation, tribe, tongue, and people— 7 saying with a loud voice, [a]"Fear God and give glory to Him, for the hour of His judgment has
come; [b]and worship Him who made heaven
and earth, the sea and springs of water."
8 And another angel followed, saying,
[a]"Babylon[1] is fallen, is fallen, that great city,
because [b]she has made all nations drink of
the wine of the wrath of her fornication."
9 Then a third angel followed them, saying
with a loud voice, [a]"If anyone worships the
beast and his image, and receives *his* [b]mark
on his forehead or on his hand, 10 he himself
[a]shall also drink of the wine of the wrath of
God, which is [b]poured out full strength into
[c]the cup of His indignation. [d]He shall be
tormented with [e]fire and brimstone in the

13:3 [a] Rev. 13:12, 14 [b] Rev. 17:8 **13:4** [a] Rev. 18:18 **13:5** [a] Dan. 7:8, 11, 20, 25; 11:36 [b] Rev. 11:2 [1] M-Text reads *make war.* **13:6** [a] [Col. 2:9] **13:7** [a] Dan. 7:21 [b] Rev. 11:18 [1] NU-Text and M-Text add *and people.* **13:8** [a] Ex. 32:32 [b] Rev. 17:8 **13:9** [a] Rev. 2:7 **13:10** [a] Is. 33:1 [b] Gen. 9:6 [c] Rev. 14:12 **13:11** [a] Rev. 11:7 **13:12** [a] Rev. 13:3, 4 **13:13** [a] Matt. 24:24 [b] 1 Kin. 18:38 **13:14** [a] Rev. 12:9 [b] 2 Thess. 2:9 [c] 2 Kin. 20:7 [1] M-Text reads *my own people.* **13:15** [a] Rev. 16:2 **13:16** [a] Rev. 7:3; 14:9; 20:4 **13:17** [a] Rev. 14:9–11 [b] Rev. 15:2 [1] NU-Text and M-Text omit *or.* **13:18** [a] Rev. 17:9 [b] [1 Cor. 2:14] [c] Rev. 15:2 [d] Rev. 21:17 **14:1** [a] Rev. 5:6 [b] Rev. 7:4; 14:3 [c] Rev. 7:3; 22:4 [1] NU-Text and M-Text read *the.* [2] NU-Text and M-Text add *His name and.* **14:2** [a] Rev. 1:15; 19:6 [b] Rev. 5:8 **14:3** [a] Rev. 5:9 **14:4** [a] [2 Cor. 11:2] [b] Rev. 3:4; 7:17 [c] Rev. 5:9 [d] James 1:18 [1] M-Text adds *by Jesus.* **14:5** [a] Ps. 32:2 [b] Eph. 5:27 [1] NU-Text and M-Text read *falsehood.* [2] NU-Text and M-Text omit *before the throne of God.* **14:6** [a] Rev. 8:13 [b] Eph. 3:9 [c] Rev. 13:7 **14:7** [a] Rev. 11:18 [b] Neh. 9:6 **14:8** [a] Is. 21:9 [b] Jer. 51:7 [1] NU-Text reads *Babylon the great is fallen, is fallen, which has made;* M-Text reads *Babylon the great is fallen. She has made.* **14:9** [a] Rev. 13:14, 15; 14:11 [b] Rev. 13:16 **14:10** [a] Ps. 75:8 [b] Rev. 18:6 [c] Rev. 16:19 [d] Rev. 20:10 [e] 2 Thess. 1:7

presence of the holy angels and in the presence of the Lamb. 11 And [a]the smoke of their
torment ascends forever and ever; and they
have no rest day or night, who worship the
beast and his image, and whoever receives
the mark of his name."

12 [a]Here is the patience of the saints; [b]here
are those[1] who keep the commandments of
God and the faith of Jesus.

13 Then I heard a voice from heaven saying
to me,[1] "Write: [a]'Blessed *are* the dead [b]who
die in the Lord from now on.' "

"Yes," says the Spirit, [c]"that they may rest
from their labors, and their works follow
[d]them."

Reaping the Earth's Harvest

14 Then I looked, and behold, a white cloud,
and on the cloud sat *One* like the Son of Man,
having on His head a golden crown, and in
His hand a sharp sickle. 15 And another angel
[a]came out of the temple, crying with a loud
voice to Him who sat on the cloud, [b]"Thrust
in Your sickle and reap, for the time has come
for You[1] to reap, for the harvest [c]of the earth
is ripe." 16 So He who sat on the cloud thrust
in His sickle on the earth, and the earth was
reaped.

Reaping the Grapes of Wrath

17 Then another angel came out of the
temple which is in heaven, he also having
a sharp sickle.

18 And another angel came out from the
altar, [a]who had power over fire, and he cried
with a loud cry to him who had the sharp sickle, saying, [b]"Thrust in your sharp sickle and
gather the clusters of the vine of the earth,
for her grapes are fully ripe." 19 So the angel
thrust his sickle into the earth and gathered
the vine of the earth, and threw *it* into [a]the
great winepress of the wrath of God. 20 And
[a]the winepress was trampled [b]outside the
city, and blood came out of the winepress,
[c]up to the horses' bridles, for one thousand
six hundred furlongs.

Prelude to the Bowl Judgments

15 Then [a]I saw another sign in heaven,
great and marvelous: [b]seven angels
having the seven last plagues, [c]for in them
the wrath of God is complete.

2 And I saw *something* like [a]a sea of glass
[b]mingled with fire, and those who have the
victory over the beast, [c]over his image and
over his mark[1] *and* over the [d]number of his
name, standing on the sea of glass, [e]hav-
ing harps of God. 3 They sing [a]the song of
Moses, the servant of God, and the song of
the [b]Lamb, saying:

[c]"Great and marvelous *are* Your works,
Lord God Almighty!
[d]Just and true *are* Your ways,
O King of the saints![1]
4 [a]Who shall not fear You, O Lord, and
glorify Your name?
For *You* alone *are* [b]holy.
For [c]all nations shall come and worship
before You,
For Your judgments have been
manifested."

PEACE NOTE

Experience peace today by reminding yourself of the heavenly city where you will spend eternity. Imagine majestic angels praising God's power!

REVELATION 15:3

5 After these things I looked, and behold,[1]
[a]the temple of the tabernacle of the testimony in heaven was opened. 6 And out of the
temple came the seven angels having the
seven plagues, [a]clothed in pure bright linen,
and having their chests girded with golden
bands. 7 [a]Then one of the four living creatures
gave to the seven angels seven golden bowls
full of the wrath of God [b]who lives forever
and ever. 8 [a]The temple was filled with smoke
[b]from the glory of God and from His power,
and no one was able to enter the temple till
the seven plagues of the seven angels were
completed.

14:11 [a] Is. 34:8–10 **14:12** [a] Rev. 13:10 [b] Rev. 12:17 [1] NU-Text and M-Text omit *here are those.* **14:13** [a] Eccl. 4:1, 2 [b] 1 Cor. 15:18 [c] Heb. 4:9, 10 [d] [1 Cor. 3:11–15; 15:58] [1] NU-Text and M-Text omit *to me.* **14:15** [a] Rev. 16:17 [b] Joel 3:13 [c] Jer. 51:33 [1] NU-Text and M-Text omit *for You.* **14:18** [a] Rev. 16:8 [b] Joel 3:13 **14:19** [a] Rev. 19:15 **14:20** [a] Is. 63:3 [b] Heb. 13:12 [c] Is. 34:3 **15:1** [a] Rev. 12:1, 3 [b] Rev. 21:9 [c] Rev. 14:10 **15:2** [a] Rev. 4:6 [b] [Matt. 3:11] [c] Rev. 13:14, 15 [d] Rev. 13:17 [e] Rev. 5:8 [1] NU-Text and M-Text omit *over his mark.* **15:3** [a] Ex. 15:1–21 [b] Rev. 15:3 [c] Deut. 32:3, 4 [d] Ps. 145:17 [1] NU-Text and M-Text read *nations.* **15:4** [a] Ex. 15:14 [b] Lev. 11:44 [c] Is. 66:23 **15:5** [a] Num. 1:50 [1] NU-Text and M-Text omit *behold.* **15:6** [a] Ex. 28:6 **15:7** [a] Rev. 4:6 [b] 1 Thess. 1:9 **15:8** [a] Ex. 19:18; 40:34 [b] 2 Thess. 1:9

16 Then I heard a loud voice from the temple saying [a]to the seven angels, "Go and pour out the bowls[1] [b]of the wrath of God on the earth."

First Bowl: Loathsome Sores

2 So the first went and poured out his bowl [a]upon the earth, and a foul and [b]loathsome sore came upon the men [c]who had the mark of the beast and those [d]who worshiped his image.

Second Bowl: The Sea Turns to Blood

3 Then the second angel poured out his bowl [a]on the sea, and [b]it became blood as of a dead *man;* [c]and every living creature in the sea died.

Third Bowl: The Waters Turn to Blood

4 Then the third angel poured out his bowl [a]on the rivers and springs of water, [b]and they became blood. 5 And I heard the angel of the waters saying:

[a]"You are righteous, O Lord,[1]
The One [b]who is and who was and who
is to be,[2]
Because You have judged these things.
6 For [a]they have shed the blood [b]of
saints and prophets,
[c]And You have given them blood to drink.
For[1] it is their just due."

7 And I heard another from[1] the altar saying, "Even so, [a]Lord God Almighty, [b]true and righteous *are* Your judgments."

Fourth Bowl: Men Are Scorched

8 Then the fourth angel poured out his bowl [a]on the sun, [b]and power was given to him to scorch men with fire. 9 And men were scorched with great heat, and they [a]blasphemed the name of God who has power over these plagues; [b]and they did not repent [c]and give Him glory.

Fifth Bowl: Darkness and Pain

10 Then the fifth angel poured out his bowl [a]on the throne of the beast, [b]and his kingdom became full of darkness; [c]and they gnawed their tongues because of the pain. 11 They blasphemed the God of heaven because of their pains and their sores, and did not repent of their deeds.

Sixth Bowl: Euphrates Dried Up

12 Then the sixth angel poured out his bowl [a]on the great river Euphrates, [b]and its water was dried up, [c]so that the way of the kings from the east might be prepared. 13 And I saw three unclean [a]spirits like frogs *coming* out of the mouth of [b]the dragon, out of the mouth of the beast, and out of the mouth of [c]the false prophet. 14 For they are spirits of demons, [a]performing signs, *which* go out to the kings of the earth and[1] of [b]the whole world, to gather them to [c]the battle of that great day of God Almighty.

15 [a]"Behold, I am coming as a thief. Blessed *is* he who watches, and keeps his garments, [b]lest he walk naked and they see his shame."

16 [a]And they gathered them together to the place called in Hebrew, Armageddon.[1]

Seventh Bowl: The Earth Utterly Shaken

17 Then the seventh angel poured out his bowl into the air, and a loud voice came out of the temple of heaven, from the throne, saying, [a]"It is done!" 18 And [a]there were noises and thunderings and lightnings; [b]and there was a great earthquake, such a mighty and great earthquake [c]as had not occurred since men were on the earth. 19 Now [a]the great city was divided into three parts, and the cities of the nations fell. And [b]great Babylon [c]was remembered before God, [d]to give her the cup of the wine of the fierceness of His wrath. 20 Then [a]every island fled away, and the mountains were not found. 21 And great hail from heaven fell upon men, *each hailstone* about the weight of a talent. Men blasphemed God because of the plague of the hail, since that plague was exceedingly great.

The Scarlet Woman and the Scarlet Beast

17 Then [a]one of the seven angels who had the seven bowls came and talked with me, saying to me,[1] "Come, [b]I will show you the judgment of [c]the great harlot [d]who sits on many waters, 2 [a]with whom the kings of the earth committed fornication, and [b]the

16:1 [a] Rev. 15:1 [b] Rev. 14:10 [1] NU-Text and M-Text read *seven bowls.* **16:2** [a] Rev. 8:7 [b] Ex. 9:9–11 [c] Rev. 13:15–17; 14:9 [d] Rev. 13:14 **16:3** [a] Rev. 8:8; 11:6 [b] Ex. 7:17–21 [c] Rev. 8:9 **16:4** [a] Rev. 8:10 [b] Ex. 7:17–20 **16:5** [a] Rev. 15:3, 4 [b] Rev. 1:4, 8 [1] NU-Text and M-Text omit *O Lord.* [2] NU-Text and M-Text read *who was, the Holy One.* **16:6** [a] Matt. 23:34 [b] Rev. 11:18 [c] Is. 49:26 [1] NU-Text and M-Text omit *For.* **16:7** [a] Rev. 15:3 [b] Rev. 13:10; 19:2 [1] NU-Text and M-Text omit *another from.* **16:8** [a] Rev. 8:12 [b] Rev. 9:17, 18 **16:9** [a] Rev. 16:11 [b] Dan. 5:22 [c] Rev. 11:13 **16:10** [a] Rev. 13:2 [b] Rev. 8:12; 9:2 [c] Rev. 11:10 **16:12** [a] Rev. 9:14 [b] Jer. 50:38 [c] Is. 41:2, 25; 46:11 **16:13** [a] 1 John 4:1 [b] Rev. 12:3, 9 [c] Rev. 13:11, 14; 19:20; 20:10 **16:14** [a] 2 Thess. 2:9 [b] Luke 2:1 [c] Rev. 17:14; 19:19; 20:8 [1] NU-Text and M-Text omit *of the earth and.* **16:15** [a] Matt. 24:43 [b] 2 Cor. 5:3 **16:16** [a] Rev. 19:19 [1] M-Text reads *Megiddo.* **16:17** [a] Rev. 10:6; 21:6 **16:18** [a] Rev. 4:5 [b] Rev. 11:13 [c] Dan. 12:1 **16:19** [a] Rev. 14:8 [b] Rev. 17:5, 18 [c] Rev. 14:8; 18:5 [d] Is. 51:17 **16:20** [a] Rev. 6:14; 20:11 **17:1** [a] Rev. 1:1; 21:9 [b] Rev. 16:19 [c] Nah. 3:4 [d] Jer. 51:13 [1] NU-Text and M-Text omit *to me.* **17:2** [a] Rev. 2:22; 18:3, 9 [b] Jer. 51:7

inhabitants of the earth were made drunk with the wine of her fornication."

3 So he carried me away in the Spirit [a]into the wilderness. And I saw a woman sitting [b]on a scarlet beast *which was* full of [c]names of blasphemy, having seven heads and ten horns. 4 The woman [a]was arrayed in purple and scarlet, [b]and adorned with gold and precious stones and pearls, [c]having in her hand a golden cup [d]full of abominations and the filthiness of her fornication.[1] 5 And on her forehead a name *was* written:

[a]MYSTERY, BABYLON THE GREAT,
THE MOTHER OF HARLOTS
AND OF THE ABOMINATIONS
OF THE EARTH.

6 I saw [a]the woman, drunk [b]with the blood of the saints and with the blood of [c]the martyrs of Jesus. And when I saw her, I marveled with great amazement.

The Meaning of the Woman and the Beast

7 But the angel said to me, "Why did you marvel? I will tell you the mystery of the woman and of the beast that carries her, which has the seven heads and the ten horns. 8 The beast that you saw was, and is not, and [a]will ascend out of the bottomless pit and [b]go to perdition. And those who [c]dwell on the earth [d]will marvel, [e]whose names are not written in the Book of Life from the foundation of the world, when they see the beast that was, and is not, and yet is.[1]

9 [a]"Here *is* the mind which has wisdom: [b]The seven heads are seven mountains on which the woman sits. 10 There are also seven kings. Five have fallen, one is, *and* the other has not yet come. And when he comes, he must [a]continue a short time. 11 The [a]beast that was, and is not, is himself also the eighth, and is of the seven, and is going to perdition.

12 [a]"The ten horns which you saw are ten kings who have received no kingdom as yet, but they receive authority for one hour as kings with the beast. 13 These are of one mind, and they will give their power and authority to the beast. 14 [a]These will make war with the Lamb, and the Lamb will [b]overcome them, [c]for He is Lord of lords and King of kings; [d]and those *who are* with Him *are* called, chosen, and faithful."

15 Then he said to me, [a]"The waters which you saw, where the harlot sits, [b]are peoples, multitudes, nations, and tongues. 16 And the ten horns which you saw on[1] the beast, [a]these will hate the harlot, make her [b]desolate [c]and naked, eat her flesh and [d]burn her with fire. 17 [a]For God has put it into their hearts to fulfill His purpose, to be of one mind, and to give their kingdom to the beast, [b]until the words of God are fulfilled. 18 And the woman whom you saw [a]is that great city [b]which reigns over the kings of the earth."

The Fall of Babylon the Great

18 After[a] these things I saw another angel coming down from heaven, having great authority, [b]and the earth was illuminated with his glory. 2 And he cried mightily[1] with a loud voice, saying, [a]"Babylon the great is fallen, is fallen, and [b]has become a dwelling place of demons, a prison for every foul spirit, and [c]a cage for every unclean and hated bird! 3 For all the nations [a]have drunk of the wine of the wrath of her fornication, the kings of the earth have committed fornication with her, [b]and the merchants of the earth have become rich through the abundance of her luxury."

4 And I heard another voice from heaven saying, [a]"Come out of her, my people, lest you share in her sins, and lest you receive of her plagues. 5 [a]For her sins have reached[1] to heaven, and [b]God has remembered her iniquities.

PEACE NOTE

You may be the first person willing to pray for a hurting person's peace with God through Christ.

17:3 [a] Rev. 12:6, 14; 21:10 [b] Rev. 12:3 [c] Rev. 13:1 **17:4** [a] Rev. 18:12, 16 [b] Dan. 11:38 [c] Jer. 51:7 [d] Rev. 14:8 [1] M-Text reads *the filthiness of the fornication of the earth.* **17:5** [a] 2 Thess. 2:7 **17:6** [a] Rev. 18:24 [b] Rev. 13:15 [c] Rev. 6:9, 10 **17:8** [a] Rev. 11:7 [b] Rev. 13:10; 17:11 [c] Rev. 3:10 [d] Rev. 13:3 [e] Rev. 13:8 [1] NU-Text and M-Text read *and shall be present.* **17:9** [a] Rev. 13:18 [b] Rev. 13:1 **17:10** [a] Rev. 13:5 **17:11** [a] Rev. 13:3, 12, 14; 17:8 **17:12** [a] Dan. 7:20 **17:14** [a] Rev. 16:14; 19:19 [b] Rev. 19:20 [c] 1 Tim. 6:15 [d] Jer. 50:44 **17:15** [a] Is. 8:7 [b] Rev. 13:7 **17:16** [a] Jer. 50:41 [b] Rev. 18:17, 19 [c] Ezek. 16:37, 39 [d] Rev. 18:8 [1] NU-Text and M-Text read *saw, and the beast.* **17:17** [a] 2 Thess. 2:11 [b] Rev. 10:7 **17:18** [a] Rev. 11:8; 16:19 [b] Rev. 12:4 **18:1** [a] Rev. 17:1, 7 [b] Ezek. 43:2 **18:2** [a] Is. 13:19; 21:9 [b] Is. 13:21; 34:11, 13–15 [c] Is. 14:23 [1] NU-Text and M-Text omit *mightily.* **18:3** [a] Rev. 14:8 [b] Is. 47:15 **18:4** [a] Is. 48:20 **18:5** [a] Gen. 18:20 [b] Rev. 16:19 [1] NU-Text and M-Text read *have been heaped up.*

6 [a]Render to her just as she rendered to you,[1]
and repay her double according to her works;
[b]in the cup which she has mixed, [c]mix double
for her. 7 [a]In the measure that she glorified
herself and lived luxuriously, in the same
measure give her torment and sorrow; for she
says in her heart, 'I sit *as* [b]queen, and am no
widow, and will not see sorrow.' 8 Therefore
her plagues will come [a]in one day—death
and mourning and famine. And [b]she will
be utterly burned with fire, [c]for strong *is* the
Lord God who judges[1] her.

The World Mourns Babylon's Fall

9 [a]"The kings of the earth who committed
fornication and lived luxuriously with her
[b]will weep and lament for her, [c]when they see
the smoke of her burning, 10 standing at a distance for fear of her torment, saying, [a]'Alas,
alas, that great city Babylon, that mighty city!
[b]For in one hour your judgment has come.'

11 "And [a]the merchants of the earth will weep
and mourn over her, for no one buys their
merchandise anymore: 12 [a]merchandise of
gold and silver, precious stones and pearls,
fine linen and purple, silk and scarlet, every
kind of citron wood, every kind of object of
ivory, every kind of object of most precious
wood, bronze, iron, and marble; 13 and cinnamon and incense, fragrant oil and frankincense, wine and oil, fine flour and wheat,
cattle and sheep, horses and chariots, and
bodies and [a]souls of men. 14 The fruit that your
soul longed for has gone from you, and all the
things which are rich and splendid have gone
from you,[1] and you shall find them no more
at all. 15 The merchants of these things, who
became rich by her, will stand at a distance
for fear of her torment, weeping and wailing,
16 and saying, 'Alas, alas, [a]that great city [b]that
was clothed in fine linen, purple, and scarlet,
and adorned with gold and precious stones
and pearls! 17 [a]For in one hour such great
riches came to nothing.' [b]Every shipmaster,
all who travel by ship, sailors, and as many
as trade on the sea, stood at a distance 18 [a]and
cried out when they saw the smoke of her
burning, saying, [b]'What *is* like this great city?'
19 [a]"They threw dust on their heads and
cried out, weeping and wailing, and saying,
'Alas, alas, that great city, in which all who had
ships on the sea became rich by her wealth!
[b]For in one hour she is made desolate.'

20 [a]"Rejoice over her, O heaven, and *you*
holy apostles[1] and prophets, for [b]God has
avenged you on her!"

Finality of Babylon's Fall

21 Then a mighty angel took up a stone like
a great millstone and threw *it* into the sea,
saying, [a]"Thus with violence the great city
Babylon shall be thrown down, and [b]shall not
be found anymore. 22 [a]The sound of harpists,
musicians, flutists, and trumpeters shall not
be heard in you anymore. No craftsman of
any craft shall be found in you anymore, and
the sound of a millstone shall not be heard
in you anymore. 23 [a]The light of a lamp shall
not shine in you anymore, [b]and the voice of
bridegroom and bride shall not be heard in
you anymore. For [c]your merchants were the
great men of the earth, [d]for by your sorcery
all the nations were deceived. 24 And [a]in her
was found the blood of prophets and saints,
and of all who [b]were slain on the earth."

Heaven Exults over Babylon

19 After these things [a]I heard[1] a loud voice
of a great multitude in heaven, saying,
"Alleluia! [b]Salvation and glory and honor and
power *belong* to the Lord[2] our God! 2 For [a]true
and righteous *are* His judgments, because He
has judged the great harlot who corrupted
the earth with her fornication; and He [b]has
avenged on her the blood of His servants
shed by her." 3 Again they said, "Alleluia! [a]Her
smoke rises up forever and ever!" 4 And [a]the
twenty-four elders and the four living creatures fell down and worshiped God who sat
on the throne, saying, [b]"Amen! Alleluia!"
5 Then a voice came from the throne, saying,
[a]"Praise our God, all you His servants and
those who fear Him, [b]both[1] small and great!"

6 [a]And I heard, as it were, the voice of a
great multitude, as the sound of many waters
and as the sound of mighty thunderings, saying, "Alleluia! For [b]the[1] Lord God Omnipotent
reigns! 7 Let us be glad and rejoice and give
Him glory, for [a]the marriage of the Lamb has
come, and His wife has made herself ready."

18:6 [a] Ps. 137:8 [b] Rev. 14:10 [c] Rev. 16:19 [1] NU-Text and M-Text omit *to you.* **18:7** [a] Ezek. 28:2–8 [b] Is. 47:7, 8 **18:8** [a] Rev. 18:10 [b] Rev. 17:16 [c] Jer. 50:34 [1] NU-Text and M-Text read *has judged.* **18:9** [a] Ezek. 26:16; 27:35 [b] Jer. 50:46 [c] Rev. 19:3 **18:10** [a] Is. 21:9 [b] Rev. 18:17, 19 **18:11** [a] Ezek. 27:27–34 **18:12** [a] Rev. 17:4 **18:13** [a] Ezek. 27:13 **18:14** [1] NU-Text and M-Text read *been lost to you.* **18:16** [a] Rev. 17:18 [b] Rev. 17:4 **18:17** [a] Rev. 18:10 [b] Is. 23:14 **18:18** [a] Ezek. 27:30 [b] Rev. 13:4 **18:19** [a] Josh. 7:6 [b] Rev. 18:8 **18:20** [a] Jer. 51:48 [b] Luke 11:49 [1] NU-Text and M-Text read *saints and apostles.* **18:21** [a] Jer. 51:63, 64 [b] Rev. 12:8; 16:20 **18:22** [a] Jer. 7:34; 16:9; 25:10 **18:23** [a] Jer. 25:10 [b] Jer. 7:34; 16:9 [c] Is. 23:8 [d] 2 Kin. 9:22 **18:24** [a] Rev. 16:6; 17:6 [b] Jer. 51:49 **19:1** [a] Rev. 11:15; 19:6 [b] Rev. 4:11 [1] NU-Text and M-Text add *something like.* [2] NU-Text and M-Text omit *the Lord.* **19:2** [a] Rev. 15:3; 16:7 [b] Deut. 32:43 **19:3** [a] Is. 34:10 **19:4** [a] Rev. 4:4, 6, 10 [b] 1 Chr. 16:36 **19:5** [a] Ps. 134:1 [b] Rev. 11:18 [1] NU-Text and M-Text omit *both.* **19:6** [a] Ezek. 1:24 [b] Rev. 11:15 [1] NU-Text and M-Text read *our.* **19:7** [a] [Matt. 22:2; 25:10]

8 And [a]to her it was granted to be arrayed in fine linen, clean and bright, [b]for the fine linen is the righteous acts of the saints.

9 Then he said to me, "Write: [a]'Blessed *are* those who are called to the marriage supper of the Lamb!' " And he said to me, [b]"These are the true sayings of God." 10 And [a]I fell at his feet to worship him. But he said to me, [b]"See *that you do* not *do that!* I am your [c]fellow servant, and of your brethren [d]who have the testimony of Jesus. Worship God! For the [e]testimony of Jesus is the spirit of prophecy."

Christ on a White Horse

11 [a]Now I saw heaven opened, and behold, [b]a white horse. And He who sat on him *was* called [c]Faithful and True, and [d]in righteousness He judges and makes war. 12 [a]His eyes *were* like a flame of fire, and on His head *were* many crowns. [b]He had[1] a name written that no one knew except Himself. 13 [a]He *was* clothed with a robe dipped in blood, and His name is called [b]The Word of God. 14 [a]And the armies in heaven, [b]clothed in fine linen, white and clean,[1] followed Him on white horses. 15 Now [a]out of His mouth goes a sharp[1] sword, that with it He should strike the nations. And [b]He Himself will rule them with a rod of iron. [c]He Himself treads the winepress of the fierceness and wrath of Almighty God. 16 And [a]He has on *His* robe and on His thigh a name written:

[b]KING OF KINGS AND
LORD OF LORDS.

The Beast and His Armies Defeated

17 Then I saw an angel standing in the sun; and he cried with a loud voice, saying to all the birds that fly in the midst of heaven, [a]"Come and gather together for the supper of the great God,[1] 18 [a]that you may eat the flesh of kings, the flesh of captains, the flesh of mighty men, the flesh of horses and of those who sit on them, and the flesh of all *people,* free[1] and slave, both small and great."

19 [a]And I saw the beast, the kings of the earth, and their armies, gathered together to make war against Him who sat on the horse and against His army. 20 [a]Then the beast was captured, and with him the false prophet who worked signs in his presence, by which he deceived those who received the mark of the beast and [b]those who worshiped his image. [c]These two were cast alive into the lake of fire [d]burning with brimstone. 21 And the rest [a]were killed with the sword which proceeded from the mouth of Him who sat on the horse. [b]And all the birds [c]were filled with their flesh.

Satan Bound 1,000 Years

20 Then I saw an angel coming down from heaven, [a]having the key to the bottomless pit and a great chain in his hand. 2 He laid hold of [a]the dragon, that serpent of old, who is *the* Devil and Satan, and bound him for a thousand years; 3 and he cast him into the bottomless pit, and shut him up, and [a]set a seal on him, [b]so that he should deceive the nations no more till the thousand years were finished. But after these things he must be released for a little while.

The Saints Reign with Christ 1,000 Years

4 And I saw [a]thrones, and they sat on them, and [b]judgment was committed to them. Then *I saw* [c]the souls of those who had been beheaded for their witness to Jesus and for the word of God, [d]who had not worshiped the beast [e]or his image, and had not received *his* mark on their foreheads or on their hands. And they [f]lived and [g]reigned with Christ for a[1] thousand years. 5 But the rest of the dead did not live again until the thousand years were finished. This *is* the first resurrection. 6 Blessed and holy *is* he who has part in the first resurrection. Over such [a]the second death has no power, but they shall be [b]priests of God and of Christ, [c]and shall reign with Him a thousand years.

Satanic Rebellion Crushed

7 Now when the thousand years have expired, Satan will be released from his prison 8 and will go out [a]to deceive the nations which are in the four corners of the earth, [b]Gog and Magog, [c]to gather them together to battle, whose number *is* as the sand of the sea. 9 [a]They went up on the breadth of the earth and surrounded the camp of the saints and the beloved city. And fire came down from

19:8 [a] Ezek. 16:10 [b] Ps. 132:9 **19:9** [a] Luke 14:15 [b] Rev. 22:6 **19:10** [a] Rev. 22:8 [b] Acts 10:26 [c] [Heb. 1:14] [d] 1 John 5:10 [e] Luke 24:27 **19:11** [a] Rev. 15:5 [b] Rev. 6:2; 19:19, 21 [c] Rev. 3:7, 14 [d] Is. 11:4 **19:12** [a] Rev. 1:14 [b] Rev. 2:17; 19:16 [1] M-Text adds *names written, and.* **19:13** [a] Is. 63:2, 3 [b] [John 1:1, 14] **19:14** [a] Rev. 14:20 [b] Matt. 28:3 [1] NU-Text and M-Text read *pure white linen.* **19:15** [a] Is. 11:4 [b] Ps. 2:8, 9 [c] Is. 63:3–6 [1] M-Text adds *two-edged.* **19:16** [a] Rev. 2:17; 19:12 [b] Dan. 2:47 **19:17** [a] Ezek. 39:17 [1] NU-Text and M-Text read *the great supper of God.* **19:18** [a] Ezek. 39:18–20 [1] NU-Text and M-Text read *both free.* **19:19** [a] Rev. 16:13–16 **19:20** [a] Rev. 16:13 [b] Rev. 13:8, 12, 13 [c] Dan. 7:11 [d] Rev. 14:10 **19:21** [a] Rev. 19:15 [b] Rev. 19:17, 18 [c] Rev. 17:16 **20:1** [a] Rev. 1:18; 9:1 **20:2** [a] 2 Pet. 2:4 **20:3** [a] Dan. 6:17 [b] Rev. 12:9; 20:8, 10 **20:4** [a] Dan. 7:9 [b] [1 Cor. 6:2, 3] [c] Rev. 6:9 [d] Rev. 13:12 [e] Rev. 13:15 [f] John 14:19 [g] Rom. 8:17 [1] M-Text reads *the.* **20:6** [a] [Rev. 2:11; 20:14] [b] Is. 61:6 [c] Rev. 20:4 **20:8** [a] Rev. 12:9; 20:3, 10 [b] Ezek. 38:2; 39:1, 6 [c] Rev. 16:14 **20:9** [a] Ezek. 38:9, 16

God out of heaven and devoured them. 10 The
devil, who deceived them, was cast into the
lake of fire and brimstone [a]where[1] the beast
and the false prophet *are.* And they [b]will be
tormented day and night forever and ever.

The Great White Throne Judgment

11 Then I saw a great white throne and Him
who sat on it, from whose face [a]the earth
and the heaven fled away. [b]And there was
found no place for them. 12 And I saw the
dead, [a]small and great, standing before God,[1]
[b]and books were opened. And another [c]book
was opened, which is *the Book* of Life. And
the dead were judged [d]according to their
works, by the things which were written in
the books. 13 The sea gave up the dead who
were in it, [a]and Death and Hades delivered
up the dead who were in them. [b]And they
were judged, each one according to his works.
14 Then [a]Death and Hades were cast into the
lake of fire. [b]This is the second death.[1] 15 And
anyone not found written in the Book of Life
[a]was cast into the lake of fire.

All Things Made New

21 Now [a]I saw a new heaven and a new
earth, [b]for the first heaven and the first
earth had passed away. Also there was no
more sea. 2 Then I, John,[1] saw [a]the holy city,
New Jerusalem, coming down out of heaven
from God, prepared [b]as a bride adorned for
her husband. 3 And I heard a loud voice from
heaven saying, "Behold, [a]the tabernacle of
God *is* with men, and He will dwell with them,
and they shall be His people. God Himself will
be with them *and be* their God. 4 [a]And God
will wipe away every tear from their eyes;
[b]there shall be no more death, [c]nor sorrow,
nor crying. There shall be no more pain, for
the former things have passed away."

PEACE NOTE

God shall wipe away every single tear! Heaven is beyond description and comprehension. This is your future home! Let God's peace carry you today!

REVELATION 21:4

20:10 [a] Rev. 19:20; 20:14, 15 [b] Rev. 14:10 [1] NU-Text and M-Text add *also.* **20:11** [a] 2 Pet. 3:7 [b] Dan. 2:35 **20:12** [a] Rev. 19:5 [b] Dan. 7:10 [c] Ps. 69:28 [d] Matt. 16:27 [1] NU-Text and M-Text read *the throne.* **20:13** [a] Rev. 1:18; 6:8; 21:4 [b] Rev. 2:23; 20:12 **20:14** [a] 1 Cor. 15:26 [b] Rev. 21:8 [1] NU-Text and M-Text add *the lake of fire.* **20:15** [a] Rev. 19:20 **21:1** [a] [2 Pet. 3:13] [b] Rev. 20:11 **21:2** [a] Is. 52:1 [b] 2 Cor. 11:2 [1] NU-Text and M-Text omit *John.* **21:3** [a] Lev. 26:11 **21:4** [a] Is. 25:8 [b] 1 Cor. 15:26 [c] Is. 35:10; 51:11; 65:19

THE RENEWAL OF WORLDWIDE PEACE

And I heard a loud voice from heaven saying, "Behold, the tabernacle of God is with men, and He will dwell with them."

REVELATION 21:3

I sometimes find contemporary world events discouraging. We all do. It's worse knowing that, in some cases, they will get worse before they get better. My faith assures me, though, that God is in control and that the endgame is in His hands. The Book of Revelation is our reminder that we were made for another world full of God's peace.

For now, the church embodies God's peace, a peace that Jesus will bring to the world. The author of the Book of Revelation explained how that will be. John said he heard a voice say, "Behold, the tabernacle of God is with men, and He will dwell with them" (v. 3). That's how it all started, according to John 1:14: "The Word became flesh and dwelt among us." "Dwelt" here means to live in a tent or tabernacle. The Book of Revelation says that will happen again when Jesus Christ returns. Jesus is the "tabernacle of God" (Rev. 21:3), and when He takes up residence, peace will return.

No matter how bleak our outlook, we can look forward to living with God, who is peace personified. Share that peace with someone who is discouraged.

5 Then [a]He who sat on the throne said, [b]"Behold, I make all things new." And He said to me,[1] "Write, for [c]these words are true and faithful."

6 And He said to me, [a]"It is done! [b]I am the Alpha and the Omega, the Beginning and the End. [c]I will give of the fountain of the water of life freely to him who thirsts. 7 He who overcomes shall inherit all things,[1] and [a]I will be his God and he shall be My son. 8 [a]But the cowardly, unbelieving,[1] abominable, murderers, sexually immoral, sorcerers, idolaters, and all liars shall have their part in [b]the lake which burns with fire and brimstone, which is the second death."

The New Jerusalem

9 Then one of [a]the seven angels who had the seven bowls filled with the seven last plagues came to me[1] and talked with me, saying, "Come, I will show you [b]the bride, the Lamb's wife."[2] 10 And he carried me away [a]in the Spirit to a great and high mountain, and showed me [b]the great city, the holy[1] Jerusalem, descending out of heaven from God, 11 [a]having the glory of God. Her light *was* like a most precious stone, like a jasper stone, clear as crystal. 12 Also she had a great and high wall with [a]twelve gates, and twelve angels at the gates, and names written on them, which are *the names* of the twelve tribes of the children of Israel: 13 [a]three gates on the east, three gates on the north, three gates on the south, and three gates on the west.

14 Now the wall of the city had twelve foundations, and [a]on them were the names[1] of the twelve apostles of the Lamb. 15 And he who talked with me [a]had a gold reed to measure the city, its gates, and its wall. 16 The city is laid out as a square; its length is as great as its breadth. And he measured the city with the reed: twelve thousand furlongs. Its length, breadth, and height are equal. 17 Then he measured its wall: one hundred *and* forty-four cubits, *according* to the measure of a man, that is, of an angel. 18 The construction of its wall was *of* jasper; and the city *was* pure gold, like clear glass. 19 [a]The foundations of the wall of the city *were* adorned with all kinds of precious stones: the first foundation *was* jasper, the second sapphire, the third chalcedony, the fourth emerald, 20 the fifth sardonyx, the sixth sardius, the seventh chrysolite, the eighth beryl, the ninth topaz, the tenth chrysoprase, the eleventh jacinth, and the twelfth amethyst. 21 The twelve gates *were* twelve [a]pearls: each individual gate was of one pearl. [b]And the street of the city *was* pure gold, like transparent glass.

The Glory of the New Jerusalem

22 [a]But I saw no temple in it, for the Lord God Almighty and the Lamb are its temple. 23 [a]The city had no need of the sun or of the moon to shine in it,[1] for the glory[2] of God illuminated it. The Lamb *is* its light. 24 [a]And the nations of those who are saved[1] shall walk in its light, and the kings of the earth bring their glory and honor into it.[2] 25 [a]Its gates shall not be shut at all by day [b](there shall be no night there). 26 [a]And they shall bring the glory and the honor of the nations into it.[1] 27 But [a]there shall by no means enter it anything that defiles, or causes[1] an abomination or a lie, but only those who are written in the Lamb's [b]Book of Life.

The River of Life

22 And he showed me [a]a pure[1] river of water of life, clear as crystal, proceeding from the throne of God and of the Lamb. 2 [a]In the middle of its street, and on either side of the river, *was* [b]the tree of life, which bore twelve fruits, each *tree* yielding its fruit every month. The leaves of the tree *were* [c]for the healing of the nations. 3 And [a]there shall be no more curse, [b]but the throne of God and of the Lamb shall be in it, and His [c]servants shall serve Him. 4 [a]They shall see His face, and [b]His name *shall be* on their foreheads. 5 [a]There shall be no night there: They need no lamp nor [b]light of the sun, for [c]the Lord God gives them light. [d]And they shall reign forever and ever.

The Time Is Near

6 Then he said to me, [a]"These words *are* faithful and true." And the Lord God of the holy[1] prophets [b]sent His angel to show His servants the things which must [c]shortly take place.

21:5 [a] Rev. 4:2, 9; 20:11 [b] Is. 43:19 [c] Rev. 19:9; 22:6 [1] NU-Text and M-Text omit *to me.* **21:6** [a] Rev. 10:6; 16:17 [b] Rev. 1:8; 22:13 [c] John 4:10 [1] M-Text omits *It is done.* **21:7** [a] Zech. 8:8 [1] M-Text reads *overcomes, I shall give him these things.* **21:8** [a] 1 Cor. 6:9 [b] Rev. 20:14 [1] M-Text adds *and sinners.* **21:9** [a] Rev. 15:1 [b] Rev. 19:7; 21:2 [1] NU-Text and M-Text omit *to me.* [2] M-Text reads *I will show you the woman, the Lamb's bride.* **21:10** [a] Rev. 1:10 [b] Ezek. 48 [1] NU-Text and M-Text omit *the great* and read *the holy city, Jerusalem.* **21:11** [a] Rev. 15:8; 21:23; 22:5 **21:12** [a] Ezek. 48:31–34 **21:13** [a] Ezek. 48:31–34 **21:14** [a] Eph. 2:20 [1] NU-Text and M-Text read *twelve names.* **21:15** [a] Ezek. 40:3 **21:19** [a] Is. 54:11 **21:21** [a] Matt. 13:45, 46 [b] Rev. 22:2 **21:22** [a] John 4:21, 23 **21:23** [a] Is. 24:23; 60:19, 20 [1] NU-Text and M-Text omit *in it.* [2] M-Text reads *the very glory.* **21:24** [a] Is. 60:3, 5; 66:12 [1] NU-Text and M-Text omit *of those who are saved.* [2] M-Text reads *the glory and honor of the nations to Him.* **21:25** [a] Is. 60:11 [b] Is. 60:20 **21:26** [a] Rev. 21:24 [1] M-Text adds *that they may enter in.* **21:27** [a] Joel 3:17 [b] Phil. 4:3 [1] NU-Text and M-Text read *anything profane, nor one who causes.* **22:1** [a] Ezek. 47:1 [1] NU-Text and M-Text omit *pure.* **22:2** [a] Ezek. 47:12 [b] Gen. 2:9 [c] Rev. 21:24 **22:3** [a] Zech. 14:11 [b] Ezek. 48:35 [c] Rev. 7:15 **22:4** [a] [Matt. 5:8] [b] Rev. 14:1 **22:5** [a] Rev. 21:23 [b] Rev. 7:15 [c] Ps. 36:9 [d] Dan. 7:18, 27 **22:6** [a] Rev. 19:9 [b] Rev. 1:1 [c] Heb. 10:37 [1] NU-Text and M-Text read *spirits of the prophets.*

7[a]"Behold, I am coming quickly! [b]Blessed
is he who keeps the words of the prophecy
of this book."
8Now I, John, saw and heard[1] these things.
And when I heard and saw, [a]I fell down to
worship before the feet of the angel who
showed me these things.
9Then he said to me, [a]"See *that you do* not
do that. For[1] I am your fellow servant, and of
your brethren the prophets, and of those who
keep the words of this book. Worship God."
10[a]And he said to me, "Do not seal the words
of the prophecy of this book, [b]for the time is
at hand. 11He who is unjust, let him be unjust
still; he who is filthy, let him be filthy still; he
who is righteous, let him be righteous[1] still;
he who is holy, let him be holy still."

Jesus Testifies to the Churches

12"And behold, I am coming quickly, and
[a]My reward *is* with Me, [b]to give to every one
according to his work. 13[a]I am the Alpha and
the Omega, *the* Beginning and *the* End, the
First and the Last."[1]
14[a]Blessed *are* those who do His commandments,[1] that they may have the right
[b]to the tree of life, [c]and may enter through
the gates into the city. 15But[1] [a]outside *are*
[b]dogs and sorcerers and sexually immoral
and murderers and idolaters, and whoever
loves and practices a lie.
16[a]"I, Jesus, have sent My angel to testify to
you these things in the churches. [b]I am the
Root and the Offspring of David, [c]the Bright
and Morning Star."
17And the Spirit and [a]the bride say, "Come!"
And let him who hears say, "Come!" [b]And let
him who thirsts come. Whoever desires, let
him take the water of life freely.

A Warning

18For[1] I testify to everyone who hears the
words of the prophecy of this book: [a]If anyone adds to these things, God will add[2] to
him the plagues that are written in this book;
19and if anyone takes away from the words
of the book of this prophecy, [a]God shall take
away[1] his part from the Book[2] of Life, from
the holy city, and *from* the things which are
written in this book.

I Am Coming Quickly

20He who testifies to these things says,
"Surely I am coming quickly."
Amen. Even so, come, Lord Jesus!
21The grace of our Lord Jesus Christ *be*
with you all.[1] Amen.

22:7 [a] [Rev. 3:11] [b] Rev. 1:3 **22:8** [a] Rev. 19:10 [1] NU-Text and M-Text read *am the one who heard and saw.* **22:9** [a] Rev. 19:10 [1] NU-Text and M-Text omit *For.* **22:10** [a] Dan. 8:26 [b] Rev. 1:3 **22:11** [1] NU-Text and M-Text read *do right.* **22:12** [a] Is. 40:10; 62:11 [b] Rev. 20:12 **22:13** [a] Is. 41:4 [1] NU-Text and M-Text read *the First and the Last, the Beginning and the End.* **22:14** [a] Dan. 12:12 [b] [Prov. 11:30] [c] Rev. 21:27 [1] NU-Text reads *wash their robes.* **22:15** [a] 1 Cor. 6:9 [b] Phil. 3:2 [1] NU-Text and M-Text omit *But.* **22:16** [a] Rev. 1:1 [b] Rev. 5:5 [c] Num. 24:17 **22:17** [a] [Rev. 21:2, 9] [b] Is. 55:1 **22:18** [a] Deut. 4:2; 12:32 [1] NU-Text and M-Text omit *For.* [2] M-Text reads *may God add.* **22:19** [a] Ex. 32:33 [1] M-Text reads *may God take away.* [2] NU-Text and M-Text read *tree of life.* **22:21** [1] NU-Text reads *with all;* M-Text reads *with all the saints.*

TOPICAL INDEX OF DEVOTIONS

Peace with God

Peace When You Are Tempted

Being a Person of Peace

Peace as a Family

Psalms and Proverbs of Peace

Peace in Daily Circumstances

Peace When You Suffer or Grieve

The Holy Spirit Brings Peace

Peace Because of God's Character, Presence, and Promises

- Genesis 21:1
- Exodus 3:14
- Numbers 25:12
- Joshua 1:9
- 2 Chronicles 2:6
- Psalm 23:1
- Isaiah 54:10
- Malachi 3:6–7
- Romans 15:13
- 1 Peter 1:2
- Revelation 21:3

The Prince of Peace (Character of Jesus)

- Isaiah 9:6–7
- Isaiah 53:5
- Daniel 7:13
- Zechariah 3:8
- Matthew 3:17
- Matthew 9:8
- Matthew 11:28
- Matthew 19:14
- Mark 2:17
- Luke 7:13

Peace and Our Creator

- Genesis 1:1
- Genesis 1:26–27
- Genesis 1:31
- Genesis 2:7
- Job 38:4
- Psalm 8:5
- Psalm 19:1
- Isaiah 45:7
- Habakkuk 2:14

Spiritual Practices That Bring Peace

- Genesis 24:63
- Deuteronomy 4:1
- 1 Samuel 1:17
- 1 Kings 19:12
- 2 Kings 22:20
- 2 Chronicles 30:18–19
- Psalm 1:1–2
- Micah 7:7
- Matthew 6:7–8
- Luke 10:19
- 1 Thessalonians 5:23

FEATURES INDEX

NKJV CONCISE CONCORDANCE

This concordance indexes over 3,500 words with over 9,200 context lines from verses in which they are used in the NKJV. Words are referenced with Scripture quotations, in which the first letter of the word, bolded and italicized, stands for the entire word. The first number in parenthesis following each heading indicates the times that word appears in the Bible. The second number indicates the number of verses in which it appears.

A

ABASED (1/1)
I know how to be ***a*** .... Phil. 4:12

ABBA (3/3)
And He said, "***A*** .... Mark 14:36
by whom we cry out, "***A*** .... Rom. 8:15

ABHOR (21/20)
Therefore I ***a*** myself........... Job 42:6

ABHORRED (12/12)
a His own inheritance .... Ps. 106:40

ABIDE (36/32)
LORD, who may ***a*** .... Ps. 15:1
"If you ***a*** in My word........... John 8:31
If you ***a*** in Me .... John 15:7
a in My love................... John 15:9

ABIDES (26/24)
He who ***a*** in Me .... John 15:5
will of God ***a*** forever......... 1 John 2:17

ABIDING (2/2)
not have His word ***a*** .... John 5:38

ABILITY (11/10)
according to his own ***a*** ...... Matt. 25:15
a which God supplies .... 1 Pet. 4:11

ABLE (167/163)
For who is ***a*** to judge .... 1 Kin. 3:9
God whom we serve is ***a*** .... Dan. 3:17
God is ***a*** to raise up .... Matt. 3:9
fear Him who is ***a*** .... Matt. 10:28
Are you ***a*** to drink the .... Matt. 20:22
persuaded that He is ***a*** .... 2 Tim. 1:12
learning and never ***a*** .... 2 Tim. 3:7
that God was ***a*** to............ Heb. 11:19

ABOLISHED (4/4)
having ***a*** in His flesh .... Eph. 2:15
Christ, who has ***a*** .... 2 Tim. 1:10

ABOMINABLE (21/21)
they deny Him, being ***a*** .... Titus 1:16
unbelieving, ***a***, murderers ...... Rev. 21:8

ABOMINATION (78/71)
yes, seven are an ***a*** .... Prov. 6:16
even his prayer is an ***a*** .... Prov. 28:9
and place there the ***a*** .... Dan. 11:31
the ***a*** of desolation .... Dan. 12:11
the '***a*** of desolation,' .... Matt. 24:15

ABOMINATIONS (75/73)
delights in their ***a*** .... Is. 66:3
a golden cup full of ***a*** .... Rev. 17:4

ABOUND (21/19)
the offense might ***a*** .... Rom. 5:20
sin that grace may ***a*** .... Rom. 6:1
to make all grace ***a*** .... 2 Cor. 9:8
and I know how to ***a*** .... Phil. 4:12

ABOUNDED (6/5)
But where sin ***a*** .... Rom. 5:20

ABOUNDING (6/6)
immovable, always ***a*** .... 1 Cor. 15:58

ABOVE (234/221)
that is in heaven ***a***............... Ex. 20:4
A it stood seraphim .... Is. 6:2
He who comes from ***a*** .... John 3:31
beneath; I am from ***a*** .... John 8:23
been given you from ***a*** .... John 19:11
things which are ***a*** .... Col. 3:1
perfect gift is from ***a*** .... James 1:17

ABSENT (11/11)
in the body we are ***a*** .... 2 Cor. 5:6

ABSTAIN (8/8)
we write to them to ***a*** .... Acts 15:20
A from every form .... 1 Thess. 5:22

ABUNDANCE (79/77)
put in out of their ***a*** .... Mark 12:44
not consist in the ***a*** .... Luke 12:15

ABUNDANT (23/23)
in labors more ***a*** .... 2 Cor. 11:23

ABUNDANTLY (23/23)
a satisfied with the .... Ps. 36:8
may have it more ***a*** .... John 10:10
to do exceedingly ***a*** .... Eph. 3:20

ACCEPT (35/33)
offering, I will not ***a*** .... Jer. 14:12
Should I ***a*** this from .... Mal. 1:13

ACCEPTABLE (24/24)
a time I have heard.............. Is. 49:8
proclaim the ***a*** year .... Is. 61:2
proclaim the ***a*** year .... Luke 4:19
is that good and ***a*** .... Rom. 12:2

ACCEPTABLY (1/1)
we may serve God *a* ....Heb. 12:28
ACCEPTED (26/26)
Behold, now is the *a* ....2 Cor. 6:2
by which He made us *a* ....Eph. 1:6
ACCESS (4/4)
we have *a* by faith ....Rom. 5:2
ACCOMPLISHED (16/16)
all things were now *a* ....John 19:28
ACCORD (22/22)
continued with one *a* ....Acts 1:14
ACCOUNT (28/28)
they will give *a* of it..........Matt. 12:36
put that on my *a* ....Philem. 1:18
ACCOUNTED (14/14)
and He *a* it to him..........Gen. 15:6
his faith is *a* for ....Rom. 4:5
and it was *a* to him ....Gal. 3:6
and it was *a* to him ....James 2:23
ACCURSED (24/20)
not know the law is *a* ....John 7:49
calls Jesus *a*, and no..........1 Cor. 12:3
let him be *a*..........Gal. 1:8
ACCUSATION (12/12)
over His head the *a*..........Matt. 27:37
they might find an *a*..........Luke 6:7
ACCUSE (13/13)
they began to *a* Him..........Luke 23:2
ACCUSED (13/13)
while He was being *a* ....Matt. 27:12
ACCUSER (2/2)
a of our brethren..........Rev. 12:10
ACCUSING (1/1)
their thoughts *a* or else..........Rom. 2:15
ACKNOWLEDGE (15/15)
a my transgressions..........Ps. 51:3
in all your ways *a*..........Prov. 3:6
ACKNOWLEDGES (3/3)
he who *a* the Son has..........1 John 2:23
ACQUAINT (1/1)
a yourself with Him..........Job 22:21
ACQUAINTED (2/2)
a Man of sorrows and *a*..........Is. 53:3
ACQUIT (3/3)
at all *a* the wicked ....Nah. 1:3
ACT (24/23)
adultery, in the very *a* ....John 8:4
ACTIONS (1/1)
by Him *a* are weighed ....1 Sam. 2:3
ACTS (74/72)
of Your awesome *a*..........Ps. 145:6
ADD (34/34)
Do not *a* to His words ....Prov. 30:6
ADDED (19/19)
And the Lord *a* to the..........Acts 2:47
It was *a* because of ....Gal. 3:19

ADMONISH (5/5)
a him as a brother..........2 Thess. 3:15
ADMONITION (3/3)
were written for our *a* ....1 Cor. 10:11
in the training and *a* ....Eph. 6:4
ADOPTION (5/5)
received the Spirit of *a* ....Rom. 8:15
waiting for the *a* ....Rom. 8:23
to whom pertain the *a*..........Rom. 9:4
ADORN (5/5)
also, that the women *a* ....1 Tim. 2:9
ADORNED (13/13)
also *a* themselves ....1 Pet. 3:5
prepared as a bride *a*..........Rev. 21:2
ADRIFT (1/1)
A among the dead..........Ps. 88:5
ADULTERER (3/3)
The eye of the *a*..........Job 24:15
ADULTERERS (9/9)
nor idolaters, nor *a*..........1 Cor. 6:9
a God will judge..........Heb. 13:4
ADULTEROUS (6/6)
evil and *a* generation..........Matt. 12:39
ADULTERY (40/33)
You shall not commit *a*..........Ex. 20:14
already committed *a* ....Matt. 5:28
is divorced commits *a* ....Matt. 5:32
another commits *a*..........Mark 10:11
those who commit *a*..........Rev. 2:22
ADVANTAGE (11/11)
a that I go away..........John 16:7
Satan should take *a* ....2 Cor. 2:11
ADVERSARIES (35/35)
and there are many *a*..........1 Cor. 16:9
terrified by your *a*..........Phil. 1:28
ADVERSARY (21/20)
Agree with your *a*..........Matt. 5:25
opportunity to the *a*..........1 Tim. 5:14
your *a* the devil walks ....1 Pet. 5:8
ADVERSITY (20/20)
I shall never be in *a* ....Ps. 10:6
the day of *a* consider ....Eccl. 7:14
ADVICE (29/26)
in this I give my *a*..........2 Cor. 8:10
ADVOCATE (1/1)
we have an *A* with the ....1 John 2:1
AFAR (54/54)
and not a God *a*..........Jer. 23:23
to you who were *a*..........Eph. 2:17
but having seen them *a*..........Heb. 11:13
AFFAIRS (9/9)
himself with the *a*..........2 Tim. 2:4
AFFECTION (4/4)
to his wife the *a*..........1 Cor. 7:3
AFFECTIONATE (1/1)
Be kindly *a* to one..........Rom. 12:10

AFFIRM (4/4)
you to ***a*** constantly . . . . . Titus 3:8
AFFLICT (31/30)
a Your heritage . . . . . Ps. 94:5
For He does not ***a*** . . . . . Lam. 3:33
AFFLICTED (49/48)
To him who is ***a*** . . . . . Job 6:14
hears the cry of the ***a*** . . . . . Job 34:28
days of the ***a*** are evil. . . . . Prov. 15:15
Smitten by God, and ***a*** . . . . . Is. 53:4
oppressed and He was ***a*** . . . . . Is. 53:7
"O you ***a*** one, tossed . . . . . Is. 54:11
being destitute, ***a*** . . . . . Heb. 11:37
AFFLICTING (1/1)
A the just and taking . . . . . Amos 5:12
AFFLICTION (68/66)
the bread of ***a*** . . . . . Deut. 16:3
a take hold of me. . . . . . Job 30:16
and it is an evil ***a*** . . . . . Eccl. 6:2
For our light ***a*** . . . . . 2 Cor. 4:17
supposing to add ***a*** . . . . . Phil. 1:16
AFRAID (216/212)
garden, and I was ***a*** . . . . . Gen. 3:10
saying, "Do not be ***a*** . . . . . Gen. 15:1
none will make you ***a*** . . . . . Lev. 26:6
ungodliness made me ***a*** . . . . . Ps. 18:4
Whenever I am ***a*** . . . . . Ps. 56:3
no one will make them ***a*** . . . . . Is. 17:2
dream which made me ***a*** . . . . . Dan. 4:5
It is I; do not be ***a*** . . . . . Matt. 14:27
if you do evil, be ***a*** . . . . . Rom. 13:4
do good and are not ***a*** . . . . . 1 Pet. 3:6
AFTERWARD (86/86)
a receive me to glory . . . . . Ps. 73:24
you shall follow Me ***a*** . . . . . John 13:36
AGAIN (428/412)
'You must be born ***a*** . . . . . John 3:7
having been born ***a*** . . . . . 1 Pet. 1:23
AGAINST (1,615/1,341)
come to 'set a man ***a*** . . . . . Matt. 10:35
or house divided ***a*** . . . . . Matt. 12:25
not with Me is ***a*** Me. . . . . . Matt. 12:30
blasphemy ***a*** the Spirit . . . . . Matt. 12:31
lifted up his heel ***a*** . . . . . John 13:18
LORD and ***a*** His Christ . . . . . Acts 4:26
to kick ***a*** the goads . . . . . Acts 9:5
a the promises of God . . . . . Gal. 3:21
we do not wrestle ***a*** . . . . . Eph. 6:12
I have a few things ***a*** . . . . . Rev. 2:20
AGE (63/60)
the grave at a full ***a*** . . . . . Job 5:26
and in the ***a*** to come. . . . . . Mark 10:30
AGED (9/9)
a one as Paul, the ***a*** . . . . . Philem. 1:9
AGES (7/7)
ordained before the ***a*** . . . . . 1 Cor. 2:7

AGONY (2/2)
And being in ***a*** . . . . . Luke 22:44
AGREE (9/9)
that if two of you ***a*** . . . . . Matt. 18:19
AGREED (11/11)
unless they are ***a*** . . . . . Amos 3:3
AGREEMENT (12/11)
what ***a*** has the temple . . . . . 2 Cor. 6:16
AIR (43/43)
the birds of the ***a*** . . . . . Gen. 1:26
of the ***a*** have nests . . . . . Luke 9:58
of the power of the ***a*** . . . . . Eph. 2:2
the Lord in the ***a*** . . . . . 1 Thess. 4:17
ALIENATED (7/6)
darkened, being ***a*** . . . . . Eph. 4:18
you, who once were ***a*** . . . . . Col. 1:21
ALIENS (17/17)
A have devoured his. . . . . . Hos. 7:9
without Christ, being ***a*** . . . . . Eph. 2:12
ALIKE (14/14)
esteems every day ***a*** . . . . . Rom. 14:5
ALIVE (91/89)
I kill and I make ***a*** . . . . . Deut. 32:39
son was dead and is ***a*** . . . . . Luke 15:24
presented Himself ***a*** . . . . . Acts 1:3
dead indeed to sin, but ***a*** . . . . . Rom. 6:11
all shall be made ***a*** . . . . . 1 Cor. 15:22
that we who are ***a*** . . . . . 1 Thess. 4:15
and behold, I am ***a*** . . . . . Rev. 1:18
These two were cast ***a*** . . . . . Rev. 19:20
ALLELUIA (4/4)
Again they said, "***A*** . . . . . Rev. 19:3
ALLOW (28/28)
a Your Holy One . . . . . Ps. 16:10
a My faithfulness. . . . . . Ps. 89:33
a Your Holy One . . . . . Acts 2:27
ALLURE (3/3)
they ***a*** through the lusts . . . . . 2 Pet. 2:18
ALMOND (9/7)
a tree blossoms . . . . . Eccl. 12:5
ALMOST (10/10)
a persuade me to. . . . . . Acts 26:28
ALOES (5/5)
mixture of myrrh and ***a*** . . . . . John 19:39
ALPHA (4/4)
I am the ***A*** and the . . . . . Rev. 1:8
I am the ***A*** and the . . . . . Rev. 22:13
ALTAR (378/322)
Then Noah built an ***a*** . . . . . Gen. 8:20
An ***a*** of earth you . . . . . Ex. 20:24
it to you upon the ***a*** . . . . . Lev. 17:11
your gift to the ***a*** . . . . . Matt. 5:23
swears by the ***a*** . . . . . Matt. 23:18
I even found an ***a*** . . . . . Acts 17:23
We have an ***a*** from . . . . . Heb. 13:10
ALTARS (63/52)
Even Your ***a***, O LORD . . . . . Ps. 84:3
and torn down Your ***a*** . . . . . Rom. 11:3

ALTERED (2/2)
of His face was *a* .... Luke 9:29
ALWAYS (94/89)
delight, rejoicing *a* .... Prov. 8:30
the poor with you *a* .... Matt. 26:11
lo, I am with you *a* ....Matt. 28:20
men *a* ought to pray............Luke 18:1
immovable, *a* abounding ..... 1 Cor. 15:58
Rejoice in the Lord *a* ....Phil. 4:4
thus we shall *a*...............1 Thess. 4:17
a be ready to give a............ 1 Pet. 3:15
AM (909/835)
to Moses, "I *A* WHO I *A* .... Ex. 3:14
First and I *a* the Last ....Is. 44:6
in My name, I *a* there......... Matt. 18:20
I *a* the bread of life .... John 6:35
I *a* the light of the .... John 8:12
I *a* from above .... John 8:23
Abraham was, I *A* .... John 8:58
I *a* the door.................. John 10:9
I *a* the good shepherd ....John 10:11
I *a* the resurrection ....John 11:25
to him, "I *a* the way........... John 14:6
of God I *a* what I *a*............ 1 Cor. 15:10
AMBASSADOR (3/3)
for which I am an *a*............ Eph. 6:20
AMBASSADORS (7/7)
we are *a* for Christ............ 2 Cor. 5:20
AMBITION (2/2)
Christ from selfish *a*............. Phil. 1:16
AMEN (77/72)
are Yes, and in Him *A*..........2 Cor. 1:20
creatures said, "*A* .... Rev. 5:14
ANCHOR (1/1)
hope we have as an *a*...........Heb. 6:19
ANCIENT (23/23)
Do not remove the *a* .... Prov. 23:10
until the *A* of Days ....Dan. 7:22
ANGEL (199/190)
"Behold, I send an *A*............Ex. 23:20
the *A* of His Presence............ Is. 63:9
things, behold, an *a* .... Matt. 1:20
for an *a* of the Lord.............Matt. 28:2
Then an *a* of the Lord .... Luke 1:11
And behold, an *a*................ Luke 2:9
a appeared to Him from ...... Luke 22:43
For an *a* went down at.......... John 5:4
a has spoken to Him .... John 12:29
But at night an *a* .... Acts 5:19
A who appeared to him........Acts 7:35
Then immediately an *a* .... Acts 12:23
himself into an *a*.............. 2 Cor. 11:14
even if we, or an *a* ....Gal. 1:8
Then I saw a strong *a*............ Rev. 5:2
Jesus, have sent My *a*.......... Rev. 22:16
ANGELS (92/90)
If He charges His *a* ....Job 4:18
lower than the *a*................. Ps. 8:5
He shall give His *a* .... Ps. 91:11
He shall give His *a* .... Matt. 4:6
not even the *a* of heaven......Matt. 24:36
and all the holy *a*............. Matt. 25:31
twelve legions of *a* ....Matt. 26:53
And she saw two *a*............ John 20:12
and worship of *a* ....Col. 2:18
much better than the *a* .... Heb. 1:4
unwittingly entertained *a*....... Heb. 13:2
things which *a* desire...........1 Pet. 1:12
did not spare the *a* ....2 Pet. 2:4
a who did not keep ....Jude 1:6
ANGER (233/228)
For His *a* is but for a............. Ps. 30:5
gracious, slow to *a* .... Ps. 103:8
Nor will He keep His *a*.......... Ps. 103:9
around at them with *a*.......... Mark 3:5
bitterness, wrath, *a*............. Eph. 4:31
ANGRY (92/89)
Cain, "Why are you *a* ....Gen. 4:6
"Let not the LORD be *a*.........Gen. 18:30
the Son, lest He be *a*.............Ps. 2:12
a man stirs up strife.......... Prov. 29:22
right for you to be *a* .... Jon. 4:4
you that whoever is *a*.......... Matt. 5:22
"Be *a*, and do not sin"...........Eph. 4:26
ANGUISH (25/25)
longer remembers the *a*.......John 16:21
tribulation and *a*................Rom. 2:9
ANIMAL (45/37)
of every clean *a* .... Gen. 7:2
set him on his own *a* .... Luke 10:34
ANIMALS (39/35)
of *a* after their kind........... Gen. 6:20
of four-footed *a* .... Acts 10:12
ANNUL (3/3)
years later, cannot *a*............Gal. 3:17
ANNULS (1/1)
is confirmed, no one *a*...........Gal. 3:15
ANOINT (35/34)
a my head with oil .... Ps. 23:5
when you fast, *a*................ Matt. 6:17
a My body for burial............ Mark 14:8
a your eyes with eye............ Rev. 3:18
ANOINTED (101/99)
"Surely the LORD's *a*.......... 1 Sam. 16:6
destroy the LORD's *a*.......... 2 Sam. 1:14
"Do not touch My *a*............1 Chr. 16:22
Because He has *a* ....Luke 4:18
but this woman has *a*.......... Luke 7:46
a the eyes of the................ John 9:6
It was that Mary who *a* ....John 11:2
Jesus, whom You *a* ....Acts 4:27
and has *a* us is God............ 2 Cor. 1:21
ANOINTING (27/25)
But you have an *a* ....1 John 2:20
ANOTHER (442/401)
that you love one *a*........... John 13:34

ARMOR (30/30)
Put on the whole *a* . . . . Eph. 6:11

ARMS (33/31)
are the everlasting *a*. . . . . Deut. 33:27
took Him up in his *a* . . . . Luke 2:28

AROMA (46/45)
To the one we are the *a* . . . . 2 Cor. 2:16
for a sweet-smelling *a* . . . . Eph. 5:2

AROUSED (42/41)
the LORD was greatly *a* . . . . Num. 11:10
Then Joseph, being *a*. . . . . Matt. 1:24

ARRAYED (9/9)
his glory was not *a* . . . . Matt. 6:29
"Who are these *a*. . . . . Rev. 7:13

ARROGANCE (6/6)
Pride and *a* and the . . . . Prov. 8:13

ARROW (20/18)
a that flies by day . . . . Ps. 91:5

ARROWS (43/41)
a pierce me deeply . . . . Ps. 38:2
Like *a* in the hand of . . . . Ps. 127:4

ASCEND (19/19)
Who may *a* into the . . . . Ps. 24:3
If I *a* into heaven. . . . . Ps. 139:8
'I will *a* into heaven . . . . Is. 14:13
see the Son of Man *a* . . . . John 6:62

ASCENDED (17/17)
You have *a* on high. . . . . Ps. 68:18
No one has *a* to heaven . . . . John 3:13
"When He *a* on high. . . . . Eph. 4:8

ASCENDING (6/6)
the angels of God *a*. . . . . John 1:51

ASCRIBE (3/3)
A strength to God . . . . Ps. 68:34

ASHAMED (117/105)
Let me not be *a* . . . . Ps. 25:2
And Israel shall be *a*. . . . . Hos. 10:6
For whoever is *a* . . . . Mark 8:38
am not *a* of the gospel. . . . . Rom. 1:16
Therefore God is not *a*. . . . . Heb. 11:16

ASHES (43/41)
become like dust and *a* . . . . Job 30:19
in sackcloth and *a*. . . . . Luke 10:13

ASIDE (101/94)
lay something *a*, storing . . . . . . 1 Cor. 16:2
lay *a* all filthiness . . . . James 1:21
Therefore, laying *a* . . . . 1 Pet. 2:1

ASK (119/113)
when your children *a*. . . . . Josh. 4:6
"A a sign for yourself . . . . Is. 7:11
whatever things you *a* . . . . Matt. 21:22
a, and it will be. . . . . Luke 11:9
that whatever You *a* . . . . John 11:22
a anything in My . . . . John 14:14
in that day you will *a* . . . . John 16:23
above all that we *a* . . . . Eph. 3:20
wisdom, let him *a* . . . . James 1:5
But let him *a* in faith . . . . James 1:6
because you do not *a*. . . . . James 4:2

ASKS (18/17)
For everyone who *a* . . . . Matt. 7:8
if his son *a* for bread . . . . Matt. 7:9
Or if he *a* for a fish . . . . Luke 11:11

ASLEEP (19/19)
But He was *a*. . . . . Matt. 8:24
but some have fallen *a* . . . . 1 Cor. 15:6
those who are *a* . . . . 1 Thess. 4:15

ASSEMBLING (1/1)
not forsaking the *a*. . . . . Heb. 10:25

ASSEMBLY (132/125)
a I will praise You . . . . Ps. 22:22
fast, call a sacred *a* . . . . Joel 1:14
a I will sing praise. . . . . Heb. 2:12
to the general *a* . . . . Heb. 12:23

ASSURANCE (7/7)
riches of the full *a*. . . . . Col. 2:2
Spirit and in much *a* . . . . 1 Thess. 1:5
to the full *a* of hope . . . . Heb. 6:11

ASSURE (1/1)
a our hearts before. . . . . 1 John 3:19

ASSURED (4/4)
learned and been *a*. . . . . 2 Tim. 3:14

ASTONISHED (46/46)
Just as many were *a*. . . . . Is. 52:14
who heard Him were *a* . . . . Luke 2:47

ASTRAY (32/30)
and one of them goes *a*. . . . . . . Matt. 18:12
like sheep going *a*. . . . . 1 Pet. 2:25

ATONEMENT (99/86)
the blood that makes *a* . . . . Lev. 17:11
for it is the Day of *A* . . . . Lev. 23:28
there will be no *a*. . . . . Is. 22:14

ATTAIN (10/10)
It is high, I cannot *a* . . . . Ps. 139:6
worthy to *a* that age . . . . Luke 20:35
by any means, I may *a*. . . . . Phil. 3:11

ATTENTION (12/12)
My son, give *a* to my. . . . . Prov. 4:20

ATTENTIVE (8/8)
Let Your ears be *a* . . . . Ps. 130:2

ATTESTED (1/1)
a Man *a* by God to you . . . . Acts 2:22

AUSTERE (2/2)
because you are an *a* . . . . Luke 19:21

AUTHOR (3/3)
For God is not the *a* . . . . 1 Cor. 14:33
unto Jesus, the *a* . . . . Heb. 12:2

AUTHORITIES (6/5)
a that exist are . . . . Rom. 13:1

AUTHORITY (90/85)
them as one having *a*. . . . . Matt. 7:29
"All *a* has been given . . . . Matt. 28:18
a I will give You . . . . Luke 4:6
and has given Him *a* . . . . John 5:27
You have given Him *a* . . . . John 17:2
defile the flesh, reject *a*. . . . . Jude 1:8

B

Arise and be *b*, and wash ...... Acts 22:16
were *b* into Christ .... Rom. 6:3
I thank God that I *b*............. 1 Cor. 1:14
Spirit we were all *b* .... 1 Cor. 12:13

BAPTIZING (7/7)
b them in the name of .... Matt. 28:19

BARBARIAN (1/1)
nor uncircumcised, *b*............ Col. 3:11

BARLEY (36/35)
who has five *b* loaves .... John 6:9

BARN (5/5)
the wheat into my *b* .... Matt. 13:30

BARNS (5/5)
reap nor gather into *b* .... Matt. 6:26
I will pull down my *b* .... Luke 12:18

BARREN (24/24)
But Sarai was *b*.............. Gen. 11:30
"Sing, O *b*, you who have.......... Is. 54:1

BASE (26/26)
and the *b* things of .... 1 Cor. 1:28

BASIN (3/2)
poured water into a *b*.......... John 13:5

BASKET (32/29)
and put it under a *b* .... Matt. 5:15
I was let down in a *b*.......... 2 Cor. 11:33

BASKETS (15/15)
they took up twelve *b*......... Matt. 14:20

BATHED (4/4)
to him, "He who is *b* .... John 13:10

BATS (1/1)
To the moles and *b* .... Is. 2:20

BATTLE (184/171)
b is the LORD's .... 1 Sam. 17:47
became valiant in *b* .... Heb. 11:34

BEAR (225/215)
greater than I can *b* .... Gen. 4:13
whom Sarah shall *b* .... Gen. 17:21
not *b* false witness .... Ex. 20:16
b their iniquities .... Is. 53:11
child, and *b* a Son .... Matt. 1:23
A good tree cannot *b* .... Matt. 7:18
how long shall I *b* .... Matt. 17:17
by, to *b* His cross .... Mark 15:21
And whoever does not *b*........ Luke 14:27
are strong ought to *b* .... Rom. 15:1
B one another's .... Gal. 6:2
b the sins of many............... Heb. 9:28

BEARD (15/14)
the edges of your *b* .... Lev. 19:27
Running down on the *b*......... Ps. 133:2

BEARING (25/25)
goes forth weeping, *b*........... Ps. 126:6
And He, *b* His cross .... John 19:17
the camp, *b* His reproach ...... Heb. 13:13

BEARS (27/25)
Every branch that *b* .... John 15:2

BEAST (127/117)
You preserve man and *b* .... Ps. 36:6
And I saw a *b* rising .... Rev. 13:1
the mark of the *b*.............. Rev. 19:20

BEASTS (100/97)
naturally, like brute *b*........... Jude 1:10

BEAT (40/40)
b their swords into .... Is. 2:4
spat in His face and *b*.......... Matt. 26:67

BEATEN (27/26)
Three times I was *b*........... 2 Cor. 11:25

BEAUTIFUL (53/53)
B in elevation, the joy .... Ps. 48:2
has made everything *b* .... Eccl. 3:11
my love, you are as *b* .... Song 6:4
How *b* upon the .... Is. 52:7
indeed appear *b*.............. Matt. 23:27

BEAUTIFY (4/4)
b the place of My .... Is. 60:13

BEAUTY (49/49)
"The *b* of Israel is .... 2 Sam. 1:19
To behold the *b* .... Ps. 27:4
see the King in His *b*............. Is. 33:17
no *b* that we should .... Is. 53:2

BECAME (269/263)
man *b* a living being.............. Gen. 2:7
to the Jews I *b* as a Jew .... 1 Cor. 9:20

BED (89/87)
I remember You on my *b* .... Ps. 63:6
if I make my *b* in hell .... Ps. 139:8
"Arise, take up your *b*............ Matt. 9:6
be two men in one *b*........... Luke 17:34
and the *b* undefiled .... Heb. 13:4

BEDS (10/10)
sing aloud on their *b* .... Ps. 149:5

BEFOREHAND (13/13)
do not worry *b* .... Mark 13:11
told you all things *b* .... Mark 13:23
when He testified *b*.............. 1 Pet. 1:11

BEG (16/16)
b you as sojourners .... 1 Pet. 2:11

BEGAN (131/129)
since the world *b*................ Luke 1:70

BEGGAR (3/3)
there was a certain *b* .... Luke 16:20

BEGGARLY (1/1)
weak and *b* elements .... Gal. 4:9

BEGINNING (105/103)
b God created the .... Gen. 1:1
In the *b* was the Word .... John 1:1
a murderer from the *b*........... John 8:44
True Witness, the *B*............... Rev. 3:14
and the Omega, the *B*............ Rev. 21:6

BEGOTTEN (18/18)
today I have *b* You................ Ps. 2:7
glory as of the only *b* .... John 1:14
loves him who is *b* .... 1 John 5:1

BIRDS (87/85)
b make their nests . . . Ps. 104:17
Look at the *b* of the air . . . Matt. 6:26
"Foxes have holes and *b* . . . Matt. 8:20

BIRTH (48/46)
the day of one's *b* . . . Eccl. 7:1
Now the *b* of Jesus . . . Matt. 1:18
will rejoice at his *b* . . . Luke 1:14
conceived, it gives *b* . . . James 1:15

BIRTHDAY (3/3)
which was Pharaoh's *b* . . . Gen. 40:20

BIRTHRIGHT (10/9)
Esau despised his *b* . . . Gen. 25:34

BISHOP (3/3)
the position of a *b* . . . 1 Tim. 3:1
b must be blameless . . . Titus 1:7

BIT (3/3)
and they *b* the people . . . Num. 21:6

BITE (4/4)
A serpent may *b* . . . Eccl. 10:11
But if you *b* and . . . Gal. 5:15

BITTER (43/41)
b herbs they shall eat it . . . Ex. 12:8
and do not be *b* . . . Col. 3:19
But if you have *b* . . . James 3:14

BITTERLY (20/20)
And Hezekiah wept *b* . . . 2 Kin. 20:3
he went out and wept *b* . . . Matt. 26:75

BITTERNESS (21/21)
you are poisoned by *b* . . . Acts 8:23
b springing up cause . . . Heb. 12:15

BLACK (16/15)
one hair white or *b* . . . Matt. 5:36
a *b* horse and he who sat . . . Rev. 6:5
and the sun became *b* . . . Rev. 6:12

BLACKNESS (6/6)
whom is reserved the *b* . . . Jude 1:13

BLACKSMITH (3/3)
I have created the *b* . . . Is. 54:16

BLADE (4/3)
first the *b*, then the head . . . Mark 4:28

BLAME (4/4)
be holy and without *b* . . . Eph. 1:4

BLAMELESS (47/45)
and that man was *b* . . . Job 1:1
body be preserved *b* . . . 1 Thess. 5:23

BLAMELESSLY (2/2)
b we behaved . . . 1 Thess. 2:10

BLASPHEME (6/6)
b Your name forever . . . Ps. 74:10
compelled them to *b* . . . Acts 26:11
b that noble name . . . James 2:7

BLASPHEMED (23/23)
who passed by *b* Him . . . Matt. 27:39
great heat, and they *b* . . . Rev. 16:9

BLASPHEMER (1/1)
I was formerly a *b* . . . 1 Tim. 1:13

BLASPHEMES (5/4)
b the name of the LORD . . . Lev. 24:16
"This Man *b!*" . . . Matt. 9:3

BLASPHEMIES (7/7)
is this who speaks *b* . . . Luke 5:21

BLASPHEMY (13/11)
but the *b* against . . . Matt. 12:31
was full of names of *b* . . . Rev. 17:3

BLEATING (1/1)
"What then is this *b* . . . 1 Sam. 15:14

BLEMISH (56/50)
be holy and without *b* . . . Eph. 5:27
as of a lamb without *b* . . . 1 Pet. 1:19

BLEMISHED (1/1)
to the Lord what is *b* . . . Mal. 1:14

BLESS (133/123)
b those who *b* you . . . Gen. 12:3
You go unless You *b* . . . Gen. 32:26
"The LORD *b* you and . . . Num. 6:24
b the LORD at all . . . Ps. 34:1
b You while I live . . . Ps. 63:4
b His holy name . . . Ps. 103:1
b those who curse . . . Luke 6:28
B those who persecute . . . Rom. 12:14
Being reviled, we *b* . . . 1 Cor. 4:12

BLESSED (303/287)
B is the man who walks . . . Ps. 1:1
B is the man to whom . . . Ps. 32:2
B is the nation whose . . . Ps. 33:12
B is he who comes . . . Ps. 118:26
rise up and call her *b* . . . Prov. 31:28
B are the poor in . . . Matt. 5:3
B are those who mourn . . . Matt. 5:4
B are the meek . . . Matt. 5:5
B are those who hunger . . . Matt. 5:6
B are the merciful . . . Matt. 5:7
B are the pure in . . . Matt. 5:8
B are the peacemakers . . . Matt. 5:9
B are those who are . . . Matt. 5:10
B is He who comes . . . Matt. 21:9
'It is more *b* to give . . . Acts 20:35
B be the God and . . . Eph. 1:3
'*B* are the dead who . . . Rev. 14:13

BLESSING (67/64)
and you shall be a *b* . . . Gen. 12:2
before you today a *b* . . . Deut. 11:26
shall be showers of *b* . . . Ezek. 34:26
and you shall be a *b* . . . Zech. 8:13
that the *b* of Abraham . . . Gal. 3:14
with every spiritual *b* . . . Eph. 1:3

BLIND (82/73)
To open *b* eyes . . . Is. 42:7
His watchmen are *b* . . . Is. 56:10
if the *b* leads the *b* . . . Matt. 15:14
to Him, "Are we *b* . . . John 9:40
miserable, poor, *b* . . . Rev. 3:17

BLINDED (6/6)
and the rest were *b* . . . Rom. 11:7

BLINDS (2/2)
a bribe, for a bribe ***b*** .... Deut. 16:19

BLOOD (424/357)
of your brother's ***b*** .... Gen. 4:10
b shall be shed .... Gen. 9:6
b that makes atonement .... Lev. 17:11
hands are full of ***b*** .... Is. 1:15
And the moon into ***b*** .... Joel 2:31
For this is My ***b*** .... Matt. 26:28
betraying innocent ***b*** .... Matt. 27:4
new covenant in My ***b*** .... Luke 22:20
were born, not of ***b*** .... John 1:13
b has eternal life .... John 6:54
with His own ***b*** .... Acts 20:28
propitiation by His ***b*** .... Rom. 3:25
justified by His ***b*** .... Rom. 5:9
redemption through His ***b*** .... Eph. 1:7
brought near by the ***b*** .... Eph. 2:13
against flesh and ***b*** .... Eph. 6:12
peace through the ***b*** .... Col. 1:20
with the precious ***b*** .... 1 Pet. 1:19
b of Jesus Christ His .... 1 John 1:7
our sins in His own ***b*** .... Rev. 1:5
us to God by Your ***b*** .... Rev. 5:9
them white in the ***b*** .... Rev. 7:14
overcame him by the ***b*** .... Rev. 12:11
a robe dipped in ***b*** .... Rev. 19:13

BLOODSHED (24/23)
me from the guilt of ***b*** .... Ps. 51:14

BLOODTHIRSTY (9/9)
The LORD abhors the ***b*** .... Ps. 5:6

BLOSSOM (9/9)
and ***b*** as the rose .... Is. 35:1

BLOT (11/11)
from my sins, and ***b*** .... Ps. 51:9
and I will not ***b*** .... Rev. 3:5

BLOTTED (8/8)
your sins may be ***b*** .... Acts 3:19

BLOW (35/34)
with a very severe ***b*** .... Jer. 14:17

BLOWS (13/12)
The wind ***b*** where it .... John 3:8

BOAST (46/41)
puts on his armor ***b*** .... 1 Kin. 20:11
and make your ***b*** .... Rom. 2:17
lest anyone should ***b*** .... Eph. 2:9

BOASTERS (2/2)
God, violent, proud, ***b*** .... Rom. 1:30

BOASTING (14/14)
Where is ***b*** then .... Rom. 3:27

BODIES (38/35)
b a living sacrifice .... Rom. 12:1
not know that your ***b*** .... 1 Cor. 6:15
wives as their own ***b*** .... Eph. 5:28

BODILY (4/4)
b form like a dove .... Luke 3:22
of the Godhead ***b*** .... Col. 2:9

BODY (224/196)
of the ***b*** is the eye .... Matt. 6:22
those who kill the ***b*** .... Matt. 10:28
Take, eat; this is My ***b*** .... Matt. 26:26
of the temple of His ***b*** .... John 2:21
deliver me from this ***b*** .... Rom. 7:24
redemption of our ***b*** .... Rom. 8:23
members in one ***b*** .... Rom. 12:4
But I discipline my ***b*** .... 1 Cor. 9:27
b which is broken .... 1 Cor. 11:24
baptized into one ***b*** .... 1 Cor. 12:13
are the ***b*** of Christ .... 1 Cor. 12:27
though I give my ***b*** .... 1 Cor. 13:3
It is sown a natural ***b*** .... 1 Cor. 15:44
in the ***b*** of His flesh .... Col. 1:22
our sins in His own ***b*** .... 1 Pet. 2:24

BOILS (7/6)
Job with painful ***b*** .... Job 2:7

BOLDLY (12/12)
therefore come ***b*** .... Heb. 4:16

BOLDNESS (12/12)
in whom we have ***b*** .... Eph. 3:12
that we may have ***b*** .... 1 John 4:17

BOND (9/9)
love, which is the ***b*** .... Col. 3:14

BONDAGE (42/41)
out of the house of ***b*** .... Ex. 13:14
again with a yoke of ***b*** .... Gal. 5:1

BONDS (17/17)
"Let us break Their ***b*** .... Ps. 2:3

BONDSERVANTS (9/9)
B, be obedient to .... Eph. 6:5
Masters, give your ***b*** .... Col. 4:1

BONDWOMAN (9/7)
the one by a ***b*** .... Gal. 4:22

BONE (16/15)
b clings to my skin .... Job 19:20

BONES (94/81)
I can count all My ***b*** .... Ps. 22:17
and my ***b*** waste away .... Ps. 31:10
I kept silent, my ***b*** .... Ps. 32:3
the wind, or how the ***b*** .... Eccl. 11:5
say to them, 'O dry ***b*** .... Ezek. 37:4
of dead men's ***b*** .... Matt. 23:27
b shall be broken .... John 19:36

BOOK (178/165)
are written in the ***b*** .... Gal. 3:10
in the Lamb's ***B*** .... Rev. 21:27
the prophecy of this ***b*** .... Rev. 22:18

BOOKS (8/7)
b there is no end .... Eccl. 12:12
not contain the ***b*** .... John 21:25
God, and ***b*** were opened .... Rev. 20:12

BOOTH (2/2)
of Zion is left as a ***b*** .... Is. 1:8

BORDERS (22/22)
and enlarge the ***b*** .... Matt. 23:5

BORE (148/143)
And to Sarah who *b* . . . . Is. 51:2
b the sin of many. . . . . Is. 53:12
b our sicknesses. . . . . Matt. 8:17
who Himself *b* our sins . . . . 1 Pet. 2:24
b a male Child who was . . . . Rev. 12:5

BORN (144/138)
A time to be *b* . . . . Eccl. 3:2
unto us a Child is *b* . . . . Is. 9:6
b Jesus who is called . . . . Matt. 1:16
unless one is *b* again . . . . John 3:3
That which is *b*. . . . . John 3:6
having been *b* again . . . . 1 Pet. 1:23
who loves is *b* of God . . . . 1 John 4:7

BORROWER (2/2)
b is servant to the . . . . Prov. 22:7

BORROWS (2/2)
The wicked *b* and does. . . . . Ps. 37:21

BOSOM (35/31)
angels to Abraham's *b* . . . . Luke 16:22
Son, who is in the *b*. . . . . John 1:18

BOTTOMLESS (7/7)
ascend out of the *b* . . . . Rev. 17:8
the key to the *b*. . . . . Rev. 20:1

BOUGHT (44/44)
b the threshing floor . . . . 2 Sam. 24:24
all that he had and *b*. . . . . Matt. 13:46
For you were *b* at a . . . . 1 Cor. 6:20
denying the Lord who *b* . . . . 2 Pet. 2:1

BOUND (91/89)
on earth will be *b*. . . . . Matt. 16:19
And see, now I go *b*. . . . . Acts 20:22
who has a husband is *b* . . . . Rom. 7:2
Are you *b* to a wife . . . . 1 Cor. 7:27
Devil and Satan, and *b* . . . . Rev. 20:2

BOUNTIFULLY (8/7)
and he who sows *b* . . . . 2 Cor. 9:6

BOW (98/94)
You shall not *b* . . . . Ex. 23:24
let us worship and *b* . . . . Ps. 95:6
who sat on it had a *b*. . . . . Rev. 6:2

BOWED (75/73)
stood all around and *b*. . . . . Gen. 37:7
And they *b* the knee . . . . Matt. 27:29

BOWL (31/30)
and poured out his *b* . . . . Rev. 16:2

BOWLS (32/29)
Go and pour out the *b* . . . . Rev. 16:1

BOX (4/4)
Judas had the money *b* . . . . John 13:29

BOYS (3/3)
Shall be full of *b*. . . . . Zech. 8:5

BRAIDED (9/8)
not with *b* hair or . . . . 1 Tim. 2:9

BRANCH (34/30)
raise to David a *B*. . . . . Jer. 23:5
forth My Servant the *B*. . . . . Zech. 3:8
b that bears fruit He . . . . John 15:2

BRANCHES (84/67)
vine, you are the *b*. . . . . John 15:5

BRASS (4/4)
become sounding *b* . . . . 1 Cor. 13:1

BRAVE (1/1)
in the faith, be *b*. . . . . 1 Cor. 16:13

BREAD (346/315)
of Salem brought out *b* . . . . Gen. 14:18
shall eat unleavened *b*. . . . . Ex. 23:15
not live by *b* alone. . . . . Deut. 8:3
b eaten in secret is . . . . Prov. 9:17
B gained by deceit is . . . . Prov. 20:17
Cast your *b* upon the . . . . Eccl. 11:1
for what is not *b*. . . . . Is. 55:2
these stones become *b* . . . . Matt. 4:3
not live by *b* alone. . . . . Matt. 4:4
this day our daily *b*. . . . . Matt. 6:11
eating, Jesus took *b* . . . . Matt. 26:26
I am the *b* of life . . . . John 6:48
He was betrayed took *b* . . . . 1 Cor. 11:23

BREADTH (7/6)
is as great as its *b*. . . . . Rev. 21:16

BREAK (138/131)
covenant I will not *b*. . . . . Ps. 89:34
together to *b* bread . . . . Acts 20:7

BREAKING (20/20)
in the *b* of bread . . . . Acts 2:42
b bread from house to . . . . Acts 2:46

BREAKS (31/31)
Until the day *b* . . . . Song 2:17

BREAST (16/15)
back on Jesus' *b*. . . . . John 13:25

BREASTPLATE (28/24)
righteousness as a *b*. . . . . Is. 59:17
having put on the *b* . . . . Eph. 6:14

BREASTS (27/27)
Your two *b* are like . . . . Song 4:5
b which nursed You . . . . Luke 11:27

BREATH (54/51)
nostrils the *b* of life. . . . . Gen. 2:7
that there was no *b* . . . . 1 Kin. 17:17
Man is like a *b*. . . . . Ps. 144:4
everything that has *b* . . . . Ps. 150:6
"Surely I will cause *b* . . . . Ezek. 37:5
gives to all life, *b* . . . . Acts 17:25
power to give *b*. . . . . Rev. 13:15

BREATHES (2/2)
indeed he *b* his last. . . . . Job 14:10

BRETHREN (398/389)
and you are all *b* . . . . Matt. 23:8
least of these My *b*. . . . . Matt. 25:40
firstborn among many *b*. . . . . Rom. 8:29
thus sin against the *b*. . . . . 1 Cor. 8:12
over five hundred *b* . . . . 1 Cor. 15:6
perils among false *b*. . . . . 2 Cor. 11:26
sincere love of the *b* . . . . 1 Pet. 1:22
because we love the *b*. . . . . 1 John 3:14
our lives for the *b* . . . . 1 John 3:16

BRIBE (15/13)
you shall take no *b* . . . . Ex. 23:8
b blinds the eyes . . . . Deut. 16:19

BRIBES (9/9)
hand is full of *b* . . . . Ps. 26:10

BRICK (9/9)
people straw to make *b* . . . . Ex. 5:7

BRICKS (5/5)
"Come, let us make *b* . . . . Gen. 11:3

BRIDE (14/14)
I will show you the *b*. . . . . Rev. 21:9
the Spirit and the *b* . . . . Rev. 22:17

BRIDEGROOM (26/20)
and as the *b* rejoices. . . . . Is. 62:5
mourn as long as the *b* . . . . Matt. 9:15
went out to meet the *b*. . . . . Matt. 25:1
the friend of the *b* . . . . John 3:29

BRIDLE (8/8)
b the whole body. . . . . James 3:2

BRIER (3/3)
b shall come up the . . . . Is. 55:13

BRIERS (11/11)
there shall come up *b*. . . . . Is. 5:6

BRIGHTER (4/4)
a light from heaven, *b* . . . . Acts 26:13

BRIGHTNESS (19/19)
and kings to the *b* . . . . Is. 60:3
who being the *b* . . . . Heb. 1:3

BRIMSTONE (14/14)
the lake of fire and *b*. . . . . Rev. 20:10

BRING (710/677)
b back his soul . . . . Job 33:30
b My righteousness. . . . . Is. 46:13
Who shall *b* a charge . . . . Rom. 8:33
b Christ down from. . . . . Rom. 10:6
even so God will *b* . . . . 1 Thess. 4:14

BROAD (16/16)
b is the way that. . . . . Matt. 7:13

BROKE (79/76)
b them at the foot of. . . . . Ex. 32:19
He blessed and *b* . . . . Matt. 14:19
b the legs of the . . . . John 19:32

BROKEN (166/160)
this stone will be *b* . . . . Matt. 21:44
Scripture cannot be *b*. . . . . John 10:35
is My body which is *b* . . . . 1 Cor. 11:24

BROKENHEARTED (3/3)
He heals the *b* and . . . . Ps. 147:3

BRONZE (161/138)
So Moses made a *b* . . . . Num. 21:9
b walls against the. . . . . Jer. 1:18
a *third kingdom* of *b* . . . . Dan. 2:39

BROOD (8/8)
B of vipers . . . . Matt. 12:34
hen gathers her *b* . . . . Luke 13:34

BROOK (50/47)
disciples over the *B*. . . . . John 18:1

BROOKS (14/14)
for the water *b* . . . . Ps. 42:1

BROTHER (357/322)
"Where is Abel your *b* . . . . Gen. 4:9
b offended is harder. . . . . Prov. 18:19
b will deliver up. . . . . Matt. 10:21
how often shall my *b* . . . . Matt. 18:21
b will rise again . . . . John 11:23
b goes to law against . . . . 1 Cor. 6:6
Whoever hates his *b*. . . . . 1 John 3:15

BROTHERHOOD (4/4)
Love the *b* . . . . 1 Pet. 2:17

BROTHERLY (5/4)
b love continue . . . . Heb. 13:1

BROTHER'S (34/30)
Am I my *b* keeper . . . . Gen. 4:9
at the speck in your *b*. . . . . Matt. 7:3

BROTHERS (173/164)
is My mother, or My *b* . . . . Mark 3:33
b are these who hear . . . . Luke 8:21

BRUISE (4/3)
He shall *b* your head. . . . . Gen. 3:15
the LORD to *b* Him . . . . Is. 53:10

BRUISED (4/4)
He was *b* for our . . . . Is. 53:5
b reed He will not . . . . Matt. 12:20

BUCKLER (4/4)
be your shield and *b*. . . . . Ps. 91:4

BUFFET (1/1)
of Satan to *b* me. . . . . 2 Cor. 12:7

BUILD (161/153)
b ourselves a city. . . . . Gen. 11:4
"Would you *b* a house . . . . 2 Sam. 7:5
labor in vain who *b*. . . . . Ps. 127:1
down, and a time to *b*. . . . . Eccl. 3:3
'This man began to *b* . . . . Luke 14:30
What house will you *b* . . . . Acts 7:49
For if I *b* again . . . . Gal. 2:18

BUILDER (2/2)
foundations, whose *b*. . . . . Heb. 11:10

BUILDING (31/30)
in whom the whole *b* . . . . Eph. 2:21

BUILDS (12/11)
one take heed how he *b*. . . . . 1 Cor. 3:10

BUILT (214/197)
Wisdom has *b* her house. . . . . Prov. 9:1
to a wise man who *b*. . . . . Matt. 7:24
having been *b* on the . . . . Eph. 2:20

BULLS (59/56)
For if the blood of *b* . . . . Heb. 9:13

BULWARKS (2/2)
Mark well her *b* . . . . Ps. 48:13

BUNDLE (4/4)
each man's *b* of money . . . . Gen. 42:35

BURDEN (56/56)
Cast your *b* on the. . . . . Ps. 55:22
easy and My *b* is light. . . . . Matt. 11:30

we might not be a *b* ... 1 Thess. 2:9
on you no other *b* ... Rev. 2:24

BURDENS (19/18)
For they bind heavy *b*. ... Matt. 23:4
Bear one another's *b* ... Gal. 6:2

BURDENSOME (9/9)
I myself was not *b*. ... 2 Cor. 12:13
commandments are not *b* ... 1 John 5:3

BURIAL (17/16)
she did it for My *b* ... Matt. 26:12
for the day of My *b* ... John 12:7

BURIED (104/101)
Therefore we were *b*. ... Rom. 6:4
and that He was *b* ... 1 Cor. 15:4
b with Him in baptism. ... Col. 2:12

BURN (144/137)
the bush does not *b* ... Ex. 3:3
"Did not our heart *b* ... Luke 24:32

BURNED (167/159)
If anyone's work is *b*. ... 1 Cor. 3:15
my body to be *b* ... 1 Cor. 13:3

BURNING (58/55)
b torch that passed ... Gen. 15:17
b fire shut up in my ... Jer. 20:9
plucked from the *b* ... Amos 4:11

BURNT (294/267)
lamb for a *b* offering ... Gen. 22:7
delight in *b* offering ... Ps. 51:16

BURST (10/10)
the new wine will *b*. ... Luke 5:37

BURY (39/36)
and let the dead *b* ... Matt. 8:22

BUSH (11/9)
from the midst of a *b* ... Ex. 3:2

BUSINESS (20/19)
about My Father's *b* ... Luke 2:49

BUSYBODIES (2/2)
at all, but are *b* ... 2 Thess. 3:11

BUTLER (9/9)
b did not remember ... Gen. 40:23

BUTTER (3/3)
were smoother than *b* ... Ps. 55:21

BUY (58/53)
Yes, come, *b* wine and ... Is. 55:1
I counsel you to *b* ... Rev. 3:18
and that no one may *b*. ... Rev. 13:17

BUYS (4/4)
has and *b* that field ... Matt. 13:44

BYWORD (10/10)
But He has made me a *b* ... Job 17:6

C

CAGE (4/4)
foul spirit, and a *c* ... Rev. 18:2

CAKE (13/12)
Ephraim is a *c*. ... Hos. 7:8

CALAMITY (49/46)
will laugh at your *c* ... Prov. 1:26

CALCULATED (1/1)
c the dust of the ... Is. 40:12

CALDRON (5/5)
this city is the *c* ... Ezek. 11:3

CALF (31/31)
and made a molded *c*. ... Ex. 32:4
And bring the fatted *c* ... Luke 15:23

CALL (187/182)
c upon Him while He ... Is. 55:6
c His name Jesus ... Matt. 1:21
c the righteous ... Matt. 9:13
Lord our God will *c* ... Acts 2:39
you must not *c* common. ... Acts 10:15
c and election sure ... 2 Pet. 1:10

CALLED (619/593)
c the light Day ... Gen. 1:5
c his wife's name Eve ... Gen. 3:20
I have *c* you by your ... Is. 43:1
"Out of Egypt I *c* ... Matt. 2:15
a city *c* Nazareth ... Matt. 2:23
For many are *c* ... Matt. 20:16
to those who are the *c* ... Rom. 8:28
these He also *c* ... Rom. 8:30
c children of God ... 1 John 3:1

CALLING (29/29)
the gifts and the *c* ... Rom. 11:29
For you see your *c*. ... 1 Cor. 1:26
remain in the same *c* ... 1 Cor. 7:20

CALLS (33/32)
c them all by name ... Ps. 147:4
David himself *c* ... Mark 12:37
c his own sheep ... John 10:3

CALM (6/6)
there was a great *c* ... Matt. 8:26

CAMEL (9/9)
it is easier for a *c* ... Matt. 19:24

CAMP (181/164)
to Him, outside the *c* ... Heb. 13:13

CAN (344/309)
I *c* do all things ... Phil. 4:13

CANCER (1/1)
will spread like *c* ... 2 Tim. 2:17

CANOPY (4/4)
His *c* around Him was ... Ps. 18:11

CAPSTONE (1/1)
bring forth the *c* ... Zech. 4:7

CAPTAIN (72/71)
which, having no *c* ... Prov. 6:7

CAPTIVE (88/82)
and be led away *c*. ... Luke 21:24
He led captivity *c*. ... Eph. 4:8

CAPTIVES (54/49)
make *c* of gullible women. ... 2 Tim. 3:6

CAPTIVITY (106/98)
every thought into *c*. ... 2 Cor. 10:5

CARCASS (20/16)
For wherever the *c* . . . . Matt. 24:28
CARE (32/30)
"Lord, do You not *c* . . . . Luke 10:40
how will he take *c* . . . . 1 Tim. 3:5
CARED (3/3)
he said, not that he *c* . . . . John 12:6
CAREFULLY (26/26)
I shall walk *c* all my . . . . Is. 38:15
CARELESS (2/2)
but he who is *c* . . . . Prov. 19:16
CARES (11/10)
no one *c* for my soul . . . . Ps. 142:4
for He *c* for you . . . . 1 Pet. 5:7
CARNAL (7/6)
c mind is enmity . . . . Rom. 8:7
CARNALLY (6/6)
c minded is death . . . . Rom. 8:6
CAROUSE (1/1)
count it pleasure to *c* . . . . 2 Pet. 2:13
CARPENTER (1/1)
Is this not the *c* . . . . Mark 6:3
CARRIED (153/141)
and *c* our sorrows . . . . Is. 53:4
CARRY (80/77)
for you to *c* your bed . . . . John 5:10
it is certain we can *c* . . . . 1 Tim. 6:7
CARRYING (17/15)
a man will meet you *c* . . . . Mark 14:13
CASE (34/33)
Festus laid Paul's *c* . . . . Acts 25:14
CASSIA (3/3)
myrrh and aloes and *c* . . . . Ps. 45:8
CAST (323/307)
Why are you *c* down . . . . Ps. 42:5
whole body to be *c* . . . . Matt. 5:29
In My name they will *c* . . . . Mark 16:17
by no means *c* out . . . . John 6:37
c their crowns before . . . . Rev. 4:10
the great dragon was *c* . . . . Rev. 12:9
CASTING (15/15)
c down arguments . . . . 2 Cor. 10:5
c all your care . . . . 1 Pet. 5:7
CASTS (12/12)
perfect love *c* out . . . . 1 John 4:18
CATCH (17/17)
c Him in His words . . . . Mark 12:13
From now on you will *c* . . . . Luke 5:10
CATCHES (6/6)
and the wolf *c* the . . . . John 10:12
c the wise in their . . . . 1 Cor. 3:19
CAUGHT (44/44)
behind him was a ram *c* . . . . Gen. 22:13
her Child was *c* up . . . . Rev. 12:5
CAUSE (219/210)
hated Me without a *c* . . . . John 15:25
For this *c* I was born . . . . John 18:37
CAVES (8/8)
in dens and *c* of the . . . . Heb. 11:38
CEASE (72/72)
and night shall not *c* . . . . Gen. 8:22
He makes wars *c* . . . . Ps. 46:9
tongues, they will *c* . . . . 1 Cor. 13:8
CEDAR (52/49)
dwell in a house of *c* . . . . 2 Sam. 7:2
CEDARS (22/21)
the LORD breaks the *c* . . . . Ps. 29:5
CELESTIAL (2/1)
but the glory of the *c* . . . . 1 Cor. 15:40
CENSER (12/10)
Aaron, each took his *c* . . . . Lev. 10:1
CERTAINTY (3/3)
you may know the *c* . . . . Luke 1:4
CERTIFICATE (7/7)
a man to write a *c* . . . . Mark 10:4
CHAFF (15/15)
be chased like the *c* . . . . Is. 17:13
He will burn up the *c* . . . . Matt. 3:12
CHAIN (10/10)
pit and a great *c* . . . . Rev. 20:1
CHAINED (3/3)
of God is not *c* . . . . 2 Tim. 2:9
CHAINS (49/47)
And his *c* fell off . . . . Acts 12:7
am, except for these *c* . . . . Acts 26:29
CHAMBERS (58/48)
brought me into his *c* . . . . Song 1:4
CHAMPION (3/3)
And a *c* went out from . . . . 1 Sam. 17:4
CHANGE (23/23)
now and to *c* my tone . . . . Gal. 4:20
there is also a *c* . . . . Heb. 7:12
CHANGED (37/36)
c the glory of the . . . . Rom. 1:23
but we shall all be *c* . . . . 1 Cor. 15:51
CHANGERS' (1/1)
and poured out the *c* . . . . John 2:15
CHANGES (12/11)
c the times and the . . . . Dan. 2:21
CHANNELS (4/4)
c of the sea were seen . . . . Ps. 18:15
CHARIOT (62/54)
that suddenly a *c* . . . . 2 Kin. 2:11
CHARIOTS (110/101)
Some trust in *c* . . . . Ps. 20:7
CHARITABLE (5/5)
you do not do your *c* . . . . Matt. 6:1
c deeds which she . . . . Acts 9:36
CHARM (1/1)
C is deceitful and . . . . Prov. 31:30
CHARMS (4/4)
who sew magic *c* . . . . Ezek. 13:18

COBRA (3/3)
the lion and the *c*. . . . . .Ps. 91:13
COBRA'S (1/1)
shall play by the *c* . . . . Is. 11:8
COFFIN (3/3)
and he was put in a *c* . . . . Gen. 50:26
touched the open *c*. . . . . .Luke 7:14
COIN (2/2)
if she loses one *c* . . . . .Luke 15:8
COLD (17/16)
and harvest, *c* and. . . . . .Gen. 8:22
of many will grow *c*. . . . . Matt. 24:12
that you are neither *c*. . . . . Rev. 3:15
COLLECTION (4/4)
concerning the *c* . . . . 1 Cor. 16:1
COLT (15/14)
on a donkey, a *c* . . . . .Zech. 9:9
on a donkey, a *c* . . . . Matt. 21:5
COME (1,702/1,588)
He will *c* and save you . . . . .Is. 35:4
who have no money, *C*. . . . . Is. 55:1
Your kingdom *c*. . . . . Matt. 6:10
C to Me . . . . Matt. 11:28
I have *c* in My . . . . John 5:43
and I have not *c*. . . . . John 7:28
thirsts, let him *c*. . . . . John 7:37
c as a light into the . . . . John 12:46
O Lord, *c*. .1 Cor. 16:22
the door, I will *c*. . . . . .Rev. 3:20
COMELINESS (1/1)
He has no form or *c* . . . . .Is. 53:2
COMES (272/257)
Lord's death till He *c*. . . . . 1 Cor. 11:26
COMFORT (59/55)
and Your staff, they *c* . . . . Ps. 23:4
yes, *c* My people. . . . . .Is. 40:1
c each other and edify . . . . . . 1 Thess. 5:11
COMFORTED (31/31)
So Isaac was *c* after. . . . . .Gen. 24:67
refusing to be *c* . . . . Jer. 31:15
COMFORTER (4/3)
She had no *c* . . . . .Lam. 1:9
COMFORTS (10/10)
I, even I, am He who *c* . . . . Is. 51:12
COMING (260/254)
see the Son of Man *c*. . . . . .Mark 13:26
mightier than I is *c* . . . . .Luke 3:16
are Christ's at His *c* . . . . 1 Cor. 15:23
Behold, I am *c* . . . . .Rev. 3:11
"Surely I am *c*. . . . . .Rev. 22:20
COMMAND (202/195)
c I have received . . . . John 10:18
And I know that His *c* . . . . John 12:50
if you do whatever I *c*. . . . . .John 15:14
COMMANDED (450/437)
not endure what was *c*. . . . . .Heb. 12:20
COMMANDMENT (112/108)
c of the LORD is pure . . . . Ps. 19:8
which is the great *c*. . . . . .Matt. 22:36
A new *c* I give to. . . . . John 13:34
which is the first *c*. . . . . .Eph. 6:2
And this is His *c*. . . . . .1 John 3:23
COMMANDMENTS (159/156)
covenant, the Ten *C* . . . . .Ex. 34:28
as doctrines the *c* . . . . Matt. 15:9
c hang all the Law . . . . .Matt. 22:40
He who has My *c* . . . . .John 14:21
COMMANDS (20/20)
with authority He *c*. . . . . Mark 1:27
COMMEND (7/7)
But food does not *c*. . . . . .1 Cor. 8:8
COMMENDABLE (2/2)
patiently, this is *c*. . . . . .1 Pet. 2:20
COMMENDED (8/8)
c the unjust steward . . . . Luke 16:8
COMMENDS (2/1)
but whom the Lord *c* . . . . .2 Cor. 10:18
COMMIT (65/60)
"You shall not *c* . . . . Ex. 20:14
into Your hands I *c* . . . . Luke 23:46
COMMITS (30/26)
sin also *c* lawlessness. . . . . .1 John 3:4
COMMITTED (112/106)
c Himself to Him who . . . . 1 Pet. 2:23
COMMON (28/28)
c people heard Him . . . . Mark 12:37
had all things in *c* . . . . .Acts 2:44
concerning our *c*. . . . . .Jude 1:3
COMMOTION (3/3)
there arose a great *c*. . . . . Acts 19:23
COMMUNED (1/1)
I *c* with my heart . . . . Eccl. 1:16
COMMUNION (4/3)
c of the Holy Spirit . . . . 2 Cor. 13:14
COMPANION (25/25)
a man my equal, My *c*. . . . . .Ps. 55:13
COMPANY (51/47)
great was the *c* . . . . .Ps. 68:11
to an innumerable *c*. . . . . .Heb. 12:22
COMPARE (6/6)
c ourselves with those . . . . 2 Cor. 10:12
COMPARED (4/4)
are not worthy to be *c* . . . . Rom. 8:18
COMPASSION (47/44)
are a God full of *c*. . . . . Ps. 86:15
He was moved with *c* . . . . .Matt. 9:36
whomever I will have *c* . . . . Rom. 9:15
He can have *c* on those . . . . .Heb. 5:2
COMPASSIONATE (2/2)
the Lord is very *c*. . . . . .James 5:11
COMPASSIONS (1/1)
because His *c* fail not. . . . . Lam. 3:22

CONSENTING (2/2)
Now Saul was *c* to his . . . . Acts 8:1
CONSIDER (84/83)
When I *c* Your heavens . . . . Ps. 8:3
My people do not *c* . . . . Is. 1:3
C the lilies of the . . . . Matt. 6:28
C the ravens . . . . Luke 12:24
c Him who endured . . . . Heb. 12:3
CONSIST (2/2)
in Him all things *c* . . . . Col. 1:17
CONSOLATION (14/13)
if there is any *c*. . . . . Phil. 2:1
given us everlasting *c*. . . . . . . .2 Thess. 2:16
CONSOLE (2/2)
c those who mourn. . . . . .Is. 61:3
CONSTANT (1/1)
c prayer was offered . . . . Acts 12:5
CONSUME (41/39)
whom the Lord will *c* . . . . 2 Thess. 2:8
CONSUMED (74/73)
but the bush was not *c*. . . . . Ex. 3:2
mercies we are not *c*. . . . . Lam. 3:22
beware lest you be *c* . . . . .Gal. 5:15
CONSUMING (8/8)
our God is a *c* fire. . . . . .Heb. 12:29
CONTAIN (4/4)
of heavens cannot *c* . . . . .2 Chr. 2:6
c the books that . . . . John 21:25
CONTEMPT (14/14)
and be treated with *c* . . . . Mark 9:12
CONTEMPTIBLE (4/4)
and his speech *c* . . . . .2 Cor. 10:10
CONTEND (21/20)
c earnestly for the . . . . .Jude 1:3
CONTENT (10/10)
state I am, to be *c* . . . . Phil. 4:11
covetousness; be *c* . . . . .Heb. 13:5
CONTENTIONS (8/8)
sorcery, hatred, *c*. . . . . Gal. 5:20
CONTENTIOUS (6/6)
anyone seems to be *c*. . . . . .1 Cor. 11:16
CONTENTMENT (1/1)
c is great gain . . . . 1 Tim. 6:6
CONTINUAL (10/10)
a merry heart has a *c* . . . . .Prov. 15:15
c coming she weary me. . . . . .Luke 18:5
CONTINUALLY (75/75)
heart was only evil *c*. . . . . .Gen. 6:5
will give ourselves *c* . . . . .Acts 6:4
remains a priest *c* . . . . .Heb. 7:3
CONTINUE (46/45)
Shall we *c* in sin that. . . . . Rom. 6:1
C earnestly in prayer . . . . Col. 4:2
Let brotherly love *c*. . . . . .Heb. 13:1
CONTINUED (37/37)
c steadfastly in the . . . . .Acts 2:42
CONTRADICTIONS (1/1)
idle babblings and *c* . . . . 1 Tim. 6:20
CONTRARY (29/29)
to worship God *c* . . . . Acts 18:13
CONTRIBUTION (2/2)
to make a certain *c* . . . . Rom. 15:26
CONTRITE (5/4)
a broken and a *c*. . . . . Ps. 51:17
poor and of a *c* spirit . . . . Is. 66:2
CONTROVERSY (6/6)
For the LORD has a *c*. . . . . .Jer. 25:31
CONVERSION (1/1)
describing the *c*. . . . . Acts 15:3
CONVERTED (3/3)
unless you are *c*. . . . . Matt. 18:3
CONVICT (3/3)
He has come, He will *c*. . . . . John 16:8
CONVICTS (1/1)
Which of you *c*. . . . . John 8:46
CONVINCED (7/7)
Let each be fully *c* . . . . Rom. 14:5
COOKED (3/3)
c their own children . . . . Lam. 4:10
COOL (4/4)
and *c* my tongue . . . . Luke 16:24
COPIES (2/2)
necessary that the *c* . . . . Heb. 9:23
COPPER (7/7)
sold for two *c* coins. . . . . .Luke 12:6
COPPERSMITH (1/1)
c did me much harm . . . . 2 Tim. 4:14
COPY (10/10)
who serve the *c* . . . . .Heb. 8:5
CORD (11/11)
this line of scarlet *c*. . . . . Josh. 2:18
And a threefold *c*. . . . . Eccl. 4:12
before the silver *c* . . . . .Eccl. 12:6
CORDS (24/24)
had made a whip of *c*. . . . . John 2:15
CORNER (23/21)
was not done in a *c*. . . . . .Acts 26:26
CORNERSTONE (11/11)
become the chief *c* . . . . Matt. 21:42
in Zion a chief *c* . . . . 1 Pet. 2:6
CORRECT (9/9)
C your son, and he will. . . . . Prov. 29:17
CORRECTED (3/3)
human fathers who *c*. . . . . .Heb. 12:9
CORRECTION (18/18)
Do not withhold *c* . . . . Prov. 23:13
for reproof, for *c* . . . . 2 Tim. 3:16
CORRECTS (5/5)
the LORD loves He *c* . . . . Prov. 3:12
CORRODED (1/1)
and silver are *c*. . . . . James 5:3

CORRUPT (20/19)
in these things they *c* .... Jude 1:10
CORRUPTED (12/12)
for all flesh had *c* .... Gen. 6:12
Your riches are *c* .... James 5:2
CORRUPTIBLE (5/5)
redeemed with *c* things.......... 1 Pet. 1:18
CORRUPTION (18/18)
Your Holy One to see *c*.......... Ps. 16:10
c inherit incorruption .... 1 Cor. 15:50
having escaped the *c* .... 2 Pet. 1:4
COST (4/4)
and count the *c* .... Luke 14:28
COULD (230/218)
c remove mountains .... 1 Cor. 13:2
which no one *c* number .... Rev. 7:9
COUNCILS (2/2)
deliver you up to *c* .... Mark 13:9
COUNSEL (90/89)
who walks not in the *c* .... Ps. 1:1
We took sweet *c* .... Ps. 55:14
guide me with Your *c* .... Ps. 73:24
according to the *c* .... Eph. 1:11
immutability of His *c*............ Heb. 6:17
I *c* you to buy from .... Rev. 3:18
COUNSELOR (12/12)
be called Wonderful, *C*.............. Is. 9:6
COUNSELORS (21/21)
c there is safety .... Prov. 11:14
COUNT (42/40)
c my life dear to .... Acts 20:24
His promise, as some *c* .... 2 Pet. 3:9
COUNTED (35/35)
Even a fool is *c* .... Prov. 17:28
who rule well be *c* .... 1 Tim. 5:17
COUNTENANCE (39/38)
The LORD lift up His *c* .... Num. 6:26
hypocrites, with a sad *c*.......... Matt. 6:16
His *c* was like .... Matt. 28:3
of the glory of his *c* .... 2 Cor. 3:7
COUNTRY (159/155)
"Get out of your *c*............... Gen. 12:1
that is, a heavenly *c*............ Heb. 11:16
COUNTRYMEN (8/8)
for my brethren, my *c* .... Rom. 9:3
COURAGE (22/22)
strong and of good *c*........... Deut. 31:6
COURT (131/108)
They zealously *c* you .... Gal. 4:17
COURTEOUS (1/1)
be tenderhearted, be *c* .... 1 Pet. 3:8
COURTS (26/26)
and into His *c* .... Ps. 100:4
COVENANT (313/293)
I will establish My *c* .... Gen. 6:18
the LORD made a *c* .... Gen. 15:18
will show them His *c* .... Ps. 25:14
sons will keep My *c* .... Ps. 132:12
I will make a new *c* .... Jer. 31:31
the Messenger of the *c*........... Mal. 3:1
cup is the new *c* .... Luke 22:20
He says, "A new *c*.............. Heb. 8:13
Mediator of the new *c*.......... Heb. 12:24
of the everlasting *c* .... Heb. 13:20
COVENANTS (3/3)
the glory, the *c* .... Rom. 9:4
COVER (73/72)
He shall *c* you with .... Ps. 91:4
c a multitude of sins........... James 5:20
COVERED (99/95)
Whose sin is *c*.................... Ps. 32:1
You have *c* all their sin........... Ps. 85:2
For there is nothing *c*.......... Matt. 10:26
COVERING (43/38)
spread a cloud for a *c* .... Ps. 105:39
COVERINGS (2/2)
and made themselves *c*.......... Gen. 3:7
COVET (10/9)
"You shall not *c* .... Ex. 20:17
COVETED (2/2)
c no one's silver .... Acts 20:33
COVETOUS (6/6)
nor thieves, nor *c*............. 1 Cor. 6:10
COVETOUSNESS (17/17)
heed and beware of *c* .... Luke 12:15
COWARDLY (1/1)
the *c*, unbelieving .... Rev. 21:8
CRAFTINESS (6/6)
not walking in *c* .... 2 Cor. 4:2
in the cunning *c*................ Eph. 4:14
CRAFTSMAN (10/10)
instructor of every *c*........... Gen. 4:22
CRAFTY (7/7)
the devices of the *c*.............. Job 5:12
Nevertheless, being *c* .... 2 Cor. 12:16
CREAM (3/3)
were bathed with *c* .... Job 29:6
CREATE (11/9)
peace and *c* calamity .... Is. 45:7
CREATED (46/40)
So God *c* man in His .... Gen. 1:27
Has not one God *c*............... Mal. 2:10
c in Christ Jesus................ Eph. 2:10
new man which was *c* .... Eph. 4:24
CREATION (13/13)
know that the whole *c* .... Rom. 8:22
Christ, he is a new *c* .... 2 Cor. 5:17
anything, but a new *c*............ Gal. 6:15
CREATOR (7/7)
Remember now your *C* .... Eccl. 12:1
God, the LORD, the *C*.............. Is. 40:28
rather than the *C* .... Rom. 1:25
CREATURE (30/26)
the gospel to every *c*........... Mark 16:15

D

DELIVERER (12/12)
D will come out of . . . . Rom. 11:26
DELIVERS (22/22)
even Jesus who ***d*** . . . . 1 Thess. 1:10
DELUSION (2/2)
send them strong ***d*** . . . . 2 Thess. 2:11
DEMON (20/18)
Jesus rebuked the ***d*** . . . . Matt. 17:18
and have a ***d*** . . . . John 8:48
DEMONIC (1/1)
is earthly, sensual, ***d*** . . . . James 3:15
DEMONS (49/42)
authority over all ***d*** . . . . Luke 9:1
the ***d*** are subject . . . . Luke 10:17
Even the ***d*** believe . . . . James 2:19
DEMONSTRATE (2/2)
faith, to ***d*** His . . . . Rom. 3:25
DEMONSTRATES (2/2)
d His own love toward . . . . Rom. 5:8
DEN (19/17)
cast him into the ***d*** . . . . Dan. 6:16
it a '***d*** of thieves . . . . Matt. 21:13
DENARIUS (9/8)
the laborers for a ***d*** . . . . Matt. 20:2
DENIED (17/17)
before men will be ***d*** . . . . Luke 12:9
Peter then ***d*** again . . . . John 18:27
d the Holy One and the . . . . Acts 3:14
things cannot be ***d*** . . . . Acts 19:36
household, he has ***d*** . . . . 1 Tim. 5:8
DENIES (5/4)
But whoever ***d*** Me . . . . Matt. 10:33
d that Jesus is the . . . . 1 John 2:22
DENY (26/25)
let him ***d*** himself . . . . Matt. 16:24
He cannot ***d*** Himself . . . . 2 Tim. 2:13
DENYING (3/3)
but ***d*** its power . . . . 2 Tim. 3:5
d the Lord who bought . . . . 2 Pet. 2:1
DEPART (125/122)
scepter shall not ***d*** . . . . Gen. 49:10
on the left hand, '***D*** . . . . Matt. 25:41
will ***d*** from the faith . . . . 1 Tim. 4:1
DEPARTING (8/8)
heart of unbelief in ***d*** . . . . Heb. 3:12
DEPARTURE (4/4)
d savage wolves will . . . . Acts 20:29
and the time of my ***d*** . . . . 2 Tim. 4:6
DEPRESSION (1/1)
of man causes ***d*** . . . . Prov. 12:25
DEPTH (9/9)
nor height nor ***d*** . . . . Rom. 8:39
Oh, the ***d*** of the . . . . Rom. 11:33
DEPTHS (31/31)
our sins into the ***d*** . . . . Mic. 7:19
DERISION (12/12)
shall hold them in ***d*** . . . . Ps. 2:4
DESCEND (10/10)
d now from the cross . . . . Mark 15:32
Lord Himself will ***d*** . . . . 1 Thess. 4:16
DESCENDANTS (157/143)
"We are Abraham's ***d*** . . . . John 8:33
DESCENDED (19/18)
He who ***d*** is also the . . . . Eph. 4:10
DESCENDING (11/11)
God ascending and ***d*** . . . . John 1:51
the holy Jerusalem, ***d*** . . . . Rev. 21:10
DESERT (28/28)
and rivers in the ***d*** . . . . Is. 43:19
'Look, He is in the ***d*** . . . . Matt. 24:26
DESERTED (15/15)
d place by Himself . . . . Matt. 14:13
DESERTS (6/6)
They wandered in ***d*** . . . . Heb. 11:38
DESIGN (11/9)
with an artistic ***d*** . . . . Ex. 26:31
DESIRABLE (9/9)
the eyes, and a tree ***d*** . . . . Gen. 3:6
DESIRE (122/121)
d shall be for your . . . . Gen. 3:16
Behold, You ***d*** truth in . . . . Ps. 51:6
"Father, I ***d*** that . . . . John 17:24
all manner of evil ***d*** . . . . Rom. 7:8
Brethren, my heart's ***d*** . . . . Rom. 10:1
d the best gifts . . . . 1 Cor. 12:31
the two, having a ***d*** . . . . Phil. 1:23
DESIRED (28/28)
d are they than gold . . . . Ps. 19:10
One thing I have ***d*** . . . . Ps. 27:4
DESIRES (43/41)
shall give you the ***d*** . . . . Ps. 37:4
the devil, and the ***d*** . . . . John 8:44
not come from your ***d*** . . . . James 4:1
DESOLATE (147/132)
any more be termed ***D*** . . . . Is. 62:4
house is left to you ***d*** . . . . Matt. 23:38
DESOLATION (45/45)
the 'abomination of ***d*** . . . . Matt. 24:15
DESPAIRED (2/2)
strength, so that we ***d*** . . . . 2 Cor. 1:8
DESPISE (40/40)
one and ***d*** the other . . . . Matt. 6:24
d the riches of His . . . . Rom. 2:4
DESPISED (58/57)
He is ***d*** and rejected . . . . Is. 53:3
the things which are ***d*** . . . . 1 Cor. 1:28
DESPISES (12/12)
d his neighbor sins . . . . Prov. 14:21
DESPISING (1/1)
the cross, ***d*** the shame . . . . Heb. 12:2
DESTITUTE (7/7)
of corrupt minds and ***d*** . . . . 1 Tim. 6:5
DESTROY (270/252)
Why should you ***d*** . . . . Eccl. 7:16

shall not hurt nor *d*. . . . . Is. 11:9
I did not come to *d* . . . . Matt. 5:17
Him who is able to *d*. . . . . Matt. 10:28
Barabbas and *d* Jesus. . . . . Matt. 27:20
to save life or to *d* . . . . Luke 6:9
d men's lives but to. . . . . Luke 9:56
d the wisdom of the . . . . 1 Cor. 1:19
able to save and to *d*. . . . . James 4:12

DESTROYED (171/166)
d all living things. . . . . Gen. 7:23
house, this tent, is *d* . . . . 2 Cor. 5:1

DESTRUCTION (108/106)
You turn man to *d*. . . . . Ps. 90:3
d that lays waste . . . . Ps. 91:6
your life from *d* . . . . Ps. 103:4
Pride goes before *d*. . . . . Prov. 16:18
whose end is *d* . . . . Phil. 3:19
with everlasting *d* . . . . 2 Thess. 1:9

DESTRUCTIVE (2/2)
bring in *d* heresies . . . . 2 Pet. 2:1

DETERMINED (41/41)
d their preappointed . . . . Acts 17:26
For I *d* not to know . . . . 1 Cor. 2:2

DEVICE (1/1)
there is no work or *d* . . . . Eccl. 9:10

DEVICES (3/3)
not ignorant of his *d* . . . . 2 Cor. 2:11

DEVIL (35/33)
to be tempted by the *d*. . . . . Matt. 4:1
prepared for the *d*. . . . . Matt. 25:41
of your father the *d*. . . . . John 8:44
give place to the *d* . . . . Eph. 4:27
the snare of the *d* . . . . 2 Tim. 2:26
the works of the *d* . . . . 1 John 3:8

DEVIOUS (3/3)
crooked, and who are *d* . . . . Prov. 2:15

DEVISES (9/9)
d wickedness on his . . . . Ps. 36:4
But a generous man *d* . . . . Is. 32:8

DEVOID (6/6)
He who is *d* of wisdom. . . . . Prov. 11:12

DEVOTED (7/6)
Your servant, who is *d* . . . . Ps. 119:38

DEVOUR (66/65)
For you *d* widows' . . . . Matt. 23:14
bite and *d* one another . . . . Gal. 5:15
seeking whom he may *d* . . . . 1 Pet. 5:8
d her Child as . . . . Rev. 12:4

DEVOURED (50/49)
Some wild beast has *d* . . . . Gen. 37:20
birds came and *d* them . . . . Matt. 13:4
of heaven and *d* them . . . . Rev. 20:9

DEVOUT (9/9)
man was just and *d*. . . . . Luke 2:25
d soldier from among . . . . Acts 10:7

DEW (37/36)
God give you of the *d* . . . . Gen. 27:28

DIADEMS (1/1)
ten horns, and seven *d* . . . . Rev. 12:3

DIAMOND (4/4)
d it is engraved. . . . . Jer. 17:1

DICTATES (9/9)
according to the *d*. . . . . Jer. 23:17

DIE (290/271)
it you shall surely *d*. . . . . Gen. 2:17
I shall not *d*, but live. . . . . Ps. 118:17
born, and a time to *d* . . . . Eccl. 3:2
eat of it and not *d* . . . . John 6:50
to you that you will *d* . . . . John 8:24
though he may *d* . . . . John 11:25
that one man should *d* . . . . John 11:50
the flesh you will *d* . . . . Rom. 8:13
For as in Adam all *d* . . . . 1 Cor. 15:22
and to *d* is gain. . . . . Phil. 1:21
for men to *d* once . . . . Heb. 9:27
are the dead who *d* . . . . Rev. 14:13

DIED (229/216)
And all flesh *d* . . . . Gen. 7:21
in due time Christ *d* . . . . Rom. 5:6
Christ *d* for us. . . . . Rom. 5:8
Now if we *d* with . . . . Rom. 6:8
and He *d* for all . . . . 2 Cor. 5:15
for if we *d* with Him . . . . 2 Tim. 2:11

DIES (56/49)
made alive unless it *d* . . . . 1 Cor. 15:36

DIFFERS (1/1)
for one star *d* from . . . . 1 Cor. 15:41

DILIGENCE (9/9)
d it produced in you. . . . . 2 Cor. 7:11

DILIGENT (17/16)
hand of the *d* makes rich . . . . . . Prov. 10:4

DILIGENTLY (23/23)
he sought it *d* with tears . . . . Heb. 12:17

DIM (10/10)
His eyes were not *d*. . . . . Deut. 34:7

DIMLY (1/1)
we see in a mirror, *d*. . . . . 1 Cor. 13:12

DINE (4/4)
come in to him and *d*. . . . . Rev. 3:20

DINNER (5/5)
invites you to *d* . . . . 1 Cor. 10:27

DIP (10/10)
d your piece of bread . . . . Ruth 2:14

DIPPED (10/9)
clothed with a robe *d*. . . . . Rev. 19:13

DIRECT (12/12)
Now may the Lord *d*. . . . . 2 Thess. 3:5

DIRT (4/4)
cast up mire and *d* . . . . Is. 57:20

DISARMED (1/1)
d principalities. . . . . Col. 2:15

DISASTER (39/37)
voyage will end with *d*. . . . . Acts 27:10

"Sirs, what must I ***d*** . . . Acts 16:30
d evil that good may . . . Rom. 3:8
or whatever you ***d***, ***d*** . . . 1 Cor. 10:31

DOCTRINE (37/36)
What new ***d*** is this . . . Mark 1:27
"My ***d*** is not Mine . . . John 7:16
with every wind of ***d*** . . . Eph. 4:14
is contrary to sound ***d*** . . . 1 Tim. 1:10
is profitable for ***d*** . . . 2 Tim. 3:16
not endure sound ***d*** . . . 2 Tim. 4:3

DOCTRINES (5/5)
the commandments and ***d*** . . . Col. 2:22
various and strange ***d*** . . . Heb. 13:9

DOERS (2/2)
But be ***d*** of the word . . . James 1:22

DOG (15/15)
d is better than a . . . Eccl. 9:4
d returns to his own . . . 2 Pet. 2:22

DOGS (24/23)
what is holy to the ***d*** . . . Matt. 7:6
d eat the crumbs which . . . Matt. 15:27
But outside are ***d*** . . . Rev. 22:15

DOMINION (56/50)
let them have ***d*** . . . Gen. 1:26
d is an everlasting . . . Dan. 4:34
sin shall not have ***d*** . . . Rom. 6:14
glory and majesty, ***d*** . . . Jude 1:25

DONKEY (84/75)
d its master's crib . . . Is. 1:3
and riding on a ***d*** . . . Zech. 9:9
colt, the foal of a ***d*** . . . Matt. 21:5
d speaking with a . . . 2 Pet. 2:16

DOOM (15/15)
for the day of ***d*** . . . Prov. 16:4

DOOR (163/155)
stone against the ***d*** . . . Matt. 27:60
to you, I am the ***d*** . . . John 10:7
before you an open ***d*** . . . Rev. 3:8
I stand at the ***d*** . . . Rev. 3:20

DOORKEEPER (3/3)
I would rather be a ***d*** . . . Ps. 84:10

DOORPOSTS (17/17)
write them on the ***d*** . . . Deut. 6:9

DOORS (70/67)
up, you everlasting ***d*** . . . Ps. 24:7

DOUBLE (24/22)
from the LORD's hand ***d*** . . . Is. 40:2
worthy of ***d*** honor . . . 1 Tim. 5:17

DOUBLE-MINDED (3/3)
he is a ***d*** man . . . James 1:8

DOUBT (9/9)
faith, why did you ***d*** . . . Matt. 14:31

DOUBTING (4/4)
in faith, with no ***d*** . . . James 1:6

DOUBTS (4/4)
And why do ***d*** arise in . . . Luke 24:38
for I have ***d*** about you . . . Gal. 4:20

DOVE (20/20)
d found no resting . . . Gen. 8:9
descending like a ***d*** . . . Matt. 3:16

DOVES (10/10)
and harmless as ***d*** . . . Matt. 10:16

DOWNCAST (1/1)
who comforts the ***d*** . . . 2 Cor. 7:6

DRAGNET (3/3)
d that was cast . . . Matt. 13:47

DRAGON (13/12)
they worshiped the ***d*** . . . Rev. 13:4
He laid hold of the ***d*** . . . Rev. 20:2

DRAINED (6/6)
all faces are ***d*** . . . Joel 2:6

DRANK (47/46)
them, and they all ***d*** . . . Mark 14:23

DRAW (65/64)
d honey from the rock . . . Deut. 32:13
me to ***d*** near to God . . . Ps. 73:28
and the years ***d*** . . . Eccl. 12:1
will ***d*** all peoples . . . John 12:32
D near to God and He . . . James 4:8

DRAWS (12/12)
your redemption ***d*** . . . Luke 21:28

DREAM (72/59)
Now Joseph had a ***d*** . . . Gen. 37:5
your old men shall ***d*** . . . Joel 2:28
to Joseph in a ***d*** . . . Matt. 2:13
things today in a ***d*** . . . Matt. 27:19

DREAMERS (2/2)
d defile the flesh . . . Jude 1:8

DREAMS (26/25)
Nebuchadnezzar had ***d*** . . . Dan. 2:1

DRIED (36/35)
of her blood was ***d*** . . . Mark 5:29
saw the fig tree ***d*** . . . Mark 11:20

DRIFT (1/1)
have heard, lest we ***d*** . . . Heb. 2:1

DRINK (347/307)
gave me vinegar to ***d*** . . . Ps. 69:21
lest they ***d*** and forget . . . Prov. 31:5
follow intoxicating ***d*** . . . Is. 5:11
d the milk of the . . . Is. 60:16
bosom, that you may ***d*** . . . Is. 66:11
"Bring wine, let us ***d*** . . . Amos 4:1
that day when I ***d*** . . . Matt. 26:29
mingled with gall to ***d*** . . . Matt. 27:34
with myrrh to ***d*** . . . Mark 15:23
to her, "Give Me a ***d*** . . . John 4:7
him come to Me and ***d*** . . . John 7:37
do, as often as you ***d*** . . . 1 Cor. 11:25
No longer ***d*** only water . . . 1 Tim. 5:23

DRINKS (21/20)
to her, "Whoever ***d*** . . . John 4:13
d My blood has eternal . . . John 6:54
For he who eats and ***d*** . . . 1 Cor. 11:29

E

heaven and *e* pass away .... Matt. 5:18
e as it is in heaven............. Matt. 6:10
treasures on *e*, where.......... Matt. 6:19
then shook the *e* ....Heb. 12:26
new heaven and a new *e* ....Rev. 21:1

EARTHLY (6/6)
If I have told you *e* .... John 3:12
that if our *e* house.............. 2 Cor. 5:1
their mind on *e* things.......... Phil. 3:19
from above, but is *e* .... James 3:15

EARTHQUAKE (17/14)
LORD was not in the *e* ....1 Kin. 19:11
there was a great *e* ....Matt. 28:2

EARTHQUAKES (3/3)
And there will be *e* .... Mark 13:8

EASIER (8/8)
Which is *e*, to say............... Mark 2:9
It is *e* for a camel............ Mark 10:25

EAST (169/161)
goes toward the *e* .... Gen. 2:14
wise men from the *E* .... Matt. 2:1
many will come from *e* ....Matt. 8:11
will come from the *e* .... Luke 13:29

EAT (554/494)
you may freely *e* .... Gen. 2:16
'You shall not *e*................. Gen. 3:17
e this scroll .... Ezek. 3:1
life, what you will *e*............ Matt. 6:25
give us His flesh to *e*..........John 6:52
one believes he may *e* .... Rom. 14:2
e meat nor drink wine .... Rom. 14:21
I will never again *e* .... 1 Cor. 8:13
neither shall he *e*........... 2 Thess. 3:10

EATEN (96/90)
Have you *e* from the........... Gen. 3:11
And he was *e* by worms........ Acts 12:23

EATS (47/42)
receives sinners and *e* ....Luke 15:2
Whoever *e* My flesh .... John 6:54
e this bread will live .... John 6:58
He who *e*, *e* to the .... Rom. 14:6
an unworthy manner *e* .... 1 Cor. 11:29

EDIFICATION (10/10)
has given me for *e*............2 Cor. 13:10
rather than godly *e* ....1 Tim. 1:4

EDIFIES (3/2)
puffs up, but love *e* .... 1 Cor. 8:1

EDIFY (3/3)
but not all things *e* ....1 Cor. 10:23

EDIFYING (2/2)
of the body for the *e*............Eph. 4:16

ELDER (12/12)
against an *e* except ....1 Tim. 5:19

ELDERS (199/194)
the tradition of the *e* .... Matt. 15:2
be rejected by the *e*............. Luke 9:22
they had appointed *e*........... Acts 14:23
e who rule well be ....1 Tim. 5:17
lacking, and appoint *e* ....Titus 1:5
e obtained a good .... Heb. 11:2
e who are among you I ....1 Pet. 5:1
I saw twenty-four *e* .... Rev. 4:4

ELDERSHIP (1/1)
of the hands of the *e*............1 Tim. 4:14

ELECT (20/20)
gather together His *e* .... Matt. 24:31
e have obtained it ....Rom. 11:7
e according to the .... 1 Pet. 1:2
a chief cornerstone, *e*........... 1 Pet. 2:6

ELECTION (5/5)
call and *e* sure .... 2 Pet. 1:10

ELEMENTS (4/4)
weak and beggarly *e*............. Gal. 4:9
e will melt with ....2 Pet. 3:10

ELEVEN (24/24)
numbered with the *e* .... Acts 1:26

ELOQUENT (2/2)
an *e* man and mighty.......... Acts 18:24

EMBALM (1/1)
to *e* his father ....Gen. 50:2

ENCOURAGED (14/14)
is, that I may be *e* .... Rom. 1:12
and all may be *e*.............. 1 Cor. 14:31

END (256/239)
make me to know my *e* .... Ps. 39:4
shall keep it to the *e* ....Ps. 119:33
e is the way of death...........Prov. 14:12
There was no *e* of all............Eccl. 4:16
Declaring the *e*...................Is. 46:10
what shall be the *e* ....Dan. 12:8
the harvest is the *e* .... Matt. 13:39
always, even to the *e*..........Matt. 28:20
He loved them to the *e*..........John 13:1
For Christ is the *e* .... Rom. 10:4
But the *e* of all .... 1 Pet. 4:7
the latter *e* is worse.............2 Pet. 2:20
My works until the *e*.............Rev. 2:26
Beginning and the *E*............Rev. 22:13

ENDLESS (2/2)
and *e* genealogies ....1 Tim. 1:4
to the power of an *e* .... Heb. 7:16

ENDURANCE (2/2)
run with *e* the race that......... Heb. 12:1

ENDURE (42/40)
as the sun and moon *e*........... Ps. 72:5
His name shall *e* ....Ps. 72:17
persecuted, we *e* .... 1 Cor. 4:12

ENDURED (7/7)
he had patiently *e* ....Heb. 6:15
e as seeing Him who .... Heb. 11:27
For consider Him who *e* ....Heb. 12:3

ENDURES (64/64)
And His truth *e* .... Ps. 100:5
For His mercy *e* ....Ps. 136:1

F

FAR (293/280)
Your judgments are *f* . . . . Ps. 10:5
Be not *f* from Me . . . . Ps. 22:11
The LORD is *f* from the. . . . . Prov. 15:29
their heart is *f* from . . . . Matt. 15:8
going to a *f* country . . . . Mark 13:34
though He is not *f* . . . . Acts 17:27
you who once were *f*. . . . . Eph. 2:13

FARMER (6/6)
The hard-working *f*. . . . . 2 Tim. 2:6
See how the *f* waits . . . . James 5:7

FASHIONED (7/7)
have made me and *f*. . . . . Job 10:8

FASHIONS (3/3)
He *f* their hearts. . . . . Ps. 33:15

FAST (81/72)
of your *f* you find pleasure . . . . Is. 58:3
f that I have chosen . . . . Is. 58:5
"Moreover, when you *f*. . . . . Matt. 6:16
disciples do not *f*. . . . . Matt. 9:14
I *f* twice a week. . . . . Luke 18:12

FASTED (15/15)
'When you *f* and. . . . . Zech. 7:5
And when He had *f*. . . . . Matt. 4:2

FASTING (20/20)
except by prayer and *f* . . . . Matt. 17:21
give yourselves to *f*. . . . . 1 Cor. 7:5

FASTINGS (3/3)
in sleeplessness, in *f*. . . . . 2 Cor. 6:5

FAT (110/85)
and you will eat the *f* . . . . Gen. 45:18
f is the LORD's. . . . . Lev. 3:16

FATHER (943/820)
man shall leave his *f*. . . . . Gen. 2:24
and you shall be a *f*. . . . . Gen. 17:4
I was a *f* to the poor . . . . Job 29:16
A *f* of the fatherless. . . . . Ps. 68:5
f pities his children. . . . . Ps. 103:13
God, Everlasting *F*. . . . . Is. 9:6
You, O LORD, are our *F*. . . . . Is. 63:16
time cry to Me, My *F*. . . . . Jer. 3:4
for I am a *F* to Israel. . . . . Jer. 31:9
"A son honors his *f* . . . . Mal. 1:6
Have we not all one *F*. . . . . Mal. 2:10
your *F* who sees in secret . . . . Matt. 6:4
He who loves *f* . . . . Matt. 10:37
does anyone know the *F* . . . . Matt. 11:27
'He who curses *f*. . . . . Matt. 15:4
for One is your *F* . . . . Matt. 23:9
F will be divided . . . . Luke 12:53
F loves the Son. . . . . John 3:35
F raises the dead . . . . John 5:21
F judges no one . . . . John 5:22
He has seen the *F* . . . . John 6:46
F who sent Me bears. . . . . John 8:18
we have one *F*. . . . . John 8:41
he is a liar and the *f* of it . . . . . . John 8:44
I and My *F* are one . . . . John 10:30
'I am going to the *F*. . . . . John 14:28
came forth from the *F*. . . . . John 16:28
that he might be the *f*. . . . . Rom. 4:11
one God and *F* of all . . . . Eph. 4:6
"I will be to Him a *F* . . . . Heb. 1:5
comes down from the *F* . . . . James 1:17
if you call on the *F*. . . . . 1 Pet. 1:17
and testify that the *F* . . . . 1 John 4:14

FATHERLESS (40/40)
the helper of the *f* . . . . Ps. 10:14
He relieves the *f*. . . . . Ps. 146:9
do not defend the *f* . . . . Is. 1:23
they may rob the *f*. . . . . Is. 10:2
You the *f* finds mercy. . . . . Hos. 14:3

FATHER'S (166/157)
you in My *F* kingdom . . . . Matt. 26:29
I must be about My *F* . . . . Luke 2:49
F house are many . . . . John 14:2
that a man has his *f* . . . . 1 Cor. 5:1

FATHERS (435/411)
the LORD God of our *f*. . . . . Ezra 7:27
f trusted in You . . . . Ps. 22:4
our ears, O God, our *f* . . . . Ps. 44:1
f ate the manna . . . . John 6:31
of whom are the *f* . . . . Rom. 9:5
unaware that all our *f*. . . . . 1 Cor. 10:1

FATNESS (9/9)
of the root and *f*. . . . . Rom. 11:17

FAULT (18/17)
I have found no *f*. . . . . Luke 23:14
does He still find *f*. . . . . Rom. 9:19
of God without *f*. . . . . Phil. 2:15

FAULTLESS (2/2)
covenant had been *f*. . . . . Heb. 8:7
to present you *f* . . . . Jude 1:24

FAULTS (3/3)
"I remember my *f* . . . . Gen. 41:9
me from secret *f* . . . . Ps. 19:12

FAVOR (96/96)
granted me life and *f* . . . . Job 10:12
His *f* is for life. Ps. 30:5
A good man obtains *f*. . . . . Prov. 12:2
and stature, and in *f* . . . . Luke 2:52
God and having *f* . . . . Acts 2:47

FAVORED (4/4)
"Rejoice, highly *f* . . . . Luke 1:28

FAVORITISM (2/2)
do not show personal *f* . . . . Luke 20:21
God shows personal *f*. . . . . Gal. 2:6

FEAR (366/353)
this and live, for I *f* God. . . . . Gen. 42:18
to put the dread and *f*. . . . . Deut. 2:25
said, "Does Job *f* . . . . Job 1:9
Yes, you cast off *f*. . . . . Job 15:4
of death, I will *f* . . . . Ps. 23:4
whom shall I *f*. . . . . Ps. 27:1
Oh, *f* the LORD . . . . Ps. 34:9
there is no *f* of God . . . . Ps. 36:1

FIGHT (102/98)
The LORD will *f* for you .... Ex. 14:14
Our God will *f* for us .... Neh. 4:20
My servants would *f* .... John 18:36
to him, let us not *f* .... Acts 23:9
F the good *f* .... 1 Tim. 6:12
have fought the good *f* .... 2 Tim. 4:7

FIGHTS (6/6)
your God is He who *f* .... Josh. 23:10
because my lord *f* .... 1 Sam. 25:28
f come from among .... James 4:1

FIGS (25/22)
from thornbushes or *f* .... Matt. 7:16
or a grapevine bear *f* .... James 3:12

FILL (52/52)
f the earth and subdue .... Gen. 1:28
"Do I not *f* heaven .... Jer. 23:24
f this temple with .... Hag. 2:7
"*F* the waterpots .... John 2:7
that He might *f* .... Eph. 4:10

FILLED (159/157)
the whole earth be *f* .... Ps. 72:19
for they shall be *f* .... Matt. 5:6
"Let the children be *f* .... Mark 7:27
he would gladly have *f* .... Luke 15:16
being *f* with all .... Rom. 1:29
but be *f* with the Spirit .... Eph. 5:18
peace, be warmed and *f* .... James 2:16

FILTHY (9/8)
with *f* garments .... Zech. 3:3
poor man in *f* clothes .... James 2:2
oppressed by the *f* .... 2 Pet. 2:7
let him be *f* .... Rev. 22:11

FIND (171/164)
sure your sin will *f* .... Num. 32:23
that no one can *f* .... Eccl. 3:11
seek, and you will *f* .... Matt. 7:7
f a Babe wrapped .... Luke 2:12
f no fault in this Man .... Luke 23:4
f grace to help in .... Heb. 4:16

FINDS (30/28)
whoever *f* me *f* life .... Prov. 8:35
f a wife *f* a good .... Prov. 18:22
and he who seeks *f* .... Matt. 7:8
f his life will lose .... Matt. 10:39
and he who seeks *f* .... Luke 11:10

FINGER (26/24)
written with the *f* .... Ex. 31:18
dip the tip of his *f* .... Luke 16:24
"Reach your *f* .... John 20:27

FINISH (15/15)
he has enough to *f* .... Luke 14:28
has given Me to *f* .... John 5:36

FINISHED (90/89)
f the work which You .... John 17:4
He said, "It is *f* .... John 19:30
I have *f* the race .... 2 Tim. 4:7

FIRE (543/503)
rained brimstone and *f* .... Gen. 19:24
to him in a flame of *f* .... Ex. 3:2
God, who answers by *f* .... 1 Kin. 18:24
LORD was not in the *f* .... 1 Kin. 19:12
we went through *f* .... Ps. 66:12
f goes before Him .... Ps. 97:3
burns as the *f* .... Is. 9:18
you walk through the *f* .... Is. 43:2
f that burns all the .... Is. 65:5
He break out like *f* .... Amos 5:6
for conflict by *f* .... Amos 7:4
like a refiner's *f* .... Mal. 3:2
the Holy Spirit and *f* .... Matt. 3:11
f is not quenched .... Mark 9:44
"I came to send *f* .... Luke 12:49
tongues, as of *f* .... Acts 2:3
f taking vengeance .... 2 Thess. 1:8
and that burned with *f* .... Heb. 12:18
And the tongue is a *f* .... James 3:6
vengeance of eternal *f* .... Jude 1:7
into the lake of *f* .... Rev. 20:14

FIRM (13/13)
of the hope *f* to the .... Heb. 3:6

FIRMAMENT (17/15)
Thus God made the *f* .... Gen. 1:7
f shows His handiwork .... Ps. 19:1

FIRST (443/415)
f father sinned .... Is. 43:27
desires to be *f* .... Matt. 20:27
f shall be slave .... Mark 10:44
And the gospel must *f* .... Mark 13:10
evil, of the Jew *f* .... Rom. 2:9
f man Adam became a .... 1 Cor. 15:45
that we who *f* trusted .... Eph. 1:12
love Him because He *f* .... 1 John 4:19
I am the *F* and the .... Rev. 1:17
you have left your *f* .... Rev. 2:4
is the *f* resurrection .... Rev. 20:5

FIRSTBORN (141/114)
LORD struck all the *f* .... Ex. 12:29
brought forth her *f* .... Matt. 1:25
that He might be the *f* .... Rom. 8:29
invisible God, the *f* .... Col. 1:15
the beginning, the *f* .... Col. 1:18
witness, the *f* from .... Rev. 1:5

FIRSTFRUITS (33/31)
also who have the *f* .... Rom. 8:23
and has become the *f* .... 1 Cor. 15:20
order: Christ the *f* .... 1 Cor. 15:23

FISH (61/56)
had prepared a great *f* .... Jon. 1:17
belly of the great *f* .... Matt. 12:40
five loaves and two *f* .... Matt. 14:17
and likewise the *f* .... John 21:13

FISHERS (2/2)
and I will make you *f* .... Matt. 4:19

FIVE (256/194)
- *f* smooth stones ... 1 Sam. 17:40
- about *f* thousand men ... Matt. 14:21
- and *f* were foolish ... Matt. 25:2

FIXED (6/6)
- is a great gulf *f* ... Luke 16:26

FLAME (32/31)
- *f* will dry out his ... Job 15:30
- am tormented in this *f* ... Luke 16:24
- and His ministers a *f* ... Heb. 1:7
- and His eyes like a *f* ... Rev. 1:14

FLAMES (5/4)
- the LORD divides the *f* ... Ps. 29:7

FLAMING (8/8)
- *f* sword which turned ... Gen. 3:24
- in *f* fire taking ... 2 Thess. 1:8

FLATTER (3/3)
- They *f* with their ... Ps. 5:9

FLATTERED (1/1)
- Nevertheless they *f* ... Ps. 78:36

FLATTERING (9/9)
- *f* speech deceive ... Rom. 16:18
- swelling words, *f* ... Jude 1:16

FLATTERS (6/6)
- *f* his neighbor spreads ... Prov. 29:5

FLATTERY (2/2)
- shall corrupt with *f* ... Dan. 11:32

FLAVOR (3/3)
- the salt loses its *f* ... Matt. 5:13

FLAX (9/8)
- *f* He will not quench ... Matt. 12:20

FLEE (100/95)
- Or where can I *f* ... Ps. 139:7
- And the shadows *f* ... Song 2:17
- who are in Judea *f* ... Matt. 24:16
- *F* sexual immorality ... 1 Cor. 6:18
- *f* these things and ... 1 Tim. 6:11
- devil and he will *f* ... James 4:7

FLESH (337/300)
- bone of my bones and *f* ... Gen. 2:23
- shall become one *f* ... Gen. 2:24
- *f* had corrupted their ... Gen. 6:12
- *f* I shall see God ... Job 19:26
- My *f* also will rest in ... Ps. 16:9
- is wearisome to the *f* ... Eccl. 12:12
- And all *f* shall see it ... Is. 40:5
- "All *f* is grass ... Is. 40:6
- out My Spirit on all *f* ... Joel 2:28
- two shall become one *f* ... Matt. 19:5
- were shortened, no *f* ... Matt. 24:22
- shall become one *f* ... Mark 10:8
- And the Word became *f* ... John 1:14
- I shall give is My *f* ... John 6:51
- unless you eat the *f* ... John 6:53
- of God, but with the *f* ... Rom. 7:25
- on the things of the *f* ... Rom. 8:5
- to the *f* you will die ... Rom. 8:13
- *f* should glory in His ... 1 Cor. 1:29
- "shall become one *f* ... 1 Cor. 6:16
- For the *f* lusts ... Gal. 5:17
- have crucified the *f* ... Gal. 5:24
- may boast in your *f* ... Gal. 6:13
- the lust of the *f* ... 1 John 2:16
- has come in the *f* ... 1 John 4:2

FLESHLY (6/6)
- *f* wisdom but by the ... 2 Cor. 1:12
- *f* lusts which war against ... 1 Pet. 2:11

FLIES (15/13)
- Dead *f* putrefy the ... Eccl. 10:1

FLOAT (2/2)
- and he made the iron *f* ... 2 Kin. 6:6

FLOCK (121/108)
- lead Joseph like a *f* ... Ps. 80:1
- He will feed His *f* ... Is. 40:11
- you do not feed the *f* ... Ezek. 34:3
- my God, "Feed the *f* ... Zech. 11:4
- sheep of the *f* will be ... Matt. 26:31
- "Do not fear, little *f* ... Luke 12:32
- there will be one *f* ... John 10:16
- Shepherd the *f* of God ... 1 Pet. 5:2
- examples to the *f* ... 1 Pet. 5:3

FLOOD (33/31)
- the waters of the *f* ... Gen. 7:10
- them away like a *f* ... Ps. 90:5
- the days before the *f* ... Matt. 24:38
- bringing in the *f* ... 2 Pet. 2:5
- of his mouth like a *f* ... Rev. 12:15

FLOODS (12/10)
- me, and the *f* of ... Ps. 18:4
- *f* on the dry ground ... Is. 44:3
- rain descended, the *f* ... Matt. 7:25

FLOURISH (12/12)
- the righteous shall *f* ... Ps. 72:7

FLOW (26/24)
- of his heart will *f* ... John 7:38

FLOWER (21/18)
- as a *f* of the field ... Ps. 103:15
- beauty is a fading *f* ... Is. 28:4
- grass withers, the *f* ... Is. 40:7
- of man as the *f* ... 1 Pet. 1:24

FLOWERS (10/10)
- *f* appear on the earth ... Song 2:12

FLOWING (27/26)
- 'a land *f* with milk ... Deut. 6:3
- the Gentiles like a *f* ... Is. 66:12

FLUTE (14/14)
- play the harp and *f* ... Gen. 4:21

FLUTES (5/4)
- instruments and *f* ... Ps. 150:4

FLUTISTS (1/1)
- harpists, musicians, *f* ... Rev. 18:22

FLY (17/17)
- soon cut off, and we *f* ... Ps. 90:10

FOLLOW (95/92)
f You wherever You go . . . . Matt. 8:19
He said to him, "*F* . . . . Matt. 9:9
up his cross, and *f* . . . . Mark 8:34
will by no means *f* . . . . John 10:5
serves Me, let him *f* . . . . John 12:26
that you should *f* . . . . 1 Pet. 2:21
f the Lamb wherever He . . . . Rev. 14:4
and their works *f* . . . . Rev. 14:13

FOLLOWED (117/115)
f the LORD my God . . . . Josh. 14:8
we have left all and *f* . . . . Mark 10:28

FOLLOWS (14/14)
f Me shall not walk . . . . John 8:12

FOLLY (28/28)
taken much notice of *f* . . . . Job 35:15
not turn back to *f* . . . . Ps. 85:8
F is joy to him who is . . . . Prov. 15:21
F is set in great . . . . Eccl. 10:6

FOOD (212/196)
you it shall be for *f* . . . . Gen. 1:29
that lives shall be *f* . . . . Gen. 9:3
f which you eat shall . . . . Ezek. 4:10
the fields yield no *f* . . . . Hab. 3:17
that there may be *f* . . . . Mal. 3:10
to give them *f* in due . . . . Matt. 24:45
and you gave Me *f* . . . . Matt. 25:35
and he who has *f* . . . . Luke 3:11
have you any *f* . . . . John 21:5
they ate their *f* . . . . Acts 2:46
our hearts with *f* . . . . Acts 14:17
destroy with your *f* . . . . Rom. 14:15
f makes my brother . . . . 1 Cor. 8:13
the same spiritual *f* . . . . 1 Cor. 10:3
sower, and bread for *f* . . . . 2 Cor. 9:10
And having *f* and . . . . 1 Tim. 6:8
and not solid *f* . . . . Heb. 5:12
But solid *f* belongs to . . . . Heb. 5:14
of *f* sold his birthright . . . . Heb. 12:16
destitute of daily *f* . . . . James 2:15

FOODS (6/5)
f which God created . . . . 1 Tim. 4:3

FOOL (68/65)
f has said in his . . . . Ps. 14:1
is like sport to a *f* . . . . Prov. 10:23
f is right in his own . . . . Prov. 12:15
is too lofty for a *f* . . . . Prov. 24:7
whoever says, 'You *f* . . . . Matt. 5:22
I have become a *f* . . . . 2 Cor. 12:11

FOOLISH (54/53)
I was so *f* and . . . . Ps. 73:22
f pulls it down with . . . . Prov. 14:1
f man squanders it . . . . Prov. 21:20
Has not God made *f* . . . . 1 Cor. 1:20
O *f* Galatians . . . . Gal. 3:1
were also once *f* . . . . Titus 3:3
But avoid *f* disputes . . . . Titus 3:9

FOOLISHLY (9/9)
I speak *f*—I am bold . . . . 2 Cor. 11:21

FOOLISHNESS (23/23)
F is bound up in the . . . . Prov. 22:15
devising of *f* is sin . . . . Prov. 24:9
of the cross is *f* . . . . 1 Cor. 1:18
Because the *f* of God . . . . 1 Cor. 1:25

FOOLS (40/40)
f despise wisdom . . . . Prov. 1:7
folly of *f* is deceit . . . . Prov. 14:8
F mock at sin . . . . Prov. 14:9
We are *f* for Christ's . . . . 1 Cor. 4:10

FOOT (93/89)
will not allow your *f* . . . . Ps. 121:3
f will not stumble . . . . Prov. 3:23
From the sole of the *f* . . . . Is. 1:6
you turn away your *f* . . . . Is. 58:13
f causes you to sin . . . . Matt. 18:8
you dash your *f* . . . . Luke 4:11
If the *f* should say . . . . 1 Cor. 12:15

FOOTSTOOL (16/16)
Your enemies Your *f* . . . . Ps. 110:1
Your enemies Your *f* . . . . Matt. 22:44

FORBID (13/13)
said, "Do not *f* him . . . . Mark 9:39
"Can anyone *f* water . . . . Acts 10:47
f that I should boast . . . . Gal. 6:14

FORBIDDING (4/4)
f to marry . . . . 1 Tim. 4:3

FOREFATHERS (4/4)
conscience, as my *f* . . . . 2 Tim. 1:3

FOREHEADS (8/8)
put a mark on the *f* . . . . Ezek. 9:4
seal of God on their *f* . . . . Rev. 9:4
his mark on their *f* . . . . Rev. 20:4

FOREIGNER (26/24)
"I am a *f* and a . . . . Gen. 23:4
of me, since I am a *f* . . . . Ruth 2:10
to God except this *f* . . . . Luke 17:18

FOREIGNERS (18/18)
f who were there . . . . Acts 17:21
longer strangers and *f* . . . . Eph. 2:19

FOREKNEW (2/2)
For whom He *f* . . . . Rom. 8:29
His people whom He *f* . . . . Rom. 11:2

FOREKNOWLEDGE (2/2)
purpose and *f* of God . . . . Acts 2:23

FOREORDAINED (1/1)
He indeed was *f* . . . . 1 Pet. 1:20

FORESAW (1/1)
'I *f* the LORD . . . . Acts 2:25

FORESEEING (2/2)
f that God would . . . . Gal. 3:8

FORESEES (2/2)
A prudent man *f* . . . . Prov. 22:3

FORETOLD (3/3)
have also *f* these days . . . . Acts 3:24
killed those who *f* . . . . Acts 7:52

FORSAKEN (75/73)
My God, why have You *f*. . . . . .Ps. 22:1
seen the righteous *f* . . . . Ps. 37:25
My God, why have You *f*. . . . . . . Matt. 27:46
persecuted, but not *f* . . . . .2 Cor. 4:9
for Demas has *f* . . . . 2 Tim. 4:10
FORSAKING (1/1)
f the assembling . . . . .Heb. 10:25
FORSOOK (16/16)
f God who made him . . . . Deut. 32:15
all the disciples *f* . . . . .Matt. 26:56
with me, but all *f* . . . . 2 Tim. 4:16
FORTRESS (20/20)
LORD is my rock, my *f* . . . . .2 Sam. 22:2
my rock of refuge, a *f* . . . . .Ps. 31:2
FOUND (398/384)
f a helper comparable . . . . Gen. 2:20
a thousand I have *f* . . . . .Eccl. 7:28
LORD while He may be *f* . . . . .Is. 55:6
fruit on it and *f* none . . . . .Luke 13:6
he was lost and is *f* . . . . .Luke 15:24
f the Messiah" (which . . . . .John 1:41
and be *f* in Him . . . . .Phil. 3:9
FOUNDATION (56/55)
Of old You laid the *f* . . . . Ps. 102:25
the earth without a *f*. . . . . Luke 6:49
loved Me before the *f* . . . . John 17:24
I have laid the *f* . . . . 1 Cor. 3:10
f can anyone lay than . . . . .1 Cor. 3:11
us in Him before the *f* . . . . Eph. 1:4
not laying again the *f* . . . . Heb. 6:1
Lamb slain from the *f* . . . . Rev. 13:8
FOUNDATIONS (32/32)
when I laid the *f*. . . . . Job 38:4
The *f* of the wall . . . . .Rev. 21:19
FOUNTAIN (26/26)
will become in him a *f* . . . . John 4:14
FOUNTAINS (8/8)
on that day all the *f*. . . . . Gen. 7:11
lead them to living *f* . . . . .Rev. 7:17
FRAGRANCE (11/10)
was filled with the *f*. . . . . John 12:3
we are to God the *f* . . . . 2 Cor. 2:15
FREE (73/71)
'You will be made *f* . . . . John 8:33
And having been set *f* . . . . Rom. 6:18
Jesus has made me *f* . . . . Rom. 8:2
is neither slave nor *f*. . . . . Gal. 3:28
Christ has made us *f*. . . . . .Gal. 5:1
he is a slave or *f* . . . . Eph. 6:8
FREED (3/3)
has died has been f . . . . Rom. 6:7
FREEDMAN (1/1)
slave is the Lord's *f* . . . . 1 Cor. 7:22
FREELY (22/21)
the garden you may *f*. . . . . Gen. 2:16
F you have received . . . . Matt. 10:8

f give us all things . . . . .Rom. 8:32
the water of life *f* . . . . Rev. 22:17
FRIEND (55/51)
of Abraham Your *f* . . . . 2 Chr. 20:7
a *f* of tax collectors . . . . .Matt. 11:19
of you shall have a *f* . . . . Luke 11:5
f Lazarus sleeps . . . . John 11:11
he was called the *f*. . . . . .James 2:23
wants to be a *f*. . . . . .James 4:4
FRIENDS (56/55)
My *f* scorn me. . . . . Job 16:20
the rich has many *f*. . . . . Prov. 14:20
one's life for his *f*. . . . . .John 15:13
I have called you *f*. . . . . .John 15:15
to forbid any of his *f* . . . . .Acts 24:23
FROGS (14/14)
your territory with *f* . . . . Ex. 8:2
f coming out of the . . . . Rev. 16:13
FRUIT (189/175)
and showed them the *f* . . . . .Num. 13:26
brings forth its *f*. . . . . .Ps. 1:3
f is better than gold. . . . . Prov. 8:19
with good by the *f* . . . . .Prov. 12:14
like the first *f* .Is. 28:4
does not bear good *f*. . . . . Matt. 3:10
good tree bears good *f* . . . . .Matt. 7:17
not drink of this *f* . . . . .Matt. 26:29
and blessed is the *f* . . . . .Luke 1:42
life, and bring no *f*. . . . . .Luke 8:14
and he came seeking *f* . . . . .Luke 13:6
And if it bears *f*. . . . . .Luke 13:9
branch that bears *f* . . . . John 15:2
that you bear much *f* . . . . John 15:8
should go and bear *f*. . . . . .John 15:16
God, you have your *f*. . . . . .Rom. 6:22
that we should bear *f* . . . . Rom. 7:4
But the *f* of the Spirit is . . . . Gal. 5:22
yields the peaceable *f*. . . . . Heb. 12:11
Now the *f* of. . . . . James 3:18
autumn trees without *f* . . . . Jude 1:12
tree yielding its *f* . . . . Rev. 22:2
FRUITFUL (37/34)
them, saying, "Be *f* . . . . Gen. 1:22
wife shall be like a *f*. . . . . Ps. 128:3
pleasing Him, being *f*. . . . . Col. 1:10
FRUITS (20/20)
Therefore bear *f*. . . . . Matt. 3:8
know them by their *f* . . . . Matt. 7:16
of mercy and good *f* . . . . James 3:17
which bore twelve *f*. . . . . Rev. 22:2
FULFILL (34/33)
for us to *f* all . . . . Matt. 3:15
f the law of Christ . . . . Gal. 6:2
f my joy by being . . . . .Phil. 2:2
and *f* all the good. . . . . 2 Thess. 1:11
If you really *f* . . . . James 2:8
FULFILLED (75/75)
the law till all is *f*. . . . . Matt. 5:18

I do not seek My own *g* .... John 8:50
"Give God the *g*............... John 9:24
g which I had with You .... John 17:5
g which You gave Me I........ John 17:22
he did not give *g* .... Acts 12:23
doing good seek for *g*........... Rom. 2:7
in faith, giving *g*................ Rom. 4:20
the adoption, the *g* .... Rom. 9:4
the riches of His *g*.............. Rom. 9:23
God, alone wise, be *g* .... Rom. 16:27
who glories, let him *g*.......... 1 Cor. 1:31
to His riches in *g* .... Phil. 4:19
appear with Him in *g*............ Col. 3:4
For you are our *g*........... 1 Thess. 2:20
many sons to *g*.................. Heb. 2:10
grass, and all the *g* .... 1 Pet. 1:24
to whom belong the *g* .... 1 Pet. 4:11
for the Spirit of *g*............. 1 Pet. 4:14
the presence of His *g* .... Jude 1:24
O Lord, to receive *g*.............. Rev. 4:11

GLORYING (1/1)
Your *g* is not good.............. 1 Cor. 5:6

GLUTTON (4/4)
you say, 'Look, a *g* .... Luke 7:34

GLUTTONS (2/2)
companion of *g* shames .... Prov. 28:7
evil beasts, lazy *g*............... Titus 1:12

GNASHING (7/7)
will be weeping and *g*.......... Matt. 8:12

GO (1,487/1,358)
'Let My people *g*.................. Ex. 5:1
for wherever you *g* .... Ruth 1:16
Those who *g* down to.......... Ps. 107:23
Where can I *g* from............. Ps. 139:7
to whom shall we *g*............. John 6:68
g you cannot come .... John 8:21
I *g* to prepare a place .... John 14:2
and he shall *g* out no more...... Rev. 3:12

GOADS (4/4)
to kick against the *g*............. Acts 9:5

GOAL (1/1)
I press toward the *g* .... Phil. 3:14

GOATS (52/48)
his sheep from the *g*.......... Matt. 25:32
with the blood of *g* .... Heb. 9:12
g could take away .... Heb. 10:4

GOD (4,393/3,841)
G created the heavens .... Gen. 1:1
Abram of *G* Most High......... Gen. 14:19
and I will be their *G*.............. Gen. 17:8
"I am the LORD your *G*........... Ex. 20:2
G is a consuming fire.......... Deut. 4:24
If the LORD is *G* .... 1 Kin. 18:21
G is greater than all............ 2 Chr. 2:5
You have been My *G* .... Ps. 22:10
G is our refuge .... Ps. 46:1
G is in the midst of .... Ps. 46:5
me a clean heart, O *G* .... Ps. 51:10
Our *G* is the *G* .... Ps. 68:20
Who is so great a *G* .... Ps. 77:13
Restore us, O *G*................... Ps. 80:7
You alone are *G* .... Ps. 86:10
Exalt the LORD our *G* .... Ps. 99:9
Yes, our *G* is merciful.......... Ps. 116:5
For *G* is in heaven .... Eccl. 5:2
Counselor, Mighty *G*.............. Is. 9:6
G is my salvation .... Is. 12:2
stricken, smitten by *G* .... Is. 53:4
translated, "*G* with us."......... Matt. 1:23
in *G* my Savior .... Luke 1:47
the Word was with *G*............. John 1:1
For *G* so loved the .... John 3:16
G is Spirit, and those........... John 4:24
"My Lord and my *G*.......... John 20:28
Christ is the Son of *G*.......... Acts 8:37
Indeed, let *G* be true.......... Rom. 3:4
If *G* is for us...................... Rom. 8:31
G is faithful .... 1 Cor. 1:9
G shall supply all .... Phil. 4:19
and I will be their *G*............ Heb. 8:10
G is a consuming fire .... Heb. 12:29
for *G* is love .... 1 John 4:8
No one has seen *G*............ 1 John 4:12
G Himself will be .... Rev. 21:3
and I will be his *G* .... Rev. 21:7

GODDESS (5/5)
after Ashtoreth the *g* .... 1 Kin. 11:5
of the great *g* Diana .... Acts 19:35

GODHEAD (2/2)
eternal power and *G*........... Rom. 1:20
the fullness of the *G* .... Col. 2:9

GODLINESS (16/16)
is the mystery of *g*............ 1 Tim. 3:16
Now *g* with contentment .... 1 Tim. 6:6
having a form of *g*.............. 2 Tim. 3:5
to perseverance *g* .... 2 Pet. 1:6

GODLY (16/16)
who desire to live *g*........... 2 Tim. 3:12
reverence and *g* fear........... Heb. 12:28
to deliver the *g*.................. 2 Pet. 2:9

GODS (235/207)
your God is God of *g*......... Deut. 10:17
I said, "You are *g* .... Ps. 82:6
yourselves with *g* .... Is. 57:5
If He called them *g* .... John 10:35
g have come down to .... Acts 14:11

GOLD (452/394)
g I do not have .... Acts 3:6
with braided hair or *g* .... 1 Tim. 2:9
a man with *g* rings .... James 2:2
Your *g* and silver are............ James 5:3
more precious than *g*............. 1 Pet. 1:7
like silver or *g*.................... 1 Pet. 1:18
of the city was pure *g*.......... Rev. 21:21

GONE (221/217)
like sheep have *g*.................. Is. 53:6

GOOD (700/643)
God saw that it was *g* ... Gen. 1:10
but God meant it for *g* ... Gen. 50:20
Shall we indeed accept *g* ... Job 2:10
is none who does *g* ... Ps. 14:1
Truly God is *g* to ... Ps. 73:1
g word makes it glad ... Prov. 12:25
on the evil and the *g* ... Prov. 15:3
A merry heart does *g* ... Prov. 17:22
learn to do *g* ... Is. 1:17
talked to me, with *g* ... Zech. 1:13
A *g* man out of the ... Matt. 12:35
No one is *g* but One ... Matt. 19:17
For she has done a *g* ... Matt. 26:10
who went about doing *g* ... Acts 10:38
g man someone would ... Rom. 5:7
in my flesh) nothing *g* ... Rom. 7:18
overcome evil with *g* ... Rom. 12:21
fruitful in every *g* ... Col. 1:10
know that the law is *g* ... 1 Tim. 1:8
For this is *g* and ... 1 Tim. 2:3
bishop, he desires a *g* ... 1 Tim. 3:1
for this is *g* and ... 1 Tim. 5:4
prepared for every *g* ... 2 Tim. 2:21
Every *g* gift and every ... James 1:17

GOODNESS (45/42)
"I will make all My *g* ... Ex. 33:19
and abounding in *g* ... Ex. 34:6
"You are my Lord, my *g* ... Ps. 16:2
Surely *g* and mercy ... Ps. 23:6
that I would see the *g* ... Ps. 27:13
the riches of His *g* ... Rom. 2:4
kindness, *g* ... Gal. 5:22

GOSPEL (100/94)
The beginning of the *g* ... Mark 1:1
and believe in the *g* ... Mark 1:15
g must first be preached ... Mark 13:10
to testify to the *g* ... Acts 20:24
separated to the *g* ... Rom. 1:1
not ashamed of the *g* ... Rom. 1:16
to a different *g* ... Gal. 1:6
the everlasting *g* ... Rev. 14:6

GOVERNMENT (2/2)
and the *g* will be upon ... Is. 9:6

GRACE (148/137)
But Noah found *g* ... Gen. 6:8
G is poured upon Your ... Ps. 45:2
The LORD will give *g* ... Ps. 84:11
the Spirit of *g* ... Zech. 12:10
and the *g* of God was ... Luke 2:40
g and truth came ... John 1:17
And great *g* was upon ... Acts 4:33
receive abundance of *g* ... Rom. 5:17
g is no longer *g* ... Rom. 11:6
For you know the *g* ... 2 Cor. 8:9
"My *g* is sufficient ... 2 Cor. 12:9
The *g* of the Lord ... 2 Cor. 13:14
you have fallen from *g* ... Gal. 5:4
to the riches of His *g* ... Eph. 1:7
g you have been saved ... Eph. 2:8
g was given according ... Eph. 4:7
G be with all those ... Eph. 6:24
shaken, let us have *g* ... Heb. 12:28
But He gives more *g* ... James 4:6
but grow in the *g* ... 2 Pet. 3:18

GRACIOUS (32/31)
he said, "God be *g* ... Gen. 43:29
I will be *g* to whom I ... Ex. 33:19
at the *g* words which ... Luke 4:22
that the Lord is *g* ... 1 Pet. 2:3

GRAFTED (5/4)
in unbelief, will be *g* ... Rom. 11:23

GRAIN (251/229)
it treads out the *g* ... Deut. 25:4
be revived like *g* ... Hos. 14:7
to pluck heads of *g* ... Matt. 12:1
unless a *g* of wheat ... John 12:24

GRAPES (38/35)
brought forth wild *g* ... Is. 5:2
have eaten sour *g* ... Ezek. 18:2
Do men gather *g* ... Matt. 7:16
g are fully ripe ... Rev. 14:18

GRASS (63/56)
The *g* withers ... Is. 40:7
so clothes the *g* ... Matt. 6:30
"All flesh is as *g* ... 1 Pet. 1:24

GRAVE (53/50)
my soul up from the *g* ... Ps. 30:3
And they made His *g* ... Is. 53:9
the power of the *g* ... Hos. 13:14

GRAVES (19/17)
and the *g* were opened ... Matt. 27:52
g which are not ... Luke 11:44
g will hear His voice ... John 5:28

GRAY (10/10)
the man of *g* hairs ... Deut. 32:25

GREAT (837/803)
and make your name *g* ... Gen. 12:2
For the LORD is *g* ... 1 Chr. 16:25
Who does *g* things ... Job 5:9
g is the Holy One ... Is. 12:6
g is Your faithfulness ... Lam. 3:23
he shall be called *g* ... Matt. 5:19
one pearl of *g* price ... Matt. 13:46
desires to become *g* ... Matt. 20:26
g drops of blood ... Luke 22:44
appearing of our *g* ... Titus 2:13
g men, the rich men ... Rev. 6:15
Babylon the *G* ... Rev. 17:5
the dead, small and *g* ... Rev. 20:12

GREATER (82/78)
kingdom of heaven is *g* ... Matt. 11:11
place there is One *g* ... Matt. 12:6
g than Jonah is here ... Matt. 12:41
g than Solomon is here ... Matt. 12:42
a servant is not *g* ... John 13:16

H

if your right *h* causes .... Matt. 5:30
do not let your left *h* .... Matt. 6:3
h causes you to sin .... Mark 9:43
sitting at the right *h* .... Mark 14:62
at the right *h* of God .... Acts 7:55
The Lord is at *h* .... Phil. 4:5
"Sit at My right *h* .... Heb. 1:13
down at the right *h* .... Heb. 10:12

HANDIWORK (2/2)
firmament shows His *h* .... Ps. 19:1

HANDLE (11/10)
H Me and see .... Luke 24:39
do not taste, do not *h* .... Col. 2:21

HANDLED (2/2)
and our hands have *h* .... 1 John 1:1

HANDS (456/434)
took his life in his *h* .... 1 Sam. 19:5
but His *h* make whole .... Job 5:18
They pierced My *h* .... Ps. 22:16
h formed the dry land .... Ps. 95:5
than having two *h* .... Matt. 18:8
Behold My *h* and My .... Luke 24:39
h the print of the .... John 20:25
his *h* what is good .... Eph. 4:28
the laying on of the *h* .... 1 Tim. 4:14
to fall into the *h* .... Heb. 10:31

HANDWRITING (1/1)
having wiped out the *h* .... Col. 2:14

HANGED (19/19)
went and *h* himself .... Matt. 27:5

HANGS (2/2)
h the earth on nothing .... Job 26:7
is everyone who *h* .... Gal. 3:13

HAPPY (24/21)
H is the man who has .... Ps. 127:5

HARD (54/53)
I knew you to be a *h* .... Matt. 25:24
"This is a *h* saying .... John 6:60
are some things *h* .... 2 Pet. 3:16

HARDEN (12/12)
But I will *h* his heart .... Ex. 4:21
h your hearts as .... Heb. 3:8

HARDENED (22/22)
But Pharaoh *h* his .... Ex. 8:32
their heart was *h* .... Mark 6:52
eyes and *h* their hearts .... John 12:40
lest any of you be *h* .... Heb. 3:13

HARDENS (5/5)
whom He wills He *h* .... Rom. 9:18

HARLOT (76/71)
of a *h* named Rahab .... Josh. 2:1
h is one body with .... 1 Cor. 6:16
of the great *h* who .... Rev. 17:1

HARLOTRIES (5/4)
Let her put away her *h* .... Hos. 2:2

HARLOTRY (50/44)
are the children of *h* .... Hos. 2:4
for the spirit of *h* .... Hos. 5:4

HARLOTS (9/9)
h enter the kingdom .... Matt. 21:31
Great, The Mother of *H* .... Rev. 17:5

HARP (34/33)
Lamb, each having a *h* .... Rev. 5:8

HARPS (19/19)
We hung our *h* upon the .... Ps. 137:2

HARVEST (68/58)
seedtime and *h* .... Gen. 8:22
"The *h* is past .... Jer. 8:20
h truly is plentiful .... Matt. 9:37
sickle, because the *h* .... Mark 4:29
already white for *h* .... John 4:35

HASTENS (8/8)
and he sins who *h* .... Prov. 19:2

HASTILY (5/5)
utter anything *h* .... Eccl. 5:2

HASTY (4/4)
Do you see a man *h* .... Prov. 29:20

HATE (86/83)
love the LORD, *h* evil .... Ps. 97:10
h every false way .... Ps. 119:104
h the double-minded .... Ps. 119:113
I *h* and abhor lying .... Ps. 119:163
love, and a time to *h* .... Eccl. 3:8
You who *h* good and .... Mic. 3:2
either he will *h* the one .... Matt. 6:24

HATED (53/51)
but Esau I have *h* .... Mal. 1:3
And you will be *h* .... Matt. 10:22
have seen and also *h* .... John 15:24
but Esau I have *h* .... Rom. 9:13
For no one ever *h* .... Eph. 5:29

HATEFUL (2/2)
h woman when she is .... Prov. 30:23
in malice and envy, *h* .... Titus 3:3

HATERS (2/2)
backbiters, *h* of God .... Rom. 1:30

HATES (37/36)
six things the LORD *h* .... Prov. 6:16
lose it, and he who *h* .... John 12:25
"If the world *h* .... John 15:18
h his brother is .... 1 John 2:11

HAUGHTY (18/18)
bring down *h* looks .... Ps. 18:27
my heart is not *h* .... Ps. 131:1
h spirit before a fall .... Prov. 16:18

HEAD (361/331)
He shall bruise your *h* .... Gen. 3:15
you swear by your *h* .... Matt. 5:36
and gave Him to be *h* .... Eph. 1:22
For the husband is *h* .... Eph. 5:23

HEAL (46/45)
O LORD, *h* me .... Ps. 6:2
h your backslidings .... Jer. 3:22
torn, but He will *h* .... Hos. 6:1

JUDGES (69/67)
He makes the *j* of the .... Is. 40:23
For the Father *j* .... John 5:22
he who is spiritual *j* .... 1 Cor. 2:15
j me is the Lord .... 1 Cor. 4:4
Him who *j* righteously........ 1 Pet. 2:23

JUDGMENT (190/186)
Teach me good *j*. .... Ps. 119:66
from prison and from *j* .... Is. 53:8
be in danger of the *j* .... Matt. 5:21
shall not come into *j*. .... John 5:24
and My *j* is righteous .... John 5:30
if I do judge, My *j*. .... John 8:16
Now is the *j* of this............. John 12:31
the righteous *j* of God .... Rom. 1:32
j which came from one.......... Rom. 5:16
appear before the *j* .... 2 Cor. 5:10
after this the *j*................... Heb. 9:27
time has come for *j*. .... 1 Pet. 4:17
a long time their *j* .... 2 Pet. 2:3
darkness for the *j* .... Jude 1:6

JUDGMENTS (122/120)
I dread, for Your *j* .... Ps. 119:39
unsearchable are His *j*.......... Rom. 11:33

JUST (262/256)
Noah was a *j* man .... Gen. 6:9
j man who perishes .... Eccl. 7:15
j shall live by his .... Hab. 2:4
her husband, being a *j* .... Matt. 1:19
resurrection of the *j* .... Luke 14:14
j persons who need no........... Luke 15:7
the Holy One and the *J* .... Acts 3:14
dead, both of the *j* .... Acts 24:15
j shall live by faith............... Rom. 1:17
that He might be *j*.............. Rom. 3:26
j men made perfect .... Heb. 12:23
have murdered the *j*............. James 5:6
He is faithful and *j* .... 1 John 1:9

JUSTICE (130/129)
j as the noonday .... Ps. 37:6
and Your poor with *j*............. Ps. 72:2
j the measuring line.............. Is. 28:17
the LORD is a God of *j*............ Is. 30:18
He will bring forth *j* .... Is. 42:1
J is turned back .... Is. 59:14
I, the LORD, love *j* .... Is. 61:8
truth, and His ways *j*. .... Dan. 4:37
'Execute true *j* .... Zech. 7:9
"Where is the God of *j* .... Mal. 2:17
And He will declare *j* .... Matt. 12:18
His humiliation His *j* .... Acts 8:33

JUSTIFICATION (3/3)
because of our *j* .... Rom. 4:25
offenses resulted in *j* .... Rom. 5:16

JUSTIFIED (37/33)
Me that you may be *j* .... Job 40:8
words you will be *j* .... Matt. 12:37
But wisdom is *j* .... Luke 7:35
j rather than the.................. Luke 18:14
who believes is *j*.................. Acts 13:39
"That You may be *j* .... Rom. 3:4
law no flesh will be *j*............ Rom. 3:20
j freely by His grace .... Rom. 3:24
having been *j* by .... Rom. 5:1
these He also *j* .... Rom. 8:30
that we might be *j*................. Gal. 2:16
the harlot also *j* .... James 2:25

JUSTIFIES (4/4)
He who *j* the wicked .... Prov. 17:15
It is God who *j*.................... Rom. 8:33

JUSTIFY (9/9)
wanting to *j* himself .... Luke 10:29
"You are those who *j*. .... Luke 16:15
is one God who will *j*............ Rom. 3:30

K

KEEP (371/362)
k you wherever you .... Gen. 28:15
day, to *k* it holy.................... Ex. 20:8
Let all the earth *k*................. Hab. 2:20
k the commandments .... Matt. 19:17
If you love Me, *k*.................. John 14:15
k through Your name .... John 17:11
orderly and *k* the law .... Acts 21:24
k the unity of the................. Eph. 4:3
k His commandments........... 1 John 2:3

KEEPER (19/19)
Am I my brother's *k* .... Gen. 4:9
The LORD is your *k* .... Ps. 121:5

KEEPS (42/40)
k truth forever .... Ps. 146:6
k the commandment .... Prov. 19:16
none of you *k* the law............ John 7:19
born of God *k* himself .... 1 John 5:18
and *k* his garments.............. Rev. 16:15

KEPT (170/165)
For I have *k* the ways .... 2 Sam. 22:22
these things I have *k*........... Matt. 19:20
love, just as I have *k* .... John 15:10
k back part of the.................. Acts 5:2
I have *k* the faith .... 2 Tim. 4:7
who are *k* by the power .... 1 Pet. 1:5

KEY (6/6)
have taken away the *k* .... Luke 11:52
"He who has the *k*................. Rev. 3:7

KEYS (2/2)
I will give you the *k*. .... Matt. 16:19
And I have the *k*.................... Rev. 1:18

KILL (196/184)
k the Passover lamb .... Ex. 12:21
I *k* and I make alive............ Deut. 32:39
"Am I God, to *k*................... 2 Kin. 5:7
a time to *k* .... Eccl. 3:3
of them they will *k* .... Luke 11:49
afraid of those who *k* .... Luke 12:4
Why do you seek to *k* .... John 7:19
"Rise, Peter; *k* and eat .... Acts 10:13

k the love of Christ . . . . Eph. 3:19
k whom I have believed. . . . . . . .2 Tim. 1:12
this we *k* that we *k* Him . . . . 1 John 2:3
and you *k* all things . . . . .1 John 2:20
By this we *k* love . . . . 1 John 3:16
k that He abides. . . . . .1 John 3:24
k that we are of God . . . . 1 John 5:19
"I *k* your works. . . . . Rev. 2:2

KNOWLEDGE (164/161)
and the tree of the *k* . . . . .Gen. 2:9
unto night reveals *k* . . . . Ps. 19:2
k is too wonderful. . . . . Ps. 139:6
Wise people store up *k*. . . . . .Prov. 10:14
k spares his words. . . . . .Prov. 17:27
and he who increases *k* . . . . Eccl. 1:18
k is that wisdom. . . . . Eccl. 7:12
k shall increase . . . . Dan. 12:4
having more accurate *k*. . . . . . . .Acts 24:22
having the form of *k*. . . . . .Rom. 2:20
by the law is the *k* of sin. . . . . .Rom. 3:20
whether there is *k* . . . . 1 Cor. 13:8
Christ which passes *k*. . . . . .Eph. 3:19
is falsely called *k* . . . . .1 Tim. 6:20
in the grace and *k* . . . . 2 Pet. 3:18

KNOWN (229/218)
If you had *k* Me . . . . John 8:19
My sheep, and am *k* . . . . .John 10:14
The world has not *k* . . . . .John 17:25
peace they have not *k*. . . . . Rom. 3:17
"For who has *k* . . . . Rom. 11:34
after you have *k* . . . . Gal. 4:9
requests be made *k*. . . . . .Phil. 4:6
k the Holy Scriptures . . . . 2 Tim. 3:15

KNOWS (82/80)
For God *k* that in . . . . .Gen. 3:5
k what is in the. . . . . Dan. 2:22
k the things you have. . . . . Matt. 6:8
and hour no one *k*. . . . . .Matt. 24:36
but God *k* your hearts. . . . . .Luke 16:15
searches the hearts *k* . . . . Rom. 8:27
k the things of God . . . . .1 Cor. 2:11
k those who are His . . . . 2 Tim. 2:19
to him who *k* to do . . . . James 4:17
and *k* all things. . . . . .1 John 3:20

L

LABOR (109/105)
Six days you shall *l* . . . . .Ex. 20:9
things are full of *l* . . . . Eccl. 1:8
has man for all his *l* . . . . Eccl. 2:22
He shall see the *l* . . . . Is. 53:11
to Me, all you who *l*. . . . . Matt. 11:28
Do not *l* for the. . . . . .John 6:27
knowing that your *l* . . . . 1 Cor. 15:58
but rather let him *l* . . . . .Eph. 4:28
mean fruit from my *l* . . . . .Phil. 1:22
your work of faith, *l* . . . . 1 Thess. 1:3
forget your work and *l* . . . . .Heb. 6:10
your works, your *l* . . . . Rev. 2:2

LABORED (24/22)
l more abundantly than . . . . . . 1 Cor. 15:10
for you, lest I have *l* . . . . Gal. 4:11

LABORERS (13/12)
but the *l* are few. . . . . Matt. 9:37

LABORING (4/4)
l night and day . . . . .1 Thess. 2:9

LABORS (18/16)
entered into their *l* . . . . John 4:38
creation groans and *l* . . . . .Rom. 8:22
l more abundant . . . . 2 Cor. 11:23
may rest from their *l* . . . . .Rev. 14:13

LACK (39/37)
What do I still *l*. . . . . Matt. 19:20
"One thing you *l*. . . . . Mark 10:21

LADDER (1/1)
and behold, a *l* . . . . .Gen. 28:12

LAID (211/206)
the place where they *l* . . . . Mark 16:6
"Where have you *l*. . . . . .John 11:34

LAKE (10/10)
cast alive into the *l* . . . . Rev. 19:20

LAMB (102/95)
but where is the *l*. . . . . Gen. 22:7
He was led as a *l*. . . . . Is. 53:7
The *L* of God who takes . . . . John 1:29
the elders, stood a *L* . . . . Rev. 5:6
"Worthy is the *L* . . . . Rev. 5:12
by the blood of the *L*. . . . . Rev. 12:11

LAME (34/32)
l shall leap like a . . . . .Is. 35:6
blind see and the *l*. . . . . .Matt. 11:5
And a certain man *l* . . . . Acts 3:2

LAMENTATION (24/23)
was heard in Ramah, *l* . . . . Matt. 2:18
and made great *l* . . . . Acts 8:2

LAMP (34/34)
Your word is a *l* . . . . Ps. 119:105
the *l* of the wicked. . . . . Prov. 13:9
his *l* will be put out . . . . .Prov. 20:20
Nor do they light a *l* . . . . Matt. 5:15
"The *l* of the body . . . . Matt. 6:22
when he has lit a *l* . . . . Luke 8:16
l gives you light . . . . .Luke 11:36
does not light a *l* . . . . .Luke 15:8
burning and shining *l* . . . . John 5:35

LAMPS (35/29)
he made its seven *l* . . . . Ex. 37:23
and trimmed their *l* . . . . Matt. 25:7

LAMPSTAND (41/34)
branches of the *l* . . . . Ex. 25:32
a basket, but on a *l*. . . . . Matt. 5:15
and remove your *l*. . . . . Rev. 2:5

LAND (1,745/1,511)
l that I will show you . . . . Gen. 12:1
l flowing with milk . . . . Ex. 3:8
they will see the *l*. . . . . Is. 33:17
Bethlehem, in the *l* . . . . Matt. 2:6

LANGUAGE (38/33)
whole earth had one *l* ....Gen. 11:1
speak in his own *l* ....Acts 2:6
blasphemy, filthy *l*. ....Col. 3:8
LANGUAGES (9/9)
according to their *l* ....Gen. 10:20
LAST (107/101)
He shall stand at *l* ....Job 19:25
First and I am the *L* ....Is. 44:6
l will be first ....Matt. 20:16
the First and the *L*. ....Rev. 1:11
LATTER (40/39)
l times some will ....1 Tim. 4:1
LAUGH (15/13)
Why did Sarah *l* .... Gen. 18:13
Woe to you who *l*. ....Luke 6:25
LAUGHS (4/4)
The Lord *l* at him. ....Ps. 37:13
LAUGHTER (7/7)
your *l* be turned to ....James 4:9
LAW (441/388)
stones a copy of the *l* ....Josh. 8:32
The *l* of the LORD is. ....Ps. 19:7
I delight in Your *l* ....Ps. 119:70
The *l* of Your mouth is ....Ps. 119:72
Oh, how I love Your *l* ....Ps. 119:97
And Your *l* is truth ....Ps. 119:142
l will proceed from Me. .... Is. 51:4
in whose heart is My *l* .... Is. 51:7
the *L* is no more. ....Lam. 2:9
The *l* of truth was in ....Mal. 2:6
to destroy the *L* ....Matt. 5:17
for this is the *L*. .... Matt. 7:12
hang all the *L* and the ....Matt. 22:40
one tittle of the *l* to fail ....Luke 16:17
l was given through ....John 1:17
"Does our *l* judge a ....John 7:51
l is the knowledge ....Rom. 3:20
because the *l* brings .... Rom. 4:15
when there is no *l* .... Rom. 5:13
you are not under *l*. ....Rom. 6:14
For what the *l* could ....Rom. 8:3
l that I might live. ....Gal. 2:19
under guard by the *l*. .... Gal. 3:23
l is fulfilled in one. ....Gal. 5:14
into the perfect *l* .... James 1:25
fulfill the royal *l*. ....James 2:8
LAWFUL (38/36)
Is it *l* to pay taxes. .... Matt. 22:17
All things are *l* ....1 Cor. 6:12
LAWGIVER (6/6)
There is one *L*. .... James 4:12
LAWLESS (9/9)
l one will be revealed .... 2 Thess. 2:8
LAWLESSNESS (11/9)
Me, you who practice *l*. .... Matt. 7:23
l is already at work ....2 Thess. 2:7
LAWYERS (5/5)
Woe to you also, *l*. ....Luke 11:46
LAY (203/196)
nowhere to *l* His head ....Matt. 8:20
l hands may receive ....Acts 8:19
LAZINESS (2/2)
l the building decays ....Eccl. 10:18
LAZY (16/16)
l man will be put to. .... Prov. 12:24
wicked and *l* servant. ....Matt. 25:26
liars, evil beasts, *l* ....Titus 1:12
LEAD (62/62)
L me in Your truth and .... Ps. 25:5
And do not *l* us into .... Matt. 6:13
"Can the blind *l* ....Luke 6:39
LEADS (22/22)
He *l* me in the paths ....Ps. 23:3
And if the blind *l* ....Matt. 15:14
LEAF (9/9)
plucked olive *l* .... Gen. 8:11
LEAN (6/6)
all your heart, and *l*. .... Prov. 3:5
LEAP (9/9)
Then the lame shall *l* ....Is. 35:6
LEARN (35/35)
l to do good .... Is. 1:17
My yoke upon you and *l* ...... Matt. 11:29
LEARNED (21/19)
Me the tongue of the *l* ....Is. 50:4
have not so *l* Christ .... Eph. 4:20
in all things I have *l* .... Phil. 4:12
LEARNING (7/7)
l is driving you mad ....Acts 26:24
LEAST (42/40)
so, shall be called *l* .... Matt. 5:19
LEAVE (107/106)
a man shall *l* his. ....Gen. 2:24
For You will not *l*. ....Ps. 16:10
"I will never *l* .... Heb. 13:5
LEAVEN (24/21)
of heaven is like *l*. .... Matt. 13:33
l leavens the whole .... Gal. 5:9
LEAVES (23/20)
and they sewed fig *l* ....Gen. 3:7
The *l* of the tree ....Rev. 22:2
LED (89/89)
l them forth by the ....Ps. 107:7
For as many as are *l* .... Rom. 8:14
LEFT (335/324)
l hand know what your .... Matt. 6:3
LEND (15/12)
And if you *l* to those .... Luke 6:34
LENDER (2/2)
is servant to the *l*. .... Prov. 22:7
LENDS (3/3)
ever merciful, and *l*. .... Ps. 37:26

LENGTH (73/69)
is your life and the *l* ... Deut. 30:20
LEOPARD (6/6)
or the *l* its spots ... Jer. 13:23
LEPERS (6/6)
And many *l* were in ... Luke 4:27
LET (1,557/1,272)
"*L* there be light" ... Gen. 1:3
LETTER (38/36)
for the *l* kills ... 2 Cor. 3:6
or by word or by *l* ... 2 Thess. 2:2
LETTERS (34/32)
does this Man know *l* ... John 7:15
LEVIATHAN (6/5)
"Can you draw out *L* ... Job 41:1
LEVITE (28/28)
Likewise a *L*, when he ... Luke 10:32
LEWDNESS (23/22)
wickedness, deceit, *l* ... Mark 7:22
LIAR (12/12)
for he is a *l* and the ... John 8:44
but every man a *l* ... Rom. 3:4
we make Him a *l* ... 1 John 1:10
his brother, he is a *l* ... 1 John 4:20
LIARS (5/5)
"All men are *l* ... Ps. 116:11
l shall have their ... Rev. 21:8
LIBERALITY (3/3)
he who gives, with *l* ... Rom. 12:8
LIBERALLY (2/2)
who gives to all *l* ... James 1:5
LIBERTY (26/23)
year, and proclaim *l* ... Lev. 25:10
to proclaim *l* to the ... Luke 4:18
into the glorious *l* ... Rom. 8:21
Lord is, there is *l* ... 2 Cor. 3:17
therefore in the *l* ... Gal. 5:1
LIE (151/149)
Do not *l* to one ... Col. 3:9
God, who cannot *l* ... Titus 1:2
an abomination or a *l* ... Rev. 21:27
LIED (4/4)
You have not *l* to men ... Acts 5:4
LIES (121/115)
sin *l* at the door ... Gen. 4:7
speaking *l* in hypocrisy ... 1 Tim. 4:2
LIFE (495/449)
the breath of *l* ... Gen. 2:7
For the *l* of the ... Lev. 17:11
before you today *l* ... Deut. 30:15
He will redeem their *l* ... Ps. 72:14
word has given me *l* ... Ps. 119:50
She is a tree of *l* ... Prov. 3:18
finds me finds *l* ... Prov. 8:35
L is more than food ... Luke 12:23
l was the light ... John 1:4
so the Son gives *l* ... John 5:21
spirit, and they are *l* ... John 6:63
have the light of *l* ... John 8:12
and I lay down My *l* ... John 10:15
resurrection and the *l* ... John 11:25
you lay down your *l* ... John 13:38
l which I now live ... Gal. 2:20
l is hidden with ... Col. 3:3
For what is your *l* ... James 4:14
l was manifested ... 1 John 1:2
and the pride of *l* ... 1 John 2:16
has given us eternal *l* ... 1 John 5:11
the Lamb's Book of *L* ... Rev. 21:27
right to the tree of *l* ... Rev. 22:14
the water of *l* freely ... Rev. 22:17
from the Book of *L* ... Rev. 22:19
LIFT (94/91)
I will *l* up my eyes to ... Ps. 121:1
Lord, and He will *l* ... James 4:10
LIFTED (133/128)
your heart is *l* up ... Ezek. 28:2
in Hades, he *l* up his ... Luke 16:23
the Son of Man be *l* ... John 3:14
And I, if I am *l* ... John 12:32
LIGHT (253/221)
"Let there be *l* ... Gen. 1:3
The LORD is my *l* ... Ps. 27:1
and a *l* to my path ... Ps. 119:105
The *l* of the righteous ... Prov. 13:9
The LORD gives *l* ... Prov. 29:13
Truly the *l* is sweet ... Eccl. 11:7
let us walk in the *l* ... Is. 2:5
l shall break forth ... Is. 58:8
"You are the *l* ... Matt. 5:14
Let your *l* so shine ... Matt. 5:16
than the sons of *l* ... Luke 16:8
and the life was the *l* ... John 1:4
darkness rather than *l* ... John 3:19
saying, "I am the *l* ... John 8:12
God who commanded *l* ... 2 Cor. 4:6
Walk as children of *l* ... Eph. 5:8
You are all sons of *l* ... 1 Thess. 5:5
into His marvelous *l* ... 1 Pet. 2:9
to you, that God is *l* ... 1 John 1:5
l as He is in the ... 1 John 1:7
says he is in the *l* ... 1 John 2:9
The Lamb is its *l* ... Rev. 21:23
LIGHTNING (18/18)
For as the *l* comes ... Matt. 24:27
countenance was like *l* ... Matt. 28:3
LIGHTNINGS (10/10)
the throne proceeded *l* ... Rev. 4:5
LIGHTS (10/10)
"Let there be *l* ... Gen. 1:14
whom you shine as *l* ... Phil. 2:15
LIKENESS (36/30)
according to Our *l* ... Gen. 1:26
carved image—any *l* ... Ex. 20:4
when I awake in Your *l* ... Ps. 17:15
and coming in the *l* ... Phil. 2:7

LILY (6/6)
the *l* of the valleys . . . . Song 2:1
LIMIT (6/6)
to the sea its *l* . . . . Prov. 8:29
LINE (42/33)
upon precept, *l* upon *l* . . . . Is. 28:10
I am setting a plumb *l* . . . . Amos 7:8
LINEN (105/93)
wrapped Him in the *l* . . . . Mark 15:46
LINGER (3/3)
salvation shall not *l* . . . . Is. 46:13
LION (97/82)
l shall eat straw . . . . Is. 11:7
LIONS (43/39)
the mouths of *l* . . . . Heb. 11:33
LIPS (118/117)
off all flattering *l* . . . . Ps. 12:3
The *l* of the righteous . . . . Prov. 10:21
but the *l* of knowledge . . . . Prov. 20:15
am a man of unclean *l* . . . . Is. 6:5
other *l* I will speak . . . . 1 Cor. 14:21
from evil, and his *l* . . . . 1 Pet. 3:10
LISTEN (112/109)
you are not able to *l* . . . . John 8:43
you who fear God, *l* . . . . Acts 13:16
LISTENS (4/4)
but whoever *l* to me . . . . Prov. 1:33
LITTLE (231/215)
though you are *l* . . . . Mic. 5:2
l ones only a cup . . . . Matt. 10:42
"O you of *l* faith . . . . Matt. 14:31
to whom *l* is forgiven . . . . Luke 7:47
faithful in a very *l* . . . . Luke 19:17
LIVE (272/254)
eat, and *l* forever . . . . Gen. 3:22
a man does, he shall *l* . . . . Lev. 18:5
"Seek Me and *l* . . . . Amos 5:4
but the just shall *l* . . . . Hab. 2:4
l by bread alone . . . . Matt. 4:4
for in Him we *l* . . . . Acts 17:28
l peaceably with all . . . . Rom. 12:18
the life which I now *l* . . . . Gal. 2:20
If we *l* in the Spirit . . . . Gal. 5:25
to me, to *l* is Christ . . . . Phil. 1:21
LIVED (65/65)
died and rose and *l* . . . . Rom. 14:9
And they *l* and reigned . . . . Rev. 20:4
LIVES (138/125)
but man *l* by every . . . . Deut. 8:3
but Christ *l* in me . . . . Gal. 2:20
to lay down our *l* . . . . 1 John 3:16
I am He who *l* . . . . Rev. 1:18
LIVING (179/168)
and man became a *l* . . . . Gen. 2:7
in the light of the *l* . . . . Ps. 56:13
the dead, but of the *l* . . . . Matt. 22:32
Why do you seek the *l* . . . . Luke 24:5
the word of God is *l* . . . . Heb. 4:12
l creature was like a . . . . Rev. 4:7
LOATHSOME (4/4)
but a wicked man is *l* . . . . Prov. 13:5
LOAVES (32/30)
have here only five *l* . . . . Matt. 14:17
you ate of the *l* . . . . John 6:26
LOCUST (22/12)
What the chewing *l* . . . . Joel 1:4
LOCUSTS (24/22)
and his food was *l* . . . . Matt. 3:4
LOFTY (10/10)
Wisdom is too *l* . . . . Prov. 24:7
LONG (236/227)
your days may be *l* . . . . Deut. 5:16
who *l* for death . . . . Job 3:21
I *l* for Your salvation . . . . Ps. 119:174
go around in *l* robes . . . . Mark 12:38
LONGSUFFERING (16/16)
is love, joy, peace, *l* . . . . Gal. 5:22
and gentleness, with *l* . . . . Eph. 4:2
for all patience and *l* . . . . Col. 1:11
might show all *l* . . . . 1 Tim. 1:16
when once the Divine *l* . . . . 1 Pet. 3:20
and consider that the *l* . . . . 2 Pet. 3:15
LOOK (295/287)
A proud *l*, a lying . . . . Prov. 6:17
"*L* to Me, and be saved . . . . Is. 45:22
l on Me whom they . . . . Zech. 12:10
say to you, '*L* here . . . . Luke 17:23
while we do not *l* . . . . 2 Cor. 4:18
LOOKED (146/144)
For He *l* down from the . . . . Ps. 102:19
He *l* for justice . . . . Is. 5:7
the Lord turned and *l* . . . . Luke 22:61
for he *l* to the reward . . . . Heb. 11:26
LOOKING (41/35)
the plow, and *l* back . . . . Luke 9:62
l for the blessed hope . . . . Titus 2:13
l unto Jesus, the author . . . . Heb. 12:2
l carefully lest . . . . Heb. 12:15
l for the mercy of . . . . Jude 1:21
LOOKS (27/26)
The lofty *l* of man . . . . Is. 2:11
to you that whoever *l* . . . . Matt. 5:28
LOOSE (27/27)
and whatever you *l* . . . . Matt. 16:19
said to them, "*L* him . . . . John 11:44
LOOSED (18/17)
the silver cord is *l* . . . . Eccl. 12:6
LORD (7,773/6,614)
L is my strength . . . . Ex. 15:2
L our God, the *L* . . . . Deut. 6:4
You alone are the *L* . . . . Neh. 9:6
The *L* of hosts . . . . Ps. 24:10
Gracious is the *L* . . . . Ps. 116:5
L surrounds His people . . . . Ps. 125:2

The *L* is righteous . . . Ps. 129:4
L is near to all who . . . Ps. 145:18
L is a God of justice . . . Is. 30:18
L Our Righteousness . . . Jer. 23:6
"The *L* is one . . . Zech. 14:9
shall not tempt the *L* . . . Matt. 4:7
shall worship the *L* . . . Matt. 4:10
Son of Man is also *L* . . . Mark 2:28
who is Christ the *L* . . . Luke 2:11
L is risen indeed . . . Luke 24:34
call Me Teacher and *L* . . . John 13:13
He is *L* of all . . . Acts 10:36
with your mouth the *L* . . . Rom. 10:9
say that Jesus is *L* . . . 1 Cor. 12:3
second Man is the *L* . . . 1 Cor. 15:47
the Spirit of the *L* . . . 2 Cor. 3:17
that Jesus Christ is *L* . . . Phil. 2:11
and deny the only *L* . . . Jude 1:4
L God Omnipotent . . . Rev. 19:6

LORDS (40/38)
for He is Lord of *l* . . . Rev. 17:14

LOSE (18/18)
save his life will *l* . . . Matt. 16:25

LOSES (11/11)
but if the salt *l* . . . Matt. 5:13
and *l* his own soul . . . Matt. 16:26

LOSS (15/14)
count all things *l* . . . Phil. 3:8

LOST (34/33)
save that which was *l* . . . Matt. 18:11
and none of them is *l* . . . John 17:12
You gave Me I have *l* . . . John 18:9

LOTS (25/22)
garments, casting *l* . . . Mark 15:24
And they cast their *l* . . . Acts 1:26

LOUD (72/72)
cried out with a *l* . . . Matt. 27:46
I heard behind me a *l* . . . Rev. 1:10

LOVE (361/322)
l your neighbor as . . . Lev. 19:18
l the LORD your God . . . Deut. 6:5
Oh, *l* the LORD . . . Ps. 31:23
he has set his *l* . . . Ps. 91:14
Oh, how I *l* Your law . . . Ps. 119:97
l covers all sins . . . Prov. 10:12
a time to *l* . . . Eccl. 3:8
banner over me was *l* . . . Song 2:4
l is as strong as death . . . Song 8:6
do justly, to *l* mercy . . . Mic. 6:8
to you, *l* your enemies . . . Matt. 5:44
which of them will *l* . . . Luke 7:42
you do not have the *l* . . . John 5:42
if you have *l* for one . . . John 13:35
"If you *l* Me, keep My . . . John 14:15
and My Father will *l* . . . John 14:23
l one another as I . . . John 15:12
l has no one than this . . . John 15:13
because the *l* of God . . . Rom. 5:5
to *l* one another . . . Rom. 13:8
greatest of these is *l* . . . 1 Cor. 13:13
For the *l* of Christ . . . 2 Cor. 5:14
of the Spirit is *l* . . . Gal. 5:22
Husbands, *l* your wives . . . Eph. 5:25
the commandment is *l* . . . 1 Tim. 1:5
For the *l* of money is . . . 1 Tim. 6:10
Let brotherly *l* . . . Heb. 13:1
having not seen you *l* . . . 1 Pet. 1:8
for "*l* will cover a . . . 1 Pet. 4:8
brotherly kindness *l* . . . 2 Pet. 1:7
By this we know *l* . . . 1 John 3:16
Beloved, let us *l* . . . 1 John 4:7
know God, for God is *l* . . . 1 John 4:8
There is no fear in *l* . . . 1 John 4:18
l Him because He first . . . 1 John 4:19
who loves God must *l* . . . 1 John 4:21
For this is the *l* . . . 1 John 5:3
have left your first *l* . . . Rev. 2:4

LOVED (96/86)
L one and friend You . . . Ps. 88:18
Yet Jacob I have *l* . . . Mal. 1:2
forgiven, for she *l* . . . Luke 7:47
so *l* the world that . . . John 3:16
whom Jesus *l* . . . John 13:23
"As the Father *l* . . . John 15:9
l them as You have . . . John 17:23
the Son of God, who *l* . . . Gal. 2:20
l the church and gave . . . Eph. 5:25
Beloved, if God so *l* . . . 1 John 4:11
To Him who *l* us and . . . Rev. 1:5

LOVELY (19/19)
he is altogether *l* . . . Song 5:16
whatever things are *l* . . . Phil. 4:8

LOVES (65/57)
He who *l* father or . . . Matt. 10:37
l his life will lose . . . John 12:25
l Me will be loved . . . John 14:21
l a cheerful giver . . . 2 Cor. 9:7
If anyone *l* the world . . . 1 John 2:15
l God must love his . . . 1 John 4:21

LOVINGKINDNESS (29/29)
to declare Your *l* . . . Ps. 92:2

LOWER (29/28)
made him a little *l* . . . Heb. 2:7

LOWLINESS (2/2)
with all *l* and . . . Eph. 4:2

LOWLY (14/14)
for I am gentle and *l* . . . Matt. 11:29
in presence am *l* . . . 2 Cor. 10:1
l brother glory . . . James 1:9

LUKEWARM (1/1)
because you are *l* . . . Rev. 3:16

LUST (15/14)
looks at a woman to *l* . . . Matt. 5:28
not fulfill the *l* . . . Gal. 5:16
You *l* and do not have . . . James 4:2
the *l* of the flesh . . . 1 John 2:16

LUSTS (19/19)
to fulfill its *l*. . . . . Rom. 13:14
also youthful *l* . . . . 2 Tim. 2:22
and worldly *l*. . . . . Titus 2:12
to the former *l* . . . . 1 Pet. 1:14
abstain from fleshly *l*. . . . . 1 Pet. 2:11
to their own ungodly *l* . . . . Jude 1:18

LUTE (6/6)
Praise Him with the *l*. . . . . Ps. 150:3

LUXURY (8/8)
in pleasure and *l* . . . . James 5:5
the abundance of her *l*. . . . . Rev. 18:3

LYING (76/76)
I hate and abhor *l* . . . . Ps. 119:163
righteous man hates *l* . . . . Prov. 13:5
not trust in these *l*. . . . . Jer. 7:4
signs, and *l* wonders. . . . . 2 Thess. 2:9

M

MADE (1,316/1,236)
m the stars also . . . . Gen. 1:16
things My hand has *m*. . . . . Is. 66:2
All things were *m* . . . . John 1:3

MADNESS (11/11)
m is in their hearts . . . . Eccl. 9:3

MAGIC (3/3)
m brought their books. . . . . Acts 19:19

MAGNIFIED (9/9)
So let Your name be *m*. . . . . 2 Sam. 7:26
the Lord Jesus was *m*. . . . . Acts 19:17
also Christ will be *m*. . . . . Phil. 1:20

MAGNIFIES (1/1)
"My soul *m* the Lord. . . . . Luke 1:46

MAGNIFY (7/7)
m the LORD with me. . . . . Ps. 34:3

MAIDSERVANT (40/35)
""Behold the *m* . . . . Luke 1:38

MAIDSERVANTS (13/12)
m I will pour out My. . . . . Acts 2:18

MAJESTY (32/32)
right hand of the *M*. . . . . Heb. 1:3
eyewitnesses of His *m*. . . . . 2 Pet. 1:16
wise, be glory and *m*. . . . . Jude 1:25

MAKE (1,012/947)
"Let Us *m* man in Our . . . . Gen. 1:26
m you a great nation . . . . Gen. 12:2
"You shall not *m* . . . . Ex. 20:4
m Our home with him. . . . . John 14:23

MAKER (22/21)
M is your husband . . . . Is. 54:5
has forgotten his *M*. . . . . Hos. 8:14
builder and *m* is God . . . . Heb. 11:10

MALICE (6/6)
in *m* be babes . . . . 1 Cor. 14:20
laying aside all *m* . . . . 1 Pet. 2:1

MAN (2,081/1,872)
"Let Us make *m* . . . . Gen. 1:26
m that You are mindful. . . . . Ps. 8:4
coming of the Son of *M*. . . . . Matt. 24:27
"Behold the *M* . . . . John 19:5
since by *m* came death . . . . 1 Cor. 15:21
though our outward *m* . . . . 2 Cor. 4:16
that the *m* of God may. . . . . 2 Tim. 3:17
is the number of a *m* . . . . Rev. 13:18

MANGER (4/4)
and laid Him in a *m* . . . . Luke 2:7

MANIFEST (15/14)
m Myself to him. . . . . John 14:21

MANIFESTATION (3/3)
But the *m* of the. . . . . 1 Cor. 12:7

MANIFESTED (13/12)
"I have *m* Your name . . . . John 17:6
God was *m* in the flesh. . . . . 1 Tim. 3:16
the life was *m*. . . . . 1 John 1:2

MANIFOLD (5/5)
the *m* wisdom of God. . . . . Eph. 3:10

MANNA (18/16)
of Israel ate *m* . . . . Ex. 16:35
Our fathers ate the *m*. . . . . John 6:31

MANNER (94/91)
Is this the *m* of man . . . . 2 Sam. 7:19
in an unworthy *m* . . . . 1 Cor. 11:27
Behold what *m* of love. . . . . 1 John 3:1

MANSIONS (1/1)
house are many *m* . . . . John 14:2

MANTLE (7/7)
Then he took the *m* . . . . 2 Kin. 2:14

MARK (24/23)
And the LORD set a *m*. . . . . Gen. 4:15
whoever receives the *m*. . . . . Rev. 14:11

MARRED (3/3)
so His visage was *m* . . . . Is. 52:14

MARRIAGE (17/16)
M is honorable among . . . . Heb. 13:4

MARRIED (32/31)
But he who is *m*. . . . . 1 Cor. 7:33

MARRY (21/19)
they neither *m* nor are. . . . . Matt. 22:30
forbidding to *m* . . . . 1 Tim. 4:3

MARRYING (2/2)
and drinking, *m*. . . . . Matt. 24:38

MARTYRS (1/1)
the blood of the *m*. . . . . Rev. 17:6

MARVELED (34/34)
Jesus heard it, He *m*. . . . . Matt. 8:10
so that Pilate *m* . . . . Mark 15:5

MARVELOUS (21/19)
It is *m* in our eyes . . . . Ps. 118:23
of darkness into His *m* . . . . 1 Pet. 2:9

MASTER (159/148)
a servant like his *m*. . . . . Matt. 10:25
greater than his *m*. . . . . John 15:20
and useful for the *M*. . . . . 2 Tim. 2:21

MASTERS (17/16)
can serve two *m*. . . . . Luke 16:13
who have believing *m* . . . . 1 Tim. 6:2
MATTERS (21/20)
the weightier *m* . . . . Matt. 23:23
MATURE (3/3)
understanding be *m*. . . . . 1 Cor. 14:20
us, as many as are *m* . . . . Phil. 3:15
MEANT (6/5)
but God *m* it for good. . . . . Gen. 50:20
MEASURE (57/53)
a perfect and just *m* . . . . Deut. 25:15
give the Spirit by *m*. . . . . John 3:34
to each one a *m* . . . . Rom. 12:3
MEASURED (52/49)
m heaven with a span . . . . Is. 40:12
you use, it will be *m* . . . . Matt. 7:2
MEASURES (9/9)
your house differing *m* . . . . Deut. 25:14
MEASURING (17/16)
behold, a man with a *m*. . . . . Zech. 2:1
m themselves by . . . . 2 Cor. 10:12
MEAT (56/47)
will never again eat *m* . . . . 1 Cor. 8:13
MEDIATOR (8/8)
by the hand of a *m* . . . . Gal. 3:19
is one God and one *M*. . . . . 1 Tim. 2:5
to Jesus the *M* of the . . . . Heb. 12:24
MEDICINE (2/2)
does good, like *m* . . . . Prov. 17:22
MEDICINES (2/2)
you will use many *m* . . . . Jer. 46:11
MEDITATE (18/18)
but you shall *m* . . . . Josh. 1:8
M within your heart on . . . . Ps. 4:4
I will *m* on Your . . . . Ps. 119:15
m beforehand on what . . . . Luke 21:14
m on these things . . . . Phil. 4:8
MEDITATES (2/2)
in His law he *m* . . . . Ps. 1:2
MEDITATION (9/9)
O LORD, consider my *m*. . . . . Ps. 5:1
It is my *m* all the day . . . . Ps. 119:97
MEDIUM (5/4)
a woman who is a *m*. . . . . Lev. 20:27
MEDIUM'S (1/1)
shall be like a *m*. . . . . Is. 29:4
MEDIUMS (9/9)
"Seek those who are *m* . . . . Is. 8:19
MEEK (5/5)
with equity for the *m* . . . . Is. 11:4
Blessed are the *m* . . . . Matt. 5:5
MEEKNESS (5/5)
are done in the *m* . . . . James 3:13
MEET (115/111)
prepare to *m* your God . . . . Amos 4:12
m the Lord in the air . . . . 1 Thess. 4:17

MELODY (5/5)
singing and making *m*. . . . . Eph. 5:19
MELT (16/15)
the elements will *m* . . . . 2 Pet. 3:10
MEMBER (8/7)
body is not one *m* . . . . 1 Cor. 12:14
MEMBERS (32/24)
you that one of your *m* . . . . Matt. 5:29
do not present your *m*. . . . . Rom. 6:13
neighbor, for we are *m*. . . . . Eph. 4:25
MEMORIAL (26/25)
and this is My *m* . . . . Ex. 3:15
also be told as a *m*. . . . . Matt. 26:13
MEMORY (9/9)
The *m* of the righteous . . . . Prov. 10:7
MEN (1,592/1,428)
m began to call on the . . . . Gen. 4:26
make you fishers of *m* . . . . Matt. 4:19
goodwill toward *m* . . . . Luke 2:14
from heaven or from *m*. . . . . Luke 20:4
Likewise also the *m* . . . . Rom. 1:27
the Lord, and not to *m*. . . . . Eph. 6:7
between God and *m* . . . . 1 Tim. 2:5
MENSERVANTS (2/2)
And also on My *m*. . . . . Joel 2:29
And on My *m* and on My. . . . . Acts 2:18
MERCHANDISE (14/14)
house a house of *m*. . . . . John 2:16
MERCIES (35/35)
give you the sure *m* . . . . Acts 13:34
MERCIFUL (39/35)
LORD, the LORD God, *m* . . . . Ex. 34:6
He is ever *m* . . . . Ps. 37:26
Blessed are the *m* . . . . Matt. 5:7
saying, 'God be *m* . . . . Luke 18:13
For I will be *m* . . . . Heb. 8:12
MERCY (282/269)
but showing *m* to . . . . Ex. 20:6
and abundant in *m*. . . . . Num. 14:18
m endures forever . . . . 1 Chr. 16:34
M and truth have met . . . . Ps. 85:10
m is everlasting . . . . Ps. 100:5
Let not *m* and truth . . . . Prov. 3:3
For I desire *m* and not . . . . Hos. 6:6
do justly, to love *m* . . . . Mic. 6:8
'I desire *m* and not . . . . Matt. 9:13
And His *m* is on those . . . . Luke 1:50
"I will have *m* . . . . Rom. 9:15
that He might have *m* . . . . Rom. 11:32
m has made trustworthy. . . . . . . 1 Cor. 7:25
God, who is rich in *m* . . . . Eph. 2:4
but I obtained *m* . . . . 1 Tim. 1:13
that he may find *m* . . . . 2 Tim. 1:18
to His *m* He saved us . . . . Titus 3:5
that we may obtain *m* . . . . Heb. 4:16
MERRY (21/21)
m heart makes a . . . . Prov. 15:13
we should make *m* . . . . Luke 15:32

MOTHER (240/225)
because she was the *m* .... Gen. 3:20
leave his father and *m* .... Matt. 19:5
"Behold your *m* .... John 19:27
The *M* of Harlots .... Rev. 17:5

MOUNT (154/148)
come up to *M* Sinai.............. Ex. 19:23
they shall *m* up with............. Is. 40:31

MOUNTAIN (208/181)
to Horeb, the *m* .... Ex. 3:1
let us go up to the *m*............... Is. 2:3
image became a great *m*........ Dan. 2:35
Who are you, O great *m*.......... Zech. 4:7
you will say to this *m* .... Matt. 17:20
with Him on the holy *m* .... 2 Pet. 1:18

MOUNTAINS (235/221)
m were brought forth .... Ps. 90:2
m shall depart and the........... Is. 54:10
in Judea flee to the *m* .... Matt. 24:16
that I could remove *m* .... 1 Cor. 13:2

MOURN (46/45)
a time to *m* .... Eccl. 3:4
are those who *m* .... Matt. 5:4
of the earth will *m*................. Rev. 1:7

MOURNED (24/24)
and have not rather *m*........... 1 Cor. 5:2

MOURNING (52/48)
shall be a great *m* .... Zech. 12:11
be turned to *m* and............ James 4:9

MOUTH (394/374)
"Who has made man's *m* .... Ex. 4:11
Out of the *m* of babes............. Ps. 8:2
knowledge, but the *m* .... Prov. 10:14
The *m* of an immoral......... Prov. 22:14
and a flattering *m* .... Prov. 26:28
m speaking pompous .... Dan. 7:8
m defiles a man .... Matt. 15:11
m I will judge you .... Luke 19:22
I will give you a *m*............. Luke 21:15
m confession is made .... Rom. 10:10
m great swelling words .... Jude 1:16
vomit you out of My *m* .... Rev. 3:16

MOVED (92/91)
she shall not be *m*............... Ps. 46:5
spoke as they were *m*........... 2 Pet. 1:21

MUCH (218/208)
m study is wearisome .... Eccl. 12:12
to whom *m* is given .... Luke 12:48

MULTIPLIED (43/42)
of the disciples *m* .... Acts 6:7
word of God grew and *m*....... Acts 12:24

MULTIPLY (48/44)
"Be fruitful and *m*.............. Gen. 1:22
m the descendants .... Jer. 33:22

MULTITUDE (222/215)
stars of heaven in *m*........... Deut. 1:10
In the *m* of words sin.......... Prov. 10:19
compassion on the *m* .... Matt. 15:32
with the angel a *m*................ Luke 2:13
"love will cover a *m*.............. 1 Pet. 4:8
and behold, a great *m* .... Rev. 7:9

MURDER (21/20)
"You shall not *m* .... Ex. 20:13
'You shall not *m*................. Matt. 5:21
You *m* and covet and .... James 4:2

MURDERED (13/13)
Jesus whom you *m*.............. Acts 5:30

MURDERER (21/16)
He was a *m* from the .... John 8:44
his brother is a *m* .... 1 John 3:15

MURDERERS (9/8)
and profane, for *m* .... 1 Tim. 1:9
abominable, *m*.................. Rev. 21:8

MURDERS (6/6)
evil thoughts, *m*................ Matt. 15:19

MUSING (1/1)
while I was *m*, the fire .... Ps. 39:3

MUTILATION (2/2)
beware of the *m*................... Phil. 3:2

MUZZLE (4/4)
"You shall not *m* .... 1 Tim. 5:18

MYSTERIES (5/5)
to you to know the *m* .... Matt. 13:11
and understand all *m*.......... 1 Cor. 13:2

MYSTERY (22/22)
given to know the *m*............ Mark 4:11
wisdom of God in a *m* .... 1 Cor. 2:7
Behold, I tell you a *m*.......... 1 Cor. 15:51
made known to us the *m* .... Eph. 1:9
the *m* of godliness .... 1 Tim. 3:16

N

NAILED (1/1)
n it to the cross .... Col. 2:14

NAKED (41/40)
And they were both *n*........... Gen. 2:25
knew that they were *n* .... Gen. 3:7
"*N* I came from my................ Job 1:21
I was *n* and you .... Matt. 25:36
but all things are *n* .... Heb. 4:13
brother or sister is *n*......... James 2:15
poor, blind, and *n* .... Rev. 3:17

NAKEDNESS (57/43)
or famine, or *n*................. Rom. 8:35
n may not be revealed .... Rev. 3:18

NAME (930/835)
Abram called on the *n* .... Gen. 13:4
This is My *n* forever .... Ex. 3:15
shall not take the *n*............... Ex. 20:7
glorious and awesome *n*...... Deut. 28:58
excellent is Your *n*................. Ps. 8:1
n will put their trust .... Ps. 9:10
be His glorious *n*................ Ps. 72:19
do not call on Your *n* .... Ps. 79:6
to Your *n* give glory .... Ps. 115:1

above all Your *n* .... Ps. 138:2
A good *n* is to be .... Prov. 22:1
what is His Son's *n* .... Prov. 30:4
be called by a new *n* .... Is. 62:2
Everlasting is Your *n* .... Is. 63:16
They will call on My *n* .... Zech. 13:9
to you who fear My *n* .... Mal. 4:2
hallowed be Your *n* .... Matt. 6:9
prophesied in Your *n* .... Matt. 7:22
n Gentiles will trust .... Matt. 12:21
together in My *n* .... Matt. 18:20
will come in My *n* .... Matt. 24:5
who believe in His *n* .... John 1:12
comes in his own *n* .... John 5:43
his own sheep by *n* .... John 10:3
through faith in His *n* .... Acts 3:16
there is no other *n* .... Acts 4:12
which is above every *n* .... Phil. 2:9
deed, do all in the *n* .... Col. 3:17
a more excellent *n* .... Heb. 1:4
you hold fast to My *n* .... Rev. 2:13
n that you are alive .... Rev. 3:1
having His Father's *n* .... Rev. 14:1
and glorify Your *n* .... Rev. 15:4
n written that no one .... Rev. 19:12

NAME'S (29/29)
saved them for His *n* .... Ps. 106:8

NARROW (8/8)
"Enter by the *n* gate .... Matt. 7:13

NATION (151/132)
make you a great *n* .... Gen. 12:2
Righteousness exalts a *n* ...... Prov. 14:34
n that was not called .... Is. 65:1
I will make them one *n* .... Ezek. 37:22
since there was a *n* .... Dan. 12:1
n will rise against .... Matt. 24:7
for he loves our *n* .... Luke 7:5
those who are not a *n* .... Rom. 10:19
tribe, tongue, and *n* .... Rev. 13:7

NATIONS (445/426)
Why do the *n* rage .... Ps. 2:1
I will give You the *n* .... Ps. 2:8
n shall serve Him .... Ps. 72:11
disciples of all the *n* .... Matt. 28:19
who was to rule all *n* .... Rev. 12:5
the healing of the *n* .... Rev. 22:2

NATURAL (11/10)
women exchanged the *n* .... Rom. 1:26
the men, leaving the *n* .... Rom. 1:27
did not spare the *n* .... Rom. 11:21
n man does not receive .... 1 Cor. 2:14
It is sown a *n* body .... 1 Cor. 15:44

NATURE (13/12)
We who are Jews by *n* .... Gal. 2:15
by *n* children of wrath .... Eph. 2:3
of the divine *n* .... 2 Pet. 1:4

NEAR (309/295)
But the word is very *n* .... Deut. 30:14
upon Him while He is *n* .... Is. 55:6
know that it is *n* .... Matt. 24:33
kingdom of God is *n* .... Luke 21:31
"The word is *n* .... Rom. 10:8
to those who were *n* .... Eph. 2:17
for the time is *n* .... Rev. 1:3

NEARER (1/1)
now our salvation is *n* .... Rom. 13:11

NEED (72/70)
the things you have *n* .... Matt. 6:8
supply all your *n* .... Phil. 4:19
to help in time of *n* .... Heb. 4:16

NEGLECT (5/5)
if we *n* so great a .... Heb. 2:3

NEGLECTED (2/2)
n the weightier .... Matt. 23:23

NEIGHBOR (100/95)
you shall love your *n* .... Lev. 19:18
'You shall love your *n* .... Matt. 5:43
"And who is my *n* .... Luke 10:29
"You shall love your *n* .... Rom. 13:9

NEVER (123/114)
in Me shall *n* thirst .... John 6:35
in Me shall *n* die .... John 11:26
Love *n* fails .... 1 Cor. 13:8
n take away sins .... Heb. 10:11
"I will *n* leave you .... Heb. 13:5
prophecy *n* came by .... 2 Pet. 1:21

NEW (173/153)
and there is nothing *n* .... Eccl. 1:9
For behold, I create *n* .... Is. 65:17
n every morning .... Lam. 3:23
wine into *n* wineskins .... Matt. 9:17
of the *n* covenant .... Matt. 26:28
n commandment I give .... John 13:34
he is a *n* creation .... 2 Cor. 5:17
when I will make a *n* .... Heb. 8:8
n heavens and a *n* .... 2 Pet. 3:13
n name written which .... Rev. 2:17
And they sang a *n* .... Rev. 5:9
And I saw a *n* heaven .... Rev. 21:1
I make all things *n* .... Rev. 21:5

NEWNESS (2/2)
also should walk in *n* .... Rom. 6:4

NIGHT (305/293)
darkness He called *N* .... Gen. 1:5
It is a *n* of solemn .... Ex. 12:42
pillar of fire by *n* .... Ex. 13:22
gives songs in the *n* .... Job 35:10
and continued all *n* .... Luke 6:12
man came to Jesus by *n* .... John 3:2
n is coming when no .... John 9:4
came to Jesus by *n* .... John 19:39
as a thief in the *n* .... 1 Thess. 5:2
there shall be no *n* .... Rev. 21:25

NINETY-NINE (6/6)
he not leave the *n* .... Matt. 18:12

NOTHING (286/280)
I can of Myself do *n* .... John 5:30
Me you can do *n* .... John 15:5
men, it will come to *n* .... Acts 5:38
have not love, I am *n* .... 1 Cor. 13:2
Be anxious for *n* .... Phil. 4:6
For we brought *n* .... 1 Tim. 6:7

NOURISHED (6/6)
"I have *n* and .... Is. 1:2

NOURISHES (2/2)
n and cherishes it .... Eph. 5:29

NUMBER (174/162)
if a man could *n* .... Gen. 13:16
teach us to *n* our days .... Ps. 90:12
which no one could *n* .... Rev. 7:9
His *n* is 666 .... Rev. 13:18

O

OATH (100/92)
for the sake of your *o* .... Eccl. 8:2
he denied with an *o* .... Matt. 26:72
o which He swore .... Luke 1:73

OATHS (8/8)
shall perform your *o* .... Matt. 5:33

OBEDIENCE (14/14)
o many will be made .... Rom. 5:19
captivity to the *o* .... 2 Cor. 10:5
for *o* and sprinkling .... 1 Pet. 1:2

OBEDIENT (14/14)
you are willing and *o* .... Is. 1:19
of the priests were *o* .... Acts 6:7
make the Gentiles *o* .... Rom. 15:18
Himself and became *o* .... Phil. 2:8
as *o* children .... 1 Pet. 1:14

OBEY (108/104)
God and *o* His voice .... Deut. 4:30
His voice we will *o* .... Josh. 24:24
o is better than .... 1 Sam. 15:22
o God rather than men .... Acts 5:29
and do not *o* the truth .... Rom. 2:8
yourselves slaves to *o* .... Rom. 6:16
o your parents in all .... Col. 3:20
Bondservants, *o* in all .... Col. 3:22
on those who do not *o* .... 2 Thess. 1:8
O those who rule .... Heb. 13:17

OBEYED (43/43)
of sin, yet you *o* .... Rom. 6:17
they have not all *o* .... Rom. 10:16
By faith Abraham *o* .... Heb. 11:8

OBSERVATION (1/1)
does not come with *o* .... Luke 17:20

OBSERVE (85/81)
teaching them to *o* all .... Matt. 28:20

OBTAIN (13/13)
they also may *o* mercy .... Rom. 11:31
o salvation through .... 1 Thess. 5:9

OBTAINED (27/25)
o a part in this .... Acts 1:17
yet have now *o* mercy .... Rom. 11:30
endured, he *o* the .... Heb. 6:15

OBTAINS (3/3)
o favor from the LORD .... Prov. 8:35

OFFEND (7/7)
lest we *o* them .... Matt. 17:27
than that he should *o* .... Luke 17:2
them, "Does this *o* .... John 6:61

OFFENDED (15/15)
So they were *o* at Him .... Matt. 13:57

OFFENSE (21/20)
and a rock of *o* .... Is. 8:14
You are an *o* to Me .... Matt. 16:23
by the one man's *o* .... Rom. 5:17
the *o* of the cross .... Gal. 5:11
sincere and without *o* .... Phil. 1:10
and a rock of *o* .... 1 Pet. 2:8

OFFENSES (8/7)
For *o* must come .... Matt. 18:7
impossible that no *o* .... Luke 17:1

OFFER (217/196)
come and *o* your gift .... Matt. 5:24
let us continually *o* .... Heb. 13:15

OFFERED (129/123)
to eat those things *o* .... 1 Cor. 8:10
so Christ was *o* .... Heb. 9:28
o one sacrifice .... Heb. 10:12

OFFERING (803/547)
o You did not require .... Ps. 40:6
You make His soul an *o* .... Is. 53:10
Himself for us, an *o* .... Eph. 5:2
o You did not .... Heb. 10:5
o He has perfected .... Heb. 10:14

OFFERINGS (279/210)
and offered burnt *o* .... Gen. 8:20
In burnt *o* and .... Heb. 10:6

OFFICE (11/11)
sitting at the tax *o* .... Matt. 9:9

OFFSPRING (41/41)
wife and raise up *o* .... Matt. 22:24
For we are also His *o* .... Acts 17:28
am the Root and the *O* .... Rev. 22:16

OFTEN (33/31)
o I wanted to gather .... Luke 13:34
as *o* as you eat this .... 1 Cor. 11:26

OIL (222/204)
a bin, and a little *o* .... 1 Kin. 17:12
very costly fragrant *o* .... Matt. 26:7
anointing him with *o* .... James 5:14
and do not harm the *o* .... Rev. 6:6

OLD (339/310)
young, and now am *o* .... Ps. 37:25
was said to those of *o* .... Matt. 5:21
but when you are *o* .... John 21:18
Your *o* men shall dream .... Acts 2:17
o man was crucified .... Rom. 6:6
o things have passed .... 2 Cor. 5:17
have put off the *o* man .... Col. 3:9

that serpent of *o* ... Rev. 20:2

OLDER (16/16)

o shall serve the ... Gen. 25:23
not rebuke an *o* man ... 1 Tim. 5:1

OLDEST (9/9)

beginning with the *o* ... John 8:9

OLIVE (41/38)

a freshly plucked *o* ... Gen. 8:11
o tree which is wild ... Rom. 11:24

OMNIPOTENT (1/1)

For the Lord God *O* ... Rev. 19:6

ONCE (83/81)

died, He died to sin *o* ... Rom. 6:10
for this He did *o* for all ... Heb. 7:27
also suffered *o* ... 1 Pet. 3:18

ONE (2,611/2,242)

"*O* thing you lack ... Mark 10:21
o thing is needed ... Luke 10:42
I and My Father are *o* ... John 10:30
Me, that they may be *o* ... John 17:11
o accord in the temple ... Acts 2:46
for you are all *o* ... Gal. 3:28
to create in Himself *o* ... Eph. 2:15
o Lord, *o* faith, *o* ... Eph. 4:5
o God and Father of ... Eph. 4:6
O Mediator between God ... 1 Tim. 2:5
a thousand years as *o* ... 2 Pet. 3:8

OPENED (128/122)

o not His mouth ... Is. 53:7
o the Scriptures ... Luke 24:32
o their understanding ... Luke 24:45
Now I saw heaven *o* ... Rev. 19:11

OPENS (18/17)

him the doorkeeper *o* ... John 10:3
and shuts and no one *o* ... Rev. 3:7

OPINION (5/5)

be wise in your own *o* ... Rom. 11:25

OPINIONS (1/1)

falter between two *o* ... 1 Kin. 18:21

OPPORTUNITY (13/12)

But sin, taking *o* ... Rom. 7:8
as we have *o* ... Gal. 6:10
but you lacked *o* ... Phil. 4:10

OPPRESS (27/27)

he loves to *o* ... Hos. 12:7
o the widow or the ... Zech. 7:10
Do not the rich *o* ... James 2:6

OPPRESSED (44/44)

for all who are *o* ... Ps. 103:6
The tears of the *o* ... Eccl. 4:1
He was *o* and He was ... Is. 53:7
healing all who were *o* ... Acts 10:38

OPPRESSES (5/5)

o the poor reproaches ... Prov. 14:31

OPPRESSION (27/27)

have surely seen the *o* ... Ex. 3:7
their life from *o* ... Ps. 72:14
brought low through *o* ... Ps. 107:39
Redeem me from the *o* ... Ps. 119:134
considered all the *o* ... Eccl. 4:1
o destroys a wise ... Eccl. 7:7
justice, but behold, *o* ... Is. 5:7
surely seen the *o* ... Acts 7:34

ORACLES (5/5)

received the living *o* ... Acts 7:38
were committed the *o* ... Rom. 3:2
principles of the *o* ... Heb. 5:12

ORDAINED (10/10)

o you a prophet ... Jer. 1:5
the Man whom He has *o* ... Acts 17:31

ORDER (73/72)

done decently and in *o* ... 1 Cor. 14:40

ORDERS (6/6)

o his conduct aright I ... Ps. 50:23

ORDINANCE (42/41)

resists the *o* of God ... Rom. 13:2

ORDINANCES (29/28)

and fleshly *o* imposed ... Heb. 9:10

ORPHANS (4/4)

I will not leave you *o* ... John 14:18
to visit *o* and widows ... James 1:27

OUGHT (52/52)

These you *o* to have ... Matt. 23:23
pray for as we *o* ... Rom. 8:26
persons *o* you to be ... 2 Pet. 3:11

OUTCAST (3/3)

they called you an *o* ... Jer. 30:17

OUTCASTS (7/7)

will assemble the *o* ... Is. 11:12

OUTRAN (2/2)

the other disciple *o* ... John 20:4

OUTSIDE (138/136)

and dish, that the *o* ... Matt. 23:26
Pharisees make the *o* ... Luke 11:39
toward those who are *o* ... Col. 4:5
to Him, *o* the camp ... Heb. 13:13
But *o* are dogs and ... Rev. 22:15

OUTSTRETCHED (18/18)

and with an *o* arm ... Deut. 26:8

OUTWARD (6/6)

at the *o* appearance ... 1 Sam. 16:7
adornment be merely *o* ... 1 Pet. 3:3

OUTWARDLY (3/3)

not a Jew who is one *o* ... Rom. 2:28

OVERCAME (2/2)

My throne, as I also *o* ... Rev. 3:21
And they *o* him by ... Rev. 12:11

OVERCOME (21/20)

good cheer, I have *o* ... John 16:33
and the Lamb will *o* ... Rev. 17:14

OVERCOMES (11/11)

of God *o* the world ... 1 John 5:4
o I will give to eat ... Rev. 2:7
o shall not be hurt ... Rev. 2:11
o shall inherit all ... Rev. 21:7

When you *p* through the..........Is. 43:2
and earth will *p* ....Matt. 24:35

PASSED (113/105)
forbearance God had *p* ....Rom. 3:25
High Priest who has *p* ....Heb. 4:14
know that we have *p*.........1 John 3:14

PASSES (29/29)
of Christ which *p*...............Eph. 3:19

PASSION (3/3)
uncleanness, *p*, evil ....Col. 3:5

PASSIONS (3/3)
gave them up to vile *p*........Rom. 1:26

PASSOVER (79/73)
It is the LORD's *P*...............Ex. 12:11
I will keep the *P*..............Matt. 26:18
indeed Christ, our *P*...........1 Cor. 5:7
By faith he kept the *P*..........Heb. 11:28

PASTORS (1/1)
and some *p* and................Eph. 4:11

PASTURE (24/22)
the sheep of Your *p*...............Ps. 74:1
in and out and find *p*..........John 10:9

PASTURES (14/14)
to lie down in green *p* ....Ps. 23:2

PATH (28/28)
You will show me the *p*..........Ps. 16:11

PATHS (41/41)
He leads me in the *p*...............Ps. 23:3
Make His *p* straight ....Matt. 3:3
and make straight *p*..........Heb. 12:13

PATIENCE (25/25)
'Master, have *p*................Matt. 18:26
and bear fruit with *p*..........Luke 8:15
labor of love, and *p*...........1 Thess. 1:3
faith, love, *p* ....1 Tim. 6:11
your faith produces *p*...........James 1:3
p have its perfect...............James 1:4
in the kingdom and *p*............Rev. 1:9

PATIENT (7/7)
rejoicing in hope, *p*...........Rom. 12:12
uphold the weak, be *p* ....1 Thess. 5:14

PATIENTLY (7/6)
if you take it *p*...................1 Pet. 2:20

PATRIARCHS (2/2)
begot the twelve *p*...............Acts 7:8

PATTERN (13/12)
p which you were ....Ex. 26:30
as you have us for a *p*...........Phil. 3:17
p shown you on the ....Heb. 8:5

PEACE (396/368)
you, and give you *p*...........Num. 6:26
both lie down in *p*..................Ps. 4:8
p have those who...............Ps. 119:165
I am for *p*...........................Ps. 120:7
war, and a time of *p* ....Eccl. 3:8
Father, Prince of *P* ....Is. 9:6
keep him in perfect *p*...............Is. 26:3
p they have not ....Is. 59:8
slightly, saying, '*P* ....Jer. 6:14
place I will give *p*.................Hag. 2:9
is worthy, let your *p* ....Matt. 10:13
that I came to bring *p* ....Matt. 10:34
and on earth *p* ....Luke 2:14
if a son of *p* is there ....Luke 10:6
that make for your *p*...........Luke 19:42
I leave with you, My *p* ....John 14:27
in Me you may have *p* ....John 16:33
Grace to you and *p* ....Rom. 1:7
by faith, we have *p*................Rom. 5:1
God has called us to *p* ....1 Cor. 7:15
p will be with you ....2 Cor. 13:11
Spirit is love, joy, *p* ....Gal. 5:22
He Himself is our *p*..............Eph. 2:14
and the *p* of God ....Phil. 4:7
And let the *p* of God ....Col. 3:15
faith, love, *p* ....2 Tim. 2:22
meaning "king of *p*,"..............Heb. 7:2

PEACEABLE (5/5)
is first pure, then *p*...........James 3:17

PEACEABLY (11/10)
on you, live *p* ....Rom. 12:18

PEACEFUL (4/4)
in a *p* habitation ....Is. 32:18

PEACEMAKERS (1/1)
Blessed are the *p*..................Matt. 5:9

PEARL (2/2)
had found one *p* ....Matt. 13:46

PEARLS (7/7)
nor cast your *p*......................Matt. 7:6
gates were twelve *p*..............Rev. 21:21

PENTECOST (3/3)
P had fully come ....Acts 2:1

PEOPLE (2,136/1,908)
will take you as My *p* ....Ex. 6:7
p shall be my *p*......................Ruth 1:16
p who know the joyful ....Ps. 89:15
We are His *p* and the ....Ps. 100:3
"Blessed is Egypt My *p*............Is. 19:25
to make ready a *p* ....Luke 1:17
take out of them a *p* ....Acts 15:14
who were not My *p* ....Rom. 9:25
and they shall be My *p*..........2 Cor. 6:16
LORD will judge His *p*.........Heb. 10:30
but are now the *p*..................1 Pet. 2:10
tribe and tongue and *p* ....Rev. 5:9
they shall be His *p*.................Rev. 21:3

PERCEIVE (23/23)
seeing, but do not *p* ....Is. 6:9
may see and not *p*................Mark 4:12

PERDITION (8/8)
except the son of *p* ....John 17:12
revealed, the son of *p*........2 Thess. 2:3
who draw back to *p*...........Heb. 10:39

PERFECT (61/56)
Noah was a just man, *p* ....Gen. 6:9

Father in heaven is *p* .... Matt. 5:48
they may be made *p* .... John 17:23
and *p* will of God .... Rom. 12:2
when that which is *p* .... 1 Cor. 13:10
present every man *p* .... Col. 1:28
good gift and every *p* .... James 1:17
in word, he is a *p* .... James 3:2
p love casts out fear .... 1 John 4:18

PERFECTED (11/11)
third day I shall be *p* .... Luke 13:32
or am already *p* .... Phil. 3:12
the Son who has been *p* .... Heb. 7:28

PERFECTION (7/7)
let us go on to *p* .... Heb. 6:1

PERISH (110/108)
so that we may not *p* .... Jon. 1:6
little ones should *p* .... Matt. 18:14
in Him should not *p* .... John 3:16
they shall never *p* .... John 10:28
among those who *p* .... 2 Thess. 2:10
that any should *p* .... 2 Pet. 3:9

PERISHABLE (1/1)
do it to obtain a *p* .... 1 Cor. 9:25

PERISHED (28/28)
Truth has *p* and has .... Jer. 7:28

PERISHING (11/11)
We are *p* .... Matt. 8:25

PERMIT (14/14)
I do not *p* a woman .... 1 Tim. 2:12

PERMITS (2/2)
we will do if God *p* .... Heb. 6:3

PERMITTED (12/12)
p no one to do them .... Ps. 105:14

PERSECUTE (19/19)
when they revile and *p* .... Matt. 5:11

PERSECUTED (18/18)
If they *p* Me .... John 15:20
p, but not forsaken .... 2 Cor. 4:9

PERSECUTES (1/1)
wicked in his pride *p* .... Ps. 10:2

PERSECUTION (9/9)
p arises because of .... Matt. 13:21
At that time a great *p* .... Acts 8:1
do I still suffer *p* .... Gal. 5:11

PERSECUTOR (1/1)
a blasphemer, a *p* .... 1 Tim. 1:13

PERSEVERANCE (9/8)
tribulation produces *p* .... Rom. 5:3

PERSEVERE (1/1)
kept My command to *p* .... Rev. 3:10

PERSISTENCE (1/1)
p he will rise and .... Luke 11:8

PERSON (100/94)
do not regard the *p* .... Matt. 22:16
express image of His *p* .... Heb. 1:3

PERSUADE (14/14)
"You almost *p* me .... Acts 26:28

PERSUADED (21/21)
neither will they be *p* .... Luke 16:31
p that He is able .... 2 Tim. 1:12

PERSUASIVE (2/2)
p words of human .... 1 Cor. 2:4

PERVERSE (33/33)
your way is *p* .... Num. 22:32
p man sows strife .... Prov. 16:28
from this *p* generation .... Acts 2:40

PERVERT (11/11)
You shall not *p* .... Deut. 16:19
p the gospel of Christ .... Gal. 1:7

PERVERTING (2/2)
will you not cease *p* .... Acts 13:10

PERVERTS (3/3)
p his ways will become .... Prov. 10:9

PESTILENCE (42/41)
from the perilous *p* .... Ps. 91:3
Before Him went *p* .... Hab. 3:5

PESTILENCES (2/2)
will be famines, *p* .... Matt. 24:7

PETITIONS (4/4)
p that we have asked .... 1 John 5:15

PHARISEE (11/10)
temple to pray, one a *P* .... Luke 18:10

PHILOSOPHERS (1/1)
p encountered him .... Acts 17:18

PHILOSOPHY (1/1)
cheat you through *p* .... Col. 2:8

PHYSICIAN (6/6)
have no need of a *p* .... Matt. 9:12

PHYSICIANS (6/5)
her livelihood on *p* .... Luke 8:43

PIECES (118/107)
they took the thirty *p* .... Matt. 27:9

PIERCE (9/9)
a sword will *p* .... Luke 2:35

PIERCED (9/9)
p My hands and My feet .... Ps. 22:16
Me whom they have *p* .... Zech. 12:10
of the soldiers *p* .... John 19:34
p themselves through .... 1 Tim. 6:10
and they also who *p* .... Rev. 1:7

PIERCING (1/1)
p even to the division .... Heb. 4:12

PILGRIMAGE (5/4)
heart is set on *p* .... Ps. 84:5
In the house of my *p* .... Ps. 119:54

PILGRIMS (4/4)
we are aliens and *p* .... 1 Chr. 29:15
were strangers and *p* .... Heb. 11:13

PILLAR (51/39)
and she became a *p* .... Gen. 19:26
and by night in a *p* .... Ex. 13:21
the living God, the *p* .... 1 Tim. 3:15

PILLARS (105/90)
break their sacred *p* .... Ex. 34:13

blood and fire and *p* . . . . Joel 2:30
and his feet like *p* . . . . Rev. 10:1

PIT (89/81)
who go down to the *p* . . . . Ps. 28:1
a harlot is a deep *p* . . . . Prov. 23:27
my life in the *p* . . . . Lam. 3:53
up my life from the *p* . . . . Jon. 2:6
into the bottomless *p* . . . . Rev. 20:3

PITIABLE (1/1)
of all men the most *p* . . . . 1 Cor. 15:19

PITS (6/6)
The proud have dug *p* . . . . Ps. 119:85

PITY (33/32)
for someone to take *p* . . . . Ps. 69:20
p He redeemed them . . . . Is. 63:9
just as I had *p* . . . . Matt. 18:33

PLACE (845/798)
Come, see the *p* . . . . Matt. 28:6
My word has no *p* . . . . John 8:37
I go to prepare a *p* . . . . John 14:2
might go to his own *p* . . . . Acts 1:25

PLACES (196/183)
and the rough *p* . . . . Is. 40:4
They love the best *p* . . . . Matt. 23:6
in the heavenly *p* . . . . Eph. 1:3

PLAGUE (75/64)
bring yet one more *p* . . . . Ex. 11:1

PLAGUES (22/21)
p that are written . . . . Rev. 22:18

PLANK (6/5)
First remove the *p* . . . . Matt. 7:5

PLANS (22/22)
He makes the *p* of the . . . . Ps. 33:10
that devises wicked *p* . . . . Prov. 6:18

PLANT (50/48)
A time to *p* . . . . Eccl. 3:2
Him as a tender *p* . . . . Is. 53:2
p of an alien vine . . . . Jer. 2:21
p which My heavenly . . . . Matt. 15:13

PLANTED (41/41)
shall be like a tree *p* . . . . Ps. 1:3
by the roots and be *p* . . . . Luke 17:6
I *p*, Apollos watered . . . . 1 Cor. 3:6

PLANTS (12/12)
neither he who *p* . . . . 1 Cor. 3:7

PLATTER (17/17)
head here on a *p* . . . . Matt. 14:8

PLEASANT (47/47)
food, that it was *p* . . . . Gen. 3:6
they despised the *p* . . . . Ps. 106:24

PLEASANTNESS (1/1)
Her ways are ways of *p* . . . . Prov. 3:17

PLEASE (220/214)
in the flesh cannot *p* . . . . Rom. 8:8
p his neighbor for his . . . . Rom. 15:2
how he may *p* the Lord . . . . 1 Cor. 7:32
is impossible to *p* Him . . . . Heb. 11:6

PLEASED (60/59)
Then You shall be *p* . . . . Ps. 51:19
in whom I am well *p* . . . . Matt. 3:17
God was not well *p* . . . . 1 Cor. 10:5
testimony, that he *p* . . . . Heb. 11:5

PLEASES (23/23)
Whatever the LORD *p* . . . . Ps. 135:6

PLEASURE (55/54)
Do good in Your good *p* . . . . Ps. 51:18
p will be a poor man . . . . Prov. 21:17
shall perform all My *p* . . . . Is. 44:28
your Father's good *p* . . . . Luke 12:32
to the good *p* of His . . . . Eph. 1:5
for sin You had no *p* . . . . Heb. 10:6
back, My soul has no *p* . . . . Heb. 10:38
p that war in your . . . . James 4:1

PLEASURES (8/8)
Your right hand are *p* . . . . Ps. 16:11
cares, riches, and *p* . . . . Luke 8:14
to enjoy the passing *p* . . . . Heb. 11:25

PLOW (10/9)
put his hand to the *p* . . . . Luke 9:62

PLOWED (6/6)
You have *p* wickedness . . . . Hos. 10:13

PLOWMAN (2/2)
p shall overtake the . . . . Amos 9:13

PLUCK (22/21)
p the heads of grain . . . . Mark 2:23

PLUCKED (14/14)
cheeks to those who *p* . . . . Is. 50:6
And His disciples *p* . . . . Luke 6:1
you would have *p* . . . . Gal. 4:15

PLUNDER (71/61)
p the Egyptians . . . . Ex. 3:22
The *p* of the poor is . . . . Is. 3:14
house and *p* his goods . . . . Matt. 12:29

PLUNDERED (39/36)
a people robbed and *p* . . . . Is. 42:22
"And when you are *p* . . . . Jer. 4:30

PLUNDERING (9/9)
me because of the *p* . . . . Is. 22:4
accepted the *p* of your . . . . Heb. 10:34

POETS (1/1)
some of your own *p* . . . . Acts 17:28

POISON (9/8)
"The *p* of asps is . . . . Rom. 3:13

POISONED (2/2)
p by bitterness . . . . Acts 8:23

POLLUTIONS (1/1)
have escaped the *p* . . . . 2 Pet. 2:20

POMP (5/5)
had come with great *p* . . . . Acts 25:23

POMPOUS (4/4)
and a mouth speaking *p* . . . . Dan. 7:8

PONDER (2/2)
P the path of your . . . . Prov. 4:26

PONDERED (2/2)
p them in her heart............Luke 2:19

PONDERS (1/1)
p all his paths..................Prov. 5:21

POOR (201/194)
p will never cease ....Deut. 15:11
So the *p* have hope ....Job 5:16
I delivered the *p*...............Job 29:12
p shall eat and be..............Ps. 22:26
But I am *p* and needy...........Ps. 40:17
Let the *p* and needy ....Ps. 74:21
He raises the *p* ....Ps. 113:7
a slack hand becomes *p*........Prov. 10:4
p man is hated even ....Prov. 14:20
p reproaches his Maker.........Prov. 17:5
remembered that same *p*.......Eccl. 9:15
the alien or the *p* ....Zech. 7:10
"Blessed are the *p* ....Matt. 5:3
p have the gospel.................Matt. 11:5
For you have the *p* ....Matt. 26:11
your sakes He became *p* ....2 Cor. 8:9
should remember the *p*.........Gal. 2:10
God not chosen the *p* ....James 2:5
wretched, miserable, *p* ....Rev. 3:17

PORTION (64/61)
O LORD, You are the *p* ....Ps. 16:5
heart and my *p* forever ....Ps. 73:26
You are my *p*.....................Ps. 119:57
I will divide Him a *p*.............Is. 53:12
rejoice in their *p* ....Is. 61:7
The *P* of Jacob is not ....Jer. 10:16
"The LORD is my *p*...............Lam. 3:24
and appoint him his *p* ....Matt. 24:51
to give them their *p* ....Luke 12:42
give me the *p* ....Luke 15:12

POSSESS (101/92)
descendants shall *p* ....Gen. 22:17
p the land which ....Josh. 1:11
By your patience *p* ....Luke 21:19
p his own vessel..............1 Thess. 4:4

POSSESSED (14/14)
"The LORD *p* me at ....Prov. 8:22

POSSESSING (2/2)
and yet *p* all things ....2 Cor. 6:10

POSSESSION (105/94)
as an everlasting *p* ....Gen. 17:8
and an enduring *p* ....Heb. 10:34

POSSESSIONS (39/38)
and sold their *p* ....Acts 2:45

POSSIBLE (15/15)
God all things are *p*...........Matt. 19:26
p that the blood ....Heb. 10:4

POUR (67/66)
p My Spirit on your................Is. 44:3
P out Your fury ....Jer. 10:25
that I will *p* out My ....Joel 2:28
"And I will *p* ....Zech. 12:10
angels, "Go and *p*....................Rev. 16:1

POURED (86/82)
I am *p* out like water ....Ps. 22:14
grace is *p* upon Your ....Ps. 45:2
strong, because He *p* ....Is. 53:12
and My fury will be *p* ....Jer. 7:20
broke the flask and *p* ....Mark 14:3
I am already being *p*............2 Tim. 4:6
whom He *p* out on us...............Titus 3:6

POVERTY (21/21)
leads only to *p* ....Prov. 14:23
p put in all the ....Luke 21:4
and their deep *p* ....2 Cor. 8:2
p might become rich ....2 Cor. 8:9
tribulation, and *p* ....Rev. 2:9

POWER (245/237)
that I may show My *p*...............Ex. 9:16
him who is without *p* ....Job 26:2
p who can understand...........Job 26:14
p belongs to God ....Ps. 62:11
p Your enemies shall ....Ps. 66:3
gives strength and *p*...............Ps. 68:35
a king is, there is *p* ....Eccl. 8:4
No one has *p* over the ....Eccl. 8:8
'Not by might nor by *p*...........Zech. 4:6
the kingdom and the *p* ....Matt. 6:13
the Son of Man has *p* ....Matt. 9:6
Scriptures nor the *p* ....Matt. 22:29
p went out from Him..............Luke 6:19
you are endued with *p*........Luke 24:49
I have *p* to lay it ....John 10:18
"You could have no *p* ....John 19:11
you shall receive *p* ....Acts 1:8
as though by our own *p*.........Acts 3:12
man is the great *p* ....Acts 8:10
"Give me this *p*.........................Acts 8:19
for it is the *p* ....Rom. 1:16
saved it is the *p* ....1 Cor. 1:18
Greeks, Christ the *p*...............1 Cor. 1:24
that the *p* of Christ ....2 Cor. 12:9
greatness of His *p* ....Eph. 1:19
the Lord and in the *p* ....Eph. 6:10
to His glorious *p* ....Col. 1:11
the glory of His *p*...............2 Thess. 1:9
of fear, but of *p*.......................2 Tim. 1:7
by the word of His *p* ....Heb. 1:3
p of death, that.......................Heb. 2:14
as His divine *p* ....2 Pet. 1:3
dominion and *p*.........................Jude 1:25
to him I will give *p* ....Rev. 2:26
honor and glory and *p* ....Rev. 5:13

POWERFUL (6/6)
of the LORD is *p* ....Ps. 29:4
of God is living and *p* ....Heb. 4:12

POWERS (13/13)
principalities and *p* ....Col. 2:15
word of God and the *p* ....Heb. 6:5

PRAISE (236/205)
p shall be of You in ....Ps. 22:25
the people shall *p* ....Ps. 45:17

P is awaiting You . . . . Ps. 65:1
let all the peoples *p*. . . . . Ps. 67:3
p shall be continually. . . . . .Ps. 71:6
And the heavens will *p* . . . . Ps. 89:5
Seven times a day I *p* . . . . .Ps. 119:164
that has breath *p* . . . . Ps. 150:6
Let another man *p* . . . . Prov. 27:2
let her own works *p* . . . . .Prov. 31:31
And your gates *P*. . . . . .Is. 60:18
He makes Jerusalem a *p* . . . . .Is. 62:7
For You are my *p*. . . . . Jer. 17:14
Me a name of joy, a *p* . . . . .Jer. 33:9
give you fame and *p*. . . . . Zeph. 3:20
You have perfected *p* . . . . Matt. 21:16
of men more than the *p* . . . . . . John 12:43
p is not from men but . . . . .Rom. 2:29
Then each one's *p* . . . . .1 Cor. 4:5
should be to the *p*. . . . . Eph. 1:12
to the glory and *p* . . . . .Phil. 1:11
I will sing *p* to You . . . . .Heb. 2:12
the sacrifice of *p* . . . . Heb. 13:15
and for the *p* of those. . . . . 1 Pet. 2:14
saying, "*P* our God. . . . . Rev. 19:5

PRAISED (24/24)
daily He shall be *p*. . . . . .Ps. 72:15
LORD's name is to be *p*. . . . . Ps. 113:3
and greatly to be *p* . . . . Ps. 145:3
the Most High and *p*. . . . . Dan. 4:34

PRAISES (36/32)
it is good to sing *p*. . . . . Ps. 147:1
and he *p* her . . . . Prov. 31:28

PRAISEWORTHY (1/1)
if there is anything *p* . . . . Phil. 4:8

PRAISING (11/11)
they will still be *p* . . . . Ps. 84:4
of the heavenly host *p* . . . . .Luke 2:13
in the temple *p*. . . . . Luke 24:53

PRAY (146/139)
at noon I will *p*. . . . . .Ps. 55:17
who hate you, and *p* . . . . Matt. 5:44
"And when you *p*. . . . . Matt. 6:5
manner, therefore, *p* . . . . Matt. 6:9
Watch and *p* . . . . Matt. 26:41
"Lord, teach us to *p*. . . . . Luke 11:1
And I will *p* .John 14:16
I do not *p* for the . . . . .John 17:9
"I do not *p* for. . . . . John 17:20
p without ceasing . . . . .1 Thess. 5:17
Brethren, *p* for us . . . . .1 Thess. 5:25
Let him *p*. . . . . .James 5:13
to one another, and *p*. . . . . James 5:16
say that he should *p* . . . . .1 John 5:16

PRAYED (59/59)
p more earnestly. . . . . Luke 22:44
p earnestly that it . . . . James 5:17

PRAYER (113/108)
p made in this place . . . . 2 Chr. 7:15
And my *p* is pure . . . . Job 16:17
A *p* to the God of my. . . . . Ps. 42:8
P also will be made . . . . .Ps. 72:15
He shall regard the *p* . . . . .Ps. 102:17
to the LORD, but the *p* . . . . Prov. 15:8
not go out except by *p* . . . . .Matt. 17:21
all night in *p* to God . . . . .Luke 6:12
continually to *p* . . . . .Acts 6:4
where *p* was . . . . Acts 16:13
steadfastly in *p*. . . . . Rom. 12:12
to fasting and *p* . . . . 1 Cor. 7:5
always with all *p* . . . . .Eph. 6:18
but in everything by *p* . . . . .Phil. 4:6
the word of God and *p* . . . . 1 Tim. 4:5
And the *p* of faith . . . . James 5:15

PRAYERS (27/27)
though you make many *p*. . . . . Is. 1:15
pretense make long *p* . . . . Matt. 23:14
fervently for you in *p*. . . . . .Col. 4:12
p may not be hindered . . . . 1 Pet. 3:7
which are the *p* . . . . Rev. 5:8

PREACH (47/45)
time Jesus began to *p* . . . . Matt. 4:17
you hear in the ear, *p*. . . . . Matt. 10:27
P the gospel to the . . . . .Luke 4:18
And how shall they *p* . . . . Rom. 10:15
p Christ crucified. . . . . 1 Cor. 1:23
I or they, so we *p* . . . . .1 Cor. 15:11
P the word. . . . . 2 Tim. 4:2

PREACHED (59/59)
out and *p* everywhere . . . . Mark 16:20
of sins should be *p* . . . . Luke 24:47
p Christ to them. . . . . .Acts 8:5
lest, when I have *p* . . . . .1 Cor. 9:27
than what we have *p*. . . . . .Gal. 1:8
the gospel was *p* . . . . .Heb. 4:2
also He went and *p* . . . . 1 Pet. 3:19

PREACHER (11/11)
they hear without a *p*. . . . . Rom. 10:14
I was appointed a *p*. . . . . .1 Tim. 2:7

PREACHES (4/4)
the Jesus whom Paul *p* . . . . Acts 19:13
p another Jesus whom. . . . . 2 Cor. 11:4
p any other gospel. . . . . .Gal. 1:9
p the faith which he . . . . .Gal. 1:23

PREACHING (26/26)
p Jesus as the . . . . Acts 5:42
not risen, then our *p*. . . . . 1 Cor. 15:14

PRECEPTS (25/25)
all His *p* are sure . . . . Ps. 111:7
how I love Your *p*. . . . . Ps. 119:159

PRECIOUS (77/75)
P in the sight of the. . . . . Ps. 116:15
She is more *p* than . . . . .Prov. 3:15
p things shall not. . . . . .Is. 44:9
if you take out the *p* . . . . Jer. 15:19
farmer waits for the *p* . . . . James 5:7
more *p* than gold. . . . . .1 Pet. 1:7
who believe, He is *p* . . . . 1 Pet. 2:7
p in the sight of . . . . 1 Pet. 3:4

PREDESTINED (4/4)
He foreknew, He also *p* ....Rom. 8:29
having *p* us to....................Eph. 1:5
inheritance, being *p*............Eph. 1:11
PREEMINENCE (2/2)
He may have the *p* ....Col. 1:18
loves to have the *p* ....3 John 1:9
PREFERENCE (2/2)
in honor giving *p*..............Rom. 12:10
PREJUDICE (1/1)
these things without *p*.........1 Tim. 5:21
PREMEDITATE (1/1)
p what you will..................Mark 13:11
PREPARATION (11/10)
Now it was the *P*.................John 19:14
your feet with the *p* ....Eph. 6:15
PREPARE (97/96)
p a table before me in .... Ps. 23:5
P the way of the LORD .... Mark 1:3
p a place for you .... John 14:2
PREPARED (109/107)
for whom it is *p* ....Matt. 20:23
which You have *p* ....Luke 2:31
mercy, which He had *p* ....Rom. 9:23
things which God has *p*..........1 Cor. 2:9
Now He who has *p*...................2 Cor. 5:5
p beforehand that we................Eph. 2:10
God, for He has *p*.................Heb. 11:16
PRESENCE (156/147)
themselves from the *p*...........Gen. 3:8
went out from the *p* ....Gen. 4:16
P will go with you .... Ex. 33:14
afraid in any man's *p* ....Deut. 1:17
p is fullness of joy ....Ps. 16:11
shall dwell in Your *p*...........Ps. 140:13
not tremble at My *p* ....Jer. 5:22
shall shake at My *p* ....Ezek. 38:20
and drank in Your *p* .... Luke 13:26
full of joy in Your *p*................Acts 2:28
but his bodily *p* ....2 Cor. 10:10
obeyed, not as in my *p*...........Phil. 2:12
PRESENT (130/127)
we are all *p* before...............Acts 10:33
evil is *p* with me.....................Rom. 7:21
p your bodies a living............ Rom. 12:1
or death, or things *p*............1 Cor. 3:22
absent in body but *p*..............1 Cor. 5:3
that He might *p* ....Eph. 5:27
p you faultless ....Jude 1:24
PRESERVE (35/34)
He shall p your soul ....Ps. 121:7
The LORD shall *p* ....Ps. 121:8
loses his life will *p*.................Luke 17:33
every evil work and *p*.......... 2 Tim. 4:18
PRESERVED (16/16)
soul, and body be *p*..........1 Thess. 5:23
PRESERVES (8/8)
For the LORD *p* the .... Ps. 31:23
p the souls of His.................. Ps. 97:10
he who keeps his way *p*..........Prov. 16:17
PRETENSE (6/6)
p make long prayers...............Matt. 23:14
PRICE (26/25)
one pearl of great *p*.............Matt. 13:46
you were bought at a *p* ....1 Cor. 6:20
PRIDE (51/48)
p serves as their necklace .... Ps. 73:6
By *p* comes nothing ....Prov. 13:10
P goes before ....Prov. 16:18
and her daughter had *p*....... Ezek. 16:49
was hardened in *p*..................... Dan. 5:20
For the *p* of the.......................Zech. 11:3
evil eye, blasphemy, *p* .... Mark 7:22
p he fall into the .... 1 Tim. 3:6
eyes, and the *p* of life ....1 John 2:16
PRIEST (510/456)
he was the *p* of God............. Gen. 14:18
p forever according ....Ps. 110:4
So He shall be a *p* ....Zech. 6:13
and faithful High *P*..................Heb. 2:17
we have a great High *P* .... Heb. 4:14
p forever according ....Heb. 5:6
Christ came as High *P* .... Heb. 9:11
PRIESTHOOD (21/19)
p being changed ....Heb. 7:12
has an unchangeable *p* ....Heb. 7:24
generation, a royal *p* ....1 Pet. 2:9
PRIESTS (409/383)
to Me a kingdom of *p* .... Ex. 19:6
her *p* teach for pay ....Mic. 3:11
made us kings and *p* ....Rev. 1:6
PRINCE (54/50)
is the house of the *p*...............Job 21:28
Everlasting Father, *P* ....Is. 9:6
until Messiah the *P*................ Dan. 9:25
days without king or *p*.................Hos. 3:4
p asks for gifts ....Mic. 7:3
and killed the *P* ....Acts 3:15
His right hand to be *P* .... Acts 5:31
the *p* of the power.......................Eph. 2:2
PRINCES (173/161)
to put confidence in *p* ....Ps. 118:9
He brings the *p* ....Is. 40:23
PRISON (93/87)
and put him into the *p*........ Gen. 39:20
Bring my soul out of *p*............Ps. 142:7
in darkness from the *p* ....Is. 42:7
the opening of the *p*................... Is. 61:1
John had heard in *p* ....Matt. 11:2
I was in *p* and you..............Matt. 25:36
PRIZE (9/9)
the goal for the *p*.......................Phil. 3:14
PROCEED (17/17)
of the same mouth *p* ....James 3:10

PROCEEDED (8/8)
for I *p* forth . . . . John 8:42

PROCEEDS (12/12)
by every word that *p* . . . . Deut. 8:3
by every word that *p* . . . . Matt. 4:4
Spirit of truth who *p* . . . . John 15:26

PROCLAIM (54/52)
began to *p* it freely . . . . Mark 1:45
knowing, Him I *p* . . . . Acts 17:23
drink this cup, you *p* . . . . 1 Cor. 11:26

PROCLAIMED (33/32)
p the good news . . . . Ps. 40:9
he went his way and *p* . . . . Luke 8:39

PROCLAIMER (1/1)
"He seems to be a *p* . . . . Acts 17:18

PROCLAIMS (5/4)
good news, who *p* . . . . Is. 52:7

PRODIGAL (1/1)
with *p* living . . . . Luke 15:13

PROFANE (36/36)
and priest are *p* . . . . Jer. 23:11
tried to *p* the temple . . . . Acts 24:6
But reject *p* and old . . . . 1 Tim. 4:7

PROFANED (25/23)
and *p* My Sabbaths . . . . Ezek. 22:8

PROFANENESS (1/1)
of Jerusalem *p* has . . . . Jer. 23:15

PROFANING (2/2)
p the covenant of the . . . . Mal. 2:10

PROFESS (1/1)
They *p* to know God . . . . Titus 1:16

PROFIT (53/52)
For what *p* is it to . . . . Matt. 16:26
For what will it *p* . . . . Mark 8:36
For what *p* is it to . . . . Luke 9:25
her masters much *p* . . . . Acts 16:16
brought no small *p* . . . . Acts 19:24
what is the *p* of . . . . Rom. 3:1
not seeking my own *p* . . . . 1 Cor. 10:33
Christ will *p* you . . . . Gal. 5:2
about words to no *p* . . . . 2 Tim. 2:14
them, but He for our *p* . . . . Heb. 12:10
What does it *p* . . . . James 2:14
and sell, and make a *p* . . . . James 4:13

PROFITABLE (13/12)
It is doubtless not *p* . . . . 2 Cor. 12:1
of God, and is *p* . . . . 2 Tim. 3:16

PROFITS (7/7)
have not love, it *p* . . . . 1 Cor. 13:3

PROMISE (53/50)
Behold, I send the *P* . . . . Luke 24:49
but to wait for the *P* . . . . Acts 1:4
For the *p* is to you . . . . Acts 2:39
for the hope of the *p* . . . . Acts 26:6
p might be sure . . . . Rom. 4:16
Therefore, since a *p* . . . . Heb. 4:1
to the heirs of *p* . . . . Heb. 6:17
did not receive the *p* . . . . Heb. 11:39

PROMISED (51/50)
Him faithful who had *p* . . . . Heb. 11:11

PROMISES (13/13)
For all the *p* of God . . . . 2 Cor. 1:20
his Seed were the *p* . . . . Gal. 3:16
having received the *p* . . . . Heb. 11:13
great and precious *p* . . . . 2 Pet. 1:4

PROPER (13/13)
you, but for what is *p* . . . . 1 Cor. 7:35
but, which is *p* . . . . 1 Tim. 2:10

PROPERLY (2/2)
Let us walk *p* . . . . Rom. 13:13

PROPHECY (18/18)
miracles, to another *p* . . . . 1 Cor. 12:10
for *p* never came by . . . . 2 Pet. 1:21
is the spirit of *p* . . . . Rev. 19:10
of the book of this *p* . . . . Rev. 22:19

PROPHESIED (47/44)
Lord, have we not *p* . . . . Matt. 7:22
prophets and the law *p* . . . . Matt. 11:13

PROPHESIES (10/9)
p edifies the church . . . . 1 Cor. 14:4

PROPHESY (86/75)
prophets, "Do not *p* . . . . Is. 30:10
The prophets *p* falsely . . . . Jer. 5:31
your daughters shall *p* . . . . Joel 2:28
Who can but *p* . . . . Amos 3:8
saying, "*P* to us . . . . Matt. 26:68
your daughters shall *p* . . . . Acts 2:17
know in part and we *p* . . . . 1 Cor. 13:9

PROPHET (242/227)
raise up for you a *P* . . . . Deut. 18:15
"I alone am left a *p* . . . . 1 Kin. 18:22
I ordained you a *p* . . . . Jer. 1:5
The *p* is a fool . . . . Hos. 9:7
nor was I a son of a *p* . . . . Amos 7:14
send you Elijah the *p* . . . . Mal. 4:5
p shall receive a . . . . Matt. 10:41
p is not without honor . . . . Matt. 13:57
by Daniel the *p* . . . . Mark 13:14
is not a greater *p* . . . . Luke 7:28
it cannot be that a *p* . . . . Luke 13:33
Nazareth, who was a *P* . . . . Luke 24:19
"Are you the *P* . . . . John 1:21
"This is truly the *P* . . . . John 6:14
with him the false *p* . . . . Rev. 19:20

PROPHETIC (2/2)
p word confirmed . . . . 2 Pet. 1:19

PROPHETS (237/225)
the Law or the *P* . . . . Matt. 5:17
is the Law and the *P* . . . . Matt. 7:12
or one of the *p* . . . . Matt. 16:14
the tombs of the *p* . . . . Matt. 23:29
indeed, I send you *p* . . . . Matt. 23:34
one who kills the *p* . . . . Matt. 23:37
Then many false *p* . . . . Matt. 24:11
have Moses and the *p* . . . . Luke 16:29

You are sons of the *p* .... Acts 3:25
p did your fathers not .... Acts 7:52
To Him all the *p* .... Acts 10:43
do you believe the *p* .... Acts 26:27
by the Law and the *P* .... Rom. 3:21
have killed Your *p* .... Rom. 11:3
to be apostles, some *p* .... Eph. 4:11
this salvation the *p* .... 1 Pet. 1:10
because many false *p* .... 1 John 4:1
found the blood of *p* .... Rev. 18:24

PROPITIATION (4/4)
set forth as a *p* .... Rom. 3:25
to God, to make *p* .... Heb. 2:17
He Himself is the *p* .... 1 John 2:2
His Son to be the *p* .... 1 John 4:10

PROPRIETY (1/1)
modest apparel, with *p* .... 1 Tim. 2:9

PROSPER (49/48)
they *p* who love you .... Ps. 122:6
of the LORD shall *p* .... Is. 53:10
against you shall *p* .... Is. 54:17
storing up as he may *p* .... 1 Cor. 16:2
I pray that you may *p* .... 3 John 1:2

PROSPERED (12/12)
since the LORD has *p* .... Gen. 24:56

PROSPERING (2/2)
His ways are always *p* .... Ps. 10:5

PROSPERITY (24/24)
p all your days .... Deut. 23:6
p the destroyer .... Job 15:21
Now in my *p* I said .... Ps. 30:6
has pleasure in the *p* .... Ps. 35:27
When I saw the *p* .... Ps. 73:3
I pray, send now *p* .... Ps. 118:25
that we have our *p* .... Acts 19:25

PROSPEROUS (8/8)
will make your way *p* .... Josh. 1:8

PROSPERS (5/5)
just as your soul *p* .... 3 John 1:2

PROUD (47/47)
tongue that speaks *p* .... Ps. 12:3
and fully repays the *p* .... Ps. 31:23
does not respect the *p* .... Ps. 40:4
a haughty look and a *p* .... Ps. 101:5
p He knows from afar .... Ps. 138:6
Everyone *p* in heart .... Prov. 16:5
by wine, he is a *p* .... Hab. 2:5
He has scattered the *p* .... Luke 1:51
"God resists the *p* .... 1 Pet. 5:5

PROVERB (21/20)
of a drunkard is a *p* .... Prov. 26:9
one shall take up a *p* .... Mic. 2:4
to the true *p* .... 2 Pet. 2:22

PROVERBS (8/8)
spoke three thousand *p* .... 1 Kin. 4:32
in order many *p* .... Eccl. 12:9

PROVIDE (30/29)
"My son, God will *p* .... Gen. 22:8
P neither gold nor .... Matt. 10:9
if anyone does not *p* .... 1 Tim. 5:8

PROVIDED (21/21)
these hands have *p* .... Acts 20:34
p something better .... Heb. 11:40

PROVISION (9/9)
no *p* for the flesh .... Rom. 13:14

PROVOKE (37/36)
Do they *p* Me to .... Jer. 7:19
you, fathers, do not *p* .... Eph. 6:4

PROVOKED (30/29)
p the Most High .... Ps. 78:56
his spirit was *p* .... Acts 17:16
seek its own, is not *p* .... 1 Cor. 13:5

PRUDENCE (7/7)
To give *p* to the .... Prov. 1:4
wisdom, dwell with *p* .... Prov. 8:12
us in all wisdom and *p* .... Eph. 1:8

PRUDENT (22/22)
p man covers shame .... Prov. 12:16
A *p* man conceals .... Prov. 12:23
The wisdom of the *p* .... Prov. 14:8
p considers well .... Prov. 14:15
heart will be called *p* .... Prov. 16:21
p man foresees evil .... Prov. 22:3
Therefore the *p* .... Amos 5:13
from the wise and *p* .... Matt. 11:25

PRUDENTLY (2/2)
Servant shall deal *p* .... Is. 52:13

PRUNES (1/1)
that bears fruit He *p* .... John 15:2

PSALM (83/83)
each of you has a *p* .... 1 Cor. 14:26

PSALMIST (1/1)
And the sweet *p* .... 2 Sam. 23:1

PSALMS (10/10)
to one another in *p* .... Eph. 5:19
Let him sing *p* .... James 5:13

PUNISH (47/47)
p the righteous is .... Prov. 17:26
Shall I not *p* them for .... Jer. 5:9

PUNISHED (19/19)
p them often in every .... Acts 26:11
These shall be *p* .... 2 Thess. 1:9

PUNISHES (2/2)
will you say when He *p* .... Jer. 13:21

PUNISHMENT (46/42)
p is greater than I .... Gen. 4:13
you do in the day of *p* .... Is. 10:3
p they shall perish .... Jer. 10:15
not turn away its *p* .... Amos 1:3
into everlasting *p* .... Matt. 25:46
p which was inflicted .... 2 Cor. 2:6
Of how much worse *p* .... Heb. 10:29
sent by him for the *p* .... 1 Pet. 2:14
the unjust under *p* .... 2 Pet. 2:9

RAISED (132/127)
be killed, and be *r* . . . . Matt. 16:21
just as Christ was *r* . . . . Rom. 6:4
Spirit of Him who *r*. . . . . Rom. 8:11
"How are the dead *r* . . . . 1 Cor. 15:35
and the dead will be *r*. . . . . 1 Cor. 15:52
and *r* us up together. . . . . Eph. 2:6

RAISES (11/11)
For as the Father *r*. . . . . John 5:21
but in God who *r* . . . . 2 Cor. 1:9

RANSOM (13/13)
to give His life a *r* . . . . Mark 10:45
who gave Himself a *r* . . . . 1 Tim. 2:6

RANSOMED (3/3)
and the *r* of the LORD. . . . . Is. 35:10
redeemed Jacob, and *r* . . . . Jer. 31:11

RASH (4/4)
Do not be *r* with your. . . . . Eccl. 5:2

RASHLY (3/3)
and do nothing *r* . . . . Acts 19:36

RAVENOUS (3/3)
inwardly they are *r* . . . . Matt. 7:15

RAVENS (5/5)
Consider the *r*. . . . . Luke 12:24

REACHING (1/1)
r forward to those . . . . Phil. 3:13

READ (67/63)
day, and stood up to *r*. . . . . Luke 4:16
hearts, known and *r* . . . . 2 Cor. 3:2

READER (1/1)
let the *r* understand . . . . Mark 13:14

READINESS (2/2)
the word with all *r*. . . . . Acts 17:11

READING (10/9)
r the prophet Isaiah . . . . Acts 8:30

READS (4/4)
Blessed is he who *r*. . . . . Rev. 1:3

READY (84/82)
and those who were *r*. . . . . Matt. 25:10
"Lord, I am *r* . . . . Luke 22:33
Be *r* in season and out . . . . 2 Tim. 4:2
and always be *r* . . . . 1 Pet. 3:15

REAP (34/28)
they neither sow nor *r* . . . . Matt. 6:26
you knew that I *r*. . . . . Matt. 25:26

REAPED (4/4)
you have *r* iniquity . . . . Hos. 10:13

REAPERS (10/10)
r are the angels . . . . Matt. 13:39

REAPING (3/3)
r what I did not . . . . Luke 19:22

REAPS (4/3)
One sows and another *r* . . . . John 4:37

REASON (67/67)
Come now, and let us *r*. . . . . Is. 1:18
who asks you a *r* . . . . 1 Pet. 3:15

REASONED (14/14)
for three Sabbaths *r* . . . . Acts 17:2

REBEL (18/17)
if you refuse and *r*. . . . . Is. 1:20

REBELLING (1/1)
more against Him by *r*. . . . . Ps. 78:17

REBELLION (23/23)
hearts as in the *r* . . . . Heb. 3:8

REBELLIOUS (40/38)
day long to a *r* people. . . . . Is. 65:2

REBUILD (8/7)
God, to *r* its ruins. . . . . Ezra 9:9
r it as in the days of. . . . . Amos 9:11

REBUKE (70/69)
Turn at my *r* . . . . Prov. 1:23
r a wise man . . . . Prov. 9:8
r is better than love. . . . . Prov. 27:5
sins against you, *r*. . . . . Luke 17:3
Do not *r* an older man . . . . 1 Tim. 5:1
who are sinning *r* . . . . 1 Tim. 5:20
"The Lord *r* you . . . . Jude 1:9
As many as I love, I *r* . . . . Rev. 3:19

REBUKED (31/31)
r the winds and the. . . . . Matt. 8:26
r their unbelief. . . . . Mark 16:14
but he was *r* for his . . . . 2 Pet. 2:16

REBUKES (9/9)
ear that hears the *r*. . . . . Prov. 15:31

RECEIVE (173/167)
believing, you will *r* . . . . Matt. 21:22
and His own did not *r* . . . . John 1:11
will come again and *r*. . . . . John 14:3
the world cannot *r* . . . . John 14:17
Ask, and you will *r* . . . . John 16:24
"*R* the Holy Spirit . . . . John 20:22
"Lord Jesus, *r* . . . . Acts 7:59
r the Holy Spirit. . . . . Acts 19:2
R one who is weak. . . . . Rom. 14:1
r the Spirit by the . . . . Gal. 3:2
suppose that he will *r*. . . . . James 1:7

RECEIVED (155/153)
But as many as *r* . . . . John 1:12
for God has *r* him . . . . Rom. 14:3
For I *r* from the Lord . . . . 1 Cor. 11:23
have *r* Christ Jesus . . . . Col. 2:6
r up in glory . . . . 1 Tim. 3:16

RECEIVES (42/28)
r you *r* Me . . . . Matt. 10:40
and whoever *r* Me . . . . Mark 9:37

RECONCILE (4/4)
and that He might *r* . . . . Eph. 2:16

RECONCILED (7/6)
First be *r* to your . . . . Matt. 5:24
were enemies we were *r*. . . . . Rom. 5:10
Christ's behalf, be *r*. . . . . 2 Cor. 5:20

RECONCILIATION (4/4)
now received the *r* . . . . Rom. 5:11
to us the word of *r*. . . . . 2 Cor. 5:19

renew them again to *r* .... Heb. 6:6
found no place for *r* .... Heb. 12:17
all should come to *r* .... 2 Pet. 3:9

REPENTED (7/7)
it, because they *r* .... Matt. 12:41

REPETITIONS (1/1)
r as the heathen do .... Matt. 6:7

REPORT (41/38)
Who has believed our *r* .... Is. 53:1
things are of good *r* .... Phil. 4:8

REPROACH (89/87)
R has broken my heart .... Ps. 69:20
with dishonor comes *r* .... Prov. 18:3
not remember the *r* .... Is. 54:4
because I bore the *r* .... Jer. 31:19
these things You *r* .... Luke 11:45
lest he fall into *r* .... 1 Tim. 3:7
esteeming the *r* .... Heb. 11:26
and without *r* .... James 1:5

REPROACHED (13/12)
If you are *r* for the .... 1 Pet. 4:14

REPROACHES (14/14)
is not an enemy who *r* .... Ps. 55:12
in infirmities, in *r* .... 2 Cor. 12:10

REPROOF (1/1)
for doctrine, for *r* .... 2 Tim. 3:16

REPROOFS (1/1)
R of instruction are .... Prov. 6:23

REPUTATION (5/5)
seven men of good *r* .... Acts 6:3
made Himself of no *r* .... Phil. 2:7

REQUEST (26/26)
He gave them their *r* .... Ps. 106:15
For Jews *r* a sign .... 1 Cor. 1:22

REQUESTS (2/2)
r be made known .... Phil. 4:6

REQUIRE (26/25)
offering You did not *r* .... Ps. 40:6
what does the LORD *r* .... Mic. 6:8

REQUIRED (18/17)
your soul will be *r* .... Luke 12:20
him much will be *r* .... Luke 12:48

REQUIREMENTS (2/2)
keeps the righteous *r* .... Rom. 2:26
r that was against us .... Col. 2:14

RESERVED (15/15)
"I have *r* for Myself .... Rom. 11:4
r in heaven for you .... 1 Pet. 1:4
habitation, He has *r* .... Jude 1:6

RESIST (10/10)
r an evil person .... Matt. 5:39
r the Holy Spirit .... Acts 7:51
R the devil and he .... James 4:7

RESISTED (4/4)
For who has *r* His will .... Rom. 9:19
for he has greatly *r* .... 2 Tim. 4:15
You have not yet *r* .... Heb. 12:4

RESISTS (4/3)
"God *r* the proud .... James 4:6
for "God *r* the proud .... 1 Pet. 5:5

RESPECT (17/17)
of the law held in *r* .... Acts 5:34
and we paid them *r* .... Heb. 12:9

RESPECTED (4/4)
And the LORD *r* Abel .... Gen. 4:4

REST (305/295)
is the Sabbath of *r* .... Ex. 31:15
to build a house of *r* .... 1 Chr. 28:2
R in the LORD .... Ps. 37:7
fly away and be at *r* .... Ps. 55:6
"This is the *r* .... Is. 28:12
is the place of My *r* .... Is. 66:1
and I will give you *r* .... Matt. 11:28
shall not enter My *r* .... Heb. 3:11
remains therefore a *r* .... Heb. 4:9
that they should *r* .... Rev. 6:11
"that they may *r* .... Rev. 14:13
But the *r* of the dead .... Rev. 20:5

RESTED (55/55)
He had done, and He *r* .... Gen. 2:2
"And God *r* on the .... Heb. 4:4

RESTORATION (1/1)
until the times of *r* .... Acts 3:21

RESTORE (56/55)
R to me the joy .... Ps. 51:12
"So I will *r* to you .... Joel 2:25
and will *r* all things .... Matt. 17:11
You at this time *r* .... Acts 1:6
who are spiritual *r* .... Gal. 6:1

RESTORES (4/4)
He *r* my soul .... Ps. 23:3

RESTRAINS (5/4)
only He who now *r* .... 2 Thess. 2:7

RESTRAINT (4/4)
they break all *r* .... Hos. 4:2

RESTS (5/5)
r quietly in the heart .... Prov. 14:33

RESURRECTION (41/40)
to her, "I am the *r* .... John 11:25
them Jesus and the *r* .... Acts 17:18
the likeness of His *r* .... Rom. 6:5
say that there is no *r* .... 1 Cor. 15:12
and the power of His *r* .... Phil. 3:10
obtain a better *r* .... Heb. 11:35
This is the first *r* .... Rev. 20:5

RETAIN (9/9)
r the sins of any .... John 20:23

RETURN (282/258)
womb, naked shall he *r* .... Eccl. 5:15
let him *r* to the LORD .... Is. 55:7
me, and I will *r* .... Jer. 31:18
"*R* to Me," says the LORD .... Zech. 1:3
he says, 'I will *r* .... Matt. 12:44

ROBE (49/48)
'Bring out the best *r* . . . . Luke 15:22
on Him a purple *r* . . . . John 19:2
Then a white *r* was . . . . Rev. 6:11

ROBES (17/17)
have stained all My *r* . . . . Is. 63:3
go around in long *r* . . . . Luke 20:46
clothed with white *r* . . . . Rev. 7:9

ROCK (123/111)
you shall strike the *r* . . . . Ex. 17:6
and struck the *r* . . . . Num. 20:11
For their *r* is not . . . . Deut. 32:31
And who is a *r* . . . . 2 Sam. 22:32
Blessed be my *R* . . . . 2 Sam. 22:47
For You are my *r* . . . . Ps. 31:3
r that is higher than . . . . Ps. 61:2
been mindful of the *R* . . . . Is. 17:10
shadow of a great *r* . . . . Is. 32:2
his house on the *r* . . . . Matt. 7:24
r I will build My . . . . Matt. 16:18
stumbling stone and *r* . . . . Rom. 9:33
R that followed them . . . . 1 Cor. 10:4

ROD (93/83)
Your *r* and Your staff . . . . Ps. 23:4
shall come forth a *R* . . . . Is. 11:1
rule them with a *r* . . . . Rev. 2:27

ROOM (53/52)
you a large upper *r* . . . . Mark 14:15
no *r* for them in the . . . . Luke 2:7
into the upper *r* . . . . Acts 1:13

ROOT (36/35)
day there shall be a *R* . . . . Is. 11:10
because they had no *r* . . . . Matt. 13:6
of money is a *r* . . . . 1 Tim. 6:10
lest any *r* of . . . . Heb. 12:15
I am the *R* and the . . . . Rev. 22:16

ROOTED (3/3)
r and built up in Him . . . . Col. 2:7

ROSE (100/99)
end Christ died and *r* . . . . Rom. 14:9
buried, and that He *r* . . . . 1 Cor. 15:4
that Jesus died and *r* . . . . 1 Thess. 4:14

RULE (61/58)
and he shall *r* . . . . Gen. 3:16
puts an end to all *r* . . . . 1 Cor. 15:24
let the peace of God *r* . . . . Col. 3:15
Let the elders who *r* . . . . 1 Tim. 5:17
Remember those who *r* . . . . Heb. 13:7

RULER (77/75)
to Me the One to be *r* . . . . Mic. 5:2
by Beelzebub, the *r* . . . . Matt. 12:24
the *r* of this world . . . . John 12:31
'Who made you a *r* . . . . Acts 7:27

RULERS (81/73)
and the *r* take counsel . . . . Ps. 2:2
"You know that the *r* . . . . Matt. 20:25
which none of the *r* . . . . 1 Cor. 2:8
powers, against the *r* . . . . Eph. 6:12

RULES (16/16)
that the Most High *r* . . . . Dan. 4:17
that the Most High *r* . . . . Dan. 4:32
r his own house well . . . . 1 Tim. 3:4

RULING (4/4)
r their children . . . . 1 Tim. 3:12

RUMORS (3/3)
hear of wars and *r* . . . . Matt. 24:6

RUN (73/67)
r and not be weary . . . . Is. 40:31
us, and let us *r* . . . . Heb. 12:1

S

SABAOTH (2/2)
S had left us a . . . . Rom. 9:29
ears of the Lord of *S* . . . . James 5:4

SABBATH (132/111)
"Remember the *S* . . . . Ex. 20:8
S was made for man . . . . Mark 2:27

SABBATHS (37/35)
S you shall keep . . . . Ex. 31:13

SACRIFICE (185/175)
to the LORD than *s* . . . . Prov. 21:3
For the LORD has a *s* . . . . Is. 34:6
of My offerings they *s* . . . . Hos. 8:13
LORD has prepared a *s* . . . . Zeph. 1:7
desire mercy and not *s* . . . . Matt. 9:13
an offering and a *s* . . . . Eph. 5:2
put away sin by the *s* . . . . Heb. 9:26
no longer remains a *s* . . . . Heb. 10:26
offer the *s* of praise . . . . Heb. 13:15

SACRIFICED (35/35)
s their sons and their . . . . Ps. 106:37

SACRIFICES (106/103)
The *s* of God are a . . . . Ps. 51:17
multitude of your *s* . . . . Is. 1:11
priests, to offer up *s* . . . . Heb. 7:27
s God is well pleased . . . . Heb. 13:16

SAFE (12/12)
he has received him *s* . . . . Luke 15:27

SAFELY (28/28)
make them lie down *s* . . . . Hos. 2:18

SAFETY (18/18)
say, "Peace and *s* . . . . 1 Thess. 5:3

SAINTS (94/92)
s who are on the earth . . . . Ps. 16:3
does not forsake His *s* . . . . Ps. 37:28
is the death of His *s* . . . . Ps. 116:15
war against the *s* . . . . Dan. 7:21
Jesus, called to be *s* . . . . 1 Cor. 1:2
the least of all the *s* . . . . Eph. 3:8
be glorified in His *s* . . . . 2 Thess. 1:10
all delivered to the *s* . . . . Jude 1:3
shed the blood of *s* . . . . Rev. 16:6

SALT (42/36)
shall season with *s* . . . . Lev. 2:13
"You are the *s* . . . . Matt. 5:13
s loses its flavor . . . . Mark 9:50

SCHEMES (9/9)
sought out many *s* .... Eccl. 7:29
SCHISM (1/1)
there should be no *s* .... 1 Cor. 12:25
SCHOOL (1/1)
daily in the *s* of.......... Acts 19:9
SCOFF (3/3)
They *s* at kings .... Hab. 1:10
SCOFFER (11/11)
"He who corrects a *s* .... Prov. 9:7
s is an abomination .... Prov. 24:9
SCOFFERS (4/4)
s will come in the .... 2 Pet. 3:3
SCORCHED (4/4)
And men were *s* with .... Rev. 16:9
SCORN (9/9)
My friends *s* me .... Job 16:20
SCORNS (5/5)
He *s* the scornful .... Prov. 3:34
SCORPIONS (5/5)
on serpents and *s* .... Luke 10:19
They had tails like *s* .... Rev. 9:10
SCOURGE (11/11)
will mock Him, and *s* .... Mark 10:34
SCOURGES (6/6)
s every son whom .... Heb. 12:6
SCRIBES (67/67)
"Beware of the *s* .... Mark 12:38
SCRIPTURE (32/32)
S cannot be broken .... John 10:35
All *S* is given by .... 2 Tim. 3:16
SCRIPTURES (21/21)
S must be fulfilled .... Mark 14:49
SCROLL (35/33)
eat this *s*, and go .... Ezek. 3:1
the sky receded as a *s* .... Rev. 6:14
SEA (390/340)
drowned in the Red *S* .... Ex. 15:4
who go down to the *s* .... Ps. 107:23
and the *s* obey Him .... Matt. 8:27
throne there was a *s* .... Rev. 4:6
there was no more *s* .... Rev. 21:1
SEAL (29/28)
stands, having this *s* .... 2 Tim. 2:19
SEALED (34/24)
by whom you were *s* .... Eph. 4:30
SEAM (3/3)
tunic was without *s* .... John 19:23
SÉANCE (1/1)
"Please conduct a *s* .... 1 Sam. 28:8
SEARCH (48/46)
glory of kings is to *s* .... Prov. 25:2
s the Scriptures .... John 5:39
SEARCHED (21/21)
s the Scriptures .... Acts 17:11

SEARCHES (8/8)
For the Spirit *s* .... 1 Cor. 2:10
SEASON (31/30)
Be ready in *s* and out .... 2 Tim. 4:2
SEASONED (5/4)
how shall it be *s* .... Matt. 5:13
SEASONS (10/10)
the times and the *s* .... 1 Thess. 5:1
SEAT (62/56)
shall make a mercy *s* .... Ex. 25:17
before the judgment *s* .... 2 Cor. 5:10
SEATS (6/6)
at feasts, the best *s* .... Matt. 23:6
SECRET (59/56)
s things belong .... Deut. 29:29
in the *s* place of His .... Ps. 27:5
Father who is in the *s* .... Matt. 6:6
SECRETLY (34/34)
He lies in wait *s* .... Ps. 10:9
SECRETS (9/9)
For He knows the *s* .... Ps. 44:21
God will judge the *s* .... Rom. 2:16
SECT (6/6)
to the strictest *s* .... Acts 26:5
SECURELY (10/10)
nation that dwells *s* .... Jer. 49:31
SEDUCED (5/5)
flattering lips she *s* .... Prov. 7:21
SEE (705/662)
in my flesh I shall *s* .... Job 19:26
for they shall *s* God .... Matt. 5:8
seeing they do not *s* .... Matt. 13:13
rejoiced to *s* My day .... John 8:56
They shall *s* His face .... Rev. 22:4
SEED (113/103)
He shall see His *s* .... Is. 53:10
S were the promises .... Gal. 3:16
you are Abraham's *s* .... Gal. 3:29
SEEDS (5/5)
the good *s* are the .... Matt. 13:38
SEEK (243/229)
pray and *s* My face .... 2 Chr. 7:14
Yet they *s* Me daily .... Is. 58:2
s, and you will find .... Matt. 7:7
of Man has come to *s* .... Luke 19:10
You will *s* Me and .... John 7:34
For all *s* their own .... Phil. 2:21
s those things which .... Col. 3:1
SEEKING (38/38)
like a roaring lion, *s* .... 1 Pet. 5:8
SEEKS (41/38)
There is none who *s* .... Rom. 3:11
SEEMS (36/34)
There is a way which *s* .... Prov. 14:12
SEEN (274/259)
s God face to face .... Gen. 32:30
No one has *s* God at .... John 1:18

s Me has *s* the .... John 14:9
things which are not *s* .... 2 Cor. 4:18

SEES (55/53)
s his brother in need .... 1 John 3:17

SELF-CONFIDENT (1/1)
a fool rages and is *s*. .... Prov. 14:16

SELF-CONTROL (8/7)
gentleness, *s*. .... Gal. 5:23
to knowledge *s* .... 2 Pet. 1:6

SELF-CONTROLLED (1/1)
just, holy, *s*. .... Titus 1:8

SELF-SEEKING (3/3)
envy and *s* exist .... James 3:16

SELL (32/31)
s whatever you have .... Mark 10:21

SEND (231/222)
"Behold, I *s* you out .... Matt. 10:16
has sent Me, I also *s* .... John 20:21

SENSES (2/2)
of use have their *s* .... Heb. 5:14

SENSIBLY (1/1)
who can answer *s* .... Prov. 26:16

SENSUAL (2/2)
but is earthly, *s*. .... James 3:15

SENT (688/665)
unless they are *s* .... Rom. 10:15

SEPARATED (33/33)
it pleased God, who *s* .... Gal. 1:15

SEPARATES (4/4)
who repeats a matter *s*. .... Prov. 17:9

SEPARATION (10/8)
the middle wall of *s* .... Eph. 2:14

SERAPHIM (2/2)
Above it stood *s* .... Is. 6:2

SERIOUS (7/7)
therefore be *s* and .... 1 Pet. 4:7

SERPENT (42/39)
s was more cunning .... Gen. 3:1
"Make a fiery *s* .... Num. 21:8
Moses lifted up the *s*. .... John 3:14

SERPENTS (14/14)
be wise as *s* .... Matt. 10:16

SERVANT (508/462)
s will rule over a son. .... Prov. 17:2
good and faithful *s* .... Matt. 25:21

SERVANTS (464/430)
are unprofitable *s* .... Luke 17:10

SERVE (214/201)
to be served, but to *s*. .... Matt. 20:28
but through love *s*. .... Gal. 5:13

SERVES (10/8)
If anyone *s* Me .... John 12:26

SERVICE (105/96)
is your reasonable *s* .... Rom. 12:1
with goodwill doing *s*. .... Eph. 6:7

SERVING (20/20)
fervent in spirit, *s* .... Rom. 12:11

SET (619/596)
"See, I have *s*. .... Deut. 30:15
s aside the grace .... Gal. 2:21

SETTLE (11/11)
Therefore *s* it in .... Luke 21:14

SETTLED (15/15)
O LORD, Your word is *s*. .... Ps. 119:89

SEVEN (433/365)
s churches which are .... Rev. 1:4

SEVENTY (67/66)
S weeks are .... Dan. 9:24

SEVERE (29/29)
not to be too *s*. .... 2 Cor. 2:5

SEVERITY (2/1)
the goodness and *s* .... Rom. 11:22

SHADE (12/12)
may nest under its *s* .... Mark 4:32

SHADOW (60/58)
In the *s* of His hand .... Is. 49:2
the law, having a *s* .... Heb. 10:1

SHAKE (40/40)
s the earth .... Is. 2:19
I will *s* all nations .... Hag. 2:7

SHAKEN (32/31)
not to be soon *s* .... 2 Thess. 2:2

SHAKES (7/6)
s the Wilderness .... Ps. 29:8

SHAME (115/109)
never be put to *s* .... Joel 2:26
to put to *s* the wise .... 1 Cor. 1:27
glory is in their *s* .... Phil. 3:19

SHAMEFUL (8/8)
For it is *s* even to .... Eph. 5:12

SHARE (20/19)
to do good and to *s* .... Heb. 13:16

SHARING (3/3)
for your liberal *s* .... 2 Cor. 9:13

SHARP (23/21)
S as a two-edged sword .... Prov. 5:4

SHARPEN (5/5)
s their tongue like a .... Ps. 64:3

SHARPNESS (1/1)
I should use *s* .... 2 Cor. 13:10

SHEATH (8/8)
your sword into the *s* .... John 18:11

SHEAVES (11/10)
bringing his *s* .... Ps. 126:6
gather them like *s* .... Mic. 4:12

SHED (44/42)
which is *s* for many. .... Matt. 26:28

SHEDDING (2/2)
blood, and without *s*. .... Heb. 9:22

SHEEP (193/182)
s will be scattered .... Zech. 13:7

having a hundred *s* .... Luke 15:4
and I know My *s* .... John 10:14
"He was led as a *s* .... Acts 8:32

SHEEPFOLDS (6/6)
lie down among the *s* .... Ps. 68:13

SHEET (2/2)
object like a great *s* .... Acts 10:11

SHELTER (13/13)
the LORD will be a *s* .... Joel 3:16

SHELTERS (2/2)
s him all the day long .... Deut. 33:12

SHEOL (18/18)
not leave my soul in *S* .... Ps. 16:10
the belly of *S* I cried .... Jon. 2:2

SHEPHERD (55/52)
The LORD is my *s* .... Ps. 23:1
His flock like a *s* .... Is. 40:11
'I will strike the *S* .... Matt. 26:31
"I am the good *s* .... John 10:11
the dead, that great *S* .... Heb. 13:20
S the flock of God .... 1 Pet. 5:2
when the Chief *S* .... 1 Pet. 5:4

SHEPHERDS (43/38)
And I will give you *s* .... Jer. 3:15
s have led them astray .... Jer. 50:6

SHIELD (51/50)
I am your *s* .... Gen. 15:1
truth shall be your *s* .... Ps. 91:4
all, taking the *s* .... Eph. 6:16

SHINE (29/29)
LORD make His face *s* .... Num. 6:25
among whom you *s* .... Phil. 2:15

SHINED (1/1)
them a light has *s* .... Is. 9:2

SHINES (6/6)
And the light *s* .... John 1:5

SHINING (13/13)
light is already *s* .... 1 John 2:8

SHIPS (37/33)
down to the sea in *s* .... Ps. 107:23

SHIPWRECK (1/1)
faith have suffered *s* .... 1 Tim. 1:19

SHOOT (19/18)
they *s* out the lip .... Ps. 22:7

SHORT (18/17)
have sinned and fall *s* .... Rom. 3:23

SHORTENED (12/10)
those days were *s* .... Matt. 24:22

SHOUT (48/43)
from heaven with a *s* .... 1 Thess. 4:16

SHOW (163/155)
a land that I will *s* .... Gen. 12:1
s Him greater works .... John 5:20

SHOWBREAD (19/18)
s which was not lawful .... Matt. 12:4

SHOWERS (10/9)
make it soft with *s* .... Ps. 65:10

SHREWDLY (2/2)
because he had dealt *s* .... Luke 16:8

SHRINES (7/7)
who made silver *s* .... Acts 19:24

SHUFFLES (1/1)
with his eyes, he *s* .... Prov. 6:13

SHUNNED (2/2)
feared God and *s* evil .... Job 1:1

SHUT (82/80)
For you *s* up the .... Matt. 23:13

SHUTS (8/7)
s his eyes from seeing .... Is. 33:15
who opens and no one *s* .... Rev. 3:7

SICK (78/78)
I was *s* and you .... Matt. 25:36
faith will save the *s* .... James 5:15

SICKLE (13/12)
"Thrust in Your *s* .... Rev. 14:15

SICKNESS (17/17)
will sustain him in *s* .... Prov. 18:14
"This *s* is not unto .... John 11:4

SICKNESSES (4/4)
And bore our *s* .... Matt. 8:17

SIDE (396/310)
The LORD is on my *s* .... Ps. 118:6

SIFT (3/3)
s the nations with the .... Is. 30:28

SIGH (9/8)
our years like a *s* .... Ps. 90:9

SIGHING (10/10)
For my *s* comes before .... Job 3:24

SIGHT (318/304)
and see this great *s* .... Ex. 3:3
by faith, not by *s* .... 2 Cor. 5:7

SIGN (92/83)
will give you a *s* .... Is. 7:14
seeks after a *s* .... Matt. 12:39
For Jews request a *s* .... 1 Cor. 1:22

SIGNS (73/72)
and let them be for *s* .... Gen. 1:14
cannot discern the *s* .... Matt. 16:3
Jesus did many other *s* .... John 20:30

SILENCE (24/24)
that You may *s* .... Ps. 8:2
seal, there was *s* .... Rev. 8:1

SILENT (46/45)
season, and am not *s* .... Ps. 22:2

SILK (3/3)
and covered you with *s* .... Ezek. 16:10

SILVER (320/283)
may buy the poor for *s* .... Amos 8:6
him thirty pieces of *s* .... Matt. 26:15

SIMILITUDE (1/1)
been made in the *s* .... James 3:9

SIMPLE (21/21)
making wise the *s* .... Ps. 19:7

SPARES (4/4)
s his rod hates his . . . . Prov. 13:24
SPARK (1/1)
the work of it as a *s* . . . . Is. 1:31
SPARKLES (1/1)
it is red, when it *s*. . . . . Prov. 23:31
SPARKS (4/3)
to trouble, as the *s*. . . . . .Job 5:7
SPARROW (3/3)
s has found a home . . . . Ps. 84:3
SPARROWS (4/4)
more value than many *s* . . . . . . Matt. 10:31
SPAT (5/5)
Then they *s* on Him . . . . .Matt. 27:30
SPEAK (509/483)
only the word that I *s* . . . . .Num. 22:35
oh, that God would *s*. . . . . Job 11:5
and a time to *s* . . . . .Eccl. 3:7
s anymore in His name . . . . Jer. 20:9
or what you should *s* . . . . Matt. 10:19
to you when all men *s* . . . . Luke 6:26
s what I have seen. . . . . .John 8:38
He hears He will *s* . . . . .John 16:13
Spirit and began to *s*. . . . . Acts 2:4
SPEAKING (90/89)
envy, and all evil *s*. . . . . 1 Pet. 2:1
SPEAKS (79/72)
to face, as a man *s* . . . . Ex. 33:11
He whom God has sent *s*. . . . . . . John 3:34
When he *s* a lie. . . . . John 8:44
he being dead still *s* . . . . Heb. 11:4
of sprinkling that *s* . . . . .Heb. 12:24
SPEAR (50/43)
His side with a *s*. . . . . John 19:34
SPEARS (18/18)
and their *s* into. . . . . .Is. 2:4
SPECK (6/5)
do you look at the *s*. . . . . Matt. 7:3
SPECTACLE (4/4)
you were made a *s*. . . . . .Heb. 10:33
SPEECH (43/42)
one language and one *s*. . . . . .Gen. 11:1
and his *s* contemptible . . . . 2 Cor. 10:10
s always be with grace . . . . Col. 4:6
SPEECHLESS (5/5)
your mouth for the *s* . . . . Prov. 31:8
SPEED (3/3)
they shall come with *s* . . . . .Is. 5:26
SPEEDILY (14/14)
I call, answer me *s*. . . . . Ps. 102:2
SPEND (26/25)
Why do you *s* money for . . . . .Is. 55:2
amiss, that you may *s*. . . . . James 4:3
SPENT (23/22)
"But when he had *s*. . . . . Luke 15:14
SPIDER (1/1)
s skillfully grasps. . . . . .Prov. 30:28

SPIES (16/16)
men who had been *s*. . . . . .Josh. 6:23
SPIN (2/2)
neither toil nor *s* . . . . .Matt. 6:28
SPINDLE (1/1)
her hand holds the *s*. . . . . .Prov. 31:19
SPIRIT (576/523)
S shall not strive . . . . .Gen. 6:3
S that is upon you . . . . .Num. 11:17
portion of your *s* . . . . 2 Kin. 2:9
Then a *s* passed before . . . . Job 4:15
hand I commit my *s* . . . . .Ps. 31:5
The *s* of a man is the. . . . . Prov. 20:27
s will return to God . . . . Eccl. 12:7
S has gathered them. . . . . Is. 34:16
I have put My *S*. .Is. 42:1
S entered me when He. . . . . Ezek. 2:2
new heart and a new *s* . . . . Ezek. 18:31
I will put My *S*. . . . . .Ezek. 36:27
walk in a false *s* . . . . .Mic. 2:11
I will put My *S*. . . . . Matt. 12:18
S descending upon Him . . . . Mark 1:10
s indeed is willing . . . . Mark 14:38
go before Him in the *s* . . . . Luke 1:17
manner of *s* you are of. . . . . Luke 9:55
hands I commit My *s* . . . . Luke 23:46
they had seen a *s* . . . . Luke 24:37
God is *S*. . . . . John 4:24
I speak to you are *s*. . . . . John 6:63
but if a *s* or an angel . . . . .Acts 23:9
the flesh but in the *S*. . . . . .Rom. 8:9
s that we are children. . . . . Rom. 8:16
what the mind of the *S*. . . . . Rom. 8:27
to us through His *S* . . . . .1 Cor. 2:10
gifts, but the same *S* . . . . 1 Cor. 12:4
but the *S* gives life. . . . . .2 Cor. 3:6
Now the Lord is the *S* . . . . 2 Cor. 3:17
Having begun in the *S* . . . . Gal. 3:3
has sent forth the *S*. . . . . Gal. 4:6
with the Holy *S*. . . . . Eph. 1:13
the unity of the *S* . . . . .Eph. 4:3
stand fast in one *s* . . . . Phil. 1:27
S expressly says that. . . . . .1 Tim. 4:1
S who dwells in us. . . . . James 4:5
made alive by the *S*. . . . . 1 Pet. 3:18
do not believe every *s* . . . . 1 John 4:1
has given us of His *S*. . . . . 1 John 4:13
S who bears witness . . . . .1 John 5:6
not having the *S*. . . . . Jude 1:19
I was in the *S* on the . . . . .Rev. 1:10
him hear what the *S* . . . . Rev. 2:7
And the *S* and the . . . . Rev. 22:17
SPIRITS (41/41)
who makes His angels *s*. . . . . Ps. 104:4
heed to deceiving *s* . . . . .1 Tim. 4:1
SPIRITUAL (28/23)
s judges all things . . . . 1 Cor. 2:15
However, the *s* is not . . . . .1 Cor. 15:46

SUBDUE (9/9)
s all things to ... Phil. 3:21
SUBJECT (17/16)
for it is not *s* ... Rom. 8:7
Let every soul be *s*. ... Rom. 13:1
all their lifetime *s* ... Heb. 2:15
SUBJECTED (2/1)
because of Him who *s* ... Rom. 8:20
SUBJECTION (8/7)
put all things in *s*. ... Heb. 2:8
SUBMISSION (4/4)
his children in *s*. ... 1 Tim. 3:4
SUBMISSIVE (6/6)
Yes, all of you be *s*. ... 1 Pet. 5:5
SUBMIT (11/11)
Therefore *s* to God ... James 4:7
s yourselves to every ... 1 Pet. 2:13
SUBSIDED (4/4)
and the waters *s*. ... Gen. 8:1
SUBSTANCE (12/12)
Bless his *s* ... Deut. 33:11
SUCCESS (5/5)
please give me *s*. ... Gen. 24:12
but wisdom brings *s*. ... Eccl. 10:10
SUCCESSFUL (1/1)
Joseph, and he was a *s*. ... Gen. 39:2
SUDDENLY (72/71)
s there was with the ... Luke 2:13
SUE (1/1)
s you and take away ... Matt. 5:40
SUFFER (46/46)
for the Christ to *s*. ... Luke 24:46
Christ, if indeed we *s* ... Rom. 8:17
in Him, but also to *s* ... Phil. 1:29
SUFFERED (21/20)
s these things and to ... Luke 24:26
for whom I have *s* ... Phil. 3:8
after you have *s* ... 1 Pet. 5:10
SUFFERING (7/7)
Is anyone among you *s* ... James 5:13
SUFFERINGS (14/14)
I consider that the *s* ... Rom. 8:18
perfect through *s*. ... Heb. 2:10
SUFFERS (5/5)
Love *s* long and is ... 1 Cor. 13:4
SUFFICIENCY (2/2)
but our *s* is from God ... 2 Cor. 3:5
SUFFICIENT (15/14)
S for the day is its ... Matt. 6:34
SUM (9/9)
How great is the *s* ... Ps. 139:17
SUMMER (25/25)
and heat, winter and *s* ... Gen. 8:22
SUMPTUOUSLY (1/1)
fine linen and fared *s*. ... Luke 16:19

SUN (161/153)
So the *s* stood still ... Josh. 10:13
s shall not strike you ... Ps. 121:6
s returned ten degrees. ... Is. 38:8
the *s* and moon grow ... Joel 2:10
s shall go down on the ... Mic. 3:6
for He makes His *s* ... Matt. 5:45
the *s* was darkened ... Luke 23:45
do not let the *s* ... Eph. 4:26
s became black as ... Rev. 6:12
had no need of the *s*. ... Rev. 21:23
SUPPER (15/15)
to eat the Lord's *S* ... 1 Cor. 11:20
took the cup after *s*. ... 1 Cor. 11:25
together for the *s*. ... Rev. 19:17
SUPPLICATION (35/33)
by prayer and *s*. ... Phil. 4:6
SUPPLIES (11/11)
by what every joint *s*. ... Eph. 4:16
SUPPLY (18/16)
And my God shall *s*. ... Phil. 4:19
SUPPORT (13/13)
this, that you must *s*. ... Acts 20:35
SUPREME (1/1)
to the king as *s* ... 1 Pet. 2:13
SURE (26/26)
s your sin will find. ... Num. 32:23
call and election *s* ... 2 Pet. 1:10
SURETY (12/10)
Be *s* for Your servant ... Ps. 119:122
Jesus has become a *s* ... Heb. 7:22
SURROUND (17/17)
LORD, mercy shall *s* ... Ps. 32:10
SURROUNDED (35/34)
also, since we are *s* ... Heb. 12:1
SURVIVOR (4/4)
was no refugee or *s*. ... Lam. 2:22
SUSPICIONS (1/1)
reviling, evil *s*. ... 1 Tim. 6:4
SUSTAIN (4/4)
S me with cakes of. ... Song 2:5
SWADDLING (4/4)
Him in *s* cloths. ... Luke 2:7
SWALLOW (21/21)
a gnat and *s* a camel ... Matt. 23:24
SWEAR (48/46)
'You shall not *s*. ... Matt. 5:33
began to curse and *s*. ... Matt. 26:74
SWEARING (2/2)
By *s* and lying ... Hos. 4:2
SWEARS (18/13)
but whoever *s* by the ... Matt. 23:18
SWEAT (3/3)
Then His *s* became like ... Luke 22:44
SWEET (94/91)
s are Your words ... Ps. 119:103
but it will be as *s* ... Rev. 10:9

SWEETNESS (5/5)
mouth like honey in *s* .... Ezek. 3:3
SWELLING (10/9)
they speak great *s* .... 2 Pet. 2:18
SWIFT (22/21)
let every man be *s* .... James 1:19
SWIM (5/5)
night I make my bed *s* .... Ps. 6:6
SWOON (1/1)
as they *s* like the .... Lam. 2:12
SWORD (422/382)
s which turned every ....Gen. 3:24
The *s* of the LORD is ....Is. 34:6
'A *s*, a *s* is sharpened........... Ezek. 21:9
Bow and *s* of battle I............Hos. 2:18
to bring peace but a *s* .... Matt. 10:34
for all who take the *s* .... Matt. 26:52
the *s* of the Spirit............... Eph. 6:17
than any two-edged *s*........... Heb. 4:12
mouth goes a sharp *s* ....Rev. 19:15
SWORDS (27/27)
shall beat their *s* ....Is. 2:4
SWORE (76/76)
So I *s* in My wrath .... Heb. 3:11
SWORN (47/46)
"By Myself I have *s* ....Gen. 22:16
"The LORD has *s*................ Heb. 7:21
SYMBOLIC (2/2)
which things are *s*............... Gal. 4:24
SYMPATHIZE (1/1)
Priest who cannot *s* .... Heb. 4:15
SYMPATHY (1/1)
My *s* is stirred.................. Hos. 11:8
SYNAGOGUE (41/41)
but are a *s* of Satan .... Rev. 2:9

T

TABERNACLE (320/286)
t He shall hide me............... Ps. 27:5
I will abide in Your *t*............. Ps. 61:4
and will rebuild the *t* .... Acts 15:16
and more perfect *t* .... Heb. 9:11
TABERNACLES (13/13)
Feast of *T* was at hand .... John 7:2
TABLE (79/75)
prepare a *t* before me............ Ps. 23:5
dogs under the *t* .... Mark 7:28
of the Lord's *t* .... 1 Cor. 10:21
TABLES (18/13)
and overturned the *t* ....Matt. 21:12
TABLET (6/6)
is engraved on the *t* .... Jer. 17:1
TAIL (15/14)
t drew a third of the .... Rev. 12:4
TAKE (894/848)
t Your Holy Spirit .... Ps. 51:11
T My yoke upon................ Matt. 11:29
and *t* up his cross .... Mark 8:34
My life that I may *t* ....John 10:17
TAKEN (286/274)
He was *t* from prison ....Is. 53:8
one will be *t* and the...........Matt. 24:40
until He is *t* out of...........2 Thess. 2:7
TALEBEARER (6/6)
t reveals secrets............... Prov. 11:13
TALENT (13/13)
went and hid your *t* .... Matt. 25:25
TALK (25/25)
shall *t* of them when........... Deut. 6:7
TALKED (41/41)
within us while He *t* .... Luke 24:32
TALKERS (2/2)
both idle *t* and ....Titus 1:10
TAMBOURINE (4/4)
The mirth of the *t* ....Is. 24:8
TARES (8/8)
the *t* also appeared........... Matt. 13:26
TARGET (4/4)
You set me as Your *t*.............Job 7:20
TARRY (7/7)
come and will not *t*............Heb. 10:37
TASK (6/6)
this burdensome *t* .... Eccl. 1:13
TASTE (21/20)
Oh, *t* and see that the........... Ps. 34:8
might *t* death for................Heb. 2:9
TASTED (9/9)
t the heavenly gift...............Heb. 6:4
TAUGHT (74/72)
as His counselor has *t* ....Is. 40:13
from man, nor was I *t* .... Gal. 1:12
TAUNT (2/2)
and a byword, a *t*................Jer. 24:9
TAX (33/30)
t collectors do the............. Matt. 5:46
TAXES (12/11)
t to whom *t* .... Rom. 13:7
TEACH (106/104)
"Can anyone *t*.................Job 21:22
t me Your paths................. Ps. 25:4
t you the fear of the ....Ps. 34:11
t transgressors Your.............Ps. 51:13
So *t* us to number our .... Ps. 90:12
t you again the first ....Heb. 5:12
TEACHER (55/54)
for One is your *T* ....Matt. 23:8
know that You are a *t* .... John 3:2
named Gamaliel, a *t* ....Acts 5:34
a *t* of the Gentiles in ....1 Tim. 2:7
TEACHERS (17/16)
than all my *t* .... Ps. 119:99
prophets, third *t* ....1 Cor. 12:28
and some pastors and *t*......... Eph. 4:11
desiring to be *t*..................1 Tim. 1:7
there will be false *t* .... 2 Pet. 2:1

TEACHES (21/19)
the Holy Spirit *t* ... 1 Cor. 2:13
the same anointing *t* ... 1 John 2:27

TEACHING (42/42)
t them to observe all ... Matt. 28:20
t every man in all ... Col. 1:28

TEAR (35/34)
I, even I, will *t* ... Hos. 5:14
will wipe away every *t* ... Rev. 21:4

TEARS (37/36)
my couch with my *t* ... Ps. 6:6
mindful of your *t* ... 2 Tim. 1:4
it diligently with *t* ... Heb. 12:17

TEETH (45/43)
You have broken the *t* ... Ps. 3:7

TELL (263/256)
Who can *t* if God ... Jon. 3:9
whatever they *t* ... Matt. 23:3
He comes, He will *t* ... John 4:25

TEMPERATE (4/4)
for the prize is *t* in all ... 1 Cor. 9:25
husband of one wife, *t* ... 1 Tim. 3:2

TEMPEST (16/16)
And suddenly a great *t* ... Matt. 8:24

TEMPLE (371/326)
So Solomon built the *t* ... 1 Kin. 6:14
LORD is in His holy *t* ... Ps. 11:4
One greater than the *t* ... Matt. 12:6
"Destroy this *t* ... John 2:19
your body is the *t* ... 1 Cor. 6:19
grows into a holy *t* ... Eph. 2:21
sits as God in the *t* ... 2 Thess. 2:4
and the Lamb are its *t* ... Rev. 21:22

TEMPLES (8/8)
t made with hands ... Acts 7:48

TEMPORARY (1/1)
which are seen are *t* ... 2 Cor. 4:18

TEMPT (8/8)
t the LORD your God ... Matt. 4:7

TEMPTATION (12/11)
do not lead us into *t* ... Matt. 6:13
the man who endures *t* ... James 1:12

TEMPTED (18/15)
forty days, *t* by Satan ... Mark 1:13
lest you also be *t* ... Gal. 6:1
in all points *t* ... Heb. 4:15

TEMPTER (2/2)
Now when the *t* came ... Matt. 4:3

TENDER (33/33)
your heart was *t* ... 2 Kin. 22:19

TENDERHEARTED (2/2)
to one another, *t* ... Eph. 4:32

TENDS (2/2)
t a flock and does not ... 1 Cor. 9:7

TENT (112/101)
earthly house, this *t* ... 2 Cor. 5:1

TENTMAKERS (1/1)
occupation they were *t* ... Acts 18:3

TENTS (69/66)
than dwell in the *t* ... Ps. 84:10

TERRESTRIAL (2/1)
bodies and *t* bodies ... 1 Cor. 15:40

TERRIBLE (23/23)
is great and very *t* ... Joel 2:11

TERRIFIED (11/11)
and not in any way *t* ... Phil. 1:28

TERRIFY (6/6)
me with dreams and *t* ... Job 7:14

TERRIFYING (1/1)
t was the sight ... Heb. 12:21

TERROR (39/39)
are nothing, you see *t* ... Job 6:21
not be afraid of the *t* ... Ps. 91:5

TERRORS (15/15)
consumed with *t* ... Ps. 73:19

TEST (37/37)
said, "Why do you *t* ... Matt. 22:18
T all things ... 1 Thess. 5:21
but *t* the spirits ... 1 John 4:1

TESTAMENT (3/3)
where there is a *t* ... Heb. 9:16

TESTED (27/26)
that God *t* Abraham ... Gen. 22:1
Where your fathers *t* ... Heb. 3:9
though it is *t* by fire ... 1 Pet. 1:7

TESTIFIED (29/29)
he who has seen has *t* ... John 19:35
of God which He has *t* ... 1 John 5:9

TESTIFIES (7/7)
that the Holy Spirit *t* ... Acts 20:23

TESTIFY (30/30)
t what We have ... John 3:11
t that the Father ... 1 John 4:14

TESTIFYING (3/3)
was righteous, God *t* ... Heb. 11:4

TESTIMONIES (37/37)
those who keep His *t* ... Ps. 119:2
t are my meditation ... Ps. 119:99

TESTIMONY (96/90)
two tablets of the *T* ... Ex. 31:18
under your feet as a *t* ... Mark 6:11
no one receives His *t* ... John 3:32
not believed the *t* ... 1 John 5:10
For the *t* of Jesus is ... Rev. 19:10

TESTING (12/12)
came to Him, *t* Him ... Matt. 19:3

TESTS (6/6)
men, but God who *t* ... 1 Thess. 2:4

THANK (25/24)
"I *t* You, Father ... Matt. 11:25
t You that I am not ... Luke 18:11

THANKFUL (3/3)
Him as God, nor were *t* ... Rom. 1:21

THANKFULNESS (1/1)
Felix, with all *t* . . . . Acts 24:3
THANKS (75/72)
the cup, and gave *t* . . . . Matt. 26:27
T be to God for His . . . . 2 Cor. 9:15
THANKSGIVING (32/31)
His presence with *t*. . . . . Ps. 95:2
into His gates with *t*. . . . . Ps. 100:4
supplication, with *t*. . . . . Phil. 4:6
THEATER (2/2)
and rushed into the *t*. . . . . Acts 19:29
THIEF (25/25)
do not despise a *t* . . . . Prov. 6:30
because he was a *t*. . . . . John 12:6
Lord will come as a *t*. . . . . 2 Pet. 3:10
THIEVES (14/14)
And companions of *t* . . . . Is. 1:23
THINGS (302/290)
in heaven give good *t*. . . . . Matt. 7:11
kept all these *t* . . . . Luke 2:51
share in all good *t* . . . . Gal. 6:6
THINK (59/57)
t you have eternal . . . . John 5:39
not to *t* of himself . . . . Rom. 12:3
THINKS (10/10)
yet the LORD *t* upon me. . . . . Ps. 40:17
for as he *t* in his . . . . Prov. 23:7
t he stands take heed . . . . 1 Cor. 10:12
THIRST (29/29)
those who hunger and *t* . . . . Matt. 5:6
in Me shall never *t*. . . . . John 6:35
anymore nor *t* anymore . . . . Rev. 7:16
THIRSTS (6/6)
My soul *t* for God. . . . . Ps. 42:2
saying, "If anyone *t*. . . . . John 7:37
freely to him who *t* . . . . Rev. 21:6
THIRSTY (21/21)
I was *t* and you gave . . . . Matt. 25:35
THISTLES (3/3)
or figs from *t*. . . . . Matt. 7:16
THORN (6/6)
a *t* in the flesh was . . . . 2 Cor. 12:7
THORNBUSHES (1/1)
gather grapes from *t* . . . . Matt. 7:16
THORNS (48/45)
Both *t* and thistles it. . . . . Gen. 3:18
And some fell among *t* . . . . Matt. 13:7
wearing the crown of *t*. . . . . John 19:5
THOUGHT (51/51)
You understand my *t* . . . . Ps. 139:2
I *t* as a child. . . . . 1 Cor. 13:11
THOUGHTS (52/48)
The LORD knows the *t* . . . . Ps. 94:11
unrighteous man his *t*. . . . . Is. 55:7
For My *t* are not your . . . . Is. 55:8
Jesus, knowing their *t* . . . . Matt. 9:4
heart proceed evil *t*. . . . . Matt. 15:19
The LORD knows the *t* . . . . 1 Cor. 3:20
THREAT (3/2)
shall flee at the *t* . . . . Is. 30:17
THREATEN (2/2)
suffered, He did not *t*. . . . . 1 Pet. 2:23
THREATENING (2/2)
to them, giving up *t* . . . . Eph. 6:9
THREATS (6/6)
still breathing *t* . . . . Acts 9:1
THREE (444/390)
hope, love, these *t*. . . . . 1 Cor. 13:13
THRESH (6/6)
it is time to *t* her . . . . Jer. 51:33
THRESHING (48/48)
t shall last till the. . . . . Lev. 26:5
THROAT (7/7)
t is an open tomb . . . . Rom. 3:13
THRONE (175/159)
Your *t*, O God, is . . . . Ps. 45:6
Lord sitting on a *t* . . . . Is. 6:1
"Heaven is My *t* . . . . Is. 66:1
for it is God's *t*. . . . . Matt. 5:34
will give Him the *t*. . . . . Luke 1:32
"Your *t*, O God, is . . . . Heb. 1:8
come boldly to the *t* . . . . Heb. 4:16
My Father on His *t* . . . . Rev. 3:21
I saw a great white *t* . . . . Rev. 20:11
THRONES (13/11)
invisible, whether *t*. . . . . Col. 1:16
THRONG (3/3)
house of God in the *t* . . . . Ps. 55:14
THROW (37/37)
t Yourself down . . . . Matt. 4:6
THROWN (41/41)
neck, and he were *t*. . . . . Mark 9:42
THRUST (31/29)
and rose up and *t* . . . . Luke 4:29
THUNDER (22/22)
The voice of Your *t* . . . . Ps. 77:18
the voice of loud *t*. . . . . Rev. 14:2
THUNDERED (4/4)
"The LORD *t* from . . . . 2 Sam. 22:14
THUNDERINGS (7/7)
the sound of mighty *t* . . . . Rev. 19:6
THUNDERS (6/5)
The God of glory *t* . . . . Ps. 29:3
TIDINGS (12/11)
I bring you good *t*. . . . . Luke 2:10
TILL (150/145)
no man to *t* the ground . . . . Gen. 2:5
TILLER (1/1)
but Cain was a *t* . . . . Gen. 4:2
TILLS (2/2)
t his land will have . . . . Prov. 28:19
TIME (609/551)
pray to You in a *t*. . . . . Ps. 32:6
for the *t* is near. . . . . Rev. 1:3

TROUBLED (62/62)
You are worried and *t* ....Luke 10:41
shaken in mind or *t* .... 2 Thess. 2:2
TROUBLES (22/22)
out of all their *t* .... Ps. 25:22
will be famines and *t* .... Mark 13:8
him out of all his *t*............ Acts 7:10
TROUBLING (4/4)
wicked cease from *t* .... Job 3:17
TRUE (80/77)
He who sent Me is *t*........... John 7:28
Indeed, let God be *t*........... Rom. 3:4
whatever things are *t*...........Phil. 4:8
may know Him who is *t*.......1 John 5:20
for these words are *t*........... Rev. 21:5
TRUMPET (60/58)
deed, do not sound a *t*.......... Matt. 6:2
t makes an uncertain.......... 1 Cor. 14:8
For the *t* will sound........... 1 Cor. 15:52
TRUST (125/125)
t also in Him, and He shall....... Ps. 37:5
T in the LORD with all .... Prov. 3:5
Do not *t* in a friend .... Mic. 7:5
those who *t* in riches .... Mark 10:24
TRUSTED (32/31)
"He *t* in the LORD................ Ps. 22:8
He *t* in God .... Matt. 27:43
TRUSTS (19/19)
But he who *t* in the .... Ps. 32:10
TRUTH (223/210)
led me in the way of *t*......... Gen. 24:48
Behold, You desire *t*............ Ps. 51:6
t shall be your shield .... Ps. 91:4
and Your law is *t* ....Ps. 119:142
t is fallen in the .... Is. 59:14
called the City of *T* ....Zech. 8:3
you shall know the *t*............John 8:32
"I am the way, the *t*............ John 14:6
He, the Spirit of *t*.............John 16:13
to Him, "What is *t* .... John 18:38
who suppress the *t* .... Rom. 1:18
but, speaking the *t* .... Eph. 4:15
your waist with *t* ....Eph. 6:14
I am speaking the *t*.............1 Tim. 2:7
they may know the *t*.........2 Tim. 2:25
the knowledge of the *t*.......... 2 Tim. 3:7
that we are of the *t* .... 1 John 3:19
the Spirit is *t*...................1 John 5:6
TRY (10/10)
which is to *t* you .... 1 Pet. 4:12
TUMULT (20/20)
Your enemies make a *t* .... Ps. 83:2
TUNIC (17/13)
Also he made him a *t*...........Gen. 37:3
TUNICS (12/12)
the LORD God made *t*............ Gen. 3:21

TURBAN (16/12)
"Remove the *t*................Ezek. 21:26
TURN (288/277)
you shall not *t* ....Deut. 17:11
"Repent, *t* away from .... Ezek. 14:6
on your right cheek, *t*............ Matt. 5:39
t them from darkness ....Acts 26:18
TURNED (259/253)
The wicked shall be *t* ....Ps. 9:17
of Israel, they have *t*.............. Is. 1:4
and how you *t* to God ....1 Thess. 1:9
TURNING (14/14)
marvel that you are *t* ....Gal. 1:6
or shadow of *t*..................James 1:17
TURNS (40/40)
A soft answer *t*................. Prov. 15:1
that he who *t*.................James 5:20
TURTLEDOVE (5/5)
t is heard in our land .... Song 2:12
TUTOR (2/2)
the law was our *t* .... Gal. 3:24
TWIST (2/2)
unstable people *t* to ....2 Pet. 3:16
TWO (759/647)
T are better than one ....Eccl. 4:9
t shall become one .... Matt. 19:5
new man from the *t* .... Eph. 2:15
TYPE (1/1)
of Adam, who is a *t* .... Rom. 5:14

U

UNAFRAID (1/1)
Do you want to be *u* .... Rom. 13:3
UNBELIEF (12/12)
because of their *u* .... Matt. 13:58
help my *u*......................Mark 9:24
did it ignorantly in *u* .... 1 Tim. 1:13
enter in because of *u* ....Heb. 3:19
UNBELIEVERS (6/5)
yoked together with *u* ....2 Cor. 6:14
UNBELIEVING (6/5)
Do not be *u* ....John 20:27
u nothing is pure.................Titus 1:15
But the cowardly, *u*............. Rev. 21:8
UNCIRCUMCISED (54/47)
not the physically *u* ....Rom. 2:27
UNCLEAN (208/167)
I am a man of *u* lips ....Is. 6:5
any man common or *u* .... Acts 10:28
there is nothing *u* .... Rom. 14:14
that no fornicator, *u*............. Eph. 5:5
UNCLEANNESS (34/30)
men's bones and all *u* .... Matt. 23:27
flesh in the lust of *u* ....2 Pet. 2:10
UNCLOTHED (1/1)
we want to be *u* ....2 Cor. 5:4

VINEDRESSER (1/1)
and My Father is the *v* .... John 15:1
VINEGAR (6/5)
As *v* to the teeth and .... Prov. 10:26
VINES (12/11)
foxes that spoil the *v* .... Song 2:15
VINEYARD (70/60)
Who plants a *v* and .... 1 Cor. 9:7
VIOLENCE (60/59)
was filled with *v*. .... Gen. 6:11
of heaven suffers *v* .... Matt. 11:12
VIOLENT (16/16)
haters of God, *v* .... Rom. 1:30
VIPER (6/6)
and stings like a *v* .... Prov. 23:32
VIPERS (5/5)
to them, "Brood of *v*. .... Matt. 3:7
VIRGIN (44/44)
v shall conceive .... Is. 7:14
"Behold, the *v* shall. .... Matt. 1:23
VIRGINS (21/21)
v who took their lamps .... Matt. 25:1
women, for they are *v* .... Rev. 14:4
VIRTUE (4/3)
to your faith *v*. .... 2 Pet. 1:5
VISAGE (1/1)
v was marred more than. .... Is. 52:14
VISIBLE (2/2)
that are on earth, *v* .... Col. 1:16
VISION (77/71)
in a trance I saw a *v* .... Acts 11:5
v appeared to Paul in .... Acts 16:9
VISIONS (27/27)
young men shall see *v*. .... Joel 2:28
VISIT (27/26)
v orphans and widows. .... James 1:27
VISITATION (2/2)
God in the day of *v* .... 1 Pet. 2:12
VISITED (17/17)
Israel, for He has *v* .... Luke 1:68
VISITING (4/4)
v the iniquity of the fathers .... Ex. 20:5
VISITOR (1/1)
am a foreigner and a *v*. .... Gen. 23:4
VITALITY (1/1)
v was turned into the .... Ps. 32:4
VOICE (458/422)
fire a still small *v*. .... 1 Kin. 19:12
if you will hear His *v* .... Ps. 95:7
"The *v* of one crying .... Matt. 3:3
And suddenly a *v*. .... Matt. 3:17
for they know his *v* .... John 10:4
the truth hears My *v*. .... John 18:37
If anyone hears My *v* .... Rev. 3:20
VOICES (21/19)
And there were loud *v* .... Rev. 11:15
VOID (15/14)
they are a nation *v* .... Deut. 32:28
heirs, faith is made *v* .... Rom. 4:14
VOLUME (2/2)
in the *v* of the book. .... Heb. 10:7
VOLUNTEERS (1/1)
Your people shall be *v* .... Ps. 110:3
VOMIT (11/11)
returns to his own *v* .... 2 Pet. 2:22
VOW (36/35)
for he had taken a *v* .... Acts 18:18
VOWS (28/26)
to reconsider his *v* .... Prov. 20:25

W

WAGE (4/4)
w the good warfare. .... 1 Tim. 1:18
WAGES (40/37)
For the *w* of sin is .... Rom. 6:23
Indeed the *w* of the .... James 5:4
WAIL (31/28)
"Son of man, *w*. .... Ezek. 32:18
WAILING (24/22)
There will be *w*. .... Matt. 13:42
WAIT (94/91)
w patiently for Him .... Ps. 37:7
w shall renew their .... Is. 40:31
To those who eagerly *w*. .... Heb. 9:28
WAITED (28/27)
w patiently for the .... Ps. 40:1
Divine longsuffering *w* .... 1 Pet. 3:20
WAITING (15/15)
ourselves, eagerly *w*. .... Rom. 8:23
from that time *w*. .... Heb. 10:13
WAITS (11/11)
the creation eagerly *w*. .... Rom. 8:19
WAKE (4/4)
us, that whether we *w* .... 1 Thess. 5:10
WALK (230/220)
w before Me and be .... Gen. 17:1
Yea, though I *w* .... Ps. 23:4
W prudently when you .... Eccl. 5:1
"This is the way, *w*. .... Is. 30:21
be weary, they shall *w* .... Is. 40:31
w humbly with your God .... Mic. 6:8
W while you have the. .... John 12:35
so we also should *w* .... Rom. 6:4
For we *w* by faith. .... 2 Cor. 5:7
W in the Spirit .... Gal. 5:16
And *w* in love .... Eph. 5:2
that you may *w* worthy .... Col. 1:10
and they shall *w* .... Rev. 3:4
WALKED (103/102)
Enoch *w* with God. .... Gen. 5:22
The people who *w*. .... Is. 9:2
in which you once *w* .... Eph. 2:2

WEIGHT (45/40)
us lay aside every *w* .... Heb. 12:1
WEIGHTIER (1/1)
have neglected the *w* .... Matt. 23:23
WELFARE (2/2)
does not seek the *w* .... Jer. 38:4
WELL (267/255)
daughters have done *w* .... Prov. 31:29
wheel broken at the *w* .... Eccl. 12:6
"Those who are *w* .... Matt. 9:12
said to him, "*W* done .... Matt. 25:21
WELLS (12/11)
These are *w* without .... 2 Pet. 2:17
WENT (1,406/1,295)
They *w* out from us .... 1 John 2:19
out and *w* bitterly .... Matt. 26:75
He saw the city and *w* .... Luke 19:41
Jesus *w* .... John 11:35
WET (6/6)
his body was *w* with .... Dan. 4:33
WHEAT (49/49)
w falls into the .... John 12:24
WHEELS (29/22)
noise of rattling *w* .... Nah. 3:2
WHERE (546/497)
not knowing *w* he was .... Heb. 11:8
WHIP (3/3)
A *w* for the horse .... Prov. 26:3
WHIRLWIND (27/25)
Job out of the *w* .... Job 38:1
has His way in the *w* .... Nah. 1:3
WHISPER (5/5)
my ear received a *w* .... Job 4:12
WHISPERER (1/1)
w separates the best .... Prov. 16:28
WHISPERERS (1/1)
they are *w* .... Rom. 1:29
WHISPERINGS (1/1)
backbitings, *w* .... 2 Cor. 12:20
WHITE (71/64)
clothed in *w* garments .... Rev. 3:5
behold, a *w* horse .... Rev. 6:2
and made them *w* .... Rev. 7:14
WHOLE (237/232)
w body were an eye .... 1 Cor. 12:17
WHOLESOME (2/2)
not consent to *w* words .... 1 Tim. 6:3
WHOLLY (17/17)
w followed the LORD .... Deut. 1:36
WICKED (342/324)
w shall be silent .... 1 Sam. 2:9
w shall be no more .... Ps. 37:10
if there is any *w* .... Ps. 139:24
w forsake his way .... Is. 55:7
and desperately *w* .... Jer. 17:9
the sway of the *w* .... 1 John 5:19

WICKEDLY (21/21)
God will never do *w* .... Job 34:12
WICKEDNESS (128/121)
LORD saw that the *w* .... Gen. 6:5
in the tents of *w* .... Ps. 84:10
man repented of his *w* .... Jer. 8:6
is full of greed and *w* .... Luke 11:39
sexual immorality, *w* .... Rom. 1:29
and overflow of *w* .... James 1:21
WIDE (47/43)
shall open your hand *w* .... Deut. 15:8
w is the gate and .... Matt. 7:13
to you, our heart is *w* .... 2 Cor. 6:11
WIDOW (56/56)
the fatherless and *w* .... Ps. 146:9
How like a *w* is she .... Lam. 1:1
Then one poor *w* .... Mark 12:42
w has children or .... 1 Tim. 5:4
WIDOW'S (4/4)
and I caused the *w* .... Job 29:13
WIDOWS (26/24)
w were neglected .... Acts 6:1
to visit orphans and *w* .... James 1:27
WIFE (389/357)
and be joined to his *w* .... Gen. 2:24
w finds a good thing .... Prov. 18:22
but a prudent *w* .... Prov. 19:14
"Go, take yourself a *w* .... Hos. 1:2
divorces his *w* .... Mark 10:11
'I have married a *w* .... Luke 14:20
Remember Lot's *w* .... Luke 17:32
so love his own *w* .... Eph. 5:33
the husband of one *w* .... Titus 1:6
WILD (59/56)
olive tree which is *w* .... Rom. 11:24
WILDERNESS (306/293)
I will make the *w* .... Is. 41:18
of one crying in the *w* .... Matt. 3:3
the serpent in the *w* .... John 3:14
WILES (1/1)
to stand against the *w* .... Eph. 6:11
WILL (105/98)
w be done on earth as .... Matt. 6:10
but he who does the *w* .... Matt. 7:21
nevertheless not My *w* .... Luke 22:42
flesh, nor of the *w* .... John 1:13
not to do My own *w* .... John 6:38
w is present with me .... Rom. 7:18
acceptable and perfect *w* .... Rom. 12:2
works in you both to *w* .... Phil. 2:13
according to His own *w* .... Heb. 2:4
good work to do His *w* .... Heb. 13:21
WILLFULLY (2/2)
For if we sin *w* .... Heb. 10:26
For this they *w* .... 2 Pet. 3:5
WILLING (41/41)
If you are *w* and .... Is. 1:19

their *w* follow them ....Rev. 14:13
according to their *w*.............Rev. 20:12

WORLD (252/217)
The field is the *w*............Matt. 13:38
He was in the *w*...............John 1:10
For God so loved the *w* ....John 3:16
His Son into the *w* ....John 3:17
w cannot hate you ....John 7:7
You are of this *w*..............John 8:23
I have overcome the *w* ....John 16:33
w may become guilty..........Rom. 3:19
be conformed to this *w*........Rom. 12:2
loved this present *w*.........2 Tim. 4:10
Do not love the *w* ....1 John 2:15
w is passing away ....1 John 2:17

WORLDS (2/2)
also He made the *w* ....Heb. 1:2

WORM (11/11)
But I am a *w*...................Ps. 22:6
w does not die and the ....Mark 9:44

WORMS (7/7)
And he was eaten by *w* ....Acts 12:23

WORMWOOD (10/9)
of the star is *W*..................Rev. 8:11

WORRY (9/8)
to you, do not *w*...............Matt. 6:25

WORRYING (3/3)
by *w* can add one cubit ....Matt. 6:27

WORSE (23/22)
w than their fathers ....Jer. 7:26

WORSHIP (112/105)
and have come to *w* Him ....Matt. 2:2
w what you do not know.......John 4:22
the angels of God *w* ....Heb. 1:6

WORSHIPED (67/66)
on their faces and *w*............Rev. 11:16

WORSHIPER (1/1)
if anyone is a *w* ....John 9:31

WORTH (12/12)
and make my speech *w*........Job 24:25

WORTHLESS (18/18)
Indeed they are all *w*............Is. 41:29

WORTHLESSNESS (2/2)
long will you love *w*.............. Ps. 4:2

WORTHY (52/50)
present time are not *w* ....Rom. 8:18
to walk *w* of the calling ....Eph. 4:1
the world was not *w*...........Heb. 11:38
"*W* is the Lamb who .... Rev. 5:12

WOUND (20/17)
and my *w* incurable ....Jer. 15:18
and his deadly *w*............... Rev. 13:3

WOUNDED (34/34)
But He was *w* for our ....Is. 53:5

WOUNDING (1/1)
killed a man for *w*...............Gen. 4:23

WOUNDS (16/16)
Faithful are the *w* .... Prov. 27:6

WRANGLINGS (1/1)
useless *w* of men of .... 1 Tim. 6:5

WRATH (198/194)
speak to them in His *w* ....Ps. 2:5
Surely the *w* of man ....Ps. 76:10
So I swore in My *w* ....Ps. 95:11
W is cruel and anger a ....Prov. 27:4
in My *w* I struck you............Is. 60:10
w remember mercy ....Hab. 3:2
For the *w* of God is ....Rom. 1:18
up for yourself *w*..............Rom. 2:5
nature children of *w* ....Eph. 2:3
sun go down on your *w*..........Eph. 4:26
Let all bitterness, *w* ....Eph. 4:31
not fearing the *w*...............Heb. 11:27
for the *w* of man does ....James 1:20
of the wine of the *w*...........Rev. 14:8
for in them the *w* ....Rev. 15:1
fierceness of His *w*............ Rev. 16:19

WRATHFUL (2/2)
w man stirs up strife ....Prov. 15:18

WRESTLE (1/1)
For we do not *w*.................Eph. 6:12

WRETCHED (2/2)
w man that I am ....Rom. 7:24
know that you are *w*............ Rev. 3:17

WRETCHEDNESS (1/1)
do not let me see my *w*........Num. 11:15

WRINKLE (1/1)
not having spot or *w* ....Eph. 5:27

WRITE (89/81)
w them on their hearts ....Heb. 8:10

WRITING (22/21)
the *w* was the *w*................ Ex. 32:16

WRITINGS (1/1)
do not believe his *w*........... John 5:47

WRITTEN (280/272)
tablets of stone, *w*.............. Ex. 31:18
your names are *w*............ Luke 10:20
"What I have *w*............... John 19:22

WRONG (31/29)
has done nothing *w*.......... Luke 23:41
But he who does *w*............. Col. 3:25

WRONGED (8/8)
We have *w* no one..............2 Cor. 7:2

WRONGS (1/1)
me *w* his own soul ....Prov. 8:36

WROTE (62/61)
stooped down and *w* .... John 8:6

WROUGHT (2/2)
And skillfully *w*.................Ps. 139:15

Y

YEAR (366/320)
the acceptable *y*..................Is. 61:2
of sins every *y* ....Heb. 10:3

YEARS (528/445)
lives are seventy *y*.............. Ps. 90:10
when He was twelve *y* .... Luke 2:42
with Him a thousand *y* ....Rev. 20:6
YES (209/204)
let your '*Y*' be '*Y*,' .... Matt. 5:37
YESTERDAY (9/9)
For we were born *y*...............Job 8:9
YOKE (56/50)
Take My *y* upon you .... Matt. 11:29
YOKED (2/2)
Do not be unequally *y* ....2 Cor. 6:14
YOUNG (370/350)
I have been *y* .... Ps. 37:25
she may lay her *y*.................. Ps. 84:3
I write to you, *y* .... 1 John 2:13
YOUNGER (32/32)
Likewise you *y* people .... 1 Pet. 5:5
YOURS (73/65)
the battle is not *y*.............2 Chr. 20:15
Y is the kingdom .... Matt. 6:13
And all Mine are *Y* ....John 17:10
for I do not seek *y*............ 2 Cor. 12:14
YOUTH (70/67)
the sins of my *y* .... Ps. 25:7
in the days of your *y*............ Eccl. 11:9
I have kept from my *y* .... Matt. 19:20
YOUTHFUL (4/4)
Flee also *y* lusts .... 2 Tim. 2:22

Z

ZEAL (22/21)
The *z* of the LORD of............2 Kin. 19:31
"*Z* for Your house has...........John 2:17
that they have a *z* .... Rom. 10:2
ZEALOUS (18/17)
z for good works .... Titus 2:14

A Note Regarding the Type

This Bible was set in the Thomas Nelson NKJV Typeface, commissioned by Thomas Nelson Publishers and designed in Aarhus by Klaus Krogh and Heidi Rand Sørensen of 2K/DENMARK. The letterforms take inspiration from a distinctive typeface found in an early Thomas Nelson *Novum Testamentum*, printed in 1844 in Edinburgh—which in turn reflects the Scotch Roman typefaces created by the celebrated English punchcutter Richard Austin for the type foundry of William Miller, circa 1808–1813.

Just as the NKJV translation inherits the tradition and literary beauty *of the King James Bible while* updating the language for today's readers, so Thomas Nelson's custom NKJV font family builds on classic letterforms of the past while reflecting cutting-edge typographical design. The result is a type design that is at once beautiful and efficient, traditional and modern—ideal for presenting the sacred words of ancient Scripture to readers today.

Map 1: WORLD OF THE PATRIARCHS

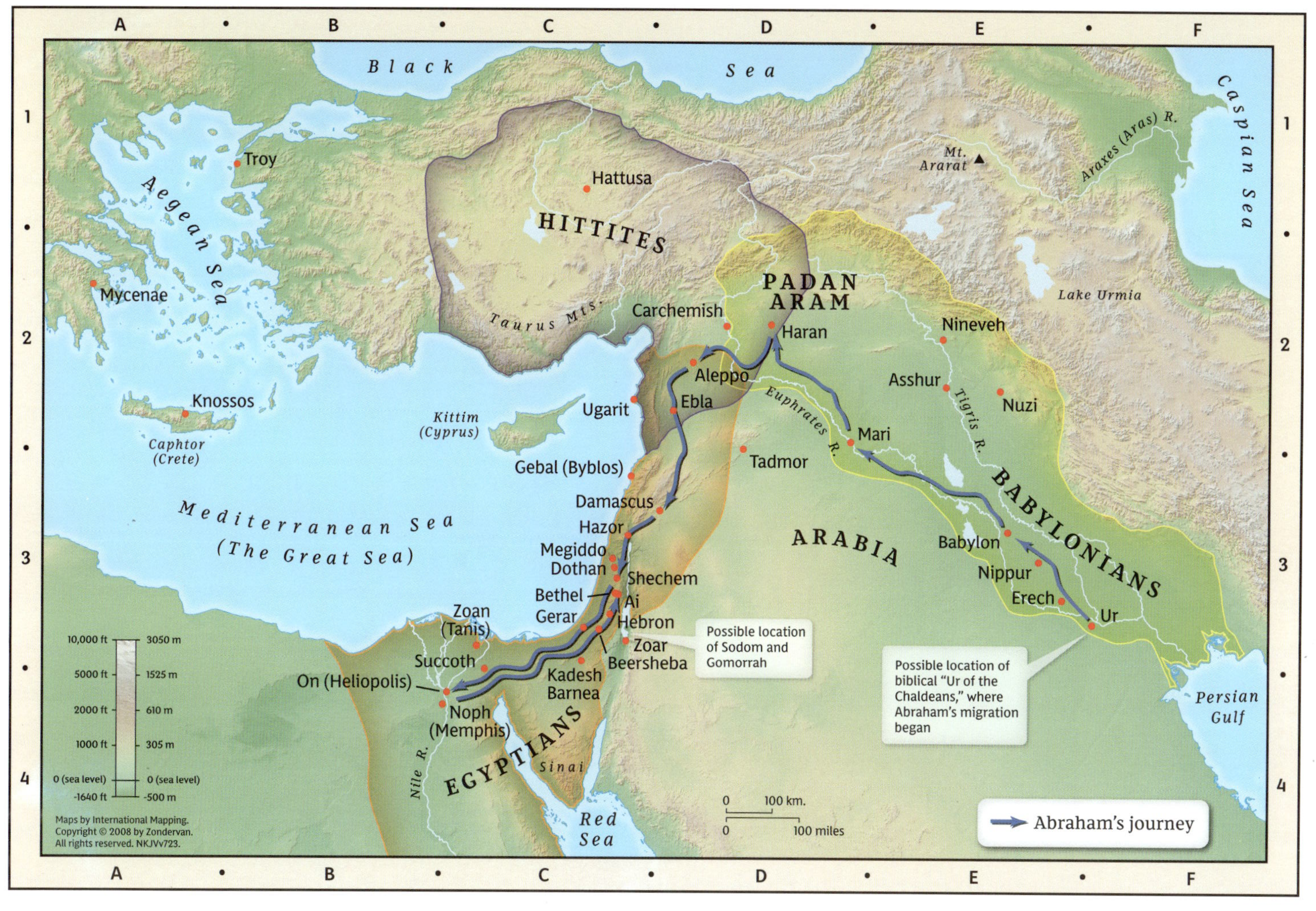

Map 2: EXODUS AND CONQUEST OF CANAAN

Map 3: LAND OF THE TWELVE TRIBES

Map 4: KINGDOM OF DAVID AND SOLOMON

Map 5: JESUS' MINISTRY

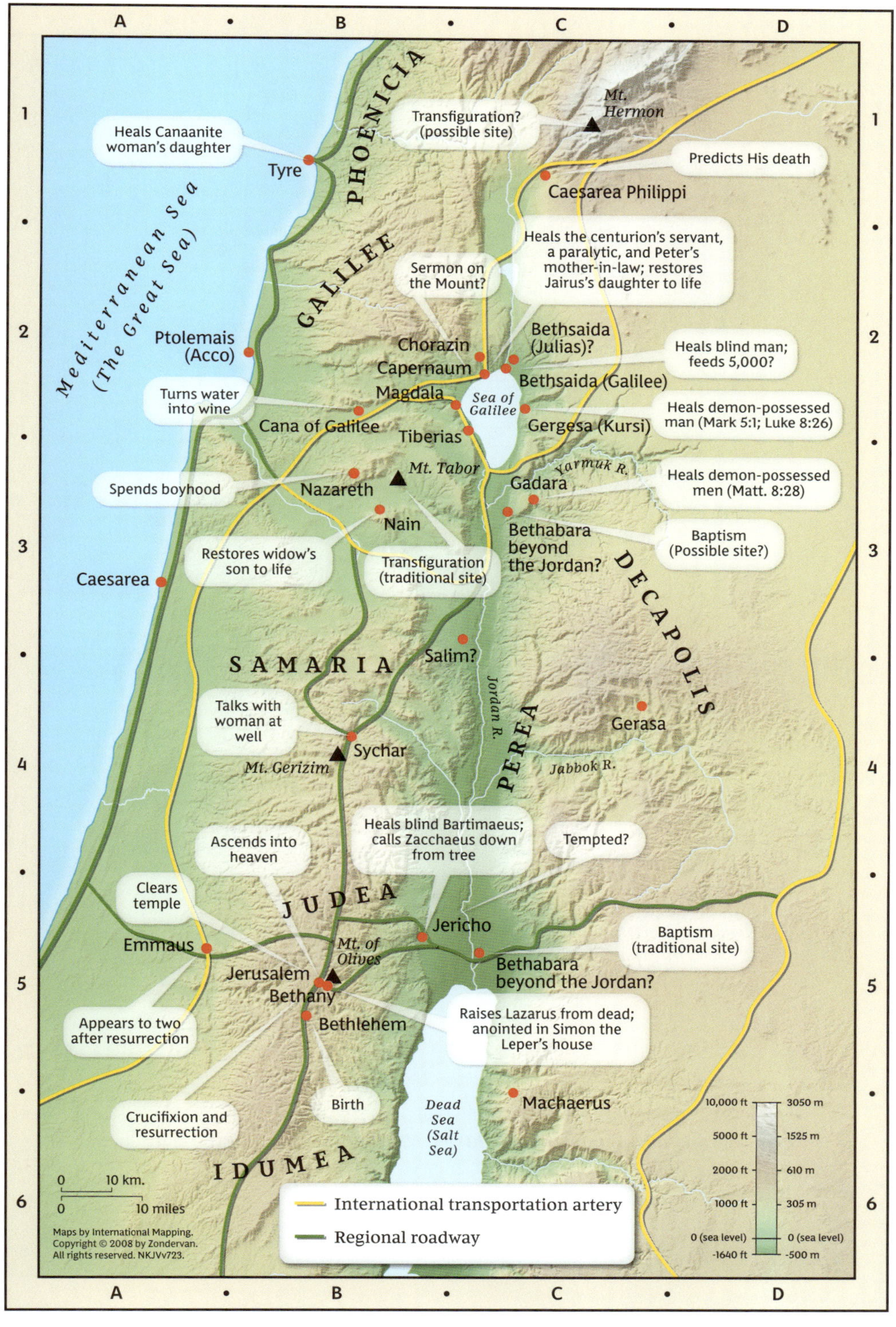

Map 6: PAUL'S MISSIONARY JOURNEYS

5
6
7
8
A
B
C
D
E
F
DACIA
MOESIA
THRACE
ONIA
Black Sea
10,000 ft
5000 ft
2000 ft
1000 ft
0 (sea level)
-1640 ft
3050 m
1525 m
610 m
305 m
0 (sea level)
-500 m
Amphipolis
Philippi
Thessalonica
Neapolis
Samothrace
Apollonia?
BITHYNIA & PONTUS
Mt. Olympus
Troas
Assos
Mitylene
Chios
Aegean Sea
MYSIA
ASIA
Pergamos
Thyatira
LYDIA
Sardis
Smyrna
Ephesus
Philadelphia
Samos
Laodicea
Colosse
Miletus
Patmos
Cos
Cnidus
GALATIA
CAPPADOCIA
LYCAONIA
Antioch (Pisidian)
PISIDIA
PAMPHYLIA
Iconium
Lystra
Derbe
COMMAGENE
Euphrates R.
CILICIA
Tarsus
Issus
SYRIA
Seleucia Pieria
Aleppo
Antioch (Syrian)
LYCIA
Attalia
Patara
Myra
Perga
Rhodes
Delphi
Athens
Cenchrea
Corinth
Sparta
Crete
Phoenix
Salmone
Lasea
Claudа
Fair Havens
Cyprus
Salamis
Paphos
ABILENE
PHOENICIA
Sidon
Tyre
Ptolemais
Damascus
Caesarea
JUDEA
Jordan R.
Jerusalem
Dead Sea
(Salt Sea)
Mediterranean Sea
(The Great Sea)
ENAICA
EGYPT
ARABIA
Nile R.
Red Sea
0
200 km.
0
200 miles
5
6
7
8

Map 7: JERUSALEM IN THE TIME OF JESUS

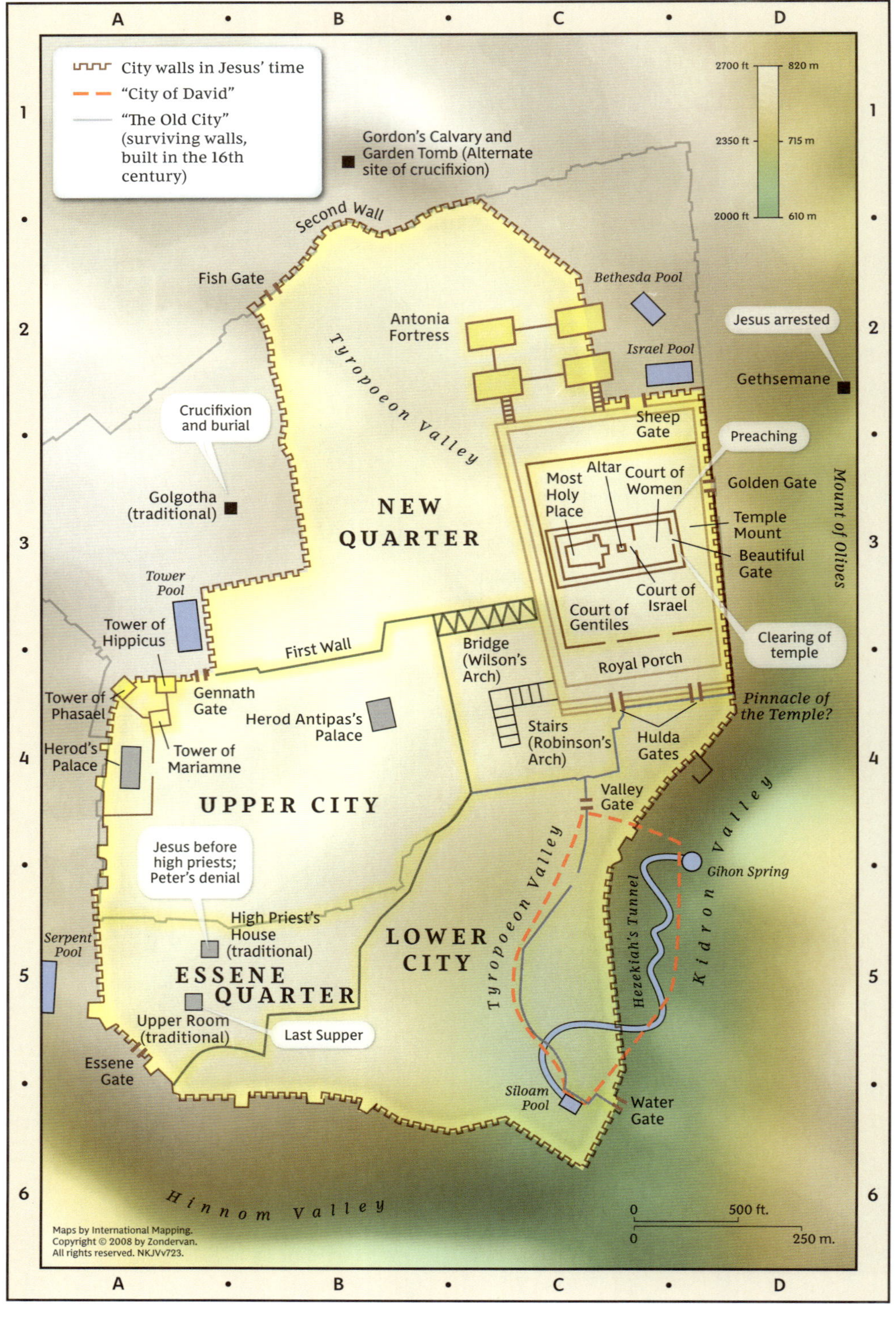